Official 1992 National Football League

Record & Fact Book

P9-DOC-049

A National Football League Book.
Workman Publishing Co., New York.

National Football League, 1992

410 Park Avenue, New York, N.Y. 10022   (212) 758-1500

Commissioner: Paul Tagliabue
President: Neil Austrian
Executive Vice President and League Counsel: Jay Moyer
Executive Vice President for Labor Relations/Chairman NFLMC: Harold Henderson
Vice President of Communications and Development: Joe Browne
Vice President of Broadcasting and Productions: Val Pinchbeck, Jr.
Vice President of Operations: Roger Goodell
Treasurer: Tom Sullivan
Executive Director for Special Events: Jim Steeg
Executive Director/General Counsel NFLMC: Dennis Curran

ADMINISTRATION
Director of Administration: John Buzzeo
Comptroller: Joe Siclare

BROADCASTING
Director of Broadcast Services: Dick Maxwell
Assistant Director of Broadcasting/Productions: Nancy Behar

COMMUNICATIONS
Director of Communications: Greg Aiello
Director of Information: Pete Abitante
Director of Information, AFC: Leslie Hammond
Director of Information, NFC: Reggie Roberts

OFFICIATING
Director of Officiating: Jerry Seeman
Assistant Director of Officiating: Jack Reader
Supervisor of Officials: Leo Miles
Supervisor of Officials: Ron DeSouza

OPERATIONS
Director of Game Operations: Jan Van Duser
Director of Planning: Don Weiss
Director of Club Administration: Joe Ellis
Assistant Director of Game Operations: Tim Davey
Special Projects: Bill Granholm

PLAYER EMPLOYMENT
Director of Labor Operations: John Jones
Director of Labor Planning and Research: Peter Ruocco
Director of Player Personnel: Joel Bussert
Director of Player Programs: Lem Burnham
Labor Relations Counsel: Lal Heneghan
Labor Relations Counsel: Rapheal Prevot

SECURITY
Director of Security: Warren Welsh
Assistant Director of Security: Charles R. Jackson, Jr.

SPECIAL EVENTS
Assistant Director of Special Events: Susan McCann Minogue

Cover Photograph by Andy Hayt

Printed in the United States of America.

A National Football League Book.
Compiled by the NFL Communications Department and Seymour Siwoff, Elias Sports Bureau.
Edited by Reggie Roberts, NFL Communications Department and Chuck Garrity, Jr., NFLP Creative Services.
Statistics by Elias Sports Bureau.
Produced by NFL Properties, Inc., Creative Services Division.

Workman Publishing Co.
708 Broadway, New York, N.Y. 10003
Manufactured in the United States of America.
First printing, July 1992.

10 9 8 7 6 5 4 3 2 1

Index

A

Active List 13
AFC vs. NFC, 1970-1991 298
All-Pro Teams, 1991 170
Atlanta Falcons 84
Attendance, NFL's 10 Biggest Weekends . . . 309
Attendance, 1991 206
Attendance, Paid 309
Awards, 1991 169

B

Buffalo Bills 26

C

Calendar, 1992-93 12
Chicago All-Star Game 297
Chicago Bears 88
Chronology of Professional Football 232
Cincinnati Bengals 30
Cleveland Browns 34
Coaches, Active, Career Victories 22
Coaches, 100 Career Victories 22

D

Dallas Cowboys 92
Denver Broncos 38
Detroit Lions 96
Draft, All-Time Number-One Choices 310
Draft, 1992 20

F

First-Round Selections 311

G

Green Bay Packers 100

H

Houston Oilers 42

I

Indianapolis Colts 46
International Games 297

K

Kansas City Chiefs 50

L

Los Angeles Raiders 54
Los Angeles Rams 104

M

Miami Dolphins 58
Minnesota Vikings 108
Monday Night Football 300

N

New England Patriots 62
New Orleans Saints 112
New York Giants 116
New York Jets 66
1991 Season Recap
   1991 Preseason Standings and Results . . . 143
   1991 Regular-Season Standings and Results . . . 144
   1991 Best Passing Performances 173
   1991 Best Pass Receiving Performances . . . 174
   1991 Best Rushing Performances 172
   1991 Best Sack Performances 175
   1991 Week by Week 146

O

Official Signals 378
Officials, 1992 Roster of 376
Overtime, History of 304

P

Passer Rating System 15
Philadelphia Eagles 120
Phoenix Cardinals 124
Pittsburgh Steelers 70

Playoff Bowl 297
Playoff Games
   AFC Championship Games 284
   AFC Divisional Playoff Games 287
   AFC First-Round Playoff Games 289
   NFC Championship Games 286
   NFC Divisional Playoff Games 288
   NFC First-Round Playoff Games 290
Pro Bowl, Game Summaries 291
Pro Bowl, Records 370
Pro Football Hall of Fame 228
Pro Football Hall of Fame Games 297

R

Records, All-Time 318
Records, Postseason 361
Reserve Lists 13
Roster Limits 13
Rules, Digest of 382

S

San Diego Chargers 74
San Francisco 49ers 128
Schedule, Figuring 1993 16
Schedule, 1992 Season 4
Scoring, Top 10 Weekends 309
Seattle Seahawks 78
Standings, 1920-1991 241
Statistics
   AFC Active Leaders 18
   Inside the Numbers, Statistical Highlights . . . 208
   NFC Active Leaders 19
   Outstanding Performers 339
   What to Look for in 1992 23
   Yearly Leaders 345
Statistics, 1991
   AFC, NFC, and NFL Summary 180
   American Football Conference Team Defense . . . 177
   American Football Conference Team Offense . . . 176
   Club Leaders 181
   Club Rankings by Yards 181
   Individual Field Goals 185
   Individual Fumbles 200
   Individual Interceptions 193
   Individual Kickoff Returns 198
   Individual Passing 188
   Individual Pass Receiving 191
   Individual Punting 195
   Individual Punt Returns 197
   Individual Rushing 186
   Individual Sacks 204
   Individual Scoring 182
   National Football Conference Team Defense . . . 179
   National Football Conference Team Offense . . . 178
   Takeaway-Giveaway Table 181
Super Bowl, Game Summaries 277
Super Bowl, Records 353

T

Tampa Bay Buccaneers 132
Team vs. Team Results 250
Television, 10 Most Watched Programs in TV History . . . 309
Television, Top 10 Televised Sports Events . . . 309
Tie-Breaking Procedures 14
Trades, 1991-92 142
Trading Period 13

W

Waivers 13
Washington Redskins 136

(All times local except Tokyo, London, and Berlin which are EDT)
Nationally televised games in parentheses.

Preseason/First Week

Saturday, August 1	Hall of Fame Game at Canton, Ohio	(ABC)	3:00
	New York Jets ___ vs. Philadelphia ___		
	American Bowl '92 at Tokyo	(ESPN)	10:00*
	Houston ___ vs. Dallas ___		
	Miami ___ vs. Washington ___		8:00
	at Orlando, Fla.		
Monday, August 3	Denver ___ at San Francisco ___		5:00
Thursday, August 6	Los Angeles Rams ___ at Seattle ___		6:00
Friday, August 7	Dallas ___ at Miami ___		8:00
Saturday, August 8	Atlanta ___ at Cleveland ___		7:00
	Buffalo ___ at Minnesota ___		7:00
	Houston ___ at Detroit ___		7:00
	Kansas City ___ at Green Bay ___		7:00
	Los Angeles Raiders ___ at San Francisco ___		5:00
	New England ___ at Indianapolis ___		6:30
	Philadelphia ___ at Pittsburgh ___		7:00
	San Diego ___ at Phoenix ___		7:30
	Tampa Bay ___ at Denver ___		4:00
	Washington ___ at New York Jets ___		8:00
Sunday, August 9	Cincinnati ___ at New York Giants ___	(TNT)	7:00
Monday, August 10	New Orleans ___ at Chicago ___	(ABC)	7:00

*Tokyo game actual kickoff 11:00 A.M. August 2.

Preseason/Second Week

Friday, August 14	San Diego ___ at New England ___		7:00
Saturday, August 15	American Bowl '92 at Berlin	(NBC)	1:00*
	Denver ___ vs. Miami ___		
	Atlanta ___ at Tampa Bay ___		7:00
	Chicago ___ at Phoenix ___		5:00
	Cincinnati ___ at Philadelphia ___		7:30
	Cleveland ___ at New York Giants ___	(CBS)	8:00
	Houston ___ at Dallas ___		8:00
	Kansas City ___ at Minnesota ___		7:30
	Los Angeles Raiders ___ at Los Angeles Rams ___		7:00
	Seattle ___ at Indianapolis ___		7:30
Sunday, August 16	New York Jets ___ vs. Green Bay ___		3:00
	at Madison, Wis.		
	American Bowl '92 at London	(NBC)	1:00*
	San Francisco ___ vs. Washington ___		
Monday, August 17	Detroit ___ at Buffalo ___	(ESPN)	8:00
	Pittsburgh ___ at New Orleans ___		7:00

*Berlin game actual kickoff 7:00 P.M. August 15;
London game actual kickoff 6:00 P.M. August 16.

Preseason/Third Week

Friday, August 21	San Francisco ___ at San Diego ___	(TNT)	5:00
Saturday, August 22	Denver ___ at Dallas ___		8:00
	Green Bay ___ at Los Angeles Rams ___		6:00
	Houston ___ at New Orleans ___	(CBS)	11:30
	Indianapolis ___ at Cincinnati ___		7:30
	New England ___ at Detroit ___		7:00
	New York Giants ___ at New York Jets ___		8:00
	Phoenix ___ at Seattle ___		7:00
	Tampa Bay ___ at Miami ___		8:00
	Washington ___ at Los Angeles Raiders ___		1:00
Sunday, August 23	Philadelphia ___ at Atlanta ___	(ABC)	1:30
	Pittsburgh ___ at Chicago ___	(TNT)	7:00
Monday, August 24	Buffalo ___ at Kansas City ___	(ABC)	7:00
	Minnesota ___ at Cleveland ___		6:00

Preseason/Fourth Week

Thursday, August 27	Los Angeles Rams ___ at San Diego ___	7:00
	New Orleans ___ vs. Miami ___	(ESPN) 8:00
	at Baltimore, Md.	
	New York Jets ___ at Philadelphia ___	7:30
Friday, August 28	Buffalo ___ at Atlanta ___	(NBC) 8:00
	Chicago ___ at Dallas ___	7:00
	Cleveland ___ at Tampa Bay ___	7:30
	Detroit ___ at Cincinnati ___	7:30
	Indianapolis ___ at Kansas City ___	7:00
	Phoenix ___ at Denver ___	7:00
	Seattle ___ at San Francisco ___	5:00
Saturday, August 29	Houston ___ at Los Angeles Raiders ___	1:00
	Minnesota ___ at Washington ___	(CBS) 8:00
	New England ___ vs. Green Bay ___	7:00
	at Milwaukee, Wis.	
	New York Giants ___ at Pittsburgh ___	7:00

First Week

Sunday, September 6	Cincinnati ___ at Seattle ___	1:00
(CBS-TV National Weekend)	Cleveland ___ at Indianapolis ___	12:00
	Detroit ___ at Chicago ___	12:00
	Kansas City ___ at San Diego ___	1:00
	Los Angeles Rams ___ at Buffalo ___	1:00
	Minnesota ___ at Green Bay ___	12:00
	New England ___ at Miami ___	4:00
	New Orleans ___ at Philadelphia ___	1:00
	New York Jets ___ at Atlanta ___	1:00
	Phoenix ___ at Tampa Bay ___	4:00
	Pittsburgh ___ at Houston ___	12:00
	San Francisco ___ at New York Giants ___	4:00
Sunday Night	Los Angeles Raiders ___ at Denver ___	(TNT) 6:00
Monday, September 7	Washington ___ at Dallas ___	(ABC) 8:00

Second Week

Sunday, September 13	Atlanta ___ at Washington ___	1:00
(NBC-TV National Weekend)	Buffalo ___ at San Francisco ___	1:00
	Chicago ___ at New Orleans ___	12:00
	Dallas ___ at New York Giants ___	1:00
	Green Bay ___ at Tampa Bay ___	1:00
	Houston ___ at Indianapolis ___	3:00
	Los Angeles Raiders ___ at Cincinnati ___	1:00
	Minnesota ___ at Detroit ___	1:00
	New England ___ at Los Angeles Rams ___	1:00
	New York Jets ___ at Pittsburgh ___	4:00
	San Diego ___ at Denver ___	2:00
	Seattle ___ at Kansas City ___	12:00
Sunday Night	Philadelphia ___ at Phoenix ___	(TNT) 5:00
Monday, September 14	Miami ___ at Cleveland ___	(ABC) 9:00

Third Week

Sunday, September 20	Cincinnati ___ at Green Bay ___	12:00
(CBS-TV National Weekend)	Cleveland ___ at Los Angeles Raiders ___	1:00
	Denver ___ at Philadelphia ___	1:00
	Detroit ___ at Washington ___	4:00
	Kansas City ___ at Houston ___	12:00
	Los Angeles Rams ___ at Miami ___	4:00
	New Orleans ___ at Atlanta ___	1:00
	Phoenix ___ at Dallas ___	3:00
	Pittsburgh ___ at San Diego ___	1:00
	San Francisco ___ at New York Jets ___	1:00
	Seattle ___ at New England ___	1:00
	Tampa Bay ___ at Minnesota ___	12:00
Sunday Night	Indianapolis ___ at Buffalo ___	(TNT) 8:00
Monday, September 21	New York Giants ___ at Chicago ___	(ABC) 8:00

Fourth Week
Open Date: Five NFC East Teams;
AFC East Fifth-Place Team

Sunday, September 27	Atlanta ___ at Chicago ___	12:00
(NBC-TV National Weekend)	Buffalo ___ at New England ___	1:00
	Denver ___ at Cleveland ___	1:00
	Miami ___ at Seattle ___	1:00
	Minnesota ___ at Cincinnati ___	1:00
	New York Jets ___ at Los Angeles Rams ___	1:00
	Pittsburgh ___ at Green Bay ___	3:00
	San Diego ___ at Houston ___	12:00
	Tampa Bay ___ at Detroit ___	1:00
Sunday Night	San Francisco ___ at New Orleans ___	(TNT) 7:00
Monday, September 28	Los Angeles Raiders ___ at Kansas City ___	(ABC) 8:00

Fifth Week
Open Date: Four AFC Central Teams

Sunday, October 4	Chicago ___ at Minnesota ___	12:00
(CBS-TV National Weekend)	Green Bay ___ at Atlanta ___	1:00
	Indianapolis ___ at Tampa Bay ___	1:00
	Kansas City ___ at Denver ___	2:00
	Los Angeles Rams ___ at San Francisco ___	1:00
	Miami ___ at Buffalo ___	1:00
	New Orleans ___ at Detroit ___	1:00
	New York Giants ___ at Los Angeles Raiders ___	1:00
	Seattle ___ at San Diego ___	1:00
	Washington ___ at Phoenix ___	1:00
Sunday Night	New England ___ at New York Jets ___	(TNT) 8:00
Monday, October 5	Dallas ___ at Philadelphia ___	(ABC) 9:00

Sixth Week
Open Date: Five NFC Central Teams;
AFC West Fifth-Place Team

Sunday, October 11	Atlanta ___ at Miami ___	1:00
(NBC-TV National Weekend)	Buffalo ___ at Los Angeles Raiders ___	1:00
	Houston ___ at Cincinnati ___	4:00
	New York Jets ___ at Indianapolis ___	3:00
	Philadelphia ___ at Kansas City ___	12:00
	Phoenix ___ at New York Giants ___	1:00
	Pittsburgh ___ at Cleveland ___	1:00
	San Francisco ___ at New England ___	1:00
	Seattle ___ at Dallas ___	12:00
Sunday Night	Los Angeles Rams ___ at New Orleans ___	(TNT) 6:30
Monday, October 12	Denver ___ at Washington ___	(ABC) 9:00

Seventh Week
Open Date: Four AFC East Teams

Thursday, October 15	Detroit ___ at Minnesota ___	(TNT) 6:30
Sunday, October 18	Atlanta ___ at San Francisco ___	1:00
(CBS-TV National Weekend)	Green Bay ___ at Cleveland ___	1:00
	Houston ___ at Denver ___	2:00
	Kansas City ___ at Dallas ___	12:00
	Los Angeles Raiders ___ at Seattle ___	1:00
	New Orleans ___ at Phoenix ___	1:00
	New York Giants ___ at Los Angeles Rams ___	1:00
	Philadelphia ___ at Washington ___	1:00
	San Diego ___ at Indianapolis ___	12:00
	Tampa Bay ___ at Chicago ___	12:00
Monday, October 19	Cincinnati ___ at Pittsburgh ___	(ABC) 9:00

Eighth Week
Open Date: Four NFC West Teams

Sunday, October 25	Chicago ___ at Green Bay ___	12:00
(NBC-TV National Weekend)	Cincinnati ___ at Houston ___	12:00
	Cleveland ___ at New England ___	4:00
	Dallas ___ at Los Angeles Raiders ___	1:00
	Denver ___ at San Diego ___	1:00
	Detroit ___ at Tampa Bay ___	1:00
	Indianapolis ___ at Miami ___	4:00
	Phoenix ___ at Philadelphia ___	1:00
	Seattle ___ at New York Giants ___	1:00
	Washington ___ at Minnesota ___	12:00
Sunday Night	Pittsburgh ___ at Kansas City ___	(TNT) 6:30
Monday, October 26	Buffalo ___ at New York Jets ___	(ABC) 9:00

Ninth Week
Open Date: Four AFC West Teams

Sunday, November 1	Cleveland ___ at Cincinnati ___	4:00
(CBS-TV National Weekend)	Green Bay ___ at Detroit ___	1:00
	Houston ___ at Pittsburgh ___	1:00
	Indianapolis ___ at San Diego ___	1:00
	Los Angeles Rams ___ at Atlanta ___	1:00
	Miami ___ at New York Jets ___	1:00
	New England ___ at Buffalo ___	1:00
	Philadelphia ___ at Dallas ___	3:00
	San Francisco ___ at Phoenix ___	2:00
	Tampa Bay ___ at New Orleans ___	12:00
Sunday Night	New York Giants ___ at Washington ___	(TNT) 8:00
Monday, November 2	Minnesota ___ at Chicago ___	(ABC) 8:00

Tenth Week

Sunday, November 8	Cleveland ___ at Houston ___	12:00
(NBC-TV National Weekend)	Dallas ___ at Detroit ___	1:00
	Green Bay ___ at New York Giants ___	1:00
	Los Angeles Raiders ___ at Philadelphia ___	1:00
	Miami ___ at Indianapolis ___	1:00
	Minnesota ___ at Tampa Bay ___	1:00
	New Orleans ___ at New England ___	1:00
	New York Jets ___ at Denver ___	2:00
	Phoenix ___ at Los Angeles Rams ___	1:00
	Pittsburgh ___ at Buffalo ___	4:00
	San Diego ___ at Kansas City ___	3:00
	Washington ___ at Seattle ___	1:00
Sunday Night	Cincinnati ___ at Chicago ___	(ESPN) 7:00
Monday, November 9	San Francisco ___ at Atlanta ___	(ABC) 9:00

Eleventh Week

Sunday, November 15	Chicago ___ at Tampa Bay ___	4:00
(CBS-TV National Weekend)	Cincinnati ___ at New York Jets ___	1:00
	Detroit ___ at Pittsburgh ___	1:00
	Houston ___ at Minnesota ___	12:00
	Los Angeles Rams ___ at Dallas ___	12:00
	New England ___ at Indianapolis ___	1:00
	New Orleans ___ at San Francisco ___	1:00
	Philadelphia ___ vs. Green Bay ___ at Milwaukee	12:00
	Phoenix ___ at Atlanta ___	1:00
	San Diego ___ at Cleveland ___	1:00
	Seattle ___ at Los Angeles Raiders ___	1:00
	Washington ___ at Kansas City ___	12:00
Sunday Night	New York Giants ___ at Denver ___	(ESPN) 6:00
Monday, November 16	Buffalo ___ at Miami ___	(ABC) 9:00

Twelfth Week

Sunday, November 22	Atlanta ___ at Buffalo ___		1:00
(NBC-TV National Weekend)	Cleveland ___ at Minnesota ___		12:00
	Dallas ___ at Phoenix ___		2:00
	Denver ___ at Los Angeles Raiders ___		1:00
	Detroit ___ at Cincinnati ___		1:00
	Green Bay ___ at Chicago ___		12:00
	Houston ___ at Miami ___		1:00
	Indianapolis ___ at Pittsburgh ___		1:00
	New York Jets ___ at New England ___		4:00
	Philadelphia ___ at New York Giants ___		1:00
	San Francisco ___ at Los Angeles Rams ___		1:00
	Tampa Bay ___ at San Diego ___		1:00
Sunday Night	Kansas City ___ at Seattle ___	(ESPN) 5:00
Monday, November 23	Washington ___ at New Orleans ___	(ABC) 8:00

Thirteenth Week

Thursday, November 26	Houston ___ at Detroit ___	(NBC) 12:30
Thanksgiving Day	New York Giants ___ at Dallas ___	(CBS) 3:00
Sunday, November 29	Buffalo ___ at Indianapolis ___	4:00
(CBS-TV National Weekend)	Chicago ___ at Cleveland ___	1:00
	Kansas City ___ at New York Jets ___	1:00
	Miami ___ at New Orleans ___	12:00
	Minnesota ___ at Los Angeles Rams ___	1:00
	New England ___ at Atlanta ___	1:00
	Philadelphia ___ at San Francisco ___	1:00
	Phoenix ___ at Washington ___	1:00
	Pittsburgh ___ at Cincinnati ___	1:00
	Tampa Bay ___ vs. Green Bay ___ at Milwaukee	12:00
Sunday Night	Los Angeles Raiders ___ at San Diego ___	(ESPN) 5:00
Monday, November 30	Denver ___ at Seattle ___	(ABC) 6:00

Fourteenth Week

Thursday, December 3	Atlanta ___ at New Orleans ___	(ESPN) 7:00
Sunday, December 6	Cincinnati ___ at Cleveland ___	1:00
(NBC-TV National Weekend)	Dallas ___ at Denver ___	2:00
	Detroit ___ vs. Green Bay ___ at Milwaukee	12:00
	Indianapolis ___ at New England ___	1:00
	Kansas City ___ at Los Angeles Raiders ___	1:00
	Miami ___ at San Francisco ___	1:00
	Minnesota ___ at Philadelphia ___	1:00
	New York Jets ___ at Buffalo ___	1:00
	San Diego ___ at Phoenix ___	2:00
	Seattle ___ at Pittsburgh ___	1:00
	Washington ___ at New York Giants ___	4:00
Sunday Night	Los Angeles Rams ___ at Tampa Bay ___	(ESPN) 8:00
Monday, December 7	Chicago ___ at Houston ___	(ABC) 8:00

Fifteenth Week

Saturday, December 12	Denver ___ at Buffalo ___	(NBC) 12:30
	New York Giants ___ at Phoenix ___	(CBS) 2:00
Sunday, December 13	Atlanta ___ at Tampa Bay ___	1:00
(CBS-TV National Weekend)	Cincinnati ___ at San Diego ___	1:00
	Cleveland ___ at Detroit ___	1:00
	Dallas ___ at Washington ___	1:00
	Indianapolis ___ at New York Jets ___	1:00
	New England ___ at Kansas City ___	12:00
	New Orleans ___ at Los Angeles Rams ___	1:00
	Philadelphia ___ at Seattle ___	1:00
	Pittsburgh ___ at Chicago ___	12:00
	San Francisco ___ at Minnesota ___	12:00
Sunday Night	Green Bay ___ at Houston ___	(ESPN) 7:00
Monday, December 14	Los Angeles Raiders ___ at Miami ___	(ABC) 9:00

Sixteenth Week

Saturday, December 19
Kansas City ___ at New York Giants ___	(NBC)	12:30
Tampa Bay ___ at San Francisco ___	(CBS)	1:00

Sunday, December 20
(NBC-TV National Weekend)
Buffalo ___ at New Orleans ___	12:00
Chicago ___ at Detroit ___	4:00
Houston ___ at Cleveland ___	1:00
Los Angeles Rams ___ at Green Bay ___	12:00
Minnesota ___ at Pittsburgh ___	1:00
New England ___ at Cincinnati ___	1:00
Phoenix ___ at Indianapolis ___	1:00
San Diego ___ at Los Angeles Raiders ___	1:00
Seattle ___ at Denver ___	2:00
Washington ___ at Philadelphia ___	1:00

Sunday Night
New York Jets ___ at Miami ___   (ESPN) 8:00

Monday, December 21
Dallas ___ at Atlanta ___   (ABC) 9:00

Seventeenth Week

Saturday, December 26
Los Angeles Raiders ___ at Washington ___	(NBC)	4:00
New Orleans ___ at New York Jets ___	(CBS)	12:30

Sunday, December 27
(CBS-TV National Weekend)
Atlanta ___ at Los Angeles Rams ___	1:00
Chicago ___ at Dallas ___	3:00
Cleveland ___ at Pittsburgh ___	1:00
Denver ___ at Kansas City ___	12:00
Green Bay ___ at Minnesota ___	12:00
Indianapolis ___ at Cincinnati ___	1:00
Miami ___ at New England ___	1:00
New York Giants ___ at Philadelphia ___	1:00
San Diego ___ at Seattle ___	1:00
Tampa Bay ___ at Phoenix ___	2:00

Sunday Night
Buffalo ___ at Houston ___   (ESPN) 7:00

Monday, December 28
Detroit ___ at San Francisco ___   (ABC) 6:00

Wild Card Playoff Games

Site Priorities
Three Wild Card teams (division non-champions with best three records) from each conference and the division champion with the third-best record in each conference will enter the first round of the playoffs. The division champion with the third-best record will play host to the Wild Card team with the third-best record. The Wild Card team with the best record will play host to the Wild Card team with the second-best record. There are no restrictions on intra-division games.

Saturday, January 2, 1993   American Football Conference

_____ at _____ (ABC)

National Football Conference

_____ at _____ (ABC)

Sunday, January 3, 1993   American Football Conference

_____ at _____ (NBC)

National Football Conference

_____ at _____ (CBS)

Divisional Playoff Games

Site Priorities
In each conference, the two division champions with the highest won-lost-tied percentage during the regular season will play host to the Wild Card winners. The division champion with the best record in each conference is assured of playing the Wild Card survivor with the poorest record. There are no restrictions on intra-division games.

Saturday, January 9, 1993   American Football Conference

_____ at _____ (NBC)

National Football Conference

_____ at _____ (CBS)

Sunday, January 10, 1993   American Football Conference

_____ at _____ (NBC)

National Football Conference

_____ at _____ (CBS)

Conference Championship Games, Super Bowl XXVII, and AFC-NFC Pro Bowl

Site Priorities for Championship Games

The home teams will be the surviving playoff winners with the best won-lost-tied percentage during the regular season. A Wild Card team cannot play host unless two Wild Card teams are in the game, in which case the Wild Card team with the best record will play host.

Sunday, January 17, 1993   American Football Conference Championship Game

_____ at _____ (NBC)

National Football Conference Championship Game

_____ at _____ (CBS)

Sunday, January 31, 1993   Super Bowl XXVII at Rose Bowl, Pasadena, California

_____ vs. _____ (NBC)

Sunday, February 7, 1993   AFC-NFC Pro Bowl at Honolulu, Hawaii

AFC _____ vs. NFC _____ (ESPN)

Postseason Games

Saturday, January 2	AFC and NFC Wild Card Playoffs (ABC)
Sunday, January 3	AFC and NFC Wild Card Playoffs (NBC and CBS)
Saturday, January 9	AFC and NFC Divisional Playoffs (NBC and CBS)
Sunday, January 10	AFC and NFC Divisional Playoffs (NBC and CBS)
Sunday, January 17	AFC and NFC Championship Games (NBC and CBS)
Sunday, January 31	Super Bowl XXVII at Rose Bowl, Pasadena, California (NBC)
Sunday, February 7	AFC-NFC Pro Bowl at Honolulu, Hawaii (ESPN)

1992 Nationally Televised Games

(All games carried on CBS Radio Network.)

Regular Season

Sunday, September 6	Los Angeles Raiders at Denver (night, TNT)
Monday, September 7	Washington at Dallas (night, ABC)
Sunday, September 13	Philadelphia at Phoenix (night, TNT)
Monday, September 14	Miami at Cleveland (night, ABC)
Sunday, September 20	Indianapolis at Buffalo (night, TNT)
Monday, September 21	New York Giants at Chicago (night, ABC)
Sunday, September 27	San Francisco at New Orleans (night, TNT)
Monday, September 28	Los Angeles Raiders at Kansas City (night, ABC)
Sunday, October 4	New England at New York Jets (night, TNT)
Monday, October 5	Dallas at Philadelphia (night, ABC)
Sunday, October 11	Los Angeles Rams at New Orleans (night, TNT)
Monday, October 12	Denver at Washington (night, ABC)
Thursday, October 15	Detroit at Minnesota (night, TNT)
Monday, October 19	Cincinnati at Pittsburgh (night, ABC)
Sunday, October 25	Pittsburgh at Kansas City (night, TNT)
Monday, October 26	Buffalo at New York Jets (night, ABC)
Sunday, November 1	New York Giants at Washington (night, TNT)
Monday, November 2	Minnesota at Chicago (night, ABC)
Sunday, November 8	Cincinnati at Chicago (night, ESPN)
Monday, November 9	San Francisco at Atlanta (night, ABC)
Sunday, November 15	New York Giants at Denver (night, ESPN)
Monday, November 16	Buffalo at Miami (night, ABC)
Sunday, November 22	Kansas City at Seattle (night, ESPN)
Monday, November 23	Washington at New Orleans (night, ABC)
Thursday, November 26	Houston at Detroit (day, NBC)
	New York Giants at Dallas (day, CBS)
Sunday, November 29	Los Angeles Raiders at San Diego (night, ESPN)
Monday, November 30	Denver at Seattle (night, ABC)
Thursday, December 3	Atlanta at New Orleans (night, ESPN)
Sunday, December 6	Los Angeles Rams at Tampa Bay (night, ESPN)
Monday, December 7	Chicago at Houston (night, ABC)
Saturday, December 12	Denver at Buffalo (day, NBC)
	New York Giants at Phoenix (day, CBS)
Sunday, December 13	Green Bay at Houston (night, ESPN)
Monday, December 14	Los Angeles Raiders at Miami (night, ABC)
Saturday, December 19	Kansas City at New York Giants (day, NBC)
	Tampa Bay at San Francisco (day, CBS)
Sunday, December 20	New York Jets at Miami (night, ESPN)
Monday, December 21	Dallas at Atlanta (night, ABC)
Saturday, December 26	Los Angeles Raiders at Washington (day, NBC)
	New Orleans at New York Jets (day, CBS)
Sunday, December 27	Buffalo at Houston (night, ESPN)
Monday, December 28	Detroit at San Francisco (night, ABC)

1992 AFC-NFC Interconference Games

(All times local.)

September 6	Los Angeles Rams at Buffalo	1:00
	New York Jets at Atlanta	1:00
September 13	Buffalo at San Francisco	1:00
	New England at Los Angeles Rams	1:00
September 20	Cincinnati at Green Bay	12:00
	Denver at Philadelphia	1:00
	Los Angeles Rams at Miami	4:00
	San Francisco at New York Jets	1:00
September 27	Minnesota at Cincinnati	1:00
	New York Jets at Los Angeles Rams	1:00
	Pittsburgh at Green Bay	3:00
October 4	Indianapolis at Tampa Bay	1:00
	New York Giants at L.A. Raiders	1:00
October 11	Atlanta at Miami	1:00
	Philadelphia at Kansas City	12:00
	San Francisco at New England	1:00
	Seattle at Dallas	12:00
October 12	Denver at Washington	9:00
October 18	Green Bay at Cleveland	1:00
	Kansas City at Dallas	12:00
October 25	Dallas at Los Angeles Raiders	1:00
	Seattle at New York Giants	1:00
November 8	Cincinnati at Chicago	7:00
	Los Angeles Raiders at Philadelphia	1:00
	New Orleans at New England	1:00
	Washington at Seattle	1:00
November 15	Detroit at Pittsburgh	1:00
	Houston at Minnesota	12:00
	New York Giants at Denver	6:00
	Washington at Kansas City	12:00
November 22	Atlanta at Buffalo	1:00
	Cleveland at Minnesota	12:00
	Detroit at Cincinnati	1:00
	Tampa Bay at San Diego	1:00
November 26	Houston at Detroit	12:30
November 29	Chicago at Cleveland	1:00
	Miami at New Orleans	12:00
	New England at Atlanta	1:00
December 6	Dallas at Denver	2:00
	Miami at San Francisco	1:00
	San Diego at Phoenix	2:00
December 7	Chicago at Houston	8:00
December 13	Cleveland at Detroit	1:00
	Green Bay at Houston	7:00
	Philadelphia at Seattle	1:00
	Pittsburgh at Chicago	12:00
December 19	Kansas City at New York Giants	12:30
December 20	Buffalo at New Orleans	12:00
	Minnesota at Pittsburgh	1:00
	Phoenix at Indianapolis	1:00
December 26	Los Angeles Raiders at Washington	4:00
	New Orleans at New York Jets	12:30

Important Dates

1992 Season

July 7	Claiming period of 24 hours begins in waiver system. All waiver requests for the rest of the year are no-recall and no-withdrawal.
Mid-July	Preseason training camps open. Clubs are not permitted to open official preseason camp earlier than July 5.
July 15	Deadline for a player who has practiced and/or played in a minor league in 1992 to sign in the NFL without being required to clear Procedural Recall waivers.
August 1	Hall of Fame Game, Canton, Ohio: New York Jets vs. Philadelphia
August 1	American Bowl '92, Tokyo, Japan: Houston vs. Dallas
August 7-9	First preseason weekend.
August 14-16	Second preseason weekend.
August 15	American Bowl '92, Berlin, Germany: Denver vs. Miami
August 16	American Bowl '92, London, England: Washington vs. San Francisco
August 21-23	Third preseason weekend.
August 25	Roster cutdown to maximum of 60 players on Active List by 4 P.M., Eastern time.
August 26	All tryouts on this date for the remainder of the season must be reported to the league office.
August 28-30	Fourth preseason weekend.
August 31	Roster cutdown to maximum of 47 players on Active List by 12 noon, Eastern time.
September 1	All clubs are required to file a personnel (injury) report with their conference Director of Information by 1 P.M., Eastern time, on this Tuesday and thereafter on each Wednesday before a regular-season game. The report is to be updated by 1 P.M., Eastern time, each Thursday.
September 6-7	Regular season opens.
September 22	Priority on multiple waiver claims is now based on the current season's standings.
October 13	All trading ends at 4 P.M., Eastern time.
October 20-21	NFL Fall Meeting, Chicago, Illinois.
November 28	Deadline for reinstatement of players in Reserve List categories of Retired, Did Not Report, and Veteran Free Agent Asked to Re-Sign.
December 21-22	Balloting for AFC-NFC Pro Bowl.
December 25	Deadline for waiver requests in 1992, except for "special waiver requests" by teams participating in playoffs.
January 2-3	AFC and NFC Wild Card Playoff Games.
January 9-10	AFC and NFC Divisional Playoff Games.
January 17	AFC and NFC Championship Games.
January 31	Super Bowl XXVII at Rose Bowl, Pasadena, California.
February 1	Trading period begins.
February 1	Deadline for establishing Protected List of 37 players. All players who are not on Protected List will be eligible to sign as free agents with any other club through April 1.
February 7	AFC-NFC Pro Bowl at Aloha Stadium, Honolulu, Hawaii.

1993 Season

February 8	Waiver system begins for 1993.
February 10-15	Combine timing and testing of college players, Hoosier Dome, Indianapolis, Indiana.
March 14-19	NFL Annual Meeting, Palm Springs, California.
April 1	Expiration of free agency period for unprotected players.
April 25-26	58th Annual NFL Selection Meeting, New York, New York.
May 25-26	NFL Spring Meeting, Atlanta, Georgia.
July 31	Hall of Fame Game, Canton, Ohio: Los Angeles Raiders vs. Green Bay.
August 6-8	First preseason weekend.
September 5-6	Regular season opens.
January 2-3	Regular season closes.
January 8-9	AFC and NFC Wild Card Playoff Games.
January 15-16	AFC and NFC Divisional Playoff Games.
January 23	AFC and NFC Championship Games.
January 30	Super Bowl XXVIII at Georgia Dome, Atlanta, Georgia.
February 6	AFC-NFC Pro Bowl.

Future Pro Football Hall of Fame Games

1994	Denver Broncos (AFC) vs. Dallas Cowboys (NFC)
1995	San Diego Chargers (AFC) vs. Atlanta Falcons (NFC)
1996	Indianapolis Colts (AFC) vs. New Orleans Saints (NFC)
1997	Seattle Seahawks (AFC) vs. Minnesota Vikings (NFC)
1998	Pittsburgh Steelers (AFC) vs. Tampa Bay Buccaneers (NFC)

Waivers

The waiver system is a procedure by which player contracts or NFL rights to players are made available by a club to other clubs in the League. During the procedure, the 27 other clubs either file claims to obtain the players or waive the opportunity to do so—thus the term "waiver." Claiming clubs are assigned players on a priority based on the inverse of won-and-lost standing. The claiming period normally is 10 days during the offseason and 24 hours from early July through December. In some circumstances, another 24 hours is added on to allow the original club to rescind its action (known as a recall of a waiver request) and/or the claiming club to do the same (known as withdrawal of a claim). If a player passes through waivers unclaimed and is not recalled by the original club, he becomes a free agent. All waivers from July through December are no recall and no withdrawal. Under the Collective Bargaining Agreement, from the beginning of the waiver system each year on the day after the Pro Bowl through the trading deadline (October 13, 1992), any veteran who has acquired four years of pension credit may, if about to be assigned to another club through the waiver system, reject such assignment and become a free agent.

Active List

The Active List is the principal status for players participating for a club. It consists of all players under contract, including option, who are eligible for preseason, regular season, and postseason games. In 1992, teams will be permitted to open training camp with no more than 80 players under contract and thereafter must meet a series of mandatory roster reductions prior to the season opener. Teams will be permitted an Active List of 45 players and an Inactive List of two players for each regular-season and postseason game during the 1992 season. Provided that a club has two quarterbacks on its 45-player Active List, a third quarterback from its Inactive List is permitted to dress for the game, but if he participates in the game, the other two quarterbacks are thereafter prohibited from playing.

August 25 . . . . active list of 60 players
August 31 . . . . active list of 45 players (plus two-player Inactive List)

In addition to the Active List limits described above, there also is an overall roster limit of 80 players that is applicable to players on a club's Active, Inactive, or Exempt Lists, and any players on Reserve as Injured, Physically Unable to Perform, Non-Football Illness/Injury, and Suspended.

Reserve List

The Reserve List is a status for players who, for reasons of injury, retirement, military service, or other circumstances, are not immediately available for participation with a club. Players on Reserve/Injured are not eligible to practice or return to the Active List until four regular-season games have been played.

Each club will have five free activations for players placed on Reserve/Injured after the final cutdown. Players also can be returned to the club's Active List if they clear Procedural Recall waivers. Any player placed on Reserve/Injured prior to or concurrent with the final cutdown on August 31 may not return to the club nor practice with the team that year. Clubs participating in postseason competition will be granted an additional activation for each postseason game, provided they have exhausted all previous activations.

Players in the category of Reserve/Retired, Reserve/Did Not Report, or Reserve/Veteran Free Agent Asked to Re-Sign may not be reinstated during the period from 30 days before the end of the regular season through the postseason.

Trades

Unrestricted trading between the AFC and NFC is allowed in 1992 through October 13, after which trading will end until February 1, 1993.

Annual Active Player Limits

NFL

Year(s)	Limit
1985-92	45
1983-84	49
1982	45†-49
1978-81	45
1975-77	43
1974	47
1964-73	40
1963	37
1961-62	36
1960	38
1959	36
1957-58	35
1951-56	33
1949-50	32
1948	35
1947	35*-34
1945-46	33
1943-44	28
1940-42	33
1938-39	30
1936-37	25
1935	24
1930-34	20
1926-29	18
1925	16

†45 for first two games
*35 for first three games

AFL

Year(s)	Limit
1966-69	40
1965	38
1964	34
1962-63	33
1960-61	35

Tie-Breaking Procedures

The following procedures will be used to break standings ties for postseason playoffs and to determine regular-season schedules.

To Break a Tie Within a Division

If, at the end of the regular season, two or more clubs in the same division finish with identical won-lost-tied percentages, the following steps will be taken until a champion is determined.

Two Clubs

1. Head-to-head (best won-lost-tied percentage in games between the clubs).
2. Best won-lost-tied percentage in games played within the division.
3. Best won-lost-tied percentage in games played within the conference.
4. Best won-lost-tied percentage in common games, if applicable.
5. Best net points in division games.
6. Best net points in all games.
7. Strength of schedule.
8. Best net touchdowns in all games.
9. Coin toss.

Three or More Clubs

(Note: If one team wins multiple-team tiebreaker to advance to playoff round, remaining teams revert to step 1 of applicable two-club format, i.e., either in division tiebreaker or Wild Card tiebreaker. If two teams in a multiple-team tie possess superior marks in a tiebreaking step, this pair of teams revert to top of applicable two-club format to break tie. One team advances to playoff round, while other returns to original group and step 1 of applicable tiebreaker).

1. Head-to-head (best won-lost-tied percentage in games among the clubs).
2. Best won-lost-tied percentage in games played within the division.
3. Best won-lost-tied percentage in games played within the conference.
4. Best won-lost-tied percentage in common games.
5. Best net points in division games.
6. Best net points in all games.
7. Strength of schedule.
8. Best net touchdowns in all games.
9. Coin toss.

To Break a Tie for the Wild Card Team

If it is necessary to break ties to determine the three Wild Card clubs from each conference, the following steps will be taken.
1. If the tied clubs are from the same division, apply division tiebreaker.
2. If the tied clubs are from different divisions, apply the following steps.

Two Clubs

1. Head-to-head, if applicable.
2. Best won-lost-tied percentage in games played within the conference.
3. Best won-lost-tied percentage in common games, minimum of four.
4. Best average net points in conference games.
5. Best net points in all games.
6. Strength of schedule.
7. Best net touchdowns in all games.
8. Coin toss.

Three or More Clubs

(Note: If two clubs remain tied after third or other clubs are eliminated, tiebreaker reverts to step 1 of applicable two-club format.)

When the first Wild Card team has been identified, the procedure is repeated to name the second Wild Card, i.e., eliminate all but the highest-ranked club in each division prior to proceeding to step two, and repeated a third time, if necessary, to identify the third Wild Card. In situations where three or more teams from the same division are involved in the procedure, the original seeding of the teams remains the same for subsequent applications of the tiebreaker if the top-ranked team in that division qualifies for a Wild Card berth.

1. Apply division tiebreaker to eliminate all but highest-ranked club in each division prior to proceeding to step 2. The original seeding within a division upon application of the division tiebreaker remains the same for all subsequent applications of the procedure that are necessary to identify the three Wild Card participants.
2. Head-to-head sweep (Applicable only if one club has defeated each of the others or one club has lost to each of the others.)
3. Best won-lost-tied percentage in games played within the conference.
4. Best won-lost-tied percentage in common games, minimum of four.
5. Best average net points in conference games.
6. Best net points in all games.
7. Strength of schedule.
8. Best net touchdowns in all games.
9. Coin toss.

Other Tie-Breaking Procedures

1. Only one team advances to the playoffs in any tie-breaking step. Remaining tied teams revert to the first step of the division or Wild Card tiebreakers.
2. In comparing division and conference records or records against common opponents among tied teams, the best won-lost-tied percentage is the deciding factor since teams may have played an unequal number of games.
3. To determine home-field priority among division titlists, apply Wild Card tiebreakers.
4. To determine home-field priority for Wild Card qualifiers, apply division tiebreakers (if teams are from the same division) or Wild Card tiebreakers (if teams are from different divisions).

Tie-Breaking Procedure for Selection Meeting

If two or more clubs are tied for selection order, the conventional strength of schedule tiebreaker will be applied, subject to the following exceptions for all playoff teams.

1. The Super Bowl winner will be last and the Super Bowl loser will be next-to-last.
2. Any non-Super Bowl playoff team involved in the tie moves down in drafting priority as follows:
   A. Participation by a club in the playoffs without a victory adds one-half victory to the club's regular-season won-lost-tied record.
   B. For each victory in the playoffs, one full victory will be added to the club's regular-season won-lost-tied record.
3. Clubs with the best won-lost-tied records after these steps are applied will drop to their appropriate spots at the bottom of the tied segment. In no case will the above process move a club lower than the segment in which it was initially tied.
4. Tied clubs will alternate priority throughout the 12 rounds of the draft. In case of a tie involving three or more teams, the club with priority in the first round will drop to the bottom of the tied segment in the second round and move its way back to the top of the segment in each succeeding round.

NFL Passer Rating System

The NFL rates its forward passers for statistical purposes against a pre-fixed performance standard based on statistical achievements of all qualified pro passers since 1960. The system now being used replaced one that rated passers in relation to their position in a total group based on various criteria. The current system, which was adopted in 1973, removes inequities that existed in the former method and, at the same time, provides a means of comparing passing performances from one season to the next.

It is important to remember that the system is used to rate **passers,** not **quarterbacks.** Statistics do not reflect leadership, play-calling, and other intangible factors that go into making a successful professional quarterback. Four categories are used as a basis for compiling a rating:

— Percentage of touchdown passes per attempt
— Percentage of completions per attempt
— Percentage of interceptions per attempt
— Average yards gained per attempt

The base, or **average** standard, is 1.000. The bottom is .000. To earn a 2.000 rating, a passer must perform at exceptional levels, i.e., 70 percent in completions, 10 percent in touchdowns, 1.5 percent in interceptions, and 11 yards average gain per pass attempt. The **maximum** a passer can receive in any category is 2.375.

For example, to gain a 2.375 in completion percentage, a passer would have to complete 77.5 percent of his passes. The NFL record is 70.55 by Ken Anderson (Cincinnati, 1982). To gain 2.375 in percentage of interceptions, a passer would have to go the entire season without an interception. The 2.375 figure in average yards is 12.50, compared with the NFL record of 11.17 by Tommy O'Connell (Cleveland, 1957). To earn a 2.375 in percentage of touchdowns, a passer would have to achieve an 11.9. The record is 13.9 by Sid Luckman (Chicago, 1943).

In order to make the rating more understandable, the point rating is then converted into a scale of 100. For instance, if a passer completes 11 of 23 passes for 114 yards, with one touchdown and no interceptions, the four components would be:

— **Percentage of Completions**— 11 of 23 is 47.8 percent. The point rating is 0.890.

— **Percentage of Touchdown Passes**— 1 touchdown in 23 attempts works out to 4.3 percent for a rating of 0.860.

— **Percentage of Interceptions**— You can't do better than zero, so the passer receives a maximum rating of 2.375.

— **Average Yards Gained Per Attempt**— 23 attempts divided into 114 yards equals 4.96 yards per attempt for a corresponding rating of 0.490.

The sum of the four components is 4.615, which converts to a rating of 76.9. In order for a passer to achieve 100, his points would have to total 6.000. In rare cases, where statistical performance has been superior, it is possible for a passer to go over 100. However, such an instance is rare. The leading passers each year were checked from 1932 when the NFL began keeping official statistics, and only 12 passers in history have scored over 100 in the year they led the league in passing. The most recent passer to lead the league and score over 100 was San Francisco quarterback Steve Young, who achieved a 101.8 rating in 1991.

Figuring the 1993 NFL Schedule

As soon as the final game of the 1992 NFL regular season (Detroit at San Francisco on December 28) has been completed, it will be possible to determine the 1993 opponents of the 28 teams.

At the March, 1990, Owners' Meeting, the NFL announced it would play its 16-game schedule over 17 weeks. The 16-over-17 format provided each team one open weekend.

Each 1992 team schedule is based on a "common opponent" formula initiated for the 1978 season and most recently modified in 1987. Under the common opponent format, the first- through fourth-place teams in a division play at least 12 of their 16 games the following season against common opponents, and the fifth-place team in the division plays at least 10 common opponent games. It is not a position scheduling format in which the strong play the strong and the weak play the weak.

For years, the NFL had been seeking a more easily understood and balanced schedule that would provide both competitive equality and a variety of opponents. Under the old rotation scheduling system in effect from 1970-77, non-division opponents were determined by a pre-set formula. This often resulted in competitive imbalances.

With common opponents as the basis for scheduling, a more competitive and equitable method of determining division champions and postseason playoff representatives has developed. Teams battling for a division title are playing at least 75 percent of their games against common opponents.

In 1987, NFL owners passed a bylaw proposal designed to modify the common opponent scheduling format in the hopes of creating even more equity. Since then, the pairings with non-division opponents have been:

Prior Year's Finish in Division	Pairings in Non-Division Games Within Conference	Previous Pairings 1978-86
1	1-1-2-3	1-1-4-4
2	1-2-2-4	2-2-3-3
3	1-3-3-4	2-2-3-3
4	2-3-4-4	1-1-4-4

Under the common opponent format, schedules of any NFL team are figured according to one of the following three formulas. (The reference point for the figuring is the team's final division standing. Ties for a position in divisions are broken according to the tie-breaking procedures outlined on page 14. The chart on the following page is included for use as you go through each step.)

A. First- through fourth-place teams in a five-team division (AFC East, AFC West, NFC East, NFC Central).

1. Home-and-home round-robin within the division (8 games).
2. One game each with the first- through fourth-place teams in a division of the other conference (4 games). In 1993, the AFC East will play the NFC East, the AFC Central will play the NFC West, and the AFC West will play the NFC Central.
3. The first-place team plays the first-place teams in the other divisions within the conference plus a second- and third-place team within the conference. The second-place team plays the second-place teams in the other divisions within the conference plus a first- and fourth-place team within the conference. The third-place team plays the third-place teams in the other divisions within the conference plus a first- and fourth-place team within the conference. The fourth-place team plays the fourth-place teams in the other divisions within the conference plus a second- and third-place team within the conference (4 games).

This completes the 16-game schedule.

B. First- through fourth-place teams in a four-team division (AFC Central, NFC West).

1. Home-and-home round-robin within the division (6 games).
2. One game with each of the fifth-place teams in the conference (2 games).
3. The same procedure that is listed in step A2 (4 games).
4. The same procedure that is listed in step A3 (4 games).

This completes the 16-game schedule.

C. The fifth-place teams in a division (AFC East, AFC West, NFC East, NFC Central).

1. Home-and-home round-robin within the division (8 games).
2. One game with each team in the four-team division of the conference (4 games).
3. A home-and-home with the other fifth-place team in the conference (2 games).
4. One game each with the fifth-place teams in the other conference (2 games).

This completes the 16-game schedule.

The 1993 Opponent Breakdown chart on the following page does not include the round-robin games within the division. Those are automatically scheduled on a home-and-away basis.

1992 NFL Standings

A Team's 1993 Schedule

AFC　　　NFC

EAST AE　　　**EAST NE**

Team Name
_____

EAST AE

1 _____

2 _____

3 _____

4 _____

5 _____

EAST NE

1 _____

2 _____

3 _____

4 _____

5 _____

CENTRAL AC

1 _____

2 _____

3 _____

4 _____

WEST NW

1 _____

2 _____

3 _____

4 _____

WEST AW

1 _____

2 _____

3 _____

4 _____

5 _____

CENTRAL NC

1 _____

2 _____

3 _____

4 _____

5 _____

1993 Opponent Breakdown

(Certain game sites for interconference opponents are subject to change under NFL scheduling formulas.)

AE AFC EAST HOME	AWAY	AC AFC CENTRAL HOME	AWAY	AW AFC WEST HOME	AWAY	NE NFC EAST HOME	AWAY	NC NFC CENTRAL HOME	AWAY	NW NFC WEST HOME	AWAY
AE1 AC1	AW1	**AC1** AW1	AE1	**AW1** AE1	AC1	**NE1** NW1	NC1	**NC1** NE1	NW1	**NW1** NC1	NE1
AW2	AC3	AE2	AW3	AC2	AE3	NC2	NW3	NW2	NE3	NE2	NC3
NE1	NE2	AE5	AW5	NC1	NC2	AE2	AE1	AW2	AW1	NE5	NC5
NE3	NE4	NW1	NW2	NC3	NC4	AE4	AE3	AW4	AW3	AC2	AC1
		NW3	NW4							AC4	AC3
AE2 AC2	AW2	**AC2** AW2	AE2	**AW2** AE2	AC2	**NE2** NW2	NC2	**NC2** NE2	NW2	**NW2** NC2	NE2
AW4	AC1	AE4	AW1	AC4	AE1	NC4	NW1	NW4	NE1	NE4	NC1
NE2	NE1	AW5	AE5	NC2	NC1	AE1	AE2	AW1	AW2	NC5	NE5
NE4	NE3	NW2	NW1	NC4	NC3	AE3	AE1	AW3	AW4	AC1	AC2
		NW4	NW3							AC3	AC4
AE3 AC3	AW3	**AC3** AW3	AE3	**AW3** AE3	AC3	**NE3** NW3	NC3	**NC3** NE3	NW3	**NW3** NC3	NE3
AW1	AC4	AE1	AW4	AC1	AE4	NC1	NW4	NW1	NE4	NE1	NC4
NE1	NE2	AE5	AW5	NC1	NC2	AE2	AE1	AW2	AW1	NE5	NC5
NE3	NE4	NW1	NW2	NC3	NC4	AE4	AE3	AW4	AW3	AC2	AC1
		NW3	NW4							AC4	AC3
AE4 AC4	AW4	**AC4** AW4	AE4	**AW4** AE4	AC4	**NE4** NW4	NC4	**NC4** NE4	NW4	**NW4** NC4	NE4
AW3	AC2	AE3	AW2	AC3	AE2	NC3	NW2	NW3	NE2	NE3	NC2
NE2	NE1	AW5	AE5	NC2	NC1	AE1	AE2	AW1	AW2	NC5	NE5
NE4	NE3	NW2	NW1	NC4	NC3	AE3	AE4	AW3	AW4	AC1	AC2
		NW4	NW3							AC3	AC4
AE5 AC2	AC1			**AW5** AC1	AC2	**NE5** NW2	NW1	**NC5** NW1	NW2		
AC4	AC3			AC3	AC4	NW4	NW3	NW3	NW4		
AW5	AW5			AE5	AE5	NC5	NC5	NE5	NE5		
NC5	NE5			NE5	NC5	AE5	AW5	AW5	AE5		

AFC ACTIVE STATISTICAL LEADERS

LEADING ACTIVE PASSERS, AMERICAN FOOTBALL CONFERENCE
1,000 or more attempts

	Yrs.	Att.	Comp.	Pct. Comp.	Yards	Avg. Gain	TD	Pct. TD	Had Int.	Pct. Int.	Rate Pts.
Dan Marino, Mia.	9	4730	2798	59.2	35386	7.48	266	5.6	149	3.2	88.2
Jim Kelly, Buff.	6	2562	1555	60.7	19574	7.64	138	5.4	89	3.5	88.0
Boomer Esiason, Cin.	8	3100	1753	56.5	24264	7.83	163	5.3	114	3.7	84.0
Dave Krieg, K.C.	12	3576	2096	58.6	26132	7.31	195	5.5	148	4.1	82.3
Bernie Kosar, Clev.	7	2857	1671	58.5	19937	6.98	103	3.6	71	2.5	81.6
Ken O'Brien, N.Y.J.	8	3367	1984	58.9	23744	7.05	119	3.5	89	2.6	81.3
Warren Moon, Hou.	8	3680	2105	57.2	27679	7.52	157	4.3	133	3.6	80.3
John Elway, Den.	9	4023	2201	54.7	27974	6.95	148	3.7	140	3.5	74.4
Jay Schroeder, Raiders	7	2158	1092	50.6	16245	7.53	94	4.4	88	4.1	73.1
Bubby Brister, Pitt.	6	1361	713	52.4	9385	6.90	49	3.6	52	3.8	70.6
Jack Trudeau, Ind.	6	1193	622	52.1	7384	6.19	35	2.9	47	3.9	64.7
Vince Evans, Raiders	11	1053	512	48.6	7015	6.66	37	3.5	59	5.6	58.7

TOP 10 ACTIVE RUSHERS, AFC
2,000 or more yards

	Yrs.	Att.	Yards	TD
1. Eric Dickerson, Raiders	9	2783	12439	88
2. Marcus Allen, Raiders	10	2023	8244	77
3. James Brooks, Clev.	11	1667	7918	49
4. Freeman McNeil, N.Y.J.	11	1755	7904	38
5. Joe Morris, Clev.	8	1411	5585	50
6. Thurman Thomas, Buff.	3	1064	4829	26
7. Kevin Mack, Clev.	7	1112	4547	39
8. Christian Okoye, K.C.	5	1102	4449	34
9. Johnny Hector, N.Y.J.	9	1027	4213	41
10. John L. Williams, Sea.	6	952	3869	13

Other Leading Rushers

James Jones, Sea.	9	1010	3626	26
Rueben Mayes, Sea.	4	837	3408	23
John Stephens, N.E.	4	816	2972	15
Marion Butts, S.D.	3	628	2742	23
Merril Hoge, Pitt.	5	727	2716	20
Bobby Humphrey, Mia.	3	593	2386	14
Albert Bentley, Ind.	7	526	2355	19
John Elway, Den.	9	460	2188	20
Kenneth Davis, Buff.	6	484	2128	13

TOP 10 ACTIVE PASS RECEIVERS, AFC
275 or more receptions

	Yrs.	No.	Yards	TD
1. James Lofton, Buff.	14	699	13035	69
2. Mark Clayton, Mia.	9	507	8024	78
3. Al Toon, N.Y.J.	7	486	6294	29
4. Andre Reed, Buff.	7	469	6466	49
5. Mark Duper, Mia.	10	467	8107	52
6. Marcus Allen, Raiders	10	418	3981	17
7. James Brooks, Clev.	11	381	3622	30
8. Stephone Paige, K.C.	9	377	6341	49
9. Ernest Givins, Hou.	6	371	5740	31
10. Bill Brooks, Ind.	6	367	5350	27

Other Leading Receivers

Eddie Brown, Cin.	7	363	6134	41
Louis Lipps, Pitt.	8	358	6018	39
Vance Johnson, Den.	7	343	4714	30
Pete Holohan, Clev.	11	343	3811	16
John L. Williams, Sea.	6	339	3145	13
Irving Fryar, N.E.	8	308	4935	34
Webster Slaughter, Clev.	6	305	4834	27
Willie Gault, Raiders	9	298	6063	40
James Jones, Sea.	9	297	2451	10
Rodney Holman, Cin.	10	292	4063	32
Freeman McNeil, N.Y.J.	11	279	2807	12

TOP 10 ACTIVE SCORERS, AFC
250 or more points

	Yrs.	TD	FG	PAT	TP
1. Pat Leahy, N.Y.J.	18	0	304	558	1470
2. Nick Lowery, K.C.	13	0	284	410	1262
3. Jim Breech, Cin.	13	0	224	486	1158
4. Gary Anderson, Pitt.	10	0	229	323	1010
5. Scott Norwood, Buff.	7	0	133	271	670
6. Raul Allegre, N.Y.J.	9	0	137	183	594
7. Marcus Allen, Raiders	10	95	0	0	570
Al Del Greco, Hou.	8	0	111	237	570
9. Eric Dickerson, Raiders	9	93	0	0	558
10. Dean Biasucci, Ind.	7	0	118	179	553

Other Leading Scorers

James Brooks, Clev.	11	79	0	0	474
Mark Clayton, Mia.	9	79	0	0	474
James Lofton, Buff.	14	70	0	0	420
Jeff Jaeger, Raiders	4	0	81	136	379
David Treadwell, Den.	3	0	79	104	341
Pete Stoyanovich, Mia.	3	0	71	103	316
Mark Duper, Mia.	10	52	0	0	312
Joe Morris, Clev.	8	52	0	0	312
Freeman McNeil, N.Y.J.	11	50	0	0	300
Andre Reed, Buff.	7	50	0	0	300
Stephone Paige, K.C.	9	49	0	0	294
Kevin Mack, Clev.	7	47	0	0	282
Louis Lipps, Pitt.	8	46	0	0	276
Johnny Hector, N.Y.J.	9	44	0	0	264

TOP 10 ACTIVE INTERCEPTORS, AFC
20 or more interceptions

	Yrs.	No.	Yards	TD
1. Ronnie Lott, Raiders	11	59	695	5
2. Deron Cherry, K.C.	11	50	688	1
3. David Waymer, Raiders	12	48	536	0
4. Gill Byrd, S.D.	9	38	458	2
5. Vann McElroy, Sea.	9	31	296	1
Albert Lewis, K.C.	9	31	268	0
7. Fred Marion, N.E.	10	29	457	1
8. David Fulcher, Cin.	6	28	246	2
9. Kevin Ross, K.C.	8	27	403	1
10. Lionel Washington, Raiders	9	26	271	2

Other Leading Interceptors

Eugene Daniel, Ind.	8	25	223	1
Ronnie Lippett, N.E.	8	24	420	2
Dennis Smith, Den.	11	23	364	0
Mark Kelso, Buff.	6	23	306	1
Erik McMillan, N.Y.J.	4	22	608	5
Jerry Gray, Hou.	7	22	350	3
Eugene Robinson, Sea.	7	22	330	0
Mike Prior, Ind.	6	21	307	1
Terry Taylor, Clev.	8	20	228	2
Cedric Mack, S.D.	9	20	178	0

TOP 10 ACTIVE QUARTERBACK SACKERS, AFC
(since 1982)

	No.
1. Jacob Green, Sea.	97.5
2. Greg Townsend, Raiders	95
3. Andre Tippett, N.E.	84.5
4. Bruce Smith, Buff.	78
5. Howie Long, Raiders	69
6. Lee Williams, Hou.	68.5
7. Sean Jones, Hou.	67
8. Karl Mecklenburg, Den.	61
9. Jeff Bryant, Sea.	57.5
10. Simon Fletcher, Den.	56

Other Leading Sackers

Bill Pickel, N.Y.J.	55
Keith Millard, Sea.	53
Leslie O'Neal, S.D.	51.5

TOP 10 ACTIVE PUNT RETURNERS, AFC
40 or more punt returns

	Yrs.	No.	Yards	Avg.	TD
1. Louis Lipps, Pitt.	8	107	1212	11.3	3
2. James Brooks, Clev.	11	52	565	10.9	0
Clarence Verdin, Ind.	6	101	1096	10.9	2
4. Mitchell Price, Cin.	2	43	454	10.6	2
5. Irving Fryar, N.E.	8	206	2055	10.0	3
6. Tim Brown, Raiders	4	116	1112	9.6	1
7. Chris Warren, Sea.	2	60	567	9.5	1
8. Jeff Query, Hou.	3	76	712	9.4	0
9. Mark Clayton, Mia.	9	52	485	9.3	1
Rod Woodson, Pitt.	5	144	1341	9.3	1

Other Leading Punt Returners

Clifford Hicks, Buff.	5	54	496	9.2	0
Paul Skansi, Sea.	9	96	863	9.0	0
Vance Johnson, Den.	7	81	689	8.5	0
Nesby Glasgow, Sea.	13	80	651	8.1	1
Bill Brooks, Ind.	6	43	292	6.8	0

TOP 10 ACTIVE KICKOFF RETURNERS, AFC
40 or more kickoff returns

	Yrs.	No.	Yards	Avg.	TD
1. Tim Brown, Raiders	4	45	1190	26.4	1
2. Anthony Miller, S.D.	4	47	1194	25.4	1
3. Nate Lewis, S.D.	2	40	961	24.0	1
4. Sammy Martin, Ind.	4	100	2317	23.2	1
5. Rod Woodson, Pitt.	5	165	3766	22.8	2
Vance Johnson, Den.	7	45	1027	22.8	0
7. Ron Brown, Raiders	8	199	4493	22.6	4
8. Nesby Glasgow, Sea.	13	85	1906	22.4	0
9. Chris Warren, Sea.	2	58	1270	21.9	0
10. Gaston Green, Den.	4	42	905	21.5	1
Tim McGee, Cin.	6	58	1249	21.5	0
Albert Bentley, Ind.	7	148	3175	21.5	0

Other Leading Kickoff Returners

Steve Tasker, Buff.	7	42	896	21.3	0
Jamie Holland, Clev.	5	133	2806	21.1	1
James Brooks, Clev.	11	129	2713	21.0	0
Leonard Harris, Hou.	6	57	1193	20.9	0
Al Edwards, Buff.	2	42	879	20.9	1
Ronnie Harmon, S.D.	6	50	1034	20.7	0
Don Smith, Mia.	3	41	831	20.3	0
Donnie Elder, S.D.	6	150	3040	20.3	0
Dwight Stone, Pitt.	5	75	1517	20.2	1
Eric Metcalf, Clev.	3	106	2121	20.0	2
Marvin Allen, N.E.	4	43	844	19.6	0
Clarence Verdin, Ind.	6	104	2039	19.6	1
Alton Montgomery, Den.	2	40	774	19.4	0
Terance Mathis, N.Y.J.	2	72	1386	19.3	0
Joe Morris, Clev.	8	40	659	16.5	0

TOP 10 ACTIVE PUNTERS, AFC
50 or more punts

	Yrs.	No.	Avg.	LG
1. Rohn Stark, Ind.	10	746	43.9	72
2. Reggie Roby, Mia.	9	520	43.4	77
3. Greg Montgomery, Hou.	4	203	42.3	63
4. Mike Horan, Den.	8	520	42.1	75
5. Brian Hansen, Clev.	7	533	42.0	69
6. Lee Johnson, Cin.	7	441	41.4	70
7. Rick Tuten, Sea.	3	109	41.0	60
Jeff Gossett, Raiders	10	625	41.0	64
9. John Kidd, S.D.	8	583	40.4	67
10. Shawn McCarthy, N.E.	1	66	40.2	93

Other Leading Punters

Bryan Barker, K.C.	2	121	39.5	57
Louie Aguiar, N.Y.J.	1	64	39.4	61
Chris Mohr, Buff.	2	138	39.1	58

NFC ACTIVE STATISTICAL LEADERS

LEADING ACTIVE PASSERS, NATIONAL FOOTBALL CONFERENCE
1,000 or more attempts

	Yrs.	Att.	Comp.	Pct. Comp.	Yards	Avg. Gain	TD	Pct. TD	Had Int.	Pct. Int.	Rate Pts.
Joe Montana, S.F.	12	4579	2914	63.6	34998	7.64	242	5.3	123	2.7	93.4
Mark Rypien, Wash.	4	1409	809	57.4	11132	7.90	84	6.0	48	3.4	88.5
Steve Young, S.F.	7	1104	640	58.0	8412	7.62	51	4.6	35	3.2	84.3
Jim Everett, Rams	6	2528	1431	56.6	18783	7.43	112	4.4	93	3.7	79.7
Jim McMahon, Phil.	10	2151	1243	57.8	15637	7.27	89	4.1	77	3.6	79.4
Randall Cunningham, Phil.	7	2257	1231	54.5	15418	6.83	107	4.7	71	3.1	78.7
Bobby Hebert, N.O.	6	1633	953	58.4	11343	6.95	66	4.0	59	3.6	78.1
Phil Simms, N.Y.G.	12	4110	2246	54.6	29512	7.18	179	4.4	145	3.5	77.4
Steve DeBerg, T.B.	14	4613	2632	57.1	31455	6.82	183	4.0	189	4.1	74.2
Jim Harbaugh, Chi.	5	1076	621	57.7	7079	6.58	30	2.8	33	3.1	74.1
Wade Wilson, Minn.	10	1665	929	55.8	12135	7.29	66	4.0	75	4.5	73.4
Don Majkowski, G.B.	5	1552	851	54.8	10599	6.83	54	3.5	54	3.5	73.3
Chris Miller, Atl.	5	1770	945	53.4	11982	6.77	71	4.0	63	3.6	73.3
Troy Aikman, Dall.	3	1055	618	58.6	7082	6.71	31	2.9	46	4.4	70.5
Mike Tomczak, G.B.	7	1153	582	50.5	7737	6.71	44	3.8	56	4.9	64.6
Mike Pagel, Rams	10	1480	745	50.3	9292	6.28	48	3.2	60	4.1	64.1
Vinny Testaverde, T.B.	5	1802	920	51.1	12266	6.81	63	3.5	96	5.3	62.4

TOP 10 ACTIVE RUSHERS, NFC
2,000 or more yards

	Yrs.	Att.	Yards	TD
1. Ottis Anderson, N.Y.G.	13	2552	10242	81
2. Gerald Riggs, Wash.	10	1989	8188	69
3. Roger Craig, Minn.	9	1848	7654	51
4. Earnest Byner, Wash.	8	1377	5560	41
5. Neal Anderson, Chi.	6	1157	4938	42
6. Barry Sanders, Det.	3	877	4322	43
7. Dalton Hilliard, N.O.	6	961	3554	34
8. Randall Cunningham, Phil.	7	486	3437	23
9. Gary Anderson, T.B.	6	786	3159	15
10. Emmitt Smith, Dall.	2	606	2500	23

Other Leading Rushers
Keith Byars, Phil.	6	709	2496	16
Alfred Anderson, Minn.	8	626	2374	22
Allen Pinkett, N.O.	6	561	2324	21

TOP 10 ACTIVE PASS RECEIVERS, NFC
275 or more receptions

	Yrs.	No.	Yards	TD
1. Art Monk, Wash.	12	801	10984	60
2. Roy Green, Phil.	13	551	8860	66
3. Drew Hill, Atl.	12	540	8824	57
4. Jerry Rice, S.F.	7	526	9072	93
5. Roger Craig, Minn.	9	525	4578	16
6. Henry Ellard, Rams	9	485	8089	43
Gary Clark, Wash.	7	485	7830	53
8. Mickey Shuler, Phil.	14	462	5100	37
9. Steve Jordan, Minn.	10	411	5348	25
10. Eric Martin, N.O.	7	398	5863	40

Other Leading Receivers
Anthony Carter, Minn.	7	377	6281	45
Ottis Anderson, N.Y.G.	13	376	3062	5
Earnest Byner, Wash.	8	323	3079	11
Keith Byars, Phil.	6	315	3030	11
Ricky Sanders, Wash.	6	305	4509	29
Sterling Sharpe, G.B.	4	281	4280	23

TOP 10 ACTIVE SCORERS, NFC
250 or more points

	Yrs.	TD	FG	PAT	TP
1. Eddie Murray, Det.	12	0	244	381	1113
2. Matt Bahr, N.Y.G.	13	0	221	402	1065
3. Morten Andersen, N.O.	10	0	217	314	965
4. Norm Johnson, Atl.	10	0	178	371	905
5. Kevin Butler, Chi.	7	0	153	263	722
6. Tony Zendejas, Rams	7	0	134	222	624
7. Jerry Rice, S.F.	7	97	0	0	582
8. Ottis Anderson, N.Y.G.	13	86	0	0	516
9. Chip Lohmiller, Wash.	4	0	109	178	505
10. Fuad Reveiz, Minn.	6	0	83	221	470

Other Leading Scorers
Mike Cofer, S.F.	5	0	95	182	467
Roger Ruzek, Phil.	5	0	96	153	441
Roy Green, Phil.	13	69	0	0	414
Gerald Riggs, Wash.	10	69	0	0	414
Roger Craig, Minn.	9	67	0	0	402
Greg Davis, Phx.	5	0	88	115	379
Art Monk, Wash.	12	60	0	0	360
Drew Hill, Atl.	12	58	0	0	348
Neal Anderson, Chi.	6	56	0	0	336
Earnest Byner, Wash.	8	53	0	0	318
Gary Clark, Wash.	7	53	0	0	318
Chris Jacke, G.B.	3	0	63	101	290
Henry Ellard, Rams	9	47	0	0	282
Barry Sanders, Det.	3	47	0	0	282
Anthony Carter, Minn.	7	46	0	0	276
Dalton Hilliard, N.O.	6	43	0	0	258

TOP 10 ACTIVE INTERCEPTORS, NFC
20 or more interceptions

	Yrs.	No.	Yards	TD
1. Everson Walls, N.Y.G.	11	54	478	1
2. Joey Browner, Minn.	9	37	465	3
3. Darrell Green, Wash.	9	29	261	2
4. Felix Wright, Minn.	7	28	472	2
5. Bobby Butler, Atl.	11	27	222	1
6. Scott Case, Atl.	8	26	252	1
Wes Hopkins, Phil.	8	26	235	1
Tim McKyer, Atl.	6	26	126	1
9. Jerry Holmes, G.B.	10	25	306	2
10. Carl Lee, Minn.	9	24	309	2

Other Leading Interceptors
Issiac Holt, Dall.	7	21	240	2
Eric Allen, Phil.	4	21	171	1
Dave Duerson, Phx.	9	20	226	0
Mark Murphy, G.B.	11	20	194	1

TOP 10 ACTIVE QUARTERBACK SACKERS, NFC
(since 1982)

	No.
1. Lawrence Taylor, N.Y.G.	121.5
2. Reggie White, Phil.	110
3. Richard Dent, Chi.	103.5
4. Rickey Jackson, N.O.	90
5. Charles Mann, Wash.	76
Steve McMichael, Chi.	76
7. Leonard Marshall, N.Y.G.	75.5
8. Jim Jeffcoat, Dall.	70
9. Pat Swilling, N.O.	66
10. Charles Haley, S.F.	63.5

Other Leading Sackers
Kevin Greene, Rams	62.5
Chris Doleman, Minn.	61.5
Mike Cofer, Det.	60.5
Keith Willis, Wash.	59
Tim Harris, S.F.	58
Freddie Joe Nunn, Phx.	56
Clyde Simmons, Phil.	52

TOP 10 ACTIVE PUNT RETURNERS, NFC
40 or more punt returns

	Yrs.	No.	Yards	Avg.	TD
1. Mel Gray, Det.	6	119	1479	12.4	2
Brian Mitchell, Wash.	2	57	707	12.4	2
3. David Meggett, N.Y.G.	3	117	1336	11.4	3
4. Henry Ellard, Rams	9	133	1509	11.3	4
5. Darrell Green, Wash.	9	50	549	11.0	0
6. Vai Sikahema, Phil.	6	219	2391	10.9	3
7. John Taylor, S.F.	5	138	1461	10.6	2
8. Darryl Henley, Rams	3	60	571	9.5	0
9. Johnny Bailey, Phx.	2	72	680	9.4	1
Kelvin Martin, Dall.	5	96	898	9.4	1

Other Leading Punt Returners
Deion Sanders, Atl.	3	78	727	9.3	2
Derrick Shepard, Dall.	5	75	679	9.1	1
Kitrick Taylor, G.B.	4	63	568	9.0	1
Don Griffin, S.F.	6	68	598	8.8	1
Willie Drewrey, T.B.	7	144	1260	8.8	0
Vince Buck, N.O.	2	68	565	8.3	0
Eric Martin, N.O.	7	46	368	8.0	0
Ricky Nattiel, T.B.	5	55	421	7.7	0
Rod Harris, Phil.	3	108	826	7.6	0

TOP 10 ACTIVE KICKOFF RETURNERS, NFC
40 or more kickoff returns

	Yrs.	No.	Yards	Avg.	TD
1. Mel Gray, Det.	6	194	4680	24.1	1
2. James Dixon, G.B.	3	101	2315	22.9	1
Dennis Gentry, Chi.	10	176	4023	22.9	3
4. Charles Wilson, G.B.	2	58	1320	22.8	1
5. Roy Green, Phil.	13	89	2002	22.5	1
6. David Meggett, N.Y.G.	3	73	1583	21.7	0
7. Deion Sanders, Atl.	3	100	2152	21.5	1
8. Vai Sikahema, Phil.	6	179	3826	21.4	0
9. Gene Atkins, N.O.	5	71	1508	21.2	0
10. Dexter Carter, S.F.	2	78	1622	20.8	1

Other Leading Kickoff Returners
Willie Drewrey, T.B.	7	87	1804	20.7	0
Marc Logan, S.F.	5	63	1282	20.3	1
Robert Delpino, Rams	4	55	1110	20.2	0
Brian Mitchell, Wash.	2	47	948	20.2	0
Drew Hill, Atl.	12	172	3460	20.1	1
Stanford Jennings, T.B.	8	148	2965	20.0	1
Gary Anderson, T.B.	6	99	1983	20.0	1
Allen Pinkett, N.O.	6	80	1577	19.7	0
Derrick Shepard, Dall.	5	51	1007	19.7	0
Alfred Anderson, Minn.	8	42	803	19.1	0
Bobby Morse, N.O.	4	41	780	19.0	1
Thomas Sanders, Phil.	7	104	1956	18.8	1
Rod Harris, Phil.	3	49	895	18.3	0
Vince Workman, G.B.	3	55	896	16.3	0
Mark Ingram, N.Y.G.	5	47	742	15.8	0

TOP 10 ACTIVE PUNTERS, NFC
50 or more punts

	Yrs.	No.	Avg.	LG
1. Sean Landeta, N.Y.G.	7	440	43.4	71
2. Rich Camarillo, Phx.	11	727	42.8	76
3. Tommy Barnhardt, N.O.	5	243	42.2	65
4. Jim Arnold, Det.	9	683	42.1	69
Harry Newsome, Minn.	7	521	42.1	65
6. Scott Fulhage, Atl.	5	331	41.4	65
Maury Buford, Chi.	9	577	41.4	71
Mike Saxon, Dall.	7	530	41.4	64
9. Paul McJulien, G.B.	1	86	40.4	62
10. Jeff Feagles, Phil.	4	313	40.1	77

Other Leading Punters
Bryan Wagner, G.B.	5	300	40.0	71
Kelly Goodburn, Wash.	5	282	39.9	61
Joe Prokop, S.F.	6	344	39.3	76
Dan Stryzinski, T.B.	2	139	39.2	63
Barry Helton, Rams	4	213	38.9	56

57th Annual NFL Draft, April 26-27, 1992

Atlanta Falcons (Drafted alternately 19-18-17-20)

1. Bob Whitfield—8, T, Stanford
   Tony Smith—19, RB, Southern Mississippi
2. Choice to Phoenix through New England
   Chuck Smith—51, DE, Tennessee, from Dallas
3. Howard Dinkins—73, LB, Florida State
4. Frankie Smith—104, DB, Baylor
5. Choice to San Diego
6. Terry Ray—158, DB, Oklahoma
7. Tim Paulk—182, LB, Florida, from Miami
   Choice to Los Angeles Raiders through Miami
8. Derrick Moore—216, RB, Northeast Oklahoma
   Reggie Dwight—217, TE, Troy State, from Dallas
9. Keith Alex—243, T, Texas A&M
10. Darryl Hardy—270, LB, Tennessee
11. Robin Jones—297, DE, Baylor
12. Choice to Miami

Buffalo Bills (Drafted 27th)

1. John Fina—27, T, Arizona
2. James Patton—55, NT, Texas
3. Keith Goganious—83, LB, Penn State
4. Frank Kmet—111, DE, Purdue
5. Matt Darby—139, DB, UCLA
6. Nate Turner—167, TE, Nebraska
7. Kurt Schulz—195, DB, Eastern Washington
8. Leonard Humphries—223, DB, Penn State
9. Chris Walsh—251, WR, Stanford
10. Barry Rose—279, WR, Wisconsin-Stevens Point
11. Vince Marrow—307, TE, Toledo
12. Matt Rodgers—335, QB, Iowa

Chicago Bears (Drafted alternately 22-21-24-23)

1. Alonzo Spellman—22, DE, Ohio State
2. Troy Auzenne—49, T, California
3. Jeremy Lincoln—80, DB, Tennessee
4. Will Furrer—107, QB, Virginia Tech
5. Todd Harrison—134, TE, North Carolina State
6. Mark Berry—161, DB, Texas
7. John Brown—192, WR, Houston
8. Choice to New York Jets
9. Mirko Jurkovic—246, G, Notre Dame
10. Nikki Fisher—273, RB, Virginia
11. Louis Age—304, T, Southwestern Louisiana
12. Chris Wilson—331, LB, Oklahoma

Cincinnati Bengals (Drafted alternately 4-3-2)

1. Choice to Washington
   David Klingler—6, QB, Houston, from San Diego through Washington
   Darryl Williams—28, DB, Miami, from Washington
2. Carl Pickens—31, WR, Tennessee
3. Choice to Dallas through Washington
   Leonard Wheeler—84, DB, Troy State, from Washington
4. Ricardo McDonald—88, LB, Pittsburgh
5. Craig Thompson—115, TE, North Carolina A&T
6. Chris Burns—142, DT, Middle Tennessee State
7. Lance Olberding—172, T, Iowa
8. Roosevelt Nix—199, DE, Central State, Ohio
9. Ostell Miles—226, RB, Houston
10. Horace Smith—256, DB, Oregon Tech
11. John Earle—283, T, Western Illinois
12. Eric Shaw—310, LB, Louisiana Tech

Cleveland Browns (Drafted alternately 9-8)

1. Tommy Vardell—9, RB, Stanford
2. Choice to Dallas
   Patrick Rowe—52, WR, San Diego State, from New Orleans through Dallas
3. Bill Johnson—65, DT, Michigan State
   Gerald Dixon—78, LB, South Carolina, from Dallas
4. Choice to Philadelphia
5. Choice to Dallas
6. Rico Smith—143, WR, Colorado, from Tampa Bay
   Choice to Tampa Bay
   George Williams—163, DT, Notre Dame, from Dallas
7. Selwyn Jones—177, DB, Colorado State
8. Choice to New England
9. Tim Hill—233, DB, Kansas
10. Marcus Lowe—260, DT, Baylor
11. Augustin Olobia—289, WR, Washington State
12. Keithen McCant—316, QB, Nebraska
    Tim Simpson—329, C-G, Illinois, from Dallas

Dallas Cowboys (Drafted alternately 24-23-22-21)

1. Kevin Smith—17, DB, Texas A&M, from Philadelphia through Green Bay and Atlanta
   Robert Jones—24, LB, East Carolina
2. Jimmy Smith—36, WR, Jackson State, from Cleveland
   Darren Woodson—37, DB, Arizona State, from New England
   Choice to Atlanta
3. Clayton Holmes—58, DB, Carson-Newman, from Cincinnati through Washington
   Choice to Cleveland
   James Brown—82, T, Virginia State, from Detroit
4. Choice to Indianapolis through Los Angeles Raiders
   Tom Myslinski—109, G-C, Tennessee, from Detroit
5. Greg Briggs—120, DB, Texas Southern, from New England through Atlanta
   Rod Milstead—121, G, Delaware State, from Cleveland
   Choice to Houston
6. Fallon Wacasey—149, TE, Tulsa, from New England
   Choice to Cleveland
7. Choice to Green Bay through Los Angeles Raiders
8. Choice to Atlanta
9. Nate Kirtman—248, DB, Pomona-Pitzer
   Chris Hall—250, DB, East Carolina, from Detroit
10. John Terry—275, G, Livingstone
11. Tim Daniel—302, WR, Florida A&M
12. Don Harris—317, DB, Texas Tech, from New England
    Choice to Cleveland

Denver Broncos (Drafted alternately 25-26)

1. Tommy Maddox—25, QB, UCLA
2. Shane Dronett—54, DE, Texas
3. Choice to Detroit
4. Chuck Johnson—110, G, Texas
5. Frank Robinson—137, DB, Boise State
6. Choice to New York Jets
7. Ron Geater—170, DE, Iowa, from Tampa Bay
   Jim Johnson—181, T, Michigan State, from New York Jets
   Jon Bostick—193, WR, Nebraska
8. Dietrich Lockridge—208, G, Jackson State, from New York Jets
   Choice to Tampa Bay through Dallas and Cleveland
9. Muhammad Oliver—249, DB, Oregon
10. Bob Meek—278, C, Auburn
11. Cedric Tillman—305, WR, Alcorn State
12. John Granby—334, DB, Virginia Tech

Detroit Lions (Drafted alternately 26-25)

1. Robert Porcher—26, DE, South Carolina State
2. Tracy Scroggins—53, LB, Tulsa
   Jason Hanson—56, K, Washington State, from Washington through Dallas
3. Thomas McLemore—81, TE, Southern, from Denver
   Choice to Dallas
4. Choice to Dallas
5. Choice to New Orleans
6. Larry Tharpe—145, T, Tennessee State, from Phoenix through New England
   Choice to New England
7. Choice to New England
8. Willie Clay—221, DB, Georgia Tech
9. Choice to Dallas
10. Choice to New England
11. Ed Tillison—306, RB, Northwest Missouri
12. Choice to New England

Green Bay Packers (Drafted alternately 5-7-6)

1. Terrell Buckley—5, DB, Florida State
2. Mark D'Onofrio—34, LB, Penn State
3. Robert Brooks—62, WR, South Carolina
4. Choice to San Francisco
   Edgar Bennett—103, RB, Florida State, from San Francisco
5. Dexter McNabb—119, RB, Florida
   Orlando McKay—130, WR, Washington, from San Francisco
6. Choice to Phoenix
   Mark Chmura—157, TE, Boston College, from San Francisco
7. Choice to Los Angeles Raiders
   Christopher Holder—190, WR, Tuskegee, from Dallas through Los Angeles Raiders
8. Choice to Pittsburgh through San Francisco
9. Ty Detmer—230, QB, Brigham Young
   Shazzon Bradley—240, NT, Tennessee, from Los Angeles Raiders
10. Andrew Oberg—257, T, North Carolina
11. Gabe Mokwuah—287, LB, American International
12. Brett Collins—314, LB, Washington

Houston Oilers (Drafted alternately 23-22-21-24)

1. Choice to San Diego
2. Eddie Robinson—50, LB, Alabama State
3. Corey Harris—77, WR, Vanderbilt
4. Mike Mooney—108, T, Georgia Tech
5. Joe Bowden—133, LB, Oklahoma, from New Orleans
   Tony Brown—135, DB, Fresno State
   Tim Roberts—136, DT, Southern Mississippi, from Dallas
6. Mario Bailey—162, WR, Washington
7. Elbert Turner—189, WR, Illinois
8. Bucky Richardson—220, QB, Texas A&M
9. Bernard Dafney—247, T, Tennessee
10. Dion Johnson—274, WR, East Carolina
11. Anthony Davis—301, LB, Utah
12. Joe Wood—332, K, Air Force

Indianapolis Colts (Drafted 1st)

1. Steve Emtman—1, DT, Washington
   Quentin Coryatt—2, LB, Texas A&M, from Tampa Bay
2. Ashley Ambrose—29, DB, Mississippi Valley State
3. Choice to Los Angeles Rams
4. Rodney Culver—85, RB, Notre Dame
   Tony McCoy—105, DT, Florida, from Dallas through Los Angeles Raiders
5. Maury Toy—113, RB, UCLA
6. Shoun Habersham—141, WR, Tennessee-Chattanooga
7. Derek Steele—169, DE, Maryland
8. Jason Belser—197, DB, Oklahoma
   Ronald Humphrey—212, RB, Mississippi Valley State, from Los Angeles Raiders
9. Eddie Miller—225, WR, South Carolina
10. Steve Grant—253, LB, West Virginia
11. Choice to Los Angeles Rams
12. Mike Brandon—309, DE, Florida

Kansas City Chiefs (Drafted alternately 20-19-18-17)

1. Dale Carter—20, DB, Tennessee
2. Matt Blundin—40, QB, Virginia, from Minnesota through Dallas
   Choice to Washington through Dallas
3. Choice to Washington through Dallas
4. Mike Evans—101, DE, Michigan
5. Choice to Tampa Bay
6. Tony Smith—159, WR, Notre Dame
7. Erick Anderson—186, LB, Michigan
8. Jim Jennings—213, G, San Diego State
9. Jay Leeuwenburg—244, C, Colorado
10. Jerry Ostroski—271, G, Tulsa
11. Doug Rigby—298, DE, Wyoming
12. Corey Williams—325, DB, Oklahoma State

Los Angeles Raiders (Drafted 16th)

1. Chester McGlockton—16, DE, Clemson
2. Greg Skrepenak—32, T, Michigan, from Tampa Bay
   Choice to Tampa Bay
3. Choice to New Orleans through Tampa Bay
4. Choice to Phoenix through New England
5. Derrick Hoskins—128, DB, Southern Mississippi
6. Tony Rowell—156, C, Florida
7. Curtis Cotton—173, DB, Nebraska, from Green Bay
   Choice to Tampa Bay
   Kevin Smith—185, RB, UCLA, from Atlanta through Miami
8. Choice to Indianapolis
9. Choice to Green Bay
10. Alberto White—268, LB, Texas Southern
11. Choice to Miami
12. Tom Roth—324, G, Southern Illinois

Los Angeles Rams (Drafted alternately 3-2-4)

1. Sean Gilbert—3, DE, Pittsburgh
2. Steve Israel—30, DB, Pittsburgh
3. Marc Boutte—57, DT, Louisiana State, from Indianapolis
   Todd Kinchen—60, WR, Louisiana State
4. Shawn Harper—87, T, Indiana
5. Chris Crooms—114, DB, Texas A&M
6. Joe Campbell—144, RB, Middle Tennessee State
7. Darryl Ashmore—171, T, Northwestern
8. Ricky Jones—198, QB, Alabama State
9. T. J. Rubley—228, QB, Tulsa
10. Tim Lester—255, RB, Eastern Kentucky
11. Brian Townsend—281, LB, Michigan, from Indianapolis
    Brian Thomas—282, WR, Southern
12. Kelvin Harris—312, C, Miami

Miami Dolphins (Drafted alternately 12-15-14-13)

1. Troy Vincent—7, DB, Wisconsin, from Phoenix
   Marco Coleman—12, LB, Georgia Tech
2. Eddie Blake—43, DT, Auburn
3. Larry Webster—70, DT, Maryland
4. Dwight Hollier—97, LB, North Carolina
5. Christopher Perez—124, LB, Texas
6. Roosevelt Collins—155, LB, Texas Christian
7. Choice to Atlanta
   Dave Moore—191, TE, Pittsburgh, from New Orleans through Los Angeles Raiders
8. Andre Powell—209, LB, Penn State
9. Tony Tellington—236, DB, Youngstown
10. Raoul Spears—267, RB, Southern California
11. Lee Miles—294, WR, Baylor
    Mark Barsotti—296, QB, Fresno State, from Los Angeles Raiders
12. Milton Biggins—321, TE, Western Kentucky
    Kameno Bell—328, RB, Illinois, from Atlanta

Minnesota Vikings (Drafted alternately 13-12-15-14)

1. Choice to New England through Dallas
2. Robert Harris—39, DE, Southern, from Seattle
   Choice to Kansas City through Dallas
3. Choice to New England through Dallas
4. Roy Barker—98, DT, North Carolina
5. Ed McDaniel—125, LB, Clemson
6. Mike Gaddis—152, RB, Oklahoma
7. David Wilson—183, DB, California
8. Luke Fisher—210, TE, East Carolina
9. Brad Johnson—227, QB, Florida State, from Tampa Bay
   Ronnie West—237, WR, Pittsburg, Kansas
10. Brad Culpepper—264, DT, Florida
11. Charles Evans—295, RB, Clark, Georgia
12. Joe Randolph—322, WR, Elon

New England Patriots (Drafted alternately 8-9)

1. Choice to Atlanta
   Eugene Chung—13, T, Virginia Tech, from Minnesota through Dallas
2. Rod Smith—35, DB, Notre Dame, from Phoenix
   Choice to Dallas
3. Todd Collins—64, LB, Carson-Newman
   Kevin Turner—71, RB, Alabama, from Minnesota through Dallas
4. Dion Lambert—90, DB, UCLA, from San Diego
   Darren Anderson—93, DB, Toledo
5. Dwayne Sabb—116, LB, New Hampshire, from Tampa Bay
   Choice to Dallas through Atlanta
6. Choice to Dallas
   Tracy Boyd—165, G, Elizabeth City State, from Detroit
7. Wayne Hawkins—176, WR, Southwest Minnesota
   Jim Gray—194, DT, West Virginia, from Detroit
8. Scott Lockwood—204, RB, Southern California, from Cleveland
   Sam Gash—205, RB, Penn State
9. David Dixon—232, DT, Arizona State
10. Turner Baur—261, TE, Stanford
    Steve Gordon—277, C, California, from Detroit
11. Mike Petko—288, LB, Nebraska
12. Choice to Dallas
    Freeman Baysinger—333, WR, Humboldt State, from Detroit

New Orleans Saints (Drafted alternately 21-24-23-22)

1. Vaughn Dunbar—21, RB, Indiana
2. Choice to Cleveland through Dallas
3. Tyrone Legette—72, DB, Nebraska, from Los Angeles Raiders through Tampa Bay
   Choice to Tampa Bay
4. Gene McGuire—95, C, Notre Dame, from Seattle
   Sean Lumpkin—106, DB, Minnesota
5. Choice to Houston
   Torrance Small—138, WR, Alcorn State, from Detroit
6. Kary Vincent—164, DB, Texas A&M
7. Choice to Miami through Los Angeles Raiders
8. Robert Stewart—218, NT, Alabama
9. Donald Jones—245, LB, Washington
10. Marcus Dowdell—276, WR, Tennessee State
11. Mike Gisler—303, G, Houston
12. Scott Adell—330, T, North Carolina State

New York Giants (Drafted alternately 14-13-12-15)

1. Derek Brown—14, TE, Notre Dame
2. Phillippi Sparks—41, DB, Arizona State
3. Aaron Pierce—69, TE, Washington
4. Keith Hamilton—99, DT, Pittsburgh
5. Michael Wright—126, DB, Washington State
6. Stacey Dillard—153, NT, Oklahoma
7. Corey Widmer—180, NT, Montana State
8. Kent Graham—211, QB, Ohio State
9. Anthony Prior—238, DB, Washington State
10. George Rooks—265, NT, Syracuse
11. Nate Singleton—292, WR, Grambling
12. Charles Swann—323, WR, Indiana State

New York Jets (Drafted alternately 15-14-13-12)

1. Johnny Mitchell—15, TE, Nebraska
2. Kurt Barber—42, LB, Southern California
3. Siupeli Malamala—68, T, Washington
4. Keo Coleman—96, LB, Mississippi State
5. Cal Dixon—127, C, Florida
6. Glenn Cadrez—154, LB, Houston
   Jeff Blake—166, QB, East Carolina, from Denver
7. Choice to Denver
8. Choice to Denver
   Vincent Brownlee—219, WR, Mississippi, from Chicago
9. Choice to Phoenix
10. Mario Johnson—266, DT, Missouri
11. Eric Boles—293, WR, Central Washington
12. Choice to Seattle

Philadelphia Eagles (Drafted alternately 17-20-19-18)

1. Choice to Dallas through Green Bay and Atlanta
2. Siran Stacy—48, RB, Alabama
3. Tommy Jeter—75, DT, Texas
4. Tony Brooks—92, RB, Notre Dame, from Cleveland
   Casey Weldon—102, QB, Florida State
5. Corey Barlow—129, DB, Auburn
6. Jeff Sydner—160, WR, Hawaii
7. William Boatwright—187, G, Virginia Tech
8. Chuck Bullough—214, LB, Michigan State
9. Ephesians Bartley—241, LB, Florida
10. Mark McMillian—272, DB, Alabama
11. Pumpy Tudors—299, P, Tennessee-Chattanooga
12. Brandon Houston—326, T, Oklahoma

Phoenix Cardinals (Drafted alternately 7-6-5)

1. Choice to Miami
2. Choice to New England
   Tony Sacca—46, QB, Penn State, from Atlanta through New England
3. Ed Cunningham—61, C, Washington
4. Jeff Christy—91, T, Pittsburgh
   Michael Bankston—100, NT, Sam Houston State, from Los Angeles Raiders through New England
5. Choice to Tampa Bay through New Orleans
6. Choice to Detroit through New England
   Brian Brauninger—146, T, Oklahoma, from Green Bay
7. Derek Ware—175, TE, Central State, Oklahoma
8. Eric Blount—202, WR, North Carolina
9. David Henson—229, NT, Central Arkansas
   Tyrone Williams—239, WR, Western Ontario, from New York Jets
10. Reggie Yarbrough—259, RB, Cal State-Fullerton
11. Rob Baxley—286, T, Iowa
12. Lance Wilson—313, NT, Texas

Pittsburgh Steelers (Drafted alternately 11-10)

1. Leon Searcy—11, T, Miami
2. Levon Kirkland—38, LB, Clemson
3. Joel Steed—67, NT, Colorado
4. Charles Davenport—94, WR, North Carolina State
5. Allan Haller—123, DB, Michigan State
6. Choice to San Francisco
7. Russ Campbell—179, TE, Kansas State
   Scottie Graham—188, RB, Ohio State, from San Francisco
8. Darren Perry—203, DB, Penn State, from Green Bay through San Francisco
   Hesham Ismail—206, G, Florida
   Nate Williams—215, DT, Mississippi State, from San Francisco
9. Elnardo Webster—235, LB, Rutgers
10. Mike Saunders—262, RB, Iowa
11. Kendall Gammons—291, G, Pittsburg, Kansas
12. Cornelius Benton—318, QB, Connecticut

San Diego Chargers (Drafted alternately 6-5-7)

1. Choice to Cincinnati through Washington
   Chris Mims—23, DE, Tennessee, from Houston
2. Marquez Pope—33, DB, Fresno State
3. Ray Ethridge—63, WR, Pasadena C.C.
4. Choice to New England
5. Curtis Whitley—117, C, Clemson
   Kevin Little—131, LB, North Carolina A&T, from Atlanta
   Eric Jonassen—140, T, Bloomsburg, from Washington
6. Reggie White—147, DT, North Carolina A&T
7. Deems May—174, TE, North Carolina
8. James Fuller—201, DB, Portland State
9. Johnnie Barnes—231, WR, Hampton
10. Arthur Paul—258, DT, Arizona State
11. Keith McAfee—285, RB, Texas A&M
12. Carlos Huerta—315, K, Miami

San Francisco 49ers (Drafted alternately 18-17-20-19)

1. Dana Hall—18, DB, Washington
2. Amp Lee—45, RB, Florida State
3. Brian Bollinger—76, G, North Carolina
4. Mark Thomas—89, DE, North Carolina State, from Green Bay
   Choice to Green Bay
5. Choice to Green Bay
6. Damien Russell—151, DB, Virginia Tech, from Pittsburgh
7. Choice to Green Bay
8. Choice to Pittsburgh
9. Darian Hagan—242, QB, Colorado
10. Corey Mayfield—269, DE, Oklahoma
11. Tom Covington—300, TE, Georgia Tech
12. Matt La Bounty—327, DE, Oregon

Seattle Seahawks (Drafted alternately 10-11)

1. Ray Roberts—10, T, Virginia
2. Choice to Minnesota
3. Bobby Spitulski—66, LB, Central Florida
4. Choice to New Orleans
5. Gary Dandridge—122, DB, Appalachian State
6. Michael Bates—150, WR, Arizona
7. Mike Frier—178, DT, Appalachian State
8. Muhammad Shamsid-Deen—207, RB, Tennessee-Chattanooga
9. Larry Stayner—234, TE, Boise State
10. Anthony Hamlet—263, DE, Miami
11. Kris Rongen—290, G, Washington
12. Chico Fraley—319, LB, Washington
    John MacNeill—320, DE, Michigan State, from New York Jets

Tampa Bay Buccaneers (Drafted alternately 2-4-3)

1. Choice to Indianapolis
2. Choice to Los Angeles Raiders
   Courtney Hawkins—44, WR, Michigan State, from Los Angeles Raiders
3. Mark Wheeler—59, DT, Texas A&M
   Tyji Armstrong—79, TE, Mississippi, from New Orleans
4. Craig Erickson—86, QB, Miami
5. Choice to New England
   Rogerick Green—118, DB, Kansas State, from Phoenix through New Orleans
   Santana Dotson—132, DE, Baylor, from Kansas City
6. Choice to Cleveland
   James Malone—148, LB, UCLA, from Cleveland
7. Choice to Denver
   Ken Swilling—184, DB, Georgia Tech, from Los Angeles Raiders
8. Anthony McDowell—200, RB, Texas Tech
   Mike Pawlawski—222, QB, California, from Denver through Dallas and Cleveland
9. Choice to Minnesota
10. Elijah Alexander—254, LB, Kansas State
11. Mazio Royster—284, RB, Southern California
12. Klaus Wilmsmeyer—311, P, Louisville

Washington Redskins (Drafted 28th)

1. Desmond Howard—4, WR, Michigan, from Cincinnati
   Choice to Cincinnati
2. Shane Collins—47, DE, Arizona State, from Kansas City through Dallas
   Choice to Detroit through Dallas
3. Paul Siever—74, G, Penn State, from Kansas City through Dallas
   Choice to Cincinnati
4. Chris Hakel—112, QB, William & Mary
5. Choice to San Diego
6. Ray Rowe—168, TE, San Diego State
7. Calvin Holmes—196, DB, Southern California
8. Darryl Moore—224, G, Texas-El Paso
9. Boone Powell—252, LB, Texas
10. Tony Barker—280, LB, Rice
11. Terry Smith—308, WR, Penn State
12. Matt Elliott—336, C, Michigan

Active Coaches' Career Records (Order Based on Career Victories)

Start of 1992 Season

Coach	Team(s)	Regular Season				Postseason				Career			
		Yrs.	Won	Lost	Tied	Pct.	Won	Lost	Tied	Pct.	Won	Lost	Tied	Pct.
Don Shula	Baltimore Colts, Miami Dolphins	29	289	131	6	.685	17	14	0	.548	306	145	6	.676
Chuck Knox	Los Angeles Rams, Buffalo Bills, Seattle Seahawks	19	171	114	1	.600	7	11	0	.389	178	125	1	.587
Joe Gibbs	Washington Redskins	11	115	53	0	.685	15	4	0	.789	130	57	0	.695
Dan Reeves	Denver Broncos	11	102	65	1	.610	7	6	0	.538	109	71	1	.605
Mike Ditka	Chicago Bears	10	101	51	0	.664	6	6	0	.500	107	57	0	.652
Marv Levy	Kansas City Chiefs, Buffalo Bills	11	87	72	0	.547	5	4	0	.556	92	76	0	.548
Tom Flores	Oakland-Los Angeles Raiders, Seattle Seahawks	9	83	53	0	.610	8	3	0	.727	91	56	0	.619
Marty Schottenheimer	Cleveland Browns, Kansas City Chiefs	8	73	45	1	.618	3	6	0	.333	76	51	1	.598
Jack Pardee	Chicago Bears, Washington Redskins, Houston Oilers	8	64	58	0	.525	1	3	0	.250	65	61	0	.516
Sam Wyche	Cincinnati Bengals, Tampa Bay Buccaneers	8	61	66	0	.480	3	2	0	.600	64	68	0	.485
Jim Mora	New Orleans Saints	6	57	38	0	.600	0	3	0	.000	57	41	0	.582
Jerry Glanville	Houston Oilers, Atlanta Falcons	7	48	49	0	.495	3	4	0	.429	51	53	0	.490
George Seifert	San Francisco 49ers	3	38	10	0	.792	4	1	0	.800	42	11	0	.792
Ted Marchibroda	Baltimore-Indianapolis Colts	5	41	33	0	.554	0	3	0	.000	41	36	0	.532
Art Shell	Los Angeles Raiders	3	28	16	0	.636	1	2	0	.333	29	18	0	.617
Wayne Fontes	Detroit Lions	3	27	26	0	.509	1	1	0	.500	28	27	0	.509
Jimmy Johnson	Dallas Cowboys	3	19	29	0	.396	1	1	0	.500	20	30	0	.400
Bruce Coslet	New York Jets	2	14	18	0	.438	0	1	0	.000	14	19	0	.424
Rich Kotite	Philadelphia Eagles	1	10	6	0	.625	0	0	0	.000	10	6	0	.625
Joe Bugel	Phoenix Cardinals	2	9	23	0	.281	0	0	0	.000	9	23	0	.281
Ray Handley	New York Giants	1	8	8	0	.500	0	0	0	.000	8	8	0	.500
Bill Belichick	Cleveland Browns	1	6	10	0	.375	0	0	0	.000	6	10	0	.375
Dick MacPherson	New England Patriots	1	6	10	0	.375	0	0	0	.000	6	10	0	.375
Bill Cowher	Pittsburgh Steelers	0	0	0	0	.000	0	0	0	.000	0	0	0	.000
Dennis Green	Minnesota Vikings	0	0	0	0	.000	0	0	0	.000	0	0	0	.000
Mike Holmgren	Green Bay Packers	0	0	0	0	.000	0	0	0	.000	0	0	0	.000
Bobby Ross	San Diego Chargers	0	0	0	0	.000	0	0	0	.000	0	0	0	.000
Dave Shula	Cincinnati Bengals	0	0	0	0	.000	0	0	0	.000	0	0	0	.000

Coaches With 100 Career Victories (Order Based on Career Victories)

Start of 1992 Season

Coach	Team(s)	Regular Season				Postseason				Career			
		Yrs.	Won	Lost	Tied	Pct.	Won	Lost	Tied	Pct.	Won	Lost	Tied	Pct.
George Halas	Chicago Bears	40	319	148	31	.672	6	3	0	.667	325	151	31	.672
Don Shula	Baltimore Colts, Miami Dolphins	29	289	131	6	.685	17	14	0	.548	306	145	6	.676
Tom Landry	Dallas Cowboys	29	250	162	6	.605	20	16	0	.556	270	178	6	.601
Earl (Curly) Lambeau	Green Bay Packers, Chicago Cardinals, Washington Redskins	33	226	132	22	.624	3	2	0	.600	229	134	22	.623
Chuck Noll	Pittsburgh Steelers	23	193	148	1	.566	16	8	0	.667	209	156	1	.572
Chuck Knox	Los Angeles Rams, Buffalo Bills, Seattle Seahawks	19	171	114	1	.600	7	11	0	.389	178	125	1	.587
Paul Brown	Cleveland Browns, Cincinnati Bengals	21	166	100	6	.621	4	8	0	.333	170	108	6	.609
Bud Grant	Minnesota Vikings	18	158	96	5	.620	10	12	0	.455	168	108	5	.607
Steve Owen	New York Giants	23	151	100	17	.595	2	8	0	.200	153	108	17	.581
Hank Stram	Kansas City Chiefs, New Orleans Saints	17	131	97	10	.571	5	3	0	.625	136	100	10	.573
Weeb Ewbank	Baltimore Colts, New York Jets	20	130	129	7	.502	4	1	0	.800	134	130	7	.507
Joe Gibbs	Washington Redskins	11	115	53	0	.685	15	4	0	.789	130	57	0	.695
Sid Gillman	Los Angeles Rams, Los Angeles-San Diego Chargers, Houston Oilers	18	122	99	7	.550	1	5	0	.167	123	104	7	.541
George Allen	Los Angeles Rams, Washington Redskins	12	116	47	5	.705	2	7	0	.222	118	54	5	.681
Don Coryell	St. Louis Cardinals, San Diego Chargers	14	111	83	1	.572	3	6	0	.333	114	89	1	.561
John Madden	Oakland Raiders	10	103	32	7	.750	9	7	0	.563	112	39	7	.731
Dan Reeves	Denver Broncos	11	102	65	1	.610	7	6	0	.538	109	71	1	.605
Ray (Buddy) Parker	Chicago Cardinals, Detroit Lions, Pittsburgh Steelers	15	104	75	9	.577	3	1	0	.750	107	76	9	.581
Mike Ditka	Chicago Bears	10	101	51	0	.664	6	6	0	.500	107	57	0	.652
Vince Lombardi	Green Bay Packers, Washington Redskins	10	96	34	6	.728	9	1	0	.900	105	35	6	.740
Bill Walsh	San Francisco 49ers	10	92	59	1	.609	10	4	0	.714	102	63	1	.617

Look for in 1992

Things that could happen in 1992

• **Art Monk,** Washington, has 801 career receptions and needs 19 to break Steve Largent's NFL record of 819.

• **James Lofton,** Buffalo, has gained 13,035 career yards on 699 receptions. He needs 55 yards to surpass the NFL record total of Steve Largent (13,089).

• **Jerry Rice,** San Francisco, has caught 93 scoring passes and needs 8 touchdown receptions to break Steve Largent's NFL record of 100.

• **Dan Marino,** Miami, needs 25 touchdown passes to surpass Johnny Unitas's career total of 290 and move into second place in NFL history behind Fran Tarkenton, who had 342 career scoring passes.

• Marino has had 16 games in which he has thrown at least 4 touchdown passes and needs 2 more to become the NFL's all-time leader in that category.

• **Joe Montana,** San Francisco, and Marino, Miami, need 86 and 202 pass completions, respectively, to join Fran Tarkenton (3,686) and Dan Fouts (3,297) as the only players in NFL history with 3,000 completions.

• **Phil Simms,** New York Giants, who enters 1992 with 29,512 passing yards, needs 488 yards to reach 30,000. **John Elway,** Denver, needs 2,026 yards to reach 30,000 yards, and **Warren Moon,** Houston, needs 2,321 yards. Twelve quarterbacks in NFL history have passed for more than 30,000 yards.

• **Eric Dickerson,** Los Angeles Raiders, has 12,439 career rushing yards, 300 behind Tony Dorsett, who stands second in NFL history. The all-time rushing leader is Walter Payton (16,726).

• **James Brooks,** Cleveland, has gained 14,818 combined yards in his NFL career. He needs 642 yards to surpass Jim Brown's total of 15,459 and move into third place in NFL history.

• Rice, **Marcus Allen,** Los Angeles Raiders, and Dickerson, each have a chance to join seven other players in NFL history who have scored 100 touchdowns. Rice needs 3, Allen 5, and Dickerson 7 to reach the century mark. The seven players who have scored 100 career touchdowns are: Jim Brown, Walter Payton, John Riggins, Lenny Moore, Don Hutson, Steve Largent, and Franco Harris.

• **Nick Lowery,** Kansas City, needs 16 field goals to become the sixth player in NFL history to kick 300 field goals.

• **Morten Andersen,** New Orleans, has scored 965 points and needs 35 more to become the twentieth player in NFL history to reach the 1,000-point plateau.

• **Don Shula,** Miami's head coach, starts the season with 289 regular-season victories and needs 11 more to reach 300. George Halas (319) is the only coach in NFL history to reach that milestone.

• **Marv Levy,** Buffalo's head coach, has 92 career victories. He needs 8 more to reach 100 in his career.

• **Kevin Butler,** Chicago, has scored 722 points and needs 29 to surpass Walter Payton as the Bears' all-time leading scorer.

• **Barry Sanders,** Detroit, has gained 4,322 rushing yards and needs 785 yards to surpass Billy Sims's club record of 5,106. With Sanders's next touchdown, he will break Sims's club record of 47 career touchdowns.

• **Mark Clayton,** Miami, who has 507 career receptions, needs 4 to eclipse the Dolphins' club record established by Nat Moore.

• **Christian Okoye,** Kansas City, who has 4,449 rushing yards, only needs 3 yards to break the club record held by Ed Podolak.

• **Anthony Carter,** Minnesota, has gained 6,281 yards on receptions and has caught 45 touchdown passes. He needs 120 yards and 6 touchdown receptions to break the Vikings' records, both held by Sammy White (6,400 and 50).

• **Stephone Paige,** Kansas City, has 377 career receptions and needs 40 in 1992 to break the Chiefs' record of 416, held by Henry Marshall. With 49 touchdown receptions, Paige needs 9 more to eclipse Otis Taylor's club record of 57.

• **Ken O'Brien,** New York Jets, has passed for 23,744 yards. He needs 3,314 yards to surpass the club record of 27,057 held by Joe Namath.

• **Jim Everett,** Los Angeles Rams, has passed for 18,783 yards. He needs 3,441 yards to overtake Roman Gabriel, who holds the club record with 22,223.

• **Henry Ellard,** Los Angeles Rams, has 47 career touchdowns, 11 shy of the club record held by Eric Dickerson.

• **Vinny Testaverde,** Tampa Bay, has passed for 63 career touchdowns and needs 11 to break Doug Williams's club record of 73. Testaverde, who starts the season with 12,266 passing yards, needs 383 yards to break the club record of 12,648, also held by Williams.

• **Darrell Green,** Washington, has 29 career interceptions, 8 shy of becoming the club's all-time leader.

• **Eddie Brown,** Cincinnati, has caught 41 touchdown passes, 12 shy of the Bengals' record of 53 held by Isaac Curtis.

• **Warren Moon,** Houston, who has passed for 157 touchdowns, needs 9 to break George Blanda's club record of 165.

• **Deron Cherry,** Kansas City, has 50 career interceptions, 8 shy of the Chiefs' record held by Emmitt Thomas.

• **Earnest Byner,** Washington, needs 1,000 rushing yards in 1992 to become the first running back in Redskins' history to post three consecutive 1,000-yard seasons. Byner rushed for 1,219 in 1990 and 1,048 in 1991.

• **Randall Cunningham,** Philadelphia, has 3,437 career rushing yards, 237 shy of the NFL's all-time record for a quarterback held by Fran Tarkenton (3,674).

• **Al Toon,** New York Jets, has 486 career receptions. He needs 14 catches to join Don Maynard (627) as the only two players in club history with at least 500 receptions.

• **Eric Martin,** New Orleans, needs at least 1 reception in each of his first 7 games to eclipse the club record of 79 held by Danny Abramowicz. Martin has receptions in his last 73 games.

• **Steve DeBerg,** Tampa Bay, needs 545 passing yards to reach 32,000 for his career. DeBerg currently has 31,455 career passing yards.

• **Thurman Thomas,** Buffalo, needs 171 rushing yards to reach 5,000 for his career. Thomas currently has 4,829 career rushing yards. Thomas also will try to extend Buffalo's unbeaten streak to 20-0 when he tops the 100-yard rushing mark. The Bills have won 19 consecutive games when Thomas has rushed for 100 yards or more.

THE AFC

Buffalo Bills 26

Cincinnati Bengals 30

Cleveland Browns 34

Denver Broncos 38

Houston Oilers 42

Indianapolis Colts 46

Kansas City Chiefs 50

Los Angeles Raiders 54

Miami Dolphins 58

New England Patriots 62

New York Jets 66

Pittsburgh Steelers 70

San Diego Chargers 74

Seattle Seahawks 78

American Football Conference Eastern Division

Team Colors: Royal Blue, Scarlet Red, and White

One Bills Drive
Orchard Park, New York 14127
Telephone: (716) 648-1800

Club Officials

President: Ralph C. Wilson, Jr.
Vice President: Linda Bogdan
General Manager and Vice President-
  Administration: Bill Polian
Vice President-Head Coach: Marv Levy
Treasurer: Jeffrey C. Littmann
Executive Assistant to General Manager:
  Christy Wilson
Asst. G.M./Director of Pro Personnel: Bob Ferguson
Asst. G.M./Business Operations: Bill Munson
Director of Administration: Ed Stillwell
Business Manager: Jim Overdorf
Director of Player Personnel: John Butler
Asst. Dir./Collegiate Scouting: A.J. Smith
Director of Marketing/Sales: Jerry Foran
Director of Public/Community Relations:
  Denny Lynch
Director of Media Relations: Scott Berchtold
Director of Stadium Operations: Steve Champlin
Box Office Comptroller: June Foran
Equipment Manager: Dave Hojnowski
Strength/Conditioning Coordinator: Rusty Jones
Trainers: Ed Abramoski, Bud Carpenter, Bill Ford
Video Director: Henry Kunttu

Stadium: Rich Stadium • **Capacity:** 80,290
  One Bills Drive
  Orchard Park, New York 14127

Playing Surface: AstroTurf

Training Camp: Fredonia State University
  Fredonia, New York 14063

1992 Schedule

Preseason
Aug. 8	at Minnesota	7:00
Aug. 17	**Detroit**	8:00
Aug. 24	at Kansas City	7:00
Aug. 28	at Atlanta	8:00

Regular Season
Sept. 6	**Los Angeles Rams**	1:00
Sept. 13	at San Francisco	1:00
Sept. 20	**Indianapolis**	8:00
Sept. 27	at New England	1:00
Oct. 4	**Miami**	1:00
Oct. 11	at Los Angeles Raiders	1:00
Oct. 18	**Open Date**	
Oct. 26	at N.Y. Jets (Monday)	9:00
Nov. 1	**New England**	1:00
Nov. 8	**Pittsburgh**	4:00
Nov. 16	at Miami (Monday)	9:00
Nov. 22	**Atlanta**	1:00
Nov. 29	at Indianapolis	4:00
Dec. 6	**New York Jets**	1:00
Dec. 12	**Denver** (Saturday)	12:30
Dec. 20	at New Orleans	12:00
Dec. 27	at Houston	7:00

Bills Coaching History

(219-258-8)
1960-61	Buster Ramsey	11-16-1
1962-65	Lou Saban	38-18-3
1966-68	Joe Collier*	13-17-1
1968	Harvey Johnson	1-10-1
1969-70	John Rauch	7-20-1
1971	Harvey Johnson	1-13-0
1972-76	Lou Saban**	32-29-1
1976-77	Jim Ringo	3-20-0
1978-82	Chuck Knox	38-38-0
1983-85	Kay Stephenson***	10-26-0
1985-86	Hank Bullough****	4-17-0
1986-91	Marv Levy	61-34-0

  *Released after two games in 1968
  **Resigned after five games in 1976
  ***Released after four games in 1985
  ****Released after nine games in 1986

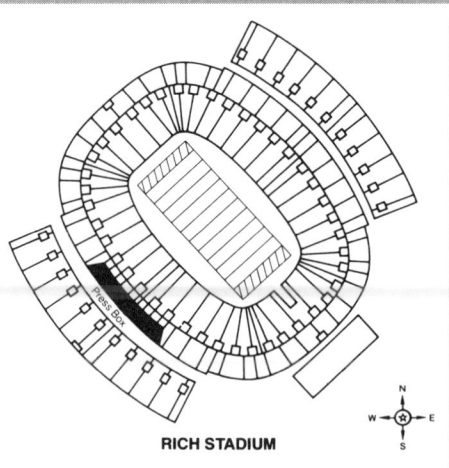

RICH STADIUM

Record Holders
Individual Records—Career
Category	Name	Performance
Rushing (Yds.)	O.J. Simpson, 1969-1977	10,183
Passing (Yds.)	Joe Ferguson, 1973-1984	27,590
Passing (TDs)	Joe Ferguson, 1973-1984	181
Receiving (No.)	Andre Reed, 1985-1991	469
Receiving (Yds.)	Andre Reed, 1985-1991	6,466
Interceptions	George (Butch) Byrd, 1964-1970	40
Punting (Avg.)	Paul Maguire, 1964-1970	42.1
Punt Return (Avg.)	Keith Moody, 1976-79	10.5
Kickoff Return (Avg.)	Wallace Francis, 1973-74	27.2
Field Goals	Scott Norwood, 1985-1991	133
Touchdowns (Tot.)	O.J. Simpson, 1969-1977	70
Points	Scott Norwood, 1985-1991	670

Individual Records—Single Season
Category	Name	Performance
Rushing (Yds.)	O.J. Simpson, 1973	2,003
Passing (Yds.)	Jim Kelly, 1991	3,844
Passing (TDs)	Jim Kelly, 1991	33
Receiving (No.)	Andre Reed, 1989	88
Receiving (Yds.)	Andre Reed, 1989	1,312
Interceptions	Billy Atkins, 1961	10
	Tom Janik, 1967	10
Punting (Avg.)	Billy Atkins, 1961	44.5
Punt Return (Avg.)	Keith Moody, 1977	13.1
Kickoff Return (Avg.)	Ed Rutkowski, 1963	30.2
Field Goals	Scott Norwood, 1988	32
Touchdowns (Tot.)	O.J. Simpson, 1975	23
Points	O.J. Simpson, 1975	138

Individual Records—Single Game
Category	Name	Performance
Rushing (Yds.)	O.J. Simpson, 11-25-76	273
Passing (Yds.)	Joe Ferguson, 10-9-83	419
Passing (TDs)	Jim Kelly, 9-8-91	6
Receiving (No.)	Greg Bell, 9-8-85	13
	Andre Reed, 9-18-89	13
	Thurman Thomas, 9-15-91	13
Receiving (Yds.)	Jerry Butler, 9-23-79	255
Interceptions	Many Times	3
	Last time by Jeff Nixon, 9-7-80	
Field Goals	Pete Gogolak, 12-5-65	5
	Scott Norwood, 9-25-88	5
Touchdowns (Tot.)	Cookie Gilchrist, 12-8-63	5
Points	Cookie Gilchrist, 12-8-63	30

1991 Team Record
Preseason (2-3)

Date	Result		Opponents
7/28	W	17-13	vs. Philadelphia at London
8/5	L	17-23	at N.Y. Giants
8/10	W	21-16	Detroit
8/17	L	24-35	vs. Green Bay at Madison, Wis.
8/24	L	13-30	at Chicago

Regular Season (13-3)

Date	Result		Opponents	Att.
9/1	W	35-31	Miami	80,252
9/8	W	52-34	Pittsburgh	79,545
9/15	W	23-20	at N.Y. Jets	65,309
9/22	W	17-10	at Tampa Bay	57,323
9/29	W	35-20	Chicago	80,366
10/7	L	6-33	at Kansas City	76,120
10/13	W	42- 6	Indianapolis	79,015
10/21	W	35-16	Cincinnati	80,131
11/3	W	22-17	New England	78,278
11/10	W	34-24	at Green Bay	52,175
11/18	W	41-27	at Miami	71,062
11/24	L	13-16	at New England	47,053
12/1	W	24-13	N.Y. Jets	80,243
12/8	W	30-27	at L.A. Raiders (OT)	85,081
12/15	W	35- 7	at Indianapolis	48,286
12/22	L	14-17	Detroit (OT)	78,059

(OT) Overtime

Postseason (2-1)

Date	Result		Opponent	Att.
1/5	W	37-14	Kansas City	80,182
1/12	W	10- 7	Denver	82,272
1/26	L	24-37	Washington	63,130

Score by Periods

Bills	82	130	106	137	3	—	458
Opponents	40	87	92	96	3	—	318

Attendance
Home 635,889   Away 502,409   Total 1,138,298
Single-game home record, 80,366 (9-29-91)
Single-season home record, 635,889 (1991)*
*NFL record

1991 Team Statistics

	Bills	Opp.
Total First Downs	359	335
Rushing	128	138
Passing	208	166
Penalty	23	31
Third Down: Made/Att.	90/191	74/218
Third Down: Pct.	47.1	33.9
Fourth Down: Made/Att.	4/12	8/20
Fourth Down: Pct.	33.3	40.0
Total Net Yards	6252	5458
Avg. Per Game	390.8	341.1
Total Plays	1056	1086
Avg. Per Play	5.9	5.0
Net Yards Rushing	2381	2044
Avg. Per Game	148.8	127.8
Total Rushes	505	519
Net Yards Passing	3871	3414
Avg. Per Game	241.9	213.4
Sacked/Yards Lost	35/269	31/246
Gross Yards	4140	3660
Att./Completions	516/332	536/299
Completion Pct.	64.3	55.8
Had Intercepted	19	23
Punts/Avg.	54/38.6	70/39.1
Net Punting Avg.	36.1	33.4
Penalties/Yards Lost	113/865	110/938
Fumbles/Ball Lost	25/16	26/14
Touchdowns	58	34
Rushing	16	20
Passing	39	12
Returns	3	2
Avg. Time of Possession	26:04	33:56

1991 Individual Statistics

Scoring

	TD R	TD P	TD Rt	PAT	FG	Saf	TP
Norwood	0	0	0	56/58	18/29	0	110
Thomas	7	5	0	0/0	0/0	0	72
Reed	0	10	0	0/0	0/0	0	60
Lofton	0	8	0	0/0	0/0	0	48
Beebe	0	6	0	0/0	0/0	0	36
K. Davis	4	1	0	0/0	0/0	0	30
Gardner	4	0	0	0/0	0/0	0	24
McKeller	0	3	0	0/0	0/0	0	18
Edwards	0	1	1	0/0	0/0	0	12
Metzelaars	0	2	0	0/0	0/0	0	12
Rolle	0	2	0	0/0	0/0	0	12
Daluiso, Atl.-Buff.	0	0	0	2/2	2/3	0	8
Bennett	0	0	1	0/0	0/0	0	6
Kelly	1	0	0	0/0	0/0	0	6
Odomes	0	0	1	0/0	0/0	0	6
Tasker	0	1	0	0/0	0/0	0	6
Bills	16	39	3	56/58	18/29	0	458
Opponents	20	12	2	33/34	27/35	0	318

Passing

	Att.	Comp.	Yds.	Pct.	TD	Int.	Tkld.	Rate
Kelly	474	304	3844	64.1	33	17	31/227	97.6
Reich	41	27	305	65.9	6	2	4/42	107.2
Mohr	1	1	-9	100.0	0	0	0/0	79.2
Bills	516	332	4140	64.3	39	19	35/269	99.0
Opponents	536	299	3660	55.8	12	23	31/246	66.6

Rushing

	Att.	Yds.	Avg.	LG	TD
Thomas	288	1407	4.9	33	7
K. Davis	129	624	4.8	78t	4
Gardner	42	146	3.5	18	4
Reed	12	136	11.3	46	0
Kelly	20	45	2.3	12	1
Edwards	1	17	17.0	17	0
Reich	13	6	0.5	8	0
Bills	505	2381	4.7	78t	16
Opponents	519	2044	3.9	56t	20

Receiving

	No.	Yds.	Avg.	LG	TD
Reed	81	1113	13.7	55	10
Thomas	62	631	10.2	50t	5
Lofton	57	1072	18.8	77t	8
McKeller	44	434	9.9	29t	3
Beebe	32	414	12.9	34t	6
Edwards	22	228	10.4	33t	1
K. Davis	20	118	5.9	14t	1
Metzelaars	5	54	10.8	51t	2
Gardner	3	20	6.7	11	0
Rolle	3	10	3.3	5	2
Tasker	2	39	19.5	20t	1
Alexander	1	7	7.0	7	0
Bills	332	4140	12.5	77t	39
Opponents	299	3660	12.2	78t	12

Interceptions

	No.	Yds.	Avg.	LG	TD
Odomes	5	120	24.0	48	1
Talley	5	45	9.0	13	0
Jackson	4	31	7.8	15	0
L. Smith	3	22	7.3	22	0
Kelso	2	0	0.0	0	0
Bentley	1	58	58.0	58	0
Hale	1	0	0.0	0	0
Hicks	1	0	0.0	0	0
Williams	1	0	0.0	0	0
Bills	23	276	12.0	58	1
Opponents	19	320	16.8	57t	2

Punting

	No.	Yds.	Avg.	In 20	LG
Mohr	54	2085	38.6	12	58
Bills	54	2085	38.6	12	58
Opponents	70	2740	39.1	19	93

Punt Returns

	No.	FC	Yds.	Avg.	LG	TD
Edwards	13	9	69	5.3	21	0
Hicks	12	7	203	16.9	59	0
Odomes	1	0	9	9.0	9	0
Bills	26	16	281	10.8	59	0
Opponents	15	17	53	3.5	20	0

Kickoff Returns

	No.	Yds.	Avg.	LG	TD
Edwards	31	623	20.1	91t	1
Fuller	8	125	15.6	22	0
Beebe	7	121	17.3	24	0
K. Davis	4	73	18.3	23	0
Gardner	1	10	10.0	10	0
Taylor	1	18	18.0	18	0
Bills	52	970	18.7	91t	1
Opponents	62	1266	20.4	54	0

Sacks

	No.
Bennett	9.0
Wright	6.0
Talley	4.0
Hansen	2.0
L. Smith	2.0
Lodish	1.5
B. Smith	1.5
Jackson	1.0
Odomes	1.0
Rogers	1.0
Seals	1.0
Bills	31.0
Opponents	35.0

1992 Draft Choices

Round	Name	Pos.	College
1.	John Fina	T	Arizona
2.	James Patton	NT	Texas
3.	Keith Goganious	LB	Penn State
4.	Frank Kmet	DE	Purdue
5.	Matt Darby	DB	UCLA
6.	Nate Turner	TE	Nebraska
7.	Kurt Schulz	DB	E. Washington
8.	Leonard Humphries	DB	Penn State
9.	Chris Walsh	WR	Stanford
10.	Barry Rose	WR	Wis.-Stevens Point
11.	Vince Marrow	TE	Toledo
12.	Matt Rodgers	QB	Iowa

Buffalo Bills 1992 Veteran Roster

No.	Name	Pos.	Ht.	Wt.	Birth-date	NFL Exp.	College	Hometown	How Acq.	'91 Games/Starts
54	Bailey, Carlton	LB	6-3	235	12/15/64	5	North Carolina	Baltimore, Md.	D9-'88	16/16
62	Baldinger, Brian	G-T	6-4	278	1/7/59	10	Duke	Massapequa, N.Y.	PB(Ind)-'92#	16/14*
92	Baldinger, Gary	NT	6-3	270	10/4/63	6	Wake Forest	Massapequa, N.Y.	FA-'90	7/0
75	Ballard, Howard	T	6-6	325	11/3/63	5	Alabama A&M	Ashland, Ala.	D11-'87	16/16
82	†Beebe, Don	WR	5-11	184	12/18/64	4	Chadron State	Sugar Grove, Ill.	D3-'89	11/7
97	†Bennett, Cornelius	LB	6-2	238	8/25/66	6	Alabama	Birmingham, Ala.	T(Ind)-'87	16/16
64	Brennan, Mike	G-T	6-5	285	3/22/67	3	Notre Dame	Baltimore, Md.	FA-'91	0*
57	Brownlow, Darrick	LB	5-10	240	12/28/68	2	Illinois	Indianapolis, Ind.	PB(Dall)-'92#	16/0*
2	Christie, Steve	K	6-0	185	11/13/67	3	William & Mary	Oakville, Canada	PB(TB)-'92#	16/0*
58	Conlan, Shane	LB	6-3	230	3/4/64	6	Penn State	Frewsburg, N.Y.	D1-'87	16/15
60	Davis, Darrell	LB	6-2	264	3/10/66	3	Texas Christian	Midland, Tex.	FA-'92	13/0*
65	Davis, John	G	6-4	310	8/22/65	6	Georgia Tech	Ellijay, Ga.	PB(Hou)-'89#	12/12
23	†Davis, Kenneth	RB	5-10	208	4/16/62	7	Texas Christian	Temple, Tex.	PB(GB)-'89#	16/1
45	Drane, Dwight	S	6-2	205	5/6/62	7	Oklahoma	Miami, Fla.	SD1-'84	14/0
85	†Edwards, Al	WR	5-8	173	5/18/67	3	Northwestern Louisiana	Kenner, La.	D11-'90	16/5
50	Fairs, Eric	LB	6-3	244	2/17/64	7	Memphis State	Memphis, Tenn.	PB(Hou)-'92#	16/0*
59	Frerotte, Mitch	G-T	6-3	285	3/30/65	4	Penn State	Kittanning, Pa.	FA-'88	16/0
33	Fuller, Eddie	RB	5-9	201	6/22/68	2	Louisiana State	Leesville, La.	D4-'90	5/0
25	Gamble, Kenny	RB	5-10	206	3/8/65	4	Colgate	Holyoke, Mass.	FA-'92	0*
35	Gardner, Carwell	RB	6-2	232	11/27/66	3	Louisville	Louisville, Ky.	D2-'90	16/5
99	Garner, Hal	LB	6-4	238	1/18/62	6	Utah State	Logan, Utah	D3b-'85	16/0
7	Gilbert, Gale	QB	6-3	210	12/20/61	5	California	Red Bluff, Calif.	FA-'89	0*
26	Hale, Chris	CB	5-7	170	1/4/66	4	Southern California	Monrovia, Calif.	D7b-'89	5/0
90	Hansen, Phil	DE	6-5	275	5/20/68	2	North Dakota State	Ellendale, N.D.	D2-'91	14/10
52	Harvey, Richard	LB	6-1	235	9/11/66	2	Tulane	Pascagoula, Miss.	FA-'92	1/0*
27	Hicks, Clifford	CB	5-10	188	8/18/64	6	Oregon	San Diego, Calif.	FA-'90	16/0
67	Hull, Kent	C	6-5	278	1/13/61	7	Mississippi State	Greenwood, Miss.	FA-'86	16/16
47	†Jackson, Kirby	CB	5-10	180	2/2/65	6	Mississippi State	Sturgis, Miss.	FA-'87	16/12
20	Jones, Henry	S	5-11	197	12/29/67	2	Illinois	St. Louis, Mo.	D1-'91	15/0
98	Jones, Marlon	DE	6-4	278	7/1/64	3	Central State, Ohio	Baltimore, Md.	FA-'92	0*
12	Kelly, Jim	QB	6-3	218	2/14/60	7	Miami	East Brady, Pa.	D1b-'83	15/15
38	Kelso, Mark	S	5-11	185	7/23/63	7	William & Mary	Pittsburgh, Pa.	FA-'86	16/16
63	Lingner, Adam	C	6-4	268	11/2/60	10	Illinois	Rock Island, Ill.	PB(KC)-'89#	16/0
73	†Lodish, Mike	NT	6-3	272	8/11/67	3	UCLA	Birmingham, Mich.	D10-'90	16/6
80	Lofton, James	WR	6-3	190	7/5/56	15	Stanford	Los Angeles, Calif.	FA-'89	15/0
84	†McKeller, Keith	TE	6-4	245	7/9/64	5	Jacksonville State	Fairfield, Ala.	D9-'87	16/14
88	Metzelaars, Pete	TE	6-7	250	5/24/60	11	Wabash	Portage, Mich.	T(Sea)-'85	16/1
9	Mohr, Chris	P	6-5	215	5/11/66	3	Alabama	Thomson, Ga.	FA-'91	16/0
41	Mueller, Jamie	RB	6-1	224	10/4/64	5	Benedictine	Fairview Park, Ohio	D3b-'87	0*
11	Norwood, Scott	K	6-0	207	7/17/60	8	James Madison	Alexandria, Va.	FA-'85	16/0
37	Odomes, Nate	CB	5-10	188	8/25/65	6	Wisconsin	Columbus, Ga.	D2a-'87	16/16
74	Parker, Glenn	G-T	6-5	305	4/22/66	3	Arizona	Huntington Beach, Calif.	D3-'90	16/5
44	Paterra, Greg	RB	5-11	220	5/11/67	3	Slippery Rock	McKeesport, Pa.	FA-'91	0*
53	Patton, Marvcus	LB	6-2	225	5/1/67	3	UCLA	Lawndale, Calif.	D8-'90	16/2
94	Pike, Mark	DE	6-4	272	12/27/63	6	Georgia Tech	Villa Hills, Ky.	D7b-'86	16/1
83	Reed, Andre	WR	6-2	190	1/29/64	8	Kutztown State	Allentown, Pa.	D4a-'85	16/16
14	Reich, Frank	QB	6-4	210	12/4/61	8	Maryland	Lebanon, Pa.	D3a-'85	16/1
51	Ritcher, Jim	G	6-3	273	5/21/58	13	North Carolina State	Medina, Ohio	D1-'80	16/16
96	†Seals, Leon	DE	6-5	270	1/30/64	6	Jackson State	Baton Rouge, La.	D4b-'87	16/16
77	Sims, Kenneth	DE	6-5	290	10/31/59	8	Texas	Kosse, Tex.	FA-'92	0*
78	Smith, Bruce	DE	6-4	273	6/18/63	8	Virginia Tech	Norfolk, Va.	D1a-'85	5/5
46	Smith, Leonard	S	5-11	202	9/2/60	10	McNeese State	Baton Rouge, La.	T(Phx)-'88	16/16
79	Staysniak, Joe	T	6-5	295	12/8/66	2	Ohio State	Elyria, Ohio	FA-'90	2/0
56	Talley, Darryl	LB	6-4	235	7/10/60	10	West Virginia	Cleveland, Ohio	D2-'83	16/16
89	Tasker, Steve	WR	5-9	183	4/10/62	8	Northwestern	Leoti, Kan.	W(Hou)-'86	16/0
21	Taylor, Brian	S	5-10	195	10/1/67	3	Oregon State	New Orleans, La.	FA-'91	3/0
87	Thomas, Ed	TE	6-3	245	5/4/66	3	Houston	New Orleans, La.	PB(TB)-'92#	6/0*
34	Thomas, Thurman	RB	5-10	198	5/16/66	5	Oklahoma State	Missouri City, Tex.	D2-'88	15/15
72	Williams, Chris	NT	6-3	304	11/23/68	2	American International	Brockton, Mass.	PB(Phx)-'92#	15/0*
31	Williams, James	CB	5-10	178	3/30/67	3	Fresno State	Coalinga, Calif.	D1-'90	8/4
69	Wolford, Will	T	6-5	297	5/18/64	7	Vanderbilt	Louisville, Ky.	D1b-'86	15/15
91	Wright, Jeff	NT	6-3	270	6/13/63	5	Central Missouri State	Lawrence, Kan.	D8b-'88	9/9

* B. Baldinger played 16 games with Indianapolis in '91; Brennan active for 1 game but did not play; Brownlow played 16 games with Dallas; Christie played 16 games with Tampa Bay; D. Davis played 13 games with N.Y. Jets; Fairs played 16 games with Houston; Gamble last active with Kansas City in '90; Gilbert active for 3 games but did not play; Harvey played 1 game with New England; M. Jones last active with Cleveland in '89; Mueller and Paterra missed '91 season due to injury; Sims last active with New England in '89; E. Thomas played 6 games with Tampa Bay; C. Williams played 15 games with Phoenix.

† Option playout; subject to developments.

Plan B unconditional free agent.

Players lost through Plan B (4): LB Ray Bentley (Cin; 16 games in '91), K Brad Daluiso (Dall; 14), WR Mike Alexander (Raid; 3), TE Butch Rolle (Phx; 16).

Also played with Bills in '91—LB David Bavaro (2 games), NT Odell Haggins (5), CB-S Chris Oldham (2), DE Reggie Rogers (2).

COACHING STAFF

Head Coach, Marv Levy

Pro Career: Begins his sixth full season as Bills head coach. Led the Bills to their second consecutive AFC championship and their fourth straight AFC East title in 1991. Under Levy, the Bills recorded 13-3 records in 1990 and 1991, the best regular-season marks in club history. He guided the Bills to their second consecutive AFC East title with a 9-7 record in 1989. Finished 1988 season with a 12-4 record and a berth in the AFC Championship Game. In his first full year with Bills in 1987, he led team to a 7-8 record. Replaced Hank Bullough on November 3, 1986, and compiled a 2-5 record over the final seven weeks of the season. Previously served as head coach of the Kansas City Chiefs from 1978-1982 and produced a 31-42 mark. Levy began his pro coaching career in 1969 as an assistant with the Philadelphia Eagles. He joined George Allen and the Los Angeles Rams as an assistant one year later and followed Allen to Washington, where he remained with the Redskins through the 1972 season when Washington played in Super Bowl VII. He was named head coach of the Montreal Alouettes (CFL) in 1973 and posted a 50-34-4 record and two Grey Cup victories (1974, 1977) in five seasons in Canada. After two seasons away from football, he became head coach of the Chicago Blitz of the USFL in 1984. No pro playing experience. Career NFL record: 92-76.

Background: Running back at Coe College 1948-1950. Coached at high school level for two years before returning to alma mater from 1953-55. Joined New Mexico staff in 1956 and served as head coach there in 1958-59. Head coach at California from 1960-63 before becoming head coach at William & Mary from 1964-68.

Personal: Born August 3, 1928, Chicago, Ill. Levy was Phi Beta Kappa at Coe College and earned master's degree in English history from Harvard. He lives in Orchard Park, N.Y.

Assistant Coaches

Tom Bresnahan, offensive coordinator-offensive line; born January 21, 1935, Springfield, Mass., lives in Hamburg, N.Y. Tackle Holy Cross 1953-55. No pro playing experience. College coach: Williams 1963-67, Columbia 1968-72, Navy 1973-80. Pro coach: Kansas City Chiefs 1981-82, New York Giants 1983-84, St. Louis/Phoenix Cardinals 1986-88, joined Bills in 1989.

Walt Corey, defensive coordinator-linebackers; born May 9, 1938, Latrobe, Pa., lives in West Seneca, N.Y. Defensive end Miami 1957-59. Pro linebacker Kansas City Chiefs 1960-66. College coach: Utah State 1967-69, Miami 1970-71. Pro coach: Kansas City Chiefs 1971-74, 1978-86, Cleveland Browns 1975-77, joined Bills in 1987.

Bruce DeHaven, special teams; born September 6, 1952, Trousdale, Kan., lives in East Aurora, N.Y. No college or pro playing experience. College coach: Kansas 1979-81, New Mexico State 1982. Pro coach: New Jersey Generals (USFL) 1983, Pittsburgh Maulers (USFL) 1984, Orlando Renegades (USFL) 1985, joined Bills in 1987.

Charlie Joiner, receivers; born October 14, 1947, Many, La., lives in Orchard Park, N.Y. Wide receiver Grambling 1965-68. Defensive back-wide receiver Houston Oilers 1969-72, Cincinnati Bengals 1972-75, San Diego Chargers 1976-86. Pro coach: San Diego Chargers 1987-91, joined Bills in 1992.

Rusty Jones, strength and conditioning; born August 14, 1953, Berwick, Maine, lives in Lakeview, N.Y. No college or pro playing experience. College coach: Springfield 1978-79. Pro coach: Pittsburgh Maulers (USFL) 1983-84, joined Bills in 1985.

Don Lawrence, offensive quality control-tight ends; born June 4, 1937, Cleveland, Ohio, lives in Orchard Park, N.Y. Offensive-defensive lineman Notre Dame 1957-59. Pro offensive-defensive lineman Washington Redskins 1959-61. College coach: Notre Dame 1961-63, Kansas State 1964-65, Cincinnati 1966, Virginia 1970-73 (head coach 1971-73), Texas Christian 1974-75, Missouri 1976-77. Pro coach: British Columbia Lions (CFL) 1978-79, Kansas City Chiefs 1980-82, 1987-88, Buffalo Bills 1983-84, Tampa Bay Buccaneers 1985-86, Winnipeg Blue Bombers (CFL) 1989, rejoined Bills in 1990.

Chuck Lester, defensive quality control-administrative assistant to head coach; born May 18, 1955, Chicago, Ill., lives in Orchard Park, N.Y. Linebacker Oklahoma 1974. No pro playing experience. College coach: Iowa State 1980-81, Oklahoma 1982-84. Pro coach: Kansas City Chiefs 1984-86 (scout), joined Bills in 1987.

Elijah Pitts, assistant head coach-running backs; born February 3, 1938, Mayflower, Ark., lives in Orchard Park, N.Y. Running back Philander Smith 1957-60. Pro running back Green Bay Packers 1961-69, 1971, Los Angeles Rams 1970, Chicago Bears 1970, New Orleans Saints 1970. Pro coach: Los Angeles Rams 1974-77, Buffalo Bills 1978-80, Houston Oilers 1981-83, Hamilton Tiger-Cats (CFL) 1984, rejoined Bills in 1985.

Dick Roach, defensive backs; born August 23, 1937, Rapid City, S.D., lives in West Seneca, N.Y. Defensive back Black Hills State 1952-55. No pro playing experience. College coach: Montana State 1966-69, Oregon State 1970, Wyoming 1971-72, Fresno State 1973, Washington State 1974-75. Pro coach: Montreal Alouettes (CFL) 1976-77, Kansas City Chiefs 1978-80, New England Patriots 1981, Michigan Panthers (USFL) 1983-84, Tampa Bay Buccaneers 1985-86, joined Bills in 1987.

Dan Sekanovich, defensive line; born July 27, 1933, West Hazleton, Pa., lives in Orchard Park, N.Y. End Tennessee 1951-53. Pro defensive end Montreal Alouettes (CFL) 1954. College coach: Susquehanna 1961-63, Connecticut 1964-67, Pittsburgh 1968, Navy 1969-70, Kentucky 1971-72. Pro coach: Montreal Alouettes (CFL) 1973-76, New York Jets 1977-82, Atlanta Falcons 1983-85, Miami Dolphins 1986-91, joined Bills in 1992.

Jim Shofner, quarterbacks; born December 18, 1935, Grapevine, Tex., lives in Orchard Park, N.Y. Running back Texas Christian 1955-57. Pro defensive back Cleveland Browns 1958-63. College coach: Texas Christian 1964-66, 1974-76 (head coach). Pro coach: San Francisco 49ers 1967-73, 1977, Cleveland Browns 1978-80, 1990-91 (head coach last 7 games in 1990), (director of player personnel in 1991), Houston Oilers 1981-82, Dallas Cowboys 1983-85, St. Louis/Phoenix Cardinals 1986-89, joined Bills in 1992.

Buffalo Bills 1992 First-Year Roster

Name	Pos.	Ht.	Wt.	Birth-date	College	Hometown	How Acq.
Childs, Jason	T	6-4	280	1/6/69	North Dakota	Crystal, Minn.	FA
Crouch, Jim	K	6-4	175	9/13/68	Cal State-Sacramento	Los Altos, Calif.	FA
Darby, Matt	S	6-1	200	11/19/68	UCLA	Virginia Beach, Va.	D5
Fina, John	G-T	6-4	282	3/11/69	Arizona	Tucson, Ariz.	D1
Goganious, Keith	LB	6-2	237	12/7/68	Penn State	Virginia Beach, Va.	D3
Griffith, Howard (1)	RB	6-0	223	11/17/67	Illinois	Chicago, Ill.	FA
Helkowski, Doug	P	6-0	195	9/10/69	Penn State	Ruffsdale, Pa.	FA
Humphries, Leonard	CB-S	5-9	170	6/19/70	Penn State	Akron, Ohio	D8
Kmet, Frank	DE-DT	6-3	289	3/13/70	Purdue	Mt. Prospect, Ill.	D4
Lamb, Brad (1)	WR	5-10	171	10/7/67	Anderson, Ind.	Middletown, Ohio	D8-'91
Maddox, Mark (1)	LB	6-1	233	3/23/68	Northern Michigan	Milwaukee, Wis.	D9-'91
Marrow, Vince	TE	6-3	251	8/17/68	Toledo	Youngstown, Ohio	D11
Mayfield, Curtis (1)	WR	5-11	174	3/23/68	Oklahoma State	Dallas, Tex.	FA
Patton, James	DE-DT	6-3	276	1/5/70	Texas	Houston, Tex.	D2
Rodgers, Matt	QB	6-4	205	1/8/69	Iowa	Walpole, Mass.	D12
Rose, Barry	WR	6-0	190	7/28/68	Wis.-Stevens Point	Baldwin, Wis.	D10
Schulz, Kurt	S	6-1	206	12/12/68	Eastern Washington	Yakima, Wash.	D7
Stephenson, Jeffrey (1)	LB	6-4	240	12/14/65	St. Cloud State	Minneapolis, Minn.	FA
Turner, Nate	TE	6-1	241	5/28/69	Nebraska	Chicago, Ill.	D6
Walsh, Chris	WR	6-1	185	12/12/68	Stanford	Concord, Calif.	D9
Wren, Darryl (1)	CB	6-0	186	1/25/67	Pittsburg, Kan.	Tulsa, Okla.	D3-'91

The term NFL Rookie is defined as a player who is in his first season of professional football and has not been on the roster of another professional football team for any regular-season or postseason games. A Rookie is designated by an "R" on NFL rosters. Players who have been active in another professional football league or players who have NFL experience, including either preseason training camp or being on an active roster for fewer than three regular-season or postseason games, are termed NFL First-Year Players. An NFL First-Year Player is designated by a "1" on NFL rosters. Thereafter, a player on an NFL active roster for at least three regular-season or postseason games is credited with an earned year of NFL playing experience.

NOTES

_____

_____

_____

_____

_____

_____

_____

_____

_____

American Football Conference Central Division

Team Colors: Black, Orange, and White

200 Riverfront Stadium
Cincinnati, Ohio 45202
Telephone: (513) 621-3550

Club Officials

President: John Sawyer
Vice President/General Manager: Michael Brown
Assistant General Manager, Director of
   Player Personnel: Pete Brown
Corporate Secretary, Legal Counsel:
   Katie Brown Blackburn
Business Manager: Bill Connelly
Director of Public Relations: Allan Heim
Accountant: Jay Reis
Ticket Manager: Paul Kelly
Consultant: John Murdough
Trainer: Paul Sparling
Equipment Manager: Tom Gray
Video Director: Al Davis

Stadium: Riverfront Stadium • **Capacity:** 60,389
   200 Riverfront Stadium
   Cincinnati, Ohio 45202

Playing Surface: AstroTurf-8

Training Camp: Wilmington College
   Wilmington, Ohio 45177

1992 Schedule

Preseason
Aug. 9	at New York Giants	7:00
Aug. 15	at Philadelphia	7:30
Aug. 22	**Indianapolis**	7:30
Aug. 28	**Detroit**	7:30

Regular Season
Sept. 6	at Seattle	1:00
Sept. 13	**Los Angeles Raiders**	1:00
Sept. 20	at Green Bay	12:00
Sept. 27	**Minnesota**	1:00
Oct. 4	**Open Date**	
Oct. 11	**Houston**	4:00
Oct. 19	at Pittsburgh (Monday)	9:00
Oct. 25	at Houston	12:00
Nov. 1	**Cleveland**	4:00
Nov. 8	at Chicago	7:00
Nov. 15	at New York Jets	1:00
Nov. 22	**Detroit**	1:00
Nov. 29	**Pittsburgh**	1:00
Dec. 6	at Cleveland	1:00
Dec. 13	at San Diego	1:00
Dec. 20	**New England**	1:00
Dec. 27	**Indianapolis**	1:00

Bengals Coaching History

(179-188-1)
1968-75	Paul Brown	55-59-1
1976-78	Bill Johnson*	18-15-0
1978-79	Homer Rice	8-19-0
1980-83	Forrest Gregg	34-27-0
1984-91	Sam Wyche	64-68-0

*Resigned after five games in 1978

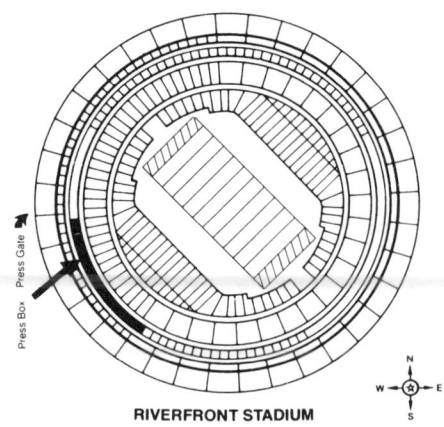

RIVERFRONT STADIUM

Record Holders

Individual Records—Career
Category	Name	Performance
Rushing (Yds.)	James Brooks, 1984-1991	6,393
Passing (Yds.)	Ken Anderson, 1971-1986	32,838
Passing (TDs)	Ken Anderson, 1971-1986	197
Receiving (No.)	Isaac Curtis, 1973-1984	420
Receiving (Yds.)	Isaac Curtis, 1973-1984	7,106
Interceptions	Ken Riley, 1969-1983	63
Punting (Avg.)	Dave Lewis, 1970-73	43.9
Punt Return (Avg.)	Mike Martin, 1983-89	9.9
Kickoff Return (Avg.)	Lemar Parrish, 1970-78	24.7
Field Goals	Jim Breech, 1980-1991	184
Touchdowns (Tot.)	Pete Johnson, 1977-1983	70
Points	Jim Breech, 1980-1991	971

Individual Records—Single Season
Category	Name	Performance
Rushing (Yds.)	James Brooks, 1989	1,239
Passing (Yds.)	Boomer Esiason, 1986	3,959
Passing (TDs)	Ken Anderson, 1981	29
Receiving (No.)	Dan Ross, 1981	71
Receiving (Yds.)	Eddie Brown, 1988	1,273
Interceptions	Ken Riley, 1976	9
Punting (Avg.)	Dave Lewis, 1970	46.2
Punt Return (Avg.)	Mike Martin, 1984	15.7
Kickoff Return (Avg.)	Lemar Parrish, 1970	30.2
Field Goals	Horst Muhlmann, 1972	27
Touchdowns (Tot.)	Pete Johnson, 1981	16
Points	Jim Breech, 1985	120

Individual Records—Single Game
Category	Name	Performance
Rushing (Yds.)	James Brooks, 12-23-90	201
Passing (Yds.)	Boomer Esiason, 10-7-90	490
Passing (TDs)	Boomer Esiason, 12-21-86	5
Receiving (No.)	Tim McGee, 11-9-89	11
Receiving (Yds.)	Eddie Brown, 11-6-88	216
Interceptions	Many times	3
	Last time by David Fulcher, 12-16-89	
Field Goals	Horst Muhlmann, 11-8-70	5
	Horst Muhlmann, 9-24-72	5
	Jim Breech, 11-1-87	5
Touchdowns (Tot.)	Larry Kinnebrew, 10-28-84	4
Points	Larry Kinnebrew, 10-28-84	24

1991 Team Record
Preseason (2-2)

Date	Result		Opponents
8/2	L	20-24	at Detroit
8/10	L	24-29	Philadelphia
8/17	W	27-24	Minnesota (OT)
8/24	W	19-16	vs. Green Bay at Mil. (OT)

Regular Season (3-13)

Date	Result		Opponents	Att.
9/1	L	14-45	at Denver	72,855
9/8	L	7-30	Houston	56,463
9/15	L	13-14	at Cleveland	78,269
9/22	L	27-34	Washington	52,038
10/6	L	7-13	Seattle	60,010
10/13	L	23-35	at Dallas	63,275
10/21	L	16-35	at Buffalo	80,131
10/27	L	3-35	at Houston	58,634
11/3	W	23-21	Cleveland	55,077
11/10	L	27-33	Pittsburgh (OT)	55,503
11/17	L	10-17	at Philadelphia	63,189
11/24	L	14-38	L.A. Raiders	52,044
12/1	W	27-24	N.Y. Giants	45,063
12/9	L	13-37	at Miami	60,616
12/15	L	10-17	at Pittsburgh	35,420
12/22	W	29- 7	New England	46,394

(OT) Overtime

Score by Periods

Bengals	57	71	64	71	0	—	263
Opponents	68	163	76	122	6	—	435

Attendance

Home 422,592   Away 512,389   Total 934,981
Single-game home record, 60,284 (10-17-71)
Single-season home record, 473,288 (1990)

1991 Team Statistics

	Bengals	Opp.
Total First Downs	286	308
Rushing	96	100
Passing	162	191
Penalty	28	17
Third Down: Made/Att.	78/212	86/194
Third Down: Pct.	36.8	44.3
Fourth Down: Made/Att.	9/20	4/8
Fourth Down: Pct.	45.0	50.0
Total Net Yards	4969	5652
Avg. Per Game	310.6	353.3
Total Plays	993	980
Avg. Per Play	5.0	5.8
Net Yards Rushing	1811	1662
Avg. Per Game	113.2	103.9
Total Rushes	449	454
Net Yards Passing	3158	3990
Avg. Per Game	197.4	249.4
Sacked/Yards Lost	33/255	21/129
Gross Yards	3413	4119
Att./Completions	511/290	505/303
Completion Pct.	56.8	60.0
Had Intercepted	22	17
Punts/Avg.	65/43.5	57/42.0
Net Punting Avg.	34.3	36.4
Penalties/Yards Lost	107/845	94/808
Fumbles/Ball Lost	31/20	23/14
Touchdowns	27	53
Rushing	11	20
Passing	14	26
Returns	2	7
Avg. Time of Possession	29:14	30:46

1991 Individual Statistics

Scoring

	TD R	TD P	TD Rt	PAT	FG	Saf	TP
Breech	0	0	0	27/27	23/29	0	96
Brooks	2	2	0	0/0	0/0	0	24
McGee	0	4	0	0/0	0/0	0	24
Woods	4	0	0	0/0	0/0	0	24
Brown	0	2	0	0/0	0/0	0	12
Green	2	0	0	0/0	0/0	0	12
Holman	0	2	0	0/0	0/0	0	12
Taylor	2	0	0	0/0	0/0	0	12
Ball	1	0	0	0/0	0/0	0	6
Barber	0	1	0	0/0	0/0	0	6
Dingle	0	1	0	0/0	0/0	0	6
Fulcher	0	0	1	0/0	0/0	0	6
James	0	1	0	0/0	0/0	0	6
Price	0	0	1	0/0	0/0	0	6
Rembert	0	1	0	0/0	0/0	0	6
Saddler, Phx.-Cin.	0	0	1	0/0	0/0	0	6
Johnson	0	0	0	0/0	1/3	0	3
Gordon	0	0	0	0/0	0/0	1	2
Bengals	11	14	2	27/27	24/32	1	263
Opponents	20	26	7	49/52	22/31	1	435

Passing

	Att.	Comp.	Yds.	Pct.	TD	Int.	Tkld.	Rate
Esiason	413	233	2883	56.4	13	16	25/190	72.5
Hollas	55	32	310	58.2	1	4	7/57	49.8
Wilhelm	42	24	217	57.1	0	2	1/8	51.4
Johnson	1	1	3	100.0	0	0	0/0	79.2
Bengals	511	290	3413	56.8	14	22	33/255	68.4
Opponents	505	303	4119	60.0	26	17	21/129	89.2

Rushing

	Att.	Yds.	Avg.	LG	TD
Green	158	731	4.6	75t	2
Brooks	152	571	3.8	25	2
Taylor	33	153	4.6	34t	2
Woods	36	97	2.7	12	4
Dingle	21	91	4.3	21	0
Esiason	24	66	2.8	16	0
Hollas	12	66	5.5	27	0
Ball	10	21	2.1	10	1
Wilhelm	1	9	9.0	9	0
Brown	1	8	8.0	8	0
Johnson	1	−2	−2.0	−2	0
Bengals	449	1811	4.0	75t	11
Opponents	454	1662	3.7	43	20

Receiving

	No.	Yds.	Avg.	LG	TD
Brown	59	827	14.0	53	2
McGee	51	802	15.7	52t	4
Brooks	40	348	8.7	40	2
Holman	31	445	14.4	39	2
Barber	23	255	11.1	42t	1
Taylor	21	122	5.8	16	0
Green	16	136	8.5	18	0
Kattus	12	136	11.3	24	0
Rembert	9	117	13.0	23t	1
James	7	103	14.7	22	1
Woods	6	36	6.0	16	0
Dingle	5	23	4.6	12	1
Riggs	4	14	3.5	7	0
Garrett	3	32	10.7	13	0
Ball	3	17	5.7	9	0
Bengals	290	3413	11.8	53	14
Opponents	303	4119	13.6	74t	26

Interceptions

	No.	Yds.	Avg.	LG	TD
Fulcher	4	51	12.8	27t	1
Thomas	3	0	0	0	0
Dixon	2	62	31.0	47	0
Bussey	2	18	9.0	18	0
Barker	1	29	29.0	29	0
Mitz	1	8	8.0	8	0
Fain	1	1	1.0	1	0
Francis	1	0	0.0	0	0
Grant	1	0	0.0	0	0
Price	1	0	0.0	0	0
Bengals	17	169	9.9	47	1
Opponents	22	331	15.0	52t	3

Punting

	No.	Yds.	Avg.	In 20	LG
Johnson	64	2795	43.7	15	62
Breech	1	33	33.0	0	33
Bengals	65	2828	43.5	15	62
Opponents	57	2394	42.0	14	59

Punt Returns

	No.	FC	Yds.	Avg.	LG	TD
Price	14	6	203	14.5	78t	1
Barber	13	5	70	5.4	15	0
Garrett	1	0	7	7.0	7	0
James	1	0	0	0.0	0	0
Bengals	29	11	280	9.7	78t	1
Opponents	38	7	456	12.0	75t	2

Kickoff Returns

	No.	Yds.	Avg.	LG	TD
Ball	13	262	20.2	24	0
Garrett	13	214	16.5	24	0
Brooks	11	190	17.3	35	0
James	8	143	17.9	26	0
Dingle	7	176	25.1	63	0
Price	5	91	18.2	22	0
Green	4	66	16.5	20	0
King	3	34	11.3	17	0
Riggs	2	28	14.0	15	0
Barber	1	7	7.0	7	0
Holman	1	15	15.0	15	0
Thomas	1	−1	−1.0	−1	0
Bengals	69	1225	17.8	63	0
Opponents	38	741	19.5	34	0

Sacks

	No.
Krumrie	4.0
Stubbs, Dall.-Cin.	4.0
Stubbs, Cin.	3.0
Francis	3.0
Williams	3.0
Gordon	2.0
Grant	2.0
Tuatagaloa	2.0
Billups	1.0
Walker	1.0
Bengals	21.0
Opponents	33.0

1992 Draft Choices

Round	Name	Pos.	College
1.	David Klingler	QB	Houston
	Darryl Williams	DB	Miami
2.	Carl Pickens	WR	Tennessee
3.	Leonard Wheeler	DB	Troy State
4.	Ricardo McDonald	LB	Pittsburgh
5.	Craig Thompson	TE	North Carolina A&T
6.	Chris Burns	DT	Middle Tenn. St.
7.	Lance Olberding	T	Iowa
8.	Roosevelt Nix	DE	Central State, Ohio
9.	Ostell Miles	RB	Houston
10.	Horace Smith	DB	Oregon Tech
11.	John Earle	T	Western Illinois
12.	Eric Shaw	LB	Louisiana Tech

Cincinnati Bengals 1992 Veteran Roster

No.	Name	Pos.	Ht.	Wt.	Birth-date	NFL Exp.	College	Hometown	How Acq.	'91 Games/Starts
65	Arthur, Mike	C	6-3	271	5/7/68	2	Texas A&M	Minneapolis, Minn.	D5-'91	7/3
42	Ball, Eric	RB	6-2	214	7/1/66	4	UCLA	Ypsilanti, Mich.	D2-'89	6/4
86	Barber, Mike	WR	5-11	172	6/19/67	4	Marshall	Charleston, W. Va.	PB(Phx)-'90#	15/2
53	Barker, Leo	LB	6-2	230	11/7/59	9	New Mexico State	Cristobal, Panama	D7-'84	16/11
35	Bennett, Antoine	CB	5-11	185	11/29/67	2	Florida A&M	Miami, Fla.	D12-'91	3/0
90	Bentley, Ray	LB	6-2	235	11/25/60	7	Central Michigan	Grand Rapids, Mich.	PB(Buff)-'92#	16/0*
3	Breech, Jim	K	5-6	161	4/11/56	14	California	Sacramento, Calif.	FA-'89	16/0
81	Brown, Eddie	WR	6-0	185	12/17/62	8	Miami	Miami, Fla.	D1-'85	13/12
27	Bussey, Barney	S	6-0	210	5/20/62	7	South Carolina State	Lincolnton, Ga.	D5-'84	12/7
38	Dingle, Mike	RB	6-2	240	1/30/69	2	South Carolina	Moncks Corner, S.C.	D8-'91	8/0
29	†Dixon, Rickey	S	5-11	191	12/26/66	5	Oklahoma	Dallas, Tex.	D1-'88	15/9
7	Esiason, Boomer	QB	6-5	220	4/17/61	9	Maryland	East Islip, N.Y.	D2-'84	14/14
26	Fenner, Derrick	RB	6-3	228	4/6/67	4	North Carolina	Oxon Hill, Md.	PB(Sea)-'92#	11/7*
50	Francis, James	LB	6-5	252	8/4/68	3	Baylor	Houston, Tex.	D1-'90	16/16
33	Fulcher, David	S	6-3	238	9/28/64	7	Arizona State	Los Angeles, Calif.	D3b-'86	16/16
89	Garrett, Shane	WR	5-11	185	11/16/67	2	Texas A&M	Lafayette, La.	D9-'91	4/0
58	Gordon, Alex	LB	6-5	245	9/14/64	6	Cincinnati	Jacksonville, Fla.	PB(Raid)-'91#	14/1
98	Grant, David	NT	6-5	278	9/17/65	5	West Virginia	Belleville, N.J.	D4-'88	13/13
28	Green, Harold	RB	6-2	222	1/29/68	3	South Carolina	Ladson, S.C.	D2-'90	14/10
45	Haddix, Wayne	CB	6-1	205	7/23/63	5	Liberty	Middleton, Tenn.	W(TB)-'91	7/7
12	Hollas, Donald	QB	6-3	215	11/22/67	2	Rice	Kingsville, Tex.	D4-'91	8/1
82	†Holman, Rodney	TE	6-3	238	4/20/60	11	Tulane	Ypsilanti, Mich.	D3-'82	16/15
11	Johnson, Lee	P-K	6-2	200	11/27/61	8	Brigham Young	Conroe, Tex.	W(Clev)-'88	16/0
25	†Jones, Rod	CB	6-0	185	3/31/64	7	Southern Methodist	Dallas, Tex.	T(TB)-'90	4/2
84	Kattus, Eric	TE	6-5	251	3/4/63	7	Michigan	Cincinnati, Ohio	D4-'86	16/2
55	Kirk, Randy	LB	6-2	231	12/27/64	5	San Diego State	San Diego, Calif.	PB(SD)-'92#	5/0*
64	†Kozerski, Bruce	C	6-4	287	4/2/62	9	Holy Cross	Plains, Pa.	D9-'84	16/16
69	Krumrie, Tim	NT	6-2	274	5/20/60	10	Wisconsin	Eau Claire, Wis.	D10-'83	16/16
85	McGee, Tim	WR	5-10	183	8/7/64	7	Tennessee	Cleveland, Ohio	D1a-'86	16/16
62	Melander, Jon	T	6-7	280	12/27/66	2	Minnesota	Fridley, Minn.	PB(NE)-'92#	10/3*
99	Mitz, Alonzo	DE	6-4	278	6/5/63	6	Florida	Ft. Pierce, Fla.	W(SF)-'91	15/13
73	Moyer, Ken	T	6-7	297	11/19/66	4	Toledo	Temperance, Mich.	FA-'89	15/10
78	Muñoz, Anthony	T	6-6	284	8/19/58	13	Southern California	Ontario, Calif.	D1-'80	13/13
32	†Price, Mitchell	CB	5-9	181	5/10/67	3	Tulane	San Antonio, Tex.	D9-'90	13/2
88	Rembert, Reggie	WR	6-5	200	12/25/66	2	West Virginia	Okeechobee, Fla.	T(NYJ)-'90	16/0
72	Ridgle, Elston	DE	6-5	277	8/24/63	4	Nevada-Reno	Valley Village, Calif.	W(GB)-'92	0*
87	Riggs, Jim	TE	6-5	245	9/29/63	6	Clemson	Laurinburg, N.C.	D4-'87	16/1
79	Rogers, Lamar	DE	6-4	290	11/5/67	2	Auburn	Opp, Ala.	D2-'91	11/3
76	Scrafford, Kirk	T	6-6	255	3/16/67	3	Montana	Billings, Mont.	FA-'90	9/5
67	Stubbs, Daniel	DE	6-4	264	1/3/65	5	Miami	Red Bank, N.J.	W(Dall)-'91	7/0
97	Stewart, Andrew	DE	6-5	265	11/20/65	2	Cincinnati	West Hempstead, N.Y.	FA-'91	0*
20	Taylor, Craig	RB	6-0	228	1/3/66	4	West Virginia	Linden, N.J.	D6-'89	12/3
22	Thomas, Eric	CB	5-11	181	9/11/64	6	Tulane	Sacramento, Calif.	D2-'87	16/16
96	†Tuatagaloa, Natu	DE	6-4	274	5/25/66	4	California	San Rafael, Calif.	D5-'89	16/4
34	Vinson, Fernandus	S	5-10	197	11/3/68	2	North Carolina State	Montgomery, Ala.	D7-'91	13/0
59	Walker, Kevin	LB	6-3	244	12/24/65	5	Maryland	West Milford, N.J.	D3-'88	5/4
63	†Walter, Joe	T	6-7	292	6/18/63	8	Texas Tech	Dallas, Tex.	D7a-'85	15/14
51	White, Leon	LB	6-3	242	10/4/63	7	Brigham Young	La Mesa, Calif.	D5-'86	16/0
4	†Wilhelm, Erik	QB	6-3	217	11/19/65	4	Oregon State	Lake Oswego, Ore.	D3-'89	4/1
94	Williams, Alfred	LB	6-6	240	11/6/68	2	Colorado	Houston, Tex.	D1-'91	16/15
60	Withycombe, Mike	T	6-5	310	11/18/64	4	Fresno State	Lemoore, Calif.	W(Pitt)-'91	3/0

* Bentley played 16 games with Buffalo in '91; Fenner played 11 games with Seattle; Kirk played 5 games with San Diego; Melander played 10 games with New England; Ridgle last active with Phoenix in '90; Stewart missed '91 season due to injury.

† Option playout; subject to developments.

Plan B unconditional free agent.

Players lost through Plan B (8): CB Lewis Billups (GB; 13 games in '91), LB Ed Brady (TB; 16), RB James Brooks (Clev; 15), LB Bernard Clark (Dall; 12), C Paul Jetton (NO; 8), G Bruce Reimers (TB; 10), G Ralph Tamm (SF; 1), LB Carl Zander (Ind; 14).

Also played with Bengals in '91—G Brian Blados (6 games), T Mike Brennan (3), CB Richard Fain (6), WR Lynn James (10), T Scott Jones (2), CB-S Joe King (6), DE Skip McClendon (5), DE Rod Saddler (2), RB Ickey Woods (9).

COACHING STAFF

Head Coach, Dave Shula

Pro Career: Shula begins his first year as head coach of the Cincinnati Bengals. He became the sixth head coach in Bengals history on December 27, 1991. Shula was offensive coordinator and quarterbacks' coach for Dallas in 1989-90 before joining Cincinnati in 1991 as receivers' coach. Shula began his coaching career with the Miami Dolphins in 1982. In 1988, Shula was named assistant head coach with the Dolphins. He was a wide receiver and kick return specialist with the Baltimore Colts in 1981.

Background: Outstanding wide receiver at Dartmouth where he was a two-time All-Ivy League selection.

Personal: Born May 28, 1959. He and his wife, Leslie, live in Lexington, Ky., and have three sons—Daniel, Christopher, and Matthew.

Assistant Coaches

Jim Anderson, running backs; born March 27, 1948, Harrisburg, Pa., lives in Cincinnati. Linebacker-defensive end Cal Western (U.S. International) 1967-70. No pro playing experience. College coach: Cal Western 1970-71, Scottsdale, Ariz., Community College 1973, Nevada-Las Vegas 1974-75, Southern Methodist 1976-80, Stanford 1981-83. Pro coach: Joined Bengals in 1984.

Dana Bible, quarterbacks; born October 30, 1953, Cincinnati, lives in Cincinnati. Defensive back Cincinnati 1972-75. No pro playing experience. College coach: Cincinnati 1976-80, Miami (Ohio) 1981-83, 1989, North Carolina State 1983-85, San Diego State 1986-88. Pro coach: Joined Bengals in 1990.

Marv Braden, special teams; born January 25, 1938, Kansas City, Mo., lives in Cincinnati. Linebacker Southwest Missouri State 1956-59. No pro playing experience. College coach: Parsons 1963-66, Northeast Missouri State 1967-68 (head coach), Cal Western (U.S. International) 1969-72, Iowa State 1973, Southern Methodist 1974-75, Michigan State 1976. Pro coach: Denver Broncos 1977-80, San Diego Chargers 1981-85, St. Louis/Phoenix Cardinals 1986-89, joined Bengals in 1990.

Mike Haluchak, linebackers; born November 28, 1949, Concord, Calif., lives in Cincinnati. Linebacker Southern California 1967-70. No pro playing experience. College coach: Southern California 1976-77, Cal State-Fullerton 1978, Pacific 1979-80, California 1981, North Carolina State 1982. Pro coach: Oakland Invaders (USFL) 1983-85; San Diego Chargers 1986-91, joined Bengals in 1992.

Bob Karmelowicz, defensive line; born July 22, 1949, New Britain, Conn., lives in Cincinnati. Nose tackle Bridgeport 1972. No pro playing experience. College coach: Arizona State 1974-79, Massachusetts 1979-80, Texas-El Paso 1980-81, Illinois 1982-87, Washington State 1987-89, Miami 1990-91. Pro coach: Joined Bengals in 1992.

Ron Lynn, defensive coordinator; born December 6, 1944, Youngstown, Ohio, lives in Cincinnati. Quarterback-defensive back Mt. Union (Ohio) 1963-65. No pro playing experience. College coach: Toledo 1966, Mt. Union (Ohio) 1967-73, Kent State 1974-76, San Jose State 1977-78, Pacific 1979, California 1980-82. Pro coach: Oakland Invaders (USFL) 1983-85, San Diego Chargers 1986-91, joined Bengals in 1992.

Jim McNally, offensive line; born December 13, 1943, Buffalo, N.Y., lives in Cincinnati. Guard Buffalo 1961-65. No pro playing experience. College coach: Buffalo 1966-69, Marshall 1973-75, Boston College 1976-78, Wake Forest 1979. Pro coach: Joined Bengals in 1980.

Cincinnati Bengals 1992 First-Year Roster

Name	Pos.	Ht.	Wt.	Birth-date	College	Hometown	How Acq.
Beckton, Sean (1)	WR	5-11	175	9/9/68	Central Florida	Ormond Beach, Fla.	FA
Benson, Mark	WR	6-5	203	3/21/69	Northwestern	Buffalo Grove, Ill.	FA
Boerboom, Brian	G-T	6-7	305	3/26/69	Nebraska	Colorado Springs, Colo.	FA
Braxton, Emery	CB	5-10	172	12/5/69	Fresno State	Detroit, Mich.	FA
Burns, Chris	DE	6-4	282	1/9/70	Middle Tennessee St.	Franklin, Tenn.	D6
Dees, Andrew	G-T	6-6	270	12/1/69	Syracuse	Babylon, N.Y.	FA
Earle, John	G-T	6-5	284	4/1/68	Western Illinois	Keyport, N.J.	D11
Germer, Chad	G-T	6-5	282	7/15/69	Montana	Three Forks, Mont.	FA
Harris, Pete	LB	6-0	240	7/4/69	Mississippi	Homestead, Fla.	FA
Isaiah, Richard (1)	WR	6-0	175	7/17/68	Toledo	Akron, Ohio	FA
Klingler, David	QB	6-2	205	2/17/69	Houston	Stratford, Tex.	D1a
Ladd, Tom	G-T	6-6	280	4/19/68	Brigham Young	Potomac, Md.	FA
McDonald, Ricardo	LB	6-2	235	11/8/69	Pittsburgh	Kingston, Jamaica	D4
Miles, Ostell	RB	6-0	236	8/6/71	Houston	Pueblo, Colo.	D9
Moore, Paul	RB	6-1	242	7/9/68	Florida State	Miami, Fla.	FA
Nix, Roosevelt	DE	6-6	315	4/17/67	Central State, Ohio	Toledo, Ohio	D8
Olberding, Lance	T	6-6	307	3/1/71	Iowa	Rochester, Minn.	D6
Pickens, Carl	WR	6-2	206	3/23/70	Tennessee	Murphy, N.C.	D2
Pitts, Larry	WR	6-1	182	8/18/69	Wash. & Jefferson	Cincinnati, Ohio	FA
Sargent, Kevin	G-T	6-6	284	3/31/69	Eastern Washington	Bremerton, Wash.	FA
Shaw, Eric	LB	6-3	248	9/17/71	Louisiana Tech	Pensacola, Fla.	D12
Shipp, Marcus	S	6-2	192	6/14/70	Southwest Missouri	Oklahoma City, Okla.	FA
Smith, Horace	CB	5-10	180	1/17/68	Oregon Tech	Los Angeles, Calif.	D10
Stegall, Milt	WR	6-0	184	1/25/70	Miami, Ohio	Cincinnati, Ohio	FA
Straughter, Lloyd	LB	6-4	241	3/18/69	Jackson State	Yazoo City, Miss.	FA
Thomason, Jeff	TE	6-4	233	12/30/69	Oregon	Newport Beach, Calif.	FA
Thompson, Craig	TE	6-2	244	1/13/69	North Carolina A&T	Hartsville, S.C.	D5
Wheeler, Leonard	CB	5-11	189	1/15/69	Troy State	Taccoa, Ga.	D3
Wiggins, Shawn (1)	WR	5-10	165	8/15/68	Wyoming	Newark, N.J.	FA
Williams, Darryl	S	6-0	191	1/7/70	Miami	Miami, Fla.	D1b
Wright, Kimble	DE	6-5	260	11/10/68	Ramapo	Newark, N.J.	FA

The term NFL Rookie is defined as a player who is in his first season of professional football and has not been on the roster of another professional football team for any regular-season or postseason games. A Rookie is designated by an "R" on NFL rosters. Players who have been active in another professional football league or players who have NFL experience, including either preseason training camp or being on an active roster for fewer than three regular-season or postseason games, are termed NFL First-Year Players. An NFL First-Year Player is designated by a "1" on NFL rosters. Thereafter, a player on an NFL active roster for at least three regular-season or postseason games is credited with an additional year of NFL playing experience.

NOTES

_____

_____

_____

_____

_____

_____

_____

_____

_____

_____

_____

Ron Meeks, defensive backfield; born August 27, 1954, Jacksonville, Fla., lives in Cincinnati. Defensive back Arkansas State 1975-76. Pro defensive back Hamilton Tiger-Cats (CFL) 1977-79, Ottawa Roughriders (CFL) 1979, Toronto Argonauts (CFL) 1980-81. College coach: Arkansas State 1984-85, Miami 1986-87, New Mexico State 1988, Fresno State 1989-90. Pro coach: Dallas Cowboys 1991, joined Bengals in 1992.

Mike Pope, tight ends; born March 15, 1942, Monroe, N.C., lives in Cincinnati. Quarterback Lenoir Rhyne 1962-64. No pro playing experience. College coach: Florida State 1970-74, Texas Tech 1975-77, Mississippi 1978-82. Pro coach: New York Giants 1983-91, joined Bengals in 1992.

Richard Williamson, wide receivers, born April 13, 1941, Ft. Deposit, Ala., lives in Cincinnati. Receiver Alabama 1961-62. No pro playing experience. College coach: Alabama 1963-67, 1970-71, Arkansas 1968-69, 1972-74, Memphis State 1975-80 (head coach). Pro coach: Kansas City Chiefs 1983-86, Tampa Bay Buccaneers 1987-91 (interim head coach final three games of 1990 season, head coach 1991), joined Bengals in 1992.

Kim Wood, strength; born July 12, 1945, Barrington, Ill., lives in Cincinnati. Running back Wisconsin 1965-68. No pro playing experience. Pro coach: Joined Bengals in 1975.

CLEVELAND BROWNS

American Football Conference
Central Division

Team Colors: Seal Brown, Orange, and White

80 First Street
Berea, Ohio 44017
Telephone: (216) 891-5000

Club Officials

President and Owner: Arthur B. Modell
Executive Vice President/Legal and Administration: Jim Bailey
Vice President/Assistant to President: David Modell
Vice President/Public Relations: Kevin Byrne
Treasurer: Mike Srsen
Director of Operations/Information: Bob Eller
Assistant Director of Public Relations: Francine Lubera
Player Relations/Media Services: Dino Lucarelli
Director of Pro Personnel: Michael Lombardi
Director of College Scouting: Dom Anile
Scouts: Tom Dimitroff, Pat Hill, Ron Marciniak, Terry McDonough, Ozzie Newsome, Ernie Plank, Ellis Rainsberger, Bill Shunkwiler, Lionel Vital
Head Trainer: Bill Tessendorf
Facilities Manager: Charley Cusick
Equipment Manager: Ed Carroll

Stadium: Cleveland Stadium • **Capacity:** 78,512
West 3rd Street
Cleveland, Ohio 44114

Playing Surface: Grass

Training Camp: 80 First Street
Berea, Ohio 44017

1992 Schedule

Preseason

Aug. 8	**Atlanta**	7:00
Aug. 15	at New York Giants	8:00
Aug. 24	**Minnesota**	6:00
Aug. 28	at Tampa Bay	7:30

Regular Season

Sept. 6	at Indianapolis	12:00
Sept. 14	**Miami** (Monday)	9:00
Sept. 20	at Los Angeles Raiders	1:00
Sept. 27	**Denver**	1:00
Oct. 4	**Open Date**	
Oct. 11	**Pittsburgh**	1:00
Oct. 18	**Green Bay**	1:00
Oct. 25	at New England	4:00
Nov. 1	at Cincinnati	4:00
Nov. 8	at Houston	12:00
Nov. 15	**San Diego**	1:00
Nov. 22	at Minnesota	12:00
Nov. 29	**Chicago**	1:00
Dec. 6	**Cincinnati**	1:00
Dec. 13	at Detroit	1:00
Dec. 20	**Houston**	1:00
Dec. 27	at Pittsburgh	1:00

Browns Coaching History

(354-250-10)

1950-62	Paul Brown	115-49-5
1963-70	Blanton Collier	79-38-2
1971-74	Nick Skorich	30-26-2
1975-77	Forrest Gregg*	18-23-0
1977	Dick Modzelewski	0-1-0
1978-84	Sam Rutigliano**	47-52-0
1984-88	Marty Schottenheimer	46-31-0
1989-90	Bud Carson***	12-14-1
1990	Jim Shofner	1-6-0
1991	Bill Belichick	6-10-0

*Resigned after 13 games in 1977
**Released after eight games in 1984
***Released after nine games in 1990

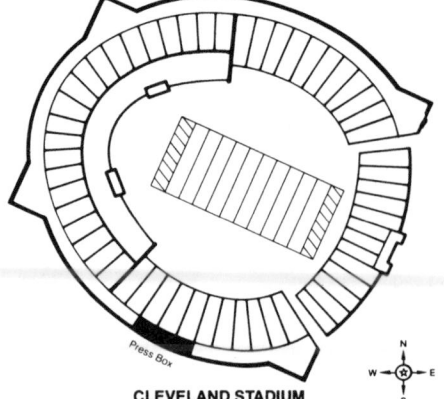

CLEVELAND STADIUM

Record Holders

Individual Records—Career

Category	Name	Performance
Rushing (Yds.)	Jim Brown, 1957-1965	12,312
Passing (Yds.)	Brian Sipe, 1974-1983	23,713
Passing (TDs)	Brian Sipe, 1974-1983	154
Receiving (No.)	Ozzie Newsome, 1978-1990	662
Receiving (Yds.)	Ozzie Newsome, 1978-1990	7,980
Interceptions	Thom Darden, 1972-74, 1976-1981	45
Punting (Avg.)	Horace Gillom, 1950-56	43.8
Punt Return (Avg.)	Greg Pruitt, 1973-1981	11.8
Kickoff Return (Avg.)	Greg Pruitt, 1973-1981	26.3
Field Goals	Lou Groza, 1950-59, 1961-67	234
Touchdowns (Tot.)	Jim Brown, 1957-1965	*126
Points	Lou Groza, 1950-59, 1961-67	1,349

Individual Records—Single Season

Category	Name	Performance
Rushing (Yds.)	Jim Brown, 1963	1,863
Passing (Yds.)	Brian Sipe, 1980	4,132
Passing (TDs)	Brian Sipe, 1980	30
Receiving (No.)	Ozzie Newsome, 1983	89
	Ozzie Newsome, 1984	89
Receiving (Yds.)	Webster Slaughter, 1989	1,236
Interceptions	Thom Darden, 1978	10
Punting (Avg.)	Gary Collins, 1965	46.7
Punt Return (Avg.)	Leroy Kelly, 1965	15.6
Kickoff Return (Avg.)	Billy Reynolds, 1954	29.5
Field Goals	Matt Bahr, 1984	24
	Matt Bahr, 1988	24
Touchdowns (Tot.)	Jim Brown, 1965	21
Points	Jim Brown, 1965	126

Individual Records—Single Game

Category	Name	Performance
Rushing (Yds.)	Jim Brown, 11-24-57	237
	Jim Brown, 11-19-61	237
Passing (Yds.)	Bernie Kosar, 1-3-87	489
Passing (TDs)	Frank Ryan, 12-12-64	5
	Bill Nelsen, 11-2-69	5
	Brian Sipe, 10-7-79	5
Receiving (No.)	Ozzie Newsome, 10-14-84	14
Receiving (Yds.)	Ozzie Newsome, 10-14-84	191
Interceptions	Many times	3
	Last time by Frank Minnifield, 11-22-87	
Field Goals	Don Cockroft, 10-19-75	5
Touchdowns (Tot.)	Dub Jones, 11-25-51	*6
Points	Dub Jones, 11-25-51	36

*NFL Record

1991 Team Record

Preseason (2-2)

Date	Result		Opponents
8/5	L	10-23	Tampa Bay
8/10	W	16-10	N.Y. Giants
8/16	W	24-21	at Washington (OT)
8/23	L	7-31	at Minnesota

Regular Season (6-10)

Date	Result		Opponents	Att.
9/1	L	14-26	Dallas	78,860
9/8	W	20- 0	at New England	35,377
9/15	W	14-13	Cincinnati	78,269
9/22	L	10-13	at N.Y. Giants	75,891
10/6	L	14-17	N.Y. Jets	71,042
10/13	L	17-42	at Washington	54,715
10/20	W	30-24	at San Diego (OT)	48,440
10/27	W	17-14	Pittsburgh	78,285
11/3	L	21-23	at Cincinnati	55,077
11/10	L	30-32	Philadelphia	72,086
11/17	L	24-28	at Houston	58,155
11/24	W	20-15	Kansas City	63,991
12/1	W	31- 0	at Indianapolis	57,539
12/8	L	7-17	Denver	73,539
12/15	L	14-17	Houston	55,680
12/22	L	10-17	at Pittsburgh	47,070

(OT) Overtime

Score by Periods

Browns	57	105	77	48	6	—	293
Opponents	25	113	51	109	0	—	298

Attendance

Home 571,752   Away 432,264   Total 1,004,016
Single-game home record, 85,073 (9-21-70)
Single-season home record, 620,496 (1980)

1991 Team Statistics

	Browns	Opp.
Total First Downs	265	298
Rushing	82	100
Passing	163	179
Penalty	20	19
Third Down: Made/Att.	74/199	97/215
Third Down: Pct.	37.2	45.1
Fourth Down: Made/Att.	9/20	9/17
Fourth Down: Pct.	45.0	52.9
Total Net Yards	4664	5084
Avg. Per Game	291.5	317.8
Total Plays	934	1004
Avg. Per Play	5.0	5.1
Net Yards Rushing	1360	1875
Avg. Per Game	85.0	117.2
Total Rushes	389	447
Net Yards Passing	3304	3209
Avg. Per Game	206.5	200.6
Sacked/Yards Lost	42/243	35/236
Gross Yards	3547	3445
Att./Completions	503/312	522/312
Completion Pct.	62.0	59.8
Had Intercepted	10	15
Punts/Avg.	80/42.5	61/41.3
Net Punting Avg.	36.1	35.2
Penalties/Yards Lost	108/872	103/770
Fumbles/Ball Lost	18/8	33/18
Touchdowns	35	33
Rushing	12	12
Passing	19	20
Returns	4	1
Avg. Time of Possession	29:00	31:00

1991 Individual Statistics

Scoring

	TD R	TD P	TD Rt	PAT	FG	Saf	TP
Stover	0	0	0	33/34	16/22	0	81
Hoard	2	9	0	0/0	0/0	0	66
Mack	8	2	0	0/0	0/0	0	60
Slaughter	0	3	0	0/0	0/0	0	18
M. Jackson	0	2	0	0/0	0/0	0	12
Langhorne	0	2	0	0/0	0/0	0	12
Morris	2	0	0	0/0	0/0	0	12
Ja. Jones	0	0	1	0/0	0/0	1	8
Brandon	0	0	1	0/0	0/0	0	6
Brennan	0	1	0	0/0	0/0	0	6
James, Cin.-Clev.	0	1	0	0/0	0/0	0	6
Newsome	0	0	1	0/0	0/0	0	6
Turner	0	0	1	0/0	0/0	0	6
Browns	12	19	4	33/34	16/22	1	293
Opponents	12	20	1	32/33	22/30	1	298

Passing

	Att.	Comp.	Yds.	Pct.	TD	Int.	Tkld.	Rate
Kosar	494	307	3487	62.1	18	9	41/232	87.8
Philcox	8	4	49	50.0	0	1	0/0	29.7
Hansen	1	1	11	100.0	1	0	0/0	152.1
Metcalf	0	0	0	—	0	0	1/11	0.0
Browns	503	312	3547	62.0	19	10	42/243	87.5
Opponents	522	312	3445	59.8	20	15	35/236	80.2

Rushing

	Att.	Yds.	Avg.	LG	TD
Mack	197	726	3.7	51t	8
Morris	93	289	3.1	15	2
Hoard	37	154	4.2	52	2
Metcalf	30	107	3.6	15	0
Kosar	26	74	2.8	14	0
Rouson	3	14	4.7	9	0
Philcox	1	-1	-1.0	-1	0
Hansen	2	-3	-1.5	0	0
Browns	389	1360	3.5	52	12
Opponents	447	1875	4.2	65t	12

Receiving

	No.	Yds.	Avg.	LG	TD
Slaughter	64	906	14.2	62t	3
Hoard	48	567	11.8	71t	9
Mack	40	255	6.4	22	2
Langhorne	39	505	12.9	40t	2
Brennan	31	325	10.5	30	1
Metcalf	29	294	10.1	45	0
Galbraith	27	328	12.1	42	0
M. Jackson	17	268	15.8	65t	2
Morris	13	76	5.8	13	0
James, Cin.-Clev.	7	103	14.7	22	1
Cox, S.D.-Mia.-Clev.	5	53	10.6	19	0
Rouson	2	9	4.5	6	0
Talley	1	13	13.0	13	0
Kosar	1	1	1.0	1	0
Browns	312	3547	11.4	71t	19
Opponents	312	3445	11.0	70t	20

Interceptions

	No.	Yds.	Avg.	LG	TD
Braggs	3	15	5.0	15	0
Brandon	2	70	35.0	40	1
Turner	2	42	21.0	42t	1
Matthews	1	35	35.0	35	0
Newsome	1	31	31.0	31	0
Ja. Jones	1	20	20.0	20t	1
Brown	1	19	19.0	19	0
Hilliard	1	19	19.0	19	0
Figaro	1	9	9.0	9	0
A. Jackson	1	0	0.0	0	0
Johnson	1	0	0.0	0	0
Browns	15	260	17.3	42t	3
Opponents	10	95	9.5	57t	1

Punting

	No.	Yds.	Avg.	In 20	LG
Hansen	80	3397	42.5	20	65
Browns	80	3397	42.5	20	65
Opponents	61	2520	41.3	16	61

Punt Returns

	No.	FC	Yds.	Avg.	LG	TD
Slaughter	17	3	112	6.6	17	0
Metcalf	12	1	100	8.3	30	0
Brennan	2	6	11	5.5	11	0
James, Cin.-Clev.	1	0	0	0.0	0	0
Minnifield	0	0	28	—	28	0
Browns	31	10	251	8.1	31	0
Opponents	40	15	388	9.7	48	0

Kickoff Returns

	No.	Yds.	Avg.	LG	TD
Metcalf	23	351	15.3	24	0
Morris	18	310	17.2	36	0
James, Cin.-Clev.	11	192	17.5	26	0
James, Clev.	3	49	16.3	21	0
Peebles	8	149	18.6	32	0
J. King, Cin.-Clev.	3	34	11.3	17	0
Galbraith	2	13	6.5	8	0
Baldwin, Minn.-Clev.	1	14	14.0	14	0
Rouson	1	16	16.0	16	0
Browns	55	888	16.1	36	0
Opponents	50	1022	20.4	47	0

Sacks

	No.
Perry	8.5
Matthews	6.5
Brandon	3.0
Burnett	3.0
Pleasant	2.5
Hilliard	2.0
Sagapolutele	1.5
Waiters	1.5
Barnett	1.0
Braggs	1.0
Conover	1.0
Ja. Jones	1.0
Thornton	1.0
Brown	0.5
Florence	0.5
Logan	0.5
Browns	35.0
Opponents	42.0

1992 Draft Choices

Round	Name	Pos.	College
1.	Tommy Vardell	RB	Stanford
2.	Patrick Rowe	WR	San Diego State
3.	Bill Johnson	DT	Michigan State
	Gerald Dixon	LB	South Carolina
6.	Rico Smith	WR	Colorado
	George Williams	DT	Notre Dame
7.	Selwyn Jones	DB	Colorado State
9.	Tim Hill	DB	Kansas
10.	Marcus Lowe	DT	Baylor
11.	Augustin Olobia	WR	Washington State
12.	Keithen McCant	QB	Nebraska
	Tim Simpson	C-G	Illinois

Cleveland Browns 1992 Veteran Roster

No.	Name	Pos.	Ht.	Wt.	Birth-date	NFL Exp.	College	Hometown	How Acq.	'91 Games/ Starts
61	Baab, Mike	C	6-4	275	12/6/59	11	Texas	Fort Worth, Tex.	PB(NE)-'90#	16/16
24	Baldwin, Randy	RB	5-10	216	8/19/67	2	Mississippi	Griffin, Ga.	FA-'91	0*
37	Barnett, Harlon	S	5-11	200	1/2/67	3	Michigan State	Cincinnati, Ohio	D4-'90	16/10
42	Berry, Latin	CB-S	5-10	196	1/13/67	3	Oregon	Lakeview Terrace, Calif.	FA-'91	15/0
36	Braggs, Stephen	CB-S	5-9	180	8/29/65	6	Texas	Houston, Tex.	D6-'87	16/10
58	†Brandon, David	LB	6-4	230	2/9/65	5	Memphis State	Memphis, Tenn.	PB(SD)-'91#	16/8
28	Brooks, James	RB	5-10	180	12/28/58	12	Auburn	Warner Robins, Ga.	PB(Cin)-'92#	15/12*
52	Brown, Richard	LB	6-3	240	9/21/65	5	San Diego State	Westminster, Calif.	PB(SD)-'91#	16/12
90	Burnett, Rob	DE-DT	6-4	270	8/27/67	3	Syracuse	Coram, N.Y.	D5-'90	13/8
71	Burton, Leonard	G-T	6-3	277	6/18/64	6	South Carolina	Memphis, Tenn.	FA-'91	0*
77	t-Childress, Freddie	T	6-4	330	9/17/66	2	Arkansas	West Helena, Ark.	T(NE)-'92	15/1
99	Cooks, Johnie	LB	6-4	251	11/23/58	11	Mississippi State	Leland, Miss.	FA-'91	2/0
74	Farren, Paul	G-T	6-6	270	12/24/60	10	Boston University	Cohasset, Mass.	D12-'83	13/0
53	Figaro, Cedric	LB	6-3	255	8/17/66	5	Notre Dame	Lafayette, La.	FA-'91	12/0
69	Fike, Dan	G	6-7	285	6/16/61	8	Florida	Pensacola, Fla.	FA-'85	16/16
81	†Galbraith, Scott	TE	6-3	260	1/7/67	3	Southern California	Sacramento, Calif.	D7-'90	16/13
30	Hampton, Alonzo	CB	5-10	190	1/19/67	3	Pittsburgh	Edgewater, Colo.	PB(TB)-'92#	15/3*
11	Hansen, Brian	P	6-4	220	10/26/60	8	Sioux Falls	Hawarden, Iowa	PB(NE)-'91#	16/0
41	Hardy, John	CB	5-10	165	6/11/68	2	California	Pasadena, Calif.	FA-'92	4/0*
23	Harper, Mark	CB	5-9	185	11/5/61	6	Alcorn State	Memphis, Tenn.	FA-'86	0*
38	Harris, Odie	CB-S	6-0	190	4/1/66	5	Sam Houston State	Bryan, Tex.	W(Dall)-'91	16/0
39	†Hilliard, Randy	CB	5-11	160	6/2/67	3	Northwestern Louisiana	Metairie, La.	D6-'90	14/10
33	Hoard, Leroy	RB	5-11	230	5/5/68	3	Michigan	New Orleans, La.	D2-'90	16/9
18	Holland, Jamie	WR	6-1	195	2/1/64	6	Ohio State	Wake Forest, N.C.	PB(Raid)-'92#	16/0*
89	Holohan, Pete	TE	6-4	247	7/25/59	12	Notre Dame	Liverpool, N.Y.	PB(KC)-'92#	16/3*
25	Jackson, Alfred	CB	6-0	180	7/10/67	4	San Diego State	Tulare, Calif.	FA-'91	6/1
1	Jackson, Michael	WR	6-4	195	4/12/69	2	Southern Mississippi	Kentwood, La.	D6-'91	16/7
80	†James, Lynn	WR	6-0	190	1/25/65	3	Arizona State	Navasota, Tex.	W(Cin)-'91	10/0
59	Johnson, Mike	LB	6-1	230	11/26/62	7	Virginia Tech	Hyattsville, Md.	SD1b-'84	5/4
96	Jones, James	DE-DT	6-2	294	2/6/69	2	Northern Iowa	Davenport, Iowa	D3-'91	16/16
66	†Jones, Tony	T	6-5	290	5/24/66	5	Western Carolina	Cannesville, Ga.	FA-'88	16/16
88	Kinchen, Brian	TE	6-2	232	8/6/65	5	Louisiana State	Baton Rouge, La.	FA-'91	14/0
68	King, Ed	G	6-4	303	12/3/69	2	Auburn	Phenix City, Ala.	D2-'91	16/15
19	Kosar, Bernie	QB	6-5	215	11/25/63	8	Miami	Boardman, Ohio	SD1-'85	16/16
97	Logan, Ernie	DE-DT	6-3	271	5/18/68	2	East Carolina	Fayetteville, N.C.	W(Atl)-'91	15/5
34	Mack, Kevin	RB	6-0	225	8/9/62	8	Clemson	Kings Mountain, N.C.	SD1a-'84	14/11
57	†Matthews, Clay	LB	6-2	245	3/15/56	15	Southern California	New Trier, Ill.	D1a-'78	15/15
21	Metcalf, Eric	RB	5-10	190	1/23/68	4	Texas	Arlington, Va.	D1-'89	8/3
31	Minnifield, Frank	CB	5-9	180	1/1/60	9	Louisville	Lexington, Ky.	FA-'84	14/11
20	Morris, Joe	RB	5-7	195	9/15/60	10	Syracuse	Ayer, Mass.	FA-'91	16/4
22	Newsome, Vince	S	6-1	185	1/22/61	10	Washington	Vacaville, Calif.	PB(Rams)-'91#	15/15
40	Perkins, Bruce	RB	6-2	225	8/14/67	3	Arizona State	Waterloo, Iowa	PB(Ind)-'92#	14/1*
92	Perry, Michael Dean	DT	6-1	285	8/27/65	5	Clemson	Aiken, S.C.	D2-'88	16/15
17	Philcox, Todd	QB	6-4	225	9/25/66	3	Syracuse	Norwalk, Conn.	PB(Cin)-'91#	4/0
98	Pleasant, Anthony	DE	6-5	258	1/27/68	3	Tennessee State	Century, Fla.	D3-'90	16/7
70	Rienstra, John	G	6-5	275	3/22/63	7	Temple	Bryn Athyne, Pa.	PB(Pitt)-'91#	16/16
75	Sagapolutele, Pio	DE-DT	6-6	297	11/28/69	2	San Diego State	Honolulu, Hawaii	D4-'91	15/8
84	†Slaughter, Webster	WR	6-1	170	10/19/64	7	San Diego State	Stockton, Calif.	D2-'86	16/16
3	Stover, Matt	K	5-11	178	1/27/68	2	Louisiana Tech	Dallas, Tex.	PB(NYG)-'91#	16/0
87	Talley, John	TE	6-5	245	12/19/64	3	West Virginia	Cleveland, Ohio	FA-'90	3/1
24	Taylor, Terry	CB	5-10	190	7/18/61	8	Southern Illinois	Warren, Ohio	PB(Det)-'92#	13/0*
67	Thome, Chris	C	6-4	280	1/15/69	2	Minnesota	West St. Paul, Minn.	W(Minn)-'91	7/0
92	Thornton, John	DE-DT	6-3	303	6/28/69	2	Cincinnati	Flint, Mich.	W(NO)-'91	5/0*
85	†Tillman, Lawyer	WR	6-5	230	5/20/66	2	Auburn	Mobile, Ala.	D2-'89	0*
29	Turner, Eric	S	6-1	207	9/20/68	2	UCLA	Ventura, Calif.	D1-'91	8/7
50	Waiters, Van	LB	6-4	250	2/27/65	5	Indiana	Coral Gables, Fla.	D3-'88	16/9
47	Wilburn, Barry	CB	6-3	186	12/9/63	6	Mississippi	Memphis, Tenn.	FA-'92	0*
93	Wise, Mike	DE	6-7	270	6/5/64	6	California-Davis	Novato, Calif.	W(Raid)-'91#	3/2
26	Wolfley, Ron	RB	6-0	230	10/14/62	8	West Virginia	Hamburg, N.Y.	PB(Phx)-'92#	16/0*
78	Woods, Rob	T	6-5	295	10/3/65	2	Arizona	Santa Barbara, Calif.	PB(Cin)-'91#	2/1

* Baldwin last active with Miami in '90; Brooks played 15 games with Cincinnati in '91; Burton, Harper, and Tillman missed '91 season due to injury; Hampton played 15 games with Tampa Bay; Hardy last active with Miami in '90; Holland played 16 games with L.A. Raiders; Holohan played 16 games with Kansas City; Perkins played 14 games with Indianapolis; Taylor played 13 games with Detroit; Thornton last active with New Orleans in '90; Wilburn last active with Washington in '89; Wolfley played 16 games with Phoenix.

† Option playout; subject to developments.

t- Browns traded for Childress (New England).

Retired—Wide receiver Danny Peebles, three-year veteran, 7 games in '91.

Plan B unconditional free agent.

Players lost through Plan B (6): T Frank Conover (GB; 4 games in '91), S Thane Gash (SF; missed '91 season due to injury), CB-S Ray Irvin (KC; missed '91 season due to injury), CB-S Joe King (TB; 7), WR Reggie Langhorne (Ind; 14), RB Mike Oliphant (Sea; 4).

Also played with Browns in '91—CB Tony Blaylock (5 games), WR Brian Brennan (15), CB Raymond Clayborn (1), TE Arthur Cox (2), CB Anthony Florence (6), CB-S Darryl Ingram (2), LB Jock Jones (9), RB Lee Rouson (16).

COACHING STAFF

Head Coach, Bill Belichick

Pro Career: Became the Browns' tenth head coach on February 5, 1991. Most recently was defensive coordinator of the New York Giants, who defeated the Buffalo Bills 20-19 in Super Bowl XXV. Also coordinated the Giants' defense that won Super Bowl XXI in 1986. Began coaching career at 23 as a special assistant to Ted Marchibroda with the Baltimore Colts in 1975. He tutored the Detroit Lions' tight ends, wide receivers, and special teams in 1976-77, before joining the Denver Broncos in 1978. He joined the Giants in 1979 as a defensive assistant and special teams coach, moved to linebackers in 1981-82, and became defensive coordinator in 1983. Career record: 6-10.

Background: Attended Annapolis (Maryland) High School and Phillips Academy in Andover, Mass. Played football and lacrosse at Wesleyan (Conn.) University. Earned a bachelor's degree in economics from Wesleyan in 1975.

Personal: Born April 16, 1952, in Nashville, Tenn. Bill and his wife, Debby, live in Brecksville, Ohio, and have three children, Amanda, Stephen, and Brian.

Assistant Coaches

Ernie Adams, offensive assistant; born March 31, 1953, Waltham, Mass., lives in Berea, Ohio. No college or pro playing experience. College coach: Northwestern 1972-75. Pro coach: New England Patriots 1975-78, New York Giants 1979-81 (Pro Personnel Director 1982-85), joined Browns in 1991.

Jim Bates, inside linebackers; born May 31, 1946, Pontiac, Mich., lives in Berea, Ohio. Linebacker Tennessee 1964-67. No pro playing experience. College coach: Tennessee 1968, 1989, Southern Mississippi 1972, Villanova 1973-74, Kansas State 1975-76, West Virginia 1977, Texas Tech 1978-83, Florida 1990. Pro coach: San Antonio Gunslingers (USFL) 1984-85 (head coach 1985), Detroit Drive (Arena Football) 1988, joined Browns in 1991.

Don Blackmon, outside linebackers; born March 14, 1958, Pompano Beach, Fla., lives in Berea, Ohio. Linebacker Tulsa 1977-80. Pro linebacker New England Patriots 1981-87. No college coaching experience. Pro coach: New England Patriots 1988-90, joined Browns in 1991.

Steve Crosby, running backs; born July 3, 1950, Great Bend, Kan., lives in Berea, Ohio. Running back Fort Hays State 1969-72. Pro running back New York Giants 1974-76. Pro coach: Miami Dolphins 1979-82, Atlanta Falcons 1983-84, 1986-89, Cleveland Browns 1985, New England Patriots 1990, rejoined Browns in 1991.

Al Groh, defensive assistant; born July 13, 1944, New York City, lives in Middleburg Heights, Ohio. Defensive end Virginia 1964-67. No pro playing experience. College coach: Army 1968-69, Virginia 1970-72, North Carolina 1973-77, Air Force 1978-79, Texas Tech 1980, Wake Forest 1981-86 (head coach), South Carolina 1988. Pro coach: Atlanta Falcons 1987, New York Giants 1989-91, joined Browns in 1992.

Hal Hunter, offensive line; born June 3, 1934, Canonsburg, Pa., lives in Hinckley, Ohio. Linebacker/guard Pittsburgh 1953-55. Pro guard Pittsburgh Steelers 1956. College coach: Richmond 1958-61, West Virginia 1962-63, Maryland 1964-65, Duke 1966-70, Kentucky 1971-72, Indiana 1973-76, California State (Pa.) 1977-80. Pro coach: Hamilton Tiger-Cats (CFL) 1981, Baltimore/Indianapolis Colts 1982-84, (interim head coach, final game in 1984), Pittsburgh Steelers 1985-88, joined Browns in 1989.

Richard Mann, receivers; born April 20, 1947, Aliquippa, Pa., lives in Strongsville, Ohio. Wide receiver Arizona State 1966-68. No pro playing experience. College coach: Arizona State 1974-79, Louisville 1980-81. Pro coach: Baltimore/Indianapolis Colts 1982-84; joined Browns in 1985.

Cleveland Browns 1992 First-Year Roster

Name	Pos.	Ht.	Wt.	Birth-date	College	Hometown	How Acq.
Brockman, Lonnie (1)	LB	6-3	230	3/14/68	West Virginia	Pittsburgh, Pa.	FA
Dahl, Bob (1)	T	6-5	285	11/5/68	Notre Dame	Chagrin Falls, Ohio	FA
Dixon, Gerald	LB	6-3	252	6/20/69	South Carolina	Rock Hill, S.C.	D3b
Foster, Sean (1)	WR	5-11	185	12/22/67	Long Beach State	Los Angeles, Calif.	FA
Francis, Jeff (1)	QB	6-4	225	7/7/66	Tennessee	Mt. Prospect, Ill.	FA
Goode, James (1)	LB	6-2	245	1/21/68	Oklahoma	Houston, Tex.	FA
Greenfield, Brian (1)	P	5-11	227	6/6/69	Pittsburgh	Sepulveda, Calif.	D10-'91
Harmon, Eric (1)	G	6-1	280	3/3/67	Clemson	Camden, N.J.	FA
Haynes, Hayward (1)	G	6-2	280	6/29/67	Florida State	Bartow, Fla.	FA
Hill, Tim	CB	5-8	176	9/16/69	Kansas	Columbus, Ohio	D9
Johnson, Bill	DE-DT	6-4	305	12/9/68	Michigan State	Chicago, Ill.	D3a
Jones, Selwyn	CB	6-0	185	5/13/70	Colorado State	Missouri City, Tex.	D7
Lowe, Marcus	DT	6-3	305	9/22/69	Baylor	Houston, Tex.	D10
McCant, Keithen	QB	6-2	205	3/8/69	Nebraska	Grand Prairie, Tex.	D12a
McCardell, Keenan (1)	WR	6-1	185	1/6/70	Nevada-Las Vegas	Houston, Tex.	FA
McGonnigal, Bruce (1)	TE	6-4	230	5/1/68	Virginia	Baltimore, Md.	FA
Olobia, Augustin	WR	5-11	195	7/18/69	Washington State	Belgin, Nigeria	D11
Quinton, Dustin (1)	T	6-6	305	9/12/68	Nevada-Las Vegas	Auburn, Calif.	FA
Rowe, Patrick	WR	6-1	195	2/17/69	San Diego State	San Diego, Calif.	D2
Shavers, Tyrone (1)	WR	6-3	210	2/9/68	Lamar	Texarkana, Tex.	FA
Simpson, Tim	G	6-1	290	3/5/69	Illinois	East Peoria, Ill.	D12b
Smith, Rico	WR	6-0	185	1/14/69	Colorado	Paramount, Calif.	D6
Trumbull, Rick (1)	T	6-6	300	12/4/67	Missouri	St. Louis, Mo.	FA
Vardell, Tommy	RB	6-2	238	2/20/69	Stanford	El Cajon, Calif.	D1
Wilkerson, Gary (1)	CB	6-0	180	10/11/65	Penn State	Sutherland, Va.	FA
Williams, George	DT	6-2	305	2/3/69	Notre Dame	Willingboro, N.J.	D6b

The term NFL Rookie is defined as a player who is in his first season of professional football and has not been on the roster of another professional football team for any regular-season or postseason games. A Rookie is designated by an "R" on NFL rosters. Players who have been active in another professional football league or players who have NFL experience, including either preseason training camp or being on an active roster for fewer than three regular-season or postseason games, are termed NFL First-Year Players. An NFL First-Year Player is designated by a "1" on NFL rosters. Thereafter, a player on an NFL active roster for at least three regular-season or postseason games is credited with an additional year of NFL playing experience.

NOTES

_____

_____

_____

_____

_____

_____

_____

_____

_____

_____

_____

John Mitchell, defensive line; born October 14, 1950, Mobile, Ala., lives in Hinckley, Ohio. Defensive end Eastern Arizona J.C. 1969-70, Alabama 1971-72. No pro playing experience. College coach: Alabama 1973-76, Arkansas 1977-82, Temple 1986, Louisiana State 1987-90. Pro coach: Birmingham Stallions (USFL) 1983-85, joined Browns in 1991.

Scott O'Brien, special teams; born June 25, 1957, Superior, Wis., lives in Berea, Ohio. Defensive end Wisconsin-Superior 1975-78. Pro defensive end Green Bay Packers 1979, Toronto Argonauts (CFL) 1979. College coach: Wisconsin-Superior 1980-82, Nevada-Las Vegas 1983-85, Rice 1986, Pittsburgh 1987-90. Pro coach: Joined Browns in 1991.

Nick Saban, defensive coordinator; born October 31, 1951, Fairmont, W. Va., lives in Berea, Ohio. Defensive back Kent State 1969-72. No pro playing experience. College coach: Kent State 1973-76, Syracuse 1977, West Virginia 1978-79, Ohio State 1980-81, Navy 1982, Michigan State 1983-87, Toledo 1990 (head coach). Pro coach: Houston Oilers 1988-89, joined Browns in 1991.

Jerry Simmons, strength and conditioning; born June 15, 1954, Elkhart, Kan., lives in Berea, Ohio. Linebacker Fort Hays State 1976-77. No pro playing experience. College coach: Fort Hays State 1978, Clemson 1980, Rice 1981-82, Southern California 1983-87. Pro coach: New England Patriots 1988-90, joined Browns in 1991.

Kevin Spencer, offensive assistant; born November 2, 1953, Queens, N.Y., lives in Bay Village, Ohio. No college or pro playing experience. College coach: State University of New York 1975-76, Cornell 1979-80, Ithaca 1981-86, Wesleyan 1987-91 (head coach). Pro coach: Joined Browns in 1991.

Gary Tranquill, quarterbacks; born April 13, 1940, Avella, Pa., lives in Berea, Ohio. Quarterback Wittenberg 1959-62. College coach: Wittenberg 1963-69, Ball State 1970, Bowling Green 1971-72, Navy 1973-76, Ohio State 1977-78, West Virginia 1979-81, Navy 1982-86 (head coach), Virginia 1987-90. Pro coach: Joined Browns in 1991.

DENVER BRONCOS

American Football Conference Western Division

Team Colors: Orange, Royal Blue, and White

13655 Broncos Parkway
Englewood, Colorado 80112
Telephone: (303) 649-9000

Club Officials

President-Chief Executive Officer:
Pat Bowlen
Vice President-Head Coach: Dan Reeves
General Manager: John Beake
Chief Financial Officer-Treasurer:
Robert M. Hurley
Director of Football Operations: Lide Huggins
Director of Player Personnel: Reed Johnson
Director of Media Relations: Jim Saccomano
Assistant to the General Manager: Fred Fleming
Ticket Manager: Gail Stuckey
Director of Operations: Bill Harpole
Director of Player and Community
Relations: Charlie Lee
Trainer: Steve Antonopulos
Equipment Manager: Dan Bill
Video Director: Kent Erickson

Stadium: Denver Mile High Stadium •
Capacity: 76,273
1900 West Eliot
Denver, Colorado 80204

Playing Surface: Grass (PAT)

Training Camp: University of Northern Colorado
Greeley, Colorado 80639

1992 Schedule

Preseason

Aug. 3	at San Francisco	5:00
Aug. 8	**Tampa Bay**	4:00
Aug. 15	vs. Miami at Berlin	1:00
Aug. 22	at Dallas	8:00
Aug. 28	**Phoenix**	7:00

Regular Season

Sept. 6	**Los Angeles Raiders**	6:00
Sept. 13	**San Diego**	2:00
Sept. 20	at Philadelphia	1:00
Sept. 27	at Cleveland	1:00
Oct. 4	**Kansas City**	2:00
Oct. 12	at Washington (Monday)	9:00
Oct. 18	**Houston**	2:00
Oct. 25	at San Diego	1:00
Nov. 1	**Open Date**	
Nov. 8	**New York Jets**	2:00
Nov. 15	**New York Giants**	6:00
Nov. 22	at Los Angeles Raiders	1:00
Nov. 30	at Seattle (Monday)	6:00
Dec. 6	**Dallas**	2:00
Dec. 12	at Buffalo (Saturday)	12:30
Dec. 20	**Seattle**	2:00
Dec. 27	at Kansas City	12:00

Broncos Coaching History

(233-243-10)

1960-61	Frank Filchock*	7-20-1
1962-64	Jack Faulkner*	9-22-1
1964-66	Mac Speedie**	6-19-1
1966	Ray Malavasi	4-8-0
1967-71	Lou Saban***	20-42-3
1971	Jerry Smith	2-3-0
1972-76	John Ralston	34-33-3
1977-80	Robert (Red) Miller	42-25-0
1981-91	Dan Reeves	109-71-1

*Released after four games in 1964
**Resigned after two games in 1966
***Resigned after nine games in 1971

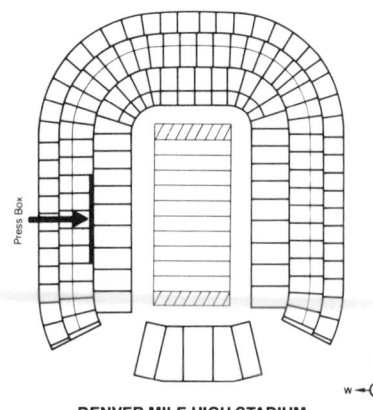

DENVER MILE HIGH STADIUM

Record Holders

Individual Records—Career

Category	Name	Performance
Rushing (Yds.)	Floyd Little, 1967-1975	6,323
Passing (Yds.)	John Elway, 1983-1991	27,974
Passing (TDs)	John Elway, 1983-1991	148
Receiving (No.)	Lionel Taylor, 1960-66	543
Receiving (Yds.)	Lionel Taylor, 1960-66	6,872
Interceptions	Steve Foley, 1976-1986	44
Punting (Avg.)	Jim Fraser, 1962-64	45.2
Punt Return (Avg.)	Rick Upchurch, 1975-1983	12.1
Kickoff Return (Avg.)	Abner Haynes, 1965-66	26.3
Field Goals	Jim Turner, 1971-79	151
Touchdowns (Tot.)	Floyd Little, 1967-1975	54
Points	Jim Turner, 1971-79	742

Individual Records—Single Season

Category	Name	Performance
Rushing (Yds.)	Otis Armstrong, 1974	1,407
Passing (Yds.)	John Elway, 1985	3,891
Passing (TDs)	Frank Tripucka, 1960	24
Receiving (No.)	Lionel Taylor, 1961	100
Receiving (Yds.)	Steve Watson, 1981	1,244
Interceptions	Goose Gonsoulin, 1960	11
Punting (Avg.)	Jim Fraser, 1963	46.1
Punt Return (Avg.)	Floyd Little, 1967	16.9
Kickoff Return (Avg.)	Bill Thompson, 1969	28.5
Field Goals	Gene Mingo, 1962	27
	David Treadwell, 1989, 1991	27
Touchdowns (Tot.)	Sammy Winder, 1986	14
Points	Gene Mingo, 1962	137

Individual Records—Single Game

Category	Name	Performance
Rushing (Yds.)	Otis Armstrong, 12-8-74	183
Passing (Yds.)	Frank Tripucka, 9-15-62	447
Passing (TDs)	Frank Tripucka, 10-28-62	5
	John Elway, 11-18-84	5
Receiving (No.)	Lionel Taylor, 11-29-64	13
	Bobby Anderson, 9-30-73	13
Receiving (Yds.)	Lionel Taylor, 11-27-60	199
Interceptions	Goose Gonsoulin, 9-18-60	*4
	Willie Brown, 11-15-64	*4
Field Goals	Gene Mingo, 10-6-63	5
	Rich Karlis, 11-20-83	5
Touchdowns (Tot.)	Many times	3
	Last time by Gaston Green, 9-22-91	
Points	Gene Mingo, 12-10-60	21

*NFL Record

1991 Team Record

Preseason (2-3)

Date	Result		Opponents
7/27	L	3-14	vs. Detroit at Canton, Ohio
8/2	W	10- 3	Indianapolis
8/7	L	6-24	at San Francisco
8/19	W	21-13	Miami
8/23	L	10-34	at Phoenix

Regular Season (12-4)

Date	Result		Opponents	Att.
9/1	W	45-14	Cincinnati	72,855
9/8	L	13-16	at L.A. Raiders	50,812
9/15	W	16-10	Seattle	74,152
9/22	W	27-19	San Diego	73,258
9/29	W	13- 6	at Minnesota	55,031
10/6	L	14-42	at Houston	59,145
10/20	W	19-16	Kansas City	75,866
10/27	W	9- 6	at New England	43,994
11/3	W	20-13	Pittsburgh	70,973
11/10	L	16-17	L.A. Raiders	75,896
11/17	W	24-20	at Kansas City	74,661
11/24	L	10-13	at Seattle	60,430
12/1	W	20- 3	New England	67,116
12/8	W	17- 7	at Cleveland	73,539
12/15	W	24-19	Phoenix	74,098
12/22	W	17-14	at San Diego	51,449

Postseason (1-1)

Date	Result		Opponent	Att.
1/4	W	26-24	Houston	75,392
1/12	L	7-10	at Buffalo	80,377

Score by Periods

Broncos	42	111	71	80	0	—	304
Opponents	43	77	49	66	0	—	235

Attendance

Home 584,214   Away 469,061   Total 1,053,275
Single-game home record, 76,105 (1-4-87)
Single-season home record, 598,224 (1981)

1991 Team Statistics

	Broncos	Opp.
Total First Downs	284	242
Rushing	117	81
Passing	150	147
Penalty	17	14
Third Down: Made/Att.	93/224	64/206
Third Down: Pct.	41.5	31.1
Fourth Down: Made/Att.	8/14	7/17
Fourth Down: Pct.	57.1	41.2
Total Net Yards	5012	4549
Avg. Per Game	313.3	284.3
Total Plays	1012	939
Avg. Per Play	5.0	4.8
Net Yards Rushing	2015	1794
Avg. Per Game	125.9	112.1
Total Rushes	507	411
Net Yards Passing	2997	2755
Avg. Per Game	187.3	172.2
Sacked/Yards Lost	46/313	52/346
Gross Yards	3310	3101
Att./Completions	459/246	476/246
Completion Pct.	53.6	51.7
Had Intercepted	12	23
Punts/Avg.	74/41.2	79/44.5
Net Punting Avg.	36.4	39.1
Penalties/Yards Lost	94/715	105/848
Fumbles/Ball Lost	31/13	26/10
Touchdowns	32	22
Rushing	16	8
Passing	13	12
Returns	3	2
Avg. Time of Possession	31:36	28:24

1991 Individual Statistics

Scoring

	TD R	TD P	TD Rt	PAT	FG	Saf	TP
Treadwell	0	0	0	31/32	27/36	0	112
Elway	6	0	0	0/0	0/0	0	36
Green	4	0	0	0/0	0/0	0	24
Lewis	4	0	0	0/0	0/0	0	24
Sewell	2	2	0	0/0	0/0	0	24
V. Johnson	0	3	0	0/0	0/0	0	18
Nattiel	0	2	0	0/0	0/0	0	12
Young	0	2	0	0/0	0/0	0	12
Braxton	0	0	1	0/0	0/0	0	6
Dimry	0	0	1	0/0	0/0	0	6
Jackson	0	1	0	0/0	0/0	0	6
R. Johnson	0	1	0	0/0	0/0	0	6
Powers	0	0	1	0/0	0/0	0	6
Russell	0	1	0	0/0	0/0	0	6
Sharpe	0	1	0	0/0	0/0	0	6
Broncos	16	13	3	31/32	27/36	0	304
Opponents	8	12	2	22/22	27/33	0	235

Passing

	Att.	Comp.	Yds.	Pct.	TD	Int.	Tkld.	Rate
Elway	451	242	3253	53.7	13	12	45/305	75.4
Kubiak	5	3	33	60.0	0	0	1/8	79.6
Sewell	3	1	24	33.3	0	0	0/0	63.2
Broncos	459	246	3310	53.6	13	12	46/313	75.3
Opponents	476	246	3101	51.7	12	23	52/346	60.6

Rushing

	Att.	Yds.	Avg.	LG	TD
Green	261	1037	4.0	63t	4
Lewis	99	376	3.8	27	4
Elway	55	255	4.6	17t	6
Sewell	50	211	4.2	26	2
Perryman	21	45	2.1	6	0
Humphrey	11	33	3.0	7	0
Jackson	2	18	9.0	21	0
Sharpe	1	15	15.0	15	0
Kubiak	3	11	3.7	12	0
Horan	2	9	4.5	9	0
Rivers	2	5	2.5	3	0
Broncos	507	2015	4.0	63t	16
Opponents	411	1794	4.4	49	8

Receiving

	No.	Yds.	Avg.	LG	TD
Young	44	629	14.3	52t	2
Sewell	38	436	11.5	60	2
Jackson	33	603	18.3	71	1
Sharpe	22	322	14.6	37	1
Russell	21	317	15.1	40	1
V. Johnson	21	208	9.9	22	3
Perryman	17	171	10.1	24	0
Nattiel	16	288	18.0	70t	2
Green	13	78	6.0	13	0
Kay	11	139	12.6	32	0
R. Johnson	6	73	12.2	31	1
Lewis	2	9	4.5	7	0
Elway	1	24	24.0	24	0
B. Johnson	1	13	13.0	13	0
Broncos	246	3310	13.5	71	13
Opponents	246	3101	12.6	63	12

Interceptions

	No.	Yds.	Avg.	LG	TD
Atwater	5	104	20.8	49	0
D. Smith	5	60	12.0	39	0
Braxton	4	55	13.8	52t	1
Dimry	3	35	11.7	26t	1
Henderson	2	53	26.5	53	0
Brooks	2	7	3.5	9	0
Robbins	1	35	35.0	35	0
Lang	1	30	30.0	30	0
Broncos	23	379	16.5	53	2
Opponents	12	101	8.4	43	0

Punting

	No.	Yds.	Avg.	In 20	LG
Horan	72	3012	41.8	24	71
Elway	1	34	34.0	0	34
Broncos	74	3046	41.2	24	71
Opponents	79	3513	44.5	17	63

Punt Returns

	No.	FC	Yds.	Avg.	LG	TD
V. Johnson	24	14	174	7.3	20	0
Nattiel	10	2	43	4.3	17	0
Clark	7	1	67	9.6	18	0
Broncos	41	17	284	6.9	20	0
Opponents	28	14	170	6.1	23	0

Kickoff Returns

	No.	Yds.	Avg.	LG	TD
Montgomery	26	488	18.8	55	0
Russell	7	120	17.1	30	0
Clark	2	45	22.5	29	0
Lewis	1	20	20.0	20	0
Sewell	1	14	14.0	14	0
Broncos	37	687	18.6	55	0
Opponents	62	1096	17.7	38	0

Sacks

	No.
Fletcher	13.5
Croel	10.0
Mecklenburg	9.0
Holmes	5.0
Kragen	3.5
Mills	3.0
Walker	3.0
Powers	2.0
Atwater	1.0
Braxton	1.0
Sochia	1.0
Broncos	52.0
Opponents	46.0

1992 Draft Choices

Round	Name	Pos.	College
1.	Tommy Maddox	QB	UCLA
2.	Shane Dronett	DE	Texas
4.	Chuck Johnson	G	Texas
5.	Frank Robinson	DB	Boise State
7.	Ron Geater	DE	Iowa
	Jim Johnson	T	Michigan State
	Jon Bostick	WR	Nebraska
8.	Dietrich Lockridge	G	Jackson State
9.	Muhammad Oliver	DB	Oregon
10.	Bob Meeks	C	Auburn
11.	Cedric Tillman	WR	Alcorn State
12.	John Granby	DB	Virginia Tech

Denver Broncos 1992 Veteran Roster

No.	Name	Pos.	Ht.	Wt.	Birth-date	NFL Exp.	College	Hometown	How Acq.	'91 Games/Starts
27	Atwater, Steve	S	6-3	217	10/28/66	4	Arkansas	Chicago, Ill.	D1-'89	16/16
87	Awalt, Rob	TE	6-5	238	4/9/64	6	San Diego State	Landsthul, Germany	PB(Dall)-'92#	12/2*
34	Braxton, Tyrone	CB	5-11	185	12/17/64	6	North Dakota State	Madison, Wis.	D12-'87	16/15
56	Brooks, Michael	LB	6-1	235	10/2/64	6	Louisiana State	Rustin, La.	D3-'87	14/14
65	Crawford, Elbert	G-T	6-3	280	6/20/66	3	Arkansas	Chicago, Ill.	PB(NE)-'92#	16/16*
51	Croel, Mike	LB	6-3	231	6/6/69	2	Nebraska	Detroit, Mich.	D1-'91	13/10
62	†Davidson, Jeff	G	6-5	309	10/3/67	3	Ohio State	Akron, Ohio	D5a-'90	16/14
29	Dimry, Charles	CB	6-0	175	1/31/66	5	Nevada-Las Vegas	San Diego, Calif.	PB(Atl)-'91#	16/1
7	Elway, John	QB	6-3	215	6/28/60	10	Stanford	Port Angeles, Wash.	T(Balt)-'83	16/16
63	Farrell, Sean	G	6-3	260	5/25/60	11	Penn State	Southampton, N.Y.	FA-'90	5/4
73	Fletcher, Simon	LB	6-5	240	2/18/62	8	Houston	Bay City, Tex.	D2b-'85	16/16
28	†Green, Gaston	RB	5-11	192	8/1/66	5	UCLA	Los Angeles, Calif.	T(Rams)-'91	13/12
93	Haliburton, Ronnie	LB	6-4	230	4/14/68	3	Louisiana State	Port Arthur, Tex.	D6-'90	8/0
24	Henderson, Wymon	CB	5-9	186	12/15/61	6	Nevada-Las Vegas	North Miami Beach, Fla.	FA-'89	16/16
90	†Holmes, Ron	DE	6-4	265	8/26/63	8	Washington	Seattle, Wash.	T(TB)-'89	15/14
2	Horan, Mike	P	5-11	190	2/1/59	9	Long Beach State	Orange, Calif.	FA-'86	16/0
80	Jackson, Mark	WR	5-9	180	7/23/63	7	Purdue	Chicago, Ill.	D6b-'86	12/10
86	Johnson, Barry	WR	6-2	197	2/1/68	2	Maryland	Baltimore, Md.	FA-'91	4/0
89	Johnson, Reggie	TE	6-2	256	1/27/68	2	Florida State	Pensacola, Fla.	D2-'91	16/3
82	Johnson, Vance	WR	5-11	185	3/13/63	8	Arizona	Trenton, N.J.	D2a-'85	10/0
66	Juriga, Jim	G-T	6-6	275	9/12/64	4	Illinois	Fort Wayne, Ind.	D4-'86	0*
72	Kartz, Keith	C	6-4	270	5/5/63	6	California	Las Vegas, Nev.	FA-'87	16/16
88	Kay, Clarence	TE	6-2	237	7/30/61	9	Georgia	Seneca, S.C.	D7-'84	16/16
68	Ker, Crawford	G	6-3	285	5/5/62	8	Florida	Philadelphia, Pa.	PB(Dall)-'91#	12/10
71	Kragen, Greg	NT	6-3	265	3/4/62	8	Utah State	Chicago, Ill.	FA-'85	16/16
21	†Lang, Le-Lo	CB-S	5-11	185	1/23/67	3	Washington	Los Angeles, Calif.	D5b-'90	16/0
76	Lanier, Ken	T	6-3	290	7/8/59	12	Florida State	Columbus, Ohio	D5-'81	16/16
41	Lewis, Greg	RB	5-10	214	8/10/69	2	Washington	Port St. Joe, Fla.	D5-'91	16/4
59	Lucas, Tim	LB	6-3	230	4/3/61	6	California	Stockton, Calif.	FA-'87	5/3
77	Mecklenburg, Karl	LB	6-3	235	9/1/60	10	Minnesota	Edina, Minn.	D12-'83	16-16
52	Mills, Jeff	LB	6-3	238	10/8/68	3	Nebraska	Montclair, N.J.	W(SD)-'90	12/3
22	Montgomery, Alton	CB-S	6-0	195	6/16/68	3	Houston	Griffin, Ga.	D2-'90	16/0
57	Murray, Mark	LB	6-2	240	10/15/67	2	Florida	Orlando, Fla.	FA-'91	6/0
11	Pelluer, Steve	QB	6-4	209	5/29/62	8	Washington	Bellevue, Wash.	PB(KC)-'92#	0*
33	Perryman, Robert	RB	6-2	233	10/16/64	6	Michigan	Raleigh, N.C.	PB(NE)-'91#	15/7
78	Pollack, Frank	G-T	6-5	285	11/5/67	3	Northern Arizona	Phoenix, Ariz.	PB(SF)-'92#	15/0*
91	Powers, Warren	DE	6-6	287	2/4/65	4	Maryland	Baltimore, Md.	D2b-'89	13/11
38	Rivers, Reggie	RB	6-1	215	2/22/68	2	Southwest Texas State	Dayton, Ohio	FA-'91	16/0
85	Russell, Derek	WR	6-0	179	6/22/69	2	Arkansas	Little Rock, Ark.	D4-'91	13/5
74	†Salem, Harvey	T	6-6	289	1/15/61	10	California	Berkeley, Calif.	T(Det)-'91	10/0
30	Sewell, Steve	RB	6-3	210	4/2/63	8	Oklahoma	San Francisco, Calif.	D1-'85	16/1
81	†Sharpe, Shannon	TE	6-2	230	6/26/68	3	Savannah State	Glennville, Ga.	D7-'90	16/9
49	†Smith, Dennis	S	6-3	200	2/3/59	12	Southern California	Santa Monica, Calif.	D1-'81	16/16
70	†Sochia, Brian	NT-DE	6-3	278	6/21/61	10	Northwestern Oklahoma	Massena, N.Y.	FA-'91	10/3
60	Subis, Nick	C-T	6-3	278	12/24/67	2	San Diego State	Inglewood, Calif.	D6-'91	16/0
54	Traylor, Keith	LB	6-2	260	9/3/69	2	Central Oklahoma	Malvern, Ark.	D3-'91	16/2
9	Treadwell, David	K	6-1	180	2/27/67	4	Clemson	Columbia, S.C.	T(Phx)-'89	16/0
96	Walker, Kenny	DE-DT	6-3	260	4/6/67	2	Nebraska	Crane, Tex.	D8-'91	16/1
79	Widell, Dave	T	6-6	292	5/14/65	5	Boston College	Hartford, Conn.	T(Dall)-'91	16/2
67	†Widell, Doug	G	6-4	287	9/23/66	4	Boston College	Hartford, Conn.	D2a-'89	16/16
83	Young, Michael	WR	6-1	183	2/21/62	8	UCLA	Hanford, Calif.	FA-'89	16/13

* Awalt played 12 games with Dallas in '91; Crawford played 16 games with New England; Juriga missed '91 season due to injury; Pelluer last active with Kansas City in '90; Pollack played 15 games with San Francisco.

† Option playout; subject to developments.

Retired—Quarterback Gary Kubiak, nine-year veteran, 16 games in '91.

Traded—Running back Bobby Humphrey to Miami, wide receiver Ricky Nattiel to Tampa Bay.

Plan B unrestricted free agent.

Players lost through Plan B (1): S Randy Robbins (NE; 16 games in '91).

Also played with Broncos in '91—DE Alphonso Carreker (6 games), CB-S Kevin Clark (4), T Darrell Hamilton (6), DE Jim Szymanski (1).

COACHING STAFF

Head Coach, Dan Reeves

Pro Career: Became ninth head coach in Broncos history on February 28, 1981, after spending entire pro career as both player and coach with the Dallas Cowboys. In 1991, Reeves led the Broncos to a 12-4 record, the AFC Western Division title, and a berth in the AFC Championship Game. Reeves has taken the Broncos to five first and three second-place finishes in the division, along with six playoff berths and four AFC Championship Game appearances. He comes into the 1992 season in seventeenth place on the all-time pro coaching victory list with 109. Denver was 5-11 in 1990, but Reeves's Broncos won the AFC Western Division title and AFC championship in 1986, 1987, and 1989, making Denver the only AFC team to reach three Super Bowls during the decade of the 1980s. Denver posted regular-season records of 11-5 (1986), 10-4-1 (1987), and 11-5 (1989) in those championship seasons. Reeves has played or coached in eight Super Bowls, the most by any single participant in the NFL's Championship Game. He led Denver to an 11-5 record in 1985, barely missing a playoff berth. Guided the Broncos to AFC West championship with a 13-3 record in 1984, and a 9-7 mark and playoff berth in 1983. His teams were 10-6 in 1981 and 2-7 in 1982. He joined the Cowboys as a free agent running back in 1965 when he undertook the dual role of player-coach for two seasons. Was the Cowboys' offensive backfield coach in 1972 and from 1974-76, and became offensive coordinator in 1977. Reeves was an all-purpose running back during his eight seasons as a player, rushing for 1,990 yards and catching 129 passes for 1,693. Career record: 109-71-1.

Background: Quarterback at South Carolina from 1962-64. He was inducted into the school's Hall of Fame in 1978.

Personal: Born January 19, 1944, Rome, Ga. Dan and his wife, Pam, live in Denver and have three children—Dana, Laura, and Lee.

Assistant Coaches

Marvin Bass, special assistant; born August 28, 1919, Norfolk, Va., lives in Denver. Tackle William & Mary 1940-42. No pro playing experience. College coach: William & Mary 1944-48, 1950-51 (head coach), North Carolina 1949, South Carolina 1956-59, 1961-65, Georgia Tech 1960, Richmond 1973. Pro coach: Washington Redskins 1952, Montreal Beavers (Continental League) 1966-67, Montreal Alouettes (CFL) 1968, Buffalo Bills 1969-71, Birmingham Americans (WFL) 1974-75, joined Broncos in 1982.

Raymond Berry, quarterbacks; born February 27, 1933, Paris, Tex., lives in Denver. Receiver Baltimore Colts 1955-67. College coach: Arkansas 1970-72. Pro coach: Dallas Cowboys 1968-69, Detroit Lions 1973-75, 1991, Cleveland Browns 1976-77, New England Patriots 1978-81, 1984-89 (head coach), joined Broncos in 1992.

Barney Chavous, defensive assistant; born March 22, 1951, Aiken, S.C., lives in Denver. Defensive end South Carolina State 1969-72. Pro defensive end Denver Broncos 1973-85. Pro coach: Joined Broncos in 1989.

Joe DeCamillis, defensive quality control; born June 29, 1965, Denver, lives in Denver. No college or pro playing experience. Wrestler Wyoming 1983-87. Pro coach: Joined Broncos in 1989.

Mo Forte, running backs; born March 1, 1947, Hannibal, Mo., lives in Denver. Running back Minnesota 1965-68. No pro playing experience. College coach: Minnesota 1970-75, Duke 1976-77, Michigan State 1978-79, Arizona State 1980-81, North Carolina A&T 1982-87 (head coach). Pro coach: Joined Broncos in 1988.

George Henshaw, offensive coordinator-wide receivers; born January 22, 1948, Richmond, Va., lives in Denver. Defensive tackle West Virginia 1967-69. No pro playing experience. College coach: West Virginia 1970-75, Florida State 1976-82, Alabama 1983-86, Tulsa 1987 (head coach). Pro coach: Joined Broncos in 1988.

Pete Mangurian, offensive line; born June 17, 1955, Los Angeles, Calif., lives in Denver. Defensive lineman Louisiana State 1975-78. No pro playing experience. College coach: Southern Methodist 1979-80, New Mexico State 1981, Stanford 1982-83, Louisiana State 1984-87. Pro coach: Joined Broncos in 1988.

Al Miller, strength and conditioning; born August 29, 1947, El Dorado, Ark., lives in Denver. Wide receiver Northeast Louisiana 1966-69. No pro playing experience. College coach: Northwestern Louisiana 1974-78, Mississippi State 1980, Northeast Louisiana 1981, Alabama 1982-84. Pro coach: Joined Broncos in 1985.

Mike Nolan, linebackers; born March 7, 1959, Baltimore, Md., lives in Denver. Safety Oregon 1977-80. No pro playing experience. College coach: Stanford 1982-83, Rice 1984-85, Louisiana State 1986. Pro coach: Joined Broncos in 1987.

Wade Phillips, defensive coordinator; born June 21, 1947, Orange, Tex., lives in Denver. Linebacker Houston 1966-68. No pro playing experience. College coach: Houston 1969, Oklahoma State 1973-74, Kansas 1975. Pro coach: Houston Oilers 1976-80, New Orleans Saints 1981-85 (head coach last four games of 1985), Philadelphia Eagles 1986-88, joined Broncos in 1989.

Harold Richardson, tight ends-special teams; born September 27, 1944, Houston, Tex., lives in Denver. Tight end Southern Methodist 1964-67. No pro playing experience. College coach: Southern Methodist 1971-72, Oklahoma State 1973-76, Texas Christian 1977-78, North Texas State 1979-80, Colorado State 1986-88. Pro coach: New Orleans Saints 1981-85, joined Broncos in 1989.

Ernie Stautner, defensive line; born April 20, 1925, Cham, Bavaria, lives in Denver. Tackle Boston College 1946-49. Pro defensive tackle Pittsburgh Steelers 1950-63 (player-coach 1963). Inducted into Pro Football Hall of Fame in 1969. Pro coach: Pittsburgh Steelers 1964, Washington Redskins 1965, Dallas Cowboys 1966-88, Dallas Texans (Arena League, head coach) 1990, joined Broncos in 1991.

Charlie Waters, defensive backs; born September 10, 1948, Miami, Fla., lives in Denver. Safety Clemson 1967-69. Pro safety Dallas Cowboys 1970-81. Pro coach: Joined Broncos in 1988.

Denver Broncos 1992 First-Year Roster

Name	Pos.	Ht.	Wt.	Birth-date	College	Hometown	How Acq.
Bostick, Jon	WR	6-2	185	10/4/69	Nebraska	El Dorado, Kan.	D7
Colar, Hesh	CB-S	5-10	188	10/15/70	San Jose State	Shreveport, La.	FA
Davis, Paschall	CB-S	6-2	220	6/5/69	Texas A&I	Bryan, Tex.	FA
Dronett, Shane	DE-NT	6-6	260	1/12/71	Texas	Orange, Tex.	D2
Dugan, Chris	K	5-10	170	5/4/65	Arizona State	Omaha, Neb.	FA
Flythe, Mark	DE-NT	6-7	290	10/4/68	Penn State	Philadelphia, Pa.	FA
Freeman, Russell	G-T	6-7	274	9/2/69	Georgia Tech	Homestead, Pa.	FA
Geater, Ron	DE-NT	6-6	270	4/23/69	Iowa	Cedar Rapids, Iowa	D7
Gibson, Don (1)	DE-NT	6-2	270	3/4/68	Southern California	Atlanta, Ga.	D9-'91
Granby, John	CB-S	6-1	198	11/11/68	Virginia Tech	Virginia Beach, Va.	D12
Johnson, Chuck	G-T	6-5	275	5/22/69	Texas	Freeport, Tex.	D4
Johnson, Jim	G-T	6-5	305	6/20/68	Michigan State	Grand Rapids, Mich.	D7
Jones, Jay	TE	6-6	245	9/3/69	Abilene Christian	Midland, Tex.	FA
Kacherski, John	LB	6-3	240	6/27/67	Ohio State	Riverhead, N.Y.	FA
Lockridge, Dietrich	G-T	6-3	325	5/9/68	Jackson State	Tupelo, Miss.	D8
Lester, Greg	WR	5-10	172	12/16/69	Georgia Tech	Daytona Beach, Fla.	FA
Maddox, Tommy	QB	6-4	195	9/2/71	UCLA	Shreveport, La.	D1
Marshall, Arthur	WR	5-11	174	4/29/69	Georgia	Ft. Gordon, Ga.	FA
McCullough, Russ	G-T	6-10	320	10/31/68	Missouri	Olathe, Kan.	FA
Meeks, Bob	G-T	6-2	279	5/28/69	Auburn	Andulisa, Ala.	D10
Moore, Shawn (1)	QB	6-2	214	4/4/68	Virginia	Martinsville, Va.	D11-'91
Oliver, Muhammed	CB-S	5-11	170	3/12/69	Oregon	Brooklyn, N.Y.	D9
Oshodin, Willie	DE-NT	6-4	240	9/16/69	Villanova	Benn City, Nigeria	FA
Reagan, Scotty (1)	DE-NT	6-5	273	7/29/67	Humboldt State	Panorama City, Calif.	FA
Robinson, Frank	CB-S	5-11	174	1/11/69	Boise State	Newark, N.J.	D5
Robinson, Harold	WR	5-11	180	2/23/70	Akron	Youngstown, Ohio	FA
Satterwhite, Stacey	DE-NT	6-6	270	7/21/70	Oklahoma State	Welch, Okla.	FA
Snow, Carlos	RB	5-9	200	10/24/68	Ohio State	Cincinnati, Ohio	FA
Sullins, John	LB	6-1	225	9/7/69	Alabama	Oxford, Miss.	FA
Tillman, Cedric	WR	6-3	195	7/22/70	Alcorn State	Gulfport, Miss.	D11
Wright, Bobby	RB	6-1	205	9/14/68	Nebraska Wesleyan	Beatrice, Neb.	FA

The term NFL Rookie is defined as a player who is in his first season of professional football and has not been on the roster of another professional football team for any regular-season or postseason games. A Rookie is designated by an "R" on NFL rosters. Players who have been active in another professional football league or players who have NFL experience, including either preseason training camp or being on an active roster for fewer than three regular-season or postseason games, are termed NFL First-Year Players. An NFL First-Year Player is designated by a "1" on NFL rosters. Thereafter, a player on an NFL active roster for at least three regular-season or postseason games is credited with an additional year of NFL playing experience.

NOTES

_____

_____

_____

_____

_____

_____

_____

_____

American Football Conference Central Division

Team Colors: Columbia Blue, Scarlet, and White

6910 Fannin Street
Houston, Texas 77030
Telephone: (713) 797-9111

Club Officials

President: K. S. (Bud) Adams, Jr.
Executive Vice President/General Manager:
  Mike Holovak
Executive Vice President/Administration:
  Mike McClure
Executive Vice President/Finance:
  Scott Thompson
Executive Assistant to President:
  Thomas S. Smith
Vice President/Marketing and Broadcasting:
  Don MacLachlan
Assistant General Manager: Floyd Reese
Director of Business Operations: Lewis Mangum
Controller: Gene Pierce
Director of Accounting Services: Marilan Logan
Director of Media Services: Chip Namias
Director of Ticket Administration Services:
  Mike Mullis
Assistant Ticket Manager: Ralph Stolarski
Director of Security: Grady Sessums
Head Trainer: Brad Brown
Assistant Trainer: Don Moseley
Equipment Manager: Gordon Batty
Video Coordinator: Ken Sparacino

Stadium: Astrodome • **Capacity:** 62,021
  Loop 610, Kirby and Fannin Streets
  Houston, Texas 77054

Playing Surface: AstroTurf-8

Training Camp: Prassel Residence Hall
  Trinity University
  San Antonio, Texas 78212

1992 Schedule

Preseason

Aug. 1	vs. Dallas at Tokyo	10:00
Aug. 7	at Detroit	7:00
Aug. 15	at Dallas	8:00
Aug. 22	at New Orleans	11:30
Aug. 29	at Los Angeles Raiders	1:00

Regular Season

Sept. 6	**Pittsburgh**	12:00
Sept. 13	at Indianapolis	3:00
Sept. 20	**Kansas City**	12:00
Sept. 27	**San Diego**	12:00
Oct. 4	**Open Date**	
Oct. 11	at Cincinnati	4:00
Oct. 18	at Denver	2:00
Oct. 25	**Cincinnati**	12:00
Nov. 1	at Pittsburgh	1:00
Nov. 8	**Cleveland**	12:00
Nov. 15	at Minnesota	12:00
Nov. 22	at Miami	1:00
Nov. 26	at Detroit (Thanksgiving)	12:30
Dec. 7	**Chicago** (Monday)	8:00
Dec. 13	**Green Bay**	7:00
Dec. 20	at Cleveland	1:00
Dec. 27	**Buffalo**	7:00

Oilers Coaching History

(221-261-6)

1960-61	Lou Rymkus*	12-7-1
1961	Wally Lemm	10-0-0
1962-63	Frank (Pop) Ivy	17-12-0
1964	Sammy Baugh	4-10-0
1965	Hugh Taylor	4-10-0
1966-70	Wally Lemm	28-40-4
1971	Ed Hughes	4-9-1
1972-73	Bill Peterson**	1-18-0
1973-74	Sid Gillman	8-15-0
1975-80	O.A. (Bum) Phillips	59-38-0
1981-83	Ed Biles***	8-23-0
1983	Chuck Studley	2-8-0
1984-85	Hugh Campbell****	8-22-0
1985-89	Jerry Glanville	35-35-0
1990-91	Jack Pardee	21-14-0

  *Released after five games in 1961
  **Released after five games in 1973
  ***Resigned after six games in 1983
  ****Released after 14 games in 1985

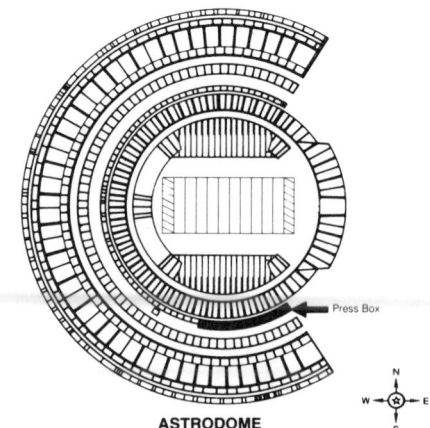

Press Box

ASTRODOME

Record Holders
Individual Records—Career

Category	Name	Performance
Rushing (Yds.)	Earl Campbell, 1978-1984	8,574
Passing (Yds.)	Warren Moon, 1984-1991	27,679
Passing (TDs)	George Blanda, 1960-66	165
Receiving (No.)	Drew Hill, 1985-1991	480
Receiving (Yds.)	Drew Hill, 1985-1991	7,477
Interceptions	Jim Norton, 1960-68	45
Punting (Avg.)	Jim Norton, 1960-68	42.3
Punt Return (Avg.)	Billy Johnson, 1974-1980	13.2
Kickoff Return (Avg.)	Bobby Jancik, 1962-67	26.4
Field Goals	Tony Zendejas, 1985-1990	117
Touchdowns (Tot.)	Earl Campbell, 1978-1984	73
Points	George Blanda, 1960-66	596

Individual Records—Single Season

Category	Name	Performance
Rushing (Yds.)	Earl Campbell, 1980	1,934
Passing (Yds.)	Warren Moon, 1991	4,690
Passing (TDs)	George Blanda, 1961	36
Receiving (No.)	Charley Hennigan, 1964	101
Receiving (Yds.)	Charley Hennigan, 1961	*1,746
Interceptions	Fred Glick, 1963	12
	Mike Reinfeldt, 1979	12
Punting (Avg.)	Greg Montgomery, 1990	45.0
Punt Return (Avg.)	Billy Johnson, 1977	15.4
Kickoff Return (Avg.)	Ken Hall, 1960	31.2
Field Goals	Tony Zendejas, 1989	25
Touchdowns (Tot.)	Earl Campbell, 1979	19
Points	George Blanda, 1960	115
	Tony Zendejas, 1989	115

Individual Records—Single Game

Category	Name	Performance
Rushing (Yds.)	Billy Cannon, 12-10-61	216
Passing (Yds.)	Warren Moon, 12-16-90	527
Passing (TDs)	George Blanda, 11-19-61	*7
Receiving (No.)	Charley Hennigan, 10-13-61	13
	Haywood Jeffires, 10-13-91	13
Receiving (Yds.)	Charley Hennigan, 10-13-61	272
Interceptions	Many times	3
	Last time by Willie Alexander, 11-14-71	
Field Goals	Skip Butler, 10-12-75	6
Touchdowns (Tot.)	Billy Cannon, 12-10-61	5
Points	Billy Cannon, 12-10-61	30

*NFL Record

1991 Team Record
Preseason (2-2)
Date	Result		Opponents
8/3	L	29-31	at San Diego
8/9	L	7-36	Atlanta
8/18	W	30-20	Dallas
8/22	W	16-13	vs. L.A. Rams at Memphis, Tenn.

Regular Season (11-5)
Date	Result		Opponents	Att.
9/1	W	47-17	L.A. Raiders	61,367
9/8	W	30- 7	at Cincinnati	56,463
9/16	W	17- 7	Kansas City	61,058
9/22	L	20-24	at New England	30,702
10/6	W	42-14	Denver	59,145
10/13	W	23-20	at N.Y. Jets	70,758
10/20	W	17-13	at Miami	60,705
10/27	W	35- 3	Cincinnati	58,634
11/3	L	13-16	at Wash. (OT)	55,096
11/10	W	26-23	Dallas (OT)	63,001
11/17	W	28-24	Cleveland	58,155
11/24	L	14-26	at Pittsburgh	45,795
12/2	L	6-13	Philadelphia	62,141
12/8	W	31- 6	Pittsburgh	59,225
12/15	W	17-14	at Cleveland	55,680
12/21	L	20-24	at N.Y. Giants	63,421

(OT) Overtime

Postseason (1-1)
Date	Result		Opponent	Att.
12/29	W	17-10	N.Y. Jets	61,485
1/4	L	24-26	at Denver	75,301

Score by Periods
Oilers	43	129	64	147	3	—	386
Opponents	53	81	59	55	3	—	251

Attendance
Home 482,726   Away 438,620   Total 921,346
Single-game home record, 63,001 (11-10-91)
Single-season home record, 482,726 (1991)

1991 Team Statistics
	Oilers	Opp.
Total First Downs	353	280
Rushing	99	94
Passing	236	163
Penalty	18	23
Third Down: Made/Att.	97/195	88/219
Third Down: Pct.	49.7	40.2
Fourth Down: Made/Att.	3/9	9/19
Fourth Down: Pct.	33.3	47.4
Total Net Yards	5987	4748
Avg. Per Game	374.2	296.8
Total Plays	1022	984
Avg. Per Play	5.9	4.8
Net Yards Rushing	1366	1540
Avg. Per Game	85.4	96.3
Total Rushes	331	407
Net Yards Passing	4621	3208
Avg. Per Game	288.8	200.5
Sacked/Yards Lost	24/183	45/314
Gross Yards	4804	3522
Att./Completions	667/411	532/310
Completion Pct.	61.6	58.3
Had Intercepted	21	20
Punts/Avg.	53/41.7	74/42.1
Net Punting Avg.	36.6	36.6
Penalties/Yards Lost	99/784	109/797
Fumbles/Ball Lost	33/19	27/18
Touchdowns	46	26
Rushing	16	8
Passing	24	17
Returns	6	1
Avg. Time of Possession	30:28	29:32

1991 Individual Statistics
Scoring
	TD R	TD P	TD Rt	PAT	FG	Saf	TP
Howfield	0	0	0	25/29	13/18	0	64
Pinkett	9	1	0	0/0	0/0	0	60
Del Greco	0	0	0	16/16	10/13	0	46
Jeffires	0	7	0	0/0	0/0	0	42
Givins	0	5	0	0/0	0/0	0	30
Duncan	0	4	0	0/0	0/0	0	24
Hill	0	4	0	0/0	0/0	0	24
White	4	0	0	0/0	0/0	0	24
T. Jones	0	2	0	0/0	0/0	0	12
Moon	2	0	0	0/0	0/0	0	12
Brown	1	0	0	0/0	0/0	0	6
Coleman	0	1	0	0/0	0/0	0	6
Dishman	0	0	1	0/0	0/0	0	6
Dumas	0	0	1	0/0	0/0	0	6
Lathon	0	0	1	0/0	0/0	0	6
Lewis	0	0	1	0/0	0/0	0	6
McDowell	0	0	1	0/0	0/0	0	6
A. Smith	0	0	1	0/0	0/0	0	6
Oilers	16	24	6	41/46	23/31	0	386
Opponents	8	17	1	26/26	23/29	0	251

Passing
	Att.	Comp.	Yds.	Pct.	TD	Int.	Tkld.	Rate
Moon	655	404	4690	61.7	23	21	23/174	81.7
Carlson	12	7	114	58.3	1	0	1/9	118.1
Oilers	667	411	4804	61.6	24	21	24/183	82.3
Opponents	532	310	3522	58.3	17	20	45/314	73.2

Rushing
	Att.	Yds.	Avg.	LG	TD
Pinkett	171	720	4.2	32	9
White	110	465	4.2	20	4
Brown	8	85	10.6	39t	1
Moon	33	68	2.1	12	2
Givins	4	30	7.5	23	0
Hill	1	1	1.0	1	0
Carlson	4	-3	-0.8	0	0
Oilers	331	1366	4.1	39t	16
Opponents	407	1540	3.8	24	8

Receiving
	No.	Yds.	Avg.	LG	TD
Jeffires	100	1181	11.8	44	7
Hill	90	1109	12.3	61t	4
Givins	70	996	14.2	49	5
Duncan	55	588	10.7	42	4
Pinkett	29	228	7.9	36t	1
White	27	211	7.8	20	0
T. Jones	19	251	13.2	68t	2
Coleman	11	138	12.5	26	1
Harris	8	101	12.6	29	0
Brown	2	1	0.5	4	0
Oilers	411	4804	11.7	68t	24
Opponents	310	3522	11.4	80t	17

Interceptions
	No.	Yds.	Avg.	LG	TD
Dishman	6	61	10.2	43	0
McDowell	4	31	7.8	23	0
Orlando	4	18	4.5	18	0
Lathon	3	77	25.7	52t	1
Lewis	1	33	33.0	33t	1
Dumas	1	19	19.0	19	0
A. Smith	1	16	16.0	16	0
Oilers	20	255	12.8	52t	2
Opponents	21	296	14.1	47	0

Punting
	No.	Yds.	Avg.	In 20	LG
Gr. Montgomery	48	2105	43.9	13	60
Sullivan	3	106	35.3	1	37
Oilers	53	2211	41.7	14	60
Opponents	74	3115	42.1	22	64

Punt Returns
	No.	FC	Yds.	Avg.	LG	TD
Coleman	22	8	138	6.3	24	0
Givins	11	0	107	9.7	29	0
Duncan	1	3	-1	-1.0	-1	0
Jackson	1	0	0	0.0	0	0
Robertson	1	0	0	0.0	0	0
Oilers	36	11	244	6.8	29	0
Opponents	29	5	192	6.6	17	0

Kickoff Returns
	No.	Yds.	Avg.	LG	TD
Pinkett	26	508	19.5	41	0
Coleman	13	256	19.7	31	0
Brown	3	30	10.0	16	0
Harris	2	34	17.0	19	0
Flannery	1	0	0.0	0	0
V. Jones	1	7	7.0	7	0
Oilers	46	835	18.2	41	0
Opponents	63	1071	17.0	42	0

Sacks
	No.
Fuller	15.0
S. Jones	10.0
Childress	7.0
L. Williams	3.0
Lathon	2.0
Alm	1.0
Jackson	1.0
Lewis	1.0
McDowell	1.0
Robertson	1.0
A. Smith	1.0
Kozak	0.5
D. Smith	0.5
Oilers	45.0
Opponents	24.0

1992 Draft Choices
Round	Name	Pos.	College
2.	Eddie Robinson	LB	Alabama State
3.	Corey Harris	WR	Vanderbilt
4.	Mike Mooney	T	Georgia Tech
5.	Joe Bowden	LB	Oklahoma
	Tony Brown	DB	Fresno State
	Tim Roberts	DT	So. Mississippi
6.	Mario Bailey	WR	Washington
7.	Elbert Turner	WR	Illinois
8.	Bucky Richardson	QB	Texas A&M
9.	Bernard Dafney	T	Tennessee
10.	Dion Johnson	WR	East Carolina
11.	Anthony Davis	LB	Utah
12.	Joe Wood	K	Air Force

Houston Oilers 1992 Veteran Roster

No.	Name	Pos.	Ht.	Wt.	Birth-date	NFL Exp.	College	Hometown	How Acq.	'91 Games/ Starts
76	Alm, Jeff	DT	6-6	269	3/31/68	3	Notre Dame	Orland Park, Ill.	D2-'90	12/1
33	Brown, Gary	RB	5-11	224	7/1/69	2	Penn State	Williamsport, Pa.	D8-'91	11/0
14	Carlson, Cody	QB	6-3	202	11/5/63	6	Baylor	San Antonio, Tex.	D3-'87	3/0
79	Childress, Ray	DT-DE	6-6	272	10/20/62	8	Texas A&M	Richardson, Tex.	D1a-'85	15/15
87	Coleman, Pat	WR	5-7	173	4/8/67	2	Mississippi	Cleveland, Miss.	D9-'90	14/0
66	Dawson, Doug	C-G	6-3	288	12/27/61	5	Texas	Houston, Tex.	FA-'91	14/10
3	Del Greco, Al	K	5-10	200	3/2/62	9	Auburn	Coral Gables, Fla.	FA-'91	7/0
28	†Dishman, Cris	CB	6-0	178	8/13/65	5	Purdue	Louisville, Ky.	D5a-'88	15/15
77	Donnalley, Kevin	T	6-5	290	6/10/68	2	North Carolina	Raleigh, N.C.	D3b-'91	16/0
38	Dumas, Mike	S	5-11	178	3/18/69	2	Indiana	Lowell, Mich.	D2a-'91	13/0
80	†Duncan, Curtis	WR	5-11	184	1/26/65	6	Northwestern	Detroit, Mich.	D10-'87	16/16
55	Flannery, John	C-G	6-3	304	1/13/69	2	Syracuse	Pottsville, Pa.	D2c-'91	16/9
95	†Fuller, William	DE	6-3	274	3/8/62	7	North Carolina	Chesapeake, Va.	T(Rams)-'86	16/16
81	Givins, Ernest	WR	5-9	172	9/3/64	7	Louisville	St. Petersburg, Fla.	D2-'86	16/16
93	Graf, Rick	LB	6-5	244	8/29/64	6	Wisconsin	Madison, Wis.	PB(Mia)-'91#	12/0
21	Gray, Jerry	CB-S	6-0	185	12/2/62	8	Texas	Lubbock, Tex.	PB(Rams)-'92#	16/9*
83	Harris, Leonard	WR	5-8	162	11/27/60	7	Texas Tech	McKinney, Tex.	FA-'87	9/0
24	Jackson, Steve	CB	5-8	182	4/8/69	2	Purdue	Houston, Tex.	D3a-'91	15/2
84	Jeffires, Haywood	WR	6-2	201	12/12/64	6	North Carolina State	Greensboro, N.C.	D1b-'87	16/16
23	†Johnson, Richard	CB	6-1	195	9/16/63	8	Wisconsin	Dixmoor, Ill.	D1b-'85	14/14
96	Jones, Sean	DE	6-7	264	12/19/62	9	Northeastern	Montclair, N.J.	T(Raid)-'88	16/12
30	Jones, Victor	RB	5-8	212	12/5/67	3	Louisiana State	Zachary, La.	FA-'91	14/0
56	†Kozak, Scott	LB	6-3	222	11/28/65	4	Oregon	Colton, Ore.	D2-'89	16/0
57	Lathon, Lamar	LB	6-3	250	12/23/67	3	Houston	Wharton, Tex.	D1-'90	16/16
29	Lewis, Darryl	CB	5-9	188	12/16/68	2	Arizona	La Puente, Calif.	D2b-'91	16/1
78	Maggs, Don	G-T	6-5	290	11/1/61	6	Tulane	Youngstown, Ohio	SD2-'84	16/15
74	Matthews, Bruce	C-G	6-5	291	8/8/61	10	Southern California	Arcadia, Calif.	D1-'83	16/16
25	†McDowell, Bubba	S	6-1	198	11/4/66	4	Miami	Merritt Island, Fla.	D3-'89	16/16
91	Meads, Johnny	LB	6-2	226	6/25/61	9	Nicholls State	Napoleonville, La.	D3-'84	16/16
94	Montgomery, Glenn	DT	6-0	272	3/31/67	4	Houston	Gretna, La.	D5-'89	16/0
9	Montgomery, Greg	P	6-4	215	10/29/64	5	Michigan State	Red Bank, N.J.	D3-'88	15/0
1	Moon, Warren	QB	6-3	212	11/18/56	9	Washington	Los Angeles, Calif.	FA-'84	16/16
63	†Munchak, Mike	G	6-3	284	3/5/60	11	Penn State	Scranton, Pa.	D1-'82	13/13
64	Norgard, Erik	C-G	6-1	282	11/4/65	2	Colorado	Arlington, Wash.	FA-'91	0*
26	†Orlando, Bo	S	5-10	180	4/3/66	3	West Virginia	Berwick, Pa.	D6-'89	16/16
72	Peguese, Willis	DE	6-4	273	12/18/66	3	Miami	Miami, Fla.	D3-'90	7/0
89	Query, Jeff	WR	6-0	165	3/7/67	4	Millikin	Maroa, Ill.	PB(GB)-'92#	16/0*
31	Robertson, Marcus	CB-S	5-11	197	10/2/69	2	Iowa State	Pasadena, Calif.	D4b-'91	16/0
53	Seale, Eugene	LB	5-10	253	6/3/64	6	Lamar	Jasper, Tex.	FA-'87	15/0
54	Smith, Al	LB	6-1	251	11/26/64	6	Utah State	Los Angeles, Calif.	D6a-'87	16/16
99	Smith, Doug	DT	6-6	309	6/13/59	8	Auburn	Bayboro, N.C.	D2a-'84	15/15
70	Steinkuhler, Dean	T	6-3	287	1/27/61	9	Nebraska	Burr, Neb.	D1-'84	16/1
32	Tillman, Spencer	RB	5-11	206	4/21/64	6	Oklahoma	Tulsa, Okla.	PB(SF)-'92#	16/0*
44	White, Lorenzo	RB	5-11	222	4/12/66	5	Michigan State	Ft. Lauderdale, Fla.	D1-'88	13/0
73	Williams, David	T	6-5	292	6/21/66	4	Florida	Lakeland, Fla.	D1-'89	16/16
97	Williams, Lee	DE-DT	6-6	271	10/15/62	9	Bethune-Cookman	Ft. Lauderdale, Fla.	T(SD)-'91	10/5

* Gray played 16 games with L.A. Rams in '91; Norgard missed '91 season due to injury; Query played 16 games with Green Bay; Tillman played 16 games with San Francisco.

† Option playout; subject to developments.

Traded—RB Allen Pinkett to New Orleans.

Retired—Ezra Johnson, 16-year defensive end, 2 games in '91.

Plan B unconditional free agent.

Players lost through Plan B (4): LB Eric Fairs (Buff; 16 games in '91), WR Drew Hill (Atl; 16), WR Alex Johnson (NE; 5), WR Tony Jones (Atl; 16).

Also played with Oilers in '91—CB Herbie Anderson (1 game), K Ian Howfield (9), WR Frank Miotke (8), P Kent Sullivan (1).

COACHING STAFF

Head Coach,
Jack Pardee

Pro Career: Named the Oilers' fourteenth head coach on January 9, 1990. Accepted post after serving three years (1987-89) as head coach at University of Houston. While at Houston, Cougars set over 100 NCAA/Southwest Conference records in 1988 and 1989. In 1986, was a scout for the Green Bay Packers. Prior to that, was head coach of successful Houston Gamblers of the USFL from 1984-85 as team led league in total offense and scoring in both seasons. Spent 1982 in private business after serving as defensive coordinator for San Diego Chargers in 1981. That season, Chargers won AFC's Western Division and advanced to AFC Championship Game. From 1978-80, was head coach of the Washington Redskins, earning NFL coach of the year honors in 1979. Was head coach of the Chicago Bears from 1975-77, earning NFC coach of the year accolades in 1976 and leading the club in 1977 to its first playoff berth in 14 years. Was general manager/head coach for Florida Blazers of the World Football League in 1974, winning division title and advancing to WFL title game. Began coaching career as Washington Redskins' assistant in 1973. Drafted by Los Angeles Rams in second round in 1957 and played 15 seasons at linebacker for Rams (1957-64, 1966-70) and Washington Redskins (1971-72). Was an all-pro selection in 1963 and 1971, and is a member of Rams' fortieth anniversary team. Career record: 65-61.

Background: Played linebacker and fullback in All-America and Academic All-America career for coach Paul (Bear) Bryant at Texas A&M (1953-56). Is a member of the Texas A&M Hall of Fame, National Football Foundation Hall of Fame, College Football Hall of Fame, Texas Sports Hall of Fame, and Senior Bowl Hall of Fame.

Personal: Born April 19, 1936, Exira, Iowa. Jack and his wife, Phyllis, live in Missouri City, Tex., and have two sons, Steven and Ted, and three daughters, Judee, Anne, and Susan.

Assistant Coaches

Jim Eddy, defensive coordinator; born May 2, 1939, Checotah, Okla., lives in Houston. Defensive back/running back New Mexico State 1956-59. No pro playing experience. College coach: New Mexico State 1965-70, Texas-El Paso 1971-72, Houston 1987-89. Pro coach: Saskatchewan Rough Riders (CFL) 1974-78 (head coach 1977-78), Hamilton Tiger-Cats (CFL) 1979-80, Montreal Alouettes (CFL) 1981 (head coach), Toronto Argonauts (CFL) 1982-83, Houston Gamblers (USFL) 1984-85, joined Oilers in 1990.

Kevin Gilbride, offensive coordinator; born August 27, 1951, New Haven, Conn., lives in Missouri City, Tex. Quarterback/tight end Southern Connecticut State 1970-73. No pro playing experience. College coach: Idaho State 1974-75, Tufts 1976-77, American International 1978-79, Southern Connecticut State 1980-84 (head coach), East Carolina 1987-88. Pro coach: Ottawa Rough Riders (CFL) 1985-86, joined Oilers in 1989.

Frank Novak, running backs; born May 18, 1938, Worcester, Mass., lives in Missouri City, Tex. Quarterback Northern Michigan 1959-61. No pro playing experience. College coach: Northern Michigan 1966-72, East Carolina 1973, Virginia 1974-75, Western Illinois 1976-77, Holy Cross 1978-83, Massachusetts 1986, Missouri 1988. Pro coach: Oklahoma Outlaws (USFL) 1984, Birmingham Stallions (USFL) 1985, joined Oilers in 1989.

Chris Palmer, receivers; born September 23, 1949, Mt. Kisco, N.Y., lives in Missouri City, Tex. Quarterback Southern Connecticut State 1968-71. No pro playing experience. College coach: Connecticut 1972-74, Lehigh 1975, Colgate 1976-82, New Haven 1986-87 (head coach), Boston University 1988-89 (head coach). Pro coach: Montreal Concordes (CFL) 1983, New Jersey Generals (USFL) 1984-85, joined Oilers in 1990.

Richard Smith, special teams-linebackers; born October 17, 1955, Los Angeles, lives in Richmond, Tex. Offensive lineman Rio Hondo (Calif.) J.C. 1975-76, Fresno State 1977-78. No pro playing experience. College coach: Rio Hondo (Calif.) J.C. 1979-80, Cal State-Fullerton 1981-83, California 1984-86, Arizona 1987. Pro coach: Joined Oilers in 1988.

Jim Stanley, defensive line; born June 22, 1934, Dunham, Ky., lives in Houston. Guard/defensive tackle Texas A&M 1954-57. No pro playing experience. College coach: Southern Methodist 1961, Texas-El Paso 1962, Oklahoma State 1963-68, 1972-78 (head coach 1973-78), Navy 1969-70. Pro coach: Winnipeg Blue Bombers (CFL) 1971, New York Giants 1979, Atlanta Falcons 1980-82, Michigan Panthers (USFL) 1983-84 (head coach), Tampa Bay Buccaneers 1986, joined Oilers in 1990.

Pat Thomas, defensive backs; born September 1, 1954, Plano, Tex., lives in Missouri City, Tex. Cornerback Texas A&M 1972-75. Pro cornerback Los Angeles Rams 1976-82. College coach: Houston 1987-89. Pro coach: Houston Gamblers (USFL) 1984-85, joined Oilers in 1990.

Steve Watterson, strength and rehabilitation; born November 27, 1956, Newport, R.I., lives in Sugar Land, Tex. Attended Rhode Island. No college or pro playing experience. Pro coach: Philadelphia Eagles 1984-85 (assistant trainer), joined Oilers in 1986 (elevated to assistant coach in 1988).

Bob Young, offensive line; born September 3, 1942, Marshall, Tex., lives in Sugar Land, Tex. Guard Texas 1960-61, Howard Payne 1962-63. Pro guard Denver Broncos 1966-70, Houston Oilers 1971, 1980, St. Louis Cardinals 1972-79, New Orleans Saints 1981. College coach: Houston 1987-89. Pro coach: Houston Gamblers (USFL) 1984-85, joined Oilers in 1990.

Houston Oilers 1992 First-Year Roster

Name	Pos.	Ht.	Wt.	Birth-date	College	Hometown	How Acq.
Bailey, Mario	WR	5-9	162	11/30/70	Washington	Seattle, Wash.	D6
Bowden, Joe	LB	5-11	227	2/25/70	Oklahoma	Mesquite, Tex.	D5a
Brown, Tony	CB	5-9	183	5/15/70	Fresno State	Granada Hills, Calif.	D5b
Dafney, Bernard	T	6-5	317	11/1/68	Tennessee	Los Angeles, Calif.	D9
Davis, Anthony	LB	6-0	231	3/7/69	Utah	Pasco, Wash.	D11
Gray, Terry (1)	G-C	6-2	280	5/25/68	Baylor	Spring, Tex.	FA
Harris, Corey	WR	5-11	195	10/15/69	Vanderbilt	Indianapolis, Ind.	D3
Hazard, Manny	WR	5-8	173	7/22/69	Houston	Pacifica, Calif.	FA
Hopkins, Wade	WR	6-2	196	8/23/68	Southwest Baptist	Pasadena, Tex.	FA
Johnson, Dion	WR	5-8	164	4/4/70	East Carolina	Newport News, Va.	D10
Long, Kevin	S	6-2	200	4/17/70	Villanova	Milford, Conn.	FA
Mooney, Mike	T	6-6	332	5/31/69	Georgia Tech	Sykesville, Md.	D4
Nee, John	T	6-5	284	11/21/67	Elon	Central Valley, N.Y.	FA
Pharms, Charles	S	5-11	185	12/15/69	Miami	Houston, Tex.	FA
Reed, Curtis (1)	WR	6-3	199	12/3/65	Millikin	McLeansboro, Ill.	FA
Richardson, Bucky	QB	6-1	221	2/7/92	Texas A&M	Baton Rouge, La.	D8
Roberts, Tim	DT	6-6	309	4/14/69	Southern Mississippi	Atlanta, Ga.	D5c
Robinson, Eddie	LB	6-1	242	4/13/70	Alabama State	New Orleans, La.	D2
Robinson, Jeroy (1)	LB	6-2	240	6/14/68	Texas A&M	Bryan, Tex.	FA
Slack, Reggie (1)	QB	6-1	221	5/2/68	Auburn	Milton, Fla.	D12-'90
Turner, Elbert	WR	5-11	165	3/19/68	Illinois	Gary, Ind.	D7
Wellman, Gary (1)	WR	5-9	175	8/9/67	Southern California	Westlake, Calif.	D5-'91
Williams, Anthony	LB	6-1	240	6/1/70	Alabama A&M	Waco, Tex.	FA
Wood, Joe	K	6-1	202	12/29/68	Air Force	Mission Viejo, Calif.	D12

The term NFL Rookie is defined as a player who is in his first season of professional football and has not been on the roster of another professional football team for any regular-season or postseason games. A Rookie is designated by an "R" on NFL rosters. Players who have been active in another professional football league or players who have NFL experience, including either preseason training camp or being on an active roster for fewer than three regular-season or post-season games, are termed NFL First-Year Players. An NFL First-Year Player is designated by a "1" on NFL rosters. Thereafter, a player on an NFL active roster for at least three regular-season or postseason games is credited with an additional year of NFL playing experience.

NOTES

INDIANAPOLIS COLTS

American Football Conference Eastern Division

Team Colors: Royal Blue and White

**P.O. Box 535000
Indianapolis, Indiana 46253
Telephone: (317) 297-2658**

Club Officials

President-Treasurer: Robert Irsay
Vice President-General Manager: James Irsay
Vice President-General Counsel:
   Michael G. Chernoff
Assistant General Manager: Bob Terpening
Director of Player Personnel: Jack Bushofsky
Controller: Kurt Humphrey
Director of Operations: Pete Ward
Director of Public Relations: Craig Kelley
Ticket Manager: Larry Hall
Assistant Directors of Public Relations:
   Rod St. Clair, Todd Stewart
Purchasing Administrator: David Filar
Equipment Manager: Jon Scott
Assistant Equipment Manager: Mike Mays
Video Director: Marty Heckscher
Assistant Video Director: John Starliper
Head Trainer: Hunter Smith
Assistant Trainer: Dave Hammer
Team Physician and Orthopedic Surgeon:
   K. Donald Shelbourne
Orthopedic Surgeon: Arthur C. Rettig

Stadium: Hoosier Dome • **Capacity:** 60,129
            100 South Capitol Avenue
            Indianapolis, Indiana 46225

Playing Surface: AstroTurf

Training Camp: Anderson University
            Anderson, Indiana 46011

1992 Schedule

Preseason
Aug. 8	**New England**	6:30
Aug. 15	**Seattle**	7:30
Aug. 22	at Cincinnati	7:30
Aug. 28	at Kansas City	7:00

Regular Season
Sept. 6	**Cleveland**	12:00
Sept. 13	**Houston**	3:00
Sept. 20	at Buffalo	8:00
Sept. 27	**Open Date**	
Oct. 4	at Tampa Bay	1:00
Oct. 11	**New York Jets**	3:00
Oct. 18	**San Diego**	12:00
Oct. 25	at Miami	4:00
Nov. 1	at San Diego	1:00
Nov. 8	**Miami**	1:00
Nov. 15	**New England**	1:00
Nov. 22	at Pittsburgh	1:00
Nov. 29	**Buffalo**	4:00
Dec. 6	at New England	1:00
Dec. 13	at New York Jets	1:00
Dec. 20	**Phoenix**	1:00
Dec. 27	at Cincinnati	1:00

Colts Coaching History

**Baltimore 1953-1983
(276-283-7)**

1953	Keith Molesworth	3-9-0
1954-62	Weeb Ewbank	61-52-1
1963-69	Don Shula	73-26-4
1970-72	Don McCafferty*	26-11-1
1972	John Sandusky	4-5-0
1973-74	Howard Schnellenberger**	4-13-0
1974	Joe Thomas	2-9-0
1975-79	Ted Marchibroda	41-36-0
1980-81	Mike McCormack	9-23-0
1982-84	Frank Kush***	11-28-1
1984	Hal Hunter	0-1-0
1985-86	Rod Dowhower****	5-24-0
1986-91	Ron Meyer#	36-36-0
1991	Rick Venturi	1-10-0

 *Released after five games in 1972
 **Released after three games in 1974
 ***Resigned after 15 games in 1984
****Released after 13 games in 1986
 #Released after 5 games in 1991

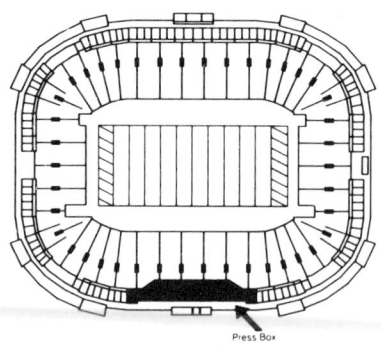

HOOSIER DOME

Record Holders
Individual Records—Career
Category	Name	Performance
Rushing (Yds.)	Lydell Mitchell, 1972-77	5,487
Passing (Yds.)	Johnny Unitas, 1956-1972	39,768
Passing (TDs)	Johnny Unitas, 1956-1972	287
Receiving (No.)	Raymond Berry, 1955-1967	631
Receiving (Yds.)	Raymond Berry, 1955-1967	9,275
Interceptions	Bob Boyd, 1960-68	57
Punting (Avg.)	Rohn Stark, 1982-1991	43.9
Punt Return (Avg.)	Wendell Harris, 1964	12.6
Kickoff Return (Avg.)	Jim Duncan, 1969-1971	32.5
Field Goals	Dean Biasucci 1984, 1986-89	118
Touchdowns (Tot.)	Lenny Moore, 1956-1967	113
Points	Lenny Moore, 1956-1967	678

Individual Records—Single Season
Category	Name	Performance
Rushing (Yds.)	Eric Dickerson, 1988	1,659
Passing (Yds.)	Johnny Unitas, 1963	3,481
Passing (TDs)	Johnny Unitas, 1959	32
Receiving (No.)	Joe Washington, 1979	82
Receiving (Yds.)	Raymond Berry, 1960	1,298
Interceptions	Tom Keane, 1953	11
Punting (Avg.)	Rohn Stark, 1985	45.9
Punt Return (Avg.)	Clarence Verdin, 1989	12.9
Kickoff Return (Avg.)	Jim Duncan, 1970	35.4
Field Goals	Raul Allegre, 1983	30
Touchdowns (Tot.)	Lenny Moore, 1964	20
Points	Lenny Moore, 1964	120

Individual Records—Single Game
Category	Name	Performance
Rushing (Yds.)	Norm Bulaich, 9-19-71	198
Passing (Yds.)	Johnny Unitas, 9-17-67	401
Passing (TDs)	Gary Cuozzo, 11-14-65	5
	Gary Hogeboom, 10-4-87	5
Receiving (No.)	Lydell Mitchell, 12-15-74	13
	Joe Washington, 9-2-79	13
Receiving (Yds.)	Raymond Berry, 11-10-57	224
Interceptions	Many times	3
	Last time by Leonard Coleman, 10-12-86	
Field Goals	Many times	5
	Last time by Dean Biasucci, 9-25-88	
Touchdowns (Tot.)	Many times	4
	Last time by Eric Dickerson, 10-31-88	
Points	Many times	24
	Last time by Eric Dickerson, 10-31-88	

1991 Team Record

Preseason (1-3)

Date	Result		Opponents
8/2	L	3-10	at Denver
8/10	L	7-17	Seattle
8/17	W	34-28	New Orleans
8/23	L	21-23	at Philadelphia

Regular Season (1-15)

Date	Result		Opponents	Att.
9/1	L	7-16	New England	49,961
9/8	L	6-17	at Miami	51,155
9/15	L	0-16	at L.A. Raiders	40,287
9/22	L	24-33	Detroit	53,396
9/29	L	3-31	at Seattle	56,656
10/6	L	3-21	Pittsburgh	55,383
10/13	L	6-42	at Buffalo	79,015
10/20	L	6-17	N.Y. Jets	53,025
11/3	L	6-10	Miami	55,899
11/10	W	28-27	at N.Y. Jets	44,792
11/17	L	17-31	Chicago	60,519
11/24	L	10-14	at Green Bay	42,132
12/1	L	0-31	Cleveland	57,539
12/8	L	17-23	at New Engl. (OT)	20,131
12/15	L	7-35	Buffalo	48,286
12/22	L	3-17	at Tampa Bay	28,043

(OT) Overtime

Score by Periods

Colts	24	54	27	38	0	—	143
Opponents	96	106	88	85	6	—	381

Attendance

Home 434,008   Away 362,211   Total 796,219
Single-game home record, 61,479 (11-13-83)
Single-season home record, 481,305 (1984)

1991 Team Statistics

	Colts	Opp.
Total First Downs	236	305
Rushing	55	140
Passing	163	152
Penalty	18	13
Third Down: Made/Att.	65/208	98/199
Third Down: Pct.	31.3	49.2
Fourth Down: Made/Att.	10/25	7/11
Fourth Down: Pct.	40.0	63.6
Total Net Yards	3748	5127
Avg. Per Game	234.3	320.4
Total Plays	923	961
Avg. Per Play	4.1	5.3
Net Yards Rushing	1169	2327
Avg. Per Game	73.1	145.4
Total Rushes	354	544
Net Yards Passing	2579	2800
Avg. Per Game	161.2	175.0
Sacked/Yards Lost	57/487	29/202
Gross Yards	3066	3002
Att./Completions	512/305	388/240
Completion Pct.	59.6	61.9
Had Intercepted	16	15
Punts/Avg.	82/42.6	59/41.4
Net Punting Avg.	34.8	36.2
Penalties/Yards Lost	85/689	88/645
Fumbles/Ball Lost	31/15	21/13
Touchdowns	14	47
Rushing	3	23
Passing	10	22
Returns	1	2
Avg. Time of Possession	28:05	31:55

1991 Individual Statistics

Scoring

	TD R	TD P	TD Rt	PAT	FG	Saf	TP
Biasucci	0	0	0	14/14	15/26	0	59
Hester	0	5	0	0/0	0/0	0	30
Brooks	0	4	0	0/0	0/0	0	24
Dickerson	2	1	0	0/0	0/0	0	18
Manoa	1	0	0	0/0	0/0	0	6
Verdin	0	0	1	0/0	0/0	0	6
Colts	3	10	1	14/14	15/26	0	143
Opponents	23	22	2	46/46	17/23	1	381

Passing

	Att.	Comp.	Yds.	Pct.	TD	Int.	Tkld.	Rate
George	485	292	2910	60.2	10	12	56/481	73.8
Herrmann	19	11	137	57.9	0	3	0/0	40.8
Trudeau	7	2	19	28.6	0	1	1/6	0.0
Hilger	1	0	0	0.0	0	0	0/0	39.6
Colts	512	305	3066	59.6	10	16	57/487	70.2
Opponents	388	240	3002	61.9	22	15	29/202	88.7

Rushing

	Att.	Yds.	Avg.	LG	TD
Dickerson	167	536	3.2	28	2
Clark	114	366	3.2	25	0
Manoa	27	144	5.3	44	1
Johnson	22	94	4.3	15	0
George	16	36	2.3	13	0
Perkins	4	11	2.8	4	0
Verdin	1	4	4.0	4	0
Herrmann	1	-1	-1.0	-1	0
Huffman	1	-8	-8.0	-8	0
Stark	1	-13	-13.0	-13	0
Colts	354	1169	3.3	44	3
Opponents	544	2327	4.3	78t	23

Receiving

	No.	Yds.	Avg.	LG	TD
Brooks	72	888	12.3	46	4
Hester	60	753	12.6	49t	5
Johnson	42	344	8.2	24	0
Dickerson	41	269	6.6	26	1
Clark	33	245	7.4	23	0
Verdin	21	214	10.2	28	0
Mrosko	8	90	11.3	20	0
Bentley	7	42	6.0	11	0
Martin	5	79	15.8	25	0
Beach	5	56	11.2	26	0
Huffman	3	14	4.7	7	0
Perkins	3	-2	-0.7	3	0
Manoa	2	5	2.5	5	0
Thornton	1	38	38.0	38	0
Cash	1	18	18.0	18	0
Coley	1	13	13.0	13	0
Colts	305	3066	10.1	49t	10
Opponents	240	3002	12.5	84t	22

Interceptions

	No.	Yds.	Avg.	LG	TD
Baylor	4	50	12.5	32	0
Prior	3	50	16.7	37	0
Daniel	3	22	7.3	12	0
Goode	2	27	13.5	27	0
Radecic	1	26	26.0	26	0
Herrod	1	25	25.0	25	0
Holloway	1	4	4.0	4	0
Taylor	0	-2	—	-2	0
Colts	15	202	13.5	37	0
Opponents	16	184	11.5	58	1

Punting

	No.	Yds.	Avg.	In 20	LG
Stark	82	3492	42.6	14	65
Colts	82	3492	42.6	14	65
Opponents	59	2444	41.4	16	63

Punt Returns

	No.	FC	Yds.	Avg.	LG	TD
Verdin	25	10	165	6.6	22	0
Grant	2	2	6	3.0	6	0
Prior	0	2	0	—	0	0
Colts	27	14	171	6.3	22	0
Opponents	47	14	516	11.0	59t	1

Kickoff Returns

	No.	Yds.	Avg.	LG	TD
Martin, N.E.-Ind.	20	483	24.2	38	0
Martin, Ind.	12	305	25.4	38	0
Verdin	36	689	19.1	88t	1
Grant	3	20	6.7	10	0
McCloughan	2	35	17.5	19	0
McDonald	1	3	3.0	3	0
Mrosko	1	9	9.0	9	0
Colts	55	1061	19.3	88t	1
Opponents	33	573	17.4	50	0

Sacks

	No.
Bickett	5.0
Hand	5.0
Thompson	5.0
Clancy	2.5
Herrod	2.5
Goode	2.0
Siragusa	2.0
Ball	1.0
Banks	1.0
Baylor	1.0
Curry	1.0
Holloway	1.0
Colts	29.0
Opponents	57.0

1992 Draft Choices

Round	Name	Pos.	College
1.	Steve Emtman	DT	Washington
	Quentin Coryatt	LB	Texas A&M
2.	Ashley Ambrose	DB	Mississippi Valley St.
4.	Rodney Culver	RB	Notre Dame
	Tony McCoy	DT	Florida
5.	Maury Toy	RB	UCLA
6.	Shoun Habersham	WR	Tenn.-Chattanooga
7.	Derek Steele	DE	Maryland
8.	Jason Belser	DB	Oklahoma
	Ronald Humphrey	RB	Mississippi Valley St.
9.	Eddie Miller	WR	South Carolina
10.	Steve Grant	LB	West Virginia
12.	Mike Brandon	DE	Florida

Indianapolis Colts 1992 Veteran Roster

No.	Name	Pos.	Ht.	Wt.	Birth-date	NFL Exp.	College	Hometown	How Acq.	'91 Games/ Starts
90	Agee, Mel	DE	6-5	290	11/22/68	2	Illinois	Chicago, Ill.	D6-'91	16/2
31	Ball, Michael	CB-S	6-0	220	8/5/64	5	Southern	New Orleans, La.	D4-'88	15/14
51	Banks, Chip	LB	6-4	254	9/18/59	10	Southern California	Augusta, Ga.	T(SD)-'89	11/9
36	†Baylor, John	CB-S	6-0	203	3/5/65	3	Southern Mississippi	Meridian, Miss.	D5-'88	16/3
20	Bentley, Albert	RB	5-11	217	8/15/60	7	Miami	Immokalee, Fla.	SD2-'84	1/0
4	Biasucci, Dean	K	6-0	190	7/25/62	8	Western Carolina	Niagara Falls, N.Y.	FA-'86	16/0
50	Bickett, Duane	LB	6-5	251	12/1/62	8	Southern California	Los Angeles, Calif.	D1-'85	16/16
80	Brooks, Bill	WR	6-0	189	4/6/64	7	Boston University	Milton, Mass.	D4-'86	16/16
71	Call, Kevin	T	6-7	308	11/13/61	9	Colorado State	Boulder, Colo.	D5b-'84	16/16
88	Cash, Kerry	TE	6-4	247	8/7/69	2	Texas	San Antonio, Tex.	D5-'91	4/2
76	Clancy, Sam	DE	6-7	290	5/29/58	9	Pittsburgh	Pittsburgh, Pa.	PB(Clev)-'89#	16/1
32	Clark, Ken	RB	5-9	204	6/11/66	3	Nebraska	Evergreen, Ala.	FA-'91	16/7
67	Conlin, Chris	G-T	6-4	287	6/7/65	3	Penn State	Philadelphia, Pa.	FA-'90	8/2
38	Daniel, Eugene	CB-S	5-11	188	5/4/61	9	Louisiana State	Baton Rouge, La.	D8-'84	16/16
95	Davis, Travis	NT	6-2	274	5/10/66	3	Michigan State	Warren, Ohio	PB(NO)-'91#	16/8
69	Dixon, Randy	G	6-3	302	3/12/65	6	Pittsburgh	Clewiston, Fla.	D4-'87	12/11
53	Donaldson, Ray	C	6-3	300	5/18/58	13	Georgia	Rome, Ga.	D2a-'80	3/3
64	Garalczyk, Mark	DE-DT	6-6	281	8/12/64	3	Western Michigan	Detroit, Mich.	FA-'91	0*
11	George, Jeff	QB	6-4	221	12/8/67	3	Illinois	Indianapolis, Ind.	D1-'90	16/16
37	Goode, Chris	CB-S	6-0	196	9/17/63	5	Alabama	Town Creek, Ala.	D10-'87	15/15
26	Grant, Alan	CB-S	5-10	187	10/1/66	3	Stanford	Pasadena, Calif.	D4c-'90	16/1
78	Hand, Jon	DE	6-7	301	11/13/63	7	Alabama	Sylacauga, Ala.	D1-'86	16/16
9	Herrmann, Mark	QB	6-4	220	1/8/59	11	Purdue	Carmel, Ind.	W(Rams)-'90	2/0
54	Herrod, Jeff	LB	6-0	246	7/29/66	5	Mississippi	Birmingham, Ala.	D9-'88	14/14
84	Hester, Jessie	WR	5-11	172	1/21/63	7	Florida State	Belle Glade, Fla.	FA-'90	16/16
25	Holloway, Cornell	CB-S	5-11	182	1/30/66	3	Pittsburgh	Alliance, Ohio	FA-'90	10/0
1	Huffman, Darvell	WR	5-8	158	5/5/67	2	Boston University	Boston, Mass.	FA-'91	3/0
23	Johnson, Anthony	RB	6-0	222	10/25/67	3	Notre Dame	Indianapolis, Ind.	D2-'90	9/6
85	Langhorne, Reggie	WR	6-2	205	4/7/63	8	Elizabeth City State	Carrollton, Va.	PB(Clev)-'92#	14/9*
44	Manoa, Tim	RB	6-1	245	9/4/64	5	Penn State	Pittsburgh, Pa.	FA-'91	9/5
86	†Martin, Sammy	WR	5-11	175	8/21/65	5	Louisiana State	New Orleans, La.	W(NE)-'91	8/0
63	Matich, Trevor	G-T	6-4	297	10/9/61	8	Brigham Young	Sacramento, Calif.	PB(NYJ)-'92#	15/0*
42	McCloughan, Dave	CB-S	6-1	180	11/20/66	2	Colorado	San Leandro, Calif.	D3-'91	15/0
96	†McDonald, Quintus	LB	6-3	263	12/14/66	4	Penn State	Rockingham, N.C.	D6-'89	16/9
73	Moss, Zefross	T	6-6	338	8/17/66	3	Alabama State	Tuscaloosa, Ala.	T(Dall)-'89	11/10
49	Mrosko, Bob	TE	6-5	260	11/13/65	4	Penn State	Cleveland, Ohio	FA-'91	11/4
75	Pankey, Irv	T	6-5	295	2/15/58	12	Penn State	Aberdeen, Pa.	T(Rams)-'91	3/3
39	Prior, Mike	S	6-0	210	11/14/63	7	Illinois State	Chicago Heights, Ill.	FA-'87	9/7
97	Radecic, Scott	LB	6-3	236	6/14/62	9	Penn State	Pittsburgh, Pa.	W(Buff)-'90	14/9
74	Schultz, William	T	6-5	293	5/1/67	3	Southern California	Granada Hills, Calif.	D4b-'90	10/9
65	Shoulders, Darin	T	6-3	288	5/23/68	2	Tulane	Jackson, Miss.	FA-'91	1/0
98	Siragusa, Tony	NT	6-3	291	5/14/67	3	Pittsburgh	Kenilworth, N.J.	FA-'90	13/6
66	Solt, Ron	G	6-3	280	5/19/62	8	Maryland	Wilkes-Barre, Pa.	PB(Phil)-'92#	15/15*
3	Stark, Rohn	P	6-3	203	5/4/59	11	Florida State	Minneapolis, Minn.	D2b-'82	16/0
68	Tomberlin, Pat	T	6-2	330	1/29/66	2	Florida State	Jacksonville, Fla.	D4-'89	0*
10	†Trudeau, Jack	QB	6-3	219	9/9/62	7	Illinois	Livermore, Calif.	D2-'86	2/0
7	Tupa, Tom	QB	6-4	225	2/6/66	5	Ohio State	Brecksville, Ohio	PB(Phx)-'92#	11/11*
72	Vander Poel, Mark	T	6-7	303	3/5/68	2	Michigan State	Holland, Mich.	FA-'91	5/1
58	Vanderbeek, Matt	LB	6-3	258	8/16/67	3	Colorado	Upland, Calif.	D4-'91	10/1
83	Verdin, Clarence	WR	5-8	162	6/14/63	7	Southwestern Louisiana	New Orleans, La.	T(Wash)-'88	16/0
92	†Walker, Tony	LB	6-3	235	4/2/68	3	Southeastern Missouri	Birmingham, Ala.	D6-'90	16/0
93	Zander, Carl	LB	6-2	235	4/12/63	8	Tennessee	Mendham, N.J.	PB(Cin)-'92#	14/14*

* Garalczyk and Tomberlin missed '91 season due to injury; Langhorne played 14 games with Cleveland in '91; Matich played 15 games with N.Y. Jets; Solt played 15 games with Philadelphia; Tupa played 11 games with Phoenix; Zander played 14 games with Cincinnati.

† Option playout; subject to developments.

Traded—RB Eric Dickerson to L.A. Raiders.

Retired—Donnell Thompson, 11-year defensive end, 14 games in '91.

Plan B unconditional free agent.

Players lost through Plan B (9): G Brian Baldinger (Buff; 16 games in '91), TE Pat Beach (NYJ; 12), G Brian Blados (Sea; 7), QB Rusty Hilger (Sea; 1), LB Matt Jaworski (Pitt; 8), LB Brian Jones (Mia; 11), RB Bruce Perkins (Clev; 14), CB-S Keith Taylor (NO; 10).

Also played with Colts in '91—C Mark Cannon (4 games), TE James Coley (7), DE Shane Curry (9), LB Cedric Figaro (1), LB Frank Giannetti (3), RB Brian Lattimore (3), T Jack Linn (1), T William (Bubba) Paris (13), C Pat Snyder (1), WR Reggie Thornton (5).

COACHING STAFF

Head Coach, Ted Marchibroda

Pro Career: Marchibroda, the third-winningest head coach in Colts history, returned to the organization on January 28, 1992. He originally joined the Colts as head coach on February 15, 1975, and served through the 1979 season. His tenure produced a 41-36 record and three consecutive AFC Eastern Division titles (1975, 10-4; 1976, 11-3; and 1977, 10-4). Marchibroda took a Colts' team that was 2-12 in 1974 and engineered the greatest one-season turnaround in NFL history, producing a 10-4 record in 1975, the first time in league history a club moved from last to first. His three divisional championships represent the most titles won by a Colts head coach. Prior to returning to the Colts, Marchibroda served five years as an assistant with the Buffalo Bills, the last three as offensive coordinator. Marchibroda began his career as backfield coach with the Washington Redskins in 1961. He joined George Allen's staff with the Los Angeles Rams in 1965. He moved with Allen to the Redskins in 1971, where he served as offensive coordinator through the 1974 season. After his stint with the Colts, Marchibroda served as quarterback coach with Chicago in 1981, then moved on to Detroit as offensive coordinator from 1982-83. He served that same role in Philadelphia from 1984-85 before joining Buffalo in 1987. Marchibroda was the first draft pick of the Pittsburgh Steelers in 1953 and played one year before serving in the Army. He returned to Pittsburgh for the 1955-56 seasons. His top season was 1956, completing 124 of 275 passes for 1,585 yards and 12 touchdowns. Marchibroda's playing career ended with the Chicago Cardinals in 1957. Career record 41-36.

Background: Quarterback at St. Bonaventure 1950-51 and University of Detroit 1952. Led nation in total offense at Detroit. He was a football, basketball (where he was all-state), and baseball player at Franklin (Pa.) High School.

Personal: Born March 15, 1931, Franklin, Pa. Ted and his wife, Ann, reside in Indianapolis. They have two daughters, Jodi and Lonni, and two sons, Ted Jr. and Robert.

Assistant Coaches

Ron Blackledge, offensive assistant; born April 15, 1938, Canton, Ohio, lives in Indianapolis. Tight end-defensive end Bowling Green 1957-59. No pro playing experience. College coach: Ashland 1968-69, Cincinnati 1970-72, Kentucky 1973-75, Princeton 1976, Kent State 1977-81 (head coach 1979-81). Pro coach: Pittsburgh Steelers 1982-91, joined Colts in 1992.

George Catavolos, secondary; born May 8, 1945, Chicago, Ill., lives in Indianapolis. Defensive back Purdue 1964-66. No pro playing experience. College coach: Purdue 1967-68, 1971-76, Middle Tennessee State 1969, Louisville 1970, Kentucky 1977-81, Tennessee 1982-83. Pro coach: Joined Colts in 1984.

Alex Gibbs, offensive line; born February 11, 1941, Morganton, N.C., lives in Indianapolis. Running back-defensive back Davidson College 1959-63. No pro playing experience. College coach: Duke 1969-70, Kentucky 1971-72, West Virginia 1973-74, Ohio State 1975-78, Auburn 1979-81, Georgia 1982-83. Pro coach: Denver Broncos 1984-87, Los Angeles Raiders 1988-89, San Diego Chargers 1990-91, joined Colts in 1992.

Gene Huey, running backs; born July 20, 1947, Uniontown, Pa., lives in Indianapolis. Defensive back-wide receiver Wyoming 1966-69. No pro playing experience. College coach: Wyoming 1970-74, New Mexico 1975-77, Nebraska 1977-87, Ohio State 1988-91. Pro coach: Joined Colts in 1992.

Indianapolis Colts 1992 First-Year Roster

Name	Pos.	Ht.	Wt.	Birth-date	College	Hometown	How Acq.
Ambrose, Ashley	CB-S	5-10	177	9/17/70	Mississippi Valley St.	New Orleans, La.	D2
Arbuckle, Charles (1)	TE	6-3	240	9/13/68	UCLA	Beaumont, Tex.	FA
Belser, Jason	CB-S	5-9	187	4/28/70	Oklahoma	Kansas City, Mo.	D8a
Brandon, Michael	DE	6-4	290	6/30/68	Florida	Berry, Fla.	D12
Britton, Eddie (1)	WR	5-10	160	12/1/68	Central State, Ohio	Chicago, Ill.	FA
Coryatt, Quentin	LB	6-3	237	8/1/70	Texas A&M	St. Croix, Virgin Islands	D1b
Culver, Rodney	RB	5-9	221	12/23/69	Notre Dame	Detroit, Mich.	D4a
Emtman, Steve	DT	6-4	290	4/16/70	Washington	Spokane, Wash.	D1a
Grant, Stephen	LB	6-0	227	12/23/69	West Virginia	Miami, Fla.	D10
Habersham, Shoun	WR	5-10	180	12/12/68	Tenn.-Chattanooga	Brooklyn, N.Y.	D6
Heldt, Michael (1)	C	6-2	285	1/2/70	Notre Dame	Cedar Rapids, Iowa	FA
Humphrey, Ronald	RB	5-10	201	3/3/69	Mississippi Valley St.	Marland, Tex.	D8b
Luedeke, Rob (1)	C	6-5	271	9/26/67	Penn State	Bridgewater, N.J.	FA
McCoy, Anthony	NT	6-0	279	6/10/69	Florida	Orlando, Fla.	D4b
Miller, Eddie	WR	6-0	181	6/20/69	South Carolina	Tumison, Ga.	D9
Steele, Derek	DE	6-3	265	12/27/68	Maryland	Newport News, Va.	D7
Thorson, Chad (1)	LB	6-2	240	7/6/67	Wheaton College	Columbus, Ohio	FA
Toner, Ed (1)	RB	6-0	240	3/22/68	Boston College	Lynn, Mass.	FA
Toy, Maury	RB	6-0	231	1/27/69	UCLA	Chicago, Ill.	D5
Tucker, Mark (1)	G-T	6-2	279	4/29/68	Southern California	Spokane, Wash.	FA

The term NFL Rookie is defined as a player who is in his first season of professional football and has not been on the roster of another professional football team for any regular-season or postseason games. A Rookie is designated by an "R" on NFL rosters. Players who have been active in another professional football league or players who have NFL experience, including either preseason training camp or being on an active roster for fewer than three regular-season or postseason games, are termed NFL First-Year Players. An NFL First-Year Player is designated by a "1" on NFL rosters. Thereafter, a player on an NFL active roster for at least three regular-season or postseason games is credited with an additional year of NFL playing experience.

NOTES

_____

_____

_____

_____

_____

_____

_____

_____

_____

_____

_____

_____

Nick Nicolau, offensive coordinator; born May 5, 1933, New York, N.Y., lives in Indianapolis. Running back Southern Connecticut 1957-59. No pro playing experience. College coach: Southern Connecticut 1960, Springfield 1961, Bridgeport 1962-69 (head coach 1965-69), Massachusetts 1970, Connecticut 1971-72, Kentucky 1973-75, Kent State 1976. Pro coach: Hamilton Tiger-Cats (CFL) 1977, Montreal Alouettes (CFL) 1978-79, New Orleans Saints 1980, Denver Broncos 1981-87, Los Angeles Raiders 1988, Buffalo Bills 1989-91, joined Colts in 1992.

Dwain Painter, receivers; born February 13, 1942, Monroeville, Pa., lives in Indianapolis. Quarterback-defensive back Rutgers 1961-64. No pro playing experience. College coach: San Jose State 1971-72, College of San Mateo 1973, Brigham Young 1974-75, UCLA 1976-78, Northern Arizona 1979-81 (head coach), Georgia Tech 1982-85, Texas 1986, Illinois 1987. Pro coach: Pittsburgh Steelers 1988-91, joined Colts in 1992.

Francis Peay, defensive line; born May 23, 1944, Pittsburgh, Pa., lives in Indianapolis. Tackle Missouri 1963-66. Pro tackle New York Giants 1966-67, Green Bay Packers 1968-72, Kansas City Chiefs 1973-74. College coach: Notre Dame 1976-77, California 1978-79, Northwestern 1980-81, 1986-91 (head coach). Pro coach: Joined Colts in 1992.

Jay Robertson, defensive assistant; born February 20, 1940, Chicago, Ill., lives in Indianapolis. Center Northwestern 1959-62. No pro playing experience. College coach: Northwestern 1967-75, Northern Illinois 1976-79, Wisconsin 1980-81, Notre Dame 1982-83, Army 1988-91. Pro coach: Joined Colts in 1992.

Brad Seely, special teams-tight ends; born September 6, 1956, Vinton, Iowa, lives in Indianapolis. Tackle-guard South Dakota State 1974-77. No pro playing experience. College coach: Colorado State 1980, Southern Methodist 1981, North Carolina State 1982, Pacific 1983, Oklahoma State 1984-88. Pro coach: Joined Colts in 1989.

Rick Venturi, defensive coordinator-linebackers; born February 23, 1946, Taylorville, Ill., lives in Indianapolis. Quarterback-defensive back Northwestern 1965-67. No pro playing experience. College coach: Northwestern 1968-72, 1978-80 (head coach), Purdue 1973-76, Illinois 1977. Pro coach: Hamilton Tiger-Cats (CFL) 1981, joined Colts in 1982 (head coach for 11 games in 1991).

Tom Zupancic, strength and conditioning; born September 14, 1955, Indianapolis, lives in Indianapolis. Defensive tackle-offensive tackle Indiana Central 1975-78. No pro playing experience. Pro coach: Joined Colts in 1984.

Chiefs Coaching History

Dallas Texans 1960-62
(240-228-12)

1960-74	Hank Stram	129-79-10
1975-77	Paul Wiggin*	11-24-0
1977	Tom Bettis	1-6-0
1978-82	Marv Levy	31-42-0
1983-86	John Mackovic	30-35-0
1987-88	Frank Gansz	8-22-1
1989-91	Marty Schottenheimer	30-20-1

*Released after seven games in 1977

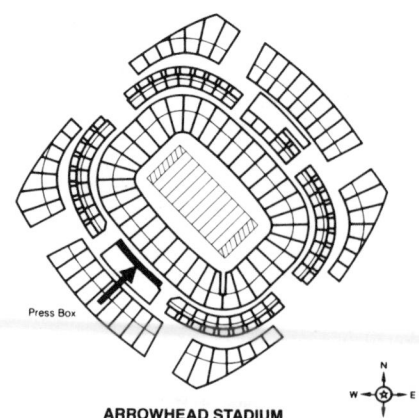

ARROWHEAD STADIUM

American Football Conference
Western Division

Team Colors: Red, Gold, and White

One Arrowhead Drive
Kansas City, Missouri 64129
Telephone: (816) 924-9300

Club Officials

Founder: Lamar Hunt
Chairman of the Board: Jack Steadman
President/General Manager and Chief Operating
    Officer: Carl Peterson
Executive Vice President: Tim Connolly
Assistant General Manager: Dennis Thum
Secretary: Jim Seigfreid
Director of Finance/Treasurer: Dale Young
Director of Public Relations: Bob Moore
Director of Operations: Jeff Klein
Director of Marketing & Sales: Dennis Watley
Director of Development: Ken Blume
Player Personnel Director: Whitey Dovell
Player Personnel Consultant: Lynn Stiles
Assistant Director of Public Relations:
    Jim Carr
Director of Promotions: Phil Thomas
Community Relations Manager: Brenda Boatright
Ticket Manager: Phil Youtsey
Equipment Manager: Mike Davidson
Assistant Equipment Manager: Allen Wright
Trainer: Dave Kendall
Assistant Trainer: Bud Epps
Video Coordinator: Mike Dennis
Assistant Video Coordinator: Mike Kirk

Stadium: Arrowhead Stadium • **Capacity:** 78,067
    One Arrowhead Drive
    Kansas City, Missouri 64129

Playing Surface: AstroTurf-8

Training Camp: University of
    Wisconsin-River Falls
    River Falls, Wisconsin 54022

1992 Schedule

Preseason

Aug. 8	at Green Bay	7:00
Aug. 15	at Minnesota	7:30
Aug. 24	**Buffalo**	7:00
Aug. 28	**Indianapolis**	7:00

Regular Season

Sept. 6	at San Diego	1:00
Sept. 13	**Seattle**	12:00
Sept. 20	at Houston	12:00
Sept. 28	**L.A. Raiders** (Monday)	8:00
Oct. 4	at Denver	2:00
Oct. 11	**Philadelphia**	12:00
Oct. 18	at Dallas	12:00
Oct. 25	**Pittsburgh**	6:30
Nov. 1	**Open Date**	
Nov. 8	**San Diego**	3:00
Nov. 15	**Washington**	12:00
Nov. 22	at Seattle	5:00
Nov. 29	at New York Jets	1:00
Dec. 6	at Los Angeles Raiders	1:00
Dec. 13	**New England**	12:00
Dec. 19	at N.Y. Giants (Saturday)	12:30
Dec. 27	**Denver**	12:00

Record Holders

Individual Records—Career

Category	Name	Performance
Rushing (Yds.)	Ed Podolak, 1969-1977	4,451
Passing (Yds.)	Len Dawson, 1962-1975	28,507
Passing (TDs)	Len Dawson, 1962-1975	237
Receiving (No.)	Henry Marshall, 1976-1987	416
Receiving (Yds.)	Otis Taylor, 1965-1975	7,306
Interceptions	Emmitt Thomas, 1966-1978	58
Punting (Avg.)	Jerrel Wilson, 1963-1977	43.5
Punt Return (Avg.)	J.T. Smith, 1979-1984	10.6
Kickoff Return (Avg.)	Noland Smith, 1967-69	26.8
Field Goals	Nick Lowery, 1980-1991	284
Touchdowns (Tot.)	Otis Taylor, 1965-1975	60
Points	Nick Lowery, 1980-1991	1,255

Individual Records—Single Season

Category	Name	Performance
Rushing (Yds.)	Christian Okoye, 1989	1,480
Passing (Yds.)	Bill Kenney, 1983	4,348
Passing (TDs)	Len Dawson, 1964	30
Receiving (No.)	Carlos Carson, 1983	80
Receiving (Yds.)	Carlos Carson, 1983	1,351
Interceptions	Emmitt Thomas, 1974	12
Punting (Avg.)	Jerrel Wilson, 1965	46.0
Punt Return (Avg.)	Abner Haynes, 1960	15.4
Kickoff Return (Avg.)	Dave Grayson, 1962	29.7
Field Goals	Nick Lowery, 1990	34
Touchdowns (Tot.)	Abner Haynes, 1962	19
Points	Nick Lowery, 1990	139

Individual Records—Single Game

Category	Name	Performance
Rushing (Yds.)	Barry Word, 10-14-90	200
Passing (Yds.)	Len Dawson, 11-1-64	435
Passing (TDs)	Len Dawson, 11-1-64	6
Receiving (No.)	Ed Podolak, 10-7-73	12
Receiving (Yds.)	Stephone Paige, 12-22-85	309
Interceptions	Bobby Ply, 12-16-62	*4
	Bobby Hunt, 12-4-64	*4
	Deron Cherry, 9-29-85	*4
Field Goals	Many times	5
	Last time by Nick Lowery, 12-29-90	
Touchdowns (Tot.)	Abner Haynes, 11-26-61	5
Points	Abner Haynes, 11-26-61	30

*NFL Record

1991 Team Record
Preseason (2-2)

Date	Result		Opponents
8/3	L	14-24	Dallas
8/10	W	19-10	vs. N.Y. Jets at St. Louis
8/17	W	38-14	Detroit
8/23	L	7-20	at Tampa Bay

Regular Season (10-6)

Date	Result		Opponents	Att.
9/1	W	14- 3	Atlanta	74,246
9/8	L	10-17	New Orleans	74,816
9/16	L	7-17	at Houston	61,058
9/22	W	20-13	Seattle	71,789
9/29	W	14-13	at San Diego	44,907
10/7	W	33- 6	Buffalo	76,120
10/13	W	42- 7	Miami	76,021
10/20	L	16-19	at Denver	75,866
10/28	W	24-21	L.A. Raiders	77,111
11/10	W	27-20	at L.A. Rams	52,511
11/17	L	20-24	Denver	74,661
11/24	L	15-20	at Cleveland	63,991
12/1	W	19- 6	at Seattle	57,248
12/8	W	20-17	San Diego (OT)	73,330
12/14	L	14-28	at San Francisco	62,672
12/22	W	27-21	at L.A. Raiders	65,144

(OT) Overtime

Postseason (1-1)

Date	Result		Opponent	Att.
12/28	W	10- 6	L.A. Raiders	77,130
1/5	L	14-37	at Buffalo	79,731

Score by Periods

Chiefs	44	91	79	105	3	—	322
Opponents	58	85	50	59	0	—	252

Attendance
Home 598,094   Away 483,397   Total 1,081,491
Single-game home record, 82,094 (11-5-72)
Single-season home record, 598,094 (1991)

1991 Team Statistics

	Chiefs	Opp.
Total First Downs	322	275
Rushing	127	88
Passing	172	168
Penalty	23	19
Third Down: Made/Att.	92/205	76/191
Third Down: Pct.	44.9	39.8
Fourth Down: Made/Att.	12/20	11/18
Fourth Down: Pct.	60.0	61.1
Total Net Yards	5321	4998
Avg. Per Game	332.6	312.4
Total Plays	1021	927
Avg. Per Play	5.2	5.4
Net Yards Rushing	2217	1770
Avg. Per Game	138.6	110.6
Total Rushes	521	417
Net Yards Passing	3104	3228
Avg. Per Game	194.0	201.8
Sacked/Yards Lost	21/177	39/304
Gross Yards	3281	3532
Att./Completions	479/284	471/279
Completion Pct.	59.3	59.2
Had Intercepted	14	15
Punts/Avg.	57/40.4	60/42.5
Net Punting Avg.	35.0	36.5
Penalties/Yards Lost	94/724	110/827
Fumbles/Ball Lost	22/8	27/18
Touchdowns	35	27
Rushing	14	8
Passing	19	17
Returns	2	2
Avg. Time of Possession	31:16	28:44

1991 Individual Statistics

Scoring

	TD R	TD P	TD Rt	PAT	FG	Saf	TP
Lowery	0	0	0	35/35	25/30	0	110
Okoye	9	0	0	0/0	0/0	0	54
Barnett	0	5	0	0/0	0/0	0	30
Word	4	0	0	0/0	0/0	0	24
Harry	0	3	0	0/0	0/0	0	18
Williams	1	2	0	0/0	0/0	0	18
Birden	0	2	0	0/0	0/0	0	12
Hayes	0	2	0	0/0	0/0	0	12
Holohan	0	2	0	0/0	0/0	0	12
B. Jones	0	1	0	0/0	0/0	0	6
Martin	0	0	1	0/0	0/0	0	6
McNair	0	1	0	0/0	0/0	0	6
D. Thomas	0	0	1	0/0	0/0	0	6
R. Thomas	0	1	0	0/0	0/0	0	6
Saleaumua	0	0	0	0/0	0/0	1	2
Chiefs	14	19	2	35/35	25/30	1	322
Opponents	8	17	2	25/27	21/28	1	252

Passing

	Att.	Comp.	Yds.	Pct.	TD	Int.	Tkld.	Rate
DeBerg	434	256	2965	59.0	17	14	19/161	79.3
Vlasic	44	28	316	63.6	2	0	2/16	100.2
Williams	1	0	0	0.0	0	0	0/0	39.6
Chiefs	479	284	3281	59.3	19	14	21/177	81.1
Opponents	471	279	3532	59.2	17	15	39/304	81.5

Rushing

	Att.	Yds.	Avg.	LG	TD
Okoye	225	1031	4.6	48	9
Word	160	684	4.3	37	4
Williams	97	447	4.6	21	1
McNair	10	51	5.1	11	0
Saxon	6	13	2.2	8	0
Stradford	1	7	7.0	7	0
Vlasic	1	−1	−1.0	−1	0
DeBerg	21	−15	−0.7	0	0
Chiefs	521	2217	4.3	48	14
Opponents	417	1770	4.2	60t	8

Receiving

	No.	Yds.	Avg.	LG	TD
R. Thomas	43	495	11.5	39	1
Barnett	41	564	13.8	63	5
McNair	37	342	9.2	36	1
Harry	35	431	12.3	36	3
Birden	27	465	17.2	57t	2
Hayes	19	208	10.9	23	2
Williams	16	147	9.2	17	2
B. Jones	14	97	6.9	14	1
Holohan	13	113	8.7	26	2
Paige	9	111	12.3	26	0
Stradford	9	91	10.1	17	0
F. Jones	8	85	10.6	23	0
Saxon	6	55	9.2	22	0
Okoye	3	34	11.3	13	0
Anders	2	30	15.0	23	0
Word	2	13	6.5	8	0
Chiefs	284	3281	11.6	63	19
Opponents	279	3532	12.7	71t	17

Interceptions

	No.	Yds.	Avg.	LG	TD
Cherry	4	31	7.8	16	0
Pearson	3	43	14.3	43	0
Lewis	3	21	7.0	21	0
Burruss	1	83	83.0	83	0
Washington	1	34	34.0	34	0
B. Bell	1	4	4.0	4	0
Martin	1	0	0.0	0	0
Ross	1	0	0.0	0	0
Chiefs	15	216	14.4	83	0
Opponents	14	251	17.9	71t	2

Punting

	No.	Yds.	Avg.	In 20	LG
Barker	57	2303	40.4	11	57
Chiefs	57	2303	40.4	11	57
Opponents	60	2549	42.5	18	62

Punt Returns

	No.	FC	Yds.	Avg.	LG	TD
Stradford	22	4	150	6.8	18	0
F. Jones	12	2	108	9.0	25	0
Chiefs	34	6	258	7.6	25	0
Opponents	27	16	190	7.0	19	0

Kickoff Returns

	No.	Yds.	Avg.	LG	TD
Williams	24	524	21.8	76	0
Stradford	14	292	20.9	38	0
McNair	4	66	16.5	18	0
Saxon	4	56	14.0	23	0
F. Jones	2	40	20.0	26	0
Chiefs	48	978	20.4	76	0
Opponents	57	1171	20.5	55	0

Sacks

	No.
D. Thomas	13.5
Smith	8.0
Martin	5.0
Maas	4.0
Simien	2.0
Saleaumua	1.5
Everett	1.0
Hackett	1.0
Marts	1.0
Pearson	1.0
Porter	1.0
Chiefs	39.0
Opponents	21.0

1992 Draft Choices

Round	Name	Pos.	College
1.	Dale Carter	DB	Tennessee
2.	Matt Blundin	QB	Virginia
4.	Mike Evans	DE	Michigan
6.	Tony Smith	WR	Notre Dame
7.	Erick Anderson	LB	Michigan
8.	Jim Jennings	G	San Diego State
9.	Jay Leeuwenburg	C	Colorado
10.	Jerry Ostroski	G	Tulsa
11.	Doug Rigby	DE	Wyoming
12.	Corey Williams	DB	Oklahoma State

Kansas City Chiefs 1992 Veteran Roster

No.	Name	Pos.	Ht.	Wt.	Birth-date	NFL Exp.	College	Hometown	How Acq.	'91 Games/ Starts
68	Allen, Kevin	T	6-5	310	6/21/63	2	Indiana	Cincinnati, Ohio	FA-'92	0*
76	Alt, John	T	6-8	296	5/30/62	9	Iowa	Columbia Heights, Minn.	D1b-'84	16/16
77	Baldinger, Rich	T	6-4	293	12/31/59	11	Wake Forest	Long Island, N.Y.	FA-'83	16/15
4	Barker, Bryan	P	6-1	187	6/28/64	3	Santa Clara	Kirkland, Wash.	FA-'90	16/0
82	Barnett, Tim	WR	6-1	209	4/19/68	2	Jackson State	Rosedale, Miss.	D3-'91	16/8
60	Beavers, Scott	G	6-4	277	2/17/67	2	Georgia Tech	Fairburn, Ga.	FA-'92	0*
88	Birden, J.J.	WR	5-9	170	6/16/65	3	Oregon	Portland, Ore.	FA-'90	15/0
89	Cash, Keith	TE	6-4	235	8/7/69	2	Texas	San Antonio, Tex.	PB(Pitt)-'92#	5/0*
20	Cherry, Deron	S	5-11	203	9/12/59	12	Rutgers	Palmyra, N.J.	FA-'81	16/5
49	Coleman, Eric	CB	6-0	190	12/27/66	3	Wyoming	Denver, Colo.	FA-'92	0*
39	Everett, Eric	CB	5-10	170	7/13/66	5	Texas Tech	Daingerfield, Tex.	FA-'91	11/0
74	Graham, Derrick	T	6-4	306	3/18/67	3	Appalachian State	Groveland, Fla.	D5a-'90	16/1
67	Grant, Darryl	DT	6-1	275	11/22/59	11	Rice	San Antonio, Tex.	FA-'92	2/0*
98	Griffin, Leonard	DE	6-4	278	9/22/62	7	Grambling	Lake Providence, La.	D3-'86	16/2
61	Grunhard, Tim	C	6-2	299	5/17/68	3	Notre Dame	Chicago, Ill.	D2-'90	16/16
56	Hackett, Dino	LB	6-3	230	6/28/64	7	Appalachian State	Greensboro, N.C.	D2-'86	16/14
22	Hagy, John	S	6-0	190	12/9/65	4	Texas	San Antonio, Tex.	FA-'92	0*
86	Harry, Emile	WR	5-11	186	4/5/63	6	Stanford	Los Angeles, Calif.	FA-'86	12/8
85	†Hayes, Jonathan	TE	6-5	248	8/11/62	8	Iowa	Pittsburgh, Pa.	D2-'85	16/16
43	Jones, Bill	RB	5-11	227	9/10/66	3	Southwest Texas State	Corsicana, Tex.	D12-'89	15/14
80	Jones, Fred	WR	5-9	182	3/6/67	3	Grambling	Decatur, Ga.	D4-'90	11/0
12	Krieg, Dave	QB	6-1	192	10/20/58	13	Milton	Schofield, Wis.	PB(Sea)-'92#	10/9*
1	Lansford, Mike	K	6-0	190	7/20/58	10	Washington	Arcadia, Calif.	FA-'92	0*
29	Lewis, Albert	CB	6-2	195	10/6/60	10	Grambling	Mansfield, La.	D3-'83	8/6
8	†Lowery, Nick	K	6-4	205	5/27/56	13	Dartmouth	Washington, D.C.	FA-'80	16/0
72	Lutz, David	G	6-6	305	12/30/59	10	Georgia Tech	Peachland, N.C.	D2-'83	16/16
63	Maas, Bill	DE	6-5	275	12/19/62	9	Pittsburgh	Newtown Square, Pa.	D1a-'84	16/16
57	Martin, Chris	LB	6-2	241	12/19/60	10	Auburn	Huntsville, Ala.	FA-'88	16/15
51	Marts, Lonnie	LB	6-1	243	11/10/68	2	Tulane	New Orleans, La.	FA-'90	16/2
48	McNair, Todd	RB	6-1	191	10/7/65	4	Temple	Pennsauken, N.J.	D8b-'89	14/0
35	†Okoye, Christian	RB	6-1	260	8/16/61	6	Azusa Pacific	Enugu, Nigeria	D2-'87	14/12
83	†Paige, Stephone	WR	6-2	188	10/15/61	10	Fresno State	Long Beach, Calif.	FA-'83	3/2
24	Pearson, Jayice	CB	5-11	186	8/17/63	7	Washington	Oceanside, Calif.	FA-'86	14/12
27	Porter, Kevin	S	5-10	214	4/11/66	5	Auburn	Warner Robins, Ga.	D3-'88	16/15
55	†Randle, Ervin	LB	6-1	250	10/12/62	8	Baylor	Hearne, Tex.	T(TB)-'91	12/1
52	Rogers, Tracy	LB	6-2	241	8/13/67	3	Fresno State	Taft, Calif.	FA-'90	10/1
31	Ross, Kevin	CB	5-9	182	1/16/62	9	Temple	Paulsboro, N.J.	D7-'84	14/13
97	Saleaumua, Dan	NT	6-0	295	11/25/64	6	Arizona State	San Diego, Calif.	PB(Det)-'89#	16/16
54	Simien, Tracy	LB	6-1	245	5/21/67	2	Texas Christian	Bay City, Tex.	FA-'91	15/12
95	†Sims, Tom	NT	6-2	285	4/18/67	2	Pittsburgh	Detroit, Mich.	D6-'90	14/0
90	Smith, Neil	DE	6-4	275	4/10/66	5	Nebraska	New Orleans, La.	D1-'88	16/16
59	Snow, Percy	LB	6-2	250	11/5/67	2	Michigan State	Canton, Ohio	D1-'90	15/9
25	Stradford, Troy	RB-WR	5-9	194	9/11/64	6	Boston College	Linden, N.J.	PB(Mia)-'91#	10/0
79	Szott, David	G	6-4	275	12/12/67	3	Penn State	Clifton, N.J.	D7-'90	1/0
94	Szymanski, Jim	DE	6-5	262	9/7/67	2	Michigan State	Sterling Heights, Mich.	FA-'92	1/0*
19	Taylor, Gene	WR	6-2	182	11/12/62	3	Fresno State	Berkeley, Calif.	FA-'92	1/0*
58	Thomas, Derrick	LB	6-3	236	1/1/67	4	Alabama	Miami, Fla.	D1-'89	16/15
81	†Thomas, Robb	WR	5-11	175	3/29/66	4	Oregon State	Corvallis, Ore.	D6-'89	15/12
46	Thompson, Bennie	S	6-0	200	2/10/63	3	Grambling	New Orleans, La.	PB(NO)-'92#	16/0*
73	Valerio, Joe	T	6-5	293	2/11/69	2	Pennsylvania	Ridley, Pa.	D2-'91	6/0
13	Vlasic, Mark	QB	6-3	205	10/25/63	5	Iowa	Monaca, Pa.	PB(SD)-'91#	6/0*
44	Williams, Harvey	RB	6-2	222	4/22/67	2	Louisiana State	Hempstead, Tex.	D1-'91	14/1
23	Word, Barry	RB	6-2	242	7/17/64	4	Virginia	Long Island, Va.	FA-'90	16/3

* Allen last active with Philadelphia in '85; Beavers last active with Denver in '90; Cash played 5 games with Pittsburgh in '91; Coleman last active with New England in '90; Grant played 2 games with Tampa Bay; Hagy last active with Buffalo in '90; Krieg played 10 games with Seattle; Lansford last active with L.A. Rams in '90; Szymanski played 1 game with Denver; Taylor played 1 game with New England; Thompson played 16 games with New Orleans; Vlasic played 6 games with Kansas City.

† Option playout; subject to developments.

Retired—Lloyd Burruss, 11-year safety, 16 games in '91.

Plan B unconditional free agent.

Players lost through Plan B (7): QB Steve DeBerg (TB; 16 games in '91), CB-S Bernard Ellison (Raid; did not play in '91), TE Pete Holohan (Clev; 16), CB-S Anthony Parker (Minn; 2), QB Steve Pelluer (Den; active for 1 game but did not play); RB James Saxon (Mia; 16), C Frank Winters (GB; 16).

Also played with Chiefs in '91—CB Billy Bell (8 games), CB Stan Petry (2), TE Troy Sadowski (14), DE Pat Swoopes (14), CB Charles Washington (16).

COACHING STAFF

Head Coach,
Marty Schottenheimer

Pro Career: In three seasons as head coach of the Kansas City Chiefs, Schottenheimer has established the highest winning percentage in franchise history (.615). Moreover, his .618 career winning percentage is fourth highest among active NFL coaches with at least 50 games coached. He has directed the Chiefs to three of their five winning seasons since 1974 and has taken Kansas City to the NFL playoffs two consecutive years, their first back-to-back playoff appearances since 1968-69. Schottenheimer has led his teams to the playoffs six of his seven full seasons as an NFL head coach and has coached six consecutive teams to winning records. As head coach of the Cleveland Browns from midseason in 1984 through 1988, he led the Browns to four playoff berths, three AFC Central Division titles, two AFC Championship Game appearances, and captured AFC coach of the year honors (1986). He first joined the Browns in 1980 as defensive coordinator after serving as linebackers coach of the Detroit Lions in 1978-79. His first NFL coaching job came with the New York Giants, where he was linebackers coach and offensive coordinator from 1975-77. He served as an assistant coach with the Portland Storm (WFL) in 1974. A seventh-round draft choice of the Buffalo Bills in 1965, he played linebacker with the Bills until 1968 and finished his pro playing career with the Boston Patriots in 1969-70. Career record: 76-51-1.

Background: Schottenheimer was an All-America linebacker at University of Pittsburgh 1962-64. Following his retirement from pro football, he worked as a real estate developer in both Miami and Denver from 1971-74.

Personal: Born September 23, 1943, Canonsburg, Pa. Marty and his wife, Patricia, live in Overland Park, Kan., and have one daughter, Kristen, and one son, Brian.

Assistant Coaches

Dave Adolph, defensive coordinator-linebackers; born June 6, 1937, Akron, Ohio, lives in Kansas City. Guard-linebacker Akron 1955-58. No pro playing experience. College coach: Akron 1963-64, Connecticut 1965-68, Kentucky 1969-72, Illinois 1973-76, Ohio State 1977-78. Pro coach: Cleveland Browns 1979-84, 1986-88, San Diego Chargers 1985, Los Angeles Raiders 1989-91, joined Chiefs in 1992.

Bruce Arians, running backs; born October 3, 1952, York, Pa., lives in Kansas City. Quarterback Virginia Tech 1971-74. No pro playing experience. College coach: Virginia Tech 1975-77, Mississippi State 1978-80, Alabama 1981-82, Temple 1983-88 (head coach). Pro coach: Joined Chiefs in 1989.

Russ Ball, assistant strength and conditioning; born August 28, 1959, Moberly, Mo., lives in Kansas City. Center Central Missouri State 1977-80. No pro playing experience. College coach: Missouri 1981-88. Pro coach: Joined Chiefs in 1989.

Herman Edwards, defensive backs; born April 27, 1954, Ft. Monmouth, N.J., lives in Blue Springs, Mo. Defensive back California 1972-75, San Diego State 1976-77. Pro cornerback Philadelphia Eagles 1977-86, Los Angeles Rams 1986, Atlanta Falcons 1986. Pro scout: Kansas City Chiefs 1989-91. Pro coach: Joined Chiefs in 1992.

Howard Mudd, offensive line; born February 10, 1942, Midland, Mich., lives in Kansas City. Guard Hillsdale 1961-63. Pro guard San Francisco 49ers 1964-69, Chicago Bears 1970-71. College coach: California 1972-73. Pro coach: San Diego Chargers 1974-76, San Francisco 49ers 1977, Seattle Seahawks 1978-82, Cleveland Browns 1983-88, joined Chiefs in 1989.

Joe Pendry, offensive coordinator-quarterbacks; born August 5, 1947, Matheny, W. Va., lives in Lakewood, Mo. Tight end West Virginia 1966-67. No pro playing experience. College coach: West Virginia 1967-74, 1976-77, Kansas State 1975, Pittsburgh 1978-79, Michigan State 1980-81. Pro coach: Philadelphia Stars (USFL) 1983, Pittsburgh Maulers (USFL) 1984 (head coach), Cleveland Browns 1985-88, joined Chiefs in 1989.

Tom Pratt, defensive line; born June 21, 1935, Edgerton, Wis., lives in Overland Park, Kan. Linebacker Miami 1953-56. No pro playing experience. College coach: Miami 1957-59, Southern Mississippi 1960-62. Pro coach: Kansas City Chiefs 1963-77, New Orleans Saints 1978-80, Cleveland Browns 1981-88, rejoined Chiefs in 1989.

Dave Redding, strength and conditioning; born June 14, 1952, North Platte, Neb., lives in Kansas City. Defensive end Nebraska 1972-75. No pro playing experience. College coach: Nebraska 1976, Washington State 1977, Missouri 1978-81. Pro coach: Cleveland Browns 1982-88, joined Chiefs in 1989.

Al Saunders, assistant head coach-receivers; born February 1, 1947, London, England, lives in Kansas City. Defensive back San Jose State 1966-68. No pro playing experience. College coach: Southern California 1970-71, Missouri 1972, Utah State 1973-75, California 1976-81, Tennessee 1982. Pro coach: San Diego Chargers 1983-88 (head coach 1986-88), joined Chiefs in 1989.

Kurt Schottenheimer, special teams; born October 1, 1949, McDonald, Pa., lives in Kansas City. Defensive back Miami 1969-70. No pro playing experience. College coach: William Patterson 1974, Michigan State 1978-82, Tulane 1983, Louisiana State 1984-85, Notre Dame 1986. Pro coach: Cleveland Browns 1987-88, joined Chiefs in 1989.

Darvin Wallis, special assistant-quality control; born February 14, 1949, Ft. Branch, Ind., lives in Overland Park, Kan. Defensive end Arizona 1970-71. No pro playing experience. College coach: Adams State 1976-77, Tulane 1978-79, Mississippi 1980-81. Pro coach: Cleveland Browns 1982-88, joined Chiefs in 1989.

Kansas City Chiefs 1992 First-Year Roster

Name	Pos.	Ht.	Wt.	Birth-date	College	Hometown	How Acq.
Anderson, Erick	LB	6-1	241	10/7/68	Michigan	Glenbrook, Ill.	D7
Blundin, Matt	QB	6-6	228	3/7/69	Virginia	Ridley, Pa.	D2
Bradley, James (1)	WR	6-0	196	11/24/68	Michigan State	Orrville, Ohio	FA
Brown, Dean (1)	G	6-3	311	9/7/68	Notre Dame	Canton, Ohio	FA
Bryant, Phil	RB	5-10	213	3/27/70	Virginia Tech	Landover, Md.	FA
Carter, Dale	CB-S-KR	6-1	181	11/28/69	Tennessee	Covington, Ga.	D1
Davis, Willie (1)	WR	6-0	170	10/10/67	Central Arkansas	Altheimer, Ark.	FA
DeArmus, Dan	P	5-10	199	10/26/69	Maryland	Miami, Fla.	FA
Dohring, Tom (1)	T	6-6	290	5/24/68	Michigan	Dearborn, Mich.	D8-'91
Evans, Mike	DT	6-3	269	6/2/67	Michigan	Roxbury, Mass.	D4
Grant, Marcus	WR	5-9	172	9/12/70	Houston	Dallas, Tex.	FA
Hargain, Tony (1)	WR	6-0	188	12/26/67	Oregon	North Highlands, Calif.	FA
Hemingway, George (1)	RB	6-0	236	5/3/68	Colorado	Colton, Calif.	FA
Hudson, Craig (1)	TE	6-3	245	5/7/67	Wisconsin	East Aurora, Ill.	FA
Jackson, Byron	WR	5-7	160	2/16/68	San Jose State	Landover, Md.	FA
Jennings, Jim	C-G	6-4	295	4/4/69	San Diego State	San Marcos, Calif.	D8
Leeuwenburg, Jay	C	6-2	267	6/18/69	Colorado	Kirkwood, Mo.	D9
Lewis, Tauhan (1)	CB	5-10	176	9/29/68	Nebraska	Colorado Springs, Colo.	FA
Malone, Darrell (1)	S	5-10	177	11/23/67	Jacksonville State	Jacksonville, Ala.	FA
Mincy, Charles (1)	S	5-11	187	12/16/69	Washington	Los Angeles, Calif.	D5-'91
Ostroski, Jerry	G	6-3	310	6/12/70	Tulsa	Pottstown, Pa.	D10
Pupunu, Alfred	TE	6-2	242	10/17/69	Weber State	Salt Lake City, Utah	FA
Rigby, Doug	DE	6-6	276	4/4/69	Wyoming	Crete, Neb.	D11
Shropshire, Ed	DE	6-4	276	12/30/68	Virginia State	Alexandria, Va.	FA
Smith, Michael	WR	5-8	160	11/21/70	Kansas State	New Orleans, La.	FA
Smith, Tony	WR	6-2	185	10/2/69	Notre Dame	Gary, Ind.	D6
Starcevich, Steve	K	6-4	225	10/21/66	Philadelphia Textile	Northville, Mich.	FA
Stephens, Santo	LB	6-4	232	6/16/69	Temple	Capital Heights, Md.	FA
Terry, Doug	CB-S	5-11	188	12/12/69	Kansas	Liberal, Kan.	FA
Thompson, Kevin (1)	S	5-10	190	4/17/66	Oklahoma	Houston, Tex.	FA
Weatherspoon, Stephon (1)	LB	6-2	245	6/15/66	Texas Tech	Lubbock, Tex.	FA
Williams, Corey	CB-S	6-2	190	4/24/70	Oklahoma State	Macon, Ga.	D12
Young, Todd (1)	TE	6-5	257	2/2/67	Penn State	Tempe, Ariz.	FA

The term NFL Rookie is defined as a player who is in his first season of professional football and has not been on the roster of another professional football team for any regular-season or postseason games. A Rookie is designated by an "R" on NFL rosters. Players who have been active in another professional football league or players who have NFL experience, including either preseason training camp or being on an active roster for fewer than three regular-season or postseason games, are termed NFL First-Year Players. An NFL First-Year Player is designated by a "1" on NFL rosters. Thereafter, a player on an NFL active roster for at least three regular-season or postseason games is credited with an additional year of NFL playing experience.

NOTES

American Football Conference
Western Division

Team Colors: Silver and Black

332 Center Street
El Segundo, California 90245
Telephone: (310) 322-3451

Club Officials

President of the Managing General Partner:
Al Davis
Executive Assistant: Al LoCasale
Pro Football Scout: George Karras
Finance: Gary Huff
Legal Affairs: Jeff Birren, Amy Trask
Senior Executive: John Herrera
Senior Administrator: Morris Bradshaw
Business Manager: John Novak
Publications: Mike Taylor
Administrative Assistant: John Walsh
Ticket Operations: Peter Eiges
Trainers: George Anderson, H. Rod Martin,
  Todd Sperber
Equipment Manager: Richard Romanski
Assistant Equipment Manager: Bob Romanski

Stadium: Los Angeles Memorial Coliseum •
  Capacity: 92,488
  3911 South Figueroa Street
  Los Angeles, California 90037

Playing Surface: Grass

Training Camp: Radisson Hotel
  Oxnard, California 93030

1992 Schedule

Preseason
Aug. 8	at San Francisco	5:00
Aug. 15	at Los Angeles Rams	7:00
Aug. 22	**Washington**	1:00
Aug. 29	Houston	1:00

Regular Season
Sept. 6	at Denver	6:00
Sept. 13	at Cincinnati	1:00
Sept. 20	**Cleveland**	1:00
Sept. 28	at Kansas City (Monday)	8:00
Oct. 4	**New York Giants**	1:00
Oct. 11	**Buffalo**	1:00
Oct. 18	at Seattle	1:00
Oct. 25	**Dallas**	1:00
Nov. 1	**Open Date**	
Nov. 8	at Philadelphia	1:00
Nov. 15	**Seattle**	1:00
Nov. 22	**Denver**	1:00
Nov. 29	at San Diego	5:00
Dec. 6	**Kansas City**	1:00
Dec. 14	at Miami (Monday)	9:00
Dec. 20	**San Diego**	1:00
Dec. 26	at Washington (Saturday)	4:00

Raiders Coaching History

Oakland 1960-1981
(307-184-11)

1960-61	Eddie Erdelatz*	6-10-0
1961-62	Marty Feldman**	2-15-0
1962	Red Conkright	1-8-0
1963-65	Al Davis	23-16-3
1966-68	John Rauch	35-10-1
1969-78	John Madden	112-39-7
1979-87	Tom Flores	91-56-0
1988-89	Mike Shanahan***	8-12-0
1989-91	Art Shell	29-18-0

*Released after two games in 1961
**Released after five games in 1962
***Released after four games in 1989

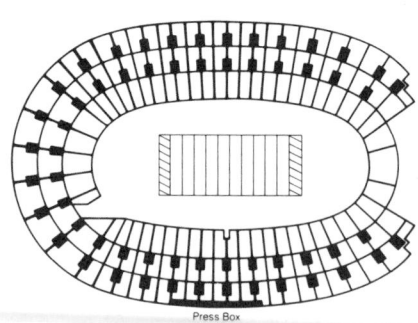

MEMORIAL COLISEUM

Record Holders
Individual Records—Career

Category	Name	Performance
Rushing (Yds.)	Marcus Allen, 1982-1991	8,244
Passing (Yds.)	Ken Stabler, 1970-79	19,078
Passing (TDs)	Ken Stabler, 1970-79	150
Receiving (No.)	Fred Biletnikoff, 1965-1978	589
Receiving (Yds.)	Fred Biletnikoff, 1965-1978	8,974
Interceptions	Willie Brown, 1967-1978	39
	Lester Hayes, 1977-1986	39
Punting (Avg.)	Ray Guy, 1973-1986	42.5
Punt Return (Avg.)	Claude Gibson, 1963-65	12.6
Kickoff Return (Avg.)	Jack Larscheid, 1960-61	28.4
Field Goals	George Blanda, 1967-1975	156
Touchdowns (Tot.)	Marcus Allen, 1982-1991	95
Points	George Blanda, 1967-1975	863

Individual Records—Single Season

Category	Name	Performance
Rushing (Yds.)	Marcus Allen, 1985	1,759
Passing (Yds.)	Ken Stabler, 1979	3,615
Passing (TDs)	Daryle Lamonica, 1969	34
Receiving (No.)	Todd Christensen, 1986	95
Receiving (Yds.)	Art Powell, 1964	1,361
Interceptions	Lester Hayes, 1980	13
Punting (Avg.)	Ray Guy, 1973	45.3
Punt Return (Avg.)	Claude Gibson, 1964	14.4
Kickoff Return (Avg.)	Harold Hart, 1975	30.5
Field Goals	Jeff Jaeger, 1991	29
Touchdowns (Tot.)	Marcus Allen, 1984	18
Points	George Blanda, 1968	117

Individual Records—Single Game

Category	Name	Performance
Rushing (Yds.)	Bo Jackson, 11-30-87	221
Passing (Yds.)	Cotton Davidson, 10-25-64	427
Passing (TDs)	Tom Flores, 12-22-63	6
	Daryle Lamonica, 10-19-69	6
Receiving (No.)	Dave Casper, 10-3-76	12
Receiving (Yds.)	Art Powell, 12-22-63	247
Interceptions	Many times	3
	Last time by Charles Phillips, 12-8-75	
Field Goals	Many times	4
	Last time by Jeff Jaeger, 9-29-91	
Touchdowns (Tot.)	Art Powell, 12-22-63	4
	Marcus Allen, 9-24-84	4
Points	Art Powell, 12-22-63	24
	Marcus Allen, 9-24-84	24

1991 Team Record

Preseason (3-2)

Date	Result		Opponents
7/27	L	17-24	San Francisco
8/3	L	17-19	vs. Miami at Tokyo
8/12	W	17-12	at Dallas
8/17	W	13-10	Chicago
8/23	W	17- 7	at San Diego

Regular Season (9-7)

Date	Result		Opponents	Att.
9/1	L	17-47	at Houston	61,367
9/8	W	16-13	Denver	50,812
9/15	W	16- 0	Indianapolis	40,287
9/22	L	17-21	at Atlanta	53,615
9/29	W	12- 6	San Francisco	91,494
10/6	L	13-21	San Diego	42,787
10/13	W	23-20	at Seattle (OT)	61,974
10/20	W	20-17	L.A. Rams	85,102
10/28	L	21-24	at Kansas City	77,111
11/10	W	17-16	at Denver	75,896
11/17	W	31- 7	Seattle	49,317
11/24	W	38-14	at Cincinnati	52,044
12/1	W	9- 7	at San Diego	56,780
12/8	L	27-30	Buffalo (OT)	85,081
12/16	L	0-27	at New Orleans	68,625
12/22	L	21-27	Kansas City	65,144

(OT) Overtime

Postseason (0-1)

Date	Result		Opponent	Att.
12/28	L	6-10	at Kansas City	75,827

Score by Periods

Raiders	58	108	63	66	3	—	298
Opponents	49	89	52	104	3	—	297

Attendance

Home 510,024   Away 507,412   Total 1,017,436
Single-game home record, 91,494 (9-29-91)
Single-season home record, 516,205 (1986)

1991 Team Statistics

	Raiders	Opp.
Total First Downs	248	305
Rushing	97	108
Passing	132	176
Penalty	19	21
Third Down: Made/Att.	75/195	94/211
Third Down: Pct.	38.5	44.5
Fourth Down: Made/Att.	7/12	10/19
Fourth Down: Pct.	58.3	52.6
Total Net Yards	4425	5165
Avg. Per Game	276.6	322.8
Total Plays	893	1002
Avg. Per Play	5.0	5.2
Net Yards Rushing	1706	1889
Avg. Per Game	106.6	118.1
Total Rushes	446	447
Net Yards Passing	2719	3276
Avg. Per Game	169.9	204.8
Sacked/Yards Lost	33/258	42/283
Gross Yards	2977	3559
Att./Completions	414/220	513/295
Completion Pct.	53.1	57.5
Had Intercepted	18	18
Punts/Avg.	67/44.2	61/38.7
Net Punting Avg.	38.5	31.0
Penalties/Yards Lost	117/1013	111/905
Fumbles/Ball Lost	20/13	24/13
Touchdowns	30	36
Rushing	8	13
Passing	20	18
Returns	2	5
Avg. Time of Possession	29:10	30:50

1991 Individual Statistics

Scoring

	TD R	TD P	TD Rt	PAT	FG	Saf	TP
Jaeger	0	0	0	29/30	29/34	0	116
Brown	0	5	1	0/0	0/0	0	36
Horton	0	5	0	0/0	0/0	0	30
Gault	0	4	0	0/0	0/0	0	24
Bell	3	0	0	0/0	0/0	0	18
Glover	0	3	0	0/0	0/0	0	18
Allen	2	0	0	0/0	0/0	0	12
S. Smith	1	1	0	0/0	0/0	0	12
Craig	1	0	0	0/0	0/0	0	6
Fernandez	0	1	0	0/0	0/0	0	6
Graddy	0	1	0	0/0	0/0	0	6
McCallum	1	0	0	0/0	0/0	0	6
Patterson	0	0	1	0/0	0/0	0	6
Dorn	0	0	0	0/0	0/0	1	2
Raiders	8	20	2	29/30	29/34	1	298
Opponents	13	18	5	33/36	16/28	0	297

Passing

	Att.	Comp.	Yds.	Pct.	TD	Int.	Tkld.	Rate
Schroeder	357	189	2562	52.9	15	16	31/238	71.4
Marinovich	40	23	243	57.5	3	0	0/0	100.3
Evans	14	6	127	42.9	1	2	2/20	59.8
Allen	2	1	11	50.0	1	0	0/0	106.3
Gossett	1	1	34	100.0	0	0	0/0	118.8
Raiders	414	220	2977	53.1	20	18	33/258	74.3
Opponents	513	295	3559	57.5	18	18	42/283	76.0

Rushing

	Att.	Yds.	Avg.	LG	TD
Craig	162	590	3.6	15	1
Bell	78	307	3.9	15	3
Allen	63	287	4.6	26	2
S. Smith	62	265	4.3	19	1
McCallum	31	110	3.5	9	1
Schroeder	28	76	2.7	15	0
Wilson	6	21	3.5	8	0
Evans	8	20	2.5	11	0
Brown	5	16	3.2	9	0
Marinovich	3	14	4.7	11	0
Raiders	446	1706	3.8	26	8
Opponents	447	1889	4.2	39t	13

Receiving

	No.	Yds.	Avg.	LG	TD
Horton	53	650	12.3	52	5
Fernandez	46	694	15.1	59	1
Brown	36	554	15.4	78t	5
Gault	20	346	17.3	59t	4
Craig	17	136	8.0	20	0
Allen	15	131	8.7	25	0
S. Smith	15	130	8.7	37t	1
Graddy	6	195	32.5	80t	1
Bell	6	62	10.3	24	0
Glover	5	45	9.0	18	3
Patterson	1	34	34.0	34	0
Raiders	220	2977	13.5	80t	20
Opponents	295	3559	12.1	57t	18

Interceptions

	No.	Yds.	Avg.	LG	TD
Lott	8	52	6.5	27	0
Washington	5	22	4.4	16	0
Anderson	2	14	7.0	14	0
Townsend	1	31	31.0	31	0
Benson	1	25	25.0	25	0
Long	1	11	11.0	11	0
Raiders	18	155	8.6	31	0
Opponents	18	374	20.8	83	2

Punting

	No.	Yds.	Avg.	In 20	LG
Gossett	67	2961	44.2	26	61
Raiders	67	2961	44.2	26	61
Opponents	61	2361	38.7	8	60

Punt Returns

	No.	FC	Yds.	Avg.	LG	TD
Brown	29	10	330	11.4	75t	1
Raiders	29	10	330	11.4	75t	1
Opponents	41	8	341	8.3	59	0

Kickoff Returns

	No.	Yds.	Avg.	LG	TD
Holland	22	421	19.1	27	0
Graddy	22	373	17.0	37	0
McCallum	5	105	21.0	25	0
Brown	1	29	29.0	29	0
S. Smith	1	0	0.0	0	0
Turk	1	0	0.0	0	0
Raiders	52	928	17.8	37	0
Opponents	58	1059	18.3	91t	1

Sacks

	No.
Townsend	13.0
A. Smith	10.5
Davis	6.5
Long	3.0
Moss	3.0
Wallace	2.0
Benson	1.0
Golic	1.0
Harrison	1.0
Lott	1.0
Raiders	42.0
Opponents	33.0

1992 Draft Choices

Round	Name	Pos.	College
1.	Chester McGlockton	DE	Clemson
2.	Greg Skrepenak	T	Michigan
5.	Derrick Hoskins	DB	So. Mississippi
6.	Tony Rowell	C	Florida
7.	Curtis Cotton	DB	Nebraska
	Kevin Smith	RB	UCLA
10.	Alberto White	LB	Texas Southern
12.	Tom Roth	G	Southern Illinois

Los Angeles Raiders 1992 Veteran Roster

No.	Name	Pos.	Ht.	Wt.	Birth-date	NFL Exp.	College	Hometown	How Acq.	'91 Games/ Starts
45	Adams, Stefon	WR	5-10	185	8/11/63	6	East Carolina	High Point, N.C.	FA-'92	0*
80	Alexander, Mike	WR	6-3	185	3/19/65	3	Penn State	Piscataway, N.J.	PB(Buff)-'92#	3/1*
32	†Allen, Marcus	RB	6-2	210	3/26/60	11	Southern California	San Diego, Calif.	D1-'82	8/2
33	Anderson, Eddie	S	6-1	210	7/22/63	7	Fort Valley State	Warner Robins, Ga.	FA-'87	16/16
59	Bell, Anthony	LB	6-3	235	7/2/64	7	Michigan State	Fort Lauderdale, Fla.	PB(Det)-'92#	10/0*
38	Bell, Nick	RB	6-2	255	8/19/68	2	Iowa	Las Vegas, Nev.	D2-'91	9/1
54	†Benson, Tom	LB	6-2	240	9/6/61	9	Oklahoma	Ardmore, Tex.	PB(NE)-'89#	16/14
97	Broughton, Willie	DT	6-5	280	9/9/64	5	Miami	Fort Pierce, Fla.	FA-'92	0*
24	Brown, Ron	WR	5-11	185	3/3/61	9	Arizona State	Baldwin Park, Calif.	PB(Rams)-'92#	6/0*
81	†Brown, Tim	WR	6-0	195	7/22/66	4	Notre Dame	Dallas, Tex.	D1-'88	16/1
56	Bruce, Aundray	LB	6-5	250	1/30/66	5	Auburn	Montgomery, Ala.	PB(Atl)-'92#	14/2*
70	Davis, Scott	DE	6-7	275	8/7/65	5	Illinois	Plainfield, Ill.	D1-'88	16/16
29	t-Dickerson, Eric	RB	6-3	224	9/2/60	10	Southern Methodist	Sealy, Tex.	T(Ind)-'92	10/9*
8	Dilweg, Anthony	QB	6-3	200	3/28/65	3	Duke	Bethesda, Md.	FA-'92	0*
46	†Dorn, Torin	CB	6-0	195	2/29/68	3	North Carolina	Southfield, Mich.	D4-'90	16/1
50	Ellison, Riki	LB	6-2	225	8/15/60	9	Southern California	Tucson, Ariz.	FA-'90	16/15
11	†Evans, Vince	QB	6-2	210	6/14/55	13	Southern California	Greensboro, N.C.	FA-'90	4/0
86	Fernandez, Mervyn	WR	6-3	200	12/29/59	6	San Jose State	San Jose, Calif.	D10-'83	16/13
73	†FitzPatrick, James	G	6-7	320	2/1/64	7	Southern California	Beaverton, Ore.	PB(SD)-'90#	16/4
27	Gainer, Derrick	RB	5-11	240	8/15/66	2	Florida A&M	Plant City, Fla.	FA-'92	0*
83	Gault, Willie	WR	6-1	175	9/5/60	10	Tennessee	Griffin, Ga.	T(Chi)-'88	16/15
87	Glover, Andrew	TE	6-6	240	8/12/67	2	Grambling	Geismar, La.	D10-'91	16/1
79	Golic, Bob	DT	6-2	275	10/26/57	13	Notre Dame	Cleveland, Ohio	PB(Clev)-'89#	16/14
7	Gossett, Jeff	P	6-2	195	1/25/57	11	Eastern Illinois	Charleston, Ill.	T(Hou)-'88	16/0
85	Graddy, Sam	WR	5-10	175	2/10/64	5	Tennessee	Gaffney, S.C.	PB(Den)-'89#	12/0
60	Graves, Rory	T	6-6	295	7/21/63	5	Ohio State	Decatur, Ga.	FA-'88	3/0
74	Harrison, Nolan	DT	6-5	285	1/25/69	2	Indiana	Flossmoor, Ill.	D6-'91	14/3
88	Horton, Ethan	TE	6-4	240	12/19/62	6	North Carolina	Kannapolis, N.C.	FA-'89	16/16
18	Jaeger, Jeff	K	5-11	195	11/26/64	5	Washington	Kent, Wash.	PB(Clev)-'89#	16/0
58	Jimerson, A.J.	DE	6-3	235	5/12/68	3	Norfolk State	Chesapeake, Va.	D8-'90	13/0
52	Jones, Mike	LB	6-1	225	4/15/69	2	Missouri	Kansas City, Mo.	FA-'91	16/0
25	Land, Dan	S	6-0	195	7/3/65	5	Albany State	Donalsonville, Ga.	FA-'89	16/0
75	Long, Howie	DE	6-5	270	1/6/60	12	Villanova	Charleston, Mass.	D2-'81	14/13
42	Lott, Ronnie	S	6-0	205	5/8/59	12	Southern California	Rialto, Calif.	PB(SF)-'91#	16/16
12	Marinovich, Todd	QB	6-4	215	7/4/69	2	Southern California	Mission Viejo, Calif.	D1-'91	1/1
41	McCallum, Napoleon	RB	6-2	225	10/6/63	4	Navy	Milford, Ohio	T(SD)-'90	16/0
36	†McDaniel, Terry	CB	5-10	180	2/8/65	4	Tennessee	Saginaw, Mich.	D1-'88	16/16
77	†McElroy, Reggie	T	6-6	290	3/4/60	9	West Texas State	Beaumont, Tex.	FA-'91	16/5
65	†Montoya, Max	G	6-5	290	5/2/56	14	UCLA	La Puente, Calif.	PB(Cin)-'90#	11/10
72	Mosebar, Don	C	6-6	285	9/11/61	10	Southern California	Visalia, Calif.	D1-'83	16/16
99	†Moss, Winston	LB	6-3	240	12/24/65	6	Miami	Miami, Fla.	T(TB)-'91	16/16
31	Mueller, Vance	RB	6-0	220	5/5/64	6	Occidental	Jackson, Calif.	D4-'86	0*
53	Noga, Niko	LB	6-1	235	3/1/62	9	Hawaii	Honolulu, Hawaii	PB(Det)-'92#	16/0*
71	Patten, Joel	T	6-7	290	2/7/58	6	Duke	Fairfax, Va.	PB(SD)-'91#	1/0
43	†Patterson, Elvis	S	5-11	195	10/21/60	9	Kansas	Houston, Tex.	PB(SD)-'90#	16/0
64	Peat, Todd	G	6-2	325	5/20/64	5	Northern Illinois	Champaign, Ill.	FA-'92	0*
10	†Schroeder, Jay	QB	6-4	215	6/28/61	9	UCLA	Pacific Palisades, Calif.	T(Wash)-'88	15/15
23	Seale, Sam	CB	5-9	185	10/6/62	9	Western State, Colo.	Orange, N.J.	PB(SD)-'92#	16/16*
94	Smith, Anthony	DE	6-3	265	6/28/67	2	Arizona	Elizabeth City, N.C.	D1-'90	16/2
35	Smith, Steve	RB	6-1	240	8/30/64	6	Penn State	Clinton, Md.	D3-'87	16/16
93	Townsend, Greg	DE	6-3	270	11/3/61	10	Texas Christian	Compton, Calif.	D4-'83	16/16
67	Turk, Dan	C	6-4	285	6/25/62	7	Wisconsin	Milwaukee, Wis.	FA-'89	16/0
51	Wallace, Aaron	LB	6-3	235	4/17/67	3	Texas A&M	New Orleans, La.	D2-'90	16/0
48	†Washington, Lionel	CB	6-0	185	10/21/60	10	Tulane	New Orleans, La.	T(StL)-'87	16/16
44	Waymer, Dave	S	6-1	190	7/1/58	13	Notre Dame	Mooresville, N.C.	PB(SF)-'92#	16/15*
68	Wilkerson, Bruce	T	6-5	295	7/28/64	6	Tennessee	Philadelphia, Tenn.	D2-'87	16/16
76	Wisniewski, Steve	G	6-4	285	4/7/67	4	Penn State	Houston, Tex.	D2-'89	15/15
66	Wright, Steve	T	6-6	280	4/18/59	10	Northern Illinois	Wayzata, Minn.	FA-'88	16/16

* Adams last active with Miami in '90; Alexander played 3 games with Buffalo in '91; A. Bell played 10 games with Detroit; Broughton last active with Dallas in '90; R. Brown played 6 games with L.A. Rams; Bruce played 14 games with Atlanta; Dickerson played 10 games with Indianapolis; Dilweg last active with Green Bay in '90; Gainer last active with Cleveland in '90; Mueller missed '91 season due to injury; Noga played 16 games with Detroit; Peat last active with L.A. Raiders in '90; Seale played 16 games with San Diego; Waymer played 16 games with San Francisco.

† Option playout; subject to developments.

t- Raiders traded for Dickerson (Indianapolis).

Traded—CB Garry Lewis to Dallas.

Plan B unconditional free agent.

Players lost through Plan B (6): RB Roger Craig (Minn; 15 games in '91), S Derrick Crudup (SF; 16), TE Mike Dyal (KC; last active in '90), DT Roy Hart (NYJ; 1), WR Jamie Holland (Clev; 16), CB-S Tahaun Lewis (KC; 0).

Also played with Raiders in '91—RB Doug Lloyd (1 game), LB Jerry Robinson (16), RB Marcus Wilson (1).

COACHING STAFF

Head Coach, Art Shell

Pro Career: Named ninth head coach in Raiders' history on October 3, 1989. Had been Raiders' offensive line coach for seven years, including 1983 world championship season. He first joined the coaching staff in 1983 after 15 seasons as one of the greatest offensive tackles in pro football history. Came to Raiders in 1968 as a third-round draft choice out of Maryland State (now Maryland-Eastern Shore). Went on to play in 207 league games, including first 156 in a row, and 24 playoff games for the Raiders. Starting left tackle in Super Bowl XI and XV victories. Selected to Pro Bowl eight times—most by any Raiders player. Inducted into Pro Football Hall of Fame on August 5, 1989. Also named to state of South Carolina Sports Hall of Fame. Career record: 29-18-0.

Background: All-America tackle as junior and senior and three-year All-Conference on both offense and defense at Maryland State 1965-67. Also lettered in basketball.

Personal: Born November 26, 1946, Charleston, S.C. Art and wife, Janice, live in Palos Verdes, California with their sons Arthur III and Christopher.

Assistant Coaches

Fred Biletnikoff, wide receivers; born February 23, 1943, Erie, Pa., lives in El Segundo, Calif. Wide receiver Florida State 1962-64. Pro wide receiver Oakland Raiders 1965-78, Montreal Alouettes (CFL) 1980. College coach: Palomar, Calif., J.C. 1983, Diablo Valley, Calif., J.C. 1984, 1986. Pro coach: Oakland Invaders (USFL) 1985, Calgary Stampeders (CFL) 1987-88, joined Raiders in 1989.

Gunther Cunningham, defense-linebackers; born June 19, 1946, Munich, Germany, lives in El Segundo, Calif. Linebacker Oregon 1965-67. No pro playing experience. College coach: Oregon 1969-71, Arkansas 1972, Stanford 1973-76, California 1977-80. Pro coach: Hamilton Tiger-Cats (CFL) 1981, Baltimore/Indianapolis Colts 1982-84, San Diego Chargers 1985-90, joined Raiders in 1991.

Kim Helton, offensive line; born July 28, 1948, Pensacola, Fla., lives in Rancho Palos Verdes, Calif. Center Florida 1967-69. No pro playing experience. College coach: Florida 1972-78, Miami 1979-82. Pro coach: Tampa Bay Buccaneers 1983-86, Houston Oilers 1987-89, joined Raiders in 1990.

Ronnie Jones, linebackers; born October 17, 1955, Dumas, Tex., lives in El Segundo, Calif. Running back Northwestern State (Okla.) 1974-77. No pro playing experience. College coach: Northeastern State (Okla.) 1979-83, Tulsa 1984, Arizona State 1985-86. Pro coach: Philadelphia Eagles 1987-90, Los Angeles Rams 1991, joined Raiders in 1992.

Earl Leggett, defensive line; born May 5, 1933, Jacksonville, Fla., lives in Redondo Beach, Calif. Tackle Hinds J.C. 1953-54, Louisiana State 1955-56. Pro defensive tackle Chicago Bears 1957-65, Los Angeles Rams 1966, New Orleans Saints 1967-68. College coach: Nicholls State 1971, Texas Christian 1972-73. Pro coach: Southern California Sun (WFL) 1974-75, Seattle Seahawks 1976-77, San Francisco 49ers 1978, Oakland/Los Angeles Raiders 1980-88, Denver Broncos 1989-90, rejoined Raiders in 1991.

Odis McKinney, defensive backs; born May 19, 1957, Detroit, Mich., lives in Woodland Hills, Calif. Defensive back Colorado 1976-77. Pro defensive back New York Giants 1978-79, Oakland/Los Angeles Raiders 1980-85, Kansas City Chiefs 1985, Los Angeles Raiders 1986. Pro coach: Joined Raiders in 1990.

Steve Ortmayer, football operations-special teams; born February 13, 1944, Painesville, Ohio, lives in Palos Verdes Estates, Calif. La Verne College 1966. No college or pro playing experience. College coach: Colorado 1967-73, Georgia Tech 1974. Pro coach: Kansas City Chiefs 1975-77, Oakland/Los Angeles Raiders 1978-86, San Diego Chargers 1987-89 (Director of Football Operations), rejoined Raiders in 1990.

Terry Robiskie, tight ends; born November 12, 1954, New Orleans, La., lives in Beverly Hills, Calif. Running back Louisiana State 1973-76. Pro running back Oakland Raiders 1977-79, Miami Dolphins 1980-81. Pro coach: Joined Raiders in 1982.

Joe Scannella, offensive backfield; born May 22, 1932, Passaic, N.J., lives in El Segundo, Calif. Quarterback Lehigh 1947-50. Pro safety Saskatchewan Roughriders (CFL) 1951-52. College coach: Cornell 1960, C.W. Post 1963-68 (head coach 1964-68), Vermont 1970-71. Pro coach: Montreal Alouettes (CFL) 1969, 1978-81 (head coach), Oakland Raiders 1972-77, Cleveland Browns 1982-84, rejoined Raiders in 1987.

Jack Stanton, defensive backs; born June 6, 1938, Bridgeville, Pa., lives in El Segundo, Calif. Running back North Carolina State 1959-60. Pro running back Pittsburgh Steelers 1961, Toronto Argonauts (CFL) 1962-63. College coach: George Washington 1966, North Carolina State 1968-72, Florida State 1973, 1976-83, North Carolina 1974-75, Purdue 1986, New Mexico 1987-88. Pro coach: Atlanta Falcons 1984-85, joined Raiders in 1989.

Tom Walsh, offense; born April 16, 1949, Vallejo, Calif., lives in Manhattan Beach, Calif. UC-Santa Barbara 1971. No college or pro playing experience. College coach: University of San Diego 1972-76, U.S. International 1979, Murray State 1980, Cincinnati 1981. Pro coach: Joined Raiders in 1982.

Mike White, quarterbacks; born January 4, 1936, Berkeley, Calif., lives in Newport Beach, Calif. Offensive end California 1955-57. No pro playing experience. College coach: California 1958-63, 1972-77 (head coach), Stanford 1964-71, Illinois 1980-87 (head coach). Pro coach: San Francisco 49ers 1978-79, joined Raiders in 1990.

Los Angeles Raiders 1992 First-Year Roster

Name	Pos.	Ht.	Wt.	Birth-date	College	Hometown	How Acq.
Cotton, Curtis	S	6-0	205	9/16/69	Nebraska	Omaha, Neb.	D7
Ellison, Bernard (1)	S	6-1	205	1/2/67	Nevada-Reno	Milpitas, Calif.	FA
Freeman, Kyle (1)	LB	6-1	225	11/22/65	Angelo State	Snyder, Tex.	FA
Harrell, Greg (1)	TE	6-5	245	4/22/62	Maryland	Harrellsville, N.C.	FA
Hinchcliff, William (1)	WR	6-0	195	9/13/60	Auckland Institute	Phoenix, Ariz.	FA
Hobbs, Daryl	WR	6-1	175	5/23/71	Pacific	Los Angeles, Calif.	FA
Hoskins, Derrick	S	6-2	200	11/16/70	Southern Mississippi	Philadelphia, Miss.	D5
Johnson, Dennis (1)	CB	6-1	200	8/22/67	Winston-Salem State	Harrels, N.C.	D12-'91
Jones, David (1)	TE	6-3	225	11/9/68	Delaware State	Hillside, N.J.	FA
McGlockton, Chester	DE	6-4	335	9/16/69	Clemson	Whiteville, N.C.	D1
Montgomery, Tyrone	WR	5-11	185	8/3/70	Mississippi	Greenville, Miss.	FA
Reddick, Michael (1)	WR	5-8	165	11/7/67	Nevada-Las Vegas	Miami, Fla.	FA
Richardson, Paul	WR	6-4	205	2/25/69	UCLA	Los Angeles, Calif.	FA
Roth, Tom	G	6-5	275	9/19/68	Southern Illinois	Godfrey, Ill.	D12
Rowell, Tony	C	6-4	295	7/24/69	Florida	Melbourne, Fla.	D6
Showell, Malcolm (1)	DT	6-6	270	10/1/68	Delaware State	Baltimore, Md.	FA
Skrepenak, Greg	T	6-6	315	1/31/70	Michigan	Wilkes-Barre, Pa.	D2
Smith, Kevin	RB	6-4	250	7/25/69	UCLA	Oakland, Calif.	D7
Taotoai, Josh (1)	C	6-6	315	1/20/68	Florida	Wilmington, Calif.	FA
White, Alberto	LB	6-3	245	4/8/71	Texas Southern	Miami, Fla.	D10
Wood, Scott	QB	6-5	215	12/13/69	St. Mary's, Calif.	Anaheim, Calif.	FA

The term NFL Rookie is defined as a player who is in his first season of professional football and has not been on the roster of another professional football team for any regular-season or postseason games. A Rookie is designated by an "R" on NFL rosters. Players who have been active in another professional football league or players who have NFL experience, including either preseason training camp or being on an active roster for fewer than three regular-season or postseason games, are termed NFL First-Year Players. An NFL First-Year Player is designated by a "1" on NFL rosters. Thereafter, a player on an NFL active roster for at least three regular-season or postseason games is credited with an additional year of NFL playing experience.

NOTES

MIAMI DOLPHINS

American Football Conference Eastern Division

Team Colors: Aqua, Coral, and White

Joe Robbie Stadium
2269 N.W. 199th Street
Miami, Florida 33056
Telephone: (305) 620-5000

Club Officials

President: Timothy J. Robbie
Executive Vice President: Daniel T. Robbie
Executive Vice President: Janet Robbie
Executive V.P./General Manager:
　Eddie J. Jones
General Counsel: Jann M. Iliff
Assistant General Manager: Bryan Wiedmeier
Head Coach: Don Shula
Director of Player Personnel: Charley Winner
Director of College Scouting: Tom Heckert
Director of Media Relations: Harvey Greene
Media Relations Assistant: Scott Stone
Director of Sales: P.J. Wright
Marketing Director: David Evans
Community Relations Director: Fudge Browne
Treasurer: Jill R. Strafaci
Trainer: Ryan Vermillion
Equipment Manager: Bob Monica

Stadium: Joe Robbie Stadium •
　　　　　Capacity: 73,000
　　　　　2269 N.W. 199th Street
　　　　　Miami, Florida 33056

Playing Surface: Grass (PAT)

Training Camp: St. Thomas University
　　　　　16400-D N.W. 32nd Avenue
　　　　　Miami, Florida 33054

1992 Schedule

Preseason
Aug. 1	vs. Washington at Orlando	8:00
Aug. 7	**Dallas**	8:00
Aug. 15	vs. Denver at Berlin	1:00
Aug. 22	**Tampa Bay**	8:00
Aug. 27	vs. New Orleans at Baltimore	8:00

Regular Season
Sept. 6	**New England**	4:00
Sept. 14	at Cleveland (Monday)	9:00
Sept. 20	**Los Angeles Rams**	4:00
Sept. 27	at Seattle	1:00
Oct. 4	at Buffalo	1:00
Oct. 11	**Atlanta**	1:00
Oct. 18	**Open Date**	
Oct. 25	**Indianapolis**	4:00
Nov. 1	at New York Jets	1:00
Nov. 8	at Indianapolis	1:00
Nov. 16	**Buffalo** (Monday)	9:00
Nov. 22	**Houston**	1:00
Nov. 29	at New Orleans	12:00
Dec. 6	at San Francisco	1:00
Dec. 14	**L.A. Raiders** (Monday)	9:00
Dec. 20	**New York Jets**	8:00
Dec. 27	at New England	1:00

Dolphins Coaching History

(248-158-4)

1966-69	George Wilson	15-39-2
1970-91	Don Shula	233-119-2

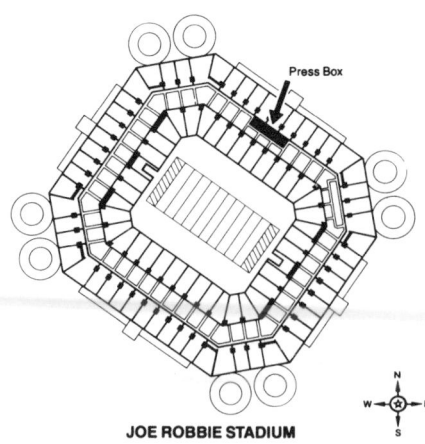

JOE ROBBIE STADIUM

Record Holders

Individual Records—Career
Category	Name	Performance
Rushing (Yds.)	Larry Csonka, 1968-1974, 1979	6,737
Passing (Yds.)	Dan Marino, 1983-1991	35,386
Passing (TDs)	Dan Marino, 1983-1991	266
Receiving (No.)	Nat Moore, 1974-1986	510
Receiving (Yds.)	Mark Duper, 1982-1991	8,107
Interceptions	Jake Scott, 1970-75	35
Punting (Avg.)	Reggie Roby, 1983-1991	43.4
Punt Return (Avg.)	Freddie Solomon, 1975-77	11.4
Kickoff Return (Avg.)	Mercury Morris, 1969-1975	26.5
Field Goals	Garo Yepremian, 1970-78	165
Touchdowns (Tot.)	Mark Clayton, 1983-1991	79
Points	Garo Yepremian, 1970-78	830

Individual Records—Single Season
Category	Name	Performance
Rushing (Yds.)	Delvin Williams, 1978	1,258
Passing (Yds.)	Dan Marino, 1984	*5,084
Passing (TDs)	Dan Marino, 1984	*48
Receiving (No.)	Mark Clayton, 1988	86
Receiving (Yds.)	Mark Clayton, 1984	1,389
Interceptions	Dick Westmoreland, 1967	10
Punting (Avg.)	Reggie Roby, 1991	45.7
Punt Return (Avg.)	Freddie Solomon, 1975	12.3
Kickoff Return (Avg.)	Duriel Harris, 1976	32.9
Field Goals	Pete Stoyanovich, 1991	31
Touchdowns (Tot.)	Mark Clayton, 1984	18
Points	Pete Stoyanovich, 1991	121

Individual Records—Single Game
Category	Name	Performance
Rushing (Yds.)	Mercury Morris, 9-30-73	197
Passing (Yds.)	Dan Marino, 10-23-88	521
Passing (TDs)	Bob Griese, 11-24-77	6
	Dan Marino, 9-21-86	6
Receiving (No.)	Jim Jensen, 11-6-88	12
Receiving (Yds.)	Mark Duper, 11-10-85	217
Interceptions	Dick Anderson, 12-3-73	*4
Field Goals	Garo Yepremian, 9-26-71	5
Touchdowns (Tot.)	Paul Warfield, 12-15-73	4
Points	Paul Warfield, 12-15-73	24

*NFL Record

1991 Team Record
Preseason (3-2)

Date	Result		Opponents
7/26	L	0- 6	Chicago
8/3	W	19-17	vs. L.A. Raiders at Tokyo
8/10	W	29-13	at Tampa Bay
8/19	L	13-21	at Denver
8/24	W	28-24	New Orleans

Regular Season (8-8)

Date	Result		Opponents	Att.
9/1	L	31-35	at Buffalo	80,252
9/8	W	17- 6	Indianapolis	51,155
9/15	L	13-17	at Detroit	56,896
9/22	W	16-13	Green Bay	56,583
9/29	L	23-41	at N.Y. Jets	71,170
10/6	W	20-10	at New England	49,749
10/13	L	7-42	at Kansas City	76,021
10/20	L	13-17	Houston	60,705
11/3	W	10- 6	at Indianapolis	55,899
11/10	W	30-20	New England	56,065
11/18	L	27-41	Buffalo	71,062
11/24	W	16-13	at Chicago (OT)	58,288
12/1	W	33-14	Tampa Bay	51,036
12/9	W	37-13	Cincinnati	60,616
12/15	L	30-38	at San Diego	47,731
12/22	L	20-23	N.Y. Jets (OT)	69,636

(OT) Overtime

Score by Periods

Dolphins	55	119	51	115	3	—	343
Opponents	65	100	75	106	3	—	349

Attendance
Home 476,858   Away 496,006   Total 972,864
Single-game home record, 71,062 (11-18-91)
Single-season home record, 510,359 (1990)

1991 Team Statistics

	Dolphins	Opp.
Total First Downs	312	327
Rushing	91	133
Passing	205	177
Penalty	16	17
Third Down: Made/Att.	84/205	103/210
Third Down: Pct.	41.0	49.0
Fourth Down: Made/Att.	10/13	6/10
Fourth Down: Pct.	76.9	60.0
Total Net Yards	5241	5406
Avg. Per Game	327.6	337.9
Total Plays	970	1019
Avg. Per Play	5.4	5.3
Net Yards Rushing	1352	2301
Avg. Per Game	84.5	143.8
Total Rushes	379	499
Net Yards Passing	3889	3105
Avg. Per Game	243.1	194.1
Sacked/Yards Lost	28/188	35/248
Gross Yards	4077	3353
Att./Completions	563/327	485/300
Completion Pct.	58.1	61.9
Had Intercepted	14	12
Punts/Avg.	57/44.8	65/39.8
Net Punting Avg.	36.5	34.3
Penalties/Yards Lost	62/516	91/684
Fumbles/Ball Lost	23/14	19/9
Touchdowns	35	40
Rushing	8	17
Passing	26	18
Returns	1	5
Avg. Time of Possession	29:08	30:52

1991 Individual Statistics

Scoring

	TD R	TD P	TD Rt	PAT	FG	Saf	TP
Stoyanovich	0	0	0	28/29	31/37	0	121
Clayton	0	12	0	0/0	0/0	0	72
Duper	0	5	0	0/0	0/0	0	30
Higgs	4	0	0	0/0	0/0	0	24
Baumann	0	0	0	6/6	2/2	0	12
Edmunds	0	2	0	0/0	0/0	0	12
Jensen	0	2	0	0/0	0/0	0	12
Martin	0	2	0	0/0	0/0	0	12
Banks	0	1	0	0/0	0/0	0	6
Baty	0	1	0	0/0	0/0	0	6
Craver	1	0	0	0/0	0/0	0	6
Klingbeil	0	0	1	0/0	0/0	0	6
Marino	1	0	0	0/0	0/0	0	6
Paige	0	1	0	0/0	0/0	0	6
S. Smith	1	0	0	0/0	0/0	0	6
Secules	1	0	0	0/0	0/0	0	6
Dolphins	8	26	1	34/35	33/39	0	343
Opponents	17	18	5	40/40	23/33	0	349

Passing

	Att.	Comp.	Yds.	Pct.	TD	Int.	Tkld.	Rate
Marino	549	318	3970	57.9	25	13	27/182	85.8
Secules	13	8	90	61.5	1	1	1/6	75.8
Jensen	1	1	17	100.0	0	0	0/0	118.8
Dolphins	563	327	4077	58.1	26	14	28/188	85.7
Opponents	485	300	3353	61.9	18	12	35/248	84.5

Rushing

	Att.	Yds.	Avg.	LG	TD
Higgs	231	905	3.9	24	4
S. Smith	83	297	3.6	18	1
Craver	20	58	2.9	7t	1
Marino	27	32	1.2	11	1
Secules	4	30	7.5	12	1
Paige	10	25	2.5	6	0
Logan	4	5	1.3	2	0
Dolphins	379	1352	3.6	24	8
Opponents	499	2301	4.6	63t	17

Receiving

	No.	Yds.	Avg.	LG	TD
Duper	70	1085	15.5	43t	5
Clayton	70	1053	15.0	43t	12
Paige	57	469	8.2	26	1
Martin	27	434	16.1	54	2
Jensen	21	183	8.7	19	2
Baty	20	269	13.5	30	1
S. Smith	14	95	6.8	12	0
Edmunds	11	118	10.7	22	2
Higgs	11	80	7.3	13	0
Banks	9	119	13.2	25	1
Craver	8	67	8.4	25	0
Miller	4	49	12.3	15	0
Pruitt	2	30	15.0	24	0
Henry	2	17	8.5	9	0
Sims	1	9	9.0	9	0
Dolphins	327	4077	12.5	54	26
Opponents	300	3353	11.2	54t	18

Interceptions

	No.	Yds.	Avg.	LG	TD
Oliver	5	80	16.0	37	0
Harden	2	39	19.5	22	0
Lee	1	14	14.0	14	0
Reichenbach	1	2	2.0	2	0
Brown	1	0	0.0	0	0
J. Williams	1	0	0.0	0	0
Odom	1	0	0.0	0	0
Dolphins	12	135	11.3	37	0
Opponents	14	217	15.5	83t	2

Punting

	No.	Yds.	Avg.	In 20	LG
Roby	54	2466	45.7	17	64
Stoyanovich	2	85	42.5	1	49
Dolphins	57	2551	44.8	18	64
Opponents	65	2588	39.8	10	61

Punt Returns

	No.	FC	Yds.	Avg.	LG	TD
Miller	28	10	248	8.9	32	0
Junior	1	0	0	0.0	0	0
Martin	1	0	10	10.0	10	0
J. Williams	0	2	0	—	0	0
Dolphins	30	12	258	8.6	32	0
Opponents	30	8	332	11.1	39	0

Kickoff Returns

	No.	Yds.	Avg.	LG	TD
Craver	32	615	19.2	49	0
Logan	12	191	15.9	31	0
Paige	2	31	15.5	16	0
Dellenbach	1	0	0.0	0	0
Henry	1	13	13.0	13	0
Hill	1	33	33.0	33	0
J. Williams	1	7	7.0	7	0
Dolphins	50	890	17.8	49	0
Opponents	66	1270	19.2	39	0

Sacks

	No.
Cross	7.0
Griggs	5.5
Junior	5.0
Klingbeil	5.0
Turner	4.0
B. Cox	2.0
Offerdahl	1.5
Gardner	1.0
H. Green	1.0
Harden	1.0
Odom	1.0
Dolphins	35.0
Opponents	28.0

1992 Draft Choices

Round	Name	Pos.	College
1.	Troy Vincent	DB	Wisconsin
	Marco Coleman	LB	Georgia Tech
2.	Eddie Blake	DT	Auburn
3.	Larry Webster	DT	Maryland
4.	Dwight Hollier	LB	North Carolina
5.	Christopher Perez	T	Kansas
6.	Roosevelt Collins	LB	Texas Christian
7.	Dave Moore	TE	Pittsburgh
8.	Andre Powell	LB	Penn State
9.	Tony Tellington	DB	Youngstown State
10.	Raoul Spears	RB	Southern California
11.	Lee Miles	WR	Baylor
	Mark Barsotti	QB	Fresno State
12.	Milton Biggins	TE	Western Kentucky
	Kameno Bell	RB	Illinois

Miami Dolphins 1992 Veteran Roster

No.	Name	Pos.	Ht.	Wt.	Birth-date	NFL Exp.	College	Hometown	How Acq.	'91 Games/ Starts
40	Alexander, Bruce	CB	5-9	169	9/17/65	3	Stephen F. Austin	Lufkin, Tex.	PB(Det)-'92#	9/0*
86	Banks, Fred	WR	5-10	185	5/26/62	7	Liberty	Columbus, Ga.	FA-'87	7/0
84	Baty, Greg	TE	6-5	240	8/28/64	5	Stanford	Sparta, N.J.	FA-'90	16/8
53	Bolcar, Ned	LB	6-1	235	1/12/67	3	Notre Dame	Phillipsburg, N.J.	PB(Sea)-'91#	8/0
37	Brown, J.B.	CB	6-0	192	1/5/67	4	Maryland	Washington, D.C.	D12-'89	15/11
81	Clark, Robert	WR	5-11	173	8/6/65	5	North Carolina Central	Richmond, Va.	PB(Det)-'92#	14/14*
83	Clayton, Mark	WR	5-9	185	4/8/61	10	Louisville	Indianapolis, Ind.	D8-'83	16/16
50	Cooper, Louis	LB	6-2	238	8/5/63	8	Western Carolina	Marion, S.C.	PB(KC)-'91#	12/0
51	Cox, Bryan	LB	6-3	235	2/17/68	2	Western Illinois	St. Louis, Mo.	D5a-'91	13/13
34	Craver, Aaron	RB	5-11	215	12/18/69	2	Fresno State	Compton, Calif.	D3-'91	14/0
91	†Cross, Jeff	DE	6-4	272	3/25/66	5	Missouri	Blythe, Calif.	D9-'88	16/16
65	†Dellenbach, Jeff	T-C	6-6	285	2/14/63	8	Wisconsin	Wausau, Wis.	D4b-'85	15/2
74	Dennis, Mark	T	6-6	295	4/15/65	6	Illinois	Washington, Ill.	D8b-'87	16/16
85	†Duper, Mark	WR	5-9	192	1/25/59	11	Northwestern Louisiana	Moreauville, La.	D2-'82	16/16
80	Edmunds, Ferrell	TE	6-6	254	4/16/65	5	Maryland	Danville, Va.	D3-'88	8/6
62	Galbreath, Harry	G	6-2	275	1/1/65	5	Tennessee	Clarksville, Tenn.	D8a-'88	16/16
35	Glenn, Kerry	CB	5-9	178	1/3/62	6	Minnesota	East St. Louis, Ill.	PB(NYJ)-'90#	3/0
42	Green, Chris	CB	5-11	188	2/26/68	2	Illinois	Lawrenceburg, Ind.	D6-'91	16/0
55	Green, Hugh	LB	6-2	230	7/27/59	12	Pittsburgh	Natchez, Miss.	T(TB)-'85	11/3
92	†Griggs, David	LB	6-3	248	2/5/67	4	Virginia	Pennsauken, N.J.	FA-'89	16/16
59	Grimsley, John	LB	6-2	238	2/25/62	8	Kentucky	Canton, Ohio	T(Hou)-'91	0*
97	Hall, Mark	DE	6-4	280	8/21/65	3	Southwestern Louisiana	Patterson, La.	FA-'92	0*
45	†Harden, Bobby	S	6-0	192	2/8/67	2	Miami	Ft. Lauderdale, Fla.	D12-'90	16/5
21	†Higgs, Mark	RB	5-7	195	4/11/66	5	Kentucky	Owensboro, Ky.	PB(Phil)-'90#	14/10
29	Hobley, Liffort	S	6-0	202	5/12/62	6	Louisiana State	Shreveport, La.	FA-'87	0*
	t-Humphrey, Bobby	RB	6-1	201	10/11/66	4	Alabama	Birmingham, Ala.	T(Den)-'92	4/0*
48	Iaquaniello, Mike	S	6-3	208	2/13/68	2	Michigan State	Dearborn, Mich.	FA-'91	15/0
24	†Jackson, Vestee	CB	6-0	186	8/14/63	7	Washington	Fresno, Calif.	T(Chi)-'91	16/16
11	Jensen, Jim	WR	6-4	224	11/14/58	12	Boston University	Doylestown, Pa.	D11-'81	16/0
90	Jones, Brian	LB	6-1	240	1/22/68	2	Texas	Lubbock, Tex.	PB(Ind)-'92#	11/1*
54	Junior, E.J.	LB	6-3	242	12/8/59	12	Alabama	Nashville, Tenn.	PB(Phx)-'89#	16/0
99	Klingbeil, Chuck	NT	6-1	260	11/2/65	2	Northern Michigan	Houghton, Mich.	FA-'91	15/4
44	Lankford, Paul	CB	6-1	191	6/15/58	11	Penn State	Farmingdale, N.Y.	D3-'82	15/0
98	†Lee, Shawn	NT	6-2	285	10/24/66	5	North Alabama	Brooklyn, N.Y.	T(Atl)-'90	3/2
32	Limbrick, Garrett	RB	6-2	240	11/16/65	2	Oklahoma State	Northbrook, Tex.	FA-'90	0*
13	Marino, Dan	QB	6-4	224	9/15/61	10	Pittsburgh	Pittsburgh, Pa.	D1-'83	16/16
89	Martin, Tony	WR	6-0	180	9/5/65	3	Mesa, Colo.	Miami, Fla.	FA-'89	16/0
28	†McGruder, Michael	CB	5-11	190	5/6/62	2	Kent State	Cleveland Heights, Ohio	FA-'90	16/5
43	McNorton, Bruce	CB	5-11	175	2/28/59	10	Georgetown, Ky.	Daytona Beach, Fla.	FA-'90	0*
82	Miller, Scott	WR	5-10	179	10/20/68	2	UCLA	El Toro, Calif.	D9-'91	16/0
77	Nichols, Gerald	NT	6-2	267	2/10/64	6	Florida State	Clearwater, Fla.	PB(TB)-'92#	16/5*
93	†Odom, Cliff	LB	6-2	243	8/15/58	12	Texas-Arlington	Beaumont, Tex.	PB(Ind)-'90#	14/11
56	Offerdahl, John	LB	6-3	238	8/17/64	7	Western Michigan	Fort Atkinson, Wis.	D2-'86	6/6
96	Oglesby, Alfred	NT	6-3	278	1/27/67	3	Houston	Weimer, Tex.	D3-'90	12/12
25	Oliver, Louis	S	6-2	226	3/9/66	4	Florida	Belle Glade, Fla.	D1b-'89	16/16
49	†Paige, Tony	RB	5-10	235	10/14/62	9	Virginia Tech	Washington, D.C.	PB(Det)-'90#	16/16
71	Robbins, Kevin	T	6-6	300	12/12/66	2	Michigan State	Washington, D.C.	FA-'92	0*
4	Roby, Reggie	P	6-2	246	7/30/61	10	Iowa	East Waterloo, Iowa	D6-'83	16/0
41	Rogers, Glenn	CB	6-0	185	6/8/69	2	Memphis State	Memphis, Tenn.	FA-'92	5/1*
22	Saxon, James	RB	5-11	234	3/23/66	5	San Jose State	Burton, S.C.	PB(KC)-'92#	16/0*
9	Secules, Scott	QB	6-3	220	11/8/64	5	Virginia	Centreville, Va.	T(Dall)-'89	14/0
69	Sims, Keith	G	6-2	305	6/17/67	3	Iowa State	Watchung, N.J.	D2-'90	12/12
30	Smith, Don	RB	5-11	200	10/30/63	4	Mississippi State	Hamilton, Miss.	PB(Buff)-'91#	0*
10	Stoyanovich, Pete	K	5-10	185	4/28/67	4	Indiana	Dearborn Heights, Mich.	D8-'89	14/0
67	†Swoopes, Pat	DE	6-3	277	3/4/64	4	Mississippi State	Florence, Ala.	FA-'91	7/0*
95	Turner, T.J.	DE	6-4	280	5/16/63	7	Houston	Lufkin, Tex.	D3-'86	13/12
63	Uhlenhake, Jeff	C	6-3	284	1/28/66	4	Ohio State	Newark, Ohio	D5-'89	13/10
78	Webb, Richmond	T	6-6	298	1/11/67	3	Texas A&M	Dallas, Tex.	D1-'90	14/14
60	†Weidner, Bert	C-G	6-3	284	11/20/66	3	Kent State	Eden, N.Y.	D11-'89	15/10
88	Wellsandt, Doug	TE	6-3	248	2/9/67	2	Washington State	Ritzville, Wash.	FA-'92	0*
61	Williams, Gene	G	6-2	308	10/14/68	2	Iowa State	Omaha, Neb.	D5b-'91	10/10
26	Williams, Jarvis	S	5-11	200	5/16/65	5	Florida	Palatka, Fla.	D2-'88	11/11
87	Williams, Mike	WR	5-10	177	10/9/66	2	Northeastern	Katonah, N.Y.	FA-'91	3/0

* Alexander played 9 games with Detroit in '91; Clark played 14 games with Detroit; Grimsley, Hobley, Limbrick, McNorton, and D. Smith missed '91 season due to injury; Hall last active with Green Bay in '90; Humphrey played 4 games with Denver; Jones played 11 games with Indianapolis; Nichols played 16 games with Tampa Bay; Robbins active for 8 games with Atlanta but did not play; Rogers played 5 games with Tampa Bay; Saxon played 16 games with Kansas City; Swoopes played 4 games with Kansas City, 3 with Miami; Wellsandt last active with N.Y. Jets in '90.

† Option playout; subject to developments.

Traded—RB Sammie Smith to Denver.

t- Dolphins traded for Humphrey (Denver).

Plan B unconditional free agent.

Players lost through Plan B (6): DE Donnie Gardner (NYJ; 10), RB Marc Logan (SF; 16), S Stevon Moore (Clev; 0), T James Parrish (SD; 0), DE Terry Price (SD; 0), LB Mike Reichenbach (SF; 16).

Also played with Dolphins in '91—K Charlie Baumann (2 games), TE Arthur Cox (2), TE Charles Henry (6), WR Randal Hill (1), QB Scott Mitchell (2), WR James Pruitt (5), RB Sammie Smith (12), NT Brian Sochia (3), T Dave Zawatson (2).

COACHING STAFF

Head Coach, Don Shula

Pro Career: Begins his thirtieth season as an NFL head coach, and twenty-third with the Dolphins. Miami has won or shared first place in the AFC East in 13 of his 22 years and has earned 13 playoff berths in that span. Has most wins (306) among active NFL coaches and is second only to George Halas's 325. Captured back-to-back NFL championships, defeating Washington 14-7 in Super Bowl VII and Minnesota 24-7 in Super Bowl VIII. Lost to Dallas 24-3 in Super Bowl VI, to Washington 27-17 in Super Bowl XVII, and to San Francisco 38-16 in Super Bowl XIX. His 17-0 team in 1972 is the only team in NFL history to go undefeated throughout the regular season and postseason. Started his pro playing career with Cleveland Browns as defensive back in 1951. After two seasons with Browns, spent 1953-56 with Baltimore Colts and 1957 with Washington Redskins. Joined Detroit Lions as defensive coach in 1960 and was named head coach of the Colts in 1963. Baltimore had a 13-1 record in 1968 and captured NFL championship before losing to New York Jets in Super Bowl III. Career record: 306-145-6.

Background: Outstanding offensive player at John Carroll University in Cleveland before becoming defensive specialist as a pro. His alma mater awarded him a doctorate in humanities in May, 1973. Served as assistant coach at Virginia in 1958 and at Kentucky in 1959.

Personal: Born January 4, 1930, in Painesville, Ohio. Don lives in Miami Lakes, Fla., and has five children—Dave, Donna, Sharon, Annie, and Mike. Dave is Cincinnati's head coach and Mike is a coaches' assistant with Miami.

Assistant Coaches

Joe Greene, defensive line; born September 24, 1946, Temple, Tex., lives in Miami. Defensive tackle North Texas State 1966-68. Pro defensive tackle Pittsburgh Steelers 1969-81. Inducted into Pro Football Hall of Fame in 1987. Pro coach: Pittsburgh Steelers 1987-91, joined Dolphins in 1992.

George Hill, linebackers; born April 28, 1933, Bay Village, Ohio, lives in Miami. Tackle-fullback Denison 1954-57. No pro playing experience. College coach: Findlay 1959, Denison 1960-64, Cornell 1965, Duke 1966-70, Ohio State 1971-78. Pro coach: Philadelphia Eagles 1979-84, Indianapolis Colts 1985-88, joined Dolphins in 1989.

Tony Nathan, coaches' assistant; born December 14, 1956, Birmingham, Ala., lives in Miami. Running back Alabama 1975-78. Pro running back Miami Dolphins 1979-87. Pro coach: Joined Dolphins in 1988.

Tom Olivadotti, defense; born September 22, 1945, Long Branch, N.J., lives in Cooper City, Fla. Defensive back-wide receiver Upsala 1963-66. No pro playing experience. College coach: Princeton 1975-77, Boston College 1978-79, Miami 1980-83. Pro coach: Cleveland Browns 1985-86, joined Dolphins in 1987.

Mel Phillips, defensive backs; born January 6, 1942, Shelby, N.C., lives in Miami Lakes, Fla. Defensive back-running back North Carolina A&T 1964-65. Pro defensive back San Francisco 49ers 1966-77. Pro coach: Detroit Lions 1980-84, joined Dolphins in 1985.

John Sandusky, assistant head coach-offensive line-run offense; born December 28, 1925, Philadelphia, lives in Hollywood, Fla. Tackle Villanova 1946-49. Pro tackle Cleveland Browns 1950-55, Green Bay Packers 1956. College coach: Villanova 1957-58. Pro coach: Baltimore Colts 1959-72 (head coach 1972), Philadelphia Eagles 1973-75, joined Dolphins in 1976.

Larry Seiple, receivers; born February 14, 1945, Allentown, Pa., lives in Miami Lakes, Fla. Running back-receiver-punter Kentucky 1964-66. Pro punter-tight end-receiver-running back Miami Dolphins 1967-77. College coach: Miami 1978-79. Pro coach: Detroit Lions 1980-84, Tampa Bay Buccaneers 1985-86, joined Dolphins in 1988.

Mike Shula, coaches' assistant; born June 23, 1965, Baltimore, Md., lives in Miami. Quarterback Alabama 1984-87. Pro quarterback Tampa Bay Buccaneers 1987. Pro coach: Tampa Bay Buccaneers 1988-90, joined Dolphins in 1991.

Dwight Stephenson, assistant offensive line; born November 20, 1957, Murfreesboro, N.C., lives in Miami Lakes, Fla. Center Alabama 1976-79. Pro center Miami Dolphins 1980-88. Pro coach: Joined Dolphins in 1992.

Gary Stevens, quarterbacks-pass offense; born March 19, 1943, Cleveland, Ohio, lives in Kendall, Fla. Running back John Carroll 1963-65. No pro playing experience. College coach: Louisville 1971-74, Kent State 1975, West Virginia 1976-79, Miami 1980-88. Pro coach: Joined Dolphins in 1989.

Carl Taseff, offensive backs; born September 28, 1928, Cleveland, Ohio, lives in Miami. Back John Carroll 1947-50. Pro defensive back Cleveland Browns 1951, Baltimore Colts 1953-61, Philadelphia Eagles 1961, Buffalo Bills 1962. Pro coach: Boston Patriots 1964, Detroit Lions 1965-66, joined Dolphins in 1970.

Junior Wade, strength and conditioning; born February 2, 1947, Bath, S.C., lives in Miami. South Carolina State 1969. No college or pro playing experience. Pro coach: Joined Dolphins in 1975, coach since 1983.

Mike Westhoff, special teams; born January 10, 1948, Pittsburgh, Pa., lives in Ft. Lauderdale, Fla. Center-linebacker Wichita State 1967-69. No pro playing experience. College coach: Indiana 1974-75, Dayton 1976, Indiana State 1977, Northwestern 1978-80, Texas Christian 1981. Pro coach: Baltimore/Indianapolis Colts 1982-84, Arizona Outlaws (USFL) 1985, joined Dolphins in 1986.

Miami Dolphins 1992 First-Year Roster

Name	Pos.	Ht.	Wt.	Birth-date	College	Hometown	How Acq.
Barsotti, Mark	QB	6-1	207	3/4/69	Fresno State	Fresno, Calif.	D11b
Bell, Kameno	RB	5-11	221	4/5/69	Illinois	Chicago, Ill.	D12b
Biggins, Milton	TE	6-4	273	12/29/69	Western Kentucky	Chicago, Ill.	D12a
Blackshear, Rodney	WR	5-11	178	7/25/69	Texas Tech	Houston, Tex.	FA
Blake, Eddie	NT	6-3	321	12/18/68	Auburn	Fayetteville, Tenn.	D2
Brown, Harry	WR	6-2	202	1/16/68	Florida A&M	Miami, Fla.	FA
Brunson, Joe (1)	DE	6-4	270	10/15/68	Tenn.-Chattanooga	Elberton, Ga.	FA
Burkhead, Rick	RB	6-1	235	3/22/69	Eastern Kentucky	Winchester, Ky.	FA
Carruthers, Kirk	LB	6-2	203	7/15/70	Florida State	East Lansing, Mich.	FA
Carswell, Chuck	CB	5-9	195	10/13/69	Georgia	Marietta, Ga.	FA
Citizen, Tony (1)	RB	5-8	204	5/25/66	McNeese State	Church Point, La.	FA
Coleman, Marco	LB	6-3	259	12/18/69	Georgia Tech	Dayton, Ohio	D1b
Collins, Brent (1)	LB	6-2	235	4/27/68	Carson-Newman	Johnson City, Tenn.	FA
Collins, Roosevelt	LB	6-4	235	1/25/68	Texas Christian	Shreveport, La.	D6
Downing, Tim (1)	DE	6-5	280	4/9/67	Washington State	Durham, Calif.	FA
Ekonomou, Nick (1)	C-G	6-3	291	11/3/67	Florida State	Melbourne, Fla.	FA
Flowers, Leodis	RB	5-11	204	8/21/69	Nebraska	Omaha, Neb.	FA
Gray, Chris	QB	6-4	207	2/4/68	West Virginia	West Mifflin, Pa.	FA
Hart, Kevin	RB	6-0	230	6/29/69	Western Illinois	Clinton, Iowa	FA
Hochertz, Martin (1)	DE	6-5	245	10/21/68	Southern Illinois	Chicago, Ill.	FA
Hollier, Dwight	LB	6-2	242	4/21/69	North Carolina	Hampton, Va.	D4
Hope, Charles	G	6-3	284	3/12/70	Central State, Ohio	New Castle, Del.	FA
Humphreys, Matt	G	6-1	279	5/6/68	Slippery Rock	Antioch, Ill.	FA
Kouri, Chris	RB	5-11	195	12/1/69	Yale	Charlotte, N.C.	FA
Lewis, Tyrone	CB	5-9	190	12/17/68	West Virginia	Winston-Salem, N.C.	FA
Long, Ted	WR	5-9	189	1/21/69	Oklahoma	Waco, Tex.	FA
Miles, Lee	WR	5-6	156	9/18/69	Baylor	Mart, Tex.	D11a
Mitchell, Scott (1)	QB	6-6	236	1/2/68	Utah	Springville, Utah	D4-'90
Moore, Dave	TE	6-2	247	11/11/69	Pittsburgh	Roxbury, N.J.	D7
Moronta, Horacio (1)	NT	6-1	295	9/6/66	Wagner	Pemberton, N.J.	FA
Ostaszewski, Joe	NT	6-3	272	5/17/69	Florida State	Lantana, Fla.	FA
Paramalee, Bernie	RB	5-11	190	9/16/67	Ball State	Jersey City, N.J.	FA
Perez, Christopher	T	6-5	285	6/21/69	Kansas	Palantine, Ill.	D5
Polly, Eddie	CB	5-10	190	9/6/69	Iowa	Oklahoma City, Okla.	FA
Powell, Andre	LB	6-1	226	6/1/69	Penn State	York, Pa.	D8
Rose, Blaine (1)	G	6-5	271	6/13/66	Maryland	Stanton, Ohio	FA
Rose, Curtis	G	6-3	295	6/8/70	Edinboro	Logan, Ohio	FA
Sander, Mark (1)	LB	6-2	232	3/21/68	Louisville	Louisville, Ky.	FA
Spears, Raoul	RB	5-11	240	10/23/69	Southern California	Long Beach, Calif.	D10
Tellington, Tony	CB	5-9	175	10/9/68	Youngstown State	Youngstown, Ohio	D9
Vincent, Troy	CB	6-0	191	6/8/70	Wisconsin	Trenton, N.J.	D1
Waits, Alex (1)	P	6-2	204	6/21/68	Texas	East Plano, Tex.	FA
Ware, Larry	RB	5-9	180	3/2/68	Georgia	Montgomery, Ala.	FA
Webster, Larry	DE	6-5	285	1/18/69	Maryland	Elkton, Md.	D3

The term NFL Rookie is defined as a player who is in his first season of professional football and has not been on the roster of another professional football team for any regular-season or postseason games. A Rookie is designated by an "R" on NFL rosters. Players who have been active in another professional football league or players who have NFL experience, including either preseason training camp or being on an active roster for fewer than three regular-season or postseason games, are termed NFL First-Year Players. An NFL First-Year Player is designated by a "1" on NFL rosters. Thereafter, a player on an NFL active roster for at least three regular-season or postseason games is credited with an additional year of NFL playing experience.

NOTES

_____

_____

_____

_____

NEW ENGLAND PATRIOTS

American Football Conference Eastern Division

Team Colors: Red, White, and Blue

Foxboro Stadium
Route 1
Foxboro, Massachusetts 02035
Telephone: (508) 543-8200

Club Officials

Chairman of the Board: James B. Orthwein
President: Francis W. Murray
Chief Executive Officer: Sam Jankovich
Vice President: Francis J. Kilroy
Vice President-Player Operations: Joe Mendes
Vice President-Administration: Patrick Forté
Vice President-Pro Personnel/Player Asst.:
Tom Bass
Vice President-Public Relations: Pat Hanlon
Assistant Director of Player Operations:
Charles Armey
Coordinator of College Scouting: Charles Garcia
Personnel Scouts: Larry Cook, Mike Pollom,
Bob Teahan
Executive Director of Marketing: Anne Parry
Director of Data Processing: Peg Myers
Director of Operations: Mike Quashie
Director of Ticket Sales: Ken Sternfeld
Director of Publications: Mike Hanson
Director of Community Relations: Nadine Jackson
Director of Special Events: Mitch Hardin
Controller: Virginia Widmann
Head Trainer: Ron O'Neil
Equipment Manager: George Luongo
Video Director: Ken Deininger

Stadium: Foxboro Stadium • **Capacity:** 60,794
Route 1
Foxboro, Massachusetts 02035

Playing Surface: Grass

Training Camp: Bryant College
Route 7
Smithfield, Rhode Island 02917

1992 Schedule

Preseason
Aug. 8	at Indianapolis	6:30
Aug. 14	**San Diego**	7:00
Aug. 22	at Detroit	7:00
Aug. 29	vs. Green Bay at Milw.	7:00

Regular Season
Sept. 6	at Miami	4:00
Sept. 13	at Los Angeles Rams	1:00
Sept. 20	**Seattle**	1:00
Sept. 27	**Buffalo**	1:00
Oct. 4	at New York Jets	8:00
Oct. 11	**San Francisco**	1:00
Oct. 18	**Open Date**	
Oct. 25	**Cleveland**	4:00
Nov. 1	at Buffalo	1:00
Nov. 8	**New Orleans**	1:00
Nov. 15	at Indianapolis	1:00
Nov. 22	**New York Jets**	4:00
Nov. 29	at Atlanta	1:00
Dec. 6	**Indianapolis**	1:00
Dec. 13	at Kansas City	12:00
Dec. 20	at Cincinnati	1:00
Dec. 27	**Miami**	1:00

Patriots Coaching History

Boston 1960-1970
(218-251-9)
1960-61	Lou Saban*	7-12-0
1961-68	Mike Holovak	53-47-9
1969-70	Clive Rush**	5-16-0
1970-72	John Mazur***	9-21-0
1972	Phil Bengtson	1-4-0
1973-78	Chuck Fairbanks****	46-41-0
1978	Hank Bullough-Ron Erhardt#	0-1-0
1979-81	Ron Erhardt	21-27-0
1982-84	Ron Meyer##	18-16-0
1984-89	Raymond Berry	51-41-0
1990	Rod Rust	1-15-0
1991	Dick MacPherson	6-10-0

*Released after five games in 1961
**Released after seven games in 1970
***Resigned after nine games in 1972
****Suspended for final regular season game in 1978
#Co-coaches
##Released after eight games in 1984

Record Holders
Individual Records—Career
Category	Name	Performance
Rushing (Yds.)	Sam Cunningham, 1973-79, 1981-82	5,453
Passing (Yds.)	Steve Grogan, 1975-1990	26,886
Passing (TDs)	Steve Grogan, 1975-1990	182
Receiving (No.)	Stanley Morgan, 1977-1989	534
Receiving (Yds.)	Stanley Morgan, 1977-1989	10,352
Interceptions	Raymond Clayborn, 1977-1989	36
Punting (Avg.)	Rich Camarillo, 1981-87	42.6
Punt Return (Avg.)	Mack Herron, 1973-75	12.0
Kickoff Return (Avg.)	Horace Ivory, 1977-1981	27.6
Field Goals	Gino Cappelletti, 1960-1970	176
Touchdowns (Tot.)	Stanley Morgan, 1977-1989	68
Points	Gino Cappelletti, 1960-1970	1,130

Individual Records—Single Season
Category	Name	Performance
Rushing (Yds.)	Jim Nance, 1966	1,458
Passing (Yds.)	Vito (Babe) Parilli, 1964	3,465
Passing (TDs)	Vito (Babe) Parilli, 1964	31
Receiving (No.)	Stanley Morgan, 1986	84
Receiving (Yds.)	Stanley Morgan, 1986	1,491
Interceptions	Ron Hall, 1964	11
Punting (Avg.)	Rich Camarillo, 1983	44.6
Punt Return (Avg.)	Mack Herron, 1974	14.8
Kickoff Return (Avg.)	Raymond Clayborn, 1977	31.0
Field Goals	Tony Franklin, 1986	32
Touchdowns (Tot.)	Steve Grogan, 1976	13
	Stanley Morgan, 1979	13
Points	Gino Cappelletti, 1964	155

Individual Records—Single Game
Category	Name	Performance
Rushing (Yds.)	Tony Collins, 9-18-83	212
Passing (Yds.)	Tony Eason, 9-21-86	414
Passing (TDs)	Vito (Babe) Parilli, 11-15-64	5
	Vito (Babe) Parilli, 10-15-67	5
	Steve Grogan, 9-9-79	5
Receiving (No.)	Art Graham, 11-20-66	11
	Tony Collins, 11-29-87	11
Receiving (Yds.)	Stanley Morgan, 11-8-81	182
Interceptions	Many times	3
	Last time by Roland James, 10-23-83	
Field Goals	Gino Cappelletti, 10-4-64	6
Touchdowns (Tot.)	Many times	3
	Last time by Stanley Morgan, 9-21-86	
Points	Gino Cappelletti, 12-18-65	28

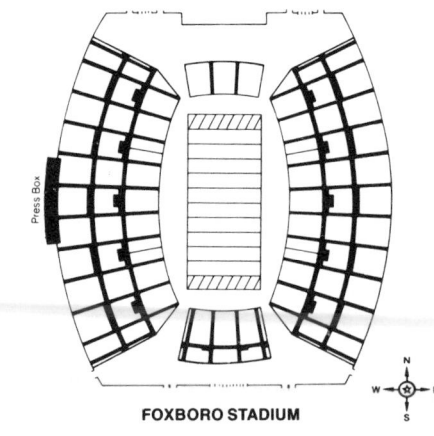

FOXBORO STADIUM

1991 Team Record
Preseason (1-3)

Date	Result		Opponents
8/3	L	7-28	at Green Bay
8/10	L	6-27	Washington
8/17	L	0-46	at Phoenix
8/24	W	24- 3	N.Y. Giants

Regular Season (6-10)

Date	Result		Opponents	Att.
9/1	W	16- 7	at Indianapolis	49,961
9/8	L	0-20	Cleveland	35,377
9/15	L	6-20	at Pittsburgh	53,703
9/22	W	24-20	Houston	30,702
9/29	L	10-24	at Phoenix	26,043
10/6	L	10-20	Miami	49,749
10/20	W	26-23	Minnesota (OT)	45,367
10/27	L	6- 9	Denver	43,994
11/3	L	17-22	at Buffalo	78,278
11/10	L	20-30	at Miami	56,065
11/17	L	21-28	N.Y. Jets	30,743
11/24	W	16-13	Buffalo	47,053
12/1	L	3-20	at Denver	67,116
12/8	W	23-17	Indianapolis (OT)	20,131
12/15	W	6- 3	at N.Y. Jets	55,689
12/22	L	7-29	at Cincinnati	46,394

(OT) Overtime

Score by Periods

Patriots	40	55	23	84	9	—	211
Opponents	53	122	32	98	0	—	305

Attendance
Home 303,116   Away 433,249   Total 736,365
Single-game home record, 61,457 (12-5-71)
Single-season home record, 482,572 (1986)

1991 Team Statistics

	Patriots	Opp.
Total First Downs	259	312
Rushing	93	94
Passing.	155	199
Penalty	11	19
Third Down: Made/Att.	72/213	95/228
Third Down: Pct.	33.8	41.7
Fourth Down: Made/Att.	6/13	4/14
Fourth Down: Pct.	46.2	28.6
Total Net Yards	4473	5431
Avg. Per Game	279.6	339.4
Total Plays	977	1050
Avg. Per Play	4.6	5.2
Net Yards Rushing	1467	1579
Avg. Per Game	91.7	98.7
Total Rushes	433	460
Net Yards Passing	3006	3852
Avg. Per Game	187.9	240.8
Sacked/Yards Lost	63/436	25/183
Gross Yards	3442	4035
Att./Completions	481/284	565/335
Completion Pct.	59.0	59.3
Had Intercepted	22	12
Punts/Avg.	82/39.0	69/42.2
Net Punting Avg.	34.6	36.2
Penalties/Yards Lost	97/667	83/608
Fumbles/Ball Lost	34/20	32/19
Touchdowns	22	31
Rushing	9	5
Passing.	11	25
Returns	2	1
Avg. Time of Possession	29:27	30:33

1991 Individual Statistics

Scoring

	TD R	TD P	TD Rt	PAT	FG	Saf	TP
Staurovsky	0	0	0	10/11	13/19	0	49
Baumann, Mia.-N.E.	0	0	0	15/16	9/12	0	42
Baumann, N.E.	0	0	0	9/10	7/10	0	30
Russell	4	0	0	0/0	0/0	0	24
Cook	0	3	0	0/0	0/0	0	18
Fryar	0	3	0	0/0	0/0	0	18
Vaughn	2	0	1	0/0	0/0	0	18
McMurtry	0	2	0	0/0	0/0	0	12
Stephens	2	0	0	0/0	0/0	0	12
Timpson	0	2	0	0/0	0/0	0	12
Childress	0	0	1	0/0	0/0	0	6
Coates	0	1	0	0/0	0/0	0	6
Millen	1	0	0	0/0	0/0	0	6
Patriots	9	11	2	19/21	20/29	0	211
Opponents	5	25	1	30/31	29/42	1	305

Passing

	Att.	Comp.	Yds.	Pct.	TD	Int.	Tkld.	Rate
Millen	409	246	3073	60.1	9	18	54/379	72.5
Hodson	68	36	345	52.9	1	4	9/57	47.7
Vaughn	2	1	13	50.0	1	0	0/0	110.4
Fryar	1	0	0	0	0	0	0/0	39.6
McCarthy	1	1	11	100.0	0	0	0/0	112.5
Patriots	481	284	3442	59.0	11	22	63/436	69.7
Opponents	565	335	4035	59.3	25	12	25/183	87.1

Rushing

	Att.	Yds.	Avg.	LG	TD
Russell	266	959	3.6	24	4
Stephens	63	163	2.6	13	2
Vaughn	31	146	4.7	23	2
Millen	31	92	3.0	14	1
Hunter	18	53	2.9	9	0
Allen	13	50	3.8	11	0
Fryar	2	11	5.5	9	0
Adams	2	3	1.5	2	0
Chilton	1	0	0.0	0	0
Hodson	4	0	0.0	1	0
Timpson	1	−4	−4.0	−4	0
Coates	1	−6	−6.0	−6	0
Patriots	433	1467	3.4	24	9
Opponents	460	1579	3.4	31	5

Receiving

	No.	Yds.	Avg.	LG	TD
Cook	82	808	9.9	49	3
Fryar	68	1014	14.9	56t	3
McMurtry	41	614	15.0	40	2
Timpson	25	471	18.8	60t	2
Russell	18	81	4.5	18	0
Stephens	16	119	7.4	24	0
Hunter	11	97	8.8	25	0
Coates	10	95	9.5	17	1
Vaughn	9	89	9.9	32	0
Carpenter	3	45	15.0	23	0
Allen	1	9	9.0	9	0
Patriots	284	3442	12.1	60t	11
Opponents	335	4035	12.0	65t	25

Interceptions

	No.	Yds.	Avg.	LG	TD
Hurst	3	21	7.0	21	0
Marion	2	33	16.5	33	0
Lippett	2	27	13.5	27	0
Henderson	2	2	1.0	2	0
Washington	2	0	0.0	0	0
Tippett	1	10	10.0	10	0
Patriots	12	93	7.8	33	0
Opponents	22	154	7.0	27	0

Punting

	No.	Yds.	Avg.	In 20	LG
McCarthy	66	2650	40.2	17	93
Wagner	14	548	39.1	0	54
Patriots	80	3198	39.9	17	93
Opponents	69	2909	42.2	16	71

Punt Returns

	No.	FC	Yds.	Avg.	LG	TD
Henderson	27	10	201	7.4	39	0
Fryar	2	4	10	5.0	10	0
Pool	1	0	0	0.0	0	0
Zackery	1	0	0	0.0	0	0
Patriots	31	14	211	6.8	39	0
Opponents	37	20	303	8.2	40	1

Kickoff Returns

	No.	Yds.	Avg.	LG	TD
Vaughn	34	717	21.1	99t	1
Allen	8	161	20.1	31	0
Martin	8	178	22.3	26	0
Hobby	2	0	0.0	0	0
Timpson	2	37	18.5	21	0
Coates	1	6	6.0	6	0
Rakoczy	1	9	9.0	9	0
Patriots	56	1108	19.8	99t	1
Opponents	51	850	16.7	49	0

Sacks

	No.
Tippett	8.5
Veris	4.0
Williams	3.5
Brown	3.0
Agnew	2.0
Hobby	2.0
Howard	1.0
Singleton	1.0
Patriots	25.0
Opponents	63.0

1992 Draft Choices

Round	Name	Pos.	College
1.	Eugene Chung	T	Virginia Tech
2.	Rod Smith	DB	Notre Dame
3.	Todd Collins	LB	Carson-Newman
	Kevin Turner	RB	Alabama
4.	Dion Lambert	DB	UCLA
	Darren Anderson	DB	Toledo
5.	Dwayne Sabb	LB	New Hampshire
6.	Tracy Boyd	G	Elizabeth City State
7.	Wayne Hawkins	WR	S.W. Minnesota
	Jim Gray	DT	West Virginia
8.	Scott Lockwood	RB	Southern California
	Sam Gash	RB	Penn State
9.	David Dixon	DT	Arizona State
10.	Turner Baur	TE	Stanford
	Steve Gordon	C	California
11.	Mike Petko	LB	Nebraska
12.	Freeman Baysinger	WR	Humboldt State

New England Patriots 1992 Veteran Roster

No.	Name	Pos.	Ht.	Wt.	Birth-date	NFL Exp.	College	Hometown	How Acq.	'91 Games/ Starts
92	Agnew, Ray	DE	6-3	272	12/9/67	3	North Carolina State	Winston-Salem, N.C.	D1b-'90	13/10
39	Allen, Marvin	RB	5-10	208	11/23/65	5	Tulane	Wichita Falls, Tex.	FA-'90	15/0
78	Armstrong, Bruce	T	6-4	284	9/7/65	6	Louisville	Miami, Fla.	D1-'87	16/16
8	Baumann, Charlie	K	6-1	203	8/25/67	2	West Virginia	Erie, Pa.	FA-'91	9/0*
43	Bergeson, Eric	S	6-0	194	1/1/66	2	Brigham Young	Provo, Utah	FA-'92	0*
59	†Brown, Vincent	LB	6-2	245	1/9/65	5	Mississippi Valley State	Decatur, Ga.	D2-'88	16/15
63	†Chilton, Gene	C	6-3	286	3/27/64	6	Texas	Houston, Tex.	FA-'90	16/16
87	Coates, Ben	TE	6-4	245	8/16/69	2	Livingstone College	Greenwood, S.C.	D5b-'91	16/2
85	Cook, Marv	TE	6-4	234	2/24/66	4	Iowa	West Branch, Iowa	D3a-'89	16/16
88	Dykes, Hart Lee	WR	6-4	218	9/2/66	3	Oklahoma State	Bay City, Tex.	D1-'89	0*
80	Fryar, Irving	WR	6-0	200	9/28/62	9	Nebraska	Mount Holly, N.J.	D1-'84	16/15
91	Gannon, Chris	DE	6-6	260	1/20/66	4	Southwestern Louisiana	Orange Park, Fla.	PB(SD)-'90#	8/0
72	Goad, Tim	NT	6-3	280	2/28/66	5	North Carolina	Stuart, Va.	D4a-'88	16/15
41	†Gordon, Tim	S	6-0	188	5/7/65	6	Tulsa	Ardmore, Okla.	FA-'90	11/7
77	Harlow, Pat	T	6-6	290	3/16/69	2	Southern California	Norco, Calif.	D1a-'91	16/16
36	Henderson, Jerome	CB	5-10	189	8/8/69	2	Clemson	Statesville, N.C.	D2-'91	16/1
60	Hobby, Marion	DE	6-4	277	11/7/66	3	Tennessee	Birmingham, Ala.	FA-'90	15/1
13	Hodson, Tom	QB	6-3	195	1/28/67	3	Louisiana State	Matthews, La.	D3-'90	16/3
99	Howard, David	LB	6-1	230	12/8/61	8	Long Beach State	Long Beach, Calif.	T(Dall)-'91	16/5
45	Hunter, Ivy Joe	RB	6-1	248	11/16/66	4	Kentucky	Gainesville, Fla.	PB(Ind)-'91#	13/11
37	Hurst, Maurice	CB	5-10	185	9/17/67	4	Southern	New Orleans, La.	D4a-'89	15/14
50	Jarostchuk, Ilia	LB	6-3	245	8/1/64	5	New Hampshire	Utica, N.Y.	FA-'91	0*
82	Johnson, Alex	WR	5-9	167	8/18/68	2	Miami	West Covina, Calif.	PB(Hou)-'92#	5/0*
26	Key, David	S	5-10	198	3/27/68	2	Michigan	Columbus, Ohio	D6-'91	3/0
42	†Lippett, Ronnie	CB	5-11	180	12/10/60	9	Miami	Sebring, Fla.	D8-'83	16/13
51	Lockhart, Eugene	LB	6-2	233	3/8/61	9	Houston	Crockett, Tex.	T(Dall)-'91	16/13
31	†Marion, Fred	S	6-2	191	1/2/59	11	Miami	Gainesville, Fla.	D5-'82	11/11
11	McCarthy, Shawn	P	6-6	227	2/22/68	2	Purdue	Freemont, Ohio	FA-'91	13/0
58	McGovern, Rob	LB	6-2	234	10/1/66	4	Holy Cross	Oradell, N.J.	PB(Pitt)-'92#	15/0*
86	†McMurtry, Greg	WR	6-2	207	10/15/67	3	Michigan	Brockton, Mass.	D3-'90	15/13
7	†Millen, Hugh	QB	6-5	216	11/22/63	5	Washington	Seattle, Wash.	PB(Atl)-'91#	13/13
27	†Pool, David	CB	5-9	182	12/20/66	3	Carson-Newman	Cincinnati, Ohio	FA-'91	15/3
71	Rakoczy, Gregg	C-G	6-5	280	5/18/65	6	Miami	Medford Lakes, N.J.	FA-'91	5/2
61	t-Redding, Reggie	G	6-4	305	9/22/68	2	Cal State-Fullerton	Cincinnati, Ohio	T(Atl)-'92	13/0*
52	†Rembert, Johnny	LB	6-3	234	1/19/61	10	Clemson	DeSoto, Fla.	D4-'83	12/1
48	Robbins, Randy	S	6-2	189	9/14/62	9	Arizona	Casa Grande, Ariz.	PB(Den)-'92#	16/2*
32	Russell, Leonard	RB	6-2	235	11/17/69	2	Arizona State	Long Beach, Calif.	D1b-'91	16/15
55	Singleton, Chris	LB	6-2	247	2/20/67	3	Arizona	Parsippany, N.J.	D1a-'90	12/11
76	Smerlas, Fred	NT	6-4	291	4/8/57	14	Boston College	Waltham, Mass.	FA-'91	16/1
44	Stephens, John	RB	6-1	215	2/23/66	5	Northwestern Louisiana	Springhill, La.	D1-'88	14/3
53	Tardits, Richard	LB	6-2	235	7/30/65	2	Georgia	Biarritz, France	FA-'90	16/0
83	†Timpson, Michael	WR	5-10	175	6/6/67	3	Penn State	Hialeah, Fla.	D4-'89	16/2
56	Tippett, Andre	LB	6-3	241	12/27/59	10	Iowa	Newark, N.J.	D2b-'82	16/16
24	Vaughn, Jon	RB	5-9	203	3/12/70	2	Michigan	Florissant, Mo.	D5a-'91	16/2
90	†Veris, Garin	DE	6-4	255	2/27/63	7	Stanford	Chillicothe, Ohio	D2-'85	16/4
21	†Washington, Mickey	CB	5-9	187	7/8/68	3	Texas A&M	Beaumont, Tex.	FA-'90	16/4
96	Williams, Brent	DE	6-4	275	10/23/64	7	Toledo	Flint, Mich.	D7b-'86	16/16
75	Williams, Larry	G	6-5	294	7/3/63	5	Notre Dame	Santa Ana, Calif.	PB(NO)-'92#	6/2*

* Baumann played 2 games with Miami in '91, 7 with New England; Bergeson last active with Atlanta in '90; Dykes and Jarostchuk missed '91 season due to injury; Johnson played 5 games with Houston; McGovern played 15 games with Pittsburgh; Redding played 13 games with Atlanta; Robbins played 16 games with Denver; Williams played 6 games with New Orleans.

† Option playout; subject to developments.

t- Patriots traded for Redding (Atlanta).

Plan B unconditional free agent.

Players lost through Plan B (10): WR Rob Carpenter (NYJ; 8 games in '91), G-T Stan Clayton (Pitt; 0), S Harry Colon (Det; 16), G Elbert Crawford (Den; 16), WR Millard Hamilton (NYG; 0), G Jon Melander (Cin; 10), LB Ed Reynolds (NYG; 9), K Jason Staurovsky (NYJ; 9), T David Viaene (GB; 0), S Tony Zackery (Clev; 16).

Also played with Patriots in '91—RB George Adams (2 games), G Fred Childress (15), WR Sean Foster (active for 1 game but did not play), S Darrell Fullington (5), LB Richard Harvey (1), WR Sammy Martin (4), DE Sean Smith (2), WR Gene Taylor (1), G Danny Villa (10), P Bryan Wagner (3).

COACHING STAFF

Head Coach,
Dick MacPherson

Pro Career: Led New England to 6-10 record in his first season as the Patriots' head coach. Named the Patriots' eleventh head coach on January 7, 1991. Accepted post after serving 10 years (1981-90) as head coach at Syracuse University. While at Syracuse, MacPherson compiled a record of 66-46-4 (.586) and appeared in five bowl games, including the 1990 Aloha Bowl. Was linebackers coach with Cleveland Browns under Sam Rutigliano from 1978-80. Prior to that, was head coach at Massachusetts and led Minutemen to 45-27-1 record in seven years (1971-77). Was defensive backs coach and later defensive coordinator with Denver Broncos from 1967-70. Before that, was assistant coach at Maryland (1966) and Cincinnati (1961-65). Began coaching career at Massachusetts as freshman coach from 1959-60. Compiled collegiate coaching record of 111-73-5 (.600). Career record: 6-10.

Background: Entered Maine Maritime Academy in 1948, but left after two years to join the Air Force. Spent four years in the service, then enrolled at Springfield (Massachusetts) College and received bachelor of science degree in 1958. Was center on football team at Springfield and earned three letters. Was standout on 1956 undefeated squad and was team captain as a senior. Received master's degree in 1959 from Illinois.

Personal: Born November 4, 1930, Old Town, Maine. Dick and his wife, Sandra, live in Foxboro, Mass., and have two daughters—Maureen and Janet.

Assistant Coaches

Joe Collier, defensive coordinator; born June 7, 1932, Rock Island, Ill., lives in Foxboro, Mass. Defensive end Northwestern 1950-53. No pro playing experience. Pro coach: Boston Patriots 1960-61, Buffalo Bills 1962-68 (head coach 1966-68), Denver Broncos 1969-88, rejoined Patriots in 1991.

Joel Collier, assistant running backs-assistant wide receivers; born December 25, 1963, Buffalo, N.Y., lives in Foxboro, Mass. Linebacker Northern Colorado 1983-86. No pro playing experience. College coach: Syracuse 1988-89 (graduate assistant). Pro coach: Tampa Bay Buccaneers 1990, joined Patriots in 1991.

Dick Coury, offensive coordinator; born September 29, 1929, Athens, Ohio, lives in Foxboro, Mass. Quarterback Notre Dame 1950-54. No pro playing experience. College coach: Southern California 1967-69, Cal State-Fullerton 1970-71. Pro coach: Denver Broncos 1972-73, Portland Storm (WFL) 1974, San Diego Chargers 1975, Philadelphia Eagles 1976-82, Boston/New Orleans/Portland Breakers (USFL) 1983-85 (head coach), Los Angeles Rams 1986-90, joined Patriots in 1991.

Ivan Fears, wide receivers; born November 15, 1954, Portsmouth, Va., lives in Franklin, Mass. Running back William and Mary 1973-76. No pro playing experience. College coach: William and Mary 1977-80, Syracuse 1981-90. Pro coach: Joined Patriots in 1991.

Norm Gerber, inside linebackers; born August 11, 1935, Manchester, N.H., lives in Hopedale, Mass. Tackle Connecticut 1953-56. No pro playing experience. College coach: Central Connecticut State 1965-69, Columbia 1969-73, Boston College 1974-78, Dartmouth 1978-80, Syracuse 1980-90. Pro coach: Joined Patriots in 1991.

Bobby Grier, running backs; born November 10, 1942, Detroit, Mich., lives in Holliston, Mass. Running back Iowa 1961-64. No pro playing experience. College coach: Eastern Michigan 1974-77, Boston College 1978-80. Pro coach: New England Patriots 1981-91 (scout 1982-84).

New England Patriots 1992 First-Year Roster

Name	Pos.	Ht.	Wt.	Birth-date	College	Hometown	How Acq.
Anderson, Darren	CB	5-10	179	1/11/69	Toledo	Cincinnati, Ohio	D4b
Austin, Randy (1)	TE	6-2	245	12/14/67	UCLA	Granada Hills, Calif.	FA
Baur, Turner	TE	6-4	247	11/19/68	Stanford	St. Louis, Mo.	D10a
Baysinger, Freeman	WR	5-9	164	12/22/69	Humboldt State	Oakland, Calif.	D12
Bowles, Scott (1)	G-T	6-5	280	12/20/67	North Texas State	Wichita Falls, Tex.	FA
Boyd, Tracy	G	6-4	296	8/27/67	Elizabeth City State	Crowley, La.	D6
Chung, Eugene	G	6-4	295	6/14/69	Virginia Tech	Oakton, Va.	D1
Clark, Reggie (1)	LB	6-2	226	10/17/67	North Carolina	Charlotte, N.C.	FA-'91
Clark, Waldy	CB	5-11	183	4/21/69	Boston College	Cambridge, Mass.	FA
Collins, Todd	LB	6-2	242	5/27/70	Carson-Newman	New Market, Tenn.	D3a
Dixon, David	DT	6-4	320	1/5/69	Arizona State	Auckland, New Zealand	D9
Esty, Chuck	G	6-5	285	12/30/68	St. Lawrence	Framingham, Mass.	FA
Gash, Sam	RB	5-11	224	3/7/69	Penn State	Hendersonville, N.C.	D8b
Gordon, Steve	C	6-3	279	4/14/69	California	Nevada City, Calif.	D10b
Gray, Jim	DT	6-2	285	7/5/69	West Virginia	West Mifflin, Pa.	D7b
Hawkins, Wayne	WR	5-10	176	10/27/69	Southwest Minnesota	Columbia Heights, Minn.	D7a
Lahr, Greg	T	6-5	290	12/9/69	Kentucky	Columbus, Ohio	FA
Lambert, Dion	CB	6-0	185	2/12/69	UCLA	Lakeview Terrace, Calif.	D4a
Lockwood, Scott	RB	5-10	196	3/23/68	Southern California	Pasadena, Calif.	D8a
Means, Kelvin	WR	6-0	180	10/27/69	Fresno State	Compton, Calif.	FA
Petko, Mike	LB	6-2	232	10/2/69	Nebraska	Anaheim, Calif.	D11
Price, William	CB	6-1	200	3/30/70	Kansas State	Akron, Ohio	FA
Sabb, Dwayne	LB	6-4	248	10/9/69	New Hampshire	Union, N.J.	D5
Smith, Jeff (1)	WR	6-4	180	5/28/63	Cal Poly-SLO	Poway, Calif.	FA
Smith, Rod	CB	5-11	187	3/12/70	Notre Dame	Roseville, Minn.	D2
Stephens, Calvin (1)	G	6-2	285	10/25/67	South Carolina	Kings Mountain, N.C.	D3-'91
Tappin, John	WR	5-8	158	6/16/70	N.W. Louisiana	Bastrop, La.	FA
Tucker, Greg	S	6-2	205	12/23/68	Northern Colorado	Colorado Springs, Colo.	FA
Turner, Kevin	RB	6-0	224	6/12/69	Alabama	Prattville, Ala.	D3b
Whitley, Kevin	CB	5-10	190	2/26/70	Georgia Southern	Lakeside, Ga.	FA
Wilkes, Troy	LB	6-4	230	9/16/68	C.W. Post	Westmoreland, N.H.	FA
Zolak, Scott (1)	QB	6-5	222	12/13/67	Maryland	Monongahela, Pa.	D4-'91

The term NFL Rookie is defined as a player who is in his first season of professional football and has not been on the roster of another professional football team for any regular-season or postseason games. A Rookie is designated by an "R" on NFL rosters. Players who have been active in another professional football league or players who have NFL experience, including either preseason training camp or being on an active roster for fewer than three regular-season or postseason games, are termed NFL First-Year Players. An NFL First-Year Player is designated by a "1" on NFL rosters. Thereafter, a player on an NFL active roster for at least three regular-season or postseason games is credited with an additional year of NFL playing experience.

NOTES

_____

_____

_____

_____

_____

_____

_____

_____

_____

Rod Humenuik, offensive line; born June 17, 1938, Detroit, Mich., lives in Foxboro, Mass. Guard Southern California 1956-58. Pro guard Winnipeg Blue Bombers (CFL) 1960-62. College coach: Fullerton, Calif., J.C. 1964-65, Southern California 1966-70, Cal State-Northridge 1971-72 (head coach). Pro coach: Toronto Argonauts (CFL) 1973-74, Cleveland Browns 1975-82, Kansas City Chiefs 1983-84, New England Patriots 1985-88, New York Jets 1989, rejoined Patriots in 1990.

Stan Jones, defensive line; born November 24, 1931, Altoona, Pa., lives in Walpole, Mass. Tackle Maryland 1949-53. Pro guard/defensive tackle Chicago Bears 1954-65, Washington Redskins 1966. Inducted into Pro Football Hall of Fame in 1991. Pro coach: Denver Broncos 1967-71, 1976-88, Buffalo Bills 1972-75, Cleveland Browns 1989-90, joined Patriots in 1991.

Myrel Moore, outside linebackers; born March 9, 1934, Sebastopol, Calif., lives in Foxboro, Mass. Tight end/linebacker California-Davis 1954-57. Pro linebacker Washington Redskins 1958-59. College coach: Santa Ana, Calif., J.C. 1959, California 1963. Pro coach: Denver Broncos 1972, 1981-88 (scout 1981), Oakland Raiders 1978-80, joined Patriots in 1991.

Dante Scarnecchia, tight ends-special teams; born February 15, 1948, Los Angeles, Calif., lives in Wrentham, Mass. Center/guard California Western 1968-70. No pro playing experience. College coach: California Western (now U.S. International) 1970-72, Iowa State 1973, Southern Methodist 1975-76, 1980-81, Pacific 1977-78, Northern Arizona 1979. Pro coach: New England Patriots 1982-89, Indianapolis Colts 1990, rejoined Patriots in 1991.

Dave Uyrus, assistant defensive line-assistant special teams; born August 19, 1952, Adams, Mass., lives in Wrentham, Mass. Tackle Middlebury College 1970-74. No pro playing experience. College coach: Middlebury College 1974-76, Massachusetts 1977-78, American International 1979, Merchant Marine Academy 1980, Syracuse 1981-90. Pro coach: Joined Patriots in 1991.

Charlie West, defensive backs; born August 31, 1946, Terrell, Tex., lives in North Attleboro, Mass. Defensive back Texas-El Paso 1965-68. Pro defensive back Minnesota Vikings 1968-73, Detroit Lions 1974-77, Denver Broncos 1978-79. College coach: Macalester College 1981, California 1982, Howard 1989. Pro coach: Denver Broncos 1983-88, joined Patriots in 1991.

American Football Conference
Eastern Division

Team Colors: Kelly Green and White

1000 Fulton Avenue
Hempstead, New York 11550
Telephone: (516) 538-6600

Club Officials

Chairman of the Board: Leon Hess
President: Steve Gutman
Vice President & General Manager:
  Dick Steinberg
Director of Player Personnel: Dick Haley
Pro Personnel Director: Jim Royer
Talent Scouts: Joe Collins, Don Grammer,
  Sid Hall, Ron Nay, Marv Sunderland
College Scouting Assistant: John Griffin
Director of Public Relations: Frank Ramos
Public Relations Assistant: Eileen Walker
Public Relations Assistant: Brooks Thomas
Comptroller: Mike Gerstle
Director of Operations: Mike Kensil
Director of Business Relations: Bob Parente
Ticket Manager: Gerry Parravano
Video Director: Jim Pons
Assistant Video Director: John Seiter
Trainer: Bob Reese
Assistant Trainers: Pepper Burruss, Joe Patten
Equipment Manager: Bill Hampton
Assistant Equipment Managers: Bill Hampton, Jr.,
  Mickey Rendine

Stadium: Giants Stadium • **Capacity:** 76,891
  East Rutherford, New Jersey 07073

Playing Surface: AstroTurf

Training Center: 1000 Fulton Avenue
  Hempstead, New York 11550
  (516) 538-6600

1992 Schedule

Preseason
Aug. 1	vs. Philadelphia at Canton	3:00
Aug. 8	**Washington**	8:00
Aug. 16	vs. Green Bay at Madison	3:00
Aug. 22	**New York Giants**	8:00
Aug. 27	at Philadelphia	7:30

Regular Season
Sept. 6	at Atlanta	1:00
Sept. 13	at Pittsburgh	4:00
Sept. 20	**San Francisco**	1:00
Sept. 27	at Los Angeles Rams	1:00
Oct. 4	**New England**	8:00
Oct. 11	at Indianapolis	3:00
Oct. 18	**Open Date**	
Oct. 26	**Buffalo** (Monday)	9:00
Nov. 1	**Miami**	1:00
Nov. 8	at Denver	2:00
Nov. 15	**Cincinnati**	1:00
Nov. 22	at New England	4:00
Nov. 29	**Kansas City**	1:00
Dec. 6	at Buffalo	1:00
Dec. 13	**Indianapolis**	1:00
Dec. 20	at Miami	8:00
Dec. 26	**New Orleans** (Saturday)	12:30

Jets Coaching History

New York Titans 1960-62
(214-257-8)
1960-61	Sammy Baugh	14-14-0
1962	Clyde (Bulldog) Turner	5-9-0
1963-73	Weeb Ewbank	73-78-6
1974-75	Charley Winner*	9-14-0
1975	Ken Shipp	1-4-0
1976	Lou Holtz**	3-10-0
1976	Mike Holovak	0-1-0
1977-82	Walt Michaels	41-49-1
1983-89	Joe Walton	54-59-1
1990-91	Bruce Coslet	14-19-0

*Released after nine games in 1975
**Resigned after 13 games in 1976

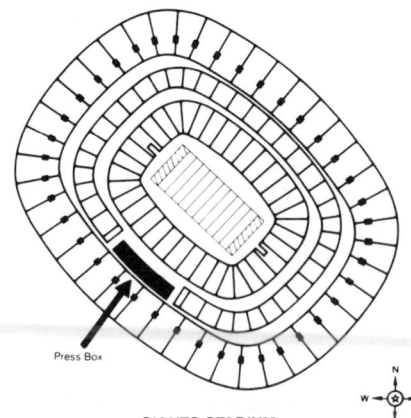

Press Box

GIANTS STADIUM

Record Holders
Individual Records—Career
Category	Name	Performance
Rushing (Yds.)	Freeman McNeil, 1981-1991	7,904
Passing (Yds.)	Joe Namath, 1965-1976	27,057
Passing (TDs)	Joe Namath, 1965-1976	170
Receiving (No.)	Don Maynard, 1960-1972	627
Receiving (Yds.)	Don Maynard, 1960-1972	11,732
Interceptions	Bill Baird, 1963-69	34
Punting (Avg.)	Curley Johnson, 1961-68	42.8
Punt Return (Avg.)	Dick Christy, 1961-63	16.2
Kickoff Return (Avg.)	Bobby Humphery, 1984-89	22.8
Field Goals	Pat Leahy, 1974-1991	304
Touchdowns (Tot.)	Don Maynard, 1960-1972	88
Points	Pat Leahy, 1974-1991	1,470

Individual Records—Single Season
Category	Name	Performance
Rushing (Yds.)	Freeman McNeil, 1985	1,331
Passing (Yds.)	Joe Namath, 1967	4,007
Passing (TDs)	Al Dorow, 1960	26
	Joe Namath, 1967	26
Receiving (No.)	Al Toon, 1988	93
Receiving (Yds.)	Don Maynard, 1967	1,434
Interceptions	Dainard Paulson, 1964	12
Punting (Avg.)	Curley Johnson, 1965	45.3
Punt Return (Avg.)	Dick Christy, 1961	21.3
Kickoff Return (Avg.)	Bobby Humphery, 1984	30.7
Field Goals	Jim Turner, 1968	34
Touchdowns (Tot.)	Art Powell, 1960	14
	Don Maynard, 1965	14
	Emerson Boozer, 1972	14
Points	Jim Turner, 1968	145

Individual Records—Single Game
Category	Name	Performance
Rushing (Yds.)	Freeman McNeil, 9-15-85	192
Passing (Yds.)	Joe Namath, 9-24-72	496
Passing (TDs)	Joe Namath, 9-24-72	6
Receiving (No.)	Clark Gaines, 9-21-80	17
Receiving (Yds.)	Don Maynard, 11-17-68	228
Interceptions	Many times	3
	Last time by Erik McMillan, 10-23-88	
Field Goals	Jim Turner, 11-3-68	6
	Bobby Howfield, 12-3-72	6
Touchdowns (Tot.)	Wesley Walker, 9-21-86	4
Points	Wesley Walker, 9-21-86	24

1991 Team Record

Preseason (1-3)

Date	Result		Opponents
8/3	L	10-24	Philadelphia
8/10	L	10-19	vs. Kansas City at St. Louis
8/17	L	10-24	at N.Y. Giants
8/24	W	13- 9	vs. Washington at Columbia, S.C.

Regular Season (8-8)

Date	Result		Opponents	Att.
9/1	W	16-13	Tampa Bay	61,204
9/8	L	13-20	at Seattle	56,770
9/15	L	20-23	Buffalo	65,309
9/23	L	13-19	at Chicago (OT)	65,255
9/29	W	41-23	Miami	71,170
10/6	W	17-14	at Cleveland	71,042
10/13	L	20-23	Houston	70,758
10/20	W	17- 6	at Indianapolis	53,025
11/3	W	19-16	Green Bay (OT)	67,435
11/10	L	27-28	Indianapolis	44,792
11/17	W	28-21	at New England	30,743
11/24	W	24- 3	San Diego	59,025
12/1	L	13-24	at Buffalo	80,243
12/8	L	20-34	at Detroit	69,304
12/15	L	3- 6	New England	55,689
12/22	W	23-20	at Miami (OT)	69,636

(OT) Overtime

Postseason (0-1)

Date	Result		Opponent	Att.
12/29	L	10-17	at Houston	62,838

Score by Periods

Jets	93	84	53	78	6	—	314
Opponents	36	78	91	82	6	—	293

Attendance

Home 495,382   Away 496,018   Total 991,400
Single-game home record, 74,975 (12-2-84)
Single-season home record, 541,832 (1985)

1991 Team Statistics

	Jets	Opp.
Total First Downs	331	298
Rushing	133	94
Passing	169	185
Penalty	29	19
Third Down: Made/Att.	81/214	71/193
Third Down: Pct.	37.9	36.8
Fourth Down: Made/Att.	12/21	10/19
Fourth Down: Pct.	57.1	52.6
Total Net Yards	5316	4981
Avg. Per Game	332.3	311.3
Total Plays	1059	954
Avg. Per Play	5.0	5.2
Net Yards Rushing	2160	1442
Avg. Per Game	135.0	90.1
Total Rushes	523	379
Net Yards Passing	3156	3539
Avg. Per Game	197.3	221.2
Sacked/Yards Lost	33/273	35/226
Gross Yards	3429	3765
Att./Completions	503/295	540/331
Completion Pct.	58.6	61.3
Had Intercepted	12	18
Punts/Avg.	64/39.4	56/40.6
Net Punting Avg.	34.6	35.6
Penalties/Yards Lost	103/814	93/774
Fumbles/Ball Lost	28/13	38/19
Touchdowns	32	31
Rushing	17	8
Passing	12	21
Returns	3	2
Avg. Time of Possession	33:25	26:35

1991 Individual Statistics

Scoring

	TD R	TD P	TD Rt	PAT	FG	Saf	TP
Leahy	0	0	0	30/30	26/37	0	108
Baxter	11	0	0	0/0	0/0	0	66
Burkett	0	4	1	0/0	0/0	0	30
Moore	0	5	0	0/0	0/0	0	30
Thomas	3	1	0	0/0	0/0	0	24
Allegre, NYG-NYJ	0	0	0	7/7	5/6	0	22
Allegre, Jets	0	0	0	2/2	3/4	0	11
McMillan	0	0	2	0/0	0/0	0	12
McNeil	2	0	0	0/0	0/0	0	12
Brown	1	0	0	0/0	0/0	0	6
Mathis	0	1	0	0/0	0/0	0	6
Matich	0	1	0	0/0	0/0	0	6
Aguiar	0	0	0	0/0	1/2	0	3
Jets	17	12	3	32/32	30/43	0	314
Opponents	8	21	2	29/30	26/38	0	293

Passing

	Att.	Comp.	Yds.	Pct.	TD	Int.	Tkld.	Rate
O'Brien	489	287	3300	58.7	10	11	33/273	76.6
Taylor	10	5	76	50.0	1	1	0/0	69.2
Nagle	2	1	10	50.0	0	0	0/0	64.6
Thomas	1	1	16	100.0	1	0	0/0	158.3
Toon	1	1	27	100.0	0	0	0/0	118.8
Jets	503	295	3429	58.6	12	12	33/273	77.4
Opponents	540	331	3765	61.3	21	18	35/226	81.3

Rushing

	Att.	Yds.	Avg.	LG	TD
Thomas	189	728	3.9	25	3
Baxter	184	666	3.6	31	11
Hector	62	345	5.6	47	0
McNeil	51	300	5.9	58	2
O'Brien	23	60	2.6	13	0
Taylor	7	23	3.3	13	0
Mathis	1	19	19.0	19	0
Aguiar	1	18	18.0	18	0
Brown	3	4	1.3	2	1
Nagle	1	-1	-1.0	-1	0
Burkett	1	-2	-2.0	-2	0
Jets	523	2160	4.1	58	17
Opponents	379	1442	3.8	51t	8

Receiving

	No.	Yds.	Avg.	LG	TD
Toon	74	963	13.0	32	0
Moore	70	987	14.1	53	5
Thomas	30	195	6.5	18	1
Mathis	28	329	11.8	39	1
Burkett	23	327	14.2	50t	4
Dressel	17	122	7.2	22	0
Boyer	16	153	9.6	22	0
Baxter	12	124	10.3	34	0
McNeil	7	56	8.0	13	0
Hector	7	51	7.3	16	0
Whisenhunt	4	34	8.5	16	0
Dawkins	3	38	12.7	24	0
Matich	3	23	7.7	14	1
O'Brien	1	27	27.0	27	0
Jets	295	3429	11.6	53	12
Opponents	331	3765	11.4	73t	21

Interceptions

	No.	Yds.	Avg.	LG	TD
Brim	4	52	13.0	24	0
McMillan	3	168	56.0	83t	2
Hasty	3	39	13.0	39	0
J. Kelly	2	6	3.0	6	0
Mersereau	2	0	0.0	0	0
Young	1	15	15.0	15	0
Clifton	1	3	3.0	3	0
B. Washington	1	0	0.0	0	0
Kors	1	0	0.0	0	0
Jets	18	283	15.7	83t	2
Opponents	12	105	8.8	40	0

Punting

	No.	Yds.	Avg.	In 20	LG
Aguiar	64	2521	39.4	14	61
Jets	64	2521	39.4	14	61
Opponents	56	2271	40.6	15	57

Punt Returns

	No.	FC	Yds.	Avg.	LG	TD
Mathis	23	10	157	6.8	25	0
Jets	23	10	157	6.8	25	0
Opponents	29	13	164	5.7	21	0

Kickoff Returns

	No.	Yds.	Avg.	LG	TD
Mathis	29	599	20.7	50	0
Brown	10	100	10.0	31	0
Hector	8	172	21.5	53	0
Odegard	6	106	17.7	32	0
Dawkins	2	22	11.0	12	0
Boyer	1	0	0.0	0	0
Dressel	1	0	0.0	0	0
P. Kelly	1	4	4.0	4	0
Jets	58	1003	17.3	53	0
Opponents	60	921	15.4	88t	1

Sacks

	No.
Lageman	10.0
Byrd	7.0
M. Washington	6.0
Mersereau	2.0
Pickel	2.0
B. Washington	2.0
Brim	1.0
Clifton	1.0
Davis	1.0
Houston	1.0
Lewis	1.0
McMillan	1.0
Jets	35.0
Opponents	33.0

1992 Draft Choices

Round	Name	Pos.	College
1.	Johnny Mitchell	TE	Nebraska
2.	Kurt Barber	LB	Southern California
3.	Siupeli Malamala	T	Washington
4.	Keo Coleman	LB	Mississippi State
5.	Cal Dixon	C	Florida
6.	Glenn Cadrez	LB	Houston
	Jeff Blake	QB	East Carolina
8.	Vincent Brownlee	WR	Mississippi
10.	Mario Johnson	DT	Missouri
11.	Eric Boles	WR	Central Washington

New York Jets 1992 Veteran Roster

No.	Name	Pos.	Ht.	Wt.	Birth-date	NFL Exp.	College	Hometown	How Acq.	'91 Games/ Starts
4	Aguiar, Louie	P	6-2	200	6/30/66	2	Utah State	Livermore, Calif.	FA-'91	16/0
2	Allegre, Raul	K	5-10	167	6/15/59	10	Texas	Shelton, Wash.	FA-'91	1/0
30	Baxter, Brad	RB	6-1	235	5/5/67	3	Alabama State	Slocomb, Ala.	FA-'89	16/14
46	Beach, Pat	TE	6-4	250	12/28/59	10	Washington State	Pullman, Wash.	PB(Ind)-'92#	12/10*
80	†Boyer, Mark	TE	6-4	242	9/16/62	8	Southern California	Huntington Beach, Calif.	PB(Ind)-'90#	11/10
43	Brim, Mike	CB	6-0	192	1/23/66	5	Virginia Union	Danville, Va.	PB(Minn)-'91#	16/12
29	Brown, A.B.	RB	5-9	215	12/4/65	3	West Virginia	Salem, N.J.	D8-'89	9/0
87	Burkett, Chris	WR	6-4	200	8/21/62	8	Jackson State	Collins, Miss.	FA-'89	15/1
90	Byrd, Dennis	DT	6-5	266	10/5/66	4	Tulsa	Mustang, Okla.	D2-'89	16/16
66	†Cadigan, Dave	G	6-4	285	4/6/65	5	Southern California	Newport Beach, Calif.	D1-'88	15/10
83	Carpenter, Rob	WR	6-2	215	8/1/68	2	Syracuse	Amityville, N.Y.	PB(NE)-'92#	8/1*
28	Chaffey, Pat	RB	6-1	218	4/19/67	2	Oregon State	North Marion, Ore.	FA-'92	14/2*
59	Clifton, Kyle	LB	6-4	236	8/23/62	9	Texas Christian	Bridgeport, Tex.	D3-'84	16/16
69	Criswell, Jeff	T	6-7	291	3/7/64	6	Graceland	Searsboro, Iowa	FA-'88	16/16
89	Dawkins, Dale	WR	6-1	190	10/30/66	3	Miami	Vero Beach, Fla.	D9-'90	15/0
62	†Duffy, Roger	C	6-3	285	7/16/67	3	Penn State	Canton, Ohio	D8-'90	12/0
75	Eatman, Irv	T	6-7	298	1/1/61	7	UCLA	Dayton, Ohio	T(KC)-'91	16/16
36	Fishback, Joe	S	5-11	200	11/29/67	2	Carson-Newman	Knoxville, Tenn.	PB(Atl)-'92#	14/0*
91	†Frase, Paul	DE-DT	6-5	270	5/5/65	4	Syracuse	Barrington, N.H.	D6-'88	16/2
92	Gardner, Donnie	DE	6-3	260	2/17/68	2	Kentucky	Louisville, Ky.	PB(Mia)-'92#	10/0*
96	Gunn, Mark	DE	6-5	292	7/24/68	2	Pittsburgh	Cleveland, Ohio	D4-'91	15/1
79	Haight, Mike	G-T	6-4	291	10/6/62	7	Iowa	Dyersville, Iowa	D1-'86	7/6
61	Hart, Roy	DT	6-0	285	7/10/65	2	South Carolina	Tifton, Ga.	PB(Raid)-'92#	1/0
40	Hasty, James	CB	6-0	201	5/23/65	5	Washington State	Seattle, Wash.	D3b-'88	16/16
34	†Hector, Johnny	RB	5-11	214	11/26/60	10	Texas A&M	New Iberia, La.	D2-'83	14/1
55	Houston, Bobby	LB	6-2	235	10/26/67	2	North Carolina State	Hyattsville, Md.	PB(Atl)-'91#	14/0
95	Johnson, Troy	LB	6-2	236	11/10/64	5	Oklahoma	Houston, Tex.	W(Chi)-'90	16/0
58	Kelly, Joe	LB	6-2	235	12/11/64	7	Washington	Los Angeles, Calif.	T(Cin)-'90	16/12
82	Kelly, Pat	TE	6-6	252	10/29/65	2	Syracuse	Webster, N.Y.	PB(Den)-'90#	8/0
25	Kors, R.J.	S	6-0	195	6/27/66	2	Long Beach State	Woodland Hills, Calif.	PB(Sea)-'91#	16/0
56	Lageman, Jeff	DE	6-5	266	7/18/67	4	Virginia	Great Falls, Va.	D1-'89	16/16
5	Leahy, Pat	K	6-0	200	3/19/51	19	St. Louis	St. Louis, Mo.	FA-'74	15/0
57	Lewis, Mo	LB	6-3	240	10/21/69	2	Georgia	Peachtree, Ga.	D3-'91	16/15
81	Mathis, Terance	WR-KR	5-10	170	6/7/67	3	New Mexico	Stone Mountain, Ga.	D6-'90	16/1
22	McMillan, Erik	S	6-2	200	5/3/65	5	Missouri	Silver Spring, Md.	D3a-'88	16/6
24	†McNeil, Freeman	RB	5-11	208	4/22/59	12	UCLA	Carson, Calif.	D1-'81	13/1
94	Mersereau, Scott	DT	6-3	275	4/8/65	6	Southern Connecticut	Riverhead, N.Y.	FA-'87	13/13
72	Miller, Brett	T	6-7	286	10/2/58	10	Iowa	Glendale, Calif.	PB(SD)-'90#	15/0
85	Moore, Rob	WR	6-3	205	9/27/68	3	Syracuse	Hempstead, N.Y.	SD1-'90	16/16
51	Mott, Joe	LB	6-4	234	10/6/65	3	Iowa	Endicott, N.Y.	D3-'89	0*
8	Nagle, Browning	QB	6-3	225	4/29/68	2	Louisville	Largo, Fla.	D2-'91	1/0
7	†O'Brien, Ken	QB	6-4	212	11/27/60	10	California-Davis	Sacramento, Calif.	D1-'83	16/16
21	Odegard, Don Boyd	CB-KR	6-0	180	11/22/66	3	Nevada-Las Vegas	Kennewick, Wash.	FA-'90	16/1
71	Pickel, Bill	DT	6-5	265	11/5/59	10	Rutgers	Maspeth, N.Y.	PB(Raid)-'91#	15/1
20	Price, Dennis	CB	6-1	175	6/14/65	3	UCLA	Long Beach, Calif.	T(Raid)-'90	0*
49	Sadowski, Troy	TE	6-6	260	12/8/65	3	Georgia	Chamblee, Ga.	FA-'92	14/1*
45	Stargell, Tony	CB	5-11	180	8/7/66	3	Tennessee State	LaGrange, Ga.	D3-'90	16/7
10	Staurovsky, Jason	K	5-9	170	3/23/63	5	Tulsa	Tulsa, Okla.	PB(NE)-'92#	9/0*
53	Sweeney, Jim	C-G	6-4	286	8/8/62	9	Pittsburgh	Pittsburgh, Pa.	D2a-'84	16/16
11	†Taylor, Troy	QB	6-4	200	4/5/68	3	California	Sacramento, Calif.	D4-'90	5/0
32	Thomas, Blair	RB	5-10	195	10/7/67	3	Penn State	Philadelphia, Pa.	D1-'90	16/12
88	†Toon, Al	WR	6-4	205	4/30/63	8	Wisconsin	Newport News, Va.	D1-'85	15/15
23	Turner, Marcus	CB-S	6-0	185	1/13/66	4	UCLA	Long Beach, Calif.	PB(Phx)-'92#	3/0*
48	Washington, Brian	S	6-1	212	9/10/65	4	Nebraska	Richmond, Va.	W(Clev)-'89	16/16
97	Washington, Marvin	DE	6-6	272	10/22/65	4	Idaho	Dallas, Tex.	D6a-'89	15/15
86	Whisenhunt, Ken	TE	6-3	240	2/28/62	6	Georgia Tech	Augusta, Ga.	W(Wash)-'91	7/2
67	White, Dwayne	G	6-2	305	2/10/67	3	Alcorn State	Philadelphia, Pa.	D7a-'90	16/16
31	†Young, Lonnie	CB-S	6-1	192	7/18/63	8	Michigan State	Flint, Mich.	T(Phx)-'91	12/11

* Beach played 12 games with Indianapolis in '91; Carpenter played 8 games with New England; Chaffey played 14 games with Atlanta; Fishback played 14 games with Atlanta; Gardner played 10 games with Miami; Hart played 1 game with L.A. Raiders; Mott and Price missed '91 season due to injury; Sadowski played 14 games with Kansas City; Staurovsky played 9 games with New England; Turner played 3 games with Phoenix.

† Option playout; subject to developments.

Plan B unconditional free agent.

Players lost through Plan B (1): C-G-T-TE Trevor Matich (Ind; 15 games in '91).

Also played with Jets in '91 — DE Darrell Davis (13 games), TE Chris Dressel (15), LB John Galvin (9).

COACHING STAFF

Head Coach, Bruce Coslet

Pro Career: Begins third year as head coach of the Jets. In only his second season, the Jets improved from 6-10 to post an 8-8 record and earn their first playoff berth in five years. In 1991, the Jets finished fourth in total offense (332.3 yards per game) in the AFC and led the AFC in defensing the run (90.1). The offense, defense, and special teams combined for a positive turnover edge of plus 12, second in the AFC and fourth in the NFL. Coslet entered the pro coaching ranks as tight ends and special teams coach with the San Francisco 49ers in 1980. He joined the Cincinnati Bengals in 1981 in the same capacity. In 1983, he was given the added responsibility of the Bengals' passing game. Coslet tutored Cincinnati's receivers in 1984-85 before being named offensive coordinator (1986-89). The Bengals had the NFL's top-ranked offense in three of those seasons and went to Super Bowl XXIII. He played tight end for Cincinnati in 1969-76. Career record: 14-19.

Background: Tight end at the University of the Pacific from 1965-67.

Personal: Born August 5, 1946, in Oakdale, Calif. Bruce and his wife, Kathy, live on Long Island, and have two children—J.J. and Amy.

Assistant Coaches

Paul Alexander, offensive assistant-tight ends; born February 12, 1960, Rochester, N.Y., lives on Long Island. Tackle Cortland State 1978-81. No pro playing experience. College coach: Penn State 1982-84, Michigan 1985-86, Central Michigan 1987-91. Pro coach: Joined Jets in 1992.

Larry Beightol, offensive line; born November 21, 1942, Morrisdale, Pa., lives on Long Island. Guard-linebacker Catawba College 1961-63. No pro playing experience. College coach: William & Mary 1968-71, North Carolina State 1972-75, Auburn 1976, Arkansas 1977-78, 1980-82, Louisiana Tech 1979 (head coach), Missouri 1983-84. Pro coach: Atlanta Falcons 1985-86, Tampa Bay Buccaneers 1987-88, San Diego Chargers 1989, joined Jets in 1990.

Kippy Brown, running backs; born March 6, 1955, Sweetwater, Tenn., lives on Long Island. Quarterback Memphis State 1973-77. No pro playing experience. College coach: Memphis State 1978-80, Louisville 1981, Tennessee 1982-89. Pro coach: Joined Jets in 1990.

Pete Carroll, defensive coordinator; born September 15, 1951, San Francisco, Calif., lives on Long Island. Defensive back Pacific 1969-72. No pro playing experience. College coach: Arkansas 1977, Iowa State 1978, Ohio State 1979, North Carolina State 1980-82, Pacific 1983. Pro coach: Buffalo Bills 1984, Minnesota Vikings 1985-89, joined Jets in 1990.

Ed Donatell, defensive assistant-secondary; born February 4, 1957, Akron, Ohio, lives on Long Island. Safety Glenville State 1975-78. No pro playing experience. College coach: Kent State 1979-80, Washington 1981-82, Pacific 1983-85, Idaho 1986-88, Cal State-Fullerton 1989. Pro coach: Joined Jets in 1990.

Foge Fazio, linebackers; born February 22, 1939, Dawmont, W. Va., lives on Long Island. Linebacker-center Pittsburgh 1957-60. Pro linebacker Boston Patriots 1961. College coach: Boston University 1967, Harvard 1968, Pittsburgh 1969-72, 1977-81 (head coach), Cincinnati 1973-76, Notre Dame 1986-87. Pro coach: Atlanta Falcons 1988-89, joined Jets in 1990.

Walt Harris, quarterbacks; born November 9, 1946, Modesto, Calif., lives on Long Island. Defensive back Pacific 1966-67. No pro playing experience. College coach: Pacific 1970-73, 1988-91 (head coach), California 1974-77, Michigan State 1978-79, Illinois 1980-82, Tennessee 1983-88. Pro coach: Joined Jets in 1992.

New York Jets 1992 First-Year Roster

Name	Pos.	Ht.	Wt.	Birth-date	College	Hometown	How Acq.
Anthony, Corwin (1)	TE	6-3	240	10/8/68	UCLA	Bakersfield, Calif.	FA
Barber, Kurt	LB	6-4	241	1/5/69	Southern California	Paducah, Ky.	D2
Blake, Jeff	QB	6-0	202	12/4/70	East Carolina	Sanford, Fla.	D6
Boles, Eric	WR	6-3	195	4/29/70	Central Washington	Tacoma, Wash.	D11
Brownlee, Vincent	WR-KR	5-11	191	12/20/69	Mississippi	Amory, Miss.	D8
Bryant, Blaise (1)	RB	5-11	203	11/23/69	Iowa State	Huntington Bch., Calif.	D6-'91
Cadrez, Glenn	LB	6-3	235	1/20/70	Houston	El Centro, Calif.	D6
Coleman, Keo	LB	6-1	255	5/1/70	Mississippi State	Milwaukee, Wis.	D4
Dixon, Cal	C	6-4	284	10/11/69	Florida	Merritt Island, Fla.	D5
Fisher, Kelvin	RB	5-10	214	9/12/68	Arizona State	Ambridge, Pa.	FA
Hayes, Mark (1)	T	6-6	295	6/19/68	Arizona State	San Diego, Calif.	D12-'91
Holt, Richard	S	6-2	190	9/10/69	Arizona	Carson, Calif.	FA
Jenkins, Pepper (1)	LB	6-4	216	3/7/68	Long Beach State	Los Angeles, Calif.	FA
Johnson, Mario	DT-G	6-3	313	1/30/70	Missouri	Florissant, Mo.	D10
Jones, Claude	G	6-2	289	9/12/69	Miami	Ft. Lauderdale, Fla.	FA
Kinard, Leroy (1)	RB	5-9	200	2/24/69	Liberty	Winter Garden, Fla.	FA
Malamala, Siupeli	T	6-5	313	1/15/69	Washington	Kalaheo, Hawaii	D3
McAlister, Scott	P	6-2	226	3/30/69	North Carolina	Greensboro, N.C.	FA
Miller, Clarence	WR	6-1	185	9/27/67	Illinois State	Rockford, Ill.	FA
Mitchell, Johnny	TE	6-3	263	1/20/71	Nebraska	Chicago, Ill.	D1
Moore, Reggie (1)	WR	5-9	175	3/23/68	UCLA	Houston, Tex.	FA-'91
Nelson, Patrick	WR	5-10	175	6/12/69	Liberty	Wildwood, Fla.	FA
Sullivan, Brad	G-T	6-5	275	9/10/70	New Mexico	El Paso, Tex.	FA
Wicka, Wayne	DT	6-5	275	5/31/66	Winona	Dodge, Wis.	FA
Willig, Matt	DT	6-8	255	1/21/69	Southern California	Santa Fe Springs, Calif.	FA

The term NFL Rookie is defined as a player who is in his first season of professional football and has not been on the roster of another professional football team for any regular-season or postseason games. A Rookie is designated by an "R" on NFL rosters. Players who have been active in another professional football league or players who have NFL experience, including either preseason training camp or being on an active roster for fewer than three regular-season or postseason games, are termed NFL First-Year Players. An NFL First-Year Player is designated by a "1" on NFL rosters. Thereafter, a player on an NFL active roster for at least three regular-season or postseason games is credited with an additional year of NFL playing experience.

NOTES

_____

_____

_____

_____

_____

_____

_____

_____

_____

_____

_____

_____

_____

_____

Greg Mackrides, strength and conditioning; born July 9, 1954, Philadelphia, Pa., lives on Long Island. No college or pro playing experience. College coach: Villanova 1985-88, Fairfield 1986-88. U.S. Olympic Wrestling team 1988, U.S. Pan American and World touring teams 1986-88. Pro coach: New York Knicks (NBA) 1987-90, joined Jets in 1990.

Chip Myers, receivers; born July 9, 1945, Panama City, Fla., lives on Long Island. Receiver Northwest Oklahoma 1964-66. Pro receiver San Francisco 1967, Cincinnati Bengals 1969-76. College coach: Illinois 1980-82. Pro coach: Tampa Bay Buccaneers 1983-84, Indianapolis Colts 1985-88, joined Jets in 1990.

Al Roberts, special teams coordinator; born January 6, 1944, Fresno, Calif., lives on Long Island. Running back Washington 1964-65, Puget Sound 1967-68. No pro playing experience. College coach: Washington 1977-82, Purdue 1986, Wyoming 1987. Pro coach: Los Angeles Express (USFL) 1983-84, Houston Oilers 1984-85, Philadelphia Eagles 1988-90, joined Jets in 1991.

Greg Robinson, defensive line; born October 9, 1951, Los Angeles, Calif., lives on Long Island. Linebacker-tight end Pacific 1972-73. No pro playing experience. College coach: Cal State-Fullerton 1977-79, North Carolina State 1980-81, UCLA 1982-89. Pro coach: Joined Jets in 1990.

American Football Conference Central Division

Team Colors: Black and Gold

Three Rivers Stadium
300 Stadium Circle
Pittsburgh, Pennsylvania 15212
Telephone: (412) 323-1200
FAX: (412) 323-1393

Club Officials

President: Daniel M. Rooney
Vice President: John R. McGinley
Vice President: Arthur J. Rooney, Jr.
Secretary and Counsel: Arthur J. Rooney II
Administration Advisor: Charles H. Noll
Director of Communications: Joe Gordon
Director of Public Relations: Dan Edwards
P.R. Assistant/Community Relations: Ron Miller
Controller: Dan McGrogan
Assistant Controller: Dan Ferens
Assistant Controller: Jim Ellenberger
Director of Football Operations: Tom Donahoe
Football Business Manager: James A. Boston
College Scouting Coordinator: Tom Modrak
East Talent Scout: Charles Bailey
BLESTO Scout: Bob Lane
Midwest Talent Scout: Max McCartney
West Talent Scout: Bob Schmitz
Ticket Sales Manager: Geraldine R. Glenn
Player Relations: Anthony Griggs
Head Trainer: John Norwig
Administrative Trainer: Ralph Berlin
Equipment Manager: Anthony Parisi
Field Manager: Rodgers Freyvogel

Stadium: Three Rivers Stadium •
Capacity: 59,600
300 Stadium Circle
Pittsburgh, Pennsylvania 15212

Playing Surface: AstroTurf

Training Camp: St. Vincent College
Latrobe, Pennsylvania 15650

1992 Schedule

Preseason
Aug. 8	**Philadelphia**	7:00
Aug. 17	at New Orleans	7:00
Aug. 23	at Chicago	7:30
Aug. 29	**New York Giants**	7:00

Regular Season
Sept. 6	at Houston	12:00
Sept. 13	**New York Jets**	4:00
Sept. 20	at San Diego	1:00
Sept. 27	at Green Bay	3:00
Oct. 4	**Open Date**	
Oct. 11	at Cleveland	1:00
Oct. 19	**Cincinnati** (Monday)	9:00
Oct. 25	at Kansas City	6:30
Nov. 1	**Houston**	1:00
Nov. 8	at Buffalo	4:00
Nov. 15	**Detroit**	1:00
Nov. 22	**Indianapolis**	1:00
Nov. 29	at Cincinnati	1:00
Dec. 6	**Seattle**	1:00
Dec. 13	at Chicago	12:00
Dec. 20	**Minnesota**	1:00
Dec. 27	**Cleveland**	1:00

Steelers Coaching History

Pittsburgh Pirates 1933-1940
(370-411-20)

1933	Forrest (Jap) Douds	3-6-2
1934	Luby DiMelio	2-10-0
1935-36	Joe Bach	10-14-0
1937-39	Johnny Blood (McNally)*	6-19-0
1939-40	Walt Kiesling	3-13-3
1941	Bert Bell**	0-2-0
	Aldo (Buff) Donelli***	0-5-0
1941-44	Walt Kiesling****	13-20-2
1945	Jim Leonard	2-8-0
1946-47	Jock Sutherland	13-10-1
1948-51	Johnny Michelosen	20-26-2
1952-53	Joe Bach	11-13-0
1954-56	Walt Kiesling	14-22-0
1957-64	Raymond (Buddy) Parker	51-47-6
1965	Mike Nixon	2-12-0
1966-68	Bill Austin	11-28-3
1969-91	Chuck Noll	209-156-1

*Released after three games in 1939
**Resigned after two games in 1941
***Released after five games in 1941
****Co-coach with Earle (Greasy) Neale in Philadelphia-Pittsburgh merger in 1943 and with Phil Handler in Chicago Cardinals-Pittsburgh merger in 1944

Record Holders

Individual Records—Career

Category	Name	Performance
Rushing (Yds.)	Franco Harris, 1972-1983	11,950
Passing (Yds.)	Terry Bradshaw, 1970-1983	27,989
Passing (TDs)	Terry Bradshaw, 1970-1983	212
Receiving (No.)	John Stallworth, 1974-1987	537
Receiving (Yds.)	John Stallworth, 1974-1987	8,723
Interceptions	Mel Blount, 1970-1983	57
Punting (Avg.)	Bobby Joe Green, 1960-61	45.7
Punt Return (Avg.)	Bobby Gage, 1949-1950	14.9
Kickoff Return (Avg.)	Lynn Chandnois, 1950-56	29.6
Field Goals	Gary Anderson, 1982-1991	229
Touchdowns (Tot.)	Franco Harris, 1972-1983	100
Points	Gary Anderson, 1982-1991	1,010

Individual Records—Single Season

Category	Name	Performance
Rushing (Yds.)	Franco Harris, 1975	1,246
Passing (Yds.)	Terry Bradshaw, 1979	3,724
Passing (TDs)	Terry Bradshaw, 1978	28
Receiving (No.)	John Stallworth, 1984	80
Receiving (Yds.)	John Stallworth, 1984	1,395
Interceptions	Mel Blount, 1975	11
Punting (Avg.)	Bobby Joe Green, 1961	47.0
Punt Return (Avg.)	Bobby Gage, 1949	16.0
Kickoff Return (Avg.)	Lynn Chandnois, 1952	35.2
Field Goals	Gary Anderson, 1985	33
Touchdowns (Tot.)	Louis Lipps, 1985	15
Points	Gary Anderson, 1985	139

Individual Records—Single Game

Category	Name	Performance
Rushing (Yds.)	John Fuqua, 12-20-70	218
Passing (Yds.)	Bobby Layne, 12-3-58	409
Passing (TDs)	Terry Bradshaw, 11-15-81	5
	Mark Malone, 9-8-85	5
Receiving (No.)	J.R. Wilburn, 10-22-67	12
Receiving (Yds.)	Buddy Dial, 10-22-61	235
Interceptions	Jack Butler, 12-13-53	*4
Field Goals	Gary Anderson, 10-23-88	6
Touchdowns (Tot.)	Ray Mathews, 10-17-54	4
	Roy Jefferson, 11-3-68	4
Points	Ray Mathews, 10-17-54	24
	Roy Jefferson, 11-3-68	24

*NFL Record

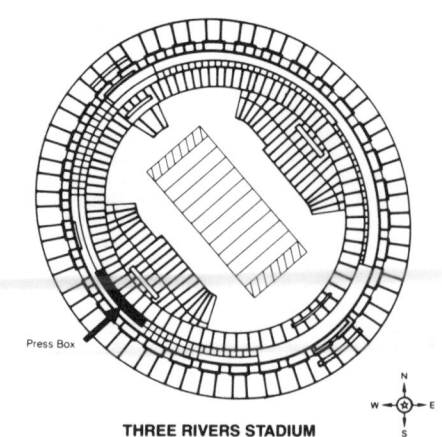

Press Box

THREE RIVERS STADIUM

1991 Team Record
Preseason (2-2)

Date	Result		Opponents
8/4	W	16- 7	Washington
8/10	L	24-34	at Minnesota
8/17	L	20-21	at Philadelphia
8/23	W	16- 3	at Detroit

Regular Season (7-9)

Date	Result		Opponents	Att.
9/1	W	26-20	San Diego	55,848
9-8	L	34-52	at Buffalo	79,545
9/15	W	20- 6	New England	53,703
9/22	L	14-23	at Philadelphia	65,511
10/6	W	21- 3	at Indianapolis	55,383
10/14	L	20-23	N.Y. Giants	57,608
10/20	L	7-27	Seattle	54,678
10/27	L	14-17	at Cleveland	78,285
11/3	L	13-20	at Denver	70,973
11/10	W	33-27	at Cincinnati (OT)	55,503
11/17	L	14-41	Washington	56,813
11/24	W	26-14	Houston	45,795
11/28	L	10-20	at Dallas	62,253
12/8	L	6-31	at Houston	59,225
12/15	W	17-10	Cincinnati	35,420
12/22	W	17-10	Cleveland	47,070

(OT) Overtime

Score by Periods

Steelers	42	53	67	124	6	—	292
Opponents	61	116	54	113	0	—	344

Attendance

Home 406,935   Away 526,678   Total 933,613
Single-game home record, 59,541 (9-30-85)
Single-season home record, 462,567 (1983)

1991 Team Statistics

	Steelers	Opp.
Total First Downs	254	320
Rushing	82	98
Passing	158	194
Penalty	14	28
Third Down: Made/Att.	62/197	94/218
Third Down: Pct.	31.5	43.1
Fourth Down: Made/Att.	6/17	4/9
Fourth Down: Pct.	35.3	44.4
Total Net Yards	4581	5168
Avg. Per Game	286.3	323.0
Total Plays	915	1039
Avg. Per Play	5.0	5.0
Net Yards Rushing	1627	1582
Avg. Per Game	101.7	98.9
Total Rushes	394	466
Net Yards Passing	2954	3586
Avg. Per Game	184.6	224.1
Sacked/Yards Lost	45/359	38/257
Gross Yards	3313	3843
Att./Completions	476/259	535/334
Completion Pct.	54.4	62.4
Had Intercepted	16	19
Punts/Avg.	75/39.9	65/41.6
Net Punting Avg.	36.3	35.3
Penalties/Yards Lost	116/933	84/685
Fumbles/Ball Lost	37/14	27/11
Touchdowns	32	38
Rushing	8	14
Passing	20	21
Returns	4	3
Avg. Time of Possession	27:06	32:54

1991 Individual Statistics

Scoring

	TD R	TD P	TD Rt	PAT	FG	Saf	TP
Anderson	0	0	0	31/31	23/33	0	100
Green	0	6	0	0/0	0/0	0	36
Stone	0	5	0	0/0	0/0	0	30
W. Williams	4	0	0	0/0	0/0	0	24
Hoge	2	1	0	0/0	0/0	0	18
Cooper	0	2	0	0/0	0/0	0	12
Foster	1	1	0	0/0	0/0	0	12
Lipps	0	2	0	0/0	0/0	0	12
Mills	0	1	1	0/0	0/0	0	12
Calloway	0	1	0	0/0	0/0	0	6
Cash	0	1	0	0/0	0/0	0	6
Hinkle	0	0	1	0/0	0/0	0	6
O'Donnell	1	0	0	0/0	0/0	0	6
Shelton	0	0	1	0/0	0/0	0	6
J. Williams	0	0	1	0/0	0/0	0	6
Steelers	8	20	4	31/31	23/33	0	292
Opponents	14	21	3	38/38	26/41	0	344

Passing

	Att.	Comp.	Yds.	Pct.	TD	Int.	Tkld.	Rate
O'Donnell	286	156	1963	54.5	11	7	30/214	78.8
Brister	190	103	1350	54.2	9	9	15/145	72.9
Steelers	476	259	3313	54.4	20	16	45/359	76.4
Opponents	535	334	3843	62.4	21	19	38/257	82.3

Rushing

	Att.	Yds.	Avg.	LG	TD
Hoge	165	610	3.7	24	2
Foster	96	488	5.1	56t	1
W. Williams	57	262	4.6	21	4
Worley	22	117	5.3	16	0
O'Donnell	18	82	4.6	22	1
Thompson	20	60	3.0	14	0
Brister	11	17	1.5	8	0
Stone	1	2	2.0	2	0
Stryzinski	4	-11	-2.8	0	0
Steelers	394	1627	4.1	56t	8
Opponents	466	1582	3.4	33	14

Receiving

	No.	Yds.	Avg.	LG	TD
Lipps	55	671	12.2	35	2
Hoge	49	379	7.7	25	1
Green	41	582	14.2	49	6
Stone	32	649	20.3	89t	5
Calloway	15	254	16.9	33t	1
W. Williams	15	139	9.3	29	0
Thompson	14	118	8.4	32	0
Cooper	11	147	13.4	47t	2
Foster	9	117	13.0	31	1
Cash	7	90	12.9	20	1
Mularkey	6	67	11.2	21	0
Mills	3	79	26.3	35t	1
Graham	2	21	10.5	15	0
Steelers	259	3313	12.8	89t	20
Opponents	334	3843	11.5	66t	21

Interceptions

	No.	Yds.	Avg.	LG	TD
Everett	4	53	13.3	27	0
Woodson	3	72	24.0	41	0
Shelton	3	57	19.0	57t	1
Hinkle	2	68	34.0	57t	1
Vincent	2	52	26.0	27	0
Griffin	1	22	22.0	22	0
Little	1	5	5.0	5	0
G. Jones	1	0	0.0	0	0
Johnson	1	0	0.0	0	0
Lloyd	1	0	0.0	0	0
Steelers	19	329	17.3	57t	2
Opponents	16	182	11.4	40	2

Punting

	No.	Yds.	Avg.	In 20	LG
Stryzinski	74	2996	40.5	10	63
Steelers	75	2996	39.9	10	63
Opponents	65	2705	41.6	17	59

Punt Returns

	No.	FC	Yds.	Avg.	LG	TD
Woodson	28	12	320	11.4	40	0
Graham	8	2	46	5.8	13	0
Cash	1	0	6	6.0	6	0
Mills	1	0	0	0.0	0t	1
Vincent	1	0	1	1.0	1	0
Steelers	39	14	373	9.6	40	1
Opponents	29	27	210	7.2	24	0

Kickoff Returns

	No.	Yds.	Avg.	LG	TD
Woodson	44	880	20.0	47	0
Mills	11	284	25.8	54	0
Stone	6	75	12.5	25	0
Graham	3	48	16.0	23	0
McGovern	1	0	0.0	0	0
Thompson	1	8	8.0	8	0
J. Williams	1	19	19.0	19	0
Steelers	67	1314	19.6	54	0
Opponents	43	825	19.2	63	0

Sacks

	No.
J. Williams	9.0
Lloyd	8.0
Willis	7.0
Evans	2.0
Hinkle	2.0
A. Jones	2.0
Veasey	2.0
G. Williams	2.0
Johnson	1.0
Lake	1.0
Nickerson	1.0
Woodson	1.0
Steelers	38.0
Opponents	45.0

1992 Draft Choices

Round	Name	Pos.	College
1.	Leon Searcy	T	Miami
2.	Levon Kirkland	LB	Clemson
3.	Joel Steed	NT	Colorado
4.	Charles Davenport	WR	North Carolina St.
5.	Alan Haller	DB	Michigan State
7.	Russ Campbell	TE	Kansas State
	Scottie Graham	RB	Ohio State
8.	Darren Perry	DB	Penn State
	Hesham Ismail	G	Florida
	Nate Williams	DT	Mississippi State
9.	Elnardo Webster	LB	Rutgers
10.	Mike Saunders	RB	Iowa
11.	Kendall Gammons	G	Pittsburg, Kan.
12.	Cornelius Benton	QB	Connecticut

Pittsburgh Steelers 1992 Veteran Roster

No.	Name	Pos.	Ht.	Wt.	Birth-date	NFL Exp.	College	Hometown	How Acq.	'91 Games/Starts
1	Anderson, Gary	K	5-11	179	7/16/59	11	Syracuse	Durban, South Africa	W(Buff)-'82	16/0
60	Blankenship, Brian	G	6-1	280	4/7/63	6	Nebraska	Omaha, Neb.	FA-'87	3/3
6	†Brister, Bubby	QB	6-3	217	8/15/62	7	Northeast Louisiana	Alexandria, La.	D3-'86	8/8
61	Caliguire, Dean	G-C	6-2	280	3/2/67	2	Pittsburgh	Pittsburgh, Pa.	FA-'91	7/0
74	Clayton, Stan	T	6-3	265	1/31/65	4	Penn State	Cherry Hill, N.J.	PB(NE)-'92#	0*
87	Cooper, Adrian	TE	6-5	259	4/27/68	2	Oklahoma	Denver, Colo.	D4b-'91	16/8
64	Davidson, Kenny	DE	6-5	264	8/17/67	3	Louisiana State	Shreveport, La.	D2-'90	13/1
63	Dawson, Dermontti	C	6-2	275	6/17/65	5	Kentucky	Lexington, Ky.	D2-'88	16/16
36	Drummond, Robert	RB	6-1	205	6/21/67	4	Syracuse	Jamesville, N.Y.	PB(Phil)-'92#	16/0*
66	Evans, Donald	DE	6-2	258	3/14/64	4	Winston-Salem State	Raleigh, N.C.	FA-'90	16/14
27	†Everett, Thomas	S	5-9	183	11/21/64	6	Baylor	Daingerfield, Tex.	D4-'87	16/16
29	Foster, Barry	RB	5-10	218	12/8/68	3	Arkansas	Duncanville, Tex.	D5-'90	10/9
96	Gibson, Tom	DE	6-8	275	12/20/63	4	Northern Arizona	San Fernando, Calif.	PB(Rams)-'92#	4/1*
81	Graham, Jeff	WR	6-1	195	2/14/69	2	Ohio State	Dayton, Ohio	D2-'91	13/1
86	Green, Eric	TE	6-5	280	6/22/67	3	Liberty	Savannah, Ga.	D1-'90	11/11
22	Griffin, Larry	S	6-0	202	1/11/63	7	North Carolina	Chesapeake, Va.	FA-'87	6/0
77	Haselrig, Carlton	G	6-1	295	1/22/66	3	Pittsburgh-Johnstown	Johnstown, Pa.	D12-'89	16/16
53	Hinkle, Bryan	LB	6-2	224	6/4/59	11	Oregon	Silverdale, Wash.	D6-'81	14/14
33	Hoge, Merril	RB	6-2	222	1/26/65	6	Idaho State	Pocatello, Idaho	D10-'87	16/16
62	†Ilkin, Tunch	T	6-3	273	9/23/57	13	Indiana State	Highland Park, Ill.	D6-'80	16/16
65	Jackson, John	T	6-6	289	1/4/65	5	Eastern Kentucky	Cincinnati, Ohio	D10-'88	16/16
56	Jaworski, Matt	LB	6-1	226	10/23/67	2	Colgate	Buffalo, N.Y.	PB(Ind)-'92#	8/3*
44	Johnson, David	CB	6-0	181	4/14/66	4	Kentucky	Louisville, Ky.	D7-'89	16/16
97	†Jones, Aaron	DE	6-5	257	12/18/66	5	Eastern Kentucky	Orlando, Fla.	D1-'88	16/7
25	Jones, Gary	S	6-1	208	11/30/67	3	Texas A&M	Tyler, Tex.	D9-'90	9/1
37	†Lake, Carnell	S	6-1	207	7/15/67	4	UCLA	Inglewood, Calif.	D2-'89	16/16
83	†Lipps, Louis	WR	5-10	185	8/9/62	9	Southern Mississippi	Reserve, La.	D1-'84	15/14
50	Little, David	LB	6-1	236	1/3/59	12	Florida	Miami, Fla.	D7-'81	14/10
95	Lloyd, Greg	LB	6-2	223	5/26/65	5	Fort Valley State	Fort Valley, Ga.	D6b-'87	16/16
67	Love, Duval	G-T	6-3	287	6/24/63	8	UCLA	Fountain Valley, Calif.	PB(Rams)-'92#	16/13*
89	Mills, Ernie	WR	5-11	178	10/28/68	2	Florida	Dunnellon, Fla.	D3-'91	16/2
84	Mularkey, Mike	TE	6-4	240	11/19/61	10	Florida	Ft. Lauderdale, Fla.	PB(Minn)-'89#	9/6
54	†Nickerson, Hardy	LB	6-2	227	9/1/65	6	California	Los Angeles, Calif.	D5-'87	16/14
14	O'Donnell, Neil	QB	6-3	223	7/3/66	3	Maryland	Madison, N.J.	D3a-'90	12/8
55	Olsavsky, Jerry	LB	6-1	219	3/29/67	3	Pittsburgh	Youngstown, Ohio	D10-'89	16/4
90	Richardson, Huey	LB	6-5	233	2/2/68	2	Florida	Atlanta, Ga.	D1-'91	5/0
71	Ricketts, Tom	T	6-5	288	11/21/65	4	Pittsburgh	Murrysville, Pa.	D1b-'89	14/8
3	Royals, Mark	P	6-5	215	6/22/64	3	Appalachian State	Mathews, Va.	PB(TB)-'92#	16/0*
24	Shelton, Richard	CB	5-9	196	1/2/66	3	Liberty	Marietta, Ga.	FA-'91	14/2
40	Smagala, Stan	S	5-10	184	4/6/68	3	Notre Dame	Burbank, Ill.	PB(Dall)-'92#	8/0*
41	Smith, Kevin	S	5-11	204	4/2/67	2	Rhode Island	Newport, R.I.	FA-'91	16/1
69	Solomon, Ariel	T	6-5	271	7/16/68	2	Colorado	Boulder, Colo.	D10-'91	5/2
20	†Stone, Dwight	RB-WR	6-0	190	1/28/64	6	Middle Tennessee State	Florala, Ala.	FA-'87	16/8
11	Strom, Rick	QB	6-2	197	3/11/65	4	Georgia Tech	Pittsburgh, Pa.	FA-'89	0*
73	Strzelczyk, Justin	T	6-5	297	8/18/68	3	Maine	Seneca, N.Y.	D11-'90	16/0
34	Thompson, Leroy	RB	5-10	215	2/3/69	2	Penn State	Knoxville, Tenn.	D6-'91	13/0
91	Veasey, Craig	DE-DT	6-2	285	12/25/66	3	Houston	Clear Lake City, Tex.	D3b-'90	13/2
43	Vincent, Shawn	CB	5-10	180	6/2/68	2	Akron	St. Clairsville, Ohio	FA-'91	10/1
23	Walker, Sammy	CB	5-11	197	1/20/69	2	Texas Tech	McKinney, Tex.	D4a-'91	2/0
98	†Williams, Gerald	NT	6-3	282	9/8/63	7	Auburn	Lanett, Ala.	D2-'86	16/15
57	Williams, Jerrol	LB	6-5	237	7/5/67	4	Purdue	Las Vegas, Nev.	D4-'89	16/4
42	Williams, Warren	RB	6-0	213	7/29/65	5	Miami	Fort Myers, Fla.	D6-'88	16/3
26	Woodson, Rod	CB	6-0	197	3/10/65	6	Purdue	Fort Wayne, Ind.	D1-'87	15/15

* Clayton active for 5 games with New England but did not play; Drummond played 16 games with Philadelphia; Gibson played 4 games with L.A. Rams; Jaworski played 8 games with Indianapolis; Love played 16 games with L.A. Rams; Royals played 16 games with Tampa Bay; Smagala played 8 games with Dallas; Strom active for 3 games but did not play.

† Option playout; subject to developments.

Plan B unconditional free agent.

Players lost through Plan B (7): LB Jeff Brady (GB; 16 games in '91), WR Chris Calloway (NYG; 12), TE Keith Cash (KC; 5), CB Delton Hall (SD; 6), LB Rob McGovern (NE; 15), P Dan Stryzinski (TB; 16), DE Keith Willis (Wash; 16).

Also played with Steelers in '91—G Terry Long (8 games), C-G Mike Withycombe (2), RB Tim Worley (2).

COACHING STAFF

Head Coach, Bill Cowher

Pro Career: Became the fifteenth head coach in Steelers' history on January 21, 1992, succeeding the retired Chuck Noll. Cowher is the second-youngest head coach in the NFL. Most recently was defensive coordinator-linebackers coach for the Kansas City Chiefs from 1988-1991. Began his NFL career as a free agent linebacker with the Philadelphia Eagles in 1979, and then signed with the Cleveland Browns the following year. Cowher played three seasons (1980-82) in Cleveland before being traded back to the Philadelphia Eagles, where he played two more years (1983-84). Cowher began his coaching career in 1985 at age 28 under Marty Schottenheimer at the Cleveland Browns. He was the Browns' special teams coach in 1985-86 and secondary coach in 1987-88 before following Schottenheimer to the Kansas City Chiefs in 1989 as defensive coordinator.

Background: Excelled in football, basketball, and track for Carlynton High in Crafton, Pa. Was a three-year starter at linebacker for North Carolina State, serving as captain and earning team MVP honors as senior. Graduated in 1979 with education degree.

Personal: Born in Pittsburgh, Pa., on May 8, 1957. His wife Kaye, also a North Carolina State graduate, played professional basketball for the New York Stars of the Women's Professional Basketball League with twin sister Faye. Bill and Kaye live in Pittsburgh and have three daughters—Meagan Lyn, Lauren Marie, and Lindsay Morgan.

Assistant Coaches

Dom Capers, defensive coordinator; born August 7, 1950, Cambridge, Ohio, lives in Pittsburgh. Defensive back Mount Union College 1968-71. No pro playing experience. College coach: Hawaii 1975-76, San Jose State 1977, California 1978-79, Tennessee 1980-81, Ohio State 1982-83. Pro coach: Philadelphia/Baltimore Stars (USFL) 1984-85, New Orleans Saints 1986-91, joined Steelers in 1992.

Ron Erhardt, offensive coordinator; born February 27, 1931, Mandan, N.D., lives in Pittsburgh. Quarterback Jamestown (N.D.) College 1951-54. No pro playing experience. College coach: North Dakota State 1963-72 (head coach 1966-72). Pro coach: New England Patriots 1973-81 (head coach 1979-81), New York Giants 1982-91, joined Steelers in 1992.

Steve Furness, defensive line; born December 5, 1950, Warwick, R.I., lives in Pittsburgh. Defensive tackle Rhode Island 1968-71. Pro defensive tackle Pittsburgh Steelers 1972-80, Detroit Lions 1981. College coach: Michigan State 1983-90. Pro coach: Indianapolis Colts 1991, joined Steelers in 1992.

John Guy, special teams; born May 26, 1951, Greensboro, N.C., lives in Pittsburgh. Defensive back-kicker North Carolina A&T 1969-72. No pro playing experience. College coach: North Carolina 1973-77, Virginia Tech 1978, Duke 1978-80, Georgia Tech 1981-86, Alabama 1987-89, Kentucky 1990-91. Pro coach: Joined Steelers in 1992.

Bob Harrison, wide receivers; born September 9, 1941, Cleveland, Ohio, lives in Pittsburgh. Wide receiver Kent State 1960-63. No pro playing experience. College coach: Kent State 1969-70, Iowa 1971-73, Cornell 1974, North Carolina State 1975-76, Tennessee 1977-82, Georgia 1989-91. Pro coach: Atlanta Falcons 1983-86, joined Steelers in 1992.

Dick Hoak, running backs; born December 8, 1939, Jeannette, Pa., lives in Greensburg, Pa. Halfback-quarterback Penn State 1958-60. Pro running back Pittsburgh Steelers 1961-70. Pro coach: Joined Steelers in 1972.

Pittsburgh Steelers 1992 First-Year Roster

Name	Pos.	Ht.	Wt.	Birth-date	College	Hometown	How Acq.
Benton, Cornelius	QB	6-3	209	10/21/69	Connecticut	Ft. Lauderdale, Fla.	D12
Black, Johnnie	DE-DT	6-1	275	11/26/68	Sam Houston State	Waco, Tex.	FA
Campbell, Russ	TE	6-5	252	4/2/69	Kansas State	Wichita, Kan.	D7a
Chandler, Darrin (1)	WR	5-9	170	3/29/67	Georgia Southern	Atlanta, Ga.	FA
Collins, Gerry	RB	5-7	195	6/4/69	Penn State	Cinnaminson, N.J.	FA
Daniels, David	RB	5-10	220	11/14/69	East Carolina	Greenville, N.C.	FA
Davenport, Charles	WR	6-3	206	11/22/68	North Carolina State	Fayetteville, N.C.	D4
Didio, Mark	WR	5-11	170	2/17/69	Connecticut	Syracuse, N.Y.	FA
Dingman, Dean (1)	G	6-2	270	9/27/68	Michigan	Troy, Wis.	D8-'91
Fair, Ron (1)	WR	5-11	195	10/28/66	Arizona State	Asheville, N.C.	FA
Gammon, Kendall	G	6-4	273	10/28/68	Pittsburg, Kan.	Wichita, Kan.	D11
Graham, Scottie	RB	5-9	222	3/28/69	Ohio State	Long Beach, N.Y.	D7b
Haller, Alan	CB	5-11	177	8/9/70	Michigan State	Lansing, Mich.	D5
Hargett, David	S	6-1	200	12/2/68	Georgia	Valdosta, Ga.	FA
Hill, Andrew	WR	6-3	204	6/1/70	Indiana, Pa.	New Brighton, Pa.	FA
Howe, Garry (1)	NT	6-1	277	6/20/68	Colorado	Spencer, Iowa	FA-'91
Ismail, Hesham	G	6-2	291	6/11/69	Florida	Lake Alfred, Fla.	D8b
Kirkland, Levon	LB	6-0	240	2/17/69	Clemson	Lamar, S.C.	D2
Ostaszewski, Henry	DE-DT	6-3	264	5/17/69	Florida State	Boynton Beach, Fla.	FA
Owens, Darrick	WR	6-2	195	11/5/70	Mississippi	Tallahassee, Fla.	FA
Perry, Darren	S	5-10	190	12/29/68	Penn State	Deep Creek, Va.	D8a
Rodgers, Kacy	LB	6-2	253	6/24/69	Tennessee	Humboldt, Tenn.	FA
Saunders, Mike	RB	5-11	206	10/3/69	Iowa	Milton, Wis.	D10
Searcy, Leon	T	6-3	295	12/21/69	Miami	Orlando, Fla.	D1
Siffri, Paul	TE	6-4	245	12/5/69	Furman	Atlanta, Ga.	FA
Steed, Joel	NT	6-2	285	2/17/69	Colorado	Denver, Colo.	D3
Thomas, Derrick	LB	6-2	230	9/24/69	Kentucky	Lexington, Ky.	FA
Webster, Elnardo	LB	6-2	246	12/23/69	Rutgers	Jersey City, N.J.	D9
Williams, Nate	DE-DT	6-3	291	6/11/68	Mississippi State	Houston, Tex.	D8c

The term NFL Rookie is defined as a player who is in his first season of professional football and has not been on the roster of another professional football team for any regular-season or postseason games. A Rookie is designated by an "R" on NFL rosters. Players who have been active in another professional football league or players who have NFL experience, including either preseason training camp or being on an active roster for fewer than three regular-season or postseason games, are termed NFL First-Year Players. An NFL First-Year Player is designated by a "1" on NFL rosters. Thereafter, a player on an NFL active roster for at least three regular-season or postseason games is credited with an additional year of NFL playing experience.

NOTES

_____

_____

_____

_____

_____

_____

_____

_____

_____

_____

_____

_____

Pat Hodgson, tight ends; born January 30, 1944, Columbus, Ga., lives in Pittsburgh. Tight end Georgia 1963-65. Pro tight end Washington Redskins 1966, Minnesota Vikings 1967. College coach: Georgia 1968-70, 1972-77, Florida State 1971, Texas Tech 1978. Pro coach: San Diego Chargers 1978, New York Giants 1979-87, joined Steelers in 1992.

Dick LeBeau, defensive backs; born September 9, 1937, London, Ohio, lives in Pittsburgh. Defensive back-offensive back Ohio State 1954-57. Pro cornerback Detroit Lions 1959-72. Pro coach: Philadelphia Eagles 1973-75, Green Bay Packers 1976-79, Cincinnati Bengals 1980-91, joined Steelers in 1992.

Marvin Lewis, linebackers; born September 23, 1958, McDonald, Pa., lives in Pittsburgh. Linebacker Idaho State 1977-80. No pro playing experience. College coach: Idaho State 1981-84, Long Beach State 1985-86, New Mexico 1987-89, Pittsburgh 1990-91. Pro coach: Joined Steelers in 1992.

Kent Stephenson, offensive line; born February 4, 1942, Anita, Iowa, lives in Pittsburgh. Guard-nose tackle Northern Iowa 1962-64. No pro playing experience. College coach: Wayne State 1965-68, North Dakota 1969-71, Southern Methodist 1972-73, Iowa 1974-76, Oklahoma 1977-78, Kansas 1979-82. Pro coach: Michigan Panthers (USFL) 1983-84, Seattle Seahawks 1985-91, joined Steelers in 1992.

SAN DIEGO CHARGERS

American Football Conference Western Division

Team Colors: Navy Blue, White, and Gold

San Diego Jack Murphy Stadium
P.O. Box 609609
San Diego, California 92160-9609
Telephone: (619) 280-2111

Club Officials

Chairman of the Board/President: Alex G. Spanos
Vice Chairman: Dean A. Spanos
General Manager: Bobby Beathard
Vice President-Finance: Jeremiah T. Murphy
Assistant General Manager: Dick Daniels
Director of Player Personnel: Billy Devaney
Director of Pro Personnel: Rudy Feldman
Director of College Scouting: John Hinek
Coordinator of Football Operations: Marty Hurney
Director of Public Relations: Bill Johnston
Chief Financial Officer: Jeanne Bonk
Business Manager: Pat Curran
Director of Marketing: Rich Israel
Director of Ticket Operations: Joe Scott
Assistant Director of Public Relations:
    Rob Boulware
Video Director: Gene Leff
Head Trainer: Keoki Kamau
Equipment Manager: Sid Brooks

Stadium: San Diego Jack Murphy Stadium •
    Capacity: 60,836
    9449 Friars Road
    San Diego, California 92108

Playing Surface: Grass

Training Camp: University of California-
    San Diego
    Third College
    La Jolla, California 92037

1992 Schedule

Preseason

Aug. 8	at Phoenix	7:30
Aug. 14	at New England	7:00
Aug. 21	**San Francisco**	5:00
Aug. 27	**Los Angeles Rams**	7:00

Regular Season

Sept. 6	**Kansas City**	1:00
Sept. 13	at Denver	2:00
Sept. 20	**Pittsburgh**	1:00
Sept. 27	at Houston	12:00
Oct. 4	**Seattle**	1:00
Oct. 11	**Open Date**	
Oct. 18	at Indianapolis	12:00
Oct. 25	**Denver**	1:00
Nov. 1	**Indianapolis**	1:00
Nov. 8	at Kansas City	3:00
Nov. 15	at Cleveland	1:00
Nov. 22	**Tampa Bay**	1:00
Nov. 29	**Los Angeles Raiders**	5:00
Dec. 6	at Phoenix	2:00
Dec. 13	**Cincinnati**	1:00
Dec. 20	at Los Angeles Raiders	1:00
Dec. 27	at Seattle	1:00

Chargers Coaching History

(230-239-11)

1960-69	Sid Gillman*	83-51-6
1969-70	Charlie Waller	9-7-3
1971	Sid Gillman**	4-6-0
1971-73	Harland Svare***	7-17-2
1973	Ron Waller	1-5-0
1974-78	Tommy Prothro****	21-39-0
1978-86	Don Coryell#	72-60-0
1986-88	Al Saunders	17-22-0
1989-91	Dan Henning	16-32-0

*Retired after nine games in 1969
**Resigned after 10 games in 1971
***Resigned after eight games in 1973
****Resigned after four games in 1978
#Resigned after eight games in 1986

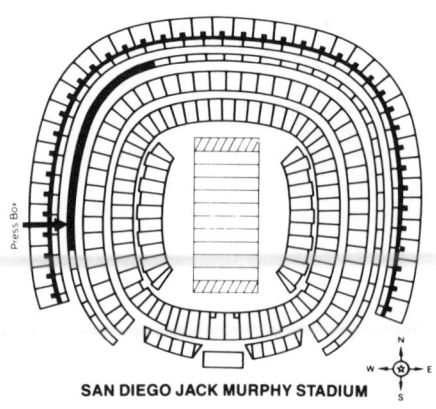

SAN DIEGO JACK MURPHY STADIUM

Record Holders

Individual Records—Career

Category	Name	Performance
Rushing (Yds.)	Paul Lowe, 1960-67	4,963
Passing (Yds.)	Dan Fouts, 1973-1987	43,040
Passing (TDs)	Dan Fouts, 1973-1987	254
Receiving (No.)	Charlie Joiner, 1976-1986	586
Receiving (Yds.)	Lance Alworth, 1962-1970	9,585
Interceptions	Gill Byrd, 1983-1991	38
Punting (Avg.)	Maury Buford, 1982-84	42.7
Punt Return (Avg.)	Leslie (Speedy) Duncan, 1964-1970	12.3
Kickoff Return (Avg.)	Leslie (Speedy) Duncan, 1964-1970	25.2
Field Goals	Rolf Benirschke, 1977-1986	146
Touchdowns (Tot.)	Lance Alworth, 1962-1970	83
Points	Rolf Benirschke, 1977-1986	766

Individual Records—Single Season

Category	Name	Performance
Rushing (Yds.)	Marion Butts, 1990	1,225
Passing (Yds.)	Dan Fouts, 1981	4,802
Passing (TDs)	Dan Fouts, 1981	33
Receiving (No.)	Kellen Winslow, 1980	89
Receiving (Yds.)	Lance Alworth, 1965	1,602
Interceptions	Charlie McNeil, 1961	9
Punting (Avg.)	Dennis Partee, 1969	44.6
Punt Return (Avg.)	Leslie (Speedy) Duncan, 1965	15.5
Kickoff Return (Avg.)	Keith Lincoln, 1962	28.4
Field Goals	Rolf Benirschke, 1980	24
Touchdowns (Tot.)	Chuck Muncie, 1981	19
Points	Rolf Benirschke, 1980	118

Individual Records—Single Game

Category	Name	Performance
Rushing (Yds.)	Gary Anderson, 12-18-88	217
Passing (Yds.)	Dan Fouts, 10-19-80	444
	Dan Fouts, 12-11-82	444
Passing (TDs)	Dan Fouts, 11-22-81	6
Receiving (No.)	Kellen Winslow, 10-7-84	15
Receiving (Yds.)	Wes Chandler, 12-20-82	260
Interceptions	Many times	3
	Last time by Pete Shaw, 11-2-80	
Field Goals	Many times	4
	Last time by John Carney, 9-22-91	
Touchdowns (Tot.)	Kellen Winslow, 11-22-81	5
Points	Kellen Winslow, 11-22-81	30

1991 Team Record

Preseason (1-3)

Date	Result		Opponents
8/3	W	31-29	Houston
8/12	L	3-24	at L.A. Rams
8/19	L	13-24	at San Francisco
8/23	L	7-17	L.A. Raiders

Regular Season (4-12)

Date	Result		Opponents	Att.
9/1	L	20-26	at Pittsburgh	55,848
9/8	L	14-34	at San Francisco	60,753
9/15	L	10-13	Atlanta	44,804
9/22	L	19-27	at Denver	73,258
9/29	L	13-14	Kansas City	44,907
10/6	W	21-13	at L.A. Raiders	42,787
10/13	L	24-30	at L.A. Rams	47,433
10/20	L	24-30	Cleveland (OT)	48,440
10/27	L	9-20	at Seattle	58,025
11/10	W	17-14	Seattle	43,597
11/17	W	24-21	New Orleans	48,420
11/24	L	3-24	at N.Y. Jets	59,025
12/1	L	7- 9	L.A. Raiders	56,780
12/8	L	17-20	at K.C. (OT)	73,330
12/15	W	38-30	Miami	47,731
12/22	L	14-17	Denver	51,449

(OT) Overtime

Score by Periods

Chargers	41	95	37	101	0	—	274
Opponents	63	97	73	100	9	—	342

Attendance

Home 368,128   Away 470,459   Total 856,587
Single-game home record, 61,880 (11-29-87)
Single-season home record, 415,626 (1985)

1991 Team Statistics

	Chargers	Opp.
Total First Downs	285	292
Rushing	114	94
Passing	155	181
Penalty	16	17
Third Down: Made/Att.	76/217	68/189
Third Down: Pct.	35.0	36.0
Fourth Down: Made/Att.	13/25	6/8
Fourth Down: Pct.	52.0	75.0
Total Net Yards	4995	5111
Avg. Per Game	312.2	319.4
Total Plays	1010	961
Avg. Per Play	4.9	5.3
Net Yards Rushing	2248	1666
Avg. Per Game	140.5	104.1
Total Rushes	464	430
Net Yards Passing	2747	3445
Avg. Per Game	171.7	215.3
Sacked/Yards Lost	35/236	28/183
Gross Yards	2983	3628
Att./Completions	511/272	503/300
Completion Pct.	53.2	59.6
Had Intercepted	16	19
Punts/Avg.	77/39.8	76/40.3
Net Punting Avg.	34.8	35.2
Penalties/Yards Lost	96/799	87/718
Fumbles/Ball Lost	24/12	22/9
Touchdowns	31	39
Rushing	16	15
Passing	13	22
Returns	2	2
Avg. Time of Possession	30:02	29:58

1991 Individual Statistics

Scoring

	TD R	TD P	TD Rt	PAT	FG	Saf	TP
Carney	0	0	0	31/31	19/29	0	88
Bernstine	8	0	0	0/0	0/0	0	48
Butts	6	1	0	0/0	0/0	0	42
Lewis	0	3	1	0/0	0/0	0	24
McEwen	0	3	0	0/0	0/0	0	18
Miller	0	3	0	0/0	0/0	0	18
Harmon	1	1	0	0/0	0/0	0	12
Hendrickson	1	1	0	0/0	0/0	0	12
Frank	0	0	1	0/0	0/0	0	6
Jefferson	0	1	0	0/0	0/0	0	6
Chargers	16	13	2	31/31	19/29	0	274
Opponents	15	22	2	37/38	23/29	1	342

Passing

	Att.	Comp.	Yds.	Pct.	TD	Int.	Tkld.	Rate
Friesz	487	262	2896	53.8	12	15	32/214	67.1
Gagliano	23	9	76	39.1	0	1	3/22	30.3
Bernstine	1	1	11	100.0	0	0	0/0	152.1
Chargers	511	272	2983	53.2	13	16	35/236	66.2
Opponents	503	300	3628	59.6	22	19	28/183	80.7

Rushing

	Att.	Yds.	Avg.	LG	TD
Butts	193	834	4.3	44	6
Bernstine	159	766	4.8	63t	8
Harmon	89	544	6.1	33	1
Jefferson	1	27	27.0	27	0
Gagliano	3	19	6.3	16	0
Friesz	10	18	1.8	11	0
Bieniemy	3	17	5.7	15	0
Lewis	3	10	3.3	9	0
Samuels	2	10	5.0	6	0
Hendrickson	1	3	3.0	3t	1
Chargers	464	2248	4.8	63t	16
Opponents	430	1666	3.9	63t	15

Receiving

	No.	Yds.	Avg.	LG	TD
Harmon	59	555	9.4	36	1
Miller	44	649	14.8	58	3
Lewis	42	554	13.2	49t	3
McEwen	37	399	10.8	30	3
Taylor	24	218	9.1	27	0
Walker	20	134	6.7	14	0
Jefferson	12	125	10.4	29	1
Bernstine	11	124	11.3	25	0
Butts	10	91	9.1	46	1
Cox	5	53	10.6	19	0
Hendrickson	4	36	9.0	20	1
Samuels	2	33	16.5	29	0
Young	2	12	6.0	6	0
Chargers	272	2983	11.0	58	13
Opponents	300	3628	12.1	89t	22

Interceptions

	No.	Yds.	Avg.	LG	TD
Byrd	6	48	8.0	22	0
Carrington	3	30	10.0	19	0
Rolling	2	54	27.0	47	0
Richard	2	5	2.5	3	0
Smith	2	0	0.0	0	0
Frank	1	71	71.0	71t	1
Shelton	1	19	19.0	19	0
Bayless	1	0	0.0	0	0
Elder	1	0	0.0	0	0
Chargers	19	227	11.9	71t	1
Opponents	16	183	11.4	49	1

Punting

	No.	Yds.	Avg.	In 20	LG
Kidd	76	3064	40.3	22	60
Chargers	77	3064	39.8	22	60
Opponents	76	3064	40.3	18	60

Punt Returns

	No.	FC	Yds.	Avg.	LG	TD
Taylor	28	18	269	9.6	48	0
Lewis	5	5	59	11.8	26	0
Byrd	0	2	0	—	0	0
Chargers	33	25	328	9.9	48	0
Opponents	32	25	267	8.3	32	0

Kickoff Returns

	No.	Yds.	Avg.	LG	TD
Lewis	23	578	25.1	95t	1
Elder	27	535	19.8	42	0
Harmon	2	25	12.5	14	0
Benson	1	2	2.0	2	0
Bernstine	1	7	7.0	7	0
Butts	1	0	0.0	0	0
Carrington	0	24	—	24	0
Chargers	55	1171	21.3	95t	1
Opponents	52	1034	19.9	76	0

Sacks

	No.
O'Neal	9.0
Seau	7.0
Grossman	5.5
Benson	1.0
Elder	1.0
Phillips	1.0
Plummer	1.0
Rolling	1.0
Shelton	1.0
Hinkle	0.5
Chargers	28.0
Opponents	35.0

1992 Draft Choices

Round	Name	Pos.	College
1.	Chris Mims	DE	Tennessee
2.	Marquez Pope	DB	Fresno State
3.	Ray Ethridge	WR	Pasadena C.C.
5.	Curtis Whitley	C	Clemson
	Kevin Little	LB	North Carolina A&T
	Eric Jonassen	T	Bloomsburg
6.	Reggie White	DT	North Carolina A&T
7.	Deems May	TE	North Carolina
8.	James Fuller	DB	Portland State
9.	Johnnie Barnes	WR	Hampton
10.	Arthur Paul	DT	Arizona State
11.	Keith McAfee	RB	Texas A&M
12.	Carlos Huerta	K	Miami

San Diego Chargers 1992 Veteran Roster

No.	Name	Pos.	Ht.	Wt.	Birth-date	NFL Exp.	College	Hometown	How Acq.	'91 Games/ Starts
85	Affholter, Eric	WR	6-0	187	4/10/66	2	Southern California	Agoura, Calif.	PB(GB)-'92#	4/0*
52	Anno, Sam	LB	6-3	240	1/26/65	6	Southern California	Santa Monica, Calif.	PB(TB)-'92#	16/0*
95	Benson, Mitchell	DT	6-4	300	5/30/67	4	Texas Christian	Ft. Worth, Tex.	FA-'91	16/0
82	†Bernstine, Rod	RB	6-3	238	2/8/65	6	Texas A&M	Bryan, Tex.	D1-'87	13/8
32	Bieniemy, Eric	RB	5-7	210	8/15/69	2	Colorado	West Covina, Calif.	D2b-'91	15/0
37	Blaylock, Tony	CB	5-10	190	2/21/65	5	Winston-Salem State	Garner, N.C.	W(Clev)-'91	7/1*
35	Butts, Marion	RB	6-1	248	8/1/66	4	Florida State	Sylvester, Ga.	D7a-'89	16/8
22	Byrd, Gill	CB-S	5-11	198	2/20/61	10	San Jose State	San Francisco, Calif.	D1c-'83	15/15
3	†Carney, John	K	5-11	170	4/20/64	4	Notre Dame	West Palm Beach, Fla.	FA-'90	16/0
29	Carrington, Darren	S	6-2	200	10/10/66	4	Northern Arizona	Bronx, N.Y.	FA-'91	16/1
59	Clark, Greg	LB	6-0	226	3/5/65	5	Arizona State	Torrance, Calif.	W(GB)-'91	14/0
28	Elder, Donnie	CB	5-9	178	12/13/63	7	Memphis State	Chattanooga, Tenn.	FA-'90	16/1
88	Faison, Derrick	WR	6-4	200	8/24/67	2	Howard	Lake City, S.C.	FA-'92	0*
27	Frank, Donald	CB	6-0	192	10/24/65	3	Winston-Salem State	Tarboro, N.C.	FA-'90	16/1
17	†Friesz, John	QB	6-4	218	5/19/67	2	Idaho	Coeur d'Alene, Idaho	D6a-'90	16/16
16	Gagliano, Bob	QB	6-3	205	9/5/58	8	Utah State	Glendale, Calif.	PB(Det)-'91#	2/0
67	†Goeas, Leo	G-T	6-4	292	8/15/66	3	Hawaii	Honolulu, Hawaii	D3b-'90	9/4
58	Grayson, David	LB	6-3	233	2/27/64	5	Fresno State	San Diego, Calif.	FA-'91	1/0
92	Grossman, Burt	DE	6-4	255	4/10/67	4	Pittsburgh	Bala-Cynwyd, Pa.	D1-'89	16/16
53	†Hall, Courtney	C-G	6-1	281	8/26/68	4	Rice	Wilmington, Del.	D2a-'89	16/16
36	Hall, Delton	S	6-1	211	1/16/65	6	Clemson	Greensboro, N.C.	PB(Pitt)-'92#	6/0*
33	Harmon, Ronnie	RB	5-11	207	5/7/64	7	Iowa	Queens, N.Y.	PB(Buff)-'90#	16/0
34	Hendrickson, Steve	RB-LB	6-0	258	8/30/66	4	California	Napa, Calif.	FA-'90	15/4
39	Jackson, Cedric	RB	6-0	235	1/13/68	2	Texas Christian	Texarkana, Tex.	PB(Det)-'92#	8/1*
80	Jefferson, Shawn	WR	5-11	172	2/22/69	2	Central Flordia	Jacksonville, Fla.	T(Hou)-'91	16/3
98	Joelson, Greg	DE	6-3	270	8/22/66	2	Arizona State	Coos Bay, Ore.	PB(SF)-'92#	4/0*
10	†Kidd, John	P	6-3	208	8/22/61	9	Northwestern	Findlay, Ohio	PB(Buff)-'90#	16/0
81	Lewis, Nate	WR	5-11	198	10/19/66	3	Oregon Tech	Moultrie, Ga.	D7c-'90	16/9
47	†Mack, Cedric	CB	5-11	190	9/14/60	10	Baylor	Freeport, Tex.	W(Phx)-'91	7/1
99	Marve, Eugene	LB	6-2	240	8/14/60	11	Saginaw Valley State	Flint, Mich.	PB(TB)-'92#	16/6*
31	McEwen, Craig	RB	6-1	226	12/16/65	6	Utah	Northport, N.Y.	FA-'91	16/6
83	Miller, Anthony	WR	5-11	189	4/15/65	5	Tennessee	Pasadena, Calif.	D1-'88	13/12
77	Moten, Eric	G	6-2	306	4/11/68	2	Michigan State	Cleveland Heights, Ohio	D2c-'91	16/11
91	†O'Neal, Leslie	DE	6-4	259	5/7/64	6	Oklahoma State	Little Rock, Ark.	D1a-'86	16/16
38	Oldham, Chris	CB	5-9	183	10/26/68	3	Oregon	Sacramento, Calif.	FA-'92	4/0*
75	†Phillips, Joe	NT	6-5	315	7/15/63	7	Southern Methodist	Vancouver, Wash.	FA-'87	16/15
50	†Plummer, Gary	LB	6-2	244	1/26/60	7	California	Fremont, Calif.	FA-'86	16/15
24	Richard, Stanley	S	6-2	197	10/21/67	2	Texas	Hawkins, Tex.	D1-'91	15/14
65	†Richards, David	G-T	6-4	310	4/11/66	5	UCLA	Dallas, Tex.	D4c-'88	16/16
57	†Rolling, Henry	LB	6-2	225	9/8/65	5	Nevada-Reno	Henderson, Nev.	FA-'90	15/13
20	Samuels, Chris	RB	5-10	202	5/16/69	2	Texas	San Antonio, Tex.	D12-'91	3/0
55	Seau, Junior	LB	6-3	250	1/19/69	3	Southern California	Oceanside, Calif.	D1-'90	16/16
23	†Shelton, Anthony	S	6-1	195	9/4/67	3	Tennessee State	Fayetteville, Tenn.	W(SF)-'90	11/4
54	Smith, Billy Ray	LB	6-3	236	8/10/61	10	Arkansas	Plano, Tex.	D1a-'83	14/3
72	Swayne, Harry	T	6-5	290	2/2/65	6	Rutgers	Philadelphia, Pa.	PB(TB)-'91#	12/12
56	Thaxton, Galand	LB	6-1	240	10/23/64	3	Wyoming	Denver, Colo.	PB(Atl)-'91#	14/0
84	Thigpen, Yancey	WR	6-0	208	8/15/69	2	Winston-Salem State	Tarboro, N.C.	D4-'91	4/1
76	†Thompson, Broderick	G-T	6-4	295	8/14/60	7	Kansas	Cerritos, Calif.	FA-'87	16/16
93	Thornton, George	DT	6-3	300	4/28/68	2	Alabama	Montgomery, Ala.	D2a-'91	16/3
86	Verhulst, Chris	TE	6-3	245	5/16/66	3	Chico State	San Ramon, Calif.	FA-'92	0*
89	Walker, Derrick	TE	6-0	250	6/23/67	3	Michigan	Chicago Heights, Ill.	D6d-'90	16/16
73	Walker, Jeff	G-T	6-4	286	1/22/63	3	Memphis State	Olive Branch, Miss.	FA-'92	0*
87	Young, Duane	TE	6-1	276	5/29/68	2	Michigan State	Kalamazoo, Mich.	D5-'91	7/5
70	†Zandofsky, Mike	C-G	6-2	305	11/30/65	4	Washington	Corvallis, Ore.	T(Phx)-'90	10/5

* Affholter played 4 games with Green Bay in '91; Anno played 16 games with Tampa Bay; Blaylock played 5 games with Cleveland, 2 with San Diego; Faison last active with L.A. Rams in '90; Hall played 6 games with Pittsburgh; Jackson played 8 games with Detroit; Joelson played 4 games with San Francisco; Marve played 16 games with Tampa Bay; Oldham played 2 games with Buffalo, 2 with Phoenix; Verhulst last active with Denver in '90; J. Walker last active with New Orleans in '89.

† Option playout; subject to developments.

Plan B unconditional free agent.

Players lost through Plan B (11): S Martin Bayless (KC; 16 games in '91), C Frank Cornish (Dall; 16), T Eric Floyd (Phil; 2), DE George Hinkle (Wash; 13), WR David Jones (Raid; 0), LB Randy Kirk (Cin; 5), G Mark May (Phx; 9), DE Skip McClendon (Minn; 2), C Mark Rodenhauser (Chi; 10), CB Sam Seale (Raid; 16), WR Kitrick Taylor (GB; 12).

Also played with Chargers in '91—TE Arthur Cox (8 games), S Floyd Fields (1), TE Mark Walczak (1), LB Mike Wilcher (2).

COACHING STAFF

Head Coach, Bobby Ross

Pro Career: Begins first season as San Diego's head coach. Named ninth head coach in Chargers' history January 2, 1992. Ross began his pro coaching career in 1978 as an assistant with the Kansas City Chiefs, where he coached special teams and defense in 1978-79 and offensive backs in 1980-81. No pro playing experience.

Background: Played quarterback and defensive back for Virginia Military Institute. Began coaching career in 1965 at VMI. Moved on as an assistant at William & Mary 1967-70, Rice 1971, and Maryland 1972. Head coach at The Citadel 1973-77. Compiled 39-19-1 (.672) record as he led Maryland (1982-86) to three Atlantic Coast Conference titles and made four bowl game appearances in five seasons. Guided Georgia Tech (1987-91) to first ACC title in school history. Under Ross, the Yellow Jackets won first national championship as country's only undefeated team (11-0-1) in 1990. Named consensus national coach of the year in 1990. Career collegiate head coaching record: 94-76-2.

Personal: Born December 23, 1936, Richmond, Va. Bobby and wife, Alice, live in San Diego and have five children—Chris, Kevin, Robbie, Mary, and Teresa.

Assistant Coaches

Bill Arnsparger, defensive coordinator; born December 16, 1926, Paris, Ky., lives in San Diego. Tackle Miami (Ohio) 1946-49. No pro playing experience. College coach: Miami (Ohio) 1950, Ohio State 1951-53, Kentucky 1954-61, Tulane 1962-63, Louisiana State 1984-86, Florida 1987-91 (athletic director). Pro coach: Baltimore Colts 1964-69, Miami Dolphins 1970-73, 1976-83, New York Giants 1974-76 (head coach), joined Chargers in 1992.

Sylvester Croom, offensive backs; born September 25, 1954, Tuscaloosa, Ala., lives in San Diego. Center Alabama 1971-74. Pro center New Orleans Saints 1975. College coach: Alabama 1976-86. Pro coach: Tampa Bay Buccaneers 1987-90, Indianapolis Colts 1991, joined Chargers in 1992.

John Dunn, strength and conditioning; born July 22, 1956, Hillsdale, N.Y., lives in San Diego. Guard Penn State 1974-77. No pro playing experience. College coach: Penn State 1978. Pro coach: Washington Redskins 1984-86, Los Angeles Raiders 1987-89, joined Chargers in 1990.

John Fox, defensive backs; born February 8, 1955, Virginia Beach, Va., lives in San Diego. Defensive back San Diego State 1975-77. No pro playing experience. College coach: U.S. International 1979, Boise State 1980, Long Beach State 1981, Utah 1982, Kansas 1983, 1985, Iowa State 1984, Pittsburgh 1986-88. Pro coach: Los Angeles Express (USFL) 1985, Pittsburgh Steelers 1989-91, joined Chargers in 1992.

Ralph Friedgen, tight ends-running game coordinator; born April 4, 1947, Harrison, N.Y., lives in San Diego. Guard Maryland 1967-68. No pro playing experience. College coach: The Citadel 1973-79, William & Mary 1980, Murray State 1981, Maryland 1982-86, Georgia Tech 1987-91. Pro coach: Joined Chargers in 1992.

Dale Lindsey, linebackers; born January 18, 1943, Bedford, Ind., lives in San Diego. Linebacker Western Kentucky 1961-64. Pro linebacker Cleveland Browns 1965-73. College coach: Southern Methodist 1988-89. Pro coach: Cleveland Browns 1974, Portland Storm (WFL) 1975, Toronto Argonauts (CFL) 1979-82, Boston Breakers (USFL) 1983, New Jersey Generals (USFL) 1984-85, Green Bay Packers 1986-87, New England Patriots 1990, Tampa Bay Buccaneers 1991, joined Chargers in 1992.

Carl Mauck, offensive line; born July 7, 1947, McLeansboro, Ill., lives in San Diego. Linebacker-center Southern Illinois 1966-68. Pro center Baltimore Colts 1969, Miami Dolphins 1970, San Diego Chargers 1971-74, Houston Oilers 1975-81. Pro coach: New Orleans Saints 1982-85, Kansas City Chiefs 1986-88, Tampa Bay Buccaneers 1991, joined Chargers in 1992.

John Misciagna, quality control; born December 11, 1954, Brooklyn, N.Y., lives in San Diego. Guard Dickinson College 1973-76. No pro playing experience. College coach: Indiana (Pa.) University 1977, Columbia 1978-79, Maryland 1980-88, Georgia Tech 1989-91. Pro coach: Joined Chargers in 1992.

George O'Leary, defensive line; born August 17, 1946, New York, N.Y., lives in San Diego. Offensive lineman-fullback New Hampshire 1964-67. No pro playing experience. College coach: Syracuse 1980-86, Georgia Tech 1987-91. Pro coach: Joined Chargers in 1992.

Chuck Priefer, special teams; born July 26, 1941, Cleveland, Ohio, lives in San Diego. No college or pro playing experience. College coach: Miami (Ohio) 1977, North Carolina 1978-83, Kent State 1986, Georgia Tech 1987-91. Pro coach: Green Bay Packers 1984-85, joined Chargers in 1992.

Jack Reilly, quarterbacks-passing game coordinator; born May 22, 1945, Boston, Mass., lives in San Diego. Quarterback Washington State 1963, Santa Monica, Calif., College 1964, Long Beach State 1965-66. No pro playing experience. College coach: El Camino, Calif., J.C. 1980-84, Utah 1985-89 (head coach). Pro coach: Joined Chargers in 1990.

Jerry Sullivan, wide receivers; born July 13, 1944, Miami, Fla., lives in San Diego. Quarterback Florida State 1963-64. No pro playing experience. College coach: Kansas State 1971-72, Texas Tech 1973-75, South Carolina 1976-82, Indiana 1983, Louisiana State 1984-90, Ohio State 1991. Pro coach: Joined Chargers in 1992.

San Diego Chargers 1992 First-Year Roster

Name	Pos.	Ht.	Wt.	Birth-date	College	Hometown	How Acq.
Andrews, Rich (1)	K	5-11	175	3/11/69	Florida State	Ft. Lauderdale, Fla.	FA
Barnes, Johnnie	WR	6-1	173	7/21/68	Hampton	Suffolk, Va.	D9
Beauford, Terry (1)	G	6-1	296	3/27/68	Florida A&M	Ft. Pierce, Fla.	D7b-'91
Brown, Leon	RB	5-10	213	5/12/68	Temple	Ocean City, N.J.	FA
Collins, Chris	LB	6-2	233	11/1/68	Southern Methodist	Dallas, Tex.	FA
Doggette, Cecil	CB	5-9	183	11/15/70	West Virginia	Queens, N.Y.	FA
Ethridge, Ray (1)	WR	5-10	180	9/11/68	Pasadena City Col.	San Diego, Calif.	D3
Fields, Floyd (1)	S	6-0	208	1/7/69	Arizona State	South Holland, Ill.	D5b-'91
Fuller, James	S	5-11	208	8/5/69	Portland State	Tacoma, Wash.	D8
Graham, Jeff (1)	QB	6-6	220	2/5/66	Long Beach State	Costa Mesa, Calif.	FA-'91
Huerta, Carlos	K	5-7	172	6/29/69	Miami	Coral Gables, Fla.	D12
Jenkins, Darryl (1)	T	6-4	310	5/3/67	Georgia Tech	Jacksonville, Fla.	FA
Johnson, Jarrod (1)	C	6-1	280	3/29/69	Lehigh	West Orange, N.J.	FA
Jonassen, Eric	T	6-5	310	8/16/68	Bloomsburg	Glen Burnie, Md.	D5c
Jones, Kenneth (1)	CB-S	6-1	205	9/12/68	Tennessee State	Nashville, Tenn.	FA
Jones, Richard (1)	P	6-3	200	3/25/65	Arizona State	Scottsdale, Ariz.	FA
Kaaialii, Mitch	G	6-4	292	10/28/68	Hawaii	Las Vegas, Nev.	FA
Katoa, Andy (1)	LB	6-2	238	8/18/65	Southern Oregon St.	Millbrae, Calif.	D9-'91
Kelson, Derrick (1)	CB-S	6-0	187	5/14/68	Purdue	Warren, Ohio	FA
Laister, Jimmy	G-T	6-6	305	4/12/69	Oregon Tech	Maplesville, Ala.	D6
Lenseigne, Tony	RB	6-4	240	8/7/69	Eastern Washington	Yakima, Wash.	FA
Little, Kevin	LB	6-2	251	12/19/69	North Carolina A&T	Charleston, N.C.	D5b
May, Deems	TE	6-4	250	3/6/69	North Carolina	Lexington, N.C.	D7
McAfee, Keith	RB	6-0	214	2/21/69	Texas A&M	Sugerland, Tex.	D11
Mims, Chris	DE	6-5	270	9/29/70	Tennessee	Los Angeles, Calif.	D1
O'Hara, Pat (1)	QB	6-3	205	9/27/68	Southern California	Santa Monica, Calif.	FA
Parrish, James (1)	T	6-5	292	5/19/68	Temple	Baltimore, Md.	FA
Paul, Arthur	DT	6-6	307	8/23/68	Arizona State	Washington, D.C.	D10
Pope, Marquez	CB	5-10	188	10/29/70	Fresno State	Moreno Valley, Calif.	D2
Price, Terry (1)	DE	6-4	272	4/5/68	Texas A&M	Plano, Tex.	FA
Raye, Jimmy (1)	WR	5-9	165	11/24/68	San Diego State	Irvine, Calif.	FA
Savage, Tony (1)	DT	6-3	300	7/7/67	Washington State	San Francisco, Calif.	FA
Vanhorse, Sean (1)	CB	5-10	180	7/22/68	Howard	Baltimore, Md.	FA
Walkinshaw, Don	G	6-4	285	12/26/69	Portland State	Spanaway, Wash.	FA
White, Reggie	DT	6-4	291	3/22/70	North Carolina A&T	Mulford Mills, Md.	D6
Whitley, Curtis	C	6-1	288	5/10/69	Clemson	Smithfield, N.C.	D5a
Williams, Wayne	CB	5-9	175	10/14/69	Louisiana State	West Columbia, Tex.	FA

The term NFL Rookie is defined as a player who is in his first season of professional football and has not been on the roster of another professional football team for any regular-season or postseason games. A Rookie is designated by an "R" on NFL rosters. Players who have been active in another professional football league or players who have NFL experience, including either preseason training camp or being on an active roster for fewer than three regular-season or postseason games, are termed NFL First-Year Players. An NFL First-Year Player is designated by a "1" on NFL rosters. Thereafter, a player on an NFL active roster for at least three regular-season or postseason games is credited with an additional year of NFL playing experience.

NOTES

_____

_____

_____

_____

_____

_____

_____

SEATTLE SEAHAWKS

American Football Conference
Western Division

Team Colors: Blue, Green, and Silver

11220 N.E. 53rd Street
Kirkland, Washington 98033
Telephone: (206) 827-9777

Club Officials

Owner: Ken Behring
President/Head Coach: Tom Flores
Executive Vice President: Mickey Loomis
Vice President/Football Operations:
  Chuck Allen
Vice President/Administration and Public
  Relations: Gary Wright
Player Personnel Director: Mike Allman
Publicity Director: Dave Neubert
Community Relations Director: Sandy Gregory
Sales and Marketing Director: Reggie McKenzie
Data Processing Director: Tom Monroe
Ticket Manager: James Nagaoka
Trainer: Jim Whitesel
Equipment Manager: Walt Loeffler
Team Physicians: Dr. Kevin Auld, Dr. Pierce
Scranton, Dr. James Trombold,
  Dr. Pete Van Patten

Stadium: Kingdome • Capacity: 64,400
  201 South King Street
  Seattle, Washington 98104

Playing Surface: AstroTurf

Training Camp: 11220 N.E. 53rd Street
  Kirkland, Washington 98033

1992 Schedule

Preseason
Aug. 6	**Los Angeles Rams**	6:00
Aug. 15	at Indianapolis	7:30
Aug. 22	**Phoenix**	7:00
Aug. 28	at San Francisco	5:00

Regular Season
Sept. 6	**Cincinnati**	1:00
Sept. 13	at Kansas City	12:00
Sept. 20	at New England	1:00
Sept. 27	**Miami**	1:00
Oct. 4	at San Diego	1:00
Oct. 11	at Dallas	12:00
Oct. 18	**Los Angeles Raiders**	1:00
Oct. 25	at New York Giants	1:00
Nov. 1	**Open Date**	
Nov. 8	**Washington**	1:00
Nov. 15	at Los Angeles Raiders	1:00
Nov. 22	**Kansas City**	5:00
Nov. 30	**Denver** (Monday)	6:00
Dec. 6	at Pittsburgh	1:00
Dec. 13	**Philadelphia**	1:00
Dec. 20	at Denver	2:00
Dec. 27	**San Diego**	1:00

Seahawks Coaching History
(122-129-0)

1976-82	Jack Patera*		35-59-0
1982	Mike McCormack		4-3-0
1983-91	Chuck Knox		83-67-0

*Released after two games in 1982

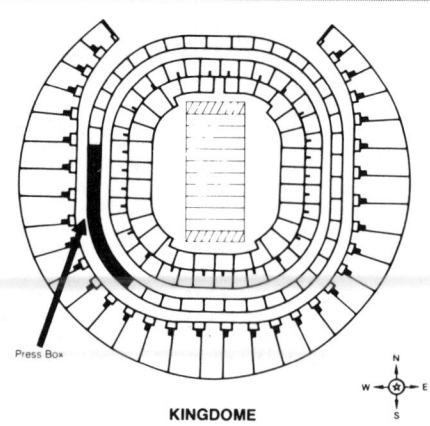

Press Box

KINGDOME

Record Holders
Individual Records—Career

Category	Name	Performance
Rushing (Yds.)	Curt Warner, 1983-89	6,705
Passing (Yds.)	Dave Krieg, 1980-1991	26,132
Passing (TDs)	Dave Krieg, 1980-1991	195
Receiving (No.)	Steve Largent, 1976-1989	*819
Receiving (Yds.)	Steve Largent, 1976-1989	*13,089
Interceptions	Dave Brown, 1976-1986	50
Punting (Avg.)	Ruben Rodriguez, 1987-89	40.3
Punt Return (Avg.)	Paul Johns, 1981-84	11.4
Kickoff Return (Avg.)	Bobby Joe Edmonds, 1986-88	22.1
Field Goals	Norm Johnson, 1982-1990	159
Touchdowns (Tot.)	Steve Largent, 1976-1989	101
Points	Norm Johnson, 1982-1990	810

Individual Records—Single Season

Category	Name	Performance
Rushing (Yds.)	Curt Warner, 1986	1,481
Passing (Yds.)	Dave Krieg, 1984	3,671
Passing (TDs)	Dave Krieg, 1984	32
Receiving (No.)	Steve Largent, 1985	79
Receiving (Yds.)	Steve Largent, 1985	1,287
Interceptions	John Harris, 1981	10
	Kenny Easley, 1984	10
Punting (Avg.)	Rick Tuten, 1991	43.0
Punt Return (Avg.)	Bobby Joe Edmonds, 1987	12.6
Kickoff Return (Avg.)	Al Hunter, 1978	24.1
Field Goals	John Kasay, 1991	25
Touchdowns (Tot.)	David Sims, 1978	15
	Sherman Smith, 1979	15
	Derrick Fenner, 1990	15
Points	Norm Johnson, 1984	110

Individual Records—Single Game

Category	Name	Performance
Rushing (Yds.)	Curt Warner, 11-27-83	207
Passing (Yds.)	Dave Krieg, 11-20-83	418
Passing (TDs)	Dave Krieg, 12-2-84	5
	Dave Krieg, 9-15-85	5
	Dave Krieg, 11-28-88	5
Receiving (No.)	Steve Largent, 10-18-87	15
Receiving (Yds.)	Steve Largent, 10-18-87	261
Interceptions	Kenny Easley, 9-3-84	3
Field Goals	Norm Johnson, 9-20-87	5
	Norm Johnson, 12-18-88	5
Touchdowns (Tot.)	Daryl Turner, 9-15-85	4
	Curt Warner, 12-11-88	4
Points	Daryl Turner, 9-15-85	24
	Curt Warner, 12-11-88	24

*NFL Record

1991 Team Record

Preseason (2-2)

Date	Result		Opponents
8/3	L	13-31	Phoenix
8/10	W	17- 7	at Indianapolis
8/17	W	23- 7	at L.A. Rams
8/23	L	16-28	San Francisco

Regular Season (7-9)

Date	Result		Opponents	Att.
9/1	L	24-27	at New Orleans	68,492
9/8	W	20-13	N.Y. Jets	56,770
9/15	L	10-16	at Denver	74,152
9/22	L	13-20	at Kansas City	71,789
9/29	W	31- 3	Indianapolis	56,656
10/6	W	13- 7	at Cincinnati	60,010
10/13	L	20-23	L.A. Raiders (OT)	61,974
10/20	W	27- 7	at Pittsburgh	54,678
10/27	W	20- 9	San Diego	58,025
11/10	L	14-17	at San Diego	43,597
11/17	L	7-31	at L.A. Raiders	49,317
11/24	W	13-10	Denver	60,430
12/1	L	6-19	Kansas City	57,248
12/8	L	22-24	San Francisco	56,711
12/15	L	13-26	at Atlanta	53,834
12/22	W	23- 9	L.A. Rams	51,100

(OT) Overtime

Score by Periods

Seahawks	39	78	79	80	0	—	276
Opponents	25	112	47	74	3	—	261

Attendance

Home 484,914   Away 475,869   Total 934,783
Single-game home record, 64,411 (12-15-84)
Single-season home record, 494,103 (1988)

1991 Team Statistics

	Seahawks	Opp.
Total First Downs	253	262
Rushing	80	91
Passing	159	159
Penalty	14	12
Third Down: Made/Att.	67/193	78/220
Third Down: Pct.	34.7	35.5
Fourth Down: Made/Att.	2/9	9/20
Fourth Down: Pct.	22.2	45.0
Total Net Yards	4534	4703
Avg. Per Game	283.4	293.9
Total Plays	924	988
Avg. Per Play	4.9	4.8
Net Yards Rushing	1426	1684
Avg. Per Game	89.1	105.3
Total Rushes	394	435
Net Yards Passing	3108	3019
Avg. Per Game	194.3	188.7
Sacked/Yards Lost	42/263	36/269
Gross Yards	3371	3288
Att./Completions	488/290	517/296
Completion Pct.	59.4	57.3
Had Intercepted	26	18
Punts/Avg.	76/40.6	79/39.1
Net Punting Avg.	35.7	33.0
Penalties/Yards Lost	85/682	108/845
Fumbles/Ball Lost	26/17	34/21
Touchdowns	29	25
Rushing	11	4
Passing	15	18
Returns	3	3
Avg. Time of Possession	29:27	30:33

1991 Individual Statistics

Scoring

	TD R	TD P	TD Rt	PAT	FG	Saf	TP
Kasay	0	0	0	27/28	25/31	0	102
Williams	4	1	0	0/0	0/0	0	30
Fenner	4	0	0	0/0	0/0	0	24
Tice	0	4	0	0/0	0/0	0	24
Chadwick	0	3	0	0/0	0/0	0	18
Jones	3	0	0	0/0	0/0	0	18
Blades	0	2	0	0/0	0/0	0	12
L. Clark	0	2	0	0/0	0/0	0	12
Kane	0	2	0	0/0	0/0	0	12
B. Davis	0	0	1	0/0	0/0	0	6
Hunter	0	0	1	0/0	0/0	0	6
McNeal	0	1	0	0/0	0/0	0	6
Warren	0	0	1	0/0	0/0	0	6
Seahawks	11	15	3	27/29	25/31	0	276
Opponents	4	18	3	25/25	28/32	1	261

Passing

	Att.	Comp.	Yds.	Pct.	TD	Int.	Tkld.	Rate
Krieg	285	187	2080	65.6	11	12	32/216	82.5
Kemp	181	94	1207	51.9	4	12	8/38	52.9
Stouffer	15	6	57	40.0	0	1	2/9	23.5
McGwire	7	3	27	42.9	0	1	0/0	14.3
Seahawks	488	290	3371	59.4	15	26	42/263	68.4
Opponents	517	296	3288	57.3	18	18	36/269	73.4

Rushing

	Att.	Yds.	Avg.	LG	TD
Williams	188	741	3.9	42	4
Fenner	91	267	2.9	15	4
Jones	45	154	3.4	22	3
Kemp	22	106	4.8	18	0
Loville	22	69	3.1	22	0
Krieg	13	59	4.5	24	0
Blades	2	17	8.5	11	0
Warren	11	13	1.2	7	0
Seahawks	394	1426	3.6	42	11
Opponents	435	1684	3.9	32	4

Receiving

	No.	Yds.	Avg.	LG	TD
Blades	70	1003	14.3	52	2
Williams	61	499	8.2	35	1
Kane	50	763	15.3	60	2
Chadwick	22	255	11.6	29	3
L. Clark	21	228	10.9	24t	2
McNeal	17	208	12.2	36	1
Fenner	11	72	6.5	15	0
Jones	10	103	10.3	29	0
Tice	10	70	7.0	16	4
Skansi	9	96	10.7	21	0
Daniels	4	38	9.5	19	0
Thomas	3	27	9.0	11	0
Warren	2	9	4.5	12	0
Seahawks	290	3371	11.6	60	15
Opponents	296	3288	11.1	61t	18

Interceptions

	No.	Yds.	Avg.	LG	TD
Robinson	5	56	11.2	27	0
Harper	4	84	21.0	43	0
Blackmon	3	59	19.7	29	0
B. Davis	1	40	40.0	40t	1
Hunter	1	32	32.0	32t	1
Glasgow	1	28	28.0	28	0
Cain	1	5	5.0	5	0
Porter	1	0	0.0	0	0
Green	1	−2	−2.0	−2	0
Seahawks	18	302	16.8	43	2
Opponents	26	334	12.8	58	2

Punting

	No.	Yds.	Avg.	In 20	LG
Tuten	49	2106	43.0	8	60
Donnelly	13	505	38.8	1	57
Waits	14	474	33.9	2	50
Seahawks	76	3085	40.6	11	60
Opponents	79	3089	39.1	20	65

Punt Returns

	No.	FC	Yds.	Avg.	LG	TD
Warren	32	19	298	9.3	59t	1
Loville	3	1	16	5.3	18	0
B. Davis	1	0	1	1.0	1	0
Harper	1	0	5	5.0	5	0
Skansi	1	0	5	5.0	5	0
Seahawks	38	20	325	8.6	59t	1
Opponents	40	18	289	7.2	29	0

Kickoff Returns

	No.	Yds.	Avg.	LG	TD
Warren	35	792	22.6	55	0
Loville	18	412	22.9	50	0
McNeal	4	30	7.5	15	0
Tice	3	46	15.3	20	0
Seahawks	60	1280	21.3	55	0
Opponents	51	858	16.8	38	0

Sacks

	No.
Porter	10.0
Kennedy	6.5
Green	6.0
Bryant	3.0
Glasgow	2.5
Wooden	2.0
Woods	2.0
Blackmon	1.0
Jefferson	1.0
Robinson	1.0
Comeaux	0.5
Skow	0.5
Seahawks	36.0
Opponents	42.0

1992 Draft Choices

Round	Name	Pos.	College
1.	Ray Roberts	T	Virginia
3.	Bobby Spitulski	LB	Central Florida
5.	Gary Dandridge	DB	Appalachian State
6.	Michael Bates	WR	Arizona
7.	Mike Frier	DT	Appalachian State
8.	Muhammad Shamsid-Deen	RB	Tenn.-Chattanooga
9.	Larry Stayner	TE	Boise State
10.	Anthony Hamlet	DE	Miami
11.	Kris Rongen	G	Washington
12.	Chico Fraley	LB	Washington
	John MacNeill	DE	Michigan State

Seattle Seahawks 1992 Veteran Roster

No.	Name	Pos.	Ht.	Wt.	Birth-date	NFL Exp.	College	Hometown	How Acq.	'91 Games/ Starts
65	Bailey, Edwin	G	6-4	284	5/15/59	12	South Carolina State	Savannah, Ga.	D5-'81	3/3
25	Blackmon, Robert	S	6-0	197	5/12/67	3	Baylor	Van Vleck, Tex.	D2b-'90	16/16
89	†Blades, Brian	WR	5-11	189	7/24/65	5	Miami	Ft. Lauderdale, Fla.	D2-'88	16/16
60	Blados, Brian	C-G	6-5	296	1/11/62	9	North Carolina	Arlington, Va.	PB(Ind)-'92#	13/6*
64	Brilz, Darrick	G	6-3	287	2/14/64	6	Oregon State	Pinole Valley, Calif.	FA-'89	16/7
77	Bryant, Jeff	DT	6-5	281	5/22/60	11	Clemson	Decatur, Ga.	D1-'82	16/14
59	Cain, Joe	LB	6-1	233	6/11/65	4	Oregon Tech	Compton, Calif.	FA-'89	16/0
84	Clark, Louis	WR	6-0	198	7/3/64	6	Mississippi State	Shannon, Miss.	D10-'87	16/0
53	Comeaux, Darren	LB	6-1	239	4/15/60	11	Arizona State	San Diego, Calif.	FA-'91	16/11
51	Cotton, Marcus	LB	6-3	233	8/11/66	5	Southern California	Oakland, Calif.	PB(Clev)-'91#	3/0
88	Daniels, David	WR	6-1	190	9/16/69	2	Penn State	Sarasota, Fla.	D3-'91	16/0
34	Davis, Brian	CB	6-2	187	8/31/63	6	Nebraska	Phoenix, Ariz.	W(Wash)-'90	16/2
33	Dodge, Dedrick	S	6-2	184	6/14/67	2	Florida State	Mulberry, Fla.	FA-'91	11/0
54	Feasel, Grant	C	6-7	283	6/28/60	8	Abilene Christian	Barstow, Calif.	FA-'87	15/15
18	Gelbaugh, Stan	QB	6-3	207	12/4/62	5	Maryland	Mechanicsburg, Pa.	PB(Phx)-'92#	6/3*
22	Glasgow, Nesby	S	5-10	187	4/15/57	14	Washington	Gardena, Calif.	FA-'88	16/1
79	†Green, Jacob	DE	6-3	263	1/21/57	13	Texas A&M	Houston, Tex.	D1-'80	16/16
29	†Harper, Dwayne	CB	5-11	174	3/29/66	5	South Carolina State	Orangeburg, S.C.	D11b-'88	16/16
78	Hayes, Eric	DT	6-3	288	11/12/67	3	Florida State	Tampa, Fla.	D5-'90	5/3
66	Heck, Andy	T	6-6	289	1/1/67	4	Notre Dame	Fairfax, Va.	D1-'89	16/16
82	Heller, Ron	TE	6-3	242	9/18/63	5	Oregon State	Clark Fork, Idaho	FA-'92	0*
16	Hilger, Rusty	QB	6-4	209	5/9/62	6	Oklahoma State	Oklahoma City, Okla.	PB(Ind)-'92#	1/0*
76	Hitchcock, Bill	T	6-6	291	8/26/65	2	Purdue	Kirkland, Canada	FA-'91	16/9
27	Hunter, Patrick	CB	5-11	186	10/24/64	7	Nevada	San Francisco, Calif.	D3-'86	15/15
20	Jefferson, James	CB	6-1	199	11/18/63	4	Texas A&I	Kingsville, Tex.	FA-'89	16/0
43	Johnson, Tracy	RB	6-0	230	11/29/66	4	Clemson	Kannapolis, N.C.	PB(Atl)-'92#	16/5*
30	†Jones, James	RB	6-3	232	3/21/61	10	Florida	Pompano Beach, Fla.	T(Det)-'89	16/6
83	Junkin, Trey	TE	6-2	237	1/23/61	10	Louisiana Tech	Winfield, La.	FA-'90	16/0
81	Kane, Tommy	WR	5-11	181	1/14/64	5	Syracuse	Montreal, Canada	D3-'88	16/15
4	Kasay, John	K	5-10	189	10/27/69	2	Georgia	Athens, Ga.	D4-'91	16/0
96	Kennedy, Cortez	DT	6-3	293	8/23/68	3	Miami	Rivercrest, Ark.	D1-'90	16/16
63	Lee, Ronnie	T	6-3	296	12/24/56	14	Baylor	Tyler, Tex.	T(Atl)-'90	10/7
62	Leggett, Brad	C	6-4	270	1/16/66	2	Southern California	Fountain Valley, Calif.	PB(NO)-'92#	4/2*
36	t-Mayes, Rueben	RB	5-11	200	6/6/63	5	Washington State	North Battleford, Canada	T(NO)-'92	0*
26	McElroy, Vann	S	6-2	199	1/13/60	10	Baylor	Uvalde, Tex.	T(Raid)-'90	0*
10	McGwire, Dan	QB	6-8	243	12/18/67	2	San Diego State	Claremont, Calif.	D1-'91	1/1
86	†McNeal, Travis	TE	6-3	244	1/10/67	4	Tennessee-Chattanooga	Birmingham, Ala.	D4a-'89	16/4
71	Millard, Bryan	G	6-5	277	12/2/60	9	Texas	Dumas, Tex.	FA-'84	16/16
75	t-Millard, Keith	DT	6-5	268	3/18/62	7	Washington State	Pleasanton, Calif.	T(Minn)-'92	0*
72	Nash, Joe	DT	6-3	278	10/11/60	11	Boston College	Dorchester, Mass.	FA-'82	16/0
58	Newbill, Richard	LB	6-1	248	2/8/68	2	Miami	Clearview, N.J.	FA-'91	1/0
21	Oliphant, Mike	RB	5-9	171	5/19/63	4	Puget Sound	Federal Way, Wash.	PB(Clev)-'92#	4/0*
97	Porter, Rufus	LB	6-1	227	5/18/65	5	Southern	Baton Rouge, La.	FA-'88	15/15
41	Robinson, Eugene	S	6-0	191	5/28/63	8	Colgate	Hartford, Conn.	FA-'85	16/16
73	Singer, Curt	G	6-5	281	11/4/61	5	Tennessee	Aliquippa, Pa.	FA-'91	13/0
94	Stephens, Rod	LB	6-1	237	6/14/66	4	Georgia Tech	Atlanta, Ga.	FA-'90	16/0
11	Stouffer, Kelly	QB	6-3	214	7/6/64	4	Colorado State	Rushville, Neb.	T(Phx)-'88	2/1
85	Thomas, Doug	WR	5-10	178	9/18/69	2	Clemson	Hamlet, N.C.	D2-'91	11/0
56	†Tofflemire, Joe	C	6-3	273	7/7/65	3	Arizona	Post Falls, Idaho	D2-'89	0*
14	Tuten, Rick	P	6-2	218	1/5/65	4	Florida State	Ocala, Fla.	FA-'91	10/0
42	Warren, Chris	RB	6-2	225	1/24/67	3	Ferrum	Burke, Va.	D4-'90	16/1
74	Wheat, Warren	G	6-6	286	5/13/67	3	Brigham Young	Phoenix, Ariz.	W(Rams)-'89	14/7
32	Williams, John L.	RB	5-11	231	11/23/64	7	Florida	Palatka, Fla.	D1-'86	16/16
90	Wooden, Terry	LB	6-3	236	1/14/67	3	Syracuse	Farmington, Conn.	D2a-'90	16/15
57	†Woods, Tony	DE	6-4	269	9/11/65	6	Pittsburgh	Newark, N.J.	D1-'87	14/14
92	†Wyman, David	LB	6-2	248	3/31/64	6	Stanford	Reno, Nev.	D2-'87	6/5

* Blados played 6 games with Cincinnati, 7 with Indianapolis in '91; Gelbaugh played 6 games with Phoenix; Heller last active with Atlanta in '90; Hilger played 1 game with Indianapolis; Johnson played 16 games with Atlanta; Leggett played 4 games with New Orleans; Mayes last active with New Orleans in '90; McElroy and K. Millard missed '91 season due to injury; Oliphant played 4 games with Cleveland; Tofflemire active for 1 game but did not play.

† Option playout; subject to developments.

t- Seahawks traded for Mayes (New Orleans) and K. Millard (Minnesota).

Plan B unconditional free agent.

Players lost through Plan B (6): WR Jeff Chadwick (Rams; 12 games in '91), RB Derrick Fenner (Cin; 11), QB Dave Krieg (KC; 10), RB Derek Loville (Rams; 16), DE Jim Skow (Rams; 11), TE Mike Tice (Minn; 16).

Also played with Seahawks in '91—LB Bernard Clark (2 games); P Rick Donnelly (3); QB Jeff Kemp (7); WR Paul Skansi (5); P Alex Waits (3).

COACHING STAFF

President/Head Coach, Tom Flores

Pro Career: Named the fourth head coach in the history of the Seahawks on January 6, 1992. Had served as president and general manager from February 22, 1989. Flores previously served as the head coach of the Oakland/Los Angeles Raiders from 1979 through 1987. He won two Super Bowl titles with the Raiders, 27-10 over the Philadelphia Eagles in Super Bowl XV after the 1980 season, and 38-9 over the Washington Redskins in Super Bowl XVIII in 1983. Those are the only Super Bowl triumphs by an AFC team in the 1980s. The 1980 Raiders are the only Wild Card team to win the Super Bowl. Flores was a member of the Raiders' organization for 22 seasons, as a quarterback (1960-61, 1963-66), assistant coach (1972-78), and head coach (1979-87). Also played for the Buffalo Bills (1967-68) and Kansas City Chiefs (1969-70), and coached with the Bills (1971) before returning to the Raiders as a coach. Is one of two players in league history to have Super Bowl rings as a player (Kansas City, Super Bowl IV), assistant coach (Raiders, Super Bowl XI) and head coach (Raiders, Super Bowls XV and XVIII). Still holds the Raiders' record with six touchdown passes in a 1963 game. Career record: 91-56-0.

Background: Quarterback at Fresno, California, Junior College 1954-55 and the College of the Pacific 1956-57. Coached at his alma mater in 1959 before joining the Raiders as a quarterback in 1960.

Personal: Born March 21, 1937, in Fresno, California. Tom and his wife, Barbara, live in Kirkland, Washington, and have twin sons, Mark and Scott, and a daughter, Kim.

Assistant Coaches

Tommy Brasher, defensive line; born December 30, 1940, El Dorado, Ark., lives in Redmond, Wash. Linebacker Arkansas 1962-63. No pro playing experience. College coach: Arkansas 1970, Virginia Tech 1971, Northeast Louisiana 1974, 1976, Southern Methodist 1977-81. Pro coach: Shreveport Steamer (WFL) 1975, New England Patriots 1982-84, Philadelphia Eagles 1985, Atlanta Falcons 1986-89, Tampa Bay Buccaneers 1990, joined Seahawks in 1992.

Bob Bratkowski, wide receivers; born December 2, 1955, San Angelo, Tex., lives in Redmond, Wash. Wide receiver Washington State 1974, 1976-77. No pro playing experience. College coach: Missouri 1978-80, Weber State 1981-85, Wyoming 1986, Washington State 1987-88, Miami 1989-91. Pro coach: Joined Seahawks in 1992.

Dave Brown, defensive assistant; born January 16, 1953, Akron, Ohio, lives in Seattle. Defensive back Michigan 1972-74. Pro defensive back Pittsburgh Steelers 1975, Seattle Seahawks 1976-86, Green Bay Packers 1987-90. Pro coach: Joined Seahawks in 1992.

Tom Catlin, assistant head coach-defense; born September 8, 1931, Ponca City, Okla., lives in Redmond, Wash. Center-linebacker Oklahoma 1950-52. Pro linebacker Cleveland Browns 1953-54, 1957-58, Philadelphia Eagles 1959. College coach: Army 1956. Pro coach: Dallas Texans-Kansas City Chiefs 1960-65, Los Angeles Rams 1966-77, Buffalo Bills 1978-82, joined Seahawks in 1983.

Hudson Houck, offensive line; born January 7, 1943, Los Angeles, lives in Kirkland, Wash. Center Southern California 1962-64. No pro playing experience. College coach: Southern California 1970-72, 1976-82, Stanford 1973-75. Pro coach: Los Angeles Rams 1983-91, joined Seahawks in 1992.

Seattle Seahawks 1992 First-Year Roster

Name	Pos.	Ht.	Wt.	Birth-date	College	Hometown	How Acq.
Adams, Theo (1)	T	6-4	298	4/24/63	Hawaii	Honolulu, Hawaii	FA
Bates, Michael	WR	5-10	189	12/19/69	Arizona	Tucson, Ariz.	D6
Brewer, Derwin (1)	WR	5-8	165	5/26/68	Middle Tennessee St.	LaGrange, Ga.	FA
Cole, Randy	LB	6-1	235	2/21/66	UCLA	Junction City, Ariz.	FA
Conner, Andy	LB	6-3	236	12/27/68	Oregon	Klamath River, Calif.	FA
Dandridge, Gary	S	6-0	213	12/14/68	Appalachian State	Bristol, Tenn.	D5
Ellison, Clifford	CB	5-11	200	10/20/69	Baylor	San Antonio, Tex.	FA
Flesch, Jeb	C	6-2	273	2/21/69	Clemson	Morrow, Ga.	FA
Fraley, Chico	LB	6-1	210	4/21/69	Washington	Rowland Heights, Calif.	D12a
Frier, Mike	DT	6-5	300	3/20/69	Appalachian State	Jacksonville, N.C.	D7
Hamlet, Anthony	DE	6-3	260	6/21/69	Miami	Delray Beach, Fla.	D10
Harris, James	DE	6-7	267	5/3/68	Temple	East St. Louis, Ill.	FA
Holt, Leroy (1)	RB	5-10	224	2/7/67	Southern California	Los Angeles, Calif.	FA
Jovanovich, Mike	T	6-4	278	5/11/67	Boston College	Ontario, Canada	FA
MacNeill, John	DE	6-4	250	11/15/68	Michigan State	Marshfield, Mass.	D12b
May, Bryan	G	6-6	291	1/7/67	Brigham Young	Salt Lake City, Utah	FA
Mero, Joe	CB	5-11	184	2/18/68	Louisiana State	New Orleans, La.	FA
Moore, Rod	WR	6-0	192	12/16/68	Utah State	Richmond, Calif.	FA
Roberts, Ray	T	6-6	304	6/3/69	Virginia	Asheville, N.C.	D1
Robinson, James	T	6-4	293	5/3/68	Texas Southern	Corpus Christi, Tex.	FA
Robinson, Rafael	S	5-11	200	6/19/69	Wisconsin	Jefferson, Tex.	FA
Rodgers, Tyrone	DE	6-3	266	4/27/69	Washington	Carson, Calif.	FA
Rongen, Kris	G	6-5	284	8/20/69	Washington	Federal Way, Wash.	D11
Shamsid-Deen, Muhammad	RB	5-11	200	11/16/69	Tenn.-Chattanooga	Decatur, Ga.	D8
Silvestri, Don	K	6-4	205	12/25/68	Pittsburgh	Perkasie, Pa.	FA
Sinclair, Michael (1)	DE	6-4	255	1/31/68	Eastern New Mexico	Beaumont, Tex.	D6-'91
Spitulski, Bob	LB	6-3	235	9/10/69	Central Florida	Orlando, Fla.	D3
Stayner, Larry	TE	6-5	241	6/6/69	Boise State	Marysville, Wash.	D9
Stephens, Ralph (1)	P	6-3	210	12/17/64	Georgia Southern	Atlanta, Ga.	FA
Sturdivant, Michael	WR	6-2	195	4/19/69	Virginia Tech	New Haven, Conn.	FA
Thomas, Greg	S	6-1	221	9/11/69	Colorado	Rancho Palos Verdes, Calif.	FA
Treggs, Brian	WR	5-9	161	6/11/70	California	Carson, Calif.	FA
Wilborn, Jason	LB	6-3	235	1/10/69	California	Anaheim Hills, Calif.	FA
Wilks, Steve	CB	6-0	184	8/8/69	Appalachian State	Charlotte, N.C.	FA

The term NFL Rookie is defined as a player who is in his first season of professional football and has not been on the roster of another professional football team for any regular-season or postseason games. A Rookie is designated by an "R" on NFL rosters. Players who have been active in another professional football league or players who have NFL experience, including either preseason training camp or being on an active roster for fewer than three regular-season or postseason games, are termed NFL First-Year Players. An NFL First-Year Player is designated by a "1" on NFL rosters. Thereafter, a player on an NFL active roster for at least three regular-season or postseason games is credited with an additional year of NFL playing experience.

NOTES

_____

_____

_____

_____

_____

_____

_____

Larry Kennan, offensive coordinator-quarterbacks; born June 13, 1944, Pomona, Calif., lives in Kirkland, Wash. Quarterback La Verne College 1962-65. No pro playing experience. College coach: Colorado 1969-71, Nevada-Las Vegas 1973-75, Southern Methodist 1976-78, Lamar 1979-81 (head coach). Pro coach: Los Angeles Raiders 1982-87, Denver Broncos 1988, Indianapolis Colts 1989-90, London Monarchs (World League) 1991 (head coach), joined Seahawks in 1992.

Paul Moyer, defensive backfield; born July 26, 1961, Villa Park, Calif., lives in Renton, Wash. Safety Fullerton, Calif., J.C. 1979-80, Arizona State 1981-82. Pro safety Seattle Seahawks 1983-89. Pro coach: Joined Seahawks in 1990.

Russ Purnell, special teams-tight ends; born June 12, 1948, Chicago, Ill., lives in Bellevue, Wash. Center Orange Coast, Calif., J.C. 1966-67, Whittier College 1968-69. No pro playing experience. College coach: Whittier 1970-71, Southern California 1982-85. Pro coach: Joined Seahawks in 1986.

Frank Raines, strength and conditioning; born November 29, 1960, Portsmouth, Va., lives in Kirkland, Wash. No college or pro playing experience. Pro coach: Washington Redskins 1986-89, joined Seahawks in 1990.

Clarence Shelmon, running backs; born September 17, 1952, Bossier, La., lives in Kirkland, Wash. Running back Houston 1971-75. No pro playing experience. College coach: Army 1978-80, Indiana 1981-83, Arizona 1984-86, Southern California 1987-90. Pro coach: Los Angeles Rams 1991, joined Seahawks in 1992.

Rusty Tillman, defensive coordinator-linebackers; born February 27, 1948, Beloit, Wis., lives in Bellevue, Wash. Linebacker Northern Arizona 1967-69. Pro linebacker Washington Redskins 1970-77. Pro coach: Joined Seahawks in 1979.

THE NFC

Atlanta Falcons 84

Chicago Bears 88

Dallas Cowboys 92

Detroit Lions 96

Green Bay Packers 100

Los Angeles Rams 104

Minnesota Vikings 108

New Orleans Saints 112

New York Giants 116

Philadelphia Eagles 120

Phoenix Cardinals 124

San Francisco 49ers 128

Tampa Bay Buccaneers 132

Washington Redskins 136

National Football Conference Western Division

Team Colors: Black, Red, Silver, and White

Suwanee Road at I-85
Suwanee, Georgia 30174
Telephone: (404) 945-1111

Club Officials

Chairman of the Board: Rankin M. Smith, Sr.
President: Taylor Smith
Vice President & Chief Financial Officer: Jim Hay
Vice President of Player Personnel:
　Ken Herock
Director of Marketing: Tommy Nobis
Director of Public Relations: Charlie Taylor
Asst. Director of Public Relations: Frank Kleha
Public Relations Assistant: Todd Marble
Director of Community Relations: Carol Breeding
Director of Ticket Operations: Jack Ragsdale
Asst. Director of Ticket Operations: Luci Bailey
Administrative Assistant/Player Personnel:
　Danny Mock
Scouts: Bill Baker, Scott Campbell,
　Dick Corrick, Elbert Dubenion, Bill Groman
Director of Pro Personnel: Chuck Connor
Controller: Wallace Norman
Trainer: Jerry Rhea
Assistant Trainer: Billy Brooks
Equipment Manager: Whitey Zimmerman
Assistant Equipment Manager: Horace Daniel
Video Director: Tom Atcheson

Stadium: Georgia Dome •
　Capacity: 70,500
　285 International Boulevard
　Atlanta, Georgia 30313

Playing Surface: Artificial turf

Training Camp: Suwanee Road at I-85
　　　　　　Suwanee, Georgia 30174

1992 Schedule

Preseason
Aug. 8	at Cleveland	7:00
Aug. 15	at Tampa Bay	7:00
Aug. 23	**Philadelphia**	1:30
Aug. 28	**Buffalo**	8:00

Regular Season
Sept. 6	**New York Jets**	1:00
Sept. 13	at Washington	1:00
Sept. 20	**New Orleans**	1:00
Sept. 27	at Chicago	12:00
Oct. 4	**Green Bay**	1:00
Oct. 11	at Miami	1:00
Oct. 18	at San Francisco	1:00
Oct. 25	**Open Date**	
Nov. 1	**Los Angeles Rams**	1:00
Nov. 9	**San Francisco** (Monday)	9:00
Nov. 15	**Phoenix**	1:00
Nov. 22	at Buffalo	1:00
Nov. 29	**New England**	1:00
Dec. 3	at New Orleans (Thursday)	7:00
Dec. 13	at Tampa Bay	1:00
Dec. 21	**Dallas** (Monday)	9:00
Dec. 27	at Los Angeles Rams	1:00

Falcons Coaching History

(146-239-5)

1966-68	Norb Hecker*	4-26-1
1968-74	Norm Van Brocklin**	37-49-3
1974-76	Marion Campbell***	6-19-0
1976	Pat Peppler	3-6-0
1977-82	Leeman Bennett	47-44-0
1983-86	Dan Henning	22-41-1
1987-89	Marion Campbell****	11-32-0
1989	Jim Hanifan	0-4-0
1990-91	Jerry Glanville	16-18-0

*Released after three games in 1968
**Released after eight games in 1974
***Released after five games in 1976
****Retired after 12 games in 1989

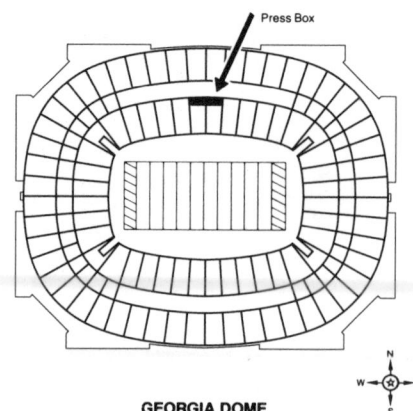

Press Box

GEORGIA DOME

Record Holders

Individual Records—Career
Category	Name	Performance
Rushing (Yds.)	Gerald Riggs, 1982-88	6,631
Passing (Yds.)	Steve Bartkowski, 1975-1985	23,468
Passing (TDs)	Steve Bartkowski, 1975-1985	154
Receiving (No.)	Alfred Jenkins, 1975-1983	359
Receiving (Yds.)	Alfred Jenkins, 1975-1983	6,257
Interceptions	Rolland Lawrence, 1973-1980	39
Punting (Avg.)	Rick Donnelly, 1985-89	42.6
Punt Return (Avg.)	Al Dodd, 1973-74	11.8
Kickoff Return (Avg.)	Ron Smith, 1966-67	24.3
Field Goals	Mick Luckhurst, 1981-87	115
Touchdowns (Tot.)	Gerald Riggs, 1982-88	48
Points	Mick Luckhurst, 1981-87	558

Individual Records—Single Season
Category	Name	Performance
Rushing (Yds.)	Gerald Riggs, 1985	1,719
Passing (Yds.)	Steve Bartkowski, 1981	3,830
Passing (TDs)	Steve Bartkowski, 1980	31
Receiving (No.)	Andre Rison, 1990	82
Receiving (Yds.)	Alfred Jenkins, 1981	1,358
Interceptions	Scott Case, 1988	10
Punting (Avg.)	Billy Lothridge, 1968	44.3
Punt Return (Avg.)	Gerald Tinker, 1974	13.9
Kickoff Return (Avg.)	Sylvester Stamps, 1987	27.5
Field Goals	Nick Mike-Mayer, 1973	26
Touchdowns (Tot.)	Alfred Jenkins, 1981	13
	Gerald Riggs, 1984	13
Points	Mick Luckhurst, 1981	114

Individual Records—Single Game
Category	Name	Performance
Rushing (Yds.)	Gerald Riggs, 9-2-84	202
Passing (Yds.)	Steve Bartkowski, 11-15-81	416
Passing (TDs)	Randy Johnson, 11-16-69	4
	Steve Bartkowski, 10-19-80	4
	Steve Bartkowski, 10-18-81	4
Receiving (No.)	William Andrews, 11-15-81	15
Receiving (Yds.)	Alfred Jackson, 12-2-84	193
Interceptions	Many times	2
	Last time by Deion Sanders, 12-15-91	
Field Goals	Nick Mike-Mayer, 11-4-73	5
	Tim Mazzetti, 10-30-78	5
Touchdowns (Tot.)	Many times	3
	Last time by Andre Rison, 11-17-91	
Points	Many times	18
	Last time by Andre Rison, 11-17-91	

1991 Team Record
Preseason (2-2)

Date	Result		Opponents
8/3	W	38-17	vs. L.A. Rams at Jacksonville, Fla.
8/9	W	36- 7	at Houston
8/17	L	7-12	Tampa Bay
8/23	L	17-20	at Dallas (OT)

Regular Season (10-6)

Date	Result		Opponents	Att.
9/1	L	3-14	at Kansas City	74,246
9/8	L	19-20	Minnesota	50,936
9/15	W	13-10	at San Diego	44,804
9/22	W	21-17	L.A. Raiders	53,615
9/29	L	6-27	New Orleans	56,556
10/13	W	39-34	at San Francisco	66,210
10/20	L	10-16	at Phoenix	24,124
10/27	W	31-14	L.A. Rams	50,187
11/3	W	17-14	San Francisco	51,259
11/10	L	17-56	at Washington	52,461
11/17	W	43- 7	Tampa Bay	41,274
11/24	W	23-20	at N.O. (OT)	68,591
12/1	W	35-31	Green Bay	43,270
12/8	W	31-14	at L.A. Rams	35,315
12/15	W	26-13	Seattle	53,834
12/22	L	27-31	at Dallas	60,962

(OT) Overtime

Postseason (1-1)

Date	Result		Opponent	Att.
12/28	W	27-20	at New Orleans	68,299
1/4	L	7-24	at Washington	55,177

Score by Periods

Falcons	84	102	88	84	3	—	361
Opponents	48	94	70	126	0	—	338

Attendance
Home 400,931   Away 426,713   Total 827,644
Single-game home record, 59,257 (10-30-77)
Single-season home record, 442,457 (1980)

1991 Team Statistics

	Falcons	Opp.
Total First Downs	258	278
Rushing	82	94
Passing	162	157
Penalty	14	27
Third Down: Made/Att.	69/194	82/210
Third Down: Pct.	35.6	39.0
Fourth Down: Made/Att.	5/9	2/9
Fourth Down: Pct.	55.6	22.2
Total Net Yards	5113	5248
Avg. Per Game	319.6	328.0
Total Plays	941	976
Avg. Per Play	5.4	5.4
Net Yards Rushing	1664	1953
Avg. Per Game	104.0	122.1
Total Rushes	410	466
Net Yards Passing	3449	3295
Avg. Per Game	215.6	205.9
Sacked/Yards Lost	31/185	29/237
Gross Yards	3634	3532
Att./Completions	500/260	481/252
Completion Pct.	52.0	52.4
Had Intercepted	22	19
Punts/Avg.	82/42.6	79/40.3
Net Punting Avg.	36.4	35.5
Penalties/Yards Lost	113/929	100/802
Fumbles/Ball Lost	19/14	27/16
Touchdowns	42	43
Rushing	6	13
Passing	30	28
Returns	6	2
Avg. Time of Possession	29:13	30:47

1991 Individual Statistics

Scoring

	TD R	TD P	TD Rt	PAT	FG	Saf	TP
N. Johnson	0	0	0	38/39	19/23	0	95
Rison	0	12	0	0/0	0/0	0	72
Haynes	0	11	0	0/0	0/0	0	66
Broussard	4	1	0	0/0	0/0	0	30
Pritchard	0	2	0	0/0	0/0	0	12
Sanders	0	0	2	0/0	0/0	0	12
Thomas	0	2	0	0/0	0/0	0	12
Daluiso	0	0	0	2/2	2/3	0	8
Barnett	0	0	1	0/0	0/0	0	6
Chaffey	1	0	0	0/0	0/0	0	6
Dixon	0	1	0	0/0	0/0	0	6
Fishback	0	0	1	0/0	0/0	0	6
Pegram	1	0	0	0/0	0/0	0	6
Tippins	0	0	1	0/0	0/0	0	6
Tuggle	0	0	1	0/0	0/0	0	6
Wilkins	0	1	0	0/0	0/0	0	6
Jordan	0	0	0	0/0	0/0	2	4
Falcons	6	30	6	40/42	21/26	3	361
Opponents	13	28	2	41/43	13/26	0	338

Passing

	Att.	Comp.	Yds.	Pct.	TD	Int.	Tkld.	Rate
Miller	413	220	3103	53.3	26	18	23/145	80.6
Tolliver	82	40	531	48.8	4	2	7/29	75.8
Favre	5	0	0	0.0	0	2	1/11	0.0
Falcons	500	260	3634	52.0	30	22	31/185	77.4
Opponents	481	252	3532	52.4	28	19	29/237	79.3

Rushing

	Att.	Yds.	Avg.	LG	TD
Broussard	99	449	4.5	36	4
Rozier	96	361	3.8	19	0
Pegram	101	349	3.5	34	1
Miller	32	229	7.2	20	0
Chaffey	29	127	4.4	27	1
Jones	35	126	3.6	14	0
T. Johnson	8	26	3.3	6	0
Tolliver	9	6	0.7	7	0
Rison	1	−9	−9.0	−9	0
Falcons	410	1664	4.1	36	6
Opponents	466	1953	4.2	65t	13

Receiving

	No.	Yds.	Avg.	LG	TD
Rison	81	976	12.0	39t	12
Haynes	50	1122	22.4	80t	11
Pritchard	50	624	12.5	29	2
Thomas	28	365	13.0	37	2
Dixon	12	146	12.2	23	1
Broussard	12	120	10.0	25t	1
Phillips	6	73	12.2	24	0
Jones	6	58	9.7	15	0
Collins	3	37	12.3	21	0
T. Johnson	3	27	9.0	13	0
Wilkins	3	22	7.3	12	1
Rozier	2	15	7.5	9	0
Ruether	1	22	22.0	22	0
Sanders	1	17	17.0	17	0
Bruce	1	11	11.0	11	0
Pegram	1	−1	−1.0	−1	0
Falcons	260	3634	14.0	80t	30
Opponents	252	3532	14.0	97t	28

Interceptions

	No.	Yds.	Avg.	LG	TD
Sanders	6	119	19.8	55t	1
McKyer	6	24	4.0	24	0
Case	2	23	11.5	17	0
Jordan	2	3	1.5	3	0
Tippins	1	35	35.0	35	0
Tuggle	1	21	21.0	21	0
Gann	1	0	0.0	0	0
Falcons	19	225	11.8	55t	1
Opponents	22	279	12.7	51	1

Punting

	No.	Yds.	Avg.	In 20	LG
Fulhage	81	3470	42.8	21	60
N. Johnson	1	21	21.0	1	21
Falcons	82	3491	42.6	22	60
Opponents	79	3187	40.3	27	64

Punt Returns

	No.	FC	Yds.	Avg.	LG	TD
Sanders	21	9	170	8.1	23	0
Jordan	14	9	116	8.3	13	0
Falcons	35	18	286	8.2	23	0
Opponents	45	18	387	8.6	29	0

Kickoff Returns

	No.	Yds.	Avg.	LG	TD
Sanders	26	576	22.2	100t	1
Pegram	16	260	16.3	30	0
Jordan	5	100	20.0	29	0
Fishback	3	29	9.7	19	0
Chaffey	1	14	14.0	14	0
Pritchard	1	18	18.0	18	0
Falcons	52	997	19.2	100t	1
Opponents	67	1419	21.2	102t	1

Sacks

	No.
Green	5.0
Jordan	4.0
Conner	3.5
Bryan	3.0
Gardner	3.0
Mitchell	2.0
Shelley	2.0
Epps	1.5
Barnett	1.0
Donaldson	1.0
Sanders	1.0
Tippins	1.0
Tuggle	1.0
Falcons	29.0
Opponents	31.0

1992 Draft Choices

Round	Name	Pos.	College
1.	Bob Whitfield	T	Stanford
	Tony Smith	RB	So. Mississippi
2.	Chuck Smith	DE	Tennessee
3.	Howard Dinkins	LB	Florida State
4.	Frankie Smith	DB	Baylor
6.	Terry Ray	DB	Oklahoma
7.	Tim Paulk	LB	Florida
8.	Derrick Moore	RB	N.E. Oklahoma
	Reggie Dwight	TE	Troy State
9.	Keith Alex	T	Texas A&M
10.	Darryl Hardy	LB	Tennessee
11.	Robin Jones	DE	Baylor

Atlanta Falcons 1992 Veteran Roster

No.	Name	Pos.	Ht.	Wt.	Birth-date	NFL Exp.	College	Hometown	How Acq.	'91 Games/ Starts
72	Barnett, Oliver	NT	6-3	285	4/9/66	3	Kentucky	Louisville, Ky.	D3-'90	15/2
33	Bratton, Melvin	RB	6-1	225	2/2/65	3	Miami	Miami, Fla.	FA-'92	0*
34	Broussard, Steve	RB	5-7	201	2/22/67	3	Washington State	Los Angeles, Calif.	D1-'90	14/5
77	Bryan, Rick	DE	6-4	265	3/20/62	8	Oklahoma	Coweta, Okla.	D1-'84	16/12
23	Butler, Bobby	CB	5-11	175	5/28/59	12	Florida State	Delray Beach, Fla.	D1-'81	15/2
25	Case, Scott	S	6-1	188	5/17/62	9	Oklahoma	Edmond, Okla.	D2a-'84	16/16
85	Collins, Shawn	WR	6-2	204	2/20/67	4	Northern Arizona	San Diego, Calif.	D1b-'89	4/1
56	Conner, Darion	LB	6-2	250	9/28/67	3	Jackson State	Prairie Point, Miss.	D2-'90	15/14
42	Donaldson, Jeff	S	6-0	190	4/19/62	9	Colorado	Ft. Collins, Colo.	PB(KC)-'91#	16/0
64	†Dukes, Jamie	C	6-1	285	6/14/64	7	Florida State	Orlando, Fla.	FA-'86	16/16
32	Eaton, Tracey	S	6-1	195	7/19/65	5	Portland State	Medford, Ore.	PB(Phx)-'91#	16/0
74	†Epps, Tory	NT	6-0	270	5/28/67	3	Memphis State	Uniontown, Pa.	D8-'90	16/2
51	Faryniarz, Brett	LB	6-3	235	7/23/65	5	San Diego State	Rancho Cordova, Calif.	PB(Rams)-'92#	12/8*
53	Forde, Brian	LB	6-3	235	11/1/63	5	Washington State	Montreal, Canada	PB(NO)-'92#	16/0*
68	Fortin, Roman	G	6-5	270	2/26/67	2	San Diego State	Ventura, Calif.	PB(Det)-'92#	16/0*
79	†Fralic, Bill	G	6-5	280	10/31/62	8	Pittsburgh	Penn Hills, Pa.	D1-'85	12/12
17	†Fulhage, Scott	P	6-0	193	11/17/61	6	Kansas State	Beloit, Kan.	FA-'89	16/0
76	Gann, Mike	DE	6-5	270	10/19/63	8	Notre Dame	Lakewood, Colo.	D2-'85	5/5
67	Gardner, Moe	NT	6-2	258	8/10/68	2	Illinois	Indianapolis, Ind.	D4-'91	16/13
99	Green, Tim	DE	6-2	245	12/16/63	7	Syracuse	Liverpool, N.Y.	D1b-'86	16/16
98	Hamilton, Darrell	T	6-5	298	5/11/65	4	North Carolina	Washington, D.C.	FA-'92	6/0*
81	Haynes, Michael	WR	6-0	180	12/24/65	5	Northern Arizona	New Orleans, La.	D7-'88	16/16
86	Hill, Drew	WR	5-9	172	10/5/56	13	Georgia Tech	Newnan, Ga.	PB(Hou)-'92#	16/16*
75	Hinton, Chris	T	6-4	300	7/31/61	10	Northwestern	Chicago, Ill.	T(Ind)-'90	16/16
69	†Hoover, Houston	G	6-2	295	2/6/65	5	Jackson State	Yazoo City, Miss.	D6-'88	16/16
9	†Johnson, Norm	K	6-2	203	5/31/60	11	UCLA	Garden Grove, Calif.	FA-'91	14/0
38	†Jones, Keith	RB	6-1	210	3/20/66	4	Illinois	Rock Hills, Mo.	D3-'89	5/3
83	Jones, Tony	WR	5-7	145	12/30/65	3	Texas	Grapeland, Tex.	PB(Hou)-'92#	16/0*
40	†Jordan, Brian	S	6-1	205	3/29/67	4	Richmond	Baltimore, Md.	FA-'89	16/15
78	Kenn, Mike	T	6-7	280	2/9/56	15	Michigan	Evanston, Ill.	D1-'78	16/15
88	Le Bel, Harper	TE	6-4	245	7/14/63	4	Colorado State	Sherman Oaks, Calif.	PB(Phil)-'91#	3/0
54	Lyles, Robert	LB	6-1	230	3/21/61	9	Texas Christian	Los Angeles, Calif.	FA-'90	16/14
22	McKyer, Tim	CB	6-0	174	9/5/63	7	Texas-Arlington	Port Arthur, Tex.	T(Mia)-'91	16/16
12	Miller, Chris	QB	6-2	205	8/9/65	6	Oregon	Eugene, Ore.	D1-'87	15/14
87	Milling, James	WR	5-9	160	2/14/65	3	Maryland	Oxon Hill, Md.	PB(NYG)-'92#	1/0*
41	Pegram, Erric	RB	5-9	188	1/7/69	2	North Texas State	Dallas, Tex.	D6-'91	16/7
82	Phillips, Jason	WR	5-7	168	10/11/68	4	Houston	Houston, Tex.	PB(Det)-'91#	11/0
39	Pickens, Bruce	CB	5-11	190	5/9/68	2	Nebraska	Kansas City, Mo.	D1-'91	7/0
35	Pritchard, Mike	WR	5-11	180	10/25/69	2	Colorado	Las Vegas, Nev.	D1b-'91	16/11
59	Rade, John	LB	6-2	240	8/31/60	10	Boise State	Ceres, Calif.	D8-'83	11/10
95	†Reid, Michael	LB	6-2	235	6/25/64	6	Wisconsin	Albany, Ga.	D7-'87	3/0
80	Rison, Andre	WR	6-0	188	3/18/67	4	Michigan State	Flint, Mich.	T(Ind)-'90	16/15
55	Ruether, Mike	C	6-4	286	9/20/62	7	Texas	Shawnee Mission, Kan.	FA-'90	16/6
94	Saddler, Rod	DE	6-5	280	12/8/65	6	Texas A&M	Decatur, Ga.	FA-'92	6/0*
21	Sanders, Deion	CB	6-0	185	8/9/67	4	Florida State	Ft. Myers, Fla.	D1a-'89	15/15
37	†Shelley, Elbert	CB	5-11	185	12/24/64	6	Arkansas State	Tyronza, Ark.	D11-'87	11/0
66	Sims, Joe	T	6-3	294	3/1/69	2	Nebraska	Sudbury, Mass.	D11-'91	6/0
71	Smith, Sean	DE	6-7	280	5/29/67	2	Georgia Tech	Wyoming, Ohio	FA-'92	2/0*
89	†Thomas, George	WR	5-9	169	7/11/64	4	Nevada-Las Vegas	Riverside, Calif.	D6-'88	12/6
52	Tippins, Ken	LB	6-1	230	7/22/66	4	Middle Tennessee State	Adel, Ga.	FA-'90	16/7
11	Tolliver, Billy Joe	QB	6-1	218	2/7/66	4	Texas Tech	Boyd, Tex.	T(SD)-'91	7/2
58	Tuggle, Jessie	LB	5-11	230	2/14/65	6	Valdosta State	Spalding, Ga.	FA-'87	16/16
92	Zawatson, Dave	G-T	6-5	288	4/13/66	3	California	Concord, Calif.	FA-'92	2/0*

* Bratton last active with Denver in '90; Faryniarz played 12 games with L.A. Rams in '91; Forde played 16 games with New Orleans; Fortin played 16 games with Detroit; Hamilton played 6 games with Denver; Hill played 16 games with Houston; Jones played 16 games with Houston; Milling played 1 game with N.Y. Giants; Saddler played 4 games with Phoenix, 2 with Cincinnati; Smith played 2 games with New England; Zawatson played 2 games with Miami.

† Option playout; subject to developments.

Plan B unconditional free agent.

Players lost through Plan B (9): C Guy Bingham (Phil; 13 games in '91), LB Aundray Bruce (Raid; 14), RB Pat Chaffey (NYJ; 14), WR Floyd Dixon (Phil; 10), CB-S Joe Fishback (NYJ; 14), T John Hunter (TB; 2), RB Tracy Johnson (Sea; 16), CB-S Brian Mitchell (Dall; 15), TE Gary Wilkins (Wash; 5).

Also played with Falcons in '91—TE Rich Bartlewski (1 game), K Brad Daluiso (2), CB William Evers (2), LB Wes Pritchett (3), T Reggie Redding (13), RB Mike Rozier (11).

COACHING STAFF

Head Coach, Jerry Glanville

Pro Career: Led Atlanta to a 10-6 regular-season record in 1991 and a spot in the NFC playoffs for first time since 1982. Named Falcons' head coach on January 14, 1990. Served as Houston Oilers' head coach from the last two games of the 1985 season through 1989. Guided Oilers to three consecutive playoff berths (1987-89), posting a 28-19 mark in the process. Under his direction, Houston was one of only four NFL teams to make the playoffs during those years. The 50-year-old Glanville took over a team that had suffered five consecutive losing seasons and turned the club into winners in his second season at the helm. As an assistant coach, he was part of three playoff teams and one division title winner in Atlanta. He helped the 1977 team establish the modern-day record for fewest points allowed in a season (129 over 14 games) with his attacking "Gritz Blitz" defense. Career record: 51-53.

Background: Attended Montana State in 1960 before transferring to Northern Michigan, where he played linebacker from 1961-63. He coached in the Ohio high school system from 1964-66 before accepting an assistant coaching post at Western Kentucky in 1967. From 1968-73, he was an assistant at Georgia Tech, helping the Yellow Jackets to three bowl games.

Personal: Born October 14, 1941, in Detroit, Mich. Jerry and his wife, Brenda, live in Roswell, Ga., with their son, Justin.

Assistant Coaches

Bobby April, Jr., special teams, tight ends; born April 15, 1953, New Orleans, La., lives in Atlanta. Linebacker Nicholls State 1972-75. No pro playing experience. College coach: Tulane 1979, Arizona 1980-86, Southern California 1987-90. Pro coach: Joined Falcons in 1991.

Jimmy Carr, secondary; born March 25, 1933, Kayford, W. Va., lives in Atlanta. Running back-defensive back-linebacker Morris Harvey (now University of Charleston, W. Va.) 1951-54. Pro running back-defensive back-linebacker Chicago Cardinals 1955-57, Montreal Alouettes (CFL) 1958, Philadelphia Eagles 1959-63, Washington Redskins 1964-65. Pro coach: Minnesota Vikings 1966-68, 1979-81, Chicago Bears 1969, 1973-74, Philadelphia Eagles 1970-72, Detroit Lions 1975-76, Buffalo Bills 1977, San Francisco 49ers 1978, Denver Gold (USFL) 1983-84, New England Patriots 1985-89, joined Falcons in 1990.

June Jones, assistant head coach-offense; born February 19, 1953, Portland, Ore., lives in Atlanta. Quarterback Hawaii 1973-74, Portland State 1975-76. Pro quarterback Atlanta Falcons 1977-81, Toronto Argonauts (CFL) 1982. College coach: Hawaii 1983. Pro coach: Toronto Argonauts (CFL) 1982, Houston Gamblers (USFL) 1984, Denver Gold (USFL) 1985, Houston Oilers 1987-88, Detroit Lions 1989-90, joined Falcons in 1991.

Tim Jorgensen, strength and conditioning; born April 21, 1955, St. Louis, Mo., lives in Snellville, Ga. Guard Southwest Missouri State 1974-76. No pro playing experience. College coach: Southwest Missouri State 1977-78, Alabama 1979, Louisiana State 1980-83. Pro coach: Philadelphia Eagles 1984-86, joined Falcons in 1987.

Bill Kollar, defensive line; born November 12, 1952, Warren, Ohio, lives in Atlanta. Defensive end Montana State 1971-74. Pro defensive end Cincinnati Bengals 1974-76, Tampa Bay Buccaneers 1977-81. College coach: Illinois 1985-87, Purdue 1988-89. Pro coach: Tampa Bay Buccaneers 1984, joined Falcons in 1990.

Jimmy Robinson, wide receivers; born January 3, 1953, Atlanta, lives in Atlanta. Wide receiver Georgia Tech 1972-74. Pro wide receiver Atlanta Falcons 1975, New York Giants 1976-79, San Francisco 49ers 1980, Denver Broncos 1981. College coach: Georgia Tech 1986-89. Pro coach: Memphis Showboats (USFL) 1984-85, joined Falcons in 1990.

Keith Rowen, offensive line; born September 2, 1952, New York, N.Y., lives in Atlanta. Offensive tackle Stanford 1972-74. No pro playing experience. College coach: Stanford 1975-76, Long Beach State 1977-78, Arizona 1979-82. Pro coach: Boston/New Orleans Breakers (USFL) 1983-84, Cleveland Browns 1984, Indianapolis Colts 1985-88, New England Patriots 1989, joined Falcons in 1990.

Doug Shively, assistant head coach-defense; born March 18, 1938, Lexington, Ky., lives in Atlanta. End Kentucky 1955-58. No pro playing experience. College coach: Virginia Tech 1960-66, Kentucky 1967-70, Clemson 1971-72, North Carolina 1973. Pro coach: New Orleans Saints 1974-76, Atlanta Falcons 1977-82, Arizona Wranglers (USFL) 1983 (head coach), San Diego Chargers 1984, Tampa Bay Buccaneers 1985, Houston Oilers 1986-89, rejoined Falcons in 1990.

Ollie Wilson, running backs; born March 31, 1951, Worcester, Mass., lives in Atlanta. Wide receiver Springfield 1971-73. No pro playing experience. College coach: Springfield 1975, Northeastern 1976-82, California 1983-90. Pro coach: Joined Falcons in 1991.

Atlanta Falcons 1992 First-Year Roster

Name	Pos.	Ht.	Wt.	Birth-date	College	Hometown	How Acq.
Alex, Keith	G-T	6-4	312	6/9/69	Texas A&M	Beaumont, Tex.	D9
Ashe, Richard (1)	TE	6-4	260	3/14/67	Humboldt State	Moreno Valley, Calif.	FA
Brown, Kevin	LB	6-2	248	5/26/70	Youngstown	Youngstown, Ohio	FA
Bullock, Randy	LB	6-1	234	11/23/69	N.W. Louisiana	Jonesboro, Ark.	FA
Dinkins, Howard	LB	6-1	223	4/26/69	Florida State	Jacksonville, Fla.	D3
Dwight, Reggie	TE	6-4	266	4/4/70	Troy State	Cordele, Ga.	D8b
Evans, Scott (1)	DE	6-4	260	3/29/68	Oklahoma	Edmond, Okla.	FA
Giles, Oscar (1)	DE	6-2	246	9/27/68	Texas	Dallas, Tex.	FA
Hamm, Horace	WR	5-11	170	12/20/69	Lehigh	Lauderdale Lakes, Fla.	FA
Hardy, Darryl	LB	6-2	220	11/22/68	Tennessee	Cincinnati, Ohio	D10
Johnson, Michael (1)	WR	6-0	190	1/14/69	Cal St.-Sacramento	Fairfield, Calif.	FA
Jones, Robin	DE	6-2	266	6/19/69	Baylor	Dallas, Tex.	D11
Miller, Karl (1)	WR	5-10	183	1/24/69	Georgia Southern	College Park, Ga.	FA
Moore, Derrick	RB	6-1	227	10/13/67	N.E. Oklahoma State	Albany, Ga.	D8a
Olive, Bobby (1)	WR	5-11	160	4/22/69	Ohio State	Atlanta, Ga.	FA
Paulk, Tim	LB	6-1	229	4/3/68	Florida	Miami, Fla.	D7
Ray, Terry	S	6-1	187	10/12/69	Oklahoma	Killeen, Tex.	D6
Reynolds, Don	DT	6-3	274	11/11/69	Virginia	Martinsville, Va.	FA
Smith, Chuck	DE	6-2	242	12/21/69	Tennessee	Athens, Ga.	D2
Smith, Frankie	CB	5-9	177	10/8/68	Baylor	Groesbeck, Tex.	D4
Smith, Hosie	G	6-2	317	7/5/68	Central State, Ohio	Franklin, La.	FA
Smith, Tony	RB	6-1	214	6/29/70	Southern Mississippi	Vicksburg, Miss.	D1b
Thomas, Mick	LB	6-2	233	6/14/69	Arkansas	Bakersfield, Calif.	FA
Truitt, Leroy (1)	T	6-3	308	5/23/69	Houston	La Marque, Tex.	FA
Washington, Sharron	CB	5-10	199	1/15/69	Missouri	Hazelwood, Mo.	FA
Whitfield, Bob	T	6-5	291	10/18/71	Stanford	Carson, Calif.	D1a

The term NFL Rookie is defined as a player who is in his first season of professional football and has not been on the roster of another professional football team for any regular-season or postseason games. A Rookie is designated by an "R" on NFL rosters. Players who have been active in another professional football league or players who have NFL experience, including either preseason training camp or being on an active roster for fewer than three regular-season or postseason games, are termed NFL First-Year Players. An NFL First-Year Player is designated by a "1" on NFL rosters. Thereafter, a player on an NFL active roster for at least three regular-season or postseason games is credited with an actual year of NFL playing experience.

NOTES

_____
_____
_____
_____
_____
_____
_____
_____
_____
_____
_____

National Football Conference Central Division

Team Colors: Navy Blue, Orange, and White

Corporate Headquarters:
Halas Hall, 250 North Washington
Lake Forest, Illinois 60045
Telephone: (708) 295-6600

Club Officials

Chairman of the Board: Edward W. McCaskey
President and CEO: Michael B. McCaskey
Secretary: Virginia H. McCaskey
Vice President-Player Personnel: Bill Tobin
Director of Administration: Tim LeFevour
Director of Com. Relations: Pat McCaskey
Director of Finance: Ted Phillips
Director of Marketing and Communications:
  Ken Valdiserri
Director of Public Relations: Bryan Harlan
Asst. Director of Public Relations: John Bostrom
Public Relations Assistant: Doug Green
Ticket Manager: George McCaskey
Computer Systems: Greg Gershuny
Video Director: Mitch Friedman
Trainer: Fred Caito
Assistant Trainer: Brian McCaskey
Strength Coordinator: Clyde Emrich
Physical Dev. Coordinator: Russ Reiderer
Equipment Manager: Gary Haeger
Assistant Equipment Manager: Tony Medlin
Scouts: Gary Smith, Rod Graves, Ken Geiger,
  Jeff Shiver, Charlie Mackey

Stadium: Soldier Field • **Capacity:** 66,946
  425 McFetridge Place
  Chicago, Illinois 60605

Playing Surface: Grass

Training Camp: University of
  Wisconsin-Platteville
  Platteville, Wisconsin 53818

1992 Schedule

Preseason
Aug. 8	**New Orleans**	7:00
Aug. 15	at Phoenix	5:00
Aug. 23	**Pittsburgh**	7:00
Aug. 28	at Dallas	7:00

Regular Season
Sept. 6	**Detroit**	12:00
Sept. 13	at New Orleans	12:00
Sept. 21	**N.Y. Giants** (Monday)	8:00
Sept. 27	**Atlanta**	12:00
Oct. 4	at Minnesota	12:00
Oct. 11	**Open Date**	
Oct. 18	**Tampa Bay**	12:00
Oct. 25	at Green Bay	12:00
Nov. 2	**Minnesota** (Monday)	8:00
Nov. 8	**Cincinnati**	7:00
Nov. 15	at Tampa Bay	4:00
Nov. 22	**Green Bay**	12:00
Nov. 29	at Cleveland	1:00
Dec. 7	at Houston (Monday)	8:00
Dec. 13	**Pittsburgh**	12:00
Dec. 20	at Detroit	4:00
Dec. 27	at Dallas	3:00

Bears Coaching History

Decatur Staleys 1920
Chicago Staleys 1921
(574-364-42)

1920-29	George Halas	84-31-19
1930-32	Ralph Jones	24-10-7
1933-42	George Halas*	89-24-4
1942-45	Hunk Anderson-Luke Johnsos**	23-12-2
1946-55	George Halas	76-43-2
1956-57	John (Paddy) Driscoll	14-10-1
1958-67	George Halas	76-53-6
1968-71	Jim Dooley	20-36-0
1972-74	Abe Gibron	11-30-1
1975-77	Jack Pardee	20-23-0
1978-81	Neill Armstrong	30-35-0
1982-91	Mike Ditka	107-57-0

*Retired after six games to enter U.S. Navy
**Co-coaches

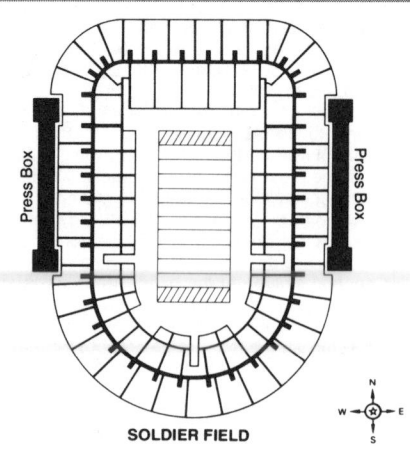

SOLDIER FIELD

Record Holders

Individual Records—Career
Category	Name	Performance
Rushing (Yds.)	Walter Payton, 1975-1987	*16,726
Passing (Yds.)	Sid Luckman, 1939-1950	14,686
Passing (TDs)	Sid Luckman, 1939-1950	137
Receiving (No.)	Walter Payton, 1975-1987	492
Receiving (Yds.)	Johnny Morris, 1958-1967	5,059
Interceptions	Gary Fencik, 1976-1987	38
Punting (Avg.)	George Gulyanics, 1947-1952	44.5
Punt Return (Avg.)	Ray (Scooter) McLean, 1940-47	14.8
Kickoff Return (Avg.)	Gale Sayers, 1965-1971	30.6
Field Goals	Kevin Butler, 1985-1991	153
Touchdowns (Tot.)	Walter Payton, 1975-1987	125
Points	Walter Payton, 1975-1987	750

Individual Records—Single Season
Category	Name	Performance
Rushing (Yds.)	Walter Payton, 1977	1,852
Passing (Yds.)	Bill Wade, 1962	3,172
Passing (TDs)	Sid Luckman, 1943	28
Receiving (No.)	Johnny Morris, 1964	93
Receiving (Yds.)	Johnny Morris, 1964	1,200
Interceptions	Mark Carrier, 1990	10
Punting (Avg.)	Bobby Joe Green, 1963	46.5
Punt Return (Avg.)	Harry Clark, 1943	15.8
Kickoff Return (Avg.)	Gale Sayers, 1967	37.7
Field Goals	Kevin Butler, 1985	31
Touchdowns (Tot.)	Gale Sayers, 1965	**22
Points	Kevin Butler, 1985	**144

Individual Records—Single Game
Category	Name	Performance
Rushing (Yds.)	Walter Payton, 11-20-77	*275
Passing (Yds.)	Johnny Lujack, 12-11-49	468
Passing (TDs)	Sid Luckman, 11-14-43	*7
Receiving (No.)	Jim Keane, 10-23-49	14
Receiving (Yds.)	Harlon Hill, 10-31-54	214
Interceptions	Many times	3
	Last time by Mark Carrier, 12-9-90	
Field Goals	Roger LeClerc, 12-3-61	5
	Mac Percival, 10-20-68	5
Touchdowns (Tot.)	Gale Sayers, 12-12-65	*6
Points	Gale Sayers, 12-12-65	36

*NFL Record
**NFL Rookie Record

1991 Team Record
Preseason (2-3)

Date	Result		Opponents
7/26	W	6- 0	at Miami
8/3	L	7-21	vs. San Francisco at Berlin
8/11	L	10-12	Phoenix
8/17	L	10-13	at L.A. Raiders
8/24	W	30-13	Buffalo

Regular Season (11-5)

Date	Result		Opponents	Att.
9/1	W	10- 6	Minnesota	64,112
9/8	W	21-20	at Tampa Bay	62,409
9/15	W	20-17	N.Y. Giants	64,829
9/23	W	19-13	N.Y. Jets (OT)	65,255
9/29	L	20-35	at Buffalo	80,366
10/6	L	7-20	Washington	64,941
10/17	W	10- 0	at Green Bay	58,435
10/27	W	20-17	at New Orleans	68,591
11/3	W	20-10	Detroit	57,281
11/11	W	34-17	at Minnesota	59,001
11/17	W	31-17	at Indianapolis	60,519
11/24	L	13-16	Miami (OT)	58,288
11/28	L	6-16	at Detroit	78,879
12/8	W	27-13	Green Bay	62,353
12/14	W	27- 0	Tampa Bay	54,719
12/23	L	14-52	at San Francisco	60,419

(OT) Overtime

Postseason (0-1)

Date	Result		Opponent	Att.
12/29	L	13-17	Dallas	66,213

Score by Periods

Bears	40	96	71	86	6	—	299
Opponents	57	72	51	86	3	—	269

Attendance

Home 491,778   Away 528,619   Total 1,020,397
Single-game home record, 66,475 (9-17-89)
Single-season home record, 495,484 (1986)

1991 Team Statistics

	Bears	Opp.
Total First Downs	317	254
Rushing	120	77
Passing	168	164
Penalty	29	13
Third Down: Made/Att.	95/221	69/208
Third Down: Pct.	43.0	33.2
Fourth Down: Made/Att.	7/18	10/21
Fourth Down: Pct.	38.9	47.6
Total Net Yards	5069	4507
Avg. Per Game	316.8	281.7
Total Plays	1025	942
Avg. Per Play	4.9	4.8
Net Yards Rushing	1949	1580
Avg. Per Game	121.8	98.8
Total Rushes	502	389
Net Yards Passing	3120	2927
Avg. Per Game	195.0	182.9
Sacked/Yards Lost	26/172	40/257
Gross Yards	3292	3184
Att./Completions	497/286	513/286
Completion Pct.	57.5	55.8
Had Intercepted	17	17
Punts/Avg.	70/40.2	81/41.3
Net Punting Avg.	35.0	35.8
Penalties/Yards Lost	80/662	94/891
Fumbles/Ball Lost	25/16	25/13
Touchdowns	35	29
Rushing	18	9
Passing	16	19
Returns	1	1
Avg. Time of Possession	33:01	26:59

1991 Individual Statistics

Scoring

	TD R	TD P	TD Rt	PAT	FG	Saf	TP
Butler	0	0	0	32/34	19/29	0	89
Anderson	6	3	0	0/0	0/0	0	54
Muster	6	1	0	0/0	0/0	0	42
Davis	0	6	0	0/0	0/0	0	36
Green	3	0	0	0/0	0/0	0	18
Waddle	0	3	0	0/0	0/0	0	18
Harbaugh	2	0	0	0/0	0/0	0	12
Morgan	0	2	0	0/0	0/0	0	12
Bailey	1	0	0	0/0	0/0	0	6
Stinson	0	0	1	0/0	0/0	0	6
Thornton	0	1	0	0/0	0/0	0	6
Bears	18	16	1	32/34	19/29	0	299
Opponents	9	19	1	29/29	22/30	0	269

Passing

	Att.	Comp.	Yds.	Pct.	TD	Int.	Tkld.	Rate
Harbaugh	478	275	3121	57.5	15	16	24/163	73.7
Willis	18	11	171	61.1	1	1	2/9	88.0
Anderson	1	0	0	0.0	0	0	0/0	39.6
Bears	497	286	3292	57.5	16	17	26/172	74.1
Opponents	513	286	3184	55.8	19	17	40/257	72.9

Rushing

	Att.	Yds.	Avg.	LG	TD
Anderson	210	747	3.6	42t	6
Muster	90	412	4.6	24	6
Harbaugh	70	338	4.8	20	2
Green	61	217	3.6	18	3
Rouse	27	74	2.7	10	0
Gentry	9	58	6.4	17	0
Bailey	15	43	2.9	11	1
Lewis	15	36	2.4	9	0
Morgan	3	18	6.0	13	0
Willis	2	6	3.0	8	0
Bears	502	1949	3.9	42t	18
Opponents	389	1580	4.1	64t	9

Receiving

	No.	Yds.	Avg.	LG	TD
Davis	61	945	15.5	75t	6
Waddle	55	599	10.9	37t	3
Anderson	47	368	7.8	26t	3
Muster	35	287	8.2	21	1
Thornton	17	278	16.4	33	1
Gentry	16	149	9.3	18	0
Rouse	15	93	6.2	14	0
Morgan	13	211	16.2	84t	2
Morris	8	147	18.4	33	0
Jennings	8	109	13.6	19	0
Green	6	54	9.0	15	0
Boso	3	36	12.0	22	0
Kozlowski	2	16	8.0	11	0
Bears	286	3292	11.5	84t	16
Opponents	286	3184	11.1	77t	19

Interceptions

	No.	Yds.	Avg.	LG	TD
Stinson	4	69	17.3	34t	1
Paul	3	21	7.0	10	0
Carrier	2	54	27.0	39	0
Tate	2	35	17.5	28	0
Woolford	2	21	10.5	16	0
Gayle	1	11	11.0	11	0
Mangum	1	5	5.0	5	0
Morrissey	1	5	5.0	5	0
Dent	1	4	4.0	4	0
Bears	17	225	13.2	39	1
Opponents	17	145	8.5	23	0

Punting

	No.	Yds.	Avg.	In 20	LG
Buford	69	2814	40.8	13	64
Bears	70	2814	40.2	13	64
Opponents	81	3343	41.3	26	61

Punt Returns

	No.	FC	Yds.	Avg.	LG	TD
Bailey	36	11	281	7.8	37	0
Waddle	5	3	31	6.2	11	0
Green	3	1	9	3.0	8	0
Morgan	3	0	19	6.3	11	0
Bears	47	15	340	7.2	37	0
Opponents	28	12	205	7.3	18	0

Kickoff Returns

	No.	Yds.	Avg.	LG	TD
Bailey	16	311	19.4	31	0
Gentry	13	227	17.5	27	0
Morgan	8	133	16.6	29	0
Green	4	69	17.3	29	0
Lewis	2	13	6.5	13	0
Rouse	2	10	5.0	10	0
Bears	45	763	17.0	31	0
Opponents	58	1134	19.6	47	0

Sacks

	No.
Dent	10.5
McMichael	9.0
Roper	8.0
Perry	5.5
Armstrong	1.5
Ryan	1.5
Cox	1.0
Mangum	1.0
Williams	1.0
Woolford	1.0
Bears	40.0
Opponents	26.0

1992 Draft Choices

Round	Name	Pos.	College
1.	Alonzo Spellman	DE	Ohio State
2.	Troy Auzenne	T	California
3.	Jeremy Lincoln	DB	Tennessee
4.	Will Furrer	QB	Virginia Tech
5.	Todd Harrison	TE	North Carolina St.
6.	Mark Berry	DB	Texas
7.	John Brown	WR	Houston
9.	Mirko Jurkovic	G	Notre Dame
10.	Nikki Fisher	RB	Virginia
11.	Louis Age	T	S.W. Louisiana
12.	Chris Wilson	LB	Oklahoma

Chicago Bears 1992 Veteran Roster

No.	Name	Pos.	Ht.	Wt.	Birth-date	NFL Exp.	College	Hometown	How Acq.	'91 Games/ Starts
35	Anderson, Neal	RB	5-11	210	8/14/64	7	Florida	Graceville, Fla.	D1-'86	13/12
93	Armstrong, Trace	DE	6-4	259	10/5/65	4	Florida	Birmingham, Ala.	D1b-'89	12/12
62	†Bortz, Mark	G	6-6	272	2/12/61	10	Iowa	Pardeeville, Wis.	D8-'83	9/9
8	Buford, Maury	P	6-0	198	2/18/60	11	Texas Tech	Mt. Pleasant, Tex.	W(GB)-'89	16/0
6	Butler, Kevin	K	6-1	190	7/24/62	8	Georgia	Redan, Ga.	D4-'85	16/0
20	Carrier, Mark	S	6-1	180	4/28/68	3	Southern California	Long Beach, Calif.	D1-'90	16/16
54	Cox, Ron	LB	6-2	242	2/27/68	3	Fresno State	Fresno, Calif.	D2b-'90	6/0
82	†Davis, Wendell	WR	5-11	188	1/3/66	5	Louisiana State	Shreveport, La.	D1-'88	16/16
95	Dent, Richard	DE	6-5	268	12/13/60	10	Tennessee State	Atlanta, Ga.	D8-'83	16/16
37	Douglass, Maurice	CB	5-11	200	2/12/64	7	Kentucky	Dayton, Ohio	D8-'86	16/0
24	Fain, Richard	CB	5-10	180	2/29/68	2	Florida	Ft. Myers, Fla.	PB(Phx)-'92#	6/2*
67	Fontenot, Jerry	C	6-3	272	11/21/66	4	Texas A&M	Lafayette, La.	D3-'89	16/7
17	Gardocki, Chris	K-P	6-1	194	2/7/70	2	Clemson	Stone Mountain, Ga.	D3-'91	4/0
23	Gayle, Shaun	S	5-11	194	3/8/62	9	Ohio State	Bethel, Va.	D10-'84	12/9
29	Gentry, Dennis	WR	5-8	180	2/10/59	11	Baylor	Lubbock, Tex.	D4-'82	15/0
31	Green, Mark	RB	5-11	195	3/22/67	4	Notre Dame	Riverside, Calif.	D5a-'89	16/4
4	Harbaugh, Jim	QB	6-3	220	12/23/64	6	Michigan	Ann Arbor, Mich.	D1-'87	16/16
63	†Hilgenberg, Jay	C	6-3	260	3/21/60	12	Iowa	Iowa City, Iowa	FA-'81	16/16
85	†Jennings, Keith	TE	6-4	251	5/19/66	3	Clemson	Summerville, S.C.	FA-'91	10/3
53	†Jones, Dante	LB	6-1	236	3/23/65	5	Oklahoma	Dallas, Tex.	D2-'88	16/0
88	Kozlowski, Glen	WR	6-1	205	12/31/62	6	Brigham Young	Honolulu, Hawaii	D11-'86	16/0
92	Kumerow, Eric	DE-DT	6-7	270	4/17/65	4	Ohio State	Oak Park, Ill.	T(Mia)-'91	0*
33	Lewis, Darren	RB	5-10	230	11/7/68	2	Texas A&M	Henderson, Tex.	D6-'91	15/0
26	Mangum, John	CB	5-10	173	3/16/67	3	Alabama	Magee, Miss.	FA-'90	16/1
75	Mattes, Ron	T	6-6	300	8/8/63	7	Virginia	Ringtown, Pa.	T(NYJ)-'91	15/0
76	McMichael, Steve	DT	6-2	268	10/17/57	13	Texas	Houston, Tex.	FA-'81	16/16
81	Morgan, Anthony	WR	6-1	195	11/15/67	2	Tennessee	Cleveland, Ohio	D5-'91	14/2
84	Morris, Ron	WR	6-1	195	11/4/64	6	Southern Methodist	Cooper, Tex.	D2-'87	3/1
51	Morrissey, Jim	LB	6-3	227	12/24/62	8	Michigan State	Flint, Mich.	D11-'85	16/11
25	Muster, Brad	RB	6-3	231	4/11/65	5	Stanford	Novato, Calif.	D1-'88	11/11
36	†Paul, Markus	S	6-2	199	4/1/66	4	Syracuse	Kissimmee, Fla.	D4-'89	14/7
72	†Perry, William	DT	6-2	360	12/16/62	8	Clemson	Aiken, S.C.	D1-'85	16/16
59	Rivera, Ron	LB	6-3	240	1/7/62	9	California	Monterey, Calif.	D2-'84	16/5
52	Rodenhauser, Mark	C	6-5	265	6/1/61	5	Illinois State	Addison, Ill.	PB(SD)-'92#	10/0*
55	Roper, John	LB	6-1	228	10/4/65	4	Texas A&M	Houston, Tex.	D2a-'89	16/16
30	Rouse, James	RB	6-0	220	12/18/66	3	Arkansas	Little Rock, Ark.	D8b-'89	14/4
96	Ryan, Tim	DT	6-4	268	9/8/67	3	Southern California	Memphis, Tenn.	D3a-'90	16/4
50	Singletary, Mike	LB	6-0	230	10/9/58	12	Baylor	Houston, Tex.	D2-'81	16/16
32	Stinson, Lemuel	CB	5-9	159	5/10/66	5	Texas Tech	Houston, Tex.	D6-'88	16/16
58	Stonebreaker, Mike	LB	6-0	226	1/14/67	2	Notre Dame	Baltimore, Md.	D9-'91	16/0
49	Tate, David	S	6-0	177	11/22/64	5	Colorado	Denver, Colo.	D8-'88	16/0
57	Thayer, Tom	G	6-4	270	8/16/61	8	Notre Dame	Joliet, Ill.	D4-'83	16/16
60	Thomas, Stan	T	6-5	302	10/28/68	2	Texas	El Centro, Calif.	D1-'91	15/7
80	Thornton, James	TE	6-2	242	2/8/65	5	Cal State-Fullerton	Santa Rosa, Calif.	D4-'88	16/13
78	Van Horne, Keith	T	6-6	283	11/6/57	12	Southern California	Mt. Lebanon, Pa.	D1-'81	16/16
87	Waddle, Tom	WR	6-0	181	2/20/67	4	Boston College	Cincinnati, Ohio	FA-'89	16/13
71	Williams, James	DE	6-7	305	3/29/68	2	Cheyney State	Pittsburgh, Pa.	FA-'91	14/0
10	Willis, Peter Tom	QB	6-2	188	1/4/67	3	Florida State	Morris, Ala.	D3b-'90	4/0
73	Wojciechowski, John	G	6-4	270	7/30/63	6	Michigan State	Detroit, Mich.	FA-'87	16/9
21	Woolford, Donnell	CB	5-9	187	1/6/66	4	Clemson	Fayetteville, N.C.	D1a-'89	15/15
97	Zorich, Chris	DT	6-1	267	3/13/69	2	Notre Dame	Chicago, Ill.	D2-'91	12/0

* Fain played 6 games with Phoenix in '91; Kumerow missed '91 season due to injury; Rodenhauser played 10 games with San Diego.

† Option playout; subject to developments.

Retired—Tackle Jim Covert, nine-year veteran, missed '91 season due to injury.

Plan B unconditional free agent.

Player lost through Plan B (1): RB Johnny Bailey (Phx; 14 games in '91).

Also played with Bears in '91—TE Cap Boso (6 games), CB John Hardy (4).

COACHING STAFF

Head Coach, Mike Ditka

Pro Career: Became Bears' tenth head coach on January 20, 1982, after serving nine years as an offensive assistant with Dallas. Led Bears to first Super Bowl title following 15-1 1985 season. Bears shut out New York Giants and Los Angeles Rams in playoffs before routing New England 46-10 in Super Bowl XX. Rebounded from 6-10 season in 1989 and led Bears to 11-5 mark in 1990 which won NFC Central Division for sixth time in seven years. Repeated 11-5 record in 1991, which qualified Chicago for a Wild Card playoff spot. Under his leadership, the Bears have made the playoffs in seven of his 10 seasons and have advanced to the NFC Championship Game on three occasions. Ditka is a 30-year veteran of the NFL as both a player and coach. He had a 12-year playing career as a tight end with Chicago (1961-66), Philadelphia (1967-68), and Dallas (1969-72). A first-round draft choice by Chicago in 1961, Ditka was NFL rookie of the year, all-NFL (1961-64), and played in five Pro Bowls (1962-66). He joined Cowboys' coaching staff in 1973. In addition to working with Dallas special teams, Ditka coached Cowboys' receivers. During his NFL career, he has been in the playoffs 17 times and has been a member of five NFC champions and three NFL champions. He became the first tight end to be inducted into the Pro Football Hall of Fame in July, 1988. Career record: 107-57.

Background: Played at University of Pittsburgh from 1958-60 and was a unanimous All-America his senior year. A two-way performer, he played both tight end and linebacker. He also was one of the nation's leading punters with a 40-plus-yard average over three years.

Personal: Born October 18, 1939, Carnegie, Pa. Mike and his wife, Diana, live in Bannockburn, Ill., and have four children—Michael, Mark, Megan, and Matt.

Assistant Coaches

Danny Abramowicz, special teams; born July 13, 1945, Steubenville, Ohio, lives in Vernon Hills, Ill. Wide receiver Xavier 1964-66. Pro wide receiver New Orleans Saints 1967-73, San Francisco 49ers 1973-74. Pro coach: Joined Bears in 1992.

Steve Kazor, tight ends; born February 24, 1948, New Kensington, Pa., lives in Vernon Hills, Ill. Nose tackle Westminister College 1967-70. No pro playing experience. College coach: Emporia State 1973 (head coach), Texas-Arlington 1974, Colorado State 1975, Wyoming 1976, Texas 1977-78, Texas-El Paso 1979-80. Pro coach: Joined Bears in 1982.

Greg Landry, offensive coordinator; born December 18, 1946, Nashua, N.H., lives in Libertyville, Ill. Quarterback Massachusetts 1965-67. Pro quarterback Detroit Lions 1968-78, Baltimore Colts 1979-81, Chicago Blitz/Arizona Wranglers (USFL) 1983-84, Chicago Bears 1984. Pro coach: Cleveland Browns 1985, joined Bears in 1986.

John Levra, defensive line; born October 2, 1937, Arma, Kan., lives in Libertyville, Ill. Guard-linebacker Pittsburg (Kan.) State 1963-65. No pro playing experience. College coach: Stephen F. Austin 1971-74, Kansas 1975-78, North Texas State 1979. Pro coach: British Columbia Lions (CFL) 1980, New Orleans Saints 1981-85, joined Bears in 1986.

David McGinnis, linebackers; born August 7, 1951, Independence, Kan., lives in Lake Forest, Ill. Defensive back Texas Christian 1970-72. No pro playing experience. College coach: Texas Christian 1973-74, 1982, Missouri 1975-77, Indiana State 1978-81, Kansas State 1983-85. Pro coach: Joined Bears in 1986.

Vic Rapp, wide receivers; born December 23, 1935, Marionville, Mo., lives in Rochester, Mich. Running back Southwest Missouri State 1954-57. No pro playing experience. College coach: Arizona 1965-66, Missouri 1967-71. Pro coach: Edmonton Eskimos (CFL) 1972-76, British Columbia Lions (CFL) 1977-82 (head coach), Houston Oilers 1983, Los Angeles Rams 1984, Tampa Bay Buccaneers 1985-86, Detroit Lions 1987, joined Bears in 1989.

Johnny Roland, running backs; born May 21, 1943, Corpus Christi, Tex., lives in Vernon Hills, Ill. Running back Missouri 1963-65. Pro running back St. Louis Cardinals 1966-72, New York Giants 1973. College coach: Notre Dame 1975. Pro coach: Green Bay Packers 1974, Philadelphia Eagles 1976-78, joined Bears in 1983.

Dick Stanfel, offensive line; born July 20, 1927, San Francisco, Calif., lives in Libertyville, Ill. Guard San Francisco 1948-50. Pro guard Detroit Lions 1952-55, Washington Redskins 1956-58. College coach: Notre Dame 1959-62, California 1963. Pro coach: Philadelphia Eagles 1964-70, San Francisco 49ers 1971-75, New Orleans Saints 1976-80 (head coach, 4 games in 1980), joined Bears in 1981.

Vince Tobin, defensive coordinator; born September 29, 1943, Burlington Junction, Mo., lives in Libertyville, Ill. Defensive back-running back Missouri 1961-64. No pro playing experience. College coach: Missouri 1967-76. Pro coach: British Columbia Lions (CFL) 1977-82, Philadelphia/Baltimore Stars (USFL) 1983-85, joined Bears in 1986.

Zaven Yaralian, defensive backs; born February 5, 1952, Syria, lives in Lake Forest, Ill. Defensive back Nebraska 1972-73. Pro defensive back Green Bay Packers 1974, Philadelphia Bell (WFL) 1975. College coach: Nebraska 1975, Washington State 1976-77, Missouri 1978-83, Florida 1984-87, Colorado 1988-89. Pro coach: Joined Bears in 1990.

Chicago Bears 1992 First-Year Roster

Name	Pos.	Ht.	Wt.	Birth-date	College	Hometown	How Acq.
Age, Louis	T	6-7	340	2/1/70	S.W. Louisiana	New Orleans, La.	D11
Ashley, Tyrone	RB	6-1	198	5/3/70	Mississippi	Hialeah, Fla.	FA
Auzenne, Troy	T	6-7	282	6/26/69	California	Baldwin Park, Calif.	D2
Backes, Tom (1)	G-T	6-4	273	3/19/68	Oklahoma	El Paso, Tex.	D10-'91
Berry, Mark	CB	5-11	180	12/29/68	Texas	Dallas, Tex.	D6
Blackwell, Kelly	TE	6-1	255	2/13/69	Texas Christian	Ft. Worth, Tex.	FA
Bounds, Mark	P	5-10	186	6/30/69	Texas Tech	Stamford, Tex.	FA
Boyce, Charles	CB	5-11	180	4/27/69	Sam Houston State	DeSoto, Tex.	FA
Brown III, John	WR	6-1	199	7/7/68	Houston	Dodge City, Kan.	FA
Deter, Charles	DT	6-2	274	2/19/69	Penn State	DuBois, Pa.	FA
Fisher, Nikki	RB	5-10	227	12/26/69	Virginia	Martinsville, Va.	FA
Furrer, Will	QB	6-3	208	2/5/68	Virginia Tech	Pullman, Wash.	FA
Graham, Maxie	DE	6-4	277	2/28/70	Western Illinois	Miami, Fla.	FA
Harrison, Todd	TE	6-4	260	3/20/69	North Carolina State	Gainesville, Fla.	FA
Inhat, Eric (1)	TE	6-4	245	8/18/68	Marshall	Columbus, Ohio	FA
Johnson, Darron	WR	6-0	188	4/26/69	Angelo State	Austin, Tex.	FA
Johnson, Eric	DE	6-2	240	3/11/70	Stephen F. Austin	Hooks, Tex.	FA
Jones, Walter	WR	5-10	180	7/18/70	Duke	Roanoake Rapids, N.C.	FA
Jurkovic, Mirko	G	6-3	282	5/19/70	Notre Dame	Calumet City, Ill.	D9
Justin, Paul (1)	QB	6-4	202	5/19/68	Arizona State	Shaumburg, Ill.	D7-'91
Lincoln, Jeremy	CB	5-10	180	4/7/69	Tennessee	Toledo, Ohio	D3
Lott, James (1)	CB	5-9	181	1/8/67	Clemson	Brown, N.C.	FA
Lynch, Brendan	LB	6-1	236	11/8/68	Wisconsin	Hinsdale, Ill.	FA
Mickel, Marcus	WR	5-9	184	12/15/69	Virginia Tech	Newport News, Va.	FA
Minter, Peyton	DE	6-5	269	9/8/69	Purdue	Chicago, Ill.	FA
Nobbe, David	G-T	6-6	281	2/12/70	Indianapolis College	Greensburg, Ind.	FA
O'Bradovich, Ed	LB	6-0	247	7/28/69	Michigan State	Palatine, Ind.	FA
Primous, Marlon	S	6-3	224	12/12/68	Illinois	Carson, Calif.	FA
Rankin, Alex	G-T	6-9	312	11/24/68	Angelo State	Laredo, Tex.	FA
Schwantz, Jim	LB	6-2	231	1/23/70	Purdue	Palatine, Ill.	FA
Taylor, Robert	LB	6-3	279	2/19/69	Mississippi College	Long Beach, Miss.	FA
Thomas, Gene	WR	5-10	167	8/18/70	Maryland	Rockville, Md.	FA
Williams, Arnie	LB	6-1	226	8/4/70	Southern Mississippi	Bayminette, Ala.	FA
Wright, Eric	WR	6-0	197	8/4/69	Stephen F. Austin	Pittsburg, Tex.	FA
Wilson, Chris	LB	6-0	227	1/8/69	Oklahoma	Dallas, Tex.	FA

The term NFL Rookie is defined as a player who is in his first season of professional football and has not been on the roster of another professional football team for any regular-season or postseason games. A Rookie is designated by an "R" on NFL rosters. Players who have been active in another professional football league or players who have NFL experience, including either preseason training camp or being on an active roster for fewer than three regular-season or postseason games, are termed NFL First-Year Players. An NFL First-Year Player is designated by a "1" on NFL rosters. Thereafter, a player on an NFL active roster for at least three regular-season or postseason games is credited with an additional year of NFL playing experience.

NOTES

National Football Conference Eastern Division

Team Colors: Royal Blue, Metallic Silver Blue, and White

Cowboys Center
One Cowboys Parkway
Irving, Texas 75063
Telephone: (214) 556-9900

Club Officials

Owner/President/General Manager:
  Jerry Jones
Vice President: Stephen Jones
Vice President: Mike McCoy
Vice President/Marketing: George Hays
Treasurer: Jack Dixon
Director of Administrative Personnel: Steve Orsini
Marketing and Special Events Coordinator:
  Charlotte Anderson
Public Relations Director: Rich Dalrymple
Director of Operations: Bruce Mays
Trainer: Kevin O'Neill
Equipment Manager: Buck Buchanan
Video Director: Robert Blackwell
Cheerleader Director: Kelli McGonagill

Stadium: Texas Stadium • **Capacity:** 65,024
  Irving, Texas 75062

Playing Surface: Texas Turf

Training Camp: St. Edward's University
  Austin, Texas 78704

1992 Schedule

Preseason
Aug. 1	vs. Houston at Tokyo	10:00
Aug. 7	at Miami	8:00
Aug. 15	**Houston**	8:00
Aug. 22	**Denver**	8:00
Aug. 28	**Chicago**	7:00

Regular Season
Sept. 7	**Washington** (Monday)	8:00
Sept. 13	at New York Giants	1:00
Sept. 20	**Phoenix**	3:00
Sept. 27	**Open Date**	
Oct. 5	at Philadelphia (Monday)	9:00
Oct. 11	**Seattle**	12:00
Oct. 18	**Kansas City**	12:00
Oct. 25	at Los Angeles Raiders	1:00
Nov. 1	**Philadelphia**	3:00
Nov. 8	at Detroit	1:00
Nov. 15	**Los Angeles Rams**	12:00
Nov. 22	at Phoenix	2:00
Nov. 26	**N.Y. Giants** (Thanksgiving)	3:00
Dec. 6	at Denver	2:00
Dec. 13	at Washington	1:00
Dec. 21	at Atlanta (Monday)	9:00
Dec. 27	**Chicago**	3:00

Cowboys Coaching History

(290-208-6)

1960-88	Tom Landry	270-178-6
1989-91	Jimmy Johnson	20-30-0

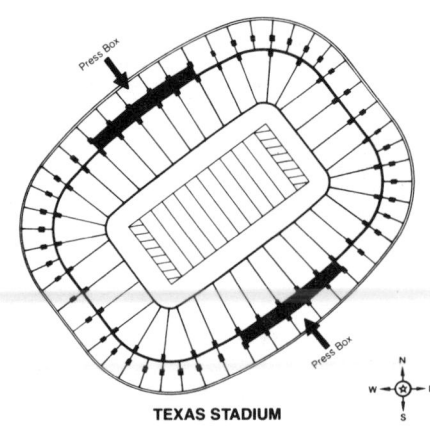

TEXAS STADIUM

Record Holders

Individual Records—Career

Category	Name	Performance
Rushing (Yds.)	Tony Dorsett, 1977-1987	12,036
Passing (Yds.)	Roger Staubach, 1969-1979	22,700
Passing (TDs)	Danny White, 1976-1988	155
Receiving (No.)	Drew Pearson, 1973-1983	489
Receiving (Yds.)	Tony Hill, 1977-1986	7,988
Interceptions	Mel Renfro, 1964-1977	52
Punting (Avg.)	Mike Saxon, 1985-1991	41.4
Punt Return (Avg.)	Bob Hayes, 1965-1974	11.1
Kickoff Return (Avg.)	Mel Renfro, 1964-1977	26.4
Field Goals	Rafael Septien, 1978-1986	162
Touchdowns (Tot.)	Tony Dorsett, 1977-1987	86
Points	Rafael Septien, 1978-1986	874

Individual Records—Single Season

Category	Name	Performance
Rushing (Yds.)	Tony Dorsett, 1981	1,646
Passing (Yds.)	Danny White, 1983	3,980
Passing (TDs)	Danny White, 1983	29
Receiving (No.)	Michael Irvin, 1991	93
Receiving (Yds.)	Michael Irvin, 1991	1,523
Interceptions	Everson Walls, 1981	11
Punting (Avg.)	Sam Baker, 1962	45.4
Punt Return (Avg.)	Bob Hayes, 1968	20.8
Kickoff Return (Avg.)	Mel Renfro, 1965	30.0
Field Goals	Rafael Septien, 1981	27
	Ken Willis, 1991	27
Touchdowns (Tot.)	Dan Reeves, 1966	16
Points	Rafael Septien, 1983	123

Individual Records—Single Game

Category	Name	Performance
Rushing (Yds.)	Tony Dorsett, 12-4-77	206
Passing (Yds.)	Don Meredith, 11-10-63	460
Passing (TDs)	Many times	5
	Last time by Danny White, 10-30-83	
Receiving (No.)	Lance Rentzel, 11-19-67	13
Receiving (Yds.)	Bob Hayes, 11-13-66	246
Interceptions	Herb Adderley, 9-26-71	3
	Lee Roy Jordan, 11-4-73	3
	Dennis Thurman, 12-13-81	3
Field Goals	Roger Ruzek, 12-21-87	5
Touchdowns (Tot.)	Many times	4
	Last time by Emmitt Smith, 11-18-90	
Points	Many times	24
	Last time by Emmitt Smith, 11-18-90	

1991 Team Record
Preseason (2-2)

Date	Result		Opponents
8/3	W	24-14	at Kansas City
8/12	L	12-17	L.A. Raiders
8/18	L	20-30	at Houston
8/23	W	20-17	Atlanta (OT)

Regular Season (11-5)

Date	Result		Opponents	Att.
9/1	W	26-14	at Cleveland	78,860
9/9	L	31-33	Washington	63,025
9/15	L	0-24	Philadelphia	62,656
9/22	W	17- 9	at Phoenix	68,814
9/29	W	21-16	N.Y. Giants	64,010
10/6	W	20-17	at Green Bay	53,695
10/13	W	35-23	Cincinnati	63,275
10/27	L	10-34	at Detroit	74,906
11/3	W	27- 7	Phoenix	61,190
11/10	W	23-26	at Houston (OT)	63,001
11/17	L	9-22	at N.Y. Giants	76,410
11/24	W	24-21	at Washington	55,561
11/28	W	20-10	Pittsburgh	62,253
12/8	W	23-14	New Orleans	64,530
12/15	W	25-13	at Philadelphia	65,854
12/22	W	31-27	Atlanta	60,962

(OT) Overtime

Postseason (1-1)

Date	Result		Opponent	Att.
12/29	W	17-13	at Chicago	66,213
1/5	L	6-38	at Detroit	79,166

Score by Periods

Cowboys	91	105	35	111	0	—	342
Opponents	61	89	66	91	3	—	310

Attendance

Home 501,901 Away 537,101 Total 1,039,002
Single-game home record, 80,259 (11-24-66)
Single-season home record, 511,541 (1981)

1991 Team Statistics

	Cowboys	Opp.
Total First Downs	304	299
Rushing	89	103
Passing	191	180
Penalty	24	16
Third Down: Made/Att.	74/196	76/194
Third Down: Pct.	37.8	39.2
Fourth Down: Made/Att.	6/14	7/17
Fourth Down: Pct.	42.9	41.2
Total Net Yards	5101	5066
Avg. Per Game	318.8	316.6
Total Plays	971	963
Avg. Per Play	5.3	5.3
Net Yards Rushing	1711	1571
Avg. Per Game	106.9	98.2
Total Rushes	433	400
Net Yards Passing	3390	3495
Avg. Per Game	211.9	218.4
Sacked/Yards Lost	38/273	23/151
Gross Yards	3663	3646
Att./Completions	500/305	540/320
Completion Pct.	61.0	59.3
Had Intercepted	12	12
Punts/Avg.	57/42.6	61/38.8
Net Punting Avg.	36.8	32.4
Penalties/Yards Lost	74/610	97/801
Fumbles/Ball Lost	23/12	23/11
Touchdowns	37	32
Rushing	15	11
Passing	16	17
Returns	6	4
Avg. Time of Possession	30:06	29:54

1991 Individual Statistics

Scoring

	TD R	TD P	TD Rt	PAT	FG	Saf	TP
Willis	0	0	0	37/37	27/39	0	118
E. Smith	12	1	0	0/0	0/0	0	78
Irvin	0	8	0	0/0	0/0	0	48
Novacek	0	4	0	0/0	0/0	0	24
Horton	0	0	2	0/0	0/0	0	12
Agee	1	0	0	0/0	0/0	0	6
Aikman	1	0	0	0/0	0/0	0	6
Blake	1	0	0	0/0	0/0	0	6
Edwards	0	0	1	0/0	0/0	0	6
Harper	0	1	0	0/0	0/0	0	6
Johnston	0	1	0	0/0	0/0	0	6
Martin	0	0	1	0/0	0/0	0	6
Roberts	0	1	0	0/0	0/0	0	6
R. Williams	0	0	1	0/0	0/0	0	6
Wright	0	0	1	0/0	0/0	0	6
Hendrix	0	0	0	0/0	0/0	1	2
Cowboys	15	16	6	37/37	27/39	1	342
Opponents	11	17	4	31/32	29/39	0	310

Passing

	Att.	Comp.	Yds.	Pct.	TD	Int.	Tkld.	Rate
Aikman	363	237	2754	65.3	11	10	32/224	86.7
Beuerlein	137	68	909	49.6	5	2	6/49	77.2
Kupp, Phx.-Dall.	7	3	23	42.9	0	0	2/23	51.5
Cowboys	500	305	3663	61.0	16	12	38/273	84.1
Opponents	540	320	3646	59.3	17	12	23/151	80.8

Rushing

	Att.	Yds.	Avg.	LG	TD
E. Smith	365	1563	4.3	75t	12
Blake	15	80	5.3	30t	1
Johnston	17	54	3.2	10	0
Agee	9	20	2.2	8	1
Aikman	16	5	0.3	9	1
Kupp, Phx.-Dall.	1	5	5.0	5	0
Richards	2	4	2.0	3	0
Wright	2	-1	-0.5	3	0
Beuerlein	7	-14	-2.0	-1	0
Cowboys	433	1711	4.0	75t	15
Opponents	400	1571	3.9	75t	11

Receiving

	No.	Yds.	Avg.	LG	TD
Irvin	93	1523	16.4	66t	8
Novacek	59	664	11.3	49	4
E. Smith	49	258	5.3	14	1
Johnston	28	244	8.7	22	1
Harper	20	326	16.3	39	1
Martin	16	243	15.2	27	0
Roberts	16	136	8.5	21	1
Wright	10	170	17.0	53	1
Agee	7	43	6.1	9	0
Awalt	5	57	11.4	20	0
Blake	1	5	5.0	5	0
Aikman	1	-6	-6.0	-6	0
Cowboys	305	3663	12.0	66t	16
Opponents	320	3646	11.4	67t	17

Interceptions

	No.	Yds.	Avg.	LG	TD
Holt	4	2	0.5	2	0
Brown	2	31	15.5	20	0
Washington	2	9	4.5	9	0
Horton	1	65	65.0	65t	1
Edwards	1	36	36.0	36t	1
R. Williams	1	24	24.0	24	0
Gant	1	0	0.0	0	0
Cowboys	12	167	13.9	65t	2
Opponents	12	244	20.3	96t	2

Punting

	No.	Yds.	Avg.	In 20	LG
Saxon	57	2426	42.6	16	64
Cowboys	57	2426	42.6	16	64
Opponents	61	2364	38.8	14	77

Punt Returns

	No.	FC	Yds.	Avg.	LG	TD
Martin	21	8	244	11.6	85t	1
Shepard	6	3	57	9.5	14	0
Brownlow	1	0	0	0.0	0	0
Horton	1	0	8	8.0	8	0
Wright	0	1	0	—	0	0
Cowboys	29	12	309	10.7	85t	1
Opponents	28	10	231	8.3	34	0

Kickoff Returns

	No.	Yds.	Avg.	LG	TD
Wright	21	514	24.5	102t	1
Dixon	18	398	22.1	39	0
Gant	6	114	19.0	26	0
Martin	3	47	15.7	25	0
Shepard	3	54	18.0	21	0
Horton	1	0	0.0	0	0
Cowboys	52	1127	21.7	102t	1
Opponents	69	1169	16.9	82t	1

Sacks

	No.
Tolbert	7.0
Maryland	4.5
Jeffcoat	4.0
Casillas	2.5
Jones	2.0
Noonan	1.0
Stubbs	1.0
R. Williams	1.0
Cowboys	23.0
Opponents	38.0

1992 Draft Choices

Round	Name	Pos.	College
1.	Kevin Smith	DB	Texas A&M
	Robert Jones	LB	East Carolina
2.	Jimmy Smith	WR	Jackson State
	Darren Woodson	DB	Arizona State
3.	Clayton Holmes	DB	Carson-Newman
	James Brown	T	Virginia State
4.	Tom Myslinski	C-G	Tennessee
5.	Greg Briggs	DB	Texas Southern
	Rod Milstead	G	Delaware State
6.	Fallon Wacasey	TE	Tulsa
9.	Nate Kirtman	DB	Pomona-Pitzer
	Chris Hall	DB	East Carolina
10.	John Terry	G	Livingstone
11.	Tim Daniel	WR	Florida A&M
12.	Don Harris	DB	Texas Tech

Dallas Cowboys 1992 Veteran Roster

No.	Name	Pos.	Ht.	Wt.	Birth-date	NFL Exp.	College	Hometown	How Acq.	'91 Games/ Starts
34	Agee, Tommie	RB	6-0	225	2/22/64	5	Auburn	Maplesville, Ala.	PB(KC)-'90#	16/0
8	Aikman, Troy	QB	6-4	222	11/21/66	4	UCLA	Henryetta, Okla.	D1-'89	12/12
36	Albritton, Vince	S	6-2	216	7/23/62	9	Washington	Oakland, Calif.	FA-'84	6/0
86	Alphin, Gerald	WR	6-3	220	5/21/64	3	Kansas State	St. Louis, Mo.	FA-'92	5/0*
40	†Bates, Bill	S	6-1	205	6/6/61	10	Tennessee	Knoxville, Tenn.	FA-'83	16/0
7	Beuerlein, Steve	QB	6-2	209	3/7/65	4	Notre Dame	Anaheim, Calif.	T(Raid)-'91	8/4
46	Blake, Ricky	RB	6-2	244	7/15/67	2	Alabama A&M	Lincoln County, Tenn.	FA-'91	2/0
32	Brooks, Michael	S	6-0	189	3/12/67	2	North Carolina State	Greensboro, N.C.	FA-'90	0*
24	Brown, Larry	CB	5-11	182	11/30/69	2	Texas Christian	Los Angeles, Calif.	D12-'91	16/13
75	Casillas, Tony	DT	6-3	277	10/26/63	7	Oklahoma	Tulsa, Okla.	T(Atl)-'91	16/16
59	Clark, Bernard	LB	6-2	248	1/12/67	3	Miami	Tampa, Fla.	PB(Cin)-'92#	14/0*
93	Cooper, Reggie	LB	6-2	215	7/11/68	2	Nebraska	Slidell, La.	FA-'91	2/0
68	Cornish, Frank	C-G	6-4	295	9/24/67	3	UCLA	Chicago, Ill.	PB(SD)-'92#	16/0*
5	Daluiso, Brad	K	6-2	207	12/31/67	2	UCLA	San Diego, Calif.	PB(Buff)-'92#	16/0*
58	Edwards, Dixon	LB	6-1	224	3/25/68	2	Michigan State	Cincinnati, Ohio	D2-'91	12/1
29	Gant, Kenneth	CB	5-11	188	4/18/67	3	Albany State	Lakeland, Fla.	D9-'90	16/1
63	Gesek, John	G	6-5	279	2/18/63	6	Cal State-Sacramento	Danville, Calif.	T(Raid)-'90	16/15
66	Gogan, Kevin	G	6-7	317	11/2/64	6	Washington	Pacifica, Calif.	D8-'87	16/16
80	Harper, Alvin	WR	6-3	203	7/6/67	2	Tennessee	Frostproof, Fla.	D1b-'91	15/5
70	Hellestrae, Dale	C-G	6-5	285	7/11/62	6	Southern Methodist	Scottsdale, Ariz.	T(Raid)-'90	16/0
90	Hill, Tony	DE	6-6	242	10/23/68	2	Tennessee-Chattanooga	Warren County, Ga.	D4c-'91	8/0
30	Holt, Issiac	CB	6-2	201	10/4/62	8	Alcorn State	Birmingham, Ala.	T(Minn)-'89	15/15
20	Horton, Ray	S	5-11	190	4/12/60	10	Washington	Tacoma, Wash.	PB(Cin)-'89#	16/16
88	†Irvin, Michael	WR	6-2	199	3/5/66	5	Miami	Ft. Lauderdale, Fla.	D1-'88	16/16
77	†Jeffcoat, Jim	DE	6-5	274	4/1/61	10	Arizona State	Cliffwood, N.J.	D1-'83	16/16
48	Johnston, Daryl	RB	6-2	236	2/10/66	4	Syracuse	Youngstown, N.Y.	D2-'89	16/14
97	Jones, Jimmie	DE-DT	6-4	276	1/9/66	3	Miami	Okeechobee, Fla.	D3-'90	16/6
35	Jordan, Tony	RB	6-2	220	5/5/65	3	Kansas State	Rochester, N.Y.	FA-'92	0*
9	Kupp, Craig	QB	6-4	215	4/14/67	2	Pacific	Selah, Wash.	W(Phx)-'91	1/0*
78	Lett, Leon	DE-DT	6-6	287	10/12/68	2	Emporia State	Fair Hope, Ala.	D7-'91	5/0
21	t-Lewis, Garry	CB	5-11	185	8/25/67	3	Alcorn State	New Orleans, La.	T(Raid)-'92	16/2*
85	Lomack, Tony	WR	5-8	180	4/27/68	2	Florida	Tallahassee, Fla.	FA-'92	1/0*
83	Martin, Kelvin	WR	5-9	162	5/14/65	6	Boston College	Jacksonville, Fla.	D4-'87	16/0
67	Maryland, Russell	DT	6-1	277	3/22/69	2	Miami	Chicago, Ill.	D1a-'91	16/7
25	Mitchell, Brian	CB	5-9	164	12/13/68	2	Brigham Young	Waco, Tex.	PB(Atl)-'92#	15/0*
98	Myles, Godfrey	LB	6-1	241	9/22/68	2	Florida	Miami, Fla.	D3a-'91	3/0
61	Newton, Nate	T	6-3	332	12/20/61	7	Florida A&M	Orlando, Fla.	FA-'86	14/14
73	Noonan, Danny	DT	6-4	275	7/14/65	6	Nebraska	Lincoln, Neb.	D1-'87	15/3
51	†Norton, Ken	LB	6-2	238	9/29/66	5	UCLA	Los Angeles, Calif.	D2-'88	16/16
84	†Novacek, Jay	TE	6-4	231	10/24/62	8	Wyoming	Gothenburg, Neb.	PB(Phx)-'90#	16/12
52	Pruitt, Mickey	LB	6-1	218	1/10/65	5	Colorado	Chicago, Ill.	W(Chi)-'91	12/1
87	Roberts, Alfredo	TE	6-3	252	3/1/65	5	Miami	Hollywood, Fla.	PB(KC)-'91#	16/10
4	Saxon, Mike	P	6-3	202	7/10/62	8	San Diego State	Arcadia, Calif.	FA-'85	16/0
82	†Shepard, Derrick	WR	5-10	183	1/22/64	5	Oklahoma	Odessa, Tex.	FA-'91	6/0
22	Smith, Emmitt	RB	5-9	203	5/15/69	3	Florida	Escambia, Fla.	D1-'90	16/16
57	†Smith, Vinson	LB	6-2	231	7/3/65	4	East Carolina	Statesville, N.C.	PB(Pitt)-'90#	13/12
53	†Stepnoski, Mark	C	6-2	269	1/20/67	4	Pittsburgh	Erie, Pa.	D3a-'89	16/16
92	†Tolbert, Tony	DE	6-6	265	12/29/67	4	Texas-El Paso	Englewood, N.J.	D4-'89	16/16
71	Tuinei, Mark	T	6-5	299	3/31/60	10	Hawaii	Honolulu, Hawaii	FA-'83	12/12
76	Veingrad, Alan	G-T	6-5	280	7/24/63	6	East Texas State	Miami, Fla.	PB(GB)-'91#	16/4
37	†Washington, James	S	6-1	197	1/10/65	5	UCLA	Los Angeles, Calif.	PB(Rams)-'90#	16/16
28	Weatherspoon, Chuck	RB	5-7	229	7/31/68	2	Houston	La Habra, Calif.	FA-'92	4/0*
79	Williams, Erik	T	6-6	319	9/7/68	2	Central State, Ohio	Philadelphia, Pa.	D3c-'91	11/3
23	Williams, Robert	CB	5-10	190	10/2/62	6	Baylor	Galveston, Tex.	FA-'87	16/2
81	Wright, Alexander	WR	6-0	190	7/19/67	3	Auburn	Albany, Ga.	D2-'90	16/5

* Alphin played 5 games with New Orleans in '91; Brooks missed '91 season due to injury; Clark played 12 games with Cincinnati, 2 with Seattle; Cornish played 16 games with San Diego; Daluiso played 2 games with Atlanta, 14 with Buffalo; Jordan active with Houston for 1 game but did not play; Kupp played 1 game with Phoenix; Lewis played 16 games with L.A. Raiders; Lomack played 1 game with Phoenix; Mitchell played 15 games with Atlanta; Weatherspoon played 4 games with Tampa Bay.

† Option playout; subject to developments.

Plan B unconditional free agent.

t- Cowboys traded for Lewis (L.A. Raiders).

Players lost through Plan B (6): TE Robert Awalt (Den; 12 games in '91), LB Darrick Brownlow (Buff; 16), LB Jack Del Rio (Minn; 16), CB Manny Hendrix (SF; 16), S Stan Smagala (Pitt; 8), K Ken Willis (TB; 16).

Also played with Cowboys in '91—WR James Dixon (7 games), RB Alonzo Highsmith (2), RB Curvin Richards (2), CB-S Donald Smith (3), DE Daniel Stubbs (9).

COACHING STAFF

Head Coach,
Jimmy Johnson

Pro Career: Named second head coach in Cowboys' history on February 25, 1989. Named NFL coach of the year in 1990. No pro playing experience. Career record: 20-30.

Background: All-Southwest Conference defensive lineman on Arkansas's 1964 undefeated national championship team. Began coaching career in 1965 at Louisiana Tech. Moved on as an assistant at Wichita State 1967, Iowa State 1968-69, Oklahoma 1970-72, Arkansas 1973-76, and Pittsburgh 1977-78. Head coach at Oklahoma State from 1979-83. Compiled 52-9 (.853) record in five seasons as head coach at the University of Miami. Under Johnson, the Hurricanes won the national championship in 1987 and 34 of 36 games from 1986-88. Career collegiate record: 81-34-3.

Personal: Born July 16, 1943, Port Arthur, Tex. Jimmy lives in Irving, Tex., and has two sons, Brent and Chad.

Assistant Coaches

Hubbard Alexander, wide receivers; born February 14, 1939, Winston-Salem, N.C., lives in Coppell, Tex. Center Tennessee State 1958-61. No pro playing experience. College coach: Tennessee State 1962-63, Vanderbilt 1974-78, Miami 1979-88. Pro coach: Joined Cowboys in 1989.

Joe Avezzano, special teams; born November 17, 1943, Yonkers, N.Y., lives in Coppell, Tex. Guard Florida State 1961-65. Pro center Boston Patriots 1966. College coach: Florida State 1968, Iowa State 1969-72, Pittsburgh 1973-76, Tennessee 1977-79, Oregon State 1980-84 (head coach), Texas 1985-88. Pro coach: Joined Cowboys in 1990.

Joe Brodsky, running backs; born June 9, 1934, Miami, Fla., lives in Irving, Tex. Fullback/linebacker Florida 1953-56. No pro playing experience. College coach: Miami 1978-88. Pro coach: Joined Cowboys in 1989.

Dave Campo, defensive backs; born July 18, 1947, New London, Conn., lives in Coppell, Tex. Defensive back Central Connecticut State 1967-70. No pro playing experience. College coach: Central Connecticut State 1971-72, Albany State 1973, Bridgeport 1974, Pittsburgh 1975, Washington State 1976, Boise State 1977-79, Oregon State 1980, Weber State 1981-82, Iowa State 1983, Syracuse 1984-86, Miami 1987-88. Pro coach: Joined Cowboys in 1989.

Butch Davis, defensive line; born November 17, 1951, Tahlequah, Okla., lives in Coppell, Tex. Defensive end Arkansas 1971-74. No pro playing experience. College coach: Oklahoma State 1979-83, Miami 1984-88. Pro coach: Joined Cowboys in 1989.

Robert Ford, tight ends; born June 21, 1951, Belton, Tex., lives in Irving, Tex. Wide receiver Houston 1970-72. No pro playing experience. College coach: Western Illinois 1974-76, New Mexico 1977-79, Oregon State 1980-81, Mississippi State 1982-83, Kansas 1986, Texas Tech 1987-88, Texas A&M 1989-90. Pro coach: Houston Gamblers (USFL) 1985, joined Cowboys in 1991.

Steve Hoffman, kickers-research and development; born September 8, 1958, Camden, N.J., lives in Coppell, Tex. Quarterback-running back-wide receiver Dickinson College 1979-82. Pro punter Washington Federals (USFL) 1983. College coach: Miami 1985-87. Pro coach: Joined Cowboys in 1989.

Norv Turner, offensive coordinator-quarterbacks; born May 17, 1952, Martinez, Calif., lives in Irving, Tex. Quarterback Oregon 1972-74. No pro playing experience. College coach: Oregon 1975, Southern California 1976-84. Pro coach: L.A. Rams 1985-90, joined Cowboys in 1991.

Dallas Cowboys 1992 First-Year Roster

Name	Pos.	Ht.	Wt.	Birth-date	College	Hometown	How Acq.
Beasley, Michael	RB	5-10	203	5/27/69	West Virginia	Pottstown, Pa.	FA
Boles, Tony (1)	RB	6-1	196	12/11/67	Michigan	Detroit, Mich.	FA
Briggs, Greg	S	6-3	209	10/19/68	Texas Southern	Meadville, Miss.	D5a
Brown, James	T	6-6	331	1/3/70	Virginia State	Philadelphia, Pa.	D3b
Burch, Swift	DE-DT	6-4	272	5/8/69	Temple	Washington, D.C.	FA
Crum, Maurice (1)	LB	6-0	220	4/19/69	Miami	Tampa, Fla.	FA
Daniel, Tim	WR	5-11	184	9/14/69	Florida A&M	Atlanta, Ga.	D11
Elliott, Lin	K	6-0	180	11/11/68	Texas Tech	Waco, Tex.	FA
Evans, Melvin	G	6-2	316	1/29/69	Texas Southern	Trenton, N.J.	FA
Evans, Patt	T	6-6	261	3/14/69	Minnesota	Wallingford, Conn.	FA
Garrett, Jason (1)	QB	6-2	195	3/28/66	Princeton	Chagrin, Ohio	FA
Graham, Lorenzo (1)	RB	5-11	200	3/25/65	Livingston	Perdido, Ala.	FA
Hall, Chris	S	6-2	184	4/25/70	East Carolina	Pemberton, N.J.	D9b
Harris, Donald	S	6-0	185	11/12/67	Texas Tech	Waco, Tex.	D12
Harris, Kevin (1)	DE	6-5	251	10/21/69	Texas Southern	Dallas, Tex.	D4d-'91
Heath, Harold	TE	6-3	249	7/9/68	Jackson State	Canton, Miss.	FA
Hennings, Chad	DE	6-6	272	10/20/65	Air Force	Elberon, Iowa	D11-'88
Holmes, Clayton	CB	5-10	178	8/23/69	Carson-Newman	Florence, S.C.	D3a
James, Michael	CB-S	5-11	184	1/1/69	Arkansas	Pine Bluff, Ark.	FA
Jones, Robert	LB	6-2	236	9/27/69	East Carolina	Nottoway, Va.	D1b
Kirtman, Nate	S	6-1	186	6/6/71	Pomona-Pitzer	Berkeley, Calif.	D9a
Milstead, Rod	G	6-2	293	11/10/69	Delaware State	Indian Head, Md.	D5b
Myslinski, Tom	G	6-2	291	12/7/68	Tennessee	Rome, N.Y.	D4
Richards, Curvin (1)	RB	5-9	195	12/26/68	Pittsburgh	LaPorte, Tex.	D4a-'91
Smith, Jimmy	WR	6-1	200	2/9/69	Jackson State	Jackson, Miss.	D2a
Smith, Kevin	CB	5-11	173	4/7/70	Texas A&M	Orange, Tex.	D1a
Terry, John	G-T	6-4	292	8/30/68	Livingstone College	Greenwood, S.C.	D10
Tilton, Terry	LB	6-1	230	6/6/68	Angelo State	Waco, Tex.	FA
Wacasey, Fallon	TE	6-7	241	2/8/69	Tulsa	Kansas City, Kan.	D6
Woodson, Darren	S	6-1	216	4/25/69	Arizona State	Phoenix, Ariz.	D2b

The term NFL Rookie is defined as a player who is in his first season of professional football and has not been on the roster of another professional football team for any regular-season or postseason games. A Rookie is designated by an "R" on NFL rosters. Players who have been active in another professional football league or players who have NFL experience, including either preseason training camp or being on an active roster for fewer than three regular-season or postseason games, are termed NFL First-Year Players. An NFL First-Year Player is designated by a "1" on NFL rosters. Thereafter, a player on an NFL active roster for at least three regular-season or postseason games is credited with an additional year of NFL playing experience.

NOTES

_____

_____

_____

_____

_____

_____

_____

_____

_____

_____

_____

_____

Dave Wannstedt, assistant head coach-defensive coordinator-linebackers; born May 21, 1952, Pittsburgh, Pa., lives in Coppell, Tex. Offensive tackle Pittsburgh 1970-73. No pro playing experience. College coach: Pittsburgh 1975-78, Oklahoma State 1979-82, Southern California 1983-85, Miami 1986-88. Pro coach: Joined Cowboys in 1989.

Tony Wise, offensive line; born December 28, 1951, Albany, N.Y., lives in Coppell, Tex. Offensive lineman Ithaca College 1971-72. No pro playing experience. College coach: Albany State 1973, Bridgeport 1974, Central Connecticut State 1975, Washington State 1976, Pittsburgh 1977-78, Oklahoma State 1979-83, Syracuse 1984, Miami 1985-88. Pro coach: Joined Cowboys in 1989.

Mike Woicik, strength and conditioning; born September 26, 1956, Westwood, Mass., lives in Coppell, Tex. Boston College 1974-78. No college or pro playing experience. College coach: Springfield 1978-80, Syracuse 1980-89. Pro coach: Joined Cowboys in 1990.

National Football Conference Central Division

Team Colors: Honolulu Blue and Silver

Pontiac Silverdome
1200 Featherstone Road
Pontiac, Michigan 48342
Telephone: (313) 335-4131

Club Officials

President-Owner: William Clay Ford
Executive Vice President-CEO:
   Chuck Schmidt
Director of Player Personnel: Ron Hughes
Director of Pro Personnel: Kevin Colbert
Scouts: Milt Davis, Dirk Dierking, Allen Hughes,
   Scott McEwen, Jim Owens, Rick Spielman,
   John Trump
Director of Player Relations: Otis Canty
Controller/Travel Coordinator: Tom Lesnau
Director of Marketing, Broadcasting, and
   Communications: Bill Keenist
Director of Marketing, Sales, and
   Ticket Operations: Fred Otto
Director of Community Relations and Detroit Lions
   Charities: Tim Pendell
Media Relations Coordinator: Mike Murray
Media Relations Assistant: James Petrylka
Strength and Conditioning: Bert Hill
Trainer: Kent Falb
Equipment Manager: Dan Jaroshewich
Video Director: Steve Hermans

Stadium: Pontiac Silverdome • **Capacity:** 80,500
   1200 Featherstone Road
   Pontiac, Michigan 48342

Playing Surface: AstroTurf

Training Camp: Pontiac Silverdome
   1200 Featherstone Road
   Pontiac, Michigan 48342

1992 Schedule

Preseason
Aug. 8	**Houston**	7:00
Aug. 17	at Buffalo	8:00
Aug. 22	**New England**	7:00
Aug. 28	at Cincinnati	7:30

Regular Season
Sept. 6	at Chicago	12:00
Sept. 13	**Minnesota**	1:00
Sept. 20	at Washington	4:00
Sept. 27	**Tampa Bay**	1:00
Oct. 4	**New Orleans**	1:00
Oct. 11	**Open Date**	
Oct. 15	at Minnesota (Thursday)	6:30
Oct. 25	at Tampa Bay	1:00
Nov. 1	**Green Bay**	1:00
Nov. 8	**Dallas**	1:00
Nov. 15	at Pittsburgh	1:00
Nov. 22	at Cincinnati	1:00
Nov. 26	**Houston** (Thanksgiving)	12:30
Dec. 6	vs. Green Bay at Milw.	12:00
Dec. 13	**Cleveland**	1:00
Dec. 20	**Chicago**	4:00
Dec. 28	at San Francisco (Monday)	6:00

Lions Coaching History

Portsmouth Spartans 1930-33
(394-403-32)

1930	Hal (Tubby) Griffen	5-6-3
1931-36	George (Potsy) Clark	49-20-6
1937-38	Earl (Dutch) Clark	14-8-0
1939	Elmer (Gus) Henderson	6-5-0
1940	George (Potsy) Clark	5-5-1
1941-42	Bill Edwards*	4-9-1
1942	John Karcis	0-8-0
1943-47	Charles (Gus) Dorais	20-31-2
1948-50	Alvin (Bo) McMillin	12-24-0
1951-56	Raymond (Buddy) Parker	50-24-2
1957-64	George Wilson	55-45-6
1965-66	Harry Gilmer	10-16-2
1967-72	Joe Schmidt	43-35-7
1973	Don McCafferty	6-7-1
1974-76	Rick Forzano**	15-17-0
1976-77	Tommy Hudspeth	11-13-0
1978-84	Monte Clark	43-63-1
1985-88	Darryl Rogers***	18-40-0
1988-91	Wayne Fontes	28-27-0

*Released after three games in 1942
**Resigned after four games in 1976
***Released after 11 games in 1988

Record Holders
Individual Records—Career

Category	Name	Performance
Rushing (Yds.)	Billy Sims, 1980-84	5,106
Passing (Yds.)	Bobby Layne, 1950-58	15,710
Passing (TDs)	Bobby Layne, 1950-58	118
Receiving (No.)	Charlie Sanders, 1968-1977	336
Receiving (Yds.)	Gail Cogdill, 1960-68	5,220
Interceptions	Dick LeBeau, 1959-1972	62
Punting (Avg.)	Yale Lary, 1952-53, 1956-1964	44.3
Punt Return (Avg.)	Jack Christiansen, 1951-58	12.8
Kickoff Return (Avg.)	Pat Studstill, 1961-67	25.7
Field Goals	Eddie Murray, 1980-1991	243
Touchdowns (Tot.)	Billy Sims, 1980-84	47
	Barry Sanders, 1989-1991	47
Points	Eddie Murray, 1980-1991	1,113

Individual Records—Single Season

Category	Name	Performance
Rushing (Yds.)	Barry Sanders, 1991	1,548
Passing (Yds.)	Gary Danielson, 1980	3,223
Passing (TDs)	Bobby Layne, 1951	26
Receiving (No.)	James Jones, 1984	77
Receiving (Yds.)	Pat Studstill, 1966	1,266
Interceptions	Don Doll, 1950	12
	Jack Christiansen, 1953	12
Punting (Avg.)	Yale Lary, 1963	48.9
Punt Return (Avg.)	Jack Christiansen, 1952	21.5
Kickoff Return (Avg.)	Tom Watkins, 1965	34.4
Field Goals	Eddie Murray, 1980	27
Touchdowns (Tot.)	Barry Sanders, 1991	17
Points	Doak Walker, 1950	128

Individual Records—Single Game

Category	Name	Performance
Rushing (Yds.)	Barry Sanders, 11-24-91	220
Passing (Yds.)	Bobby Layne, 11-5-50	374
Passing (TDs)	Gary Danielson, 12-9-78	5
Receiving (No.)	Cloyce Box, 12-3-50	12
	James Jones, 9-28-86	12
Receiving (Yds.)	Cloyce Box, 12-3-50	302
Interceptions	Don Doll, 10-23-49	*4
Field Goals	Garo Yepremian, 11-13-66	6
Touchdowns (Tot.)	Cloyce Box, 12-3-50	4
Points	Cloyce Box, 12-3-50	24

*NFL Record

PONTIAC SILVERDOME

1991 Team Record

Preseason (2-3)

Date	Result		Opponents
7/27	W	14- 3	vs. Denver at Canton, Ohio
8/2	W	24-20	Cincinnati
8/10	L	16-21	at Buffalo
8/17	L	14-38	at Kansas City
8/23	L	3-16	Pittsburgh

Regular Season (12-4)

Date	Result		Opponents	Att.
9/1	L	0-45	at Washington	52,958
9/8	W	23-14	Green Bay	43,132
9/15	W	17-13	Miami	56,896
9/22	W	33-24	at Indianapolis	53,396
9/29	W	31- 3	Tampa Bay	48,784
10/6	W	24-20	Minnesota	63,423
10/20	L	3-35	at San Francisco	61,240
10/27	W	34-10	Dallas	74,906
11/3	L	10-20	at Chicago	57,281
11/10	L	21-30	at Tampa Bay	37,742
11/17	W	21-10	L.A. Rams	60,873
11/24	W	34-14	at Minnesota	51,644
11/28	W	16- 6	Chicago	78,879
12/8	W	34-20	N.Y. Jets	69,304
12/15	W	21-17	at Green Bay	43,881
12/22	W	17-14	at Buffalo (OT)	78,059

(OT) Overtime

Postseason (1-1)

Date	Result		Opponent	Att.
1/5	W	38- 6	Dallas	79,166
1/12	L	10-41	at Washington	55,585

Score by Periods

Lions	72	67	77	120	3	—	339
Opponents	75	108	58	54	0	—	295

Attendance

Home 496,197   Away 436,201   Total 932,398
Single-game home record, 80,444 (12-20-81)
Single-season home record, 622,593 (1980)

1991 Team Statistics

	Lions	Opp.
Total First Downs	280	305
Rushing	116	93
Passing	148	189
Penalty	16	23
Third Down: Made/Att.	72/197	80/203
Third Down: Pct.	36.5	39.4
Fourth Down: Made/Att.	3/6	9/20
Fourth Down: Pct.	50.0	45.0
Total Net Yards	4788	5046
Avg. Per Game	299.3	315.4
Total Plays	938	1008
Avg. Per Play	5.1	5.0
Net Yards Rushing	1930	1760
Avg. Per Game	120.6	110.0
Total Rushes	454	444
Net Yards Passing	2858	3286
Avg. Per Game	178.6	205.4
Sacked/Yards Lost	25/116	30/237
Gross Yards	2974	3523
Att./Completions	459/252	534/315
Completion Pct.	54.9	59.0
Had Intercepted	17	19
Punts/Avg.	75/41.2	67/39.2
Net Punting Avg.	35.4	31.7
Penalties/Yards Lost	93/799	94/704
Fumbles/Ball Lost	25/13	32/17
Touchdowns	40	34
Rushing	19	16
Passing	16	16
Returns	5	2
Avg. Time of Possession	28:39	31:21

1991 Individual Statistics

Scoring

	TD R	TD P	TD Rt	PAT	FG	Saf	TP
B. Sanders	16	1	0	0/0	0/0	0	102
Murray	0	0	0	40/40	19/28	0	97
Green	0	7	0	0/0	0/0	0	42
Clark	0	6	0	0/0	0/0	0	36
Peete	2	0	0	0/0	0/0	0	12
Crockett	0	0	1	0/0	0/0	0	6
Farr	0	1	0	0/0	0/0	0	6
Gray	0	0	1	0/0	0/0	0	6
Hayworth	0	0	1	0/0	0/0	0	6
Kramer	1	0	0	0/0	0/0	0	6
Perriman	0	1	0	0/0	0/0	0	6
S. White	0	0	1	0/0	0/0	0	6
W. White	0	0	1	0/0	0/0	0	6
Ball	0	0	0	0/0	0/0	1	2
Lions	19	16	5	40/40	19/28	1	339
Opponents	16	16	2	34/34	19/28	0	295

Passing

	Att.	Comp.	Yds.	Pct.	TD	Int.	Tkld.	Rate
Kramer	265	136	1635	51.3	11	8	14/74	71.8
Peete	194	116	1339	59.8	5	9	11/42	69.9
Lions	459	252	2974	54.9	16	17	25/116	71.0
Opponents	534	315	3523	59.0	16	19	30/237	73.9

Rushing

	Att.	Yds.	Avg.	LG	TD
B. Sanders	342	1548	4.5	69t	16
Peete	25	125	5.0	26	2
Overton	14	59	4.2	9	0
Jackson	17	55	3.2	10	0
Dozier	9	48	5.3	29	0
Arnold	2	42	21.0	21	0
Kramer	35	26	0.7	12	1
Gray	2	11	5.5	6	0
Perriman	4	10	2.5	6	0
Ware	4	6	1.5	10	0
Lions	454	1930	4.3	69t	19
Opponents	444	1760	4.0	59t	16

Receiving

	No.	Yds.	Avg.	LG	TD
Perriman	52	668	12.8	42	1
Clark	47	640	13.6	68t	6
Farr	42	431	10.3	34t	1
B. Sanders	41	307	7.5	34	1
Green	39	592	15.2	73t	7
Moore	11	135	12.3	21	0
Tennell	4	43	10.8	18	0
Overton	4	38	9.5	14	0
Gray	3	42	14.0	31	0
Matthews	3	21	7.0	11	0
Campbell	2	49	24.5	28	0
Fortin	1	4	4.0	4	0
Dozier	1	3	3.0	3	0
Riley	1	3	3.0	3	0
Jackson	1	-2	-2.0	-2	0
Lions	252	2974	11.8	73t	16
Opponents	315	3523	11.2	51	16

Interceptions

	No.	Yds.	Avg.	LG	TD
Crockett	6	141	23.5	96t	1
Taylor	4	26	6.5	23	0
Jamison	3	52	17.3	19	0
W. White	2	35	17.5	28	0
S. White	1	18	18.0	18t	1
Blades	1	14	14.0	14	0
Alexander	1	0	0.0	0	0
Hayworth	1	0	0.0	0	0
Lions	19	286	15.1	96t	2
Opponents	17	229	13.5	57t	1

Punting

	No.	Yds.	Avg.	In 20	LG
Arnold	75	3092	41.2	27	63
Lions	75	3092	41.2	27	63
Opponents	67	2629	33.2	16	56

Punt Returns

	No.	FC	Yds.	Avg.	LG	TD
Gray	25	14	385	15.4	78t	1
Jenkins	1	0	0	0.0	0	0
Lions	26	14	385	14.8	78t	1
Opponents	35	10	340	9.7	69t	1

Kickoff Returns

	No.	Yds.	Avg.	LG	TD
Gray	36	929	25.8	71	0
Campbell	9	85	9.4	18	0
Dozier	4	60	15.0	38	0
Overton	4	71	17.8	23	0
Bell	1	0	0.0	0	0
Clark	1	0	0.0	0	0
Jackson	1	9	9.0	9	0
Scott	1	16	16.0	16	0
Lions	57	1170	20.5	71	0
Opponents	63	1095	17.4	53	0

Sacks

	No.
Hunter	6.0
Owens	5.5
Jamison	4.0
Spindler	3.5
Ball	2.0
Hayworth	2.0
Pete	1.5
Pritchett	1.5
Cofer	1.0
Crockett	1.0
Jenkins	1.0
Spielman	1.0
Lions	30.0
Opponents	25.0

1992 Draft Choices

Round	Name	Pos.	College
1.	Robert Porcher	DE	South Carolina St.
2.	Tracy Scroggins	LB	Tulsa
	Jason Hanson	K	Washington State
3.	Thomas McLemore	TE	Southern University
6.	Larry Tharpe	T	Tennessee State
8.	Willie Clay	DB	Georgia Tech
11.	Ed Tillison	RB	Northwest Missouri

Detroit Lions 1992 Veteran Roster

No.	Name	Pos.	Ht.	Wt.	Birth-date	NFL Exp.	College	Hometown	How Acq.	'91 Games/ Starts
65	†Andolsek, Eric	G	6-2	286	8/22/66	5	Louisiana State	Thibodaux, La.	D5-'88	16/16
6	Arnold, Jim	P	6-3	211	1/31/61	10	Vanderbilt	Dalton, Ga.	FA-'86	16/0
93	Ball, Jerry	NT	6-1	298	12/15/64	6	Southern Methodist	Beaumont, Tex.	D3-'87	13/13
40	Barrett, Reggie	WR	6-3	215	8/14/69	2	Texas-El Paso	Corpus Christi, Tex.	D3-'91	2/0
36	†Blades, Bennie	S	6-1	221	9/3/66	5	Miami	Ft. Lauderdale, Fla.	D1-'88	16/16
66	Bouwens, Shawn	G	6-4	280	5/25/68	2	Nebraska-Wesleyan	Lincoln, Neb.	FA-'91	16/0
75	Brown, Lomas	T	6-4	287	3/30/63	8	Florida	Miami, Fla.	D1-'85	15/15
87	†Campbell, Jeff	WR	5-8	167	3/29/68	3	Colorado	Vail, Colo.	D5-'90	14/1
50	†Caston, Toby	LB	6-1	243	7/17/65	6	Louisiana State	Monroe, La.	PB(Hou)-'89#	16/0
55	Cofer, Michael	LB	6-5	244	4/7/60	9	Tennessee	Knoxville, Tenn.	D3-'83	2/2
21	Colon, Harry	S	5-11	203	2/14/69	2	Missouri	Kansas City, Kan.	PB(NE)-'92#	16/14*
76	Conover, Scott	T	6-4	285	9/27/68	2	Purdue	Freehold, N.J.	D5-'91	16/3
39	Crockett, Ray	CB	5-9	181	1/5/67	4	Baylor	Duncanville, Tex.	D4-'89	16/16
67	Dallafior, Ken	G-C	6-4	279	8/26/59	8	Minnesota	Madison Heights, Mich.	PB(SD)-'89#	6/5
42	†Dozier, D.J.	RB	6-0	205	9/21/65	6	Penn State	Norfolk, Va.	W(Minn)-'92	6/0
81	†Farr, Mike	WR	5-10	192	8/8/67	3	UCLA	Birmingham, Mich.	FA-'90	16/13
98	†Gibson, Dennis	LB	6-2	243	2/8/64	6	Iowa State	Ankeny, Iowa	D8-'87	16/16
53	†Glover, Kevin	C	6-2	282	6/17/63	8	Maryland	Upper Marlboro, Md.	D2-'85	16/16
23	†Gray, Mel	WR-KR	5-9	162	3/16/61	7	Purdue	Williamsburg, Va.	PB(NO)-'89#	16/0
86	†Green, Willie	WR	6-2	179	4/2/66	2	Mississippi	Athens, Ga.	D8a-'90	16/15
99	†Hayworth, Tracy	LB	6-3	260	12/18/67	3	Tennessee	Franklin, Tenn.	D7-'90	16/14
97	Hunter, Jeff	DE	6-5	285	4/12/66	3	Albany State	Augusta, Ga.	FA-'90	16/0
58	†Jamison, George	LB	6-1	228	9/30/62	6	Cincinnati	Bridgeton, N.J.	SD2-'84	16/16
24	Jenkins, Melvin	CB	5-10	173	3/16/62	6	Cincinnati	Jackson, Miss.	PB(Sea)-'91#	16/16
48	Johnson, Jimmie	TE	6-2	248	10/6/66	4	Howard	Augusta, Ga.	PB(Wash)-'92#	6/0*
57	Jones, Victor	LB	6-2	240	10/19/66	5	Virginia Tech	Rockville, Md.	PB(TB)-'89#	10/0
12	Kramer, Erik	QB	6-1	195	11/6/64	3	North Carolina State	Encino, Calif.	FA-'91	13/8
89	Little, David	TE	6-2	226	4/18/61	9	Middle Tennessee State	Selma, Calif.	FA-'91	2/0
16	Long, Chuck	QB	6-4	217	2/18/63	6	Iowa	Wheaton, Ill.	FA-'91	0*
83	Matthews, Aubrey	WR	5-7	165	9/15/62	7	Delta State	Pascagoula, Miss.	PB(GB)-'90#	1/1
79	Milburn, Darryl	DE	6-3	260	10/25/68	2	Grambling	Baton Rouge, La.	D9-'91	2/0
84	Moore, Herman	WR	6-3	205	10/20/69	2	Virginia	Danville, Va.	D1-'91	13/1
3	Murray, Eddie	K	5-10	180	8/29/56	13	Tulane	Halifax, Nova Scotia	D7-'80	16/0
70	Owens, Dan	DE	6-3	268	3/16/67	3	Southern California	Whittier, Calif.	D2-'90	16/16
77	Paris, Bubba	T	6-6	315	10/6/60	10	Michigan	Louisville, Ky.	FA-'91	0*
9	†Peete, Rodney	QB	6-0	193	3/16/66	4	Southern California	Tucson, Ariz.	D6-'89	8/8
80	†Perriman, Brett	WR	5-9	180	10/10/65	5	Miami	Miami, Fla.	T(NO)-'91	15/14
96	†Pete, Lawrence	NT	6-0	282	1/18/66	4	Nebraska	Wichita, Kan.	D5-'89	14/3
94	Pritchett, Kelvin	DE	6-2	281	10/24/69	2	Mississippi	Atlanta, Ga.	T(Dall)-'91	16/0
44	Riley, Eugene	TE	6-3	238	10/9/66	2	Ball State	Cincinnati, Ohio	FA-'92	5/1
20	Sanders, Barry	RB	5-8	203	7/16/68	4	Oklahoma State	Wichita, Kan.	D1-'89	15/15
64	†Sanders, Eric	T-G	6-7	286	10/22/58	12	Nevada-Reno	Reno, Nev.	W(Atl)-'86	14/14
38	Scott, Kevin	CB	5-9	175	5/19/69	2	Stanford	Phoenix, Ariz.	D4-'91	16/0
54	Spielman, Chris	LB	6-0	247	10/11/65	5	Ohio State	Massillon, Ohio	D2b-'88	16/16
92	Spindler, Marc	NT-DE	6-5	277	11/28/69	3	Pittsburgh	West Scranton, Pa.	D3-'90	16/16
46	Tennell, Derek	TE	6-5	270	2/12/64	5	UCLA	Los Angeles, Calif.	FA-'91	15/2
11	Ware, Andre	QB	6-2	205	7/31/68	3	Houston	Dickinson, Tex.	D1-'90	1/0
28	Welch, Herb	S	5-11	180	1/12/61	6	UCLA	Watchung, N.J.	PB(Wash)-'90#	10/0
25	†White, Sheldon	CB	5-11	188	3/1/65	5	Miami, Ohio	Dayton, Ohio	W(NYG)-'90	16/0
35	White, William	CB-S	5-10	191	2/19/66	5	Ohio State	Lima, Ohio	D4-'88	16/16

* Colon played 16 games with New England in '91; Johnson played 6 games with Washington; Long last active with Detroit in '90; Paris active for 2 games but did not play.

† Option playout; subject to developments.

Plan B unconditional free agent.

Players lost through Plan B (9): CB Bruce Alexander (Mia; 9 games in '91), LB Anthony Bell (Raid; 10), WR Robert Clark (Mia; 14), T Roman Fortin (Atl; 16), RB Cedric Jackson (SD; 8), LB Niko Noga (Raid; 16), RB Don Overton (Phil; 14), CB Terry Taylor (Clev; 11), CB Sean Vanhorse (SD; 0).

Also played with Lions in '91—LB Mark Brown (2 games), G Mike Utley (9).

COACHING STAFF

Head Coach, Wayne Fontes

Pro Career: Became the Lions' seventeenth head coach on December 22, 1988, after serving five weeks as interim head coach (2-3 record). Fontes led the Lions to a 7-9 record in 1989, including five consecutive season-ending wins, and a 6-10 record in 1990. Under Fontes, the Lions finished 12-4 and won the NFC Central Division in 1991. The Lions notched their first playoff victory since 1957 and made their first appearance in the NFC Championship Game in 1991. He began the 1988 season as Detroit's defensive coordinator and secondary coach, following a nine-year stint with the Tampa Bay Buccaneers. A former defensive back with the New York Jets, Fontes advanced from secondary coach to defensive coordinator to assistant head coach of the Buccaneers during his years with Tampa Bay. As a player with the Jets, his brief pro career was cut short by a broken leg after two seasons (1963-64). However, his 83-yard interception return against Houston (12-15-63) did stand as the Jets' team record until it was broken in 1989 by Erik McMillan's 93-yard return. Career record: 28-27.

Background: A former two-sport star (football and baseball) at Michigan State, Fontes earned all-Big Ten honors at defensive back for the Spartans. He earned his bachelor's degree in education and biological science and later earned his master's degree in administration, all from Michigan State. After directing the freshman team at Michigan State in 1965, Fontes became defensive backfield coach at Dayton in 1968. He also served in the same capacity at Iowa (1969-71) and Southern California (1972-75).

Personal: Born February 17, 1939, New Bedford, Mass. Fontes and his wife, Evelyn, live in Rochester Hills, Mich., and have three children—Mike, Scott, and Kim.

Assistant Coaches

Don Clemons, administrative assistant; born February 15, 1954, Newark, N.J., lives in Rochester, Mich. Defensive end Muehlenberg College 1973-76. No pro playing experience. College coach: Kutztown State 1977-78, New Mexico 1979, Arizona State 1980-84. Pro coach: Detroit Lions 1985-90, rejoined Lions in 1992.

Frank Gansz, special teams; born November 22, 1938, Altoona, Pa., lives in Auburn Hills, Mich. Center-linebacker Navy 1957-59. No pro playing experience. College coach: Air Force 1964, Colgate 1968, Navy 1969, Oklahoma State 1973, 1975, Army 1974, UCLA 1976-77. Pro coach: San Francisco 49ers 1978, Cincinnati Bengals 1979-80, Kansas City Chiefs 1981-82, 1986-88 (head coach 1987-88), Philadelphia Eagles 1983-85, joined Lions in 1989.

Dan Henning, offensive coordinator; born June 21, 1942, Bronx, N.Y., lives in Rochester Hills, Mich. Quarterback William & Mary 1960-63. Pro quarterback San Diego Chargers 1966. College coach: Florida State 1968-70, 1974, Virginia Tech 1971, 1973. Pro coach: Houston Oilers 1972, New York Jets 1976-78, Miami Dolphins 1979-80, Washington Redskins 1981-82, 1987-88, Atlanta Falcons 1983-86 (head coach), San Diego Chargers 1988-91 (head coach), joined Lions in 1992.

Lamar Leachman, defensive line; born August 7, 1934, Cartersville, Ga., lives in Pontiac, Mich. Center-linebacker Tennessee 1952-55. No pro playing experience. College coach: Richmond 1966-67, Georgia Tech 1968-71, Memphis State 1972, South Carolina 1973. Pro coach: New York Stars (WFL) 1974, Toronto Argonauts (CFL) 1975-77, Montreal Alouettes (CFL) 1978-79, New York Giants 1980-89, joined Lions in 1990.

Dave Levy, assistant head coach; born October 25, 1932, Carrollton, Mo., lives in Lake Orion, Mich. Guard UCLA 1952-53. No pro playing experience. College coach: UCLA 1954, Long Beach City College 1955, Southern California 1960-75. Pro coach: San Diego Chargers 1980-88, joined Lions in 1989.

Billie Matthews, running backs; born March 15, 1930, Houston, Tex., lives in Rochester, Mich. Quarterback Southern University 1948-51. No pro playing experience. College coach: Kansas 1970, UCLA 1971-78. Pro coach: San Francisco 49ers 1979-82, Philadelphia Eagles 1983-84, Indianapolis Colts 1985-86, Kansas City Chiefs 1987-88, joined Lions in 1989.

Herb Paterra, inside linebackers; born November 8, 1940, Glassport, Pa., lives in Rochester Hills, Mich. Offensive guard-linebacker Michigan State 1960-62. Pro linebacker Buffalo Bills 1963-64, Hamilton Tiger-Cats (CFL) 1965-68. College coach: Michigan State 1969-71, Wyoming 1972-74. Pro coach: Charlotte Hornets (WFL) 1975, Hamilton Tiger-Cats (CFL) 1978-79, Los Angeles Rams 1980-82, Edmonton Eskimos (CFL) 1983, Green Bay Packers 1984-85, Buffalo Bills 1986, Tampa Bay Buccaneers 1987-88, joined Lions in 1989.

Charlie Sanders, receivers; born August 25, 1946, Greensboro, N.C., lives in Rochester, Mich. Tight end Minnesota 1966-67. Pro tight end Detroit Lions 1968-77. Pro coach: Joined Lions in 1989.

Jerry Wampfler, offensive line; born August 6, 1932, New Philadelphia, Ohio, lives in Lake Orion, Mich. Tackle Miami, Ohio 1951-54. No pro playing experience. College coach: Presbyterian 1955, Miami, Ohio 1963-65, Notre Dame 1966-69, Colorado State 1970-72 (head coach). Pro coach: Philadelphia Eagles 1973-75, 1979-83, Buffalo Bills 1976-77, New York Giants 1978, Green Bay Packers 1984-87, San Diego Chargers 1988, joined Lions in 1989.

Woody Widenhofer, defensive coordinator, outside linebackers; born January 20, 1943, Riverview, Mich., lives in Rochester Hills, Mich. Linebacker Missouri 1961-64. No pro playing experience. College coach: Michigan State 1969-70, Eastern Michigan 1971, Minnesota 1972, Missouri 1985-88 (head coach). Pro coach: Pittsburgh Steelers 1973-83, Oklahoma Outlaws (USFL) 1984 (head coach), joined Lions in 1989.

Detroit Lions 1992 First-Year Roster

Name	Pos.	Ht.	Wt.	Birth-date	College	Hometown	How Acq.
Brooks, Darrell	C	6-3	323	5/6/70	Tennessee State	Memphis, Tenn.	FA
Clay, Willie	CB	5-9	184	9/5/70	Georgia Tech	Pittsburgh, Pa.	D8
Crutchfield, Tony	CB-S	5-9	188	9/24/69	Brigham Young	Pasadena, Calif.	FA
Ealy, Ken	WR	5-10	177	5/20/69	Central Michigan	College Park, Ga.	FA
Eaton, Darrin	WR	6-0	197	3/21/69	Michigan State	Camden, N.J.	FA
Fields, Earnest	LB	5-11	236	10/15/68	Tennessee	Milan, Tenn.	FA
Ford, Darryl (1)	LB	6-1	225	6/22/66	New Mexico State	Dallas, Tex.	FA
Gicewicz, Rich (1)	TE	6-3	246	12/4/65	Michigan State	Getzville, N.Y.	FA
Griffin, Willie (1)	DE	6-3	286	3/24/66	Nebraska	Jackson, Miss.	FA
Haliburton, Sheldon (1)	T	6-6	315	1/31/68	Texas A&I	Los Angeles, Calif.	FA
Hanson, Jason	K	5-11	183	6/17/70	Washington State	Spokane, Wash.	D2b
Kent, Phillip	LB	6-1	244	9/19/70	Mississippi	Kansas City, Mo.	FA
Linn, Jack (1)	T	6-5	278	6/10/67	West Virginia	Rochester, Pa.	FA
McGill, Reggie (1)	RB	5-10	195	7/11/69	Arizona	Phoenix, Ariz.	FA
McLemore, Thomas	TE	6-5	245	3/24/70	Southern	Shreveport, La.	D3
Miller, Blake (1)	G-T	6-1	282	8/23/68	Louisiana State	Baton Rouge, La.	FA
Porcher, Robert	DE	6-3	283	7/30/69	South Carolina State	Wando, S.C.	D1
Scroggins, Tracy	LB	6-2	255	9/11/69	Tulsa	Checotah, Okla.	D2a
Tharpe, Larry	T	6-4	299	11/19/70	Tennessee State	Macon, Ga.	D6
Tillison, Ed	RB	6-0	255	2/12/69	N.W. Missouri State	Pearl River, La.	D8
Wilson, Bernard	DT	6-2	295	8/17/70	Tennessee State	Nashville, Tenn.	FA

The term NFL Rookie is defined as a player who is in his first season of professional football and has not been on the roster of another professional football team for any regular-season or postseason games. A Rookie is designated by an "R" on NFL rosters. Players who have been active in another professional football league or players who have NFL experience, including either preseason training camp or being on an active roster for fewer than three regular-season or postseason games, are termed NFL First-Year Players. An NFL First-Year Player is designated by a "1" on NFL rosters. Thereafter, a player on an NFL active roster for at least three regular-season or postseason games is credited with an additional year of NFL playing experience.

NOTES

National Football Conference Central Division

Team Colors: Dark Green, Gold, and White

1265 Lombardi Avenue
Green Bay, Wisconsin 54307-0628
Telephone: (414) 496-5700

Club Officials

President, CEO: Bob Harlan
Vice President: John Fabry
Secretary: Peter M. Platten III
Treasurer: John R. Underwood
Chief Financial Officer: Michael R. Reinfeldt
Exec. V.P. and General Manager: Ron Wolf
Exec. Assistant to the President: Phil Pionek
Exec. Director of Public Relations: Lee Remmel
Director of Marketing: Jeff Cieply
Asst. Director of Public Relations: Jeff Blumb
Director of Community Relations:
  Mark Schiefelbein
Director of Pro Personnel: Jesse Kaye
Green Bay Ticket Director: Mark Wagner
Milwaukee Ticket Director: Marge Paget
Controller: Dick Blasczyk
Video Director: Al Treml
Trainer: Domenic Gentile
Equipment Manager: Bob Noel
Corporate Security Officer: Jerry Parins
Stadium Supervisor: Ted Eisenreich

Stadium: Lambeau Field • **Capacity:** 59,543
  P.O. Box 10628
  1265 Lombardi Avenue
  Green Bay, Wisconsin 54307-0628

  Milwaukee County Stadium •
  Capacity: 56,051
  Highway I-94
  Milwaukee, Wisconsin 53214

Playing Surfaces: Grass

Training Camp: St. Norbert College
  West DePere, Wisconsin 54115

1992 Schedule

Preseason
Aug. 8	**Kansas City**	7:00
Aug. 16	vs. N.Y. Jets at Madison	3:00
Aug. 22	at Los Angeles Rams	6:00
Aug. 29	**New England** at Milw.	7:00

Regular Season
Sept. 6	**Minnesota**	12:00
Sept. 13	at Tampa Bay	1:00
Sept. 20	**Cincinnati**	12:00
Sept. 27	**Pittsburgh**	3:00
Oct. 4	at Atlanta	1:00
Oct. 11	**Open Date**	
Oct. 18	at Cleveland	1:00
Oct. 25	**Chicago**	12:00
Nov. 1	at Detroit	1:00
Nov. 8	at New York Giants	1:00
Nov. 15	**Philadelphia** at Milwaukee	12:00
Nov. 22	at Chicago	12:00
Nov. 29	**Tampa Bay** at Milwaukee	12:00
Dec. 6	**Detroit** at Milwaukee	12:00
Dec. 13	at Houston	7:00
Dec. 20	**Los Angeles Rams**	12:00
Dec. 27	at Minnesota	12:00

Packers Coaching History
(489-413-36)

1921-49	Earl (Curly) Lambeau	212-106-21
1950-53	Gene Ronzani*	14-31-1
1953	Hugh Devore- Ray (Scooter) McLean**	0-2-0
1954-57	Lisle Blackbourn	17-31-0
1958	Ray (Scooter) McLean	1-10-1
1959-67	Vince Lombardi	98-30-4
1968-70	Phil Bengtson	20-21-1
1971-74	Dan Devine	25-28-4
1975-83	Bart Starr	53-77-3
1984-87	Forrest Gregg	25-37-1
1988-91	Lindy Infante	24-40-0

*Released after 10 games in 1953
**Co-coaches

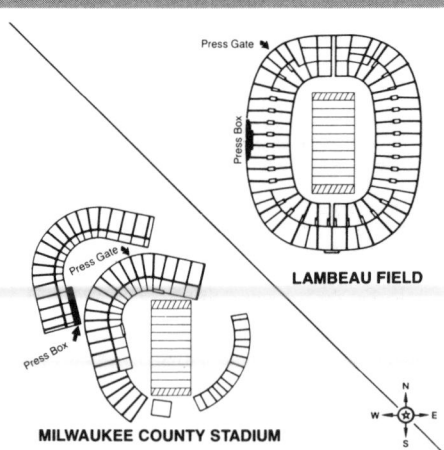

LAMBEAU FIELD

MILWAUKEE COUNTY STADIUM

Record Holders
Individual Records—Career

Category	Name	Performance
Rushing (Yds.)	Jim Taylor, 1958-1966	8,207
Passing (Yds.)	Bart Starr, 1956-1971	23,718
Passing (TDs)	Bart Starr, 1956-1971	152
Receiving (No.)	James Lofton, 1978-1986	530
Receiving (Yds.)	James Lofton, 1978-1986	9,656
Interceptions	Bobby Dillon, 1952-59	52
Punting (Avg.)	Dick Deschaine, 1955-57	42.6
Punt Return (Avg.)	Billy Grimes, 1950-52	13.2
Kickoff Return (Avg.)	Travis Williams, 1967-1970	26.7
Field Goals	Chester Marcol, 1972-1980	120
Touchdowns (Tot.)	Don Hutson, 1935-1945	105
Points	Don Hutson, 1935-1945	823

Individual Records—Single Season

Category	Name	Performance
Rushing (Yds.)	Jim Taylor, 1962	1,407
Passing (Yds.)	Lynn Dickey, 1983	4,458
Passing (TDs)	Lynn Dickey, 1983	32
Receiving (No.)	Sterling Sharpe, 1989	90
Receiving (Yds.)	Sterling Sharpe, 1989	1,423
Interceptions	Irv Comp, 1943	10
Punting (Avg.)	Jerry Norton, 1963	44.7
Punt Return (Avg.)	Billy Grimes, 1950	19.1
Kickoff Return (Avg.)	Travis Williams, 1967	41.1
Field Goals	Chester Marcol, 1972	33
Touchdowns (Tot.)	Jim Taylor, 1962	19
Points	Paul Hornung, 1960	*176

Individual Records—Single Game

Category	Name	Performance
Rushing (Yds.)	Jim Taylor, 12-3-61	186
Passing (Yds.)	Lynn Dickey, 10-12-80	418
Passing (TDs)	Many times	5
	Last time by Lynn Dickey, 9-4-83	
Receiving (No.)	Don Hutson, 11-22-42	14
Receiving (Yds.)	Bill Howton, 10-21-56	257
Interceptions	Bobby Dillon, 11-26-53	*4
	Willie Buchanon, 9-24-78	*4
Field Goals	Chris Jacke, 11-11-90	5
Touchdowns (Tot.)	Paul Hornung, 12-12-65	5
Points	Paul Hornung, 10-8-61	33

*NFL Record

1991 Team Record
Preseason (2-2)

Date	Result		Opponents
8/3	W	28- 7	New England
8/10	L	20-31	at New Orleans
8/17	W	35-24	vs. Buffalo at Madison, Wis.
8/24	L	16-19	Cincinnati (OT)

Regular Season (4-12)

Date	Result		Opponents	Att.
9/1	L	3-20	Philadelphia	58,991
9/8	L	14-23	at Detroit	43,132
9/15	W	15-13	Tampa Bay	58,114
9/22	L	13-16	at Miami	56,583
9/29	L	21-23	at L.A. Rams	54,736
10/6	L	17-20	Dallas	53,695
10/17	L	0-10	Chicago	58,435
10/27	W	27- 0	at Tampa Bay	40,275
11/3	L	16-19	at N.Y. Jets (OT)	67,435
11/10	L	24-34	Buffalo	52,175
11/17	L	21-35	Minnesota	57,614
11/24	W	14-10	Indianapolis	42,132
12/1	L	31-35	at Atlanta	43,270
12/8	L	13-27	at Chicago	62,353
12/15	L	17-21	Detroit	43,881
12/21	W	27- 7	at Minnesota	52,860

(OT) Overtime

Score by Periods

Packers	68	78	55	72	0	—	273
Opponents	47	102	49	112	3	—	313

Attendance
Home 425,037   Away 420,644   Total 845,681
Single-game home record, 56,895 (11-3-85, Lambeau Field), 56,258 (9-28-80, Milwaukee County Stadium)
Single-season home record, 445,335 (1989)

1991 Team Statistics

	Packers	Opp.
Total First Downs	259	298
Rushing	88	99
Passing	150	177
Penalty	21	22
Third Down: Made/Att.	77/207	85/220
Third Down: Pct.	37.2	38.6
Fourth Down: Made/Att.	8/14	10/19
Fourth Down: Pct.	57.1	52.6
Total Net Yards	4332	4812
Avg. Per Game	270.8	300.8
Total Plays	940	1033
Avg. Per Play	4.6	4.7
Net Yards Rushing	1389	1546
Avg. Per Game	86.8	96.6
Total Rushes	381	457
Net Yards Passing	2943	3266
Avg. Per Game	183.9	204.1
Sacked/Yards Lost	45/270	45/307
Gross Yards	3213	3573
Att./Completions	514/272	531/305
Completion Pct.	52.9	57.4
Had Intercepted	19	15
Punts/Avg.	86/40.4	76/42.1
Net Punting Avg.	34.4	34.5
Penalties/Yards Lost	98/834	106/777
Fumbles/Ball Lost	41/17	31/14
Touchdowns	31	35
Rushing	12	10
Passing	17	20
Returns	2	5
Avg. Time of Possession	28:15	31:45

1991 Individual Statistics

Scoring

	TD R	TD P	TD Rt	PAT	FG	Saf	TP
Jacke	0	0	0	31/31	18/24	0	85
Workman	7	4	0	0/0	0/0	0	66
Sharpe	0	4	0	0/0	0/0	0	24
Harris	0	3	0	0/0	0/0	0	18
West	0	3	0	0/0	0/0	0	18
Kemp	0	2	0	0/0	0/0	0	12
Majkowski	2	0	0	0/0	0/0	0	12
Wilson	0	1	0	0/0	0/0	0	12
Noble	0	0	1	0/0	0/0	0	6
Thompson	1	0	0	0/0	0/0	0	6
Tomczak	1	0	0	0/0	0/0	0	6
Woodside	1	0	0	0/0	0/0	0	6
Paup	0	0	0	0/0	0/0	1	2
Packers	12	17	2	31/31	18/24	1	273
Opponents	10	20	5	34/35	23/31	0	313

Passing

	Att.	Comp.	Yds.	Pct.	TD	Int.	Tkld.	Rate
Tomczak	238	128	1490	53.8	11	9	13/105	72.6
Majkowski	226	115	1362	50.9	3	8	30/152	59.3
Kiel	50	29	361	58.0	3	2	2/13	83.8
Packers	514	272	3213	52.9	17	19	45/270	67.9
Opponents	531	305	3573	57.4	20	15	45/307	78.8

Rushing

	Att.	Yds.	Avg.	LG	TD
Thompson	141	471	3.3	40t	1
Woodside	84	326	3.9	29	1
Workman	71	237	3.3	30t	7
Majkowski	25	108	4.3	15	2
Rice	30	100	3.3	21	0
Tomczak	17	93	5.5	48	1
Kiel	4	46	11.5	26	0
Sharpe	4	4	1.0	12	0
Wilson	3	3	1.0	5	0
Harris	1	1	1.0	1	0
McJulien	1	0	0.0	0	0
Packers	381	1389	3.6	48	12
Opponents	457	1546	3.4	27	10

Receiving

	No.	Yds.	Avg.	LG	TD
Sharpe	69	961	13.9	58t	4
Workman	46	371	8.1	25	4
Kemp	42	583	13.9	39	2
Harris	24	264	11.0	35	3
Woodside	22	185	8.4	28	0
Wilson	19	305	16.1	75t	1
West	15	151	10.1	21	3
Weathers	12	150	12.5	22	0
Query	7	94	13.4	26	0
Thompson	7	71	10.1	18	0
Affholter	7	68	9.7	20	0
Rice	2	10	5.0	7	0
Packers	272	3213	11.8	75t	17
Opponents	305	3573	11.7	87t	20

Interceptions

	No.	Yds.	Avg.	LG	TD
Cecil	3	76	25.3	32	0
Murphy	3	27	9.0	16	0
Butler	3	6	2.0	6	0
Clark	2	42	21.0	22	0
Brown	1	37	37.0	37	0
Stephen	1	23	23.0	23	0
Tuaolo	1	23	23.0	23	0
Holmes	1	0	0.0	0	0
Packers	15	234	15.6	37	0
Opponents	19	185	9.7	65t	1

Punting

	No.	Yds.	Avg.	In 20	LG
McJulien	86	3473	40.4	22	62
Packers	86	3473	40.4	22	62
Opponents	76	3199	42.1	19	61

Punt Returns

	No.	FC	Yds.	Avg.	LG	TD
Sikahema	26	4	239	9.2	62	0
Query	14	3	157	11.2	28	0
Workman	1	0	0	0.0	0	0
Packers	41	7	396	9.7	62	0
Opponents	35	24	375	10.7	78t	1

Kickoff Returns

	No.	Yds.	Avg.	LG	TD
Wilson	23	522	22.7	82t	1
Sikahema	15	325	21.7	35	0
Workman	8	139	17.4	26	0
Thompson	7	127	18.1	30	0
Rice	3	36	12.0	15	0
Webb	2	40	20.0	23	0
Davey	1	8	8.0	8	0
Dean	1	0	0.0	0	0
Packers	60	1197	20.0	82t	1
Opponents	46	942	20.5	56	0

Sacks

	No.
Bennett	13.0
Paup	7.5
Archambeau	4.5
Brown	4.0
Tuaolo	3.5
Brock	2.5
Noble	2.5
Dent	1.5
Patterson	1.5
Stephen	1.5
Mitchell	1.0
Murphy	1.0
Packers	45.0
Opponents	45.0

1992 Draft Choices

Round	Name	Pos.	College
1.	Terrell Buckley	DB	Florida State
2.	Mark D'Onofrio	LB	Penn State
3.	Robert Brooks	WR	South Carolina
4.	Edgar Bennett	RB	Florida State
5.	Dexter McNabb	RB	Florida
	Orlando McKay	WR	Washington
6.	Mark Chmura	TE	Boston College
7.	Christopher Holder	WR	Tuskegee
9.	Ty Detmer	QB	Brigham Young
	Shazzon Bradley	NT	Tennessee
10.	Andrew Oberg	T	North Carolina
11.	Gabe Mokwuah	LB	American Int'l.
12.	Brett Collins	LB	Washington

Green Bay Packers 1992 Veteran Roster

No.	Name	Pos.	Ht.	Wt.	Birth-date	NFL Exp.	College	Hometown	How Acq.	'91 Games/Starts
74	†Archambeau, Lester	DE	6-5	271	6/27/67	3	Stanford	Montville, N.J.	D7-'90	16/0
67	Ard, Billy	G	6-3	273	3/12/59	12	Wake Forest	Watchung, N.J.	PB(NYG)-'89#	5/2
82	Beach, Sanjay	WR	6-1	190	2/21/66	2	Colorado State	Chandler, Ariz.	PB(SF)-'92#	16/0*
90	Bennett, Tony	LB	6-2	242	7/1/67	3	Mississippi	Alligator, Miss.	D1a-'90	16/16
34	Billups, Lewis	CB	5-11	182	10/10/63	7	North Alabama	Niceville, Fla.	PB(Cin)-'92#	13/7*
51	Brady, Jeff	LB	6-1	230	11/9/68	2	Kentucky	Melbourne, Ky.	PB(Pitt)-'92#	16/0*
62	Brock, Matt	DE	6-5	290	1/14/66	4	Oregon	San Diego, Calif.	D3a-'89	16/16
93	†Brown, Robert	DE	6-3	278	5/21/60	11	Virginia Tech	Edenton, N.C.	D4-'82	16/16
36	Butler, LeRoy	CB	6-0	195	7/19/68	3	Florida State	Jacksonville, Fla.	D2-'90	16/16
63	Campen, James	C	6-2	275	6/11/64	6	Tulane	Sacramento, Calif.	PB(NO)-'89#	13/13
26	Cecil, Chuck	S	6-0	190	11/8/64	5	Arizona	San Diego, Calif.	D4a-'88	16/16
78	Cheek, Louis	T-G	6-7	286	10/6/64	5	Texas A&M	Fairfield, Tex.	PB(Phil)-'91#	12/9
25	Clark, Vinnie	CB	6-0	194	1/22/69	2	Ohio State	Cincinnati, Ohio	D1-'91	16/4
77	Conover, Frank	NT	6-5	325	4/6/68	2	Syracuse	Englishtown, N.J.	PB(Clev)-'92#	4/1*
99	Davey, Don	DE	6-4	273	4/8/68	2	Wisconsin	Manitowoc, Wis.	D3a-'91	16/0
42	Dean, Walter	RB	5-10	216	5/1/68	2	Grambling	Grambling, La.	D6a-'91	9/0
56	Dent, Burnell	LB	6-1	233	3/16/63	7	Tulane	New Orleans, La.	D6-'86	14/1
41	Dixon, James	WR	5-10	184	2/2/67	4	Houston	Vernon, Tex.	FA-'92	7/0*
4	t-Favre, Brett	QB	6-2	220	10/10/69	2	Southern Mississippi	Kiln, Miss.	T(Atl)-'92	2/0*
21	†Fuller, Joe	CB	5-10	186	9/25/64	3	Northern Iowa	Minneapolis, Minn.	FA-'91	16/0
65	†Hallstrom, Ron	G	6-6	305	6/11/59	11	Iowa	Moline, Ill.	D1-'82	16/16
80	†Harris, Jackie	TE	6-3	243	1/4/68	3	Northeast Louisiana	Pine Bluff, Ark.	D4-'90	16/6
24	Hauck, Tim	S	5-10	181	12/20/66	3	Montana	Big Timber, Mont.	PB(NE)-'91#	16/0
50	Holland, Johnny	LB	6-2	232	3/11/65	6	Texas A&M	Hempstead, Tex.	D2-'87	16/14
44	†Holmes, Jerry	CB	6-1	178	12/22/57	11	West Virginia	Hampton, Va.	PB(Det)-'90#	13/12
48	Ingram, Darryl	TE	6-3	245	5/2/66	2	California	Newhall, Calif.	FA-'92	2/0*
13	Jacke, Chris	K	6-0	197	3/12/66	4	Texas-El Paso	Richardson, Tex.	D6-'89	16/0
92	Jurkovic, John	NT	6-2	297	8/18/67	2	Eastern Illinois	Calumet City, Ill.	FA-'91	5/0
81	†Kemp, Perry	WR	5-11	163	12/31/61	6	California, Pa.	Westland, Pa.	FA-'88	16/12
59	Larson, Kurt	LB	6-4	241	2/25/66	4	Michigan State	Waukesha, Wis.	PB(Ind)-'91#	13/0
7	†Majkowski, Don	QB	6-2	206	2/25/64	6	Virginia	Depew, N.Y.	D10-'87	9/8
79	Mandarich, Tony	T-G	6-5	310	9/23/66	4	Michigan State	Kent, Ohio	D1-'89	15/15
97	McDonald, Mike	LB	6-1	240	6/22/58	8	Southern California	Burbank, Calif.	PB(Rams)-'92#	16/0*
16	McJulien, Paul	P	5-10	190	2/24/65	2	Jackson State	Baker, La.	W(SF)-'91	16/0
47	Mitchell, Roland	CB-S	5-11	198	3/15/64	6	Texas Tech	Bay City, Tex.	PB(Atl)-'91#	16/0
57	†Moran, Rich	G	6-3	280	3/19/62	8	San Diego State	Pleasanton, Calif.	D3-'85	16/16
37	†Murphy, Mark	S	6-2	209	4/22/58	11	West Liberty State	Canton, Ohio	FA-'80	16/16
91	†Noble, Brian	LB	6-4	250	9/6/62	8	Arizona State	Anaheim, Calif.	D5-'85	16/16
96	Patterson, Shawn	DE	6-5	273	6/13/64	5	Arizona State	Tempe, Ariz.	D2-'88	11/0
95	†Paup, Bryce	LB	6-5	247	2/29/68	3	Northern Iowa	Scranton, Iowa	D6-'90	12/1
31	Rice, Allen	RB	5-10	206	4/5/62	9	Baylor	Houston, Tex.	PB(Minn)-'91#	6/3
73	t-Robbins, Tootie	T	6-5	310	6/2/58	11	East Carolina	Windsor, N.C.	T(Phx)-'92	16/16*
75	†Ruettgers, Ken	T	6-6	286	8/20/62	8	Southern California	Bakersfield, Calif.	D1-'85	4/4
84	Sharpe, Sterling	WR	6-1	205	4/6/65	5	South Carolina	Glennville, Ga.	D1-'88	16/16
68	†Singletary, Reggie	T	6-4	296	1/17/64	6	North Carolina State	Cerro Gerdo, N.C.	FA-'91	0*
54	Stephen, Scott	LB	6-2	243	6/18/64	6	Arizona State	Los Angeles, Calif.	D3b-'87	16/16
85	Taylor, Kitrick	WR	5-11	189	7/22/64	5	Washington State	Pomona, Calif.	PB(SD)-'92#	12/0*
39	Thompson, Darrell	RB	6-0	227	11/23/67	3	Minnesota	Rochester, Minn.	D1b-'90	13/13
18	†Tomczak, Mike	QB	6-1	204	10/23/62	8	Ohio State	Calumet City, Ill.	PB(Chi)-'91#	12/7
61	Townsend, Andre	DE	6-3	265	10/8/62	8	Mississippi	Aberdeen, Miss.	FA-'92	0*
98	Tuaolo, Esera	NT	6-2	284	7/11/68	2	Oregon State	Chino, Calif.	D2-'91	16/16
76	Viaene, David	G-T	6-5	300	7/14/63	3	Minnesota-Duluth	Kaukauna, Wis.	PB(NE)-'92#	0*
35	Washington, Charles	S	6-1	220	10/8/66	4	Cameron	Dallas, Tex.	PB(Ind)-'92#	16/1*
30	Webb, Chuck	RB	5-9	201	11/17/69	2	Tennessee	Toledo, Ohio	D3b-'91	2/0
86	†West, Ed	TE	6-1	244	8/2/61	9	Auburn	Leighton, Ala.	FA-'84	16/16
38	White, Adrian	S	6-0	205	4/6/64	5	Florida	Orange Park, Fla.	PB(NYG)-'92#	14/0*
88	†Wilson, Charles	WR	5-9	178	7/1/68	3	Memphis State	Tallahassee, Fla.	D5-'90	15/2
52	Winters, Frank	C-G	6-3	285	1/23/64	6	Western Illinois	Union City, N.J.	PB(KC)-'92#	16/0*
33	Woodside, Keith	RB	6-0	217	7/29/64	5	Texas A&M	Vidalia, La.	D3-'88	16/12
46	Workman, Vince	RB	5-10	201	5/9/68	4	Ohio State	Dublin, Ohio	D5b-'89	16/0

* Beach played 16 games with San Francisco in '91; Billups played 13 games with Cincinnati; Brady played 16 games with Pittsburgh; Conover played 4 games with Cleveland; Dixon played 7 games with Dallas; Favre played 2 games with Atlanta; Ingram played 2 games with Cleveland; McDonald played 16 games with L.A. Rams; Robbins played 16 games with Phoenix; Singletary active for 6 games but did not play; Taylor played 12 games with San Diego; Townsend last active with Denver in '90; Viaene last active with New England in '90; Washington played 16 games with Indianapolis; White played 14 games with N.Y. Giants; Winters played 16 games with Kansas City.

† Option playout; subject to developments.

t- Packers traded for Favre (Atlanta), Robbins (Phoenix).

Plan B unconditional free agent.

Traded—Quarterback Blair Kiel to Atlanta.

Players lost through Plan B (6): WR Erik Affholter (SD; 4 games in '91), LB Reggie Burnett (TB; 3), C Blair Bush (Rams; 16), T Steve Gabbard (Wash; 4), WR Jeff Query (Hou; 16), RB-KR Vai Sikahema (Phil; 11).

Also played with Packers in '91—RB Steve Avery (1 game), LB Greg Clark (2), T Scott Jones (2), T Keith Uecker (14), WR Clarence Weathers (14).

COACHING STAFF

Head Coach,
Mike Holmgren

Pro Career: Named head coach on January 11, 1992. Became the eleventh head coach in the history of the franchise. Offensive coordinator the past three years (1989-1991) for the San Francisco 49ers under George Seifert after spending previous three seasons (1986-88) as quarterbacks coach under Bill Walsh. During his six-year tenure, the 49ers won five consecutive NFC Western Division championships (1986-1990) and back-to-back Super Bowls (XXIII and XXIV). In that span, San Francisco compiled the NFL's best overall record (71-23-1, a .753 percentage). The 49ers' offense never ranked lower than third overall in his three years as coordinator.

Background: Quarterback at Southern California (1966-69) and was drafted by the St. Louis Cardinals in the eighth round of the 1970 NFL draft. He served as an assistant coach at San Francisco State (1981) and Brigham Young (1982-85) before his tenure with the 49ers. Earned his bachelor of science degree in business finance at Southern California (1970).

Personal: Born June 15, 1948, in San Francisco. He and his wife, Kathy, live in Green Bay and have four daughters—Calla, Jenny, Emily, and Gretchen.

Assistant Coaches

Greg Blache, defensive line; born March 9, 1949, New Orleans, La., lives in Green Bay. No college or pro playing experience. College coach: Notre Dame 1973-75, 1981-83, Tulane 1976-80, Southern University 1986, Kansas 1987. Pro coach: Jacksonville Bulls (USFL) 1984-85, joined Packers in 1988.

Nolan Cromwell, special teams; born January 30, 1955, Smith Center, Kan., lives in Green Bay. Quarterback-safety Kansas 1973-76. Pro defensive back Los Angeles Rams 1977-87. Pro coach: Los Angeles Rams 1991, joined Packers in 1992.

Jon Gruden, offensive assistant-quality control; born August 17, 1963, Sandusky, Ohio, lives in Green Bay. Quarterback Dayton 1983-85. No pro playing experience. College coach: Tennessee 1986-87, Southeast Missouri 1988, Pacific 1989, Pittsburgh 1991. Pro coach: San Francisco 49ers 1990, joined Packers in 1992.

Gil Haskell, running backs; born September 24, 1943, San Francisco, Calif., lives in Green Bay. Defensive back San Francisco State 1961, 1963-65. No pro playing experience. College coach: Southern California 1978-82. Pro coach: Los Angeles Rams 1983-91, joined Packers in 1992.

Dick Jauron, defensive backs; born October 7, 1950, Peoria, Ill., lives in Green Bay. Defensive back Yale 1970-72. Pro defensive back Detroit Lions 1973-77, Cincinnati Bengals 1978-80. Pro coach: Buffalo Bills 1985, joined Packers in 1986.

Kent Johnston, strength and conditioning; born February 21, 1956, Mexia, Tex., lives in Green Bay. Defensive back Stephen F. Austin 1974-77. No pro playing experience. College coach: Northeast Louisiana 1979, Northwestern Louisiana 1980-81, Alabama 1983-86. Pro coach: Tampa Bay Buccaneers 1987-91, joined Packers in 1992.

Sherman Lewis, offensive coordinator-receivers; born June 29, 1942, Louisville, Ky., lives in Green Bay. Running back Michigan State 1961-63. Pro running back Toronto Argonauts (CFL) 1964-65, New York Jets 1966. College coach: Michigan State 1969-82. Pro coach: San Francisco 49ers 1983-91, joined Packers in 1992.

Jim Lind, defensive assistant-quality control; born November 11, 1947, Isle, Minn., lives in Green Bay. Linebacker Bethel College 1965-66; defensive back Bemidji State 1971-72. No pro playing experience. College coach: St. Cloud State 1977-78, St. John's (Minn.) 1979-80, Brigham Young 1981-82, Minnesota-Morris 1983-86 (head coach), Wisconsin-Eau Claire 1987-91 (head coach). Pro coach: Joined Packers in 1992.

Tom Lovat, offensive line; born December 28, 1938, Bingham, Utah, lives in Green Bay. Guard-linebacker Utah 1958-60. No pro playing experience. College coach: Utah 1967, 1972-76 (head coach 1974-76), Idaho State 1968-70, Stanford 1977-79, Wyoming 1989. Pro coach: Saskatchewan Roughriders (CFL) 1971, Green Bay Packers 1980, St. Louis-Phoenix Cardinals 1981-84, 1990-91, Indianapolis Colts 1985-88, rejoined Packers in 1992.

Steve Mariucci, quarterbacks; born November 4, 1955, Iron Mountain, Mich., lives in Green Bay. Quarterback Northern Michigan 1974-77. No pro playing experience. College coach: Northern Michigan 1978-79, Cal State-Fullerton 1980-82, Louisville 1983-84, Southern California 1986, California 1987-89. Pro coach: Orlando Renegades (USFL) 1985, Los Angeles Rams 1985, joined Packers in 1992.

Andy Reid, tight ends-offensive line assistant; born March 19, 1958, Los Angeles, Calif., lives in Green Bay. Offensive tackle-guard Brigham Young 1978-80. No pro playing experience. College coach: San Francisco State 1983-85, Northern Arizona 1986, Texas-El Paso 1987, Missouri 1988-91. Pro coach: Joined Packers in 1992.

Ray Rhodes, defensive coordinator; born October 20, 1950, Mexia, Tex., lives in Green Bay. Running back-wide receiver Texas Christian 1969-70, Tulsa 1972-73. Pro defensive back New York Giants 1974-79, San Francisco 49ers 1980. Pro coach: San Francisco 49ers 1981-91, joined Packers in 1992.

Bob Valesente, linebackers; born July 19, 1940, Seneca Falls, N.Y., lives in Green Bay. Halfback Ithaca College 1958-61. No pro playing experience. College coach: Cornell 1964-74, Cincinnati 1975-76, Arizona 1977-79, Mississippi State 1980-81, Kansas 1984-87 (head coach, 1986-87), Maryland 1988, Pittsburgh 1989. Pro coach: Baltimore Colts 1982-83, Pittsburgh Steelers 1990-91, joined Packers in 1992.

Green Bay Packers 1992 First-Year Roster

Name	Pos.	Ht.	Wt.	Birth-date	College	Hometown	How Acq.
Avery, Steve (1)	RB	6-1	225	8/18/66	Northern Michigan	Brookfield, Wis.	FA-'91
Barrie, Sebastian	DE	6-2	273	5/28/70	Liberty	Dallas, Tex.	FA
Bennett, Edgar	RB	6-0	208	2/15/69	Florida State	Jacksonville, Fla.	D4
Booker, Anthony	T	6-4	263	7/23/69	Indiana State	Cincinnati, Ohio	FA
Bradley, Shazzon	NT	6-1	272	2/22/70	Tennessee	Athens, Tenn.	D9b
Bridewell, Jeff (1)	QB	6-5	217	5/13/67	California-Davis	Napa, Calif.	FA
Brooks, Robert	WR	6-0	175	6/23/70	South Carolina	Greenwood, S.C.	D3
Buckley, Terrell	CB	5-9	174	6/7/71	Florida State	Pascagoula, Miss.	D1
Chmura, Mark	TE	6-5	236	2/22/69	Boston College	South Deerfield, Mass.	D6
Collins, Brett	LB	6-1	226	10/8/68	Washington	Portland, Ore.	D12
Collins, Linzy (1)	WR	6-0	190	1/24/69	Missouri	St. Louis, Mo.	D12-'91
Cullinane, Gene	C-G	6-3	271	11/10/66	Washburn	Omaha, Neb.	FA
Detmer, Ty	QB	6-0	182	10/30/67	Brigham Young	San Antonio, Tex.	D9a
D'Onofrio, Mark	LB	6-2	231	3/17/69	Penn State	North Bergen, N.J.	D2
Evans, Jerry (1)	TE	6-4	250	9/28/68	Toledo	Lorain, Ohio	FA
Garten, Joe (1)	C-G	6-2	289	8/13/68	Colorado	Placentia, Calif.	D6b-'91
Holder, Chris	WR	6-0	182	10/23/69	Tuskegee	Mobile, Ala.	D7
Jackson, Pat (1)	WR	5-9	175	7/8/69	Kansas State	Columbus, Ohio	FA
Lauscher, Jon	LB	6-2	250	3/31/70	Wisconsin-LaCrosse	Green Bay, Wis.	FA
Lloyd, Doug (1)	RB	6-1	230	8/31/65	North Dakota State	Beaver Dam, Wis.	FA
McKay, Orlando	WR	5-10	175	10/2/69	Washington	Mesa, Ariz.	D5b
McNabb, Dexter	RB	6-1	244	7/9/69	Florida	De Funiak Springs, Fla.	D5a
Mokwuah, Gabe	LB	6-2	254	11/28/70	American Int'l.	Staten Island, N.Y.	D11
Oberg, Andrew	T	6-7	300	2/2/69	North Carolina	Rochester, Pa.	D10
Porter, Rapier	G	6-3	276	8/14/66	Arkansas-Pine Bluff	Mobile, Ala.	D10
Wilson, Marcus (1)	RB	6-1	210	4/16/68	Virginia	Rochester, N.Y.	FA
Young, Ron (1)	WR	6-3	208	3/15/68	Washington State	San Diego, Calif.	FA

The term NFL Rookie is defined as a player who is in his first season of professional football and has not been on the roster of another professional football team for any regular-season or postseason games. A Rookie is designated by an "R" on NFL rosters. Players who have been active in another professional football league or players who have NFL experience, including either preseason training camp or being on an active roster for fewer than three regular-season or postseason games, are termed NFL First-Year Players. An NFL First-Year Player is designated by a "1" on NFL rosters. Thereafter, a player on an NFL active roster for at least three regular-season or postseason games is credited with an additional year of NFL playing experience.

NOTES

_____

_____

_____

_____

_____

_____

_____

_____

_____

LOS ANGELES RAMS

National Football Conference Western Division

Team Colors: Royal Blue, Gold, and White

Business Address:
2327 West Lincoln Avenue
Anaheim, California 92801
Telephone: (714) 535-7267

Ticket Office:
Anaheim Stadium
1900 State College Boulevard
Anaheim, California 92806
Telephone: (714) 937-6767

Club Officials

Owner/President: Georgia Frontiere
Executive Vice President: John Shaw
Senior Vice President: Jay Zygmunt
Vice President-Media and Community Relations:
   Marshall Klein
Vice President-Head Coach: Chuck Knox
Administrator, Football Operations: Jack Faulkner
General Counsel: Steve Novak
Director of Player Personnel: John Becker
Director of Player Relations: Paul (Tank) Younger
Director of Promotions/Sales: Pete Donovan
Director of Public Relations: Rick Smith
Trainers: George Menefee, Jim Anderson,
   Blynn DeNiro
Equipment Managers: Don Hewitt, Todd Hewitt

Stadium: Anaheim Stadium • **Capacity:** 69,008
   Anaheim, California 92806

Playing Surface: Grass

Training Camp: University of California-Irvine
   Irvine, California 92717

1992 Schedule

Preseason

Aug. 6	at Seattle	6:00
Aug. 15	**Los Angeles Raiders**	7:00
Aug. 22	**Green Bay**	6:00
Aug. 27	at San Diego	7:00

Regular Season

Sept. 6	at Buffalo	1:00
Sept. 13	**New England**	1:00
Sept. 20	at Miami	4:00
Sept. 27	**New York Jets**	1:00
Oct. 4	at San Francisco	1:00
Oct. 11	at New Orleans	6:30
Oct. 18	**New York Giants**	1:00
Oct. 25	**Open Date**	
Nov. 1	at Atlanta	1:00
Nov. 8	**Phoenix**	1:00
Nov. 15	at Dallas	12:00
Nov. 22	**San Francisco**	1:00
Nov. 29	**Minnesota**	1:00
Dec. 6	at Tampa Bay	8:00
Dec. 13	**New Orleans**	1:00
Dec. 20	at Green Bay	12:00
Dec. 27	**Atlanta**	1:00

Rams Coaching History

Cleveland 1937-1945
(396-336-20)

1937-38	Hugo Bezdek*	1-13-0
1938	Art Lewis	4-4-0
1939-42	Earl (Dutch) Clark	16-26-2
1944	Aldo (Buff) Donelli	4-6-0
1945-46	Adam Walsh	16-5-1
1947	Bob Snyder	6-6-0
1948-49	Clark Shaughnessy	14-8-3
1950-52	Joe Stydahar**	19-9-0
1952-54	Hamp Pool	23-11-2
1955-59	Sid Gillman	28-32-1
1960-62	Bob Waterfield***	9-24-1
1962-65	Harland Svare	14-31-3
1966-70	George Allen	49-19-4
1971-72	Tommy Prothro	14-12-2
1973-77	Chuck Knox	57-20-1
1978-82	Ray Malavasi	43-36-0
1983-91	John Robinson	79-74-0

*Released after three games in 1938
**Resigned after one game in 1952
***Resigned after eight games in 1962

Record Holders
Individual Records—Career

Category	Name	Performance
Rushing (Yds.)	Eric Dickerson, 1983-87	7,245
Passing (Yds.)	Roman Gabriel, 1962-1972	22,223
Passing (TDs)	Roman Gabriel, 1962-1972	154
Receiving (No.)	Henry Ellard, 1983-1991	485
Receiving (Yds.)	Henry Ellard, 1983-1991	8,089
Interceptions	Ed Meador, 1959-1970	46
Punting (Avg.)	Danny Villanueva, 1960-64	44.2
Punt Return (Avg.)	Henry Ellard, 1983-1990	11.3
Kickoff Return (Avg.)	Tom Wilson, 1956-1961	27.1
Field Goals	Mike Lansford, 1982-1990	158
Touchdowns (Tot.)	Eric Dickerson, 1983-87	58
Points	Mike Lansford, 1982-1990	789

Individual Records—Single Season

Category	Name	Performance
Rushing (Yds.)	Eric Dickerson, 1984	*2,105
Passing (Yds.)	Jim Everett, 1989	4,310
Passing (TDs)	Jim Everett, 1988	31
Receiving (No.)	Henry Ellard, 1988	86
Receiving (Yds.)	Elroy (Crazylegs) Hirsch, 1951	1,425
Interceptions	Dick (Night Train) Lane, 1952	*14
Punting (Avg.)	Danny Villanueva, 1962	45.5
Punt Return (Avg.)	Woodley Lewis, 1952	18.5
Kickoff Return (Avg.)	Verda (Vitamin T) Smith, 1950	33.7
Field Goals	David Ray, 1973	30
Touchdowns (Tot.)	Eric Dickerson, 1983	20
Points	David Ray, 1973	130

Individual Records—Single Game

Category	Name	Performance
Rushing (Yds.)	Eric Dickerson, 1-4-86	248
Passing (Yds.)	Norm Van Brocklin, 9-28-51	*554
Passing (TDs)	Many times	5
	Last time by Jim Everett, 9-25-88	
Receiving (No.)	Tom Fears, 12-3-50	*18
Receiving (Yds.)	Willie Anderson, 11-26-89	*336
Interceptions	Many times	3
	Last time by Pat Thomas, 10-7-79	
Field Goals	Bob Waterfield, 12-9-51	5
Touchdowns (Tot.)	Bob Shaw, 12-11-49	4
	Elroy (Crazylegs) Hirsch, 9-28-51	4
	Harold Jackson, 10-14-73	4
Points	Bob Shaw, 12-11-49	24
	Elroy (Crazylegs) Hirsch, 9-28-51	24
	Harold Jackson, 10-14-73	24

*NFL Record

ANAHEIM STADIUM

1991 Team Record
Preseason (1-3)

Date	Result		Opponents
8/3	L	17-38	vs. Atlanta at Jacksonville, Fla.
8/12	W	24- 3	San Diego
8/17	L	7-23	Seattle
8/22	L	13-16	vs. Houston at Memphis, Tenn.

Regular Season (3-13)

Date	Result		Opponents	Att.
9/1	L	14-24	Phoenix	47,069
9/8	W	19-13	at N.Y. Giants	76,541
9/15	L	7-24	at New Orleans	68,583
9/22	L	10-27	at San Francisco	63,871
9/29	W	23-21	Green Bay	54,736
10/13	W	30-24	San Diego	47,433
10/20	L	17-20	at L.A. Raiders	85,102
10/27	L	14-31	at Atlanta	50,187
11/3	L	17-24	New Orleans	58,713
11/10	L	20-27	Kansas City	52,511
11/17	L	10-21	at Detroit	60,873
11/25	L	10-33	San Francisco	61,881
12/1	L	6-27	Washington	55,027
12/8	L	14-31	Atlanta	35,315
12/15	L	14-20	at Minnesota	61,518
12/22	L	9-23	at Seattle	51,100

Score by Periods

Rams	22	103	55	54	0	— 234
Opponents	95	114	76	105	0	— 390

Attendance
Home 412,685   Away 517,775   Total 930,460
Single-game home record, 67,037 (12-23-84)
Single-season home record, 500,403 (1980)

1991 Team Statistics

	Rams	Opp.
Total First Downs	270	286
Rushing	75	105
Passing	180	162
Penalty	15	19
Third Down: Made/Att.	75/198	73/184
Third Down: Pct.	37.9	39.7
Fourth Down: Made/Att.	9/19	5/8
Fourth Down: Pct.	47.4	62.5
Total Net Yards	4695	5204
Avg. Per Game	293.4	325.3
Total Plays	936	920
Avg. Per Play	5.0	5.7
Net Yards Rushing	1285	1659
Avg. Per Game	80.3	103.7
Total Rushes	388	469
Net Yards Passing	3410	3545
Avg. Per Game	213.1	221.6
Sacked/Yards Lost	30/200	17/112
Gross Yards	3610	3657
Att./Completions	518/289	434/259
Completion Pct.	55.8	59.7
Had Intercepted	20	11
Punts/Avg.	75/38.1	68/41.6
Net Punting Avg.	32.3	34.8
Penalties/Yards Lost	108/774	83/743
Fumbles/Ball Lost	32/20	17/8
Touchdowns	26	47
Rushing	11	19
Passing	13	25
Returns	2	3
Avg. Time of Possession	29:03	30:57

1991 Individual Statistics

Scoring

	TD R	TD P	TD Rt	PAT	FG	Saf	TP
Zendejas	0	0	0	25/26	17/17	0	76
Delpino	9	1	0	0/0	0/0	0	60
Ellard	0	3	0	0/0	0/0	0	18
Carter	0	2	0	0/0	0/0	0	12
Johnson	0	2	0	0/0	0/0	0	12
Price	0	2	0	0/0	0/0	0	12
Anderson	0	1	0	0/0	0/0	0	6
Dupree	1	0	0	0/0	0/0	0	6
Gary	1	0	0	0/0	0/0	0	6
Gray	0	0	1	0/0	0/0	0	6
Newman	0	0	1	0/0	0/0	0	6
Thompson	0	1	0	0/0	0/0	0	6
Turner	0	1	0	0/0	0/0	0	6
Greene	0	0	0	0/0	0/0	1	2
Rams	11	13	2	25/26	17/17	1	234
Opponents	19	25	3	46/47	20/28	1	390

Passing

	Att.	Comp.	Yds.	Pct.	TD	Int.	Tkld.	Rate
Everett	490	277	3438	56.5	11	20	30/200	68.9
Pagel	27	11	150	40.7	2	0	0/0	83.9
Helton	1	1	22	100.0	0	0	0/0	118.8
Rams	518	289	3610	55.8	13	20	30/200	69.9
Opponents	434	259	3657	59.7	25	11	17/112	95.6

Rushing

	Att.	Yds.	Avg.	LG	TD
Delpino	214	688	3.2	36	9
Gary	68	245	3.6	14	1
Dupree	49	179	3.7	24	1
McGee	19	65	3.4	9	0
Everett	27	44	1.6	10	0
Turner	7	44	6.3	11	0
Brown	2	11	5.5	11	0
Thompson	2	9	4.5	9	0
Rams	388	1285	3.3	36	11
Opponents	469	1659	3.5	26	19

Receiving

	No.	Yds.	Avg.	LG	TD
Ellard	64	1052	16.4	38	3
Delpino	55	617	11.2	78	1
Price	35	410	11.7	27	2
Anderson	32	530	16.6	54	1
Johnson	32	253	7.9	27	2
McGee	20	160	8.0	20	0
Cox	15	216	14.4	39	0
Gary	13	110	8.5	22	0
Carter	8	69	8.6	18t	2
Dupree	6	46	7.7	21	0
Brown	3	52	17.3	21	0
Turner	3	41	13.7	19t	1
Thompson	2	35	17.5	22	1
Raye	1	19	19.0	19	0
Rams	289	3610	12.5	78	13
Opponents	259	3657	14.1	78	25

Interceptions

	No.	Yds.	Avg.	LG	TD
Gray	3	83	27.7	59t	1
Henley	3	22	7.3	22	0
Stewart	2	8	4.0	8	0
Newman	1	58	58.0	58	0
Terrell	1	4	4.0	4	0
Lyght	1	0	0.0	0	0
Rams	11	175	15.9	59t	1
Opponents	20	297	14.9	97t	1

Punting

	No.	Yds.	Avg.	In 20	LG
Helton	11	453	41.2	2	46
Hatcher	63	2403	38.1	16	52
Rams	75	2856	38.1	18	52
Opponents	68	2829	41.6	20	62

Punt Returns

	No.	FC	Yds.	Avg.	LG	TD
Turner	23	4	201	8.7	29	0
Henley	13	4	110	8.5	16	0
Gray	1	1	9	9.0	9	0
Rams	37	9	320	8.6	29	0
Opponents	33	21	292	8.8	42	0

Kickoff Returns

	No.	Yds.	Avg.	LG	TD
Turner	24	457	19.0	36	0
Brown	12	256	21.3	39	0
Lang	12	194	16.2	34	0
Delpino	4	54	13.5	19	0
McDonald	3	32	10.7	16	0
Raye	2	57	28.5	48	0
Carter	1	18	18.0	18	0
Sanders	1	2	2.0	2	0
Rams	59	1070	18.1	48	0
Opponents	39	671	17.2	35	0

Sacks

	No.
Greene	3.0
Robinson	3.0
Kelm	2.0
Phifer	2.0
Wilson	2.0
Newman	1.0
Piel	1.0
Stewart	1.0
Strickland	1.0
Young	1.0
Rams	17.0
Opponents	30.0

1992 Draft Choices

Round	Name	Pos.	College
1.	Sean Gilbert	DE	Pittsburgh
2.	Steve Israel	DB	Pittsburgh
3.	Marc Boutte	DT	Louisiana State
	Todd Kinchen	WR	Louisiana State
4.	Shawn Harper	T	Indiana
5.	Chris Crooms	DB	Texas A&M
6.	Joe Campbell	RB	Middle Tenn. St.
7.	Darryl Ashmore	T	Northwestern
8.	Ricky Jones	QB	Alabama State
9.	T.J. Rubley	QB	Tulsa
10.	Tim Lester	RB	Eastern Kentucky
11.	Brian Townsend	LB	Michigan
	Brian Thomas	WR	Southern
12.	Kelvin Harris	C	Miami

Los Angeles Rams 1992 Veteran Roster

No.	Name	Pos.	Ht.	Wt.	Birth-date	NFL Exp.	College	Hometown	How Acq.	'91 Games/Starts
83	Anderson, Willie	WR	6-0	175	3/7/65	5	UCLA	Paulsboro, N.J.	D2b-'88	12/10
28	Bailey, Robert	CB	5-9	176	9/3/68	2	Miami	Miami, Fla.	D4-'91	6/0
17	Bracken, Don	P	6-1	211	2/16/62	8	Michigan	Thermopolis, Wyo.	FA-'92	0*
61	Brostek, Bern	C-G	6-3	300	9/11/66	3	Washington	Honolulu, Hawaii	D1-'90	14/8
51	Bush, Blair	C	6-3	275	11/25/56	15	Washington	Palos Verdes, Calif.	PB(GB)-'92#	16/3*
59	Butcher, Paul	LB	6-0	230	11/8/63	6	Wayne State	Detroit, Mich.	FA-'90	16/3
88	†Carter, Pat	TE	6-3	255	8/1/66	5	Florida State	Riverview, Fla.	T(Det)-'89	16/5
89	Chadwick, Jeff	WR	6-3	185	12/16/60	10	Grand Valley State	Dearborn, Mich.	PB(Sea)-'92#	12/0*
79	Charles, Mike	DT	6-4	305	9/23/62	10	Syracuse	Newark, N.J.	FA-'91	7/4
84	†Cox, Aaron	WR	5-10	178	3/13/65	5	Arizona State	Los Angeles, Calif.	D1b-'88	15/5
39	Delpino, Robert	RB	6-0	205	11/2/65	5	Missouri	Dodge City, Kan.	D5-'88	16/15
22	Dupree, Marcus	RB	6-2	225	5/22/64	3	Oklahoma	Philadelphia, Miss.	FA-'90	8/1
80	Ellard, Henry	WR	5-11	182	7/21/61	10	Fresno State	Fresno, Calif.	D2-'83	16/16
11	Everett, Jim	QB	6-5	212	1/3/63	7	Purdue	Albuquerque, N.M.	T(Hou)-'86	16/16
43	Gary, Cleveland	RB	6-0	226	5/4/66	4	Miami	Indiantown, Fla.	D1b-'89	10/2
91	Greene, Kevin	LB-DE	6-3	247	7/31/62	8	Auburn	Granite City, Ill.	D5-'85	16/16
70	Hawkins, Bill	DE	6-6	269	5/9/66	4	Miami	Miami, Fla.	D1a-'89	6/0
9	Helton, Barry	P	6-3	205	1/2/65	5	Colorado	Simla, Colo.	FA-'91	3/0
20	Henley, Darryl	CB	5-9	172	10/30/66	4	UCLA	La Verne, Calif.	D2c-'89	16/15
65	Jenkins, A.J.	DE	6-2	240	4/12/66	3	Cal State-Fullerton	Havelock, N.C.	FA-'92	0*
72	Jenkins, Robert	T	6-5	285	12/30/63	7	UCLA	Dublin, Calif.	D6-'86	12/8
86	†Johnson, Damone	TE	6-4	250	3/2/62	7	Cal Poly-SLO	Santa Monica, Calif.	D6-'85	16/16
52	Kelm, Larry	LB	6-4	240	11/29/64	6	Texas A&M	Corpus Christi, Tex.	D4-'87	16/15
38	Lang, David	RB	5-11	201	3/28/67	2	Northern Arizona	San Bernardino, Calif.	D12-'90	16/0
21	Loville, Derek	RB	5-9	196	7/4/68	3	Oregon	San Francisco, Calif.	PB(Sea)-'92#	16/0*
41	Lyght, Todd	CB	6-0	186	2/9/69	2	Notre Dame	Germantown, Md.	D1-'91	12/8
24	McGee, Buford	RB	6-0	210	8/16/60	9	Mississippi	Durant, Miss.	T(SD)-'87	16/4
71	Milinichik, Joe	G	6-5	290	3/30/63	6	North Carolina State	Emmaus, Pa.	PB(Det)-'90#	5/5
66	Newberry, Tom	C-G	6-2	285	12/20/62	7	Wisconsin-LaCrosse	Onalaska, Wis.	D2-'86	16/16
26	†Newman, Anthony	S	6-0	199	11/25/65	5	Oregon	Beaverton, Ore.	D2a-'88	16/1
14	†Pagel, Mike	QB	6-2	220	9/13/60	11	Arizona State	Phoenix, Ariz.	FA-'91	16/0
69	Pahukoa, Jeff	G-T	6-2	298	2/2/69	2	Washington	Vancouver, Wash.	D12a-'91	7/0
64	Perry, Gerald	T	6-6	305	11/12/64	5	Southern	Columbia, S.C.	T(Den)-'91	11/9
58	Phifer, Roman	LB	6-2	230	3/5/68	2	UCLA	Pineville, N.C.	D2-'91	12/5
95	Piel, Mike	DT	6-4	270	9/21/65	4	Illinois	El Toro, Calif.	D3-'88	6/3
87	Price, Jim	TE	6-4	247	10/2/66	2	Stanford	Englewood, N.J.	FA-'91	12/6
97	Robinson, Gerald	DE	6-3	262	5/4/63	5	Auburn	Notasulga, Ala.	PB(SD)-'91#	15/4
92	Rocker, David	DT	6-4	267	3/12/69	2	Auburn	Atlanta, Ga.	FA-'92	6/3
55	Sanders, Glenell	LB	6-0	224	11/4/66	3	Louisiana Tech	Clinton, La.	PB(Chi)-'91#	16/1
68	Skow, Jim	DE	6-3	250	6/29/63	7	Nebraska	Omaha, Neb.	PB(Sea)-'92#	11/1*
78	†Slater, Jackie	T	6-4	287	5/27/54	17	Jackson State	Jackson, Miss.	D3-'76	13/13
56	Smith, Doug	C	6-3	272	11/25/56	15	Bowling Green	Columbus, Ohio	FA-'78	15/8
50	Stams, Frank	LB	6-2	237	7/17/65	4	Notre Dame	Akron, Ohio	D2a-'89	5/0
23	†Stewart, Michael	S	6-0	199	7/12/65	6	Fresno State	Bakersfield, Calif.	D8-'87	16/16
53	Strickland, Fred	LB	6-2	250	8/15/66	5	Purdue	Wanaque, N.J.	D2c-'88	14/10
37	Terrell, Pat	S	6-0	195	3/18/68	3	Notre Dame	Memphis, Tenn.	D2-'90	16/16
32	Thompson, Ernie	RB	5-11	230	10/25/69	2	Indiana	Terre Haute, Ind.	D12b-'91	3/0
30	Turner, Vernon	WR	5-8	185	1/6/67	2	Carson-Newman	Brooklyn, N.Y.	W(Buff)-'91	15/0
77	Wilson, Karl	DE	6-4	275	3/10/64	6	Louisiana State	Baton Rouge, La.	PB(Mia)-'91#	13/10
99	Wright, Alvin	DT	6-2	285	2/5/61	7	Jacksonville State	Wedonee, Ala.	FA-'86	13/11
76	Young, Robert	DT	6-6	273	1/29/69	2	Mississippi State	Jackson, Miss.	D5-'91	16/13
10	Zendejas, Tony	K	5-8	165	5/15/60	8	Nevada-Reno	Chino, Calif.	PB(Hou)-'91#	16/0

* Bracken last active with Green Bay in '90; Bush played 16 games with Green Bay in '91; Chadwick played 12 games with Seattle; A.J. Jenkins last active with Pittsburgh in '90; Loville played 16 games with Seattle; Skow played 11 games with Seattle.

† Option playout; subject to developments.

Players lost through Plan B (7): WR-KR Ron Brown (Raid; 6 games in '91), LB Brett Faryniarz (Atl; 12), DE Tom Gibson (Pitt; 5), CB Jerry Gray (Hou; 16), CB-S Sammy Lilly (TB; 16), G Duval Love (Pitt; 16), LB Mike McDonald (GB; 16).

Also played with Rams in '91—LB Terry Crews (6 games), P Dale Hatcher (13), DT Chris Pike (8), WR Jimmy Raye (2), RB Mosi Tatupu (5), DE Ben Thomas (2), CB Rodney Thomas (3).

COACHING STAFF

Head Coach, Chuck Knox

Pro Career: Starts his second tour of duty as Rams head coach. Named to the post on January 8, 1992, after serving as Seattle's head coach from 1983-91 and leading the Seahawks into the playoffs four times. Previously served as head coach of Buffalo Bills 1978-82, leading them to the AFC East title in 1980. Led the Rams to five consecutive NFC West titles (1973-77) before taking over Bills. Pro assistant with New York Jets 1963-66, coaching offensive line, before moving to Detroit in 1967. Served Lions as offensive line coach until named head coach of Rams in 1973. No pro playing experience. Career record: 178-125-1.

Background: Played tackle for Juniata College in Huntingdon, Pa., 1950-53. Was an assistant coach at his alma mater in 1954, then spent 1955 season at Tyrone High in Tyrone, Pa. Was head coach at Ellwood City (Pa.) High School from 1956-58. Moved to Wake Forest as an assistant coach in 1959-60, then Kentucky in 1961-62.

Personal: Born April 27, 1932, in Sewickley, Pa. Chuck and his wife, Shirley live in Anaheim, Calif., and have four children—Chris, Kathy, Colleen, and Chuck.

Assistant Coaches

John Becker, administrative assistant; born February 16, 1943, Alexandria, Va., lives in Huntington Beach, Calif. Cal State-Northridge. No college or pro playing experience. College coach: UCLA 1970, New Mexico State 1971, New Mexico 1972-73, Los Angeles Valley J.C. 1974-76 (head coach), Oregon 1977-79. Pro coach: Philadelphia Eagles 1980-83, Buffalo Bills 1984, Indianapolis Colts 1985-86, Seattle Seahawks 1989-91, joined Rams in 1992.

George Dyer, defensive coordinator; born May 4, 1940, Alhambra, Calif., lives in Villa Park, Calif. Center-linebacker U.C. Santa Barbara 1961-63. No pro playing experience. College coach: Humboldt State 1964-66, Coalinga (Calif.) J.C. 1967 (head coach), Portland State 1968-71, Idaho 1972, San Jose State 1973, Michigan State 1977-79, Arizona State 1980-81. Pro coach: Winnipeg Blue Bombers (CFL) 1974-76, Buffalo Bills 1982, Seattle Seahawks 1983-91, joined Rams in 1992.

Jim Erkenbeck, offensive line; born September 10, 1929, Los Angeles, Calif., lives in Anaheim Hills, Calif. Linebacker-end San Diego State 1949-52. No pro playing experience. College coach: San Diego State 1960-63, Grossmont (Calif.) J.C. 1964-67, Utah State 1968, Washington State 1969-71, California 1972-76. Pro coach: Winnipeg Blue Bombers (CFL) 1977, Montreal Alouettes (CFL) 1978-81, Calgary Stampeders (CFL) 1982, Philadelphia/Baltimore Stars (USFL) 1983-85, New Orleans Saints 1986, Dallas Cowboys 1987-88, Kansas City Chiefs 1989-91, joined Rams in 1992.

Chick Harris, running backs; born September 21, 1945, Durham, N.C., lives in Irvine, Calif. Running back Northern Arizona 1966-69. No pro playing experience. College coach: Colorado State 1970-72, Long Beach State 1973-74, Washington 1975-80. Pro coach: Buffalo Bills 1981-82, Seattle Seahawks 1983-91, joined Rams in 1992.

Milt Jackson, receivers; born October 16, 1943, Groesbeck, Tex., lives in Anaheim, Calif. Defensive back Tulsa 1965-66. Pro defensive back San Francisco 49ers 1967. College coach: Oregon State 1973, Rice 1974, California 1975-76, Oregon 1977-78, UCLA 1979. Pro coach: San Francisco 49ers 1980-82, Buffalo Bills 1983-84, Philadelphia Eagles 1985, Houston Oilers 1986-88, Indianapolis Colts 1989-91, joined Rams in 1992.

Pat Perles, coach assistant-defense; born October 2, 1963, East Detroit, Mich., lives in Anaheim, Calif. Nose tackle Kent State 1983, linebacker Michigan State 1984-86. No pro playing experience. College coach: Michigan State 1988, Toledo 1989-91. Pro coach: Joined Rams in 1992.

Rod Perry, defensive backfield; born September 11, 1953, Fresno, Calif., lives in Anaheim Hills, Calif. Defensive back Colorado 1972-74. Pro cornerback Los Angeles Rams 1975-82, Cleveland Browns 1983-84. College coach: Columbia 1985, Fresno City College 1986, Fresno State 1987-88. Pro coach: Seattle Seahawks 1989-91, joined Rams in 1992.

Howard Tippett, special teams-tight ends; born September 23, 1938, Tallassee, Ala., lives in Huntington Beach, Calif. Quarterback-safety East Tennessee State 1956-58. No pro playing experience. College coach: Tulane 1963-65, West Virginia 1966, 1970-71, Houston 1967-69, Wake Forest 1972, Mississippi State 1973, Washington State 1976, Oregon 1977-78, UCLA 1980, Illinois 1987. Pro coach: Jacksonville, Express (WFL) 1974-75, Tampa Bay Buccaneers 1981-86, Green Bay Packers 1988-91, joined Rams in 1992.

Ted Tollner, quarterbacks; born May 29, 1940, San Francisco, Calif., lives in Anaheim, Calif. Quarterback Cal Poly-SLO 1959-61. No pro playing experience. College coach: College of San Mateo 1971-72 (head coach), San Diego State 1973-80, Brigham Young 1981, Southern California 1982-86 (head coach 1983-86). Pro coach: Buffalo Bills 1987-88, San Diego Chargers 1989-91, joined Rams in 1992.

Joe Vitt, assistant head coach-safeties; born August 23, 1954, Camden, N.J., lives in Mission Viejo, Calif. Linebacker Towson State 1973-75. No pro playing experience. Pro coach: Baltimore Colts 1979-81, Seattle Seahawks 1982-91, joined Rams in 1992.

Ernie Zampese, offensive coordinator; born March 12, 1936, Santa Barbara, Calif., lives in El Toro, Calif. Halfback Southern California 1956-58. No pro playing experience. College coach: Hancock, Calif., J.C. 1962-65, Cal Poly-SLO 1966, San Diego State 1967-75. Pro coach: San Diego Chargers 1976, 1979-86, New York Jets 1977-78 (scout), joined Rams in 1987.

Los Angeles Rams 1992 First-Year Roster

Name	Pos.	Ht.	Wt.	Birth-date	College	Hometown	How Acq.
Ashmore, Darryl	T	6-7	300	11/1/69	Northwestern	Franklin, Tenn.	D7
Boutte, Marc	DT-DE	6-4	298	7/26/69	Louisiana State	Lake Charles, La.	D3a
Buckley, Eric	S	5-11	212	6/4/69	Central Florida	Merritt Island, Fla.	FA
Campbell, Joe	RB	5-9	180	1/14/70	Middle Tenn. State	Nashville, Tenn.	D6
Carr, Derrick (1)	T	6-6	270	3/14/67	Humboldt State	Detroit, Mich.	FA-'91
Chavis, Jessie	CB-S	6-0	195	10/13/69	Norfolk State	Richmond, Va.	FA
Crooms, Chris	S	6-0	211	2/4/69	Texas A&M	Baytown, Tex.	D5
Fisher, John	G	6-4	282	9/4/69	Tennessee	Milan, Tenn.	FA
Fort, Neal (1)	T	6-5	279	4/12/68	Brigham Young	El Centro, Calif.	D6-'91
Franks, Charles	CB	5-10	188	1/11/70	Oklahoma	Oklahoma City, Okla.	FA
Gilbert, Sean	DT-DE	6-4	315	4/10/70	Pittsburgh	Aliquippa, Pa.	D1
Hammond, Vance	DT	6-6	295	12/4/67	Clemson	Spartanburg, S.C.	FA
Harper, Shawn	T	6-3	292	7/9/68	Indiana	Columbus, Ohio	D4
Harris, Kelvin	C	6-2	272	5/17/69	Miami	Ft. Myers, Fla.	D12
Hartley, Frank	TE	6-3	275	12/15/67	Illinois	Chicago, Ill.	FA
Hornco, Thomas	LB	6-0	245	1/8/70	Northwestern	Highland, Ind.	FA
Israel, Steve	CB	5-10	186	3/16/69	Pittsburgh	Lawnside, N.J.	D2
Johnson, Hendricks	WR	6-2	185	7/31/68	Northern Arizona	Indianapolis, Ind.	FA
Jones, Ricky	QB	6-0	185	2/12/70	Alabama State	Jackson, Miss.	D8
Kinchen, Todd	WR	5-11	187	1/7/69	Louisiana State	Baton Rouge, La.	D3b
Lester, Tim	RB	5-9	215	6/15/68	Eastern Kentucky	Miami, Fla.	D10
McKinney, Darian	TE	6-6	240	9/11/69	Central Michigan	Lansing, Mich.	FA
Nicholas, Everett	S	6-1	190	12/24/68	Miss. Valley State	Houston, Tex.	FA
Pinckney, Jonathan	WR	6-2	190	5/6/69	Stanford	Bethlehem, Pa.	FA
Rubley, T.J.	QB	6-3	205	11/29/68	Tulsa	Davenport, Iowa	D9
Schneider, Randy	T	6-6	290	4/30/69	Indiana	Mishawaka, Ind.	FA
Sims, John	DE	6-4	275	10/14/67	Miss. Valley State	Columbia, Miss.	FA
Thomas, Brian	WR	6-3	195	3/14/70	Southern	New Orleans, La.	D11b
Thompson, Ernie (1)	RB	5-11	230	10/25/69	Indiana	Terre Haute, Ind.	D12b-'91
Townsend, Brian	LB	6-3	242	11/7/68	Michigan	Cincinnati, Ohio	D11a
Veatch, Matt	QB	6-3	216	6/7/69	San Jose State	Manhattan, Kan.	FA

The term NFL Rookie is defined as a player who is in his first season of professional football and has not been on the roster of another professional football team for any regular-season or postseason games. A Rookie is designated by an "R" on NFL rosters. Players who have been active in another professional football league or players who have NFL experience, including either preseason training camp or being on an active roster for fewer than three regular-season or postseason games, are termed NFL First-Year Players. An NFL First-Year Player is designated by a "1" on NFL rosters. Thereafter, a player on an NFL active roster for at least three regular-season or postseason games is credited with an additional year of NFL playing experience.

NOTES

MINNESOTA VIKINGS

National Football Conference Central Division

Team Colors: Purple, Gold, and White

9520 Viking Drive
Eden Prairie, Minnesota 55344
Telephone: (612) 828-6500

Club Officers
Chairman of the Board: John C. Skoglund
Vice Chairmen: Jaye F. Dyer, Philip S. Maas
Directors: N. Bud Grossman, Roger L. Headrick,
  Elizabeth MacMillan, Carol S. Sperry,
  Wheelock Whitney

Club Officials
President, Chief Executive Officer:
  Roger L. Headrick
Vice President, Administration/Team Operations:
  Jeff Diamond
Vice President, Finance/Commercial Operations:
  Jim Miller
Assistant to the President, Football: Bob Hollway
Director of Finance: Harley Peterson
Director of Research and Dev.: Mike Eayrs
Director of Marketing: Kernal Buhler
Community Relations Coordinator: Mary Bednarz
Director of Public Relations: Merrill Swanson
Director of Team Operations: Dan Endy
Ticket Manager: Harry Randolph
Asst. G.M., Player Personnel: Jerry Reichow
Director of Player Personnel: Frank Gilliam
Director of Pro Personnel: Paul Wiggin
Player Personnel Coordinator: Scott Studwell
Equipment Manager: Dennis Ryan
Trainer: Fred Zamberletti
Video Director: Larry Kohout

Stadium: Hubert H. Humphrey Metrodome •
  Capacity: 63,000
    500 11th Avenue South
    Minneapolis, Minnesota 55415

Playing Surface: AstroTurf

Training Camp: Mankato State University
    Mankato, Minnesota 56001

1992 Schedule

Preseason
Aug. 8	**Buffalo**	7:00
Aug. 15	**Kansas City**	7:00
Aug. 24	at Cleveland	6:00
Aug. 29	at Washington	8:00

Regular Season
Sept. 6	at Green Bay	12:00
Sept. 13	at Detroit	1:00
Sept. 20	**Tampa Bay**	12:00
Sept. 27	at Cincinnati	1:00
Oct. 4	**Chicago**	12:00
Oct. 11	**Open Date**	
Oct. 15	**Detroit** (Thursday)	6:30
Oct. 25	**Washington**	12:00
Nov. 2	at Chicago (Monday)	8:00
Nov. 8	at Tampa Bay	1:00
Nov. 15	**Houston**	12:00
Nov. 22	**Cleveland**	12:00
Nov. 29	at Los Angeles Rams	1:00
Dec. 6	at Philadelphia	1:00
Dec. 13	**San Francisco**	12:00
Dec. 20	at Pittsburgh	1:00
Dec. 27	**Green Bay**	12:00

Vikings Coaching History
(255-218-9)

1961-66	Norm Van Brocklin	29-51-4
1967-83	Bud Grant	161-99-5
1984	Les Steckel	3-13-0
1985	Bud Grant	7-9-0
1986-91	Jerry Burns	55-46-0

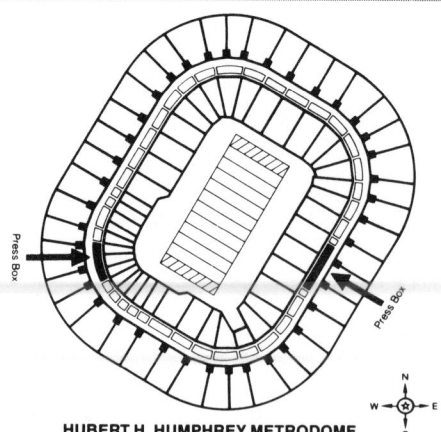

HUBERT H. HUMPHREY METRODOME

Record Holders
Individual Records—Career

Category	Name	Performance
Rushing (Yds.)	Chuck Foreman, 1973-79	5,879
Passing (Yds.)	Fran Tarkenton, 1961-66, 1972-78	33,098
Passing (TDs)	Fran Tarkenton, 1961-66, 1972-78	239
Receiving (No.)	Steve Jordan 1982-1991	411
Receiving (Yds.)	Sammy White, 1976-1985	5,925
Interceptions	Paul Krause, 1968-1979	53
Punting (Avg.)	Bobby Walden, 1964-67	42.9
Punt Return (Avg.)	Tommy Mason, 1961-66	10.4
Kickoff Return (Avg.)	Bob Reed, 1962-63	27.1
Field Goals	Fred Cox, 1963-1977	282
Touchdowns (Tot.)	Bill Brown, 1962-1974	76
Points	Fred Cox, 1963-1977	1,365

Individual Records—Single Season

Category	Name	Performance
Rushing (Yds.)	Chuck Foreman, 1976	1,155
Passing (Yds.)	Tommy Kramer, 1981	3,912
Passing (TDs)	Tommy Kramer, 1981	26
Receiving (No.)	Rickey Young, 1978	88
Receiving (Yds.)	Anthony Carter, 1988	1,225
Interceptions	Paul Krause, 1975	10
Punting (Avg.)	Bobby Walden, 1964	46.4
Punt Return (Avg.)	Leo Lewis, 1987	12.5
Kickoff Return (Avg.)	John Gilliam, 1972	26.3
Field Goals	Rich Karlis, 1989	31
Touchdowns (Tot.)	Chuck Foreman, 1975	22
Points	Chuck Foreman, 1975	132

Individual Records—Single Game

Category	Name	Performance
Rushing (Yds.)	Chuck Foreman, 10-24-76	200
Passing (Yds.)	Tommy Kramer, 11-2-86	490
Passing (TDs)	Joe Kapp, 9-28-69	*7
Receiving (No.)	Rickey Young, 12-16-79	15
Receiving (Yds.)	Sammy White, 11-7-76	210
Interceptions	Many times	3
	Last time by Willie Teal, 11-28-82	
Field Goals	Rich Karlis, 11-5-89	*7
Touchdowns (Tot.)	Chuck Foreman, 12-20-75	4
	Ahmad Rashad, 9-2-79	4
Points	Chuck Foreman, 12-20-75	24
	Ahmad Rashad, 9-2-79	24

*NFL Record

1991 Team Record

Preseason (2-2)

Date	Result		Opponents
8/3	L	3-18	at New Orleans
8/10	W	34-24	Pittsburgh
8/17	L	24-27	at Cincinnati (OT)
8/23	W	31- 7	Cleveland

Regular Season (8-8)

Date	Result		Opponents	Att.
9/1	L	6-10	at Chicago	64,112
9/8	W	20-19	at Atlanta	50,936
9/15	W	17-14	San Francisco	59,148
9/22	L	0-26	at New Orleans	68,591
9/29	L	6-13	Denver	55,031
10/6	L	20-24	at Detroit	63,423
10/13	W	34- 7	Phoenix	51,209
10/20	L	23-26	at New Eng. (OT)	45,367
10/27	W	28- 0	at Phoenix	45,447
11/3	W	28-13	Tampa Bay	35,737
11/11	L	17-34	Chicago	59,001
11/17	W	35-21	at Green Bay	57,614
11/24	L	14-34	Detroit	51,644
12/8	W	26-24	at Tampa Bay	41,091
12/15	W	20-14	L.A. Rams	61,518
12/21	L	7-27	Green Bay	52,860

(OT) Overtime

Score by Periods

Vikings	51	91	67	92	0	—	301
Opponents	51	77	51	124	3	—	306

Attendance

Home 426,148   Away 436,581   Total 862,729
Single-game home record, 62,851 (10-19-86)
Single-season home record, 464,902 (1983)

1991 Team Statistics

	Vikings	Opp.
Total First Downs	300	301
Rushing	125	106
Passing	158	172
Penalty	17	23
Third Down: Made/Att.	78/197	97/215
Third Down: Pct.	39.6	45.1
Fourth Down: Made/Att.	6/15	6/12
Fourth Down: Pct.	40.0	50.0
Total Net Yards	5084	5016
Avg. Per Game	317.8	313.5
Total Plays	969	988
Avg. Per Play	5.2	5.1
Net Yards Rushing	2201	1837
Avg. Per Game	137.6	114.8
Total Rushes	464	456
Net Yards Passing	2883	3179
Avg. Per Game	180.2	198.7
Sacked/Yards Lost	28/133	33/217
Gross Yards	3016	3396
Att./Completions	477/284	499/286
Completion Pct.	59.5	57.3
Had Intercepted	16	17
Punts/Avg.	68/45.5	67/42.7
Net Punting Avg.	36.3	36.7
Penalties/Yards Lost	88/675	92/709
Fumbles/Ball Lost	21/10	24/11
Touchdowns	36	35
Rushing	18	17
Passing	16	16
Returns	2	2
Avg. Time of Possession	29:35	30:25

1991 Individual Statistics

Scoring

	TD R	TD P	TD Rt	PAT	FG	Saf	TP
Reveiz	0	0	0	34/35	17/24	0	85
Walker	10	0	0	0/0	0/0	0	60
A. Carter	1	5	0	0/0	0/0	0	36
C. Carter	0	5	0	0/0	0/0	0	30
Allen	2	1	0	0/0	0/0	0	18
Gannon	2	0	0	0/0	0/0	0	12
Jordan	0	2	0	0/0	0/0	0	12
M. Jones	0	2	0	0/0	0/0	0	12
Nelson	2	0	0	0/0	0/0	0	12
Anderson	1	0	0	0/0	0/0	0	6
H. Jones	0	1	0	0/0	0/0	0	6
Merriweather	0	0	1	0/0	0/0	0	6
Rutland	0	0	1	0/0	0/0	0	6
Vikings	18	16	2	34/36	17/24	0	301
Opponents	17	16	2	34/35	20/29	1	306

Passing

	Att.	Comp.	Yds.	Pct.	TD	Int.	Tkld.	Rate
Gannon	354	211	2166	59.6	12	6	19/91	81.5
Wilson	122	72	825	59.0	3	10	8/42	53.5
Nelson	1	1	25	100.0	1	0	0/0	158.3
H. Jones	0	0	0	—	0	0	1/0	0.0
Vikings	477	284	3016	59.5	16	16	28/133	75.2
Opponents	499	286	3396	57.3	16	17	33/217	74.7

Rushing

	Att.	Yds.	Avg.	LG	TD
Walker	198	825	4.2	71t	10
Allen	120	563	4.7	55t	2
Gannon	43	236	5.5	42	2
Nelson	28	210	7.5	29	2
Anderson	26	118	4.5	19	1
A. Carter	13	117	9.0	32	1
Fenney	23	99	4.3	17	0
Wilson	13	33	2.5	15	0
Vikings	464	2201	4.7	71t	18
Opponents	456	1837	4.0	54	17

Receiving

	No.	Yds.	Avg.	LG	TD
C. Carter	72	962	13.4	50	5
Jordan	57	638	11.2	25	2
A. Carter	51	553	10.8	46t	5
Walker	33	204	6.2	19	0
H. Jones	32	384	12.0	43	1
Nelson	19	142	7.5	13	0
Allen	6	49	8.2	21	1
Lewis	4	36	9.0	11	0
Novoselsky	4	27	6.8	8	0
Fenney	2	11	5.5	8	0
M. Jones	2	8	4.0	5t	2
Anderson	1	2	2.0	2	0
Gannon	1	0	0.0	0	0
Vikings	284	3016	10.6	50	16
Opponents	286	3396	11.9	75t	16

Interceptions

	No.	Yds.	Avg.	LG	TD
Browner	5	97	19.4	45	0
McMillian	4	5	1.3	3	0
Rutland	3	104	34.7	97t	1
Wright	2	3	1.5	3	0
Merriweather	1	22	22.0	22t	1
Berry	1	11	11.0	11	0
Lee	1	0	0.0	0	0
Vikings	17	242	14.2	97t	2
Opponents	16	203	12.7	35	1

Punting

	No.	Yds.	Avg.	In 20	LG
Newsome	68	3095	45.5	17	65
Vikings	68	3095	45.5	17	65
Opponents	67	2861	42.7	13	62

Punt Returns

	No.	FC	Yds.	Avg.	LG	TD
Lewis	30	15	225	7.5	44	0
Vikings	30	15	225	7.5	44	0
Opponents	42	5	426	10.1	33	0

Kickoff Returns

	No.	Yds.	Avg.	LG	TD
Nelson	31	682	22.0	50	0
Eilers	5	99	19.8	26	0
Walker	5	83	16.6	21	0
Allen	1	14	14.0	14	0
Anderson	1	7	7.0	7	0
Baldwin	1	14	14.0	14	0
Vikings	44	899	20.4	50	0
Opponents	43	851	19.8	71	0

Sacks

	No.
Randle	9.5
Thomas	8.0
Doleman	7.0
Noga	3.0
Strauthers	2.5
Berry	1.0
Mayes	1.0
Merriweather	1.0
Vikings	33.0
Opponents	28.0

1992 Draft Choices

Round	Name	Pos.	College
2.	Robert Harris	DE	Southern
4.	Roy Barker	DT	North Carolina
5.	Ed McDaniel	LB	Clemson
6.	Mike Gaddis	RB	Oklahoma
7.	David Wilson	DB	California
8.	Luke Fisher	TE	East Carolina
9.	Brad Johnson	QB	Florida State
	Ronnie West	WR	Pittsburg, Kan.
10.	Brad Culpepper	DT	Florida
11.	Charles Evans	RB	Clark, Ga.
12.	Joe Randolph	WR	Elon

Minnesota Vikings 1992 Veteran Roster

No.	Name	Pos.	Ht.	Wt.	Birth-date	NFL Exp.	College	Hometown	How Acq.	'91 Games/ Starts
21	Allen, Terry	RB	5-10	189	2/21/68	2	Clemson	Commerce, Ga.	D9-'80	15/6
46	†Anderson, Alfred	RB	6-1	219	8/4/61	9	Baylor	Waco, Tex.	D3-'84	16/5
50	†Berry, Ray	LB	6-2	227	10/28/63	6	Baylor	Abilene, Tex.	D2-'87	16/16
47	Browner, Joey	S	6-2	231	5/15/60	10	Southern California	Atlanta, Ga.	D1-'83	14/14
53	Caesar, Ivan	LB	6-1	226	1/7/67	2	Boston College	Boynton Beach, Fla.	D11-'91	14/2
81	Carter, Anthony	WR	5-11	176	9/17/60	8	Michigan	Riviera Beach, Fla.	T(Mia)-'85	15/15
80	†Carter, Cris	WR	6-3	198	11/25/65	6	Ohio State	Middletown, Ohio	W(Phil)-'90	16/16
33	Craig, Roger	RB	6-0	225	7/10/60	10	Nebraska	Davenport, Iowa	PB(Raid)-'92#	15/13*
55	Del Rio, Jack	LB	6-4	240	4/4/63	8	Southern California	Castro Valley, Pa.	PB(Dall)-'92#	16/16*
56	Doleman, Chris	DE	6-5	266	10/16/61	8	Pittsburgh	York, Pa.	D1-'86	16/16
59	Dusbabek, Mark	LB	6-3	224	6/23/64	3	Minnesota	Fairbault, Minn.	FA-'89	1/1
31	Fenney, Rick	RB	6-1	233	12/7/64	6	Washington	Everett, Wash.	D8-'87	11/0
78	Freeman, Lorenzo	DE-DT	6-5	319	5/23/64	6	Pittsburgh	East Camden, N.J.	PB(NYG)-'92#	16/4*
16	†Gannon, Rich	QB	6-3	203	12/20/65	6	Delaware	Philadelphia, Pa.	T(NE)-'87	15/11
25	Glenn, Vencie	S	6-0	190	10/26/64	7	Indiana State	Silver Spring, Md.	PB(NO)-'92#	16/1*
74	†Habib, Brian	T	6-7	292	12/2/64	4	Washington	Ellensburg, Wash.	D10-'88	16/8
76	Irwin, Tim	T	6-7	301	12/13/58	12	Tennessee	Knoxville, Tenn.	D3-'81	16/16
51	Jenkins, Carlos	LB	6-3	219	7/12/68	2	Michigan State	Lantana, Fla.	D3a-'91	3/0
84	Jones, Hassan	WR	6-0	196	7/2/64	7	Florida State	Clearwater, Fla.	D5-'86	16/7
82	Jones, Mike	TE	6-3	256	11/10/66	3	Texas A&M	Bridgeport, Conn.	D3-'90	16/0
83	Jordan, Steve	TE	6-3	238	1/10/61	11	Brown	Phoenix, Ariz.	D7-'82	16/16
69	†Kalis, Todd	G	6-5	285	5/10/65	5	Arizona State	Phoenix, Ariz.	D1-'88	16/8
39	Lee, Carl	CB	5-11	182	4/6/61	10	Marshall	South Charleston, Va.	D7-'83	14/14
63	Lowdermilk, Kirk	C	6-3	270	4/10/63	8	Ohio State	Canton, Ohio	D3a-'85	16/16
91	Manusky, Greg	LB	6-1	236	8/12/66	5	Colgate	Wilkes-Barre, Pa.	PB(Wash)-'90#	16/0
23	†Mayes, Mike	CB	5-10	179	8/17/66	3	Louisiana State	DeRidder, La.	FA-'91	9/0
96	McClendon, Skip	DE	6-7	287	4/9/64	6	Arizona State	Detroit, Mich.	PB(SD)-'91#	9/0
64	McDaniel, Randall	G	6-3	271	12/19/64	5	Arizona State	Avondale, Ariz.	D1-'88	16/16
26	McMillian, Audray	CB	6-0	190	8/13/62	7	Houston	Carthage, Tex.	PB(Hou)-'89#	16/7
57	Merriweather, Mike	LB	6-2	226	11/26/60	10	Pacific	Vallejo, Calif.	T(Pitt)-'89	16/16
68	Morris, Mike	C	6-5	268	2/22/61	5	Northeast Missouri State	Centerville, Iowa	FA-'91	16/0
18	†Newsome, Harry	P	6-0	189	1/25/63	8	Wake Forest	Cheraw, S.C.	PB(Pitt)-'90#	16/0
99	Noga, Al	DE	6-1	264	9/16/65	5	Hawaii	Honolulu, Hawaii	D3-'88	16/8
85	Novoselsky, Brent	TE	6-2	236	1/8/66	5	Pennsylvania	Niles, Ill.	FA-'89	16/0
42	Parker, Anthony	CB	5-10	180	2/11/66	2	Arizona State	Tempe, Ariz.	PB(KC)-'92#	2/0*
93	Randle, John	DT	6-1	264	12/12/67	3	Texas A&I	Hearne, Tex.	FA-'90	16/8
7	Reveiz, Fuad	K	5-11	225	2/24/63	7	Tennessee	Miami, Fla.	FA-'90	16/0
48	Rutland, Reggie	CB	6-1	191	6/20/64	6	Georgia Tech	East Point, Ga.	D4-'87	13/12
12	†Salisbury, Sean	QB	6-5	213	3/9/63	4	Southern California	Escondido, Calif.	FA-'90	0*
60	Schreiber, Adam	C-G	6-4	280	2/20/62	9	Texas	Huntsville, Ala.	PB(NYJ)-'90#	15/0
38	Scott, Todd	CB	5-10	190	1/23/68	2	Southwestern Louisiana	Galveston, Tex.	D6-'91	16/1
17	Smith, Kendal	WR	5-10	189	11/23/65	3	Utah State	Mountain View, Calif.	FA-'92	0*
67	Teeter, Mike	DT	6-2	269	10/4/67	2	Michigan	Fruitport, Mich.	FA-'91	1/0
97	Thomas, Henry	DT	6-2	269	1/12/65	6	Louisiana State	Houston, Tex.	D3-'87	16/15
87	Tice, Mike	TE	6-7	247	2/2/59	12	Michigan	Central Islip, N.Y.	PB(Sea)-'92#	16/15*
41	Wilcots, Solomon	S	5-11	200	10/3/64	6	Colorado	Compton, Calif.	PB(Cin)-'91#	16/1
11	Wilson, Wade	QB	6-3	205	2/1/59	12	East Texas State	Greenville, Tex.	D8-'81	5/5
22	Wright, Felix	S	6-2	197	6/22/59	8	Drake	Carthage, Mo.	PB(Clev)-'91#	16/16
65	Zimmerman, Gary	T	6-6	286	12/13/61	7	Oregon	Walnut, Calif.	T(NYG)-'86	16/16

* Craig played 15 games with L.A. Raiders in '91; Del Rio played 16 games with Dallas; Freeman played 16 games with N.Y. Giants; Glenn played 16 games with New Orleans; McClendon played 9 games with San Diego; Parker played 2 games with Kansas City; Salisbury last active with Minnesota in '90; Smith last active with Cincinnati in '90; Tice played 16 games with Seattle.

† Option playout; subject to developments.

Traded—Defensive tackle Keith Millard to Seattle, linebacker Jimmy Williams to Tampa Bay.

Retired—Chris Foote, nine-year center, 0 games in '91; Leo Lewis, 11-year wide receiver-kick returner, 16 games in '91; Craig Wolfley, 12-year guard, 16 games in '91.

Plan B unconditional free agent.

Players lost through Plan B (1): S Pat Eilers (Phx; 16 games in '91).

Also played with Vikings in '91—RB Randy Baldwin (4 games), DT Ken Clarke (16), WR Terry Obee (1), WR Jake Reed (1), LB Mac Stephens (3), DE Thomas Strauthers (15), RB Herschel Walker (15).

COACHING STAFF

Head Coach,
Dennis Green

Pro Career: Named the fifth head coach in Vikings history on January 10, 1992. Coached special teams and receivers in 1979 for San Francisco 49ers. Returned to San Francisco from 1986-88 as receivers coach. Credited with the development of two of the game's premier wide receivers—Jerry Rice and John Taylor. Coached in Super Bowl XXIII. Played one season for British Columbia Lions (CFL).

Background: Running back at Iowa 1968-70. Began coaching career at Iowa as a graduate assistant in 1972. Moved to Dayton in 1973 as running backs and receivers coach before returning to Iowa from 1974-76 to coach receivers and quarterbacks. Running backs coach at Stanford from 1977-78. Returned to Stanford in 1980 as offensive coordinator. Head coach at Northwestern from 1981-85. Green earned Big Ten coach-of-the-year honors in 1982. In 1989, Green was named head coach at Stanford where he was 16-16 in three seasons.

Personal: Born February 17, 1949, in Harrisburg, Pa. Graduated from Iowa with bachelor of science degree in recreation. Dennis, and his wife, Margie, live in Eden Prairie, Minn., and have two children—Patti and Jeremy.

Assistant Coaches

Tom Batta, special teams; born October 6, 1942, Youngstown, Ohio, lives in Bloomington, Minn. Offensive-defensive lineman Kent State 1961-63. No pro playing experience. College coach: Akron 1973, Colorado 1974-78, Kansas 1979-82, North Carolina State 1983. Pro coach: Joined Vikings in 1984.

Brian Billick, tight ends; born February 28, 1954, Redlands, Calif., lives in Eden Prairie, Minn. Tight end Brigham Young 1974-76. Pro tight end Dallas Cowboys 1977. College coach: Redlands 1977, Brigham Young 1978, San Diego State 1981-85, Utah State 1986-88, Stanford 1989-91. Pro coach: Joined Vikings in 1992.

Jack Burns, offensive coordinator; born January 3, 1949, Tampa, Fla., lives in Eden Prairie, Minn. Safety Florida 1967-71. No pro playing experience. College coach: Florida 1971-73, 1975, Louisville 1974, 1985-88, Texas 1976, Vanderbilt 1977-78, Auburn 1979-80. Pro coach: Tampa Bay Bandits (USFL) 1981-83 (scout), Washington Redskins 1989-91, joined Vikings in 1992.

Tony Dungy, defensive coordinator; born October 6, 1955, Jackson, Mich., lives in Eden Prairie, Minn. Quarterback Minnesota 1973-76. Pro safety Pittsburgh Steelers 1977-78, San Francisco 49ers 1979. College coach: Minnesota 1980. Pro coach: Pittsburgh Steelers 1981-88, Kansas City Chiefs 1989-91, joined Vikings in 1992.

Monte Kiffin, inside linebackers; born February 29, 1940, Lexington, Ky., lives in Bloomington, Minn. Offensive-defensive tackle Nebraska 1958-61. Pro defensive end Winnipeg Blue Bombers (CFL) 1965-66. College coach: Nebraska 1966-76, Arkansas 1977-79, North Carolina State 1980-82 (head coach). Pro coach: Green Bay Packers 1983, Buffalo Bills 1984-85, Minnesota Vikings 1985-89, New York Jets 1990, rejoined Vikings in 1991.

John Michels, offensive line; born February 15, 1931, Philadelphia, Pa., lives in Bloomington, Minn. Guard Tennessee 1949-52. Pro guard Philadelphia Eagles 1953, 1956, Winnipeg Blue Bombers (CFL) 1957. College coach: Texas A&M 1958. Pro coach: Winnipeg Blue Bombers (CFL) 1959-66, joined Vikings in 1967.

Tom Moore, wide receivers; born November 7, 1938, Owatanna, Minn., lives in Bloomington, Minn. Quarterback Iowa 1957-60. No pro playing experience. College coach: Iowa 1961-62, Dayton 1965-68, Wake Forest 1969, Georgia Tech 1970-71, Minnesota 1972-73, 1975-76. Pro coach: New York Stars (WFL) 1974, Pittsburgh Steelers 1977-89, joined Vikings in 1990.

Minnesota Vikings 1992 First-Year Roster

Name	Pos.	Ht.	Wt.	Birth-date	College	Hometown	How Acq.
Adams, Scott (1)	G	6-5	281	9/28/66	Georgia	Lake City, Fla.	FA
Banks, Curtis	CB	5-11	192	9/6/68	Arkansas	Dallas, Tex.	FA
Barker, Roy	DT	6-4	292	2/14/69	North Carolina	Central Islip, N.Y.	D4
Culpepper, Brad	DT	6-1	267	5/8/68	Florida	Tallahassee, Fla.	D10
Dahl, Brian	LB	6-4	241	1/10/70	Moorhead State	Kennedy, Minn.	FA
Evans, Chuck	RB	6-1	217	4/16/67	Clark, Ga.	Augusta, Ga.	D11
Fisher, Luke	TE	6-2	235	11/21/68	East Carolina	Mt. Holly, N.J.	D8
Gaddis, Mike	RB	6-0	217	3/4/69	Oklahoma	Midwest City, Okla.	D6
Griffith, Brent (1)	T	6-6	310	4/28/69	Minnesota-Duluth	Little Falls, Minn.	FA
Hall, Victor	TE	6-2	244	12/4/68	Auburn	Anniston, Ala.	FA
Harris, Robert	DT	6-4	285	6/13/69	Southern	Riviera Beach, Fla.	D2
Hughes, Darren	WR	6-1	175	6/3/67	Carson-Newman	Harbor City, Tenn.	D12
Johnson, Brad	QB	6-4	218	9/13/68	Florida State	Black Mountain, N.C.	D9a
Lyles, Del	LB	6-1	215	9/7/70	Utah State	Richmond, Calif.	FA
McDaniel, Ed	LB	5-11	232	2/2/69	Clemson	Leesville, S.C.	D5
Miller, Eric	DT	6-3	265	5/13/69	Miami	Palm Beach Garden, Fla.	FA
Randolph, Joe	WR	5-7	155	4/30/71	Elon	Washington, N.Y.	D12
Simmons, Randy	RB	6-0	225	3/1/69	Texas A&M	McKinney, Tex.	FA
Sutter, Ed	LB	6-3	235	10/3/69	Northwestern	Peoria, Ill.	FA
Welborne, Tripp (1)	S	6-0	205	11/20/68	Michigan	Reidsville, N.C.	D7b-'91
Wenzel, Eric	T	6-5	278	4/28/69	Northwestern	Cottage Grove, Minn.	FA
West, Ronnie	WR	6-2	215	6/23/68	Pittsburg, Kan.	Wilcox, Ga.	D9b
Wilson, David	S	5-11	201	6/10/70	California	Los Angeles, Calif.	D7
Wise, Brian	S	6-1	225	7/24/69	Iowa	Tinley Park, Ill.	FA

The term NFL Rookie is defined as a player who is in his first season of professional football and has not been on the roster of another professional football team for any regular-season or postseason games. A Rookie is designated by an "R" on NFL rosters. Players who have been active in another professional football league or players who have NFL experience, including either preseason training camp or being on an active roster for fewer than three regular-season or postseason games, are termed NFL First-Year Players. An NFL First-Year Player is designated by a "1" on NFL rosters. Thereafter, a player on an NFL active roster for at least three regular-season or postseason games is credited with an additional year of NFL playing experience.

NOTES

_____

_____

_____

_____

_____

_____

_____

_____

_____

_____

John Teerlinck, defensive line; born April 9, 1951, Rochester, N.Y., lives in Eden Prairie, Minn. Defensive lineman Western Illinois 1970-73. Pro defensive tackle San Diego Chargers 1974-76. College coach: Iowa Lakes J.C. 1977, Eastern Illinois 1978-79, Illinois 1980-82. Pro coach: Chicago Blitz (USFL) 1984, Cleveland Browns 1989-90, Los Angeles Rams 1991, joined Vikings in 1992.

Willie Shaw, defensive backs; born January 11, 1944, San Diego, Calif., lives in Eden Prairie, Minn. Cornerback New Mexico 1966-68. No pro playing experience. College coach: San Diego City College 1970-73, Stanford 1974-76, 1989-91, Long Beach State 1977-78, Oregon 1979, Arizona State 1980-84. Pro coach: Detroit Lions 1985-88, joined Vikings in 1992.

Richard Solomon, outside linebackers; born December 8, 1949, New Orleans, La., lives in Eden Prairie, Minn. Running back-defensive back Iowa 1970-73. No pro playing experience. College coach: Dubuque 1973-75, Southern Illinois 1976, Iowa 1977-78, Syracuse 1979, Illinois 1980-86. Pro coach: New York Giants 1987-91 (scout), joined Vikings in 1992.

Tyrone Willingham, running backs; born December 30, 1953, Jacksonville, N.C., lives in Deephaven, Minn. Quarterback Michigan State 1974-77. No pro playing experience. College coach: Michigan State 1977, 1980-82, Central Michigan 1978-79, North Carolina State 1983-85, Rice 1986-88, Stanford 1989-91. Pro coach: Joined Vikings in 1992.

Steve Wetzel, strength and conditioning; born May 11, 1963, Washington D.C., lives in Eden Prairie, Minn. No college or pro playing experience. College coach: Maryland 1985-89, George Mason 1990. Pro coach: Washington Redskins 1990-91, joined Vikings in 1992.

NEW ORLEANS SAINTS

National Football Conference Western Division

Team Colors: Old Gold, Black, and White

1500 Poydras Street
New Orleans, Louisiana 70112
Telephone: (504) 733-0255

Club Officials

Owner/General Partner: Tom Benson
President/General Manager: Jim Finks
Vice President/Administration: Jim Miller
Business Manager/Controller: Bruce Broussard
Director of Player Personnel: Bill Kuharich
Director of Marketing: Greg Suit
Assistant Director of Marketing: Bill Ferrante
Director of Media Relations: Rusty Kasmiersky
Assistant Director of Media Relations: Neal Gulkis
Director of Travel/Entertainment: Barra Birrcher
Director of Community Relations: Chanel Lagarde
Player Personnel Scouts: Bill Baker, Hamp Cook,
   Hokie Gajan, Tom Marino, Carmen Piccone
Ticket Manager: Sandy King
Trainer: Dean Kleinschmidt
Equipment Manager: Dan Simmons
Video Director: Albert Aucoin

Stadium: Louisiana Superdome •
   Capacity: 69,065
   1500 Poydras Street
   New Orleans, Louisiana 70112

Playing Surface: AstroTurf

Training Camp: University of Wisconsin-La Crosse
   La Crosse, Wisconsin 54601

1992 Schedule

Preseason
Aug. 10	at Chicago	7:00
Aug. 17	**Pittsburgh**	7:00
Aug. 22	**Houston**	11:30
Aug. 27	vs. Miami at Baltimore	8:00

Regular Season
Sept. 6	at Philadelphia	1:00
Sept. 13	**Chicago**	12:00
Sept. 20	at Atlanta	1:00
Sept. 27	**San Francisco**	7:00
Oct. 4	at Detroit	1:00
Oct. 11	**Los Angeles Rams**	6:30
Oct. 18	at Phoenix	1:00
Oct. 25	**Open Date**	
Nov. 1	**Tampa Bay**	12:00
Nov. 8	at New England	1:00
Nov. 15	at San Francisco	1:00
Nov. 23	**Washington** (Monday)	8:00
Nov. 29	**Miami**	12:00
Dec. 3	**Atlanta** (Thursday)	7:00
Dec. 13	at Los Angeles Rams	1:00
Dec. 20	**Buffalo**	12:00
Dec. 26	at N.Y. Jets (Saturday)	12:30

Saints Coaching History

(140-228-5)
1967-70	Tom Fears*	13-34-2
1970-72	J.D. Roberts	7-25-3
1973-75	John North**	11-23-0
1975	Ernie Hefferle	1-7-0
1976-77	Hank Stram	7-21-0
1978-80	Dick Nolan***	15-29-0
1980	Dick Stanfel	1-3-0
1981-85	O.A. (Bum) Phillips****	27-42-0
1985	Wade Phillips	1-3-0
1986-91	Jim Mora	57-41-0

*Released after seven games in 1970
**Released after six games in 1975
***Released after 12 games in 1980
****Resigned after 12 games in 1985

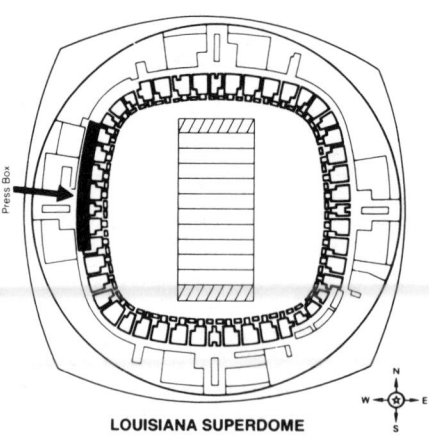

LOUISIANA SUPERDOME

Record Holders
Individual Records—Career
Category	Name	Performance
Rushing (Yds.)	George Rogers, 1981-84	4,267
Passing (Yds.)	Archie Manning, 1971-1982	21,734
Passing (TDs)	Archie Manning, 1971-1982	115
Receiving (No.)	Eric Martin, 1985-1991	398
Receiving (Yds.)	Eric Martin, 1985-1991	5,863
Interceptions	Dave Waymer, 1980-89	37
Punting (Avg.)	Tommy Barnhardt, 1987, 1989-1991	42.3
Punt Return (Avg.)	Mel Gray, 1986-88	13.4
Kickoff Return (Avg.)	Walter Roberts, 1967	26.3
Field Goals	Morten Andersen, 1982-1991	317
Touchdowns (Tot.)	Dalton Hilliard, 1986-1991	43
Points	Morten Andersen, 1982-1991	965

Individual Records—Single Season
Category	Name	Performance
Rushing (Yds.)	George Rogers, 1981	1,674
Passing (Yds.)	Archie Manning, 1980	3,716
Passing (TDs)	Archie Manning, 1980	23
Receiving (No.)	Eric Martin, 1988	85
Receiving (Yds.)	Eric Martin, 1989	1,090
Interceptions	Dave Whitsell, 1967	10
Punting (Avg.)	Brian Hansen, 1984	43.8
Punt Return (Avg.)	Mel Gray, 1987	14.7
Kickoff Return (Avg.)	Don Shy, 1969	27.9
Field Goals	Morten Andersen, 1985	31
Touchdowns (Tot.)	Dalton Hilliard, 1989	18
Points	Morten Andersen, 1987	121

Individual Records—Single Game
Category	Name	Performance
Rushing (Yds.)	George Rogers, 9-4-83	206
Passing (Yds.)	Archie Manning, 12-7-80	377
Passing (TDs)	Billy Kilmer, 11-2-69	6
Receiving (No.)	Tony Galbreath, 9-10-78	14
Receiving (Yds.)	Wes Chandler, 9-2-79	205
Interceptions	Tommy Myers, 9-3-78	3
	Dave Waymer, 10-6-85	3
	Reggie Sutton, 10-18-87	3
	Gene Atkins, 12-22-91	3
Field Goals	Morten Andersen, 12-1-85	5
	Morten Andersen, 11-15-87	5
Touchdowns (Tot.)	Many times	3
	Last time by Rueben Mayes, 9-23-90	
Points	Many times	18
	Last time by Rueben Mayes, 9-23-90	

1991 Team Record
Preseason (2-2)

Date	Result		Opponents
8/3	W	18- 3	Minnesota
8/10	W	31-20	Green Bay
8/17	L	28-34	at Indianapolis
8/24	L	24-28	at Miami

Regular Season (11-5)

Date	Result		Opponents	Att.
9/1	W	27-24	Seattle	68,492
9/8	W	17-10	at Kansas City	74,816
9/15	W	24- 7	L.A. Rams	68,583
9/22	W	26- 0	Minnesota	68,591
9/29	W	27- 6	at Atlanta	56,556
10/13	W	13- 6	at Philadelphia	64,224
10/20	W	23- 7	Tampa Bay	68,591
10/27	L	17-20	Chicago	68,591
11/3	W	24-17	at L.A. Rams	58,713
11/10	W	10- 3	San Francisco	68,591
11/17	L	21-24	at San Diego	48,420
11/24	W	20-23	Atlanta (OT)	68,591
12/1	L	24-38	at San Francisco	62,092
12/8	L	14-23	at Dallas	64,530
12/16	W	27- 0	L.A. Raiders	68,625
12/22	W	27- 3	at Phoenix	30,928

(OT) Overtime

Postseason (0-1)

Date	Result		Opponent	Att.
12/28	L	20-27	Atlanta	68,299

Score by Periods

Saints	61	120	75	85	0	—	341
Opponents	23	59	54	72	3	—	211

Attendance
Home 548,655   Away 460,279   Total 1,018,934
Single-game home record, 70,940 (11-4-79)
Single-season home record, 548,655 (1991)

1991 Team Statistics

	Saints	Opp.
Total First Downs	267	214
Rushing	93	63
Passing	157	139
Penalty	17	12
Third Down: Made/Att.	86/228	49/188
Third Down: Pct.	37.7	26.1
Fourth Down: Made/Att.	5/10	4/13
Fourth Down: Pct.	50.0	30.8
Total Net Yards	4968	3933
Avg. Per Game	310.5	245.8
Total Plays	1008	875
Avg. Per Play	4.9	4.5
Net Yards Rushing	1709	1213
Avg. Per Game	106.8	75.8
Total Rushes	483	334
Net Yards Passing	3259	2720
Avg. Per Game	203.7	170.0
Sacked/Yards Lost	19/160	50/337
Gross Yards	3419	3057
Att./Completions	506/292	491/259
Completion Pct.	57.7	52.7
Had Intercepted	15	29
Punts/Avg.	87/43.0	88/42.3
Net Punting Avg.	35.3	37.1
Penalties/Yards Lost	101/801	95/711
Fumbles/Ball Lost	24/15	34/19
Touchdowns	38	23
Rushing	15	6
Passing	20	12
Returns	3	5
Avg. Time of Possession	33:58	26:02

1991 Individual Statistics

Scoring

	TD R	TD P	TD Rt	PAT	FG	Saf	TP
Andersen	0	0	0	38/38	25/32	0	113
Turner	0	8	0	0/0	0/0	0	48
Fenerty	3	2	0	0/0	0/0	0	30
Heyward	4	1	0	0/0	0/0	0	30
Hilliard	4	1	0	0/0	0/0	0	30
E. Martin	0	4	0	0/0	0/0	0	24
Jordan	2	1	0	0/0	0/0	0	18
Early	0	2	0	0/0	0/0	0	12
McAfee	2	0	0	0/0	0/0	0	12
Carroll	0	1	0	0/0	0/0	0	6
Maxie	0	0	1	0/0	0/0	0	6
Swilling	0	0	1	0/0	0/0	0	6
Warren	0	0	1	0/0	0/0	0	6
Saints	15	20	3	38/38	25/32	0	341
Opponents	6	12	5	22/23	17/21	0	211

Passing

	Att.	Comp.	Yds.	Pct.	TD	Int.	Tkld.	Rate
Hebert	248	149	1676	60.1	9	8	16/134	79.0
Walsh	255	141	1638	55.3	11	6	3/26	79.5
M. Buck	2	1	61	50.0	0	1	0/0	56.3
Heyward	1	1	44	100.0	0	0	0/0	118.8
Saints	506	292	3419	57.7	20	15	19/160	79.2
Opponents	491	259	3057	52.7	12	29	50/337	55.5

Rushing

	Att.	Yds.	Avg.	LG	TD
McAfee	109	494	4.5	34	2
Fenerty	139	477	3.4	54	3
Heyward	76	260	3.4	15	4
Hilliard	79	252	3.2	65t	4
Jordan	47	150	3.2	25	2
Hebert	18	56	3.1	16	0
Early	3	13	4.3	6	0
Morse	3	7	2.3	8	0
Barnhardt	1	0	0.0	0	0
Walsh	8	0	0.0	3	0
Saints	483	1709	3.5	65t	15
Opponents	334	1213	3.6	33	6

Receiving

	No.	Yds.	Avg.	LG	TD
E. Martin	66	803	12.2	30	4
Turner	64	927	14.5	65t	8
Early	32	541	16.9	52	2
Fenerty	26	235	9.0	50t	2
Tice	22	230	10.5	22	0
Hilliard	21	127	6.0	14t	1
Carroll	18	184	10.2	31t	1
Brenner	16	179	11.2	21	0
Jordan	15	92	6.1	19	1
Heyward	4	34	8.5	22t	1
Newman	3	33	11.0	14	0
Scales	3	23	7.7	14	0
McAfee	1	8	8.0	8	0
Wainright	1	3	3.0	3	0
Saints	292	3419	11.7	65t	20
Opponents	259	3057	11.8	80t	12

Interceptions

	No.	Yds.	Avg.	LG	TD
Atkins	5	198	39.6	79	0
V. Buck	5	12	2.4	12	0
Glenn	4	35	8.8	18	0
Jones	3	61	20.3	51	0
Cook	3	54	18.0	22	0
Maxie	3	33	11.0	31t	1
Mills	2	13	6.5	8	0
Swilling	1	39	39.0	39t	1
Johnson	1	19	19.0	19	0
Thompson	1	14	14.0	14	0
Lee, S.F.-N.O.	1	5	5.0	5	0
Petry	1	4	4.0	4	0
Saints	29	482	16.6	79	2
Opponents	15	257	17.1	59t	2

Punting

	No.	Yds.	Avg.	In 20	LG
Barnhardt	86	3743	43.5	20	61
Saints	87	3743	43.0	20	61
Opponents	88	3725	42.3	20	64

Punt Returns

	No.	FC	Yds.	Avg.	LG	TD
V. Buck	31	13	260	8.4	52	0
Fenerty	12	6	55	4.6	13	0
Morse	1	0	2	2.0	2	0
Saints	44	19	317	7.2	52	0
Opponents	50	11	470	9.4	40	0

Kickoff Returns

	No.	Yds.	Avg.	LG	TD
Atkins	20	368	18.4	27	0
Jennings	12	213	17.8	24	0
Early	9	168	18.7	34	0
Morse	3	60	20.0	21	0
Fenerty	2	28	14.0	14	0
Jordan	2	18	9.0	18	0
Glenn	1	10	10.0	10	0
McAfee	1	14	14.0	14	0
Saints	50	879	17.6	34	0
Opponents	35	851	24.3	98t	2

Sacks

	No.
Swilling	17.0
Jackson	11.5
Warren	7.0
W. Martin	3.5
Atkins	3.0
Goff	2.0
Wilks	2.0
Miller	1.0
Mills	1.0
Turnbull	1.0
J. Williams	1.0
Florence, Clev.-N.O.	0.5
Saints	50.0
Opponents	19.0

1992 Draft Choices

Round	Name	Pos.	College
1.	Vaughn Dunbar	RB	Indiana
3.	Tyrone Legette	DB	Nebraska
4.	Gene McGuire	C	Notre Dame
	Sean Lumpkin	DB	Minnesota
5.	Torrance Small	WR	Alcorn State
6.	Kary Vincent	DB	Texas A&M
8.	Robert Stewart	NT	Alabama
9.	Donald Jones	LB	Washington
10.	Marcus Dowdell	WR	Tennessee State
11.	Mike Gisler	G	Houston
12.	Scott Adell	T	North Carolina St.

New Orleans Saints 1992 Veteran Roster

No.	Name	Pos.	Ht.	Wt.	Birth-date	NFL Exp.	College	Hometown	How Acq.	'91 Games/ Starts
7	Andersen, Morten	K	6-2	221	8/19/60	11	Michigan State	Indianapolis, Ind.	D4-'82	16/0
28	†Atkins, Gene	S	6-1	200	11/22/64	6	Florida A&M	Tallahassee, Fla.	D7-'87	16/16
6	Barnhardt, Tommy	P	6-2	207	6/11/63	6	North Carolina	China Grove, N.C.	FA-'89	16/0
85	Brenner, Hoby	TE	6-5	245	6/2/59	12	Southern California	Fullerton, Calif.	D3b-'81	16/16
67	Brock, Stan	T	6-6	278	6/8/58	13	Colorado	Beaverton, Ore.	D1-'80	16/16
16	†Buck, Mike	QB	6-3	227	4/22/67	3	Maine	Sayville, N.Y.	D6a-'90	2/0
26	Buck, Vince	CB	6-0	198	1/12/68	3	Central State, Ohio	Owensboro, Ky.	D2-'90	13/13
80	Carroll, Wesley	WR	6-0	183	9/6/67	2	Miami	Cleveland, Ohio	D2-'91	12/0
41	†Cook, Toi	CB	5-11	188	12/3/64	6	Stanford	Van Nuys, Calif.	D8-'87	14/14
71	Cooper, Richard	T	6-5	290	11/1/64	3	Tennessee	Memphis, Tenn.	FA-'89	15/11
72	Dombrowski, Jim	T	6-5	298	10/19/63	7	Virginia	Williamsville, N.Y.	D1-'86	16/16
89	Early, Quinn	WR	6-0	188	4/13/65	5	Iowa	South Great Neck, N.Y.	PB(SD)-'91#	15/12
22	†Fenerty, Gill	RB	6-0	205	8/24/63	3	Holy Cross	New Orleans, La.	D7-'86	16/12
33	Florence, Anthony	CB	5-11	180	12/11/66	2	Bethune-Cookman	Delray Beach, Fla.	FA-'92	6/0*
91	Goff, Robert	NT	6-3	270	10/2/65	5	Auburn	Bradenton, Fla.	T(TB)-'90	15/0
74	Haverdink, Kevin	T	6-5	285	10/20/65	4	Western Michigan	Hamilton, Mich.	D5-'89	10/5
3	Hebert, Bobby	QB	6-4	215	8/19/60	7	Northwestern Louisiana	Cut Off, La.	FA-'85	9/9
34	Heyward, Craig	RB	5-11	260	9/26/66	5	Pittsburgh	Passaic, N.J.	D1-'88	7/4
61	Hilgenberg, Joel	C-G	6-2	252	7/10/62	9	Iowa	Iowa City, Iowa	D4-'84	16/14
21	†Hilliard, Dalton	RB	5-8	204	1/21/64	7	Louisiana State	Patterson, La.	D2-'86	10/3
57	†Jackson, Rickey	LB	6-2	243	3/20/58	12	Pittsburgh	Pahokee, Fla.	D2-'81	16/16
68	Jetton, Paul	C-G	6-4	288	10/6/64	4	Texas	Houston, Tex.	PB(Cin)-'92#	8/8*
53	Johnson, Vaughan	LB	6-3	235	3/24/62	7	North Carolina State	Morehead City, N.C.	SD1-'84	13/11
27	Jones, Reginald	CB	6-1	202	1/11/69	2	Memphis State	West Memphis, Ark.	D5-'91	13/1
23	Jordan, Buford	RB	6-0	223	6/26/62	7	McNeese State	Iota, La.	FA-'90	14/6
60	†Kennard, Derek	G	6-3	300	9/9/62	7	Nevada-Reno	Stockton, Calif.	T(Phx)-'91	3/3
84	†Martin, Eric	WR	6-1	207	11/8/61	8	Louisiana State	Van Vleck, Tex.	D7-'85	16/13
93	Martin, Wayne	DE	6-5	275	10/26/65	4	Arkansas	Cherry Valley, Ark.	D1-'89	16/16
39	†Maxie, Brett	S	6-2	194	1/13/62	8	Texas Southern	Dallas, Tex.	FA-'85	16/16
25	McAfee, Fred	RB	5-10	193	6/20/68	2	Mississippi College	Philadelphia, Miss.	D6-'91	9/0
69	Miller, Les	DE	6-7	285	3/1/65	6	Fort Hays State	Arkansas City, Kan.	PB(SD)-'91#	16/0
51	Mills, Sam	LB	5-9	225	6/3/59	7	Montclair State	Long Branch, N.J.	FA-'86	16/16
35	†Morse, Bobby	RB	5-10	213	10/3/65	5	Michigan State	Muskegon, Mich.	FA-'89	6/0
86	†Newman, Patrick	WR	5-11	189	9/10/68	2	Utah State	San Diego, Calif.	PB(Minn)-'91#	7/0
45	Petry, Stan	CB	5-11	180	8/14/66	4	Texas Christian	Fort Bend, Tex.	FA-'91	2/0*
20	t-Pinkett, Allen	RB	5-9	196	1/25/64	7	Notre Dame	Sterling, Va.	T(Hou)-'92	16/16*
70	Port, Chris	G	6-5	290	11/2/67	2	Duke	Wanaque, N.J.	D12-'90	14/11
55	Ross, Scott	LB	6-1	235	12/7/68	2	Southern California	El Toro, Calif.	D11-'91	4/0
83	Scales, Greg	TE	6-4	253	5/9/66	4	Wake Forest	Winston-Salem, N.C.	D5a-'88	2/1
99	Smeenge, Joel	DE	6-5	250	4/1/68	2	Western Michigan	Grand Rapids, Mich.	D3-'90	14/0
30	Smith, Cedric	RB	5-10	223	5/27/68	3	Florida	Enterprise, Ala.	FA-'91	6/0
43	Spears, Ernest	S	5-11	192	11/6/67	2	Southern California	Oceanside, Calif.	FA-'92	0*
56	Swilling, Pat	LB	6-3	242	10/25/64	7	Georgia Tech	Toccoa, Ga.	D3b-'86	16/16
29	Taylor, Keith	S	5-11	206	12/21/64	5	Illinois	Pennsauken, N.J.	PB(Ind)-'92#	16/10*
82	Tice, John	TE	6-5	249	6/22/60	10	Maryland	Central Islip, N.Y.	D3a-'83	15/7
65	Trapilo, Steve	G	6-5	281	9/20/64	5	Boston College	Dorchester, Mass.	D4-'87	0*
97	Turnbull, Renaldo	DE	6-4	255	1/5/66	3	West Virginia	St. Thomas, Virgin Islands	D1-'90	16/0
88	Turner, Floyd	WR	5-11	188	5/29/66	4	Northwestern Louisiana	Mansfield, La.	D6-'89	16/4
87	Wainright, Frank	TE	6-3	236	10/10/67	2	Northern Colorado	Arvada, Colo.	D8-'91	14/2
4	Walsh, Steve	QB	6-3	204	12/1/66	4	Miami	St. Paul, Minn.	T(Dall)-'90	8/7
73	Warren, Frank	DE	6-4	290	9/14/59	11	Auburn	Birmingham, Ala.	D3a-'81	16/16
94	Wilks, Jim	NT	6-5	275	3/12/58	12	San Diego State	Pasadena, Calif.	D12-'81	16/15
90	Williams, James	LB	6-0	230	10/10/68	3	Mississippi State	North Natchez, Miss.	D6b-'90	16/4
92	†Winston, DeMond	LB	6-2	239	9/14/68	2	Vanderbilt	Lansing, Mich.	D4-'90	0*

* Florence played 6 games with Cleveland in '91; Jetton played 8 games with Cincinnati; Petry played 2 games with Kansas City; Pinkett played 16 games with Houston; Spears last active with New Orleans in '90; Taylor played 16 games with Indianapolis; Trapilo and Winston missed '91 season due to injury.

† Option playout; subject to developments.

t- Saints traded for Pinkett (Houston).

Plan B unconditional free agent.

Players lost through Plan B (6): LB Brian Forde (Atl; 16 games in '91), S Vencie Glenn (Minn; 16), C Brad Leggett (Sea; 4), CB Milton Mack (TB; 8), S Bennie Thompson (KC; 16), G Larry Williams (NE; 6).

Also played with Saints in '91—WR Gerald Alphin (5 games), RB Stanford Jennings (5), T Mike Keim (1), CB Mark Lee (3), CB Calvin Nicholson (8).

COACHING STAFF

Head Coach, Jim Mora

Pro Career: Begins seventh year as an NFL head coach, after leading Saints to first-ever NFC Western Division title and third playoff appearance in club history in 1991 with an 11-5 mark. Was named 1987 NFL coach of the year after leading Saints to a 12-4 record and the team's first playoff appearance. Came to New Orleans following a three-year career as the winningest coach in USFL history as head coach of the Philadelphia/Baltimore Stars. Directed Stars to championship game in each of his three seasons and won league championship in 1984 and 1985. He won USFL coach of the year honors following the 1984 season. Mora began his pro coaching career in 1978 as defensive line coach of the Seattle Seahawks. In 1982, he became defensive coordinator of the New England Patriots and played a vital role in the Patriots' march to the playoffs that year. No pro playing experience. Career record: 57-41.

Background: Played tight end and defensive end at Occidental College. Assistant coach at Occidental from 1960-63 and head coach from 1964-66. Linebacker coach at Stanford (1967) on a staff that included former Eagles head coach Dick Vermeil. Defensive assistant at Colorado 1968-73. Linebacker coach under Vermeil at UCLA 1974. Defensive coordinator at Washington 1975-77. Received bachelor's degree in physical education from Occidental in 1957. Also holds master's degree in education from Southern California.

Personal: Born May 24, 1935, in Glendale, Calif. Jim and his wife, Connie, live in Metairie, La., and have three sons—Michael, Stephen, and Jim (defensive backs coach for the Saints).

Assistant Coaches

Paul Boudreau, offensive line; born December 30, 1949, Somerville, Mass., lives in Destrehan, La. Guard Boston College 1971-73. No pro playing experience. College coach: Boston College 1974-76, Maine 1977-78, Dartmouth 1979-81, Navy 1983. Pro coach: Edmonton Eskimos (CFL) 1983-86, joined Saints in 1987.

Vic Fangio, outside linebackers; born August 22, 1958, Dunmore, Pa., lives in Destrehan, La. Defensive back East Stroudsburg 1976-78. No pro playing experience. College coach: North Carolina 1983. Pro coach: Philadelphia/Baltimore Stars (USFL) 1984-85, joined Saints in 1986.

Joe Marciano, tight ends-special teams; born February 10, 1954, Scranton, Pa., lives in Kenner, La. Quarterback Temple 1972-75. No pro playing experience. College coach: East Stroudsburg 1977, Rhode Island 1978-79, Villanova 1980, Penn State 1981, Temple 1982. Pro coach: Philadelphia/Baltimore Stars (USFL) 1983-85, joined Saints in 1986.

Jim Mora, defensive backs; born November 19, 1961, Los Angeles, Calif., lives in Metairie, La. Defensive back Washington 1980-83. No pro playing experience. College coach: Washington 1984. Pro coach: San Diego Chargers 1985-91, joined Saints in 1992.

Russell Paternostro, strength and conditioning; born July 21, 1940, New Orleans, La., lives in Covington, La. San Diego State. No college or pro playing experience. Pro coach: Joined Saints in 1981.

John Pease, defensive line; born October 14, 1943, Pittsburgh, Pa., lives in Kenner, La. Wingback Utah 1963-64. No pro playing experience. College coach: Fullerton, Calif., J.C. 1970-73, Long Beach State 1974-76, Utah 1977, Washington 1978-83. Pro coach: Philadelphia/Baltimore Stars (USFL) 1983-85, joined Saints in 1986.

Steve Sidwell, defensive coordinator-inside linebackers; born August 30, 1944, Winfield, Kan., lives in Destrehan, La. Linebacker Colorado 1962-65. No pro playing experience. College coach: Colorado 1966-73, Nevada-Las Vegas 1974-75, Southern Methodist 1976-81. Pro coach: New England Patriots 1982-84, Indianapolis Colts 1985, joined Saints in 1986.

Jim Skipper, running backs; born January 23, 1949, Breaux Bridge, La., lives in Kenner, La. Defensive back Whittier College 1971-72. No pro playing experience. College coach: Cal Poly-Pomona 1974-76, San Jose State 1977-78, Pacific 1979, Oregon 1980-82. Pro coach: Philadelphia/Baltimore Stars (USFL) 1983-85, joined Saints in 1986.

Carl Smith, offensive coordinator-quarterbacks; born April 26, 1948, Wasco, Calif., lives in Kenner, La. Defensive back Cal Poly-SLO 1968-70. No pro playing experience. College coach: Cal Poly-SLO 1971, Colorado 1972-73, Southwestern Louisiana 1974-78, Lamar 1979-81, North Carolina State 1982. Pro coach: Philadelphia/Baltimore Stars (USFL) 1983-85, joined Saints in 1986.

Steve Walters, wide receivers; born June 16, 1948, Jonesboro, Ark., lives in Destrehan, La. Quarterback-defensive back Arkansas 1967-70. No pro playing experience. College coach: Tampa 1973, Northeast Louisiana 1974-75, Morehead State 1976, Tulsa 1977-78, Memphis State 1979, Southern Methodist 1980-81, Alabama 1985. Pro coach: New England Patriots 1982-84, joined Saints in 1986.

New Orleans Saints 1992 First-Year Roster

Name	Pos.	Ht.	Wt.	Birth-date	College	Hometown	How Acq.
Adell, Scott	T	6-4	279	2/25/69	North Carolina State	Fletcher, N.C.	D12
Bolton, Nathaniel (1)	WR	5-11	189	7/1/68	Mississippi College	McLain, Miss.	FA
Dowdell, Marcus	WR	5-10	179	5/22/70	Tennessee State	Birmingham, Ala.	D10
Dunbar, Vaughn	RB	5-10	204	9/4/69	Indiana	Fort Wayne, Ind.	D1
Gisler, Mike	G	6-3	305	8/26/69	Houston	Runge, Tex.	D11
Jones, Donald	LB	6-0	231	3/26/69	Washington	Gladys, Va.	D9
Keim, Mike (1)	T	6-7	285	11/12/65	Brigham Young	Eagar, Ariz.	FA-'91
Legette, Tyrone	CB	5-9	177	2/15/70	Nebraska	Columbia, S.C.	D3
Lumpkin, Sean	S	6-0	206	1/4/70	Minnesota	Golden Valley, Minn.	D4b
McGuire, Gene	C	6-2	284	7/17/70	Notre Dame	Panama City, Fla.	D4a
Small, Torrance	WR	6-3	201	9/6/70	Alcorn State	Tampa, Fla.	D5
Spencer, Jimmy (1)	CB	5-9	180	3/29/69	Florida	South Bay, Fla.	FA
Stewart, Robert	NT	5-11	292	4/12/67	Alabama	Ashford, Ala.	D8
Vincent, Kary	CB	5-10	178	9/19/69	Texas A&M	Port Arthur, Tex.	D6

The term NFL Rookie is defined as a player who is in his first season of professional football and has not been on the roster of another professional football team for any regular-season or postseason games. A Rookie is designated by an "R" on NFL rosters. Players who have been active in another professional football league or players who have NFL experience, including either preseason training camp or being on an active roster for fewer than three regular-season or postseason games, are termed NFL First-Year Players. An NFL First-Year Player is designated by a "1" on NFL rosters. Thereafter, a player on an NFL active roster for at least three regular-season or postseason games is credited with an additional year of NFL playing experience.

NOTES

National Football Conference Eastern Division

Team Colors: Blue, Red, and White

Giants Stadium
East Rutherford, New Jersey 07073
Telephone: (201) 935-8111

Club Officials

President/Co-CEO: Wellington T. Mara
Chairman/Co-CEO: Preston Robert Tisch
Executive Vice President/General Counsel:
 John K. Mara, Esq.
Treasurer: Jonathan Tisch
Vice President-General Manager: George Young
Assistant General Manager: Harry Hulmes
Controller: John Pasquali
Director of Player Personnel: Tom Boisture
Director of Pro Personnel: Tim Rooney
Director of Media Services: Ed Croke
Director of Administration: Tom Power
Senior Director of Marketing: Rusty Hawley
Director of Promotion: Frank Mara
Ticket Manager: John Gorman
Head Trainer: Ronnie Barnes
Assistant Trainers: John Johnson, Mike Ryan
Equipment Manager: Ed Wagner, Jr.

Stadium: Giants Stadium • **Capacity:** 77,311
 East Rutherford, New Jersey 07073

Playing Surface: AstroTurf

Training Camp: Fairleigh Dickinson-Madison
 Florham Park, N.J. 07932

1992 Schedule

Preseason
Aug. 9	**Cincinnati**	7:00
Aug. 15	**Cleveland**	8:00
Aug. 22	at New York Jets	8:00
Aug. 29	at Pittsburgh	7:00

Regular Season
Sept. 6	**San Francisco**	4:00
Sept. 13	**Dallas**	1:00
Sept. 21	at Chicago (Monday)	8:00
Sept. 27	**Open Date**	
Oct. 4	at Los Angeles Raiders	1:00
Oct. 11	**Phoenix**	1:00
Oct. 18	at Los Angeles Rams	1:00
Oct. 25	**Seattle**	1:00
Nov. 1	at Washington	8:00
Nov. 8	**Green Bay**	1:00
Nov. 15	at Denver	6:00
Nov. 22	**Philadelphia**	1:00
Nov. 26	at Dallas (Thanksgiving)	3:00
Dec. 6	**Washington**	4:00
Dec. 12	at Phoenix (Saturday)	2:00
Dec. 19	**Kansas City** (Saturday)	12:30
Dec. 27	at Philadelphia	1:00

Giants Coaching History
(488-398-32)
1925	Bob Folwell	8-4-0
1926	Joe Alexander	8-4-1
1927-28	Earl Potteiger	15-8-3
1929-30	LeRoy Andrews*	24-5-1
1930	Benny Friedman	2-0-0
1931-53	Steve Owen	153-108-17
1954-60	Jim Lee Howell	54-29-4
1961-68	Allie Sherman	57-54-4
1969-73	Alex Webster	29-40-1
1974-76	Bill Arnsparger**	7-28-0
1976-78	John McVay	14-23-0
1979-82	Ray Perkins	24-35-0
1983-90	Bill Parcells	85-52-1
1991	Ray Handley	8-8-0

*Released after 15 games in 1930
**Released after seven games in 1976

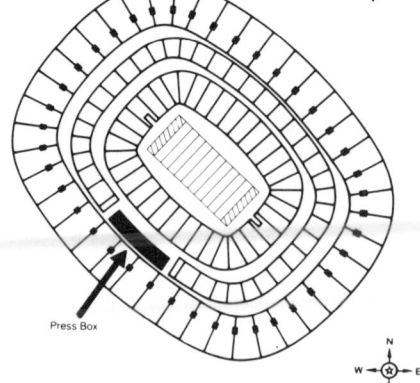

Press Box

GIANTS STADIUM

Record Holders
Individual Records—Career
Category	Name	Performance
Rushing (Yds.)	Joe Morris, 1982-88	5,296
Passing (Yds.)	Phil Simms, 1979-1991	29,512
Passing (TDs)	Phil Simms, 1979-1991	179
Receiving (No.)	Joe Morrison, 1959-1972	395
Receiving (Yds.)	Frank Gifford, 1952-1960, 1962-64	5,434
Interceptions	Emlen Tunnell, 1948-1958	74
Punting (Avg.)	Don Chandler, 1956-1964	43.8
Punt Return (Avg.)	David Meggett, 1989-1991	11.4
Kickoff Return (Avg.)	Rocky Thompson, 1971-72	27.2
Field Goals	Pete Gogolak, 1966-1974	126
Touchdowns (Tot.)	Frank Gifford, 1952-1960, 1962-64	78
Points	Pete Gogolak, 1966-1974	646

Individual Records—Single Season
Category	Name	Performance
Rushing (Yds.)	Joe Morris, 1986	1,516
Passing (Yds.)	Phil Simms, 1984	4,044
Passing (TDs)	Y.A. Tittle, 1963	36
Receiving (No.)	Earnest Gray, 1983	78
Receiving (Yds.)	Homer Jones, 1967	1,209
Interceptions	Otto Schnellbacher, 1951	11
	Jim Patton, 1958	11
Punting (Avg.)	Don Chandler, 1959	46.6
Punt Return (Avg.)	Merle Hapes, 1942	15.5
Kickoff Return (Avg.)	John Salscheider, 1949	31.6
Field Goals	Ali Haji-Sheikh, 1983	*35
Touchdowns (Tot.)	Joe Morris, 1985	21
Points	Ali Haji-Sheikh, 1983	127

Individual Records—Single Game
Category	Name	Performance
Rushing (Yds.)	Gene Roberts, 11-12-50	218
Passing (Yds.)	Phil Simms, 10-13-85	513
Passing (TDs)	Y.A. Tittle, 10-28-62	*7
Receiving (No.)	Mark Bavaro, 10-13-85	12
Receiving (Yds.)	Del Shofner, 10-28-62	269
Interceptions	Many times	3
	Last time by Terry Kinard, 9-27-87	
Field Goals	Joe Danelo, 10-18-81	6
Touchdowns (Tot.)	Ron Johnson, 10-2-72	4
	Earnest Gray, 9-7-80	4
Points	Ron Johnson, 10-2-72	24
	Earnest Gray, 9-7-80	24

*NFL Record

1991 Team Record
Preseason (2-2)

Date	Result		Opponents
8/5	W	23-17	Buffalo
8/10	L	10-16	at Cleveland
8/17	W	24-10	N.Y. Jets
8/24	L	3-24	at New England

Regular Season (8-8)

Date	Result		Opponents	Att.
9/2	W	16-14	San Francisco	76,319
9/8	L	13-19	L.A. Rams	76,541
9/15	L	17-20	at Chicago	64,829
9/22	W	13-10	Cleveland	75,891
9/29	L	16-21	at Dallas	64,010
10/6	W	20- 9	Phoenix	75,891
10/14	W	23-20	at Pittsburgh	57,608
10/27	L	13-17	Washington	76,627
11/4	L	7-30	at Philadelphia	65,816
11/10	W	21-14	at Phoenix	50,048
11/17	W	22- 9	Dallas	76,410
11/24	W	21-14	at Tampa Bay	63,698
12/1	L	24-27	at Cincinnati	45,063
12/8	L	14-19	Philadelphia	76,099
12/15	L	17-34	at Washington	54,722
12/21	W	24-20	Houston	63,421

Score by Periods

Giants	81	89	58	53	0	—	281
Opponents	24	93	51	129	0	—	297

Attendance
Home 597,199   Away 465,794   Total 1,062,993
Single-game home record, 77,025 (1-13-91)
Single-season home record, 599,570 (1990)

1991 Team Statistics

	Giants	Opp.
Total First Downs	280	257
Rushing	120	103
Passing	148	138
Penalty	12	16
Third Down: Made/Att.	86/202	67/191
Third Down: Pct.	42.6	35.1
Fourth Down: Made/Att.	7/16	6/9
Fourth Down: Pct.	43.8	66.7
Total Net Yards	4908	4600
Avg. Per Game	306.8	287.5
Total Plays	951	888
Avg. Per Play	5.2	5.2
Net Yards Rushing	2064	1726
Avg. Per Game	129.0	107.9
Total Rushes	487	414
Net Yards Passing	2844	2874
Avg. Per Game	177.8	179.6
Sacked/Yards Lost	36/181	34/254
Gross Yards	3025	3128
Att./Completions	428/261	440/251
Completion Pct.	61.0	57.0
Had Intercepted	8	12
Punts/Avg.	64/43.3	74/40.5
Net Punting Avg.	35.3	34.6
Penalties/Yards Lost	92/719	80/622
Fumbles/Ball Lost	33/15	27/9
Touchdowns	30	30
Rushing	16	11
Passing	13	17
Returns	1	2
Avg. Time of Possession	31:47	28:13

1991 Individual Statistics

Scoring

	TD R	TD P	TD Rt	PAT	FG	Saf	TP
Bahr	0	0	0	24/25	22/29	0	90
Hampton	10	0	0	0/0	0/0	0	60
Meggett	1	3	1	0/0	0/0	0	30
Baker	0	4	0	0/0	0/0	0	24
Ingram	0	3	0	0/0	0/0	0	18
Cross	0	2	0	0/0	0/0	0	12
Hostetler	2	0	0	0/0	0/0	0	12
Allegre	0	0	0	5/5	2/2	0	11
Anderson	1	0	0	0/0	0/0	0	6
Mowatt	0	1	0	0/0	0/0	0	6
Simms	1	0	0	0/0	0/0	0	6
Tillman	1	0	0	0/0	0/0	0	6
Giants	16	13	1	29/30	24/31	0	281
Opponents	11	17	2	30/30	29/30	0	297

Passing

	Att.	Comp.	Yds.	Pct.	TD	Int.	Tkld.	Rate
Hostetler	285	179	2032	62.8	5	4	20/100	84.1
Simms	141	82	993	58.2	8	4	14/79	87.0
Ingram	1	0	0	0.0	0	0	1/2	39.6
Meggett	1	0	0	0.0	0	0	1/0	39.6
Giants	428	261	3025	61.0	13	8	36/181	84.7
Opponents	440	251	3128	57.0	17	12	34/254	80.8

Rushing

	Att.	Yds.	Avg.	LG	TD
Hampton	256	1059	4.1	44	10
Tillman	65	287	4.4	17	1
Hostetler	42	273	6.5	47t	2
Meggett	29	153	5.3	30t	1
Anderson	53	141	2.7	9	1
Carthon	32	109	3.4	10	0
Simms	9	42	4.7	19	1
Bunch	1	0	0.0	0	0
Giants	487	2064	4.2	47t	16
Opponents	414	1726	4.2	42t	11

Receiving

	No.	Yds.	Avg.	LG	TD
Ingram	51	824	16.2	41	3
Meggett	50	412	8.2	22	3
Hampton	43	283	6.6	19	0
Baker	30	525	17.5	52	4
Turner	21	356	17.0	55	0
Cross	20	283	14.2	30	2
McCaffrey	16	146	9.1	26	0
Anderson	11	41	3.7	13	0
Carthon	7	39	5.6	9	0
Mowatt	5	78	15.6	33	1
Tillman	5	30	6.0	12	0
Bunch	2	8	4.0	6	0
Giants	261	3025	11.6	55	13
Opponents	251	3128	12.5	75t	17

Interceptions

	No.	Yds.	Avg.	LG	TD
Collins	4	77	19.3	41	0
Walls	4	7	1.8	5	0
Johnson	2	5	2.5	5	0
White	1	30	30.0	30	0
Jackson	1	3	3.0	3	0
Giants	12	122	10.2	41	0
Opponents	8	36	4.5	22	0

Punting

	No.	Yds.	Avg.	In 20	LG
Landeta	64	2768	43.3	16	61
Giants	64	2768	43.3	16	61
Opponents	74	2999	40.5	21	60

Punt Returns

	No.	FC	Yds.	Avg.	LG	TD
Meggett	28	9	287	10.3	70t	1
Ingram	8	1	49	6.1	13	0
Giants	36	10	336	9.3	70t	1
Opponents	35	10	350	10.0	78t	1

Kickoff Returns

	No.	Yds.	Avg.	LG	TD
Meggett	25	514	20.6	42	0
Hampton	10	204	20.4	51	0
Ingram	8	125	15.6	25	0
Smith	3	34	11.3	18	0
Tillman	2	29	14.5	19	0
Cross	1	11	11.0	11	0
Freeman	1	0	0.0	0	0
Giants	50	917	18.3	51	0
Opponents	55	940	17.1	36	0

Sacks

	No.
Marshall	11.0
Taylor	7.0
Johnson	6.5
Banks	4.0
Miller	2.5
Howard	1.5
Dorsey	0.5
Freeman	0.5
Walls	0.5
Giants	34.0
Opponents	36.0

1992 Draft Choices

Round	Name	Pos.	College
1.	Derek Brown	TE	Notre Dame
2.	Phillippi Sparks	DB	Arizona State
3.	Aaron Pierce	TE	Washington
4.	Keith Hamilton	DT	Pittsburgh
5.	Michael Wright	DB	Washington State
6.	Stacey Dillard	DT	Oklahoma
7.	Corey Widmer	NT	Montana State
8.	Kent Graham	QB	Ohio State
9.	Anthony Prior	DB	Washington State
10.	George Rooks	NT	Syracuse
11.	Nate Singleton	WR	Grambling
12.	Charles Swann	WR	Indiana State

New York Giants 1992 Veteran Roster

No.	Name	Pos.	Ht.	Wt.	Birth-date	NFL Exp.	College	Hometown	How Acq.	'91 Games/ Starts
51	†Abrams, Bobby	LB	6-3	230	4/12/67	3	Michigan	Detroit, Mich.	FA-'90	16/2
24	Anderson, Ottis	RB	6-2	225	1/19/57	14	Miami	West Palm Beach, Fla.	T(StL)-'86	10/1
9	Bahr, Matt	K	5-10	175	7/6/56	14	Penn State	Langhorne, Pa.	FA-'90	13/0
85	Baker, Stephen	WR	5-8	160	8/30/64	6	Fresno State	San Antonio, Tex.	D3-'87	15/13
58	†Banks, Carl	LB	6-4	235	8/29/62	9	Michigan State	Flint, Mich.	D1-'84	16/15
46	†Brown, Roger	CB	6-0	196	12/16/66	3	Virginia Tech	Baltimore, Md.	FA-'90	16/1
33	Bunch, Jarrod	RB	6-2	248	8/9/68	2	Michigan	Ashtabula, Ohio	D1-'91	16/1
90	Calloway, Chris	WR	5-10	185	3/29/68	3	Michigan	Chicago, Ill.	FA-'92	12/0*
17	Carlson, Jeff	QB	6-3	215	5/23/66	3	Weber State	Cypress, Calif.	PB(TB)-'92#	3/1*
6	Cavanaugh, Matt	QB	6-2	210	10/27/56	15	Pittsburgh	Youngstown, Ohio	FA-'90	4/0
25	†Collins, Mark	CB	5-10	190	1/16/64	7	Cal State-Fullerton	San Bernardino, Calif.	D2-'86	16/15
87	Cross, Howard	TE	6-5	245	8/8/67	4	Alabama	Huntsville, Ala.	D6-'89	16/16
99	DeOssie, Steve	LB	6-2	248	11/22/62	9	Boston College	Tacoma, Wash.	T(Dall)-'89	16/2
77	†Dorsey, Eric	DE	6-5	280	8/5/64	7	Notre Dame	McLean, Va.	D1-'86	11/10
76	Elliott, John	T	6-7	305	4/1/65	5	Michigan	Lake Ronkonkoma, N.Y.	D2-'88	16/16
93	Fox, Mike	DE	6-6	275	8/5/67	3	West Virginia	Akron, Ohio	D2-'90	15/5
29	Guyton, Myron	S	6-1	205	8/26/67	4	Eastern Kentucky	Metcalf, Ga.	D8-'89	16/16
27	Hampton, Rodney	RB	5-11	215	4/3/69	3	Georgia	Houston, Tex.	D1-'90	14/14
15	Hostetler, Jeff	QB	6-3	212	4/22/61	8	West Virginia	Johnston, Pa.	D3-'84	12/12
74	†Howard, Erik	NT	6-4	268	11/12/64	7	Washington State	San Jose, Calif.	D2a-'86	6/4
82	Ingram, Mark	WR	5-10	188	8/23/65	6	Michigan State	Rockford, Ill.	D1-'87	16/13
47	†Jackson, Greg	S	6-1	200	8/20/66	4	Louisiana State	Hialeah, Fla.	D3a-'89	13/12
52	Johnson, Pepper	LB	6-3	248	6/29/64	7	Ohio State	Detroit, Mich.	D2b-'86	16/16
68	Jones, Clarence	T	6-6	280	5/6/68	2	Maryland	Brooklyn, N.Y.	D4-'91	3/0
49	Kaumeyer, Thom	S	5-11	190	3/17/67	5	Oregon	La Jolla, Calif.	PB(Sea)-'91#	0*
61	†Kratch, Bob	G	6-3	288	1/6/66	4	Iowa	Mahwah, N.J.	D3-'89	15/1
5	Landeta, Sean	P	6-0	210	1/6/62	8	Towson State	Baltimore, Md.	FA-'85	15/0
70	Marshall, Leonard	DE	6-3	285	10/22/61	10	Louisiana State	Franklin, La.	D2-'83	16/16
81	McCaffrey, Ed	WR	6-5	215	8/17/68	2	Stanford	Allentown, Pa.	D3-'91	16/0
96	McGhee, Kanavis	LB	6-4	257	10/4/68	2	Colorado	Houston, Tex.	D2-'91	16/0
38	McGriggs, Lamar	CB-S	6-3	210	5/9/68	2	Western Illinois	Chicago, Ill.	D8-'91	16/0
30	Meggett, David	RB	5-7	180	4/30/66	4	Towson State	Charleston, S.C.	D5-'89	16/2
57	Miller, Corey	LB	6-2	255	10/25/68	2	South Carolina	Pageland, S.C.	D6-'91	16/1
60	†Moore, Eric	T	6-5	290	1/21/65	5	Indiana	Berkeley, Mo.	D1-'88	16/16
65	†Oates, Bart	C	6-3	265	12/16/58	8	Brigham Young	Albany, Ga.	FA-'85	16/16
12	Perez, Mike	QB	6-1	210	3/7/65	3	San Jose State	Denver, Colo.	FA-'91	0*
55	Reasons, Gary	LB	6-4	234	2/18/62	9	Northwestern Louisiana	Cowely, Tex.	D4a-'84	16/15
95	Reynolds, Ed	LB	6-5	242	9/23/61	10	Virginia	Ridgeway, Va.	PB(NE)-'92#	9/0*
72	Riesenberg, Doug	T	6-5	275	7/22/65	6	California	Moscow, Idaho	D6a-'87	15/15
66	Roberts, William	T	6-5	280	8/5/62	8	Ohio State	Miami, Fla.	D1a-'84	16/16
11	†Simms, Phil	QB	6-3	214	11/3/55	13	Morehead State	Louisville, Ky.	D1-'79	6/4
88	Smith, Joey	WR	5-10	177	5/30/69	2	Louisville	Knoxville, Tenn.	FA-'91	1/0
56	Taylor, Lawrence	LB	6-3	243	2/4/59	12	North Carolina	Williamsburg, Va.	D1-'81	14/14
21	Thompson, Reyna	CB	6-0	193	8/28/63	7	Baylor	Dallas, Tex.	FA-'89	12/1
34	†Tillman, Lewis	RB	6-0	195	4/16/66	4	Jackson State	Oklahoma City, Okla.	D4-'89	16/1
28	Walls, Everson	CB	6-1	194	12/28/59	12	Grambling	Dallas, Tex.	FA-'90	14/13
73	Washington, John	DE	6-4	275	2/20/63	7	Oklahoma State	Houston, Tex.	D3-'86	12/8
59	Williams, Brian	C-G	6-5	300	6/8/66	4	Minnesota	Mt. Lebanon, Pa.	D1-'89	14/0
23	Williams, Perry	CB	6-2	203	5/12/61	9	North Carolina State	Hamlet, N.C.	D7-'83	16/7

* Calloway played 12 games with Pittsburgh in '91; Carlson played 3 games with Tampa Bay; Kaumeyer last active with Seattle in '90; Perez last active with N.Y. Giants in '90; Reynolds played 9 games with New England.

† Option playout; subject to developments.

Plan B unconditional free agent.

Players lost through Plan B (6): DE Tim Downing (Mia; did not play in '91), NT Lorenzo Freeman (Minn; 16), WR James Milling (Atl; active for 1 game but did not play), LB Anthony Moss (Clev; 0), WR Odessa Turner (SF; 16), CB-S Adrian White (GB; 13).

Also played with Giants in '91—K Raul Allegre (3 games), RB Maurice Carthon (16), CB A.J. Greene (2), NT Greg Meisner (4), TE Zeke Mowatt (16).

COACHING STAFF

Head Coach, Ray Handley

Pro Career: Became thirteenth head coach in New York Giants history on May 15, 1991. Had served as running backs coach with Giants since 1984, and was then named offensive coordinator in February, 1991, before replacing Bill Parcells, who resigned as head coach on May 15, 1991. Career record: 8-8.

Background: Running back at Stanford 1963-65. No pro playing experience. College assistant at Stanford 1967, 1971-74, 1979-83, Army 1968-69, and Air Force 1975-78.

Personal: Born October 8, 1944, Artesia, N.M. Ray and his wife, JoAnne, live in West Orange, N.J., and have a son, Donnie, and a daughter, Cami.

Assistant Coaches

Dave Brazil, linebackers; born March 25, 1936, Detroit, Mich., lives in East Rutherford, N.J. No college or pro playing experience. College coach: Holy Cross 1968-69, Tulsa 1970-71, Eastern Michigan 1972-74, Boston College 1978-79, Kent State 1980-82. Pro coach: Detroit Wheel (WFL) 1975, Chicago Fire (WFL) 1976, Kansas City Chiefs 1984-88, Pittsburgh Steelers 1989-91, joined Giants in 1992.

Fred Bruney, defensive backs; born December 30, 1931, Martins Ferry, Ohio, lives in Chatham, N.J. Running back Ohio State 1950-52. Pro defensive back San Francisco 49ers 1953-56, Pittsburgh Steelers 1957, Los Angeles Rams 1958, Boston Patriots 1960-62. College coach: Ohio State 1959. Pro coach: Boston Patriots 1963, Philadelphia Eagles 1964-68, 1977-85, Atlanta Falcons 1969-76, 1986-89, Tampa Bay Buccaneers 1990, joined Giants in 1991.

Romeo Crennell, defensive line; born June 18, 1947, Lynchburg, Va., lives in Montvale, N.J. Defensive lineman Western Kentucky 1966-69. No pro playing experience. College coach: Western Kentucky 1970-74, Texas Tech 1975-77, Mississippi 1978-79, Georgia Tech 1980. Pro coach: Joined Giants in 1981.

Jim Fassel, offensive coordinator; born August 31, 1949, Anaheim, Calif., lives in East Rutherford, N.J. Quarterback Southern California 1969-70, Long Beach State 1971. Pro quarterback Chicago Bears 1972, Houston Oilers 1972, San Diego Chargers 1972. College coach: Fullerton (Calif.) J.C. 1973, Utah 1976, 1985-89 (head coach), Weber State 1977-78, Stanford 1979-83. Pro coach: Hawaii (WFL) 1974, Portland Breakers (USFL) 1984, joined Giants in 1991.

Fred Hoaglin, offensive line; born January 28, 1944, Alliance, Ohio, lives in Sparta, N.J. Center Pittsburgh 1962-65. Pro center Cleveland Browns 1966-72, Baltimore Colts 1973, Houston Oilers 1974-75, Seattle Seahawks 1976. Pro coach: Detroit Lions 1978-84, joined Giants in 1985.

Johnny Parker, strength and conditioning; born February 1, 1947, Greenville, S.C., lives in Montvale, N.J. Graduate of Mississippi, master's degree from Delta State University. No college or pro playing experience. College coach: South Carolina 1974-76, Indiana 1977-79, Louisiana State 1980, Mississippi 1981-83. Pro coach: Joined Giants in 1984.

Dick Rehbein, tight ends; born November 22, 1955, Green Bay, Wis., lives in East Rutherford, N.J. Center Ripon 1973-77. No pro playing experience. Pro coach: Green Bay Packers 1979-83, Los Angeles Express (USFL) 1984, Minnesota Vikings 1984-91, joined Giants in 1992.

Rod Rust, defensive coordinator; born August 2, 1928, Cedar Rapids, Iowa, lives in East Rutherford, N.J. Center-linebacker Iowa State 1947-49. No pro playing experience. College coach: New Mexico 1960-62, Stanford 1963-66, North Texas State 1967-72 (head coach). Pro coach: Montreal Alouettes (CFL) 1973-75, Philadelphia Eagles 1976-77, Kansas City Chiefs 1978-82, 1988, New England Patriots 1983-87, 1990 (head coach), Pittsburgh Steelers 1989, joined Giants in 1992.

George Sefcik, wide receivers; born December 27, 1939, Cleveland, Ohio, lives in East Rutherford, N.J. Halfback Notre Dame 1959-61. No pro playing experience. College coach: Notre Dame 1963-68, Kentucky 1969-72. Pro coach: Baltimore Colts 1973-74, Cleveland Browns 1975-77, 1989-90, Cincinnati Bengals 1979-83, Green Bay Packers 1984-87, Kansas City Chiefs 1988, joined Giants in 1991.

Mike Sweatman, special teams; born October 23, 1946, Kansas City, Mo., lives in Wayne, N.J. Linebacker Kansas 1964-67. No pro playing experience. College coach: Kansas 1973-74, 1979-82, Tulsa 1977-78, Tennessee 1983. Pro coach: Minnesota Vikings 1984, joined Giants in 1985.

Bob Trott, defensive assistant; born March 19, 1954, Kannapolis, N.C., lives in East Rutherford, N.J. Defensive back North Carolina 1973-75. No pro playing experience. College coach: North Carolina 1976-77, Air Force 1978-83, Arkansas 1984-89, Clemson 1990. Pro coach: Joined Giants in 1991.

Charlie Weis, running backs, born March 30, 1956, Trenton, N.J., lives in Middlesex, N.J. No college or pro playing experience. College coach: South Carolina 1985-88. Pro coach: Joined Giants in 1990.

New York Giants 1992 First-Year Roster

Name	Pos.	Ht.	Wt.	Birth-date	College	Hometown	How Acq.
Bradberry, Ramsey	S	6-2	198	3/10/69	Texas A&M	Dallas, Tex.	FA
Brown, Derek	TE	6-6	252	3/31/70	Notre Dame	Fairfax, Va.	D1
Bruun, Eric	P	6-2	215	11/16/68	Purdue	Oakland, Calif.	FA
Carroll, Kevin	LB	6-3	258	6/17/69	Knoxville	Hempstead, Tex.	FA
Dillard, Stacy	NT	6-5	288	9/17/68	Oklahoma	Clarksville, Tex.	D6
Dressel, Robert	C	6-4	300	8/19/69	Purdue	Phoenix, Ariz.	FA
Fineanganofo, Nick	T	6-5	315	5/23/68	Arizona	Tonga	FA
Graham, Kent	QB	6-5	220	11/1/68	Ohio State	Wheaton, Ill.	D8
Haley, Micah	NT	6-2	282	11/9/68	East Texas State	Little Rock, Ark.	FA
Hamilton, Keith	DE	6-6	280	5/5/71	Pittsburgh	Lynchburg, Va.	D4
Johnson, Adam	G	6-4	300	2/26/70	S.W. Louisiana	Baton Rouge, La.	FA
Lynn, Anthony	RB	6-2	220	12/21/68	Texas Tech	McKinney, Tex.	FA
Mancini, Kevin	G	6-3	280	4/16/70	Florida State	Troy, Mich.	FA
Pierce, Aaron	TE	6-5	246	9/6/69	Washington	Seattle, Wash.	D3
Poloskey, Mike	LB	6-2	255	9/17/69	Illinois	Joliet, Ill.	FA
Prior, Anthony	S	5-11	185	3/27/70	Washington State	Mira Loma, Calif.	D9
Raymond, Corey	CB	5-11	180	7/28/69	Louisiana State	New Iberia, La.	FA
Rooks, George	NT	6-4	275	8/9/70	Syracuse	White Plains, N.Y.	D10
Singleton, Nate	WR	6-0	190	7/5/68	Grambling	New Orleans, La.	D11
Sparks, Phillippi	CB	5-11	186	4/15/69	Arizona State	Glendale, Calif.	D2
Swann, Charles	WR	6-1	195	10/29/70	Indiana State	South Bend, Ind.	D12
Van Bellinger, Scott	LB	6-4	248	5/26/69	Northern Illinois	Green Bay, Wis.	FA
Wallace, Randall	C	6-4	280	12/17/68	Oklahoma	Midwest City, Okla.	FA
Widmer, Corey	NT	6-3	276	12/25/68	Montana State	Bozeman, Mont.	D7
Wright, Mike	CB	6-0	182	9/25/69	Washington State	Seattle, Wash.	D5
Wright, T.C.	RB	5-9	187	12/18/69	San Diego State	Phoenix, Ariz.	FA
Zizakovic, Lubo	DE	6-8	270	2/28/68	Maryland	Toronto, Canada	FA

The term NFL Rookie is defined as a player who is in his first season of professional football and has not been on the roster of another professional football team for any regular-season or postseason games. A Rookie is designated by an "R" on NFL rosters. Players who have been active in another professional football league or players who have NFL experience, including either preseason training camp or being on an active roster for fewer than three regular-season or postseason games, are termed NFL First-Year Players. An NFL First-Year Player is designated by a "1" on NFL rosters. Thereafter, a player on an NFL active roster for at least three regular-season or postseason games is credited with an additional year of NFL playing experience.

NOTES

_____

_____

_____

_____

_____

_____

_____

_____

_____

_____

_____

_____

_____

_____

National Football Conference Eastern Division

Team Colors: Kelly Green, Silver, and White

Veterans Stadium
Broad Street and Pattison Avenue
Philadelphia, Pennsylvania 19148
Telephone: (215) 463-2500

Club Officials
Owner: Norman Braman
President-Chief Operating Officer: Harry Gamble
Vice President: Suzi Braman
V.P.-Chief Financial Officer: Mimi Box
V.P.-Marketing and Development: Decker Uhlhorn
Asst. to the President: George Azar
Asst. to the President-General Counsel:
 Bob Wallace
Director of Player Personnel: Joe Woolley
Director of Pro Scouting: Tom Gamble
Director of Public Relations: Ron Howard
Assistant Director of Public Relations:
 Michael Gilbert
Assoc. Director of Sales and Marketing:
 Leslie Stephenson
Dir. of Alumni Relations/Traveling Sec.:
 Jim Gallagher
Director of Administration: Vicki Chatley
Ticket Manager: Leo Carlin
Director of Sales: Lou Scheinfeld
Asst. Director of Penthouse Sales: Ken Iman
Trainer: Otho Davis
Asst. Trainer: David Price
Equipment Manager: Rusty Sweeney
Video Director: Mike Dougherty

Stadium: Veterans Stadium •
 Capacity: 65,178
 3501 South Broad Street
 Philadelphia, Pennsylvania 19148
Playing Surface: AstroTurf-8
Training Camp: West Chester University
 West Chester, Pennsylvania 19382

1992 Schedule

Preseason
Aug. 1	vs. N.Y. Jets at Canton	3:00
Aug. 8	at Pittsburgh	7:00
Aug. 15	**Cincinnati**	7:30
Aug. 23	at Atlanta	1:30

Regular Season
Sept. 6	**New Orleans**	1:00
Sept. 13	at Phoenix	5:00
Sept. 20	**Denver**	1:00
Sept. 27	**Open Date**	
Oct. 5	**Dallas** (Monday)	9:00
Oct. 11	at Kansas City	12:00
Oct. 18	at Washington	1:00
Oct. 25	**Phoenix**	1:00
Nov. 1	at Dallas	3:00
Nov. 8	**Los Angeles Raiders**	1:00
Nov. 15	vs. Green Bay at Milw.	12:00
Nov. 22	at New York Giants	1:00
Nov. 29	at San Francisco	1:00
Dec. 6	**Minnesota**	1:00
Dec. 13	at Seattle	1:00
Dec. 20	**Washington**	1:00
Dec. 27	**New York Giants**	1:00

Eagles Coaching History

(343-420-24)
1933-35	Lud Wray	9-21-1
1936-40	Bert Bell	10-44-2
1941-50	Earle (Greasy) Neale*	66-44-5
1951	Alvin (Bo) McMillin**	2-0-0
1951	Wayne Millner	2-8-0
1952-55	Jim Trimble	25-20-3
1956-57	Hugh Devore	7-16-1
1958-60	Lawrence (Buck) Shaw	20-16-1
1961-63	Nick Skorich	15-24-3
1964-68	Joe Kuharich	28-41-1
1969-71	Jerry Williams***	7-22-2
1971-72	Ed Khayat	8-15-2
1973-75	Mike McCormack	16-25-1
1976-82	Dick Vermeil	57-51-0
1983-85	Marion Campbell****	17-29-1
1985	Fred Bruney	1-0-0
1986-90	Buddy Ryan	43-38-1
1991	Rich Kotite	10-6-0

*Co-coach with Walt Kiesling in Philadelphia-Pittsburgh
 merger in 1943
**Retired after two games in 1951
***Released after three games in 1971
****Released after 15 games in 1985

Record Holders
Individual Records—Career
Category	Name	Performance
Rushing (Yds.)	Wilbert Montgomery, 1977-1984	6,538
Passing (Yds.)	Ron Jaworski, 1977-1986	26,963
Passing (TDs)	Ron Jaworski, 1977-1986	175
Receiving (No.)	Harold Carmichael, 1971-1983	589
Receiving (Yds.)	Harold Carmichael, 1971-1983	8,978
Interceptions	Bill Bradley, 1969-1976	34
Punting (Avg.)	Joe Muha, 1946-1950	42.9
Punt Return (Avg.)	Steve Van Buren, 1944-1951	13.9
Kickoff Return (Avg.)	Steve Van Buren, 1944-1951	26.7
Field Goals	Paul McFadden, 1984-87	91
Touchdowns (Tot.)	Harold Carmichael, 1971-1983	79
Points	Bobby Walston, 1951-1962	881

Individual Records—Single Season
Category	Name	Performance
Rushing (Yds.)	Wilbert Montgomery, 1979	1,512
Passing (Yds.)	Randall Cunningham, 1988	3,808
Passing (TDs)	Sonny Jurgensen, 1961	32
Receiving (No.)	Keith Jackson, 1988	81
	Keith Byars, 1990	81
Receiving (Yds.)	Mike Quick, 1983	1,409
Interceptions	Bill Bradley, 1971	11
Punting (Avg.)	Joe Muha, 1948	47.2
Punt Return (Avg.)	Steve Van Buren, 1944	15.3
Kickoff Return (Avg.)	Al Nelson, 1972	29.1
Field Goals	Paul McFadden, 1984	30
Touchdowns (Tot.)	Steve Van Buren, 1945	18
Points	Paul McFadden, 1984	116

Individual Records—Single Game
Category	Name	Performance
Rushing (Yds.)	Steve Van Buren, 11-27-49	205
Passing (Yds.)	Bobby Thomason, 11-18-53	437
Passing (TDs)	Adrian Burk, 10-17-54	*7
Receiving (No.)	Don Looney, 12-1-40	14
Receiving (Yds.)	Tommy McDonald, 12-10-60	237
Interceptions	Russ Craft, 9-24-50	*4
Field Goals	Tom Dempsey, 11-12-72	6
Touchdowns (Tot.)	Many times	4
	Last time by Wilbert Montgomery, 10-7-79	
Points	Bobby Walston, 10-17-54	25

*NFL Record

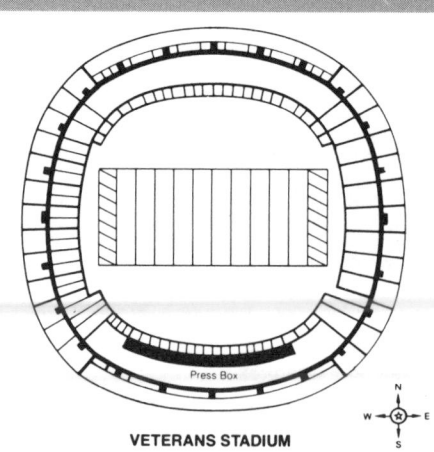

VETERANS STADIUM

Press Box

1991 Team Record

Preseason (4-1)

Date	Result		Opponents
7/28	L	13-17	vs. Buffalo at London
8/3	W	24-10	at N.Y. Jets
8/10	W	29-24	at Cincinnati
8/17	W	21-20	Pittsburgh
8/23	W	23-21	Indianapolis

Regular Season (10-6)

Date	Result		Opponents	Att.
9/1	W	20- 3	at Green Bay	58,991
9/8	L	10-26	Phoenix	63,818
9/15	W	24- 0	at Dallas	62,656
9/22	W	23-14	Pittsburgh	65,511
9/30	L	0-23	at Washington	55,198
10/6	L	13-14	at Tampa Bay	41,219
10/13	L	6-13	New Orleans	64,224
10/27	L	7-23	San Francisco	65,796
11/4	W	30- 7	N.Y. Giants	65,816
11/10	W	32-30	at Cleveland	72,086
11/17	W	17-10	Cincinnati	63,189
11/24	W	34-14	at Phoenix	37,307
12/2	W	13- 6	at Houston	62,141
12/8	W	19-14	at N.Y. Giants	76,099
12/15	L	13-25	Dallas	65,854
12/22	W	24-22	Washington	58,988

Score by Periods

Eagles	41	109	53	82	0	—	285
Opponents	72	71	38	63	0	—	244

Attendance

Home 513,196   Away 465,697   Total 978,893
Single-game home record, 72,111 (11-1-81)
Single-season home record, 557,325 (1980)

1991 Team Statistics

	Eagles	Opp.
Total First Downs	249	206
Rushing	86	53
Passing	142	133
Penalty	21	20
Third Down: Made/Att.	73/223	62/208
Third Down: Pct.	32.7	29.8
Fourth Down: Made/Att.	8/13	2/13
Fourth Down: Pct.	61.5	15.4
Total Net Yards	4302	3549
Avg. Per Game	268.9	221.8
Total Plays	1004	905
Avg. Per Play	4.3	3.9
Net Yards Rushing	1396	1136
Avg. Per Game	87.3	71.0
Total Rushes	446	383
Net Yards Passing	2906	2413
Avg. Per Game	181.6	150.8
Sacked/Yards Lost	45/263	55/394
Gross Yards	3169	2807
Att./Completions	513/285	467/206
Completion Pct.	55.6	44.1
Had Intercepted	27	26
Punts/Avg.	88/41.4	86/42.7
Net Punting Avg.	34.0	37.4
Penalties/Yards Lost	111/839	105/881
Fumbles/Ball Lost	34/16	43/22
Touchdowns	29	24
Rushing	8	4
Passing	17	16
Returns	4	4
Avg. Time of Possession	33:25	26:35

1991 Individual Statistics

Scoring

	TD R	TD P	TD Rt	PAT	FG	Saf	TP
Ruzek	0	0	0	27/29	28/33	0	111
Kei. Jackson	0	5	0	0/0	0/0	0	30
Barnett	0	4	0	0/0	0/0	0	24
Byars	1	3	0	0/0	0/0	0	24
Joseph	3	0	0	0/0	0/0	0	18
Williams	0	3	0	0/0	0/0	0	18
Drummond	2	0	0	0/0	0/0	0	12
Joyner	0	0	2	0/0	0/0	0	12
M. Johnson	0	2	0	0/0	0/0	0	12
McMahon	1	0	0	0/0	0/0	0	6
O. Smith	0	0	1	0/0	0/0	0	6
Sanders	1	0	0	0/0	0/0	0	6
Simmons	0	0	1	0/0	0/0	0	6
Eagles	8	17	4	27/29	28/33	0	285
Opponents	4	16	4	23/24	25/33	1	244

Passing

	Att.	Comp.	Yds.	Pct.	TD	Int.	Tkld.	Rate
McMahon	311	187	2239	60.1	12	11	21/128	80.3
Kemp, Sea.-Phil.	295	151	1753	51.2	9	17	20/99	55.7
Kemp, Phil.	114	57	546	50.0	5	5	12/61	60.1
Goebel	56	30	267	53.6	0	6	6/37	27.0
Ryan	26	10	98	38.5	0	4	4/21	10.3
Cunningham	4	1	19	25.0	0	0	2/16	46.9
Byars	2	0	0	0.0	0	1	0/0	0.0
Eagles	513	285	3169	55.6	17	27	45/263	63.2
Opponents	467	206	2807	44.1	16	26	55/394	52.1

Rushing

	Att.	Yds.	Avg.	LG	TD
Joseph	135	440	3.3	24	3
Byars	94	383	4.1	28	1
Sherman	106	279	2.6	12	0
Kemp, Sea.-Phil.	38	179	4.7	18	0
Kemp, Phil.	16	73	4.6	18	0
Sanders	54	122	2.3	16	1
McMahon	22	55	2.5	12	1
Drummond	12	27	2.3	7	2
Ken. Jackson	1	18	18.0	18	0
Goebel	1	2	2.0	2	0
Barnett	1	0	0.0	0	0
Feagles	3	-1	-0.3	11	0
Ryan	1	-2	-2.0	-2	0
Eagles	446	1396	3.1	28	8
Opponents	383	1136	3.0	34	4

Receiving

	No.	Yds.	Avg.	LG	TD
Barnett	62	948	15.3	75t	4
Byars	62	564	9.1	37	3
Kei. Jackson	48	569	11.9	73t	5
Williams	33	326	9.9	30	3
Green	29	364	12.6	42	0
Sherman	14	59	4.2	11	0
Joseph	10	64	6.4	13	0
Sanders	8	62	7.8	14	0
Shuler	6	91	15.2	21	0
M. Johnson	6	70	11.7	31t	2
Ken. Jackson	4	29	7.3	9	0
Harris	2	28	14.0	22	0
McMahon	1	-5	-5.0	-5	0
Eagles	285	3169	11.1	75t	17
Opponents	206	2807	13.6	75	16

Interceptions

	No.	Yds.	Avg.	LG	TD
Hopkins	5	26	5.2	14	0
Allen	5	20	4.0	8	0
Joyner	3	41	13.7	41	0
Miano	3	30	10.0	18	0
O. Smith	2	74	37.0	74t	1
Evans	2	46	23.0	31	0
B. Smith	2	6	3.0	6	0
Booty	1	24	24.0	24	0
Golic	1	13	13.0	13	0
Waters	1	0	0.0	0	0
White	1	0	0.0	0	0
Eagles	26	280	10.8	74t	1
Opponents	27	432	16.0	59	2

Punting

	No.	Yds.	Avg.	In 20	LG
Feagles	87	3640	41.8	29	77
Eagles	88	3640	41.4	29	77
Opponents	86	3670	42.7	19	65

Punt Returns

	No.	FC	Yds.	Avg.	LG	TD
Harris	53	9	416	7.8	40	0
Eagles	53	9	416	7.8	40	0
Opponents	42	11	431	10.3	85t	1

Kickoff Returns

	No.	Yds.	Avg.	LG	TD
Harris	28	473	16.9	33	0
Sanders	10	160	16.0	31	0
Green	5	70	14.0	21	0
Sherman	4	61	15.3	20	0
Eagles	47	764	16.3	33	0
Opponents	60	1146	19.1	51	0

Sacks

	No.
White	15.0
Simmons	13.0
Brown	9.0
Joyner	6.5
Golic	2.5
Hopkins	2.0
Pitts	2.0
Thomas	2.0
Booty	1.0
Jenkins	1.0
Eagles	55.0
Opponents	45.0

1992 Draft Choices

Round	Name	Pos.	College
2.	Siran Stacy	RB	Alabama
3.	Tommy Jeter	DT	Texas
4.	Tony Brooks	RB	Notre Dame
	Casey Weldon	QB	Florida State
5.	Corey Barlow	DB	Auburn
6.	Jeff Sydner	WR	Hawaii
7.	William Boatwright	G	Virginia Tech
8.	Chuck Bullough	LB	Michigan State
9.	Ephesians Bartley	LB	Florida
10.	Mark McMillian	DB	Alabama
11.	Pumpy Tudors	P	Tenn.-Chattanooga
12.	Brandon Houston	T	Oklahoma

Philadelphia Eagles 1992 Veteran Roster

No.	Name	Pos.	Ht.	Wt.	Birth-date	NFL Exp.	College	Hometown	How Acq.	'91 Games/Starts
72	Alexander, David	C	6-3	275	7/28/64	6	Tulsa	Broken Arrow, Okla.	D5-'87	16/16
21	†Allen, Eric	CB	5-10	180	11/22/65	5	Arizona State	San Diego, Calif.	D2-'88	16/16
18	†Archer, Dave	QB	6-2	208	2/15/62	7	Iowa State	Norcross, Ga.	FA-'91	0*
86	Barnett, Fred	WR	6-0	199	6/17/66	3	Arkansas State	Gunnison, Miss.	D3-'90	15/15
65	Bingham, Guy	C	6-3	260	2/25/58	13	Montana	Aberdeen, Wash.	PB(Atl)-'92#	13/0*
42	Booty, John	CB-S	6-0	180	10/9/65	5	Texas Christian	Carthage, Tex.	PB(NYJ)-'91#	13/1
99	Brown, Jerome	DT	6-2	295	2/4/65	6	Miami	Brooksville, Fla.	D1-'87	16/11
67	Bruhin, John	G	6-3	285	12/9/64	5	Tennessee	Knoxville, Tenn.	PB(TB)-'92#	10/5*
41	Byars, Keith	RB	6-1	238	10/14/63	7	Ohio State	Dayton, Ohio	D1-'86	16/16
12	Cunningham, Randall	QB	6-4	205	3/27/63	7	Nevada-Las Vegas	Santa Barbara, Calif.	D2-'85	1/1
78	Davis, Antone	T	6-4	325	2/28/67	2	Tennessee	Fort Valley, Ga.	D1-'91	16/15
84	Dixon, Floyd	WR	5-9	170	4/9/64	7	Stephen F. Austin	Beaumont, Tex.	PB(Atl)-'92#	11/3*
56	†Evans, Byron	LB	6-2	235	2/23/64	6	Arizona	Phoenix, Ariz.	W(NE)-'90	16/15
5	Feagles, Jeff	P	6-1	205	3/7/66	5	Miami	Phoenix, Ariz.	D4-'87	16/0
95	Flores, Mike	DE	6-3	256	12/1/66	2	Louisville	Youngstown, Ohio	D11-'91	4/0
61	Floyd, Eric	G-T	6-5	310	10/28/65	3	Auburn	Rome, Ga.	PB(SD)-'92#	2/0*
8	Goebel, Brad	QB	6-3	198	10/13/67	2	Baylor	Cuero, Tex.	FA-'91	4/2
90	Golic, Mike	DT	6-5	275	12/12/62	7	Notre Dame	Cleveland, Ohio	FA-'87	16/6
71	†Gray, Cecil	G-T	6-4	275	2/16/68	2	North Carolina	Virginia Beach, Va.	D9-'90	2/2
81	†Green, Roy	WR	6-1	195	6/30/57	14	Henderson State	Magnolia, Ark.	FA-'91	13/3
54	†Hager, Britt	LB	6-1	225	2/20/66	4	Texas	Odessa, Tex.	D3-'89	16/0
91	Harmon, Andy	DE	6-4	265	4/6/69	2	Kent State	Centerville, Ohio	D6-'91	16/0
80	Harris, Rod	WR	5-10	185	11/14/66	4	Texas A&M	Dallas, Tex.	W(Dall)-'90	16/0
73	Heller, Ron	T	6-6	280	8/25/62	9	Penn State	Farmingdale, N.Y.	T(Sea)-'88	16/14
48	Hopkins, Wes	S	6-1	215	9/26/61	9	Southern Methodist	Birmingham, Ala.	D2a-'83	16/16
76	†Hudson, John	G-C	6-2	275	1/29/68	2	Auburn	Memphis, Tenn.	D11a-'90	16/0
88	†Jackson, Keith	TE	6-2	250	4/19/65	5	Oklahoma	Little Rock, Ark.	D1-'88	16/16
83	†Jackson, Kenny	WR	6-0	180	2/15/62	9	Penn State	South River, N.J.	FA-'91	16/2
46	†Jenkins, Izel	CB	5-10	190	5/27/64	5	North Carolina State	Wilson, N.C.	D11-'88	14/5
87	Johnson, Maurice	TE	6-2	243	1/9/67	2	Temple	Washington, D.C.	FA-'91	12/6
32	Joseph, James	RB	6-0	222	10/28/67	2	Auburn	Phenix City, Ala.	D7-'91	16/3
59	Joyner, Seth	LB	6-2	235	11/18/64	7	Texas-El Paso	El Paso, Tex.	D8-'86	16/16
16	†Kemp, Jeff	QB	6-0	201	7/11/59	12	Dartmouth	Bethesda, Md.	W(Sea)-'91	16/2*
57	Kowalkowski, Scott	LB	6-2	228	8/23/68	2	Notre Dame	Orchard Lake, Mich.	D8-'91	16/0
62	McKnight, Dennis	C-G	6-3	280	9/12/59	10	Drake	Staten Island, N.Y.	PB(Det)-'91#	16/13
9	†McMahon, Jim	QB	6-1	195	8/21/59	11	Brigham Young	Northbrook, Ill.	FA-'91	12/11
38	Miano, Rich	CB-S	6-1	200	9/3/62	6	Hawaii	Honolulu, Hawaii	FA-'91	16/1
25	Overton, Don	RB	6-0	221	9/24/67	3	Fairmont State	Columbus, Ohio	PB(Det)-'92#	16/0*
74	Pitts, Mike	DT	6-5	280	9/25/60	10	Alabama	Baltimore, Md.	T(Atl)-'87	16/15
55	†Rose, Ken	LB	6-1	215	6/9/62	6	Nevada-Las Vegas	Sacramento, Calif.	FA-'90	16/0
7	†Ruzek, Roger	K	6-1	200	12/17/60	6	Weber State	San Francisco, Calif.	FA-'89	16/0
45	Sanders, Thomas	RB	5-11	202	1/4/62	8	Texas A&M	Giddings, Tex.	FA-'90	5/3
79	Schad, Mike	G	6-5	290	10/2/63	4	Queens College, Canada	Bellville, Ontario	PB(Rams)-'89#	0*
75	Selby, Rob	G-T	6-3	286	10/11/67	2	Auburn	Birmingham, Ala.	D3-'91	13/0
23	Sherman, Heath	RB	6-0	205	3/27/67	4	Texas A&I	El Campo, Tex.	D6-'89	16/5
82	Shuler, Mickey	TE	6-3	230	8/21/56	15	Penn State	Enola, Pa.	FA-'90	4/0
22	Sikahema, Vai	WR	5-9	196	8/29/62	7	Brigham Young	Mesa, Ariz.	PB(GB)-'92#	11/0*
96	Simmons, Clyde	DE	6-6	280	8/4/64	7	Western Carolina	Wilmington, N.C.	D9-'86	16/16
26	Smith, Ben	CB-S	5-11	185	5/14/67	3	Georgia	Warner Robins, Ga.	D1-'90	10/10
63	†Smith, Daryle	T	6-5	276	1/18/64	6	Tennessee	Powell, Tenn.	FA-'91	14/1
30	†Smith, Otis	CB	5-11	184	10/22/65	2	Missouri	Metairie, La.	FA-'90	15/1
51	Thomas, William	LB	6-2	218	8/13/68	2	Texas A&M	Amarillo, Tex.	D4-'91	16/7
20	†Waters, Andre	S	5-11	200	3/10/62	9	Cheyney State	Pahokee, Fla.	FA-'84	16/16
92	White, Reggie	DE	6-5	285	12/19/61	8	Tennessee	Chattanooga, Tenn.	SD1-'84	16/16
89	†Williams, Calvin	WR	5-11	190	3/3/67	3	Purdue	Baltimore, Md.	D5-'90	12/11

* Archer active for 2 games but did not play; Bingham played 13 games with Atlanta in '91; Bruhin played 10 games with Tampa Bay; Dixon played 11 games with Atlanta; Floyd played 2 games with San Diego; Kemp played 9 games with Seattle and 7 games with Philadelphia; Overton played 16 games with Detroit; Schad missed '91 season due to injury; Sikahema played 11 games with Green Bay.

† Option playout; subject to developments.

Plan B unconditional free agent.

Players lost through Plan B (3): RB Robert Drummond (Pitt; 16 games in '91), LB Jessie Small (Phx; 16), G Ron Solt (Ind; 15).

Also played with the Eagles in '91 — G Bruce Collie (5 games), QB Pat Ryan (4).

COACHING STAFF

Head Coach, Rich Kotite

Pro Career: Became the eighteenth head coach in Eagles' history on January 8, 1991. After a 3-5 start, marked by a season-ending injury to quarterback Randall Cunningham on opening day, and subsequent injuries to backup Jim McMahon, Kotite rallied the Eagles. Philadelphia narrowly missed the playoffs after winning seven of their last eight games on the strength of the league's best defense. He originally served as the team's offensive coordinator in 1990 when the club led the NFL in rushing and time of possession, and also led the NFC in scoring and touchdown passes. Kotite had previously served as the New York Jets' offensive coordinator and receivers coach from 1985-89 after originally joining the club as receivers coach in 1983. In each of Kotite's years at the helm of the New York offense, the Jets finished near the top in the AFC in total offense, including a third-place ranking in 1985. Kotite began his pro coaching career with New Orleans in 1977 before joining Cleveland the following year. Kotite was the Browns' receivers coach from 1978-82. He aided in the development of Cleveland's perennial all-pro tight end Ozzie Newsome. During his playing career, he was known as a scrappy tight end and outstanding special teams performer with the New York Giants (1967, 1969-72) and Steelers (1968). Career record: 10-6.

Background: Attended Poly Prep in Brooklyn, N.Y. After a brief boxing career at the University of Miami where he was the school's heavyweight champ, he served as a sparring partner for Cassius Clay, later known as Muhammad Ali. Kotite became a Little All-America tight end at Wagner College in Staten Island, N.Y.

Personal: Born in Brooklyn on October 13, 1942. He and his wife, Elizabeth, live in Mt. Laurel, N.J. and have one daughter—Alexandra.

Assistant Coaches

Dave Atkins, tight ends; born May 18, 1949, Victoria, Tex., lives in Marlton, N.J. Running back Texas-El Paso 1970-72. Pro running back San Francisco 49ers 1973, Honolulu (WFL) 1974, San Diego Chargers 1975. College coach: Texas-El Paso 1979-80, San Diego State 1981-85. Pro coach: Joined Eagles in 1986.

Zeke Bratkowski, quarterbacks; born October 20, 1931, Danville, Ill., lives in Mt. Laurel, N.J. Quarterback Georgia 1951-53. Pro quarterback Chicago Bears 1954, 1957-60, Los Angeles Rams 1961-63, Green Bay Packers 1963-68, 1971. Pro coach: Green Bay Packers 1969-70, 1975-81, Chicago Bears 1972-74, Baltimore-Indianapolis Colts 1982-84, New York Jets 1985-89, Cleveland Browns 1990, joined Eagles in 1991.

Lew Carpenter, receivers; born January 12, 1932, Hayti, Mo., lives in Mt. Laurel, N.J. Running back Arkansas 1950-52. Pro running back-defensive back-end Detroit Lions 1953-55, Cleveland Browns 1957-58, Green Bay Packers 1959-63. College coach: Southwest Texas State 1989. Pro coach: Minnesota Vikings 1964-66, Atlanta Falcons 1967-68, Washington Redskins 1969-70, St. Louis Cardinals 1971-72, Houston Oilers 1973-74, Green Bay Packers 1975-85, Detroit Lions 1986-88, joined Eagles in 1990.

Bud Carson, defensive coordinator-secondary; born April 28, 1931, Freeport, Pa., lives in Mt. Laurel, N.J. Defensive back North Carolina 1950-52. No pro playing experience. College coach: North Carolina 1957-64, South Carolina 1965, Georgia Tech 1966-71, Kansas 1984. Pro coach: Pittsburgh Steelers 1972-77, Los Angeles Rams 1978-81, Baltimore Colts 1982, Kansas City Chiefs 1983, New York Jets 1985-88, Cleveland Browns 1989-90 (head coach), joined Eagles in 1991.

Peter Giunta, defensive assistant; born August 11, 1956, Salem, Mass., lives in Bensalem, Pa. Running back-defensive back Northeastern 1974-77. No pro playing experience. College coach: Penn State 1981-83, Brown 1984-87, Lehigh 1988-90. Pro coach: Joined Eagles in 1991.

Dale Haupt, defensive line; born April 12, 1929, Manitowoc, Wis., lives in Cherry Hill, N.J. Defensive lineman-linebacker Wyoming 1950-53. No pro playing experience. College coach: Tennessee 1960-63, Iowa State 1964-65, Richmond 1966-71, North Carolina State 1972-76, Duke 1977. Pro coach: Chicago Bears 1978-85, joined Eagles in 1986.

Bill Muir, offensive line; born October 26, 1942, Pittsburgh, Pa., lives in Mt. Laurel, N.J. Tackle Susquehanna 1962-64. No pro playing experience. College coach: Susquehanna 1965, Delaware Valley 1966-67, Rhode Island 1970-71, Idaho State 1972-73, Southern Methodist 1976-77. Pro coach: Orlando (Continental Football League) 1968-69, Houston-Shreveport Steamer (WFL) 1975, New England Patriots 1982-84, Detroit Lions 1985-88, Indianapolis Colts 1989-91, joined Eagles in 1992.

Larry Pasquale, special teams coordinator; born April 21, 1941, Brooklyn, N.Y., lives in Mt. Laurel, N.J. Quarterback Bridgeport 1961-63. No pro playing experience. College coach: Slippery Rock State 1967, Boston University 1968, Navy 1969-70, Massachusetts 1971-75, Idaho State 1976. Pro coach: Montreal Alouettes (CFL) 1977-78, Detroit Lions 1979, New York Jets 1980-89, San Diego Chargers 1990-91, joined Eagles in 1992.

Jim Vechiarella, linebackers; born February 20, 1937, Youngstown, Ohio, lives in Mt. Laurel, N.J. Linebacker Youngstown State 1955-57. No pro playing experience. College coach: Youngstown State 1964-74, Southern Illinois 1976-77, Tulane 1978-80. Pro coach: Charlotte (WFL) 1975, Los Angeles Rams 1981-82, Kansas City Chiefs 1983-85, New York Jets 1986-89, Cleveland Browns 1990, joined Eagles in 1991.

Jim Williams, strength and conditioning; born March 29, 1948, Kingston, Pa., lives in Mt. Laurel, N.J. No college or pro playing experience. College coach: Nebraska 1972-74, Arkansas 1974-77, Wyoming 1977-79. Pro coach: New York Giants 1979-81, New York Jets 1982-89, joined Eagles in 1991.

Richard Wood, running backs; born February 2, 1936, Lanett, Ala., lives in Mt. Laurel, N.J. Quarterback Auburn 1956-59. Pro quarterback Baltimore Colts 1960-61, San Diego Chargers 1962, Denver Broncos 1962, New York Jets 1963-64, Oakland Raiders 1965, Miami Dolphins 1966. College coach: Georgia 1967-68, Mississippi 1971-73, Auburn 1986. Pro coach: Oakland Raiders 1969-70, Cleveland Browns 1974, New Orleans Saints 1976-77, Atlanta Falcons 1978-82, Philadelphia Eagles 1983, Kansas City Chiefs 1987-88, New England Patriots 1989-90, rejoined Eagles in 1991.

Philadelphia Eagles 1992 First-Year Roster

Name	Pos.	Ht.	Wt.	Birth-date	College	Hometown	How Acq.
Allen, Ron	CB-S	5-7	167	1/4/69	Rutgers	Iselin, N.J.	FA
Anderson, Preston	DE-D1	6-4	265	3/28/69	Duke	Norwalk, Conn.	FA
Barlow, Corey	CB	5-9	182	11/1/70	Auburn	Atlanta, Ga.	D5
Bartley, Ephesians	LB	6-2	213	8/9/69	Florida	Jacksonville, Fla.	D9
Boatwright, William	G	6-2	307	10/24/69	Virginia Tech	Northampton, Va.	D7
Brooks, Tony	RB	6-0	230	8/17/69	Notre Dame	Tulsa, Okla.	D4a
Bullough, Chuck	LB	6-1	226	3/3/69	Michigan State	Orchard Park, N.Y.	D8
Campbell, Jesse (1)	S	6-1	215	4/11/69	North Carolina State	Vanceboro, N.C.	D2-'91
Christ, Tim	T	6-5	280	4/19/69	Rutgers	Morrisville, N.J.	FA
Graham, Peter	QB	6-3	207	7/25/67	Notre Dame	Rumson, N.J.	FA
Graves, Broderick (1)	RB	5-11	202	4/7/68	Winston-Salem State	Charlotte, N.C.	FA
Hess, Bill (1)	WR	5-8	171	2/6/66	West Chester	West Chester, Pa.	FA
Houston, Brandon	T	6-4	284	4/2/69	Oklahoma	Abernathy, Tex.	D12
Hunter, Stacy	TE	6-4	284	11/1/68	Northeastern	Jacksonville, Tex.	FA
Jeter, Tommy	DT	6-5	282	9/20/69	Texas	Nacogdoches, Tex.	D3
Kovell, Paul (1)	TE	6-2	233	4/28/68	Indiana, Pa.	Uniontown, Pa.	FA
McMillan, Chad	C	6-3	273	9/13/68	Texas	Katy, Tex.	FA
McMillian, Mark	CB-S	5-7	162	4/29/70	Alabama	Los Angeles, Calif.	D10
Mitchell, Chris (1)	CB-S	6-1	197	11/26/67	Mississippi	Town Creek, Ala.	FA
Patterson, Melvin (1)	WR	6-1	190	9/7/65	Stephen F. Austin	Killeen, Tex.	FA
Smith, Carl	RB	5-9	188	4/24/68	Maine	Riverhead, N.Y.	FA
Stacy, Siran	RB	5-11	203	8/6/68	Alabama	Geneva, Ala.	D2
Sydner, Jeff	WR-KR	5-7	170	11/11/69	Hawaii	Columbus, Ohio	D6
Tudors, Pumpy	P	5-7	203	11/3/68	Tenn.-Chattanooga	Jasper, Tenn.	D11
Weldon, Casey	QB	6-0	200	2/3/69	Florida State	Tallahassee, Fla.	D4b

The term NFL Rookie is defined as a player who is in his first season of professional football and has not been on the roster of another professional football team for any regular-season or postseason games. A Rookie is designated by an "R" on NFL rosters. Players who have been active in another professional football league or players who have NFL experience, including either preseason training camp or being on an active roster for fewer than three regular-season or postseason games, are termed NFL First-Year Players. An NFL First-Year Player is designated by a "1" on NFL rosters. Thereafter, a player on an NFL active roster for at least three regular-season or postseason games is credited with an additional year of NFL playing experience.

NOTES

_____

_____

_____

_____

_____

_____

_____

_____

PHOENIX CARDINALS

National Football Conference Eastern Division

Team Colors: Cardinal Red, Black, and White

P.O. Box 888
Phoenix, Arizona 85001-0888
Telephone: (602) 379-0101

Club Officials

President: William V. Bidwill
Executive Vice President: Joe Rhein
Vice President/General Manager: Larry Wilson
Secretary and General Counsel:
   Thomas J. Guilfoil
Treasurer and Chief Financial Officer:
   Charley Schlegel
Director of Pro Personnel: Erik Widmark
Director of Player Personnel: George Boone
Public Relations Director: Paul Jensen
Media Coordinator: Greg Gladysiewski
Director of Community Relations: Adele Harris
Director of Marketing: Joe Castor
Ticket Manager: Steve Walsh
Trainer: John Omohundro
Assistant Trainers: Jim Shearer, Jeff Herndon
Equipment Manager: Mark Ahlemeier
Assistant Equipment Manager: Steve Christensen

Stadium: Sun Devil Stadium • **Capacity:** 73,473
   Fifth Street
   Tempe, Arizona 85287

Playing Surface: Grass

Training Camp: Northern Arizona University
   Flagstaff, Arizona 86011

1992 Schedule

Preseason
Aug. 8	**San Diego**	7:30
Aug. 15	**Chicago**	5:00
Aug. 22	at Seattle	7:00
Aug. 28	at Denver	7:00

Regular Season
Sept. 6	at Tampa Bay	4:00
Sept. 13	**Philadelphia**	5:00
Sept. 20	at Dallas	3:00
Sept. 27	**Open Date**	
Oct. 4	**Washington**	1:00
Oct. 11	at New York Giants	1:00
Oct. 18	**New Orleans**	1:00
Oct. 25	at Philadelphia	1:00
Nov. 1	**San Francisco**	2:00
Nov. 8	at Los Angeles Rams	1:00
Nov. 15	at Atlanta	1:00
Nov. 22	**Dallas**	2:00
Nov. 29	at Washington	1:00
Dec. 6	**San Diego**	2:00
Dec. 12	**N.Y. Giants** (Saturday)	2:00
Dec. 20	at Indianapolis	1:00
Dec. 27	**Tampa Bay**	2:00

Cardinals Coaching History

Chicago 1920-1959
St. Louis 1960-1987
(375-505-39)

1920-22	John (Paddy) Driscoll	17-8-4
1923-24	Arnold Horween	13-8-1
1925-26	Norman Barry	16-8-2
1927	Guy Chamberlin	3-7-1
1928	Fred Gillies	1-5-0
1929	Dewey Scanlon	6-6-1
1930	Ernie Nevers	5-6-2
1931	LeRoy Andrews*	0-1-0
1931	Ernie Nevers	5-3-0
1932	Jack Chevigny	2-6-2
1933-34	Paul Schissler	6-15-1
1935-38	Milan Creighton	16-26-4
1939	Ernie Nevers	1-10-0
1940-42	Jimmy Conzelman	8-22-3
1943-45	Phil Handler**	1-29-0
1946-48	Jimmy Conzelman	27-10-0
1949	Phil Handler-Buddy Parker***	2-4-0
1949	Raymond (Buddy) Parker	4-1-1
1950-51	Earl (Curly) Lambeau****	7-15-0
1951	Phil Handler-Cecil Isbell#	1-1-0
1952	Joe Kuharich	4-8-0
1953-54	Joe Stydahar	3-20-1
1955-57	Ray Richards	14-21-1
1958-61	Frank (Pop) Ivy##	17-29-2
1961	Chuck Drulis-Ray Prochaska-Ray Willsey###	2-0-0
1962-65	Wally Lemm	27-26-3
1966-70	Charley Winner	35-30-5
1971-72	Bob Hollway	8-18-2
1973-77	Don Coryell	42-29-1
1978-79	Bud Wilkinson####	9-20-0
1979	Larry Wilson	2-1-0
1980-85	Jim Hanifan	39-50-1
1986-89	Gene Stallings(α	23-34-1
1989	Hank Kuhlmann	0-5-0
1990-91	Joe Bugel	9-23-0

*Resigned after one game in 1931
**Co-coach with Walt Kiesling in Chicago Cardinals-Pittsburgh merger in 1944
***Co-coaches for first six games in 1949
****Resigned after 10 games in 1951
#Co-coaches
##Resigned after 12 games in 1961
###Co-coaches
####Released after 13 games in 1979
(α Released after 11 games in 1989

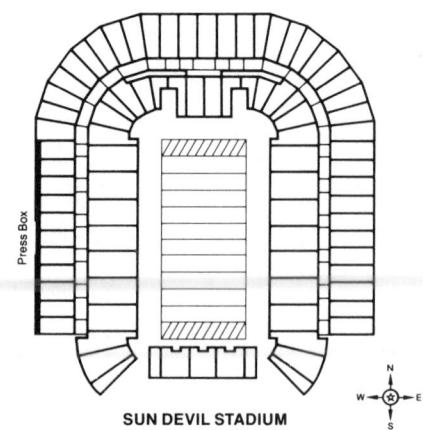

SUN DEVIL STADIUM

Record Holders

Individual Records—Career
Category	Name	Performance
Rushing (Yds.)	Ottis Anderson, 1979-1986	7,999
Passing (Yds.)	Jim Hart, 1966-1983	34,639
Passing (TDs)	Jim Hart, 1966-1983	209
Receiving (No.)	Roy Green, 1979-1990	522
Receiving (Yds.)	Roy Green, 1979-1990	8,497
Interceptions	Larry Wilson, 1960-1972	52
Punting (Avg.)	Jerry Norton, 1959-1961	44.9
Punt Return (Avg.)	Charley Trippi, 1947-1955	13.7
Kickoff Return (Avg.)	Ollie Matson, 1952, 1954-58	28.5
Field Goals	Jim Bakken, 1962-1978	282
Touchdowns (Tot.)	Roy Green, 1979-1990	70
Points	Jim Bakken, 1962-1978	1,380

Individual Records—Single Season
Category	Name	Performance
Rushing (Yds.)	Ottis Anderson, 1979	1,605
Passing (Yds.)	Neil Lomax, 1984	4,614
Passing (TDs)	Charley Johnson, 1963	28
	Neil Lomax, 1984	28
Receiving (No.)	J.T. Smith, 1987	91
Receiving (Yds.)	Roy Green, 1984	1,555
Interceptions	Bob Nussbaumer, 1949	12
Punting (Avg.)	Jerry Norton, 1960	45.6
Punt Return (Avg.)	John (Red) Cochran, 1949	20.9
Kickoff Return (Avg.)	Ollie Matson, 1958	35.5
Field Goals	Jim Bakken, 1967	27
Touchdowns (Tot.)	John David Crow, 1962	17
Points	Jim Bakken, 1967	117
	Neil O'Donoghue, 1984	117

Individual Records—Single Game
Category	Name	Performance
Rushing (Yds.)	John David Crow, 12-18-60	203
Passing (Yds.)	Neil Lomax, 12-16-84	468
Passing (TDs)	Jim Hardy, 10-2-50	6
	Charley Johnson, 9-26-65	6
	Charley Johnson, 11-2-69	6
Receiving (No.)	Sonny Randle, 11-4-62	16
Receiving (Yds.)	Sonny Randle, 11-4-62	256
Interceptions	Bob Nussbaumer, 11-13-49	*4
	Jerry Norton, 11-20-60	*4
Field Goals	Jim Bakken, 9-24-67	*7
Touchdowns (Tot.)	Ernie Nevers, 11-28-29	*6
Points	Ernie Nevers, 11-28-29	*40

*NFL Record

1991 Team Record
Preseason (4-0)

Date	Result		Opponents
8/3	W	31-13	at Seattle
8/11	W	12-10	at Chicago
8/17	W	46- 0	New England
8/23	W	34-10	Denver

Regular Season (4-12)

Date	Result		Opponents	Att.
9/1	W	24-14	at L.A. Rams	47,069
9/8	W	26-10	at Philadelphia	63,818
9/15	L	0-34	at Washington	54,662
9/22	L	9-17	Dallas	68,814
9/29	W	24-10	New England	26,043
10/6	L	9-20	at N.Y. Giants	75,891
10/13	L	7-34	at Minnesota	51,209
10/20	W	16-10	Atlanta	29,804
10/27	L	0-28	Minnesota	45,447
11/3	L	7-27	at Dallas	61,190
11/10	L	14-21	N.Y. Giants	50,048
11/17	L	10-14	at San Francisco	50,180
11/24	L	14-34	Philadelphia	37,307
12/8	L	14-20	Washington	48,373
12/15	L	19-24	at Denver	74,098
12/22	L	3-27	New Orleans	30,928

Score by Periods

Cardinals	43	68	32	53	0	—	196
Opponents	93	87	84	80	0	—	344

Attendance
Home 336,764   Away 478,117   Total 814,881
Single-game home record, 68,814 (9-22-91)
Single-season home record, 472,937 (1988)

1991 Team Statistics

	Cardinals	Opp.
Total First Downs	237	301
Rushing	73	132
Passing	143	156
Penalty	21	13
Third Down: Made/Att.	68/204	76/190
Third Down: Pct.	33.3	40.0
Fourth Down: Made/Att.	4/17	5/7
Fourth Down: Pct.	23.5	71.4
Total Net Yards	3962	5052
Avg. Per Game	247.6	315.8
Total Plays	926	965
Avg. Per Play	4.3	5.2
Net Yards Rushing	1295	2136
Avg. Per Game	80.9	133.5
Total Rushes	391	493
Net Yards Passing	2667	2916
Avg. Per Game	166.7	182.3
Sacked/Yards Lost	43/372	25/153
Gross Yards	3039	3069
Att./Completions	492/254	447/268
Completion Pct.	51.6	60.0
Had Intercepted	25	17
Punts/Avg.	77/44.7	71/45.2
Net Punting Avg.	38.9	37.7
Penalties/Yards Lost	78/661	94/734
Fumbles/Ball Lost	31/14	37/21
Touchdowns	19	43
Rushing	6	27
Passing	10	12
Returns	3	4
Avg. Time of Possession	29:01	30:59

1991 Individual Statistics

Scoring

	TD R	TD P	TD Rt	PAT	FG	Saf	TP
G. Davis	0	0	0	19/19	21/30	0	82
Johnson	4	2	0	0/0	0/0	0	36
E. Jones	0	4	0	0/0	0/0	0	24
Proehl	0	2	0	0/0	0/0	0	12
E. Hill	0	0	1	0/0	0/0	0	6
R. Hill	0	1	0	0/0	0/0	0	6
Lynch	0	0	1	0/0	0/0	0	6
Saddler	0	0	1	0/0	0/0	0	6
Thompson	1	0	0	0/0	0/0	0	6
Tupa	1	0	0	0/0	0/0	0	6
W. Williams	0	1	0	0/0	0/0	0	6
Cardinals	6	10	3	19/19	21/30	0	196
Opponents	27	12	4	41/43	15/23	0	344

Passing

	Att.	Comp.	Yds.	Pct.	TD	Int.	Tkld.	Rate
Tupa	315	165	2053	52.4	6	13	24/197	62.0
Chandler, T.B.-Phx.	154	78	846	50.6	5	10	17/134	50.9
Chandler, Phx.	50	25	289	50.0	1	2	7/58	57.8
Gelbaugh	118	61	674	51.7	3	10	10/94	42.1
Kupp	7	3	23	42.9	0	0	2/23	51.5
Camarillo	1	0	0	0.0	0	0	0/0	39.6
Thompson	1	0	0	0.0	0	0	0/0	39.6
Cardinals	492	254	3039	51.6	10	25	43/372	56.4
Opponents	447	268	3069	60.0	12	17	25/153	73.8

Rushing

	Att.	Yds.	Avg.	LG	TD
Johnson	196	666	3.4	21	4
Thompson	126	376	3.0	22	1
Chandler, T.B.-Phx.	26	111	4.3	12	0
Chandler, Phx.	8	32	4.0	12	0
Tupa	28	97	3.5	17	1
Centers	14	44	3.1	8	0
E. Jones	5	24	4.8	9	0
Gelbaugh	9	23	2.6	13	0
Proehl	3	21	7.0	17	0
Flagler	1	7	7.0	7	0
Kupp	1	5	5.0	5	0
Cardinals	391	1295	3.3	22	6
Opponents	493	2136	4.3	60t	27

Receiving

	No.	Yds.	Avg.	LG	TD
E. Jones	61	957	15.7	53	4
Proehl	55	766	13.9	62t	2
R. Hill	43	495	11.5	31t	1
Johnson	29	225	7.8	51t	2
Centers	19	176	9.3	23	0
Jorden	15	127	8.5	19	0
Jackson	8	108	13.5	30	0
Flagler	8	85	10.6	17	0
Reeves	8	45	5.6	13	0
Thompson	7	52	7.4	14	0
W. Williams	1	3	3.0	3t	1
Cardinals	254	3039	12.0	62t	10
Opponents	268	3069	11.5	43	12

Interceptions

	No.	Yds.	Avg.	LG	TD
A. Williams	6	60	10.0	32	0
McDonald	5	36	7.2	13	0
Lynch	3	59	19.7	35t	1
Zordich	1	27	27.0	27	0
Duerson	1	5	5.0	5	0
Fain, Cin.-Phx.	1	1	1.0	1	0
Patterson	1	0	0.0	0	0
Cardinals	17	187	11.0	35t	1
Opponents	25	399	16.0	79	1

Punting

	No.	Yds.	Avg.	In 20	LG
Camarillo	76	3445	45.3	19	60
Cardinals	77	3445	44.7	19	60
Opponents	71	3207	45.2	24	65

Punt Returns

	No.	FC	Yds.	Avg.	LG	TD
Jackson	31	3	244	7.9	19	0
Centers	5	2	30	6.0	12	0
Proehl	4	0	26	6.5	14	0
Edwards	1	1	7	7.0	7	0
Cardinals	41	6	307	7.5	19	0
Opponents	48	12	313	6.5	24	0

Kickoff Returns

	No.	Yds.	Avg.	LG	TD
Centers	16	330	20.6	39	0
Edwards	13	261	20.1	36	0
Flagler	12	208	17.3	32	0
R. Hill, Mia.-Phx.	9	146	16.2	33	0
R. Hill, Phx.	8	113	14.1	25	0
Jackson	2	41	20.5	21	0
Lomack	1	19	19.0	19	0
Cardinals	52	972	18.7	39	0
Opponents	42	958	22.8	99t	1

Sacks

	No.
Harvey	9.0
Nunn	7.0
Swann	4.0
Faulkner	2.0
Braxton	1.0
E. Hill	1.0
Wahler	1.0
Cardinals	25.0
Opponents	43.0

1992 Draft Choices

Round	Name	Pos.	College
2.	Tony Sacca	QB	Penn State
3.	Ed Cunningham	C	Washington
4.	Jeff Christy	T	Pittsburgh
	Michael Bankston	NT	Sam Houston State
6.	Brian Brauninger	T	Oklahoma
7.	Derek Ware	TE	Central State, Okla.
8.	Eric Blount	WR	North Carolina
9.	David Henson	NT	Central Arkansas
	Tyrone Williams	WR	Western Ontario
10.	Reggie Yarbrough	RB	Cal State-Fullerton
11.	Rob Baxley	T	Iowa
12.	Lance Wilson	NT	Texas

Phoenix Cardinals 1992 Veteran Roster

No.	Name	Pos.	Ht.	Wt.	Birth-date	NFL Exp.	College	Hometown	How Acq.	'91 Games/Starts
20	Bailey, Johnny	RB	5-8	180	3/17/67	3	Texas A&I	Houston, Tex.	PB(Chi)-'92#	14/0*
54	†Braxton, David	LB	6-2	230	5/26/65	4	Wake Forest	Jacksonville, N.C.	FA-'90	16/2
16	†Camarillo, Rich	P	5-11	195	11/29/59	12	Washington	Pico Rivera, Calif.	FA-'89	16/0
37	†Centers, Larry	RB	6-0	200	6/1/68	3	Stephen F. Austin	Tatum, Tex.	D5-'90	9/2
17	Chandler, Chris	QB	6-4	220	10/12/65	4	Washington	Everett, Wash.	W(TB)-'91	3/2
93	Coleman, Sidney	LB	6-2	250	1/14/64	5	Southern Mississippi	Gulfport, Miss.	PB(TB)-'91#	16/2
21	Davis, Dexter	CB	5-10	190	3/20/70	2	Clemson	Brooklyn, N.Y.	D4-'91	11/0
5	Davis, Greg	K	6-0	200	10/29/65	6	Citadel	Atlanta, Ga.	PB(Atl)-'91#	16/0
22	†Duerson, Dave	S	6-1	208	11/28/60	10	Notre Dame	Muncie, Ind.	FA-'91	11/4
81	Edwards, Anthony	WR	5-9	190	5/26/66	4	New Mexico Highlands	Casa Grande, Ariz.	FA-'91	13/0
24	Eilers, Pat	S	5-11	195	9/3/66	3	Notre Dame	St. Paul, Minn.	PB(Minn)-'92#	16/0*
94	Faulkner, Jeff	DE	6-4	305	4/4/64	4	Southern	Miami, Fla.	PB(Ind)-'91#	16/14
56	†Harvey, Ken	LB	6-3	230	5/6/65	5	California	Austin, Tex.	D1-'88	16/16
58	Hill, Eric	LB	6-2	250	11/14/66	4	Louisiana State	Galveston, Tex.	D1-'89	16/15
81	Hill, Randal	WR	5-10	177	9/21/69	2	Miami	Miami, Fla.	T(Mia)-'91	15/4
97	Hyche, Steve	LB	6-2	226	6/12/63	3	Livingston	Cordova, Ala.	FA-'91	16/0
80	Jackson, John	WR	6-0	183	1/2/67	3	Southern California	Diamond Bar, Calif.	FA-'90	16/3
53	Jax, Garth	LB	6-3	240	9/16/63	7	Florida State	Houston, Tex.	PB(Dall)-'89#	12/9
39	†Johnson, Johnny	RB	6-3	220	6/11/68	3	San Jose State	Santa Cruz, Calif.	D7-'90	15/14
86	Jones, Ernie	WR	6-0	200	12/15/64	5	Indiana	Elkhart, Ind.	D7-'88	16/16
55	Jones, Jock	LB	6-2	227	3/13/68	3	Virginia Tech	Ashland, Va.	FA-'91	5/0
75	Jones, Mike	DE-DT	6-4	285	8/25/69	2	North Carolina State	Columbia, S.C.	D2-'91	16/1
85	†Jorden, Tim	TE	6-3	235	10/30/66	3	Indiana	Westchester, Ohio	FA-'89	16/9
57	†Kauahi, Kani	C	6-3	275	9/6/59	10	Hawaii	Kekaha, Hawaii	PB(GB)-'89#	16/0
51	†Lewis, Bill	C	6-6	290	7/12/63	7	Nebraska	Sioux City, Iowa	PB(Raid)-'90#	16/16
28	Lofton, Steve	CB	5-9	180	11/26/68	2	Texas A&M	Jacksonville, Miss.	FA-'91	11/1
29	†Lynch, Lorenzo	CB	5-10	200	4/6/63	5	Cal State-Sacramento	Oakland, Calif.	PB(Chi)-'90#	16/14
40	Massey, Robert	CB	5-10	185	2/17/67	4	North Carolina Central	Charlotte, N.C.	T(NO)-'91	12/5
73	May, Mark	G-T	6-6	290	11/2/59	11	Pittsburgh	Oneonta, N.Y.	PB(SD)-'92#	9/0*
46	McDonald, Tim	S	6-2	215	1/6/65	6	Southern California	Fresno, Calif.	D2-'87	13/13
50	Nunn, Freddie Joe	LB	6-4	250	4/9/62	8	Mississippi	Louisville, Miss.	D1-'85	16/16
76	Patterson, Craig	NT	6-4	317	7/18/64	2	Brigham Young	Castle Dale, Utah	FA-'90	16/13
87	Proehl, Ricky	WR	6-0	190	3/7/68	3	Wake Forest	Hillsborough, N.J.	D3-'90	16/16
89	Reeves, Walter	TE	6-3	266	12/15/65	4	Auburn	Eufala, Ala.	D2-'89	15/13
82	Rolle, Butch	TE	6-4	245	8/19/64	7	Michigan State	Hallandale, Fla.	PB(Buff)-'92#	16/0*
3	Rosenbach, Timm	QB	6-1	210	10/27/66	3	Washington State	Pullman, Wash.	SD1-'89	0*
67	Sharpe, Luis	T	6-5	295	6/16/60	11	UCLA	Detroit, Mich.	D1-'82	16/16
52	Small, Jessie	LB	6-3	240	11/30/66	4	Eastern Kentucky	Boston, Ga.	PB(Phil)-'92#	16/8*
61	†Smith, Lance	G	6-3	290	11/1/63	8	Louisiana State	Kannapolis, N.C.	D3-'85	16/16
69	Smith, Vernice	G-T	6-3	298	10/24/65	3	Florida A&M	Orlando, Fla.	FA-'89	14/7
90	Stowe, Tyronne	LB	6-1	249	5/30/65	6	Rutgers	Passaic, N.J.	PB(Pitt)-'91#	13/4
98	Swann, Eric	DE-DT	6-4	310	8/16/70	2	No College	Swann Station, N.C.	D1-'91	12/3
27	Taylor, Jay	CB	5-10	175	11/8/67	4	San Jose State	San Diego, Calif.	D6-'89	16/1
34	Thompson, Anthony	RB	6-0	210	4/8/67	3	Indiana	Terre Haute, Ind.	D2-'90	16/4
74	t-Villa, Danny	G	6-5	305	9/21/64	6	Arizona State	Nogales, Ariz.	T(NE)-'92	10/10*
66	†Wahler, Jim	NT	6-4	275	7/29/66	4	UCLA	San Jose, Calif.	D4-'89	15/14
35	Williams, Aeneas	CB	5-10	187	1/29/69	2	Southern	New Orleans, La.	D3-'91	16/15
60	Williams, Willie	T	6-6	300	8/6/67	2	Louisiana State	Houston, Tex.	SD9-'90	16/3
68	Wolf, Joe	G	6-6	295	12/28/66	4	Boston College	Allentown, Pa.	D1b-'89	8/6
38	Zordich, Michael	S	6-1	200	10/12/63	6	Penn State	Youngstown, Ohio	PB(NYJ)-'89#	16/16

* Bailey played 14 games with Chicago in '91; Eilers played 16 games with Minnesota; May played 9 games with San Diego; Rolle played 16 games with Buffalo; Rosenbach missed '91 season due to injury; Small played 16 games with Philadelphia; Villa played 10 games with New England.

† Option playout; subject to developments.

t- Cardinals traded for Villa (New England).

Traded—T Tootie Robbins to Green Bay.

Plan B unconditional free agent.

Players lost through Plan B (7): RB Greg Amsler (NYG; 0 games in '91), CB Richard Fain (Chi; 2), QB Stan Gelbaugh (Sea; 6), QB Tom Tupa (Ind; 11), CB-S Marcus Turner (NYJ; 3), NT Chris Williams (Buff; 15), RB Ron Wolfley (Clev; 16).

Also played with Cardinals in 1991—G Mike Brennan (active for 8 games but did not play), LB Scott Evans (1), WR Amod Field (2), RB Terrence Flagler (7), QB Craig Kupp (1), WR Tony Lomack (1), CB-S Chris Oldham (2), DE Rod Saddler (4).

Coaching Staff

Head Coach, Joe Bugel

Pro Career: Named head coach on February 7, 1990. Became thirty-first head coach in the history of the franchise dating back to 1920. Assistant head coach-offense under Joe Gibbs with Washington Redskins from 1981-89. Tutored the famous "Hogs" as Redskins' offensive line coach during his tenure with Washington. The Redskins reached the playoffs five times in nine seasons, posting an 11-3 (.786) postseason record. Washington won three NFL championships and four division titles in that span. Four Redskin offensive linemen earned Pro Bowl recognition under Bugel's tutelage—Jeff Bostic, Russ Grimm, Joe Jacoby, and Mark May. He coached Houston Oilers' offensive line from 1977-80 when team set rushing and passing records (1980). He began his professional coaching career with the Detroit Lions in 1975-76. Career record: 9-23.

Background: Offensive guard at Western Kentucky (1960-62). He served as an assistant coach at Western Kentucky (1964-68), Navy (1969), Iowa State (1973), and Ohio State (1974).

Personal: Born March 10, 1940, in Pittsburgh, Pa. Joe and wife Brenda, live in Phoenix, and have three daughters—Angie, Holly, and Jennifer.

Assistant Coaches

Ted Cottrell, defensive line; born June 13, 1947, Chester, Pa., lives in Phoenix. Linebacker Delaware Valley College 1966-68. Pro linebacker Atlanta Falcons 1969-70, Winnipeg Blue Bombers (CFL) 1971. College coach: Rutgers 1973-80, 1983. Pro coach: Kansas City Chiefs 1981-82, New Jersey Generals (USFL) 1983-84, Buffalo Bills 1986-89, joined Cardinals in 1990.

Bobby Jackson, running backs; born February 16, 1940, Forsyth, Ga., lives in Phoenix. Linebacker-running back Samford (Ga.) 1959-62. No pro playing experience. College coach: Florida State 1965-69, Kansas State 1970-74, Louisville 1975-76, Tennessee 1977-82. Pro coach: Atlanta Falcons 1983-86, San Diego Chargers 1987-91, joined Cardinals in 1992.

Jim Johnson, defensive secondary; born May 26, 1941, Maywood, Ill., lives in Phoenix. Quarterback Missouri 1959-62. Pro tight end Buffalo Bills 1963-64. College coach: Missouri Southern 1967-68 (head coach), Drake 1969-72, Indiana 1973-76, Notre Dame 1977-80. Pro coach: Oklahoma Outlaws (USFL) 1984, Jacksonville Bulls (USFL) 1985, joined Cardinals in 1986.

John Matsko, offensive line; born February 2, 1951, Cleveland, Ohio, lives in Phoenix. Fullback Kent State 1970-73. No pro playing experience. College coach: Kent State 1973, Miami, Ohio 1974-75, 1977, North Carolina 1978-84, Navy 1985, Arizona 1986, Southern California 1987-91. Pro coach: Joined Cardinals in 1992.

Mike Murphy, defensive assistant-quality control; born September 25, 1944, New York, N.Y., lives in Phoenix. Guard-linebacker Huron, S.D., College 1962-65. No pro playing experience. College coach: Vermont 1970-73, Idaho State 1974-76, Western Illinois 1977-78. Pro coach: Saskatchewan Roughriders (CFL) 1979-83, Chicago Blitz (USFL) 1984, Detroit Lions 1985-89, joined Cardinals in 1990.

Joe Pascale, outside linebackers; born April 4, 1946, New York, N.Y., lives in Phoenix. Linebacker Connecticut 1963-66. No pro playing experience. College coach: Connecticut 1967-68, Rhode Island 1969-73, Idaho State 1974-76 (head coach 1976), Princeton 1977-79. Pro coach: Montreal Alouettes (CFL) 1980-81, Ottawa Rough Riders (CFL) 1982-83, New Jersey Generals (USFL) 1984-85, joined Cardinals in 1986.

Ted Plumb, receivers; born August 20, 1939, Reno, Nev., lives in Phoenix. Wide receiver Baylor 1960-61. Pro wide receiver Buffalo Bills 1962. College coach: Cerritos, Calif., J.C. 1966-67, Texas Christian 1968-70, Tulsa 1971, Kansas 1972-73. Pro coach: New York Giants 1974-76, Atlanta Falcons 1977-79, Chicago Bears 1980-85, Philadelphia Eagles 1986-89, joined Cardinals in 1990.

Jerry Rhome, offensive coordinator; born March 6, 1942, Dallas, Tex., lives in Phoenix. Quarterback Southern Methodist 1960-61, Tulsa 1963-64. Pro quarterback Dallas Cowboys 1965-68, Cleveland Browns 1969, Houston Oilers 1970, Los Angeles Rams 1971-72. College coach: Tulsa 1973-75. Pro coach: Seattle Seahawks 1976-82, Washington Redskins 1983-87, San Diego Chargers 1988, Dallas Cowboys 1989, joined Cardinals in 1990.

Pete Rodriguez, special teams; born July 25, 1940, Chicago, Ill., lives in Phoenix. Guard-linebacker Denver University 1959-60, Western State, Colo. 1961-63. No pro playing experience. College coach: Western State, Colo. 1964, Arizona 1968-69, Western Illinois 1970-73, 1979-82 (head coach), Florida State 1974-75, Iowa State 1976-78, Northern Iowa 1986. Pro coach: Michigan Panthers (USFL) 1983-84, Denver Gold (USFL) 1985, Jacksonville Bulls (USFL) 1986, Ottawa Rough Riders (CFL) 1987, Los Angeles Raiders 1988-89, joined Cardinals in 1990.

Bob Rogucki, strength and conditioning; born September 27, 1953, Clarksburg, W. Va., lives in Phoenix. No college or pro playing experience. College coach: Penn State 1981, Weber State 1982, Army 1983-89. Pro coach: Joined Cardinals in 1990.

Fritz Shurmur, defensive coordinator; born July 15, 1932, Riverview, Mich., lives in Phoenix. Center Albion 1951-53. No pro playing experience. College coach: Albion 1956-61, Wyoming 1962-74 (head coach 1971-74). Pro coach: Detroit Lions 1975-77, New England Patriots 1978-81, Los Angeles Rams 1982-90, joined Cardinals in 1991.

Phoenix Cardinals 1992 First-Year Roster

Name	Pos.	Ht.	Wt.	Birth-date	College	Hometown	How Acq.
Bankston, Michael	NT	6-1	285	3/12/70	Sam Houston State	East Bernard, Tex.	D4b
Baxley, Rob	T	6-5	285	3/14/69	Iowa	Oswego, Ill.	D11
Blount, Eric	WR	5-9	192	9/22/70	North Carolina	Ayden, N.C.	D8
Brauninger, Brian	T	6-5	279	1/18/69	Oklahoma	Arlington, Tex.	D5
Brown, Eddie (1)	WR	5-11	192	10/2/69	Louisiana Tech	Miami, Fla.	FA-'91
Brown, Ivory Lee (1)	RB	6-2	230	8/17/69	Arkansas-Pine Bluff	Palestine, Tex.	D7-'91
Brown, Verlond	WR	6-1	175	11/26/68	Houston	Forrest City, Ark.	FA
Christy, Jeff	G-T	6-3	294	2/2/69	Pittsburgh	Freeport, Pa.	D4a
Coleman, Roderick	TE	6-5	250	12/4/68	Indiana	Albany, Ga.	FA
Cunningham, Ed	C	6-3	289	8/17/69	Washington	Alexandria, Va.	D3
Dutton, Doug	NT	6-4	265	8/13/69	Indiana State	Mahomet, Ill.	FA
Edwards, Bernard	WR	6-5	205	2/24/69	Ohio State	Ft. Myers, Fla.	FA
Henson, David	NT	6-2	280	11/28/67	Central Arkansas	Maumelle, Ark.	D9a
Jackson, Robert	WR	6-1	196	6/10/69	Central State, Ohio	Gaithersburg, Md.	FA
Kelly, Andy	QB	6-3	211	5/6/68	Tennessee	Dayton, Tenn.	FA
Nord, Mike (1)	T	6-7	290	11/23/67	North Alabama	Lexington, Ky.	FA-'91
Richards, James (1)	G	6-4	289	11/7/69	California	Antelope Valley, Calif.	FA
Rucker, Keith	NT	6-3	348	11/20/68	Ohio Wesleyan	University Park, Ill.	FA
Sacca, Tony	QB	6-5	234	4/17/70	Penn State	Delran, N.J.	D2
Sands, Tony	RB	5-6	175	10/24/68	Kansas	Ft. Lauderdale, Fla.	FA
Simms, Kelly	CB	5-10	200	11/10/70	Cincinnati	St. Petersburg, Fla.	FA
Taylor, Alphonso	NT	6-1	350	9/7/69	Temple	Trenton, N.J.	FA
Ware, Derek	TE	6-2	245	9/17/67	Central State, Okla.	Sacramento, Calif.	D7
Williams, Tyrone	WR	6-5	207	3/26/70	Western Ontario	Halifax, Nova Scotia	D9b
Wilson, Lance	NT	6-2	265	5/14/69	Texas	San Antonio, Tex.	D12
Wright, Willie (1)	LB	6-4	239	3/9/68	Wyoming	Riverton, Wyo.	FA-'91
Yarbrough, Reggie	RB	6-1	215	1/18/69	Cal State-Fullerton	Denver, Colo.	D10

The term NFL Rookie is defined as a player who is in his first season of professional football and has not been on the roster of another professional football team for any regular-season or postseason games. A Rookie is designated by an "R" on NFL rosters. Players who have been active in another professional football league or players who have NFL experience, including either preseason training camp or being on an active roster for fewer than three regular-season or post-season games, are termed NFL First-Year Players. An NFL First-Year Player is designated by a "1" on NFL rosters. Thereafter, a player on an NFL active roster for at least three regular-season or postseason games is credited with an additional year of NFL playing experience.

NOTES

SAN FRANCISCO 49ERS

National Football Conference Western Division

Team Colors: Forty Niners Gold and Scarlet

4949 Centennial Boulevard Santa Clara, California 95054 Telephone: (408) 562-4949

Club Officials

Owner: Edward J. DeBartolo, Jr.
President: Carmen Policy
Vice President-Football Administration:
John McVay
Vice President-Business Operations & C.F.O.:
Keith Simon
Coordinator of Football Operations/Player
Personnel: Dwight Clark
Director of Pro Personnel: Allan Webb
Director of Publications/Club Relations:
Jerry Walker
Director of Public/Community Relations:
Rodney Knox
Director of Marketing/Promotions:
Laurie Albrecht
Coordinator of Football Operations: Neal Dahlen
Ticket Manager: Lynn Carrozzi
Director of Stadium Operations:
Murlan (Mo) Fowell
Video Director: Robert Yanagi
Trainer: Lindsy McLean
Equipment Manager: Bronco Hinek

Stadium: Candlestick Park • **Capacity:** 66,513
San Francisco, California 94124

Playing Surface: Grass

Training Camp: Sierra Community College
Rocklin, California 95677

1992 Schedule

Preseason
Aug. 3	**Denver**	5:00
Aug. 8	**Los Angeles Raiders**	5:00
Aug. 16	vs. Washington at London	1:00
Aug. 21	at San Diego	5:00
Aug. 28	**Seattle**	5:00

Regular Season
Sept. 6	at New York Giants	4:00
Sept. 13	**Buffalo**	1:00
Sept. 20	at New York Jets	1:00
Sept. 27	at New Orleans	7:00
Oct. 4	**Los Angeles Rams**	1:00
Oct. 11	at New England	1:00
Oct. 18	**Atlanta**	1:00
Oct. 25	**Open Date**	
Nov. 1	at Phoenix	2:00
Nov. 9	at Atlanta (Monday)	9:00
Nov. 15	**New Orleans**	1:00
Nov. 22	at Los Angeles Rams	1:00
Nov. 29	**Philadelphia**	1:00
Dec. 6	**Miami**	1:00
Dec. 13	at Minnesota	12:00
Dec. 19	**Tampa Bay** (Saturday)	1:00
Dec. 28	**Detroit** (Monday)	6:00

49ers Coaching History
(324-274-13)

1950-54	Lawrence (Buck) Shaw	33-25-2
1955	Norman (Red) Strader	4-8-0
1956-58	Frankie Albert	19-17-1
1959-63	Howard (Red) Hickey*	27-27-1
1963-67	Jack Christiansen	26-38-3
1968-75	Dick Nolan	56-56-5
1976	Monte Clark	8-6-0
1977	Ken Meyer	5-9-0
1978	Pete McCulley**	1-8-0
1978	Fred O'Connor	1-6-0
1979-88	Bill Walsh	102-63-1
1989-91	George Seifert	42-11-0

*Resigned after three games in 1963
**Released after nine games in 1978

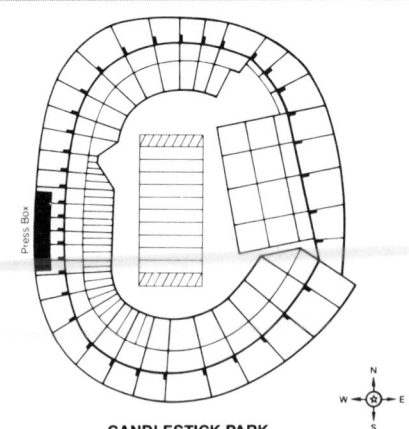

CANDLESTICK PARK

Record Holders

Individual Records—Career
Category	Name	Performance
Rushing (Yds.)	Joe Perry, 1950-1960, 1963	7,344
Passing (Yds.)	Joe Montana, 1979-1991	34,998
Passing (TDs)	Joe Montana, 1979-1991	242
Receiving (No.)	Jerry Rice, 1985-1991	526
Receiving (Yds.)	Jerry Rice, 1985-1991	9,072
Interceptions	Ronnie Lott, 1981-1990	51
Punting (Avg.)	Tommy Davis, 1959-1969	44.7
Punt Return (Avg.)	Manfred Moore, 1974-75	14.7
Kickoff Return (Avg.)	Abe Woodson, 1958-1964	29.4
Field Goals	Ray Wersching, 1977-1987	190
Touchdowns (Tot.)	Jerry Rice, 1985-1991	97
Points	Ray Wersching, 1977-1987	979

Individual Records—Single Season
Category	Name	Performance
Rushing (Yds.)	Roger Craig, 1988	1,502
Passing (Yds.)	Joe Montana, 1990	3,944
Passing (TDs)	Joe Montana, 1987	31
Receiving (No.)	Jerry Rice, 1990	100
Receiving (Yds.)	Jerry Rice, 1986	1,570
Interceptions	Dave Baker, 1960	10
	Ronnie Lott, 1986	10
Punting (Avg.)	Tommy Davis, 1965	45.8
Punt Return (Avg.)	Dana McLemore, 1982	22.3
Kickoff Return (Avg.)	Joe Arenas, 1953	34.4
Field Goals	Mike Cofer, 1989	29
Touchdowns (Tot.)	Jerry Rice, 1987	23
Points	Jerry Rice, 1987	138

Individual Records—Single Game
Category	Name	Performance
Rushing (Yds.)	Delvin Williams, 10-31-76	194
Passing (Yds.)	Joe Montana, 10-14-90	476
Passing (TDs)	Joe Montana, 10-14-90	6
Receiving (No.)	Jerry Rice, 10-14-90	13
Receiving (Yds.)	John Taylor, 12-11-89	286
Interceptions	Dave Baker, 12-4-60	*4
Field Goals	Ray Wersching, 10-16-83	6
Touchdowns (Tot.)	Jerry Rice, 10-14-90	5
Points	Jerry Rice, 10-14-90	30

*NFL Record

1991 Team Record
Preseason (5-0)

Date	Result		Opponents
7/27	W	24-17	at L.A. Raiders
8/3	W	21-7	vs. Chicago
			at Berlin
8/7	W	24- 6	Denver
8/19	W	24-13	San Diego
8/23	W	28-16	at Seattle

Regular Season (10-6)

Date	Result		Opponents	Att.
9/2	L	14-16	at N.Y. Giants	76,319
9/8	W	34-14	San Diego	60,753
9/15	L	14-17	at Minnesota	59,148
9/22	W	27-10	L.A. Rams	63,871
9/29	L	6-12	at L.A. Raiders	91,494
10/13	L	34-39	Atlanta	66,210
10/20	W	35- 3	Detroit	61,240
10/27	W	23- 7	at Philadelphia	65,796
11/3	L	14-17	at Atlanta	51,259
11/10	L	3-10	at New Orleans	68,591
11/17	W	14-10	Phoenix	50,180
11/25	W	33-10	at L.A. Rams	61,881
12/1	W	38-24	New Orleans	62,092
12/8	W	24-22	at Seattle	56,711
12/14	W	28-14	Kansas City	62,672
12/23	W	52-14	Chicago	60,419

Score by Periods

49ers	63	139	64	127	0	—	393
Opponents	30	89	64	56	0	—	239

Attendance
Home 487,437   Away 531,199   Total 1,018,636
Single-game home record, 66,334 (1-20-91)
Single-season home record, 506,186 (1990)

1991 Team Statistics

	49ers	Opp.
Total First Downs	336	260
Rushing	112	86
Passing	197	155
Penalty	27	19
Third Down: Made/Att.	92/193	71/201
Third Down: Pct.	47.7	35.3
Fourth Down: Made/Att.	3/8	9/17
Fourth Down: Pct.	37.5	52.9
Total Net Yards	5858	4554
Avg. Per Game	366.1	284.6
Total Plays	986	929
Avg. Per Play	5.9	4.9
Net Yards Rushing	1861	1512
Avg. Per Game	116.3	94.5
Total Rushes	440	399
Net Yards Passing	3997	3042
Avg. Per Game	249.8	190.1
Sacked/Yards Lost	24/170	31/212
Gross Yards	4167	3254
Att./Completions	522/325	499/267
Completion Pct.	62.3	53.5
Had Intercepted	12	12
Punts/Avg.	56/39.2	82/41.0
Net Punting Avg.	33.2	34.7
Penalties/Yards Lost	114/902	84/782
Fumbles/Ball Lost	33/19	32/16
Touchdowns	50	25
Rushing	19	8
Passing	29	16
Returns	2	1
Avg. Time of Possession	31:34	28:26

1991 Individual Statistics

Scoring

	TD R	TD P	TD Rt	PAT	FG	Saf	TP
Cofer	0	0	0	49/50	14/28	0	91
Rice	0	14	0	0/0	0/0	0	84
Taylor	0	9	0	0/0	0/0	0	54
Sydney	5	2	0	0/0	0/0	0	42
Rathman	6	0	0	0/0	0/0	0	36
D. Carter	2	1	1	0/0	0/0	0	24
Young	4	0	0	0/0	0/0	0	24
Henderson	2	0	0	0/0	0/0	0	12
Sherrard	0	2	0	0/0	0/0	0	12
Griffin	0	0	1	0/0	0/0	0	6
Williams	0	1	0	0/0	0/0	0	6
Jordan	0	0	0	0/0	0/0	1	2
49ers	19	29	2	49/50	14/28	1	393
Opponents	8	16	1	23/25	22/25	0	239

Passing

	Att.	Comp.	Yds.	Pct.	TD	Int.	Tkld.	Rate
Young	279	180	2517	64.5	17	8	13/79	101.8
Bono	237	141	1617	59.5	11	4	11/91	88.5
Musgrave	5	4	33	80.0	1	0	0/0	133.8
Sydney	1	0	0	0.0	0	0	0/0	39.6
49ers	522	325	4167	62.3	29	12	24/170	96.2
Opponents	499	267	3254	53.5	16	12	31/212	74.5

Rushing

	Att.	Yds.	Avg.	LG	TD
Henderson	137	561	4.1	25	2
Young	66	415	6.3	21	4
D. Carter	85	379	4.5	53t	2
Sydney	57	245	4.3	32	5
Rathman	63	183	2.9	16	6
Bono	17	46	2.7	18	0
Tillman	13	40	3.1	8	0
Rice	1	2	2.0	2	0
Prokop	1	-10	-10.0	-10	0
49ers	440	1861	4.2	53t	19
Opponents	399	1512	3.8	37	8

Receiving

	No.	Yds.	Avg.	LG	TD
Rice	80	1206	15.1	73t	14
Taylor	64	1011	15.8	97t	9
Rathman	34	286	8.4	32	0
Henderson	30	303	10.1	23	0
Jones	27	417	15.4	41	0
Sherrard	24	296	12.3	31	2
D. Carter	23	253	11.0	26	1
Williams	22	235	10.7	21	1
Sydney	13	90	6.9	19	2
Beach	4	43	10.8	20	0
Walls	2	24	12.0	21	0
Tillman	2	3	1.5	3	0
49ers	325	4167	12.8	97t	29
Opponents	267	3254	12.2	51	16

Interceptions

	No.	Yds.	Avg.	LG	TD
Waymer	4	77	19.3	42	0
K. Lewis	2	20	10.0	20	0
Jackson	1	11	11.0	11	0
Romanowski	1	7	7.0	7	0
Lee	1	5	5.0	5	0
Whitmore	1	5	5.0	5	0
Bowles	1	0	0.0	0	0
Griffin	1	0	0.0	0	0
49ers	12	125	10.4	42	0
Opponents	12	82	6.8	37	0

Punting

	No.	Yds.	Avg.	In 20	LG
Mojsiejenko	16	656	41.0	0	55
Prokop	40	1541	38.5	8	58
49ers	56	2197	39.2	8	58
Opponents	82	3365	41.0	17	58

Punt Returns

	No.	FC	Yds.	Avg.	LG	TD
Taylor	31	14	267	8.6	24	0
Beach	10	0	53	5.3	15	0
K. Lewis	1	0	0	0.0	0	0
Griffin	0	1	0	—	0	0
49ers	42	15	320	7.6	24	0
Opponents	30	6	239	8.0	23	0

Kickoff Returns

	No.	Yds.	Avg.	LG	TD
D. Carter	37	839	22.7	98t	1
Tillman	9	132	14.7	27	0
Beach	2	37	18.5	23	0
Sydney	1	13	13.0	13	0
Whitmore	1	7	7.0	7	0
49ers	50	1028	20.6	98t	1
Opponents	66	1288	19.5	100t	1

Sacks

	No.
Haley	7.0
Roberts	7.0
Brown	3.0
Harris	3.0
Holt	3.0
Fagan	2.0
DeLong	1.0
Romanowski	1.0
Washington	1.0
Waymer	1.0
Whitmore	1.0
49ers	31.0
Opponents	24.0

1992 Draft Choices

Round	Name	Pos.	College
1.	Dana Hall	DB	Washington
2.	Amp Lee	RB	Florida State
3.	Brian Bollinger	G	North Carolina
4.	Mark Thomas	DE	North Carolina St.
6.	Damien Russell	DB	Virginia Tech
9.	Darian Hagan	QB	Colorado
10.	Corey Mayfield	DE	Oklahoma
11.	Tom Covington	TE	Georgia Tech
12.	Matt LaBounty	DE	Oregon

San Francisco 49ers 1992 Veteran Roster

No.	Name	Pos.	Ht.	Wt.	Birth-date	NFL Exp.	College	Hometown	How Acq.	'91 Games/ Starts
79	Barton, Harris	G	6-4	280	4/19/64	6	North Carolina	Atlanta, Ga.	D1a-'87	16/16
13	Bono, Steve	QB	6-4	215	5/11/62	8	UCLA	Norristown, Pa.	FA-'89	9/6
22	Bowles, Todd	S	6-2	205	11/18/63	7	Temple	Elizabeth, N.J.	PB(Wash)-'91#	16/14
96	Brown, Dennis	DE	6-4	290	11/6/67	3	Washington	Long Beach, Calif.	D2a-'90	16/4
64	Burt, Jim	NT	6-1	270	6/7/59	12	Miami	Waldwick, N.J.	FA-'89	4/1
35	Carter, Dexter	RB	5-9	170	9/15/67	3	Florida State	Appling County, Ga.	D1-'90	16/15
95	Carter, Michael	NT	6-2	285	10/29/60	9	Southern Methodist	Dallas, Tex.	D5a-'84	15/15
6	Cofer, Mike	K	6-1	190	2/19/64	8	North Carolina State	Charlotte, N.C.	FA-'88	16/0
27	Crudup, Derrick	S	6-3	219	2/15/65	3	Oklahoma	Boca Raton, Fla.	PB(Raid)-'92#	16/0*
25	Davis, Eric	CB	5-11	178	1/26/68	2	Jacksonville State	Anniston, Ala.	D2b-'90	2/2
59	†DeLong, Keith	LB	6-2	235	8/14/67	4	Tennessee	Knoxville, Tenn.	D1-'89	15/14
54	Donahue, Mitch	LB	6-2	254	2/4/68	2	Wyoming	Billings, Mont.	D4a-'91	13/0
75	Fagan, Kevin	DE	6-4	265	4/25/63	6	Miami	Lake Worth, Fla.	D4c-'86	8/7
67	Foster, Roy	G	6-4	290	5/24/60	11	Southern California	Shawnee Mission, Kan.	PB(Mia)-'91#	16/16
31	Gash, Thane	S	5-11	198	9/1/65	4	East Tennessee State	Hendersonville, N.C.	PB(Clev)-'92#	0*
98	Goss, Antonio	LB	6-4	228	8/11/66	4	North Carolina	Randleman, N.C.	D12a-'89	14/0
29	Griffin, Don	CB	6-0	176	3/17/64	7	Middle Tennessee State	Pelham, Ga.	D6-'86	16/16
93	Haggins, Odell	NT	6-2	275	2/27/67	2	Florida State	Bartow, Fla.	FA-'92	5/0*
94	Haley, Charles	LB-DE	6-5	230	1/6/64	7	James Madison	Campbell County, Va.	D4a-'86	14/14
63	Hamel, Dean	DE	6-3	271	7/7/61	7	Tulsa	Warren, Mich.	FA-'92	0*
36	Hanks, Merton	CB	6-2	185	3/12/68	2	Iowa	Lake Highlands, Tex.	D5a-'91	13/8
92	Harris, Tim	LB-DE	6-6	258	9/10/64	7	Memphis State	Memphis, Tenn.	T(GB)-'91	11/4
5	Hatcher, Dale	P	6-2	230	4/5/63	7	Clemson	Cheraw, S.C.	FA-'92	13/0*
30	†Henderson, Keith	RB	6-1	220	8/4/66	4	Georgia	Carterville, Ga.	D3-'89	14/1
47	Hendrix, Manny	CB	5-10	188	10/20/64	7	Utah	Phoenix, Ariz.	PB(Dall)-'92#	16/3*
78	Holt, Pierce	DE	6-4	280	1/1/62	5	Angelo State	Houston, Tex.	D2b-'88	13/11
40	Jackson, Johnnie	S	6-1	204	1/11/67	4	Houston	Harlingen, Tex.	D5a-'89	16/4
55	Johnson, John	LB	6-3	230	5/8/68	2	Clemson	LaGrange, Ga.	D2c-'91	9/0
84	†Jones, Brent	TE	6-4	230	2/12/63	6	Santa Clara	San Jose, Calif.	FA-'87	10/9
90	Jordan, Darin	LB	6-2	245	12/4/64	3	Northeastern	Stroughton, Mass.	PB(Raid)-'91#	15/4
21	Kyles, Troy	WR	6-1	185	8/13/68	2	Howard	Detroit, Mich.	FA-'92	0*
45	Lewis, Kevin	CB	5-11	173	11/14/66	3	Northwestern Louisiana	New Orleans, La.	FA-'90	16/3
83	†Lewis, Ronald	WR	5-11	173	3/25/68	2	Florida State	Jacksonville, Fla.	D3a-'90	0*
43	Logan, Marc	RB	6-0	212	5/9/65	6	Kentucky	Lexington, Ky.	PB(Mia)-'92#	16/0*
62	McIntyre, Guy	G	6-3	265	2/17/61	9	Georgia	Thomasville, Ga.	D3-'84	16/16
16	Montana, Joe	QB	6-2	195	6/11/56	13	Notre Dame	New Eagle, Pa.	D3-'79	0*
69	Neville, Tom	G	6-5	298	9/4/61	4	Fresno State	Fairbanks, Alaska	FA-'91	12/0
26	Pollard, Darryl	CB	5-11	187	5/11/65	5	Weber State	Colorado Springs, Colo.	FA-'88	0*
4	†Prokop, Joe	P	6-2	225	7/7/60	7	Cal Poly-Pomona	White Bear Lake, Minn.	FA-'91	11/0
44	Rathman, Tom	RB	6-1	232	10/7/62	7	Nebraska	Grand Island, Neb.	D3a-'86	16/16
52	Reichenbach, Mike	LB	6-2	240	9/14/61	9	East Stroudsburg	Bethlehem, Pa.	PB(Mia)-'92#	16/15*
80	†Rice, Jerry	WR	6-2	200	10/13/62	8	Mississippi Valley State	Crawford, Miss.	D1-'85	16/16
91	†Roberts, Larry	DE	6-3	275	6/2/63	7	Alabama	Dothan, Ala.	D2-'86	16/9
53	Romanowski, Bill	LB	6-4	231	4/2/66	5	Boston College	Vernon, Conn.	D3-'88	16/16
61	Sapolu, Jesse	C	6-2	260	3/10/61	7	Hawaii	Honolulu, Hawaii	D11-'83	16/16
88	†Sherrard, Mike	WR	6-2	187	6/21/63	5	UCLA	Los Angeles, Calif.	PB(Dall)-'89#	16/0
92	Siglar, Ricky	T	6-7	296	6/14/66	2	San Jose State	Albuquerque, N.M.	FA-'89	0*
24	Sydney, Harry	RB	6-0	217	6/26/59	6	Kansas	Fayetteville, N.C.	FA-'87	16/0
64	Tamm, Ralph	C-G	6-4	280	3/11/66	3	West Chester	Bensalem, Pa.	PB(Cin)-'92#	4/0*
82	Taylor, John	WR	6-1	185	3/31/62	6	Delaware State	Pennsauken, N.J.	D3c-'86	16/16
60	Thomas, Chuck	C	6-3	280	12/24/60	7	Oklahoma	Houston, Tex.	FA-'87	12/0
32	Thomas, Rodney	CB	5-10	190	12/21/65	5	Brigham Young	Ontario, Calif.	FA-'92	3/0*
38	Toney, Anthony	RB	6-0	233	9/23/62	6	Texas A&M	Salinas, Calif.	FA-'92	0*
23	Turner, Odessa	WR	6-3	215	10/12/64	6	Northwestern Louisiana	Monroe, La.	PB(NYG)-'92#	16/0*
74	†Wallace, Steve	T	6-5	276	12/27/64	7	Auburn	Atlanta, Ga.	D4b-'86	16/16
89	†Walls, Wesley	TE	6-5	246	2/26/66	4	Mississippi	Pontotoc, Miss.	D2-'89	15/0
99	†Walter, Michael	LB	6-3	238	11/30/60	10	Oregon	Eugene, Ore.	W(Dall)-'84	11/11
97	Washington, Ted	NT-DE	6-4	299	4/13/68	2	Louisville	Tampa, Fla.	D1-'91	16/0
41	Whitmore, David	S	6-0	235	7/6/67	3	Stephen F. Austin	Daingerfield, Tex.	PB(NYG)-'91#	11/0
81	†Williams, Jamie	TE	6-4	245	2/25/60	10	Nebraska	Houston, Tex.	PB(Hou)-'89#	16/7
8	Young, Steve	QB	6-2	200	10/11/61	8	Brigham Young	Greenwich, Conn.	T(TB)-'87	11/10

* Crudup played 16 games with L.A. Raiders in '91; Gash missed '91 season due to injury; Haggins played 5 games with Buffalo; Hamel last active with Dallas in '90; Hatcher played 13 games with L.A. Rams; Hendrix played 16 games with Dallas; Kyles last active with N.Y. Giants in '90; R. Lewis, Montana, Pollard, and Siglar missed '91 season due to injury; Logan played 16 games with Miami; Reichenbach played 16 games with Miami; Tamm played 1 game with Cleveland, 2 games with Washington, and 1 game with Cincinnati; R. Thomas played 3 games with L.A. Rams; Toney last active with Philadelphia in '90; Turner played 16 games with N.Y. Giants.

† Option playout; subject to developments.

Plan B unconditional free agent.

Players lost through Plan B (7): WR Sanjay Beach (GB; 16 games in '91), T Scott Bowles (NE; did not play in '91), WR Tony Hargain (KC; did not play in '91), DE Greg Joelson (SD; 4), T Frank Pollack (Den; 15), RB Spencer Tillman (Hou; 16), S Dave Waymer (Raid; 16).

Also played with 49ers in '91—C Dean Caliguire (2 games), S Greg Cox (11), CB Mark Lee (5), P Ralf Mojsiejenko (5), QB Bill Musgrave (1).

COACHING STAFF

Head Coach, George Seifert

Pro Career: Named 49ers' head coach on January 26, 1989, after serving as the team's defensive coordinator since 1983. Immediately earned a place in league history, winning a record 17 games his first year and becoming only the second rookie head coach to lead his team to a Super Bowl title (Don McCafferty of Baltimore in 1970 was the first). Recorded the NFL's best won-loss mark in 1990, posting a 14-2 record and guided San Francisco to its fifth consecutive NFC West title. In 1991, the 49ers recorded a 10-6 mark, missing the playoffs for the first time since 1982. Joined 49ers as secondary coach in 1980. In only his second season in the pro ranks, San Francisco had the second best defense in the league and won a Super Bowl (XVI) title, despite starting three rookies in the defensive backfield. Appointed the team's defensive coordinator in 1983. Finished 1987 with the top defense in the NFL and a 13-2 record. In 1988, San Francisco's defense ranked third en route to the Super Bowl XXIII title. No pro playing experience. Career record: 42-11.

Background: Linebacker at University of Utah (1960-62). Served a six-month tour of duty with the U.S. Army following graduation. Returned to Utah as a graduate assistant in 1964. Named head coach at Westminster College in Salt Lake City in 1965. Assistant at Iowa (1966), Oregon (1967-71), and Stanford (1972-74). Left Stanford to become head coach at Cornell (1975-76). Joined Bill Walsh's staff at Stanford in 1977 and helped the Cardinal to a two-year mark of 17-7, including victories in the Sun and Bluebonnet Bowls. Received bachelor's degree in zoology (1963) and master's degree in physical education (1966) from Utah.

Personal: Born January 22, 1940, in San Francisco. He and his wife, Linda, have two children—Eve and Jason—and live in Los Altos, Calif.

Assistant Coaches

Jerry Attaway, conditioning; born January 3, 1946, Susanville, Calif., lives in San Jose, Calif. Defensive back Yuba, Calif., J.C. 1964-65, Cal-Davis 1967. No pro playing experience. College coach: Cal-Davis 1970-71, Idaho 1972-74, Utah State 1975-77, Southern California 1978-82. Pro coach: Joined 49ers in 1983.

Dwaine Board, defensive assistant; born November 29, 1956, Rocky Mount, Va., lives in Redwood City, Calif. Defensive lineman North Carolina A&T 1974-77. Pro defensive lineman San Francisco 49ers 1979-87, New Orleans Saints 1988. Pro coach: Joined 49ers in 1991.

Jeff Fisher, defensive backs; born February 25, 1958, Culver City, Calif., lives in Santa Clara, Calif. Defensive back Southern California 1978-80. Pro defensive back-punt returner Chicago Bears 1981-85. Pro coach: Philadelphia Eagles 1986-90, Los Angeles Rams 1991, joined 49ers in 1992.

Carl Jackson, running backs; born August 16, 1940, Bay City, Tex., lives in Santa Clara, Calif. Quarterback Prairie View A&M 1959-62. No pro playing experience. College coach: North Texas State 1976-78, Iowa 1979-91. Pro coach: Joined 49ers in 1992.

Alan Lowry, special teams; born November 21, 1950, Irving, Tex., lives in Santa Clara, Calif. Defensive back-quarterback Texas 1970-72. No pro playing experience. College coach: Virginia Tech 1974, Wyoming 1975, Texas 1976-81. Pro coach: Dallas Cowboys 1982-90, Tampa Bay Buccaneers 1991, joined 49ers in 1992.

John Marshall, defensive line; born October 2, 1945, Arroyo Grande, Calif., lives in Pleasanton, Calif. Linebacker Washington State 1964. No pro playing experience. College coach: Oregon 1970-76, Southern California 1977-79. Pro coach: Green Bay Packers 1980-82, Atlanta Falcons 1983-85, Indianapolis Colts 1986-88, joined 49ers in 1989.

San Francisco 49ers 1992 First-Year Roster

Name	Pos.	Ht.	Wt.	Birth-date	College	Hometown	How Acq.
Asman, Scott (1)	TE	6-4	245	6/28/69	West Chester	Philadelphia, Pa.	FA
Bates, Steve (1)	DE-LB	6-4	240	6/28/66	James Madison	Pittsburgh, Pa.	FA
Boatswain, Harry (1)	T	6-4	295	6/26/69	New Haven	Brooklyn, N.Y.	D5b-'91
Bollinger, Brian	G	6-5	285	11/21/68	North Carolina	Indialantic, Fla.	D3
Canley, Sheldon (1)	RB	5-9	195	4/19/68	San Jose State	Lompoc, Calif.	D7-'91
Covington, Tom	TE.	6-3	241	5/1/69	Georgia Tech	Hempstead, N.Y.	D11
Deese, Derrick	G	6-3	270	5/17/70	Southern California	Culver City, Calif.	FA
Dickson, Joel (1)	DE	6-3	280	12/16/67	California	Vallejo, Calif.	FA
Ford, Chris (1)	WR	6-1	185	5/20/67	Lamar	Houston, Tex.	FA
Evans, Kevin (1)	WR	6-4	190	8/16/68	San Jose State	Ft. Worth, Tex.	FA
Hagan, Darien	WR	5-9	191	2/1/70	Colorado	Los Angeles, Calif.	D9
Hall, Dana	S	6-2	206	7/8/69	Washington	Diamond Bar, Calif.	D1
Harrison, Martin (1)	LB	6-4	240	9/20/67	Washington	Bellevue, Wash.	D10
Keen, Robbie (1)	K-P	6-4	225	8/2/68	California	Orangevale, Calif.	FA
LaBounty, Matt	DE	6-4	254	1/3/69	Oregon	Novato, Calif.	D12
Lee, Amp	RB	5-11	200	10/1/71	Florida State	Chipley, Fla.	D2
Mayfield, Corey	NT	6-2	280	2/25/70	Oklahoma	Tyler, Tex.	D10
Musgrave, Bill (1)	QB	6-2	196	11/11/67	Oregon	Grand Junction, Colo.	FA-'91
Renna, Mike (1)	DE	6-4	270	7/26/67	Delaware	Princeton Junction, N.J.	FA
Russell, Damien	S	6-1	204	8/20/70	Virginia Tech	Baltimore, Md.	D6
Sanfratello, Mike (1)	DE	6-4	265	5/28/68	Northern Arizona	Scottsdale, Ariz.	FA
Seay, Mark	WR	6-0	175	4/11/67	Long Beach State	San Bernardino, Calif.	FA
Siler, Clarence	DE-LB	6-4	250	3/11/67	Cal State-Fullerton	Daytona Beach, Fla.	FA
Smith, Freddie	CB	6-1	188	9/22/69	San Jose State	San Bernardino, Calif.	FA
Smith, Leroy	LB	6-2	214	1/6/69	Iowa	Sicklerville, N.J.	FA
Thomas, Mark	DE	6-5	259	5/6/69	North Carolina State	Lilburn, Ga.	D4
Walker, Adam (1)	RB	6-1	210	6/7/68	Pittsburgh	Munhall, Pa.	FA
Watters, Ricky (1)	RB	6-1	212	4/7/69	Notre Dame	Harrisburg, Pa.	D2a-'91
Wilkins, David	DE-LB	6-4	240	2/24/69	Eastern Kentucky	Cincinnati, Ohio	FA

The term NFL Rookie is defined as a player who is in his first season of professional football and has not been on the roster of another professional football team for any regular-season or postseason games. A Rookie is designated by an "R" on NFL rosters. Players who have been active in another professional football league or players who have NFL experience, including either preseason training camp or being on an active roster for fewer than three regular-season or postseason games, are termed NFL First-Year Players. An NFL First-Year Player is designated by a "1" on NFL rosters. Thereafter, a player on an NFL active roster for at least three regular-season or postseason games is credited with an additional year of NFL playing experience.

NOTES

_____

_____

_____

_____

_____

_____

_____

Bobb McKittrick, offensive line; born December 29, 1935, Baker, Ore., lives in San Mateo, Calif. Guard Oregon State 1955-57. No pro playing experience. College coach: Oregon State 1961-64, UCLA 1965-70. Pro coach: Los Angeles Rams 1971-72, San Diego Chargers 1974-78, joined 49ers in 1979.

Bill McPherson, defensive coordinator; born October 24, 1931, Santa Clara, Calif., lives in San Jose, Calif. Tackle Santa Clara 1950-52. No pro playing experience. College coach: Santa Clara 1963-74, UCLA 1975-77. Pro coach: Philadelphia Eagles 1978, joined 49ers in 1979.

Mike Shanahan, offensive coordinator-quarterbacks; born August 24, 1952, Oak Park, Ill., lives in Santa Clara, Calif. Quarterback Eastern Illinois 1970-73. No pro playing experience. College coach: Oklahoma 1975-76, Northern Arizona 1977, Eastern Illinois 1978, Minnesota 1979, Florida 1980-83. Pro coach: Denver Broncos 1984-87, 1989-91, Los Angeles Raiders 1988-89 (head coach), joined 49ers in 1992.

Ray Sherman, receivers; born November 27, 1951, Berkeley, Calif., lives in Dublin, Calif. Wide receiver Laney, Calif., J.C. 1969-70, Fresno State 1971-72. Pro defensive back Green Bay Packers 1973. College coach: San Jose State 1974, California 1975, 1981, Michigan State 1976-77, Wake Forest 1978-80, Purdue 1982-85, Georgia 1986-87. Pro coach: Houston Oilers 1988-89, Atlanta Falcons 1990, joined 49ers in 1991.

Mike Solari, tight ends-offensive line assistant; born January 16, 1955, Daly City, Calif., lives in Santa Clara, Calif. Offensive lineman San Diego State 1975-76. No pro playing experience. College coach: Mira Vista, Calif., J.C. 1977-78, U.S. International 1979, Boise State 1980, Cincinnati 1981-82, Kansas 1983-85, Pittsburgh 1986, Alabama 1990-91. Pro coach: Dallas Cowboys 1987-88, Phoenix Cardinals 1989, joined 49ers in 1992.

Eric Wright, defensive backs assistant; born April 18, 1959, St. Louis, Mo., lives in Santa Clara, Calif. Defensive back Missouri 1978-80. Pro defensive back San Francisco 49ers 1981-90. Pro coach: Joined 49ers in 1991.

Bob Zeman, linebackers; born February 22, 1937, Wheaton, Ill., lives in Boulder Creek, Calif. Fullback/halfback Wisconsin 1957-59. Pro defensive back Los Angeles/San Diego Chargers 1960-61, 1965-66, Denver Broncos 1962-63. College coach: Northwestern 1968-69, Wisconsin 1970. Pro coach: Oakland Raiders 1971-77, 1984-86, Denver Broncos 1978-82, Buffalo Bills 1983, joined 49ers in 1989.

TAMPA BAY BUCCANEERS

National Football Conference
Central Division

Team Colors: Florida Orange, White, and Red

One Buccaneer Place
Tampa, Florida 33607
Telephone: (813) 870-2700

Club Officials

Owner: Hugh F. Culverhouse
President: Gay Culverhouse
Vice President-Football Administration:
  Rich McKay
Assistant to the President/Director of Ticket
  Operations: Terry Wooten
Director of Public Relations: Rick Odioso
Director of Corporate Sales: Jim Overton
Controller: Patrick Smith
Manager of Advertising & Sales: Paul Sickmon
Manager of Operations: Paul Royak
Asst. Director/Ticket Operations: Lori Grimm
Asst. Director/Public Relations: Cheryl Harden
Computer Services Coordinator: Terri Kimbell
Community Relations Representative:
  Tara Trousdell-Bassett
Media Relations Assistant: Scott Smith
Advertising Sales Assistant: Jayne Portnoy
Corporate Sales Assistant: Clay Marafiote
Trainer: Chris Smith
Assistant Trainer: Joe Joe Petrone
Equipment Manager: Frank Pupello
Assistant Equipment Manager: Carl Melchior
Video Director: Davy Levy
Assistant Video Director: Pat Brazil

Stadium: Tampa Stadium • **Capacity:** 74,292
  North Dale Mabry
  Tampa, Florida 33607

Playing Surface: Grass

Training Camp: University of Tampa
  401 West Kennedy Boulevard
  Tampa, Florida 33606

1992 Schedule

Preseason
Aug. 8	at Denver	4:00
Aug. 15	**Atlanta**	7:00
Aug. 22	at Miami	8:00
Aug. 28	**Cleveland**	7:30

Regular Season
Sept. 6	**Phoenix**	4:00
Sept. 13	**Green Bay**	1:00
Sept. 20	at Minnesota	12:00
Sept. 27	at Detroit	1:00
Oct. 4	**Indianapolis**	1:00
Oct. 11	**Open Date**	
Oct. 18	at Chicago	12:00
Oct. 25	**Detroit**	1:00
Nov. 1	at New Orleans	12:00
Nov. 8	**Minnesota**	1:00
Nov. 15	**Chicago**	4:00
Nov. 22	at San Diego	1:00
Nov. 29	vs. Green Bay at Milw.	12:00
Dec. 6	**Los Angeles Rams**	8:00
Dec. 13	**Atlanta**	1:00
Dec. 19	at San Francisco (Saturday)	1:00
Dec. 27	at Phoenix	2:00

Buccaneers Coaching History

(72-175-1)
1976-84	John McKay	45-91-1
1985-86	Leeman Bennett	4-28-0
1987-90	Ray Perkins*	19-41-0
1990-91	Richard Williamson	4-15-0

*Released after 13 games in 1990

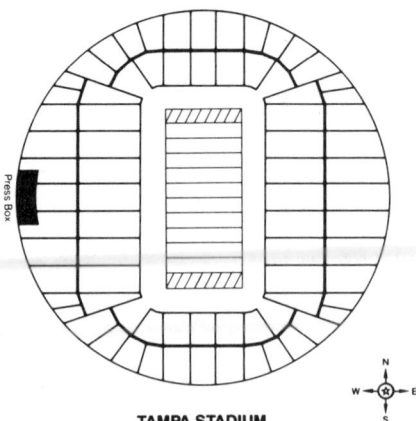

TAMPA STADIUM

Record Holders
Individual Records—Career
Category	Name	Performance
Rushing (Yds.)	James Wilder, 1981-89	5,957
Passing (Yds.)	Doug Williams, 1978-1982	12,648
Passing (TDs)	Doug Williams, 1978-1982	73
Receiving (No.)	James Wilder, 1981-89	430
Receiving (Yds.)	Kevin House, 1980-86	4,928
Interceptions	Cedric Brown, 1977-1984	29
Punting (Avg.)	Frank Garcia, 1983-87	41.1
Punt Return (Avg.)	Willie Drewrey, 1989-1991	9.4
Kickoff Return (Avg.)	Isaac Hagins, 1976-1980	21.9
Field Goals	Donald Igwebuike, 1985-89	94
Touchdowns (Tot.)	James Wilder, 1981-89	46
Points	Donald Igwebuike, 1985-89	416

Individual Records—Single Season
Category	Name	Performance
Rushing (Yds.)	James Wilder, 1984	1,544
Passing (Yds.)	Doug Williams, 1981	3,563
Passing (TDs)	Doug Williams, 1980	20
	Vinny Testaverde, 1989	20
Receiving (No.)	James Wilder, 1984	85
Receiving (Yds.)	Kevin House, 1981	1,176
Interceptions	Cedric Brown, 1981	9
Punting (Avg.)	Larry Swider, 1981	42.7
Punt Return (Avg.)	Willie Drewrey, 1989	11.0
Kickoff Return (Avg.)	Isaac Hagins, 1977	23.5
Field Goals	Steve Christie, 1990	23
Touchdowns (Tot.)	James Wilder, 1984	13
Points	Donald Igwebuike, 1989	99

Individual Records—Single Game
Category	Name	Performance
Rushing (Yds.)	James Wilder, 11-6-83	219
Passing (Yds.)	Doug Williams, 11-16-80	486
Passing (TDs)	Steve DeBerg, 9-13-87	5
Receiving (No.)	James Wilder, 9-15-85	13
Receiving (Yds.)	Mark Carrier, 12-6-87	212
Interceptions	Many times	2
	Last time by Harry Hamilton, 12-23-90	
Field Goals	Many times	4
	Last time by Steve Christie, 12-16-90	4
Touchdowns (Tot.)	Jimmie Giles, 10-20-85	4
Points	Jimmie Giles, 10-20-85	24

1991 Team Record

Preseason (3-1)

Date	Result		Opponents
8/5	W	23-10	at Cleveland
8/10	L	13-29	Miami
8/17	W	12- 7	at Atlanta
8/23	W	20- 7	Kansas City

Regular Season (3-13)

Date	Result		Opponents	Att.
9/1	L	13-16	at N.Y. Jets	61,204
9/8	L	20-21	Chicago	62,409
9/15	L	13-15	at Green Bay	58,114
9/22	L	10-17	Buffalo	57,323
9/29	L	3-31	at Detroit	48,784
10/6	W	14-13	Philadelphia	41,219
10/20	L	7-23	at New Orleans	68,591
10/27	L	0-27	Green Bay	40,275
11/3	L	13-28	at Minnesota	35,737
11/10	W	30-21	Detroit	37,742
11/17	L	7-43	at Atlanta	41,274
11/24	L	14-21	N.Y. Giants	63,698
12/1	L	14-33	at Miami	51,036
12/8	L	24-26	Minnesota	41,091
12/14	L	0-27	at Chicago	54,719
12/22	W	17- 3	Indianapolis	28,043

Score by Periods

Buccaneers	30	49	41	79	0	—	199
Opponents	82	111	77	95	0	—	365

Attendance

Home 371,800   Away 419,459   Total 791,259
Single-game home record, 72,077 (10-8-89)
Single-season home record, 545,980 (1979)

1991 Team Statistics

	Buccaneers	Opp.
Total First Downs	249	295
Rushing	79	120
Passing	147	147
Penalty	23	28
Third Down: Made/Att.	60/190	79/209
Third Down: Pct.	31.6	37.8
Fourth Down: Made/Att.	7/14	6/13
Fourth Down: Pct.	50.0	46.2
Total Net Yards	4001	4979
Avg. Per Game	250.1	311.2
Total Plays	922	989
Avg. Per Play	4.3	5.0
Net Yards Rushing	1429	2107
Avg. Per Game	89.3	131.7
Total Rushes	371	512
Net Yards Passing	2572	2872
Avg. Per Game	160.8	179.5
Sacked/Yards Lost	56/383	39/258
Gross Yards	2955	3130
Att./Completions	495/250	438/257
Completion Pct.	50.5	58.7
Had Intercepted	29	11
Punts/Avg.	84/40.3	71/42.9
Net Punting Avg.	32.3	36.5
Penalties/Yards Lost	88/780	110/925
Fumbles/Ball Lost	30/18	27/16
Touchdowns	22	41
Rushing	9	21
Passing	13	15
Returns	0	5
Avg. Time of Possession	26:57	33:03

1991 Individual Statistics

Scoring

	TD R	TD P	TD Rt	PAT	FG	Saf	TP
Christie	0	0	0	22/22	15/20	0	67
Cobb	7	0	0	0/0	0/0	0	42
Dawsey	1	3	0	0/0	0/0	0	24
J. Anderson	0	2	0	0/0	0/0	0	12
Carrier	0	2	0	0/0	0/0	0	12
Drewrey	0	2	0	0/0	0/0	0	12
Hill	0	2	0	0/0	0/0	0	12
Wilson	0	2	0	0/0	0/0	0	12
G. Anderson	1	0	0	0/0	0/0	0	6
Buccaneers	9	13	0	22/22	15/20	0	199
Opponents	21	15	5	40/41	25/35	2	365

Passing

	Att.	Comp.	Yds.	Pct.	TD	Int.	Tkld.	Rate
Testaverde	326	166	1994	50.9	8	15	35/234	59.0
Chandler	104	53	557	51.0	4	8	10/76	47.6
Carlson	65	31	404	47.7	1	6	11/73	34.4
Buccaneers	495	250	2955	50.5	13	29	56/383	53.4
Opponents	438	257	3130	58.7	15	11	39/258	81.7

Rushing

	Att.	Yds.	Avg.	LG	TD
Cobb	196	752	3.8	59t	7
G. Anderson	72	263	3.7	64t	1
Wilson	42	179	4.3	20	0
Testaverde	32	101	3.2	19	0
Chandler	18	79	4.4	12	0
Carlson	5	25	5.0	11	0
Highsmith	5	21	4.2	10	0
Dawsey	1	9	9.0	9t	1
Buccaneers	371	1429	3.9	64t	9
Opponents	512	2107	4.1	71t	21

Receiving

	No.	Yds.	Avg.	LG	TD
Dawsey	55	818	14.9	65t	3
Carrier	47	698	14.9	35	2
Ro. Hall	31	284	9.2	24	0
Drewrey	26	375	14.4	87t	2
G. Anderson	25	184	7.4	21	0
Wilson	20	121	6.1	15	2
Hill	17	185	10.9	18	2
Cobb	15	111	7.4	21	0
J. Anderson	6	73	12.2	34	2
E. Thomas	4	55	13.8	19	0
Anthony	4	51	12.8	14	0
Buccaneers	250	2955	11.8	87t	13
Opponents	257	3130	12.2	51	15

Interceptions

	No.	Yds.	Avg.	LG	TD
Covington	3	21	7.0	18	0
Fullington	2	13	6.5	10	0
Reynolds	2	7	3.5	7	0
Hampton	1	12	12.0	12	0
M. Carter	1	5	5.0	5	0
C. Carter	1	4	4.0	4	0
Marve	1	1	1.0	1	0
Buccaneers	11	63	5.7	18	0
Opponents	29	349	12.0	32	1

Punting

	No.	Yds.	Avg.	In 20	LG
Royals	84	3389	40.3	22	56
Buccaneers	84	3389	40.3	22	56
Opponents	71	3049	42.9	18	63

Punt Returns

	No.	FC	Yds.	Avg.	LG	TD
Drewrey	38	15	360	9.5	33	0
C. Carter	1	0	1	1.0	1	0
Buccaneers	39	15	361	9.3	33	0
Opponents	49	11	559	11.4	70t	1

Kickoff Returns

	No.	Yds.	Avg.	LG	TD
G. Anderson	34	643	18.9	39	0
Drewrey	12	246	20.5	43	0
Hardy	8	119	14.9	26	0
Cobb	2	15	7.5	15	0
Wilson	2	19	9.5	11	0
Ro. Hall	1	1	1.0	1	0
Ryan	1	4	4.0	4	0
Buccaneers	60	1047	17.5	43	0
Opponents	32	720	22.5	55	0

Sacks

	No.
B. Thomas	11.0
Manley	6.5
McCants	5.0
Newton	5.0
Davis	3.5
Chamblee	1.0
Covington	1.0
Rh. Hall	1.0
Murphy	1.0
Nichols	1.0
Reynolds	1.0
Seals	1.0
Tiggle	1.0
Buccaneers	39.0
Opponents	56.0

1992 Draft Choices

Round	Name	Pos.	College
2.	Courtney Hawkins	WR	Michigan State
3.	Mark Wheeler	DT	Texas A&M
	Tyji Armstrong	TE	Mississippi
4.	Craig Erickson	QB	Miami
5.	Rogerick Green	DB	Kansas State
	Santana Dotson	DE	Baylor
6.	James Malone	LB	UCLA
7.	Ken Swilling	DB	Georgia Tech
8.	Anthony McDowell	RB	Texas Tech
	Mike Pawlawski	QB	California
10.	Elijah Alexander	LB	Kansas State
11.	Mazio Royster	RB	Southern California
12.	Klaus Wilmsmeyer	P	Louisville

Tampa Bay Buccaneers 1992 Veteran Roster

No.	Name	Pos.	Ht.	Wt.	Birth-date	NFL Exp.	College	Hometown	How Acq.	'91 Games/ Starts
40	Anderson, Gary	RB	6-1	190	4/18/61	7	Arkansas	Columbia, Mo.	T(SD)-'90	16/5
89	Anderson, Jesse	TE	6-2	245	7/26/66	3	Mississippi State	West Point, Miss.	D4-'90	15/2
62	†Beckles, Ian	G	6-1	295	7/20/67	3	Indiana	Montreal, Canada	D5-'90	16/16
53	Brady, Ed	LB	6-2	235	6/17/62	9	Illinois	Morris, Ill.	PB(Cin)-'92#	16/0*
47	Burnette, Reggie	LB	6-2	240	10/4/68	2	Houston	Rayville, La.	PB(GB)-'92#	3/0*
88	Carrier, Mark	WR	6-0	185	10/28/65	6	Nicholls State	Church Point, La.	D3-'87	16/16
44	†Carter, Carl	CB	5-11	180	4/7/64	7	Texas Tech	Ft. Worth, Tex.	FA-'91	11/10
23	Carter, Marty	S	6-1	200	12/17/69	2	Middle Tennessee State	LaGrange, Ga.	D8-'91	14/11
57	Chamblee, Al	DE	6-1	240	11/17/68	2	Virginia Tech	Virginia Beach, Va.	FA-'91	9/0
34	†Cobb, Reggie	RB	6-0	215	7/7/68	3	Tennessee	Knoxville, Tenn.	D2-'90	16/11
25	Covington, Tony	S	5-11	190	12/26/67	2	Virginia	Winston-Salem, N.C.	D4-'91	16/12
79	†Davis, Reuben	DE-DT	6-4	295	5/7/65	5	North Carolina	Greensboro, N.C.	D9-'88	12/11
80	Dawsey, Lawrence	WR	6-0	195	11/16/67	2	Florida State	Dothan, Ala.	D3a-'91	16/10
17	DeBerg, Steve	QB	6-3	215	1/19/54	16	San Jose State	Anaheim, Calif.	PB(KC)-'92#	16/15*
76	†Dill, Scott	T	6-5	285	4/5/66	5	Memphis State	Birmingham, Ala.	PB(Phx)-'90#	8/0
87	†Drewrey, Willie	WR	5-7	170	4/28/63	8	West Virginia	Columbus, N.J.	PB(Hou)-'89#	16/0
95	Duckens, Mark	DE-DT	6-4	270	3/4/65	3	Arizona State	Wichita, Kan.	FA-'92	0*
33	Frizzell, William	S	6-3	205	9/8/62	9	North Carolina Central	Greenville, N.C.	PB(Phil)-'91#	16/4
27	Fullington, Darrell	S	6-1	195	4/17/64	5	Miami	Smyrna Beach, Fla.	FA-'91	11/0*
60	Grimes, Randy	C	6-4	275	7/20/60	9	Baylor	Tyler, Tex.	D2-'83	0*
74	Gruber, Paul	T	6-5	290	2/24/65	5	Wisconsin	Prairie Du Sac, Wis.	D1-'88	16/16
91	Hall, Rhett	DE-DT	6-2	260	12/5/68	2	California	Morgan Hill, Calif.	D6-'91	16/0
82	Hall, Ron	TE	6-4	245	3/15/64	6	Hawaii	Escondido, Calif.	D4-'87	15/15
36	Hardy, Robert	RB	5-10	210	9/1/67	2	Carson-Newman	Gaffney, S.C.	FA-'91	16/0
32	Highsmith, Alonzo	RB	6-1	235	2/26/65	6	Miami	Miami, Fla.	FA-'91	11/0*
84	†Hill, Bruce	WR	6-0	180	2/29/64	6	Arizona State	Lancaster, Calif.	D4c-'87	6/6
62	Hunter, John	C-G	6-8	300	8/16/65	4	Brigham Young	North Bend, Ore.	PB(Atl)-'92#	2/0*
28	Jennings, Stanford	RB	6-1	210	3/12/62	9	Furman	Summerville, S.C.	FA-'92	5/0*
24	Jones, Roger	CB	5-9	175	4/22/69	2	Tennessee State	Nashville, Tenn.	FA-'91	6/0*
41	King, Joe	CB	6-2	200	5/7/68	2	Oklahoma State	Dallas, Tex.	PB(Clev)-'92#	13/0*
22	Lilly, Sammy	CB-S	5-11	175	2/12/65	4	Georgia Tech	Augusta, Ga.	PB(Rams)-'92#	16/1*
21	Mack, Milton	CB	5-11	180	9/20/63	6	Alcorn State	Jackson, Miss.	PB(NO)-'92#	14/6*
78	Maxey, Curtis	DE-DT	6-3	300	6/28/65	3	Grambling	Indianapolis, Ind.	FA-'92	0*
61	Mayberry, Tony	C	6-4	285	12/8/67	3	Wake Forest	Springfield, Va.	D4-'90	16/16
52	McCants, Keith	DE	6-3	265	4/19/68	3	Alabama	Mobile, Ala.	D1-'90	16/16
73	†McHale, Tom	G	6-4	280	2/25/63	6	Cornell	Gaithersburg, Md.	FA-'87	15/11
70	McRae, Charles	T	6-7	290	9/16/68	2	Tennessee	Clinton, Tenn.	D1-'91	16/4
59	†Murphy, Kevin	LB	6-2	235	9/8/63	7	Oklahoma	Richardson, Tex.	D2-'86	16/14
83	t-Nattiel, Ricky	WR	5-9	180	1/25/66	6	Florida	Gainesville, Fla.	T(Den)-'92	16/0*
96	†Newton, Tim	DE-DT	6-0	275	3/23/63	8	Florida	Orlando, Fla.	FA-'90	16/16
66	Reimers, Bruce	G	6-7	300	9/28/60	9	Iowa State	Humboldt, Iowa	PB(Cin)-'92#	10/8*
29	†Reynolds, Ricky	CB	5-11	190	1/19/65	6	Washington State	Sacramento, Calif.	D2-'87	16/16
30	Robinson, Mark	S	5-11	200	9/13/62	8	Penn State	Silver Spring, Md.	T(KC)-'88	0*
75	Rogers, Reggie	DE	6-6	280	1/21/64	3	Washington	Sacramento, Calif.	FA-'92	2/0*
64	Ryan, Tim	G	6-2	280	9/2/68	2	Notre Dame	Kansas City, Mo.	D5b-'91	15/1
98	†Seals, Ray	DE	6-3	270	6/17/65	3	No College	Syracuse, N.Y.	FA-'90	10/9
19	Simmons, Stacy	WR	5-9	180	8/5/68	2	Florida	Clearwater, Fla.	FA-'92	14/0*
55	†Solomon, Jesse	LB	6-0	235	11/4/63	7	Florida State	Madison, Fla.	T(NE)-'91	13/12
4	Stryzinski, Dan	P	6-1	195	5/15/65	3	Indiana	Indianapolis, Ind.	PB(Pitt)-'92#	16/0
72	Taylor, Rob	T	6-6	290	11/14/60	7	Northwestern	Fairmont, Ohio	FA-'86	16/12
14	Testaverde, Vinny	QB	6-5	215	11/13/63	6	Miami	Elmont, N.Y.	D1-'87	13/12
51	Thomas, Broderick	LB	6-4	245	2/20/67	4	Nebraska	Houston, Tex.	D1-'89	16/16
58	Tiggle, Calvin	LB	6-1	235	11/10/68	2	Georgia Tech	Ft. Washington, Md.	D7-'91	16/0
54	t-Williams, Jimmy	LB	6-3	230	11/15/60	11	Nebraska	Washington, D.C.	T(Minn)-'92	12/12*
1	Willis, Ken	K	5-11	190	10/6/66	3	Kentucky	Owensboro, Ky.	PB(Dall)-'92#	16/0*
20	Wilson, Robert	RB	6-0	240	1/13/69	2	Texas A&M	Houston, Tex.	D3b-'91	16/15

* Brady played 16 games with Cincinnati in '91; Burnette played 3 games with Green Bay; DeBerg played 16 games with Kansas City; Duckens last active with Detroit in '90, Fullington played 5 games with New England, 6 with Tampa Bay; Grimes and Robinson missed '91 season due to injury; Highsmith played 2 games with Dallas, 9 with Tampa Bay; Hunter played 2 games with Atlanta; Jennings played 5 games with New Orleans; Jones played 6 games with Tampa Bay; King played 6 games with Cincinnati, 7 with Cleveland; Lilly played 16 games with L.A. Rams; Mack played 14 games with New Orleans; Maxey last active with Atlanta in '89; Nattiel played 16 games with Denver; Reimers played 10 games with Cincinnati; Rogers played 2 games with Buffalo; Simmons played 14 games with Indianapolis; Stryzinski played 16 games with Pittsburgh; Williams played 12 games with Minnesota; Willis played 16 games with Dallas.

† Option playout; subject to developments.

t- Buccaneers traded for Nattiel (Denver) and Williams (Minnesota)

Plan B unconditional free agent.

Players lost through Plan B (10): LB Sam Anno (SD; 16 games in '91), G John Bruhin (Phil; 10), QB Jeff Carlson (NYG; 3), K Steve Christie (Buff; 16), CB-S Anthony Hampton (Clev; 15), LB Eugene Marve (SD; 16), DE-DT Gerald Nichols (Mia; 16), QB Pat O'Hara (SD; 0), P Mark Royals (Pitt; 16), TE Ed Thomas (Buff; 6).

Also played with Buccaneers in '91 — WR Terry Anthony (9 games), QB Chris Chandler (6), DT Darryl Grant (2), CB-S Wayne Haddix (6), S Harry Hamilton (7), DE Dexter Manley (14), LB Maurice Oliver (3), CB-S Glen Rogers (5), RB Chuck Weatherspoon (4).

COACHING STAFF

Head Coach, Sam Wyche

Pro Career: Became the Buccaneers' fifth head coach on January 10, 1992, after eight seasons with the Cincinnati Bengals. Led the Bengals to the AFC championship in 1988 and Super Bowl XXIII against the San Francisco 49ers. Played quarterback with the Bengals 1968-70, Washington Redskins 1971-73, Detroit Lions 1974-75, St. Louis Cardinals 1976, and Buffalo Bills 1977. Quarterback coach with the San Francisco 49ers 1979-82. Career record 64-68.

Background: Attended North Fulton High School in Atlanta. Quarterback at Furman University from 1963-65. Assistant coach at South Carolina in 1967. Head coach at Indiana in 1983.

Personal: Born January 5, 1945, in Atlanta, Georgia. Sam and wife, Jane, live in Tampa, and have two children—Zak and Kerry.

Assistant Coaches

Maxie Baughan, linebackers; born August 3, 1938, Forkland, Ala., lives in Tampa. Center-linebacker Georgia Tech 1956-60. Pro linebacker Philadelphia Eagles 1960-65, Los Angeles Rams 1966-70, Washington Redskins 1971, 1974. College coach: Georgia Tech 1972-73, Cornell 1983-88 (head coach). Pro coach: Baltimore Colts 1975-79, Detroit Lions 1980-82, Minnesota Vikings 1990-91, joined Buccaneers in 1992.

Harold Jackson, receivers; born January 6, 1946, Quincy, Miss., lives in Tampa. Wide receiver Jackson State 1964-67. Pro wide receiver Los Angeles Rams 1968, 1973-77, Philadelphia Eagles 1969-72, New England Patriots 1978-81, Seattle Seahawks 1983. Pro coach: New England Patriots 1985-89, joined Buccaneers in 1992.

Ed Khayat, defensive line; born September 14, 1935, Moss Point, Miss., lives in Tampa. Offensive-defensive end Millsaps 1953, Perkinston J.C. 1954, Tulane 1955-56. Pro defensive end-tackle Washington Redskins 1957, 1962-63, Philadelphia Eagles 1958-61, 1964-65, Boston Patriots 1966. Pro coach: New Orleans Saints 1967-70, Philadelphia Eagles 1971-72 (head coach), Detroit Lions 1973-74, 1982-84, Atlanta Falcons 1975-76, Baltimore Colts 1977-81, New England Patriots 1985-89, joined Buccaneers in 1992.

Ray Oliver, strength and conditioning; born June 19, 1961, Cincinnati, Ohio, lives in Tampa. Defensive back Ohio State 1980-81. No pro playing experience. College coach: Cincinnati 1981-82, Kansas 1983-86, Pittsburgh 1986-89, Kentucky 1989-91. Pro coach: Joined Buccaneers in 1992.

Willie Peete, running backs; born July 14, 1937, Mesa, Ariz., lives in Tampa. Fullback Arizona 1956-59. No pro playing experience. College coach: Arizona 1960-62, 1971-82. Pro coach: Kansas City Chiefs 1983-86, Green Bay Packers 1987-91, joined Buccaneers in 1992.

Turk Schonert, quarterbacks; born January 15, 1957, Placentia, Calif., lives in Tampa. Quarterback Stanford 1976-79. Pro quarterback Cincinnati Bengals 1981-85, 1988-89, Atlanta Falcons 1986. Pro coach: Joined Buccaneers in 1992.

George Stewart, special teams; born December 29, 1958, Little Rock, Ark., lives in Tampa. Guard Arkansas 1977-80. No pro playing experience. College coach: Minnesota 1984-85, Notre Dame 1986-88. Pro coach: Pittsburgh Steelers 1989-91, joined Buccaneers in 1992.

Bob Wylie, offensive line; born February 16, 1951, Providence, R.I., lives in Tampa. Linebacker Colorado 1969-71. No pro playing experience. College coach: Brown 1980-82, Holy Cross 1983-84, Ohio University 1985-87, Colorado State 1988-89. Pro coach: New York Jets 1990-91, joined Buccaneers in 1992.

Tampa Bay Buccaneers 1992 First-Year Roster

Name	Pos.	Ht.	Wt.	Birth-date	College	Hometown	How Acq.
Alexander, Elijah	LB	6-2	230	8/8/70	Kansas State	Ft. Worth, Tex.	D10
Armstrong, Tyji	LB	6-4	255	10/3/70	Mississippi	Inkster, Mich.	D3b
Culpepper, Willie	WR	5-11	155	3/27/67	S.W. Louisiana	Jacksonville, Fla.	FA
Dotson, Santana	DE	6-5	270	12/19/69	Baylor	Houston, Tex.	D5b
Erickson, Craig	QB	6-2	206	5/17/69	Miami	West Palm Beach, Fla.	D4
Garrett, John (1)	WR	5-11	170	3/2/65	Princeton	Chagrin, Ohio	FA
Green, Rogerick	CB-S	5-10	180	12/15/69	Kansas State	San Antonio, Tex.	D5a
Hawkins, Courtney	WR	5-9	180	12/12/69	Michigan State	Flint, Mich.	D2
Hickson, Hyland (1)	RB	5-9	220	2/25/69	Michigan State	Ft. Lauderdale, Fla.	FA
Hopkins, Marcus (1)	CB-S	6-0	190	9/11/69	Southern California	San Diego, Calif.	FA
Kirkland, Dean (1)	G	6-2	290	1/4/68	Washington	Vancouver, Wash.	FA
Malone, James	LB	6-2	235	3/13/69	UCLA	Shaker Heights, Ohio	D6
McDowell, Anthony	RB	5-11	230	11/12/68	Texas Tech	Killeen, Tex.	D8a
Pawlawski, Mike	QB	6-1	205	7/18/69	California	Los Angeles, Calif.	D8b
Royster, Mazio	RB	6-1	205	8/3/70	Southern California	Pomona, Calif.	D11
Swilling, Ken	S	6-2	245	11/25/70	Georgia Tech	Toccoa, Ga.	D7
Sullivan, Mike (1)	G	6-3	280	12/22/67	Miami	Chicago, Ill.	FA
Wheeler, Mark	NT	6-2	290	4/1/70	Texas A&M	San Marcos, Tex.	D3a
Wilmsmeyer, Klaus	P-K	6-1	210	12/4/67	Louisville	Mississauga, Canada	D12

The term NFL Rookie is defined as a player who is in his first season of professional football and has not been on the roster of another professional football team for any regular-season or postseason games. A Rookie is designated by an "R" on NFL rosters. Players who have been active in another professional football league or players who have NFL experience, including either preseason training camp or being on an active roster for fewer than three regular-season or postseason games, are termed NFL First-Year Players. An NFL First-Year Player is designated by a "1" on NFL rosters. Thereafter, a player on an NFL active roster for at least three regular-season or postseason games is credited with an additional year of NFL playing experience.

NOTES

WASHINGTON REDSKINS

National Football Conference Eastern Division

Team Colors: Burgundy and Gold

Redskin Park, P.O. Box 17247
Dulles International Airport
Washington, D.C. 20041
Telephone: (703) 478-8900

Club Officials

Chairman of the Board-CEO: Jack Kent Cooke
Executive Vice President: John Kent Cooke
Secretary: Stuart Haney
Controller: Gregory Dillon
Board of Directors: Jack Kent Cooke, John Kent
  Cooke, James Lacher
General Manager: Charley Casserly
Assistant General Manager: Bobby Mitchell
Director of Pro Player Personnel: Kirk Mee
Director of Pro Scouting: Joe Mack
Director of College Scouting: George Saimes
Scouts: Chuck Banker, Gene Bates, Larry Bryan,
  Mike Hagen, Mel Kaufman, Miller McCalmon
V.P./Communications: Charlie Dayton
Director of Media Relations: Mike McCall
Director of Information: John Autry
Director of Stadium Operations/Club Promotions:
  John Kent Cooke, Jr.
Video Director: Donnie Schoenmann
Ticket Manager: Sue Barton
Asst. Ticket Mgrs.: Larry Desautels, Tony Lyman,
  Kathy Shumate
Head Trainer: Bubba Tyer
Assistant Trainers: Al Bellamy, Kevin Bastin
Equipment Manager: Jay Brunetti

Stadium: RFK Stadium • **Capacity:** 55,677
  East Capitol Street
  Washington, D.C. 20003

Playing Surface: Grass

Training Camp: Dickinson College
  Carlisle, Pennsylvania 17013

1992 Schedule

Preseason
Aug. 1	vs. Miami at Orlando	8:00
Aug. 8	at New York Jets	8:00
Aug. 16	vs. San Francisco at London	1:00
Aug. 22	at Los Angeles Raiders	1:00
Aug. 29	**Minnesota**	8:00

Regular Season
Sept. 7	at Dallas (Monday)	8:00
Sept. 13	**Atlanta**	1:00
Sept. 20	**Detroit**	4:00
Sept. 27	**Open Date**	
Oct. 4	at Phoenix	1:00
Oct. 12	**Denver** (Monday)	9:00
Oct. 18	**Philadelphia**	1:00
Oct. 25	at Minnesota	12:00
Nov. 1	**New York Giants**	8:00
Nov. 8	at Seattle	1:00
Nov. 15	at Kansas City	12:00
Nov. 23	at New Orleans (Monday)	8:00
Nov. 29	**Phoenix**	1:00
Dec. 6	at New York Giants	4:00
Dec. 13	**Dallas**	1:00
Dec. 20	at Philadelphia	1:00
Dec. 26	**L.A. Raiders** (Saturday)	4:00

Redskins Coaching History

Boston 1932-36
(436-357-26)

1932	Lud Wray	4-4-2
1933-34	William (Lone Star) Dietz	11-11-2
1935	Eddie Casey	2-8-1
1936-42	Ray Flaherty	56-23-3
1943	Arthur (Dutch) Bergman	7-4-1
1944-45	Dudley DeGroot	14-6-1
1946-48	Glen (Turk) Edwards	16-18-1
1949	John Whelchel*	3-3-1
1949-51	Herman Ball**	4-16-0
1951	Dick Todd	5-4-0
1952-53	Earl (Curly) Lambeau	10-13-1
1954-58	Joe Kuharich	26-32-2
1959-60	Mike Nixon	4-18-2
1961-65	Bill McPeak	21-46-3
1966-68	Otto Graham	17-22-3
1969	Vince Lombardi	7-5-2
1970	Bill Austin	6-8-0
1971-77	George Allen	69-35-1
1978-80	Jack Pardee	24-24-0
1981-91	Joe Gibbs	130-57-0

*Released after seven games in 1949
**Released after three games in 1951

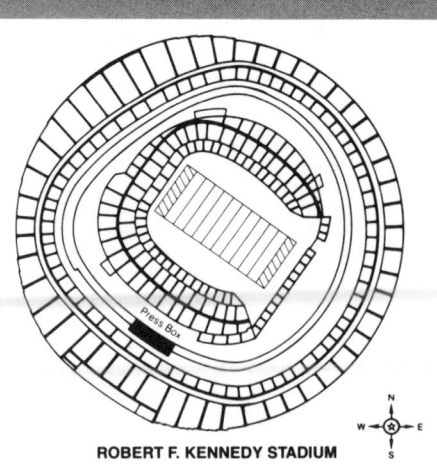

ROBERT F. KENNEDY STADIUM

Record Holders
Individual Records—Career
Category	Name	Performance
Rushing (Yds.)	John Riggins, 1976-79, 1981-85	7,472
Passing (Yds.)	Joe Theismann, 1974-1985	25,206
Passing (TDs)	Sammy Baugh, 1937-1952	187
Receiving (No.)	Art Monk, 1980-1991	801
Receiving (Yds.)	Art Monk, 1980-1991	10,984
Interceptions	Brig Owens, 1966-1977	36
Punting (Avg.)	Sammy Baugh, 1937-1952	*45.1
Punt Return (Avg.)	Johnny Williams, 1952-53	12.8
Kickoff Return (Avg.)	Bobby Mitchell, 1962-68	28.5
Field Goals	Mark Moseley, 1974-1986	263
Touchdowns (Tot.)	Charley Taylor, 1964-1977	90
Points	Mark Moseley, 1974-1986	1,206

Individual Records—Single Season
Category	Name	Performance
Rushing (Yds.)	John Riggins, 1983	1,347
Passing (Yds.)	Jay Schroeder, 1986	4,109
Passing (TDs)	Sonny Jurgensen, 1967	31
Receiving (No.)	Art Monk, 1984	*106
Receiving (Yds.)	Bobby Mitchell, 1963	1,436
Interceptions	Dan Sandifer, 1948	13
Punting (Avg.)	Sammy Baugh, 1940	*51.4
Punt Return (Avg.)	Johnny Williams, 1952	15.3
Kickoff Return (Avg.)	Mike Nelms, 1981	29.7
Field Goals	Mark Moseley, 1983	33
Touchdowns (Tot.)	John Riggins, 1983	*24
Points	Mark Moseley, 1983	161

Individual Records—Single Game
Category	Name	Performance
Rushing (Yds.)	Gerald Riggs, 9-17-89	221
Passing (Yds.)	Sammy Baugh, 10-31-43	446
Passing (TDs)	Sammy Baugh, 10-31-43	6
	Sammy Baugh, 11-23-47	6
	Mark Rypien, 11-10-91	6
Receiving (No.)	Art Monk, 12-15-85	13
	Kelvin Bryant, 12-7-86	13
	Art Monk, 11-4-90	13
Receiving (Yds.)	Anthony Allen, 10-4-87	255
Interceptions	Sammy Baugh, 11-14-43	*4
	Dan Sandifer, 10-31-48	*4
Field Goals	Many times	5
	Last time by Chip Lohmiller, 12-22-91	
Touchdowns (Tot.)	Dick James, 12-17-61	4
	Larry Brown, 12-4-73	4
Points	Dick James, 12-17-61	24
	Larry Brown, 12-4-73	24

*NFL Record

1991 Team Record

Preseason (1-3)

Date	Result		Opponents
8/4	L	7-16	at Pittsburgh
8/10	W	27- 6	at New England
8/16	L	21-24	Cleveland (OT)
8/24	L	9-13	vs. N.Y. Jets at
			Columbia, S.C.

Regular Season (14-2)

Date	Result		Opponents	Att.
9/1	W	45- 0	Detroit	52,958
9/9	W	33-31	at Dallas	63,025
9/15	W	34- 0	Phoenix	54,662
9/22	W	34-27	at Cincinnati	52,038
9/30	W	23-0	Philadelphia	55,198
10/6	W	20- 7	at Chicago	64,941
10/13	W	42-17	Cleveland	54,715
10/27	W	17-13	at N.Y. Giants	76,627
11/3	W	16-13	Houston (OT)	55,096
11/10	W	56-17	Atlanta	52,461
11/17	W	41-14	at Pittsburgh	56,813
11/24	L	21-24	Dallas	55,561
12/1	W	27- 6	at L.A. Rams	55,027
12/8	W	20-14	at Phoenix	48,373
12/15	W	34-17	N.Y. Giants	54,722
12/22	L	22-24	at Philadelphia	58,988

(OT) Overtime

Postseason (3-0)

Date	Result		Opponent	Att.
1/4	W	24- 7	Atlanta	55,181
1/12	W	41-10	Detroit	55,585
1/26	W	37-24	Buffalo	63,130

Score by Periods

Redskins	83	150	101	148	3	—	485
Opponents	54	57	55	58	0	—	224

Attendance

Home 435,373   Away 475,832   Total 911,205
Single-game home record, 55,750 (11-10-85)
Single-season home record, 437,540 (1986)

1991 Team Statistics

	Redskins	Opp.
Total First Downs	302	242
Rushing	107	72
Passing	179	151
Penalty	16	19
Third Down: Made/Att.	111/220	70/206
Third Down: Pct.	50.5	34.0
Fourth Down: Made/Att.	4/7	8/23
Fourth Down: Pct.	57.1	34.8
Total Net Yards	5741	4293
Avg. Per Game	358.8	268.3
Total Plays	996	947
Avg. Per Play	5.8	4.5
Net Yards Rushing	2049	1346
Avg. Per Game	128.1	84.1
Total Rushes	540	348
Net Yards Passing	3692	2947
Avg. Per Game	230.8	184.2
Sacked/Yards Lost	9/79	50/345
Gross Yards	3771	3292
Att./Completions	447/261	549/292
Completion Pct.	58.4	53.2
Had Intercepted	11	27
Punts/Avg.	55/37.6	85/41.7
Net Punting Avg.	33.1	33.4
Penalties/Yards Lost	90/798	94/767
Fumbles/Ball Lost	26/12	22/14
Touchdowns	56	26
Rushing	21	11
Passing	30	13
Returns	5	2
Avg. Time of Possession	31:51	28:09

1991 Individual Statistics

Scoring

	TD R	TD P	TD Rt	PAT	FG	Saf	TP
Lohmiller	0	0	0	56/56	31/43	0	149
Riggs	11	0	0	0/0	0/0	0	66
Clark	0	10	0	0/0	0/0	0	60
Monk	0	8	0	0/0	0/0	0	48
Sanders	1	5	0	0/0	0/0	0	36
Byner	5	0	0	0/0	0/0	0	30
Ervins	3	1	0	0/0	0/0	0	24
Orr	0	4	0	0/0	0/0	0	24
Ji. Johnson	0	2	0	0/0	0/0	0	12
Mitchell	0	0	2	0/0	0/0	0	12
Collins	0	0	1	0/0	0/0	0	6
Marshall	0	0	1	0/0	0/0	0	6
Mayhew	0	0	1	0/0	0/0	0	6
Rypien	1	0	0	0/0	0/0	0	6
Redskins	21	30	5	56/56	31/43	0	485
Opponents	11	13	2	26/26	14/18	0	224

Passing

	Att.	Comp.	Yds.	Pct.	TD	Int.	Tkld.	Rate
Rypien	421	249	3564	59.1	28	11	7/59	97.9
Rutledge	22	11	189	50.0	1	0	2/20	94.7
Byner	4	1	18	25.0	1	0	0/0	85.4
Redskins	447	261	3771	58.4	30	11	9/79	98.0
Opponents	549	292	3292	53.2	13	27	50/345	58.8

Rushing

	Att.	Yds.	Avg.	LG	TD
Byner	274	1048	3.8	32	5
Ervins	145	680	4.7	65t	3
Riggs	78	248	3.2	32	11
Sanders	7	47	6.7	17	1
Monk	9	19	2.1	14	0
Mitchell	3	14	4.7	8	0
Rypien	15	6	0.4	11	1
Clark	1	0	0.0	0	0
Rutledge	8	-13	-1.6	-1	0
Redskins	540	2049	3.8	65t	21
Opponents	348	1346	3.9	75t	11

Receiving

	No.	Yds.	Avg.	LG	TD
Monk	71	1049	14.8	64t	8
Clark	70	1340	19.1	82t	10
Sanders	45	580	12.9	45	5
Byner	34	308	9.1	31	0
Ervins	16	181	11.3	28	1
Orr	10	201	20.1	47t	4
Warren	5	51	10.2	17	0
Middleton	3	25	8.3	11	0
Hobbs	3	24	8.0	10	0
Ji. Johnson	3	7	2.3	4t	2
Riggs	1	5	5.0	5	0
Redskins	261	3771	14.4	82t	30
Opponents	292	3292	11.3	75t	13

Interceptions

	No.	Yds.	Avg.	LG	TD
Marshall	5	75	15.0	54t	1
Green	5	47	9.4	24	0
Edwards	4	52	13.0	27	0
Mayhew	3	31	10.3	31t	1
Collins	2	33	16.5	18	1
S. Johnson	2	5	2.5	5	0
Gouveia	1	22	22.0	22	0
T. Johnson	1	14	14.0	14	0
Coleman	1	0	0.0	0	0
Copeland	1	0	0.0	0	0
Mays	1	0	0.0	0	0
Stokes	1	0	0.0	0	0
Redskins	27	279	10.3	54t	3
Opponents	11	109	9.9	74t	1

Punting

	No.	Yds.	Avg.	In 20	LG
Goodburn	52	2070	39.8	16	61
Redskins	55	2070	37.6	16	61
Opponents	85	3548	41.7	13	58

Punt Returns

	No.	FC	Yds.	Avg.	LG	TD
Mitchell	45	21	600	13.3	69t	2
Hobbs	1	0	10	10.0	10	0
Redskins	46	21	610	13.3	69t	2
Opponents	31	7	190	6.1	20	0

Kickoff Returns

	No.	Yds.	Avg.	LG	TD
Mitchell	29	583	20.1	35	0
Ervins	11	232	21.1	46	0
Jo. Johnson	5	83	16.6	25	0
Gouveia	3	12	4.0	9	0
Hobbs	1	16	16.0	16	0
Redskins	49	926	18.9	46	0
Opponents	66	1153	17.5	39	0

Sacks

	No.
Mann	11.5
Stokes	6.5
Marshall	5.5
Geathers	4.5
Wilson	4.5
Coleman	3.5
T. Johnson	3.5
Collins	3.0
Williams	3.0
Buck	1.5
A. Johnson	1.0
S. Johnson	1.0
Koch	1.0
Redskins	50.0
Opponents	9.0

1992 Draft Choices

Round	Name	Pos.	College
1.	Desmond Howard	WR	Michigan
2.	Shane Collins	DE	Arizona State
3.	Paul Siever	G	Penn State
4.	Chris Hakel	QB	William & Mary
6.	Ray Rowe	TE	San Diego State
7.	Calvin Holmes	DB	Southern California
8.	Darryl Moore	G	Texas-El Paso
9.	Boone Powell	LB	Texas
10.	Tony Barker	LB	Rice
11.	Terry Smith	WR	Penn State
12.	Matt Elliott	C	Michigan

Washington Redskins 1992 Veteran Roster

No.	Name	Pos.	Ht.	Wt.	Birth-date	NFL Exp.	College	Hometown	How Acq.	'91 Games/ Starts
61	Adickes, Mark	G	6-4	285	4/22/61	7	Baylor	Richardson, Tex.	PB(KC)-'90#	16/0
53	Bostic, Jeff	C	6-2	278	9/18/58	13	Clemson	Greensboro, N.C.	FA-'80	16/16
82	Brandes, John	TE	6-2	249	4/2/64	6	Cameron University	Arlington, Tex.	PB(Ind)-'90#	16/0
67	Brown, Ray	T	6-5	280	12/12/62	5	Arkansas State	Marion, Ark.	PB(Phx)-'89#	0*
99	Buck, Jason	DE	6-4	264	7/27/63	6	Brigham Young	St. Anthony, Idaho	FA-'91	8/1
21	Byner, Earnest	RB	5-10	218	9/15/62	9	East Carolina	Milledgeville, Ga.	T(Clev)-'89	16/16
50	Caldwell, Ravin	LB	6-3	240	8/4/63	6	Arkansas	Ft. Smith, Ark.	D5-'86	16/0
84	Clark, Gary	WR	5-9	173	5/1/62	8	James Madison	Dublin, Va.	SD2-'84	16/16
51	Coleman, Monte	LB	6-2	245	11/4/57	14	Central Arkansas	Pine Bluff, Ark.	D11-'79	16/1
55	Collins, Andre	LB	6-1	233	5/4/68	3	Penn State	Cinnaminson, N.J.	D2-'90	16/16
26	Copeland, Danny	S	6-2	213	1/24/66	4	Eastern Kentucky	Thomasville, Ga.	PB(KC)-'91#	16/14
27	Edwards, Brad	S	6-2	207	3/22/66	5	South Carolina	Fayetteville, N.C.	PB(Minn)-'90#	16/16
32	Ervins, Ricky	RB	5-7	200	12/7/68	2	Southern California	Pasadena, Calif.	D3-'91	15/0
74	Gabbard, Steve	T	6-4	297	7/19/66	2	Florida State	Charlotte, N.C.	PB(GB)-'92#	4/0*
97	Geathers, James	DT	6-7	289	6/26/60	8	Wichita State	Georgetown, S.C.	PB(NO)-'90#	16/0
2	Goodburn, Kelly	P	6-2	199	4/14/62	6	Emporia State	Correctionville, Iowa	FA-'90	16/0
54	Gouveia, Kurt	LB	6-1	228	9/14/64	6	Brigham Young	Honolulu, Hawaii	D8-'86	14/1
28	†Green, Darrell	CB	5-8	170	2/15/60	10	Texas A&I	Houston, Tex.	D1-'83	16/16
91	Hinkle, George	DE	6-5	269	3/17/65	5	Arizona	Pacific, Mo.	PB(SD)-'92#	13/13*
34	Hoage, Terry	S	6-2	201	4/11/62	9	Georgia	Huntsville, Tex.	PB(Phil)-'91#	6/0
86	Hobbs, Stephen	WR	5-11	200	11/14/65	3	North Alabama	Mendenhall, Miss.	PB(KC)-'89#	16/0
16	Humphries, Stan	QB	6-2	224	4/14/65	3	Northeast Louisiana	Shreveport, La.	D6-'88	0*
66	Jacoby, Joe	T	6-6	314	7/6/59	12	Louisville	Louisville, Ky.	FA-'81	16/16
36	Jenkins, James	TE	6-2	234	8/17/67	2	Rutgers	Staten Island, N.Y.	FA-'91	4/0
47	Johnson, Anthony	CB	5-8	170	6/22/67	4	Southwest Texas State	San Antonio, Tex.	D6-'89	11/0
80	Johnson, Joe	WR	5-8	170	12/21/62	9	Notre Dame	Washington, D.C.	FA-'89	2/0
45	Johnson, Sidney	CB	5-9	175	3/7/65	4	California	Cerritos, Calif.	FA-'90	15/0
78	Johnson, Tim	DT	6-3	283	1/29/65	6	Penn State	Sarasota, Fla.	T(Pitt)-'90	16/16
79	†Lachey, Jim	T	6-6	294	6/4/63	8	Ohio State	St. Henry, Ohio	T(Raid)-'88	15/15
8	Lohmiller, Chip	K	6-3	210	7/16/66	5	Minnesota	Minneapolis, Minn.	D2-'88	16/0
71	Mann, Charles	DE	6-6	272	4/12/61	10	Nevada-Reno	Sacramento, Calif.	D3-'83	15/15
58	Marshall, Wilber	LB	6-1	231	4/18/62	9	Florida	Titusville, Fla.	FA-'88	16/16
35	Mayhew, Martin	CB	5-8	172	10/8/65	4	Florida State	Tallahassee, Fla.	PB(Buff)-'89#	16/16
20	Mays, Alvoid	CB	5-9	180	7/10/66	3	West Virginia	Bradenton, Fla.	FA-'90	13/0
63	†McKenzie, Raleigh	C-G	6-2	279	2/8/63	8	Tennessee	Knoxville, Tenn.	D11-'85	16/14
87	Middleton, Ron	TE	6-2	270	7/17/65	6	Auburn	Atmore, Ala.	PB(Clev)-'90#	12/12
30	†Mitchell, Brian	RB	5-10	209	8/18/68	3	Southwestern Louisiana	Plaquemine, La.	D5-'90	16/0
81	Monk, Art	WR	6-3	210	12/5/57	13	Syracuse	White Plains, N.Y.	D1-'80	16/16
89	Orr, Terry	TE	6-2	235	9/27/61	7	Texas	Savannah, Ga.	FA-'91	16/6
37	Riggs, Gerald	RB	6-1	240	11/6/60	11	Arizona State	Las Vegas, Nev.	T(Atl)-'89	16/0
10	Rutledge, Jeff	QB	6-1	193	1/22/57	14	Alabama	Birmingham, Ala.	PB(NYG)-'90#	16/0
11	†Rypien, Mark	QB	6-4	234	10/2/62	5	Washington State	Spokane, Wash.	D6-'86	16/16
83	†Sanders, Ricky	WR	5-11	180	8/30/62	7	Southwest Texas State	Temple, Tex.	T(NE)-'86	16/7
69	Schlereth, Mark	G	6-3	283	1/25/66	4	Idaho	Anchorage, Alaska	D10-'89	16/16
23	Settle, John	RB	5-9	210	6/2/65	5	Appalachian State	Ruffin, N.C.	PB(Atl)-'91#	0*
76	Simmons, Ed	T	6-5	300	12/31/63	6	Eastern Washington	Seattle, Wash.	D6-'87	6/2
60	Stokes, Fred	DE	6-3	274	3/14/64	6	Georgia Southern	Vidalia, Ga.	PB(Rams)-'89#	16/11
31	Vaughn, Clarence	S	6-0	202	7/17/64	5	Northern Illinois	Chicago, Ill.	D8-'87	12/0
40	Walton, Alvin	S	6-0	180	3/14/64	7	Kansas	Banning, Calif.	D3-'86	4/2
85	Warren, Don	TE	6-4	242	5/5/56	14	San Diego State	Covina, Calif.	D4-'79	10/7
98	Wilkins, Gary	TE	6-2	248	11/23/63	6	Georgia Tech	West Palm Beach, Fla.	PB(Atl)-'92#	6/0*
93	Willis, Keith	DE	6-1	263	7/29/59	10	Northeastern	Newark, N.J.	PB(Pitt)-'92#	16/7*
75	Williams, Eric	DT	6-4	290	2/24/62	9	Washington State	Stockton, Calif.	T(Det)-'90	15/15
94	Wilson, Bobby	DT	6-2	283	3/4/68	2	Michigan State	Chicago, Ill.	D1-'91	16/1

* Brown and Settle missed '91 season due to injury; Gabbard played 4 games with Green Bay in '91; Hinkle played 13 games with San Diego; Humphries active for 2 games but did not play; Wilkins played 6 games with Atlanta; Willis played 16 games with Pittsburgh.

† Option playout; subject to developments.

Retired—Matt Millen, 12-year linebacker, 16 games in '91.

Plan B unconditional free agent.

Players lost through Plan B (2): TE Jimmy Johnson (Det; 6 games in '91), WR Keenan McCardell (Clev; 0).

Also played with Redskins in '91—S Travis Curtis (1 game), DE Markus Koch (6), G Ralph Tamm (2).

COACHING STAFF

Head Coach,
Joe Gibbs

Pro Career: Enters twelfth season as Redskins' all-time leader in wins. He is the third-winningest coach among active NFL coaches with 130 career wins. Has led Redskins to three Super Bowl titles and four Super Bowl appearances. Washington has appeared in postseason play 7 of last 10 seasons under Gibbs. Named head coach on January 13, 1981, after spending eight years as an NFL assistant coach and nine seasons on the collegiate level. Came to Redskins from San Diego Chargers, where he was offensive coordinator in 1979 and 1980. Prior to that, he was offensive coordinator for the Tampa Bay Buccaneers in 1978 and offensive backfield coach for the St. Louis Cardinals from 1973-77. While he was with San Diego, the Chargers won the AFC West title and led the NFL in passing two consecutive years. No pro playing experience. Career record: 130-57.

College: Played tight end, linebacker, and guard under Don Coryell at San Diego State in 1961 and 1962 after spending two years at Cerritos, Calif., J.C. 1959-60. Started college coaching career at San Diego State 1964-66, followed by Florida State 1967-68, Southern California 1969-70, and Arkansas 1971-72.

Personal: Born November 25, 1940, in Mocksville, N.C. Graduated from Santa Fe Springs, Calif., High School. Two-time national racquetball champion and ranked second in the over-35 category in 1978. He and his wife, Pat, live in Vienna, Va., and have two sons—J.D. and Coy.

Assistant Coaches

Jason Arapoff, assistant conditioning; born July 8, 1965, Weymouth, Mass., lives in Centreville, Va. Defensive back Springfield College 1985-88. No pro playing experience. Pro coach: Joined Redskins in 1992.

Don Breaux, running backs; born August 3, 1940, Jennings, La., lives in Centreville, Va. Quarterback McNeese State 1959-61. Pro quarterback Denver Broncos 1963, San Diego Chargers 1964-65. College coach: Florida State 1966-67, Arkansas 1968-71, 1977-80, Florida 1973-74, Texas 1975-76. Pro coach: Joined Redskins in 1981.

Bobby DePaul, administrative assistant-defensive line; born January 29, 1963, Cheverly, Md., lives in Bowie, Md. Linebacker Maryland 1982-83. No pro playing experience. College coach: Catholic University 1986-88. Pro coach: Joined Redskins in 1989.

Rod Dowhower, quarterbacks-passing game; born April 15, 1943, Ord, Neb., lives in Ashburn, Va. Quarterback San Diego State 1963-65. No pro playing experience. College coach: San Diego State 1966-72, UCLA 1974-75, Boise State 1976, Stanford 1977-79 (head coach 1979). Pro coach: St. Louis Cardinals 1973, 1982-84, Denver Broncos 1980-81, Indianapolis Colts 1985-86 (head coach), Atlanta Falcons 1987-89, joined Redskins in 1990.

Jim Hanifan, offensive line; born September 21, 1933, Compton, Calif., lives in Reston, Va. Tight end California 1952-54. Pro tight end Toronto Argonauts (CFL) 1955. College coach: Glendale, Calif., J.C. 1964-66, Utah 1967-70, California 1971-72, San Diego State 1972-73. Pro coach: St. Louis Cardinals 1974-85 (head coach 1980-85), Atlanta Falcons 1987-89 (interim head coach last four games of 1989), joined Redskins in 1990.

Larry Peccatiello, defensive coordinator; born December 21, 1935, Newark, N.J., lives in Warrenton, Va. Receiver William & Mary 1955-58. No pro playing experience. College coach: William & Mary 1961-68, Navy 1969-70, Rice 1971. Pro coach: Houston Oilers 1972-75, Seattle Seahawks 1976-80, joined Redskins in 1981.

Richie Petitbon, assistant head coach-defense; born April 18, 1938, New Orleans, La., lives in Vienna, Va. Quarterback-defensive back Tulane 1955-58. Pro defensive back Chicago Bears 1959-67, Los Angeles Rams 1969-70, Washington Redskins 1971-73. Pro coach: Houston Oilers 1974-77, joined Redskins in 1978.

Dan Riley, conditioning; born October 19, 1949, Syracuse, N.Y., lives in Ashburn, Va. No college or pro playing experience. College coach: Army 1973-76, Penn State 1977-81. Pro coach: Joined Redskins in 1982.

Wayne Sevier, special teams; born July 3, 1941, San Diego, Calif., lives in Broad Run, Va. Quarterback Chaffey, Calif., J.C. 1960, San Diego State 1961-62. No pro playing experience. College coach: California Western 1968-69. Pro coach: St. Louis Cardinals 1974-75, Atlanta Falcons 1976, San Diego Chargers 1979-80, 1987-88, Washington Redskins 1981-86, rejoined Redskins in 1989.

Warren Simmons, offensive line; born February 25, 1942, Poughkeepsie, N.Y., lives in Ashburn, Va. Center San Diego State 1963-65. No pro playing experience. College coach: Cal State-Fullerton 1972-75, Cerritos, Calif., J.C. 1976-80. Pro coach: Joined Redskins in 1981.

Charley Taylor, research and development-receivers; born September 28, 1942, Grand Prairie, Tex., lives in Reston, Va. Running back Arizona State 1961-63. Pro running back-wide receiver Washington Redskins 1964-76. Pro coach: Joined Redskins in 1982.

Emmitt Thomas, defensive backs; born June 4, 1943, Angleton, Tex., lives in Reston, Va. Quarterback-wide receiver Bishop (Tex.) College 1963-65. Pro defensive back Kansas City Chiefs 1966-78. College coach: Central Missouri State 1979-80. Pro coach: St. Louis Cardinals 1981-85, joined Redskins in 1986.

LaVern Torgeson, defensive line; born February 28, 1929, LaCrosse, Wash., lives in Fairfax, Va. Center-linebacker Washington State 1948-50. Pro linebacker Detroit Lions 1951-54, Washington Redskins 1955-58. Pro coach: Washington Redskins 1959-61, 1971-77, Pittsburgh Steelers 1962-68, Los Angeles Rams 1969-70, 1978-80, rejoined Redskins in 1981.

Washington Redskins 1992 First-Year Roster

Name	Pos.	Ht.	Wt.	Birth-date	College	Hometown	How Acq.
Barker, Tony	LB	6-2	230	9/9/68	Rice	Wichita, Kan.	D10
Brothen, Kevin	G	6-1	284	11/16/69	Vanderbilt	Oaklawn, Ill.	FA
Brown, Hurlie	CB-S	6-0	195	6/21/69	Miami	Merritt Island, Fla.	FA
Cahoon, Victor	WR	5-10	180	12/20/68	Arizona State	Manassas, Va.	FA
Collins, Shane	DE	6-3	267	4/11/69	Arizona State	Bozeman, Mont.	D2
Conklin, Cary (1)	QB	6-4	233	2/29/68	Washington	Yakima, Wash.	D4-'91
Elewonibi, Mo (1)	T	6-4	282	12/16/65	Brigham Young	British Columbia, Can.	D3-'90
Elliott, Matt	C	6-1	265	10/1/68	Michigan	Carmel, Ind.	D12
Fuller, Thomas	DT	6-4	280	3/4/69	Tennessee	Crystal Lake, Ill.	FA
Greene, Robert	RB	5-8	207	9/10/70	William & Mary	Ft. Washington, Md.	FA
Gulledge, David (1)	S	6-1	203	10/26/67	Jacksonville State	Pell City, Ala.	D11-'91
Hakel, Chris	QB	6-2	230	8/8/69	William & Mary	Mechanicsburg, Pa.	D4
Holmes, Calvin	CB	5-8	183	1/4/70	Southern California	Carson, Calif.	D7
Howard, Desmond	WR	5-9	183	5/15/70	Michigan	Cleveland, Ohio	D1
Moore, Darryl	G	6-2	294	1/27/69	Texas-El Paso	Minden, La.	D8
Powell, Boone	LB	6-3	237	9/4/68	Texas	Duncanville, Tex.	D9
Rowe, Ray	TE	6-2	256	7/28/69	San Diego State	San Diego, Calif.	D6
Siever, Paul	G	6-5	293	8/10/69	Penn State	Coatesville, Pa.	D3
Smith, Terry	WR	5-9	170	7/29/69	Penn State	Monroeville, Pa.	D11
Thomas, Robert	RB	6-0	215	1/14/69	Carson-Newman	Reddick, Fla.	FA

The term NFL Rookie is defined as a player who is in his first season of professional football and has not been on the roster of another professional football team for any regular-season or postseason games. A Rookie is designated by an "R" on NFL rosters. Players who have been active in another professional football league or players who have NFL experience, including either preseason training camp or being on an active roster for fewer than three regular-season or post-season games, are termed NFL First-Year Players. An NFL First-Year Player is designated by a "1" on NFL rosters. Thereafter, a player on an NFL active roster for at least three regular-season or postseason games is credited with an additional year of NFL playing experience.

NOTES

_____

_____

_____

_____

_____

_____

_____

_____

_____

_____

_____

1991 SEASON IN REVIEW

Trades 142

Preseason Standings and Results 143

Regular Season Standings and Results 144

Week by Week Game Summaries 146

Pro Football Awards 169

All-Pro Teams 170

Rushing, Passing, Receiving
  and Sack Leaders 172

Team and Individual Statistics 176

Paid Attendance Breakdown 206

Trades

1991 Interconference Trades

Defensive tackle **Dick Chapura** from Philadelphia to Houston for a draft choice. (8/8)

Defensive back **Vencie Glenn** from the Los Angeles Raiders to New Orleans for a draft choice. (8/14)

Tackle **Ron Mattes** from the New York Jets to Chicago for a draft choice. (8/19)

Quarterback **Steve Beuerlein** from the Los Angeles Raiders to Dallas for a draft choice. (8/26)

Linebacker **Ervin Randle** from Tampa Bay to Kansas City for a draft choice. (8/27)

Quarterback **Billy Joe Tolliver** from San Diego to Atlanta for a draft choice. (8/28)

Wide receiver **Randal Hill** from Miami to Phoenix for a draft choice. (9/3)

Tackle **Irv Pankey** from the Los Angeles Rams to Indianapolis for the Colts' third-round and eleventh-round selections in 1992. (9/5)

Linebacker **Jesse Solomon** from Dallas to New England for a draft choice. (9/17)

Linebacker **Jesse Solomon** from New England to Tampa Bay for a draft choice. (9/18)

Tackle **Harvey Salem** from Detroit to Denver for a draft choice. (10/8)

1992 Interconference Trades

Guard **Reggie Redding** from Atlanta to New England for a draft choice. (1/27)

Wide receiver **Ricky Nattiel** from Denver to Tampa Bay for a draft choice. (1/30)

Guard **Danny Villa** from New England to Phoenix for a draft choice. (1/30)

Running back **Allen Pinkett** from Houston to New Orleans for a draft choice. (1/31)

Defensive back **Garry Lewis** from the Los Angeles Raiders to Dallas for a draft choice. (2/1)

Defensive tackle **Keith Millard** from Minnesota to Seattle for the Seahawks' second-round choice in 1992 and a future choice. Minnesota selected defensive end **Robert Harris** (Southern). (4/26)

Cleveland's second- and fifth-round choices in 1992 to Dallas for New Orleans's second-round choice in 1992, Denver's eighth-round choice in 1992 (both previously obtained by Dallas), and the Cowboys' third-, sixth-, and twelfth-round choices in 1992. Cleveland selected wide receiver **Patrick Rowe** (San Diego State), linebacker **Gerald Dixon** (South Carolina), defensive tackle **George Williams** (Notre Dame), and center-guard **Tim Simpson** (Illinois), and traded the eighth-round choice to Tampa Bay. Dallas selected wide receiver **Jimmy Smith** (Jackson State) and guard **Rod Milstead** (Delaware State). (4/26)

Running back **Rueben Mayes** from New Orleans to Seattle for the Seahawks' fourth-round choice in 1992. New Orleans selected center **Gene McGuire** (Notre Dame). (4/26)

Cincinnati's first- and third-round choices in 1992 to Washington for San Diego's first-round choice in 1992 plus the Redskins' first- and third-round choices in 1992. Washington selected wide receiver **Desmond Howard** (Michigan) and defensive back **Clayton Holmes** (Carson-Newman). Cincinnati selected quarterback **David Klingler** (Houston), defensive back **Darryl Williams** (Miami), and defensive back **Leonard Wheeler** (Troy State). (4/26)

New England's first-round choice in 1992 to Atlanta for the Falcons' first-, second-, and fifth-round choices in 1992. Atlanta selected tackle **Bob Whitfield** (Stanford). New England subsequently traded its choices to Dallas, Phoenix, and Dallas, respectively. (4/26)

Minnesota's first- and third-round choices from Dallas to New England for Atlanta's first- and fourth-round choices and the Patriots' second-round choice. New England selected tackle **Eugene Chung** (Virginia Tech) and running back **Kevin Turner** (Alabama). Dallas subsequently traded Atlanta's choices and selected defensive back **Darren Woodson** (Arizona State) with New England's second-round choice. (4/26)

Tampa Bay's second-round choice in 1992 to the Los Angeles Raiders for the Raiders' second-, third-, and seventh-round choices in 1992. Los Angeles selected tackle **Greg Skrepenak** (Michigan). Tampa Bay selected wide receiver **Courtney Hawkins** (Michigan State), traded the Raiders' third-round choice in 1992 to New Orleans, and selected defensive back **Ken Swilling** (Georgia Tech). (4/26)

Phoenix's second-round choice in 1992 to New England for Atlanta's second-round choice in 1992 and the Los Angeles Raiders' fourth-round choice in 1992. Phoenix selected quarterback **Tony Sacca** (Penn State) and nose tackle **Michael Bankston** (Sam Houston State). New England selected defensive back **Rod Smith** (Notre Dame). (4/26)

Minnesota's second-round choice in 1992 from Dallas to Kansas City for the Chiefs' second- and third-round choices in 1992. Dallas subsequently traded Kansas City's choices to Washington. Kansas City selected quarterback **Matt Blundin** (Virginia). (4/26)

Tampa Bay's sixth-round choice in 1992 to Cleveland for the Browns' sixth-round choice and Denver's eighth-round choice in 1992 obtained from Dallas. Cleveland selected wide receiver **Rico Smith** (Colorado). Tampa Bay selected linebacker **James Malone** (UCLA) and quarterback **Mike Pawlawski** (California). (4/27)

Phoenix's sixth-round choice in 1992, which had been obtained by New England, to Detroit for the Lions' sixth-, seventh-, tenth-, and twelfth-round choices in 1992. New England selected guard **Tracy Boyd** (Elizabeth City State), offensive tackle **Jim Gray** (West Virginia), center **Steve Gordon** (California), and wide receiver **Freeman Baysinger** (Humboldt State). Detroit selected tackle **Larry Tharpe** (Tennessee State). (4/27)

Pittsburgh's sixth-round choice in 1992 to San Francisco for the 49ers' seventh- and eighth-round choices in 1992 and Green Bay's eighth-round choice in 1992. Pittsburgh selected running back **Scottie Graham** (Ohio State), defensive back **Darren Perry** (Penn State), and defensive tackle **Nate Williams** (Mississippi State). San Francisco selected defensive back **Damien Russell** (Virginia Tech). (4/27)

Green Bay's seventh-round choice in 1992 to the Los Angeles Raiders for Dallas's seventh-round choice, previously obtained by Los Angeles, and the Raiders' ninth-round choice in 1992. Los Angeles selected defensive back **Curtis Cotton** (Nebraska). Green Bay selected wide receiver **Christopher Holder** (Tuskegee) and nose tackle **Shazzon Bradley** (Tennessee). (4/27)

Miami's seventh-round choice in 1992 to Atlanta for the Falcons' seventh- and twelfth-round choices in 1992. Atlanta selected linebacker **Tim Paulk** (Florida). Miami traded the seventh-round choice to the Los Angeles Raiders and selected running back **Kameno Bell** (Illinois). (4/27)

1991 AFC Trades

Tight end **Robert Tyler** from the Los Angeles Raiders to Indianapolis for a draft choice. (8/20)

Defensive end **Lee Williams** from San Diego to Houston for wide receiver **Shawn Jefferson** and the Oilers' first-round selection in 1992. (8/23)

Guard **Newt Harrell** from the Los Angeles Raiders to Cleveland for a draft choice. (8/26)

1992 AFC Trades

Guard **Freddie Childress** from New England to Cleveland for a draft choice. (1/30)

Running back **Eric Dickerson** from Indianapolis to the Los Angeles Raiders for Dallas's fourth-round choice in 1992 and the Raiders' eighth-round choice in 1992. Indianapolis selected defensive tackle **Tony McCoy** (Florida) and running back **Ronald Humphrey** (Mississippi Valley State). (4/26)

New Orleans's seventh-round choice in 1992 (previously obtained by the Los Angeles Raiders) and the Raiders' eleventh-round choice in 1992 to Miami for Atlanta's seventh-round choice in 1992 previously obtained by the Dolphins. Los Angeles selected running back **Kevin Smith** (UCLA). Miami selected tight end **Dave Moore** (Pittsburgh) and quarterback **Mark Barsotti** (Fresno State). (4/27)

Denver's sixth-round choice in 1992 to the New York Jets for the Jets' seventh- and eighth-round choices in 1992. New York selected quarterback **Jeff Blake** (East Carolina). Denver selected tackle **Jim Johnson** (Michigan State) and guard **Dietrich Lockridge** (Jackson State). (4/27)

1991 NFC Trades

Running back **Terrence Flagler** from Phoenix to San Francisco for a draft choice. (8/12)

Defensive back **Robert Massey** from New Orleans to Phoenix for guard **Derek Kennard** and the Cardinals' fifth-round selection in 1992. (8/19)

Wide receiver **Brett Perriman** from New Orleans to Detroit for a draft choice. (8/21)

Kicker **Brad Daluiso** from Green Bay to Atlanta for a draft choice. (8/27)

Linebacker **Tim Harris** from Green Bay to San Francisco for the 49ers' second-round selections in 1992 and 1993. (9/30)

1992 NFC Trades

Tackle **Tootie Robbins** from Phoenix to Green Bay for a draft choice. (2/1)

Linebacker **Jimmy Williams** from Minnesota to Tampa Bay for a draft choice. (2/1)

Quarterback **Brett Favre** from Atlanta to Green Bay for Philadelphia's first-round choice in 1992, which had been previously obtained by the Packers. (2/12)

Atlanta reacquired its own first- and fourth-round choices in 1992 which Dallas had obtained from New England after the Patriots had acquired the picks from the Falcons, for Philadelphia's first-round choice in 1992, which had previously been obtained by Atlanta, and New England's fifth-round choice, previously obtained by Atlanta. The Falcons selected running back **Tony Smith** (Southern Mississippi) and defensive back **Frankie Smith** (Baylor). The Cowboys selected defensive back **Kevin Smith** (Texas A&M) and defensive back **Greg Briggs** (Texas Southern). (4/26)

Washington's second-round choice in 1992 from Dallas to Detroit for the Lions' third-, fourth-, and ninth-round choices in 1992. Dallas selected tackle **James Brown** (Virginia State), guard-center **Tom Myslinski** (Tennessee), and defensive back **Chris Hall** (East Carolina). Detroit selected kicker **Jason Hanson** (Washington State). (4/26)

Kansas City's second- and third-round choices in 1992 from Dallas to Washington for the Redskins' second-round choice in 1992 and Cincinnati's third-round choice in 1992 previously obtained by Washington. Dallas traded Washington's second-round choice in 1992 to Detroit and selected defensive back **Clayton Holmes** (Carson-Newman). Washington selected defensive end **Shane Collins** (Arizona State) and guard **Paul Siever** (Penn State). (4/26)

The Los Angeles Raiders' third-round choice in 1992 from Tampa Bay to New Orleans for the Saints' third-round choice in 1992 and the Cardinals' fifth-round choice in 1992, previously obtained by the Saints. Tampa Bay selected tight end **Tyji Armstrong** (Mississippi) and defensive back **Rogerick Green** (Kansas State). New Orleans selected defensive back **Tyrone Legette** (Nebraska). (4/26)

Green Bay's fourth- and eighth-round choices in 1992 to San Francisco for the 49ers' fourth-, fifth-, and sixth-round choices in 1992. Green Bay selected running back **Edgar Bennett** (Florida State), wide receiver **Orlando McKay** (Washington), and tight end **Mark Chmura** (Boston College). San Francisco selected defensive end **Mark Thomas** (North Carolina State) and traded Green Bay's eighth-round selection to Pittsburgh. (4/26)

American Football Conference

Eastern Division

	W	L	T	Pct.	Pts.	OP
Miami†	3	2	0	.600	89	81
Buffalo**	2	3	0	.400	92	117
Indianapolis	1	3	0	.250	65	78
New England	1	3	0	.250	37	104
N.Y. Jets	1	3	0	.250	43	76

Central Division

	W	L	T	Pct.	Pts.	OP
Cincinnati	2	2	0	.500	90	93
Cleveland	2	2	0	.500	57	85
Houston	2	2	0	.500	82	100
Pittsburgh	2	2	0	.500	76	65

Western Division

	W	L	T	Pct.	Pts.	OP
L.A. Raiders†	3	2	0	.600	81	72
Kansas City	2	2	0	.500	78	68
Seattle	2	2	0	.500	69	73
Denver*	2	3	0	.400	50	88
San Diego	1	3	0	.250	54	94

*Includes Hall of Fame Game
**Includes American Bowl '91 in London
***Includes American Bowl '91 in Berlin
†Includes American Bowl '91 in Tokyo

National Football Conference

Eastern Division

	W	L	T	Pct.	Pts.	OP
Phoenix	4	0	0	1.000	123	33
Philadelphia**	4	1	0	.800	110	92
Dallas	2	2	0	.500	76	78
N.Y. Giants	2	2	0	.500	60	67
Washington	1	3	0	.250	64	59

Central Division

	W	L	T	Pct.	Pts.	OP
Tampa Bay	3	1	0	.750	68	53
Green Bay	2	2	0	.500	99	81
Minnesota	2	2	0	.500	92	76
Chicago***	2	3	0	.400	63	59
Detroit*	2	3	0	.400	71	98

Western Division

	W	L	T	Pct.	Pts.	OP
San Fran.***	5	0	0	1.000	121	59
Atlanta	2	2	0	.500	98	56
New Orleans	2	2	0	.500	101	85
L.A. Rams	1	3	0	.250	61	80

AFC Preseason Results—Team By Team

Eastern Division

BUFFALO (2-3)

17	Phil. (ABL)	13
17	N.Y. Giants	23
21	*Detroit	16
24	Green Bay	35
13	Chicago	30
92		117

INDIANAPOLIS (1-3)

3	Denver	10
7	*Seattle	17
34	*New Orleans	28
21	Philadelphia	23
65		78

MIAMI (3-2)

0	*Chicago	6
19	L.A. Raid. (ABT)	17
29	Tampa Bay	13
13	Denver	21
28	*New Orleans	24
89		81

NEW ENGLAND (1-3)

7	Green Bay	28
6	*Washington	27
0	Phoenix	46
24	*N.Y. Giants	3
37		104

N.Y. JETS (1-3)

10	*Philadelphia	24
10	Kansas City	19
10	N.Y. Giants	24
13	Washington	9
43		76

Central Division

CINCINNATI (2-2)

20	Detroit	24
24	*Philadelphia	29
27	*Minnesota (OT)	24
19	Green Bay (OT)	16
90		93

CLEVELAND (2-2)

10	*Tampa Bay	23
16	*N.Y. Giants	10
24	Washington (OT)	21
7	Minnesota	31
57		85

HOUSTON (2-2)

29	San Diego	31
7	*Atlanta	36
30	*Dallas	20
16	L.A. Rams	13
82		100

PITTSBURGH (2-2)

16	*Washington	7
24	Minnesota	34
20	Philadelphia	21
16	Detroit	3
76		65

Western Division

DENVER (2-3)

3	Detroit (HOF)	14
10	*Indianapolis	3
6	San Francisco	24
21	*Miami	13
10	Phoenix	34
50		88

KANSAS CITY (2-2)

14	*Dallas	24
19	N.Y. Jets	10
38	*Detroit	14
7	Tampa Bay	20
78		68

L.A. RAIDERS (3-2)

17	*San Francisco	24
17	Miami (ABT)	19
17	Dallas	12
13	*Chicago	10
17	San Diego	7
81		72

SAN DIEGO (1-3)

31	*Houston	29
3	L.A. Rams	24
13	San Francisco	24
7	*L.A. Raiders	17
54		94

SEATTLE (2-2)

13	*Phoenix	31
17	Indianapolis	7
23	L.A. Rams	7
16	*San Francisco	28
69		73

NFC Preseason Results —Team By Team

Eastern Division

DALLAS (2-2)

24	Kansas City	14
12	*L.A. Raiders	17
20	Houston	30
20	*Atlanta (OT)	17
76		78

N.Y. GIANTS (2-2)

23	*Buffalo	17
10	Cleveland	16
24	*N.Y. Jets	10
3	New England	24
60		67

PHILADELPHIA (4-1)

13	Buffalo (ABL)	17
24	N.Y. Jets	10
29	Cincinnati	24
21	*Pittsburgh	20
23	*Indianapolis	21
110		92

PHOENIX (4-0)

31	Seattle	13
12	Chicago	10
46	*New England	0
34	*Denver	10
123		33

WASHINGTON (1-3)

7	Pittsburgh	16
27	New England	6
21	*Cleveland (OT)	24
9	N.Y. Jets	13
64		59

Central Division

CHICAGO (2-3)

6	Miami	0
7	San Fran. (ABB)	21
10	*Phoenix	12
10	*L.A. Raiders	13
30	*Buffalo	13
63		59

DETROIT (2-3)

14	Denver (HOF)	3
24	*Cincinnati	20
16	Buffalo	21
14	Kansas City	38
3	*Pittsburgh	16
71		98

GREEN BAY (2-2)

28	*New England	7
20	New Orleans	31
35	Buffalo	24
16	*Cincinnati (OT)	19
99		81

MINNESOTA (2-2)

3	New Orleans	18
34	*Pittsburgh	24
24	Cincinnati (OT)	27
31	*Cleveland	7
92		76

TAMPA BAY (3-1)

23	Cleveland	10
13	*Miami	29
12	Atlanta	7
20	*Kansas City	7
68		53

Western Division

ATLANTA (2-2)

38	L.A. Rams	17
36	Houston	7
7	*Tampa Bay	12
17	Dallas (OT)	20
98		56

L.A. RAMS (1-3)

17	Atlanta	38
24	*San Diego	3
7	*Seattle	23
13	Houston	16
61		80

NEW ORLEANS (2-2)

18	*Minnesota	3
31	*Green Bay	20
28	Indianapolis	34
24	Miami	28
101		85

SAN FRANCISCO (5-0)

24	L.A. Raiders	17
21	Chicago (ABB)	7
24	*Denver	6
24	*San Diego	13
28	Seattle	16
121		59

*denotes home game
(OT) denotes overtime
(HOF) denotes Hall of Fame Game
(ABT) denotes American Bowl '91 in Tokyo
(ABB) denotes American Bowl '91 in Berlin
(ABL) denotes American Bowl '91 in London

1991 NFL STANDINGS

American Football Conference

Eastern Division
	W	L	T	Pct.	Pts.	OP
Buffalo	13	3	0	.813	458	318
N.Y. Jets*	8	8	0	.500	314	293
Miami	8	8	0	.500	343	349
New England	6	10	0	.375	211	305
Indianapolis	1	15	0	.063	143	381

Central Division
	W	L	T	Pct.	Pts.	OP
Houston	11	5	0	.688	386	251
Pittsburgh	7	9	0	.438	292	344
Cleveland	6	10	0	.375	293	298
Cincinnati	3	13	0	.188	263	435

Western Division
	W	L	T	Pct.	Pts.	OP
Denver	12	4	0	.750	304	235
Kansas City*	10	6	0	.625	322	252
L.A. Raiders*	9	7	0	.563	298	297
Seattle	7	9	0	.438	276	261
San Diego	4	12	0	.250	274	342

*Wild Card Team

The New York Jets finished ahead of Miami based on a head-to-head sweep (2-0). Atlanta finished ahead of San Francisco based on a head-to-head sweep (2-0).

National Football Conference

Eastern Division
	W	L	T	Pct.	Pts.	OP
Washington	14	2	0	.875	485	224
Dallas*	11	5	0	.688	342	310
Philadelphia	10	6	0	.625	285	244
N.Y. Giants	8	8	0	.500	281	297
Phoenix	4	12	0	.250	196	344

Central Division
	W	L	T	Pct.	Pts.	OP
Detroit	12	4	0	.750	339	295
Chicago*	11	5	0	.688	299	269
Minnesota	8	8	0	.500	301	306
Green Bay	4	12	0	.250	273	313
Tampa Bay	3	13	0	.188	199	365

Western Division
	W	L	T	Pct.	Pts.	OP
New Orleans	11	5	0	.688	341	211
Atlanta*	10	6	0	.625	361	338
San Francisco	10	6	0	.625	393	239
L.A. Rams	3	13	0	.188	234	390

Wild Card Playoffs
AFC .... Kansas City 10, L.A. Raiders 6, December 28, at Kansas City
Houston 17, N.Y. Jets 10, December 29, at Houston
NFC .... Atlanta 27, New Orleans 20, December 28, at New Orleans
Dallas 17, Chicago 13, December 29, at Chicago

Divisional Playoffs
AFC .... Denver 26, Houston 24, January 4, at Denver
Buffalo 37, Kansas City 14, January 5, at Buffalo
NFC .... Washington 24, Atlanta 7, January 4, at Washington
Detroit 38, Dallas 6, January 5, at Detroit

Championship Games
AFC .... Buffalo 10, Denver 7, January 12, at Buffalo
NFC .... Washington 41, Detroit 10, January 12, at Washington
SUPER BOWL XXVI .... Washington 37, Buffalo 24, January 26, at Hubert H. Humphrey Metrodome, Minneapolis, Minnesota
AFC-NFC PRO BOWL .... NFC 21, AFC 15, February 2, at Aloha Stadium, Honolulu, Hawaii

AFC Season Records—Team by Team

BUFFALO (13-3)
35	*Miami	31
52	*Pittsburgh	34
23	at N.Y. Jets	20
17	at Tampa Bay	10
35	*Chicago	20
6	at Kansas City	33
42	*Indianapolis	6
35	*Cincinnati	16
	OPEN DATE	
22	*New England	17
34	vs. G.B. at Mil.	24
41	at Miami	27
13	at New England	16
24	*N.Y. Jets	13
30	at L.A. Raid. (OT)	27
35	at Indianapolis	7
17	*Detroit (OT)	17
458		**318**

CINCINNATI (3-13)
14	at Denver	45
7	*Houston	30
13	at Cleveland	14
27	*Washington	34
	OPEN DATE	
7	*Seattle	13
23	at Dallas	35
16	at Buffalo	35
3	at Houston	35
23	*Cleveland	21
27	*Pittsburgh (OT)	33
10	at Philadelphia	17
14	*L.A. Raiders	38
27	*N.Y. Giants	24
13	at Miami	37
10	at Pittsburgh	17
29	*New England	7
263		**435**

CLEVELAND (6-10)
14	*Dallas	26
20	at New England	0
14	*Cincinnati	13
10	at N.Y. Giants	13
	OPEN DATE	
14	*N.Y. Jets	17
17	at Washington	42
30	at San Diego (OT)	24
17	*Pittsburgh	14
21	at Cincinnati	23
30	*Philadelphia	32
24	at Houston	28
20	*Kansas City	15
31	at Indianapolis	0
7	*Denver	17
14	*Houston	17
10	at Pittsburgh	17
293		**298**

DENVER (12-4)
45	*Cincinnati	14
13	at L.A. Raiders	16
16	*Seattle	10
27	*San Diego	19
13	at Minnesota	6
14	at Houston	42
	OPEN DATE	
19	*Kansas City	16
9	at New England	6
20	*Pittsburgh	13
16	*L.A. Raiders	17
24	at Kansas City	20
10	at Seattle	13
20	*New England	3
17	at Cleveland	7
24	*Phoenix	19
17	at San Diego	14
304		**235**

HOUSTON (11-5)
47	*L.A. Raiders	17
30	at Cincinnati	7
17	*Kansas City	7
20	at New England	24
	OPEN DATE	
42	*Denver	14
23	at N.Y. Jets	20
17	at Miami	13
35	*Cincinnati	3
13	at Wash. (OT)	16
26	*Dallas (OT)	23
28	*Cleveland	24

INDIANAPOLIS (1-15)
7	*New England	16
6	at Miami	17
0	at L.A. Raiders	16
24	*Detroit	33
3	at Seattle	31
3	*Pittsburgh	21
6	at Buffalo	42
6	*N.Y. Jets	17
	OPEN DATE	
6	*Miami	10
28	at N.Y. Jets	27
17	*Chicago	31
10	vs. G.B. at Mil.	14
0	*Cleveland	31
17	at New Eng. (OT)	23
7	*Buffalo	35
3	at Tampa Bay	17
143		**381**

KANSAS CITY (10-6)
14	*Atlanta	3
10	*New Orleans	17
7	at Houston	17
20	*Seattle	13
14	at San Diego	13
33	*Buffalo	6
42	*Miami	7
16	at Denver	19
24	*L.A. Raiders	21
	OPEN DATE	
27	at L.A. Rams	20
20	*Denver	24
15	at Cleveland	20
19	at Seattle	6
20	*San Diego (OT)	17
14	at San Francisco	28
27	at L.A. Raiders	21
322		**252**

L.A. RAIDERS (9-7)
17	at Houston	47
16	*Denver	13
16	*Indianapolis	0
17	at Atlanta	21
12	*San Francisco	6
13	*San Diego	21
23	at Seattle (OT)	20
20	*L.A. Rams	17
21	at Kansas City	24
	OPEN DATE	
17	at Denver	16
31	*Seattle	7
38	at Cincinnati	14
9	at San Diego	7
27	*Buffalo (OT)	30
0	at New Orleans	27
21	*Kansas City	27
298		**297**

MIAMI (8-8)
31	at Buffalo	35
17	*Indianapolis	6
13	at Detroit	17
16	*Green Bay	13
23	at N.Y. Jets	41
20	at New England	10
7	at Kansas City	42
13	*Houston	17
	OPEN DATE	
10	at Indianapolis	6
30	*New England	20
27	*Buffalo	41
16	at Chicago (OT)	13
33	*Tampa Bay	14
37	*Cincinnati	13
30	at San Diego	38
20	*N.Y. Jets (OT)	23
343		**349**

NEW ENGLAND (6-10)
16	at Indianapolis	7
0	*Cleveland	20
6	at Pittsburgh	20
24	*Houston	20
10	at Phoenix	24
10	*Miami	20
	OPEN DATE	

PITTSBURGH (7-9)
26	*San Diego	20
34	at Buffalo	52
20	*New England	6
14	at Philadelphia	23
	OPEN DATE	
21	at Indianapolis	3
20	*N.Y. Giants	23
21	*Seattle	27
14	at Cleveland	17
13	at Denver	20
33	at Cincinnati (OT)	27
14	*Washington	41
26	*Houston	14
10	at Dallas	20
6	at Houston	31
17	*Cincinnati	10
17	*Cleveland	10
292		**344**

SAN DIEGO (4-12)
20	at Pittsburgh	26
14	at San Francisco	34
10	*Atlanta	13
19	at Denver	27
13	*Kansas City	14
21	at L.A. Raiders	13
24	at L.A. Rams	30
24	*Cleveland (OT)	30
9	at Seattle	20
	OPEN DATE	
17	*Seattle	24
24	*New Orleans	21
3	at N.Y. Jets	24
7	*L.A. Raiders	9
17	at K.C. (OT)	20
38	*Miami	30
14	*Denver	17
274		**342**

SEATTLE (7-9)
24	at New Orleans	27
20	*N.Y. Jets	13
10	at Denver	16
13	at Kansas City	20
31	*Indianapolis	3
13	at Cincinnati	7
20	*L.A. Raiders (OT)	23
27	at Pittsburgh	7
20	*San Diego	9
	OPEN DATE	
14	at San Diego	17
7	at L.A. Raiders	31
13	*Denver	10
6	*Kansas City	19
22	*San Francisco	24
13	at Atlanta	26
23	*L.A. Rams	9
276		**261**

N.Y. JETS (8-8)
16	*Tampa Bay	13
13	at Seattle	20
20	*Buffalo	23
13	at Chicago (OT)	19
41	*Miami	23
17	at Cleveland	14
20	*Houston	23
17	at Indianapolis	6
	OPEN DATE	
19	*Green Bay (OT)	16
27	*Indianapolis	28
28	at New England	21
24	*San Diego	3
13	at Buffalo	24
20	at Detroit	34
3	*New England	6
23	at Miami (OT)	20
314		**293**

HOUSTON (11-5) (continued)
	OPEN DATE	
42	*Denver	14
23	at N.Y. Jets	20
17	at Miami	13
35	*Cincinnati	3
13	at Wash. (OT)	16
26	*Dallas (OT)	23
28	*Cleveland	24

NEW ENGLAND (6-10) (continued)
6	at Pittsburgh	20
24	*Houston	20
10	at Phoenix	24
10	*Miami	20
	OPEN DATE	

144

NFC Season Records—Team by Team

ATLANTA (10-6)

3	at Kansas City	14
19	*Minnesota	20
13	at San Diego	10
21	*L.A. Raiders	17
6	*New Orleans	27
	OPEN DATE	
39	at San Francisco	34
10	at Phoenix	16
31	*L.A. Rams	14
17	*San Francisco	14
17	at Washington	56
43	*Tampa Bay	7
23	at N.O. (OT)	20
35	*Green Bay	31
31	at L.A. Rams	14
26	*Seattle	13
27	at Dallas	31
361		**338**

CHICAGO (11-5)

10	*Minnesota	6
21	at Tampa Bay	20
20	*N.Y. Giants	17
19	*N.Y. Jets (OT)	13
20	at Buffalo	35
7	*Washington	20
	OPEN DATE	
10	at Green Bay	0
20	at New Orleans	17
20	*Detroit	10
34	at Minnesota	17
31	at Indianapolis	17
13	*Miami (OT)	16
6	at Detroit	16
27	*Green Bay	13
27	*Tampa Bay	0
14	at San Francisco	52
299		**269**

DALLAS (11-5)

26	at Cleveland	14
31	*Washington	33
0	*Philadelphia	24
17	at Phoenix	9
21	*N.Y. Giants	16
20	vs. G.B. at Mil.	17
35	*Cincinnati	23
	OPEN DATE	
10	at Detroit	34
27	*Phoenix	7
23	at Houston (OT)	26
9	at N.Y. Giants	22
24	at Washington	21
20	*Pittsburgh	10
23	*New Orleans	14
25	at Philadelphia	13
31	*Atlanta	27
342		**310**

DETROIT (12-4)

0	at Washington	45
23	*Green Bay	14
17	*Miami	13
33	at Indianapolis	24
31	*Tampa Bay	3
24	*Minnesota	20
	OPEN DATE	
3	at San Francisco	35
34	*Dallas	10
10	at Chicago	20
21	at Tampa Bay	30
21	*L.A. Rams	10
34	at Minnesota	14
16	*Chicago	6
34	*N.Y. Jets	20
21	at Green Bay	17
17	at Buffalo (OT)	14
339		**295**

GREEN BAY (4-12)

3	*Philadelphia	20
14	at Detroit	23
15	*Tampa Bay	13
13	at Miami	16
21	at L.A. Rams	23
17	*Dallas at Mil.	20
	OPEN DATE	
0	*Chicago	10
27	at Tampa Bay	0
16	at N.Y. Jets (OT)	19
24	*Buffalo at Mil.	34
21	*Minnesota	35
14	*Ind. at Mil.	10
31	at Atlanta	35
13	at Chicago	27
17	*Detroit	21
27	at Minnesota	7
273		**313**

L.A. RAMS (3-13)

14	*Phoenix	24
19	at N.Y. Giants	13
7	at New Orleans	24
10	at San Francisco	27
23	*Green Bay	21
	OPEN DATE	
30	*San Diego	24
17	at L.A. Raiders	20
14	at Atlanta	31
17	*New Orleans	24
20	*Kansas City	27
10	at Detroit	21
10	*San Francisco	33
6	*Washington	27
14	*Atlanta	31
14	at Minnesota	20
9	at Seattle	23
234		**390**

MINNESOTA (8-8)

6	at Chicago	10
20	at Atlanta	19
17	*San Francisco	14
0	at New Orleans	26
6	*Denver	13
20	at Detroit	24
34	*Phoenix	7
23	at New Eng. (OT)	26
28	at Phoenix	0
28	*Tampa Bay	13
17	*Chicago	34
35	at Green Bay	21
14	*Detroit	34
	OPEN DATE	
26	at Tampa Bay	24
20	*L.A. Rams	14
7	*Green Bay	27
301		**306**

NEW ORLEANS (11-5)

27	*Seattle	24
17	at Kansas City	10
24	*L.A. Rams	7
26	*Minnesota	0
27	at Atlanta	6
	OPEN DATE	
13	at Philadelphia	6
23	*Tampa Bay	7
17	*Chicago	20
24	at L.A. Rams	17
10	*San Francisco	3
21	at San Diego	24
20	*Atlanta (OT)	23
24	at San Francisco	38
14	at Dallas	23
27	*L.A. Raiders	0
27	at Phoenix	3
341		**211**

N.Y. GIANTS (8-8)

16	*San Francisco	14
13	*L.A. Rams	19
17	at Chicago	20
13	*Cleveland	10
16	at Dallas	21
20	*Phoenix	9
23	at Pittsburgh	20
	OPEN DATE	
13	*Washington	17
7	at Philadelphia	30
21	at Phoenix	14
22	*Dallas	9
21	at Tampa Bay	14
24	at Cincinnati	27
14	*Philadelphia	19
17	at Washington	34
24	*Houston	20
281		**297**

PHILADELPHIA (10-6)

20	at Green Bay	3
10	*Phoenix	26
24	at Dallas	0
23	*Pittsburgh	14
0	at Washington	23
13	at Tampa Bay	14
6	*New Orleans	13
	OPEN DATE	
7	*San Francisco	23
30	*N.Y. Giants	7
32	at Cleveland	30
17	*Cincinnati	10
34	at Phoenix	14
13	at Houston	6
19	at N.Y. Giants	14
13	*Dallas	25
24	*Washington	22
285		**244**

PHOENIX (4-12)

24	at L.A. Rams	14
26	at Philadelphia	10
0	at Washington	34
9	*Dallas	17
24	*New England	10
9	at N.Y. Giants	20
7	at Minnesota	34
16	*Atlanta	10
0	*Minnesota	28
7	at Dallas	27
14	*N.Y. Giants	21
10	at San Francisco	14
14	*Philadelphia	34
	OPEN DATE	
14	*Washington	20
19	at Denver	24
3	*New Orleans	27
196		**344**

SAN FRANCISCO (10-6)

14	at N.Y. Giants	16
34	*San Diego	14
14	at Minnesota	17
27	*L.A. Rams	10
6	at L.A. Raiders	12
	OPEN DATE	
34	*Atlanta	39
35	*Detroit	3
23	at Philadelphia	7
14	at Atlanta	17
3	at New Orleans	10
14	*Phoenix	10
33	at L.A. Rams	10
38	*New Orleans	24
24	at Seattle	22
28	*Kansas City	14
52	*Chicago	14
393		**239**

TAMPA BAY (3-13)

13	at N.Y. Jets	16
20	*Chicago	21
13	at Green Bay	15
10	*Buffalo	17
3	at Detroit	31
14	*Philadelphia	13
	OPEN DATE	
7	at New Orleans	23
0	*Green Bay	27
13	at Minnesota	28
30	*Detroit	21
7	at Atlanta	43
14	*N.Y. Giants	21
14	at Miami	33
24	*Minnesota	26
0	at Chicago	27
17	*Indianapolis	3
199		**365**

WASHINGTON (14-2)

45	*Detroit	0
33	at Dallas	31
34	*Phoenix	0
34	at Cincinnati	27
23	*Philadelphia	0
20	at Chicago	7
42	*Cleveland	17
	OPEN DATE	
17	at N.Y. Giants	13
16	*Houston (OT)	13
56	*Atlanta	17
41	at Pittsburgh	14
21	*Dallas	24
27	at L.A. Rams	6
20	at Phoenix	14
34	*N.Y. Giants	17
22	at Philadelphia	24
485		**224**

* denotes home game
(OT) denotes overtime

Attendance figures as they appear in the following, and in the club-by-club sections starting on page 26, are turnstile counts and not paid attendance. Paid attendance totals are on page 206.

First Week Summaries

Standings

American Football Conference

Eastern Division

	W	L	T	Pct.	Pts.	OP
Buffalo	1	0	0	1.000	35	31
New England	1	0	0	1.000	16	7
N.Y. Jets	1	0	0	1.000	16	13
Indianapolis	0	1	0	.000	7	16
Miami	0	1	0	.000	31	35

Central Division

	W	L	T	Pct.	Pts.	OP
Houston	1	0	0	1.000	47	17
Pittsburgh	1	0	0	1.000	26	20
Cincinnati	0	1	0	.000	14	45
Cleveland	0	1	0	.000	14	26

Western Division

	W	L	T	Pct.	Pts.	OP
Denver	1	0	0	1.000	45	14
Kansas City	1	0	0	1.000	14	3
L.A. Raiders	0	1	0	.000	17	47
San Diego	0	1	0	.000	20	26
Seattle	0	1	0	.000	24	27

National Football Conference

Eastern Division

	W	L	T	Pct.	Pts.	OP
Dallas	1	0	0	1.000	26	14
N.Y. Giants	1	0	0	1.000	16	14
Philadelphia	1	0	0	1.000	20	3
Phoenix	1	0	0	1.000	24	14
Washington	1	0	0	1.000	45	0

Central Division

	W	L	T	Pct.	Pts.	OP
Chicago	1	0	0	1.000	10	6
Detroit	0	1	0	.000	0	45
Green Bay	0	1	0	.000	3	20
Minnesota	0	1	0	.000	6	10
Tampa Bay	0	1	0	.000	13	16

Western Division

	W	L	T	Pct.	Pts.	OP
New Orleans	1	0	0	1.000	27	24
Atlanta	0	1	0	.000	3	14
L.A. Rams	0	1	0	.000	14	24
San Francisco	0	1	0	.000	14	16

Sunday, September 1

Kansas City 14, Atlanta 3 — at Arrowhead Stadium, attendance 74,246. Christian Okoye ran for 143 yards and 1 touchdown and helped set up the Chiefs' other score as Kansas City downed the Falcons. After Deron Cherry recovered Chris Miller's fumble at the Falcons' 27-yard line in the third quarter, Okoye carried the ball on four consecutive plays, the last a 4-yard touchdown run to give the Chiefs a 7-3 lead. In the fourth quarter, he ran 48 yards on third-and-1 to position Kansas City for Steve DeBerg's 6-yard touchdown pass to Emile Harry. The Chiefs kept the Falcons out of the end zone by intercepting 4 of Miller's passes. Cornerback Albert Lewis accounted for 3 of the thefts.

Atlanta	3	0	0	0	—	3
Kansas City	0	0	7	7	—	14

Atl — FG Daluiso 20
KC— Okoye 4 run (Lowery kick)
KC— Harry 6 pass from DeBerg (Lowery kick)

Denver 45, Cincinnati 14 — at Mile High Stadium, attendance 72,855. John Elway passed for 2 touchdowns and ran for 2 more as the Broncos, last in the AFC Western Division in 1990, overwhelmed the defending AFC Central Division-champion Bengals. Elway, who completed 18 of 28 passes for 262 yards, started the scoring with a 52-yard touchdown pass to Michael Young just 3:33 into the game. His 3-yard run in the second quarter broke a 7-7 tie, and when he tossed a 1-yard touchdown pass to Reggie Johnson with 15 seconds left in the first half, Denver led 28-7. Newly acquired running back Gaston Green ran for 116 yards on 24 carries for the Broncos, who amassed 471 total yards. Boomer Esiason passed for 206 yards and 2 touchdowns for Cincinnati, but was intercepted 3 times.

Cincinnati	7	0	7	0	—	14
Denver	7	21	7	10	—	45

Den — Young 52 pass from Elway (Treadwell kick)
Cin — Barber 42 pass from Esiason (Breech kick)
Den — Elway 3 run (Treadwell kick)
Den — Lewis 1 run (Treadwell kick)
Den — R. Johnson 1 pass from Elway (Treadwell kick)
Cin — McGee 52 pass from Esiason (Breech kick)
Den — Braxton 52 interception return (Treadwell kick)
Den — Elway 5 run (Treadwell kick)
Den — FG Treadwell 19

Dallas 26, Cleveland 14 — at Cleveland Stadium, attendance 78,860. Troy Aikman passed for 274 yards and 2 touchdowns and Emmitt Smith ran for 112 yards as the Cowboys won on opening day for the twenty-fourth time in their 32-year history and ruined the head-coaching debut of the Browns' Bill Belichick. Dallas scored on all four of its first-half possessions to take a 20-7 lead at halftime. The final touchdown came on a 4-yard pass from Aikman to Michael Irvin with 19 seconds left. But Cleveland got back in it early in the second half, pulling within 20-14 on a 62-yard pass from Bernie Kosar to Webster Slaughter just 27 seconds into the third quarter. The Cowboys secured the victory when Ken Willis kicked 2 field goals in the fourth quarter, the latter a club record-tying 54-yarder. Aikman completed 24 of 37 passes and was not intercepted. Irvin caught 9 passes for 123 yards.

Dallas	3	17	0	6	—	26
Cleveland	7	0	7	0	—	14

Dall — FG Willis 38
Cleve — Mack 1 run (Stover kick)
Dall — FG Willis 25
Dall — Novacek 3 pass from Aikman (Willis kick)
Dall — Irvin 4 pass from Aikman (Willis kick)
Cleve — Slaughter 62 pass from Kosar (Stover kick)
Dall — FG Willis 22
Dall — FG Willis 54

Houston 47, L.A. Raiders 17 — at Astrodome, attendance 61,367. Warren Moon passed for 250 yards and 2 touchdowns and Allen Pinkett rushed for 144 yards and 1 score as the Oilers defeated the Raiders. Houston jumped to a 16-0 lead, then put the game away with a third-quarter spurt. Los Angeles's Jeff Jaeger kicked a 39-yard field goal midway through the period to pull the Raiders within 23-10, but the Oilers countered with a seven-play, 82-yard drive that ended with a 28-yard touchdown pass from Moon to Tony Jones. Sam Graddy fumbled the ensuing kickoff, and Houston's Mike Dumas recovered, returning it 19 yards for a touchdown to make the score 37-10. The Oilers' Run-and-Shoot offense piled up 459 total yards against the Raiders.

L.A. Raiders	0	7	3	7	—	17
Houston	6	10	21	10	—	47

Hou — Pinkett 8 run (kick failed)
Hou — Moon 1 run (Howfield kick)
Hou — FG Howfield 34
Raiders — Gault 59 pass from Schroeder (Jaeger kck)
Hou — Givins 22 pass from Moon (Howfield kick)
Raiders — FG Jaeger 39
Hou — T. Jones 28 pass from Moon (Howfield kick)
Hou — Dumas 19 fumble recovery return (Howfield kick)
Hou — FG Howfield 46
Raiders — Graddy 80 pass from Evans (Jaeger kick)
Hou — G. Brown 39 run (Howfield kick)

Buffalo 35, Miami 31 — at Rich Stadium, attendance 80,252. Jim Kelly passed for 381 yards and the Bills amassed a club-record 593 yards of total offense while beating the Dolphins. Kelly completed 29 of 39 passes and threw for 2 touchdowns, and also got help from Thurman Thomas, who rushed for 165 yards and 1 touchdown on 25 carries and caught 8 passes for 103 yards and another score. Still, it was Miami, behind Dan Marino's 267 yards and 3 touchdowns passing, which took an early 14-0 lead and still had a 24-14 advantage in the fourth quarter. But Carwell Gardner gave Buffalo the lead when he capped a 70-yard drive with a 1-yard touchdown run with 9:08 left in the game. Thomas's 7-yard touchdown with 3:55 left eventually stood up as the game-winner. Andre Reed had 11 catches for 154 yards for the Bills. The Dolphins' Mark Clayton caught 6 passes for 138 yards and Mark Higgs, playing in place of injured Sammie Smith, carried 30 times for 146 yards.

Miami	7	7	3	14	—	31
Buffalo	0	7	14	14	—	35

Mia — Clayton 43 pass from Marino (Baumann kick)
Mia — Higgs 3 run (Baumann kick)
Buff — Reed 54 pass from Kelly (Norwood kick)
Mia — FG Baumann 21
Buff — Rolle 3 pass from Reich (Norwood kick)
Buff — Thomas 50 pass from Kelly (Norwood kick)
Mia — Clayton 5 pass from Marino (Baumann kick)
Buff — Gardner 1 run (Norwood kick)
Buff — Thomas 7 run (Norwood kick)
Mia — Duper 3 pass from Marino (Baumann kick)

Chicago 10, Minnesota 6 — at Soldier Field, attendance 64,112. Markus Paul's second interception of the game, on the Bears' 11-yard line with 1:19 left to play, secured Chicago's win over the Vikings. Tom Waddle, cut by the Bears earlier in the week but re-signed, caught a 37-yard pass from Jim Harbaugh with 55 seconds to go in the first half for the game's only touchdown. Wade Wilson completed 21 of 37 passes for 248 yards for the Vikings, but was intercepted 3 times. The Bears won for the eighth consecutive time on opening day, the longest current streak in the NFL.

Minnesota	3	0	3	0	—	6
Chicago	0	7	0	3	—	10

Minn — FG Reveiz 26
Chi — Waddle 37 pass from Harbaugh (Butler kick)
Minn — FG Reveiz 24
Chi — FG Butler 22

New England 16, Indianapolis 7 — at Hoosier Dome, attendance 49,961. Jason Staurovsky kicked 3 field goals and the Patriots, winners of just one game a year ago, beat the Colts to snap a 14-game regular-season losing streak in Dick MacPherson's coaching debut. Ironically, New England's last victory also came against Indianapolis in the Hoosier Dome, and Staurovsky's 3 field goals made the difference in that 16-14 win. The Patriots' Tommy Hodson completed 13 of 18 passes for 136 yards, including a 23-yard touchdown to tight end Marv Cook in the first quarter. The Colts' Jeff George was 27 of 42 for 301 yards, but was intercepted twice as Indianapolis lost its eighth straight opener.

New England	7	3	3	3	—	16
Indianapolis	7	0	0	0	—	7

NE — Cook 23 pass from Hodson (Staurovsky kick)
Ind — Brooks 24 pass from George (Biasucci kick)
NE — FG Staurovsky 35
NE — FG Staurovsky 39
NE — FG Staurovsky 36

Philadelphia 20, Green Bay 3 — at Lambeau Field, attendance 58,991. Jim McMahon came off the bench to throw for 257 yards and 2 touchdowns, and lead the Eagles to the victory in Rich Kotite's debut as head coach. Philadelphia suffered a severe blow when quarterback Randall Cunningham injured a knee in the second quarter and was lost for the season. But McMahon came on to pass 32 yards to Keith Byars for a second-quarter touchdown and 75 yards to Fred Barnett for a score in the fourth period. The Eagles' defense limited Green Bay to only 44 rushing yards, had 4 sacks, and forced 5 turnovers. Don Majkowski, attempting to rebound from rotator cuff surgery, completed 16 of 42 passes for 201 yards with 3 interceptions for the Packers.

Philadelphia	0	13	0	7	—	20
Green Bay	0	0	3	0	—	3

Phil — FG Ruzek 37
Phil — Byars 32 pass from McMahon (Ruzek kick)
Phil — FG Ruzek 40
GB — FG Jacke 21
Phil — Barnett 75 pass from McMahon (Ruzek kick)

Phoenix 24, L.A. Rams 14 — at Anaheim Stadium, attendance 47,069. Tom Tupa, pressed into action at quarterback after starter Timm Rosenbach was lost for the season to injury, passed for 1 touchdown, ran for 1, and directed an error-free offense to lead the Cardinals over the Rams. Phoenix took advantage of 5 lost fumbles and 2 interceptions to upset favored Los Angeles. Eric Hill picked up a mishandled snap on the Rams' first possession and ran 85 yards for a touchdown just 2:01 into the game. Later in the quarter, Tupa threw a 28-yard touchdown pass to Ernie Jones, and before the half was over, he ran 1 yard for a score to cap a 45-yard drive. That came after punter Rich Camarillo recovered Vernon Turner's fumble on a punt return. Jim Everett passed for 290 yards for the Rams, who had 375 total yards. Robert Delpino rushed for 81 yards and 2 touchdowns and caught 10 passes for 113 yards.

Phoenix	14	7	0	3	—	24
L.A. Rams	0	7	7	0	—	14

Phx — Hill 85 fumble recovery return (G. Davis kick)
Phx — E. Jones 28 pass from Tupa (G. Davis kick)
Rams — Delpino 1 run (Zendejas kick)
Phx — Tupa 1 run (G. Davis kick)
Rams — Delpino 1 run (Zendejas kick)
Phx — FG G. Davis 32

Pittsburgh 26, San Diego 20 — at Three Rivers Stadium, attendance 55,848. Dwight Stone took a screen pass from backup quarterback Neil O'Donnell and turned it into an 89-yard touchdown for the clinching score in the Steelers' victory. Bubby Brister passed for 189 yards and a touchdown for Pittsburgh, which led 19-3 early in the fourth quarter. But the Chargers made it close when Nate Lewis caught an 11-yard touchdown pass from Rod Bernstine on a halfback-option play, and John Carney kicked a 35-

yard field goal to make it 19-13 with 2:14 to play. But on the Steelers' next possession, O'Donnell, in the game because Brister suffered a mild concussion midway through the fourth quarter, and Stone teamed for the clinching score.

San Diego	0	3	0	17	—	20
Pittsburgh	3	7	6	10	—	26

Pitt — FG Anderson 38
SD — FG Carney 48
Pitt — Calloway 33 pass from Brister (Anderson kick)
Pitt — FG Anderson 29
Pitt — FG Anderson 31
Pitt — FG Anderson 39
SD — Lewis 11 pass from Bernstine (Carney kick)
SD — FG Carney 35
Pitt — Stone 89 pass from O'Donnell (Anderson kick)
SD — Jefferson 5 pass from Friesz (Carney kick)

New Orleans 27, Seattle 24 — at Louisiana Superdome, attendance 68,492. Bobby Hebert, playing in his first game since missing the entire 1990 season, threw a 10-yard touchdown pass to Floyd Turner with 1:11 left in the game to lift the Saints to a dramatic victory. New Orleans let an early 17-point lead slip away, and fell behind 24-20 when Brian Davis intercepted Hebert's pass and returned it 40 yards for a touchdown with 14 seconds left in the third quarter. But Hebert marched his team 68 yards to the winning touchdown in a 14-play, six-minute drive. Seattle had a chance to tie the game, but John Kasay's 37-yard field-goal try with 14 seconds left failed.

Seattle	0	7	17	0	—	24
New Orleans	7	13	0	7	—	27

NO — Fenerty 50 pass from Hebert (Andersen kick)
NO — FG Andersen 47
NO — Swilling 39 interception return (Andersen kick)
Sea— Blades 10 pass from Krieg (Kasay kick)
NO — FG Andersen 31
Sea— Blades 25 pass from Krieg (Kasay kick)
Sea— FG Kasay 37
Sea— Davis 40 interception return (Kasay kick)
NO — Turner 10 pass from Hebert (Andersen kick)

N.Y. Jets 16, Tampa Bay 13 — at Giants Stadium, attendance 61,204. Pat Leahy's third field goal of the game, a 40-yarder with 1:22 remaining, was the difference in the Jets' victory over the Buccaneers. Leahy, at 40 the league's oldest player, capped a nine-play, 48-yard drive that won the game for New York. Tampa Bay had tied it at 13-13 on a 65-yard touchdown pass from Vinny Testaverde to rookie Lawrence Dawsey with 5:57 to go. Blair Thomas ran for 92 yards on 23 carries for the Jets, who used their ground-oriented attack to control the ball for more than 39 minutes.

Tampa Bay	3	3	0	7	—	13
N.Y. Jets	7	3	0	6	—	16

TB — FG Christie 29
Jets— McNeil 1 run (Leahy kick)
TB — FG Christie 38
Jets— FG Leahy 30
Jets— FG Leahy 25
TB — Dawsey 65 pass from Testaverde (Christie kick)
Jets— FG Leahy 40

Sunday Night, September 1

Washington 45, Detroit 0 — at RFK Stadium, attendance 55,671. Quarterback Mark Rypien passed for 2 touchdowns and Earnest Byner ran for 1 and passed for 1 on a halfback-option play to power the Redskins past the Lions. Rypien completed 15 of 19 passes for 183 yards as Washington amassed 392 yards of total offense. Brian Mitchell added to the onslaught with a 69-yard punt return for a touchdown in the first quarter, which helped stake the Redskins to a 35-0 lead by halftime. Detroit, meanwhile, managed only 9 first downs and 154 total yards while running just 41 plays from scrimmage. Cornerback Darrell Green had 2 of Washington's 3 interceptions of the Lions' Rodney Peete.

Detroit	0	0	0	0	—	0
Washington	21	14	7	3	—	45

Wash— Riggs 1 run (Lohmiller kick)
Wash— J. Johnson 4 pass from Rypien (Lohmiller kick)
Wash— Mitchell 69 punt return (Lohmiller kick)
Wash— Sanders 18 pass from Byner (Lohmiller kick)
Wash— Byner 6 run (Lohmiller kick)
Wash— Clark 38 pass from Rypien (Lohmiller kick)
Wash— FG Lohmiller 26

Monday, September 2

N.Y. Giants 16, San Francisco 14 — at Giants Stadium, attendance 76,319. Matt Bahr's 35-yard field goal with five seconds remaining in the game gave the defending Super Bowl-champion Giants a 16-14 victory over the 49ers. New York, which defeated San Francisco 15-13 in the 1990 NFC Championship Game when Bahr kicked 5 field goals, including the game-winner as time ran out, snapped the 49ers' NFL-record 18-game regular-season road winning streak. San Francisco had taken a 14-13 lead early in the fourth quarter when Steve Young, starting in place of injured Joe Montana, ran 5 yards for a touchdown with 13:37 to play. But Jeff Hostetler marched the Giants 60 yards to the winning field goal, making the key play by completing an 11-yard pass to Mark Ingram on third-and-10 from the 49ers' 37. The win gave Ray Handley a successful debut as head coach.

San Francisco	7	0	0	7	—	14
N.Y. Giants	3	10	0	3	—	16

Giants— FG Bahr 35
SF — Rice 73 pass from Young (Cofer kick)
Giants— Anderson 1 run (Bahr kick)
Giants— FG Bahr 28
SF — Young 5 run (Cofer kick)
Giants— FG Bahr 35

Second Week Summaries

Standings

American Football Conference

Eastern Division

	W	L	T	Pct.	Pts.	OP
Buffalo	2	0	0	1.000	87	65
Miami	1	1	0	.500	48	41
New England	1	1	0	.500	16	27
N.Y. Jets	1	1	0	.500	29	33
Indianapolis	0	2	0	.000	13	33
Central Division						
Houston	2	0	0	1.000	77	24
Cleveland	1	1	0	.500	34	26
Pittsburgh	1	1	0	.500	60	72
Cincinnati	0	2	0	.000	21	75
Western Division						
Denver	1	1	0	.500	58	30
Kansas City	1	1	0	.500	24	20
L.A. Raiders	1	1	0	.500	33	60
Seattle	1	1	0	.500	44	40
San Diego	0	2	0	.000	34	60

National Football Conference

Eastern Division

	W	L	T	Pct.	Pts.	OP
Phoenix	2	0	0	1.000	50	24
Washington	2	0	0	1.000	78	31
Dallas	1	1	0	.500	57	47
N.Y. Giants	1	1	0	.500	29	33
Philadelphia	1	1	0	.500	30	29
Central Division						
Chicago	2	0	0	1.000	31	26
Detroit	1	1	0	.500	23	59
Minnesota	1	1	0	.500	26	29
Green Bay	0	2	0	.000	17	43
Tampa Bay	0	2	0	.000	33	37
Western Division						
New Orleans	2	0	0	1.000	44	34
L.A. Rams	1	1	0	.500	33	37
San Francisco	1	1	0	.500	48	30
Atlanta	0	2	0	.000	22	34

Sunday, September 8

Chicago 21, Tampa Bay 20 — at Tampa Stadium, attendance 62,409. Jim Harbaugh passed for 2 touchdowns and running back Neal Anderson scored twice in the Bears' victory. Anderson caught a 7-yard pass from Harbaugh midway through the second quarter to put Chicago ahead for good at 14-10. Earlier, Anderson scored on a 12-yard run. Harbaugh's 43-yard touchdown pass to Wendell Davis early in the second half proved to be the game-winner. The Bears turned the ball over 4 times—twice in their own territory—but held off the Buccaneers on the strength of their defense. John Roper, Steve McMichael, and Richard Dent each had 2 sacks.

Chicago	7	7	7	0	—	21
Tampa Bay	10	3	0	7	—	20

TB — FG Christie 31
Chi— N. Anderson 12 run (Butler kick)
TB — G. Anderson 64 run (Christie kick)
Chi— N. Anderson 7 pass from Harbaugh (Butler kick)
TB — FG Christie 36
Chi— Davis 43 pass from Harbaugh (Butler kick)
TB — Hill 15 pass from Chandler (Christie kick)

Cleveland 20, New England 0 — at Foxboro Stadium, attendance 35,377. Bernie Kosar threw 2 touchdown passes and the Browns' defense shut down the Patriots en route to the victory. Kosar, who completed 15 of 22 passes for 187 yards, threw scoring passes of 7 yards to Leroy Hoard in the second quarter and 65 yards to Michael Jackson in the fourth. In between, Matt Stover booted a pair of field goals. Meanwhile, Cleveland limited the Patriots to only 9 first downs and 143 yards in total offense while forcing 4 turnovers.

Cleveland	0	7	3	10	—	20
New England	0	0	0	0	—	0

Cleve — Hoard 7 pass from Kosar (Stover kick)
Cleve — FG Stover 30
Cleve — FG Stover 32
Cleve — Jackson 65 pass from Kosar (Stover kick)

L.A. Raiders 16, Denver 13 — at Los Angeles Memorial Coliseum, attendance 48,569. Jay Schroeder passed for 168 yards and 1 touchdown, but the Raiders mostly kept the ball on the ground to defeat the Broncos. Los Angeles ran 38 times while putting the ball in the air only 19 times and maintained possession for more than 35 minutes. Roger Craig, acquired as a Plan B free agent from the 49ers in the offseason, ran for 99 yards on 27 carries. The Raiders outgained Denver on the ground 133-33. Jeff Jaeger's 3 field goals and Schroeder's 16-yard touchdown pass to Willie Gault in the third quarter put the Raiders ahead 16-6. John Elway's 3-yard touchdown pass to Steve Sewell in the final minute could only make it close.

Denver	3	3	0	7	—	13
L.A. Raiders	0	3	7	6	—	16

Den — FG Treadwell 22
Den — FG Treadwell 47
Raiders— FG Jaeger 29
Raiders— Gault 16 pass from Schroeder (Jaeger kick)
Raiders— FG Jaeger 23
Raiders— FG Jaeger 34
Den — Sewell 3 pass from Elway (Treadwell kick)

Detroit 23, Green Bay 14 — at Pontiac Silverdome, attendance 43,132. Rodney Peete passed for 271 yards and 1 touchdown as the Lions rebounded from their disastrous opening-day loss to Washington by beating the Packers. Detroit got things started by marching 83 yards to a touchdown on its first possession. Barry Sanders capped the 16-play, 10-minute drive with a 4-yard touchdown run. Sanders was back in the lineup after missing the opener with a rib injury. The game was tied 7-7 until Eddie Murray gave the Lions the lead for good with a 41-yard field goal as time ran out in the first half. Peete, who completed 25 of 38 passes, fired a 12-yard touchdown to Willie Green early in the third quarter, and Murray added field goals of 27 and 36 yards. Robert Clark caught 10 passes for 143 yards for Detroit.

Green Bay	0	7	7	0	—	14
Detroit	7	3	10	3	—	23

Det— Sanders 4 run (Murray kick)
GB— Workman 1 run (Jacke kick)
Det— FG Murray 41
Det— Green 12 pass from Peete (Murray kick)
Det— FG Murray 27
GB— Majkowski 2 run (Jacke kick)
Det— FG Murray 36

Miami 17, Indianapolis 6 — at Joe Robbie Stadium, attendance 51,155. Mark Higgs rushed for 111 yards and the Dolphins' defense, burned by Buffalo for nearly 600 total yards in the season opener, limited the Colts to only 150 yards of total offense in the victory. Higgs, who had a combined 251 rushing yards in his first three NFL seasons, upped his total to 257 in two games this year while filling in for injured Sammie Smith. It was rookie Aaron Craver, however, who scored on a 7-yard run in the third quarter that broke a 7-7 tie. Dan Marino's 9-yard touchdown pass to Jim Jensen with 6:47 to go secured the win.

Indianapolis	0	3	0	3	—	6
Miami	3	0	7	7	—	17

Mia— FG Baumann 48
Ind — FG Biasucci 48
Mia— Craver 7 run (Baumann kick)
Ind — FG Biasucci 21
Mia— Jensen 9 pass from Marino (Baumann kick)

L.A. Rams 19, N.Y. Giants 13 — at Giants Stadium, attendance 76,541. Robert Delpino rushed for 116 yards and 1 touchdown and Tony Zendejas kicked 4 field goals as the Rams surprised the Giants. Delpino's touchdown came on fourth-and-goal from the 1-yard line with 4:58 left in the first half and put the Rams ahead 10-3, a lead they never relinquished. Zendejas booted 3 field goals in the second half, and punter Dale Hatcher dropped 2 kicks inside New York's 5-yard line to keep the Giants pinned deep in their own territory. Los Angeles built its advantage to 19-6 before New York made it close on a 1-yard pass from Jeff Hostetler to David Meggett with 1:58 left in the game.

L.A. Rams	0	10	3	6	—	19
N.Y. Giants	0	6	0	7	—	13

Rams — FG Zendejas 29
Giants— FG Bahr 46
Rams — Delpino 1 run (Zendejas kick)
Giants— FG Bahr 40
Rams — FG Zendejas 50
Rams — FG Zendejas 32
Rams — FG Zendejas 33
Giants — Meggett 1 pass from Hostetler (Bahr kick)

Minnesota 20, Atlanta 19 — at Atlanta-Fulton County Stadium, attendance 50,936. Cris Carter caught a pair of touchdown passes and Herschel Walker ran for 125 yards to lead the Vikings past the Falcons. Atlanta led 10-7 until

early in the third quarter, when Anthony Carter scored on a 14-yard run. Cris Carter's acrobatic, one-handed grab of a Wade Wilson pass with 11:23 to go in the game put Minnesota ahead 20-10 and stood up as the winning points. Chris Miller completed 27 of 41 passes for 300 yards and 2 touchdowns for the Falcons, who amassed 439 yards of total offense. Atlanta's George Thomas had 128 yards on 7 catches, including a 20-yard touchdown with 53 seconds left to make it close. Wilson completed 13 of 18 passes for 157 yards and 2 scores for the Vikings.

Minnesota	7	0	7	6	—	20
Atlanta	3	7	0	9	—	19

Atl —FG Daluiso 23
Minn—C. Carter 25 pass from Wilson (Reveiz kick)
Atl —Wilkins 3 pass from Miller (Daluiso kick)
Minn—A. Carter 14 run (Reveiz kick)
Minn—C. Carter 39 pass from Wilson (kick failed)
Atl —Safety, Wilson ran out of end zone
Atl —Thomas 20 pass from Miller (Daluiso kick)

New Orleans 17, Kansas City 10 — at Arrowhead Stadium, attendance 74,916. The Saints dominated the first half, building a 17-0 lead, then held on in the second half to beat the Chiefs and up their record to 2-0 for the first time in the 25-year history of the franchise. New Orleans scored on its first two possessions, with Morten Andersen kicking a 40-yard field goal and Bobby Hebert throwing a 13-yard touchdown pass to Eric Martin. Before halftime, Hebert completed another touchdown pass, a 45-yarder to Quinn Early. By intermission, the Saints had 13 first downs and 235 total yards; Kansas City just 1 first down and 30 yards. But the second half was a complete reversal with the Chiefs picking up 16 first downs to New Orleans's 2 and 242 yards to only 24. Nick Lowery kicked a 23-yard field goal on the Chiefs' first possession of the half and Steve DeBerg threw a 7-yard touchdown pass to Jonathan Hayes on the second, which came with 13:52 to play in the game. But Reggie Jones and linebacker Sam Mills ended subsequent threats with interceptions and Kansas City's final drive, which began at its own 21, ended on the Saints' 10 as time ran out.

New Orleans	10	7	0	0	—	17
Kansas City	0	0	3	7	—	10

NO—FG Andersen 40
NO—Martin 13 pass from Hebert (Andersen kick)
NO—Early 45 pass from Hebert (Andersen kick)
KC—FG Lowery 23
KC—Hayes 7 pass from DeBerg (Lowery kick)

Seattle 20, N.Y. Jets 13 — at Kingdome, attendance 56,770. Jeff Kemp threw 2 touchdown passes in the third quarter to break open a close contest and the Seahawks went on to defeat the Jets. Kemp, making his first start in three years because Dave Krieg was injured in Seattle's opener, completed 17 of 28 passes for 182 yards. With the Seahawks leading just 6-3 in the third quarter, Kemp passed 12 yards to Travis McNeal for a touchdown and followed that with a 15-yard score to Tommy Kane 2:27 later for a 20-3 lead. A 6-yard touchdown pass from Troy Taylor to Rob Moore with 1:14 left pulled New York within seven points, but that was as close as the Jets could get. Seattle's Dwayne Harper helped secure the win with two fourth-quarter interceptions.

N.Y. Jets	0	3	0	10	—	13
Seattle	0	3	17	0	—	20

Jets—FG Leahy 29
Sea—FG Kasay 23
Sea—FG Kasay 34
Sea—McNeal 12 pass from Kemp (Kasay kick)
Sea—Kane 15 pass from Kemp (Kasay kick)
Jets—FG Leahy 30
Jets—Moore 6 pass from Taylor (Leahy kick)

Phoenix 26, Philadelphia 10 — at Veterans Stadium, attendance 63,818. Tom Tupa passed for 218 yards and 1 touchdown and the Cardinals, who forced 7 turnovers in a season-opening victory over the Rams, had 6 more as they upset the Eagles. Tupa completed only 6 of 19 passes, but included was a 51-yard touchdown to Johnny Johnson as Phoenix built a 16-0 first-half lead. Philadelphia pulled within 19-10 in the third quarter and was threatening to score, but the Cardinals' Freddie Joe Nunn forced Philadelphia's Fred Barnett to fumble near the goal line and Aeneas Williams recovered. Phoenix recovered 5 fumbles in all, including one that defensive end Rod Saddler ran 7 yards with for the final touchdown with 2:48 left in the game. That one was also forced by Nunn, who sacked Jim McMahon on the play.

Phoenix	13	3	3	7	—	26
Philadelphia	0	10	0	0	—	10

Phx—FG Davis 52
Phx—Johnson 51 pass from Tupa (Davis kick)
Phx—FG Davis 28
Phx—FG Davis 22
Phil—Sanders 3 run (Ruzek kick)
Phil—FG Ruzek 47
Phx—FG Davis 42
Phx—Saddler 7 fumble recovery return (Davis kick)

Buffalo 52, Pittsburgh 34 — at Rich Stadium, attendance 79,545. Jim Kelly passed for 363 yards and 6 touchdowns and the Bills rolled up 537 yards in total offense to beat the Steelers. Pittsburgh had the top-rated defense in the league in 1990, when it allowed only 9 touchdown passes all season, but Buffalo was unstoppable as it eclipsed the 500-yard mark for the second consecutive week. Still, the Steelers were in this one until early in the fourth quarter. A 57-yard interception return for a touchdown by Bryan Hinkle helped Pittsburgh trim a 31-10 deficit to 31-27. But with 13:09 left in the game, Kelly passed 11 yards to Don Beebe for a touchdown. The pair teamed again on a 4-yarder at the 7:57 mark, and 45 seconds later, Nate Odomes returned an interception 32 yards for a touchdown to break the game open at 52-27. Beebe caught 10 pases for 112 yards in all, while Andre Reed added 118 yards and 1 touchdown on 9 receptions. Kelly completed 31 of his 43 attempts, and Thurman Thomas ran for 104 yards on 15 carries. Pittsburgh's Barry Foster gained 121 yards on only 9 attempts, and broke loose for a 56-yard touchdown run in the second quarter.

Pittsburgh	0	10	17	7	—	34
Buffalo	10	14	7	21	—	52

Buff—Lofton 53 pass from Kelly (Norwood kick)
Buff—FG Norwood 50
Pitt—FG Anderson 25
Buff—Beebe 34 pass from Kelly (Norwood kick)
Buff—Beebe 14 pass from Kelly (Norwood kick)
Pitt—Foster 56 run (Anderson kick)
Buff—Reed 14 pass from Kelly (Norwood kick)
Pitt—W. Williams 1 run (Anderson kick)
Pitt—Hinkle 57 interception return (Anderson kick)
Pitt—FG Anderson 27
Buff—Beebe 11 pass from Kelly (Norwood kick)
Buff—Beebe 4 pass from Kelly (Norwood kick)
Buff—Odomes 32 interception return (Norwood kick)
Pitt—Hoge 1 run (Anderson kick)

San Francisco 34, San Diego 14 — at Candlestick Park, attendance 60,753. Jerry Rice caught 9 passes for 150 yards and 2 touchdowns, including a 70-yarder that helped break the game open in the third quarter as the 49ers pulled away for the victory. Rice caught a 32-yard touchdown pass from Steve Young early in the second quarter to give San Francisco its first lead at 10-7. It was 17-14 at halftime, but Rice grabbed Young's pass at midfield, 1:49 into the third quarter, and raced to the end zone to make it 24-14. Keith Henderson's 6-yard touchdown run later in the quarter effectively put the game out of reach. Young completed 26 of 36 passes for 348 yards and 3 touchdowns as the 49ers had 458 yards of total offense.

San Diego	7	7	0	0	—	14
San Francisco	3	14	14	3	—	34

SD—McEwen 1 pass from Friesz (Carney kick)
SF—FG Cofer 34
SF—Rice 32 pass from Young (Cofer kick)
SD—Miller 9 pass from Friesz (Carney kick)
SF—Taylor 1 pass from Young (Cofer kick)
SF—Rice 70 pass from Young (Cofer kick)
SF—Henderson 6 run (Cofer kick)
SF—FG Cofer 28

Sunday Night, September 8

Houston 30, Cincinnati 7 — at Riverfront Stadium, attendance 56,463. Warren Moon passed for 315 yards and Allen Pinkett ran for 101 to lead the Oilers over the Bengals. After Cincinnati pulled within 13-7 late in the third quarter, Moon completed 6 of 7 passes on a 90-yard touchdown drive—all of it through the air—that culminated in his 22-yard scoring toss to Haywood Jeffires. Just 1:01 later, Lamar Lathon returned a tipped pass 52 yards for the touchdown that put the game out of reach at 27-7.

Houston	0	6	7	17	—	30
Cincinnati	0	0	7	0	—	7

Hou—FG Howfield 19
Hou—FG Howfield 21
Hou—Pinkett 31 run (Howfield kick)
Cin—James 18 pass from Esiason (Breech kick)
Hou—Jeffires 22 pass from Moon (Howfield kick)
Hou—Lathon 52 interception return (Howfield kick)
Hou—FG Howfield 37

Monday, September 9

Washington 33, Dallas 31 — at Texas Stadium, attendance 63,025. Mark Rypien passed for 2 touchdowns and Chip Lohmiller kicked 4 long-distance field goals to rally the Redskins past the Cowboys. Dallas led 21-10 in the first half, but Washington came back to take the lead on 2 kicks by Lohmiller and Rypien's 37-yard touchdown pass to Art Monk. The Cowboys forged ahead again at 24-23 on a 51-yard field goal by Ken Willis. Gerald Riggs's 1-yard touchdown run and Lohmiller's fourth field goal rendered Troy Aikman's 6-yard touchdown pass to Michael Irvin with two seconds left meaningless. Lohmiller booted field goals of 53 and 52 yards in the second quarter, and added 45- and 46-yarders after halftime. Earnest Byner rushed for 101 yards for the Redskins, while Dallas's Emmitt Smith had 112 yards, including a 75-yard touchdown run in the first quarter.

Washington	7	13	3	10	—	33
Dallas	14	7	3	7	—	31

Dall—Novacek 3 pass from Aikman (Willis kick)
Wash—Johnson 3 pass from Rypien (Lohmiller kick)
Dall—E. Smith 75 run (Willis kick)
Wash—FG Lohmiller 53
Dall—E. Smith 5 pass from Aikman (Willis kick)
Wash—Monk 37 pass from Rypien (Lohmiller kick)
Wash—FG Lohmiller 52
Wash—FG Lohmiller 45
Dall—FG Willis 51
Wash—Riggs 1 run (Lohmiller kick)
Wash—FG Lohmiller 46
Dall—Irvin 6 pass from Aikman (Willis kick)

Third Week Summaries

Standings

American Football Conference

Eastern Division	W	L	T	Pct.	Pts.	OP
Buffalo	3	0	0	1.000	110	85
Miami	1	2	0	.333	61	58
New England	1	2	0	.333	22	47
N.Y. Jets	1	2	0	.333	49	56
Indianapolis	0	3	0	.000	13	49
Central Division						
Houston	3	0	0	1.000	94	31
Cleveland	2	1	0	.667	48	39
Pittsburgh	2	1	0	.667	80	78
Cincinnati	0	3	0	.000	34	89
Western Division						
Denver	2	1	0	.667	74	40
L.A. Raiders	2	1	0	.667	49	60
Kansas City	1	2	0	.333	31	37
Seattle	1	2	0	.333	54	56
San Diego	0	3	0	.000	44	73

National Football Conference

Eastern Division	W	L	T	Pct.	Pts.	OP
Washington	3	0	0	1.000	112	31
Philadelphia	2	1	0	.667	54	29
Phoenix	2	1	0	.667	50	58
Dallas	1	2	0	.333	57	71
N.Y. Giants	1	2	0	.333	46	53
Central Division						
Chicago	3	0	0	1.000	51	43
Detroit	2	1	0	.667	40	72
Minnesota	2	1	0	.667	43	43
Green Bay	1	2	0	.333	32	56
Tampa Bay	0	3	0	.000	46	52
Western Division						
New Orleans	3	0	0	1.000	68	41
Atlanta	1	2	0	.333	35	44
L.A. Rams	1	2	0	.333	40	61
San Francisco	1	2	0	.333	62	47

Sunday, September 15

Atlanta 13, San Diego 10 — at San Diego Jack Murphy Stadium, attendance 44,804. Steve Broussard rushed for 101 yards and newly signed Norm Johnson kicked a pair of field goals as the Falcons snapped their 19-game road losing string by defeating the Chargers in San Diego. Atlanta hadn't won away from home since beating the Raiders in the Los Angeles Memorial Coliseum on November 30, 1988. But Mike Pritchard caught a 14-yard touchdown pass from Chris Miller in the first quarter and Johnson, the longtime Seahawks kicker who was signed as a free agent earlier in the week, added field goals of 28 and 36 yards. The Chargers had a chance to tie the game in the final seconds, but John Carney was wide left on a 47-yard field-goal try. Carney, who missed only 2 three-point attempts all of the 1990 season, missed 3 lengthy tries against the Falcons.

Atlanta	7	3	3	0	—	13
San Diego	0	7	0	3	—	10

Atl—Pritchard 14 pass from C. Miller (Johnson kick)
Atl—FG Johnson 28
SD—A. Miller 15 pass from Friesz (Carney kick)
Atl—FG Johnson 36
SD—FG Carney 39

Buffalo 23, N.Y. Jets 20 — at Giants Stadium, attendance 65,309. Jim Kelly's 15-yard touchdown pass to Thurman Thomas with 4:14 left in the game rallied the Bills to the victory. After the touchdown pass, the Jets moved into position for a potential game-tying field goal, but Pat Leahy's 51-yard attempt was short with 23 seconds left. Kelly completed 27 of 37 passes for 275 yards and 2 touchdowns. He teamed with James Lofton for a 10-yard completion on fourth-and-6 from New York's 30-yard line on the winning drive. Thomas, held to under 100 yards rushing for the first time this season (he had 62),

caught 13 passes for 112 yards. Scott Norwood kicked 3 field goals for the Bills, including a career-long 52-yarder in the second quarter.

Buffalo	0	10	6	7	—	23
N.Y. Jets	0	10	7	3	—	20

Jets— McNeil 1 run (Leahy kick)
Buff— FG Norwood 52
Jets— FG Leahy 32
Buff— Reed 7 pass from Kelly (Norwood kick)
Buff— FG Norwood 25
Jets— B. Thomas 5 pass from O'Brien (Leahy kick)
Buff— FG Norwood 44
Jets— FG Leahy 39
Buff— T. Thomas 15 pass from Kelly (Norwood kick)

Cleveland 14, Cincinnati 13 — at Cleveland Stadium, attendance 78,269. Matt Stover kicked 4 field goals, including a 45-yarder with four seconds remaining as the Browns, just 3-13 a season ago, raised their record to 2-1. The defending AFC Central Division-champion Bengals, meanwhile, fell to 0-3. Cleveland started its winning drive at its own 12-yard line with just over three minutes to go and marched 60 yards in 14 plays. Cincinnati, which lost 3 fumbles, each leading to earlier Stover field goals, had erased an 11-3 deficit with a 26-yard touchdown pass from Boomer Esiason to Tim McGee and a 36-yard field goal by Jim Breech with 6:41 left. James Brooks rushed for 111 yards on 18 carries for the Bengals. Webster Slaughter had 107 yards on 8 catches for the Browns.

Cincinnati	3	0	0	10	—	13
Cleveland	0	5	6	3	—	14

Cin — FG Breech 21
Cleve— Safety, J. Jones tackled Brooks in end zone
Cleve— FG Stover 30
Cleve— FG Stover 42
Cleve— FG Stover 38
Cin — McGee 26 pass from Esiason (Breech kick)
Cin — FG Breech 36
Cleve— FG Stover 45

L.A. Raiders 16, Indianapolis 0 — at Los Angeles Memorial Coliseum, attendance 40,287. Mervyn Fernandez caught a touchdown pass and Jeff Jaeger kicked 3 field goals as the Raiders methodically beat the Colts, posting their first shutout since the opening game of the 1987 season. Fernandez, who caught 7 passes for 90 yards, grabbed a 16-yard pass from Jay Schroeder early in the second quarter to give Los Angeles all the points it needed. The Raiders totaled only 268 yards in the game, but the Colts missed a pair of field-goal tries and lost 2 fumbles, 1 by Eric Dickerson at the Los Angeles 12-yard line. The Raiders improved their record to 14-2 at home under head coach Art Shell.

Indianapolis	0	0	0	0	—	0
L.A. Raiders	0	13	3	0	—	16

Raiders— Fernandez 16 pass from Schroeder (Jaeger kick)
Raiders— FG Jaeger 33
Raiders— FG Jaeger 41
Raiders— FG Jaeger 33

Detroit 17, Miami 13 — at Pontiac Silverdome, attendance 56,896. Rodney Peete ran for 1 touchdown and passed for another and the Lions executed a fourth-quarter goal-line stand to beat the Dolphins. Peete threw a 26-yard touchdown pass to Willie Green to tie the game at 10-10 in the second quarter, then ran six yards to put Detroit ahead in the third period. But with the Lions ahead 17-13 late in the game, Peete's pass was intercepted by Miami's Shawn Lee and returned 14 yards to the Lions' 3-yard line. On third down from the 3, Dan Owens threw Mark Higgs for a 3-yard loss, and on fourth down from the 6, Dan Marino's pass in the end zone was broken up by Ray Crockett with 2:58 remaining in the game. Detroit then ran out the clock. The Lions' Barry Sanders finished with 143 yards on 32 carries.

Miami	3	7	0	3	—	13
Detroit	3	7	7	0	—	17

Det— FG Murray 46
Mia— FG Stoyanovich 18
Mia— Higgs 4 run (Stoyanovich kick)
Det— Green 26 pass from Peete (Murray kick)
Det— Peete 6 run (Murray kick)
Mia— FG Stoyanovich 47

Pittsburgh 20, New England 6 — at Three Rivers Stadium, attendance 53,703. Bubby Brister completed 22 of 29 passes for 262 yards and 1 touchdown as the Steelers beat the Patriots. Pittsburgh, which had given up 52 points and 537 total yards to Buffalo one week earlier, held New England without a touchdown and to only 174 total yards. The game was tied 6-6 until Pittsburgh's Thomas Everett intercepted a Tommy Hodson pass and returned it 27 yards, setting up Brister's 32-yard touchdown pass to Eric Green with 13:41 left in the game. The clinching touchdown came with 3:18 to go, when Bryan Wagner kicked the ball into the back of one of his own blockers and Ernie Mills recovered in the end zone for Pittsburgh.

New England	0	6	0	0	—	6
Pittsburgh	3	3	0	14	—	20

Pitt— FG Anderson 49
NE— FG Staurovsky 33
NE— FG Staurovsky 28
Pitt— FG Anderson 32
Pitt— Green 32 pass from Brister (Anderson kick)
Pitt— Mills recovered blocked punt in end zone (Anderson kick)

Chicago 20, N.Y. Giants 17 — at Soldier Field, attendance 64,829. The Bears remained unbeaten when Neal Anderson ran 42 yards for a fourth-quarter touchdown and William Perry blocked Matt Bahr's 35-yard field-goal attempt in the closing seconds. The Giants had rallied from a 13-0 halftime deficit on a field goal by Bahr and a pair of scoring runs by Rodney Hampton, the last a 3-yarder with 10:09 to play for a 17-13 lead. But Chicago responded with a 76-yard drive, with Anderson's touchdown coming with 6:39 remaining. Finally, Perry blocked Bahr's game-tying attempt with 15 seconds to go. The Bears' Jim Harbaugh completed 15 of 25 passes for 221 yards, including a 75-yard touchdown pass to Wendell Davis in the second quarter. New York's Jeff Hostetler was 25 of 35 for 209 yards.

N.Y. Giants	0	0	10	7	—	17
Chicago	0	13	0	7	—	20

Chi — FG Butler 46
Chi — Davis 75 pass from Harbaugh (Butler kick)
Chi — FG Butler 20
Giants— FG Bahr 35
Giants— Hampton 6 run (Bahr kick)
Giants— Hampton 3 run (Bahr kick)
Chi — Anderson 42 run (Butler kick)

Philadelphia 24, Dallas 0 — at Texas Stadium, attendance 62,656. Clyde Simmons posted 4½ of a club-record 11 sacks as the Eagles overwhelmed the Cowboys. Jerome Brown added 2½ sacks and Mike Golic had 2 more for Philadelphia, which limited Dallas to only 8 first downs and 90 total yards. The Cowboys' Troy Aikman, the victim of all 11 sacks, completed 11 of 25 passes for 112 yards with 3 interceptions. Jim McMahon completed 18 of 29 passes for 207 yards for the Eagles. He had an 11-yard touchdown pass to Fred Barnett on Philadelphia's second possession, and added a 6-yard scoring toss to Keith Byars to close the scoring in the fourth quarter. Barnett caught 7 passes for 111 yards.

Philadelphia	7	10	0	7	—	24
Dallas	0	0	0	0	—	0

Phil— Barnett 11 pass from McMahon (Ruzek kick)
Phil— FG Ruzek 42
Phil— Drummond 1 run (Ruzek kick)
Phil— Byars 6 pass from McMahon (Ruzek kick)

Washington 34, Phoenix 0 — at RFK Stadium, attendance 54,622. The Redskins scored on their first two possessions and dominated the Cardinals en route to posting their second consecutive shutout at home and moving into first place in the NFC Eastern Division. Earnest Byner rushed for 109 yards, including a 2-yard touchdown to open the scoring. Wilber Marshall had a pair of interceptions for the Redskins, one at the Washington goal line and one in the third quarter that he returned 55 yards for a touchdown. The Redskins, who outgained Phoenix 350 to 165, posted 4 sacks and intercepted the Cardinals' Tom Tupa 3 times.

Phoenix	0	0	0	0	—	0
Washington	7	7	14	6	—	34

Wash— Byner 2 run (Lohmiller kick)
Wash— Sanders 10 run (Lohmiller kick)
Wash— Clark 28 pass from Rypien (Lohmiller kick)
Wash— Marshall 55 interception return (Lohmiller kick)
Wash— FG Lohmiller 30
Wash— FG Lohmiller 48

Minnesota 17, San Francisco 14 — at Metrodome, attendance 59,148. The Vikings scored all of their points in the second quarter and made the big plays defensively deep in their own territory to beat the 49ers. San Francisco led 7-0 on the first of 2 touchdown passes from Steve Young to Jerry Rice until Anthony Carter turned a short pass from Wade Wilson into a 46-yard touchdown early in the second quarter. Later in the period, Audray McMillian intercepted Young's pass in the end zone and Minnesota drove 98 yards to Herschel Walker's 1-yard touchdown run and a 14-7 lead with 2:25 left in the first half. Fuad Reveiz kicked a 31-yard field goal on the final play of the half and the Vikings made the 17-7 advantage stand up. Late in the third quarter, Ken Clarke forced a fumble that Ray Berry recovered at the Minnesota 12-yard line, and one series later, Todd Scott blocked a 35-yard field-goal attempt.

San Francisco	7	0	0	7	—	14
Minnesota	0	17	0	0	—	17

SF — Rice 15 pass from Young (Cofer kick)
Minn— A. Carter 46 pass from Wilson (Reveiz kick)
Minn— Walker 1 run (Reveiz kick)
Minn— FG Reveiz 31
SF — Rice 21 pass from Young (Cofer kick)

Denver 16, Seattle 10 — at Mile High Stadium, attendance 74,152. The Broncos built a 16-0 lead, then barely held on to defeat the Seahawks. Three field goals by David Treadwell and a 61-yard touchdown pass from John Elway to Ricky Nattiel staked Denver to its lead in the fourth quarter. But with 7:30 left in the game, Seattle's John Kasay kicked a 28-yard field goal, and 3:26 later, Derrick Fenner scored on a 1-yard run to trim the Seahawks' deficit to 16-10. The Broncos failed to make a first down the entire fourth quarter, and when they punted again, Seattle marched to a first down at the Denver 14. But from there, Jeff Kemp threw 4 incompletions in the end zone, the last with 43 seconds left. Kemp completed 21 of 50 passes for 322 yards in all. Tommy Kane had 122 yards on 6 catches and Brian Blades had 107 on 5 for Seattle. Elway was 19 of 32 for 252 yards for the Broncos. Gaston Green rushed for 92 yards for Denver.

Seattle	0	0	0	10	—	10
Denver	0	10	3	3	—	16

Den— FG Treadwell 17
Den— Nattiel 61 pass from Elway (Treadwell kick)
Den— FG Treadwell 25
Den— FG Treadwell 35
Sea— FG Kasay 28
Sea— Fenner 1 run (Kasay kick)

Green Bay 15, Tampa 13 — at Lambeau Field, attendance 58,114. Chris Jacke kicked a 22-yard field goal with 22 seconds remaining, and the Packers rallied from eight points down in the final 2:03 to beat the winless Buccaneers. Tampa Bay had taken a 13-5 lead on an 87-yard touchdown pass from Vinny Testaverde to Willie Drewrey with 3:59 left in the game. But Green Bay quarterback Don Majkowski marched his team 76 yards in less than two minutes, throwing an 8-yard scoring pass to Vince Workman to trim the deficit to 13-12 with 2:03 to go. After the Buccaneers punted, Majkowski passed 36 yards to Perry Kemp for the key play on a 40-yard drive to Jacke's winning field goal. Majkowski completed 20 of 38 passes for 258 yards. Testaverde was 19 of 30 for 278 yards.

Tampa Bay	0	0	3	10	—	13
Green Bay	0	5	0	10	—	15

GB— Safety, Paup tackled Testaverde in end zone
GB— FG Jacke 24
TB — FG Christie 31
TB — FG Christie 22
TB — Drewrey 87 pass from Testaverde (Christie kick)
GB— Workman 8 pass from Majkowski (Jacke kick)
GB— FG Jacke 22

Sunday Night, September 15

New Orleans 24, L.A. Rams 7 — at Louisiana Superdome, attendance 68,583. Craig Heyward scored on a pair of 1-yard runs in the second half and the Saints' defense shut out the Rams' offense as New Orleans continued its best-ever start. The game was tied 7-7 in the third quarter after Los Angeles' Jerry Gray intercepted a Bobby Hebert pass and returned it 59 yards for a touchdown. But the Saints answered that with a nine-play, 87-yard drive that ended with the first of Heyward's short scoring bursts with 3:31 left in the third quarter. Heyward made it 21-7 with another touchdown with 10:29 to go in the game. Rickey Jackson had 2 of his team's 5 sacks for New Orleans, which limited the Rams to only 120 total yards. Los Angeles had just 6 first downs and failed to convert any of its 10 third-down opportunities.

L.A. Rams	0	0	7	0	—	7
New Orleans	7	0	7	10	—	24

NO — Hilliard 1 run (Andersen kick)
Rams— Gray 59 interception return (Zendejas kick)
NO — Heyward 1 run (Andersen kick)
NO — Heyward 1 run (Andersen kick)
NO — FG Andersen 42

Monday, September 16

Houston 17, Kansas City 7 — at Astrodome, attendance 61,058. Warren Moon's 4-yard touchdown pass to Haywood Jeffires late in the third quarter broke a 7-7 tie and lifted the Oilers past the Chiefs. Moon, who completed 29 of 38 passes for 233 yards and was not intercepted, capped the 93-yard drive with his touchdown to Jeffires with nine seconds left in the period. Houston then got an end zone interception by Cris Dishman with 9:40 remaining in the game to help preserve the victory. Ian Howfield kicked a 23-yard field goal with 21 seconds left for the game's final points. Kansas City's lone score came on a 2-yard run by Christian Okoye with 27 seconds left in the first half. The Oilers raised their record to 3-0 for the first time in franchise history.

Kansas City	0	7	0	0	—	7
Houston	7	0	7	3	—	17

Hou— Pinkett 1 run (Howfield kick)
KC — Okoye 2 run (Lowery kick)
Hou— Jeffires 4 pass from Moon (Howfield kick)
Hou— FG Howfield 23

Fourth Week Summaries

Standings

American Football Conference

Eastern Division

	W	L	T	Pct.	Pts.	OP
Buffalo	4	0	0	1.000	127	95
Miami	2	2	0	.500	77	71
New England	2	2	0	.500	46	67
N.Y. Jets	1	3	0	.250	62	75
Indianapolis	0	4	0	.000	37	82

Central Division

	W	L	T	Pct.	Pts.	OP
Houston	4	0	0	1.000	114	55
Cleveland	2	2	0	.500	57	52
Pittsburgh	2	2	0	.500	94	101
Cincinnati	0	4	0	.000	61	123

Western Division

	W	L	T	Pct.	Pts.	OP
Denver	3	1	0	.750	101	59
Kansas City	2	2	0	.500	51	50
L.A. Raiders	2	2	0	.500	66	81
Seattle	1	3	0	.250	67	76
San Diego	0	4	0	.000	63	100

National Football Conference

Eastern Division

	W	L	T	Pct.	Pts.	OP
Washington	4	0	0	1.000	146	58
Philadelphia	3	1	0	.750	77	43
Dallas	2	2	0	.500	74	80
N.Y. Giants	2	2	0	.500	59	63
Phoenix	2	2	0	.500	59	75

Central Division

	W	L	T	Pct.	Pts.	OP
Chicago	4	0	0	1.000	70	56
Detroit	3	1	0	.750	73	96
Minnesota	2	2	0	.500	43	69
Green Bay	1	3	0	.250	45	72
Tampa Bay	0	4	0	.000	56	69

Western Division

	W	L	T	Pct.	Pts.	OP
New Orleans	4	0	0	1.000	94	41
Atlanta	2	2	0	.500	56	61
San Francisco	2	2	0	.500	89	57
L.A. Rams	1	3	0	.250	50	88

Sunday, September 22

Buffalo 17, Tampa Bay 10 — at Tampa Stadium, attendance 57,323. Jim Kelly's 29-yard touchdown pass to Keith McKeller with 5:21 left in the game gave the Bills the victory. Kelly completed 20 of 35 passes for 322 yards for the Bills, whose league-leading offense continued to flourish, amassing 421 total yards. But the winless Buccaneers still had a chance to tie until Chris Chandler's pass in the end zone from the Buffalo 8-yard line fell incomplete as time expired.

Buffalo	7	0	3	7	—	17
Tampa Bay	0	0	7	3	—	10

Buff— Gardner 1 run (Norwood kick)
TB — Cobb 1 run (Christie kick)
Buff— FG Norwood 33
TB — FG Christie 19
Buff— McKeller 29 pass from Kelly (Norwood kick)

N.Y. Giants 13, Cleveland 10 — at Giants Stadium, attendance 75,891. The Giants built a 13-0 first-half lead, then left the game in the hands of their defense to escape with a 13-10 victory. New York allowed the Browns only 10 first downs and 145 total yards. Cleveland is coached by former Giants defensive coordinator Bill Belichick. The defending Super Bowl champions also got 4 sacks, including a key 7-yarder by Carl Banks after Cleveland had driven to New York's 38-yard line late in the game. Rodney Hampton ran for 104 yards, including a 28-yard touchdown in the second quarter, and Lewis Tillman had 90 for the Giants, who rushed for 212 yards. Matt Bahr had a pair of field goals and became only the eighteenth player in NFL history to surpass the 1,000-point mark for his career.

Cleveland	0	0	3	7	—	10
N.Y. Giants	3	10	0	0	—	13

Giants— FG Bahr 44
Giants— FG Bahr 48
Giants— Hampton 28 run (Bahr kick)
Cleve — FG Stover 30
Cleve — Mack 7 pass from Kosar (Stover kick)

Detroit 33, Indianapolis 24 — at Hoosier Dome, attendance 53,396. Barry Sanders rushed for 179 yards and 2 touchdowns and the Lions rallied from an early 10-0 deficit to defeat the Colts. Indianapolis still led 10-7 in the third quarter until Rohn Stark was tackled for a 13-yard loss while attempting to punt. Detroit took over on the Colts' 16-yard line, and after a 14-yard run by Rodney Peete, Sanders scored from two yards out to give the Lions the lead for good. Sanders added a 23-yard touchdown with 2:57 left in the fourth quarter to put the game out of reach at 33-17. Peete completed 17 of 23 passes for 167 yards. Backup Erik Kramer threw an 11-yard touchdown pass to Willie Green to put Detroit ahead 23-10 while Peete was out of the game for an equipment adjustment. The Lions ran for 208 yards and had 402 yards of total offense while limiting Indianapolis to a franchise-low 4 rushing yards. Eric Dickerson scored 2 touchdowns for the Colts, but rushed 13 times for only 17 yards, the lowest single-game output of his career.

Detroit	0	7	16	10	—	33
Indianapolis	10	0	0	14	—	24

Ind — Dickerson 2 run (Biasucci kick)
Ind — FG Biasucci 20
Det— Peete 7 run (Murray kick)
Det— Sanders 2 run (Murray kick)
Det— Safety, Ball tackled Dickerson in end zone
Det— Green 11 pass from Kramer (Murray kick)
Det— FG Murray 19
Ind — Dickerson 2 pass from George (Biasucci kick)
Det— Sanders 23 run (Murray kick)
Ind — Hester 12 pass from George (Biasucci kick)

Miami 16, Green Bay 13 — at Joe Robbie Stadium, attendance 56,583. Pete Stoyanovich kicked a 31-yard field goal with 8:21 left in the game to give Dolphins head coach Don Shula his 300th career coaching victory. Stoyanovich's field goal was his third of the game and capped Miami's fourth-quarter comeback. The Dolphins trailed 13-6 until Chuck Klingbeil fell on Don Majkowski's fumble in the end zone on the first play of the fourth quarter. Vestee Jackson secured the win when he fell on another Majkowski fumble at the Green Bay 24-yard line in the closing moments. With the triumph, Shula joined the legendary George Halas as the only NFL coaches to post 300 victories. Halas won a league-record 325 games in 40 seasons spread over four different coaching stints with the Chicago Bears. Shula won 73 games in seven seasons as Baltimore's head coach from 1963-69, then joined the Dolphins in 1970.

Green Bay	0	13	0	0	—	13
Miami	6	0	0	10	—	16

Mia— FG Stoyanovich 43
Mia— FG Stoyanovich 52
GB — FG Jacke 28
GB — FG Jacke 34
GB — West 14 pass from Majkowski (Jacke kick)
Mia— Klingbeil fumble recovery in end zone (Stoyanovich kick)
Mia— FG Stoyanovich 31

New England 24, Houston 20 — at Foxboro Stadium, attendance 30,702. Hugh Millen's 34-yard touchdown pass to Greg McMurtry with six seconds remaining lifted the Patriots to a stunning upset of the previously unbeaten Oilers. Millen, making his first start of the season after New England's offense had sputtered through the first three games, completed 22 of 33 passes for 244 yards and directed his team to a 17-6 lead through three quarters. But Warren Moon, who passed for 268 yards, threw a pair of fourth-quarter touchdown passes to Curtis Duncan, the last a five-yarder with 1:52 left in the game, to give the Oilers a 20-17 lead. Millen then marched his team 83 yards to the winning score. Marv Cook caught 10 passes for 99 yards, including a 13-yard halfback option pass from Jon Vaughn for a touchdown in the second quarter.

Houston	3	3	0	14	—	20
New England	3	14	0	7	—	24

NE — FG Staurovsky 33
Hou— FG Howfield 28
NE — Cook 13 pass from Vaughn (Staurovsky kick)
Hou— FG Howfield 38
NE — Russell 2 run (Staurovsky kick)
Hou— Duncan 35 pass from Moon (Howfield kick)
Hou— Duncan 5 pass from Moon (Howfield kick)
NE — McMurtry 34 pass from Millen (Staurovsky kick)

Atlanta 21, L.A. Raiders 17 — at Atlanta-Fulton County Stadium, attendance 53,615. Chris Miller passed for 242 yards and 2 touchdowns and the Falcons limited the Raiders to only 159 total yards to win. Atlanta scored just three plays into the game when Deion Sanders sacked Jay Schroeder, forcing a fumble that Jessie Tuggle scooped up and raced 18 yards with for a touchdown. After the Raiders had rallied for a 14-7 lead in the third quarter, Miller threw a 25-yard touchdown pass to Steve Broussard to tie it, then a 46-yard scoring toss to Michael Haynes on the first play of the fourth quarter to put the Falcons ahead 21-14. The lead held up when Sanders intercepted Schroeder's fourth-down pass in the end zone with 1:36 remaining.

L.A. Raiders	0	7	7	3	—	17
Atlanta	7	0	7	7	—	21

Atl — Tuggle 18 fumble recovery return (Johnson kick)
Raiders— Glover 4 pass from Schroeder (Jaeger kick)
Raiders— Horton 5 pass from Schroeder (Jaeger kick)
Atl — Broussard 25 pass from Miller (Johnson kick)
Atl — Haynes 46 pass from Miller (Johnson kick)
Raiders— FG Jaeger 49

San Francisco 27, L.A. Rams 10 — at Candlestick Park, attendance 63,871. San Francisco's Jerry Rice broke the game open when he caught a short pass from Steve Young in the fourth quarter and turned it into a 62-yard touchdown. Rice's score came with 8:54 remaining in the game and turned The 49ers' 3-point lead into a 20-10 advantage. Five minutes later, Harry Sydney put the game out of reach by scoring on a 25-yard run. Young completed 21 of 31 passes for 288 yards and 2 touchdowns, including a 12-yarder to John Taylor with 18 seconds left in the first half to forge a 10-10 tie. That came only 23 seconds after Tony Zendejas's 22-yard field goal had given the Rams a 10-3 lead. But it took Young only four plays to move the 49ers 65 yards to the tying touchdown. San Francisco amassed 422 total yards in the game, including 149 on the ground.

L.A. Rams	0	10	0	0	—	10
San Francisco	3	7	3	14	—	27

SF — FG Cofer 22
Rams— Delpino 1 run (Zendejas kick)
Rams— FG Zendejas 22
SF — Taylor 12 pass from Young (Cofer kick)
SF — FG Cofer 47
SF — Rice 62 pass from Young (Cofer kick)
SF — Sydney 25 run (Cofer kick)

New Orleans 26, Minnesota 0 — at Louisiana Superdome, attendance 68,591. The unbeaten Saints continued their torrid start by completely shutting down the Vikings en route to the victory. New Orleans allowed Minnesota only 6 first downs and 151 total yards on just 41 plays from scrimmage. The Vikings crossed midfield only once, that on a desperation pass at the end of the first half, and maintained possession for only 19:12. The Saints, on the other hand, totaled 341 yards, and scored on a pair of 8-yard runs by Craig Heyward and 4 Morten Andersen field goals. Gill Fenerty had 106 yards and Heyward 72 as New Orleans rushed for 196 yards.

Minnesota	0	0	0	0	—	0
New Orleans	0	13	0	13	—	26

NO— Heyward 8 run (Andersen kick)
NO— FG Andersen 34
NO— FG Andersen 30
NO— FG Andersen 38
NO— Heyward 8 run (Andersen kick)
NO— FG Andersen 26

Philadelphia 23, Pittsburgh 14 — at Veterans Stadium, attendance 65,511. Jim McMahon passed for 286 yards and ran for 1 touchdown as the Eagles dominated the final three quarters to beat Pittsburgh. The Steelers marched 91 and 60 yards to touchdowns on their first two possessions for a 14-7 lead. But Pittsburgh managed only 4 first downs and 75 total yards after that as Philadelphia played ball-control football. Trailing 14-13 at halftime, the Eagles maintained possession for 22:26 the rest of the way, and took the lead for good on Robert Drummond's 2-yard run with 5:46 left in the third quarter. McMahon completed 21 of 31 passes, with 6 completions for 114 yards to Roy Green, the longtime Cardinals receiver who was signed as a free agent just four days earlier. Eric Green had 8 catches for 158 yards for the Steelers. With the victory, Philadelphia raised its record to 3-1, its best start since 1981.

Pittsburgh	14	0	0	0	—	14
Philadelphia	7	6	7	3	—	23

Pitt — Hoge 12 pass from Brister (Anderson kick)
Phil— McMahon 1 run (Ruzek kick)
Pitt — E. Green 8 pass from Brister (Anderson kick)
Phil— FG Ruzek 27
Phil— FG Ruzek 34
Phil— Drummond 2 run (Ruzek kick)
Phil— FG Ruzek 20

Denver 27, San Diego 19 — at Mile High Stadium, attendance 73,258. Gaston Green ran for 127 yards and 3 touchdowns to power the Broncos past the Chargers and into sole possession of first place in the AFC Western Division. After the two teams traded field goals for a 6-6 tie at the end of the first half, Green scored on a five-yard run midway through the third quarter to give Denver a 13-6 lead. It was 13-12 early in the fourth quarter when Green broke loose for a 63-yard touchdown, and after San Diego pulled within a point again, Green secured the win with a 20-yard touchdown spurt with 2:46 left in the game. John Carney kicked 4 field goals for the Chargers, who ran for 171 yards but could score just 1 touchdown. San Diego's Rod Bernstine had 103 yards on 18 carries. John Elway passed for 218 yards for Denver.

San Diego	3	3	3	10	—	19
Denver	3	3	7	14	—	27

SD — FG Carney 41
Den— FG Treadwell 34
SD — FG Carney 43
Den— FG Treadwell 23
Den— Green 5 run (Treadwell kick)
SD — FG Carney 43
SD — FG Carney 36

Den— Green 63 run (Treadwell kick)
SD — Butts 27 run (Carney kick)
Den— Green 20 run (Treadwell kick)

Kansas City 20, Seattle 13 — at Arrowhead Stadium, attendance 57,323. Steve DeBerg passed for 2 touchdowns and the Chiefs held off the Seahawks to win. DeBerg's second touchdown pass, a 15-yarder to Harvey Williams, gave Kansas City a 20-3 lead with 10:31 to go in the game. But Seattle rallied, trimming the deficit to 7 points on a field goal by John Kasay and Derrick Fenner's 1-yard run with 1:29 remaining. The Seahawks recovered the onside kick attempt and moved to the Chiefs' 34-yard line, but Chris Martin intercepted Jeff Kemp's pass with 1:08 left to preserve the win. Missed opportunities were the norm for Seattle, which turned the ball over 4 times and failed to score the first five times it moved inside the Chiefs' 20. Kemp finished 18 of 30 for 232 yards but was intercepted twice. DeBerg completed 21 of 32 passes for 214 yards.

Seattle	0	0	3	10	—	13
Kansas City	0	10	0	10	—	20

KC — FG Lowery 37
KC — Barnett 18 pass from DeBerg (Lowery kick)
Sea— FG Kasay 45
KC — FG Lowery 39
KC — H. Williams 15 pass from DeBerg (Lowery kick)
Sea— FG Kasay 38
Sea— Fenner 1 run (Kasay kick)

Washington 34, Cincinnati 27 — at Riverfront Stadium, attendance 52,038. Gerald Riggs ran for 3 touchdowns, including a 7-yarder with 2:02 remaining, to negate a 17-point second-half comeback by the Bengals. Washington led 27-10 after a 26-yard field goal by Chip Lohmiller early in the third quarter. But Cincinnati rallied on 1- and 34-yard touchdown runs by Craig Taylor and a 25-yard field goal by Jim Breech with 9:48 to go. The Redskins won the game by marching 53 yards in six plays, all on the ground, to the winning touchdown. Earnest Byner ran for 75 yards and Riggs had 61, while Mark Rypien passed for 217 yards for Washington. The Bengals' Boomer Esiason passed for 212 yards.

Washington	3	21	3	7	—	34
Cincinnati	7	3	14	3	—	27

Wash— FG Lohmiller 40
Cin — Brooks 5 run (Breech kick)
Wash— Riggs 1 run (Lohmiller kick)
Cin — FG Breech 46
Wash— Riggs 1 run (Lohmiller kick)
Wash— Mitchell 66 punt return (Lohmiller kick)
Wash— FG Lohmiller 26
Cin — Taylor 1 run (Breech kick)
Cin — Taylor 34 run (Breech kick)
Cin — FG Breech 25
Wash— Riggs 7 run (Lohmiller kick)

Sunday Night, September 22

Dallas 17, Phoenix 9 — at Sun Devil Stadium, attendance 68,814. Emmitt Smith ran for 182 yards on 23 carries and scored 2 first-quarter touchdowns to lift the Cowboys to victory. Smith raced 60 yards for a score on Dallas's third play of the game, then went 12 yards for a touchdown the next time the Cowboys had the ball. He also set up Ken Willis's 41-yard field goal in the fourth quarter with a 37-yard run. The Cardinals' Tom Tupa completed 24 of 38 passes for 242 yards and moved his team inside the Dallas 20-yard line three times, but Phoenix had to settle for Greg Davis field goals each time.

Dallas	14	0	0	3	—	17
Phoenix	0	6	0	3	—	9

Dall— Smith 60 run (Willis kick)
Dall— Smith 12 run (Willis kick)
Phx— FG Davis 32
Phx— FG Davis 32
Phx— FG Davis 29
Dall— FG Willis 41

Monday, September 23

Chicago 19, N.Y. Jets 13 — at Soldier Field, attendance 65,256. Jim Harbaugh's 1-yard touchdown run with 18 seconds left in overtime gave the Bears a dramatic victory over the Jets. Before Harbaugh's winning run, Chicago apparently won the game on a touchdown pass to tight end Cap Boso. But Boso was ruled down inches short of the goal line, and Harbaugh snuck the final yard for the score. Earlier, Harbaugh's 5-yard touchdown pass to Neal Anderson tied the game with no time left in regulation. New York had a pair of chances to win the game. First, the Jets stopped Harbaugh inches short of the goal line on fourth-and-goal while ahead 13-6 with 3:32 left in the fourth quarter. But while attempting to run out the clock, Blair Thomas was stripped of the ball by the Bears' Steve McMichael at New York's 36-yard line. Then in overtime, Pat Leahy missed a game-winning 28-yard field-goal try.

N.Y. Jets	3	3	7	0	0	—	13
Chicago	3	0	0	10	6	—	19

Chi — FG Butler 33
Jets— FG Leahy 19
Jets— FG Leahy 34
Jets— Baxter 1 run (Leahy kick)
Chi — FG Butler 44
Chi — Anderson 5 pass from Harbaugh (Butler kick)
Chi — Harbaugh 1 run (Butler kick)

Fifth Week Summaries

Standings

American Football Conference

Eastern Division

	W	L	T	Pct.	Pts.	OP
Buffalo	5	0	0	1.000	162	115
Miami	2	3	0	.400	100	112
New England	2	3	0	.400	56	91
N.Y. Jets	2	3	0	.400	103	98
Indianapolis	0	5	0	.000	40	113
Central Division						
Houston	3	1	0	.750	114	55
Cleveland	2	2	0	.500	94	101
Pittsburgh	2	2	0	.500	58	52
Cincinnati	0	4	0	.000	61	123
Western Division						
Denver	4	1	0	.800	114	65
Kansas City	3	2	0	.600	65	63
L.A. Raiders	3	2	0	.600	78	87
Seattle	2	3	0	.400	98	79
San Diego	0	5	0	.000	76	114

National Football Conference

Eastern Division

	W	L	T	Pct.	Pts.	OP
Washington	5	0	0	1.000	169	58
Dallas	3	2	0	.600	95	96
Philadelphia	3	2	0	.600	77	66
Phoenix	3	2	0	.600	83	85
N.Y. Giants	2	3	0	.400	75	84
Central Division						
Chicago	4	1	0	.800	90	91
Detroit	4	1	0	.800	104	99
Minnesota	2	3	0	.400	49	82
Green Bay	1	4	0	.200	66	95
Tampa Bay	0	5	0	.000	59	100
Western Division						
New Orleans	5	0	0	1.000	121	47
Atlanta	2	3	0	.400	62	88
L.A. Rams	2	3	0	.400	73	109
San Francisco	2	3	0	.400	95	69

Sunday, September 29

Buffalo 35, Chicago 20 — at Rich Stadium, attendance 80,366. Jim Kelly passed for 303 yards and 3 touchdowns and Buffalo broke open a close game in the second half to cruise to its fifth consecutive victory. The Bears led 6-0 until Kelly teamed with Al Edwards on a 33-yard scoring pass just 12 seconds before halftime to give the Bills the lead for good. In the third quarter, Carwell Gardner recovered his own fumble in the end zone for a touchdown, and Kelly threw a 2-yard scoring strike to Butch Rolle (his tenth consecutive reception for a touchdown) to make it 21-6. Buffalo's James Lofton caught 4 passes for 122 yards, including a 77-yard touchdown in the fourth quarter. Thurman Thomas ran for 117 yards and a touchdown on 25 carries for the Bills.

Chicago	0	6	0	14	—	20
Buffalo	0	7	14	14	—	35

Chi — FG Butler 28
Chi — FG Butler 42
Buff— Edwards 33 pass from Kelly (Norwood kick)
Buff— Gardner fumble recovery in end zone (Norwood kick)
Buff— Rolle 2 pass from Kelly (Norwood kick)
Chi — Anderson 2 run (Butler kick)
Buff— Lofton 77 pass from Kelly (Norwood kick)
Buff— Thomas 11 run (Norwood kick)
Chi — Green 1 run (Butler kick)

L.A. Rams 23, Green Bay 21 — at Anaheim Stadium, attendance 54,736. The Rams scored a pair of touchdowns only 7 seconds apart late in the second quarter, built up a 23-7 lead, and then held on for the victory. Los Angeles trailed 7-6 until Robert Delpino scored on a 2-yard run with just 40 seconds left in the first half, the touchdown coming five plays after Paul Butcher recovered a fumble on the Green Bay 20. On the ensuing kickoff, Butcher forced a fumble that teammate Anthony Newman recovered and ran 17 yards for another score. After extending their lead to 23-7 on Tony Zendejas's third field goal of the game, the Rams withstood a Packers' charge that included a pair of fourth-quarter touchdown passes from backup Blair Kiel. Green Bay starter Don Majkowski scored on a 2-yard touchdown run in the second quarter but injured his shoulder on the play and had to leave the game.

Green Bay	0	7	0	14	—	21
L.A. Rams	3	17	3	0	—	23

Rams— FG Zendejas 30
GB — Majkowski 2 run (Jacke kick)
Rams— FG Zendejas 32
Rams— Delpino 2 run (Zendejas kick)
Rams— Newman 17 fumble recovery return (Zendejas kick)
Rams— FG Zendejas 28
GB — Kemp 2 pass from Kiel (Jacke kick)
GB — Workman 5 pass from Kiel (Jacke kick)

Seattle 31, Indianapolis 3 — at Kingdome, attendance 56,656. John L. Williams and Derrick Fenner each ran for touchdowns as the Seahawks powered past the Colts, handing Indianapolis its fifth consecutive loss. With Williams gaining 80 yards and Fenner 69, the Seahawks rushed for 168 yards and controlled the ball on the ground, maintaining possession for more than 37 of the game's 60 minutes. The Colts, meanwhile, were limited to 9 first downs and 137 yards of total offense. Dan McGwire made his first career start for the Seahawks and completed 3 of 7 passes in the first half. He was replaced in the second half by veteran Jeff Kemp, who threw a 7-yard touchdown pass to Tommy Kane.

Indianapolis	0	3	0	0	—	3
Seattle	7	10	7	7	—	31

Sea— Williams 6 run (Kasay kick)
Sea— FG Kasay 41
Sea— Warren 59 punt return (Kasay kick)
Ind — FG Biasucci 54
Sea— Kane 7 pass from Kemp (Kasay kick)
Sea— Fenner 10 run (Kasay kick)

Kansas City 14, San Diego 13 — at San Diego Jack Murphy Stadium, attendance 44,907. Christian Okoye scored on a 1-yard run just 1:19 into the game and the Chiefs went on to hand the Chargers their fifth consecutive loss of the season, their eighth straight dating back to the 1990 season. San Diego held Kansas City to only 182 yards of total offense, including just 86 rushing. Chiefs rookie Harvey Williams returned the opening kickoff 76 yards to set up Okoye's score. Steve DeBerg's 11-yard touchdown pass to Robb Thomas in the second quarter proved to be the deciding score. John Carney kicked a pair of second-half field goals to pull the Chargers within one point, but also had a 36-yard attempt at the end of the first half misfire when it hit the upright. Rod Bernstine ran for 112 yards and a touchdown for San Diego.

Kansas City	7	7	0	0	—	14
San Diego	7	0	3	3	—	13

KC — Okoye 1 run (Lowery kick)
SD — Bernstine 2 run (Carney kick)
KC — Thomas 11 pass from DeBerg (Lowery kick)
SD — FG Carney 26
SD — FG Carney 37

N.Y. Jets 41, Miami 23 — at Giants Stadium, attendance 71,170. Ken O'Brien passed for 221 yards and the Jets' running backs combined for 206, but the game's biggest plays came from the special teams and the defense as New York snapped a 3-game losing streak by defeating the Dolphins. The Jets led just 14-10 before Chris Burkett blocked Reggie Roby's punt and returned it 11 yards for a touchdown with 12 seconds left in the first half for a 21-10 lead. In the fourth quarter, Erik McMillan sealed the victory when he intercepted a Dan Marino pass and returned it 83 yards for a touchdown, the fourth scoring return of his career. Freeman McNeil ran for 69 yards, Blair Thomas had 67, and Brad Baxter 46 and 2 touchdowns for the Jets, who averaged 5.6 yards per rushing attempt.

Miami	3	10	3	7	—	23
N.Y. Jets	7	14	3	17	—	41

Jets— Moore 17 pass from O'Brien (Leahy kick)
Mia — FG Stoyanovich 33
Mia — Duper 30 pass from Marino (Stoyanovich kick)
Jets— Baxter 2 run (Leahy kick)
Jets— Burkett 11 blocked punt return (Leahy kick)
Mia — FG Stoyanovich 53
Jets— FG Leahy 25
Mia — FG Stoyanovich 33
Jets— Baxter 3 run (Leahy kick)
Jets— FG Leahy 27
Jets— McMillan 83 interception return (Leahy kick)
Mia — Clayton 10 pass from Secules (Stoyanovich kick)

Phoenix 24, New England 10 — at Sun Devil Stadium, attendance 26,043. Tom Tupa passed for 312 yards and 3 touchdowns to lift the Cardinals over the Patriots. Phoenix was clinging to a 14-10 lead late in the fourth quarter when Tupa connected with Ricky Proehl on a 62-yard touchdown pass for the clinching score. Earlier, Tupa teamed with Ernie Jones (17 yards) and Johnny Johnson (15) on touchdown passes. New England scored its only touchdown when Jon Vaughn returned a second-quarter kickoff 99 yards.

New England	0	7	0	3	—	10
Phoenix	0	14	0	10	—	24

Phx— Jones 17 pass from Tupa (Davis kick)
NE — Vaughn 99 kickoff return (Staurovsky kick)
Phx— Johnson 15 pass from Tupa (Davis kick)
NE — FG Staurovsky 39
Phx— Proehl 62 pass from Tupa (Davis kick)
Phx— FG Davis 47

New Orleans 27, Atlanta 6 — at Atlanta-Fulton County Stadium, attendance 56,556. Bobby Hebert passed for 2 touchdowns to Floyd Turner and the Saints' defense stifled the Falcons' offense as New Orleans improved its club-record start to 5-0. The Saints limited Atlanta to only 8 first downs and 162 total yards, had 5 sacks and a pair of fumble recoveries, and extended its string of not allowing a touchdown (the Falcons' lone score came on a fumble recovery return) to 12 consecutive quarters. Hebert's first touchdown pass to Turner was a 47-yarder that gave New Orleans the lead for good at 10-6 with 1:08 left in the first half. The pair also teamed for a 17-yard score midway through the third quarter. Morten Andersen had a pair of field goals to extend his string to 10 straight without a miss in 1991. Dalton Hilliard closed the scoring with a career-best 65-yard run.

New Orleans	3	7	10	7	—	27
Atlanta	0	6	0	0	—	6

NO — FG Andersen 23
Atl — Tippins 23 fumble recovery return (kick failed)
NO — Turner 47 pass from Hebert (Andersen kick)
NO — Turner 17 pass from Hebert (Andersen kick)
NO — FG Andersen 31
NO — Hilliard 65 run (Andersen kick)

Dallas 21, N.Y. Giants 16 — at Texas Stadium, attendance 64,010. Troy Aikman's 23-yard touchdown pass to Michael Irvin with just 2:13 left lifted the Cowboys to the victory over the Giants, snapping Dallas's six-game losing streak to New York. After the go-ahead touchdown pass, Jeff Hostetler drove the Giants into scoring position, but Issiac Holt's interception in the end zone with 1:11 to go secured the victory. That spoiled a dramatic comeback attempt for New York, which earlier had rallied from a 14-3 deficit to take a 16-14 lead on a 19-yard touchdown pass from Hostetler to Stephen Baker with 5:41 remaining. But Aikman, who completed 20 of 27 passes for 277 yards with no interceptions, moved the Cowboys 84 yards in 8 plays for the winning score. Hostetler completed 28 of 34 passes for 368 yards as the Giants amassed 487 yards of total offense. New York's Mark Ingram had 6 catches for 142 yards.

N.Y. Giants	0	3	3	10	—	16
Dallas	0	7	7	7	—	21

Giants — FG Bahr 43
Dall — Smith 3 run (Willis kick)
Dall — Horton 20 fumble recovery return (Willis kick)
Giants — FG Bahr 29
Giants — FG Bahr 25
Giants — Baker 19 pass from Hostetler (Bahr kick)
Dall — Irvin 23 pass from Aikman (Willis kick)

L.A. Raiders 12, San Francisco 6 — at Los Angeles Memorial Coliseum, attendance 91,494. Jeff Jaeger kicked a club record-tying 4 field goals and the Raiders kept the 49ers' high-powered offense in check to win a taut defensive struggle. Los Angeles managed only 93 rushing yards and 220 total yards, but positioned Jaeger for field goals of 44, 20, 49, and 41 yards. The Raiders' pass rush snuffed San Francisco's final drive by pressuring quarterback Steve Young into throwing an incompletion on fourth down from the Los Angeles 19-yard line with 1:48 left.

San Francisco	3	0	0	3	—	6
L.A. Raiders	0	6	3	3	—	12

SF — FG Cofer 23
Raiders — FG Jaeger 44
Raiders — FG Jaeger 20
Raiders — FG Jaeger 49
Raiders — FG Jaeger 41
SF — FG Cofer 25

Detroit 31, Tampa Bay 3 — at Pontiac Silverdome, attendance 44,479. Barry Sanders rushed for 160 yards and 3 touchdowns as the Lions moved into a tie for first place in the NFC Central by beating the Buccaneers. Sanders scored on a 7-yard run midway through the first quarter and Detroit never trailed. His 69-yard run in the fourth quarter to close the scoring was the longest touchdown run of his career. Winless Tampa Bay managed only 187 yards in total offense. Quarterback Chris Chandler completed 10 of 26 passes for 64 yards before leaving the game with a concussion in the third quarter.

Tampa Bay	0	3	0	0	—	3
Detroit	14	7	0	10	—	31

Det — Sanders 7 run (Murray kick)
Det — Green 26 pass from Peete (Murray kick)
Det — Sanders 1 run (Murray kick)
TB — FG Christie 32
Det — FG Murray 38
Det — Sanders 69 run (Murray kick)

Sunday Night, September 29

Denver 13, Minnesota 6 — at Metrodome, attendance 55,031. John Elway ran 17 yards for the game's only touchdown to lead the Broncos past the Vikings. With Minnesota leading 6-3 late in the third quarter, Elway took off on a quarterback draw and bulled his way into the end zone, running over Vikings cornerback Audrey McMillan at the goal line. Elway completed only 8 of 22 passes for 84 yards, but running back Gaston Green rushed for a career-high 158 yards on 26 carries, his third 100-yard rushing game of the season. Minnesota's Rich Gannon relieved starter Wade Wilson and drove the Vikings to Denver's 13-yard line in the final minute before the drive stalled.

Denver	0	3	7	3	—	13
Minnesota	3	0	3	0	—	6

Minn — FG Reveiz 49
Den — FG Treadwell 37
Minn — FG Reveiz 25
Den — Elway 17 run (Treadwell kick)
Den — FG Treadwell 32

Monday, September 30

Washington 23, Philadelphia 0 — at RFK Stadium, attendance 55,198. The Redskins joined the Saints and Bills as the NFL's only unbeaten teams through week 5 by posting their third consecutive home shutout of the season. Washington's defense was dominant, limiting the Eagles to only 4 first downs and 89 yards in total offense, while intercepting 3 passes. Philadelphia, which already had lost Randall Cunningham to injury in the first game of the season, lost another signal caller when Jim McMahon injured a knee on the final play of the first quarter and had to leave the game. Earnest Byner ran for 95 yards and Gerald Riggs added 70 for the Redskins, who controlled the ball on the ground, rushing for 173 yards and maintaining possession for 38:40. Chip Lohmiller kicked three field goals.

Philadelphia	0	0	0	0	—	0
Washington	0	10	3	10	—	23

Wash — Monk 19 pass from Rypien (Lohmiller kick)
Wash — FG Lohmiller 37
Wash — FG Lohmiller 35
Wash — Byner 7 run (Lohmiller kick)
Wash — FG Lohmiller 27

Sixth Week Summaries

Standings

American Football Conference

Eastern Division

	W	L	T	Pct.	Pts.	OP
Buffalo	5	1	0	.833	168	148
Miami	3	3	0	.500	120	122
N.Y. Jets	3	3	0	.500	120	112
New England	2	4	0	.333	66	111
Indianapolis	0	6	0	.000	43	136

Central Division

	W	L	T	Pct.	Pts.	OP
Houston	4	1	0	.800	156	69
Pittsburgh	3	2	0	.600	117	104
Cleveland	2	3	0	.400	72	69
Cincinnati	0	5	0	.000	68	136

Western Division

	W	L	T	Pct.	Pts.	OP
Denver	4	2	0	.667	128	107
Kansas City	4	2	0	.667	98	69
L.A. Raiders	3	3	0	.500	91	108
Seattle	3	3	0	.500	111	86
San Diego	1	5	0	.167	97	127

National Football Conference

Eastern Division

	W	L	T	Pct.	Pts.	OP
Washington	6	0	0	1.000	189	65
Dallas	4	2	0	.667	115	113
N.Y. Giants	3	3	0	.500	95	93
Philadelphia	3	3	0	.500	90	80
Phoenix	3	3	0	.500	92	105

Central Division

	W	L	T	Pct.	Pts.	OP
Detroit	5	1	0	.833	128	119
Chicago	4	2	0	.667	97	111
Minnesota	2	4	0	.333	69	106
Green Bay	1	5	0	.167	83	115
Tampa Bay	1	5	0	.167	73	113

Western Division

	W	L	T	Pct.	Pts.	OP
New Orleans	5	0	0	1.000	121	47
Atlanta	2	3	0	.400	62	88
L.A. Rams	2	3	0	.400	73	109
San Francisco	2	3	0	.400	95	69

Sunday, October 6

Dallas 20, Green Bay 17 — at Milwaukee County Stadium, attendance 53,695. The Cowboys turned 2 interceptions into a pair of touchdowns just 1:14 apart in the second quarter and held on for the victory. Safety Ray Horton broke a scoreless tie with a 65-yard interception return for a touchdown with 1:54 left in the first half. Ten seconds later, Issiac Holt picked off another of Blair Kiel's passes, giving the Cowboys the ball on the Packers' 38. The short touchdown drive ended with a 13-yard pass from Troy Aikman to Jay Novacek 41 seconds before halftime. Green Bay's Charles Wilson returned the second-half kickoff 82 yards for a touchdown, but Dallas controlled the ball for 23 minutes in the second half and got a pair of field goals from Ken Willis to secure the victory. Emmitt Smith helped the Cowboys maintain possession by rushing for 122 yards on 32 carries. Novacek had 121 yards on 11 catches, 7 of which resulted in first downs.

Dallas	0	14	3	3	—	20
Green Bay	0	3	7	7	—	17

Dall — Horton 65 interception return (Willis kick)
Dall — Novacek 13 pass from Aikman (Willis kick)
GB — FG Jacke 42
GB — Wilson 82 kickoff return (Jacke kick)
Dall — FG Willis 23
Dall — FG Willis 39
GB — Sharpe 13 pass from Kiel (Jacke kick)

Houston 42, Denver 14 — at Astrodome, attendance 59,145. Warren Moon passed for 334 yards and 2 touchdowns, but it was the Oilers' defense that provided the impetus for a 35-0 halftime lead before Houston coasted to the victory. The Oilers' defense set the tone early, sacking John Elway on the first play of the game. One minute later, Bo Orlando blocked Mike Horan's punt and Bubba McDowell recovered in the end zone for a Houston touchdown. In the second quarter, Cris Dishman picked off an Elway pass and returned it 43 yards to the 1, setting up Allen Pinkett's touchdown run. Moments later, Elway fumbled when sacked by Sean Jones and William Fuller recovered for Houston to set up another touchdown. Dishman completed the 3-touchdown outburst in less than four minutes when he picked up a fumble forced by Fuller and ran 19 yards for a touchdown for a 28-0 advantage. In all, Houston's defense had 6 sacks and forced 3 turnovers.

Denver	0	0	7	7	—	14
Houston	7	28	0	7	—	42

Hou — McDowell blocked punt recovery in end zone (Howfield kick)
Hou — Pinkett 1 run (Howfield kick)
Hou — White 1 run (Howfield kick)
Hou — Dishman 19 fumble recovery return (Howfield kick)
Hou — Jeffires 3 pass from Moon (Howfield kick)
Den — Sewell 3 pass from Elway (Treadwell kick)
Den — Nattiel 70 pass from Elway (Treadwell kick)
Hou — Pinkett 36 pass from Moon (Howfield kick)

Miami 20, New England 10 — at Foxboro Stadium, attendance 55,075. Dan Marino passed for 224 yards and 2 touchdowns in the second quarter alone to lead the Dolphins past the Patriots. Marino, who completed 25 of 38 passes for 331 yards in all—his first 300-yard passing performance of the season—helped Miami overcome an early 7-0 deficit by throwing scoring passes of 24 yards to Mark Clayton and 5 yards to Jim Jensen. The Patriots scored on their first possession after a 40-yard punt return by Jerome Henderson, but managed only 195 total yards and could not score again until the Dolphins had a 20-7 lead. Miami's E.J. Junior posted 4 of the Dolphins' season-high 6 sacks.

Miami	0	17	0	3	—	20
New England	7	0	0	3	—	10

NE — Stephens 1 run (Staurovsky kick)
Mia — FG Stoyanovich 47
Mia — Clayton 24 pass from Marino (Stoyanovich kick)
Mia — Jensen 5 pass from Marino (Stoyanovich kick)
Mia — FG Stoyanovich 25
NE — FG Staurovsky 37

Detroit 24, Minnesota 20 — at Pontiac Silverdome, attendance 63,423. Barry Sanders's 15-yard touchdown run with 36 seconds left in the game capped a 21-point fourth-quarter rally and gave the Lions their fifth consecutive victory and sole possession of first place in the NFC Central Division. Detroit trailed 20-3 until cutting into the deficit on a 68-yard touchdown pass from Rodney Peete to Robert Clark with 6:50 remaining. After the Lions recovered an onside kick, Peete teamed with Willie Green on a 16-yard scoring pass to make it 20-17 with 4:22 to go. The winning drive started from the Lions' 28 with less than three minutes to go, and 10 plays later Sanders scored on a third-and-1 play. The third-year running back eclipsed the 100-yard rushing barrier for the fourth straight week, running for 116, and also caught a team-high 9 passes for 76 yards. Peete completed 24 of 38 passes for 281 yards. The Vikings' Herschel Walker did not play because of a shoulder injury.

Minnesota	7	7	3	3	—	20
Detroit	0	3	0	21	—	24

Minn — Nelson 11 run (Reveiz kick)
Minn — Jordan 2 pass from Gannon (Reveiz kick)
Det — FG Murray 47
Minn — FG Reveiz 42
Minn — FG Reveiz 25
Det — Clark 68 pass from Peete (Murray kick)
Det — Green 16 pass from Peete (Murray kick)
Det — Sanders 15 run (Murray kick)

N.Y. Jets 17, Cleveland 14 — at Cleveland Stadium, attendance 71,042. Pat Leahy's 28-yard field goal early in the fourth quarter proved to be the difference as the Jets edged the Browns. Cleveland rallied from a 14-0 halftime deficit to tie the score before Leahy's winning kick with 10:45 to go. The Browns had a chance to win in the final moments, but their last drive ended when New York's James Hasty recovered a Bernie Kosar fumble on the

Jets' 39-yard line with 1:14 left. Despite entering the game with the NFL's top-ranked rushing offense, New York ran for only 76 yards. But Ken O'Brien completed 19 of 23 passes for 195 yards, and Blair Thomas threw a 16-yard touchdown pass to Rob Moore on a halfback-option play.

N.Y. Jets	0	14	0	3	—	17
Cleveland	0	0	14	0	—	14

Jets — Moore 16 pass from Thomas (Leahy kick)
Jets — Baxter 1 run (Leahy kick)
Cleve — Mack 1 run (Stover kick)
Cleve — Hoard 4 pass from Kosar (Stover kick)
Jets — FG Leahy 28

Tampa Bay 14, Philadelphia 13 — at Tampa Stadium, attendance 41,219. Chris Chandler came off the bench to replace the injured Vinny Testaverde and threw a pair of touchdown passes in the final 4:19, lifting the Buccaneers to their first win of the season. With his team trailing 13-0 late in the fourth quarter, Tampa Bay's Broderick Thomas tackled Eagles punter Jeff Feagles at the Philadelphia 8-yard line after he bobbled the snap from center. Two plays later, Chandler teamed with Robert Wilson to cut the deficit to 13-7. The winning score came on a 5-yard pass to Bruce Hill with 1:09 remaining. That capped a 54-yard, 6-play drive on which Chandler also had completions of 19 and 17 yards to Lawrence Dawsey. Philadelphia's Brad Goebel, subbing for injured Randall Cunningham and Jim McMahon, completed 9 of 20 passes for 62 yards and was intercepted twice in his starting debut. Testaverde completed just 5 of 18 passes for 52 yards for the Buccaneers before injuring the thumb on his throwing hand in the third quarter.

Philadelphia	0	0	13	0	—	13
Tampa Bay	0	0	0	14	—	14

Phil — FG Ruzek 18
Phil — FG Ruzek 45
Phil — Joyner fumble recovery in end zone (Ruzek kick)
TB — Wilson 8 pass from Chandler (Christie kick)
TB — Hill 5 pass from Chandler (Christie kick)

N.Y. Giants 20, Phoenix 9 — at Giants Stadium, attendance 75,891. Rodney Hampton rushed for a career-high 137 yards and 1 touchdown on 22 carries to lead the Giants past the Cardinals. New York scored on its first three possessions, built a 17-3 halftime advantage, and never was seriously threatened en route to its sixth consecutive victory over Phoenix. The Giants' Jeff Hostetler completed 14 of 18 passes for 200 yards and 1 touchdown. Greg Davis kicked 3 field goals to account for all of the Cardinals' scoring.

Phoenix	3	0	6	0	—	9
N.Y. Giants	14	3	0	3	—	20

Giants — Hampton 12 run (Bahr kick)
Phx — FG Davis 52
Giants — Mowatt 7 pass from Hostetler (Bahr kick)
Giants — FG Bahr 42
Phx — FG Davis 40
Phx — FG Davis 29
Giants — FG Bahr 27

San Diego 21, L.A. Raiders 13 — at Los Angeles Memorial Coliseum, attendance 42,787. The Chargers' defense forced 3 critical fourth-quarter turnovers and San Diego ended an 8-game losing streak dating back to 1990 by beating the Raiders. The Chargers led just 14-13 before Henry Rolling scooped up a Roger Craig fumble early in the fourth quarter and returned it 53 yards to Los Angeles's 13-yard line. Four plays later, Marion Butts caught a 2-yard touchdown pass from John Friesz for the clinching score. Earlier, Butts scored on a 1-yard run on fourth-and-goal just two seconds before halftime to give San Diego the lead for good. The Chargers kept the game out of reach by intercepting Jay Schroeder on each of Los Angeles's final two possessions.

San Diego	0	14	0	7	—	21
L.A. Raiders	3	7	3	0	—	13

Raiders — FG Jaeger 39
SD — Bernstine 4 run (Carney kick)
Raiders — Horton 11 pass from Schroeder (Jaeger kick)
SD — Butts 1 run (Carney kick)
Raiders — FG Jaeger 34
SD — Butts 2 pass from Friesz (Carney kick)

Seattle 13, Cincinnati 7 — at Riverfront Stadium, attendance 60,010. The Seahawks forced 5 turnovers en route to keeping the defending Central Division-champion Bengals winless. John Kasay's third-quarter field goals of 36 and 31 yards broke a 7-7 tie and provided the margin of victory. Cincinnati had a chance to win the game late in the fourth quarter after Eric Thomas intercepted a Jeff Kemp pass with 2:09 left, but the Bengals' final drive stalled inside Seattle's 20-yard line when Boomer Esiason's fourth-down pass to James Brooks was inches short of a first down.

Seattle	7	0	6	0	—	13
Cincinnati	0	7	0	0	—	7

Sea — Williams 35 run (Kasay kick)
Cin — Ball 1 run (Breech kick)
Sea — FG Kasay 36
Sea — FG Kasay 31

Washington 20, Chicago 7 — at Soldier Field, attendance 64,941. Mark Rypien threw a pair of touchdown passes to Art Monk and the Redskins remained unbeaten by defeating the Bears. Washington's 10-0 halftime lead was trimmed to 10-7 on a 1-yard run by Neal Anderson late in the third quarter, but end Fred Stokes made the defensive play of the game to restore momentum to the Redskins. He intercepted a tipped pass early in the fourth period to give Washington possession at Chicago's 36-yard line. Nine plays later, Rypien and Monk teamed for the clinching score.

Washington	0	10	0	10	—	20
Chicago	0	0	7	0	—	7

Wash — FG Lohmiller 47
Wash — Monk 26 pass from Rypien (Lohmiller kick)
Chi — Anderson 1 run (Butler kick)
Wash — Monk 5 pass from Rypien (Lohmiller kick)
Wash — FG Lohmiller 23

Sunday Night, October 6

Pittsburgh 21, Indianapolis 3 — at Hoosier Dome, attendance 55,383. Bubby Brister threw a pair of second-half touchdown passes to help spoil the head coaching debut of the Colts' Rick Venturi. Winless Indianapolis led 3-0 until Brister, who was 8-for-8 passing in the second half and 13 of 16 in the game, teamed with Eric Green on a 21-yard touchdown pass midway through the third quarter to give Pittsburgh the lead for good. Venturi, formerly the Colts' defensive coordinator, took over as head coach earlier in the week after Ron Meyer was fired from the post.

Pittsburgh	0	0	7	14	—	21
Indianapolis	0	3	0	0	—	3

Ind — FG Biasucci 19
Pitt — Green 21 pass from Brister (Anderson kick)
Pitt — Foster 24 pass from Brister (Anderson kick)
Pitt — Hoge 1 run (Anderson kick)

Monday, October 7

Kansas City 33, Buffalo 6 — at Arrowhead Stadium, attendance 76,120. Christian Okoye ran for 130 yards and 2 touchdowns and the Chiefs broke open a close game with 17 points in a span of 3:27 late in the third quarter to hand the defending AFC-champion Bills their first defeat of the season. Derrick Thomas had 4 sacks and forced 2 of the 5 fumbles that the Chiefs recovered as Kansas City limited the high-powered Buffalo offense to only 211 yards and no touchdowns. Each of Okoye's short third-quarter touchdown runs came following fumble recoveries. Harvey Williams gave the Chiefs a pair of 100-yard rushers when he gained 103. In all, Kansas City rushed for 247 yards, had 26 first downs to the Bills' 11, ran 77 plays to 43, and maintained possession for more than 44 minutes.

Buffalo	0	6	0	0	—	6
Kansas City	3	10	17	3	—	33

KC — FG Lowery 41
KC — Holohan 1 pass from DeBerg (Lowery kick)
Buff — FG Norwood 44
Buff — FG Norwood 25
KC — FG Lowery 40
KC — FG Lowery 24
KC — Okoye 5 run (Lowery kick)
KC — Okoye 2 run (Lowery kick)
KC — FG Lowery 22

Seventh Week Summaries

Standings

American Football Conference

Eastern Division

	W	L	T	Pct.	Pts.	OP
Buffalo	6	1	0	.857	210	154
Miami	3	4	0	.429	127	164
N.Y. Jets	3	4	0	.429	140	135
New England	2	4	0	.333	66	111
Indianapolis	0	7	0	.000	49	176

Central Division

	W	L	T	Pct.	Pts.	OP
Houston	5	1	0	.833	179	89
Pittsburgh	3	3	0	.500	137	127
Cleveland	2	4	0	.333	89	111
Cincinnati	0	6	0	.000	91	171

Western Division

	W	L	T	Pct.	Pts.	OP
Kansas City	5	2	0	.714	140	76
Denver	4	2	0	.667	128	107
L.A. Raiders	4	3	0	.571	114	128
Seattle	3	4	0	.429	131	109
San Diego	1	6	0	.143	121	157

National Football Conference

Eastern Division

	W	L	T	Pct.	Pts.	OP
Washington	7	0	0	1.000	231	82
Dallas	5	2	0	.714	150	136
N.Y. Giants	4	3	0	.571	118	113
Philadelphia	3	4	0	.429	96	93
Phoenix	3	4	0	.429	99	139

Central Division

	W	L	T	Pct.	Pts.	OP
Detroit	5	1	0	.833	128	119
Chicago	4	2	0	.667	97	111
Minnesota	3	4	0	.429	103	113
Green Bay	1	5	0	.167	83	115
Tampa Bay	1	5	0	.167	73	113

Western Division

	W	L	T	Pct.	Pts.	OP
New Orleans	6	0	0	1.000	134	53
Atlanta	3	3	0	.500	101	122
L.A. Rams	3	3	0	.500	103	133
San Francisco	2	4	0	.333	129	108

Sunday, October 13

Dallas 35, Cincinnati 23 — at Texas Stadium, attendance 63,275. Emmitt Smith ran 2 yards for the go-ahead touchdown on the first play of the fourth quarter and the Cowboys' defense forced 3 consecutive turnovers, including an interception that was returned 36 yards for a touchdown by Dixon Edwards, to beat the Bengals. Winless Cincinnati re-took the lead at 23-21 in the see-saw game on a 26-yard field goal by Jim Breech late in the third quarter. But the advantage was short-lived as Troy Aikman teamed with Michael Irvin on a 61-yard pass play to set up Smith's touchdown run just 2:05 later. Aikman passed for 276 yards and Ricky Blake ran 30 yards for a touchdown on his first NFL carry for the Cowboys, who improved to 5-2, their best start since 1986. Harold Green had a 75-yard touchdown run and rushed for 124 yards on only 12 carries for the Bengals, 0-6 for the first time since 1979.

Cincinnati	10	0	13	0	—	23
Dallas	0	21	0	14	—	35

Cin — FG Breech 45
Cin — Brooks 3 run (Breech kick)
Dall — Aikman 2 run (Willis kick)
Dall — Blake 30 run (Willis kick)
Dall — Novacek 26 pass from Aikman (Willis kick)
Cin — Green 75 run (Breech kick)
Cin — FG Breech 24
Cin — FG Breech 26
Dall — Smith 2 run (Willis kick)
Dall — Edwards 36 interception return (Willis kick)

Washington 42, Cleveland 17 — at RFK Stadium, attendance 54,715. Ricky Ervins came off the bench to rush for 133 yards and 2 touchdowns on 13 carries as the Redskins remained unbeaten by routing the Browns. After Cleveland had trimmed a 21-7 halftime deficit to 21-17 in the third quarter, Ervins returned a kickoff 46 yards. Two plays later, he was inserted into the lineup and later capped the drive with a 12-yard touchdown run to make it 28-17. Ervins, in the game because Earnest Byner injured his right ring finger, also closed the scoring with a 65-yard scoring run in the fourth quarter. The Redskins' Art Monk caught 7 passes for 106 yards and 1 touchdown and moved into second place on the NFL's all-time list with 756 career receptions. For the Browns, Bernie Kosar completed 21 of 29 passes for 266 yards. Cleveland's first touchdown came on an 11-yard pass from punter Brian Hansen, the holder on placekicks, to Webster Slaughter on a fake field-goal attempt. The Redskins' 7-0 start matched their best in 51 seasons.

Cleveland	7	0	10	0	—	17
Washington	7	14	7	14	—	42

Wash — Monk 14 pass from Rypien (Lohmiller kick)
Cleve — Slaughter 11 pass from Hansen (Stover kick)
Wash — Riggs 1 run (Lohmiller kick)
Wash — Byner 21 run (Lohmiller kick)
Cleve — FG Stover 26
Cleve — Newsome 37 fumble recovery return (Stover kick)
Wash — Ervins 12 run (Lohmiller kick)
Wash — Riggs 1 run (Lohmiller kick)
Wash — Ervins 65 run (Lohmiller kick)

Houston 23, N.Y. Jets 20 — at Giants Stadium, attendance 70,758. Warren Moon completed 35 of 50 passes for 423 yards and a pair of touchdowns as the Oilers beat the Jets to match their best start in franchise history. Houston fell behind early 10-0 but rallied as its defense shut down the Jets' potent rushing attack. New York, which entered the game averaging 149.3 yards per game on the ground, rushed for 41 yards in the first quarter, but for only 2 after that. The Oilers' Ian Howfield broke a 13-13 tie early in the fourth quarter with a 23-yard field goal, and Moon's 37-yard touchdown pass to Drew Hill with 2:09 left was the clinching score. For Hill, it was the 411th reception of his career with Houston, making him the club's all-time leading pass catcher. The Jets made it close when Ken O'Brien passed 18 yards to Chris Burkett for a touch-

down on the final play of the game.

Houston	0	13	0	10	—	23
N.Y. Jets	10	0	3	7	—	20

Jets — Baxter 3 run (Leahy kick)
Jets — FG Leahy 21
Hou — Duncan 3 pass from Moon (kick failed)
Hou — White 1 run (Howfield kick)
Jets — FG Leahy 31
Hou — FG Howfield 23
Hou — Hill 37 pass from Moon (Howfield kick)
Jets — Burkett 18 pass from O'Brien (Leahy kick)

Buffalo 42, Indianapolis 6 — at Rich Stadium, attendance 79,015. Jim Kelly passed for only 44 yards and left the game in the first half with a mild concussion, so the Bills used their rushing attack to overwhelm the Colts. Buffalo piled up 276 yards rushing, 117 by Thurman Thomas, who had 107 yards by halftime. His backup, Kenneth Davis, rushed for 108 yards in the second half, including a 78-yard touchdown run early in the fourth quarter. Frank Reich replaced Kelly late in the first half and completed 6 of 7 passes for 76 yards and a pair of touchdowns. The Colts, who failed to score a touchdown for the third consecutive game overall and fifth straight on the road, played without Eric Dickerson, who was sidelined with a hamstring injury.

Indianapolis	0	6	0	0	—	6
Buffalo	14	14	7	7	—	42

Buff — Thomas 14 run (Norwood kick)
Buff — Gardner 3 run (Norwood kick)
Ind — FG Biasucci 26
Ind — FG Biasucci 29
Buff — Thomas 7 run (Norwood kick)
Buff — McKeller 5 pass from Reich (Norwood kick)
Buff — Lofton 11 pass from Reich (Norwood kick)
Buff — Davis 78 run (Norwood kick)

Kansas City 42, Miami 7 — at Arrowhead Stadium, attendance 76,021. Christian Okoye ran for 153 yards and 2 touchdowns and Chris Martin returned a fumble 100 yards for a score in the Chiefs' rout of the Dolphins. Okoye got Kansas City started with a 38-yard touchdown run on its first series. Miami threatened to tie the game the next time it had the ball, but the Chiefs' Tracy Simien forced Sammie Smith to fumble near the goal line and Martin, another linebacker, recovered and returned it the length of the field. Kansas City was never threatened after that, building a 42-0 advantage before the Dolphins could score. The Chiefs finished the game with 221 yards rushing and 452 total yards. Steve DeBerg completed 9 of 12 passes for 177 yards and 3 touchdowns.

Miami	0	0	0	7	—	7
Kansas City	14	14	14	0	—	42

KC — Okoye 38 run (Lowery kick)
KC — Martin 100 fumble recovery return (Lowery kick)
KC — Barnett 7 pass from DeBerg (Lowery kick)
KC — Okoye 1 run (Lowery kick)
KC — McNair 14 pass from DeBerg (Lowery kick)
KC — Barnett 41 pass from DeBerg (Lowery kick)
Mia — Secules 4 run (Stoyanovich kick)

New Orleans 13, Philadelphia 6 — at Veterans Stadium, attendance 64,224. Steve Walsh threw a 14-yard touchdown pass to Dalton Hilliard and the Saints' defense was dominant in shutting down the Eagles and extending its string to 16 quarters without allowing a touchdown. Walsh replaced Bobby Hebert, who had suffered a mild concussion, in the second quarter and in the third period teamed with Hilliard for the touchdown that gave undefeated New Orleans the lead for good at 10-6. But the real story was the Saints' defense, which forced 6 fumbles, intercepted 5 passes, and posted 5 sacks, 2 by Pat Swilling. Philadelphia's Brad Goebel completed 12 of 22 passes for 106 yards but was intercepted 4 times. Pat Ryan replaced Goebel and was 6 of 12 for 74 yards and was picked off once.

New Orleans	0	3	7	3	—	13
Philadelphia	0	6	0	0	—	6

Phil — FG Ruzek 38
Phil — FG Ruzek 41
NO — FG Andersen 36
NO — Hilliard 14 pass from Walsh (Andersen kick)
NO — FG Andersen 26

Minnesota 34, Phoenix 7 — at Metrodome, attendance 51,029. Rich Gannon passed for 254 yards and 2 touchdowns and scored on an 18-yard run to propel the Vikings past the Cardinals. Minnesota, which had scored only 69 points in its first six games of the season, led 13-0 late in the second quarter until Gannon effectively put the game out of reach by scrambling for his touchdown only 15 seconds before halftime. The Vikings went on to lead 34-0 before Phoenix scored a late touchdown. Tom Tupa passed for 240 yards for the Cardinals but was sacked 5 times, including 3 by John Randle.

Phoenix	0	0	0	7	—	7
Minnesota	7	13	7	7	—	34

Minn — C. Carter 42 pass from Gannon (Reveiz kick)
Minn — Walker 1 run (Reveiz kick)
Minn — Gannon 18 run (kick failed)
Minn — A. Carter 3 pass from Gannon (Reveiz kick)
Minn — Anderson 6 run (Reveiz kick)
Phx — Thompson 1 run (G. Davis kick)

L.A. Rams 30, San Diego 24 — at Anaheim Stadium, attendance 47,433. Jim Everett ended a personal touchdown drought by throwing his first 2 scoring passes of the year and leading the Rams past the Chargers. Everett, who completed 19 of 25 passes for 219 yards, teamed with Jim Price for an 18-yard touchdown pass early in the second period. In the fourth quarter, he hooked up with Price again, this time from 12 yards, for the clinching score. The Rams also were aided by a key safety scored on the final play of the first half. After Los Angeles tied the game at 14-14 on a 1-yard run by Robert Delpino 19 seconds before halftime, a muffed kickoff gave the Chargers possession at their own 1-yard line. With no time left on the clock, Kevin Greene tackled Marion Butts in the end zone for the safety that put the Rams ahead for good.

San Diego	7	7	7	3	—	24
L.A. Rams	0	16	7	7	—	30

SD — Miller 30 pass from Friesz (Carney kick)
Rams — Price 18 pass from Everett (Zendejas kick)
SD — Lewis 49 pass from Friesz (Carney kick)
Rams — Delpino 1 run (Zendejas kick)
Rams — Safety, Greene tackled Butts in end zone
Rams — Delpino 1 run (Zendejas kick)
SD — Bernstine 1 run (Carney kick)
Rams — Price 12 pass from Everett (Zendejas kick)
SD — FG Carney 27

Atlanta 39, San Francisco 34 — at Candlestick Park, attendance 57,343. Chris Miller passed for 3 touchdowns and Deion Sanders returned a kickoff 100 yards for a score to spark the Falcons past the 49ers. Atlanta led 14-0 before the game was five minutes old and still held a 27-20 advantage after Sanders's return in the third quarter. But San Francisco battled back, taking a 34-33 lead on Steve Young's 7-yard run with 12 minutes left. Norm Johnson's 2 field goals after that provided the winning points for the Falcons, and former 49er Tim McKyer secured the victory with a pair of interceptions in the final 2:23. The wild game featured 805 yards of total offense, 437 by San Francisco. Atlanta's Steve Broussard led all rushers with 104 yards on 10 carries. The 49ers' Young passed for 348 yards and 2 touchdowns but was intercepted 3 times.

Atlanta	14	6	13	6	—	39
San Francisco	0	14	13	7	—	34

Atl — Haynes 27 pass from Miller (Johnson kick)
Atl — Rison 7 pass from Miller (Johnson kick)
Atl — FG Johnson 29
SF — Young 6 run (Cofer kick)
Atl — FG Johnson 43
SF — Taylor 54 pass from Young (Cofer kick)
SF — Rice 57 pass from Young (kick failed)
Atl — Sanders 100 kickoff return (Johnson kick)
SF — Sydney 5 run (Cofer kick)
Atl — Rison 1 pass from Miller (kick failed)
SF — Young 7 run (Cofer kick)
Atl — FG Johnson 44
Atl — FG Johnson 30

Sunday Night, October 13

L.A. Raiders 23, Seattle 20 — at Kingdome, attendance 61,974. Jeff Jaeger's 49-yard field goal with one second remaining tied the game in regulation, then his 37-yard kick 6:37 into overtime won it for the Raiders. Jaeger's kicks capped a remarkable comeback for Los Angeles, which trailed 17-0 at halftime. The Raiders tied the score at 17-17 on a 12-yard touchdown pass from Jay Schroeder to Tim Brown with 6 minutes left. Seattle regained the lead on John Kasay's 45-yard field goal with 2:04 to go, but Schroeder, who completed 28 of a club-record-tying 52 pass attempts for 274 yards and 2 touchdowns, directed a 53-yard drive to the tying field goal. In overtime, the Raiders' Ronnie Lott picked off a Jeff Kemp pass at the Seahawks' 22-yard line to set up the winning field goal.

L.A. Raiders	0	0	7	13	3	— 23
Seattle	3	14	0	3	0	— 20

Sea — FG Kasay 36
Sea — Clark 11 pass from Kemp (Kasay kick)
Sea — Hunter 32 interception return (Kasay kick)
Raiders — Horton 8 pass from Schroeder (Jaeger kick)
Raiders — FG Jaeger 47
Raiders — T. Brown 12 pass from Schroeder (Jaeger kick)
Sea — FG Kasay 45
Raiders — FG Jaeger 49
Raiders — FG Jaeger 37

Monday, October 14

N.Y. Giants 23, Pittsburgh 20 — at Three Rivers Stadium, attendance 57,608. Matt Bahr's 44-yard field goal with 4 seconds remaining lifted the Giants to the victory and spoiled a dramatic rally by the Steelers. New York led 13-0 at halftime, then increased its advantage to 20-0 midway through the third quarter on a 30-yard touchdown run by David Meggett. But at that point, Pittsburgh replaced ailing Bubby Brister with Neil O'Donnell and the Steelers mounted their comeback. O'Donnell directed Pittsburgh on four consecutive scoring drives, and tied the game with a 5-yard touchdown pass to Eric Green with 50 seconds left. But the Giants started their next possession on their own 40 and drove to the winning field goal. Jeff Hostetler's 18-yard scramble to the Steelers' 26 was the key play.

N.Y. Giants	7	6	7	3	—	23
Pittsburgh	0	0	3	17	—	20

Giants — Cross 12 pass from Hostetler (Bahr kick)
Giants — FG Bahr 45
Giants — FG Bahr 40
Giants — Meggett 30 run (Bahr kick)
Pitt — FG Anderson 26
Pitt — FG Anderson 39
Pitt — Lipps 16 pass from O'Donnell (Anderson kick)
Pitt — Green 5 pass from O'Donnell (Anderson kick)
Giants — FG Bahr 44

Eighth Week Summaries

Standings

American Football Conference

Eastern Division

	W	L	T	Pct.	Pts.	OP
Buffalo	7	1	0	.875	245	170
N.Y. Jets	4	4	0	.500	157	141
New England	3	4	0	.429	92	134
Miami	3	5	0	.375	140	181
Indianapolis	0	8	0	.000	55	193
Central Division						
Houston	6	1	0	.857	196	102
Cleveland	3	4	0	.429	119	135
Pittsburgh	3	4	0	.429	142	154
Cincinnati	0	7	0	.000	107	206
Western Division						
Denver	5	2	0	.714	147	123
Kansas City	5	3	0	.625	156	95
L.A. Raiders	5	3	0	.625	134	145
Seattle	4	4	0	.500	158	116
San Diego	1	7	0	.125	145	187

National Football Conference

Eastern Division

	W	L	T	Pct.	Pts.	OP
Washington	7	0	0	1.000	231	82
Dallas	5	2	0	.714	150	136
N.Y. Giants	4	3	0	.571	118	113
Phoenix	4	4	0	.500	115	149
Philadelphia	3	4	0	.429	96	93
Central Division						
Chicago	5	2	0	.714	107	111
Detroit	5	2	0	.714	131	154
Minnesota	3	5	0	.375	126	139
Green Bay	1	6	0	.143	83	125
Tampa Bay	1	6	0	.143	80	136
Western Division						
New Orleans	7	0	0	1.000	157	60
Atlanta	3	4	0	.429	111	138
L.A. Rams	3	4	0	.429	120	153
San Francisco	3	4	0	.429	164	111

Thursday, October 17

Chicago 10, Green Bay 0 — at Lambeau Field, attendance 58,435. Jim Harbaugh threw an 8-yard touchdown pass to tight end James Thornton and the Bears' defense limited the Packers to 5 first downs and 138 total yards to win the contest. Chicago kept the ball on the ground most of the night, rushing for 161 yards and maintaining possession for 39 minutes, 27 seconds while running 72 plays to Green Bay's 47. The Bears' Neal Anderson rushed for 81 yards on 16 carries. Don Majkowski returned to the Packers' lineup after missing a week with a bruised shoulder, but completed only 3 of 16 passes for 32 yards.

Chicago	0	7	0	3	—	10
Green Bay	0	0	0	0	—	0

Chi — Thornton 8 pass from Harbaugh (Butler kick)
Chi — FG Butler 22

Sunday, October 20

Phoenix 16, Atlanta 10 — at Sun Devil Stadium, attendance 24,124. Greg Davis kicked 3 field goals and Tim McDonald intercepted a pair of passes in the final 3:37 as the Cardinals rallied in the second half to beat the Falcons. Atlanta led 10-3 at halftime, but Phoenix tied it in the third quarter as rookie Randal Hill caught his first NFL touchdown pass, a 31-yarder from Tom Tupa. Davis, who scored 106 points for the Falcons in 1990 but was left unprotected under Plan B and signed with the Cardinals, then broke the tie with field goals of 51 and 49 yards. McDonald's thefts were 2 of the 5 turnovers Phoenix forced,

4 of them in the second half.

Atlanta	7	3	0	0	—	10
Phoenix	3	0	10	3	—	16

Phx—FG Davis 29
Atl —Pritchard 21 pass from Miller (N. Johnson kick)
Atl —FG N. Johnson 29
Phx—Hill 31 pass from Tupa (Davis kick)
Phx—FG Davis 51
Phx—FG Davis 49

Cleveland 30, San Diego 24 — at San Diego Jack Murphy Stadium, attendance 48,440. Former Charger David Brandon returned an interception 30 yards for a touchdown 7:40 into overtime to give the Browns a come-from-behind victory. Cleveland trailed 17-3 before scoring 2 touchdowns in a span of 2:26 late in the third quarter and early in the fourth to tie the game. Later, Bernie Kosar's 15-yard touchdown pass to Leroy Hoard with 4:09 left tied the game again at 24-24. San Diego had a chance to win it in regulation, but John Carney missed a 49-yard field-goal try as time ran out. For the Browns, Kosar completed 26 of 42 passes for 303 yards and 2 touchdowns. The Chargers' John Friesz was 33 of 54 for a career-high 321 yards and 1 touchdown, but was intercepted twice. Brandon, who spent four years with San Diego, was left unprotected following the 1990 season and was signed by the Browns as a Plan B free agent.

Cleveland	0	3	7	14	6	—	30
San Diego	3	0	14	7	0	—	24

SD —FG Carney 27
Cleve—FG Stover 30
SD —Harmon 11 run (Carney kick)
SD —Butts 2 run (Carney kick)
Cleve—Hoard 6 pass from Kosar (Stover kick)
Cleve—Morris 1 run (Stover kick)
SD —Hendrickson 2 pass from Friesz (Carney kick)
Cleve—Hoard 15 pass from Kosar (Stover kick)
Cleve—Brandon 30 interception return

San Francisco 35, Detroit 3 — at Candlestick Park, attendance 61,240. Steve Young completed his first 16 passes, Keith Henderson ran for 104 yards, and the 49ers overwhelmed the Lions en route to snapping Detroit's five-game winning streak. Young, who finished the day completing 18 of 20 for 237 yards, threw touchdown passes of 2 yards to Jerry Rice and 22 yards to Mike Sherrard, the former coming with 39 seconds left in the first half and effectively putting the game out of reach at 21-3. Barry Sanders, who entered the game with a string of four consecutive 100-yard rushing games, managed only 26 yards on 7 carries for Detroit. San Francisco had 29 first downs to the Lions' 10, outgained its opponent 505-207, and maintained possession for 77 plays and an astounding 45:04 to Detroit's 35 and 14:56.

Detroit	0	3	0	0	—	3
San Francisco	0	21	14	0	—	35

SF —Rathman 1 run (Cofer kick)
Det—FG Murray 37
SF —Sydney 11 run (Cofer kick)
SF —Rice 2 pass from Young (Cofer kick)
SF —Rathman 2 run (Cofer kick)
SF —Sherrard 22 pass from Young (Cofer kick)

Houston 17, Miami 13 — at Joe Robbie Stadium, attendance 60,705. Warren Moon threw a 1-yard touchdown pass to Curtis Duncan in the fourth quarter and Oilers cornerback Cris Dishman recovered a fumble in his own end zone with 3:10 remaining to preserve Houston's victory over the Dolphins. The go-ahead touchdown pass came with 9:30 left. But the win wasn't secured until Lamar Lathon forced Sammie Smith to fumble on first-and-goal from the 1-yard line and Dishman recovered when the ball rolled into the end zone. It was the sixth consecutive game that Dishman was responsible for an opponent's turnover, either by intercepting a pass or recovering a fumble. The game was highlighted by a bizarre second quarter in which the two teams combined for 7 turnovers. Moon was intercepted twice and Dan Marino three times, while both teams also lost a fumble. In all, the Dolphins turned over the ball 5 times, the Oilers 4.

Houston	0	7	3	7	—	17
Miami	3	7	3	0	—	13

Mia —FG Stoyanovich 34
Hou—Lewis 33 interception return (Howfield kick)
Mia —Clayton 19 pass from Marino (Stoyanovich kick)
Hou—FG Howfield 26
Mia —FG Stoyanovich 46
Hou—Duncan 1 pass from Moon (Howfield kick)

Denver 19, Kansas City 16 — at Mile High Stadium, attendance 75,866. David Treadwell's 27-yard field goal with 2:37 left in the game broke a 16-16 tie and gave the Broncos the victory and sole possession of first place in the AFC Western Division. Treadwell's kick was set up by a 71-yard pass from John Elway to Mark Jackson on third-and-17 from the Denver 13. The Broncos played without leading rusher Gaston Green (bruised thigh) and instead relied on the arm of Elway, who completed 14 of 27 passes for 270 yards. Included was a 22-yard scoring toss to Derek Russell just 11 seconds before halftime to give Denver a 13-6 lead at the intermission. Steve DeBerg passed for 241 yards and drove the Chiefs into Broncos' territory in the closing moments before the drive stalled.

Kansas City	3	3	3	7	—	16
Denver	0	13	3	3	—	19

KC —FG Lowery 32
Den—FG Treadwell 39
Den—FG Treadwell 30
KC —FG Lowery 48
Den—Russell 22 pass from Elway (Treadwell kick)
KC —FG Lowery 25
Den—FG Treadwell 25
KC —Williams 14 run (Lowery kick)
Den—FG Treadwell 27

L.A. Raiders 20, L.A. Rams 17 — at Los Angeles Memorial Coliseum, attendance 85,102. Jeff Jaeger kicked a 34-yard field goal with just two seconds left to give the Raiders the victory over the Rams. Jaeger's kick was set up when Ronnie Lott intercepted a Jim Everett pass at the Rams' 39 with 3:08 to go. Earlier, Lott picked off a pass in the end zone as the Rams, ahead 17-10, were driving for the apparent clinching score with 6:22 remaining. The Raiders then drove 80 yards to tie the score at 17-17 on Nick Bell's 1-yard touchdown run, the team's first rushing score of the season. Jay Schroeder completed 15 of 26 passes for 271 yards for the Raiders, including 45- and 24-yard completions on the tying touchdown drive. Everett finished 22 of 35 for 300 yards and 2 touchdowns.

L.A. Rams	7	3	7	0	—	17
L.A. Raiders	7	0	3	10	—	20

Rams —Delpino 4 pass from Everett (Zendejas kick)
Raiders—Gault 9 pass from Schroeder (Jaeger kick)
Rams —FG Zendejas 37
Raiders—FG Jaeger 35
Rams —Turner 19 pass from Everett (Zendejas kick)
Raiders—N. Bell 1 run (Jaeger kick)
Raiders—FG Jaeger 34

New England 26, Minnesota 23 — at Foxboro Stadium, attendance 45,367. Jason Staurovsky's 42-yard field goal as time ran out in overtime gave the Patriots the victory over the Vikings. The winning kick came eight plays after New England's David Pool recovered Steve Jordan's fumble at the Patriots' 20. Hugh Millen, who completed 22 of 32 passes for 326 yards, got the winning drive started with a 17-yard pass to Ben Coates, and later threw 27 yards to Greg McMurtry to put the ball in Vikings' territory. Minnesota had rallied to tie the game with 10 points in the final 1:37 of regulation. Fuad Reveiz's 23-yard field goal with 20 seconds to go made it 23-23 after Rich Gannon threw a 4-yard touchdown pass to Anthony Carter and the Vikings recovered a subsequent onside kick. Gannon completed 35 of a club-record 63 passes for 317 yards and was not intercepted. Staurovsky, who missed a fourth-quarter extra-point attempt, also missed a 36-yard field-goal try with 10:45 left in the extra session before making his winning three-pointer.

Minnesota	0	10	3	10	0	— 23
New England	7	7	0	9	3	— 26

NE —McMurtry 18 pass from Millen (Staurovsky kick)
Minn—Walker 1 run (Reveiz kick)
NE —Russell 1 run (Staurovsky kick)
Minn—FG Reveiz 23
Minn—FG Reveiz 32
NE —Childress fumble recovery in end zone (kick failed)
NE —FG Staurovsky 38
Minn—A.Carter 4 pass from Gannon (Reveiz kick)
Minn—FG Reveiz 23
NE —FG Staurovsky 42

N.Y. Jets 17, Indianapolis 6 — at Hoosier Dome, attendance 53,025. Ken O'Brien's 47-yard touchdown pass to Rob Moore on a flea-flicker play in the first quarter proved to be all the points the Jets needed as the winless Colts failed to score a touchdown for the fourth consecutive game. O'Brien completed 14 of 19 passes for 205 yards and New York rushed for 138 yards. Indianapolis ran only 43 plays and totaled 170 yards. For the second week in a row, the Colts played without Eric Dickerson, sidelined with a hamstring injury.

N.Y. Jets	7	7	3	0	—	17
Indianapolis	0	6	0	0	—	6

Jets—Moore 47 pass from O'Brien (Leahy kick)
Ind —FG Biasucci 42
Jets—Baxter 1 run (Leahy kick)
Ind —FG Biasucci 34
Jets—FG Leahy 19

Seattle 27, Pittsburgh 7 — at Three Rivers Stadium, attendance 54,678. Dave Krieg, out since the first week of the season with a broken thumb, returned to the lineup and passed for 266 yards and a pair of touchdowns to lead the Seahawks past the Steelers. Krieg, showing no ill effects from the layoff, completed his first 9 passes, and completed 25 of 31. He threw a 14-yard touchdown pass to Jeff Chadwick to give Seattle a 17-0 lead 18 seconds before halftime, then added a 1-yard toss to Mike Tice to put the game out of reach in the fourth quarter. Neil O'Donnell, who rallied Pittsburgh from a 20-point deficit against the Giants six days earlier, made his first start in place of injured Bubby Brister. He passed for 184 yards, including a 57-yard touchdown to Dwight Stone, but was victimized by 4 sacks and an interception.

Seattle	3	14	3	7	—	27
Pittsburgh	0	0	7	0	—	7

Sea—FG Kasay 36
Sea—Williams 1 run (Kasay kick)
Sea—Chadwick 14 pass from Krieg (Kasay kick)
Pitt —Stone 57 pass from O'Donnell (Anderson kick)
Sea—FG Kasay 21
Sea—Tice 1 pass from Krieg (Kasay kick)

New Orleans 23, Tampa Bay 7 — at Louisiana Superdome, attendance 68,591. The Saints used their familiar blend of an efficient offense with a stifling defense to post their seventh consecutive victory of the season. Steve Walsh, subbing for injured starter Bobby Hebert, passed for 205 yards and an 8-yard touchdown to Eric Martin in the fourth quarter to secure the win. Though the Buccaneers did score the first touchdown against New Orleans's defense in 18 quarters, they could manage only 46 rushing yards and 219 total yards while committing 3 turnovers.

Tampa Bay	0	0	7	0	—	7
New Orleans	7	9	0	7	—	23

NO—Fenerty 1 run (Andersen kick)
NO—FG Andersen 32
NO—FG Andersen 28
NO—FG Andersen 48
TB —Wilson 5 pass from Chandler (Christie kick)
NO—E. Martin 8 pass from Walsh (Andersen kick)

Monday, October 21

Buffalo 35, Cincinnati 16 — at Rich Stadium, attendance 80,131. Jim Kelly overcame a shaky start to pass for 392 yards and 5 touchdowns as the Bills handed the Bengals their seventh consecutive defeat. Kelly threw 3 interceptions in the first quarter, but Cincinnati could convert them into only 3 points. Then, on the first play of the second quarter, he teamed with James Lofton on a 71-yard scoring bomb to put Buffalo ahead for good. In all, Kelly completed 18 of 27 passes and Lofton had 8 receptions for 220 yards. The Bills gained 487 total yards and averaged 9 yards per play. Harold Green ran for 141 yards on 26 carries for the Bengals, who amassed 411 yards of total offense themselves.

Cincinnati	3	0	10	3	—	16
Buffalo	0	14	14	7	—	35

Cin —FG Breech 32
Buff—Lofton 74 pass from Kelly (Norwood kick)
Buff—Metzelaars 51 pass from Kelly (Norwood kick)
Cin —Brown 19 pass from Esiason (Breech kick)
Buff—Lofton 48 pass from Kelly (Norwood kick)
Cin —FG Johnson 53
Buff—Reed 24 pass from Kelly (Norwood kick)
Cin —FG Breech 42
Buff—Thomas 5 pass from Kelly (Norwood kick)

Ninth Week Summaries

Standings

American Football Conference

Eastern Division

	W	L	T	Pct.	Pts.	OP
Buffalo	7	1	0	.875	245	170
N.Y. Jets	4	4	0	.500	157	141
Miami	3	5	0	.375	140	181
New England	3	5	0	.375	98	143
Indianapolis	0	8	0	.000	55	193

Central Division

	W	L	T	Pct.	Pts.	OP
Houston	7	1	0	.875	231	105
Cleveland	4	4	0	.500	136	149
Pittsburgh	3	5	0	.375	156	171
Cincinnati	0	8	0	.000	110	241

Western Division

	W	L	T	Pct.	Pts.	OP
Denver	6	2	0	.750	156	129
Kansas City	6	3	0	.667	180	116
L.A. Raiders	5	4	0	.556	155	169
Seattle	5	4	0	.556	178	125
San Diego	1	8	0	.111	154	207

National Football Conference

Eastern Division

	W	L	T	Pct.	Pts.	OP
Washington	8	0	0	1.000	248	95
Dallas	5	3	0	.625	160	170
N.Y. Giants	4	4	0	.500	131	130
Phoenix	4	5	0	.444	115	177
Philadelphia	3	5	0	.375	103	116

Central Division

Chicago	6	2	0	.750	127	128
Detroit	6	2	0	.750	165	164
Minnesota	4	5	0	.444	154	139
Green Bay	2	6	0	.250	110	125
Tampa Bay	1	7	0	.125	80	163

Western Division

New Orleans	7	1	0	.875	174	80
Atlanta	4	4	0	.500	142	152
San Francisco	4	4	0	.500	187	118
L.A. Rams	3	5	0	.375	134	184

Sunday, October 27

Chicago 20, New Orleans 17 — at Louisiana Superdome, attendance 68,591. Jim Harbaugh, who had completed only 2 of his first 19 passes under heavy pressure from the Saints' defense, completed all 3 of his attempts on the Bears' final drive, including the game-winning 12-yard touchdown to Tom Waddle with 54 seconds remaining. The loss, which dropped New Orleans from the ranks of the undefeated, was the Saints' first since suffering a 16-6 setback to Chicago in a 1990 NFC First-Round Playoff Game. Stymied most of the game and limited to only 126 total yards to that point, the Bears took possession on their own 48-yard line with less than two minutes to go after a 12-yard punt. The key play of the 52-yard drive was a 27-yard pass from Harbaugh to Wendell Davis. New Orleans had forged a 17-13 lead behind 2 touchdown passes by Bobby Hebert and a 60-yard field goal by Morten Andersen—to equal the second longest three-pointer in league history—on the final play of the first half.

Chicago	0	6	7	7	—	20
New Orleans	7	3	7	0	—	17

NO—Turner 65 pass from Hebert (Andersen kick)
Chi—FG Butler 34
Chi—FG Butler 48
NO—FG Andersen 60
Chi—Muster 6 run (Butler kick)
NO—Turner 8 pass from Hebert (Andersen kick)
Chi—Waddle 12 pass from Harbaugh (Butler kick)

Houston 35, Cincinnati 3 — at Astrodome, attendance 58,634. Warren Moon threw 3 touchdown passes in the first half and the Oilers breezed to victory over the Bengals. Moon completed 24 of 37 passes for 289 yards before giving way to Cody Carlson midway through the fourth quarter. Carlson passed for another 92 yards, including a 68-yard touchdown to Tony Jones. In all, the Oilers amassed 486 yards in total offense to just 183 for Cincinnati. Erik Wilhelm, subbing for injured Boomer Esiason, made his first career start, completing 12 of 24 passes for 106 yards, with 2 interceptions. Cris Dishman, whose third-quarter interception set up a touchdown, created a turnover for the seventh consecutive game.

Cincinnati	0	3	0	0	—	3
Houston	13	10	6	6	—	35

Hou—Jeffires 6 pass from Moon (Howfield kick)
Hou—Hill 61 pass from Moon (kick failed)
Hou—Givins 14 pass from Moon (Howfield kick)
Hou—FG Howfield 33
Cin—FG Breech 20
Hou—Pinkett 2 run (kick failed)
Hou—Jones 68 pass from Carlson (kick failed)

Detroit 34, Dallas 10 — at Pontiac Silverdome, attendance 74,506. Erik Kramer, who came off the bench to throw his first 2 NFL touchdown passes, helped the Lions keep pace with the Bears atop the NFC Central Division by beating the Cowboys. Dallas lost despite compiling 22 first downs to Detroit's 13 and outgaining the Lions 415-208. The Cowboys were victimized by four turnovers, including an interception that Ray Crockett returned 96 yards for a touchdown, and a blocked field goal that was scooped up and returned 55 yards for a score by William White. Kramer, who completed 9 of 16 passes for 108 yards and 2 touchdowns, was in the game because Rodney Peete suffered a torn Achilles' tendon in the first quarter and was lost for the season.

Dallas	0	10	0	0	—	10
Detroit	3	7	10	14	—	34

Det—FG Murray 44
Dall—Roberts 1 pass from Aikman (Willis kick)
Det—White 55 blocked field goal return (Murray kick)
Dall—FG Willis 35
Det—Green 26 pass from Kramer (Murray kick)
Det—FG Murray 32
Det—Sanders 10 pass from Kramer (Murray kick)
Det—Crockett 96 interception return (Murray kick)

Denver 9, New England 6 — at Foxboro Stadium, attendance 43,994. David Treadwell kicked 3 field goals, including the game-winner from 34 yards with 1:56 remaining, to lift the Broncos past the Patriots. Jason Staurovsky accounted for New England's points with a pair of field goals, but was denied a chance at a third when time ran out with the Patriots in possession of the ball on Denver's 6-yard line. After Treadwell's third field goal, Hugh Millen completed 6 of 9 passes for 69 yards to put the Patriots at the 15 with 14 seconds left. But with his team out of timeouts, Millen was tackled after a 9-yard scramble and New England didn't have time to run another play or bring on the field goal unit.

Denver	3	3	0	3	—	9
New England	0	3	0	3	—	6

Den—FG Treadwell 35
NE—FG Staurovsky 20
Den—FG Treadwell 18
NE—FG Staurovsky 17
Den—FG Treadwell 34

Green Bay 27, Tampa Bay 0 — at Tampa Stadium, attendance 40,275. Don Majkowski passed for 223 yards and 1 touchdown and the Packers' defense had 6 sacks and forced 8 turnovers en route to the shutout victory. Green Bay set the tone early, scoring first on Brian Noble's 1-yard return of quarterback Chris Chandler's fumble less than six minutes into the game. Turnovers also led to a pair of Chris Jacke field goals and Majkowski's 10-yard scoring pass to tight end Ed West. Chandler and rookie Jeff Carlson—in his NFL debut—combined to complete 14 of 38 passes, with 5 interceptions. The Packers limited Tampa Bay to 170 total yards.

Green Bay	10	3	7	7	—	27
Tampa Bay	0	0	0	0	—	0

GB—Noble 1 fumble recovery return (Jacke kick)
GB—FG Jacke 34
GB—FG Jacke 46
GB—West 10 pass from Majkowski (Jacke kick)
GB—Workman 4 run (Jacke kick)

Atlanta 31, L.A. Rams 14 — at Atlanta-Fulton County Stadium, attendance 50,187. Chris Miller completed 14 of 19 passes for 237 yards and 2 touchdowns to lead the Falcons past the Rams. Miller posted those numbers despite suffering bruised ribs in the second quarter and a bruised knee in the third period, after which he left the game for good. But by that time, Atlanta had a 28-0 lead, which they stretched to 31-0 before allowing a pair of fourth-quarter touchdowns. The Falcons outgained the Rams 399-209.

L.A. Rams	0	0	0	14	—	14
Atlanta	7	14	10	0	—	31

Atl—Dixon 19 pass from Miller (N. Johnson kick)
Atl—Chaffey 5 run (N. Johnson kick)
Atl—Rison 20 pass from Miller (N. Johnson kick)
Atl—Haynes 55 pass from Miller (N. Johnson kick)
Atl—FG N. Johnson 44
Rams—Delpino 9 run (Zendejas kick)
Rams—Carter 18 pass from Pagel (Zendejas kick)

Minnesota 28, Phoenix 0 — at Sun Devil Stadium, attendance 45,447. Herschel Walker ran for 3 touchdowns in the second half as the Vikings shut out the Cardinals. Walker, who gained 79 yards on 17 carries, broke open a close game with a 16-yard touchdown early in the third quarter, then added short scoring bursts of 1 and 5 yards in the fourth quarter. Minnesota's defense did the rest, limiting Phoenix to only 7 first downs, 32 yards rushing, and 158 total yards.

Minnesota	0	7	7	14	—	28
Phoenix	0	0	0	0	—	0

Minn—H. Jones 5 pass from Gannon (Reveiz kick)
Minn—Walker 16 run (Reveiz kick)
Minn—Walker 1 run (Reveiz kick)
Minn—Walker 5 run (Reveiz kick)

Cleveland 17, Pittsburgh 14 — at Cleveland Stadium, attendance 78,285. Bernie Kosar completed 21 of 29 passes for 179 yards and 1 touchdown to lead the Browns past the Steelers. Kosar's touchdown pass was a strange one. His short pass intended for Scott Galbraith was tipped in the air by a Pittsburgh defender and floated to Leroy Hoard, who was lying on his back in the end zone, having been tripped up while running a pass route. That gave the Browns a 10-0 lead in the second quarter. The Steelers rallied and had a chance to tie the game midway through the fourth period, but Gary Anderson's 52-yard field goal try hit the upright and bounced away. Kosar extended his string of consecutive pass attempts without an interception to 262, second only to former Packer Bart Starr's NFL-record 294.

Pittsburgh	0	7	0	7	—	14
Cleveland	3	7	7	0	—	17

Cleve—FG Stover 34
Cleve—Hoard 2 pass from Kosar (Stover kick)
Pitt—O'Donnell 1 run (Anderson kick)
Cleve—Mack 1 run (Stover kick)
Pitt—Williams 1 run (Anderson kick)

Seattle 20, San Diego 9 — at Kingdome, attendance 58,025. The Seahawks were limited to only 202 total yards, but used a 55-yard kickoff return and a club record-tying 54-yard field goal to help beat the Chargers. San Diego pulled within 10-9 on John Carney's third field goal of the game late in the third quarter. But Chris Warren returned the ensuing kickoff from his own 5-yard line to the Chargers' 40, and seven plays later Dave Krieg threw a 5-yard touchdown pass to Mike Tice. John Kasay's 54-yard field goal—his eighth successful try in a row and his second of more than 50 yards in the game—with six minutes remaining put the game out of reach.

San Diego	0	6	3	0	—	9
Seattle	7	3	0	10	—	20

Sea—Fenner 1 run (Kasay kick)
SD—FG Carney 29
Sea—FG Kasay 51
SD—FG Carney 24
SD—FG Carney 36
Sea—Tice 5 pass from Krieg (Kasay kick)
Sea—FG Kasay 54

San Francisco 23, Philadelphia 7 — at Veterans Stadium, attendance 65,796. Charles Haley posted 3 sacks and Don Griffin intercepted a pass and recovered a fumble as the 49ers' defense paved the way for the victory over the Eagles. Larry Roberts added a pair of sacks for San Francisco, which had 6 in all and forced 5 turnovers. The 49ers' offense, meanwhile, uncharacteristically attempted only 15 passes—Steve Young completed 10 for 96 yards—and had more rushing yards (137) than passing yards (85). Jim McMahon returned to Philadelphia's lineup and completed 19 of 28 passes for 222 yards and 1 touchdown in his first start since missing two games with a knee injury. But he reinjured the knee late in the first half, returning only after backup Jeff Kemp suffered a concussion in the third quarter. The 49ers, who had their NFL-record 18-game road winning streak snapped in the season opener, won on the road for the first time in four tries.

San Francisco	7	7	3	6	—	23
Philadelphia	0	7	0	0	—	7

SF—Taylor 21 pass from Young (Cofer kick)
Phil—Byars 19 pass from McMahon (Ruzek kick)
SF—Rathman 2 run (Cofer kick)
SF—FG Cofer 45
SF—FG Cofer 25
SF—FG Cofer 50

Sunday Night, October 27

Washington 17, N.Y. Giants 13 — at Giants Stadium, attendance 76,627. The Redskins spotted the Giants a 13-point lead in the first half, then stormed back with 17 unanswered points in the second to win and raise their record to 8-0 for the first time in the 60-year history of the franchise. Washington rallied on a pair of touchdown passes from Mark Rypien to Gary Clark just 2:52 apart late in the third quarter and early in the fourth. Chip Lohmiller added a 35-yard field goal in the final minute to secure the victory. The Giants scored on their first two possessions of the game and outgained the Redskins 207 yards to 35 in the first half. But Washington reversed that in the second half, outgaining New York 219-64 to help snap its six-game losing streak to the Giants.

Washington	0	0	7	10	—	17
N.Y. Giants	10	3	0	0	—	13

Giants—FG Allegre 23
Giants—Hampton 1 run (Allegre kick)
Giants—FG Allegre 36
Wash—Clark 7 pass from Rypien (Lohmiller kick)
Wash—Clark 54 pass from Rypien (Lohmiller kick)
Wash—FG Lohmiller 35

Monday, October 28

Kansas City 24, L.A. Raiders 21 — at Arrowhead Stadium, attendance 77,111. Steve DeBerg's 6-yard touchdown pass to Tim Barnett capped a fourth-quarter comeback and lifted the Chiefs past the Raiders. Kansas City trailed 21-10 and Los Angeles was driving for the apparent clinching score when Lloyd Burruss intercepted a Jay Schroeder pass near the goal line and returned it 83 yards. Six plays later, on fourth-and-goal from the 1, Christian Okoye scored to trim the deficit to 21-17. After the Raiders punted, the Chiefs drove 57 yards to the winning touchdown, sustaining the drive when DeBerg passed 5 yards to Todd McNair on fourth-and-4.

L.A. Raiders	11	7	3	0	—	21
Kansas City	0	7	3	14	—	24

Raiders—FG Jaeger 18
Raiders—Safety, Dorn tackled Barnett in end zone
Raiders—Bell 1 run (kick blocked)
KC—B. Jones 8 pass from DeBerg (Lowery kick)
Raiders—S. Smith 37 pass from Schroeder (Jaeger kick)
KC—FG Lowery 33
Raiders—FG Jaeger 22
KC—Okoye 1 run (Lowery kick)
KC—Barnett 6 pass from DeBerg (Lowery kick)

Tenth Week Summaries

Standings

American Football Conference

Eastern Division

	W	L	T	Pct.	Pts.	OP
Buffalo	8	1	0	.889	267	187
N.Y. Jets	5	4	0	.556	176	156
Miami	4	5	0	.444	150	187
New England	3	6	0	.333	115	165
Indianapolis	0	9	0	.000	61	203

Central Division

	W	L	T	Pct.	Pts.	OP
Houston	7	2	0	.778	244	121
Cleveland	4	5	0	.444	157	172
Pittsburgh	3	6	0	.333	169	191
Cincinnati	1	8	0	.111	133	262

Western Division

	W	L	T	Pct.	Pts.	OP
Denver	7	2	0	.778	176	142
Kansas City	6	3	0	.667	180	116
L.A. Raiders	5	4	0	.556	155	169
Seattle	5	4	0	.556	178	125
San Diego	1	8	0	.111	154	207

National Football Conference

Eastern Division

	W	L	T	Pct.	Pts.	OP
Washington	9	0	0	1.000	264	108
Dallas	6	3	0	.667	187	177
N.Y. Giants	4	5	0	.444	138	160
Philadelphia	4	5	0	.444	133	123
Phoenix	4	6	0	.400	122	204

Central Division

	W	L	T	Pct.	Pts.	OP
Chicago	7	2	0	.778	147	138
Detroit	6	3	0	.667	175	184
Minnesota	5	5	0	.500	182	152
Green Bay	2	7	0	.222	126	144
Tampa Bay	1	8	0	.111	93	191

Western Division

	W	L	T	Pct.	Pts.	OP
New Orleans	8	1	0	.889	198	97
Atlanta	5	4	0	.556	159	166
San Francisco	4	5	0	.444	201	135
L.A. Rams	3	6	0	.333	151	208

Sunday, November 3

Cincinnati 23, Cleveland 21 — at Riverfront Stadium, attendance 55,077. Eric Thomas blocked Matt Stover's 34-yard field goal try on the final play of the game to help the Bengals snap their club record-tying losing streak at eight games. Jim Breech's third field goal, a 38-yarder with 13:41 to play, proved to be the game-winner, but Cincinnati survived some anxious moments before notching its first victory of the season. First, the Browns' Kevin Mack, who rushed for 78 yards and 3 touchdowns, fumbled the ball away to the Bengals on the Cincinnati 15-yard line with 5:15 remaining. Then Stover had a 47-yard field-goal attempt hit the left upright and bounce away with 2:02 left, and normally sure-handed Brian Brennan dropped the potential game-winning touchdown pass in the end zone with 42 seconds to go. The Bengals fell behind 14-3 in the second quarter but rallied behind a pair of touchdown passes by Boomer Esiason, who completed 18 of 30 passes for 185 yards. Cincinnati's Harold Green rushed for 135 yards on 24 carries.

Cleveland	0	14	7	0	—	21
Cincinnati	3	10	7	3	—	23

Cin — FG Breech 23
Cleve — Mack 4 run (Stover kick)
Cleve — Mack 2 run (Stover kick)
Cin — Dingle 2 pass from Esiason (Breech kick)
Cin — FG Breech 38
Cin — Brown 34 pass from Esiason (Breech kick)
Cleve — Mack 2 run (Stover kick)
Cin — FG Breech 38

Chicago 20, Detroit 10 — at Soldier Field, attendance 57,281. Wendell Davis caught a pair of scoring passes in the second half to rally the Bears past the Lions in a battle between the leaders of the NFC Central Division. Erik Kramer threw an 11-yard touchdown pass to Brett Perriman in the second quarter to help stake Detroit to a 10-3 lead at halftime. But after Kevin Butler kicked a 25-yard field goal to trim the deficit to 10-6, Jim Harbaugh and Davis teamed on a 22-yard touchdown pass with 26 seconds left in the third quarter to put the Bears ahead for good. Harbaugh's 8-yard pass to Davis with 3:53 left in the fourth quarter put the game out of reach.

Detroit	0	10	0	0	—	10
Chicago	3	0	10	7	—	20

Chi — FG Butler 21
Det — Perriman 11 pass from Kramer (Murray kick)
Det — FG Murray 31
Chi — FG Butler 25
Chi — Davis 22 pass from Harbaugh (Butler kick)
Chi — Davis 8 pass from Harbaugh (Butler kick)

N.Y. Jets 19, Green Bay 16 — at Giants Stadium, attendance 67,435. After tying the game on a 22-yard field goal with 1 minute left in regulation, the Jets' Pat Leahy won it with a 37-yard field goal 9:40 into overtime. Leahy, who booted 4 field goals in all, made his winning kick three plays after Bobby Houston recovered a muffed punt at the Packers' 23-yard line. Earlier, the Jets got another big score after safety R.J. Kors recovered a fumble with the score tied at 6-6 in the closing seconds of the first half. With the ball at midfield and time for only one more play, New York's Ken O'Brien lofted a desperation pass toward the end zone. It was tipped by three players before settling in the hands of Chris Burkett to give New York a 13-6 lead. Backup Mike Tomczak completed 8 of 11 passes for 73 yards and led the Packers to a pair of scores after taking over for injured starter Don Majkowski in the third quarter.

Green Bay	3	3	7	3	0	—	16
N.Y. Jets	3	10	0	3	3	—	19

Jets — FG Leahy 30
GB — FG Jacke 53
GB — FG Jacke 41
Jets — FG Leahy 39
Jets — Burkett 50 pass from O'Brien (Leahy kick)
GB — West 1 pass from Tomczak (Jacke kick)
GB — FG Jacke 34
Jets — FG Leahy 22
Jets — FG Leahy 37

Washington 16, Houston 13 — at RFK Stadium, attendance 55,096. The 8-0 Redskins outlasted the 7-1 Oilers in overtime as Chip Lohmiller kicked a 41-yard field goal 4:01 into the extra period. Houston had a chance to win it in regulation, but Ian Howfield's 33-yard field goal try with one second remaining was no good. In the overtime, Darrell Green made a diving interception at the Oilers' 33-yard line, and Lohmiller made his winning kick four plays later. Houston had tied the game in the fourth quarter on Lorenzo White's 1-yard run with 1:42 to play. Earlier in the fourth period, Earnest Byner, who rushed for 112 yards on 21 carries, scored on a 23-yard run to put the Redskins ahead 13-6.

Houston	0	6	0	7	0	—	13
Washington	0	3	3	7	3	—	16

Wash — FG Lohmiller 21
Hou — FG Howfield 24
Hou — FG Howfield 23
Wash — FG Lohmiller 20
Wash — Byner 23 run (Lohmiller kick)
Hou — White 1 run (Howfield kick)
Wash — FG Lohmiller 41

Miami 10, Indianapolis 6 — at Hoosier Dome, attendance 55,899. Dan Marino's 12-yard touchdown pass to Mark Duper on the Dolphins' first possession proved to be all the points Miami needed to beat the winless Colts. Later in the first quarter, Marino, who completed 21 of 37 passes for 231 yards, and Duper teamed on a 37-yard pass to set up Pete Stoyanovich's 35-yard field goal. Indianapolis could counter only with a pair of Dean Biasucci field goals, stretching their touchdown drought to five games. Duper, who had 64 receiving yards, moved into a tie for first place with Nat Moore on the club's career list with 7,547 yards.

Miami	10	0	0	0	—	10
Indianapolis	0	3	3	0	—	6

Mia — Duper 12 pass from Marino (Stoyanovich kick)
Mia — FG Stoyanovich 35
Ind — FG Biasucci 47
Ind — FG Biasucci 25

Buffalo 22, New England 17 — at Rich Stadium, attendance 78,278. Thurman Thomas rushed for 126 yards and the clinching touchdown to lead the Bills to their sixteenth consecutive victory at home. The upstart Patriots trailed just 16-10 until Buffalo recovered a fumble at the New England 25-yard line. Three plays later, Thomas bolted 15 yards for a touchdown. Leonard Russell, who rushed for 106 yards (his second consecutive 100-yard outing), scored on a 3-yard run with 4:36 remaining to make it close. But New England's final threat was snuffed when the Bills' Darryl Talley intercepted a Hugh Millen pass at the Buffalo 30 with 15 seconds remaining.

New England	0	3	7	7	—	17
Buffalo	3	3	7	9	—	22

Buff — FG Norwood 19
Buff — FG Norwood 21
NE — FG Staurovsky 36
Buff — Beebe 13 pass from Kelly (Norwood kick)
NE — Russell 1 run (Staurovsky kick)
Buff — FG Norwood 42
Buff — Thomas 15 run (kick blocked)
NE — Russell 3 run (Staurovsky kick)

New Orleans 24, L.A. Rams 17 — at Anaheim Stadium, attendance 58,713. Steve Walsh passed for 269 yards and 2 touchdowns to lead the Saints past the Rams. With Bobby Hebert nursing a sore shoulder, Walsh stepped in and completed 17 of 33 passes, including a 31-yard touchdown to Wesley Carroll with three seconds left in the first half to break a 10-10 tie. That came 19 seconds after Gene Atkins stripped the Rams' Jim Price of the ball at the New Orleans 44-yard line and Vencie Glenn recovered for the Saints. Los Angeles managed 381 total yards against New Orleans's top-ranked defense, but committed 5 turnovers. Jim Everett completed 18 of 31 passes for 346 yards for Los Angeles, but was victimized by 3 interceptions and 3 sacks.

New Orleans	10	7	0	7	—	24
L.A. Rams	3	7	0	7	—	17

NO — FG Andersen 45
NO — Heyward 22 pass from Walsh (Andersen kick)
Rams — FG Zendejas 31
Rams — Delpino 2 run (Zendejas kick)
NO — Carroll 31 pass from Walsh (Andersen kick)
NO — Jordan 11 run (Andersen kick)
Rams — Anderson 15 pass from Everett (Zendejas kick)

Dallas 27, Phoenix 7 — at Texas Stadium, attendance 61,190. Emmitt Smith rushed for 3 touchdowns as the Cowboys defeated the Cardinals. Dallas struck early, as Alexander Wright returned the opening kickoff 71 yards to set up a field goal. The Cowboys took a 10-0 lead when Troy Aikman completed passes of 25 yards to Michael Irvin and 37 yards to Alvin Harper to set up Smith's 3-yard touchdown run. Smith scored on runs of 1 and 3 yards in the second half. Aikman completed 17 of 23 passes for 191 yards. Phoenix's Johnny Johnson, who rushed for 89 yards, capped an 84-yard drive with a 1-yard run for the Cardinals' only touchdown.

Phoenix	0	7	0	0	—	7
Dallas	10	0	7	10	—	27

Dall — FG Willis 36
Dall — Smith 3 run (Willis kick)
Phx — Johnson 1 run (Davis kick)
Dall — Smith 1 run (Willis kick)
Dall — FG Willis 27
Dall — Smith 3 run (Willis kick)

Atlanta 17, San Francisco 14 — at Atlanta-Fulton County Stadium, attendance 51,259. Michael Haynes caught Billy Joe Tolliver's 44-yard desperation pass with 1 second remaining to give the Falcons a come-from-behind victory over the 49ers. The win gave Atlanta a season sweep of San Francisco for the first time since 1980, and was the Falcons' first over the 49ers in Atlanta since winning on a similar play in 1983. San Francisco appeared to have rallied for the victory when Steve Bono, in the game because starter Steve Young sprained knee ligaments in the second quarter, hit John Taylor with a 30-yard touchdown pass with only 53 seconds to go. But Tolliver, also a backup who replaced injured Chris Miller in the first half, moved the Falcons 80 yards in 7 plays, the key play a 19-yard completion to Andre Rison on fourth-and-six. Earlier, Young and Taylor teamed on a 97-yard touchdown pass, the longest in club history.

San Francisco	0	7	0	7	—	14
Atlanta	0	0	0	17	—	17

SF — Taylor 97 pass from Young (Cofer kick)
Atl — Rison 3 pass from Tolliver (N. Johnson kick)
Atl — FG N. Johnson 29
SF — Taylor 30 pass from Bono (Cofer kick)
Atl — M. Haynes 44 pass from Tolliver (N. Johnson kick)

Minnesota 28, Tampa Bay 13 — at Metrodome, attendance 35,737. Terry Allen rushed for 127 yards and 2 touchdowns on 14 carries and the Vikings overcame a sluggish first half to beat the Buccaneers. Tampa Bay led 6-0 in the third quarter after a pair of field goals by Steve Christie. But Allen, a first-year player who was inactive all of the 1990 season while rehabilitating an injured knee, scored on a 15-yard run with 4:40 left in the quarter to give the Vikings the lead. After Mike Merriweather returned an interception 22 yards for a touchdown, Allen put the game out of reach by breaking loose for a 55-yard touchdown run. The Vikings' Rich Gannon completed 19 of 28 passes for 160 yards and had a 2-yard touchdown completion to Steve Jordan.

Tampa Bay	0	3	3	7	—	13
Minnesota	0	0	14	14	—	28

TB — FG Christie 49
TB — FG Christie 40
Minn — Allen 15 run (Reveiz kick)
Minn — Merriweather 22 interception return (Reveiz kick)
Minn — Allen 55 run (Reveiz kick)
Minn — Jordan 2 pass from Gannon (Reveiz kick)
TB — J. Anderson 1 pass from Testaverde (Christie kick)

Sunday Night, November 3

Denver 20, Pittsburgh 13 — at Mile High Stadium, attendance 70,973. Greg Lewis rushed for 111 yards and 1 touchdown to help the Broncos maintain sole possession of first place in the AFC West by holding off a late Steelers' comeback attempt. Lewis, starting in place of the injured Gaston Green, carried 19 times and scored on a 1-yard run in the second quarter to cut an early Pittsburgh lead to 10-7. Six minutes later, John Elway ran 4 yards for a score to put Denver ahead for good. After falling behind 20-10, the Steelers tried to rally, but Gary Anderson missed a 24-yard field-goal attempt midway through the fourth quarter—his first miss from inside 35 yards in 57 tries—and Eric Green dropped a potential game-tying touchdown pass on a fourth-down play with 41 seconds left.

Pittsburgh	3	7	0	3	—	13
Denver	0	17	3	0	—	20

Pitt — FG Anderson 26
Pitt — Green 23 pass from O'Donnell (Anderson kick)
Den — Lewis 1 run (Treadwell kick)

Den	—	Elway 4 run (Treadwell kick)
Den	—	FG Treadwell 28
Den	—	FG Treadwell 21
Pitt	—	FG Anderson 39

Monday, November 4

Philadelphia 30, N.Y. Giants 7 — at Veterans Stadium, attendance 65,816. Jim McMahon threw a 73-yard touchdown pass to Keith Jackson and the Eagles' defense limited the Giants to 180 total yards as Philadelphia defeated the Giants. New York entered the game averaging more than 150 rushing yards per game, but could manage only 46 in this one. When the Giants turned to the pass, they fared no better, as the Eagles sacked New York quarterback Jeff Hostetler 4 times and held him to 9 completions in 17 attempts for 142 yards. McMahon completed 16 of 26 passes for 229 yards. His second-quarter bomb to Jackson gave Philadelphia a 10-0 lead and all the points it would need.

N.Y. Giants	0	0	7	0	—	7
Philadelphia	0	13	7	10	—	30

Phil	—	FG Ruzek 38
Phil	—	Jackson 73 pass from McMahon (Ruzek kick)
Phil	—	FG Ruzek 36
Phil	—	Joseph 11 run (Ruzek kick)
Giants	—	Hampton 1 run (Allegre kick)
Phil	—	FG Ruzek 25
Phil	—	Joseph 1 run (Ruzek kick)

Eleventh Week Summaries

Standings

American Football Conference

Eastern Division

	W	L	T	Pct.	Pts.	OP
Buffalo	9	1	0	.900	301	211
Miami	5	5	0	.500	180	207
N.Y. Jets	5	5	0	.500	203	185
New England	3	7	0	.300	135	195
Indianapolis	1	9	0	.100	89	230

Central Division

	W	L	T	Pct.	Pts.	OP
Houston	8	2	0	.800	270	144
Cleveland	4	6	0	.400	187	204
Pittsburgh	4	6	0	.400	202	218
Cincinnati	1	9	0	.100	160	295

Western Division

	W	L	T	Pct.	Pts.	OP
Denver	7	3	0	.700	192	159
Kansas City	7	3	0	.700	207	136
L.A. Raiders	6	4	0	.600	172	185
Seattle	5	5	0	.500	192	142
San Diego	2	8	0	.200	171	221

National Football Conference

Eastern Division

	W	L	T	Pct.	Pts.	OP
Washington	10	0	0	1.000	320	125
Dallas	6	4	0	.600	210	203
N.Y. Giants	5	5	0	.500	159	174
Philadelphia	5	5	0	.500	165	153
Phoenix	4	7	0	.364	136	225

Central Division

	W	L	T	Pct.	Pts.	OP
Chicago	8	2	0	.800	181	155
Detroit	6	4	0	.600	196	214
Minnesota	5	6	0	.455	196	186
Green Bay	2	8	0	.200	150	178
Tampa Bay	2	8	0	.200	123	212

Western Division

	W	L	T	Pct.	Pts.	OP
New Orleans	9	1	0	.900	208	100
Atlanta	5	5	0	.500	176	222
San Francisco	4	6	0	.400	204	145
L.A. Rams	3	7	0	.300	171	235

Sunday, November 10

Washington 56, Atlanta 17 — at RFK Stadium, attendance 52,641. Mark Rypien equaled a club-record with 6 touchdown passes and ran for another as the Redskins beat the Falcons. Rypien passed for 442 yards on only 16 completions (in 31 attempts), burning Atlanta's man-to-man coverage for touchdown bombs covering 82, 64, and 61 yards. Art Monk caught 7 passes for 164 yards and 2 touchdowns and Gary Clark had 203 yards and 3 touchdowns on just 4 catches. With the victory, the Redskins became only the fourteenth team in NFL history to start a season 10-0. Washington's 56 points was its most since a 72-41 drubbing of the New York Giants in 1966.

Atlanta	3	0	14	0	—	17
Washington	7	21	7	21	—	56

Atl	—	FG Johnson 31
Wash	—	Orr 9 pass from Rypien (Lohmiller kick)
Wash	—	Clark 61 pass from Rypien (Lohmiller kick)
Wash	—	Rypien 4 run (Lohmiller kick)
Wash	—	Clark 19 pass from Rypien (Lohmiller kick)
Atl	—	Haynes 75 pass from Tolliver (Johnson kick)
Atl	—	Rison 15 pass from Tolliver (Johnson kick)
Wash	—	Monk 19 pass from Rypien (Lohmiller kick)
Wash	—	Clark 82 pass from Rypien (Lohmiller kick)
Wash	—	Monk 64 pass from Rypien (Lohmiller kick)
Wash	—	Collins 15 interception return (Lohmiller kick)

Buffalo 34, Green Bay 24 — at Milwaukee County Stadium, attendance 52,175. Jim Kelly passed for 232 yards and 2 touchdowns and ran for 1 score to lead the Bills past the Packers. Green Bay had first-half leads of 7-0 and 10-7, but Buffalo rallied to take the lead for good with an 80-yard drive late in the second quarter, capped by a 12-yard scoring pass from Kelly to Don Beebe 1:48 before halftime. The Bills then took the second-half kickoff and marched 78 yards to another touchdown on Thurman Thomas's 5-yard run. Thomas ran for 106 yards on 24 carries, while James Lofton caught 6 passes for 114 yards. Mike Tomczak, making his first-ever start for the Packers, completed 23 of 38 passes for 317 yards and 2 touchdowns. Green Bay's Sterling Sharpe had 8 receptions for 133 yards.

Buffalo	0	14	10	10	—	34
Green Bay	7	3	7	7	—	24

GB	—	Workman 1 run (Jacke kick)
Buff	—	Reed 6 pass from Kelly (Norwood kick)
GB	—	FG Jacke 25
Buff	—	Beebe 12 pass from Kelly (Norwood kick)
Buff	—	Thomas 5 run (Norwood kick)
GB	—	Sharpe 58 pass from Tomczak (Jacke kick)
Buff	—	FG Norwood 38
Buff	—	Kelly 1 run (Norwood kick)
Buff	—	FG Norwood 21
GB	—	Harris 1 pass from Tomczak (Jacke kick)

Houston 26, Dallas 23 — at Astrodome, attendance 63,001. Al Del Greco, signed only five days earlier to strengthen the Oilers' ineffective kicking game, kicked 4 field goals, including a 23-yarder with 29 seconds left in overtime, to give Houston the victory. The Oilers drove 80 yards to the winning field goal after Bubba McDowell recovered Emmitt Smith's first fumble of the season. Earlier, Del Greco had a chance to win the game in regulation, but his 41-yard attempt in the final minute hit the upright and bounced away. In the second quarter, he was successful on a career-best 52-yarder. The Cowboys jumped to a 10-0 lead in the first quarter after blocking each of Houston punter Greg Montgomery's first two punts. Robert Williams scooped up the first one and ran 18 yards for a touchdown. The Oilers rallied and took their first lead of the game on a 4-yard run by Lorenzo White with 4:46 left in the fourth quarter. Dallas tied it 23-23 on a 10-yard pass from Troy Aikman to Michael Irvin with 2:45 left. Houston quarterback Warren Moon completed 41 of 56 passes for 432 yards as the Oilers amassed 583 total yards. The intrastate rivalry was witnessed by 63,001 fans, the largest crowd ever to see a football game in the Astrodome.

Dallas	10	3	3	7	0	—	23
Houston	0	10	3	10	3	—	26

Dall	—	Williams 18 blocked punt return (Willis kick)
Dall	—	FG Willis 35
Hou	—	Pinkett 1 run (Del Greco kick)
Hou	—	FG Del Greco 52
Dall	—	FG Willis 37
Hou	—	FG Del Greco 19
Dall	—	FG Willis 45
Hou	—	FG Del Greco 22
Hou	—	White 4 run (Del Greco kick)
Dall	—	Irvin 10 pass from Aikman (Willis kick)
Hou	—	FG Del Greco 23

Tampa Bay 30, Detroit 21 — at Tampa Stadium, attendance 37,742. Reggie Cobb rushed for a career-high 139 yards and 3 touchdowns as the Buccaneers upset the Lions. Steve Christie added 3 field goals, all within a span of 4:03 at the end of the second quarter, as Tampa Bay built a 23-7 halftime advantage. Cobb's 59-yard touchdown run late in the third quarter gave the Buccaneers a 30-14 lead. Barry Sanders ran for 118 yards and 2 touchdowns for the Lions. Erik Kramer passed for 248 yards but was intercepted twice and lost a pair of fumbles.

Detroit	7	0	7	7	—	21
Tampa Bay	7	16	7	0	—	30

TB	—	Cobb 1 run (Christie kick)
Det	—	Sanders 1 run (Murray kick)
TB	—	Cobb 3 run (Christie kick)
TB	—	FG Christie 29
TB	—	FG Christie 33
TB	—	FG Christie 30
Det	—	Sanders 5 run (Murray kick)
TB	—	Cobb 59 run (Christie kick)
Det	—	Kramer 1 run (Murray kick)

Indianapolis 28, N.Y. Jets 27 — at Giants Stadium, attendance 44,792. Jeff George passed for 239 yards and 3 touchdowns and Clarence Verdin returned the second-half kickoff 88 yards for a touchdown to lead the Colts to their first victory of the season. The Jets led 14-0 in the second quarter and threatened to break the game open but could not convert on a pair of scoring opportunities, settling for field-goal attempts that failed. With 1:07 left in the first half, Indianapolis snapped a touchdown drought of more than five games when George completed a 49-yard touchdown pass to Jessie Hester. George later threw 7-yard scoring passes to Hester and Bill Brooks just 1:30 apart in the third quarter, the latter coming after New York fumbled a kickoff. Ken O'Brien passed for 329 yards for the Jets, who had 436 yards of total offense, but had two drives stall inside the Colts' 10-yard line in the fourth quarter, forcing them to kick field goals.

Indianapolis	0	7	21	0	—	28
N.Y. Jets	7	7	7	6	—	27

Jets	—	Baxter 4 run (Leahy kick)
Jets	—	Burkett 15 pass from O'Brien (Leahy kick)
Ind	—	Hester 49 pass from George (Biasucci kick)
Ind	—	Verdin 88 kickoff return (Biasucci kick)
Jets	—	Baxter 1 run (Leahy kick)
Ind	—	Hester 7 pass from George (Biasucci kick)
Ind	—	Brooks 7 pass from George (Biasucci kick)
Jets	—	FG Leahy 22
Jets	—	FG Leahy 25

Kansas City 27, L.A. Rams 20 — at Anaheim Stadium, attendance 52,511. Derrick Thomas picked up a fumble and ran 23 yards for a touchdown late in the fourth quarter, then forced and recovered a fumble in the final minute to preserve the Chiefs' victory over the Rams. Los Angeles had tied the game 20-20 on a 17-yard touchdown pass from Jim Everett to Damone Johnson midway through the fourth quarter. But the Rams missed an opportunity to take the lead when Tony Zendejas—who had not missed a kick of any kind all season—failed to convert the extra point. With 2:25 left in the game, Kansas City's Deron Cherry forced the fumble by Robert Delpino that Thomas returned for the game-winning score. Everett, who completed 26 of 37 passes for 329 yards and 3 touchdowns, then drove the Rams to the Chiefs' 16-yard line with 40 seconds remaining. But on first down, Thomas sacked him, stripped the ball, and recovered.

Kansas City	7	7	6	7	—	27
L.A. Rams	0	14	0	6	—	20

KC	—	Hayes 6 pass from DeBerg (Lowery kick)
Rams	—	Johnson 1 pass from Everett (Zendejas kick)
KC	—	Word 1 run (Lowery kick)
Rams	—	Ellard 14 pass from Everett (Zendejas kick)
KC	—	FG Lowery 20
KC	—	FG Lowery 44
Rams	—	Johnson 17 pass from Everett (kick failed)
KC	—	D. Thomas 23 fumble recovery return (Lowery kick)

L.A. Raiders 17, Denver 16 — at Mile High Stadium, attendance 75,896. Scott Davis blocked an extra-point attempt midway through the fourth quarter and James FitzPatrick batted away a 48-yard field-goal try on the last play of the game as the Raiders held on to defeat the Broncos. Los Angeles, which was outgained 383-244, rallied from a 10-7 halftime deficit with 10 points in the third quarter, the key play a 23-yard touchdown pass from Jay Schroeder to Tim Brown. A 10-yard scoring pass from John Elway to Vance Johnson pulled Denver within a point with 8:37 left in the game, but Davis kept the Broncos from tying it when he swatted the extra-point try. After Karl Mecklenburg blocked a 36-yard field goal attempt by the Raiders' Jeff Jaeger at the 1:55 mark, Elway marched Denver into position for David Treadwell's ill-fated 3-point attempt as time ran out.

L.A. Raiders	7	0	10	0	—	17
Denver	3	7	0	6	—	16

Den	—	FG Treadwell 19
Raiders	—	Glover 11 pass from Allen (Jaeger kick)
Den	—	Elway 7 run (Treadwell kick)
Raiders	—	T. Brown 23 pass from Schroeder (Jaeger kick)
Raiders	—	FG Jaeger 20
Den	—	V. Johnson 10 pass from Elway (kick blocked)

N.Y. Giants 21, Phoenix 14 — at Sun Devil Stadium, attendance 50,048. Jeff Hostetler ran for 2 touchdowns as the defending Super Bowl-champion Giants snapped a two-game losing streak and kept their playoff hopes alive. Hostetler's first touchdown came on a 47-yard scramble in the first quarter. His second was a 4-yarder that culminated a 91-yard, 18-play drive that consumed 11:14 at the outset of the third quarter and gave New York a 21-7 lead. Stan Gelbaugh, the World League's offensive most valuable player in 1991, relieved starter Tom Tupa for Phoenix, and completed back-to-back passes, the second a 34-yard touchdown to Ricky Proehl, for a 2-play, 57-yard scoring drive that pulled Phoenix within 21-14 with 2:24 left. But when the Cardinals got the ball back with 1:53 remaining, Gelbaugh's first pass was intercepted by the Giants' Everson Walls at the New York 47. Rodney Hampton ran for 99 yards on 24 carries for the Giants.

N.Y. Giants	7	7	7	0	—	21
Phoenix	0	7	0	7	—	14

Giants	—	Hostetler 47 run (Allegre kick)
Giants	—	Hampton 1 run (Allegre kick)
Phx	—	Johnson 3 run (Davis kick)
Giants	—	Hostetler 4 run (Allegre kick)
Phx	—	Proehl 34 pass from Gelbaugh (Davis kick)

Philadelphia 32, Cleveland 30 — at Cleveland Stadium,

attendance 72,086. Jim McMahon completed a 5-yard touchdown pass to Calvin Williams with 5:19 remaining and the Eagles wiped out a 23-0 deficit to rally past the Browns. Matt Stover made a career-best 50-yard field goal early in the game, and before the first quarter was over, Cleveland also had scored on a 42-yard interception return by Eric Turner and a screen pass that Leroy Hoard turned into a 65-yard touchdown. The Browns scored again in the opening seconds of the second quarter, and by halftime had 30 points against Philadelphia's top-ranked defense. But Philadelphia rallied behind McMahon, whose status was questionable up until game time because of a sore arm. The veteran quarterback completed 26 of 43 passes for 341 yards and 3 touchdowns. The game-winner came three plays after Britt Hager recovered Webster Slaughter's fumbled punt at Cleveland's 2-yard line. Bernie Kosar passed for 246 yards and 3 touchdowns for the Browns. He also extended his streak of consecutive passes without an interception to 308, breaking Bart Starr's NFL record of 294. The streak ended when Ben Smith intercepted one of Kosar's passes in the second quarter.

Philadelphia	0	17	6	9	—	32
Cleveland	16	14	0	0	—	30

Cleve— FG Stover 50
Cleve— Turner 42 interception return (Stover kick)
Cleve— Hoard 65 pass from Kosar (kick failed)
Cleve— Slaughter 18 pass from Kosar (Stover kick)
Phil — Jackson 18 pass from McMahon (Ruzek kick)
Phil — Barnett 70 pass from McMahon (Ruzek kick)
Phil — FG Ruzek 21
Cleve— Langhorne 24 pass from Kosar (Stover kick)
Phil — FG Ruzek 37
Phil — FG Ruzek 24
Phil — FG Ruzek 19
Phil — Williams 5 pass from McMahon (kick failed)

Pittsburgh 33, Cincinnati 27 — at Riverfront Stadium, attendance 55,503. Eric Green caught a 26-yard touchdown pass from Neil O'Donnell 6:32 into overtime to give the Steelers the victory. The winning score came three plays after linebacker Greg Lloyd stripped the ball from the Bengals' Ickey Woods and returned the fumble 19 yards to the Cincinnati 44-yard line. The Bengals, who led at one point in the first half 17-3, still had a 24-13 advantage midway through the fourth quarter, until O'Donnell tossed a 35-yard touchdown pass to Ernie Mills. O'Donnell, who completed 24 of 39 passes for 309 yards and 3 touchdowns and was not intercepted, then passed 12 yards to Louis Lipps with 1:24 left to give Pittsburgh the lead for the first time. Cincinnati forced the extra session when Jim Breech kicked a 47-yard field goal with five seconds to go. Boomer Esiason completed 32 of 43 passes for 361 yards and 1 touchdown for the Bengals. Eddie Brown had 10 receptions for Cincinnati.

Pittsburgh	0	6	7	14	6	—	33
Cincinnati	10	7	0	10	0	—	27

Cin— FG Breech 29
Cin— Woods 4 run (Breech kick)
Pitt— FG Anderson 44
Cin— Holman 18 pass from Esiason (Breech kick)
Pitt— FG Anderson 46
Pitt— J. Williams 38 fumble recovery return (Anderson kick)
Cin— Woods 1 run (Breech kick)
Pitt— Mills 35 pass from O'Donnell (Anderson kick)
Pitt— Lipps 12 pass from O'Donnell (Anderson kick)
Cin— FG Breech 47
Pitt— E. Green 26 pass from O'Donnell

New Orleans 10, San Francisco 3 — at Louisiana Superdome, attendance 68,591. Steve Walsh threw an 8-yard touchdown pass to Eric Martin for the only touchdown of the game as the Saints beat the 49ers in a defensive struggle. New Orleans managed only 10 first downs and 191 yards of total offense, but the second-quarter touchdown and Morten Andersen's 21-yard field goal in the third quarter provided the margin of difference as the Saints' relentless defense limited San Francisco to only 216 total yards. The 49ers, playing with third-string quarterback Steve Bono, scored their only points on a 32-yard field goal by Mike Cofer. That came on a 2-yard drive after former Saint Dave Waymer intercepted a pass and returned it 42 yards.

San Francisco	3	0	0	0	—	3
New Orleans	0	7	3	0	—	10

SF — FG Cofer 32
NO— E. Martin 8 pass from Walsh (Andersen kick)
NO— FG Andersen 21

San Diego 17, Seattle 14 — at San Diego Jack Murphy Stadium, attendance 43,597. John Carney kicked a club-record 54-yard field goal with 18 seconds to go in the game to give the Chargers the victory. Carney's kick spoiled a fourth-quarter comeback by the Seahawks, who had rallied from a 14-0 deficit to tie the game on a pair of touchdown passes from Dave Krieg, the second of which was a 20-yarder to Jeff Chadwick with 5:09 left. But Kitrick Taylor's 29-yard punt return to the Seattle 33-yard line positioned San Diego for Carney's game-winning kick. Krieg completed 28 of 38 passes for 376 yards and became the thirty-first quarterback in league history to surpass the 25,000-yard mark in career passing. Brian Blades caught 8 of Krieg's passes for 131 yards, while the Chargers' Anthony Miller had 5 receptions for 124 yards.

Seattle	0	0	0	14	—	14
San Diego	7	7	0	3	—	17

SD — Butts 17 run (Carney kick)
SD — Butts 1 run (Carney kick)
Sea— Williams 13 pass from Krieg (Kasay kick)
Sea— Chadwick 20 pass from Krieg (Kasay kick)
SD — FG Carney 54

Sunday Night, November 10

Miami 30, New England 20 — at Joe Robbie Stadium, attendance 56,065. Dan Marino's 32-yard touchdown pass to Mark Clayton broke a 20-20 tie with 1:47 left in the game to help the Dolphins beat the Patriots. Pete Stoyanovich added a 44-yard field goal in the final minute after New England gave up possession on downs. Miami led at one point 20-6, but the Patriots rallied to tie the game on Hugh Millen touchdown passes of 40 yards to Irving Fryar and 5 yards to Marv Cook. Millen completed 20 of 26 passes for 257 yards. Marino was 19 of 29 for 263 yards. Stoyanovich kicked 3 field goals.

New England	3	3	7	7	—	20
Miami	7	10	3	10	—	30

NE — FG Baumann 44
Mia— Clayton 31 pass from Marino (Stoyanovich kick)
Mia— Banks 5 pass from Marino (Stoyanovich kick)
Mia— FG Stoyanovich 21
NE — FG Baumann 37
Mia— FG Stoyanovich 42
NE — Fryar 40 pass from Millen (Baumann kick)
NE — Cook 5 pass from Millen (Baumann kick)
Mia— Clayton 32 pass from Marino (Stoyanovich kick)
Mia— FG Stoyanovich 44

Monday, November 11

Chicago 34, Minnesota 17 — at Metrodome, attendance 59,001. Neal Anderson rushed for a pair of touchdowns and the Bears strengthened their lead in the NFC Central Division by defeating the Vikings. After a 29-yard touchdown pass from Rich Gannon to Anthony Carter pulled the Vikings to within 20-17 late in the third quarter, the Bears broke the game open. Anderson scored on a 24-yard touchdown run early in the fourth quarter, and two plays later, Lemuel Stinson intercepted Gannon's pass and returned it 34 yards for a touchdown. Anderson rushed for 91 yards and Brad Muster had 56 for the Bears, who ran for 191 yards and maintained possession for 38:20 to the Vikings' 21:40.

Chicago	0	17	3	14	—	34
Minnesota	7	3	7	0	—	17

Minn— Nelson 6 run (Reveiz kick)
Chi — N. Anderson 6 run (Butler kick)
Chi — Morgan 7 pass from Harbaugh (Butler kick)
Minn— FG Reveiz 20
Chi — FG Butler 50
Chi — FG Butler 41
Minn— A. Carter 29 pass from Gannon (Reveiz kick)
Chi — N. Anderson 24 run (Butler kick)
Chi — Stinson 34 interception return (Butler kick)

Twelfth Week Summaries

Standings

American Football Conference

Eastern Division

	W	L	T	Pct.	Pts.	OP
Buffalo	10	1	0	.909	342	238
N.Y. Jets	6	5	0	.545	231	206
Miami	5	6	0	.455	207	248
New England	3	8	0	.273	156	223
Indianapolis	1	10	0	.091	106	261
Central Division						
Houston	9	2	0	.818	298	168
Cleveland	4	7	0	.364	211	232
Pittsburgh	4	7	0	.364	216	259
Cincinnati	1	10	0	.091	170	312
Western Division						
Denver	8	3	0	.727	216	179
Kansas City	7	4	0	.636	227	160
L.A. Raiders	7	4	0	.636	203	192
Seattle	5	6	0	.455	199	173
San Diego	3	8	0	.273	195	242

National Football Conference

Eastern Division

	W	L	T	Pct.	Pts.	OP
Washington	11	0	0	1.000	361	139
Dallas	6	5	0	.545	219	225
N.Y. Giants	6	5	0	.545	181	183
Philadelphia	6	5	0	.545	182	163
Phoenix	4	8	0	.333	146	239
Central Division						
Chicago	9	2	0	.818	212	172
Detroit	7	4	0	.636	217	224
Minnesota	6	6	0	.500	234	207
Green Bay	2	9	0	.182	171	213
Tampa Bay	2	9	0	.182	130	255
Western Division						
New Orleans	9	2	0	.818	229	124
Atlanta	6	5	0	.545	219	229
San Francisco	5	6	0	.455	218	155
L.A. Rams	3	8	0	.273	181	256

Sunday, November 17

Chicago 31, Indianapolis 17 — at Hoosier Dome, attendance 60,519. Jim Harbaugh threw a pair of touchdown passes in the third quarter to break a 10-10 tie and lead the Bears to the victory. Dean Biasucci's 56-yard field goal with three seconds left in the first half gave the Colts a tie at the intermission. But with 6:34 left in the third quarter, Harbaugh completed a 13-yard touchdown pass to Brad Muster to give Chicago a 17-10 lead. Less than three minutes later, Harbaugh hit Anthony Morgan on a quick slant pass for an 84-yard scoring play. Muster ran for 101 yards on 15 carries and caught 6 passes for the Bears. Harbaugh completed 18 of 32 passes for 287 yards. Bill Brooks caught 7 passes for 106 yards for the Colts.

Chicago	7	3	14	7	—	31
Indianapolis	7	3	0	7	—	17

Ind— Hester 4 pass from George (Biasucci kick)
Chi— Harbaugh 6 run (Butler kick)
Chi— FG Butler 21
Ind— FG Biasucci 56
Chi— Muster 13 pass from Harbaugh (Butler kick)
Chi— Morgan 84 pass from Harbaugh (Butler kick)
Ind— Brooks 9 pass from George (Biasucci kick)
Chi— Muster 9 run (Butler kick)

Philadelphia 17, Cincinnati 10 — at Veterans Stadium, attendance 63,189. The Eagles' defense intercepted 3 passes, recovered a fumble, and posted 6 sacks in Philadelphia's third consecutive victory. James Joseph ran 1 yard for a touchdown early in the fourth quarter to break a 7-7 tie and provide the winning points. Reggie White intercepted a pass and Wes Hopkins intercepted 2 passes for Philadelphia. The win moved the Eagles into a three-way tie for second place in the NFC Eastern Division and vaulted them back into playoff contention after a 3-5 start.

Cincinnati	0	7	0	3	—	10
Philadelphia	0	7	0	10	—	17

Cin— Brooks 16 pass from Esiason (Breech kick)
Phil— Williams 10 pass from McMahon (Ruzek kick)
Phil— Joseph 1 run (Ruzek kick)
Phil— FG Ruzek 37
Cin— FG Breech 38

N.Y. Giants 22, Dallas 9 — at Giants Stadium, attendance 76,410. The Giants, using the same formula that propelled them to a Super Bowl victory one year earlier, pounded out a convincing win over the Cowboys. New York rushed for 138 yards, maintained possession for more than 36 minutes, and kept Dallas out of the end zone. The Giants also got 3 field goals from Matt Bahr and a 1-yard touchdown run by Rodney Hampton as they forged a 16-3 lead at halftime. Jeff Hostetler's 35-yard touchdown pass to Mark Ingram with 10:08 remaining effectively put the game out of reach. Lawrence Taylor recovered a pair of fumbles to set up field goals in the first half.

Dallas	0	3	6	0	—	9
N.Y. Giants	6	10	0	6	—	22

Giants— FG Bahr 27
Giants— FG Bahr 37
Dall — FG Willis 22
Giants— Hampton 1 run (Bahr kick)
Giants— FG Bahr 22
Dall — FG Willis 31
Dall — FG Willis 18
Giants— Ingram 35 pass from Hostetler (kick failed)

Denver 24, Kansas City 20 — at Arrowhead Stadium, attendance 74,661. Gaston Green ran for 133 yards, including 60 on a second-quarter touchdown run, and the Broncos completed a season sweep of the Chiefs and moved back into sole possession of first place in the AFC Western Division. Denver trailed 13-10 in the third quarter until John Elway threw a 29-yard touchdown pass to Mark Jackson. Fifty-nine seconds later, Charles Dimry intercepted a Steve DeBerg pass and returned it 26 yards for the touchdown that gave the Broncos a 24-13 lead. DeBerg, who passed for 207 yards but was intercepted 4 times, was replaced at that point by Mark Vlasic, who threw a touchdown pass midway through the fourth quarter to make the score close. Derrick Thomas had 3 sacks for Kansas City.

Denver	3	7	14	0	—	24
Kansas City	0	10	3	7	—	20

Den— FG Treadwell 37
KC — Okoye 7 run (Lowery kick)
Den— Green 60 run (Treadwell kick)

KC —FG Lowery 19
KC —FG Lowery 27
Den—Jackson 29 pass from Elway (Treadwell kick)
Den—Dimry 26 interception return (Treadwell kick)
KC —Barnett 8 pass from Vlasic (Lowery kick)

Detroit 21, L.A. Rams 10 — at Pontiac Silverdome, attendance 60,873. Erik Kramer threw 3 touchdown passes, 2 of them in the fourth quarter, as the Lions rallied to hand the Rams their fifth consecutive defeat. Los Angeles took a 10-7 lead through three quarters, but on the first play of the fourth period, Kramer completed an 11-yard touchdown pass to Robert Clark, his second of the day, to put Detroit ahead. On the next series, Ray Crockett intercepted Jim Everett's pass and returned it 42 yards to the Rams' 33. Three plays later, Kramer teamed with Mike Farr for a 34-yard touchdown. Kramer completed 15 of 25 passes for 185 yards. Everett was 26 of 45 for 308 yards, including a 19-yard touchdown to Henry Ellard in the third quarter.

L.A. Rams	3	0	7	0	—	10
Detroit	0	7	0	14	—	21

Rams—FG Zendejas 27
Det —Clark 6 pass from Kramer (Murray kick)
Rams—Ellard 19 pass from Everett (Zendejas kick)
Det —Clark 11 pass from Kramer (Murray kick)
Det —Farr 34 pass from Kramer (Murray kick)

Minnesota 35, Green Bay 21 — at Lambeau Field, attendance 57,614. Down 21-14 at halftime, the Vikings dominated the second half to rally past the Packers. Minnesota pieced together lengthy, time-consuming touchdown drives of 79, 80, and 98 yards after the intermission and controlled the ball for more than 24 of the game's final 30 minutes. Green Bay, which had 262 total yards in the first half, ran only three plays in the third quarter and finished with just 38 total yards in the second half. Herschel Walker, who rushed for 95 yards, ran five yards for a score to break a 21-21 tie 49 seconds into the fourth quarter. The Vikings then drove nearly the length of the field to Rich Gannon's game-clinching, 5-yard touchdown run with 4:26 left in the game.

Minnesota	7	7	7	14	—	35
Green Bay	14	7	0	0	—	21

GB —Workman 1 run (Jacke kick)
Minn—C. Carter 29 pass from Gannon (Reveiz kick)
GB —Wilson 75 pass from Tomczak (Jacke kick)
Minn—M. Jones 3 pass from Gannon (Reveiz kick)
GB —Harris 1 pass from Tomczak (Jacke kick)
Minn—C. Carter 17 pass from Gannon (Reveiz kick)
Minn—Walker 5 run (Reveiz kick)
Minn—Gannon 5 run (Reveiz kick)

San Diego 24, New Orleans 21 — at San Diego Jack Murphy Stadium, attendance 48,420. John Carney kicked a 19-yard field goal with five seconds left—his second game-winner in the final minute in as many weeks—to lift the Chargers past the Saints. New Orleans, behind 2 touchdown passes from Steve Walsh and Frank Warren's 37-yard return of a blocked punt by teammate Wayne Martin, led 21-14 late in the game. But San Diego's Marion Butts, who gained 92 yards on 15 carries, ran five yards for the tying touchdown with 3:04 remaining. After forcing the Saints to punt, the Chargers marched 70 yards in 1:24, with John Friesz's 29-yard pass to Chris Samuels positioning them for Carney's winning kick. One week earlier, Carney beat the Seattle Seahawks with a club-record 54-yard field goal with 18 seconds remaining. Nate Lewis returned a second-quarter kickoff 95 yards for a touchdown for San Diego.

New Orleans	7	14	0	0	—	21
San Diego	7	7	0	10	—	24

NO—Jordan 1 pass from Walsh (Andersen kick)
SD—Hendrickson 3 run (Carney kick)
NO—Warren 37 blocked punt return (Andersen kick)
SD—Lewis 95 kickoff return (Carney kick)
NO—Early 38 pass from Walsh (Andersen kick)
SD—Butts 5 run (Carney kick)
SD—FG Carney 19

N.Y. Jets 28, New England 21 — at Foxboro Stadium, attendance 30,743. Kyle Clifton led a swarm of Jets who stopped the Patriots' Jon Vaughn on the 1-yard line as time ran out, and New York held off a furious fourth-quarter rally to defeat New England. The Jets led 21-0 until the Patriots exploded for 3 touchdowns in the final period. The final 2 scores came on short touchdown runs by Vaughn just 1:48 apart, and each after New York's Brad Baxter lost fumbles deep in Jets' territory. But Ken O'Brien, who passed for 309 yards and 3 touchdowns, marched New York 71 yards to the winning score, a 3-yard touchdown pass to Trevor Matich with 57 seconds left. Matich, an offensive lineman, lined up at tight end because of injuries to other players. Hugh Millen passed for 372 yards and 1 touchdown and tried to rally New England again after the tying score, driving the Patriots from their own 27 to the Jets' 1 with one second left before Vaughn was stopped on the final play. Al Toon caught 9 passes for 127 yards for New York. Irving Fryar had 143 yards on 8 receptions for New England.

N.Y. Jets	7	7	7	7	—	28
New England	0	0	0	21	—	21

Jets—A. Brown 1 run (Leahy kick)
Jets—Burkett 7 pass from O'Brien (Leahy kick)
Jets—Mathis 35 pass from O'Brien (Leahy kick)
NE —Fryar 56 pass from Millen (Baumann kick)
NE —Vaughn 3 run (Baumann kick)
NE —Vaughn 2 run (Baumann kick)
Jets—Matich 3 pass from O'Brien (Leahy kick)

San Francisco 14, Phoenix 10 — at Candlestick Park, attendance 50,180. Todd Bowles broke up Stan Gelbaugh's pass in the end zone on fourth down with 30 seconds remaining and the 49ers held off the Cardinals, dealing Phoenix its fourth consecutive defeat. Neither team was productive offensively, but San Francisco got short touchdown runs from Keith Henderson and Tom Rathman to take a 14-3 lead into the final minutes. But Gelbaugh, the former World League offensive most valuable player making his first NFL start, passed 26 yards to Ernie Jones to pull the Cardinals within 14-10 with 6:07 left in the game. After a 49ers punt, Phoenix moved from its own 41-yard line to the San Francisco 9 before a holding penalty and 3 incompletions in the end zone stalled the drive.

Phoenix	0	0	3	7	—	10
San Francisco	0	7	0	7	—	14

SF —Henderson 2 run (Cofer kick)
Phx—FG Davis 35
SF —Rathman 1 run (Cofer kick)
Phx—E. Jones 26 pass from Gelbaugh (Davis kick)

L.A. Raiders 31, Seattle 7 — at Los Angeles Memorial Coliseum, attendance 49,317. Jay Schroeder completed 16 of 19 passes for 237 yards and 3 touchdowns as the Raiders easily handled the Seahawks. Jeff Jaeger kicked a 51-yard field goal on Los Angeles's first possession, and the Raiders scored touchdowns each of the next three times they had the ball to take a 24-7 lead at halftime. The last touchdown of the half came on a screen pass to tight end Ethan Horton. A converted running back, Horton raced 51 yards to score with 33 seconds to go in the second quarter. He had 7 catches for 123 yards in the game. Anthony Smith and Scott Davis each had 2½ sacks for the Raiders.

Seattle	0	7	0	0	—	7
L.A. Raiders	3	21	0	7	—	31

Raiders—FG Jaeger 51
Raiders—Gault 4 pass from Schroeder (Jaeger kick)
Raiders—Glover 1 pass from Schroeder (Jaeger kick)
Sea —Tice 6 pass from Krieg (Kasay kick)
Raiders—Horton 51 pass from Schroeder (Jaeger kick)
Raiders—McCallum 1 run (Jaeger kick)

Atlanta 43, Tampa Bay 7 — at Atlanta-Fulton County Stadium, attendance 41,274. Chris Miller threw 3 touchdown passes to Andre Rison in a span of less than six minutes as the Falcons erupted for a club-record 33 points in the second quarter en route to an easy victory over the Buccaneers. Atlanta had only 3 points in the period until Steve Broussard started the onslaught with a 5-yard touchdown run 7:06 before halftime. Just 21 seconds later, Brian Jordan sacked Tampa Bay's Vinny Testaverde, forcing a fumble that rolled out of the end zone for a safety and a 12-0 lead. Miller then passed 39 yards for a touchdown to Rison at the 5:49 mark, and connected twice more, from 12 and 15 yards, in the final minute of the half. Atlanta's Deion Sanders returned an interception 31 yards to set up the latter touchdown. Oliver Barnett ran 75 yards with a recovered fumble for a touchdown in the fourth quarter for the Falcons.

Tampa Bay	0	0	0	7	—	7
Atlanta	0	33	3	7	—	43

Atl—FG Johnson 31
Atl—Broussard 5 run (Johnson kick)
Atl—Safety, Testaverde fumbled out of end zone
Atl—Rison 39 pass from Miller (Johnson kick)
Atl—Rison 12 pass from Miller (Johnson kick)
Atl—Rison 15 pass from Miller (Johnson kick)
Atl—FG Johnson 49
Atl—Barnett 75 fumble recovery return (Johnson kick)
TB—Dawsey 4 pass from Carlson (Christie kick)

Washington 41, Pittsburgh 14 — at Three Rivers Stadium, attendance 56,813. Mark Rypien passed for 325 yards and 2 touchdowns and the Redskins became the first team to clinch a playoff berth by raising their record to 11-0 with a rout of the Steelers. Washington became the ninth NFL team in all and the first since the Chicago Bears in 1985 to win each of its first 11 games. The Redskins amassed 462 total yards and led 27-0 after three quarters. Ricky Ervins ran for 84 yards and Art Monk caught 8 passes for 130 yards for Washington. Pittsburgh's Neil O'Donnell completed 23 of 36 passes for 289 yards and had 2 touchdown passes in the fourth quarter.

Washington	7	10	10	14	—	41
Pittsburgh	0	0	0	14	—	14

Wash—Riggs 1 run (Lohmiller kick)
Wash—FG Lohmiller 36
Wash—Monk 11 pass from Rypien (Lohmiller kick)
Wash—FG Lohmiller 41
Wash—Riggs 1 run (Lohmiller kick)
Pitt —Cooper 5 pass from O'Donnell (Anderson kick)
Pitt —Stone 40 pass from O'Donnell (Anderson kick)
Wash—Clark 49 pass from Rypien (Lohmiller kick)
Wash—Sanders 40 pass from Rutledge (Lohmiller kick)

Sunday Night, November 17

Houston 28, Cleveland 24 — at Astrodome, attendance 58,155. Warren Moon threw a 1-yard touchdown pass to Drew Hill with nine seconds left, giving the Oilers the victory over the Browns. Moon's pass was his eighth consecutive completion on the 11-play, 84-yard drive. He finished with 31 completions in 44 attempts for 399 yards and 3 touchdowns. Cleveland led 17-7 until Moon passed 40 yards to Hill for a touchdown late in the third quarter, then connected with Pat Coleman for a 4-yard score and a 21-17 lead with 9:06 left in the game. But Bernie Kosar, who was 21 of 34 for 279 yards and 2 touchdowns, completed a 40-yard scoring pass to Reggie Langhorne with 4:17 remaining to put Cleveland back ahead. Hill finished with 11 catches for 144 yards. Leroy Hoard had 10 catches for 107 yards for the Browns.

Cleveland	7	7	3	7	—	24
Houston	0	7	7	14	—	28

Cleve—Hoard 14 pass from Kosar (Stover kick)
Hou —Pinkett 5 run (Del Greco kick)
Cleve—Morris 5 run (Stover kick)
Cleve—FG Stover 55
Hou —Hill 40 pass from Moon (Del Greco kick)
Hou —Coleman 4 pass from Moon (Del Greco kick)
Cleve—Langhorne 40 pass from Kosar (Stover kick)
Hou —Hill 1 pass from Moon (Del Greco kick)

Monday, November 18

Buffalo 41, Miami 27 — at Joe Robbie Stadium, attendance 71,062. Thurman Thomas ran for 135 yards and scored 2 touchdowns to power the Bills past the Dolphins. Buffalo also got considerable help from its defense, which forced 5 turnovers, 3 of which led to 17 points. The game was tied 10-10 in the second quarter when Cornelius Bennett sacked Miami's Dan Marino, forcing a fumble that Bennett picked up and ran six yards for the touchdown that put the Bills ahead to stay. Marino's pass on the next play was intercepted by Kirby Jackson to set up Scott Norwood's 21-yard field goal to give Buffalo a 20-13 halftime lead. Things got worse for Miami as Aaron Craver fumbled the second-half kickoff which Hal Garner recovered to set up a 5-yard touchdown pass from Jim Kelly to Andre Reed. Kelly completed 20 of 28 passes for 185 yards and 3 touchdowns. Kenneth Davis added 98 rushing yards as the Bills amassed 262 yards on the ground. Marino passed for 326 yards and 2 touchdowns.

Buffalo	10	10	14	7	—	41
Miami	3	10	7	7	—	27

Mia—FG Stoyanovich 33
Buff—Thomas 10 pass from Kelly (Norwood kick)
Buff—FG Norwood 42
Mia—Smith 1 run (Stoyanovich kick)
Buff—Bennett 6 fumble recovery return (Norwood kick)
Buff—FG Norwood 21
Mia—FG Stoyanovich 28
Buff—Reed 5 pass from Kelly (Norwood kick)
Buff—Thomas 1 run (Norwood kick)
Mia—Baty 1 pass from Marino (Stoyanovich kick)
Buff—Reed 23 pass from Kelly (Norwood kick)
Mia—Martin 8 pass from Marino (Stoyanovich kick)

Thirteenth Week Summaries

Standings

American Football Conference

Eastern Division

	W	L	T	Pct.	Pts.	OP
Buffalo	10	2	0	.833	355	254
N.Y. Jets	7	5	0	.583	255	209
Miami	6	6	0	.500	223	261
New England	4	8	0	.333	172	236
Indianapolis	1	11	0	.083	116	275

Central Division

Houston	9	3	0	.750	312	194
Cleveland	5	7	0	.417	231	247
Pittsburgh	5	7	0	.417	242	273
Cincinnati	1	11	0	.083	184	350

Western Division

Denver	8	4	0	.667	226	192
L.A. Raiders	8	4	0	.667	241	206
Kansas City	7	5	0	.583	242	180
Seattle	6	6	0	.500	212	183
San Diego	3	9	0	.250	198	266

National Football Conference

Eastern Division

	W	L	T	Pct.	Pts.	OP
Washington	11	1	0	.917	382	163
Dallas	7	5	0	.583	243	246
N.Y. Giants	7	5	0	.583	202	197
Philadelphia	7	5	0	.583	216	177
Phoenix	4	9	0	.308	160	273
Central Division						
Chicago	9	3	0	.750	225	188
Detroit	8	4	0	.667	251	238
Minnesota	6	7	0	.462	248	241
Green Bay	3	9	0	.250	185	223
Tampa Bay	2	10	0	.167	144	276
Western Division						
New Orleans	9	3	0	.750	249	147
Atlanta	7	5	0	.583	242	249
San Francisco	6	6	0	.500	251	165
L.A. Rams	3	9	0	.250	191	289

Sunday, November 24

New England 16, Buffalo 13 — at Foxboro Stadium, attendance 47,053. Hugh Millen's 2-yard touchdown run with 11:40 left in the game stood up as the Patriots stunned the AFC East-leading Bills. The victory snapped New England's four-game losing streak and stopped Buffalo's winning string at five. After falling behind 10-0 in the first half, the Patriots rallied, and trailed just 10-9 at halftime after a 50-yard touchdown pass from Millen to Irving Fryar with 27 seconds to go in the second quarter. Millen's 34-yard pass to Fryar was the key play on the game-winning 65-yard drive. The Bills had a chance to win or tie in the final minute, driving from their own 20 to the New England 35. But Jim Kelly, who was intercepted 4 times and sacked 4 times, was sacked on third down and threw incomplete on fourth down.

Buffalo	3	7	3	0	—	13
New England	0	9	0	7	—	16

Buff— FG Norwood 23
Buff— Thomas 10 pass from Kelly (Norwood kick)
NE — FG Baumann 46
NE — Fryar 50 pass from Millen (kick blocked)
Buff— FG Norwood 29
NE — Millen 2 run (Baumann kick)

Dallas 24, Washington 21 — at RFK Stadium, attendance 55,561. Steve Beuerlein came off the bench to lead two fourth-quarter scoring drives as the Cowboys handed the Redskins their first defeat of the season. Starter Troy Aikman passed for 204 yards in just over one half of play, and his 34-yard desperation pass to Alvin Harper with four seconds left in the first half gave Dallas a 14-7 lead. But in the third quarter, Aikman sprained a knee and was replaced by Beuerlein. Early in the fourth period, Beuerlein threw a 24-yard touchdown pass to Michael Irvin. After Washington pulled within 21-14 with 8:21 remaining, the Cowboys consumed more than seven of the remaining minutes on a 15-play drive that ended with Ken Willis's 42-yard field goal with 1:14 to go. Beuerlein completed 7 of 12 passes for 109 yards. Emmitt Smith ran for 132 yards on 34 carries for Dallas, which totaled 399 yards and maintained possession for nearly 39 minutes.

Dallas	0	14	0	10	—	24
Washington	7	0	0	14	—	21

Wash— Mayhew 31 interception return (Lohmiller kick)
Dall — Smith 32 run (Willis kick)
Dall — Harper 34 pass from Aikman (Willis kick)
Dall — Irvin 24 pass from Beuerlein (Willis kick)
Wash— Riggs 1 run (Lohmiller kick)
Dall — FG Willis 42
Wash— Sanders 29 pass from Rypien (Lohmiller kick)

Seattle 13, Denver 10 — at Kingdome, attendance 60,430. John L. Williams ran for 109 yards on 17 carries, but it was the defense that dominated in the Seahawks' victory. Seattle forged a 13-0 halftime advantage on 2 John Kasay field goals and a 4-yard touchdown pass from Dave Krieg to Jeff Chadwick. The Seahawks drove only two and four yards to Kasay's field goals, which came after a fumble recovery by Jacob Green and an interception by Robert Blackmon. Denver got back in the game when Mike Croel sacked Krieg, forcing a fumble that Warren Powers scooped up and returned 22 yards for a touchdown just 52 seconds into the third quarter. David Treadwell's field goal midway through the period trimmed the Broncos' deficit to 13-10, but the Seahawks' defense held down the stretch, twice stopping Denver on downs in Seattle territory in the final five minutes.

Denver	0	0	10	0	—	10
Seattle	3	10	0	0	—	13

Sea— FG Kasay 36
Sea— Chadwick 4 pass from Krieg (Kasay kick)
Sea— FG Kasay 42
Den— Powers 22 fumble recovery return (Treadwell kick)
Den— FG Treadwell 23

Detroit 34, Minnesota 14 — at Metrodome, attendance 51,644. Barry Sanders led the Lions by rushing for a club-record 220 yards and 4 touchdowns and in the process became only the eighth player in NFL history to rush for more than 1,000 yards in each of his first three seasons. Detroit led just 10-7 in the third quarter when Sanders scored on a 45-yard run with 6:51 remaining in the period. After Ray Crockett intercepted a Rich Gannon pass on the next series—1 of 5 Minnesota turnovers in Lions territory—Sanders scored from four yards out to make it 24-7. Sanders also had scoring runs of 17 yards in the first quarter and nine yards in the fourth period. Cris Carter totaled 116 yards on 7 catches for the Vikings. Minnesota's Steve Jordan caught 3 passes to give him a club-record 401 for his career. By winning, the Lions moved within one game of first-place Chicago in the NFC Central Division, and severely hampered the Vikings' playoff chances.

Detroit	7	3	14	10	—	34
Minnesota	0	7	0	7	—	14

Det — Sanders 17 run (Murray kick)
Minn— A. Carter 25 pass from Nelson (Reveiz kick)
Det — FG Murray 37
Det — Sanders 45 run (Murray kick)
Det — Sanders 4 run (Murray kick)
Minn— Walker 1 run (Reveiz kick)
Det — Sanders 9 run (Murray kick)
Det — FG Murray 50

Pittsburgh 26, Houston 14 — at Three Rivers Stadium, attendance 45,795. The Steelers' defense intercepted 5 of Warren Moon's passes and forced him to fumble once, as Pittsburgh kept the Oilers from clinching the AFC Central Division title. The Steelers' offense then converted those turnovers into 16 points. Gary Anderson kicked 4 field goals, and Neil O'Donnell threw a 43-yard touchdown pass to Dwight Stone with 51 seconds left in the first half to give Pittsburgh a 16-7 lead. Thomas Everett and Shawn Vincent each had 2 interceptions for the Steelers. Moon completed 24 of 48 passes for 324 yards and 2 touchdowns, but 20 mile-per-hour winds and a temperature of 12 degrees with the wind-chill factor contributed to his 5 interceptions.

Houston	0	7	0	7	—	14
Pittsburgh	6	10	7	3	—	26

Pitt — FG Anderson 20
Pitt — FG Anderson 28
Hou— Givins 10 pass from Moon (Del Greco kick)
Pitt — FG Anderson 33
Pitt — Stone 43 pass from O'Donnell (Anderson kick)
Pitt — W. Williams 1 run (Anderson kick)
Hou— Jeffires 15 pass from Moon (Del Greco kick)
Pitt — FG Anderson 24

Green Bay 14, Indianapolis 10 — at Milwaukee County Stadium, attendance 42,132. Mike Tomczak ran 2 yards for a touchdown early in the second half and the Packers held on to beat the Colts. Vince Workman's 1-yard run in the first quarter gave Green Bay the lead and Tomczak, who set up his own score with a 48-yard run, made it 14-3 with 9:08 left in the third quarter. Indianapolis's Jeff George passed 6 yards to Bill Brooks with 4:46 left in the game to make it 14-10, but after the Colts drove to the Packers' 20-yard line in the final moments, Mark Murphy sacked George for a 13-yard loss on third down and George threw incomplete on fourth down. Brooks had 10 catches for 70 yards for Indianapolis. Green Bay totaled only 192 yards, the Colts just 189.

Indianapolis	0	3	0	7	—	10
Green Bay	7	0	7	0	—	14

GB— Workman 1 run (Jacke kick)
Ind— FG Biasucci 35
GB— Tomczak 2 run (Jacke kick)
Ind— Brooks 6 pass from George (Biasucci kick)

Cleveland 20, Kansas City 15 — at Cleveland Stadium, attendance 63,991. Running back Leroy Hoard scored 2 touchdowns as the Browns beat the Chiefs. Hoard ran 1 yard for a touchdown in the first quarter, then took a short pass from Bernie Kosar and went 71 yards for the score that gave Cleveland a 17-0 lead early in the third quarter. Kansas City rallied, and eventually pulled within five points on a 5-yard touchdown pass from Steve DeBerg to Emile Harry with 2:52 remaining in the game, but could get no closer. The Chiefs amassed 389 total yards to only 281 for the Browns, but were victimized by their own mistakes. DeBerg, who passed for 319 yards, threw 3 interceptions, and Kansas City lost 3 fumbles—2 inside the Browns' 5-yard line. Harry caught 11 passes for 159 yards.

Kansas City	0	0	3	12	—	15
Cleveland	0	10	10	0	—	20

Cleve— Hoard 1 run (Stover kick)
Cleve— FG Stover 34
Cleve— Hoard 71 pass from Kosar (Stover kick)
KC — FG Lowery 34
Cleve— FG Stover 21
KC — FG Lowery 22
KC — Safety, Lewis tackled Kosar in end zone
KC — Harry 5 pass from DeBerg (Lowery kick)

L.A. Raiders 38, Bengals 14 — at Riverfront Stadium, attendance 52,044. Ronnie Lott intercepted 2 passes and the Raiders' defense forced 5 turnovers in a rout of the Bengals. Los Angeles managed only 19 net yards passing and 176 total yards, but got a pair of big plays on special teams to move into a tie for first place in the AFC Western Division. Tim Brown returned a second-quarter punt 75 yards for a touchdown and Elvis Patterson returned a fumble three yards for a score after a bad snap on a punt attempt as the Raiders built a 28-0 first-half advantage. Lott set up Los Angeles's first touchdown with a 20-yard interception return in the first quarter, and had a 27-yard return of a theft in the fourth quarter to position the Raiders for a field goal. Tom Benson also intercepted a pass that led to a touchdown for Los Angeles. Cincinnati's Donald Hollas, making his first NFL start in place of injured Boomer Esiason, completed 17 of 31 passes for 141 yards and 1 touchdown, but suffered 3 interceptions.

L.A. Raiders	7	21	7	3	—	38
Cincinnati	0	7	0	7	—	14

Raiders— Smith 1 run (Jaeger kick)
Raiders— Craig 5 run (Jaeger kick)
Raiders— Brown 75 punt return (Jaeger kick)
Raiders— Patterson 3 fumble recovery return (Jaeger kick)
Cin — Woods 1 run (Breech kick)
Raiders— Allen 3 run (Jaeger kick)
Raiders— FG Jaeger 28
Cin — Rembert 24 pass from Hollas (Breech kick)

Miami 16, Chicago 13 — at Soldier Field, attendance 58,288. Pete Stoyanovich's 27-yard field goal 4:11 into overtime capped a rally from 10 points down and gave the Dolphins the victory over the Bears. Miami trailed 13-3 entering the fourth quarter, but Stoyanovich kicked a 22-yard field goal and Dan Marino passed 2 yards to Ferrell Edmunds with 1:51 left to force the extra session. The tying score came two plays after a bad snap allowed Marc Logan to block Maury Buford's punt, setting the Dolphins up at the 4-yard line. In overtime, a 31-yard pass from Marino to Mark Clayton, who slipped but still caught the ball while on the ground, positioned Miami for the winning kick. With the loss, Chicago had its five-game winning streak snapped.

Miami	0	3	0	10	3	—	16
Chicago	7	3	3	0	0	—	13

Chi— Muster 3 run (Butler kick)
Mia— FG Stoyanovich 35
Chi— FG Butler 32
Chi— FG Butler 19
Mia— FG Stoyanovich 22
Mia— Edmunds 2 pass from Marino (Stoyanovich kick)
Mia— FG Stoyanovich 27

Tampa Bay 21, N.Y. Giants 14 — at Tampa Stadium, attendance 63,698. Phil Simms, in the game because starter Jeff Hostetler injured his back in the third quarter, threw a 30-yard touchdown pass to Stephen Baker with 16 seconds remaining in the game to lift the Giants over the Buccaneers. Tampa Bay had tied the game on a 19-yard touchdown pass from Vinny Testaverde to Willie Drewrey with 5:59 left. But on the winning drive, Simms moved his team 90 yards in eight plays, completing seven consecutive passes for 85 yards along the way. Playing extensively for the first time all season, Simms completed 10 of 14 passes for 100 yards. Reggie Cobb ran for 110 yards on 22 carries for the Buccaneers.

N.Y. Giants	7	0	7	7	—	21
Tampa Bay	0	7	0	7	—	14

Giants— Meggett 70 punt return (Bahr kick)
TB — Cobb 27 run (Christie kick)
Giants— Hampton 5 run (Bahr kick)
TB — Drewrey 19 pass from Testaverde (Christie kick)
Giants— Baker 30 pass from Simms (Bahr kick)

Philadelphia 34, Phoenix 14 — at Sun Devil Stadium, attendance 32,568. Seth Joyner returned a fumble 34 yards for a touchdown, forced another fumble that was recovered for a score, and caused an interception that led to a touchdown in the Eagles' defense-dominated victory over the Cardinals. Philadelphia forced 7 turnovers in all, intercepting 4 passes and recovering 3 fumbles, while adding 4 sacks. Joyner hit Stan Gelbaugh as he was throwing in the first quarter, and John Booty intercepted the pass, which set up an 18-yard touchdown pass from Jim McMahon to Fred Barnett. Two plays later, Joyner returned Anthony Thompson's fumble for a touchdown. Still in the first quarter, Joyner sacked Gelbaugh and knocked the ball loose. Clyde Simmons recovered in the end zone for a touchdown and a 20-7 Philadelphia lead. The Cardinals got a defensive touchdown of their own when Lorenzo Lynch returned an interception 35 yards for a score, but the Eagles put the game out of reach with a pair of second-half touchdowns.

Philadelphia	20	0	7	7	—	34
Phoenix	7	7	0	0	—	14

Phil— Barnett 18 pass from McMahon (Ruzek kick)
Phil— Joyner 34 fumble recovery return (kick failed)
Phx— W. Williams 3 pass from Gelbaugh (Davis kick)
Phil— Simmons fumble recovery in end zone (Ruzek kick)

Phx— Lynch 35 interception return (Davis kick)
Phil— Keith Jackson 29 pass from McMahon (Ruzek kick)
Phil— Byars 14 run (Ruzek kick)

N.Y. Jets 24, San Diego 3 — at Giants Stadium, attendance 59,025. Blair Thomas rushed for 2 touchdowns to lead the Jets to the victory. New York took a 7-0 lead just 1:45 into the game on a 6-yard touchdown pass from Ken O'Brien to Rob Moore. The Jets went 29 yards after San Diego's Mitchell Benson fumbled a short opening kickoff. Chris Burkett recovered for New York. Thomas capped a 75-yard drive with a 1-yard touchdown run late in the first quarter, and added a 22-yard score on the first play of the fourth quarter. John Friesz completed 7 of 9 passes in the first half for San Diego but left the game after injuring an ankle on the Chargers' lone scoring drive.

San Diego	0	3	0	0	—	3
N.Y. Jets	14	0	3	7	—	24

Jets— Moore 6 pass from O'Brien (Leahy kick)
Jets— Thomas 1 run (Leahy kick)
SD — FG Carney 53
Jets— FG Leahy 28
Jets— Thomas 22 run (Leahy kick)

Sunday Night, November 24

Atlanta 23, New Orleans 20 — at Louisiana Superdome, attendance 68,591. Norm Johnson kicked a 50-yard field goal with 1:57 remaining in overtime as the Falcons remained alive in the NFC Western Division title race by beating the Saints. New Orleans, which would have clinched its first-ever division championship with a victory, led 20-10 late in the game. But Johnson's 27-yard field goal with 5:02 left in regulation pulled Atlanta within a touchdown, and Chris Miller's 18-yard touchdown pass to Michael Haynes with 1:53 remaining tied it. Haynes, who also caught an 80-yard touchdown pass in the third quarter and finished with 187 yards on 6 receptions, got the Falcons out of a hole in overtime by grabbing a 57-yard pass from Miller when they were on their own 2-yard line. Four plays later, Johnson kicked the game-winner.

Atlanta	0	3	7	10	3	—	23
New Orleans	0	7	6	7	0	—	20

Atl — FG N. Johnson 25
NO— Fenerty 2 run (Andersen kick)
NO— FG Andersen 39
Atl — Haynes 80 pass from Miller (N. Johnson kick)
NO— FG Andersen 31
NO— McAfee 1 run (Andersen kick)
Atl — FG N. Johnson 27
Atl — Haynes 18 pass from Miller (N. Johnson kick)
Atl — FG N. Johnson 50

Monday, November 25

San Francisco 33, L.A. Rams 10 — at Anaheim Stadium, attendance 61,881. Steve Bono passed for a career-high 306 yards and the 49ers built a 30-0 first-half lead en route to an easy victory over the Rams. Bono had completions of 41 yards to Brent Jones and 78 yards to John Taylor to set up 1-yard scoring runs by Harry Sydney and Tom Rathman in the first quarter, and San Francisco was never threatened after that. Taylor finished with 6 catches for 121 yards. Jim Everett completed 20 of 32 passes for 249 yards for the Rams. With the victory, the 49ers stayed alive in the NFC playoff chase.

San Francisco	16	14	0	3	—	33
L.A. Rams	0	3	7	0	—	10

SF — Sydney 1 run (Cofer kick)
SF — Rathman 1 run (Cofer kick)
SF — Safety, Jordan tackled Turner in end zone
SF — Sydney 2 pass from Bono (Cofer kick)
SF — Carter 3 run (Cofer kick)
Rams— FG Zendejas 37
Rams— Dupree 1 run (Zendejas kick)
SF — FG Cofer 39

Fourteenth Week Summaries

Standings

American Football Conference

Eastern Division	W	L	T	Pct.	Pts.	OP
Buffalo	11	2	0	.846	379	267
Miami	7	6	0	.538	256	275
N.Y. Jets	7	6	0	.538	268	233
New England	4	9	0	.308	175	256
Indianapolis	1	12	0	.077	116	306
Central Division						
Houston	9	4	0	.692	318	207
Cleveland	6	7	0	.462	262	247
Pittsburgh	5	8	0	.385	252	293
Cincinnati	2	11	0	.154	211	374
Western Division						
Denver	9	4	0	.692	246	195
L.A. Raiders	9	4	0	.692	250	213
Kansas City	8	5	0	.615	261	186
Seattle	6	7	0	.462	218	202
San Diego	3	10	0	.231	205	275

National Football Conference

Eastern Division	W	L	T	Pct.	Pts.	OP
Washington	12	1	0	.923	409	169
Dallas	8	5	0	.615	263	256
Philadelphia	8	5	0	.615	229	183
N.Y. Giants	7	6	0	.538	226	224
Phoenix	4	9	0	.308	160	273
Central Division						
Chicago	9	4	0	.692	231	204
Detroit	9	4	0	.692	267	244
Minnesota	6	7	0	.462	248	241
Green Bay	3	10	0	.231	216	258
Tampa Bay	2	11	0	.154	158	309
Western Division						
New Orleans	9	4	0	.692	273	185
Atlanta	8	5	0	.615	277	280
San Francisco	7	6	0	.538	289	189
L.A. Rams	3	10	0	.231	197	316

Thursday, November 28

Detroit 16, Chicago 6 — at Pontiac Silverdome, attendance 78,879. The Lions' defense intercepted 4 passes and recovered a pair of fumbles to lead Detroit past the Bears on Thanksgiving Day. Chicago outgained the Lions 319 total yards to 208, but could manage only a pair of Kevin Butler field goals as other potential scoring drives were stopped by the miscues. Eddie Murray kicked 3 field goals for Detroit, including a 37-yarder with 2:50 remaining to put the game out of reach. With the victory, the Lions assured themselves of their first winning season since 1983.

Chicago	0	6	0	0	—	6
Detroit	10	0	3	3	—	16

Det— FG Murray 21
Det— Clark 9 pass from Kramer (Murray kick)
Chi— FG Butler 27
Chi— FG Butler 22
Det— FG Murray 50
Det— FG Murray 37

Dallas 20, Pittsburgh 10 — at Texas Stadium, attendance 62,253. Steve Beuerlein threw a 66-yard touchdown pass to Michael Irvin midway through the fourth quarter to secure the victory for the Cowboys. The Steelers had trimmed a 13-3 deficit to 13-10 on Warren Williams's 3-yard touchdown run with 7:54 remaining in the game. But three plays later, Beuerlein and Irvin teamed for the clinching touchdown. Emmitt Smith ran for 109 yards and 1 touchdown on 32 carries, and Irvin caught 8 passes for 157 yards for Dallas. Beuerlein, subbing for the injured Troy Aikman, completed 14 of 25 passes for 217 yards and was not intercepted. The Cowboys raised their record to 16-7-1 on Thanksgiving Day.

Pittsburgh	0	0	3	7	—	10
Dallas	7	3	0	10	—	20

Dall— E. Smith 6 run (Willis kick)
Dall— FG Willis 19
Pitt — FG Anderson 42
Dall— FG Willis 43
Pitt — W. Williams 3 run (Anderson kick)
Dall— Irvin 66 pass from Beuerlein (Willis kick)

Sunday, December 1

Cleveland 31, Indianapolis 0 — at Hoosier Dome, attendance 57,539. The opportunistic Browns scored 24 first-half points following Colts' turnovers and coasted to the victory. Cleveland, which entered the game tops in the league with a turnover ratio of plus-16, intercepted a pair of Jeff George passes and recovered 2 fumbles while not committing any miscues. Interceptions by Stephen Braggs and James Jones (he returned his 20 yards for a touchdown) resulted in second-quarter touchdowns, and fumble recoveries by Clay Matthews and Alfred Jackson also set up scores. The Browns kept the pressure on George in the second half and finished with 6 sacks, including 3 by David Brandon and 2 by Matthews. Indianapolis's Eric Dickerson returned from a three-game suspension and ran for 117 yards on 16 carries.

Cleveland	3	28	0	0	—	31
Indianapolis	0	0	0	0	—	0

Cleve— FG Stover 41
Cleve— Mack 3 pass from Kosar (Stover kick)
Cleve— Mack 51 run (Stover kick)
Cleve— Hoard 2 run (Stover kick)
Cleve— J. Jones 20 interception return (Stover kick)

Atlanta 35, Green Bay 31 — at Atlanta-Fulton County Stadium, attendance 43,270. Chris Miller, fighting off the effects of the flu, threw a 16-yard touchdown pass to Andre Rison with 41 seconds left to give the Falcons the come-from-behind victory. Green Bay led 28-14 early in the fourth quarter until Miller, who did not start the game because of a high temperature and was fed intraveneous fluids in the locker room during the first half, passed 20 yards for a touchdown to Rison. Atlanta then tied the game on the ensuing kickoff when Joe Fishback recovered a fumble and returned it 16 yards for a touchdown. The Packers regained the lead on a 27-yard field goal by Chris Jacke with 4:21 to play and were in position to win until punter Paul McJulien bobbled a snap from center and was thrown for a 2-yard loss on his own 41-yard line with 1:22 remaining. Miller then directed the winning four-play drive, passing for 21 yards to Rison in addition to the game-winner. The fifth-year veteran completed 12 of 18 passes for 186 yards in all. Rison caught 8 passes for 124 yards.

Green Bay	7	14	0	10	—	31
Atlanta	7	0	7	21	—	35

Atl — Pegram 4 run (Johnson kick)
GB— Sharpe 4 pass from Tomczak (Jacke kick)
GB— Thompson 40 run (Jacke kick)
GB— Kemp 13 pass from Tomczak (Jacke kick)
Atl — Broussard 3 run (Johnson kick)
GB— Sharpe 20 pass from Tomczak (Jacke kick)
Atl — Rison 20 pass from Miller (Johnson kick)
Atl — Fishback 16 fumble recovery return (Johnson kick)
GB— FG Jacke 27
Atl — Rison 16 pass from Miller (Johnson kick)

Kansas City 19, Seattle 6 — at Kingdome, attendance 57,248. Nick Lowery kicked 4 field goals to become the Chiefs' all-time scoring leader and Kansas City stayed alive in the AFC Western Division race by beating the Seahawks. The Chiefs' running game suffered apparent blows when Christian Okoye (sprained knee) and Harvey Williams (hamstring) were injured. But Barry Word stepped in and ran for 96 yards on 26 carries to pace their efficient ball-control attack. Steve DeBerg completed 17 of 26 passes for 154 yards for Kansas City, which ran 69 plays to Seattle's 45 and maintained possession for nearly 36 minutes. Lowery, who raised his career totals to 1,236 points and 280 field goals to establish club records formerly held by Pro Football Hall of Fame member Jan Stenerud, accounted for all the Chiefs' points as they built a 12-3 lead after three quarters. DeBerg then put the game out of reach by passing 8 yards for a touchdown to Pete Holohan midway through the fourth period.

Kansas City	3	6	3	7	—	19
Seattle	3	0	0	3	—	6

Sea— FG Kasay 19
KC — FG Lowery 20
KC — FG Lowery 28
KC — FG Lowery 36
KC — FG Lowery 39
KC — Holohan 8 pass from DeBerg (Lowery kick)
Sea— FG Kasay 26

Denver 20, New England 3 — at Mile High Stadium, attendance 67,116. John Elway, playing despite a sore shoulder, completed 18 of 25 passes for 215 yards and 1 touchdown to lead the Broncos past the Patriots and keep Denver tied for the AFC Western Division lead. Elway directed three first-half scoring drives as the Broncos built a 17-0 advantage at the intermission. He completed 4 passes on the opening drive of the game, including a 21-yard touchdown to Vance Johnson. Denver's defense sacked Hugh Millen 5 times, including twice by Karl Mecklenburg. Millen completed 19 of 36 passes for 247 yards but was intercepted twice by the Broncos' Dennis Smith.

New England	0	0	3	0	—	3
Denver	10	7	3	0	—	20

Den— V. Johnson 21 pass from Elway (Treadwell kick)
Den— FG Treadwell 20
Den— Lewis 12 run (Treadwell kick)
NE — FG Baumann 23
Den— FG Treadwell 24

San Francisco 38, New Orleans 24 — at Candlestick Park, attendance 62,092. Steve Bono passed for 347 yards and 3 touchdowns and the 49ers scored three times in the last 4:09 to rally past the Saints and keep their playoff hopes alive. Trailing 24-17 midway through the fourth quarter, San Francisco had an apparent touchdown run by Tom Rathman reversed by instant replay, and New Orleans held with a goal-line stand. But minutes later, Dexter Carter, who earlier had scored on a 98-yard kickoff return, tied the game when he caught an 11-yard touchdown pass from Bono. After forcing a punt, the 49ers took the lead for good when Jerry Rice turned a short pass from Bono into a 47-yard touchdown with 1:36 left. Rathman scored the final touchdown on a 1-yard run with four seconds to go, one play after Johnnie Jackson recovered Steve Walsh's fumble and returned it 49 yards. Bono completed 27 of 41 passes and Rice caught 9 passes for 154 yards for the 49ers. Walsh was 25 of 42 for 317 yards and 2 touchdowns. Floyd Turner caught 10 passes for 132 yards for the Saints.

New Orleans	0	10	14	0	—	24
San Francisco	0	14	3	21	—	38

SF — Taylor 19 pass from Bono (Cofer kick)
NO— Turner 6 pass from Walsh (Andersen kick)
SF — D. Carter 98 kickoff return (Cofer kick)
NO— FG Andersen 52
SF — FG Cofer 42
NO— McAfee 12 run (Andersen kick)
NO— Turner 3 pass from Walsh (Andersen kick)
SF — D. Carter 11 pass from Bono (Cofer kick)

SF —Rice 47 pass from Bono (Cofer kick)
SF —Rathman 1 run (Cofer kick)

Cincinnati 27, N.Y. Giants 24 — at Riverfront Stadium, attendance 45,063. Jim Breech kicked a 35-yard field goal to break a 17-17 tie midway through the fourth quarter and Mitchell Price returned a punt 78 yards for the game-clinching touchdown as the Bengals severely hampered the Giants' playoff hopes by upsetting the defending Super Bowl champions. After Price's touchdown, which came with 4:17 to go, the Giants scored on a 19-yard pass from Phil Simms to Mark Ingram with 1:02 left to pull within three points. But Cincinnati recovered the ensuing onside kickoff attempt and held on for the victory. Simms, making his first start of the season, completed 26 of 44 passes for 296 yards and helped stake New York to a 17-7 lead in the third quarter. But the Bengals erased that deficit on a field goal by Breech and a 1-yard touchdown run by Harold Green.

N.Y. Giants	7	7	3	7	—	24
Cincinnati	7	0	3	17	—	27

Giants— Baker 15 pass from Simms (Bahr kick)
Cin —McGee 41 pass from Esiason (Breech kick)
Giants— Baker 13 pass from Simms (Bahr kick)
Giants— FG Bahr 37
Cin —FG Breech 35
Cin —Green 1 run (Breech kick)
Cin —FG Breech 35
Cin —Price 78 punt return (Breech kick)
Giants— Ingram 19 pass from Simms (Bahr kick)

Buffalo 24, N.Y. Jets 13 — at Rich Stadium, attendance 80,243. Jim Kelly passed for 251 yards, Thurman Thomas ran for 124, and the Bills wrapped up their fourth consecutive AFC Eastern Division title by beating the Jets. New York trailed just 17-13 and was driving for the potential go-ahead touchdown midway through the fourth quarter when Rob Moore's fumble at the Buffalo 7-yard line was recovered by the Bills' Mark Kelso. Kelly then directed a 93-yard scoring march. He passed 54 yards to James Lofton and capped the drive with a 27-yard touchdown to Lofton for the clinching score with 4:21 left in the game. Lofton caught 5 passes for 109 yards and Al Edwards had 9 receptions for 78 yards for Buffalo. Bruce Smith, who had missed all but one of the previous 12 games while recovering from knee surgery, returned and had 5 tackles and 1 sack for Buffalo, which won for the seventeenth consecutive time at home. Kelly, who completed 21 of 38 passes, also had a 16-yard touchdown pass to Andre Reed in the first quarter and set a club record with his twenty-seventh and twenty-eighth scoring passes of the season.

N.Y. Jets	7	3	3	0	—	13
Buffalo	7	3	7	7	—	24

Jets— Baxter 3 run (Leahy kick)
Buff— Reed 16 pass from Kelly (Norwood kick)
Jets— FG Leahy 19
Buff— FG Norwood 31
Buff— Davis 4 run (Norwood kick)
Jets— FG Leahy 23
Buff— Lofton 27 pass from Kelly (Norwood kick)

Miami 33, Tampa Bay 14 — at Joe Robbie Stadium, attendance 51,036. Dan Marino passed for 307 yards and 2 touchdowns and Mark Higgs ran for 131 yards and another score as the Dolphins easily defeated the Buccaneers. Tampa Bay led 7-0 after the first period, but Miami scored 24 unanswered points in the second quarter to put the game away. Marino, who completed 20 of 32 passes, surpassed the 3,000-yard mark for an NFL-record eighth time. Tony Martin caught 5 passes for 106 yards for the Dolphins, who amassed 468 total yards. Vinny Testaverde completed 21 of 39 passes for 224 yards for the Buccaneers. Lawrence Dawsey had 8 catches for 100 yards for Tampa Bay, including a 17-yard touchdown in the fourth quarter.

Tampa Bay	7	0	0	7	—	14
Miami	0	24	6	3	—	33

TB —Cobb 2 run (Christie kick)
Mia— Duper 6 pass from Marino (Stoyanovich kick)
Mia— FG Stoyanovich 41
Mia— Higgs 19 run (Stoyanovich kick)
Mia— Martin 26 pass from Marino (Stoyanovich kick)
Mia— FG Stoyanovich 24
Mia— FG Stoyanovich 19
Mia— FG Stoyanovich 30
TB —Dawsey 17 pass from Testaverde (Christie kick)

Washington 27, L.A. Rams 6 — at Anaheim Stadium, attendance 55,027. Mark Rypien threw a pair of third-quarter touchdown passes and the Redskins broke open a close game in the second half to beat the Rams and clinch their first NFC Eastern Division title since 1987. Rypien, who completed 15 of 24 passes for 269 yards, also threw a 47-yard scoring pass to Terry Orr in the first half. With his team leading only 7-6 early in the third quarter, Rypien passed 30 yards to Ricky Sanders and 24 yards to Ricky Ervins for touchdowns to put the game out of reach. Los Angeles lost its seventh consecutive game.

Washington	7	0	14	6	—	27
L.A. Rams	3	3	0	0	—	6

Rams— FG Zendejas 41
Wash— Orr 47 pass from Rypien (Lohmiller kick)
Rams— FG Zendejas 34
Wash— Sanders 30 pass from Rypien (Lohmiller kick)
Wash— Ervins 24 pass from Rypien (Lohmiller kick)
Wash— FG Lohmiller 35
Wash— FG Lohmiller 35

Sunday Night, December 1

L.A. Raiders 9, San Diego 7 — at San Diego Jack Murphy Stadium, attendance 56,780. Jeff Jaeger kicked 3 first-half field goals and Scott Davis blocked a field goal attempt with 1:57 remaining in the game to lift the Raiders past the Chargers. Los Angeles, which remained tied with Denver for the AFC Western Division lead with the victory, built a 9-0 advantage at halftime on the strength of Jaeger's field goals, one of which was a career-long 53-yarder with eight seconds left in the half, and a stifling defense that allowed only 5 total yards. But San Diego made it close on a 1-yard run by Rod Bernstine in the third quarter, and had an apparent go-ahead touchdown pass from John Friesz to Derrick Walker nullified by a holding penalty late in the game. Two plays later, Davis blocked John Carney's 44-yard field-goal try to preserve the win.

L.A. Raiders	3	6	0	0	—	9
San Diego	0	0	7	0	—	7

Raiders— FG Jaeger 37
Raiders— FG Jaeger 19
Raiders— FG Jaeger 53
SD —Bernstine 1 run (Carney kick)

Monday, December 2

Philadelphia 13, Houston 6 — at Astrodome, attendance 62,141. Seth Joyner forced 2 fumbles, recovered 2, and had a pair of sacks as the Eagles improved their playoff chances and kept the Oilers from clinching the AFC Central Division title. Philadelphia's defense was dominant, forcing 6 fumbles, recovering 5, and posting 4 sacks while holding Houston's high-powered offense without a touchdown for the first time in 33 games. Jeff Kemp, who came off the bench when Jim McMahon injured an elbow, passed 24 yards to Keith Jackson for the game's only touchdown. The Oilers' Warren Moon completed 24 of 46 passes for 262 yards and drove his team to the Eagles' 24-yard line in the closing seconds, but threw incomplete passes in the end zone on the final three plays of the game.

Philadelphia	0	0	10	3	—	13
Houston	0	3	3	0	—	6

Hou— FG Del Greco 42
Phil —FG Ruzek 23
Phil —Keith Jackson 21 pass from Kemp (Ruzek kick)
Hou— FG Del Greco 47
Phil —FG Ruzek 29

Fifteenth Week Summaries

Standings

American Football Conference

Eastern Division

	W	L	T	Pct.	Pts.	OP
Buffalo	12	2	0	.857	409	294
Miami	8	6	0	.571	293	288
N.Y. Jets	7	7	0	.500	288	267
New England	5	9	0	.357	198	273
Indianapolis	1	13	0	.071	133	329

Central Division

	W	L	T	Pct.	Pts.	OP
Houston	10	4	0	.714	349	213
Cleveland	6	8	0	.429	269	264
Pittsburgh	5	9	0	.357	258	324
Cincinnati	2	12	0	.143	224	411

Western Division

	W	L	T	Pct.	Pts.	OP
Denver	10	4	0	.714	263	202
Kansas City	9	5	0	.643	281	203
L.A. Raiders	9	5	0	.643	277	243
Seattle	6	8	0	.429	240	226
San Diego	3	11	0	.214	222	295

National Football Conference

Eastern Division

	W	L	T	Pct.	Pts.	OP
Washington	13	1	0	.929	429	183
Dallas	9	5	0	.643	286	270
Philadelphia	9	5	0	.643	248	197
N.Y. Giants	7	7	0	.500	240	243
Phoenix	4	10	0	.286	174	293

Central Division

	W	L	T	Pct.	Pts.	OP
Chicago	10	4	0	.714	258	217
Detroit	10	4	0	.714	301	264
Minnesota	7	7	0	.500	274	265
Green Bay	3	11	0	.214	229	285
Tampa Bay	2	12	0	.143	182	335

Western Division

	W	L	T	Pct.	Pts.	OP
Atlanta	9	5	0	.643	308	294
New Orleans	9	5	0	.643	287	208
San Francisco	8	6	0	.571	313	211
L.A. Rams	3	11	0	.214	211	347

Sunday, December 8

Atlanta 31, L.A. Rams 14 — at Anaheim Stadium, attendance 35,315. Chris Miller passed for 271 yards and 2 touchdowns as the Falcons beat the Rams and moved into a first-place tie with New Orleans in the NFC Western Division. The victory was the fourth in a row and sixth in seven games for surging Atlanta, while Los Angeles lost its eighth straight. Steve Broussard scored on a pair of 1-yard runs as Atlanta built a 24-7 halftime advantage and won handily. The Falcons kept the game out of reach by sacking Jim Everett 3 times and limiting him to only 7 completions in 16 attempts for 109 yards.

Atlanta	10	14	7	0	—	31
L.A. Rams	0	7	0	7	—	14

Atl —FG Johnson 21
Atl —Broussard 1 run (Johnson kick)
Rams— Carter 6 pass from Everett (Zendejas kick)
Atl —Broussard 1 run (Johnson kick)
Atl —Rison 6 pass from Miller (Johnson kick)
Atl —Haynes 9 pass from Miller (Johnson kick)
Rams— Thompson 13 pass from Pagel (Zendejas kick)

Buffalo 30, L.A. Raiders 27 — at Los Angeles Memorial Coliseum, attendance 85,081. Scott Norwood kicked a 42-yard field goal 2:34 into overtime and the Bills overcame a 13-point, fourth-quarter deficit to beat the Raiders. Norwood's kick came five plays after Mark Kelso intercepted Jay Schroeder's pass at the Bills' 36. Jim Kelly's 31-yard pass to Andre Reed positioned Buffalo for the winning field goal. The Raiders had built a 27-14 advantage through three quarters on the passing of Schroeder, who threw for 252 yards, including a 78-yard bomb to Tim Brown in the first quarter. But the Bills rallied, tying the score on a 1-yard run by Kenneth Davis with 4:06 left and a 9-yard pass from Kelly to James Lofton with 1:00 to go. Kelly completed 33 of 52 passes for 347 yards and 2 touchdowns. Keith McKeller caught 10 passes for 57 yards, while Reed totaled 107 yards on 8 receptions for Buffalo. Norwood, who missed a 36-yard field-goal try with 11 seconds left in regulation and an extra point in the fourth quarter, also missed two other field-goal attempts before redeeming himself in the extra session. The victory clinched the home-field advantage for Buffalo throughout the AFC playoffs. Despite the defeat, the Raiders learned later in the day that they had qualified for postseason play.

Buffalo	7	7	0	13	3	—	30
L.A. Raiders	10	10	7	0	0	—	27

Raiders— FG Jaeger 19
Raiders— T. Brown 78 pass from Schroeder (Jaeger kick)
Buff —Edwards 91 kickoff return (Norwood kick)
Raiders— Bell 12 run (Jaeger kick)
Buff —McKeller 9 pass from Kelly (Norwood kick)
Raiders— FG Jaeger 28
Raiders— Allen 1 run (Jaeger kick)
Buff —K. Davis 1 run (kick failed)
Buff —Lofton 9 pass from Kelly (Norwood kick)
Buff —FG Norwood 42

Denver 17, Cleveland 7 — at Cleveland Stadium, attendance 73,539. The Broncos clinched at least a wild-card playoff spot and moved back into first place in the AFC Western Division while crushing the Browns' playoff hopes with the victory. John Elway's 6-yard touchdown pass to Vance Johnson broke a 7-7 tie with 8:54 remaining, and moments later Elway set up David Treadwell's 37-yard field goal with a 60-yard completion to Steve Sewell. Elway finished with 16 completions in 29 attempts for 221 yards. Jeff Mills, who was replacing the injured Mike Croel, had 2 sacks for the Broncos, who got to Bernie Kosar 5 times and limited the Browns to 9 first downs and 181 total yards. The victory was the 100th regular-season win for Denver head coach Dan Reeves.

Denver	0	7	0	10	—	17
Cleveland	7	0	0	0	—	7

Cleve— Mack 3 run (Stover kick)
Den —Young 30 pass from Elway (Treadwell kick)
Den —V. Johnson 6 pass from Elway (Treadwell kick)
Den —FG Treadwell 37

Chicago 27, Green Bay 13 — at Soldier Field, attendance 62,353. Brad Muster and Wendell Davis each had 2 touchdowns and scored just 10 seconds apart in the second quarter to lead the Bears past the Packers. With the victory, Chicago kept pace with Detroit atop the NFC Central Division and gave head coach Mike Ditka his 100th regular-season win. The Packers led 10-7 until Muster ran 6 yards for a touchdown with 3:37 left in the first half. On the next play from scrimmage, The Bears' Jim Morrissey intercepted a Mike Tomczak pass and returned it 5 yards. Jim Harbaugh then fired a 20-yard touchdown pass to Davis one play later to make it 21-10. The pair also

teamed for a 35-yard score in the fourth quarter.

Green Bay	3	10	0	0	—	13
Chicago	7	14	6	0	—	27

Chi — Muster 8 run (Butler kick)
GB — FG Jacke 25
GB — Harris 1 pass from Tomczak (Jacke kick)
Chi — Muster 6 run (Butler kick)
Chi — Davis 20 pass from Harbaugh (Butler kick)
GB — FG Jacke 25
Chi — Davis 35 pass from Harbaugh (Butler kick)

New England 23, Indianapolis 17 — at Foxboro Stadium, attendance 20,131. Hugh Millen's 45-yard touchdown pass to Michael Timpson 8:55 into overtime gave the Patriots a come-from-behind victory. New England trailed 17-3 in the fourth quarter until John Stephens ran 1 yard for a touchdown early in the period and Millen tossed a 2-yard touchdown pass to tight end Ben Coates to tie the score with seven seconds remaining. Millen was sacked 8 times, but completed 21 of 40 passes for 330 yards. Greg McMurtry had 119 yards on 8 catches for the Patriots, who amassed 400 total yards.

Indianapolis	0	14	3	0	0	—	17
New England	3	0	0	14	6	—	23

NE — FG Baumann 24
Ind — Hester 13 pass from George (Biasucci kick)
Ind — Dickerson 1 run (Biasucci kick)
Ind — FG Biasucci 40
NE — Stephens 1 run (Baumann kick)
NE — Coates 2 pass from Millen (Baumann kick)
NE — Timpson 45 pass from Millen

Dallas 23, New Orleans 14 — at Texas Stadium, attendance 64,530. Emmitt Smith rushed for 112 yards and the Cowboys edged closer to a playoff berth by handing the slumping Saints their fourth consecutive loss. Smith's 100-yard outing was the tenth of his 30-game career, and was the first allowed by the New Orleans defense all season. He carried 27 times, including 9 times for 50 yards on a 63-yard, 12-play touchdown drive in the final minutes that clinched the win. The Cowboys had regained the lead earlier in the fourth quarter on Ken Willis's third field goal of the game, a 40-yarder. That was set up by a 29-yard pass from Steve Beuerlein to Michael Irvin. On the play, Irvin established club single-season records for receptions (he finished the day at 78) and receiving yards (1,262). He broke records formerly held by Herschel Walker and Bob Hayes, respectively.

New Orleans	0	7	7	0	—	14
Dallas	7	3	3	10	—	23

Dall — Johnston 1 pass from Beuerlein (Willis kick)
Dall — FG Willis 50
NO — Martin 8 pass from Walsh (Andersen kick)
Dall — FG Willis 41
NO — Fenerty 4 pass from Walsh (Andersen kick)
Dall — FG Willis 40
Dall — Agee 4 run (Willis kick)

Detroit 34, N.Y. Jets 20 — at Pontiac Silverdome, attendance 69,304. Barry Sanders rushed for 114 yards and 2 touchdowns to lead the Lions past the Jets. Sanders scored on runs of 14 and 51 yards in the first quarter to equal Billy Sims's club records of 16 touchdowns in a season and 42 rushing touchdowns in a career. After New York tied the game 14-14, a 73-yard touchdown pass from Erik Kramer to Willie Green midway through the second quarter put Detroit ahead for good. With the victory, the Lions remained tied with Chicago for first place in the NFC Central Division. The Lions also reached the 10-win plateau for the first time since 1970, and completed an 8-0 season at home.

N.Y. Jets	14	0	3	3	—	20
Detroit	14	10	10	0	—	34

Det — Sanders 14 run (Murray kick)
Det — Sanders 51 run (Murray kick)
Jets — Thomas 6 run (Leahy kick)
Jets — McMillan 57 interception return (Leahy kick)
Det — Green 73 pass from Kramer (Murray kick)
Det — FG Murray 43
Jets — FG Leahy 22
Det — FG Murray 37
Det — Hayworth 28 fumble recovery return (Murray kick)
Jets — FG Leahy 25

Philadelphia 19, N.Y. Giants 14 — at Giants Stadium, attendance 76,099. Roger Ruzek kicked 4 field goals as the Eagles won their sixth consecutive game and eliminated the defending Super Bowl-champion Giants from playoff contention. New York's Phil Simms completed only 7 of 23 passes for 100 yards, but did stake the Giants to a 14-3 lead in the first half with a pair of touchdown passes to David Meggett. Philadelphia rallied, pulling within 14-10 on an 8-yard pass from Jeff Kemp to Calvin Williams with 42 seconds left in the first half. Kemp, who passed for 146 yards and ran for 45, replaced Jim McMahon, who suffered bruised ribs while scrambling on a pass play in the second quarter. Ruzek booted 3 field goals in the second half, including a 51-yarder 55 seconds into the fourth quarter to put the Eagles ahead. Matt Bahr, one of the heroes in the Giants' drive to Super Bowl XXV, missed 2 field goals, including a 32-yarder that would have given his team the lead with 7:20 remaining.

Philadelphia	0	10	3	6	—	19
N.Y. Giants	7	7	0	0	—	14

Giants — Meggett 8 pass from Simms (Bahr kick)
Phil — FG Ruzek 46
Giants — Meggett 14 pass from Simms (Bahr kick)
Phil — C. Williams 8 pass from Kemp (Ruzek kick)
Phil — FG Ruzek 21
Phil — FG Ruzek 51
Phil — FG Ruzek 36

Houston 31, Pittsburgh 6 — at Astrodome, attendance 59,225. Allen Pinkett rushed for 2 touchdowns as the Oilers routed the Steelers to clinch their first-ever AFC Central Division title. Warren Moon passed for 254 yards and 1 touchdown and Houston's defense harassed Pittsburgh's Neil O'Donnell all afternoon. O'Donnell was sacked 7 times, 2 each by Ray Childress and Sean Jones, and fumbled after 2 of them. The second was scooped up by Al Smith and returned 70 yards for a touchdown. Pinkett, who began the scoring with a 7-yard run in the first quarter and added an 11-yard touchdown in the fourth period, ran for 98 yards on 16 carries to revive the Oilers' running attack. Houston had rushed for a total of only 90 yards in its previous three games.

Pittsburgh	0	3	3	0	—	6
Houston	7	3	7	14	—	31

Hou — Pinkett 7 run (Del Greco kick)
Hou — FG Del Greco 24
Pitt — FG Anderson 54
Hou — Jeffires 16 pass from Moon (Del Greco kick)
Pitt — FG Anderson 36
Hou — Pinkett 11 run (Del Greco kick)
Hou — A. Smith 70 fumble recovery return (Del Greco kick)

Kansas City 20, San Diego 17 — at Arrowhead Stadium, attendance 73,330. Former Chargers quarterback Mark Vlasic came off the bench to rally the Chiefs from a 14-point halftime deficit to an overtime victory over his ex-team. The victory clinched at least a wild-card playoff spot for Kansas City. Vlasic, a Plan B free agent who signed with the Chiefs after four years with San Diego, replaced an ineffective Steve DeBerg and completed 12 of 18 passes for 150 yards and 1 touchdown in the second half. His 16-yard touchdown pass to Harvey Williams with 3:00 left in regulation gave Kansas City a 17-14 lead, but the Chargers forced the extra session when John Carney kicked a 27-yard field goal with 11 seconds to go. The Chiefs won it on Nick Lowery's 18-yard field goal 11:26 into overtime. It was Lowery's twentieth consecutive successful field goal.

San Diego	0	14	0	3	0	—	17
Kansas City	0	0	10	7	3	—	20

SD — Lewis 6 pass from Friesz (Carney kick)
SD — Frank 71 interception return (Carney kick)
KC — FG Lowery 29
KC — Word 1 run (Lowery kick)
KC — Williams 16 pass from Vlasic (Lowery kick)
SD — FG Carney 27
KC — FG Lowery 18

San Francisco 24, Seattle 22 — at Kingdome, attendance 64,677. Steve Bono's 15-yard touchdown pass to John Taylor with 1:08 remaining lifted the 49ers to the victory and kept San Francisco's playoff hopes alive while eliminating the Seahawks. Bono, who completed 25 of 44 passes for 280 yards and 3 touchdowns, set up the winning score with a 41-yard pass to Taylor. After the touchdown pass, Seattle still had a chance to win the game with a field goal, but Dave Krieg lost a fumble at the 49ers' 49 with 43 seconds to go when he was hit from behind by Tim Harris after a lengthy scramble. That set a dubious mark for Krieg, who lost his NFL-record 107th career fumble on the play. Taylor totaled 113 yards on 7 catches for San Francisco, which won despite turning over the ball 5 times. The Seahawks converted 3 fumble recoveries into 13 points.

San Francisco	0	10	7	7	—	24
Seattle	6	3	7	6	—	22

Sea — J. Jones 1 run (kick failed)
SF — Sydney 3 pass from Bono (Cofer kick)
Sea — FG Kasay 37
SF — FG Cofer 50
SF — Rice 9 pass from Bono (Cofer kick)
Sea — J.L. Williams 5 run (Kasay kick)
Sea — FG Kasay 25
Sea — FG Kasay 38
SF — Taylor 15 pass from Bono (Cofer kick)

Washington 20, Phoenix 14 — at Sun Devil Stadium, attendance 48,373. Mark Rypien passed for 2 third-quarter touchdowns and Chip Lohmiller kicked 2 fourth-quarter field goals as the Redskins erased a 14-0 halftime deficit to win for the thirteenth time in 14 outings and clinch the home-field advantage throughout the NFC playoffs. The Cardinals took their halftime lead on a pair of short touchdown runs by Johnny Johnson. But Washington, limited to 121 total yards in the first half, totaled 263 yards in the second half, and scored on touchdown drives of 80 and 71 yards. Rypien completed 22 of 33 passes for 256 yards and Earnest Byner rushed for 116 yards on 25 carries for the Redskins.

Washington	0	0	14	6	—	20
Phoenix	0	14	0	0	—	14

Phx — J. Johnson 1 run (Davis kick)
Phx — J. Johnson 3 run (Davis kick)
Wash — Orr 4 pass from Rypien (Lohmiller kick)
Wash — Sanders 17 pass from Rypien (Lohmiller kick)
Wash — FG Lohmiller 42
Wash — FG Lohmiller 27

Sunday Night, December 8

Minnesota 26, Tampa Bay 24 — at Tampa Stadium, attendance 41,091. Herschel Walker rushed for 126 yards on only 16 carries, one a 71-yard touchdown run in the first quarter, to lead the Vikings to the victory. Fuad Reveiz kicked 4 field goals, including a pair of 50-yarders, for Minnesota, which built a 20-3 first-half advantage and held on for the win. The second of Reveiz's 50-yard field goals, midway through the fourth quarter, provided the eventual winning points. Vinny Testaverde brought the Buccaneers close by passing for 330 yards and 2 touchdowns. The Vikings piled up 296 yards rushing and 436 total yards.

Minnesota	10	10	3	3	—	26
Tampa Bay	3	7	7	7	—	24

Minn — FG Reveiz 50
TB — FG Christie 40
Minn — Walker 71 run (Reveiz kick)
Minn — M. Jones 5 pass from Gannon (Reveiz kick)
Minn — FG Reveiz 40
TB — J. Anderson 1 pass from Testaverde (Christie kick)
TB — Cobb 1 run (Christie kick)
Minn — FG Reveiz 32
Minn — FG Reveiz 50
TB — Carrier 21 pass from Testaverde (Christie kick)

Monday, December 9

Miami 37, Cincinnati 13 — at Joe Robbie Stadium, attendance 60,616. Dan Marino completed 24 of 33 passes for 281 yards and 3 touchdowns to lead the Dolphins over the Bengals. The victory was the fifth in six games for Miami, which edged closer to a wild-card playoff berth. The Dolphins jumped out to a 17-3 lead but Cincinnati pulled within 20-13 early in the fourth quarter on a 1-yard run by Ickey Woods. Then Miami, aided by a pair of Bengals' fumbles, put the game away by scoring 17 points in a span of 3:29 on Mark Higgs's 3-yard run, Marino's 16-yard scoring pass to Mark Clayton, and Pete Stoyanovich's third field goal of the game. Marino's 3 touchdown passes gave him 20 for the season, marking an NFL-record ninth time he had reached that plateau. He also moved past Jim Hart into the fifth spot on the NFL's career passing chart with 34,818 passing yards.

Cincinnati	0	6	0	7	—	13
Miami	7	10	3	17	—	37

Mia — Duper 43 pass from Marino (Stoyanovich kick)
Mia — FG Stoyanovich 50
Cin — FG Breech 27
Mia — Clayton 18 pass from Marino (Stoyanovich kick)
Cin — FG Breech 50
Mia — FG Stoyanovich 22
Cin — Woods 1 run (Breech kick)
Mia — Higgs 3 run (Stoyanovich kick)
Mia — Clayton 16 pass from Marino (Stoyanovich kick)
Mia — FG Stoyanovich 36

Sixteenth Week Summaries

Standings

American Football Conference

Eastern Division	W	L	T	Pct.	Pts.	OP
Buffalo	13	2	0	.867	444	301
Miami	8	7	0	.533	323	326
N.Y. Jets	7	8	0	.467	291	273
New England	6	9	0	.400	204	276
Indianapolis	1	14	0	.067	140	364
Central Division						
Houston	11	4	0	.733	366	227
Cleveland	6	9	0	.400	283	281
Pittsburgh	6	9	0	.400	275	334
Cincinnati	2	13	0	.133	234	428
Western Division						
Denver	11	4	0	.733	287	221
Kansas City	9	6	0	.600	295	231
L.A. Raiders	9	6	0	.600	277	270
Seattle	6	9	0	.400	253	252
San Diego	4	11	0	.267	260	325

National Football Conference

Eastern Division	**W**	**L**	**T**	**Pct.**	**Pts.**	**OP**
Washington	14	1	0	.933	463	200
Dallas	10	5	0	.667	311	283
Philadelphia	9	6	0	.600	261	222
N.Y. Giants	7	8	0	.467	257	277
Phoenix	4	11	0	.267	193	317
Central Division						
Chicago	11	4	0	.733	285	217
Detroit	11	4	0	.733	322	281
Minnesota	8	7	0	.533	294	279
Green Bay	3	12	0	.200	246	306
Tampa Bay	2	13	0	.133	182	362
Western Division						
Atlanta	10	5	0	.667	334	307
New Orleans	10	5	0	.667	314	208
San Francisco	9	6	0	.600	341	225
L.A. Rams	3	12	0	.200	225	367

Saturday, December 14

Chicago 27, Tampa Bay 0 — at Soldier Field, attendance 54,719. Richard Dent posted 3 sacks and intercepted a pass as the Bears shut out the Buccaneers to clinch a playoff berth. Chicago used a powerful ground game combined with a stifling defense to overwhelm Tampa Bay. The Bears rushed for 182 yards, limited the Buccaneers to 7 first downs and 106 total yards, and controlled the ball for more than 40 of the game's 60 minutes. Mark Green, playing for injured starter Neal Anderson, rushed for a career-high 82 yards and 2 touchdowns. His first score was set up by Dent's interception.

Tampa Bay	0	0	0	0	—	0
Chicago	6	7	7	7	—	27

Chi—Muster 1 run (kick failed)
Chi—Green 2 run (Butler kick)
Chi—Green 1 run (Butler kick)
Chi—Bailey 1 run (Butler kick)

San Francisco 28, Kansas City 14 — at Candlestick Park, attendance 62,672. Steve Bono passed for 220 yards and 3 touchdowns before leaving the game in the third quarter with a sprained knee as the 49ers won their fifth consecutive game. Bono's third touchdown pass was a 20-yarder to Jerry Rice that gave San Francisco an insurmountable 21-0 lead midway though the third quarter. But Bono also became the third 49ers quarterback to go down with an injury this season. Joe Montana was lost for the year with torn tendons in his right elbow and backup Steve Young suffered a knee injury November 3. Young led San Francisco to its final touchdown in the fourth quarter. Kansas City's Nick Lowery kicked 2 extra points to give him 101 points for the season. It marked the ninth time in his career that he'd surpassed the 100-point mark, an NFL record. Despite the victory, the 49ers' hopes for an NFL record-tying ninth consecutive season in the playoffs were dashed by results later in the weekend.

Kansas City	0	0	7	7	—	14
San Francisco	7	7	7	7	—	28

SF—Rice 1 pass from Bono (Cofer kick)
SF—Taylor 9 pass from Bono (Cofer kick)
SF—Rice 20 pass from Bono (Cofer kick)
KC—Word 11 run (Lowery kick)
SF—Carter 53 run (Cofer kick)
KC—Harry 17 pass from DeBerg (Lowery kick)

Sunday, December 15

Pittsburgh 17, Cincinnati 10 — at Three Rivers Stadium, attendance 35,420. Bubby Brister, playing in his first game in more than two months, completed 15 of 28 passes for 184 yards and 2 touchdowns to lead the Steelers to the victory. Brister's 19-yard touchdown pass to Keith Cash on the first play of the final quarter provided the margin of victory. He also completed a pair of crucial third-down passes on the 61-yard drive. Merril Hoge ran for 79 yards and caught 4 passes for Pittsburgh, which outgained Cincinnati 326 to 195. David Fulcher returned a second-quarter interception 27 yards for a touchdown for the Bengals.

Cincinnati	0	7	3	0	—	10
Pittsburgh	10	0	0	7	—	17

Pitt—Cooper 47 pass from Brister (Anderson kick)
Pitt—FG Anderson 47
Cin—Fulcher 27 interception return (Breech kick)
Cin—FG Breech 39
Pitt—Cash 19 pass from Brister (Anderson kick)

Dallas 25, Philadelphia 13 — at Veterans Stadium, attendance 65,854. Kelvin Martin returned a fourth-quarter punt 85 yards for a touchdown as the Cowboys snapped the Eagles' six-game winning streak and clinched their first playoff berth since 1985. Martin's return gave Dallas a 15-10 lead 45 seconds into the fourth quarter. After Philadelphia trimmed the deficit to 15-13, Steve Beuerlein passed four yards to Michael Irvin for the clinching score with 6:02 remaining. Beuerlein, who completed 9 of 31 passes for 145 yards but didn't turn the ball over against the Eagles' top-ranked defense, passed 32 yards to Jay Novacek and 36 yards to Irvin on the 80-yard drive. Beuerlein was sacked just once, while the Cowboys got to Jeff Kemp 7 times. Jimmie Jones had 2½ sacks and Ken Norton added 2 for Dallas.

Dallas	5	0	3	17	—	25
Philadelphia	0	10	0	3	—	13

Dall—FG Willis 50
Dall—Safety, Hendrix tackled Booty in end zone
Phil—Johnson 31 pass from Kemp (Ruzek kick)
Phil—FG Ruzek 37
Dall—FG Willis 32
Dall—Martin 85 punt return (Willis kick)
Phil—FG Ruzek 47
Dall—Irvin 4 pass from Beuerlein (Willis kick)
Dall—FG Willis 37

Detroit 21, Green Bay 17 — at Lambeau Field, attendance 43,881. Erik Kramer threw a pair of touchdown passes to Robert Clark and Mel Gray returned a fourth-quarter punt 78 yards for a touchdown as the Lions clinched at least a wild-card playoff berth with the victory. The win was the first outdoors all season for the Lions, who play their home games in the Pontiac Silverdome, and they did it in temperatures that reached 18 below with the wind-chill factor. Detroit remained tied with the Bears for first place in the NFC Central Division and equaled a club record with their eleventh victory. The Lions also made the playoffs for the first time since 1983. The Packers led 10-7 until Kramer capped a 60-yard touchdown drive with a 3-yard pass to Clark with 11:48 remaining in the game. Just 1:48 later, Gray's punt return provided the eventual winning points. Green Bay amassed 367 total yards to just 206 for Detroit, but the Lions' Jim Arnold kept the Packers in poor field position with four kicks inside the 20.

Detroit	7	0	0	14	—	21
Green Bay	7	3	0	7	—	17

GB —Workman 30 run (Jacke kick)
Det —R. Clark 19 pass from Kramer (Murray kick)
GB —FG Jacke 23
Det —R. Clark 3 pass from Kramer (Murray kick)
Det —Gray 78 punt return (Murray kick)
GB —Workman 12 pass from Tomczak (Jacke kick)

Houston 17, Cleveland 14 — at Cleveland Stadium, attendance 55,680. Warren Moon completed a 2-yard touchdown pass to Haywood Jeffires with 2:19 left in the game to give the Oilers the victory. After the go-ahead touchdown, Bernie Kosar moved his team to the Houston 1-yard line with four seconds remaining, but Matt Stover missed the potential game-tying 19-yard field-goal try on the last play of the game. Moon, who completed 26 of 40 passes for 250 yards and 2 touchdowns, set an NFL record for most completions in a season. He finished the game at 382, breaking Dan Marino's previous mark of 378. Kosar was 28 of 40 for 258 yards and 2 touchdowns. Leroy Hoard caught 10 passes for the Browns. The Oilers equaled a franchise record with their eleventh victory of the season.

Houston	0	10	0	7	—	17
Cleveland	7	7	0	0	—	14

Cleve—Hoard 8 pass from Kosar (Stover kick)
Hou —Givins 7 pass from Moon (Del Greco kick)
Cleve—Brennan 8 pass from Kosar (Stover kick)
Hou —FG Del Greco 27
Hou —Jeffires 2 pass from Moon (Del Greco kick)

Minnesota 20, L.A. Rams 14 — at Metrodome, attendance 46,312. Reggie Rutland returned a fourth-quarter interception a club-record 97 yards for a touchdown and the Vikings handed the Rams their ninth consecutive defeat. Los Angeles, which never led, was trailing just 13-7 and driving for the potential go-ahead touchdown when Jim Everett's pass for Henry Ellard at the goal line was returned by Rutland for the clinching score. His 97-yard return eclipsed Minnesota's old record of 94, set by Walker Lee Ashley against Chicago in 1988. Everett completed 26 of 43 passes for 263 yards but was intercepted 4 times. The Rams also lost their last chance to win the game on a fumbled snap on their final possession.

L.A. Rams	0	0	7	7	—	14
Minnesota	0	10	3	7	—	20

Minn —Walker 2 run (Reveiz kick)
Minn —FG Reveiz 20
Rams—Gary 1 run (Zendejas kick)
Minn —FG Reveiz 22
Minn —Rutland 97 interception return (Reveiz kick)
Rams—Ellard 8 pass from Everett (Zendejas kick)

San Diego 38, Miami 30 — at San Diego Jack Murphy Stadium, attendance 47,731. Rod Bernstine ran for 104 yards and 3 fourth-quarter touchdowns as the Chargers stunned the Dolphins. Miami, which led 23-10 entering the final period, was on the verge of clinching a playoff berth after hearing that the Jets had lost to the Patriots. But a 25-yard touchdown pass from John Friesz to Ronnie Harmon trimmed the Dolphins' lead to 23-17, and moments later Joe Phillips recovered Dan Marino's fumble at the Dolphins' 13. Three plays later, Bernstine ran 5 yards for his first touchdown, putting the Chargers ahead 24-23. After rookie safety Stanley Richard intercepted a Marino pass later in the quarter, Bernstine capped a 43-yard drive with a 1-yard touchdown run. He put the game out of reach with a 63-yard spurt with 1:38 left, just moments after Miami had closed to within one point at 31-30. Marino passed for 313 yards and 3 touchdowns for the Dolphins. Mark Duper caught 9 passes for 123 yards.

Miami	3	7	13	7	—	30
San Diego	0	10	0	28	—	38

Mia—FG Stoyanovich 34
SD —FG Carney 35
Mia—Marino 10 run (Stoyanovich kick)
SD —McEwen 12 pass from Friesz (Carney kick)
Mia—Paige 9 pass from Marino (kick failed)
Mia—Clayton 10 pass from Marino (Stoyanovich kick)
SD —Harmon 25 pass from Friesz (Carney kick)
SD —Bernstine 5 run (Carney kick)
SD —Bernstine 1 run (Carney kick)
Mia—Clayton 8 pass from Marino (Stoyanovich kick)
SD —Bernstine 63 run (Carney kick)

New England 6, N.Y. Jets 3 — at Giants Stadium, attendance 55,869. Charlie Baumann's 2 field goals provided the Patriots with all the points they needed in wind-swept Giants Stadium. New England totaled just 226 yards in the game, but drove 41 yards to Baumann's 45-yard field goal in the first quarter and 77 yards to his 41-yarder, which proved to be the game-winner, in the third quarter. The Jets missed a pair of short field-goal attempts. Pat Leahy, bothered by hip and hamstring injuries, missed a 23-yarder. He was replaced by punter Luis Aguiar, who converted a 23-yard try in the second quarter for New York's only points, but Aguiar also misfired on a 27-yard effort. Leonard Russell rushed for 112 yards on 26 carries for the Patriots.

New England	3	0	3	0	—	6
N.Y. Jets	0	3	0	0	—	3

NE —FG Baumann 45
Jets—FG Aguiar 23
NE —FG Baumann 41

Washington 34, N.Y. Giants 17 — at RFK Stadium, attendance 54,722. Mark Rypien passed for 230 yards and 3 touchdowns and Danny Copeland intercepted a pass and recovered a fumble as the Redskins won for the fourteenth time in 15 games. The Giants led 10-7 in the second quarter until Copeland recovered a Phil Simms fumble at New York's 17-yard line. Two plays later, Gerald Riggs scored on a 1-yard run to give the Redskins the lead for good. Copeland intercepted Simms on the Giants' next possession, and Rypien passed 22 yards to Terry Orr for a 21-10 lead. Ricky Ervins gained 85 yards for Washington and Earnest Byner had 68, which was good enough to give him his second consecutive 1,000-yard season. Gary Clark totaled 129 yards and scored 2 touchdowns on 3 receptions for Washington. Simms passed for 288 yards and 1 touchdown for the Giants.

N.Y. Giants	3	7	7	0	—	17
Washington	7	17	3	7	—	34

Giants—FG Bahr 36
Wash —Clark 65 pass from Rypien (Lohmiller kick)
Giants—Simms 1 run (Bahr kick)
Wash —Riggs 1 run (Lohmiller kick)
Wash —Orr 22 pass from Rypien (Lohmiller kick)
Wash —FG Lohmiller 36
Wash —FG Lohmiller 36
Giants—Ingram 18 pass from Simms (Bahr kick)
Wash —Clark 50 pass from Rypien (Lohmiller kick)

Denver 24, Phoenix 19 — at Mile High Stadium, attendance 74,098. John Elway's 4-yard touchdown run with 1:46 left in the game rallied the Broncos past the Cardinals. Denver's victory, coupled with the Raiders' loss the next night, gave the Broncos the AFC Western Division title, one year after finishing in last place. Elway, who completed 19 of 33 passes for 245 yards, was intercepted 3 times in the second half, and Phoenix converted all 3 into field goals by Greg Davis for a 19-17 lead. But Elway came back and completed 22-yard passes to Vance Johnson and Shannon Sharpe on the winning drive, which covered 66 yards in 6 plays. The loss was the ninth in a row for the Cardinals.

Phoenix	0	3	10	6	—	19
Denver	7	3	7	7	—	24

Den—Sharpe 3 pass from Elway (Treadwell kick)
Den—FG Treadwell 18
Phx —FG Davis 33
Phx —FG Davis 45
Den—Sewell 8 run (Treadwell kick)
Phx —Jones 45 pass from Chandler (Davis kick)
Phx —FG Davis 28
Phx —FG Davis 38
Den—Elway 4 run (Treadwell kick)

Atlanta 26, Seattle 13 — at Atlanta-Fulton County Stadium, attendance 55,834. The Falcons, last-place finishers in the NFC Western Division for four consecutive seasons, clinched their first playoff berth since 1982. Chris Miller threw a pair of touchdown passes and Deion Sanders intercepted 2 passes for Atlanta, which won its fifth consecutive game. Sanders also took a lateral after teammate

Tim McKyer's third-quarter interception and raced 48 yards for a score to give the Falcons a 19-0 lead. Atlanta, which built a 12-0 advantage in the first half while allowing the Seahawks only 37 total yards, was never threatened.

Seattle	0	0	3	10	—	13
Atlanta	2	10	7	7	—	26

Atl —Safety, Jordan tackled Stouffer in end zone
Atl —FG Johnson 42
Atl —Thomas 4 pass from Miller (Johnson kick)
Atl —Sanders 48 interception return (Johnson kick)
Sea—FG Kasay 43
Sea—FG Kasay 43
Atl —Haynes 30 pass from Miller (Johnson kick)
Sea—Clark 24 pass from Krieg (Kasay kick)

Sunday Night, December 15

Buffalo 35, Indianapolis 7 — at Hoosier Dome, attendance 48,286. The Bills secured the home-field advantage throughout the AFC playoffs by easily beating the Colts. Jim Kelly passed for 3 touchdowns in the first half, and Buffalo scored on each of its first three possessions to breeze to the victory. Kelly completed 9 of 11 passes for 119 yards before giving way to backup Frank Reich, who also threw a touchdown pass in the fourth quarter. Kenneth Davis ran for 90 yards and a score on 22 carries and also caught a 14-yard touchdown pass from Kelly. The Colts completed an 0-8 year at home and equaled the franchise record for most losses in a season (14).

Buffalo	21	7	0	7	—	35
Indianapolis	0	0	0	7	—	7

Buff—K. Davis 1 run (Norwood kick)
Buff—Lofton 11 pass from Kelly (Norwood kick)
Buff—K. Davis 14 pass from Kelly (Norwood kick)
Buff—Reed 23 pass from Kelly (Norwood kick)
Ind —Manoa 1 run (Biasucci kick)
Buff—Metzelaars 4 pass from Reich (Norwood kick)

Monday, December 16

New Orleans 27, L.A. Raiders 0 — at Louisiana Superdome, attendance 68,625. Bobby Hebert, out six weeks with an injured right shoulder, returned to the lineup to pass for 320 yards and help the Saints snap a four-game losing streak and clinch a spot in the playoffs. Hebert completed 28 of 39 passes to spark New Orleans, which also got a dominating performance out of its defense. The Raiders managed only 6 first downs and 117 total yards, and had their offense on the field for only 19:24. The Saints missed scoring opportunities early, but broke the game open late with 17 points in a span of 1:41 in the fourth quarter. Gill Fenerty's 2-yard touchdown run and Brett Maxie's 31-yard interception return with 1:54 left in the game provided the final points.

L.A. Raiders	0	0	0	0	—	0
New Orleans	3	0	7	17	—	27

NO—FG Andersen 37
NO—Hilliard 1 run (Andersen kick)
NO—FG Andersen 42
NO—Fenerty 2 run (Andersen kick)
NO—Maxie 31 interception return (Andersen kick)

Seventeenth Week Summaries

Standings

American Football Conference

Eastern Division

	W	L	T	Pct.	Pts.	OP
Buffalo	13	3	0	.813	458	318
N.Y. Jets	8	8	0	.500	314	293
Miami	8	8	0	.500	343	349
New England	6	10	0	.375	211	305
Indianapolis	1	15	0	.063	143	381
Central Division						
Houston	11	5	0	.688	386	251
Pittsburgh	7	9	0	.438	292	344
Cleveland	6	10	0	.375	293	298
Cincinnati	3	13	0	.188	263	435
Western Division						
Denver	12	4	0	.750	304	235
Kansas City	10	6	0	.625	322	252
L.A. Raiders	9	7	0	.563	298	297
Seattle	7	9	0	.438	276	261
San Diego	4	12	0	.250	274	342

National Football Conference

Eastern Division

	W	L	T	Pct.	Pts.	OP
Washington	14	2	0	.875	485	224
Dallas	11	5	0	.688	342	310
Philadelphia	10	6	0	.625	285	244
N.Y. Giants	8	8	0	.500	281	297
Phoenix	4	12	0	.250	196	344
Central Division						
Detroit	12	4	0	.750	339	295
Chicago	11	5	0	.688	299	269
Minnesota	8	8	0	.500	301	306
Green Bay	4	12	0	.250	273	313
Tampa Bay	3	13	0	.188	199	365
Western Division						
New Orleans	11	5	0	.688	341	211
Atlanta	10	6	0	.625	361	338
San Francisco	10	6	0	.625	393	239
L.A. Rams	3	13	0	.188	234	390

Saturday, December 21

Green Bay 27, Minnesota 7 — at Metrodome, attendance 52,860. Vince Workman scored 2 touchdowns to lead the Packers to the victory over the Vikings. Workman caught a 12-yard touchdown pass from Mike Tomczak late in the first quarter to put Green Bay ahead 10-0, then ran 1 yard for the touchdown that made it 20-0 late in the third quarter, effectively putting the game out of reach. The Packers totaled just 188 yards in the game, but converted 3 Minnesota turnovers into 17 points. The Vikings averted a shutout when Rich Gannon passed 9 yards to Terry Allen for a touchdown with 1:22 to play.

Green Bay	10	0	10	7	—	27
Minnesota	0	0	0	7	—	7

GB —FG Jacke 42
GB —Workman 12 pass from Tomczak (Jacke kick)
GB —FG Jacke 39
GB —Workman 1 run (Jacke kick)
GB —Woodside 10 run (Jacke kick)
Minn—Allen 9 pass from Gannon (Reveiz kick)

N.Y. Giants 24, Houston 20 — at Giants Stadium, attendance 63,421. The defending Super Bowl-champion Giants, already eliminated from the playoff race and facing the possibility of a losing season, upset the Oilers, costing Houston a franchise-record twelfth victory and a bye in the first round of the playoffs. New York's Phil Simms completed 15 of 17 passes for 200 yards and Rodney Hampton rushed for a career-high 140 yards to help New York finish the season 8-8. Hampton scored on a 2-yard run in the first quarter and Simms threw a 12-yard touchdown pass to tight end Howard Cross in the second period as New York built a 24-6 advantage through three quarters. The Oilers tried to rally, but Warren Moon's 6-yard touchdown run with 6:06 remaining and his 5-yard touchdown pass to Ernest Givins with 1:28 left could only make it close.

Houston	0	6	0	14	—	20
N.Y. Giants	7	10	7	0	—	24

Giants—Hampton 2 run (Bahr kick)
Hou —FG Del Greco 37
Giants—Cross 12 pass from Simms (Bahr kick)
Giants—FG Bahr 54
Hou —FG Del Greco 34
Giants—Tillman 4 run (Bahr kick)
Hou —Moon 6 run (Del Greco kick)
Hou —Givins 5 pass from Moon (Del Greco kick)

Sunday, December 22

Dallas 31, Atlanta 27 — at Texas Stadium, attendance 60,962. Emmitt Smith ran for 160 yards to win the league's rushing title and scored on a 6-yard run early in the fourth quarter to give the Cowboys the victory. The loss kept the Falcons from winning the NFC Western Division title as they entered the playoffs as a wild-card team. Despite Smith's big day, he also lost a fumble at Atlanta's 18-yard line with 1:54 left in the game. The Falcons' Chris Miller, who passed for 325 yards and 3 touchdowns, marched his team 66 yards to the Dallas 16, but then threw 4 consecutive incompletions. Larry Brown tipped away the final pass, which was intended for Deion Sanders, normally a cornerback who was in the game as an extra wide receiver. Michael Irvin caught 10 passes for 169 yards for the Cowboys. Alexander Wright had a 102-yard kickoff return for a touchdown for Dallas. Michael Haynes totaled 148 yards and scored twice on 5 receptions for the Falcons.

Atlanta	14	3	10	0	—	27
Dallas	21	3	0	7	—	31

Dall—Irvin 58 pass from Beuerlein (Willis kick)
Atl —Haynes 67 pass from Miller (Johnson kick)
Dall—E. Smith 4 run (Willis kick)
Atl —Rison 28 pass from Miller (Johnson kick)
Dall—Wright 102 kickoff return (Willis kick)
Dall—FG Willis 20
Atl —FG Johnson 25
Atl —FG Johnson 29
Atl —Haynes 43 pass from Miller (Johnson kick)
Dall—E. Smith 6 run (Willis kick)

Pittsburgh 17, Cleveland 10 — at Three Rivers Stadium, attendance 47,070. Bubby Brister threw a 65-yard touchdown pass to Dwight Stone and the Steelers stopped a pair of Browns' drives in the final minutes to preserve the win. Brister's touchdown pass gave Pittsburgh a 10-3 lead in the third quarter. Richard Shelton then returned an interception 57 yards for a touchdown to give Pittsburgh a 17-3 lead with 9:28 left in the game. Cleveland threatened after that, but Shelton made his third interception of the game in the end zone with 2:06 remaining, and Greg Lloyd sacked Bernie Kosar on the game's final play from the Steelers' 13-yard line to seal the victory. Kosar completed 28 of 49 passes for 335 yards and 1 touchdown for Cleveland. Webster Slaughter caught 11 of Kosar's passes for 138 yards.

Cleveland	0	3	0	7	—	10
Pittsburgh	3	0	7	7	—	17

Pitt —FG Anderson 34
Cleve—FG Stover 19
Pitt —Stone 65 pass from Brister (Anderson kick)
Pitt —Shelton 57 interception return (Anderson kick)
Cleve—M. Jackson 27 pass from Kosar (Stover kick)

Denver 17, San Diego 14 — at San Diego Jack Murphy Stadium, attendance 51,449. The AFC Western Division-champion Broncos turned 2 first-half turnovers into 10 points, then got a 2-yard touchdown run from Greg Lewis in the fourth quarter to win their fourth consecutive game and secure a first-round bye in the playoffs. Gaston Green had 90 yards as Denver rushed for 148 yards and maintained possession for more than 36 minutes. The Broncos also forced 4 turnovers, intercepting San Diego's John Friesz 3 times and recovering 1 fumble.

Denver	3	7	0	7	—	17
San Diego	0	7	0	7	—	14

Den—FG Treadwell 42
Den—Sewell 2 run (Treadwell kick)
SD —McEwen 1 pass from Friesz (Carney kick)
Den—G. Lewis 2 run (Treadwell kick)
SD —Bernstine 1 run (Carney kick)

Detroit 17, Buffalo 14 — at Rich Stadium, attendance 78,059. Eddie Murray's 21-yard field goal 4:23 into overtime gave the Lions the victory over the shorthanded Bills. With the AFC Eastern Division title and home-field advantage already secured, Buffalo rested offensive stars Jim Kelly, Thurman Thomas, and James Lofton. But backup Frank Reich threw 2 touchdown passes, including a 20-yarder to backup Steve Tasker to tie the game at 14-14 with 2:33 left in regulation. Detroit had rallied from a 7-0 deficit to take the lead on a 1-yard run by Barry Sanders and an 18-yard interception return by William White. But Sanders, who rushed for 108 yards, fumbled at the Lions' 20-yard line with 2:38 left and one play later, Reich and Tasker teamed for the tying score. In overtime, the Lions won the toss and marched 61 yards to the Buffalo 4 before Murray's kick. Kenneth Davis ran for 118 yards for the Bills. Though the fans saw Buffalo's 17-game winning streak at Rich Stadium snapped, the crowd of 78,059 enabled the Bills to set an NFL single-season home attendance record of 635,889.

Detroit	0	0	0	14	3	—	17
Buffalo	0	7	0	7	0	—	14

Buff—Reed 7 pass from Reich (Norwood kick)
Det —Sanders 1 run (Murray kick)
Det —White 18 interception return (Murray kick)
Buff—Tasker 20 pass from Reich (Norwood kick)
Det —FG Murray 21

Tampa Bay 17, Indianapolis 3 — at Tampa Stadium, attendance 28,043. The Buccaneers snapped a five-game losing streak and extended the Colts' winless string to six games with the victory. Vinny Testaverde passed 29 yards to Mark Carrier for the touchdown that gave Tampa Bay the lead for good with 21 seconds remaining in the first half. Wide receiver Lawrence Dawsey ran 9 yards for the Buccaneers' other touchdown. Indianapolis's Jeff George passed for 203 yards but was sacked 5 times. The Colts also lost 4 fumbles.

Indianapolis	0	3	0	0	—	3
Tampa Bay	0	7	7	3	—	17

Ind—FG Biasucci 39
TB —Carrier 29 pass from Testaverde (Christie kick)
TB —Dawsey 9 run (Christie kick)
TB —FG Christie 28

Kansas City 27, L.A. Raiders 21 — at Los Angeles Memorial Coliseum, attendance 65,144. Barry Word rushed 35 times for 152 yards and 1 touchdown as the Chiefs ground out the victory over the Raiders, setting up a wild-card playoff game between the same teams one week later in Kansas City. Had Los Angeles won, the rematch would have been played in the Coliseum. Kansas City controlled the game by running the football, rushing 48 times for 206 yards, and maintaining possession for more than 39 minutes. But it was two quick strikes through the air that secured the victory. Steve DeBerg's 57-yard touchdown pass to J.J. Birden at the start of the second quarter gave the Chiefs the lead for good, and his 53-yarder to Birden with 7:00 left increased the lead to 27-14 after the Raiders had closed to within six points. Los Angeles's Todd Marinovich, making his first NFL start in place of injured Jay Schroeder, kept the Raiders in it by completing 23 of 40 passes for 243 yards and 3 touchdowns, including 2 in the fourth quarter. DeBerg was 14 of 20 for 277 yards and 2 scores for Kansas City. Birden caught 8 passes for 188 yards.

Kansas City	7	10	0	10	—	27
L.A. Raiders	7	0	0	14	—	21

KC —Word 1 run (Lowery kick)
Raiders—Brown 26-yard pass from Marinovich (Jaeger kick)
KC —Birden 57 pass from DeBerg (Lowery kick)
KC —FG Lowery 33

KC — FG Lowery 25
Raiders— Horton 7 pass from Marinovich (Jaeger kick)
KC — Birden 53 pass from DeBerg (Lowery kick)
Raiders— Brown 23 pass from Marinovich (Jaeger kick)

Cincinnati 29, New England 7 — at Riverfront Stadium, attendance 46,394. Boomer Esiason passed for 333 yards and 3 touchdowns to lead the Bengals over the Patriots. After New England got a 60-yard touchdown pass from Hugh Millen to Michael Timpson on its first possession, Esiason tied the game with a 21-yard touchdown pass to Rodney Holman. In the second quarter, he added touchdown passes of 12 yards to Tim McGee and 36 yards to James Brooks just 1:52 apart for a 21-7 lead at halftime. Esiason completed 20 of 40 passes and was not intercepted. Millen passed for 271 yards for the Patriots. Timpson caught 7 passes for 150 yards.

New England	7	0	0	0	—	7
Cincinnati	7	14	0	8	—	29

NE — Timpson 60 pass from Millen (Baumann kick)
Cin — Holman 21 pass from Esiason (Breech kick)
Cin — McGee 12 pass from Esiason (Breech kick)
Cin — Brooks 36 pass from Esiason (Breech kick)
Cin — FG Breech 49
Cin — FG Breech 25
Cin — Safety, Gordon tackled Millen in end zone

New Orleans 27, Phoenix 3 — at Sun Devil Stadium, attendance 30,928. The Saints won their first NFC Western Division title in the history of the franchise by beating the Cardinals. New Orleans only had 12 first downs and 190 total yards in the game, but intercepted 5 passes and forced 2 fumbles to win. Gene Atkins had 3 interceptions in the second half, and would have had a fourth that he returned 55 yards for a touchdown had it not been negated by a penalty. Dalton Hilliard and Buford Jordan scored on short touchdown runs and Bobby Hebert passed 19 yards to Floyd Turner for a score in the fourth quarter.

New Orleans	0	13	7	7	—	27
Phoenix	3	0	0	0	—	3

Phx— FG Davis 38
NO — FG Andersen 27
NO — Hilliard 2 run (Andersen kick)
NO — FG Andersen 39
NO — Jordan 3 run (Andersen kick)
NO — Turner 19 pass from Hebert (Andersen kick)

N.Y. Jets 23, Miami 20 — at Joe Robbie Stadium, attendance 69,636. Raul Allegre, signed only five days earlier to replace injured Pat Leahy, tied the game with a 44-yard field goal on the final play of regulation, then won it with a 30-yarder 7:33 into overtime, giving the Jets the last playoff berth in the AFC. The Dolphins, who needed a win or a tie to advance to postseason play, took a 20-17 lead on a fourth-down, 1-yard pass from Dan Marino to Ferrell Edmunds with 44 seconds remaining. But New York drove to Miami's 26-yard line to position Allegre for his tying kick. The key gains were Ken O'Brien's passes to Rob Moore (23 yards) and Terance Mathis (14 yards). In overtime, the Dolphins won the coin toss but had to punt after their first possession, and the Jets then marched 65 yards in 11 plays. O'Brien had a 29-yard completion to Moore on that drive. Johnny Hector ran for 132 yards for the Jets, who amassed 231 yards on the ground. For the Dolphins, Marino completed 27 of 45 passes for 282 yards and 2 touchdowns, including an 18-yard score to Mark Clayton on the final play of the first half.

N.Y. Jets	7	0	7	6	3	—	23
Miami	0	7	3	10	0	—	20

Jets— Baxter 1 run (Allegre kick)
Mia — Clayton 18 pass from Marino (Stoyanovich kick)
Mia — FG Stoyanovich 23
Jets— Baxter 1 run (Allegre kick)
Mia — FG Stoyanovich 33
Jets— FG Allegre 25
Mia — Edmunds 1 pass from Marino (Stoyanovich kick)
Jets— FG Allegre 44
Jets— FG Allegre 30

Philadelphia 24, Washington 22 — at Veterans Stadium, attendance 58,988. Roger Ruzek kicked a 38-yard field goal with 13 seconds left to give the Eagles the win over the Redskins. Washington led 19-7 before Philadelphia exploded for 17 fourth-quarter points. Jeff Kemp threw short touchdown passes to Keith Jackson and Maurice Johnson to erase the deficit and give the Eagles a 21-19 lead. But Chip Lohmiller kicked his fifth field goal of the day, a 35-yarder with 2:34 left, to put the Redskins back ahead. Kemp then marched his team 58 yards to Ruzek's winning field goal.

Washington	3	10	3	6	—	22
Philadelphia	7	0	0	17	—	24

Phil — O. Smith 74 interception return (Ruzek kick)
Wash — FG Lohmiller 21
Wash — Ervins 1 run (Lohmiller kick)
Wash — FG Lohmiller 47
Wash — FG Lohmiller 47
Wash — FG Lohmiller 38
Phil — Keith Jackson 2 pass from Kemp (Ruzek kick)
Phil — M. Johnson 6 pass from Kemp (Ruzek kick)
Wash — FG Lohmiller 35
Phil — FG Ruzek 38

Sunday Night, December 21

Seattle 23, L.A. Rams 9 — at Kingdome, attendance 51,100. The Seahawks scored 16 points in a span of 6:20 in the third quarter to rally past the Rams, handing Los Angeles its tenth consecutive defeat. John Kasay's 35-yard field goal with 12:11 left in the third period put Seattle ahead 10-9. After a short punt and Chris Warren's 29-yard punt return, the Seahawks drove 9 yards to James Jones's 1-yard touchdown at the 9:10 mark. Jones then scored on a 6-yard run with 5:51 left in period, capping a 19-yard drive after Terry Wooden recovered Jim Everett's fumble. Tony Zendejas, who kicked 3 field goals to account for all the Rams' points, finished the season an NFL-record 17 of 17 on three-point tries.

L.A. Rams	3	6	0	0	—	9
Seattle	0	7	16	0	—	23

Rams— FG Zendejas 44
Rams— FG Zendejas 46
Sea — Tice 4 pass from Krieg (Kasay kick)
Rams— FG Zendejas 50
Sea — FG Kasay 35
Sea — Jones 1 run (Kasay kick)
Sea — Jones 6 run (kick failed)

Monday, December 23

San Francisco 52, Chicago 14 — at Candlestick Park, attendance 60,419. Steve Young, returning to the starting lineup for the first time since injuring a knee six weeks earlier, completed 21 of 32 passes for 338 yards and 3 touchdowns to lead the 49ers to the easy victory over the playoff-bound Bears. San Francisco, which finished with a 10-6 record, failed to make the playoffs for the first time since 1982. Chicago ended the season 11-5 and earned a wild-card spot in the playoffs. The 49ers jumped to a 24-0 halftime advantage on scoring passes by Young of 2 yards to Jamie Williams and 3 and 69 yards to Jerry Rice, and Mike Cofer's 41 yard field goal. San Francisco outgained the Bears 355-134 in total yardage in the first half. Don Griffin's 99-yard fumble return for a touchdown highlighted the 49ers' second-half scoring.

Chicago	0	0	7	7	—	14
San Francisco	7	17	0	28	—	52

SF — Williams 2 pass from Young (Cofer kick)
SF — Rice 3 pass from Young (Cofer kick)
SF — Rice 69 pass from Young (Cofer kick)
SF — FG Cofer 41
Chi— Anderson 26 pass from Harbaugh (Butler kick)
SF — Young 2 run (Cofer kick)
SF — Griffin 99 fumble recovery return (Cofer kick)
SF — Sydney 2 run (Cofer kick)
Chi— Waddle 11 pass from Willis (Butler kick)
SF — Sherrard 15 pass from Musgrave (Cofer kick)

Eighteenth Week Summaries

Saturday, December 28

Atlanta 27, New Orleans 20 — at Louisiana Superdome, attendance 68,794. Michael Haynes caught a short pass from Chris Miller and turned it into the game-winning 61-yard touchdown for the Falcons with 2:41 left in the game. The Saints, who won their first NFC Western Division title and made the playoffs for the third time in five years, remained winless in postseason games in franchise history. Atlanta rallied from a 10-0 second-quarter deficit behind 3 touchdown passes by Miller, who completed 18 of 30 passes for 291 yards. Haynes had 6 receptions for 144 yards and 2 touchdowns, including a 20-yarder that gave the Falcons their first lead at 17-13 early in the third quarter. New Orleans regained the lead on Dalton Hilliard's 1-yard run 50 seconds into the fourth quarter, but Atlanta tied it at 20-20 on Norm Johnson's 36-yard field goal with 7:43 remaining. After Haynes's go-ahead touchdown, Bobby Hebert drove the Saints to the Falcons' 35-yard line, but was intercepted by Atlanta's Tim McKyer.

Atlanta	0	10	7	10	—	27
New Orleans	7	6	0	7	—	20

NO — Turner 26 pass from Hebert (Andersen kick)
NO — FG Andersen 45
Atl — Rison 24 pass from Miller (Johnson kick)
Atl — FG Johnson 44
NO — FG Andersen 35
Atl — Haynes 20 pass from Miller (Johnson kick)
NO — Hilliard 1 run (Andersen kick)
Atl — FG Johnson 36
Atl — Haynes 61 pass from Miller (Johnson kick)

Kansas City 10, L.A. Raiders 6 — at Arrowhead Stadium, attendance 75,827. Steve DeBerg passed 11 yards to Fred Jones for the game's only touchdown and the Chiefs forced 6 turnovers to hang on and beat the Raiders. The Raiders' Todd Marinovich, who passed for 243 yards and 3 touchdowns in a narrow loss to Kansas City one week earlier, completed 12 of 23 passes for 140 yards, but was intercepted 4 times. Deron Cherry had 2 of the thefts, the second of which he returned 29 yards to the Los Angeles 11-yard line in the second quarter. DeBerg and Jones connected for the touchdown on the next play, 5:07 before halftime. The Raiders drove to the Chiefs' 24-yard line in the final minutes, but were whistled for 4 penalties in a 5-play span before reserve linebacker Lonnie Marts ended the threat with an interception. Barry Word rushed for 130 yards on 33 carries for Kansas City, which ran the ball 39 times and passed only 14. Nick Bell carried 20 times for 107 yards for Los Angeles, which outgained the Chiefs 276 yards to 204.

L.A. Raiders	0	3	3	0	—	6
Kansas City	0	7	0	3	—	10

KC — F. Jones 11 pass from DeBerg (Lowery kick)
Raiders — FG Jaeger 32
Raiders — FG Jaeger 26
KC — FG Lowery 18

Sunday, December 29

Dallas 17, Chicago 13 — at Soldier Field, attendance 62,594. Emmitt Smith rushed for 105 yards and 1 touchdown on 26 carries to lead the Cowboys to their first postseason victory since the 1982 season. Smith's touchdown gave Dallas a 10-0 lead and came 5 plays after Dallas linebacker Darrick Brownlow blocked Maury Buford's punt and teammate Ken Norton recovered at the Bears' 10-yard line. In the third quarter, Dallas' Steve Beuerlein capped a 75-yard drive with a 3-yard touchdown pass to Jay Novacek for a 17-6 lead, and the Cowboys made the advantage stand up. Smith carried 26 times in the game and became the first player ever to eclipse the 100-yard plateau against Chicago in postseason play. Jim Harbaugh passed for 218 yards for Chicago, which outgained Dallas 372 total yards to 288. Tom Waddle caught 9 passes for 104 yards and 1 touchdown, a 6-yarder with 2:42 left in the game to make it close, for the Bears.

Dallas	10	0	7	0	—	17
Chicago	0	3	3	7	—	13

Dall— FG Willis 27
Dall— E. Smith 1 run (Willis kick)
Chi — FG Butler 19
Chi — FG Butler 43
Dall— Novacek 3 pass from Beuerlein (Willis kick)
Chi — Waddle 6 pass from Harbaugh (Butler kick)

Houston 17, N.Y. Jets 10 — at Astrodome, attendance 61,485. Warren Moon threw a pair of touchdown passes to Ernest Givins and the Oilers' defense stopped the Jets inside Houston's 5-yard line twice in the second half to preserve the victory. The Oilers led 14-10 entering the third quarter, when the Jets took the second-half kickoff and consumed more than eight minutes while driving to the Houston 8-yard line. On third down, Ken O'Brien's pass was intercepted by safety Bubba McDowell at the 2. After Al Del Greco's 53-yard field goal put the Oilers ahead 17-10 early in the fourth quarter, New York drove to the Houston 3. But on third down, Al Smith stopped Brad Baxter for no gain, and on fourth-and-inches, a trio of players, including Smith, stopped Freeman McNeil for no gain. The Jets had one more chance after recovering Moon's fumble at the Oilers' 26 with 4:59 left in the game, but New York could not convert a first down. For Houston, Moon completed 28 of 40 passes for 271 yards. Drew Hill had 9 catches for 77 yards for Houston. The Jets' O'Brien was 21 of 31 for 221 yards but was intercepted 3 times. Al Toon caught 8 passes for 96 yards and 1 touchdown.

N.Y. Jets	0	10	0	0	—	10
Houston	7	7	0	3	—	17

Hou — Givins 5 pass from Moon (Del Greco kick)
Jets — Toon 10 pass from O'Brien (Allegre kick)
Hou — Givins 20 pass from Moon (Del Greco kick)
Jets — FG Allegre 33
Hou — FG Del Greco 53

Nineteenth Week Summaries

Saturday, January 4, 1992

Washington 24, Atlanta 7 — at RFK Stadium, attendance 55,181. The Redskins overcame poor weather conditions by rushing for 162 yards, while the Falcons succumbed to the wind, rain, and mud by turning the ball over 6 times. Rookie Ricky Ervins gained 104 yards on 23 carries as Washington maintained possession for more than 36 minutes. Gerald Riggs had a pair of short touchdown runs for the Redskins. Washington scored all the points it needed in a span of 3:11 of the second quarter. Ervins capped an 81-yard drive with a 17-yard touchdown run and Riggs scored on a 2-yard run four plays after James Geathers recovered a fumble at Atlanta's 39-yard line.

Atlanta	0	7	0	0	—	7
Washington	0	14	3	7	—	24

Wash— Ervins 17 run (Lohmiller kick)
Wash— Riggs 2 run (Lohmiller kick)
Atl — T. Johnson 1 run (N. Johnson kick)
Wash— FG Lohmiller 24
Wash— Riggs 1 run (Lohmiller kick)

Denver 26, Houston 24 — at Mile High Stadium, attendance 75,301. David Treadwell's 28-yard field goal with 16 seconds remaining in the game capped a dramatic 87-yard drive in the closing moments to lift the Broncos over the Oilers. Treadwell's winning kick came shortly after

John Elway's 44-yard completion to Vance Johnson on fourth-and-10 from the Denver 35-yard line. Earlier on the drive, Elway scrambled 7 yards for a first down on fourth-and-6 from the 28. And it was Elway's 22-yard completion to Michael Young that got the Broncos out of a hole at their own 2-yard line. Denver started the winning drive there with no time outs left after Houston's Greg Montgomery dropped his punt out of bounds with 2:07 left in the game. Warren Moon passed for 3 touchdowns as Houston built first-half leads of 14-0 and 21-6. But the Broncos' defense stiffened, allowing only a field goal in the second half. That came 1:35 into the fourth quarter and gave the Oilers a 24-16 lead. Elway, who passed for 257 yards and 1 touchdown, then directed an 80-yard touchdown march that trimmed the deficit to 24-23 with 6:53 to go. Moon finished with 27 completions in 36 attempts for 325 yards. Ernest Givins had 111 yards on 6 catches for Houston.

Houston	14	7	0	3	24
Denver	6	7	3	10	26

Hou — Jeffires 15 pass from Moon (Del Greco kick)
Hou — Hill 9 pass from Moon (Del Greco kick)
Den — V. Johnson 10 pass from Elway (kick failed)
Hou — Duncan 6 pass from Moon (Del Greco kick)
Den — Lewis 1 run (Treadwell kick)
Den — FG Treadwell 49
Hou — FG Del Greco 25
Den — Lewis 1 run (Treadwell kick)
Den — FG Treadwell 28

Sunday, January 5, 1992
NFC Divisional Playoff Game

Detroit 38, Dallas 6 — at Pontiac Silverdome, attendance 79,835. Erik Kramer completed 29 of 38 passes for 341 yards and 3 touchdowns as the ground-oriented Lions took to the air to beat the Cowboys. Barry Sanders, the NFL's second-leading rusher with 1,548 yards during the regular season, carried only 12 times for 69 yards (47 coming on a fourth-quarter touchdown run), but Detroit still piled up 421 yards of total offense. Two of Kramer's scoring passes went Willie Green, who had 4 catches for 115 yards, and Melvin Jenkins returned a second-quarter interception 41 yards for a touchdown for the Lions. Jenkins's touchdown gave Detroit a 14-3 lead, and the Lions put the game away by scoring 2 touchdowns in a span of 1:05 of the third quarter. Green's second touchdown catch, a 9-yarder, gave Detroit a 24-6 advantage, and after Victor Jones recovered Troy Aikman's fumble at the Dallas 27-yard line, Herman Moore caught a 7-yard touchdown pass to put the game away.

Dallas	3	3	0	0	6
Detroit	7	10	14	7	38

Det — Green 31 pass from Kramer (Murray kick)
Dall — FG Willis 28
Det — Jenkins 41 interception return (Murray kick)
Dall — FG Willis 28
Det — FG Murray 36
Det — Green 9 pass from Kramer (Murray kick)
Det — Moore 7 pass from Kramer (Murray kick)
Det — Sanders 47 run (Murray kick)

Sunday, January 5, 1992
AFC Divisional Playoff Game

Buffalo 37, Kansas City 14 — at Rich Stadium, attendance 80,182. Jim Kelly threw 3 touchdown passes and the Bills avenged a 33-6 loss to the Chiefs in the regular season by breezing to the victory. Kelly, who completed 23 of 35 passes for 273 yards, teamed with Andre Reed for scoring passes of 25 and 53 yards as Buffalo built a 17-0 advantage at halftime. Kelly's 10-yard touchdown pass to James Lofton early in the third quarter put the game out of reach at 24-0. Thurman Thomas rushed for 100 yards on 22 carries for the Bills, marking the fourth consecutive postseason game that he eclipsed the century mark. Reed had 100 yards on 4 catches as Buffalo amassed 448 total yards to Kansas City's 213. The Chiefs' Steve DeBerg was knocked out of the game in the second quarter with a strained thumb. Backup Mark Vlasic passed for 124 yards and 1 touchdown for Kansas City, but was intercepted 4 times.

Kansas City	0	0	7	7	14
Buffalo	7	10	7	13	37

Buff — Reed 25 pass from Kelly (Norwood kick)
Buff — Reed 53 pass from Kelly (Norwood kick)
Buff — FG Norwood 33
Buff — Lofton 10 pass from Kelly (Norwood kick)
KC — Word 3 run (Lowery kick)
Buff — FG Norwood 20
Buff — FG Norwood 47
Buff — Davis 5 run (Norwood kick)
KC — F. Jones 20 pass from Vlasic (Lowery kick)

Twentieth Week Summaries

Sunday, January 12, 1992
AFC Championship Game

Buffalo 10, Denver 7 — at Rich Stadium, attendance 80,272. Carlton Bailey returned an interception 11 yards for a touchdown and Scott Norwood's fourth-quarter field goal provided the margin of difference as the Bills won their second consecutive AFC championship. The game was scoreless until Buffalo's Jeff Wright tipped John El-

way's screen pass over the middle and Bailey returned it for a touchdown with 5:28 left in the third quarter. After Norwood's 44-yard field goal with 4:18 left in the game, Denver's Gary Kubiak capped an 85-yard drive with a 3-yard touchdown run with 1:43 remaining. Denver recovered the ensuing onside kick at its own 49-yard line, but turned the ball over one play later when running back Steve Sewell fumbled after being hit by the Bills' Kirby Jackson after catching a pass. Jackson recovered to end the Broncos' final threat. Kubiak, who entered the game in the fourth quarter when Elway could not continue because of a thigh bruise suffered earlier in the game, completed 11 of 12 passes for 136 yards after announcing he would retire at the end of the season. Denver held Buffalo's explosive offense in check, limiting the Bills to only 12 first downs and 213 total yards. But the Broncos, who had 20 first downs and 304 yards, managed only 1 touchdown despite good field position and nine trips inside Buffalo's territory. Kicker David Treadwell missed 3 field-goal tries, including 2 that bounced off the uprights.

Denver	0	0	0	7	7
Buffalo	0	0	7	3	10

Buff — Bailey 11 interception return (Norwood kick)
Buff — FG Norwood 44
Den — Kubiak 3 run (Treadwell kick)

Sunday, January 12, 1992
NFC Championship Game

Washington 41, Detroit 10 — at RFK Stadium, attendance 55,585. The Redskins turned a pair of turnovers into 10 points less than five minutes into the game and coasted to the victory to earn a record-tying fifth Super Bowl berth. Washington's Charles Mann forced the Lions' Erik Kramer to fumble on the first play from scrimmage, and Gerald Riggs capped a two-play, 10-yard drive with a 2-yard touchdown run just 1:06 into the game. Less than three minutes later, the Redskins scored again when Kurt Gouveia's 38-yard interception return set up Chip Lohmiller's 20-yard field goal. Detroit briefly pulled within three points on an 18-yard touchdown pass from Kramer to Willie Green, but Riggs added a 3-yard touchdown run, and Mark Rypien passed 45 yards to Gary Clark and 21 yards to Art Monk for touchdowns in the second half to put the game out of reach. Rypien completed 12 of 17 passes for 228 yards for Washington, which beat the Lions 45-0 on the same field on the opening day of the season. Kramer completed 21 of 33 passes for 249 yards for Detroit.

Detroit	0	10	0	0	10
Washington	10	7	10	14	41

Wash — Riggs 2 run (Lohmiller kick)
Wash — FG Lohmiller 20
Det — W. Green 18 pass from Kramer (Murray kick)
Wash — Riggs 3 run (Lohmiller kick)
Det — FG Murray 30
Wash — FG Lohmiller 28
Wash — Clark 45 pass from Rypien (Lohmiller kick)
Wash — Monk 21 pass from Rypien (Lohmiller kick)
Wash — D. Green 32 interception return (Lohmiller kick)

Twenty-First Week Summaries

Sunday, January 26, 1992
Super Bowl XXVI
Minneapolis, Minnesota

Washington 37, Buffalo 24 — at Metrodome, attendance 63,130. Mark Rypien passed for 292 yards and 2 touchdowns as the Redskins overwhelmed the Bills to win their third Super Bowl in the past 10 years. Rypien, the game's most valuable player, completed 18 of 33 passes, including a 10-yard scoring strike to Earnest Byner and a 30-yard touchdown to Gary Clark. The latter came late in the third quarter, after Buffalo had trimmed a 24-0 deficit to 24-10, and effectively put the game out of reach. Washington went on to lead by as much as 37-10 before the Bills made it close with a pair of touchdowns in the final six minutes. Though the Redskins struggled early, converting their first three drives inside the Bills' 20-yard line into only 3 points, they built a 17-0 halftime lead. And they made it 24-0 just 16 seconds into the second half, after Kurt Gouveia intercepted Buffalo quarterback Jim Kelly's pass on the first play of the third quarter and returned it 23 yards to the Bills' 2. One play later, Gerald Riggs scored his second touchdown of the game to make it 24-0. Kelly, forced to bring Buffalo from behind, completed 28 of a Super Bowl-record 58 passes for 275 yards and 2 touchdowns, but was intercepted 4 times. Bills running back Thurman Thomas, who had an AFC-high 1,407 yards rushing and an NFL-best 2,038 total yards from scrimmage during the regular season, ran for only 13 yards on 10 carries and was limited to 27 yards on 4 receptions. Clark had 7 catches for 114 yards and Art Monk added 7 for 113 for the Redskins, who amassed 417 yards of total offense while limiting the explosive Bills to 283. Washington's Joe Gibbs became only the third head coach to win as many as three Super Bowls.

Washington	0	17	14	6	37
Buffalo	0	0	10	14	24

Wash — FG Lohmiller 34
Wash — Byner 10 pass from Rypien (Lohmiller kick)
Wash — Riggs 1 run (Lohmiller kick)
Wash — Riggs 2 run (Lohmiller kick)

Buff — FG Norwood 21
Buff — Thomas 1 run (Norwood kick)
Wash — Clark 30 pass from Rypien (Lohmiller kick)
Wash — FG Lohmiller 25
Wash — FG Lohmiller 39
Buff — Metzelaars 2 pass from Kelly (Norwood kick)
Buff — Beebe 4 pass from Kelly (Norwood kick)

Twenty-Second Week Summaries

Sunday, February 2, 1992
AFC-NFC Pro Bowl
Honolulu, Hawaii

NFC 21, AFC 15—at Aloha Stadium, attendance 50,209. Atlanta's Chris Miller threw an 11-yard touchdown pass to San Francisco's Jerry Rice with 4:04 remaining in the game to lift the NFC to victory over the AFC. It was the NFC's thirteenth victory in the 22-game series. The AFC had taken a 15-14 lead when the Raiders' Jeff Jaeger kicked a 27-yard field goal 1:49 into the fourth quarter. But the NFC, aided by a key roughing-the-passer penalty on a third-down incompletion from the AFC 24-yard line, drove 85 yards to the winning score. The Cowboy's Michael Irvin, playing in his first Pro Bowl, caught 8 passes for 125 yards, including a 13-yard touchdown in the first quarter, and was named the player of the game. Rice had 7 catches for 77 yards. Mark Rypien of Washington, the Super Bowl most valuable player one week earlier, completed 11 of 18 passes for 165 yards and 2 touchdowns for the NFC, including a 35-yarder to Redskins teammate Gary Clark just 26 seconds before halftime. Miller completed 7 of his 10 attempts for 85 yards.

NFC	7	7	0	7	21
AFC	7	5	0	3	15

AFC—Clayton 4 pass from Kelly (Jaeger kick)
NFC—Irvin 13 pass from Rypien (Lohmiller kick)
AFC—Safety, Byner tackled in end zone
AFC—FG Jaeger 48
NFC—Clark 35 pass from Rypien (Lohmiller kick)
AFC—FG Jaeger 27
NFC—Rice 11 pass from Miller (Lohmiller kick)

1991 Professional Football Awards

	NFL	AFC	NFC
Professional Football Writers of America			
Most Valuable Player	Thurman Thomas		
Rookie of the Year	Mike Croel		
Coach of the Year	Wayne Fontes		
Associated Press			
Most Valuable Player	Thurman Thomas		
Offensive Player of the Year	Thurman Thomas		
Defensive Player of the Year	Pat Swilling		
Rookie of the Year—Offensive	Leonard Russell		
Rookie of the Year—Defensive	Mike Croel		
Coach of the Year	Wayne Fontes		
United Press International			
Offensive Player of the Year		Thurman Thomas	Mark Rypien
Defensive Player of the Year		Cornelius Bennett	Reggie White
Coach of the Year		Dan Reeves	Wayne Fontes
Rookie of the Year		Mike Croel	Lawrence Dawsey
The Sporting News			
Player of the Year	Thurman Thomas		
Rookie of the Year	Mike Croel		
Coach of the Year	Joe Gibbs		
Football News			
Player of the Year		Thurman Thomas	Mark Rypien
Coach of the Year		Dan Reeves	Wayne Fontes
Pro Football Weekly			
Offensive Player of the Year	Thurman Thomas		
Defensive Player of the Year	Reggie White		
Rookie of the Year—Offensive	Leonard Russell		
Rookie of the Year—Defensive	Mike Croel		
Coach of the Year	Wayne Fontes		
Football Digest			
Player of the Year	Barry Sanders		
Rookie of the Year—Offensive	Leonard Russell		
Rookie of the Year—Defensive	Mike Croel		
Coach of the Year	Jimmy Johnson		
Maxwell Club			
Player of the Year (Bert Bell Trophy)	Barry Sanders		
Super Bowl XXVI Most Valuable Player			
(Pete Rozelle Trophy)	Mark Rypien		
AFC-NFC Pro Bowl Player of the Game			
(Dan McGuire Award)	Michael Irvin		

AFC-NFC Players of the Week:

	AFC Offense	**AFC Defense**	**NFC Offense**	**NFC Defense**
Week 1	RB Thurman Thomas, Buff.	CB Albert Lewis, K.C.	QB Jim McMahon, Phil.	DE Reggie White, Phil.
Week 2	QB Jim Kelly, Buff.	LB Lamar Lathon, Hou.	K Chip Lohmiller, Wash.	LB John Roper, Chi.
Week 3	RB Thuman Thomas, Buff.	S Steve Atwater, Den.	WR Anthony Carter, Minn.	DE Clyde Simmons, Phil.
				LB Bryce Paup, G.B.
Week 4	TE Marv Cook, N.E.	LB Cornelius Bennett, Buff.	RB Emmitt Smith, Dall.	CB Deion Sanders, Atl.
Week 5	RB Gaston Green, Den.	CB Nate Odomes, Buff.	QB Troy Aikman, Dall.	LB Rickey Jackson, N.O.
Week 6	WR Ernest Givins, Hou.	LB Derrick Thomas, K.C.	RB Rodney Hampton, N.Y.G.	LB Wilber Marshall, Wash.
Week 7	WR Haywood Jeffires, Hou.	CB Lionel Washington, Raiders	WR Art Monk, Wash.	DE Chris Doleman, Minn.
Week 8	WR James Lofton, Buff.	S Ronnie Lott, Raiders	QB Steve Young, S.F.	S Tim McDonald, Phx.
Week 9	QB Steve DeBerg, K.C.	LB Clay Matthews, Clev.	QB Chris Miller, Atl.	CB Ray Crockett, Det.
Week 10	QB Boomer Esiason, Cin.	DE Jeff Lageman, N.Y.J.	RB Terry Allen, Minn.	LB Pat Swilling, N.O.
Week 11	QB Jeff George, Ind.	LB Derrick Thomas, K.C.	QB Mark Rypien, Wash.	LB Broderick Thomas, T.B.
Week 12	QB Warren Moon, Hou.	LB Billy Ray Smith, S.D.	WR Art Monk, Wash.	CB Deion Sanders, Atl.
Week 13	WR Irving Fryar, N.E.	LB Rufus Porter, Sea.	RB Barry Sanders, Det.	LB Pepper Johnson, N.Y.G.
Week 14	QB Dan Marino, Mia.	LB Tracy Simien, K.C.	QB Steve Bono, S.F.	LB Seth Joyner, Phil.
Week 15	QB Jim Kelly, Buff.	DT Ray Childress, Hou.	WR John Taylor, S.F.	S Brian Jordan, Atl.
Week 16	RB Rod Bernstine, S.D.	DE William Fuller, Hou.	QB Bobby Hebert, N.O.	DE Richard Dent, Chi.
Week 17	WR J.J. Birden, K.C.	CB Richard Shelton, Pitt.	WR Michael Irvin, Dall.	S Gene Atkins, N.O.

AFC-NFC Players of the Month:

	AFC Offense	**AFC Defense**	**NFC Offense**	**NFC Defense**
Sept.	QB Jim Kelly, Buff. RB Thurman Thomas, Buff.	DE Neil Smith, K.C.	RB Barry Sanders, Det.	LB Sam Mills, N.O.
Oct.	RB Christian Okoye, K.C.	CB Cris Dishman, Hou.	QB Steve Young, S.F.	LB Wilber Marshall, Wash.
Nov.	RB Thurman Thomas, Buff.	S Ronnie Lott, Raiders	WR Gary Clark, Wash.	CB Ray Crockett, Det.
Dec.	RB Barry Word, K.C.	LB Simon Fletcher, Den.	RB Emmitt Smith, Dall.	LB Jessie Tuggle, Atl.

1991 ALL-PRO TEAMS

1991 PFWA All-Pro Team

Selected by the Professional Football Writers of America

Offense

Michael Irvin, Dallas . . . . Wide Receiver
Haywood Jeffires, Houston . . . . Wide Receiver
Marv Cook, New England . . . . Tight End
Jim Lachey, Washington . . . . Tackle
Mike Kenn, Atlanta . . . . Tackle
Steve Wisniewski, Los Angeles Raiders . . . . Guard
Mike Munchak, Houston . . . . Guard
Kent Hull, Buffalo . . . . Center
Jim Kelly, Buffalo . . . . Quarterback
Thurman Thomas, Buffalo . . . . Running Back
Barry Sanders, Detroit . . . . Running Back
Jeff Jaeger, Los Angeles Raiders . . . . Kicker

Defense

Reggie White, Philadelphia . . . . Defensive End
Clyde Simmons, Philadelphia . . . . Defensive End
Jerome Brown, Philadelphia . . . . Defensive Tackle
Jerry Ball, Detroit . . . . Defensive Tackle
Seth Joyner, Philadelphia . . . . Outside Linebacker
Pat Swilling, New Orleans . . . . Outside Linebacker
Sam Mills, New Orleans . . . . Inside Linebacker
Al Smith, Houston . . . . Inside Linebacker
Darrell Green, Washington . . . . Cornerback
Deion Sanders, Atlanta . . . . Cornerback
Ronnie Lott, Los Angeles Raiders . . . . Safety
Steve Atwater, Denver . . . . Safety
Jeff Gossett, Los Angeles Raiders . . . . Punter
Mel Gray, Detroit . . . . Kick Returner/Punt Returner

1991 Associated Press All-Pro Team

Offense

Michael Irvin, Dallas . . . . Wide Receiver
Haywood Jeffires, Houston . . . . Wide Receiver
Marv Cook, New England . . . . Tight End
Jim Lachey, Washington . . . . Tackle
Mike Kenn, Atlanta . . . . Tackle
Steve Wisniewski, Los Angeles Raiders . . . . Guard
Mike Munchak, Houston . . . . Guard
Kent Hull, Buffalo . . . . Center
Jim Kelly, Buffalo . . . . Quarterback
Barry Sanders, Detroit . . . . Running Back
Thurman Thomas, Buffalo . . . . Running Back
Jeff Jaeger, Los Angeles Raiders . . . . Kicker
Mel Gray, Detroit . . . . Kick Returner

Defense

Reggie White, Philadelphia . . . . Defensive End
Clyde Simmons, Philadelphia . . . . Defensive End
Jerome Brown, Philadelphia . . . . Defensive Tackle
Jerry Ball, Detroit . . . . Defensive Tackle
Pat Swilling, New Orleans . . . . Outside Linebacker
Derrick Thomas, Kansas City . . . . Outside Linebacker
Mike Singletary, Chicago . . . . Inside Linebacker
Chris Spielman, Detroit . . . . Inside Linebacker
Darrell Green, Washington . . . . Cornerback
Cris Dishman, Houston . . . . Cornerback
Steve Atwater, Denver . . . . Safety
Ronnie Lott, Los Angeles Raiders . . . . Safety
Jeff Gossett, Los Angeles Raiders . . . . Punter

1991 All-NFL Team

Selected by the Associated Press and Professional Football Writers of America

Offense

Michael Irvin, Dallas (AP, PFWA) . . . . Wide Receiver
Haywood Jeffires, Houston (AP, PFWA) . . . . Wide Receiver
Marv Cook, New England (AP, PFWA) . . . . Tight End
Jim Lachey, Washington (AP, PFWA) . . . . Tackle
Mike Kenn, Atlanta (AP, PFWA) . . . . Tackle
Steve Wisniewski, Los Angeles Raiders (AP, PFWA) . . . . Guard
Mike Munchak, Houston (AP, PFWA) . . . . Guard
Kent Hull, Buffalo (AP, PFWA) . . . . Center
Jim Kelly, Buffalo (AP, PFWA) . . . . Quarterback
Thurman Thomas, Buffalo (AP, PFWA) . . . . Running Back
Barry Sanders, Detroit (AP, PFWA) . . . . Running Back

Defense

Reggie White, Philadelphia (AP, PFWA) . . . . Defensive End
Clyde Simmons, Philadelphia (AP, PFWA) . . . . Defensive End
Jerome Brown, Philadelphia (AP, PFWA) . . . . Defensive Tackle
Jerry Ball, Detroit (AP, PFWA) . . . . Defensive Tackle
Pat Swilling, New Orleans (AP, PFWA) . . . . Outside Linebacker
Seth Joyner, Philadelphia (PFWA) . . . . Outside Linebacker
Derrick Thomas, Kansas City (AP) . . . . Outside Linebacker
Sam Mills, New Orleans (PFWA) . . . . Inside Linebacker
Chris Spielman, Detroit (AP) . . . . Inside Linebacker
Mike Singletary, Chicago (AP) . . . . Inside Linebacker
Al Smith, Houston (PFWA) . . . . Inside Linebacker
Darrell Green, Washington (AP, PFWA) . . . . Cornerback
Deion Sanders, Atlanta (PFWA) . . . . Cornerback
Cris Dishman, Houston (AP) . . . . Cornerback
Ronnie Lott, Los Angeles Raiders (AP, PFWA) . . . . Safety
Steve Atwater, Denver (AP, PFWA) . . . . Safety

Specialists

Jeff Jaeger, Los Angeles Raiders (AP, PFWA) . . . . Kicker
Jeff Gossett, Los Angeles Raiders (AP, PFWA) . . . . Punter
Mel Gray, Detroit (AP, PFWA) . . . . Kick Returner/Punt Returner

1991 UPI All-AFC Team

Selected by United Press International

Offense

Andre Reed, Buffalo . . . . Wide Receiver
Haywood Jeffires, Houston . . . . Wide Receiver
Marv Cook, New England . . . . Tight End
John Alt, Kansas City . . . . Tackle
Bruce Armstrong, New England . . . . Tackle
Mike Munchak, Houston . . . . Guard
Steve Wisniewski, Los Angeles Raiders . . . . Guard
Kent Hull, Buffalo . . . . Center
Jim Kelly, Buffalo . . . . Quarterback
Thurman Thomas, Buffalo . . . . Running Back
Gaston Green, Denver . . . . Running Back
Jeff Jaeger, Los Angeles Raiders . . . . Kicker

Defense

Greg Townsend, Los Angeles Raiders . . . . Defensive End
William Fuller, Houston . . . . Defensive End
Greg Kragen, Denver . . . . Defensive Tackle
Ray Childress, Houston . . . . Defensive Tackle
Cornelius Bennett, Buffalo . . . . Outside Linebacker
Derrick Thomas, Kansas City . . . . Outside Linebacker
Al Smith, Houston . . . . Inside Linebacker
Karl Mecklenburg, Denver . . . . Inside Linebacker
Cris Dishman, Houston . . . . Cornerback
Nate Odomes, Buffalo . . . . Cornerback
Ronnie Lott, Los Angeles Raiders . . . . Safety
Steve Atwater, Denver . . . . Safety
Reggie Roby, Miami . . . . Punter

1991 UPI All-NFC Team

Selected by United Press International

Offense

Michael Irvin, Dallas . . . . Wide Receiver
Gary Clark, Washington . . . . Wide Receiver
Jay Novacek, Dallas . . . . Tight End
Jim Lachey, Washington . . . . Tackle
Mike Kenn, Atlanta . . . . Tackle
Raleigh McKenzie, Washington . . . . Guard
Guy McIntyre, San Francisco . . . . Guard
Jay Hilgenberg, Chicago . . . . Center
Mark Rypien, Washington . . . . Quarterback
Barry Sanders, Detroit . . . . Running Back
Emmitt Smith, Dallas . . . . Running Back
Chip Lohmiller, Washington . . . . Kicker

Defense

Reggie White, Philadelphia . . . . Defensive End
Clyde Simmons, Philadelphia . . . . Defensive End
Jerry Ball, Detroit . . . . Defensive Tackle
Pat Swilling, New Orleans . . . . Outside Linebacker
Wilber Marshall, Washington . . . . Outside Linebacker
Jessie Tuggle, Atlanta . . . . Inside Linebacker
Mike Singletary, Chicago . . . . Inside Linebacker
Darrell Green, Washington . . . . Cornerback
Deion Sanders, Atlanta . . . . Cornerback
Andre Waters, Philadelphia . . . . Safety
Bennie Blades, Detroit . . . . Safety
Rich Camarillo, Phoenix . . . . Punter

1991 PFWA All-Rookie Team

Selected by the Professional Football Writers of America

Offense

Lawrence Dawsey, Tampa Bay . . . . Wide Receiver
Mike Pritchard, Atlanta . . . . Wide Receiver
Adrian Cooper, Pittsburgh . . . . Tight End
Pat Harlow, New England . . . . Tackle
Antone Davis, Philadelphia . . . . Tackle
Ed King, Cleveland . . . . Guard
Eric Moten, San Diego . . . . Guard
John Flannery, Houston . . . . Center
No Selection . . . . Quarterback
Leonard Russell, New England . . . . Running Back
Ricky Ervins, Washington . . . . Running Back
John Kasay, Seattle . . . . Kicker

Defense

Kenny Walker, Denver . . . . Defensive End
Phil Hansen, Buffalo . . . . Defensive End
Russell Maryland, Dallas . . . . Defensive Tackle
Moe Gardner, Atlanta . . . . Defensive Tackle
Mike Croel, Denver . . . . Outside Linebacker
Mo Lewis, New York Jets . . . . Outside Linebacker
Keith Traylor, Denver . . . . Inside Linebacker
Darrick Brownlow, Dallas . . . . Inside Linebacker
Aeneas Williams, Phoenix . . . . Cornerback
Larry Brown, Dallas . . . . Cornerback
Eric Turner, Cleveland . . . . Safety
Stanley Richard, San Diego . . . . Safety

Ten Best Rushing Performances, 1991

	Attempts	Yards	TD
1. Barry Sanders Detroit vs. Minnesota, November 24	23	220	4
2. Emmitt Smith Dallas vs. Phoenix, September 22	23	182	2
3. Barry Sanders Detroit vs. Indianapolis, September 22	30	179	2
4. Thurman Thomas Buffalo vs. Miami, September 1	25	165	1
5. Barry Sanders Detroit vs. Tampa Bay, September 29	27	160	3
Emmitt Smith Dallas vs. Atlanta, December 22	32	160	2
7. Gaston Green Denver vs. Minnesota, September 29	26	158	0
8. Christian Okoye Kansas City vs. Miami, October 13	23	153	2
9. Barry Word Kansas City vs. L.A. Raiders, December 22	35	152	1
10. Mark Higgs Miami vs. Buffalo, September 1	30	146	1

100-Yard Rushing Performances, 1991

First Week
Thurman Thomas, Buffalo	165 yards vs. Miami
Mark Higgs, Miami	146 yards vs. Buffalo
Allen Pinkett, Houston	144 yards vs. L.A. Raiders
Christian Okoye, Kansas City	143 yards vs. Atlanta
Gaston Green, Denver	116 yards vs. Cincinnati
Emmitt Smith, Dallas	112 yards vs. Cleveland

Second Week
Herschel Walker, Minnesota	125 yards vs. Atlanta
Barry Foster, Pittsburgh	121 yards vs. Buffalo
Robert Delpino, L.A. Rams	116 yards vs. N.Y. Giants
Emmitt Smith, Dallas	112 yards vs. Washington
Mark Higgs, Miami	111 yards vs. Indianapolis
Thurman Thomas, Buffalo	107 yards vs. Pittsburgh
James Brooks, Cincinnati	101 yards vs. Houston
Earnest Byner, Washington	101 yards vs. Dallas
Allen Pinkett, Houston	101 yards vs. Cincinnati

Third Week
Barry Sanders, Detroit	143 yards vs. Miami
James Brooks, Cincinnati	111 yards vs. Cleveland
Earnest Byner, Washington	109 yards vs. Phoenix
Steve Broussard, Atlanta	101 yards vs. San Diego

Fourth Week
Emmitt Smith, Dallas	182 yards vs. Phoenix
Barry Sanders, Detroit	179 yards vs. Indianapolis
Gaston Green, Denver	127 yards vs. San Diego
Blair Thomas, N.Y. Jets	125 yards vs. Chicago
Gill Fenerty, New Orleans	106 yards vs. Minnesota
Rodney Hampton, N.Y. Giants	104 yards vs. Cleveland
Rod Bernstine, San Diego	103 yards vs. Denver

Fifth Week
Barry Sanders, Detroit	160 yards vs. Tampa Bay
Gaston Green, Denver	158 yards vs. Minnesota
Thurman Thomas, Buffalo	117 yards vs. Chicago
Rod Bernstine, San Diego	112 yards vs. Kansas City
Herschel Walker, Minnesota	103 yards vs. Denver

Sixth Week
Rodney Hampton, N.Y. Giants	137 yards vs. Phoenix
Christian Okoye, Kansas City	130 yards vs. Buffalo
Emmitt Smith, Dallas	122 yards vs. Green Bay
Barry Sanders, Detroit	116 yards vs. Minnesota
Harvey Williams, Kansas City	103 yards vs. Buffalo

Seventh Week
Christian Okoye, Kansas City	153 yards vs. Miami
Ricky Ervins, Washington	133 yards vs. Cleveland
Harold Green, Cincinnati	124 yards vs. Dallas
Thurman Thomas, Buffalo	117 yards vs. Indianapolis
Kenneth Davis, Buffalo	108 yards vs. Indianapolis
Steve Broussard, Atlanta	104 yards vs. San Francisco

Eighth Week
Harold Green, Cincinnati	141 yards vs. Buffalo
Keith Henderson, San Francisco	104 yards vs. Detroit

Ninth Week
None

Tenth Week
Harold Green, Cincinnati	135 yards vs. Cleveland
Terry Allen, Minnesota	127 yards vs. Tampa Bay
Thurman Thomas, Buffalo	126 yards vs. New England
Earnest Byner, Washington	112 yards vs. Houston
Greg Lewis, Denver	111 yards vs. Pittsburgh
Leonard Russell, New England	106 yards vs. Buffalo

Eleventh Week
Reggie Cobb, Tampa Bay	139 yards vs. Detroit
Barry Sanders, Detroit	118 yards vs. Tampa Bay
Thurman Thomas, Buffalo	106 yards vs. Green Bay
Gaston Green, Denver	103 yards vs. L.A. Raiders

Twelfth Week
Thurman Thomas, Buffalo	135 yards vs. Miami
Gaston Green, Denver	133 yards vs. Kansas City
Brad Muster, Chicago	101 yards vs. Indianapolis

Thirteenth Week
Barry Sanders, Detroit	220 yards vs. Minnesota
Fred McAfee, New Orleans	138 yards vs. Atlanta
Emmitt Smith, Dallas	132 yards vs. Washington
Reggie Cobb, Tampa Bay	110 yards vs. N.Y. Giants
John L. Williams, Seattle	109 yards vs. Denver

Fourteenth Week
Mark Higgs, Miami	131 yards vs. Tampa Bay
Thurman Thomas, Buffalo	124 yards vs. N.Y. Jets
Eric Dickerson, Indianapolis	117 yards vs. Cleveland
Emmitt Smith, Dallas	109 yards vs. Pittsburgh

Fifteenth Week
Herschel Walker, Minnesota	126 yards vs. Tampa Bay
Earnest Byner, Washington	116 yards vs. Phoenix
Barry Sanders, Detroit	114 yards vs. N.Y. Jets
Emmitt Smith, Dallas	112 yards vs. New Orleans

Sixteenth Week
Barry Word, Kansas City	115 yards vs. San Francisco
Leonard Russell, New England	112 yards vs. N.Y. Jets
Rod Bernstine, San Diego	104 yards vs. Miami

Seventeenth Week
Emmitt Smith, Dallas	160 yards vs. Atlanta
Barry Word, Kansas City	152 yards vs. L.A. Raiders
Rodney Hampton, N.Y. Giants	140 yards vs. Houston
Johnny Hector, N.Y. Jets	132 yards vs. Miami
Kenneth Davis, Buffalo	118 yards vs. Detroit
Barry Sanders, Detroit	108 yards vs. Buffalo

> **Times 100 or More (79)**
> Sanders, E. Smith, 8; Thomas, 7; G. Green, 5; Byner, 4; Bernstine, H. Green, Hampton, Higgs, Okoye, Walker, 3; Brooks, Broussard, Cobb, Davis, Pinkett, Russell, Word, 2.

Ten Best Passing Performances, 1991

	Att.	Comp.	Yards	TD
1. Mark Rypien Washington vs. Atlanta, November 10	31	16	442	6
2. Warren Moon Houston vs. Dallas, November 10	56	41	432	0
3. Warren Moon Houston vs. N.Y. Jets, October 13	50	35	423	2
4. Warren Moon Houston vs. Cleveland, November 17	44	31	399	3
5. Jim Kelly Buffalo vs. Cincinnati, October 21	27	18	392	5
6. Jim Kelly Buffalo vs. Miami, September 1	39	29	381	2
7. Dave Krieg Seattle vs. San Diego, November 10	38	28	376	2
8. Hugh Millen New England vs. N.Y. Jets, November 17	43	30	372	1
9. Jeff Hostetler N.Y. Giants vs. Dallas, September 29	34	28	368	1
10. Jim Kelly Buffalo vs. Pittsburgh, September 8	43	31	363	6

300-Yard Passing Performances, 1991

First Week
Jim Kelly, Buffalo — 381 yards vs. Miami
Jeff George, Indianapolis — 301 yards vs. New England

Second Week
Jim Kelly, Buffalo — 363 yards vs. Pittsburgh
Steve Young, San Francisco — 348 yards vs. San Diego
Warren Moon, Houston — 315 yards vs. Cincinnati
Chris Miller, Atlanta — 300 yards vs. Minnesota

Third Week
Jeff Kemp, Seattle — 322 yards vs. Denver

Fourth Week
Jeff George, Indianapolis — 348 yards vs. Detroit
Jim Kelly, Buffalo — 322 yards vs. Tampa Bay
Jim Harbaugh, Chicago — 303 yards vs. N.Y. Jets

Fifth Week
Jeff Hostetler, N.Y. Giants — 368 yards vs. Dallas
Tom Tupa, Phoenix — 312 yards vs. New England
Jim Kelly, Buffalo — 303 yards vs. Chicago

Sixth Week
Warren Moon, Houston — 334 yards vs. Denver
Dan Marino, Miami — 321 yards vs. New England
John Elway, Denver — 301 yards vs. Houston

Seventh Week
Warren Moon, Houston — 423 yards vs. N.Y. Jets
Steve Young, San Francisco — 348 yards vs. Atlanta
John Friesz, San Diego — 306 yards vs. L.A. Rams

Eighth Week
Jim Kelly, Buffalo — 392 yards vs. Cincinnati
Hugh Millen, New England — 326 yards vs. Minnesota
John Friesz, San Diego — 321 yards vs. Cleveland
Rich Gannon, Minnesota — 317 yards vs. New England
Jim Everett, L.A. Rams — 300 yards vs. L.A. Raiders

Ninth Week
Troy Aikman, Dallas — 331 yards vs. Detroit

Tenth Week
Jim Everett, L.A. Rams — 346 yards vs. New Orleans

Eleventh Week
Mark Rypien, Washington — 442 yards vs. Atlanta
Warren Moon, Houston — 432 yards vs. Dallas
Dave Krieg, Seattle — 376 yards vs. San Diego
Boomer Esiason, Cincinnati — 361 yards vs. Pittsburgh
Jim McMahon, Philadelphia — 341 yards vs. Cleveland
Jim Everett, L.A. Rams — 329 yards vs. Kansas City
Ken O'Brien, N.Y. Jets — 329 yards vs. Indianapolis
Mike Tomczak, Green Bay — 317 yards vs. Buffalo
Neil O'Donnell, Pittsburgh — 309 yards vs. Cincinnati

Twelfth Week
Warren Moon, Houston — 399 yards vs. Cleveland
Hugh Millen, New England — 372 yards vs. N.Y. Jets
Dan Marino, Miami — 326 yards vs. Buffalo
Mark Rypien, Washington — 325 yards vs. Pittsburgh
Ken O'Brien, N.Y. Jets — 309 yards vs. New England
Jim Everett, L.A. Rams — 308 yards vs. Detroit

Thirteenth Week
Warren Moon, Houston — 324 yards vs. Pittsburgh
Steve DeBerg, Kansas City — 319 yards vs. Cleveland
Steve Bono, San Francisco — 306 yards vs. L.A. Rams

Fourteenth Week
Steve Bono, San Francisco — 347 yards vs. New Orleans
Steve Walsh, New Orleans — 317 yards vs. San Francisco
Dan Marino, Miami — 307 yards vs. Tampa Bay

Fifteenth Week
Jim Kelly, Buffalo — 347 yards vs. L.A. Raiders
Hugh Millen, New England — 330 yards vs. Indianapolis
Vinny Testaverde, Tampa Bay — 330 yards vs. Minnesota

Sixteenth Week
Bobby Hebert, New Orleans — 320 yards vs. L.A. Raiders
Dan Marino, Miami — 313 yards vs. San Diego

Seventeenth Week
Steve Young, San Francisco — 338 yards vs. Chicago
Bernie Kosar, Cleveland — 335 yards vs. Pittsburgh
Boomer Esiason, Cincinnati — 333 yards vs. New England
Chris Miller, Atlanta — 325 yards vs. Dallas

Times 300 or More (56)
Kelly, Moon, 6; Everett, Marino, 4; Millen, Young, 3; Bono, Esiason, Friesz, George, Miller, O'Brien, Rypien, Young, 2.

Ten Best Receiving Performances, 1991

	Yards	No.	TD
1. James Lofton Buffalo vs. Cincinnati, October 21	220	8	2
2. Gary Clark Washington vs. Atlanta, November 10	203	4	3
3. J.J. Birden Kansas City vs. L.A. Raiders, December 22	188	8	2
4. Michael Haynes Atlanta vs. New Orleans, November 24	187	6	2
5. Haywood Jeffires Houston vs. N.Y. Jets, October 13	186	13	0
6. Floyd Turner New Orleans vs. Chicago, October 27	179	9	2
7. Michael Irvin Dallas vs. Atlanta, December 22	169	10	1
8. Art Monk Washington vs. Atlanta, November 10	164	7	1
9. Irving Fryar New England vs. Minnesota, October 20	161	9	0
10. Brian Blades Seattle vs. New Orleans, September 1	160	12	2
Henry Ellard L.A. Rams vs. Kansas City, November 10	160	8	1

100-Yard Receiving Performances, 1991
(Number in parentheses is receptions.)

First Week
Brian Blades, Seattle — 160 yards (12) vs. New Orleans
Andre Reed, Buffalo — 154 yards (11) vs. Miami
Mark Clayton, Miami — 138 yards (6) vs. Buffalo
Dwight Stone, Pittsburgh — 124 yards (4) vs. San Diego
Michael Irvin, Dallas — 123 yards (9) vs. Cleveland
Henry Ellard, L.A. Rams — 116 yards (7) vs. Phoenix
Robert Delpino, L.A. Rams — 113 yards (10) vs. Phoenix
Keith Byars, Philadelphia — 111 yards (8) vs. Green Bay
Gary Clark, Washington — 107 yards (6) vs. Detroit
Thurman Thomas, Buffalo — 103 yards (8) vs. Miami
Sam Graddy, L.A. Raiders — 102 yards (3) vs. Houston

Second Week
Jerry Rice, San Francisco — 150 yards (9) vs. San Diego
Robert Clark, Detroit — 143 yards (10) vs. Green Bay
George Thomas, Atlanta — 128 yards (7) vs. Minnesota
Andre Reed, Buffalo — 118 yards (9) vs. Pittsburgh
Don Beebe, Buffalo — 112 yards (10) vs. Pittsburgh

Third Week
Tommy Kane, Seattle — 122 yards (6) vs. Denver
Thurman Thomas, Buffalo — 112 yards (13) vs. N.Y. Jets
Fred Barnett, Philadelphia — 111 yards (7) vs. Dallas
Brian Blades, Seattle — 107 yards (5) vs. Denver
Webster Slaughter, Cleveland — 107 yards (8) vs. Cincinnati

Fourth Week
Eric Green, Pittsburgh — 158 yards (8) vs. Philadelphia
Roy Green, Philadelphia — 114 yards (6) vs. Pittsburgh
Anthony Johnson, Indianapolis — 105 yards (9) vs. Detroit
Tom Waddle, Chicago — 102 yards (8) vs. N.Y. Jets

Fifth Week
Ernie Jones, Phoenix — 145 yards (8) vs. New England
Mark Ingram, N.Y. Giants — 142 yards (6) vs. Dallas
James Lofton, Buffalo — 122 yards (4) vs. Chicago
Ricky Proehl, Phoenix — 107 yards (4) vs. New England
Mark Clayton, Miami — 100 yards (7) vs. N.Y. Jets

Sixth Week
Ernest Givins, Houston — 151 yards (5) vs. Denver
Jay Novacek, Dallas — 121 yards (11) vs. Green Bay
Eddie Brown, Cincinnati — 117 yards (7) vs. Seattle
Mark Jackson, Denver — 111 yards (7) vs. Houston
Ron Morris, Chicago — 106 yards (5) vs. Washington

Seventh Week
Haywood Jeffires, Houston — 186 yards (13) vs. N.Y. Jets
Anthony Miller, San Diego — 149 yards (7) vs. L.A. Rams
Michael Irvin, Dallas — 148 yards (6) vs. Cincinnati
Jerry Rice, San Francisco — 138 yards (7) vs. Atlanta
Cris Carter, Minnesota — 118 yards (6) vs. Phoenix
Art Monk, Washington — 106 yards (7) vs. Cleveland
Tony Martin, Miami — 104 yards (4) vs. Kansas City

Eighth Week
James Lofton, Buffalo — 220 yards (8) vs. Cincinnati
Irving Fryar, New England — 161 yards (9) vs. Minnesota
Robert Delpino, L.A. Rams — 118 yards (8) vs. L.A. Raiders
Cris Carter, Minnesota — 114 yards (10) vs. New England
Tommy Kane, Seattle — 102 yards (6) vs. Pittsburgh

Ninth Week
Floyd Turner, New Orleans — 179 yards (9) vs. Chicago
Michael Irvin, Dallas — 143 yards (8) vs. Detroit
Jay Novacek, Dallas — 131 yards (10) vs. Detroit
Drew Hill, Houston — 129 yards (6) vs. Cincinnati
Michael Haynes, Atlanta — 110 yards (4) vs. L.A. Rams
Mervyn Fernandez, L.A. Raiders — 107 yards (3) vs. Kansas City

Tenth Week
John Taylor, San Francisco — 127 yards (2) vs. Atlanta
Andre Reed, Buffalo — 121 yards (5) vs. New England
Al Toon, N.Y. Jets — 109 yards (8) vs. Green Bay
Webster Slaughter, Cleveland — 107 yards (5) vs. Cincinnati

Eleventh Week
Gary Clark, Washington — 203 yards (4) vs. Atlanta
Art Monk, Washington — 164 yards (7) vs. Atlanta
Henry Ellard, L.A. Rams — 160 yards (8) vs. Kansas City
Fred Barnett, Philadelphia — 146 yards (8) vs. Cleveland
Sterling Sharpe, Green Bay — 133 yards (8) vs. Buffalo
Brian Blades, Seattle — 131 yards (8) vs. San Diego
Brett Perriman, Detroit — 127 yards (6) vs. Tampa Bay
Anthony Miller, San Diego — 124 yards (5) vs. Seattle
James Lofton, Buffalo — 114 yards (6) vs. Green Bay
Michael Haynes, Atlanta — 105 yards (2) vs. Washington
Tim McGee, Cincinnati — 101 yards (3) vs. Pittsburgh
Jessie Hester, Indianapolis — 100 yards (5) vs. N.Y. Jets

Twelfth Week
Drew Hill, Houston — 144 yards (11) vs. Cleveland
Irving Fryar, New England — 143 yards (8) vs. N.Y. Jets
Art Monk, Washington — 130 yards (8) vs. Pittsburgh
Al Toon, N.Y. Jets — 127 yards (9) vs. New England
Ethan Horton, L.A. Raiders — 123 yards (7) vs. Seattle
Fred Barnett, Philadelphia — 108 yards (6) vs. Cincinnati
Leroy Hoard, Cleveland — 107 yards (10) vs. Houston
Billy Brooks, Indianapolis — 106 yards (7) vs. Chicago
Mark Carrier, Tampa Bay — 104 yards (6) vs. Atlanta

Thirteenth Week
Michael Haynes, Atlanta — 187 yards (6) vs. New Orleans
Emile Harry, Kansas City — 159 yards (11) vs. Cleveland
Irving Fryar, New England — 134 yards (6) vs. Buffalo
Michael Irvin, Dallas — 130 yards (9) vs. Washington
Haywood Jeffires, Houston — 122 yards (8) vs. Pittsburgh
John Taylor, San Francisco — 121 yards (6) vs. L.A. Rams
Cris Carter, Minnesota — 116 yards (7) vs. Detroit
Floyd Turner, New Orleans — 115 yards (5) vs. Atlanta
Alvin Harper, Dallas — 101 yards (4) vs. Washington

Fourteenth Week
Michael Irvin, Dallas — 157 yards (8) vs. Pittsburgh
Jerry Rice, San Francisco — 154 yards (9) vs. New Orleans
Floyd Turner, New Orleans — 132 yards (10) vs. San Francisco
Andre Rison, Atlanta — 124 yards (8) vs. Green Bay
Mark Ingram, N.Y. Giants — 116 yards (7) vs. Cincinnati
James Lofton, Buffalo — 109 yards (5) vs. N.Y. Jets
Tony Martin, Miami — 106 yards (5) vs. Tampa Bay
Lawrence Dawsey, Tampa Bay — 100 yards (8) vs. Miami

Fifteenth Week
Mark Duper, Miami — 134 yards (7) vs. Cincinnati
Greg McMurtry, New England — 119 yards (8) vs. Indianapolis
John Taylor, San Francisco — 113 yards (7) vs. Seattle
Michael Haynes, Atlanta — 112 yards (6) vs. L.A. Rams
Mark Carrier, Tampa Bay — 110 yards (6) vs. Minnesota
Andre Reed, Buffalo — 107 yards (8) vs. L.A. Raiders
Tim Brown, L.A. Raiders — 106 yards (2) vs. Buffalo
Michael Irvin, Dallas — 101 yards (5) vs. New Orleans

Sixteenth Week

Gary Clark, Washington	129 yards (3) vs. N.Y. Giants
Quinn Early, New Orleans	127 yards (4) vs. L.A. Raiders
Mark Duper, Miami	123 yards (9) vs. San Diego
Willie Anderson, L.A. Rams	103 yards (7) vs. Minnesota

Seventeenth Week

J.J. Birden, Kansas City	188 yards (8) vs. L.A. Raiders
Michael Irvin, Dallas	169 yards (10) vs. Atlanta
Michael Timpson, New England	150 yards (7) vs. Cincinnati
Michael Haynes, Atlanta	148 yards (5) vs. Dallas
Webster Slaughter, Cleveland	138 yards (11) vs. Pittsburgh
Wendell Davis, Chicago	136 yards (6) vs. San Francisco
Jerry Rice, San Francisco	125 yards (5) vs. Chicago
Cris Carter, Minnesota	112 yards (7) vs. Green Bay

Times 100 or More (115)

Irvin, 7; Haynes, 5; C. Carter, Lofton, Reed, Rice, 4; Barnett, Blades, G. Clark, Fryar, Monk, Slaughter, J. Taylor, Turner, 3; Carrier, Clayton, Delpino, Duper, Ellard, Hill, Ingram, Jeffires, Kane, T. Martin, A. Miller, Novacek, T. Thomas, Toon, 2.

Top Quarterback Sack Performances, 1991
(2.5 or More Sacks Per Game Needed to Qualify)

First Week

Reggie White, Philadelphia	3.0 vs. Green Bay

Second Week

Andre Tippett, New England	2.5 vs. Cleveland

Third Week

Bryce Paup, Green Bay	4.5 vs. Tampa Bay
Clyde Simmons, Philadelphia	4.5 vs. Dallas
Jerome Brown, Philadelphia	2.5 vs. Dallas

Fourth Week

None

Fifth Week

Rickey Jackson, New Orleans	3.0 vs. Atlanta

Sixth Week

E.J. Junior, Miami	4.0 vs. New England
Derrick Thomas, Kansas City	4.0 vs. Buffalo
William Fuller, Houston	3.0 vs. Denver

Seventh Week

John Randle, Minnesota	3.0 vs. Phoenix

Eighth Week

Henry Thomas, Minnesota	3.0 vs. New England
Pat Swilling, New Orleans	2.5 vs. Tampa Bay
Frank Warren, New Orleans	2.5 vs. Tampa Bay

Ninth Week

Charles Haley, San Francisco	3.0 vs. Philadelphia

Tenth Week

Ken Harvey, Phoenix	3.0 vs. Dallas
Pat Swilling, New Orleans	3.0 vs. L.A. Rams

Eleventh Week

Leonard Marshall, N.Y. Giants	3.0 vs. Phoenix

Twelfth Week

Derrick Thomas, Kansas City	3.0 vs. Denver
Scott Davis, L.A. Raiders	2.5 vs. Seattle

Thirteenth Week

Pepper Johnson, N.Y. Giants	4.5 vs. Tampa Bay

Fourteenth Week

David Brandon, Cleveland	3.0 vs. Indianapolis

Fifteenth Week

None

Sixteenth Week

Richard Dent, Chicago	3.0 vs. Tampa Bay
Jimmie Jones, Dallas	2.5 vs. Philadelphia

Seventeenth Week

Leslie O'Neal, San Diego	4.5 vs. Denver
Jerrol Williams, Pittsburgh	4.0 vs. Cleveland
Dennis Byrd, N.Y. Jets	2.5 vs. Miami

American Football Conference Offense

	Buff.	Cin.	Clev.	Den.	Hou.	Ind.	K.C.	Raid.	Mia.	N.E.	N.Y.J.	Pitt.	S.D.	Sea.
First Downs	359	286	265	284	353	236	322	248	312	259	331	254	285	253
Rushing	128	96	82	117	99	55	127	97	91	93	133	82	114	80
Passing	208	162	163	150	236	163	172	132	205	155	169	158	155	159
Penalty	23	28	20	17	18	18	23	19	16	11	29	14	16	14
Rushes	505	449	389	507	331	354	521	446	379	433	523	394	464	394
Net Yds. Gained	2381	1811	1360	2015	1366	1169	2217	1706	1352	1467	2160	1627	2248	1426
Avg. Gain	4.7	4.0	3.5	4.0	4.1	3.3	4.3	3.8	3.6	3.4	4.1	4.1	4.8	3.6
Avg. Yds. per Game	148.8	113.2	85.0	125.9	85.4	73.1	138.6	106.6	84.5	91.7	135.0	101.7	140.5	89.1
Passes Attempted	516	511	503	459	667	512	479	414	563	481	503	476	511	488
Completed	332	290	312	246	411	305	284	220	327	284	295	259	272	290
% Completed	64.3	56.8	62.0	53.6	61.6	59.6	59.3	53.1	58.1	59.0	58.6	54.4	53.2	59.4
Total Yds. Gained	4140	3413	3547	3310	4804	3066	3281	2977	4077	3442	3429	3313	2983	3371
Times Sacked	35	33	42	46	24	57	21	33	28	63	33	45	35	42
Yds. Lost	269	255	243	313	183	487	177	258	188	436	273	359	236	263
Net Yds. Gained	3871	3158	3304	2997	4621	2579	3104	2719	3889	3006	3156	2954	2747	3108
Avg. Yds. per Game	241.9	197.4	206.5	187.3	288.8	161.2	194.0	169.9	243.1	187.9	197.3	184.6	171.7	194.3
Net Yds. per Pass Play	7.03	5.81	6.06	5.93	6.69	4.53	6.21	6.08	6.58	5.53	5.89	5.67	5.03	5.86
Yds. Gained per Comp.	12.47	11.77	11.37	13.46	11.69	10.05	11.55	13.53	12.47	12.12	11.62	12.79	10.97	11.62
Combined Net Yds. Gained	6252	4969	4664	5012	5987	3748	5321	4425	5241	4473	5316	4581	4995	4534
% Total Yds. Rushing	38.1	36.4	29.2	40.2	22.8	31.2	41.7	38.6	25.8	32.8	40.6	35.5	45.0	31.5
% Total Yds. Passing	61.9	63.6	70.8	59.8	77.2	68.8	58.3	61.4	74.2	67.2	59.4	64.5	55.0	68.5
Avg. Yds. per Game	390.8	310.6	291.5	313.3	374.2	234.3	332.6	276.6	327.6	279.6	332.3	286.3	312.2	283.4
Ball Control Plays	1056	993	934	1012	1022	923	1021	893	970	977	1059	915	1010	924
Avg. Yds. per Play	5.9	5.0	5.0	5.0	5.9	4.1	5.2	5.0	5.4	4.6	5.0	5.0	4.9	4.9
Avg. Time of Poss.	26:04	29:14	29:00	31:36	30:28	28:05	31:16	29:10	29:08	29:27	33:25	27:06	30:02	29:27
Third Down Efficiency	47.1	36.8	37.2	41.5	49.7	31.3	44.9	38.5	41.0	33.8	37.9	31.5	35.0	34.7
Had Intercepted	19	22	10	12	21	16	14	18	14	22	12	16	16	26
Yds. Opp. Returned	320	331	95	101	296	184	251	374	217	154	105	182	183	334
Ret. by Opp. for TD	2	3	1	0	0	1	2	2	2	0	0	2	1	2
Punts	54	65	80	74	53	82	57	67	57	82	64	75	77	76
Yds. Punted	2085	2828	3397	3046	2211	3492	2303	2961	2551	3198	2521	2996	3064	3085
Avg. Yds. per Punt	38.6	43.5	42.5	41.2	41.7	42.6	40.4	44.2	44.8	39.0	39.4	39.9	39.8	40.6
Punt Returns	26	29	31	41	36	27	34	29	30	31	23	39	33	38
Yds. Returned	281	280	251	284	244	171	258	330	258	211	157	373	328	325
Avg. Yds. per Return	10.8	9.7	8.1	6.9	6.8	6.3	7.6	11.4	8.6	6.8	6.8	9.6	9.9	8.6
Returned for TD	0	1	0	0	0	0	0	1	0	0	0	1	0	1
Kickoff Returns	52	69	55	37	46	55	48	52	50	56	58	67	55	60
Yds. Returned	970	1225	888	687	835	1061	978	928	890	1108	1003	1314	1171	1280
Avg. Yds. per Return	18.7	17.8	16.1	18.6	18.2	19.3	20.4	17.8	17.8	19.8	17.3	19.6	21.3	21.3
Returned for TD	1	0	0	0	0	1	0	0	0	1	0	0	1	0
Fumbles	25	31	18	31	33	31	22	20	23	34	28	37	24	26
Lost	16	20	8	13	19	15	8	13	14	20	13	14	12	17
Out of Bounds	1	2	0	4	2	2	1	2	1	1	1	5	1	0
Own Rec. for TD	0	0	0	0	0	0	0	0	0	1	0	0	0	0
Opp. Rec. by	14	14	18	10	18	13	18	13	9	19	19	11	9	21
Opp. Rec. for TD	1	0	1	1	3	0	2	1	1	0	0	1	0	0
Penalties	113	107	108	94	99	85	94	117	62	97	103	116	96	85
Yds. Penalized	865	845	872	715	784	689	724	1013	516	667	814	933	799	682
Total Points Scored	458	263	293	304	386	143	322	298	343	211	314	292	274	276
Total TDs	58	27	35	32	46	14	35	30	35	22	32	32	31	29
TDs Rushing	16	11	12	16	16	3	14	8	8	9	17	8	16	11
TDs Passing	39	14	19	13	24	10	19	20	26	11	12	20	13	15
TDs on Ret. and Rec.	3	2	4	3	6	1	2	2	1	2	3	4	2	3
Extra Points	56	27	33	31	41	14	35	29	34	19	32	31	31	27
Safeties	0	1	1	0	0	0	1	1	0	0	0	0	0	0
Field Goals Made	18	24	16	27	23	15	25	29	33	20	30	23	19	25
Field Goals Attempted	29	32	22	36	31	26	30	34	39	29	43	33	29	31
% Successful	62.1	75.0	72.7	75.0	74.2	57.7	83.3	85.3	84.6	69.0	69.8	69.7	65.5	80.6

American Football Conference Defense

	Buff.	Cin.	Clev.	Den.	Hou.	Ind.	K.C.	Raid.	Mia.	N.E.	N.Y.J.	Pitt.	S.D.	Sea.
First Downs	335	308	298	242	280	305	275	305	327	312	298	320	292	262
Rushing	138	100	100	81	94	140	88	108	133	94	94	98	94	91
Passing	166	191	179	147	163	152	168	176	177	199	185	194	181	159
Penalty	31	17	19	14	23	13	19	21	17	19	19	28	17	12
Rushes	519	454	447	411	407	544	417	447	499	460	379	466	430	435
Net Yds. Gained	2044	1662	1875	1794	1540	2327	1770	1889	2301	1579	1442	1582	1666	1684
Avg. Gain	3.9	3.7	4.2	4.4	3.8	4.3	4.2	4.2	4.6	3.4	3.8	3.4	3.9	3.9
Avg. Yds. per Game	127.8	103.9	117.2	112.1	96.3	145.4	110.6	118.1	143.8	98.7	90.1	98.9	104.1	105.3
Passes Attempted	536	505	522	476	532	388	471	513	485	565	540	535	503	517
Completed	299	303	312	246	310	240	279	295	300	335	331	334	300	296
% Completed	55.8	60.0	59.8	51.7	58.3	61.9	59.2	57.5	61.9	59.3	61.3	62.4	59.6	57.3
Total Yds. Gained	3660	4119	3445	3101	3522	3002	3532	3559	3353	4035	3765	3843	3628	3288
Times Sacked	31	21	35	52	45	29	39	42	35	25	35	38	28	36
Yds. Lost	246	129	236	346	314	202	304	283	248	183	226	257	183	269
Net Yds. Gained	3414	3990	3209	2755	3208	2800	3228	3276	3105	3852	3539	3586	3445	3019
Avg. Yds. per Game	213.4	249.4	200.6	172.2	200.5	175.0	201.8	204.8	194.1	240.8	221.2	224.1	215.3	188.7
Net Yds. per Pass Play	6.02	7.59	5.76	5.22	5.56	6.71	6.33	5.90	5.97	6.53	6.15	6.26	6.49	5.46
Yds. Gained per Comp.	12.24	13.59	11.04	12.61	11.36	12.51	12.66	12.06	11.18	12.04	11.37	11.51	12.09	11.11
Combined Net Yds. Gained	5458	5652	5084	4549	4748	5127	4998	5165	5406	5431	4981	5168	5111	4703
% Total Yds. Rushing	37.4	29.4	36.9	39.4	32.4	45.4	35.4	36.6	42.6	29.1	29.0	30.6	32.6	35.8
% Total Yds. Passing	62.6	70.6	63.1	60.6	67.6	54.6	64.6	63.4	57.4	70.9	71.0	69.4	67.4	64.2
Avg. Yds. per Game	341.1	353.3	317.8	284.3	296.8	320.4	312.4	322.8	337.9	339.4	311.3	323.0	319.4	293.9
Ball Control Plays	1086	980	1004	939	984	961	927	1002	1019	1050	954	1039	961	988
Avg. Yds. per Play	5.0	5.8	5.1	4.8	4.8	5.3	5.4	5.2	5.3	5.2	5.2	5.0	5.3	4.8
Avg. Time of Poss.	33:56	30:46	31:00	28:24	29:32	31:55	28:44	30:50	30:52	30:33	26:35	32:55	29:58	30:33
Third Down Efficiency	33.9	44.3	45.1	31.1	40.2	49.2	39.8	44.5	49.0	41.7	36.8	43.1	36.0	35.5
Intercepted by	23	17	15	23	20	15	15	18	12	12	18	19	19	18
Yds. Returned by	276	169	260	379	255	202	216	155	135	93	283	329	227	302
Returned for TD	1	1	3	2	2	0	0	0	0	0	2	2	1	2
Punts	70	57	61	79	74	59	60	61	65	69	56	65	76	79
Yds. Punted	2740	2394	2520	3513	3115	2444	2549	2361	2588	2909	2271	2705	3064	3089
Avg. Yds. per Punt	39.1	42.0	41.3	44.5	42.1	41.4	42.5	38.7	39.8	42.2	40.6	41.6	40.3	39.1
Punt Returns	15	38	40	28	29	47	27	41	30	37	29	29	32	40
Yds. Returned	53	456	388	170	192	516	190	341	332	303	164	210	267	289
Avg. Yds. per Return	3.5	12.0	9.7	6.1	6.6	11.0	7.0	8.3	11.1	8.2	5.7	7.2	8.3	7.2
Returned for TD	0	2	0	0	0	1	0	0	0	1	0	0	0	0
Kickoff Returns	62	38	50	62	63	33	57	58	66	51	60	43	52	51
Yds. Returned	1266	741	1022	1096	1071	573	1171	1059	1270	850	921	825	1034	858
Avg. Yds. per Return	20.4	19.5	20.4	17.7	17.0	17.4	20.5	18.3	19.2	16.7	15.4	19.2	19.9	16.8
Returned for TD	0	0	0	0	0	0	0	1	0	0	1	0	0	0
Fumbles	26	23	33	26	27	21	27	24	19	32	38	27	22	34
Lost	14	14	18	10	18	13	18	13	9	19	19	11	9	21
Out of Bounds	2	1	1	0	1	1	1	3	1	2	0	5	2	3
Own Rec. for TD	0	0	0	0	0	0	0	0	0	0	0	0	0	0
Opp. Rec. by	16	20	7	13	19	15	8	13	14	20	13	14	12	17
Opp. Rec. for TD	0	2	0	1	0	0	0	2	2	0	1	1	0	1
Penalties	110	94	103	105	109	88	110	111	91	83	93	84	87	108
Yds. Penalized	938	808	770	848	797	645	827	905	684	608	774	685	718	845
Total Points Scored	318	435	298	235	251	381	252	297	349	305	293	344	342	261
Total TDs	34	53	33	22	26	47	27	36	40	31	31	38	39	25
TDs Rushing	20	20	12	8	8	23	8	13	17	5	8	14	15	4
TDs Passing	12	26	20	12	17	22	17	18	18	25	21	21	22	18
TDs on Ret. and Rec.	2	7	1	2	1	2	2	5	5	1	2	3	2	3
Extra Points	33	49	32	22	26	46	25	33	40	30	29	38	37	25
Safeties	0	1	1	0	0	1	1	0	0	1	0	0	1	1
Field Goals Made	27	22	22	27	23	17	21	16	23	29	26	26	23	28
Field Goals Attempted	35	31	30	33	29	23	28	28	33	42	38	41	29	32
% Successful	77.1	71.0	73.3	81.8	79.3	73.9	75.0	57.1	69.7	69.0	68.4	63.4	79.3	87.5

National Football Conference Offense

	Atl.	Chi.	Dall.	Det.	G.B.	Rams	Minn.	N.O.	N.Y.G.	Phil.	Phx.	S.F.	T.B.	Wash.
First Downs	258	317	304	280	259	270	300	267	280	249	237	336	249	302
Rushing	82	120	89	116	88	75	125	93	120	86	73	112	79	107
Passing	162	168	191	148	150	180	158	157	148	142	143	197	147	179
Penalty	14	29	24	16	21	15	17	17	12	21	21	27	23	16
Rushes	410	502	433	454	381	388	464	483	487	446	391	440	371	540
Net Yds. Gained	1664	1949	1711	1930	1389	1285	2201	1709	2064	1396	1295	1861	1429	2049
Avg. Gain	4.1	3.9	4.0	4.3	3.6	3.3	4.7	3.5	4.2	3.1	3.3	4.2	3.9	3.8
Avg. Yds. per Game	104.0	121.8	106.9	120.6	86.8	80.3	137.6	106.8	129.0	87.3	80.9	116.3	89.3	128.1
Passes Attempted	500	497	500	459	514	518	477	506	428	513	492	522	495	447
Completed	260	286	305	252	272	289	284	292	261	285	254	325	250	261
% Completed	52.0	57.5	61.0	54.9	52.9	55.8	59.5	57.7	61.0	55.6	51.6	62.3	50.5	58.4
Total Yds. Gained	3634	3292	3663	2974	3213	3610	3016	3419	3025	3169	3039	4167	2955	3771
Times Sacked	31	26	38	25	45	30	28	19	36	45	43	24	56	9
Yds. Lost	185	172	273	116	270	200	133	160	181	263	372	170	383	79
Net Yds. Gained	3449	3120	3390	2858	2943	3410	2883	3259	2844	2906	2667	3997	2572	3692
Avg. Yds. per Game	215.6	195.0	211.9	178.6	183.9	213.1	180.2	203.7	177.8	181.6	166.7	249.8	160.8	230.8
Net Yds. per Pass Play	6.50	5.97	6.30	5.90	5.26	6.22	5.71	6.21	6.13	5.21	4.99	7.32	4.67	8.10
Yds. Gained per Comp.	13.98	11.51	12.01	11.80	11.81	12.49	10.62	11.71	11.59	11.12	11.96	12.82	11.82	14.45
Combined Net Yds. Gained	5113	5069	5101	4788	4332	4695	5084	4968	4908	4302	3962	5858	4001	5741
% Total Yds. Rushing	32.5	38.4	33.5	40.3	32.1	27.4	43.3	34.4	42.1	32.5	32.7	31.8	35.7	35.7
% Total Yds. Passing	67.5	61.6	66.5	59.7	67.9	72.6	56.7	65.6	57.9	67.5	67.3	68.2	64.3	64.3
Avg. Yds. per Game	319.6	316.8	318.8	299.3	270.8	293.4	317.8	310.5	306.8	268.9	247.6	366.1	250.1	358.8
Ball Control Plays	941	1025	971	938	940	936	969	1008	951	1004	926	986	922	996
Avg. Yds. per Play	5.4	4.9	5.3	5.1	4.6	5.0	5.2	4.9	5.2	4.3	4.3	5.9	4.3	5.8
Avg. Time of Poss.	29:13	33:01	30:06	28:39	28:15	29:03	29:35	33:58	31:47	33:25	29:01	31:34	26:57	31:51
Third Down Efficiency	35.6	43.0	37.8	36.5	37.2	37.9	39.6	37.7	42.6	32.7	33.3	47.7	31.6	50.5
Had Intercepted	22	17	12	17	19	20	16	15	8	27	25	12	29	11
Yds. Opp. Returned	279	145	244	229	185	297	203	257	36	432	399	82	349	109
Ret. by Opp. for TD	1	0	2	1	1	1	1	2	0	2	1	0	1	1
Punts	82	70	57	75	86	75	68	87	64	88	77	56	84	55
Yds. Punted	3491	2814	2426	3092	3473	2856	3095	3743	2768	3640	3445	2197	3389	2070
Avg. Yds. per Punt	42.6	40.2	42.6	41.2	40.4	38.1	45.5	43.0	43.3	41.4	44.7	39.2	40.3	37.6
Punt Returns	35	47	29	26	41	37	30	44	36	53	41	42	39	46
Yds. Returned	286	340	309	385	396	320	225	317	336	416	307	320	361	610
Avg. Yds. per Return	8.2	7.2	10.7	14.8	9.7	8.6	7.5	7.2	9.3	7.8	7.5	7.6	9.3	13.3
Returned for TD	0	0	1	1	0	0	0	0	1	0	0	0	0	2
Kickoff Returns	52	45	52	57	60	59	44	50	50	47	52	50	60	49
Yds. Returned	997	763	1127	1170	1197	1070	899	879	917	764	972	1028	1047	926
Avg. Yds. per Return	19.2	17.0	21.7	20.5	20.0	18.1	20.4	17.6	18.3	16.3	18.7	20.6	17.5	18.9
Returned for TD	1	0	1	0	1	0	0	0	0	0	0	1	0	0
Fumbles	19	25	23	25	41	32	21	24	33	34	31	33	30	26
Lost	14	16	12	13	17	20	10	15	15	16	14	19	18	12
Out of Bounds	0	0	3	0	2	2	3	0	2	3	0	4	2	3
Own Rec. for TD	0	0	0	0	0	0	0	0	0	0	0	0	0	0
Opp. Rec. by	16	13	11	17	14	8	11	19	9	22	21	16	16	13
Opp. Rec. for TD	4	0	1	1	1	1	0	0	0	3	2	1	0	0
Penalties	113	80	74	93	98	108	88	101	92	111	78	114	88	90
Yds. Penalized	929	662	610	799	834	774	675	801	719	839	661	902	780	798
Total Points Scored	361	299	342	339	273	234	301	341	281	285	196	393	199	485
Total TDs	42	35	37	40	31	26	36	38	30	29	19	50	22	56
TDs Rushing	6	18	15	19	12	18	15	16	8	6	19	19	9	21
TDs Passing	30	16	16	16	17	13	16	20	13	17	10	29	13	30
TDs on Ret. and Rec.	6	1	6	5	2	2	2	3	1	4	3	2	0	5
Extra Points	40	32	37	40	31	25	34	38	29	27	19	49	22	56
Safeties	3	0	1	1	1	1	0	0	0	0	0	1	0	0
Field Goals Made	21	19	27	19	18	17	17	25	24	28	21	14	15	31
Field Goals Attempted	26	29	39	28	24	17	24	32	31	33	30	28	20	43
% Successful	80.8	65.5	69.2	67.9	75.0	100.0	70.8	78.1	77.4	84.8	70.0	50.0	75.0	72.1

National Football Conference Defense

	Atl.	Chi.	Dall.	Det.	G.B.	Rams	Minn.	N.O.	N.Y.G.	Phil.	Phx.	S.F.	T.B.	Wash.
First Downs	278	254	299	305	298	286	301	214	257	206	301	260	295	242
Rushing	94	77	103	93	99	105	106	63	103	53	132	86	120	72
Passing	157	164	180	189	177	162	172	139	138	133	156	155	147	151
Penalty	27	13	16	23	22	19	23	12	16	20	13	19	28	19
Rushes	466	389	400	444	457	469	456	334	414	383	493	399	512	348
Net Yds. Gained	1953	1580	1571	1760	1546	1659	1837	1213	1726	1136	2136	1512	2107	1346
Avg. Gain	4.2	4.1	3.9	4.0	3.4	3.5	4.0	3.6	4.2	3.0	4.3	3.8	4.1	3.9
Avg. Yds. per Game	122.1	98.8	98.2	110.0	96.6	103.7	114.8	75.8	107.9	71.0	133.5	94.5	131.7	84.1
Passes Attempted	481	513	540	534	531	434	499	491	440	467	447	499	438	549
Completed	252	286	320	315	305	259	286	259	251	206	268	267	257	292
% Completed	52.4	55.8	59.3	59.0	57.4	59.7	57.3	52.7	57.0	44.1	60.0	53.5	58.7	53.2
Total Yds. Gained	3532	3184	3646	3523	3573	3657	3396	3057	3128	2807	3069	3254	3130	3292
Times Sacked	29	40	23	30	45	17	33	50	34	55	25	31	39	50
Yds. Lost	237	257	151	237	307	112	217	337	254	394	153	212	258	345
Net Yds. Gained	3295	2927	3495	3286	3266	3545	3179	2720	2874	2413	2916	3042	2872	2947
Avg. Yds. per Game	205.9	182.9	218.4	205.4	204.1	221.6	198.7	170.0	179.6	150.8	182.3	190.1	179.5	184.2
Net Yds. per Pass Play	6.46	5.29	6.21	5.83	5.67	7.86	5.98	5.03	6.06	4.62	6.18	5.74	6.02	4.92
Yds. Gained per Comp.	14.02	11.13	11.39	11.18	11.71	14.12	11.87	11.80	12.46	13.63	11.45	12.19	12.18	11.27
Combined Net Yds. Gained	5248	4507	5066	5046	4812	5204	5016	3933	4600	3549	5052	4554	4979	4293
% Total Yds. Rushing	37.2	35.1	31.0	34.9	32.1	31.9	36.6	30.8	37.5	32.0	42.3	33.2	42.3	31.4
% Total Yds. Passing	62.8	64.9	69.0	65.1	67.9	68.1	63.4	69.2	62.5	68.0	57.7	66.8	57.7	68.6
Avg. Yds. per Game	328.0	281.7	316.6	315.4	300.8	325.3	313.5	245.8	287.5	221.8	315.8	284.6	311.2	268.3
Ball Control Plays	976	942	963	1008	1033	920	988	875	888	905	965	929	989	947
Avg. Yds. per Play	5.4	4.8	5.3	5.0	4.7	5.7	5.1	4.5	5.2	3.9	5.2	4.9	5.0	4.5
Avg. Time of Poss.	30:47	26:59	29:54	31:21	31:45	30:57	30:25	26:02	28:13	26:35	30:59	28:26	33:03	28:09
Third Down Efficiency	39.0	33.2	39.2	39.4	38.6	39.7	45.1	26.1	35.1	29.8	40.0	35.3	37.8	34.0
Intercepted by	19	17	12	19	15	11	17	29	12	26	17	12	11	27
Yds. Returned by	225	225	167	286	234	175	242	482	122	280	187	125	63	279
Returned for TD	1	1	2	2	0	1	2	2	0	1	1	0	0	3
Punts	79	81	61	67	76	68	67	88	74	86	71	82	71	85
Yds. Punted	3187	3343	2364	2629	3199	2829	2861	3725	2999	3670	3207	3365	3049	3548
Avg. Yds. per Punt	40.3	41.3	38.8	39.2	42.1	41.6	42.7	42.3	40.5	42.7	45.2	41.0	42.9	41.7
Punt Returns	45	28	28	35	35	33	42	50	35	42	48	30	49	31
Yds. Returned	387	205	231	340	375	292	426	470	350	431	313	239	559	190
Avg. Yds. per Return	8.6	7.3	8.3	9.7	10.7	8.8	10.1	9.4	10.0	10.3	6.5	8.0	11.4	6.1
Returned for TD	0	0	0	1	1	0	0	0	1	1	0	0	1	0
Kickoff Returns	67	58	69	63	46	39	43	35	55	60	42	66	32	66
Yds. Returned	1419	1134	1169	1095	942	671	851	851	940	1146	958	1288	720	1153
Avg. Yds. per Return	21.2	19.6	16.9	17.4	20.5	17.2	19.8	24.3	17.1	19.1	22.8	19.5	22.5	17.5
Returned for TD	1	0	1	0	0	0	0	2	0	0	1	1	0	0
Fumbles	27	25	23	32	31	17	24	34	27	43	37	32	27	22
Lost	16	13	11	17	14	8	11	19	9	22	21	16	16	14
Out of Bounds	1	1	0	1	2	0	2	1	1	1	5	2	3	4
Own Rec. for TD	0	0	0	0	0	0	1	0	0	0	0	0	0	0
Opp. Rec. by	14	16	12	13	17	20	10	15	15	16	14	19	18	12
Opp. Rec. for TD	0	1	0	0	3	2	0	1	1	1	2	0	3	1
Penalties	100	94	97	94	106	83	92	95	80	105	94	84	110	94
Yds. Penalized	802	891	801	704	777	743	709	711	622	881	734	782	925	767
Total Points Scored	338	269	310	295	313	390	306	211	297	244	344	239	365	224
Total TDs	43	29	32	34	35	47	35	23	30	24	43	25	41	26
TDs Rushing	13	9	11	16	10	19	17	6	11	4	27	8	21	11
TDs Passing	28	19	17	16	20	25	16	12	17	16	12	16	15	13
TDs on Ret. and Rec.	2	1	4	2	5	3	2	5	2	4	4	1	5	2
Extra Points	41	29	31	34	34	46	34	22	30	23	41	23	40	26
Safeties	0	0	0	0	0	1	1	0	0	1	0	0	2	0
Field Goals Made	13	22	29	19	23	20	20	17	29	25	15	22	25	14
Field Goals Attempted	26	30	39	28	31	28	29	21	30	33	23	25	35	18
% Successful	50.0	73.3	74.4	67.9	74.2	71.4	69.0	81.0	96.7	75.8	65.2	88.0	71.4	77.8

AFC, NFC, and NFL Summary

	AFC Offense Total	AFC Offense Average	AFC Defense Total	AFC Defense Average	NFC Offense Total	NFC Offense Average	NFC Defense Total	NFC Defense Average	NFL Total	NFL Average
First Downs	4047	289.1	4159	297.1	3908	279.1	3796	271.1	7955	284.1
Rushing	1394	99.6	1453	103.8	1365	97.5	1306	93.3	2759	98.5
Passing	2387	170.5	2437	174.1	2270	162.1	2220	158.6	4657	166.3
Penalty	266	19.0	269	19.2	273	19.5	270	19.3	539	19.3
Rushes	6089	434.9	6315	451.1	6190	442.1	5964	426.0	12279	438.5
Net Yds. Gained	24305	1736.1	25155	1796.8	23932	1709.4	23082	1648.7	48237	1722.8
Avg. Gain	——	4.0	——	4.0	——	3.9	——	3.9	——	3.9
Avg. Yds. per Game	——	108.5	——	112.3	——	106.8	——	103.0	——	107.7
Passes Attempted	7083	505.9	7088	506.3	6868	490.6	6863	490.2	13951	498.3
Completed	4127	294.8	4180	298.6	3876	276.9	3823	273.1	8003	285.8
% Completed	——	58.3	——	59.0	——	56.4	——	55.7	——	57.4
Total Yds. Gained	49153	3510.9	49852	3560.9	46947	3353.4	46248	3303.4	96100	3432.1
Times Sacked	537	38.4	491	35.1	455	32.5	501	35.8	992	35.4
Yds. Lost	3940	281.4	3426	244.7	2957	211.2	3471	247.9	6897	246.3
Net Yds. Gained	45213	3229.5	46426	3316.1	43990	3142.1	42777	3055.5	89203	3185.8
Avg. Yds. per Game	——	201.8	——	207.3	——	196.4	——	191.0	——	199.1
Net Yds. per Pass Play	——	5.93	——	6.13	——	6.01	——	5.81	——	5.97
Yds. Gained per Comp.	——	11.91	——	11.93	——	12.11	——	12.10	——	12.01
Combined Net Yds. Gained	69518	4965.6	71581	5112.9	67922	4851.6	65859	4704.2	137440	4908.6
% Total Yds. Rushing	——	35.0	——	35.1	——	35.2	——	35.0	——	35.1
% Total Yds. Passing	——	65.0	——	64.9	——	64.8	——	65.0	——	64.9
Avg. Yds. per Game	——	310.3	——	319.6	——	303.2	——	294.0	——	306.8
Ball Control Plays	13709	979.2	13894	992.4	13513	965.2	13328	952.0	27222	972.2
Avg. Yds. per Play	——	5.1	——	5.2	——	5.0	——	4.9	——	5.0
Third Down Efficiency	——	38.6	——	40.7	——	38.9	——	36.7	——	38.7
Interceptions	238	17.0	244	17.4	250	17.9	244	17.4	488	17.4
Yds. Returned	3127	223.4	3281	234.4	3246	231.9	3092	220.9	6373	227.6
Returned for TD	18	1.3	16	1.1	14	1.0	16	1.1	32	1.1
Punts	963	68.8	931	66.5	1024	73.1	1056	75.4	1987	71.0
Yds. Punted	39738	2838.4	38262	2733.0	42499	3035.6	43975	3141.1	82237	2937.0
Avg. Yds. per Punt	——	41.3	——	41.1	——	41.5	——	41.6	——	41.4
Punt Returns	447	31.9	462	33.0	546	39.0	531	37.9	993	35.5
Yds. Returned	3751	267.9	3871	276.5	4928	352.0	4808	343.4	8679	310.0
Avg. Yds. per Return	——	8.4	——	8.4	——	9.0	——	9.1	——	8.7
Returned for TD	4	0.3	4	0.3	5	0.4	5	0.4	9	0.3
Kickoff Returns	760	54.3	747	53.4	728	52.0	741	52.9	1488	53.1
Yds. Returned	14338	1024.1	13757	982.6	13756	982.6	14337	1024.1	28094	1003.4
Avg. Yds. per Return	——	18.9	——	18.4	——	18.9	——	19.3	——	18.9
Returned for TD	4	0.3	2	0.1	4	0.3	6	0.4	8	0.3
Fumbles	383	27.4	379	27.1	397	28.4	401	28.6	780	27.9
Lost	202	14.4	206	14.7	211	15.1	207	14.8	413	14.8
Out of Bounds	23	1.6	23	1.6	24	1.7	24	1.7	47	1.7
Own Rec. for TD	1	0.1	0	0.0	0	0.0	1	0.1	1	0.0
Opp. Rec.	206	14.7	201	14.4	206	14.7	211	15.1	412	14.7
Opp. Rec. for TD	11	0.8	10	0.7	14	1.0	15	1.1	25	0.9
Penalties	1376	98.3	1376	98.3	1328	94.9	1328	94.9	2704	96.6
Yds. Penalized	10918	779.9	10852	775.1	10783	770.2	10849	775.0	21701	775.0
Total Points Scored	4177	298.4	4361	311.5	4329	309.2	4145	296.1	8506	303.8
Total TDs	458	32.7	482	34.4	491	35.1	467	33.4	949	33.9
TDs Rushing	165	11.8	175	12.5	193	13.8	183	13.1	358	12.8
TDs Passing	255	18.2	269	19.2	256	18.3	242	17.3	511	18.3
TDs on Ret. and Rec.	38	2.7	38	2.7	42	3.0	42	3.0	80	2.9
Extra Points	440	31.4	465	33.2	479	34.2	454	32.4	919	32.8
Safeties	4	0.3	7	0.5	8	0.6	5	0.4	12	0.4
Field Goals Made	327	23.4	330	23.6	296	21.1	293	20.9	623	22.3
Field Goals Attempted	444	31.7	452	32.3	404	28.9	396	28.3	848	30.3
% Successful	——	73.6	——	73.0	——	73.3	——	74.0	—	73.5

Club Leaders

First Downs	Offense	Defense
	Buff. 359	Phil. 206
Rushing	N.Y.J. 133	Phil. 53
Passing	Hou. 236	Phil. 133
Penalty	Chi. & N.Y.J. 29	N.O.& Sea. 12

Rushes		
	Wash. 540	N.O. 334
Net Yds. Gained	Buff. 2381	Phil. 1136
Avg. Gain	S.D. 4.8	Phil. 2.97

Passes Attempted		
	Hou. 667	Ind. 388
Completed	Hou. 411	Phil. 206
% Completed	Buff. 64.3	Phil. 44.1
Total Yds. Gained	Hou. 4804	Phil. 2807
Times Sacked	Wash. 9	Phil. 55
Yds. Lost	Wash. 79	Phil. 394
Net Yds. Gained	Hou. 4621	Phil. 2413
Net Yds. per Pass Play	Wash. 8.10	Phil. 4.62
Yds. Gained per Comp.	Wash. 14.45	Clev. 11.04

Combined Net Yds. Gained		
	Buff. 6252	Phil. 3549
% Total Yds. Rushing	S.D. 45.0	N.Y.J. 29.0
% Total Yds. Passing	Hou. 77.2	Ind. 54.6

Ball Control Plays		
	N.Y.J. 1059	N.O. 875
Avg. Yds. per Play	S.F. 5.94	Phil. 3.92
Avg. Time of Poss.	N.O. 33:58	—

Third Down Efficiency	Wash. 50.5	N.O. 26.1

Interceptions		
	—	N.O. 29
Yds. Returned	—	N.O. 482
Returned for TD	—	Clev. & Wash. 3

Punts		
	Phil. 88	—
Yds. Punted	N.O. 3743	—
Avg. Yds. per Punt	Minn. 45.5	—

Punt Returns		
	Phil. 53	Buff. 15
Yds. Returned	Wash. 610	Buff. 53
Avg. Yds. per Return	Det. 14.8	Buff. 3.5
Returned for TD	Wash. 2	—

Kickoff Returns		
	Cin. 69	T.B. 32
Yds. Returned	Pitt. 1314	Ind. 573
Avg. Yds. per Return	Dall. 21.7	N.Y.J. 15.4
Returned for TD	Eight with 1	—

Total Points Scored		
	Wash. 485	N.O. 211
Total TDs	Buff. 58	Den. 22
TDs Rushing	Wash. 21	Phil. & Sea. 4
TDs Passing	Buff. 39	Four with 12
TDs on Ret. and Rec.	Atl., Dall. & Hou. 6	Five with 1
Extra Points	Buff. & Wash. 56	Den. & N.O. 22
Safeties	Atl. 3	—
Field Goals Made	Mia. 33	Atl. 13
Field Goals Attempted	N.Y.J. & Wash. 43	Wash. 18
% Successful	Rams 100.0	Atl. 50.0

National Football League Club Rankings By Yards

Team	Offense Total	Rush	Pass	Defense Total	Rush	Pass
Atlanta	8	16	6	24	23	20
Buffalo	*1	*1	4	27	24	21
Chicago	11	9	13	4	10	8
Cincinnati	14	12	11	28	13	28
Cleveland	19	24	9	18	21	15
Dallas	9	13	8	17	8	23
Denver	12	8	17	5	19	3
Detroit	17	10	22	15	17	19
Green Bay	24	22	19	10	7	17
Houston	2	23	*1	9	6	14
Indianapolis	28	28	27	20	28	4
Kansas City	5	3	15	13	18	16
L.A. Raiders	23	15	25	21	22	18
L.A. Rams	18	27	7	23	12	25
Miami	7	25	3	25	27	12
Minnesota	10	4	21	14	20	13
New England	22	18	16	26	9	27
New Orleans	15	14	10	2	2	2
N.Y. Giants	16	6	23	7	16	6
N.Y. Jets	6	5	12	12	4	24
Philadelphia	25	21	20	*1	*1	*1
Phoenix	27	26	26	16	26	7
Pittsburgh	20	17	18	22	11	26
San Diego	13	2	24	19	14	22
San Francisco	3	11	2	6	5	11
Seattle	21	20	14	8	15	10
Tampa Bay	26	19	28	11	25	5
Washington	4	7	5	3	3	9

* = League leader

AFC Takeaways/Giveaways

	Takeaways Int.	Fum.	Total	Giveaways Int.	Fum.	Total	Net Diff.
Cleveland	15	18	33	10	8	18	15
N.Y. Jets	18	19	37	12	13	25	12
Kansas City	15	18	33	14	8	22	11
Denver	23	10	33	12	13	25	8
Buffalo	23	14	37	19	16	35	2
Pittsburgh	19	11	30	16	14	30	0
L.A. Raiders	18	13	31	18	13	31	0
San Diego	19	9	28	16	12	28	0
Houston	20	18	38	21	19	40	-2
Indianapolis	15	13	28	16	15	31	-3
Seattle	18	21	39	26	17	43	-4
Miami	12	9	21	14	14	28	-7
Cincinnati	17	14	31	22	20	42	-11
New England	12	19	31	22	20	42	-11

NFC Takeaways/Giveaways

	Takeaways Int.	Fum.	Total	Giveaways Int.	Fum.	Total	Net Diff.
New Orleans	29	19	48	15	15	30	18
Washington	27	14	41	11	12	23	18
Detroit	19	17	36	17	13	30	6
Philadelphia	26	22	48	27	16	43	5
Minnesota	17	11	28	16	10	26	2
Atlanta	19	16	35	22	14	36	-1
Dallas	12	11	23	12	12	24	-1
Phoenix	17	21	38	25	14	39	-1
N.Y. Giants	12	9	21	8	15	23	-2
Chicago	17	13	30	17	16	33	-3
San Francisco	12	16	28	12	19	31	-3
Green Bay	15	14	29	19	17	36	-7
Tampa Bay	11	16	27	29	18	47	-20
L.A. Rams	11	8	19	20	20	40	-21

Scoring

Points
NFC: 149 Chip Lohmiller, Washington
AFC: 121 Pete Stoyanovich, Miami

Touchdowns
NFC: 17 Barry Sanders, Detroit
AFC: 12 Mark Clayton, Miami
        Thurman Thomas, Buffalo

Extra Points
AFC: 56 Scott Norwood, Buffalo
NFC: 56 Chip Lohmiller, Washington

Field Goals
AFC: 31 Pete Stoyanovich, Miami
NFC: 31 Chip Lohmiller, Washington

Fielf Goal Attempts
NFC: 43 Chip Lohmiller, Washington
AFC: 37 Pat Leahy, Jets
        Pete Stoyanovich, Miami

Longest Field Goal
NFC: 60 Morten Andersen, New Orleans vs. Chicago, October 27
AFC: 55 Matt Stover, Cleveland at Houston, November 17

Most Points, Game
AFC: 24 Don Beebe, Buffalo vs. Pittsburgh, September 8 (4 TD)
NFC: 24 Barry Sanders, Detroit at Minnesota, November 24 (4 TD)

Team Leaders, Points
AFC: BUFFALO: 110, Scott Norwood; CINCINNATI: 96, Jim Breech; CLEVELAND: 81, Matt Stover; DENVER: 112, David Treadwell; HOUSTON: 64, Ian Howfield; INDIANAPOLIS: 59, Dean Biasucci; KANSAS CITY: 110, Nick Lowery; RAIDERS: 116, Jeff Jaeger, MIAMI: 121, Pete Stoyanovich; NEW ENGLAND: 49, Jason Staurovsky; JETS: 108, Pat Leahy; PITTSBURGH: 100, Gary Anderson; SAN DIEGO: 88, John Carney; SEATTLE: 102, John Kasay.
NFC: ATLANTA: 95, Norm Johnson; CHICAGO: 89, Kevin Butler; DALLAS: 118, Ken Willis; DETROIT: 102, Barry Sanders; GREEN BAY: 85, Chris Jacke; RAMS: 76, Tony Zendejas; MINNESOTA: 85, Fuad Reveiz; NEW ORLEANS: 113, Morten Andersen; GIANTS: 90, Matt Bahr; PHILADELPHIA: 111, Roger Ruzek; PHOENIX: 82, Greg Davis; SAN FRANCISCO: 91, Mike Cofer; TAMPA BAY: 67, Steve Christie; WASHINGTON: 149, Chip Lohmiller

Team Champion
NFC: 485—Washington
AFC: 458—Buffalo

AFC Scoring—Team

	TD	TDR	TDP	TD Misc.	PAT	PAT Att.	FG	FG Att.	SAF	TP
Buffalo	58	16	39	3	56	58	18	29	0	458
Houston	46	16	24	6	41	46	23	31	0	386
Miami	35	8	26	1	34	35	33	39	0	343
Kansas City	35	14	19	2	35	35	25	30	1	322
N.Y. Jets	32	17	12	3	32	32	30	43	0	314
Denver	32	16	13	3	31	32	27	36	0	304
L.A. Raiders	30	8	20	2	29	30	29	34	1	298
Cleveland	35	12	19	4	33	34	16	22	1	293
Pittsburgh	32	8	20	4	31	31	23	33	0	292
Seattle	29	11	15	3	27	29	25	31	0	276
San Diego	31	16	13	2	31	31	19	29	0	274
Cincinnati	27	11	14	2	27	27	24	32	1	263
New England	22	9	11	2	19	21	20	29	0	211
Indianapolis	14	3	10	1	14	14	15	26	0	143
AFC Total	458	165	255	38	440	455	327	444	4	4177
AFC Average	32.7	11.8	18.2	2.7	31.4	32.5	23.4	31.7	0.3	298.4

NFC Scoring—Team

	TD	TDR	TDP	TD Misc.	PAT	PAT Att.	FG	FG Att.	SAF	TP
Washington	56	21	30	5	56	56	31	43	0	485
San Francisco	50	19	29	2	49	50	14	28	1	393
Atlanta	42	6	30	6	40	42	21	26	3	361
Dallas	37	15	16	6	37	37	27	39	1	342
New Orleans	38	15	20	3	38	38	25	32	0	341
Detroit	40	19	16	5	40	40	19	28	1	339
Minnesota	36	18	16	2	34	36	17	24	0	301
Chicago	35	18	16	1	32	34	19	29	0	299
Philadelphia	29	8	17	4	27	29	28	33	0	285
N.Y. Giants	30	16	13	1	29	30	24	31	0	281
Green Bay	31	12	17	2	31	31	18	24	1	273
L.A. Rams	26	11	13	2	25	26	17	17	1	234

	TD	TDR	TDP	TD Misc.	PAT	PAT Att.	FG	FG Att.	SAF	TP
Tampa Bay	22	9	13	0	22	22	15	20	0	199
Phoenix	19	6	10	3	19	19	21	30	0	196
NFC Total	491	193	256	42	479	490	296	404	8	4329
NFC Average	35.1	13.8	18.3	3.0	34.2	35.0	21.1	28.9	0.6	309.2
NFL Total	949	358	511	80	919	945	623	848	12	8506
NFL Average	33.9	12.8	18.3	2.9	32.8	33.8	22.3	30.3	0.4	303.8

NFL Top 10 Scorers—Touchdowns

	TD	TDR	TDP	TD Misc.	TP
Sanders, Barry, Det.	17	16	1	0	102
Rice, Jerry, S.F.	14	0	14	0	84
Smith, Emmitt, Dall.	13	12	1	0	78
Clayton, Mark, Mia.	12	0	12	0	72
Rison, Andre, Atl.	12	0	12	0	72
Thomas, Thurman, Buff.	12	7	5	0	72
Baxter, Brad, Jets	11	11	0	0	66
Haynes, Michael, Atl.	11	0	11	0	66
Hoard, Leroy, Clev.	11	2	9	0	66
Riggs, G sderald, Wash.	11	11	0	0	66
Workman, Vince, G.B.	11	7	4	0	66

NFL Top 10 Scorers—Kicking

	PAT	PAT Att.	FG	FG Att.	TP
Lohmiller, Chip, Wash.	56	56	31	43	149
Stoyanovich, Pete, Mia.	28	29	31	37	121
Willis, Ken, Dall.	37	37	27	39	118
Jaeger, Jeff, Raiders	29	30	29	34	116
Andersen, Morten, N.O.	38	38	25	32	113
Treadwell, David, Den.	31	32	27	36	112
Ruzek, Roger, Phil.	27	29	28	33	111
Lowery, Nick, K.C.	35	35	25	30	110
Norwood, Scott, Buff.	56	58	18	29	110
Leahy, Pat, Jets	30	30	26	37	108

AFC Scoring—Individual

Kickers	PAT	PAT Att.	FG	FG Att.	TP
Stoyanovich, Pete, Mia.	28	29	31	37	121
Jaeger, Jeff, Raiders	29	30	29	34	116
Treadwell, David, Den.	31	32	27	36	112
Lowery, Nick, K.C.	35	35	25	30	110
Norwood, Scott, Buff.	56	58	18	29	110
Leahy, Pat, Jets	30	30	26	37	108
Kasay, John, Sea.	27	28	25	31	102
Anderson, Gary, Pitt.	31	31	23	33	100
Breech, Jim, Cin.	27	27	23	29	96
Carney, John, S.D.	31	31	19	29	88
Stover, Matt, Clev.	33	34	16	22	81
Howfield, Ian, Hou.	25	29	13	18	64
Biasucci, Dean, Ind.	14	14	15	26	59
Staurovsky, Jason, N.E.	10	11	13	19	49
Del Greco, Al, Hou.	16	16	10	13	46
Baumann, Charlie, Mia.-N.E.	15	16	9	12	42
Allegre, Raul, Giants-Jets	7	7	5	6	22
Aguiar, Louie, Jets	0	0	1	2	3
Johnson, Lee, Cin.	0	0	1	3	3

Non-Kickers	TD	TDR	TDP	TD Misc.	TP
Clayton, Mark, Mia.	12	0	12	0	72
Thomas, Thurman, Buff.	12	7	5	0	72
Baxter, Brad, Jets	11	11	0	0	66
Hoard, Leroy, Clev.	11	2	9	0	66
Mack, Kevin, Clev.	10	8	2	0	60
Pinkett, Allen, Hou.	10	9	1	0	60
Reed, Andre, Buff.	10	0	10	0	60
Okoye, Christian, K.C.	9	9	0	0	54
Bernstine, Rod, S.D.	8	8	0	0	48
Lofton, James, Buff.	8	0	8	0	48
Butts, Marion, S.D.	7	6	1	0	42
Jeffires, Haywood, Hou.	7	0	7	0	42
Beebe, Don, Buff.	6	0	6	0	36
Brown, Tim, Raiders	6	0	5	1	36
Elway, John, Den.	6	6	0	0	36
Green, Eric, Pitt.	6	0	6	0	36
Barnett, Tim, K.C.	5	0	5	0	30
Burkett, Chris, Jets	5	0	5	0	30
Davis, Kenneth, Buff.	5	4	1	0	30
Duper, Mark, Mia.	5	0	5	0	30
Givins, Ernest, Hou.	5	0	5	0	30

Name	TD	TDR	TDP	TD Misc.	TP
Hester, Jessie, Ind.	5	0	5	0	30
Horton, Ethan, Raiders	5	0	5	0	30
Moore, Rob, Jets	5	0	5	0	30
Stone, Dwight, Pitt.	5	0	5	0	30
Williams, John L., Sea.	5	4	1	0	30
Brooks, Bill, Ind.	4	0	4	0	24
Brooks, James, Cin.	4	2	2	0	24
Duncan, Curtis, Hou.	4	0	4	0	24
Fenner, Derrick, Sea.	4	4	0	0	24
Gardner, Carwell, Buff.	4	4	0	0	24
Gault, Willie, Raiders	4	0	4	0	24
Green, Gaston, Den.	4	4	0	0	24
Higgs, Mark, Mia.	4	4	0	0	24
Hill, Drew, Hou.	4	0	4	0	24
Lewis, Greg, Den.	4	4	0	0	24
Lewis, Nate, S.D.	4	0	3	1	24
McGee, Tim, Cin.	4	0	4	0	24
Russell, Leonard, N.E.	4	4	0	0	24
Sewell, Steve, Den.	4	2	2	0	24
Thomas, Blair, Jets	4	3	1	0	24
Tice, Mike, Sea.	4	0	4	0	24
White, Lorenzo, Hou.	4	4	0	0	24
Williams, Warren, Pitt.	4	4	0	0	24
Woods, Ickey, Cin.	4	4	0	0	24
Word, Barry, K.C.	4	4	0	0	24
Bell, Nick, Raiders	3	3	0	0	18
Chadwick, Jeff, Sea.	3	0	3	0	18
Cook, Marv, N.E.	3	0	3	0	18
Dickerson, Eric, Ind.	3	2	1	0	18
Fryar, Irving, N.E.	3	0	3	0	18
Glover, Andrew, Raiders	3	0	3	0	18
Harry, Emile, K.C.	3	0	3	0	18
Hoge, Merril, Pitt.	3	2	1	0	18
Johnson, Vance, Den.	3	0	3	0	18
Jones, James, Sea.	3	3	0	0	18
McEwen, Craig, S.D.	3	0	3	0	18
McKeller, Keith, Buff.	3	0	3	0	18
Miller, Anthony, S.D.	3	0	3	0	18
Slaughter, Webster, Clev.	3	0	3	0	18
Vaughn, Jon, N.E.	3	2	0	1	18
Williams, Harvey, K.C.	3	1	2	0	18
Allen, Marcus, Raiders	2	2	0	0	12
Birden, J.J., K.C.	2	0	2	0	12
Blades, Brian, Sea.	2	0	2	0	12
Brown, Eddie, Cin.	2	0	2	0	12
Clark, Louis, Sea.	2	0	2	0	12
Cooper, Adrian, Pitt.	2	0	2	0	12
Edmunds, Ferrell, Mia.	2	0	2	0	12
Edwards, Al, Buff.	2	0	1	1	12
Foster, Barry, Pitt.	2	1	1	0	12
Green, Harold, Cin.	2	2	0	0	12
Harmon, Ronnie, S.D.	2	1	1	0	12
Hayes, Jonathan, K.C.	2	0	2	0	12
Hendrickson, Steve, S.D.	2	1	1	0	12
Holman, Rodney, Cin.	2	0	2	0	12
Holohan, Pete, K.C.	2	0	2	0	12
Jackson, Michael, Clev.	2	0	2	0	12
Jensen, Jim, Mia.	2	0	2	0	12
Jones, Tony, Hou.	2	0	2	0	12
Kane, Tommy, Sea.	2	0	2	0	12
Langhorne, Reggie, Clev.	2	0	2	0	12
Lipps, Louis, Pitt.	2	0	2	0	12
Martin, Tony, Mia.	2	0	2	0	12
McMillan, Erik, Jets	2	0	0	2	12
McMurtry, Greg, N.E.	2	0	2	0	12
McNeil, Freeman, Jets	2	2	0	0	12
Metzelaars, Pete, Buff.	2	0	2	0	12
Mills, Ernie, Pitt.	2	0	1	1	12
Moon, Warren, Hou.	2	2	0	0	12
Morris, Joe, Clev.	2	2	0	0	12
Nattiel, Ricky, Den.	2	0	2	0	12
Rolle, Butch, Buff.	2	0	2	0	12
Smith, Steve, Raiders	2	1	1	0	12
Stephens, John, N.E.	2	2	0	0	12
Taylor, Craig, Cin.	2	2	0	0	12
Timpson, Michael, N.E.	2	0	2	0	12
Young, Mike, Den.	2	0	2	0	12
Jones, James, Clev.	1	0	0	1	*8
Ball, Eric, Cin.	1	1	0	0	6
Banks, Fred, Mia.	1	0	1	0	6
Barber, Mike, Cin.	1	0	1	0	6
Baty, Greg, Mia.	1	0	1	0	6
Bennett, Cornelius, Buff.	1	0	0	1	6
Brandon, David, Clev.	1	0	0	1	6
Braxton, Tyrone, Den.	1	0	0	1	6
Brennan, Brian, Clev.	1	0	1	0	6
Brown, A.B., Jets	1	1	0	0	6
Brown, Gary, Hou.	1	1	0	0	6

Name	TD	TDR	TDP	TD Misc.	TP
Calloway, Chris, Pitt.	1	0	1	0	6
Cash, Keith, Pitt.	1	0	1	0	6
Childress, Freddie, N.E.	1	0	0	1	6
Coates, Ben, N.E.	1	0	1	0	6
Coleman, Patrick, Hou.	1	0	1	0	6
Craig, Roger, Raiders	1	1	0	0	6
Craver, Aaron, Mia.	1	1	0	0	6
Davis, Brian, Sea.	1	0	0	1	6
Dimry, Charles, Den.	1	0	0	1	6
Dingle, Mike, Cin.	1	0	1	0	6
Dishman, Cris, Hou.	1	0	0	1	6
Dumas, Mike, Hou.	1	0	0	1	6
Fernandez, Mervyn, Raiders	1	0	1	0	6
Frank, Donald, S.D.	1	0	0	1	6
Fulcher, David, Cin.	1	0	0	1	6
Graddy, Sam, Raiders	1	0	1	0	6
Hinkle, Bryan, Pitt.	1	0	0	1	6
Hunter, Patrick, Sea.	1	0	0	1	6
Jackson, Mark, Den.	1	0	1	0	6
James, Lynn, Cin.	1	0	1	0	6
Jefferson, Shawn, S.D.	1	0	1	0	6
Johnson, Reggie, Den.	1	0	1	0	6
Jones, Bill, K.C.	1	0	1	0	6
Kelly, Jim, Buff.	1	1	0	0	6
Klingbeil, Chuck, Mia.	1	0	0	1	6
Lathon, Lamar, Hou.	1	0	0	1	6
Lewis, Darryll, Hou.	1	0	0	1	6
Manoa, Tim, Ind.	1	1	0	0	6
Marino, Dan, Mia.	1	1	0	0	6
Martin, Chris, K.C.	1	0	0	1	6
Mathis, Terance, Jets	1	0	1	0	6
Matich, Trevor, Jets	1	0	1	0	6
McCallum, Napoleon, Raiders	1	1	0	0	6
McDowell, Bubba, Hou.	1	0	0	1	6
McNair, Todd, K.C.	1	0	1	0	6
McNeal, Travis, Sea.	1	0	1	0	6
Millen, Hugh, N.E.	1	1	0	0	6
Newsome, Vince, Clev.	1	0	0	1	6
O'Donnell, Neil, Pitt.	1	1	0	0	6
Odomes, Nate, Buff.	1	0	0	1	6
Paige, Tony, Mia.	1	0	1	0	6
Patterson, Elvis, Raiders	1	0	0	1	6
Powers, Warren, Den.	1	0	0	1	6
Price, Mitchell, Cin.	1	0	0	1	6
Rembert, Reggie, Cin.	1	0	1	0	6
Russell, Derek, Den.	1	0	1	0	6
Secules, Scott, Mia.	1	1	0	0	6
Sharpe, Shannon, Den.	1	0	1	0	6
Shelton, Richard, Pitt.	1	0	0	1	6
Smith, Al, Hou.	1	0	0	1	6
Smith, Sammie, Mia.	1	1	0	0	6
Tasker, Steve, Buff.	1	0	1	0	6
Thomas, Derrick, K.C.	1	0	0	1	6
Thomas, Robb, K.C.	1	0	1	0	6
Turner, Eric, Clev.	1	0	0	1	6
Verdin, Clarence, Ind.	1	0	0	1	6
Warren, Chris, Sea.	1	0	0	1	6
Williams, Jerrol, Pitt.	1	0	0	1	6
Dorn, Torin, Raiders	0	0	0	0	*2
Gordon, Alex, Cin.	0	0	0	0	*2
Saleaumua, Dan, K.C.	0	0	0	0	*2

* Indicates safety scored
# Indicates safety scored

NFC Scoring—Individual

Kickers	PAT	PAT Att.	FG	FG Att.	TP
Lohmiller, Chip, Wash.	56	56	31	43	149
Willis, Ken, Dall.	37	37	27	39	118
Andersen, Morten, N.O.	38	38	25	32	113
Ruzek, Roger, Phil.	27	29	28	33	111
Murray, Eddie, Det.	40	40	19	28	97
Johnson, Norm, Atl.	38	39	19	23	95
Cofer, Mike, S.F.	49	50	14	28	91
Bahr, Matt, Giants	24	25	22	29	90
Butler, Kevin, Chi.	32	34	19	29	89
Jacke, Chris, G.B.	31	31	18	24	85
Reveiz, Fuad, Minn.	34	35	17	24	85
Davis, Greg, Phx.	19	19	21	30	82
Zendejas, Tony, Rams	25	26	17	17	76
Christie, Steve, T.B.	22	22	15	20	67
Daluiso, Brad, Atl.	2	2	2	3	8

Non-Kickers	TD	TDR	TDP	TD Misc.	TP
Sanders, Barry, Det.	17	16	1	0	102

	TD	TDR	TDP	TD Misc.	TP
Rice, Jerry, S.F.	14	0	14	0	84
Smith, Emmitt, Dall.	13	12	1	0	78
Rison, Andre, Atl.	12	0	12	0	72
Haynes, Michael, Atl.	11	0	11	0	66
Riggs, Gerald, Wash.	11	11	0	0	66
Workman, Vince, G.B.	11	7	4	0	66
Clark, Gary, Wash.	10	0	10	0	60
Delpino, Robert, Rams	10	9	1	0	60
Hampton, Rodney, Giants	10	10	0	0	60
Walker, Herschel, Minn.	10	10	0	0	60
Anderson, Neal, Chi.	9	6	3	0	54
Taylor, John, S.F.	9	0	9	0	54
Irvin, Michael, Dall.	8	0	8	0	48
Monk, Art, Wash.	8	0	8	0	48
Turner, Floyd, N.O.	8	0	8	0	48
Cobb, Reggie, T.B.	7	7	0	0	42
Green, Willie, Det.	7	0	7	0	42
Muster, Brad, Chi.	7	6	1	0	42
Sydney, Harry, S.F.	7	5	2	0	42
Carter, Anthony, Minn.	6	1	5	0	36
Clark, Robert, Det.	6	0	6	0	36
Davis, Wendell, Chi.	6	0	6	0	36
Johnson, Johnny, Phx.	6	4	2	0	36
Rathman, Tom, S.F.	6	6	0	0	36
Sanders, Ricky, Wash.	6	1	5	0	36
Broussard, Steve, Atl.	5	4	1	0	30
Byner, Earnest, Wash.	5	5	0	0	30
Carter, Cris, Minn.	5	0	5	0	30
Fenerty, Gill, N.O.	5	3	2	0	30
Heyward, Craig, N.O.	5	4	1	0	30
Hilliard, Dalton, N.O.	5	4	1	0	30
Jackson, Keith, Phil.	5	0	5	0	30
Meggett, David, Giants	5	1	3	1	30
Baker, Stephen, Giants	4	0	4	0	24
Barnett, Fred, Phil.	4	0	4	0	24
Byars, Keith, Phil.	4	1	3	0	24
Carter, Dexter, S.F.	4	2	1	1	24
Dawsey, Lawrence, T.B.	4	1	3	0	24
Ervins, Ricky, Wash.	4	3	1	0	24
Jones, Ernie, Phx.	4	0	4	0	24
Martin, Eric, N.O.	4	0	4	0	24
Novacek, Jay, Dall.	4	0	4	0	24
Orr, Terry, Wash.	4	0	4	0	24
Sharpe, Sterling, G.B.	4	0	4	0	24
Young, Steve, S.F.	4	4	0	0	24
Allen, Terry, Minn.	3	2	1	0	18
Ellard, Henry, Rams	3	0	3	0	18
Green, Mark, Chi.	3	3	0	0	18
Harris, Jackie, G.B.	3	0	3	0	18
Ingram, Mark, Giants	3	0	3	0	18
Jordan, Buford, N.O.	3	2	1	0	18
Joseph, James, Phil.	3	3	0	0	18
Waddle, Tom, Chi.	3	0	3	0	18
West, Ed, G.B.	3	0	3	0	18
Williams, Calvin, Phil.	3	0	3	0	18
Anderson, Jesse, T.B.	2	0	2	0	12
Carrier, Mark, T.B.	2	0	2	0	12
Carter, Pat, Rams	2	0	2	0	12
Cross, Howard, Giants	2	0	2	0	12
Drewrey, Willie, T.B.	2	0	2	0	12
Drummond, Robert, Phil.	2	2	0	0	12
Early, Quinn, N.O.	2	0	2	0	12
Gannon, Rich, Minn.	2	2	0	0	12
Harbaugh, Jim, Chi.	2	2	0	0	12
Henderson, Keith, S.F.	2	2	0	0	12
Hill, Bruce, T.B.	2	0	2	0	12
Horton, Ray, Dall.	2	0	0	2	12
Hostetler, Jeff, Giants	2	2	0	0	12
Johnson, Damone, Rams	2	0	2	0	12
Johnson, Jimmie, Wash.	2	0	2	0	12
Johnson, Maurice, Phil.	2	0	2	0	12
Jones, Mike, Minn.	2	0	2	0	12
Jordan, Steve, Minn.	2	0	2	0	12
Joyner, Seth, Phil.	2	0	0	2	12
Kemp, Perry, G.B.	2	0	2	0	12
Majkowski, Don, G.B.	2	2	0	0	12
McAfee, Fred, N.O.	2	2	0	0	12
Mitchell, Brian, Wash.	2	0	0	2	12
Morgan, Anthony, Chi.	2	0	2	0	12
Nelson, Darrin, Minn.	2	2	0	0	12
Peete, Rodney, Det.	2	2	0	0	12
Price, Jim, Rams	2	0	2	0	12
Pritchard, Mike, Atl.	2	0	2	0	12
Proehl, Ricky, Phx.	2	0	2	0	12
Sanders, Deion, Atl.	2	0	0	2	12
Sherrard, Mike, S.F.	2	0	2	0	12
Thomas, George, Atl.	2	0	2	0	12
Wilson, Charles, G.B.	2	0	1	1	12

	TD	TDR	TDP	TD Misc.	TP
Wilson, Robert, T.B.	2	0	2	0	12
Agee, Tommie, Dall.	1	1	0	0	6
Aikman, Troy, Dall.	1	1	0	0	6
Anderson, Alfred, Minn.	1	1	0	0	6
Anderson, Gary, T.B.	1	1	0	0	6
Anderson, Ottis, Giants	1	1	0	0	6
Anderson, Willie, Rams	1	0	1	0	6
Bailey, Johnny, Chi.	1	1	0	0	6
Barnett, Oliver, Atl.	1	0	0	1	6
Blake, Ricky, Dall.	1	1	0	0	6
Carroll, Wesley, N.O.	1	0	1	0	6
Chaffey, Pat, Atl.	1	1	0	0	6
Collins, Andre, Wash.	1	0	0	1	6
Crockett, Ray, Det.	1	0	0	1	6
Dixon, Floyd, Atl.	1	0	1	0	6
Dupree, Marcus, Rams	1	1	0	0	6
Edwards, Dixon, Dall.	1	0	0	1	6
Farr, Mike, Det.	1	0	1	0	6
Fishback, Joe, Atl.	1	0	0	1	6
Gary, Cleveland, Rams	1	1	0	0	6
Gray, Jerry, Rams	1	0	0	1	6
Gray, Mel, Det.	1	0	0	1	6
Griffin, Don, S.F.	1	0	0	1	6
Harper, Alvin, Dall.	1	0	1	0	6
Hayworth, Tracy, Det.	1	0	0	1	6
Hill, Eric, Phx.	1	0	0	1	6
Hill, Randal, Phx.	1	0	1	0	6
Johnston, Daryl, Dall.	1	0	1	0	6
Jones, Hassan, Minn.	1	0	1	0	6
Kramer, Erik, Det.	1	1	0	0	6
Lynch, Lorenzo, Phx.	1	0	0	1	6
Marshall, Wilber, Wash.	1	0	0	1	6
Martin, Kelvin, Dall.	1	0	0	1	6
Maxie, Brett, N.O.	1	0	0	1	6
Mayhew, Martin, Wash.	1	0	0	1	6
McMahon, Jim, Phil.	1	1	0	0	6
Merriweather, Mike, Minn.	1	0	0	1	6
Mowatt, Zeke, Giants	1	0	1	0	6
Newman, Anthony, Rams	1	0	0	1	6
Noble, Brian, G.B.	1	0	0	1	6
Pegram, Erric, Atl.	1	1	0	0	6
Perriman, Brett, Det.	1	0	1	0	6
Roberts, Alfredo, Dall.	1	0	1	0	6
Rutland, Reggie, Minn.	1	0	0	1	6
Rypien, Mark, Wash.	1	1	0	0	6
Saddler, Rod, Phx.	1	0	0	1	6
Sanders, Thomas, Phil.	1	1	0	0	6
Simmons, Clyde, Phil.	1	0	0	1	6
Simms, Phil, Giants	1	1	0	0	6
Smith, Otis, Phil.	1	0	0	1	6
Stinson, Lemuel, Chi.	1	0	0	1	6
Swilling, Pat, N.O.	1	0	0	1	6
Thompson, Anthony, Phx.	1	1	0	0	6
Thompson, Darrell, G.B.	1	1	0	0	6
Thompson, Ernie, Rams	1	0	1	0	6
Thornton, James, Chi.	1	0	1	0	6
Tillman, Lewis, Giants	1	1	0	0	6
Tippins, Kenny, Atl.	1	0	0	1	6
Tomczak, Mike, G.B.	1	1	0	0	6
Tuggle, Jessie, Atl.	1	0	0	1	6
Tupa, Tom, Phx.	1	1	0	0	6
Turner, Vernon, Rams	1	0	1	0	6
Warren, Frank, N.O.	1	0	0	1	6
White, Sheldon, Det.	1	0	0	1	6
White, William, Det.	1	0	0	1	6
Wilkins, Gary, Atl.	1	0	1	0	6
Williams, Jamie, S.F.	1	0	1	0	6
Williams, Robert, Dall.	1	0	0	1	6
Williams, Willie, Phx.	1	0	1	0	6
Woodside, Keith, G.B.	1	1	0	0	6
Wright, Alexander, Dall.	1	0	0	1	6
Jordan, Brian, Atl.	0	0	0	0	*4
Ball, Jerry, Det.	0	0	0	0	*2
Greene, Kevin, Rams	0	0	0	0	*2
Hendrix, Manuel, Dall.	0	0	0	0	*2
Jordan, Darin, S.F.	0	0	0	0	*2
Paup, Bryce, G.B.	0	0	0	0	*2

* indicates safety scored
# indicates extra point scored

Field Goals

Best Percentage
NFC: 1.000 Tony Zendejas, Rams
AFC: .853 Jeff Jaeger, Raiders

Made
AFC: 31 Pete Stoyanovich, Miami
NFC: 31 Chip Lohmiller, Washington

Attempts
NFC: 43 Chip Lohmiller, Washington
AFC: 37 Pat Leahy, Jets
Pete Stoyanovich, Miami

Longest
NFC: 60 Morten Andersen, New Orleans
AFC: 55 Matt Stover, Cleveland

Average Yards Made
NFC: 37.3 Greg Davis, Phoenix
AFC: 36.0 John Kasay, Seattle

AFC Field Goals—Team

	FG	FG Att.	Pc.	Long
L.A. Raiders	29	34	.853	53
Miami	33	39	.846	53
Kansas City	25	30	.833	48
Seattle	25	31	.806	54
Cincinnati	24	32	.750	53
Denver	27	36	.750	47
Houston	23	31	.742	52
Cleveland	16	22	.727	55
N.Y. Jets	30	43	.698	44
Pittsburgh	23	33	.697	54
New England	20	29	.690	46
San Diego	19	29	.655	54
Buffalo	18	29	.621	52
Indianapolis	15	26	.577	54
AFC Total	327	444	——	55
AFC Average	23.4	31.7	.736	—

NFC Field Goals—Team

	FG	FG Att.	Pct.	Long
L.A. Rams	17	17	1.000	50
Philadelphia	28	33	.848	51
Atlanta	21	26	.808	50
New Orleans	25	32	.781	60
N.Y. Giants	24	31	.774	54
Green Bay	18	24	.750	53
Tampa Bay	15	20	.750	49
Washington	31	43	.721	53
Minnesota	17	24	.708	50
Phoenix	21	30	.700	52
Dallas	27	39	.692	54
Detroit	19	28	.679	50
Chicago	19	29	.655	50
San Francisco	14	28	.500	50
NFC Total	296	404	——	60
NFC Average	21.1	28.9	.733	—
NFL Total	623	848	——	60
NFL Average	22.3	30.3	.735	—

AFC Field Goals—Individual

	1-19 Yards	20-29 Yards	30-39 Yards	40-49 Yards	50 & More	Totals	Avg. Yds. Att.	Avg. Yds. Made	Avg. Yds. Miss	Long
Jaeger, Jeff, Raiders	3-3 1.000	7-7 1.000	10-13 .769	7-7 1.000	2-4 .500	29-34 .853	35.7	34.7	41.8	53
Stoyanovich, Pete, Mia.	2-2 1.000	8-8 1.000	11-12 .917	7-10 .700	3-5 .600	31-37 .838	36.3	34.2	47.2	53
Lowery, Nick, K.C.	2-2 1.000	11-11 1.000	8-8 1.000	4-7 .571	0-2 .000	25-30 .833	33.1	30.3	46.8	48
Kasay, John, Sea.	1-1 1.000	5-6 .833	11-14 .786	6-7 .857	2-3 .667	25-31 .806	36.3	36.0	37.5	54
Breech, Jim, Cin.	0-0 ——	9-10 .900	8-10 .800	5-6 .833	1-3 .333	23-29 .793	35.7	34.3	41.0	50
Treadwell, David, Den.	5-5 1.000	10-10 1.000	9-12 .750	3-9 .333	0-0 ——	27-36 .750	31.9	28.8	41.1	47
Stover, Matt, Clev.	1-2 .500	2-3 .667	8-9 .889	3-6 .500	2-2 1.000	16-22 .727	35.0	34.8	35.7	55
Howfield, Ian, Hou.	1-1 1.000	7-7 1.000	4-6 .667	1-2 .500	0-2 .000	13-18 .722	32.9	28.8	43.8	46
Leahy, Pat, Jets	3-3 1.000	13-16 .813	9-11 .818	1-5 .200	0-2 .000	26-37 .703	31.0	27.7	38.7	40
Anderson, Gary, Pitt.	0-0 ——	8-10 .800	9-11 .818	5-6 .833	1-6 .167	23-33 .697	37.4	35.1	42.6	54
Staurovsky, Jason, N.E.	1-1 1.000	2-3 .667	9-12 .750	1-3 .333	0-0 ——	13-19 .684	34.6	33.3	37.5	42
Carney, John, S.D.	1-1 1.000	6-6 1.000	6-8 .750	4-10 .400	2-4 .500	19-29 .655	39.3	35.7	46.0	54
Norwood, Scott, Buff.	1-1 1.000	7-8 .875	3-7 .429	5-9 .556	2-4 .500	18-29 .621	36.7	33.4	41.9	52
Biasucci, Dean, Ind.	1-1 1.000	5-5 1.000	3-4 .750	5-13 .385	1-3 .333	15-26 .577	39.5	35.1	45.5	54
Non-Qualifiers (Less than 15 attempts)										
Allegre, Raul, Giants-Jets	0-0 ——	2-2 1.000	2-2 1.000	1-2 .500	0-0 ——	5-6 .833	33.5	31.6	43.0	44
Del Greco, Al, Hou.	1-1 1.000	4-5 .800	2-3 .667	2-3 .667	1-1 1.000	10-13 .769	32.9	32.7	33.7	52
Baumann, Charlie, Mia.-N.E.	0-0 ——	3-3 1.000	1-3 .333	5-5 1.000	0-1 .000	9-12 .750	37.5	36.6	40.3	48
Daluiso, Brad, Atl.-Buff.	0-0 ——	2-3 .667	0-0 ——	0-0 ——	0-0 ——	2-3 .667	23.0	21.5	26.0	23
Aguiar, Louie, Jets	0-0 ——	1-2 .500	0-0 ——	0-0 ——	0-0 ——	1-2 .500	25.0	23.0	27.0	23
Johnson, Lee, Cin.	0-0 ——	0-0 ——	0-0 ——	0-0 ——	1-3 .333	1-3 .333	53.3	53.0	53.5	53
AFC Total	23-24 .958	109-121 .901	112-144 .778	65-110 .591	18-45 .400	327-444 .736	35.4	33.1	41.9	55
League Total	30-31 .968	205-221 .928	205-262 .782	141-240 .588	42-94 .447	623-848 .735	36.3	33.9	42.8	60

Leader based on percentage, minimum 16 field-goal attempts

NFC Field Goals—Individual

	1-19 Yards	20-29 Yards	30-39 Yards	40-49 Yards	50 & Over	Totals	Avg. Yds. Att.	Avg. Yds. Made	Avg. Yds. Miss	Long
Zendejas, Tony, Rams	0-0	4-4	8-8	3-3	2-2	17-17	35.5	35.5	—	50
	—	1.000	1.000	1.000	1.000	1.000				
Ruzek, Roger, Phil.	2-2	8-8	9-10	8-10	1-3	28-33	36.2	34.4	46.4	51
	1.000	1.000	.900	.800	.333	.848				
Johnson, Norm, Atl.	0-0	9-9	4-4	5-8	1-2	19-23	36.5	33.8	49.5	50
	—	1.000	1.000	.625	.500	.826				
Andersen, Morten, N.O.	0-0	6-6	11-13	6-9	2-4	25-32	37.9	36.2	44.1	60
	—	1.000	.846	.667	.500	.781				
Bahr, Matt, Giants	0-0	6-6	6-8	9-12	1-3	22-29	38.5	37.3	42.4	54
	—	1.000	.750	.750	.333	.759				
Jacke, Chris, G.B.	0-0	9-9	4-5	4-9	1-1	18-24	35.1	32.4	43.2	53
	—	1.000	.800	.444	1.000	.750				
Christie, Steve, T.B.	1-1	4-4	7-11	3-4	0-0	15-20	34.0	32.5	38.6	49
	1.000	1.000	.636	.750	—	.750				
Lohmiller, Chip, Wash.	0-0	9-9	10-12	10-17	2-5	31-43	39.1	36.4	46.3	53
	—	1.000	.833	.588	.400	.721				
Reveiz, Fuad, Minn.	0-0	9-9	3-3	3-7	2-5	17-24	36.5	31.4	48.9	50
	—	1.000	1.000	.429	.400	.708				
Davis, Greg, Phx.	0-0	6-6	7-7	5-10	3-7	21-30	40.5	37.3	47.9	52
	—	1.000	1.000	.500	.429	.700				
Willis, Ken, Dall.	2-2	6-6	9-11	6-13	4-7	27-39	38.4	35.3	45.4	54
	1.000	1.000	.818	.462	.571	.692				
Murray, Eddie, Det.	1-1	3-4	8-10	5-9	2-4	19-28	38.3	36.5	42.1	50
	1.000	.750	.800	.556	.500	.679				
Butler, Kevin, Chi.	1-1	9-11	3-5	5-9	1-3	19-29	34.3	31.4	39.9	50
	1.000	.818	.600	.556	.333	.655				
Cofer, Mike, S.F.	0-0	5-5	3-10	4-10	2-3	14-28	38.1	35.9	40.2	50
	—	1.000	.300	.400	.667	.500				
NFC Total	7-7	96-100	93-118	76-130	24-49	296-404	37.2	34.8	43.8	60
	1.000	.960	.788	.585	.490	.733				
League Total	30-31	205-221	205-262	141-240	42-946	23-848	36.3	33.9	42.8	60
	.968	.928	.782	.588	.447	.735				

Leader based on percentage, minimum 16 field goal attempts

Rushing

Individual Champions
- **NFC:** 1563—Emmitt Smith, Dallas
- **AFC:** 1407—Thurman Thomas, Buffalo

Most Yards, Game
- **NFC:** 220—Barry Sanders, Detroit at Minnesota, November 24, (23 attempts, 4 TD)
- **AFC:** 165—Thurman Thomas, Buffalo vs. Miami, September 1, (25 attempts, TD)

Longest
- **AFC:** 78—Kenneth Davis, Buffalo vs. Indianapolis, October 13, -TD
- **NFC:** 75—Emmitt Smith, Dallas vs. Washington, September 9, -TD

Attempts
- **NFC:** 365—Emmitt Smith, Dallas
- **AFC:** 288—Thurman Thomas, Buffalo

Most Attempts, Game
- **NFC:** 35—Heath Sherman, Philadelphia at Tampa Bay, October 6 (89 yards)
- **AFC:** 35—Barry Word, Kansas City at Raiders, December 22 (152 yards)

Yards Per Attempt
- **AFC:** 4.9—Thurman Thomas, Buffalo
- **NFC:** 4.7—Terry Allen, Minnesota

Touchdowns
- **NFC:** 16—Barry Sanders, Detroit
- **AFC:** 11—Brad Baxter, Jets

Team Leaders, Yards
- **AFC:** BUFFALO: 1407, Thurman Thomas; CINCINNATI: 731, Harold Green; CLEVELAND: 726, Kevin Mack; DENVER: 1037, Gaston Green; HOUSTON: 720, Allen Pinkett; INDIANAPOLIS: 536, Eric Dickerson; KANSAS CITY: 1031, Christian Okoye; RAIDERS: 590, Roger Craig; MIAMI: 905, Mark Higgs; NEW ENGLAND: 959, Leonard Russell; JETS: 728, Blair Thomas; PITTSBURGH: 610, Merril Hoge; SAN DIEGO: 834, Marion Butts; SEATTLE: 741, John L. Williams
- **NFC:** ATLANTA: 449, Steve Broussard; CHICAGO: 747, Neal Anderson; DALLAS: 1563, Emmitt Smith; DETROIT: 1548, Barry Sanders; GREEN BAY: 471, Darrell Thompson; RAMS: 688, Robert Delpino; MINNESOTA: 825, Herschel Walker; NEW ORLEANS: 494, Fred McAfee; GIANTS: 1059, Rodney Hampton; PHILADELPHIA: 440, James Joseph; PHOENIX: 666, Johnny Johnson; SAN FRANCISCO: 561, Keith Henderson; TAMPA BAY: 752, Reggie Cobb; WASHINGTON: 1048, Earnest Byner

Team Champions
- **AFC:** 2381 — Buffalo
- **NFC:** 2201 — Minnesota

AFC Rushing—Team

	Att	Yards	Avg	Long	TD
Buffalo	505	2381	4.7	t78	16
San Diego	464	2248	4.8	t63	16
Kansas City	521	2217	4.3	48	14
N.Y. Jets	523	2160	4.1	58	17
Denver	507	2015	4.0	t63	16
Cincinnati	449	1811	4.0	t75	11
L.A. Raiders	446	1706	3.8	26	8
Pittsburgh	394	1627	4.1	t56	8
New England	433	1467	3.4	24	9
Seattle	394	1426	3.6	42	11
Houston	331	1366	4.1	t39	16
Cleveland	389	1360	3.5	52	12
Miami	379	1352	3.6	24	8
Indianapolis	354	1169	3.3	44	3
AFC Total	6089	24305	—	t78	165
AFC Average	434.9	1736.1	4.0	—	11.8

NFC Rushing—Team

	Att	Yards	Avg	Long	TD
Minnesota	464	2201	4.7	t71	18
N.Y. Giants	487	2064	4.2	t47	16
Washington	540	2049	3.8	t65	21
Chicago	502	1949	3.9	t42	18
Detroit	454	1930	4.3	t69	19
San Francisco	440	1861	4.2	t53	19
Dallas	433	1711	4.0	t75	15
New Orleans	483	1709	3.5	t65	15
Atlanta	410	1664	4.1	36	6
Tampa Bay	371	1429	3.9	t64	9
Philadelphia	446	1396	3.1	28	8
Green Bay	381	1389	3.6	48	12
Phoenix	391	1295	3.3	22	6
L.A. Rams	388	1285	3.3	36	11
NFC Total	6190	23932	—	t75	193
NFC Average	442.1	1709.4	3.9	—	13.8
League Total	12279	48237	—	t78	358
League Average	438.5	1722.8	3.9	—	12.8

NFL Top 10 Rushers

	Att	Yards	Avg	Long	TD
Smith, Emmitt, Dall.	365	1563	4.3	t75	12
Sanders, Barry, Det.	343	1548	4.5	t69	16
Thomas, Thurman, Buff.	288	1407	4.9	33	7
Hampton, Rodney, Giants	256	1059	4.1	44	10
Byner, Earnest, Wash.	274	1048	3.8	32	5
Green, Gaston, Den.	261	1037	4.0	t63	4
Okoye, Christian, K.C.	225	1031	4.6	48	9
Russell, Leonard, N.E.	266	959	3.6	24	4
Higgs, Mark, Mia.	231	905	3.9	24	4
Butts, Marion, S.D.	193	834	4.3	44	6

AFC Rushing—Individual

	Att.	Yards	Avg.	Long	TD
Thomas, Thurman, Buff.	288	1407	4.9	33	7
Green, Gaston, Den.	261	1037	4.0	t63	4
Okoye, Christian, K.C.	225	1031	4.6	48	9
Russell, Leonard, N.E.	266	959	3.6	24	4
Higgs, Mark, Mia.	231	905	3.9	24	4
Butts, Marion, S.D.	193	834	4.3	44	6
Bernstine, Rod, S.D.	159	766	4.8	t63	8
Williams, John L., Sea.	188	741	3.9	42	4
Green, Harold, Cin.	158	731	4.6	t75	2
Thomas, Blair, Jets	189	728	3.9	25	3
Mack, Kevin, Clev.	197	726	3.7	t51	8
Pinkett, Allen, Hou.	171	720	4.2	32	9
Word, Barry, K.C.	160	684	4.3	37	4
Baxter, Brad, Jets	184	666	3.6	31	11
Davis, Kenneth, Buff.	129	624	4.8	t78	4
Hoge, Merril, Pitt.	165	610	3.7	24	2
Craig, Roger, Raiders	162	590	3.6	15	1
Brooks, James, Cin.	152	571	3.8	25	2
Harmon, Ronnie, S.D.	89	544	6.1	33	1
Dickerson, Eric, Ind.	167	536	3.2	28	2
Foster, Barry, Pitt.	96	488	5.1	t56	1
White, Lorenzo, Hou.	110	465	4.2	20	4
Williams, Harvey, K.C.	97	447	4.6	21	1
Lewis, Greg, Den.	99	376	3.8	27	4
Clark, Ken, Ind.	114	366	3.2	25	0
Hector, Johnny, Jets	62	345	5.6	47	0
Bell, Nick, Raiders	78	307	3.9	15	3
McNeil, Freeman, Jets	51	300	5.9	58	2
Smith, Sammie, Mia.	83	297	3.6	18	1
Morris, Joe, Clev.	93	289	3.1	15	2
Allen, Marcus, Raiders	63	287	4.6	26	2
Fenner, Derrick, Sea.	91	267	2.9	15	4
Smith, Steve, Raiders	62	265	4.3	19	1
Williams, Warren, Pitt.	57	262	4.6	21	4
Elway, John, Den.	55	255	4.6	t17	6
Sewell, Steve, Den.	50	211	4.2	26	2
Stephens, John, N.E.	63	163	2.6	13	2
Hoard, Leroy, Clev.	37	154	4.2	52	2
Jones, James, Sea.	45	154	3.4	22	3
Taylor, Craig, Cin.	33	153	4.6	t34	2
Gardner, Carwell, Buff.	42	146	3.5	18	4
Vaughn, Jon, N.E.	31	146	4.7	23	2
Manoa, Tim, Ind.	27	144	5.3	44	1
Reed, Andre, Buff.	12	136	11.3	46	0
Worley, Tim, Pitt.	22	117	5.3	16	0
McCallum, Napoleon, Raiders	31	110	3.5	9	1
Metcalf, Eric, Clev.	30	107	3.6	15	0
Woods, Ickey, Cin.	36	97	2.7	12	4
Johnson, Anthony, Ind.	22	94	4.3	15	0
Millen, Hugh, N.E.	31	92	3.0	14	1
Dingle, Mike, Cin.	21	91	4.3	21	0
Brown, Gary, Hou.	8	85	10.6	t39	1
O'Donnell, Neil, Pitt.	18	82	4.6	22	1
Schroeder, Jay, Raiders	28	76	2.7	15	0
Kosar, Bernie, Clev.	26	74	2.8	14	0
Loville, Derek, Sea.	22	69	3.1	22	0
Moon, Warren, Hou.	33	68	2.1	12	2
Esiason, Boomer, Cin.	24	66	2.8	16	0
Hollas, Donald, Cin.	12	66	5.5	27	0
O'Brien, Ken, Jets	23	60	2.6	13	0
Thompson, Leroy, Pitt.	20	60	3.0	14	0
Krieg, Dave, Sea.	13	59	4.5	24	0
Craver, Aaron, Mia.	20	58	2.9	t7	1
Hunter, Ivy Joe, N.E.	18	53	2.9	9	0
McNair, Todd, K.C.	10	51	5.1	11	0
Allen, Marvin, N.E.	13	50	3.8	11	0
Kelly, Jim, Buff.	20	45	2.3	12	1
Perryman, Bob, Den.	21	45	2.1	6	0
George, Jeff, Ind.	16	36	2.3	13	0
Humphrey, Bobby, Den.	11	33	3.0	7	0
Marino, Dan, Mia.	27	32	1.2	11	1
Givins, Ernest, Hou.	4	30	7.5	23	0
Secules, Scott, Mia.	4	30	7.5	12	1
Jefferson, Shawn, S.D.	1	27	27.0	27	0

	Att.	Yards	Avg.	Long	TD
Paige, Tony, Mia.	10	25	2.5	6	0
Taylor, Troy, Jets	7	23	3.3	13	0
Ball, Eric, Cin.	10	21	2.1	10	1
Wilson, Marcus, Raiders	6	21	3.5	8	0
Evans, Vince, Raiders	8	20	2.5	11	0
Gagliano, Bob, S.D.	3	19	6.3	16	0
Mathis, Terance, Jets	1	19	19.0	19	0
Aguiar, Louie, Jets	1	18	18.0	18	0
Friesz, John, S.D.	10	18	1.8	11	0
Jackson, Mark, Den.	2	18	9.0	21	0
Bieniemy, Eric, S.D.	3	17	5.7	15	0
Blades, Brian, Sea.	2	17	8.5	11	0
Brister, Bubby, Pitt.	11	17	1.5	8	0
Edwards, Al, Buff.	1	17	17.0	17	0
Brown, Tim, Raiders	5	16	3.2	9	0
Sharpe, Shannon, Den.	1	15	15.0	15	0
Marinovich, Todd, Raiders	3	14	4.7	11	0
Rouson, Lee, Clev.	3	14	4.7	9	0
Saxon, James, K.C.	6	13	2.2	8	0
Warren, Chris, Sea.	11	13	1.2	7	0
Fryar, Irving, N.E.	2	11	5.5	9	0
Kubiak, Gary, Den.	3	11	3.7	12	0
Perkins, Bruce, Ind.	4	11	2.8	4	0
Lewis, Nate, S.D.	3	10	3.3	9	0
Samuels, Chris, S.D.	2	10	5.0	6	0
Horan, Mike, Den.	2	9	4.5	9	0
Wilhelm, Erik, Cin.	1	9	9.0	9	0
Brown, Eddie, Cin.	1	8	8.0	8	0
Stradford, Troy, K.C.	1	7	7.0	7	0
Reich, Frank, Buff.	13	6	0.5	8	0
Logan, Marc, Mia.	4	5	1.3	2	0
Rivers, Reggie, Den.	2	5	2.5	3	0
Brown, A.B., Jets	3	4	1.3	2	1
Verdin, Clarence, Ind.	1	4	4.0	4	0
Adams, George, N.E.	2	3	1.5	2	0
Hendrickson, Steve, S.D.	1	3	3.0	t3	1
Stone, Dwight, Pitt.	1	2	2.0	2	0
Hill, Drew, Hou.	1	1	1.0	1	0
Chilton, Gene, N.E.	1	0	0.0	0	0
Hodson, Tom, N.E.	4	0	0.0	1	0
Herrmann, Mark, Ind.	1	-1	-1.0	-1	0
Nagle, Browning, Jets	1	-1	-1.0	-1	0
Philcox, Todd, Clev.	1	-1	-1.0	-1	0
Vlasic, Mark, K.C.	1	-1	-1.0	-1	0
Burkett, Chris, Jets	1	-2	-2.0	-2	0
Johnson, Lee, Cin.	1	-2	-2.0	-2	0
Carlson, Cody, Hou.	4	-3	-0.8	0	0
Hansen, Brian, Clev.	2	-3	-1.5	0	0
Timpson, Michael, N.E.	1	-4	-4.0	-4	0
Coates, Ben, N.E.	1	-6	-6.0	-6	0
Huffman, Darvell, Ind.	1	-8	-8.0	-8	0
Stryzinski, Dan, Pitt.	4	-11	-2.8	0	0
Stark, Rohn, Ind.	1	-13	-13.0	-13	0
DeBerg, Steve, K.C.	21	-15	-0.7	0	0

t indicates touchdown.
Leader based on most yards gained

NFC Rushing—Individual

	Att.	Yards	Avg.	Long	TD
Smith, Emmitt, Dall.	365	1563	4.3	t75	12
Sanders, Barry, Det.	342	1548	4.5	t69	16
Hampton, Rodney, Giants	256	1059	4.1	44	10
Byner, Earnest, Wash.	274	1048	3.8	32	5
Walker, Herschel, Minn.	198	825	4.2	t71	10
Cobb, Reggie, T.B.	196	752	3.8	t59	7
Anderson, Neal, Chi.	210	747	3.6	t42	6
Delpino, Robert, Rams	214	688	3.2	36	9
Ervins, Ricky, Wash.	145	680	4.7	t65	3
Johnson, Johnny, Phx.	196	666	3.4	21	4
Allen, Terry, Minn.	120	563	4.7	t55	2
Henderson, Keith, S.F.	137	561	4.1	25	2
McAfee, Fred, N.O.	109	494	4.5	34	2
Fenerty, Gill, N.O.	139	477	3.4	54	3
Thompson, Darrell, G.B.	141	471	3.3	t40	1
Broussard, Steve, Atl.	99	449	4.5	36	4
Joseph, James, Phil.	135	440	3.3	24	3
Young, Steve, S.F.	66	415	6.3	21	4
Muster, Brad, Chi.	90	412	4.6	24	6
Byars, Keith, Phil.	94	383	4.1	28	1
Carter, Dexter, S.F.	85	379	4.5	t53	2
Thompson, Anthony, Phx.	126	376	3.0	22	1
Rozier, Mike, Atl.	96	361	3.8	19	0
Pegram, Erric, Atl.	101	349	3.5	34	1
Harbaugh, Jim, Chi.	70	338	4.8	20	2
Woodside, Keith, G.B.	84	326	3.9	29	1
Tillman, Lewis, Giants	65	287	4.4	17	1
Sherman, Heath, Phil.	106	279	2.6	12	0

	Att.	Yards	Avg.	Long	TD
Hostetler, Jeff, Giants	42	273	6.5	t47	2
Anderson, Gary, T.B.	72	263	3.7	t64	1
Heyward, Craig, N.O.	76	260	3.4	15	4
Hilliard, Dalton, N.O.	79	252	3.2	t65	4
Riggs, Gerald, Wash.	78	248	3.2	32	11
Gary, Cleveland, Rams	68	245	3.6	14	1
Sydney, Harry, S.F.	57	245	4.3	32	5
Workman, Vince, G.B.	71	237	3.3	t30	7
Gannon, Rich, Minn.	43	236	5.5	42	2
Miller, Chris, Atl.	32	229	7.2	20	0
Green, Mark, Chi.	61	217	3.6	18	3
Nelson, Darrin, Minn.	28	210	7.5	29	2
Rathman, Tom, S.F.	63	183	2.9	16	6
Dupree, Marcus, Rams	49	179	3.7	24	1
Kemp, Jeff, Sea.-Phil.	38	179	4.7	18	0
Wilson, Robert, T.B.	42	179	4.3	20	0
Meggett, David, Giants	29	153	5.3	t30	1
Jordan, Buford, N.O.	47	150	3.2	25	2
Anderson, Ottis, Giants	53	141	2.7	9	1
Chaffey, Pat, Atl.	29	127	4.4	27	1
Jones, Keith, Atl.	35	126	3.6	14	0
Peete, Rodney, Det.	25	125	5.0	26	2
Sanders, Thomas, Phil.	54	122	2.3	16	1
Anderson, Alfred, Minn.	26	118	4.5	19	1
Carter, Anthony, Minn.	13	117	9.0	32	1
Chandler, Chris, T.B.-Phx.	26	111	4.3	12	0
Carthon, Maurice, Giants	32	109	3.4	10	0
Majkowski, Don, G.B.	25	108	4.3	15	2
Testaverde, Vinny, T.B.	32	101	3.2	19	0
Rice, Allen, G.B.	30	100	3.3	21	0
Fenney, Rick, Minn.	23	99	4.3	17	0
Tupa, Tom, Phx.	28	97	3.5	17	1
Tomczak, Mike, G.B.	17	93	5.5	48	1
Blake, Ricky, Dall.	15	80	5.3	t30	1
Rouse, James, Chi.	27	74	2.7	10	0
McGee, Buford, Rams	19	65	3.4	9	0
Overton, Don, Det.	14	59	4.2	9	0
Gentry, Dennis, Chi.	9	58	6.4	17	0
Hebert, Bobby, N.O.	18	56	3.1	16	0
Jackson, Cedric, Det.	17	55	3.2	10	0
McMahon, Jim, Phil.	22	55	2.5	12	1
Johnston, Daryl, Dall.	17	54	3.2	10	0
Dozier, D.J., Det.	9	48	5.3	29	0
Sanders, Ricky, Wash.	7	47	6.7	17	1
Bono, Steve, S.F.	17	46	2.7	18	0
Kiel, Blair, G.B.	4	46	11.5	26	0
Centers, Larry, Phx.	14	44	3.1	8	0
Everett, Jim, Rams	27	44	1.6	10	0
Turner, Vernon, Rams	7	44	6.3	11	0
Bailey, Johnny, Chi.	15	43	2.9	11	1
Arnold, Jim, Det.	2	42	21.0	21	0
Simms, Phil, Giants	9	42	4.7	19	1
Tillman, Spencer, S.F.	13	40	3.1	8	0
Lewis, Darren, Chi.	15	36	2.4	9	0
Wilson, Wade, Minn.	13	33	2.5	15	0
Drummond, Robert, Phil.	12	27	2.3	7	2
Johnson, Tracy, Atl.	8	26	3.3	6	0
Kramer, Erik, Det.	35	26	0.7	12	1
Carlson, Jeff, T.B.	5	25	5.0	11	0
Jones, Ernie, Phx.	5	24	4.8	9	0
Gelbaugh, Stan, Phx.	9	23	2.6	13	0
Highsmith, Alonzo, T.B.	5	21	4.2	10	0
Proehl, Ricky, Phx.	3	21	7.0	17	0
Agee, Tommie, Dall.	9	20	2.2	8	1
Monk, Art, Wash.	9	19	2.1	14	0
Jackson, Kenny, Phil.	1	18	18.0	18	0
Morgan, Anthony, Chi.	3	18	6.0	13	0
Mitchell, Brian, Wash.	3	14	4.7	8	0
Early, Quinn, N.O.	3	13	4.3	6	0
Brown, Ron, Rams	2	11	5.5	11	0
Gray, Mel, Det.	2	11	5.5	6	0
Perriman, Brett, Det.	4	10	2.5	6	0
Dawsey, Lawrence, T.B.	1	9	9.0	t9	1
Thompson, Ernie, Rams	2	9	4.5	9	0
Flagler, Terrence, Phx.	1	7	7.0	7	0
Morse, Bobby, N.O.	3	7	2.3	8	0
Rypien, Mark, Wash.	15	6	0.4	11	1
Tolliver, Billy Joe, Atl.	9	6	0.7	7	0
Ware, Andre, Det.	4	6	1.5	10	0
Willis, Peter Tom, Chi.	2	6	3.0	8	0
Aikman, Troy, Dall.	16	5	0.3	9	1
Kupp, Craig, Phx.	1	5	5.0	5	0
Richards, Curvin, Dall.	2	4	2.0	3	0
Sharpe, Sterling, G.B.	4	4	1.0	12	0
Wilson, Charles, G.B.	3	3	1.0	5	0
Goebel, Brad, Phil.	1	2	2.0	2	0
Rice, Jerry, S.F.	1	2	2.0	2	0
Harris, Jackie, G.B.	1	1	1.0	1	0

	Att	Yards	Avg	Long	TD
Barnett, Fred, Phil.	1	0	0.0	0	0
Barnhardt, Tommy, N.O.	1	0	0.0	0	0
Bunch, Jarrod, Giants	1	0	0.0	0	0
Clark, Gary, Wash.	1	0	0.0	0	0
McJulien, Paul, G.B.	1	0	0.0	0	0
Walsh, Steve, N.O.	8	0	0.0	3	0
Feagles, Jeff, Phil.	3	-1	-0.3	11	0
Wright, Alexander, Dall.	2	-1	-0.5	3	0
Ryan, Pat, Phil.	1	-2	-2.0	-2	0
Rison, Andre, Atl.	1	-9	-9.0	-9	0
Prokop, Joe, S.F.	1	-10	-10.0	-10	0
Rutledge, Jeff, Wash.	8	-13	-1.6	-1	0
Beuerlein, Steve, Dall.	7	-14	-2.0	-1	0

t indicates touchdown
Leader based on mosts yards gained

Passing

Individual Champions (Rating Points)
NFC: 101.8—Steve Young, San Francisco
AFC: 97.6—Jim Kelly, Buffalo

Completion Percentage
AFC: 65.6—Dave Krieg, Seattle
NFC: 65.3—Troy Aikman, Dallas

Attempts
AFC: 655—Warren Moon, Houston
NFC: 490—Jim Everett, Rams

Completions
AFC: 404—Warren Moon, Houston
NFC: 277—Jim Everett, Rams

Yards
AFC: 4690—Warren Moon, Houston
NFC: 3564—Mark Rypien, Washington

Most Yards, Game
NFC: 442—Mark Rypien, Washington vs. Atlanta, November 10, (16-31, 6 TD)
AFC: 432—Warren Moon, Houston vs. Dallas, November 10, (41-56) (OT)

Longest
NFC: 97—Steve Young (to John Taylor), San Francisco at Atlanta, November 3 - TD
AFC: 89—Neil O'Donnell (to Dwight Stone), Pittsburgh vs. San Diego, September 1 - TD

Yards Per Attempt
NFC: 9.02—Steve Young, San Francisco
AFC: 8.11—Jim Kelly, Buffalo

Touchdown Passes
AFC: 33—Jim Kelly, Buffalo
NFC: 28—Mark Rypien, Washington

Most Touchdown Passes, Game
AFC: 6—Jim Kelly, Buffalo vs. Pittsburgh, September 8, (31-43, 363 yards)
NFC: 6—Mark Rypien, Washington vs. Atlanta, November 10, (16-31, 442 yards)

Lowest Interception Percentage
NFC: 1.4—Jeff Hostetler, Giants
AFC: 1.8—Bernie Kosar, Cleveland

Team Champions
AFC: 4621—Houston
NFC: 3997—San Francisco

AFC Passing—Team

	Att.	Comp.	Pct. Comp.	Gross Yards	Sacked	Yards Lost	Net Yards	Avg. Yds. Att.	Att. Yds. Comp	TD	Pct. TD	Long	Int.	Pct. Int.
Houston	667	411	61.6	4804	24	183	4621	7.20	11.69	24	3.6	t68	21	3.1
Miami	563	327	58.1	4077	28	188	3889	7.24	12.47	26	4.6	54	14	2.5
Buffalo	516	332	64.3	4140	35	269	3871	8.02	12.47	39	7.6	t77	19	3.7
Cleveland	503	312	62.0	3547	42	243	3304	7.05	11.37	19	3.8	t71	10	2.0
Cincinnati	511	290	56.8	3413	33	255	3158	6.68	11.77	14	2.7	53	22	4.3
N.Y. Jets	503	295	58.6	3429	33	273	3156	6.82	11.62	12	2.4	53	12	2.4
Seattle	488	290	59.4	3371	42	263	3108	6.91	11.62	15	3.1	60	26	5.3
Kansas City	479	284	59.3	3281	21	177	3104	6.85	11.55	19	4.0	63	14	2.9
New England	481	284	59.0	3442	63	436	3006	7.16	12.12	11	2.3	t60	22	4.6
Denver	459	246	53.6	3310	46	313	2997	7.21	13.46	13	2.8	71	12	2.6
Pittsburgh	476	259	54.4	3313	45	359	2954	6.96	12.79	20	4.2	t89	16	3.4
San Diego	511	272	53.2	2983	35	236	2747	5.84	10.97	13	2.5	58	16	3.1
L.A. Raiders	414	220	53.1	2977	33	258	2719	7.19	13.53	20	4.8	t80	18	4.3
Indianapolis	512	305	59.6	3066	57	487	2579	5.99	10.05	10	2.0	t49	16	3.1
AFC Total	7083	4127	——	49153	537	3940	45213	——	——	255	——	t89	238	——
AFC Average	505.9	294.8	58.3	3510.9	38.4	281.4	3229.5	6.94	11.91	18.2	3.6	——	17.0	3.4

NFC Passing—Team

	Att.	Comp.	Pct. Comp.	Gross Yards	Sacked	Yards Lost	Net Yards	Avg. Yds. Att.	Att. Yds. Comp	TD	Pct. TD	Long	Int.	Pct. Int.
San Francisco	522	325	62.3	4167	24	170	3997	7.98	12.82	29	5.6	t97	12	2.3
Washington	447	261	58.4	3771	9	79	3692	8.44	14.45	30	6.7	t82	11	2.5
Atlanta	500	260	52.0	3634	31	185	3449	7.27	13.98	30	6.0	t80	22	4.4
L.A. Rams	518	289	55.8	3610	30	200	3410	6.97	12.49	13	2.5	78	20	3.9
Dallas	500	305	61.0	3663	38	273	3390	7.33	12.01	16	3.2	t66	12	2.4
New Orleans	506	292	57.7	3419	19	160	3259	6.76	11.71	20	4.0	t65	15	3.0
Chicago	497	286	57.5	3292	26	172	3120	6.62	11.51	16	3.2	t84	17	3.4
Green Bay	514	272	52.9	3213	45	270	2943	6.25	11.81	17	3.3	t75	19	3.7
Philadelphia	513	285	55.6	3169	45	263	2906	6.18	11.12	17	3.3	t75	27	5.3
Minnesota	477	284	59.5	3016	28	133	2883	6.32	10.62	16	3.4	50	16	3.4
Detroit	459	252	54.9	2974	25	116	2858	6.48	11.80	16	3.5	t73	17	3.7
N.Y. Giants	428	261	61.0	3025	36	181	2844	7.07	11.59	13	3.0	55	8	1.9
Phoenix	492	254	51.6	3039	43	372	2667	6.18	11.96	10	2.0	t62	25	5.1
Tampa Bay	495	250	50.5	2955	56	383	2572	5.97	11.82	13	2.6	t87	29	5.9
NFC Total	6868	3876	——	46947	455	2957	43990	——	——	256	——	t97	250	——
NFC Average	490.6	276.9	56.4	3353.4	32.5	211.2	3142.1	6.84	12.11	18.3	3.7	—	17.9	3.6
League Total	13951	8003	——	96100	992	6897	89203	——	——	511	——	t97	488	——
League Average	498.3	285.8	57.4	3432.1	35.4	246.3	3185.8	6.89	12.01	18.3	3.7	——	17.4	3.5

Leader based on net yards

NFL Top 10 Individual Qualifiers

	Att.	Comp.	Pct. Comp.	Yards	Avg. Gain	TD	Pct. TD	Long	Int.	Pct. Int.	Sacked	Yards Lost	Rating Points
Young, Steve, S.F.	279	180	64.5	2517	9.02	17	6.1	t97	8	2.9	13	79	101.8
Rypien, Mark, Wash.	421	249	59.1	3564	8.47	28	6.7	t82	11	2.6	7	59	97.9
Kelly, Jim, Buff.	474	304	64.1	3844	8.11	33	7.0	t77	17	3.6	31	227	97.6
Bono, Steve, S.F.	237	141	59.5	1617	6.82	11	4.6	78	4	1.7	11	91	88.5
Kosar, Bernie, Clev.	494	307	62.1	3487	7.06	18	3.6	t71	9	1.8	41	232	87.8
Aikman, Troy, Dall.	363	237	65.3	2754	7.59	11	3.0	61	10	2.8	32	224	86.7
Marino, Dan, Mia.	549	318	57.9	3970	7.23	25	4.6	54	13	2.4	27	182	85.8
Hostetler, Jeff, Giants	285	179	62.8	2032	7.13	5	1.8	55	4	1.4	20	100	84.1
Krieg, Dave, Sea.	285	187	65.6	2080	7.30	11	3.9	60	12	4.2	32	216	82.5
Moon, Warren, Hou.	655	404	61.7	4690	7.16	23	3.5	t61	21	3.2	23	174	81.7

AFC Passing—Individual Qualifiers

	Att.	Comp.	Pct. Comp.	Yards	Avg. Gain	TD	Pct. TD	Long	Int.	Pct. Int.	Tkd.	Yards Lost	Rating Points
Kelly, Jim, Buff.	474	304	64.1	3844	8.11	33	7.0	t77	17	3.6	31	227	97.6
Kosar, Bernie, Clev.	494	307	62.1	3487	7.06	18	3.6	t71	9	1.8	41	232	87.8
Marino, Dan, Mia.	549	318	57.9	3970	7.23	25	4.6	54	13	2.4	27	182	85.8
Krieg, Dave, Sea.	285	187	65.6	2080	7.30	11	3.9	60	12	4.2	32	216	82.5
Moon, Warren, Hou.	655	404	61.7	4690	7.16	23	3.5	t61	21	3.2	23	174	81.7
DeBerg, Steve, K.C.	434	256	59.0	2965	6.83	17	3.9	63	14	3.2	19	161	79.3
O'Donnell, Neil, Pitt.	286	156	54.5	1963	6.86	11	3.8	t89	7	2.4	30	214	78.8
O'Brien, Ken, Jets	489	287	58.7	3300	6.75	10	2.0	53	11	2.2	33	273	76.6
Elway, John, Den.	451	242	53.7	3253	7.21	13	2.9	71	12	2.7	45	305	75.4
George, Jeff, Ind.	485	292	60.2	2910	6.00	10	2.1	t49	12	2.5	56	481	73.8
Esiason, Boomer, Cin.	413	233	56.4	2883	6.98	13	3.1	53	16	3.9	25	190	72.5
Millen, Hugh, N.E.	409	246	60.1	3073	7.51	9	2.2	t60	18	4.4	54	379	72.5
Schroeder, Jay, Raiders	357	189	52.9	2562	7.18	15	4.2	t78	16	4.5	31	238	71.4
Friesz, John, S.D.	487	262	53.8	2896	5.95	12	2.5	58	15	3.1	32	214	67.1

	Att.	Comp	Pct. Comp.	Yards	Avg. Gain	TD	Pct. TD	Long	Int.	Pct. Int.	Tkd.	Yards Lost	Rating Points
Non-Qualifiers													
Carlson, Cody, Hou.	12	7	58.3	114	9.50	1	8.3	t68	0	0.0	1	9	118.1
Reich, Frank, Buff.	41	27	65.9	305	7.44	6	14.6	29	2	4.9	4	42	107.2
Marinovich, Todd, Raiders	40	23	57.5	243	6.08	3	7.5	t26	0	0.0	0	0	100.3
Vlasic, Mark, K.C.	44	28	63.6	316	7.18	2	4.5	30	0	0.0	2	16	100.2
Secules, Scott, Mia.	13	8	61.5	90	6.92	1	7.7	17	1	7.7	1	6	75.8
Brister, Bubby, Pitt.	190	103	54.2	1350	7.11	9	4.7	t65	9	4.7	15	145	72.9
Taylor, Troy, Jets	10	5	50.0	76	7.60	1	10.0	51	1	10.0	0	0	69.2
Evans, Vince, Raiders	14	6	42.9	127	9.07	1	7.1	t80	2	14.3	2	20	59.8
Wilhelm, Erik, Cin.	42	24	57.1	217	5.17	0	0.0	29	2	4.8	1	8	51.4
Hollas, Donald, Cin.	55	32	58.2	310	5.64	1	1.8	t23	4	7.3	7	57	49.8
Hodson, Tom, N.E.	68	36	52.9	345	5.07	1	1.5	32	4	5.9	9	57	47.7
Herrmann, Mark, Ind.	19	11	57.9	137	7.21	0	0.0	26	3	15.8	0	0	40.8
Gagliano, Bob, S.D.	23	9	39.1	76	3.30	0	0.0	17	1	4.3	3	22	30.3
Stouffer, Kelly, Sea.	15	6	40.0	57	3.80	0	0.0	19	1	6.7	2	9	23.5
Less than 10 attempts													
Allen, Marcus, Raiders	2	1	50.0	11	5.50	1	50.0	t11	0	0.0	0	0	106.3
Bernstine, Rod, S.D.	1	1	100.0	11	11.00	1	100.0	t11	0	0.0	0	0	152.1
Fryar, Irving, N.E.	1	0	0.0	0	0.00	0	0.0	0	0	0.0	0	0	39.6
Gossett, Jeff, Raiders	1	1	100.0	34	34.00	0	0.0	34	0	0.0	0	0	118.8
Hansen, Brian, Clev.	1	1	100.0	11	11.00	1	100.0	t11	0	0.0	0	0	152.1
Hilger, Rusty, Ind.	1	0	0.0	0	0.00	0	0.0	0	0	0.0	0	0	39.6
Jensen, Jim, Mia.	1	1	100.0	17	17.00	0	0.0	17	0	0.0	0	0	118.8
Johnson, Lee, Cin.	1	1	100.0	3	3.00	0	0.0	3	0	0.0	0	0	79.2
Kubiak, Gary, Den.	5	3	60.0	33	6.60	0	0.0	14	0	0.0	1	8	79.6
McCarthy, Shawn, N.E.	1	1	100.0	11	11.00	0	0.0	11	0	0.0	0	0	112.5
McGwire, Dan, Sea.	7	3	42.9	27	3.86	0	0.0	13	1	14.3	0	0	14.3
Metcalf, Eric, Clev.	0	0	—	0	—	0	—	0	0	—	1	11	0.0
Mohr, Chris, Buff.	1	1	100.0	-9	-9.00	0	0.0	-9	0	0.0	0	0	79.2
Nagle, Browning, Jets	2	1	50.0	10	5.00	0	0.0	10	0	0.0	0	0	64.6
Philcox, Todd, Clev.	8	4	50.0	49	6.13	0	0.0	28	1	12.5	0	0	29.7
Sewell, Steve, Den.	3	1	33.3	24	8.00	0	0.0	24	0	0.0	0	0	63.2
Thomas, Blair, Jets	1	1	100.0	16	16.00	1	100.0	t16	0	0.0	0	0	158.3
Toon, Al, Jets	1	1	100.0	27	27.00	0	0.0	27	0	0.0	0	0	118.8
Trudeau, Jack, Ind.	7	2	28.6	19	2.71	0	0.0	11	1	14.3	1	6	0.0
Vaughn, Jon, N.E.	2	1	50.0	13	6.50	1	50.0	t13	0	0.0	0	0	110.4
Williams, Harvey, K.C.	1	0	0.0	0	0.00	0	0.0	0	0	0.0	0	0	39.6

t indicates touchdown
Leader based on rating points, minimum 224 attempts

NFC Passing—Individual Qualifiers

	Att.	Comp	Pct. Comp.	Yds	Avg. Gain	TD	Pct. TD	Long	Int.	Pct. Int.	Tkd.	Yards Lost	Rating Points
Young, Steve, S.F.	279	180	64.5	2517	9.02	17	6.1	t97	8	2.9	13	79	101.8
Rypien, Mark, Wash.	421	249	59.1	3564	8.47	28	6.7	t82	11	2.6	7	59	97.9
Bono, Steve, S.F.	237	141	59.5	1617	6.82	11	4.6	78	4	1.7	11	91	88.5
Aikman, Troy, Dall.	363	237	65.3	2754	7.59	11	3.0	61	10	2.8	32	224	86.7
Hostetler, Jeff, Giants	285	179	62.8	2032	7.13	5	1.8	55	4	1.4	20	100	84.1
Gannon, Rich, Minn.	354	211	59.6	2166	6.12	12	3.4	50	6	1.7	19	91	81.5
Miller, Chris, Atl.	413	220	53.3	3103	7.51	26	6.3	t80	18	4.4	23	145	80.6
McMahon, Jim, Phil.	311	187	60.1	2239	7.20	12	3.9	t75	11	3.5	21	128	80.3
Walsh, Steve, N.O.	255	141	55.3	1638	6.42	11	4.3	41	6	2.4	3	26	79.5
Hebert, Bobby, N.O.	248	149	60.1	1676	6.76	9	3.6	t65	8	3.2	16	134	79.0
Harbaugh, Jim, Chi.	478	275	57.5	3121	6.53	15	3.1	t84	16	3.3	24	163	73.7
Tomczak, Mike, G.B.	238	128	53.8	1490	6.26	11	4.6	t75	9	3.8	13	105	72.6
Kramer, Erik, Det.	265	136	51.3	1635	6.17	11	4.2	t73	8	3.0	14	74	71.8
Everett, Jim, Rams	490	277	56.5	3438	7.02	11	2.2	78	20	4.1	30	200	68.9
Tupa, Tom, Phx.	315	165	52.4	2053	6.52	6	1.9	t62	13	4.1	24	197	62.0
Majkowski, Don, G.B.	226	115	50.9	1362	6.03	3	1.3	39	8	3.5	30	152	59.3
Testaverde, Vinny, T.B.	326	166	50.9	1994	6.12	8	2.5	t87	15	4.6	35	234	59.0
Kemp, Jeff, Sea.-Phil.	295	151	51.2	1753	5.94	9	3.1	57	17	5.8	20	99	55.7
Non-Qualifiers													
Rutledge, Jeff, Wash.	22	11	50.0	189	8.59	1	4.5	t40	0	0.0	2	20	94.7
Willis, Peter Tom, Chi.	18	11	61.1	171	9.50	1	5.6	42	1	5.6	2	9	88.0
Simms, Phil, Giants	141	82	58.2	993	7.04	8	5.7	38	4	2.8	14	79	87.0
Pagel, Mike, Rams	27	11	40.7	150	5.56	2	7.4	30	0	0.0	0	0	83.9
Kiel, Blair, G.B.	50	29	58.0	361	7.22	3	6.0	35	2	4.0	2	13	83.8
Beuerlein, Steve, Dall.	137	68	49.6	909	6.64	5	3.6	t66	2	1.5	6	49	77.2
Tolliver, Billy Joe, Atl.	82	40	48.8	531	6.48	4	4.9	t75	2	2.4	7	29	75.8
Peete, Rodney, Det.	194	116	59.8	1339	6.90	5	2.6	t68	9	4.6	11	42	69.9
Wilson, Wade, Minn.	122	72	59.0	825	6.76	3	2.5	t46	10	8.2	8	42	53.5
Chandler, Chris, T.B.-Phx.	154	78	50.6	846	5.49	5	3.2	t45	10	6.5	17	134	50.9
Gelbaugh, Stan, Phx.	118	61	51.7	674	5.71	3	2.5	t34	10	8.5	10	94	42.1
Carlson, Jeff, T.B.	65	31	47.7	404	6.22	1	1.5	36	6	9.2	11	73	34.4
Goebel, Brad, Phil.	56	30	53.6	267	4.77	0	0.0	26	6	10.7	6	37	27.0
Ryan, Pat, Phil.	26	10	38.5	98	3.77	0	0.0	32	4	15.4	4	21	10.3
Less than 10 attempts													
Anderson, Neal, Chi.	1	0	0.0	0	0.00	0	0.0	0	0	0.0	0	0	39.6
Buck, Mike, N.O.	2	1	50.0	61	30.50	0	0.0	61	1	50.0	0	0	56.3
Byars, Keith, Phil.	2	0	0.0	0	0.00	0	0.0	0	1	50.0	0	0	0.0
Byner, Earnest, Wash.	4	1	25.0	18	4.50	1	25.0	t18	0	0.0	0	0	85.4
Camarillo, Rich, Phx.	1	0	0.0	0	0.00	0	0.0	0	0	0.0	0	0	39.6
Cunningham, Randall, Phil.	4	1	25.0	19	4.75	0	0.0	19	0	0.0	2	16	46.9
Favre, Brett, Atl.	5	0	0.0	0	0.00	0	0.0	0	2	40.0	1	11	0.0

	Att.	Comp	Pct. Comp.	Yards	Avg. Gain	TD	Pct. TD	Long	Int.	Pct. Int.	Tkd.	Yards Lost	Rating Points
Helton, Barry, Rams	1	1	100.0	22	22.00	0	0.0	22	0	0.0	0	0	118.8
Heyward, Craig, N.O.	1	1	100.0	44	44.00	0	0.0	44	0	0.0	0	0	118.8
Ingram, Mark, Giants	1	0	0.0	0	0.00	0	0.0	0	0	0.0	1	2	39.6
Jones, Hassan, Minn.	0	0	—	0	—	0	—	0	0	—	1	0	0
Kupp, Craig, Phx.	7	3	42.9	23	3.29	0	0.0	11	0	0.0	2	23	51.5
Meggett, David, Giants	1	0	0.0	0	0.00	0	0.0	0	0	0.0	1	0	39.6
Musgrave, Bill, S.F.	5	4	80.0	33	6.60	1	20.0	t15	0	0.0	0	0	133.8
Nelson, Darrin, Minn.	1	1	100.0	25	25.00	1	100.0	t25	0	0.0	0	0	158.3
Sydney, Harry, S.F.	1	0	0.0	0	0.00	0	0.0	0	0	0.0	0	0	39.6
Thompson, Anthony, Phx.	1	0	0.0	0	0.00	0	0.0	0	0	0.0	0	0	39.6

t indicates touchdown
Leader based on rating points, minimum 224 attempts

Pass Receiving

Individual Champions
AFC: 100—Haywood Jeffires, Houston
NFC: 93—Michael Irvin, Dallas

Most Receptions, Game
AFC: 13—Thurman Thomas, Buffalo at Jets, September 15 (112 yards, TD)
Haywood Jeffires, Houston at Jets, October 13 (186 yards)
NFC: 11—Jay Novacek, Dallas at Green Bay, October 6 (121 yards, TD)

Yards
NFC: 1523—Michael Irvin, Dallas
AFC: 1181—Haywood Jeffires, Houston

Most Yards, Game
AFC: 220—James Lofton, Buffalo vs. Cincinnati, October 21 (8 receptions, 2 TD)
NFC: 203—Gary Clark, Washington vs. Atlanta, November 10 (4 receptions, 3 TD)

Longest
NFC: 97—John Taylor (from Steve Young) San Francisco at Atlanta, November 3 (TD)
AFC: 89—Dwight Stone (from Neil O'Donnell) Pittsburgh vs. San Diego, September 1 (TD)

Yards Per Reception
NFC: 22.4—Michael Haynes, Atlanta
AFC: 20.3—Dwight Stone, Pittsburgh

Touchdowns
NFC: 14—Jerry Rice, San Francisco
AFC: 12—Mark Clayton, Miami

Team Leaders, Receptions
AFC: BUFFALO: 81, Andre Reed; CINCINNATI: 59, Eddie Brown; CLEVELAND: 64, Webster Slaughter; DENVER: 44, Mike Young; HOUSTON: 100, Haywood Jeffires; INDIANAPOLIS: 72, Bill Brooks; KANSAS CITY: 43, Robb Thomas; RAIDERS: 53, Ethan Horton; MIAMI: 70, Mark Clayton, Mark Duper; NEW ENGLAND: 82, Marv Cook; JETS: 74, Al Toon; PITTSBURGH: 55, Louis Lipps; SAN DIEGO: 59, Ronnie Harmon; SEATTLE: 70, Brian Blades

NFC: ATLANTA: 81, Andre Rison; CHICAGO: 61, Wendell Davis; DALLAS: 93, Michael Irvin; DETROIT: 52, Brett Perriman; GREEN BAY: 69, Sterling Sharpe; RAMS: 64, Henry Ellard; MINNESOTA: 72, Cris Carter; NEW ORLEANS: 66, Eric Martin; GIANTS: 51, Mark Ingram; PHILADELPHIA: 62, Fred Barnett, Keith Byars; PHOENIX: 61, Ernie Jones; SAN FRANCISCO: 80, Jerry Rice; TAMPA BAY: 55, Lawrence Dawsey; WASHINGTON: 71, Art Monk

NFL Top 10 Pass Receivers
	No.	Yards	Avg.	Long	TD
Jeffires, Haywood, Hou.	100	1181	11.8	44	7
Irvin, Michael, Dall.	93	1523	16.4	t66	8
Hill, Drew, Hou.	90	1109	12.3	t61	4
Cook, Marv, N.E.	82	808	9.9	49	3
Reed, Andre, Buff.	81	1113	13.7	55	10
Rison, Andre, Atl.	81	976	12.0	t39	12
Rice, Jerry, S.F.	80	1206	15.1	t73	14
Toon, Al, Jets	74	963	13.0	32	0
Carter, Cris, Minn.	72	962	13.4	50	5
Brooks, Bill, Ind.	72	888	12.3	46	4

NFL Top 10 Pass Receivers By Yards
	Yards	No.	Avg.	Long	TD
Irvin, Michael, Dall.	1523	93	16.4	t66	8
Clark, Gary, Wash.	1340	70	19.1	t82	10
Rice, Jerry, S.F.	1206	80	15.1	t73	14
Jeffires, Haywood, Hou.	1181	100	11.8	44	7
Haynes, Michael, Atl.	1122	50	22.4	t80	11
Reed, Andre, Buff.	1113	81	13.7	55	10
Hill, Drew, Hou.	1109	90	12.3	t61	4
Duper, Mark, Mia.	1085	70	15.5	t43	5
Lofton, James, Buff.	1072	57	18.8	t77	8
Clayton, Mark, Mia.	1053	70	15.0	t43	12

AFC Pass Receiving—Individual
	No.	Yards	Avg.	Long	TD
Jeffires, Haywood, Hou.	100	1181	11.8	44	7
Hill, Drew, Hou.	90	1109	12.3	t61	4

	No.	Yards	Avg.	Long	TD
Cook, Marv, N.E.	82	808	9.9	49	3
Reed, Andre, Buff.	81	1113	13.7	55	10
Toon, Al, Jets	74	963	13.0	32	0
Brooks, Bill, Ind.	72	888	12.3	46	4
Duper, Mark, Mia.	70	1085	15.5	t43	5
Clayton, Mark, Mia.	70	1053	15.0	t43	12
Blades, Brian, Sea.	70	1003	14.3	52	2
Givins, Ernest, Hou.	70	996	14.2	49	5
Moore, Rob, Jets	70	987	14.1	53	5
Fryar, Irving, N.E.	68	1014	14.9	t56	3
Slaughter, Webster, Clev.	64	906	14.2	t62	3
Thomas, Thurman, Buff.	62	631	10.2	t50	5
Williams, John L., Sea.	61	499	8.2	35	1
Hester, Jessie, Ind.	60	753	12.6	t49	5
Brown, Eddie, Cin.	59	827	14.0	53	2
Harmon, Ronnie, S.D.	59	555	9.4	36	1
Lofton, James, Buff.	57	1072	18.8	t77	8
Paige, Tony, Mia.	57	469	8.2	26	1
Lipps, Louis, Pitt.	55	671	12.2	35	2
Duncan, Curtis, Hou.	55	588	10.7	42	4
Horton, Ethan, Raiders	53	650	12.3	52	5
McGee, Tim, Cin.	51	802	15.7	t52	4
Kane, Tommy, Sea.	50	763	15.3	60	2
Hoge, Merril, Pitt.	49	379	7.7	25	1
Hoard, Leroy, Clev.	48	567	11.8	t71	9
Fernandez, Mervyn, Raiders	46	694	15.1	59	1
Miller, Anthony, S.D.	44	649	14.8	58	3
Young, Mike, Den.	44	629	14.3	t52	2
McKeller, Keith, Buff.	44	434	9.9	t29	3
Thomas, Robb, K.C.	43	495	11.5	39	1
Lewis, Nate, S.D.	42	554	13.2	t49	3
Johnson, Anthony, Ind.	42	344	8.2	24	0
McMurtry, Greg, N.E.	41	614	15.0	40	2
Green, Eric, Pitt.	41	582	14.2	49	6
Barnett, Tim, K.C.	41	564	13.8	63	5
Dickerson, Eric, Ind.	41	269	6.6	26	1
Brooks, James, Cin.	40	348	8.7	40	2
Mack, Kevin, Clev.	40	255	6.4	22	2
Langhorne, Reggie, Clev.	39	505	12.9	t40	2
Sewell, Steve, Den.	38	436	11.5	60	2
McEwen, Craig, S.D.	37	399	10.8	30	3
McNair, Todd, K.C.	37	342	9.2	36	1
Brown, Tim, Raiders	36	554	15.4	t78	5
Harry, Emile, K.C.	35	431	12.3	36	3
Jackson, Mark, Den.	33	603	18.3	71	1
Clark, Ken, Ind.	33	245	7.4	23	0
Stone, Dwight, Pitt.	32	649	20.3	t89	5
Beebe, Don, Buff.	32	414	12.9	t34	6
Holman, Rodney, Cin.	31	445	14.4	39	2
Brennan, Brian, Clev.	31	325	10.5	30	1
Thomas, Blair, Jets	30	195	6.5	18	1
Metcalf, Eric, Clev.	29	294	10.1	45	0
Pinkett, Allen, Hou.	29	228	7.9	t36	1
Mathis, Terance, Jets	28	329	11.8	39	1
Birden, J.J., K.C.	27	465	17.2	t57	2
Martin, Tony, Mia.	27	434	16.1	54	2
Galbraith, Scott, Clev.	27	328	12.1	42	0
White, Lorenzo, Hou.	27	211	7.8	20	0
Timpson, Michael, N.E.	25	471	18.8	t60	2
Taylor, Kitrick, S.D.	24	218	9.1	27	0
Burkett, Chris, Jets	23	327	14.2	t50	4
Barber, Mike, Cin.	23	255	11.1	t42	1
Sharpe, Shannon, Den.	22	322	14.6	37	1
Chadwick, Jeff, Sea.	22	255	11.6	29	3
Edwards, Al, Buff.	22	228	10.4	t33	1
Russell, Derek, Den.	21	317	15.1	40	1
Clark, Louis, Sea.	21	228	10.9	t24	2
Verdin, Clarence, Ind.	21	214	10.2	28	0
Johnson, Vance, Den.	21	208	9.9	22	3
Jensen, Jim, Mia.	21	183	8.7	19	2

191

	No.	Yards	Avg.	Long	TD
Taylor, Craig, Cin.	21	122	5.8	16	0
Gault, Willie, Raiders	20	346	17.3	t59	4
Baty, Greg, Mia.	20	269	13.5	30	1
Walker, Derrick, S.D.	20	134	6.7	14	0
Davis, Kenneth, Buff.	20	118	5.9	t14	1
Jones, Tony, Hou.	19	251	13.2	t68	2
Hayes, Jonathan, K.C.	19	208	10.9	23	2
Russell, Leonard, N.E.	18	81	4.5	18	0
Jackson, Michael, Clev.	17	268	15.8	t65	2
McNeal, Travis, Sea.	17	208	12.2	36	1
Perryman, Bob, Den.	17	171	10.1	24	0
Craig, Roger, Raiders	17	136	8.0	20	0
Dressel, Chris, Jets	17	122	7.2	22	0
Nattiel, Ricky, Den.	16	288	18.0	t70	2
Boyer, Mark, Jets	16	153	9.6	22	0
Williams, Harvey, K.C.	16	147	9.2	17	2
Green, Harold, Cin.	16	136	8.5	18	0
Stephens, John, N.E.	16	119	7.4	24	0
Calloway, Chris, Pitt.	15	254	16.9	t33	1
Williams, Warren, Pitt.	15	139	9.3	29	0
Allen, Marcus, Raiders	15	131	8.7	25	0
Smith, Steve, Raiders	15	130	8.7	t37	1
Thompson, Leroy, Pitt.	14	118	8.4	32	0
Jones, Bill, K.C.	14	97	6.9	14	1
Smith, Sammie, Mia.	14	95	6.8	12	0
Holohan, Pete, K.C.	13	113	8.7	26	2
Green, Gaston, Den.	13	78	6.0	13	0
Morris, Joe, Clev.	13	76	5.8	13	0
Kattus, Eric, Cin.	12	136	11.3	24	0
Jefferson, Shawn, S.D.	12	125	10.4	29	1
Baxter, Brad, Jets	12	124	10.3	34	0
Cooper, Adrian, Pitt.	11	147	13.4	t47	2
Kay, Clarence, Den.	11	139	12.6	32	0
Coleman, Patrick, Hou.	11	138	12.5	26	1
Bernstine, Rod, S.D.	11	124	11.3	25	0
Edmunds, Ferrell, Mia.	11	118	10.7	22	2
Hunter, Ivy Joe, N.E.	11	97	8.8	25	0
Higgs, Mark, Mia.	11	80	7.3	13	0
Fenner, Derrick, Sea.	11	72	6.5	15	0
Jones, James, Sea.	10	103	10.3	29	0
Coates, Ben, N.E.	10	95	9.5	17	1
Butts, Marion, S.D.	10	91	9.1	46	1
Tice, Mike, Sea.	10	70	7.0	16	4
Banks, Fred, Mia.	9	119	13.2	25	1
Foster, Barry, Pitt.	9	117	13.0	31	1
Rembert, Reggie, Cin.	9	117	13.0	t23	1
Paige, Stephone, K.C.	9	111	12.3	26	0
Skansi, Paul, Sea.	9	96	10.7	21	0
Stradford, Troy, K.C.	9	91	10.1	17	0
Vaughn, Jon, N.E.	9	89	9.9	32	0
Harris, Leonard, Hou.	8	101	12.6	29	0
Mrosko, Bob, Ind.	8	90	11.3	20	0
Jones, Fred, K.C.	8	85	10.6	23	0
Craver, Aaron, Mia.	8	67	8.4	25	0
James, Lynn, Cin.	7	103	14.7	22	1
Cash, Keith, Pitt.	7	90	12.9	20	1
McNeil, Freeman, Jets	7	56	8.0	13	0
Hector, Johnny, Jets	7	51	7.3	16	0
Bentley, Albert, Ind.	7	42	6.0	11	0
Graddy, Sam, Raiders	6	195	32.5	t80	1
Johnson, Reggie, Den.	6	73	12.2	31	1
Mularkey, Mike, Pitt.	6	67	11.2	21	0
Bell, Nick, Raiders	6	62	10.3	24	0
Saxon, James, K.C.	6	55	9.2	22	0
Woods, Ickey, Cin.	6	36	6.0	16	0
Martin, Sammy, Ind.	5	79	15.8	25	0
Beach, Pat, Ind.	5	56	11.2	26	0
Metzelaars, Pete, Buff.	5	54	10.8	t51	2
Cox, Arthur, S.D.	5	53	10.6	19	0
Glover, Andrew, Raiders	5	45	9.0	18	3
Dingle, Mike, Cin.	5	23	4.6	12	1
Miller, Scott, Mia.	4	49	12.3	15	0
Daniels, David, Sea.	4	38	9.5	19	0
Hendrickson, Steve, S.D.	4	36	9.0	20	1
Whisenhunt, Ken, Jets	4	34	8.5	16	0
Riggs, Jim, Cin.	4	14	3.5	7	0
Mills, Ernie, Pitt.	3	79	26.3	t35	1
Carpenter, Rob, N.E.	3	45	15.0	23	0
Dawkins, Dale, Jets	3	38	12.7	24	0
Okoye, Christian, K.C.	3	34	11.3	13	0
Garrett, Shane, Cin.	3	32	10.7	13	0
Thomas, Doug, Sea.	3	27	9.0	11	0
Matich, Trevor, Jets	3	23	7.7	14	1
Gardner, Carwell, Buff.	3	20	6.7	11	0
Ball, Eric, Cin.	3	17	5.7	9	0
Huffman, Darvell, Ind.	3	14	4.7	7	0
Rolle, Butch, Buff.	3	10	3.3	5	2
Perkins, Bruce, Ind.	3	-2	-0.7	3	0

	No.	Yards	Avg.	Long	TD
Tasker, Steve, Buff.	2	39	19.5	t20	1
Samuels, Chris, S.D.	2	33	16.5	29	0
Anders, Kimble, K.C.	2	30	15.0	23	0
Pruitt, James, Mia.	2	30	15.0	24	0
Graham, Jeff, Pitt.	2	21	10.5	15	0
Henry, Charles, Mia.	2	17	8.5	9	0
Word, Barry, K.C.	2	13	6.5	8	0
Young, Duane, S.D.	2	12	6.0	6	0
Lewis, Greg, Den.	2	9	4.5	7	0
Rouson, Lee, Clev.	2	9	4.5	6	0
Warren, Chris, Sea.	2	9	4.5	12	0
Manoa, Tim, Ind.	2	5	2.5	5	0
Brown, Gary, Hou.	2	1	0.5	4	0
Thornton, Reginald, Ind.	1	38	38.0	38	0
Patterson, Elvis, Raiders	1	34	34.0	34	0
O'Brien, Ken, Jets	1	27	27.0	27	0
Elway, John, Den.	1	24	24.0	24	0
Cash, Kerry, Ind.	1	18	18.0	18	0
Coley, James, Ind.	1	13	13.0	13	0
Johnson, Barry, Den.	1	13	13.0	13	0
Talley, John, Clev.	1	13	13.0	13	0
Allen, Marvin, N.E.	1	9	9.0	9	0
Sims, Keith, Mia.	1	9	9.0	9	0
Alexander, Mike, Buffalo	1	7	7.0	7	0
Kosar, Bernie, Clev.	1	1	1.0	1	0

t indicates touchdown.

Leader based on most passes caught

NFC Pass Receiving—Individual

	No.	Yards	Avg.	Long	TD
Irvin, Michael, Dall.	93	1523	16.4	t66	8
Rison, Andre, Atl.	81	976	12.0	t39	12
Rice, Jerry, S.F.	80	1206	15.1	t73	14
Carter, Cris, Minn.	72	962	13.4	50	5
Monk, Art, Wash.	71	1049	14.8	t64	8
Clark, Gary, Wash.	70	1340	19.1	t82	10
Sharpe, Sterling, G.B.	69	961	13.9	t58	4
Martin, Eric, N.O.	66	803	12.2	30	4
Ellard, Henry, Rams	64	1052	16.4	38	3
Taylor, John, S.F.	64	1011	15.8	t97	9
Turner, Floyd, N.O.	64	927	14.5	t65	8
Barnett, Fred, Phil.	62	948	15.3	t75	4
Byars, Keith, Phil.	62	564	9.1	37	3
Jones, Ernie, Phx.	61	957	15.7	53	4
Davis, Wendell, Chi.	61	945	15.5	t75	6
Novacek, Jay, Dall.	59	664	11.3	49	4
Jordan, Steve, Minn.	57	638	11.2	25	2
Dawsey, Lawrence, T.B.	55	818	14.9	t65	3
Proehl, Ricky, Phx.	55	766	13.9	t62	2
Delpino, Robert, Rams	55	617	11.2	78	1
Waddle, Tom, Chi.	55	599	10.9	t37	3
Perriman, Brett, Det.	52	668	12.8	42	1
Ingram, Mark, Giants	51	824	16.2	41	3
Carter, Anthony, Minn.	51	553	10.8	t46	5
Haynes, Michael, Atl.	50	1122	22.4	t80	11
Pritchard, Mike, Atl.	50	624	12.5	29	2
Meggett, David, Giants	50	412	8.2	22	3
Smith, Emmitt, Dall.	49	258	5.3	14	1
Jackson, Keith, Phil.	48	569	11.9	t73	5
Carrier, Mark, T.B.	47	698	14.9	35	2
Clark, Robert, Det.	47	640	13.6	t68	6
Anderson, Neal, Chi.	47	368	7.8	t26	3
Workman, Vince, G.B.	46	371	8.1	25	4
Sanders, Ricky, Wash.	45	580	12.9	45	5
Hill, Randal, Phx.	43	495	11.5	t31	1
Hampton, Rodney, Giants	43	283	6.6	19	0
Kemp, Perry, G.B.	42	583	13.9	39	2
Farr, Mike, Det.	42	431	10.3	t34	1
Sanders, Barry, Det.	41	307	7.5	34	1
Green, Willie, Det.	39	592	15.2	t73	7
Price, Jim, Rams	35	410	11.7	27	2
Muster, Brad, Chi.	35	287	8.2	21	1
Byner, Earnest, Wash.	34	308	9.1	31	0
Rathman, Tom, S.F.	34	286	8.4	32	0
Williams, Calvin, Phil.	33	326	9.9	30	3
Walker, Herschel, Minn.	33	204	6.2	19	0
Early, Quinn, N.O.	32	541	16.9	52	2
Anderson, Willie, Rams	32	530	16.6	54	1
Jones, Hassan, Minn.	32	384	12.0	43	1
Johnson, Damone, Rams	32	253	7.9	27	2
Hall, Ron, T.B.	31	284	9.2	24	0
Baker, Stephen, Giants	30	525	17.5	52	4
Henderson, Keith, S.F.	30	303	10.1	23	0
Green, Roy, Phil.	29	364	12.6	42	0
Johnson, Johnny, Phx.	29	225	7.8	t51	2
Thomas, George, Atl.	28	365	13.0	37	2
Johnston, Daryl, Dall.	28	244	8.7	22	1

	No.	Yards	Avg.	Long	TD
Jones, Brent, S.F.	27	417	15.4	41	0
Drewrey, Willie, T.B.	26	375	14.4	t87	2
Fenerty, Gill, N.O.	26	235	9.0	t50	2
Anderson, Gary, T.B.	25	184	7.4	21	0
Sherrard, Mike, S.F.	24	296	12.3	31	2
Harris, Jackie, G.B.	24	264	11.0	35	3
Carter, Dexter, S.F.	23	253	11.0	26	1
Williams, Jamie, S.F.	22	235	10.7	21	1
Tice, John, N.O.	22	230	10.5	22	0
Woodside, Keith, G.B.	22	185	8.4	28	0
Turner, Odessa, Giants	21	356	17.0	55	0
Hilliard, Dalton, N.O.	21	127	6.0	t14	1
Harper, Alvin, Dall.	20	326	16.3	39	1
Cross, Howard, Giants	20	283	14.2	30	2
McGee, Buford, Rams	20	160	8.0	20	0
Wilson, Robert, T.B.	20	121	6.1	15	2
Wilson, Charles, G.B.	19	305	16.1	t75	1
Centers, Larry, Phx.	19	176	9.3	23	0
Nelson, Darrin, Minn.	19	142	7.5	13	0
Carroll, Wesley, N.O.	18	184	10.2	t31	1
Thornton, James, Chi.	17	278	16.4	33	1
Hill, Bruce, T.B.	17	185	10.9	18	2
Martin, Kelvin, Dall.	16	243	15.2	27	0
Ervins, Ricky, Wash.	16	181	11.3	28	1
Brenner, Hoby, N.O.	16	179	11.2	21	0
Gentry, Dennis, Chi.	16	149	9.3	18	0
McCaffrey, Ed, Giants	16	146	9.1	26	0
Roberts, Alfredo, Dall.	16	136	8.5	21	1
Cox, Aaron, Rams	15	216	14.4	39	0
West, Ed, G.B.	15	151	10.1	21	3
Jorden, Tim, Phx.	15	127	8.5	19	0
Cobb, Reggie, T.B.	15	111	7.4	21	0
Rouse, James, Chi.	15	93	6.2	14	0
Jordan, Buford, N.O.	15	92	6.1	19	1
Sherman, Heath, Phil.	14	59	4.2	11	0
Morgan, Anthony, Chi.	13	211	16.2	t84	2
Gary, Cleveland, Rams	13	110	8.5	22	0
Sydney, Harry, S.F.	13	90	6.9	19	2
Weathers, Clarence, G.B.	12	150	12.5	22	0
Dixon, Floyd, Atl.	12	146	12.2	23	1
Broussard, Steve, Atl.	12	120	10.0	t25	1
Moore, Herman, Det.	11	135	12.3	21	0
Anderson, Ottis, Giants	11	41	3.7	13	0
Orr, Terry, Wash.	10	201	20.1	t47	4
Wright, Alexander, Dall.	10	170	17.0	53	0
Joseph, James, Phil.	10	64	6.4	13	0
Morris, Ron, Chi.	8	147	18.4	33	0
Jennings, Keith, Chi.	8	109	13.6	19	0
Jackson, John, Phx.	8	108	13.5	30	0
Flagler, Terrence, Phx.	8	85	10.6	17	0
Carter, Pat, Rams	8	69	8.6	t18	2
Sanders, Thomas, Phil.	8	62	7.8	14	0
Reeves, Walter, Phx.	8	45	5.6	13	0
Query, Jeff, G.B.	7	94	13.4	26	0
Thompson, Darrell, G.B.	7	71	10.1	18	0
Affholter, Erik, G.B.	7	68	9.7	20	0
Thompson, Anthony, Phx.	7	52	7.4	14	0
Agee, Tommie, Dall.	7	43	6.1	9	0
Carthon, Maurice, Giants	7	39	5.6	9	0
Shuler, Mickey, Phil.	6	91	15.2	21	0
Anderson, Jesse, T.B.	6	73	12.2	34	2
Phillips, Jason, Atl.	6	73	12.2	24	0
Johnson, Maurice, Phil.	6	70	11.7	t31	2
Jones, Keith, Atl.	6	58	9.7	15	0
Green, Mark, Chi.	6	54	9.0	15	0
Allen, Terry, Minn.	6	49	8.2	21	1
Dupree, Marcus, Rams	6	46	7.7	21	0
Mowatt, Zeke, Giants	5	78	15.6	33	1
Awalt, Robert, Dall.	5	57	11.4	20	0
Warren, Don, Wash.	5	51	10.2	17	0
Tillman, Lewis, Giants	5	30	6.0	12	0
Thomas, Ed, T.B.	4	55	13.8	19	0
Anthony, Terry, T.B.	4	51	12.8	14	0
Beach, Sanjay, S.F.	4	43	10.8	20	0
Tennell, Derek, Det.	4	43	10.8	18	0
Overton, Don, Det.	4	38	9.5	14	0
Lewis, Leo, Minn.	4	36	9.0	11	0
Heyward, Craig, N.O.	4	34	8.5	t22	1
Jackson, Kenny, Phil.	4	29	7.3	9	0
Novoselsky, Brent, Minn.	4	27	6.8	8	0
Brown, Ron, Rams	3	52	17.3	21	0
Gray, Mel, Det.	3	42	14.0	31	0
Turner, Vernon, Rams	3	41	13.7	t19	1
Collins, Shawn, Atl.	3	37	12.3	21	0
Boso, Cap, Chi.	3	36	12.0	22	0
Newman, Pat, N.O.	3	33	11.0	14	0

	No.	Yards	Avg.	Long	TD
Johnson, Tracy, Atl.	3	27	9.0	13	0
Middleton, Ron, Wash.	3	25	8.3	11	0
Hobbs, Stephen, Wash.	3	24	8.0	10	0
Scales, Greg, N.O.	3	23	7.7	14	0
Wilkins, Gary, Atl.	3	22	7.3	12	1
Matthews, Aubrey, Det.	3	21	7.0	11	0
Johnson, Jimmie, Wash.	3	7	2.3	t4	2
Campbell, Jeff, Det.	2	49	24.5	28	0
Thompson, Ernie, Rams	2	35	17.5	22	1
Harris, Rod, Phil.	2	28	14.0	22	0
Walls, Wesley, S.F.	2	24	12.0	21	0
Kozlowski, Glen, Chi.	2	16	8.0	11	0
Rozier, Mike, Atl.	2	15	7.5	9	0
Fenney, Rick, Minn.	2	11	5.5	8	0
Rice, Allen, G.B.	2	10	5.0	7	0
Bunch, Jarrod, Giants	2	8	4.0	6	0
Jones, Mike, Minn.	2	8	4.0	t5	2
Tillman, Spencer, S.F.	2	3	1.5	3	0
Ruether, Mike, Atl.	1	22	22.0	22	0
Raye, Jimmy, Rams	1	19	19.0	19	0
Sanders, Deion, Atl.	1	17	17.0	17	0
Bruce, Aundray, Atl.	1	11	11.0	11	0
McAfee, Fred, N.O.	1	8	8.0	8	0
Blake, Ricky, Dall.	1	5	5.0	5	0
Riggs, Gerald, Wash.	1	5	5.0	5	0
Fortin, Roman, Det.	1	4	4.0	4	0
Dozier, D.J., Det.	1	3	3.0	3	0
Riley, Eugene, Det.	1	3	3.0	3	0
Wainright, Frank, N.O.	1	3	3.0	3	0
Williams, Willie, Phx.	1	3	3.0	t3	1
Anderson, Alfred, Minn.	1	2	2.0	2	0
Gannon, Rich, Minn.	1	0	0.0	0	0
Pegram, Erric, Atl.	1	-1	-1.0	-1	0
Jackson, Cedric, Det.	1	-2	-2.0	-2	0
McMahon, Jim, Phil.	1	-5	-5.0	-5	0
Aikman, Troy, Dall.	1	-6	-6.0	-6	0

t indicates touchdown
Leader based on most passes caught

Interceptions

Individual Champions
    AFC: 8—Ronnie Lott, Raiders
    NFC: 6—Ray Crockett, Detroit
            Tim McKyer, Atlanta
            Deion Sanders, Atlanta
            Aeneas Williams, Phoenix
Most Interceptions, Game
    AFC: 3—Albert Lewis, Kansas City vs. Atlanta, September 1
            Richard Shelton, Pittsburgh vs. Cleveland, December 22 (1 TD)
    NFC: 3—Gene Atkins, New Orleans at Phoenix, December 22
Yards
    NFC: 198—Gene Atkins, New Orleans
    AFC: 168—Erik McMillan, Jets
Longest
    NFC: 97—Reggie Rutland, Minnesota vs. Rams, December 15 (TD)
    AFC: 83—Erik McMillan, Jets vs. Miami, September 29 (TD)
            Lloyd Burruss, Kansas City vs. Raiders, October 28
Touchdowns
    AFC: 2—Erik McMillan, Jets
    NFC: 1—By 16 players
Team Leaders, Interceptions
AFC: BUFFALO: 5, Nate Odomes, Darryl Talley; CINCINNATI: 4, David Fulcher;
    CLEVELAND: 3, Stephen Braggs; DENVER: 5, Steve Atwater, Dennis
    Smith; HOUSTON: 6, Cris Dishman; INDIANAPOLIS: 4, John Baylor;
    KANSAS CITY: 4, Deron Cherry; RAIDERS: 8, Ronnie Lott; MIAMI: 5,
    Louis Oliver; NEW ENGLAND: 4, Maurice Hurst; JETS: 5, Mike Brim;
    PITTSBURGH: 4, Thomas Everett; SAN DIEGO: 6, Gill Byrd; SEATTLE: 5,
    Eugene Robinson
NFC: ATLANTA: 6, Tim McKyer, Deion Sanders; CHICAGO: 4, Lemuel Stinson;
    DALLAS: 4, Issiac Holt; DETROIT: 6, Ray Crockett; GREEN BAY: 3, LeRoy
    Butler, Chuck Cecil, Mark Murphy; RAMS: 3, Jerry Gray, Darryl Henley;
    MINNESOTA: 5, Joey Browner; NEW ORLEANS: 5, Gene Atkins, Vince
    Buck; GIANTS: 4, Mark Collins, Everson Walls; PHILADELPHIA: 5, Eric
    Allen, Wes Hopkins; PHOENIX: 6, Aeneas Williams; SAN FRANCISCO: 4,
    Dave Waymer; TAMPA BAY: 3, Tony Covington; WASHINGTON: 5, Darrell
    Green, Wilber Marshall

Team Champions
    NFC: 29—Philadelphia
    AFC: 23—Buffalo, Denver

AFC Interceptions—Team

	No.	Yards	Avg.	Long	TD
Denver	23	379	16.5	53	2
Buffalo	23	276	12.0	58	1
Houston	20	255	12.8	t52	2
Pittsburgh	19	329	17.3	t57	2
San Diego	19	227	11.9	t71	1
Seattle	18	302	16.8	43	2
N.Y. Jets	18	283	15.7	t83	2
L.A. Raiders	18	155	8.6	31	0
Cincinnati	17	169	9.9	47	1
Cleveland	15	260	17.3	t42	3
Kansas City	15	216	14.4	83	0
Indianapolis	15	202	13.5	37	0
Miami	12	135	11.3	37	0
New England	12	93	7.8	33	0
AFC Total	244	3281	——	t83	16
AFC Average	17.4	234.4	13.4	—	1.1

NFC Interceptions—Team

	No.	Yards	Avg.	Long	TD
New Orleans	29	482	16.6	79	2
Washington	27	279	10.3	t54	3
Philadelphia	26	280	10.8	t74	1
Detroit	19	286	15.1	t96	2
Atlanta	19	225	11.8	t55	1
Minnesota	17	242	14.2	t97	2
Chicago	17	225	13.2	39	1
Phoenix	17	187	11.0	t35	1
Green Bay	15	234	15.6	37	0
Dallas	12	167	13.9	t65	2
San Francisco	12	125	10.4	42	0
N.Y. Giants	12	122	10.2	41	0
L.A. Rams	11	175	15.9	t59	1
Tampa Bay	11	63	5.7	18	0
NFC Total	244	3092	——	t97	16
NFC Average	17.4	220.9	12.7	—	1.1
NFL Total	488	6373	——	t97	32
NFL Average	17.4	227.6	13.1	—	1.1

NFL Top 10 Interceptors

	No.	Yards	Avg.	Long	TD
Lott, Ronnie, Raiders	8	52	6.5	27	0
Crockett, Ray, Det.	6	141	23.5	t96	1
Sanders, Deion, Atl.	6	119	19.8	t55	1
Dishman, Cris, Hou.	6	61	10.2	43	0
Williams, Aeneas, Phx.	6	60	10.0	32	0
Byrd, Gill, S.D.	6	48	8.0	22	0
McKyer, Tim, Atl.	6	24	4.0	24	0
Atkins, Gene, N.O.	5	198	39.6	79	0
Odomes, Nate, Buff.	5	120	24.0	48	1
Atwater, Steve, Den.	5	104	20.8	49	0
Browner, Joey, Minn.	5	97	19.4	45	0
Oliver, Louis, Mia.	5	80	16.0	37	0
Marshall, Wilber, Wash.	5	75	15.0	t54	1
Smith, Dennis, Den.	5	60	12.0	39	0
Robinson, Eugene, Sea.	5	56	11.2	27	0
Green, Darrell, Wash.	5	47	9.4	24	0
Talley, Darryl, Buff.	5	45	9.0	13	0
McDonald, Tim, Phx.	5	36	7.2	13	0
Hopkins, Wes, Phil.	5	26	5.2	14	0
Washington, Lionel, Raiders	5	22	4.4	16	0
Allen, Eric, Phil.	5	20	4.0	8	0
Buck, Vince, N.O.	5	12	2.4	12	0

AFC Interceptions—Individual

	No.	Yards	Avg.	Long	TD
Lott, Ronnie, Raiders	8	52	6.5	27	0
Dishman, Cris, Hou.	6	61	10.2	43	0
Byrd, Gill, S.D.	6	48	8.0	22	0
Odomes, Nate, Buff.	5	120	24.0	48	1
Atwater, Steve, Den.	5	104	20.8	49	0
Oliver, Louis, Mia.	5	80	16.0	37	0
Smith, Dennis, Den.	5	60	12.0	39	0
Robinson, Eugene, Sea.	5	56	11.2	27	0
Talley, Darryl, Buff.	5	45	9.0	13	0
Washington, Lionel, Raiders	5	22	4.4	16	0
Harper, Dwayne, Sea.	4	84	21.0	43	0
Braxton, Tyrone, Den.	4	55	13.8	t52	1
Everett, Thomas, Pitt.	4	53	13.3	27	0
Brim, Michael, Cin.	4	52	13.0	24	0
Fulcher, David, Cin.	4	51	12.8	t27	1
Baylor, John, Ind.	4	50	12.5	32	0

	No.	Yards	Avg.	Long	TD
Cherry, Deron, K.C.	4	31	7.8	16	0
Jackson, Kirby, Buff.	4	31	7.8	15	0
McDowell, Bubba, Hou.	4	31	7.8	23	0
Orlando, Bo, Hou.	4	18	4.5	18	0
McMillan, Erik, Jets	3	168	56.0	t83	2
Lathon, Lamar, Hou.	3	77	25.7	t52	1
Woodson, Rod, Pitt.	3	72	24.0	41	0
Blackmon, Robert, Sea.	3	59	19.7	29	0
Shelton, Richard, Pitt.	3	57	19.0	t57	1
Prior, Mike, Ind.	3	50	16.7	37	0
Pearson, Jayice, K.C.	3	43	14.3	43	0
Hasty, James, Jets	3	39	13.0	39	0
Dimry, Charles, Den.	3	35	11.7	t26	1
Carrington, Darren, S.D.	3	30	10.0	19	0
Daniel, Eugene, Ind.	3	22	7.3	12	0
Smith, Leonard, Buff.	3	22	7.3	22	0
Hurst, Maurice, N.E.	3	21	7.0	21	0
Lewis, Albert, K.C.	3	21	7.0	21	0
Braggs, Stephen, Clev.	3	15	5.0	15	0
Thomas, Eric, Cin.	3	0	0.0	0	0
Brandon, David, Clev.	2	70	35.0	40	1
Hinkle, Bryan, Pitt.	2	68	34.0	t57	1
Dixon, Rickey, Cin.	2	62	31.0	47	0
Rolling, Henry, S.D.	2	54	27.0	47	0
Henderson, Wymon, Den.	2	53	26.5	53	0
Vincent, Shawn, Pitt.	2	52	26.0	27	0
Turner, Eric, Clev.	2	42	21.0	t42	1
Harden, Bobby, Mia.	2	39	19.5	22	0
Marion, Fred, N.E.	2	33	16.5	33	0
Goode, Chris, Ind.	2	27	13.5	27	0
Lippett, Ronnie, N.E.	2	27	13.5	27	0
Bussey, Barney, Cin.	2	18	9.0	18	0
Anderson, Eddie, Raiders	2	14	7.0	14	0
Brooks, Michael, Den.	2	7	3.5	9	0
Kelly, Joe, Jets	2	6	3.0	6	0
Richard, Stanley, S.D.	2	5	2.5	3	0
Henderson, Jerome, N.E.	2	2	1.0	2	0
Kelso, Mark, Buff.	2	0	0.0	0	0
Mersereau, Scott, Jets	2	0	0.0	0	0
Smith, Billy Ray, S.D.	2	0	0.0	0	0
Washington, Mickey, N.E.	2	0	0.0	0	0
Burruss, Lloyd, K.C.	1	83	83.0	83	0
Frank, Donald, S.D.	1	71	71.0	t71	1
Bentley, Ray, Buff.	1	58	58.0	58	0
Davis, Brian, Sea.	1	40	40.0	t40	1
Matthews, Clay, Clev.	1	35	35.0	35	0
Robbins, Randy, Den.	1	35	35.0	35	0
Washington, Charles, K.C.	1	34	34.0	34	0
Lewis, Darryll, Hou.	1	33	33.0	t33	1
Hunter, Patrick, Sea.	1	32	32.0	t32	1
Newsome, Vince, Clev.	1	31	31.0	31	0
Townsend, Greg, Raiders	1	31	31.0	31	0
Lang, Le-Lo, Den.	1	30	30.0	30	0
Barker, Leo, Cin.	1	29	29.0	29	0
Glasgow, Nesby, Sea.	1	28	28.0	28	0
Radecic, Scott, Ind.	1	26	26.0	26	0
Benson, Thomas, Raiders	1	25	25.0	25	0
Herrod, Jeff, Ind.	1	25	25.0	25	0
Griffin, Larry, Pitt.	1	22	22.0	22	0
Jones, James, Clev.	1	20	20.0	t20	1
Brown, Richard, Clev.	1	19	19.0	19	0
Dumas, Mike, Hou.	1	19	19.0	19	0
Hilliard, Randy, Clev.	1	19	19.0	19	0
Shelton, Anthony, S.D.	1	19	19.0	19	0
Smith, Al, Hou.	1	16	16.0	16	0
Young, Lonnie, Jets	1	15	15.0	15	0
Lee, Shawn, Mia.	1	14	14.0	14	0
Long, Howie, Raiders	1	11	11.0	11	0
Tippett, Andre, N.E.	1	10	10.0	10	0
Figaro, Cedric, Clev.	1	9	9.0	9	0
Mitz, Alonzo, Cin.	1	8	8.0	8	0
Cain, Joe, Sea.	1	5	5.0	5	0
Little, David, Pitt.	1	5	5.0	5	0
Bell, Billy, K.C.	1	4	4.0	4	0
Holloway, Cornell, Ind.	1	4	4.0	4	0
Clifton, Kyle, Jets	1	3	3.0	3	0
Reichenbach, Mike, Mia.	1	2	2.0	2	0
Fain, Richard, Cin.	1	1	1.0	1	0
Bayless, Martin, S.D.	1	0	0.0	0	0
Brown, J.B., Mia.	1	0	0.0	0	0
Elder, Donnie, S.D.	1	0	0.0	0	0
Francis, James, Cin.	1	0	0.0	0	0
Grant, David, Cin.	1	0	0.0	0	0
Hale, Chris, Buff.	1	0	0.0	0	0
Hicks, Clifford, Buff.	1	0	0.0	0	0
Jackson, Alfred, Clev.	1	0	0.0	0	0
Johnson, David, Pitt.	1	0	0.0	0	0
Johnson, Mike, Clev.	1	0	0.0	0	0

	No.	Yards	Avg.	Long	TD
Jones, Gary, Pitt.	1	0	0.0	0	0
Kors, R.J., Jets	1	0	0.0	0	0
Lloyd, Greg, Pitt.	1	0	0.0	0	0
Martin, Chris, K.C.	1	0	0.0	0	0
Odom, Cliff, Mia.	1	0	0.0	0	0
Porter, Rufus, Sea.	1	0	0.0	0	0
Price, Mitchell, Cin.	1	0	0.0	0	0
Ross, Kevin, K.C.	1	0	0.0	0	0
Washington, Brian, Jets	1	0	0.0	0	0
Williams, James, Buff.	1	0	0.0	0	0
Williams, Jarvis, Mia.	1	0	0.0	0	0
Green, Jacob, Sea.	1	-2	-2.0	-2	0
Taylor, Keith, Ind.	0	-2	—	-2	0

t indicates touchdown
Leader based on most interceptions

NFC Interceptions—Individual

	No.	Yards	Avg.	Long	TD
Crockett, Ray, Det.	6	141	23.5	t96	1
Sanders, Deion, Atl.	6	119	19.8	t55	1
Williams, Aeneas, Phx.	6	60	10.0	32	0
McKyer, Tim, Atl.	6	24	4.0	24	0
Atkins, Gene, N.O.	5	198	39.6	79	0
Browner, Joey, Minn.	5	97	19.4	45	0
Marshall, Wilber, Wash.	5	75	15.0	t54	1
Green, Darrell, Wash.	5	47	9.4	24	0
McDonald, Tim, Phx.	5	36	7.2	13	0
Hopkins, Wes, Phil.	5	26	5.2	14	0
Allen, Eric, Phil.	5	20	4.0	8	0
Buck, Vince, N.O.	5	12	2.4	12	0
Collins, Mark, Giants	4	77	19.3	41	0
Waymer, Dave, S.F.	4	77	19.3	42	0
Stinson, Lemuel, Chi.	4	69	17.3	t34	1
Edwards, Brad, Wash.	4	52	13.0	27	0
Glenn, Vencie, N.O.	4	35	8.8	18	0
Taylor, Terry, Det.	4	26	6.5	23	0
Walls, Everson, Giants	4	7	1.8	5	0
McMillian, Audrey, Minn.	4	5	1.3	3	0
Holt, Issiac, Dall.	4	2	0.5	2	0
Rutland, Reggie, Minn.	3	104	34.7	t97	1
Gray, Jerry, Rams	3	83	27.7	t59	1
Cecil, Chuck, G.B.	3	76	25.3	32	0
Jones, Reggie, N.O.	3	61	20.3	51	0
Lynch, Lorenzo, Phx.	3	59	19.7	t35	1
Cook, Toi, N.O.	3	54	18.0	22	0
Jamison, George, Det.	3	52	17.3	19	0
Joyner, Seth, Phil.	3	41	13.7	41	0
Maxie, Brett, N.O.	3	33	11.0	t31	1
Mayhew, Martin, Wash.	3	31	10.3	t31	1
Miano, Rich, Phil.	3	30	10.0	18	0
Murphy, Mark, G.B.	3	27	9.0	16	0
Henley, Darryl, Rams	3	22	7.3	22	0
Covington, Tony, T.B.	3	21	7.0	18	0
Paul, Markus, Chi.	3	21	7.0	10	0
Butler, LeRoy, G.B.	3	6	2.0	6	0
Smith, Otis, Phil.	2	74	37.0	t74	1
Carrier, Mark, Chi.	2	54	27.0	39	0
Evans, Byron, Phil.	2	46	23.0	31	0
Clark, Vinnie, G.B.	2	42	21.0	22	0
Tate, David, Chi.	2	35	17.5	28	0
White, William, Det.	2	35	17.5	28	0
Collins, Andre, Wash.	2	33	16.5	18	1
Brown, Larry, Dall.	2	31	15.5	20	0
Case, Scott, Atl.	2	23	11.5	17	0
Woolford, Donnell, Chi.	2	21	10.5	16	0
Lewis, Kevin, S.F.	2	20	10.0	20	0
Fullington, Darrell, T.B.	2	13	6.5	10	0
Mills, Sam, N.O.	2	13	6.5	8	0
Washington, James, Dall.	2	9	4.5	9	0
Stewart, Michael, Rams	2	8	4.0	8	0
Reynolds, Ricky, T.B.	2	7	3.5	7	0
Smith, Ben, Phil.	2	6	3.0	6	0
Johnson, Pepper, Giants	2	5	2.5	5	0
Johnson, Sidney, Wash.	2	5	2.5	5	0
Jordan, Brian, Atl.	2	3	1.5	3	0
Wright, Felix, Minn.	2	3	1.5	3	0
Horton, Ray, Dall.	1	65	65.0	t65	1
Newman, Anthony, Rams	1	58	58.0	58	0
Swilling, Pat, N.O.	1	39	39.0	t39	1
Brown, Robert, G.B.	1	37	37.0	37	0
Edwards, Dixon, Dall.	1	36	36.0	t36	1
Tippins, Kenny, Atl.	1	35	35.0	35	0
White, Adrian, Giants	1	30	30.0	30	0
Zordich, Mike, Phx.	1	27	27.0	27	0
Booty, John, Phil.	1	24	24.0	24	0
Williams, Robert, Dall.	1	24	24.0	24	0
Stephen, Scott, G.B.	1	23	23.0	23	0

	No.	Yards	Avg.	Long	TD
Tuaolo, Esera, G.B.	1	23	23.0	23	0
Gouveia, Kurt, Wash.	1	22	22.0	22	0
Merriweather, Mike, Minn.	1	22	22.0	t22	1
Tuggle, Jessie, Atl.	1	21	21.0	21	0
Johnson, Vaughan, N.O.	1	19	19.0	19	0
White, Sheldon, Det.	1	18	18.0	t18	1
Blades, Bennie, Det.	1	14	14.0	14	0
Johnson, Tim, Wash.	1	14	14.0	14	0
Thompson, Bennie, N.O.	1	14	14.0	14	0
Golic, Mike, Phil.	1	13	13.0	13	0
Hampton, Alonzo, T.B.	1	12	12.0	12	0
Berry, Ray, Minn.	1	11	11.0	11	0
Gayle, Shaun, Chi.	1	11	11.0	11	0
Jackson, Johnny, S.F.	1	11	11.0	11	0
Romanowski, Bill, S.F.	1	7	7.0	7	0
Carter, Marty, T.B.	1	5	5.0	5	0
Duerson, Dave, Phx.	1	5	5.0	5	0
Lee, Mark, S.F.	1	5	5.0	5	0
Mangum, John, Chi.	1	5	5.0	5	0
Morrissey, Jim, Chi.	1	5	5.0	5	0
Whitmore, David, S.F.	1	5	5.0	5	0
Carter, Carl, T.B.	1	4	4.0	4	0
Dent, Richard, Chi.	1	4	4.0	4	0
Petry, Stan, N.O.	1	4	4.0	4	0
Terrell, Pat, Rams	1	4	4.0	4	0
Jackson, Greg, Giants	1	3	3.0	3	0
Marve, Eugene, T.B.	1	1	1.0	1	0
Alexander, Bruce, Det.	1	0	0.0	0	0
Bowles, Todd, S.F.	1	0	0.0	0	0
Coleman, Monte, Wash.	1	0	0.0	0	0
Copeland, Danny, Wash.	1	0	0.0	0	0
Gann, Mike, Atl.	1	0	0.0	0	0
Gant, Kenneth, Dall.	1	0	0.0	0	0
Griffin, Don, S.F.	1	0	0.0	0	0
Hayworth, Tracy, Det.	1	0	0.0	0	0
Holmes, Jerry, G.B.	1	0	0.0	0	0
Lee, Carl, Minn.	1	0	0.0	0	0
Lyght, Todd, Rams	1	0	0.0	0	0
Mays, Alvoid, Wash.	1	0	0.0	0	0
Patterson, Craig, Phx.	1	0	0.0	0	0
Stokes, Fred, Wash.	1	0	0.0	0	0
Waters, Andre, Phil.	1	0	0.0	0	0
White, Reggie, Phil.	1	0	0.0	0	0

t indicates touchdown
Leader based on most interceptions

Punting

Average Yards Per Punt
  AFC: 45.7—Reggie Roby, Miami
  NFC: 45.5—Harry Newsome, Minnesota

Net Average Yards Per Punt
  NFC: 38.9—Rich Camarillo, Phoenix
  AFC: 38.5—Jeff Gossett, Raiders

Longest
  AFC: 93—Shawn McCarthy, New England at Buffalo, November 3
  NFC: 77—Jeff Feagles, Philadelphia at Dallas, September 15

Punts
  NFC: 87—Jeff Feagles, Philadelphia
  AFC: 82—Rohn Stark, Indianapolis

Punts, Game
  AFC: 10—Rohn Stark, Indianapolis at New England, December 8 (413 yards)
  NFC: 10—Dale Hatcher, Rams at New Orleans, September 15 (384 yards)
       Jim Arnold, Detroit at Green Bay, December 15 (391 yards)

Team Champions
  NFC: 45.5—Minnesota
  AFC: 44.8—Miami

AFC Punting—Team

	Net Punts	Gross Yards	Long	Gross Avg.	TB	Blk.	Opp. Ret.	Ret. Yards	In 20	Net Avg.
Miami	57	2551	64	44.8	7	1	30	332	18	36.5
L.A. Raiders	67	2961	61	44.2	2	0	41	341	26	38.5
Cincinnati	65	2828	62	43.5	7	0	38	456	15	34.3
Indianapolis	82	3492	65	42.6	6	0	47	516	14	34.8
Cleveland	80	3397	65	42.5	6	0	40	388	20	36.1
Houston	53	2211	60	41.7	4	2	29	192	14	36.6
Denver	74	3046	71	41.2	9	1	28	170	24	36.4
Seattle	76	3085	60	40.6	4	0	40	289	11	35.7
Kansas City	57	2303	57	40.4	6	0	27	190	11	35.0
Pittsburgh	75	2996	63	39.9	3	1	29	210	10	36.3
San Diego	77	3064	60	39.8	6	1	32	267	22	34.8
N.Y. Jets	64	2521	61	39.4	7	0	29	164	14	34.6
New England	82	3198	93	39.0	3	2	37	303	17	34.6
Buffalo	54	2085	58	38.6	4	0	15	53	12	36.1
AFC Total	963	39738	93	——	74	8	462	3871	228	——
AFC Average	68.8	2838.4	—	41.3	5.3	0.6	33.0	276.5	16.3	35.7

NFC Punting—Team

	Net Punts	Gross Yards	Long	Gross Avg.	TB	Blk.	Opp. Ret.	Ret. Yards	In 20	Net Avg.
Minnesota	68	3095	65	45.5	10	0	42	426	17	36.3
Phoenix	77	3445	60	44.7	7	1	48	313	19	38.9
N.Y. Giants	64	2768	61	43.3	8	0	35	350	16	35.3
New Orleans	87	3743	61	43.0	10	1	50	470	20	35.3
Atlanta	82	3491	60	42.6	6	0	45	387	22	36.4
Dallas	57	2426	64	42.6	5	0	28	231	16	36.8
Philadelphia	88	3640	77	41.4	11	1	42	431	29	34.0
Detroit	75	3092	63	41.2	5	0	35	340	27	35.4
Green Bay	86	3473	62	40.4	7	0	35	375	22	34.4
Tampa Bay	84	3389	56	40.3	6	0	49	559	22	32.3
Chicago	70	2814	64	40.2	8	1	28	205	13	35.0
San Francisco	56	2197	58	39.2	5	0	30	239	8	33.2
L.A. Rams	75	2856	52	38.1	7	1	33	292	18	32.5
Washington	55	2070	61	37.6	3	3	31	190	16	33.1
NFC Total	1024	42499	77	——	98	8	531	4808	265	——
NFC Average	73.1	3035.6	—	41.5	7.0	0.6	37.9	343.4	18.9	34.9
NFL Total	1987	82237	93	——	172	16	993	8679	493	——
NFL Average	71.0	2937.0	—	41.4	6.1	0.6	35.5	310.0	17.6	35.3

NFL Top 10 Punters

	Net Punts	Gross Yards	Long	Gross Avg.	Total Punts	TB	Blk.	Opp. Ret.	Ret. Yards	In 20	Net Avg.
Roby, Reggie, Mia.	54	2466	64	45.7	55	7	1	29	324	17	36.4
Newsome, Harry, Minn.	68	3095	65	45.5	68	10	0	42	426	17	36.3
Camarillo, Rich, Phx.	76	3445	60	45.3	77	7	1	48	313	19	38.9
Gossett, Jeff, Raiders	67	2961	61	44.2	67	2	0	41	341	26	38.5
Montgomery, Greg, Hou.	48	2105	60	43.9	50	4	2	28	183	13	36.8
Johnson, Lee, Cin.	64	2795	62	43.7	64	6	0	38	456	15	34.7
Barnhardt, Tommy, N.O.	86	3743	61	43.5	87	10	1	50	470	20	35.3
Landeta, Sean, Giants	64	2768	61	43.3	64	8	0	35	350	16	35.3
Tuten, Rick, Sea.	49	2106	60	43.0	49	3	0	29	239	8	36.9
Fulhage, Scott, Atl.	81	3470	60	42.8	81	6	0	45	387	21	36.6

AFC Punting—Individual

	Net Punts	Gross Yards	Long	Gross Avg.	Total Punts	TB	Blk.	Opp. Ret.	Ret. Yards	In 20	Net Avg.
Roby, Reggie, Mia.	54	2466	64	45.7	55	7	1	29	324	17	36.4
Gossett, Jeff, Raiders	67	2961	61	44.2	67	2	0	41	341	26	38.5
Montgomery, Greg, Hou.	48	2105	60	43.9	50	4	2	28	183	13	36.8
Johnson, Lee, Cin.	64	2795	62	43.7	64	6	0	38	456	15	34.7
Tuten, Rick, Sea.	49	2106	60	43.0	49	3	0	29	239	8	36.9
Stark, Rohn, Ind.	82	3492	65	42.6	82	6	0	47	516	14	34.8
Hansen, Brian, Clev.	80	3397	65	42.5	80	6	0	40	388	20	36.1
Horan, Mike, Den.	72	3012	71	41.8	73	8	1	28	170	24	36.7
Stryzinski, Dan, Pitt.	74	2996	63	40.5	75	3	1	29	210	10	36.3
Barker, Bryan, K.C	57	2303	57	40.4	57	6	0	27	190	11	35.0
Kidd, John, S.D.	76	3064	60	40.3	77	6	1	32	267	22	34.8
McCarthy, Shawn, N.E.	66	2650	93	40.2	68	3	2	26	163	17	35.7
Aguiar, Louie, Jets	64	2521	61	39.4	64	7	0	29	164	14	34.6
Mohr, Chris, Buff.	54	2085	58	38.6	54	4	0	15	53	12	36.1
Nonqualifiers											
Wagner, Bryan, N.E.	14	548	54	39.1	14	0	0	11	140	0	29.1
Waits, Alex, Sea.	14	474	50	33.9	14	0	0	5	4	2	33.6
Donnelly, Rick, Sea.	13	505	57	38.8	13	1	0	6	46	1	33.8
Sullivan, Kent, Hou.	3	106	37	35.3	3	0	0	1	9	1	32.3
Stoyanovich, Pete, Mia.	2	85	49	42.5	2	0	0	1	8	1	38.5
Breech, Jim, Cin.	1	33	33	33.0	1	1	0	0	0	0	13.0
Elway, John, Den.	1	34	34	34.0	1	1	0	0	0	0	14.0

Leader based on average, minimum 40 punts.

NFC Punting—Individual

	Net Punts	Gross Yards	Long	Gross Avg.	Total Punts	TB	Blk.	Opp. Ret.	Ret. Yards	In 20	Net Avg.
Newsome, Harry, Minn.	68	3095	65	45.5	68	10	0	42	426	17	36.3
Camarillo, Rich, Phx.	76	3445	60	45.3	77	7	1	48	313	19	38.9
Barnhardt, Tommy, N.O.	86	3743	61	43.5	87	10	1	50	470	20	35.3
Landeta, Sean, Giants	64	2768	61	43.3	64	8	0	35	350	16	35.3
Fulhage, Scott, Atl.	81	3470	60	42.8	81	6	0	45	387	21	36.6
Saxon, Mike, Dall.	57	2426	64	42.6	57	5	0	28	231	16	36.8
Feagles, Jeff, Phil.	87	3640	77	41.8	88	11	1	42	431	29	34.0
Arnold, Jim, Det.	75	3092	63	41.2	75	5	0	35	340	27	35.4
Buford, Maury, Chi.	69	2814	64	40.8	70	8	1	28	205	13	35.0
McJulien, Paul, G.B.	86	3473	62	40.4	86	7	0	35	375	22	34.4
Royals, Mark, T.B.	84	3389	56	40.3	84	6	0	49	559	22	32.3
Goodburn, Kelly, Wash.	52	2070	61	39.8	55	3	3	31	190	16	33.1
Prokop, Joe, S.F.	40	1541	58	38.5	40	1	0	21	138	8	34.6
Hatcher, Dale, Rams	63	2403	52	38.1	63	5	0	29	231	16	32.9
Nonqualifiers											
Mojsiejenko, Ralf, S.F.	16	656	55	41.0	16	4	0	9	101	0	29.7
Helton, Barry, Rams	11	453	46	41.2	12	2	1	4	61	2	29.3
Johnson, Norm, Atl.	1	21	21	21.0	1	0	0	0	0	1	21.0

Leader based on gross average, minimum 40 punts.

Punt Returns

Yards Per Return
- **NFC:** 15.4—Mel Gray, Detroit
- **AFC:** 11.4—Rod Woodson, Pittsburgh

Yards
- **NFC:** 600—Brian Mitchell, Washington
- **AFC:** 330—Tim Brown, Raiders

Yards, Game
- **NFC:** 116—Kelvin Martin, Dallas at Philadelphia, December 15 (5 returns)
- **AFC:** 87—Chris Warren, Seattle vs. Indianapolis, September 29 (4 returns)

Longest
- **NFC:** 85—Kelvin Martin, Dallas at Philadelphia, December 15 (TD)
- **AFC:** 78—Mitchell Price, Cincinnati vs. Giants, December 1 (TD)

Returns
- **NFC:** 53—Rod Harris, Philadelphia
- **AFC:** 32—Chris Warren, Seattle

Returns, Game
- **NFC:** 6—Rod Harris, Philadelphia at Green Bay, September 1 (49 yards)
  David Meggett, Giants vs. Cleveland, September 22 (79 yards)
  Vince Buck, New Orleans vs. Minnesota, September 22 (37 yards)
  Leo Lewis, Minnesota at Phoenix, October 27 (31 yards)
- **AFC:** 5—Fred Jones, Kansas City vs. New Orleans, September 8 (61 yards)
  Kitrick Taylor, San Diego vs. Cleveland, October 20 (79 yards)
  Scott Miller, Miami vs. Tampa Bay, December 1 (51 yards)
  Clarence Verdin, Indianapolis at New England, December 8 (10 yards)
  Jerome Henderson, New England vs. Indianapolis, December 8 (50 yards)
  Vance Johnson, Denver at San Diego, December 22 (17 yards)

Fair Catches
- **NFC:** 21—Brian Mitchell, Washington
- **AFC:** 19—Chris Warren, Seattle

Touchdowns
- **NFC:** 2—Brian Mitchell, Washington
- **AFC:** 1—Tim Brown, Raiders
  Ernie Mills, Pittsburgh
  Mitchell Price, Cincinnati
  Chris Warren, Seattle

Team Champion
- **NFC:** 14.8—Detroit
- **AFC:** 11.4—Raiders

AFC Punt Returns—Team

	No.	FC	Yards	Avg.	Long	TD
L.A. Raiders	29	10	330	11.4	t75	1
Buffalo	26	16	281	10.8	59	0
San Diego	33	25	328	9.9	48	0
Cincinnati	29	11	280	9.7	t78	1
Pittsburgh	39	14	373	9.6	40	1
Miami	30	12	258	8.6	32	0
Seattle	38	20	325	8.6	t59	1
Cleveland	31	10	251	8.1	31	0
Kansas City	34	6	258	7.6	25	0
Denver	41	17	284	6.9	20	0
N.Y. Jets	23	10	157	6.8	25	0
New England	31	14	211	6.8	39	0
Houston	36	11	244	6.8	29	0
Indianapolis	27	14	171	6.3	22	0
AFC Total	447	190	3751	——	t78	4
AFC Average	31.9	13.6	267.9	8.4	—	0.3

NFC Punt Returns—Team

	No.	FC	Yards	Avg.	Long	TD
Detroit	26	14	385	14.8	t78	1
Washington	46	21	610	13.3	t69	2
Dallas	29	12	309	10.7	t85	1
Green Bay	41	7	396	9.7	62	0
N.Y. Giants	36	10	336	9.3	t70	1
Tampa Bay	39	15	361	9.3	33	0
L.A. Rams	37	9	320	8.6	29	0
Atlanta	35	18	286	8.2	23	0
Philadelphia	53	9	416	7.8	40	0
San Francisco	42	15	320	7.6	24	0
Minnesota	30	15	225	7.5	44	0
Phoenix	41	6	307	7.5	19	0
Chicago	47	15	340	7.2	37	0
New Orleans	44	19	317	7.2	52	0
NFC Total	546	185	4928	——	t85	5
NFC Average	39.0	13.2	352.0	9.0	—	0.4
NFL Total	993	375	8679	——	t85	9
NFL Average	35.5	13.4	310.0	8.7	—	0.3

NFL Top 10 Punt Returners

	No.	FC	Yards	Avg.	Long	TD
Gray, Mel, Det.	25	14	385	15.4	t78	1
Mitchell, Brian, Wash.	45	21	600	13.3	t69	2
Martin, Kelvin, Dall.	21	8	244	11.6	t85	1
Woodson, Rod, Pitt.	28	12	320	11.4	40	0
Brown, Tim, Raiders	29	10	330	11.4	t75	1
Meggett, David, Giants	28	9	287	10.3	t70	1
Taylor, Kitrick, S.D.	28	18	269	9.6	48	0
Drewrey, Willie, T.B.	38	15	360	9.5	33	0
Warren, Chris, Sea.	32	19	298	9.3	t59	1
Sikahema, Vai, G.B.	26	4	239	9.2	62	0

AFC Punt Returns—Individual

	No.	FC	Yards	Avg.	Long	TD
Woodson, Rod, Pitt.	28	12	320	11.4	40	0
Brown, Tim, Raiders	29	10	330	11.4	t75	1
Taylor, Kitrick, S.D.	28	18	269	9.6	48	0
Warren, Chris, Sea.	32	19	298	9.3	t59	1
Miller, Scott, Mia.	28	10	248	8.9	32	0
Henderson, Jerome, N.E.	27	10	201	7.4	39	0
Johnson, Vance, Den.	24	14	174	7.3	20	0
Mathis, Terance, Jets	23	10	157	6.8	25	0
Stradford, Troy, K.C.	22	4	150	6.8	18	0
Verdin, Clarence, Ind.	25	10	165	6.6	22	0
Coleman, Patrick, Hou.	22	8	138	6.3	24	0
Nonqualifiers						
Slaughter, Webster, Clev.	17	3	112	6.6	17	0
Price, Mitchell, Cin.	14	6	203	14.5	t78	1
Barber, Mike, Cin.	13	5	70	5.4	15	0
Edwards, Al, Buff.	13	9	69	5.3	21	0
Hicks, Clifford, Buff.	12	7	203	16.9	59	0
Jones, Fred, K.C.	12	2	108	9.0	25	0
Metcalf, Eric, Clev.	12	1	100	8.3	30	0
Givins, Ernest, Hou.	11	0	107	9.7	29	0
Nattiel, Ricky, Den.	10	2	43	4.3	17	0
Graham, Jeff, Pitt.	8	2	46	5.8	13	0
Clark, Kevin, Den.	7	1	67	9.6	18	0
Lewis, Nate, S.D.	5	5	59	1.8	26	0
Loville, Derek, Sea.	3	1	16	5.3	18	0
Brennan, Brian, Clev.	2	6	11	5.5	11	0
Fryar, Irving, N.E.	2	4	10	5.0	10	0
Grant, Alan, Ind.	2	2	6	3.0	6	0
Martin, Tony, Mia.	1	0	10	10.0	10	0
Odomes, Nate, Buff.	1	0	9	9.0	9	0
Garrett, Shane, Cin.	1	0	7	7.0	7	0
Cash, Keith, K.C.	1	0	6	6.0	6	0
Harper, Dwayne, Sea.	1	0	5	5.0	5	0
Skansi, Paul, Sea.	1	0	5	5.0	5	0
Davis, Brian, Sea.	1	0	1	1.0	1	0
Vincent, Shawn, Pitt.	1	0	1	1.0	1	0
Jackson, Steve, Hou.	1	0	0	0.0	0	0
James, Lynn, Cin.	1	0	0	0.0	0	0
Junior, E.J., Mia.	1	0	0	0.0	0	0
Mills, Ernie, Pitt.	1	0	0	0.0	t0	1
Pool, David, N.E.	1	0	0	0.0	0	0
Robertson, Marcus, Hou.	1	0	0	0.0	0	0
Zackery, Tony, N.E.	1	0	0	0.0	0	0
Duncan, Curtis, Hou.	1	3	-1	-1.0	-1	0
Minnifield, Frank, Clev.	0	0	28	——	28	0
Byrd, Gill, S.D.	0	2	0	——	0	0
Prior, Mike, Ind.	0	2	0	——	0	0
Williams, Jarvis, Mia.	0	2	0	——	0	0

t indicates touchdown
Leader based on average return, minimum 20 returns

NFC Punt Returns—Individual

	No.	FC	Yards	Avg.	Long	TD
Gray, Mel, Det.	25	14	385	15.4	t78	1
Mitchell, Brian, Wash.	45	21	600	13.3	t69	2
Martin, Kelvin, Dall.	21	8	244	11.6	t85	1
Meggett, David, Giants	28	9	287	10.3	t70	1
Drewrey, Willie, T.B.	38	15	360	9.5	33	0
Sikahema, Vai, G.B.	26	4	239	9.2	62	0
Turner, Vernon, Rams	23	4	201	8.7	29	0
Taylor, John, S.F.	31	14	267	8.6	24	0
Buck, Vince, N.O.	31	13	260	8.4	52	0
Sanders, Deion, Atl.	21	9	170	8.1	23	0
Jackson, John, Phx.	31	3	244	7.9	19	0
Harris, Rod, Phil.	53	9	416	7.8	40	0
Bailey, Johnny, Chi.	36	11	281	7.8	37	0
Lewis, Leo, Minn.	30	15	225	7.5	44	0
Nonqualifiers						
Query, Jeff, G.B.	14	3	157	11.2	28	0
Jordan, Brian, Atl.	14	9	116	8.3	13	0
Henley, Darryl, Rams	13	4	110	8.5	16	0
Fenerty, Gill, N.O.	12	6	55	4.6	13	0
Beach, Sanjay, S.F.	10	0	53	5.3	15	0
Ingram, Mark, Giants	8	1	49	6.1	13	0

	No.	FC	Yards	Avg.	Long	TD
Shepard, Derrick, Dall.	6	3	57	9.5	14	0
Waddle, Tom, Chi.	5	3	31	6.2	11	0
Centers, Larry, Phx.	5	2	30	6.0	12	0
Proehl, Ricky, Phx.	4	0	26	6.5	14	0
Morgan, Anthony, Chi.	3	0	19	6.3	11	0
Green, Mark, Chi.	3	1	9	3.0	8	0
Hobbs, Stephen, Wash.	1	0	10	10.0	10	0
Gray, Jerry, Rams	1	1	9	9.0	9	0
Horton, Ray, Dall.	1	0	8	8.0	8	0
Edwards, Anthony, Phx.	1	1	7	7.0	7	0
Morse, Bobby, N.O.	1	0	2	2.0	2	0
Carter, Carl, T.B.	1	0	1	1.0	1	0
Brownlow, Darrick, Dall.	1	0	0	0.0	0	0
Jenkins, Mel, Det.	1	0	0	0.0	0	0
Lewis, Kevin, S.F.	1	0	0	0.0	0	0
Workman, Vince, G.B.	1	0	0	0.0	0	0
Griffin, Don, S.F.	0	1	0	——	0	0
Wright, Alexander, Dall.	0	1	0	——	0	0

t indicates touchdown
Leader based on average return, minimum 20 returns

Kickoff Returns

Yards Per Return
  NFC: 25.8—Mel Gray, Detroit
  AFC: 25.1—Nate Lewis, San Diego
Yards
  NFC: 929—Mel Gray, Detroit
  AFC: 880—Rod Woodson, Pittsburgh
Yards, Game
  NFC: 193—Alexander Wright, Dallas vs. Atlanta, December 22 (6 returns)
  AFC: 134—Jon Vaughn, New England at Phoenix, September 29 (2 returns)
Longest
  NFC: 102—Alexander Wright, Dallas vs. Atlanta, December 22 (TD)
  AFC: 99—Jon Vaughn, New England at Phoenix, September 29 (TD)
Returns
  AFC: 44—Rod Woodson, Pittsburgh
  NFC: 37—Dexter Carter, San Francisco
Returns, Game
  NFC: 8—Erric Pegram, Atlanta at Washington, November 10 (138 yards)
  AFC: 7—Shane Garrett, Cincinnati at Miami, December 9 (105 yards)
Touchdowns
  AFC: 1—Al Edwards, Buffalo
    Nate Lewis, San Diego
    Jon Vaughn, New England
    Clarence Verdin, Indianapolis
  NFC: 1—Dexter Carter, San Francisco
    Deion Sanders, Atlanta
    Charles Wilson, Green Bay
    Alexander Wright, Dallas
Team Champion
  NFC: 21.7—Dallas
  AFC: 21.3—Seattle

AFC Kickoff Returns—Team

	No.	Yards	Avg.	Long	TD
Seattle	60	1280	21.3	55	0
San Diego	55	1171	21.3	t95	1
Kansas City	48	978	20.4	76	0
New England	56	1108	19.8	t99	1
Pittsburgh	67	1314	19.6	54	0
Indianapolis	55	1061	19.3	t88	1
Buffalo	52	970	18.7	t91	1
Denver	37	687	18.6	55	0
Houston	46	835	18.2	41	0
L.A. Raiders	52	928	17.8	37	0
Miami	50	890	17.8	49	0
Cincinnati	69	1225	17.8	63	0
N.Y. Jets	58	1003	17.3	53	0
Cleveland	55	888	16.1	36	0
AFC Total	760	14338	—	t99	4
AFC Average	54.3	1024.1	18.9	—	0.3

NFC Kickoff Returns—Team

	No.	Yards	Avg.	Long	TD
Dallas	52	1127	21.7	t102	1
San Francisco	50	1028	20.6	t98	1
Detroit	57	1170	20.5	71	0
Minnesota	44	899	20.4	50	0
Green Bay	60	1197	20.0	t82	1
Atlanta	52	997	19.2	t100	1
Washington	49	926	18.9	46	0
Phoenix	52	972	18.7	39	0
N.Y. Giants	50	917	18.3	51	0

	No.	Yards	Avg.	Long	TD
L.A. Rams	59	1070	18.1	48	0
New Orleans	50	879	17.6	34	0
Tampa Bay	60	1047	17.5	43	0
Chicago	45	763	17.0	31	0
Philadelphia	47	764	16.3	33	0
NFC Total	727	13756	——	t102	4
NFC Average	51.9	982.6	18.9	—	0.3
NFL Total	1487	28094	——	t102	8
NFL Average	53.1	1003.4	18.9	—	0.3

NFL Top 10 Kickoff Returners

	No.	Yards	Avg.	Long	TD
Gray, Mel, Det.	36	929	25.8	71	0
Lewis, Nate, S.D.	23	578	25.1	t95	1
Wright, Alexander, Dall.	21	514	24.5	t102	1
Martin, Sammy, N.E.-Ind.	20	483	24.2	38	0
Wilson, Charles, G.B.	23	522	22.7	t82	1
Carter, Dexter, S.F.	37	839	22.7	t98	1
Warren, Chris, Sea.	35	792	22.6	55	0
Sanders, Deion, Atl.	26	576	22.2	t100	1
Nelson, Darrin, Minn.	31	682	22.0	50	0
Williams, Harvey, K.C.	24	524	21.8	76	0

AFC Kickoff Returns—Individual

	No.	Yards	Avg.	Long	TD
Lewis, Nate, S.D.	23	578	25.1	t95	1
Martin, Sammy, N.E.-Ind.	20	483	24.2	38	0
Warren, Chris, Sea.	35	792	22.6	55	0
Williams, Harvey, K.C.	24	524	21.8	76	0
Vaughn, Jon, N.E.	34	717	21.1	t99	1
Mathis, Terance, Jets	29	599	20.7	50	0
Edwards, Al, Buff.	31	623	20.1	t91	1
Woodson, Rod, Pitt.	44	880	20.0	47	0
Elder, Donnie, S.D.	27	535	19.8	42	0
Pinkett, Allen, Hou.	26	508	19.5	41	0
Craver, Aaron, Mia.	32	615	19.2	49	0
Verdin, Clarence, Ind.	36	689	19.1	t88	1
Holland, Jamie, Raiders	22	421	19.1	27	0
Montgomery, Alton, Den.	26	488	18.8	55	0
Graddy, Sam, Raiders	22	373	17.0	37	0
Metcalf, Eric, Clev.	23	351	15.3	24	0
Nonqualifiers					
Loville, Derek, Sea.	18	412	22.9	50	0
Morris, Joe, Clev.	18	310	17.2	36	0
Stradford, Troy, K.C.	14	292	20.9	38	0
Ball, Eric, Cin.	13	262	20.2	24	0
Coleman, Patrick, Hou.	13	256	19.7	31	0
Garrett, Shane, Cin.	13	214	16.5	24	0
Logan, Marc, Mia.	12	191	15.9	31	0
Mills, Ernie, Pitt.	11	284	25.8	54	0
James, Lynn, Cin.-Clev.	11	192	17.5	26	0
Brooks, James, Cin.	f11	190	17.3	35	0
Brown, A.B., Jets	10	100	10.0	31	0
Hector, Johnny, Jets	8	172	21.5	53	0
Allen, Marvin, N.E.	8	161	20.1	31	0
Peebles, Danny, Clev.	8	149	18.6	32	0
Fuller, Eddie, Buff.	8	125	15.6	22	0
Dingle, Mike, Cin.	7	176	25.1	63	0
Beebe, Don, Buff.	7	121	17.3	24	0
Russell, Derek, Den.	7	120	17.1	30	0
Odegard, Don, Jets	6	106	17.7	32	0
Stone, Dwight, Pitt.	6	75	12.5	25	0
McCallum, Napoleon, Raiders	5	105	21.0	25	0
Price, Mitchell, Cin.	5	91	18.2	22	0
Davis, Kenneth, Buff.	4	73	18.3	23	0
Green, Harold, Cin.	4	66	16.5	20	0
McNair, Todd, K.C.	4	66	16.5	18	0
Saxon, James, K.C.	4	56	14.0	23	0
McNeal, Travis, Sea.	4	30	7.5	15	0
Graham, Jeff, Pitt.	3	48	16.0	23	0
Tice, Mike, Sea.	3	46	15.3	20	0
King, Joe, Cin.	3	34	11.3	17	0
Brown, Gary, Hou.	3	30	10.0	16	0
Grant, Alan, Ind.	3	20	6.7	10	0
Clark, Kevin, Den.	2	45	22.5	29	0
Jones, Fred, K.C.	2	40	20.0	26	0
Timpson, Michael, N.E.	2	37	18.5	21	0
McCloughan, Dave, Ind.	2	35	17.5	19	0
Harris, Leonard, Hou.	2	34	17.0	19	0
Paige, Tony, Mia.	2	31	15.5	16	0
Riggs, Jim, Cin.	2	28	14.0	15	0
Harmon, Ronnie, S.D.	2	25	12.5	14	0
Dawkins, Dale, Jets	2	22	11.0	12	0

	No.	Yards	Avg.	Long	TD
Galbraith, Scott, Clev.	2	13	6.5	8	0
Hobby, Marion, N.E.	2	0	0.0	0	0
Brown, Tim, Raiders	1	29	29.0	29	0
Lewis, Greg, Den.	1	20	20.0	20	0
Williams, Jerrol, Pitt.	1	19	19.0	19	0
Taylor, Brian, Buff.	1	18	18.0	18	0
Rouson, Lee, Clev.	1	16	16.0	16	0
Holman, Rodney, Cin.	1	15	15.0	15	0
Sewell, Steve, Den.	1	14	14.0	14	0
Henry, Charles, Mia.	1	13	13.0	13	0
Gardner, Carwell, Buff.	1	10	10.0	10	0
Mrosko, Bob, Ind.	1	9	9.0	9	0
Rakoczy, Gregg, N.E.	1	9	9.0	9	0
Thompson, Leroy, Pitt.	1	8	8.0	8	0
Barber, Mike, Cin.	1	7	7.0	7	0
Bernstine, Rod, S.D.	f1	7	7.0	7	0
Jones, Victor, Hou.	1	7	7.0	7	0
Williams, Jarvis, Mia.	1	7	7.0	7	0
Coates, Ben, N.E.	f1	6	6.0	6	0
Kelly, Pat, Jets	1	4	4.0	4	0
McDonald, Quintus, Ind.	1	3	3.0	3	0
Benson, Mitchell, S.D.	f1	2	2.0	2	0
Boyer, Mark, Jets	1	0	0.0	0	0
Butts, Marion, S.D.	1	0	0.0	0	0
Dellenbach, Jeff, Mia.	1	0	0.0	0	0
Dressel, Chris, Jets	f1	0	0.0	0	0
Flannery, John, Hou.	1	0	0.0	0	0
McGovern, Rob, Pitt.	1	0	0.0	0	0
Smith, Steve, Raiders	1	0	0.0	0	0
Turk, Dan, Raiders	1	0	0.0	0	0
Thomas, Eric, Cin.	1	-1	-1.0	-1	0
Carrington, Darren, S.D.	0	24	——	24	0
Bienemy, Eric, S.D.	f0	0	——	0	0
McEwen, Craig, S.D.	f0	0	——	0	0
Rembert, Johnny, N.E.	f0	0	——	0	0
Rolle, Butch, Buff.	f0	0	——	0	0

t indicates touchdown
* indicates fair catch
Leader based on average return, minimum 20 returns

NFC Kickoff Returns—Individual

	No.	Yards	Avg.	Long	TD
Gray, Mel, Det.	36	929	25.8	71	0
Wright, Alexander, Dall.	21	514	24.5	t102	1
Wilson, Charles, G.B.	23	522	22.7	t82	1
Carter, Dexter, S.F.	37	839	22.7	t98	1
Sanders, Deion, Atl.	26	576	22.2	t100	1
Nelson, Darrin, Minn.	31	682	22.0	50	0
Meggett, David, Giants	25	514	20.6	42	0
Mitchell, Brian, Wash.	29	583	20.1	35	0
Turner, Vernon, Rams	24	457	19.0	36	0
Anderson, Gary, T.B.	34	643	18.9	39	0
Atkins, Gene, N.O.	20	368	18.4	27	0
Harris, Rod, Phil.	28	473	16.9	33	0
Nonqualifiers					
Dixon, James, Dall.	18	398	22.1	39	0
Centers, Larry, Phx.	16	330	20.6	39	0
Bailey, Johnny, Chi.	f16	311	19.4	31	0
Pegram, Erric, Atl.	16	260	16.3	30	0
Sikahema, Vai, G.B.	15	325	21.7	35	0
Edwards, Anthony, Phx.	13	261	20.1	36	0
Gentry, Dennis, Chi.	13	227	17.5	27	0
Brown, Ron, Rams	12	256	21.3	39	0
Drewrey, Willie, T.B.	12	246	20.5	43	0
Jennings, Stanford, N.O.	12	213	17.8	24	0
Flagler, Terrence, Phx.	12	208	17.3	32	0
Lang, David, Rams	12	194	16.2	34	0
Ervins, Ricky, Wash.	11	232	21.1	46	0
Hampton, Rodney, Giants	10	204	20.4	51	0
Sanders, Thomas, Phil.	10	160	16.0	31	0
Early, Quinn, N.O.	9	168	18.7	34	0
Hill, Randal, Mia.-Phx.	9	146	16.2	33	0
Tillman, Spencer, S.F.	9	132	14.7	27	0
Campbell, Jeff, Det.	9	85	9.4	18	0
Workman, Vince, G.B.	8	139	17.4	26	0
Morgan, Anthony, Chi.	8	133	16.6	29	0
Ingram, Mark, Giants	8	125	15.6	25	0
Hardy, Robert, T.B.	8	119	14.9	26	0
Thompson, Darrell, G.B.	7	127	18.1	30	0
Gant, Kenneth, Dall.	6	114	19.0	26	0
Jordan, Brian, Atl.	5	100	20.0	29	0
Eilers, Pat, Minn.	5	99	19.8	26	0
Johnson, Joe, Wash.	f5	83	16.6	25	0
Walker, Herschel, Minn.	5	83	16.6	21	0
Green, Roy, Phil.	5	70	14.0	21	0
Overton, Don, Det.	4	71	17.8	23	0
Green, Mark, Chi.	4	69	17.3	29	0
Sherman, Heath, Phil.	4	61	15.3	20	0
Dozier, D.J., Det.	4	60	15.0	38	0
Delpino, Robert, Rams	4	54	13.5	19	0
Morse, Bobby, N.O.	3	60	20.0	21	0
Shepard, Derrick, Dall.	3	54	18.0	21	0
Martin, Kelvin, Dall.	3	47	15.7	25	0
Rice, Allen, G.B.	3	36	12.0	15	0
Smith, Joey, Giants	3	34	11.3	18	0
McDonald, Mike, Rams	3	32	10.7	16	0
Fishback, Joe, Atl.	3	29	9.7	19	0
Gouveia, Kurt, Wash.	3	12	4.0	9	0
Raye, Jimmy, Rams	2	57	28.5	48	0
Jackson, John, Phx.	2	41	20.5	21	0
Webb, Chuck, G.B.	2	40	20.0	23	0
Beach, Sanjay, S.F.	2	37	18.5	23	0
Tillman, Lewis, Giants	2	29	14.5	19	0
Fenerty, Gill, N.O.	2	28	14.0	14	0
Wilson, Robert, T.B.	2	19	9.5	11	0
Jordan, Buford, N.O.	2	18	9.0	18	0
Cobb, Reggie, T.B.	2	15	7.5	15	0
Lewis, Darren, Chi.	2	13	6.5	13	0
Rouse, James, Chi.	2	10	5.0	10	0
Lomack, Tony, Phx.	1	19	19.0	19	0
Carter, Pat, Rams	f1	18	18.0	18	0
Pritchard, Mike, Atl.	1	18	18.0	18	0
Hobbs, Stephen, Wash.	1	16	16.0	16	0
Scott, Kevin, Det.	1	16	16.0	16	0
Allen, Terry, Minn.	1	14	14.0	14	0
Baldwin, Randy, Minn.	1	14	14.0	14	0
Chaffey, Pat, Atl.	1	14	14.0	14	0
McAfee, Fred, N.O.	1	14	14.0	14	0
Sydney, Harry, S.F.	1	13	13.0	13	0
Cross, Howard, Giants	1	11	11.0	11	0
Glenn, Vencie, N.O.	1	10	10.0	10	0
Jackson, Cedric, Det.	1	9	9.0	9	0
Davey, Don, G.B.	1	8	8.0	8	0
Anderson, Alfred, Minn.	1	7	7.0	7	0
Whitmore, David, S.F.	1	7	7.0	7	0
Ryan, Tim, T.B.	1	4	4.0	4	0
Sanders, Glenell, Rams	1	2	2.0	2	0
Hall, Ron, T.B.	1	1	1.0	1	0
Bell, Anthony, Det.	1	0	0.0	0	0
Clark, Robert, Det.	1	0	0.0	0	0
Dean, Walter, G.B.	1	0	0.0	0	0
Freeman, Lorenzo, Giants	1	0	0.0	0	0
Horton, Ray, Dall.	1	0	0.0	0	0
Donaldson, Jeff, Atl.	f0	0	——	0	0
Weathers, Clarence, G.B.	f0	0	——	0	0

t indicates touchdown
* indicates fair catch
Leader based on average return, minimum 20 returns

Fumbles

Most Fumbles
- **AFC:** 12—John Elway, Denver
- **NFC:** 12—Jim Everett, Rams

Most Fumbles, Game
- **NFC:** 4—Mark Rypien, Washington vs. Philadelphia, September 30
- **AFC:** 3—Jeff Kemp, Seattle at Denver, September 15
  - Jim Kelly, Buffalo at Kansas City, October 7
  - Warren Moon, Houston vs. Philadelphia, December 2
  - Neil O'Donnell, Pittsburgh at Houston, December 8

Own Fumbles Recovered
- **NFC:** 6—Jeff Hostetler, Giants
- **AFC:** 4—Steve DeBerg, Kansas City
  - Keith Kartz, Denver
  - Hugh Millen, New England
  - Warren Moon, Houston

Most Own Fumbles Recovered, Game
- **AFC:** 2—Steve DeBerg, Kansas City vs. Atlanta, September 1
  - Warren Moon, Houston at Pittsburgh, November 24
  - William Schultz, Indianapolis at Green Bay, November 24
  - Dan Stryzinski, Pittsburgh at Dallas, November 28
  - Todd McNair, Kansas City at San Francisco, December 14
  - Boomer Esiason, Cincinnati at Pittsburgh, December 15
- **NFC:** 2—Mel Gray, Detroit at Indianapolis, September 22
  - Tom Tupa, Phoenix at Giants, October 6
  - Vinny Testaverde, Tampa Bay vs. Giants, November 24
  - Erik Kramer, Detroit vs. Chicago, November 28
  - Vince Workman, Green Bay vs. Detroit, December 15

Opponents' Fumbles Recovered
- **AFC:** 4—Chris Burkett, Jets
  - James Hasty, Jets
  - Vince Newsome, Cleveland
  - Derrick Thomas, Kansas City
  - Terry Wooden, Seattle
  - Tony Woods, Seattle
- **NFC:** 4—Johnny Holland, Green Bay
  - Rickey Jackson, New Orleans
  - Seth Joyner, Philadelphia

Most Opponents' Fumbles Recovered, Game
- **AFC:** 2—Vince Newsome, Cleveland vs. Cincinnati, September 15
  - Terry Wooden, Seattle at Denver, September 15
  - Derrick Thomas, Kansas City at Rams, November 10
  - James Jones, Cleveland vs. Kansas City, November 24
- **NFC:** 2—Wes Hopkins, Philadelphia at Tampa Bay, October 6
  - Lawrence Taylor, Giants vs. Dallas, November 17
  - Seth Joyner, Philadelphia at Houston, December 2
  - Scott Case, Atlanta at Dallas, December 22
  - Don Griffin, San Francisco vs. Chicago, December 23

Yards
- **AFC:** 100—Chris Martin , Kansas City
- **NFC:** 99—Don Griffin, San Francisco

Longest
- **AFC:** 100—Chris Martin, Kansas City vs. Miami, October 13 (TD)
- **NFC:** 99—Don Griffin, San Francisco vs. Chicago, December 23 (TD)

AFC Fumbles—Team

	Fum.	Own Rec.	Fum. OB	TD	Opp. Rec.	TD	Yds	Tot. Rec.
Cleveland	18	10	0	0	18	1	40	28
L.A. Raiders	20	5	2	0	13	1	7	18
Kansas City	22	13	1	0	18	2	127	31
Miami	23	8	1	0	9	1	-7	17
San Diego	24	11	1	0	9	0	31	20
Buffalo	25	8	1	0	14	1	8	22
Seattle	26	9	0	0	21	0	2	30
N.Y. Jets	28	14	1	0	19	0	11	33
Cincinnati	31	9	2	0	14	0	38	23
Denver	31	14	4	0	10	1	29	24
Indianapolis	31	14	2	0	13	0	16	27
Houston	33	12	2	0	18	3	108	30
New England	34	13	1	1	19	0	-30	32
Pittsburgh	37	18	5	0	11	1	73	29
AFC Total	383	158	23	1	206	11	453	364
AFC Average	27.4	11.3	1.6	0.1	14.7	0.8	32.4	26.0

NFC Fumbles—Team

	Fum.	Own Rec.	Fum. OB	TD	Opp. Rec.	TD	Yds	Tot. Rec.
Atlanta	19	5	0	0	16	4	180	21
Minnesota	21	8	3	0	11	0	-5	19
Dallas	23	8	3	0	11	1	52	19
New Orleans	24	9	0	0	19	0	-38	28
Chicago	25	9	0	0	13	0	27	22
Detroit	25	12	0	0	17	1	43	29
Washington	26	11	3	0	13	0	15	24
Tampa Bay	30	10	2	0	16	0	-5	26
Phoenix	31	17	0	0	21	2	146	38
L.A. Rams	32	10	2	0	8	1	17	18
N.Y. Giants	33	16	2	0	9	0	-25	25
San Francisco	33	10	4	0	16	1	140	26
Philadelphia	34	15	3	0	22	3	55	37
Green Bay	41	22	2	0	14	1	19	36
NFC Total	397	162	24	0	206	14	621	368
NFC Average	28.4	11.6	1.7	0.0	14.7	1.0	44.4	26.3
NFL Total	780	320	47	1	412	25	1074	732
NFL Average	27.9	11.4	1.7	0.1	14.7	0.9	38.4	26.1

Fumbled though the end zone, ball awarded to opponents: None.
Fum OB = Fumbled out of bounds.
Yards includes aborted plays, own recoveries, and opponents' recoveries

AFC Fumbles—Individual

	Fum.	Own Rec.	Opp. Rec.	Yds	Tot. Rec.
Aguiar, Louie, Jets	0	1	0	0	1
Allen, Marcus, Raiders	1	0	0	0	0
Allen, Marvin, N.E.	0	0	1	0	1
Anderson, Eddie, Raiders	0	0	1	0	1
Arthur, Mike, Cin.	0	1	0	0	1
Atwater, Steve, Den.	0	0	1	0	1
Baab, Mike, Clev.	0	1	0	0	1
Bailey, Carlton, Buff.	0	0	1	0	1
Bailey, Edwin, Sea.	0	1	0	0	1
Baldinger, Brian, Ind.	3	0	0	0	0
Baldinger, Rich, K.C.	0	1	0	0	1
Ball, Eric, Cin.	1	0	0	0	0
Barnett, Tim, K.C.	0	1	0	0	1
Baty, Greg, Mia.	1	0	0	0	0
Baxter, Brad, Jets	6	1	0	0	1
Bayless, Martin, S.D.	0	0	1	0	1
Baylor, John, Ind.	0	0	1	0	1
Beebe, Don, Buff.	3	0	0	0	0
Bell, Nick, Raiders	2	0	0	0	0
Bennett, Cornelius, Buff.	0	0	2	9	2
Benson, Mitchell, S.D.	1	0	0	0	0
Bernstine, Rod, S.D.	1	0	0	0	0
Billups, Lewis, Cin.	0	0	1	7	1
Birden, J.J., K.C.	1	0	0	0	0
Blackmon, Robert, Sea.	0	0	1	0	1
Blades, Brian, Sea.	1	0	0	0	0
Braxton, Tyrone, Den.	1	0	1	0	1
Brennan, Brian, Clev.	1	0	0	0	0
Brilz, Darrick, Sea.	0	1	0	0	1
Brim, Michael, Jets	0	1	0	0	1
Brister, Bubby, Pitt.	4	2	0	0	2
Brooks, Bill, Ind.	0	1	0	0	1
Brooks, James, Cin.	5	0	0	0	0
Brown, A.B., Jets	2	1	0	0	1
Brown, Richard, Clev.	0	0	1	0	1
Brown, Tim, Raiders	1	0	0	0	0
Brown, Vincent, N.E.	0	0	1	0	1
Burkett, Chris, Jets	0	0	4	0	4
Burnett, Rob, Clev.	0	0	1	9	1
Burruss, Lloyd, K.C.	0	0	1	0	1
Bussey, Barney, Cin.	0	0	1	0	1
Butts, Marion, S.D.	3	0	0	0	0
Calloway, Chris, Pitt.	0	1	0	0	1
Carlson, Cody, Hou.	1	0	0	0	0
Chadwick, Jeff, Sea.	0	0	1	0	1
Cherry, Deron, K.C.	0	0	1	0	1
Childress, Freddie, N.E.	0	1	0	0	1
Childress, Ray, Hou.	0	0	1	0	1
Chilton, Gene, N.E.	1	0	0	-16	0
Clark, Ken, Ind.	4	1	0	0	1
Clark, Kevin, Den.	1	0	0	0	0
Coleman, Patrick, Hou.	3	0	0	0	0
Colon, Harry, N.E.	0	0	2	-8	2
Conlan, Shane, Buff.	0	0	2	0	2
Cook, Marv, N.E.	2	1	1	0	2
Craig, Roger, Raiders	2	0	0	0	0
Craver, Aaron, Mia.	2	1	1	0	2
Daniels, David, Sea.	1	0	2	0	2
Davis, Darrell, Jets	0	0	1	0	1
Dawkins, Dale, Jets	0	0	1	0	1
Dawson, Dermontti, Pitt.	2	1	0	2	1
DeBerg, Steve, K.C.	6	4	0	-19	4
Dennis, Mark, Mia.	0	1	0	0	1
Dickerson, Eric, Ind.	6	1	0	0	1
Dimry, Charles, Den.	0	0	1	0	1

	Fum.	Own Rec.	Opp. Rec.	Yds.	Tot. Rec.
Dishman, Cris, Hou.	0	0	3	19	3
Dixon, Randy, Ind.	0	1	0	0	1
Donaldson, Ray, Ind.	0	1	0	0	1
Dorn, Torin, Raiders	0	1	0	0	1
Dumas, Mike, Hou.	0	0	3	19	3
Duncan, Curtis, Hou.	1	0	0	0	0
Eatman, Irv, Jets	0	1	0	0	1
Edwards, Al, Buff.	2	0	0	0	0
Elder, Donnie, S.D.	1	0	0	0	0
Ellison, Riki, Raiders	0	0	2	0	2
Elway, John, Den.	12	2	0	0	2
Esiason, Boomer, Cin.	10	3	0	-5	3
Evans, Donald, Pitt.	0	0	1	0	1
Everett, Thomas, Pitt.	0	0	2	18	2
Fenner, Derrick, Sea.	2	0	0	0	0
Figaro, Cedric, Clev.	0	0	1	0	1
Flannery, John, Hou.	0	1	0	0	1
Fletcher, Simon, Den.	0	0	1	0	1
Foster, Barry, Pitt.	5	1	0	1	1
Francis, James, Cin.	0	0	1	0	1
Frase, Paul, Jets	1	0	0	0	0
Friesz, John, S.D.	10	2	0	-21	2
Fryar, Irving, N.E.	2	0	0	0	0
Fulcher, David, Cin.	1	0	3	12	3
Fuller, William, Hou.	0	0	2	3	2
Gagliano, Bob, S.D.	2	1	0	-3	1
Galbraith, Scott, Clev.	0	0	1	0	1
Galvin, John, Jets	0	0	1	0	1
Gannon, Chris, N.E.	0	0	1	0	1
Gardner, Carwell, Buff.	4	2	1	0	3
Garrett, Shane, Cin.	1	0	0	0	0
George, Jeff, Ind.	8	2	0	-4	2
Givins, Ernest, Hou.	3	0	0	0	0
Glasgow, Nesby, Sea.	0	0	1	12	1
Golic, Bob, Raiders	0	0	1	0	1
Gordon, Alex, Cin.	0	0	1	0	1
Gordon, Tim, N.E.	0	0	2	0	2
Graddy, Sam, Raiders	1	0	0	0	0
Green, Eric, Pitt.	2	0	0	0	0
Green, Gaston, Den.	4	0	0	0	0
Green, Harold, Cin.	2	0	0	0	0
Green, Jacob, Sea.	0	0	2	0	2
Grossman, Burt, S.D.	0	0	2	0	2
Grunhard, Tim, K.C.	0	1	0	0	1
Hall, Courtney, S.D.	0	2	0	0	2
Hand, Jon, Ind.	0	0	1	2	1
Hansen, Brian, Clev.	0	1	0	0	1
Hansen, Phil, Buff.	0	0	1	0	1
Harden, Bobby, Mia.	0	0	1	0	1
Harmon, Ronnie, S.D.	2	0	0	0	0
Harris, Odie, Clev.	0	0	1	0	1
Haselrig, Carlton, Pitt.	0	1	0	2	1
Hasty, James, Jets	0	0	4	7	4
Hayes, Eric, Sea.	0	0	1	0	1
Hayes, Jonathan, K.C.	1	0	0	0	0
Henderson, Jerome, N.E.	2	1	0	0	1
Hendrickson, Steve, S.D.	0	0	1	0	1
Herrod, Jeff, Ind.	0	0	3	0	3
Hester, Jessie, Ind.	3	1	0	0	1
Hicks, Cliff, Buff.	1	0	0	0	0
Higgs, Mark, Mia.	3	0	0	0	0
Hill, Drew, Hou.	2	0	0	0	0
Hilliard, Randy, Clev.	0	0	1	0	1
Hinkle, Bryan, Pitt.	0	0	1	0	1
Hinkle, George, S.D.	0	0	1	0	1
Hoard, Leroy, Clev.	1	1	0	4	1
Hobby, Marion, N.E.	0	0	1	0	1
Hodson, Tom, N.E.	2	0	0	0	0
Hoge, Merril, Pitt.	3	1	0	0	1
Hollas, Donald, Cin.	3	0	0	0	0
Holman, Rodney, Cin.	1	0	0	0	0
Horan, Mike, Den.	0	1	0	0	1
Horton, Ethan, Raiders	1	0	0	0	0
Houston, Bobby, Jets	0	0	1	0	1
Hull, Kent, Buff.	0	1	0	0	1
Hunter, Ivy Joe, N.E.	0	1	1	0	2
Jackson, Alfred, Clev.	0	0	2	0	2
Jackson, John, Pitt.	0	1	0	0	1
Jackson, Kirby, Buff.	0	1	0	0	1
Jackson, Mark, Den.	1	0	0	0	0
Jackson, Steve, Hou.	1	1	1	0	2
Jackson, Vestee, Mia.	0	0	1	0	1
James, Lynn, Cin.	1	0	0	0	0
Jefferson, James, Sea.	1	0	1	6	1
Jeffires, Haywood, Hou.	3	1	0	0	1
Johnson, Anthony, Ind.	2	0	0	0	0
Johnson, Lee, Cin.	1	0	0	0	0
Johnson, Reggie, Den.	0	1	0	0	1
Johnson, Troy, Jets	0	0	1	0	1
Johnson, Vance, Den.	1	1	0	0	1
Jones, Fred, K.C.	3	2	1	0	3
Jones, Henry, Buff.	0	1	0	0	1
Jones, James, Clev.	0	0	3	15	3
Jones, James, Sea.	2	0	1	0	1
Jones, Jock, Clev.	0	1	0	0	1
Jones, Tony, Clev.	0	1	0	0	1
Jones, Tony, Hou.	1	0	0	0	0
Kane, Tommy, Sea.	1	0	0	0	0
Kartz, Keith, Den.	0	4	0	11	4
Kelly, Jim, Buff.	6	2	0	-4	2
Kelly, Joe, Jets	1	0	0	0	0
Kelly, Pat, Jets	0	1	0	0	1
Kelso, Mark, Buff.	0	0	3	3	3
Kemp, Jeff, Sea.	5	0	0	-23	0
Kennedy, Cortez, Sea.	0	0	1	0	1
Key, David, N.E.	0	0	1	0	1
Kinchen, Brian, Clev.	1	0	0	-11	0
King, Ed, Clev.	0	1	0	0	1
Klingbeil, Chuck, Mia.	0	0	1	0	1
Kors, R.J., Jets	0	0	1	8	1
Kosar, Bernie, Clev.	10	2	0	-18	2
Kozerski, Bruce, Cin.	0	1	0	0	1
Krieg, Dave, Sea.	6	0	0	0	0
Krumrie, Tim, Cin.	0	0	1	0	1
Kubiak, Gary, Den.	1	0	0	0	0
Lanier, Ken, Den.	0	1	0	0	1
Lattimore, Brian, Ind.	0	0	1	0	1
Lewis, Darryll, Hou.	0	1	0	0	1
Lewis, Greg, Den.	3	0	0	0	0
Lewis, Mo, Jets	0	0	1	0	1
Lewis, Nate, S.D.	0	1	0	2	1
Lippett, Ronnie, N.E.	0	1	0	-8	1
Lipps, Louis, Pitt.	1	0	0	0	0
Lloyd, Greg, Pitt.	1	0	2	0	2
Lofton, James, Buff.	2	1	0	0	1
Logan, Ernie, Clev.	0	0	1	0	1
Logan, Marc, Mia.	1	0	0	0	0
Long, Terry, Pitt.	0	1	0	0	1
Lott, Ronnie, Raiders	0	0	1	4	1
Loville, Derek, Sea.	0	1	0	0	1
Lutz, Dave, K.C.	0	1	0	0	1
Maas, Bill, K.C.	0	0	1	0	1
Mack, Kevin, Clev.	1	0	0	0	0
Maggs, Don, Hou.	0	2	0	0	2
Manoa, Tim, Ind.	1	2	0	0	2
Marino, Dan, Mia.	6	3	0	-8	3
Martin, Chris, K.C.	0	0	1	100	1
Martin, Sammy, Ind.	1	0	0	0	0
Martin, Tony, Mia.	2	0	0	0	0
Marts, Lonnie, K.C.	0	0	1	0	1
Mathis, Terance, Jets	4	1	0	0	1
Matthews, Bruce, Hou.	1	1	0	-3	1
McCallum, Napoleon, Raiders	1	0	0	0	0
McDaniel, Terry, Raiders	0	0	1	0	1
McDowell, Bubba, Hou.	0	0	2	0	2
McGee, Tim, Cin.	1	0	0	0	0
McGruder, Michael, Mia.	0	0	1	0	1
McMillan, Erik, Jets	0	0	1	0	1
McMurtry, Greg, N.E.	1	0	0	0	0
McNair, Todd, K.C.	2	2	0	0	2
McNeal, Travis, Sea.	1	2	0	0	2
McNeil, Freeman, Jets	1	1	0	0	1
Mersereau, Scott, Jets	0	0	1	0	1
Metcalf, Eric, Clev.	1	0	0	0	0
Millard, Bryan, Sea.	0	1	0	0	1
Millen, Hugh, N.E.	10	4	0	-17	4
Miller, Anthony, S.D.	1	1	0	0	2
Miller, Scott, Mia.	4	3	0	0	3
Mills, Ernie, Pitt.	0	0	1	0	1
Mitz, Alonzo, Cin.	0	0	1	0	1
Montgomery, Alton, Den.	1	0	1	0	1
Montgomery, Glenn, Hou.	0	0	1	0	1
Moon, Warren, Hou.	11	4	0	-4	4
Moore, Rob, Jets	2	0	0	0	0
Morris, Joe, Clev.	2	1	0	0	1
Mosebar, Don, Raiders	0	1	0	0	1
Moss, Winston, Raiders	0	0	2	0	2
Moyer, Ken, Cin.	0	1	0	0	1
Muñoz, Anthony, Cin.	0	1	0	0	1
Nattiel, Ricky, Den.	2	0	0	0	0
Newsome, Vince, Clev.	0	0	4	37	4
O'Brien, Ken, Jets	6	1	0	-4	1
O'Donnell, Neil, Pitt.	11	2	0	-3	2
Odegard, Don, Jets	1	0	0	0	0

	Fum.	Own Rec.	Opp. Rec.	Yds.	Tot. Rec.
Odom, Cliff, Mia.	0	0	1	0	1
Odomes, Nate, Buff.	1	0	1	0	1
Okoye, Christian, K.C.	5	0	0	0	0
Oliver, Louis, Mia.	0	0	1	0	1
Orlando, Bo, Hou.	0	0	2	0	2
Paige, Tony, Mia.	1	0	0	0	0
Patterson, Elvis, Raiders	0	0	2	3	2
Perryman, Rob, Den.	1	1	0	1	1
Phillips, Joe, S.D.	0	0	1	0	1
Pinkett, Allen, Hou.	2	0	0	0	0
Pleasant, Anthony, Clev.	0	0	1	4	1
Plummer, Gary, S.D.	0	0	1	0	1
Pool, David, N.E.	1	0	1	0	1
Porter, Kevin, K.C.	0	0	1	0	1
Powers, Warren, Den.	0	0	2	27	2
Price, Mitchell, Cin.	0	0	1	0	1
Prior, Mike, Ind.	0	0	1	0	1
Rakoczy, Gregg, N.E.	1	0	0	0	0
Reed, Andre, Buff.	1	0	0	0	0
Reimers, Bruce, Cin.	0	0	0	0	0
Rienstra, John, Clev.	0	1	0	0	1
Robbins, Randy, Den.	0	0	1	0	1
Robertson, Marcus, Hou.	1	0	0	0	0
Robinson, Eugene, Sea.	0	0	1	0	1
Robinson, Jerry, Raiders	0	0	1	0	1
Rolling, Henry, S.D.	1	1	1	53	2
Ross, Kevin, K.C.	0	0	1	13	1
Russell, Leonard, N.E.	8	0	0	0	0
Saleaumua, Dan, K.C.	0	0	2	0	2
Saxon, James, K.C.	1	0	0	0	0
Schroeder, Jay, Raiders	7	1	0	0	1
Schultz, William, Ind.	0	2	0	0	2
Sewell, Steve, Den.	1	1	0	0	1
Sharpe, Shannon, Den.	0	1	0	0	1
Shelton, Richard, Pitt.	0	2	0	0	2
Simien, Tracy, K.C.	0	0	1	0	1
Singleton, Chris, N.E.	0	0	1	21	1
Siragusa, Tony, Ind.	0	0	1	5	1
Skansi, Paul, Sea.	1	0	0	0	0
Slaughter, Webster, Clev.	1	0	0	0	0
Smith, Al, Hou.	0	0	1	70	1
Smith, Anthony, Raiders	0	0	1	0	1
Smith, Billy Ray, S.D.	0	0	1	0	1
Smith, Dennis, Den.	0	0	1	5	1
Smith, Doug, Hou.	0	0	1	0	1
Smith, Leonard, Buff.	0	0	1	0	1
Smith, Neil, K.C.	0	0	2	10	2
Smith, Sammie, Mia.	3	0	0	0	0
Smith, Steve, Raiders	4	2	0	0	2
Sochia, Brian, Den.	0	0	1	0	1
Stargell, Tony, Jets	0	1	0	0	1
Stark, Rohn, Ind.	1	1	1	0	2
Stephens, John, N.E.	0	1	0	0	1
Stephens, Rod, Sea.	0	0	1	0	1
Stryzinski, Dan, Pitt.	1	2	0	0	2
Szott, David, K.C.	0	1	0	0	1
Talley, Darryl, Buff.	0	0	2	0	2
Tardits, Richard, N.E.	0	1	0	0	1
Taylor, Craig, Cin.	1	0	0	0	0
Taylor, Keith, Ind.	0	0	1	13	1
Taylor, Kitrick, S.D.	2	1	0	0	1
Thomas, Blair, Jets	3	0	0	0	0
Thomas, Derrick, K.C.	0	0	4	23	4
Thomas, Eric, Cin.	0	0	1	0	1
Thomas, Thurman, Buff.	5	0	0	0	0
Thompson, Broderick, S.D.	0	1	0	0	1
Thompson, Donnell, Ind.	0	0	1	0	1
Thompson, Leroy, Pitt.	1	1	0	0	1
Tice, Mike, Sea.	0	1	0	0	1
Timpson, Michael, N.E.	2	0	0	0	0
Tippett, Andre, N.E.	0	0	3	0	3
Toon, Al, Jets	0	1	0	0	1
Townsend, Greg, Raiders	0	0	1	0	1
Turner, Eric, Clev.	0	0	1	0	1
Turner, T.J., Mia.	0	0	2	1	2
Vaughn, Jon, N.E.	1	1	0	-2	1
Verdin, Clarence, Ind.	2	1	1	0	2
Villa, Danny, N.E.	0	1	1	0	2
Vlasic, Mark, K.C.	1	0	0	0	0
Walker, Derrick, S.D.	0	1	0	0	1
Walker, Tony, Ind.	0	0	1	0	1
Walter, Joe, Cin.	0	1	0	0	1
Warren, Chris, Sea.	3	1	0	0	1
Washington, Brian, Jets	1	0	1	0	1
Washington, Charles, K.C.	0	0	1	0	1
White, Dwayne, Jets	0	1	0	0	1
White, Lorenzo, Hou.	3	0	0	0	0

	Fum.	Own Rec.	Opp. Rec.	Yds.	Tot. Rec.
Widell, Dave, Den.	1	0	0	-15	0
Widell, Doug, Den.	0	1	0	0	1
Wilhelm, Erik, Cin.	1	0	0	0	0
Williams, Alfred, Cin.	0	0	2	24	2
Williams, Brent, N.E.	0	0	2	0	2
Williams, David, Hou.	0	1	0	0	1
Williams, Harvey, K.C.	1	0	0	0	0
Williams, Jerrol, Pitt.	0	0	1	38	1
Williams, John L., Sea.	2	1	0	0	1
Williams, Lee, Hou.	0	0	1	4	1
Williams, Warren, Pitt.	2	1	0	0	1
Willis, Keith, Pitt.	0	0	1	0	1
Wooden, Terry, Sea.	0	0	4	5	4
Woods, Ickey, Cin.	2	0	0	0	0
Woods, Tony, Sea.	0	0	4	2	4
Woodson, Rod, Pitt.	3	1	2	15	3
Word, Barry, K.C.	1	0	0	0	0
Worley, Tim, Pitt.	1	0	0	0	0
Young, Lonnie, Jets	0	0	1	0	1
Young, Mike, Den.	1	0	0	0	0
Zackery, Tony, N.E.	1	0	0	0	0
Zander, Carl, Cin.	0	0	1	0	1

Yards includes aborted plays, own recoveries, and opponents' recoveries

NFC Fumbles—Individual

	Fum.	Own Rec.	Opp. Rec.	Yds.	Tot. Rec.
Aikman, Troy, Dall.	4	0	0	0	0
Alexander, David, Phil.	0	2	0	4	2
Allen, Eric, Phil.	0	0	1	0	1
Allen, Terry, Minn.	4	1	0	0	1
Anderson, Gary, T.B.	4	0	0	0	0
Anderson, Neal, Chi.	5	1	0	0	1
Anderson, Willie, Rams	2	1	0	0	1
Anno, Sam, T.B.	0	0	1	0	1
Ard, Bill, G.B.	0	2	0	0	2
Atkins, Gene, N.O.	0	0	2	0	2
Awalt, Robert, Dall.	1	0	0	0	0
Bailey, Johnny, Chi.	4	2	0	0	2
Baker, Stephen, Giants	0	1	0	0	1
Barnett, Fred, Phil.	2	1	0	0	1
Barnett, Oliver, Atl.	0	0	1	75	1
Barton, Harris, S.F.	0	1	0	0	1
Bates, Bill, Dall.	0	0	2	0	2
Beach, Sanjay, S.F.	1	0	0	0	0
Bell, Anthony, Det.	0	0	1	0	1
Berry, Ray, Minn.	0	0	1	0	1
Blades, Bennie, Det.	0	0	3	21	3
Bono, Steve, S.F.	7	0	0	-8	0
Booty, John, Phil.	0	1	0	0	1
Bostic, Jeff, Wash.	1	1	0	0	1
Bowles, Todd, S.F.	0	1	1	0	2
Brandes, John, Wash.	0	1	0	0	1
Braxton, David, Phx.	0	0	1	7	1
Brenner, Hoby, N.O.	0	1	0	4	1
Broussard, Steve, Atl.	1	0	0	0	0
Brown, Jerome, Phil.	0	0	2	0	2
Brown, Larry, Dall.	0	0	1	0	1
Brown, Lomas, Det.	0	1	0	0	1
Brown, Robert, G.B.	0	0	1	0	1
Buck, Vince, N.O.	0	0	3	0	3
Bunch, Jarrod, Giants	1	0	0	0	0
Bush, Blair, G.B.	0	0	1	0	1
Butcher, Paul, Rams	0	0	1	0	1
Butler, Bobby, Atl.	0	0	1	39	1
Butler, LeRoy, G.B.	0	0	1	0	1
Byars, Keith, Phil.	5	0	0	0	0
Byner, Earnest, Wash.	3	1	0	0	1
Caesar, Ivan, Minn.	0	0	2	0	2
Caldwell, Ravin, Wash.	0	0	1	0	1
Camarillo, Rich, Phx.	0	0	1	0	1
Campbell, Jeff, Det.	1	0	0	0	0
Carlson, Jeff, T.B.	2	1	0	0	1
Carrier, Mark, Chi.	0	0	1	2	1
Carrier, Mark, T.B.	2	1	0	0	1
Carter, Cris, Minn.	1	0	0	0	0
Carter, Dexter, S.F.	5	1	0	0	1
Carter, Pat, Rams	1	0	0	0	0
Carthon, Maurice, Giants	1	0	0	0	0
Case, Scott, Atl.	0	0	2	2	2
Casillas, Tony, Dall.	0	0	1	0	1
Centers, Larry, Phx.	4	2	0	0	2
Chaffey, Pat, Atl.	1	0	0	0	0
Chandler, Chris, T.B.-Phx.	6	2	0	-7	2
Clark, Robert, Det.	0	1	0	0	1
Cobb, Reggie, T.B.	3	0	0	0	0
Coleman, Monte, Wash.	0	0	1	0	1
Collins, Andre, Wash.	1	0	1	0	1

| | | Own | Opp. | | Tot. |
	Fum.	Rec.	Rec.	Yds.	Rec.
Collins, Mark, Giants	0	1	1	0	2
Conner, Darion, Atl.	1	0	1	5	1
Cooper, Richard, N.O.	0	1	0	0	1
Copeland, Danny, Wash.	0	1	2	0	3
Covington, Tony, T.B.	0	0	1	0	1
Cox, Aaron, Rams	1	0	0	0	0
Cross, Howard, Giants	1	0	0	0	0
Davis, Dexter, Phx.	0	1	1	0	2
DeLong, Keith, S.F.	0	0	1	0	1
Dean, Walter, G.B.	1	0	0	0	0
Del Rio, Jack, Dall.	0	1	0	0	1
Delpino, Robert, Rams	3	1	0	0	1
Dent, Burnell, G.B.	0	0	1	0	1
Dent, Richard, Chi.	0	0	1	0	1
Dixon, James, Dall.	1	0	0	0	0
Doleman, Chris, Minn.	0	0	2	7	2
Douglass, Maurice, Chi.	0	0	2	0	2
Drewrey, Willie, T.B.	3	1	0	0	1
Drummond, Robert, Phil.	1	0	0	0	0
Dukes, Jamie, Atl.	0	1	0	0	1
Dupree, Marcus, Rams	1	0	0	0	0
Early, Quinn, N.O.	2	0	0	0	0
Eilers, Pat, Minn.	0	0	2	0	2
Ellard, Henry, Rams	1	1	0	0	1
Epps, Tory, Atl.	0	0	1	0	1
Ervins, Ricky, Wash.	1	1	0	0	1
Evans, Byron, Phil.	1	0	2	0	2
Everett, Jim, Rams	12	1	0	-4	1
Farr, Mike, Det.	1	0	0	0	0
Faryniarz, Brett, Rams	0	0	1	0	1
Feagles, Jeff, Phil.	1	1	0	0	1
Fenerty, Gill, N.O.	1	0	0	0	0
Fishback, Joe, Atl.	0	0	2	16	2
Foster, Roy, S.F.	0	1	0	0	1
Gannon, Rich, Minn.	2	0	0	0	0
Gant, Kenneth, Dall.	0	0	1	0	1
Gary, Cleveland, Rams	1	0	0	0	0
Gelbaugh, Stan, Phx.	4	1	0	0	1
Gentry, Dennis, Chi.	1	0	0	0	0
Glenn, Vencie, N.O.	0	0	1	0	1
Goebel, Brad, Phil.	2	0	0	0	0
Gray, Jerry, Rams	0	0	1	4	1
Gray, Mel, Det.	3	2	0	0	2
Green, Mark, Chi.	4	0	0	0	0
Green, Tim, Atl.	0	1	2	0	3
Griffin, Don, S.F.	0	0	3	99	3
Gruber, Paul, T.B.	0	0	1	0	1
Guyton, Myron, Giants	0	0	1	0	1
Hager, Britt, Phil.	0	0	1	0	1
Haley, Charles, S.F.	0	0	1	3	1
Hall, Ron, T.B.	1	0	0	0	0
Hallstrom, Ron, G.B.	0	1	0	0	1
Hamilton, Harry, T.B.	0	0	1	0	1
Hampton, Rodney, Giants	5	1	0	0	1
Hanks, Merton, S.F.	0	0	2	0	2
Harbaugh, Jim, Chi.	6	0	0	-3	0
Hardy, Robert, T.B.	1	2	0	0	2
Harris, Jackie, G.B.	1	0	1	0	1
Harris, Rod, Phil.	6	1	0	0	1
Harris, Tim, S.F.	0	0	1	0	1
Harvey, Ken, Phx.	0	0	2	0	2
Hauck, Tim, G.B.	0	0	1	0	1
Hawkins, Bill, Rams	0	0	1	0	1
Hayworth, Tracy, Det.	0	0	2	28	2
Hebert, Bobby, N.O.	5	2	0	-19	2
Heller, Ron, Phil.	0	1	0	0	1
Henderson, Keith, S.F.	4	0	0	0	0
Henley, Darryl, Rams	1	1	0	0	1
Hilgenberg, Joel, N.O.	1	0	0	-12	0
Hill, Eric, Phx.	0	0	1	85	1
Hilliard, Dalton, N.O.	3	1	0	0	1
Holland, Johnny, G.B.	0	0	4	3	4
Holmes, Jerry, G.B.	0	0	1	12	1
Hoover, Houston, Atl.	0	1	0	0	1
Hopkins, Wes, Phil.	0	0	3	0	3
Horton, Ray, Dall.	1	1	2	37	3
Hostetler, Jeff, Giants	7	6	0	-9	6
Howard, Erik, Giants	0	0	1	0	1
Hudson, John, Phil.	1	0	0	0	0
Hunter, Jeff, Det.	0	0	1	0	1
Hyche, Steve, Phx.	0	0	2	0	2
Ingram, Mark, Giants	3	1	0	0	1
Irvin, Michael, Dall.	3	1	0	0	1
Irwin, Tim, Minn.	0	1	0	0	1
Jackson, Cedric, Det.	1	0	0	0	0
Jackson, Greg, Giants	1	0	0	0	0
Jackson, John, Phx.	3	1	0	0	1
Jackson, Johnny, S.F.	0	0	2	49	2
Jackson, Keith, Phil.	2	0	0	0	0
Jackson, Rickey, N.O.	0	0	4	4	4
Jamison, George, Det.	1	0	1	0	1
Jenkins, Mel, Det.	1	1	0	15	1
Jennings, Stanford, N.O.	1	0	0	0	0
Johnson, A.J., Wash.	0	0	1	10	1
Johnson, Johnny, Phx.	2	0	0	0	0
Johnson, Maurice, Phil.	0	1	0	3	1
Johnson, Tracy, Atl.	0	0	1	0	1
Johnson, Vaughan, N.O.	0	0	1	0	1
Jones, Brent, S.F.	2	1	0	0	1
Jones, Ernie, Phx.	1	0	0	0	0
Jones, Hassan, Minn.	1	0	0	0	0
Jones, Jimmie, Dall.	0	0	2	15	2
Jones, Mike, Minn.	0	0	1	0	1
Jones, Roger, T.B.	0	0	1	0	1
Jones, Victor, Det.	0	0	1	0	1
Jordan, Brian, Atl.	0	0	1	0	1
Jordan, Buford, N.O.	2	1	0	0	1
Jordan, Steve, Minn.	2	1	0	0	1
Jorden, Tim, Phx.	0	1	0	0	1
Joseph, James, Phil.	2	0	0	0	0
Joyner, Seth, Phil.	0	0	4	47	4
Kemp, Perry, G.B.	2	0	0	0	0
Kiel, Blair, G.B.	2	1	0	0	1
Koch, Markus, Wash.	0	0	2	0	2
Kowalkowski, Scott, Phil.	0	1	0	0	1
Kozlowski, Glen, Chi.	0	0	1	0	1
Kramer, Erik, Det.	8	4	0	-5	4
Kupp, Craig, Phx.	1	0	0	0	0
Lang, David, Rams	1	0	0	0	0
Lee, Carl, Minn.	0	0	1	0	1
Lewis, Bill, Phx.	0	1	0	0	1
Lewis, Kevin, S.F.	1	0	0	0	0
Lewis, Leo, Minn.	3	1	0	0	1
Love, Duval, Rams	0	2	0	0	2
Lowdermilk, Kirk, Minn.	1	1	0	-22	1
Lyght, Todd, Rams	1	0	1	0	1
Lyles, Robert, Atl.	0	0	1	0	1
Lynch, Lorenzo, Phx.	0	0	1	17	1
Majkowski, Don, G.B.	10	4	0	-3	4
Mangum, John, Chi.	0	1	1	0	2
Manley, Dexter, T.B.	0	0	1	0	1
Mann, Charles, Wash.	0	0	1	0	1
Marshall, Wilber, Wash.	0	0	1	0	1
Martin, Eric, N.O.	2	0	0	0	0
Martin, Kelvin, Dall.	2	1	0	0	1
Martin, Wayne, N.O.	0	0	1	0	1
Marve, Eugene, T.B.	0	0	1	0	1
Massey, Robert, Phx.	0	0	1	2	1
Maxie, Brett, N.O.	0	0	1	0	1
Mayberry, Tony, T.B.	3	0	0	-17	0
Mayhew, Martin, Wash.	0	0	1	0	1
Mays, Alvoid, Wash.	0	1	0	0	1
McAfee, Fred, N.O.	2	0	0	0	0
McCants, Keith, T.B.	0	0	1	0	1
McDaniel, Randall, Minn.	0	1	0	0	1
McDonald, Tim, Phx.	0	0	1	0	1
McGee, Buford, Rams	1	0	0	0	0
McGriggs, Lamar, Giants	0	0	1	0	1
McIntyre, Guy, S.F.	0	1	0	0	1
McJulien, Paul, G.B.	1	1	0	-2	1
McKnight, Dennis, Phil.	1	0	0	-7	0
McKyer, Tim, Atl.	0	0	0	6	0
McMahon, Jim, Phil.	2	2	0	0	2
McMichael, Steve, Chi.	0	0	2	0	2
McMillian, Audrey, Minn.	0	0	1	13	1
Meggett, David, Giants	8	3	0	0	3
Miller, Chris, Atl.	5	0	0	0	0
Miller, Corey, Giants	0	1	0	0	1
Mills, Sam, N.O.	0	0	2	0	2
Mitchell, Brian, Wash.	8	1	0	0	1
Monk, Art, Wash.	2	0	0	0	0
Morgan, Anthony, Chi.	1	0	0	0	0
Murphy, Kevin, T.B.	0	0	1	0	1
Murphy, Mark, G.B.	0	0	1	0	1
Muster, Brad, Chi.	0	2	0	0	2
Nelson, Darrin, Minn.	2	0	0	0	0
Newman, Anthony, Rams	0	0	1	17	1
Newton, Nate, Dall.	0	1	0	0	1
Newton, Tim, T.B.	0	0	2	0	2
Noble, Brian, G.B.	0	0	1	1	1
Noga, Niko, Det.	0	0	1	0	1
Novacek, Jay, Dall.	3	1	0	0	1
Nunn, Freddie Joe, Phx.	0	0	2	1	2
Orr, Terry, Wash.	0	1	0	0	1
Overton, Don, Det.	1	0	0	0	0
Owens, Dan, Det.	0	0	2	0	2

	Fum.	Own Rec.	Opp. Rec.	Yds.	Tot. Rec.
Patterson, Craig, Phx.	0	0	1	0	1
Peete, Rodney, Det.	2	1	0	-1	1
Pegram, Erric, Atl.	1	0	0	0	0
Pitts, Mike, Phil.	0	0	1	0	1
Price, Jim, Rams	2	0	1	0	1
Pritchard, Mike, Atl.	2	0	0	0	0
Proehl, Ricky, Phx.	0	1	0	0	1
Prokop, Joe, S.F.	1	0	0	0	0
Query, Jeff, G.B.	1	1	0	0	1
Rathman, Tom, S.F.	2	2	0	0	2
Redding, Reggie, Atl.	1	1	0	0	1
Reeves, Walter, Phx.	1	1	0	0	1
Rice, Allen, G.B.	2	0	0	0	0
Rice, Jerry, S.F.	1	0	0	0	0
Riggs, Gerald, Wash.	1	0	0	0	0
Rison, Andre, Atl.	1	0	0	0	0
Robbins, Tootie, Phx.	0	1	0	0	1
Rocker, David, Rams	0	0	1	1	1
Romanowski, Bill, S.F.	0	0	2	0	2
Rouse, James, Chi.	1	0	0	0	0
Rozier, Mike, Atl.	2	0	0	0	0
Ruettgers, Ken, G.B.	0	1	0	0	1
Ryan, Pat, Phil.	2	0	0	0	0
Ryan, Tim, Chi.	0	0	2	0	2
Rypien, Mark, Wash.	9	3	0	-5	3
Saddler, Rod, Phx.	0	0	1	7	1
Sanders, Barry, Det.	5	1	0	0	1
Sanders, Deion, Atl.	1	1	0	0	1
Sanders, Thomas, Phil.	2	0	0	0	0
Seals, Ray, T.B.	0	0	2	0	2
Sharpe, Sterling, G.B.	1	2	0	0	2
Sherman, Heath, Phil.	3	1	0	0	1
Sikahema, Vai, G.B.	3	0	0	0	0
Simmons, Clyde, Phil.	0	0	3	0	3
Simms, Phil, Giants	4	2	0	-16	2
Smeenge, Joel, N.O.	0	1	0	0	1
Smith, Daryle, Phil.	0	1	0	0	1
Smith, Emmitt, Dall.	8	1	0	0	1
Smith, Lance, Phx.	0	2	0	5	2
Smith, Otis, Phil.	0	0	1	0	1
Solomon, Jesse, T.B.	0	0	1	0	1
Solt, Ron, Phil.	0	1	0	0	1
Spielman, Chris, Det.	0	0	3	0	3
Spindler, Marc, Det.	0	0	1	0	1
Stephen, Scott, G.B.	0	0	1	0	1
Stinson, Lemuel, Chi.	0	0	2	0	2
Stokes, Fred, Wash.	0	0	2	10	2
Stowe, Tyronne, Phx.	0	0	1	0	1
Stubbs, Danny, Dall.	0	0	1	0	1
Swilling, Pat, N.O.	0	0	1	5	1
Sydney, Harry, S.F.	3	1	0	0	1
Taylor, Jay, Phx.	0	0	1	0	1
Taylor, John, S.F.	1	0	0	0	0
Taylor, Lawrence, Giants	0	0	2	0	2
Taylor, Terry, Det.	0	0	1	0	1
Terrell, Pat, Rams	0	1	0	0	1
Testaverde, Vinny, T.B.	5	3	0	0	3
Thayer, Tom, Chi.	0	1	0	0	1
Thomas, Broderick, T.B.	0	0	2	12	2
Thomas, Henry, Minn.	0	0	1	0	1
Thomas, William, Phil.	0	1	0	0	1
Thompson, Anthony, Phx.	3	0	0	0	0
Thompson, Bennie, N.O.	0	1	1	0	2
Thompson, Darrell, G.B.	1	1	0	0	1
Thornton, James, Chi.	1	0	0	0	0
Tice, John, N.O.	1	0	0	0	0
Tillman, Lewis, Giants	2	0	0	0	0
Tillman, Spencer, S.F.	2	0	1	0	1
Tippins, Kenny, Atl.	0	0	1	23	1
Tolbert, Tony, Dall.	0	0	1	0	1
Tolliver, Billy Joe, Atl.	3	0	0	-4	0
Tomczak, Mike, G.B.	5	2	0	-1	2
Tuggle, Jessie, Atl.	0	0	2	18	2
Tupa, Tom, Phx.	8	2	0	0	2
Turnbull, Renaldo, N.O.	0	0	1	0	1
Turner, Floyd, N.O.	1	0	0	0	0
Turner, Marcus, Phx.	0	0	1	0	1
Turner, Vernon, Rams	4	2	1	-1	2
Utley, Mike, Det.	0	1	0	0	1
Van Horne, Keith, Chi.	0	1	0	0	1
Waddle, Tom, Chi.	2	0	0	0	0
Walker, Herschel, Minn.	2	1	0	0	1
Walls, Everson, Giants	0	0	2	0	2
Walsh, Steve, N.O.	3	1	0	-20	1
Ware, Andre, Det.	1	0	0	-15	0
Waters, Andre, Phil.	0	0	1	0	1
Waymer, Dave, S.F.	0	0	2	3	2
Weathers, Clarence, G.B.	1	0	0	0	0
White, Reggie, Phil.	0	0	3	8	3
Williams, Aeneas, Phx.	1	1	1	10	2
Williams, Calvin, Phil.	1	0	0	0	0
Williams, Erik, Dall.	0	1	0	0	1
Williams, James, N.O.	0	0	1	0	1
Williams, Perry, Giants	0	0	1	0	1
Wilson, Bobby, Wash.	0	0	1	0	1
Wilson, Charles, G.B.	4	1	0	0	1
Wilson, Robert, T.B.	3	1	0	0	1
Wilson, Wade, Minn.	3	1	0	-3	1
Wojciechowski, John, Chi.	0	1	0	0	1
Woodside, Keith, G.B.	3	1	0	0	1
Woolford, Donnell, Chi.	0	0	1	28	1
Workman, Vince, G.B.	3	4	0	9	4
Young, Steve, S.F.	3	1	0	-6	1
Zordich, Mike, Phx.	0	1	2	19	3

Yards includes aborted plays, own recoveries, and opponents' recoveries

Sacks

Most Sacks
- **NFC:** 17.0—Pat Swilling, New Orleans
- **AFC:** 15.0—William Fuller, Houston

Most Sacks, Game
- **NFC:** 4.5—Bryce Paup, Green Bay vs. Tampa Bay, September 15
  Clyde Simmons, Philadelphia at Dallas, September 15
  Pepper Johnson, Giants at Tampa Bay, November 24
- **AFC:** 4.0—E.J. Junior, Miami at New England, October 6
  Derrick Thomas, Kansas City vs. Buffalo, October 7
  Jerrol Williams, Pittsburgh vs. Cleveland, December 22
  Leslie O'Neal, San Diego vs. Denver, December 22

Team Champion
- **NFC:** 55—Philadelphia
- **AFC:** 52—Denver

AFC Sacks—Team

	Sacks	Yards
Denver	52	346
Houston	45	314
L.A. Raiders	42	283
Kansas City	39	304
Pittsburgh	38	257
Seattle	36	269
Cleveland	35	236
N.Y. Jets	35	226
Miami	35	248
Buffalo	31	246
Indianapolis	29	202
San Diego	28	183
New England	25	183
Cincinnati	21	129
AFC Total	491	3426
AFC Average	35.1	244.7

NFC Sacks—Team

	Sacks	Yards
Philadelphia	55	394
New Orleans	50	337
Washington	50	345
Green Bay	45	307
Chicago	40	257
Tampa Bay	39	258
N.Y. Giants	34	254
Minnesota	33	217
San Francisco	31	212
Detroit	30	237
Atlanta	29	237
Phoenix	25	153
Dallas	23	151
L.A. Rams	17	112
NFC Total	501	3471
NFC Average	35.8	247.9
NFL Total	992	6897
NFL Average	35.4	246.3

NFL Top 10 Individual Leaders in Sacks

	Total		Total
Swilling, Pat, N.O.	17.0	Bennett, Tony, G.B.	13.0
Fuller, William, Hou.	15.0	Simmons, Clyde, Phil.	13.0
White, Reggie, Phil.	15.0	Townsend, Greg, Raiders	13.0
Fletcher, Simon, Den.	13.5	Jackson, Rickey, N.O.	11.5
Thomas, Derrick, K.C.	13.5	Mann, Charles, Wash.	11.5

AFC Sacks—Individual

Fuller, William, Hou.	15.0
Fletcher, Simon, Den.	13.5
Thomas, Derrick, K.C.	13.5
Townsend, Greg, Raiders	13.0
Smith, Anthony, Raiders	10.5
Croel, Mike, Den.	10.0
Jones, Sean, Hou.	10.0
Lageman, Jeff, Jets	10.0
Porter, Rufus, Sea.	10.0
Bennett, Cornelius, Buff.	9.0
Mecklenburg, Karl, Den.	9.0
O'Neal, Leslie, S.D.	9.0
Williams, Jerrol, Pitt.	9.0
Perry, Michael Dean, Clev.	8.5
Tippett, Andre, N.E.	8.5
Lloyd, Greg, Pitt.	8.0
Smith, Neil, K.C.	8.0
Byrd, Dennis, Jets	7.0
Childress, Ray, Hou.	7.0
Cross, Jeff, Mia.	7.0
Seau, Junior, S.D.	7.0
Willis, Keith, Pitt.	7.0
Davis, Scott, Raiders	6.5
Kennedy, Cortez, Sea.	6.5
Matthews, Clay, Clev.	6.5
Green, Jacob, Sea.	6.0
Washington, Marvin, Jets	6.0
Wright, Jeff, Buff.	6.0
Griggs, David, Mia.	5.5
Grossman, Burt, S.D.	5.5
Bickett, Duane, Ind.	5.0
Hand, Jon, Ind.	5.0
Holmes, Ron, Den.	5.0
Junior, E.J., Mia.	5.0
Klingbeil, Chuck, Mia.	5.0
Martin, Chris, K.C.	5.0
Thompson, Donnell, Ind.	5.0
Krumrie, Tim, Cin.	4.0
Maas, Bill, K.C.	4.0
Stubbs, Danny, Dall.-Cin.	4.0
Talley, Darryl, Buff.	4.0
Turner, T.J., Mia.	4.0
Veris, Garin, N.E.	4.0
Kragen, Greg, Den.	3.5
Williams, Brent, N.E.	3.5
Brandon, David, Clev.	3.0
Brown, Vincent, N.E.	3.0
Bryant, Jeff, Sea.	3.0
Burnett, Rob, Clev.	3.0
Francis, James, Cin.	3.0
Long, Howie, Raiders	3.0
Mills, Jeff, Den.	3.0
Moss, Winston, Raiders	3.0
Walker, Kenny, Den.	3.0
Williams, Alfred, Cin.	3.0
Williams, Lee, Hou.	3.0
Clancy, Sam, Ind.	2.5
Glasgow, Nesby, Sea.	2.5
Herrod, Jeff, Ind.	2.5
Pleasant, Anthony, Clev.	2.5
Agnew, Ray, N.E.	2.0
Cox, Bryan, Mia.	2.0
Evans, Donald, Pitt.	2.0
Goode, Chris, Ind.	2.0
Gordon, Alex, Cin.	2.0
Grant, David, Cin.	2.0
Hansen, Phil, Buff.	2.0
Hilliard, Randy, Clev.	2.0
Hinkle, Bryan, Pitt.	2.0
Hobby, Marion, N.E.	2.0
Jones, Aaron, Pitt.	2.0
Lathon, Lamar, Hou.	2.0
Mersereau, Scott, Jets	2.0
Pickel, Bill, Jets	2.0
Powers, Warren, Den.	2.0
Simien, Tracy, K.C.	2.0
Siragusa, Tony, Ind.	2.0
Smith, Leonard, Buff.	2.0
Tuatagaloa, Natu, Cin.	2.0
Veasey, Craig, Pitt.	2.0
Wallace, Aaron, Raiders	2.0
Washington, Brian, Jets	2.0
Williams, Gerald, Pitt.	2.0
Wooden, Terry, Sea.	2.0
Woods, Tony, Sea.	2.0
Lodish, Mike, Buff.	1.5
Offerdahl, John, Mia.	1.5
Sagapolutele, Pio, Clev.	1.5
Saleaumua, Dan, K.C.	1.5
Smith, Bruce, Buff.	1.5
Waiters, Van, Clev.	1.5
Alm, Jeff, Hou.	1.0
Atwater, Steve, Den.	1.0
Ball, Michael, Ind.	1.0
Banks, Chip, Ind.	1.0
Barnett, Harlon, Clev.	1.0
Baylor, John, Ind.	1.0
Benson, Mitchell, S.D.	1.0
Benson, Thomas, Raiders	1.0
Billups, Lewis, Cin.	1.0
Blackmon, Robert, Sea.	1.0
Braggs, Stephen, Clev.	1.0
Braxton, Tyrone, Den.	1.0
Brim, Michael, Jets	1.0
Clifton, Kyle, Jets	1.0
Conover, Frank, Clev.	1.0
Curry, Shane, Ind.	1.0
Davis, Darrell, Jets	1.0
Elder, Donnie, S.D.	1.0
Everett, Eric, K.C.	1.0
Gardner, Donnie, Mia.	1.0
Golic, Bob, Raiders	1.0
Green, Hugh, Mia.	1.0
Hackett, Dino, K.C.	1.0
Harden, Bobby, Mia.	1.0
Harrison, Nolan, Raiders	1.0
Holloway, Cornell, Ind.	1.0
Houston, Bobby, Jets	1.0
Howard, David, N.E.	1.0
Jackson, Kirby, Buff.	1.0
Jackson, Steve, Hou.	1.0
Jefferson, James, Sea.	1.0
Johnson, David, Pitt.	1.0
Jones, James, Clev.	1.0
Lake, Carnell, Pitt.	1.0
Lewis, Darryll, Hou.	1.0
Lewis, Mo, Jets	1.0
Lott, Ronnie, Raiders	1.0
Marts, Lonnie, K.C.	1.0
McDowell, Bubba, Hou.	1.0
McMillan, Erik, Jets	1.0
Nickerson, Hardy, Pitt.	1.0
Odom, Cliff, Mia.	1.0
Odomes, Nate, Buff.	1.0
Pearson, J.C., K.C.	1.0
Phillips, Joe, S.D.	1.0
Plummer, Gary, S.D.	1.0
Porter, Kevin, K.C.	1.0
Robertson, Marcus, Hou.	1.0
Robinson, Eugene, Sea.	1.0
Rogers, Reggie, Buff.	1.0
Rolling, Henry, S.D.	1.0
Seals, Leon, Buff.	1.0
Shelton, Anthony, S.D.	1.0
Singleton, Chris, N.E.	1.0
Smith, Al, Hou.	1.0
Sochia, Brian, Den.	1.0
Thornton, John, Clev.	1.0
Walker, Kevin, Cin.	1.0
Woodson, Rod, Pitt.	1.0
Brown, Richard, Clev.	0.5
Comeaux, Darren, Sea.	0.5
Florence, Anthony, Clev.	0.5
Hinkle, George, S.D.	0.5
Kozak, Scott, Hou.	0.5
Logan, Ernie, Clev.	0.5
Skow, Jim, Sea.	0.5
Smith, Doug, Hou.	0.5

NFC Sacks—Individual

Swilling, Pat, N.O.	17.0
White, Reggie, Phil.	15.0
Bennett, Tony, G.B.	13.0
Simmons, Clyde, Phil.	13.0
Jackson, Rickey, N.O.	11.5
Mann, Charles, Wash.	11.5
Marshall, Leonard, Giants	11.0
Thomas, Broderick, T.B.	11.0
Dent, Richard, Chi.	10.5
Randle, John, Minn.	9.5
Brown, Jerome, Phil.	9.0
Harvey, Ken, Phx.	9.0
McMichael, Steve, Chi.	9.0
Roper, John, Chi.	8.0
Thomas, Henry, Minn.	8.0
Paup, Bryce, G.B.	7.5
Doleman, Chris, Minn.	7.0
Haley, Charles, S.F.	7.0
Nunn, Freddie Joe, Phx.	7.0
Roberts, Larry, S.F.	7.0
Taylor, Lawrence, Giants	7.0
Tolbert, Tony, Dall.	7.0
Warren, Frank, N.O.	7.0
Johnson, Pepper, Giants	6.5
Joyner, Seth, Phil.	6.5
Manley, Dexter, T.B.	6.5
Stokes, Fred, Wash.	6.5
Hunter, Jeff, Det.	6.0
Marshall, Wilber, Wash.	5.5
Owens, Dan, Det.	5.5
Perry, William, Chi.	5.5
Green, Tim, Atl.	5.0
McCants, Keith, T.B.	5.0
Newton, Tim, T.B.	5.0
Archambeau, Lester, G.B.	4.5
Geathers, James, Wash.	4.5
Maryland, Russell, Dall.	4.5
Wilson, Bobby, Wash.	4.5
Banks, Carl, Giants	4.0
Brown, Robert, G.B.	4.0
Jamison, George, Det.	4.0
Jeffcoat, Jim, Dall.	4.0
Jordan, Brian, Atl.	4.0
Swann, Eric, Phx.	4.0
Coleman, Monte, Wash.	3.5
Conner, Darion, Atl.	3.5
Davis, Reuben, T.B.	3.5
Johnson, Tim, Wash.	3.5
Martin, Wayne, N.O.	3.5
Spindler, Marc, Det.	3.5
Tuaolo, Esera, G.B.	3.5
Atkins, Gene, N.O.	3.0
Brown, Dennis, S.F.	3.0
Bryan, Rick, Atl.	3.0
Collins, Andre, Wash.	3.0
Gardner, Moe, Atl.	3.0
Greene, Kevin, Rams	3.0
Harris, Tim, S.F.	3.0
Holt, Pierce, S.F.	3.0
Noga, Al, Minn.	3.0
Robinson, Gerald, Rams	3.0
Williams, Eric, Wash.	3.0
Brock, Matt, G.B.	2.5
Casillas, Tony, Dall.	2.5
Golic, Mike, Phil.	2.5
Miller, Corey, Giants	2.5
Noble, Brian, G.B.	2.5
Strauthers, Tom, Minn.	2.5
Ball, Jerry, Det.	2.0
Fagan, Kevin, S.F.	2.0
Faulkner, Jeff, Phx.	2.0
Goff, Robert, N.O.	2.0
Hayworth, Tracy, Det.	2.0
Hopkins, Wes, Phil.	2.0
Jones, Jimmie, Dall.	2.0
Kelm, Larry, Rams	2.0
Mitchell, Brian, Atl.	2.0
Phifer, Roman, Rams	2.0
Pitts, Mike, Phil.	2.0
Shelley, Elbert, Atl.	2.0
Thomas, William, Phil.	2.0
Wilks, Jim, N.O.	2.0
Wilson, Karl, Rams	2.0
Armstrong, Trace, Chi.	1.5
Buck, Jason, Wash.	1.5
Dent, Burnell, G.B.	1.5
Epps, Tory, Atl.	1.5
Howard, Erik, Giants	1.5
Patterson, Shawn, G.B.	1.5
Pete, Lawrence, Det.	1.5
Pritchett, Kelvin, Det.	1.5
Ryan, Tim, Chi.	1.5
Stephen, Scott, G.B.	1.5
Barnett, Oliver, Atl.	1.0
Berry, Ray, Minn.	1.0
Booty, John, Phil.	1.0
Braxton, David, Phx.	1.0
Chamblee, Al, T.B.	1.0
Cofer, Mike, Det.	1.0
Covington, Tony, T.B.	1.0
Cox, Ron, Chi.	1.0
Crockett, Ray, Det.	1.0
DeLong, Keith, S.F.	1.0
Donaldson, Jeff, Atl.	1.0
Hall, Rhett, T.B.	1.0
Hill, Eric, Phx.	1.0
Jenkins, Izel, Phil.	1.0
Jenkins, Mel, Det.	1.0
Johnson, A.J., Wash.	1.0
Johnson, Sidney, Wash.	1.0
Koch, Markus, Wash.	1.0
Mangum, John, Chi.	1.0
Mayes, Michael, Minn.	1.0
Merriweather, Mike, Minn.	1.0
Miller, Les, N.O.	1.0
Mills, Sam, N.O.	1.0
Mitchell, Roland, G.B.	1.0
Murphy, Kevin, T.B.	1.0
Murphy, Mark, G.B.	1.0
Newman, Anthony, Rams	1.0
Nichols, Gerald, T.B.	1.0
Noonan, Danny, Dall.	1.0
Piel, Mike, Rams	1.0
Reynolds, Ricky, T.B.	1.0
Romanowski, Bill, S.F.	1.0
Sanders, Deion, Atl.	1.0
Seals, Ray, T.B.	1.0
Spielman, Chris, Det.	1.0
Stewart, Michael, Rams	1.0
Strickland, Fred, Rams	1.0
Tiggle, Calvin, T.B.	1.0
Tippins, Kenny, Atl.	1.0
Tuggle, Jessie, Atl.	1.0
Turnbull, Renaldo, N.O.	1.0
Wahler, Jim, Phx.	1.0
Washington, Ted, S.F.	1.0
Waymer, Dave, S.F.	1.0
Whitmore, Dave, S.F.	1.0
Williams, James, Chi.	1.0
Williams, James, N.O.	1.0
Williams, Robert, Dall.	1.0
Woolford, Donnell, Chi.	1.0
Young, Robert, Rams	1.0
Dorsey, Eric, Giants	0.5
Freeman, Lorenzo, Giants	0.5
Walls, Everson, Giants	0.5

1991 NFL Paid Attendance Breakdown

	Games	Attendance	Average
AFC Preseason	7	379,728	54,247
NFC Preseason	7	396,865	56,695
AFC-NFC Preseason, Interconference	46	2,320,840	50,453
NFL Preseason Total	**60**	**3,097,433**	**51,624**
AFC Regular Season	86	5,368,197	62,421
NFC Regular Season	86	5,202,915	60,499
AFC-NFC Regular Season, Interconference	52	3,270,347	62,891
NFL Regular Season Total	**224**	**13,841,459**	**61,792**
AFC Wild Card Playoffs	2		
(L.A. Raiders at Kansas City)		77,130	
(N.Y. Jets at Houston)		62,838	
AFC Divisional Playoffs	2		
(Houston at Denver)		75,392	
(Kansas City at Buffalo)		79,731	
AFC Championship Game	1		
(Denver at Buffalo)		80,377	
NFC Wild Card Playoffs	2		
(Atlanta at New Orleans)		68,299	
(Dallas at Chicago)		66,213	
NFC Divisional Playoffs	2		
(Atlanta at Washington)		55,177	
(Dallas at Detroit)		79,166	
NFC Championship Game	1		
(Detroit at Washington)		55,585	
Super Bowl XXVI at Minneapolis, Minnesota	1		
(Washington vs. Buffalo)		63,130	
AFC-NFC Pro Bowl at Honolulu, Hawaii	1	50,209	
NFL Postseason Total	**12**	**813,247**	**67,771**
NFL All Games	**296**	**17,752,139**	**59,973**

One Million Plus Club

During the 1991 season, 14 clubs drew a combined home and away paid attendance of more than 1 million. The Buffalo Bills drew an NFL-leading 1,154,362 fans in 1991.

Team	Total Paid Home Attendance	Total Paid Visiting Attendance	Total Paid Attendance
Buffalo	631,786	522,576	1,154,362
Kansas City	610,844	495,087	1,105.931
New York Jets	602,255	503,577	1,105,832
New York Giants	608,953	491,220	1,100,173
Denver	595,276	481,372	1,076,648
San Francisco	522,759	548,003	1,070,762
Chicago	529,230	539,178	1,068,408
Dallas	493,177	541,207	1,034,384
Cleveland	575,711	454,973	1,030,684
New Orleans	540,740	475,062	1,015,802
Miami	499,613	515,428	1,015,041
Cincinnati	465,205	542,577	1,007,782
Los Angeles Raiders	487,829	519,769	1,007,598
Pittsburgh	472,352	533,674	1,006,026

INSIDE THE NUMBERS

The NFL A to Z—Regular Season 208

The NFL A to Z—Postseason 208

Joe Montana's Career Passing Statistics 209

Joe Montana's Career Postseason Passing Statistics 209

All-Time Passer Rankings in Different Categories 210

Records of NFL Teams, 1981-1991 210

Most Points in a Game By Each NFL Team 212

Teams That Have Scored Sixty Points in a Game 213

NFL's Oldest/Youngest Starters in 1991 213

Eric Dickerson's Career Rushing vs. Each Opponent 213

Roger Craig's Career Rushing vs. Each Opponent 213

Joe Montana's Career Passing vs. Each Opponent 214

Phil Simms's Career Passing vs. Each Opponent 214

Dan Marino's Career Passing vs. Each Opponent 214

John Elway's Career Passing vs. Each Opponent 214

Boomer Esiason's Career Passing vs. Each Opponent 214

Warren Moon's Career Passing vs. Each Opponent 214

Jim Kelly's Career Passing vs. Each Opponent 215

Jerry Rice's Career Receiving vs. Each Opponent 215

Art Monk's Career Receiving vs. Each Opponent 215

Starting Records of Active NFL Quarterbacks 216

Individual Leaders Over Last Two, Three, Four Seasons . . . 216

Team Leaders Over Last Two, Three, Four Seasons 216

Opening Day Records, 1933-1991 217

Oldest NFL Records 217

Largest Trades in NFL History 217

Retired Uniform Numbers 217

1991 Score By Quarters 218

Greatest Comebacks in NFL History 219

Teams' Records Since AFL-NFL Merger 220

Longest Winning Streaks Since 1970 221

NFL Playoff Appearances By Seasons 221

Teams in Super Bowl Contention, 1978-1991 221

Games Decided by 7 Points or Less and 3 Points or Less 221

All-Time Records of Current NFL Teams 222

The NFL A to Z—Regular Season

AFC Central Division teams won only two of their 16 games against NFC East Division teams in 1991. Overall, NFC teams held a 33-19 advantage over the AFC in last year's interconference games, the NFC's third consecutive year winning more than 60 percent of those meetings.

Bernie Kosar avoids interceptions better than any quarterback in NFL history. His career rate of 2.49 interceptions per 100 passes is the lowest ever, and last season he completed a streak of 308 consecutive passes without an interception.

Chris Martin's 100-yard run with a recovered fumble last October 13 vs. Miami was the second-longest such play in NFL history. Jack Tatum of Oakland went 104 yards after recovering a Green Bay fumble in 1972.

Dan Marino has become the first player in NFL history to pass for 3,000 or more yards in eight different seasons, and he has done it in eight consecutive years.

Erik McMillan of the Jets was the only NFL player to return two interceptions for touchdowns last season. Touchdown returns are a specialty of his—in his four years in the NFL, McMillan has scored seven touchdowns (five on interception returns and two on returns of recovered fumbles).

Fifty percent of all NFL regular-season games last season—that's 112 of 224—were decided by seven points or fewer. The New York Giants played the most such games, splitting 12 games with a final margin in that range.

Going into the 1992 season, Steve Largent holds the all-time NFL career records for receptions (819), yards on receptions (13,089), and touchdown receptions (100). However, he is under challenge in all three categories, by three different receivers. Washington's Art Monk has 801 receptions, Buffalo's James Lofton has 13,035 yards on receptions, and San Francisco's Jerry Rice has caught 93 touchdown passes.

Head coaches who will make their NFL debuts in 1992: Bill Cowher (Pittsburgh), Dennis Green (Minnesota), Mike Holmgren (Green Bay), Bobby Ross (San Diego), and Dave Shula (Cincinnati). Four other head coaches start the 1992 season with new teams: Tom Flores (Seattle), Chuck Knox (Los Angeles Rams), Ted Marchibroda (Indianapolis), and Sam Wyche (Tampa Bay).

Irving Fryar, New England's wide receiver and kick returner, is the American Football Conference's active leader in total punt return yardage with 2,055.

Jeff George of Indianapolis was the seventh quarterback to be the top selection in the NFL draft since 1970, and the first to throw more touchdown passes than interceptions in his first two seasons.

Kurt Gouveia of the Washington Redskins, who has only two interceptions in 72 regular-season NFL games, intercepted a pass in each of Washington's three 1991 postseason games.

Longest regular-season consecutive scoring streak belongs to Cincinnati Bengals kicker Jim Breech, who has scored in each of his 181 regular-season games.

Miami led the NFL in fewest penalties (62) last season, the twelfth time in the past 16 years that the Dolphins have paced the league in that category.

No NFL team has a better record on Monday night than the Los Angeles Raiders, who are 29-8-1 entering the 1992 season. The Raiders will make two Monday night appearances this season—September 28 at Kansas City and December 14 at Miami.

Oilers quarterback Warren Moon completed 41 passes against the Dallas Cowboys on November 10, 1991. The NFL record for most completions in a single game (42) is held by former New York Jets quarterback Richard Todd vs. San Francisco on September 21, 1980.

Philadelphia last season became only the seventh team in history, and only the second since the 1970 merger, to allow the fewest rushing yards, the fewest passing yards, and the fewest overall yards in the same season. Minnesota accomplished it in 1975; before that, it was done by the 1954 Browns, the 1959 Giants, the 1963 Bears, the 1965 Chargers, and the 1969 Chiefs.

Quick quiz: Who is the only player in NFL history to amass 5,000 yards rushing and 5,000 yards on receptions? It's Hall-of-Famer Lenny Moore, who gained 5,174 yards rushing and 6,039 on receptions for the Baltimore Colts, 1956-67.

Referee Pat Haggerty is entering his twenty-eighth season as an NFL official, the longest tenure of any active on-field official.

Steve Young (101.8) of the 49ers led the NFL in passing last season, while teammate Steve Bono (88.5) finished fourth. You have to go back to 1956 to find the last time that two teammates finished among the league's top five passers; that year, the Rams' Bill Wade ranked second and Norm Van Brocklin finished fourth.

The 49ers have not been shut out in their last 226 regular-season games, the second-longest such streak in NFL history. The Browns set the all-time mark of 274 consecutive games without being shut out from 1950 to 1971.

Under the NFL's passer rating system, 10 of the top 20 quarterbacks in the history of the league are still active, including the top four: Joe Montana (93.4), Dan Marino (88.2), Jim Kelly (88.0), and Boomer Esiason (84.0).

Vai Sikahema, Philadelphia's running back and kick returner, was the last NFL player to return two punts for touchdowns in a game (December 21, 1986). Sikahema, who played for the St. Louis Cardinals at the time of the record, had two touchdown returns against the Tampa Bay Buccaneers. His touchdown returns covered 71 and 60 yards. Sikahema is the NFL's active punt return yardage leader with 2,391.

When Mike Ditka starts his eleventh consecutive season as the Chicago Bears' head coach in 1992, he will set a club record in that category. How can that be when George Halas was the Bears' head coach for an NFL-record 40 years? Halas served his 40 years as head coach in four 10-year segments.

XXV most valuable player Ottis Anderson of the Super Bowl XXV champion New York Giants enters the 1992 NFL season as the leading active rusher in the National Football Conference with 10,242 yards.

Youngest regular starter in the NFL last season? Ed King, a rookie guard with the Cleveland Browns, who was born on December 3, 1969. The oldest was Kansas City Chiefs quarterback Steve DeBerg, born on January 19, 1954.

Zendejas has been a popular name for kickers in recent years; no fewer than four family members have kicked in the NFL. Last year, Tony Zendejas of the Los Angeles Rams became the first kicker in NFL history to go through an entire season without missing a field-goal attempt. He went 17 for 17.

The NFL A to Z—Postseason

Attendance for the first 26 Super Bowls has totaled 2,090,633 for an average of 80,409.

Buffalo Bills seek a record-tying third consecutive conference title. Should the Bills win the AFC crown in 1992, they would match the Miami Dolphins (1971, 1972, and 1973) as the only teams to win three consecutive AFC titles.

Chicago Bears coach Mike Ditka is the NFC's only head coach who has won a Super Bowl as a player, assistant coach, and head coach. Ditka is also the only coach in club history to lead the Bears to five straight postseason appearances (1984-88). Seattle Seahawks coach Tom Flores is the only AFC coach who has won Super Bowl titles as a player, assistant coach, and head coach.

Dan McGuire Award winner for the 1992 AFC-NFC Pro Bowl was wide receiver Michael Irvin of the Dallas Cowboys. The award is presented annually to the Pro Bowl's player of the game.

Every Super Bowl champion, since the AFL-NFL merger in 1970, with the exception of the Oakland Raiders in 1981, has also been an AFC or NFC division champion. The Raiders, who qualified for the playoffs as a Wild Card in 1981, defeated the Philadelphia Eagles 27-10 in Super Bowl XV.

For the first time in 34 years, the Detroit Lions played a playoff game at their home stadium during the 1991 postseason. Detroit faced the Dallas Cowboys in the NFC Divisional Playoffs and came away a 38-6 winner. The Lions met the Washington Redskins in the NFC Championship Game and fell 41-10. In 1991, Detroit, 12-4, captured its first NFC Central Division title since 1983.

Going into the 1992 season, the Dallas Cowboys are the winningest team in postseason play with a 21-17 record. Dallas made the playoffs for the first time since 1985 last season and defeated the Chicago Bears 17-13 in an NFC Wild Card Game before losing to the Detroit Lions 38-6 in the NFC Divisional Playoffs.

Home team in Super Bowl XXVII will be the National Football Conference champion. The American Football Conference Buffalo Bills were the home team at Super Bowl XXVI played in Minneapolis. The home team has won 11 Super Bowls; visiting teams have won 15.

In the Raiders' first-round playoff game against the Chiefs on December 28, Ronnie Lott intercepted a pass, moving him into a tie with Charlie Waters and Bill Simpson for the most career interceptions (nine) in postseason play. Lott's next postseason interception would make him the NFL's all-time postseason leader with 10.

January 31, 1993, is the date for Super Bowl XXVII, which will match the latest date ever for a Super Bowl. On January 31, 1988, Washington defeated Denver 42-10 in Super Bowl XXII at San Diego Jack Murphy Stadium.

Kansas City's Mike Mercer kicked the first field goal in Super Bowl history, a 31-yarder against Green Bay in Super Bowl I on January 15, 1967.

Longest field goal in postseason play was a 58-yarder by Miami Dolphins kicker Pete Stoyanovich against the Kansas City Chiefs in a 1990 AFC Wild Card game.

Mark Rypien of the world champion Washington Redskins won the Pete Rozelle Trophy as the most valuable player of Super Bowl XXVI. Rypien completed 18 of 33 passes for 292 yards and had touchdown passes of 10 and 30 yards in his club's 37-24 victory over Buffalo. The Super Bowl MVP Trophy was renamed the Pete Rozelle Trophy in November, 1990, and was awarded for the first time to Ottis Anderson of the New York Giants following Super Bowl XXV.

NFC teams have won the last eight Super Bowls to take a 14-12 lead over the AFC in Super Bowl competition.

One hundred twenty million people in the United States and 750 million in more than 60 countries worldwide watched Super Bowl XXVI last year. The audience was the third highest in television history, behind Super Bowl XX (127 million) and the final episode of M·A·S·H. (121 million).

Pasadena's Rose Bowl is the site for Super Bowl XXVII. It will mark the fifth time that the NFL Championship Game will be played in the southern California city. Past Super Bowls played in Pasadena were XI, XIV, XVII, and XXI.

Quiz time. Who is the only player in NFL history to be a member of three different Super Bowl winning franchises? Answer—Matt Millen. Along with being a member of Super Bowl XXVI champion Washington Redskins, he was also a part of the championship Raiders' teams in Super Bowls XV and XVIII and with the San Francisco 49ers in Super Bowl XXIV.

Rice, as in San Francisco 49ers Pro Bowl wide receiver Jerry Rice, currently has 61 receptions in 11 postseason games and needs 13 catches to become the NFL's all-time leading postseason receiver. Former Raiders wide receiver Cliff Branch is the NFL's all-time leader with 73 receptions in 22 postseason games.

Super Bowl XXVII will be televised by NBC. It will be the twelfth Super Bowl broadcast by the network. NBC has televised Super Bowls I, III, V, VII, IX, XI, XIII, XV, XVII, XX, and XXIII.

Ten-and-a-half quarterback sacks in the playoffs by Chicago's Richard Dent equal the most by a player in NFL postseason history. Dent has accomplished the record in 10 postseason games.

Under Los Angeles Raiders head coach Art Shell, the AFC defeated the NFC 23-21 in the 1991 AFC-NFC Pro Bowl. Shell, an eight-time Pro Bowl tackle with the Raiders, the most in club history, became the first former AFC-NFC Pro Bowl player ever to coach a winning Pro Bowl team.

Victories in all three of the Washington Redskins' postseason games, culminating in Super Bowl XXVI, increased Joe Gibbs's career total of postseason wins to 15. Only Tom Landry (20), Don Shula (17), and Chuck Noll (16) have won more postseason games.

Winning shares for NFL players participating in the 1991 postseason totaled $14.9 million. The Super Bowl champion Redskins each received $64,000, while the AFC champion Bills each received $46,000.

XXVI marked the first Super Bowl to be played in a stadium (Metrodome in Minneapolis, Minnesota) that hosted the World Series three months earlier. Two other facilities (Los Angeles Memorial Coliseum and San Diego Jack Murphy Stadium) have hosted both a Super Bowl and a World Series, but in different seasons.

Yet another Super Bowl appearance by the Washington Redskins or the Miami Dolphins in 1993 would give both teams an NFL-high six appearances in the league's championship game. Washington's five previous trips to the Super Bowl were in January of 1973, 1983, 1984, 1988, and 1992. Miami made it to Super Bowls in January of 1972, 1973, 1974, 1983, and 1985.

Zero. The number of games the 1972 Miami Dolphins lost en route to winning Super Bowl VII. It was 20 years ago that Don Shula's Dolphins became the first team to go undefeated and untied in an NFL season.

Comparison of Joe Montana's Career Statistics With Hall of Fame Quarterbacks Whose Careers Ended Since 1945

Passing

	Att.	Comp.	Pct.	Yds.	Avg.	Lng.	TD	Pct.	Int.	Pct.	Rating
Joe Montana	4579	2914	63.6	34,998	7.64	96t	242	5.3	123	2.7	93.4
Sammy Baugh	2995	1693	56.5	21,886	7.31	86t	187	6.2	203	6.8	72.0
George Blanda	4007	1911	47.7	26,920	6.72	95t	236	5.9	277	6.9	60.8
Terry Bradshaw	3901	2025	51.9	27,989	7.17	90t	212	5.4	210	5.4	70.9
Len Dawson	3741	2136	57.1	28,711	7.67	92t	239	6.4	183	4.9	82.6
Otto Graham	1565	872	55.7	13,499	8.63	81t	88	5.6	94	6.0	78.1
Bob Griese	3429	1926	56.2	25,092	7.32	86t	192	5.6	172	5.0	77.1
Arnie Herber*	1175	481	40.9	8,041	6.84	92t	78	6.6	106	9.0	49.3
Sonny Jurgensen	4262	2433	57.1	32,224	7.56	99t	255	6.0	189	4.4	82.8
Bobby Layne	3700	1814	49.0	26,768	7.23	97t	196	5.3	243	6.6	63.4
Sid Luckman	1744	904	51.8	14,686	8.42	86t	137	7.9	132	7.6	75.0
Joe Namath	3762	1886	50.1	27,663	7.35	91	173	4.6	220	5.8	65.6
Bart Starr	3149	1808	57.4	24,718	7.85	91t	152	4.8	138	4.4	80.5
Roger Staubach	2958	1685	57.0	22,700	7.67	91t	153	5.2	109	3.7	83.4
Fran Tarkenton	6467	3686	57.0	47,003	7.27	89t	342	5.3	266	4.1	80.4
Y.A. Tittle	3817	2118	55.5	28,339	7.42	78t	212	5.6	221	5.8	73.8
Johnny Unitas	5186	2830	54.6	40,239	7.76	89t	290	5.6	253	4.9	78.2
Norm Van Brocklin	2895	1553	53.6	23,611	8.16	91t	173	6.0	178	6.1	75.3
Bob Waterfield	1617	814	50.3	11,849	7.33	91t	97	6.0	128	7.9	61.6

Rushing

	Yrs.	Last Year	G	Att.	Yds.	Avg.	Lng.	TD
Joe Montana	12	1990	166	411	1567	3.8	21	20
Sammy Baugh	16	1952	165	324	325	1.0	41t	9
George Blanda	26	1975	340	135	344	2.5	19	9
Terry Bradshaw	14	1983	168	444	2257	5.1	39	32
Len Dawson	19	1975	211	294	1293	4.4	43	9
Otto Graham	6	1955	72	306	682	2.2	36	33
Bob Griese	14	1980	161	261	994	3.8	35	7
Arnie Herber*	13	1945	x	250	116	0.5	x	2
Sonny Jurgensen	18	1974	218	181	492	2.7	33	15
Bobby Layne	15	1962	175	611	2451	4.0	36	25
Sid Luckman	12	1950	128	204	−239	−1.2	40t	4
Joe Namath	13	1977	140	71	140	2.0	39	7
Bart Starr	16	1971	196	247	1308	5.3	39	15
Roger Staubach	11	1979	131	410	2264	5.5	33	20
Fran Tarkenton	18	1978	246	675	3674	5.4	52t	32
Y.A. Tittle	15	1964	178	291	999	3.4	45	33
Johnny Unitas	18	1973	211	450	1777	3.9	34	13
Norm Van Brocklin	12	1960	140	102	40	0.4	16	11
Bob Waterfield	8	1952	91	75	21	0.3	25	13

*statistics do not include 1930-31 seasons. xUnavailable.

Joe Montana's Game-by-Game Postseason Career

Date	Game	Opponent	Att.	Comp.	Pct.	Yds.	Avg.	TD	Int.	Rating
Jan. 3, 1982	NFC Divisional Playoff	N.Y. Giants	31	20	64.5	304	9.81	2	1	104.8
Jan. 10, 1982	NFC Championship Game	Dallas	35	22	62.9	286	8.17	3	3	81.4
Jan. 24, 1982	Super Bowl XVI	Cincinnati	22	14	63.6	157	7.14	1	0	100.0
Dec. 31, 1983	NFC Divisional Playoff	Detroit	31	18	58.1	201	6.48	1	1	74.8
Jan. 8, 1984	NFC Championship Game	Washington	48	27	56.3	347	7.23	3	1	91.2
Dec. 29, 1984	NFC Divisional Playoff	N.Y. Giants	39	25	64.1	309	7.92	3	3	82.1
Jan. 6, 1985	NFC Championship Game	Chicago	34	18	52.9	233	6.85	1	2	60.0
Jan. 20, 1985	Super Bowl XIX	Miami	35	24	68.6	331	9.46	3	0	127.2
Dec. 29, 1985	NFC First-Round Game	N.Y. Giants	47	26	55.3	296	6.30	0	1	65.6
Jan. 4, 1987	NFC Divisional Playoff	N.Y. Giants	15	8	53.3	98	6.53	0	2	34.2
Jan. 9, 1988	NFC Divisional Playoff	Minnesota	26	12	46.2	109	4.19	0	1	42.0
Jan. 1, 1989	NFC Divisional Playoff	Minnesota	27	16	59.3	178	6.59	3	1	100.5
Jan. 8, 1989	NFC Championship Game	Chicago	27	17	63.0	288	10.67	3	0	136.0

Date	Game	Opponent	Att.	Comp.	Pct.	Yds.	Avg.	TD	Int.	Rating
Jan. 22, 1989	Super Bowl XXIII	Cincinnati	36	23	63.9	357	9.92	2	0	115.2
Jan. 6, 1990	NFC Divisional Playoff	Minnesota	24	17	70.8	241	10.04	4	0	142.5
Jan. 14, 1990	NFC Championship Game	L.A. Rams	30	26	86.7	262	8.73	2	0	125.3
Jan. 28, 1990	Super Bowl XXIV	Denver	29	22	75.9	297	10.24	5	0	147.6
Jan. 12, 1991	NFC Divisional Playoff	Washington	31	22	71.0	274	8.84	2	1	106.1
Jan. 20, 1991	NFC Championship Game	N.Y. Giants	26	18	69.2	190	7.31	1	0	103.0
Totals (19 games)			593	375	63.2	4758	8.02	39	17	98.2

Highest NFL Postseason Passer Ratings (Minimum: 100 Attempts)

	Games	Att.	Comp.	Pct.	Yds.	Avg. Gain	TD	Int.	Rating
Bart Starr	10	213	130	61.0	1753	8.23	15	3	104.8
Joe Montana	19	593	375	63.2	4758	8.02	39	17	98.2
Ken Anderson	6	166	110	66.3	1321	7.96	9	6	93.5
Joe Theismann	10	211	128	60.7	1782	8.45	11	7	91.4
Ken Stabler	13	351	203	57.8	2641	7.52	19	13	84.2
Warren Moon	7	258	162	62.8	1901	7.37	10	9	83.5
Terry Bradshaw	19	456	261	57.2	3833	8.41	30	26	83.0
Phil Simms	8	228	128	56.1	1461	6.41	10	4	82.9
Jim Plunkett	10	272	162	59.6	2293	8.43	11	12	81.9
Bernie Kosar	7	260	146	56.2	1860	7.15	15	10	81.9

Highest NFL Postseason Passer Ratings, Active Players (Minimum: 100 Attempts)

	Games	Att.	Comp.	Pct.	Yds.	Avg. Gain	TD	Int.	Rating
Joe Montana	19	593	375	63.2	4758	8.02	39	17	98.2
Warren Moon	7	258	162	62.8	1901	7.37	10	9	83.5
Phil Simms	8	228	128	56.1	1461	6.41	10	4	82.9
Bernie Kosar	7	260	146	56.2	1860	7.15	15	10	81.9
Dan Marino	8	313	173	55.3	2224	7.11	18	12	80.9
Mark Rypien	5	158	86	54.4	1257	7.96	7	6	79.5
Dave Krieg	7	183	94	51.4	1242	6.79	9	6	75.9
Wade Wilson	6	185	99	53.5	1322	7.15	7	6	75.6
Jim McMahon	7	130	70	53.8	967	7.44	4	4	75.4
John Elway	13	384	200	52.1	3019	7.86	16	17	73.7

All-Time Rankings of Players in Four Categories That Determine NFL Passer Rating
Minimum: 1500 Attempts

Completion Percentage

	Pct.	Att.	Comp.
Joe Montana	63.64	4579	2914
Jim Kelly	60.69	2562	1555
Ken Stabler	59.85	3793	2270
Danny White	59.69	2950	1761
Ken Anderson	59.31	4475	2654
Dan Marino	59.15	4730	2798
Ken O'Brien	58.92	3367	1984
Dan Fouts	58.83	5604	3297
Dave Krieg	58.61	3576	2096
Bernie Kosar	58.49	2857	1671

Touchdown Percentage

	Pct.	Att.	TD
Sid Luckman	7.86	1744	137
Frank Ryan	6.99	2133	149
Len Dawson	6.39	3741	239
Daryle Lamonica	6.31	2601	164
Sammy Baugh	6.24	2995	187
Charley Conerly	6.11	2833	173
Bob Waterfield	6.00	1617	97
Earl Morrall	5.99	2689	161
Sonny Jurgensen	5.98	4262	255
Norm Van Brocklin	5.98	2895	173

Average Yards Per Pass

	Avg.	Att.	Yards
Otto Graham	8.63	1565	13,499
Sid Luckman	8.42	1744	14,686
Norm Van Brocklin	8.16	2895	23,611
Ed Brown	7.85	1987	15,600
Bart Starr	7.85	3149	24,718
Boomer Esiason	7.83	3100	24,264
Johnny Unitas	7.76	5186	40,239
Earl Morrall	7.74	2689	20,809
Dan Fouts	7.68	5604	43,040
Len Dawson	7.67	3741	28,711

Interception Percentage

	Pct.	Att.	Int.
Bernie Kosar	2.49	2857	71
Ken O'Brien	2.64	3367	89
Joe Montana	2.69	4579	123
Neil Lomax	2.85	3153	90
Randall Cunningham	3.15	2257	71
Dan Marino	3.15	4730	149
Tony Eason	3.26	1564	51
Roman Gabriel	3.31	4498	149
Jim Kelly	3.47	2562	89
Don Majkowski	3.48	1552	54

Teams That Finished In First Place In Their Division the Season After Finishing in Last Place

Season	Team	Record	Previous Season
1967	Houston	9-4-1	*3-11
1968	Minnesota	8-6	3-8-3
1970	Cincinnati	8-6	4-9-1
1970	San Francisco	10-3-1	4-8-2
1972	Green Bay	10-4	4-8-2
1975	Baltimore	10-4	2-12
1979	Tampa Bay	10-6	5-11
1981	Cincinnati	12-4	6-10
1987	Indianapolis	9-6	3-13
1988	Cincinnati	12-4	4-11
1990	Cincinnati	9-7	8-8
1991	Denver	12-4	5-11

*tied for last place

Records of NFL Teams, 1982-91

AFC	W - L - T	Pct.	Division Titles	Playoff Berths	Postseason Record	Super Bowl Record
Miami	95-57-0	.625	3	5	7-5	0-2
Denver	92-59-1	.609	5	6	7-6	0-3
L.A. Raiders	92-60-0	.605	3	6	5-5	1-0
Seattle	84-68-0	.553	1	4	3-4	0-0
Cleveland	76-75-1	.503	4	6	3-6	0-0
Pittsburgh	76-76-0	.500	2	4	2-4	0-0
Cincinnati	75-77-0	.493	2	3	3-3	0-1
Buffalo	74-78-0	.487	4	4	5-4	0-2
N.Y. Jets	73-78-1	.484	0	4	3-4	0-0
New England	73-79-0	.480	1	3	3-3	0-1
Kansas City	70-80-2	.467	0	3	1-3	0-0
Houston	64-88-0	.421	1	5	3-5	0-0
San Diego	61-91-0	.401	0	1	1-1	0-0
Indianapolis	53-98-1	.352	1	1	0-1	0-0

NFC	W - L - T	Pct.	Division Titles	Playoff Berths	Postseason Record	Super Bowl Record
San Francisco	109-42-1	.720	7	8	11-5	3-0
Washington	107-45-0	.704	4	7	15-4	3-1
Chicago	101-51-0	.664	6	7	6-6	1-0
N.Y. Giants	89-62-1	.589	3	5	8-3	2-0
New Orleans	81-71-0	.533	1	3	0-3	0-0
L.A. Rams	77-75-0	.507	1	6	4-6	0-0
Minnesota	75-77-0	.493	1	4	4-4	0-0
Philadelphia	74-76-2	.493	1	3	0-3	0-0
Dallas	73-79-0	.480	1	4	3-4	0-0
Green Bay	62-88-2	.414	0	1	1-1	0-0

NFC	W - L - T	Pct.	Division Titles	Playoff Berths	Postseason Record	Super Bowl Record
Detroit	62-89-1	.411	2	3	1-3	0-0
Phoenix	59-91-2	.395	0	1	0-1	0-0
Atlanta	53-98-1	.352	0	2	1-2	0-0
Tampa Bay	40-112-0	.263	0	1	0-1	0-0

Indianapolis totals include Baltimore, 1982-83
Phoenix totals include St. Louis, 1982-87

In 1982, due to players' strike, the divisional format was abandoned.
(L.A. Raiders and Washington won regular-season conference titles, not included in "Division Titles" totals listed above. Sixteen teams were awarded playoff berths, included in totals listed above.)

Home Records, 1982-91

AFC	W - L - T	Pct.	NFC	W - L - T	Pct.
Denver	57-20-0	.740	Chicago	58-18-0	.763
Miami	54-21-0	.720	Washington	57-18-0	.760
Seattle	51-26-0	.662	N.Y. Giants	52-25-0	.675
L.A. Raiders	50-26-0	.658	San Francisco	51-25-0	.671
Kansas City	47-28-0	.627	Minnesota	46-31-0	.597
Pittsburgh	46-29-0	.613	New Orleans	44-32-0	.579
Buffalo	47-30-0	.610	L.A. Rams	40-36-0	.526
Cincinnati	46-30-0	.605	Dallas	39-37-0	.513
Houston	44-32-0	.579	Philadelphia	38-38-1	.500
Cleveland	42-32-1	.567	Detroit	35-40-1	.467
New England	43-33-0	.566	Green Bay	34-41-1	.454
N.Y. Jets	37-38-0	.493	Phoenix	32-42-1	.433
San Diego	36-39-0	.480	Atlanta	31-45-1	.409
Indianapolis	29-46-1	.388	Tampa Bay	28-48-0	.368

Road Records, 1982-91

AFC	W - L - T	Pct.	NFC	W - L - T	Pct.
L.A. Raiders	42-34-0	.553	San Francisco	58-17-0	.770
Miami	41-36-0	.532	Washington	50-27-0	.649
N.Y. Jets	36-40-0	.474	Chicago	43-33-0	.566
Denver	35-39-1	.473	N.Y. Giants	37-37-1	.500
Cleveland	34-43-0	.442	L.A. Rams	37-39-0	.487
Seattle	33-42-0	.440	New Orleans	37-39-0	.487
New England	30-46-0	.395	Philadelphia	36-38-1	.487
Pittsburgh	30-47-0	.390	Dallas	34-42-0	.447
Cincinnati	29-47-0	.382	Minnesota	29-46-0	.387
Buffalo	27-48-0	.360	Green Bay	28-47-1	.375
San Diego	25-52-0	.325	Phoenix	27-49-1	.357
Indianapolis	24-52-0	.316	Detroit	27-49-0	.355
Kansas City	23-52-2	.312	Atlanta	22-53-0	.293
Houston	20-56-0	.263	Tampa Bay	12-64-0	.158

Records by Months, 1982-91

AFC	Sept. W - L - T	Oct. W - L - T	Nov. W - L - T	*Dec. W - L - T	Total W - L - T	Pct.
Miami	22-15	23-14	25-15	25-13	95-57-0	.625
Denver	24-12-1	26-11	22-18	20-18	92-59-1	.609
L.A. Raiders	25-12	23-15	21-18	23-15	92-60-0	.605
Seattle	17-19	25-14	20-19	22-16	84-68-0	.553
Cleveland	17-19	20-19	21-17-1	18-20	76-75-1	.503
Pittsburgh	15-20	21-19	19-21	21-16	76-76-0	.500
Cincinnati	15-19	19-22	18-21	23-15	75-77-0	.493
Buffalo	21-16	20-17	20-20	13-25	74-78-0	.487
N.Y. Jets	22-15	18-19-1	20-21	13-23	73-78-1	.484
New England	16-21	19-18	20-20	18-20	73-79-0	.480
Kansas City	20-17	13-24-1	13-25-1	24-14	70-80-2	.467
Houston	13-23	17-22	19-20	15-23	64-88-0	.421
San Diego	13-24	12-27	20-19	16-21	61-91-0	.401
Indianapolis	8-29	16-21	14-26	15-22-1	53-98-1	.352

NFC	Sept. W - L - T	Oct. W - L - T	Nov. W - L - T	*Dec. W - L - T	Total W - L - T	Pct.
San Francisco	25-11	27-10-1	25-14	32-7	109-42-1	.720
Washington	25-12	25-12	29-12	28-9	107-45-0	.704
Chicago	27-10	26-11	30-11	18-19	101-51-0	.664
N.Y. Giants	22-15	21-15-1	24-15	22-17	89-62-1	.589
New Orleans	20-16	19-19	24-16	18-20	81-71-0	.533
L.A. Rams	22-14	19-19	20-20	16-22	77-75-0	.507
Minnesota	21-16	15-23	22-19	17-19	75-77-0	.493
Philadelphia	14-23	20-17	21-18-1	19-18-1	74-76-2	.493
Dallas	22-15	18-20	19-23	14-21	73-79-0	.480
Green Bay	10-26-1	16-21	18-22	18-19-1	62-88-2	.414
Detroit	14-23	16-21	16-25	16-20	62-89-1	.411
Phoenix	16-21	15-22-1	14-27	14-21-1	59-91-2	.395
Atlanta	15-21	12-25-1	12-28	14-24	53-98-1	.352
Tampa Bay	10-27	7-31	12-28	11-26	40-112-0	.263

Indianapolis totals include Baltimore, 1982-83
Phoenix totals include St. Louis, 1982-87

*Includes for each team one game played during January.

Takeaways/Giveaways in 1982-91

	Takeaways			Giveaways			
AFC	Int.	Fum.	Total	Int.	Fum.	Total	Net Diff.
Kansas City	209	165	374	170	142	312	62
Denver	210	159	369	188	142	330	39
Seattle	201	186	387	204	151	355	32
Pittsburgh	227	143	370	200	144	344	26
N.Y. Jets	189	145	334	160	156	316	18
Cincinnati	187	139	326	174	147	321	5
New England	173	166	339	191	145	336	3
Cleveland	193	126	319	168	149	317	2
Indianapolis	155	159	314	190	133	323	−9
Miami	183	123	306	180	144	324	−18
Houston	168	156	324	205	160	365	−41
L.A. Raiders	180	138	318	204	157	361	−43
Buffalo	168	145	313	211	161	372	−59
San Diego	181	142	323	226	156	382	−59

	Takeaways			Giveaways			
NFC	Int.	Fum.	Total	Int.	Fum.	Total	Net Diff.
San Francisco	212	137	349	134	141	275	74
Washington	220	142	362	169	136	305	57
Philadelphia	212	163	375	182	141	323	52
Minnesota	213	157	370	205	120	323	47
Chicago	233	132	365	182	161	343	22
N.Y. Giants	194	134	328	165	145	310	18
New Orleans	197	161	358	200	151	351	7
L.A. Rams	191	149	340	174	171	345	−5
Atlanta	176	148	324	181	157	338	−14
Detroit	180	156	336	209	154	363	−27
Dallas	183	147	330	224	144	368	−38
Phoenix	157	142	299	187	153	340	−41
Green Bay	187	163	350	232	168	400	−50
Tampa Bay	179	166	343	243	160	403	−60

Indianapolis totals include Baltimore, 1982-83
Phoenix totals include St. Louis, 1982-87

High and Low Single-Game Yardage Totals, 1982-91

Most Total Yards, Game
676 Washington vs. Detroit, Nov. 4, 1990 (OT)
661 San Diego vs. Cincinnati, Dec. 20, 1982
621 Cincinnati vs. N.Y. Jets, Dec. 21, 1986
597 N.Y. Jets vs. Miami, Nov. 27, 1988
593 San Diego vs. L.A. Raiders, Nov. 10, 1985 (OT)

Fewest Total Yards, Game
53 Pittsburgh vs. Cleveland, Sept. 10, 1989
57 New England vs. N.Y. Jets, Sept. 19, 1982
60 Detroit vs. Minnesota, Nov. 24, 1988
65 Tampa Bay vs. Green Bay, Dec. 1, 1985
65 Seattle vs. New England, Dec. 4, 1988

Most Yards Rushing, Game
356 L.A. Raiders vs. Seattle, Nov. 30, 1987
328 New England vs. N.Y. Jets, Sept. 18, 1983
310 Kansas City vs. Detroit, Oct. 14, 1990
307 Washington vs. Atlanta, Nov. 3, 1985
305 Pittsburgh vs. Miami, Dec. 18, 1988

Fewest Yards Rushing, Game
0 Buffalo vs. Chicago, Oct. 2, 1988
1 Tampa Bay vs. Washington, Oct. 22, 1989
2 New England vs. New Orleans, Nov. 30, 1986
4 Indianapolis vs. Detroit, Sept. 22, 1991
6 N.Y. Giants vs. L.A. Rams, Nov. 12, 1989

Most Yards Passing, Game
521 Miami vs. N.Y. Jets, Oct. 23, 1988
506 L.A. Rams vs. Chicago, Dec. 26, 1982
505 Houston vs. Kansas City, Dec. 16, 1990
494 San Diego vs. Seattle, Sept. 15, 1985
486 San Diego vs. Cincinnati, Dec. 20, 1982

Fewest Yards Passing, Game
−22 Atlanta vs. Chicago, Nov. 24, 1985
−13 Cincinnati vs. San Diego, Oct. 4, 1987
−4 New England vs. N.Y. Jets, Sept. 19, 1982
−2 Pittsburgh vs. Buffalo, Dec. 12, 1982
1 Denver vs. Pittsburgh, Sept. 4, 1983

NFL Individual Leaders, 1982-91

Points	Touchdowns	Field Goals
1043, Nick Lowery	97, Jerry Rice	238, Nick Lowery
1010, Gary Anderson	95, Marcus Allen	229, Gary Anderson
965, Morten Andersen	93, Eric Dickerson	217, Morten Andersen
925, Jim Breech	79, Mark Clayton	192, Eddie Murray
922, Pat Leahy	73, James Brooks	190, Pat Leahy

Rushes	Rushing Yards	Rushing TDs	TD Passes	Receptions	Reception Yards
2783, Eric Dickerson	12439, Eric Dickerson	88, Eric Dickerson	266, Dan Marino	687, Art Monk	9293, Art Monk
2023, Marcus Allen	8244, Marcus Allen	77, Marcus Allen	207, Joe Montana	526, Jerry Rice	9072, Jerry Rice
1989, Gerald Riggs	8188, Gerald Riggs	69, Gerald Riggs	188, Dave Krieg	525, Roger Craig	8729, James Lofton
1848, Roger Craig	7654, Roger Craig	56, Curt Warner	163, Boomer Esiason	517, Roy Green	8137, Roy Green
1698, Curt Warner	7393, James Brooks	55, Ottis Anderson	157, Warren Moon	507, Mark Clayton	8107, Mark Duper

Passes	Completions	Passing Yards	Receiving TDs	Interceptions	Sacks
4730, Dan Marino	2798, Dan Marino	35,386, Dan Marino	93, Jerry Rice	52, Ronnie Lott	121.5, Lawrence Taylor
4023, John Elway	2414, Joe Montana	29,542, Joe Montana	78, Mark Clayton	49, Deron Cherry	110.0, Reggie White
3795, Joe Montana	2201, John Elway	27,974, John Elway	62, Roy Green	44, Dave Waymer	103.5, Richard Dent
3680, Warren Moon	2105, Warren Moon	27,679, Warren Moon	61, Mike Quick	43, Everson Walls	97.5, Jacob Green
3462, Dave Krieg	2032, Dave Krieg	25,289, Dave Krieg	54, Steve Largent	38, Dave Brown	97.5, Dexter Manley
				38, Gill Byrd	

Records for Each Current NFL Team for Most Points in a Game (Regular Season Only)

Note: When the record has been achieved more than once, only the most recent game is shown; summaries are listed in alphabetical order by conference. Bold face indicates team holding record.

BUFFALO BILLS
September 18, 1966, at Buffalo

Miami . . . . 3 7 0 14 — 24
Buffalo . . . . 21 23 3 7 — 58
TDs: Buff—Bobby Burnett 2, Butch Byrd 2, Jack Spikes 2, Bobby Crockett, Jack Kemp; Mia—Dave Kocourek, Bo Roberson, John Roderick. TD Passes: Buff—Jack Kemp, Daryle Lamonica; Mia—George Wilson 3. FGs: Buff—Booth Lusteg; Mia—Gene Mingo.

CINCINNATI BENGALS
December 17, 1989, at Cincinnati

Houston . . . . 0 0 7 — 7
Cincinnati . . . . 21 10 21 9 — 61
TDs: Cin—Eddie Brown 2, Eric Ball, James Brooks, Ira Hillary, Rodney Holman, Tim McGee, Craig Taylor; Hou—Lorenzo White. TD Passes: Cin—Boomer Esiason 4, Erik Wilhelm. FGs: Cin—Jim Breech 2.

CLEVELAND BROWNS
November 7, 1954, at Cleveland

Washington . . . . 0 3 0 0 — 3
Cleveland . . . . 13 14 21 14 — 62
TDs: Clev—Darrell Brewster 2, Mo Bassett, Ken Gorgal, Otto Graham, Dub Jones, Dante Lavelli, Curley Morrison. TD Passes: Clev—George Ratterman 3, Otto Graham. FGs: Clev—Lou Groza 2; Wash—Vic Janowicz.

DENVER BRONCOS
October 6, 1963, at Denver

San Diego . . . . 13 7 0 14 — 34
Denver . . . . 3 14 9 24 — 50
TDs: Den—Lionel Taylor 2, Goose Gonsoulin, Gene Prebola, Donnie Stone; SD—Keith Lincoln 2, Lance Alworth, Paul Lowe, Jacque MacKinnon. TD Passes: Den—John McCormick 3; SD—Tobin Rote 3, John Hadl 2. FGs: Den—Gene Mingo 5.

HOUSTON OILERS
December 9, 1990, at Houston

Cleveland . . . . 0 7 7 0 — 14
Houston . . . . 14 31 7 6 — 58
TDs: Hou—Lorenzo White 4, Ernest Givins, Leonard Harris, Tony Jones, Terry Kinard; Clev—Eric Metcalf 2. TD Passes: Hou—Warren Moon 2, Cody Carlson; Clev—Bernie Kosar. FG: Hou—Teddy Garcia.

INDIANAPOLIS COLTS
December 12, 1976, at Baltimore

Buffalo . . . . 3 3 7 7 — 20
Baltimore Colts . . . . . . 7 13 28 10 — 58
TDs: Balt—Roger Carr, Raymond Chester, Glenn Doughty, Roosevelt Leaks, Derrel Luce, Lydell Mitchell, Howard Stevens; Buff—Bob Chandler, O. J. Simpson. TD Passes: Balt—Bert Jones 3; Buff—Gary Marangi. FGs: Balt—Toni Linhart 3; Buff—George Jakowenko 2.

KANSAS CITY CHIEFS
September 7, 1963, at Denver

Kansas City . . . . 14 14 21 10 — 59
Denver . . . . 0 7 0 0 — 7
TDs: KC—Chris Burford 2, Frank Jackson 2, Dave Grayson, Abner Haynes, Sherrill Headrick, Curtis McClinton; Den—Lionel Taylor. TD Passes: KC—Len Dawson 4, Curtis McClinton; Den—Mickey Slaughter. FG: KC—Tommy Brooker.

LOS ANGELES RAIDERS
December 22, 1963, at Oakland

Houston . . . . 14 21 14 0 — 49
Oakland Raiders . . . . . . 7 28 7 10 — 52
TDs: Oak—Art Powell 4, Clem Daniels, Claude Gibson, Ken Herock; Hou—Willard Dewveall 2, Dave Smith 2, Charley Hennigan, Bob McLeod, Charley Tolar. TD Passes: Oak—Tom Flores 6; Hou—George Blanda 5. FG: Oak—Mike Mercer.

MIAMI DOLPHINS
November 24, 1977, at St. Louis

Miami . . . . 14 14 20 7 — 55
St. Louis . . . . 7 0 0 7 — 14
TDs: Mia—Nat Moore 3, Gary Davis, Duriel Harris, Leroy Harris, Benny Malone, Andre Tillman; StL—Ike Harris, Terry Metcalf. TD Passes: Mia—Bob Griese 6; StL—Jim Hart.

NEW ENGLAND PATRIOTS
September 9, 1979, at New England

New York Jets . . . . 3 0 0 0 — 3
New England . . . . 14 21 7 14 — 56
TDs: NE—Harold Jackson 3, Stanley Morgan 2, Allan Clark, Andy Johnson, Don Westbrook. TD Passes: NE—Steve Grogan 5, Tom Owen. FG: NYJ—Pat Leahy.

NEW YORK JETS
November 17, 1985, at New York

Tampa Bay . . . . 14 7 0 0 — 28
New York Jets . . . . 17 24 14 7 — 62
TDs: NYJ—Mickey Shuler 3, Johnny Hector 2, Tony Paige, Al Toon, Wesley Walker 2, Freeman McNeil 2, Kevin House, Calvin Magee. TD Passes: NYJ—Ken O'Brien 5; TB—Steve DeBerg 2. FGs: NYJ—Pat Leahy 2.

PITTSBURGH STEELERS
November 30, 1952, at Pittsburgh

New York Giants . . . . 0 0 7 0 — 7
Pittsburgh . . . . 14 14 7 28 — 63
TDs: Pitt—Lynn Chandnois 2, Dick Hensley 2, Jack Butler, George Hays, Ray Mathews, Ed Modzelewski, Elbie Nickel; NYG—Bill Stribling. TD Passes: Pitt—Jim Finks 4; Gary Kerkorian; NYG—Tom Landry.

SAN DIEGO CHARGERS
December 22, 1963, at San Diego

Denver . . . . 7 10 3 0 — 20
San Diego . . . . 10 16 10 22 — 58
TDs: SD—Paul Lowe 2, Chuck Allen, Bobby Jackson, Dave Kocourek, Keith Lincoln, Jacque MacKinnon; Den—Billy Joe, Donnie Stone. TD Passes: SD—John Hadl, Tobin Rote; Den—Don Breaux. FGs: SD—George Blair 3; Den—Gene Mingo 2.

SEATTLE SEAHAWKS
October 30, 1977, at Seattle

Buffalo . . . . 3 0 7 7 — 17
Seattle . . . . 14 28 7 7 — 56
TDs: Sea—Steve Largent 2, Duke Fergerson, Al Hunter, David Sims, Sherman Smith, Don Testerman, Jim Zorn; Buff—Joe Ferguson, John Kimbrough. TD Passes: Sea—Jim Zorn 4; Buff—Joe Ferguson 2. FG: Buff—Carson Long.

ATLANTA FALCONS
September 16, 1973, at New Orleans

Atlanta . . . . 0 24 21 17 — 62
New Orleans . . . . 0 0 7 0 — 7
TDs: Atl—Ken Burrow 2, Eddie Ray 2, Wes Chesson, Tom Hayes, Art Malone, Joe Profit; NO—Bill Butler. TD Passes: Atl—Dick Shiner 3, Bob Lee; NO—Archie Manning. FGs: Atl—Nick Mike-Mayer.

CHICAGO BEARS
December 7, 1980, at Chicago

Green Bay . . . . 0 7 0 0 — 7
Chicago . . . . 0 28 13 20 — 61
TDs: Chi—Walter Payton 3, Brian Baschnagel, Robin Earl, Roland Harper, Willie McClendon, Len Walterscheid, Rickey Watts; GB—James Lofton. TD Passes: Chi—Vince Evans 3; GB—Lynn Dickey.

DALLAS COWBOYS
October 12, 1980, at Dallas

San Francisco . . . . 0 7 0 7 — 14
Dallas . . . . 14 24 14 7 — 59
TDs: Dall—Drew Pearson 3, Ron Springs 2, Tony Dorsett, Billy Joe DuPree, Robert Newhouse; SF—Dwight Clark 2. TD Passes: Dall—Danny White 4; SF—Steve DeBerg 2. FG: Dall—Rafael Septien.

DETROIT LIONS
October 26, 1952, at Green Bay

Detroit . . . . 14 14 14 10 — 52
Green Bay . . . . 7 3 7 0 — 17
TDs: Det—Jug Girard 2, Bob Hoernschemeyer 2, Jack Christiansen, Jim Smith, Bill Swiacki; GB—Billy Howton, Jim Keane. TD Passes: Det—Bobby Layne 3; GB—Babe Parilli, Tobin Rote. FGs: Det—Pat Harder; GB—Bill Reichardt.

GREEN BAY PACKERS
October 7, 1945, at Milwaukee

Detroit . . . . 0 7 7 7 — 21
Green Bay . . . . 0 41 9 7 — 57
TDs: GB—Don Hutson 4, Charley Brock, Irv Comp, Ted Fritsch, Clyde Goodnight; Det—Chuck Fenenbock, John Greene, Bob Westfall. TD Passes: GB—Tex McKay 4, Lou Brock, Irv Comp; Det—Dave Ryan.

LOS ANGELES RAMS
October 22, 1950, at Los Angeles

Baltimore . . . . 13 0 7 7 — 27
Los Angeles . . . . 21 14 14 21 — 70
TDs: LA—Bob Boyd 2, Vitamin T. Smith 2, Tom Fears, Elroy (Crazylegs) Hirsch, Dick Hoerner, Ralph Pasquariello, Dan Towler, Bob Waterfield; Balt—Chet Mutryn 2, Adrian Burk, Billy Stone. TD Passes: LA—Norm Van Brocklin 2, Bob Waterfield 2, Glenn Davis; Balt—Adrian Burk 3.

MINNESOTA VIKINGS
October 18, 1970, at Minnesota

Dallas . . . . 3 3 0 7 — 13
Minnesota . . . . 14 20 17 3 — 54
TDs: Minn—Clint Jones 2, Ed Sharockman 2, John Beasley, Dave Osborn; Dall—Calvin Hill. TD Pass: Minn—Gary Cuozzo. FGs: Minn—Fred Cox 4; Dall—Mike Clark 2.

NEW ORLEANS SAINTS
November 21, 1976, at Seattle

New Orleans . . . . 3 17 28 3 — 51
Seattle . . . . 6 0 14 7 — 27
TDs: NO—Bobby Douglass 2, Tony Galbreath, Chuck Muncie, Tom Myers, Elex Price; Sea—Sherman Smith 2, Steve Largent, Jim Zorn. TD Pass: Sea—Bill Munson 2. FGs: NO—Rich Szaro 3.

NEW YORK GIANTS
November 26, 1972, at New York

Philadelphia . . . . 3 7 0 0 — 10
New York Giants . . . . . . 14 24 10 14 — 62
TDs: NYG—Don Herrmann 2, Ron Johnson 2, Bob Tucker 2, Randy Johnson; Phil—Harold Jackson. TD Passes: NYG—Norm Snead 3, Randy Johnson 2; Phil—John Reaves. FGs: NYG—Pete Gogolak 2; Phil—Tom Dempsey.

PHILADELPHIA EAGLES
November 6, 1934, at Philadelphia

```
Cincinnati Reds ........ 0  0  0  0 —  0
Philadelphia ........... 26  6 12 20 — 64
```
TDs: Phil—Joe Carter 3, Swede Hanson 3, Marvin Ellstrom, Roger Kirkman, Ed Matesic, Ed Storm. TD Passes: Phil—Ed Matesic 2, Albert Weiner 2, Marvin Elstrom.

PHOENIX CARDINALS
November 13, 1949, at New York

```
Chicago Cardinals ..... 7 31 14 13 — 65
New York Bulldogs ..... 7  0  6  7 — 20
```
TDs: Chi—Red Cochran 2, Pat Harder 2, Bill Dewell, Mel Kutner, Bob Ravensburg, Vic Schwall, Charlie Trippi; NY—Joe Golding, Frank Muehlheuser, Johnny Rauch. TD Passes: Chi—Paul Christman 3, Jim Hardy 3; NY—Bobby Layne. FG: Chi—Pat Harder.

SAN FRANCISCO 49ERS
December 23, 1991, at San Francisco

```
Chicago ........... 0  0  7  7 — 14
San Francisco ..... 7 17  0 28 — 52
```
TDs: SF—Jerry Rice 2, Don Griffin, Mike Sherrard, Harry Sydney, Jamie Williams, Steve Young; Chi—Neal Anderson, Tom Waddle. TD Passes: SF—Steve Young 3, Bill Musgrave; Chi—Jim Harbaugh, Peter Tom Willis. FG: SF—Mike Cofer.

TAMPA BAY BUCCANEERS
September 13, 1987, at Tampa Bay

```
Atlanta ............. 0  3  0  7 — 10
Tampa Bay ........... 14 13  7 14 — 48
```
TDs: TB—Gerald Carter 2, Cliff Austin, Steve Bartalo, Mark Carrier, Phil Freeman, Calvin Magee; Atl—Stacey Bailey. TD Passes: TB—Steve DeBerg 5; Atl—Scott Campbell. FG: Atl—Mick Luckhurst.

WASHINGTON REDSKINS
November 27, 1966, at Washington

```
New York Giants ....... 0 14 14 13 — 41
Washington .......... 13 21 14 24 — 72
```
TDs: Wash—A.D. Whitfield 3, Brig Owens 2, Charley Taylor 2, Rickie Harris, Joe Don Looney, Bobby Mitchell; NYG—Allen Jacobs, Homer Jones, Dan Lewis, Joe Morrison, Aaron Thomas, Gary Wood. TD Passes: Wash—Sonny Jurgensen 3; NYG—Gary Wood 2, Tom Kennedy. FG: Wash—Charlie Gogolak.

NFL Games In Which a Team Has Scored 60 or More Points

(Home team in capitals)

Regular Season

WASHINGTON 72, New York Giants 41 .... November 27, 1966
LOS ANGELES RAMS 70, Baltimore 27 .... October 22, 1950
Chicago Cardinals 65, NEW YORK BULLDOGS 20 ... November 13, 1949
LOS ANGELES RAMS 65, Detroit 24 .... October 29, 1950
PHILADELPHIA 64, Cincinnati 0 .... November 6, 1934
CHICAGO CARDINALS 63, New York Giants 35 .... October 17, 1948
AKRON 62, Oorang 0 .... October 29, 1922
PITTSBURGH 62, New York Giants 7 .... November 30, 1952
CLEVELAND 62, New York Giants 14 .... December 6, 1953
CLEVELAND 62, Washington 3 .... November 7, 1954
NEW YORK GIANTS 62, Philadelphia 10 .... November 26, 1972
Atlanta 62, NEW ORLEANS 7 .... September 16, 1973
NEW YORK JETS 62, Tampa Bay 28 .... November 17, 1985
CHICAGO 61, San Francisco 20 .... December 12, 1965
Cincinnati 61, HOUSTON 17 .... December 17, 1972
CHICAGO 61, Green Bay 7 .... December 7, 1980
CINCINNATI 61, Houston 7 .... December 17, 1989
ROCK ISLAND 60, Evansville 0 .... October 15, 1922
CHICAGO CARDINALS 60, Rochester 0 .... October 7, 1923

Postseason

Chicago Bears 73, WASHINGTON 0 .... December 8, 1940

Youngest and Oldest Regular Starters in NFL in 1991

Minimum: 8 Games Started

Five Youngest Regular Starters

	Birthdate	Starts	Position
Ed King, Cleveland	12/3/69	15	G
Larry Brown, Dallas	11/30/69	13	CB
Pio Sagapolutele, Cleveland	11/28/69	8	DE
Marc Spindler, Detroit	11/28/69	16	DT
Leonard Russell, New England	11/17/69	15	RB

Five Oldest Regular Starters

	Birthdate	Starts	Position
Steve DeBerg, Kansas City	1/19/54	15	QB
Jackie Slater, L.A. Rams	5/27/54	13	T
Mike Kenn, Atlanta	2/9/56	15	T
Clay Matthews, Cleveland	3/15/56	15	LB
Max Montoya, L.A. Raiders	5/12/56	10	G

Youngest and Oldest Regular Starters By Position in 1991

Minimum: 8 Games Started

	Youngest	Oldest
QB	12/8/67 Jeff George, Ind.	1/19/54 Steve DeBerg, K.C.
RB	11/17/69 Leonard Russell, N.E.	12/28/58 James Brooks, Cin.
WR	10/25/69 Mike Pritchard, Atl.	7/5/56 James Lofton, Buff.
TE	4/27/68 Adrian Cooper, Pitt.	2/2/59 Mike Tice, Sea.
C	8/26/68 Courtney Hall, S.D.	11/25/56 Doug Smith, Rams
G	12/3/69 Ed King, Clev.	5/12/56 Max Montoya, Raiders
T	3/16/69 Pat Harlow, N.E.	5/27/54 Jackie Slater, Rams
DE	11/28/69 Pio Sagapolutele, Clev.	1/21/57 Jacob Green, Sea.
DT	2/6/69 James Jones, Clev.	8/26/56 Ken Clarke, Minn.
LB	10/21/69 Mo Lewis, Jets	3/15/56 Clay Matthews, Clev.
CB	11/30/69 Larry Brown, Dall.	12/22/57 Jerry Holmes, G.B.
S	2/14/69 Harry Colon, N.E.	4/22/58 Mark Murphy, G.B.

Eric Dickerson's Career Rushing vs. Each Opponent

Opponent	Games	Rushes	Yards	Yards Per Rush	Yards Per Game	TD
Atlanta	9	179	852	4.8	94.7	9
Buffalo	7	150	580	3.9	82.9	3
Chicago	4	115	482	4.2	120.5	5
Cincinnati	3	75	384	5.1	128.0	3
Cleveland	6	125	609	4.9	101.5	2
Dallas	2	49	244	5.0	122.0	1
Denver	3	43	249	5.8	83.0	4
Detroit	3	67	346	5.2	115.3	5
Green Bay	4	95	426	4.5	106.5	2
Houston	4	105	609	5.8	152.3	4
Indianapolis	1	25	121	4.8	121.0	1
Kansas City	1	26	68	2.6	68.0	1
L.A. Raiders	2	45	175	3.9	87.5	0
L.A. Rams	1	21	116	5.5	116.0	1
Miami	10	220	1040	4.7	104.0	6
Minnesota	3	73	217	3.0	72.3	1
New England	10	224	758	3.4	75.8	4
New Orleans	9	192	907	4.7	100.8	6
N.Y. Giants	4	86	338	3.9	84.5	1
N.Y. Jets	9	196	787	4.0	87.4	8
Philadelphia	2	45	161	3.6	80.5	0
Phoenix	4	96	585	6.1	146.3	4
Pittsburgh	2	36	73	2.0	36.5	0
San Diego	4	105	452	4.3	113.0	0
San Francisco	9	170	832	4.9	92.4	3
Seattle	2	44	192	4.4	96.0	3
Tampa Bay	6	154	768	5.0	128.0	10
Washington	2	22	68	3.1	34.0	1
Totals	126	2783	12,439	4.5	98.7	88

Phoenix totals include three games vs. St. Louis.

Roger Craig's Career Rushing vs. Each Opponent

Opponent	Games	Rushes	Yards	Yards Per Rush	Yards Per Game	TD
Atlanta	16	214	1012	4.7	63.3	6
Buffalo	3	49	190	3.9	63.3	1
Chicago	5	46	176	3.8	35.2	0
Cincinnati	4	55	217	3.9	54.3	1
Cleveland	2	22	71	3.2	35.5	2
Dallas	4	57	235	4.1	58.8	2
Denver	4	87	417	4.8	104.3	0
Detroit	3	42	185	4.4	61.7	1
Green Bay	4	39	136	3.5	34.0	0
Houston	4	36	145	4.0	36.3	1
Indianapolis	3	45	210	4.7	70.0	2
Kansas City	2	32	114	3.6	57.0	1
L.A. Raiders	2	27	92	3.4	46.0	0
L.A. Rams	17	248	1026	4.1	60.4	9
Miami	2	29	154	5.3	77.0	2
Minnesota	5	71	247	3.5	49.4	3
New England	3	56	206	3.7	68.7	2
New Orleans	16	200	796	4.0	49.8	5
N.Y. Giants	5	66	256	3.9	51.2	0
N.Y. Jets	3	42	190	4.5	63.3	2
Philadelphia	4	50	186	3.7	46.5	0
Phoenix	4	51	277	5.1	69.3	2
Pittsburgh	2	16	45	2.8	22.5	0
San Diego	2	24	126	5.3	63.0	2
San Francisco	1	13	44	3.4	44.0	0
Seattle	3	48	190	4.0	63.3	0
Tampa Bay	6	84	339	4.0	56.5	7
Washington	5	87	322	3.7	64.4	0
Totals	136	1848	7654	4.1	56.3	51

Phoenix totals include three games vs. St. Louis.

Joe Montana's Career Passing vs. Each Opponent

Opponent	Games	Att.	Cmp.	Pct.	Yards	Avg. Gain	TD	Int.	Sacked
Atlanta	21	567	370	65.3	4436	7.82	36	17	33/235
Buffalo	2	64	43	67.2	381	5.95	2	0	6/46
Chicago	7	162	90	55.6	1023	6.31	5	4	20/144
Cincinnati	4	141	90	63.8	923	6.55	7	6	9/75
Cleveland	4	140	88	62.9	1003	7.16	7	6	6/48
Dallas	5	126	84	66.7	1114	8.84	9	3	7/48
Denver	4	106	58	54.7	779	7.35	4	3	6/50
Detroit	5	120	74	61.7	713	5.94	2	2	9/55
Green Bay	5	149	104	69.8	1264	8.48	7	2	8/50
Houston	4	135	95	70.4	1164	8.62	10	4	5/31
Indianapolis	1	26	15	57.7	233	8.96	1	0	3/29
Kansas City	2	69	43	62.3	488	7.07	2	2	3/16
L.A. Raiders	4	96	51	53.1	659	6.86	4	1	11/92
L.A. Rams	23	693	446	64.4	5632	8.13	37	15	47/297
Miami	2	30	19	63.3	267	8.90	1	0	3/22
Minnesota	5	104	66	63.5	829	7.97	9	3	7/28
New England	4	108	69	63.9	791	7.32	6	2	6/39
New Orleans	20	508	314	61.8	3704	7.29	31	14	38/225
N.Y. Giants	8	210	132	62.9	1435	6.83	10	3	7/38
N.Y. Jets	3	79	48	60.8	538	6.81	3	3	3/17
Philadelphia	3	54	35	64.8	546	10.11	5	2	9/52
Phoenix	6	141	95	67.4	1389	9.85	13	5	7/53
Pittsburgh	4	150	100	66.7	919	6.13	4	8	3/20
San Diego	3	68	45	66.2	627	9.22	6	2	2/13
Seattle	3	62	37	59.7	539	8.69	6	4	3/17
Tampa Bay	8	254	176	69.3	1860	7.32	8	6	11/70
Washington	6	217	127	58.5	1742	8.03	7	6	9/84
Totals	166	4579	2914	63.6	34,998	7.64	242	123	281/1894

L.A. Raiders totals include one game vs. Oakland
Phoenix totals include six games vs. St. Louis

Phil Simms's Career Passing vs. Each Opponent

Opponent	Games	Att.	Cmp.	Pct.	Yards	Avg. Gain	TD	Int.	Sacked
Atlanta	4	116	66	56.9	910	7.84	4	3	12/81
Buffalo	1	10	6	60.0	59	5.90	0	0	1/0
Chicago	1	28	15	53.6	181	6.46	1	0	8/53
Cincinnati	2	106	66	62.3	809	7.63	4	2	10/88
Cleveland	1	37	23	62.2	289	7.81	1	2	4/22
Dallas	20	516	269	52.1	4169	8.08	33	30	50/376
Denver	3	78	43	55.1	519	6.65	1	1	8/64
Detroit	4	112	78	69.6	935	8.35	6	0	11/73
Green Bay	5	156	97	62.2	1302	8.35	11	4	16/111
Houston	2	41	28	68.3	434	10.59	3	1	1/8
Indianapolis	2	35	24	68.6	239	6.83	1	5	5/33
Kansas City	3	82	42	51.2	587	7.16	5	5	7/52
L.A. Raiders	2	55	31	56.4	408	7.42	2	2	5/39
L.A. Rams	7	235	131	55.7	1565	6.66	7	6	27/224
Miami	1	25	13	52.0	182	7.28	0	0	1/3
Minnesota	3	58	33	56.9	428	7.38	1	2	4/27
New Orleans	5	155	90	58.1	1011	6.52	5	7	13/88
N.Y. Jets	4	135	78	57.8	928	6.87	5	2	21/167
Philadelphia	19	551	272	49.4	3776	6.85	22	20	55/381
Phoenix	16	438	220	50.2	2853	6.51	28	10	44/275
Pittsburgh	1	16	10	62.5	106	6.63	1	1	3/24
San Diego	3	99	54	54.5	667	6.74	1	4	8/72
San Francisco	7	258	143	55.4	1802	6.98	8	8	31/185
Seattle	3	78	43	55.1	487	6.24	3	5	9/59
Tampa Bay	7	191	111	58.1	1060	5.55	6	5	19/197
Washington	18	499	260	52.1	3806	7.63	22	22	57/432
Totals	144	4110	2246	54.6	29,512	7.18	179	145	430/3134

Indianapolis totals include one game vs. Baltimore
Phoenix totals include 12 games vs. St. Louis

Dan Marino's Career Passing vs. Each Opponent

Opponent	Games	Att.	Cmp.	Pct.	Yards	Avg. Gain	TD	Int.	Sacked
Atlanta	1	40	20	50.0	303	7.58	2	4	0/0
Buffalo	17	583	369	63.3	4490	7.70	33	24	20/168
Chicago	3	79	39	49.4	566	7.16	5	3	6/36
Cincinnati	4	136	84	61.8	1026	7.54	7	1	5/39
Cleveland	4	151	87	57.6	1178	7.80	9	5	0/0
Dallas	3	115	66	57.4	860	7.48	6	3	4/36
Denver	1	43	25	58.1	390	9.07	3	0	3/25
Detroit	2	78	39	50.0	421	5.40	2	2	3/28
Green Bay	4	146	95	65.1	1151	7.88	9	6	4/22
Houston	6	180	97	53.9	1227	6.82	9	10	3/20
Indianapolis	18	574	343	59.8	4272	7.44	30	7	14/104
Kansas City	4	148	84	56.8	1031	6.97	8	3	2/20
L.A. Raiders	5	178	100	56.2	1235	6.94	11	5	7/64
L.A. Rams	2	84	54	64.3	682	8.12	7	2	1/4
Minnesota	1	37	20	54.1	264	7.14	2	3	0/0
New England	17	580	334	57.6	4033	6.95	26	27	11/95
New Orleans	2	63	39	61.9	391	6.21	4	1	1/6
N.Y. Giants	1	30	14	46.7	115	3.83	0	2	1/7

Opponent	Games	Att.	Cmp.	Pct.	Yards	Avg. Gain	TD	Int.	Sacked
N.Y. Jets	16	627	369	58.9	5007	7.99	43	20	21/119
Philadelphia	3	127	72	56.7	987	7.77	6	2	5/45
Phoenix	2	61	42	68.9	634	10.39	5	0	1/9
Pittsburgh	6	175	110	62.9	1333	7.62	9	9	1/4
San Diego	4	163	103	63.2	1243	7.63	9	2	6/42
San Francisco	2	75	42	56.0	495	6.60	3	4	3/29
Seattle	1	29	17	58.6	250	8.62	2	1	1/8
Tampa Bay	3	117	74	63.2	875	7.48	7	1	1/10
Washington	3	111	60	54.1	927	8.35	9	2	1/2
Totals	135	4730	2798	59.2	35,386	7.48	266	149	125/942

Indianapolis totals include two games vs. Baltimore
Phoenix totals include one game vs. St. Louis

John Elway's Career Passing vs. Each Opponent

Opponent	Games	Att.	Cmp.	Pct.	Yards	Avg. Gain	TD	Int.	Sacked
Atlanta	2	64	35	54.7	526	8.22	4	2	4/26
Buffalo	4	109	55	50.5	739	6.78	5	4	8/70
Chicago	4	94	51	54.3	650	6.91	3	4	9/65
Cincinnati	3	75	48	64.0	617	8.23	6	1	2/13
Cleveland	6	170	90	52.9	1255	7.38	9	6	9/64
Dallas	1	24	12	50.0	200	8.33	3	0	1/2
Detroit	3	88	56	63.6	699	7.94	2	2	7/72
Green Bay	3	94	55	58.5	546	5.81	1	4	1/4
Houston	2	77	41	53.2	557	7.23	5	4	7/69
Indianapolis	6	183	98	53.6	1315	7.19	6	2	16/127
Kansas City	16	481	254	52.8	3268	6.79	10	24	39/283
L.A. Raiders	16	470	255	54.3	3091	6.58	17	21	40/332
L.A. Rams	2	74	39	52.7	501	6.77	5	2	3/24
Miami	1	37	18	48.6	250	6.76	0	1	3/24
Minnesota	4	90	54	60.0	633	7.03	8	1	9/60
New England	6	192	108	56.3	1286	6.70	7	4	8/54
New Orleans	2	79	46	58.2	519	6.57	4	2	4/35
N.Y. Giants	2	94	52	55.3	628	6.68	1	2	3/19
N.Y. Jets	1	28	13	46.4	145	5.18	0	1	5/27
Philadelphia	3	84	44	52.4	567	6.75	4	5	13/104
Phoenix	2	62	39	62.9	492	7.94	3	5	3/16
Pittsburgh	6	167	87	52.1	1090	6.53	5	5	12/90
San Diego	17	517	284	54.9	3416	6.61	11	20	42/272
San Francisco	2	81	41	50.6	425	5.25	3	3	5/43
Seattle	17	554	306	55.2	4277	7.72	25	15	39/287
Washington	1	35	20	57.1	282	8.06	1	0	3/23
Totals	132	4023	2201	54.7	27,974	6.95	148	140	295/2205

Boomer Esiason's Career Passing vs. Each Opponent

Opponent	Games	Att.	Cmp.	Pct.	Yards	Avg. Gain	TD	Int.	Sacked
Atlanta	3	67	34	50.7	367	5.48	1	2	3/3
Buffalo	6	127	73	57.5	989	7.79	6	4	5/42
Chicago	2	66	32	48.5	396	6.00	2	4	6/56
Cleveland	15	345	185	53.6	2369	6.87	15	13	19/134
Dallas	3	85	48	56.5	661	7.78	4	2	4/22
Denver	2	50	32	64.0	512	10.24	4	4	2/17
Detroit	2	66	43	65.2	566	8.58	3	2	2/3
Green Bay	1	24	15	62.5	207	8.63	3	0	3/24
Houston	14	391	230	58.8	3331	8.52	22	17	28/201
Indianapolis	3	92	51	55.4	658	7.15	4	3	9/72
Kansas City	4	121	67	55.4	940	7.77	5	3	7/71
L.A. Raiders	4	80	44	55.0	659	8.24	4	2	5/44
L.A. Rams	1	45	31	68.9	490	10.89	3	0	1/7
Miami	3	86	47	54.7	617	7.17	2	1	6/69
Minnesota	2	79	48	60.8	619	7.84	4	4	7/62
New England	6	190	101	53.2	1571	8.27	12	7	10/71
New Orleans	2	75	33	44.0	309	4.12	3	2	9/71
N.Y. Giants	2	54	32	59.3	397	7.35	4	0	4/36
N.Y. Jets	6	147	82	55.8	1301	8.85	12	6	13/93
Philadelphia	2	50	30	60.0	473	9.46	5	3	5/45
Phoenix	2	38	24	63.2	356	9.37	4	1	3/22
Pittsburgh	15	415	250	60.2	3503	8.44	18	17	26/226
San Diego	3	97	56	57.7	748	7.71	8	5	10/84
San Francisco	2	49	26	53.1	294	6.00	2	2	5/28
Seattle	5	138	72	52.2	978	7.09	4	6	12/96
Tampa Bay	1	28	17	60.7	197	7.04	5	0	1/1
Washington	3	95	50	52.6	756	7.96	4	3	8/65
Totals	115	3100	1753	56.5	24,264	7.83	163	114	211/1665

Phoenix totals include one game vs. St. Louis

Warren Moon's Career Passing vs. Each Opponent

Opponent	Games	Att.	Cmp.	Pct.	Yards	Avg. Gain	TD	Int.	Sacked
Atlanta	3	114	63	55.3	847	7.43	8	5	7/37
Buffalo	5	134	74	55.2	1010	7.54	5	6	9/73
Chicago	2	55	28	50.9	521	9.47	3	3	5/49
Cincinnati	15	469	262	55.9	3572	7.62	22	18	32/279
Cleveland	15	468	272	58.1	3636	7.77	21	18	36/277

Opponent	Games	Att.	Cmp.	Pct.	Yards	Avg. Gain	TD	Int.	Sacked
Dallas	3	111	67	60.4	873	7.86	2	4	16/105
Denver	2	48	27	56.3	456	9.50	3	1	5/43
Detroit	2	76	51	67.1	743	9.78	3	4	0/0
Green Bay	1	21	14	66.7	218	10.38	2	1	0/0
Indianapolis	6	216	131	60.6	1795	8.31	11	7	12/86
Kansas City	6	204	125	61.3	1523	7.77	7	4	22/152
L.A. Raiders	4	138	68	49.3	1004	7.28	6	5	13/115
L.A. Rams	3	115	66	57.4	853	7.42	3	5	6/49
Miami	5	111	76	68.5	910	8.20	5	6	9/97
Minnesota	2	57	30	52.6	349	6.12	1	1	9/65
New England	2	73	34	46.6	495	6.78	3	4	3/25
New Orleans	3	81	42	51.9	496	6.12	2	2	5/37
N.Y. Giants	2	83	48	57.8	566	6.82	3	2	5/46
N.Y. Jets	3	121	85	70.2	1011	8.36	6	2	7/60
Philadelphia	1	46	24	52.2	262	5.70	0	0	4/36
Phoenix	2	61	31	50.8	453	7.43	4	2	3/21
Pittsburgh	15	455	251	55.2	3211	7.06	18	21	36/278
San Diego	4	136	72	52.9	988	7.27	5	2	7/53
San Francisco	3	102	60	58.8	745	7.30	6	5	6/39
Seattle	2	60	37	61.7	414	6.90	2	2	2/12
Tampa Bay	1	23	14	60.9	149	6.48	2	0	0/0
Washington	3	102	53	52.0	579	5.68	4	3	6/46
Totals	115	3680	2105	57.2	27,679	7.52	157	133	265/2080

Phoenix totals include one game vs. St. Louis

Jim Kelly's Career Passing vs. Each Opponent

Opponent	Games	Att.	Cmp.	Pct.	Yards	Avg. Gain	TD	Int.	Sacked
Atlanta	1	22	17	77.3	231	10.50	2	1	3/18
Chicago	2	66	39	59.1	576	8.73	3	1	9/79
Cincinnati	4	99	65	65.7	1008	10.18	10	7	5/49
Cleveland	3	93	56	60.2	737	7.93	5	0	6/31
Denver	3	101	58	57.4	600	5.94	2	5	7/55
Green Bay	2	49	27	55.1	312	6.37	3	2	5/23
Houston	4	145	90	62.1	1141	7.87	11	5	16/128
Indianapolis	11	293	179	61.1	2221	7.58	20	7	11/91
Kansas City	3	95	58	61.1	670	7.05	3	4	10/82
L.A. Raiders	4	133	79	59.4	972	7.31	7	3	7/45
Miami	10	301	202	67.1	2396	7.96	14	5	17/140
Minnesota	1	31	17	54.8	204	6.58	0	1	1/8
New England	11	305	173	56.7	2238	7.34	10	16	36/294
New Orleans	1	35	17	48.6	211	6.03	2	3	2/7
N.Y. Giants	1	11	7	63.6	115	10.46	1	0	0/0
N.Y. Jets	11	342	204	59.6	2644	7.73	23	11	20/132
Philadelphia	2	71	39	54.9	488	6.87	4	3	2/20
Phoenix	2	26	17	65.4	270	10.39	4	1	5/34
Pittsburgh	1	43	31	72.1	363	8.44	6	2	2/20
San Francisco	1	42	26	61.9	265	6.31	0	3	2/10
Seattle	2	48	26	54.2	324	6.75	1	2	2/21
Tampa Bay	3	114	72	63.2	913	8.01	4	3	5/54
Washington	1	43	25	58.1	292	6.79	1	3	3/33
Totals	86	2562	1555	60.7	19,574	7.64	138	89	181/1399

Phoenix totals include one game vs. St. Louis

Jerry Rice's Career Receiving vs. Each Opponent

Opponent	Games	Rec.	Yards	Yards Per Rec.	Yards Per Game	TD
Atlanta	13	69	1157	16.8	89.0	14
Buffalo	1	3	46	15.3	46.0	1
Chicago	5	24	424	17.7	84.8	7
Cincinnati	2	12	187	15.6	93.5	2
Cleveland	2	13	193	14.8	96.5	4
Dallas	3	21	286	13.6	95.3	2
Denver	2	7	145	20.7	72.5	0
Detroit	3	8	73	9.1	24.3	1
Green Bay	4	23	432	18.8	108.0	4
Houston	2	13	155	11.9	77.5	2
Indianapolis	2	12	335	27.9	167.5	4
Kansas City	2	8	100	12.5	50.0	2
L.A. Raiders	3	11	193	17.5	64.3	0
L.A. Rams	14	61	1148	18.8	82.0	8
Miami	1	3	76	25.3	76.0	2
Minnesota	5	25	436	17.4	87.2	5
New England	2	10	147	14.7	73.5	2
New Orleans	14	65	1050	16.2	75.0	7
N.Y. Giants	5	22	398	18.1	79.6	4
N.Y. Jets	2	10	192	19.2	96.0	1
Philadelphia	3	11	238	21.6	79.3	3
Phoenix	3	10	223	22.3	74.3	3
Pittsburgh	2	11	137	12.5	68.5	1
San Diego	2	15	321	21.4	160.5	4
Seattle	3	14	272	19.4	90.7	4
Tampa Bay	4	24	325	13.5	81.3	4
Washington	4	21	383	18.2	95.8	2
Totals		108	526	9072	17.2	84.0	93

Phoenix totals include one game vs. St. Louis

James Lofton's Career Receiving vs. Each Opponent

Opponent	Games	Rec.	Yards	Yards Per Rec.	Yards Per Game	TD
Atlanta	6	25	595	23.8	99.2	4
Buffalo	4	14	343	24.5	85.8	2
Chicago	18	72	1312	18.2	72.9	5
Cincinnati	6	23	443	19.3	73.8	4
Cleveland	5	16	295	18.4	59.0	2
Dallas	3	4	37	9.3	12.3	0
Denver	6	23	378	16.4	63.0	1
Detroit	19	68	1123	16.5	59.1	5
Green Bay	2	8	146	18.3	73.0	0
Houston	5	14	230	16.4	46.0	1
Indianapolis	8	19	256	13.5	32.0	2
Kansas City	4	12	220	18.3	55.0	0
L.A. Raiders	4	11	193	17.5	48.3	2
L.A. Rams	9	34	648	19.1	72.0	3
Miami	8	22	367	16.7	45.9	2
Minnesota	18	68	1312	19.3	72.9	7
New England	8	16	328	20.5	41.0	0
New Orleans	8	26	528	20.3	66.0	6
N.Y. Giants	7	27	524	19.4	74.9	1
N.Y. Jets	10	27	565	20.9	56.5	3
Philadelphia	3	12	269	22.4	89.7	2
Phoenix	3	16	244	15.3	81.3	1
Pittsburgh	4	15	344	22.9	86.0	4
San Diego	5	15	337	22.5	67.4	2
San Francisco	5	18	270	15.0	54.0	0
Seattle	8	21	448	21.3	56.0	6
Tampa Bay	17	63	1089	17.3	64.1	4
Washington	4	10	191	19.1	47.8	0
Totals	207	699	13,035	18.6	63.0	69

Indianapolis totals include one game vs. Baltimore
L.A. Raiders totals include one game vs. Oakland
Phoenix totals include two games vs. St. Louis

Art Monk's Career Receiving vs. Each Opponent

Opponent	Games	Rec.	Yards	Yards Per Rec.	Yards Per Game	TD
Atlanta	7	33	539	16.3	77.0	7
Buffalo	4	28	263	9.4	65.8	2
Chicago	7	36	496	13.8	70.9	4
Cincinnati	3	21	366	17.4	122.0	1
Cleveland	3	11	146	13.3	48.7	1
Dallas	20	87	1212	13.9	60.6	2
Denver	3	14	192	13.7	64.0	2
Detroit	7	38	414	10.9	59.1	2
Green Bay	3	10	148	14.8	49.3	1
Houston	3	16	147	9.2	49.0	0
Indianapolis	3	19	340	17.9	113.3	5
L.A. Raiders	4	11	161	14.6	40.3	0
L.A. Rams	4	15	306	20.4	76.5	2
Miami	3	17	188	11.1	62.7	2
Minnesota	3	16	201	12.6	67.0	1
New England	3	9	100	11.1	33.3	0
New Orleans	6	29	413	14.2	68.8	2
N.Y. Giants	22	89	1148	12.9	52.2	2
N.Y. Jets	1	3	70	23.3	70.0	0
Philadelphia	23	89	1138	12.8	49.5	8
Phoenix	23	101	1416	14.0	61.6	13
Pittsburgh	3	23	281	12.2	93.7	1
San Diego	4	23	361	15.7	90.3	0
San Francisco	6	40	583	14.6	97.2	2
Seattle	3	11	217	19.7	72.3	0
Tampa Bay	2	12	138	11.5	69.0	0
Totals	173	801	10,984	13.7	63.5	60

Indianapolis totals include one game vs. Baltimore
L.A. Raiders totals include one game vs. Oakland
Phoenix totals include 15 games vs. St. Louis

Starting Records of Active NFL Quarterbacks
Minimum: 10 starts

	W-L-T	Pct.
Joe Montana	100-39	.719
Mark Rypien	33-13	.717
Jim McMahon	58-25	.699
Jeff Hostetler	11-5	.688
Jay Schroeder	53-26	.671
Steve Beuerlein	12-7	.632
Bobby Hebert	37-22	.627
John Elway	81-48-1	.627
Jim Harbaugh	23-14	.622
Dan Marino	82-51	.617
Jim Kelly	53-33	.616
Mike Tomczak	23-15	.605
Phil Simms	83-56	.597
Randall Cunningham	41-28-1	.593
Dave Krieg	70-49	.588
Bob Gagliano	7-5	.583
Jeff Kemp	16-12-1	.569
Wade Wilson	27-21	.563
Bernie Kosar	48-43-1	.527
Boomer Esiason	54-53	.505
Erik Kramer	5-5	.500
Bubby Brister	26-27	.491
Rodney Peete	13-14	.481
Ken O'Brien	49-53-1	.481
Rich Gannon	11-12	.478
Warren Moon	54-61	.470
Don Majkowski	21-24-1	.467
Jim Everett	37-43	.463
Hugh Millen	7-9	.438
Steve Walsh	10-13	.435
Billy Joe Tolliver	9-12	.429
Chris Chandler	10-14	.417
Steve DeBerg	51-80-1	.390
Steve Young	15-24	.385
Jack Trudeau	14-23	.378
Troy Aikman	14-24	.368
Chris Miller	20-36	.357
Steve Pelluer	9-19-1	.328
Vinny Testaverde	19-39	.328
Mike Pagel	17-36-1	.324
Tom Tupa	4-9	.308
Timm Rosenbach	5-12	.294
Jeff Rutledge	2-7-1	.250
John Friesz	4-13	.235
Jeff George	6-22	.214
Chuck Long	4-17	.190
Mark Herrmann	2-9	.182

Individual NFL Leaders Over Recent Seasons

Last 2 Seasons	Last 3 Seasons	Last 4 Seasons
Points		
280, Chip Lohmiller	408, Chip Lohmiller	505, Chip Lohmiller
249, Nick Lowery	355, Nick Lowery	464, Scott Norwood
221, Pete Stoyanovich	341, David Treadwell	459, Mike Cofer
221, David Treadwell	338, Mike Cofer	459, Nick Lowery
220, Scott Norwood	335, Scott Norwood	419, Morten Andersen
Touchdowns		
33, Barry Sanders	47, Barry Sanders	54, Jerry Rice
27, Jerry Rice	44, Jerry Rice	49, Neal Anderson
25, Thurman Thomas	37, Neal Anderson	47, Barry Sanders
24, Emmitt Smith	37, Thurman Thomas	39, Thurman Thomas
22, Neal Anderson	29, Herschel Walker	38, Mark Clayton
22, Andre Rison		
Field Goals		
61, Chip Lohmiller	90, Chip Lohmiller	110, Nick Lowery
59, Nick Lowery	83, Nick Lowery	109, Chip Lohmiller
52, Pete Stoyanovich	79, David Treadwell	94, Mike Cofer
52, David Treadwell	71, Pete Stoyanovich	93, Scott Norwood
49, Pat Leahy	67, Mike Cofer	92, Morten Andersen
49, Roger Ruzek	67, Jeff Jaeger	92, Gary Anderson
Rushes		
606, Emmitt Smith	877, Barry Sanders	1064, Thurman Thomas
597, Barry Sanders	857, Thurman Thomas	1035, Eric Dickerson
571, Earnest Byner	840, Christian Okoye	993, Neal Anderson
559, Thurman Thomas	744, Neal Anderson	993, Herschel Walker
470, Neal Anderson	705, Earnest Byner	945, Christian Okoye
470, Christian Okoye		
Rushing Yards		
2852, Barry Sanders	4322, Barry Sanders	4829, Thurman Thomas
2704, Thurman Thomas	3948, Thurman Thomas	4322, Barry Sanders
2500, Emmitt Smith	3316, Christian Okoye	4206, Neal Anderson
2267, Earnest Byner	3100, Neal Anderson	4183, Eric Dickerson
2059, Marion Butts	2847, Earnest Byner	4024, Herschel Walker

Last 2 Seasons	Last 3 Seasons	Last 4 Seasons
Rushing TDs		
29, Barry Sanders	43, Barry Sanders	43, Barry Sanders
23, Emmitt Smith	28, Christian Okoye	39, Neal Anderson
18, Derrick Fenner	27, Neal Anderson	34, Ottis Anderson
18, Thurman Thomas	26, Ottis Anderson	32, Greg Bell
17, Brad Baxter	24, Thurman Thomas	31, Christian Okoye
17, Gerald Riggs		
Passes		
1239, Warren Moon	1703, Warren Moon	2236, Dan Marino
1080, Dan Marino	1630, Dan Marino	2079, Jim Everett
1044, Jim Everett	1562, Jim Everett	1997, Warren Moon
953, John Elway	1430, Bernie Kosar	1865, John Elway
917, Bernie Kosar	1377, Ken O'Brien	1801, Ken O'Brien
Completions		
766, Warren Moon	1046, Warren Moon	1286, Dan Marino
624, Dan Marino	932, Dan Marino	1206, Warren Moon
584, Jim Everett	888, Jim Everett	1196, Jim Everett
537, Bernie Kosar	840, Bernie Kosar	1037, Ken O'Brien
536, John Elway	801, Ken O'Brien	1033, John Elway
Passing Yards		
9379, Warren Moon	13010, Warren Moon	15964, Dan Marino
7533, Dan Marino	11737, Jim Everett	15701, Jim Everett
7427, Jim Everett	11530, Dan Marino	15337, Warren Moon
6779, John Elway	9830, John Elway	13183, Jim Kelly
6673, Jim Kelly	9803, Jim Kelly	13139, John Elway
TD Passes		
57, Jim Kelly	82, Jim Kelly	98, Dan Marino
56, Warren Moon	79, Warren Moon	97, Jim Kelly
46, Dan Marino	70, Dan Marino	96, Warren Moon
44, Mark Rypien	66, Mark Rypien	94, Jim Everett
43, Chris Miller	65, Boomer Esiason	93, Boomer Esiason
Receptions		
180, Jerry Rice	262, Jerry Rice	326, Jerry Rice
174, Haywood Jeffires	240, Andre Reed	311, Andre Reed
164, Drew Hill	230, Drew Hill	302, Drew Hill
163, Andre Rison	226, Sterling Sharpe	297, Art Monk
152, Andre Reed	225, Art Monk	296, Henry Ellard
Reception Yards		
2708, Jerry Rice	4191, Jerry Rice	5497, Jerry Rice
2452, Gary Clark	3728, Henry Ellard	5142, Henry Ellard
2346, Henry Ellard	3681, Gary Clark	4573, Gary Clark
2229, Haywood Jeffires	3489, Sterling Sharpe	4338, Andre Reed
2184, Andre Rison	3370, Andre Reed	4280, Sterling Sharpe
Receiving TDs		
27, Jerry Rice	44, Jerry Rice	53, Jerry Rice
22, Andre Rison	27, Gary Clark	38, Mark Clayton
18, Gary Clark	27, Andre Reed	34, Gary Clark
18, Andre Reed	26, Andre Rison	33, Andre Reed
16, John Taylor	26, John Taylor	28, John Taylor
Interceptions		
13, Gill Byrd	20, Gill Byrd	27, Gill Byrd
12, Joey Browner	17, Joey Browner	22, Joey Browner
12, Mark Carrier	17, Dave Waymer	22, Erik McMillan
11, Ronnie Lott	16, Eric Allen	21, Eric Allen
11, Dave Waymer	16, David Fulcher	21, David Fulcher
	16, Ronnie Lott	21, Ronnie Lott
	16, Tim McDonald	
Sacks		
33.5, Derrick Thomas	44.5, Pat Swilling	58.0, Reggie White
29.0, Reggie White	43.5, Derrick Thomas	51.5, Pat Swilling
28.0, Pat Swilling	40.0, Reggie White	49.0, Kevin Greene
25.5, Greg Townsend	39.0, Chris Doleman	48.0, Lawrence Taylor
24.5, Simon Fletcher	36.5, Simon Fletcher	47.5, Greg Townsend

NFL Team Leaders Over Recent Seasons

Last 2 Seasons	Last 3 Seasons	Last 4 Seasons
Highest Won-Lost Percentage		
.813, Buffalo	.792, San Francisco	.750, San Francisco
.750, San Francisco	.729, Buffalo	.734, Buffalo
.750, Washington	.708, Washington	.672, N.Y. Giants
.688, Chicago	.688, N.Y. Giants	.641, Philadelphia
.656, three teams	.646, Philadelphia	.641, Washington
Most Points		
886, Buffalo	1295, Buffalo	1624, Buffalo
866, Washington	1252, Washington	1597, Washington
791, Houston	1188, San Francisco	1580, Houston
746, San Francisco	1156, Houston	1557, San Francisco
712, Detroit	1027, Cincinnati	1475, Cincinnati
Most Total Yards		
12209, Houston	18021, San Francisco	23921, San Francisco
11753, San Francisco	17636, Houston	23235, Washington
11528, Buffalo	17556, Washington	22841, Houston
11303, Washington	17381, Buffalo	22696, Buffalo
10536, Kansas City	16167, L.A. Rams	22190, Cincinnati

Last 2 Seasons	Last 3 Seasons	Last 4 Seasons
Most Rushing Yards		
4505, San Diego	6725, Buffalo	9124, Cincinnati
4461, Buffalo	6672, Chicago	8991, Chicago
4385, Chicago	6414, Cincinnati	8858, Buffalo
4287, N.Y. Jets	6392, Kansas City	8419, San Diego
4165, Kansas City	6378, San Diego	8105, Kansas City
		8105, N.Y. Jets
Most Passing Yards		
9426, Houston	12925, Houston	16133, Miami
8174, San Francisco	12476, San Francisco	15881, Houston
7401, Miami	11617, Miami	15853, San Francisco
7228, L.A. Rams	11520, Washington	15656, Washington
7171, Washington	11361, L.A. Rams	15166, L.A. Rams
Fewest Turnovers		
37, N.Y. Giants	67, N.Y. Giants	94, N.Y. Giants
41, Kansas City	82, Kansas City	112, San Francisco
49, N.Y. Jets	86, San Francisco	115, Kansas City
51, Washington	88, Washington	117, N.Y. Jets
55, L.A. Raiders	89, Denver	119, Indianapolis
55, Miami	89, Indianapolis	
	89, L.A. Raiders	
Fewest Points Allowed		
478, San Francisco	731, San Francisco	1025, San Francisco
486, New Orleans	760, N.Y. Giants	1064, N.Y. Giants
508, N.Y. Giants	787, New Orleans	1070, New Orleans
509, Kansas City	795, Kansas City	1115, Kansas City
525, Washington	817, Philadelphia	1135, Buffalo
Fewest Total Yards Allowed		
8209, Philadelphia	13103, Philadelphia	18008, Minnesota
8806, N.Y. Giants	13445, San Francisco	18020, San Francisco
8811, New Orleans	13470, N.Y. Giants	18556, N.Y. Giants
8827, San Francisco	13917, Minnesota	18902, Philadelphia
8999, Chicago	13938, Washington	19088, Chicago
Fewest Rushing Yards Allowed		
2305, Philadelphia	3910, Philadelphia	5562, Philadelphia
2770, San Francisco	4098, New Orleans	5741, San Francisco
2772, New Orleans	4153, San Francisco	5877, New Orleans
2933, Washington	4277, Washington	6022, Washington
3115, Houston	4724, N.Y. Giants	6375, Chicago
Fewest Passing Yards Allowed		
5621, N.Y. Giants	8323, Minnesota	10812, Minnesota
5814, Phoenix	8746, N.Y. Giants	11430, Kansas City
5821, Miami	8964, Denver	11897, Denver
5822, Minnesota	8996, Kansas City	12073, N.Y. Giants
5847, Chicago	9036, L.A. Raiders	12143, Buffalo
Most Opponents' Turnovers		
78, Kansas City	134, Philadelphia	178, Philadelphia
78, Philadelphia	116, Washington	150, Houston
75, Chicago	114, New Orleans	150, Minnesota
75, New Orleans	114, Pittsburgh	148, Chicago
74, Washington	113, Chicago	147, Pittsburgh

Records of Teams on Opening Day, 1933-91

AFC	W	L	T	Pct.	Longest W Strk.	Longest L Strk.	Current Streak
Denver	19	12	1	.613	3	4	W-1
L.A. Raiders	19	13	0	.594	5	5	L-1
Cleveland	24	18	0	.571	5	5	L-1
San Diego	18	14	0	.563	6	5	L-5
Houston	17	15	0	.531	4	3	W-1
Kansas City	17	15	0	.531	5	4	W-2
Pittsburgh	28	25	4	.528	4	3	W-1
Indianapolis	20	19	0	.513	8	8	L-8
Cincinnati	12	12	0	.500		4	L-1
New England	16	16	0	.500	5	3	W-1
Miami	11	14	1	.440	4	5	L-1
N.Y. Jets	14	18	0	.438	3	5	W-1
Buffalo	13	19	0	.406	4	5	W-4
Seattle	4	12	0	.250	3	8	L-3

NFC	W	L	T	Pct.	Longest W Strk.	Longest L Strk.	Current Streak
Dallas	24	7	1	.774	17	3	W-2
N.Y. Giants	33	22	4	.600	4	3	W-4
Chicago	34	24	4	.586	8	6	W-8
Minnesota	17	13	1	.567	4	2	L-2
Atlanta	14	12	0	.538	5	3	L-1
L.A. Rams	29	25	0	.537	5	6	L-2
Washington	29	26	4	.527	6	5	W-2
Detroit	30	27	2	.526	7	4	L-3
Green Bay	29	27	3	.518	5	6	L-1
San Francisco	19	22	1	.463	4	3	L-1
Phoenix	26	31	1	.456	6	6	W-1
Philadelphia	23	34	1	.404	5	9	W-1
Tampa Bay	6	10	0	.375	3	5	L-1
New Orleans	6	19	0	.240	1	6	W-1

NOTE: All ties occurred prior to 1972, when calculation of ties in percentages as half-win, half-loss was begun.

Oldest Individual Single-Season or Single-Game Records in NFL Record & Fact Book
Regular-Season Records That Have Not Been Surpassed or Tied

Most Points, Game—40, Ernie Nevers, Chi. Cardinals vs. Chi. Bears, Nov. 28, 1929 (6-td, 4-pat)

Most Touchdowns Rushing, Game—6, Ernie Nevers, Chi. Cardinals vs. Chi. Bears, Nov. 28, 1929

Highest Punting Average, Season (Qualifiers)—51.40, Sammy Baugh, Washington, 1940 (35-1,799)

Highest Punting Average, Game (minimum: 4 punts)—61.75, Bob Cifers, Detroit vs. Chi. Bears, Nov. 24, 1946 (4-247)

Highest Average Gain, Pass Receptions, Season (minimum: 24 receptions)—32.58, Don Currivan, Boston, 1947 (24-782)

Highest Average Gain, Passing, Game (minimum: 20 passes)—18.58, Sammy Baugh, Washington vs. Boston, Oct. 31, 1948 (24-446)

Most Touchdowns, Fumble Recoveries, Game—2, Fred (Dippy) Evans, Chi. Bears vs. Washington, Nov. 28, 1948

Most Yards Gained, Intercepted Passes, Rookie, Season—301, Don Doll, Detroit, 1949

Most Passes Had Intercepted, Game—8, Jim Hardy, Chi. Cardinals vs. Philadelphia, Sept. 24, 1950

Highest Average Gain, Rushing, Game (minimum: 10 attempts)—17.09, Marion Motley, Cleveland vs. Pittsburgh, Oct. 29, 1950 (11-188)

Most Yards Gained, Kickoff Returns, Game—294, Wally Triplett, Detroit vs. Los Angeles, Oct. 29, 1950

Highest Kickoff Return Average, Game (minimum: 3 returns)—73.50, Wally Triplett, Detroit vs. Los Angeles, Oct. 29, 1950 (4-294)

Most Pass Receptions, Game—18, Tom Fears, Los Angeles vs. Green Bay, Dec. 3, 1950

Highest Punt Return Average, Season (Qualifiers)—23.00, Herb Rich, Baltimore, 1950 (12-276)

Highest Punt Return Average, Rookie, Season (Qualifiers)—23.00, Herb Rich, Baltimore, 1950 (12-276)

Most Yards Passing, Game—554, Norm Van Brocklin, Los Angeles vs. N.Y. Yanks, Sept. 28, 1951

Most Touchdowns, Punt Returns, Rookie, Season—4, Jack Christiansen, Detroit, 1951

Most Interceptions By, Season—14, Dick (Night Train) Lane, Los Angeles, 1952

Most Interceptions By, Rookie, Season—14, Dick (Night Train) Lane, Los Angeles, 1952

Highest Average Gain, Passing, Season (Qualifiers)—11.17, Tommy O'Connell, Cleveland, 1957 (110-1,229)

Most Points, Season—176, Paul Hornung, Green Bay, 1960 (15-td, 41-pat, 15-fg)

Most Yards Gained, Pass Receptions, Rookie, Season—1,473, Bill Groman, Houston, 1960

Largest Trades in NFL History
(Based on number of players or draft choices involved)

15—March 26, 1953—T Mike McCormack, DT Don Colo, LB Tom Catlin, DB John Petitbon, and G Herschell Forester from Baltimore to Cleveland for DB Don Shula, DB Bert Rechichar, DB Carl Taseff, LB Ed Sharkey, E Gern Nagler, QB Harry Agganis, T Dick Batten, T Stu Sheets, G Art Spinney, and G Elmer Willhoite.

15—January 28, 1971—LB Marlin McKeever, first- and third-round choices in 1971, and third-, fourth-, fifth-, sixth-, and seventh-round choices in 1972 from Washington to the Los Angeles Rams for LB Maxie Baughan, LB Jack Pardee, LB Myron Pottios, RB Jeff Jordan, G John Wilbur, DT Diron Talbert, and a fifth-round choice in 1971.

12—June 13, 1952—Selection rights to Les Richter from the Dallas Texans to the Los Angeles Rams for RB Dick Hoerner, DB Tom Keane, DB George Sims, C Joe Reid, HB Billy Baggett, T Jack Halliday, FB Dick McKissack, LB Vic Vasicek, E Richard Wilkins, C Aubrey Phillips, and RB Dave Anderson.

10—March 23, 1959—HB Ollie Matson from the Chicago Cardinals to the Los Angeles Rams for T Frank Fuller, DE Glenn Holtzman, T Ken Panfil, DT Art Hauser, E John Tracey, FB Larry Hickman, HB Don Brown, the Rams second-round choice in 1960, and a player to be delivered during the 1959 training camp.

10—October 31, 1987—RB Eric Dickerson from the Los Angeles Rams to Indianapolis. The rights to LB Cornelius Bennett from Indianapolis to Buffalo. Indianapolis running back Owen Gill and the Colts' first- and second-round choices in 1988 and second-round choice in 1989, plus Bills running back Greg Bell and Buffalo's first-round choice in 1988 and first- and second-round choices in 1989 to the Rams.

Retired Uniform Numbers in NFL
AFC

Buffalo:	None	
Cincinnati:	Bob Johnson	54
Cleveland:	Otto Graham	14
	Jim Brown	32
	Ernie Davis	45
	Don Fleming	46
	Lou Groza	76
Denver:	Frank Tripucka	18
	Floyd Little	44

Houston: . . . . .Earl Campbell 34
Jim Norton 43
Elvin Bethea 65
Indianapolis: . . . . . . .Johnny Unitas 19
Buddy Young 22
Lenny Moore 24
Art Donovan 70
Jim Parker 77
Raymond Berry 82
Gino Marchetti 89
Kansas City: . . . . . . .Len Dawson 16
Abner Haynes 28
Stone Johnson 33
Mack Lee Hill 36
Bobby Bell 78
Los Angeles Raiders: . . . .None
Miami: . . . . .Bob Griese 12
New England: . . . . . . .Gino Cappelletti 20
Steve Nelson 57
John Hannah 73
Jim Hunt 79
Bob Dee 89
New York Jets: . . . . . .Joe Namath 12
Don Maynard 13
Pittsburgh: . . . . .None
San Diego: . . . . .Dan Fouts 14
Seattle: . . . ."Fans/the twelfth man" 12
NFC
Atlanta: . . . . .William Andrews 31
Jeff Van Note 57
Tommy Nobis 60
Chicago: . . . . .Bronko Nagurski 3
George McAfee 5
Willie Galimore 28
Walter Payton 34
Brian Piccolo 41
Sid Luckman 42
Bill Hewitt 56
Bill George 61
Bulldog Turner 66
Red Grange 77
Dallas: . . . . .None
Detroit: . . . . .Dutch Clark 7
Bobby Layne 22
Doak Walker 37
Joe Schmidt 56
Chuck Hughes 85
Charlie Sanders 88
Green Bay: . . . . .Tony Canadeo 3
Don Hutson 14
Bart Starr 15
Ray Nitschke 66
Los Angeles Rams: . .Bob Waterfield 7
Merlin Olsen 74
Minnesota: . . . . .Fran Tarkenton 10
Alan Page 88
New Orleans: . . . . . . .Jim Taylor 31
Doug Atkins 81
New York Giants: . . . .Ray Flaherty 1
Mel Hein 7
Y. A. Tittle 14
Al Blozis 32
Joe Morrison 40
Charlie Conerly 42
Ken Strong 50
Philadelphia: . . . . . . .Steve Van Buren 15
Tom Brookshier 40
Pete Retzlaff 44
Chuck Bednarik 60
Al Wistert 70
Phoenix: . . . . .Larry Wilson 8
Stan Mauldin 77
J.V. Cain 88
Marshall Goldberg 99
San Francisco: . . . . .John Brodie 12
Joe Perry 34
Jimmy Johnson 37
Hugh McElhenny 39
Charlie Krueger 70
Leo Nomellini 73
Dwight Clark 87
Tampa Bay: . . . . .Lee Roy Selmon 63
Washington: . . . . . . .Sammy Baugh 33

1991 NFL Score by Quarters

AFC Offense	1	2	3	4	OT	PTS
Buffalo	82	130	106	137	3	458
Houston	43	129	64	147	3	386
Miami	55	119	51	115	3	343
Kansas City	44	91	79	105	3	322
N.Y. Jets	93	84	53	78	6	314
Denver	42	111	71	80	0	304
L.A. Raiders	58	108	63	66	3	298
Cleveland	57	105	77	48	6	293
Pittsburgh	42	53	67	124	6	292
Seattle	39	78	79	80	0	276
San Diego	41	95	37	101	0	274
Cincinnati	57	71	64	71	0	263
New England	40	55	23	84	9	211
Indianapolis	24	54	27	38	0	143

NFC Offense	1	2	3	4	OT	PTS
Washington	83	150	101	148	3	485
San Francisco	63	139	64	127	0	393
Atlanta	84	102	88	84	3	361
Dallas	91	105	35	111	0	342
New Orleans	61	120	75	85	0	341
Detroit	72	67	77	120	3	339
Minnesota	51	91	67	92	0	301
Chicago	40	96	71	86	6	299
Philadelphia	41	109	53	82	0	285
N.Y. Giants	81	89	58	53	0	281
Green Bay	68	78	55	72	0	273
L.A. Rams	22	103	55	54	0	234
Tampa Bay	30	49	41	79	0	199
Phoenix	43	68	32	53	0	196

AFC Defense	1	2	3	4	OT	PTS
Denver	43	77	49	66	0	235
Houston	53	81	59	55	3	251
Kansas City	58	85	50	59	0	252
Seattle	25	112	47	74	3	261
N.Y. Jets	36	78	91	82	6	293
L.A. Raiders	49	89	52	104	3	297
Cleveland	25	113	51	109	0	298
New England	53	122	32	98	0	305
Buffalo	40	87	92	96	3	318
San Diego	63	97	73	100	9	342
Pittsburgh	61	116	54	113	0	344
Miami	65	100	75	106	3	349
Indianapolis	96	106	88	85	6	381
Cincinnati	68	163	76	122	6	435

NFC Defense	1	2	3	4	OT	PTS
New Orleans	23	59	54	72	3	211
Washington	54	57	55	58	0	224
San Francisco	30	89	64	56	0	239
Philadelphia	72	71	38	63	0	244
Chicago	57	72	51	86	3	269
Detroit	75	108	58	54	0	295
N.Y. Giants	24	93	51	129	0	297
Minnesota	51	77	51	124	3	306
Dallas	61	89	66	91	3	310
Green Bay	47	102	49	112	3	313
Atlanta	48	94	70	126	0	338
Phoenix	93	87	84	80	0	344
Tampa Bay	82	111	77	95	0	365
L.A. Rams	95	114	76	105	0	390

NFL TOTALS	1	2	3	4	OT	PTS
	1547	2649	1733	2520	57	8506

Team Leaders

Offense

	Most Scored	Fewest Scored
1st Quarter	93, N.Y. Jets	22, L.A. Rams
2nd Quarter	150, Washington	49, Tampa Bay
3rd Quarter	106, Buffalo	23, New England
4th Quarter	148, Washington	38, Indianapolis

Defense

	Most Allowed	Fewest Allowed
1st Quarter	96, Indianapolis	23, New Orleans
2nd Quarter	163, Cincinnati	57, Washington
3rd Quarter	92, Buffalo	32, New England
4th Quarter	129, N.Y. Giants	54, Detroit

Greatest Comebacks in NFL History
(Most Points Overcome To Win Game)

Regular-Season Games

From 28 points behind to win:
December 7, 1980, at San Francisco

New Orleans	14	21	0	0	0	— 35
San Francisco	0	7	14	14	3	— 38

NO —Harris 33 pass from Manning (Ricardo kick)
NO —Childs 21 pass from Manning (Ricardo kick)
NO —Holmes 1 run (Ricardo kick)
SF —Solomon 57 punt return (Wersching kick)
NO —Holmes 1 run (Ricardo kick)
NO —Harris 41 pass from Manning (Ricardo kick)
SF —Montana 1 run (Wersching kick)
SF —Clark 71 pass from Montana (Wersching kick)
SF —Solomon 14 pass from Montana (Wersching kick)
SF —Elliott 7 run (Wersching kick)
SF —FG Wersching 36

	N.O.	S.F.
First Downs	27	24
Total Yards	519	430
Yards Rushing	143	176
Yards Passing	376	254
Turnovers	3	0

From 25 points behind to win:
November 8, 1987, at St. Louis

Tampa Bay	7	7	14	0	— 28
St. Louis	0	3	0	28	— 31

TB —Carrier 5 pass from DeBerg (Igwebuike kick)
TB —Carter 3 pass from DeBerg (Igwebuike kick)
StL —FG Gallery 31
TB —Smith 34 pass from DeBerg (Igwebuike kick)
TB —Smith 3 run (Igwebuike kick)
StL —Awalt 4 pass from Lomax (Gallery kick)
StL —Noga 23 fumble recovery (Gallery kick)
StL —J. Smith 11 pass from Lomax (Gallery kick)
StL —J. Smith 17 pass from Lomax (Gallery kick)

	T.B.	St.L.
First Downs	26	26
Total Yards	377	415
Yards Rushing	83	137
Yards Passing	294	278
Turnovers	1	2

From 24 points behind to win:
October 27, 1946, at Washington

Philadelphia	0	0	14	14	— 28
Washington	10	14	0	0	— 24

Wash —Rosato 2 run (Poillon kick)
Wash —FG Poillon 28
Wash —Rosato 4 run (Poillon kick)
Wash —Lapka recovered fumble in end zone (Poillon kick)
Phil —Steele 1 run (Lio kick)
Phil —Pritchard 45 pass from Thompson (Lio kick)
Phil —Steinke 7 pass from Thompson (Lio kick)
Phil —Ferrante 30 pass from Thompson (Lio kick)

	Phil.	Wash.
First Downs	14	8
Total Yards	262	127
Yards Rushing	34	66
Yards Passing	228	61
Turnovers	6	3

From 24 points behind to win:
October 20, 1957, at Detroit

Baltimore	7	14	6	0	— 27
Detroit	0	3	7	21	— 31

Balt —Mutscheller 15 pass from Unitas (Rechichar kick)
Det —FG Martin 47
Balt —Moore 72 pass from Unitas (Rechichar kick)
Balt —Mutscheller 52 pass from Unitas (Rechichar kick)
Balt —Moore 4 pass from Unitas (kick failed)
Det —Junker 14 pass from Rote (Layne kick)
Det —Cassady 26 pass from Layne (Layne kick)
Det —Johnson 1 run (Layne kick)
Det —Cassady 29 pass from Layne (Layne kick)

	Balt.	Det.
First Downs	15	20
Total Yards	322	369
Yards Rushing	117	178
Yards Passing	205	191
Turnovers	6	4

From 24 points behind to win:
October 25, 1959, at Chicago

Philadelphia	0	0	21	7	— 28
Chi. Cardinals	7	10	7	0	— 24

Chi —Crow 10 pass from Roach (Conrad kick)
Chi —J. Hill 77 blocked field goal return (Conrad kick)
Chi —FG Conrad 15
Chi —Lane 37 interception return (Conrad kick)
Phil —Barnes 1 run (Walston kick)
Phil —McDonald 29 pass from Van Brocklin (Walston kick)
Phil —Barnes 2 run (Walston kick)
Phil —McDonald 22 pass from Van Brocklin (Walston kick)

	Phil.	Chi.
First Downs	22	14
Total Yards	399	313
Yards Rushing	168	163
Yards Passing	231	150
Turnovers	2	6

From 24 points behind to win:
October 23, 1960, at Denver

Boston	10	7	7	0	— 24
Denver	0	0	14	17	— 31

Bos —FG Cappelletti 12
Bos —Colclough 10 pass from Songin (Cappelletti kick)
Bos —Wells 6 pass from Songin (Cappelletti kick)
Bos —Miller 47 pass from Songin (Cappelletti kick)
Den —Carmichael 21 pass from Tripucka (Mingo kick)
Den —Jessup 19 pass from Tripucka (Mingo kick)
Den —Carmichael 35 lateral from Taylor, pass from Tripucka (Mingo kick)
Den —Taylor 8 pass from Tripucka (Mingo kick)
Den —FG Mingo 9

	Bos.	Den.
First Downs	19	16
Total Yards	434	326
Yards Rushing	211	65
Yards Passing	223	261
Turnovers	7	4

From 24 points behind to win:
December 15, 1974, at Miami

New England	21	3	0	3	— 27
Miami	0	17	7	10	— 34

NE —Hannah recovered fumble in end zone (J. Smith kick)
NE —Sanders 23 interception return (J. Smith kick)
NE —Herron 4 pass from Plunkett (J. Smith kick)
NE —FG J. Smith 46
Mia —Nottingham 1 run (Yepremian kick)
Mia —Baker 37 pass from Morrall (Yepremian kick)
Mia —FG Yepremian 28
Mia —Baker 46 pass from Morrall (Yepremian kick)
NE —FG J. Smith 34
Mia —Nottingham 2 run (Yepremian kick)
Mia —FG Yepremian 40

	N.E.	Mia.
First Downs	18	18
Total Yards	333	333
Yards Rushing	114	61
Yards Passing	219	272
Turnovers	3	4

From 24 points behind to win:
December 4, 1977, at Minnesota

San Francisco	0	10	14	3	— 27
Minnesota	0	0	7	21	— 28

SF —Delvin Williams 2 run (Wersching kick)
SF —FG Wersching 31
SF —Dave Williams 80 kickoff return (Wersching kick)
SF —Delvin Williams 5 run (Wersching kick)
Minn —McClanahan 15 pass from Lee (Cox kick)
Minn —Rashad 8 pass from Kramer (Cox kick)
Minn —Tucker 9 pass from Kramer (Cox kick)
SF —FG Wersching 31
Minn —S. White 69 pass from Kramer (Cox kick)

	S.F.	Minn.
First Downs	19	18
Total Yards	243	309
Yards Rushing	196	52
Yards Passing	47	257
Turnovers	2	5

From 24 points behind to win:
September 23, 1979, at Denver

Seattle	10	10	14	0	— 34
Denver	0	10	21	6	— 37

Sea —FG Herrera 28
Sea —Doornink 5 run (Herrera kick)
Den —FG Turner 27
Sea —Doornink 5 run (Herrera kick)
Den —Armstrong 2 run (Turner kick)
Sea —FG Herrera 22
Sea —McCullum 13 pass from Zorn (Herrera kick)
Sea —Smith 1 run (Herrera kick)
Den —Studdard 2 pass from Morton (Turner kick)
Den —Moses 11 pass from Morton (Turner kick)

Den—Upchurch 35 pass from Morton (Turner kick)
Den—Lytle 1 run (kick failed)

	Sea.	Den.
First Downs	22	23
Total Yards	350	344
Yards Rushing	153	90
Yards Passing	197	254
Turnovers	4	3

From 24 points behind to win:
September 23, 1979, at Cincinnati

Houston	0	10	17	0	3 — 30
Cincinnati	14	10	0	3	0 — 27

Cin —Johnson 1 run (Bahr kick)
Cin —Alexander 2 run (Bahr kick)
Cin —Johnson 1 run (Bahr kick)
Cin —FG Bahr 52
Hou—Burrough 35 pass from Pastorini (Fritsch kick)
Hou—FG Fritsch 33
Hou—Campbell 8 run (Fritsch kick)
Hou—Caster 22 pass from Pastorini (Fritsch kick)
Hou—FG Fritsch 47
Cin —FG Bahr 55
Hou—FG Fritsch 29

	Hou.	Cin.
First Downs	19	21
Total Yards	361	265
Yards Rushing	177	165
Yards Passing	184	100
Turnovers	3	2

From 24 points behind to win:
November 22, 1982, at Los Angeles

San Diego	10	14	0	0 — 24
L.A. Raiders	0	7	14	7 — 28

SD —FG Benirschke 19
SD —Scales 29 pass from Fouts (Benirschke kick)
SD —Muncie 2 run (Benirschke kick)
SD —Muncie 1 run (Benirschke kick)
Raiders —Christensen 1 pass from Plunkett (Bahr kick)
Raiders —Allen 3 run (Bahr kick)
Raiders —Allen 6 run (Bahr kick)
Raiders —Hawkins 1 run (Bahr kick)

	S.D.	Raiders
First Downs	26	23
Total Yards	411	326
Yards Rushing	72	181
Yards Passing	339	145
Turnovers	4	2

From 24 points behind to win:
September 26, 1988, at Denver

L.A. Raiders	0	0	14	13	3 — 30
Denver	7	17	0	3	0 — 27

Den —Dorsett 1 run (Karlis kick)
Den —Dorsett 1 run (Karlis kick)
Den —Sewell 7 pass from Elway (Karlis kick)
Den —FG Karlis 39
Raiders —Smith 40 pass from Schroeder (Bahr kick)
Raiders —Smith 42 pass from Schroeder (Bahr kick)
Raiders —FG Bahr 28
Raiders —Allen 4 run (Bahr kick)
Den —FG Karlis 25
Raiders —FG Bahr 44
Raiders —FG Bahr 35

	Raiders	Den.
First Downs	20	23
Total Yards	363	398
Yards Rushing	128	189
Yards Passing	235	209
Turnovers	1	5

Postseason Games

From 20 points behind to win:
Western Conference Playoff Game
December 22, 1957, at San Francisco

Detroit	0	7	14	10 — 31
San Francisco	14	10	3	0 — 27

SF —Owens 34 pass from Tittle (Soltau kick)
SF —McElhenny 47 pass from Tittle (Soltau kick)
Det—Junker 4 pass from Rote (Martin kick)
SF —Wilson 12 pass from Tittle (Soltau kick)
SF —FG Soltau 25
SF —FG Soltau 10
Det—Tracy 2 run (Martin kick)
Det—Tracy 58 run (Martin kick)
Det—Gedman 3 run (Martin kick)
Det—FG Martin 14

	Det.	S.F.
First Downs	22	20
Total Yards	324	351
Yards Rushing	129	127
Yards Passing	195	224
Turnovers	5	4

From 18 points behind to win:
NFC Divisional Playoff Game
December 23, 1972, at San Francisco

Dallas	3	10	0	17 — 30
San Francisco	7	14	7	0 — 28

SF —Washington 97 kickoff return (Gossett kick)
Dall—FG Fritsch 37
SF —Schreiber 1 run (Gossett kick)
SF —Schreiber 1 run (Gossett kick)
Dall—FG Fritsch 45
Dall—Alworth 28 pass from Morton (Fritsch kick)
SF —Schreiber 1 run (Gossett kick)
Dall—FG Fritsch 27
Dall—Parks 20 pass from Staubach (Fritsch kick)
Dall—Sellers 10 pass from Staubach (Fritsch kick)

	Dall.	S.F.
First Downs	22	13
Total Yards	402	255
Yards Rushing	165	105
Yards Passing	237	150
Turnovers	5	3

From 18 points behind to win:
AFC Divisional Playoff Game
January 4, 1986, at Miami

Cleveland	7	7	7	0 — 21
Miami	3	0	14	7 — 24

Mia —FG Reveiz 51
Clev—Newsome 16 pass from Kosar (Bahr kick)
Clev—Byner 21 run (Bahr kick)
Clev—Byner 66 run (Bahr kick)
Mia —Moore 6 pass from Marino (Reveiz kick)
Mia —Davenport 31 run (Reveiz kick)
Mia —Davenport 1 run (Reveiz kick)

	Clev.	Mia.
First Downs	17	20
Total Yards	313	330
Yards Rushing	251	92
Yards Passing	62	238
Turnovers	1	1

From 15 points behind to win:
AFC Divisional Playoff Game
January 4, 1992, at Denver

Houston	14	7	0	3 — 24
Denver	6	7	3	10 — 26

Hou —Jeffires 15 pass from Moon (Del Greco kick)
Hou —Hill 9 pass from Moon (Del Greco kick)
Den —V. Johnson 10 pass from Elway (kick failed)
Hou —Duncan 6 pass from Moon (Del Greco kick)
Den —Lewis 1 run (Treadwell kick)
Den —FG Treadwell 49
Hou —FG Del Greco 25
Den —Lewis 1 run (Treadwell kick)
Den —FG Treadwell 28

	Hou.	Den.
First Downs	23	26
Total Yards	422	418
Yards Rushing	97	151
Yards Passing	325	267
Turnovers	1	1

Records of NFL Teams Since 1970 AFL-NFL Merger

AFC	W - L - T	Pct.	Division Titles	Playoff Berths	Postseason Record	Super Bowl Record
Miami	218-108-2	.668	9	13	15-11	2-3
L.A. Raiders	210-112-6	.651	9	14	17-11	3-0
Pittsburgh	192-135-1	.587	9	12	16-8	4-0
Denver	185-137-6	.574	7	9	9-9	0-4
Cincinnati	167-161-0	.509	5	7	5-7	0-2
Cleveland	164-161-3	.505	6	9	3-9	0-0
Seattle*	119-125-0	.488	1	4	3-4	0-0
New England	151-177-0	.460	2	5	3-5	0-1
Kansas City	147-174-7	.458	1	4	1-4	0-0
Buffalo	146-180-2	.448	5	7	6-7	0-2
Houston	142-184-2	.436	1	8	7-8	0-0
San Diego	140-183-5	.434	3	4	3-4	0-0
N.Y. Jets	140-186-2	.430	0	5	3-5	0-0
Indianapolis	135-191-2	.414	5	6	4-5	1-0

NFC	W - L - T	Pct.	Division Titles	Playoff Berths	Post-season Record	Super Bowl Record
Washington	212-115-1	.648	5	12	17-9	3-2
Dallas	202-126-0	.616	9	15	20-13	2-3
L.A. Rams	192-132-4	.592	8	14	10-14	0-1
Minnesota	190-136-2	.582	10	13	11-13	0-3
San Francisco	188-137-3	.578	11	12	16-8	4-0
Chicago	174-153-1	.532	6	9	6-8	1-0
Philadelphia	152-170-6	.472	2	7	3-7	0-1
N.Y. Giants	152-174-2	.466	3	6	9-4	2-0
Detroit	145-179-4	.448	2	4	1-4	0-0
Phoenix	140-182-6	.436	2	3	0-3	0-0
Green Bay	132-188-8	.414	1	2	1-2	0-0
Atlanta	132-192-4	.408	1	4	2-4	0-0
New Orleans	128-196-4	.395	1	3	0-3	0-0
Tampa Bay*	71-172-1	.293	2	3	1-3	0-0

*entered NFL in 1976.
Indianapolis totals include Baltimore, 1970-83.
L.A. Raiders totals include Oakland, 1970-81.
Phoenix totals include St. Louis, 1970-87.

Tie games before 1972 are not calculated in won-lost percentage.

In 1982, due to players' strike, the divisional format was abandoned. (L.A. Raiders and Washington won regular-season conference titles, not included in "Division Titles" totals listed above. Sixteen teams were awarded playoff berths, included in totals listed above.)

Longest Winning Streaks Since 1970

Regular-season games

16	Miami, 1971-73	(1 in 1971, 14 in 1972, 1 in 1973)
16	Miami, 1983-84	(5 in 1983, 11 in 1984)
15	San Francisco, 1989-90	(5 in 1989, 10 in 1990)
14	Oakland, 1976-77	(10 in 1976, 4 in 1977)
13	Chicago, 1984-85	(1 in 1984, 12 in 1985)
13	Minnesota, 1974-75	(3 in 1974, 10 in 1975)
13	N.Y. Giants, 1989-90	(3 in 1989, 10 in 1990)
12	Washington, 1990-91	(1 in 1990, 11 in 1991)
11	Pittsburgh, 1975	
11	Baltimore, 1975-76	(9 in 1975, 2 in 1976)
11	Chicago, 1986-87	(7 in 1986, 4 in 1987)
10	Miami, 1973	
10	Pittsburgh, 1976-77	(9 in 1976, 1 in 1977)
10	Denver, 1984	

NFL Playoff Appearances by Seasons

Team	Number of Seasons in Playoffs
Cleveland	22
Los Angeles Rams	22
New York Giants	22
Chicago	20
Dallas	19
Washington	18
Los Angeles Raiders	17
Minnesota	15
Green Bay	13
Houston	13
Miami	13
Pittsburgh	13
San Francisco	13
Buffalo	11
Indianapolis	11
Philadelphia	11
Denver	9
Detroit	9
San Diego	9
Kansas City	8
Cincinnati	7
New York Jets	7
New England	6
Phoenix	5
Atlanta	4
Seattle	4
New Orleans	3
Tampa Bay	3

Teams in Super Bowl Contention, 1978-91

	With 3 Weeks to Play	With 2 Weeks to Play	With 1 Week to Play
1991	20	18	13
1990	23	20	15
1989	21	18	17
1988	21	18	15
1987	19	19	15
1986	19	17	14
1985	21	18	13
1984	18	14	13

1983	24	19	15
1982	20	17	12
1981	21	20	16
1980	20	14	12
1979	19	15	13
1978	20	17	12

Games Decided by 7 Points or Less and 3 Points or Less (1970-91)

	Games Decided by 7 Points or Less	Games Decided by 3 Points or Less
1970	59 of 182 (32.4%)	34 of 182 (18.7%)
1971	76 of 182 (41.8%)	35 of 182 (19.2%)
1972	71 of 182 (39.0%)	38 of 182 (20.9%)
1973	60 of 182 (32.9%)	28 of 182 (15.4%)
1974	91 of 182 (50.0%)	37 of 182 (20.3%)
1975	62 of 182 (34.1%)	35 of 182 (19.2%)
1976	73 of 196 (37.2%)	38 of 196 (19.4%)
1977	85 of 196 (43.4%)	36 of 196 (18.4%)
1978	108 of 224 (48.2%)	49 of 224 (21.9%)
1979	104 of 224 (46.4%)	51 of 224 (22.8%)
1980	108 of 224 (48.2%)	58 of 224 (25.9%)
1981	91 of 224 (40.6%)	60 of 224 (26.8%)
1982	61 of 126 (48.4%)	33 of 126 (26.2%)
1983	106 of 224 (47.3%)	54 of 224 (24.1%)
1984	95 of 224 (42.4%)	58 of 224 (25.9%)
1985	87 of 224 (38.8%)	38 of 224 (17.0%)
1986	106 of 224 (47.3%)	48 of 224 (21.4%)
1987	99 of 210 (47.1%)	40 of 210 (19.0%)
1988	113 of 224 (50.4%)	62 of 224 (27.7%)
1989	107 of 224 (47.8%)	55 of 224 (24.6%)
1990	97 of 224 (43.3%)	54 of 224 (24.1%)
1991	112 of 224 (50.0%)	57 of 224 (25.4%)

1991 Records of Teams in Close Games

AFC	Overall Record	Decided by 7 Pts. or Less	Decided By 3 Pts. or Less
Buffalo	13-3	5-2	2-2
Cincinnati	3-13	2-6	2-1
Cleveland	6-10	4-7	2-5
Denver	12-4	8-3	3-3
Houston	11-5	5-4	3-1
Indianapolis	1-15	1-3	1-0
Kansas City	10-6	6-4	3-1
L.A. Raiders	9-7	6-4	5-2
Miami	8-8	3-4	2-1
New England	6-10	5-3	3-1
N.Y. Jets	8-8	5-6	4-4
Pittsburgh	7-9	4-3	0-2
San Diego	4-12	2-8	2-5
Seattle	7-9	3-6	1-4

NFC	Overall Record	Decided by 7 Pts. or Less	Decided By 3 Pts. or Less
Atlanta	10-6	6-3	3-1
Chicago	11-5	5-1	3-1
Dallas	11-5	4-2	2-2
Detroit	12-4	4-0	1-0
Green Bay	4-12	2-6	1-4
L.A. Rams	3-13	3-4	1-1
Minnesota	8-8	4-4	3-1
New Orleans	11-5	5-3	1-3
N.Y. Giants	8-8	6-6	3-2
Philadelphia	10-6	5-2	2-1
Phoenix	4-12	1-4	0-0
San Francisco	10-6	2-6	1-3
Tampa Bay	3-13	1-6	1-4
Washington	14-2	5-2	2-2

Super Bowl Champions Who Did Not Make Playoffs The Following Year

N.Y. Giants—Super Bowl XXV champions did not make playoffs in the 1991 season.

Washington—Super Bowl XXII champions did not make playoffs in the 1988 season.

N.Y. Giants—Super Bowl XXI champions did not make playoffs in the 1987 season.

San Francisco—Super Bowl XVI champions did not make playoffs in the 1982 season.

Oakland—Super Bowl XV champions did not make playoffs in the 1981 season.

Pittsburgh—Super Bowl XIV champions did not make playoffs in the 1980 season.

Kansas City—Super Bowl IV champions did not make playoffs in the 1970 season.

Green Bay—Super Bowl II champions did not make playoffs in the 1968 season.

All-Time Records of Current NFL Teams

Buffalo Bills

Season	All Games			Home Games			Road Games		
	W	L	T	W	L	T	W	L	T
1960	5	8	1	3	4		2	4	1
1961	6	8		2	5		4	3	
1962	7	6	1	3	3	1	4	3	
1963	7	6	1	4	2	1	3	4	
1964	12	2		6	1		6	1	
1965	10	3	1	5	2		5	1	1
1966	9	4	1	4	2	1	5	2	
1967	4	10		2	5		2	5	
1968	1	12	1	1	6		0	6	1
1969	4	10		4	3		0	7	
1970	3	10	1	1	6		2	4	1
1971	1	13		1	6		0	7	
1972	4	9	1	2	4	1	2	5	
1973	9	5		5	2		4	3	
1974	9	5		5	2		4	3	
1975	8	6		3	4		5	2	
1976	2	12		1	6		1	6	
1977	3	11		1	6		2	5	
1978	5	11		4	4		1	7	
1979	7	9		3	5		4	4	
1980	11	5		6	2		5	3	
1981	10	6		7	1		3	5	
1982	4	5		4	1		0	4	
1983	8	8		3	5		5	3	
1984	2	14		2	6		0	8	
1985	2	14		2	6		0	8	
1986	4	12		3	5		1	7	
1987	7	8		4	4		3	4	
1988	12	4		8	0		4	4	
1989	9	7		6	2		3	5	
1990	13	3		8	0		5	3	
1991	13	3		7	1		6	2	
Total	211	249	8	120	111	4	91	138	4

Cincinnati Bengals

Season	All Games			Home Games			Road Games		
	W	L	T	W	L	T	W	L	T
1968	3	11		2	5		1	6	
1969	4	9	1	4	3		0	6	1
1970	8	6		5	2		3	4	
1971	4	10		3	4		1	6	
1972	8	6		4	3		4	3	
1973	10	4		7	0		3	4	
1974	7	7		4	3		3	4	
1975	11	3		6	1		5	2	
1976	10	4		6	1		4	3	
1977	8	6		5	2		3	4	
1978	4	12		3	5		1	7	
1979	4	12		4	4		0	8	
1980	6	10		3	5		3	5	
1981	12	4		6	2		6	2	
1982	7	2		4	0		3	2	
1983	7	9		4	4		3	5	
1984	8	8		5	3		3	5	
1985	7	9		5	3		2	6	
1986	10	6		6	2		4	4	
1987	4	11		1	7		3	4	
1988	12	4		8	0		4	4	
1989	8	8		5	3		3	5	
1990	9	7		5	3		4	4	
1991	3	13		3	5		0	8	
Total	174	181	1	108	70		66	111	1

Cleveland Browns

Season	All Games			Home Games			Road Games		
	W	L	T	W	L	T	W	L	T
1950	10	2		5	1		5	1	
1951	11	1		6	0		5	1	
1952	8	4		4	2		4	2	
1953	11	1		6	0		5	1	
1954	9	3		5	1		4	2	
1955	9	2	1	5	1		4	1	1
1956	5	7		1	5		4	2	
1957	9	2	1	6	0		3	2	1
1958	9	3		4	2		5	1	
1959	7	5		3	3		4	2	
1960	8	3	1	4	2		4	1	1
1961	8	5	1	4	3		4	2	1
1962	7	6	1	4	2	1	3	4	
1963	10	4		5	2		5	2	
1964	10	3	1	5	1	1	5	2	
1965	11	3		5	2		6	1	
1966	9	5		5	2		4	3	
1967	9	5		6	1		3	4	
1968	10	4		5	2		5	2	
1969	10	3	1	5	1	1	5	2	
1970	7	7		4	3		3	4	
1971	9	5		4	3		5	2	
1972	10	4		4	3		6	1	
1973	7	5	2	5	1	1	2	4	1
1974	4	10		3	4		1	6	
1975	3	11		3	4		0	7	
1976	9	5		6	1		3	4	
1977	6	8		2	5		4	3	
1978	8	8		5	3		3	5	
1979	9	7		5	3		4	4	
1980	11	5		6	2		5	3	
1981	5	11		3	5		2	6	
1982	4	5		2	2		2	3	
1983	9	7		6	2		3	5	
1984	5	11		2	6		3	5	
1985	8	8		5	3		3	5	
1986	12	4		6	2		6	2	
1987	10	5		5	2		5	3	
1988	10	6		6	2		4	4	
1989	9	6	1	5	2	1	4	4	
1990	3	13		2	6		1	7	
1991	6	10		3	5		3	5	
Total	344	232	10	185	102	5	159	130	5

Denver Broncos

Season	All Games			Home Games			Road Games		
	W	L	T	W	L	T	W	L	T
1960	4	9	1	2	4	1	2	5	
1961	3	11		2	5		1	6	
1962	7	7		3	4		4	3	
1963	2	11	1	2	5		0	6	1
1964	2	11	1	2	4	1	0	7	
1965	4	10		2	5		2	5	
1966	4	10		3	4		1	6	
1967	3	11		1	6		2	5	
1968	5	9		3	4		2	5	
1969	5	8	1	4	2	1	1	6	
1970	5	8	1	3	3	1	2	5	
1971	4	9	1	2	4	1	2	5	
1972	5	9		3	4		2	5	
1973	7	5	2	3	3	1	4	2	1
1974	7	6	1	3	3	1	4	3	
1975	6	8		5	2		1	6	
1976	9	5		6	1		3	4	
1977	12	2		6	1		6	1	
1978	10	6		6	2		4	4	
1979	10	6		6	2		4	4	
1980	8	8		4	4		4	4	
1981	10	6		8	0		2	6	
1982	2	7		1	4		1	3	
1983	9	7		6	2		3	5	
1984	13	3		7	1		6	2	
1985	11	5		6	2		5	3	
1986	11	5		7	1		4	4	
1987	10	4	1	7	1		3	3	1
1988	8	8		6	2		2	6	
1989	11	5		6	2		5	3	
1990	5	11		4	4		1	7	
1991	12	4		7	1		5	3	
Total	224	234	10	136	92	7	88	142	3

Houston Oilers

Season	All Games			Home Games			Road Games		
	W	L	T	W	L	T	W	L	T
1960	10	4		6	1		4	3	
1961	10	3	1	6	1		4	2	1
1962	11	3		6	1		5	2	
1963	6	8		4	3		2	5	
1964	4	10		3	4		1	6	
1965	4	10		3	4		1	6	
1966	3	11		3	4		0	7	
1967	9	4	1	5	2		4	2	1
1968	7	7		3	4		4	3	
1969	6	6	2	4	2	1	2	4	1
1970	3	10	1	1	6		2	4	1
1971	4	9	1	3	3	1	1	6	
1972	1	13		1	6		0	7	
1973	1	13		0	7		1	6	
1974	7	7		3	4		4	3	
1975	10	4		5	2		5	2	
1976	5	9		3	4		2	5	
1977	8	6		5	2		3	4	
1978	10	6		5	2		5	3	
1979	11	5		6	2		5	3	
1980	11	5		6	2		5	3	
1981	7	9		5	3		2	6	
1982	1	8		1	4		0	4	
1983	2	14		2	6		0	8	
1984	3	13		2	6		1	7	
1985	5	11		4	4		1	7	
1986	5	11		4	4		1	7	
1987	9	6		5	2		4	4	
1988	10	6		7	1		3	5	
1989	9	7		6	2		3	5	
1990	9	7		6	2		3	5	
1991	11	5		7	1		4	4	
Total	212	250	6	130	102	2	82	148	4

Indianapolis Colts*

Season	All Games			Home Games			Road Games		
	W	L	T	W	L	T	W	L	T
1953	3	9		2	4		1	5	
1954	3	9		2	4		1	5	
1955	5	6	1	4	1	1	1	5	
1956	5	7		4	2		1	5	
1957	7	5		4	2		3	3	
1958	9	3		6	0		3	3	
1959	9	3		4	2		5	1	
1960	6	6		4	2		2	4	
1961	8	6		5	2		3	4	
1962	7	7		3	4		4	3	
1963	8	6		4	3		4	3	
1964	12	2		7	1		5	1	
1965	10	3	1	5	2		5	1	1
1966	9	5		5	2		4	3	
1967	11	1	2	6	0	1	5	1	1
1968	13	1		6	1		7	0	
1969	8	5	1	4	2	1	4	3	
1970	11	2	1	5	1	1	6	1	
1971	10	4		5	2		5	2	
1972	5	9		2	5		3	4	
1973	4	10		3	4		1	6	
1974	2	12		0	7		2	5	
1975	10	4		5	2		5	2	
1976	11	3		6	1		5	2	
1977	10	4		6	1		4	3	
1978	5	11		2	6		3	5	
1979	5	11		3	5		2	6	
1980	7	9		2	6		5	3	
1981	2	14		1	7		1	7	
1982	0	8	1	0	3	1	0	5	
1983	7	9		3	5		4	4	
1984	4	12		2	6		2	6	
1985	5	11		4	4		1	7	
1986	3	13		1	7		2	6	
1987	9	6		4	4		5	2	
1988	9	7		6	2		3	5	
1989	8	8		6	2		2	6	
1990	7	9		3	5		4	4	
1991	1	15		0	8		1	7	
Total	268	275	7	144	127	5	124	148	2

*includes Baltimore Colts (1953-83).

Kansas City Chiefs*

Season	All Games			Home Games			Road Games		
	W	L	T	W	L	T	W	L	T
1960	8	6		5	2		3	4	
1961	6	8		4	3		2	5	
1962	11	3		6	1		5	2	
1963	5	7	2	4	3		1	4	2
1964	7	7		4	3		3	4	
1965	7	5	2	5	2		2	3	2
1966	11	2	1	4	2	1	7	0	
1967	9	5		4	3		5	2	
1968	12	2		6	1		6	1	
1969	11	3		6	1		5	2	
1970	7	5	2	4	1	2	3	4	
1971	10	3	1	7	0		3	3	1
1972	8	6		4	3		4	3	
1973	7	5	2	5	1	1	2	4	1
1974	5	9		1	6		4	3	
1975	5	9		3	4		2	5	
1976	5	9		1	6		4	3	
1977	2	12		1	6		1	6	
1978	4	12		3	5		1	7	
1979	7	9		3	5		4	4	
1980	8	8		3	5		5	3	
1981	9	7		5	3		4	4	
1982	3	6		2	2		1	4	
1983	6	10		5	3		1	7	
1984	8	8		5	3		3	5	
1985	6	10		5	3		1	7	
1986	10	6		6	2		4	4	
1987	4	11		3	4		1	7	
1988	4	11	1	4	4		0	7	1
1989	8	7	1	5	3		3	4	1
1990	11	5		6	2		5	3	
1991	10	6		6	2		4	4	
Total	234	222	12	134	95	4	100	127	8

*includes Dallas Texans (1960-62).

Los Angeles Raiders*

Season	All Games			Home Games			Road Games		
	W	L	T	W	L	T	W	L	T
1960	6	8		3	4		3	4	
1961	2	12		1	6		1	6	

[Los Angeles Raiders*] (continued)

Season	W	L	T	W	L	T	W	L	T
1962	1	13		1	6		0	7	
1963	10	4		6	1		4	3	
1964	5	7	2	5	2		0	5	2
1965	8	5	1	5	2		3	3	1
1966	8	5	1	3	3	1	5	2	
1967	13	1		7	0		6	1	
1968	12	2		6	1		6	1	
1969	12	1	1	7	0		5	1	1
1970	8	4	2	6	1		2	3	2
1971	8	4	2	5	1	1	3	3	1
1972	10	3	1	5	1	1	5	2	
1973	9	4	1	5	2		4	2	1
1974	12	2		6	1		6	1	
1975	11	3		6	1		5	2	
1976	13	1		7	0		6	1	
1977	11	3		6	1		5	2	
1978	9	7		4	4		5	3	
1979	9	7		6	2		3	5	
1980	11	5		6	2		5	3	
1981	7	9		4	4		3	5	
1982	8	1		4	0		4	1	
1983	12	4		6	2		6	2	
1984	11	5		6	2		5	3	
1985	12	4		7	1		5	3	
1986	8	8		3	5		5	3	
1987	5	10		3	5		2	5	
1988	7	9		3	5		4	4	
1989	8	8		7	1		1	7	
1990	12	4		6	2		6	2	
1991	9	7		5	3		4	4	
Total	287	170	11	160	71	3	127	99	8

*includes Oakland Raiders (1960-81).

Miami Dolphins

	All Games			Home Games			Road Games		
Season	W	L	T	W	L	T	W	L	T
1966	3	11		2	5		1	6	
1967	4	10		4	3		0	7	
1968	5	8	1	1	5	1	4	3	
1969	3	10	1	2	4	1	1	6	
1970	10	4		6	1		4	3	
1971	10	3	1	6	1		4	2	1
1972	14	0		7	0		7	0	
1973	12	2		7	0		5	2	
1974	11	3		7	0		4	3	
1975	10	4		5	2		5	2	
1976	6	8		3	4		3	4	
1977	10	4		6	1		4	3	
1978	11	5		7	1		4	4	
1979	10	6		6	2		4	4	
1980	8	8		5	3		3	5	
1981	11	4	1	6	1	1	5	3	
1982	7	2		4	0		3	2	
1983	12	4		7	1		5	3	
1984	14	2		7	1		7	1	
1985	12	4		8	0		4	4	
1986	8	8		4	4		4	4	
1987	8	7		4	3		4	4	
1988	6	10		4	4		2	6	
1989	8	8		4	4		4	4	
1990	12	4		7	1		5	3	
1991	8	8		5	3		3	5	
Total	233	147	4	134	54	3	99	93	1

New England Patriots*

	All Games			Home Games			Road Games		
Season	W	L	T	W	L	T	W	L	T
1960	5	9		3	4		2	5	
1961	9	4	1	4	2	1	5	2	
1962	9	4	1	6	1		3	3	1
1963	7	6	1	5	1	1	2	5	
1964	10	3	1	4	2	1	6	1	
1965	4	8	2	1	4	2	3	4	
1966	8	4	2	4	2	1	4	2	1
1967	3	10	1	2	4		1	6	1
1968	4	10		2	5		2	5	
1969	4	10		2	5		2	5	
1970	2	12		1	6		1	6	
1971	6	8		5	2		1	6	
1972	3	11		2	5		1	6	
1973	5	9		3	4		2	5	
1974	7	7		3	4		4	3	
1975	3	11		2	5		1	6	
1976	11	3		6	1		5	2	
1977	9	5		6	1		3	4	
1978	11	5		5	3		6	2	
1979	9	7		6	2		3	5	
1980	10	6		6	2		4	4	
1981	2	14		2	6		0	8	
1982	5	4		3	1		2	3	
1983	8	8		5	3		3	5	
1984	9	7		5	3		4	4	
1985	11	5		7	1		4	4	
1986	11	5		4	4		7	1	
1987	8	7		5	3		3	4	
1988	9	7		7	1		2	6	
1989	5	11		3	5		2	6	
1990	1	15		0	8		1	7	
1991	6	10		4	4		2	6	
Total	214	245	9	123	104	6	91	141	3

*includes Boston Patriots (1960-70).

New York Jets*

	All Games			Home Games			Road Games		
Season	W	L	T	W	L	T	W	L	T
1960	7	7		3	4		4	3	
1961	7	7		5	2		2	5	
1962	5	9		2	5		3	4	
1963	5	8	1	4	2	1	1	6	
1964	5	8	1	5	1	1	0	7	
1965	5	8	1	3	3	1	2	5	
1966	6	6	2	4	3		2	3	2
1967	8	5	1	4	2	1	4	3	
1968	11	3		6	1		5	2	
1969	10	4		5	2		5	2	
1970	4	10		2	5		2	5	
1971	6	8		4	3		2	5	
1972	7	7		4	3		3	4	
1973	4	10		2	4		2	6	
1974	7	7		3	4		4	3	
1975	3	11		1	6		2	5	
1976	3	11		2	5		1	6	
1977	3	11		1	6		2	5	
1978	8	8		4	4		4	4	
1979	8	8		6	2		2	6	
1980	4	12		2	6		2	6	
1981	10	5	1	6	2		4	3	1
1982	6	3		3	1		3	2	
1983	7	9		2	6		5	3	
1984	7	9		3	5		4	4	
1985	11	5		7	1		4	4	
1986	10	6		5	3		5	3	
1987	6	9		4	4		2	5	
1988	8	7	1	5	2	1	3	5	
1989	4	12		1	7		3	5	
1990	6	10		3	5		3	5	
1991	8	8		4	4		4	4	
Total	209	251	8	115	113	5	94	138	3

*includes New York Titans (1960-62).

Pittsburgh Steelers*

	All Games			Home Games			Road Games		
Season	W	L	T	W	L	T	W	L	T
1933	3	6	2	2	3		1	3	2
1934	2	10		1	5		1	5	
1935	4	8		2	5		2	3	
1936	6	6		4	1		2	5	
1937	4	7		2	4		2	3	
1938	2	9		0	5		2	4	
1939	1	9	1	1	4		0	5	1
1940	2	7	2	1	2	2	1	5	
1941	1	9	1	1	4		0	5	1
1942	7	4		3	2		4	2	
1945	2	8		1	4		1	4	
1946	5	5	1	4	1		1	4	1
1947	8	4		5	1		3	3	
1948	4	8		4	2		0	6	
1949	6	5	1	3	2		3	3	
1950	6	6		2	4		4	2	
1951	4	7	1	1	4	1	3	3	
1952	5	7		2	4		3	3	
1953	6	6		3	3		3	3	
1954	5	7		4	2		1	5	
1955	4	8		3	2		1	6	
1956	5	7		3	3		2	4	
1957	6	6		4	2		2	4	
1958	7	4	1	5	1		2	3	1
1959	6	5	1	3	2	1	3	3	
1960	5	6	1	4	2		1	4	1
1961	6	8		4	3		2	5	
1962	9	5		4	3		5	2	
1963	7	4	3	5	0	2	2	4	1
1964	5	9		2	5		3	4	
1965	2	12		1	6		1	6	
1966	5	8	1	3	3	1	2	5	
1967	4	9	1	1	6		3	3	1
1968	2	11	1	1	6		1	5	1
1969	1	13		1	6		0	7	
1970	5	9		4	3		1	6	
1971	6	8		5	2		1	6	
1972	11	3		7	0		4	3	
1973	10	4		7	0		3	4	
1974	10	3	1	5	1	1	5	2	
1975	12	2		6	1		6	1	
1976	10	4		6	1		4	3	
1977	9	5		6	1		3	4	
1978	14	2		7	1		7	1	
1979	12	4		8	0		4	4	
1980	9	7		6	2		3	5	
1981	8	8		5	3		3	5	
1982	6	3		4	0		2	3	
1983	10	6		4	4		6	2	
1984	9	7		6	2		3	5	
1985	7	9		5	3		2	6	
1986	6	10		4	4		2	6	
1987	8	7		4	3		4	4	
1988	5	11		4	4		1	7	
1989	9	7		4	4		5	3	
1990	9	7		6	2		3	5	
1991	7	9		5	3		2	6	
Total	349	388	19	208	158	8	141	230	11

*includes Pittsburgh Pirates (1933-40).

San Diego Chargers*

	All Games			Home Games			Road Games		
Season	W	L	T	W	L	T	W	L	T
1960	10	4		5	2		5	2	
1961	12	2		6	1		6	1	
1962	4	10		3	4		1	6	
1963	11	3		6	1		5	2	
1964	8	5	1	4	3		4	2	1
1965	9	2	3	4	1	2	5	1	1
1966	7	6	1	5	2		2	4	1
1967	8	5	1	5	2	1	3	3	
1968	9	5		4	3		5	2	
1969	8	6		6	2		3	4	
1970	5	6	3	2	3	2	3	3	1
1971	6	8		6	1		0	7	
1972	4	9	1	2	5		2	4	1
1973	2	11	1	2	5		0	6	1
1974	5	9		3	4		2	5	
1975	2	12		1	6		1	6	
1976	6	8		3	4		3	4	
1977	7	7		3	4		4	3	
1978	9	7		5	3		4	4	
1979	12	4		7	1		5	3	
1980	11	5		6	2		5	3	
1981	10	6		5	3		5	3	
1982	6	3		3	1		3	2	
1983	6	10		4	4		2	6	
1984	7	9		4	4		3	5	
1985	8	8		6	2		2	6	
1986	4	12		2	6		2	6	
1987	8	7		4	3		4	4	
1988	6	10		3	5		3	5	
1989	6	10		4	4		2	6	
1990	6	10		3	5		3	5	
1991	4	12		2	6		2	6	
Total	226	231	11	128	101	5	98	130	6

*includes Los Angeles Chargers (1960).

Seattle Seahawks

	All Games			Home Games			Road Games		
Season	W	L	T	W	L	T	W	L	T
1976	2	12		1	6		1	6	
1977	5	9		3	4		2	5	
1978	9	7		5	3		4	4	
1979	9	7		5	3		4	4	
1980	4	12		0	8		4	4	
1981	6	10		5	3		1	7	
1982	4	5		3	2		1	3	
1983	9	7		5	3		4	4	
1984	12	4		7	1		5	3	
1985	8	8		5	3		3	5	
1986	10	6		7	1		3	5	
1987	9	6		6	2		3	4	
1988	9	7		5	3		4	4	
1989	7	9		5	3		2	6	
1990	9	7		5	3		4	4	
1991	7	9		5	3		2	6	
Total	119	125		70	53		49	72	

Atlanta Falcons

	All Games			Home Games			Road Games		
Season	W	L	T	W	L	T	W	L	T
1966	3	11		1	6		2	5	
1967	1	12	1	1	5	1	0	7	
1968	2	12		1	6		1	6	
1969	6	8		4	3		2	5	
1970	4	8	2	3	4		1	4	2
1971	7	6	1	4	3		3	3	1
1972	7	7		4	3		3	4	
1973	9	5		5	2		4	3	
1974	3	11		2	5		1	6	
1975	4	10		3	4		1	6	
1976	4	10		3	4		1	6	
1977	7	7		4	3		3	4	
1978	9	7		7	1		2	6	
1979	6	10		3	5		3	5	

(continued)

Season	All Games W	L	T	Home Games W	L	T	Road Games W	L	T
1980	12	4		6	2		6	2	
1981	7	9		4	4		3	5	
1982	5	4		2	3		3	1	
1983	7	9		4	4		3	5	
1984	4	12		2	6		2	6	
1985	4	12		3	5		1	7	
1986	7	8	1	2	5	1	5	3	
1987	3	12		2	6		1	6	
1988	5	11		2	6		3	5	
1989	3	13		3	5		0	8	
1990	5	11		5	3		0	8	
1991	10	6		6	2		4	4	
Total	144	235	5	85	106	2	59	129	3

Chicago Bears*

Season	All Games W	L	T	Home Games W	L	T	Road Games W	L	T
1920	10	1	2	6	0	1	4	1	1
1921	9	1	1	9	1	1	0	0	
1922	9	3		7	1		2	2	
1923	9	2	1	7	1	1	2	1	
1924	6	1	4	5	0	3	1	1	1
1925	9	5	3	7	1	1	2	4	2
1926	12	1	3	10	0	2	2	1	1
1927	9	3	2	7	1	1	2	2	1
1928	7	5	1	6	3		1	2	1
1929	4	9	2	1	5	2	3	4	
1930	9	4	1	5	1		4	2	
1931	8	5		6	3		2	2	
1932	7	1	6	6	1	1	1	0	5
1933	10	2	1	6	0		4	2	1
1934	13	0		5	0		8	0	
1935	6	4	2	1	2	2	5	2	
1936	9	3		3	1		6	2	
1937	9	1	1	4	1		5	0	1
1938	6	5		2	3		4	2	
1939	8	3		4	1		4	2	
1940	8	3		5	0		3	3	
1941	10	1		5	1		5	0	
1942	11	0		6	0		5	0	
1943	8	1	1	5	0		3	1	1
1944	6	3	1	4	0	1	2	3	
1945	3	7		2	3		1	4	
1946	8	2	1	4	1	1	4	1	
1947	8	4		4	2		4	2	
1948	10	2		5	1		5	1	
1949	9	3		5	1		4	2	
1950	9	3		6	0		3	3	
1951	7	5		3	3		4	2	
1952	5	7		3	3		2	4	
1953	3	8	1	1	4	1	2	4	
1954	8	4		4	2		4	2	
1955	8	4		5	1		3	3	
1956	9	2	1	6	0		3	2	1
1957	5	7		2	4		3	3	
1958	8	4		5	1		3	3	
1959	8	4		4	2		4	2	
1960	5	6	1	4	2		1	4	1
1961	8	6		5	2		3	4	
1962	9	5		4	3		5	2	
1963	11	1	2	6	0	1	5	1	1
1964	5	9		2	5		3	4	
1965	9	5		5	2		4	3	
1966	5	7	2	4	1	2	1	6	
1967	7	6	1	3	3	1	4	3	
1968	7	7		2	5		5	2	
1969	1	13		1	6		0	7	
1970	6	8		3	4		3	4	
1971	6	8		4	3		2	5	
1972	4	9	1	1	5	1	3	4	
1973	3	11		1	6		2	5	
1974	4	10		4	3		0	7	
1975	4	10		3	4		1	6	
1976	7	7		4	3		3	4	
1977	9	5		5	2		4	3	
1978	7	9		4	4		3	5	
1979	10	6		6	2		4	4	
1980	7	9		5	3		2	6	
1981	6	10		4	4		2	6	
1982	3	6		2	2		1	4	
1983	8	8		5	3		3	5	
1984	10	6		6	2		4	4	
1985	15	1		8	0		7	1	
1986	14	2		7	1		7	1	
1987	11	4		6	2		5	2	
1988	12	4		7	1		5	3	
1989	6	10		4	4		2	6	
1990	11	5		7	1		4	4	
1991	11	5		6	2		5	3	
Total	561	351	42	329	146	24	232	205	18

*includes Decatur Staleys (1920) and Chicago Staleys (1921).

Dallas Cowboys

Season	All Games W	L	T	Home Games W	L	T	Road Games W	L	T
1960	0	11	1	0	6		0	5	1
1961	4	9	1	2	4	1	2	5	
1962	5	8	1	2	4	1	3	4	
1963	4	10		3	4		1	6	
1964	5	8	1	2	4	1	3	4	
1965	7	7		5	2		2	5	
1966	10	3	1	6	1		4	2	1
1967	9	5		5	2		4	3	
1968	12	2		5	2		7	0	
1969	11	2	1	6	0	1	5	2	
1970	10	4		6	1		4	3	
1971	11	3		6	1		5	2	
1972	10	4		5	2		5	2	
1973	10	4		6	1		4	3	
1974	8	6		5	2		3	4	
1975	10	4		5	2		5	2	
1976	11	3		6	1		5	2	
1977	12	2		6	1		6	1	
1978	12	4		7	1		5	3	
1979	11	5		6	2		5	3	
1980	12	4		8	0		4	4	
1981	12	4		8	0		4	4	
1982	6	3		3	2		3	1	
1983	12	4		6	2		6	2	
1984	9	7		5	3		4	4	
1985	10	6		7	1		3	5	
1986	7	9		3	5		4	4	
1987	7	8		3	4		4	4	
1988	3	13		1	7		2	6	
1989	1	15		0	8		1	7	
1990	7	9		5	3		2	6	
1991	11	5		6	2		5	3	
Total	269	191	6	149	80	4	120	111	2

Detroit Lions*

Season	All Games W	L	T	Home Games W	L	T	Road Games W	L	T
1930	5	6	3	5	1	2	0	5	1
1931	11	3		8	0		3	3	
1932	6	2	4	3	0	2	3	2	2
1933	6	5		4	1		2	4	
1934	10	3		6	2		4	1	
1935	7	3	2	5	0	1	2	3	1
1936	8	4		5	1		3	3	
1937	7	4		4	2		3	2	
1938	7	4		4	3		3	1	
1939	6	5		4	2		2	3	
1940	5	5	1	3	3		2	2	1
1941	4	6	1	3	2		1	4	1
1942	0	11		0	7		0	4	
1943	3	6	1	2	2	1	1	4	
1944	6	3	1	4	2		2	1	1
1945	7	3		4	1		3	2	
1946	1	10		1	5		0	5	
1947	3	9		2	4		1	5	
1948	2	10		2	4		0	6	
1949	4	8		2	4		2	4	
1950	6	6		4	2		2	4	
1951	7	4	1	3	3	1	4	1	
1952	9	3		6	1		3	2	
1953	10	2		5	1		5	1	
1954	9	2	1	5	0	1	4	2	
1955	3	9		3	4		0	5	
1956	9	3		5	1		4	2	
1957	8	4		5	1		3	3	
1958	4	7	1	2	4		2	3	1
1959	3	8	1	2	4		1	4	1
1960	7	5		5	1		2	4	
1961	8	5	1	2	5		6	0	1
1962	11	3		7	0		4	3	
1963	5	8	1	3	3	1	2	5	
1964	7	5	2	3	3	1	4	2	1
1965	6	7	1	2	4	1	4	3	
1966	4	9	1	3	4		1	5	1
1967	5	7	2	3	4		2	3	2
1968	4	8	2	1	4	2	3	4	
1969	9	4	1	5	2		4	2	1
1970	10	4		6	1		4	3	
1971	7	6	1	3	4		4	2	1
1972	8	5	1	5	2		3	3	1
1973	6	7	1	4	3		2	4	1
1974	7	7		5	2		2	5	
1975	7	7		4	3		3	4	
1976	6	8		5	2		1	6	
1977	6	8		5	2		1	6	
1978	7	9		5	3		2	6	
1979	2	14		2	6		0	8	
1980	9	7		6	2		3	5	

(continued)

Season	All Games W	L	T	Home Games W	L	T	Road Games W	L	T
1981	8	8		7	1		1	7	
1982	4	5		2	3		2	2	
1983	9	7		6	2		3	5	
1984	4	11	1	2	5	1	2	6	
1985	7	9		6	2		1	7	
1986	5	11		1	7		4	4	
1987	4	11		1	6		3	5	
1988	4	12		2	6		2	6	
1989	7	9		4	4		3	5	
1990	6	10		3	5		3	5	
1991	12	4		8	0		4	4	
Total	387	398	32	237	168	14	150	230	18

*includes Portsmouth Spartans (1930-33)

Green Bay Packers

Season	All Games W	L	T	Home Games W	L	T	Road Games W	L	T
1921	3	2	1	2	1		1	1	1
1922	4	3	3	4	1	1	0	2	2
1923	7	2	1	4	2	1	3	0	
1924	7	4		5	0		2	4	
1925	8	5		6	0		2	5	
1926	7	3	3	4	1	2	3	2	1
1927	7	2	1	6	1		1	1	1
1928	6	4	3	2	2	2	4	2	1
1929	12	0	1	5	0		7	0	1
1930	10	3	1	6	0		4	3	1
1931	12	2		8	0		4	2	
1932	10	3	1	5	0	1	5	3	
1933	5	7	1	3	2	1	2	5	
1934	7	6		4	2		3	4	
1935	8	4		5	2		3	2	
1936	10	1	1	5	1		5	0	1
1937	7	4		3	2		4	2	
1938	8	3		4	2		4	1	
1939	9	2		4	1		5	1	
1940	6	4	1	4	2		2	2	1
1941	10	1		4	1		6	0	
1942	8	2	1	4	1		4	1	1
1943	7	2	1	2	1	1	5	1	
1944	8	2		5	0		3	2	
1945	6	4		4	1		2	3	
1946	6	5		2	3		4	2	
1947	6	5	1	4	2		2	3	1
1948	3	9		2	4		1	5	
1949	2	10		1	5		1	5	
1950	3	9		3	3		0	6	
1951	3	9		2	4		1	5	
1952	6	6		3	3		3	3	
1953	2	9	1	1	5		1	4	1
1954	4	8		2	4		2	4	
1955	6	6		5	1		1	5	
1956	4	8		2	4		2	4	
1957	3	9		1	5		2	4	
1958	1	10	1	1	4	1	0	6	
1959	7	5		4	2		3	3	
1960	8	4		4	2		4	2	
1961	11	3		6	1		5	2	
1962	13	1		7	0		6	1	
1963	11	2	1	6	1		5	1	1
1964	8	5	1	4	3		4	2	1
1965	10	3	1	6	1		4	2	1
1966	12	2		6	1		6	1	
1967	9	4	1	4	2	1	5	2	
1968	6	7	1	2	5		4	2	1
1969	8	6		5	2		3	4	
1970	6	8		4	3		2	5	
1971	4	8	2	3	3	1	1	5	1
1972	10	4		4	3		6	1	
1973	5	7	2	3	2	2	2	5	
1974	6	8		4	3		2	5	
1975	4	10		3	4		1	6	
1976	5	9		4	3		1	6	
1977	4	10		2	5		2	5	
1978	8	7	1	5	2	1	3	5	
1979	5	11		4	4		1	7	
1980	5	10	1	4	4		1	6	1
1981	8	8		4	4		4	4	
1982	5	3	1	3	1		2	2	1
1983	8	8		5	3		3	5	
1984	8	8		5	3		3	5	
1985	8	8		5	3		3	5	
1986	4	12		1	7		3	5	
1987	5	9	1	2	5	1	3	4	
1988	4	12		2	6		2	6	
1989	10	6		6	2		4	4	
1990	6	10		3	5		3	5	
1991	4	12		2	6		2	6	
Total	476	408	36	269	174	16	207	234	20

Los Angeles Rams*

Season	All Games W	L	T	Home Games W	L	T	Road Games W	L	T
1937	1	10		0	5		1	5	
1938	4	7		2	2		2	5	
1939	5	5	1	3	2	1	2	3	
1940	4	6	1	3	1	1	1	5	
1941	2	9		1	4		1	5	
1942	5	6		3	2		2	4	
1944	4	6		1	2		3	4	
1945	9	1		4	0		5	1	
1946	6	4	1	3	2		3	2	1
1947	6	6		3	3		3	3	
1948	6	5	1	3	2	1	3	3	
1949	8	2	2	5	1		3	1	2
1950	9	3		5	1		4	2	
1951	8	4		5	2		3	2	
1952	9	3		5	1		4	2	
1953	8	3	1	5	1		3	2	1
1954	6	5	1	3	2	1	3	3	
1955	8	3	1	5	1		3	2	1
1956	4	8		4	2		0	6	
1957	6	6		5	1		1	5	
1958	8	4		4	2		4	2	
1959	2	10		0	6		2	4	
1960	4	7	1	2	3	1	2	4	
1961	4	10		4	3		0	7	
1962	1	12	1	0	7		1	5	1
1963	5	9		3	4		2	5	
1964	5	7	2	3	2	2	2	5	
1965	4	10		3	4		1	6	
1966	8	6		5	2		3	4	
1967	11	1	2	5	1	1	6	0	1
1968	10	3	1	5	2		5	1	1
1969	11	3		5	2		6	1	
1970	9	4	1	3	3	1	6	1	
1971	8	5	1	4	2	1	4	3	
1972	6	7	1	4	3		2	4	1
1973	12	2		7	0		5	2	
1974	10	4		6	1		4	3	
1975	12	2		6	1		6	1	
1976	10	3	1	5	2		5	1	1
1977	10	4		7	0		3	4	
1978	12	4		6	2		6	2	
1979	9	7		4	4		5	3	
1980	11	5		6	2		5	3	
1981	6	10		4	4		2	6	
1982	2	7		1	4		1	3	
1983	9	7		5	3		4	4	
1984	10	6		5	3		5	3	
1985	11	5		6	2		5	3	
1986	10	6		6	2		4	4	
1987	6	9		3	4		3	5	
1988	10	6		4	4		6	2	
1989	11	5		6	2		5	3	
1990	5	11		2	6		3	5	
1991	3	13		2	6		1	7	
Total	383	316	20	209	135	10	174	181	10

*includes Cleveland Rams (1937-42, 1944-45)

Minnesota Vikings

Season	All Games W	L	T	Home Games W	L	T	Road Games W	L	T
1961	3	11		3	4		0	7	
1962	2	11	1	1	5	1	1	6	
1963	5	8	1	3	4		2	4	1
1964	8	5	1	4	3		4	2	1
1965	7	7		2	5		5	2	
1966	4	9	1	2	5		2	4	1
1967	3	8	3	1	4	2	2	4	1
1968	8	6		4	3		4	3	
1969	12	2		7	0		5	2	
1970	12	2		7	0		5	2	
1971	11	3		5	2		6	1	
1972	7	7		3	4		4	3	
1973	12	2		7	0		5	2	
1974	10	4		4	3		6	1	
1975	12	2		7	0		5	2	
1976	11	2	1	6	0	1	5	2	
1977	9	5		5	2		4	3	
1978	8	7	1	5	3		3	4	1
1979	7	9		5	3		2	6	
1980	9	7		5	3		4	4	
1981	7	9		5	3		2	6	
1982	5	4		4	1		1	3	
1983	8	8		3	5		5	3	
1984	3	13		2	6		1	7	
1985	7	9		4	4		3	5	
1986	9	7		5	3		4	4	
1987	8	7		5	3		3	4	
1988	11	5		7	1		4	4	

New Orleans Saints

Season	All Games W	L	T	Home Games W	L	T	Road Games W	L	T
1967	3	11		2	5		1	6	
1968	4	9	1	3	4		1	5	1
1969	5	9		3	4		2	5	
1970	2	11	1	2	5		0	6	1
1971	4	8	2	2	3	1	2	4	1
1972	2	11	1	2	5		0	6	1
1973	5	9		5	2		0	7	
1974	5	9		4	3		1	6	
1975	2	12		2	5		0	7	
1976	4	10		2	5		2	5	
1977	3	11		2	5		1	6	
1978	7	9		3	5		4	4	
1979	8	8		3	5		5	3	
1980	1	15		0	8		1	7	
1981	4	12		2	6		2	6	
1982	4	5		2	3		2	2	
1983	8	8		5	3		3	5	
1984	7	9		3	5		4	4	
1985	5	11		3	5		2	6	
1986	7	9		4	4		3	5	
1987	12	3		6	1		6	2	
1988	10	6		5	3		5	3	
1989	9	7		5	3		4	4	
1990	8	8		5	3		3	5	
1991	11	5		6	2		5	3	
Total	140	225	5	81	103		59	122	4

New York Giants

Season	All Games W	L	T	Home Games W	L	T	Road Games W	L	T
1925	8	4		7	2		1	2	
1926	8	4	1	5	2	1	3	2	
1927	11	1	1	7	1		4	0	1
1928	4	7	2	1	2	2	3	5	
1929	13	1	1	7	1		6	0	1
1930	13	4		6	2		7	2	
1931	7	6	1	4	2	1	3	4	
1932	4	6	2	3	2	1	1	4	1
1933	11	3		7	0		4	3	
1934	8	5		5	1		3	4	
1935	9	3		4	2		5	1	
1936	5	6	1	3	3	1	2	3	
1937	6	3	2	4	2	1	2	1	1
1938	8	2	1	6	1		2	1	1
1939	9	1	1	6	0		3	1	1
1940	6	4	1	4	3		2	1	1
1941	8	3		5	2		3	1	
1942	5	5	1	3	2	1	2	3	
1943	6	3	1	4	2		2	1	1
1944	8	1	1	5	1		3	0	1
1945	3	6	1	2	4		1	2	1
1946	7	3	1	5	1	1	2	2	
1947	2	8	2	2	3	1	0	5	1
1948	4	8		2	4		2	4	
1949	6	6		2	4		4	2	
1950	10	2		5	1		5	1	
1951	9	2	1	5	1		4	1	1
1952	7	5		2	4		5	1	
1953	3	9		2	4		1	5	
1954	7	5		4	2		3	3	
1955	6	5	1	4	1	1	2	4	
1956	8	3	1	4	1	1	4	2	
1957	7	5		3	3		4	2	
1958	9	3		5	1		4	2	
1959	10	2		5	1		5	1	
1960	6	4	2	1	3	2	5	1	
1961	10	3	1	4	2	1	6	1	
1962	12	2		6	1		6	1	
1963	11	3		5	2		6	1	
1964	2	10	2	2	5		0	5	2
1965	7	7		3	4		4	3	
1966	1	12	1	1	6		0	6	1
1967	7	7		5	2		2	5	
1968	7	7		3	4		4	3	
1969	6	8		5	2		1	6	
1970	9	5		5	2		4	3	
1971	4	10		1	6		3	4	
1972	8	6		4	3		4	3	
1973	2	11	1	2	4	1	0	7	
1974	2	12		0	7		2	5	
1975	5	9		2	5		3	4	
1976	3	11		3	4		0	7	
1977	5	9		3	4		2	5	
1978	6	10		5	3		1	7	
1979	6	10		4	4		2	6	
1980	4	12		2	6		2	6	
1981	9	7		4	4		5	3	
1982	4	5		2	3		2	2	
1983	3	12	1	1	7		2	5	1
1984	9	7		6	2		3	5	
1985	10	6		6	2		4	4	
1986	14	2		8	0		6	2	
1987	6	9		5	3		1	6	
1988	10	6		5	3		5	3	
1989	12	4		7	1		5	3	
1990	13	3		7	1		6	2	
1991	8	8		5	3		3	5	
Total	476	381	32	270	176	16	206	205	16

Philadelphia Eagles

Season	All Games W	L	T	Home Games W	L	T	Road Games W	L	T
1933	3	5	1	2	3	1	1	2	
1934	4	7		2	4		2	3	
1935	2	9		0	5		2	4	
1936	1	11		1	6		0	5	
1937	2	8	1	0	5	1	2	3	
1938	5	6		2	3		3	3	
1939	1	9	1	1	3	1	0	6	
1940	1	10		1	4		0	6	
1941	2	8	1	1	4	1	1	4	
1942	2	9		0	5		2	4	
1944	7	1	2	3	1	2	4	0	
1945	7	3		6	0		1	3	
1946	6	5		3	2		3	3	
1947	8	4		6	1		2	3	
1948	9	2	1	6	0		3	2	1
1949	11	1		6	0		5	1	
1950	6	6		2	4		4	2	
1951	4	8		1	5		3	3	
1952	7	5		4	2		3	3	
1953	7	4	1	5	0	1	2	4	
1954	7	4	1	5	1		2	3	1
1955	4	7	1	4	2		0	5	1
1956	3	8	1	2	3	1	1	5	
1957	4	8		3	3		1	5	
1958	2	9	1	2	4		0	5	1
1959	6	5		4	1		2	4	
1960	10	2		5	1		5	1	
1961	10	4		5	2		5	2	
1962	3	10	1	2	5		1	5	1
1963	2	10	2	1	5	1	1	5	1
1964	6	8		3	4		3	4	
1965	5	9		2	5		3	4	
1966	9	5		5	2		4	3	
1967	6	7	1	5	2		1	5	1
1968	2	12		1	6		1	6	
1969	4	9	1	2	5		2	4	1
1970	3	10	1	3	3	1	0	7	
1971	6	7	1	3	4		3	3	1
1972	2	11	1	0	6	1	2	5	
1973	5	8	1	4	3		1	5	1
1974	7	7		5	2		2	5	
1975	4	10		2	5		2	5	
1976	4	10		2	5		2	5	
1977	5	9		4	3		1	6	
1978	9	7		5	3		4	4	
1979	11	5		5	3		6	2	
1980	12	4		7	1		5	3	
1981	10	6		6	2		4	4	
1982	3	6		1	4		2	2	
1983	5	11		1	7		4	4	
1984	6	9	1	5	3		1	6	1
1985	7	9		4	4		3	5	
1986	5	10	1	2	5	1	3	5	
1987	7	8		4	4		3	4	
1988	10	6		5	3		5	3	
1989	11	5		6	2		5	3	
1990	10	6		6	2		4	4	
1991	10	6		4	4		6	2	
Total	330	408	23	187	186	12	143	222	11

Phoenix Cardinals*

Season	All Games W	L	T	Home Games W	L	T	Road Games W	L	T
1920	6	2	2	5	1	1	1	1	
1921	3	3	2	3	3	1	0	0	1
1922	8	3		8	3		0	0	
1923	8	4		8	3		0	1	
1924	5	4	1	5	3	1	0	1	
1925	11	2	1	11	2		0	0	1
1926	5	6	1	3	3		2	3	1
1927	3	7	1	2	3		1	4	
1928	1	5		1	1		0	4	
1929	6	6	1	3	2		3	4	1
1930	5	6	2	3	2		2	4	2

Season	All Games W	L	T	Home Games W	L	T	Road Games W	L	T
1931	5	4		3	0		2	4	
1932	2	6	2	1	2	1	1	4	1
1933	1	9	1	0	4	1	1	5	
1934	5	6		2	2		3	4	
1935	6	4	2	2	2		4	2	2
1936	3	8	1	3	1	1	0	7	
1937	5	5	1	1	3		4	2	1
1938	2	9		1	4		1	5	
1939	1	10		0	4		1	6	
1940	2	7	2	2	1	1	0	6	1
1941	3	7	1	0	3	1	3	4	
1942	3	8		2	2		1	6	
1943	0	10		0	3		0	7	
1945	1	9		0	3		1	6	
1946	6	5		2	2		4	3	
1947	9	3		5	0		4	3	
1948	11	1		5	1		6	0	
1949	6	5	1	2	3	1	4	2	
1950	5	7		3	3		2	4	
1951	3	9		1	5		2	4	
1952	4	8		2	4		2	4	
1953	1	10	1	0	5	1	1	5	
1954	2	10		2	4		0	6	
1955	4	7	1	3	2	1	1	5	
1956	7	5		4	2		3	3	
1957	3	9		0	6		3	3	
1958	2	9	1	1	4	1	1	5	
1959	2	10		2	4		0	6	
1960	6	5	1	3	2	1	3	3	
1961	7	7		3	4		4	3	
1962	4	9	1	2	4	1	2	5	
1963	9	5		3	4		6	1	
1964	9	3	2	4	1	1	5	2	1
1965	5	9		2	5		3	4	
1966	8	5	1	5	1	1	3	4	
1967	6	7	1	3	3	1	3	4	
1968	9	4	1	4	2	1	5	2	
1969	4	9	1	3	4		1	5	1
1970	8	5	1	6	1		2	4	1
1971	4	9	1	1	5	1	3	4	
1972	4	9	1	2	5		2	4	1
1973	4	9	1	2	4	1	2	5	
1974	10	4		5	2		5	2	
1975	11	3		6	1		5	2	
1976	10	4		6	1		4	3	
1977	7	7		4	3		3	4	
1978	6	10		3	5		3	5	
1979	5	11		3	5		2	6	
1980	5	11		2	6		3	5	
1981	7	9		5	3		2	6	
1982	5	4		1	3		4	1	
1983	8	7	1	4	3	1	4	4	
1984	9	7		5	3		4	4	
1985	5	11		4	4		1	7	
1986	4	11	1	3	5		1	6	1
1987	7	8		4	3		3	5	
1988	7	9		4	4		3	5	
1989	5	11		2	6		3	5	
1990	5	11		3	5		2	6	
1991	4	12		2	6		2	6	
Total	372	493	39	210	218	22	162	275	17

*includes Chicago Cardinals (1920-59) and St. Louis Cardinals (1960-87).

San Francisco 49ers

Season	All Games W	L	T	Home Games W	L	T	Road Games W	L	T
1950	3	9		3	3		0	6	
1951	7	4	1	5	1		2	3	1
1952	7	5		3	3		4	2	
1953	9	3		5	1		4	2	
1954	7	4	1	4	2		3	2	1
1955	4	8		2	4		2	4	
1956	5	6	1	3	3		2	3	1
1957	8	4		5	1		3	3	
1958	6	6		4	2		2	4	
1959	7	5		4	2		3	3	
1960	7	5		3	3		4	2	
1961	7	6	1	5	1	1	2	5	
1962	6	8		1	6		5	2	
1963	2	12		2	5		0	7	
1964	4	10		3	4		1	6	
1965	7	6	1	4	2	1	3	4	
1966	6	6	2	4	2	1	2	4	1
1967	7	7		3	4		4	3	
1968	7	6	1	3	3	1	4	3	
1969	4	8	2	3	3	1	1	5	1
1970	10	3	1	5	1	1	5	2	
1971	9	5		4	3		5	2	
1972	8	5	1	4	2	1	4	3	
1973	5	9		3	4		2	5	
1974	6	8		3	4		3	4	
1975	5	9		2	5		3	4	
1976	8	6		4	3		4	3	
1977	5	9		3	4		2	5	
1978	2	14		2	6		0	8	
1979	2	14		2	6		0	8	
1980	6	10		4	4		2	6	
1981	13	3		7	1		6	2	
1982	3	6		0	5		3	1	
1983	10	6		4	4		6	2	
1984	15	1		7	1		8	0	
1985	10	6		5	3		5	3	
1986	10	5	1	6	2		4	3	1
1987	13	2		6	1		7	1	
1988	10	6		4	4		6	2	
1989	14	2		6	2		8	0	
1990	14	2		6	2		8	0	
1991	10	6		7	1		3	5	
Total	308	265	13	163	123	7	145	142	6

Tampa Bay Buccaneers

Season	All Games W	L	T	Home Games W	L	T	Road Games W	L	T
1976	0	14		0	7		0	7	
1977	2	12		1	6		1	6	
1978	5	11		3	5		2	6	
1979	10	6		5	3		5	3	
1980	5	10	1	2	5	1	3	5	
1981	9	7		6	2		3	5	
1982	5	4		4	1		1	3	
1983	2	14		1	7		1	7	
1984	6	10		6	2		0	8	
1985	2	14		2	6		0	8	
1986	2	14		1	7		1	7	
1987	4	11		2	5		2	6	
1988	5	11		3	5		2	6	
1989	5	11		2	6		3	5	
1990	6	10		4	4		2	6	
1991	3	13		3	5		0	8	
Total	71	172	1	45	76	1	26	96	

Washington Redskins*

Season	All Games W	L	T	Home Games W	L	T	Road Games W	L	T
1932	4	4	2	2	3	1	2	1	1
1933	5	5	2	4	2		1	3	2
1934	6	6		4	3		2	3	
1935	2	8	1	2	5		0	3	1
1936	7	5		4	3		3	2	
1937	8	3		4	2		4	1	
1938	6	3	2	3	1	1	3	2	1
1939	8	2	1	5	0	1	3	2	
1940	9	2		6	0		3	2	
1941	6	5		4	2		2	3	
1942	10	1		5	1		5	0	
1943	6	3	1	4	2		2	1	1
1944	6	3	1	4	2		2	1	1
1945	8	2		6	0		2	2	
1946	5	5	1	3	2	1	2	3	
1947	4	8		4	2		0	6	
1948	7	5		4	2		3	3	
1949	4	7	1	3	3		1	4	1
1950	3	9		1	5		2	4	
1951	5	7		2	4		3	3	
1952	4	8		1	5		3	3	
1953	6	5	1	3	3		3	2	1
1954	3	9		3	3		0	6	
1955	8	4		3	3		5	1	
1956	6	6		4	2		2	4	
1957	5	6	1	2	3	1	3	3	
1958	4	7	1	3	2	1	1	5	
1959	4	8		2	4		2	4	
1960	1	9	2	1	4	1	0	5	1
1961	1	12	1	1	6		0	6	1
1962	5	7	2	3	4		2	3	2
1963	3	11		1	6		2	5	
1964	6	8		4	3		2	5	
1965	6	8		3	4		3	4	
1966	7	7		4	3		3	4	
1967	5	6	3	2	4	1	3	2	2
1968	5	9		3	4		2	5	
1969	7	5	2	4	2	1	3	3	1
1970	6	8		4	3		2	5	
1971	9	4	1	4	2	1	5	2	
1972	11	3		6	1		5	2	
1973	10	4		7	0		3	4	
1974	10	4		6	1		4	3	
1975	8	6		5	2		3	4	
1976	10	4		5	2		5	2	
1977	9	5		5	2		4	3	
1978	8	8		5	3		3	5	
1979	10	6		6	2		4	4	
1980	6	10		4	4		2	6	
1981	8	8		5	3		3	5	
1982	8	1		3	1		5	0	
1983	14	2		7	1		7	1	
1984	11	5		7	1		4	4	
1985	10	6		5	3		5	3	
1986	12	4		7	1		5	3	
1987	11	4		6	1		5	3	
1988	7	9		4	4		3	5	
1989	10	6		4	4		6	2	
1990	10	6		7	1		3	5	
1991	14	2		7	1		7	1	
Total	417	343	26	240	152	10	177	191	16

*includes Boston Braves (1932) and Boston Redskins (1933-36).

HISTORY

Pro Football Hall of Fame 228

Chronology 232

Past NFL Standings 241

All-Time Team vs. Team Results 250

Super Bowl Game Summaries 277

Playoff Game Summaries 284

AFC-NFC Pro Bowl Game Summaries 291

All-Time Pro Bowl Results 296

Chicago All-Star Games 297

NFL Playoff Bowls 297

Pro Football Hall of Fame Games 297

NFL International Games 297

AFC-NFC Interconference Games 298

Monday Night Results 300

Thursday-Sunday Night Results 303

History of Overtime Games 304

NFL Paid Attendance 309

NFL's 10 Biggest Attendance Weekends 309

NFL's 10 Highest Scoring Weekends 309

Top 10 Televised Sports Events of All Time . . 309

Ten Most Watched Programs in TV History . . 309

Number-One Draft Choices 310

First-Round Selections 311

PRO FOOTBALL HALL OF FAME

The Professional Football Hall of Fame is located in Canton, Ohio, site of the organizational meeting on September 17, 1920, from which the National Football League evolved. The NFL recognized Canton as the Hall of Fame site on April 27, 1961. Canton area individuals, foundations, and companies donated almost $400,000 in cash and services to provide funds for the construction of the original two-building complex, which was dedicated on September 7, 1963. The original Hall of Fame complex was almost doubled in size with the completion of a $620,000 expansion project that was dedicated on May 10, 1971. A second expansion project was completed on November 20, 1978. It now features four exhibition areas and a theater twice the size of the original one.

The Hall represents the sport of pro football in many ways—through four large and colorful exhibition galleries, in the twin enshrinement halls, with numerous fan-participation electronic devices, a research library, and a museum store.

In recent years, the Pro Football Hall of Fame has become an extremely popular tourist attraction. At the end of 1991, a total of 5,081,854 fans had visited the Hall of Fame.

New members of the Pro Football Hall of Fame are elected annually by a 31-member National Board of Selectors, made up of media representatives from every league city, two at-large representatives, and a representative of the Pro Football Writers of America. Between four and seven new members are elected each year. An affirmative vote of approximately 80 percent is needed for election.

Any fan may nominate any eligible player or contributor simply by writing to the Pro Football Hall of Fame. Players must be retired five years to be eligible, while a coach need only be retired with no time limit specified. Contributors (administrators, owners, et al.) may be elected while they are still active.

The charter class of 17 enshrinees was elected in 1963 and the honor roll now stands at 164 with the election of a four-man class in 1992. That class consists of Lem Barney, Al Davis, John Mackey, and John Riggins.

Roster of Members

HERB ADDERLEY
Defensive back. 6-1, 200. Born in Philadelphia, Pennsylvania, June 8, 1939. Michigan State. Inducted in 1980. 1961-69 Green Bay Packers, 1970-72 Dallas Cowboys.

LANCE ALWORTH
Wide receiver. 6-0, 184. Born in Houston, Texas, August 3, 1940. Arkansas. Inducted in 1978. 1962-70 San Diego Chargers, 1971-72 Dallas Cowboys.

DOUG ATKINS
Defensive end. 6-8, 275. Born in Humboldt, Tennessee, May 8, 1930. Tennessee. Inducted in 1982. 1953-54 Cleveland Browns, 1955-66 Chicago Bears, 1967-69 New Orleans Saints.

MORRIS (RED) BADGRO
End. 6-0, 190. Born in Orilla, Washington, December 1, 1902. Southern California. Inducted in 1981. 1927 New York Yankees, 1930-35 New York Giants, 1936 Brooklyn Dodgers.

LEM BARNEY
Cornerback. 6-0, 190. Born in Gulfport, Mississippi, September 9, 1945. Jackson State. Inducted in 1992. 1967-77 Detroit Lions.

CLIFF BATTLES
Halfback. 6-1, 201. Born in Akron, Ohio, May 1, 1910. Died April 28, 1981. West Virginia Wesleyan. Inducted in 1968. 1932 Boston Braves, 1933-36 Boston Redskins, 1937 Washington Redskins.

SAMMY BAUGH
Quarterback. 6-2, 180. Born in Temple, Texas, March 17, 1914. Texas Christian. Inducted in 1963. 1937-52 Washington Redskins.

CHUCK BEDNARIK
Center-linebacker. 6-3, 230. Born in Bethlehem, Pennsylvania, May 1, 1925. Pennsylvania. Inducted in 1967. 1949-62 Philadelphia Eagles.

BERT BELL
Team owner. Commissioner. Born in Philadelphia, Pennsylvania, February 25, 1895. Died October 11, 1959. Pennsylvania. Inducted in 1963. 1933-40 Philadelphia Eagles, 1941-42 Pittsburgh Steelers, 1943 Phil-Pitt, 1944-46 Pittsburgh Steelers. Commissioner, 1946-59.

BOBBY BELL
Linebacker. 6-4, 225. Born in Shelby, North Carolina, June 17, 1940. Minnesota. Inducted in 1983. 1963-74 Kansas City Chiefs.

RAYMOND BERRY
End. 6-2, 187. Born in Corpus Christi, Texas, February 27, 1933. Southern Methodist. Inducted in 1973. 1955-67 Baltimore Colts.

CHARLES W. BIDWILL, SR.
Team owner. Born in Chicago, Illinois, September 16, 1895. Died April 19, 1947. Loyola of Chicago. Inducted in 1967. 1933-43 Chicago Cardinals, 1944 Card-Pitt, 1945-47 Chicago Cardinals.

FRED BILETNIKOFF
Wide receiver. 6-1, 190. Born in Erie, Pennsylvania, February 23, 1943. Florida State. Inducted in 1988. 1965-78 Oakland Raiders.

GEORGE BLANDA
Quarterback-kicker. 6-2, 215. Born in Youngwood, Pennsylvania, September 17, 1927. Kentucky. Inducted in 1981. 1949-58 Chicago Bears, 1950 Baltimore Colts, 1960-66 Houston Oilers, 1967-75 Oakland Raiders.

MEL BLOUNT
Cornerback. 6-3, 205. Born in Vidalia, Georgia, April 10, 1948. Southern University. Inducted in 1989. 1970-83 Pittsburgh Steelers.

TERRY BRADSHAW
Quarterback. 6-3, 210. Born in Shreveport, Louisiana, September 2, 1948. Louisiana Tech. Inducted in 1989. 1970-83 Pittsburgh Steelers.

JIM BROWN
Fullback. 6-2, 232. Born in St. Simons, Georgia, February 17, 1936. Syracuse. Inducted in 1971. 1957-65 Cleveland Browns.

PAUL BROWN
Coach. Born in Norwalk, Ohio, September 7, 1908. Died August 5, 1991. Miami, Ohio. Inducted in 1967. 1946-49 Cleveland Browns (AAFC), 1950-62 Cleveland Browns, 1968-75 Cincinnati Bengals.

ROOSEVELT BROWN
Tackle. 6-3, 255. Born in Charlottesville, Virginia, October 20, 1932. Morgan State. Inducted in 1975. 1953-65 New York Giants.

WILLIE BROWN
Defensive back. 6-1, 210. Born in Yazoo City, Mississippi, December 2, 1940. Grambling. Inducted in 1984. 1963-66 Denver Broncos, 1967-78 Oakland Raiders.

BUCK BUCHANAN
Defensive tackle. 6-7, 274. Born in Gainesville, Alabama, September 10, 1940. Grambling. Inducted in 1990. 1963-75 Kansas City Chiefs.

DICK BUTKUS
Linebacker. 6-3, 245. Born in Chicago, Illinois, December 9, 1942. Illinois. Inducted in 1979. 1965-73 Chicago Bears.

EARL CAMPBELL
Running back. 5-11, 233. Born in Tyler, Texas, March 29, 1955. Texas. Inducted in 1991. 1978-84 Houston Oilers, 1984-85 New Orleans Saints.

TONY CANADEO
Halfback. 5-11, 195. Born in Chicago, Illinois, May 5, 1919. Gonzaga. Inducted in 1974. 1941-44, 1946-52 Green Bay Packers.

JOE CARR
NFL president. Born in Columbus, Ohio, October 22, 1880. Died May 20, 1939. Did not attend college. Inducted in 1963. President, 1921-39 National Football League.

GUY CHAMBERLIN
End. Coach. 6-2, 210. Born in Blue Springs, Nebraska, January 16, 1894. Died April 4, 1967. Nebraska. Inducted in 1965. 1920 Decatur Staleys, 1921 Chicago Staleys, player-coach 1922-23 Canton Bulldogs, 1924 Cleveland Bulldogs, 1925-26 Frankford Yellow Jackets, 1927 Chicago Cardinals.

JACK CHRISTIANSEN
Defensive back. 6-1, 185. Born in Sublette, Kansas, December 20, 1928. Died June 29, 1986. Colorado State. Inducted in 1970. 1951-58 Detroit Lions.

EARL (DUTCH) CLARK
Quarterback. 6-0, 185. Born in Fowler, Colorado, October 11, 1906. Died August 5, 1978. Colorado College. Inducted in 1963. 1931-32 Portsmouth Spartans, 1934-38 Detroit Lions.

GEORGE CONNOR
Tackle-linebacker. 6-3, 240. Born in Chicago, Illinois, January 21, 1925. Holy Cross, Notre Dame. Inducted in 1975. 1948-55 Chicago Bears.

JIMMY CONZELMAN
Quarterback. Coach. Team owner. 6-0, 180. Born in St. Louis, Missouri, March 6, 1898. Died July 31, 1970. Washington, Missouri. Inducted in 1964. 1920 Decatur Staleys, 1921-22 Rock Island, Ill., Independents, 1923-24 Milwaukee Badgers; owner-coach, 1925-26 Detroit Panthers; player-coach 1927-29, coach 1930 Providence Steam Roller; coach, 1940-42 Chicago Cardinals, 1946-48 Chicago Cardinals.

LARRY CSONKA
Running back. 6-3, 235. Born in Stow, Ohio, December 25, 1946. Syracuse. Inducted in 1987. Miami Dolphins 1968-74, 1979, New York Giants 1976-78.

AL DAVIS
Team, League Administrator. Born in Brockton, Massachusetts, July 4, 1929. Wittenberg, Syracuse. Inducted in 1992. 1963-81 Oakland Raiders, 1982-92 Los Angeles Raiders, 1966 American Football League.

WILLIE DAVIS
Defensive end. 6-3, 245. Born in Lisbon, Louisiana, July 24, 1934. Grambling. Inducted in 1981. 1958-59 Cleveland Browns, 1960-69 Green Bay Packers.

LEN DAWSON
Quarterback. 6-0, 190. Born in Alliance, Ohio, June 20, 1935. Purdue. Inducted in 1987. Pittsburgh Steelers 1957-59, Cleveland Browns 1960-61, Dallas Texans 1962, Kansas City Chiefs 1963-75.

MIKE DITKA
Tight end. 6-3, 225. Born in Carnegie, Pennsylvania, October 18, 1939. Pittsburgh. Inducted in 1988. 1961-66 Chicago Bears, 1967-68 Philadelphia Eagles, 1969-72 Dallas Cowboys.

ART DONOVAN
Defensive tackle. 6-3, 265. Born in Bronx, New York, June 5, 1925. Boston College. Inducted in 1968. 1950 Baltimore Colts, 1951 New York Yanks, 1952 Dallas Texans, 1953-61 Baltimore Colts.

JOHN (PADDY) DRISCOLL
Quarterback. 5-11, 160. Born in Evanston, Illinois, January 11, 1896. Died June 29, 1968. Northwestern. Inducted in 1965. 1920 Decatur Staleys, 1920-25 Chicago Cardinals, 1926-29 Chicago Bears. Coach, 1956-57 Chicago Bears.

BILL DUDLEY
Halfback. 5-10, 176. Born in Bluefield, Virginia, December 24, 1921. Virginia. Inducted in 1966. 1942, 1945-46 Pittsburgh Steelers, 1947-49 Detroit Lions, 1950-51, 1953 Washington Redskins.

GLEN (TURK) EDWARDS
Tackle. 6-2, 260. Born in Mold, Washington, September 28, 1907. Died January 12, 1973. Washington State. Inducted in 1969. 1932 Boston Braves, 1933-36 Boston Redskins, 1937-40 Washington Redskins.

WEEB EWBANK
Coach. Born in Richmond, Indiana, May 6, 1907. Miami, Ohio. Inducted in 1978. 1954-62 Baltimore Colts, 1963-73 New York Jets.

TOM FEARS
End. 6-2, 215. Born in Los Angeles, California, December 3, 1923. Santa Clara, UCLA. Inducted in 1970. 1948-56 Los Angeles Rams.

RAY FLAHERTY
End. Coach. Born in Spokane, Washington, September 1, 1904. Gonzaga. Inducted in 1976. 1926 Los Angeles Wildcats (AFL), 1927-28 New York Yankees, 1928-29, 1931-35 New York Giants. Coach, 1936 Boston Redskins, 1937-42 Washington Redskins, 1946-48 New York Yankees (AAFC), 1949 Chicago Hornets (AAFC).

LEN FORD
End. 6-5, 260. Born in Washington, D.C., February 18, 1926. Died March 14, 1972. Michigan. Inducted in 1976. 1948-49 Los Angeles Dons (AAFC), 1950-57 Cleveland Browns, 1958 Green Bay Packers.

DAN FORTMANN
Guard. 6-0, 207. Born in Pearl River, New York, April 11, 1916. Colgate. Inducted in 1965. 1936-43 Chicago Bears.

FRANK GATSKI
Center. 6-3, 240. Born in Farmington, West Virginia, March 18, 1922. Marshall, Auburn. Inducted in 1985. 1946-49 Cleveland Browns (AAFC), 1950-56 Cleveland Browns, 1957 Detroit Lions.

BILL GEORGE
Linebacker. 6-2, 230. Born in Waynesburg, Pennsylvania, October 27, 1930. Died September 30, 1982. Wake Forest. Inducted in 1974. 1952-65 Chicago Bears, 1966 Los Angeles Rams.

FRANK GIFFORD
Halfback. 6-1, 195. Born in Santa Monica, California, August 16, 1930. Southern California. Inducted in 1977. 1952-60, 1962-64 New York Giants.

SID GILLMAN
Coach. Born in Minneapolis, Minnesota, October 26, 1911. Ohio State. Inducted in 1983. 1955-59 Los Angeles Rams, 1960 Los Angeles Chargers, 1961-69 San Diego Chargers, 1973-74 Houston Oilers.

OTTO GRAHAM
Quarterback. 6-1, 195. Born in Waukegan, Illinois, December 6, 1921. Northwestern. Inducted in 1965. 1946-49 Cleveland Browns (AAFC), 1950-55 Cleveland Browns.

HAROLD (RED) GRANGE
Halfback. 6-0, 185. Born in Forksville, Pennsylvania, June 13, 1903. Died January 28, 1991. Illinois. Inducted in 1963. 1925 Chicago Bears, 1926 New York Yankees (AFL), 1927 New York Yankees, 1929-34 Chicago Bears.

JOE GREENE
Defensive tackle. 6-4, 260. Born in Temple, Texas, September 24, 1946. North Texas State. Inducted in 1987. 1969-81 Pittsburgh Steelers.

FORREST GREGG
Tackle. 6-4, 250. Born in Birthright, Texas, October 18, 1933. Southern Methodist. Inducted in 1977. 1956, 1958-70 Green Bay Packers, 1971 Dallas Cowboys.

BOB GRIESE
Quarterback. 6-1, 190. Born in Evansville, Indiana, February 3, 1945. Purdue. Inducted in 1990. 1967-80 Miami Dolphins.

LOU GROZA
Tackle-kicker. 6-3, 250. Born in Martin's Ferry, Ohio, January 25, 1924. Ohio State. Inducted in 1974. 1946-49 Cleveland Browns (AAFC), 1950-59, 1961-67 Cleveland Browns.

JOE GUYON
Halfback. 6-1, 180. Born in Mahnomen, Minnesota, November 26, 1892. Died November 27, 1971. Carlisle, Georgia Tech. Inducted in 1966. 1920 Canton Bulldogs, 1921 Cleveland Indians, 1922-23 Oorang Indians, 1924 Rock Island, Ill., Independents, 1924-25 Kansas City Cowboys, 1927 New York Giants.

GEORGE HALAS
End. Coach. Team owner. Born in Chicago, Illinois, February 2, 1895. Died October 31, 1983. Illinois. Inducted in 1963. 1920 Decatur Staleys, 1921 Chicago Staleys, 1922-29 Chicago Bears; coach, 1933-42, 1946-55, 1958-67 Chicago Bears.

JACK HAM
Linebacker. 6-1, 225. Born in Johnstown, Pennsylvania, December 23, 1948. Penn State. Inducted in 1988. 1971-82 Pittsburgh Steelers.

JOHN HANNAH
Guard. 6-3, 265. Born in Canton, Georgia, April 4, 1951. Alabama. Inducted in 1991. 1973-85 New England Patriots.

FRANCO HARRIS
Running back. 6-2, 225. Born in Fort Dix, New Jersey, March 7, 1950. Penn State. Inducted in 1990. 1972-83 Pittsburgh Steelers, 1984 Seattle Seahawks.

ED HEALEY
Tackle. 6-3, 220. Born in Indian Orchard, Massachusetts, December 28, 1894. Died December 9, 1978. Dartmouth. Inducted in 1964. 1920-22 Rock Island, Ill., Independents, 1922-27 Chicago Bears.

MEL HEIN
Center. 6-2, 225. Born in Redding, California, August 22, 1909. Died January 31, 1992. Washington State. Inducted in 1963. 1931-45 New York Giants.

TED HENDRICKS
Linebacker. 6-7, 235. Born in Guatemala City, Guatemala, November 1, 1947. Miami. Inducted in 1990. 1969-73 Baltimore Colts, 1974 Green Bay Packers, 1975-81 Oakland Raiders, 1982-83 Los Angeles Raiders.

WILBUR (PETE) HENRY
Tackle. 6-0, 250. Born in Mansfield, Ohio, October 31, 1897. Died February 7, 1952. Washington & Jefferson. Inducted in 1963. 1920-23, 1925-26 Canton Bulldogs, 1927 New York Giants, 1927-28 Pottsville Maroons.

ARNIE HERBER
Quarterback. 6-1, 200. Born in Green Bay, Wisconsin, April 2, 1910. Died October 14, 1969. Wisconsin, Regis College. Inducted in 1966. 1930-40 Green Bay Packers, 1944-45 New York Giants.

BILL HEWITT
End. 5-11, 191. Born in Bay City, Michigan, October 8, 1909. Died January 14, 1947. Michigan. Inducted in 1971. 1932-36 Chicago Bears, 1937-39 Philadelphia Eagles, 1943 Phil-Pitt.

CLARKE HINKLE
Fullback. 5-11, 201. Born in Toronto, Ohio, April 10, 1909. Died November 9, 1988. Bucknell. Inducted in 1964. 1932-41 Green Bay Packers.

ELROY (CRAZYLEGS) HIRSCH
Halfback-end. 6-2, 190. Born in Wausau, Wisconsin, June 17, 1923. Wisconsin, Michigan. Inducted in 1968. 1946-48 Chicago Rockets (AAFC), 1949-57 Los Angeles Rams.

PAUL HORNUNG
Halfback. 6-2, 220. Born in Louisville, Kentucky, December 23, 1935. Notre Dame. Inducted in 1986. 1957-62, 1964-66 Green Bay Packers.

KEN HOUSTON
Safety. 6-3, 198. Born in Lufkin, Texas, November 12, 1944. Prairie View A&M. Inducted in 1986. 1967-72 Houston Oilers, 1973-80 Washington Redskins.

CAL HUBBARD
Tackle. 6-5, 250. Born in Keytesville, Missouri, October 31, 1900. Died October 17, 1977. Centenary, Geneva. Inducted in 1963. 1927-28 New York Giants, 1929-33, 1935 Green Bay Packers, 1936 New York Giants, 1936 Pittsburgh Pirates.

SAM HUFF
Linebacker. 6-1, 230. Born in Morgantown, West Virginia, October 4, 1934. West Virginia. Inducted in 1982. 1956-63 New York Giants, 1964-67, 1969 Washington Redskins.

LAMAR HUNT
Team owner. Born in El Dorado, Arkansas, August 2, 1932. Southern Methodist. Inducted in 1972. 1960-62 Dallas Texans, 1963-90 Kansas City Chiefs.

DON HUTSON
End. 6-1, 180. Born in Pine Bluff, Arkansas, January 31, 1913. Alabama. Inducted in 1963. 1935-45 Green Bay Packers.

JOHN HENRY JOHNSON
Fullback. 6-2, 225. Born in Waterproof, Louisiana, November 24, 1929. St. Mary's, Arizona State. Inducted in 1987. San Francisco 49ers 1954-56, Detroit Lions 1957-59, Pittsburgh Steelers 1960-65, Houston Oilers 1966.

DAVID (DEACON) JONES
Defensive end. 6-5, 250. Born in Eatonville, Florida, December 9, 1938. Mississippi Vocational. Inducted in 1980. 1961-71 Los Angeles Rams, 1972-73 San Diego Chargers, 1974 Washington Redskins.

STAN JONES
Guard-defensive tackle. 6-1, 250. Born in Altoona, Pennsylvania, November 24, 1931. Maryland. Inducted in 1991. 1954-65 Chicago Bears, 1966 Washington Redskins.

SONNY JURGENSEN
Quarterback. 6-0, 203. Born in Wilmington, North Carolina, August 23, 1934. Duke. Inducted in 1983. 1957-63 Philadelphia Eagles, 1964-74 Washington Redskins.

WALT KIESLING
Guard. Coach. 6-2, 245. Born in St. Paul, Minnesota, March 27, 1903. Died March 2, 1962. St. Thomas (Minnesota). Inducted in 1966. 1926-27 Duluth Eskimos, 1928 Pottsville Maroons, 1929-33 Chicago Cardinals, 1934 Chicago Bears, 1935-36 Green Bay Packers, 1937-38 Pittsburgh Pirates; coach, 1939-42 Pittsburgh Steelers; co-coach, 1943 Phil-Pitt, 1944 Card-Pitt; coach, 1954-56 Pittsburgh Steelers.

FRANK (BRUISER) KINARD
Tackle. 6-1, 210. Born in Pelahatchie, Mississippi, October 23, 1914. Died September 7, 1985. Mississippi. Inducted in 1971. 1938-44 Brooklyn Dodgers-Tigers, 1946-47 New York Yankees (AAFC).

EARL (CURLY) LAMBEAU
Coach. Born in Green Bay, Wisconsin, April 9, 1898. Died June 1, 1965. Notre Dame. Inducted in 1963. 1919-49 Green Bay Packers, 1950-51 Chicago Cardinals, 1952-53 Washington Redskins.

JACK LAMBERT
Linebacker. 6-4, 220. Born in Mantua, Ohio, July 8, 1952. Kent State. Inducted in 1990. 1974-84 Pittsburgh Steelers.

TOM LANDRY
Coach. Born in Mission, Texas, September 11, 1924. Texas. Inducted in 1990. 1960-88 Dallas Cowboys.

DICK (NIGHT TRAIN) LANE
Defensive back. 6-2, 210. Born in Austin, Texas, April 16, 1928. Scottsbluff Junior College. Inducted in 1974. 1952-53 Los Angeles Rams, 1954-59 Chicago Cardinals, 1960-65 Detroit Lions.

JIM LANGER
Center. 6-2, 255. Born in Little Falls, Minnesota, May 16, 1948. South Dakota State. Inducted in 1987. Miami Dolphins 1970-79, Minnesota Vikings 1980-81.

WILLIE LANIER
Linebacker. 6-1, 245. Born in Clover, Virginia, August 21, 1945. Morgan State. Inducted in 1986. 1967-77 Kansas City Chiefs.

YALE LARY
Defensive back-punter. 5-11, 189. Born in Fort Worth, Texas, November 24, 1930. Texas A&M. Inducted in 1979. 1952-53, 1956-64 Detroit Lions.

DANTE LAVELLI
End. 6-0, 199. Born in Hudson, Ohio, February 23, 1923. Ohio State. Inducted in 1975. 1946-49 Cleveland Browns (AAFC), 1950-56 Cleveland Browns.

BOBBY LAYNE
Quarterback. 6-2, 190. Born in Santa Anna, Texas, December 19, 1926. Died December 1, 1986. Texas. Inducted in 1967. 1948 Chicago Bears, 1949 New York Bulldogs, 1950-58 Detroit Lions, 1958-62 Pittsburgh Steelers.

ALPHONSE (TUFFY) LEEMANS
Fullback. 6-0, 200. Born in Superior, Wisconsin, November 12, 1912. Died January 19, 1979. George Washington. Inducted in 1978. 1936-43 New York Giants.

BOB LILLY
Defensive tackle. 6-5, 260. Born in Olney, Texas, July 26, 1939. Texas Christian. Inducted in 1980. 1961-74 Dallas Cowboys.

VINCE LOMBARDI
Coach. Born in Brooklyn, New York, June 11, 1913. Died September 3, 1970. Fordham. Inducted in 1971. 1959-67 Green Bay Packers, 1969 Washington Redskins.

SID LUCKMAN
Quarterback. 6-0, 195. Born in Brooklyn, New York, November 21, 1916. Columbia. Inducted in 1965. 1939-50 Chicago Bears.

ROY (LINK) LYMAN
Tackle. 6-2, 252. Born in Table Rock, Nebraska, November 30, 1898. Died December 16, 1972. Nebraska. Inducted in 1964. 1922-23, 1925 Canton Bulldogs, 1924 Cleveland Bulldogs, 1925 Frankford Yellow Jackets, 1926-28, 1930-31, 1933-34 Chicago Bears.

JOHN MACKEY
Tight end. 6-2, 224. Born in New York, New York, September 24, 1941. Syracuse. Inducted in 1992. 1963-71 Baltimore Colts, 1972 San Diego Chargers.

TIM MARA
Team owner. Born in New York, New York, July 29, 1887. Died February 17, 1959. Did not attend college. Inducted in 1963. 1925-59 New York Giants.

GINO MARCHETTI
Defensive end. 6-4, 245. Born in Smithers, West Virginia, January 2, 1927. San Francisco. Inducted in 1972. 1952 Dallas Texans, 1953-64, 1966 Baltimore Colts.

GEORGE PRESTON MARSHALL
Team owner. Born in Grafton, West Virginia, October 11, 1897. Died August 9, 1969. Randolph-Macon. Inducted in 1963. 1932 Boston Braves, 1933-36 Boston Redskins, 1937-69 Washington Redskins.

OLLIE MATSON
Halfback. 6-2, 220. Born in Trinity, Texas, May 1, 1930. San Francisco. Inducted in 1972. 1952, 1954-58 Chicago Cardinals, 1959-62 Los Angeles Rams, 1963 Detroit Lions, 1964-66 Philadelphia Eagles.

DON MAYNARD
Wide receiver. 6-1, 175. Born in Crosbyton, Texas, January 25, 1935. Texas Western. Inducted in 1987. New York Giants 1958, New York Titans 1960-62, New York Jets 1963-72, St. Louis Cardinals 1973.

GEORGE McAFEE
Halfback. 6-0, 177. Born in Ironton, Ohio, March 13, 1918. Duke. Inducted in 1966. 1940-41, 1945-50 Chicago Bears.

MIKE McCORMACK
Tackle. 6-4, 248. Born in Chicago, Illinois, June 21, 1930. Kansas. Inducted in 1984. 1951 New York Yanks, 1954-62 Cleveland Browns.

HUGH McELHENNY
Halfback. 6-1, 198. Born in Los Angeles, California, December 31, 1928. Washington. Inducted in 1970. 1952-60 San Francisco 49ers, 1961-62 Minnesota Vikings, 1963 New York Giants, 1964 Detroit Lions.

JOHNNY BLOOD (McNALLY)
Halfback. 6-0, 185. Born in New Richmond, Wisconsin, November 27, 1903. Died November 28, 1985. St. John's (Minnesota). Inducted in 1963. 1925-26 Milwaukee Badgers, 1926-27 Duluth Eskimos, 1928 Pottsville Maroons, 1929-33, 1935-36 Green Bay Packers, 1934 Pittsburgh Pirates; player-coach, 1937-39 Pittsburgh Pirates.

MIKE MICHALSKE
Guard. 6-0, 209. Born in Cleveland, Ohio, April 24, 1903. Died October 26, 1983. Penn State. Inducted in 1964. 1926 New York Yankees (AFL), 1927-28 New York Yankees, 1929-35, 1937 Green Bay Packers.

WAYNE MILLNER
End. 6-0, 191. Born in Roxbury, Massachusetts, January 31, 1913. Died November 19, 1976. Notre Dame. Inducted in 1968. 1936 Boston Redskins, 1937-41, 1945 Washington Redskins.

BOBBY MITCHELL
Running back-wide receiver. 6-0, 195. Born in Hot Springs, Arkansas, June 6, 1935. Illinois. Inducted in 1983. 1958-61 Cleveland Browns, 1962-68 Washington Redskins.

RON MIX
Tackle. 6-4, 250. Born in Los Angeles, California, March 10, 1938. Southern California. Inducted in 1979. 1960 Los Angeles Chargers, 1961-69 San Diego Chargers, 1971 Oakland Raiders.

LENNY MOORE
Back. 6-1, 198. Born in Reading, Pennsylvania, November 25, 1933. Penn State. Inducted in 1975. 1956-67 Baltimore Colts.

MARION MOTLEY
Fullback. 6-1, 238. Born in Leesburg, Georgia, June 5, 1920. South Carolina State, Nevada. Inducted in 1968. 1946-49 Cleveland Browns (AAFC), 1950-53 Cleveland Browns, 1955 Pittsburgh Steelers.

GEORGE MUSSO
Guard-tackle. 6-2, 270. Born in Collinsville, Illinois. April 8, 1910. Millikin. Inducted in 1982. 1933-44 Chicago Bears.

BRONKO NAGURSKI
Fullback. 6-2, 225. Born in Rainy River, Ontario, Canada, November 3, 1908. Died January 7, 1990. Minnesota. Inducted in 1963. 1930-37, 1943 Chicago Bears.

JOE NAMATH
Quarterback. 6-2, 200. Born in Beaver Falls, Pennsylvania, May 31, 1943. Alabama. Inducted in 1985. 1965-76 New York Jets, 1977 Los Angeles Rams.

EARLE (GREASY) NEALE
Coach. Born in Parkersburg, West Virginia, November 5, 1891. Died November 2, 1973. West Virginia Wesleyan. Inducted in 1969. 1941-42, 1944-50 Philadelphia Eagles; co-coach, Phil-Pitt 1943.

ERNIE NEVERS
Fullback. 6-1, 205. Born in Willow River, Minnesota, June 11, 1903. Died May 3, 1976. Stanford. Inducted in 1963. 1926-27 Duluth Eskimos, 1929-31 Chicago Cardinals.

RAY NITSCHKE
Linebacker. 6-3, 235. Born in Elmwood Park, Illinois, December 29, 1936. Illinois. Inducted in 1978. 1958-72 Green Bay Packers.

LEO NOMELLINI
Defensive tackle. 6-3, 250. Born in Lucca, Italy, June 19, 1924. Minnesota. Inducted in 1969. 1950-63 San Francisco 49ers.

MERLIN OLSEN
Defensive tackle. 6-5, 270. Born in Logan, Utah, September 15, 1940. Utah State. Inducted in 1982. 1962-76 Los Angeles Rams.

JIM OTTO
Center. 6-2, 255. Born in Wausau, Wisconsin, January 5, 1938. Miami. Inducted in 1980. 1960-74 Oakland Raiders.

STEVE OWEN
Tackle. Coach. 6-0, 235. Born in Cleo Springs, Oklahoma, April 21, 1898. Died May 17, 1964. Phillips. Inducted in 1966. 1924-25 Kansas City Cowboys, 1926-30 New York Giants; coach, 1931-53 New York Giants.

ALAN PAGE
Defensive tackle. 6-4, 225. Born in Canton, Ohio, August 7, 1945. Notre Dame. Inducted in 1988. 1967-78 Minnesota Vikings, 1978-81 Chicago Bears.

CLARENCE (ACE) PARKER
Quarterback. 5-11, 168. Born in Portsmouth, Virginia, May 17, 1912. Duke. Inducted in 1972. 1937-41 Brooklyn Dodgers, 1945 Boston Yanks, 1946 New York Yankees (AAFC).

JIM PARKER
Guard-tackle. 6-3, 273. Born in Macon, Georgia, April 3, 1934. Ohio State. Inducted in 1973. 1957-67 Baltimore Colts.

JOE PERRY
Fullback. 6-0, 200. Born in Stevens, Arkansas, January 22, 1927. Compton Junior College. Inducted in 1969. 1948-49 San Francisco 49ers (AAFC), 1950-60, 1963 San Francisco 49ers, 1961-62 Baltimore Colts.

PETE PIHOS
End. 6-1, 210. Born in Orlando, Florida, October 22, 1923. Indiana. Inducted in 1970. 1947-55 Philadelphia Eagles.

HUGH (SHORTY) RAY
Supervisor of officials 1938-56. Born in Highland Park, Illinois, September 21, 1884. Died September 16, 1956. Illinois. Inducted in 1966.

DAN REEVES
Team owner. Born in New York, New York, June 30, 1912. Died April 15, 1971. Georgetown. Inducted in 1967. 1941-45 Cleveland Rams, 1946-71 Los Angeles Rams.

JOHN RIGGINS
Running back. 6-2, 240. Born in Seneca, Kansas, August 4, 1949. Kansas. Inducted in 1992. 1971-75 New York Jets, 1976-79, 1981-85 Washington Redskins.

JIM RINGO
Center. 6-1, 235. Born in Orange, New Jersey, November 21, 1931. Syracuse. Inducted in 1981. 1953-63 Green Bay Packers, 1964-67 Philadelphia Eagles.

ANDY ROBUSTELLI
Defensive end. 6-0, 230. Born in Stamford, Connecticut, December 6, 1925. Arnold College. Inducted in 1971. 1951-55 Los Angeles Rams, 1956-64 New York Giants.

ART ROONEY
Team owner. Born in Coulterville, Pennsylvania, January 27, 1901. Died August 25, 1988. Georgetown, Duquesne. Inducted in 1964. 1933-40 Pittsburgh Pirates, 1941-42, 1945-88 Pittsburgh Steelers, 1943 Phil-Pitt, 1944 Card-Pitt.

PETE ROZELLE
Commissioner. Born in South Gate, California, March 1, 1926. San Francisco. Inducted in 1985. Commissioner, 1960-89.

BOB ST. CLAIR
Tackle. 6-9, 265. Born in San Francisco, California, February 18, 1931. San Francisco, Tulsa. Inducted in 1990. 1953-63 San Francisco 49ers.

GALE SAYERS
Running back. 6-0, 200. Born in Wichita, Kansas, May 30, 1943. Kansas. Inducted in 1977. 1965-71 Chicago Bears.

JOE SCHMIDT
Linebacker. 6-0, 222. Born in Pittsburgh, Pennsylvania, January 19, 1932. Pittsburgh. Inducted in 1973. 1953-65 Detroit Lions.

TEX SCHRAMM
Team president-general manager. Born in San Gabriel, California, June 2, 1920. Texas. Inducted in 1991. 1947-57 Los Angeles Rams. 1960-88 Dallas Cowboys.

ART SHELL
Tackle. 6-5, 285. Born in Charleston, South Carolina, November 25, 1946. Maryland State-Eastern Shore. Inducted in 1989. 1968-81 Oakland Raiders, 1982 Los Angeles Raiders.

O.J. SIMPSON
Running back. 6-1, 212. Born in San Francisco, California, July 9, 1947. Southern California. Inducted in 1985. 1969-77 Buffalo Bills, 1978-79 San Francisco 49ers.

BART STARR
Quarterback. 6-1, 200. Born in Montgomery, Alabama, January 9, 1934. Alabama. Inducted in 1977. 1956-71 Green Bay Packers.

ROGER STAUBACH
Quarterback. 6-3, 202. Born in Cincinnati, Ohio, February 5, 1942. Navy. Inducted in 1985. 1969-79 Dallas Cowboys.

ERNIE STAUTNER
Defensive tackle. 6-2, 235. Born in Prinzing-by-Cham, Bavaria, Germany, April 20, 1925. Boston College. Inducted in 1969. 1950-63 Pittsburgh Steelers.

JAN STENERUD
Kicker. 6-2, 190. Born in Fetsund, Norway, November 26, 1942. Montana State. Inducted in 1991. 1967-79 Kansas City Chiefs, 1980-83 Green Bay Packers, 1984-85 Minnesota Vikings.

KEN STRONG
Halfback. 5-11, 210. Born in New Haven, Connecticut, August 6, 1906. Died October 5, 1979. New York University. Inducted in 1967. 1929-32 Staten Island Stapletons, 1933-35, 1939, 1944-47 New York Giants, 1936-37 New York Yanks (AFL).

JOE STYDAHAR
Tackle. 6-4, 230. Born in Kaylor, Pennsylvania, March 3, 1912. Died March 23, 1977. West Virginia. Inducted in 1967. 1936-42, 1945-46 Chicago Bears.

FRAN TARKENTON
Quarterback. 6-0, 185. Born in Richmond, Virginia, February 3, 1940. Georgia. Inducted in 1986. 1961-66, 1972-78 Minnesota Vikings, 1967-71 New York Giants.

CHARLEY TAYLOR
Running back-wide receiver. 6-3, 210. Born in Grand Prairie, Texas, September 28, 1941. Arizona State. Inducted in 1984. 1964-75, 1977 Washington Redskins.

JIM TAYLOR
Fullback. 6-0, 216. Born in Baton Rouge, Louisiana, September 20, 1935. Louisiana State. Inducted in 1976. 1958-66 Green Bay Packers, 1967 New Orleans Saints.

JIM THORPE
Halfback. 6-1, 190. Born in Prague, Oklahoma, May 28, 1888. Died March 28, 1953. Carlisle. Inducted in 1963. 1915-17, 1919-20, 1926 Canton Bulldogs, 1921 Cleveland Indians, 1922-23 Oorang Indians, 1924 Rock Island, Ill., Independents, 1925 New York Giants, 1928 Chicago Cardinals.

Y.A. TITTLE
Quarterback. 6-0, 200. Born in Marshall, Texas, October 24, 1926. Louisiana State. Inducted in 1971. 1948-49 Baltimore Colts (AAFC), 1950 Baltimore Colts, 1951-60 San Francisco 49ers, 1961-64 New York Giants.

GEORGE TRAFTON
Center. 6-2, 235. Born in Chicago, Illinois, December 6, 1896. Died September 5, 1971. Notre Dame. Inducted in 1964. 1920 Decatur Staleys, 1921 Chicago Staleys, 1922-32 Chicago Bears.

CHARLEY TRIPPI
Halfback. 6-0, 185. Born in Pittston, Pennsylvania, December 14, 1922. Georgia. Inducted in 1968. 1947-55 Chicago Cardinals.

EMLEN TUNNELL
Safety. 6-1, 200. Born in Bryn Mawr, Pennsylvania, March 29, 1925. Died July 23, 1975. Toledo, Iowa. Inducted in 1967. 1948-58 New York Giants, 1959-61 Green Bay Packers.

CLYDE (BULLDOG) TURNER
Center. 6-2, 235. Born in Sweetwater, Texas, November 10, 1919. Hardin-Simmons. Inducted in 1966. 1940-52 Chicago Bears.

JOHNNY UNITAS
Quarterback. 6-1, 195. Born in Pittsburgh, Pennsylvania, May 7, 1933. Louisville. Inducted in 1979. 1956-72 Baltimore Colts, 1973 San Diego Chargers.

GENE UPSHAW
Guard. 6-5, 255. Born in Robstown, Texas, August 15, 1945. Texas A & I. Inducted in 1987. Oakland Raiders 1967-81.

NORM VAN BROCKLIN
Quarterback. 6-1, 190. Born in Eagle Butte, South Dakota, March 15, 1926. Died May 2, 1983. Oregon. Inducted in 1971. 1949-57 Los Angeles Rams, 1958-60 Philadelphia Eagles.

STEVE VAN BUREN
Halfback. 6-1, 200. Born in La Ceiba, Honduras, December 28, 1920. Louisiana State. Inducted in 1965. 1944-51 Philadelphia Eagles.

DOAK WALKER
Halfback. 5-10, 172. Born in Dallas, Texas, January 1, 1927. Southern Methodist. Inducted in 1986. 1950-55 Detroit Lions.

PAUL WARFIELD
Wide receiver. 6-0, 188. Born in Warren, Ohio, November 28, 1942. Ohio State. Inducted in 1983. 1964-69, 1976-77 Cleveland Browns, 1970-74 Miami Dolphins.

BOB WATERFIELD
Quarterback. 6-2, 200. Born in Elmira, New York, July 26, 1920. Died March 25, 1983. UCLA. Inducted in 1965. 1945 Cleveland Rams, 1946-52 Los Angeles Rams.

ARNIE WEINMEISTER
Defensive tackle. 6-4, 235. Born in Rhein, Saskatchewan, Canada, March 23, 1923. Washington. Inducted in 1984. 1948-49 New York Yankees (AAFC), 1950-53 New York Giants.

BILL WILLIS
Guard. 6-2, 215. Born in Columbus, Ohio, October 5, 1921. Ohio State. Inducted in 1977. 1946-49 Cleveland Browns (AAFC), 1950-53 Cleveland Browns.

LARRY WILSON
Safety. 6-0, 190. Born in Rigby, Idaho, March 24, 1938. Utah. Inducted in 1978. 1960-72 St. Louis Cardinals.

ALEX WOJCIECHOWICZ
Center. 6-0, 235. Born in South River, New Jersey, August 12, 1915. Fordham. Inducted in 1968. 1938-46 Detroit Lions, 1946-50 Philadelphia Eagles.

WILLIE WOOD
Safety. 5-10, 190. Born in Washington, D.C., December 23, 1936. Southern California. Inducted in 1989. 1960-71 Green Bay Packers.

1869 Rutgers and Princeton played a college soccer football game, the first ever, November 6. The game used modified London Football Association rules. During the next seven years, rugby gained favor with the major eastern schools over soccer, and modern football began to develop from rugby.

1876 At the Massasoit convention, the first rules for American football were written. Walter Camp, who would become known as the father of American football, first became involved with the game.

1892 In an era in which football was a major attraction of local athletic clubs, an intense competition between two Pittsburgh-area clubs, the Allegheny Athletic Association (AAA) and the Pittsburgh Athletic Club (PAC), led to the making of the first professional football player. Former Yale All-America guard William (Pudge) Heffelfinger was paid $500 by the AAA to play in a game against the PAC, becoming the first person to be paid to play football, November 12. The AAA won the game 4-0 when Heffelfinger picked up a PAC fumble and ran 35 yards for a touchdown.

1893 The Pittsburgh Athletic Club signed one of its players, probably halfback Grant Dibert, to the first-known pro football contract, which covered all of the PAC's games for the year.

1895 John Brallier became the first football player to openly turn pro, accepting $10 and expenses to play for the Latrobe YMCA against the Jeannette Athletic Club.

1896 The Allegheny Athletic Association team fielded the first completely professional team for its abbreviated two-game season.

1897 The Latrobe Athletic Association football team went entirely professional, becoming the first team to play a full season with only professionals.

1898 A touchdown was changed from four points to five.

1899 Chris O'Brien formed a neighborhood team, which played under the name the Morgan Athletic Club, on the south side of Chicago. The team later became known as the Normals, then the Racine (for a street in Chicago) Cardinals, the Chicago Cardinals, the St. Louis Cardinals, and, in 1988, the Phoenix Cardinals. The team remains the oldest continuing operation in pro football.

1900 William C. Temple took over the team payments for the Duquesne Country and Athletic Club, becoming the first known individual club owner.

1902 Baseball's Philadelphia Athletics, managed by Connie Mack, and the Philadelphia Phillies formed professional football teams, joining the Pittsburgh Stars in the first attempt at a pro football league, named the National Football League. The Athletics won the first night football game ever played, 39-0 over Kanaweola AC at Elmira, New York, November 21.

All three teams claimed the pro championship for the year, but the league president, Dave Berry, named the Stars the champions. Pitcher Rube Waddell was with the Athletics, and pitcher Christy Matthewson a fullback for Pittsburgh.

The first World Series of pro football, actually a five-team tournament, was played among a team made up of players from both the Athletics and the Phillies, but simply named New York; the New York Knickerbockers; the Syracuse AC; the Warlow AC; and the Orange (New Jersey) AC at New York's original Madison Square Garden. New York and Syracuse played the first indoor football game before 3,000, December 28. Syracuse, with Glen (Pop) Warner at guard, won 6-0 and went on to win the tournament.

1903 The Franklin (Pa.) Athletic Club won the second and last World Series of pro football over the Oreos AC of Asbury Park, New Jersey; the Watertown Red and Blacks; and the Orange AC.

Pro football was popularized in Ohio when the Massillon Tigers, a strong amateur team, hired four Pittsburgh pros to play in the season-ending game against Akron. At the same time, pro football declined in the Pittsburgh area, and the emphasis on the pro game moved west from Pennsylvania to Ohio.

1904 A field goal was changed from five points to four.

Ohio had at least seven pro teams, with Massillon winning the Ohio Independent Championship, that is, the pro title. Talk surfaced about forming a state-wide league to end spiraling salaries brought about by constant bidding for players and to write universal rules for the game. The feeble attempt to start the league failed.

Halfback Charles Follis signed a contract with the Shelby AC, making him the first-known black pro football player.

1905 The Canton AC, later to become known as the Bulldogs, became a professional team. Massillon again won the Ohio League championship.

1906 The forward pass was legalized. The first authenticated pass completion in a pro game came on October 27, when George (Peggy) Parratt of Massillon threw a completion to Dan (Bullet) Riley in a victory over a combined Benwood-Moundsville team.

Arch-rivals Canton and Massillon, the two best pro teams in America, played twice, with Canton winning the first game but Massillon winning the second and the Ohio League championship. A betting scandal and the financial disaster wrought upon the two clubs by paying huge salaries caused a temporary decline in interest in pro football in the two cities and, somewhat, throughout Ohio.

1909 A field goal dropped from four points to three.

1912 A touchdown was increased from five points to six.

Jack Cusack revived a strong pro team in Canton.

1913 Jim Thorpe, a former football and track star at the Carlisle Indian School (Pa.) and a double gold medal winner at the 1912 Olympics in Stockholm, played for the Pine Village Pros in Indiana.

1915 Massillon again fielded a major team, reviving the old rivalry with Canton. Cusack signed Thorpe to play for Canton for $250 a game.

1916 With Thorpe and former Carlisle teammate Pete Calac starring, Canton went 9-0-1, won the Ohio League championship, and was acclaimed the pro football champion.

1917 Despite an upset by Massillon, Canton again won the Ohio League championship.

1919 Canton again won the Ohio League championship, despite the team having been turned over from Cusack to Ralph Hay. Thorpe and Calac were joined in the backfield by Joe Guyon.

Earl (Curly) Lambeau and George Calhoun organized the Green Bay Packers. Lambeau's employer at the Indian Packing Company provided $500 for equipment and allowed the team to use the company field for practices. The Packers went 10-1.

1920 Pro football was in a state of confusion due to three major problems: dramatically rising salaries; players continually jumping from one team to another following the highest offer; and the use of college players still enrolled in school. A league in which all the members would follow the same rules seemed the answer. An organizational meeting, at which the Akron Pros, Canton Bulldogs, Cleveland Indians, and Dayton Triangles were represented, was held in Canton, Ohio, August 20. This meeting resulted in the formation of the American Professional Football Conference.

A second organizational meeting was held in Canton, September 17. The teams were from four states—Akron, Canton, Cleveland, and Dayton from Ohio; the Hammond Pros and Muncie Flyers from Indiana; the Rochester Jeffersons from New York; and the Rock Island Independents, Decatur Staleys, and Racine Cardinals from Illinois. The name of the league was changed to the American Professional Football Association. Hoping to capitalize on his fame, the members elected Thorpe president; Stanley Cofall of Cleveland was elected vice president. A membership fee of $100 per team was charged to give an appearance of respectability, but no team ever paid it. Scheduling was left up to the teams, and there were wide variations, both in the overall number of games played and in the number played against APFA member teams.

Four other teams—the Buffalo All-Americans, Chicago Tigers, Columbus Panhandles, and Detroit Heralds—joined the league sometime during the year. On September 26, the first game featuring an APFA team was played at Rock Island's Douglas Park. A crowd of 800 watched the Independents defeat the St. Paul Ideals 48-0. A week later, October 3, the first game matching two APFA teams was held. At Triangle Park, Dayton defeated Columbus 14-0, with Lou Partlow of Dayton scoring the first touchdown in a game between Association teams. The same day, Rock Island defeated Muncie 45-0.

By the beginning of December, most of the teams in the APFA had abandoned their hopes for a championship, and some of them, including the Chicago Tigers and the Detroit Heralds, had finished their seasons, disbanded, and had their franchises canceled by the Association. Four teams—Akron, Buffalo, Canton, and Decatur—still had championship as-pirations, but a series of late-season games among them left Akron as the only undefeated team in the Association. At one of these games, Akron sold tackle Bob Nash to Buffalo for $300 and five percent of the gate receipts—the first APFA player deal.

1921 At the league meeting in Akron, April 30, the championship of the 1920 season was awarded to the Akron Pros. The APFA was reorganized, with Joe Carr of the Columbus Panhandles named president and Carl Storck of Dayton secretary-treasurer. Carr moved the Association's headquarters to Columbus, drafted a league constitution and by-laws, gave teams territorial rights, restricted player movements, developed membership criteria for the franchises, and issued standings for the first time, so that the APFA would have a clear champion.

The Association's membership increased to 22 teams, including the Green Bay Packers, who were awarded to John Clair of the Acme Packing Company.

Thorpe moved from Canton to the Cleveland Indians, but he was hurt early in the season and played very little.

A.E. Staley turned the Decatur Staleys over to player-coach George Halas, who moved the team to Cubs Park in Chicago. Staley paid Halas $5,000 to keep the name Staleys for one more year. Halas made halfback Ed (Dutch) Sternaman his partner.

The Staleys claimed the APFA championship with a 9-1-1 record, as did Buffalo at 9-1-2. Carr ruled in favor of the Staleys, giving Halas his first championship.

1922 After admitting the use of players who had college eligibility remaining during the 1921 season, Clair and the Green Bay management withdrew from the APFA, January 28. Curly Lambeau promised to obey league rules and then used $50 of his own money to buy back the franchise. Bad weather and low attendance plagued the Packers, and Lambeau went broke, but local merchants arranged a $2,500 loan for the club. A public nonprofit corporation was set up to operate the team, with Lambeau as head coach and manager.

The American Professional Football Association changed its name to the National Football League, June 24. The Chicago Staleys became the Chicago Bears.

The NFL fielded 18 teams, including the new Oorang Indians of Marion, Ohio, an all-Indian team featuring Thorpe, Joe Guyon, and Pete Calac, and sponsored by the Oorang dog kennels.

Canton, led by player-coach Guy Chamberlin and tackles Link Lyman and Wilbur (Pete) Henry, emerged as the league's first true powerhouse, going 10-0-2.

1923 For the first time, all of the franchises considered to be part of the NFL fielded teams. Thorpe played first for Oorang, then for the Toledo Maroons. Against the Bears, Thorpe fumbled, and Halas picked up the ball and returned it 98 yards for a touchdown, a record that would last until 1972.

Canton had its second consecutive undefeated season, going 11-0-1

for the NFL title.

1924 The league had 18 franchises, including new ones in Kansas City, Kenosha, and Frankford, a section of Philadelphia. League champion Canton, successful on the field but not at the box office, was purchased by the owner of the Cleveland franchise, who kept the Canton franchise inactive, while using the best players for his Cleveland team, which he renamed the Bulldogs. Cleveland won the title with a 7-1-1 record.

1925 Five new franchises were admitted to the NFL—the New York Giants, who were awarded to Tim Mara and Billy Gibson for $500; the Detroit Panthers, featuring Jimmy Conzelman as owner, coach, and tailback; the Providence Steam Roller; a new Canton Bulldogs team; and the Pottsville Maroons, who had been perhaps the most successful independent pro team. The NFL established its first player limit, at 16 players.

Late in the season, the NFL made its greatest coup in gaining national recognition. Shortly after the University of Illinois season ended in November, All-America halfback Harold (Red) Grange signed a contract to play with the Chicago Bears. On Thanksgiving Day, a crowd of 36,000—the largest in pro football history—watched Grange and the Bears play the Chicago Cardinals to a scoreless tie at Wrigley Field. At the beginning of December, the Bears left on a barnstorming tour that saw them play eight games in 12 days, in St. Louis, Philadelphia, New York City, Washington, Boston, Pittsburgh, Detroit, and Chicago. A crowd of 73,000 watched the game against the Giants at the Polo Grounds, helping assure the future of the troubled NFL franchise in New York. The Bears then played nine more games in the South and West, including a game in Los Angeles, in which 75,000 fans watched them defeat the Los Angeles Tigers in the Los Angeles Memorial Coliseum.

Pottsville and the Chicago Cardinals were the top contenders for the league title, with Pottsville winning a late-season meeting 21-7. Pottsville scheduled a game against a team of former Notre Dame players for Shibe Park in Philadelphia. Frankford lodged a protest not only because the game was in Frankford's protected territory, but because it was being played the same day as a Yellow Jackets home game. Carr gave three different notices forbidding Pottsville to play the game, but Pottsville played anyway, December 12. That day, Carr fined the club, suspended it from all rights and privileges (including the right to play for the NFL championship), and returned its franchise to the league. The Cardinals, who ended the season with the best record in the league, were named the 1925 champions.

1926 Grange's manager, C.C. Pyle, told the Bears that Grange wouldn't play for them unless he was paid a five-figure salary and given one-third ownership of the team. The Bears refused. Pyle leased Yankee Stadium in New York City, then petitioned for an NFL franchise. After he was refused, he started the first American Football League. It lasted one season and included Grange's New York Yankees and eight other teams. The AFL champion Philadelphia Quakers played a December game against the New York Giants, seventh in the NFL, and the Giants won 31-0. At the end of the season, the AFL folded.

Halas pushed through a rule that prohibited any team from signing a player whose college class had not graduated.

The NFL grew to 22 teams, including the Duluth Eskimos, who signed All-America fullback Ernie Nevers of Stanford, giving the league a gate attraction to rival Grange. The 15-member Eskimos, dubbed the Iron Men of the North, played 29 exhibition and league games, 28 on the road, and Nevers played in all but 29 minutes of them.

Frankford edged the Bears for the championship, despite Halas having obtained John (Paddy) Driscoll from the Cardinals. On December 4, the Yellow Jackets scored in the final two minutes to defeat the Bears 7-6 and move ahead of them in the standings.

1927 At a special meeting in Cleveland, April 23, Carr decided to secure the NFL's future by eliminating the financially weaker teams and consolidating the quality players onto a limited number of more successful teams. The new-look NFL dropped to 12 teams, and the center of gravity of the league left the Midwest, where the NFL had started, and began to emerge in the large cities of the East. One of the new teams was Grange's New York Yankees, but Grange suffered a knee injury and the Yankees finished in the middle of the pack. The NFL championship was won by the cross-town rival New York Giants, who posted 10 shutouts in 13 games.

1928 Grange and Nevers both retired from pro football, and Duluth disbanded, as the NFL was reduced to only 10 teams. The Providence Steam Roller of Jimmy Conzelman and Pearce Johnson won the championship, playing in the Cycledrome, a 10,000-seat oval that had been built for bicycle races.

1929 Chris O'Brien sold the Chicago Cardinals to David Jones, July 27.

The NFL added a fourth official, the field judge, July 28.

Grange and Nevers returned to the NFL. Nevers scored six rushing touchdowns and four extra points as the Cardinals beat Grange's Bears 40-6, November 28. The 40 points set a record that remains the NFL's oldest.

Providence became the first NFL team to host a game at night under floodlights, against the Cardinals, November 3.

The Packers added back Johnny Blood (McNally), tackle Cal Hubbard, and guard Mike Michalske, and won their first NFL championship, edging the Giants, who featured quarterback Benny Friedman.

1930 Dayton, the last of the NFL's original franchises, was purchased by John Dwyer, moved to Brooklyn, and renamed the Dodgers. The Portsmouth, Ohio, Spartans entered the league.

The Packers edged the Giants for the title, but the most improved team was the Bears. Halas retired as a player and replaced himself as coach of the Bears with Ralph Jones, who refined the T-formation by introducing wide ends and a halfback in motion. Jones also introduced rookie All-America fullback-tackle Bronko

Nagurski.

The Giants defeated a team of former Notre Dame players coached by Knute Rockne 22-0 before 55,000 at the Polo Grounds, December 14. The proceeds went to the New York Unemployment Fund to help those suffering because of the Great Depression, and the easy victory helped give the NFL credibility with the press and the public.

1931 The NFL decreased to 10 teams, and halfway through the season the Frankford franchise folded. Carr fined the Bears, Packers, and Portsmouth $1,000 each for using players whose college classes had not graduated.

The Packers won an unprecedented third consecutive title, beating out the Spartans, who were led by rookie backs Earl (Dutch) Clark and Glenn Presnell.

1932 George Preston Marshall, Vincent Bendix, Jay O'Brien, and M. Dorland Doyle were awarded a franchise for Boston, July 9. Despite the presence of two rookies—halfback Cliff Battles and tackle Glen (Turk) Edwards—the new team, named the Braves, lost money and Marshall was left as the sole owner at the end of the year.

NFL membership dropped to eight teams, the lowest in history. Official statistics were kept for the first time. The Bears and the Spartans finished the season in the first-ever tie for first place. After the season finale, the league office arranged for the first playoff game in NFL history. The game was moved indoors to Chicago Stadium because of bitter cold and heavy snow. The arena allowed only an 80-yard field that came right to the walls. The goal posts were moved from the end lines to the goal lines and, for safety, inbounds lines or hashmarks where the ball would be put in play were drawn 10 yards from the walls that butted against the sidelines. The Bears won 9-0, December 18, scoring the winning touchdown on a two-yard pass from Nagurski to Grange. The Spartans claimed Nagurski's pass was thrown from less than five yards behind the line of scrimmage, violating the existing passing rule, but the play stood.

1933 The NFL, which long had followed the rules of college football, made a number of significant changes from the college game for the first time and began to independently develop rules serving its needs and the style of play it preferred. The innovations from the 1932 championship game—inbounds line or hashmarks and goal posts on the goal lines—were adopted. Also the forward pass was legalized from anywhere behind the line of scrimmage, February 25.

Marshall and Halas pushed through a proposal that divided the NFL into two divisions, with the winners to meet in an annual championship game, July 8.

Three new franchises joined the league—the Pittsburgh Pirates of Art Rooney, the Philadelphia Eagles of Bert Bell and Lud Wray, and the Cincinnati Reds. The Staten Island Stapletons suspended operations for a year, but never returned to the league.

Halas bought out Sternaman, became sole owner of the Bears, and reinstated himself as head coach. Marshall changed the name of the

Boston Braves to the Redskins. David Jones sold the Chicago Cardinals to Charles W. Bidwill.

In the first NFL Championship Game scheduled before the season, the Western Division champion Bears defeated the Eastern Division champion Giants 23-21 at Wrigley Field, December 17.

1934 G.A. (Dick) Richards purchased the Portsmouth Spartans, moved them to Detroit, and renamed them the Lions.

Professional football gained new prestige when the Bears were matched against the best college football players in the first Chicago College All-Star Game, August 31. The game ended in a scoreless tie before 79,432 at Soldier Field.

The Cincinnati Reds lost their first eight games, then were suspended from the league for defaulting on payments. The St. Louis Gunners, an independent team, joined the NFL by buying the Cincinnati franchise and went 1-2 the last three weeks.

Rookie Beattie Feathers of the Bears became the NFL's first 1,000-yard rusher, gaining 1,004 on 101 carries. The Thanksgiving Day game between the Bears and the Lions became the first NFL game broadcast nationally, with Graham McNamee the announcer for CBS radio.

In the championship game, on an extremely cold and icy day at the Polo Grounds, the Giants trailed the Bears 13-3 in the third quarter before changing to basketball shoes for better footing. The Giants won 30-13 in what has come to be known as the Sneakers Game, December 9.

The player waiver rule was adopted, December 10.

1935 The NFL adopted Bert Bell's proposal to hold an annual draft of college players, to begin in 1936, with teams selecting in an inverse order of finish, May 19. The inbounds line or hashmarks were moved nearer the center of the field, 15 yards from the sidelines.

All-America end Don Hutson of Alabama joined Green Bay. The Lions defeated the Giants 26-7 in the NFL Championship Game, December 15.

1936 There were no franchise transactions for the first year since the formation of the NFL. It also was the first year in which all member teams played the same number of games.

The Eagles made University of Chicago halfback and Heisman Trophy winner Jay Berwanger the first player ever selected in the NFL draft, February 8. The Eagles traded his rights to the Bears, but Berwanger never played pro football. The first player selected to actually sign was the number-two pick, Riley Smith of Alabama, who was selected by Boston.

A rival league was formed, and it became the second to call itself the American Football League. The Boston Shamrocks were its champions.

Due to poor attendance, Marshall, the owner of the host team, moved the Championship Game from Boston to the Polo Grounds in New York. Green Bay defeated the Redskins 21-6, December 13.

1937 Homer Marshman was granted a Cleveland franchise, named the Rams, February 12. Marshall moved the Redskins to Washington, D.C., February 13. The Redskins signed

TCU All-America tailback Sammy Baugh, who led them to a 28-21 victory over the Bears in the NFL Championship Game, December 12.

The Los Angeles Bulldogs had an 8-0 record to win the AFL title, but then the two-year-old league folded.

1938 At the suggestion of Halas, Hugh (Shorty) Ray became a technical advisor on rules and officiating to the NFL. A new rule called for a 15-yard penalty for roughing the passer.

Rookie Byron (Whizzer) White of the Pittsburgh Pirates led the NFL in rushing. The Giants defeated the Packers 23-17 for the NFL title, December 11.

Marshall, *Los Angeles Times* sports editor Bill Henry, and promoter Tom Gallery established the Pro Bowl game between the NFL champion and a team of pro all-stars.

1939 The New York Giants defeated the Pro All-Stars 13-10 in the first Pro Bowl, at Wrigley Field, Los Angeles, January 15.

Carr, NFL president since 1921, died in Columbus, May 20. Carl Storck was named acting president, May 25.

An NFL game was televised for the first time when NBC broadcast the Brooklyn Dodgers-Philadelphia Eagles game from Ebbets Field to the approximately 1,000 sets then in New York.

Green Bay defeated New York 27-0 in the NFL Championship Game, December 10 at Milwaukee. NFL attendance exceeded one million in a season for the first time, reaching 1,071,200.

1940 A six-team rival league, the third to call itself the American Football League, was formed, and the Columbus Bullies won its championship.

Halas's Bears, with additional coaching by Clark Shaughnessy of Stanford, defeated the Redskins 73-0 in the NFL Championship Game, December 8. The game, which was the most decisive victory in NFL history, popularized the Bears' T-formation with a man-in-motion. It was the first championship carried on network radio, broadcast by Red Barber to 120 stations of the Mutual Broadcasting System, which paid $2,500 for the rights.

Art Rooney sold the Pittsburgh franchise to Alexis Thompson, December 9, then bought part interest in the Philadelphia Eagles.

1941 Elmer Layden was named the first Commissioner of the NFL, March 1; Storck, the acting president, resigned, April 5. NFL headquarters were moved to Chicago.

Bell and Rooney traded the Eagles to Thompson for the Pirates, then renamed their new team the Steelers. Homer Marshman sold the Rams to Daniel F. Reeves and Fred Levy, Jr.

The league by-laws were revised to provide for playoffs in case there were ties in division races, and sudden-death overtimes in case a playoff game was tied after four quarters. An official *NFL Record Manual* was published for the first time.

Columbus again won the championship of the AFL, but the two-year-old league then folded.

The Bears and the Packers finished in a tie for the Western Division championship, setting up the first divisional playoff game in league history. The Bears won 33-14, then defeated the Giants 37-9 for the

NFL championship, December 21.

1942 Players departing for service in World War II depleted the rosters of NFL teams. Halas left the Bears in midseason to join the Navy, and Luke Johnsos and Heartley (Hunk) Anderson served as co-coaches as the Bears went 11-0 in the regular season. The Redskins defeated the Bears 14-6 in the NFL Championship Game, December 13.

1943 The Cleveland Rams, with co-owners Reeves and Levy in the service, were granted permission to suspend operations for one season, April 6. Levy transferred his stock in the team to Reeves, April 16.

The NFL adopted free substitution, April 7. The league also made the wearing of helmets mandatory and approved a 10-game schedule for all teams.

Philadelphia and Pittsburgh were granted permission to merge for one season, June 19. The team, known as Phil-Pitt (and called the Steagles by fans), divided home games between the two cities, and Earle (Greasy) Neale of Philadelphia and Walt Kiesling of Pittsburgh served as co-coaches. The merger automatically dissolved the last day of the season, December 5.

Ted Collins was granted a franchise for Boston, to become active in 1944.

Sammy Baugh led the league in passing, punting, and interceptions. He led the Redskins to a tie with the Giants for the Eastern Division title, and then to a 28-0 victory in a divisional playoff game. The Bears beat the Redskins 41-21 in the NFL Championship Game, December 26.

1944 Collins, who had wanted a franchise in Yankee Stadium in New York, named his new team in Boston the Yanks. Cleveland resumed operations. The Brooklyn Dodgers changed their name to the Tigers.

Coaching from the bench was legalized, April 20.

The Cardinals and the Steelers were granted permission to merge for one year under the name Card-Pitt, April 21. Phil Handler of the Cardinals and Walt Kiesling of the Steelers served as co-coaches. The merger automatically dissolved the last day of the season, December 3.

In the NFL Championship Game, Green Bay defeated the New York Giants 14-7, December 17.

1945 The inbounds lines or hash-marks were moved from 15 yards away from the sidelines to nearer the center of the field—20 yards from the sidelines.

Brooklyn and Boston merged into a team that played home games in both cities and was known simply as The Yanks. The team was coached by former Boston head coach Herb Kopf. In December, the Brooklyn franchise withdrew from the NFL to join the new All-America Football Conference; all the players on its active and reserve lists were assigned to The Yanks, who once again became the Boston Yanks.

Halas rejoined the Bears late in the season after service with the U.S. Navy. Although Halas took over much of the coaching duties, Anderson and Johnsos remained the coaches of record throughout the season.

Steve Van Buren of Philadelphia led the NFL in rushing, kickoff returns, and scoring.

After the Japanese surrendered

ending World War II, a count showed that the NFL service roster, limited to men who had played in league games, totaled 638, 21 of whom had died in action.

Rookie quarterback Bob Waterfield led Cleveland to a 15-14 victory over Washington in the NFL Championship Game, December 16.

1946 The contract of Commissioner Layden was not renewed, and Bert Bell, the co-owner of the Steelers, replaced him, January 11. Bell moved the league headquarters from Chicago to the Philadelphia suburb of Bala-Cynwyd.

Free substitution was withdrawn and substitutions were limited to no more than three men at a time. Forward passes were made automatically incomplete upon striking the goal posts, January 11.

The NFL took on a truly national appearance for the first time when Reeves was granted permission by the league to move his NFL champion Rams to Los Angeles.

The rival All-America Football Conference began play with eight teams. The Cleveland Browns, coached by Paul Brown, won the AAFC's first championship, defeating the New York Yankees 14-9.

Bill Dudley of the Steelers led the NFL in rushing, interceptions, and punt returns, and won the league's most valuable player award.

Backs Frank Filchock and Merle Hapes of the Giants were questioned about an attempt by a New York man to fix the championship game with the Bears. Bell suspended Hapes but allowed Filchock to play; he played well, but Chicago won 24-14, December 15.

1947 The NFL added a fifth official, the back judge.

A bonus choice was made for the first time in the NFL draft. One team each year would select the special choice before the first round began. The Chicago Bears won a lottery and the rights to the first choice and drafted back Bob Fenimore of Oklahoma A&M.

The Cleveland Browns again won the AAFC title, defeating the New York Yankees 14-3.

Charles Bidwill, Sr., owner of the Cardinals, died April 19, but his wife and sons retained ownership of the team. On December 28, the Cardinals won the NFL Championship Game 28-21 over the Philadelphia Eagles, who had beaten Pittsburgh 21-0 in a playoff.

1948 Plastic helmets were prohibited. A flexible artificial tee was permitted at the kickoff. Officials other than the referee were equipped with whistles, not horns, January 14.

Fred Mandel sold the Detroit Lions to a syndicate headed by D. Lyle Fife, January 15.

Halfback Fred Gehrke of the Los Angeles Rams painted horns on the Rams' helmets, the first modern helmet emblems in pro football.

The Cleveland Browns won their third straight championship in the AAFC, going 14-0 and then defeating the Buffalo Bills 49-7.

In a blizzard, the Eagles defeated the Cardinals 7-0 in the NFL Championship Game, December 19.

1949 Alexis Thompson sold the champion Eagles to a syndicate headed by James P. Clark, January 15. The Boston Yanks became the New York Bulldogs, sharing the Polo

Grounds with the Giants.

Free substitution was adopted for one year, January 20.

The NFL had two 1,000-yard rushers in the same season for the first time—Steve Van Buren of Philadelphia and Tony Canadeo of Green Bay.

The AAFC played its season with a one-division, seven-team format. On December 9, Bell announced a merger agreement in which three AAFC franchises—Cleveland, San Francisco, and Baltimore—would join the NFL in 1950. The Browns won their fourth consecutive AAFC title, defeating the 49ers 21-7, December 11.

In a heavy rain, the Eagles defeated the Rams 14-0 in the NFL Championship Game, December 18.

1950 Unlimited free substitution was restored, opening the way for the era of two platoons and specialization in pro football, January 20.

Curly Lambeau, founder of the franchise and Green Bay's head coach since 1921, resigned under fire, February 1.

The name National Football League was restored after about three months as the National-American Football League. The American and National conferences were created to replace the Eastern and Western divisions, March 3.

The New York Bulldogs became the Yanks and divided the players of the former AAFC Yankees with the Giants. A special allocation draft was held in which the 13 teams drafted the remaining AAFC players, with special consideration for Baltimore, which received 15 choices compared to 10 for other teams.

The Los Angeles Rams became the first NFL team to have all of its games—both home and away—televised. The Washington Redskins followed the Rams in arranging to televise their games; other teams made deals to put selected games on television.

In the first game of the season, former AAFC champion Cleveland defeated NFL champion Philadelphia 35-10. For the first time, deadlocks occurred in both conferences and playoffs were necessary. The Browns defeated the Giants in the American and the Rams defeated the Bears in the National. Cleveland defeated Los Angeles 30-28 in the NFL Championship Game, December 24.

1951 The Pro Bowl game, dormant since 1942, was revived under a new format matching the all-stars of each conference at the Los Angeles Memorial Coliseum. The American Conference defeated the National Conference 28-27, January 14.

Abraham Watner returned the Baltimore franchise and its player contracts back to the NFL for $50,000. Baltimore's former players were made available for drafting at the same time as college players, January 18.

A rule was passed that no tackle, guard, or center would be eligible to catch a forward pass, January 18.

The Rams reversed their television policy and televised only road games.

The NFL Championship Game was televised coast-to-coast for the first time, December 23. The DuMont Network paid $75,000 for the rights to the game, in which the Rams

defeated the Browns 24-17.

1952 Ted Collins sold the New York Yanks' franchise back to the NFL, January 19. A new franchise was awarded to a group in Dallas after it purchased the assets of the Yanks, January 24. The new Texans went 1-11, with the owners turning the franchise back to the league in midseason. For the last five games of the season, the commissioner's office operated the Texans as a road team, using Hershey, Pennsylvania, as a home base. At the end of the season the franchise was canceled, the last time an NFL team failed.

The Pittsburgh Steelers abandoned the Single-Wing for the T-formation, the last pro team to do so.

The Detroit Lions won their first NFL championship in 17 years, defeating the Browns 17-7 in the title game, December 28.

1953 A Baltimore group headed by Carroll Rosenbloom was granted a franchise and was awarded the holdings of the defunct Dallas organization, January 23. The team, named the Colts, put together the largest trade in league history, acquiring 10 players from Cleveland in exchange for five.

The names of the American and National conferences were changed to the Eastern and Western conferences, January 24.

Jim Thorpe died, March 28.

Mickey McBride, founder of the Cleveland Browns, sold the franchise to a syndicate headed by Dave R. Jones, June 10.

The NFL policy of blacking out home games was upheld by Judge Allan K. Grim of the U.S. District Court in Philadelphia, November 12.

The Lions again defeated the Browns in the NFL Championship Game, winning 17-16, December 27.

1954 The Canadian Football League began a series of raids on NFL teams, signing quarterback Eddie LeBaron and defensive end Gene Brito of Washington and defensive tackle Arnie Weinmeister of the Giants, among others.

Fullback Joe Perry of the 49ers became the first player in league history to gain 1,000 yards rushing in consecutive seasons.

Cleveland defeated Detroit 56-10 in the NFL Championship Game, December 26.

1955 The sudden-death overtime rule was used for the first time in a preseason game between the Rams and Giants at Portland, Oregon, August 28. The Rams won 23-17 three minutes into overtime.

A rule change declared the ball dead immediately if the ball carrier touched the ground with any part of his body except his hands or feet while in the grasp of an opponent.

The NFL Players Association was founded.

The Baltimore Colts made an 80-cent phone call to Johnny Unitas and signed him as a free agent. Another quarterback, Otto Graham, played his last game as the Browns defeated the Rams 38-14 in the NFL Championship Game, December 26. Graham had quarterbacked the Browns to 10 championship-game appearances in 10 years.

NBC replaced DuMont as the network for the title game, paying a rights fee of $100,000.

1956 Grabbing an opponent's facemask (other than the ball carrier) was made illegal. Using radio receivers to communicate with players on the field was prohibited. A natural leather ball with white end stripes replaced the white ball with black stripes for night games.

The Giants moved from the Polo Grounds to Yankee Stadium.

Halas retired as coach of the Bears, and was replaced by Paddy Driscoll.

CBS became the first network to broadcast some NFL regular-season games to selected television markets across the nation.

The Giants routed the Bears 47-7 in the NFL Championship Game, December 30.

1957 Pete Rozelle was named general manager of the Rams. Anthony J. Morabito, founder and co-owner of the 49ers, died of a heart attack during a game against the Bears at Kezar Stadium, October 28. An NFL-record crowd of 102,368 saw the 49ers-Rams game at the Los Angeles Memorial Coliseum, November 10.

The Lions came from 20 points down to post a 31-27 playoff victory over the 49ers, December 22. Detroit defeated Cleveland 59-14 in the NFL Championship Game, December 29.

1958 The bonus selection in the draft was eliminated, January 29. The last selection was quarterback King Hill of Rice by the Chicago Cardinals.

Halas reinstated himself as coach of the Bears.

Jim Brown of Cleveland gained an NFL-record 1,527 yards rushing. In a divisional playoff game, the Giants held Brown to eight yards and defeated Cleveland 10-0.

Baltimore, coached by Weeb Ewbank, defeated the Giants 23-17 in the first sudden-death overtime in an NFL Championship Game, December 28. The game ended when Colts fullback Alan Ameche scored on a one-yard touchdown run after 8:15 of overtime.

1959 Vince Lombardi was named head coach of the Green Bay Packers, January 28. Tim Mara, the co-founder of the Giants, died, February 17.

Lamar Hunt of Dallas announced his intentions for a second pro football league. The first meeting was held in Chicago, August 14, and consisted of Hunt representing Dallas; Bob Howsam, Denver; K.S. (Bud) Adams, Houston; Barron Hilton, Los Angeles; Max Winter and Bill Boyer, Minneapolis; and Harry Wismer, New York City. They made plans to begin play in 1960.

The new league was named the American Football League, August 22. Buffalo, owned by Ralph Wilson, became the seventh franchise, October 28. Boston, owned by William H. Sullivan, became the eighth team, November 22. The first AFL draft, lasting 33 rounds, was held, November 22. Joe Foss was named AFL Commissioner, November 30. An additional draft of 20 rounds was held by the AFL, December 2.

NFL Commissioner Bert Bell died of a heart attack suffered at Franklin Field, Philadelphia, during the last two minutes of a game between the Eagles and the Steelers, October 11. Treasurer Austin Gunsel was named president in the office of the commissioner, October 14.

The Colts again defeated the Giants in the NFL Championship Game, 31-16, December 27.

1960 Pete Rozelle was elected NFL Commissioner as a compromise choice on the twenty-third ballot, January 26. Rozelle moved the league offices to New York City.

Hunt was elected AFL president for 1960, January 26. Minneapolis withdrew from the AFL, January 27, and the same ownership was given an NFL franchise for Minnesota (to start in 1961), January 28. Dallas received an NFL franchise for 1960, January 28. Oakland received an AFL franchise, January 30.

The AFL adopted the two-point option on points after touchdown, January 28. A no-tampering verbal pact, relative to players' contracts, was agreed to between the NFL and AFL, February 9.

The NFL owners voted to allow the transfer of the Chicago Cardinals to St. Louis, March 13.

The AFL signed a five-year television contract with ABC, June 9.

The Boston Patriots defeated the Buffalo Bills 28-7 before 16,000 at Buffalo in the first AFL preseason game, July 30. The Denver Broncos defeated the Patriots 13-10 before 21,597 at Boston in the first AFL regular-season game, September 9. Philadelphia defeated Green Bay 17-13 in the NFL Championship Game, December 26.

1961 The Houston Oilers defeated the Los Angeles Chargers 24-16 before 32,183 in the first AFL Championship Game, January 1.

Detroit defeated Cleveland 17-16 in the first Playoff Bowl, or Bert Bell Benefit Bowl, between second-place teams in each conference in Miami, January 7.

End Willard Dewveall of the Bears played out his option and joined the Oilers, becoming the first player to deliberately move from one league to the other, January 14.

Ed McGah, Wayne Valley, and Robert Osborne bought out their partners in the ownership of the Raiders, January 17. The Chargers were transferred to San Diego, February 10. Dave R. Jones sold the Browns to a group headed by Arthur B. Modell, March 22. The Howsam brothers sold the Broncos to a group headed by Calvin Kunz and Gerry Phipps, May 26.

NBC was awarded a two-year contract for radio and television rights to the NFL Championship Game for $615,000 annually, $300,000 of which was to go directly into the NFL Player Benefit Plan, April 5.

Canton, Ohio, where the league that became the NFL was formed in 1920, was chosen as the site of the Pro Football Hall of Fame, April 27. Dick McCann, a former Redskins executive, was named executive director.

A bill legalizing single-network television contracts by professional sports leagues was introduced in Congress by Representative Emanuel Celler. It passed the House and Senate and was signed into law by President John F. Kennedy, September 30.

Houston defeated San Diego 10-3 for the AFL championship, December 24. Green Bay won its first NFL championship since 1944, defeating the New York Giants 37-0, December 31.

1962 The Western Division defeated the Eastern Division 47-27 in the first AFL All-Star Game, played before 20,973 in San Diego, January 7.

Both leagues prohibited grabbing any player's facemask. The AFL voted to make the scoreboard clock the official timer of the game.

The NFL entered into a single-network agreement with CBS for telecasting all regular-season games for $4,650,000 annually, January 10.

Judge Roszel Thompson of the U.S. District Court in Baltimore ruled against the AFL in its antitrust suit against the NFL, May 21. The AFL had charged the NFL with monopoly and conspiracy in areas of expansion, television, and player signings. The case lasted two and a half years, the trial two months.

McGah and Valley acquired controlling interest in the Raiders, May 24. The AFL assumed financial responsibility for the New York Titans, November 8. With Commissioner Rozelle as referee, Daniel F. Reeves regained the ownership of the Rams, outbidding his partners in sealed-envelope bidding for the team, November 27.

The Dallas Texans defeated the Oilers 20-17 for the AFL championship at Houston after 17 minutes, 54 seconds of overtime on a 25-yard field goal by Tommy Brooker, December 23. The game lasted a record 77 minutes, 54 seconds.

Judge Edward Weinfeld of the U.S. District Court in New York City upheld the legality of the NFL's television blackout within a 75-mile radius of home games and denied an injunction that would have forced the championship game between the Giants and the Packers to be televised in the New York City area, December 28. The Packers beat the Giants 16-7 for the NFL title, December 30.

1963 The Dallas Texans transferred to Kansas City, becoming the Chiefs, February 8. The New York Titans were sold to a five-man syndicate headed by David (Sonny) Werblin, March 28. Weeb Ewbank became the Titans' new head coach and the team's name was changed to the Jets, April 15. They began play in Shea Stadium.

NFL Properties, Inc., was founded to serve as the licensing arm of the NFL.

Rozelle indefinitely suspended Green Bay halfback Paul Hornung and Detroit defensive tackle Alex Karras for placing bets on their own teams and on other NFL games; he also fined five other Detroit players $2,000 each for betting on one game in which they did not participate, and the Detroit Lions Football Company $2,000 on each of two counts for failure to report information promptly and for lack of sideline supervision.

Paul Brown, head coach of the Browns since its inception, was fired and replaced by Blanton Collier. Don Shula replaced Weeb Ewbank as head coach of the Colts.

The AFL allowed the Jets and Raiders to select players from other franchises in hopes of giving the league more competitive balance, May 11.

NBC was awarded exclusive network broadcasting rights for the 1963 AFL Championship Game for $926,000, May 23.

The Pro Football Hall of Fame was dedicated at Canton, Ohio, September 7.

The U.S. Fourth Circuit Court of Appeals reaffirmed the lower court's finding for the NFL in the $10-million suit brought by the AFL, ending three and a half years of litigation, November 21.

Jim Brown of Cleveland rushed for an NFL single-season record 1,863 yards.

Boston defeated Buffalo 26-8 in the first divisional playoff game in AFL history, December 28.

The Bears defeated the Giants 14-10 in the NFL Championship Game, a record sixth and last title for Halas in his thirty-sixth season as the Bears' coach, December 29.

1964 The Chargers defeated the Patriots in the AFL Championship Game, January 5.

William Clay Ford, the Lions' president since 1961, purchased the team, January 10. A group representing the late James P. Clark sold the Eagles to a group headed by Jerry Wolman, January 21. Carroll Rosenbloom, the majority owner of the Colts since 1953, acquired complete ownership of the team, January 23.

CBS submitted the winning bid of $14.1 million per year for the NFL regular-season television rights for 1964 and 1965, January 24. CBS acquired the rights to the championship games for 1964 and 1965 for $1.8 million per game, April 17.

The AFL signed a five-year, $36-million television contract with NBC to begin with the 1965 season, January 29.

Hornung and Karras were reinstated by Rozelle, March 16.

Pete Gogolak of Cornell signed a contract with Buffalo, becoming the first soccer-style kicker in pro football.

Buffalo defeated San Diego 20-7 in the AFL Championship Game, December 26. Cleveland defeated Baltimore 27-0 in the NFL Championship Game, December 27.

1965 The NFL teams pledged not to sign college seniors until completion of all their games, including bowl games, and empowered the Commissioner to discipline the clubs up to as much as the loss of an entire draft list for a violation of the pledge, February 15.

The NFL added a sixth official, the line judge, February 19. The color of the officials' penalty flags was changed from white to bright gold, April 5.

Atlanta was awarded an NFL franchise for 1966, with Rankin Smith, Sr., as owner, June 30. Miami was awarded an AFL franchise for 1966, with Joe Robbie and Danny Thomas as owners, August 16.

Green Bay defeated Baltimore 13-10 in sudden-death overtime in a Western Conference playoff game. Don Chandler kicked a 25-yard field goal for the Packers after 13 minutes, 39 seconds of overtime, December 26. The Packers then defeated the Browns 23-12 in the NFL Championship Game, January 2.

In the AFL Championship Game, the Bills again defeated the Chargers, 23-0, December 26.

CBS acquired the rights to the NFL regular-season games in 1966 and 1967, with an option for 1968, for $18.8 million per year, December 29.

1966 The AFL-NFL war reached its peak, as the leagues spent a combined $7 million to sign their 1966 draft choices. The NFL signed 75 percent of its 232 draftees, the AFL 46 percent of its 181. Of the 111 common draft choices, 79 signed with the NFL, 28 with the AFL, and 4 went unsigned.

The rights to the 1966 and 1967 NFL Championship Games were sold to CBS for $2 million per game, February 14.

Foss resigned as AFL Commissioner, April 7. Al Davis, the head coach and general manager of the Raiders, was named to replace him, April 8.

Goal posts offset from the goal line, painted bright yellow, and with uprights 20 feet above the crossbar were made standard in the NFL, May 16.

A series of secret meetings regarding a possible AFL-NFL merger were held in the spring between Hunt of Kansas City and Tex Schramm of Dallas. Rozelle announced the merger, June 8. Under the agreement, the two leagues would combine to form an expanded league with 24 teams, to be increased to 26 in 1968 and to 28 by 1970 or soon thereafter. All existing franchises would be retained, and no franchises would be transferred outside their metropolitan areas. While maintaining separate schedules through 1969, the leagues agreed to play an annual AFL-NFL World Championship Game beginning in January, 1967, and to hold a combined draft, also beginning in 1967. Preseason games would be held between teams of each league starting in 1967. Official regular-season play would start in 1970 when the two leagues would officially merge to form one league with two conferences. Rozelle was named Commissioner of the expanded league setup.

Davis rejoined the Raiders, and Milt Woodard was named president of the AFL, July 25.

The St. Louis Cardinals moved into newly constructed Busch Memorial Stadium.

Barron Hilton sold the Chargers to a group headed by Eugene Klein and Sam Schulman, August 25.

Congress approved the AFL-NFL merger, passing legislation exempting the agreement itself from antitrust action, October 21.

New Orleans was awarded an NFL franchise to begin play in 1967, November 1. John Mecom, Jr., of Houston was designated majority stockholder and president of the franchise, December 15.

The NFL was realigned for the 1967-69 seasons into the Capitol and Century Divisions in the Eastern Conference and the Central and Coastal Divisions in the Western Conference, December 2. New Orleans and the New York Giants agreed to switch divisions in 1968 and return to the 1967 alignment in 1969.

The rights to the Super Bowl for four years were sold to CBS and NBC for $9.5 million, December 13.

1967 Green Bay earned the right to represent the NFL in the first AFL-NFL World Championship Game by defeating Dallas 34-27, January 1. The same day, Kansas City defeated Buffalo 31-7 to represent the AFL. The Packers defeated the Chiefs 35-10 before 61,946 fans at the Los Angeles Memorial Coliseum in the first game between AFL and NFL teams, January 15. The winning players' share for the Packers was $15,000 each, and the losing players' share for the Chiefs was $7,500 each. The game was televised by both CBS and NBC.

The "sling-shot" goal post and a six-foot-wide border around the field were made standard in the NFL, February 22.

Baltimore made Bubba Smith, a Michigan State defensive lineman, the first choice in the first combined AFL-NFL draft, March 14.

The AFL awarded a franchise to begin play in 1968 to Cincinnati, May 24. A group with Paul Brown as part owner, general manager, and head coach, was awarded the Cincinnati franchise, September 27.

Arthur B. Modell, the president of the Cleveland Browns, was elected president of the NFL, May 28.

An AFL team defeated an NFL team for the first time, when Denver beat Detroit 13-7 in a preseason game, August 5.

Green Bay defeated Dallas 21-17 for the NFL championship on a last-minute one-yard quarterback sneak by Bart Starr in 13-below-zero temperature at Green Bay, December 31. The same day, Oakland defeated Houston 40-7 for the AFL championship.

1968 Green Bay defeated Oakland 33-14 in Super Bowl II at Miami, January 14. The game had the first $3-million gate in pro football history.

Vince Lombardi resigned as head coach of the Packers, but remained as general manager, January 28.

Werblin sold his shares in the Jets to his partners Don Lillis, Leon Hess, Townsend Martin, and Phil Iselin, May 21. Lillis assumed the presidency of the club, but then died July 23. Iselin was appointed president, August 6.

Halas retired for the fourth and last time as head coach of the Bears, May 27.

The Oilers left Rice Stadium for the Astrodome and became the first NFL team to play its home games in a domed stadium.

The movie "Heidi" became a footnote in sports history when NBC didn't show the last 1:05 of the Jets-Raiders game in order to permit the children's special to begin on time. The Raiders scored two touchdowns in the last 42 seconds to win 43-32, November 17.

Ewbank became the first coach to win titles in both the NFL and AFL when his Jets defeated the Raiders 27-23 for the AFL championship, December 29. The same day, Baltimore defeated Cleveland 34-0.

1969 The AFL established a playoff format for the 1969 season, with the winner in one division playing the runner-up in the other, January 11.

An AFL team won the Super Bowl for the first time, as the Jets defeated the Colts 16-7 at Miami, January 12 in Super Bowl III. The title Super Bowl was recognized by the NFL for the first time.

Vince Lombardi became part owner, executive vice-president, and head coach of the Washington Redskins, Feb. 7.

Wolman sold the Eagles to Leonard Tose, May 1.

Baltimore, Cleveland, and Pittsburgh agreed to join the AFL teams to form the 13-team American Football Conference of the NFL in 1970, May 17. The NFL also agreed on a playoff format that would include one "wild-card" team per conference—the second-place team with the best record.

Monday Night Football was signed for 1970. ABC acquired the rights to televise 13 NFL regular-season Monday night games in 1970, 1971, and 1972.

George Preston Marshall, president emeritus of the Redskins, died at 72, August 9.

The NFL marked its fiftieth year by the wearing of a special patch by each of the 16 teams.

1970 Kansas City defeated Minnesota 23-7 in Super Bowl IV at New Orleans, January 11. The gross receipts of approximately $3.8 million were the largest ever for a one-day sports event.

Four-year television contracts, under which CBS would televise all NFC games and NBC all AFC games (except Monday night games) and the two would divide televising the Super Bowl and AFC-NFC Pro Bowl games, were announced, January 26.

Art Modell resigned as president of the NFL, March 12. Milt Woodard resigned as president of the AFL, March 13. Lamar Hunt was elected president of the AFC and George Halas was elected president of the NFC, March 19.

The merged 26-team league adopted rules changes putting names on the backs of players' jerseys, making a point after touchdown worth only one point, and making the scoreboard clock the official timing device of the game, March 18.

The Players Negotiating Committee and the NFL Players Association announced a four-year agreement guaranteeing approximately $4,535,000 annually to player pension and insurance benefits, August 3. The owners also agreed to contribute $250,000 annually to improve or implement items such as disability payments, widows' benefits, maternity benefits, and dental benefits. The agreement also provided for increased preseason game and per diem payments, averaging approximately $2.6 million annually.

The Pittsburgh Steelers moved into Three Rivers Stadium. The Cincinnati Bengals moved to Riverfront Stadium.

Lombardi died of cancer at 57, September 3.

Tom Dempsey of New Orleans kicked a game-winning NFL-record 63-yard field goal against Detroit, November 8.

1971 Baltimore defeated Dallas 16-13 on Jim O'Brien's 32-yard field goal with five seconds to go in Super Bowl V at Miami, January 17. The NBC telecast was viewed in an estimated 23,980,000 homes, the largest audience ever for a one-day sports event.

The NFC defeated the AFC 27-6 in the first AFC-NFC Pro Bowl at Los Angeles, January 24.

The Boston Patriots changed their name to the New England Patriots, March 25. Their new stadium, Schaefer Stadium, was dedicated in a 20-14 preseason victory over the Giants.

The Philadelphia Eagles left Franklin Field and played their games at the new Veterans Stadium.

The San Francisco 49ers left Kezar Stadium and moved their games to Candlestick Park.

Daniel F. Reeves, the president

and general manager of the Rams, died at 58, April 15.

The Dallas Cowboys moved from the Cotton Bowl into their new home, Texas Stadium, October 24.

Miami defeated Kansas City 27-24 in sudden-death overtime in an AFC Divisional Playoff Game, December 25. Garo Yepremian kicked a 37-yard field goal for the Dolphins after 22 minutes, 40 seconds of overtime, as the game lasted 82 minutes, 40 seconds overall, making it the longest game in history.

1972 Dallas defeated Miami 24-3 in Super Bowl VI at New Orleans, January 16. The CBS telecast was viewed in an estimated 27,450,000 homes, the top-rated one-day telecast ever.

The inbounds lines or hashmarks were moved nearer the center of the field, 23 yards, 1 foot, 9 inches from the sidelines, March 23. The method of determining won-lost percentage in standings changed. Tie games, previously not counted in the standings, were made equal to a half-game won and a half-game lost, May 24.

Robert Irsay purchased the Los Angeles Rams and transferred ownership of the club to Carroll Rosenbloom in exchange for the Baltimore Colts, July 13.

William V. Bidwill purchased the stock of his brother Charles (Stormy) Bidwill to become the sole owner of the St. Louis Cardinals, September 2.

The National District Attorneys Association endorsed the position of professional leagues in opposing proposed legalization of gambling on professional team sports, September 28.

Franco Harris's "Immaculate Reception" gave the Steelers their first postseason win ever, 13-7 over the Raiders, December 23.

1973 Rozelle announced that all Super Bowl VII tickets were sold and that the game would be telecast in Los Angeles, the site of the game, on an experimental basis, January 3.

Miami defeated Washington 14-7 in Super Bowl VII at Los Angeles, completing a 17-0 season, the first perfect-record regular-season and postseason mark in NFL history, January 14. The NBC telecast was viewed by approximately 75 million people.

The AFC defeated the NFC 33-28 in the Pro Bowl in Dallas, the first time since 1942 that the game was played outside Los Angeles, January 21.

A jersey numbering system was adopted, April 5: 1-19 for quarterbacks and specialists, 20-49 for running backs and defensive backs, 50-59 for centers and linebackers, 60-79 for defensive linemen and interior offensive linemen other than centers, and 80-89 for wide receivers and tight ends. Players who had been in the NFL in 1972 could continue to use old numbers.

NFL Charities, a nonprofit organization, was created to derive an income from monies generated from NFL Properties' licensing of NFL trademarks and team names, June 26. NFL Charities was set up to support education and charitable activities and to supply economic support to persons formerly associated with professional football who are no longer able to support themselves.

Congress adopted experimental legislation (for three years) requiring any NFL game that had been

declared a sellout 72 hours prior to kickoff to be made available for local televising, September 14. The legislation provided for an annual review to be made by the Federal Communications Commission.

The Buffalo Bills moved their home games from War Memorial Stadium to Rich Stadium in nearby Orchard Park. The Giants tied the Eagles 23-23 in the final game in Yankee Stadium, September 23. The Giants played the rest of their home games at the Yale Bowl in New Haven, Connecticut.

A rival league, the World Football League, was formed and was reported in operation, October 2. It had plans to start play in 1974.

O.J. Simpson of Buffalo became the first player to rush for more than 2,000 yards in a season, gaining 2,003.

1974 Miami defeated Minnesota 24-7 in Super Bowl VIII at Houston, the second consecutive Super Bowl championship for the Dolphins, January 13. The CBS telecast was viewed by approximately 75 million people.

Rozelle was given a 10-year contract effective January 1, 1973, February 27.

Tampa Bay was awarded a franchise to begin operation in 1976, April 24.

Sweeping rules changes were adopted to add action and tempo to games: one sudden-death overtime period was added for preseason and regular-season games; the goal posts were moved from the goal line to the end lines; kickoffs were moved from the 40- to the 35-yard line; after missed field goals from beyond the 20, the ball was to be returned to the line of scrimmage; restrictions were placed on members of the punting team to open up return possibilities; roll-blocking and cutting of wide receivers was eliminated; the extent of downfield contact a defender could have with an eligible receiver was restricted; the penalties for offensive holding, illegal use of the hands, and tripping were reduced from 15 to 10 yards; wide receivers blocking back toward the ball within three yards of the line of scrimmage were prevented from blocking below the waist, April 25.

The Toronto Northmen of the WFL signed Larry Csonka, Jim Kiick, and Paul Warfield of Miami, March 31.

Seattle was awarded an NFL franchise to begin play in 1976, June 4. Lloyd W. Nordstrom, president of the Seattle Seahawks, and Hugh Culverhouse, president of the Tampa Bay Buccaneers, signed franchise agreements, December 5.

The Birmingham Americans defeated the Florida Blazers 22-21 in the WFL World Bowl, winning the league championship, December 5.

1975 Pittsburgh defeated Minnesota 16-6 in Super Bowl IX at New Orleans, the Steelers' first championship since entering the NFL in 1933. The NBC telecast was viewed by approximately 78 million people.

The divisional winners with the highest won-loss percentage were made the home team for the divisional playoffs, and the surviving winners with the highest percentage made home teams for the championship games, June 26.

Referees were equipped with wireless microphones for all preseason, regular-season, and playoff games.

The Lions moved to the new Pontiac Silverdome. The Giants played their home games in Shea Stadium. The Saints moved into the Louisiana Superdome.

The World Football League folded, October 22.

1976 Pittsburgh defeated Dallas 21-17 in Super Bowl X in Miami. The Steelers joined Green Bay and Miami as the only teams to win two Super Bowls; the Cowboys became the first wild-card team to play in the Super Bowl. The CBS telecast was viewed by an estimated 80 million people, the largest television audience in history.

Lloyd Nordstrom, the president of the Seahawks, died at 66, January 20. His brother Elmer succeeded him as majority representative of the team.

The owners awarded Super Bowl XII, to be played on January 15, 1978, to New Orleans. They also adopted the use of two 30-second clocks for all games, visible to both players and fans to note the official time between the ready-for-play signal and snap of the ball, March 16.

A veteran player allocation was held to stock the Seattle and Tampa Bay franchises with 39 players each, March 30-31. In the college draft, Seattle and Tampa Bay each received eight extra choices, April 8-9.

The Giants moved into new Giants Stadium in East Rutherford, New Jersey.

The Steelers defeated the College All-Stars in a storm-shortened Chicago College All-Star Game, the last of the series, July 23. St. Louis defeated San Diego 20-10 in a preseason game before 38,000 in Korakuen Stadium, Tokyo, in the first NFL game outside of North America, August 16.

1977 Oakland defeated Minnesota 32-14 before a record crowd of 100,421 in Super Bowl XI at Pasadena, January 9. The paid attendance was a pro record 103,438. The NBC telecast was viewed by 81.9 million people, the largest ever to view a sports event. The victory was the fifth consecutive for the AFC in the Super Bowl.

The NFL Players Association and the NFL Management Council ratified a collective bargaining agreement extending until 1982, covering five football seasons while continuing the pension plan—including years 1974, 1975, and 1976—with contributions totaling more than $55 million. The total cost of the agreement was estimated at $107 million. The agreement called for a college draft at least through 1986; contained a no-strike, no-suit clause; established a 43-man active player limit; reduced pension vesting to four years; provided for increases in minimum salaries and preseason and postseason pay; improved insurance, medical, and dental benefits; modified previous practices in player movement and control; and reaffirmed the NFL Commissioner's disciplinary authority. Additionally, the agreement called for the NFL member clubs to make payments totaling $16 million the next 10 years to settle various legal disputes, February 25.

The San Francisco 49ers were sold to Edward J. DeBartolo, Jr., March 28.

A 16-game regular season,

4-game preseason was adopted to begin in 1978, March 29. A second wild-card team was adopted for the playoffs beginning in 1978, with the wild-card teams to play each other and the winners advancing to a round of eight postseason series.

The Seahawks were permanently aligned in the AFC Western Division and the Buccaneers in the NFC Central Division, March 31.

The owners awarded Super Bowl XIII, to be played on January 21, 1979, to Miami, to be played in the Orange Bowl; Super Bowl XIV, to be played January 20, 1980, was awarded to Pasadena, to be played in the Rose Bowl, June 14.

Rules changes were adopted to open up the passing game and to cut down on injuries. Defenders were permitted to make contact with eligible receivers only once; the head slap was outlawed; offensive linemen were prohibited from thrusting their hands to an opponent's neck, face, or head; and wide receivers were prohibited from clipping, even in the legal clipping zone.

Rozelle negotiated contracts with the three television networks to televise all NFL regular-season and postseason games, plus selected preseason games, for four years beginning with the 1978 season. ABC was awarded yearly rights to 16 Monday night games, four prime-time games, the AFC-NFC Pro Bowl, and the Hall of Fame games. CBS received the rights to all NFC regular-season and postseason games (except those in the ABC package) and to Super Bowls XIV and XVI. NBC received the rights to all AFC regular-season and postseason games (except those in the ABC package) and to Super Bowls XIII and XV. Industry sources considered it the largest single television package ever negotiated, October.

Chicago's Walter Payton set a single-game rushing record with 275 yards (40 carries) against Minnesota, November 20.

1978 Dallas defeated Denver 27-10 in Super Bowl XII, held indoors for the first time, at the Louisiana Superdome in New Orleans, January 15. The CBS telecast was viewed by more than 102 million people, meaning the game was watched by more viewers than any other show of any kind in the history of television. Dallas's victory was the first for the NFC in six years.

According to a Louis Harris Sports Survey, 70 percent of the nation's sports fans said they followed football, compared to 54 percent who followed baseball. Football increased its lead as the country's favorite, 26 percent to 16 percent for baseball, January 19.

A seventh official, the side judge, was added to the officiating crew, March 14.

The NFL continued a trend toward opening up the game. Rules changes permitted a defender to maintain contact with a receiver within five yards of the line of scrimmage, but restricted contact beyond that point. The pass-blocking rule was interpreted to permit the extending of arms and open hands, March 17.

A study on the use of instant replay as an officiating aid was made during seven nationally televised preseason games.

The NFL played for the first time in

Mexico City, with the Saints defeating the Eagles 14-7 in a preseason game, August 5.

Bolstered by the expansion of the regular-season schedule from 14 to 16 weeks, NFL paid attendance exceeded 12 million (12,771,800) for the first time. The per-game average of 57,017 was the third-highest in league history and the most since 1973.

1979 Pittsburgh defeated Dallas 35-31 in Super Bowl XIII at Miami to become the first team ever to win three Super Bowls, January 21. The NBC telecast was viewed in 35,090,000 homes, by an estimated 96.6 million fans.

The owners awarded three future Super Bowl sites: Super Bowl XV to the Louisiana Superdome in New Orleans, to be played on January 25, 1981; Super Bowl XVI to the Pontiac Silverdome in Pontiac, Michigan, to be played on January 24, 1982; and Super Bowl XVII to Pasadena's Rose Bowl, to be played on January 30, 1983, March 13.

NFL rules changes emphasized additional player safety. The changes prohibited players on the receiving team from blocking below the waist during kickoffs, punts, and field-goal attempts; prohibited the wearing of torn or altered equipment and exposed pads that could be hazardous; extended the zone in which there could be no crackback blocks; and instructed officials to quickly whistle a play dead when a quarterback was clearly in the grasp of a tackler, March 16.

Rosenbloom, the president of the Rams, drowned at 72, April 2. His widow, Georgia, assumed control of the club.

1980 Pittsburgh defeated the Los Angeles Rams 31-19 in Super Bowl XIV at Pasadena to become the first team to win four Super Bowls, January 20. The game was viewed in a record 35,330,000 homes.

The AFC-NFC Pro Bowl, won 37-27 by the NFC, was played before 48,060 fans at Aloha Stadium in Honolulu, Hawaii. It was the first time in the 30-year history of the Pro Bowl that the game was played in a non-NFL city.

Rules changes placed greater restrictions on contact in the area of the head, neck, and face. Under the heading of "personal foul," players were prohibited from directly striking, swinging, or clubbing on the head, neck, or face. Starting in 1980, a penalty could be called for such contact whether or not the initial contact was made below the neck area.

CBS, with a record bid of $12 million, won the national radio rights to 26 NFL regular-season games and all 10 postseason games for the 1980-83 seasons.

The Los Angeles Rams moved their home games to Anaheim Stadium in nearby Orange County, California.

The Oakland Raiders joined the Los Angeles Coliseum Commission's antitrust suit against the NFL. The suit contended the league violated antitrust laws in declining to approve a proposed move by the Raiders from Oakland to Los Angeles.

NFL regular-season attendance of nearly 13.4 million set a record for the third year in a row. The average paid attendance for the 224-game 1980 regular season was 59,787, the high-

est in the league's 61-year history. NFL games in 1980 were played before 92.4 percent of total stadium capacity.

Television ratings in 1980 were the second-best in NFL history, trailing only the combined ratings of the 1976 season. All three networks posted gains, and NBC's 15.0 rating was its best ever. CBS and ABC had their best ratings since 1977, with 15.3 and 20.8 ratings, respectively. CBS Radio reported a record audience of 7 million for Monday night and special games.

1981 Oakland defeated Philadelphia 27-10 in Super Bowl XV at the Louisiana Superdome in New Orleans, to become the first wild-card team to win a Super Bowl, January 25.

Edgar F. Kaiser, Jr., purchased the Denver Broncos from Gerald and Allan Phipps, February 26.

The owners adopted a disaster plan for re-stocking a team should the club be involved in a fatal accident, March 20.

The owners awarded Super Bowl XVIII to Tampa, to be played in Tampa Stadium on January 22, 1984, June 3.

A CBS-New York Times poll showed that 48 percent of sports fans preferred football to 31 percent for baseball.

The NFL teams hosted 167 representatives from 44 predominantly black colleges during training camps for a total of 289 days. The program was adopted for renewal during each training camp period.

NFL regular-season attendance—13.6 million for an average of 60,745—set a record for the fourth year in a row. It also was the first time the per-game average exceeded 60,000. NFL games in 1981 were played before 93.8 percent of total stadium capacity.

ABC and CBS set all-time rating highs. ABC finished with a 21.7 rating and CBS with a 17.5 rating. NBC was down slightly to 13.9.

1982 San Francisco defeated Cincinnati 26-21 in Super Bowl XVI at the Pontiac Silverdome, in the first Super Bowl held in the North, January 24. The CBS telecast achieved the highest rating of any televised sports event ever, 49.1 with a 73.0 share. The game was viewed by a record 110.2 million fans. CBS Radio reported a record 14 million listeners for the game.

The NFL signed a five-year contract with the three television networks (ABC, CBS, and NBC) to televise all NFL regular-season and postseason games starting with the 1982 season.

The owners awarded the 1983, 1984, and 1985 AFC-NFC Pro Bowls to Honolulu's Aloha Stadium.

A jury ruled against the NFL in the antitrust trial brought by the Los Angeles Coliseum Commission and the Oakland Raiders, May 7. The verdict cleared the way for the Raiders to move to Los Angeles, where they defeated Green Bay 24-3 in their first preseason game, August 29.

The 1982 season was reduced from a 16-game schedule to nine as the result of a 57-day players' strike. The strike was called by the NFLPA at midnight on Monday, September 20, following the Green Bay at New York Giants game. Play resumed November 21-22 following ratification of the Collective Bargaining Agreement by

NFL owners, November 17 in New York.

Under the Collective Bargaining Agreement, which was to run through the 1986 season, the NFL draft was extended through 1992 and the veteran free-agent system was left basically unchanged. A minimum salary schedule for years of experience was established; training camp and postseason pay were increased; players' medical, insurance, and retirement benefits were increased; and a severance-pay system was introduced to aid in career transition, a first in professional sports.

Despite the players' strike, the average paid attendance in 1982 was 58,472, the fifth-highest in league history.

The owners awarded the sites of two Super Bowls, December 14: Super Bowl XIX, to be played on January 20, 1985, to Stanford University Stadium in Stanford, California, with San Francisco as host team; and Super Bowl XX, to be played on January 26, 1986, to the Louisiana Superdome in New Orleans.

1983 Because of the shortened season, the NFL adopted a format of 16 teams competing in a Super Bowl Tournament for the 1982 playoffs. The NFC's number-one seed, Washington, defeated the AFC's number-two seed, Miami, 27-17 in Super Bowl XVII at the Rose Bowl in Pasadena, January 30.

Super Bowl XVII was the second-highest rated live television program of all time, giving the NFL a sweep of the top 10 live programs in television history. The game was viewed in more than 40 million homes, the largest ever for a live telecast.

Halas, the owner of the Bears and the last surviving member of the NFL's second organizational meeting, died at 88, October 31.

1984 The Los Angeles Raiders defeated Washington 38-9 in Super Bowl XVIII at Tampa Stadium, January 22. The game achieved a 46.4 rating and 71.0 share.

An 11-man group headed by H.R. (Bum) Bright purchased the Dallas Cowboys from Clint Murchison, Jr., March 20. Club president Tex Schramm was designated as managing general partner.

Patrick Bowlen purchased a majority interest in the Denver Broncos from Edgar Kaiser, Jr., March 21.

The Colts relocated to Indianapolis, March 28. Their new home became the Hoosier Dome.

The owners awarded two Super Bowl sites at their May 23-25 meetings: Super Bowl XXI, to be played on January 25, 1987, to the Rose Bowl in Pasadena; and Super Bowl XXII, to be played on January 31, 1988, to San Diego Jack Murphy Stadium.

The New York Jets moved their home games to Giants Stadium in East Rutherford, New Jersey.

Alex G. Spanos purchased a majority interest in the San Diego Chargers from Eugene V. Klein, August 28.

Houston defeated Pittsburgh 23-20 to mark the one-hundredth overtime game in regular-season play since overtime was adopted in 1974, December 2.

On the field, many all-time records were set: Dan Marino of Miami passed for 5,084 yards and 48 touchdowns; Eric Dickerson of the

Los Angeles Rams rushed for 2,105 yards; Art Monk of Washington caught 106 passes; and Walter Payton of Chicago broke Jim Brown's career rushing mark, finishing the season with 13,309 yards.

According to a CBS Sports/New York Times survey, 53 percent of the nation's sports fans said they most enjoyed watching football, compared to 18 percent for baseball, December 2-4.

NFL paid attendance exceeded 13 million for the fifth consecutive complete regular season when 13,398,112, an average of 59,813, attended games. The figure was the second-highest in league history. Teams averaged 42.4 points per game, the second-highest total since the 1970 merger.

1985 San Francisco defeated Miami 38-16 in Super Bowl XIX at Stanford Stadium in Stanford, California, January 20. The game was viewed on television by more people than any other live event in history. President Ronald Reagan, who took his second oath of office before tossing the coin for the game, was one of 115,936,000 viewers. The game drew a 46.4 rating and a 63.0 share. In addition, 6 million people watched the Super Bowl in the United Kingdom and a similar number in Italy. Super Bowl XIX had a direct economic impact of $113.5 million on the San Francisco Bay area.

NBC Radio and the NFL entered into a two-year agreement granting NBC the radio rights to a 37-game package in each of the 1985-86 seasons, March 6. The package included 27 regular-season games and 10 postseason games.

The owners awarded two Super Bowl sites at their annual meeting, March 10-15: Super Bowl XXIII, to be played on January 22, 1989, to the proposed Dolphins Stadium in Miami; and Super Bowl XXIV, to be played on January 28, 1990, to the Louisiana Superdome in New Orleans.

Norman Braman, in partnership with Edward Leibowitz, bought the Philadelphia Eagles from Leonard Tose, April 29.

Bruce Smith, a Virginia Tech defensive lineman selected by Buffalo, was the first player chosen in the fiftieth NFL draft, April 30.

A group headed by Tom Benson, Jr., was approved to purchase the New Orleans Saints from John W. Mecom, Jr., June 3.

The NFL owners adopted a resolution calling for a series of overseas preseason games, beginning in 1986, with one game to be played in England/Europe and/or one game in Japan each year. The game would be a fifth preseason game for the clubs involved and all arrangements and selection of the clubs would be under the control of the Commissioner, May 23.

The league-wide conversion to videotape from movie film for coaching study was approved.

Commissioner Rozelle was authorized to extend the commitment to Honolulu's Aloha Stadium for the AFC-NFC Pro Bowl for 1988, 1989, and 1990, October 15.

The NFL set a single-weekend paid attendance record when 902,657 tickets were sold for the weekend of October 27-28.

A Louis Harris poll in December revealed that pro football remained

the sport most followed by Americans. Fifty-nine percent of those surveyed followed pro football, compared with 54 percent who followed baseball.

The Chicago-Miami Monday game had the highest rating, 29.6, and share, 46.0, of any prime-time game in NFL history, December 2. The game was viewed in more than 25 million homes.

The NFL showed a ratings increase on all three networks for the season, gaining 4 percent on NBC, 10 on CBS, and 16 on ABC.

1986 Chicago defeated New England 46-10 in Super Bowl XX at the Louisiana Superdome, January 26. The Patriots had earned the right to play the Bears by becoming the first wild-card team to win three consecutive games on the road. The NBC telecast replaced the final episode of M*A*S*H as the most-viewed television program in history, with an audience of 127 million viewers, according to A.C. Nielsen figures. In addition to drawing a 48.3 rating and a 70 percent share in the United States, Super Bowl XX was televised to 59 foreign countries and beamed via satellite to the QE II. An estimated 300 million Chinese viewed a tape delay of the game in March. NBC Radio figures indicated an audience of 10 million for the game.

Super Bowl XX injected more than $100 million into the New Orleans-area economy, and fans spent $250 per day and a record $17.69 per person on game day.

The owners adopted limited use of instant replay as an officiating aid, prohibited players from wearing or otherwise displaying equipment, apparel, or other items that carry commercial names, names of organizations, or personal messages of any type, March 11.

After an 11-week trial, a jury in U.S. District Court in New York awarded the United States Football League one dollar in its $1.7 billion antitrust suit against the NFL. The jury rejected all of the USFL's television-related claims, which were the self-proclaimed heart of the USFL's case, July 29.

Chicago defeated Dallas 17-6 at Wembley Stadium in London in the first American Bowl. The game drew a sellout crowd of 82,699 and the NBC national telecast in this country produced a 12.4 rating and 36 percent share, making it the second-highest-rated daytime preseason game and highest daytime preseason television audience ever with 10,650,000 viewers, August 3.

Monday Night Football became the longest-running prime-time series in the history of the ABC network.

Instant replay was used to reverse two plays in 31 preseason games. During the regular season, 374 plays were closely reviewed by replay officials, leading to 38 reversals in 224 games. Eighteen plays were closely reviewed by instant replay in 10 postseason games with three reversals.

1987 The New York Giants defeated Denver 39-20 in Super Bowl XXI and captured their first NFL title since 1956. The game, played in Pasadena's Rose Bowl, drew a sellout crowd of 101,063. According to A.C. Nielsen figures, the CBS broadcast of the game was viewed in the U.S. on television by 122,640,000 people,

making the telecast the second most-watched television show of all-time behind Super Bowl XX. The game was watched live or on tape in 55 foreign countries and NBC Radio's broadcast of the game was heard by a record 10.1 million people.

The NFL set an all-time paid attendance mark of 17,304,463 for all games, including preseason, regular-season, and postseason. Average regular-season game attendance (60,663) exceeded the 60,000 figure for only the second time in league history.

New three-year TV contracts with ABC, CBS, and NBC were announced for 1987-89 at the NFL annual meeting in Maui, Hawaii, March 15. Commissioner Rozelle and Broadcast Committee Chairman Art Modell also announced a three-year contract with ESPN to televise 13 prime-time games each season. The ESPN contract was the first with a cable network. However, NFL games on ESPN also were scheduled for regular television in the city of the visiting team and in the home city if the game was sold out 72 hours in advance.

Owners also voted to continue in effect for one year the instant replay system used during the 1986 season.

A special payment program was adopted to benefit nearly 1,000 former NFL players who participated in the League before the current Bert Bell NFL Pension Plan was created and made retroactive to the 1959 season. Players covered by the new program spent at least five years in the League and played all or part of their career prior to 1959. Each vested player would receive $60 per month for each year of service in the League for life.

Possible sites for Super Bowl XXV were reduced to five locations by the NFL Super Bowl XXV Site Selection Committee: Anaheim Stadium, Los Angeles Memorial Coliseum, Joe Robbie Stadium, San Diego Jack Murphy Stadium, and Tampa Stadium.

NFL and CBS Radio jointly announced agreement granting CBS the radio rights to a 40-game package in each of the next three NFL seasons, 1987-89, April 7.

NFL owners awarded Super Bowl XXV, to be played on January 27, 1991, to Tampa Stadium, May 20.

Over 400 former NFL players from the pre-1959 era received first payments from NFL owners, July 1.

The NFL's debut on ESPN produced the two highest-rated and most-watched sports programs in basic cable history. The Chicago at Miami game on August 16 drew an 8.9 rating in 3.81 million homes. Those records fell two weeks later when the Los Angeles Raiders at Dallas game achieved a 10.2 cable rating in 4.36 million homes.

Fifty-eight preseason games drew a record paid attendance of 3,116,870.

The 1987 season was reduced from a 16-game season to 15 as the result of a 24-day players' strike. The strike was called by the NFLPA on Tuesday, September 22, following the New England at New York Jets game. Games scheduled for the third weekend were canceled but the games of weeks four, five, and six were played with replacement

teams. Striking players returned for the seventh week of the season, October 25.

In a three-team deal involving 10 players and/or draft choices, the Los Angeles Rams traded running back Eric Dickerson to the Indianapolis Colts for six draft choices and two players. Buffalo obtained the rights to linebacker Cornelius Bennett from Indianapolis, sending Greg Bell and three draft choices to the Rams. The Colts added Owen Gill and three draft choices of their own to complete the deal with the Rams, October 31.

The Chicago at Minnesota game became the highest-rated and most-watched sports program in basic cable history when it drew a 14.4 cable rating in 6.5 million homes, December 6.

Instant replay was used to reverse eight plays in 52 preseason games. During the strike-shortened 210-game regular season, 490 plays were closely reviewed by replay officials, leading to 57 reversals. Eighteen plays were closely reviewed by instant replay in 10 postseason games, with three reversals.

1988 Washington defeated Denver 42-10 in Super Bowl XXII to earn its second victory this decade in the NFL Championship Game. The game, played for the first time in San Diego Jack Murphy Stadium, drew a sellout crowd of 73,302. According to A.C. Nielsen figures, the ABC broadcast of the game was viewed in the U.S. on television by 115,000,000 people. The game was seen live or on tape in 60 foreign countries, including the People's Republic of China, and CBS's radio broadcast of the game was heard by 13.7 million people.

A total of 811 players shared in the postseason pool of $16.9 million, the most ever distributed in a single season.

In a unanimous 3-0 decision, the 2nd Circuit Court of Appeals in New York upheld the verdict of the jury that in July, 1986, had awarded the United States Football League one dollar in its $1.7 billion antitrust suit against the NFL. In a 91-page opinion, Judge Ralph K. Winter said the USFL sought through court decree the success it failed to gain among football fans, March 10.

By a 23-5 margin, owners voted to continue the instant replay system for the third consecutive season with the Instant Replay Official to be assigned to a regular seven-man, on-the-field crew. At the NFL annual meeting in Phoenix, Arizona, a 45-second clock was also approved to replace the 30-second clock. For a normal sequence of plays, the interval between plays was changed to 45 seconds from the time the ball is signaled dead until it is snapped on the succeeding play.

NFL owners approved the transfer of the Cardinals' franchise from St. Louis to Phoenix; approved two Supplemental Drafts each year—one prior to training camp and one prior to the regular season; and voted to initiate an annual series of games in Japan/Asia as early as the 1989 preseason, March 14-18.

The NFL Annual Selection Meeting returned to a separate two-day format and for the first time originated on a Sunday. ESPN drew a 3.6 rating during their seven-hour coverage of

the draft, which was viewed in 1.6 million homes, April 24-25.

Art Rooney, founder and owner of the Steelers, died at 87, August 25.

Paid and average attendance of 934,271 and 66,734 at 14 games on October 16-17 set single weekend records.

Commissioner Rozelle announced that two teams would play a preseason game as part of the American Bowl series on August 6, 1989, in the Korakuen Tokyo Dome in Japan, December 16.

NFL regular-season paid attendance of 13,535,335 and the average of 60,427 was the third highest all-time. Buffalo set an NFL team single-season, in-house attendance mark of 622,793.

1989 San Francisco defeated Cincinnati 20-16 in Super Bowl XXIII. The game, played for the first time at Joe Robbie Stadium in Miami, was attended by a sellout crowd of 75,129. NBC's telecast of the game was watched by an estimated 110,780,000 viewers, according to A.C. Nielsen, making it the sixth most-watched program in television history. The game was seen live or on tape in 60 foreign countries, including an estimated 300 million in China. The CBS Radio broadcast of the game was heard by 11.2 million people.

Commissioner Rozelle announced his retirement, pending the naming of a successor, March 22 at the NFL annual meeting in Palm Desert, California.

Following the announcement, AFC president Lamar Hunt and NFC president Wellington Mara announced the formation of a six-man search committee composed of Art Modell, Robert Parins, Dan Rooney, and Ralph Wilson. Hunt and Mara served as co-chairmen.

By a 24-4 margin, owners voted to continue the instant replay system for the fourth straight season. A strengthened policy regarding anabolic steroids and masking agents was announced by Commissioner Rozelle. NFL clubs called for strong disciplinary measures in cases of feigned injuries and adopted a joint proposal by the Long-Range Planning and Finance committees regarding player personnel rules, March 19-23.

Two hundred twenty-nine unconditional free agents signed with new teams under management's Plan B system, April 1.

Jerry Jones purchased a majority interest in the Dallas Cowboys from H.R. (Bum) Bright, April 18.

Tex Schramm was named president of the new World League of American Football to work with a six-man committee of Dan Rooney, chairman; Norman Braman, Lamar Hunt, Victor Kiam, Mike Lynn, and Bill Walsh, April 18.

NFL and CBS Radio jointly announced agreement extending CBS's radio rights to an annual 40-game package through the 1994 season, April 18.

NFL owners awarded Super Bowl XXVI, to be played on January 26, 1992, to Minneapolis, May 24.

As of opening day, September 10, of the 229 Plan B free agents, 111 were active and 23 others were on teams' reserve lists. Ninety-two others were waived and three retired.

Art Shell was named head coach

of the Los Angeles Raiders making him the NFL's first black head coach since Fritz Pollard coached the Akron Pros in 1921, October 3.

The site of the New England Patriots at San Francisco 49ers game scheduled for Candlestick Park on October 22 was switched to Stanford Stadium in the aftermath of the Bay Area Earthquake of October 17. The change was announced on October 19.

Paul Tagliabue became the seventh chief executive of the NFL on October 26 when he was chosen to succeed Commissioner Pete Rozelle on the sixth ballot of a three-day meeting in Cleveland, Ohio.

In all, 12 ballots were required to select Tagliabue. Two were conducted at a meeting in Chicago on July 6, and four at a meeting in Dallas on October 10-11. On the twelfth ballot, with Seattle absent, Tagliabue received more than the 19 affirmative votes required for election from among the 27 clubs present.

The transfer from Commissioner Rozelle to Commissioner Tagliabue took place at 12:01 A.M. on Sunday, November 5.

NFL Charities donated $1 million through United Way to benefit Bay Area earthquake victims, November 6.

NFL paid attendance of 17,399,538 was the highest total in league history. This included a total of 13,625,662 for an average of 60,829—both NFL records—for the 224-game regular season.

1990 San Francisco defeated Denver 55-10 in Super Bowl XXIV at the Louisiana Superdome, January 28. San Francisco joined Pittsburgh as the NFL's only teams to win four Super Bowls.

The NFL announced revisions in its 1990 Draft eligibility rules. College juniors became eligible but must renounce their collegiate football eligibility before applying for the NFL Draft, February 16.

Commissioner Tagliabue announced NFL teams will play their 16-game schedule over 17 weeks in 1990 and 1991 and 16 games over 18 weeks in 1992 and 1993, February 27.

The NFL revised its playoff format to include two additional wild-card teams (one per conference).

Commissioner Tagliabue and Broadcast Committee Chairman Art Modell announced a four-year contract with Turner Broadcasting to televise nine Sunday-night games.

New four-year TV agreements were ratified for 1990-93 for ABC, CBS, NBC, ESPN, and TNT at the NFL annual meeting in Orlando, Florida, March 12. The contracts totaled $3.6 billion, the largest in TV history.

The NFL announced plans to expand its American Bowl series of preseason games. In addition to games in London and Tokyo, American Bowl games were scheduled for Berlin, Germany, and Montreal, Canada, in 1990.

For the fifth straight year, NFL owners voted to continue a limited system of Instant Replay. Beginning in 1990, the replay official will have a two-minute time limit to make a decision. The vote was 21-7, March 12.

Commissioner Tagliabue announced the formation of a Committee on Expansion and Realignment, March 13. He also named a Player Advisory Council, comprised of 12 former NFL players, March 14.

One-hundred eighty-four Plan B unconditional free agents signed with new teams, April 2.

Commissioner Tagliabue appointed Dr. John Lombardo as the League's Drug Advisor for anabolic steroids, April 25 and named Dr. Lawrence Brown as the League's Advisor for Drugs of Abuse, May 17.

NFL owners awarded Super Bowl XXVIII, to be played in 1994, to the proposed Georgia Dome, May 23.

Commissioner Tagliabue named NFL referee Jerry Seeman as NFL Director of Officiating, replacing Art McNally, who announced his retirement, July 12.

NFL International Week was celebrated with four preseason games in seven days in Tokyo, London, Berlin, and Montreal. More than 200,000 fans on three continents attended the four games, August 4-11.

Commissioner Tagliabue announced the NFL Teacher of the Month program in which the League furnishes grants and scholarships in recognition of teachers who provided a positive influence upon NFL players in elementary and secondary schools, Sept. 20.

For the first time since 1957, every NFL club won at least one of its first four games, Oct. 1.

NFL total paid attendance of 17,665,671 was the highest total in League history. The regular-season total paid attendance of 13,959,896 and average of 62,321 for 224 games were the highest ever, surpassing the previous records set in the 1989 season.

1991 The New York Giants defeated Buffalo 20-19 in Super Bowl XXV to capture their second title in five years. The game was played before a sellout crowd of 73,813 at Tampa Stadium and became the first Super Bowl decided by one point, January 27. The ABC broadcast of the game was seen by more than 112,000,000 people in the United States and was seen live or taped in 60 other countries.

NFL playoff games earned the top television rating spot of the week for each week of the month-long playoffs, January 29.

A total of 693 players shared in the postseason pool of $14.9 million.

New York businessman Robert Tisch purchased a 50 percent interest in the New York Giants from Mrs. Helen Mara Nugent and her children, Tim Mara and Maura Mara Concannon, February 2.

Commissioner Tagliabue named Neil Austrian to the newly created position of President of the NFL to be chief operating officer for League-wide business and financial operations, February 27.

NFL owners voted to continue a limited system of Instant Replay for the sixth consecutive year. The vote was 21-7, March 19.

The NFL launched the World League of American Football, the first sports league to operate on a weekly basis on two separate continents, March 23.

One-hundred thirty-nine Plan B unconditional free agents signed with new teams, April 1.

NFL Charities presented a $250,000 donation to the United Service Organization. The donation was the second largest single grant ever by NFL Charities, April 5.

Commissioner Tagliabue named Harold Henderson as Executive Vice President for Labor Relations and Chairman of the NFL Management Council Executive Committee, April 8.

Russell Maryland, a University of Miami defensive lineman, was selected by Dallas, becoming the first player chosen in the 1991 NFL Draft, April 21.

NFL owners approved a recommendation by the Expansion and Realignment Committee to add two teams for the 1994 season, resulting in six divisions of five teams each, May 22.

NFL owners awarded Super Bowl XXIX, to be played on January 29, 1995, to Miami, May 23.

"NFL International Week" featured six 1990 playoff teams playing nationally televised games in London, Berlin, and Tokyo on July 28 and August 3-4. The games drew more than 150,000 fans.

Paul Brown, founder of the Cleveland Browns and Cincinnati Bengals, died at age 82, August 5.

NFL owners approved a resolution establishing an international division, reporting to the President of the NFL. A three-year financial plan for the World League was approved by NFL clubs at a meeting in Dallas, October 23.

1992 The NFL agreed to provide a minimum of $2.5 million in financial support to the NFL Alumni Association and assistance to NFL Alumni-related programs. The agreement included contributions from NFL Charities to the Pre-59ers and Dire Need Programs for former players, January 25.

The Washington Redskins defeated the Buffalo Bills 37-24 in Super Bowl XXVI to capture their third world championship in 10 years, January 27. The game was played before a sellout crowd of 63,130 at the Hubert H. Humphrey Metrodome in Minneapolis and attracted the second largest television audience in Super Bowl history. The CBS broadcast was seen by more than 120,000,000 people nationally, second only to the 127,000,000 who viewed Super Bowl XX.

For the third consecutive season, NFL total paid attendance reached a record level. Total paid attendance was 17,752,139 for the 296 preseason, regular-season, and postseason games, February 3.

The use in officiating of a limited system of Instant Replay for a seventh consecutive year was not approved. The vote was 17-11, March 18.

One-hundred sixty-six Plan B unconditional free agents signed with new teams, April 1.

Steve Emtman, a University of Washington defensive lineman, was selected by Indianapolis, becoming the first player chosen in the 1992 NFL draft, April 26.

St. Louis businessman James Orthwein purchased controlling interest of the New England Patriots from Victor Kiam, May 11.

NFL COMMISSIONERS AND PRESIDENTS*

1920	Jim Thorpe, President
1921-39	Joe Carr, President
1939-41	Carl Storck, President
1941-46	Elmer Layden, Commissioner
1946-59	Bert Bell, Commissioner
1960-89	Pete Rozelle, Commissioner
1989-present	Paul Tagliabue, Commissioner

*NFL treasurer Austin Gunsel served as president in the office of the commissioner following the death of Bert Bell (Oct. 11, 1959) until the election of Pete Rozelle (Jan. 26, 1960).

1991

American Conference

Eastern Division

	W	L	T	Pct.	Pts.	OP
Buffalo	13	3	0	.813	458	318
N.Y. Jets*	8	8	0	.500	314	293
Miami	8	8	0	.500	343	349
New England	6	10	0	.375	211	305
Indianapolis	1	15	0	.063	143	381

Central Division

	W	L	T	Pct.	Pts.	OP
Houston	11	5	0	.688	386	251
Pittsburgh	7	9	0	.438	292	344
Cleveland	6	10	0	.375	293	298
Cincinnati	3	13	0	.188	263	435

Western Division

	W	L	T	Pct.	Pts.	OP
Denver	12	4	0	.750	304	235
Kansas City*	10	6	0	.625	322	252
L.A. Raiders*	9	7	0	.563	298	297
Seattle	7	9	0	.438	276	261
San Diego	4	12	0	.250	274	342

National Conference

Eastern Division

	W	L	T	Pct.	Pts.	OP
Washington	14	2	0	.875	485	224
Dallas*	11	5	0	.688	342	310
Philadelphia	10	6	0	.625	285	244
N.Y. Giants	8	8	0	.500	281	297
Phoenix	4	12	0	.250	196	344

Central Division

	W	L	T	Pct.	Pts.	OP
Detroit	12	4	0	.750	339	295
Chicago*	11	5	0	.688	299	269
Minnesota	8	8	0	.500	301	306
Green Bay	4	12	0	.250	273	313
Tampa Bay	3	13	0	.188	199	365

Western Division

	W	L	T	Pct.	Pts.	OP
New Orleans	11	5	0	.688	341	211
Atlanta*	10	6	0	.625	361	338
San Francisco	10	6	0	.625	393	239
L.A. Rams	3	13	0	.188	234	390

Wild Card qualifiers for playoffs

New York Jets finished ahead of Miami based on head-to-head sweep (2-0). Atlanta finished ahead of San Francisco based on head-to-head sweep (2-0).
First round playoffs: KANSAS CITY 10, Los Angeles Raiders 6; HOUSTON 17, N.Y. Jets 10
Divisional playoffs: DENVER 26, Houston 24; BUFFALO 37, Kansas City 14
AFC championship: BUFFALO 10, Denver 7
First round playoffs: Atlanta 27, NEW ORLEANS 20; Dallas 17, CHICAGO 13
Divisional playoffs: WASHINGTON 24, Atlanta 7; DETROIT 38, Dallas 6
NFC championship: WASHINGTON 41, Detroit 10
Super Bowl XXVI: Washington (NFC) 37, Buffalo (AFC) 24, at Hubert H. Humphrey Metrodome, Minneapolis, Minnesota.
In the Past Standings section, home teams in playoff games are indicated by capital LETTERS.

1990

American Conference

Eastern Division

	W	L	T	Pct.	Pts.	OP
Buffalo	13	3	0	.813	428	263
Miami*	12	4	0	.750	336	242
Indianapolis	7	9	0	.438	281	353
N.Y. Jets	6	10	0	.375	295	345
New England	1	15	0	.063	181	446

Central Division

	W	L	T	Pct.	Pts.	OP
Cincinnati	9	7	0	.563	360	352
Houston*	9	7	0	.563	405	307
Pittsburgh	9	7	0	.563	292	240
Cleveland	3	13	0	.188	228	462

Western Division

	W	L	T	Pct.	Pts.	OP
L.A. Raiders	12	4	0	.750	337	268
Kansas City*	11	5	0	.688	369	257
Seattle	9	7	0	.563	306	286
San Diego	6	10	0	.375	315	281
Denver	5	11	0	.313	331	374

National Conference

Eastern Division

	W	L	T	Pct.	Pts.	OP
N.Y. Giants	13	3	0	.813	335	211
Philadelphia*	10	6	0	.625	396	299
Washington*	10	6	0	.625	381	301
Dallas	7	9	0	.438	244	308
Phoenix	5	11	0	.313	268	396

Central Division

	W	L	T	Pct.	Pts.	OP
Chicago	11	5	0	.688	348	280
Tampa Bay	6	10	0	.375	264	367
Detroit	6	10	0	.375	373	413
Green Bay	6	10	0	.375	271	347
Minnesota	6	10	0	.375	351	326

Western Division

	W	L	T	Pct.	Pts.	OP
San Francisco	14	2	0	.875	353	239
New Orleans*	8	8	0	.500	274	275
L.A. Rams	5	11	0	.313	345	412
Atlanta	5	11	0	.313	348	365

Wild Card qualifiers for playoffs

Cincinnati won AFC Central title based on best head-to-head record (3-1) vs. Houston (2-2) and Pittsburgh (1-3). Houston was Wild Card based on better conference record (8-4) than Seattle (7-5) and Pittsburgh (6-6). Philadelphia finished second in the NFC East based on better division record (5-3) than Washington (4-4). Tampa Bay was second in NFC Central based on 5-1 record vs. Detroit, Green Bay, and Minnesota. Detroit finished third based on best net division points (minus 8) vs. Green Bay (minus 40) in fourth. Minnesota was fifth based on 4-8 conference record. The Los Angeles Rams finished third in NFC West based on net points in division (plus 1) vs. Atlanta (minus 31).
First round playoffs: MIAMI 17, Kansas City 16; CINCINNATI 41, Houston 14
Divisional playoffs: BUFFALO 44, Miami 34; L.A. RAIDERS 20, Cincinnati 10
AFC championship: BUFFALO 51, L.A. Raiders 3
First round playoffs: Washington 20, PHILADELPHIA 6; CHICAGO 16, New Orleans 6
Divisional playoffs: SAN FRANCISCO 28, Washington 10; N.Y. GIANTS 31, Chicago 3
NFC championship: N.Y. Giants 15, SAN FRANCISCO 13
Super Bowl XXV: N.Y. Giants (NFC) 20, Buffalo (AFC) 19, at Tampa Stadium, Tampa, Florida.

1989

American Conference

Eastern Division

	W	L	T	Pct.	Pts.	OP
Buffalo	9	7	0	.563	409	317
Indianapolis	8	8	0	.500	298	301
Miami	8	8	0	.500	331	379
New England	5	11	0	.313	297	391
N.Y. Jets	4	12	0	.250	253	411

Central Division

	W	L	T	Pct.	Pts.	OP
Cleveland	9	6	1	.594	334	254
Houston*	9	7	0	.563	365	412
Pittsburgh*	9	7	0	.563	265	326
Cincinnati	8	8	0	.500	404	285

Western Division

	W	L	T	Pct.	Pts.	OP
Denver	11	5	0	.688	362	226
Kansas City	8	7	1	.531	318	286
L.A. Raiders	8	8	0	.500	315	297
Seattle	7	9	0	.438	241	327
San Diego	6	10	0	.375	266	290

National Conference

Eastern Division

	W	L	T	Pct.	Pts.	OP
N.Y. Giants	12	4	0	.750	348	252
Philadelphia*	11	5	0	.688	342	274
Washington	10	6	0	.625	386	308
Phoenix	5	11	0	.313	258	377
Dallas	1	15	0	.063	204	393

Central Division

	W	L	T	Pct.	Pts.	OP
Minnesota	10	6	0	.625	351	275
Green Bay	10	6	0	.625	362	356
Detroit	7	9	0	.438	312	364
Chicago	6	10	0	.375	358	377
Tampa Bay	5	11	0	.313	320	419

Western Division

	W	L	T	Pct.	Pts.	OP
San Francisco	14	2	0	.875	442	253
L.A. Rams*	11	5	0	.688	426	344
New Orleans	9	7	0	.563	386	301
Atlanta	3	13	0	.188	279	437

Wild Card qualifiers for playoffs

Indianapolis finished ahead of Miami in AFC East because of better conference record (7-5 vs. 6-8). Houston finished ahead of Pittsburgh in AFC Central because of head-to-head sweep (2-0). Minnesota finished ahead of Green Bay in NFC Central because of better division record (6-2 vs. 5-3).
First round playoff: Pittsburgh 26, HOUSTON 23 (OT)
Divisional playoffs: CLEVELAND 34, Buffalo 30; DENVER 24, Pittsburgh 23
AFC championship: DENVER 37, Cleveland 21
First round playoff: L.A. Rams 21, PHILADELPHIA 7
Divisional playoffs: L.A. Rams 19, N.Y. GIANTS 13 (OT); SAN FRANCISCO 41, Minnesota 13
NFC championship: SAN FRANCISCO 30, L.A. Rams 3
Super Bowl XXIV: San Francisco (NFC) 55, Denver (AFC) 10, at Louisiana Superdome, New Orleans, Louisiana.

1988

American Conference

Eastern Division

	W	L	T	Pct.	Pts.	OP
Buffalo	12	4	0	.750	329	237
Indianapolis	9	7	0	.563	354	315
New England	9	7	0	.563	250	284
N.Y. Jets	8	7	1	.531	372	354
Miami	6	10	0	.375	319	380

Central Division

	W	L	T	Pct.	Pts.	OP
Cincinnati	12	4	0	.750	448	329
Cleveland*	10	6	0	.625	304	288
Houston*	10	6	0	.625	424	365
Pittsburgh	5	11	0	.313	336	421

Western Division

	W	L	T	Pct.	Pts.	OP
Seattle	9	7	0	.563	339	329
Denver	8	8	0	.500	327	352
L.A. Raiders	7	9	0	.438	325	369
San Diego	6	10	0	.375	231	332
Kansas City	4	11	1	.281	254	320

National Conference

Eastern Division

	W	L	T	Pct.	Pts.	OP
Philadelphia	10	6	0	.625	379	319
N.Y. Giants	10	6	0	.625	359	304
Washington	7	9	0	.438	345	387
Phoenix	7	9	0	.438	344	398
Dallas	3	13	0	.188	265	381

Central Division

	W	L	T	Pct.	Pts.	OP
Chicago	12	4	0	.750	312	215
Minnesota*	11	5	0	.688	406	233
Tampa Bay	5	11	0	.313	261	350
Detroit	4	12	0	.250	220	313
Green Bay	4	12	0	.250	240	315

Western Division

	W	L	T	Pct.	Pts.	OP
San Francisco	10	6	0	.625	369	294
L.A. Rams*	10	6	0	.625	407	293
New Orleans	10	6	0	.625	312	283
Atlanta	5	11	0	.313	244	315

Wild Card qualifiers for playoffs

Indianapolis finished second in AFC East on basis of better record versus common opponents (7-5) over New England (6-6). Cleveland gained first AFC Wild Card position based on better division record (4-2) over Houston (3-3). Philadelphia finished first in NFC East on basis of head-to-head sweep over New York Giants. Washington finished third in NFC East on basis of better division record (4-4) over Phoenix (3-5). Detroit finished fourth in NFC Central on basis of head-to-head sweep over Green Bay. San Francisco finished first in NFC West based on better head-to-head record (3-1) over Los Angeles Rams (2-2) and New Orleans (1-3). Los Angeles Rams finished second in NFC West on basis of better division record (4-2) over New Orleans (3-3) and earned Wild Card position based on better conference record (8-4) over New York Giants (9-5) and New Orleans (6-6).
First round playoff: Houston 24, CLEVELAND 23
Divisional playoffs: CINCINNATI 21, Seattle 13; BUFFALO 17, Houston 10
AFC championship: CINCINNATI 21, Buffalo 10
First round playoff: MINNESOTA 28, Los Angeles Rams 17
Divisional playoffs: CHICAGO 20, Philadelphia 12; SAN FRANCISCO 34, Minnesota 9
NFC championship: San Francisco 28, CHICAGO 3
Super Bowl XXIII: San Francisco (NFC) 20, Cincinnati (AFC) 16, at Joe Robbie Stadium, Miami, Florida.

1987
American Conference
Eastern Division

	W	L	T	Pct.	Pts.	OP
Indianapolis	9	6	0	.600	300	238
New England	8	7	0	.533	320	293
Miami	8	7	0	.533	362	335
Buffalo	7	8	0	.467	270	305
N.Y. Jets	6	9	0	.400	334	360

Central Division

	W	L	T	Pct.	Pts.	OP
Cleveland	10	5	0	.667	390	239
Houston*	9	6	0	.600	345	349
Pittsburgh	8	7	0	.533	285	299
Cincinnati	4	11	0	.267	285	370

Western Division

	W	L	T	Pct.	Pts.	OP
Denver	10	4	1	.700	379	288
Seattle*	9	6	0	.600	371	314
San Diego	8	7	0	.533	253	317
L.A. Raiders	5	10	0	.333	301	289
Kansas City	4	11	0	.267	273	388

National Conference
Eastern Division

	W	L	T	Pct.	Pts.	OP
Washington	11	4	0	.733	379	285
Dallas	7	8	0	.467	340	348
St. Louis	7	8	0	.467	362	368
Philadelphia	7	8	0	.467	337	380
N.Y. Giants	6	9	0	.400	280	312

Central Division

	W	L	T	Pct.	Pts.	OP
Chicago	11	4	0	.733	356	282
Minnesota*	8	7	0	.533	336	335
Green Bay	5	9	1	.367	255	300
Tampa Bay	4	11	0	.267	286	360
Detroit	4	11	0	.267	269	384

Western Division

	W	L	T	Pct.	Pts.	OP
San Francisco	13	2	0	.867	459	253
New Orleans*	12	3	0	.800	422	283
L.A. Rams	6	9	0	.400	317	361
Atlanta	3	12	0	.200	205	436

*Wild Card qualifiers for playoffs

Houston gained first AFC Wild Card position on better conference record (7-4) over Seattle (5-6).

First round playoff: HOUSTON 23, Seattle 20 (OT)
Divisional playoffs: CLEVELAND 38, Indianapolis 21
　DENVER 34, Houston 10
AFC championship: DENVER 38, Cleveland 33
First round playoff: Minnesota 44, NEW ORLEANS 10
Divisional playoffs: Minnesota 36, SAN FRANCISCO 24
　Washington 21, CHICAGO 17
NFC championship: WASHINGTON 17, Minnesota 10
Super Bowl XXII: Washington (NFC) 42, Denver (AFC) 10, at San Diego Jack Murphy Stadium, San Diego, California.
Note: 1987 regular season was reduced from 16 to 15 games for each team due to players' strike.

1986
American Conference
Eastern Division

	W	L	T	Pct.	Pts.	OP
New England	11	5	0	.688	412	307
N.Y. Jets*	10	6	0	.625	364	386
Miami	8	8	0	.500	430	405
Buffalo	4	12	0	.250	287	348
Indianapolis	3	13	0	.188	229	400

Central Division

	W	L	T	Pct.	Pts.	OP
Cleveland	12	4	0	.750	391	310
Cincinnati	10	6	0	.625	409	394
Pittsburgh	6	10	0	.375	307	336
Houston	5	11	0	.313	274	329

Western Division

	W	L	T	Pct.	Pts.	OP
Denver	11	5	0	.688	378	327
Kansas City*	10	6	0	.625	358	326
Seattle	10	6	0	.625	366	293
L.A. Raiders	8	8	0	.500	323	346
San Diego	4	12	0	.250	335	396

National Conference
Eastern Division

	W	L	T	Pct.	Pts.	OP
N.Y. Giants	14	2	0	.875	371	236
Washington*	12	4	0	.750	368	296
Dallas	7	9	0	.438	346	337
Philadelphia	5	10	1	.344	256	312
St. Louis	4	11	1	.281	218	351

Central Division

	W	L	T	Pct.	Pts.	OP
Chicago	14	2	0	.875	352	187
Minnesota	9	7	0	.563	398	273
Detroit	5	11	0	.313	277	326
Green Bay	4	12	0	.250	254	418
Tampa Bay	2	14	0	.125	239	473

Western Division

	W	L	T	Pct.	Pts.	OP
San Francisco	10	5	1	.656	374	247
L.A. Rams*	10	6	0	.625	309	267
Atlanta	7	8	1	.469	280	280
New Orleans	7	9	0	.438	288	287

*Wild Card qualifiers for playoffs

New York Jets gained first AFC Wild Card position on better conference record (8-4) over Kansas City (9-5), Seattle (7-5), and Cincinnati (7-5). Kansas City gained second Wild Card based on better conference record (9-5) over Seattle (7-5) and Cincinnati (7-5).

First round playoff: NEW YORK JETS 35, Kansas City 15
Divisional playoffs: CLEVELAND 23, New York Jets 20 (OT)
　DENVER 22, New England 17
AFC championship: Denver 23, CLEVELAND 20 (OT)
First round playoff: WASHINGTON 19, Los Angeles Rams 7
Divisional playoffs: Washington 27, CHICAGO 13
　NEW YORK GIANTS 49, San Francisco 3
NFC championship: NEW YORK GIANTS 17, Washington 0
Super Bowl XXI: New York Giants (NFC) 39, Denver (AFC) 20, at Rose Bowl, Pasadena, California.

1985
American Conference
Eastern Division

	W	L	T	Pct.	Pts.	OP
Miami	12	4	0	.750	428	320
N.Y. Jets*	11	5	0	.688	393	264
New England*	11	5	0	.688	362	290
Indianapolis	5	11	0	.313	320	386
Buffalo	2	14	0	.125	200	381

Central Division

	W	L	T	Pct.	Pts.	OP
Cleveland	8	8	0	.500	287	294
Cincinnati	7	9	0	.438	441	437
Pittsburgh	7	9	0	.438	379	355
Houston	5	11	0	.313	284	412

Western Division

	W	L	T	Pct.	Pts.	OP
L.A. Raiders	12	4	0	.750	354	308
Denver	11	5	0	.688	380	329
Seattle	8	8	0	.500	349	303
San Diego	8	8	0	.500	467	435
Kansas City	6	10	0	.375	317	360

National Conference
Eastern Division

	W	L	T	Pct.	Pts.	OP
Dallas	10	6	0	.625	357	333
N.Y. Giants*	10	6	0	.625	399	283
Washington	10	6	0	.625	297	312
Philadelphia	7	9	0	.438	286	310
St. Louis	5	11	0	.313	278	414

Central Division

	W	L	T	Pct.	Pts.	OP
Chicago	15	1	0	.938	456	198
Green Bay	8	8	0	.500	337	355
Minnesota	7	9	0	.438	346	359
Detroit	7	9	0	.438	307	366
Tampa Bay	2	14	0	.125	294	448

Western Division

	W	L	T	Pct.	Pts.	OP
L.A. Rams	11	5	0	.688	340	277
San Francisco*	10	6	0	.625	411	263
New Orleans	5	11	0	.313	294	401
Atlanta	4	12	0	.250	282	452

*Wild Card qualifiers for playoffs

New York Jets gained first AFC Wild Card position on better conference record (9-3) over New England (8-4) and Denver (8-4). New England gained second AFC Wild Card position based on better record vs. common opponents (4-2) than Denver (3-3). Dallas won NFC Eastern Division title based on better record (4-0) vs. New York Giants (1-3) and Washington (1-3). New York Giants gained first NFC Wild Card position based on better conference record (7-5) over San Francisco (7-5) and Washington (6-6). San Francisco gained second NFC Wild Card position based on head-to-head victory over Washington.

First round playoff: New England 26, NEW YORK JETS 14
Divisional playoffs: MIAMI 24, Cleveland 21;
　New England 27, LOS ANGELES RAIDERS 20
AFC championship: New England 31, MIAMI 14
First round playoff: NEW YORK GIANTS 17, San Francisco 3
Divisional playoffs: LOS ANGELES RAMS 20, Dallas 0;
　CHICAGO 21, New York Giants 0
NFC championship: CHICAGO 24, Los Angeles Rams 0
Super Bowl XX: Chicago (NFC) 46, New England (AFC) 10, at Louisiana Superdome, New Orleans, Louisiana.

1984
American Conference
Eastern Division

	W	L	T	Pct.	Pts.	OP
Miami	14	2	0	.875	513	298
New England	9	7	0	.563	362	352
N.Y. Jets	7	9	0	.438	332	364
Indianapolis	4	12	0	.250	239	414
Buffalo	2	14	0	.125	250	454

Central Division

	W	L	T	Pct.	Pts.	OP
Pittsburgh	9	7	0	.563	387	310
Cincinnati	8	8	0	.500	339	339
Cleveland	5	11	0	.313	250	297
Houston	3	13	0	.188	240	437

Western Division

	W	L	T	Pct.	Pts.	OP
Denver	13	3	0	.813	353	241
Seattle*	12	4	0	.750	418	282
L.A. Raiders*	11	5	0	.688	368	278
Kansas City	8	8	0	.500	314	324
San Diego	7	9	0	.438	394	413

National Conference
Eastern Division

	W	L	T	Pct.	Pts.	OP
Washington	11	5	0	.688	426	310
N.Y. Giants*	9	7	0	.563	299	301
St. Louis	9	7	0	.563	423	345
Dallas	9	7	0	.563	308	308
Philadelphia	6	9	1	.406	278	320

Central Division

	W	L	T	Pct.	Pts.	OP
Chicago	10	6	0	.625	325	248
Green Bay	8	8	0	.500	390	309
Tampa Bay	6	10	0	.375	335	380
Detroit	4	11	1	.281	283	408
Minnesota	3	13	0	.188	276	484

Western Division

	W	L	T	Pct.	Pts.	OP
San Francisco	15	1	0	.938	475	227
L.A. Rams*	10	6	0	.625	346	316
New Orleans	7	9	0	.438	298	361
Atlanta	4	12	0	.250	281	382

*Wild Card qualifiers for playoffs

New York Giants clinched Wild Card berth based on 3-1 record vs. St. Louis's 2-2 and Dallas's 1-3. St. Louis finished ahead of Dallas based on better division record (5-3 to 3-5).

First round playoff: SEATTLE 13, Los Angeles Raiders 7
Divisional playoffs: MIAMI 31, Seattle 10; Pittsburgh 24, DENVER 17
AFC championship: MIAMI 45, Pittsburgh 28
First round playoff: New York Giants 16, LOS ANGELES RAMS 13
Divisional playoffs: SAN FRANCISCO 21, New York Giants 10;
　Chicago 23, WASHINGTON 19
NFC championship: SAN FRANCISCO 23, Chicago 0
Super Bowl XIX: San Francisco (NFC) 38, Miami (AFC) 16, at Stanford Stadium, Stanford, California.

1983

American Conference

Eastern Division

	W	L	T	Pct.	Pts.	OP
Miami	12	4	0	.750	389	250
New England	8	8	0	.500	274	289
Buffalo	8	8	0	.500	283	351
Baltimore	7	9	0	.438	264	354
N.Y. Jets	7	9	0	.438	313	331

Central Division

	W	L	T	Pct.	Pts.	OP
Pittsburgh	10	6	0	.625	355	303
Cleveland	9	7	0	.563	356	342
Cincinnati	7	9	0	.438	346	302
Houston	2	14	0	.125	288	460

Western Division

	W	L	T	Pct.	Pts.	OP
L.A. Raiders	12	4	0	.750	442	338
Seattle*	9	7	0	.563	403	397
Denver*	9	7	0	.563	302	327
San Diego	6	10	0	.375	358	462
Kansas City	6	10	0	.375	386	367

National Conference

Eastern Division

	W	L	T	Pct.	Pts.	OP
Washington	14	2	0	.875	541	332
Dallas*	12	4	0	.750	479	360
St. Louis	8	7	1	.531	374	428
Philadelphia	5	11	0	.313	233	322
N.Y. Giants	3	12	1	.219	267	347

Central Division

	W	L	T	Pct.	Pts.	OP
Detroit	9	7	0	.563	347	286
Green Bay	8	8	0	.500	429	439
Chicago	8	8	0	.500	311	301
Minnesota	8	8	0	.500	316	348
Tampa Bay	2	14	0	.125	241	380

Western Division

	W	L	T	Pct.	Pts.	OP
San Francisco	10	6	0	.625	432	293
L.A. Rams*	9	7	0	.563	361	344
New Orleans	8	8	0	.500	319	337
Atlanta	7	9	0	.438	370	389

*Wild Card qualifiers for playoffs
Seattle and Denver gained Wild Card berths over Cleveland because of their victories over the Browns.
First round playoff: SEATTLE 31, Denver 7
Divisional playoffs: Seattle 27, MIAMI 20; LOS ANGELES RAIDERS 38, Pittsburgh 10
AFC championship: LOS ANGELES RAIDERS 30, Seattle 14
First round playoff: Los Angeles Rams 24, DALLAS 17
Divisional playoffs: SAN FRANCISCO 24, Detroit 23; WASHINGTON 51, L.A. Rams 7
NFC championship: WASHINGTON 24, San Francisco 21
Super Bowl XVIII: Los Angeles Raiders (AFC) 38, Washington (NFC) 9, at Tampa Stadium, Tampa, Florida.

1982

American Conference

	W	L	T	Pct.	Pts.	OP
L.A. Raiders	8	1	0	.889	260	200
Miami	7	2	0	.778	198	131
Cincinnati	7	2	0	.778	232	177
Pittsburgh	6	3	0	.667	204	146
San Diego	6	3	0	.667	288	221
N.Y. Jets	6	3	0	.667	245	166
New England	5	4	0	.556	143	157
Cleveland	4	5	0	.444	140	182
Buffalo	4	5	0	.444	150	154
Seattle	4	5	0	.444	127	147
Kansas City	3	6	0	.333	176	184
Denver	2	7	0	.222	148	226
Houston	1	8	0	.111	136	245
Baltimore	0	8	1	.056	113	236

National Conference

	W	L	T	Pct.	Pts.	OP
Washington	8	1	0	.889	190	128
Dallas	6	3	0	.667	226	145
Green Bay	5	3	1	.611	226	169
Minnesota	5	4	0	.556	187	198
Atlanta	5	4	0	.556	183	199
St. Louis	5	4	0	.556	135	170
Tampa Bay	5	4	0	.556	158	178
Detroit	4	5	0	.444	181	176
New Orleans	4	5	0	.444	129	160
N.Y. Giants	4	5	0	.444	164	160
San Francisco	3	6	0	.333	209	206
Chicago	3	6	0	.333	141	174
Philadelphia	3	6	0	.333	191	195
L.A. Rams	2	7	0	.222	200	250

As the result of a 57-day players' strike, the 1982 NFL regular season schedule was reduced from 16 weeks to 9. At the conclusion of the regular season, the NFL conducted a 16-team postseason Super Bowl Tournament. Eight teams from each conference were seeded 1-8 based on their records during the season.

Miami finished ahead of Cincinnati based on better conference record (6-1 to 6-2). Pittsburgh won common games tie-breaker with San Diego (3-1 to 2-1) after New York Jets were eliminated from three-way tie based on conference record (Pittsburgh and San Diego 5-3 vs. Jets 2-3). Cleveland finished ahead of Buffalo and Seattle based on better conference record (4-3 to 3-3 to 3-5). Minnesota (4-1), Atlanta (4-3), St. Louis (5-4), Tampa Bay (3-3) seeds were determined by best won-lost record in conference games. Detroit finished ahead of New Orleans and the New York Giants based on better conference record (4-4 to 3-5 to 3-5).

First round playoff: MIAMI 28, New England 13
LOS ANGELES RAIDERS 27, Cleveland 10
New York Jets 44, CINCINNATI 17
San Diego 31, PITTSBURGH 28
Second round playoff: New York Jets 17, LOS ANGELES RAIDERS 14
MIAMI 34, San Diego 13
AFC championship: MIAMI 14, New York Jets 0
First round playoff: WASHINGTON 31, Detroit 7
GREEN BAY 41, St. Louis 16
MINNESOTA 30, Atlanta 24
DALLAS 30, Tampa Bay 17
Second round playoff: WASHINGTON 21, Minnesota 7
DALLAS 37, Green Bay 26
NFC championship: WASHINGTON 31, Dallas 17
Super Bowl XVII: Washington (NFC) 27, Miami (AFC) 17, at Rose Bowl, Pasadena, California.

1981

American Conference

Eastern Division

	W	L	T	Pct.	Pts.	OP
Miami	11	4	1	.719	345	275
N.Y. Jets*	10	5	1	.656	355	287
Buffalo*	10	6	0	.625	311	276
Baltimore	2	14	0	.125	259	533
New England	2	14	0	.125	322	370

Central Division

	W	L	T	Pct.	Pts.	OP
Cincinnati	12	4	0	.750	421	304
Pittsburgh	8	8	0	.500	356	297
Houston	7	9	0	.438	281	355
Cleveland	5	11	0	.313	276	375

Western Division

	W	L	T	Pct.	Pts.	OP
San Diego	10	6	0	.625	478	390
Denver	10	6	0	.625	321	289
Kansas City	9	7	0	.563	343	290
Oakland	7	9	0	.438	273	343
Seattle	6	10	0	.375	322	388

National Conference

Eastern Division

	W	L	T	Pct.	Pts.	OP
Dallas	12	4	0	.750	367	277
Philadelphia*	10	6	0	.625	368	221
N.Y. Giants*	9	7	0	.563	295	257
Washington	8	8	0	.500	347	349
St. Louis	7	9	0	.438	315	408

Central Division

	W	L	T	Pct.	Pts.	OP
Tampa Bay	9	7	0	.563	315	268
Detroit	8	8	0	.500	397	322
Green Bay	8	8	0	.500	324	361
Minnesota	7	9	0	.438	325	369
Chicago	6	10	0	.375	253	324

Western Division

	W	L	T	Pct.	Pts.	OP
San Francisco	13	3	0	.813	357	250
Atlanta	7	9	0	.438	426	355
Los Angeles	6	10	0	.375	303	351
New Orleans	4	12	0	.250	207	378

*Wild Card qualifiers for playoffs
San Diego won AFC Western title over Denver on the basis of a better division record (6-2 to 5-3). Buffalo won a Wild Card playoff berth over Denver as the result of a 9-7 victory in head-to-head competition.
First round playoff: Buffalo 31, NEW YORK JETS 27
Divisional playoffs: San Diego 41, MIAMI 38 (OT); CINCINNATI 28, Buffalo 21
AFC championship: CINCINNATI 27, San Diego 7
First round playoff: New York Giants 27, PHILADELPHIA 21
Divisional playoffs: DALLAS 38, Tampa Bay 0; SAN FRANCISCO 38, New York Giants 24
NFC championship: SAN FRANCISCO 28, Dallas 27
Super Bowl XVI: San Francisco (NFC) 26, Cincinnati (AFC) 21, at Silverdome, Pontiac, Michigan.

1980

American Conference

Eastern Division

	W	L	T	Pct.	Pts.	OP
Buffalo	11	5	0	.688	320	260
New England	10	6	0	.625	441	325
Miami	8	8	0	.500	266	305
Baltimore	7	9	0	.438	355	387
N.Y. Jets	4	12	0	.250	302	395

Central Division

	W	L	T	Pct.	Pts.	OP
Cleveland	11	5	0	.688	357	310
Houston	11	5	0	.688	295	251
Pittsburgh	9	7	0	.563	352	313
Cincinnati	6	10	0	.375	244	312

Western Division

	W	L	T	Pct.	Pts.	OP
San Diego	11	5	0	.688	418	327
Oakland*	11	5	0	.688	364	306
Kansas City	8	8	0	.500	319	336
Denver	8	8	0	.500	310	323
Seattle	4	12	0	.250	291	408

National Conference

Eastern Division

	W	L	T	Pct.	Pts.	OP
Philadelphia	12	4	0	.750	384	222
Dallas*	12	4	0	.750	454	311
Washington	6	10	0	.375	261	293
St. Louis	5	11	0	.313	299	350
N.Y. Giants	4	12	0	.250	249	425

Central Division

	W	L	T	Pct.	Pts.	OP
Minnesota	9	7	0	.563	317	308
Detroit	9	7	0	.563	334	272
Chicago	7	9	0	.438	304	264
Tampa Bay	5	10	1	.344	271	341
Green Bay	5	10	1	.344	231	371

Western Division

	W	L	T	Pct.	Pts.	OP
Atlanta	12	4	0	.750	405	272
Los Angeles*	11	5	0	.688	424	289
San Francisco	6	10	0	.375	320	415
New Orleans	1	15	0	.063	291	487

*Wild Card qualifiers for playoffs
Philadelphia won division title over Dallas on the basis of best net points in division games (plus 84 net points to plus 50). Minnesota won division title because of a better conference record than Detroit (8-4 to 9-5). Cleveland won division title because of a better conference record than Houston (8-4 to 7-5). San Diego won division title over Oakland on the basis of best net points in division games (plus 60 net points to plus 37).
First round playoff: OAKLAND 27, Houston 7
Divisional playoffs: SAN DIEGO 20, Buffalo 14; Oakland 14, CLEVELAND 12
AFC championship: Oakland 34, SAN DIEGO 27
First round playoff: DALLAS 34, Los Angeles 13
Divisional playoffs: PHILADELPHIA 31, Minnesota 16; Dallas 30, ATLANTA 27
NFC championship: PHILADELPHIA 20, Dallas 7
Super Bowl XV: Oakland (AFC) 27, Philadelphia (NFC) 10, at Louisiana Superdome, New Orleans, Louisiana.

1979

American Conference

Eastern Division

	W	L	T	Pct.	Pts.	OP
Miami	10	6	0	.625	341	257
New England	9	7	0	.563	411	326
N.Y. Jets	8	8	0	.500	337	383
Buffalo	7	9	0	.438	268	279
Baltimore	5	11	0	.313	271	351

Central Division

	W	L	T	Pct.	Pts.	OP
Pittsburgh	12	4	0	.750	416	262
Houston*	11	5	0	.688	362	331
Cleveland	9	7	0	.563	359	352
Cincinnati	4	12	0	.250	337	421

Western Division

	W	L	T	Pct.	Pts.	OP
San Diego	12	4	0	.750	411	246
Denver*	10	6	0	.625	289	262
Seattle	9	7	0	.563	378	372
Oakland	9	7	0	.563	365	337
Kansas City	7	9	0	.438	238	262

National Conference

Eastern Division

	W	L	T	Pct.	Pts.	OP
Dallas	11	5	0	.688	371	313
Philadelphia*	11	5	0	.688	339	282
Washington	10	6	0	.625	348	295
N.Y. Giants	6	10	0	.375	237	323
St. Louis	5	11	0	.313	307	358

Central Division

	W	L	T	Pct.	Pts.	OP
Tampa Bay	10	6	0	.625	273	237
Chicago*	10	6	0	.625	306	249
Minnesota	7	9	0	.438	259	337
Green Bay	5	11	0	.313	246	316
Detroit	2	14	0	.125	219	365

Western Division

	W	L	T	Pct.	Pts.	OP
Los Angeles	9	7	0	.563	323	309
New Orleans	8	8	0	.500	370	360
Atlanta	6	10	0	.375	300	388
San Francisco	2	14	0	.125	308	416

*Wild Card qualifiers for playoffs

Dallas won division title because of a better conference record than Philadelphia (10-2 to 9-3). Tampa Bay won division title because of a better division record than Chicago (6-2 to 5-3). Chicago won a Wild Card berth over Washington on the basis of best net points in all games (plus 57 net points to plus 53).

First round playoff: HOUSTON 13, Denver 7
Divisional playoffs: Houston 17, SAN DIEGO 14; PITTSBURGH 34, Miami 14
AFC championship: PITTSBURGH 27, Houston 13
First round playoff: PHILADELPHIA 27, Chicago 17
Divisional playoffs: TAMPA BAY 24, Philadelphia 17; Los Angeles 21, DALLAS 19
NFC championship: Los Angeles 9, TAMPA BAY 0
Super Bowl XIV: Pittsburgh (AFC) 31, Los Angeles (NFC) 19, at Rose Bowl, Pasadena, California.

1978

American Conference

Eastern Division

	W	L	T	Pct.	Pts.	OP
New England	11	5	0	.688	358	286
Miami*	11	5	0	.688	372	254
N.Y. Jets	8	8	0	.500	359	364
Buffalo	5	11	0	.313	302	354
Baltimore	5	11	0	.313	239	421

Central Division

	W	L	T	Pct.	Pts.	OP
Pittsburgh	14	2	0	.875	356	195
Houston*	10	6	0	.625	283	298
Cleveland	8	8	0	.500	334	356
Cincinnati	4	12	0	.250	252	284

Western Division

	W	L	T	Pct.	Pts.	OP
Denver	10	6	0	.625	282	198
Oakland	9	7	0	.563	311	283
Seattle	9	7	0	.563	345	358
San Diego	9	7	0	.563	355	309
Kansas City	4	12	0	.250	243	327

National Conference

Eastern Division

	W	L	T	Pct.	Pts.	OP
Dallas	12	4	0	.750	384	208
Philadelphia*	9	7	0	.563	270	250
Washington	8	8	0	.500	273	283
St. Louis	6	10	0	.375	248	296
N.Y. Giants	6	10	0	.375	264	298

Central Division

	W	L	T	Pct.	Pts.	OP
Minnesota	8	7	1	.531	294	306
Green Bay	8	7	1	.531	249	269
Detroit	7	9	0	.438	290	300
Chicago	7	9	0	.438	253	274
Tampa Bay	5	11	0	.313	241	259

Western Division

	W	L	T	Pct.	Pts.	OP
Los Angeles	12	4	0	.750	316	245
Atlanta*	9	7	0	.563	240	290
New Orleans	7	9	0	.438	281	298
San Francisco	2	14	0	.125	219	350

*Wild Card qualifiers for playoffs

New England won division title on the basis of a better division record than Miami (6-2 to 5-3). Minnesota won division title because of a better head-to-head record against Green Bay (1-0-1).

First round playoff: Houston 17, MIAMI 9
Divisional playoffs: Houston 31, NEW ENGLAND 14; PITTSBURGH 33, Denver 10
AFC championship: PITTSBURGH 34, Houston 5
First round playoff: ATLANTA 14, Philadelphia 13
Divisional playoffs: DALLAS 27, Atlanta 20; LOS ANGELES 34, Minnesota 10
NFC championship: Dallas 28, LOS ANGELES 0
Super Bowl XIII: Pittsburgh (AFC) 35, Dallas (NFC) 31, at Orange Bowl, Miami, Florida.

1977

American Conference

Eastern Division

	W	L	T	Pct.	Pts.	OP
Baltimore	10	4	0	.714	295	221
Miami	10	4	0	.714	313	197
New England	9	5	0	.643	278	217
N.Y. Jets	3	11	0	.214	191	300
Buffalo	3	11	0	.214	160	313

Central Division

	W	L	T	Pct.	Pts.	OP
Pittsburgh	9	5	0	.643	283	243
Houston	8	6	0	.571	299	230
Cincinnati	8	6	0	.571	238	235
Cleveland	6	8	0	.429	269	267

Western Division

	W	L	T	Pct.	Pts.	OP
Denver	12	2	0	.857	274	148
Oakland*	11	3	0	.786	351	230
San Diego	7	7	0	.500	222	205
Seattle	5	9	0	.357	282	373
Kansas City	2	12	0	.143	225	349

National Conference

Eastern Division

	W	L	T	Pct.	Pts.	OP
Dallas	12	2	0	.857	345	212
Washington	9	5	0	.643	196	189
St. Louis	7	7	0	.500	272	287
Philadelphia	5	9	0	.357	220	207
N.Y. Giants	5	9	0	.357	181	265

Central Division

	W	L	T	Pct.	Pts.	OP
Minnesota	9	5	0	.643	231	227
Chicago*	9	5	0	.643	255	253
Detroit	6	8	0	.429	183	252
Green Bay	4	10	0	.286	134	219
Tampa Bay	2	12	0	.143	103	223

Western Division

	W	L	T	Pct.	Pts.	OP
Los Angeles	10	4	0	.714	302	146
Atlanta	7	7	0	.500	179	129
San Francisco	5	9	0	.357	220	260
New Orleans	3	11	0	.214	232	336

*Wild Card qualifier for playoffs

Baltimore won division title on the basis of a better conference record than Miami (9-3 to 8-4). Chicago won a Wild Card berth over Washington on the basis of best net points in conference games (plus 48 net points to plus 4).

Divisional playoffs: DENVER 34, Pittsburgh 21; Oakland 37, BALTIMORE 31 (OT)
AFC championship: DENVER 20, Oakland 17
Divisional playoffs: DALLAS 37, Chicago 7; Minnesota 14, LOS ANGELES 7
NFC championship: DALLAS 23, Minnesota 6
Super Bowl XII: Dallas (NFC) 27, Denver (AFC) 10, at Louisiana Superdome, New Orleans, Louisiana.

1976

American Conference

Eastern Division

	W	L	T	Pct.	Pts.	OP
Baltimore	11	3	0	.786	417	246
New England*	11	3	0	.786	376	236
Miami	6	8	0	.429	263	264
N.Y. Jets	3	11	0	.214	169	383
Buffalo	2	12	0	.143	245	363

Central Division

	W	L	T	Pct.	Pts.	OP
Pittsburgh	10	4	0	.714	342	138
Cincinnati	10	4	0	.714	335	210
Cleveland	9	5	0	.643	267	287
Houston	5	9	0	.357	222	273

Western Division

	W	L	T	Pct.	Pts.	OP
Oakland	13	1	0	.929	350	237
Denver	9	5	0	.643	315	206
San Diego	6	8	0	.429	248	285
Kansas City	5	9	0	.357	290	376
Tampa Bay	0	14	0	.000	125	412

National Conference

Eastern Division

	W	L	T	Pct.	Pts.	OP
Dallas	11	3	0	.786	296	194
Washington*	10	4	0	.714	291	217
St. Louis	10	4	0	.714	309	267
Philadelphia	4	10	0	.286	165	286
N.Y. Giants	3	11	0	.214	170	250

Central Division

	W	L	T	Pct.	Pts.	OP
Minnesota	11	2	1	.821	305	176
Chicago	7	7	0	.500	253	216
Detroit	6	8	0	.429	262	220
Green Bay	5	9	0	.357	218	299

Western Division

	W	L	T	Pct.	Pts.	OP
Los Angeles	10	3	1	.750	351	190
San Francisco	8	6	0	.571	270	190
Atlanta	4	10	0	.286	172	312
New Orleans	4	10	0	.286	253	346
Seattle	2	12	0	.143	229	429

*Wild Card qualifier for playoffs

Baltimore won division title on the basis of a better division record than New England (7-1 to 6-2). Pittsburgh won division title because of a two-game sweep over Cincinnati. Washington won Wild Card berth over St. Louis because of a two-game sweep over Cardinals.

Divisional playoffs: OAKLAND 24, New England 21; Pittsburgh 40, BALTIMORE 14
AFC championship: OAKLAND 24, Pittsburgh 7
Divisional playoffs: MINNESOTA 35, Washington 20; Los Angeles 14, DALLAS 12
NFC championship: MINNESOTA 24, Los Angeles 13
Super Bowl XI: Oakland (AFC) 32, Minnesota (NFC) 14, at Rose Bowl, Pasadena, California.

1975

American Conference

Eastern Division

	W	L	T	Pct.	Pts.	OP
Baltimore	10	4	0	.714	395	269
Miami	10	4	0	.714	357	222
Buffalo	8	6	0	.571	420	355
New England	3	11	0	.214	258	358
N.Y. Jets	3	11	0	.214	258	433

Central Division

	W	L	T	Pct.	Pts.	OP
Pittsburgh	12	2	0	.857	373	162
Cincinnati*	11	3	0	.786	340	246
Houston	10	4	0	.714	293	226
Cleveland	3	11	0	.214	218	372

Western Division

	W	L	T	Pct.	Pts.	OP
Oakland	11	3	0	.786	375	255
Denver	6	8	0	.429	254	307
Kansas City	5	9	0	.357	282	341
San Diego	2	12	0	.143	189	345

National Conference

Eastern Division

	W	L	T	Pct.	Pts.	OP
St. Louis	11	3	0	.786	356	276
Dallas*	10	4	0	.714	350	268
Washington	8	6	0	.571	325	276
N.Y. Giants	5	9	0	.357	216	306
Philadelphia	4	10	0	.286	225	302

Central Division

	W	L	T	Pct.	Pts.	OP
Minnesota	12	2	0	.857	377	180
Detroit	7	7	0	.500	245	262
Chicago	4	10	0	.286	191	379
Green Bay	4	10	0	.286	226	285

Western Division

	W	L	T	Pct.	Pts.	OP
Los Angeles	12	2	0	.857	312	135
San Francisco	5	9	0	.357	255	286
Atlanta	4	10	0	.286	240	289
New Orleans	2	12	0	.143	165	360

*Wild Card qualifier for playoffs

Baltimore won division title on the basis of a two-game sweep over Miami.

Divisional playoffs: PITTSBURGH 28, Baltimore 10; OAKLAND 31, Cincinnati 28
AFC championship: PITTSBURGH 16, Oakland 10
Divisional playoffs: LOS ANGELES 35, St. Louis 23; Dallas 17, MINNESOTA 14
NFC championship: Dallas 37, LOS ANGELES 7
Super Bowl X: Pittsburgh (AFC) 21, Dallas (NFC) 17, at Orange Bowl, Miami, Florida.

1974

American Conference
Eastern Division

	W	L	T	Pct.	Pts.	OP
Miami	11	3	0	.786	327	216
Buffalo*	9	5	0	.643	264	244
New England	7	7	0	.500	348	289
N.Y. Jets	7	7	0	.500	279	300
Baltimore	2	12	0	.143	190	329

Central Division

	W	L	T	Pct.	Pts.	OP
Pittsburgh	10	3	1	.750	305	189
Cincinnati	7	7	0	.500	283	259
Houston	7	7	0	.500	236	282
Cleveland	4	10	0	.286	251	344

Western Division

	W	L	T	Pct.	Pts.	OP
Oakland	12	2	0	.857	355	228
Denver	7	6	1	.536	302	294
Kansas City	5	9	0	.357	233	293
San Diego	5	9	0	.357	212	285

National Conference
Eastern Division

	W	L	T	Pct.	Pts.	OP
St. Louis	10	4	0	.714	285	218
Washington*	10	4	0	.714	320	196
Dallas	8	6	0	.571	297	235
Philadelphia	7	7	0	.500	242	217
N.Y. Giants	2	12	0	.143	195	299

Central Division

	W	L	T	Pct.	Pts.	OP
Minnesota	10	4	0	.714	310	195
Detroit	7	7	0	.500	256	270
Green Bay	6	8	0	.429	210	206
Chicago	4	10	0	.286	152	279

Western Division

	W	L	T	Pct.	Pts.	OP
Los Angeles	10	4	0	.714	263	181
San Francisco	6	8	0	.429	226	236
New Orleans	5	9	0	.357	166	263
Atlanta	3	11	0	.214	111	271

*Wild Card qualifier for playoffs
St. Louis won division title because of a two-game sweep over Washington.
Divisional playoffs: OAKLAND 28, Miami 26; PITTSBURGH 32, Buffalo 14
AFC championship: Pittsburgh 24, OAKLAND 13
Divisional playoffs: MINNESOTA 30, St. Louis 14; LOS ANGELES 19, Washington 10
NFC championship: MINNESOTA 14, Los Angeles 10
Super Bowl IX: Pittsburgh (AFC) 16, Minnesota (NFC) 6, at Tulane Stadium, New Orleans, Louisiana.

1973

American Conference
Eastern Division

	W	L	T	Pct.	Pts.	OP
Miami	12	2	0	.857	343	150
Buffalo	9	5	0	.643	259	230
New England	5	9	0	.357	258	300
Baltimore	4	10	0	.286	226	341
N.Y. Jets	4	10	0	.286	240	306

Central Division

	W	L	T	Pct.	Pts.	OP
Cincinnati	10	4	0	.714	286	231
Pittsburgh*	10	4	0	.714	347	210
Cleveland	7	5	2	.571	234	255
Houston	1	13	0	.071	199	447

Western Division

	W	L	T	Pct.	Pts.	OP
Oakland	9	4	1	.679	292	175
Denver	7	5	2	.571	354	296
Kansas City	7	5	2	.571	231	192
San Diego	2	11	1	.179	188	386

National Conference
Eastern Division

	W	L	T	Pct.	Pts.	OP
Dallas	10	4	0	.714	382	203
Washington*	10	4	0	.714	325	198
Philadelphia	5	8	1	.393	310	393
St. Louis	4	9	1	.321	286	365
N.Y. Giants	2	11	1	.179	226	362

Central Division

	W	L	T	Pct.	Pts.	OP
Minnesota	12	2	0	.857	296	168
Detroit	6	7	1	.464	271	247
Green Bay	5	7	2	.429	202	259
Chicago	3	11	0	.214	195	334

Western Division

	W	L	T	Pct.	Pts.	OP
Los Angeles	12	2	0	.857	388	178
Atlanta	9	5	0	.643	318	224
New Orleans	5	9	0	.357	163	312
San Francisco	5	9	0	.357	262	319

*Wild Card qualifier for playoffs
Cincinnati won division title on the basis of a better conference record than Pittsburgh (8-3 to 7-4). Dallas won division title on the basis of a better point differential vs. Washington (net 13 points).
Divisional playoffs: OAKLAND 33, Pittsburgh 14; MIAMI 34, Cincinnati 16
AFC championship: MIAMI 27, Oakland 10
Divisional playoffs: MINNESOTA 27, Washington 20; DALLAS 27, Los Angeles 16
NFC championship: Minnesota 27, DALLAS 10
Super Bowl VIII: Miami (AFC) 24, Minnesota (NFC) 7, at Rice Stadium, Houston, Texas.

1972

American Conference
Eastern Division

	W	L	T	Pct.	Pts.	OP
Miami	14	0	0	1.000	385	171
N.Y. Jets	7	7	0	.500	367	324
Baltimore	5	9	0	.357	235	252
Buffalo	4	9	1	.321	257	377
New England	3	11	0	.214	192	446

Central Division

	W	L	T	Pct.	Pts.	OP
Pittsburgh	11	3	0	.786	343	175
Cleveland*	10	4	0	.714	268	249
Cincinnati	8	6	0	.571	299	229
Houston	1	13	0	.071	164	380

Western Division

	W	L	T	Pct.	Pts.	OP
Oakland	10	3	1	.750	365	248
Kansas City	8	6	0	.571	287	254
Denver	5	9	0	.357	325	350
San Diego	4	9	1	.321	264	344

National Conference
Eastern Division

	W	L	T	Pct.	Pts.	OP
Washington	11	3	0	.786	336	218
Dallas*	10	4	0	.714	319	240
N.Y. Giants	8	6	0	.571	331	247
St. Louis	4	9	1	.321	193	303
Philadelphia	2	11	1	.179	145	352

Central Division

	W	L	T	Pct.	Pts.	OP
Green Bay	10	4	0	.714	304	226
Detroit	8	5	1	.607	339	290
Minnesota	7	7	0	.500	301	252
Chicago	4	9	1	.321	225	275

Western Division

	W	L	T	Pct.	Pts.	OP
San Francisco	8	5	1	.607	353	249
Atlanta	7	7	0	.500	269	274
Los Angeles	6	7	1	.464	291	286
New Orleans	2	11	1	.179	215	361

*Wild Card qualifier for playoffs
Divisional playoffs: PITTSBURGH 13, Oakland 7; MIAMI 20, Cleveland 14
AFC championship: Miami 21, PITTSBURGH 17
Divisional playoffs: Dallas 30, SAN FRANCISCO 28; WASHINGTON 16, Green Bay 3
NFC championship: WASHINGTON 26, Dallas 3
Super Bowl VII: Miami (AFC) 14, Washington (NFC) 7, at Memorial Coliseum, Los Angeles, California.

1971

American Conference
Eastern Division

	W	L	T	Pct.	Pts.	OP
Miami	10	3	1	.769	315	174
Baltimore*	10	4	0	.714	313	140
New England	6	8	0	.429	238	325
N.Y. Jets	6	8	0	.429	212	299
Buffalo	1	13	0	.071	184	394

Central Division

	W	L	T	Pct.	Pts.	OP
Cleveland	9	5	0	.643	285	273
Pittsburgh	6	8	0	.429	246	292
Houston	4	9	1	.308	251	330
Cincinnati	4	10	0	.286	284	265

Western Division

	W	L	T	Pct.	Pts.	OP
Kansas City	10	3	1	.769	302	208
Oakland	8	4	2	.667	344	278
San Diego	6	8	0	.429	311	341
Denver	4	9	1	.308	203	275

National Conference
Eastern Division

	W	L	T	Pct.	Pts.	OP
Dallas	11	3	0	.786	406	222
Washington*	9	4	1	.692	276	190
Philadelphia	6	7	1	.462	221	302
St. Louis	4	9	1	.308	231	279
N.Y. Giants	4	10	0	.286	228	362

Central Division

	W	L	T	Pct.	Pts.	OP
Minnesota	11	3	0	.786	245	139
Detroit	7	6	1	.538	341	286
Chicago	6	8	0	.429	185	276
Green Bay	4	8	2	.333	274	298

Western Division

	W	L	T	Pct.	Pts.	OP
San Francisco	9	5	0	.643	300	216
Los Angeles	8	5	1	.615	313	260
Atlanta	7	6	1	.538	274	277
New Orleans	4	8	2	.333	266	347

*Wild Card qualifier for playoffs
Divisional playoffs: Miami 27, KANSAS CITY 24 (OT); Baltimore 20, CLEVELAND 3
AFC championship: MIAMI 21, Baltimore 0
Divisional playoffs: Dallas 20, MINNESOTA 12; SAN FRANCISCO 24, Washington 20
NFC championship: DALLAS 14, San Francisco 3
Super Bowl VI: Dallas (NFC) 24, Miami (AFC) 3, at Tulane Stadium, New Orleans, Louisiana.

1970

American Conference
Eastern Division

	W	L	T	Pct.	Pts.	OP
Baltimore	11	2	1	.846	321	234
Miami*	10	4	0	.714	297	228
N.Y. Jets	4	10	0	.286	255	286
Buffalo	3	10	1	.231	204	337
Boston Patriots	2	12	0	.143	149	361

Central Division

	W	L	T	Pct.	Pts.	OP
Cincinnati	8	6	0	.571	312	255
Cleveland	7	7	0	.500	286	265
Pittsburgh	5	9	0	.357	210	272
Houston	3	10	1	.231	217	352

Western Division

	W	L	T	Pct.	Pts.	OP
Oakland	8	4	2	.667	300	293
Kansas City	7	5	2	.583	272	244
San Diego	5	6	3	.455	282	278
Denver	5	8	1	.385	253	264

National Conference
Eastern Division

	W	L	T	Pct.	Pts.	OP
Dallas	10	4	0	.714	299	221
N.Y. Giants	9	5	0	.643	301	270
St. Louis	8	5	1	.615	325	228
Washington	6	8	0	.429	297	314
Philadelphia	3	10	1	.231	241	332

Central Division

	W	L	T	Pct.	Pts.	OP
Minnesota	12	2	0	.857	335	143
Detroit*	10	4	0	.714	347	202
Chicago	6	8	0	.429	256	261
Green Bay	6	8	0	.429	196	293

Western Division

	W	L	T	Pct.	Pts.	OP
San Francisco	10	3	1	.769	352	267
Los Angeles	9	4	1	.692	325	202
Atlanta	4	8	2	.333	206	261
New Orleans	2	11	1	.154	172	347

*Wild Card qualifier for playoffs
Divisional playoffs: BALTIMORE 17, Cincinnati 0; OAKLAND 21, Miami 14
AFC championship: BALTIMORE 27, Oakland 17
Divisional playoffs: DALLAS 5, Detroit 0; San Francisco 17, MINNESOTA 14
NFC championship: Dallas 17, SAN FRANCISCO 10
Super Bowl V: Baltimore (AFC) 16, Dallas (NFC) 13, at Orange Bowl, Miami, Florida.

1969 NFL

Eastern Conference
Capitol Division

	W	L	T	Pct.	Pts.	OP
Dallas	11	2	1	.846	369	223
Washington	7	5	2	.583	307	319
New Orleans	5	9	0	.357	311	393
Philadelphia	4	9	1	.308	279	377

Century Division

	W	L	T	Pct.	Pts.	OP
Cleveland	10	3	1	.769	351	300
N.Y. Giants	6	8	0	.429	264	298
St. Louis	4	9	1	.308	314	389
Pittsburgh	1	13	0	.071	218	404

Western Conference
Coastal Division

	W	L	T	Pct.	Pts.	OP
Los Angeles	11	3	0	.786	320	243
Baltimore	8	5	1	.615	279	268
Atlanta	6	8	0	.429	276	268
San Francisco	4	8	2	.333	277	319

Central Division

	W	L	T	Pct.	Pts.	OP
Minnesota	12	2	0	.857	379	133
Detroit	9	4	1	.692	259	188
Green Bay	8	6	0	.571	269	221
Chicago	1	13	0	.071	210	339

Conference championships: Cleveland 38, DALLAS 14; MINNESOTA 23, Los Angeles 20
NFL championship: MINNESOTA 27, Cleveland 7
Super Bowl IV: Kansas City (AFL) 23, Minnesota (NFL) 7, at Tulane Stadium, New Orleans, Louisiana.

1969 AFL

Eastern Division

	W	L	T	Pct.	Pts.	OP
N.Y. Jets	10	4	0	.714	353	269
Houston	6	6	2	.500	278	279
Boston Patriots	4	10	0	.286	266	316
Buffalo	4	10	0	.286	230	359
Miami	3	10	1	.231	233	332

Western Division

	W	L	T	Pct.	Pts.	OP
Oakland	12	1	1	.923	377	242
Kansas City	11	3	0	.786	359	177
San Diego	8	6	0	.571	288	276
Denver	5	8	1	.385	297	344
Cincinnati	4	9	1	.308	280	367

Divisional Playoffs: Kansas City 13, N.Y. JETS 6; OAKLAND 56, Houston 7
AFL championship: Kansas City 17, OAKLAND 7

1968 NFL

Eastern Conference

Capitol Division

	W	L	T	Pct.	Pts.	OP
Dallas	12	2	0	.857	431	186
N.Y. Giants	7	7	0	.500	294	325
Washington	5	9	0	.357	249	358
Philadelphia	2	12	0	.143	202	351

Century Division

	W	L	T	Pct.	Pts.	OP
Cleveland	10	4	0	.714	394	273
St. Louis	9	4	1	.692	325	289
New Orleans	4	9	1	.308	246	327
Pittsburgh	2	11	1	.154	244	397

Western Conference

Coastal Division

	W	L	T	Pct.	Pts.	OP
Baltimore	13	1	0	.929	402	144
Los Angeles	10	3	1	.769	312	200
San Francisco	7	6	1	.538	303	310
Atlanta	2	12	0	.143	170	389

Central Division

	W	L	T	Pct.	Pts.	OP
Minnesota	8	6	0	.571	282	242
Chicago	7	7	0	.500	250	333
Green Bay	6	7	1	.462	281	227
Detroit	4	8	2	.333	207	241

Conference championships: CLEVELAND 31, Dallas 20; BALTIMORE 24, Minnesota 14
NFL championship: Baltimore 34, CLEVELAND 0
Super Bowl III: N.Y. Jets (AFL) 16, Baltimore (NFL) 7, at Orange Bowl, Miami, Florida.

1968 AFL

Eastern Division

	W	L	T	Pct.	Pts.	OP
N.Y. Jets	11	3	0	.786	419	280
Houston	7	7	0	.500	303	248
Miami	5	8	1	.385	276	355
Boston Patriots	4	10	0	.286	229	406
Buffalo	1	12	1	.077	199	367

Western Division

	W	L	T	Pct.	Pts.	OP
Oakland	12	2	0	.857	453	233
Kansas City	12	2	0	.857	371	170
San Diego	9	5	0	.643	382	310
Denver	5	9	0	.357	255	404
Cincinnati	3	11	0	.214	215	329

Western Division playoff: OAKLAND 41, Kansas City 6
AFL championship: N.Y. JETS 27, Oakland 23

1967 NFL

Eastern Conference

Capitol Division

	W	L	T	Pct.	Pts.	OP
Dallas	9	5	0	.643	342	268
Philadelphia	6	7	1	.462	351	409
Washington	5	6	3	.455	347	353
New Orleans	3	11	0	.214	233	379

Century Division

	W	L	T	Pct.	Pts.	OP
Cleveland	9	5	0	.643	334	297
N.Y. Giants	7	7	0	.500	369	379
St. Louis	6	7	1	.462	333	356
Pittsburgh	4	9	1	.308	281	320

Western Conference

Coastal Division

	W	L	T	Pct.	Pts.	OP
Los Angeles	11	1	2	.917	398	196
Baltimore	11	1	2	.917	394	198
San Francisco	7	7	0	.500	273	337
Atlanta	1	12	1	.077	175	422

Central Division

	W	L	T	Pct.	Pts.	OP
Green Bay	9	4	1	.692	332	209
Chicago	7	6	1	.538	239	218
Detroit	5	7	2	.417	260	259
Minnesota	3	8	3	.273	233	294

Los Angeles won division title on the basis of advantage in points (58-34) in two games vs. Baltimore.
Conference championships: DALLAS 52, Cleveland 14; GREEN BAY 28, Los Angeles 7
NFL championship: GREEN BAY 21, Dallas 17
Super Bowl II: Green Bay (NFL) 33, Oakland (AFL) 14, at Orange Bowl, Miami, Florida.

1967 AFL

Eastern Division

	W	L	T	Pct.	Pts.	OP
Houston	9	4	1	.692	258	199
N.Y. Jets	8	5	1	.615	371	329
Buffalo	4	10	0	.286	237	285
Miami	4	10	0	.286	219	407
Boston Patriots	3	10	1	.231	280	389

Western Division

	W	L	T	Pct.	Pts.	OP
Oakland	13	1	0	.929	468	233
Kansas City	9	5	0	.643	408	254
San Diego	8	5	1	.615	360	352
Denver	3	11	0	.214	256	409

AFL championship: OAKLAND 40, Houston 7

1966 NFL

Eastern Conference

	W	L	T	Pct.	Pts.	OP
Dallas	10	3	1	.769	445	239
Cleveland	9	5	0	.643	403	259
Philadelphia	9	5	0	.643	326	340
St. Louis	8	5	1	.615	264	265
Washington	7	7	0	.500	351	355
Pittsburgh	5	8	1	.385	316	347
Atlanta	3	11	0	.214	204	437
N.Y. Giants	1	12	1	.077	263	501

Western Conference

	W	L	T	Pct.	Pts.	OP
Green Bay	12	2	0	.857	335	163
Baltimore	9	5	0	.643	314	226
Los Angeles	8	6	0	.571	289	212
San Francisco	6	6	2	.500	320	325
Chicago	5	7	2	.417	234	272
Detroit	4	9	1	.308	206	317
Minnesota	4	9	1	.308	292	304

NFL championship: Green Bay 34, DALLAS 27
Super Bowl I: Green Bay (NFL) 35, Kansas City (AFL) 10, at Memorial Coliseum, Los Angeles, California.

1966 AFL

Eastern Division

	W	L	T	Pct.	Pts.	OP
Buffalo	9	4	1	.692	358	255
Boston Patriots	8	4	2	.677	315	283
N.Y. Jets	6	6	2	.500	322	312
Houston	3	11	0	.214	335	396
Miami	3	11	0	.214	213	362

Western Division

	W	L	T	Pct.	Pts.	OP
Kansas City	11	2	1	.846	448	276
Oakland	8	5	1	.615	315	288
San Diego	7	6	1	.538	335	284
Denver	4	10	0	.286	196	381

AFL championship: Kansas City 31, BUFFALO 7

1965 NFL

Eastern Conference

	W	L	T	Pct.	Pts.	OP
Cleveland	11	3	0	.786	363	325
Dallas	7	7	0	.500	325	280
N.Y. Giants	7	7	0	.500	270	338
Washington	6	8	0	.429	257	301
Philadelphia	5	9	0	.357	363	359
St. Louis	5	9	0	.357	296	309
Pittsburgh	2	12	0	.143	202	397

Western Conference

	W	L	T	Pct.	Pts.	OP
Green Bay	10	3	1	.769	316	224
Baltimore	10	3	1	.769	389	284
Chicago	9	5	0	.643	409	275
San Francisco	7	6	1	.538	421	402
Minnesota	7	7	0	.500	383	403
Detroit	6	7	1	.462	257	295
Los Angeles	4	10	0	.286	269	328

Western Conference playoff: GREEN BAY 13, Baltimore 10 (OT)
NFL championship: GREEN BAY 23, Cleveland 12

1965 AFL

Eastern Division

	W	L	T	Pct.	Pts.	OP
Buffalo	10	3	1	.769	313	226
N.Y. Jets	5	8	1	.385	285	303
Boston Patriots	4	8	2	.333	244	302
Houston	4	10	0	.286	298	429

Western Division

	W	L	T	Pct.	Pts.	OP
San Diego	9	2	3	.818	340	227
Oakland	8	5	1	.615	298	239
Kansas City	7	5	2	.583	322	285
Denver	4	10	0	.286	303	392

AFL championship: Buffalo 23, SAN DIEGO 0

1964 NFL

Eastern Conference

	W	L	T	Pct.	Pts.	OP
Cleveland	10	3	1	.769	415	293
St. Louis	9	3	2	.750	357	331
Philadelphia	6	8	0	.429	312	313
Washington	6	8	0	.429	307	305
Dallas	5	8	1	.385	250	289
Pittsburgh	5	9	0	.357	253	315
N.Y. Giants	2	10	2	.167	241	399

Western Conference

	W	L	T	Pct.	Pts.	OP
Baltimore	12	2	0	.857	428	225
Green Bay	8	5	1	.615	342	245
Minnesota	8	5	1	.615	355	296
Detroit	7	5	2	.583	280	260
Los Angeles	5	7	2	.417	283	339
Chicago	5	9	0	.357	260	379
San Francisco	4	10	0	.286	236	330

NFL championship: CLEVELAND 27, Baltimore 0

1964 AFL

Eastern Division

	W	L	T	Pct.	Pts.	OP
Buffalo	12	2	0	.857	400	242
Boston Patriots	10	3	1	.769	365	297
N.Y. Jets	5	8	1	.385	278	315
Houston	4	10	0	.286	310	355

Western Division

	W	L	T	Pct.	Pts.	OP
San Diego	8	5	1	.615	341	300
Kansas City	7	7	0	.500	366	306
Oakland	5	7	2	.417	303	350
Denver	2	11	1	.154	240	438

AFL championship: BUFFALO 20, San Diego 7

1963 NFL

Eastern Conference

	W	L	T	Pct.	Pts.	OP
N.Y. Giants	11	3	0	.786	448	280
Cleveland	10	4	0	.714	343	262
St. Louis	9	5	0	.643	341	283
Pittsburgh	7	4	3	.636	321	295
Dallas	4	10	0	.286	305	378
Washington	3	11	0	.214	279	398
Philadelphia	2	10	2	.167	242	381

Western Conference

	W	L	T	Pct.	Pts.	OP
Chicago	11	1	2	.917	301	144
Green Bay	11	2	1	.846	369	206
Baltimore	8	6	0	.571	316	285
Detroit	5	8	1	.385	326	265
Minnesota	5	8	1	.385	309	390
Los Angeles	5	9	0	.357	210	350
San Francisco	2	12	0	.143	198	391

NFL championship: CHICAGO 14, N.Y. Giants 10

1963 AFL

Eastern Division

	W	L	T	Pct.	Pts.	OP
Boston Patriots	7	6	1	.538	327	257
Buffalo	7	6	1	.538	304	291
Houston	6	8	0	.429	302	372
N.Y. Jets	5	8	1	.385	249	399

Western Division

	W	L	T	Pct.	Pts.	OP
San Diego	11	3	0	.786	399	256
Oakland	10	4	0	.714	363	288
Kansas City	5	7	2	.417	347	263
Denver	2	11	1	.154	301	473

Eastern Division playoff: Boston 26, BUFFALO 8
AFL championship: SAN DIEGO 51, Boston 10

1962 NFL

Eastern Conference

	W	L	T	Pct.	Pts.	OP
N.Y. Giants	12	2	0	.857	398	283
Pittsburgh	9	5	0	.643	312	363
Cleveland	7	6	1	.538	291	257
Washington	5	7	2	.417	305	376
Dallas Cowboys	5	8	1	.385	398	402
St. Louis	4	9	1	.308	287	361
Philadelphia	3	10	1	.231	282	356

Western Conference

	W	L	T	Pct.	Pts.	OP
Green Bay	13	1	0	.929	415	148
Detroit	11	3	0	.786	315	177
Chicago	9	5	0	.643	321	287
Baltimore	7	7	0	.500	293	288
San Francisco	6	8	0	.429	282	331
Minnesota	2	11	1	.154	254	410
Los Angeles	1	12	1	.077	220	334

NFL championship: Green Bay 16, N.Y. GIANTS 7

1962 AFL

Eastern Division

	W	L	T	Pct.	Pts.	OP
Houston	11	3	0	.786	387	270
Boston Patriots	9	4	1	.692	346	295
Buffalo	7	6	1	.538	309	272
N.Y. Titans	5	9	0	.357	278	423

Western Division

	W	L	T	Pct.	Pts.	OP
Dallas Texans	11	3	0	.786	389	233
Denver	7	7	0	.500	353	334
San Diego	4	10	0	.286	314	392
Oakland	1	13	0	.071	213	370

AFL championship: Dallas Texans 20, HOUSTON 17 (OT)

1961 NFL

Eastern Conference

	W	L	T	Pct.	Pts.	OP
N.Y. Giants	10	3	1	.769	368	220
Philadelphia	10	4	0	.714	361	297
Cleveland	8	5	1	.615	319	270
St. Louis	7	7	0	.500	279	267
Pittsburgh	6	8	0	.429	295	287
Dallas Cowboys	4	9	1	.308	236	380
Washington	1	12	1	.077	174	392

Western Conference

	W	L	T	Pct.	Pts.	OP
Green Bay	11	3	0	.786	391	223
Detroit	8	5	1	.615	270	258
Baltimore	8	6	0	.571	302	307
Chicago	8	6	0	.571	326	302
San Francisco	7	6	1	.538	346	272
Los Angeles	4	10	0	.286	263	333
Minnesota	3	11	0	.214	285	407

NFL championship: GREEN BAY 37, N.Y. Giants 0

1961 AFL

Eastern Division

	W	L	T	Pct.	Pts.	OP
Houston	10	3	1	.769	513	242
Boston Patriots	9	4	1	.692	413	313
N.Y. Titans	7	7	0	.500	301	390
Buffalo	6	8	0	.429	294	342

Western Division

	W	L	T	Pct.	Pts.	OP
San Diego	12	2	0	.857	396	219
Dallas Texans	6	8	0	.429	334	343
Denver	3	11	0	.214	251	432
Oakland	2	12	0	.143	237	458

AFL championship: Houston 10, SAN DIEGO 3

1960 NFL

Eastern Conference	W	L	T	Pct.	Pts.	OP
Philadelphia	10	2	0	.833	321	246
Cleveland	8	3	1	.727	362	217
N.Y. Giants	6	4	2	.600	271	261
St. Louis	6	5	1	.545	288	230
Pittsburgh	5	6	1	.455	240	275
Washington	1	9	2	.100	178	309

Western Conference	W	L	T	Pct.	Pts.	OP
Green Bay	8	4	0	.667	332	209
Detroit	7	5	0	.583	239	212
San Francisco	7	5	0	.583	208	205
Baltimore	6	6	0	.500	288	234
Chicago	5	6	1	.455	194	299
L.A. Rams	4	7	1	.364	265	297
Dallas Cowboys	0	11	1	.000	177	369

NFL championship: PHILADELPHIA 17, Green Bay 13

1960 AFL

Eastern Conference	W	L	T	Pct.	Pts.	OP
Houston	10	4	0	.714	379	285
N.Y. Titans	7	7	0	.500	382	399
Buffalo	5	8	1	.385	296	303
Boston	5	9	0	.357	286	349

Western Conference	W	L	T	Pct.	Pts.	OP
L.A. Chargers	10	4	0	.714	373	336
Dallas Texans	8	6	0	.571	362	253
Oakland	6	8	0	.429	319	388
Denver	4	9	1	.308	309	393

AFL championship: HOUSTON 24, L.A. Chargers 16

1959

Eastern Conference	W	L	T	Pct.	Pts.	OP
N.Y. Giants	10	2	0	.833	284	170
Cleveland	7	5	0	.583	270	214
Philadelphia	7	5	0	.583	268	278
Pittsburgh	6	5	1	.545	257	216
Washington	3	9	0	.250	185	350
Chi. Cardinals	2	10	0	.167	234	324

Western Conference	W	L	T	Pct.	Pts.	OP
Baltimore	9	3	0	.750	374	251
Chi. Bears	8	4	0	.667	252	196
Green Bay	7	5	0	.583	248	246
San Francisco	7	5	0	.583	255	237
Detroit	3	8	1	.273	203	275
Los Angeles	2	10	0	.167	242	315

NFL championship: BALTIMORE 31, N.Y. Giants 16

1958

Eastern Conference	W	L	T	Pct.	Pts.	OP
N.Y. Giants	9	3	0	.750	246	183
Cleveland	9	3	0	.750	302	217
Pittsburgh	7	4	1	.636	261	230
Washington	4	7	1	.364	214	268
Chi. Cardinals	2	9	1	.182	261	356
Philadelphia	2	9	1	.182	235	306

Western Conference	W	L	T	Pct.	Pts.	OP
Baltimore	9	3	0	.750	381	203
Chi. Bears	8	4	0	.667	298	230
Los Angeles	8	4	0	.667	344	278
San Francisco	6	6	0	.500	257	324
Detroit	4	7	1	.364	261	276
Green Bay	1	10	1	.091	193	382

Eastern Conference playoff: N.Y. GIANTS 10, Cleveland 0
NFL championship: Baltimore 23, N.Y. GIANTS 17 (OT)

1957

Eastern Conference	W	L	T	Pct.	Pts.	OP
Cleveland	9	2	1	.818	269	172
N.Y. Giants	7	5	0	.583	254	211
Pittsburgh	6	6	0	.500	161	178
Washington	5	6	1	.455	251	230
Philadelphia	4	8	0	.333	173	230
Chi. Cardinals	3	9	0	.250	200	299

Western Conference	W	L	T	Pct.	Pts.	OP
Detroit	8	4	0	.667	251	231
San Francisco	8	4	0	.667	260	264
Baltimore	7	5	0	.583	303	235
Los Angeles	6	6	0	.500	307	278
Chi. Bears	5	7	0	.417	203	211
Green Bay	3	9	0	.250	218	311

Western Conference playoff: Detroit 31, SAN FRANCISCO 27
NFL championship: DETROIT 59, Cleveland 14

1956

Eastern Conference	W	L	T	Pct.	Pts.	OP
N.Y. Giants	8	3	1	.727	264	197
Chi. Cardinals	7	5	0	.583	240	182
Washington	6	6	0	.500	183	225
Cleveland	5	7	0	.417	167	177
Pittsburgh	5	7	0	.417	217	250
Philadelphia	3	8	1	.273	143	215

Western Conference	W	L	T	Pct.	Pts.	OP
Chi. Bears	9	2	1	.818	363	246
Detroit	9	3	0	.750	300	188
San Francisco	5	6	1	.455	233	284
Baltimore	5	7	0	.417	270	322
Green Bay	4	8	0	.333	264	342
Los Angeles	4	8	0	.333	291	307

NFL championship: N.Y. GIANTS 47, Chi. Bears 7

1955

Eastern Conference	W	L	T	Pct.	Pts.	OP
Cleveland	9	2	1	.818	349	218
Washington	8	4	0	.667	246	222
N.Y. Giants	6	5	1	.545	267	223
Chi. Cardinals	4	7	1	.364	224	252
Philadelphia	4	7	1	.364	248	231
Pittsburgh	4	8	0	.333	195	285

Western Conference	W	L	T	Pct.	Pts.	OP
Los Angeles	8	3	1	.727	260	231
Chi. Bears	8	4	0	.667	294	251
Green Bay	6	6	0	.500	258	276
Baltimore	5	6	1	.455	214	239
San Francisco	4	8	0	.333	216	298
Detroit	3	9	0	.250	230	275

NFL championship: Cleveland 38, LOS ANGELES 14

1954

Eastern Conference	W	L	T	Pct.	Pts.	OP
Cleveland	9	3	0	.750	336	162
Philadelphia	7	4	1	.636	284	230
N.Y. Giants	7	5	0	.583	293	184
Pittsburgh	5	7	0	.417	219	263
Washington	3	9	0	.250	207	432
Chi. Cardinals	2	10	0	.167	183	347

Western Conference	W	L	T	Pct.	Pts.	OP
Detroit	9	2	1	.818	337	189
Chi. Bears	8	4	0	.667	301	279
San Francisco	7	4	1	.636	313	251
Los Angeles	6	5	1	.545	314	285
Green Bay	4	8	0	.333	234	251
Baltimore	3	9	0	.250	131	279

NFL championship: CLEVELAND 56, Detroit 10

1953

Eastern Conference	W	L	T	Pct.	Pts.	OP
Cleveland	11	1	0	.917	348	162
Philadelphia	7	4	1	.636	352	215
Washington	6	5	1	.545	208	215
Pittsburgh	6	6	0	.500	211	263
N.Y. Giants	3	9	0	.250	179	277
Chi. Cardinals	1	10	1	.091	190	337

Western Conference	W	L	T	Pct.	Pts.	OP
Detroit	10	2	0	.833	271	205
San Francisco	9	3	0	.750	372	237
Los Angeles	8	3	1	.727	366	236
Chi. Bears	3	8	1	.273	218	262
Baltimore	3	9	0	.250	182	350
Green Bay	2	9	1	.182	200	338

NFL championship: DETROIT 17, Cleveland 16

1952

American Conference	W	L	T	Pct.	Pts.	OP
Cleveland	8	4	0	.667	310	213
N.Y. Giants	7	5	0	.583	234	231
Philadelphia	7	5	0	.583	252	271
Pittsburgh	5	7	0	.417	300	273
Chi. Cardinals	4	8	0	.333	172	221
Washington	4	8	0	.333	240	287

National Conference	W	L	T	Pct.	Pts.	OP
Detroit	9	3	0	.750	344	192
Los Angeles	9	3	0	.750	349	234
San Francisco	7	5	0	.583	285	221
Green Bay	6	6	0	.500	295	312
Chi. Bears	5	7	0	.417	245	326
Dallas Texans	1	11	0	.083	182	427

National Conference playoff: DETROIT 31, Los Angeles 21
NFL championship: Detroit 17, CLEVELAND 7

1951

American Conference	W	L	T	Pct.	Pts.	OP
Cleveland	11	1	0	.917	331	152
N.Y. Giants	9	2	1	.818	254	161
Washington	5	7	0	.417	183	296
Pittsburgh	4	7	1	.364	183	235
Philadelphia	4	8	0	.333	234	264
Chi. Cardinals	3	9	0	.250	210	287

National Conference	W	L	T	Pct.	Pts.	OP
Los Angeles	8	4	0	.667	392	261
Detroit	7	4	1	.636	336	259
San Francisco	7	4	1	.636	255	205
Chi. Bears	7	5	0	.583	286	282
Green Bay	3	9	0	.250	254	375
N.Y. Yanks	1	9	2	.100	241	382

NFL championship: LOS ANGELES 24, Cleveland 17

1950

American Conference	W	L	T	Pct.	Pts.	OP
Cleveland	10	2	0	.833	310	144
N.Y. Giants	10	2	0	.833	268	150
Philadelphia	6	6	0	.500	254	141
Pittsburgh	6	6	0	.500	180	195
Chi. Cardinals	5	7	0	.417	233	287
Washington	3	9	0	.250	232	326

National Conference	W	L	T	Pct.	Pts.	OP
Los Angeles	9	3	0	.750	466	309
Chi. Bears	9	3	0	.750	279	207
N.Y. Yanks	7	5	0	.583	366	367
Detroit	6	6	0	.500	321	285
Green Bay	3	9	0	.250	244	406
San Francisco	3	9	0	.250	213	300
Baltimore	1	11	0	.083	213	462

American Conference playoff: CLEVELAND 8, N.Y. Giants 3
National Conference playoff: LOS ANGELES 24, Chi. Bears 14
NFL championship: CLEVELAND 30, Los Angeles 28

1949

Eastern Division	W	L	T	Pct.	Pts.	OP
Philadelphia	11	1	0	.917	364	134
Pittsburgh	6	5	1	.545	224	214
N.Y. Giants	6	6	0	.500	287	298
Washington	4	7	1	.364	268	339
N.Y. Bulldogs	1	10	1	.091	153	365

Western Division	W	L	T	Pct.	Pts.	OP
Los Angeles	8	2	2	.800	360	239
Chi. Bears	9	3	0	.750	332	218
Chi. Cardinals	6	5	1	.545	360	301
Detroit	4	8	0	.333	237	259
Green Bay	2	10	0	.167	114	329

NFL championship: Philadelphia 14, LOS ANGELES 0

1948

Eastern Division	W	L	T	Pct.	Pts.	OP
Philadelphia	9	2	1	.818	376	156
Washington	7	5	0	.583	291	287
N.Y. Giants	4	8	0	.333	297	388
Pittsburgh	4	8	0	.333	200	243
Boston	3	9	0	.250	174	372

Western Division	W	L	T	Pct.	Pts.	OP
Chi. Cardinals	11	1	0	.917	395	226
Chi. Bears	10	2	0	.833	375	151
Los Angeles	6	5	1	.545	327	269
Green Bay	3	9	0	.250	154	290
Detroit	2	10	0	.167	200	407

NFL championship: PHILADELPHIA 7, Chi. Cardinals 0

1947

Eastern Division	W	L	T	Pct.	Pts.	OP
Philadelphia	8	4	0	.667	308	242
Pittsburgh	8	4	0	.667	240	259
Boston	4	7	1	.364	168	256
Washington	4	8	0	.333	295	367
N.Y. Giants	2	8	2	.200	190	309

Western Division	W	L	T	Pct.	Pts.	OP
Chi. Cardinals	9	3	0	.750	306	231
Chi. Bears	8	4	0	.667	363	241
Green Bay	6	5	1	.545	274	210
Los Angeles	6	6	0	.500	259	214
Detroit	3	9	0	.250	231	305

Eastern Division playoff: Philadelphia 21, PITTSBURGH 0
NFL championship: CHI. CARDINALS 28, Philadelphia 21

1946

Eastern Division	W	L	T	Pct.	Pts.	OP
N.Y. Giants	7	3	1	.700	236	162
Philadelphia	6	5	0	.545	231	220
Washington	5	5	1	.500	171	191
Pittsburgh	5	5	1	.500	136	117
Boston	2	8	1	.200	189	273

Western Division	W	L	T	Pct.	Pts.	OP
Chi. Bears	8	2	1	.800	289	193
Los Angeles	6	4	1	.600	277	257
Green Bay	6	5	0	.545	148	158
Chi. Cardinals	6	5	0	.545	260	198
Detroit	1	10	0	.091	142	310

NFL championship: Chi. Bears 24, N.Y. GIANTS 14

1945

Eastern Division

	W	L	T	Pct.	Pts.	OP
Washington	8	2	0	.800	209	121
Philadelphia	7	3	0	.700	272	133
N.Y. Giants	3	6	1	.333	179	198
Boston	3	6	1	.333	123	211
Pittsburgh	2	8	0	.200	79	220

Western Division

	W	L	T	Pct.	Pts.	OP
Cleveland	9	1	0	.900	244	136
Detroit	7	3	0	.700	195	194
Green Bay	6	4	0	.600	258	173
Chi. Bears	3	7	0	.300	192	235
Chi. Cardinals	1	9	0	.100	98	228

NFL championship: CLEVELAND 15, Washington 14

1944

Eastern Division

	W	L	T	Pct.	Pts.	OP
N.Y. Giants	8	1	1	.889	206	75
Philadelphia	7	1	2	.875	267	131
Washington	6	3	1	.667	169	180
Boston	2	8	0	.200	82	233
Brooklyn	0	10	0	.000	69	166

Western Division

	W	L	T	Pct.	Pts.	OP
Green Bay	8	2	0	.800	238	141
Chi. Bears	6	3	1	.667	258	172
Detroit	6	3	1	.667	216	151
Cleveland	4	6	0	.400	188	224
Card-Pitt	0	10	0	.000	108	328

NFL championship: Green Bay 14, N.Y. GIANTS 7

1943

Eastern Division

	W	L	T	Pct.	Pts.	OP
Washington	6	3	1	.667	229	137
N.Y. Giants	6	3	1	.667	197	170
Phil-Pitt	5	4	1	.556	225	230
Brooklyn	2	8	0	.200	65	234

Western Division

	W	L	T	Pct.	Pts.	OP
Chi. Bears	8	1	1	.889	303	157
Green Bay	7	2	1	.778	264	172
Detroit	3	6	1	.333	178	218
Chi. Cardinals	0	10	0	.000	95	238

Eastern Division playoff: Washington 28, N.Y. GIANTS 0
NFL championship: CHI. BEARS 41, Washington 21

1942

Eastern Division

	W	L	T	Pct.	Pts.	OP
Washington	10	1	0	.909	227	102
Pittsburgh	7	4	0	.636	167	119
N.Y. Giants	5	5	1	.500	155	139
Brooklyn	3	8	0	.273	100	168
Philadelphia	2	9	0	.182	134	239

Western Division

	W	L	T	Pct.	Pts.	OP
Chi. Bears	11	0	0	1.000	376	84
Green Bay	8	2	1	.800	300	215
Cleveland	5	6	0	.455	150	207
Chi. Cardinals	3	8	0	.273	98	209
Detroit	0	11	0	.000	38	263

NFL championship: WASHINGTON 14, Chi. Bears 6

1941

Eastern Division

	W	L	T	Pct.	Pts.	OP
N.Y. Giants	8	3	0	.727	238	114
Brooklyn	7	4	0	.636	158	127
Washington	6	5	0	.545	176	174
Philadelphia	2	8	1	.200	119	218
Pittsburgh	1	9	1	.100	103	276

Western Division

	W	L	T	Pct.	Pts.	OP
Chi. Bears	10	1	0	.909	396	147
Green Bay	10	1	0	.909	258	120
Detroit	4	6	1	.400	121	195
Chi. Cardinals	3	7	1	.300	127	197
Cleveland	2	9	0	.182	116	244

Western Division playoff: CHI. BEARS 33, Green Bay 14
NFL championship: CHI. BEARS 37, N.Y. Giants 9

1940

Eastern Division

	W	L	T	Pct.	Pts.	OP
Washington	9	2	0	.818	245	142
Brooklyn	8	3	0	.727	186	120
N.Y. Giants	6	4	1	.600	131	133
Pittsburgh	2	7	2	.222	60	178
Philadelphia	1	10	0	.091	111	211

Western Division

	W	L	T	Pct.	Pts.	OP
Chi. Bears	8	3	0	.727	238	152
Green Bay	6	4	1	.600	238	155
Detroit	5	5	1	.500	138	153
Cleveland	4	6	1	.400	171	191
Chi. Cardinals	2	7	2	.222	139	222

NFL championship: Chi. Bears 73, WASHINGTON 0

1939

Eastern Division

	W	L	T	Pct.	Pts.	OP
N.Y. Giants	9	1	1	.900	168	85
Washington	8	2	1	.800	242	94
Brooklyn	4	6	1	.400	108	219
Philadelphia	1	9	1	.100	105	200
Pittsburgh	1	9	1	.100	114	216

Western Division

	W	L	T	Pct.	Pts.	OP
Green Bay	9	2	0	.818	233	153
Chi. Bears	8	3	0	.727	298	157
Detroit	6	5	0	.545	145	150
Cleveland	5	5	1	.500	195	164
Chi. Cardinals	1	10	0	.091	84	254

NFL championship: GREEN BAY 27, N.Y. Giants 0

1938

Eastern Division

	W	L	T	Pct.	Pts.	OP
N.Y. Giants	8	2	1	.800	194	79
Washington	6	3	2	.667	148	154
Brooklyn	4	4	3	.500	131	161
Philadelphia	5	6	0	.455	154	164
Pittsburgh	2	9	0	.182	79	169

Western Division

	W	L	T	Pct.	Pts.	OP
Green Bay	8	3	0	.727	223	118
Detroit	7	4	0	.636	119	108
Chi. Bears	6	5	0	.545	194	148
Cleveland	4	7	0	.364	131	215
Chi. Cardinals	2	9	0	.182	111	168

NFL championship: N.Y. GIANTS 23, Green Bay 17

1937

Eastern Division

	W	L	T	Pct.	Pts.	OP
Washington	8	3	0	.727	195	120
N.Y. Giants	6	3	2	.667	128	109
Pittsburgh	4	7	0	.364	122	145
Brooklyn	3	7	1	.300	82	174
Philadelphia	2	8	1	.200	86	177

Western Division

	W	L	T	Pct.	Pts.	OP
Chi. Bears	9	1	1	.900	201	100
Green Bay	7	4	0	.636	220	122
Detroit	7	4	0	.636	180	105
Chi. Cardinals	5	5	1	.500	135	165
Cleveland	1	10	0	.091	75	207

NFL championship: Washington 28, CHI. BEARS 21

1936

Eastern Division

	W	L	T	Pct.	Pts.	OP
Boston	7	5	0	.583	149	110
Pittsburgh	6	6	0	.500	98	187
N.Y. Giants	5	6	1	.455	115	163
Brooklyn	3	8	1	.273	92	161
Philadelphia	1	11	0	.083	51	206

Western Division

	W	L	T	Pct.	Pts.	OP
Green Bay	10	1	1	.909	248	118
Chi. Bears	9	3	0	.750	222	94
Detroit	8	4	0	.667	235	102
Chi. Cardinals	3	8	1	.273	74	143

NFL championship: Green Bay 21, Boston 6, at Polo Grounds, N.Y.

1935

Eastern Division

	W	L	T	Pct.	Pts.	OP
N. Y. Giants	9	3	0	.750	180	96
Brooklyn	5	6	1	.455	90	141
Pittsburgh	4	8	0	.333	100	209
Boston	2	8	1	.200	65	123
Philadelphia	2	9	0	.182	60	179

Western Division

	W	L	T	Pct.	Pts.	OP
Detroit	7	3	2	.700	191	111
Green Bay	8	4	0	.667	181	96
Chi. Bears	6	4	2	.600	192	106
Chi. Cardinals	6	4	2	.600	99	97

NFL championship: DETROIT 26, N.Y. Giants 7
One game between Boston and Philadelphia was canceled.

1934

Eastern Division

	W	L	T	Pct.	Pts.	OP
N.Y. Giants	8	5	0	.615	147	107
Boston	6	6	0	.500	107	94
Brooklyn	4	7	0	.364	61	153
Philadelphia	4	7	0	.364	127	85
Pittsburgh	2	10	0	.167	51	206

Western Division

	W	L	T	Pct.	Pts.	OP
Chi. Bears	13	0	0	1.000	286	86
Detroit	10	3	0	.769	238	59
Green Bay	7	6	0	.538	156	112
Chi. Cardinals	5	6	0	.455	80	84
St. Louis	1	2	0	.333	27	61
Cincinnati	0	8	0	.000	10	243

NFL championship: N.Y. GIANTS 30, Chi. Bears 13

1933

Eastern Division

	W	L	T	Pct.	Pts.	OP
N.Y. Giants	11	3	0	.786	244	101
Brooklyn	5	4	1	.556	93	54
Boston	5	5	2	.500	103	97
Philadelphia	3	5	1	.375	77	158
Pittsburgh	3	6	2	.333	67	208

Western Division

	W	L	T	Pct.	Pts.	OP
Chi. Bears	10	2	1	.833	133	82
Portsmouth	6	5	0	.545	128	87
Green Bay	5	7	1	.417	170	107
Cincinnati	3	6	1	.333	38	110
Chi. Cardinals	1	9	1	.100	52	101

NFL championship: CHI. BEARS 23, N.Y. Giants 21

1932

	W	L	T	Pct.
Chicago Bears	7	1	6	.875
Green Bay Packers	10	3	1	.769
Portsmouth Spartans	6	2	4	.750
Boston Braves	4	4	2	.500
New York Giants	4	6	2	.400
Brooklyn Dodgers	3	9	0	.250
Chicago Cardinals	2	6	2	.250
Staten Island Stapletons	2	7	3	.222

Chicago Bears and Portsmouth finished regularly scheduled games tied for first place. Bears won playoff game, which counted in standings, 9-0.

1931

	W	L	T	Pct.
Green Bay Packers	12	2	0	.857
Portsmouth Spartans	11	3	0	.786
Chicago Bears	8	5	0	.615
Chicago Cardinals	5	4	0	.556
New York Giants	7	6	1	.538
Providence Steam Roller	4	4	3	.500
Staten Island Stapletons	4	6	1	.400
Cleveland Indians	2	8	0	.200
Brooklyn Dodgers	2	12	0	.143
Frankford Yellow Jackets	1	6	1	.143

1930

	W	L	T	Pct.
Green Bay Packers	10	3	1	.769
New York Giants	13	4	0	.765
Chicago Bears	9	4	1	.692
Brooklyn Dodgers	7	4	1	.636
Providence Steam Roller	6	4	1	.600
Staten Island Stapletons	5	5	2	.500
Chicago Cardinals	5	6	2	.455
Portsmouth Spartans	5	6	3	.455
Frankford Yellow Jackets	4	13	1	.222
Minneapolis Red Jackets	1	7	1	.125
Newark Tornadoes	1	10	1	.091

1929

	W	L	T	Pct.
Green Bay Packers	12	0	1	1.000
New York Giants	13	1	1	.929
Frankford Yellow Jackets	9	4	5	.692
Chicago Cardinals	6	6	1	.500
Boston Bulldogs	4	4	0	.500
Orange Tornadoes	3	4	4	.429
Staten Island Stapletons	3	4	3	.429
Providence Steam Roller	4	6	2	.400
Chicago Bears	4	9	2	.308
Buffalo Bisons	1	7	1	.125
Minneapolis Red Jackets	1	9	0	.100
Dayton Triangles	0	6	0	.000

1928

	W	L	T	Pct.
Providence Steam Roller	8	1	2	.889
Frankford Yellow Jackets	11	3	2	.786
Detroit Wolverines	7	2	1	.778
Green Bay Packers	6	4	3	.600
Chicago Bears	7	5	1	.583
New York Giants	4	7	2	.364
New York Yankees	4	8	1	.333
Pottsville Maroons	2	8	0	.200
Chicago Cardinals	1	5	0	.167
Dayton Triangles	0	7	0	.000

1927

	W	L	T	Pct.
New York Giants	11	1	1	.917
Green Bay Packers	7	2	1	.778
Chicago Bears	9	3	2	.750
Cleveland Bulldogs	8	4	1	.667
Providence Steam Roller	8	5	1	.615
New York Yankees	7	8	1	.467
Frankford Yellow Jackets	6	9	3	.400
Pottsville Maroons	5	8	0	.385
Chicago Cardinals	3	7	1	.300
Dayton Triangles	1	6	1	.143
Duluth Eskimos	1	8	0	.111
Buffalo Bisons	0	5	0	.000

1926

	W	L	T	Pct.
Frankford Yellow Jackets	14	1	1	.933
Chicago Bears	12	1	3	.923
Pottsville Maroons	10	2	1	.833
Kansas City Cowboys	8	3	0	.727
Green Bay Packers	7	3	3	.700
Los Angeles Buccaneers	6	3	1	.667
New York Giants	8	4	1	.667
Duluth Eskimos	6	5	3	.545
Buffalo Rangers	4	4	2	.500
Chicago Cardinals	5	6	1	.455
Providence Steam Roller	5	7	1	.417
Detroit Panthers	4	6	2	.400
Hartford Blues	3	7	0	.300
Brooklyn Lions	3	8	0	.273
Milwaukee Badgers	2	7	0	.222
Akron Pros	1	4	3	.200
Dayton Triangles	1	4	1	.200
Racine Tornadoes	1	4	0	.200
Columbus Tigers	1	6	0	.143
Canton Bulldogs	1	9	3	.100
Hammond Pros	0	4	0	.000
Louisville Colonels	0	4	0	.000

1925

	W	L	T	Pct.
Chicago Cardinals	11	2	1	.846
Pottsville Maroons	10	2	0	.833
Detroit Panthers	8	2	2	.800
New York Giants	8	4	0	.667
Akron Indians	4	2	2	.667
Frankford Yellow Jackets	13	7	0	.650
Chicago Bears	9	5	3	.643
Rock Island Independents	5	3	3	.625
Green Bay Packers	8	5	0	.615
Providence Steam Roller	6	5	1	.545
Canton Bulldogs	4	4	0	.500
Cleveland Bulldogs	5	8	1	.385
Kansas City Cowboys	2	5	1	.286
Hammond Pros	1	4	0	.250
Buffalo Bisons	1	6	2	.143
Duluth Kelleys	0	3	0	.000
Rochester Jeffersons	0	6	1	.000
Milwaukee Badgers	0	6	0	.000
Dayton Triangles	0	7	1	.000
Columbus Tigers	0	9	0	.000

1924

	W	L	T	Pct.
Cleveland Bulldogs	7	1	1	.875
Chicago Bears	6	1	4	.857
Frankford Yellow Jackets	11	2	1	.846
Duluth Kelleys	5	1	0	.833
Rock Island Independents	6	2	2	.750
Green Bay Packers	7	4	0	.636
Racine Legion	4	3	3	.571
Chicago Cardinals	5	4	1	.556
Buffalo Bisons	6	5	0	.545
Columbus Tigers	4	4	0	.500
Hammond Pros	2	2	1	.500
Milwaukee Badgers	5	8	0	.385
Akron Indians	2	6	0	.333
Dayton Triangles	2	6	0	.333
Kansas City Blues	2	7	0	.222
Kenosha Maroons	0	5	1	.000
Minneapolis Marines	0	6	0	.000
Rochester Jeffersons	0	7	0	.000

1923

	W	L	T	Pct.
Canton Bulldogs	11	0	1	1.000
Chicago Bears	9	2	1	.818
Green Bay Packers	7	2	1	.778
Milwaukee Badgers	7	2	3	.778
Cleveland Indians	3	1	3	.750
Chicago Cardinals	8	4	0	.667
Duluth Kelleys	4	3	0	.571
Columbus Tigers	5	4	1	.556
Buffalo All-Americans	4	4	3	.500
Racine Legion	4	4	2	.500
Toledo Maroons	2	3	2	.400
Rock Island Independents	2	3	3	.400
Minneapolis Marines	2	5	2	.286
St. Louis All-Stars	1	4	2	.200
Hammond Pros	1	5	1	.167
Dayton Triangles	1	6	1	.143
Akron Indians	1	6	0	.143
Oorang Indians	1	10	0	.091
Rochester Jeffersons	0	2	0	.000
Louisville Brecks	0	3	0	.000

1922

	W	L	T	Pct.
Canton Bulldogs	10	0	2	1.000
Chicago Bears	9	3	0	.750
Chicago Cardinals	8	3	0	.727
Toledo Maroons	5	2	2	.714
Rock Island Independents	4	2	1	.667
Racine Legion	6	4	1	.600
Dayton Triangles	4	3	1	.571
Green Bay Packers	4	3	3	.571
Buffalo All-Americans	5	4	1	.556
Akron Pros	3	5	2	.375
Milwaukee Badgers	2	4	3	.333
Oorang Indians	2	6	0	.250
Minneapolis Marines	1	3	0	.250
Louisville Brecks	1	3	0	.250
Evansville Crimson Giants	0	3	0	.000
Rochester Jeffersons	0	4	1	.000
Hammond Pros	0	5	1	.000
Columbus Panhandles	0	7	0	.000

1921

	W	L	T	Pct.
Chicago Staleys	9	1	1	.900
Buffalo All-Americans	9	1	2	.900
Akron Pros	8	3	1	.727
Canton Bulldogs	5	2	3	.714
Rock Island Independents	4	2	1	.667
Evansville Crimson Giants	3	2	0	.600
Green Bay Packers	3	2	1	.600
Dayton Triangles	4	4	1	.500
Chicago Cardinals	3	3	2	.500
Rochester Jeffersons	2	3	0	.400
Cleveland Indians	3	5	0	.375
Washington Senators	1	2	0	.333
Cincinnati Celts	1	3	0	.250
Hammond Pros	1	3	1	.250
Minneapolis Marines	1	3	1	.250
Detroit Heralds	1	5	1	.167
Columbus Panhandles	1	8	0	.111
Tonawanda Kardex	0	1	0	.000
Muncie Flyers	0	2	0	.000
Louisville Brecks	0	2	0	.000
New York Giants	0	2	0	.000

1920

	W	L	T	Pct.
Akron Pros	8	0	3	1.000
Decatur Staleys	10	1	2	.909
Buffalo All-Americans	9	1	1	.900
Chicago Cardinals	6	2	2	.750
Rock Island Independents	6	2	2	.750
Dayton Triangles	5	2	2	.714
Rochester Jeffersons	6	3	2	.667
Canton Bulldogs	7	4	2	.636
Detroit Heralds	2	3	3	.400
Cleveland Tigers	2	4	2	.333
Chicago Tigers	2	5	1	.286
Hammond Pros	2	5	0	.286
Columbus Panhandles	2	6	2	.250
Muncie Flyers	0	1	0	.000

RS = REGULAR SEASON
PS = POSTSEASON

ATLANTA vs. BUFFALO
RS: Falcons lead series, 3-2
1973—Bills, 17-6 (A)
1977—Bills, 3-0 (B)
1980—Falcons, 30-14 (B)
1983—Falcons, 31-14 (A)
1989—Falcons, 30-28 (A)
(RS Pts.—Falcons 97, Bills 76)

ATLANTA vs. CHICAGO
RS: Falcons lead series, 9-7
1966—Bears, 23-6 (C)
1967—Bears, 23-14 (A)
1968—Bears, 16-13 (C)
1969—Falcons, 48-31 (A)
1970—Bears, 23-14 (A)
1972—Falcons, 37-21 (C)
1973—Falcons, 46-6 (A)
1974—Falcons, 13-10 (A)
1976—Falcons, 10-0 (C)
1977—Falcons, 16-10 (A)
1978—Bears, 13-7 (C)
1980—Falcons, 28-17 (A)
1983—Falcons, 20-17 (C)
1985—Bears, 36-0 (C)
1986—Bears, 13-10 (A)
1990—Bears, 30-24 (C)
(RS Pts.—Falcons 309, Bears 286)

ATLANTA vs. CINCINNATI
RS: Bengals lead series, 5-2
1971—Falcons, 9-6 (C)
1975—Bengals, 21-14 (A)
1978—Bengals, 37-7 (C)
1981—Bengals, 30-28 (A)
1984—Bengals, 35-14 (C)
1987—Bengals, 16-10 (A)
1990—Falcons, 38-17 (A)
(RS Pts.—Bengals 162, Falcons 120)

ATLANTA vs. CLEVELAND
RS: Browns lead series, 8-1
1966—Browns, 49-17 (A)
1968—Browns, 30-7 (C)
1971—Falcons, 31-14 (C)
1976—Browns, 20-17 (A)
1978—Browns, 24-16 (A)
1981—Browns, 28-17 (C)
1984—Browns, 23-7 (A)
1987—Browns, 38-3 (C)
1990—Browns, 13-10 (C)
(RS Pts.—Browns 239, Falcons 125)

ATLANTA vs. DALLAS
RS: Cowboys lead series, 8-5
PS: Cowboys lead series, 2-0
1966—Cowboys, 47-14 (A)
1967—Cowboys, 37-7 (D)
1969—Cowboys, 24-17 (A)
1970—Cowboys, 13-0 (D)
1974—Cowboys, 24-0 (A)
1976—Cowboys, 17-10 (A)
1978—*Cowboys, 27-20 (D)
1980—*Cowboys, 30-27 (A)
1985—Cowboys, 24-10 (D)
1986—Falcons, 37-35 (A)
1987—Falcons, 21-10 (D)
1988—Cowboys, 26-20 (D)
1989—Falcons 27-21 (A)
1990—Falcons, 26-7 (A)
1991—Cowboys, 31-27 (D)
(RS Pts.—Cowboys 309, Falcons 223)
(PS Pts.—Cowboys 57, Falcons 47)
*NFC Divisional Playoff

ATLANTA vs. DENVER
RS: Broncos lead series, 4-3
1970—Broncos, 24-10 (D)
1972—Falcons, 23-20 (A)
1975—Falcons, 35-21 (A)
1979—Falcons, 20-17 (A) OT
1982—Falcons, 34-27 (D)
1985—Broncos, 44-28 (A)
1988—Broncos, 30-14 (A)
(RS Pts.—Broncos 186, Falcons 161)

ATLANTA vs. DETROIT
RS: Lions lead series, 16-5
1966—Lions, 28-10 (D)
1967—Lions, 24-3 (D)
1968—Lions, 24-7 (A)
1969—Lions, 27-21 (D)
1971—Lions, 41-38 (D)
1972—Lions, 26-23 (A)
1973—Lions, 31-6 (D)
1975—Lions, 17-14 (A)
1976—Lions, 24-10 (D)
1977—Falcons, 17-6 (A)
1978—Lions, 14-0 (A)
1979—Lions, 24-23 (D)
1980—Falcons, 43-28 (A)
1983—Falcons, 30-14 (D)
1984—Lions, 27-24 (A) OT
1985—Lions, 28-27 (A)
1986—Falcons, 20-6 (D)
1987—Lions, 30-13 (A)
1988—Lions, 31-17 (D)
1989—Lions, 31-24 (A)
1990—Lions, 21-14 (D)
(RS Pts.—Lions 488, Falcons 398)

ATLANTA vs. GREEN BAY
RS: Packers lead series, 9-8
1966—Packers, 56-3 (Mil)
1967—Packers, 23-0 (Mil)
1968—Packers, 38-7 (A)
1969—Packers, 28-10 (GB)
1970—Packers, 27-24 (GB)
1971—Falcons, 28-21 (A)
1972—Falcons, 10-9 (Mil)
1974—Falcons, 10-3 (A)
1975—Packers, 22-13 (GB)
1976—Packers, 24-20 (A)
1979—Falcons, 25-7 (A)
1981—Falcons, 31-17 (GB)
1982—Packers, 38-7 (A)
1983—Falcons, 47-41 (A) OT
1988—Falcons, 20-0 (A)
1989—Packers, 23-21 (Mil)
1991—Falcons, 35-31 (A)
(RS Pts.—Packers 408, Falcons 311)

ATLANTA vs. HOUSTON
RS: Falcons lead series, 5-2
1972—Falcons, 20-10 (A)
1976—Oilers, 20-14 (H)
1978—Falcons, 20-14 (A)
1981—Falcons, 31-27 (H)
1984—Falcons, 42-10 (A)
1987—Oilers, 37-33 (H)
1990—Falcons, 47-27 (A)
(RS Pts.—Falcons 207, Oilers 145)

ATLANTA vs. *INDIANAPOLIS
RS: Colts lead series, 10-0
1966—Colts, 19-7 (A)
1967—Colts, 38-31 (B)
      Colts, 49-7 (A)
1968—Colts, 28-20 (A)
      Colts, 44-0 (B)
1969—Colts, 21-14 (A)
      Colts, 13-6 (B)
1974—Colts, 17-7 (A)
1986—Colts, 28-23 (A)
1989—Colts, 13-9 (I)
(RS Pts.—Colts 270, Falcons 124)
*Franchise in Baltimore prior to 1984

ATLANTA vs. KANSAS CITY
RS: Chiefs lead series, 3-0
1972—Chiefs, 17-14 (A)
1985—Chiefs, 38-10 (KC)
1991—Chiefs, 14-3 (KC)
(RS Pts.—Chiefs 69, Falcons 27)

ATLANTA vs. *L.A. RAIDERS
RS: Raiders lead series, 4-3
1971—Falcons, 24-13 (A)
1975—Raiders, 37-34 (O) OT
1979—Raiders, 50-19 (O)
1982—Raiders, 38-14 (A)
1985—Raiders, 34-24 (A)
1988—Falcons, 12-6 (LA)
1991—Falcons, 21-17 (A)
(RS Pts.—Raiders 195, Falcons 148)
*Franchise in Oakland prior to 1982

ATLANTA vs. L.A. RAMS
RS: Rams lead series, 35-13-2
1966—Rams, 19-14 (A)
1967—Rams, 31-3 (A)
      Rams, 20-3 (LA)
1968—Rams, 27-14 (LA)
      Rams, 17-10 (A)
1969—Rams, 17-7 (LA)
      Rams, 38-6 (A)
1970—Tie, 10-10 (A)
      Rams, 17-7 (A)
1971—Tie, 20-20 (LA)
      Rams, 24-16 (A)
1972—Falcons, 31-3 (A)
      Rams, 20-7 (LA)
1973—Rams, 31-0 (LA)
      Falcons, 15-13 (A)
1974—Rams, 21-0 (LA)
      Rams, 30-7 (A)
1975—Rams, 22-7 (LA)
      Rams, 16-7 (A)
1976—Rams, 30-14 (A)
      Rams, 59-0 (LA)
1977—Falcons, 17-6 (A)
      Rams, 23-7 (LA)
1978—Rams, 10-0 (LA)
      Rams, 15-7 (A)
1979—Rams, 20-14 (LA)
      Rams, 34-13 (A)
1980—Falcons, 13-10 (A)
      Rams, 20-17 (LA) OT
1981—Rams, 37-35 (A)
      Rams, 21-16 (LA)
1982—Rams, 34-17 (A)
1983—Rams, 27-21 (LA)
      Rams, 36-13 (A)
1984—Rams, 30-28 (LA)
      Rams, 24-10 (A)
1985—Rams, 17-6 (LA)
      Falcons, 30-14 (A)
1986—Rams, 26-14 (A)
      Rams, 14-7 (LA)
1987—Falcons, 24-20 (A)
      Rams, 33-0 (LA)
1988—Rams, 33-0 (A)
      Rams, 22-7 (LA)
1989—Rams, 31-21 (A)
      Rams, 26-14 (LA)
1990—Rams, 44-24 (LA)
      Falcons, 20-13 (A)
1991—Falcons, 31-14 (A)
      Falcons, 31-14 (LA)
(RS Pts.—Rams 1,114, Falcons 694)

ATLANTA vs. MIAMI
RS: Dolphins lead series, 4-1
1970—Dolphins, 20-7 (A)
1974—Dolphins, 42-7 (M)
1980—Dolphins, 20-17 (A)
1983—Dolphins, 31-24 (M)
1986—Falcons, 20-14 (M)
(RS Pts.—Dolphins 127, Falcons 75)

ATLANTA vs. MINNESOTA
RS: Vikings lead series, 11-6
PS: Vikings lead series, 1-0
1966—Falcons, 20-13 (A)
1967—Falcons, 21-20 (A)
1968—Vikings, 47-7 (M)
1969—Falcons, 10-3 (A)
1970—Vikings, 37-7 (A)
1971—Vikings, 24-7 (M)
1973—Falcons, 20-14 (A)
1974—Falcons, 23-10 (M)
1975—Vikings, 38-0 (M)
1977—Vikings, 14-7 (A)
1980—Vikings, 24-23 (M)
1981—Falcons, 31-30 (A)
1982—*Vikings, 30-24 (M)
1984—Vikings, 27-20 (M)
1985—Falcons, 14-13 (A)
1987—Vikings, 24-13 (M)
1989—Vikings, 43-17 (M)
1991—Vikings, 20-19 (A)
(RS Pts.—Vikings 414, Falcons 246)
(PS Pts.—Vikings 30, Falcons 24)
*NFC First Round Playoff

ATLANTA vs. NEW ENGLAND
RS: Series tied, 3-3
1972—Patriots, 21-20 (NE)
1977—Patriots, 16-10 (A)
1980—Falcons, 37-21 (NE)
1983—Falcons, 24-13 (A)
1986—Patriots, 25-17 (NE)
1989—Falcons, 16-15 (A)
(RS Pts.—Falcons 124, Patriots 111)

ATLANTA vs. NEW ORLEANS
RS: Falcons lead series, 26-19
PS: Falcons lead series, 1-0
1967—Saints, 27-24 (NO)
1969—Falcons, 45-17 (A)
1970—Falcons, 14-3 (NO)
      Falcons, 32-14 (A)
1971—Falcons, 28-6 (A)
      Falcons, 24-20 (NO)
1972—Falcons, 21-14 (NO)
      Falcons, 36-20 (A)
1973—Falcons, 62-7 (NO)
      Falcons, 14-10 (A)
1974—Saints, 14-13 (NO)
      Saints, 13-3 (A)
1975—Falcons, 14-7 (A)
      Saints, 23-7 (NO)
1976—Saints, 30-0 (NO)
      Falcons, 23-20 (A)
1977—Saints, 21-20 (NO)
      Saints, 35-7 (A)
1978—Falcons, 20-17 (NO)
      Falcons, 20-17 (A)
1979—Falcons, 40-34 (NO) OT
      Saints, 37-6 (A)
1980—Falcons, 41-14 (NO)
      Falcons, 31-13 (A)
1981—Falcons, 27-0 (A)
      Falcons, 41-10 (NO)
1982—Falcons, 35-0 (A)
      Saints, 35-6 (NO)
1983—Saints, 19-17 (A)
      Saints, 27-10 (NO)
1984—Falcons, 36-28 (NO)
      Saints, 17-13 (A)
1985—Falcons, 31-24 (A)
      Falcons, 16-10 (NO)
1986—Falcons, 31-10 (NO)
      Saints, 14-9 (A)
1987—Saints, 38-0 (A)
1988—Saints, 29-21 (A)
      Saints, 10-9 (NO)
1989—Saints, 20-13 (NO)
      Saints, 26-17 (A)
1990—Falcons, 28-27 (A)
      Saints, 10-7 (NO)
1991—Saints, 27-6 (A)
      Falcons, 23-20 (NO) OT
      *Falcons, 27-20 (NO)
(RS Pts.—Falcons 969, Saints 806)
(PS Pts.—Falcons 27, Saints 20)
*NFC First Round Playoff

ATLANTA vs. N. Y. GIANTS
RS: Series tied, 6-6
1966—Falcons, 27-16 (NY)
1968—Falcons, 24-21 (A)
1971—Giants, 21-17 (A)
1974—Falcons, 14-7 (New Haven)
1977—Falcons, 17-3 (A)
1978—Falcons, 23-20 (A)
1979—Giants, 24-3 (NY)
1981—Giants, 27-24 (A) OT
1982—Falcons, 16-14 (NY)
1983—Giants, 16-13 (A) OT
1984—Giants, 19-7 (A)
1988—Giants, 23-16 (A)
(RS Pts.—Giants 211, Falcons 201)

ATLANTA vs. N. Y. JETS
RS: Jets lead series, 3-2
1973—Falcons, 28-20 (NY)
1980—Jets, 14-7 (A)
1983—Falcons, 27-21 (NY)
1986—Jets, 28-14 (A)
1989—Jets, 27-7 (NY)
(RS Pts.—Jets 110, Falcons 83)

ATLANTA vs. PHILADELPHIA
RS: Eagles lead series, 8-6-1
PS: Falcons lead series, 1-0
1966—Eagles, 23-10 (P)
1967—Eagles, 38-7 (A)
1969—Falcons, 27-3 (P)
1970—Tie, 13-13 (P)
1973—Falcons, 44-27 (P)
1976—Eagles, 14-13 (A)
1978—*Falcons, 14-13 (A)
1979—Falcons, 14-10 (P)
1980—Falcons, 20-17 (P)
1981—Eagles, 16-13 (P)
1983—Eagles, 28-24 (A)
1984—Falcons, 26-10 (A)
1985—Eagles, 23-17 (P) OT
1986—Falcons, 16-0 (A)
1988—Falcons, 27-24 (P)
1990—Eagles, 24-23 (A)
(RS Pts.—Eagles 286, Falcons 278)
(PS Pts.—Falcons 14, Eagles 13)
*NFC First Round Playoff

ATLANTA vs. *PHOENIX
RS: Cardinals lead series, 10-4
1966—Falcons, 16-10 (A)
1968—Cardinals, 17-12 (StL)
1971—Cardinals, 26-9 (A)
1973—Cardinals, 32-10 (A)
1975—Cardinals, 23-20 (StL)
1978—Cardinals, 42-21 (StL)
1980—Falcons, 33-27 (StL) OT
1981—Cardinals, 41-20 (A)
1982—Cardinals, 23-20 (A)
1986—Cardinals, 33-13 (A)
1987—Cardinals, 34-21 (A)
1989—Cardinals, 34-20 (P)
1990—Cardinals, 24-13 (A)
1991—Cardinals, 16-10 (P)
(RS Pts.—Cardinals 341, Falcons 279)
*Franchise in St. Louis prior to 1988

ATLANTA vs. PITTSBURGH
RS: Steelers lead series, 8-1
1966—Steelers, 57-33 (A)
1968—Steelers, 41-21 (A)
1970—Falcons, 27-16 (A)
1974—Steelers, 24-17 (P)
1978—Steelers, 31-7 (P)
1981—Steelers, 34-20 (A)
1984—Steelers, 35-10 (P)
1987—Steelers, 28-12 (A)
1990—Steelers, 21-9 (P)
(RS Pts.—Steelers 287, Falcons 156)

ATLANTA vs. SAN DIEGO
RS: Falcons lead series, 3-1
1973—Falcons, 41-0 (SD)
1979—Falcons, 28-26 (SD)
1988—Chargers, 10-7 (A)
1991—Falcons, 13-10 (SD)
(RS Pts.—Falcons 89, Chargers 46)

ATLANTA vs. SAN FRANCISCO
RS: 49ers lead series, 29-20-1
1966—49ers, 44-7 (A)
1967—49ers, 38-7 (SF)
   49ers, 34-28 (A)
1968—49ers, 28-13 (SF)
   49ers, 14-12 (A)
1969—Falcons, 24-12 (A)
   Falcons, 21-7 (SF)
1970—Falcons, 21-20 (A)
   49ers, 24-20 (SF)
1971—Falcons, 20-17 (A)
   49ers, 24-3 (SF)
1972—49ers, 49-14 (A)
   49ers, 20-0 (SF)
1973—49ers, 13-9 (A)
   Falcons, 17-3 (SF)
1974—49ers, 16-10 (A)
   49ers, 27-0 (SF)
1975—Falcons, 17-3 (SF)
   Falcons, 31-9 (A)
1976—49ers, 15-0 (SF)
   Falcons, 21-16 (A)
1977—Falcons, 7-0 (SF)
   49ers, 10-3 (A)
1978—Falcons, 20-17 (SF)
   Falcons, 21-10 (A)
1979—49ers, 20-15 (SF)
   Falcons, 31-21 (A)
1980—Falcons, 20-17 (SF)
   Falcons, 35-10 (A)
1981—Falcons, 34-17 (A)
   49ers, 17-14 (SF)
1982—Falcons, 17-7 (SF)
1983—49ers, 24-20 (SF)
   Falcons, 28-24 (A)
1984—49ers, 14-5 (SF)
   49ers, 35-17 (A)
1985—49ers, 35-16 (A)
   49ers, 38-17 (A)
1986—Tie, 10-10 (A) OT
   49ers, 20-0 (SF)
1987—49ers, 25-17 (A)
   49ers, 35-7 (SF)
1988—49ers, 34-17 (SF)
   49ers, 13-3 (A)
1989—49ers, 45-3 (SF)
   49ers, 23-10 (A)
1990—49ers, 19-13 (SF)
   49ers, 45-35 (A)
1991—Falcons, 39-34 (SF)
   Falcons, 17-14 (A)
(RS Pts.—49ers 1,049, Falcons 803)
ATLANTA vs. SEATTLE
RS: Seahawks lead series, 4-1
1976—Seahawks, 30-13 (S)
1979—Seahawks, 31-28 (A)
1985—Seahawks, 30-26 (S)
1988—Seahawks, 31-20 (A)
1991—Falcons, 26-13 (A)
(RS Pts.—Seahawks 135, Falcons 113)
ATLANTA vs. TAMPA BAY
RS: Series tied, 5-5
1977—Falcons, 17-0 (TB)
1978—Buccaneers, 14-9 (TB)
1979—Falcons, 17-14 (A)
1981—Buccaneers, 24-23 (TB)
1984—Buccaneers, 23-6 (TB)
1986—Falcons, 23-20 (TB) OT
1987—Buccaneers, 48-10 (TB)
1988—Falcons, 17-10 (A)
1990—Buccaneers, 23-17 (TB)
1991—Falcons, 43-7 (A)
(RS Pts.—Buccaneers 183, Falcons 182)
ATLANTA vs. WASHINGTON
RS: Redskins lead series, 11-3-1
PS: Redskins lead series, 1-0
1966—Redskins, 33-20 (W)
1967—Tie, 20-20 (A)
1969—Redskins, 27-20 (W)
1972—Redskins, 24-13 (W)
1975—Redskins, 30-27 (A)
1977—Redskins, 10-6 (W)
1978—Falcons, 20-17 (A)
1979—Redskins, 16-7 (A)
1980—Falcons, 10-6 (A)
1983—Redskins, 37-21 (W)
1984—Redskins, 27-14 (W)
1985—Redskins, 44-10 (A)
1987—Falcons, 21-20 (A)
1989—Redskins, 31-30 (A)
1991—Falcons, 56-17 (W)
   *Redskins, 24-7 (W)
(RS Pts.—Redskins 398, Falcons 256)
(PS Pts.—Redskins 24, Falcons 7)
*NFC Divisional Playoff

BUFFALO vs. ATLANTA
RS: Falcons lead series, 3-2;
See Atlanta vs. Buffalo
BUFFALO vs. CHICAGO
RS: Bears lead series, 3-2
1970—Bears, 31-13 (C)

BUFFALO vs. HOUSTON (column 3)

1974—Bills, 16-6 (B)
1979—Bears, 7-0 (B)
1988—Bears, 24-3 (C)
1991—Bills, 35-20 (B)
(RS Pts.—Bears 88, Bills 67)
BUFFALO vs. CINCINNATI
RS: Bengals lead series, 9-7
PS: Bengals lead series, 2-0
1968—Bengals, 34-23 (C)
1969—Bills, 16-13 (B)
1970—Bengals, 43-14 (B)
1973—Bengals, 16-13 (B)
1975—Bengals, 33-24 (C)
1978—Bills, 5-0 (B)
1979—Bills, 51-24 (B)
1980—Bills, 14-0 (C)
1981—Bengals, 27-24 (C) OT
   *Bengals, 28-21 (C)
1983—Bills, 10-6 (C)
1984—Bengals, 52-21 (C)
1985—Bengals, 23-17 (B)
1986—Bengals, 36-33 (C) OT
1988—Bengals, 35-21 (C)
   **Bengals, 21-10 (C)
1989—Bills, 24-7 (B)
1991—Bills, 35-16 (B)
(RS Pts.—Bengals 365, Bills 345)
(PS Pts.—Bengals 49, Bills 31)
*AFC Divisional Playoff
**AFC Championship
BUFFALO vs. CLEVELAND
RS: Browns lead series, 7-3
PS: Browns lead series, 1-0
1972—Browns, 27-10 (C)
1974—Bills, 15-10 (C)
1977—Browns, 27-16 (B)
1978—Browns, 41-20 (C)
1981—Bills, 22-13 (B)
1984—Browns, 13-10 (B)
1985—Browns, 17-7 (C)
1986—Browns, 21-17 (B)
1987—Browns, 27-21 (C)
1989—*Browns, 34-30 (C)
1990—Bills, 42-0 (C)
(RS Pts.—Browns 196, Bills 180)
(PS Pts.—Browns 34, Bills 30)
*AFC Divisional Playoff
BUFFALO vs. DALLAS
RS: Cowboys lead series, 3-1
1971—Cowboys, 49-37 (B)
1976—Cowboys, 17-10 (D)
1981—Cowboys, 27-14 (D)
1984—Bills, 14-3 (D)
(RS Pts.—Cowboys 96, Bills 75)
BUFFALO vs. DENVER
RS: Bills lead series, 15-10-1
PS: Bills lead series, 1-0
1960—Broncos, 27-21 (B)
   Tie, 38-38 (B)
1961—Broncos, 22-10 (B)
   Bills, 23-10 (D)
1962—Broncos, 23-20 (B)
   Bills, 45-38 (D)
1963—Bills, 30-28 (B)
   Bills, 27-17 (B)
1964—Bills, 30-13 (B)
   Bills, 30-19 (D)
1965—Bills, 30-15 (B)
   Bills, 31-13 (B)
1966—Bills, 38-21 (B)
1967—Bills, 17-16 (B)
   Broncos, 21-20 (B)
1968—Broncos, 34-32 (D)
1969—Bills, 41-28 (B)
1970—Broncos, 25-10 (B)
1975—Bills, 38-14 (B)
1977—Broncos, 26-6 (D)
1979—Broncos, 19-16 (B)
1981—Bills, 9-7 (B)
1984—Broncos, 37-7 (B)
1987—Bills, 21-14 (B)
1989—Broncos, 28-14 (B)
1990—Bills, 29-28 (B)
1991—*Bills, 10-7 (B)
(RS Pts.—Bills 633, Broncos 581)
(PS Pts.—Bills 10, Broncos 7)
*AFC Championship
BUFFALO vs. DETROIT
RS: Lions lead series, 2-1-1
1972—Tie, 21-21 (B)
1976—Lions, 27-14 (D)
1979—Bills, 20-17 (D)
1991—Lions, 17-14 (B) OT
(RS Pts.—Lions 82, Bills 69)
BUFFALO vs. GREEN BAY
RS: Bills lead series, 4-1
1974—Bills, 27-7 (GB)
1979—Bills, 19-12 (B)
1982—Packers, 33-21 (Mil)
1988—Bills, 28-0 (B)
1991—Bills, 34-24 (Mil)
(RS Pts.—Bills 129, Packers 76)

BUFFALO vs. HOUSTON
RS: Oilers lead series, 19-11
PS: Bills lead series, 1-0
1960—Bills, 25-24 (B)
   Oilers, 31-23 (H)
1961—Oilers, 22-12 (H)
   Oilers, 28-16 (B)
1962—Oilers, 28-23 (B)
   Oilers, 17-14 (H)
1963—Oilers, 31-20 (B)
   Oilers, 28-14 (H)
1964—Bills, 48-17 (H)
   Bills, 24-10 (B)
1965—Oilers, 19-17 (B)
   Bills, 29-18 (H)
1966—Bills, 27-20 (B)
   Bills, 42-20 (H)
1967—Oilers, 20-3 (B)
   Oilers, 10-3 (H)
1968—Oilers, 30-7 (B)
   Oilers, 35-6 (H)
1969—Oilers, 17-3 (B)
   Oilers, 28-14 (H)
1971—Oilers, 20-14 (B)
1974—Oilers, 21-9 (B)
1976—Oilers, 13-3 (B)
1978—Oilers, 17-10 (H)
1983—Bills, 30-13 (B)
1985—Bills, 20-0 (B)
1986—Oilers, 16-7 (H)
1987—Bills, 34-30 (B)
1988—*Bills, 17-10 (B)
1989—Bills, 47-41 (H) OT
1990—Oilers, 27-24 (H)
(RS Pts.—Oilers 641, Bills 578)
(PS Pts.—Bills 17, Oilers 10)
*AFC Divisional Playoff
BUFFALO vs. *INDIANAPOLIS
RS: Bills lead series, 23-19-1
1970—Tie, 17-17 (Balt)
   Colts, 20-14 (Buff)
1971—Colts, 43-0 (Buff)
   Colts, 24-0 (Balt)
1972—Colts, 17-0 (Buff)
   Colts, 35-7 (Balt)
1973—Bills, 31-13 (Buff)
   Bills, 24-17 (Balt)
1974—Bills, 27-14 (Balt)
   Bills, 6-0 (Buff)
1975—Bills, 38-31 (Balt)
   Colts, 42-35 (Buff)
1976—Colts, 31-13 (Buff)
   Colts, 58-20 (Balt)
1977—Colts, 17-14 (Balt)
   Colts, 31-13 (Buff)
1978—Bills, 24-17 (Balt)
   Bills, 21-14 (Balt)
1979—Bills, 31-13 (Balt)
   Colts, 14-13 (Buff)
1980—Colts, 17-12 (Buff)
   Colts, 28-24 (Balt)
1981—Bills, 35-3 (Balt)
   Bills, 23-17 (Buff)
1982—Bills, 20-0 (Buff)
1983—Bills, 28-23 (Buff)
   Bills, 30-7 (Balt)
1984—Colts, 31-17 (I)
   Bills, 21-15 (Buff)
1985—Colts, 49-17 (I)
   Bills, 21-9 (Buff)
1986—Bills, 24-13 (Buff)
   Colts, 24-14 (I)
1987—Colts, 47-6 (Buff)
   Bills, 27-3 (I)
1988—Bills, 34-23 (Buff)
   Colts, 17-14 (I)
1989—Colts, 37-14 (I)
   Bills, 30-7 (Buff)
1990—Bills, 26-10 (Buff)
   Bills, 31-7 (I)
1991—Bills, 42-6 (Buff)
   Bills, 35-7 (I)
(RS Pts.—Bills 893, Colts 868)
*Franchise in Baltimore prior to 1984
BUFFALO vs. *KANSAS CITY
RS: Bills lead series, 15-12-1
PS: Series tied, 1-1
1960—Texans, 45-28 (B)
   Texans, 24-7 (D)
1961—Bills, 27-24 (B)
   Bills, 30-20 (D)
1962—Texans, 41-21 (D)
   Bills, 23-14 (B)
1963—Tie, 27-27 (B)
   Bills, 35-26 (B)
1964—Bills, 34-17 (B)
   Bills, 35-22 (KC)
1965—Bills, 23-7 (KC)
   Bills, 34-25 (B)
1966—Chiefs, 42-20 (B)
   Bills, 29-14 (KC)
   **Chiefs, 31-7 (B)
1967—Chiefs, 23-13 (KC)

1968—Chiefs, 18-7 (B)
1969—Chiefs, 29-7 (B)
   Chiefs, 22-19 (KC)
1971—Chiefs, 22-9 (KC)
1973—Bills, 23-14 (B)
1976—Bills, 50-17 (B)
1978—Bills, 28-13 (B)
   Chiefs, 14-10 (KC)
1982—Bills, 14-9 (B)
1983—Bills, 14-9 (KC)
1986—Chiefs, 20-17 (B)
   Bills, 17-14 (KC)
1991—Chiefs, 33-6 (KC)
   ***Bills, 37-14 (B)
(RS Pts.—Chiefs 610, Bills 602)
(PS Pts.—Chiefs 45, Bills 44)
*Franchise in Dallas prior to 1963 and
known as Texans
**AFL Championship
***AFC Divisional Playoff
BUFFALO vs. *L.A. RAIDERS
RS: Bills lead series, 14-13
PS: Bills lead series, 1-0
1960—Bills, 38-9 (B)
   Raiders, 20-7 (O)
1961—Raiders, 31-22 (B)
   Bills, 26-21 (O)
1962—Bills, 14-6 (B)
   Bills, 10-6 (O)
1963—Raiders, 35-17 (O)
   Bills, 12-0 (B)
1964—Bills, 23-20 (B)
   Raiders, 16-13 (O)
1965—Bills, 17-12 (B)
   Bills, 17-14 (O)
1966—Bills, 31-10 (O)
1967—Raiders, 24-20 (B)
   Raiders, 28-21 (O)
1968—Raiders, 48-6 (B)
   Raiders, 13-10 (O)
1969—Raiders, 50-21 (O)
1972—Raiders, 28-16 (O)
1974—Bills, 21-20 (B)
1977—Raiders, 34-13 (O)
1980—Bills, 24-7 (B)
1983—Raiders, 27-24 (B)
1987—Raiders, 34-21 (LA)
1988—Bills, 37-21 (B)
1990—Bills, 38-24 (B)
   **Bills, 51-3 (B)
1991—Bills, 30-27 (LA) OT
(RS Pts.—Raiders 585, Bills 549)
(PS Pts.—Bills 51, Raiders 3)
*Franchise in Oakland prior to 1982
**AFC Championship
BUFFALO vs. L.A. RAMS
RS: Rams lead series, 3-2
1970—Rams, 19-0 (B)
1974—Rams, 19-14 (LA)
1980—Bills, 10-7 (B) OT
1983—Rams, 41-17 (LA)
1989—Bills, 23-20 (B)
(RS Pts.—Rams 106, Bills 64)
BUFFALO vs. MIAMI
RS: Dolphins lead series, 35-16-1
PS: Bills lead series, 1-0
1966—Bills, 58-24 (B)
   Bills, 29-0 (M)
1967—Bills, 35-13 (B)
   Dolphins, 17-14 (M)
1968—Tie, 14-14 (B)
   Dolphins, 21-17 (B)
1969—Dolphins, 24-6 (M)
   Bills, 28-3 (B)
1970—Dolphins, 33-14 (B)
   Dolphins, 45-7 (M)
1971—Dolphins, 29-14 (B)
   Dolphins, 34-0 (M)
1972—Dolphins, 24-23 (B)
   Dolphins, 30-16 (M)
1973—Dolphins, 27-6 (M)
   Dolphins, 17-0 (B)
1974—Dolphins, 24-16 (B)
   Dolphins, 35-28 (M)
1975—Dolphins, 35-30 (B)
   Dolphins, 31-21 (M)
1976—Dolphins, 30-21 (B)
   Dolphins, 45-27 (M)
1977—Dolphins, 13-0 (B)
   Dolphins, 31-14 (M)
1978—Dolphins, 31-24 (M)
   Dolphins, 25-24 (B)
1979—Dolphins, 9-7 (B)
   Dolphins, 17-7 (M)
1980—Dolphins, 17-7 (B)
   Dolphins, 17-14 (M)
1981—Bills, 31-21 (B)
   Dolphins, 16-6 (M)
1982—Dolphins, 9-7 (M)
   Dolphins, 27-10 (M)
1983—Dolphins, 12-0 (B)
   Bills, 38-35 (M) OT
1984—Dolphins, 21-17 (B)

251

Dolphins, 38-7 (M)
1985—Dolphins, 23-14 (B)
 Dolphins, 28-0 (M)
1986—Dolphins, 27-14 (M)
 Dolphins, 34-24 (B)
1987—Bills, 34-31 (M) OT
 Bills, 27-0 (B)
1988—Bills, 9-6 (B)
 Bills, 31-6 (M)
1989—Bills, 27-24 (M)
 Bills, 31-17 (B)
1990—Dolphins, 30-7 (M)
 Bills, 24-14 (B)
 *Bills, 44-34 (B)
1991—Bills, 35-31 (B)
 Bills, 41-27 (M)
(RS Pts.—Dolphins 1,182, Bills 965)
(PS Pts.—Bills 44, Dolphins 34)
*AFC Divisional Playoff

BUFFALO vs. MINNESOTA
RS: Vikings lead series, 4-2
1971—Vikings, 19-0 (M)
1975—Vikings, 35-13 (B)
1979—Vikings, 10-3 (M)
1982—Bills, 23-22 (B)
1985—Vikings, 27-20 (B)
1988—Bills, 13-10 (B)
(RS Pts.—Vikings 123, Bills 72)

BUFFALO vs. *NEW ENGLAND
RS: Patriots lead series, 33-29-1
PS: Patriots lead series, 1-0
1960—Bills, 13-0 (Bos)
 Bills, 38-14 (Buff)
1961—Patriots, 23-21 (Buff)
 Patriots, 52-21 (Bos)
1962—Tie, 28-28 (Buff)
 Patriots, 21-10 (Bos)
1963—Bills, 28-21 (Buff)
 Patriots, 17-7 (Bos)
 **Patriots, 26-8 (Buff)
1964—Patriots, 36-28 (Buff)
 Bills, 24-14 (Bos)
1965—Bills, 24-7 (Buff)
 Bills, 23-7 (Bos)
1966—Patriots, 20-10 (Buff)
 Patriots, 14-3 (Bos)
1967—Patriots, 23-0 (Buff)
 Bills, 44-16 (Bos)
1968—Patriots, 16-7 (Buff)
 Patriots, 23-6 (Bos)
1969—Bills, 23-16 (Buff)
 Patriots, 35-21 (Bos)
1970—Bills, 45-10 (Bos)
 Patriots, 14-10 (Buff)
1971—Patriots, 38-33 (NE)
 Bills, 27-20 (Buff)
1972—Bills, 38-14 (Buff)
 Bills, 27-24 (NE)
1973—Bills, 31-13 (NE)
 Bills, 37-13 (Buff)
1974—Bills, 30-28 (Buff)
 Bills, 29-28 (NE)
1975—Bills, 45-31 (Buff)
 Bills, 34-14 (NE)
1976—Patriots, 26-22 (Buff)
 Patriots, 20-10 (NE)
1977—Bills, 24-14 (NE)
 Patriots, 20-7 (Buff)
1978—Patriots, 14-10 (Buff)
 Patriots, 26-24 (NE)
1979—Patriots, 26-6 (Buff)
 Bills, 16-13 (NE) OT
1980—Bills, 31-13 (Buff)
 Patriots, 24-2 (NE)
1981—Bills, 20-17 (Buff)
 Bills, 19-10 (NE)
1982—Patriots, 30-19 (NE)
1983—Bills, 31-0 (NE)
 Patriots, 21-7 (NE)
1984—Patriots, 21-17 (Buff)
 Bills, 38-10 (NE)
1985—Patriots, 17-14 (Buff)
 Patriots, 14-3 (NE)
1986—Patriots, 23-3 (NE)
 Patriots, 22-19 (NE)
1987—Patriots, 14-7 (NE)
 Bills, 13-7 (Buff)
1988—Bills, 16-14 (NE)
 Bills, 23-20 (Buff)
1989—Bills, 31-10 (Buff)
 Patriots, 33-24 (NE)
1990—Bills, 27-10 (NE)
 Bills, 14-0 (Buff)
1991—Bills, 22-17 (Buff)
 Patriots, 16-13 (NE)
(RS Pts.—Patriots 1,237, Bills 1,232)
(PS Pts.—Patriots 26, Bills 8)
*Franchise in Boston prior to 1971
**Division Playoff

BUFFALO vs. NEW ORLEANS
RS: Series tied, 2-2
1973—Saints, 13-0 (NO)
1980—Bills, 35-26 (NO)

1983—Bills, 27-21 (B)
1989—Saints, 22-19 (B)
(RS Pts.—Saints 82, Bills 81)

BUFFALO vs. N.Y. GIANTS
RS: Bills lead series, 3-2
PS: Giants lead series, 1-0
1970—Giants, 20-6 (NY)
1975—Giants, 17-14 (B)
1978—Bills, 41-17 (B)
1987—Bills, 6-3 (B) OT
1990—Bills, 17-13 (NY)
 *Giants, 20-19 (Tampa)
(RS Pts.—Bills 84, Giants 70)
(PS Pts.—Giants 20, Bills 19)
*Super Bowl XXV

BUFFALO vs. *N.Y. JETS
RS: Bills lead series, 34-28
PS: Bills lead series, 1-0
1960—Titans, 27-3 (NY)
 Titans, 17-13 (B)
1961—Bills, 41-31 (B)
 Titans, 21-14 (NY)
1962—Titans, 17-6 (B)
 Bills, 20-3 (NY)
1963—Bills, 45-14 (B)
 Bills, 19-10 (NY)
1964—Bills, 34-24 (B)
 Bills, 20-7 (NY)
1965—Bills, 33-21 (B)
 Jets, 14-12 (NY)
1966—Bills, 33-23 (NY)
 Bills, 14-3 (B)
1967—Jets, 20-17 (B)
 Jets, 20-10 (NY)
1968—Bills, 37-35 (B)
 Jets, 25-21 (NY)
1969—Jets, 33-19 (B)
 Bills, 16-6 (NY)
1970—Bills, 34-31 (B)
 Bills, 10-6 (NY)
1971—Jets, 28-17 (NY)
 Jets, 20-7 (B)
1972—Jets, 41-24 (B)
 Jets, 41-3 (NY)
1973—Bills, 9-7 (B)
 Bills, 34-14 (NY)
1974—Bills, 16-12 (B)
 Jets, 20-10 (NY)
1975—Bills, 42-14 (B)
 Bills, 24-23 (NY)
1976—Jets, 17-14 (NY)
 Bills, 19-14 (B)
1977—Jets, 24-19 (B)
 Bills, 14-10 (NY)
1978—Bills, 21-20 (B)
 Jets, 45-14 (NY)
1979—Bills, 46-31 (B)
 Bills, 14-12 (NY)
1980—Bills, 20-10 (B)
 Bills, 31-24 (NY)
1981—Bills, 31-0 (B)
 Jets, 33-14 (NY)
 **Jets, 31-27 (NY)
1983—Jets, 34-10 (B)
 Bills, 24-17 (NY)
1984—Jets, 28-26 (B)
 Jets, 21-17 (NY)
1985—Jets, 42-3 (NY)
 Jets, 27-7 (B)
1986—Jets, 28-24 (B)
 Jets, 14-13 (NY)
1987—Jets, 31-28 (B)
 Bills, 17-14 (NY)
1988—Bills, 37-14 (NY)
 Bills, 9-6 (B) OT
1989—Bills, 34-3 (B)
 Bills, 37-0 (NY)
1990—Bills, 30-7 (NY)
 Bills, 30-27 (B)
1991—Bills, 23-20 (NY)
 Bills, 24-13 (B)
(RS Pts.—Bills, 1,294, Jets 1,227)
(PS Pts.—Bills 31, Jets 27)
*Jets known as Titans prior to 1963
**AFC First Round Playoff

BUFFALO vs. PHILADELPHIA
RS: Eagles lead series, 4-2
1973—Bills, 27-26 (B)
1981—Eagles, 20-14 (B)
1984—Eagles, 27-17 (B)
1985—Bills, 21-17 (P)
1987—Eagles, 17-7 (P)
1990—Bills, 30-23 (B)
(RS Pts.—Eagles 134, Bills 112)

BUFFALO vs. *PHOENIX
RS: Series tied, 3-3
1971—Cardinals, 28-23 (B)
1975—Bills, 32-14 (StL)
1981—Cardinals, 24-0 (StL)
1984—Cardinals, 37-7 (StL)
1986—Bills, 17-10 (B)
1990—Bills, 45-14 (B)
(RS Pts.—Cardinals 127, Bills 124)

*Franchise in St. Louis prior to 1988

BUFFALO vs. PITTSBURGH
RS: Bills lead series, 6-5
PS: Steelers lead series, 1-0
1970—Steelers, 23-10 (P)
1972—Steelers, 38-21 (B)
1974—*Steelers, 32-14 (P)
1975—Bills, 30-21 (P)
1978—Steelers, 28-17 (B)
1979—Steelers, 28-0 (P)
1980—Bills, 28-13 (B)
1982—Bills, 13-0 (B)
1985—Steelers, 30-24 (P)
1986—Bills, 16-12 (B)
1988—Bills, 36-28 (B)
1991—Bills, 52-34 (B)
(RS Pts.—Steelers 255, Bills 247)
(PS Pts.—Steelers 32, Bills 14)
*AFC Divisional Playoff

BUFFALO vs. *SAN DIEGO
RS: Chargers lead series, 16-7-2
PS: Bills lead series, 2-1
1960—Chargers, 24-10 (B)
 Bills, 32-3 (LA)
1961—Chargers, 19-11 (B)
 Chargers, 28-10 (SD)
1962—Bills, 35-10 (B)
 Bills, 40-20 (SD)
1963—Chargers, 14-10 (SD)
 Chargers, 23-13 (B)
1964—Bills, 30-3 (B)
 Bills, 27-24 (SD)
 **Bills, 20-7 (B)
1965—Chargers, 34-3 (B)
 Tie, 20-20 (SD)
 **Bills, 23-0 (SD)
1966—Chargers, 27-7 (SD)
 Tie, 17-17 (B)
1967—Chargers, 37-17 (B)
1968—Chargers, 21-6 (B)
1969—Chargers, 45-6 (SD)
1971—Chargers, 20-3 (B)
1973—Chargers, 34-7 (SD)
1976—Chargers, 34-13 (B)
1979—Chargers, 27-19 (SD)
1980—Bills, 26-24 (SD)
 ***Chargers, 20-14 (SD)
1981—Bills, 28-27 (SD)
1985—Chargers, 14-9 (B)
 Chargers, 40-7 (SD)
(RS Pts.—Chargers 589, Bills 406)
(PS Pts.—Bills 57, Chargers 27)
*Franchise in Los Angeles prior to 1961
**AFL Championship
***AFC Divisional Playoff

BUFFALO vs. SAN FRANCISCO
RS: Series tied, 2-2
1972—Bills, 27-20 (B)
1980—Bills, 18-13 (SF)
1983—49ers, 23-10 (B)
1989—49ers, 21-10 (SF)
(RS Pts.—49ers 77, Bills 65)

BUFFALO vs. SEATTLE
RS: Seahawks lead series, 3-1
1977—Seahawks, 56-17 (S)
1984—Seahawks, 31-28 (S)
1988—Bills, 13-3 (S)
1989—Seahawks, 17-16 (S)
(RS Pts.—Seahawks 107, Bills 74)

BUFFALO vs. TAMPA BAY
RS: Buccaneers lead series, 4-2
1976—Bills, 14-9 (TB)
1978—Buccaneers, 31-10 (TB)
1982—Buccaneers, 24-23 (TB)
1986—Buccaneers, 34-28 (B)
1988—Buccaneers, 10-5 (TB)
1991—Bills, 17-10 (TB)
(RS Pts.—Buccaneers 118, Bills 97)

BUFFALO vs. WASHINGTON
RS: Redskins lead series, 4-2
PS: Redskins lead series, 1-0
1972—Bills, 24-17 (W)
1977—Redskins, 10-0 (B)
1981—Bills, 21-14 (B)
1984—Redskins, 41-14 (W)
1987—Redskins, 27-7 (B)
1990—Redskins, 29-14 (W)
1991—*Redskins, 37-24 (Minneapolis)
(RS Pts.—Redskins 138, Bills 80)
(PS Pts.—Redskins 37, Bills 24)
*Super Bowl XXVI

CHICAGO vs. ATLANTA
RS: Falcons lead series, 9-7;
See Atlanta vs. Chicago

CHICAGO vs. BUFFALO
RS: Bears lead series, 3-2;
See Buffalo vs. Chicago

CHICAGO vs. CINCINNATI
RS: Series tied, 2-2
1972—Bengals, 13-3 (Chi)
1980—Bengals, 17-14 (Chi) OT
1986—Bears, 44-7 (Cin)

1989—Bears, 17-14 (Chi)
(RS Pts.—Bears 78, Bengals 51)

CHICAGO vs. CLEVELAND
RS: Browns lead series, 7-3
1951—Browns, 42-21 (Cle)
1954—Browns, 39-10 (Chi)
1960—Browns, 42-0 (Chi)
1961—Bears, 17-14 (Chi)
1967—Browns, 24-0 (Cle)
1969—Browns, 28-24 (Chi)
1972—Bears, 17-0 (Cle)
1980—Browns, 27-21 (Cle)
1986—Bears, 41-31 (Cle)
1989—Browns, 27-7 (Cle)
(RS Pts.—Browns 274, Bears 158)

CHICAGO vs. DALLAS
RS: Cowboys lead series, 7-6
PS: Cowboys lead series, 2-0
1960—Bears, 17-7 (C)
1962—Bears, 34-33 (D)
1964—Cowboys, 24-10 (C)
1968—Cowboys, 34-3 (C)
1971—Bears, 23-19 (C)
1973—Cowboys, 20-17 (C)
1976—Cowboys, 31-21 (D)
1977—*Cowboys, 37-7 (D)
1979—Cowboys, 24-20 (D)
1981—Cowboys, 10-9 (D)
1984—Cowboys, 23-14 (C)
1985—Bears, 44-0 (D)
1986—Bears, 24-10 (C)
1988—Bears, 17-7 (C)
1991—**Cowboys, 17-13 (C)
(RS Pts.—Bears 253, Cowboys 242)
(PS Pts.—Cowboys 54, Bears 20)
*NFC Divisional Playoff
**NFC First Round Playoff

CHICAGO vs. DENVER
RS: Bears lead series, 5-4
1971—Broncos, 6-3 (D)
1973—Bears, 33-14 (D)
1976—Broncos, 28-14 (C)
1978—Broncos, 16-7 (C)
1981—Bears, 35-24 (C)
1983—Bears, 31-14 (C)
1984—Bears, 27-0 (C)
1987—Broncos, 31-29 (D)
1990—Bears, 16-13 (D) OT
(RS Pts.—Bears 195, Broncos 146)

CHICAGO vs. *DETROIT
RS: Bears lead series, 72-47-5
1930—Spartans, 7-6 (P)
 Bears, 14-6 (C)
1931—Bears, 9-6 (C)
 Spartans, 3-0 (P)
1932—Tie, 13-13 (C)
 Tie, 7-7 (P)
 Bears, 9-0 (C)
1933—Bears, 17-14 (C)
 Bears, 17-7 (P)
1934—Bears, 19-16 (C)
 Bears, 10-7 (C)
1935—Tie, 20-20 (C)
 Lions, 14-2 (D)
1936—Bears, 12-10 (C)
 Lions, 13-7 (D)
1937—Bears, 28-20 (C)
 Bears, 13-0 (D)
1938—Bears, 13-7 (C)
 Lions, 14-7 (D)
1939—Lions, 10-0 (D)
 Bears, 23-13 (D)
1940—Bears, 7-0 (C)
 Lions, 17-14 (D)
1941—Bears, 49-0 (C)
 Bears, 24-7 (D)
1942—Bears, 16-0 (C)
 Bears, 42-0 (D)
1943—Bears, 27-21 (D)
 Bears, 35-14 (C)
1944—Tie, 21-21 (C)
 Lions, 41-21 (D)
1945—Lions, 16-10 (D)
 Lions, 35-28 (C)
1946—Bears, 42-6 (C)
 Bears, 45-24 (D)
1947—Bears, 33-24 (C)
 Bears, 34-14 (D)
1948—Bears, 28-0 (C)
 Bears, 42-14 (D)
1949—Bears, 27-24 (C)
 Bears, 28-7 (D)
1950—Bears, 35-21 (D)
 Bears, 6-3 (C)
1951—Bears, 28-23 (D)
 Lions, 41-28 (C)
1952—Lions, 24-23 (D)
 Lions, 45-21 (C)
1953—Lions, 20-16 (C)
 Lions, 13-7 (D)
1954—Lions, 48-23 (D)
 Bears, 28-24 (C)
1955—Bears, 24-14 (D)

Bears, 21-20 (C)
1956—Lions, 42-10 (D)
Bears, 38-21 (C)
1957—Bears, 27-7 (D)
Lions, 21-13 (C)
1958—Bears, 20-7 (D)
Bears, 21-16 (C)
1959—Bears, 24-14 (D)
Bears, 25-14 (C)
1960—Bears, 28-7 (C)
Lions, 36-0 (D)
1961—Bears, 31-17 (D)
Lions, 16-15 (C)
1962—Lions, 11-3 (D)
Bears, 3-0 (C)
1963—Bears, 37-21 (D)
Bears, 24-14 (C)
1964—Lions, 10-0 (C)
Bears, 27-24 (D)
1965—Bears, 38-10 (C)
Bears, 17-10 (D)
1966—Lions, 14-3 (D)
Tie, 10-10 (C)
1967—Bears, 14-3 (C)
Bears, 27-13 (D)
1968—Lions, 42-0 (D)
Lions, 28-10 (C)
1969—Lions, 13-7 (D)
Lions, 20-3 (C)
1970—Lions, 28-14 (D)
Lions, 16-10 (C)
1971—Bears, 28-23 (D)
Lions, 28-3 (C)
1972—Lions, 38-24 (C)
Lions, 14-0 (D)
1973—Lions, 30-7 (C)
Lions, 40-7 (D)
1974—Bears, 17-9 (C)
Lions, 34-17 (D)
1975—Lions, 27-7 (D)
Bears, 25-21 (C)
1976—Bears, 10-3 (C)
Lions, 14-10 (D)
1977—Bears, 30-20 (C)
Bears, 31-14 (D)
1978—Bears, 19-0 (D)
Lions, 21-17 (C)
1979—Bears, 35-7 (C)
Lions, 20-0 (D)
1980—Bears, 24-7 (C)
Bears, 23-17 (D) OT
1981—Lions, 48-17 (D)
Lions, 23-7 (C)
1982—Lions, 17-10 (D)
Bears, 20-17 (C)
1983—Lions, 31-17 (D)
Lions, 38-17 (C)
1984—Bears, 16-14 (C)
Bears, 30-13 (D)
1985—Bears, 24-3 (C)
Bears, 37-17 (D)
1986—Bears, 13-7 (C)
Bears, 16-13 (D)
1987—Bears, 30-10 (C)
Bears, 27-7 (D)
1988—Bears, 24-7 (C)
Bears, 13-12 (D)
1989—Bears, 47-27 (D)
Lions, 27-17 (C)
1990—Bears, 23-17 (C) OT
Lions, 38-21 (D)
1991—Bears, 20-10 (C)
Lions, 16-6 (D)
(RS Pts.—Bears 2,332, Lions 2,090)
*Franchise in Portsmouth prior to 1934
and known as the Spartans
CHICAGO vs. GREEN BAY
RS: Bears lead series, 79-57-6
PS: Bears lead series, 1-0
1921—Staleys, 20-0 (C)
1923—Bears, 3-0 (GB)
1924—Bears, 3-0 (C)
1925—Packers, 14-10 (GB)
Bears, 21-0 (C)
1926—Tie, 6-6 (GB)
Bears, 19-13 (C)
Tie, 3-3 (C)
1927—Bears, 7-6 (GB)
Bears, 14-6 (C)
1928—Tie, 12-12 (GB)
Packers, 16-6 (C)
Packers, 6-0 (C)
1929—Packers, 23-0 (GB)
Packers, 14-0 (C)
Packers, 25-0 (C)
1930—Packers, 7-0 (GB)
Packers, 13-12 (C)
Bears, 21-0 (C)
1931—Packers, 7-0 (GB)
Packers, 6-2 (C)
Bears, 7-6 (C)
1932—Tie, 0-0 (GB)
Packers, 2-0 (C)
Bears, 9-0 (C)

1933—Bears, 14-7 (GB)
Bears, 10-7 (C)
Bears, 7-6 (C)
1934—Bears, 24-10 (GB)
Bears, 27-14 (C)
1935—Packers, 7-0 (GB)
Packers, 17-14 (C)
1936—Bears, 30-3 (GB)
Packers, 21-10 (C)
1937—Bears, 14-2 (GB)
Packers, 24-14 (C)
1938—Bears, 2-0 (GB)
Packers, 24-17 (C)
1939—Packers, 21-16 (GB)
Bears, 30-27 (C)
1940—Bears, 41-10 (GB)
Bears, 14-7 (C)
1941—Bears, 25-17 (GB)
Packers, 16-14 (C)
**Bears, 33-14 (C)
1942—Packers, 44-28 (GB)
Bears, 38-7 (C)
1943—Tie, 21-21 (GB)
Bears, 21-7 (C)
1944—Packers, 42-28 (GB)
Bears, 21-0 (C)
1945—Packers, 31-21 (GB)
Bears, 28-24 (C)
1946—Bears, 30-7 (GB)
Bears, 10-7 (C)
1947—Packers, 29-20 (GB)
Bears, 20-17 (C)
1948—Bears, 45-7 (GB)
Bears, 7-6 (C)
1949—Bears, 17-0 (GB)
Bears, 24-3 (C)
1950—Packers, 31-21 (GB)
Bears, 28-14 (C)
1951—Bears, 31-20 (GB)
Bears, 24-13 (C)
1952—Bears, 24-14 (GB)
Packers, 41-28 (C)
1953—Bears, 17-13 (GB)
Tie, 21-21 (C)
1954—Bears, 10-3 (GB)
Bears, 28-23 (C)
1955—Packers, 24-3 (GB)
Bears, 52-31 (C)
1956—Packers, 37-21 (GB)
Bears, 38-14 (C)
1957—Packers, 21-17 (GB)
Bears, 21-14 (C)
1958—Bears, 34-20 (GB)
Bears, 24-10 (C)
1959—Packers, 9-6 (GB)
Bears, 28-17 (C)
1960—Bears, 17-14 (GB)
Packers, 41-13 (C)
1961—Packers, 24-0 (GB)
Bears, 31-28 (C)
1962—Packers, 49-0 (GB)
Packers, 38-7 (C)
1963—Bears, 10-3 (GB)
Bears, 26-7 (C)
1964—Packers, 23-12 (GB)
Packers, 17-3 (C)
1965—Packers, 23-14 (GB)
Bears, 31-10 (C)
1966—Packers, 17-0 (C)
Packers, 13-6 (GB)
1967—Packers, 13-10 (GB)
Packers, 17-13 (C)
1968—Packers, 13-10 (GB)
Packers, 28-27 (C)
1969—Packers, 17-0 (GB)
Packers, 21-3 (C)
1970—Packers, 20-19 (GB)
Bears, 35-17 (C)
1971—Packers, 17-14 (GB)
Packers, 31-10 (GB)
1972—Packers, 20-17 (GB)
Bears, 23-17 (C)
1973—Bears, 31-17 (GB)
Packers, 21-0 (C)
1974—Bears, 10-9 (C)
Packers, 20-3 (Mil)
1975—Bears, 27-14 (C)
Packers, 28-7 (GB)
1976—Bears, 24-13 (C)
Bears, 16-10 (GB)
1977—Bears, 26-0 (GB)
Bears, 21-10 (C)
1978—Bears, 24-14 (GB)
Bears, 14-0 (C)
1979—Bears, 6-3 (C)
Bears, 15-14 (GB)
1980—Packers, 12-6 (GB) OT
Bears, 61-7 (C)
1981—Packers, 16-9 (C)
Packers, 21-17 (GB)
1983—Packers, 31-28 (GB)
Bears, 23-21 (C)
1984—Bears, 9-7 (GB)

Packers, 20-14 (C)
1985—Bears, 23-7 (C)
Bears, 16-10 (GB)
1986—Bears, 25-12 (GB)
Bears, 12-10 (C)
1987—Bears, 26-24 (GB)
Bears, 23-10 (C)
1988—Bears, 24-6 (GB)
Bears, 16-0 (C)
1989—Packers, 14-13 (GB)
Packers, 40-28 (C)
1990—Bears, 31-13 (GB)
Bears, 27-13 (C)
1991—Bears, 10-0 (GB)
Bears, 27-13 (C)
(RS Pts.—Bears 2,412, Packers 2,069)
(PS Pts.—Bears 33, Packers 14)
*Bears known as Staleys prior to 1922
**Division Playoff
CHICAGO vs. HOUSTON
RS: Oilers lead series, 3-2
1973—Bears, 35-14 (C)
1977—Oilers, 47-0 (H)
1980—Oilers, 10-6 (C)
1986—Bears, 20-7 (H)
1989—Oilers, 33-28 (C)
(RS Pts.—Oilers 111, Bears 89)
CHICAGO vs. *INDIANAPOLIS
RS: Colts lead series, 21-16
1953—Colts, 13-9 (B)
Colts, 16-14 (C)
1954—Bears, 28-9 (C)
Bears, 28-13 (B)
1955—Colts, 23-17 (B)
Bears, 38-10 (C)
1956—Colts, 28-21 (B)
Bears, 58-27 (C)
1957—Colts, 21-10 (B)
Colts, 29-14 (C)
1958—Colts, 51-38 (B)
Colts, 17-0 (C)
1959—Bears, 26-21 (B)
Colts, 21-7 (C)
1960—Colts, 42-7 (B)
Colts, 24-20 (C)
1961—Bears, 24-10 (C)
Bears, 21-20 (B)
1962—Bears, 35-15 (C)
Bears, 57-0 (B)
1963—Bears, 10-3 (C)
Bears, 17-7 (B)
1964—Colts, 52-0 (B)
Colts, 40-24 (C)
1965—Colts, 26-21 (C)
Bears, 13-0 (B)
1966—Colts, 27-17 (C)
Colts, 21-16 (B)
1967—Colts, 24-3 (C)
1968—Colts, 28-7 (B)
1969—Colts, 24-21 (C)
1970—Colts, 21-20 (B)
1975—Colts, 35-7 (C)
1983—Colts, 22-19 (B) OT
1985—Bears, 17-10 (C)
1988—Bears, 17-13 (I)
1991—Bears, 31-17 (I)
(RS Pts.—Colts 770, Bears 742)
*Franchise in Baltimore prior to 1984
**Conference Playoff
CHICAGO vs. KANSAS CITY
RS: Bears lead series, 3-2
1973—Chiefs, 19-7 (KC)
1977—Bears, 28-27 (C)
1981—Bears, 16-13 (KC) OT
1987—Bears, 31-28 (C)
1990—Chiefs, 21-10 (C)
(RS Pts.—Chiefs 108, Bears 92)
CHICAGO vs. *L.A. RAIDERS
RS: Raiders lead series, 4-3
1972—Raiders, 28-21 (O)
1976—Raiders, 28-27 (C)
1978—Raiders, 25-19 (C) OT
1981—Bears, 23-6 (O)
1984—Bears, 17-6 (C)
1987—Bears, 6-3 (LA)
1990—Raiders, 24-10 (LA)
(RS Pts.—Bears 123, Raiders 120)
*Franchise in Oakland prior to 1982
CHICAGO vs. *L.A. RAMS
RS: Bears lead series, 44-28-3
PS: Series tied, 1-1
1937—Bears, 20-2 (Clev)
Bears, 15-7 (C)
1938—Rams, 14-7 (C)
Rams, 23-21 (Clev)
1939—Bears, 30-21 (Clev)
Bears, 35-21 (C)
1940—Bears, 21-14 (Clev)
Bears, 47-25 (C)
1941—Bears, 48-21 (Clev)
Bears, 31-13 (C)
1942—Bears, 21-7 (Clev)
Bears, 47-0 (C)
1944—Rams, 19-7 (Clev)

Bears, 28-21 (C)
1945—Rams, 17-0 (Clev)
Rams, 41-21 (C)
1946—Tie, 28-28 (C)
Bears, 27-21 (LA)
1947—Bears, 41-21 (C)
Rams, 17-14 (C)
1948—Bears, 42-21 (C)
Bears, 21-6 (LA)
1949—Bears, 31-16 (C)
Rams, 27-24 (LA)
1950—Bears, 24-20 (C)
Bears, 24-14 (C)
**Rams, 24-14 (LA)
1951—Rams, 42-17 (C)
1952—Rams, 31-7 (LA)
Rams, 40-24 (C)
1953—Bears, 38-24 (LA)
Bears, 24-21 (C)
1954—Rams, 42-38 (LA)
Bears, 24-13 (C)
1955—Bears, 31-20 (LA)
Bears, 24-3 (C)
1956—Bears, 35-24 (C)
Bears, 30-21 (C)
1957—Bears, 34-26 (C)
Bears, 16-10 (LA)
1958—Bears, 31-10 (C)
Rams, 41-35 (LA)
1959—Bears, 28-21 (C)
Bears, 26-21 (LA)
1960—Bears, 34-27 (C)
Tie, 24-24 (LA)
1961—Bears, 21-17 (LA)
Bears, 28-24 (C)
1962—Bears, 27-23 (LA)
Bears, 30-14 (C)
1963—Bears, 52-14 (LA)
Bears, 6-0 (C)
1964—Bears, 38-17 (C)
Bears, 34-24 (LA)
1965—Rams, 30-28 (C)
Bears, 31-6 (C)
1966—Bears, 31-17 (LA)
Bears, 17-10 (C)
1967—Rams, 28-17 (C)
1968—Bears, 17-16 (LA)
1969—Rams, 9-7 (C)
1971—Rams, 17-3 (LA)
1972—Tie, 13-13 (C)
1973—Bears, 26-0 (C)
1975—Rams, 38-10 (LA)
1976—Rams, 20-12 (LA)
1977—Bears, 24-23 (C)
1979—Bears, 27-23 (C)
1981—Rams, 24-7 (C)
1982—Rams, 34-26 (LA)
1983—Rams, 21-14 (LA)
1984—Rams, 29-13 (LA)
1985—***Bears, 24-0 (C)
1986—Bears, 20-17 (C)
1988—Rams, 23-3 (LA)
1989—Bears, 20-10 (C)
1990—Bears, 38-9 (C)
(RS Pts.—Bears 1,764, Rams 1,539)
(PS Pts.—Bears 38, Rams 24)
*Franchise in Cleveland prior to 1946
**Conference Playoff
***NFC Championship
CHICAGO vs. MIAMI
RS: Dolphins lead series, 5-1
1971—Dolphins, 34-3 (M)
1975—Dolphins, 46-13 (C)
1979—Dolphins, 31-16 (M)
1985—Dolphins, 38-24 (M)
1988—Bears, 34-7 (C)
1991—Dolphins, 16-13 (C) OT
(RS Pts.—Dolphins 172, Bears 103)
CHICAGO vs. MINNESOTA
RS: Vikings lead series, 30-29-2
1961—Vikings, 37-13 (M)
Bears, 52-35 (C)
1962—Bears, 13-0 (M)
Bears, 31-30 (C)
1963—Bears, 28-7 (M)
Tie, 17-17 (C)
1964—Bears, 34-28 (M)
Vikings, 41-14 (C)
1965—Bears, 45-37 (M)
Vikings, 24-17 (C)
1966—Bears, 13-10 (M)
Bears, 41-28 (C)
1967—Bears, 17-7 (M)
Tie, 10-10 (C)
1968—Bears, 27-17 (M)
Bears, 26-24 (C)
1969—Vikings, 31-0 (C)
Vikings, 31-14 (M)
1970—Vikings, 24-0 (C)
Vikings, 16-13 (M)
1971—Bears, 20-17 (M)
Vikings, 27-10 (C)
1972—Bears, 13-10 (C)

253

Vikings, 23-10 (M)
1973—Vikings, 22-13 (C)
Vikings, 31-13 (M)
1974—Vikings, 11-7 (M)
Vikings, 17-0 (C)
1975—Vikings, 28-3 (M)
Vikings, 13-9 (C)
1976—Vikings, 20-19 (M)
Bears, 14-13 (C)
1977—Vikings, 22-16 (M) OT
Bears, 10-7 (C)
1978—Vikings, 24-20 (C)
Vikings, 17-14 (M)
1979—Bears, 26-7 (C)
Vikings, 30-27 (M)
1980—Vikings, 34-14 (C)
Vikings, 13-7 (M)
1981—Vikings, 24-21 (M)
Bears, 10-9 (C)
1982—Vikings, 35-7 (M)
1983—Vikings, 23-14 (C)
Bears, 19-13 (M)
1984—Bears, 16-7 (C)
Bears, 34-3 (M)
1985—Bears, 33-24 (M)
Bears, 27-9 (C)
1986—Bears, 23-0 (C)
Vikings, 23-7 (M)
1987—Bears, 27-7 (C)
Bears, 30-24 (M)
1988—Vikings, 31-7 (C)
Vikings, 28-27 (M)
1989—Bears, 38-7 (C)
Vikings, 27-16 (M)
1990—Bears, 19-16 (C)
Vikings, 41-13 (M)
1991—Bears, 10-6 (C)
Bears, 34-17 (M)
(RS Pts.—Vikings 1,214, Bears 1,122)

CHICAGO vs. NEW ENGLAND
RS: Patriots lead series, 3-2
PS: Bears lead series, 1-0
1973—Patriots, 13-10 (C)
1979—Patriots, 27-7 (C)
1982—Bears, 26-13 (C)
1985—Bears, 20-7 (C)
*Bears, 46-10 (New Orleans)
1988—Patriots, 30-7 (NE)
(RS Pts.—Patriots 100, Bears 70)
(PS Pts.—Bears 46, Patriots 10)
*Super Bowl XX

CHICAGO vs. NEW ORLEANS
RS: Bears lead series, 8-5
PS: Bears lead series, 1-0
1968—Bears, 23-17 (NO)
1970—Bears, 24-3 (NO)
1971—Bears, 35-14 (C)
1973—Saints, 21-16 (NO)
1974—Bears, 24-10 (C)
1975—Bears, 42-17 (NO)
1977—Saints, 42-24 (C)
1980—Bears, 22-3 (C)
1982—Saints, 10-0 (C)
1983—Saints, 34-31 (NO) OT
1984—Bears, 20-7 (C)
1987—Saints, 19-17 (C)
1990—*Bears, 16-6 (C)
1991—Bears, 20-17 (NO)
(RS Pts.—Bears 298, Saints 214)
(PS Pts.—Bears 16, Saints 6)
*NFC First Round Playoff

CHICAGO vs. N.Y. GIANTS
RS: Bears lead series, 24-14-2
PS: Bears lead series, 5-3
1925—Bears, 19-7 (NY)
Giants, 9-0 (C)
1926—Bears, 7-0 (C)
1927—Giants, 13-7 (NY)
1928—Bears, 13-0 (C)
1929—Giants, 26-14 (C)
Giants, 34-0 (NY)
Giants, 14-9 (C)
1930—Giants, 12-0 (C)
Bears, 12-0 (NY)
1931—Bears, 6-0 (C)
Bears, 12-6 (NY)
Giants, 25-6 (C)
1932—Bears, 28-8 (NY)
Bears, 6-0 (C)
1933—Bears, 14-10 (C)
Giants, 3-0 (NY)
*Bears, 23-21 (C)
1934—Bears, 27-7 (C)
Bears, 10-9 (NY)
*Giants, 30-13 (NY)
1935—Bears, 20-3 (NY)
Giants, 3-0 (C)
1936—Bears, 25-7 (NY)
1937—Tie, 3-3 (NY)
1939—Giants, 16-13 (NY)
1940—Bears, 37-21 (NY)
1941—*Bears, 37-9 (C)
1942—Bears, 26-7 (NY)

1943—Bears, 56-7 (NY)
1946—Giants, 14-0 (NY)
*Bears, 24-14 (NY)
1948—Bears, 35-14 (C)
1949—Giants, 35-28 (NY)
1956—Tie, 17-17 (NY)
*Giants, 47-7 (NY)
1962—Giants, 26-24 (C)
1963—*Bears, 14-10 (C)
1965—Bears, 35-14 (NY)
1967—Bears, 34-7 (C)
1969—Giants, 28-24 (NY)
1970—Bears, 24-16 (NY)
1974—Bears, 16-13 (C)
1977—Bears, 12-9 (NY) OT
1985—**Bears, 21-0 (C)
1987—Bears, 34-19 (C)
1990—**Giants, 31-3 (NY)
1991—Bears, 20-17 (C)
(RS Pts.—Bears 673, Giants 479)
(PS Pts.—Giants 162, Bears 142)
*NFL Championship
**NFC Divisional Playoff

CHICAGO vs. N.Y. JETS
RS: Bears lead series, 3-1
1974—Jets, 23-21 (C)
1979—Bears, 23-13 (C)
1985—Bears, 19-6 (NY)
1991—Bears, 19-13 (C) OT
(RS Pts.—Bears 82, Jets 55)

CHICAGO vs. PHILADELPHIA
RS: Bears lead series, 22-3-1
PS: Series tied, 1-1
1933—Tie, 3-3 (P)
1935—Bears, 39-0 (P)
1936—Bears, 17-0 (P)
Bears, 28-7 (P)
1938—Bears, 28-6 (P)
1939—Bears, 27-14 (C)
1941—Bears, 49-14 (P)
1942—Bears, 45-14 (P)
1944—Bears, 28-7 (P)
1946—Bears, 21-14 (C)
1947—Bears, 40-7 (C)
1948—Eagles, 12-7 (P)
1949—Bears, 38-21 (C)
1955—Bears, 17-10 (C)
1961—Eagles, 16-14 (P)
1963—Bears, 16-7 (C)
1968—Bears, 29-16 (P)
1970—Bears, 20-16 (C)
1972—Bears, 21-12 (P)
1975—Bears, 15-13 (C)
1979—*Eagles, 27-17 (P)
1980—Eagles, 17-14 (P)
1983—Bears, 7-6 (P)
Bears, 17-14 (C)
1986—Bears, 13-10 (C) OT
1987—Bears, 35-3 (P)
1988—**Bears, 20-12 (C)
1989—Bears, 27-13 (C)
(RS Pts.—Bears 615, Eagles 272)
(PS Pts.—Eagles 39, Bears 37)
*NFC First Round Playoff
**NFC Divisional Playoff

*CHICAGO vs. **PHOENIX
RS: Bears lead series, 51-25-6
(NP denotes Normal Park;
Wr denotes Wrigley Field;
Co denotes Comiskey Park;
So denotes Soldier Field;
all Chicago)
1920—Cardinals, 7-6 (NP)
Staleys, 10-0 (Wr)
1921—Tie, 0-0 (Wr)
1922—Cardinals, 6-0 (Co)
Cardinals, 9-0 (Co)
1923—Bears, 3-0 (Wr)
1924—Bears, 6-0 (Wr)
Bears, 21-0 (Co)
1925—Cardinals, 9-0 (Co)
Tie, 0-0 (Wr)
1926—Bears, 16-0 (Wr)
Bears, 10-0 (So)
Tie, 0-0 (Wr)
1927—Bears, 9-0 (NP)
Cardinals, 3-0 (Wr)
1928—Bears, 15-0 (NP)
Bears, 34-0 (Wr)
1929—Tie, 0-0 (Wr)
Cardinals, 40-6 (Co)
1930—Bears, 32-6 (Co)
Bears, 6-0 (Wr)
1931—Bears, 26-13 (Wr)
Bears, 18-7 (Wr)
1932—Tie, 0-0 (Wr)
Bears, 34-0 (Wr)
1933—Bears, 12-9 (Wr)
Bears, 22-6 (Wr)
1934—Bears, 20-0 (Wr)
Bears, 17-6 (Wr)
1935—Tie, 7-7 (Wr)
Bears, 13-0 (Wr)

1936—Bears, 7-3 (Wr)
Cardinals, 14-7 (Wr)
1937—Bears, 16-7 (Wr)
Bears, 42-28 (Wr)
1938—Bears, 16-13 (So)
Bears, 34-28 (Wr)
1939—Bears, 44-7 (Wr)
Bears, 48-7 (Co)
1940—Cardinals, 21-7 (Co)
Bears, 31-23 (Wr)
1941—Bears, 53-7 (Wr)
Bears, 34-24 (Co)
1942—Bears, 41-14 (Wr)
Bears, 21-7 (Co)
1943—Bears, 20-0 (Wr)
Bears, 35-24 (Co)
1945—Cardinals, 16-7 (Wr)
Bears, 28-20 (Co)
1946—Bears, 34-17 (Co)
Cardinals, 35-28 (Wr)
1947—Cardinals, 31-7 (Co)
Cardinals, 30-21 (Wr)
1948—Cardinals, 28-17 (Co)
Cardinals, 24-21 (Wr)
1949—Bears, 17-7 (Co)
Bears, 52-21 (Wr)
1950—Bears, 27-6 (Wr)
Cardinals, 20-10 (Co)
1951—Cardinals, 28-14 (Co)
Cardinals, 24-14 (Wr)
1952—Cardinals, 21-10 (Co)
Bears, 10-7 (Wr)
1953—Cardinals, 24-17 (Wr)
1954—Bears, 29-7 (Co)
1955—Cardinals, 53-14 (Co)
1956—Bears, 10-3 (Wr)
1957—Bears, 14-6 (Co)
1958—Bears, 30-14 (Wr)
1959—Bears, 31-7 (So)
1965—Bears, 34-13 (Wr)
1966—Cardinals, 24-17 (StL)
1967—Bears, 30-3 (Wr)
1969—Cardinals, 20-17 (StL)
1972—Bears, 27-10 (C)
1975—Cardinals, 34-20 (St)
1977—Cardinals, 16-13 (StL)
1978—Bears, 17-10 (So)
1979—Bears, 42-6 (So)
1982—Cardinals, 10-7 (So)
1984—Cardinals, 38-21 (StL)
1990—Bears, 31-21 (P)
(RS Pts.—Bears 1,548, Cardinals 998)
*Franchise in Decatur prior to 1921; Bears known as Staleys prior to 1922
**Franchise in St. Louis prior to 1988 and in Chicago prior to 1960

CHICAGO vs. *PITTSBURGH
RS: Bears lead series, 15-4-1
1934—Bears, 28-0 (P)
1935—Bears, 23-7 (P)
1936—Bears, 27-9 (P)
Bears, 26-6 (C)
1937—Bears, 7-0 (P)
1939—Bears, 32-0 (P)
1941—Bears, 34-7 (C)
1945—Bears, 28-7 (P)
1947—Bears, 49-7 (C)
1949—Bears, 30-21 (C)
1958—Steelers, 24-10 (P)
1959—Bears, 27-21 (C)
1963—Tie, 17-17 (P)
1967—Steelers, 41-13 (P)
1969—Bears, 38-7 (C)
1971—Bears, 17-15 (C)
1975—Steelers, 34-3 (P)
1980—Steelers, 38-3 (P)
1986—Bears, 13-10 (C) OT
1989—Bears, 20-0 (P)
(RS Pts.—Bears 445, Steelers 271)
*Steelers known as Pirates prior to 1941

CHICAGO vs. SAN DIEGO
RS: Chargers lead series, 4-1
1970—Chargers, 20-7 (C)
1974—Chargers, 28-21 (SD)
1978—Chargers, 40-7 (SD)
1981—Bears, 20-17 (C) OT
1984—Chargers, 20-7 (SD)
(RS Pts.—Chargers 125, Bears 62)

CHICAGO vs. SAN FRANCISCO
RS: Series tied, 25-25-1
PS: 49ers lead series, 2-0
1950—Bears, 32-20 (SF)
Bears, 17-0 (C)
1951—Bears, 13-7 (C)
1952—49ers, 40-16 (C)
Bears, 20-17 (SF)
1953—49ers, 35-28 (C)
49ers, 24-14 (SF)
1954—49ers, 31-24 (C)
Bears, 31-27 (SF)
1955—49ers, 20-19 (C)
Bears, 34-23 (SF)
1956—Bears, 31-7 (C)

Bears, 38-21 (SF)
1957—49ers, 21-17 (C)
49ers, 21-17 (SF)
1958—Bears, 28-6 (C)
Bears, 27-14 (SF)
1959—49ers, 20-17 (SF)
Bears, 14-3 (C)
1960—Bears, 27-10 (C)
49ers, 25-7 (SF)
1961—Bears, 31-0 (C)
49ers, 41-31 (SF)
1962—Bears, 30-14 (SF)
49ers, 34-27 (C)
1963—Bears, 20-14 (SF)
Bears, 27-7 (C)
1964—49ers, 31-21 (SF)
Bears, 23-21 (C)
1965—49ers, 52-24 (SF)
Bears, 61-20 (C)
1966—Tie, 30-30 (C)
49ers, 41-14 (SF)
1967—Bears, 28-19 (C)
1968—Bears, 27-19 (C)
1969—49ers, 42-21 (SF)
1970—49ers, 37-16 (C)
1971—49ers, 13-0 (C)
1972—49ers, 34-21 (C)
1974—49ers, 34-0 (C)
1975—49ers, 31-3 (SF)
1976—Bears, 19-12 (SF)
1978—Bears, 16-13 (SF)
1979—Bears, 28-27 (SF)
1981—49ers, 28-17 (SF)
1983—Bears, 13-3 (C)
1984—*49ers, 23-0 (SF)
1985—Bears, 26-10 (SF)
1987—49ers, 41-0 (SF)
1988—Bears, 10-9 (C)
*49ers, 28-3 (C)
1989—49ers, 26-0 (C)
1991—49ers, 52-14 (SF)
(RS Pts.—49ers 1,148, Bears 1,063)
(PS Pts.—49ers 51, Bears 3)
*NFC Championship

CHICAGO vs. SEATTLE
RS: Seahawks lead series, 4-2
1976—Bears, 34-7 (S)
1978—Seahawks, 31-29 (C)
1982—Seahawks, 20-14 (S)
1984—Seahawks, 38-9 (C)
1987—Seahawks, 34-21 (C)
1990—Bears, 17-0 (C)
(RS Pts.—Seahawks 130, Bears 124)

CHICAGO vs. TAMPA BAY
RS: Bears lead series, 22-6
1977—Bears, 10-0 (TB)
1978—Buccaneers, 33-19 (TB)
Bears, 14-3 (C)
1979—Buccaneers, 17-13 (C)
Bears, 14-0 (TB)
1980—Bears, 23-0 (C)
Bears, 14-13 (TB)
1981—Bears, 28-17 (C)
Buccaneers, 20-10 (TB)
1982—Buccaneers, 26-23 (TB) OT
1983—Bears, 17-10 (C)
Bears, 27-0 (TB)
1984—Bears, 34-14 (C)
Bears, 44-9 (TB)
1985—Bears, 38-28 (C)
Bears, 27-19 (TB)
1986—Bears, 23-3 (TB)
Bears, 48-14 (C)
1987—Bears, 20-3 (C)
Bears, 27-26 (TB)
1988—Bears, 28-10 (C)
Bears, 27-15 (TB)
1989—Buccaneers, 42-35 (TB)
Buccaneers, 32-31 (C)
1990—Bears, 26-6 (TB)
Bears, 27-14 (C)
1991—Bears, 21-20 (TB)
Bears, 27-0 (C)
(RS Pts.—Bears 695, Buccaneers 394)

CHICAGO vs. *WASHINGTON
RS: Bears lead series, 18-12-1
PS: Redskins lead series, 4-3
1932—Tie, 7-7 (B)
1933—Bears, 7-0 (C)
Redskins, 10-0 (B)
1934—Bears, 21-0 (B)
1935—Bears, 30-14 (B)
1936—Bears, 26-0 (C)
1937—**Redskins, 28-21 (C)
1938—Bears, 31-7 (C)
1940—Redskins, 7-3 (W)
**Bears, 73-0 (W)
1941—Bears, 35-21 (C)
1942—**Redskins, 14-6 (W)
1943—Redskins, 21-7 (W)
**Bears, 41-21 (C)
1945—Redskins, 28-21 (W)
1946—Bears, 24-20 (C)

1947—Bears, 56-20 (W)
1948—Bears, 48-13 (C)
1949—Bears, 31-21 (W)
1951—Bears, 27-0 (W)
1953—Bears, 27-24 (W)
1957—Redskins, 14-3 (C)
1964—Redskins, 27-20 (W)
1968—Bears, 38-28 (C)
1971—Bears, 16-15 (C)
1974—Redskins, 42-0 (W)
1976—Bears, 33-7 (C)
1978—Bears, 14-10 (W)
1980—Bears, 35-21 (C)
1981—Redskins, 24-7 (C)
1984—***Bears, 23-19 (W)
1985—Bears, 45-10 (C)
1986—***Redskins, 27-13 (C)
1987—***Redskins, 21-17 (C)
1988—Bears, 34-14 (W)
1989—Redskins, 38-14 (W)
1990—Redskins, 10-9 (W)
1991—Bears, 20-7 (C)
(RS Pts.—Bears 666, Redskins 503)
(PS Pts.—Bears 194, Redskins 130)
*Franchise in Boston prior to 1937 and known as Braves prior to 1933
**NFL Championship
***NFC Divisional Playoff

CINCINNATI vs. ATLANTA
RS: Bengals lead series, 5-2;
See Atlanta vs. Cincinnati
CINCINNATI vs. BUFFALO
RS: Bengals lead series, 9-7
PS: Bengals lead series, 2-0;
See Buffalo vs. Cincinnati
CINCINNATI vs. CHICAGO
RS: Series tied, 2-2;
See Chicago vs. Cincinnati
CINCINNATI vs. CLEVELAND
RS: Bengals lead series, 23-20
1970—Browns, 30-27 (Cle)
Bengals, 14-10 (Cin)
1971—Browns, 27-24 (Cin)
Browns, 31-27 (Cle)
1972—Browns, 27-6 (Cle)
Browns, 27-24 (Cin)
1973—Browns, 17-10 (Cle)
Bengals, 34-17 (Cin)
1974—Bengals, 33-7 (Cin)
Bengals, 34-24 (Cle)
1975—Bengals, 24-17 (Cin)
Browns, 35-23 (Cle)
1976—Bengals, 45-24 (Cle)
Bengals, 21-6 (Cin)
1977—Browns, 13-3 (Cin)
Browns, 10-7 (Cle)
1978—Browns, 13-10 (Cle) OT
Bengals, 48-16 (Cin)
1979—Browns, 28-27 (Cle)
Bengals, 16-12 (Cin)
1980—Browns, 31-7 (Cle)
Browns, 27-24 (Cin)
1981—Bengals, 20-17 (Cin)
Bengals, 41-21 (Cle)
1982—Bengals, 23-10 (Cin)
1983—Browns, 17-7 (Cle)
Bengals, 28-21 (Cin)
1984—Bengals, 12-9 (Cin)
Bengals, 20-17 (Cle) OT
1985—Bengals, 27-10 (Cin)
Browns, 24-6 (Cle)
1986—Bengals, 30-13 (Cin)
Browns, 34-3 (Cin)
1987—Browns, 34-0 (Cin)
Browns, 38-24 (Cle)
1988—Bengals, 24-17 (Cin)
Browns, 23-16 (Cle)
1989—Bengals, 21-14 (Cin)
Bengals, 21-0 (Cle)
1990—Bengals, 34-13 (Cle)
Bengals, 21-14 (Cin)
1991—Browns, 14-13 (Cle)
Bengals, 23-21 (Cin)
(RS Pts.—Bengals 902, Browns 830)
CINCINNATI vs. DALLAS
RS: Cowboys lead series, 3-2
1973—Cowboys, 38-10 (D)
1979—Cowboys, 38-13 (D)
1985—Bengals, 50-24 (C)
1988—Bengals, 38-24 (D)
1991—Cowboys, 35-23 (D)
(RS Pts.—Cowboys 159, Bengals 134)
CINCINNATI vs. DENVER
RS: Broncos lead series, 10-6
1968—Bengals, 24-10 (C)
Broncos, 10-7 (C)
1969—Broncos, 30-23 (C)
Broncos, 27-16 (D)
1971—Bengals, 24-10 (D)
1972—Bengals, 21-10 (C)
1973—Broncos, 28-10 (D)
1975—Bengals, 17-16 (D)

1976—Bengals, 17-7 (C)
1977—Broncos, 24-13 (C)
1979—Broncos, 10-0 (D)
1981—Bengals, 38-21 (C)
1983—Broncos, 24-17 (D)
1984—Broncos, 20-17 (D)
1986—Broncos, 34-28 (D)
1991—Broncos, 45-14 (D)
(RS Pts.—Broncos 326, Bengals 286)
CINCINNATI vs. DETROIT
RS: Bengals lead series, 3-2
1970—Lions, 38-3 (D)
1974—Lions, 23-19 (C)
1983—Bengals, 17-9 (C)
1986—Bengals, 24-17 (D)
1989—Bengals, 42-7 (C)
(RS Pts.—Bengals 105, Lions 94)
CINCINNATI vs. GREEN BAY
RS: Bengals lead series, 4-2
1971—Packers, 20-17 (GB)
1976—Bengals, 28-7 (C)
1977—Bengals, 17-7 (Mil)
1980—Packers, 14-9 (GB)
1983—Bengals, 34-14 (C)
1986—Bengals, 34-28 (Mil)
(RS Pts.—Bengals 139, Packers 90)
CINCINNATI vs. HOUSTON
RS: Bengals lead series, 24-21-1
PS: Bengals lead series, 1-0
1968—Oilers, 27-17 (C)
1969—Tie, 31-31 (H)
1970—Oilers, 20-13 (C)
Bengals, 30-20 (H)
1971—Oilers, 10-6 (H)
Bengals, 28-13 (C)
1972—Bengals, 30-7 (C)
Bengals, 61-17 (H)
1973—Bengals, 24-10 (C)
Bengals, 27-24 (H)
1974—Bengals, 34-21 (C)
Oilers, 20-3 (H)
1975—Bengals, 21-19 (H)
Bengals, 23-19 (C)
1976—Bengals, 27-7 (H)
Bengals, 31-27 (C)
1977—Bengals, 13-10 (C) OT
Oilers, 21-16 (H)
1978—Bengals, 28-13 (C)
Oilers, 17-10 (H)
1979—Oilers, 30-27 (C) OT
Oilers, 42-21 (H)
1980—Oilers, 13-10 (C)
Oilers, 23-3 (H)
1981—Oilers, 17-10 (H)
Bengals, 34-21 (C)
1982—Bengals, 27-6 (C)
Bengals, 35-27 (H)
1983—Bengals, 55-14 (H)
Bengals, 38-10 (C)
1984—Bengals, 13-3 (C)
Bengals, 31-13 (H)
1985—Oilers, 44-27 (H)
Bengals, 45-27 (C)
1986—Bengals, 31-28 (C)
Oilers, 32-28 (H)
1987—Oilers, 31-29 (C)
Oilers, 21-17 (H)
1988—Bengals, 44-21 (C)
Oilers, 41-6 (H)
1989—Oilers, 26-24 (H)
Bengals, 61-7 (C)
1990—Oilers, 48-17 (H)
Bengals, 40-20 (C)
*Bengals, 41-14 (C)
1991—Oilers, 30-7 (C)
Oilers, 35-3 (H)
(RS Pts.—Bengals 1,143, Oilers 996)
(PS Pts.—Bengals 41, Oilers 14)
*AFC First Round Playoff
CINCINNATI vs.*INDIANAPOLIS
RS: Colts lead series, 6-5
PS: Colts lead series, 1-0
1970—**Colts, 17-0 (B)
1972—Colts, 20-19 (C)
1974—Colts, 24-14 (B)
1976—Colts, 28-27 (B)
1979—Colts, 38-28 (B)
1980—Bengals, 34-33 (B)
1981—Bengals, 41-19 (B)
1982—Colts, 20-17 (B)
1983—Colts, 34-31 (C)
1987—Bengals, 23-21 (I)
1989—Colts, 23-12 (C)
1990—Colts, 34-20 (C)
(RS Pts.—Colts 281, Bengals 279)
(PS Pts.—Colts 17, Bengals 0)
*Franchise in Baltimore prior to 1984
**AFC Divisional Playoff
CINCINNATI vs. KANSAS CITY
RS: Chiefs lead series, 10-9
1968—Chiefs, 13-3 (KC)
Chiefs, 16-9 (C)
1969—Bengals, 24-19 (C)

Chiefs, 42-22 (KC)
1970—Chiefs, 27-19 (C)
1972—Bengals, 23-16 (KC)
1973—Bengals, 14-6 (C)
1974—Bengals, 33-6 (C)
1976—Bengals, 27-24 (KC)
1977—Bengals, 27-7 (KC)
1978—Chiefs, 24-23 (C)
1979—Chiefs, 10-7 (C)
1980—Bengals, 20-6 (C)
1983—Chiefs, 20-15 (C)
1984—Chiefs, 27-22 (C)
1986—Chiefs, 24-14 (KC)
1987—Bengals, 30-27 (C) OT
1988—Chiefs, 31-28 (KC)
1989—Bengals, 21-17 (KC)
(RS Pts.—Bengals 381, Chiefs 362)
CINCINNATI vs. *L.A. RAIDERS
RS: Raiders lead series, 14-5
PS: Raiders lead series, 2-0
1968—Raiders, 31-10 (O)
Raiders, 34-0 (C)
1969—Bengals, 31-17 (C)
Raiders, 37-17 (O)
1970—Bengals, 31-21 (C)
1971—Bengals, 31-27 (C)
1972—Raiders, 20-14 (C)
1974—Raiders, 30-27 (C)
1975—Bengals, 14-10 (C)
**Raiders, 31-28 (O)
1976—Raiders, 35-20 (O)
1978—Raiders, 34-21 (C)
1980—Raiders, 28-17 (O)
1982—Raiders, 31-17 (C)
1983—Raiders, 20-10 (C)
1985—Raiders, 13-6 (LA)
1988—Bengals, 45-21 (LA)
1989—Bengals, 28-7 (LA)
1990—Raiders, 24-7 (LA)
**Raiders, 20-10 (LA)
1991—Raiders, 38-14 (C)
(RS Pts.—Raiders 489, Bengals 349)
(PS Pts.—Raiders 51, Bengals 38)
*Franchise in Oakland prior to 1982
**AFC Divisional Playoff
CINCINNATI vs. L.A. RAMS
RS: Bengals lead series, 4-2
1972—Rams, 15-12 (LA)
1976—Bengals, 20-12 (C)
1978—Bengals, 20-19 (LA)
1981—Bengals, 24-10 (C)
1984—Rams, 24-14 (C)
1990—Bengals, 34-31 (LA) OT
(RS Pts.—Bengals 124, Rams 111)
CINCINNATI vs. MIAMI
RS: Dolphins lead series, 9-3
PS: Dolphins lead series, 1-0
1968—Dolphins, 24-22 (C)
Bengals, 38-21 (M)
1969—Bengals, 27-21 (C)
1971—Dolphins, 23-13 (C)
1973—*Dolphins, 34-16 (M)
1974—Dolphins, 24-3 (M)
1977—Bengals, 23-17 (C)
1978—Dolphins, 21-0 (M)
1980—Dolphins, 17-16 (M)
1983—Dolphins, 38-14 (M)
1987—Dolphins, 20-14 (C)
1989—Dolphins, 20-13 (C)
1991—Dolphins, 37-13 (M)
(RS Pts.—Dolphins 317, Bengals 212)
(PS Pts.—Dolphins 34, Bengals 16)
*AFC Divisional Playoff
CINCINNATI vs. MINNESOTA
RS: Series tied, 3-3
1973—Bengals, 27-0 (C)
1977—Vikings, 42-10 (M)
1980—Bengals, 14-0 (C)
1983—Vikings, 20-14 (M)
1986—Bengals, 24-20 (C)
1989—Vikings, 29-21 (M)
(RS Pts.—Vikings 111, Bengals 110)
CINCINNATI vs. *NEW ENGLAND
RS: Patriots lead series, 7-6
1968—Patriots, 33-14 (B)
1969—Patriots, 25-14 (C)
1970—Bengals, 45-7 (C)
1972—Bengals, 31-7 (NE)
1975—Bengals, 27-10 (C)
1978—Patriots, 10-3 (C)
1979—Patriots, 20-14 (C)
1984—Patriots, 20-14 (NE)
1985—Patriots, 34-23 (NE)
1986—Bengals, 31-7 (NE)
1988—Patriots, 27-21 (NE)
1990—Bengals, 41-7 (C)
1991—Bengals, 29-7 (C)
(RS Pts.—Bengals 307, Patriots 214)
*Franchise in Boston prior to 1971
CINCINNATI vs. NEW ORLEANS
RS: Saints lead series, 4-3
1970—Bengals, 26-6 (C)
1975—Bengals, 21-0 (NO)

1978—Saints, 20-18 (C)
1981—Saints, 17-7 (NO)
1984—Bengals, 24-21 (NO)
1987—Saints, 41-24 (C)
1990—Saints, 21-7 (C)
(RS Pts.—Bengals 127, Saints 126)
CINCINNATI vs. N.Y. GIANTS
RS: Bengals lead series, 4-0
1972—Bengals, 13-10 (C)
1977—Bengals, 30-13 (C)
1985—Bengals, 35-30 (C)
1991—Bengals, 27-24 (C)
(RS Pts.—Bengals 105, Giants 77)
CINCINNATI vs. N.Y. JETS
RS: Jets lead series, 7-6
PS: Jets lead series, 1-0
1968—Jets, 27-14 (NY)
1969—Jets, 21-7 (C)
Jets, 40-7 (NY)
1971—Jets, 35-21 (NY)
1973—Bengals, 20-14 (C)
1976—Bengals, 42-3 (NY)
1981—Bengals, 31-30 (NY)
1982—*Jets, 44-17 (C)
1984—Jets, 43-23 (NY)
1985—Jets, 29-20 (C)
1986—Bengals, 52-21 (C)
1987—Jets, 27-20 (NY)
1988—Bengals, 36-19 (C)
1990—Bengals, 25-20 (C)
(RS Pts.—Jets 329, Bengals 318)
(PS Pts.—Jets 44, Bengals 17)
*AFC First Round Playoff
CINCINNATI vs. PHILADELPHIA
RS: Bengals lead series, 5-1
1971—Bengals, 37-14 (C)
1975—Bengals, 31-0 (C)
1979—Bengals, 37-13 (C)
1982—Bengals, 18-14 (P)
1988—Bengals, 28-24 (P)
1991—Eagles, 17-10 (P)
(RS Pts.—Bengals 161, Eagles 82)
CINCINNATI vs. *PHOENIX
RS: Bengals lead series, 3-1
1973—Bengals, 42-24 (C)
1979—Bengals, 34-28 (C)
1985—Cardinals, 41-27 (StL)
1988—Bengals, 21-14 (C)
(RS Pts.—Bengals 124, Cardinals 107)
*Franchise in St. Louis prior to 1988
CINCINNATI vs. PITTSBURGH
RS: Steelers lead series, 22-21
1970—Steelers, 21-10 (P)
Bengals, 34-7 (C)
1971—Bengals, 21-10 (P)
Steelers, 21-13 (C)
1972—Bengals, 15-10 (C)
Steelers, 40-17 (P)
1973—Bengals, 19-7 (C)
Steelers, 20-13 (P)
1974—Bengals, 17-10 (C)
Steelers, 27-3 (P)
1975—Bengals, 30-24 (C)
Steelers, 35-14 (P)
1976—Steelers, 23-6 (P)
Steelers, 7-3 (C)
1977—Steelers, 20-14 (P)
Steelers, 17-10 (C)
1978—Steelers, 28-3 (C)
Steelers, 7-6 (P)
1979—Bengals, 34-10 (C)
Steelers, 37-17 (P)
1980—Bengals, 30-28 (P)
Bengals, 17-16 (P)
1981—Bengals, 34-7 (C)
Bengals, 17-10 (P)
1982—Steelers, 26-20 (P) OT
1983—Steelers, 24-14 (C)
Bengals, 23-10 (P)
1984—Bengals, 38-17 (C)
Bengals, 22-20 (P)
1985—Bengals, 37-24 (P)
Bengals, 26-21 (C)
1986—Bengals, 24-22 (C)
Steelers, 30-9 (P)
1987—Steelers, 23-20 (P)
Steelers, 30-16 (C)
1988—Steelers, 17-12 (P)
Bengals, 42-7 (C)
1989—Bengals, 41-10 (C)
Bengals, 26-16 (P)
1990—Bengals, 27-3 (C)
Bengals, 16-12 (P)
1991—Steelers, 33-27 (C) OT
Steelers, 17-10 (P)
(RS Pts.—Steelers 830, Bengals 821)
CINCINNATI vs. SAN DIEGO
RS: Chargers lead series, 11-8
PS: Bengals lead series, 1-0
1968—Chargers, 29-13 (SD)
Chargers, 31-10 (C)
1969—Bengals, 34-20 (C)
Chargers, 21-14 (SD)

1970—Bengals, 17-14 (SD)
1971—Bengals, 31-0 (C)
1973—Bengals, 20-13 (SD)
1974—Chargers, 20-17 (C)
1975—Bengals, 47-17 (C)
1977—Chargers, 24-3 (SD)
1978—Chargers, 22-13 (SD)
1979—Chargers, 26-24 (C)
1980—Chargers, 31-14 (C)
1981—Bengals, 40-17 (SD)
   *Bengals, 27-7 (C)
1982—Chargers, 50-34 (SD)
1985—Chargers, 44-41 (C)
1987—Chargers, 10-9 (C)
1988—Bengals, 27-10 (C)
1990—Bengals, 21-16 (SD)
(RS Pts.—Bengals 429, Chargers 415)
(PS Pts.—Bengals 27, Chargers 7)
*AFC Championship

CINCINNATI vs. SAN FRANCISCO
RS: 49ers lead series, 5-1
PS: 49ers lead series, 2-0
1974—49ers, 21-3 (SF)
1978—49ers, 28-12 (SF)
1981—49ers, 21-3 (C)
   *49ers, 26-21 (Detroit)
1984—49ers, 23-17 (SF)
1987—49ers, 27-26 (C)
1988—**49ers, 20-16 (Miami)
1990—49ers, 20-17 (C)
(RS Pts.—49ers 122, Bengals 96)
(PS Pts.—49ers 46, Bengals 37)
*Super Bowl XVI
**Super Bowl XXIII

CINCINNATI vs. SEATTLE
RS: Series tied, 5-5
PS: Bengals lead series, 1-0
1977—Bengals, 42-20 (C)
1981—Bengals, 27-21 (C)
1982—Bengals, 24-10 (C)
1984—Seahawks, 26-6 (C)
1985—Seahawks, 28-24 (C)
1986—Bengals, 34-7 (C)
1987—Bengals, 17-10 (C)
1988—*Bengals, 21-13 (C)
1989—Seahawks, 24-17 (C)
1990—Seahawks, 31-16 (S)
1991—Seahawks, 13-7 (C)
(RS Pts.—Bengals 214, Seahawks 190)
(PS Pts.—Bengals 21, Seahawks 13)
*AFC Divisional Playoff

CINCINNATI vs. TAMPA BAY
RS: Bengals lead series, 3-1
1976—Bengals, 21-0 (C)
1980—Buccaneers, 17-12 (C)
1983—Bengals, 23-17 (TB)
1989—Bengals, 56-23 (C)
(RS Pts.—Bengals 112, Buccaneers 57)

CINCINNATI vs. WASHINGTON
RS: Redskins lead series, 4-2
1970—Redskins, 20-0 (W)
1974—Bengals, 28-17 (C)
1979—Redskins, 28-14 (W)
1985—Redskins, 27-24 (W)
1988—Bengals, 20-17 (C) OT
1991—Redskins, 34-27 (C)
(RS Pts.—Redskins 143, Bengals 113)

CLEVELAND vs. ATLANTA
RS: Browns lead series, 8-1;
See Atlanta vs. Cleveland
CLEVELAND vs. BUFFALO
RS: Browns lead series, 7-3
PS: Browns lead series, 1-0;
See Buffalo vs. Cleveland
CLEVELAND vs. CHICAGO
RS: Browns lead series, 7-3;
See Chicago vs. Cleveland
CLEVELAND vs. CINCINNATI
RS: Bengals lead series, 23-20;
See Cincinnati vs. Cleveland
CLEVELAND vs. DALLAS
RS: Browns lead series, 14-9
PS: Browns lead series, 2-1
1960—Browns, 48-7 (D)
1961—Browns, 25-7 (C)
   Browns, 38-17 (D)
1962—Browns, 19-10 (C)
   Cowboys, 45-21 (D)
1963—Browns, 41-24 (D)
   Browns, 27-17 (C)
1964—Browns, 27-6 (C)
   Browns, 20-16 (D)
1965—Browns, 23-17 (C)
   Browns, 24-17 (D)
1966—Browns, 30-21 (C)
   Cowboys, 26-14 (D)
1967—Cowboys, 21-14 (C)
   *Cowboys, 52-14 (D)
1968—Cowboys, 28-7 (C)
   *Browns, 31-20 (C)
1969—Browns, 42-10 (C)
   *Browns, 38-14 (D)

1970—Cowboys, 6-2 (C)
1974—Cowboys, 41-17 (D)
1979—Browns, 26-7 (C)
1982—Cowboys, 31-14 (D)
1985—Cowboys, 20-7 (D)
1988—Browns, 24-21 (C)
1991—Cowboys, 26-14 (C)
(RS Pts.—Browns 524, Cowboys 441)
(PS Pts.—Cowboys 86, Browns 83)
*Conference Championship
CLEVELAND vs. DENVER
RS: Broncos lead series, 10-5
PS: Broncos lead series, 3-0
1970—Browns, 27-13 (D)
1971—Broncos, 27-0 (C)
1972—Browns, 27-20 (D)
1974—Browns, 23-21 (C)
1975—Broncos, 16-15 (D)
1976—Broncos, 44-13 (D)
1978—Broncos, 19-7 (C)
1980—Broncos, 19-16 (C)
1981—Broncos, 23-20 (D) OT
1983—Broncos, 27-6 (D)
1984—Broncos, 24-14 (C)
1986—*Broncos, 23-20 (C) OT
1987—*Broncos, 38-33 (D)
1988—Broncos, 30-7 (C)
1989—Browns, 16-13 (C)
   *Broncos, 37-21 (D)
1990—Browns, 30-29 (D)
1991—Broncos, 17-7 (C)
(RS Pts.—Broncos 342, Browns 228)
(PS Pts.—Broncos 98, Browns 74)
*AFC Championship
CLEVELAND vs. DETROIT
RS: Lions lead series, 10-3
PS: Lions lead series, 3-1
1952—Lions, 17-6 (D)
   *Lions, 17-7 (C)
1953—*Lions, 17-16 (D)
1954—Lions, 14-10 (C)
   *Browns, 56-10 (C)
1957—Lions, 20-7 (D)
   *Lions, 59-14 (D)
1958—Lions, 30-10 (C)
1963—Lions, 38-10 (D)
1964—Browns, 37-21 (C)
1967—Lions, 31-14 (D)
1969—Lions, 28-21 (C)
1970—Lions, 41-24 (C)
1975—Lions, 21-10 (D)
1983—Browns, 31-26 (D)
1986—Browns, 24-21 (D)
1989—Lions, 13-10 (D)
(RS Pts.—Lions 321, Browns 214)
(PS Pts.—Lions 103, Browns 93)
*NFL Championship
CLEVELAND vs. GREEN BAY
RS: Packers lead series, 7-5
PS: Packers lead series, 1-0
1953—Browns, 27-0 (Mil)
1955—Browns, 41-10 (C)
1956—Browns, 24-7 (Mil)
1961—Packers, 49-17 (C)
1964—Packers, 28-21 (Mil)
1965—*Packers, 23-12 (GB)
1966—Packers, 21-20 (C)
1967—Packers, 55-7 (Mil)
1969—Browns, 20-7 (C)
1972—Packers, 26-10 (C)
1980—Browns, 26-21 (C)
1983—Packers, 35-21 (Mil)
1986—Packers, 17-14 (C)
(RS Pts.—Packers 276, Browns 248)
(PS Pts.—Packers 23, Browns 12)
*NFL Championship
CLEVELAND vs. HOUSTON
RS: Browns lead series, 26-17
PS: Oilers lead series, 1-0
1970—Browns, 28-14 (C)
   Browns, 21-10 (H)
1971—Browns, 31-0 (C)
   Browns, 37-24 (H)
1972—Browns, 23-17 (H)
   Browns, 20-0 (C)
1973—*Browns, 42-13 (C)
   Browns, 23-13 (H)
1974—Browns, 20-7 (C)
   Oilers, 28-24 (H)
1975—Oilers, 40-10 (C)
   Oilers, 21-10 (H)
1976—Browns, 21-7 (H)
   Browns, 13-10 (C)
1977—Browns, 24-23 (H)
   Oilers, 19-15 (C)
1978—Oilers, 16-13 (C)
   Oilers, 14-10 (H)
1979—Oilers, 31-10 (H)
   Browns, 14-7 (C)
1980—Oilers, 16-7 (C)
   Browns, 17-14 (H)
1981—Oilers, 9-3 (C)
   Oilers, 17-13 (H)

1982—Browns, 20-14 (H)
1983—Browns, 25-19 (C) OT
   Oilers, 34-27 (H)
1984—Browns, 27-10 (C)
   Browns, 27-20 (H)
1985—Browns, 21-6 (H)
   Browns, 28-21 (C)
1986—Browns, 23-20 (H)
   Browns, 13-10 (C) OT
1987—Oilers, 15-10 (C)
   Browns, 40-7 (H)
1988—Oilers, 24-17 (H)
   Browns, 28-23 (C)
   *Oilers, 24-23 (C)
1989—Browns, 28-17 (C)
   Browns, 24-20 (H)
1990—Browns 35-23 (C)
   Oilers 58-14 (H)
1991—Oilers, 28-24 (H)
   Oilers, 17-14 (C)
(RS Pts.—Browns 882, Oilers 768)
(PS Pts.—Oilers 24, Browns 23)
*AFC First Round Playoff
CLEVELAND vs. *INDIANAPOLIS
RS: Browns lead series, 12-5
PS: Series tied, 2-2
1956—Colts, 21-7 (C)
1959—Browns, 38-31 (B)
1962—Colts, 36-14 (C)
1964—**Browns, 27-0 (C)
1968—Browns, 30-20 (B)
   **Colts, 34-0 (C)
1971—Browns, 14-13 (B)
   ***Colts, 20-3 (C)
1973—Browns, 24-14 (C)
1975—Colts, 21-7 (B)
1978—Browns, 45-24 (B)
1979—Browns, 13-10 (C)
1980—Browns, 28-27 (B)
1981—Browns, 42-28 (C)
1983—Browns, 41-23 (C)
1986—Browns, 24-9 (I)
1987—Colts, 9-7 (C)
   ***Browns, 38-21 (C)
1988—Browns, 23-17 (C)
1989—Colts, 23-17 (I) OT
1991—Browns, 31-0 (I)
(RS Pts.—Browns 405, Colts 326)
(PS Pts.—Colts 75, Browns 68)
*Franchise in Baltimore prior to 1984
**NFL Championship
***AFC Divisional Playoff
CLEVELAND vs. KANSAS CITY
RS: Browns lead series, 7-6-2
1971—Chiefs, 13-7 (KC)
1972—Chiefs, 31-7 (C)
1973—Tie, 20-20 (KC)
1975—Browns, 40-14 (C)
1976—Chiefs, 39-14 (KC)
1977—Browns, 44-7 (C)
1978—Chiefs, 17-3 (KC)
1979—Browns, 27-24 (KC)
1980—Browns, 20-13 (C)
1984—Chiefs, 10-6 (KC)
1986—Browns, 20-7 (C)
1988—Browns, 6-3 (KC)
1989—Tie, 10-10 (C) OT
1990—Chiefs, 34-0 (KC)
1991—Browns, 20-15 (C)
(RS Pts.—Chiefs 257, Browns 244)
CLEVELAND vs. *L.A. RAIDERS
RS: Raiders lead series, 8-2
PS: Raiders lead series, 2-0
1970—Raiders, 23-20 (O)
1971—Raiders, 34-20 (C)
1973—Browns, 7-3 (O)
1974—Raiders, 40-24 (C)
1975—Raiders, 38-17 (O)
1977—Raiders, 26-10 (C)
1979—Raiders, 19-14 (O)
1980—**Raiders, 14-12 (C)
1982—***Raiders, 27-10 (LA)
1985—Raiders, 21-20 (C)
1986—Raiders, 27-14 (LA)
1987—Browns, 24-17 (LA)
(RS Pts.—Raiders 248, Browns 170)
(PS Pts.—Raiders 41, Browns 22)
*Franchise in Oakland prior to 1982
**AFC Divisional Playoff
***AFC First Round Playoff
CLEVELAND vs. L.A. RAMS
RS: Series tied, 7-7
PS: Browns lead series, 2-1
1950—*Browns, 30-28 (C)
1951—Browns, 38-23 (LA)
   *Rams, 24-17 (LA)
1952—Browns, 37-7 (C)
1955—*Browns, 38-14 (LA)
1957—Browns, 45-31 (C)
1958—Browns, 30-27 (LA)
1963—Browns, 20-6 (LA)
1965—Rams, 42-7 (LA)
1968—Rams, 24-6 (C)

1973—Rams, 30-17 (LA)
1977—Rams, 9-0 (C)
1978—Browns, 30-19 (C)
1981—Rams, 27-16 (LA)
1984—Rams, 20-17 (LA)
1987—Browns, 30-17 (C)
1990—Rams, 38-23 (C)
(RS Pts.—Rams 320, Browns 316)
(PS Pts.—Browns 85, Rams 66)
*NFL Championship
CLEVELAND vs. MIAMI
RS: Series tied, 4-4
PS: Dolphins lead series, 2-0
1970—Browns, 28-0 (H)
1972—*Dolphins, 20-14 (M)
1973—Dolphins, 17-9 (C)
1976—Browns, 17-13 (C)
1979—Browns, 30-24 (C) OT
1985—*Dolphins, 24-21 (M)
1986—Browns, 26-16 (C)
1988—Dolphins, 38-31 (M)
1989—Dolphins, 13-10 (M) OT
1990—Dolphins, 30-13 (C)
(RS Pts.—Browns 164, Dolphins 151)
(PS Pts.—Dolphins 44, Browns 35)
*AFC Divisional Playoff
CLEVELAND vs. MINNESOTA
RS: Vikings lead series, 6-3
PS: Vikings lead series, 1-0
1965—Vikings, 27-17 (C)
1967—Browns, 14-10 (C)
1969—Vikings, 51-3 (M)
   *Vikings, 27-7 (M)
1973—Vikings, 26-3 (M)
1975—Vikings, 42-10 (C)
1980—Vikings, 28-23 (M)
1983—Vikings, 27-21 (C)
1986—Browns, 23-20 (M)
1989—Browns, 23-17 (C) OT
(RS Pts.—Vikings 248, Browns 137)
(PS Pts.—Vikings 27, Browns 7)
*NFL Championship
CLEVELAND vs. NEW ENGLAND
RS: Browns lead series, 8-2
1971—Browns, 27-7 (C)
1974—Browns, 21-14 (NE)
1977—Browns, 30-27 (C) OT
1980—Patriots, 34-17 (NE)
1982—Browns, 10-7 (C)
1983—Browns, 30-0 (NE)
1984—Patriots, 17-16 (C)
1985—Browns, 24-20 (C)
1987—Browns, 20-10 (NE)
1991—Browns, 20-0 (NE)
(RS Pts.—Browns 215, Patriots 136)
CLEVELAND vs. NEW ORLEANS
RS: Browns lead series, 8-3
1967—Browns, 42-7 (NO)
1968—Browns, 24-10 (NO)
   Browns, 35-17 (C)
1969—Browns, 27-17 (NO)
1971—Browns, 21-17 (NO)
1975—Browns, 17-16 (C)
1978—Browns, 24-16 (NO)
1981—Browns, 20-17 (C)
1984—Saints, 16-14 (C)
1987—Saints, 28-21 (NO)
1990—Saints, 25-20 (NO)
(RS Pts.—Browns 265, Saints 186)
CLEVELAND vs. N.Y. GIANTS
RS: Browns lead series, 25-16-2
PS: Series tied, 1-1
1950—Giants, 6-0 (C)
   Giants, 17-13 (NY)
   *Browns, 8-3 (C)
1951—Browns, 14-13 (C)
   Browns, 10-0 (NY)
1952—Giants, 17-9 (C)
   Giants, 37-34 (NY)
1953—Browns, 7-0 (NY)
   Browns, 62-14 (C)
1954—Browns, 24-14 (C)
   Browns, 16-7 (NY)
1955—Browns, 24-14 (C)
   Tie, 35-35 (NY)
1956—Giants, 21-9 (C)
   Browns, 24-7 (NY)
1957—Browns, 6-3 (C)
   Browns, 34-28 (NY)
1958—Giants, 21-17 (C)
   Giants, 13-10 (NY)
   *Giants, 10-0 (NY)
1959—Giants, 10-6 (C)
   Giants, 48-7 (NY)
1960—Browns, 17-13 (C)
   Browns, 48-34 (NY)
1961—Giants, 37-21 (C)
   Tie, 7-7 (NY)
1962—Browns, 17-7 (C)
   Giants, 17-13 (NY)
1963—Browns, 35-24 (NY)
   Giants, 33-6 (C)
1964—Browns, 42-20 (C)

Browns, 52-20 (NY)
1965—Browns, 38-14 (NY)
Browns, 34-21 (C)
1966—Browns, 28-7 (NY)
Browns, 49-40 (C)
1967—Giants, 38-34 (NY)
Browns, 24-14 (C)
1968—Browns, 45-10 (C)
1969—Browns, 28-17 (C)
Giants, 27-14 (NY)
1973—Browns, 12-10 (C)
1977—Browns, 21-7 (NY)
1985—Browns, 35-33 (NY)
1991—Giants, 13-10 (NY)
(RS Pts.—Browns 987, Giants 792)
(PS Pts.—Giants 13, Browns 8)
*Conference Playoff

CLEVELAND vs. N.Y. JETS
RS: Browns lead series, 8-6
PS: Browns lead series, 1-0
1970—Browns, 31-21 (C)
1972—Browns, 26-10 (NY)
1976—Browns, 38-17 (C)
1978—Browns, 37-34 (C) OT
1979—Browns, 25-22 (NY) OT
1980—Browns, 17-14 (C)
1981—Jets, 14-13 (C)
1983—Browns, 10-7 (C)
1984—Jets, 24-20 (C)
1985—Jets, 37-10 (NY)
1986—*Browns, 23-20 (C) OT
1988—Jets, 23-3 (C)
1989—Browns, 38-24 (C)
1990—Jets, 24-21 (NY)
1991—Jets, 17-14 (C)
(RS Pts.—Browns 303, Jets 288)
(PS Pts.—Browns 23, Jets 20)
*AFC Divisional Playoff

CLEVELAND vs. PHILADELPHIA
RS: Browns lead series, 30-12-1
1950—Browns, 35-10 (P)
Browns, 13-7 (C)
1951—Browns, 20-17 (C)
Browns, 24-9 (NY)
1952—Browns, 49-7 (P)
Eagles, 28-20 (C)
1953—Browns, 37-13 (C)
Eagles, 42-27 (P)
1954—Eagles, 28-10 (P)
Browns, 6-0 (C)
1955—Browns, 21-17 (C)
Eagles, 33-17 (P)
1956—Browns, 16-0 (P)
Browns, 17-14 (C)
1957—Browns, 24-7 (C)
Eagles, 17-7 (P)
1958—Browns, 28-14 (C)
Browns, 21-14 (P)
1959—Browns, 28-7 (C)
Browns, 28-21 (P)
1960—Browns, 41-24 (P)
Eagles, 31-29 (C)
1961—Eagles, 27-20 (P)
Browns, 45-24 (C)
1962—Eagles, 35-7 (P)
Tie, 14-14 (C)
1963—Browns, 37-7 (C)
Browns, 23-17 (P)
1964—Browns, 28-20 (P)
Browns, 38-24 (C)
1965—Browns, 35-17 (P)
Browns, 38-34 (C)
1966—Browns, 27-7 (C)
Eagles, 33-21 (P)
1967—Eagles, 28-24 (P)
1968—Browns, 47-13 (C)
1969—Browns, 27-20 (P)
1972—Browns, 27-17 (C)
1976—Browns, 24-3 (C)
1979—Browns, 24-19 (C)
1982—Eagles, 24-21 (C)
1988—Browns, 19-3 (C)
1991—Eagles, 32-30 (C)
(RS Pts.—Browns 1,094, Eagles 778)

CLEVELAND vs. *PHOENIX
RS: Browns lead series, 31-10-3
1950—Browns, 34-24 (Cle)
Browns, 10-7 (Chi)
1951—Browns, 34-17 (Chi)
Browns, 49-28 (Cle)
1952—Browns, 28-13 (Cle)
Browns, 10-0 (Chi)
1953—Browns, 27-7 (Chi)
Browns, 27-16 (Cle)
1954—Browns, 31-7 (Cle)
Browns, 35-3 (Chi)
1955—Browns, 26-20 (Chi)
Browns, 35-24 (Cle)
1956—Cardinals, 9-7 (Chi)
Cardinals, 24-7 (Cle)
1957—Browns, 17-7 (Chi)
Browns, 31-0 (Cle)
1958—Browns, 35-28 (Cle)

Browns, 38-24 (Chi)
1959—Browns, 34-7 (Chi)
Browns, 17-7 (Cle)
1960—Browns, 28-27 (Cle)
Tie, 17-17 (StL)
1961—Browns, 20-17 (Cle)
Browns, 21-10 (StL)
1962—Browns, 34-7 (StL)
Browns, 38-14 (Cle)
1963—Cardinals, 20-14 (Cle)
Browns, 24-10 (StL)
1964—Tie, 33-33 (Cle)
Cardinals, 28-19 (StL)
1965—Cardinals, 49-13 (Cle)
Browns, 27-24 (Cle)
1966—Cardinals, 34-28 (Cle)
Browns, 38-10 (StL)
1967—Browns, 20-16 (Cle)
Browns, 20-16 (StL)
1968—Cardinals, 27-21 (Cle)
Cardinals, 27-16 (StL)
1969—Tie, 21-21 (Cle)
Browns, 27-21 (StL)
1974—Cardinals, 29-7 (StL)
1979—Browns, 38-20 (StL)
1985—Cardinals, 27-24 (Cle) OT
1988—Browns, 29-21 (C)
(RS Pts.—Browns 1,109, Cardinals 797)
*Franchise in St. Louis prior to 1988,
and in Chicago prior to 1960

CLEVELAND vs. PITTSBURGH
RS: Browns lead series, 50-34
1950—Browns, 30-17 (P)
Browns, 45-7 (C)
1951—Browns, 17-0 (C)
Browns, 28-0 (P)
1952—Browns, 21-20 (P)
Browns, 29-28 (C)
1953—Browns, 34-16 (C)
Browns, 20-16 (P)
1954—Steelers, 55-27 (P)
Browns, 42-7 (C)
1955—Browns, 41-14 (C)
Browns, 30-7 (P)
1956—Browns, 14-10 (P)
Steelers, 24-16 (C)
1957—Browns, 23-12 (P)
Browns, 24-0 (C)
1958—Browns, 45-12 (P)
Browns, 27-10 (C)
1959—Steelers, 17-7 (P)
Steelers, 21-20 (C)
1960—Browns, 28-20 (C)
Steelers, 14-10 (P)
1961—Browns, 30-28 (P)
Steelers, 17-13 (C)
1962—Browns, 41-14 (P)
Browns, 35-14 (C)
1963—Browns, 35-23 (C)
Steelers, 9-7 (P)
1964—Steelers, 23-7 (C)
Browns, 30-17 (P)
1965—Browns, 24-19 (C)
Browns, 42-21 (P)
1966—Browns, 41-10 (C)
Steelers, 16-6 (P)
1967—Browns, 21-10 (C)
Browns, 34-14 (P)
1968—Browns, 31-24 (C)
Browns, 45-24 (P)
1969—Browns, 42-31 (C)
Browns, 24-3 (P)
1970—Browns, 15-7 (C)
Steelers, 28-9 (P)
1971—Browns, 27-17 (C)
Steelers, 26-9 (P)
1972—Browns, 26-24 (C)
Steelers, 30-0 (P)
1973—Steelers, 33-6 (P)
Browns, 21-16 (C)
1974—Steelers, 20-16 (P)
Steelers, 26-16 (C)
1975—Steelers, 42-6 (C)
Steelers, 31-17 (P)
1976—Steelers, 31-14 (C)
Browns, 18-16 (C)
1977—Steelers, 28-14 (C)
Steelers, 35-31 (P)
1978—Steelers, 15-9 (P) OT
Steelers, 34-14 (C)
1979—Steelers, 51-35 (C)
Steelers, 33-30 (P) OT
1980—Browns, 27-26 (C)
Steelers, 16-13 (P)
1981—Steelers, 13-7 (C)
Steelers, 32-10 (P)
1982—Browns, 10-9 (C)
Steelers, 37-21 (P)
1983—Steelers, 44-17 (P)
Browns, 30-17 (C)
1984—Browns, 20-10 (C)
Steelers, 23-20 (P)
1985—Browns, 17-7 (C)

Steelers, 10-9 (P)
1986—Browns, 27-24 (P)
Browns, 37-31 (C) OT
1987—Browns, 34-10 (C)
Browns, 19-13 (P)
1988—Browns, 23-9 (P)
Browns, 27-7 (C)
1989—Browns, 51-0 (P)
Steelers, 17-7 (C)
1990—Browns, 13-3 (P)
Steelers, 35-0 (P)
1991—Browns, 17-14 (C)
Steelers, 17-10 (P)
(RS Pts.—Browns 1,885, Steelers 1,611)

CLEVELAND vs. SAN DIEGO
RS: Chargers lead series, 7-6-1
1970—Chargers, 27-10 (C)
1972—Chargers, 21-17 (SD)
1973—Tie, 16-16 (C)
1974—Chargers, 36-35 (SD)
1976—Browns, 21-17 (C)
1977—Chargers, 37-14 (SD)
1981—Chargers, 44-14 (C)
1982—Chargers, 30-13 (C)
1983—Browns, 30-24 (SD) OT
1985—Browns, 21-7 (SD)
1986—Browns, 47-17 (C)
1987—Chargers, 27-24 (SD) OT
1990—Chargers, 24-14 (C)
1991—Browns, 30-24 (SD) OT
(RS Pts.—Chargers 347, Browns 310)

CLEVELAND vs. SAN FRANCISCO
RS: Browns lead series, 8-6
1950—Browns, 34-14 (C)
1951—49ers, 24-10 (SF)
1953—Browns, 23-21 (C)
1955—Browns, 38-3 (SF)
1959—49ers, 21-20 (C)
1962—Browns, 13-10 (SF)
1968—Browns, 33-21 (SF)
1970—49ers, 34-31 (SF)
1974—Browns, 7-0 (C)
1978—Browns, 24-7 (C)
1981—Browns, 15-12 (SF)
1984—49ers, 41-7 (C)
1987—49ers, 38-24 (SF)
1990—49ers, 20-17 (SF)
(RS Pts.—Browns 296, 49ers 266)

CLEVELAND vs. SEATTLE
RS: Seahawks lead series, 8-3
1977—Seahawks, 20-19 (S)
1978—Seahawks, 47-24 (S)
1979—Seahawks, 29-24 (C)
1980—Browns, 27-3 (S)
1981—Seahawks, 42-21 (S)
1982—Browns, 21-7 (S)
1983—Seahawks, 24-9 (C)
1984—Seahawks, 33-0 (S)
1985—Seahawks, 31-13 (S)
1988—Seahawks, 16-10 (C)
1989—Browns, 17-7 (S)
(RS Pts.—Seahawks 259, Browns 185)

CLEVELAND vs. TAMPA BAY
RS: Browns lead series, 4-0
1976—Browns, 24-7 (TB)
1980—Browns, 34-27 (TB)
1983—Browns, 20-0 (C)
1989—Browns, 42-31 (TB)
(RS Pts.—Browns 120, Buccaneers 65)

CLEVELAND vs. WASHINGTON
RS: Browns lead series, 32-9-1
1950—Browns, 20-14 (C)
Browns, 45-21 (W)
1951—Browns, 45-0 (C)
1952—Browns, 19-15 (C)
Browns, 48-24 (W)
1953—Browns, 30-14 (W)
Browns, 27-3 (C)
1954—Browns, 62-3 (C)
Browns, 34-14 (W)
1955—Redskins, 27-17 (C)
Browns, 24-14 (W)
1956—Redskins, 20-9 (W)
Redskins, 20-17 (C)
1957—Browns, 21-17 (C)
Tie, 30-30 (W)
1958—Browns, 20-10 (W)
Browns, 21-14 (C)
1959—Browns, 34-7 (C)
Browns, 31-17 (W)
1960—Browns, 31-10 (W)
Browns, 27-16 (C)
1961—Browns, 31-7 (C)
Browns, 17-6 (W)
1962—Redskins, 17-16 (C)
Redskins, 17-9 (W)
1963—Browns, 37-14 (C)
Browns, 27-20 (W)
1964—Browns, 27-13 (C)
Browns, 34-24 (C)
1965—Browns, 17-7 (W)
Browns, 24-16 (C)
1966—Browns, 38-14 (W)

Browns, 14-3 (C)
1967—Browns, 42-37 (C)
1968—Browns, 24-21 (W)
1969—Browns, 27-23 (W)
1971—Browns, 20-13 (W)
1975—Redskins, 23-7 (C)
1979—Redskins, 13-9 (C)
1985—Redskins, 14-7 (C)
1988—Browns, 17-13 (W)
1991—Redskins, 42-17 (W)
(RS Pts.—Browns 1,073, Redskins 667)

DALLAS vs. ATLANTA
RS: Cowboys lead series, 8-5
PS: Cowboys lead series, 2-0;
See Atlanta vs. Dallas
DALLAS vs. BUFFALO
RS: Cowboys lead series, 3-1;
See Buffalo vs. Dallas
DALLAS vs. CHICAGO
RS: Cowboys lead series, 7-6
PS: Cowboys lead series, 2-0;
See Chicago vs. Dallas
DALLAS vs. CINCINNATI
RS: Cowboys lead series, 3-2;
See Cincinnati vs. Dallas
DALLAS vs. CLEVELAND
RS: Browns lead series, 14-9
PS: Browns lead series, 2-1;
See Cleveland vs. Dallas
DALLAS vs. DENVER
RS: Series tied, 2-2
PS: Cowboys lead series, 1-0
1973—Cowboys, 22-10 (Den)
1977—Cowboys, 14-6 (Dal)
*Cowboys, 27-10 (New Orleans)
1980—Broncos, 41-20 (Den)
1986—Broncos, 29-14 (Den)
(RS Pts.—Broncos 86, Cowboys 70)
(PS Pts.—Cowboys 27, Broncos 10)
*Super Bowl XII
DALLAS vs. DETROIT
RS: Cowboys lead series, 6-5
PS: Series tied, 1-1
1960—Lions, 23-14 (Det)
1963—Cowboys, 17-14 (Dal)
1968—Cowboys, 59-13 (Det)
1970—*Cowboys, 5-0 (Dal)
1972—Cowboys, 28-24 (Dal)
1975—Cowboys, 36-10 (Dal)
1977—Cowboys, 37-0 (Dal)
1981—Lions, 27-24 (Det)
1985—Lions, 26-21 (Det)
1986—Cowboys, 31-7 (Det)
1987—Lions, 27-17 (Det)
1991—Lions, 34-10 (Det)
*Lions, 38-6 (Det)
(RS Pts.—Cowboys 294, Lions 205)
(PS Pts.—Lions 38, Cowboys 11)
*NFC Divisional Playoff
DALLAS vs. GREEN BAY
RS: Packers lead series, 8-5
PS: Packers lead series, 2-1
1960—Packers, 41-7 (GB)
1964—Packers, 45-21 (D)
1965—Packers, 13-3 (Mil)
1966—*Packers, 34-27 (D)
1967—*Packers, 21-17 (GB)
1968—Packers, 28-17 (D)
1970—Cowboys, 16-3 (D)
1972—Packers, 16-13 (Mil)
1975—Cowboys, 19-17 (D)
1978—Cowboys, 42-14 (Mil)
1980—Cowboys, 28-7 (Mil)
1982—**Cowboys, 37-26 (D)
1984—Cowboys, 20-6 (D)
1989—Packers, 31-13 (GB)
Packers, 20-10 (D)
1991—Cowboys, 20-17 (Mil)
(RS Pts.—Packers 260, Cowboys 227)
(PS Pts.—Cowboys 81, Packers 81)
*NFL Championship
**NFC Second Round Playoff
DALLAS vs. HOUSTON
RS: Cowboys lead series, 4-3
1970—Cowboys, 52-10 (H)
1974—Cowboys, 10-0 (H)
1979—Oilers, 30-24 (D)
1982—Cowboys, 37-7 (H)
1985—Cowboys, 17-10 (H)
1988—Oilers, 25-17 (D)
1991—Oilers, 26-23 (D) OT
(RS Pts.—Cowboys 180, Oilers 108)
DALLAS vs. *INDIANAPOLIS
RS: Cowboys lead series, 6-2
PS: Colts lead series, 1-0
1960—Colts, 45-7 (D)
1967—Colts, 23-17 (B)
1969—Cowboys, 27-10 (D)
1970—**Colts, 16-13 (Miami)
1972—Cowboys, 21-0 (B)
1976—Cowboys, 30-27 (D)
1978—Cowboys, 38-0 (D)

1981—Cowboys, 37-13 (B)
1984—Cowboys, 22-3 (D)
(RS Pts.—Cowboys 199, Colts 121)
(PS Pts.—Colts 16, Cowboys 13)
*Franchise in Baltimore prior to 1984
**Super Bowl V

DALLAS vs. KANSAS CITY
RS: Series tied, 2-2
1970—Cowboys, 27-16 (KC)
1975—Chiefs, 34-31 (D)
1983—Cowboys, 41-21 (D)
1989—Chiefs, 36-28 (KC)
(RS Pts.—Cowboys 127, Chiefs 107)

DALLAS vs. *L.A. RAIDERS
RS: Raiders lead series, 3-1
1974—Raiders, 27-23 (D)
1980—Cowboys, 19-13 (O)
1983—Raiders, 40-38 (D)
1986—Raiders, 17-13 (D)
(RS Pts.—Raiders 97, Cowboys 93)
*Franchise in Oakland prior to 1982

DALLAS vs. L.A. RAMS
RS: Series tied, 8-8
PS: Series tied, 4-4
1960—Rams, 38-13 (D)
1962—Cowboys, 27-17 (LA)
1967—Rams, 35-13 (D)
1969—Rams, 24-23 (LA)
1971—Cowboys, 28-21 (D)
1973—Rams, 37-31 (LA)
    *Cowboys, 27-16 (D)
1975—Cowboys, 18-7 (D)
    **Cowboys, 37-7 (LA)
1976—*Rams, 14-12 (D)
1978—Rams, 27-14 (LA)
    **Cowboys, 28-0 (LA)
1979—Cowboys, 30-6 (D)
    *Rams, 21-19 (D)
1980—Rams, 38-14 (LA)
    ***Cowboys, 34-13 (D)
1981—Cowboys, 29-17 (D)
1983—***Rams, 24-17 (D)
1984—Cowboys, 20-13 (LA)
1985—*Rams, 20-0 (LA)
1986—Rams, 29-10 (LA)
1987—Cowboys, 29-21 (LA)
1989—Rams, 35-31 (LA)
1990—Cowboys, 24-21 (LA)
(RS Pts.—Rams 386, Cowboys 354)
(PS Pts.—Cowboys 174, Rams 115)
*NFC Divisional Playoff
**NFC Championship
***NFC First Round Playoff

DALLAS vs. MIAMI
RS: Dolphins lead series, 5-1
PS: Cowboys lead series, 1-0
1971—*Cowboys, 24-3 (New Orleans)
1973—Dolphins, 14-7 (D)
1978—Dolphins, 23-16 (M)
1981—Dolphins, 28-27 (M)
1984—Dolphins, 28-21 (M)
1987—Dolphins, 20-14 (D)
1989—Dolphins, 17-14 (D)
(RS Pts.—Dolphins 129, Cowboys 100)
(PS Pts.—Cowboys 24, Dolphins 3)
*Super Bowl VI

DALLAS vs. MINNESOTA
RS: Cowboys lead series, 7-6
PS: Cowboys lead series, 3-1
1961—Cowboys, 21-7 (D)
    Cowboys, 28-0 (M)
1966—Cowboys, 28-17 (D)
1968—Cowboys, 20-7 (M)
1970—Vikings, 54-13 (M)
1971—*Cowboys, 20-12 (M)
1973—**Vikings, 27-10 (D)
1974—Vikings, 23-21 (D)
1975—*Cowboys, 17-14 (M)
1977—Cowboys, 16-10 (M) OT
    **Cowboys, 23-6 (D)
1978—Vikings, 21-10 (D)
1979—Cowboys, 36-20 (M)
1982—Vikings, 31-27 (M)
1983—Cowboys, 37-24 (M)
1987—Vikings, 44-38 (D) OT
1988—Vikings, 43-3 (D)
(RS Pts.—Vikings 301, Cowboys 298)
(PS Pts.—Cowboys 70, Vikings 59)
*NFC Divisional Playoff
**NFC Championship

DALLAS vs. NEW ENGLAND
RS: Cowboys lead series, 6-0
1971—Cowboys, 44-21 (D)
1975—Cowboys, 34-31 (NE)
1978—Cowboys, 17-10 (D)
1981—Cowboys, 35-21 (NE)
1984—Cowboys, 20-17 (D)
1987—Cowboys, 23-17 (NE) OT
(RS Pts.—Cowboys 173, Patriots 117)

DALLAS vs. NEW ORLEANS
RS: Cowboys lead series, 13-3
1967—Cowboys, 14-10 (D)
    Cowboys, 27-10 (NO)

1968—Cowboys, 17-3 (NO)
1969—Cowboys, 21-17 (NO)
    Cowboys, 33-17 (D)
1971—Saints, 24-14 (NO)
1973—Cowboys, 40-3 (D)
1976—Cowboys, 24-6 (NO)
1978—Cowboys, 27-7 (D)
1982—Cowboys, 21-7 (D)
1983—Cowboys, 21-20 (D)
1984—Cowboys, 30-27 (D) OT
1988—Saints, 20-17 (NO)
1989—Saints, 28-0 (NO)
1990—Cowboys, 17-13 (D)
1991—Cowboys, 23-14 (D)
(RS Pts.—Cowboys 346, Saints 226)

DALLAS vs. N.Y. GIANTS
RS: Cowboys lead series, 36-21-2
1960—Tie, 31-31 (NY)
1961—Giants, 31-10 (D)
    Cowboys, 17-16 (NY)
1962—Giants, 41-10 (D)
    Giants, 41-31 (NY)
1963—Giants, 37-21 (NY)
    Giants, 34-27 (D)
1964—Tie, 13-13 (D)
    Cowboys, 31-21 (NY)
1965—Cowboys, 31-2 (D)
    Cowboys, 38-20 (NY)
1966—Cowboys, 52-7 (D)
    Cowboys, 17-7 (NY)
1967—Cowboys, 38-24 (D)
1968—Giants, 27-21 (D)
    Cowboys, 28-10 (NY)
1969—Cowboys, 25-3 (D)
1970—Cowboys, 28-10 (D)
    Giants, 23-20 (NY)
1971—Cowboys, 20-13 (D)
    Cowboys, 42-14 (NY)
1972—Cowboys, 23-14 (NY)
    Giants, 23-3 (D)
1973—Cowboys, 45-28 (D)
    Cowboys, 23-10 (New Haven)
1974—Giants, 14-6 (D)
    Cowboys, 21-7 (New Haven)
1975—Cowboys, 13-7 (NY)
    Cowboys, 14-3 (D)
1976—Cowboys, 24-14 (NY)
    Cowboys, 9-3 (D)
1977—Cowboys, 41-21 (D)
    Cowboys, 24-10 (NY)
1978—Cowboys, 34-24 (NY)
    Cowboys, 24-3 (D)
1979—Cowboys, 16-14 (NY)
    Cowboys, 28-7 (D)
1980—Cowboys, 24-3 (D)
    Giants, 38-35 (NY)
1981—Cowboys, 18-10 (D)
    Giants, 13-10 (NY) OT
1983—Cowboys, 28-13 (D)
    Cowboys, 38-20 (NY)
1984—Giants, 28-7 (NY)
    Giants, 19-7 (D)
1985—Cowboys, 30-29 (NY)
    Cowboys, 28-21 (D)
1986—Cowboys, 31-28 (D)
    Giants, 17-14 (NY)
1987—Cowboys, 16-14 (NY)
    Cowboys, 33-24 (D)
1988—Cowboys, 12-10 (D)
    Giants, 29-21 (NY)
1989—Giants, 30-13 (D)
    Giants, 15-0 (NY)
1990—Giants, 28-7 (D)
    Giants, 31-17 (NY)
1991—Cowboys, 21-16 (D)
    Giants, 22-9 (NY)
(RS Pts.—Cowboys 1,316, Giants 1,087)

DALLAS vs. N.Y. JETS
RS: Cowboys lead series, 4-1
1971—Cowboys, 52-10 (D)
1975—Cowboys, 31-21 (D)
1978—Cowboys, 30-7 (NY)
1987—Cowboys, 38-24 (NY)
1990—Jets, 24-9 (NY)
(RS Pts.—Cowboys 160, Jets 86)

DALLAS vs. PHILADELPHIA
RS: Cowboys lead series, 37-25
PS: Eagles lead series, 1-0
1960—Eagles, 27-25 (D)
1961—Eagles, 43-7 (D)
    Eagles, 35-13 (P)
1962—Cowboys, 41-19 (D)
    Eagles, 28-14 (P)
1963—Eagles, 24-21 (P)
    Cowboys, 27-20 (D)
1964—Eagles, 17-14 (D)
    Eagles, 24-14 (P)
1965—Eagles, 35-24 (D)
    Cowboys, 21-19 (P)
1966—Cowboys, 56-7 (D)
    Eagles, 24-23 (P)
1967—Eagles, 21-14 (P)
    Cowboys, 38-17 (D)

1968—Cowboys, 45-13 (P)
    Cowboys, 34-14 (D)
1969—Cowboys, 38-7 (P)
    Cowboys, 49-14 (D)
1970—Cowboys, 17-7 (P)
    Cowboys, 21-17 (D)
1971—Cowboys, 42-7 (P)
    Cowboys, 20-7 (D)
1972—Cowboys, 28-6 (D)
    Cowboys, 28-7 (P)
1973—Eagles, 30-16 (P)
    Cowboys, 31-10 (D)
1974—Eagles, 13-10 (P)
    Cowboys, 31-24 (D)
1975—Cowboys, 20-17 (P)
    Cowboys, 27-17 (D)
1976—Cowboys, 27-7 (D)
    Cowboys, 26-7 (P)
1977—Cowboys, 16-10 (P)
    Cowboys, 24-14 (D)
1978—Cowboys, 14-7 (D)
    Cowboys, 31-13 (P)
1979—Eagles, 31-21 (D)
    Cowboys, 24-17 (P)
1980—Cowboys, 17-10 (P)
    Cowboys, 35-27 (D)
    *Eagles, 20-7 (P)
1981—Cowboys, 17-14 (P)
    Cowboys, 21-10 (D)
1982—Eagles, 24-20 (D)
1983—Cowboys, 37-7 (D)
    Cowboys, 27-20 (P)
1984—Cowboys, 23-17 (D)
    Cowboys, 26-10 (P)
1985—Eagles, 16-14 (P)
    Cowboys, 34-17 (D)
1986—Cowboys, 17-14 (P)
    Eagles, 23-21 (D)
1987—Cowboys, 41-22 (D)
    Eagles, 37-20 (P)
1988—Eagles, 24-23 (P)
    Eagles, 23-7 (D)
1989—Eagles, 27-0 (D)
    Eagles, 20-10 (P)
1990—Eagles, 21-20 (D)
    Eagles, 17-3 (P)
1991—Eagles, 24-0 (D)
    Cowboys, 25-13 (P)
(RS Pts.—Cowboys 1,443, Eagles 1,120)
(PS Pts.—Eagles 20, Cowboys 7)
*NFC Championship

DALLAS vs. *PHOENIX
RS: Cowboys lead series, 36-22-1
1960—Cardinals, 12-10 (StL)
1961—Cowboys, 31-17 (D)
    Cardinals, 31-13 (StL)
1962—Cardinals, 28-24 (D)
    Cardinals, 52-20 (StL)
1963—Cardinals, 34-7 (D)
    Cowboys, 28-24 (StL)
1964—Cardinals, 16-6 (D)
    Cowboys, 31-13 (StL)
1965—Cardinals, 20-13 (StL)
    Cowboys, 27-13 (D)
1966—Tie, 10-10 (StL)
    Cowboys, 31-17 (D)
1967—Cowboys, 46-21 (D)
1968—Cowboys, 27-10 (StL)
1969—Cowboys, 24-3 (D)
1970—Cardinals, 20-7 (StL)
    Cardinals, 38-0 (D)
1971—Cowboys, 16-13 (StL)
    Cowboys, 31-12 (D)
1972—Cowboys, 33-24 (D)
    Cowboys, 27-6 (StL)
1973—Cowboys, 45-10 (D)
    Cowboys, 30-3 (StL)
1974—Cardinals, 31-28 (StL)
    Cowboys, 17-14 (D)
1975—Cowboys, 37-31 (D) OT
    Cardinals, 31-17 (StL)
1976—Cardinals, 21-17 (StL)
    Cowboys, 19-14 (D)
1977—Cowboys, 30-24 (StL)
    Cardinals, 24-17 (D)
1978—Cowboys, 21-12 (D)
    Cowboys, 24-21 (StL) OT
1979—Cowboys, 22-21 (StL)
    Cowboys, 22-13 (D)
1980—Cowboys, 27-24 (StL)
    Cowboys, 31-21 (D)
1981—Cowboys, 30-17 (D)
    Cardinals, 20-17 (StL)
1982—Cowboys, 24-7 (D)
1983—Cowboys, 34-17 (StL)
    Cowboys, 35-17 (D)
1984—Cardinals, 31-20 (D)
    Cowboys, 24-17 (StL)
1985—Cardinals, 21-10 (StL)
    Cowboys, 35-17 (D)
1986—Cowboys, 31-7 (StL)
    Cowboys, 37-6 (D)
1987—Cardinals, 24-13 (StL)

    Cowboys, 21-16 (D)
1988—Cowboys, 17-14 (P)
    Cardinals, 16-10 (D)
1989—Cardinals, 19-10 (D)
    Cardinals, 24-20 (P)
1990—Cardinals, 20-3 (P)
    Cowboys, 41-10 (D)
1991—Cowboys, 17-9 (P)
    Cowboys, 27-7 (D)
(RS Pts.—Cowboys 1,328, Cardinals 1,099)
*Franchise in St. Louis prior to 1988

DALLAS vs. PITTSBURGH
RS: Cowboys lead series, 12-11
PS: Steelers lead series, 2-0
1960—Steelers, 35-28 (D)
1961—Cowboys, 27-24 (D)
    Steelers, 37-7 (D)
1962—Steelers, 30-28 (D)
    Cowboys, 42-27 (P)
1963—Steelers, 27-21 (P)
    Steelers, 24-19 (D)
1964—Cowboys, 23-17 (P)
    Cowboys, 17-14 (D)
1965—Steelers, 22-13 (P)
    Cowboys, 24-17 (D)
1966—Cowboys, 52-21 (D)
    Cowboys, 20-7 (P)
1967—Cowboys, 24-21 (P)
1968—Cowboys, 28-7 (D)
1969—Cowboys, 10-7 (P)
1972—Cowboys, 17-13 (D)
1975—*Steelers, 21-17 (Miami)
1977—Steelers, 28-13 (P)
1978—**Steelers, 35-31 (Miami)
1979—Steelers, 14-3 (P)
1982—Steelers, 36-28 (D)
1985—Cowboys, 27-13 (D)
1988—Steelers, 24-21 (P)
1991—Cowboys, 20-10 (D)
(RS Pts.—Cowboys 506, Steelers 481)
(PS Pts.—Steelers 56, Cowboys 48)
*Super Bowl X
**Super Bowl XIII

DALLAS vs. SAN DIEGO
RS: Cowboys lead series, 4-1
1972—Cowboys, 34-28 (SD)
1980—Cowboys, 42-31 (D)
1983—Chargers, 24-23 (SD)
1986—Cowboys, 24-21 (D)
1990—Cowboys, 17-14 (D)
(RS Pts.—Cowboys 140, Chargers 118)

DALLAS vs. SAN FRANCISCO
RS: 49ers lead series, 9-5-1
PS: Cowboys lead series, 3-1
1960—49ers, 26-14 (D)
1963—49ers, 31-24 (SF)
1965—49ers, 39-31 (D)
1967—49ers, 24-16 (SF)
1969—Tie, 24-24 (D)
1970—*Cowboys, 17-10 (SF)
1971—*Cowboys, 14-3 (D)
1972—49ers, 31-10 (D)
    **Cowboys, 30-28 (SF)
1974—Cowboys, 20-14 (D)
1977—Cowboys, 42-35 (SF)
1979—Cowboys, 21-13 (SF)
1980—Cowboys, 59-14 (D)
1981—49ers, 45-14 (SF)
    *49ers, 28-27 (SF)
1983—49ers, 42-17 (SF)
1985—49ers, 31-16 (SF)
1989—49ers, 31-14 (D)
1990—49ers, 24-6 (D)
(RS Pts.—49ers 416, Cowboys 336)
(PS Pts.—Cowboys 88, 49ers 69)
*NFC Championship
**NFC Divisional Playoff

DALLAS vs. SEATTLE
RS: Cowboys lead series, 3-1
1976—Cowboys, 28-13 (S)
1980—Cowboys, 51-7 (D)
1983—Cowboys, 35-10 (S)
1986—Seahawks, 31-14 (D)
(RS Pts.—Cowboys 128, Seahawks 61)

DALLAS vs. TAMPA BAY
RS: Cowboys lead series, 6-0
PS: Cowboys lead series, 2-0
1977—Cowboys, 23-7 (D)
1980—Cowboys, 28-17 (D)
1981—*Cowboys, 38-0 (D)
1982—Cowboys, 14-9 (D)
    **Cowboys, 30-17 (D)
1983—Cowboys, 27-24 (D) OT
1990—Cowboys, 14-10 (D)
    Cowboys 17-13 (TB)
(RS Pts.—Cowboys 123, Buccaneers 80)
(PS Pts.—Cowboys 68, Buccaneers 17)
*NFC Divisional Playoff
**NFC First Round Playoff

DALLAS vs. WASHINGTON
RS: Cowboys lead series, 35-25-2
PS: Redskins lead series, 2-0
1960—Redskins, 26-14 (W)

1961—Tie, 28-28 (D)
Redskins, 34-24 (W)
1962—Tie, 35-35 (D)
Cowboys, 38-10 (W)
1963—Redskins, 21-17 (W)
Cowboys, 35-20 (D)
1964—Cowboys, 24-18 (D)
Redskins, 28-16 (W)
1965—Cowboys, 27-7 (D)
Redskins, 34-31 (W)
1966—Cowboys, 31-30 (W)
Redskins, 34-31 (W)
1967—Cowboys, 17-14 (W)
Redskins, 27-20 (D)
1968—Cowboys, 44-24 (W)
Cowboys, 29-20 (D)
1969—Cowboys, 41-28 (W)
Cowboys, 20-10 (D)
1970—Cowboys, 45-21 (W)
Cowboys, 34-0 (D)
1971—Redskins, 20-16 (D)
Cowboys, 13-0 (W)
1972—Redskins, 24-20 (W)
Cowboys, 34-24 (D)
*Redskins, 26-3 (W)
1973—Redskins, 14-7 (W)
Cowboys, 27-7 (D)
1974—Redskins, 28-21 (W)
Cowboys, 24-23 (D)
1975—Redskins, 30-24 (W) OT
Cowboys, 31-10 (D)
1976—Cowboys, 20-7 (W)
Redskins, 27-14 (D)
1977—Cowboys, 34-16 (D)
Cowboys, 14-7 (W)
1978—Redskins, 9-5 (W)
Cowboys, 37-10 (D)
1979—Redskins, 34-20 (W)
Cowboys, 35-34 (W)
1980—Cowboys, 17-3 (W)
Cowboys, 14-10 (D)
1981—Cowboys, 26-10 (W)
Cowboys, 24-10 (D)
1982—Cowboys, 24-10 (W)
*Redskins, 31-17 (W)
1983—Cowboys, 31-30 (W)
Redskins, 31-10 (D)
1984—Cowboys, 34-14 (W)
Redskins, 30-28 (D)
1985—Cowboys, 44-14 (D)
Cowboys, 13-7 (W)
1986—Cowboys, 30-6 (D)
Redskins, 41-14 (W)
1987—Redskins, 13-7 (D)
Redskins, 24-20 (W)
1988—Redskins, 35-17 (D)
Cowboys, 24-17 (W)
1989—Redskins, 30-7 (D)
Cowboys, 13-3 (W)
1990—Redskins, 19-15 (W)
Cowboys, 27-17 (D)
1991—Redskins, 33-31 (D)
Cowboys, 24-21 (W)
(RS Pts.—Cowboys, 1,471, Redskins 1,241)
(PS Pts.—Redskins 57, Cowboys 20)
*NFC Championship
———————————————
DENVER vs. ATLANTA
RS: Broncos lead series, 4-3;
See Atlanta vs. Denver
DENVER vs. BUFFALO
RS: Bills lead series, 15-10-1;
PS: Bills lead series, 1-0;
See Buffalo vs. Denver
DENVER vs. CHICAGO
RS: Bears lead series, 5-4;
See Chicago vs. Denver
DENVER vs. CINCINNATI
RS: Broncos lead series, 10-6;
See Cincinnati vs. Denver
DENVER vs. CLEVELAND
RS: Broncos lead series, 10-5
PS: Broncos lead series, 3-0;
See Cleveland vs. Denver
DENVER vs. DALLAS
RS: Series tied, 2-2
PS: Cowboys lead series, 1-0;
See Dallas vs. Denver
DENVER vs. DETROIT
RS: Broncos lead series, 4-3
1971—Lions, 24-20 (Den)
1974—Broncos, 31-27 (Den)
1978—Lions, 17-14 (Det)
1981—Broncos, 27-21 (Den)
1984—Broncos, 28-7 (Den)
1987—Broncos, 34-0 (Den)
1990—Lions, 40-27 (Det)
(RS Pts.—Broncos 181, Lions 136)
DENVER vs. GREEN BAY
RS: Broncos lead series, 4-1-1
1971—Packers, 34-13 (Mil)
1975—Broncos, 23-13 (D)
1978—Broncos, 16-3 (D)

1984—Broncos, 17-14 (D)
1987—Tie, 17-17 (Mil) OT
1990—Broncos, 22-13 (D)
(RS Pts.—Broncos 108, Packers 94)
DENVER vs. HOUSTON
RS: Oilers lead series, 19-10-1
PS: Broncos lead series, 2-1
1960—Oilers, 45-25 (D)
Oilers, 20-10 (H)
1961—Oilers, 55-14 (D)
Oilers, 45-14 (H)
1962—Broncos, 20-10 (D)
Oilers, 34-17 (H)
1963—Oilers, 20-14 (H)
Oilers, 33-24 (D)
1964—Oilers, 38-17 (H)
Oilers, 34-15 (H)
1965—Broncos, 28-17 (D)
Broncos, 31-21 (H)
1966—Oilers, 45-7 (H)
Broncos, 40-38 (D)
1967—Oilers, 10-6 (H)
Oilers, 20-18 (D)
1968—Oilers, 38-17 (H)
Oilers, 24-21 (H)
1969—Oilers, 24-21 (H)
Tie, 20-20 (D)
1970—Oilers, 31-21 (H)
1972—Broncos, 30-17 (D)
1973—Broncos, 48-20 (H)
1974—Broncos, 37-14 (D)
1976—Oilers, 17-3 (H)
1977—Broncos, 24-14 (H)
1979—*Oilers, 13-7 (H)
1980—Oilers, 20-16 (H)
1983—Broncos, 26-14 (H)
1985—Broncos, 31-20 (H)
1987—Oilers, 40-10 (D)
**Broncos, 34-10 (D)
1991—Oilers, 42-14 (H)
**Broncos, 26-24 (D)
(RS Pts.—Oilers 816, Broncos 618)
(PS Pts.—Broncos 67, Oilers 47)
*AFC First Round Playoff
**AFC Divisional Playoff
DENVER vs. *INDIANAPOLIS
RS: Broncos lead series, 8-2
1974—Broncos, 17-6 (B)
1977—Broncos, 27-13 (D)
1978—Colts, 7-6 (B)
1981—Broncos, 28-10 (D)
1983—Broncos, 17-10 (B)
Broncos, 21-19 (D)
1985—Broncos, 15-10 (I)
1988—Colts, 55-23 (I)
1989—Broncos, 14-3 (D)
1990—Broncos, 27-17 (I)
(RS Pts.—Broncos 195, Colts 150)
*Franchise in Baltimore prior to 1984
DENVER vs. *KANSAS CITY
RS: Chiefs lead series, 36-27
1960—Texans, 17-14 (D)
Texans, 34-7 (Da)
1961—Texans, 19-12 (D)
Texans, 49-21 (Da)
1962—Texans, 24-3 (D)
Texans, 17-10 (Da)
1963—Chiefs, 59-7 (D)
Chiefs, 52-21 (KC)
1964—Broncos, 33-27 (D)
Chiefs, 49-39 (KC)
1965—Chiefs, 31-23 (D)
Chiefs, 45-35 (KC)
1966—Chiefs, 37-10 (KC)
Chiefs, 56-10 (D)
1967—Chiefs, 52-9 (KC)
Chiefs, 38-24 (D)
1968—Chiefs, 34-2 (KC)
Chiefs, 30-7 (D)
1969—Chiefs, 26-13 (D)
Chiefs, 31-17 (KC)
1970—Broncos, 26-13 (D)
Chiefs, 16-0 (KC)
1971—Chiefs, 16-3 (D)
Chiefs, 28-10 (KC)
1972—Chiefs, 45-24 (D)
Chiefs, 24-21 (KC)
1973—Chiefs, 16-14 (KC)
Broncos, 14-10 (D)
1974—Broncos, 17-14 (KC)
Chiefs, 42-34 (D)
1975—Broncos, 37-33 (D)
Chiefs, 26-13 (KC)
1976—Broncos, 35-26 (KC)
Broncos, 17-16 (D)
1977—Broncos, 23-7 (D)
Broncos, 14-7 (KC)
1978—Broncos, 23-17 (KC) OT
Broncos, 24-3 (D)
1979—Broncos, 24-10 (KC)
Broncos, 20-3 (D)
1980—Chiefs, 23-17 (D)
Chiefs, 31-14 (KC)
1981—Chiefs, 28-14 (KC)

Broncos, 16-13 (D)
1982—Chiefs, 37-16 (D)
1983—Broncos, 27-24 (D)
Chiefs, 48-17 (KC)
1984—Broncos, 21-0 (D)
Chiefs, 16-13 (KC)
1985—Broncos, 30-10 (KC)
Broncos, 14-13 (D)
1986—Broncos, 38-17 (D)
Chiefs, 37-10 (KC)
1987—Broncos, 26-17 (KC)
Broncos, 20-17 (D)
1988—Chiefs, 20-13 (KC)
Broncos, 17-11 (D)
1989—Broncos, 34-20 (D)
Broncos, 16-13 (KC)
1990—Broncos, 24-23 (D)
Chiefs, 31-20 (KC)
1991—Broncos, 19-16 (D)
Broncos, 24-20 (KC)
(RS Pts.—Chiefs 1,584, Broncos 1,170)
*Franchise in Dallas prior to 1963 and known as Texans
DENVER vs. *L.A. RAIDERS
RS: Raiders lead series, 43-18-2
PS: Broncos lead series, 1-0
1960—Broncos, 31-14 (D)
Raiders, 48-10 (O)
1961—Raiders, 33-19 (O)
Broncos, 27-24 (D)
1962—Broncos, 44-7 (D)
Broncos, 23-6 (O)
1963—Raiders, 26-10 (O)
Raiders, 35-31 (O)
1964—Raiders, 40-7 (O)
Tie, 20-20 (D)
1965—Raiders, 28-20 (D)
Raiders, 24-13 (O)
1966—Raiders, 17-3 (D)
Raiders, 28-10 (O)
1967—Raiders, 51-0 (O)
Raiders, 21-17 (D)
1968—Raiders, 43-7 (D)
Raiders, 33-27 (O)
1969—Raiders, 24-14 (D)
Raiders, 41-10 (O)
1970—Raiders, 35-23 (O)
Raiders, 24-19 (D)
1971—Raiders, 27-16 (D)
Raiders, 21-13 (O)
1972—Broncos, 30-23 (O)
Raiders, 37-20 (D)
1973—Tie, 23-23 (D)
Raiders, 21-17 (O)
1974—Raiders, 28-17 (D)
Raiders, 20-17 (O)
1975—Raiders, 42-17 (O)
Raiders, 17-10 (O)
1976—Raiders, 17-10 (O)
Raiders, 19-6 (O)
1977—Broncos, 30-7 (O)
Raiders, 24-14 (O)
**Broncos, 20-17 (D)
1978—Broncos, 14-6 (D)
Broncos, 21-6 (O)
1979—Raiders, 27-3 (O)
Raiders, 14-10 (D)
1980—Raiders, 9-3 (O)
Raiders, 24-21 (D)
1981—Broncos, 9-7 (D)
Broncos, 17-0 (O)
1982—Raiders, 27-10 (LA)
1983—Raiders, 22-7 (D)
Raiders, 22-20 (LA)
1984—Broncos, 16-13 (D)
Broncos, 22-19 (LA) OT
1985—Raiders, 31-28 (LA) OT
Raiders, 17-14 (D) OT
1986—Broncos, 38-36 (D)
Raiders, 21-10 (LA)
1987—Broncos, 30-14 (D)
Raiders, 23-17 (LA)
1988—Raiders, 30-27 (LA) OT
Raiders, 21-20 (LA)
1989—Broncos, 31-21 (D)
Raiders, 16-13 (LA) OT
1990—Raiders, 14-9 (LA)
Raiders, 23-20 (D)
1991—Broncos, 16-13 (LA)
Raiders, 17-16 (D)
(RS Pts.—Raiders 1,424, Broncos 1,104)
(PS Pts.—Broncos 20, Raiders 17)
*Franchise in Oakland prior to 1982
**AFC Championship
DENVER vs. L.A. RAMS
RS: Series tied, 3-3
1972—Broncos, 16-10 (LA)
1974—Rams, 17-10 (D)
1979—Rams, 13-9 (D)
1982—Broncos, 27-24 (LA)
1985—Rams, 20-16 (LA)
1988—Broncos, 35-24 (D)
(RS Pts.—Broncos 113, Rams 108)

Broncos, 16-13 (D)
1982—Chiefs, 37-16 (D)
DENVER vs. MIAMI
RS: Dolphins lead series, 5-2-1
1966—Dolphins, 24-7 (M)
Broncos, 17-7 (D)
1967—Dolphins, 35-21 (M)
1968—Broncos, 21-14 (D)
1969—Dolphins, 27-24 (M)
1971—Tie, 10-10 (D)
1975—Dolphins, 14-13 (M)
1985—Dolphins, 30-26 (M)
(RS Pts.—Dolphins 161, Broncos 139)
DENVER vs. MINNESOTA
RS: Vikings lead series, 4-3
1972—Vikings, 23-20 (D)
1978—Vikings, 12-9 (M) OT
1981—Broncos, 19-17 (D)
1984—Broncos, 42-21 (D)
1987—Vikings, 34-27 (M)
1990—Vikings, 27-22 (M)
1991—Broncos, 13-6 (M)
(RS Pts.—Broncos 152, Vikings 140)
DENVER vs. *NEW ENGLAND
RS: Broncos lead series, 16-12
PS: Broncos lead series, 1-0
1960—Broncos, 13-10 (B)
Broncos, 31-24 (D)
1961—Patriots, 45-17 (B)
Patriots, 28-24 (D)
1962—Patriots, 41-16 (B)
Patriots, 33-29 (D)
1963—Broncos, 14-10 (D)
Patriots, 40-21 (B)
1964—Patriots, 39-10 (D)
Patriots, 12-7 (B)
1965—Broncos, 27-10 (B)
Patriots, 28-20 (D)
1966—Patriots, 24-10 (D)
Broncos, 17-10 (B)
1967—Broncos, 26-21 (D)
1968—Patriots, 20-17 (D)
Broncos, 35-14 (B)
1969—Broncos, 35-7 (D)
1972—Broncos, 45-21 (D)
1976—Patriots, 38-14 (NE)
1979—Broncos, 45-10 (D)
1980—Patriots, 23-14 (NE)
1984—Broncos, 26-19 (D)
1986—Broncos, 27-20 (D)
**Broncos, 22-17 (D)
1987—Broncos, 31-20 (D)
1988—Broncos, 21-10 (D)
1991—Broncos, 9-6 (NE)
Broncos, 20-3 (D)
(RS Pts.—Broncos 621, Patriots 586)
(PS Pts.—Broncos 22, Patriots 17)
*Franchise in Boston prior to 1971
**AFC Divisional Playoff
DENVER vs. NEW ORLEANS
RS: Broncos lead series, 4-1
1970—Broncos, 31-6 (NO)
1974—Broncos, 33-17 (D)
1979—Broncos, 10-3 (D)
1985—Broncos, 34-23 (D)
1988—Saints, 42-0 (NO)
(RS Pts.—Broncos 108, Saints 91)
DENVER vs. N. Y. GIANTS
RS: Giants lead series, 3-2
PS: Giants lead series, 1-0
1972—Giants, 29-17 (NY)
1976—Broncos, 14-13 (D)
1980—Broncos, 14-9 (NY)
1986—Broncos, 19-16 (NY)
*Giants, 39-20 (Pasadena)
1989—Giants, 14-7 (D)
(RS Pts.—Giants 84, Broncos 68)
(PS Pts.—Giants 39, Broncos 20)
*Super Bowl XXI
DENVER vs. *N.Y. JETS
RS: Jets lead series, 11-10-1
1960—Titans, 28-24 (NY)
Titans, 30-27 (D)
1961—Titans, 35-28 (NY)
Broncos, 27-10 (D)
1962—Broncos, 32-10 (NY)
Titans, 46-45 (D)
1963—Tie, 35-35 (D)
Jets, 14-9 (D)
1964—Jets, 30-6 (NY)
Broncos, 20-16 (D)
1965—Broncos, 16-13 (D)
Jets, 45-10 (NY)
1966—Jets, 16-7 (D)
1967—Jets, 38-24 (D)
Broncos, 33-24 (NY)
1968—Broncos, 21-13 (NY)
1969—Broncos, 21-19 (D)
1973—Broncos, 40-28 (NY)
1976—Broncos, 46-3 (D)
1978—Jets, 31-28 (D)
1980—Broncos, 31-24 (D)
1986—Jets, 22-10 (NY)
(RS Pts.—Broncos 540, Jets 530)
*Jets known as Titans prior to 1963

259

DENVER vs. PHILADELPHIA
RS: Eagles lead series, 4-2
1971—Eagles, 17-16 (P)
1975—Broncos, 25-10 (D)
1980—Eagles, 27-6 (P)
1983—Eagles, 13-10 (D)
1986—Broncos, 33-7 (P)
1989—Eagles, 28-24 (D)
(RS Pts.—Broncos 114, Eagles 102)
DENVER vs. *PHOENIX
RS: Broncos lead series, 3-0-1
1973—Tie, 17-17 (StL)
1977—Broncos, 7-0 (D)
1989—Broncos, 37-0 (P)
1991—Broncos, 24-19 (D)
(RS Pts.—Broncos 85, Cardinals 36)
*Franchise in St. Louis prior to 1988
DENVER vs. PITTSBURGH
RS: Broncos lead series, 9-5-1
PS: Series tied, 2-2
1970—Broncos, 16-13 (D)
1971—Broncos, 22-10 (D)
1973—Broncos, 23-13 (P)
1974—Tie, 35-35 (D) OT
1975—Steelers, 20-9 (P)
1977—Broncos, 21-7 (D)
       *Broncos, 34-21 (D)
1978—Steelers, 21-17 (D)
       *Steelers, 33-10 (P)
1979—Steelers, 42-7 (P)
1983—Broncos, 14-10 (D)
1984—*Steelers, 24-17 (D)
1985—Broncos, 31-23 (P)
1986—Broncos, 21-10 (P)
1988—Steelers, 39-21 (P)
1989—Broncos, 34-7 (D)
       *Broncos, 24-23 (D)
1990—Steelers, 34-17 (D)
1991—Broncos, 20-13 (D)
(RS Pts.—Broncos 308, Steelers 297)
(PS Pts.—Steelers 101, Broncos 85)
*AFC Divisional Playoff
DENVER vs. *SAN DIEGO
RS: Broncos lead series, 33-30-1
1960—Chargers, 23-19 (D)
       Chargers, 41-33 (LA)
1961—Chargers, 37-0 (SD)
       Chargers, 19-16 (D)
1962—Chargers, 30-21 (D)
       Broncos, 23-20 (SD)
1963—Broncos, 50-34 (D)
       Chargers, 58-20 (SD)
1964—Chargers, 42-14 (SD)
       Chargers, 31-20 (D)
1965—Chargers, 34-31 (SD)
       Chargers, 33-21 (D)
1966—Chargers, 24-17 (SD)
       Broncos, 20-17 (D)
1967—Broncos, 38-21 (D)
       Chargers, 24-20 (SD)
1968—Chargers, 55-24 (SD)
       Chargers, 47-23 (D)
1969—Broncos, 13-0 (D)
       Chargers, 45-24 (SD)
1970—Chargers, 24-21 (SD)
       Tie, 17-17 (D)
1971—Broncos, 20-16 (D)
       Chargers, 45-17 (SD)
1972—Chargers, 37-14 (SD)
       Broncos, 38-13 (D)
1973—Broncos, 30-19 (D)
       Broncos, 42-28 (SD)
1974—Broncos, 27-7 (D)
       Chargers, 17-0 (SD)
1975—Broncos, 27-17 (SD)
       Broncos, 13-10 (D) OT
1976—Broncos, 26-0 (D)
       Broncos, 17-0 (SD)
1977—Broncos, 17-14 (SD)
       Broncos, 17-9 (D)
1978—Broncos, 27-14 (D)
       Chargers, 23-0 (SD)
1979—Broncos, 7-0 (D)
       Chargers, 17-7 (SD)
1980—Chargers, 30-13 (SD)
       Broncos, 20-13 (SD)
1981—Broncos, 42-24 (D)
       Chargers, 34-17 (SD)
1982—Chargers, 23-3 (D)
       Chargers, 30-20 (SD)
1983—Broncos, 14-6 (D)
       Chargers, 31-7 (SD)
1984—Broncos, 16-13 (SD)
       Broncos, 16-13 (D)
1985—Chargers, 30-10 (SD)
       Broncos, 30-24 (D) OT
1986—Broncos, 31-14 (SD)
       Chargers, 9-3 (D)
1987—Broncos, 31-17 (SD)
       Broncos, 24-0 (D)
1988—Broncos, 34-3 (D)
       Broncos, 12-0 (SD)
1989—Broncos, 16-10 (D)

Chargers, 19-16 (SD)
1990—Chargers, 19-7 (SD)
       Broncos, 20-10 (D)
1991—Chargers, 27-19 (D)
       Broncos, 17-14 (SD)
(RS Pts.—Chargers 1,375, Broncos 1,269)
*Franchise in Los Angeles prior to 1961
DENVER vs. SAN FRANCISCO
RS: Broncos lead series, 4-2
PS: 49ers lead series, 1-0
1970—49ers, 19-14 (SF)
1973—49ers, 36-34 (D)
1979—Broncos, 38-28 (SF)
1982—Broncos, 24-21 (D)
1985—Broncos, 17-16 (D)
1988—Broncos, 16-13 (SF) OT
1989—*49ers, 55-10 (New Orleans)
(RS Pts.—Broncos 143, 49ers 133)
(PS Pts.—49ers 55, Broncos 10)
*Super Bowl XXIV
DENVER vs. SEATTLE
RS: Broncos lead series, 17-12
PS: Seahawks lead series, 1-0
1977—Broncos, 24-13 (S)
1978—Broncos, 28-7 (D)
       Broncos, 20-17 (S) OT
1979—Broncos, 37-34 (D)
       Seahawks, 28-23 (S)
1980—Broncos, 36-20 (D)
       Broncos, 25-17 (S)
1981—Seahawks, 13-10 (S)
       Broncos, 23-13 (D)
1982—Seahawks, 17-10 (D)
       Seahawks, 13-11 (S)
1983—Seahawks, 27-19 (S)
       Broncos, 38-27 (D)
       *Seahawks, 31-7 (S)
1984—Seahawks, 27-24 (S)
       Broncos, 31-14 (S)
1985—Broncos, 13-10 (D) OT
       Broncos, 27-24 (S)
1986—Broncos, 20-13 (D)
       Seahawks, 41-16 (S)
1987—Broncos, 40-17 (D)
       Seahawks, 28-21 (S)
1988—Seahawks, 21-14 (D)
       Seahawks, 42-14 (S)
1989—Broncos, 24-21 (S) OT
       Broncos, 41-14 (D)
1990—Broncos, 34-31 (D) OT
       Seahawks, 17-12 (S)
1991—Broncos, 16-10 (D)
       Seahawks, 13-10 (S)
(RS Pts.—Broncos 661, Seahawks 589)
(PS Pts.—Seahawks 31, Broncos 7)
*AFC First Round Playoff
DENVER vs. TAMPA BAY
RS: Broncos lead series, 2-0
1976—Broncos, 48-13 (D)
1981—Broncos, 24-7 (TB)
(RS Pts.—Broncos 72, Buccaneers 20)
DENVER vs. WASHINGTON
RS: Broncos lead series, 3-2
PS: Redskins lead series, 1-0
1970—Redskins, 19-3 (D)
1974—Redskins, 30-3 (W)
1980—Broncos, 20-17 (D)
1986—Broncos, 31-30 (D)
1987—*Redskins, 42-10 (San Diego)
1989—Broncos, 14-10 (W)
(RS Pts.—Redskins 106, Broncos 71)
(PS Pts.—Redskins 42, Broncos 10)
*Super Bowl XXII

DETROIT vs. ATLANTA
RS: Lions lead series, 16-5;
See Atlanta vs. Detroit
DETROIT vs. BUFFALO
RS: Lions lead series, 2-1-1;
See Buffalo vs. Detroit
DETROIT vs. CHICAGO
RS: Bears lead series, 72-47-5;
See Chicago vs. Detroit
DETROIT vs. CINCINNATI
RS: Bengals lead series, 3-2;
See Cincinnati vs. Detroit
DETROIT vs. CLEVELAND
RS: Lions lead series, 10-3
PS: Lions lead series, 3-1;
See Cleveland vs. Detroit
DETROIT vs. DALLAS
RS: Cowboys lead series, 6-5
PS: Series tied, 1-1;
See Dallas vs. Detroit
DETROIT vs. DENVER
RS: Broncos lead series, 4-3;
See Denver vs. Detroit
*DETROIT vs. GREEN BAY
RS: Packers lead series, 61-55-7
1930—Packers, 47-13 (GB)
       Tie, 6-6 (P)
1932—Packers, 15-10 (GB)
       Spartans, 19-0 (P)

1933—Packers, 17-0 (GB)
       Spartans, 7-0 (P)
1934—Lions, 3-0 (GB)
       Packers, 3-0 (D)
1935—Packers, 13-9 (GB)
       Packers, 31-7 (GB)
       Lions, 20-10 (D)
1936—Packers, 20-18 (GB)
       Packers, 26-17 (D)
1937—Packers, 26-6 (GB)
       Packers, 14-13 (D)
1938—Lions, 17-7 (GB)
       Packers, 28-7 (D)
1939—Packers, 26-7 (GB)
       Packers, 12-7 (D)
1940—Lions, 23-14 (GB)
       Packers, 50-7 (D)
1941—Packers, 23-0 (GB)
       Packers, 24-7 (D)
1942—Packers, 38-7 (Mil)
       Packers, 28-7 (D)
1943—Packers, 35-14 (GB)
       Packers, 27-6 (D)
1944—Packers, 27-6 (GB)
       Packers, 14-0 (D)
1945—Packers, 57-21 (Mil)
       Lions, 14-3 (D)
1946—Packers, 10-7 (Mil)
       Packers, 9-0 (D)
1947—Packers, 34-17 (GB)
       Packers, 35-14 (D)
1948—Packers, 33-21 (GB)
       Lions, 24-20 (D)
1949—Packers, 16-14 (GB)
       Lions, 21-7 (D)
1950—Lions, 45-7 (GB)
       Lions, 24-21 (D)
1951—Lions, 24-17 (GB)
       Lions, 52-35 (D)
1952—Lions, 52-17 (GB)
       Lions, 48-24 (D)
1953—Lions, 14-7 (GB)
       Lions, 34-15 (D)
1954—Lions, 21-17 (GB)
       Lions, 28-24 (D)
1955—Packers, 20-17 (GB)
       Lions, 24-10 (D)
1956—Lions, 20-16 (GB)
       Packers, 24-20 (D)
1957—Lions, 24-14 (GB)
       Lions, 18-6 (D)
1958—Tie, 13-13 (GB)
       Lions, 24-14 (D)
1959—Packers, 28-10 (GB)
       Packers, 24-17 (D)
1960—Packers, 28-9 (GB)
       Lions, 23-10 (D)
1961—Lions, 17-13 (Mil)
       Packers, 17-9 (D)
1962—Packers, 9-7 (GB)
       Lions, 26-14 (D)
1963—Packers, 31-10 (Mil)
       Tie, 13-13 (D)
1964—Packers, 14-10 (GB)
       Packers, 30-7 (GB)
1965—Packers, 31-21 (D)
       Lions, 12-7 (GB)
1966—Packers, 23-14 (GB)
       Packers, 31-7 (D)
1967—Tie, 17-17 (GB)
       Packers, 27-17 (D)
1968—Lions, 23-17 (GB)
       Tie, 14-14 (D)
1969—Packers, 28-17 (GB)
       Lions, 16-10 (GB)
1970—Lions, 40-0 (GB)
       Lions, 20-0 (D)
1971—Lions, 31-28 (D)
       Tie, 14-14 (Mil)
1972—Lions, 24-23 (D)
       Packers, 33-7 (GB)
1973—Tie, 13-13 (GB)
       Lions, 34-0 (D)
1974—Packers, 21-19 (Mil)
       Lions, 19-17 (D)
1975—Lions, 30-16 (Mil)
       Lions, 13-10 (D)
1976—Packers, 24-14 (GB)
       Lions, 27-6 (D)
1977—Lions, 10-6 (D)
       Packers, 10-9 (GB)
1978—Lions, 13-7 (GB)
       Packers, 35-14 (Mil)
1979—Packers, 24-16 (Mil)
       Packers, 18-13 (D)
1980—Lions, 29-7 (Mil)
       Lions, 24-3 (D)
1981—Lions, 31-27 (D)
       Packers, 31-17 (GB)
1982—Lions, 30-10 (D)
       Lions, 27-24 (D)
1983—Lions, 38-14 (D)
       Lions, 23-20 (Mil) OT

1984—Packers, 41-9 (GB)
       Lions, 31-28 (D)
1985—Packers, 43-10 (GB)
       Packers, 26-23 (D)
1986—Lions, 21-14 (GB)
       Packers, 44-40 (D)
1987—Lions, 19-16 (GB) OT
       Packers, 34-33 (D)
1988—Lions, 19-9 (Mil)
       Lions, 30-14 (D)
1989—Packers, 23-20 (Mil) OT
       Lions, 31-22 (D)
1990—Packers, 24-21 (D)
       Lions, 24-17 (GB)
1991—Lions, 23-14 (D)
       Lions, 21-17 (GB)
(RS Pts.—Packers 2,376, Lions 2,201)
*Franchise in Portsmouth prior to 1934
and known as the Spartans
DETROIT vs. HOUSTON
RS: Oilers lead series, 3-2
1971—Lions, 31-7 (H)
1975—Oilers, 24-8 (H)
1983—Oilers, 27-17 (H)
1986—Lions, 24-13 (D)
1989—Oilers, 35-31 (H)
(RS Pts.—Lions 111, Oilers 106)
DETROIT vs. *INDIANAPOLIS
RS: Series tied, 17-17-2
1953—Lions, 27-17 (B)
       Lions, 17-7 (D)
1954—Lions, 35-0 (B)
       Lions, 27-3 (D)
1955—Colts, 28-13 (B)
       Lions, 24-14 (D)
1956—Lions, 31-14 (B)
       Lions, 27-3 (D)
1957—Colts, 34-14 (B)
       Lions, 31-27 (D)
1958—Colts, 28-15 (B)
       Colts, 40-14 (D)
1959—Colts, 21-9 (B)
       Colts, 31-24 (D)
1960—Lions, 30-17 (B)
       Lions, 20-15 (D)
1961—Lions, 16-15 (B)
       Colts, 17-14 (D)
1962—Lions, 29-20 (B)
       Lions, 21-14 (D)
1963—Colts, 25-21 (B)
       Colts, 24-21 (B)
1964—Colts, 34-0 (D)
       Lions, 31-14 (D)
1965—Colts, 31-7 (B)
       Tie, 24-24 (D)
1966—Colts, 45-14 (B)
       Lions, 20-14 (D)
1967—Colts, 41-7 (B)
1968—Colts, 27-10 (D)
1969—Tie, 17-17 (B)
1973—Colts, 29-27 (D)
1977—Lions, 13-10 (B)
1980—Colts, 10-9 (D)
1985—Lions, 14-6 (I)
1991—Lions, 33-24 (I)
(RS Pts.—Colts 748, Lions 698)
*Franchise in Baltimore prior to 1984
DETROIT vs. KANSAS CITY
RS: Chiefs lead series, 4-3
1971—Lions, 32-21 (D)
1975—Chiefs, 24-21 (KC) OT
1980—Chiefs, 20-17 (KC)
1981—Lions, 27-10 (D)
1987—Chiefs, 27-20 (D)
1988—Lions, 7-6 (KC)
1990—Chiefs, 43-24 (KC)
(RS Pts.—Chiefs 151, Lions 148)
DETROIT vs. *L.A. RAIDERS
RS: Raiders lead series, 5-2
1970—Lions, 28-14 (O)
1974—Raiders, 35-13 (O)
1978—Raiders, 29-17 (O)
1981—Lions, 16-0 (D)
1984—Raiders, 24-3 (D)
1987—Raiders, 27-7 (LA)
1990—Raiders, 38-31 (D)
(RS Pts.—Raiders 167, Lions 115)
*Franchise in Oakland prior to 1982
DETROIT vs. *L.A. RAMS
RS: Rams lead series, 39-34-1
PS: Lions lead series, 1-0
1937—Lions, 28-0 (D)
       Lions, 27-7 (D)
1938—Rams, 21-17 (C)
       Lions, 6-0 (D)
1939—Lions, 15-7 (D)
       Rams, 14-3 (C)
1940—Lions, 6-0 (D)
       Rams, 24-0 (C)
1941—Lions, 17-7 (D)
       Lions, 14-0 (C)
1942—Rams, 14-0 (D)
       Rams, 27-7 (C)

1944—Rams, 20-17 (D)
    Lions, 26-14 (C)
1945—Rams, 28-21 (D)
1946—Rams, 35-14 (LA)
    Rams, 41-20 (D)
1947—Rams, 27-13 (D)
    Rams, 28-17 (LA)
1948—Rams, 44-7 (LA)
    Rams, 34-27 (D)
1949—Rams, 27-24 (LA)
    Rams, 21-10 (D)
1950—Rams, 30-28 (D)
    Rams, 65-24 (LA)
1951—Rams, 27-21 (D)
    Lions, 24-22 (LA)
1952—Lions, 17-14 (LA)
    Lions, 24-16 (D)
    **Lions, 31-21 (D)
1953—Lions, 31-19 (D)
    Rams, 37-24 (LA)
1954—Lions, 21-3 (D)
    Lions, 27-24 (LA)
1955—Rams, 17-10 (D)
    Rams, 24-13 (LA)
1956—Lions, 24-21 (D)
    Lions, 16-7 (LA)
1957—Lions, 10-7 (D)
    Rams, 35-17 (LA)
1958—Rams, 42-28 (D)
    Lions, 41-24 (LA)
1959—Lions, 17-7 (LA)
    Lions, 23-17 (D)
1960—Rams, 48-35 (LA)
    Lions, 12-10 (D)
1961—Lions, 14-13 (D)
    Lions, 28-10 (LA)
1962—Lions, 13-10 (D)
    Lions, 12-3 (LA)
1963—Lions, 23-2 (LA)
    Rams, 28-21 (D)
1964—Tie, 17-17 (LA)
    Lions, 37-17 (D)
1965—Lions, 20-0 (D)
    Lions, 31-7 (LA)
1966—Rams, 14-7 (D)
    Rams, 23-3 (LA)
1967—Rams, 31-7 (D)
1968—Rams, 10-7 (LA)
1969—Rams, 28-0 (D)
1970—Lions, 28-23 (LA)
1971—Rams, 21-13 (D)
1972—Lions, 34-17 (LA)
1974—Lions, 16-13 (LA)
1975—Rams, 20-0 (D)
1976—Lions, 20-17 (D)
1980—Lions, 41-20 (LA)
1981—Rams, 20-13 (LA)
1982—Lions, 19-14 (LA)
1983—Rams, 21-10 (LA)
1986—Rams, 14-10 (LA)
1987—Lions, 37-16 (D)
1988—Rams, 17-10 (LA)
1991—Lions, 21-10 (D)
(RS Pts.—Rams 1,423, Lions 1,324)
(PS Pts.—Lions 31, Rams 21)
*Franchise in Cleveland prior to 1946
**Conference Playoff

DETROIT vs. MIAMI
RS: Series tied, 2-2
1973—Dolphins, 34-7 (M)
1979—Dolphins, 28-10 (D)
1985—Lions, 31-21 (D)
1991—Lions, 17-13 (D)
(RS Pts.—Dolphins 96, Lions 65)

DETROIT vs. MINNESOTA
RS: Vikings lead series, 38-21-2
1961—Lions, 37-10 (M)
    Lions, 13-7 (D)
1962—Lions, 17-6 (M)
    Lions, 37-23 (D)
1963—Lions, 28-10 (D)
    Vikings, 34-31 (M)
1964—Lions, 24-20 (M)
    Tie, 23-23 (D)
1965—Lions, 31-29 (M)
    Vikings, 29-7 (D)
1966—Lions, 32-31 (M)
    Vikings, 28-16 (D)
1967—Tie, 10-10 (M)
    Lions, 14-3 (D)
1968—Vikings, 24-10 (M)
    Vikings, 13-6 (D)
1969—Vikings, 24-10 (M)
    Vikings, 27-0 (D)
1970—Vikings, 30-17 (D)
    Vikings, 24-20 (M)
1971—Vikings, 16-13 (D)
    Vikings, 29-10 (M)
1972—Vikings, 34-10 (D)
    Vikings, 16-14 (M)
1973—Vikings, 23-9 (D)
    Vikings, 28-7 (M)
1974—Vikings, 7-6 (D)

Lions, 20-16 (M)
1975—Vikings, 25-19 (M)
    Lions, 17-10 (D)
1976—Vikings, 10-9 (D)
    Vikings, 31-23 (M)
1977—Vikings, 14-7 (M)
    Vikings, 30-21 (D)
1978—Vikings, 17-7 (M)
    Lions, 45-14 (D)
1979—Vikings, 13-10 (D)
    Vikings, 14-7 (M)
1980—Lions, 27-7 (D)
    Vikings, 34-0 (M)
1981—Vikings, 26-24 (M)
    Lions, 45-7 (D)
1982—Vikings, 34-31 (D)
1983—Vikings, 20-17 (M)
    Lions, 13-2 (D)
1984—Vikings, 29-28 (D)
    Lions, 16-14 (M)
1985—Lions, 16-13 (M)
    Lions, 41-21 (D)
1986—Lions, 13-10 (M)
    Vikings, 24-10 (D)
1987—Vikings, 34-19 (M)
    Vikings, 17-14 (D)
1988—Lions, 44-17 (M)
    Vikings, 23-0 (D)
1989—Vikings, 24-17 (M)
    Vikings, 20-7 (D)
1990—Lions, 34-27 (M)
    Vikings, 17-7 (D)
1991—Lions, 24-20 (D)
    Lions, 34-14 (M)
(RS Pts.—Vikings 1,239, Lions 1,088)

DETROIT vs. NEW ENGLAND
RS: Series tied, 2-2
1971—Lions, 34-7 (NE)
1976—Lions, 30-10 (D)
1979—Patriots, 24-17 (NE)
1985—Patriots, 23-6 (NE)
(RS Pts.—Lions 87, Patriots 64)

DETROIT vs. NEW ORLEANS
RS: Lions lead series, 6-5-1
1968—Tie, 20-20 (D)
1970—Saints, 19-17 (NO)
1972—Lions, 27-14 (D)
1973—Saints, 20-13 (NO)
1974—Lions, 19-14 (D)
1976—Saints, 17-16 (NO)
1977—Lions, 23-19 (D)
1979—Saints, 17-7 (NO)
1980—Lions, 24-13 (D)
1988—Saints, 22-14 (D)
1989—Lions, 21-14 (D)
1990—Lions, 27-10 (NO)
(RS Pts.—Lions 228, Saints 199)

*DETROIT vs. N.Y. GIANTS
RS: Lions lead series, 17-15-1
PS: Lions lead series, 1-0
1930—Giants, 19-6 (P)
1931—Spartans, 14-6 (P)
    Giants, 14-0 (NY)
1932—Spartans, 7-0 (P)
    Spartans, 6-0 (NY)
1933—Spartans, 17-7 (P)
    Giants, 13-10 (NY)
1934—Lions, 9-0 (D)
1935—**Lions, 26-7 (D)
1936—Giants, 14-7 (NY)
    Lions, 38-0 (D)
1937—Lions, 17-0 (NY)
1939—Lions, 18-14 (D)
1941—Lions, 20-13 (NY)
1943—Tie, 0-0 (D)
1945—Giants, 35-14 (NY)
1947—Lions, 35-7 (D)
1949—Lions, 45-21 (NY)
1953—Lions, 27-16 (NY)
1955—Giants, 24-19 (D)
1958—Giants, 19-17 (D)
1962—Giants, 17-14 (NY)
1964—Lions, 26-3 (D)
1967—Lions, 30-7 (NY)
1969—Lions, 24-0 (D)
1972—Lions, 30-16 (D)
1974—Lions, 20-19 (D)
1976—Giants, 24-10 (NY)
1982—Giants, 13-6 (D)
1983—Lions, 15-9 (D)
1988—Giants, 30-10 (NY)
    Giants, 13-10 (D) OT
1989—Giants, 24-14 (NY)
1990—Giants, 20-0 (NY)
(RS Pts.—Lions 528, Giants 424)
(PS Pts.—Lions 26, Giants 7)
*Franchise in Portsmouth prior to 1934
and known as the Spartans
**NFL Championship

DETROIT vs. N.Y. JETS
RS: Series tied, 3-3
1972—Lions, 37-20 (D)
1979—Jets, 31-10 (NY)

1982—Jets, 28-13 (D)
1985—Lions, 31-20 (D)
1988—Jets, 17-10 (D)
1991—Lions, 34-20 (D)
(RS Pts.—Jets 136, Lions 135)

*DETROIT vs. PHILADELPHIA
RS: Lions lead series, 12-9-2
1933—Spartans, 25-0 (P)
1934—Lions, 10-0 (P)
1935—Lions, 35-0 (P)
1936—Lions, 23-0 (P)
1938—Eagles, 21-7 (D)
1940—Lions, 21-0 (P)
1941—Lions, 21-17 (D)
1945—Lions, 28-24 (D)
1948—Eagles, 45-21 (P)
1949—Eagles, 22-14 (D)
1951—Lions, 28-10 (P)
1954—Tie, 13-13 (D)
1957—Lions, 27-16 (P)
1960—Eagles, 28-10 (P)
1961—Eagles, 27-24 (D)
1965—Lions, 35-28 (P)
1968—Eagles, 12-0 (D)
1971—Eagles, 23-20 (P)
1974—Eagles, 28-17 (D)
1977—Lions, 17-13 (D)
1979—Eagles, 44-7 (P)
1984—Tie, 23-23 (D) OT
1986—Lions, 13-11 (P)
(RS Pts.—Lions 439, Eagles 405)
*Franchise in Portsmouth prior to 1934
and known as the Spartans

*DETROIT vs. **PHOENIX
RS: Lions lead series, 25-16-5
1930—Lions, 0-0 (P)
    Cardinals, 23-0 (C)
1931—Cardinals, 20-19 (C)
1932—Tie, 7-7 (P)
1933—Spartans, 7-6 (P)
1934—Lions, 6-0 (D)
    Lions, 10-0 (P)
1935—Tie, 10-10 (D)
    Lions, 7-6 (C)
1936—Lions, 39-0 (D)
    Lions, 14-7 (C)
1937—Lions, 16-7 (C)
    Lions, 16-7 (D)
1938—Lions, 10-0 (D)
    Lions, 7-3 (C)
1939—Lions, 21-3 (D)
    Lions, 17-3 (C)
1940—Tie, 0-0 (Buffalo)
    Lions, 43-14 (C)
1941—Tie, 14-14 (C)
    Lions, 21-3 (D)
1942—Cardinals, 13-0 (C)
    Cardinals, 7-0 (D)
1943—Lions, 35-17 (D)
    Lions, 7-0 (C)
1945—Lions, 10-0 (C)
    Lions, 26-0 (D)
1946—Cardinals, 34-14 (C)
    Cardinals, 36-14 (D)
1947—Cardinals, 45-21 (C)
    Cardinals, 17-7 (D)
1948—Cardinals, 56-20 (C)
    Cardinals, 28-14 (D)
1949—Lions, 24-7 (C)
    Cardinals, 42-19 (D)
1959—Lions, 45-21 (D)
1961—Lions, 45-14 (StL)
1967—Cardinals, 38-28 (StL)
1969—Lions, 20-0 (D)
1970—Lions, 16-3 (D)
1973—Lions, 20-16 (StL)
1975—Cardinals, 24-13 (D)
1978—Cardinals, 21-14 (StL)
1980—Lions, 20-7 (D)
    Cardinals, 24-23 (StL)
1989—Cardinals, 16-13 (D)
(RS Pts.—Lions 759, Cardinals 642)
*Franchise in Portsmouth prior to 1934
and known as the Spartans
**Franchise in St. Louis prior to 1988
and in Chicago prior to 1960

DETROIT vs. *PITTSBURGH
RS: Lions lead series, 13-10-1
1934—Lions, 40-7 (D)
1936—Lions, 28-3 (D)
1937—Lions, 7-3 (D)
1938—Lions, 16-7 (D)
1940—Pirates, 10-7 (D)
1942—Steelers, 35-7 (D)
1946—Lions, 17-7 (D)
1947—Steelers, 17-10 (P)
1948—Lions, 17-14 (D)
1949—Steelers, 14-7 (P)
1950—Lions, 10-7 (D)
1952—Lions, 31-6 (P)
1953—Lions, 38-21 (D)
1955—Lions, 31-28 (D)
1956—Lions, 45-7 (D)

1959—Tie, 10-10 (P)
1962—Lions, 45-7 (D)
1966—Steelers, 17-3 (P)
1967—Lions, 24-14 (D)
1969—Steelers, 16-13 (P)
1973—Steelers, 24-10 (D)
1983—Lions, 45-3 (D)
1986—Steelers, 27-17 (P)
1989—Steelers, 23-3 (D)
(RS Pts.—Lions 471, Steelers 337)
*Steelers known as Pirates prior to 1941

DETROIT vs. SAN DIEGO
RS: Lions lead series, 3-2
1972—Lions, 34-20 (D)
1977—Lions, 20-0 (D)
1978—Lions, 31-14 (D)
1981—Chargers, 28-23 (SD)
1984—Chargers, 27-24 (SD)
(RS Pts.—Lions 132, Chargers 89)

DETROIT vs. SAN FRANCISCO
RS: Lions lead series, 25-24-1
PS: Series tied, 1-1
1950—Lions, 24-7 (D)
    49ers, 28-27 (SF)
1951—49ers, 20-10 (D)
    49ers, 21-17 (SF)
1952—Lions, 17-3 (SF)
    49ers, 28-0 (D)
1953—Lions, 24-21 (D)
    Lions, 14-10 (SF)
1954—49ers, 37-31 (SF)
    Lions, 48-7 (D)
1955—Lions, 27-24 (D)
    49ers, 38-21 (SF)
1956—Lions, 20-17 (D)
    Lions, 17-13 (SF)
1957—49ers, 35-31 (SF)
    Lions, 31-10 (D)
    *Lions, 31-27 (SF)
1958—49ers, 24-21 (SF)
    Lions, 35-21 (D)
1959—49ers, 34-13 (D)
    49ers, 33-7 (SF)
1960—49ers, 14-10 (D)
    Lions, 24-0 (SF)
1961—49ers, 49-0 (D)
    Tie, 20-20 (SF)
1962—49ers, 45-24 (D)
    Lions, 38-24 (SF)
1963—Lions, 26-3 (D)
    Lions, 45-7 (SF)
1964—Lions, 26-17 (D)
    Lions, 24-7 (SF)
1965—49ers, 27-21 (D)
    49ers, 17-14 (SF)
1966—49ers, 27-24 (D)
    49ers, 41-14 (SF)
1967—Lions, 45-3 (SF)
1968—49ers, 14-7 (D)
1969—Lions, 26-14 (SF)
1970—Lions, 28-7 (D)
1971—49ers, 31-27 (SF)
1973—Lions, 30-20 (D)
1974—Lions, 17-13 (D)
1975—Lions, 28-17 (SF)
1977—49ers, 28-7 (SF)
1978—Lions, 33-14 (D)
1980—Lions, 17-13 (D)
1981—Lions, 24-17 (D)
1983—**49ers, 24-23 (SF)
1984—49ers, 30-27 (D)
1985—49ers, 23-21 (D)
1988—49ers, 20-13 (SF)
1991—49ers, 35-3 (SF)
(RS Pts.—Lions 1,104, 49ers 1,022)
(PS Pts.—Lions 54, 49ers 51)
*Conference Playoff
**NFC Divisional Playoff

DETROIT vs. SEATTLE
RS: Seahawks lead series, 4-1
1976—Lions, 41-14 (S)
1978—Seahawks, 28-16 (S)
1984—Seahawks, 38-17 (S)
1987—Seahawks, 37-14 (S)
1990—Seahawks, 30-10 (S)
(RS Pts.—Seahawks 147, Lions 98)

DETROIT vs. TAMPA BAY
RS: Series tied, 14-14
1977—Lions, 16-7 (D)
1978—Lions, 15-7 (TB)
    Lions, 34-23 (D)
1979—Buccaneers, 31-16 (TB)
    Buccaneers, 16-14 (D)
1980—Lions, 24-10 (TB)
    Lions, 27-14 (D)
1981—Buccaneers, 28-10 (TB)
    Buccaneers, 20-17 (D)
1982—Buccaneers, 23-21 (TB)
1983—Lions, 11-0 (TB)
    Lions, 23-20 (D)
1984—Buccaneers, 21-17 (TB)
    Lions, 13-7 (D) OT
1985—Lions, 30-9 (D)

Buccaneers, 19-16 (TB) OT
1986—Buccaneers, 24-20 (D)
Lions, 38-17 (TB)
1987—Buccaneers, 31-27 (D)
Lions, 20-10 (TB)
1988—Buccaneers, 23-20 (D)
Buccaneers, 21-10 (TB)
1989—Lions, 17-16 (TB)
Lions, 33-7 (D)
1990—Buccaneers, 38-21 (D)
Buccaneers, 23-20 (TB)
1991—Lions, 31-3 (D)
Buccaneers, 30-21 (TB)
(RS Pts.—Lions 582, Buccaneers 498)

*DETROIT vs. **WASHINGTON
RS: Redskins lead series, 21-8
PS: Redskins lead series, 2-0
1932—Spartans, 10-0 (P)
1933—Spartans, 13-0 (B)
1934—Lions, 24-0 (D)
1935—Lions, 17-7 (B)
Lions, 14-0 (D)
1938—Redskins, 7-5 (D)
1939—Redskins, 31-7 (W)
1940—Redskins, 20-14 (D)
1942—Redskins, 15-3 (D)
1943—Redskins, 42-20 (W)
1946—Redskins, 17-16 (W)
1947—Lions, 38-21 (D)
1948—Redskins, 46-21 (W)
1951—Lions, 35-17 (D)
1956—Redskins, 18-17 (W)
1965—Lions, 14-10 (D)
1968—Redskins, 14-3 (W)
1970—Redskins, 31-10 (W)
1973—Redskins, 20-0 (D)
1976—Redskins, 20-7 (W)
1978—Redskins, 21-19 (D)
1979—Redskins, 27-24 (D)
1981—Redskins, 33-31 (W)
1982—***Redskins, 31-7 (W)
1983—Redskins, 38-17 (W)
1984—Redskins, 28-14 (W)
1985—Redskins, 24-3 (W)
1987—Redskins, 20-13 (W)
1990—Redskins, 41-38 (D)
1991—Redskins, 45-0 (W)
****Redskins, 41-10 (W)
(RS Pts.—Redskins 613, Lions 447)
(PS Pts.—Redskins 72, Lions 17)
*Franchise in Portsmouth prior to 1934
and known as the Spartans.
**Franchise in Boston prior to 1937
***NFC First Round Playoff
****NFC Championship

GREEN BAY vs. ATLANTA
RS: Packers lead series, 9-8;
See Atlanta vs. Green Bay
GREEN BAY vs. BUFFALO
RS: Bills lead series, 4-1;
See Buffalo vs. Green Bay
GREEN BAY vs. CHICAGO
RS: Bears lead series, 79-57-6
PS: Bears lead series, 1-0;
See Chicago vs. Green Bay
GREEN BAY vs. CINCINNATI
RS: Bengals lead series, 4-2;
See Cincinnati vs. Green Bay
GREEN BAY vs. CLEVELAND
RS: Packers lead series, 7-5
PS: Packers lead series, 1-0;
See Cleveland vs. Green Bay
GREEN BAY vs. DALLAS
RS: Packers lead series, 8-5
PS: Packers lead series, 2-1;
See Dallas vs. Green Bay
GREEN BAY vs. DENVER
RS: Broncos lead series, 4-1-1;
See Denver vs. Green Bay
GREEN BAY vs. DETROIT
RS: Packers lead series, 61-55-7;
See Detroit vs. Green Bay
GREEN BAY vs. HOUSTON
RS: Oilers lead series, 3-2
1972—Packers, 23-10 (H)
1977—Oilers, 16-10 (GB)
1980—Oilers, 22-3 (GB)
1983—Packers, 41-38 (H) OT
1986—Oilers, 31-3 (GB)
(RS Pts.—Oilers 117, Packers 80)
GREEN BAY vs. *INDIANAPOLIS
RS: Series tied, 18-18-1
PS: Packers lead series, 1-0
1953—Packers, 37-14 (GB)
Packers, 35-24 (B)
1954—Packers, 7-6 (B)
Packers, 24-13 (Mil)
1955—Colts, 24-20 (Mil)
Colts, 14-10 (B)
1956—Packers, 38-33 (Mil)
Colts, 28-21 (B)
1957—Colts, 45-17 (Mil)

Packers, 24-21 (B)
1958—Colts, 24-17 (Mil)
Colts, 56-0 (B)
1959—Colts, 38-21 (B)
Colts, 28-24 (Mil)
1960—Packers, 35-21 (GB)
Colts, 38-24 (B)
1961—Packers, 45-7 (GB)
Colts, 45-21 (B)
1962—Packers, 17-6 (B)
Packers, 17-13 (GB)
1963—Packers, 31-20 (GB)
Packers, 34-20 (B)
1964—Colts, 21-20 (GB)
Colts, 24-21 (B)
1965—Packers, 20-17 (Mil)
Packers, 42-27 (B)
**Packers, 13-10 (GB) OT
1966—Packers, 24-3 (Mil)
Packers, 14-10 (B)
1967—Colts, 13-10 (B)
1968—Colts, 16-3 (GB)
1969—Colts, 14-6 (B)
1970—Colts, 13-10 (Mil)
1974—Packers, 20-13 (B)
1982—Tie, 20-20 (B) OT
1985—Colts, 37-10 (I)
1988—Colts, 20-13 (GB)
1991—Packers, 14-10 (Mil)
(RS Pts.—Colts 796, Packers 766)
(PS Pts.—Packers 13, Colts 10)
*Franchise in Baltimore prior to 1984
**Conference Playoff
GREEN BAY vs. KANSAS CITY
RS: Chiefs lead series, 3-1-1
PS: Packers lead series, 1-0
1966—*Packers, 35-10 (Los Angeles)
1973—Tie, 10-10 (Mil)
1977—Chiefs, 20-10 (KC)
1987—Packers, 23-3 (KC)
1989—Chiefs, 21-3 (GB)
1990—Chiefs, 17-3 (GB)
(RS Pts.—Chiefs 71, Packers 49)
(PS Pts.—Packers 35, Chiefs 10)
*Super Bowl I
GREEN BAY vs. *L.A. RAIDERS
RS: Raiders lead series, 5-1
PS: Packers lead series, 1-0
1967—**Packers, 33-14 (Miami)
1972—Raiders, 20-14 (GB)
1976—Raiders, 18-14 (O)
1978—Raiders, 28-3 (GB)
1984—Raiders, 28-7 (LA)
1987—Raiders, 20-0 (GB)
1990—Raiders, 29-16 (LA)
(RS Pts.—Raiders 130, Packers 67)
(PS Pts.—Packers 33, Raiders 14)
*Franchise in Oakland prior to 1982
**Super Bowl II
GREEN BAY vs. *L.A. RAMS
RS: Rams lead series, 42-34-2
PS: Packers lead series, 1-0
1937—Packers, 35-10 (C)
Packers, 35-7 (GB)
1938—Packers, 26-17 (GB)
Packers, 28-7 (C)
1939—Rams, 27-24 (GB)
Packers, 7-6 (C)
1940—Packers, 31-14 (GB)
Tie, 13-13 (C)
1941—Packers, 24-7 (Mil)
Packers, 17-14 (C)
1942—Packers, 45-28 (GB)
Packers, 30-12 (C)
1944—Packers, 30-21 (GB)
Packers, 42-7 (C)
1945—Rams, 27-14 (GB)
Rams, 20-7 (C)
1946—Rams, 21-17 (Mil)
Rams, 38-17 (LA)
1947—Packers, 17-14 (Mil)
Packers, 30-10 (LA)
1948—Packers, 16-0 (GB)
Rams, 24-10 (LA)
1949—Rams, 48-7 (GB)
Rams, 35-7 (LA)
1950—Rams, 45-14 (Mil)
Rams, 51-14 (LA)
1951—Rams, 28-0 (Mil)
Rams, 42-14 (LA)
1952—Rams, 30-28 (Mil)
Rams, 45-27 (LA)
1953—Rams, 38-20 (Mil)
Rams, 33-17 (LA)
1954—Rams, 35-17 (Mil)
Rams, 35-27 (LA)
1955—Rams, 30-28 (Mil)
Rams, 31-17 (LA)
1956—Rams, 42-17 (Mil)
Rams, 49-21 (LA)
1957—Rams, 31-27 (Mil)
Rams, 42-17 (LA)
1958—Rams, 20-7 (GB)

Rams, 34-20 (LA)
1959—Rams, 45-6 (Mil)
Packers, 38-20 (LA)
1960—Rams, 33-31 (Mil)
Rams, 35-21 (LA)
1961—Packers, 35-17 (GB)
Packers, 24-17 (LA)
1962—Packers, 41-10 (Mil)
Packers, 20-17 (LA)
1963—Packers, 42-10 (GB)
Packers, 31-14 (LA)
1964—Rams, 27-17 (Mil)
Tie, 24-24 (LA)
1965—Packers, 6-3 (Mil)
Rams, 21-10 (LA)
1966—Packers, 24-13 (GB)
Packers, 27-23 (LA)
1967—Rams, 27-24 (LA)
**Packers, 28-7 (Mil)
1968—Rams, 16-14 (GB)
1969—Rams, 34-21 (LA)
1970—Rams, 31-21 (GB)
1971—Rams, 30-13 (LA)
1973—Rams, 24-7 (LA)
1974—Packers, 17-6 (Mil)
1975—Rams, 22-5 (LA)
1977—Rams, 24-6 (Mil)
1978—Rams, 31-14 (LA)
1980—Rams, 51-21 (LA)
1981—Rams, 35-23 (LA)
1982—Packers, 35-23 (Mil)
1983—Packers, 27-24 (Mil)
1984—Packers, 31-6 (Mil)
1985—Packers, 34-17 (LA)
1988—Rams, 34-7 (GB)
1989—Rams, 41-38 (LA)
1990—Packers, 36-24 (GB)
1991—Rams, 23-21 (LA)
(RS Pts.—Rams 1,898, Packers 1,715)
(PS Pts.—Packers 28, Rams 7)
*Franchise in Cleveland prior to 1946
**Conference Championship
GREEN BAY vs. MIAMI
RS: Dolphins lead series, 7-0
1971—Dolphins, 27-6 (Mia)
1975—Dolphins, 31-7 (GB)
1979—Dolphins, 27-7 (Mia)
1985—Dolphins, 34-24 (GB)
1988—Dolphins, 24-17 (Mia)
1989—Dolphins, 23-20 (Mil)
1991—Dolphins, 16-13 (Mia)
(RS Pts.—Dolphins 182, Packers 94)
GREEN BAY vs. MINNESOTA
RS: Packers lead series, 31-29-1
1961—Packers, 33-7 (Minn)
Packers, 28-10 (Mil)
1962—Packers, 34-7 (GB)
Packers, 48-21 (Mil)
1963—Packers, 37-28 (Minn)
Packers, 28-7 (GB)
1964—Vikings, 24-23 (GB)
Packers, 42-13 (Minn)
1965—Packers, 38-13 (GB)
Packers, 24-19 (GB)
1966—Vikings, 20-17 (GB)
Packers, 28-16 (Minn)
1967—Vikings, 10-7 (Mil)
Packers, 30-27 (Minn)
1968—Vikings, 26-13 (Mil)
Vikings, 14-10 (Minn)
1969—Vikings, 19-7 (Minn)
Vikings, 9-7 (Mil)
1970—Packers, 13-10 (GB)
Vikings, 10-3 (Minn)
1971—Vikings, 24-13 (GB)
Vikings, 3-0 (Minn)
1972—Vikings, 27-13 (GB)
Packers, 23-7 (Minn)
1973—Vikings, 11-3 (Mil)
Vikings, 31-7 (GB)
1974—Vikings, 32-17 (GB)
Packers, 19-7 (Minn)
1975—Vikings, 28-17 (GB)
Vikings, 24-3 (Minn)
1976—Vikings, 17-10 (Mil)
Vikings, 20-9 (Minn)
1977—Vikings, 19-7 (Mil)
Vikings, 13-6 (GB)
1978—Vikings, 21-7 (Minn)
Tie, 10-10 (GB) OT
1979—Vikings, 27-21 (Minn) OT
Packers, 19-7 (Mil)
1980—Packers, 16-3 (GB)
Packers, 25-13 (Minn)
1981—Vikings, 30-13 (Mil)
Packers, 35-23 (Minn)
1982—Packers, 26-7 (Mil)
1983—Vikings, 20-17 (GB) OT
Packers, 29-21 (Minn)
1984—Packers, 45-17 (Mil)
Packers, 38-14 (Minn)
1985—Packers, 20-17 (GB)
Packers, 27-17 (Minn)

1986—Vikings, 42-7 (Minn)
Vikings, 32-6 (GB)
1987—Packers, 23-16 (Minn)
Packers, 16-10 (GB)
1988—Packers, 34-14 (Minn)
Packers, 18-6 (GB)
1989—Vikings, 26-14 (Minn)
Packers, 20-19 (GB)
1990—Packers, 24-10 (Mil)
Vikings, 23-7 (Minn)
1991—Vikings, 35-21 (GB)
Packers, 27-7 (Minn)
(RS Pts.—Packers 1,182, Vikings 1,060)
GREEN BAY vs. NEW ENGLAND
RS: Series tied, 2-2
1973—Patriots, 33-24 (NE)
1979—Packers, 27-14 (GB)
1985—Patriots, 26-20 (NE)
1988—Packers, 45-3 (GB)
(RS Pts.—Packers 116, Patriots 76)
GREEN BAY vs. NEW ORLEANS
RS: Packers lead series, 11-4
1968—Packers, 29-7 (Mil)
1971—Saints, 29-21 (Mil)
1972—Packers, 30-20 (NO)
1973—Packers, 30-10 (Mil)
1975—Saints, 20-19 (NO)
1976—Packers, 32-27 (Mil)
1977—Packers, 24-20 (NO)
1978—Packers, 28-17 (Mil)
1979—Packers, 28-19 (Mil)
1981—Packers, 35-7 (NO)
1984—Packers, 23-13 (NO)
1985—Packers, 38-14 (Mil)
1986—Saints, 24-10 (NO)
1987—Saints, 33-24 (NO)
1989—Packers, 35-34 (GB)
(RS Pts.—Packers 406, Saints 294)
GREEN BAY vs. N.Y. GIANTS
RS: Packers lead series, 21-19-2
PS: Packers lead series, 4-1
1928—Giants, 6-0 (GB)
Packers, 7-0 (NY)
1929—Packers, 20-6 (NY)
1930—Packers, 14-7 (GB)
Giants, 13-6 (NY)
1931—Packers, 27-7 (GB)
Packers, 14-10 (NY)
1932—Packers, 13-0 (GB)
Giants, 6-0 (NY)
1933—Giants, 10-7 (Mil)
Giants, 17-6 (NY)
1934—Packers, 20-6 (Mil)
Giants, 17-3 (NY)
1935—Packers, 16-7 (GB)
1936—Packers, 26-14 (NY)
1937—Giants, 10-0 (NY)
1938—Giants, 15-3 (NY)
*Giants, 23-17 (NY)
1939—*Packers, 27-0 (Mil)
1940—Packers, 7-3 (NY)
1942—Tie, 21-21 (NY)
1943—Packers, 35-21 (NY)
1944—Giants, 24-0 (NY)
*Packers, 14-7 (NY)
1945—Packers, 23-14 (NY)
1947—Tie, 24-24 (NY)
1948—Giants, 49-3 (Mil)
1949—Giants, 30-10 (GB)
1952—Packers, 17-3 (NY)
1957—Giants, 31-17 (GB)
1959—Giants, 20-3 (NY)
1961—Packers, 20-17 (Mil)
*Packers, 37-0 (GB)
1962—*Packers, 16-7 (NY)
1967—Packers, 48-21 (Mil)
1969—Packers, 20-10 (Mil)
1971—Giants, 42-40 (GB)
1973—Packers, 16-14 (New Haven)
1975—Packers, 40-14 (Mil)
1980—Giants, 27-21 (NY)
1981—Packers, 27-14 (NY)
Packers, 26-24 (Mil)
1982—Packers, 27-19 (NY)
1983—Giants, 27-3 (NY)
1985—Packers, 23-20 (GB)
1986—Giants, 55-24 (NY)
1987—Giants, 20-10 (NY)
(RS Pts.—Giants 719, Packers 683)
(PS Pts.—Packers 111, Giants 37)
*NFL Championship
GREEN BAY vs. N.Y. JETS
RS: Jets lead series, 5-1
1973—Packers, 23-7 (Mil)
1979—Jets, 27-22 (GB)
1981—Jets, 28-3 (NY)
1982—Jets, 15-13 (NY)
1985—Jets, 24-3 (Mil)
1991—Jets, 19-16 (NY) OT
(RS Pts.—Jets 120, Packers 80)
GREEN BAY vs. PHILADELPHIA
RS: Packers lead series, 18-6
PS: Eagles lead series, 1-0

1933—Packers, 35-9 (GB)
　　　　Packers, 10-0 (P)
1934—Packers, 19-6 (GB)
1935—Packers, 13-6 (P)
1937—Packers, 37-7 (Mil)
1939—Packers, 23-16 (P)
1940—Packers, 27-20 (GB)
1942—Packers, 7-0 (P)
1946—Packers, 19-7 (P)
1947—Eagles, 28-14 (P)
1951—Packers, 37-24 (GB)
1952—Packers, 12-10 (Mil)
1954—Packers, 37-14 (P)
1958—Packers, 38-35 (GB)
1960—*Eagles, 17-13 (P)
1962—Packers, 49-0 (P)
1968—Packers, 30-13 (GB)
1970—Packers, 30-17 (Mil)
1974—Eagles, 36-14 (P)
1976—Packers, 28-13 (GB)
1978—Eagles, 10-3 (P)
1979—Eagles, 21-10 (GB)
1987—Packers, 16-10 (GB) OT
1990—Eagles, 31-0 (P)
1991—Eagles, 20-3 (GB)
(RS Pts.—Packers 511, Eagles 353)
(PS Pts.—Eagles 17, Packers 13)
*NFL Championship
GREEN BAY vs. *PHOENIX
RS: Packers lead series, 39-21-4
PS: Packers lead series, 1-0
1921—Tie, 3-3 (C)
1922—Cardinals, 16-3 (C)
1924—Cardinals, 3-0 (C)
1925—Cardinals, 9-6 (C)
1926—Cardinals, 13-7 (GB)
　　　　Packers, 3-0 (C)
1927—Packers, 13-0 (GB)
　　　　Tie, 6-6 (C)
1928—Packers, 20-0 (GB)
1929—Packers, 9-2 (GB)
　　　　Packers, 7-6 (C)
　　　　Packers, 12-0 (C)
1930—Packers, 14-0 (GB)
　　　　Cardinals, 13-6 (C)
1931—Packers, 26-7 (GB)
　　　　Cardinals, 21-13 (C)
1932—Packers, 15-7 (GB)
　　　　Packers, 19-9 (C)
1933—Packers, 14-6 (C)
1934—Packers, 15-0 (GB)
　　　　Cardinals, 9-0 (Mil)
　　　　Cardinals, 6-0 (C)
1935—Cardinals, 7-6 (GB)
　　　　Cardinals, 3-0 (Mil)
　　　　Cardinals, 9-7 (C)
1936—Packers, 10-7 (GB)
　　　　Packers, 24-0 (Mil)
　　　　Tie, 0-0 (C)
1937—Cardinals, 14-7 (GB)
　　　　Packers, 34-13 (Mil)
1938—Packers, 28-7 (Mil)
　　　　Packers, 24-22 (Buffalo)
1939—Packers, 14-10 (GB)
　　　　Packers, 27-20 (Mil)
1940—Packers, 31-6 (Mil)
　　　　Packers, 28-7 (C)
1941—Packers, 14-13 (Mil)
　　　　Packers, 17-9 (C)
1942—Packers, 17-13 (C)
　　　　Packers, 55-24 (GB)
1943—Packers, 28-7 (C)
　　　　Packers, 35-14 (Mil)
1945—Packers, 33-14 (Mil)
1946—Packers, 19-7 (C)
　　　　Cardinals, 24-6 (GB)
1947—Cardinals, 14-10 (C)
　　　　Cardinals, 21-20 (C)
1948—Cardinals, 17-7 (Mil)
　　　　Cardinals, 42-7 (C)
1949—Cardinals, 39-17 (Mil)
　　　　Cardinals, 41-21 (C)
1955—Packers, 31-14 (GB)
1956—Packers, 24-21 (C)
1962—Packers, 17-0 (Mil)
1963—Packers, 30-7 (StL)
1967—Packers, 31-23 (StL)
1969—Packers, 45-28 (GB)
1971—Tie, 16-16 (StL)
1973—Packers, 25-21 (GB)
1976—Cardinals, 29-0 (StL)
1982—**Packers, 41-16 (GB)
1984—Packers, 24-23 (GB)
1985—Cardinals, 43-28 (StL)
1988—Packers, 26-17 (P)
1990—Packers, 24-21 (P)
(RS Pts.—Packers 1,082, Cardinals 823)
(PS Pts.—Packers 41, Cardinals 16)
*Franchise in St. Louis prior to 1988,
and in Chicago prior to 1960
**NFC First Round Playoff
GREEN BAY vs. *PITTSBURGH
RS: Packers lead series, 16-11

1933—Packers, 47-0 (GB)
1935—Packers, 27-0 (GB)
　　　　Packers, 34-14 (P)
1936—Packers, 42-10 (Mil)
1938—Packers, 20-0 (GB)
1940—Packers, 24-3 (Mil)
1941—Packers, 54-7 (P)
1942—Packers, 24-21 (Mil)
1946—Packers, 17-7 (GB)
1947—Steelers, 18-17 (Mil)
1948—Steelers, 38-7 (P)
1949—Steelers, 30-7 (Mil)
1951—Packers, 35-33 (Mil)
　　　　Steelers, 28-7 (P)
1953—Packers, 31-14 (P)
1954—Steelers, 21-20 (GB)
1957—Packers, 27-10 (P)
1960—Packers, 19-13 (P)
1963—Packers, 33-14 (Mil)
1965—Packers, 41-9 (P)
1967—Steelers, 24-17 (GB)
1969—Packers, 38-34 (P)
1970—Packers, 20-12 (P)
1975—Steelers, 16-13 (Mil)
1980—Steelers, 22-20 (P)
1983—Steelers, 25-21 (GB)
1986—Steelers, 27-3 (P)
(RS Pts.—Packers 648, Steelers 467)
*Steelers known as Pirates prior to 1941
GREEN BAY vs. SAN DIEGO
RS: Packers lead series, 3-1
1970—Packers, 22-20 (SD)
1974—Packers, 34-0 (GB)
1978—Packers, 24-3 (SD)
1984—Chargers, 34-28 (GB)
(RS Pts.—Packers 108, Chargers 57)
GREEN BAY vs. SAN FRANCISCO
RS: 49ers lead series, 25-21-1
1950—Packers, 25-21 (GB)
　　　　49ers, 30-14 (SF)
1951—49ers, 31-19 (SF)
1952—49ers, 24-14 (SF)
1953—49ers, 37-7 (Mil)
　　　　49ers, 48-14 (SF)
1954—49ers, 23-17 (Mil)
　　　　49ers, 35-0 (SF)
1955—Packers, 27-21 (Mil)
　　　　Packers, 28-7 (SF)
1956—49ers, 17-16 (GB)
　　　　49ers, 38-20 (SF)
1957—49ers, 24-14 (Mil)
　　　　49ers, 27-20 (SF)
1958—49ers, 33-12 (Mil)
　　　　49ers, 48-21 (SF)
1959—Packers, 21-20 (GB)
　　　　Packers, 36-14 (SF)
1960—Packers, 41-14 (Mil)
　　　　Packers, 13-0 (SF)
1961—Packers, 30-10 (GB)
　　　　49ers, 22-21 (SF)
1962—Packers, 31-13 (Mil)
　　　　Packers, 31-21 (SF)
1963—Packers, 28-10 (Mil)
　　　　Packers, 21-17 (SF)
1964—Packers, 24-14 (Mil)
　　　　49ers, 24-14 (SF)
1965—Packers, 27-10 (GB)
　　　　Tie, 24-24 (SF)
1966—49ers, 21-20 (SF)
　　　　Packers, 20-7 (Mil)
1967—49ers, 13-0 (GB)
1968—49ers, 27-20 (SF)
1969—Packers, 14-7 (Mil)
1970—49ers, 26-10 (SF)
1972—Packers, 34-24 (GB)
1973—49ers, 20-6 (SF)
1974—49ers, 7-6 (SF)
1976—49ers, 26-14 (GB)
1977—Packers, 16-14 (Mil)
1980—Packers, 23-16 (Mil)
1981—49ers, 13-3 (Mil)
1986—49ers, 31-17 (Mil)
1987—49ers, 23-12 (GB)
1989—Packers, 21-17 (SF)
1990—49ers, 24-20 (GB)
(RS Pts.—49ers 980, Packers 899)
GREEN BAY vs. SEATTLE
RS: Series tied, 3-3
1976—Packers, 27-20 (Mil)
1978—Packers, 45-28 (Mil)
1981—Packers, 34-24 (GB)
1984—Seahawks, 30-24 (Mil)
1987—Seahawks, 24-13 (S)
1990—Seahawks, 20-14 (Mil)
(RS Pts.—Packers 157, Seahawks 146)
GREEN BAY vs. TAMPA BAY
RS: Packers lead series, 14-11-1
1977—Packers, 13-0 (TB)
1978—Packers, 9-7 (GB)
　　　　Packers, 17-7 (TB)
1979—Buccaneers, 21-10 (GB)
　　　　Buccaneers, 21-3 (TB)
1980—Tie, 14-14 (TB) OT

Buccaneers, 20-17 (Mil)
1981—Buccaneers, 21-10 (GB)
　　　　Buccaneers, 37-3 (TB)
1983—Packers, 55-14 (GB)
　　　　Packers, 12-9 (TB) OT
1984—Buccaneers, 30-27 (TB) OT
　　　　Packers, 27-14 (GB)
1985—Packers, 21-0 (GB)
　　　　Packers, 20-17 (TB)
1986—Packers, 31-7 (Mil)
　　　　Packers, 21-7 (TB)
1987—Buccaneers, 23-17 (Mil)
1988—Buccaneers, 13-10 (GB)
　　　　Buccaneers, 27-24 (TB)
1989—Buccaneers, 23-21 (GB)
　　　　Packers, 17-16 (TB)
1990—Buccaneers, 26-14 (TB)
　　　　Packers, 20-10 (GB)
1991—Packers, 15-13 (GB)
　　　　Packers, 27-0 (TB)
(RS Pts.—Packers 475, Buccaneers 396)
GREEN BAY vs. *WASHINGTON
RS: Packers lead series, 13-12-1
PS: Series tied, 1-1
1932—Packers, 21-0 (B)
1933—Tie, 7-7 (GB)
　　　　Packers, 20-7 (B)
1934—Packers, 10-0 (B)
1936—Packers, 31-2 (GB)
　　　　Packers, 7-3 (B)
　　　　**Packers, 21-6 (New York)
1937—Redskins, 14-6 (W)
1939—Packers, 24-14 (Mil)
1941—Packers, 22-17 (W)
1943—Redskins, 33-7 (Mil)
1946—Packers, 20-7 (W)
1947—Packers, 27-10 (Mil)
1948—Packers, 23-7 (W)
1949—Redskins, 30-0 (W)
1950—Packers, 35-21 (Mil)
1952—Packers, 35-20 (Mil)
1958—Redskins, 37-21 (W)
1959—Packers, 21-0 (GB)
1968—Packers, 27-7 (W)
1972—Redskins, 21-16 (W)
　　　　***Redskins, 16-3 (W)
1974—Redskins, 17-6 (GB)
1977—Redskins, 10-9 (W)
1979—Redskins, 38-21 (W)
1983—Packers, 48-47 (GB)
1986—Redskins, 16-7 (GB)
1988—Redskins, 20-17 (Mil)
(RS Pts.—Packers 459, Redskins 434)
(PS Pts.—Packers 24, Redskins 22)
*Franchise in Boston prior to 1937 and
known as Braves prior to 1933
**NFL Championship
***NFC Divisional Playoff

HOUSTON vs. ATLANTA
RS: Falcons lead series, 5-2;
See Atlanta vs. Houston
HOUSTON vs. BUFFALO
RS: Oilers lead series, 19-11
PS: Bills lead series, 1-0;
See Buffalo vs. Houston
HOUSTON vs. CHICAGO
RS: Oilers lead series, 3-2;
See Chicago vs. Houston
HOUSTON vs. CINCINNATI
RS: Bengals lead series, 24-21-1
PS: Bengals lead series, 1-0;
See Cincinnati vs. Houston
HOUSTON vs. CLEVELAND
RS: Browns lead series, 26-17
PS: Oilers lead series, 1-0;
See Cleveland vs. Houston
HOUSTON vs. DALLAS
RS: Cowboys lead series, 4-3;
See Dallas vs. Houston
HOUSTON vs. DENVER
RS: Oilers lead series, 19-10-1
PS: Broncos lead series, 2-1;
See Denver vs. Houston
HOUSTON vs. DETROIT
RS: Oilers lead series, 3-2;
See Detroit vs. Houston
HOUSTON vs. GREEN BAY
RS: Oilers lead series, 3-2;
See Green Bay vs. Houston
HOUSTON vs. *INDIANAPOLIS
RS: Series tied, 6-6
1970—Colts, 24-20 (H)
1973—Oilers, 31-27 (B)
1976—Colts, 38-14 (B)
1979—Oilers, 28-16 (B)
1980—Oilers, 21-16 (H)
1983—Colts, 20-10 (H)
1984—Colts, 35-21 (H)
1985—Colts, 34-16 (I)
1986—Colts, 31-17 (H)
1987—Colts, 51-27 (H)
1988—Oilers, 17-14 (I) OT

1990—Oilers 24-10 (H)
(RS Pts.—Colts 302, Oilers 260)
*Franchise in Baltimore prior to 1984
HOUSTON vs. *KANSAS CITY
RS: Chiefs lead series, 21-15
PS: Chiefs lead series, 1-0
1960—Oilers, 20-10 (H)
　　　　Texans, 24-0 (D)
1961—Texans, 26-21 (D)
　　　　Oilers, 38-7 (H)
1962—Texans, 31-7 (H)
　　　　Oilers, 14-6 (D)
　　　　**Texans, 20-17 (H) OT
1963—Chiefs, 28-7 (KC)
　　　　Oilers, 28-7 (H)
1964—Chiefs, 28-7 (KC)
　　　　Chiefs, 28-19 (H)
1965—Chiefs, 52-21 (KC)
　　　　Oilers, 38-36 (H)
1966—Chiefs, 48-23 (KC)
1967—Chiefs, 25-20 (H)
　　　　Oilers, 24-19 (KC)
1968—Chiefs, 26-21 (H)
　　　　Chiefs, 24-10 (KC)
1969—Chiefs, 24-0 (KC)
1970—Chiefs, 24-9 (H)
1971—Oilers, 20-16 (H)
1973—Chiefs, 38-14 (KC)
1974—Chiefs, 17-7 (H)
1975—Oilers, 17-13 (KC)
1977—Oilers, 34-20 (H)
1978—Oilers, 20-17 (KC)
1979—Oilers, 20-6 (H)
1980—Chiefs, 21-20 (KC)
1981—Chiefs, 23-10 (KC)
1983—Chiefs, 13-10 (H) OT
1984—Oilers, 17-16 (KC)
1985—Oilers, 23-20 (H)
1986—Chiefs, 27-13 (KC)
1988—Oilers, 7-6 (H)
1989—Chiefs, 34-0 (KC)
1990—Oilers, 27-10 (KC)
1991—Oilers, 17-7 (H)
(RS Pts.—Chiefs 781, Oilers 599)
(PS Pts.—Chiefs 20, Oilers 17)
*Franchise in Dallas prior to 1963 and
known as Texans
**AFL Championship
HOUSTON vs. *L.A. RAIDERS
RS: Raiders lead series, 19-13
PS: Raiders lead series, 3-0
1960—Oilers, 37-22 (O)
　　　　Raiders, 14-13 (H)
1961—Oilers, 55-0 (H)
　　　　Oilers, 47-16 (O)
1962—Oilers, 28-20 (O)
　　　　Oilers, 32-17 (H)
1963—Raiders, 24-13 (H)
　　　　Raiders, 52-49 (O)
1964—Oilers, 42-28 (H)
　　　　Raiders, 20-10 (O)
1965—Raiders, 21-17 (H)
　　　　Raiders, 33-21 (O)
1966—Oilers, 31-0 (H)
　　　　Raiders, 38-23 (O)
1967—Raiders, 19-7 (H)
　　　　**Raiders, 40-7 (O)
1968—Raiders, 24-15 (H)
1969—Raiders, 21-17 (O)
　　　　***Raiders, 56-7 (O)
1971—Raiders, 41-21 (O)
1972—Raiders, 34-0 (H)
1973—Raiders, 17-6 (H)
1975—Oilers, 27-26 (O)
1976—Raiders, 14-13 (H)
1977—Raiders, 34-29 (H)
1978—Raiders, 21-17 (O)
1979—Oilers, 31-17 (H)
1980—****Raiders, 27-7 (O)
1981—Oilers, 17-16 (H)
1983—Raiders, 20-6 (LA)
1984—Raiders, 24-14 (H)
1986—Raiders, 28-17 (H)
1988—Oilers, 38-35 (H)
1989—Oilers, 23-7 (H)
1991—Oilers, 47-17 (H)
(RS Pts.—Oilers 763, Raiders 720)
(PS Pts.—Raiders 123, Oilers 21)
*Franchise in Oakland prior to 1982
**AFL Championship
***Inter-Divisional Playoff
****AFC First Round Playoff
HOUSTON vs. L.A. RAMS
RS: Rams lead series, 4-2
1973—Rams, 31-26 (H)
1978—Rams, 10-6 (H)
1981—Oilers, 27-20 (LA)
1984—Rams, 27-16 (LA)
1987—Oilers, 20-16 (H)
1990—Rams, 17-13 (LA)
(RS Pts.—Rams 121, Oilers 108)
HOUSTON vs. MIAMI
RS: Oilers lead series, 11-10

PS: Oilers lead series, 1-0
1966—Dolphins, 20-13 (H)
    Dolphins, 29-28 (M)
1967—Oilers, 17-14 (H)
    Oilers, 41-10 (M)
1968—Oilers, 24-10 (M)
    Dolphins, 24-7 (H)
1969—Oilers, 22-10 (H)
    Oilers, 32-7 (M)
1970—Dolphins, 20-10 (H)
1972—Dolphins, 34-13 (M)
1975—Oilers, 20-19 (H)
1977—Dolphins, 27-7 (M)
1978—Dolphins, 35-30 (H)
    *Oilers, 17-9 (M)
1979—Oilers, 9-6 (M)
1981—Dolphins, 16-10 (H)
1983—Dolphins, 24-17 (H)
1984—Dolphins, 28-10 (H)
1985—Oilers, 26-23 (H)
1986—Dolphins, 28-7 (M)
1989—Oilers, 39-7 (H)
1991—Oilers, 17-13 (M)
(RS Pts.—Oilers 404, Dolphins 399)
(PS Pts.—Oilers 17, Dolphins 9)
*AFC First Round Playoff

HOUSTON vs. MINNESOTA
RS: Vikings lead series, 3-2
1974—Vikings, 51-10 (H)
1980—Oilers, 20-16 (H)
1983—Vikings, 34-14 (M)
1986—Oilers, 23-10 (H)
1989—Vikings, 38-7 (M)
(RS Pts.—Vikings 149, Oilers 74)

HOUSTON vs. *NEW ENGLAND
RS: Patriots lead series, 17-13-1
PS: Oilers lead series, 1-0
1960—Oilers, 24-10 (B)
    Oilers, 37-21 (H)
1961—Tie, 31-31 (B)
    Oilers, 27-15 (H)
1962—Patriots, 34-21 (B)
    Oilers, 21-17 (H)
1963—Patriots, 45-3 (B)
    Patriots, 46-28 (H)
1964—Patriots, 25-24 (B)
    Patriots, 34-17 (H)
1965—Oilers, 31-10 (H)
    Patriots, 42-14 (B)
1966—Patriots, 27-21 (B)
    Patriots, 38-14 (H)
1967—Patriots, 18-7 (B)
    Oilers, 27-6 (H)
1968—Oilers, 16-0 (B)
    Oilers, 45-17 (H)
1969—Patriots, 24-0 (B)
    Oilers, 27-23 (H)
1971—Patriots, 28-20 (NE)
1973—Patriots, 32-0 (H)
1975—Oilers, 7-0 (NE)
1978—Oilers, 26-23 (H)
    **Oilers, 31-14 (NE)
1980—Oilers, 38-34 (H)
1981—Patriots, 38-10 (NE)
1982—Patriots, 29-21 (NE)
1987—Patriots, 21-7 (H)
1988—Oilers, 31-6 (H)
1989—Patriots, 23-13 (NE)
1991—Patriots, 24-20 (NE)
(RS Pts.—Patriots 741, Oilers 628)
(PS Pts.—Oilers 31, Patriots 14)
*Franchise in Boston prior to 1971
**AFC Divisional Playoff

HOUSTON vs. NEW ORLEANS
RS: Series tied, 3-3-1
1971—Tie, 13-13 (H)
1976—Oilers, 31-26 (NO)
1978—Oilers, 17-12 (NO)
1981—Saints, 27-24 (H)
1984—Saints, 27-10 (H)
1987—Saints, 24-10 (NO)
1990—Oilers 23-10 (H)
(RS Pts.—Saints 139, Oilers 128)

HOUSTON vs. N.Y. GIANTS
RS: Giants lead series, 4-0
1973—Giants, 34-14 (NY)
1982—Giants, 17-14 (NY)
1985—Giants, 35-14 (H)
1991—Giants, 24-20 (NY)
(RS Pts.—Giants 110, Oilers 62)

HOUSTON vs. *N.Y. JETS
RS: Oilers lead series, 16-12-1
PS: Oilers lead series, 1-0
1960—Oilers, 27-21 (H)
    Oilers, 42-28 (NY)
1961—Oilers, 49-13 (H)
    Oilers, 48-21 (NY)
1962—Oilers, 56-17 (H)
    Oilers, 44-10 (NY)
1963—Jets, 24-17 (NY)
    Oilers, 31-27 (H)
1964—Jets, 24-21 (NY)
    Oilers, 33-17 (H)

1965—Oilers, 27-21 (H)
    Jets, 41-14 (NY)
1966—Jets, 52-13 (NY)
    Oilers, 24-0 (H)
1967—Tie, 28-28 (NY)
1968—Jets, 20-14 (H)
    Jets, 26-7 (NY)
1969—Jets, 26-17 (NY)
    Jets, 34-26 (H)
1972—Oilers, 26-20 (H)
1974—Oilers, 27-22 (NY)
1977—Oilers, 20-0 (H)
1979—Oilers, 27-24 (H) OT
1980—Jets, 31-28 (NY) OT
1981—Jets, 33-17 (NY)
1984—Jets, 31-20 (H)
1988—Jets, 45-3 (NY)
1990—Jets, 17-12 (H)
1991—Oilers, 23-20 (NY)
    **Oilers, 17-10 (H)
(RS Pts.—Oilers 752, Jets 682)
(PS Pts.—Oilers 17, Jets 10)
*Jets known as Titans prior to 1963
**AFC First Round Playoff

HOUSTON vs. PHILADELPHIA
RS: Eagles lead series, 5-0
1972—Eagles, 18-17 (H)
1979—Eagles, 26-20 (H)
1982—Eagles, 35-14 (P)
1988—Eagles, 32-23 (P)
1991—Eagles, 13-6 (H)
(RS Pts.—Eagles 124, Oilers 80)

HOUSTON vs. *PHOENIX
RS: Cardinals lead series, 3-2
1970—Cardinals, 44-0 (StL)
1974—Cardinals, 31-27 (H)
1979—Cardinals, 24-17 (H)
1985—Oilers, 20-10 (StL)
1988—Oilers, 38-20 (H)
(RS Pts.—Cardinals 129, Oilers 102)
*Franchise in St. Louis prior to 1988

HOUSTON vs. PITTSBURGH
RS: Steelers lead series, 27-16
PS: Steelers lead series, 3-0
1970—Oilers, 19-7 (P)
    Steelers, 7-3 (H)
1971—Steelers, 23-16 (P)
    Oilers, 29-3 (H)
1972—Oilers, 24-7 (P)
    Steelers, 9-3 (H)
1973—Steelers, 36-7 (H)
    Steelers, 33-7 (P)
1974—Steelers, 13-7 (H)
    Oilers, 13-10 (P)
1975—Steelers, 24-17 (H)
    Steelers, 32-9 (H)
1976—Steelers, 32-16 (P)
    Steelers, 21-0 (H)
1977—Oilers, 27-10 (H)
    Steelers, 27-10 (P)
1978—Oilers, 24-17 (P)
    Steelers, 13-3 (H)
    *Steelers, 34-5 (P)
1979—Steelers, 38-7 (P)
    Oilers, 20-17 (H)
    *Steelers, 27-13 (P)
1980—Steelers, 31-17 (P)
    Oilers, 6-0 (H)
1981—Steelers, 26-13 (H)
    Oilers, 21-20 (P)
1982—Steelers, 24-10 (H)
1983—Steelers, 40-28 (H)
    Steelers, 17-10 (P)
1984—Steelers, 35-7 (P)
    Oilers, 23-20 (H) OT
1985—Steelers, 20-0 (H)
    Steelers, 30-7 (H)
1986—Steelers, 22-16 (H) OT
    Steelers, 21-10 (P)
1987—Oilers, 23-3 (P)
    Oilers, 24-16 (H)
1988—Oilers, 34-14 (P)
    Steelers, 37-34 (H)
1989—Oilers, 27-0 (H)
    Oilers, 23-16 (H)
    **Steelers, 26-23 (H)
1990—Steelers, 20-9 (P)
    Oilers 34-14 (H)
1991—Steelers, 26-14 (P)
    Oilers, 31-6 (H)
(RS Pts.—Steelers 854, Oilers 665)
(PS Pts.—Steelers 87, Oilers 41)
*AFC Championship
**AFC First Round Playoff

HOUSTON vs. *SAN DIEGO
RS: Chargers lead series, 17-12-1
PS: Oilers lead series, 3-0
1960—Oilers, 38-28 (H)
    Chargers, 24-21 (LA)
    **Oilers, 24-16 (H)
1961—Chargers, 34-24 (SD)
    Oilers, 33-13 (H)
    **Oilers, 10-3 (SD)

1962—Oilers, 42-17 (SD)
    Oilers, 33-27 (H)
1963—Chargers, 27-0 (SD)
    Chargers 20-14 (H)
1964—Chargers, 27-21 (SD)
    Chargers, 20-17 (H)
1965—Chargers, 31-14 (SD)
    Chargers, 37-26 (H)
1966—Chargers, 28-22 (H)
1967—Chargers, 13-3 (SD)
    Oilers, 24-17 (H)
1968—Chargers, 30-14 (SD)
1969—Chargers, 21-17 (H)
1970—Tie, 31-31 (SD)
1971—Oilers, 49-33 (H)
1972—Chargers, 34-20 (SD)
1974—Oilers, 21-14 (H)
1975—Oilers, 33-17 (H)
1976—Chargers, 30-27 (SD)
1978—Chargers, 45-24 (H)
1979—***Oilers, 17-14 (SD)
1984—Chargers, 31-14 (SD)
1985—Oilers, 37-35 (H)
1986—Chargers, 27-0 (SD)
1987—Chargers, 33-18 (H)
1989—Oilers, 34-27 (SD)
1990—Oilers 17-7 (SD)
(RS Pts.—Chargers 763, Oilers 703)
(PS Pts.—Oilers 51, Chargers 33)
*Franchise in Los Angeles prior to 1961
**AFL Championship
***AFC Divisional Playoff

HOUSTON vs. SAN FRANCISCO
RS: 49ers lead series, 5-2
1970—49ers, 30-20 (H)
1975—Oilers, 27-13 (SF)
1978—Oilers, 20-19 (H)
1981—49ers, 28-6 (SF)
1984—49ers, 34-21 (H)
1987—49ers, 27-20 (SF)
1990—49ers, 24-21 (H)
(RS Pts.—49ers 175, Oilers 135)

HOUSTON vs. SEATTLE
RS: Seahawks lead series, 4-3
PS: Oilers lead series, 1-0
1977—Oilers, 22-10 (S)
1979—Seahawks, 34-14 (S)
1980—Seahawks, 26-7 (H)
1981—Oilers, 35-17 (H)
1982—Oilers, 23-21 (H)
1987—*Oilers, 23-20 (H) OT
1988—Seahawks, 27-24 (S)
1990—Seahawks, 13-10 (S) OT
(RS Pts.—Seahawks 148, Oilers 135)
(PS Pts.—Oilers 23, Seahawks 20)
*AFC First Round Playoff

HOUSTON vs. TAMPA BAY
RS: Oilers lead series, 3-1
1976—Oilers, 20-0 (H)
1980—Oilers, 20-14 (H)
1983—Buccaneers, 33-24 (TB)
1989—Oilers, 20-17 (H)
(RS Pts.—Oilers 84, Buccaneers 64)

HOUSTON vs. WASHINGTON
RS: Series tied, 3-3
1971—Redskins, 22-13 (W)
1975—Oilers, 13-10 (H)
1979—Oilers, 29-27 (W)
1985—Redskins, 16-13 (W)
1988—Oilers, 41-17 (H)
1991—Redskins, 16-13 (W) OT
(RS Pts.—Oilers 122, Redskins 108)

INDIANAPOLIS vs. ATLANTA
RS: Colts lead series, 10-0;
See Atlanta vs. Indianapolis
INDIANAPOLIS vs. BUFFALO
RS: Bills lead series, 23-19-1;
See Buffalo vs. Indianapolis
INDIANAPOLIS vs. CHICAGO
RS: Colts lead series, 21-16;
See Chicago vs. Indianapolis
INDIANAPOLIS vs. CINCINNATI
RS: Colts lead series, 6-5
PS: Colts lead series, 1-0;
See Cincinnati vs. Indianapolis
INDIANAPOLIS vs. CLEVELAND
RS: Browns lead series, 12-5
PS: Series tied, 2-2;
See Cleveland vs. Indianapolis
INDIANAPOLIS vs. DALLAS
RS: Cowboys lead series, 6-2
PS: Colts lead series, 1-0;
See Dallas vs. Indianapolis
INDIANAPOLIS vs. DENVER
RS: Broncos lead series, 8-2;
See Denver vs. Indianapolis
INDIANAPOLIS vs. DETROIT
RS: Series tied, 17-17-2;
See Detroit vs. Indianapolis
INDIANAPOLIS vs. GREEN BAY
RS: Series tied, 18-18-1
PS: Packers lead series, 1-0;

See Green Bay vs. Indianapolis
INDIANAPOLIS vs. HOUSTON
RS: Series tied, 6-6;
See Houston vs. Indianapolis
INDIANAPOLIS vs. KANSAS CITY
RS: Chiefs lead series, 6-4
1970—Chiefs, 44-24 (B)
1972—Chiefs, 24-10 (KC)
1975—Colts, 28-14 (B)
1977—Colts, 17-6 (B)
1979—Chiefs, 14-0 (KC)
    Chiefs, 10-7 (B)
1980—Colts, 31-24 (KC)
    Chiefs, 38-28 (B)
1985—Chiefs, 20-7 (KC)
1990—Colts, 23-19 (I)
(RS Pts.—Chiefs 213, Colts 175)
*Franchise in Baltimore prior to 1984

INDIANAPOLIS vs. **L.A. RAIDERS
RS: Raiders lead series, 4-2
PS: Series tied, 1-1
1970—***Colts, 27-17 (B)
1971—Colts, 37-14 (O)
1973—Raiders, 34-21 (B)
1975—Raiders, 31-20 (B)
1977—****Raiders, 37-31 (B) OT
1984—Raiders, 21-7 (LA)
1986—Colts, 30-24 (LA)
1991—Raiders, 16-0 (LA)
(RS Pts.—Raiders 140, Colts 115)
(PS Pts.—Colts 58, Raiders 54)
*Franchise in Baltimore prior to 1984
**Franchise in Oakland prior to 1982
***AFC Championship
****AFC Divisional Playoff

INDIANAPOLIS vs. L.A. RAMS
RS: Colts lead series, 20-16-2
1953—Rams, 21-13 (B)
    Rams, 45-2 (LA)
1954—Rams, 48-0 (B)
    Colts, 22-21 (LA)
1955—Tie, 17-17 (B)
    Rams, 20-14 (LA)
1956—Colts, 56-21 (B)
    Rams, 31-7 (LA)
1957—Colts, 31-14 (B)
    Rams, 37-21 (LA)
1958—Colts, 34-7 (B)
    Rams, 30-28 (LA)
1959—Colts, 35-21 (B)
    Colts, 45-26 (LA)
1960—Colts, 31-17 (B)
    Rams, 10-3 (LA)
1961—Colts, 27-24 (B)
    Rams, 34-17 (LA)
1962—Colts, 30-27 (B)
    Colts, 14-2 (LA)
1963—Rams, 17-16 (LA)
    Colts, 19-16 (B)
1964—Colts, 35-20 (B)
    Colts, 24-7 (LA)
1965—Colts, 35-20 (B)
    Colts, 20-17 (LA)
1966—Colts, 17-3 (LA)
    Rams, 23-7 (B)
1967—Tie, 24-24 (B)
    Rams, 34-10 (LA)
1968—Colts, 27-10 (B)
    Colts, 28-24 (LA)
1969—Rams, 27-20 (B)
    Colts, 13-7 (LA)
1971—Colts, 24-17 (B)
1975—Rams, 24-13 (LA)
1986—Rams, 24-7 (I)
1989—Rams, 31-17 (LA)
(RS Pts.—Rams 818, Colts 803)
*Franchise in Baltimore prior to 1984

INDIANAPOLIS vs. MIAMI
RS: Dolphins lead series, 31-13
PS: Dolphins lead series, 1-0
1970—Colts, 35-0 (B)
    Dolphins, 34-17 (M)
1971—Dolphins, 17-14 (M)
    Colts, 14-3 (B)
    **Dolphins, 21-0 (M)
1972—Dolphins, 23-0 (B)
    Dolphins, 16-0 (M)
1973—Dolphins, 44-0 (H)
    Colts, 16-3 (B)
1974—Dolphins, 17-7 (M)
    Dolphins, 17-16 (B)
1975—Colts, 33-17 (M)
    Colts, 10-7 (B) OT
1976—Colts, 28-14 (B)
    Colts, 17-16 (M)
1977—Colts, 45-28 (B)
    Dolphins, 17-6 (M)
1978—Colts, 42-0 (B)
    Dolphins, 26-8 (M)
1979—Dolphins, 19-0 (H)
    Dolphins, 28-24 (B)
1980—Colts, 30-17 (M)
    Dolphins, 24-14 (B)

1981—Dolphins, 31-28 (B)
　　　Dolphins, 27-10 (M)
1982—Dolphins, 24-20 (M)
　　　Dolphins, 34-7 (B)
1983—Dolphins, 21-7 (B)
　　　Dolphins, 37-0 (M)
1984—Dolphins, 44-7 (M)
　　　Dolphins, 35-17 (I)
1985—Dolphins, 30-13 (M)
　　　Dolphins, 34-20 (I)
1986—Dolphins, 30-10 (M)
　　　Dolphins, 17-13 (I)
1987—Dolphins, 23-10 (I)
　　　Colts, 40-21 (M)
1988—Colts, 15-13 (I)
　　　Colts, 31-28 (M)
1989—Dolphins, 19-13 (M)
　　　Colts, 42-13 (I)
1990—Dolphins, 27-7 (I)
　　　Dolphins, 23-17 (M)
1991—Dolphins, 17-6 (M)
　　　Dolphins, 10-6 (I)
(Rs Pts.—Dolphins 987, Colts 673)
(PS Pts.—Dolphins 21, Colts 0)
*Franchise in Baltimore prior to 1984
**AFC Championship
**INDIANAPOLIS vs. MINNESOTA
RS: Colts lead series, 11-6-1
PS: Colts lead series, 1-0
1961—Colts, 34-33 (B)
　　　Vikings, 28-20 (M)
1962—Colts, 34-7 (M)
　　　Colts, 42-17 (B)
1963—Colts, 37-34 (M)
　　　Colts, 41-10 (B)
1964—Vikings, 34-24 (M)
　　　Colts, 17-14 (B)
1965—Colts, 35-16 (B)
　　　Colts, 41-21 (M)
1966—Colts, 38-23 (M)
　　　Colts, 20-17 (B)
1967—Tie, 20-20 (M)
1968—Colts, 21-9 (B)
　　　**Colts, 24-14 (B)
1969—Vikings, 52-14 (M)
1971—Vikings, 10-3 (M)
1982—Vikings, 13-10 (M)
1988—Vikings, 12-3 (M)
(RS Pts.—Colts 454, Vikings 370)
(PS Pts.—Colts 24, Vikings 14)
*Franchise in Baltimore prior to 1984
**Conference Championship
**INDIANAPOLIS vs. **NEW ENGLAND
RS: Patriots lead series, 25-18
1970—Colts, 14-6 (Bos)
　　　Colts, 27-3 (Balt)
1971—Colts, 23-3 (NE)
　　　Patriots, 21-17 (Balt)
1972—Colts, 24-17 (NE)
　　　Colts, 31-0 (Balt)
1973—Patriots, 24-16 (NE)
　　　Colts, 18-13 (Balt)
1974—Patriots, 42-3 (NE)
　　　Patriots, 27-17 (Balt)
1975—Colts, 21-10 (NE)
　　　Colts, 34-21 (Balt)
1976—Colts, 27-13 (NE)
　　　Patriots, 21-14 (Balt)
1977—Patriots, 17-3 (NE)
　　　Colts, 30-24 (Balt)
1978—Colts, 34-27 (NE)
　　　Patriots, 35-14 (Balt)
1979—Colts, 31-26 (Balt)
　　　Patriots, 50-21 (NE)
1980—Patriots, 37-21 (Balt)
　　　Patriots, 47-21 (NE)
1981—Colts, 29-28 (NE)
　　　Colts, 23-21 (Balt)
1982—Patriots, 24-13 (Balt)
1983—Patriots, 29-23 (NE) OT
　　　Colts, 12-7 (I)
1984—Patriots, 50-17 (I)
　　　Colts, 16-10 (NE)
1985—Patriots, 34-15 (NE)
　　　Patriots, 38-31 (I)
1986—Patriots, 33-3 (NE)
　　　Patriots, 30-21 (I)
1987—Colts, 30-16 (I)
　　　Patriots, 24-0 (NE)
1988—Patriots, 21-17 (NE)
　　　Colts, 24-21 (I)
1989—Patriots, 23-20 (I) OT
　　　Patriots, 22-16 (NE)
1990—Patriots, 16-14 (I)
　　　Colts, 13-10 (NE)
1991—Patriots, 16-7 (I)
　　　Patriots, 23-17 (NE) OT
(RS Pts.—Patriots 991, Colts 811)
*Franchise in Baltimore prior to 1984
**Franchise in Boston prior to 1971
**INDIANAPOLIS vs. NEW ORLEANS
RS: Colts lead series, 3-2
1967—Colts, 30-10 (B)

1969—Colts, 30-10 (NO)
1973—Colts, 14-10 (B)
1986—Saints, 17-14 (I)
1989—Saints, 41-6 (NO)
(RS Pts.—Colts 94, Saints 88)
*Franchise in Baltimore prior to 1984
**INDIANAPOLIS vs. N.Y. GIANTS
RS: Colts lead series, 5-4
PS: Colts lead series, 2-0
1954—Colts, 20-14 (B)
1955—Giants, 17-7 (NY)
1958—Giants, 24-21 (NY)
　　　**Colts, 23-17 (NY) OT
1959—**Colts, 31-16 (B)
1963—Giants, 37-28 (B)
1968—Colts, 26-0 (NY)
1971—Colts, 31-7 (B)
1975—Colts, 21-0 (NY)
1979—Colts, 31-7 (NY)
1990—Giants, 24-7 (I)
(RS Pts.—Colts 192, Giants 130)
(PS Pts.—Colts 54, Giants 33)
*Franchise in Baltimore prior to 1984
**NFL Championship
**INDIANAPOLIS vs. N.Y. JETS
RS: Colts lead series, 24-19
PS: Jets lead series, 1-0
1968—**Jets 16-7 (Miami)
1970—Colts, 29-22 (NY)
　　　Colts, 35-20 (B)
1971—Colts, 22-0 (B)
　　　Colts, 14-13 (NY)
1972—Jets, 44-34 (B)
　　　Jets, 24-20 (NY)
1973—Jets, 34-10 (B)
　　　Jets, 20-17 (NY)
1974—Colts, 35-20 (NY)
　　　Jets, 45-38 (B)
1975—Colts, 45-28 (NY)
　　　Colts, 52-19 (B)
1976—Colts, 20-0 (NY)
　　　Colts, 33-16 (B)
1977—Colts, 20-12 (NY)
　　　Colts, 33-12 (B)
1978—Jets, 33-10 (B)
　　　Jets, 24-16 (NY)
1979—Colts, 10-8 (B)
　　　Jets, 30-17 (NY)
1980—Colts, 17-14 (NY)
　　　Colts, 35-21 (B)
1981—Jets, 41-14 (B)
　　　Jets, 25-0 (NY)
1982—Jets, 37-0 (NY)
1983—Colts, 17-14 (NY)
　　　Jets, 10-6 (B)
1984—Jets, 23-14 (I)
　　　Colts, 9-5 (NY)
1985—Jets, 25-20 (NY)
　　　Jets, 35-17 (I)
1986—Jets, 26-7 (I)
　　　Jets, 31-16 (NY)
1987—Colts, 6-0 (I)
　　　Colts, 19-14 (NY)
1988—Colts, 38-14 (I)
　　　Jets, 34-16 (NY)
1989—Colts, 17-10 (NY)
　　　Colts, 27-10 (I)
1990—Colts, 17-14 (I)
　　　Colts, 29-21 (NY)
1991—Jets, 17-6 (I)
　　　Colts, 28-27 (NY)
(RS Pts.—Jets 892, Colts 885)
(PS Pts.—Jets 16, Colts 7)
*Franchise in Baltimore prior to 1984
**Super Bowl III
**INDIANAPOLIS vs. PHILADELPHIA
RS: Colts lead series, 6-5
1953—Eagles, 45-14 (P)
1965—Colts, 34-24 (B)
1967—Colts, 38-6 (P)
1969—Colts, 24-20 (B)
1970—Colts, 29-10 (B)
1974—Eagles, 30-10 (P)
1978—Eagles, 17-14 (B)
1981—Eagles, 38-13 (P)
1983—Colts, 22-21 (P)
1984—Eagles, 16-7 (P)
1990—Colts, 24-23 (P)
(RS Pts.—Eagles 250, Colts 229)
*Franchise in Baltimore prior to 1984
**INDIANAPOLIS vs. **PHOENIX
RS: Cardinals lead series, 6-4
1961—Colts, 16-0 (B)
1964—Colts, 47-27 (B)
1968—Colts, 27-0 (B)
1972—Cardinals, 10-3 (B)
1976—Cardinals, 24-17 (StL)
1978—Colts, 30-17 (StL)
1980—Cardinals, 17-10 (B)
1981—Cardinals, 35-24 (B)
1984—Cardinals, 34-33 (I)
1990—Cardinals, 20-17 (P)
(RS Pts.—Colts 224, Cardinals 184)

*Franchise in Baltimore prior to 1984
**Franchise in St. Louis prior to 1988
**INDIANAPOLIS vs. PITTSBURGH
RS: Steelers lead series, 9-4
PS: Steelers lead series, 2-0
1957—Steelers, 19-13 (B)
1968—Colts, 41-7 (P)
1971—Colts, 34-21 (B)
1974—Steelers, 30-0 (B)
1975—**Steelers, 28-10 (P)
1976—**Steelers, 40-14 (B)
1977—Colts, 31-21 (B)
1978—Steelers, 35-13 (P)
1979—Steelers, 17-13 (P)
1980—Steelers, 20-17 (B)
1983—Steelers, 24-13 (B)
1984—Colts, 17-16 (I)
1985—Steelers, 45-3 (P)
1987—Steelers, 21-7 (P)
1991—Steelers, 21-3 (I)
(RS Pts.—Steelers 297, Colts 205)
(PS Pts.—Steelers 68, Colts 24)
*Franchise in Baltimore prior to 1984
**AFC Divisional Playoff
**INDIANAPOLIS vs. SAN DIEGO
RS: Chargers lead series, 6-5
1970—Colts, 16-14 (SD)
1972—Chargers, 23-20 (B)
1976—Colts, 37-21 (SD)
1981—Chargers, 43-14 (B)
1982—Chargers, 44-26 (SD)
1984—Chargers, 38-10 (I)
1986—Chargers, 17-3 (I)
1987—Chargers, 16-13 (I)
　　　Colts, 20-7 (SD)
1988—Colts, 16-0 (SD)
1989—Colts, 10-6 (I)
(RS Pts.—Chargers 229, Colts 185)
*Franchise in Baltimore prior to 1984
**INDIANAPOLIS vs. SAN FRANCISCO
RS: Colts lead series, 21-16
1953—49ers, 38-21 (B)
　　　49ers, 45-14 (SF)
1954—Colts, 17-13 (B)
　　　49ers, 10-7 (SF)
1955—Colts, 26-14 (B)
　　　49ers, 35-24 (SF)
1956—49ers, 20-17 (B)
　　　49ers, 30-17 (SF)
1957—Colts, 27-21 (B)
　　　49ers, 17-13 (SF)
1958—Colts, 35-27 (B)
　　　49ers, 21-12 (SF)
1959—Colts, 45-14 (B)
　　　Colts, 34-14 (SF)
1960—49ers, 30-22 (B)
　　　49ers, 34-10 (SF)
1961—Colts, 20-17 (B)
　　　Colts, 27-24 (SF)
1962—49ers, 21-13 (B)
　　　Colts, 22-3 (SF)
1963—Colts, 20-14 (SF)
　　　Colts, 20-3 (B)
1964—Colts, 37-7 (B)
　　　Colts, 14-3 (SF)
1965—Colts, 27-24 (B)
　　　Colts, 34-28 (SF)
1966—Colts, 36-14 (B)
　　　Colts, 30-14 (SF)
1967—Colts, 41-7 (B)
　　　Colts, 26-9 (SF)
1968—Colts, 27-10 (B)
　　　Colts, 42-14 (SF)
1969—49ers, 24-21 (B)
　　　49ers, 20-17 (SF)
1972—49ers, 24-21 (SF)
1986—49ers, 35-14 (SF)
1989—49ers, 30-24 (I)
(RS Pts.—Colts 874, 49ers 728)
*Franchise in Baltimore prior to 1984
**INDIANAPOLIS vs. SEATTLE
RS: Colts lead series, 2-1
1977—Colts, 29-14 (S)
1978—Colts, 17-14 (S)
1991—Seahawks, 31-3 (S)
(RS Pts.—Seahawks 59, Colts 49)
*Franchise in Baltimore prior to 1984
**INDIANAPOLIS vs. TAMPA BAY
RS: Colts lead series, 4-2
1976—Colts, 42-17 (B)
1979—Buccaneers, 29-26 (B) OT
1985—Colts, 31-23 (TB)
1987—Colts, 24-6 (I)
1988—Colts, 35-31 (I)
1991—Buccaneers, 17-3 (TB)
(RS Pts.—Colts 161, Buccaneers 123)
*Franchise in Baltimore prior to 1984
**INDIANAPOLIS vs. WASHINGTON
RS: Colts lead series, 16-6
1953—Colts, 27-17 (B)
1954—Redskins, 24-21 (W)
1955—Redskins, 14-13 (B)
1956—Colts, 19-17 (B)

1957—Colts, 21-17 (W)
1958—Colts, 35-10 (B)
1959—Redskins, 27-24 (W)
1960—Colts, 20-0 (B)
1961—Colts, 27-6 (W)
1962—Colts, 34-21 (B)
1963—Colts, 36-20 (W)
1964—Colts, 45-17 (B)
1965—Colts, 38-7 (W)
1966—Colts, 37-10 (B)
1967—Colts, 17-13 (W)
1969—Colts, 41-17 (B)
1973—Redskins, 22-14 (W)
1977—Colts, 10-3 (B)
1978—Colts, 21-17 (B)
1981—Redskins, 38-14 (W)
1984—Redskins, 35-7 (I)
1990—Colts, 35-28 (I)
(RS Pts.—Colts 556, Redskins 380)
*Franchise in Baltimore prior to 1984

KANSAS CITY vs. ATLANTA
RS: Chiefs lead series, 3-0;
See Atlanta vs. Kansas City
KANSAS CITY vs. BUFFALO
RS: Bills lead series, 15-12-1
PS: Series tied, 1-1;
See Buffalo vs. Kansas City
KANSAS CITY vs. CHICAGO
RS: Bears lead series, 3-2;
See Chicago vs. Kansas City
KANSAS CITY vs. CINCINNATI
RS: Chiefs lead series, 10-9;
See Cincinnati vs. Kansas City
KANSAS CITY vs. CLEVELAND
RS: Browns lead, 7-6-2;
See Cleveland vs. Kansas City
KANSAS CITY vs. DALLAS
RS: Series tied, 2-2;
See Dallas vs. Kansas City
KANSAS CITY vs. DENVER
RS: Chiefs lead series, 36-27;
See Denver vs. Kansas City
KANSAS CITY vs. DETROIT
RS: Chiefs lead series, 4-3;
See Detroit vs. Kansas City
KANSAS CITY vs. GREEN BAY
RS: Chiefs lead series, 3-1-1
PS: Packers lead series, 1-0;
See Green Bay vs. Kansas City
KANSAS CITY vs. HOUSTON
RS: Chiefs lead series, 21-15
PS: Chiefs lead series, 1-0;
See Houston vs. Kansas City
KANSAS CITY vs. INDIANAPOLIS
RS: Chiefs lead series, 6-4;
See Indianapolis vs. Kansas City
*KANSAS CITY vs. **L.A. RAIDERS**
RS: Raiders lead series, 34-27-2
PS: Chiefs lead series, 2-1
1960—Texans, 34-16 (O)
　　　Raiders, 20-19 (D)
1961—Texans, 42-35 (O)
　　　Raiders, 43-11 (D)
1962—Texans, 26-16 (O)
　　　Texans, 35-7 (D)
1963—Raiders, 10-7 (O)
　　　Raiders, 22-7 (O)
1964—Chiefs, 21-9 (O)
　　　Chiefs, 42-7 (KC)
1965—Raiders, 37-10 (O)
　　　Chiefs, 14-7 (KC)
1966—Chiefs, 32-10 (O)
　　　Raiders, 34-13 (KC)
1967—Raiders, 23-21 (O)
　　　Raiders, 44-22 (KC)
1968—Chiefs, 24-10 (KC)
　　　Raiders, 38-21 (O)
　　　***Raiders, 41-6 (O)
1969—Raiders, 27-24 (KC)
　　　Raiders, 10-6 (O)
　　　****Chiefs, 17-7 (O)
1970—Tie, 17-17 (KC)
　　　Raiders, 20-6 (O)
1971—Tie, 20-20 (O)
　　　Chiefs, 16-14 (KC)
1972—Chiefs, 27-14 (KC)
　　　Raiders, 26-3 (O)
1973—Chiefs, 16-3 (KC)
　　　Raiders, 37-7 (O)
1974—Raiders, 27-7 (O)
　　　Raiders, 7-6 (KC)
1975—Chiefs, 42-10 (KC)
　　　Raiders, 28-20 (O)
1976—Raiders, 24-21 (KC)
　　　Raiders, 21-10 (O)
1977—Raiders, 37-28 (KC)
　　　Raiders, 21-20 (O)
1978—Raiders, 28-6 (KC)
　　　Raiders, 20-10 (KC)
1979—Chiefs, 35-7 (KC)
　　　Chiefs, 24-21 (O)
1980—Raiders, 27-14 (KC)

265

Chiefs, 31-17 (O)
1981—Chiefs, 27-0 (KC)
Chiefs, 28-17 (O)
1982—Raiders, 21-16 (KC)
1983—Raiders, 21-20 (LA)
Raiders, 28-20 (KC)
1984—Raiders, 22-20 (KC)
Raiders, 17-7 (LA)
1985—Chiefs, 36-20 (KC)
Raiders, 19-10 (LA)
1986—Raiders, 24-17 (KC)
Chiefs, 20-17 (LA)
1987—Raiders, 35-17 (LA)
Chiefs, 16-10 (KC)
1988—Raiders, 27-17 (KC)
Raiders, 17-10 (LA)
1989—Chiefs, 24-19 (KC)
Raiders, 20-14 (LA)
1990—Chiefs, 9-7 (KC)
Chiefs, 27-24 (LA)
1991—Chiefs, 24-21 (KC)
Chiefs, 27-21 (LA)
†Chiefs, 10-6 (KC)
(RS Pts.—Chiefs 1,255, Raiders 1,246)
(PS Pts.—Raiders 54, Chiefs 33)
*Franchise in Dallas prior to 1963 and
known as Texans
**Franchise in Oakland prior to 1982
***Division Playoff
****AFL Championship
†AFC First Round Playoff
KANSAS CITY vs. L.A. RAMS
RS: Rams lead series, 3-1
1973—Rams, 23-13 (KC)
1982—Rams, 20-14 (LA)
1985—Rams, 16-0 (KC)
1991—Chiefs, 27-20 (LA)
(RS Pts.—Rams 79, Chiefs 54)
KANSAS CITY vs. MIAMI
RS: Chiefs lead series, 10-6
PS: Dolphins lead series, 2-0
1966—Chiefs, 34-16 (KC)
Chiefs, 19-18 (M)
1967—Chiefs, 24-0 (M)
Chiefs, 41-0 (KC)
1968—Chiefs, 48-3 (M)
1969—Chiefs, 17-10 (KC)
1971—*Dolphins, 27-24 (KC) OT
1972—Dolphins, 20-10 (KC)
1974—Dolphins, 9-3 (M)
1976—Chiefs, 20-17 (M) OT
1981—Dolphins, 17-7 (KC)
1983—Dolphins, 14-6 (M)
1985—Dolphins, 31-0 (M)
1987—Dolphins, 42-0 (M)
1989—Chiefs, 26-21 (KC)
Chiefs, 27-24 (M)
1990—**Dolphins, 17-16 (M)
1991—Chiefs, 42-7 (KC)
(RS Pts.—Chiefs 324, Dolphins 249)
(PS Pts.—Dolphins 44, Chiefs 40)
*AFC Divisional Playoff
**AFC First Round Playoff
KANSAS CITY vs. MINNESOTA
RS: Series tied, 2-2
PS: Chiefs lead series, 1-0
1969—*Chiefs, 23-7 (New Orleans)
1970—Vikings, 27-10 (M)
1974—Vikings, 35-15 (KC)
1981—Chiefs, 10-6 (M)
1990—Chiefs, 24-21 (KC)
(RS Pts.—Vikings 89, Chiefs 59)
(PS Pts.—Chiefs 23, Vikings 7)
*Super Bowl IV
KANSAS CITY vs. **NEW ENGLAND
RS: Chiefs lead series, 12-7-3
1960—Patriots, 42-14 (B)
Texans, 34-0 (D)
1961—Patriots, 18-17 (D)
Patriots, 28-21 (B)
1962—Texans, 42-28 (D)
Texans, 27-7 (B)
1963—Tie, 24-24 (B)
Chiefs, 35-3 (KC)
1964—Patriots, 24-7 (B)
Patriots, 31-24 (KC)
1965—Chiefs, 27-17 (KC)
Tie, 10-10 (B)
1966—Chiefs, 43-24 (B)
Tie, 27-27 (KC)
1967—Chiefs, 33-10 (B)
1968—Chiefs, 31-17 (KC)
1969—Chiefs, 31-0 (B)
1970—Chiefs, 23-10 (KC)
1973—Chiefs, 10-7 (NE)
1977—Patriots, 21-17 (NE)
1981—Chiefs, 33-17 (NE)
1990—Chiefs, 37-7 (NE)
(RS Pts.—Chiefs 551, Patriots 388)
*Franchise located in Dallas prior to 1963
and known as Texans
**Franchise in Boston prior to 1971

KANSAS CITY vs. NEW ORLEANS
RS: Saints lead series, 3-2
1972—Chiefs, 20-17 (NO)
1976—Saints, 27-17 (NO)
1982—Saints, 27-17 (NO)
1985—Chiefs, 47-27 (NO)
1991—Saints, 17-10 (NO)
(RS Pts.—Saints 115, Chiefs 111)
KANSAS CITY vs. N.Y. GIANTS
RS: Giants lead series, 5-1
1974—Giants, 33-27 (KC)
1978—Giants, 26-10 (NY)
1979—Giants, 21-17 (KC)
1983—Giants, 38-17 (KC)
1984—Giants, 28-27 (NY)
1988—Giants, 28-12 (NY)
(RS Pts.—Giants 153, Chiefs 131)
***KANSAS CITY vs. ****N.Y. JETS**
RS: Chiefs lead series, 13-12-1
PS: Series tied, 1-1
1960—Titans, 37-35 (D)
Titans, 41-35 (NY)
1961—Titans, 28-7 (NY)
Texans, 35-24 (D)
1962—Texans, 20-17 (D)
Texans, 52-31 (NY)
1963—Jets, 17-0 (NY)
Chiefs, 48-0 (KC)
1964—Jets, 27-14 (NY)
Chiefs, 24-7 (KC)
1965—Chiefs, 14-10 (NY)
Jets, 13-10 (KC)
1966—Chiefs, 32-24 (NY)
1967—Chiefs, 42-18 (KC)
Chiefs, 21-7 (NY)
1968—Jets, 20-19 (NY)
1969—Chiefs, 34-16 (NY)
***Chiefs, 13-6 (NY)
1971—Jets, 13-10 (NY)
1974—Chiefs, 24-16 (NY)
1975—Jets, 30-24 (KC)
1982—Chiefs, 37-13 (KC)
1984—Chiefs, 17-16 (KC)
Jets, 28-7 (NY)
1986—****Jets, 35-15 (NY)
1987—Jets, 16-9 (KC)
1988—Tie, 17-17 (NY)
Chiefs, 38-34 (KC)
(RS Pts.—Chiefs 624, Jets 521)
(PS Pts.—Jets 41, Chiefs 28)
*Franchise in Dallas prior to 1963 and
known as Texans
**Jets known as Titans prior to 1963
***Inter-Divisional Playoff
****AFC First Round Playoff
KANSAS CITY vs. PHILADELPHIA
RS: Eagles lead series, 1-0
1972—Eagles, 21-20 (KC)
KANSAS CITY vs. *PHOENIX
RS: Chiefs lead series, 3-1-1
1970—Tie, 6-6 (KC)
1974—Chiefs, 17-13 (StL)
1980—Chiefs, 21-13 (StL)
1983—Chiefs, 38-14 (KC)
1986—Cardinals, 23-14 (StL)
(RS Pts.—Chiefs 96, Cardinals 69)
*Franchise in St. Louis prior to 1988
KANSAS CITY vs. PITTSBURGH
RS: Steelers lead series, 12-5
1970—Chiefs, 31-14 (P)
1971—Chiefs, 38-16 (KC)
1972—Steelers, 16-7 (P)
1974—Steelers, 34-24 (KC)
1975—Chiefs, 28-3 (P)
1976—Steelers, 45-0 (KC)
1978—Steelers, 27-24 (P)
1979—Steelers, 30-3 (KC)
1980—Steelers, 21-16 (P)
1981—Chiefs, 37-33 (P)
1982—Steelers, 35-14 (P)
1984—Chiefs, 37-27 (P)
1985—Steelers, 36-28 (KC)
1986—Chiefs, 24-19 (P)
1987—Steelers, 17-16 (KC)
1988—Steelers, 16-10 (P)
1989—Steelers, 23-17 (P)
(RS Pts.—Steelers 437, Chiefs 329)
KANSAS CITY vs. **SAN DIEGO
RS: Series tied, 31-31-1
1960—Chargers, 21-20 (LA)
Texans, 17-0 (D)
1961—Chargers, 26-10 (D)
Chargers, 24-14 (SD)
1962—Chargers, 32-28 (SD)
Texans, 26-17 (D)
1963—Chargers, 24-10 (SD)
Chargers, 38-17 (SD)
1964—Chargers, 28-14 (KC)
Chiefs, 49-6 (SD)
1965—Tie, 10-10 (SD)
Chiefs, 31-7 (KC)
1966—Chiefs, 24-14 (KC)
Chiefs, 27-17 (SD)

1967—Chargers, 45-31 (SD)
Chargers, 17-16 (KC)
1968—Chiefs, 27-20 (KC)
Chiefs, 40-3 (SD)
1969—Chiefs, 27-9 (SD)
Chiefs, 27-3 (KC)
1970—Chiefs, 26-14 (SD)
Chargers, 31-13 (SD)
1971—Chargers, 21-14 (SD)
Chiefs, 31-10 (KC)
1972—Chiefs, 26-14 (SD)
Chargers, 27-17 (KC)
1973—Chiefs, 19-0 (SD)
Chiefs, 33-6 (KC)
1974—Chiefs, 24-14 (SD)
Chargers, 14-7 (KC)
1975—Chiefs, 12-10 (SD)
Chargers, 28-20 (KC)
1976—Chiefs, 30-16 (SD)
Chiefs, 23-20 (KC)
1977—Chargers, 23-7 (KC)
Chiefs, 21-16 (SD)
1978—Chargers, 29-23 (SD) OT
Chiefs, 23-0 (KC)
1979—Chargers, 20-14 (SD)
Chargers, 28-7 (SD)
1980—Chargers, 24-7 (KC)
Chargers, 20-7 (SD)
1981—Chargers, 42-31 (KC)
Chargers, 22-20 (SD)
1982—Chiefs, 19-12 (KC)
1983—Chargers, 17-14 (SD)
Chargers, 41-38 (SD)
1984—Chiefs, 31-13 (KC)
Chiefs, 42-21 (SD)
1985—Chargers, 31-20 (SD)
Chiefs, 38-34 (KC)
1986—Chiefs, 42-41 (KC)
Chiefs, 24-23 (SD)
1987—Chiefs, 20-13 (KC)
Chargers, 42-21 (SD)
1988—Chargers, 24-23 (KC)
Chargers, 24-13 (SD)
1989—Chargers, 21-6 (SD)
Chargers, 20-13 (KC)
1990—Chiefs, 27-10 (KC)
Chiefs, 24-21 (SD)
1991—Chiefs, 14-13 (SD)
Chiefs, 20-17 (KC) OT
(RS Pts.—Chiefs 1,355, Chargers 1,262)
*Franchise in Dallas prior to 1963 and
known as Texans
**Franchise in Los Angeles prior to 1961
KANSAS CITY vs. SAN FRANCISCO
RS: 49ers lead series, 4-1
1971—Chiefs, 26-17 (SF)
1975—49ers, 20-3 (KC)
1982—49ers, 26-13 (KC)
1985—49ers, 31-3 (SF)
1991—49ers, 28-14 (SF)
(RS Pts.—49ers 122, Chiefs 59)
KANSAS CITY vs. SEATTLE
RS: Chiefs lead series, 15-12
1977—Seahawks, 34-31 (KC)
1978—Seahawks, 13-10 (KC)
Seahawks, 23-19 (S)
1979—Chiefs, 24-6 (S)
Chiefs, 37-21 (KC)
1980—Seahawks, 17-16 (KC)
Chiefs, 31-30 (S)
1981—Chiefs, 20-14 (S)
Chiefs, 40-13 (KC)
1983—Chiefs, 17-13 (KC)
Seahawks, 51-48 (S) OT
1984—Seahawks, 45-0 (S)
Chiefs, 34-7 (KC)
1985—Chiefs, 28-7 (KC)
Seahawks, 24-6 (S)
1986—Seahawks, 23-17 (S)
Chiefs, 27-7 (KC)
1987—Seahawks, 43-14 (S)
Chiefs, 41-20 (KC)
1988—Seahawks, 31-10 (S)
Chiefs, 27-24 (KC)
1989—Chiefs, 20-16 (S)
Chiefs, 20-10 (KC)
1990—Seahawks, 19-7 (S)
Seahawks, 17-16 (KC)
1991—Chiefs, 20-13 (KC)
Chiefs, 19-6 (S)
(RS Pts.—Chiefs 599, Seahawks 547)
KANSAS CITY vs. TAMPA BAY
RS: Chiefs lead series, 4-2
1976—Chiefs, 28-19 (TB)
1978—Buccaneers, 30-13 (KC)
1979—Buccaneers, 3-0 (TB)
1981—Chiefs, 19-10 (KC)
1984—Chiefs, 24-20 (KC)
1986—Chiefs, 27-20 (KC)
(RS Pts.—Chiefs 111, Buccaneers 102)
KANSAS CITY vs. WASHINGTON
RS: Chiefs lead series, 2-1
1971—Chiefs, 27-20 (KC)

1976—Chiefs, 33-30 (W)
1983—Redskins, 27-12 (W)
(RS Pts.—Redskins 77, Chiefs 72)

L.A. RAIDERS vs. ATLANTA
RS: Raiders lead series, 4-3;
See Atlanta vs. L.A. Raiders
L.A. RAIDERS vs. BUFFALO
RS: Bills lead series, 14-13;
PS: Bills lead series, 1-0;
See Buffalo vs. L.A. Raiders
L.A. RAIDERS vs. CHICAGO
RS: Raiders lead series, 4-3;
See Chicago vs. L.A. Raiders
L.A. RAIDERS vs. CINCINNATI
RS: Raiders lead series, 14-5
PS: Raiders lead series, 2-0;
See Cincinnati vs. L.A. Raiders
L.A. RAIDERS vs. CLEVELAND
RS: Raiders lead series, 8-2
PS: Raiders lead series, 2-0;
See Cleveland vs. L.A. Raiders
L.A. RAIDERS vs. DALLAS
RS: Raiders lead series, 3-1;
See Dallas vs. L.A. Raiders
L.A. RAIDERS vs. DENVER
RS: Raiders lead series, 43-18-2
PS: Raiders lead series, 1-0;
See Denver vs. L.A. Raiders
L.A. RAIDERS vs. DETROIT
RS: Raiders lead series, 5-2;
See Detroit vs. L.A. Raiders
L.A. RAIDERS vs. GREEN BAY
RS: Raiders lead series, 5-1
PS: Packers lead series, 1-0;
See Green Bay vs. L.A. Raiders
L.A. RAIDERS vs. HOUSTON
RS: Raiders lead series, 19-13
PS: Raiders lead series, 3-0;
See Houston vs. L.A. Raiders
L.A. RAIDERS vs. INDIANAPOLIS
RS: Raiders lead series, 4-2
PS: Series tied, 1-1;
See Indianapolis vs. L.A. Raiders
L.A. RAIDERS vs. KANSAS CITY
RS: Raiders lead series, 34-27-2
PS: Chiefs lead series, 2-1;
See Kansas City vs. L.A. Raiders
***L.A. RAIDERS vs. L.A. RAMS**
RS: Raiders lead series, 5-2
1972—Raiders, 45-17 (O)
1977—Rams, 20-14 (LA)
1979—Raiders, 24-17 (LA)
1982—Raiders, 37-31 (LA Raiders)
1985—Raiders, 16-6 (LA Rams)
1988—Rams, 22-17 (LA Raiders)
1991—Raiders, 20-17 (LA Raiders)
(RS Pts.—Raiders 173, Rams 130)
*Franchise in Oakland prior to 1982
***L.A. RAIDERS vs. MIAMI**
RS: Raiders lead series, 14-3-1
PS: Raiders lead series, 2-1
1966—Raiders, 23-14 (M)
Raiders, 21-10 (O)
1967—Raiders, 31-17 (O)
1968—Raiders, 47-21 (M)
1969—Raiders, 20-17 (O)
Tie, 20-20 (M)
1970—Dolphins, 20-13 (M)
**Raiders, 21-14 (O)
1973—Raiders, 12-7 (O)
***Dolphins, 27-10 (M)
1974—**Raiders, 28-26 (O)
1975—Raiders, 31-21 (M)
1978—Dolphins, 23-6 (M)
1979—Raiders, 13-3 (O)
1980—Raiders, 16-10 (O)
1981—Raiders, 33-17 (M)
1983—Raiders, 27-14 (LA)
1984—Raiders, 45-34 (M)
1986—Raiders, 30-28 (M)
1988—Dolphins, 24-14 (LA)
1990—Raiders, 13-10 (M)
(RS Pts.—Raiders 415, Dolphins 310)
(PS Pts.—Dolphins 67, Raiders 59)
*Franchise in Oakland prior to 1982
**AFC Divisional Playoff
***AFC Championship
***L.A. RAIDERS vs. MINNESOTA**
RS: Raiders lead series, 5-2
PS: Raiders lead series, 1-0
1973—Vikings, 24-16 (M)
1976—**Raiders, 32-14 (Pasadena)
1977—Raiders, 35-13 (O)
1978—Raiders, 27-20 (O)
1981—Raiders, 36-10 (M)
1984—Raiders, 23-20 (LA)
1987—Vikings, 31-20 (M)
1990—Raiders, 28-24 (M)
(RS Pts.—Raiders 185, Vikings 142)
(PS Pts.—Raiders 32, Vikings 14)
*Franchise in Oakland prior to 1982
**Super Bowl XI

*L.A. RAIDERS vs. **NEW ENGLAND
RS: Series tied, 12-12-1
PS: Series tied, 1-1
1960—Raiders, 27-14 (O)
    Patriots, 34-28 (B)
1961—Patriots, 20-17 (B)
    Patriots, 35-21 (O)
1962—Patriots, 26-16 (B)
    Raiders, 20-0 (O)
1963—Patriots, 20-14 (O)
    Patriots, 20-14 (B)
1964—Patriots, 17-14 (O)
    Tie, 43-43 (B)
1965—Raiders, 24-10 (B)
    Raiders, 30-21 (O)
1966—Raiders, 24-21 (B)
1967—Raiders, 35-7 (O)
    Raiders, 48-14 (B)
1968—Raiders, 41-10 (O)
1969—Raiders, 38-23 (B)
1971—Patriots, 20-6 (NE)
1974—Raiders, 41-26 (O)
1976—Patriots, 48-17 (NE)
    ***Raiders, 24-21 (O)
1978—Patriots, 21-14 (O)
1981—Patriots, 27-17 (O)
1985—Raiders, 35-20 (NE)
    ***Patriots, 27-20 (LA)
1987—Patriots, 26-23 (NE)
1989—Raiders, 24-21 (LA)
(RS Pts.—Raiders 638, Patriots 537)
(PS Pts.—Patriots 48, Raiders 44)
Franchise in Oakland prior to 1982
**Franchise in Boston prior to 1971*
***AFC Divisional Playoff*

*L.A. RAIDERS vs. NEW ORLEANS
RS: Raiders lead series, 3-2-1
1971—Tie, 21-21 (NO)
1975—Raiders, 48-10 (O)
1979—Raiders, 42-35 (NO)
1985—Raiders, 23-13 (LA)
1988—Saints, 20-6 (NO)
1991—Saints, 27-0 (NO)
(RS Pts.—Raiders 140, Saints 126)
Franchise in Oakland prior to 1982

*L.A. RAIDERS vs. N.Y. GIANTS
RS: Raiders lead series, 3-2
1973—Raiders, 42-0 (O)
1980—Raiders, 33-17 (NY)
1983—Raiders, 27-12 (LA)
1986—Giants, 14-9 (LA)
1989—Giants, 34-17 (NY)
(RS Pts.—Raiders 128, Giants 77)
Franchise in Oakland prior to 1982

*L.A. RAIDERS vs. **N.Y. JETS
RS: Raiders lead series, 13-9-2
PS: Jets lead series, 2-0
1960—Raiders, 28-27 (NY)
    Titans, 31-28 (O)
1961—Titans, 14-6 (O)
    Titans, 23-12 (NY)
1962—Titans, 28-17 (O)
    Titans, 31-21 (NY)
1963—Jets, 10-7 (NY)
    Raiders, 49-26 (O)
1964—Jets, 35-13 (NY)
    Raiders, 35-26 (O)
1965—Tie, 24-24 (NY)
    Raiders, 24-14 (O)
1966—Raiders, 24-21 (NY)
    Tie, 28-28 (O)
1967—Jets, 27-14 (NY)
    Raiders, 38-29 (O)
1968—Raiders, 43-32 (NY)
    ***Jets, 27-23 (O)
1969—Raiders, 27-14 (NY)
1970—Raiders, 14-13 (NY)
1972—Raiders, 24-16 (O)
1977—Raiders, 28-27 (NY)
1979—Jets, 28-19 (NY)
1982—****Jets, 17-14 (LA)
1985—Raiders, 31-0 (LA)
1989—Raiders, 14-7 (NY)
(RS Pts.—Raiders 568, Jets 531)
(PS Pts.—Jets 44, Raiders 37)
Franchise in Oakland prior to 1982
**Jets known as Titans prior to 1963*
***AFL Championship*
****AFC Second Round Playoff*

*L.A. RAIDERS vs. PHILADELPHIA
RS: Eagles lead series, 3-2
PS: Raiders lead series, 1-0
1971—Raiders, 34-10 (O)
1976—Raiders, 26-7 (P)
1980—Eagles, 10-7 (P)
    **Raiders, 27-10 (NO)
1986—Eagles, 33-27 (LA) OT
1989—Eagles, 10-7 (P)
(RS Pts.—Raiders 101, Eagles 70)
(PS Pts.—Raiders 27, Eagles 10)
Franchise in Oakland prior to 1982
**Super Bowl XV*

*L.A. RAIDERS vs. **PHOENIX
RS: Raiders lead series, 2-1
1973—Raiders, 17-10 (StL)
1983—Cardinals, 34-24 (LA)
1989—Raiders, 16-14 (LA)
(RS Pts.—Cardinals 58, Raiders 57)
Franchise in Oakland prior to 1982
**Franchise in St. Louis prior to 1988*

*L.A. RAIDERS vs. PITTSBURGH
RS: Raiders lead series, 7-3
PS: Series tied, 3-3
1970—Raiders, 31-14 (O)
1972—Raiders, 34-28 (P)
    **Steelers, 13-7 (P)
1973—Steelers, 17-9 (O)
    **Raiders, 33-14 (O)
1974—Raiders, 17-0 (P)
    ***Steelers, 24-13 (O)
1975—***Steelers, 16-10 (P)
1976—Raiders, 31-28 (O)
    ***Raiders, 24-7 (O)
1977—Raiders, 16-7 (P)
1980—Raiders, 45-34 (P)
1981—Raiders, 30-27 (O)
1983—**Raiders, 38-10 (LA)
1984—Steelers, 13-7 (LA)
1990—Raiders, 20-3 (LA)
(RS Pts.—Raiders 234, Steelers 177)
(PS Pts.—Raiders 125, Steelers 84)
Franchise in Oakland prior to 1982
**AFC Divisional Playoff*
***AFC Championship*

*L.A. RAIDERS vs. **SAN DIEGO
RS: Raiders lead series, 40-22-2
PS: Raiders lead series, 1-0
1960—Chargers, 52-28 (LA)
    Chargers, 41-17 (O)
1961—Chargers, 44-0 (SD)
    Chargers, 41-10 (O)
1962—Chargers, 42-33 (O)
    Chargers, 31-21 (SD)
1963—Raiders, 34-33 (O)
    Raiders, 41-27 (O)
1964—Chargers, 31-17 (O)
    Raiders, 21-20 (SD)
1965—Chargers, 17-6 (O)
    Chargers, 24-14 (SD)
1966—Chargers, 29-20 (O)
    Raiders, 41-19 (SD)
1967—Raiders, 51-10 (O)
    Raiders, 41-21 (SD)
1968—Chargers, 23-14 (O)
    Raiders, 34-27 (SD)
1969—Raiders, 24-12 (SD)
    Raiders, 21-16 (O)
1970—Tie, 27-27 (SD)
    Raiders, 20-17 (O)
1971—Raiders, 34-0 (O)
    Raiders, 34-33 (SD)
1972—Tie, 17-17 (O)
    Raiders, 21-19 (SD)
1973—Raiders, 27-17 (SD)
    Raiders, 31-3 (O)
1974—Raiders, 14-10 (SD)
    Raiders, 17-10 (O)
1975—Raiders, 6-0 (SD)
    Raiders, 25-0 (O)
1976—Raiders, 27-17 (SD)
    Raiders, 24-0 (O)
1977—Raiders, 24-0 (O)
    Chargers, 12-7 (SD)
1978—Raiders, 21-20 (SD)
    Chargers, 27-23 (O)
1979—Chargers, 30-10 (SD)
    Raiders, 45-22 (O)
1980—Chargers, 30-24 (SD) OT
    Raiders, 38-24 (O)
    ***Raiders, 34-27 (SD)
1981—Raiders, 55-21 (SD)
    Chargers, 23-10 (SD)
1982—Raiders, 28-24 (LA)
    Raiders, 41-34 (SD)
1983—Raiders, 42-10 (SD)
    Raiders, 30-14 (LA)
1984—Raiders, 33-30 (LA)
    Raiders, 44-37 (SD)
1985—Raiders, 34-21 (LA)
    Chargers, 40-34 (SD) OT
1986—Raiders, 17-13 (LA)
    Raiders, 37-31 (SD) OT
1987—Chargers, 23-17 (LA)
    Chargers, 16-14 (SD)
1988—Raiders, 24-13 (LA)
    Raiders, 13-3 (SD)
1989—Raiders, 40-14 (LA)
    Chargers, 14-12 (SD)
1990—Raiders, 24-9 (SD)
    Raiders, 17-12 (LA)
1991—Raiders, 21-13 (LA)
    Raiders, 9-7 (SD)
(RS Pts.—Raiders 1,558, Chargers 1,359)
(PS Pts.—Raiders 34, Chargers 27)

Franchise in Oakland prior to 1982
**Franchise in Los Angeles prior to 1961*
***AFC Championship*

*L.A. RAIDERS vs. SAN FRANCISCO
RS: Raiders lead series, 5-2
1970—49ers, 38-7 (O)
1974—Raiders, 35-24 (SF)
1979—Raiders, 23-10 (O)
1982—Raiders, 23-17 (SF)
1985—49ers, 34-10 (LA)
1988—Raiders, 9-3 (SF)
1991—Raiders, 12-6 (LA)
(RS Pts.—49ers 132, Raiders 119)
Franchise in Oakland prior to 1982

*L.A. RAIDERS vs. SEATTLE
RS: Series tied, 14-14
PS: Series tied, 1-1
1977—Raiders, 44-7 (O)
1978—Seahawks, 27-7 (S)
    Seahawks, 17-16 (O)
1979—Seahawks, 27-10 (S)
    Seahawks, 29-24 (O)
1980—Raiders, 33-14 (O)
    Raiders, 19-17 (S)
1981—Raiders, 20-10 (O)
    Raiders, 32-31 (S)
1982—Raiders, 28-23 (LA)
1983—Seahawks, 38-36 (S)
    Seahawks, 34-21 (LA)
    **Raiders, 30-14 (LA)
1984—Raiders, 28-14 (LA)
    Seahawks, 17-14 (S)
    ***Seahawks, 13-7 (S)
1985—Seahawks, 33-3 (S)
    Raiders, 13-3 (LA)
1986—Raiders, 14-10 (LA)
    Seahawks, 37-0 (S)
1987—Seahawks, 35-13 (LA)
    Raiders, 37-14 (S)
1988—Seahawks, 35-27 (S)
    Seahawks, 43-37 (LA)
1989—Seahawks, 24-20 (LA)
    Seahawks, 23-17 (S)
1990—Raiders, 17-13 (S)
    Raiders, 24-17 (LA)
1991—Raiders, 23-20 (S) OT
    Raiders, 31-7 (LA)
(RS Pts.—Seahawks 619, Raiders 608)
(PS Pts.—Raiders 37, Seahawks 27)
Franchise in Oakland prior to 1982
**AFC Championship*
***AFC First Round Playoff*

*L.A. RAIDERS vs. TAMPA BAY
RS: Raiders lead series, 2-0
1976—Raiders, 49-16 (O)
1981—Raiders, 18-16 (O)
(RS Pts.—Raiders 67, Buccaneers 32)
Franchise in Oakland prior to 1982

*L.A. RAIDERS vs. WASHINGTON
RS: Raiders lead series, 4-2
PS: Raiders lead series, 1-0
1970—Raiders, 34-20 (O)
1975—Raiders, 26-23 (W) OT
1980—Raiders, 24-21 (O)
1983—Redskins, 37-35 (W)
    **Raiders, 38-9 (Tampa)
1986—Redskins, 10-6 (W)
1989—Raiders, 37-24 (LA)
(RS Pts.—Raiders 162, Redskins 135)
(PS Pts.—Raiders 38, Redskins 9)
Franchise in Oakland prior to 1982
**Super Bowl XVIII*

L.A. RAMS vs. ATLANTA
RS: Rams lead series, 35-13-2;
See Atlanta vs. L.A. Rams
L.A. RAMS vs. BUFFALO
RS: Rams lead series, 3-2;
See Buffalo vs. L.A. Rams
L.A. RAMS vs. CHICAGO
RS: Bears lead series, 44-28-3
PS: Series tied, 1-1;
See Chicago vs. L.A. Rams
L.A. RAMS vs. CINCINNATI
RS: Bengals lead series, 4-2;
See Cincinnati vs. L.A. Rams
L.A. RAMS vs. CLEVELAND
RS: Series tied, 7-7
PS: Browns lead series, 2-1;
See Cleveland vs. L.A. Rams
L.A. RAMS vs. DALLAS
RS: Series tied, 8-8
PS: Series tied, 4-4;
See Dallas vs. L.A. Rams
L.A. RAMS vs. DENVER
RS: Series tied, 3-3;
See Denver vs. L.A. Rams
L.A. RAMS vs. DETROIT
RS: Rams lead series, 39-34-1
PS: Lions lead series, 1-0;
See Detroit vs. L.A. Rams
L.A. RAMS vs. GREEN BAY
RS: Rams lead series, 42-34-2

PS: Packers lead series, 1-0;
See Green Bay vs. L.A. Rams
L.A. RAMS vs. HOUSTON
RS: Rams lead series, 4-2;
See Houston vs. L.A. Rams
L.A. RAMS vs. INDIANAPOLIS
RS: Colts lead series, 20-16-2;
See Indianapolis vs. L.A. Rams
L.A. RAMS vs. KANSAS CITY
RS: Rams lead series, 3-1;
See Kansas City vs. L.A. Rams
L.A. RAMS VS. L.A. RAIDERS
RS: Raiders lead series, 5-2;
See L.A. Raiders vs. L.A. Rams
L.A. RAMS vs. MIAMI
RS: Dolphins lead series, 4-1
1971—Dolphins, 20-14 (LA)
1976—Rams, 31-28 (M)
1980—Dolphins, 35-14 (LA)
1983—Dolphins, 30-14 (M)
1986—Dolphins 37-31 (LA) OT
(RS Pts.—Dolphins 150, Rams 104)

L.A. RAMS vs. MINNESOTA
RS: Vikings lead series, 14-11-2
PS: Vikings lead series, 5-1
1961—Rams, 31-17 (LA)
    Rams, 42-21 (M)
1962—Vikings, 38-14 (LA)
    Tie, 24-24 (M)
1963—Rams, 27-24 (LA)
    Vikings, 21-13 (M)
1964—Rams, 22-13 (LA)
    Vikings, 34-13 (M)
1965—Vikings, 38-35 (LA)
    Vikings, 24-13 (M)
1966—Vikings, 35-7 (M)
    Rams, 21-6 (LA)
1967—Rams, 39-3 (LA)
1968—Rams, 31-3 (M)
1969—Vikings, 20-13 (LA)
    *Vikings, 23-20 (M)
1970—Vikings, 13-3 (M)
1972—Vikings, 45-41 (LA)
1973—Vikings, 10-9 (M)
1974—Rams, 20-17 (LA)
    **Vikings, 14-10 (M)
1976—Tie, 10-10 (M) OT
    **Vikings, 24-13 (M)
1977—Rams, 35-3 (LA)
    ***Vikings, 14-7 (LA)
1978—Rams, 34-17 (M)
    ***Rams, 34-10 (LA)
1979—Rams, 27-21 (LA) OT
1985—Rams, 13-10 (LA)
1987—Vikings, 21-16 (LA)
1988—****Vikings, 28-17 (M)
1989—Vikings, 23-21 (M) OT
1991—Vikings, 20-14 (M)
(RS Pts.—Rams 567, Vikings 552)
(PS Pts.—Vikings 113, Rams 101)
Conference Championship
**NFC Championship*
***NFC Divisional Playoff*
****NFC First Round Playoff*

L.A. RAMS vs. NEW ENGLAND
RS: Patriots lead series, 3-2
1974—Patriots, 20-14 (NE)
1980—Rams, 17-14 (NE)
1983—Patriots, 21-7 (LA)
1986—Patriots, 30-28 (LA)
1989—Rams, 24-20 (NE)
(RS Pts.—Patriots 105, Rams 90)

L.A. RAMS vs. NEW ORLEANS
RS: Rams lead series, 26-18
1967—Rams, 27-13 (NO)
1969—Rams, 36-17 (LA)
1970—Rams, 30-17 (NO)
    Rams, 34-16 (LA)
1971—Saints, 24-20 (NO)
    Rams, 45-28 (LA)
1972—Rams, 34-14 (LA)
    Saints, 19-16 (NO)
1973—Rams, 29-7 (LA)
    Rams, 24-0 (LA)
1974—Rams, 24-0 (LA)
    Saints, 20-7 (NO)
1975—Rams, 38-14 (LA)
    Rams, 14-7 (NO)
1976—Rams, 16-10 (NO)
    Rams, 33-14 (LA)
1977—Rams, 14-7 (LA)
    Saints, 27-26 (NO)
1978—Rams, 26-20 (LA)
    Saints, 10-3 (LA)
1979—Rams, 35-17 (NO)
    Saints, 29-14 (LA)
1980—Rams, 45-31 (LA)
    Rams, 27-7 (NO)
1981—Saints, 23-17 (NO)
    Rams, 21-13 (LA)
1983—Rams, 30-27 (LA)
    Rams, 26-24 (NO)
1984—Rams, 28-10 (NO)

Rams, 34-21 (LA)
1985—Rams, 28-10 (LA)
Saints, 29-3 (NO)
1986—Saints, 6-0 (NO)
Rams, 6-13 (LA)
1987—Saints, 37-10 (NO)
Rams, 31-14 (LA)
1988—Rams, 12-10 (NO)
Saints, 14-10 (LA)
1989—Saints, 40-21 (LA)
Rams, 20-17 (NO) OT
1990—Saints, 24-20 (LA)
Saints, 20-17 (NO)
1991—Saints, 24-7 (NO)
Rams, 24-17 (LA)
(RS Pts.—Rams 970, Saints 806)

*L.A. RAMS vs. N.Y. GIANTS
RS: Rams lead series, 19-8
PS: Series tied, 1-1
1938—Giants, 28-0 (NY)
1940—Rams, 13-0 (NY)
1941—Giants, 49-14 (NY)
1945—Rams, 21-17 (NY)
1946—Rams, 31-21 (NY)
1947—Rams, 34-10 (NY)
1948—Rams, 52-37 (NY)
1953—Rams, 21-7 (LA)
1954—Rams, 17-16 (NY)
1959—Giants, 23-21 (LA)
1961—Giants, 24-14 (NY)
1966—Rams, 55-14 (LA)
1968—Rams, 24-21 (LA)
1970—Rams, 31-3 (NY)
1973—Rams, 40-6 (LA)
1976—Rams, 24-10 (LA)
1978—Rams, 20-17 (NY)
1979—Giants, 20-14 (LA)
1980—Rams, 28-7 (NY)
1981—Rams, 10-7 (NY)
1983—Rams, 16-6 (NY)
1984—Rams, 33-12 (LA)
**Giants, 16-13 (LA)
1985—Giants, 24-19 (NY)
1988—Rams, 45-31 (NY)
1989—Rams, 31-10 (LA)
***Rams, 19-13 (NY) OT
1990—Giants, 31-7 (LA)
1991—Rams, 19-13 (NY)
(RS Pts.—Rams 651, Giants 467)
(PS Pts.—Rams 32, Giants 29)
*Franchise in Cleveland prior to 1946
**NFC First Round Playoff
***NFC Divisional Playoff

L.A. RAMS vs. N.Y. JETS
RS: Rams lead series, 4-2
1970—Jets, 31-20 (LA)
1974—Rams, 20-13 (NY)
1980—Rams, 38-13 (LA)
1983—Jets, 27-24 (NY) OT
1986—Rams, 17-3 (NY)
1989—Rams, 38-14 (LA)
(RS Pts.—Rams 157, Jets 101)

*L.A. RAMS vs. PHILADELPHIA
RS: Rams lead series, 15-11-1
PS: Series tied, 1-1
1937—Rams, 21-3 (P)
1939—Rams, 35-13 (Colorado Springs)
1940—Rams, 21-13 (C)
1942—Rams, 24-14 (Akron)
1944—Eagles, 26-13 (P)
1945—Eagles, 28-14 (P)
1946—Eagles, 25-14 (LA)
1947—Eagles, 14-7 (P)
1948—Tie, 28-28 (LA)
1949—Eagles, 38-14 (P)
**Eagles, 14-0 (LA)
1950—Eagles, 56-20 (P)
1955—Rams, 23-21 (P)
1956—Rams, 27-7 (LA)
1957—Rams, 17-13 (LA)
1959—Eagles, 23-20 (P)
1964—Rams, 20-10 (LA)
1967—Rams, 33-17 (LA)
1969—Rams, 23-17 (P)
1972—Rams, 34-3 (P)
1975—Rams, 42-3 (P)
1977—Rams, 20-0 (LA)
1978—Rams, 16-14 (P)
1983—Eagles, 13-9 (P)
1985—Rams, 17-6 (P)
1986—Eagles, 34-20 (P)
1988—Eagles, 30-24 (LA)
1989—***Rams, 21-7 (P)
1990—Eagles, 27-21 (LA)
(RS Pts.—Rams 577, Eagles 496)
(PS Pts.—Rams 21, Eagles 21)
*Franchise in Cleveland prior to 1946
**NFL Championship
***NFC First Round Playoff

*L.A. RAMS vs. **PHOENIX
RS: Rams lead series, 22-17-2
PS: Rams lead series, 1-0
1937—Cardinals, 6-0 (Clev)

Cardinals, 13-7 (Chi)
1938—Cardinals, 7-6 (Clev)
Cardinals, 31-17 (Chi)
1939—Rams, 24-0 (Chi)
Rams, 14-0 (Clev)
1940—Rams, 26-14 (Clev)
Cardinals, 17-7 (Chi)
1941—Rams, 10-6 (Clev)
Cardinals, 7-0 (Chi)
1942—Cardinals, 7-0 (Clev)
Rams, 7-3 (Clev)
1945—Rams, 21-0 (Clev)
Rams, 35-21 (Chi)
1946—Cardinals, 34-10 (Chi)
Rams, 17-14 (LA)
1947—Rams, 27-7 (LA)
Cardinals, 17-10 (Chi)
1948—Cardinals, 27-22 (LA)
Cardinals, 27-24 (Chi)
1949—Tie, 28-28 (Chi)
Rams, 31-27 (LA)
1951—Rams, 45-21 (LA)
1953—Tie, 24-24 (Chi)
1954—Rams, 28-17 (LA)
1958—Rams, 20-14 (Chi)
1960—Cardinals, 43-21 (LA)
1965—Rams, 27-3 (StL)
1968—Rams, 24-13 (StL)
1970—Rams, 34-13 (LA)
1972—Cardinals, 24-14 (StL)
1975—***Rams, 35-23 (LA)
1976—Cardinals, 30-28 (LA)
1979—Rams, 21-0 (LA)
1980—Rams, 21-13 (StL)
1984—Rams, 16-13 (StL)
1985—Rams, 46-14 (LA)
1986—Rams, 16-10 (StL)
1987—Rams, 27-24 (StL)
1988—Cardinals, 41-27 (LA)
1989—Rams, 37-14 (LA)
1991—Cardinals, 24-14 (LA)
(RS Pts.—Rams 829, Cardinals 672)
(PS Pts.—Rams 35, Cardinals 23)
*Franchise in Cleveland prior to 1946
**Franchise in St. Louis prior to 1988
and in Chicago prior to 1960
***NFC Divisional Playoff

*L.A. RAMS vs. **PITTSBURGH
RS: Rams lead series, 13-4-2
PS: Steelers lead series, 1-0
1938—Rams, 13-7 (New Orleans)
1939—Tie, 14-14 (C)
1941—Rams, 17-14 (Akron)
1947—Rams, 48-7 (P)
1948—Rams, 31-14 (LA)
1949—Tie, 7-7 (P)
1952—Rams, 28-14 (LA)
1955—Rams, 27-26 (LA)
1956—Steelers, 30-13 (P)
1961—Rams, 24-14 (LA)
1964—Rams, 26-14 (P)
1968—Rams, 45-10 (LA)
1971—Rams, 23-14 (P)
1975—Rams, 10-3 (LA)
1978—Rams, 10-7 (LA)
1979—***Steelers, 31-19 (Pasadena)
1981—Steelers, 24-0 (P)
1984—Steelers, 24-14 (P)
1987—Rams, 31-21 (LA)
1990—Steelers, 41-10 (P)
(RS Pts.—Rams 391, Steelers 305)
(PS Pts.—Steelers 31, Rams 19)
*Franchise in Cleveland prior to 1946
**Steelers known as Pirates prior to 1941
***Super Bowl XIV

L.A. RAMS vs. SAN DIEGO
RS: Rams lead series, 3-2
1970—Rams, 37-10 (LA)
1975—Rams, 13-10 (SD) OT
1979—Chargers, 40-16 (LA)
1988—Chargers, 38-24 (LA)
1991—Rams, 30-24 (LA)
(RS Pts.—Chargers 122, Rams 120)

L.A. RAMS vs. SAN FRANCISCO
RS: Rams lead series, 48-34-2
PS: 49ers lead series, 1-0
1950—Rams, 35-14 (SF)
Rams, 28-21 (LA)
1951—49ers, 44-17 (SF)
Rams, 23-16 (LA)
1952—Rams, 35-9 (LA)
Rams, 34-21 (SF)
1953—Rams, 31-30 (SF)
49ers, 31-27 (LA)
1954—Tie, 24-24 (LA)
Rams, 42-34 (SF)
1955—Rams, 23-14 (SF)
Rams, 27-14 (LA)
1956—49ers, 33-30 (SF)
Rams, 30-6 (LA)
1957—49ers, 23-20 (SF)
Rams, 37-24 (LA)
1958—Rams, 33-3 (SF)

Rams, 56-7 (LA)
1959—49ers, 34-0 (SF)
49ers, 24-16 (LA)
1960—49ers, 13-9 (SF)
Rams, 23-7 (LA)
1961—49ers, 35-0 (SF)
Rams, 17-7 (LA)
1962—Rams, 28-14 (SF)
49ers, 24-17 (LA)
1963—Rams, 28-21 (LA)
Rams, 21-17 (SF)
1964—Rams, 42-14 (LA)
49ers, 28-7 (SF)
1965—49ers, 45-21 (LA)
49ers, 30-27 (SF)
1966—Rams, 34-3 (LA)
49ers, 21-13 (SF)
1967—49ers, 27-24 (SF)
Rams, 17-7 (SF)
1968—Rams, 24-10 (LA)
Tie, 20-20 (SF)
1969—Rams, 27-21 (SF)
Rams, 41-30 (LA)
1970—49ers, 20-6 (LA)
Rams, 30-13 (LA)
1971—Rams, 20-13 (LA)
Rams, 17-6 (LA)
1972—Rams, 31-7 (LA)
Rams, 26-16 (SF)
1973—Rams, 40-20 (SF)
Rams, 31-13 (LA)
1974—Rams, 37-14 (LA)
Rams, 15-13 (SF)
1975—Rams, 23-14 (SF)
49ers, 24-23 (LA)
1976—49ers, 16-0 (LA)
Rams, 23-3 (SF)
1977—Rams, 34-14 (LA)
Rams, 23-10 (SF)
1978—Rams, 27-10 (LA)
Rams, 31-28 (SF)
1979—Rams, 27-24 (LA)
Rams, 26-20 (SF)
1980—Rams, 48-26 (LA)
Rams, 31-17 (SF)
1981—49ers, 20-17 (SF)
49ers, 33-31 (LA)
1982—49ers, 30-24 (SF)
Rams, 21-20 (SF)
1983—Rams, 10-7 (SF)
49ers, 45-35 (LA)
1984—49ers, 33-0 (LA)
49ers, 19-16 (SF)
1985—49ers, 28-14 (LA)
Rams, 27-20 (SF)
1986—Rams, 16-13 (LA)
49ers, 24-14 (SF)
1987—49ers, 31-10 (LA)
49ers, 48-0 (SF)
1988—49ers, 24-21 (LA)
Rams, 38-16 (SF)
1989—Rams, 13-12 (SF)
49ers, 30-27 (LA)
*49ers, 30-3 (SF)
1990—Rams, 28-17 (SF)
49ers, 26-10 (LA)
1991—49ers, 27-10 (SF)
49ers, 33-10 (LA)
(RS Pts.—Rams 1,952, 49ers 1,734)
(PS Pts.—49ers 30, Rams 3)
*NFC Championship

L.A. RAMS vs. SEATTLE
RS: Rams lead series, 4-1
1976—Rams, 45-6 (LA)
1979—Rams, 24-0 (S)
1985—Rams, 35-24 (S)
1988—Rams, 31-10 (LA)
1991—Seahawks, 23-9 (S)
(RS Pts.—Rams 144, Seahawks 63)

L.A. RAMS vs. TAMPA BAY
RS: Rams lead series, 7-2
PS: Rams lead series, 1-0
1977—Rams, 31-0 (LA)
1978—Rams, 26-23 (LA)
1979—Buccaneers, 21-6 (TB)
*Rams, 9-0 (TB)
1980—Buccaneers, 10-9 (TB)
1984—Rams, 34-33 (TB)
1985—Rams, 31-27 (TB)
1986—Rams, 26-20 (LA) OT
1987—Rams, 35-3 (LA)
1990—Rams, 35-14 (TB)
(RS Pts.—Rams 233, Buccaneers 151)
(PS Pts.—Rams 9, Buccaneers 0)
*NFC Championship

*L.A. RAMS vs. WASHINGTON
RS: Redskins lead series, 14-4-1
PS: Series tied, 2-2
1937—Redskins, 16-7 (C)
1938—Redskins, 37-13 (W)
1941—Redskins, 17-13 (W)
1942—Redskins, 33-14 (W)
1944—Redskins, 14-10 (W)

1945—**Rams, 15-14 (C)
1948—Rams, 41-13 (W)
1949—Rams, 53-27 (LA)
1951—Redskins, 31-21 (W)
1962—Redskins, 20-14 (W)
1963—Redskins, 37-14 (LA)
1967—Tie, 28-28 (LA)
1969—Rams, 24-13 (W)
1971—Redskins, 38-24 (LA)
1974—Redskins, 23-17 (LA)
***Rams, 19-10 (LA)
1977—Redskins, 17-14 (W)
1981—Redskins, 30-7 (LA)
1983—Redskins, 42-20 (LA)
***Redskins, 51-7 (W)
1986—****Redskins, 19-7 (W)
1987—Rams, 30-26 (W)
1991—Redskins, 27-6 (LA)
(RS Pts.—Redskins 489, Rams 370)
(PS Pts.—Redskins 94, Rams 48)
*Franchise in Cleveland prior to 1946
**NFL Championship
***NFC Divisional Playoff
****NFC First Round Playoff

MIAMI vs. ATLANTA
RS: Dolphins lead series, 4-1;
See Atlanta vs. Miami
MIAMI vs. BUFFALO
RS: Dolphins lead series, 35-16-1
PS: Bills lead series, 1-0;
See Buffalo vs. Miami
MIAMI vs. CHICAGO
RS: Dolphins lead series, 5-1;
See Chicago vs. Miami
MIAMI vs. CINCINNATI
RS: Dolphins lead series, 9-3
PS: Dolphins lead series, 1-0;
See Cincinnati vs. Miami
MIAMI vs. CLEVELAND
RS: Series tied, 4-4
PS: Dolphins lead series, 2-0;
See Cleveland vs. Miami
MIAMI vs. DALLAS
RS: Dolphins lead series, 5-1
PS: Cowboys lead series, 1-0;
See Dallas vs. Miami
MIAMI vs. DENVER
RS: Dolphins lead series, 5-2-1;
See Denver vs. Miami
MIAMI vs. DETROIT
RS: Series tied, 2-2;
See Detroit vs. Miami
MIAMI vs. GREEN BAY
RS: Dolphins lead series, 7-0;
See Green Bay vs. Miami
MIAMI vs. HOUSTON
RS: Oilers lead series, 11-10
PS: Oilers lead series, 1-0;
See Houston vs. Miami
MIAMI vs. INDIANAPOLIS
RS: Dolphins lead series, 31-13
PS: Dolphins lead series, 1-0;
See Indianapolis vs. Miami
MIAMI vs. KANSAS CITY
RS: Chiefs lead series, 10-6
PS: Dolphins lead series, 2-0;
See Kansas City vs. Miami
MIAMI vs. L.A. RAIDERS
RS: Raiders lead series, 14-3-1
PS: Raiders lead series, 2-1;
See L.A. Raiders vs. Miami
MIAMI vs. L.A. RAMS
RS: Dolphins lead series, 4-1;
See L.A. Rams vs. Miami
MIAMI vs. MINNESOTA
RS: Dolphins lead series, 4-1
PS: Dolphins lead series, 1-0
1972—Dolphins, 16-14 (Minn)
1973—*Dolphins, 24-7 (Houston)
1976—Vikings, 29-7 (Mia)
1979—Dolphins, 27-12 (Minn)
1982—Dolphins, 22-14 (Mia)
1988—Dolphins, 24-7 (Mia)
(RS Pts.—Dolphins 96, Vikings 76)
(PS Pts.—Dolphins 24, Vikings 7)
*Super Bowl VIII

MIAMI vs. *NEW ENGLAND
RS: Dolphins lead series, 30-20
PS: Series tied, 1-1
1966—Patriots, 20-14 (M)
1967—Patriots, 41-10 (B)
Dolphins, 41-32 (M)
1968—Dolphins, 34-10 (B)
Dolphins, 38-7 (M)
1969—Dolphins, 17-16 (B)
Patriots, 38-23 (Tampa)
1970—Patriots, 27-14 (B)
Dolphins, 37-20 (M)
1971—Dolphins, 41-3 (M)
Patriots, 34-13 (NE)
1972—Dolphins, 52-0 (M)
Dolphins, 37-21 (NE)

1973—Dolphins, 44-23 (M)
Dolphins, 30-14 (NE)
1974—Patriots, 34-24 (NE)
Dolphins, 34-27 (M)
1975—Dolphins, 22-14 (NE)
Dolphins, 20-7 (M)
1976—Patriots, 30-14 (NE)
Dolphins, 10-3 (M)
1977—Dolphins, 17-5 (M)
Patriots, 14-10 (NE)
1978—Patriots, 33-24 (NE)
Dolphins, 23-3 (M)
1979—Patriots, 28-13 (NE)
Dolphins, 39-24 (M)
1980—Patriots, 34-0 (NE)
Dolphins, 16-13 (M) OT
1981—Dolphins, 30-27 (NE) OT
Dolphins, 24-14 (M)
1982—Patriots, 3-0 (NE)
**Dolphins, 28-13 (M)
1983—Dolphins, 34-24 (M)
Patriots, 17-6 (NE)
1984—Dolphins, 28-7 (M)
Dolphins, 44-24 (NE)
1985—Patriots, 17-13 (NE)
Dolphins, 30-27 (M)
***Patriots, 31-14 (M)
1986—Patriots, 34-7 (NE)
Patriots, 34-27 (M)
1987—Patriots, 28-21 (NE)
Patriots, 24-10 (M)
1988—Patriots, 21-10 (NE)
Patriots, 6-3 (M)
1989—Dolphins, 24-10 (NE)
Dolphins, 31-10 (M)
1990—Patriots, 27-24 (NE)
Dolphins, 17-10 (M)
1991—Dolphins, 20-10 (NE)
Dolphins, 30-20 (M)
(RS Pts.—Dolphins 1,147, Patriots 966)
(PS Pts.—Patriots 44, Dolphins 42)
*Franchise in Boston prior to 1971
**AFC First Round Playoff
***AFC Championship

MIAMI vs. NEW ORLEANS
RS: Dolphins lead series, 4-1
1970—Dolphins, 21-10 (M)
1974—Dolphins, 21-0 (NO)
1980—Dolphins, 21-16 (M)
1983—Saints, 17-7 (NO)
1986—Dolphins, 31-27 (NO)
(RS Pts.—Dolphins 101, Saints 70)

MIAMI vs. N.Y. GIANTS
RS: Series tied, 1-1
1972—Dolphins, 23-13 (NY)
1990—Giants, 20-3 (NY)
(RS Pts.—Giants 33, Dolphins 26)

MIAMI vs. N.Y. JETS
RS: Dolphins lead series, 26-25-1
PS: Dolphins lead series, 1-0
1966—Jets, 19-14 (M)
Jets, 30-13 (NY)
1967—Jets, 29-7 (NY)
Jets, 33-14 (M)
1968—Jets, 35-17 (NY)
Jets, 31-7 (M)
1969—Jets, 34-31 (NY)
Jets, 27-9 (M)
1970—Dolphins, 20-6 (NY)
Dolphins, 16-10 (M)
1971—Jets, 14-10 (M)
Dolphins, 30-14 (NY)
1972—Dolphins, 27-17 (NY)
Dolphins, 28-24 (M)
1973—Dolphins, 31-3 (M)
Dolphins, 24-14 (NY)
1974—Dolphins, 21-17 (M)
Jets, 17-14 (NY)
1975—Dolphins, 43-0 (NY)
Dolphins, 27-7 (M)
1976—Dolphins, 16-0 (M)
Dolphins, 27-7 (NY)
1977—Dolphins, 21-17 (M)
Dolphins, 14-10 (NY)
1978—Jets, 33-20 (NY)
Jets, 24-13 (M)
1979—Jets, 33-27 (NY)
Jets, 27-24 (M)
1980—Jets, 17-14 (NY)
Jets, 24-17 (M)
1981—Tie, 28-28 (M) OT
Jets, 16-15 (NY)
1982—Dolphins, 45-28 (NY)
Dolphins, 20-19 (M)
*Dolphins, 14-0 (M)
1983—Dolphins, 32-14 (NY)
Dolphins, 34-14 (M)
1984—Dolphins, 31-17 (M)
Dolphins, 28-17 (M)
1985—Jets, 23-7 (NY)
Dolphins, 21-17 (M)
1986—Jets, 51-45 (NY) OT
Dolphins, 45-3 (M)

1987—Jets, 37-31 (NY) OT
Dolphins, 37-28 (M)
1988—Jets, 44-30 (M)
Jets, 38-34 (NY)
1989—Jets, 40-33 (M)
Dolphins, 31-23 (NY)
1990—Dolphins, 20-16 (M)
Dolphins, 17-3 (NY)
1991—Jets, 41-23 (NY)
Jets, 23-20 (M) OT
(RS Pts.—Dolphins 1,223, Jets 1,113)
(PS Pts.—Dolphins 14, Jets 0)
*AFC Championship

MIAMI vs. PHILADELPHIA
RS: Dolphins lead series, 5-2
1970—Eagles, 24-17 (P)
1975—Dolphins, 24-16 (M)
1978—Eagles, 17-3 (P)
1981—Dolphins, 13-10 (M)
1984—Dolphins, 24-23 (M)
1987—Dolphins, 28-10 (P)
1990—Dolphins, 23-20 (M) OT
(RS Pts.—Dolphins 132, Eagles 120)

MIAMI vs. *PHOENIX
RS: Dolphins lead series, 6-0
1972—Dolphins, 31-10 (M)
1977—Dolphins, 55-14 (StL)
1978—Dolphins, 24-10 (M)
1981—Dolphins, 20-7 (StL)
1984—Dolphins, 36-28 (StL)
1990—Dolphins, 23-3 (M)
(RS Pts.—Dolphins 189, Cardinals 72)
*Franchise in St. Louis prior to 1988

MIAMI vs. PITTSBURGH
RS: Dolphins lead series, 7-4
PS: Dolphins lead series, 2-1
1971—Dolphins, 24-21 (M)
1972—*Dolphins, 21-17 (P)
1973—Dolphins, 30-26 (M)
1976—Steelers, 14-3 (P)
1979—**Steelers, 34-14 (P)
1980—Steelers, 23-10 (P)
1981—Dolphins, 30-10 (M)
1984—Dolphins, 31-7 (P)
*Dolphins, 45-28 (M)
1985—Dolphins, 24-20 (M)
1987—Dolphins, 35-24 (M)
1988—Steelers, 40-24 (P)
1989—Steelers, 34-14 (M)
1990—Dolphins, 28-6 (P)
(RS Pts.—Dolphins 253, Steelers 225)
(PS Pts.—Dolphins 80, Steelers 79)
*AFC Championship
**AFC Divisional Playoff

MIAMI vs. SAN DIEGO
RS: Chargers lead series, 9-5
PS: Series tied, 1-1
1966—Chargers, 44-10 (SD)
1967—Chargers, 24-0 (SD)
Dolphins, 41-24 (M)
1968—Chargers, 34-28 (SD)
1969—Chargers, 21-14 (M)
1972—Dolphins, 24-10 (M)
1974—Dolphins, 28-21 (SD)
1977—Chargers, 14-13 (M)
1978—Dolphins, 28-21 (SD)
1980—Chargers, 27-24 (M) OT
1981—*Chargers, 41-38 (M) OT
1982—**Dolphins, 34-13 (M)
1984—Chargers, 34-28 (SD) OT
1986—Chargers, 50-28 (SD)
1988—Dolphins, 31-28 (M)
1991—Chargers, 38-30 (SD)
(RS Pts.—Chargers 390, Dolphins 327)
(PS Pts.—Dolphins 72, Chargers 54)
*AFC Divisional Playoff
**AFC Second Round Playoff

MIAMI vs. SAN FRANCISCO
RS: Dolphins lead series, 4-1
PS: 49ers lead series, 1-0
1973—Dolphins, 21-13 (M)
1977—Dolphins, 19-15 (SF)
1980—Dolphins, 17-13 (M)
1983—Dolphins, 20-17 (SF)
1984—*49ers, 38-16 (Stanford)
1986—49ers, 31-16 (M)
(RS Pts.—Dolphins 93, 49ers 89)
(PS Pts.—49ers 38, Dolphins 16)
*Super Bowl XIX

MIAMI vs. SEATTLE
RS: Dolphins lead series, 3-1
PS: Series tied, 1-1
1977—Dolphins, 31-13 (M)
1979—Dolphins, 19-10 (M)
1983—*Seahawks, 27-20 (M)
1984—*Dolphins, 31-10 (M)
1987—Seahawks, 24-20 (S)
1990—Dolphins, 24-17 (M)
(RS Pts.—Dolphins 94, Seahawks 64)
(PS Pts.—Dolphins 51, Seahawks 37)
*AFC Divisional Playoff

MIAMI vs. TAMPA BAY
RS: Dolphins lead series, 4-1

1976—Dolphins, 23-20 (TB)
1982—Buccaneers, 23-17 (TB)
1985—Dolphins, 41-38 (M)
1988—Dolphins, 17-14 (TB)
1991—Dolphins, 33-14 (M)
(RS Pts.—Dolphins 131, Buccaneers 109)

MIAMI vs. WASHINGTON
RS: Dolphins lead series, 4-2
PS: Series tied, 1-1
1972—*Dolphins, 14-7 (Los Angeles)
1974—Redskins, 20-17 (W)
1978—Dolphins, 16-0 (W)
1981—Dolphins, 13-10 (M)
1982—**Redskins, 27-17 (Pasadena)
1984—Dolphins, 35-17 (M)
1987—Dolphins, 23-21 (M)
1990—Redskins, 42-20 (W)
(RS Pts.—Dolphins 124, Redskins 110)
(PS Pts.—Redskins 34, Dolphins 31)
*Super Bowl VII
**Super Bowl XVII

MINNESOTA vs. ATLANTA
RS: Vikings lead series, 11-6
PS: Vikings lead series, 1-0;
See Atlanta vs. Minnesota

MINNESOTA vs. BUFFALO
RS: Vikings lead series, 4-2;
See Buffalo vs. Minnesota

MINNESOTA vs. CHICAGO
RS: Vikings lead series, 30-29-2;
See Chicago vs. Minnesota

MINNESOTA vs. CINCINNATI
RS: Series tied, 3-3;
See Cincinnati vs. Minnesota

MINNESOTA vs. CLEVELAND
RS: Vikings lead series, 6-3
PS: Vikings lead series, 1-0;
See Cleveland vs. Minnesota

MINNESOTA vs. DALLAS
RS: Cowboys lead series, 7-6
PS: Cowboys lead series, 3-1;
See Dallas vs. Minnesota

MINNESOTA vs. DENVER
RS: Vikings lead series, 4-3;
See Denver vs. Minnesota

MINNESOTA vs. DETROIT
RS: Vikings lead series, 38-21-2;
See Detroit vs. Minnesota

MINNESOTA vs. GREEN BAY
RS: Packers lead series, 31-29-1;
See Green Bay vs. Minnesota

MINNESOTA vs. HOUSTON
RS: Vikings lead series, 3-2;
See Houston vs. Minnesota

MINNESOTA vs. INDIANAPOLIS
RS: Colts lead series, 11-6-1
PS: Colts lead series, 1-0;
See Indianapolis vs. Minnesota

MINNESOTA vs. KANSAS CITY
RS: Series tied, 2-2
PS: Chiefs lead series, 1-0;
See Kansas City vs. Minnesota

MINNESOTA vs. L.A. RAIDERS
RS: Raiders lead series, 5-2
PS: Raiders lead series, 1-0;
See L.A. Raiders vs. Minnesota

MINNESOTA vs. L.A. RAMS
RS: Vikings lead series, 14-11-2
PS: Vikings lead series, 5-1;
See L.A. Rams vs. Minnesota

MINNESOTA vs. MIAMI
RS: Dolphins lead series, 4-1
PS: Dolphins lead series, 1-0;
See Miami vs. Minnesota

MINNESOTA vs. *NEW ENGLAND
RS: Patriots lead series, 3-2
1970—Vikings, 35-14 (B)
1974—Patriots, 17-14 (M)
1979—Patriots, 27-23 (NE)
1988—Vikings, 36-6 (M)
1991—Patriots, 26-23 (NE) OT
(RS Pts.—Vikings 131, Patriots 90)
*Franchise in Boston prior to 1971

MINNESOTA vs. NEW ORLEANS
RS: Vikings lead series, 11-5
PS: Vikings lead series, 1-0
1968—Saints, 20-17 (NO)
1970—Vikings, 26-0 (M)
1971—Vikings, 23-10 (NO)
1972—Vikings, 37-6 (M)
1974—Vikings, 29-9 (M)
1975—Vikings, 20-7 (NO)
1976—Vikings, 40-9 (NO)
1978—Saints, 31-24 (NO)
1980—Vikings, 23-20 (NO)
1981—Vikings, 20-10 (M)
1983—Saints, 17-16 (NO)
1985—Saints, 30-23 (M)
1986—Vikings, 33-17 (M)
1987—*Vikings, 44-10 (M)
1988—Vikings, 45-3 (M)
1990—Vikings, 32-3 (M)

1991—Saints, 26-0 (NO)
(RS Pts.—Vikings 408, Saints 218)
(PS Pts.—Vikings 44, Saints 10)
*NFC First Round Playoff

MINNESOTA vs. N.Y. GIANTS
RS: Vikings lead series, 6-4
1964—Vikings, 30-21 (NY)
1965—Vikings, 40-14 (M)
1967—Vikings, 27-24 (M)
1969—Giants, 24-23 (NY)
1971—Vikings, 17-10 (NY)
1973—Vikings, 31-7 (New Haven)
1976—Vikings, 24-7 (M)
1986—Giants, 22-20 (M)
1989—Giants, 24-14 (NY)
1990—Giants, 23-15 (NY)
(RS Pts.—Vikings 241, Giants 176)

MINNESOTA vs. N.Y. JETS
RS: Jets lead series, 3-1
1970—Jets, 20-10 (NY)
1975—Vikings, 29-21 (M)
1979—Jets, 14-7 (NY)
1982—Jets, 42-14 (M)
(RS Pts.—Jets 97, Vikings 60)

MINNESOTA vs. PHILADELPHIA
RS: Vikings lead series, 10-5
PS: Eagles lead series, 1-0
1962—Vikings, 31-21 (M)
1963—Vikings, 34-13 (P)
1968—Vikings, 24-17 (P)
1971—Vikings, 13-0 (P)
1973—Vikings, 28-21 (M)
1976—Vikings, 31-12 (P)
1978—Vikings, 28-27 (M)
1980—Eagles, 42-7 (M)
*Eagles, 31-16 (P)
1981—Vikings, 35-23 (M)
1984—Eagles, 19-17 (P)
1985—Vikings, 28-23 (P)
Eagles, 37-35 (M)
1988—Vikings, 23-21 (M)
1989—Eagles, 10-9 (P)
1990—Eagles, 32-24 (P)
(RS Pts.—Vikings 367, Eagles 318)
(PS Pts.—Eagles 31, Vikings 16)
*NFC Divisional Playoff

MINNESOTA vs. *PHOENIX
RS: Cardinals lead series, 7-4
PS: Vikings lead series, 1-0
1963—Cardinals, 56-14 (M)
1967—Cardinals, 34-24 (M)
1969—Vikings, 27-10 (StL)
1972—Cardinals, 19-17 (M)
1974—Vikings, 28-24 (StL)
**Vikings, 30-14 (M)
1977—Cardinals, 27-7 (M)
1979—Cardinals, 37-7 (StL)
1981—Cardinals, 30-17 (StL)
1983—Cardinals, 41-31 (StL)
1991—Vikings, 34-7 (M)
Vikings, 28-0 (P)
(RS Pts.—Cardinals 285, Vikings 234)
(PS Pts.—Vikings 30, Cardinals 14)
*Franchise in St. Louis prior to 1988
**NFC Divisional Playoff

MINNESOTA vs. PITTSBURGH
RS: Vikings lead series, 6-4
PS: Steelers lead series, 1-0
1962—Steelers, 39-31 (P)
1964—Vikings, 30-10 (M)
1967—Vikings, 41-27 (P)
1969—Vikings, 52-14 (M)
1972—Steelers, 23-10 (P)
1974—*Steelers, 16-6 (New Orleans)
1976—Vikings, 17-6 (M)
1980—Steelers, 23-17 (P)
1983—Vikings, 17-14 (P)
1986—Vikings, 31-7 (M)
1989—Steelers, 27-14 (P)
(RS Pts.—Vikings 260, Steelers 190)
(PS Pts.—Steelers 16, Vikings 6)
*Super Bowl IX

MINNESOTA vs. SAN DIEGO
RS: Series tied, 3-3
1971—Chargers, 30-14 (SD)
1975—Vikings, 28-13 (M)
1978—Chargers, 13-7 (M)
1981—Vikings, 33-31 (SD)
1984—Chargers, 42-13 (M)
1985—Vikings, 21-17 (M)
(RS Pts.—Chargers 146, Vikings 116)

MINNESOTA vs. SAN FRANCISCO
RS: Vikings lead series, 15-13-1
PS: 49ers lead series, 3-1
1961—49ers, 38-24 (M)
49ers, 38-28 (SF)
1962—49ers, 21-7 (M)
49ers, 35-12 (M)
1963—Vikings, 24-20 (SF)
Vikings, 45-14 (M)
1964—Vikings, 27-22 (SF)
Vikings, 24-7 (M)
1965—Vikings, 42-41 (SF)

49ers, 45-24 (M)
1966—Tie, 20-20 (SF)
Vikings, 28-3 (SF)
1967—49ers, 27-21 (M)
1968—Vikings, 30-20 (SF)
1969—Vikings, 10-7 (M)
1970—*49ers, 17-14 (M)
1971—49ers, 13-9 (M)
1972—Vikings, 20-17 (SF)
1973—Vikings, 17-13 (SF)
1975—Vikings, 27-17 (M)
1976—49ers, 20-16 (SF)
1977—Vikings, 28-27 (M)
1979—Vikings, 28-22 (M)
1983—49ers, 48-17 (M)
1984—49ers, 51-7 (SF)
1985—Vikings, 28-21 (M)
1986—Vikings, 27-24 (SF) OT
1987—*Vikings, 36-24 (SF)
1988—Vikings, 24-21 (SF)
*49ers, 34-9 (SF)
1989—*49ers, 41-13 (SF)
1990—49ers, 20-17 (M)
1991—Vikings, 17-14 (M)
(RS Pts.—49ers 692, Vikings 642)
(PS Pts.—49ers 116, Vikings 72)
*NFC Divisional Playoff

MINNESOTA vs. SEATTLE
RS: Seahawks lead series, 3-2
1976—Vikings, 27-21 (M)
1978—Seahawks, 29-28 (S)
1984—Seahawks, 20-12 (M)
1987—Seahawks, 28-17 (S)
1990—Vikings, 24-21 (S)
(RS Pts.—Seahawks 119, Vikings 108)

MINNESOTA vs. TAMPA BAY
RS: Vikings lead series, 20-8
1977—Vikings, 9-3 (TB)
1978—Buccaneers, 16-10 (M)
Vikings, 24-7 (TB)
1979—Buccaneers, 12-10 (M)
Vikings, 23-22 (TB)
1980—Vikings, 38-30 (M)
Vikings, 21-10 (TB)
1981—Buccaneers, 21-13 (TB)
Vikings, 25-10 (M)
1982—Vikings, 17-10 (M)
1983—Vikings, 19-16 (TB) OT
Buccaneers, 17-12 (M)
1984—Buccaneers, 35-31 (TB)
Vikings, 27-24 (M)
1985—Vikings, 31-16 (TB)
Vikings, 26-7 (M)
1986—Vikings, 23-10 (TB)
Vikings, 45-13 (M)
1987—Buccaneers, 20-10 (TB)
Vikings, 23-17 (M)
1988—Vikings, 14-13 (M)
Vikings, 49-20 (TB)
1989—Vikings, 17-3 (M)
Vikings, 24-10 (TB)
1990—Buccaneers, 23-20 (M) OT
Buccaneers, 26-13 (TB)
1991—Vikings, 28-13 (M)
Vikings, 26-24 (TB)
(RS Pts.—Vikings 628, Buccaneers 448)

MINNESOTA vs. WASHINGTON
RS: Redskins lead series, 5-3
PS: Series tied, 2-2
1968—Vikings, 27-14 (M)
1970—Vikings, 19-10 (M)
1972—Redskins, 24-21 (M)
1973—*Vikings, 27-20 (M)
1975—Redskins, 31-30 (W)
1976—*Vikings, 35-20 (M)
1980—Vikings, 39-14 (W)
1982—**Redskins, 21-7 (W)
1984—Redskins, 31-17 (M)
1986—Redskins, 44-38 (W) OT
1987—Redskins, 27-24 (M) OT
***Redskins, 17-10 (W)
(RS Pts.—Vikings 215, Redskins 195)
(PS Pts.—Vikings 79, Redskins 78)
*NFC Divisional Playoff
**NFC Second Round Playoff
***NFC Championship

NEW ENGLAND vs. ATLANTA
RS: Series tied, 3-3;
See Atlanta vs. New England
NEW ENGLAND vs. BUFFALO
RS: Patriots lead series, 33-29-1
PS: Patriots lead series, 1-0;
See Buffalo vs. New England
NEW ENGLAND vs. CHICAGO
RS: Patriots lead series, 3-2
PS: Bears lead series, 1-0;
See Chicago vs. New England
NEW ENGLAND vs. CINCINNATI
RS: Patriots lead series, 7-6;
See Cincinnati vs. New England
NEW ENGLAND vs. CLEVELAND
RS: Browns lead series, 8-2;

See Cleveland vs. New England
NEW ENGLAND vs. DALLAS
RS: Cowboys lead series, 6-0;
See Dallas vs. New England
NEW ENGLAND vs. DENVER
RS: Broncos lead series, 16-12
PS: Broncos lead series, 1-0;
See Denver vs. New England
NEW ENGLAND vs. DETROIT
RS: Series tied, 2-2;
See Detroit vs. New England
NEW ENGLAND vs. GREEN BAY
RS: Series tied, 2-2;
See Green Bay vs. New England
NEW ENGLAND vs. HOUSTON
RS: Patriots lead series, 17-13-1
PS: Oilers lead series, 1-0;
See Houston vs. New England
NEW ENGLAND vs. INDIANAPOLIS
RS: Patriots lead series, 25-18;
See Indianapolis vs. New England
NEW ENGLAND vs. KANSAS CITY
RS: Chiefs lead series, 12-7-3;
See Kansas City vs. New England
NEW ENGLAND vs. L.A. RAIDERS
RS: Series tied, 12-12-1
PS: Series tied, 1-1;
See L.A. Raiders vs. New England
NEW ENGLAND vs. L.A. RAMS
RS: Patriots lead series, 3-2;
See L.A. Rams vs. New England
NEW ENGLAND vs. MIAMI
RS: Dolphins lead series, 30-20
PS: Series tied, 1-1;
See Miami vs. New England
NEW ENGLAND vs. MINNESOTA
RS: Patriots lead series, 3-2;
See Minnesota vs. New England
NEW ENGLAND vs. NEW ORLEANS
RS: Patriots lead series, 5-1
1972—Patriots, 17-10 (NO)
1976—Patriots, 27-6 (NE)
1980—Patriots, 38-27 (NO)
1983—Patriots, 7-0 (NE)
1986—Patriots, 21-20 (NO)
1989—Saints, 28-24 (NE)
(RS Pts.—Patriots 134, Saints 91)
***NEW ENGLAND vs. N.Y. GIANTS**
RS: Giants lead series, 3-1
1970—Giants, 16-0 (B)
1974—Patriots, 28-20 (New Haven)
1987—Giants, 17-10 (NY)
1990—Giants, 13-10 (NE)
(RS Pts.—Giants 66, Patriots 48)
*Franchise in Boston prior to 1971
***NEW ENGLAND vs. **N.Y. JETS**
RS: Jets lead series, 35-27-1
PS: Patriots lead series, 1-0
1960—Patriots, 28-24 (NY)
Patriots, 38-21 (B)
1961—Titans, 21-20 (B)
Titans, 37-30 (NY)
1962—Patriots, 43-14 (NY)
Patriots, 24-17 (B)
1963—Patriots, 38-14 (B)
Jets, 31-24 (NY)
1964—Patriots, 26-10 (B)
Jets, 35-14 (NY)
1965—Jets, 30-20 (B)
Patriots, 27-23 (NY)
1966—Tie, 24-24 (B)
Jets, 38-28 (NY)
1967—Jets, 30-23 (NY)
Jets, 29-24 (B)
1968—Jets, 47-31 (Birmingham)
Jets, 48-14 (NY)
1969—Jets, 23-14 (B)
Jets, 23-17 (NY)
1970—Jets, 31-21 (B)
Jets, 17-3 (NY)
1971—Patriots, 20-0 (NE)
Jets, 13-6 (NY)
1972—Jets, 41-13 (NE)
Jets, 34-10 (NY)
1973—Jets, 9-7 (NE)
Jets, 33-13 (NY)
1974—Patriots, 24-0 (NY)
Jets, 21-16 (NE)
1975—Jets, 36-7 (NY)
Jets, 30-28 (NE)
1976—Patriots, 41-7 (NE)
Patriots, 38-24 (NY)
1977—Jets, 30-27 (NY)
Patriots, 24-13 (NE)
1978—Patriots, 55-21 (NE)
Patriots, 19-17 (NY)
1979—Patriots, 56-3 (NE)
Jets, 27-26 (NY)
1980—Jets, 21-11 (NY)
Patriots, 34-21 (NE)
1981—Jets, 28-24 (NY)
Jets, 17-6 (NE)
1982—Jets, 31-7 (NE)

1983—Patriots, 23-13 (NE)
Jets, 26-3 (NY)
1984—Patriots, 28-21 (NY)
Patriots, 30-20 (NE)
1985—Patriots, 20-13 (NE)
Jets, 16-13 (NY) OT
***Patriots, 26-14 (NY)
1986—Patriots, 20-6 (NY)
Jets, 31-24 (NE)
1987—Jets, 43-24 (NY)
Patriots, 42-20 (NE)
1988—Patriots, 28-3 (NE)
Patriots, 14-13 (NY)
1989—Patriots, 27-24 (NY)
Jets, 27-26 (NE)
1990—Jets, 37-13 (NE)
Jets, 42-7 (NY)
1991—Jets, 28-21 (NE)
Patriots, 6-3 (NY)
(RS Pts.—Jets 1,440, Patriots 1,422)
(PS Pts.—Patriots 26, Jets 14)
*Franchise in Boston prior to 1971
**Jets known as Titans prior to 1963
***AFC First Round Playoff
NEW ENGLAND vs. PHILADELPHIA
RS: Eagles lead series, 5-2
1973—Eagles, 24-23 (P)
1977—Patriots, 14-6 (NE)
1978—Patriots, 24-14 (NE)
1981—Eagles, 13-3 (P)
1984—Eagles, 27-17 (P)
1987—Eagles, 34-31 (NE) OT
1990—Eagles, 48-20 (P)
(RS Pts.—Eagles 166, Patriots 132)
***NEW ENGLAND vs. **PHOENIX**
RS: Cardinals lead series, 6-1
1970—Cardinals, 31-0 (StL)
1975—Cardinals, 24-17 (StL)
1978—Patriots, 16-6 (StL)
1981—Cardinals, 27-20 (NE)
1984—Cardinals, 33-10 (NE)
1990—Cardinals, 34-14 (P)
1991—Cardinals, 24-10 (P)
(RS Pts.—Cardinals 179, Patriots 87)
*Franchise in Boston prior to 1971
**Franchise in St. Louis prior to 1988
NEW ENGLAND vs. PITTSBURGH
RS: Steelers lead series, 8-3
1972—Steelers, 33-3 (P)
1974—Steelers, 21-17 (NE)
1976—Patriots, 30-27 (P)
1979—Steelers, 16-13 (NE) OT
1981—Steelers, 27-21 (P) OT
1982—Steelers, 37-14 (P)
1983—Steelers, 28-23 (P)
1986—Patriots, 34-0 (P)
1989—Steelers, 28-10 (P)
1990—Steelers, 24-3 (NE)
1991—Steelers, 20-6 (P)
(RS Pts.—Steelers 256, Patriots 179)
***NEW ENGLAND vs. **SAN DIEGO**
RS: Patriots lead series, 13-11-2
PS: Chargers lead series, 1-0
1960—Patriots, 35-0 (LA)
Chargers, 45-16 (B)
1961—Chargers, 38-27 (B)
Patriots, 41-0 (SD)
1962—Patriots, 24-20 (B)
Patriots, 20-14 (SD)
1963—Chargers, 17-13 (SD)
Chargers, 7-6 (B)
***Chargers, 51-10 (SD)
1964—Chargers, 33-28 (SD)
Chargers, 26-17 (B)
1965—Tie, 10-10 (B)
Patriots, 22-6 (SD)
1966—Chargers, 24-0 (SD)
Patriots, 35-17 (B)
1967—Chargers, 28-14 (SD)
Tie, 31-31 (SD)
1968—Chargers, 27-17 (B)
1969—Chargers, 13-10 (B)
Chargers, 28-18 (SD)
1970—Chargers, 16-14 (B)
1973—Patriots, 30-14 (NE)
1975—Patriots, 33-19 (SD)
1977—Patriots, 24-20 (SD)
1978—Patriots, 28-23 (NE)
1979—Patriots, 27-21 (NE)
1983—Patriots, 37-21 (NE)
(RS Pts.—Patriots 582, Chargers 513)
(PS Pts.—Chargers 51, Patriots 10)
*Franchise in Boston prior to 1971
**Franchise in Los Angeles prior to 1961
***AFL Championship
NEW ENGLAND vs. SAN FRANCISCO
RS: 49ers lead series, 5-1
1971—49ers, 27-10 (SF)
1975—Patriots, 24-16 (NE)
1980—49ers, 21-17 (SF)
1983—49ers, 33-13 (NE)
1986—49ers, 29-24 (NE)
1989—49ers, 37-20 (SF)

(RS Pts.—49ers 163, Patriots 108)
NEW ENGLAND vs. SEATTLE
RS: Patriots lead series, 6-4
1977—Patriots, 31-0 (NE)
1980—Patriots, 37-31 (S)
1982—Patriots, 16-0 (S)
1983—Seahawks, 24-6 (S)
1984—Patriots, 38-23 (NE)
1985—Patriots, 20-13 (S)
1986—Seahawks, 38-31 (NE)
1988—Patriots, 13-7 (NE)
1989—Seahawks, 24-3 (NE)
1990—Seahawks, 33-20 (NE)
(RS Pts.—Patriots 215, Seahawks 193)
NEW ENGLAND vs. TAMPA BAY
RS: Patriots lead series, 3-0
1976—Patriots, 31-14 (TB)
1985—Patriots, 32-14 (TB)
1988—Patriots, 10-7 (NE) OT
(RS Pts.—Patriots 73, Buccaneers 35)
NEW ENGLAND vs. WASHINGTON
RS: Redskins lead series, 4-1
1972—Patriots, 24-23 (NE)
1978—Redskins, 16-14 (NE)
1981—Redskins, 24-22 (W)
1984—Redskins, 26-10 (NE)
1990—Redskins, 25-10 (NE)
(RS Pts.—Redskins 114, Patriots 80)

NEW ORLEANS vs. ATLANTA
RS: Falcons lead series, 26-19
PS: Falcons lead series, 1-0;
See Atlanta vs. New Orleans
NEW ORLEANS vs. BUFFALO
RS: Series tied, 2-2;
See Buffalo vs. New Orleans
NEW ORLEANS vs. CHICAGO
RS: Bears lead series, 8-5
PS: Bears lead series, 1-0;
See Chicago vs. New Orleans
NEW ORLEANS vs. CINCINNATI
RS: Saints lead series, 4-3
See Cincinnati vs. New Orleans
NEW ORLEANS vs. CLEVELAND
RS: Browns lead series, 8-3;
See Cleveland vs. New Orleans
NEW ORLEANS vs. DALLAS
RS: Cowboys lead series, 13-3;
See Dallas vs. New Orleans
NEW ORLEANS vs. DENVER
RS: Broncos lead series, 4-1;
See Denver vs. New Orleans
NEW ORLEANS vs. DETROIT
RS: Lions lead series, 6-5-1;
See Detroit vs. New Orleans
NEW ORLEANS vs. GREEN BAY
RS: Packers lead series, 11-4;
See Green Bay vs. New Orleans
NEW ORLEANS vs. HOUSTON
RS: Series tied, 3-3-1;
See Houston vs. New Orleans
NEW ORLEANS vs. INDIANAPOLIS
RS: Colts lead series, 3-2;
See Indianapolis vs. New Orleans
NEW ORLEANS vs. KANSAS CITY
RS: Saints lead series, 3-2;
See Kansas City vs. New Orleans
NEW ORLEANS vs. L.A. RAIDERS
RS: Raiders lead series, 3-2-1;
See L.A. Raiders vs. New Orleans
NEW ORLEANS vs. L.A. RAMS
RS: Rams lead series, 26-18;
See L.A. Rams vs. New Orleans
NEW ORLEANS vs. MIAMI
RS: Dolphins lead series, 4-1;
See Miami vs. New Orleans
NEW ORLEANS vs. MINNESOTA
RS: Vikings lead series, 11-5
PS: Vikings lead series, 1-0;
See Minnesota vs. New Orleans
NEW ORLEANS vs. NEW ENGLAND
RS: Patriots lead series, 5-1;
See New England vs. New Orleans
NEW ORLEANS vs. N.Y. GIANTS
RS: Giants lead series, 8-6
1967—Giants, 27-21 (NY)
1968—Giants, 38-21 (NY)
1969—Saints, 25-24 (NY)
1970—Saints, 14-10 (NO)
1972—Giants, 45-21 (NY)
1975—Giants, 28-14 (NY)
1978—Saints, 28-17 (NO)
1979—Saints, 24-14 (NO)
1981—Giants, 20-7 (NY)
1984—Saints, 10-3 (NY)
1985—Giants, 21-13 (NO)
1986—Giants, 20-17 (NY)
1987—Saints, 23-14 (NO)
1988—Giants, 13-12 (NY)
(RS Pts.—Giants 294, Saints 250)
NEW ORLEANS vs. N.Y. JETS
RS: Jets lead series, 4-2
1972—Jets, 18-17 (NY)

270

1977—Jets, 16-13 (NO)
1980—Saints, 21-20 (NY)
1983—Jets, 31-28 (NO)
1986—Jets, 28-23 (NY)
1989—Saints, 29-14 (NO)
(RS Pts.—Saints 131, Jets 127)
NEW ORLEANS vs. PHILADELPHIA
RS: Eagles lead series, 9-8
1967—Saints, 31-24 (NO)
     Eagles, 48-21 (P)
1968—Eagles, 29-17 (P)
1969—Eagles, 13-10 (P)
     Saints, 26-17 (NO)
1972—Saints, 21-3 (NO)
1974—Saints, 14-10 (NO)
1977—Eagles, 28-7 (P)
1978—Eagles, 24-17 (NO)
1979—Eagles, 26-14 (NO)
1980—Eagles, 34-21 (NO)
1981—Saints, 31-14 (NO)
1983—Saints, 20-17 (P) OT
1985—Saints, 23-21 (NO)
1987—Eagles, 27-17 (P)
1989—Saints, 30-20 (NO)
1991—Saints, 13-6 (P)
(RS Pts.—Eagles 378, Saints 316)
NEW ORLEANS vs. *PHOENIX
RS: Cardinals lead series, 10-7
1967—Cardinals, 31-20 (StL)
1968—Cardinals, 21-20 (NO)
     Cardinals, 31-17 (StL)
1969—Saints, 51-42 (StL)
1970—Cardinals, 24-17 (StL)
1974—Saints, 14-0 (NO)
1977—Cardinals, 49-31 (StL)
1980—Cardinals, 40-7 (NO)
1981—Cardinals, 30-3 (StL)
1982—Cardinals, 21-7 (NO)
1983—Saints, 28-17 (NO)
1984—Saints, 34-24 (NO)
1985—Cardinals, 28-16 (StL)
1986—Saints, 16-7 (StL)
1987—Cardinals, 24-19 (StL)
1990—Saints, 28-7 (NO)
1991—Saints, 27-3 (P)
(RS Pts.—Cardinals 399, Saints 355)
*Franchise in St. Louis prior to 1988
NEW ORLEANS vs. PITTSBURGH
RS: Series tied, 5-5
1967—Steelers, 14-10 (NO)
1968—Saints, 16-12 (P)
     Saints, 24-14 (NO)
1969—Saints, 27-24 (NO)
1974—Steelers, 28-7 (NO)
1978—Steelers, 20-14 (P)
1981—Steelers, 20-6 (NO)
1984—Saints, 27-24 (NO)
1987—Saints, 20-16 (P)
1990—Steelers, 9-6 (NO)
(RS Pts.—Steelers 181, Saints 157)
NEW ORLEANS vs. SAN DIEGO
RS: Chargers lead series, 4-1
1973—Chargers, 17-14 (SD)
1977—Chargers, 14-0 (NO)
1979—Chargers, 35-0 (NO)
1988—Saints, 23-17 (SD)
1991—Chargers, 24-21 (SD)
(RS Pts.—Chargers 107, Saints 58)
NEW ORLEANS vs. SAN FRANCISCO
RS: 49ers lead series, 30-13-2
1967—49ers, 27-13 (SF)
1969—Saints, 43-38 (NO)
1970—Tie, 20-20 (SF)
     49ers, 38-27 (NO)
1971—49ers, 38-20 (NO)
     Saints, 26-20 (SF)
1972—49ers, 37-2 (NO)
     Tie, 20-20 (SF)
1973—49ers, 40-0 (SF)
     Saints, 16-10 (NO)
1974—49ers, 17-13 (NO)
     49ers, 35-21 (SF)
1975—49ers, 35-21 (SF)
     49ers, 16-6 (NO)
1976—49ers, 33-3 (SF)
     49ers, 27-7 (NO)
1977—49ers, 10-7 (NO) OT
     49ers, 20-17 (SF)
1978—Saints, 14-7 (SF)
     Saints, 24-13 (NO)
1979—Saints, 30-21 (SF)
     Saints, 31-20 (NO)
1980—49ers, 26-23 (NO)
     49ers, 38-35 (SF) OT
1981—49ers, 21-14 (SF)
     49ers, 21-17 (NO)
1982—Saints, 23-20 (SF)
1983—49ers, 32-13 (NO)
     49ers, 27-0 (SF)
1984—49ers, 30-20 (SF)
     49ers, 35-3 (NO)
1985—Saints, 20-17 (SF)
     49ers, 31-19 (NO)

1986—49ers, 26-17 (SF)
     Saints, 23-10 (NO)
1987—49ers, 24-22 (NO)
     Saints, 26-24 (SF)
1988—49ers, 34-33 (NO)
     49ers, 30-17 (SF)
1989—49ers, 24-20 (NO)
     49ers, 31-13 (SF)
1990—49ers, 13-12 (NO)
     Saints, 13-10 (SF)
1991—Saints, 10-3 (NO)
     49ers, 38-24 (SF)
(RS Pts.—49ers, 1,107, Saints 798)
NEW ORLEANS vs. SEATTLE
RS: Saints lead series, 3-2
1976—Saints, 51-27 (S)
1979—Seahawks, 38-24 (S)
1985—Seahawks, 27-3 (NO)
1988—Saints, 20-19 (S)
1991—Saints, 27-24 (NO)
(RS Pts.—Seahawks 135, Saints 125)
NEW ORLEANS vs. TAMPA BAY
RS: Saints lead series, 10-4
1977—Buccaneers, 33-14 (NO)
1978—Saints, 17-10 (TB)
1979—Saints, 42-14 (TB)
1981—Buccaneers, 31-14 (NO)
1982—Buccaneers, 13-10 (NO)
1983—Saints, 24-21 (TB)
1984—Saints, 17-13 (NO)
1985—Saints, 20-13 (NO)
1986—Saints, 38-7 (NO)
1987—Saints, 44-34 (NO)
1988—Saints, 13-9 (NO)
1989—Buccaneers, 20-10 (TB)
1990—Saints, 35-7 (NO)
1991—Saints, 23-7 (NO)
(RS Pts.—Saints 321, Buccaneers 232)
NEW ORLEANS vs. WASHINGTON
RS: Redskins lead series, 11-4
1967—Saints, 30-10 (NO)
     Saints, 30-14 (W)
1968—Saints, 37-17 (NO)
1969—Redskins, 26-20 (NO)
     Redskins, 17-14 (W)
1971—Redskins, 24-14 (W)
1973—Saints, 19-3 (NO)
1975—Redskins, 41-3 (NO)
1979—Saints, 14-10 (W)
1980—Redskins, 22-14 (W)
1982—Redskins, 27-10 (NO)
1986—Redskins, 14-6 (NO)
1988—Redskins, 27-24 (NO)
1989—Redskins, 16-14 (NO)
1990—Redskins, 31-17 (W)
(RS Pts.—Redskins 319, Saints 246)

N.Y. GIANTS vs. ATLANTA
RS: Series tied, 6-6;
See Atlanta vs. N.Y. Giants
N.Y. GIANTS vs. BUFFALO
RS: Bills lead series, 3-2
PS: Giants lead series, 1-0;
See Buffalo vs. N.Y. Giants
N.Y. GIANTS vs. CHICAGO
RS: Bears lead series, 24-14-2
PS: Bears lead series, 5-3;
See Chicago vs. N.Y. Giants
N.Y. GIANTS vs. CINCINNATI
RS: Bengals lead series, 4-0;
See Cincinnati vs. N.Y. Giants
N.Y. GIANTS vs. CLEVELAND
RS: Browns lead series, 25-16-2
PS: Series tied, 1-1;
See Cleveland vs. N.Y. Giants
N.Y. GIANTS vs. DALLAS
RS: Cowboys lead series, 36-21-2;
See Dallas vs. N.Y. Giants
N.Y. GIANTS vs. DENVER
RS: Giants lead series, 3-2
PS: Giants lead series, 1-0;
See Denver vs. N.Y. Giants
N.Y. GIANTS vs. DETROIT
RS: Lions lead series, 17-15-1
PS: Lions lead series, 1-0;
See Detroit vs. N.Y. Giants
N.Y. GIANTS vs. GREEN BAY
RS: Packers lead series, 21-19-2
PS: Packers lead series, 4-1;
See Green Bay vs. N.Y. Giants
N.Y. GIANTS vs. HOUSTON
RS: Giants lead series, 4-0;
See Houston vs. N.Y. Giants
N.Y. GIANTS vs. INDIANAPOLIS
RS: Colts lead series, 5-4
PS: Colts lead series, 2-0;
See Indianapolis vs. N.Y. Giants
N.Y. GIANTS vs. KANSAS CITY
RS: Giants lead series, 5-1;
See Kansas City vs. N.Y. Giants
N.Y. GIANTS vs. L.A. RAIDERS
RS: Raiders lead series, 3-2;
See L.A. Raiders vs. N.Y. Giants

N.Y. GIANTS vs. L.A. RAMS
RS: Rams lead series, 19-8
PS: Series tied, 1-1;
See L.A. Rams vs. N.Y. Giants
N.Y. GIANTS vs. MIAMI
RS: Series tied, 1-1;
See Miami vs. N.Y. Giants
N.Y. GIANTS vs. MINNESOTA
RS: Vikings lead series, 6-4;
See Minnesota vs. N.Y. Giants
N.Y. GIANTS vs. NEW ENGLAND
RS: Giants lead series, 3-1;
See New England vs. N.Y. Giants
N.Y. GIANTS vs. NEW ORLEANS
RS: Giants lead series, 8-6;
See New Orleans vs. N.Y. Giants
N.Y. GIANTS vs. N.Y. JETS
RS: Series tied, 3-3
1970—Giants, 22-10 (NYJ)
1974—Jets, 26-20 (New Haven) OT
1981—Jets, 26-7 (NYG)
1984—Giants, 20-10 (NYJ)
1987—Giants, 20-7 (NYG)
1988—Jets, 27-21 (NYJ)
(RS Pts.—Giants 110, Jets 106)
N.Y. GIANTS vs. PHILADELPHIA
RS: Giants lead series, 60-52-2
PS: Giants lead series, 1-0
1933—Giants, 56-0 (NY)
     Giants, 20-14 (P)
1934—Giants, 17-0 (NY)
     Eagles, 6-0 (P)
1935—Giants, 10-0 (NY)
     Giants, 21-14 (P)
1936—Eagles, 10-7 (P)
     Giants, 21-17 (NY)
1937—Giants, 16-7 (P)
     Giants, 21-0 (NY)
1938—Eagles, 14-10 (P)
     Giants, 17-7 (NY)
1939—Giants, 13-3 (P)
     Giants, 27-10 (NY)
1940—Giants, 20-14 (P)
     Giants, 17-7 (NY)
1941—Giants, 24-0 (P)
     Giants, 16-0 (NY)
1942—Giants, 35-17 (P)
     Giants, 14-0 (P)
1944—Eagles, 24-17 (NY)
     Tie, 21-21 (P)
1945—Eagles, 38-17 (P)
     Giants, 28-21 (NY)
1946—Eagles, 24-14 (P)
     Giants, 45-17 (NY)
1947—Eagles, 23-0 (P)
     Eagles, 41-24 (NY)
1948—Eagles, 45-0 (P)
     Eagles, 35-14 (NY)
1949—Eagles, 24-3 (NY)
     Eagles, 17-3 (P)
1950—Giants, 7-3 (NY)
     Giants, 9-7 (P)
1951—Giants, 26-24 (NY)
     Giants, 23-7 (P)
1952—Giants, 31-7 (P)
     Eagles, 14-10 (NY)
1953—Eagles, 30-7 (P)
     Giants, 37-28 (NY)
1954—Giants, 27-14 (NY)
     Eagles, 29-14 (P)
1955—Eagles, 27-17 (P)
     Giants, 31-7 (NY)
1956—Giants, 20-3 (NY)
     Giants, 21-7 (P)
1957—Giants, 24-20 (P)
     Giants, 13-0 (NY)
1958—Eagles, 27-24 (P)
     Giants, 24-10 (NY)
1959—Eagles, 49-21 (P)
     Giants, 24-7 (NY)
1960—Eagles, 17-10 (NY)
     Eagles, 31-23 (P)
1961—Eagles, 38-21 (P)
     Giants, 28-24 (P)
1962—Giants, 29-13 (P)
     Giants, 19-14 (NY)
1963—Giants, 37-14 (P)
     Giants, 42-14 (NY)
1964—Eagles, 38-7 (P)
     Eagles, 23-17 (NY)
1965—Giants, 16-14 (P)
     Giants, 35-27 (NY)
1966—Eagles, 35-17 (P)
     Eagles, 31-3 (NY)
1967—Giants, 44-7 (NY)
1968—Giants, 34-25 (P)
     Giants, 7-6 (NY)
1969—Eagles, 23-20 (NY)
1970—Giants, 30-23 (NY)
     Giants, 23-20 (P)
1971—Eagles, 23-7 (P)
     Eagles, 41-28 (NY)
1972—Giants, 27-12 (P)

     Giants, 62-10 (NY)
1973—Tie, 23-23 (NY)
     Eagles, 20-16 (P)
1974—Eagles, 35-7 (P)
     Eagles, 20-7 (New Haven)
1975—Giants, 23-14 (P)
     Eagles, 13-10 (NY)
1976—Eagles, 20-7 (P)
     Eagles, 10-0 (NY)
1977—Eagles, 28-10 (NY)
     Eagles, 17-14 (P)
1978—Eagles, 19-17 (NY)
     Eagles, 20-3 (P)
1979—Eagles, 23-17 (P)
     Eagles, 17-13 (NY)
1980—Eagles, 35-3 (P)
     Eagles, 31-16 (NY)
1981—Eagles, 24-10 (NY)
     Giants, 20-10 (P)
     *Giants, 27-21 (P)
1982—Giants, 23-7 (NY)
     Giants, 26-24 (P)
1983—Eagles, 17-13 (NY)
     Giants, 23-0 (P)
1984—Giants, 28-27 (NY)
     Eagles, 24-10 (P)
1985—Giants, 21-0 (NY)
     Giants, 16-10 (P) OT
1986—Giants, 35-3 (P)
     Giants, 17-14 (P)
1987—Giants, 20-17 (P)
     Giants, 23-20 (NY) OT
1988—Eagles, 24-13 (P)
     Eagles, 23-17 (NY) OT
1989—Eagles, 21-19 (P)
     Giants, 24-17 (NY)
1990—Giants, 27-20 (NY)
     Eagles, 31-13 (P)
1991—Eagles, 30-7 (P)
     Eagles, 19-14 (NY)
(RS Pts.—Giants 2,176, Eagles 2,033)
(PS Pts.—Giants 27, Eagles 21)
*NFC First Round Playoff
N.Y. GIANTS vs. *PHOENIX
RS: Giants lead series, 63-33-2
1926—Giants, 20-0 (NY)
1927—Giants, 28-7 (NY)
1929—Giants, 24-21 (NY)
1930—Giants, 25-12 (NY)
     Giants, 13-7 (C)
1935—Cardinals, 14-13 (NY)
1936—Giants, 14-6 (NY)
1938—Giants, 6-0 (NY)
1939—Giants, 17-7 (NY)
1941—Cardinals, 10-7 (NY)
1942—Giants, 21-7 (NY)
1943—Giants, 24-13 (NY)
1946—Giants, 28-24 (NY)
1947—Giants, 35-31 (NY)
1948—Cardinals, 63-35 (NY)
1949—Giants, 41-38 (C)
1950—Cardinals, 17-3 (C)
     Giants, 51-21 (NY)
1951—Giants, 28-17 (NY)
     Giants, 10-0 (C)
1952—Cardinals, 24-23 (NY)
     Giants, 28-6 (C)
1953—Giants, 21-7 (NY)
     Giants, 23-20 (C)
1954—Giants, 41-10 (C)
     Giants, 31-17 (NY)
1955—Cardinals, 28-17 (C)
     Giants, 10-0 (NY)
1956—Cardinals, 35-27 (C)
     Giants, 23-10 (NY)
1957—Giants, 27-14 (NY)
     Giants, 28-21 (C)
1958—Giants, 37-7 (Buffalo)
     Cardinals, 23-6 (NY)
1959—Giants, 9-3 (NY)
     Giants, 30-20 (Minn)
1960—Giants, 35-14 (StL)
     Cardinals, 20-13 (NY)
1961—Cardinals, 21-10 (NY)
     Giants, 24-9 (StL)
1962—Giants, 31-14 (StL)
     Giants, 31-28 (NY)
1963—Giants, 38-21 (StL)
     Cardinals, 24-17 (NY)
1964—Giants, 34-17 (NY)
     Tie, 10-10 (StL)
1965—Giants, 14-10 (NY)
     Giants, 28-15 (StL)
1966—Cardinals, 24-19 (StL)
     Cardinals, 20-17 (NY)
1967—Giants, 37-20 (StL)
     Giants, 37-14 (NY)
1968—Cardinals, 28-21 (NY)
1969—Cardinals, 42-17 (StL)
     Giants, 49-6 (NY)
1970—Giants, 35-17 (NY)
     Giants, 34-17 (StL)
1971—Giants, 21-20 (StL)

Cardinals, 24-7 (NY)
1972—Giants, 27-21 (NY)
Giants, 13-7 (StL)
1973—Cardinals, 35-27 (StL)
Giants, 24-13 (New Haven)
1974—Cardinals, 23-21 (New Haven)
Cardinals, 26-14 (StL)
1975—Cardinals, 26-14 (StL)
Cardinals, 20-13 (NY)
1976—Cardinals, 27-21 (StL)
Cardinals, 17-14 (NY)
1977—Cardinals, 28-0 (StL)
Giants, 27-7 (NY)
1978—Cardinals, 20-10 (StL)
Giants, 17-0 (NY)
1979—Cardinals, 27-14 (NY)
Cardinals, 29-20 (StL)
1980—Giants, 41-35 (StL)
Cardinals, 23-7 (NY)
1981—Giants, 34-14 (NY)
Giants, 20-10 (StL)
1982—Cardinals, 24-21 (StL)
1983—Tie, 20-20 (StL) OT
Cardinals, 10-6 (NY)
1984—Giants, 16-10 (NY)
Cardinals, 31-21 (StL)
1985—Giants, 27-17 (NY)
Giants, 34-3 (StL)
1986—Giants, 13-6 (StL)
Giants, 27-7 (NY)
1987—Giants, 30-7 (NY)
Cardinals, 27-24 (StL)
1988—Cardinals, 24-17 (P)
Giants, 44-7 (NY)
1989—Giants, 35-7 (NY)
Giants, 20-13 (P)
1990—Giants, 20-19 (NY)
Giants, 24-21 (P)
1991—Giants, 20-9 (NY)
Giants, 21-14 (P)
(RS Pts.—Giants 2,221, Cardinals 1,679)
*Franchise in St. Louis prior to 1988
and in Chicago prior to 1960

N.Y. GIANTS vs. *PITTSBURGH
RS: Giants lead series, 42-26-3
1933—Giants, 23-2 (P)
Giants, 27-3 (NY)
1934—Giants, 14-12 (P)
Giants, 17-7 (NY)
1935—Giants, 42-7 (P)
Giants, 13-0 (NY)
1936—Pirates, 10-7 (P)
1937—Giants, 10-7 (P)
Giants, 17-0 (NY)
1938—Giants, 27-14 (P)
Pirates, 13-10 (NY)
1939—Giants, 14-7 (P)
Giants, 23-7 (NY)
1940—Tie, 10-10 (P)
Giants, 12-0 (NY)
1941—Giants, 37-10 (P)
Giants, 28-7 (NY)
1942—Steelers, 13-10 (P)
Steelers, 17-9 (NY)
1945—Giants, 34-6 (P)
Steelers, 21-7 (NY)
1946—Giants, 17-14 (P)
Giants, 7-0 (NY)
1947—Steelers, 38-21 (NY)
Steelers, 24-7 (P)
1948—Giants, 34-27 (NY)
Steelers, 38-28 (P)
1949—Steelers, 28-7 (P)
Steelers, 21-17 (NY)
1950—Giants, 18-7 (P)
Steelers, 17-6 (NY)
1951—Tie, 13-13 (P)
Giants, 14-0 (NY)
1952—Steelers, 63-7 (P)
1953—Steelers, 24-14 (P)
Steelers, 14-10 (NY)
1954—Giants, 30-6 (P)
Giants, 24-3 (NY)
1955—Steelers, 30-23 (P)
1956—Steelers, 19-17 (NY)
Giants, 38-10 (NY)
Giants, 17-14 (P)
1957—Giants, 35-0 (NY)
Steelers, 21-10 (P)
1958—Giants, 17-6 (NY)
Steelers, 31-10 (P)
1959—Giants, 21-16 (P)
Steelers, 14-9 (NY)
1960—Giants, 19-17 (P)
Giants, 27-24 (NY)
1961—Giants, 17-14 (P)
Giants, 42-21 (NY)
1962—Giants, 31-27 (P)
Steelers, 20-17 (NY)
1963—Giants, 31-0 (NY)
Giants, 33-17 (NY)
1964—Steelers, 27-24 (P)
Steelers, 44-17 (NY)

1965—Giants, 23-13 (P)
Giants, 35-10 (NY)
1966—Tie, 34-34 (P)
Steelers, 47-28 (NY)
1967—Giants, 27-24 (P)
Giants, 28-20 (NY)
1968—Giants, 34-20 (NY)
1969—Giants, 10-7 (NY)
Giants, 21-17 (P)
1971—Steelers, 17-13 (P)
1976—Steelers, 27-0 (NY)
1985—Giants, 28-10 (NY)
1991—Giants, 23-20 (P)
(RS Pts.—Giants 1,393, Steelers 1,179)
*Steelers known as Pirates prior to 1941

N.Y. GIANTS vs. SAN DIEGO
RS: Giants lead series, 4-2
1971—Giants, 35-17 (NY)
1975—Giants, 35-24 (NY)
1980—Chargers, 44-7 (SD)
1983—Chargers, 41-34 (NY)
1986—Giants, 20-7 (NY)
1989—Giants, 20-13 (SD)
(RS Pts.—Giants 151, Chargers 146)

N.Y. GIANTS vs. SAN FRANCISCO
RS: Giants lead series, 11-9
PS: Giants lead series, 3-2
1952—Giants, 23-14 (NY)
1956—Giants, 38-21 (SF)
1957—49ers, 27-17 (NY)
1960—Giants, 21-19 (SF)
1963—Giants, 48-14 (NY)
1968—49ers, 26-10 (NY)
1972—Giants, 23-17 (SF)
1975—Giants, 26-23 (NY)
1977—Giants, 20-17 (NY)
1978—Giants, 27-10 (NY)
1979—Giants, 32-16 (NY)
1980—49ers, 12-0 (SF)
1981—49ers, 17-10 (SF)
*49ers, 38-24 (SF)
1984—49ers, 31-10 (NY)
*49ers, 21-10 (SF)
1985—**Giants, 17-3 (NY)
1986—Giants, 21-17 (NY)
*Giants, 49-3 (NY)
1987—49ers, 41-21 (NY)
1988—49ers, 20-17 (NY)
1989—49ers, 34-24 (SF)
1990—49ers, 7-3 (SF)
***Giants, 15-13 (SF)
1991—Giants, 16-14 (NY)
(RS Pts.—Giants 407, 49ers 400)
(PS Pts.—Giants 115, 49ers 75)
*NFC Divisional Playoff
**NFC First Round Playoff
***NFC Championship

N.Y. GIANTS vs. SEATTLE
RS: Giants lead series, 4-2
1976—Giants, 28-16 (NY)
1980—Giants, 27-21 (S)
1981—Giants, 32-0 (S)
1983—Seahawks, 17-12 (NY)
1986—Seahawks, 17-12 (S)
1989—Giants, 15-3 (NY)
(RS Pts.—Giants 126, Seahawks 74)

N.Y. GIANTS vs. TAMPA BAY
RS: Giants lead series, 7-3
1977—Giants, 10-0 (TB)
1978—Giants, 19-13 (TB)
Giants, 17-14 (NY)
1979—Giants, 17-14 (NY)
Buccaneers, 31-3 (TB)
1980—Buccaneers, 30-13 (TB)
1984—Giants, 17-14 (NY)
Buccaneers, 20-17 (TB)
1985—Giants, 22-20 (NY)
1991—Giants, 21-14 (TB)
(RS Pts.—Buccaneers 170, Giants 156)

N.Y. GIANTS vs. *WASHINGTON
RS: Giants lead series, 66-49-3
PS: Series tied, 1-1
1932—Braves, 14-6 (B)
Tie, 0-0 (NY)
1933—Redskins, 21-20 (B)
Giants, 7-0 (NY)
1934—Giants, 16-13 (B)
Giants, 3-0 (NY)
1935—Giants, 20-12 (B)
Giants, 17-6 (NY)
1936—Giants, 7-0 (B)
Redskins, 14-0 (NY)
1937—Redskins, 13-3 (W)
Redskins, 49-14 (NY)
1938—Giants, 10-7 (W)
Giants, 36-0 (NY)
1939—Tie, 0-0 (NY)
Giants, 9-7 (NY)
1940—Redskins, 21-7 (W)
Giants, 21-7 (NY)
1941—Giants, 17-10 (W)
Giants, 20-13 (NY)
1942—Giants, 14-7 (W)

1943—Redskins, 14-7 (NY)
Giants, 14-10 (NY)
Giants, 31-7 (W)
**Redskins, 28-0 (NY)
1944—Giants, 16-13 (NY)
Giants, 31-0 (W)
1945—Redskins, 24-14 (NY)
Redskins, 17-0 (NY)
1946—Redskins, 24-14 (W)
Giants, 31-0 (NY)
1947—Redskins, 28-20 (W)
Giants, 35-10 (NY)
1948—Redskins, 41-10 (W)
Redskins, 28-21 (NY)
1949—Giants, 45-35 (W)
Giants, 23-7 (NY)
1950—Giants, 21-17 (W)
Giants, 24-21 (NY)
1951—Giants, 35-14 (W)
Giants, 28-14 (NY)
1952—Giants, 14-10 (W)
Redskins, 27-17 (NY)
1953—Redskins, 13-9 (W)
Redskins, 24-21 (NY)
1954—Giants, 51-21 (W)
Giants, 24-7 (NY)
1955—Giants, 35-7 (NY)
Giants, 27-20 (W)
1956—Redskins, 33-7 (W)
Giants, 28-14 (NY)
1957—Giants, 24-20 (W)
Redskins, 31-14 (NY)
1958—Giants, 21-14 (W)
Giants, 30-0 (NY)
1959—Giants, 45-14 (NY)
Giants, 24-10 (W)
1960—Tie, 24-24 (NY)
Giants, 17-3 (W)
1961—Giants, 24-21 (W)
Giants, 53-0 (NY)
1962—Giants, 49-34 (NY)
Giants, 42-24 (W)
1963—Giants, 24-14 (W)
Giants, 44-14 (NY)
1964—Giants, 13-10 (NY)
Redskins, 36-21 (W)
1965—Redskins, 23-7 (NY)
Giants, 27-10 (W)
1966—Giants, 13-10 (NY)
Redskins, 72-41 (W)
1967—Redskins, 38-34 (W)
1968—Giants, 48-21 (NY)
Giants, 13-10 (W)
1969—Redskins, 20-14 (W)
1970—Giants, 35-33 (NY)
Giants, 27-24 (W)
1971—Redskins, 30-3 (NY)
Redskins, 23-7 (W)
1972—Redskins, 23-16 (NY)
Redskins, 27-13 (W)
1973—Redskins, 21-3 (New Haven)
Redskins, 27-24 (W)
1974—Redskins, 13-10 (New Haven)
Redskins, 24-3 (W)
1975—Redskins, 49-13 (W)
Redskins, 21-13 (NY)
1976—Redskins, 19-17 (W)
Giants, 12-9 (NY)
1977—Giants, 20-17 (NY)
Giants, 17-6 (W)
1978—Giants, 17-6 (W)
Redskins, 16-13 (W) OT
1979—Redskins, 27-0 (NY)
Giants, 14-6 (W)
1980—Redskins, 23-21 (NY)
Redskins, 16-13 (W)
1981—Giants, 17-7 (W)
Redskins, 30-27 (NY) OT
1982—Redskins, 27-17 (NY)
Redskins, 15-14 (W)
1983—Redskins, 33-17 (NY)
Redskins, 31-22 (W)
1984—Redskins, 30-14 (W)
Giants, 37-13 (W)
1985—Giants, 17-3 (NY)
Redskins, 23-21 (W)
1986—Giants, 27-20 (NY)
Giants, 24-14 (W)
***Giants, 17-0 (NY)
1987—Redskins, 38-12 (NY)
Redskins, 23-19 (W)
1988—Giants, 27-20 (NY)
Giants, 24-23 (W)
1989—Giants, 27-24 (W)
Giants, 20-17 (NY)
1990—Giants, 24-20 (W)
Giants, 21-10 (NY)
1991—Redskins, 17-13 (NY)
Redskins, 34-17 (W)
(RS Pts.—Giants 2,335, Redskins 2,119)
(PS Pts.—Redskins 28, Giants 17)
*Franchise in Boston prior to 1937 and
known as Braves prior to 1933

**Division Playoff
***NFC Championship

N.Y. JETS vs. ATLANTA
RS: Jets lead series, 3-2;
See Atlanta vs. N.Y. Jets
N.Y. JETS vs. BUFFALO
RS: Bills lead series, 34-28
PS: Bills lead series, 1-0;
See Buffalo vs. N.Y. Jets
N.Y. JETS vs. CHICAGO
RS: Bears lead series, 3-1;
See Chicago vs. N.Y. Jets
N.Y. JETS vs. CINCINNATI
RS: Jets lead series, 7-6
PS: Jets lead series, 1-0;
See Cincinnati vs. N.Y. Jets
N.Y. JETS vs. CLEVELAND
RS: Browns lead series, 8-6
PS: Browns lead series, 1-0;
See Cleveland vs. N.Y. Jets
N.Y. JETS vs. DALLAS
RS: Cowboys lead series, 4-1;
See Dallas vs. N.Y. Jets
N.Y. JETS vs. DENVER
RS: Jets lead series, 11-10-1;
See Denver vs. N.Y. Jets
N.Y. JETS vs. DETROIT
RS: Series tied, 3-3;
See Detroit vs. N.Y. Jets
N.Y. JETS vs. GREEN BAY
RS: Jets lead series, 5-1;
See Green Bay vs. N.Y. Jets
N.Y. JETS vs. HOUSTON
RS: Oilers lead series, 16-12-1
PS: Oilers lead series, 1-0;
See Houston vs. N.Y. Jets
N.Y. JETS vs. INDIANAPOLIS
RS: Colts lead series, 24-19
PS: Jets lead series, 1-0;
See Indianapolis vs. N.Y. Jets
N.Y. JETS vs. KANSAS CITY
RS: Chiefs lead series, 13-12-1
PS: Series tied, 1-1;
See Kansas City vs. N.Y. Jets
N.Y. JETS vs. L.A. RAIDERS
RS: Raiders lead series, 13-9-2
PS: Jets lead series, 2-0;
See L.A. Raiders vs. N.Y. Jets
N.Y. JETS vs. L.A. RAMS
RS: Rams lead series, 4-2;
See L.A. Rams vs. N.Y. Jets
N.Y. JETS vs. MIAMI
RS: Dolphins lead series, 26-25-1
PS: Dolphins lead series, 1-0;
See Miami vs. N.Y. Jets
N.Y. JETS vs. MINNESOTA
RS: Jets lead series, 3-1;
See Minnesota vs. N.Y. Jets
N.Y. JETS vs. NEW ENGLAND
RS: Jets lead series, 35-27-1
PS: Patriots lead series, 1-0;
See New England vs. N.Y. Jets
N.Y. JETS vs. NEW ORLEANS
RS: Jets lead series, 4-2;
See New Orleans vs. N.Y. Jets
N.Y. JETS vs. N.Y. GIANTS
RS: Series tied, 3-3;
See N.Y. Giants vs. N.Y. Jets
N.Y. JETS vs. PHILADELPHIA
RS: Eagles lead series, 4-0
1973—Eagles, 24-23 (NY)
1977—Eagles, 27-0 (P)
1978—Eagles, 17-9 (P)
1987—Eagles, 38-27 (NY)
(RS Pts.—Eagles 106, Jets 59)
N.Y. JETS vs. *PHOENIX
RS: Cardinals lead series, 2-1
1971—Cardinals, 17-10 (StL)
1975—Cardinals 37-6 (NY)
1978—Jets, 23-10 (NY)
(RS Pts.—Cardinals 64, Jets 39)
*Franchise in St. Louis prior to 1988
N.Y. JETS vs. PITTSBURGH
RS: Steelers lead series, 11-1
1970—Steelers, 21-17 (P)
1973—Steelers, 26-14 (P)
1975—Steelers, 20-7 (NY)
1977—Steelers, 23-20 (NY)
1978—Steelers, 28-17 (NY)
1981—Steelers, 38-10 (P)
1983—Steelers, 34-7 (NY)
1984—Steelers, 23-17 (NY)
1986—Steelers, 45-24 (NY)
1988—Jets, 24-20 (NY)
1989—Steelers, 13-0 (NY)
1990—Steelers, 24-7 (NY)
(RS Pts.—Steelers 315, Jets 164)

N.Y. JETS vs. **SAN DIEGO
RS: Chargers lead series, 16-9-1
1960—Chargers, 21-7 (NY)
Chargers, 50-43 (LA)
1961—Chargers, 25-10 (NY)

Chargers, 48-13 (SD)
1962—Chargers, 40-14 (SD)
Titans, 23-3 (NY)
1963—Chargers, 24-20 (SD)
Chargers, 53-7 (NY)
1964—Tie, 17-17 (NY)
Chargers, 38-3 (SD)
1965—Chargers, 34-9 (NY)
Chargers, 38-7 (SD)
1966—Jets, 17-16 (NY)
Chargers, 42-27 (SD)
1967—Jets, 42-31 (NY)
1968—Jets, 23-20 (NY)
Jets, 37-15 (SD)
1969—Chargers, 34-27 (SD)
1971—Chargers, 49-21 (SD)
1974—Jets, 27-14 (NY)
1975—Chargers, 24-16 (SD)
1983—Jets, 41-29 (SD)
1989—Jets, 20-17 (SD)
1990—Chargers, 39-3 (NY)
Chargers, 38-17 (SD)
1991—Jets, 24-3 (NY)
(RS Pts.—Chargers 762, Jets 515)
*Jets known as Titans prior to 1963
**Franchise in Los Angeles prior to 1961

N.Y. JETS vs. SAN FRANCISCO
RS: 49ers lead series, 5-1
1971—49ers, 24-21 (NY)
1976—49ers, 17-6 (SF)
1980—49ers, 37-27 (NY)
1983—Jets, 27-13 (SF)
1986—49ers, 24-10 (SF)
1989—49ers, 23-10 (NY)
(RS Pts.—49ers 138, Jets 101)

N.Y. JETS vs. SEATTLE
RS: Seahawks lead series, 8-3
1977—Seahawks, 17-0 (NY)
1978—Seahawks, 24-17 (NY)
1979—Seahawks, 30-7 (S)
1980—Seahawks, 27-17 (NY)
1981—Seahawks, 19-3 (NY)
Seahawks, 27-23 (S)
1983—Seahawks, 17-10 (NY)
1985—Jets, 17-14 (NY)
1986—Jets, 38-7 (S)
1987—Jets, 30-14 (NY)
1991—Seahawks, 20-13 (S)
(RS Pts.—Seahawks 216, Jets 175)

N.Y. JETS vs. TAMPA BAY
RS: Jets lead series, 5-1
1976—Jets, 34-0 (NY)
1982—Jets, 32-17 (NY)
1984—Buccaneers, 41-21 (TB)
1985—Jets, 62-28 (NY)
1990—Jets, 16-14 (TB)
1991—Jets, 16-13 (NY)
(RS Pts.—Jets 181, Buccaneers 113)

N.Y. JETS vs. WASHINGTON
RS: Redskins lead series, 4-0
1972—Redskins, 35-17 (NY)
1976—Redskins, 37-16 (NY)
1978—Redskins, 23-3 (W)
1987—Redskins, 17-16 (W)
(RS Pts.—Redskins 112, Jets 52)

PHILADELPHIA vs. ATLANTA
RS: Eagles lead series, 8-6-1
PS: Falcons lead series, 1-0;
See Atlanta vs. Philadelphia

PHILADELPHIA vs. BUFFALO
RS: Eagles lead series, 4-2;
See Buffalo vs. Philadelphia

PHILADELPHIA vs. CHICAGO
RS: Bears lead series, 22-3-1
PS: Series tied, 1-1;
See Chicago vs. Philadelphia

PHILADELPHIA vs. CINCINNATI
RS: Bengals lead series, 5-1;
See Cincinnati vs. Philadelphia

PHILADELPHIA vs. CLEVELAND
RS: Browns lead series, 30-12-1;
See Cleveland vs. Philadelphia

PHILADELPHIA vs. DALLAS
RS: Cowboys lead series, 37-25
PS: Eagles lead series, 1-0;
See Dallas vs. Philadelphia

PHILADELPHIA vs. DENVER
RS: Eagles lead series, 4-2;
See Denver vs. Philadelphia

PHILADELPHIA vs. DETROIT
RS: Lions lead series, 12-9-2;
See Detroit vs. Philadelphia

PHILADELPHIA vs. GREEN BAY
RS: Packers lead series, 18-6
PS: Eagles lead series, 1-0;
See Green Bay vs. Philadelphia

PHILADELPHIA vs. HOUSTON
RS: Eagles lead series, 5-0;
See Houston vs. Philadelphia

PHILADELPHIA vs. INDIANAPOLIS
RS: Colts lead series, 6-5;
See Indianapolis vs. Philadelphia

PHILADELPHIA vs. KANSAS CITY
RS: Eagles lead series, 1-0;
See Kansas City vs. Philadelphia

PHILADELPHIA vs. L.A. RAIDERS
RS: Eagles lead series, 3-2
PS: Raiders lead series, 1-0;
See L.A. Raiders vs. Philadelphia

PHILADELPHIA vs. L.A. RAMS
RS: Rams lead series, 15-11-1
PS: Series tied, 1-1;
See L.A. Rams vs. Philadelphia

PHILADELPHIA vs. MIAMI
RS: Dolphins lead series, 5-2;
See Miami vs. Philadelphia

PHILADELPHIA vs. MINNESOTA
RS: Vikings lead series, 10-5
PS: Eagles lead series, 1-0;
See Minnesota vs. Philadelphia

PHILADELPHIA vs. NEW ENGLAND
RS: Eagles lead series, 5-2;
See New England vs. Philadelphia

PHILADELPHIA vs. NEW ORLEANS
RS: Eagles lead series, 9-8;
See New Orleans vs. Philadelphia

PHILADELPHIA vs. N.Y. GIANTS
RS: Giants lead series, 60-52-2
PS: Giants lead series, 1-0;
See N.Y. Giants vs. Philadelphia

PHILADELPHIA vs. N.Y. JETS
RS: Eagles lead series, 4-0;
See N.Y. Jets vs. Philadelphia

PHILADELPHIA vs. *PHOENIX
RS: Cardinals lead series, 43-40-5
PS: Series tied, 1-1
1935—Cardinals, 12-3 (C)
1936—Cardinals, 13-0 (C)
1937—Tie, 6-6 (P)
1938—Eagles, 7-0 (Erie, Pa.)
1941—Eagles, 21-14 (P)
1945—Eagles, 21-6 (P)
1947—Cardinals, 45-21 (P)
**Cardinals, 28-21 (C)
1948—Cardinals, 21-14 (C)
**Eagles, 7-0 (P)
1949—Eagles, 28-3 (P)
1950—Eagles, 45-7 (C)
Cardinals, 14-10 (P)
1951—Eagles, 17-14 (C)
1952—Eagles, 10-7 (P)
Cardinals, 28-22 (P)
1953—Eagles, 56-17 (C)
Eagles, 38-0 (P)
1954—Eagles, 35-16 (C)
Eagles, 30-14 (P)
1955—Tie, 24-24 (C)
Eagles, 27-3 (P)
1956—Cardinals, 20-6 (P)
Cardinals, 28-17 (C)
1957—Eagles, 38-21 (C)
Cardinals, 31-27 (P)
1958—Tie, 21-21 (C)
Eagles, 49-21 (P)
1959—Eagles, 28-24 (Minn)
Eagles, 27-17 (P)
1960—Eagles, 31-27 (P)
Eagles, 20-6 (StL)
1961—Cardinals, 30-27 (P)
Eagles, 20-7 (StL)
1962—Cardinals, 27-21 (P)
Cardinals, 45-35 (StL)
1963—Cardinals, 28-24 (P)
Cardinals, 38-14 (StL)
1964—Eagles, 38-13 (P)
Cardinals, 36-34 (StL)
1965—Eagles, 34-27 (P)
Eagles, 28-24 (StL)
1966—Cardinals, 16-13 (P)
Cardinals, 41-10 (P)
1967—Cardinals, 48-14 (StL)
1968—Cardinals, 45-17 (P)
1969—Eagles, 34-30 (StL)
1970—Cardinals, 35-20 (P)
Cardinals, 23-14 (StL)
1971—Eagles, 37-20 (StL)
Eagles, 19-7 (P)
1972—Tie, 6-6 (P)
Cardinals, 24-23 (StL)
1973—Cardinals, 34-23 (P)
Eagles, 27-24 (StL)
1974—Cardinals, 7-3 (StL)
Cardinals, 13-3 (P)
1975—Cardinals, 31-20 (StL)
Cardinals, 24-23 (P)
1976—Cardinals, 33-14 (StL)
Cardinals, 17-14 (P)
1977—Cardinals, 21-17 (P)
Cardinals, 21-16 (StL)
1978—Cardinals, 16-10 (P)
Eagles, 14-10 (StL)
1979—Eagles, 24-20 (StL)
Eagles, 16-13 (P)
1980—Cardinals, 24-14 (StL)
Eagles, 17-3 (P)
1981—Eagles, 52-10 (StL)
Eagles, 38-0 (P)
1982—Cardinals, 23-20 (P)
1983—Cardinals, 14-11 (P)
Cardinals, 31-7 (StL)
1984—Cardinals, 34-14 (P)
Cardinals, 17-16 (StL)
1985—Cardinals, 30-7 (P)
Eagles, 24-14 (StL)
1986—Cardinals, 13-10 (StL)
Tie, 10-10 (P) OT
1987—Cardinals, 28-23 (StL)
Cardinals, 31-19 (P)
1988—Cardinals, 31-21 (P)
Eagles, 23-17 (Phx)
1989—Eagles, 17-5 (Phx)
Eagles, 31-14 (P)
1990—Cardinals, 23-21 (P)
Eagles, 23-21 (Phx)
1991—Cardinals, 26-10 (P)
Eagles, 34-14 (Phx)
(RS Pts.—Eagles 1,908, Cardinals 1,782)
*Franchise in St. Louis prior to 1988
and in Chicago prior to 1960
**NFL Championship

PHILADELPHIA vs. *PITTSBURGH
RS: Eagles lead series, 43-25-3
PS: Eagles lead series, 1-0
1933—Eagles, 25-6 (Phila)
1934—Eagles, 17-0 (Pitt)
Pirates, 9-7 (Phila)
1935—Pirates, 17-7 (Phila)
Eagles, 17-6 (Pitt)
1936—Pirates, 17-0 (Pitt)
Pirates, 6-0 (Johnstown, Pa.)
1937—Pirates, 27-14 (Phila)
Pirates, 16-7 (Pitt)
1938—Eagles, 27-7 (Buffalo)
Eagles, 14-7 (Charleston, W. Va.)
1939—Eagles, 17-14 (Phila)
Pirates, 24-12 (Pitt)
1940—Pirates, 7-3 (Pitt)
Eagles, 7-0 (Phila)
1941—Eagles, 10-7 (Pitt)
Tie, 7-7 (Phila)
1942—Eagles, 24-14 (Pitt)
Steelers, 14-0 (Phila)
1945—Eagles, 45-3 (Pitt)
Eagles, 30-6 (Phila)
1946—Steelers, 10-7 (Pitt)
Eagles, 10-7 (Phila)
1947—Steelers, 35-24 (Pitt)
Eagles, 21-0 (Phila)
**Eagles, 21-0 (Pitt)
1948—Eagles, 34-7 (Pitt)
Eagles, 17-0 (Phila)
1949—Eagles, 38-7 (Pitt)
Eagles, 34-17 (Phila)
1950—Eagles, 17-10 (Phila)
Steelers, 9-7 (Phila)
1951—Eagles, 34-13 (Pitt)
Steelers, 17-13 (Phila)
1952—Eagles, 31-25 (Pitt)
Eagles, 26-21 (Phila)
1953—Eagles, 23-17 (Phila)
Eagles, 35-7 (Pitt)
1954—Eagles, 24-22 (Phila)
Steelers, 17-7 (Pitt)
1955—Steelers, 13-7 (Pitt)
Eagles, 24-0 (Phila)
1956—Eagles, 35-21 (Pitt)
Eagles, 14-7 (Phila)
1957—Steelers, 6-0 (Pitt)
Eagles, 7-6 (Phila)
1958—Steelers, 24-3 (Pitt)
Steelers, 31-24 (Phila)
1959—Eagles, 28-24 (Phila)
Steelers, 31-0 (Phila)
1960—Eagles, 34-7 (Phila)
Steelers, 27-21 (Pitt)
1961—Eagles, 21-16 (Phila)
Eagles, 35-24 (Phila)
1962—Steelers, 13-7 (Phila)
Steelers, 26-17 (Phila)
1963—Tie, 21-21 (Phila)
Tie, 20-20 (Pitt)
1964—Eagles, 21-7 (Phila)
Eagles, 34-10 (Pitt)
1965—Steelers, 20-14 (Phila)
Eagles, 47-13 (Pitt)
1966—Eagles, 31-14 (Phila)
Eagles, 27-23 (Phila)
1967—Eagles, 34-24 (Phila)
1968—Steelers, 6-3 (Pitt)
1969—Eagles, 41-27 (Phila)
1970—Eagles, 30-20 (Phila)
1974—Steelers, 27-0 (Pitt)
1979—Eagles, 17-14 (Phila)
1988—Eagles, 27-26 (Phila)
1991—Eagles, 23-14 (Phila)
(RS Pts.—Eagles 1,359, Steelers 1,007)
(PS Pts.—Eagles 21, Steelers 0)
*Steelers known as Pirates prior to 1941

**Division Playoff

PHILADELPHIA vs. SAN DIEGO
RS: Chargers lead series, 3-2
1974—Eagles, 13-7 (SD)
1980—Chargers, 22-21 (SD)
1985—Chargers, 20-14 (SD)
1986—Eagles, 23-7 (P)
1989—Chargers, 20-17 (SD)
(RS Pts.—Eagles 88, Chargers 76)

PHILADELPHIA vs. SAN FRANCISCO
RS: 49ers lead series, 12-4-1
1951—Eagles, 21-14 (P)
1953—49ers, 31-21 (SF)
1956—Tie, 10-10 (P)
1958—49ers, 30-24 (P)
1959—49ers, 24-14 (SF)
1964—49ers, 28-24 (P)
1966—49ers, 35-34 (SF)
1967—49ers, 28-27 (P)
1969—49ers, 14-13 (SF)
1971—49ers, 31-3 (P)
1973—49ers, 38-28 (SF)
1975—Eagles, 27-17 (P)
1983—49ers, 22-17 (SF)
1984—49ers, 21-9 (P)
1985—49ers, 24-13 (SF)
1989—49ers, 38-28 (P)
1991—49ers, 23-7 (P)
(RS Pts.—49ers 422, Eagles 326)

PHILADELPHIA vs. SEATTLE
RS: Eagles lead series, 3-1
1976—Eagles, 27-10 (P)
1980—Eagles, 27-20 (S)
1986—Seahawks, 24-20 (S)
1989—Eagles, 31-7 (P)
(RS Pts.—Eagles 105, Seahawks 61)

PHILADELPHIA vs. TAMPA BAY
RS: Eagles lead series, 3-1
PS: Buccaneers lead series, 1-0
1977—Eagles, 13-3 (P)
1979—*Buccaneers, 24-17 (TB)
1981—Eagles, 20-10 (P)
1988—Eagles, 41-14 (TB)
1991—Buccaneers, 14-13 (TB)
(RS Pts.—Eagles 87, Buccaneers 41)
(PS Pts.—Buccaneers 24, Eagles 17)
*NFC Divisional Playoff

PHILADELPHIA vs. *WASHINGTON
RS: Redskins lead series, 65-43-5
PS: Redskins lead series, 1-0
1934—Redskins, 6-0 (B)
Redskins, 14-7 (P)
1935—Eagles, 7-6 (B)
1936—Redskins, 26-3 (P)
Redskins, 17-7 (B)
1937—Eagles, 14-0 (W)
Redskins, 10-7 (P)
1938—Redskins, 26-23 (P)
Redskins, 20-14 (W)
1939—Redskins, 7-0 (P)
Redskins, 7-6 (W)
1940—Redskins, 34-17 (P)
Redskins, 13-6 (W)
1941—Redskins, 21-17 (P)
Redskins, 20-14 (W)
1942—Redskins, 14-10 (P)
Redskins, 30-27 (W)
1944—Tie, 31-31 (P)
Eagles, 37-7 (W)
1945—Redskins, 24-14 (W)
Eagles, 16-0 (P)
1946—Eagles, 28-24 (P)
Redskins, 27-10 (P)
1947—Eagles, 45-42 (P)
Eagles, 38-14 (W)
1948—Eagles, 45-0 (W)
Eagles, 42-21 (P)
1949—Eagles, 49-14 (P)
Eagles, 44-21 (W)
1950—Eagles, 35-3 (P)
Eagles, 33-0 (W)
1951—Redskins, 27-23 (P)
Eagles, 35-21 (W)
1952—Eagles, 38-20 (P)
Redskins, 27-21 (W)
1953—Tie, 21-21 (P)
Redskins, 10-0 (W)
1954—Eagles, 49-21 (W)
Eagles, 41-33 (P)
1955—Redskins, 31-30 (P)
Redskins, 34-21 (W)
1956—Eagles, 13-9 (P)
Redskins, 19-17 (W)
1957—Eagles, 21-12 (P)
Redskins, 42-7 (W)
1958—Redskins, 24-14 (P)
Redskins, 20-0 (W)
1959—Eagles, 30-23 (P)
Eagles, 34-14 (W)
1960—Eagles, 19-13 (P)
Eagles, 38-28 (W)
1961—Eagles, 14-7 (P)
Eagles, 27-24 (W)

273

1962—Redskins, 27-21 (P)
　　　　Eagles, 37-14 (W)
1963—Eagles, 37-24 (W)
　　　　Redskins, 13-10 (P)
1964—Redskins, 35-20 (W)
　　　　Redskins, 21-10 (P)
1965—Redskins, 23-21 (W)
　　　　Eagles, 21-14 (P)
1966—Redskins, 27-13 (P)
　　　　Eagles, 37-28 (W)
1967—Eagles, 35-24 (P)
　　　　Tie, 35-35 (W)
1968—Redskins, 17-14 (W)
　　　　Redskins, 16-10 (P)
1969—Tie, 28-28 (W)
　　　　Redskins, 34-29 (P)
1970—Redskins, 33-21 (P)
　　　　Redskins, 24-6 (W)
1971—Tie, 7-7 (W)
　　　　Redskins, 20-13 (P)
1972—Redskins, 14-0 (W)
　　　　Redskins, 23-7 (P)
1973—Redskins, 28-7 (P)
　　　　Redskins, 38-20 (W)
1974—Redskins, 27-20 (P)
　　　　Redskins, 26-7 (W)
1975—Eagles, 26-10 (P)
　　　　Eagles, 26-3 (W)
1976—Redskins, 20-17 (P) OT
　　　　Redskins, 24-0 (W)
1977—Redskins, 23-17 (W)
　　　　Redskins, 17-14 (P)
1978—Redskins, 35-30 (W)
　　　　Eagles, 17-10 (P)
1979—Eagles, 28-17 (P)
　　　　Redskins, 17-7 (W)
1980—Eagles, 24-14 (P)
　　　　Eagles, 24-0 (W)
1981—Eagles, 36-13 (P)
　　　　Redskins, 15-13 (W)
1982—Redskins, 37-34 (P) OT
　　　　Redskins, 13-9 (W)
1983—Redskins, 23-13 (P)
　　　　Redskins, 28-24 (W)
1984—Redskins, 20-0 (W)
　　　　Eagles, 16-10 (P)
1985—Eagles, 19-6 (W)
　　　　Redskins, 17-12 (P)
1986—Redskins, 41-14 (W)
　　　　Redskins, 21-14 (P)
1987—Redskins, 34-24 (W)
　　　　Eagles, 31-27 (P)
1988—Redskins, 17-10 (W)
　　　　Redskins, 20-19 (P)
1989—Eagles, 42-37 (W)
　　　　Redskins, 10-3 (P)
1990—Redskins, 13-7 (W)
　　　　Eagles, 28-14 (P)
　　　　**Redskins, 20-6 (P)
1991—Redskins, 23-0 (W)
　　　　Eagles, 24-22 (P)
(RS Pts.—Eagles 2,267, Redskins 2,250)
(PS Pts.—Redskins 20, Eagles 6)
*Franchise in Boston prior to 1937
**NFC First Round Playoff

PHOENIX vs. ATLANTA
RS: Cardinals lead series, 10-4;
See Atlanta vs. Phoenix
PHOENIX vs. BUFFALO
RS: Series tied, 3-3;
See Buffalo vs. Phoenix
PHOENIX vs. CHICAGO
RS: Bears lead series, 51-25-6;
See Chicago vs. Phoenix
PHOENIX vs. CINCINNATI
RS: Bengals lead series, 3-1;
See Cincinnati vs. Phoenix
PHOENIX vs. CLEVELAND
RS: Browns lead series, 31-10-3;
See Cleveland vs. Phoenix
PHOENIX vs. DALLAS
RS: Cowboys lead series, 36-22-1;
See Dallas vs. Phoenix
PHOENIX vs. DENVER
RS: Broncos lead series, 3-0-1;
See Denver vs. Phoenix
PHOENIX vs. DETROIT
RS: Lions lead series, 25-16-5;
See Detroit vs. Phoenix
PHOENIX vs. GREEN BAY
RS: Packers lead series, 39-21-4;
PS: Packers lead series, 1-0;
See Green Bay vs. Phoenix
PHOENIX vs. HOUSTON
RS: Cardinals lead series, 3-2;
See Houston vs. Phoenix
PHOENIX vs. INDIANAPOLIS
RS: Cardinals lead series, 6-4;
See Indianapolis vs. Phoenix
PHOENIX vs. KANSAS CITY
RS: Chiefs lead series, 3-1-1;
See Kansas City vs. Phoenix

PHOENIX vs. L.A. RAIDERS
RS: Raiders lead series, 2-1;
See L.A. Raiders vs. Phoenix
PHOENIX vs. L.A. RAMS
RS: Rams lead series, 22-17-2
PS: Rams lead series, 1-0;
See L.A. Rams vs. Phoenix
PHOENIX vs. MIAMI
RS: Dolphins lead series, 6-0;
See Miami vs. Phoenix
PHOENIX vs. MINNESOTA
RS: Cardinals lead series, 7-4
PS: Vikings lead series, 1-0;
See Minnesota vs. Phoenix
PHOENIX vs. NEW ENGLAND
RS: Cardinals lead series, 6-1;
See New England vs. Phoenix
PHOENIX vs. NEW ORLEANS
RS: Cardinals lead series, 10-7;
See New Orleans vs. Phoenix
PHOENIX vs. N.Y. GIANTS
RS: Giants lead series, 63-33-2;
See N.Y. Giants vs. Phoenix
PHOENIX vs. N.Y. JETS
RS: Cardinals lead series, 2-1;
See N.Y. Jets vs. Phoenix
PHOENIX vs. PHILADELPHIA
RS: Cardinals lead series, 43-40-5
PS: Series tied, 1-1;
See Philadelphia vs. Phoenix
*PHOENIX vs. **PITTSBURGH
RS: Steelers lead series, 29-21-3
1933—Pirates, 14-13 (C)
1935—Pirates, 17-13 (P)
1936—Cardinals, 14-6 (C)
1937—Cardinals, 13-7 (P)
1939—Cardinals, 10-0 (P)
1940—Tie, 7-7 (P)
1942—Steelers, 19-3 (P)
1945—Steelers, 23-0 (P)
1946—Cardinals, 14-7 (P)
1948—Cardinals, 24-7 (P)
1950—Steelers, 28-17 (C)
　　　　Steelers, 28-7 (P)
1951—Steelers, 28-14 (C)
1952—Steelers, 34-28 (C)
　　　　Steelers, 17-14 (P)
1953—Steelers, 31-28 (P)
　　　　Steelers, 21-17 (C)
1954—Cardinals, 17-14 (C)
　　　　Steelers, 20-17 (P)
1955—Steelers, 14-7 (P)
　　　　Cardinals, 27-13 (C)
1956—Steelers, 14-7 (P)
　　　　Cardinals, 38-27 (C)
1957—Steelers, 29-20 (P)
　　　　Steelers, 27-2 (C)
1958—Steelers, 27-20 (C)
　　　　Steelers, 38-21 (P)
1959—Cardinals, 45-24 (C)
　　　　Steelers, 35-20 (P)
1960—Steelers, 27-14 (P)
　　　　Steelers, 38-7 (StL)
1961—Steelers, 30-27 (P)
　　　　Cardinals, 20-0 (StL)
1962—Steelers, 26-17 (StL)
　　　　Steelers, 19-7 (P)
1963—Steelers, 23-10 (P)
　　　　Cardinals, 24-23 (StL)
1964—Cardinals, 34-30 (StL)
　　　　Cardinals, 21-20 (P)
1965—Cardinals, 20-7 (P)
　　　　Cardinals, 21-17 (P)
1966—Steelers, 30-9 (P)
　　　　Cardinals, 6-3 (StL)
1967—Cardinals, 28-14 (P)
　　　　Tie, 14-14 (StL)
1968—Tie, 28-28 (StL)
　　　　Cardinals, 20-10 (P)
1969—Cardinals, 27-14 (P)
　　　　Cardinals, 47-10 (StL)
1972—Steelers, 25-19 (StL)
1979—Steelers, 24-21 (StL)
1985—Steelers, 23-10 (P)
1988—Cardinals, 31-14 (Phx)
(RS Pts.—Steelers 1,021, Cardinals 983)
*Franchise in St. Louis prior to 1988
and in Chicago prior to 1960
**Steelers known as Pirates prior to 1941
*PHOENIX vs. SAN DIEGO
RS: Chargers lead series, 4-1
1971—Chargers, 20-17 (SD)
1976—Chargers, 43-24 (SD)
1983—Cardinals, 44-14 (StL)
1987—Chargers, 28-24 (SD)
1989—Chargers, 24-13 (P)
(RS Pts.—Chargers 129, Cardinals 122)
*Franchise in St. Louis prior to 1988
*PHOENIX vs. SAN FRANCISCO
RS: 49ers lead series, 9-8
1951—Cardinals, 27-21 (C)
1957—Cardinals, 20-10 (SF)
1962—49ers, 24-17 (StL)

1964—Cardinals, 23-13 (SF)
1968—49ers, 35-17 (StL)
1971—49ers, 26-14 (StL)
1974—Cardinals, 34-9 (SF)
1976—Cardinals, 23-20 (StL) OT
1978—Cardinals, 16-10 (SF)
1979—Cardinals, 13-10 (StL)
1980—49ers, 24-21 (StL) OT
1982—49ers, 31-20 (StL)
1983—49ers, 42-27 (StL)
1986—49ers, 43-17 (SF)
1987—49ers, 34-28 (SF)
1988—Cardinals, 24-23 (P)
1991—49ers, 14-10 (SF)
(RS Pts.—49ers 389, Cardinals 351)
*Franchise in St. Louis prior to 1988
and in Chicago prior to 1960
*PHOENIX vs. SEATTLE
RS: Cardinals lead series, 3-0
1976—Cardinals, 30-24 (S)
1983—Cardinals, 33-28 (StL)
1989—Cardinals, 34-24 (S)
(RS Pts.—Cardinals 97, Seahawks 76)
*Franchise in St. Louis prior to 1988
*PHOENIX vs. TAMPA BAY
RS: Cardinals lead series, 6-4
1977—Buccaneers, 17-7 (TB)
1981—Buccaneers, 20-10 (TB)
1983—Cardinals, 34-27 (TB)
1985—Buccaneers, 16-0 (TB)
1986—Cardinals, 30-19 (TB)
　　　　Cardinals, 21-17 (StL)
1987—Cardinals, 31-28 (StL)
　　　　Cardinals, 31-14 (TB)
1988—Cardinals, 30-24 (TB)
1989—Buccaneers, 14-13 (TB)
(RS Pts.—Cardinals 207, Buccaneers 196)
*Franchise in St. Louis prior to 1988
*PHOENIX vs. **WASHINGTON
RS: Redskins lead series, 60-33-2
1932—Cardinals, 9-0 (B)
　　　　Braves, 8-6 (C)
1933—Redskins, 10-0 (C)
　　　　Tie, 0-0 (B)
1934—Redskins, 9-0 (B)
1935—Cardinals, 6-0 (B)
1936—Redskins, 13-10 (B)
1937—Cardinals, 21-14 (W)
1939—Redskins, 28-7 (W)
1940—Redskins, 28-21 (W)
1942—Redskins, 28-0 (W)
1943—Redskins, 13-7 (W)
1945—Redskins, 24-21 (W)
1947—Redskins, 45-21 (W)
1949—Cardinals, 38-7 (C)
1950—Cardinals, 38-28 (W)
1951—Redskins, 7-3 (C)
　　　　Redskins, 20-17 (W)
1952—Redskins, 23-7 (C)
　　　　Cardinals, 17-6 (W)
1953—Cardinals, 24-13 (C)
　　　　Redskins, 28-17 (W)
1954—Cardinals, 38-16 (C)
　　　　Redskins, 37-20 (W)
1955—Cardinals, 24-10 (W)
　　　　Redskins, 31-0 (C)
1956—Cardinals, 31-3 (W)
　　　　Redskins, 17-14 (C)
1957—Cardinals, 37-14 (C)
　　　　Cardinals, 44-14 (W)
1958—Cardinals, 37-10 (C)
　　　　Redskins, 45-31 (W)
1959—Cardinals, 49-21 (C)
　　　　Redskins, 23-14 (W)
1960—Cardinals, 44-7 (StL)
　　　　Cardinals, 26-14 (W)
1961—Cardinals, 24-0 (W)
　　　　Cardinals, 38-24 (StL)
1962—Redskins, 24-14 (W)
　　　　Tie, 17-17 (StL)
1963—Cardinals, 21-7 (W)
　　　　Cardinals, 24-20 (StL)
1964—Cardinals, 23-17 (W)
　　　　Cardinals, 38-24 (StL)
1965—Cardinals, 37-16 (W)
　　　　Cardinals, 24-20 (StL)
1966—Cardinals, 23-7 (StL)
　　　　Redskins, 26-20 (W)
1967—Cardinals, 27-21 (W)
1968—Cardinals, 41-14 (StL)
1969—Redskins, 33-17 (W)
1970—Cardinals, 27-17 (StL)
　　　　Redskins, 28-27 (W)
1971—Redskins, 24-17 (StL)
　　　　Redskins, 20-0 (W)
1972—Cardinals, 24-10 (W)
　　　　Redskins, 33-3 (StL)
1973—Cardinals, 34-27 (StL)
　　　　Redskins, 31-13 (W)
1974—Cardinals, 17-10 (W)
　　　　Cardinals, 23-20 (StL)
1975—Redskins, 27-17 (W)
　　　　Cardinals, 20-17 (StL) OT

1976—Redskins, 20-10 (W)
　　　　Redskins, 16-10 (StL)
1977—Redskins, 24-14 (W)
　　　　Redskins, 26-20 (StL)
1978—Cardinals, 28-10 (StL)
　　　　Cardinals, 27-17 (W)
1979—Redskins, 17-7 (StL)
　　　　Redskins, 30-28 (W)
1980—Cardinals, 23-0 (W)
　　　　Redskins, 31-7 (StL)
1981—Cardinals, 40-30 (StL)
　　　　Redskins, 42-21 (W)
1982—Redskins, 12-7 (StL)
　　　　Redskins, 28-0 (W)
1983—Redskins, 38-14 (StL)
　　　　Redskins, 45-7 (W)
1984—Cardinals, 26-24 (StL)
　　　　Redskins, 29-27 (W)
1985—Redskins, 27-10 (W)
　　　　Redskins, 27-16 (StL)
1986—Redskins, 28-21 (W)
　　　　Redskins, 20-17 (StL)
1987—Redskins, 28-21 (W)
　　　　Redskins, 34-17 (StL)
1988—Cardinals, 30-21 (P)
　　　　Redskins, 33-17 (W)
1989—Redskins, 30-28 (W)
　　　　Redskins, 29-10 (P)
1990—Redskins, 31-0 (W)
　　　　Redskins, 38-10 (P)
1991—Redskins, 34-0 (W)
　　　　Redskins, 20-14 (P)
(RS Pts.—Redskins 2,080, Cardinals 1,743)
*Franchise in St. Louis prior to 1988
and in Chicago prior to 1960
**Franchise in Boston prior to 1937 and
known as Braves prior to 1933

PITTSBURGH vs. ATLANTA
RS: Steelers lead series, 8-1;
See Atlanta vs. Pittsburgh
PITTSBURGH vs. BUFFALO
RS: Bills lead series, 6-5
PS: Steelers lead series, 1-0;
See Buffalo vs. Pittsburgh
PITTSBURGH vs. CHICAGO
RS: Bears lead series, 15-4-1;
See Chicago vs. Pittsburgh
PITTSBURGH vs. CINCINNATI
RS: Steelers lead series, 22-21;
See Cincinnati vs. Pittsburgh
PITTSBURGH vs. CLEVELAND
RS: Browns lead series, 50-34;
See Cleveland vs. Pittsburgh
PITTSBURGH vs. DALLAS
RS: Cowboys lead series, 12-11
PS: Steelers lead series, 2-0;
See Dallas vs. Pittsburgh
PITTSBURGH vs. DENVER
RS: Broncos lead series, 9-5-1
PS: Series tied, 2-2;
See Denver vs. Pittsburgh
PITTSBURGH vs. DETROIT
RS: Lions lead series, 13-10-1;
See Detroit vs. Pittsburgh
PITTSBURGH vs. GREEN BAY
RS: Packers lead series, 16-11;
See Green Bay vs. Pittsburgh
PITTSBURGH vs. HOUSTON
RS: Steelers lead series, 27-16
PS: Steelers lead series, 3-0;
See Houston vs. Pittsburgh
PITTSBURGH vs. INDIANAPOLIS
RS: Steelers lead series, 9-4
PS: Steelers lead series, 2-0;
See Indianapolis vs. Pittsburgh
PITTSBURGH vs. KANSAS CITY
RS: Steelers lead series, 12-5;
See Kansas City vs. Pittsburgh
PITTSBURGH vs. L.A. RAIDERS
RS: Raiders lead series, 7-3
PS: Series tied, 3-3;
See L.A. Raiders vs. Pittsburgh
PITTSBURGH vs. L.A. RAMS
RS: Rams lead series, 13-4-2
PS: Steelers lead series, 1-0;
See L.A. Rams vs. Pittsburgh
PITTSBURGH vs. MIAMI
RS: Dolphins lead series, 7-4
PS: Dolphins lead series, 2-1;
See Miami vs. Pittsburgh
PITTSBURGH vs. MINNESOTA
RS: Vikings lead series, 6-4
PS: Steelers lead series, 1-0;
See Minnesota vs. Pittsburgh
PITTSBURGH vs. NEW ENGLAND
RS: Steelers lead series, 8-3;
See New England vs. Pittsburgh
PITTSBURGH vs. NEW ORLEANS
RS: Series tied, 5-5;
See New Orleans vs. Pittsburgh

PITTSBURGH vs. N.Y. GIANTS
RS: Giants lead series, 42-26-3;
See N.Y. Giants vs. Pittsburgh
PITTSBURGH vs. N.Y. JETS
RS: Steelers lead series, 11-1;
See N.Y. Jets vs. Pittsburgh
PITTSBURGH vs. PHILADELPHIA
RS: Eagles lead series, 43-25-3
PS: Eagles lead series, 1-0;
See Philadelphia vs. Pittsburgh
PITTSBURGH vs. PHOENIX
RS: Steelers lead series, 29-21-3;
See Phoenix vs. Pittsburgh
PITTSBURGH vs. SAN DIEGO
RS: Steelers lead series, 12-4
PS: Chargers lead series, 1-0
1971—Steelers, 21-17 (P)
1972—Steelers, 24-2 (SD)
1973—Steelers, 38-21 (P)
1975—Steelers, 37-0 (SD)
1976—Steelers, 23-0 (P)
1977—Steelers, 10-9 (SD)
1979—Chargers, 35-7 (SD)
1980—Chargers, 26-17 (SD)
1982—*Chargers, 31-28 (P)
1983—Steelers, 26-3 (P)
1984—Steelers, 52-24 (P)
1985—Chargers, 54-44 (SD)
1987—Steelers, 20-16 (SD)
1988—Chargers, 20-14 (SD)
1989—Steelers, 20-17 (P)
1990—Steelers, 36-14 (P)
1991—Steelers, 26-20 (P)
(RS Pts.—Steelers 415, Chargers 278)
(PS Pts.—Chargers 31, Steelers 28)
*AFC First Round Playoff
PITTSBURGH vs. SAN FRANCISCO
RS: Series tied, 7-7
1951—49ers, 28-24 (P)
1952—Steelers, 24-7 (SF)
1954—49ers, 31-3 (SF)
1958—49ers, 23-20 (SF)
1961—Steelers, 20-10 (P)
1965—49ers, 27-17 (SF)
1968—49ers, 45-28 (P)
1973—Steelers, 37-14 (SF)
1977—Steelers, 27-0 (P)
1978—49ers, 24-7 (P)
1981—49ers, 17-14 (P)
1984—Steelers, 20-17 (SF)
1987—Steelers, 30-17 (P)
1990—49ers, 27-7 (SF)
(RS Pts.—Steelers 295, 49ers 270)
PITTSBURGH vs. SEATTLE
RS: Series tied, 4-4
1977—Steelers, 30-20 (P)
1978—Steelers, 21-10 (P)
1981—Seahawks, 24-21 (S)
1982—Seahawks, 16-0 (S)
1983—Steelers, 27-21 (S)
1986—Seahawks, 30-0 (S)
1987—Steelers, 13-9 (P)
1991—Seahawks, 27-7 (S)
(RS Pts.—Seahawks 157, Steelers 119)
PITTSBURGH vs. TAMPA BAY
RS: Steelers lead series, 4-0
1976—Steelers, 42-0 (P)
1980—Steelers, 24-21 (TB)
1983—Steelers, 17-12 (P)
1989—Steelers, 31-22 (TB)
(RS Pts.—Steelers 114, Buccaneers 55)
*PITTSBURGH vs. **WASHINGTON
RS: Redskins lead series, 42-27-3
1933—Redskins, 21-6 (P)
        Pirates, 16-14 (B)
1934—Redskins, 7-0 (P)
        Redskins, 39-0 (B)
1935—Pirates, 6-0 (P)
        Redskins, 13-3 (B)
1936—Pirates, 10-0 (P)
        Redskins, 30-0 (B)
1937—Redskins, 34-20 (P)
        Pirates, 21-13 (P)
1938—Redskins, 7-0 (P)
        Redskins, 15-0 (W)
1939—Redskins, 44-14 (W)
        Redskins, 21-14 (P)
1940—Redskins, 40-10 (P)
        Redskins, 37-10 (W)
1941—Redskins, 24-20 (P)
        Redskins, 23-3 (W)
1942—Redskins, 28-14 (W)
        Redskins, 14-0 (P)
1945—Redskins, 14-0 (P)
        Redskins, 24-0 (W)
1946—Tie, 14-14 (W)
        Steelers, 14-7 (P)
1947—Redskins, 27-26 (W)
        Steelers, 21-14 (P)
1948—Redskins, 17-14 (W)
        Steelers, 10-7 (P)
1949—Redskins, 27-14 (P)
        Redskins, 27-14 (W)

1950—Steelers, 26-7 (W)
        Redskins, 24-7 (P)
1951—Redskins, 22-7 (P)
        Steelers, 20-10 (W)
1952—Redskins, 28-24 (P)
        Steelers, 24-23 (W)
1953—Redskins, 17-9 (P)
        Steelers, 14-13 (W)
1954—Steelers, 37-7 (P)
        Redskins, 17-14 (W)
1955—Redskins, 23-14 (P)
        Redskins, 28-17 (W)
1956—Steelers, 30-13 (P)
        Steelers, 23-0 (W)
1957—Steelers, 28-7 (P)
        Redskins, 10-3 (W)
1958—Steelers, 24-16 (P)
        Tie, 14-14 (W)
1959—Redskins, 23-17 (P)
        Steelers, 27-6 (W)
1960—Tie, 27-27 (W)
        Steelers, 22-10 (P)
1961—Steelers, 20-0 (P)
        Steelers, 30-14 (W)
1962—Steelers, 23-21 (P)
        Steelers, 27-24 (W)
1963—Steelers, 38-27 (P)
        Steelers, 34-28 (W)
1964—Redskins, 30-0 (P)
        Steelers, 14-7 (W)
1965—Redskins, 31-3 (P)
        Redskins, 35-14 (W)
1966—Redskins, 33-27 (P)
        Redskins, 24-10 (W)
1967—Redskins, 15-10 (P)
1968—Redskins, 16-13 (W)
1969—Redskins, 14-7 (P)
1973—Steelers, 21-16 (P)
1979—Steelers, 38-7 (P)
1985—Redskins, 30-23 (P)
1988—Redskins, 30-29 (W)
1991—Redskins, 41-14 (P)
(RS Pts.—Redskins 1,390, Steelers 1,117)
*Steelers known as Pirates prior to 1941
**Franchise in Boston prior to 1937

SAN DIEGO vs. ATLANTA
RS: Falcons lead series, 3-1;
See Atlanta vs. San Diego
SAN DIEGO vs. BUFFALO
RS: Chargers lead series, 16-7-2
PS: Bills lead series, 2-1;
See Buffalo vs. San Diego
SAN DIEGO vs. CHICAGO
RS: Chargers lead series, 4-1;
See Chicago vs. San Diego
SAN DIEGO vs. CINCINNATI
RS: Chargers lead series, 11-8
PS: Bengals lead series, 1-0;
See Cincinnati vs. San Diego
SAN DIEGO vs. CLEVELAND
RS: Chargers lead series, 7-6-1;
See Cleveland vs. San Diego
SAN DIEGO vs. DALLAS
RS: Cowboys lead series, 4-1;
See Dallas vs. San Diego
SAN DIEGO vs. DENVER
RS: Broncos lead series, 33-30-1;
See Denver vs. San Diego
SAN DIEGO vs. DETROIT
RS: Lions lead series, 3-2;
See Detroit vs. San Diego
SAN DIEGO vs. GREEN BAY
RS: Packers lead series, 3-1;
See Green Bay vs. San Diego
SAN DIEGO vs. HOUSTON
RS: Chargers lead series, 17-12-1
PS: Oilers lead series, 3-0;
See Houston vs. San Diego
SAN DIEGO vs. INDIANAPOLIS
RS: Chargers lead series, 6-5;
See Indianapolis vs. San Diego
SAN DIEGO vs. KANSAS CITY
RS: Series tied, 31-31-1;
See Kansas City vs. San Diego
SAN DIEGO vs. L.A. RAIDERS
RS: Raiders lead series, 40-22-2
PS: Raiders lead series, 1-0;
See L.A. Raiders vs. San Diego
SAN DIEGO vs. L.A. RAMS
RS: Rams lead series, 3-2;
See L.A. Rams vs. San Diego
SAN DIEGO vs. MIAMI
RS: Chargers lead series, 9-5
PS: Series tied, 1-1;
See Miami vs. San Diego
SAN DIEGO vs. MINNESOTA
RS: Series tied, 3-3;
See Minnesota vs. San Diego
SAN DIEGO vs. NEW ENGLAND
RS: Patriots lead series, 13-11-2
PS: Chargers lead series, 1-0;
See New England vs. San Diego

SAN DIEGO vs. NEW ORLEANS
RS: Chargers lead series, 4-1;
See New Orleans vs. San Diego
SAN DIEGO vs. N.Y. GIANTS
RS: Giants lead series, 4-2;
See N.Y. Giants vs. San Diego
SAN DIEGO vs. N.Y. JETS
RS: Chargers lead series, 16-9-1;
See N.Y. Jets vs. San Diego
SAN DIEGO vs. PHILADELPHIA
RS: Chargers lead series, 3-2;
See Philadelphia vs. San Diego
SAN DIEGO vs. PHOENIX
RS: Chargers lead series, 4-1;
See Phoenix vs. San Diego
SAN DIEGO vs. PITTSBURGH
RS: Steelers lead series, 12-4
PS: Chargers lead series, 1-0;
See Pittsburgh vs. San Diego
SAN DIEGO vs. SAN FRANCISCO
RS: Series tied, 3-3
1972—49ers, 34-3 (SF)
1976—Chargers, 13-7 (SD) OT
1979—Chargers, 31-9 (SD)
1982—Chargers, 41-37 (SF)
1988—49ers, 48-10 (SD)
1991—49ers, 34-14 (SF)
(RS Pts.—49ers 169, Chargers 112)
SAN DIEGO vs. SEATTLE
RS: Seahawks lead series, 14-12
1977—Chargers, 30-28 (S)
1978—Chargers, 24-20 (S)
        Chargers, 37-10 (SD)
1979—Chargers, 33-16 (S)
        Chargers, 20-10 (SD)
1980—Chargers, 34-13 (S)
        Chargers, 21-14 (SD)
1981—Chargers, 24-10 (SD)
        Seahawks, 44-23 (S)
1983—Seahawks, 34-31 (S)
        Chargers, 28-21 (SD)
1984—Seahawks, 31-17 (S)
        Seahawks, 24-0 (SD)
1985—Seahawks, 49-35 (SD)
        Seahawks, 26-21 (S)
1986—Seahawks, 33-7 (S)
        Seahawks, 34-24 (SD)
1987—Seahawks, 34-3 (S)
1988—Chargers, 17-6 (SD)
        Seahawks, 17-14 (S)
1989—Seahawks, 17-16 (SD)
        Seahawks, 10-7 (S)
1990—Chargers, 31-14 (S)
        Seahawks, 13-10 (SD) OT
1991—Seahawks, 20-9 (S)
        Chargers, 17-14 (SD)
(RS Pts.—Seahawks 562, Chargers 533)
SAN DIEGO vs. TAMPA BAY
RS: Chargers lead series, 4-0
1976—Chargers, 23-0 (TB)
1981—Chargers, 24-23 (TB)
1987—Chargers, 17-13 (TB)
1990—Chargers, 41-10 (SD)
(RS Pts.—Chargers 105, Buccaneers 46)
SAN DIEGO vs. WASHINGTON
RS: Redskins lead series, 5-0
1973—Redskins, 38-0 (W)
1980—Redskins, 40-17 (W)
1983—Redskins, 27-24 (SD)
1986—Redskins, 30-27 (SD)
1989—Redskins, 26-21 (W)
(RS Pts.—Redskins 161, Chargers 89)

SAN FRANCISCO vs. ATLANTA
RS: 49ers lead series, 29-20-1
See Atlanta vs. San Francisco
SAN FRANCISCO vs. BUFFALO
RS: Series tied, 2-2;
See Buffalo vs. San Francisco
SAN FRANCISCO vs. CHICAGO
RS: Series tied, 25-25-1
PS: 49ers lead series, 2-0;
See Chicago vs. San Francisco
SAN FRANCISCO vs. CINCINNATI
RS: 49ers lead series, 5-1
PS: 49ers lead series, 2-0;
See Cincinnati vs. San Francisco
SAN FRANCISCO vs. CLEVELAND
RS: Browns lead series, 8-6
See Cleveland vs. San Francisco
SAN FRANCISCO vs. DALLAS
RS: 49ers lead series, 9-5-1
PS: Cowboys lead series, 3-1;
See Dallas vs. San Francisco
SAN FRANCISCO vs. DENVER
RS: Broncos lead series, 4-2;
PS: 49ers lead series, 1-0;
See Denver vs. San Francisco
SAN FRANCISCO vs. DETROIT
RS: Lions lead series, 25-24-1
PS: Series tied, 1-1;
See Detroit vs. San Francisco

SAN FRANCISCO vs. GREEN BAY
RS: 49ers lead series, 25-21-1
See Green Bay vs. San Francisco
SAN FRANCISCO vs. HOUSTON
RS: 49ers lead series, 5-2;
See Houston vs. San Francisco
SAN FRANCISCO vs. INDIANAPOLIS
RS: Colts lead series, 21-15-1;
See Indianapolis vs. San Francisco
SAN FRANCISCO vs. KANSAS CITY
RS: 49ers lead series, 4-1;
See Kansas City vs. San Francisco
SAN FRANCISCO vs. L.A. RAIDERS
RS: Raiders lead series, 5-2;
See L.A. Raiders vs. San Francisco
SAN FRANCISCO vs. L.A. RAMS
RS: Rams lead series, 48-34-2
PS: 49ers lead series, 1-0;
See L.A. Rams vs. San Francisco
SAN FRANCISCO vs. MIAMI
RS: Dolphins lead series, 4-1
PS: 49ers lead series, 1-0;
See Miami vs. San Francisco
SAN FRANCISCO vs. MINNESOTA
RS: Vikings lead series, 15-13-1
PS: 49ers lead series, 3-1;
See Minnesota vs. San Francisco
SAN FRANCISCO vs. NEW ENGLAND
RS: 49ers lead series, 5-1;
See New England vs. San Francisco
SAN FRANCISCO vs. NEW ORLEANS
RS: 49ers lead series, 30-13-2;
See New Orleans vs. San Francisco
SAN FRANCISCO vs. N.Y. GIANTS
RS: Giants lead series, 11-9
PS: Giants lead series, 3-2;
See N.Y. Giants vs. San Francisco
SAN FRANCISCO vs. N.Y. JETS
RS: 49ers lead series, 5-1;
See N.Y. Jets vs. San Francisco
SAN FRANCISCO vs. PHILADELPHIA
RS: 49ers lead series, 12-4-1;
See Philadelphia vs. San Francisco
SAN FRANCISCO vs. PHOENIX
RS: 49ers lead sseries, 9-8;
See Phoenix vs. San Francisco
SAN FRANCISCO vs. PITTSBURGH
RS: Series tied, 7-7;
See Pittsburgh vs. San Francisco
SAN FRANCISCO vs. SAN DIEGO
RS: Series tied, 3-3;
See San Diego vs. San Francisco
SAN FRANCISCO vs. SEATTLE
RS: 49ers lead series, 4-1
1976—49ers, 37-21 (S)
1979—Seahawks, 35-24 (SF)
1985—49ers, 19-6 (S)
1988—49ers, 38-7 (S)
1991—49ers, 24-22 (S)
(RS Pts.—49ers 142, Seahawks 91)
SAN FRANCISCO vs. TAMPA BAY
RS: 49ers lead series, 9-1
1977—49ers, 20-10 (SF)
1978—49ers, 6-3 (SF)
1979—49ers, 23-7 (SF)
1980—Buccaneers, 24-23 (SF)
1983—49ers, 35-21 (SF)
1984—49ers, 24-17 (SF)
1986—49ers, 31-7 (TB)
1987—49ers, 24-10 (TB)
1989—49ers, 20-16 (SF)
1990—49ers, 31-7 (SF)
(RS. Pts.—49ers 237, Buccaneers 122)
SAN FRANCISCO vs. WASHINGTON
RS: 49ers lead series, 9-6-1
PS: 49ers lead series, 2-1
1952—49ers, 23-17 (W)
1954—49ers, 41-7 (SF)
1955—Redskins, 7-0 (W)
1961—49ers, 35-3 (SF)
1967—Redskins, 31-28 (W)
1969—Tie, 17-17 (SF)
1970—49ers, 26-17 (SF)
1971—*49ers, 24-20 (SF)
1973—Redskins, 33-9 (W)
1976—Redskins, 24-21 (SF)
1978—Redskins, 38-20 (W)
1981—49ers, 30-17 (W)
1983—**Redskins, 24-21 (W)
1984—49ers, 37-31 (SF)
1985—Redskins, 35-8 (W)
1986—Redskins, 14-6 (W)
1988—49ers, 37-21 (SF)
1990—49ers, 26-13 (SF)
        *49ers, 28-10 (SF)
(RS Pts.—49ers 391, Redskins 298)
(PS Pts.—49ers 73, Redskins 54)
*NFC Divisional Playoff
**NFC Championship

SEATTLE vs. ATLANTA
RS: Seahawks lead series, 4-1;
See Atlanta vs. Seattle

SEATTLE vs. BUFFALO
RS: Seahawks lead series, 3-1;
See Buffalo vs. Seattle
SEATTLE vs. CHICAGO
RS: Seahawks lead series, 4-2;
See Chicago vs. Seattle
SEATTLE vs. CINCINNATI
RS: Series tied, 5-5
PS: Bengals lead series, 1-0;
See Cincinnati vs. Seattle
SEATTLE vs. CLEVELAND
RS: Seahawks lead series, 8-3;
See Cleveland vs. Seattle
SEATTLE vs. DALLAS
RS: Cowboys lead series, 3-1;
See Dallas vs. Seattle
SEATTLE vs. DENVER
RS: Broncos lead series, 17-12
PS: Seahawks lead series, 1-0;
See Denver vs. Seattle
SEATTLE vs. DETROIT
RS: Seahawks lead series, 4-1;
See Detroit vs. Seattle
SEATTLE vs. GREEN BAY
RS: Series tied, 3-3;
See Green Bay vs. Seattle
SEATTLE vs. HOUSTON
RS: Seahawks lead series, 4-3;
PS: Oilers lead series, 1-0;
See Houston vs. Seattle
SEATTLE vs. INDIANAPOLIS
RS: Colts lead series, 2-1;
See Indianapolis vs. Seattle
SEATTLE vs. KANSAS CITY
RS: Chiefs lead series, 15-12;
See Kansas City vs. Seattle
SEATTLE vs. L.A. RAIDERS
RS: Series tied, 14-14;
PS: Series tied, 1-1;
See L.A. Raiders vs. Seattle
SEATTLE vs. L.A. RAMS
RS: Rams lead series, 4-1;
See L.A. Rams vs. Seattle
SEATTLE vs. MIAMI
RS: Dolphins lead series, 3-1
PS: Series tied, 1-1;
See Miami vs. Seattle
SEATTLE vs. MINNESOTA
RS: Seahawks lead series, 3-2;
See Minnesota vs. Seattle
SEATTLE vs. NEW ENGLAND
RS: Patriots lead series, 6-4;
See New England vs. Seattle
SEATTLE vs. NEW ORLEANS
RS: Saints lead series, 3-2;
See New Orleans vs. Seattle
SEATTLE vs. N.Y. GIANTS
RS: Giants lead series, 4-2;
See N.Y. Giants vs. Seattle
SEATTLE vs. N.Y. JETS
RS: Seahawks lead series, 8-3;
See N.Y. Jets vs. Seattle
SEATTLE vs. PHILADELPHIA
RS: Eagles lead series, 3-1;
See Philadelphia vs. Seattle
SEATTLE vs. PHOENIX
Cardinals lead series, 3-0;
See Phoenix vs. Seattle
SEATTLE vs. PITTSBURGH
RS: Series tied, 4-4;
See Pittsburgh vs. Seattle
SEATTLE vs. SAN DIEGO
RS: Seahawks lead series, 14-12;
See San Diego vs. Seattle
SEATTLE vs. SAN FRANCISCO
RS: 49ers lead series, 4-1;
See San Francisco vs. Seattle
SEATTLE vs. TAMPA BAY
RS: Seahawks lead series, 2-0
1976—Seahawks, 13-10 (TB)
1977—Seahawks, 30-23 (S)
(RS Pts.—Seahawks 43, Buccaneers 33)
SEATTLE vs. WASHINGTON
RS: Redskins lead series, 4-1
1976—Redskins, 31-7 (W)
1980—Seahawks, 14-0 (W)
1983—Redskins, 27-17 (S)
1986—Redskins, 19-14 (W)
1989—Redskins, 29-0 (S)
(RS Pts.—Redskins 106, Seahawks 52)

TAMPA BAY vs. ATLANTA
RS: Series tied, 5-5;
See Atlanta vs. Tampa Bay
TAMPA BAY vs. BUFFALO
RS: Buccaneers lead series, 4-2;
See Buffalo vs. Tampa Bay
TAMPA BAY vs. CHICAGO
RS: Bears lead series, 22-6;
See Chicago vs. Tampa Bay
TAMPA BAY vs. CINCINNATI
RS: Bengals lead series, 3-1;
See Cincinnati vs. Tampa Bay

TAMPA BAY vs. CLEVELAND
RS: Browns lead series, 4-0;
See Cleveland vs. Tampa Bay
TAMPA BAY vs. DALLAS
RS: Cowboys lead series, 6-0
PS: Cowboys lead series, 2-0;
See Dallas vs. Tampa Bay
TAMPA BAY vs. DENVER
RS: Broncos lead series, 2-0;
See Denver vs. Tampa Bay
TAMPA BAY vs. DETROIT
RS: Series tied, 14-14;
See Detroit vs. Tampa Bay
TAMPA BAY vs. GREEN BAY
RS: Packers lead series, 14-11-1;
See Green Bay vs. Tampa Bay
TAMPA BAY vs. HOUSTON
RS: Oilers lead series, 3-1;
See Houston vs. Tampa Bay
TAMPA BAY vs. INDIANAPOLIS
RS: Colts lead series, 4-2;
See Indianapolis vs. Tampa Bay
TAMPA BAY vs. KANSAS CITY
RS: Chiefs lead series, 4-2;
See Kansas City vs. Tampa Bay
TAMPA BAY vs. L.A RAIDERS
RS: Raiders lead series, 2-0;
See L.A. Raiders vs. Tampa Bay
TAMPA BAY vs. L.A. RAMS
RS: Rams lead series, 7-2
PS: Rams lead series, 1-0;
See L.A. Rams vs. Tampa Bay
TAMPA BAY vs. MIAMI
RS: Dolphins lead series, 4-1;
See Miami vs. Tampa Bay
TAMPA BAY vs. MINNESOTA
RS: Vikings lead series, 20-8;
See Minnesota vs. Tampa Bay
TAMPA BAY vs. NEW ENGLAND
RS: Patriots lead series, 3-0;
See New England vs. Tampa Bay
TAMPA BAY vs. NEW ORLEANS
RS: Saints lead series, 10-4;
See New Orleans vs. Tampa Bay
TAMPA BAY vs. N.Y. GIANTS
RS: Giants lead series, 7-3;
See N.Y. Giants vs. Tampa Bay
TAMPA BAY vs. N.Y. JETS
RS: Jets lead series, 5-1;
See N.Y. Jets vs. Tampa Bay
TAMPA BAY vs. PHILADELPHIA
RS: Eagles lead series, 3-1
PS: Buccaneers lead series, 1-0;
See Philadelphia vs. Tampa Bay
TAMPA BAY vs. PHOENIX
RS: Cardinals lead series, 6-4;
See Phoenix vs. Tampa Bay
TAMPA BAY vs. PITTSBURGH
RS: Steelers lead series, 4-0;
See Pittsburgh vs. Tampa Bay
TAMPA BAY vs. SAN DIEGO
RS: Chargers lead series, 4-0;
See San Diego vs. Tampa Bay
TAMPA BAY vs. SAN FRANCISCO
RS: 49ers lead series, 9-1;
See San Francisco vs. Tampa Bay
TAMPA BAY vs. SEATTLE
RS: Seahawks lead series, 2-0;
See Seattle vs. Tampa Bay
TAMPA BAY vs. WASHINGTON
RS: Redskins lead series, 3-0
1977—Redskins, 10-0 (TB)
1982—Redskins, 21-13 (TB)
1989—Redskins, 32-28 (W)
(RS Pts.—Redskins 63, Buccaneers 41)

WASHINGTON vs. ATLANTA
RS: Redskins lead series, 11-3-1
PS: Redskins lead series, 1-0;
See Atlanta vs. Washington
WASHINGTON vs. BUFFALO
RS: Redskins lead series, 4-2
PS: Redskins lead series, 1-0;
See Buffalo vs. Washington
WASHINGTON vs. CHICAGO
RS: Bears lead series, 18-12-1
PS: Redskins lead series, 4-3;
See Chicago vs. Washington
WASHINGTON vs. CINCINNATI
RS: Redskins lead series, 4-2;
See Cincinnati vs. Washington
WASHINGTON vs. CLEVELAND
RS: Browns lead series, 32-9-1;
See Cleveland vs. Washington
WASHINGTON vs. DALLAS
RS: Cowboys lead series, 35-25-2
PS: Redskins lead series, 2-0;
See Dallas vs. Washington
WASHINGTON vs. DENVER
RS: Broncos lead series, 3-2
PS: Redskins lead series, 1-0;
See Denver vs. Washington

WASHINGTON vs. DETROIT
RS: Redskins lead series, 21-8
PS: Redskins lead series, 2-0;
See Detroit vs. Washington
WASHINGTON vs. GREEN BAY
RS: Packers lead series, 13-12-1
PS: Series tied, 1-1;
See Green Bay vs. Washington
WASHINGTON vs. HOUSTON
RS: Series tied, 3-3;
See Houston vs. Washington
WASHINGTON vs. INDIANAPOLIS
RS: Colts lead series, 16-6;
See Indianapolis vs. Washington
WASHINGTON vs. KANSAS CITY
RS: Chiefs lead series, 2-1;
See Kansas City vs. Washington
WASHINGTON vs. L.A. RAIDERS
RS: Raiders lead series, 4-2
PS: Raiders lead series, 1-0;
See L.A. Raiders vs. Washington
WASHINGTON vs. L.A. RAMS
RS: Redskins lead series, 14-4-1
PS: Series tied, 2-2;
See L.A. Rams vs. Washington
WASHINGTON vs. MIAMI
RS: Dolphins lead series, 4-2
PS: Series tied, 1-1;
See Miami vs. Washington
WASHINGTON vs. MINNESOTA
RS: Redskins lead series, 5-3
PS: Series tied, 1-1;
See Minnesota vs. Washington
WASHINGTON vs. NEW ENGLAND
RS: Redskins lead series, 4-1;
See New England vs. Washington
WASHINGTON vs. NEW ORLEANS
RS: Redskins lead series, 11-4;
See New Orleans vs. Washington
WASHINGTON vs. N.Y. GIANTS
RS: Giants lead series, 66-49-3
PS: Series tied, 1-1;
See N.Y. Giants vs. Washington
WASHINGTON vs. N.Y. JETS
RS: Redskins lead series, 4-0;
See N.Y. Jets vs. Washington
WASHINGTON vs. PHILADELPHIA
RS: Redskins lead series, 65-43-5
PS: Redskins lead series, 1-0;
See Philadelphia vs. Washington
WASHINGTON vs. PHOENIX
RS: Redskins lead series, 60-33-2;
See Phoenix vs. Washington
WASHINGTON vs. PITTSBURGH
RS: Redskins lead series, 42-27-3;
See Pittsburgh vs. Washington
WASHINGTON vs. SAN DIEGO
RS: Redskins lead series, 5-0;
See San Diego vs. Washington
WASHINGTON vs. SAN FRANCISCO
RS: 49ers lead series, 9-6-1
PS: 49ers lead series, 2-1;
See San Francisco vs. Washington
WASHINGTON vs. SEATTLE
RS: Redskins lead series, 4-1;
See Seattle vs. Washington
WASHINGTON vs. TAMPA BAY
RS: Redskins lead series, 3-0;
See Tampa Bay vs. Washington

SUPER BOWL SUMMARIES

Results

Season	Date	Winner (Share)	Loser (Share)	Score	Site	Attendance
XXVI	1-26-92	Washington ($36,000)	Buffalo ($18,000)	37-24	Minneapolis	63,130
XXV	1-27-91	N.Y. Giants ($36,000)	Buffalo ($18,000)	20-19	Tampa	73,813
XXIV	1-28-90	San Francisco ($36,000)	Denver ($18,000)	55-10	New Orleans	72,919
XXIII	1-22-89	San Francisco ($36,000)	Cincinnati ($18,000)	20-16	Miami	75,129
XXII	1-31-88	Washington ($36,000)	Denver ($18,000)	42-10	San Diego	73,302
XXI	1-25-87	N.Y. Giants ($36,000)	Denver ($18,000)	39-20	Pasadena	101,063
XX	1-26-86	Chicago ($36,000)	New England ($18,000)	46-10	New Orleans	73,818
XIX	1-20-85	San Francisco ($36,000)	Miami ($18,000)	38-16	Stanford	84,059
XVIII	1-22-84	L.A. Raiders ($36,000)	Washington ($18,000)	38-9	Tampa	72,920
XVII	1-30-83	Washington ($36,000)	Miami ($18,000)	27-17	Pasadena	103,667
XVI	1-24-82	San Francisco ($18,000)	Cincinnati ($9,000)	26-21	Pontiac	81,270
XV	1-25-81	Oakland ($18,000)	Philadelphia ($9,000)	27-10	New Orleans	76,135
XIV	1-20-80	Pittsburgh ($18,000)	Los Angeles ($9,000)	31-19	Pasadena	103,985
XIII	1-21-79	Pittsburgh ($18,000)	Dallas ($9,000)	35-31	Miami	79,484
XII	1-15-78	Dallas ($18,000)	Denver ($9,000)	27-10	New Orleans	75,583
XI	1-9-77	Oakland ($15,000)	Minnesota ($7,500)	32-14	Pasadena	103,438
X	1-18-76	Pittsburgh ($15,000)	Dallas ($7,500)	21-17	Miami	80,187
IX	1-12-75	Pittsburgh ($15,000)	Minnesota ($7,500)	16-6	New Orleans	80,997
VIII	1-13-74	Miami ($15,000)	Minnesota ($7,500)	24-7	Houston	71,882
VII	1-14-73	Miami ($15,000)	Washington ($7,500)	14-7	Los Angeles	90,182
VI	1-16-72	Dallas ($15,000)	Miami ($7,500)	24-3	New Orleans	81,023
V	1-17-71	Baltimore ($15,000)	Dallas ($7,500)	16-13	Miami	79,204
IV	1-11-70	Kansas City ($15,000)	Minnesota ($7,500)	23-7	New Orleans	80,562
III	1-12-69	N.Y. Jets ($15,000)	Baltimore ($7,500)	16-7	Miami	75,389
II	1-14-68	Green Bay ($15,000)	Oakland ($7,500)	33-14	Miami	75,546
I	1-15-67	Green Bay ($15,000)	Kansas City ($7,500)	35-10	Los Angeles	61,946

Super Bowl Composite Standings

	W	L	Pct.	Pts.	OP
Pittsburgh Steelers	4	0	1.000	103	73
San Francisco 49ers	4	0	1.000	163	63
Green Bay Packers	2	0	1.000	68	24
New York Giants	2	0	1.000	59	39
Chicago Bears	1	0	1.000	46	10
New York Jets	1	0	1.000	16	7
Oakland/L.A. Raiders	3	1	.750	111	66
Washington Redskins	3	2	.600	122	103
Baltimore Colts	1	1	.500	23	29
Kansas City Chiefs	1	1	.500	33	42
Dallas Cowboys	2	3	.400	112	85
Miami Dolphins	2	3	.400	74	103
Los Angeles Rams	0	1	.000	19	31
New England Patriots	0	1	.000	10	46
Philadelphia Eagles	0	1	.000	10	27
Buffalo Bills	0	2	.000	43	57
Cincinnati Bengals	0	2	.000	37	46
Denver Broncos	0	4	.000	50	163
Minnesota Vikings	0	4	.000	34	95

Past Super Bowl Most Valuable Players

Super Bowl I — QB Bart Starr, Green Bay
Super Bowl II — QB Bart Starr, Green Bay
Super Bowl III — QB Joe Namath, New York Jets
Super Bowl IV — QB Len Dawson, Kansas City
Super Bowl V — LB Chuck Howley, Dallas
Super Bowl VI — QB Roger Staubach, Dallas
Super Bowl VII — S Jake Scott, Miami
Super Bowl VIII — RB Larry Csonka, Miami
Super Bowl IX — RB Franco Harris, Pittsburgh
Super Bowl X — WR Lynn Swann, Pittsburgh
Super Bowl XI — WR Fred Biletnikoff, Oakland
Super Bowl XII — DT Randy White and DE Harvey Martin, Dallas
Super Bowl XIII — QB Terry Bradshaw, Pittsburgh
Super Bowl XIV — QB Terry Bradshaw, Pittsburgh
Super Bowl XV — QB Jim Plunkett, Oakland
Super Bowl XVI — QB Joe Montana, San Francisco
Super Bowl XVII — RB John Riggins, Washington
Super Bowl XVIII — RB Marcus Allen, Los Angeles Raiders
Super Bowl XIX — QB Joe Montana, San Francisco
Super Bowl XX — DE Richard Dent, Chicago
Super Bowl XXI — QB Phil Simms, New York Giants
Super Bowl XXII — QB Doug Williams, Washington
Super Bowl XXIII — WR Jerry Rice, San Francisco
Super Bowl XXIV — QB Joe Montana, San Francisco
Super Bowl XXV — RB Ottis Anderson, New York Giants
Super Bowl XXVI — QB Mark Rypien, Washington Redskins

Super Bowl XXVI

Metrodome, Minneapolis, Minnesota — January 26, 1992
Attendance: 63,130

WASHINGTON 37, BUFFALO 24—Mark Rypien passed for 292 yards and 2 touchdowns as the Redskins overwhelmed the Bills to win their third Super Bowl in the past 10 years. Rypien, the game's most valuable player, completed 18 of 33 passes, including a 10-yard scoring strike to Earnest Byner and a 30-yard touchdown to Gary Clark. The latter came late in the third quarter after Buffalo had trimmed a 24-0 deficit to 24-10, and effectively put the game out of reach. Washington went on to lead by as much as 37-10 before the Bills made it close with a pair of touchdowns in the final six minutes. Though the Redskins struggled early, converting their first three drives inside the Bills' 20-yard line into only 3 points, they built a 17-0 halftime lead. And they made it 24-0 just 16 seconds into the second half, after Kurt Gouveia intercepted Buffalo quarterback Jim Kelly's pass on the first play of the third quarter and returned it 23 yards to the Bills' 2. One play later, Gerald Riggs scored his second touchdown of the game to make it 24-0. Kelly, forced to bring Buffalo from behind, completed 28 of a Super Bowl-record 58 passes for 275 yards and 2 touchdowns, but was intercepted 4 times. Bills running back Thurman Thomas, who had an AFC-high 1,407 yards rushing and an NFL-best 2,038 total yards from scrimmage during the regular season, ran for only 13 yards on 10 carries and was limited to 27 yards on 4 receptions. Clark had 7 catches for 114 yards and Art Monk added 7 for 113 for the Redskins, who amassed 417 yards of total offense while limiting the explosive Bills to 283. Washington's Joe Gibbs became only the third head coach to win as many as three Super Bowls.

Washington (37)	Offense	Buffalo (24)
Gary Clark	WR	James Lofton
Jim Lachey	LT	Will Wolford
Raleigh McKenzie	LG	Jim Ritcher
Jeff Bostic	C	Kent Hull
Mark Schlereth	RG	Glenn Parker
Joe Jacoby	RT	Howard Ballard
Ron Middleton	TE	Pete Metzelaars
Don Warren	TE	Keith McKeller
Art Monk	WR	Andre Reed
Mark Rypien	QB	Jim Kelly
Earnest Byner	RB	Kenneth Davis
	Defense	
Charles Mann	LE	Leon Seals
Eric Williams	LT-NT	Jeff Wright
Tim Johnson	RT-RE	Bruce Smith
Fred Stokes	RE-LOLB	Cornelius Bennett
Wilber Marshall	LLB-LILB	Shane Conlan
Kurt Gouveia	MLB-RILB	Carlton Bailey
Andre Collins	RLB-ROLB	Darryl Talley
Martin Mayhew	LCB	Kirby Jackson
Darrell Green	RCB	Nate Odomes
Danny Copeland	SS	Dwight Drane
Brad Edwards	FS	Mark Kelso

Substitutions

Washington—Offense: K—Chip Lohmiller. P—Kelly Goodburn. QB—Jeff Rutledge. RB—Ricky Ervins, Brian Mitchell, Gerald Riggs. WR—Stephen Hobbs, Ricky Sanders. TE—John Brandes, James Jenkins, Terry Orr. G—Mark Adickes, Russ Grimm. T—Ed Simmons. Defense: E—Jason Buck. T—James Geathers, Bobby Wilson. LB—Ravin Caldwell, Monte Coleman. CB—Alvoid Mays, A.J. Johnson, Sidney Johnson. S—Terry Hoage. DNP: None. Inactive: QB—Stan Humphries. LB—Matt Millen.
Buffalo—Offense: K—Brad Daluiso, Scott Norwood. P—Chris Mohr. QB—Frank Reich. RB—Carwell Gardner, Thurman Thomas. WR—Don Beebe, Al Edwards, Steve Tasker. TE—Butch Rolle. C—Adam Lingner. G—Mitch Frerotte. T—Joe Staysniak. Defense: E—Phil Hansen, Mark Pike. T—Mike Lodish. LB—Ray Bentley, Hal Garner, Marvcus Patton. CB—Chris Hale, Clifford Hicks, James Williams. S—Henry Jones. DNP: None. Inactive: QB—Gale Gilbert. T—Mike Brennan.

Officials

Referee—Jerry Markbreit. Umpire—Bob Boylston. Head Linesman—Dale Williams. Line Judge—Ron Blum. Back Judge—Paul Baetz. Field Judge—Ed Merrifield. Side Judge—Dick Creed. Replay Official—Cal Lepore.

Scoring

Washington (NFC)	0	17	14	6	— 37
Buffalo (AFC)	0	0	10	14	— 24

Wash—FG Lohmiller 34
Wash—Byner 10 pass from Rypien (Lohmiller kick)
Wash—Riggs 1 run (Lohmiller kick)
Wash—Riggs 2 run (Lohmiller kick)
Buff —FG Norwood 21
Buff —Thomas 1 run (Norwood kick)
Wash—Clark 30 pass from Rypien (Lohmiller kick)
Wash—FG Lohmiller 25
Wash—FG Lohmiller 39
Buff —Metzelaars 2 pass from Kelly (Norwood kick)
Buff —Beebe 4 pass from Kelly (Norwood kick)

Team Statistics

	Washington	Buffalo
Total First Downs	24	25
First Downs Rushing	10	4
First Downs Passing	12	18
First Downs Penalty	2	3
Total Net Yardage	417	283
Total Offensive Plays	73	82
Average Gain per Offensive Play	5.7	3.5
Rushes	40	18
Yards Gained Rushing (Net)	125	43
Average Yards per Rush	3.1	2.4
Passes Attempted	33	59
Passes Completed	18	29
Had Intercepted	1	4
Tackled Attempting to Pass	0	5
Yards Lost Attempting to Pass	0	46
Yards Gained Passing (Net)	292	240
Punts	4	6
Average Distance	37.5	35.0
Punt Returns	0	3
Punt Return Yardage	0	9
Kickoff Returns	1	4
Kickoff Return Yardage	16	77
Interception Return Yardage	79	4
Total Return Yardage	95	90
Fumbles	1	6
Own Fumbles Recovered	1	2
Opponents Fumbles Recovered	1	0
Penalties	5	6
Yards Penalized	82	50
Total Points Scored	37	24
Touchdowns	4	3
Touchdowns Rushing	2	1
Touchdowns Passing	2	2
Touchdowns Returns	0	0
Extra Points	4	3
Field Goals	3	1
Field Goals Attempted	3	1
Safeties	0	0
Third Down Efficiency	6/16	7/17
Fourth Down Efficiency	0/1	2/2
Time of Possession	33:43	26:17

Individual Statistics

Rushing

Washington	No.	Yds.	LG	TD
Ervins	13	72	21	0
Byner	14	49	19	0
Riggs	5	7	4	2
Sanders	1	1	1	0
Rutledge	1	0	0	0
Rypien	6	-4	2	0

Buffalo	No.	Yds.	LG	TD
K. Davis	4	17	13	0
Kelly	3	16	9	0
Thomas	10	13	6	1
Lofton	1	-3	-3	0

Passing

Wash.	Att.	Comp.	Yds.	TD	Int.
Rypien	33	18	292	2	1

Buffalo	Att.	Comp.	Yds.	TD	Int.
Kelly	58	28	275	2	4
Reich	1	1	11	0	0

Receiving

Washington	No.	Yds.	LG	TD
Clark	7	114	34	1
Monk	7	113	31	0
Byner	3	24	10t	1
Sanders	1	41	41	0

Buffalo	No.	Yds.	LG	TD
Lofton	7	92	18	0
Reed	5	34	12	0
Beebe	4	61	43	1
K. Davis	4	38	12	0
Thomas	4	27	8	0
McKeller	2	29	21	0
Edwards	1	11	11	0
Metzelaars	1	2	2t	1
Kelly	1	-8	-8	0

Interceptions

Washington	No.	Yds.	LG	TD
Edwards	2	56	35	0
Gouveia	1	23	23	0
Green	1	0	0	0

Buffalo	No.	Yds.	LG	TD
Jackson	1	4	4	0

Punting

Washington	No.	Avg.	LG	Blk.
Goodburn	4	37.5	45	0

Buffalo	No.	Avg.	LG	Blk.
Mohr	6	35.0	53	0

Punt Returns

Washington	No.	FC	Yds.	LG	TD
Mitchell	0	2	0	0	0

Buffalo	No.	FC	Yds.	LG	TD
Hicks	3	0	9	7	0

Kickoff Returns

Washington	No.	Yds.	LG	TD
Mitchell	1	16	16	0

Buffalo	No.	Yds.	LG	TD
Edwards	4	77	24	0

Super Bowl XXV

Tampa Stadium, Tampa, Florida   January 27, 1991
Attendance: 73,813

NEW YORK GIANTS 20, BUFFALO 19—The NFC champion New York Giants won their second Super Bowl in five years with a 20-19 victory over AFC titlist Buffalo. New York, employing its ball-control offense, had possession for 40 minutes, 33 seconds, a Super Bowl record. The Bills, who scored 95 points in their previous two playoff games leading to Super Bowl XXV, had the ball for less than eight minutes in the second half and just 19:27 for the game. Fourteen of New York's 73 plays came on its initial drive of the third quarter, which covered 75 yards and consumed a Super Bowl-record 9:29 before running back Ottis Anderson ran one yard for a touchdown. Giants quarterback Jeff Hostetler kept the long drive going by converting three third-down plays—an 11-yard pass to running back David Meggett on third-and-eight, a 14-yard toss to wide receiver Mark Ingram on third-and-13, and a nine-yard pass to Howard Cross on third-and-four—to give New York a 17-12 lead in the third quarter. Buffalo jumped to a 12-3 lead midway through the second quarter before Hostetler completed a 14-yard scoring strike to wide receiver Stephen Baker to close the score to 12-10 at halftime. Buffalo's Thurman Thomas ran 31 yards for a touchdown on the opening play of the fourth quarter to help Buffalo recapture the lead 19-17. Giants kicker Matt Bahr's 21-yard field goal gave the Giants a 20-19 lead, but Buffalo's Scott Norwood had a chance to win the game with seconds remaining before his 47-yard field-goal attempt sailed wide right. Hostetler completed 20 of 32 passes for 222 yards and one touchdown for the game. Wide receiver Mark Ingram caught five passes for 74 yards; tight end Mark Bavaro five for 50. Anderson rushed 21 times for 102 yards and one touchdown to capture the most-valuable-player honors. Thomas totaled 190 scrimmage yards, rushing 15 times for 135 yards and catching five passes for 55 yards.

Buffalo (AFC)	3	9	0	7	— 19
N.Y. Giants (NFC)	3	7	7	3	— 20

NYG—FG Bahr 28
Buff —FG Norwood 23
Buff —D. Smith, 1 run (Norwood kick)
Buff —Safety, B. Smith (tackled Hostetler in end zone)
NYG—Baker 14 pass from Hostetler (Bahr kick)
NYG—Anderson 1 run (Bahr kick)
Buff —Thomas 31 run (Norwood kick)
NYG—FG Bahr 21

Super Bowl XXIV

Louisiana Superdome, New Orleans, Louisiana   January 28, 1990
Attendance: 72,919

SAN FRANCISCO 55, DENVER 10—NFC titlist San Francisco won its fourth Super Bowl championship with a 55-10 victory over AFC champion Denver. The 49ers, who also won Super Bowls XVI, XIX, and XXIII, tied the Pittsburgh Steelers for most Super Bowl victories. The Steelers captured Super Bowls IX, X, XIII, and XIV. San Francisco's 55 points broke the previous Super Bowl scoring mark of 46 points by Chicago in Super Bowl XX. San Francisco scored touchdowns on four of its six first-half possessions to hold a 27-3 lead at halftime. The 49ers' first-half scoring drives were lengthy and time-consuming (10 plays for 66 yards, 10 for 54, 14 for 69, and 5 for 59). Interceptions by Michael Walter and Chet Brooks ended the Broncos' first two possessions of the second half. San Francisco quarterback Joe Montana was named the Super Bowl most valuable player for a record third time. Montana completed 22 of 29 passes for 297 yards and a Super Bowl-record five touchdowns (old record: four, Terry Bradshaw, Pittsburgh, Super Bowl XIII, and Doug Williams, Washington, Super Bowl XXII). Jerry Rice, Super Bowl XXIII most valuable player, caught seven passes for 148 yards and three touchdowns. The 49ers' domination included first downs (28 to 12), net yards (461 to 167), and time of possession (39:31 to 20:29).

San Francisco (NFC)	13	14	14	14	— 55
Denver (AFC)	3	0	7	0	— 10

SF —Rice 20 pass from Montana (Cofer kick)
Den—FG Treadwell 42
SF —Jones 7 pass from Montana (kick failed)
SF —Rathman 1 run (Cofer kick)
SF —Rice 38 pass from Montana (Cofer kick)
SF —Rice 28 pass from Montana (Cofer kick)

SF —Taylor 35 pass from Montana (Cofer kick)
Den—Elway 3 run (Treadwell kick)
SF —Rathman 3 run (Cofer kick)
SF —Craig 1 run (Cofer kick)

Super Bowl XXIII

Joe Robbie Stadium, Miami, Florida   January 22, 1989
Attendance: 75,129

SAN FRANCISCO 20, CINCINNATI 16—NFC champion San Francisco captured its third Super Bowl of the 1980s by defeating AFC champion Cincinnati 20-16. The 49ers, who also won Super Bowls XVI and XIX, are the first NFC team to win three Super Bowls. Pittsburgh with four Super Bowl titles (IX, X, XIII, and XIV) and the Oakland/Los Angeles Raiders with three (XI, XV, and XVIII) lead AFC franchises. Even though San Francisco held an advantage in total net yards (453 to 229), the 49ers found themselves trailing the Bengals late in the game. With the score tied 13-13, Cincinnati took a 16-13 lead on Jim Breech's 40-yard field goal with 3:20 remaining. It was Breech's third field goal of the day, following earlier successes from 34 and 43 yards. The 49ers started their winning drive at their own 8-yard line. Over the next 11 plays, San Francisco covered 92 yards with the decisive score coming on a 10-yard pass from quarterback Joe Montana to wide receiver John Taylor with 34 seconds remaining. At halftime, the score was 3-3, the first time in Super Bowl history the game was tied at intermission. After the teams traded third-period field goals, the Bengals jumped ahead 13-6 on Stanford Jennings's 93-yard kickoff return for a touchdown with 34 seconds remaining in the quarter. The 49ers didn't waste any time coming back as they covered 85 yards in four plays, concluding with Montana's 14-yard scoring pass to Rice 57 seconds into the final stanza. Rice was named the game's most valuable player after compiling 11 catches for a Super Bowl-record 215 yards. Montana completed 23 of 36 passes for a Super Bowl-record 357 yards and two touchdowns.

Cincinnati (AFC)	0	3	10	3 — 16
San Francisco (NFC)	3	0	3	14 — 20

SF —FG Cofer 41
Cin—FG Breech 34
Cin—FG Breech 43
SF —FG Cofer 32
Cin—Jennings 93 kickoff return (Breech kick)
SF —Rice 14 pass from Montana (Cofer kick)
Cin—FG Breech 40
SF —Taylor 10 pass from Montana (Cofer kick)

Super Bowl XXII

San Diego Jack Murphy Stadium, San Diego, California   January 31, 1988
Attendance: 73,302

WASHINGTON 42, DENVER 10—NFC champion Washington won Super Bowl XXII and its second NFL championship of the 1980s with a 42-10 decision over AFC champion Denver. The Redskins, who also won Super Bowl XVII, enjoyed a record-setting second quarter en route to the victory. The Broncos broke in front 10-0 when quarterback John Elway threw a 56-yard touchdown pass to wide receiver Ricky Nattiel on the Broncos' first play from scrimmage. Following a Washington punt, Denver's Rich Karlis kicked a 24-yard field goal to cap a seven-play, 61-yard scoring drive. The Redskins then erupted for 35 points on five straight possessions in the second period and coasted thereafter. The 35 points established an NFL postseason mark for most points scored in a period, bettering the previous mark of 21 by San Francisco in Super Bowl XIX and Chicago in Super Bowl XX. Redskins quarterback Doug Williams led the second-period explosion by throwing a Super Bowl record-tying four touchdown passes, including 80- and 50-yarders to wide receiver Ricky Sanders, a 27-yarder to wide receiver Gary Clark, and an 8-yarder to tight end Clint Didier. Washington scored five touchdowns in 18 plays with total time of possession of only 5:47. Overall, Williams completed 18 of 29 passes for 340 yards and was named the game's most valuable player. His pass-yardage total eclipsed the previous Super Bowl record of 331 yards by Joe Montana of San Francisco in Super Bowl XIX. Sanders ended with 193 yards on eight catches, breaking the previous Super Bowl yardage record of 161 yards by Lynn Swann of Pittsburgh in Game X. Rookie running back Timmy Smith was the game's leading rusher with 22 carries for a Super Bowl-record 204 yards, breaking the previous mark of 191 yards by Marcus Allen of the Raiders in Game XVIII. Smith also scored twice on runs of 58 and four yards. Washington's six touchdowns and 602 total yards gained also set Super Bowl records. Redskins cornerback Barry Wilburn had two of the team's three interceptions, and strong safety Alvin Walton had two of Washington's five sacks.

Washington (NFC)	0	35	0	7 — 42
Denver (AFC)	10	0	0	0 — 10

Den —Nattiel 56 pass from Elway (Karlis kick)
Den —FG Karlis 24
Wash—Sanders 80 pass from Williams (Haji-Sheikh kick)
Wash—Clark 27 pass from Williams (Haji-Sheikh kick)
Wash—Smith 58 run (Haji-Sheikh kick)
Wash—Sanders 50 pass from Williams (Haji-Sheikh kick)
Wash—Didier 8 pass from Williams (Haji-Sheikh kick)
Wash—Smith 4 run (Haji-Sheikh kick)

Super Bowl XXI

Rose Bowl, Pasadena, California   January 25, 1987
Attendance: 101,063

NEW YORK GIANTS 39, DENVER 20—The NFC champion New York Giants captured their first NFL title since 1956 when they downed the AFC champion Denver Broncos 39-20 in Super Bowl XXI. The victory marked the NFC's fifth NFL title in the past six seasons. The Broncos, behind the passing of quarterback John Elway, who was 13 of 20 for 187 yards in the first half, held a 10-9 lead at intermission, the narrowest halftime margin in Super Bowl history. Denver's Rich Karlis opened the scoring with a Super Bowl record-tying 48-yard field goal. New York drove 78 yards in nine plays on the next series to take a 7-3 lead on quarterback Phil Simms's six-yard touchdown pass to tight end Zeke Mowatt. The Broncos came right back with a 58-yard scoring drive on six plays capped by Elway's four-yard touchdown run. The only scoring in the second period was the sack of Elway in the end zone by defensive end George Martin for a New York safety. The Giants produced a key defensive stand early in the second quarter when the Broncos had a first down at the New York one-yard line, but failed to score on three running plays and Karlis's 23-yard missed field-goal attempt. The Giants took command of the game in the third period en route to a 30-point second half, the most ever scored in one half of Super Bowl play. New York took the lead for good on tight end Mark Bavaro's 13-yard touchdown catch 4:52 into the third period. The nine-play, 63-yard scoring drive included the successful conversion of a fourth down and play on the New York 46-yard line. Denver was limited to only two net yards on 10 offensive plays in the third period. Simms set Super Bowl records for most consecutive completions (10) and highest completion percentage (88 percent on 22 completions in 25 attempts). He also passed for 268 yards and three touchdowns and was named the game's most valuable player. New York running back Joe Morris was the game's leading rusher with 20 carries for 67 yards. Denver wide receiver Vance Johnson led all receivers with five catches for 121 yards. The Giants defeated their three playoff opponents by a cumulative total of 82 points (New York 105, opponents 23), the largest such margin by a Super Bowl winner.

Denver (AFC)	10	0	0	10 — 20
N.Y. Giants (NFC)	7	2	17	13 — 39

Den —FG Karlis 48
NYG—Mowatt 6 pass from Simms (Allegre kick)
Den —Elway 4 run (Karlis kick)
NYG—Safety, Martin tackled Elway in end zone
NYG—Bavaro 13 pass from Simms (Allegre kick)
NYG—FG Allegre 21
NYG—Morris 1 run (Allegre kick)
NYG—McConkey 6 pass from Simms (Allegre kick)
Den —FG Karlis 28
NYG—Anderson 2 run (kick failed)
Den —V. Johnson 47 pass from Elway (Karlis kick)

Super Bowl XX

Louisiana Superdome, New Orleans, Louisiana   January 26, 1986
Attendance: 73,818

CHICAGO 46, NEW ENGLAND 10—The NFC champion Chicago Bears, seeking their first NFL title since 1963, scored a Super Bowl-record 46 points in downing AFC champion New England 46-10 in Super Bowl XX. The previous record for most points in a Super Bowl was 38, shared by San Francisco in XIX and the Los Angeles Raiders in XVIII. The Bears' league-leading defense tied the Super Bowl record for sacks (seven) and limited the Patriots to a record-low seven yards rushing. New England took the quickest lead in Super Bowl history when Tony Franklin kicked a 36-yard field goal with 1:19 elapsed in the first period. The score came about because of Larry McGrew's fumble recovery at the Chicago 19-yard line. However, the Bears rebounded for a 23-3 first-half lead, while building a yardage advantage of 236 total yards to New England's minus 19. Running back Matt Suhey rushed eight times for 37 yards, including an 11-yard touchdown run, and caught one pass for 24 yards in the first half. After the Patriots first drive of the second half ended with a punt to the Bears' 4-yard line, Chicago marched 96 yards in nine plays with quarterback Jim McMahon's one-yard scoring run capping the drive. McMahon became the first quarterback in Super Bowl history to rush for a pair of touchdowns. The Bears completed their scoring via a 28-yard interception return by reserve cornerback Reggie Phillips, a one-yard run by defensive tackle/fullback William Perry, and a safety when defensive end Henry Waechter tackled Patriots quarterback Steve Grogan in the end zone. Bears defensive end Richard Dent became the fourth defender to be named the game's most valuable player after contributing 1½ sacks. The Bears' victory margin of 36 points was the largest in Super Bowl history, bettering the previous mark of 29 by the Los Angeles Raiders when they topped Washington 38-9 in Game XVIII. McMahon completed 12 of 20 passes for 256 yards before leaving the game in the fourth period with a wrist injury. The NFL's all-time leading rusher, Bears running back Walter Payton, carried 22 times for 61 yards. Wide receiver Willie Gault caught four passes for 129 yards, the fourth-most receiving yards in a Super Bowl. Chicago coach Mike Ditka became the second man (Tom Flores of Raiders was the other) who played in a Super Bowl and coached a team to a victory in the game.

Chicago (NFC)	13	10	21	2 — 46
New England (AFC)	3	0	0	7 — 10

NE—FG Franklin 36
Chi—FG Butler 28
Chi—FG Butler 24
Chi—Suhey 11 run (Butler kick)
Chi—McMahon 2 run (Butler kick)

Chi—FG Butler 24
Chi—McMahon 1 run (Butler kick)
Chi—Phillips 28 interception return (Butler kick)
Chi—Perry 1 run (Butler kick)
NE—Fryar 8 pass from Grogan (Franklin kick)
Chi—Safety, Waechter tackled Grogan in end zone

Super Bowl XIX

Stanford Stadium, Stanford, California   January 20, 1985
Attendance: 84,059

SAN FRANCISCO 38, MIAMI 16—The San Francisco 49ers captured their second Super Bowl title with a dominating offense and a defense that tamed Miami's explosive passing attack. The Dolphins held a 10-7 lead at the end of the first period, which represented the most points scored by two teams in an opening quarter of a Super Bowl. However, the 49ers used excellent field position in the second period to build a 28-16 halftime lead. Running back Roger Craig set a Super Bowl record by scoring three touchdowns on pass receptions of 8 and 16 yards and a run of 2 yards. San Francisco's Joe Montana was voted the game's most valuable player. He joined Green Bay's Bart Starr and Pittsburgh's Terry Bradshaw as the only two-time Super Bowl most valuable players. Montana completed 24 of 35 passes for a Super Bowl-record 331 yards and three touchdowns, and rushed five times for 59 yards, including a six-yard touchdown. Craig had 58 yards on 15 carries and caught seven passes for 77 yards. Wendell Tyler rushed 13 times for 65 yards and had four catches for 70 yards. Dwight Clark had six receptions for 77 yards, while Russ Francis had five for 60. San Francisco's 537 total net yards bettered the previous Super Bowl record of 429 yards by Oakland in Super Bowl XI. The 49ers also held a time of possession advantage over the Dolphins of 37:11 to 22:49.

Miami (AFC)	10	6	0	0 — 16	
San Francisco (NFC)	7	21	10	0 — 38	

Mia—FG von Schamann 37
SF —Monroe 33 pass from Montana (Wersching kick)
Mia—D. Johnson 2 pass from Marino (von Schamann kick)
SF —Craig 8 pass from Montana (Wersching kick)
SF —Montana 6 run (Wersching kick)
SF —Craig 2 run (Wersching kick)
Mia—FG von Schamann 31
Mia—FG von Schamann 30
SF —FG Wersching 27
SF —Craig 16 pass from Montana (Wersching kick)

Super Bowl XVIII

Tampa Stadium, Tampa, Florida   January 22, 1984
Attendance: 72,920

LOS ANGELES RAIDERS 38, WASHINGTON 9—The Los Angeles Raiders dominated the Washington Redskins from the beginning in Super Bowl XVIII and achieved the most lopsided victory in Super Bowl history, surpassing Green Bay's 35-10 win over Kansas City in Super Bowl I. The Raiders took a 7-0 lead 4:52 into the game when Derrick Jensen blocked a Jeff Hayes punt and recovered it in the end zone for a touchdown. With 9:14 remaining in the first half, Raiders quarterback Jim Plunkett threw a 12-yard touchdown pass to wide receiver Cliff Branch to complete a three-play, 65-yard drive. Washington cut the Raiders' lead to 14-3 on a 24-yard field goal by Mark Moseley. With seven seconds left in the first half, Raiders linebacker Jack Squirek intercepted a Joe Theismann pass at the Redskins' 5-yard line and ran it in for a touchdown to give Los Angeles a 21-3 halftime lead. In the third period, running back Marcus Allen, who rushed for a Super Bowl-record 191 yards on 20 carries, increased the Raiders' lead to 35-9 on touchdown runs of five and 74 yards, the latter erasing the previous Super Bowl record of 58 yards set by Baltimore's Tom Matte in Game III. Allen was named the game's most valuable player. The victory over Washington raised Raiders coach Tom Flores's playoff record to 8-1, including a 27-10 win against Philadelphia in Super Bowl XV. The 38 points scored by the Raiders were the highest total by a Super Bowl team. The previous high was 35 points by Green Bay in Game I.

Washington (NFC)	0	3	6	0 — 9	
L.A. Raiders (AFC)	7	14	14	3 — 38	

Raiders—Jensen recovered blocked punt in end zone (Bahr kick)
Raiders—Branch 12 pass from Plunkett (Bahr kick)
Wash —FG Moseley 24
Raiders—Squirek 5 interception return (Bahr kick)
Wash —Riggins 1 run (kick blocked)
Raiders—Allen 5 run (Bahr kick)
Raiders—Allen 74 run (Bahr kick)
Raiders—FG Bahr 21

Super Bowl XVII

Rose Bowl, Pasadena, California   January 30, 1983
Attendance: 103,667

WASHINGTON 27, MIAMI 17—Fullback John Riggins's Super Bowl-record 166 yards on 38 carries sparked Washington to a 27-17 victory over AFC champion Miami. It was Riggins's fourth straight 100-yard rushing game during the playoffs, also a record. The win marked Washington's first NFL title since 1942, and was only the second time in Super Bowl history NFL/NFC teams scored consecutive victories (Green Bay did it in Super Bowls I and II and San Francisco won Super Bowl XVI). The Redskins, under second-year head coach Joe Gibbs, used a balanced offense that accounted for 400 total yards (a Super Bowl-record 276 yards rushing and 124 passing), second in Super Bowl history to 429 yards by Oakland in Super Bowl XI. The Dolphins built a 17-10 halftime lead on a 76-yard touchdown pass from quarterback David Woodley to

wide receiver Jimmy Cefalo 6:49 into the first period, a 20-yard field goal by Uwe von Schamann with 6:00 left in the half, and a Super Bowl-record 98-yard kickoff return by Fulton Walker with 1:38 remaining. Washington had tied the score at 10-10 with 1:51 left on a four-yard touchdown pass from Joe Theismann to wide receiver Alvin Garrett. Mark Moseley started the Redskins' scoring with a 31-yard field goal late in the first period, and added a 20-yarder midway through the third period to cut the Dolphins' lead to 17-13. Riggins, who was given the game's most valuable player, gave Washington its first lead of the game with 10:01 left when he ran 43 yards off left tackle for a touchdown on a fourth-and-one situation. Wide receiver Charlie Brown caught a six-yard scoring pass from Theismann with 1:55 left to complete the scoring. The Dolphins managed only 176 yards (142 in the first half). Theismann completed 15 of 23 passes for 143 yards, with two touchdowns and two interceptions. For Miami, Woodley was 4 of 14 for 97 yards, with one touchdown, and one interception. Don Strock was 0 for 3 in relief.

Miami (AFC)	7	10	0	0 — 17	
Washington (NFC)	0	10	3	14 — 27	

Mia —Cefalo 76 pass from Woodley (von Schamann kick)
Wash—FG Moseley 31
Mia —FG von Schamann 20
Wash—Garrett 4 pass from Theismann (Moseley kick)
Mia —Walker 98 kickoff return (von Schamann kick)
Wash—FG Moseley 20
Wash—Riggins 43 run (Moseley kick)
Wash—Brown 6 pass from Theismann (Moseley kick)

Super Bowl XVI

Pontiac Silverdome, Pontiac, Michigan   January 24, 1982
Attendance: 81,270

SAN FRANCISCO 26, CINCINNATI 21—Ray Wersching's Super Bowl record-tying four field goals and Joe Montana's controlled passing helped lift the San Francisco 49ers to their first NFL championship with a 26-21 victory over Cincinnati. The 49ers built a game-record 20-0 halftime lead via Montana's one-yard touchdown run, which capped an 11-play, 68-yard drive; fullback Earl Cooper's 11-yard scoring pass from Montana, which climaxed a Super Bowl record 92-yard drive on 12 plays; and Wersching's 22- and 26-yard field goals. The Bengals rebounded in the second half, closing the gap to 20-14 on quarterback Ken Anderson's five-yard run and Dan Ross's four-yard reception from Anderson, who established Super Bowl passing records for completions (25) and completion percentage (73.5 percent on 25 of 34). Wersching added early fourth-period field goals of 40 and 23 yards to increase the 49ers' lead to 26-14. The Bengals managed to score on an Anderson-to-Ross three-yard pass with only 16 seconds remaining. Ross set a Super Bowl record with 11 receptions for 104 yards. Montana, the game's most valuable player, completed 14 of 22 passes for 157 yards. Cincinnati compiled 356 yards to San Francisco's 275, which marked the first time in Super Bowl history that the team that gained the most yards from scrimmage lost the game.

San Francisco (NFC)	7	13	0	6 — 26	
Cincinnati (AFC)	0	0	7	14 — 21	

SF —Montana 1 run (Wersching kick)
SF —Cooper 11 pass from Montana (Wersching kick)
SF —FG Wersching 22
SF —FG Wersching 26
Cin—Anderson 5 run (Breech kick)
Cin—Ross 4 pass from Anderson (Breech kick)
SF —FG Wersching 40
SF —FG Wersching 23
Cin—Ross 3 pass from Anderson (Breech kick)

Super Bowl XV

Louisiana Superdome, New Orleans, Louisiana   January 25, 1981
Attendance: 76,135

OAKLAND 27, PHILADELPHIA 10—Jim Plunkett threw three touchdown passes, including an 80-yarder to Kenny King, as the Raiders became the first wild-card team to win the Super Bowl. Plunkett's touchdown bomb to King—the longest play in Super Bowl history—gave Oakland a decisive 14-0 lead with nine seconds left in the first period. Linebacker Rod Martin had set up Oakland's first touchdown, a two-yard reception by Cliff Branch, with a 17-yard interception return to the Eagles' 30 yard line. The Eagles never recovered from that early deficit, managing only a Tony Franklin field goal (30 yards) and an eight-yard touchdown pass from Ron Jaworski to Keith Krepfle the rest of the game. Plunkett, who became a starter in the sixth game of the season, completed 13 of 21 for 261 yards and was named the game's most valuable player. Oakland won nine of 11 games with Plunkett starting, but that was good enough only for second place in the AFC West, although they tied division winner San Diego with an 11-5 record. The Raiders, who had previously won Super Bowl XI over Minnesota, had to win three playoff games to get to the championship game. Oakland defeated Houston 27-7 at home followed by road victories over Cleveland (14-12) and San Diego (34-27). Oakland's Mark van Eeghen was the game's leading rusher with 75 yards on 18 carries. Philadelphia's Wilbert Montgomery led all receivers with six receptions for 91 yards. Branch had five for 67 and Harold Carmichael of Philadelphia five for 83. Martin finished the game with three interceptions, a Super Bowl record.

Oakland (AFC)	14	0	10	3 — 27	
Philadelphia (NFC)	0	3	0	7 — 10	

Oak—Branch 2 pass from Plunkett (Bahr kick)
Oak—King 80 pass from Plunkett (Bahr kick)
Phil—FG Franklin 30
Oak—Branch 29 pass from Plunkett (Bahr kick)

Oak—FG Bahr 46
Phil—Krepfle 8 pass from Jaworski (Franklin kick)
Oak—FG Bahr 35

Super Bowl XIV

Rose Bowl, Pasadena, California   January 20, 1980
Attendance: 103,985

PITTSBURGH 31, LOS ANGELES 19—Terry Bradshaw completed 14 of 21 passes for 309 yards and set two passing records as the Steelers became the first team to win four Super Bowls. Despite three interceptions by the Rams, Bradshaw kept his poise and brought the Steelers from behind twice in the second half. Trailing 13-10 at halftime, Pittsburgh went ahead 17-13 when Bradshaw hit Lynn Swann with a 47-yard touchdown pass after 2:48 of the third quarter. On the Rams' next possession Vince Ferragamo completed 15 of 25 passes for 212 yards, responded with a 50-yard pass to Billy Waddy that moved Los Angeles from its own 26 to the Steelers' 24. On the following play, Lawrence McCutcheon connected with Ron Smith on a halfback option pass that gave the Rams a 19-17 lead. On Pittsburgh's initial possession of the final period, Bradshaw lofted a 73-yard scoring pass to John Stallworth to put the Steelers in front to stay, 24-19. Franco Harris scored on a one-yard run later in the quarter to seal the verdict. A 45-yard pass from Bradshaw to Stallworth was the key play in the drive to Harris's score. Bradshaw, the game's most valuable player for the second straight year, set career Super Bowl records for most touchdown passes (nine) and most passing yards (932). Larry Anderson gave the Steelers excellent field position throughout the game with five kickoff returns for a record 162 yards.

Los Angeles (NFC)	7	6	6	0 —	19
Pittsburgh (AFC)	3	7	7	14 —	31

Pitt—FG Bahr 41
LA—Bryant 1 run (Corral kick)
Pitt—Harris 1 run (Bahr kick)
LA—FG Corral 31
LA—FG Corral 45
Pitt—Swann 47 pass from Bradshaw (Bahr kick)
LA—Smith 24 pass from McCutcheon (kick failed)
Pitt—Stallworth 73 pass from Bradshaw (Bahr kick)
Pitt—Harris 1 run (Bahr kick)

Super Bowl XIII

Orange Bowl, Miami, Florida   January 21, 1979
Attendance: 79,484

PITTSBURGH 35, DALLAS 31—Terry Bradshaw threw a record four touchdown passes to lead the Steelers to victory. The Steelers became the first team to win three Super Bowls, mostly because of Bradshaw's accurate arm. Bradshaw, voted the game's most valuable player, completed 17 of 30 passes for 318 yards, a personal high. Four of those passes went for touchdowns—two to John Stallworth and the third, with 26 seconds remaining in the second period, to Rocky Bleier for a 21-14 halftime lead. The Cowboys scored twice before intermission on Roger Staubach's 39-yard pass to Tony Hill and a 37-yard fumble return by linebacker Mike Hegman, who stole the ball from Bradshaw. The Steelers broke open the contest with two touchdowns in a span of 19 seconds midway through the final period. Franco Harris rambled 22 yards up the middle to give the Steelers a 28-17 lead with 7:10 left. Pittsburgh got the ball right back when Randy White fumbled the kickoff and Dennis Winston recovered for the Steelers. On first down, Bradshaw fired his fourth touchdown pass, an 18-yarder to Lynn Swann to boost the Steelers' lead to 35-17 with 6:51 to play. The Cowboys refused to let the Steelers run away with the contest. Staubach connected with Billy Joe DuPree on a seven-yard scoring pass with 2:23 left. Then the Cowboys recovered an onside kick and Staubach took them in for another score, passing four yards to Butch Johnson with 22 seconds remaining. Bleier recovered another onside kick with 17 seconds left to seal the victory for the Steelers.

Pittsburgh (AFC)	7	14	0	14 —	35
Dallas (NFC)	7	7	3	14 —	31

Pitt—Stallworth 28 pass from Bradshaw (Gerela kick)
Dall—Hill 39 pass from Staubach (Septien kick)
Dall—Hegman 37 fumble recovery return (Septien kick)
Pitt—Stallworth 75 pass from Bradshaw (Gerela kick)
Pitt—Bleier 7 pass from Bradshaw (Gerela kick)
Dall—FG Septien 27
Pitt—Harris 22 run (Gerela kick)
Pitt—Swann 18 pass from Bradshaw (Gerela kick)
Dall—DuPree 7 pass from Staubach (Septien kick)
Dall—B. Johnson 4 pass from Staubach (Septien kick)

Super Bowl XII

Louisiana Superdome, New Orleans, Louisiana   January 15, 1978
Attendance: 75,583

DALLAS 27, DENVER 10—The Cowboys evened their Super Bowl record at 2-2 by defeating Denver before a sellout crowd of 75,583, plus 102,010,000 television viewers, the largest audience ever to watch a sporting event. Dallas converted two interceptions into 10 points and Efren Herrera added a 35-yard field goal for a 13-0 halftime advantage. In the third period Craig Morton engineered a drive to the Cowboys' 30 and Jim Turner's 47-yard field goal made the score 13-3. After an exchange of punts, Butch Johnson made a spectacular diving catch in the end zone to complete a 45-yard pass from Roger Staubach and put the Cowboys ahead 20-3. Following Rick Upchurch's 67-yard kickoff return, Norris Weese guided the Broncos to a touchdown to cut the Dallas lead to 20-10. Dallas clinched the victory when running back Robert

Newhouse threw a 29-yard touchdown pass to Golden Richards with 7:04 remaining in the game. It was the first pass thrown by Newhouse since 1975. Harvey Martin and Randy White, who were named co-most valuable players, led the Cowboys' defense, which recovered four fumbles and intercepted four passes.

Dallas (NFC)	10	3	7	7 —	27
Denver (AFC)	0	0	10	0 —	10

Dall—Dorsett 3 run (Herrera kick)
Dall—FG Herrera 35
Dall—FG Herrera 43
Den—FG Turner 47
Dall—Johnson 45 pass from Staubach (Herrera kick)
Den—Lytle 1 run (Turner kick)
Dall—Richards 29 pass from Newhouse (Herrera kick)

Super Bowl XI

Rose Bowl, Pasadena, California   January 9, 1977
Attendance: 103,438

OAKLAND 32, MINNESOTA 14—The Raiders won their first NFL championship before a record Super Bowl crowd plus 81 million television viewers, the largest audience ever to watch a sporting event. The Raiders gained a record-breaking 429 yards, including running back Clarence Davis's 137 yards rushing. Wide receiver Fred Biletnikoff made four key receptions, which earned him the game's most valuable player trophy. Oakland scored on three successive possessions in the second quarter to build a 16-0 halftime lead. Errol Mann's 24-yard field goal opened the scoring, then the AFC champions put together drives of 64 and 35 yards, scoring on a one-yard pass from Ken Stabler to Dave Casper and a one-yard run by Pete Banaszak. The Raiders increased their lead to 19-0 on a 40-yard field goal in the third quarter, but Minnesota responded with a 12-play, 58-yard drive late in the period, with Fran Tarkenton passing eight yards to wide receiver Sammy White to cut the deficit to 19-7. Two fourth-quarter interceptions clinched the title for the Raiders. One set up Banaszak's second touchdown run, the other resulted in cornerback Willie Brown's Super Bowl-record 75-yard interception return.

Oakland (AFC)	0	16	3	13 —	32
Minnesota (NFC)	0	0	7	7 —	14

Oak—FG Mann 24
Oak—Casper 1 pass from Stabler (Mann kick)
Oak—Banaszak 1 run (kick failed)
Oak—FG Mann 40
Minn—S. White 8 pass from Tarkenton (Cox kick)
Oak—Banaszak 2 run (Mann kick)
Oak—Brown 75 interception return (kick failed)
Minn—Voigt 13 pass from Lee (Cox kick)

Super Bowl X

Orange Bowl, Miami, Florida   January 18, 1976
Attendance: 80,187

PITTSBURGH 21, DALLAS 17—The Steelers won the Super Bowl for the second year in a row on Terry Bradshaw's 64-yard touchdown pass to Lynn Swann and an aggressive defense that snuffed out a late rally by the Cowboys with an end-zone interception on the final play of the game. In the fourth quarter, Pittsburgh ran on fourth down and gave the ball on the Cowboys' 39 with 1:22 to play. Roger Staubach ran and passed for two first downs but his last desperation pass was picked off by Glen Edwards. Dallas's scoring was the result of two touchdown passes by Staubach, one to Drew Pearson for 29 yards and the other to Percy Howard for 34 yards. Toni Fritsch had a 36-yard field goal. The Steelers scored on two touchdown passes by Bradshaw, one to Randy Grossman for seven yards and the long bomb to Swann. Roy Gerela had 36- and 18-yard field goals. Reggie Harrison blocked a punt through the end zone for a safety. Swann set a Super Bowl record by gaining 161 yards on his four receptions.

Dallas (NFC)	7	3	0	7 —	17
Pittsburgh (AFC)	7	0	0	14 —	21

Dall—D. Pearson 29 pass from Staubach (Fritsch kick)
Pitt—Grossman 7 pass from Bradshaw (Gerela kick)
Dall—FG Fritsch 36
Pitt—Safety, Harrison blocked Hoopes's punt through end zone
Pitt—FG Gerela 36
Pitt—FG Gerela 18
Pitt—Swann 64 pass from Bradshaw (kick failed)
Dall—P. Howard 34 pass from Staubach (Fritsch kick)

Super Bowl IX

Tulane Stadium, New Orleans, Louisiana   January 12, 1975
Attendance: 80,997

PITTSBURGH 16, MINNESOTA 6—AFC champion Pittsburgh, in its initial Super Bowl appearance, and NFC champion Minnesota, making a third bid for its first Super Bowl title, struggled through a first half in which the only score was produced by the Steelers' defense when Dwight White downed Vikings' quarterback Fran Tarkenton in the end zone for a safety 7:49 into the second period. The Steelers forced another break and took advantage on the second-half kickoff when Minnesota's Bill Brown fumbled and Marv Kellum recovered for Pittsburgh on the Vikings' 30. After Rocky Bleier failed to gain on first down, Franco Harris carried three consecutive times for 24 yards, a loss of 3, and a 9-yard touchdown and a 9-0 lead. Though its offense was completely stymied by Pittsburgh's defense, Minnesota managed to move into a threatening position after 4:27 of the final period when Matt Blair blocked Bobby Walden's punt and Terry Brown recovered the ball in the end zone for a touchdown. Fred

Cox's kick failed and the Steelers led 9-6. Pittsburgh wasted no time putting the victory away. The Steelers took the ensuing kickoff and marched 66 yards in 11 plays, climaxed by Terry Bradshaw's four-yard scoring pass to Larry Brown with 3:31 left. Pittsburgh's defense permitted Minnesota only 119 yards total offense, including a Super Bowl low of 17 rushing yards. The Steelers, meanwhile, gained 333 yards, including Harris's record 158 yards on 34 carries.

Pittsburgh (AFC)	0	2	7	7 — 16
Minnesota (NFC)	0	0	0	6 — 6

Pitt —Safety, White downed Tarkenton in end zone
Pitt —Harris 9 run (Gerela kick)
Minn—T. Brown recovered blocked punt in end zone (kick failed)
Pitt —L. Brown 4 pass from Bradshaw (Gerela kick)

Super Bowl VIII

Rice Stadium, Houston, Texas — January 13, 1974
Attendance: 71,882

MIAMI 24, MINNESOTA 7—The defending NFL champion Dolphins, representing the AFC for the third straight year, scored the first two times they had possession on marches of 62 and 56 yards while the Miami defense limited the Vikings to only seven plays in the first period. Larry Csonka climaxed the initial 10-play drive with a five-yard touchdown bolt through right guard after 5:27 had elapsed. Four plays later, Miami began another 10-play scoring drive, which ended with Jim Kiick bursting one yard through the middle for another touchdown after 13:38 of the period. Garo Yepremian added a 28-yard field goal midway in the second period for a 17-0 Miami lead. Minnesota then drove from its 20 to a second-and-two situation on the Miami 7 yard line with 1:18 left in the half. But on two plays, Miami limited Oscar Reed to one yard. On fourth-and-one from the 6, Reed went over right tackle, but Dolphins middle linebacker Nick Buoniconti jarred the ball loose and Jake Scott recovered for Miami to halt the Minnesota threat. The Vikings were unable to muster enough offense in the second half to threaten the Dolphins. Csonka rushed 33 times for a Super Bowl-record 145 yards. Bob Griese of Miami completed six of seven passes for 73 yards.

Minnesota (NFC)	0	0	0	7 — 7
Miami (AFC)	14	3	7	0 — 24

Mia —Csonka 5 run (Yepremian kick)
Mia —Kiick 1 run (Yepremian kick)
Mia —FG Yepremian 28
Mia —Csonka 2 run (Yepremian kick)
Minn—Tarkenton 4 run (Cox kick)

Super Bowl VII

Memorial Coliseum, Los Angeles, California — January 14, 1973
Attendance: 90,182

MIAMI 14, WASHINGTON 7—The Dolphins played virtually perfect football in the first half as their defense permitted the Redskins to cross midfield only once and their offense turned good field position into two touchdowns. On its third possession, Miami opened its first scoring drive from the Dolphins' 37 yard line. An 18-yard pass from Bob Griese to Paul Warfield preceded by three plays Griese's 28-yard touchdown pass to Howard Twilley. After Washington moved from its 17 to the Miami 48 with two minutes remaining in the first half, Dolphins linebacker Nick Buoniconti intercepted a Billy Kilmer pass at the Miami 41 and returned it to the Washington 27. Jim Kiick ran for three yards, Larry Csonka for three, Griese passed to Jim Mandich for 19, and Kiick gained one to the 1-yard line. With 18 seconds left until intermission, Kiick scored from the 1. Washington's only touchdown came with 2:07 left in the game and resulted from a misplayed field-goal attempt and fumble by Garo Yepremian, with the Redskins' Mike Bass picking the ball out of the air and running 49 yards for the score. Dolphins safety Jake Scott, who had two interceptions, including one in the end zone to kill a Redskins' drive, was voted the game's most valuable player.

Miami (AFC)	7	7	0	0 — 14
Washington (NFC)	0	0	0	7 — 7

Mia —Twilley 28 pass from Griese (Yepremian kick)
Mia —Kiick 1 run (Yepremian kick)
Wash—Bass 49 fumble recovery return (Knight kick)

Super Bowl VI

Tulane Stadium, New Orleans, Louisiana — January 16, 1972
Attendance: 81,023

DALLAS 24, MIAMI 3—The Cowboys rushed for a record 252 yards and their defense limited the Dolphins to a low of 185 yards while not permitting a touchdown for the first time in Super Bowl history. Dallas converted Chuck Howley's recovery of Larry Csonka's first fumble of the season into a 3-0 advantage and led at halftime 10-3. After Dallas received the second-half kickoff, Duane Thomas led a 71-yard march in eight plays for a 17-3 margin. Howley intercepted Bob Griese's pass at the 50 and returned it to the Miami 9 early in the fourth period, and three plays later Roger Staubach passed seven yards to Mike Ditka for the final touchdown. Thomas rushed for 95 yards and Walt Garrison gained 74. Staubach, voted the game's most valuable player, completed 12 of 19 passes for 119 yards and two touchdowns.

Dallas (NFC)	3	7	7	7 — 24
Miami (AFC)	0	3	0	0 — 3

Dall—FG Clark 9
Dall—Alworth 7 pass from Staubach (Clark kick)
Mia —FG Yepremian 31

Dall—D. Thomas 3 run (Clark kick)
Dall—Ditka 7 pass from Staubach (Clark kick)

Super Bowl V

Orange Bowl, Miami, Florida — January 17, 1971
Attendance: 79,204

BALTIMORE 16, DALLAS 13—A 32-yard field goal by first-year kicker Jim O'Brien brought the Baltimore Colts a victory over the Dallas Cowboys in the final five seconds of Super Bowl V. The game between the champions of the AFC and NFC was played on artificial turf for the first time. Dallas led 13-6 at the half and interceptions by Rick Volk and Mike Curtis set up a Baltimore touchdown and O'Brien's decisive kick in the fourth period. Earl Morrall relieved an injured Johnny Unitas late in the first half, although Unitas completed the Colts' only scoring pass. It caromed off receiver Eddie Hinton's fingertips, off Dallas defensive back Mel Renfro, and finally settled into the grasp of John Mackey, who went 45 yards to score on a 75-yard play.

Baltimore (AFC)	0	6	0	10 — 16
Dallas (NFC)	3	10	0	0 — 13

Dall—FG Clark 14
Dall—FG Clark 30
Balt—Mackey 75 pass from Unitas (kick blocked)
Dall—Thomas 7 pass from Morton (Clark kick)
Balt—Nowatzke 2 run (O'Brien kick)
Balt—FG O'Brien 32

Super Bowl IV

Tulane Stadium, New Orleans, Louisiana — January 11, 1970
Attendance: 80,562

KANSAS CITY 23, MINNESOTA 7—The AFL squared the Super Bowl at two games apiece with the NFL, building a 16-0 halftime lead behind Len Dawson's superb quarterbacking and a powerful defense. Dawson, the fourth consecutive quarterback to be chosen the Super Bowl's top player, called an almost flawless game, completing 12 of 17 passes and hitting Otis Taylor on a 46-yard play for the final Chiefs touchdown. The Kansas City defense limited Minnesota's strong rushing game to 67 yards and had three interceptions and two fumble recoveries. The crowd of 80,562 set a Super Bowl record, as did the gross receipts of $3,817,872.69.

Minnesota (NFL)	0	0	7	0 — 7
Kansas City (AFL)	3	13	7	0 — 23

KC —FG Stenerud 48
KC —FG Stenerud 32
KC —FG Stenerud 25
KC —Garrett 5 run (Stenerud kick)
Minn—Osborn 4 run (Cox kick)
KC —Taylor 46 pass from Dawson (Stenerud kick)

Super Bowl III

Orange Bowl, Miami, Florida — January 12, 1969
Attendance: 75,389

NEW YORK JETS 16, BALTIMORE 7—Jets quarterback Joe Namath "guaranteed" victory on the Thursday before the game, then went out and led the AFL to its first Super Bowl victory over a Baltimore team that had lost only once in 16 games all season. Namath, chosen the outstanding player, completed 17 of 28 passes for 206 yards and directed a steady attack that dominated the NFL champions after the Jets' defense had intercepted Colts quarterback Earl Morrall three times in the first half. The Jets had 337 total yards, including 121 yards rushing by Matt Snell. Johnny Unitas, who had missed most of the season with a sore elbow, came off the bench and led Baltimore to its only touchdown late in the fourth quarter after New York led 16-0.

New York Jets (AFL)	0	7	6	3 — 16
Baltimore (NFL)	0	0	0	7 — 7

NYJ—Snell 4 run (Turner kick)
NYJ—FG Turner 32
NYJ—FG Turner 30
NYJ—FG Turner 9
Balt—Hill 1 run (Michaels kick)

Super Bowl II

Orange Bowl, Miami, Florida — January 14, 1968
Attendance: 75,546

GREEN BAY 33, OAKLAND 14—Green Bay, after winning its third consecutive NFL championship, won the Super Bowl title for the second straight year 33-14 over the AFL champion Raiders in a game that drew the first $3-million gate in football history. Bart Starr again was chosen the game's most valuable player as he completed 13 of 24 passes for 202 yards and one touchdown and directed a Packers attack that was in control all the way after building a 16-7 halftime lead. Don Chandler kicked four field goals and all-pro cornerback Herb Adderley capped the Green Bay scoring with a 60-yard run with an interception. The game marked the last for Vince Lombardi as Packers coach, ending nine years at Green Bay in which he won six Western Conference championships, five NFL championships, and two Super Bowls.

Green Bay (NFL)	3	13	10	7 — 33
Oakland (AFL)	0	7	0	7 — 14

GB —FG Chandler 39
GB —FG Chandler 20
GB —Dowler 62 pass from Starr (Chandler kick)
Oak—Miller 23 pass from Lamonica (Blanda kick)
GB —FG Chandler 43

GB —Anderson 2 run (Chandler kick)
GB —FG Chandler 31
GB —Adderley 60 interception return (Chandler kick)
Oak—Miller 23 pass from Lamonica (Blanda kick)

Super Bowl I

Memorial Coliseum, Los Angeles, California   January 15, 1967
Attendance: 61,946

GREEN BAY 35, KANSAS CITY 10—The Green Bay Packers opened the
Super Bowl series by defeating Kansas City's American Football League
champions 35-10 behind the passing of Bart Starr, the receiving of Max
McGee, and a key interception by all-pro safety Willie Wood. Green Bay broke
open the game with three second-half touchdowns, the first of which was set
up by Wood's 50-yard return of an interception to the Chiefs' 5 yard line.
McGee, filling in for ailing Boyd Dowler after having caught only four passes all
season, caught seven from Starr for 138 yards and two touchdowns. Elijah Pitts
ran for two other scores. The Chiefs' 10 points came in the second quarter, the only touchdown on a seven-yard pass from Len Dawson to Curtis
McClinton. Starr completed 16 of 23 passes for 250 yards and two touchdowns
and was chosen the most valuable player. The Packers collected $15,000 per
man and the Chiefs $7,500—the largest single-game shares in the history of
team sports.

Kansas City (AFL)	0	10	0	0 —	10
Green Bay (NFL)	7	7	14	7 —	35

GB—McGee 37 pass from Starr (Chandler kick)
KC—McClinton 7 pass from Dawson (Mercer kick)
GB—Taylor 14 run (Chandler kick)
KC—FG Mercer 31
GB—Pitts 5 run (Chandler kick)
GB—McGee 13 pass from Starr (Chandler kick)
GB—Pitts 1 run (Chandler kick)

AFC Championship Game

Includes AFL Championship Games (1960-69)

Results

Season	Date	Winner (Share)	Loser (Share)	Score	Site	Attendance
1991	Jan. 12	Buffalo ($18,000)	Denver ($18,000)	10-7	Buffalo	80,272
1990	Jan. 20	Buffalo ($18,000)	L.A. Raiders ($18,000)	51-3	Buffalo	80,325
1989	Jan. 14	Denver ($18,000)	Cleveland ($18,000)	37-21	Denver	76,046
1988	Jan. 8	Cincinnati ($18,000)	Buffalo ($18,000)	21-10	Cincinnati	59,747
1987	Jan. 17	Denver ($18,000)	Cleveland ($18,000)	38-33	Denver	76,197
1986	Jan. 11	Denver ($18,000)	Cleveland ($18,000)	23-20*	Cleveland	79,973
1985	Jan. 12	New England ($18,000)	Miami ($18,000)	31-14	Miami	75,662
1984	Jan. 6	Miami ($18,000)	Pittsburgh ($18,000)	45-28	Miami	76,029
1983	Jan. 8	L.A. Raiders ($18,000)	Seattle ($18,000)	30-14	Los Angeles	91,445
1982	Jan. 23	Miami ($18,000)	N.Y. Jets ($18,000)	14-0	Miami	67,396
1981	Jan. 10	Cincinnati ($9,000)	San Diego ($9,000)	27-7	Cincinnati	46,302
1980	Jan. 11	Oakland ($9,000)	San Diego ($9,000)	34-27	San Diego	52,675
1979	Jan. 6	Pittsburgh ($9,000)	Houston ($9,000)	27-13	Pittsburgh	50,475
1978	Jan. 7	Pittsburgh ($9,000)	Houston ($9,000)	34-5	Pittsburgh	50,725
1977	Jan. 1	Denver ($9,000)	Oakland ($9,000)	20-17	Denver	75,044
1976	Dec. 26	Oakland ($8,500)	Pittsburgh ($5,500)	24-7	Oakland	53,821
1975	Jan. 4	Pittsburgh ($8,500)	Oakland ($5,500)	16-10	Pittsburgh	50,609
1974	Dec. 29	Pittsburgh ($8,500)	Oakland ($5,500)	24-13	Oakland	53,800
1973	Dec. 30	Miami ($8,500)	Oakland ($5,500)	27-10	Miami	79,325
1972	Dec. 31	Miami ($8,500)	Pittsburgh ($5,500)	21-17	Pittsburgh	50,845
1971	Jan. 2	Miami ($8,500)	Baltimore ($5,500)	21-0	Miami	76,622
1970	Jan. 3	Baltimore ($8,500)	Oakland ($5,500)	27-17	Baltimore	54,799
1969	Jan. 4	Kansas City ($7,755)	Oakland ($6,252)	17-7	Oakland	53,564
1968	Dec. 29	N.Y. Jets ($7,007)	Oakland ($5,349)	27-23	New York	62,627
1967	Dec. 31	Oakland ($6,321)	Houston ($4,996)	40-7	Oakland	53,330
1966	Jan. 1	Kansas City ($5,309)	Buffalo ($3,799)	31-7	Buffalo	42,080
1965	Dec. 26	Buffalo ($5,189)	San Diego ($3,447)	23-0	San Diego	30,361
1964	Dec. 26	Buffalo ($2,668)	San Diego ($1,738)	20-7	Buffalo	40,242
1963	Jan. 5	San Diego ($2,498)	Boston ($1,596)	51-10	San Diego	30,127
1962	Dec. 23	Dallas ($2,206)	Houston ($1,471)	20-17*	Houston	37,981
1961	Dec. 24	Houston ($1,792)	San Diego ($1,111)	10-3	San Diego	29,556
1960	Jan. 1	Houston ($1,025)	L.A. Chargers ($718)	24-16	Houston	32,183

Sudden death overtime.

AFC Championship Game
Composite Standings

	W	L	Pct.	Pts.	OP
Kansas City Chiefs*	3	0	1.000	68	31
Cincinnati Bengals	2	0	1.000	48	17
Miami Dolphins	5	1	.833	142	86
Denver Broncos	4	1	.800	125	101
Buffalo Bills	4	2	.667	121	69
Pittsburgh Steelers	4	3	.571	153	131
Baltimore Colts	1	1	.500	27	38
New England Patriots**	1	1	.500	41	65
New York Jets	1	1	.500	27	37
Houston Oilers	2	4	.333	76	140
Oakland/L.A. Raiders	4	8	.333	228	264
San Diego Chargers***	1	6	.143	111	148
Seattle Seahawks	0	1	.000	14	30
Cleveland Browns	0	3	.000	74	98

*One game played when franchise was in Dallas (Texans). (Won 20-17)
**One game played when franchise was in Boston. (Lost 51-10)
***One game played when franchise was in Los Angeles. (Lost 24-16)

1991 American Football Conference
Championship Game

Rich Stadium, Orchard Park, New York   January 12, 1992
Attendance: 80,272

BUFFALO 10, DENVER 7—Carlton Bailey returned an interception 11 yards for a touchdown and Scott Norwood's fourth-quarter field goal provided the margin of difference as the Bills won their second consecutive AFC championship. The game was scoreless until Buffalo's Jeff Wright tipped John Elway's screen pass over the middle and Bailey returned it for a touchdown with 5:28 left in the third quarter. After Norwood's 44-yard field goal with 4:18 left in the game, Denver's Gary Kubiak capped an 85-yard drive with a 3-yard touchdown run with 1:43 remaining. Denver recovered the ensuing onside kick at its own 49-yard line, but turned the ball over one play later when running back Steve Sewell fumbled after being hit by the Bills' Kirby Jackson. Jackson recovered to end the Broncos' final threat. Kubiak, who entered the game in the fourth quarter when Elway could not continue because of a thigh bruise suffered earlier in the game, completed 11 of 12 passes for 136 yards after announcing he would retire at the end of the season. Denver held Buffalo's explosive offense in check, limiting the Bills to only 12 first downs and 213 total yards. But the Broncos, who had 20 first downs and 304 yards, managed only 1 touchdown despite good field position and seven trips inside Buffalo's territory. Kicker David Treadwell missed 3 field-goal attempts, including 2 that bounced off the uprights.

Denver (7)	Offense	Buffalo (10)
Michael Young	WR	James Lofton
Jeff Davidson	LT	Will Wolford
Sean Farrell	LG	Jim Ritcher
Dave Widell	C	Kent Hull
Doug Widell	RG	Mitch Frerotte
Ken Lanier	RT	Howard Ballard
Shannon Sharpe	TE	Keith McKeller
Derek Russell	WR	Andre Reed
John Elway	QB	Jim Kelly
Gaston Green	RB	Thurman Thomas
Vance Johnson	WR	Don Beebe
	Defense	
Warren Powers	LE	Leon Seals
Greg Kragen	NT	Jeff Wright
Ron Holmes	RE	Bruce Smith
Simon Fletcher	LOLB	Cornelius Bennett
Michael Brooks	LILB	Shane Conlan
Karl Mecklenburg	RILB	Carlton Bailey
Mike Croel	ROLB	Darryl Talley
Tyrone Braxton	LCB	Kirby Jackson
Wymon Henderson	RCB	Nate Odomes
Dennis Smith	SS	Leonard Smith
Steve Atwater	FS	Mark Kelso

Substitutions

Denver—Offense: K—David Treadwell. P—Mike Horan. QB—Gary Kubiak. RB—Greg Lewis, Reggie Rivers, Steve Sewell. WR—Mark Jackson, Ricky Nattiel. TE—Clarence Kay. C—Keith Kartz. G—Crawford Ker. T—Harvey Salem, Nick Subis. Defense: DE—Kenny Walker. NT—Brian Sochia. LB—Tim Lucas, Keith Traylor. CB—Charles Dimry, Le-Lo Lang. S—Alton Montgomery, Randy Robbins. DNP: TE—Reggie Johnson. LB—Jeff Mills. Inactive: RB—Bobby Humphrey. QB—Shawn Moore.

Buffalo—Offense: K—Brad Daluiso, Scott Norwood. P—Chris Mohr. QB—Frank Reich. RB—Kenneth Davis, Carwell Gardner. WR—Al Edwards, Steve Tasker. TE—Pete Metzelaars, Butch Rolle. C—Adam Lingner. Defense: DE—Phil Hansen, Mark Pike. NT—Mike Lodish. LB—Ray Bentley, Hal Garner, Marvcus Patton. CB—Clifford Hicks, James Williams. S—Dwight Drane, Henry Jones. DNP: T—Mike Brennan, Joe Staysniak. Inactive: QB—Gale Gilbert. G—Glenn Parker.

Officials

Referee—Dale Hamer. Umpire—Al Conway. Head Linesman—Sid Semon. Line Judge—Bill Reynolds. Back Judge—Al Jury. Field Judge—Don Hakes. Side Judge—Doug Toole. Replay Official—Bill Fette.

Scoring

Denver	0	0	0	7 —	7
Buffalo	0	0	7	3 —	10

Buff—Bailey 11 interception return (Norwood kick)
Buff—FG Norwood 44
Den—Kubiak 3 run (Treadwell kick)

Team Statistics

	Denver	Buffalo
Total First Downs	20	12
First Downs Rushing	6	5
First Downs Passing	13	5
First Downs Penalty	1	2
Total Net Yardage	304	213
Total Offensive Plays	69	61
Average Gain per Offensive Play	4.4	3.5
Rushes	32	35
Yards Gained Rushing (net)	81	104
Average Yards per Rush	2.5	3.0
Passes Attempted	33	25
Passes Completed	22	13
Had Intercepted	1	2
Tackled Attempting to Pass	4	1
Yards Lost Attempting to Pass	34	8
Yards Gained Passing (net)	223	109
Punts	6	8
Average Distance	43.7	38.0
Punt Returns	3	0
Punt Return Yardage	36	0
Kickoff Returns	3	1
Kickoff Return Yardage	49	24
Interception Return Yardage	5	11
Total Return Yardage	90	35
Fumbles	4	0
Own Fumbles Recovered	3	0
Opponents Fumbles Recovered	0	1
Penalties	4	6
Yards Penalized	20	35
Total Points Scored	7	10
Touchdowns	1	1
Touchdowns Rushing	1	0
Touchdowns Passing	0	0
Touchdowns Returns	0	1
Extra Points	1	1
Field Goals	0	1
Field Goals Attempted	3	1
Safeties	0	0
Third Down Efficiency	3/14	4/15
Fourth Down Efficiency	0/1	0/0
Time of Possession	34:53	25:07

Individual Statistics

Rushing

Denver	No.	Yds.	LG	TD
Green	19	53	18	0
Kubiak	3	22	11	1
Elway	4	10	7	0
Sewell	4	3	6	0
V. Johnson	2	−7	−1	0
Buffalo	**No.**	**Yds.**	**LG**	**TD**
Thomas	26	72	9	0
Reed	1	16	16	0
Kelly	2	9	10	0
K. Davis	6	7	4	0
McKeller	3	39	25	0
Thomas	3	15	8	0
Reed	2	19	10	0
K. Davis	2	13	9	0
Metzelaars	1	14	14	0
Lofton	1	11	11	0
Beebe	1	6	6	0

Passing

Denver	Att.	Comp.	Yds.	TD	Int.
Elway	21	11	121	0	1
Kubiak	12	11	136	0	0
Buffalo	**Att.**	**Comp.**	**Yds.**	**TD**	**Int.**
Kelly	25	13	117	0	2

Receiving

Denver	No.	Yds.	LG	TD
V. Johnson	7	100	24	0
Sewell	7	78	26	0
Sharpe	3	40	15	0
Young	3	25	10	0
Nattiel	1	10	10	0
Jackson	1	4	4	0

Interceptions

Denver	No.	Yds.	LG	TD
Braxton	1	5	5	0
Kragen	1	0	0	0
Buffalo	**No.**	**Yds.**	**LG**	**TD**
Bailey	1	11	11t	1

Punting

Denver	No.	Avg.	LG	Blk.
Horan	6	43.7	76	0
Buffalo	**No.**	**Avg.**	**LG**	**Blk.**
Mohr	8	38.0	49	0

Punt Returns

Denver	No.	FC	Yds.	LG	TD
V. Johnson	3	3	36	13	0
Buffalo	**No.**	**FC**	**Yds.**	**LG**	**TD**
Hicks	0	1	0	0	0

Kickoff Returns

Denver	No.	Yds.	LG	TD
Montgomery	2	34	18	0
Russell	1	15	15	0
Buffalo	**No.**	**Yds.**	**LG**	**TD**
Edwards	1	24	24	0

NFC Championship Game

Includes NFL Championship Games (1933-69)

Results

Season	Date	Winner (Share)	Loser (Share)	Score	Site	Attendance
1991	Jan. 12	Washington ($18,000)	Detroit ($18,000)	41-10	Washington	55,585
1990	Jan. 20	N.Y. Giants ($18,000)	San Francisco ($18,000)	15-13	San Francisco	65,750
1989	Jan. 14	San Francisco ($18,000)	L.A. Rams ($18,000)	30-3	San Francisco	65,634
1988	Jan. 8	San Francisco ($18,000)	Chicago ($18,000)	28-3	Chicago	66,946
1987	Jan. 17	Washington ($18,000)	Minnesota ($18,000)	17-10	Washington	55,212
1986	Jan. 11	New York Giants ($18,000)	Washington ($18,000)	17-0	New York	76,891
1985	Jan. 12	Chicago ($18,000)	L.A. Rams ($18,000)	24-0	Chicago	66,030
1984	Jan. 6	San Francisco ($18,000)	Chicago ($18,000)	23-0	San Francisco	61,336
1983	Jan. 8	Washington ($18,000)	San Francisco ($18,000)	24-21	Washington	55,363
1982	Jan. 22	Washington ($18,000)	Dallas ($18,000)	31-17	Washington	55,045
1981	Jan. 10	San Francisco ($9,000)	Dallas ($9,000)	28-27	San Francisco	60,525
1980	Jan. 11	Philadelphia ($9,000)	Dallas ($9,000)	20-7	Philadelphia	71,522
1979	Jan. 6	Los Angeles ($9,000)	Tampa Bay ($9,000)	9-0	Tampa Bay	72,033
1978	Jan. 7	Dallas ($9,000)	Los Angeles ($9,000)	28-0	Los Angeles	71,086
1977	Jan. 1	Dallas ($9,000)	Minnesota ($9,000)	23-6	Dallas	64,293
1976	Dec. 26	Minnesota ($8,500)	Los Angeles ($5,500)	24-13	Minnesota	48,379
1975	Jan. 4	Dallas ($8,500)	Los Angeles ($5,500)	37-7	Los Angeles	88,919
1974	Dec. 29	Minnesota ($8,500)	Los Angeles ($5,500)	14-10	Minnesota	48,444
1973	Dec. 30	Minnesota ($8,500)	Dallas ($5,500)	27-10	Dallas	64,422
1972	Dec. 31	Washington ($8,500)	Dallas ($5,500)	26-3	Washington	53,129
1971	Jan. 2	Dallas ($8,500)	San Francisco ($5,500)	14-3	Dallas	63,409
1970	Jan. 3	Dallas ($8,500)	San Francisco ($5,500)	17-10	San Francisco	59,364
1969	Jan. 4	Minnesota ($7,930)	Cleveland ($5,118)	27-7	Minnesota	46,503
1968	Dec. 29	Baltimore ($9,306)	Cleveland ($5,963)	34-0	Cleveland	78,410
1967	Dec. 31	Green Bay ($7,950)	Dallas ($5,299)	21-17	Green Bay	50,861
1966	Jan. 1	Green Bay ($9,813)	Dallas ($6,527)	34-27	Dallas	74,152
1965	Jan. 2	Green Bay ($7,819)	Cleveland ($5,288)	23-12	Green Bay	50,777
1964	Dec. 27	Cleveland ($8,052)	Baltimore ($5,571)	27-0	Cleveland	79,544
1963	Dec. 29	Chicago ($5,899)	New York ($4,218)	14-10	Chicago	45,801
1962	Dec. 30	Green Bay ($5,888)	New York ($4,166)	16-7	New York	64,892
1961	Dec. 31	Green Bay ($5,195)	New York ($3,339)	37-0	Green Bay	39,029
1960	Dec. 26	Philadelphia ($5,116)	Green Bay ($3,105)	17-13	Philadelphia	67,325
1959	Dec. 27	Baltimore ($4,674)	New York ($3,083)	31-16	Baltimore	57,545
1958	Dec. 28	Baltimore ($4,718)	New York ($3,111)	23-17*	New York	64,185
1957	Dec. 29	Detroit ($4,295)	Cleveland ($2,750)	59-14	Detroit	55,263
1956	Dec. 30	New York ($3,779)	Chi. Bears ($2,485)	47-7	New York	56,836
1955	Dec. 26	Cleveland ($3,508)	Los Angeles ($2,316)	38-14	Los Angeles	85,693
1954	Dec. 26	Cleveland ($2,478)	Detroit ($1,585)	56-10	Cleveland	43,827
1953	Dec. 27	Detroit ($2,424)	Cleveland ($1,654)	17-16	Detroit	54,577
1952	Dec. 28	Detroit ($2,274)	Cleveland ($1,712)	17-7	Cleveland	50,934
1951	Dec. 23	Los Angeles ($2,108)	Cleveland ($1,483)	24-17	Los Angeles	57,522
1950	Dec. 24	Cleveland ($1,113)	Los Angeles ($686)	30-28	Cleveland	29,751
1949	Dec. 18	Philadelphia ($1,094)	Los Angeles ($739)	14-0	Los Angeles	27,980
1948	Dec. 19	Philadelphia ($1,540)	Chi. Cardinals ($874)	7-0	Philadelphia	36,309

Season	Date	Winner (Share)	Loser (Share)	Score	Site	Attendance
1947	Dec. 28	Chi. Cardinals ($1,132)	Philadelphia ($754)	28-21	Chicago	30,759
1946	Dec. 15	Chi. Bears ($1,975)	New York ($1,295)	24-14	New York	58,346
1945	Dec. 16	Cleveland ($1,469)	Washington ($902)	15-14	Cleveland	32,178
1944	Dec. 17	Green Bay ($1,449)	New York ($814)	14-7	New York	46,016
1943	Dec. 26	Chi. Bears ($1,146)	Washington ($765)	41-21	Chicago	34,320
1942	Dec. 13	Washington ($965)	Chi. Bears ($637)	14-6	Washington	36,006
1941	Dec. 21	Chi. Bears ($430)	New York ($288)	37-9	Chicago	13,341
1940	Dec. 8	Chi. Bears ($873)	Washington ($606)	73-0	Washington	36,034
1939	Dec. 10	Green Bay ($703.97)	New York ($455.57)	27-0	Milwaukee	32,279
1938	Dec. 11	New York ($504.45)	Green Bay ($368.81)	23-17	New York	48,120
1937	Dec. 12	Washington ($225.90)	Chi. Bears ($127.78)	28-21	Chicago	15,870
1936	Dec. 13	Green Bay ($250)	Boston ($180)	21-6	New York	29,545
1935	Dec. 15	Detroit ($313.35)	New York ($200.20)	26-7	Detroit	15,000
1934	Dec. 9	New York ($621)	Chi. Bears ($414.02)	30-13	New York	35,059
1933	Dec. 17	Chi. Bears ($210.34)	New York ($140.22)	23-21	Chicago	26,000

*Sudden death overtime.

NFC Championship Game
Composite Standings

	W	L	Pct.	Pts.	OP
Green Bay Packers	8	2	.800	223	116
Philadelphia Eagles	4	1	.800	79	48
Baltimore Colts	3	1	.750	88	60
Detroit Lions	4	2	.667	139	141
Minnesota Vikings	4	2	.667	108	80
Washington Redskins*	7	5	.583	222	255
Chicago Bears	7	6	.538	286	245
Phoenix Cardinals**	1	1	.500	28	28
San Francisco 49ers	4	4	.500	156	103
Dallas Cowboys	5	7	.417	227	213
Cleveland Browns	4	7	.364	224	253
New York Giants	5	11	.313	240	322
Los Angeles Rams***	3	9	.250	123	270
Tampa Bay Buccaneers	0	1	.000	0	9

*One game played when franchise was in Boston. (Lost 21-6)
**Both games played when franchise was in Chicago. (Won 28-21, lost 7-0)
***One game played when franchise was in Cleveland. (Won 15-14)

1991 National Football Conference
Championship Game

RFK Stadium, Washington, D.C.   January 12, 1992
Attendance: 55,585

WASHINGTON 41, DETROIT 10—The Redskins turned a pair of turnovers into 10 points less than five minutes into the game and coasted to victory to earn a record-tying fifth Super Bowl berth. Washington's Charles Mann forced the Lions' Erik Kramer to fumble on the first play from scrimmage, and Gerald Riggs capped a two-play, 10-yard drive with a 2-yard touchdown run just 1:06 into the game. Less than three minutes later, the Redskins scored again when Kurt Gouveia's 38-yard interception return set up Chip Lohmiller's 20-yard field goal. Detroit briefly pulled within three points on an 18-yard touchdown pass from Kramer to Willie Green, but Riggs added a 3-yard touchdown run, and Mark Rypien passed 45 yards to Gary Clark and 21 yards to Art Monk for touchdowns in the second half to put the game out of reach. Rypien completed 12 of 17 passes for 228 yards for Washington, which beat the Lions 45-0 on the same field on the opening day of the season. Kramer completed 21 of 33 passes for 249 yards for Detroit.

Detroit (10)	Offense	Washington (41)
Willie Green	WR	Gary Clark
Brett Perriman	WR-TE	Ron Middleton
Lomas Brown	LT	Jim Lachey
Eric Andolsek	LG	Raleigh McKenzie
Kevin Glover	C	Jeff Bostic
Ken Dallafior	RG	Mark Schlereth
Scott Conover	RT	Joe Jacoby
Mike Farr	WR	Art Monk
Herman Moore	WR-TE	Don Warren
Erik Kramer	QB	Mark Rypien
Barry Sanders	RB	Earnest Byner
	Defense	
Marc Spindler	LE	Charles Mann
Lawrence Pete	NT-LT	Eric Williams
Dan Owens	RE-RT	Tim Johnson
George Jamison	LOLB-RE	Fred Stokes
Chris Spielman	LILB-LLB	Wilber Marshall
Dennis Gibson	RILB-MLB	Kurt Gouveia
Tracy Hayworth	ROLB-RLB	Andre Collins
Ray Crockett	LCB	Martin Mayhew
Melvin Jenkins	RCB	Darrell Green
William White	SS	Danny Copeland
Bennie Blades	FS	Brad Edwards

Substitutions

Detroit—Offense: K—Eddie Murray. P—Jim Arnold. QB—Chuck Long, Andre Ware. RB—D. J. Dozier, Don Overton. WR—Mel Gray, Aubrey Matthews. TE—David Little, Derek Tennell. C—Roman Fortin. G—Shawn Bouwens. T—Bubba Paris. Defense: DE—Jeff Hunter, Kelvin Pritchett. LB—Anthony Bell, Toby Caston, Victor Jones, Niko Noga. CB—Bruce Alexander, Kevin Scott, Terry Taylor, Sheldon White. DNP: WR—Robert Clark. Inactive: DE—Darryl Milburn.

Washington—Offense: K—Chip Lohmiller. P—Kelly Goodburn. QB—Jeff Rutledge. RB—Ricky Ervins, Brian Mitchell, Gerald Riggs. WR—Stephen Hobbs, Ricky Sanders. TE—John Brandes, James Jenkins, Terry Orr. G—Mark Adickes, Russ Grimm. T—Ed Simmons. Defense: DE—Jason Buck. DT—James Geathers, Bobby Wilson. LB—Ravin Caldwell, Monte Coleman. CB—A. J. Johnson, Sidney Johnson. S—Alvoid Mays, Alvin Walton. DNP: None. Inactive: QB—Stan Humphries. LB—Matt Millen.

Officials

Referee—Bob McElwee. Umpire—Art Demmas. Head Linesman—Ernie Frantz. Line Judge—Dick McKenzie. Back Judge—Jim Poole. Field Judge—Donnie Hampton. Side Judge—Tom Fincken. Replay Official—George Sladky.

Scoring

Detroit	0	10	0	0	—	10
Washington	10	7	10	14	—	41

Wash—Riggs 2 run (Lohmiller kick)
Wash—FG Lohmiller 20
Det —Green 18 pass from Kramer (Murray kick)
Wash—Riggs 3 run (Lohmiller kick)
Det —FG Murray 30
Wash—FG Lohmiller 28
Wash—Clark pass 45 from Rypien (Lohmiller kick)
Wash—Monk pass 21 from Rypien (Lohmiller kick)
Wash—Green 32 interception return (Lohmiller kick)

Team Statistics

	Detroit	Washington
Total First Downs	20	17
First Downs Rushing	6	6
First Downs Passing	12	10
First Downs Penalty	2	1
Total Net Yardage	304	345
Total Offensive Plays	65	52
Average Gain per Offensive Play	4.7	6.6
Rushes	18	35
Yards Gained Rushing (net)	72	117
Average Yards per Rush	4.0	3.3
Passes Attempted	42	17
Passes Completed	25	12
Had Intercepted	2	0
Tackled Attempting to Pass	5	0
Yards Lost Attempting to Pass	32	0
Yards Gained Passing (net)	232	228
Punts	3	3
Average Distance	47.0	35.7
Punt Returns	3	1
Punt Return Yardage	13	13
Kickoff Returns	7	3
Kickoff Return Yardage	170	59
Interception Return Yardage	0	70
Total Return Yardage	183	142
Fumbles	3	0
Own Fumbles Recovered	2	0
Opponents Fumbles Recovered	0	1
Penalties	7	4
Yards Penalized	46	46
Total Points Scored	10	41
Touchdowns	1	5
Touchdowns Rushing	0	2
Touchdowns Passing	1	2
Touchdowns Returns	0	1

	Detroit	Washington
Extra Points	1	5
Field Goals	1	2
Field Goals Attempted	2	3
Safeties	0	0
Third Down Efficiency	5/13	3/10
Fourth Down Efficiency	0/2	1/1
Time of Possession	31:24	28:36

Individual Statistics

Rushing

Detroit	No.	Yds.	LG	TD
B. Sanders	11	44	23	0
Ware	2	25	14	0
Kramer	4	4	3	0
Long	1	−1	−1	0

Washington	No.	Yds.	LG	TD
Byner	17	62	9	0
Ervins	13	53	11	0
Riggs	2	5	3t	2
Rutledge	3	−3	−1	0

Passing

Detroit	Att.	Comp.	Yds.	TD	Int.
Kramer	33	21	249	1	1
Ware	9	4	15	0	1

Wash.	Att.	Comp.	Yds.	TD	Int.
Rypien	17	12	228	2	0

Receiving

Detroit	No.	Yds.	LG	TD
Farr	6	73	26	0
Perriman	5	43	14	0
Moore	4	69	21	0
Green	4	54	18t	1
B. Sanders	4	15	10	0
Overton	2	10	6	0

Washington	No.	Yds.	LG	TD
Monk	5	94	31	1
Clark	4	77	45t	1
Sanders	2	12	7	0
Orr	1	45	45	0

Interceptions

Detroit	No.	Yds.	LG	TD
None				

Washington	No.	Yds.	LG	TD
Gouveia	1	38	38	0
Green	1	32	32t	1

Punting

Detroit	No.	Avg.	LG	Blk.
Arnold	3	47.0	56	0

Washington	No.	Avg.	LG	Blk.
Goodburn	3	35.7	40	0

Punt Returns

Detroit	No.	FC	Yds.	LG	TD
Gray	3	0	13	8	0

Washington	No.	FC	Yds.	LG	TD
Mitchell	1	0	13	13	0

Kickoff Returns

Detroit	No.	Yds.	LG	TD
Gray	5	134	55	0
Dozier	1	21	21	0
Alexander	1	15	15	0

Washington	No.	Yds.	LG	TD
Ervins	3	59	21	0

AFC Divisional Playoffs

Includes Second-Round Playoff Games (1982), AFC Inter-Divisional Games (1969), and special playoff games to break ties for AFL Division Championships (1963, 1968)

Results

Season	Date	Winner (Share)	Loser (Share)	Score	Site	Attendance
1991	Jan. 5	Buffalo ($10,000)	Kansas City ($10,000)	37-14	Buffalo	80,182
	Jan. 4	Denver ($10,000)	Houston ($10,000)	26-24	Denver	75,301
1990	Jan. 13	L.A. Raiders ($10,000)	Cincinnati ($10,000)	20-10	Los Angeles	92,045
	Jan. 12	Buffalo ($10,000)	Miami ($10,000)	44-34	Buffalo	77,087
1989	Jan. 7	Denver ($10,000)	Pittsburgh ($10,000)	24-23	Denver	75,477
	Jan. 6	Cleveland ($10,000)	Buffalo ($10,000)	34-30	Cleveland	78,921
1988	Jan. 1	Buffalo ($10,000)	Houston ($10,000)	17-10	Buffalo	79,532
	Dec. 31	Cincinnati ($10,000)	Seattle ($10,000)	21-13	Cincinnati	58,560
1987	Jan. 10	Denver ($10,000)	Houston ($10,000)	34-10	Denver	75,440
	Jan. 9	Cleveland ($10,000)	Indianapolis ($10,000)	38-21	Cleveland	79,372
1986	Jan. 4	Denver ($10,000)	New England ($10,000)	22-17	Denver	75,262
	Jan. 3	Cleveland ($10,000)	N.Y. Jets ($10,000)	23-20*	Cleveland	79,720
1985	Jan. 5	New England ($10,000)	L.A. Raiders ($10,000)	27-20	Los Angeles	87,163
	Jan. 4	Miami ($10,000)	Cleveland ($10,000)	24-21	Miami	74,667
1984	Dec. 30	Pittsburgh ($10,000)	Denver ($10,000)	24-17	Denver	74,981
	Dec. 29	Miami ($10,000)	Seattle ($10,000)	31-10	Miami	73,469
1983	Jan. 1	L.A. Raiders ($10,000)	Pittsburgh ($10,000)	38-10	Los Angeles	90,380
	Dec. 31	Seattle ($10,000)	Miami ($10,000)	27-20	Miami	74,136
1982	Jan. 16	Miami ($10,000)	San Diego ($10,000)	34-13	Miami	71,383
	Jan. 15	N.Y. Jets ($10,000)	L.A. Raiders ($10,000)	17-14	Los Angeles	90,038
1981	Jan. 3	Cincinnati ($5,000)	Buffalo ($5,000)	28-21	Cincinnati	55,420
	Jan. 2	San Diego ($5,000)	Miami ($5,000)	41-38*	Miami	73,735
1980	Jan. 4	Oakland ($5,000)	Cleveland ($5,000)	14-12	Cleveland	78,245
	Jan. 3	San Diego ($5,000)	Buffalo ($5,000)	20-14	San Diego	52,253
1979	Dec. 30	Pittsburgh ($5,000)	Miami ($5,000)	34-14	Pittsburgh	50,214
	Dec. 29	Houston ($5,000)	San Diego ($5,000)	17-14	San Diego	51,192
1978	Dec. 31	Houston ($5,000)	New England ($5,000)	31-14	New England	60,735
	Dec. 30	Pittsburgh ($5,000)	Denver ($5,000)	33-10	Pittsburgh	50,230
1977	Dec. 24	Oakland ($5,000)	Baltimore ($5,000)	37-31	Baltimore	59,925
	Dec. 24	Denver ($5,000)	Pittsburgh ($5,000)	34-21	Denver	75,059
1976	Dec. 19	Pittsburgh ($)	Baltimore ($)	40-14	Baltimore	59,296
	Dec. 18	Oakland ($)	New England ($)	24-21	Oakland	53,050
1975	Dec. 28	Oakland ($)	Cincinnati ($)	31-28	Oakland	53,030
	Dec. 27	Pittsburgh ($)	Baltimore ($)	28-10	Pittsburgh	49,557
1974	Dec. 22	Pittsburgh ($)	Buffalo ($)	32-14	Pittsburgh	49,841
	Dec. 21	Oakland ($)	Miami ($)	28-26	Oakland	53,023
1973	Dec. 23	Miami ($)	Cincinnati ($)	34-16	Miami	78,928
	Dec. 22	Oakland ($)	Pittsburgh ($)	33-14	Oakland	52,646
1972	Dec. 24	Miami ($)	Cleveland ($)	20-14	Miami	78,916
	Dec. 23	Pittsburgh ($)	Oakland ($)	13-7	Pittsburgh	50,327
1971	Dec. 26	Baltimore ($)	Cleveland ($)	20-3	Cleveland	70,734
	Dec. 25	Miami ($)	Kansas City ($)	27-24*	Kansas City	45,822
1970	Dec. 27	Oakland ($)	Miami ($)	21-14	Oakland	52,594
	Dec. 26	Baltimore ($)	Cincinnati ($)	17-0	Baltimore	49,694
1969	Dec. 21	Oakland ($)	Houston ($)	56-7	Oakland	53,539
	Dec. 20	Kansas City ($)	N.Y. Jets ($)	13-6	New York	62,977
1968	Dec. 22	Oakland ($)	Kansas City ($)	41-6	Oakland	53,605
1963	Dec. 28	Boston ($)	Buffalo ($)	26-8	Buffalo	33,044

*Sudden Death Overtime.

$ Players received 1/14 of annual salary for playoff appearances.

1991 AFC Divisional Playoff Games

Mile High Stadium, Denver, Colorado   January 4, 1992
Attendance: 75,301

DENVER 26, HOUSTON 24—David Treadwell's 28-yard field goal with 16 seconds remaining in the game capped a dramatic 87-yard drive in the closing moments to lift the Broncos over the Oilers. Treadwell's winning kick came shortly after John Elway's 44-yard completion to Vance Johnson on fourth-and-10 from the Denver 35-yard line. Earlier on the drive, Elway scrambled 7 yards for a first down on fourth-and-6 from the 28. And it was Elway's 22-yard completion to Michael Young that got the Broncos out of a hole at their 2-yard line. Denver started the winning drive there with no time outs left after Houston's Greg Montgomery dropped his punt out of bounds with 2:07 left in the game. Warren Moon passed for 3 touchdowns as Houston built first-half leads of 14-0 and 21-6. But the Broncos' defense stiffened, allowing only a field goal in the second half, which came 1:35 into the fourth quarter and gave the Oilers a 24-16 lead. Elway, who passed for 257 yards and 1 touchdown, then directed an 80-yard touchdown march that trimmed the deficit to 24-23 with 6:53 to go. Moon finished with 27 completions in 36 attempts for 325 yards. Ernest Givins had 111 yards on 6 catches.

Houston	14	7	0	3	— 24
Denver	6	7	3	10	— 26

Hou—Jeffires 15 pass from Moon (Del Greco kick)
Hou—Hill 9 pass from Moon (Del Greco kick)
Den—V. Johnson 10 pass from Elway (kick failed)
Hou—Duncan 6 pass from Moon (Del Greco kick)
Den—Lewis 1 run (Treadwell kick)
Den—FG Treadwell 49
Hou—FG Del Greco 25
Den—Lewis 1 run (Treadwell kick)
Den—FG Treadwell 28

Rich Stadium, Orchard Park, New York   January 5, 1992
Attendance: 80,182

BUFFALO 37, KANSAS CITY 14—Jim Kelly threw 3 touchdown passes and the Bills avenged a 33-6 defeat to the Chiefs in the regular season by breezing to the victory. Kelly, who completed 23 of 35 passes for 273 yards, teamed with Andre Reed for scoring passes of 25 and 53 yards as Buffalo built a 17-0 advantage at halftime. Kelly's 10-yard touchdown pass to James Lofton early in the third quarter put the game out of reach at 24-0. Thurman Thomas rushed for 100 yards on 22 carries for the Bills, marking the fourth consecutive post-season game that he eclipsed the century mark. Reed had 100 yards on 4 catches as Buffalo amassed 448 total yards to Kansas City's 213. The Chiefs' Steve DeBerg was knocked out of the game in the second quarter with a sprained thumb. Backup Mark Vlasic passed for 124 yards and 1 touchdown for Kansas City, but was intercepted 4 times.

Kansas City	0	0	7	7	— 14
Buffalo	7	10	7	13	— 37

Buff—Reed 25 pass from Kelly (Norwood kick)
Buff—Reed 53 pass from Kelly (Norwood kick)
Buff—FG Norwood 33
Buff—Lofton 10 pass from Kelly (Norwood kick)
KC —Word 3 run (Lowery kick)
Buff—FG Norwood 20
Buff—FG Norwood 47
Buff—Davis 5 run (Norwood kick)
KC —F. Jones 20 pass from Vlasic (Lowery kick)

NFC Divisional Playoffs

Includes Second-Round Playoff Games (1982), NFL Conference Championship Games (1967-69), and special playoff games to break ties for NFL Division or Conference Championships (1941, 1943, 1947, 1950, 1952, 1957, 1958, 1965)

Results

Season	Date	Winner (Share)	Loser (Share)	Score	Site	Attendance
1991	Jan. 5	Detroit ($10,000)	Dallas ($10,000)	38-6	Detroit	78,290
	Jan. 4	Washington ($10,000)	Atlanta ($10,000)	24-7	Washington	55,181
1990	Jan. 13	N.Y. Giants ($10,000)	Chicago ($10,000)	31-3	East Rutherford	77,025
	Jan. 12	San Francisco ($10,000)	Washington ($10,000)	28-10	San Francisco	65,292
1989	Jan. 7	L.A. Rams ($10,000)	N.Y. Giants ($10,000)	19-13*	East Rutherford	76,526
	Jan. 6	San Francisco ($10,000)	Minnesota ($10,000)	41-13	San Francisco	64,918
1988	Jan. 1	San Francisco ($10,000)	Minnesota ($10,000)	34-9	San Francisco	61,848
	Dec. 31	Chicago ($10,000)	Philadelphia ($10,000)	20-12	Chicago	65,534
1987	Jan. 10	Washington ($10,000)	Chicago ($10,000)	21-17	Chicago	65,268
	Jan. 9	Minnesota ($10,000)	San Francisco ($10,000)	36-24	San Francisco	63,008
1986	Jan. 4	N.Y. Giants ($10,000)	San Francisco ($10,000)	49-3	East Rutherford	75,691
	Jan. 3	Washington ($10,000)	Chicago ($10,000)	27-13	Chicago	65,524
1985	Jan. 5	Chicago ($10,000)	N.Y. Giants ($10,000)	21-0	Chicago	65,670
	Jan. 4	L.A. Rams ($10,000)	Dallas ($10,000)	20-0	Anaheim	66,581
1984	Dec. 30	Chicago ($10,000)	Washington ($10,000)	23-19	Washington	55,431
	Dec. 29	San Francisco ($10,000)	N.Y. Giants ($10,000)	21-10	San Francisco	60,303
1983	Jan. 1	Washington ($10,000)	L.A. Rams ($10,000)	51-7	Washington	54,440
	Dec. 31	San Francisco ($10,000)	Detroit ($10,000)	24-23	San Francisco	59,979
1982	Jan. 16	Dallas ($10,000)	Green Bay ($10,000)	37-26	Dallas	63,972
	Jan. 15	Washington ($10,000)	Minnesota ($10,000)	21-7	Washington	54,593
1981	Jan. 3	San Francisco ($5,000)	N.Y. Giants ($5,000)	38-24	San Francisco	58,360
	Jan. 2	Dallas ($5,000)	Tampa Bay ($5,000)	38-0	Dallas	64,848
1980	Jan. 4	Dallas ($5,000)	Atlanta ($5,000)	30-27	Atlanta	59,793
	Jan. 3	Philadelphia ($5,000)	Minnesota ($5,000)	31-16	Philadelphia	70,178
1979	Dec. 30	Los Angeles ($5,000)	Dallas ($5,000)	21-19	Dallas	64,792
	Dec. 29	Tampa Bay ($5,000)	Philadelphia ($5,000)	24-17	Tampa Bay	71,402
1978	Dec. 31	Los Angeles ($5,000)	Minnesota ($5,000)	34-10	Los Angeles	70,436
	Dec. 30	Dallas ($5,000)	Atlanta ($5,000)	27-20	Dallas	63,406
1977	Dec. 26	Dallas ($5,000)	Chicago ($5,000)	37-7	Dallas	63,260
	Dec. 26	Minnesota ($5,000)	Los Angeles ($5,000)	14-7	Los Angeles	70,203
1976	Dec. 19	Los Angeles ($)	Dallas ($)	14-12	Dallas	63,283
	Dec. 18	Minnesota ($)	Washington ($)	35-20	Minnesota	47,466
1975	Dec. 28	Dallas ($)	Minnesota ($)	17-14	Minnesota	48,050
	Dec. 27	Los Angeles ($)	St. Louis ($)	35-23	Los Angeles	73,459
1974	Dec. 22	Los Angeles ($)	Washington ($)	19-10	Los Angeles	77,925
	Dec. 21	Minnesota ($)	St. Louis ($)	30-14	Minnesota	48,150
1973	Dec. 23	Dallas ($)	Los Angeles ($)	27-16	Dallas	63,272
	Dec. 22	Minnesota ($)	Washington ($)	27-20	Minnesota	48,040
1972	Dec. 24	Washington ($)	Green Bay ($)	16-3	Washington	52,321
	Dec. 23	Dallas ($)	San Francisco ($)	30-28	San Francisco	59,746
1971	Dec. 26	San Francisco ($)	Washington ($)	24-20	San Francisco	45,327
	Dec. 25	Dallas ($)	Minnesota ($)	20-12	Minnesota	47,307
1970	Dec. 27	San Francisco ($)	Minnesota ($)	17-14	Minnesota	45,103
	Dec. 26	Dallas ($)	Detroit ($)	5-0	Dallas	69,613
1969	Dec. 28	Cleveland ($)	Dallas ($)	38-14	Dallas	69,321
	Dec. 27	Minnesota ($)	Los Angeles ($)	23-20	Minnesota	47,900
1968	Dec. 22	Baltimore ($)	Minnesota ($)	24-14	Baltimore	60,238
	Dec. 21	Cleveland ($)	Dallas ($)	31-20	Cleveland	81,497
1967	Dec. 24	Dallas ($)	Cleveland ($)	52-14	Dallas	70,786
	Dec. 23	Green Bay ($)	Los Angeles ($)	28-7	Milwaukee	49,861
1965	Dec. 26	Green Bay ($)	Baltimore ($)	13-10*	Green Bay	50,484

Season	Date	Winner (Share)	Loser (Share)	Score	Site	Attendance
1958	Dec. 21	N.Y. Giants (#)	Cleveland (#)	10-0	New York	61,274
1957	Dec. 22	Detroit (#)	San Francisco (#)	31-27	San Francisco	60,118
1952	Dec. 21	Detroit (#)	Los Angeles (#)	31-21	Detroit	47,645
1950	Dec. 17	Los Angeles (#)	Chicago Bears (#)	24-14	Los Angeles	83,501
	Dec. 17	Cleveland (#)	N.Y. Giants (#)	8-3	Cleveland	33,054
1947	Dec. 21	Philadelphia (#)	Pittsburgh (#)	21-0	Pittsburgh	35,729
1943	Dec. 19	Washington (¢)	N.Y. Giants (¢)	28-0	New York	42,800
1941	Dec. 14	Chicago Bears (¢)	Green Bay (¢)	33-14	Chicago	43,425

*Sudden Death Overtime.
$ Players received 1/14 of annual salary for playoff appearances.
# Players received 1/12 of annual salary for playoff appearances.
¢ Players received 1/10 of annual salary for playoff appearances.

1991 NFC Divisional Playoff Games

RFK Stadium, Washington, D.C.   January 4, 1992
Attendance: 55,181

WASHINGTON 24, ATLANTA 7— The Redskins overcame poor weather conditions by rushing for 162 yards, while the Falcons succumbed to the wind, rain, and mud by turning the ball over 6 times. Rookie Ricky Ervins gained 104 yards on 23 carries as Washington maintained possession for more than 36 minutes. Gerald Riggs had a pair of short touchdown runs for the Redskins. Washington scored all the points it needed in a span of 3:11 of the second quarter. Ervins capped an 81-yard drive with a 17-yard touchdown run and Riggs scored on a 2-yard run four plays after James Geathers recovered a fumble at Atlanta's 39-yard line.

Atlanta	0	7	0	0	—	7
Washington	0	14	3	7	—	24

Wash—Ervins 17 run (Lohmiller kick)
Wash—Riggs 2 run (Lohmiller kick)
Atl —T. Johnson 1 run (N. Johnson kick)
Wash—FG Lohmiller 24
Wash—Riggs 1 run (Lohmiller kick)

Pontiac Silverdome, Pontiac, Michigan   January 5, 1992
Attendance: 78,290

DETROIT 38, DALLAS 6— Erik Kramer completed 29 of 38 passes for 341 yards and 3 touchdowns as the ground-oriented Lions took to the air to beat the Cowboys. Barry Sanders, the NFL's second-leading rusher with 1,548 yards during the regular season, carried only 12 times for 69 yards (47 coming on a fourth-quarter touchdown run), but Detroit still piled up 421 yards of total offense. Two of Kramer's scoring passes went to Willie Green, who had 8 catches for 115 yards. Melvin Jenkins also returned a second-quarter interception 41 yards for a touchdown for the Lions. Jenkins's touchdown gave Detroit a 14-3 lead, and the Lions put the game away by scoring 2 touchdowns in a span of 1:05 of the third quarter. Green's second touchdown catch, a 9-yarder, gave Detroit a 24-6 advantage, and after Victor Jones recovered Troy Aikman's fumble at the Dallas 27-yard line, Herman Moore caught a 7-yard touchdown pass from Kramer to put the game away.

Dallas	3	3	0	0	—	6
Detroit	7	10	14	7	—	38

Det—Green 31 pass from Kramer (Murray kick)
Dall—FG Willis 28
Det—Jenkins 41 interception return (Murray kick)
Dall—FG Willis 28
Det—FG Murray 36
Det—Green 9 pass from Kramer (Murray kick)
Det—Moore 7 pass from Kramer (Murray kick)
Det—Sanders 47 run (Murray kick)

AFC Wild Card Playoff Games
Results

Season	Date	Winner (Share)	Loser (Share)	Score	Site	Attendance
1991	Dec. 29	Houston ($10,000)	N.Y. Jets ($6,000)	17-10	Houston	61,485
	Dec. 28	Kansas City ($6,000)	L.A. Raiders ($6,000)	10-6	Kansas City	75,827
1990	Jan. 6	Cincinnati ($10,000)	Houston ($6,000)	41-14	Cincinnati	60,012
	Jan. 5	Miami ($6,000)	Kansas City ($6,000)	17-16	Miami	67,276
1989	Dec. 31	Pittsburgh ($6,000)	Houston ($6,000)	26-23*	Houston	59,406
1988	Dec. 26	Houston ($6,000)	Cleveland ($6,000)	24-23	Cleveland	75,896
1987	Jan. 3	Houston ($6,000)	Seattle ($6,000)	23-20*	Houston	50,519
1986	Dec. 28	N.Y. Jets ($6,000)	Kansas City ($6,000)	35-15	East Rutherford	75,210
1985	Dec. 28	New England ($6,000)	N.Y. Jets ($6,000)	26-14	East Rutherford	75,945
1984	Dec. 22	Seattle ($6,000)	L.A. Raiders ($6,000)	13-7	Seattle	62,049
1983	Dec. 24	Seattle ($6,000)	Denver ($6,000)	31-7	Seattle	64,275
1982	Jan. 9	N.Y. Jets ($6,000)	Cincinnati ($6,000)	44-17	Cincinnati	57,560
	Jan. 9	San Diego ($6,000)	Pittsburgh ($6,000)	31-28	Pittsburgh	53,546
	Jan. 8	L.A. Raiders ($6,000)	Cleveland ($6,000)	27-10	Los Angeles	56,555
	Jan. 8	Miami ($6,000)	New England ($6,000)	28-13	Miami	68,842
1981	Dec. 27	Buffalo ($3,000)	N.Y. Jets ($3,000)	31-27	New York	57,050
1980	Dec. 28	Oakland ($3,000)	Houston ($3,000)	27-7	Oakland	53,333
1979	Dec. 23	Houston ($3,000)	Denver ($3,000)	13-7	Houston	48,776
1978	Dec. 24	Houston ($3,000)	Miami ($3,000)	17-9	Miami	72,445

*Sudden death overtime.

1991 AFC Wild Card Playoff Games

Arrowhead Stadium, Kansas City, Missouri   December 28, 1991
Attendance: 75,827

KANSAS CITY 10, L.A. RAIDERS 6—Steve DeBerg passed 11 yards to Fred Jones for the game's only touchdown and the Chiefs forced 6 turnovers to hang on and beat the Raiders. The Raiders' Todd Marinovich, who passed for 243 yards and 3 touchdowns in a narrow loss to Kansas City one week earlier, completed 12 of 23 passes for 140 yards, but was intercepted 4 times. Deron Cherry had 2 of the thefts, the second of which he returned 29 yards to the Los Angeles 11-yard line in the second quarter. DeBerg and Jones connected for the touchdown on the next play, 5:07 before halftime. The Raiders drove to the Chiefs' 24-yard line in the final minutes, but were whistled for 4 penalties in a 5-play span before reserve linebacker Lonnie Marts ended the threat with an interception. Barry Word rushed for 130 yards on 33 carries for Kansas City, which ran the ball 39 times and passed only 14. Nick Bell carried 20 times for 107 yards for Los Angeles, which outgained the Chiefs 276 yards to 204.

L.A. Raiders	0	3	3	0 —	6
Kansas City	0	7	0	3 —	10

KC   —F. Jones 11 pass from DeBerg (Lowery kick)
Raiders—FG Jaeger 32
Raiders—FG Jaeger 26
KC   —FG Lowery 18

Astrodome, Houston, Texas   December 29, 1991
Attendance: 61,485

HOUSTON 17, N.Y. JETS 10—Warren Moon threw a pair of touchdown passes to Ernest Givins and the Oilers' defense stopped the Jets inside Houston's 5-yard line twice in the second half to preserve the victory. The Oilers led 14-10 entering the third quarter, when the Jets took the second-half kickoff and consumed more than eight minutes while driving to the Houston 8-yard line. On third down, Ken O'Brien's pass was intercepted by safety Bubba McDowell at the 2. After Al Del Greco's 53-yard field goal put the Oilers ahead 17-10 early in the fourth quarter, New York drove to the Houston 3. But on third down, Al Smith stopped Brad Baxter for no gain, and on fourth-and-inches, a trio of players, including Smith, stopped Freeman McNeil for no gain. The Jets had one more chance after recovering Moon's fumble at the Oilers' 26 with 4:59 left in the game, but New York could not convert a first down. Moon completed 28 of 40 passes for 271 yards and Drew Hill had 9 catches for 77 yards. The Jets' O'Brien was 21 of 31 for 221 yards but was intercepted 3 times. Al Toon caught 8 passes for 96 yards and 1 touchdown for New York.

N.Y. Jets	0	10	0	0 —	10
Houston	7	7	0	3 —	17

Hou—Givins 5 pass from Moon (Del Greco kick)
Jets—Toon 10 pass from O'Brien (Allegre kick)
Hou—Givins 20 pass from Moon (Del Greco kick)
Jets—FG Allegre 33
Hou—FG Del Greco 53

NFC Wild Card Playoff Games

Results

Season	Date	Winner (Share)	Loser (Share)	Score	Site	Attendance
1991	Dec. 29	Dallas ($6,000)	Chicago ($6,000)	17-13	Chicago	62,594
	Dec. 28	Atlanta ($6,000)	New Orleans ($6,000)	27-20	New Orleans	68,794
1990	Jan. 6	Chicago ($10,000)	New Orleans ($10,000)	16-6	Chicago	60,767
	Jan. 5	Washington ($6,000)	Philadelphia ($6,000)	20-6	Philadelphia	65,287
1989	Dec. 31	L.A. Rams ($6,000)	Philadelphia ($6,000)	21-7	Philadelphia	65,479
1988	Dec. 26	Minnesota ($6,000)	L.A. Rams ($6,000)	28-17	Minnesota	61,204
1987	Jan. 3	Minnesota ($6,000)	New Orleans ($6,000)	44-10	New Orleans	68,546
1986	Dec. 28	Washington ($6,000)	L.A. Rams ($6,000)	19-7	Washington	54,567
1985	Dec. 29	N.Y. Giants ($6,000)	San Francisco ($6,000)	17-3	East Rutherford	75,131
1984	Dec. 23	N.Y. Giants ($6,000)	L.A. Rams ($6,000)	16-3	Anaheim	67,037
1983	Dec. 26	L.A. Rams ($6,000)	Dallas ($6,000)	24-17	Dallas	62,118
1982	Jan. 9	Dallas ($6,000)	Tampa Bay ($6,000)	30-17	Dallas	65,042
	Jan. 9	Minnesota ($6,000)	Atlanta ($6,000)	30-24	Minnesota	60,560
	Jan. 8	Green Bay ($6,000)	St. Louis ($6,000)	41-16	Green Bay	54,282
	Jan. 8	Washington ($6,000)	Detroit ($6,000)	31-7	Washington	55,045
1981	Dec. 27	N.Y. Giants ($3,000)	Philadelphia ($3,000)	27-21	Philadelphia	71,611
1980	Dec. 28	Dallas ($3,000)	Los Angeles ($3,000)	34-13	Dallas	63,052
1979	Dec. 23	Philadelphia ($3,000)	Chicago ($3,000)	27-17	Philadelphia	69,397
1978	Dec. 24	Atlanta ($3,000)	Philadelphia ($3,000)	14-13	Atlanta	59,403

1991 NFC Wild Card Playoff Games

Louisiana Superdome, New Orleans, Louisiana   December 28, 1991
Attendance: 68,794

ATLANTA 27, NEW ORLEANS 20—Michael Haynes caught a short pass from Chris Miller and turned it into the game-winning 61-yard touchdown for the Falcons with 2:41 left in the game. The Saints, who won their first NFC Western Division title and made the playoffs for the third time in five years, remained winless in postseason games. Atlanta rallied from a 10-0 second-quarter deficit behind 3 touchdown passes from Miller, who completed 18 of 30 passes for 291 yards. Haynes had 6 receptions for 144 yards and 2 touchdowns, the first of which was a 20-yarder that gave the Falcons their first lead at 17-13 early in the third quarter. New Orleans regained the lead on Dalton Hilliard's 1-yard run 50 seconds into the fourth quarter, but Atlanta tied it at 20-20 on Norm Johnson's 36-yard field goal with 7:43 remaining. After Haynes's go-ahead touchdown, Bobby Hebert drove his team to the Falcons' 35-yard line, but was intercepted by Atlanta's Tim McKyer.

Atlanta	0	10	7	10 —	27
New Orleans	7	6	0	7 —	20

NO—Turner 26 pass from Hebert (Andersen kick)
NO—FG Andersen 45
Atl—Rison 24 pass from Miller (Johnson kick)
Atl—FG Johnson 44
NO—FG Andersen 35
Atl—Haynes 20 pass from Miller (Johnson kick)
NO—Hilliard 1 run (Andersen kick)
Atl—FG Johnson 36
Atl—Haynes 61 pass from Miller (Johnson kick)

Soldier Field, Chicago, Illinois   December 29, 1991
Attendance: 62,594

DALLAS 17, CHICAGO 13—Emmitt Smith rushed for 105 yards and 1 touchdown on 26 carries to lead the Cowboys to their first postseason victory since the 1982 season. Smith's touchdown gave Dallas a 10-0 lead and came five plays after Dallas's Darrick Brownlow blocked Maury Buford's punt and teammate Ken Norton recovered at the Bears' 10-yard line. In the third quarter, Dallas's Steve Beuerlein capped a 75-yard drive with a 3-yard touchdown pass to Jay Novacek for a 17-6 lead, and the Cowboys made the advantage stand up. Smith carried 26 times in the game and became the first player ever to eclipse the 100-yard plateau against Chicago in postseason play. Jim Harbaugh passed for 218 yards for Chicago, which outgained Dallas 372 total yards to 288. Tom Waddle caught 9 passes for 104 yards and 1 touchdown, including a 6-yarder with 2:42 left in the game.

Dallas	10	0	7	0 —	17
Chicago	0	3	3	7 —	13

Dall—FG Willis 27
Dall—E. Smith 1 run (Willis kick)
Chi—FG Butler 19
Chi—FG Butler 43
Dall—Novacek 3 pass from Beuerlein (Willis kick)
Chi—Waddle 6 pass from Harbaugh (Butler kick)

AFC-NFC Pro Bowl At A Glance (1971-1992)
NFC leads series, 13-9

Results

Year	Date	Winner (Share)	Loser (Share)	Score	Site	Attendance
1992	Feb. 2	NFC ($10,000)	AFC ($5,000)	21-15	Honolulu	50,209
1991	Feb. 3	AFC ($10,000)	NFC ($5,000)	23-21	Honolulu	50,345
1990	Feb. 4	NFC ($10,000)	AFC ($5,000)	27-21	Honolulu	50,445
1989	Jan. 29	NFC ($10,000)	AFC ($5,000)	34-3	Honolulu	50,113
1988	Feb. 7	AFC ($10,000)	NFC ($5,000)	15-6	Honolulu	50,113
1987	Feb. 1	AFC ($10,000)	NFC ($5,000)	10-6	Honolulu	50,101
1986	Feb. 2	NFC ($10,000)	AFC ($5,000)	28-24	Honolulu	50,101
1985	Jan. 27	AFC ($10,000)	NFC ($5,000)	22-14	Honolulu	50,385
1984	Jan. 29	NFC ($10,000)	AFC ($5,000)	45-3	Honolulu	50,445
1983	Feb. 6	NFC ($10,000)	AFC ($5,000)	20-19	Honolulu	49,883
1982	Jan. 31	AFC ($5,000)	NFC ($2,500)	16-13	Honolulu	50,402
1981	Feb. 1	NFC ($5,000)	AFC ($2,500)	21-7	Honolulu	50,360
1980	Jan. 27	NFC ($5,000)	AFC ($2,500)	37-27	Honolulu	49,800
1979	Jan. 29	NFC ($5,000)	AFC ($2,500)	13-7	Los Angeles	46,281
1978	Jan. 23	NFC ($5,000)	AFC ($2,500)	14-13	Tampa	51,337
1977	Jan. 17	AFC ($2,000)	NFC ($1,500)	24-14	Seattle	64,752
1976	Jan. 26	NFC ($2,000)	AFC ($1,500)	23-20	New Orleans	30,546
1975	Jan. 20	NFC ($2,000)	AFC ($1,500)	17-10	Miami	26,484
1974	Jan. 20	AFC ($2,000)	NFC ($1,500)	15-13	Kansas City	66,918
1973	Jan. 21	AFC ($2,000)	NFC ($1,500)	33-28	Irving	37,091
1972	Jan. 23	AFC ($2,000)	NFC ($1,500)	26-13	Los Angeles	53,647
1971	Jan. 24	NFC ($2,000)	AFC ($1,500)	27-6	Los Angeles	48,222

1992 AFC-NFC Pro Bowl

Aloha Stadium, Honolulu, Hawaii
Attendance: 50,209
February 2, 1992

NFC 21, AFC 15—Atlanta's Chris Miller threw an 11-yard touchdown pass to San Francisco's Jerry Rice with 4:04 remaining in the game to lift the NFC over the AFC. It was the NFC's thirteenth win in the 22-game series. The AFC had taken a 15-14 lead when the Raiders' Jeff Jaeger kicked a 27-yard field goal 1:49 into the fourth quarter. But the NFC, aided by a key roughing-the-passer penalty on a third-down incompletion from the AFC 24-yard line, drove 85 yards to the winning score. The Cowboys' Michael Irvin, playing in his first Pro Bowl, caught 8 passes for 125 yards, including a 13-yard touchdown in the first quarter, and was named the player of the game. Rice had 7 catches for 77 yards. Mark Rypien of Washington, the Super Bowl most valuable player one week earlier, completed 11 of 18 passes for 165 yards and 2 touchdowns for the NFC, including a 35-yarder to Redskins teammate Gary Clark just 26 seconds before halftime. Miller completed 7 of his 10 attempts for 85 yards.

NFC (21)	Offense	AFC (15)
Jerry Rice (San Francisco)	WR	Haywood Jeffires (Houston)
Jim Lachey (Washington)	LT	Anthony Muñoz (Cincinnati)
Guy McIntyre (San Francisco)	LG	Mike Munchak (Houston)
Jay Hilgenberg (Chicago)	C	Bruce Matthews (Houston)
Randall McDaniel (Minnesota)	RG	Steve Wisniewski (L.A. Raiders)
Lomas Brown (Detroit)	RT	Bruce Armstrong (New England)
Jay Novacek (Dallas)	TE	Marv Cook (New England)
Michael Irvin (Dallas)	WR	Mark Clayton (Miami)
Mark Rypien (Washington)	QB	Jim Kelly (Buffalo)
Barry Sanders (Detroit)	RB	Thurman Thomas (Buffalo)
Emmitt Smith (Dallas)	RB	Marion Butts (San Diego)
	Defense	
Reggie White (Philadelphia)	LE	William Fuller (Houston)
Jerome Brown (Philadelphia)	NT	Michael Dean Perry (Cleveland)
Clyde Simmons (Philadelphia)	RE	Greg Townsend (L.A. Raiders)
Seth Joyner (Philadelphia)	LOLB	Derrick Thomas (Kansas City)
Sam Mills (New Orleans)	LILB	Al Smith (Houston)
Vaughan Johnson (New Orleans)	RILB	Junior Seau (San Diego)
Pat Swilling (New Orleans)	ROLB	Cornelius Bennett (Buffalo)
Darrell Green (Washington)	LCB	Gill Byrd (San Diego)
Deion Sanders (Atlanta)	RCB	Cris Dishman (Houston)
Mark Carrier (Chicago)	FS	Steve Atwater (Denver)
Bennie Blades (Detroit)	SS	Ronnie Lott (L.A. Raiders)

Substitutions

NFC—Offense: K—Chip Lohmiller (Washington). P—Rich Camarillo (Phoenix). QB—Troy Aikman (Dallas), Chris Miller (Atlanta). RB—Neal Anderson (Chicago), Earnest Byner (Washington). WR—Gary Clark (Washington), Andre Rison (Atlanta). TE—Steve Jordan (Minnesota). KR—Mel Gray (Detroit). C—Bart Oates (N.Y. Giants). G—Mark Schlereth (Washington). T—Chris Hinton (Atlanta). Defense: E—Charles Mann (Washington). T—Henry Thomas (Minnesota). LB—Charles Haley (San Francisco), Mike Singletary (Chicago), Chris Spielman (Detroit). CB—Eric Allen (Philadelphia). S—Shaun Gayle (Chicago). ST—Bennie Thompson (New Orleans). DNP: None.
AFC—Offense: K—Jeff Jaeger (L.A. Raiders). P—Jeff Gossett (L.A. Raiders). QB—Warren Moon (Houston), Ken O'Brien (N.Y. Jets). RB—Gaston Green (Denver), John L. Williams (Seattle). WR—James Lofton (Buffalo). TE—Ethan Horton (L.A. Raiders). KR—Tim Brown (L.A. Raiders). C—Don

Mosebar (L.A. Raiders). G—Jim Ritcher (Buffalo). T—Richmond Webb (Miami). Defense: E—Neil Smith (Kansas City). T—Cortez Kennedy (Seattle). LB—Greg Lloyd (Pittsburgh), Karl Mecklenburg (Denver), Darryl Talley (Buffalo). CB—Rod Woodson (Pittsburgh). S—Dennis Smith (Denver). ST—Steve Tasker (Buffalo). DNP: WR—Andre Reed (Buffalo).

Head Coaches

NFC—Wayne Fontes (Detroit)
AFC—Dan Reeves (Denver)

Officials

Referee—Gerald Austin. Umpire—Hendi Ancich. Line Judge—Ron Baynes. Head Linesman—Paul Weidner. Back Judge—Timmie Millis. Field Judge—John Robison. Side Judge—Howard Slavin. Replay Official—Fritz Graf.

Scoring

NFC	7	7	0	7 —	21
AFC	7	5	0	3 —	15

AFC—Clayton 4 pass from Kelly (Jaeger kick)
NFC—Irvin 13 pass from Rypien (Lohmiller kick)
AFC—Safety, Townsend tackled Byner in end zone
AFC—FG Jaeger 48
NFC—Clark 35 pass from Rypien (Lohmiller kick)
AFC—FG Jaeger 27
NFC—Rice 11 pass from Miller (Lohmiller kick)

Team Statistics

	NFC	AFC
Total First Downs	22	15
First Downs Rushing	2	5
First Downs Passing	15	7
First Downs Penalty	4	3
Total Net Yardage	293	214
Total Offensive Plays	60	64
Average Gain per Offensive Play	4.9	3.3
Rushes	21	32
Yards Gained Rushing (net)	28	103
Average Yards per Rush	1.3	3.2
Passes Attempted	36	28
Passes Completed	23	14
Had Intercepted	1	1
Tackled Attempting to Pass	3	4
Yards Lost Attempting to Pass	18	23
Yards Gained Passing (net)	265	111
Punts	1	3
Average Distance	44.0	38.0
Punt Returns	2	1
Punt Return Yardage	24	10
Kickoff Returns	2	3
Kickoff Return Yardage	36	70
Interception Return Yardage	0	0
Total Return Yardage	60	80
Fumbles	6	3
Own Fumbles Recovered	4	2
Opponent Fumbles Recovered	1	2
Penalties	8	11
Yards Penalized	60	106

Total Points Scored	21	15
Touchdowns	3	1
Touchdowns Rushing	0	0
Touchdowns Passing	3	1
Touchdowns Returns	0	0
Extra Points	3	1
Field Goals	0	2
Field Goals Attempted	1	3
Safeties	0	1
Third Down Efficiency	6/11	7/15
Fourth Down Efficiency	0/1	0/1
Time of Possession	27:31	32:29

Individual Statistics

Rushing

NFC	No.	Yds.	LG	TD
E. Smith	10	33	14	0
B. Sanders	6	5	8	0
Miller	3	0	2	0
Rypien	1	0	0	0
Byner	1	-10	-10	0

AFC	No.	Yds.	LG	TD
Butts	12	63	17	0
T. Thomas	9	14	5	0
G. Green	3	10	4	0
Williams	4	8	4	0
Kelly	2	6	6	0
Clayton	1	2	2	0
O'Brien	1	0	0	0

Passing

NFC	Att.	Comp.	Yds.	TD	Int.
Rypien	18	11	165	2	1
Miller	10	7	85	1	0
Aikman	8	5	33	0	0

AFC	Att.	Comp.	Yds.	TD	Int.
Kelly	10	6	68	1	1
Moon	9	5	54	0	0
O'Brien	9	3	12	0	0

Receiving

NFC	No.	Yds.	LG	TD
Irvin	8	125	21	1
Rice	7	77	18	1
Clark	2	46	35t	1
Rison	2	29	25	0
Anderson	2	-3	-1	0
E. Smith	1	5	5	0
B. Sanders	1	4	4	0

AFC	No.	Yds.	LG	TD
T. Brown	5	74	29	0
Horton	2	24	19	0
Cook	2	17	12	0
Jeffires	1	6	6	0
Lofton	1	6	6	0
Clayton	1	4	4t	1
Butts	1	2	2	0
Williams	1	1	1	0

Interceptions

NFC	No.	Yds.	LG	TD
D. Sanders	1	0	0	0

AFC	No.	Yds.	LG	TD
Atwater	1	0	0	0

Punting

NFC	No.	Avg.	LG	Blk.
Camarillo	1	44.0	44	0

AFC	No.	Avg.	LG	Blk.
Gossett	3	38.0	44	0

Punt Returns

NFC	No.	FC	Yds.	LG	TD
Gray	2	0	24	18	0

AFC	No.	FC	Yds.	LG	TD
T. Brown	1	0	10	10	0

Kickoff Returns

NFC	No.	Yds.	LG	TD
Gray	2	36	18	0

AFC	No.	Yds.	LG	TD
Woodson	2	59	33	0
T. Brown	1	11	11	0

1991 AFC-NFC Pro Bowl

Aloha Stadium, Honolulu, Hawaii — February 3, 1991
Attendance: 50,345

AFC 23, NFC 21—Buffalo's Jim Kelly and Houston's Ernest Givins combined for a 13-yard scoring pass late in the fourth quarter to rally the AFC over the NFC. Phoenix rookie Johnny Johnson scored on runs of one and nine yards to put the NFC ahead 14-3 in the third quarter. Buffalo's Andre Reed, who led all receivers with four catches for 80 yards, caught a 20-yard scoring reception from Kelly early in the fourth quarter to move the AFC to within one point. Barry Sanders ran 22 yards for a touchdown to increase the NFC's lead to 21-13. Miami's Jeff Cross blocked a 46-yard field-goal attempt by New Orleans's Morten Andersen with seven seconds remaining to preserve the win. Buffalo's Bruce Smith recorded three sacks and also had a blocked field goal. Kelly, who completed 13 of 19 passes for 210 yards and two touchdowns, was presented the Dan McGuire Award as player of the game. The AFC's victory narrowed the NFC's Pro Bowl series lead to 12-9.

AFC	3	0	3	17	— 23
NFC	0	7	7	7	— 21

AFC—FG Lowery 26
NFC—J. Johnson 1 run (Andersen kick)
AFC—FG Lowery 43
NFC—J. Johnson 9 run (Andersen kick)
AFC—Reed 20 pass from Kelly (Lowery kick)
NFC—Sanders 22 run (Andersen kick)
AFC—FG Lowery 34
AFC—Givins 13 pass from Kelly (Lowery kick)

1990 AFC-NFC Pro Bowl

Aloha Stadium, Honolulu, Hawaii — February 4, 1990
Attendance: 50,445

NFC 27, AFC 21—The NFC captured its second straight Pro Bowl as the defense accounted for a pair of touchdowns and forced five turnovers before the eleventh consecutive sellout crowd at Aloha Stadium. The AFC held a 7-6 halftime edge on a one-yard scoring run by Christian Okoye of the Chiefs. The NFC then rallied with 21 unanswered points in the third quarter. David Meggett of the Giants began the comeback with an 11-yard touchdown reception from Philadelphia's Randall Cunningham. The Rams' Jerry Gray followed with a 51-yard interception return for a score and the Vikings' Keith Millard added an eight-yard fumble return for a touchdown four minutes later to give the NFC a commanding 27-7 lead. Seattle's Dave Krieg rallied the AFC with a five-yard touchdown pass to Miami's Ferrell Edmunds. Cleveland's Mike Johnson then returned an interception 22 yards for a score to pull the AFC to within six points

27-21. Gray, who was credited with seven tackles, was given the Dan McGuire Award as player of the game. Krieg led all quarterbacks by completing 15 of 23 for 148 yards and one touchdown. Buffalo's Thurman Thomas topped all receivers with five catches for 47 yards, while Indianapolis's Eric Dickerson led all rushers with 46 yards on 15 carries. The win gave the NFC a 12-8 advantage in Pro Bowl games since 1971.

NFC	3	3	21	0	— 27
AFC	0	7	0	14	— 21

NFC—FG Murray 23
NFC—FG Murray 41
AFC—Okoye 1 run (Treadwell kick)
NFC—Meggett 11 pass from Cunningham (Murray kick)
NFC—Gray 51 interception return (Murray kick)
NFC—Millard 8 fumble recovery return (Murray kick)
AFC—Edmunds 5 pass from Krieg (Treadwell kick)
AFC—M. Johnson 22 interception return (Treadwell kick)

1989 AFC-NFC Pro Bowl

Aloha Stadium, Honolulu, Hawaii — January 29, 1989
Attendance: 50,113

NFC 34, AFC 3—The NFC scored 34 unanswered points to snap a two-game losing streak to the AFC before the tenth straight sellout crowd in Honolulu's Aloha Stadium. Bills kicker Scott Norwood provided the AFC's only points on a 38-yard field goal 6:23 into the game. Touchdown runs by Dallas's Herschel Walker (four yards) and Atlanta's John Settle (one) brought the NFC a 14-3 half-time lead. Walker added a seven-yard scoring run, the Saints' Morten Andersen kicked field goals of 27 and 51 yards, and Los Angeles Rams' wide receiver Henry Ellard caught an eight-yard scoring pass from Minnesota quarterback Wade Wilson in the second half to complete the scoring. Chicago running back Neal Anderson and Philadelphia quarterback Randall Cunningham, who were both appearing in their first Pro Bowl, also played major roles in the NFC's victory. Anderson rushed 13 times for 85 yards and had two receptions for 17. Cunningham, who was voted the game's outstanding player, completed 10 of 14 passes for 63 yards and rushed for 49 yards. The NFC, which had five takeaways, outgained the AFC 355 yards to 167 and held a time-of-possession advantage of 35:18 to 24:42. Houston quarterback Warren Moon completed 13 of 20 passes for 134 yards for the AFC. The win gave the NFC an 11-8 advantage in Pro Bowl games.

AFC	3	0	0	0	— 3
NFC	7	7	10	10	— 34

AFC—FG Norwood 38
NFC—Walker 4 run (Andersen kick)
NFC—Settle 1 run (Andersen kick)
NFC—FG Andersen 27
NFC—Walker 7 run (Andersen kick)
NFC—FG Andersen 51
NFC—Ellard 8 pass from Wilson (Andersen kick)

1988 AFC-NFC Pro Bowl

Aloha Stadium, Honolulu, Hawaii — February 7, 1988
Attendance: 50,113

AFC 15, NFC 6—Led by a tenacious pass rush, the AFC defeated the NFC for the second consecutive year before the ninth straight sellout crowd in Honolulu's Aloha Stadium. Buffalo quarterback Jim Kelly scored the game's lone touchdown on a one-yard run for a 7-6 halftime lead. Colts kicker Dean Biasucci added field goals from 37 and 30 yards to complete the AFC's scoring. Saints kicker Morten Andersen had 25- and 36-yard field goals to account for the NFC's points. AFC defenders held the NFC to 213 yards and recorded eight sacks. Bills defensive end Bruce Smith, who had five tackles and two sacks, was voted the game's outstanding player. Oilers running back Mike Rozier led all rushers with 49 yards on nine carries. Jets wide receiver Al Toon had five receptions for 75 yards. The AFC generated 341 yards total offense and held a time-of-possession advantage of 34:14 to 25:46. By winning, the AFC cut the NFC's lead in the Pro Bowl series to 10-8.

NFC	0	6	0	0	— 6
AFC	0	7	6	2	— 15

NFC—FG Andersen 25
AFC—Kelly 1 run (Biasucci kick)
NFC—FG Andersen 36
AFC—FG Biasucci 37
AFC—FG Biasucci 30
AFC—Safety, Montana forced out of end zone

1987 AFC-NFC Pro Bowl

Aloha Stadium, Honolulu, Hawaii — February 1, 1987
Attendance: 50,101

AFC 10, NFC 6—The AFC defeated the NFC in the lowest-scoring game in AFC-NFC Pro Bowl history. The AFC took a 10-0 halftime lead on Broncos quarterback John Elway's 10-yard touchdown pass to Raiders tight end Todd Christensen and Patriots kicker Tony Franklin's 26-yard field goal. The AFC defense made the lead stand up by forcing the NFC to settle for a pair of field goals from 38 and 19 yards by Saints kicker Morten Andersen after the NFC had first downs at the AFC 31-, 7-, 16-, 15-, 5-, and 7-yard lines. Both AFC scores were set up by fumble recoveries by Seahawks linebacker Fredd Young and Dolphins linebacker John Offerdahl, respectively. Eagles defensive end Reggie White, who tied a Pro Bowl record with four sacks and also contributed seven solo tackles, was voted the game's outstanding player. The AFC victory cut the NFC's lead in the Pro Bowl series to 10-7.

AFC	7	3	0	0 — 10
NFC	0	0	3	3 — 6

AFC—Christensen 10 pass from Elway (Franklin kick)
AFC—FG Franklin 26
NFC—FG Andersen 38
NFC—FG Andersen 19

1986 AFC-NFC Pro Bowl

Aloha Stadium, Honolulu, Hawaii   February 2, 1986
Attendance: 50,101

NFC 28, AFC 24—New York Giants quarterback Phil Simms brought the NFC back from a 24-7 halftime deficit to defeat the AFC. Simms, who completed 15 of 27 passes for 212 yards and three touchdowns, was named the most valuable player of the game. The AFC had taken its first-half lead behind a two-yard run by Los Angeles Raiders running back Marcus Allen, who also threw a 51-yard scoring pass to San Diego wide receiver Wes Chandler, an 11-yard touchdown catch by Pittsburgh wide receiver Louis Lipps, and a 34-yard field goal by Steelers kicker Gary Anderson. Minnesota's Joey Browner accounted for the NFC's only score before halftime with a 48-yard interception return for a touchdown. After intermission, the NFC blanked the AFC while scoring three touchdowns via a 15-yard catch by Washington wide receiver Art Monk, a 2-yard reception by Dallas tight end Doug Cosbie, and a 15-yard catch by Tampa Bay tight end Jimmie Giles with 2:47 remaining in the game. The victory gave the NFC a 10-6 Pro Bowl record vs. the AFC.

NFC	0	7	7	14 — 28
AFC	7	17	0	0 — 24

AFC—Allen 2 run (Anderson kick)
NFC—Browner 48 interception return (Andersen kick)
AFC—Chandler 51 pass from Allen (Anderson kick)
AFC—FG Anderson 34
AFC—Lipps 11 pass from O'Brien (Anderson kick)
NFC—Monk 15 pass from Simms (Andersen kick)
NFC—Cosbie 2 pass from Simms (Andersen kick)
NFC—Giles 15 pass from Simms (Andersen kick)

1985 AFC-NFC Pro Bowl

Aloha Stadium, Honolulu, Hawaii   January 27, 1985
Attendance: 50,385

AFC 22, NFC 14—Defensive end Art Still of the Kansas City Chiefs recovered a fumble and returned it 83 yards for a touchdown to clinch the AFC's victory over the NFC. Still's touchdown came in the fourth period with the AFC trailing 14-12 and was one of several outstanding defensive plays in a Pro Bowl dominated by two record-breaking defenses. The teams combined for a Pro Bowl-record 17 sacks, including four by New York Jets defensive end Mark Gastineau, who was named the game's outstanding player. The AFC's first score came on a safety when Gastineau tackled running back Eric Dickerson of the Los Angeles Rams in the end zone. The AFC's second score, a six-yard pass from Miami's Dan Marino to Los Angeles Raiders running back Marcus Allen, was set up by a partial block of a punt by Seahawks linebacker Fredd Young. The NFC leads the series 9-6.

AFC	0	9	0	13 — 22
NFC	0	0	7	7 — 14

AFC—Safety, Gastineau tackled Dickerson in end zone
AFC—Allen 6 pass from Marino (Johnson kick)
NFC—Lofton 13 pass from Montana (Stenerud kick)
NFC—Payton 1 run (Stenerud kick)
AFC—FG Johnson 33
AFC—Still 83 fumble recovery return (Johnson kick)
AFC—FG Johnson 22

1984 AFC-NFC Pro Bowl

Aloha Stadium, Honolulu, Hawaii   January 29, 1984
Attendance: 50,445

NFC 45, AFC 3—The NFC won its sixth Pro Bowl in the last seven seasons by routing the AFC. The NFC was led by the passing of most valuable player Joe Theismann of Washington, who completed 21 of 27 passes for 242 yards and three touchdowns. Theismann set Pro Bowl records for completions and touchdown passes. The NFC established Pro Bowl marks for most points scored and fewest points allowed. Running back William Andrews of Atlanta had six carries for 43 yards and caught four passes for 49 yards, including scoring receptions of 16 and 2 yards. Los Angeles Rams rookie Eric Dickerson gained 46 yards on 11 carries, including a 14-yard touchdown run, and had 45 yards on five catches. Rams safety Nolan Cromwell had a 44-yard interception return for a touchdown early in the third period to give the NFC a commanding 24-3 lead. Green Bay wide receiver James Lofton caught an eight-yard touchdown pass, while tight end teammate Paul Coffman had a six-yard scoring catch.

NFC	3	14	14	14 — 45
AFC	0	3	0	0 — 3

NFC—FG Haji-Sheikh 23
NFC—Andrews 16 pass from Theismann (Haji-Sheikh kick)
NFC—Andrews 2 pass from Montana (Haji-Sheikh kick)
AFC—FG Anderson 43
NFC—Cromwell 44 interception return (Haji-Sheikh kick)
NFC—Lofton 8 pass from Theismann (Haji-Sheikh kick)
NFC—Coffman 6 pass from Theismann (Haji-Sheikh kick)
NFC—Dickerson 14 run (Haji-Sheikh kick)

1983 AFC-NFC Pro Bowl

Aloha Stadium, Honolulu, Hawaii   February 6, 1983
Attendance: 49,883

NFC 20, AFC 19—Dallas's Danny White threw an 11-yard touchdown pass to the Packers' John Jefferson with 35 seconds remaining to rally the NFC over the AFC. White, who completed 14 of 26 passes for 162 yards, kept the winning 65-yard drive alive with a 14-yard completion to Jefferson on a fourth-and-seven play at the AFC 25. The AFC was ahead 12-10 at halftime and increased the lead to 19-10 in the third period, when Marcus Allen scored on a one-yard run. San Diego's Dan Fouts, who attempted 30 passes, set Pro Bowl records for most completions (17) and yards (274). Pittsburgh's John Stallworth was the AFC's leading receiver with seven catches for 67 yards. William Andrews topped the NFC with five receptions for 48 yards. Fouts and Jefferson were voted co-winners of the player of the game award.

AFC	9	3	7	0 — 19
NFC	0	10	0	10 — 20

AFC—Walker 34 pass from Fouts (Benirschke kick)
AFC—Safety, Still tackled Theismann in end zone
NFC—Andrews 3 run (Moseley kick)
NFC—FG Moseley 35
AFC—FG Benirschke 29
AFC—Allen 1 run (Benirschke kick)
NFC—FG Moseley 41
NFC—Jefferson 11 pass from D. White (Moseley kick)

1982 AFC-NFC Pro Bowl

Aloha Stadium, Honolulu, Hawaii   January 31, 1982
Attendance: 50,402

AFC 16, NFC 13—Nick Lowery of Kansas City kicked a 23-yard field goal with three seconds remaining to give the AFC a last-second victory over the NFC. Lowery's kick climaxed a 69-yard drive directed by quarterback Dan Fouts. The NFC gained a 13-13 tie with 2:43 to go when Dallas's Tony Dorsett ran four yards for a touchdown. In the drive to the game-winning field goal, Fouts completed three passes, including a 23-yarder to San Diego teammate Kellen Winslow that put the ball on the NFC's 5-yard line. Two plays later, Lowery kicked the field goal. Winslow, who caught six passes for 86 yards, was named co-player of the game along with Tampa Bay defensive end Lee Roy Selmon.

NFC	0	6	0	7 — 13
AFC	0	0	13	3 — 16

NFC—Giles 4 pass from Montana (kick blocked)
AFC—Muncie 2 run (kick failed)
AFC—Campbell 1 run (Lowery kick)
NFC—Dorsett 4 run (Septien kick)
AFC—FG Lowery 23

1981 AFC-NFC Pro Bowl

Aloha Stadium, Honolulu, Hawaii   February 1, 1981
Attendance: 50,360

NFC 21, AFC 7—Ed Murray kicked four field goals and Steve Bartkowski fired a 55-yard scoring pass to Alfred Jenkins to lead the NFC to its fourth straight victory over the AFC and a 7-4 edge in the series. Murray was named the game's most valuable player and missed tying Garo Yepremian's Pro Bowl record of five field goals when a 37-yard attempt hit the crossbar with 22 seconds remaining. The AFC's only score came on a nine-yard pass from Brian Sipe to Stanley Morgan in the second period. Bartkowski completed 9 of 21 passes for 173 yards, while Sipe connected on 10 of 15 for 142 yards. Ottis Anderson led all rushers with 70 yards on 10 carries. Earl Campbell, the NFL's leading rusher in 1980, was limited to 24 yards on eight attempts.

AFC	0	7	0	0 — 7
NFC	3	6	0	12 — 21

NFC—FG Murray 31
AFC—Morgan 9 pass from Sipe (J. Smith kick)
NFC—FG Murray 31
NFC—FG Murray 34
NFC—Jenkins 55 pass from Bartkowski (Murray kick)
NFC—FG Murray 36
NFC—Safety, Shell called for holding in end zone

1980 AFC-NFC Pro Bowl

Aloha Stadium, Honolulu, Hawaii   January 27, 1980
Attendance: 49,800

NFC 37, AFC 27—Running back Chuck Muncie of New Orleans ran for two touchdowns and threw a 25-yard option pass for another score to give the NFC its third consecutive victory over the AFC. Muncie, who was selected the game's most valuable player, snapped a 3-3 tie on a one-yard touchdown run at 1:41 of the second quarter, then scored on an 11-yard run in the fourth quarter for the NFC's final touchdown. Two scoring records were set in the game—37 points by the NFC, eclipsing the 33 by the AFC in 1973, and the 64 points by both teams, surpassing the 61 scored in 1973.

NFC	3	20	7	7 — 37
AFC	3	7	10	7 — 27

NFC—FG Moseley 37
AFC—FG Fritsch 19
NFC—Muncie 1 run (Moseley kick)
AFC—Pruitt 1 pass from Bradshaw (Fritsch kick)
NFC—D. Hill 13 pass from Manning (kick failed)
NFC—T. Hill 25 pass from Muncie (Moseley kick)
NFC—Henry 86 punt return (Moseley kick)
AFC—Campbell 2 run (Fritsch kick)

AFC—FG Fritsch 29
NFC—Muncie 11 run (Moseley kick)
AFC—Campbell 1 run (Fritsch kick)

1979 AFC-NFC Pro Bowl

Memorial Coliseum, Los Angeles, California | January 29, 1979
Attendance: 46,281

NFC 13, AFC 7—Roger Staubach completed 9 of 15 passes for 125 yards, including the winning touchdown on a 19-yard strike to Dallas Cowboys teammate Tony Hill in the third period. The winning drive began at the AFC's 45 yard line after a shanked punt. Staubach hit Ahmad Rashad with passes of 15 and 17 yards to set up Hill's decisive catch. The victory gave the NFC a 5-4 advantage in Pro Bowl games. Rashad, who accounted for 89 yards on five receptions, was named the player of the game. The AFC led 7-6 at halftime on Bob Griese's eight-yard scoring toss to Steve Largent late in the second quarter. Largent finished the game with five receptions for 75 yards. The NFC scored first as Archie Manning marched his team 70 yards in 11 plays, capped by Wilbert Montgomery's two-yard touchdown run. The AFC's Earl Campbell was the game's leading rusher with 66 yards on 12 carries.

AFC	0	7	0	0	— 7
NFC	0	6	7	0	— 13

NFC—Montgomery 2 run (kick failed)
AFC—Largent 8 pass from Griese (Yepremian kick)
NFC—T. Hill 19 pass from Staubach (Corral kick)

1978 AFC-NFC Pro Bowl

Tampa Stadium, Tampa, Florida | January 23, 1978
Attendance: 51,337

NFC 14, AFC 13—Walter Payton, the NFL's leading rusher in 1977, sparked a second-half comeback to give the NFC the win and tie the series between the two conferences at four victories each. Payton, who was the game's most valuable player, gained 77 yards on 13 carries and scored the tying touchdown on a one-yard burst with 7:37 left in the game. Efren Herrera kicked the winning extra point. The AFC dominated the first half of the game, taking a 13-0 lead on field goals of 21 and 39 yards by Toni Linhart and a 10-yard touchdown pass from Ken Stabler to Oakland teammate Cliff Branch. On the NFC's first possession of the second half, Pat Haden put together the first touchdown drive after Eddie Brown returned Ray Guy's punt to the AFC 46-yard line. Haden connected on all four of his passes on that drive, finally hitting Terry Metcalf with a four-yard scoring toss. The NFC continued to rally and, with Jim Hart at quarterback, moved 63 yards in 12 plays for the go-ahead score. During the winning drive, Hart completed five of six passes for 38 yards and Payton picked up 20 more on the ground.

AFC	3	10	0	0	— 13
NFC	0	0	7	7	— 14

AFC—FG Linhart 21
AFC—Branch 10 pass from Stabler (Linhart kick)
AFC—FG Linhart 39
NFC—Metcalf 4 pass from Haden (Herrera kick)
NFC—Payton 1 run (Herrera kick)

1977 AFC-NFC Pro Bowl

Kingdome, Seattle, Washington | January 17, 1977
Attendance: 64,752

AFC 24, NFC 14—O. J. Simpson's three-yard touchdown burst at 7:03 of the first quarter gave the AFC a lead it would not surrender, the victory breaking a two-game NFC win streak and giving the American Conference stars a 4-3 series lead. The AFC took a 17-7 lead midway through the second period on the first of two Ken Anderson touchdown passes, a 12-yarder to Charlie Joiner. But the NFC mounted a 73-yard drive capped by Lawrence McCutcheon's one-yard touchdown plunge to pull within 17-14 at the half. Following a scoreless third quarter, player of the game Mel Blount thwarted a possible NFC score when he intercepted Jim Hart's pass in the end zone. Less than three minutes later, Blount again picked off a Hart pass, returning it 16 yards to the NFC 27. That set up Anderson's 27-yard touchdown strike to the Raiders' Cliff Branch for the final score.

NFC	0	14	0	0	— 14
AFC	10	7	0	7	— 24

AFC—Simpson 3 run (Linhart kick)
AFC—FG Linhart 31
NFC—Thomas 15 run (Bakken kick)
AFC—Joiner 12 pass from Anderson (Linhart kick)
NFC—McCutcheon 1 run (Bakken kick)
AFC—Branch 27 pass from Anderson (Linhart kick)

1976 AFC-NFC Pro Bowl

Superdome, New Orleans, Louisiana | January 26, 1976
Attendance: 30,546

NFC 23, AFC 20—Mike Boryla, a late substitute who did not enter the game until 5:39 remained, lifted the National Football Conference to the victory over the American Football Conference with two touchdown passes in the final minutes. It was the second straight NFC win, squaring the series at 3-3. Until Boryla started firing the ball the AFC was in control, leading 13-0 at the half. Boryla entered the game after Billy Johnson had raced 90 yards with a punt to make the score 20-9 in favor of the AFC. He floated a 14-yard pass to Terry Metcalf and later fired an eight-yarder to Mel Gray for the winner.

AFC	0	13	0	7	— 20
NFC	0	0	9	14	— 23

AFC—FG Stenerud 20
AFC—FG Stenerud 35

AFC—Burrough 64 pass from Pastorini (Stenerud kick)
NFC—FG Bakken 42
NFC—Foreman 4 pass from Hart (kick blocked)
AFC—Johnson 90 punt return (Stenerud kick)
NFC—Metcalf 14 pass from Boryla (Bakken kick)
NFC—Gray 8 pass from Boryla (Bakken kick)

1975 AFC-NFC Pro Bowl

Orange Bowl, Miami, Florida | January 20, 1975
Attendance: 26,484

NFC 17, AFC 10—Los Angeles quarterback James Harris, who took over the NFC offense after Jim Hart of St. Louis suffered a laceration above his right eye in the second period, threw a pair of touchdown passes early in the fourth period to pace the NFC to its second victory in the five-game Pro Bowl series. The NFC win snapped a three-game AFC victory string. Harris, who was named the player of the game, connected with St. Louis's Mel Gray for an eight-yard touchdown 2:03 into the final period. One minute and 24 seconds later, following a recovery by Washington's Ken Houston of a fumble by Franco Harris of Pittsburgh, Harris tossed another eight-yard scoring pass to Washington's Charley Taylor for the decisive points.

NFC	0	3	0	14	— 17
AFC	0	0	10	0	— 10

NFC—FG Marcol 33
AFC—Warfield 32 pass from Griese (Gerela kick)
AFC—FG Gerela 33
NFC—Gray 8 pass from J. Harris (Marcol kick)
NFC—Taylor 8 pass from J. Harris (Marcol kick)

1974 AFC-NFC Pro Bowl

Arrowhead Stadium, Kansas City, Missouri | January 20, 1974
Attendance: 66,918

AFC 15, NFC 13—Miami's Garo Yepremian kicked his fifth consecutive field goal, a 42-yard kick with 21 seconds remaining, to give the AFC its third straight victory since the NFC won the inaugural game following the 1970 season. The field goal by Yepremian, who was voted the game's outstanding player, offset a 21-yard field goal by Atlanta's Nick Mike-Mayer that had given the NFC a 13-12 advantage with 1:41 remaining. The only touchdown in the game was scored by the NFC on a 14-yard pass from Philadelphia's Roman Gabriel to Lawrence McCutcheon of the Los Angeles Rams.

NFC	0	10	0	3	— 13
AFC	3	3	3	6	— 15

AFC—FG Yepremian 16
NFC—FG Mike-Mayer 27
NFC—McCutcheon 14 pass from Gabriel (Mike-Mayer kick)
AFC—FG Yepremian 37
AFC—FG Yepremian 27
AFC—FG Yepremian 41
NFC—FG Mike-Mayer 21
AFC—FG Yepremian 42

1973 AFC-NFC Pro Bowl

Texas Stadium, Irving, Texas | January 21, 1973
Attendance: 37,091

AFC 33, NFC 28—Paced by the rushing and receiving of player of the game O.J. Simpson, the AFC erased a 14-0 first period deficit and built a commanding 33-14 lead midway through the fourth period before the NFC managed two touchdowns in the final minute of play. Simpson rushed for 112 yards and caught three passes for 58 more to gain unanimous recognition in the balloting for player of the game. John Brockington scored three touchdowns for the NFC.

AFC	0	10	10	13	— 33
NFC	14	0	0	14	— 28

NFC—Brockington 1 run (Marcol kick)
NFC—Brockington 3 pass from Kilmer (Marcol kick)
AFC—Simpson 7 run (Gerela kick)
AFC—FG Gerela 18
AFC—FG Gerela 22
AFC—Hubbard 11 run (Gerela kick)
AFC—O. Taylor 5 pass from Lamonica (kick failed)
AFC—Bell 12 interception return (Gerela kick)
NFC—Brockington 1 run (Marcol kick)
NFC—Kwalick 12 pass from Snead (Marcol kick)

1972 AFC-NFC Pro Bowl

Memorial Coliseum, Los Angeles, California | January 23, 1972
Attendance: 53,647

AFC 26, NFC 13—Four field goals by Jan Stenerud of Kansas City, including a 6-6 tie-breaker from 48 yards, helped lift the AFC from a 6-0 deficit to a 19-6 advantage early in the fourth period. The AFC defense picked off three interceptions. Stenerud was selected as the outstanding offensive player and his Kansas City teammate, linebacker Willie Lanier, was the game's outstanding defensive player.

AFC	0	3	13	10	— 26
NFC	0	6	0	7	— 13

NFC—Grim 50 pass from Landry (kick failed)
AFC—FG Stenerud 25
AFC—FG Stenerud 23
AFC—FG Stenerud 48
AFC—Morin 5 pass from Dawson (Stenerud kick)
AFC—FG Stenerud 42

NFC—V. Washington 2 run (Knight kick)
AFC—F. Little 6 run (Stenerud kick)

1971 AFC-NFC Pro Bowl

Memorial Coliseum, Los Angeles, California   January 24, 1971
Attendance: 48,222

NFC 27, AFC 6—Mel Renfro of Dallas broke open the first meeting between the American Football Conference and National Football Conference all-star teams as he returned a pair of punts 82 and 56 yards for touchdowns in the final period to clinch the NFC victory over the AFC. Renfro was voted the game's outstanding back and linebacker Fred Carr of Green Bay the outstanding lineman.

AFC	0	3	3	0 —	6
NFC	0	3	10	14 —	27

AFC—FG Stenerud 37
NFC—FG Cox 13
NFC—Osborn 23 pass from Brodie (Cox kick)
NFC—FG Cox 35
AFC—FG Stenerud 16
NFC—Renfro 82 punt return (Cox kick)
NFC—Renfro 56 punt return (Cox kick)

Pro Bowl All-Time Results

Date	Result	Site (attendance)	Honored players
Jan. 15, 1939	New York Giants 13, Pro All-Stars 10	Wrigley Field, Los Angeles (20,000)	
Jan. 14, 1940	Green Bay 16, NFL All-Stars 7	Gilmore Stadium, Los Angeles (18,000)	
Dec. 29, 1940	Chicago Bears 28, NFL All-Stars 14	Gilmore Stadium, Los Angeles (21,624)	
Jan. 4, 1942	Chicago Bears 35, NFL All-Stars 24	Polo Grounds, New York (17,725)	
Dec. 27, 1942	NFL All-Stars 17, Washington 14	Shibe Park, Philadelphia (18,671)	
Jan. 14, 1951	American Conf. 28, National Conf. 27	Los Angeles Memorial Coliseum (53,676)	Otto Graham, Cleveland, player of the game
Jan. 12, 1952	National Conf. 30, American Conf. 13	Los Angeles Memorial Coliseum (19,400)	Dan Towler, Los Angeles, player of the game
Jan. 10, 1953	National Conf. 27, American Conf. 7	Los Angeles Memorial Coliseum (34,208)	Don Doll, Detroit, player of the game
Jan. 17, 1954	East 20, West 9	Los Angeles Memorial Coliseum (44,214)	Chuck Bednarik, Philadelphia, player of the game
Jan. 16, 1955	West 26, East 19	Los Angeles Memorial Coliseum (43,972)	Billy Wilson, San Francisco, player of the game
Jan. 15, 1956	East 31, West 30	Los Angeles Memorial Coliseum (37,867)	Ollie Matson, Chi. Cardinals, player of the game
Jan. 13, 1957	West 19, East 10	Los Angeles Memorial Coliseum (44,177)	Bert Rechichar, Baltimore, outstanding back Ernie Stautner, Pittsburgh, outstanding lineman
Jan. 12, 1958	West 26, East 7	Los Angeles Memorial Coliseum (66,634)	Hugh McElhenny, San Francisco, outstanding back Gene Brito, Washington, outstanding lineman
Jan. 11, 1959	East 28, West 21	Los Angeles Memorial Coliseum (72,250)	Frank Gifford, N.Y. Giants, outstanding back Doug Atkins, Chi. Bears, outstanding lineman
Jan. 17, 1960	West 38, East 21	Los Angeles Memorial Coliseum (56,876)	Johnny Unitas, Baltimore, outstanding back Gene (Big Daddy) Lipscomb, Baltimore, outstanding lineman
Jan. 15, 1961	West 35, East 31	Los Angeles Memorial Coliseum (62,971)	Johnny Unitas, Baltimore, outstanding back Sam Huff, N.Y. Giants, outstanding lineman
Jan. 7, 1962	AFL West 47, East 27	Balboa Stadium, San Diego (20,973)	Cotton Davidson, Dallas Texans, player of the game
Jan. 14, 1962	NFL West 31, East 30	Los Angeles Memorial Coliseum (57,409)	Jim Brown, Cleveland, outstanding back Henry Jordan, Green Bay, outstanding lineman
Jan. 13, 1963	AFL West 21, East 14	Balboa Stadium, San Diego (27,641)	Curtis McClinton, Dallas Texans, outstanding offensive player Earl Faison, San Diego, outstanding defensive player
Jan. 13, 1963	NFL East 30, West 20	Los Angeles Memorial Coliseum (61,374)	Jim Brown, Cleveland, outstanding back Gene (Big Daddy) Lipscomb, Pittsburgh, outstanding lineman
Jan. 12, 1964	NFL West 31, East 17	Los Angeles Memorial Coliseum (67,242)	Johnny Unitas, Baltimore, player of the game Gino Marchetti, Baltimore, outstanding lineman
Jan. 19, 1964	AFL West 27, East 24	Balboa Stadium, San Diego (20,016)	Keith Lincoln, San Diego, outstanding offensive player Archie Matsos, Oakland, outstanding defensive player
Jan. 10, 1965	NFL West 34, East 14	Los Angeles Memorial Coliseum (60,598)	Fran Tarkenton, Minnesota, outstanding back Terry Barr, Detroit, outstanding lineman
Jan. 16, 1965	AFL West 38, East 14	Jeppesen Stadium, Houston (15,446)	Keith Lincoln, San Diego, outstanding offensive player Willie Brown, Denver, outstanding defensive player
Jan. 15, 1966	AFL All-Stars 30, Buffalo 19	Rice Stadium, Houston (35,572)	Joe Namath, N.Y. Jets, most valuable player, offense Frank Buncom, San Diego, most valuable player, defense
Jan. 15, 1966	NFL East 36, West 7	Los Angeles Memorial Coliseum (60,124)	Jim Brown, Cleveland, outstanding back Dale Meinert, St. Louis, outstanding lineman
Jan. 21, 1967	AFL East 30, West 23	Oakland-Alameda County Coliseum (18,876)	Babe Parilli, Boston, outstanding offensive player Verlon Biggs, N.Y. Jets, outstanding defensive player
Jan. 22, 1967	NFL East 20, West 10	Los Angeles Memorial Coliseum (15,062)	Gale Sayers, Chicago, outstanding back Floyd Peters, Philadelphia, outstanding lineman
Jan. 21, 1968	AFL East 25, West 24	Gator Bowl, Jacksonville, Fla. (40,103)	Joe Namath and Don Maynard, N.Y. Jets, out. off. players Leslie (Speedy) Duncan, San Diego, out. def. player
Jan. 21, 1968	NFL West 38, East 20	Los Angeles Memorial Coliseum (53,289)	Gale Sayers, Chicago, outstanding back Dave Robinson, Green Bay, outstanding lineman
Jan. 19, 1969	AFL West 38, East 25	Gator Bowl, Jacksonville, Fla. (41,058)	Len Dawson, Kansas City, outstanding offensive player George Webster, Houston, outstanding defensive player
Jan. 19, 1969	NFL West 10, East 7	Los Angeles Memorial Coliseum (32,050)	Roman Gabriel, Los Angeles, outstanding back Merlin Olsen, Los Angeles, outstanding lineman
Jan. 17, 1970	AFL West 26, East 3	Astrodome, Houston (30,170)	John Hadl, San Diego, player of the game
Jan. 18, 1970	NFL West 16, East 13	Los Angeles Memorial Coliseum (57,786)	Gale Sayers, Chicago, outstanding back George Andrie, Dallas, outstanding lineman
Jan. 24, 1971	NFC 27, AFC 6	Los Angeles Memorial Coliseum (48,222)	Mel Renfro, Dallas, outstanding back Fred Carr, Green Bay, outstanding lineman
Jan. 23, 1972	AFC 26, NFC 13	Los Angeles Memorial Coliseum (53,647)	Jan Stenerud, Kansas City, outstanding offensive player Willie Lanier, Kansas City, outstanding defensive player
Jan. 21, 1973	AFC 33, NFC 28	Texas Stadium, Irving (37,091)	O.J. Simpson, Buffalo, player of the game
Jan. 20, 1974	AFC 15, NFC 13	Arrowhead Stadium, Kansas City (66,918)	Garo Yepremian, Miami, player of the game
Jan. 20, 1975	NFC 17, AFC 10	Orange Bowl, Miami (26,484)	James Harris, Los Angeles, player of the game
Jan. 26, 1976	NFC 23, AFC 20	Louisiana Superdome, New Orleans (30,546)	Billy Johnson, Houston, player of the game
Jan. 17, 1977	AFC 24, NFC 14	Kingdome, Seattle (64,752)	Mel Blount, Pittsburgh, player of the game
Jan. 23, 1978	NFC 14, AFC 13	Tampa Stadium (51,337)	Walter Payton, Chicago, player of the game
Jan. 29, 1979	NFC 13, AFC 7	Los Angeles Memorial Coliseum (46,281)	Ahmad Rashad, Minnesota, player of the game
Jan. 27, 1980	NFC 37, AFC 27	Aloha Stadium, Honolulu (49,800)	Chuck Muncie, New Orleans, player of the game
Feb. 1, 1981	NFC 21, AFC 7	Aloha Stadium, Honolulu (50,360)	Eddie Murray, Detroit, player of the game
Jan. 31, 1982	AFC 16, NFC 13	Aloha Stadium, Honolulu (50,402)	Kellen Winslow, San Diego, and Lee Roy Selmon, Tampa Bay, players of the game
Feb. 6, 1983	NFC 20, AFC 19	Aloha Stadium, Honolulu (49,883)	Dan Fouts, San Diego, and John Jefferson, Green Bay, players of the game
Jan. 29, 1984	NFC 45, AFC 3	Aloha Stadium, Honolulu (50,445)	Joe Theismann, Washington, player of the game
Jan. 27, 1985	AFC 22, NFC 14	Aloha Stadium, Honolulu (50,385)	Mark Gastineau, N.Y. Jets, player of the game
Feb. 2, 1986	NFC 28, AFC 24	Aloha Stadium, Honolulu (50,101)	Phil Simms, N.Y. Giants, player of the game
Feb. 1, 1987	AFC 10, NFC 6	Aloha Stadium, Honolulu (50,101)	Reggie White, Philadelphia, player of the game
Feb. 7, 1988	AFC 15, NFC 6	Aloha Stadium, Honolulu (50,113)	Bruce Smith, Buffalo, player of the game
Jan. 29, 1989	NFC 34, AFC 3	Aloha Stadium, Honolulu (50,113)	Randall Cunningham, Philadelphia, player of the game
Feb. 4, 1990	NFC 27, AFC 21	Aloha Stadium, Honolulu (50,445)	Jerry Gray, L.A. Rams, player of the game
Feb. 3, 1991	AFC 23, NFC 21	Aloha Stadium, Honolulu (50,345)	Jim Kelly, Buffalo, player of the game
Feb. 2, 1992	NFC 21, AFC 15	Aloha Stadium, Honolulu (50,209)	Michael Irvin, Dallas, player of the game

Pro Football Hall of Fame Game

1962	New York Giants 21, St. Louis Cardinals 21
1963	Pittsburgh Steelers 16, Cleveland Browns 7
1964	Baltimore Colts 48, Pittsburgh Steelers 17
1965	Washington Redskins 20, Detroit Lions 3
1966	No game
1967	Philadelphia Eagles 28, Cleveland Browns 13
1968	Chicago Bears 30, Dallas Cowboys 24
1969	Green Bay Packers 38, Atlanta Falcons 24
1970	New Orleans Saints 14, Minnesota Vikings 13
1971	Los Angeles Rams (NFC) 17, Houston Oilers (AFC) 6
1972	Kansas City Chiefs (AFC) 23, New York Giants (NFC) 17
1973	San Francisco 49ers (NFC) 20, New England Patriots (AFC) 7
1974	St. Louis Cardinals (NFC) 21, Buffalo Bills (AFC) 13
1975	Washington Redskins (NFC) 17, Cincinnati Bengals (AFC) 9
1976	Denver Broncos (AFC) 10, Detroit Lions (NFC) 7
1977	Chicago Bears (NFC) 20, New York Jets (AFC) 6
1978	Philadelphia Eagles (NFC) 17, Miami Dolphins (AFC) 3
1979	Oakland Raiders (AFC) 20, Dallas Cowboys (NFC) 13
1980*	San Diego Chargers (AFC) 0, Green Bay Packers (NFC) 0
1981	Cleveland Browns (AFC) 24, Atlanta Falcons (NFC) 10
1982	Minnesota Vikings (NFC) 30, Baltimore Colts (AFC) 14
1983	Pittsburgh Steelers (AFC) 27, New Orleans Saints (NFC) 14
1984	Seattle Seahawks (AFC) 38, Tampa Bay Buccaneers (NFC) 0
1985	New York Giants (NFC) 21, Houston Oilers (AFC) 20
1986	New England Patriots (AFC) 21, St. Louis Cardinals (NFC) 16
1987	San Francisco 49ers (NFC) 20, Kansas City Chiefs (AFC) 7
1988	Cincinnati Bengals (AFC) 14, Los Angeles Rams (NFC) 7
1989	Washington Redskins (NFC) 31, Buffalo Bills (AFC) 6
1990	Chicago Bears (NFC) 13, Cleveland Browns (AFC) 0
1991	Detroit Lions (NFC) 14, Denver Broncos (AFC) 3

*Game called with 5:29 remaining due to severe thunder and lightning.

NFL International Games

Date	Site	Teams
Aug. 12, 1950	Ottawa, Canada	N.Y. Giants 20, Ottawa Roughriders 6
Aug. 11, 1951	Ottawa, Canada	N.Y. Giants 38, Ottawa Roughriders 6
Aug. 5, 1959	Toronto, Canada	Chi. Cardinals 55, Tor. Argonauts 26
Aug. 6, 1960	Toronto, Canada	Pittsburgh 43, Toronto Argonauts 16
Aug. 15, 1960	Toronto, Canada	Chicago Bears 16, N.Y. Giants 7
Aug. 2, 1961	Toronto, Canada	St. Louis 36, Toronto Argonauts 7
Aug. 5, 1961	Montreal, Canada	Chi. Bears 34, Montreal Allouettes 16
Aug. 8, 1961	Hamilton, Canada	Hamilton Tiger-Cats 38, Buffalo 21
Aug. 11, 1969	Montreal, Canada	Pittsburgh 17, N.Y. Giants 13
Aug. 25, 1969	Montreal, Canada	Detroit 22, Boston Patriots 9
Aug. 16, 1976	Tokyo, Japan	St. Louis 20, San Diego 10
Aug. 5, 1978	Mexico City, Mexico	New Orleans 14, Philadelphia 7
Aug. 6, 1983	London, England	Minnesota 28, St. Louis 10
Aug. 3, 1986	London, England	Chicago Bears 17, Dallas 6
Aug. 9, 1987	London, England	L.A. Rams 28, Denver 27
July 31, 1988	London, England	Miami 27, San Francisco 21
Aug. 14, 1988	Goteborg, Sweden	Minnesota 28, Chicago 21
Aug. 18, 1988	Montreal, Canada	N.Y. Jets 11, Cleveland 7
Aug. 5, 1989	Tokyo, Japan	L.A. Rams 16, San Francisco 13 (OT)
Aug. 6, 1989	London, England	Philadelphia 17, Cleveland 13
Aug. 4, 1990	Tokyo, Japan	Denver 10, Seattle 7
Aug. 5, 1990	London, England	New Orleans 17, L.A. Raiders 10
Aug. 9, 1990	Montreal, Canada	New England 30, Pittsburgh 14
Aug. 11, 1990	Berlin, Germany	L.A. Rams 19, Kansas City 3
July 28, 1991	London, England	Buffalo 17, Philadelphia 13
Aug. 3, 1991	Berlin, Germany	San Francisco 21, Chicago 7
Aug. 3, 1991	Tokyo, Japan	L.A. Raiders 19, Miami 17

Chicago All-Star Game

Pro teams won 31, lost 9, and tied 2. The game was discontinued after 1976.

Year	Date	Winner	Loser	Attendance
1976*	July 23	Pittsburgh 24	All-Stars 0	52,895
1975	Aug. 1	Pittsburgh 21	All-Stars 14	54,103
1974		No game was played		
1973	July 27	Miami 14	All-Stars 3	54,103
1972	July 28	Dallas 20	All-Stars 7	54,162
1971	July 30	Baltimore 24	All-Stars 17	52,289
1970	July 31	Kansas City 24	All-Stars 3	69,940
1969	Aug. 1	N.Y. Jets 26	All-Stars 24	74,208
1968	Aug. 2	Green Bay 34	All-Stars 17	69,917
1967	Aug. 4	Green Bay 27	All-Stars 0	70,934
1966	Aug. 5	Green Bay 38	All-Stars 0	72,000
1965	Aug. 6	Cleveland 24	All-Stars 16	68,000
1964	Aug. 7	Chicago 28	All-Stars 17	65,000
1963	Aug. 2	All-Stars 20	Green Bay 17	65,000
1962	Aug. 3	Green Bay 42	All-Stars 20	65,000
1961	Aug. 4	Philadelphia 28	All-Stars 14	66,000
1960	Aug. 12	Baltimore 32	All-Stars 7	70,000
1959	Aug. 14	Baltimore 29	All-Stars 0	70,000
1958	Aug. 15	All-Stars 35	Detroit 19	70,000
1957	Aug. 9	N.Y. Giants 22	All-Stars 12	75,000
1956	Aug. 10	Cleveland 26	All-Stars 0	75,000
1955	Aug. 12	All-Stars 30	Cleveland 27	75,000
1954	Aug. 13	Detroit 31	All-Stars 6	93,470
1953	Aug. 14	Detroit 24	All-Stars 10	93,818
1952	Aug. 15	Los Angeles 10	All-Stars 7	88,316
1951	Aug. 17	Cleveland 33	All-Stars 0	92,180
1950	Aug. 11	All-Stars 17	Philadelphia 7	88,885
1949	Aug. 12	Philadelphia 38	All-Stars 0	93,780
1948	Aug. 20	Chi. Cardinals 28	All-Stars 0	101,220
1947	Aug. 22	All-Stars 16	Chi. Bears 0	105,840
1946	Aug. 23	All-Stars 16	Los Angeles 0	97,380
1945	Aug. 30	Green Bay 19	All-Stars 7	92,753
1944	Aug. 30	Chi. Bears 24	All-Stars 21	48,769
1943	Aug. 25	All-Stars 27	Washington 7	48,471
1942	Aug. 28	Chi. Bears 21	All-Stars 0	101,100
1941	Aug. 28	Chi. Bears 37	All-Stars 13	98,203
1940	Aug. 29	Green Bay 45	All-Stars 28	84,567
1939	Aug. 30	N.Y. Giants 9	All-Stars 0	81,456
1938	Aug. 31	All-Stars 28	Washington 16	74,250
1937	Sept. 1	All-Stars 6	Green Bay 0	84,560
1936	Sept. 1	All-Stars 7	Detroit 7 (tie)	76,000
1935	Aug. 29	Chi. Bears 5	All-Stars 0	77,450
1934	Aug. 31	Chi. Bears 0	All-Stars 0 (tie)	79,432

*Game shortened due to thunderstorms.

NFL Playoff Bowl

Western Conference won 8, Eastern Conference won 2. All games played at Miami's Orange Bowl.

1970	Los Angeles Rams 31, Dallas Cowboys 0
1969	Dallas Cowboys 17, Minnesota Vikings 13
1968	Los Angeles Rams 30, Cleveland Browns 6
1967	Baltimore Colts 20, Philadelphia Eagles 14
1966	Baltimore Colts 35, Dallas Cowboys 3
1965	St. Louis Cardinals 24, Green Bay Packers 17
1964	Green Bay Packers 40, Cleveland Browns 23
1963	Detroit Lions 17, Pittsburgh Steelers 10
1962	Detroit Lions 28, Philadelphia Eagles 10
1961	Detroit Lions 17, Cleveland Browns 16

AFC VS. NFC (REGULAR SEASON), 1970-1991

	1970	1971	1972	1973	1974	1975	1976	1977	1978	1979	1980	1981	1982	1983	1984	1985	1986	1987	1988	1989	1990	1991	Totals
Miami	2-1	3-0	3-0	3-0	2-1	3-0	0-2	2-0	3-1	4-0	4-0	3-1	1-1	3-1	4-0	3-1	2-2	3-0	3-1	2-0	2-2	3-1	58-15
L.A. Raiders	1-2	1-1-1	3-0	2-1	3-0	3-0	3-0	1-1	4-0	4-0	2-2	2-2	3-0	2-2	3-1	3-1	1-3	2-2	1-3	2-2	3-1	2-2	51-26-1
Pittsburgh	0-3	1-2	2-1	3-0	3-0	2-1	1-1	2-0	3-1	3-1	4-0	3-1	1-0	2-2	3-1	1-3	2-2	2-2	1-3	3-1	3-1	0-4	45-30
Cincinnati	1-2	1-2	2-1	2-1	2-1	3-0	2-0	2-1	2-2	2-2	2-2	2-2	1-0	3-1	2-2	2-2	3-1	1-2	4-0	2-2	1-3	1-3	43-32
Denver	2-2	1-3	1-3	0-3-1	2-2	2-1	2-0	1-1	2-2	3-1	3-1	3-1	2-1	0-2	3-1	3-1	3-1	2-1-1	3-1	2-2	1-3	2-0	43-33-2
Seattle								1-0	3-1	3-1	1-3	0-2	1-0	1-3	4-0	2-2	3-1	4-0	1-3	0-4	2-2	1-3	27-25
Cleveland	0-3	2-1	1-2	1-2	1-2	1-3	2-0	1-1	4-0	3-1	3-1	3-1	0-2	2-2	1-3	1-3	2-2	2-2	4-0	3-1	1-3	0-4	38-39
Kansas City	0-2-1	2-1	2-1	1-1-1	1-2	2-1	1-1	1-1	0-2	0-2	2-0	2-2	0-3	2-2	1-1	2-2	1-1	1-2	0-2	2-0	4-0	2-2	29-31-2
San Diego	1-2	2-1	0-3	1-2	1-2	0-3	2-0	1-1	2-2	3-1	2-2	2-2	1-0	2-2	4-0	1-1	0-4	2-0	2-2	2-2	1-1	1-3	33-36
N.Y. Jets	2-1	0-3	1-2	0-3	2-1	0-3	0-2	1-1	1-3	3-1	1-3	2-0	4-0	3-1	0-2	2-2	2-2	0-4	2-0	1-3	2-0	2-2	31-39
Buffalo	0-3	0-3	2-0-1	2-1	2-1	1-2	0-2	1-1	1-1	2-2	3-1	1-3	1-2	1-3	1-3	0-2	1-1	1-2	2-2	1-3	3-1	3-1	29-40-1
Indianapolis	3-0	2-1	0-3	2-1	1-2	2-1	0-2	1-1	2-2	1-1	1-1	0-4	0-1-1	2-0	0-4	3-1	1-3	1-0	2-2	1-3	2-2	0-4	27-39-1
New England	0-3	0-3	3-0	2-1	3-0	1-2	1-1	2-0	2-2	3-1	1-3	0-4	0-1	2-2	0-4	3-1	3-1	0-3	2-2	0-4	0-4	1-1	29-43
Houston	0-3	0-2-1	0-3	0-3	0-3	3-0	2-0	2-0	2-2	2-2	4-0	1-3	0-3	1-3	0-4	1-3	2-2	2-2	3-1	3-1	1-3	1-3	30-46-1
Tampa Bay							0-1																0-1
TOTALS	12-27-1	15-23-2	20-19-1	19-19-2	23-17	23-17	16-12	19-9	31-21	36-16	33-19	24-28	15-14-1	26-26	26-26	27-25	26-26	23-22-1	30-22	24-28	26-26	19-33	513-475-8

NFC VS. AFC (REGULAR SEASON), 1970-1991

	1970	1971	1972	1973	1974	1975	1976	1977	1978	1979	1980	1981	1982	1983	1984	1985	1986	1987	1988	1989	1990	1991	Totals
Dallas	3-0	3-0	3-0	2-1	2-1	2-1	2-0	1-1	3-1	1-3	3-1	4-0	2-1	2-2	2-2	3-1	1-3	2-1	0-4	0-2	1-1	3-1	45-27
Washington	2-1	1-2	1-2	2-1	2-1	1-2	1-1	1-1	2-2	2-2	1-3	2-2		4-0	3-1	4-0	3-1	2-1	1-3	2-2	3-1	4-0	44-29
Philadelphia	2-1	1-2	2-1	2-1	2-1	0-3	0-2	1-1	3-1	2-2	3-1	3-1	2-1	1-1	3-1	1-1	2-2	3-1	2-2	3-1	1-3	4-0	43-30
San Francisco	4-0	2-1	2-1	1-2	0-3	1-2	1-1	0-2	1-3	0-4	2-2	3-1	1-3	2-2	3-1	3-1	4-0	3-1	2-2	4-0	4-0	3-1	46-33
L.A. Rams	2-1	1-2	1-2	3-0	3-1	3-0	1-1	2-0	2-2	2-2	2-2	1-3	1-2	1-3	3-1	3-1	2-2	1-2	2-2	3-1	2-2	1-3	42-35
N.Y. Giants	3-0	1-2	1-2	1-2	1-2	2-1	0-2	0-2	1-1	1-1	1-3	1-1	1-0	0-4	2-0	2-2	3-1	2-1	1-1	4-0	3-1	3-1	34-30
Minnesota	2-1	2-1	1-2	2-1	2-1	4-0	2-0	1-1	1-3	1-3	1-3	1-3	1-3	4-0	0-4	2-0	1-3	2-1	2-2	2-2	2-2	0-2	36-38
Phoenix	2-0-1	2-1	1-2	0-2-1	2-1	2-1	1-1	0-2	0-4	1-3	1-1	3-1		3-1	3-1	2-2	1-1	0-1	1-3	1-3	2-2	1-1	29-34-2
Chicago	1-2	1-2	1-2	2-2	0-3	0-3	0-2	1-1	0-4	2-2	0-4	4-0	1-1	1-1	2-2	3-1	4-0	2-2	3-1	2-2	2-2	2-2	34-41
Detroit	3-0	4-0	2-0-1	0-3	1-2	1-2	2-0	2-0	2-2	0-4	0-2	2-2	0-1	1-3	0-4	2-2	1-3	0-4	1-1	1-3	1-3	4-0	30-41-1
New Orleans	0-3	0-1-2	0-3	1-2	0-3	0-3	1-2	0-2	1-3	0-4	1-3	2-2	1-0	1-3	3-1	0-4	1-3	4-0	4-0	4-0	2-2	3-1	29-45-2
Atlanta	1-2	3-0	2-2	2-1	0-3	1-2	0-2	0-2	1-3	1-3	2-2	1-3	1-1	3-1	1-3	0-4	1-3	0-4	1-3	2-2	2-2	3-1	28-49
Green Bay	2-1	2-1	2-1	1-1-1	2-1	0-3	0-2	0-3	2-2	1-3	1-3	1-1	1-1-1	2-2	0-4	0-4	1-3	1-2-1	1-3	0-2	1-3	1-3	22-49-3
Tampa Bay							0-1	2-0	2-0	1-3	0-4	2-1	1-3	1-1	0-4	1-1	0-2	1-3	0-4	0-2	0-2	1-3	12-32
Seattle							1-0																1-0
TOTALS	27-12-1	23-15-2	19-20-1	19-19-2	17-23	17-23	12-16	9-19	21-31	16-36	19-33	28-24	14-15-1	26-26	26-26	25-27	26-26	22-23-1	22-30	28-24	26-26	33-19	475-513-8

1991 Interconference Games
(Home Team in capital letters)

NFC 33, AFC 19

AFC Victories

KANSAS CITY 14, Atlanta 3
NEW YORK JETS 16, Tampa Bay 13
Buffalo 17, TAMPA BAY 10
MIAMI 16, Green Bay 13
BUFFALO 35, Chicago 20
LOS ANGELES RAIDERS 12, San Francisco 6
Denver 13, MINNESOTA 6
LOS ANGELES RAIDERS 20, Los Angeles Rams 17
NEW ENGLAND 26, Minnesota 23
NEW YORK JETS 19, Green Bay 16
Buffalo 34, GREEN BAY 24
HOUSTON 26, Dallas 23
Kansas City 27, LOS ANGELES RAMS 20
SAN DIEGO 24, New Orleans 21
Miami 16, CHICAGO 13
CINCINNATI 27, New York Giants 24
MIAMI 33, Tampa Bay 14
DENVER 24, Phoenix 19
SEATTLE 23, Los Angeles Rams 9

NFC Victories

Dallas 26, CLEVELAND 14
NEW ORLEANS 27, Seattle 24
New Orleans 17, KANSAS CITY 10
SAN FRANCISCO 34, San Diego 14
Atlanta 13, SAN DIEGO 10
DETROIT 17, Miami 13
NEW YORK GIANTS 13, Cleveland 10
Detroit 33, INDIANAPOLIS 24
ATLANTA 21, Los Angeles Raiders 17
PHILADELPHIA 23, Pittsburgh 14
Washington 34, CINCINNATI 27
CHICAGO 19, New York Jets 13
PHOENIX 24, New England 10
DALLAS 35, Cincinnati 23
WASHINGTON 42, Cleveland 17
LOS ANGELES RAMS 30, San Diego 24
New York Giants 23, PITTSBURGH 20
WASHINGTON 16, Houston 13
Philadelphia 32, CLEVELAND 30
Chicago 31, INDIANAPOLIS 17
PHILADELPHIA 17, Cincinnati 10
Washington 41, PITTSBURGH 14
GREEN BAY 14, Indianapolis 10
DALLAS 20, Pittsburgh 10
Philadelphia 13, HOUSTON 6
DETROIT 34, New York Jets 20
San Francisco 24, SEATTLE 22
SAN FRANCISCO 28, Kansas City 14
ATLANTA 26, Seattle 13
NEW ORLEANS 27, Los Angeles Raiders 0
NEW YORK GIANTS 24, Houston 20
Detroit 17, BUFFALO 14
TAMPA BAY 17, Indianapolis 3

Regular Season Interconference Records, 1970-1991

American Football Conference

Eastern Division

	W	L	T	Pct.
Miami	58	15	0	.795
New York Jets	31	39	0	.443
Buffalo	29	40	1	.421
Indianapolis	27	39	1	.410
New England	29	43	0	.403

Central Division

	W	L	T	Pct.
Pittsburgh	45	30	0	.600
Cincinnati	43	32	0	.573
Cleveland	38	39	0	.494
Houston	30	46	1	.396

Western Division

	W	L	T	Pct.
Los Angeles Raiders	51	26	1	.660
Denver	43	33	2	.564
Seattle	27	25	0	.519
Kansas City	29	31	2	.484
San Diego	33	36	0	.478

National Football Conference

Eastern Division

	W	L	T	Pct.
Dallas	45	27	0	.625
Washington	44	29	0	.603
Philadelphia	43	30	0	.589
New York Giants	34	30	0	.531
Phoenix	29	34	2	.462

Central Division

	W	L	T	Pct.
Minnesota	36	38	0	.486
Chicago	34	41	0	.453
Detroit	30	41	1	.424
Green Bay	22	49	3	.318
Tampa Bay	12	32	0	.273

Western Division

	W	L	T	Pct.
San Francisco	46	33	0	.582
Los Angeles Rams	42	35	0	.545
New Orleans	29	45	2	.395
Atlanta	28	49	0	.364

Interconference Victories, 1970-1991

Regular Season				Preseason			
	AFC	NFC	Tie		AFC	NFC	Tie
1970	12	27	1	1970	21	28	1
1971	15	23	2	1971	28	28	3
1972	20	19	1	1972	27	25	4
1973	19	19	2	1973	23	35	2
1974	23	17	0	1974	35	25	0
1975	23	17	0	1975	30	26	1
1976	16	12	0	1976	30	31	0
1977	19	9	0	1977	38	25	0
1978	31	21	0	1978	20	19	0
1979	36	16	0	1979	25	18	0
1980	33	19	0	1980	22	20	1
1981	24	28	0	1981	18	19	0
1982	15	14	1	1982	25	16	0
1983	26	26	0	1983	15	24	0
1984	26	26	0	1984	16	19	0
1985	27	25	0	1985	10	22	1
1986	26	26	0	1986	22	17	0
1987	23	22	1	1987	22	22	0
1988	30	22	0	1988	23	16	1
1989	24	28	0	1989	16	27	0
1990	26	26	0	1990	15	29	0
1991	19	33	0	1991	19	27	0
Total	513	475	8	Total	500	518	14

Monday Night Football, 1970-1991

(Home Team in capitals, games listed in chronological order.)

1991
NEW YORK GIANTS 16, San Francisco 14
Washington 33, DALLAS 31
HOUSTON 17, Kansas City 7
CHICAGO 19, New York Jets 13 (OT)
WASHINGTON 23, Philadelphia 0
KANSAS CITY 33, Buffalo 6
New York Giants 23, PITTSBURGH 20
BUFFALO 35, Cincinnati 16
KANSAS CITY 24, Los Angeles Raiders 21
PHILADELPHIA 30, New York Giants 7
Chicago 34, MINNESOTA 17
Buffalo 41, MIAMI 27
San Francisco 33, LOS ANGELES RAMS 10
Philadelphia 13, HOUSTON 6
MIAMI 37, Cincinnati 13
NEW ORLEANS 27, Los Angeles Raiders 0
SAN FRANCISCO 52, Chicago 14

1990
San Francisco 13, NEW ORLEANS 12
DENVER 24, Kansas City 23
Buffalo 30, NEW YORK JETS 7
SEATTLE 31, Cincinnati 16
Cleveland 30, DENVER 29
PHILADELPHIA 32, Minnesota 24
Cincinnati 34, CLEVELAND 13
PITTSBURGH 41, Los Angeles Rams 10
New York Giants 24, INDIANAPOLIS 7
PHILADELPHIA 28, Washington 14
Los Angeles Raiders 13, MIAMI 10
HOUSTON 27, Buffalo 24
SAN FRANCISCO 7, New York Giants 3
Los Angeles Raiders 38, DETROIT 31
San Francisco 26, LOS ANGELES RAMS 10
NEW ORLEANS 20, Los Angeles Rams 17

1989
New York Giants 27, WASHINGTON 24
Denver 28, BUFFALO 14
CINCINNATI 21, Cleveland 14
CHICAGO 27, Philadelphia 13
Los Angeles Raiders 14, NEW YORK JETS 7
BUFFALO 23, Los Angeles Rams 20
CLEVELAND 27, Chicago 7
NEW YORK GIANTS 24, Minnesota 14
SAN FRANCISCO 31, New Orleans 13
HOUSTON 26, Cincinnati 24
Denver 14, WASHINGTON 10
SAN FRANCISCO 34, New York Giants 24
SEATTLE 17, Buffalo 16
San Francisco 30, LOS ANGELES RAMS 27
NEW ORLEANS 30, Philadelphia 20
MINNESOTA 29, Cincinnati 21

1988
NEW YORK GIANTS 27, Washington 20
Dallas 17, PHOENIX 14
CLEVELAND 23, Indianapolis 17
Los Angeles Raiders 30, DENVER 27 (OT)
NEW ORLEANS 20, Dallas 17
PHILADELPHIA 24, New York Giants 13
Buffalo 37, NEW YORK JETS 14
CHICAGO 10, San Francisco 9
INDIANAPOLIS 55, Denver 23
HOUSTON 24, Cleveland 17
Buffalo 31, MIAMI 6
SAN FRANCISCO 37, Washington 21
SEATTLE 35, Los Angeles Raiders 27
LOS ANGELES RAMS 23, Chicago 3
MIAMI 38, Cleveland 31
MINNESOTA 28, Chicago 27

1987
CHICAGO 34, New York Giants 19
NEW YORK JETS 43, New England 24
San Francisco 41, NEW YORK GIANTS 21
DENVER 30, Los Angeles Raiders 14
Washington 13, DALLAS 7
CLEVELAND 30, Los Angeles Rams 17
MINNESOTA 34, Denver 27
DALLAS 33, New York Giants 24
NEW YORK JETS 30, Seattle 14
DENVER 31, Chicago 29
Los Angeles Rams 30, WASHINGTON 26
Los Angeles Raiders 37, SEATTLE 14

MIAMI 37, New York Jets 28
SAN FRANCISCO 41, Chicago 0
Dallas 29, LOS ANGELES RAMS 21
New England 24, MIAMI 10

1986
DALLAS 31, New York Giants 28
Denver 21, PITTSBURGH 10
Chicago 25, GREEN BAY 12
Dallas 31, ST. LOUIS 7
SEATTLE 33, San Diego 7
CINCINNATI 24, Pittsburgh 22
NEW YORK JETS 22, Denver 10
NEW YORK GIANTS 27, Washington 20
Los Angeles Rams 20, CHICAGO 17
CLEVELAND 26, Miami 16
WASHINGTON 14, San Francisco 6
MIAMI 45, New York Jets 3
New York Giants 21, SAN FRANCISCO 17
SEATTLE 37, Los Angeles Raiders 0
Chicago 16, DETROIT 13
New England 34, MIAMI 27

1985
DALLAS 44, Washington 14
CLEVELAND 17, Pittsburgh 7
Los Angeles Rams 35, SEATTLE 24
Cincinnati 37, PITTSBURGH 24
WASHINGTON 27, St. Louis 10
NEW YORK JETS 23, Miami 7
CHICAGO 23, Green Bay 7
LOS ANGELES RAIDERS 34, San Diego 21
ST. LOUIS 21, Dallas 10
DENVER 17, San Francisco 16
WASHINGTON 23, New York Giants 21
SAN FRANCISCO 19, Seattle 6
MIAMI 38, Chicago 24
Los Angeles Rams 27, SAN FRANCISCO 20
MIAMI 30, New England 27
L.A. Raiders 16, L.A. RAMS 6

1984
Dallas 20, LOS ANGELES RAMS 13
SAN FRANCISCO 37, Washington 31
Miami 21, BUFFALO 17
LOS ANGELES RAIDERS 33, San Diego 30
PITTSBURGH 38, Cincinnati 17
San Francisco 31, NEW YORK GIANTS 10
DENVER 17, Green Bay 14
Los Angeles Rams 24, ATLANTA 10
Seattle 24, SAN DIEGO 0
WASHINGTON 27, Atlanta 14
SEATTLE 17, Los Angeles Raiders 14
NEW ORLEANS 27, Pittsburgh 24
MIAMI 28, New York Jets 17
SAN DIEGO 20, Chicago 7
Los Angeles Raiders 24, DETROIT 3
MIAMI 28, Dallas 21

1983
Dallas 31, WASHINGTON 30
San Diego 17, KANSAS CITY 14
LOS ANGELES RAIDERS 27, Miami 14
NEW YORK GIANTS 27, Green Bay 3
New York Jets 34, BUFFALO 10
Pittsburgh 24, CINCINNATI 14
GREEN BAY 48, Washington 47
ST. LOUIS 20, New York Giants 20 (OT)
Washington 27, SAN DIEGO 24
DETROIT 15, New York Giants 9
Los Angeles Rams 36, ATLANTA 13
New York Jets 31, NEW ORLEANS 28
MIAMI 38, Cincinnati 14
DETROIT 13, Minnesota 2
Green Bay 12, TAMPA BAY 9 (OT)
SAN FRANCISCO 42, Dallas 17

1982
Pittsburgh 36, DALLAS 28
Green Bay 27, NEW YORK GIANTS 19
LOS ANGELES RAIDERS 28, San Diego 24
TAMPA BAY 23, Miami 17
New York Jets 28, DETROIT 13
Dallas 37, HOUSTON 7
SAN DIEGO 50, Cincinnati 34
MIAMI 27, Buffalo 10
MINNESOTA 31, Dallas 27

1981
San Diego 44, CLEVELAND 14
Oakland 36, MINNESOTA 10
Dallas 35, NEW ENGLAND 21
Los Angeles 24, CHICAGO 7
PHILADELPHIA 16, Atlanta 13
BUFFALO 31, Miami 21
DETROIT 48, Chicago 17
PITTSBURGH 26, Houston 13
DENVER 19, Minnesota 17
DALLAS 27, Buffalo 14
SEATTLE 44, San Diego 23
ATLANTA 31, Minnesota 30
MIAMI 13, Philadelphia 10
OAKLAND 30, Pittsburgh 27
LOS ANGELES 21, Atlanta 16
SAN DIEGO 23, Oakland 10

1980
Dallas 17, WASHINGTON 3
Houston 16, CLEVELAND 7
PHILADELPHIA 35, New York Giants 3
NEW ENGLAND 23, Denver 14
CHICAGO 23, Tampa Bay 0
DENVER 20, Washington 17
Oakland 45, PITTSBURGH 34
NEW YORK JETS 17, Miami 14
CLEVELAND 27, Chicago 21
HOUSTON 38, New England 34
Oakland 19, SEATTLE 17
Los Angeles 27, NEW ORLEANS 7
OAKLAND 9, Denver 3
MIAMI 16, New England 13 (OT)
LOS ANGELES 38, Dallas 14
SAN DIEGO 26, Pittsburgh 17

1979
Pittsburgh 16, NEW ENGLAND 13 (OT)
Atlanta 14, PHILADELPHIA 10
WASHINGTON 27, New York Giants 0
CLEVELAND 26, Dallas 7
GREEN BAY 27, New England 14
OAKLAND 13, Miami 3
NEW YORK JETS 14, Minnesota 7
PITTSBURGH 42, Denver 7
Seattle 31, ATLANTA 28
Houston 9, MIAMI 6
Philadelphia 31, DALLAS 21
LOS ANGELES 20, Atlanta 14
SEATTLE 30, New York Jets 7
Oakland 42, NEW ORLEANS 35
HOUSTON 20, Pittsburgh 17
SAN DIEGO 17, Denver 7

1978
DALLAS 38, Baltimore 0
MINNESOTA 12, Denver 9 (OT)
Baltimore 34, NEW ENGLAND 27
Minnesota 24, CHICAGO 20
WASHINGTON 9, Dallas 5
MIAMI 21, Cincinnati 0
DENVER 16, Chicago 7
Houston 24, PITTSBURGH 17
ATLANTA 15, Los Angeles 7
BALTIMORE 21, Washington 17
Oakland 34, CINCINNATI 21
HOUSTON 35, Miami 30
Pittsburgh 24, SAN FRANCISCO 7
SAN DIEGO 40, Chicago 7
Cincinnati 20, LOS ANGELES 19
MIAMI 23, New England 3

1977
PITTSBURGH 27, San Francisco 0
CLEVELAND 30, New England 27 (OT)
Oakland 37, KANSAS CITY 28
CHICAGO 24, Los Angeles 23
PITTSBURGH 20, Cincinnati 14
LOS ANGELES 35, Minnesota 3
ST. LOUIS 28, New York Giants 0
BALTIMORE 10, Washington 3
St. Louis 24, DALLAS 17
WASHINGTON 10, Green Bay 9
OAKLAND 34, Buffalo 13
MIAMI 17, Baltimore 6
Dallas 42, SAN FRANCISCO 35

1976
Miami 30, BUFFALO 21
Oakland 24, KANSAS CITY 21
Washington 20, PHILADELPHIA 17 (OT)

MINNESOTA 17, Pittsburgh 6
San Francisco 16, LOS ANGELES 0
NEW ENGLAND 41, New York Jets 7
WASHINGTON 20, St. Louis 10
BALTIMORE 38, Houston 14
CINCINNATI 20, Los Angeles 12
DALLAS 17, Buffalo 10
Baltimore 17, MIAMI 16
SAN FRANCISCO 20, Minnesota 16
OAKLAND 35, Cincinnati 20

1975
Oakland 31, MIAMI 21
DENVER 23, Green Bay 13
Dallas 36, DETROIT 10
WASHINGTON 27, St. Louis 17
New York Giants 17, BUFFALO 14
Minnesota 13, CHICAGO 9
Los Angeles 42, PHILADELPHIA 3
Kansas City 34, DALLAS 31
CINCINNATI 33, Buffalo 24
Pittsburgh 32, HOUSTON 9
MIAMI 20, New England 7
OAKLAND 17, Denver 10
SAN DIEGO 24, New York Jets 16

1974
BUFFALO 21, Oakland 20
PHILADELPHIA 13, Dallas 10
WASHINGTON 30, Denver 3
MIAMI 21, New York Jets 17
DETROIT 17, San Francisco 13
CHICAGO 10, Green Bay 9
PITTSBURGH 24, Atlanta 17

Los Angeles 15, SAN FRANCISCO 13
Minnesota 28, ST. LOUIS 24
Kansas City 42, DENVER 34
Pittsburgh 28, NEW ORLEANS 7
MIAMI 24, Cincinnati 3
Washington 23, LOS ANGELES 17

1973
GREEN BAY 23, New York Jets 7
DALLAS 40, New Orleans 3
DETROIT 31, Atlanta 6
WASHINGTON 14, Dallas 7
Miami 17, CLEVELAND 9
DENVER 23, Oakland 23
BUFFALO 23, Kansas City 14
PITTSBURGH 21, Washington 16
KANSAS CITY 19, Chicago 7
ATLANTA 20, Minnesota 14
SAN FRANCISCO 20, Green Bay 6
MIAMI 30, Pittsburgh 26
LOS ANGELES 40, New York Giants 6

1972
Washington 24, MINNESOTA 21
Kansas City 20, NEW ORLEANS 17
New York Giants 27, PHILADELPHIA 12
Oakland 34, HOUSTON 0
Green Bay 24, DETROIT 23
CHICAGO 13, Minnesota 10
DALLAS 28, Detroit 24
Baltimore 24, NEW ENGLAND 17
Cleveland 21, SAN DIEGO 17
WASHINGTON 24, Atlanta 13

MIAMI 31, St. Louis 10
Los Angeles 26, SAN FRANCISCO 16
OAKLAND 24, New York Jets 16

1971
Minnesota 16, DETROIT 13
ST. LOUIS 17, New York Jets 10
Oakland 34, CLEVELAND 20
DALLAS 20, New York Giants 13
KANSAS CITY 38, Pittsburgh 16
MINNESOTA 10, Baltimore 3
GREEN BAY 14, Detroit 14
BALTIMORE 24, Los Angeles 17
SAN DIEGO 20, St. Louis 17
ATLANTA 28, Green Bay 21
MIAMI 34, Chicago 3
Kansas City 26, SAN FRANCISCO 17
Washington 38, LOS ANGELES 24

1970
CLEVELAND 31, New York Jets 21
Kansas City 44, BALTIMORE 24
DETROIT 28, Chicago 14
Green Bay 22, SAN DIEGO 20
OAKLAND 34, Washington 20
MINNESOTA 13, Los Angeles 3
PITTSBURGH 21, Cincinnati 10
Baltimore 13, GREEN BAY 10
St. Louis 38, DALLAS 0
PHILADELPHIA 23, New York Giants 20
Miami 20, ATLANTA 7
Cleveland 21, HOUSTON 10
Detroit 28, LOS ANGELES 23

Monday Night Syndrome

1991

Of the 16 winning teams:
8 won the next week
5 lost the next week
0 tied the next week
3 had Open Dates the next week

Of the 16 losing teams:
7 won the next week
8 lost the next week
0 tied the next week
1 had an Open Date the next week

Of the 32 NFL teams:
15 won the next week
13 lost the next week
0 tied the next week
4 had Open Dates the next week

1970-1991

Of the 305 winning teams:
176 won the next week
123 lost the next week
3 tied the next week
3 had Open Dates the next week

Of the 305 losing teams:
164 won the next week
138 lost the next week
1 tied the next week
2 had Open Dates the next week

Of the 6 tying teams:
5 won the next week
1 lost the next week
0 tied the next week

Of the 616 NFL teams:
345 won the next week
262 lost the next week
4 tied the next week
5 had Open Dates the next week

Monday Night Won-Lost Records, 1970-1991

American Football Conference

	Buff.	Cin.	Clev.	Den.	Hou.	Ind.	K.C.	Raid.	Mia.	N.E.	N.Y.J.	Pitt.	S.D.	Sea.
Total	9-13	7-15	12-8	12-13-1	10-7	9-6	9-6	29-8-1	25-16	4-12	9-15	15-14	10-9	10-5
1991	2-1	0-2			1-1		2-1	0-2	1-1		0-1	0-1		
1990	1-1	1-1	1-1	1-1	1-0	0-1	0-1	2-0	0-1		0-1	1-0		1-0
1989	1-2	1-2	1-1	2-0	1-0				1-0		0-1			1-0
1988	2-0		1-2	0-2	1-0	1-1		1-1	1-1		0-1			1-0
1987			1-0	2-1				1-1	1-1	1-1	2-1			0-2
1986		1-0	1-0	1-1				0-1	1-2	1-0	1-1	0-2	0-1	2-0
1985		1-0	1-0	1-0				2-0	2-1	0-1	1-0	0-2	0-1	0-2
1984	0-1	0-1		1-0				2-1	3-0		0-1	1-1	1-2	2-0
1983	0-1	0-2					0-1	1-0	1-1		2-0	1-0	1-1	
1982	0-1	0-1			0-1			1-0	1-1		1-0	1-0	1-1	
1981	1-1		0-1	1-0	0-1			2-1	1-1	0-1		1-1	2-1	1-0
1980		1-1	1-2	2-0				3-0	1-1	1-2	1-0	0-2	1-0	0-1
1979			1-0	0-2	2-0			2-0	0-2	0-2	1-1	2-1	1-0	2-0
1978		1-2		1-1	2-0	2-1		1-0	2-1	0-2		1-1	1-0	
1977	0-1	0-1	1-0			1-1	0-1	2-0	1-0	0-1		2-0		
1976	0-2	1-1			0-1	2-0	0-1	2-0	1-1	1-0	0-1	0-1		
1975	0-2	1-0		1-1	0-1		1-0	2-0	1-1	0-1	0-1	1-0		1-0
1974	1-0	0-1		0-2			1-0	0-1	2-0		0-1	2-0		
1973	1-0		0-1	0-0-1			1-1	0-0-1	2-0		0-1	1-1		
1972			1-0		0-1	1-0	1-0	2-0	1-0	0-1	0-1			0-1
1971			0-1		1-1	2-0		1-0	1-0		0-1	0-1	1-0	
1970		0-1	2-0		0-1	1-1	1-0	1-0	1-0		0-1	1-0	0-1	

National Football Conference

	Atl.	Chi.	Dall.	Det.	G.B.	Rams	Minn.	N.O.	N.Y.G.	Phil.	Phx.	S.F.	T.B.	Wash.
Total	5-11	12-19	19-17	7-8-1	7-10-1	17-20	12-13	5-8	11-18-1	10-8	5-8-1	18-13	1-2	20-17
1991		2-1	0-1			0-1	0-1	1-0	2-1	2-1		2-1		2-0
1990			0-1			0-3	0-1	1-1	1-1	2-0		3-0		0-1
1989		1-1				0-2	1-1	1-1	2-1	0-2		3-0		0-2
1988		1-2	1-1			1-0	1-0	1-0	1-1	1-0	0-1	1-1		0-2
1987		1-2	2-1			1-2	1-0		0-3			2-0		1-1
1986		2-1	2-0	0-1	0-1	1-0			2-1		0-1	0-2		1-1
1985		1-1	1-1		0-1	2-1			0-1		1-1	1-2		2-1
1984	0-2	0-1	1-1	0-1	0-1	1-1		1-0	0-1			2-0		1-1
1983	0-1		1-1	2-0	2-1	1-0	0-1	0-1	1-1-1		0-0-1	1-0	0-1	1-2
1982		1-2	0-1	1-0			1-0		0-1				1-0	
1981	1-2	0-2	2-0	1-0		2-0	0-3			1-1				
1980		1-1	1-1			2-0		0-1	0-1	1-0			0-1	0-2
1979	1-2		0-2		1-0	1-0	0-1	0-1	0-1	1-1				1-0
1978	1-0	0-3	1-1				0-2	2-0			2-0	0-1		1-1
1977		1-0	1-1		0-1	1-1	0-1		0-1		0-1	0-2		1-1
1976		1-0				0-2	1-1			0-1	0-1	2-0		2-0
1975		0-1	1-1	0-1	0-1	1-0	1-0		1-0	0-1	0-1			1-0
1974	0-1	1-0	0-1	1-0	0-1	1-1	1-0	0-1		1-0		0-2		2-0
1973	1-1	0-1	1-1	1-0	1-1	1-0	0-1	0-1	0-1		0-1	1-0		1-1
1972	0-1	1-0	1-0	0-2	1-0	1-0	0-2	0-1	1-0	0-1	1-1	0-1		2-0
1971	1-0	0-1	1-0	0-1-1	0-1-1	0-2	2-0		0-1		1-0	0-1		1-0
1970	0-1	0-1	0-1	2-0	1-1	0-2	1-0		0-1	1-0				0-1

Thursday-Sunday Night Football, 1974-1991

(Home Team in capitals, games listed in chronological order.)

1991
WASHINGTON 45, Detroit 0 (Sun.)
Houston 30, CINCINNATI 7 (Sun.)
NEW ORLEANS 24, Los Angeles Rams 7 (Sun.)
Dallas 17, PHOENIX 9 (Sun.)
Denver 13, MINNESOTA 6 (Sun.)
Pittsburgh 21, INDIANAPOLIS 3 (Sun.)
Los Angeles Raiders 23, SEATTLE 20 (Sun.)
Chicago 10, GREEN BAY 0 (Thurs.)
Washington 17, NEW YORK GIANTS 13 (Sun.)
DENVER 20, Pittsburgh 13 (Sun.)
MIAMI 30, New England 20 (Sun.)
HOUSTON 28, Cleveland 24 (Sun.)
Atlanta 23, NEW ORLEANS 20 (OT) (Sun.)
Los Angeles Raiders 9, SAN DIEGO 7 (Sun.)
Minnesota 26, TAMPA BAY 24 (Sun.)
Buffalo 35, INDIANAPOLIS 7 (Sun.)
SEATTLE 23, Los Angeles Rams 9 (Sun.)

1990
NEW YORK GIANTS 27, Philadelphia 20 (Sun.)
PITTSBURGH 20, Houston 9 (Sun.)
TAMPA BAY 23, Detroit 20 (Sun.)
Washington 38, PHOENIX 10 (Sun.)
BUFFALO 38, Los Angeles Raiders 24 (Sun.)
CHICAGO 38, Los Angeles Rams 9 (Sun.)
MIAMI 17, New England 10 (Thurs.)
ATLANTA 38, Cincinnati 17 (Sun.)
MINNESOTA 27, Denver 22 (Sun.)
San Francisco 24, DALLAS 6 (Sun.)
CINCINNATI 27, Pittsburgh 3 (Sun.)
Seattle 13, SAN DIEGO 10 (Sun.)
MINNESOTA 23, Green Bay 7 (Sun.)
MIAMI 23, Philadelphia 20 (Sun.)
DETROIT 38, Chicago 21 (Sun.)
INDIANAPOLIS 35, Washington 28 (Sat.)
SEATTLE 17, Denver 12 (Sun.)
HOUSTON 34, Pittsburgh 14 (Sun.)

1989
Dallas 13, WASHINGTON 3 (Sun.)
SAN DIEGO 14, Los Angeles Raiders 12 (Sun.)
INDIANAPOLIS 27, New York Jets 10 (Sun.)
Los Angeles Rams 20, NEW ORLEANS 17 (Sun.)
MINNESOTA 27, Chicago 16 (Sun.)
MIAMI 31, New England 10 (Sun.)
SEATTLE 23, Los Angeles Raiders 17 (Sun.)
Cleveland 24, HOUSTON 20 (Sat.)

1988
HOUSTON 41, Washington 17 (Sun.)
Los Angeles Raiders 13, SAN DIEGO 3 (Sun.)
Minnesota 34, DALLAS 3 (Sun.)
New England 6, MIAMI 3 (Sun.)
New York Giants 13, NEW ORLEANS 12 (Sun.)
Pittsburgh 37, HOUSTON 34 (Sun.)
SEATTLE 42, Denver 14 (Sun.)
Los Angeles Rams 38, SAN FRANCISCO 16 (Sun.)

1987
NEW YORK GIANTS 17, New England 10 (Sun.)
SAN DIEGO 16, Los Angeles Raiders 14 (Sun.)
Miami 20, DALLAS 14 (Sun.)
SAN FRANCISCO 38, Cleveland 24 (Sun.)
Chicago 30, MINNESOTA 24 (Sun.)
SEATTLE 28, Denver 21 (Sun.)
MIAMI 23, Washington 21 (Sun.)
SAN FRANCISCO 48, Los Angeles Rams 0 (Sun)

1986
New England 20, NEW YORK JETS 6 (Thurs.)
Cincinnati 30, CLEVELAND 13 (Thurs.)
Los Angeles Raiders 37, SAN DIEGO 31 (OT) (Thurs.)
LOS ANGELES RAMS 29, Dallas 10 (Sun.)
SAN FRANCISCO 24, Los Angeles Rams 14 (Fri.)

1985
KANSAS CITY 36, Los Angeles Raiders 20 (Thurs.)
Chicago 33, MINNESOTA 24 (Thurs.)
Dallas 30, NEW YORK GIANTS 29 (Sun.)
SAN DIEGO 54, Pittsburgh 44 (Sun.)
Denver 27, SEATTLE 24 (Fri.)

1984
Pittsburgh 23, NEW YORK JETS 17 (Thurs.)
Denver 24, CLEVELAND 14 (Sun.)
DALLAS 30, New Orleans 27 (Sun.)
Washington 31, MINNESOTA 17 (Thurs.)
SAN FRANCISCO 19, Los Angeles Rams 16 (Fri.)

1983
San Francisco 48, MINNESOTA 17 (Thurs.)
CLEVELAND 17, Cincinnati 7 (Thurs.)
Los Angeles Raiders 40, DALLAS 38 (Sun.)
Los Angeles Raiders 42, SAN DIEGO 10 (Thurs.)
MIAMI 34, New York Jets 14 (Fri.)

1982
BUFFALO 23, Minnesota 22 (Thurs.)
SAN FRANCISCO 30, Los Angeles Rams 24 (Thurs.)
ATLANTA 17, San Francisco 7 (Sun.)

1981
MIAMI 30, Pittsburgh 10 (Thurs.)
Philadelphia 20, BUFFALO 14 (Thurs.)
DALLAS 29, Los Angeles 17 (Sun.)
HOUSTON 17, Cleveland 13 (Thurs.)

1980
TAMPA BAY 10, Los Angeles 9 (Thurs.)
DALLAS 42, San Diego 31 (Sun.)
San Diego 27, MIAMI 24 (OT) (Thurs.)
HOUSTON 6, Pittsburgh 0 (Thurs.)

1979
Los Angeles 13, DENVER 9 (Thurs.)
DALLAS 30, Los Angeles 6 (Sun.)
OAKLAND 45, San Diego 22 (Thurs.)
MIAMI 39, New England 24 (Thurs.)

1978
New England 21, OAKLAND 14 (Sun.)
Minnesota 21, DALLAS 10 (Thurs.)
LOS ANGELES 10, Pittsburgh 7 (Sun.)
Denver 21, OAKLAND 6 (Sun.)

1977
Minnesota 30, DETROIT 21 (Sat.)

1976
Los Angeles 20, DETROIT 17 (Sat.)

1975
LOS ANGELES 10, Pittsburgh 3 (Sat.)

1974
OAKLAND 27, Dallas 23 (Sat.)

History of Overtime Games

Preseason

Aug. 28, 1955	Los Angeles 23, New York Giants 17, at Portland, Oregon
Aug. 24, 1962	Denver 27, Dallas Texans 24, at Fort Worth, Texas
Aug. 10, 1974	San Diego 20, New York Jets 14, at San Diego
Aug. 17, 1974	Pittsburgh 33, Philadelphia 30, at Philadelphia
Aug. 17, 1974	Dallas 19, Houston 13, at Dallas
Aug. 17, 1974	Cincinnati 13, Atlanta 7, at Atlanta
Sept. 6, 1974	Buffalo 23, New York Giants 17, at Buffalo
Aug. 9, 1975	Baltimore 23, Denver 20, at Denver
Aug. 30, 1975	New England 20, Green Bay 17, at Milwaukee
Sept. 13, 1975	Minnesota 14, San Diego 14, at San Diego
Aug. 1, 1976	New England 13, New York Giants 7, at New England
Aug. 2, 1976	Kansas City 9, Houston 3, at Kansas City
Aug. 20, 1976	New Orleans 26, Baltimore 20, at Baltimore
Sept. 4, 1976	Dallas 26, Houston 20, at Dallas
Aug. 13, 1977	Seattle 23, Dallas 17, at Seattle
Aug. 28, 1977	New England 13, Pittsburgh 10, at New England
Aug. 28, 1977	New York Giants 24, Buffalo 21, at East Rutherford, N.J.
Aug. 2, 1979	Seattle 12, Minnesota 9, at Minnesota
Aug. 4, 1979	Los Angeles 20, Oakland 14, at Los Angeles
Aug. 24, 1979	Denver 20, New England 17, at Denver
Aug. 23, 1980	Tampa Bay 20, Cincinnati 14, at Tampa Bay
Aug. 5, 1981	San Francisco 27, Seattle 24, at Seattle
Aug. 29, 1981	New Orleans 20, Detroit 17, at New Orleans
Aug. 28, 1982	Miami 17, Kansas City 17, at Kansas City
Sept. 3, 1982	Miami 16, New York Giants 13, at Miami
Aug. 6, 1983	L.A. Raiders 26, San Francisco 23, at Los Angeles
Aug. 6, 1983	Atlanta 13, Washington 10, at Atlanta
Aug. 13, 1983	St. Louis 27, Chicago 24, at St. Louis
Aug. 18, 1983	New York Jets 20, Cincinnati 17, at Cincinnati
Aug. 27, 1983	Chicago 20, Kansas City 17, at Chicago
Aug. 11, 1984	Pittsburgh 20, Philadelphia 17, at Pittsburgh
Aug. 9, 1985	Buffalo 10, Detroit 10, at Pontiac, Mich.
Aug. 10, 1985	Minnesota 16, Miami 13, at Miami
Aug. 17, 1985	Dallas 27, San Diego 24, at San Diego
Aug. 24, 1985	N.Y. Giants 34, N.Y. Jets 31, at East Rutherford, N.J.
Aug. 15, 1986	Washington 27, Pittsburgh 24, at Washington
Aug. 15, 1986	Detroit 30, Seattle 27, at Detroit
Aug. 23, 1986	Los Angeles Rams 20, San Diego 17, at Anaheim
Aug. 30, 1986	Minnesota 23, Indianapolis 20, at Indianapolis
Aug. 23, 1987	Philadelphia 19, New England 13, at New England
Sept. 5, 1987	Cleveland 30, Green Bay 24, at Milwaukee
Sept. 6, 1987	Kansas City 13, St. Louis 10, at Memphis, Tenn.
Aug. 11, 1988	Seattle 16, Detroit 13, at Detroit
Aug. 19, 1988	Miami 16, Denver 13, at Miami
Aug. 19, 1988	Green Bay 21, Kansas City 21, at Milwaukee
Aug. 20, 1988	Houston 20, Los Angeles Rams 17, at Anaheim
Aug. 21, 1988	Minnesota 19, Phoenix 16, at Phoenix
Aug. 5, 1989	Los Angeles Rams 16, San Francisco 13, at Tokyo, Japan
Aug. 26, 1989	Denver 24, Dallas 21, at Denver
Sept. 1, 1989	N.Y. Jets 15, Kansas City 13, at Kansas City
Aug. 24, 1990	Cincinnati 13, New England 10, at New England
Aug. 16, 1991	Cleveland 24, Washington 21, at Washington
Aug. 17, 1991	Cincinnati 27, Minnesota 24, at Cincinnati
Aug. 23, 1991	Dallas 20, Atlanta 17, at Dallas
Aug. 24, 1991	Cincinnati 19, Green Bay 16, at Green Bay

Regular Season

Sept. 22, 1974—Pittsburgh 35, Denver 35, at Denver; Steelers win toss. Gilliam's pass intercepted and returned by Rowser to Denver's 42. Turner misses 41-yard field goal. Walden punts and Greer returns to Broncos' 39. Van Heusen punts and Edwards returns to Steelers' 16. Game ends with Steelers on own 26.

Nov. 10, 1974—New York Jets 26, New York Giants 20, at New Haven, Conn.; Giants win toss. Gogolak misses 42-yard field goal. Namath passes to Boozer for five yards and touchdown at 6:53.

Sept. 28, 1975—Dallas 37, St. Louis 31, at Dallas; Cardinals win toss. Hart's pass intercepted and returned by Jordan to Cardinals' 37. Staubach passes to DuPree for three yards and touchdown at 7:53.

Oct. 12, 1975—Los Angeles 13, San Diego 10, at San Diego; Chargers win toss. Partee punts to Rams' 14. Dempsey kicks 22-yard field goal at 9:27.

Nov. 2, 1975—Washington 30, Dallas 24, at Washington; Cowboys win toss. Staubach's pass intercepted and returned by Houston to Cowboys' 35. Kilmer runs one yard for touchdown at 6:34.

Nov. 16, 1975—St. Louis 20, Washington 17, at St. Louis; Cardinals win toss. Bakken kicks 37-yard field goal at 7:00.

Nov. 23, 1975—Kansas City 24, Detroit 21, at Kansas City; Lions win toss. Chiefs take over on downs at own 38. Stenerud kicks 26-yard field goal at 6:44.

Nov. 23, 1975—Oakland 26, Washington 23, at Washington; Redskins win toss. Bragg punts to Raiders' 42. Blanda kicks 27-yard field goal at 7:13.

Nov. 30, 1975—Denver 13, San Diego 10, at Denver; Broncos win toss. Turner kicks 25-yard field goal at 4:13.

Nov. 30, 1975—Oakland 37, Atlanta 34, at Oakland; Falcons win toss. James punts to Raiders' 16. Guy punts and Herron returns to Falcons' 41. Nick Mike-Mayer misses 45-yard field goal. Guy punts into Falcons' end zone. James punts to Raiders' 39. Blanda kicks 36-yard field goal at 15:00.

Dec. 14, 1975—Baltimore 10, Miami 7, at Baltimore; Dolphins win toss. Seiple punts to Colts' 4. Linhart kicks 31-yard field goal at 12:44.

Sept. 19, 1976—Minnesota 10, Los Angeles 10, at Minnesota; Vikings win toss. Tarkenton's pass intercepted by Monte Jackson and returned to Minnesota 16. Allen blocks Dempsey's 30-yard field goal attempt, ball rolls into end zone for touchback. Clabo punts and Scribner returns to Rams' 20. Rusty Jackson punts to Vikings' 35. Tarkenton's pass intercepted by Kay at Rams' 1, no return. Game ends with Rams on own 3.

***Sept. 27, 1976—Washington 20, Philadelphia 17,** at Philadelphia; Eagles win toss. Jones punts and E. Brown loses one yard on return to Redskins' 40. Bragg punts 51 yards into end zone for touchback. Jones punts and E. Brown returns to Redskins' 42. Bragg punts and Marshall returns to Eagles' 41. Boryla's pass intercepted by Dusek at Redskins' 37, no return. Bragg punts and Bradley returns. Philadelphia holding penalty moves ball back to Eagles' 8. Boryla pass intercepted by E. Brown and returned to Eagles' 22. Moseley kicks 29-yard field goal at 12:49.

Oct. 17, 1976—Kansas City 20, Miami 17, at Miami; Chiefs win toss. Wilson punts into end zone for touchback. Bulaich fumbles into Kansas City end zone, Collier recovers for touchback. Stenerud kicks 34-yard field goal at 14:48.

Oct. 31, 1976—St. Louis 23, San Francisco 20, at St. Louis; Cardinals win toss. Joyce punts and Leonard fumbles on return, Jones recovers at 49ers' 43. Bakken kicks 21-yard field goal at 6:42.

Dec. 5, 1976—San Diego 13, San Francisco 7, at San Diego; Chargers win toss. Morris runs 13 yards for touchdown at 5:12.

Sept. 18, 1977—Dallas 16, Minnesota 10, at Minnesota; Vikings win toss. Dallas starts on Vikings' 47 after a punt early in the overtime period. Staubach scores seven plays later on a four-yard run at 6:14.

***Sept. 26, 1977—Cleveland 30, New England 27,** at Cleveland; Browns win toss. Sipe throws a 22-yard pass to Logan at Patriots' 19. Cockroft kicks 35-yard field goal at 4:45.

Oct. 16, 1977—Minnesota 22, Chicago 16, at Minnesota; Bears win toss. Parsons punts 53 yards to Vikings' 18. Minnesota drives to Bears' 11. On a first-and-10, Vikings fake a field goal and holder Krause hits Voigt with a touchdown pass at 6:45.

Oct. 30, 1977—Cincinnati 13, Houston 10, at Cincinnati; Bengals win toss. Bahr kicks a 22-yard field goal at 5:51.

Nov. 13, 1977—San Francisco 10, New Orleans 7, at New Orleans; Saints win toss. Saints fail to move ball and Blanchard punts to 49ers' 41. Wersching kicks a 33-yard field goal at 6:33.

Dec. 18, 1977—Chicago 12, New York Giants 9, at East Rutherford, N.J.; Giants win toss. The ball changes hands eight times before Thomas kicks a 28-yard field goal at 14:51.

Sept. 10, 1978—Cleveland 13, Cincinnati 10, at Cleveland; Browns win toss. Collins returns kickoff 41 yards to Browns' 47. Cockroft kicks 27-yard field goal at 4:30.

***Sept. 11, 1978—Minnesota 12, Denver 9,** at Minnesota; Vikings win toss. Danmeier kicks 44-yard field goal at 2:56.

Sept. 24, 1978—Pittsburgh 15, Cleveland 9, at Pittsburgh; Steelers win toss. Cunningham scores on a 37-yard "gadget" pass from Bradshaw at 3:43. Steelers start winning drive on their 21.

Sept. 24, 1978—Denver 23, Kansas City 17, at Kansas City; Broncos win toss. Dilts punts to Kansas City. Chiefs advance to Broncos' 40 where Reed fails to make first down on fourth-and-one situation. Broncos march downfield. Preston scores two-yard touchdown at 10:28.

Oct. 1, 1978—Oakland 25, Chicago 19, at Chicago; Bears win toss. Both teams punt on first possession. On Chicago's second offensive series, Colzie intercepts Avellini's pass and returns it to Bears' 3. Three plays later, Whittington runs two yards for a touchdown at 5:19.

Oct. 15, 1978—Dallas 24, St. Louis 21, at St. Louis; Cowboys win toss. Dallas drives from its 23 into field goal range. Septien kicks 27-yard field goal at 3:28.

Oct. 29, 1978—Denver 20, Seattle 17, at Seattle; Broncos win toss. Ball changes hands four times before Turner kicks 18-yard field goal at 12:59.

Nov. 12, 1978—San Diego 29, Kansas City 23, at San Diego; Chiefs win toss. Fouts hits Jefferson for decisive 14-yard touchdown pass on the last play (15:00) of overtime period.

Nov. 12, 1978—Washington 16, New York Giants 13, at Washington; Redskins win toss. Moseley kicks winning 45-yard field goal at 8:32 after missing first down field goal attempt of 35 yards at 4:50.

Nov. 26, 1978—Green Bay 10, Minnesota 10, at Green Bay; Packers win toss. Both teams have possession of the ball four times.

Dec. 9, 1978—Cleveland 37, New York Jets 34, at Cleveland; Browns win toss. Cockroft kicks 22-yard field goal at 3:07.

Sept. 2, 1979—Atlanta 40, New Orleans 34, at New Orleans; Falcons win toss. Bartkowski's pass intercepted by Myers and returned to Falcons' 46. Erxleben punts to Falcons' 4. James punts to Chandler on Saints' 43. Erxleben punts and Ryckman returns to Falcons' 28. James punts and Chandler returns to Saints' 36. Erxleben retrieves punt snap on Saints' 1 and attempts pass. Mayberry intercepts and returns six yards for touchdown at 8:22.

Sept. 2, 1979—Cleveland 25, New York Jets 22, at New York; Jets win toss. Leahy's 43-yard field goal attempt goes wide right at 4:41. Evans's punt blocked by Dykes is recovered by Newton. Ramsey punts into end zone for touchback. Evans punts and Harper returns to Jets' 24. Robinson's pass intercepted by Davis and returned 33 yards to Jets' 31. Cockroft kicks 27-yard field goal at 14:45.

***Sept. 3, 1979—Pittsburgh 16, New England 13,** at Foxboro; Patriots win toss. Hare punts to Swann at Steelers' 31. Bahr kicks 41-yard field goal at 5:10.

Sept. 9, 1979—Tampa Bay 29, Baltimore 26, at Baltimore; Colts win toss. Landry fumbles, recovered by Kollar at Colts' 14. O'Donoghue kicks 31-yard, first-down field goal at 1:41.

Sept. 16, 1979—Denver 20, Atlanta 17, at Atlanta; Broncos win toss. Broncos march 65 yards to Falcons' 7. Turner kicks 24-yard field goal at 6:15.

Sept. 23, 1979—Houston 30, Cincinnati 27, at Cincinnati; Oilers win toss. Parsley punts and Lusby returns to Bengals' 33. Bahr's 32-yard field goal attempt is wide right at 8:05. Parsley's punt downed on Bengals' 5. McInally punts and Ellender returns to Bengals' 42. Fritsch's third down, 29-yard field goal attempt hits left upright and bounces through at 14:28.

Sept. 23, 1979—Minnesota 27, Green Bay 21, at Minnesota; Vikings win toss. Kramer throws 50-yard touchdown pass to Rashad at 3:18.

Oct. 28, 1979—Houston 27, New York Jets 24, at Houston; Oilers win toss. Oilers march 58 yards to Jets' 18. Fritsch kicks 35-yard field goal at 5:10.

Nov. 18, 1979—Cleveland 30, Miami 24, at Cleveland; Browns win toss. Sipe passes 39 yards to Rucker for touchdown at 1:59.

Nov. 25, 1979—Pittsburgh 33, Cleveland 30, at Pittsburgh; Browns win toss. Sipe's pass intercepted by Blount on Steelers' 4. Bradshaw pass intercepted by Bolton on Browns' 12. Evans punts and Bell returns to Steelers' 17. Bahr kicks 37-yard field goal at 14:51.

Nov. 25, 1979—Buffalo 16, New England 13, at Foxboro; Patriots win toss. Hare's punt downed on Bills' 38. Jackson punts and Morgan returns to Patriots' 20. Grogan's pass intercepted by Haslett and returned to Bills' 42. Ferguson's 51-yard pass to Butler sets up N. Mike-Mayer's 29-yard field goal at 9:15.

Dec. 2, 1979—Los Angeles 27, Minnesota 21, at Los Angeles; Rams win toss. Clark punts and Miller returns to Vikings' 25. Kramer's pass intercepted by Brown and returned to Rams' 40. Cromwell, holding for 22-yard field goal attempt, runs around left end untouched for winning score at 6:53.

Sept. 7, 1980—Green Bay 12, Chicago 6, at Green Bay; Bears win toss. Parsons punts and Nixon returns 16 yards. Five plays later, Marcol returns own blocked field goal attempt 24 yards for touchdown at 6:00.

Sept. 14, 1980—San Diego 30, Oakland 24, at San Diego; Raiders win toss. Pastorini's first-down pass intercepted by Edwards. Millen intercepts Fouts' first-down pass and returns to San Diego 46. Bahr's 50-yard field goal attempt partially blocked by Williams and recovered on Chargers' 32. Eight plays later, Fouts throws 24-yard touchdown pass to Jefferson at 8:09.

Sept. 14, 1980—San Francisco 24, St. Louis 21, at San Francisco; Cardinals win toss. Swider punts and Robinson returns to 49ers' 32. San Francisco drives 52 yards to St. Louis 16, where Wersching kicks 33-yard field goal at 4:12.

Oct. 12, 1980—Green Bay 14, Tampa Bay 14, at Tampa Bay; Packers win toss. Teams trade punts twice. Lee returns second Tampa Bay punt to Green Bay 42. Dickey completes three passes to Buccaneers' 18, where Birney's 36-yard field goal attempt is wide right as time expires.

Nov. 9, 1980—Atlanta 33, St. Louis 27, at St. Louis; Falcons win toss. Strong runs 21 yards for touchdown at 4:20.

#Nov. 20, 1980—San Diego 27, Miami 24, at Miami; Chargers win toss. Partridge punts into end zone, Dolphins take over on their own 20. Woodley's pass for Nathan intercepted by Lowe and returned 28 yards to Dolphins' 12. Benirschke kicks 28-yard field goal at 7:14.

Nov. 23, 1980—New York Jets 31, Houston 28, at New York; Jets win toss. Leahy kicks 38-yard field goal at 3:58.

Nov. 27, 1980—Chicago 23, Detroit 17, at Detroit; Bears win toss. Williams returns kickoff 95 yards for touchdown at 0:21.

Dec. 7, 1980—Buffalo 10, Los Angeles 7, at Buffalo; Rams win toss. Corral punts and Hooks returns to Bills' 34. Ferguson's 30-yard pass to Lewis sets up N. Mike-Mayer's 30-yard field goal at 5:14.

Dec. 7, 1980—San Francisco 38, New Orleans 35, at San Francisco; Saints win toss. Erxleben's punt downed by Hardy on 49ers' 27. Wersching kicks 36-yard field goal at 7:40.

***Dec. 8, 1980—Miami 16, New England 13,** at Miami; Dolphins win toss. Von Schamann kicks 23-yard field goal at 3:20.

Dec. 14, 1980—Cincinnati 17, Chicago 14, at Chicago; Bengals win toss. Breech kicks 28-yard field goal at 4:23.

Dec. 21, 1980—Los Angeles 20, Atlanta 17, at Los Angeles; Rams win toss. Corral's punt downed at Rams' 37. James punts into end zone for touchback. Corral's punt downed on Falcons' 17. Bartkowski fumbles when hit by Harris, recovered by Delaney. Corral kicks 23-yard field goal on first play of possession at 7:00.

Sept. 27, 1981—Cincinnati 27, Buffalo 24, at Cincinnati; Bills win toss. Cater punts into end zone for touchback. Bengals drive to the Bills' 10 where Breech kicks 28-yard field goal at 9:33.

Sept. 27, 1981—Pittsburgh 27, New England 21, at Pittsburgh; Patriots win toss. Hubach punts and Smith returns five yards to midfield. Four plays later Bradshaw throws 24-yard touchdown pass to Swann at 3:19.

Oct. 4, 1981—Miami 28, New York Jets 28, at Miami; Jets win toss. Teams trade punts twice. Leahy's 48-yard field goal attempt is wide right as time expires.

Oct. 25, 1981—New York Giants 27, Atlanta 24, at Atlanta; Giants win toss. Jennings' punt goes out of bounds at New York 47. Bright returns Atlanta punt to Giants' 14. Woerner fair catches punt at own 28. Andrews fumbles on first play, recovered by Van Pelt. Danelo kicks 40-yard field goal four plays later at 9:20.

Oct. 25, 1981—Chicago 20, San Diego 17, at Chicago; Bears win toss. Teams trade punts. Bears' second punt returned by Brooks to Chargers' 33. Fouts pass intercepted by Fencik and returned 32 yards to San Diego 27. Roveto kicks 27-yard field goal seven plays later at 9:30.

Nov. 8, 1981—Chicago 16, Kansas City 13, at Kansas City; Bears win toss. Teams trade punts. Kansas City takes over on downs on its own 38. Fuller's fumble recovered by Harris on Chicago 36. Roveto's 37-yard field goal wide, but Chiefs penalized for leverage. Roveto's 22-yard field goal attempt three plays later is good at 13:07.

Nov. 8, 1981—Denver 23, Cleveland 20, at Denver; Browns win toss. D. Smith recovers Hill's fumble at Denver 48. Morton's 33-yard pass to Upchurch and six-yard run by Preston set up Steinfort's 30-yard field goal at 4:10.

Nov. 8, 1981—Miami 30, New England 27, at New England; Dolphins win toss. Orosz punts and Morgan returns six yards to New England 26. Grogan's pass intercepted by Brudzinski who returns 19 yards to Patriots' 26. Von Schamann kicks 30-yard field goal on first down at 7:09.

Nov. 15, 1981—Washington 30, New York Giants 27, at New York; Giants win toss. Nelms returns Giants' punt 26 yards to New York 47. Five plays later Moseley kicks 48-yard field goal at 3:44.

Dec. 20, 1981—New York Giants 13, Dallas 10, at New York; Cowboys win toss and kick off. Jennings punts to Dallas 40. Taylor recovers Dorsett's fumble on second down. Danelo's 33-yard field goal attempt hits right upright and bounces back. White's pass for Pearson intercepted by Hunt and returned seven yards to Dallas 24. Four plays later Danelo kicks 35-yard field goal at 6:19.

Sept. 12, 1982—Washington 37, Philadelphia 34, at Philadelphia; Redskins win toss. Theismann completes five passes for 63 yards to set up Moseley's 26-yard field goal at 4:47.

Sept. 19, 1982—Pittsburgh 26, Cincinnati 20, at Pittsburgh; Bengals win toss. Anderson's pass intended for Kreider intercepted by Woodruff and returned 30 yards to Cincinnati 2. Bradshaw completes two-yard touchdown pass to Stallworth on first down at 1:08.

Dec. 19, 1982—Baltimore 20, Green Bay 20, at Baltimore; Packers win toss. K. Anderson intercepts Dickey's first-down pass and returns to Packers' 42. Miller's 44-yard field goal attempt blocked by G. Lewis. Teams trade punts before Stenerud's 47-yard field goal attempt is wide right. Teams trade punts again before time expires in Colts possession.

Jan. 2, 1983—Tampa Bay 26, Chicago 23, at Tampa; Bears win toss. Parsons punts to T. Bell at Buccaneers' 40. Capece kicks 33-yard field goal at 3:14.

Sept. 4, 1983—Baltimore 29, New England 23, at New England; Patriots win toss. Cooks runs 52 yards with fumble recovery three plays into overtime at 0:30.

Sept. 4, 1983—Green Bay 41, Houston 38, at Houston; Packers win toss. Stenerud kicks 42-yard field goal at 5:55.

Sept. 11, 1983—New York Giants 16, Atlanta 13, at Atlanta; Giants win toss. Dennis returns kickoff 54 yards to Atlanta 41. Haji-Sheikh kicks 30-yard field goal at 3:38.

Sept. 18, 1983—New Orleans 34, Chicago 31, at New Orleans; Bears win toss. Parsons punts and Groth returns five yards to New Orleans 34. Stabler pass intercepted by Schmidt at Chicago 47. Parsons punt downed by Gentry at New Orleans 2. Stabler gains 36 yards in four passes; Wilson 38 on six carries. Andersen kicks 41-yard field goal at 10:57.

Sept. 18, 1983—Minnesota 19, Tampa Bay 16, at Tampa; Vikings win toss. Coleman punts and Bell returns eight yards to Tampa Bay 47. Capece's 33-yard field goal attempt sails wide at 7:26. Dils and Young combine for 48-yard gain to Tampa Bay 27. Ricardo kicks 42-yard field goal at 9:27.

Sept. 25, 1983—Baltimore 22, Chicago 19, at Baltimore; Colts win toss. Allegre kicks 33-yard field goal nine plays later at 4:51.

Sept. 25, 1983—Cleveland 30, San Diego 24, at San Diego; Browns win toss. Walker returns kickoff 33 yards to Cleveland 37. Sipe completes 48-yard touchdown pass to Holt four plays later at 1:53.

Sept. 25, 1983—New York Jets 27, Los Angeles Rams 24, at New York; Jets win toss. Ramsey punts to Irvin who returns to 25 but penalty puts Rams on own 13. Holmes 30-yard interception return sets up Leahy's 26-yard field goal at 3:22.

Oct. 9, 1983—Buffalo 38, Miami 35, at Miami; Dolphins win toss. Von Schamann's 52-yard field goal attempt goes wide at 12:36. Cater punts to Clayton who loses 11 to own 13. Von Schamann's 43-yard field goal attempt sails wide at 5:15. Danelo kicks 36-yard field goal nine plays later at 13:58.

Oct. 9, 1983—Dallas 27, Tampa Bay 24, at Dallas; Cowboys win toss. Septien's 51-yard field goal attempt goes wide but Buccaneers penalized for roughing kicker. Septien kicks 42-yard field goal at 4:38.

Oct. 23, 1983—Kansas City 13, Houston 10, at Houston; Chiefs win toss. Lowery kicks 41-yard field goal 13 plays later at 7:41.

Oct. 23, 1983—Minnesota 20, Green Bay 17, at Green Bay; Packers win toss. Scribner's punt downed on Vikings' 42. Ricardo kicks 32-yard field goal eight plays later at 5:05.

***Oct. 24, 1983—New York Giants 20, St. Louis 20,** at St. Louis; Cardinals win toss. Teams trade punts before O'Donoghue's 44-yard field goal attempt is wide left. Jennings' punt returned by Bird to St. Louis 21. Lomax pass intercepted by Haynes who loses six yards to New York 33. Jennings' punt downed on St. Louis 17. O'Donoghue's 19-yard field goal attempt is wide right. Rutledge's pass intercepted by L. Washington who returns 25 yards to New York 25. O'Donoghue's 42-yard field goal attempt is wide right. Rutledge's pass intercepted by W. Smith at St. Louis 33 to end game.

Oct. 30, 1983—Cleveland 25, Houston 19, at Cleveland; Oilers win toss. Teams trade punts. Nielsen's pass intercepted by Whitwell who returns to Houston 20. Green runs 20 yards for touchdown on first down at 6:34.

Nov. 20, 1983—Detroit 23, Green Bay 20, at Milwaukee; Packers win toss. Scribner punts and Jenkins returns 14 yards to Green Bay 45. Murray's 33-yard field goal attempt is wide left at 9:32. Whitehurst's pass intercepted by Watkins and returned to Green Bay 27. Murray kicks 37-yard field goal four plays later at 8:30.

Nov. 27, 1983—Atlanta 47, Green Bay 41, at Atlanta; Packers win toss. K. Johnson returns interception 31 yards for touchdown at 2:13.

Nov. 27, 1983—Seattle 51, Kansas City 48, at Seattle; Seahawks win toss. Dixon's 47-yard kickoff return sets up N. Johnson's 42-yard field goal at 1:36.

Dec. 11, 1983—New Orleans 20, Philadelphia 17, at Philadelphia; Eagles win toss. Runager punts to Groth who fair catches on New Orleans 32. Stabler completes two passes for 36 yards to Goodlow to set up Andersen's 50-yard field goal at 5:30.

***Dec. 12, 1983—Green Bay 12, Tampa Bay 9,** at Tampa; Packers win toss. Stenerud kicks 23-yard field goal 11 plays later at 4:07.

Sept. 9, 1984—Detroit 27, Atlanta 24, at Atlanta; Lions win toss. Murray kicks 48-yard field goal nine plays later at 5:06.

Sept. 30, 1984—Tampa Bay 30, Green Bay 27, at Tampa; Packers win toss. Scribner punts 44 yards to Tampa Bay 2. Epps returns Garcia's punt three yards to Green Bay 27. Scribner's punt downed on Buccaneers' 33. Ariri kicks 46-yard field goal 11 plays later at 10:32.

Oct. 14, 1984—Detroit 13, Tampa Bay 7, at Detroit; Buccaneers win toss. Tampa Bay drives to Lions' 39 before Wilder fumbles. Five plays later Danielson hits Thompson with 37-yard touchdown pass at 4:34.

Oct. 21, 1984—Dallas 30, New Orleans 27, at Dallas; Cowboys win toss. Septien kicks 41-yard field goal eight plays later at 3:42.

Oct. 28, 1984—Denver 22, Los Angeles Raiders 19, at Los Angeles; Raiders win toss. Hawkins fumble recovered by Foley at Denver 7. Teams trade punts. Karlis's 42-yard field goal attempt is wide left. Teams trade punts. Wilson pass

intercepted by R. Jackson at Los Angeles 45, returned 23 yards to Los Angeles 22. Karlis kicks 35-yard field goal two plays later at 15:00.

Nov. 4, 1984—Philadelphia 23, Detroit 23, at Detroit; Lions win toss. Lions drive to Eagles' 3 in eight plays. Murray's 21-yard field goal attempt hits right upright and bounces back. Jaworski's pass intercepted by Watkins at Detroit 5. Teams trade punts. Cooper returns Black's punt five yards to Eagles' 14. Time expires four plays later with Eagles on own 21.

Nov. 18, 1984—San Diego 34, Miami 28, at San Diego; Chargers win toss. McGee scores eight plays later on a 25-yard run at 3:17.

Dec. 2, 1984—Cincinnati 20, Cleveland 17, at Cleveland; Browns win toss. Simmons returns Cox's punt 30 yards to Cleveland 35. Breech kicks 35-yard field goal seven plays later at 4:34.

Dec. 2, 1984—Houston 23, Pittsburgh 20, at Houston; Oilers win toss. Cooper kicks 30-yard field goal 16 plays later at 5:53.

Sept. 8, 1985—St. Louis 27, Cleveland 24, at Cleveland; Cardinals win toss. O'Donoghue kicks 35-yard field goal nine plays later at 5:27.

Sept. 29, 1985—New York Giants 16, Philadelphia 10, at Philadelphia; Eagles win toss. Jaworski's pass tipped by Quick and intercepted by Patterson who returns 29 yards for touchdown at 0:55.

Oct. 20, 1985—Denver 13, Seattle 10, at Denver; Seahawks win toss. Teams trade punts twice. Krieg's pass intercepted by Hunter and returned to Seahawks' 15. Karlis kicks 24-yard field goal four plays later at 9:19.

Nov. 10, 1985—Philadelphia 23, Atlanta 17, at Philadelphia; Falcons win toss. Donnelly's 62-yard punt goes out of bounds at Eagles' 1. Jaworski completes 99-yard touchdown pass to Quick two plays later at 1:49.

Nov. 10, 1985—San Diego 40, Los Angeles Raiders 34, at San Diego; Chargers win toss. James scores on 17-yard run seven plays later at 3:44.

Nov. 17, 1985—Denver 30, San Diego 24, at Denver; Chargers win toss. Thomas' 40-yard field goal attempt blocked by Smith and returned 60 yards by Wright for touchdown at 4:45.

Nov. 24, 1985—New York Jets 16, New England 13, at New York; Jets win toss. Teams trade punts twice. Patriots' second punt returned 46 yards by Sohn to Patriots' 15. Leahy kicks 32-yard field goal one play later at 10:05.

Nov. 24, 1985—Tampa Bay 19, Detroit 16, at Tampa; Lions win toss. Teams trade punts. Lions' punt downed on Buccaneers' 38. Igwebuike kicks 24-yard field goal 11 plays later at 12:31.

Nov. 24, 1985—Los Angeles Raiders 31, Denver 28, at Los Angeles; Raiders win toss. Bahr kicks 32-yard field goal six plays later at 2:42.

Dec. 8, 1985—Los Angeles Raiders 17, Denver 14, at Denver; Broncos win toss. Teams trade punts twice. Elway's fumble recovered by Townsend at Broncos' 8. Bahr kicks 26-yard field goal one play later at 4:55.

Sept. 14, 1986—Chicago 13, Philadelphia 10, at Chicago; Eagles win toss. Crawford's fumble of kickoff recovered by Jackson at Eagles' 35. Butler kicks 23-yard field goal 10 plays later at 5:56.

Sept. 14, 1986—Cincinnati 36, Buffalo 33, at Cincinnati; Bills win toss. Zander intercepts Kelly's first-down pass and returns it to Bills' 17. Breech kicks 20-yard field goal two plays later at 0:56.

Sept. 21, 1986—New York Jets 51, Miami 45, at New York; Jets win toss. O'Brien completes 43-yard touchdown pass to Walker five plays later at 2:35.

Sept. 28, 1986—Pittsburgh 22, Houston 16, at Houston; Oilers win toss. Johnson's punt returned 41 yards by Woods to Oilers' 15. Abercrombie scores on three-yard run three plays later at 2:35.

Sept. 28, 1986—Atlanta 23, Tampa Bay 20, at Tampa; Falcons win toss. Teams trade punts. Luckhurst kicks 34-yard field goal 10 plays later at 12:35.

Oct. 5, 1986—Los Angeles Rams 26, Tampa Bay 20, at Anaheim; Rams win toss. Dickerson scores four plays later on 42-yard run at 2:16.

Oct. 12, 1986—Minnesota 27, San Francisco 24, at San Francisco; Vikings win toss. C. Nelson kicks 28-yard field goal nine plays later at 4:27.

Oct. 19, 1986—San Francisco 10, Atlanta 10, at Atlanta; Falcons win toss. Teams trade punts twice. Donnelly punts to 49ers' 27. The following play Wilson recovers Rice's fumble at 49ers' 46 as time expires.

Nov. 2, 1986—Washington 44, Minnesota 38, at Washington; Redskins win toss. Schroeder completes 38-yard touchdown pass to Clark four plays later at 1:46.

Nov. 20, 1986—Los Angeles Raiders 37, San Diego 31, at San Diego; Raiders win toss. Teams trade punts. Allen scores five plays later on 28-yard run at 8:33.

Nov. 23, 1986—Cleveland 37, Pittsburgh 31, at Cleveland; Browns win toss. Teams trade punts. Six plays later Kosar hits Slaughter with 36-yard touchdown pass at 6:37.

Nov. 30, 1986—Chicago 13, Pittsburgh 10, at Chicago; Bears win toss and kick off. Newsome's punt returned by Barnes to Chicago 49. Butler kicks 42-yard field goal five plays later at 3:55.

Nov. 30, 1986—Philadelphia 33, Los Angeles Raiders 27, at Los Angeles; Eagles win toss. Teams trade punts. Long recovers Cunningham's fumble at Philadelphia 42. Waters returns Allen's fumble 81 yards to Los Angeles 4. Cunningham scores on one-yard run two plays later at 6:53.

Nov. 30, 1986—Cleveland 13, Houston 10, at Cleveland; Oilers win toss and kick off. Gossett punts to Houston 39. Luck's pass intercepted by Minnifield at Cleveland 21. Gossett punts to Houston 34. Luck's pass intercepted by Minnifield at Cleveland 43 who returns 20 yards to Houston 37. Moseley kicks 29-yard field goal nine plays later at 14:44.

Dec. 7, 1986—St. Louis 10, Philadelphia 10, at Philadelphia; Cardinals win toss. White blocks Schubert's 40-yard field goal attempt. Teams trade punts. McFadden's 43-yard field goal attempt is wide left. Schubert's 37-yard field goal attempt is wide right. Cavanaugh's pass intercepted by Carter and returned to Eagles' 48 to end game.

Dec. 14, 1986—Miami 37, Los Angeles Rams 31, at Anaheim; Dolphins win toss. Marino completes 20-yard touchdown pass to Duper six plays later at 3:04.

Sept. 20, 1987—Denver 17, Green Bay 17, at Milwaukee; Packers win toss. Del Greco's 47-yard field goal attempt is short. Teams trade punts. Elway intercepted by Noble who returns 10 yards to Green Bay 34. Davis fumbles on next play and Smith recovers. Two plays later, Karlis's 40-yard field goal attempt is wide left. Time expires two plays later with Packers on own 23.

Oct. 11, 1987—Detroit 19, Green Bay 16, at Green Bay; Lions win toss. Prindle's 42-yard field goal attempt is wide left. Packers punt downed on Detroit 17. Prindle kicks 31-yard field goal 16 plays later at 12:26.

Oct. 18, 1987—New York Jets 37, Miami 31, at New York; Jets win toss. Teams trade punts. Ryan intercepted by Hooper at Jets' 47 who returns 11 yards. Mackey intercepted by Haslett at Jets' 37 who returns 9 yards. Jets punt. Mackey intercepted by Radachowsky who returns 45 yards to Miami 24. Ryan completes eight-yard touchdown pass to Hunter five plays later at 14:26.

Oct. 18, 1987—Green Bay 16, Philadelphia 10, at Green Bay; Packers win toss. Hargrove scores on seven-yard run 10 plays later at 5:04.

Oct. 18, 1987—Buffalo 6, New York Giants 3, at Buffalo; Bills win toss. Schlopy's 28-yard field goal attempt is wide left. Teams trade punts. Rutledge intercepted by Clark who returns 23 yards to Buffalo 40. Schlopy kicks 27-yard field goal nine plays later at 14:41.

Oct. 25, 1987—Buffalo 34, Miami 31, at Miami; Bills win toss. Norwood kicks 27-yard field goal seven plays later at 4:12.

Nov. 1, 1987—San Diego 27, Cleveland 24, at San Diego; Browns win toss. Kosar intercepted by Glenn who returns 20 yards to Browns' 25. Abbott kicks 33-yard field goal three plays later at 2:16.

Nov. 15, 1987—Dallas 23, New England 17, at New England; Cowboys win toss. Walker scores on 60-yard run four plays later at 1:50.

Nov. 26, 1987—Minnesota 44, Dallas 38, at Dallas; Vikings win toss. Coleman's punt downed by Hilton at Cowboys' 37. White intercepted by Studwell who returns 12 yards to Vikings' 37. D. Nelson scores on 24-yard run seven plays later at 7:51.

Nov. 29, 1987—Philadelphia 34, New England 31, at New England; Patriots win toss. Ramsey intercepted by Joyner who returns 29 yards to Eagles' 32. Fryar fair catches Teltschik's punt at Patriots' 13. Franklin's 46-yard field goal attempt is short. McFadden's 39-yard field goal attempt is wide left. Tatupu fumbles on next play and Cobb recovers. McFadden kicks 38-yard field goal four plays later at 12:16.

Dec. 6, 1987—New York Giants 23, Philadelphia 20, at New York; Giants win toss and kick off. Teams trade punts twice. Teltschik's punt is returned 16 yards by McConkey to Eagles' 33. Three plays later, Allegre's 50-yard field goal attempt is blocked by Joyner and returned 25 yards by Hoage to Eagles' 30. McConkey returns Teltschik's punt four yards to Giants' 44. Allegre kicks 28-yard field goal four plays later at 10:42.

Dec. 6, 1987—Cincinnati 30, Kansas City 27, at Cincinnati; Bengals win toss. Teams trade punts. Breech kicks 32-yard field goal 16 plays later at 9:44.

Dec. 26, 1987—Washington 27, Minnesota 24, at Minnesota; Redskins win toss. Haji-Sheikh kicks 26-yard field goal six plays later at 2:09.

Sept. 4, 1988—Houston 17, Indianapolis 14, at Indianapolis; Colts win toss. Dickerson fumble recovered by Odom who returns six yards to Colts' 42. Zendejas kicks 35-yard field goal six plays later at 3:51.

***Sept. 26, 1988—Los Angeles Raiders 30, Denver 27,** at Denver; Broncos win toss. Teams trade punts twice. Elway intercepted by Lee who returns 20 yards to Broncos' 31. Bahr kicks 35-yard field goal four plays later at 12:35.

Oct. 2, 1988—New York Jets 17, Kansas City 17, at New York; Chiefs win toss. Chiefs punt goes into end zone for touchback. Leahy's 44-yard field goal attempt is wide right. Chiefs punt is returned by Townsell to Jets' 26. Burruss recovers McNeil's fumble at Chiefs' 11. DeBerg intercepted by Humphery at Jets' 49. Three plays later, time expires.

Oct. 9, 1988—Denver 16, San Francisco 13, at San Francisco; Broncos win toss and kick off. Young intercepted by Haynes at Broncos' 32. Denver punt downed at 49ers' 5. Young intercepted by Wilson who returns seven yards to 49ers' 5. Karlis kicks 22-yard field goal two plays later at 8:11.

Oct. 30, 1988—New York Giants 13, Detroit 10, at Detroit; Lions win toss. James's fumble recovered by Taylor at Lions' 22. Three plays later, McFadden kicks 33-yard field goal at 1:13.

Nov. 20, 1988—Buffalo 9, New York Jets 6, at Buffalo; Jets win toss. Vick's fumble recovered by Bennett at Bills' 32. Norwood kicks 30-yard field goal five plays later at 3:47.

Nov. 20, 1988—Philadelphia 23, New York Giants 17, at New York; Eagles win toss. Philadelphia's punt goes into end zone for touchback. Hostetler intercepted by Hoage who returns 11 yards to Giants' 41. Six plays later, Zendejas's 30-yard field-goal attempt is blocked and ball is recovered behind line of scrimmage by Eagles' Simmons, who runs 15 yards for touchdown at 3:09.

Dec. 11, 1988—New England 10, Tampa Bay 7, at New England; Buccaneers win toss and kick off. Staurovsky kicks 27-yard field goal six plays later at 3:08.

Dec. 17, 1988—Cincinnati 20, Washington 17, at Cincinnati; Bengals win toss. Cincinnati's punt returned by Oliphant to Redskins' 16. Grant recovers Williams's fumble at Redskins' 17. Breech kicks 20-yard field goal three plays later at 7:01.

Sept. 24, 1989—Buffalo 47, Houston 41, at Houston; Oilers win toss. Johnson returns Brady's kickoff 17 yards to Oilers' 19. Oilers drive to Buffalo 25, Zendejas's 37-yard field goal blocked, but Bills offsides and Zendejas's second attempt is wide left. Bills' ball and Kelly completes series of passes, including 28-yard game-winner to Andre Reed, at 8:42.

Oct. 8, 1989—Miami 13, Cleveland 10, at Miami; Browns win toss. Metcalf returns Stoyanovich's kickoff 20 yards to Browns' 28. Browns drive ball 46 yards in eight plays; Bahr wide left on 44-yard field goal attempt. Dolphins ball. Browns called for pass interference on Marino pass to Banks at Cleveland 47. Two plays later, Banks's 20-yard reception at Browns' 23 sets up winning 35-yard field goal by Stoyanovich at 6:23.

Oct. 22, 1989—Denver 24, Seattle 21, at Seattle; Seahawks win toss. Treadwell's 56-yard kickoff returned 18 yards by Jefferson to Seahawks' 27. Seahawks drive to Broncos' 22 in 10 plays, but Johnson's 40-yard field goal attempt wide left. Smith intercepts a Krieg pass and returns it 28 yards to Seahawks' 10. Treadwell kicks winning 27-yard field goal at 7:46.

Oct. 29, 1989—New England 23, Indianapolis 20, at Indianapolis; Patriots win toss. Biasucci kickoff returned 13 yards to Patriots' 23 by Martin. Holding penalty brings ball back to Patriots' 13. After six plays, Feagles punt returned 11 yards by Verdin to Colts' 28. Six plays later, Colts punt to Martin at Patriots' 12. Grogan completes three straight passes to Patriots' 44. Five consecutive runs put New England on Colts' 33. Davis kicks a 51-yard winning field goal for Patriots at 9:46.

Oct. 29, 1989—Green Bay 23, Detroit 20, at Milwaukee; Lions win toss. Sanders touchback on Jacke kickoff. On first play, Murphy intercepts Lions' Peete and returns it three yards to Lions' 26. Fullwood gains five yards on three plays to set up Jacke's 38-yard field goal at 2:14.

Nov. 5, 1989—Minnesota 23, Los Angeles Rams 21, at Minneapolis; Rams win toss. Karlis's kick returned 18 yards by Delpino to Rams' 19. Drive stops at Rams' 28. Merriweather blocks Hatcher's punt at 12. Ball rolls out of end zone for safety.

Nov. 19, 1989—Cleveland 10, Kansas City 10, at Cleveland; Browns win toss. Browns punt three times; Chiefs twice; before Kansas City's Lowery misses 47-yard field goal with 17 seconds remaining in overtime. Kosar's pass intercepted as time expired.

Nov. 26, 1989—Los Angeles Rams 20, New Orleans 17, at New Orleans; Saints win toss. Lansford's kickoff returned 27 yards to Saints' 30. After four plays, Barnhardt punts to Rams' 15. Saints penalized 35 yards for interference to Rams' 43. Three plays later, Everett hits Anderson with 14-yard pass to Saints' 40, then 26-yarder to put Rams in field goal position. Lansford kicks 31-yard field goal at 6:38.

Dec. 3, 1989—Los Angeles Raiders 16, Denver 13, at Los Angeles; Broncos win toss. Bell returns Jaeger kickoff 14 yards to Broncos' 18. Broncos' penalized for illegal block to Broncos' 9. Elway completes three passes for two first downs. On third and eight Elway sacked for 10-yard loss. Horan punts, Adams calls for fair catch at Raiders' 29. Dyal's 26-yard reception moves Raiders to Denver 43. Raiders move ball 34 yards in three plays to set up Jaeger's 26-yard field goal at 7:02.

Dec. 10, 1989—Indianapolis 23, Cleveland 17, at Indianapolis; Browns win toss. Teams trade punts. McNeil returns Colts' punt 42 yards to 42. Seven plays later, Bahr misses 35-yard field goal attempt. Three plays later, Stark punts and McNeil returns ball to 50-yard line. Two plays later, Prior intercepts Kosar's pass at Colts' 42 and returns it 58 yards for touchdown at 10:54.

Dec. 17, 1989—Cleveland 23, Minnesota 17, at Cleveland; Browns win toss. Browns punt to Vikings' 18. Six plays later, Vikings punt to Browns' 22. Nine plays later, Bahr lines up to attempt 31-yard field goal. Holder Pagel takes snap and passes 14 yards to Waiters for touchdown at 9:30.

Sept. 23, 1990—Denver 34, Seattle 31, at Denver; Seahawks win toss. Loville returns kickoff 19 yards to Seahawks' 27. Seahawks drive to Broncos' 26, where Johnson misses 44-yard field goal wide right. Broncos take over and Elway completes series of passes to set up Treadwell's 25-yard field goal at 9:14.

Sept. 30, 1990—Tampa Bay 23, Minnesota 20, at Minnesota; Vikings win toss. Vikings drive to Buccaneers' 31; Igwebuike's 48-yard field goal attempt wide left. Buccaneers drive to Vikings' 43 and punt. Gannon's pass is intercepted at Vikings' 26 by Wayne Haddix. Buccaneers drive to Vikings' 19 to set up Christie's 36-yard field goal at 9:11.

Oct. 7, 1990—Cincinnati 34, Los Angeles Rams 31, at Anaheim; Rams win toss. Berry returns kickoff to Rams' 21. After 3 plays, English punts and Green downs ball at Bengals' 25. After 3 plays, Johnson punts and Sutton downs ball at Rams' 29-yard line. After 3 plays, English punts and Price signals fair catch at Bengals' 47. Esiason completes series of passes to 26-yard line to set up Breech's 44-yard field goal at 11:56.

Nov. 4, 1990—Washington 41, Detroit 38, at Detroit; Redskins win toss. Howard downs kickoff on Redskins' 15. After 3 plays, Mojsiejenko punts to Redskins' 45. After 3 plays, Arnold punts to Redskins' 10. Rutledge completes series of passes to set up Lohmiller's 34-yard field goal at 9:10.

Nov. 18, 1990—Chicago 16, Denver 13, at Denver; Broncos win toss. Ezor returns kickoff to Broncos' 12. Both teams have ball twice and have to punt after each possession. Broncos punt after third possession of overtime and Bailey returns 20 yards to Broncos' 34. Harbaugh completes 10-yard pass to Thornton to set up Butler's 44-yard field goal at 13:14.

Nov. 25, 1990—Seattle 13, San Diego 10, at San Diego; Chargers win toss. Lewis returns kickoff to Chargers' 22. After 2 plays, Cox fumbles and ball is recovered by Porter at Chargers' 23. After two plays, Johnson kicks 40-yard field goal at 3:01.

Dec. 2, 1990—Chicago 23, Detroit 17, at Chicago; Lions win toss. Gray returns kickoff to Lions' 35. After 10 plays, Murray misses 35-yard field goal. Bears take possession at Chicago 20. Harbaugh completes 50-yard game-winning pass to Anderson at 10:57.

Dec. 2, 1990—Seattle 13, Houston 10, at Seattle; Seahawks win toss. Warren returns kickoff to Seahawks' 13. After 5 plays, Donnelly punts to Oilers' 23-yard line. Ford's fumble recovered by Wyman. Seahawks take possession at Oilers' 27. After 2 plays, Johnson kicks 42-yard field goal at 4:25.

Dec. 9, 1990—Miami 23, Philadelphia 20, at Miami; Eagles win toss. After 11 plays, Feagles punts to Dolphins' 26. After 6 plays, Roby punts to Eagles' 14 and Harris returns to 25. After 3 plays, Feagles punts to Dolphins' 43. Marino completes series of passes to Eagles' 22. Stoyanovich kicks 39-yard field goal at 12:32.

Dec. 9, 1990—San Francisco 20, Cincinnati 17, at Cincinnati; 49ers win toss. Carter returns kickoff to 49ers' 19. After 10 plays, Cofer kicks 23-yard field goal at 6:12.

Sept. 24, 1991—Chicago 19, New York Jets 13, at Chicago; Jets win toss. Mathis returns kickoff seven yards to New York's 12. Jets drive to New York 26; Bailey returns punt to Chicago 39. Bears drive to Jets' 44-yard line and punt into the end zone. Jets drive to Bears' 11 where Leahy's 28-yard field goal attempt is wide left. Bears drive from 20 to Jets' 1 where Harbaugh runs for touchdown at 14:42.

Oct. 13, 1991—Los Angeles Raiders 23, Seattle 20, at Seattle. Seahawks win toss. Seahawks begin on 20. After 5 plays, Tuten punts and Brown signals fair catch at Raiders' 24. After 3 plays, Gossett punts and Land downs ball at Seattle 9. After 1 play, Lott intercepts at Seahawks' 19 to set up Jaeger's game-winning 37-yard field goal at 6:37.

Oct. 20, 1991—Cleveland 30, San Diego 24, at San Diego; Chargers win toss. After kickoff, Chargers drive to Browns' 45 and punt to Browns' 6 where Hendrickson downs ball. Browns drive to 38 and punt; Taylor fair catches on Chargers' 14. After 3 plays, Brandon intercepts at Chargers' 30 and scores at 5:58.

Oct. 20, 1991—New England 26, Minnesota 23, at New England; Patriots win toss. Martin returns kickoff 18 yards to New England 22. Patriots drive to Minnesota 19. Staurovsky's 36-yard field goal attempt is wide left. Minnesota drives to the 50 where Newsome punts into end zone. On first play, McMillian intercepts at the 40 for Minnesota. After 2 plays, Marion causes Jordan fumble and Pool recovers at New England 20. New England drives to Minnesota 24 where Staurovsky kicks 42-yard field goal as time expires.

Nov. 3, 1991—New York Jets 19, Green Bay 16, at New York; Packers win toss. Thompson returns kickoff 30 yards to Packers' 39. Green Bay drives to New York 24 where Jacke's 42-yard field goal attempt is wide right. Jets drive to 50. Aguiar's punt is fumbled by Sikahema and recovered by New York at Packers' 23. After 2 plays, Leahy kicks 37-yard field goal at 9:40.

Nov. 3, 1991—Washington 16, Houston 13, at Washington; Redskins win toss. Mitchell returns kickoff 9 yards to Washington 14. After 4 plays, Goodburn punts and Givens returns to Houston 31. After 1 play, Moon's pass is intercepted by Green at the Houston 35. After 3 plays, Lohmiller kicks 41-yard field goal at 4:01.

Nov. 10, 1991—Houston 26, Dallas 23, at Houston; Oilers win toss. Pinkett returns kickoff 20 yards to Houston 24. After 6 plays, Montgomery punts and Martin returns to Dallas 24. Cowboys drive to Oilers' 24 where Smith fumbles and McDowell recovers at Oilers' 15. Houston drives to Dallas 5 where Del Greco kicks 23-yard field goal at 14:31.

Nov. 10, 1991—Pittsburgh 33, Cincinnati 27, at Cincinnati; Pittsburgh wins toss. Woodson downs kickoff for touchback. After 3 plays, Stryzinski punts and Barber returns 7 yards to Cincinnati 38. Bengals drive to Pittsburgh 37 where Woods fumbles and Lloyd returns recovery to Cincinnati 44. After 2 plays, O'Donnell passes to Green for 26-yard touchdown at 6:32.

Nov. 24, 1991—Atlanta 23, New Orleans 20, at New Orleans; Atlanta wins toss. Falcons begin at 20. After 3 plays, Fulhage punts and Fenerty signals fair catch at New Orleans 43. After 3 plays, Barnhardt punts and Thompson downs ball at Atlanta 23. After 3 plays, Fulhage punts and Fenerty fair catches at New Orleans 25. Saints drive to Atlanta 38 where Andersen misses 55-yard field-goal attempt. After 1 play, Rozier fumbles and Martin recovers on 50. Saints drive to Atlanta 38 where Barnhardt punts to Falcons' 2. Atlanta drives to New Orleans 33 where Johnson kicks 50-yard field goal at 13:03.

Nov. 24, 1991—Miami 16, Chicago 13, at Chicago; Miami wins toss. Butler kicks to Miami 20 where Paige returns kickoff 15 yards to 35. Miami drives to Chicago 9 where Stoyanovich kicks 27-yard field goal at 4:11.

Dec. 8, 1991—Buffalo 30, Los Angeles Raiders 27, at Los Angeles; Raiders win toss. Daluiso kicks into end zone for touchback. On third play, Kelso intercepts for Buffalo and returns ball to Bills' 36. Bills drive to Los Angeles 24 where Norwood kicks 42-yard field goal at 2:34.

December 8, 1991—Kansas City 20, San Diego 17, at Kansas City; Chiefs win toss. Carney kicks to Kansas City 10 where Stradford returns 23 yards to 33. After 3 plays, Barker punts to San Diego 4. Chargers drive to 40 where Kidd punts 60 yards into end zone for touchback. Kansas City drives to San Diego 39 where Barker punts 38 yards to 1. After 3 plays, Kidd punts 41 yards to San Diego 42 where Stradford returns 12 yards to 30. Chiefs drive to San Diego 1 where Lowery kicks 18-yard field goal at 11:26.

Dec. 8, 1991—New England 23, Indianapolis 17, at New England; Indianapolis wins toss. Baumann kicks off to Indianapolis 2 where Martin returns 23 yards to 25. After 3 downs, Stark punts to New England 17 where Henderson returns 8 yards to 25. New England drives to 50 where McCarthy punts and Prior signals fair catch at Indianapolis 15. After 3 plays, Stark punts to New England 40 where Henderson returns 7 yards to 47. After 2 plays, Millen passes to Timpson for 45-yard touchdown at 8:55.

Dec. 22, 1991—Detroit 17, Buffalo 14, at Buffalo; Detroit wins toss. Daluiso kicks off to Detroit 20 where Dozier returns 15 yards to the 35. Lions drive to Bills' 3 where Murray kicks 21-yard field goal at 4:23.

Dec. 22, 1991—New York Jets 23, Miami 20, at Miami; Jets win toss. Aguiar kicks to Miami's 30 where Logan returns 3 yards to the 33. After 4 downs, Stoyanovich punts to Jets' 15 where Baty returns 8 yards to 23. Jets drive to Miami 12 where Allegre kicks 30-yard field goal at 6:33.

*indicates Monday night game
#indicates Thursday night game

Postseason

Dec. 28, 1958—Baltimore 23, New York Giants 17, at New York; Giants win toss. Maynard returns kickoff to Giants' 20. Chandler punts and Taseff returns one yard to Colts' 20. Colts win at 8:15 on a one-yard run by Ameche.

Dec. 23, 1962—Dallas Texans 20, Houston Oilers 17, at Houston; Texans win toss and kick off. Jancik returns kickoff to Oilers' 33. Norton punts and Jackson makes fair catch on Texans' 22. Wilson punts and Jancik makes fair catch on Oilers' 45. Robinson intercepts Blanda's pass and returns 13 yards to Oilers' 47. Wilson's punt rolls dead at Oilers' 12. Hull intercepts Blanda's pass and returns 23 yards to midfield. Texans win at 17:54 on a 25-yard field goal by Brooker.

Dec. 26, 1965—Green Bay 13, Baltimore 10, at Green Bay; Packers win toss. Moore returns kickoff to Packers' 22. Chandler punts and Haymond returns nine yards to Colts' 41. Gilburg punts and Wood makes fair catch at Packers' 21. Chandler punts and Haymond returns one yard to Colts' 41. Michaels misses 47-yard field goal. Packers win at 13:39 on 25-yard field goal by Chandler.

Dec. 25, 1971—Miami 27, Kansas City 24, at Kansas City; Chiefs win toss. Podolak, after a lateral from Buchanan, returns kickoff to Chiefs' 46. Stenerud's 42-yard field goal is blocked. Seiple punts and Podolak makes fair catch at Chiefs' 17. Wilson punts and Scott returns 18 yards to Dolphins' 39. Yepremian misses 62-yard field goal. Scott intercepts Dawson's pass and returns 13 yards to Dolphins' 46. Seiple punts and Podolak loses one yard to Chiefs' 15. Wilson punts and Scott makes fair catch on Dolphins' 30. Dolphins win at 22:40 on a 37-yard field goal by Yepremian.

Dec. 24, 1977—Oakland 37, Baltimore 31, at Baltimore; Colts win toss. Raiders start on own 42 following a punt late in the first overtime. Oakland works way into field-goal range on Stabler's 19-yard pass to Branch at Colts' 26. Four plays later, on the second play of the second overtime, Stabler hits Casper with a 10-yard touchdown pass at 15:43.

Jan. 2, 1982—San Diego 41, Miami 38, at Miami; Chargers win toss. San Diego drives from its 13 to Miami 8. On second-and-goal, Benirschke misses 27-yard field goal attempt wide left at 9:15. Miami has the ball twice and San Diego twice more before the Dolphins get their third possession. Miami drives from the San Diego 46 to Chargers' 17 and on fourth-and-two, von Schamann's 34-yard field goal attempt is blocked by San Diego's Winslow after 11:27. Fouts then completes four of five passes, including a 39-yarder to Joiner that puts the ball on Dolphins' 10. On first down, Benirschke kicks a 29-yard field goal at 13:52. San Diego's winning drive covered 74 yards in six plays.

Jan. 3, 1987—Cleveland 23, New York Jets 20, at Cleveland; Jets win toss. Jets' punt downed at Browns' 26. Moseley's 23-yard field goal attempt is wide right. Teams trade punts. Jets' second punt downed at Browns' 31. First overtime period expires eight plays later with Browns in possession at Jets' 42. Moseley kicks 27-yard field goal four plays into second overtime at 17:02.

Jan. 11, 1987—Denver 23, Cleveland 20, at Cleveland; Browns win toss. Broncos hold Browns on four downs. Browns' punt returned four yards to Denver's 25. Elway completes 22- and 28-yard passes to set up Karlis's 33-yard field goal nine plays into drive at 5:38.

Jan. 3, 1988—Houston 23, Seattle 20, at Houston; Seahawks win toss. Rodriguez punts to K. Johnson who returns one yard to Houston 15. Zendejas kicks 32-yard field goal 12 plays later at 8:05.

Dec. 31, 1989—Pittsburgh 26, Houston 23, at Houston; Steelers win toss. Steelers punt to Oilers. Oilers' fumble recovered by Woodson and returned three yards. Four plays and 13 yards later, Anderson kicks a 50-yard field goal at 3:26.

Jan. 7, 1990—Los Angeles Rams 19, New York Giants 13, at New York; Rams win toss. Everett completes two passes to move ball to Giants' 48. White called for pass interference; ball spotted on Giants' 25. Everett hits Anderson with a 30-yard touchdown pass at 1:06.

NFL Postseason Overtime Games (By Length of Game)

Dec. 25, 1971	Miami 27, KANSAS CITY 24	82:40
Dec. 23, 1962	Dallas Texans 20, HOUSTON 17	77:54
Jan. 3, 1987	CLEVELAND 23, New York Jets 20	77:02
Dec. 24, 1977	Oakland 37, BALTIMORE 31	75:43
Jan. 2, 1982	San Diego 41, MIAMI 38	73:52
Dec. 26, 1965	GREEN BAY 13, Baltimore 10	73:39
Dec. 28, 1958	Baltimore 23, N.Y. GIANTS 17	68:15
Jan. 3, 1988	HOUSTON 23, Seattle 20	68:05
Jan. 11, 1987	Denver 23, CLEVELAND 20	65:38
Dec. 31, 1989	Pittsburgh 26, HOUSTON 23	63:26
Jan. 7, 1990	Los Angeles Rams 19, N.Y. GIANTS 13	61:06

Home team in CAPS

Overtime Won-Lost Records, 1974-1991 (Regular Season)

AFC	W	L	T
Buffalo	8	3	0
Cincinnati	8	5	0
Cleveland	11	8	1
Denver	11	6	2
Houston	5	10	0
Indianapolis	4	4	1
Kansas City	4	5	2
Los Angeles Raiders	9	5	0
Miami	6	10	1
New England	4	10	0
New York Jets	8	5	2
Pittsburgh	7	3	1
San Diego	7	9	0
Seattle	3	5	0

NFC	W	L	T
Atlanta	5	7	1
Chicago	9	8	0
Dallas	6	4	0
Detroit	5	7	1
Green Bay	5	7	4
Los Angeles Rams	5	5	1
Minnesota	8	7	2
New Orleans	2	6	0
New York Giants	6	6	1
Philadelphia	4	8	2
Phoenix	3	4	2
San Francisco	4	4	1
Tampa Bay	5	7	1
Washington	9	3	0

Overtime Games By Year (Regular Season)

1991-15	1982- 4
1990-10	1981-10
1989-11	1980-13
1988- 9	1979-12
1987-13	1978-11
1986-16	1977- 6
1985-10	1976- 5
1984- 9	1975- 9
1983-19	1974- 2

Overtime Game Summary—1974-1991

There have been 184 overtime games in regular-season play since the rule was adopted in 1974 (15 in 1991). Breakdown follows:

136 (13) times both teams had at least one possession (74%)

48 (2) times the team which won the coin toss drove for winning score (33 FG, 15 TD) (26%)

88 (8) times the team which won the coin toss won the game (48%)

83 (7) times the team which lost the coin toss won the game (45%)

119 (11) games were decided by a field goal (65%)

51 (4) games were decided by a touchdown (28%)

1 (0) game was decided by a safety (.5%)

13 (0) games ended tied (7.1%). Last time: Nov. 19, 1989, Cleveland 10, Kansas City 10, at Cleveland

Note: The number in parentheses represents the 1991 season total in each category.

Most Overtime Games, Season

5   Green Bay Packers, 1983
4   Denver Broncos, 1985
4   Cleveland Browns, 1989
3   By many teams, last time: New York Jets, 1991

Longest Consecutive Game Streaks Without Overtime (current)

81 Phoenix Cardinals (last OT game, 12/7/86 vs. Philadelphia)
68 Dallas Cowboys (last OT game, 11/26/87 vs. Minnesota)
52 New York Jets (last OT game, 11/20/88 vs. Buffalo)
52 New York Giants (last OT game, 11/20/88 vs. Philadelphia)

Shortest Overtime Games

0:21 (Chicago 23, Detroit 17; 11/27/80)—only kickoff return for TD
0:30 (Baltimore 29, New England 23; 9/4/83)
0:55 (New York Giants 16, Philadelphia 10; 9/29/85)

There have been 11 overtime postseason games dating back to 1958. In 10 cases, both teams had at least one possession. Last time: 1/7/90; Los Angeles Rams 19, New York Giants 13.

Longest Overtime Games (All Postseason Games)

22:40 Miami 27, Kansas City 24; 12/25/71
17:54 Dallas Texans 20, Houston 17; 12/23/62
17:02 Cleveland 23, New York Jets 20; 1/3/87

There have been 11 postseason overtime games dating back to 1958. Ten times, both teams had at least one possession. Last postseason overtime: Los Angeles Rams 19, New York Giants 13, 1/7/90.

Overtime Scoring Summary

119 were decided by a field goal

21 were decided by a touchdown pass

17 were decided by a touchdown run

5 were decided by interceptions (Atlanta 40, New Orleans 34, 9/2/79; Atlanta 47, Green Bay 41, 11/27/83; New York Giants 16, Philadelphia 10, 9/29/85; Indianapolis 23, Cleveland 17, 12/10/89; Cleveland 30, San Diego 24, 10/20/91)

2 were decided on a fake field goal/touchdown pass (Minnesota 22, Chicago 16, 10/16/77; Cleveland 23, Minnesota 17, 12/17/89)

1 was decided by a kickoff return (Chicago 23, Detroit 17, 11/27/80)

1 was decided by a fumble recovery (Baltimore 29, New England 23, 9/4/83)

1 was decided on a fake field goal/touchdown run (Los Angeles Rams 27, Minnesota 21, 12/2/79)

1 was decided on a blocked field goal (Denver 30, San Diego 24, 11/17/85)

1 was decided on a blocked field goal/recovery by kicker (Green Bay 12, Chicago 6, 9/7/80)

1 was decided on a blocked field goal/recovery by kicking team (Philadelphia 23, New York Giants 17, 11/20/88)

1 was decided by a safety (Minnesota 23, Los Angeles Rams 21, 11/5/89)

13 ended tied

NFL Paid Attendance

Year	Regular Season	Average	Postseason	Super Bowl
1991	13,841,459 (224 games)	61,792	813,247 (12)	63,130
1990#	13,959,896 (224 games)	#62,321	847,543 (12)	73,813
1989	13,625,662 (224 games)	60,829	685,771 (10)	72,919
1988	13,539,848 (224 games)	60,446	658,317 (10)	75,129
1987*	11,406,166 (210 games)	54,315	656,977 (10)	73,302
1986	13,588,551 (224 games)	60,663	734,002 (10)	101,063
1985	13,345,047 (224 games)	59,567	710,768 (10)	73,818
1984	13,398,112 (224 games)	59,813	665,194 (10)	84,059
1983	13,277,222 (224 games)	59,273	675,513 (10)	72,932
1982**	7,367,438 (126 games)	58,472	1,033,153 (16)	103,667
1981	13,606,990 (224 games)	60,745	637,763 (10)	81,270
1980	13,392,230 (224 games)	59,787	624,430 (10)	75,500
1979	13,182,039 (224 games)	58,848	630,326 (10)	103,985
1978	12,771,800 (224 games)	57,017	624,388 (10)	79,641
1977	11,018,632 (196 games)	56,218	534,925 (8)	75,804
1976	11,070,543 (196 games)	56,482	492,884 (8)	103,438
1975	10,213,193 (182 games)	56,116	475,919 (8)	80,187
1974	10,236,322 (182 games)	56,244	438,664 (8)	80,997
1973	10,730,933 (182 games)	58,961	525,433 (8)	71,882
1972	10,445,827 (182 games)	57,395	483,345 (8)	90,182
1971	10,076,035 (182 games)	55,363	483,891 (8)	81,023
1970	9,533,333 (182 games)	52,381	458,493 (8)	79,204
1969	6,096,127 (112 games) NFL	54,430	162,279 (3)	80,562
	2,843,373 (70 games) AFL	40,620	167,088 (3)	
1968	5,882,313 (112 games) NFL	52,521	215,902 (3)	75,377
	2,635,004 (70 games) AFL	37,643	114,438 (2)	
1967	5,938,924 (112 games) NFL	53,026	166,208 (3)	75,546
	2,295,697 (63 games) AFL	36,439	53,330 (1)	
1966	5,337,044 (105 games) NFL	50,829	74,152 (1)	†61,946
	2,160,369 (63 games) AFL	34,291	42,080 (1)	
1965	4,634,021 (98 games) NFL	47,286	100,304 (2)	
	1,782,384 (56 games) AFL	31,828	30,361 (1)	
1964	4,563,049 (98 games) NFL	46,562	79,544 (1)	
	1,447,875 (56 games) AFL	25,855	40,242 (1)	
1963	4,163,643 (98 games) NFL	42,486	45,801 (1)	
	1,208,697 (56 games) AFL	21,584	63,171 (2)	
1962	4,003,421 (98 games) NFL	40,851	64,892 (1)	
	1,147,302 (56 games) AFL	20,487	37,981 (1)	
1961	3,986,159 (98 games) NFL	40,675	39,029 (1)	
	1,002,657 (56 games) AFL	17,904	29,556 (1)	
1960	3,128,296 (78 games) NFL	40,106	67,325 (1)	
	926,156 (56 games) AFL	16,538	32,183 (1)	
1959	3,140,000 (72 games)	43,617	57,545 (1)	
1958	3,006,124 (72 games)	41,752	123,659 (2)	
1957	2,836,318 (72 games)	39,393	119,579 (2)	
1956	2,551,263 (72 games)	35,434	56,836 (1)	
1955	2,521,836 (72 games)	35,026	85,693 (1)	
1954	2,190,571 (72 games)	30,425	43,827 (1)	
1953	2,164,585 (72 games)	30,064	54,577 (1)	
1952	2,052,126 (72 games)	28,502	97,507 (2)	
1951	1,913,019 (72 games)	26,570	57,522 (1)	
1950	1,977,753 (78 games)	25,356	136,647 (3)	
1949	1,391,735 (60 games)	23,196	27,980 (1)	
1948	1,525,243 (60 games)	25,421	36,309 (1)	
1947	1,837,437 (60 games)	30,624	66,268 (2)	
1946	1,732,135 (55 games)	31,493	58,346 (1)	
1945	1,270,401 (50 games)	25,408	32,178 (1)	
1944	1,019,649 (50 games)	20,393	46,016 (1)	
1943	969,128 (40 games)	24,228	71,315 (2)	
1942	887,920 (55 games)	16,144	36,006 (1)	
1941	1,108,615 (55 games)	20,157	55,870 (2)	
1940	1,063,025 (55 games)	19,328	36,034 (1)	
1939	1,071,200 (55 games)	19,476	32,279 (1)	
1938	937,197 (55 games)	17,040	48,120 (1)	
1937	963,039 (55 games)	17,510	15,878 (1)	
1936	816,007 (54 games)	15,111	29,545 (1)	
1935	638,178 (53 games)	12,041	15,000 (1)	
1934	492,684 (60 games)	8,211	35,059 (1)	

Record

*Players' 24-day strike reduced 224-game schedule to 210 games.

**Players' 57-day strike reduced 224-game schedule to 126 games.

†Only Super Bowl that did not sell out.

NFL's 10 Biggest Attendance Weekends

(Paid Count)

Weekend	Games	Attendance
October 16-17, 1988	14	934,211
September 1-2, 1991	14	923,549
November 3-4, 1990	14	916,127
October 29-30, 1989	14	915,401
November 17-18, 1990	14	905,486
October 27-28, 1985	14	902,128
October 12-13, 1980	14	898,223
September 23-24, 1984	14	894,402
November 11-12, 1979	14	890,972
October 8-9, 1989	14	888,271

NFL's 10 Highest Scoring Weekends

Point Total	Date	Weekend
761	October 16-17, 1983	7th
736	October 25-26, 1987	7th
732	November 9-10, 1980	10th
725	November 24, 27-28, 1983	13th
714	September 17-18, 1989	2nd
711	November 26, 29-30, 1987	12th
710	November 28, December 1-2, 1985	13th
696	October 2-3, 1983	5th
693	September 24-25, 1989	3rd
676	September 21-22, 1980	3rd

Top 10 Televised Sports Events

(Based on A.C. Nielsen Figures)

Program	Date	Network	Share	Rating
Super Bowl XVI	1/24/82	CBS	73.0	49.1
Super Bowl XVII	1/30/83	NBC	69.0	48.6
Super Bowl XX	1/26/86	NBC	70.0	48.3
Super Bowl XII	1/15/78	CBS	67.0	47.2
Super Bowl XIII	1/21/79	NBC	74.0	47.1
Super Bowl XVIII	1/22/84	CBS	71.0	46.4
Super Bowl XIX	1/20/85	ABC	63.0	46.4
Super Bowl XIV	1/20/80	CBS	67.0	46.3
Super Bowl XXI	1/25/87	CBS	66.0	45.8
Super Bowl XI	1/9/77	NBC	73.0	44.4

Ten Most Watched TV Programs & Estimated Total Number of Viewers

(Based on A.C. Nielsen Figures)

Program	Date	Network	†Total Viewers
Super Bowl XX	Jan. 26, 1986	NBC	127,000,000
M*A*S*H (Special)	Feb. 28, 1983	CBS	121,624,000
Super Bowl XXVI	Jan. 26, 1992	CBS	120,000,000
Super Bowl XXI	Jan. 25, 1987	CBS	119,700,000
Super Bowl XIX	Jan. 20, 1985	ABC	115,936,000
Super Bowl XXII	Jan. 31, 1988	ABC	115,000,000
Super Bowl XXV	Jan. 27, 1991	ABC	112,140,000
Super Bowl XXIII	Jan. 22, 1989	NBC	110,800,000
Super Bowl XVI	Jan. 24, 1982	CBS	110,230,000
Super Bowl XVII	Jan. 30, 1983	NBC	109,040,000

†Watched some portion of the broadcast

NUMBER-ONE DRAFT CHOICES

Season	Team	Player	Position	College
1992	Indianapolis	Steve Emtman	DT	Washington
1991	Dallas	Russell Maryland	DT	Miami
1990	Indianapolis	Jeff George	QB	Illinois
1989	Dallas	Troy Aikman	QB	UCLA
1988	Atlanta	Aundray Bruce	LB	Auburn
1987	Tampa Bay	Vinny Testaverde	QB	Miami
1986	Tampa Bay	Bo Jackson	RB	Auburn
1985	Buffalo	Bruce Smith	DE	Virginia Tech
1984	New England	Irving Fryar	WR	Nebraska
1983	Baltimore	John Elway	QB	Stanford
1982	New England	Kenneth Sims	DT	Texas
1981	New Orleans	George Rogers	RB	South Carolina
1980	Detroit	Billy Sims	RB	Oklahoma
1979	Buffalo	Tom Cousineau	LB	Ohio State
1978	Houston	Earl Campbell	RB	Texas
1977	Tampa Bay	Ricky Bell	RB	Southern California
1976	Tampa Bay	Lee Roy Selmon	DE	Oklahoma
1975	Atlanta	Steve Bartkowski	QB	California
1974	Dallas	Ed Jones	DE	Tennessee State
1973	Houston	John Matuszak	DE	Tampa
1972	Buffalo	Walt Patulski	DE	Notre Dame
1971	New England	Jim Plunkett	QB	Stanford
1970	Pittsburgh	Terry Bradshaw	QB	Louisiana Tech
1969	Buffalo (AFL)	O.J. Simpson	RB	Southern California
1968	Minnesota	Ron Yary	T	Southern California
1967	Baltimore	Bubba Smith	DT	Michigan State
1966	Atlanta	Tommy Nobis	LB	Texas
	Miami (AFL)	Jim Grabowski	RB	Illinois
1965	New York Giants	Tucker Frederickson	RB	Auburn
	Houston (AFL)	Lawrence Elkins	E	Baylor
1964	San Francisco	Dave Parks	E	Texas Tech
	Boston (AFL)	Jack Concannon	QB	Boston College
1963	Los Angeles	Terry Baker	QB	Oregon State
	Kansas City (AFL)	Buck Buchanan	DT	Grambling
1962	Washington	Ernie Davis	RB	Syracuse
	Oakland (AFL)	Roman Gabriel	QB	North Carolina State
1961	Minnesota	Tommy Mason	RB	Tulane
	Buffalo (AFL)	Ken Rice	G	Auburn
1960	Los Angeles	Billy Cannon	RB	Louisiana State
	(AFL had no formal first pick)			
1959	Green Bay	Randy Duncan	QB	Iowa
1958	Chicago Cardinals	King Hill	QB	Rice
1957	Green Bay	Paul Hornung	HB	Notre Dame
1956	Pittsburgh	Gary Glick	DB	Colorado A&M
1955	Baltimore	George Shaw	QB	Oregon
1954	Cleveland	Bobby Garrett	QB	Stanford
1953	San Francisco	Harry Babcock	E	Georgia
1952	Los Angeles	Bill Wade	QB	Vanderbilt
1951	New York Giants	Kyle Rote	HB	Southern Methodist
1950	Detroit	Leon Hart	E	Notre Dame
1949	Philadelphia	Chuck Bednarik	C	Pennsylvania
1948	Washington	Harry Gilmer	QB	Alabama
1947	Chicago Bears	Bob Fenimore	HB	Oklahoma A&M
1946	Boston	Frank Dancewicz	QB	Notre Dame
1945	Chicago Cardinals	Charley Trippi	HB	Georgia
1944	Boston	Angelo Bertelli	QB	Notre Dame
1943	Detroit	Frank Sinkwich	HB	Georgia
1942	Pittsburgh	Bill Dudley	HB	Virginia
1941	Chicago Bears	Tom Harmon	HB	Michigan
1940	Chicago Cardinals	George Cafego	HB	Tennessee
1939	Chicago Cardinals	Ki Aldrich	C	Texas Christian
1938	Cleveland	Corbett Davis	FB	Indiana
1937	Philadelphia	Sam Francis	FB	Nebraska
1936	Philadelphia	Jay Berwanger	HB	Chicago

Note: From 1947 through 1958, the first selection in the draft was a Bonus pick, awarded to the winner of a random draw. That club, in turn, forfeited its last-round draft choice. The winner of the Bonus choice was eliminated from future draws. The system was abolished after 1958, by which time all clubs had received a Bonus choice.

If club had no first-round selection, first player drafted is listed with round in parentheses.

Atlanta Falcons

Year	Player, College, Position
1966	Tommy Nobis, Texas, LB
	Randy Johnson, Texas A&I, QB
1967	Leo Carroll, San Diego State, DE (2)
1968	Claude Humphrey, Tennessee State, DE
1969	George Kunz, Notre Dame, T
1970	John Small, Citadel, LB
1971	Joe Profit, Northeast Louisiana, RB
1972	Clarence Ellis, Notre Dame, DB
1973	Greg Marx, Notre Dame, DT (2)
1974	Gerald Tinker, Kent State, WR (2)
1975	Steve Bartkowski, California, QB
1976	Bubba Bean, Texas A&M, RB
1977	Warren Bryant, Kentucky, T
	Wilson Faumuina, San Jose State, DT
1978	Mike Kenn, Michigan, T
1979	Don Smith, Miami, DE
1980	Junior Miller, Nebraska, TE
1981	Bobby Butler, Florida State, DB
1982	Gerald Riggs, Arizona State, RB
1983	Mike Pitts, Alabama, DE
1984	Rick Bryan, Oklahoma, DT
1985	Bill Fralic, Pittsburgh, T
1986	Tony Casillas, Oklahoma, NT
	Tim Green, Syracuse, LB
1987	Chris Miller, Oregon, QB
1988	Aundray Bruce, Auburn, LB
1989	Deion Sanders, Florida State, DB
	Shawn Collins, Northern Arizona, WR
1990	Steve Broussard, Washington State, RB
1991	Bruce Pickens, Nebraska, DB
	Mike Pritchard, Colorado, WR
1992	Bob Whitfield, Stanford, T
	Tony Smith, Southern Mississippi, RB

Buffalo Bills

Year	Player, College, Position
1960	Richie Lucas, Penn State, QB
1961	Ken Rice, Auburn, T
1962	Ernie Davis, Syracuse, RB
1963	Dave Behrman, Michigan State, C
1964	Carl Eller, Minnesota, DE
1965	Jim Davidson, Ohio State, T
1966	Mike Dennis, Mississippi, RB
1967	John Pitts, Arizona State, S
1968	Haven Moses, San Diego State, WR
1969	O.J. Simpson, Southern California, RB
1970	Al Cowlings, Southern California, DE
1971	J. D. Hill, Arizona State, WR
1972	Walt Patulski, Notre Dame, DE
1973	Paul Seymour, Michigan, T
	Joe DeLamielleure, Michigan State, G
1974	Reuben Gant, Oklahoma State, TE
1975	Tom Ruud, Nebraska, LB
1976	Mario Clark, Oregon, DB
1977	Phil Dokes, Oklahoma State, DT
1978	Terry Miller, Oklahoma State, RB
1979	Tom Cousineau, Ohio State, LB
	Jerry Butler, Clemson, WR
1980	Jim Ritcher, North Carolina State, C
1981	Booker Moore, Penn State, RB
1982	Perry Tuttle, Clemson, WR
1983	Tony Hunter, Notre Dame, TE
	Jim Kelly, Miami, QB
1984	Greg Bell, Notre Dame, RB
1985	Bruce Smith, Virginia Tech, DE
	Derrick Burroughs, Memphis State, DB
1986	Ronnie Harmon, Iowa, RB
	Will Wolford, Vanderbilt, T
1987	Shane Conlan, Penn State, LB
1988	Thurman Thomas, Oklahoma State, RB (2)
1989	Don Beebe, Chadron, Neb., WR (3)
1990	James Williams, Fresno State, DB
1991	Henry Jones, Illinois, DB
1992	John Fina, Arizona, T

Chicago Bears

Year	Player, College, Position
1936	Joe Stydahar, West Virginia, T
1937	Les McDonald, Nebraska, E
1938	Joe Gray, Oregon State, B
1939	Sid Luckman, Columbia, QB
	Bill Osmanski, Holy Cross, B
1940	Clyde (Bulldog) Turner, Hardin-Simmons, C
1941	Tom Harmon, Michigan, B
	Norm Standlee, Stanford, B
	Don Scott, Ohio State, B
1942	Frankie Albert, Stanford, B
1943	Bob Steber, Missouri, B
1944	Ray Evans, Kansas, B
1945	Don Lund, Michigan, B
1946	Johnny Lujack, Notre Dame, QB
1947	Bob Fenimore, Oklahoma State, B
	Don Kindt, Wisconsin, B
1948	Bobby Layne, Texas, QB
	Max Bumgardner, Texas, E
1949	Dick Harris, Texas, C
1950	Chuck Hunsinger, Florida, B
	Fred Morrison, Ohio State, B
1951	Bob Williams, Notre Dame, B
	Billy Stone, Bradley, B
	Gene Schroeder, Virginia, E
1952	Jim Dooley, Miami, B
1953	Billy Anderson, Compton (Calif.) J.C., B
1954	Stan Wallace, Illinois, B
1955	Ron Drzewiecki, Marquette, B
1956	Menan (Tex) Schriewer, Texas, E
1957	Earl Leggett, Louisiana State, T
1958	Chuck Howley, West Virginia, G
1959	Don Clark, Ohio State, B
1960	Roger Davis, Syracuse, G
1961	Mike Ditka, Pittsburgh, E
1962	Ronnie Bull, Baylor, RB
1963	Dave Behrman, Michigan State, C
1964	Dick Evey, Tennessee, DT
1965	Dick Butkus, Illinois, LB
	Gale Sayers, Kansas, RB
	Steve DeLong, Tennessee, T
1966	George Rice, Louisiana State, DT
1967	Loyd Phillips, Arkansas, DE
1968	Mike Hull, Southern California, RB
1969	Rufus Mayes, Ohio State, T
1970	George Farmer, UCLA, WR (3)
1971	Joe Moore, Missouri, RB
1972	Lionel Antoine, Southern Illinois, T
	Craig Clemons, Iowa, DB
1973	Wally Chambers, Eastern Kentucky, DE
1974	Waymond Bryant, Tennessee State, LB
	Dave Gallagher, Michigan, DT
1975	Walter Payton, Jackson State, RB
1976	Dennis Lick, Wisconsin, T
1977	Ted Albrecht, California, T
1978	Brad Shearer, Texas, DT (3)
1979	Dan Hampton, Arkansas, DT
	Al Harris, Arizona State, DE
1980	Otis Wilson, Louisville, LB
1981	Keith Van Horne, Southern California, T
1982	Jim McMahon, Brigham Young, QB
1983	Jim Covert, Pittsburgh, T
	Willie Gault, Tennessee, WR
1984	Wilber Marshall, Florida, LB
1985	William Perry, Clemson, DT
1986	Neal Anderson, Florida, RB
1987	Jim Harbaugh, Michigan, QB
1988	Brad Muster, Stanford, RB
	Wendell Davis, Louisiana State, WR
1989	Donnell Woolford, Clemson, DB
	Trace Armstrong, Florida, DE
1990	Mark Carrier, Southern California, DB
1991	Stan Thomas, Texas, T
1992	Alonzo Spellman, Ohio State, DE

Cincinnati Bengals

Year	Player, College, Position
1968	Bob Johnson, Tennessee, C
1969	Greg Cook, Cincinnati, QB
1970	Mike Reid, Penn State, DT
1971	Vernon Holland, Tennessee State, T
1972	Sherman White, California, DE
1973	Isaac Curtis, San Diego State, WR
1974	Bill Kollar, Montana State, DT
1975	Glenn Cameron, Florida, LB
1976	Billy Brooks, Oklahoma, WR
	Archie Griffin, Ohio State, RB
1977	Eddie Edwards, Miami, DT
	Wilson Whitley, Houston, DT
	Mike Cobb, Michigan State, TE
1978	Ross Browner, Notre Dame, DT
	Blair Bush, Washington, C
1979	Jack Thompson, Washington State, QB
	Charles Alexander, Louisiana State, RB
1980	Anthony Muñoz, Southern California, T
1981	David Verser, Kansas, WR
1982	Glen Collins, Mississippi State, DE
1983	Dave Rimington, Nebraska, C
1984	Ricky Hunley, Arizona, LB
	Pete Koch, Maryland, DE
	Brian Blados, North Carolina, T
1985	Eddie Brown, Miami, WR
	Emanuel King, Alabama, LB
1986	Joe Kelly, Washington, LB
	Tim McGee, Tennessee, WR
1987	Jason Buck, Brigham Young, DE
1988	Rickey Dixon, Oklahoma, DB
1989	Eric Ball, UCLA, RB (2)
1990	James Francis, Baylor, LB
1991	Alfred Williams, Colorado, LB
1992	David Klingler, Houston, QB
	Darryl Williams, Miami, DB

Cleveland Browns

Year	Player, College, Position
1950	Ken Carpenter, Oregon State, B
1951	Ken Konz, Louisiana State, B
1952	Bert Rechichar, Tennessee, DB
	Harry Agganis, Boston U., QB
1953	Doug Atkins, Tennessee, DE
1954	Bobby Garrett, Stanford, QB
	John Bauer, Illinois, G
1955	Kurt Burris, Oklahoma, C
1956	Preston Carpenter, Arkansas, B
1957	Jim Brown, Syracuse, RB
1958	Jim Shofner, Texas Christian, DB
1959	Rich Kreitling, Illinois, DE
1960	Jim Houston, Ohio State, DE
1961	Bobby Crespino, Mississippi, TE
1962	Gary Collins, Maryland, WR
	Leroy Jackson, Western Illinois, RB
1963	Tom Hutchinson, Kentucky, WR
1964	Paul Warfield, Ohio State, WR
1965	James Garcia, Purdue, T (2)
1966	Milt Morin, Massachusetts, TE
1967	Bob Matheson, Duke, LB
1968	Marvin Upshaw, Trinity, Tex., DT-DE
1969	Ron Johnson, Michigan, RB
1970	Mike Phipps, Purdue, QB
	Bob McKay, Texas, T
1971	Clarence Scott, Kansas State, CB
1972	Thom Darden, Michigan, DB
1973	Steve Holden, Arizona State, WR
	Pete Adams, Southern California, T
1974	Billy Corbett, Johnson C. Smith, T (2)
1975	Mack Mitchell, Houston, DE
1976	Mike Pruitt, Purdue, RB
1977	Robert Jackson, Texas A&M, LB
1978	Clay Matthews, Southern California, LB
	Ozzie Newsome, Alabama, TE
1979	Willis Adams, Houston, WR
1980	Charles White, Southern California, RB
1981	Hanford Dixon, Southern Mississippi, DB
1982	Chip Banks, Southern California, LB
1983	Ron Brown, Arizona State, WR (2)
1984	Don Rogers, UCLA, DB
1985	Greg Allen, Florida State, RB (2)
1986	Webster Slaughter, San Diego State, WR (2)
1987	Mike Junkin, Duke, LB
1988	Clifford Charlton, Florida, LB
1989	Eric Metcalf, Texas, RB
1990	Leroy Hoard, Michigan, RB (2)
1991	Eric Turner, UCLA, DB
1992	Tommy Vardell, Stanford, RB

Dallas Cowboys

Year	Player, College, Position
1960	None
1961	Bob Lilly, Texas Christian, DT
1962	Sonny Gibbs, Texas Christian, QB (2)
1963	Lee Roy Jordan, Alabama, LB

1964	Scott Appleton, Texas, DT
1965	Craig Morton, California, QB
1966	John Niland, Iowa, G
1967	Phil Clark, Northwestern, DB (3)
1968	Dennis Homan, Alabama, WR
1969	Calvin Hill, Yale, RB
1970	Duane Thomas, West Texas State, RB
1971	Tody Smith, Southern California, DE
1972	Bill Thomas, Boston College, RB
1973	Billy Joe DuPree, Michigan State, TE
1974	Ed (Too Tall) Jones, Tennessee State, DE
	Charley Young, North Carolina State, RB
1975	Randy White, Maryland, LB
	Thomas Henderson, Langston, LB
1976	Aaron Kyle, Wyoming, DB
1977	Tony Dorsett, Pittsburgh, RB
1978	Larry Bethea, Michigan State, DE
1979	Robert Shaw, Tennessee, C
1980	Bill Roe, Colorado, LB (3)
1981	Howard Richards, Missouri, T
1982	Rod Hill, Kentucky State, DB
1983	Jim Jeffcoat, Arizona State, DE
1984	Billy Cannon, Jr., Texas A&M, LB
1985	Kevin Brooks, Michigan, DE
1986	Mike Sherrard, UCLA, WR
1987	Danny Noonan, Nebraska, DT
1988	Michael Irvin, Miami, WR
1989	Troy Aikman, UCLA, QB
1990	Emmitt Smith, Florida, RB
1991	Russell Maryland, Miami, DT
	Alvin Harper, Tennessee, WR
	Kelvin Pritchett, Mississippi, DT
1992	Kevin Smith, Texas A&M, DB
	Robert Jones, East Carolina, LB

Denver Broncos

Year	Player, College, Position
1960	Roger LeClerc, Trinity, Conn., C
1961	Bob Gaiters, New Mexico State, RB
1962	Merlin Olsen, Utah State, DT
1963	Kermit Alexander, UCLA, CB
1964	Bob Brown, Nebraska, T
1965	Dick Butkus, Illinois, LB (2)
1966	Jerry Shay, Purdue, DT
1967	Floyd Little, Syracuse, RB
1968	Curley Culp, Arizona State, DE (2)
1969	Grady Cavness, Texas-El Paso, DB (2)
1970	Bob Anderson, Colorado, RB
1971	Marv Montgomery, Southern California, T
1972	Riley Odoms, Houston, TE
1973	Otis Armstrong, Purdue, RB
1974	Randy Gradishar, Ohio State, LB
1975	Louis Wright, San Jose State, DB
1976	Tom Glassic, Virginia, G
1977	Steve Schindler, Boston College, G
1978	Don Latimer, Miami, DT
1979	Kelvin Clark, Nebraska, T
1980	Rulon Jones, Utah State, DE (2)
1981	Dennis Smith, Southern California, DB
1982	Gerald Willhite, San Jose State, RB
1983	Chris Hinton, Northwestern, T
1984	Andre Townsend, Mississippi, DE (2)
1985	Steve Sewell, Oklahoma, RB
1986	Jim Juriga, Illinois, T (4)
1987	Ricky Nattiel, Florida, WR
1988	Ted Gregory, Syracuse, NT
1989	Steve Atwater, Arkansas, DB
1990	Alton Montgomery, Houston, DB (2)
1991	Mike Croel, Nebraska, LB
1992	Tommy Maddox, UCLA, QB

Detroit Lions

Year	Player, College, Position
1936	Sid Wagner, Michigan State, G
1937	Lloyd Cardwell, Nebraska, B
1938	Alex Wojciechowicz, Fordham, C
1939	John Pingel, Michigan State, B
1940	Doyle Nave, Southern California, B
1941	Jim Thomason, Texas A&M, B
1942	Bob Westfall, Michigan, B
1943	Frank Sinkwich, Georgia, B
1944	Otto Graham, Northwestern, B
1945	Frank Szymanski, Notre Dame, C
1946	Bill Dellastatious, Missouri, B
1947	Glenn Davis, Army, B
1948	Y. A. Tittle, Louisiana State, B
1949	John Rauch, Georgia, B
1950	Leon Hart, Notre Dame, E

1951	Joe Watson, Rice, C
1951	Dick Stanfel, San Francisco, G (2)
1952	Yale Lary, Texas A&M, B (3)
1953	Harley Sewell, Texas, G
1954	Dick Chapman, Rice, T
1955	Dave Middleton, Auburn, B
1956	Hopalong Cassady, Ohio State, B
1957	Bill Glass, Baylor, G
1958	Alex Karras, Iowa, T
1959	Nick Pietrosante, Notre Dame, B
1960	John Robinson, Louisiana State, S
1961	Danny LaRose, Missouri, T (2)
1962	John Hadl, Kansas, QB
1963	Daryl Sanders, Ohio State, T
1964	Pete Beathard, Southern California, QB
1965	Tom Nowatzke, Indiana, RB
1966	Nick Eddy, Notre Dame, RB (2)
1967	Mel Farr, UCLA, RB
1968	Greg Landry, Massachusetts, QB
	Earl McCullouch, Southern California, WR
1969	Altie Taylor, Utah State, RB (2)
1970	Steve Owens, Oklahoma, RB
1971	Bob Bell, Cincinnati, DT
1972	Herb Orvis, Colorado, DE
1973	Ernie Price, Texas A&I, DE
1974	Ed O'Neil, Penn State, LB
1975	Lynn Boden, South Dakota State, G
1976	James Hunter, Grambling, DB
	Lawrence Gaines, Wyoming, RB
1977	Walt Williams, New Mexico State, DB (2)
1978	Luther Bradley, Notre Dame, DB
1979	Keith Dorney, Penn State, T
1980	Billy Sims, Oklahoma, RB
1981	Mark Nichols, San Jose State, WR
1982	Jimmy Williams, Nebraska, LB
1983	James Jones, Florida, RB
1984	David Lewis, California, TE
1985	Lomas Brown, Florida, T
1986	Chuck Long, Iowa, QB
1987	Reggie Rogers, Washington, DE
1988	Bennie Blades, Miami, DB
1989	Barry Sanders, Oklahoma State, RB
1990	Andre Ware, Houston, QB
1991	Herman Moore, Virginia, WR
1992	Robert Porcher, South Carolina State, DE

Green Bay Packers

Year	Player, College, Position
1936	Russ Letlow, San Francisco, G
1937	Eddie Jankowski, Wisconsin, B
1938	Cecil Isbell, Purdue, B
1939	Larry Buhler, Minnesota, B
1940	Harold Van Every, Minnesota, B
1941	George Paskvan, Wisconsin, B
1942	Urban Odson, Minnesota, T
1943	Dick Wildung, Minnesota, T
1944	Merv Pregulman, Michigan, G
1945	Walt Schlinkman, Texas Tech, B
1946	Johnny (Strike) Strzykalski, Marquette, B
1947	Ernie Case, UCLA, B
1948	Earl (Jug) Girard, Wisconsin, B
1949	Stan Heath, Nevada, B
1950	Clayton Tonnemaker, Minnesota, C
1951	Bob Gain, Kentucky, T
1952	Babe Parilli, Kentucky, QB
1953	Al Carmichael, Southern California, B
1954	Art Hunter, Notre Dame, T
	Veryl Switzer, Kansas State, B
1955	Tom Bettis, Purdue, G
1956	Jack Losch, Miami, B
1957	Paul Hornung, Notre Dame, B
	Ron Kramer, Michigan, E
1958	Dan Currie, Michigan State, C
1959	Randy Duncan, Iowa, B
1960	Tom Moore, Vanderbilt, RB
1961	Herb Adderley, Michigan State, CB
1962	Earl Gros, Louisiana State, RB
1963	Dave Robinson, Penn State, LB
1964	Lloyd Voss, Nebraska, DT
1965	Donny Anderson, Texas Tech, RB
	Lawrence Elkins, Baylor, E
1966	Jim Grabowski, Illinois, RB
	Gale Gillingham, Minnesota, T
1967	Bob Hyland, Boston College, C
	Don Horn, San Diego State, QB
1968	Fred Carr, Texas-El Paso, LB
	Bill Lueck, Arizona, G
1969	Rich Moore, Villanova, DT
1970	Mike McCoy, Notre Dame, DT

1971	Rich McGeorge, Elon, TE
	John Brockington, Ohio State, RB
1972	Willie Buchanon, San Diego State, DB
	Jerry Tagge, Nebraska, QB
1973	Barry Smith, Florida State, WR
1974	Barty Smith, Richmond, RB
1975	Bill Bain, Southern California, G (2)
1976	Mark Koncar, Colorado, T
1977	Mike Butler, Kansas, DE
	Ezra Johnson, Morris Brown, DE
1978	James Lofton, Stanford, WR
	John Anderson, Michigan, LB
1979	Eddie Lee Ivery, Georgia Tech, RB
1980	Bruce Clark, Penn State, DE
	George Cumby, Oklahoma, LB
1981	Rich Campbell, California, QB
1982	Ron Hallstrom, Iowa, G
1983	Tim Lewis, Pittsburgh, DB
1984	Alphonso Carreker, Florida State, DE
1985	Ken Ruettgers, Southern California, T
1986	Kenneth Davis, Texas Christian, RB (2)
1987	Brent Fullwood, Auburn, RB
1988	Sterling Sharpe, South Carolina, WR
1989	Tony Mandarich, Michigan State, T
1990	Tony Bennett, Mississippi, LB
	Darrell Thompson, Minnesota, RB
1991	Vinnie Clark, Ohio State, DB
1992	Terrell Buckley, Florida State, DB

Houston Oilers

Year	Player, College, Position
1960	Billy Cannon, Louisiana State, RB
1961	Mike Ditka, Pittsburgh, E
1962	Ray Jacobs, Howard Payne, DT
1963	Danny Brabham, Arkansas, LB
1964	Scott Appleton, Texas, DT
1965	Lawrence Elkins, Baylor, WR
1966	Tommy Nobis, Texas, LB
1967	George Webster, Michigan State, LB
	Tom Regner, Notre Dame, G
1968	Mac Haik, Mississippi, WR (2)
1969	Ron Pritchard, Arizona State, LB
1970	Doug Wilkerson, N. Carolina Central, G
1971	Dan Pastorini, Santa Clara, QB
1972	Greg Sampson, Stanford, DE
1973	John Matuszak, Tampa, DE
	George Amundson, Iowa State, RB
1974	Steve Manstedt, Nebraska, LB (4)
1975	Robert Brazile, Jackson State, LB
	Don Hardeman, Texas A&I, RB
1976	Mike Barber, Louisiana Tech, TE (2)
1977	Morris Towns, Missouri, T
1978	Earl Campbell, Texas, RB
1979	Mike Stensrud, Iowa State, DE (2)
1980	Angelo Fields, Michigan State, T (2)
1981	Michael Holston, Morgan State, WR (3)
1982	Mike Munchak, Penn State, G
1983	Bruce Matthews, Southern California, T
1984	Dean Steinkuhler, Nebraska, T
1985	Ray Childress, Texas A&M, DE
	Richard Johnson, Wisconsin, DB
1986	Jim Everett, Purdue, QB
1987	Alonzo Highsmith, Miami, RB
	Haywood Jeffires, North Carolina St., WR
1988	Lorenzo White, Michigan State, RB
1989	David Williams, Florida, T
1990	Lamar Lathon, Houston, LB
1991	Mike Dumas, Indiana, DB (2)
1992	Eddie Robinson, Alabama State, LB (2)

Indianapolis Colts

Year	Player, College, Position
1953	Billy Vessels, Oklahoma, B
1954	Cotton Davidson, Baylor, B
1955	George Shaw, Oregon, B
	Alan Ameche, Wisconsin, FB
1956	Lenny Moore, Penn State, B
1957	Jim Parker, Ohio State, G
1958	Lenny Lyles, Louisville, B
1959	Jackie Burkett, Auburn, C
1960	Ron Mix, Southern California, T
1961	Tom Matte, Ohio State, RB
1962	Wendell Harris, Louisiana State, S
1963	Bob Vogel, Ohio State, T
1964	Marv Woodson, Indiana, CB
1965	Mike Curtis, Duke, LB
1966	Sam Ball, Kentucky, T
1967	Bubba Smith, Michigan State, DT

	Jim Detwiler, Michigan, RB
1968	John Williams, Minnesota, G
1969	Eddie Hinton, Oklahoma, WR
1970	Norman Bulaich, Texas Christian, RB
1971	Don McCauley, North Carolina, RB
	Leonard Dunlap, North Texas State, DB
1972	Tom Drougas, Oregon, T
1973	Bert Jones, Louisiana State, QB
	Joe Ehrmann, Syracuse, DT
1974	John Dutton, Nebraska, DE
	Roger Carr, Louisiana Tech, WR
1975	Ken Huff, North Carolina, G
1976	Ken Novak, Purdue, DT
1977	Randy Burke, Kentucky, WR
1978	Reese McCall, Auburn, TE
1979	Barry Krauss, Alabama, LB
1980	Curtis Dickey, Texas A&M, RB
	Derrick Hatchett, Texas, DB
1981	Randy McMillan, Pittsburgh, RB
	Donnell Thompson, North Carolina, DT
1982	Johnie Cooks, Mississippi State, LB
	Art Schlichter, Ohio State, QB
1983	John Elway, Stanford, QB
1984	Leonard Coleman, Vanderbilt, DB
	Ron Solt, Maryland, G
1985	Duane Bickett, Southern California, LB
1986	Jon Hand, Alabama, DE
1987	Cornelius Bennett, Alabama, LB
1988	Chris Chandler, Washington, QB (3)
1989	Andre Rison, Michigan State, WR
1990	Jeff George, Illinois, QB
1991	Shane Curry, Miami, DE (2)
1992	Steve Emtman, Washington, DT
	Quentin Coryatt, Texas A&M, LB

Kansas City Chiefs

Year	Player, College, Position
1960	Don Meredith, Southern Methodist, QB
1961	E.J. Holub, Texas Tech, C
1962	Ronnie Bull, Baylor, RB
1963	Buck Buchanan, Grambling, DT
	Ed Budde, Michigan State, G
1964	Pete Beathard, Southern California, QB
1965	Gale Sayers, Kansas, RB
1966	Aaron Brown, Minnesota, DE
1967	Gene Trosch, Miami, DE-DT
1968	Mo Moorman, Texas A&M, G
	George Daney, Texas-El Paso, G
1969	Jim Marsalis, Tennessee State, CB
1970	Sid Smith, Southern California, T
1971	Elmo Wright, Houston, WR
1972	Jeff Kinney, Nebraska, RB
1973	Gary Butler, Rice, TE (2)
1974	Woody Green, Arizona State, RB
1975	Elmore Stephens, Kentucky, TE (2)
1976	Rod Walters, Iowa, G
1977	Gary Green, Baylor, DB
1978	Art Still, Kentucky, DE
1979	Mike Bell, Colorado State, DE
	Steve Fuller, Clemson, QB
1980	Brad Budde, Southern California, G
1981	Willie Scott, South Carolina, TE
1982	Anthony Hancock, Tennessee, WR
1983	Todd Blackledge, Penn State, QB
1984	Bill Maas, Pittsburgh, DT
	John Alt, Iowa, T
1985	Ethan Horton, North Carolina, RB
1986	Brian Jozwiak, West Virginia, T
1987	Paul Palmer, Temple, RB
1988	Neil Smith, Nebraska, DE
1989	Derrick Thomas, Alabama, LB
1990	Percy Snow, Michigan State, LB
1991	Harvey Williams, Louisiana State, RB
1992	Dale Carter, Tennessee, DB

Los Angeles Raiders

Year	Player, College, Position
1960	Dale Hackbart, Wisconsin, CB
1961	Joe Rutgens, Illinois, DT
1962	Roman Gabriel, North Carolina State, QB
1963	George Wilson, Alabama, RB (6)
1964	Tony Lorick, Arizona State, RB
1965	Harry Schuh, Memphis State, T
1966	Rodger Bird, Kentucky, S
1967	Gene Upshaw, Texas A&I, G
1968	Eldridge Dickey, Tennessee State, QB
1969	Art Thoms, Syracuse, DT
1970	Raymond Chester, Morgan State, TE

1971	Jack Tatum, Ohio State, S
1972	Mike Siani, Villanova, WR
1973	Ray Guy, Southern Mississippi, P
1974	Henry Lawrence, Florida A&M, T
1975	Neal Colzie, Ohio State, DB
1976	Charles Philyaw, Texas Southern, DT (2)
1977	Mike Davis, Colorado, DB (2)
1978	Dave Browning, Washington, DE (2)
1979	Willie Jones, Florida State, DE (2)
1980	Marc Wilson, Brigham Young, QB
1981	Ted Watts, Texas Tech, DB
	Curt Marsh, Washington, T
1982	Marcus Allen, Southern California, RB
1983	Don Mosebar, Southern California, T
1984	Sean Jones, Northeastern, DE (2)
1985	Jessie Hester, Florida State, WR
1986	Bob Buczkowski, Pittsburgh, DE
1987	John Clay, Missouri, T
1988	Tim Brown, Notre Dame, WR
	Terry McDaniel, Tennessee, DB
	Scott Davis, Illinois, DE
1989	Jeff Francis, Tennessee, QB (6)
1990	Anthony Smith, Arizona, DE
1991	Todd Marinovich, Southern California, QB
1992	Chester McGlockton, Clemson, DE

Los Angeles Rams

Year	Player, College, Position
1937	Johnny Drake, Purdue, B
1938	Corbett Davis, Indiana, B
1939	Parker Hall, Mississippi, B
1940	Ollie Cordill, Rice, B
1941	Rudy Mucha, Washington, C
1942	Jack Wilson, Baylor, B
1943	Mike Holovak, Boston College, B
1944	Tony Butkovich, Illinois, B
1945	Elroy (Crazylegs) Hirsch, Wisconsin, B
1946	Emil Sitko, Notre Dame, B
1947	Herman Wedemeyer, St. Mary's, Calif., B
1948	Tom Keane, West Virginia, B (2)
1949	Bobby Thomason, Virginia Military, B
1950	Ralph Pasquariello, Villanova, B
	Stan West, Oklahoma, G
1951	Bud McFadin, Texas, G
1952	Bill Wade, Vanderbilt, QB
	Bob Carey, Michigan State, E
1953	Donn Moomaw, UCLA, C
	Ed Barker, Washington State, E
1954	Ed Beatty, Cincinnati, C
1955	Larry Morris, Georgia Tech, C
1956	Joe Marconi, West Virginia, B
	Charles Horton, Vanderbilt, B
1957	Jon Arnett, Southern California, B
	Del Shofner, Baylor, E
1958	Lou Michaels, Kentucky, T
	Jim Phillips, Auburn, E
1959	Dick Bass, Pacific, B
	Paul Dickson, Baylor, T
1960	Billy Cannon, Louisiana State, RB
1961	Marlin McKeever, So. California, E-LB
1962	Roman Gabriel, North Carolina State, QB
	Merlin Olsen, Utah State, DT
1963	Terry Baker, Oregon State, QB
	Rufus Guthrie, Georgia Tech, G
1964	Bill Munson, Utah State, QB
1965	Clancy Williams, Washington State, CB
1966	Tom Mack, Michigan, G
1967	Willie Ellison, Texas Southern, RB (2)
1968	Gary Beban, UCLA, QB (2)
1969	Larry Smith, Florida, RB
	Jim Seymour, Notre Dame, WR
	Bob Klein, Southern California, TE
1970	Jack Reynolds, Tennessee, LB
1971	Isiah Robertson, Southern, LB
	Jack Youngblood, Florida, DE
1972	Jim Bertelsen, Texas, RB (2)
1973	Cullen Bryant, Colorado, DB (2)
1974	John Cappelletti, Penn State, RB
1975	Mike Fanning, Notre Dame, DT
	Dennis Harrah, Miami, T
	Doug France, Ohio State, T
1976	Kevin McLain, Colorado State, LB
1977	Bob Brudzinski, Ohio State, LB
1978	Elvis Peacock, Oklahoma, RB
1979	George Andrews, Nebraska, LB
	Kent Hill, Georgia Tech, T
1980	Johnnie Johnson, Texas, DB
1981	Mel Owens, Michigan, LB
1982	Barry Redden, Richmond, RB

1983	Eric Dickerson, Southern Methodist, RB
1984	Hal Stephens, East Carolina, DE (5)
1985	Jerry Gray, Texas, DB
1986	Mike Schad, Queen's University, Canada, T
1987	Donald Evans, Winston-Salem, DE (2)
1988	Gaston Green, UCLA, RB
	Aaron Cox, Arizona State, WR
1989	Bill Hawkins, Miami, DE
	Cleveland Gary, Miami, RB
1990	Bern Brostek, Washington, C
1991	Todd Lyght, Notre Dame, DB
1992	Sean Gilbert, Pittsburgh, DE

Miami Dolphins

Year	Player, College, Position
1966	Jim Grabowski, Illinois, RB
	Rick Norton, Kentucky, QB
1967	Bob Griese, Purdue, QB
1968	Larry Csonka, Syracuse, RB
	Doug Crusan, Indiana, T
1969	Bill Stanfill, Georgia, DE
1970	Jim Mandich, Michigan, TE (2)
1971	Otto Stowe, Iowa State, WR (2)
1972	Mike Kadish, Notre Dame, DT
1973	Chuck Bradley, Oregon, C (2)
1974	Donald Reese, Jackson State, DE
1975	Darryl Carlton, Tampa, T
1976	Larry Gordon, Arizona State, LB
	Kim Bokamper, San Jose State, LB
1977	A.J. Duhe, Louisiana State, DT
1978	Guy Benjamin, Stanford, QB (2)
1979	Jon Giesler, Michigan, T
1980	Don McNeal, Alabama, DB
1981	David Overstreet, Oklahoma, RB
1982	Roy Foster, Southern California, G
1983	Dan Marino, Pittsburgh, QB
1984	Jackie Shipp, Oklahoma, LB
1985	Lorenzo Hampton, Florida, RB
1986	John Offerdahl, Western Michigan, LB (2)
1987	John Bosa, Boston College, DE
1988	Eric Kumerow, Ohio State, DE
1989	Sammie Smith, Florida State, RB
	Louis Oliver, Florida, DB
1990	Richmond Webb, Texas A&M, T
1991	Randal Hill, Miami, WR
1992	Troy Vincent, Wisconsin, DB
	Marco Coleman, Georgia Tech, LB

Minnesota Vikings

Year	Player, College, Position
1961	Tommy Mason, Tulane, RB
1962	Bill Miller, Miami, WR (3)
1963	Jim Dunaway, Mississippi, T
1964	Carl Eller, Minnesota, DE
1965	Jack Snow, Notre Dame, WR
1966	Jerry Shay, Purdue, DT
1967	Clint Jones, Michigan State, RB
	Gene Washington, Michigan State, WR
	Alan Page, Notre Dame, DT
1968	Ron Yary, Southern California, T
1969	Ed White, California, G (2)
1970	John Ward, Oklahoma State, DT
1971	Leo Hayden, Ohio State, RB
1972	Jeff Siemon, Stanford, LB
1973	Chuck Foreman, Miami, RB
1974	Fred McNeill, UCLA, LB
	Steve Riley, Southern California, T
1975	Mark Mullaney, Colorado State, DE
1976	James White, Oklahoma State, DT
1977	Tommy Kramer, Rice, QB
1978	Randy Holloway, Pittsburgh, DE
1979	Ted Brown, North Carolina State, RB
1980	Doug Martin, Washington, DT
1981	Mardye McDole, Mississippi State, WR (2)
1982	Darrin Nelson, Stanford, RB
1983	Joey Browner, Southern California, DB
1984	Keith Millard, Washington State, DE
1985	Chris Doleman, Pittsburgh, LB
1986	Gerald Robinson, Auburn, DE
1987	D.J. Dozier, Penn State, RB
1988	Randall McDaniel, Arizona State, G
1989	David Braxton, Wake Forest, LB (2)
1990	Mike Jones, Texas A&M, TE (3)
1991	Carlos Jenkins, Michigan State, LB (3)
1992	Robert Harris, Southern University, DE (2)

New England Patriots

Year	Player, College, Position
1960	Ron Burton, Northwestern, RB
1961	Tommy Mason, Tulane, RB
1962	Gary Collins, Maryland, WR
1963	Art Graham, Boston College, WR
1964	Jack Concannon, Boston College, QB
1965	Jerry Rush, Michigan State, DE
1966	Karl Singer, Purdue, T
1967	John Charles, Purdue, S
1968	Dennis Byrd, North Carolina State, DE
1969	Ron Sellers, Florida State, WR
1970	Phil Olsen, Utah State, DE
1971	Jim Plunkett, Stanford, QB
1972	Tom Reynolds, San Diego State, WR (2)
1973	John Hannah, Alabama, G
	Sam Cunningham, So. California, RB
	Darryl Stingley, Purdue, WR
1974	Steve Corbett, Boston College, G (2)
1975	Russ Francis, Oregon, TE
1976	Mike Haynes, Arizona State, DB
	Pete Brock, Colorado, C
	Tim Fox, Ohio State, DB
1977	Raymond Clayborn, Texas, DB
	Stanley Morgan, Tennessee, WR
1978	Bob Cryder, Alabama, G
1979	Rick Sanford, South Carolina, DB
1980	Roland James, Tennessee, DB
	Vagas Ferguson, Notre Dame, RB
1981	Brian Holloway, Stanford, T
1982	Kenneth Sims, Texas, DT
	Lester Williams, Miami, DT
1983	Tony Eason, Illinois, QB
1984	Irving Fryar, Nebraska, WR
1985	Trevor Matich, Brigham Young, C
1986	Reggie Dupard, Southern Methodist, RB
1987	Bruce Armstrong, Louisville, T
1988	John Stephens, Northwestern St., La., RB
1989	Hart Lee Dykes, Oklahoma State, WR
1990	Chris Singleton, Arizona, LB
	Ray Agnew, North Carolina State, DE
1991	Pat Harlow, Southern California, T
	Leonard Russell, Arizona State, RB
1992	Eugene Chung, Virginia Tech, T

New Orleans Saints

Year	Player, College, Position
1967	Les Kelley, Alabama, RB
1968	Kevin Hardy, Notre Dame, DE
1969	John Shinners, Xavier, G
1970	Ken Burrough, Texas Southern, WR
1971	Archie Manning, Mississippi, QB
1972	Royce Smith, Georgia, G
1973	Derland Moore, Oklahoma, DE (2)
1974	Rick Middleton, Ohio State, LB
1975	Larry Burton, Purdue, WR
	Kurt Schumacher, Ohio State, T
1976	Chuck Muncie, California, RB
1977	Joe Campbell, Maryland, DE
1978	Wes Chandler, Florida, WR
1979	Russell Erxleben, Texas, P-K
1980	Stan Brock, Colorado, T
1981	George Rogers, South Carolina, RB
1982	Lindsay Scott, Georgia, WR
1983	Steve Korte, Arkansas, G (2)
1984	James Geathers, Wichita State, DE
1985	Alvin Toles, Tennessee, LB
1986	Jim Dombrowski, Virginia, T
1987	Shawn Knight, Brigham Young, DT
1988	Craig Heyward, Pittsburgh, RB
1989	Wayne Martin, Arkansas, DE
1990	Renaldo Turnbull, West Virginia, DE
1991	Wesley Carroll, Miami, WR (2)
1992	Vaughn Dunbar, Indiana, RB

New York Giants

Year	Player, College, Position
1936	Art Lewis, Ohio U., T
1937	Ed Widseth, Minnesota, T
1938	George Karamatic, Gonzaga, B
1939	Walt Neilson, Arizona, B
1940	Grenville Lansdell, Southern California, B
1941	George Franck, Minnesota, B
1942	Merle Hapes, Mississippi, B
1943	Steve Filipowicz, Fordham, B
1944	Billy Hillenbrand, Indiana, B
1945	Elmer Barbour, Wake Forest, B
1946	George Connor, Notre Dame, T
1947	Vic Schwall, Northwestern, B
1948	Tony Minisi, Pennsylvania, B
1949	Paul Page, Southern Methodist, B
1950	Travis Tidwell, Auburn, B
1951	Kyle Rote, Southern Methodist, B
	Jim Spavital, Oklahoma A&M, B
1952	Frank Gifford, Southern California, B
1953	Bobby Marlow, Alabama, B
1954	Ken Buck, Pacific, C (2)
1955	Joe Heap, Notre Dame, B
1956	Henry Moore, Arkansas, B (2)
1957	Sam DeLuca, South Carolina, T (2)
1958	Phil King, Vanderbilt, B
1959	Lee Grosscup, Utah, B
1960	Lou Cordileone, Clemson, G
1961	Bruce Tarbox, Syracuse, G (2)
1962	Jerry Hillebrand, Colorado, LB
1963	Frank Lasky, Florida, T (2)
1964	Joe Don Looney, Oklahoma, RB
1965	Tucker Frederickson, Auburn, RB
1966	Francis Peay, Missouri, T
1967	Louis Thompson, Alabama, DT (4)
1968	Dick Buzin, Penn State, T (2)
1969	Fred Dryer, San Diego State, DE
1970	Jim Files, Oklahoma, LB
1971	Rocky Thompson, West Texas State, WR
1972	Eldridge Small, Texas A&I, DB
	Larry Jacobson, Nebraska, DE
1973	Brad Van Pelt, Michigan State, LB (2)
1974	John Hicks, Ohio State, G
1975	Al Simpson, Colorado State, T (2)
1976	Troy Archer, Colorado, DE
1977	Gary Jeter, Southern California, DT
1978	Gordon King, Stanford, T
1979	Phil Simms, Morehead State, QB
1980	Mark Haynes, Colorado, DB
1981	Lawrence Taylor, North Carolina, LB
1982	Butch Woolfolk, Michigan, RB
1983	Terry Kinard, Clemson, DB
1984	Carl Banks, Michigan State, LB
	William Roberts, Ohio State, T
1985	George Adams, Kentucky, RB
1986	Eric Dorsey, Notre Dame, DE
1987	Mark Ingram, Michigan State, WR
1988	Eric Moore, Indiana, T
1989	Brian Williams, Minnesota, C-G
1990	Rodney Hampton, Georgia, RB
1991	Jarrod Bunch, Michigan, RB
1992	Derek Brown, Notre Dame, TE

New York Jets

Year	Player, College, Position
1960	George Izo, Notre Dame, QB
1961	Tom Brown, Minnesota, G
1962	Sandy Stephens, Minnesota, QB
1963	Jerry Stovall, Louisiana State, B
1964	Matt Snell, Ohio State, RB
1965	Joe Namath, Alabama, QB
	Tom Nowatzke, Indiana, RB
1966	Bill Yearby, Michigan, DT
1967	Paul Seiler, Notre Dame, T
1968	Lee White, Weber State, RB
1969	Dave Foley, Ohio State, T
1970	Steve Tannen, Florida, CB
1971	John Riggins, Kansas, RB
1972	Jerome Barkum, Jackson State, WR
	Mike Taylor, Michigan, LB
1973	Burgess Owens, Miami, DB
1974	Carl Barzilauskas, Indiana, DT
1975	Anthony Davis, Southern California, RB (2)
1976	Richard Todd, Alabama, QB
1977	Marvin Powell, Southern California, T
1978	Chris Ward, Ohio State, T
1979	Marty Lyons, Alabama, DE
1980	Johnny (Lam) Jones, Texas, WR
1981	Freeman McNeil, UCLA, RB
1982	Bob Crable, Notre Dame, LB
1983	Ken O'Brien, Cal-Davis, QB
1984	Russell Carter, Southern Methodist, DB
	Ron Faurot, Arkansas, DE
1985	Al Toon, Wisconsin, WR
1986	Mike Haight, Iowa, T
1987	Roger Vick, Texas A&M, RB
1988	Dave Cadigan, Southern California, T
1989	Jeff Lageman, Virginia, LB
1990	Blair Thomas, Penn State, RB
1991	Browning Nagle, Louisville, QB (2)
1992	Johnny Mitchell, Nebraska, TE

Philadelphia Eagles

Year	Player, College, Position
1936	Jay Berwanger, Chicago, B
1937	Sam Francis, Nebraska, B
1938	Jim McDonald, Ohio State, B
1939	Davey O'Brien, Texas Christian, B
1940	George McAfee, Duke, B
1941	Art Jones, Richmond, B (2)
1942	Pete Kmetovic, Stanford, B
1943	Joe Muha, Virginia Military, B
1944	Steve Van Buren, Louisiana State, B
1945	John Yonaker, Notre Dame, E
1946	Leo Riggs, Southern California, B
1947	Neill Armstrong, Oklahoma A&M, E
1948	Clyde (Smackover) Scott, Arkansas, B
1949	Chuck Bednarik, Pennsylvania, C
	Frank Tripucka, Notre Dame, B
1950	Harry (Bud) Grant, Minnesota, E
1951	Ebert Van Buren, Louisiana State, B
	Chet Mutryn, Xavier, B
1952	Johnny Bright, Drake, B
1953	Al Conway, Army, B (2)
1954	Neil Worden, Notre Dame, B
1955	Dick Bielski, Maryland, B
1956	Bob Pellegrini, Maryland, C
1957	Clarence Peaks, Michigan State, B
1958	Walt Kowalczyk, Michigan State, B
1959	J. D. Smith, Rice, T (2)
1960	Ron Burton, Northwestern, RB
1961	Art Baker, Syracuse, RB
1962	Pete Case, Georgia, G (2)
1963	Ed Budde, Michigan State, G
1964	Bob Brown, Nebraska, T
1965	Ray Rissmiller, Georgia, T (2)
1966	Randy Beisler, Indiana, DE
1967	Harry Jones, Arkansas, RB
1968	Tim Rossovich, Southern California, DE
1969	Leroy Keyes, Purdue, RB
1970	Steve Zabel, Oklahoma, TE
1971	Richard Harris, Grambling, DE
1972	John Reaves, Florida, QB
1973	Jerry Sisemore, Texas, T
	Charle Young, Southern California, TE
1974	Mitch Sutton, Kansas, DT (3)
1975	Bill Capraun, Miami, T (7)
1976	Mike Smith, Florida, DE (4)
1977	Skip Sharp, Kansas, DB (5)
1978	Reggie Wilkes, Georgia Tech, LB (3)
1979	Jerry Robinson, UCLA, LB
1980	Roynell Young, Alcorn State, DB
1981	Leonard Mitchell, Houston, DE
1982	Mike Quick, North Carolina State, WR
1983	Michael Haddix, Mississippi State, RB
1984	Kenny Jackson, Penn State, WR
1985	Kevin Allen, Indiana, T
1986	Keith Byars, Ohio State, RB
1987	Jerome Brown, Miami, DT
1988	Keith Jackson, Oklahoma, TE
1989	Jessie Small, Eastern Kentucky, LB (2)
1990	Ben Smith, Georgia, DB
1991	Antone Davis, Tennessee, T
1992	Siran Stacy, Alabama, RB (2)

Phoenix Cardinals

Year	Player, College, Position
1936	Jim Lawrence, Texas Christian, B
1937	Ray Buivid, Marquette, B
1938	Jack Robbins, Arkansas, B
1939	Charles (Ki) Aldrich, Texas Christian, C
1940	George Cafego, Tennessee, B
1941	John Kimbrough, Texas A&M, B
1942	Steve Lach, Duke, B
1943	Glenn Dobbs, Tulsa, B
1944	Pat Harder, Wisconsin, B
1945	Charley Trippi, Georgia, B
1946	Dub Jones, Louisiana State, B
1947	DeWitt (Tex) Coulter, Army, T
1948	Jim Spavital, Oklahoma A&M, B
1949	Bill Fischer, Notre Dame, G
1950	Jack Jennings, Ohio State, T (2)
1951	Jerry Groom, Notre Dame, C
1952	Ollie Matson, San Francisco, B
1953	Johnny Olszewski, California, B
1954	Lamar McHan, Arkansas, B
1955	Max Boydston, Oklahoma, E
1956	Joe Childress, Auburn, B
1957	Jerry Tubbs, Oklahoma, C
1958	King Hill, Rice, B

	John David Crow, Texas A&M, B
1959	Bill Stacy, Mississippi State, B
1960	George Izo, Notre Dame, QB
1961	Ken Rice, Auburn, T
1962	Fate Echols, Northwestern, DT
	Irv Goode, Kentucky, C
1963	Jerry Stovall, Louisiana State, S
	Don Brumm, Purdue, DE
1964	Ken Kortas, Louisville, DT
1965	Joe Namath, Alabama, QB
1966	Carl McAdams, Oklahoma, LB
1967	Dave Williams, Washington, WR
1968	MacArthur Lane, Utah State, RB
1969	Roger Wehrli, Missouri, DB
1970	Larry Stegent, Texas A&M, RB
1971	Norm Thompson, Utah, CB
1972	Bobby Moore, Oregon, RB-WR
1973	Dave Butz, Purdue, DT
1974	J. V. Cain, Colorado, TE
1975	Tim Gray, Texas A&M, DB
1976	Mike Dawson, Arizona, DT
1977	Steve Pisarkiewicz, Missouri, QB
1978	Steve Little, Arkansas, K
	Ken Greene, Washington State, DB
1979	Ottis Anderson, Miami, RB
1980	Curtis Greer, Michigan, DE
1981	E. J. Junior, Alabama, LB
1982	Luis Sharpe, UCLA, T
1983	Leonard Smith, McNeese State, DB
1984	Clyde Duncan, Tennessee, WR
1985	Freddie Joe Nunn, Mississippi, LB
1986	Anthony Bell, Michigan State, LB
1987	Kelly Stouffer, Colorado State, QB
1988	Ken Harvey, California, LB
1989	Eric Hill, Louisiana State, LB
	Joe Wolf, Boston College, G
1990	Anthony Thompson, Indiana, RB (2)
1991	Eric Swann, No College, DE
1992	Tony Sacca, Penn State, QB (2)

Pittsburgh Steelers

Year	Player, College, Position
1936	Bill Shakespeare, Notre Dame, B
1937	Mike Basrak, Duquesne, C
1938	Byron (Whizzer) White, Colorado, B
1939	Bill Patterson, Baylor, B (3)
1940	Kay Eakin, Arkansas, B
1941	Chet Gladchuk, Boston College, C (2)
1942	Bill Dudley, Virginia, B
1943	Bill Daley, Minnesota, B
1944	Johnny Podesto, St. Mary's, Calif., B
1945	Paul Duhart, Florida, B
1946	Felix (Doc) Blanchard, Army, B
1947	Hub Bechtol, Texas, E
1948	Dan Edwards, Georgia, E
1949	Bobby Gage, Clemson, B
1950	Lynn Chandnois, Michigan State, B
1951	Butch Avinger, Alabama, B
1952	Ed Modzelewski, Maryland, B
1953	Ted Marchibroda, St. Bonaventure, B
1954	Johnny Lattner, Notre Dame, B
1955	Frank Varrichione, Notre Dame, T
1956	Gary Glick, Colorado A&M, B
	Art Davis, Mississippi State, B
1957	Len Dawson, Purdue, B
1958	Larry Krutko, West Virginia, B (2)
1959	Tom Barnett, Purdue, B (8)
1960	Jack Spikes, Texas Christian, RB
1961	Myron Pottios, Notre Dame, LB (2)
1962	Bob Ferguson, Ohio State, RB
1963	Frank Atkinson, Stanford, T (8)
1964	Paul Martha, Pittsburgh, S
1965	Roy Jefferson, Utah, WR (2)
1966	Dick Leftridge, West Virginia, RB
1967	Don Shy, San Diego State, RB (2)
1968	Mike Taylor, Southern California, T
1969	Joe Greene, North Texas State, DT
1970	Terry Bradshaw, Louisiana Tech, QB
1971	Frank Lewis, Grambling, WR
1972	Franco Harris, Penn State, RB
1973	J. T. Thomas, Florida State, DB
1974	Lynn Swann, Southern California, WR
1975	Dave Brown, Michigan, DB
1976	Bennie Cunningham, Clemson, TE
1977	Robin Cole, New Mexico, LB
1978	Ron Johnson, Eastern Michigan, DB
1979	Greg Hawthorne, Baylor, RB
1980	Mark Malone, Arizona State, QB
1981	Keith Gary, Oklahoma, DE

Year	Player, College, Position
1982	Walter Abercrombie, Baylor, RB
1983	Gabriel Rivera, Texas Tech, DT
1984	Louis Lipps, Southern Mississippi, WR
1985	Darryl Sims, Wisconsin, DE
1986	John Rienstra, Temple, G
1987	Rod Woodson, Purdue, DB
1988	Aaron Jones, Eastern Kentucky, DE
1989	Tim Worley, Georgia, RB
	Tom Ricketts, Pittsburgh, T
1990	Eric Green, Liberty, TE
1991	Huey Richardson, Florida, DE
1992	Leon Searcy, Miami, T

San Diego Chargers

Year	Player, College, Position
1960	Monty Stickles, Notre Dame, E
1961	Earl Faison, Indiana, DE
1962	Bob Ferguson, Ohio State, RB
1963	Walt Sweeney, Syracuse, G
1964	Ted Davis, Georgia Tech, LB
1965	Steve DeLong, Tennessee, DE
1966	Don Davis, Cal State-Los Angeles, DT
1967	Ron Billingsley, Wyoming, DE
1968	Russ Washington, Missouri, DT
	Jimmy Hill, Texas A&I, DB
1969	Marty Domres, Columbia, QB
	Bob Babich, Miami, Ohio, LB
1970	Walker Gillette, Richmond, WR
1971	Leon Burns, Long Beach State, RB
1972	Pete Lazetich, Stanford, DE (2)
1973	Johnny Rodgers, Nebraska, WR
1974	Bo Matthews, Colorado, RB
	Don Goode, Kansas, LB
1975	Gary Johnson, Grambling, DT
	Mike Williams, Louisiana State, DB
1976	Joe Washington, Oklahoma, RB
1977	Bob Rush, Memphis State, C
1978	John Jefferson, Arizona State, WR
1979	Kellen Winslow, Missouri, TE
1980	Ed Luther, San Jose State, QB (4)
1981	James Brooks, Auburn, RB
1982	Hollis Hall, Clemson, DB (7)
1983	Billy Ray Smith, Arkansas, LB
	Gary Anderson, Arkansas, WR
	Gill Byrd, San Jose State, DB
1984	Mossy Cade, Texas, DB
1985	Jim Lachey, Ohio State, G
1986	Leslie O'Neal, Oklahoma State, DE
	James FitzPatrick, Southern California, T
1987	Rod Bernstine, Texas A&M, TE
1988	Anthony Miller, Tennessee, WR
1989	Burt Grossman, Pittsburgh, DE
1990	Junior Seau, Southern California, LB
1991	Stanley Richard, Texas, DB
1992	Chris Mims, Tennessee, DE

San Francisco 49ers

Year	Player, College, Position
1950	Leo Nomellini, Minnesota, T
1951	Y.A. Tittle, Louisiana State, B
1952	Hugh McElhenny, Washington, B
1953	Harry Babcock, Georgia, E
	Tom Stolhandske, Texas, E
1954	Bernie Faloney, Maryland, B
1955	Dickie Moegle, Rice, B
1956	Earl Morrall, Michigan State, B
1957	John Brodie, Stanford, B
1958	Jim Pace, Michigan, B
	Charlie Krueger, Texas A&M, T
1959	Dave Baker, Oklahoma, B
	Dan James, Ohio State, C
1960	Monty Stickles, Notre Dame, E
1961	Jimmy Johnson, UCLA, CB
	Bernie Casey, Bowling Green, WR
	Bill Kilmer, UCLA, QB
1962	Lance Alworth, Arkansas, WR
1963	Kermit Alexander, UCLA, CB
1964	Dave Parks, Texas Tech, WR
1965	Ken Willard, North Carolina, RB
	George Donnelly, Illinois, DB
1966	Stan Hindman, Mississippi, DE
1967	Steve Spurrier, Florida, QB
	Cas Banaszek, Northwestern, T
1968	Forrest Blue, Auburn, C
1969	Ted Kwalick, Penn State, TE
	Gene Washington, Stanford, WR
1970	Cedrick Hardman, North Texas State, DE
	Bruce Taylor, Boston U., DB

Year	Player, College, Position
1971	Tim Anderson, Ohio State, DB
1972	Terry Beasley, Auburn, WR
1973	Mike Holmes, Texas Southern, DB
1974	Wilbur Jackson, Alabama, RB
	Bill Sandifer, UCLA, DT
1975	Jimmy Webb, Mississippi State, DT
1976	Randy Cross, UCLA, C (2)
1977	Elmo Boyd, Eastern Kentucky, WR (3)
1978	Ken MacAfee, Notre Dame, TE
	Dan Bunz, Cal State-Long Beach, LB
1979	James Owens, UCLA, WR (2)
1980	Earl Cooper, Rice, RB
	Jim Stuckey, Clemson, DT
1981	Ronnie Lott, Southern California, DB
1982	Bubba Paris, Michigan, T (2)
1983	Roger Craig, Nebraska, RB (2)
1984	Todd Shell, Brigham Young, LB
1985	Jerry Rice, Mississippi Valley State, WR
1986	Larry Roberts, Alabama, DE (2)
1987	Harris Barton, North Carolina, T
	Terrence Flagler, Clemson, RB
1988	Danny Stubbs, Miami, DE (2)
1989	Keith DeLong, Tennessee, LB
1990	Dexter Carter, Florida State, RB
1991	Ted Washington, Louisville, DT
1992	Dana Hall, Washington, DB

Seattle Seahawks

Year	Player, College, Position
1976	Steve Niehaus, Notre Dame, DT
1977	Steve August, Tulsa, G
1978	Keith Simpson, Memphis State, DB
1979	Manu Tuiasosopo, UCLA, DT
1980	Jacob Green, Texas A&M, DE
1981	Ken Easley, UCLA, DB
1982	Jeff Bryant, Clemson, DE
1983	Curt Warner, Penn State, RB
1984	Terry Taylor, Southern Illinois, DB
1985	Owen Gill, Iowa, RB (2)
1986	John L. Williams, Florida, RB
1987	Tony Woods, Pittsburgh, LB
1988	Brian Blades, Miami, WR (2)
1989	Andy Heck, Notre Dame, T
1990	Cortez Kennedy, Miami, DT
1991	Dan McGwire, San Diego State, QB
1992	Ray Roberts, Virginia, T

Tampa Bay Buccaneers

Year	Player, College, Position
1976	Lee Roy Selmon, Oklahoma, DT
1977	Ricky Bell, Southern California, RB
1978	Doug Williams, Grambling, QB
1979	Greg Roberts, Oklahoma, G (2)
1980	Ray Snell, Wisconsin, G
1981	Hugh Green, Pittsburgh, LB
1982	Sean Farrell, Penn State, G
1983	Randy Grimes, Baylor, C (2)
1984	Keith Browner, Southern California, LB (2)
1985	Ron Holmes, Washington, DE
1986	Bo Jackson, Auburn, RB
	Roderick Jones, Southern Methodist, DB
1987	Vinny Testaverde, Miami, QB
1988	Paul Gruber, Wisconsin, T
1989	Broderick Thomas, Nebraska, LB
1990	Keith McCants, Alabama, LB
1991	Charles McRae, Tennessee, T
1992	Courtney Hawkins, Michigan State, WR (2)

Washington Redskins

Year	Player, College, Position
1936	Riley Smith, Alabama, B
1937	Sammy Baugh, Texas Christian, B
1938	Andy Farkas, Detroit, B
1939	I.B. Hale, Texas Christian, T
1940	Ed Boell, New York U., B
1941	Forest Evashevski, Michigan, B
1942	Orban (Spec) Sanders, Texas, B
1943	Jack Jenkins, Missouri, B
1944	Mike Micka, Colgate, B
1945	Jim Hardy, Southern California, B
1946	Cal Rossi, UCLA, B*
1947	Cal Rossi, UCLA, B
1948	Harry Gilmer, Alabama, B
	Lowell Tew, Alabama, B
1949	Rob Goode, Texas A&M, B
1950	George Thomas, Oklahoma, B

1951 Leon Heath, Oklahoma, B
1952 Larry Isbell, Baylor, B
1953 Jack Scarbath, Maryland, B
1954 Steve Meilinger, Kentucky, E
1955 Ralph Guglielmi, Notre Dame, B
1956 Ed Vereb, Maryland, B
1957 Don Bosseler, Miami, B
1958 Mike Sommer, George Washington, B (2)
1959 Don Allard, Boston College, B
1960 Richie Lucas, Penn State, QB
1961 Norman Snead, Wake Forest, QB
     Joe Rutgens, Illinois, DT
1962 Ernie Davis, Syracuse, RB
1963 Pat Richter, Wisconsin, TE
1964 Charley Taylor, Arizona State, RB-WR
1965 Bob Breitenstein, Tulsa, T (2)
1966 Charlie Gogolak, Princeton, K
1967 Ray McDonald, Idaho, RB
1968 Jim Smith, Oregon, DB
1969 Eugene Epps, Texas-El Paso, DB (2)
1970 Bill Brundige, Colorado, DT (2)
1971 Cotton Speyrer, Texas, WR (2)
1972 Moses Denson, Maryland State, RB (8)
1973 Charles Cantrell, Lamar, G (5)
1974 Jon Keyworth, Colorado, TE (6)
1975 Mike Thomas, Nevada-Las Vegas, RB (6)
1976 Mike Hughes, Baylor, G (5)
1977 Duncan McColl, Stanford, DE (4)
1978 Tony Green, Florida, RB (6)
1979 Don Warren, San Diego State, TE (4)
1980 Art Monk, Syracuse, WR
1981 Mark May, Pittsburgh, T
1982 Vernon Dean, San Diego State, DB (2)
1983 Darrell Green, Texas A&I, DB
1984 Bob Slater, Oklahoma, DT (2)
1985 Tory Nixon, San Diego State, DB (2)
1986 Markus Koch, Boise State, DE (2)
1987 Brian Davis, Nebraska, DB (2)
1988 Chip Lohmiller, Minnesota, K (2)
1989 Tracy Rocker, Auburn, DT (3)
1990 Andre Collins, Penn State, LB (2)
1991 Bobby Wilson, Michigan State, DT
1992 Desmond Howard, Michigan, WR
*Choice lost due to ineligibility.

RECORDS

All-Time Records 318

Outstanding Performers 339

Yearly Statistical Leaders 345

Super Bowl Records 353

Postseason Game Records 361

AFC-NFC Pro Bowl Game Records 370

Compiled by Elias Sports Bureau

The following records reflect all available official information on the National Football League from its formation in 1920 to date. Also included are all applicable records from the American Football League, 1960-69.

Individual Records

Service

Most Seasons
- 26 George Blanda, Chi. Bears, 1949, 1950-58; Baltimore, 1950; Houston, 1960-66; Oakland, 1967-75
- 21 Earl Morrall, San Francisco, 1956; Pittsburgh, 1957-58; Detroit, 1958-64; N.Y. Giants, 1965-67; Baltimore, 1968-71; Miami, 1972-76
- 20 Jim Marshall, Cleveland, 1960; Minnesota, 1961-79

Most Seasons, One Club
- 19 Jim Marshall, Minnesota, 1961-79
- 18 Jim Hart, St. Louis, 1966-83
  Jeff Van Note, Atlanta, 1969-86
  Pat Leahy, N.Y. Jets, 1974-91
- 17 Lou Groza, Cleveland, 1950-59, 1961-67
  Johnny Unitas, Baltimore, 1956-72
  John Brodie, San Francisco, 1957-73
  Jim Bakken, St. Louis, 1962-78
  Mick Tingelhoff, Minnesota, 1962-78

Most Games Played, Career
- 340 George Blanda, Chi. Bears, 1949, 1950-58; Baltimore, 1950; Houston, 1960-66; Oakland, 1967-75
- 282 Jim Marshall, Cleveland, 1960; Minnesota, 1961-79
- 263 Jan Stenerud, Kansas City, 1967-79; Green Bay, 1980-83; Minnesota, 1984-85

Most Consecutive Games Played, Career
- 282 Jim Marshall, Cleveland, 1960; Minnesota, 1961-79
- 240 Mick Tingelhoff, Minnesota, 1962-78
- 234 Jim Bakken, St. Louis, 1962-78

Head Coach

Most Seasons, Head Coach
- 40 George Halas, Chi. Bears, 1920-29, 1933-42, 1946-55, 1958-67
- 33 Earl (Curly) Lambeau, Green Bay, 1921-49; Chi. Cardinals, 1950-51; Washington, 1952-53
- 29 Tom Landry, Dallas, 1960-88
  Don Shula, Baltimore, 1963-69; Miami, 1970-91

Most Games Won, Head Coach
- 319 George Halas, Chi. Bears, 1920-29, 1933-42, 1946-55, 1958-67
- 289 Don Shula, Baltimore, 1963-69; Miami, 1970-91
- 250 Tom Landry, Dallas, 1960-88

Most Games Lost, Head Coach
- 162 Tom Landry, Dallas, 1960-88
- 148 George Halas, Chi. Bears, 1920-29, 1933-42, 1946-55, 1958-67
  Chuck Noll, Pittsburgh, 1969-91
- 132 Earl (Curly) Lambeau, Green Bay, 1921-49; Chi. Cardinals, 1950-51; Washington, 1952-53

Scoring

Most Seasons Leading League
- 5 Don Hutson, Green Bay, 1940-44
  Gino Cappelletti, Boston, 1961, 1963-66
- 3 Earl (Dutch) Clark, Portsmouth, 1932; Detroit, 1935-36
  Pat Harder, Chi. Cardinals, 1947-49
  Paul Hornung, Green Bay, 1959-61
- 2 Jack Manders, Chi. Bears, 1934, 1937
  Gordy Soltau, San Francisco, 1952-53
  Doak Walker, Detroit, 1950, 1955
  Gene Mingo, Denver, 1960, 1962
  Jim Turner, N.Y. Jets, 1968-69
  Fred Cox, Minnesota, 1969-70
  Chester Marcol, Green Bay, 1972, 1974
  John Smith, New England, 1979-80

Most Consecutive Seasons Leading League
- 5 Don Hutson, Green Bay, 1940-44
- 4 Gino Cappelletti, Boston, 1963-66
- 3 Pat Harder, Chi. Cardinals, 1947-49
  Paul Hornung, Green Bay, 1959-61

Points

Most Points, Career
- 2,002 George Blanda, Chi. Bears, 1949, 1950-58; Baltimore, 1950; Houston, 1960-66; Oakland, 1967-75 (9-td, 943-pat, 335-fg)
- 1,699 Jan Stenerud, Kansas City, 1967-79; Green Bay, 1980-83; Minnesota, 1984-85 (580-pat, 373-fg)
- 1,470 Pat Leahy, N.Y. Jets, 1974-91 (558-pat, 304-fg)

Most Points, Season
- 176 Paul Hornung, Green Bay, 1960 (15-td, 41-pat, 15-fg)
- 161 Mark Moseley, Washington, 1983 (62-pat, 33-fg)
- 155 Gino Cappelletti, Boston, 1964 (7-td, 38-pat, 25-fg)

Most Points, No Touchdowns, Season
- 161 Mark Moseley, Washington, 1983 (62-pat, 33-fg)
- 149 Chip Lohmiller, Washington, 1991 (56-pat, 31-fg)
- 145 Jim Turner, N.Y. Jets, 1968 (43-pat, 34-fg)

Most Seasons, 100 or More Points
- 9 Nick Lowery, Kansas City, 1981, 1983-86, 1988-91
- 7 Jan Stenerud, Kansas City, 1967-71; Green Bay, 1981, 1983
- 6 Gino Cappelletti, Boston, 1961-66
  George Blanda, Houston, 1960-61; Oakland, 1967-69, 1973
  Bruce Gossett, Los Angeles, 1966-67, 1969; San Francisco, 1970-71, 1973
  Morten Andersen, New Orleans, 1985-89, 1991
  Pat Leahy, N.Y. Jets, 1978, 1981, 1985, 1988, 1990-91

Most Points, Rookie, Season
- 144 Kevin Butler, Chicago, 1985 (51-pat, 31-fg)

- 132 Gale Sayers, Chicago, 1965 (22-td)
- 128 Doak Walker, Detroit, 1950 (11-td, 38-pat, 8-fg)
  Cookie Gilchrist, Buffalo, 1962 (15-td, 14-pat, 8-fg)
  Chester Marcol, Green Bay, 1972 (29-pat, 33-fg)

Most Points, Game
- 40 Ernie Nevers, Chi. Cardinals vs. Chi. Bears, Nov. 28, 1929 (6-td, 4-pat)
- 36 Dub Jones, Cleveland vs. Chi. Bears, Nov. 25, 1951 (6-td)
  Gale Sayers, Chicago vs. San Francisco, Dec. 12, 1965 (6-td)
- 33 Paul Hornung, Green Bay vs. Baltimore, Oct. 8, 1961 (4-td, 6-pat, 1-fg)

Most Consecutive Games Scoring
- 181 Jim Breech, Oakland, 1979; Cincinnati, 1980-91 (current)
- 151 Fred Cox, Minnesota, 1963-73
- 133 Garo Yepremian, Miami, 1970-78; New Orleans, 1979

Touchdowns

Most Seasons Leading League
- 8 Don Hutson, Green Bay, 1935-38, 1941-44
- 3 Jim Brown, Cleveland, 1958-59, 1963
  Lance Alworth, San Diego, 1964-66
- 2 By many players

Most Consecutive Seasons Leading League
- 4 Don Hutson, Green Bay, 1935-38, 1941-44
- 3 Lance Alworth, San Diego, 1964-66
- 2 By many players

Most Touchdowns, Career
- 126 Jim Brown, Cleveland, 1957-65 (106-r, 20-p)
- 125 Walter Payton, Chicago, 1975-87 (110-r, 15-p)
- 116 John Riggins, N.Y. Jets, 1971-75; Washington, 1976-79, 1981-85 (104-r, 12-p)

Most Touchdowns, Season
- 24 John Riggins, Washington, 1983 (24-r)
- 23 O.J. Simpson, Buffalo, 1975 (16-r, 7-p)
  Jerry Rice, San Francisco, 1987 (1-r, 22-p)
- 22 Gale Sayers, Chicago, 1965 (14-r, 6-p, 2-ret)
  Chuck Foreman, Minnesota, 1975 (13-r, 9-p)

Most Touchdowns, Rookie, Season
- 22 Gale Sayers, Chicago, 1965 (14-r, 6-p, 2-ret)
- 20 Eric Dickerson, L.A. Rams, 1983 (18-r, 2-p)
- 16 Billy Sims, Detroit, 1980 (13-r, 3-p)

Most Touchdowns, Game
- 6 Ernie Nevers, Chi. Cardinals vs. Chi. Bears, Nov. 28, 1929 (6-r)
  Dub Jones, Cleveland vs. Chi. Bears, Nov. 25, 1951 (4-r, 2-p)
  Gale Sayers, Chicago vs. San Francisco, Dec. 12, 1965 (4-r, 1-p, 1-ret)
- 5 Bob Shaw, Chi. Cardinals vs. Baltimore, Oct. 2, 1950 (5-p)
  Jim Brown, Cleveland vs. Baltimore, Nov. 1, 1959 (5-r)
  Abner Haynes, Dall. Texans vs. Oakland, Nov. 26, 1961 (4-r, 1-p)
  Billy Cannon, Houston vs. N.Y. Titans, Dec. 10, 1961 (3-r, 2-p)
  Cookie Gilchrist, Buffalo vs. N.Y. Jets, Dec. 8, 1963 (5-r)
  Paul Hornung, Green Bay vs. Baltimore, Dec. 12, 1965 (3-r, 2-p)
  Kellen Winslow, San Diego vs. Oakland, Nov. 22, 1981 (5-p)
  Jerry Rice, San Francisco vs. Atlanta, Oct. 14, 1990 (5-p)
- 4 By many players

Most Consecutive Games Scoring Touchdowns
- 18 Lenny Moore, Baltimore, 1963-65
- 14 O.J. Simpson, Buffalo, 1975
- 13 John Riggins, Washington, 1982-83
  Jerry Rice, San Francisco, 1986-87

Points After Touchdown

Most Seasons Leading League
- 8 George Blanda, Chi. Bears, 1956; Houston, 1961-62; Oakland, 1967-69, 1972, 1974
- 4 Bob Waterfield, Cleveland, 1945; Los Angeles, 1946, 1950, 1952
- 3 Earl (Dutch) Clark, Portsmouth, 1932; Detroit, 1935-36
  Jack Manders, Chi. Bears, 1933-35
  Don Hutson, Green Bay, 1941-42, 1945

Most Points After Touchdown Attempted, Career
- 959 George Blanda, Chi. Bears, 1949, 1950-58; Baltimore, 1950; Houston, 1960-66; Oakland, 1967-75
- 657 Lou Groza, Cleveland, 1950-59, 1961-67
- 601 Jan Stenerud, Kansas City, 1967-79; Green Bay, 1980-83; Minnesota, 1984-85

Most Points After Touchdown Attempted, Season
- 70 Uwe von Schamann, Miami, 1984
- 65 George Blanda, Houston, 1961
- 63 Mark Moseley, Washington, 1983

Most Points After Touchdown Attempted, Game
- 10 Charlie Gogolak, Washington vs. N.Y. Giants, Nov. 27, 1966
- 9 Pat Harder, Chi. Cardinals vs. N.Y. Giants, Oct. 17, 1948; vs. N.Y. Bulldogs, Nov. 13, 1949
  Bob Waterfield, Los Angeles vs. Baltimore, Oct. 22, 1950
  Bob Thomas, Chicago vs. Green Bay, Dec. 7, 1980
- 8 By many players

Most Points After Touchdown, Career
- 943 George Blanda, Chi. Bears, 1949, 1950-58; Baltimore, 1950; Houston, 1960-66; Oakland, 1967-75
- 641 Lou Groza, Cleveland, 1950-59, 1961-67
- 580 Jan Stenerud, Kansas City, 1967-79; Green Bay, 1980-83; Minnesota, 1984-85

Most Points After Touchdown, Season
- 66 Uwe von Schamann, Miami, 1984
- 64 George Blanda, Houston, 1961
- 62 Mark Moseley, Washington, 1983

Most Points After Touchdown, Game
- 9 Pat Harder, Chi. Cardinals vs. N.Y. Giants, Oct. 17, 1948
  Bob Waterfield, Los Angeles vs. Baltimore, Oct. 22, 1950
  Charlie Gogolak, Washington vs. N.Y. Giants, Nov. 27, 1966
- 8 By many players

Most Consecutive Points After Touchdown
- 234 Tommy Davis, San Francisco, 1959-65
- 221 Jim Turner, N.Y. Jets, 1967-70; Denver, 1971-74
- 202 Gary Anderson, Pittsburgh, 1983-88

Highest Points After Touchdown Percentage, Career (200 points after touchdown)
99.43 Tommy Davis, San Francisco, 1959-69 (350-348)
99.38 Gary Anderson, Pittsburgh, 1982-91 (325-323)
99.03 Nick Lowery, New England, 1978; Kansas City, 1980-91 (414-410)

Most Points After Touchdown, No Misses, Season
56 Danny Villanueva, Dallas, 1966
   Ray Wersching, San Francisco, 1984
   Chip Lohmiller, Washington, 1991
54 Mike Clark, Dallas, 1968
   George Blanda, Oakland, 1968
53 Pat Harder, Chi. Cardinals, 1948

Most Points After Touchdown, No Misses, Game
9 Pat Harder, Chi. Cardinals vs. N.Y. Giants, Oct. 17, 1948
   Bob Waterfield, Los Angeles vs. Baltimore, Oct. 22, 1950
8 By many players

Field Goals

Most Seasons Leading League
5 Lou Groza, Cleveland, 1950, 1952-54, 1957
4 Jack Manders, Chi. Bears, 1933-34, 1936-37
   Ward Cuff, N.Y. Giants, 1938-39, 1943; Green Bay, 1947
   Mark Moseley, Washington, 1976-77, 1979, 1982
3 Bob Waterfield, Los Angeles, 1947, 1949, 1951
   Gino Cappelletti, Boston, 1961, 1963-64
   Fred Cox, Minnesota, 1965, 1969-70
   Jan Stenerud, Kansas City, 1967, 1970, 1975

Most Consecutive Seasons Leading League
3 Lou Groza, Cleveland, 1952-54
2 By many players

Most Field Goals Attempted, Career
638 George Blanda, Chi. Bears, 1949, 1950-58; Baltimore, 1950; Houston, 1960-66; Oakland, 1967-75
558 Jan Stenerud, Kansas City, 1967-79; Green Bay, 1980-83; Minnesota, 1984-85
488 Jim Turner, N.Y. Jets, 1964-70; Denver, 1971-79

Most Field Goals Attempted, Season
49 Bruce Gossett, Los Angeles, 1966
   Curt Knight, Washington, 1971
48 Chester Marcol, Green Bay, 1972
47 Jim Turner, N.Y. Jets, 1969
   David Ray, Los Angeles, 1973
   Mark Moseley, Washington, 1983

Most Field Goals Attempted, Game
9 Jim Bakken, St. Louis vs. Pittsburgh, Sept. 24, 1967
8 Lou Michaels, Pittsburgh vs. St. Louis, Dec. 2, 1962
   Garo Yepremian, Detroit vs. Minnesota, Nov. 13, 1966
   Jim Turner, N.Y. Jets vs. Buffalo, Nov. 3, 1968
7 By many players

Most Field Goals, Career
373 Jan Stenerud, Kansas City, 1967-79; Green Bay, 1980-83; Minnesota, 1984-85
335 George Blanda, Chi. Bears, 1949, 1950-58; Baltimore, 1950; Houston, 1960-66; Oakland, 1967-75
304 Jim Turner, N.Y. Jets, 1964-70; Denver, 1971-79
   Pat Leahy, N.Y. Jets, 1974-91

Most Field Goals, Season
35 Ali Haji-Sheikh, N.Y. Giants, 1983
34 Jim Turner, N.Y. Jets, 1968
   Nick Lowery, Kansas City, 1990
33 Chester Marcol, Green Bay, 1972
   Mark Moseley, Washington, 1983
   Gary Anderson, Pittsburgh, 1985

Most Field Goals, Rookie, Season
35 Ali Haji-Sheikh, N.Y. Giants, 1983
33 Chester Marcol, Green Bay, 1972
31 Kevin Butler, Chicago, 1985

Most Field Goals, Game
7 Jim Bakken, St. Louis vs. Pittsburgh, Sept. 24, 1967
   Rich Karlis, Minnesota vs. L.A. Rams, Nov. 5, 1989 (OT)
6 Gino Cappelletti, Boston vs. Denver, Oct. 4, 1964
   Garo Yepremian, Detroit vs. Minnesota, Nov. 13, 1966
   Jim Turner, N.Y. Jets vs. Buffalo, Nov. 3, 1968
   Tom Dempsey, Philadelphia vs. Houston, Nov. 12, 1972
   Bobby Howfield, N.Y. Jets vs. New Orleans, Dec. 3, 1972
   Jim Bakken, St. Louis vs. Atlanta, Dec. 9, 1973
   Joe Danelo, N.Y. Giants vs. Seattle, Oct. 18, 1981
   Ray Wersching, San Francisco vs. New Orleans, Oct. 16, 1983
   Gary Anderson, Pittsburgh vs. Denver, Oct. 23, 1988
5 By many players

Most Field Goals, One Quarter
4 Garo Yepremian, Detroit vs. Minnesota, Nov. 13, 1966 (second quarter)
   Curt Knight, Washington vs. N.Y. Giants, Nov. 15, 1970 (second quarter)
   Roger Ruzek, Dallas vs. N.Y. Giants, Nov. 2, 1987 (fourth quarter)
3 By many players

Most Consecutive Games Scoring Field Goals
31 Fred Cox, Minnesota, 1968-70
28 Jim Turner, N.Y. Jets, 1970; Denver, 1971-72
   Chip Lohmiller, Washington, 1988-90
23 Morten Andersen, New Orleans, 1986-88

Most Consecutive Field Goals
24 Kevin Butler, Chicago, 1988-89
23 Mark Moseley, Washington, 1981-82
   Tony Zendejas, Houston, 1990; L.A. Rams, 1991 (current)
22 Pat Leahy, N.Y. Jets, 1985-86

Longest Field Goal
63 Tom Dempsey, New Orleans vs. Detroit, Nov. 8, 1970
60 Steve Cox, Cleveland vs. Cincinnati, Oct. 21, 1984
   Morten Andersen, New Orleans vs. Chicago, Oct. 27, 1991
59 Tony Franklin, Philadelphia vs. Dallas, Nov. 12, 1979
   Pete Stoyanovich, Miami vs. N.Y. Jets, Nov. 12, 1989

Highest Field Goal Percentage, Career (100 field goals)
79.33 Nick Lowery, New England, 1978; Kansas City, 1980-91 (358-284)
77.22 Morten Andersen, New Orleans, 1982-91 (281-217)
76.33 Gary Anderson, Pittsburgh, 1982-91 (300-229)

Highest Field Goal Percentage, Season (Qualifiers)
100.00 Tony Zendejas, L.A. Rams, 1991 (17-17)
95.24 Mark Moseley, Washington, 1982 (21-20)
   Eddie Murray, Detroit, 1988 (21-20)
   Eddie Murray, Detroit, 1989 (21-20)
91.89 Nick Lowery, Kansas City, 1990 (37-34)

Most Field Goals, No Misses, Game
7 Rich Karlis, Minnesota vs. L.A. Rams, Nov. 5, 1989 (OT)
6 Gino Cappelletti, Boston vs. Denver, Oct. 4, 1964
   Joe Danelo, N.Y. Giants vs. Seattle, Oct. 18, 1981
   Ray Wersching, San Francisco vs. New Orleans, Oct. 16, 1983
   Gary Anderson, Pittsburgh vs. Denver, Oct. 23, 1988
5 By many players

Most Field Goals, 50 or More Yards, Career
18 Nick Lowery, New England, 1978; Kansas City, 1980-91
   Morten Andersen, New Orleans, 1982-91
17 Jan Stenerud, Kansas City, 1967-79; Green Bay, 1980-83; Minnesota, 1984-85
16 Eddie Murray, Detroit, 1980-91

Most Field Goals, 50 or More Yards, Season
6 Dean Biasucci, Indianapolis, 1988
5 Fred Steinfort, Denver, 1980
   Norm Johnson, Seattle, 1986
4 Horst Muhlmann, Cincinnati, 1970
   Mark Moseley, Washington, 1977
   Nick Lowery, Kansas City, 1980
   Raul Allegre, Baltimore, 1983
   Kevin Butler, Chicago, 1990
   Ken Willis, Dallas, 1991

Most Field Goals, 50 or More Yards, Game
2 Jim Martin, Detroit vs. Baltimore, Oct. 23, 1960
   Tom Dempsey, New Orleans vs. Los Angeles, Dec. 6, 1970
   Chris Bahr, Cincinnati vs. Houston, Sept. 23, 1979
   Nick Lowery, Kansas City vs. Seattle, Sept. 14, 1980
   Mark Moseley, Washington vs. New Orleans, Oct. 26, 1980
   Fred Steinfort, Denver vs. Seattle, Dec. 21, 1980
   Mick Luckhurst, Atlanta vs. Denver, Dec. 5, 1982
   Morten Andersen, New Orleans vs. Philadelphia, Dec. 11, 1983
   Mick Luckhurst, Atlanta vs. L.A. Rams, Oct. 7, 1984
   Paul McFadden, Philadelphia vs. Detroit, Nov. 4, 1984
   Nick Lowery, Kansas City vs. New Orleans, Sept. 8, 1985
   Pat Leahy, N.Y. Jets vs. New England, Oct. 20, 1985
   Tony Zendejas, Houston vs. San Diego, Nov. 24, 1985
   Norm Johnson, Seattle vs. L.A. Raiders, Dec. 8, 1986
   Raul Allegre, N.Y. Giants vs. Philadelphia, Nov. 15, 1987
   Nick Lowery, Kansas City vs. Detroit, Nov. 26, 1987
   Dean Biasucci, Indianapolis vs. Miami, Sept. 25, 1988
   Paul McFadden, Atlanta vs. Buffalo, Nov. 5, 1989
   Kevin Butler, Chicago vs. Minnesota, Sept. 23, 1990
   Kevin Butler, Chicago vs. Green Bay, Oct. 7, 1990
   Chip Lohmiller, Washington vs. Indianapolis, Dec. 22, 1990
   Chip Lohmiller, Washington vs. Dallas, Sept. 9, 1991
   John Kasay, Seattle vs. San Diego, October 27, 1991
   Fuad Reveiz, Minnesota vs. Tampa Bay, Dec. 8, 1991

Safeties

Most Safeties, Career
4 Ted Hendricks, Baltimore, 1969-73; Green Bay, 1974; Oakland, 1975-81; L.A. Raiders, 1982-83
   Doug English, Detroit, 1975-79, 1981-85
3 Bill McPeak, Pittsburgh, 1949-57
   Charlie Krueger, San Francisco, 1959-73
   Ernie Stautner, Pittsburgh, 1950-63
   Jim Katcavage, N.Y. Giants, 1956-68
   Roger Brown, Detroit, 1960-66; Los Angeles, 1967-69
   Bruce Maher, Detroit, 1960-67; N.Y. Giants, 1968-69
   Ron McDole, St. Louis, 1961; Houston, 1962; Buffalo, 1963-70; Washington, 1971-78
   Alan Page, Minnesota, 1967-78; Chicago, 1979-81
   Lyle Alzado, Denver, 1971-78; Cleveland, 1979-81; L.A. Raiders, 1982-85
   Rulon Jones, Denver, 1980-88
   Steve McMichael, New England, 1980; Chicago 1981-91
2 By many players

Most Safeties, Season
2 Tom Nash, Green Bay, 1932
   Roger Brown, Detroit, 1962
   Ron McDole, Buffalo, 1964
   Alan Page, Minnesota, 1971
   Fred Dryer, Los Angeles, 1973
   Benny Barnes, Dallas, 1973
   James Young, Houston, 1977
   Tom Hannon, Minnesota, 1981
   Doug English, Detroit, 1983
   Don Blackmon, New England, 1985
   Tim Harris, Green Bay, 1988
   Brian Jordan, Atlanta, 1991

Most Safeties, Game
2 Fred Dryer, Los Angeles vs. Green Bay, Oct. 21, 1973

Rushing

Most Seasons Leading League
8 Jim Brown, Cleveland, 1957-61, 1963-65
4 Steve Van Buren, Philadelphia, 1945, 1947-49
   O.J. Simpson, Buffalo, 1972-73, 1975-76
   Eric Dickerson, L.A. Rams, 1983-84, 1986; Indianapolis, 1988
3 Earl Campbell, Houston, 1978-80

Most Consecutive Seasons Leading League
5 Jim Brown, Cleveland, 1957-61
3 Steve Van Buren, Philadelphia, 1947-49
   Jim Brown, Cleveland, 1963-65
   Earl Campbell, Houston, 1978-80
2 Bill Paschal, N.Y. Giants, 1943-44
   Joe Perry, San Francisco, 1953-54
   Jim Nance, Boston, 1966-67

Leroy Kelly, Cleveland, 1967-68
O.J. Simpson, Buffalo, 1972-73; 1975-76
Eric Dickerson, L.A. Rams, 1983-84

Attempts
Most Seasons Leading League
- 6 Jim Brown, Cleveland, 1958-59, 1961, 1963-65
- 4 Steve Van Buren, Philadelphia, 1947-50
  Walter Payton, Chicago, 1976-79
- 3 Cookie Gilchrist, Buffalo, 1963-64; Denver, 1965
  Jim Nance, Boston, 1966-67, 1969
  O.J. Simpson, Buffalo, 1973-75
  Eric Dickerson, L.A. Rams, 1983, 1986; Indianapolis, 1988

Most Consecutive Seasons Leading League
- 4 Steve Van Buren, Philadelphia, 1947-50
  Walter Payton, Chicago, 1976-79
- 3 Jim Brown, Cleveland, 1963-65
  Cookie Gilchrist, Buffalo, 1963-64; Denver, 1965
  O.J. Simpson, Buffalo, 1973-75
- 2 By many players

Most Attempts, Career
- 3,838 Walter Payton, Chicago, 1975-87
- 2,949 Franco Harris, Pittsburgh, 1972-83; Seattle, 1984
- 2,936 Tony Dorsett, Dallas, 1977-87; Denver, 1988

Most Attempts, Season
- 407 James Wilder, Tampa Bay, 1984
- 404 Eric Dickerson, L.A. Rams, 1986
- 397 Gerald Riggs, Atlanta, 1985

Most Attempts, Rookie, Season
- 390 Eric Dickerson, L.A. Rams, 1983
- 378 George Rogers, New Orleans, 1981
- 335 Curt Warner, Seattle, 1983

Most Attempts, Game
- 45 Jamie Morris, Washington vs. Cincinnati, Dec. 17, 1988 (OT)
- 43 Butch Woolfolk, N.Y. Giants vs. Philadelphia, Nov. 20, 1983
  James Wilder, Tampa Bay vs. Green Bay, Sept. 30, 1984 (OT)
- 42 James Wilder, Tampa Bay vs. Pittsburgh, Oct. 30, 1983

Yards Gained
Most Yards Gained, Career
- 16,726 Walter Payton, Chicago, 1975-87
- 12,739 Tony Dorsett, Dallas, 1977-87; Denver, 1988
- 12,439 Eric Dickerson, L.A. Rams, 1983-87; Indianapolis, 1987-91

Most Seasons, 1,000 or More Yards Rushing
- 10 Walter Payton, Chicago, 1976-81, 1983-86
- 8 Franco Harris, Pittsburgh, 1972, 1974-79, 1983
  Tony Dorsett, Dallas, 1977-81, 1983-85
- 7 Jim Brown, Cleveland, 1958-61, 1963-65
  Eric Dickerson, L.A. Rams, 1983-86; L.A. Rams-Indianapolis, 1987; Indianapolis, 1988-89

Most Consecutive Seasons, 1,000 or More Yards Rushing
- 7 Eric Dickerson, L.A. Rams, 1983-86; L.A. Rams-Indianapolis, 1987; Indianapolis, 1988-89
- 6 Franco Harris, Pittsburgh, 1974-79
  Walter Payton, Chicago, 1976-81
- 5 Jim Taylor, Green Bay, 1960-64
  O.J. Simpson, Buffalo, 1972-76
  Tony Dorsett, Dallas, 1977-81

Most Yards Gained, Season
- 2,105 Eric Dickerson, L.A. Rams, 1984
- 2,003 O.J. Simpson, Buffalo, 1973
- 1,934 Earl Campbell, Houston, 1980

Most Yards Gained, Rookie, Season
- 1,808 Eric Dickerson, L.A. Rams, 1983
- 1,674 George Rogers, New Orleans, 1981
- 1,605 Ottis Anderson, St. Louis, 1979

Most Yards Gained, Game
- 275 Walter Payton, Chicago vs. Minnesota, Nov. 20, 1977
- 273 O.J. Simpson, Buffalo vs. Detroit, Nov. 25, 1976
- 250 O.J. Simpson, Buffalo vs. New England, Sept. 16, 1973

Most Games, 200 or More Yards Rushing, Career
- 6 O.J. Simpson, Buffalo, 1969-77; San Francisco, 1978-79
- 4 Jim Brown, Cleveland, 1957-65
  Earl Campbell, Houston, 1978-84; New Orleans, 1984-85
- 3 Eric Dickerson, L.A. Rams, 1983-87; Indianapolis, 1987-91

Most Games, 200 or More Yards Rushing, Season
- 4 Earl Campbell, Houston, 1980
- 3 O.J. Simpson, Buffalo, 1973
- 2 Jim Brown, Cleveland, 1963
  O.J. Simpson, Buffalo, 1976
  Walter Payton, Chicago, 1977
  Eric Dickerson, L.A. Rams, 1984
  Greg Bell, L.A. Rams, 1989

Most Consecutive Games, 200 or More Yards Rushing
- 2 O.J. Simpson, Buffalo, 1973, 1976
  Earl Campbell, Houston, 1980

Most Games, 100 or More Yards Rushing, Career
- 77 Walter Payton, Chicago, 1975-87
- 62 Eric Dickerson, L.A. Rams, 1983-87; Indianapolis, 1987-91
- 58 Jim Brown, Cleveland, 1957-65

Most Games, 100 or More Yards Rushing, Season
- 12 Eric Dickerson, L.A. Rams, 1984
- 11 O.J. Simpson, Buffalo, 1973
  Earl Campbell, Houston, 1979
  Marcus Allen, L.A. Raiders, 1985
  Eric Dickerson, L.A. Rams, 1986
- 10 Walter Payton, Chicago, 1977, 1985
  Earl Campbell, Houston, 1980

Most Consecutive Games, 100 or More Yards Rushing
- 11 Marcus Allen, L.A. Raiders, 1985-86
- 9 Walter Payton, Chicago, 1985
- 7 O.J. Simpson, Buffalo, 1972-73
  Earl Campbell, Houston, 1979

Longest Run From Scrimmage
- 99 Tony Dorsett, Dallas vs. Minnesota, Jan. 3, 1983 (TD)
- 97 Andy Uram, Green Bay vs. Chi. Cardinals, Oct. 8, 1939 (TD)
  Bob Gage, Pittsburgh vs. Chi. Bears, Dec. 4, 1949 (TD)
- 96 Jim Spavital, Baltimore vs. Green Bay, Nov. 5, 1950 (TD)
  Bob Hoernschemeyer, Detroit vs. N.Y. Yanks, Nov. 23, 1950 (TD)

Average Gain
Highest Average Gain, Career (700 attempts)
- 5.22 Jim Brown, Cleveland, 1957-65 (2,359-12,312)
- 5.14 Eugene (Mercury) Morris, Miami, 1969-75; San Diego, 1976 (804-4,133)
- 5.00 Gale Sayers, Chicago, 1965-71 (991-4,956)

Highest Average Gain, Season (Qualifiers)
- 8.44 Beattie Feathers, Chi. Bears, 1934 (119-1,004)
- 7.98 Randall Cunningham, Philadelphia 1990 (118-942)
- 6.87 Bobby Douglass, Chicago, 1972 (141-968)

Highest Average Gain, Game (10 attempts)
- 17.09 Marion Motley, Cleveland vs. Pittsburgh, Oct. 29, 1950 (11-188)
- 16.70 Bill Grimes, Green Bay vs. N.Y. Yanks, Oct. 8, 1950 (10-167)
- 16.57 Bobby Mitchell, Cleveland vs. Washington, Nov. 15, 1959 (14-232)

Touchdowns
Most Seasons Leading League
- 5 Jim Brown, Cleveland, 1957-59, 1963, 1965
- 4 Steve Van Buren, Philadelphia, 1945, 1947-49
- 3 Abner Haynes, Dall. Texans, 1960-62
  Cookie Gilchrist, Buffalo, 1962-64
  Paul Lowe, L.A. Chargers, 1960; San Diego, 1961, 1965
  Leroy Kelly, Cleveland, 1966-68

Most Consecutive Seasons Leading League
- 3 Steve Van Buren, Philadelphia, 1947-49
  Jim Brown, Cleveland, 1957-59
  Abner Haynes, Dall. Texans, 1960-62
  Cookie Gilchrist, Buffalo, 1962-64
  Leroy Kelly, Cleveland, 1966-68

Most Touchdowns, Career
- 110 Walter Payton, Chicago, 1975-87
- 106 Jim Brown, Cleveland, 1957-65
- 104 John Riggins, N.Y. Jets, 1971-75; Washington, 1976-79, 1981-85

Most Touchdowns, Season
- 24 John Riggins, Washington, 1983
- 21 Joe Morris, N.Y. Giants, 1985
- 19 Jim Taylor, Green Bay, 1962
  Earl Campbell, Houston, 1979
  Chuck Muncie, San Diego, 1981

Most Touchdowns, Rookie, Season
- 18 Eric Dickerson, L.A. Rams, 1983
- 15 Ickey Woods, Cincinnati, 1988
- 14 Gale Sayers, Chicago, 1965
  Barry Sanders, Detroit, 1989

Most Touchdowns, Game
- 6 Ernie Nevers, Chi. Cardinals vs. Chi. Bears, Nov. 28, 1929
- 5 Jim Brown, Cleveland vs. Baltimore, Nov. 1, 1959
  Cookie Gilchrist, Buffalo vs. N.Y. Jets, Dec. 8, 1963
- 4 By many players

Most Consecutive Games Rushing for Touchdowns
- 13 John Riggins, Washington, 1982-83
  George Rogers, Washington, 1985-86
- 11 Lenny Moore, Baltimore, 1963-64
- 10 Greg Bell, L.A. Rams, 1988-89

Passing
Most Seasons Leading League
- 6 Sammy Baugh, Washington, 1937, 1940, 1943, 1945, 1947, 1949
- 4 Len Dawson, Dall. Texans; 1962; Kansas City, 1964, 1966, 1968
  Roger Staubach, Dallas, 1971, 1973, 1978-79
  Ken Anderson, Cincinnati, 1974-75, 1981-82
- 3 Arnie Herber, Green Bay, 1932, 1934, 1936
  Norm Van Brocklin, Los Angeles, 1950, 1952, 1954
  Bart Starr, Green Bay, 1962, 1964, 1966

Most Consecutive Seasons Leading League
- 2 Cecil Isbell, Green Bay, 1941-42
  Milt Plum, Cleveland, 1960-61
  Ken Anderson, Cincinnati, 1974-75, 1981-82
  Roger Staubach, Dallas, 1978-79

Pass Rating
Highest Pass Rating, Career (1,500 attempts)
- 93.4 Joe Montana, San Francisco, 1979-90
- 88.2 Dan Marino, Miami, 1983-91
- 88.0 Jim Kelly, Buffalo, 1986-91

Highest Pass Rating, Season (Qualifiers)
- 112.4 Joe Montana, San Francisco, 1989
- 110.4 Milt Plum, Cleveland, 1960
- 109.9 Sammy Baugh, Washington, 1945

Highest Pass Rating, Rookie, Season (Qualifiers)
- 96.0 Dan Marino, Miami, 1983
- 88.2 Greg Cook, Cincinnati, 1969
- 84.0 Charlie Conerly, N.Y. Giants, 1948

Attempts
Most Seasons Leading League
- 4 Sammy Baugh, Washington, 1937, 1943, 1947-48
  Johnny Unitas, Baltimore, 1957, 1959-61
  George Blanda, Chi. Bears, 1953; Houston, 1963-65
- 3 Arnie Herber, Green Bay, 1932, 1934, 1936
  Sonny Jurgensen, Washington, 1966-67, 1969
  Dan Marino, Miami, 1984, 1986, 1988
- 2 By many players

Most Consecutive Seasons Leading League
- 3 Johnny Unitas, Baltimore, 1959-61
  George Blanda, Houston, 1963-65
- 2 By many players

Most Passes Attempted, Career
6,467 Fran Tarkenton, Minnesota, 1961-66, 1972-78; N.Y. Giants, 1967-71
5,604 Dan Fouts, San Diego, 1973-87
5,186 Johnny Unitas, Baltimore, 1956-72; San Diego, 1973
Most Passes Attempted, Season
655 Warren Moon, Houston, 1991
623 Dan Marino, Miami, 1986
609 Dan Fouts, San Diego, 1981
Most Passes Attempted, Rookie, Season
439 Jim Zorn, Seattle, 1976
417 Jack Trudeau, Indianapolis, 1986
375 Norm Snead, Washington, 1961
Most Passes Attempted, Game
68 George Blanda, Houston vs. Buffalo, Nov. 1, 1964
66 Chris Miller, Atlanta vs. Detroit, Dec. 24, 1989
63 Rich Gannon, Minnesota vs. New England, Oct. 20, 1991 (OT)

Completions
Most Seasons Leading League
5 Sammy Baugh, Washington, 1937, 1943, 1945, 1947-48
4 George Blanda, Chi. Bears, 1953; Houston, 1963-65
  Sonny Jurgensen, Philadelphia, 1961; Washington, 1966-67, 1969
  Dan Marino, Miami, 1984-86, 1988
3 Arnie Herber, Green Bay, 1932, 1934, 1936
  Johnny Unitas, Baltimore, 1959-60, 1963
  John Brodie, San Francisco, 1965, 1968, 1970
  Fran Tarkenton, Minnesota, 1975-76, 1978
Most Consecutive Seasons Leading League
3 George Blanda, Houston, 1963-65
  Dan Marino, Miami, 1984-86
2 By many players
Most Passes Completed, Career
3,686 Fran Tarkenton, Minnesota, 1961-66, 1972-78; N.Y. Giants, 1967-71
3,297 Dan Fouts, San Diego, 1973-87
2,914 Joe Montana, San Francisco, 1979-90
Most Passes Completed, Season
404 Warren Moon, Hosuton, 1991
378 Dan Marino, Miami, 1986
362 Dan Marino, Miami, 1984
  Warren Moon, Houston, 1990
Most Passes Completed, Rookie, Season
208 Jim Zorn, Seattle, 1976
204 Jack Trudeau, Indianapolis, 1986
183 Jeff Komlo, Detroit, 1979
Most Passes Completed, Game
42 Richard Todd, N.Y. Jets vs. San Francisco, Sept. 21, 1980
41 Warren Moon, Houston vs. Dallas, Nov. 10, 1991 (OT)
40 Ken Anderson, Cincinnati vs. San Diego, Dec. 20, 1982
  Phil Simms, N.Y. Giants vs. Cincinnati, Oct. 13, 1985
Most Consecutive Passes Completed
22 Joe Montana, San Francisco vs. Cleveland (5), Nov. 29, 1987; vs. Green Bay (17), Dec. 6, 1987
20 Ken Anderson, Cincinnati vs. Houston, Jan. 2, 1983
18 Steve DeBerg, Denver vs. L.A. Rams (17), Dec. 12, 1982; vs. Kansas City (1), Dec. 19, 1982
  Lynn Dickey, Green Bay vs. Houston, Sept. 4, 1983
  Joe Montana, San Francisco vs. L.A. Rams (13), Oct. 28, 1984; vs. Cincinnati (5), Nov. 4, 1984
  Don Majkowski, Green Bay vs. New Orleans, Sept. 18, 1989

Completion Percentage
Most Seasons Leading League
8 Len Dawson, Dall. Texans, 1962; Kansas City, 1964-69, 1975
7 Sammy Baugh, Washington, 1940, 1942-43, 1945, 1947-49
5 Joe Montana, San Francisco, 1980-81, 1985, 1987, 1989
Most Consecutive Seasons Leading League
6 Len Dawson, Kansas City, 1964-69
3 Sammy Baugh, Washington, 1947-49
  Otto Graham, Cleveland, 1953-55
  Milt Plum, Cleveland, 1959-61
2 By many players
Highest Completion Percentage, Career (1,500 attempts)
63.64 Joe Montana, San Francisco, 1979-90 (4,579-2,914)
60.69 Jim Kelly, Buffalo, 1986-91 (2,562-1,555)
59.85 Ken Stabler, Oakland, 1970-79; Houston, 1980-81; New Orleans, 1982-84 (3,793-2,270)
Highest Completion Percentage, Season (Qualifiers)
70.55 Ken Anderson, Cincinnati, 1982 (309-218)
70.33 Sammy Baugh, Washington, 1945 (182-128)
70.21 Joe Montana, San Francisco, 1989 (386-271)
Highest Completion Percentage, Rookie, Season (Qualifiers)
58.45 Dan Marino, Miami, 1983 (296-173)
57.14 Jim McMahon, Chicago, 1982 (269-181)
56.07 Fran Tarkenton, Minnesota, 1961 (280-157)
Highest Completion Percentage, Game (20 attempts)
90.91 Ken Anderson, Cincinnati vs. Pittsburgh, Nov. 10, 1974 (22-20)
90.48 Lynn Dickey, Green Bay vs. New Orleans, Dec. 13, 1981 (21-19)
90.00 Steve Young, San Francisco vs. Detroit, Oct. 20, 1991 (20-18)

Yards Gained
Most Seasons Leading League
5 Sonny Jurgensen, Philadelphia, 1961-62; Washington, 1966-67, 1969
4 Sammy Baugh, Washington, 1937, 1940, 1947-48
  Johnny Unitas, Baltimore, 1957, 1959-60, 1963
  Dan Fouts, San Diego, 1979-82
  Dan Marino, Miami, 1984-86, 1988
3 Arnie Herber, Green Bay, 1932, 1934, 1936
  Sid Luckman, Chi. Bears, 1943, 1945-46
  John Brodie, San Francisco, 1965, 1968, 1970
  John Hadl, San Diego, 1965, 1968, 1971
  Joe Namath, N.Y. Jets, 1966-67, 1972
Most Consecutive Seasons Leading League
4 Dan Fouts, San Diego, 1979-82

Most Yards Gained, Career
3 Dan Marino, Miami, 1984-86
2 By many players
Most Yards Gained, Career
47,003 Fran Tarkenton, Minnesota, 1961-66, 1972-78; N.Y. Giants, 1967-71
43,040 Dan Fouts, San Diego, 1973-87
40,239 Johnny Unitas, Baltimore, 1956-72; San Diego, 1973
Most Seasons, 3,000 or More Yards Passing
8 Dan Marino, Miami, 1984-91
7 Joe Montana, San Francisco, 1981, 1983-85, 1987, 1989-90
  John Elway, Denver, 1985-91
6 Dan Fouts, San Diego, 1979-81, 1984-86
  Boomer Esiason, Cincinnati, 1985-90
Most Yards Gained, Season
5,084 Dan Marino, Miami, 1984
4,802 Dan Fouts, San Diego, 1981
4,746 Dan Marino, Miami, 1986
Most Yards Gained, Rookie, Season
2,571 Jim Zorn, Seattle, 1976
2,507 Dennis Shaw, Buffalo, 1970
2,337 Norm Snead, Washington, 1961
Most Yards Gained, Game
554 Norm Van Brocklin, Los Angeles vs. N.Y. Yanks, Sept. 28, 1951
527 Warren Moon, Houston vs. Kansas City, Dec. 16, 1990
521 Dan Marino, Miami vs. N.Y. Jets, Oct. 23, 1988
Most Games, 400 or More Yards Passing, Career
10 Dan Marino, Miami, 1983-91
7 Joe Montana, San Francisco, 1979-90
6 Dan Fouts, San Diego, 1973-87
Most Games, 400 or More Yards Passing, Season
4 Dan Marino, Miami, 1984
3 Dan Marino, Miami, 1986
2 George Blanda, Houston, 1961
  Sonny Jurgensen, Philadelphia, 1961
  Joe Namath, N.Y. Jets, 1972
  Dan Fouts, San Diego, 1982
  Dan Fouts, San Diego, 1985
  Phil Simms, N.Y. Giants, 1985
  Ken O'Brien, N.Y. Jets, 1986
  Bernie Kosar, Cleveland, 1986
  Dan Marino, Miami, 1988
  Randall Cunningham, Philadelphia, 1989
  Joe Montana, San Francisco, 1989
  Joe Montana, San Francisco, 1990
  Warren Moon, Houston, 1991
Most Consecutive Games, 400 or More Yards Passing
2 Dan Fouts, San Diego, 1982
  Dan Marino, Miami, 1984
  Phil Simms, N.Y. Giants, 1985
Most Games, 300 or More Yards Passing, Career
51 Dan Fouts, San Diego, 1973-87
41 Dan Marino, Miami, 1983-91
35 Joe Montana, San Francisco, 1979-90
Most Games, 300 or More Yards Passing, Season
9 Dan Marino, Miami, 1984
  Warren Moon, Houston, 1990
8 Dan Fouts, San Diego, 1980
7 Dan Fouts, San Diego, 1981
  Bill Kenney, Kansas City, 1983
  Neil Lomax, St. Louis, 1984
  Dan Fouts, San Diego, 1985
Most Consecutive Games, 300 or More Yards Passing, Season
5 Joe Montana, San Francisco, 1982
4 Dan Fouts, San Diego, 1979
  Bill Kenney, Kansas City, 1983
  Joe Montana, San Francisco, 1990
  Warren Moon, Houston, 1990
3 By many players
Longest Pass Completion (All TDs except as noted)
99 Frank Filchock (to Farkas), Washington vs. Pittsburgh, Oct. 15, 1939
  George Izo (to Mitchell), Washington vs. Cleveland, Sept. 15, 1963
  Karl Sweetan (to Studstill), Detroit vs. Baltimore, Oct. 16, 1966
  Sonny Jurgensen (to Allen), Washington vs. Chicago, Sept. 15, 1968
  Jim Plunkett (to Branch), L.A. Raiders vs. Washington, Oct. 2, 1983
  Ron Jaworski (to Quick), Philadelphia vs. Atlanta, Nov. 10, 1985
98 Doug Russell (to Tinsley), Chi. Cardinals vs. Cleveland, Nov. 27, 1938
  Ogden Compton (to Lane), Chi. Cardinals vs. Green Bay, Nov. 13, 1955
  Bill Wade (to Farrington), Chicago Bears vs. Detroit, Oct. 8, 1961
  Jacky Lee (to Dewveall), Houston vs. San Diego, Nov. 25, 1962
  Earl Morrall (to Jones), N.Y. Giants vs. Pittsburgh, Sept. 11, 1966
  Jim Hart (to Moore), St. Louis vs. Los Angeles, Dec. 10, 1972 (no TD)
97 Pat Coffee (to Tinsley), Chi. Cardinals vs. Chi. Bears, Dec. 5, 1937
  Bobby Layne (to Box), Detroit vs. Green Bay, Nov. 26, 1953
  George Shaw (to Tarr), Denver vs. Boston, Sept. 21, 1962
  Bernie Kosar (to Slaughter), Cleveland vs. Chicago, Oct. 23, 1989
  Steve Young (to Taylor), San Francisco vs. Atlanta, Nov. 3, 1991

Average Gain
Most Seasons Leading League
7 Sid Luckman, Chi. Bears, 1939-43, 1946-47
3 Arnie Herber, Green Bay, 1932, 1934, 1936
  Norm Van Brocklin, Los Angeles, 1950, 1952, 1954
  Len Dawson, Dall. Texans, 1962; Kansas City, 1966, 1968
  Bart Starr, Green Bay, 1966-68
Most Consecutive Seasons Leading League
5 Sid Luckman, Chi. Bears, 1939-43
3 Bart Starr, Green Bay, 1966-68
2 Bernie Masterson, Chi. Bears, 1937-38
  Sid Luckman, Chi. Bears, 1946-47
  Johnny Unitas, Baltimore, 1964-65
  Terry Bradshaw, Pittsburgh, 1977-78
  Steve Grogan, New England, 1980-81
Highest Average Gain, Career (1,500 attempts)
8.63 Otto Graham, Cleveland, 1950-55 (1,565-13,499)

8.42 Sid Luckman, Chi. Bears, 1939-50 (1,744-14,686)
8.16 Norm Van Brocklin, Los Angeles, 1949-57; Philadelphia, 1958-60
(2,895-23,611)
Highest Average Gain, Season (Qualifiers)
11.17 Tommy O'Connell, Cleveland, 1957 (110-1,229)
10.86 Sid Luckman, Chi. Bears, 1943 (202-2,194)
10.55 Otto Graham, Cleveland, 1953 (258-2,722)
Highest Average Gain, Rookie, Season (Qualifiers)
9.411 Greg Cook, Cincinnati, 1969 (197-1,854)
9.409 Bob Waterfield, Cleveland, 1945 (171-1,609)
8.36 Zeke Bratkowski, Chi. Bears, 1954 (130-1,087)
Highest Average Gain, Game (20 attempts)
18.58 Sammy Baugh, Washington vs. Boston, Oct. 31, 1948 (24-446)
18.50 Johnny Unitas, Baltimore vs. Atlanta, Nov. 12, 1967 (20-370)
17.71 Joe Namath, N.Y. Jets vs. Baltimore, Sept. 24, 1972 (28-496)

Touchdowns
Most Seasons Leading League
4 Johnny Unitas, Baltimore, 1957-60
Len Dawson, Dall. Texans, 1962; Kansas City, 1963, 1965-66
3 Arnie Herber, Green Bay, 1932, 1934, 1936
Sid Luckman, Chi. Bears, 1943, 1945-46
Y.A. Tittle, San Francisco, 1955; N.Y. Giants, 1962-63
Dan Marino, Miami, 1984-86
2 By many players
Most Consecutive Seasons Leading League
4 Johnny Unitas, Baltimore, 1957-60
3 Dan Marino, Miami, 1984-86
2 By many players
Most Touchdown Passes, Career
342 Fran Tarkenton, Minnesota, 1961-66, 1972-78; N.Y. Giants, 1967-71
290 Johnny Unitas, Baltimore, 1956-72; San Diego, 1973
266 Dan Marino, Miami, 1983-91
Most Touchdown Passes, Season
48 Dan Marino, Miami, 1984
44 Dan Marino, Miami, 1986
36 George Blanda, Houston, 1961
Y.A. Tittle, N.Y. Giants, 1963
Most Touchdown Passes, Rookie, Season
22 Charlie Conerly, N.Y. Giants, 1948
20 Dan Marino, Miami, 1983
19 Jim Plunkett, New England, 1971
Most Touchdown Passes, Game
7 Sid Luckman, Chi. Bears vs. N.Y. Giants, Nov. 14, 1943
Adrian Burk, Philadelphia vs. Washington, Oct. 17, 1954
George Blanda, Houston vs. N.Y. Titans, Nov. 19, 1961
Y.A. Tittle, N.Y. Giants vs. Washington, Oct. 28, 1962
Joe Kapp, Minnesota vs. Baltimore, Sept. 28, 1969
6 By many players. Last time: Mark Rypien, Washington vs. Atlanta, Nov. 10, 1991
Most Games, Four or More Touchdown Passes, Career
17 Johnny Unitas, Baltimore, 1956-72; San Diego, 1973
16 Dan Marino, Miami, 1983-91
13 George Blanda, Chi. Bears, 1949, 1950-58; Baltimore, 1950; Houston, 1960-66; Oakland, 1967-75
Most Games, Four or More Touchdown Passes, Season
6 Dan Marino, Miami, 1984
5 Dan Marino, Miami, 1986
4 George Blanda, Houston, 1961
Vince Ferragamo, Los Angeles, 1980
Most Consecutive Games, Four or More Touchdown Passes
4 Dan Marino, Miami, 1984
2 By many players
Most Consecutive Games, Touchdown Passes
47 Johnny Unitas, Baltimore, 1956-60
30 Dan Marino, Miami, 1985-87
28 Dave Krieg, Seattle, 1983-85

Had Intercepted
Most Consecutive Passes Attempted, None Intercepted
308 Bernie Kosar, Cleveland, 1990-91
294 Bart Starr, Green Bay, 1964-65
233 Steve DeBerg, Kansas City, 1990
Most Passes Had Intercepted, Career
277 George Blanda, Chi. Bears, 1949, 1950-58; Baltimore, 1950; Houston, 1960-66; Oakland, 1967-75
268 John Hadl, San Diego, 1962-72; Los Angeles, 1973-74; Green Bay, 1974-75; Houston, 1976-77
266 Fran Tarkenton, Minnesota, 1961-66, 1972-78; N.Y. Giants, 1967-71
Most Passes Had Intercepted, Season
42 George Blanda, Houston, 1962
35 Vinny Testaverde, Tampa Bay, 1988
34 Frank Tripucka, Denver, 1960
Most Passes Had Intercepted, Game
8 Jim Hardy, Chi. Cardinals vs. Philadelphia, Sept. 24, 1950
7 Parker Hall, Cleveland vs. Green Bay, Nov. 8, 1942
Frank Sinkwich, Detroit vs. Green Bay, Oct. 24, 1943
Bob Waterfield, Los Angeles vs. Green Bay, Oct. 17, 1948
Zeke Bratkowski, Chicago vs. Baltimore, Oct. 2, 1960
Tommy Wade, Pittsburgh vs. Philadelphia, Dec. 12, 1965
Ken Stabler, Oakland vs. Denver, Oct. 16, 1977
Steve DeBerg, Tampa Bay vs. San Francisco, Sept. 7, 1986
6 By many players
Most Attempts, No Interceptions, Game
63 Rich Gannon, Minnesota vs. New England, Oct. 20, 1991 (OT)
60 Davey O'Brien, Philadelphia vs. Washington, Dec. 1, 1940
57 Joe Montana, San Francisco vs. Atlanta, Oct. 6, 1985

Lowest Percentage, Passes Had Intercepted
Most Seasons Leading League, Lowest Percentage, Passes Had Intercepted
5 Sammy Baugh, Washington, 1940, 1942, 1944-45, 1947
3 Charlie Conerly, N.Y. Giants, 1950, 1956, 1959
Bart Starr, Green Bay, 1962, 1964, 1966

Roger Staubach, Dallas, 1971, 1977, 1979
Ken Anderson, Cincinnati, 1972, 1981-82
Ken O'Brien, N.Y. Jets, 1985, 1987-88
2 By many players
Lowest Percentage, Passes Had Intercepted, Career (1,500 attempts)
2.49 Bernie Kosar, Cleveland, 1985-91 (2,857-71)
2.64 Ken O'Brien, N.Y. Jets, 1984-91 (3,367-89)
2.69 Joe Montana, San Francisco, 1979-90 (4,579-123)
Lowest Percentage, Passes Had Intercepted, Season (Qualifiers)
0.66 Joe Ferguson, Buffalo, 1976 (151-1)
0.90 Steve DeBerg, Kansas City, 1990 (444-4)
1.16 Steve Bartkowski, Atlanta, 1983 (432-5)
Lowest Percentage, Passes Had Intercepted, Rookie, Season (Qualifiers)
2.03 Dan Marino, Miami, 1983 (296-6)
2.10 Gary Wood, N.Y. Giants, 1964 (143-3)
2.82 Bernie Kosar, Cleveland, 1985 (248-7)

Times Sacked
Times Sacked has been compiled since 1963.
Most Times Sacked, Career
483 Fran Tarkenton, Minnesota, 1961-66, 1972-78; N.Y. Giants, 1967-71
430 Phil Simms, N.Y. Giants, 1979-81, 1983-91
405 Craig Morton, Dallas, 1965-74; N.Y. Giants, 1974-76; Denver, 1977-82
Most Times Sacked, Season
72 Randall Cunningham, Philadelphia, 1986
62 Ken O'Brien, N.Y. Jets, 1985
61 Neil Lomax, St. Louis, 1985
Most Times Sacked, Game
12 Bert Jones, Baltimore vs. St. Louis, Oct. 26, 1980
Warren Moon, Houston vs. Dallas, Sept. 29, 1985
11 Charley Johnson, St. Louis vs. N.Y. Giants, Nov. 1, 1964
Bart Starr, Green Bay vs. Detroit, Nov. 7, 1965
Jack Kemp, Buffalo vs. Oakland, Oct. 15, 1967
Bob Berry, Atlanta vs. St. Louis, Nov. 24, 1968
Greg Landry, Detroit vs. Dallas, Oct. 6, 1975
Ron Jaworski, Philadelphia vs. St. Louis, Dec. 18, 1983
Paul McDonald, Cleveland vs. Kansas City, Sept. 30, 1984
Archie Manning, Minnesota vs. Chicago, Oct. 28, 1984
Steve Pelluer, Dallas vs. San Diego, Nov. 16, 1986
Randall Cunningham, Philadelphia vs. L.A. Raiders, Nov. 30, 1986 (OT)
David Norrie, N.Y. Jets vs. Dallas, Oct. 4, 1987
Troy Aikman, Dallas vs. Philadelphia, Sept. 15, 1991
10 By many players

Pass Receiving
Most Seasons Leading League
8 Don Hutson, Green Bay, 1936-37, 1939, 1941-45
5 Lionel Taylor, Denver, 1960-63, 1965
3 Tom Fears, Los Angeles, 1948-50
Pete Pihos, Philadelphia, 1953-55
Billy Wilson, San Francisco, 1954, 1956-57
Raymond Berry, Baltimore, 1958-60
Lance Alworth, San Diego, 1966, 1968-69
Most Consecutive Seasons Leading League
5 Don Hutson, Green Bay, 1941-45
4 Lionel Taylor, Denver, 1960-63
3 Tom Fears, Los Angeles, 1948-50
Pete Pihos, Philadelphia, 1953-55
Raymond Berry, Baltimore, 1958-60
Most Pass Receptions, Career
819 Steve Largent, Seattle, 1976-89
801 Art Monk, Washington, 1980-91
750 Charlie Joiner, Houston, 1969-72; Cincinnati, 1972-75; San Diego, 1976-86
Most Seasons, 50 or More Pass Receptions
10 Steve Largent, Seattle, 1976, 1978-81, 1983-87
9 Art Monk, Washington, 1980-81, 1984-86, 1988-91
8 James Lofton, Green Bay, 1979-81, 1983-86; Buffalo, 1991
Most Pass Receptions, Season
106 Art Monk, Washington, 1984
101 Charley Hennigan, Houston, 1964
100 Lionel Taylor, Denver, 1961
Jerry Rice, San Francisco, 1990
Haywood Jeffires, Houston, 1991
Most Pass Receptions, Rookie, Season
83 Earl Cooper, San Francisco, 1980
81 Keith Jackson, Philadelphia, 1988
72 Bill Groman, Houston, 1960
Most Pass Receptions, Game
18 Tom Fears, Los Angeles vs. Green Bay, Dec. 3, 1950
17 Clark Gaines, N.Y. Jets vs. San Francisco, Sept. 21, 1980
16 Sonny Randle, St. Louis vs. N.Y. Giants, Nov. 4, 1962
Most Consecutive Games, Pass Receptions
177 Steve Largent, Seattle, 1977-89
150 Ozzie Newsome, Cleveland, 1979-89
132 Art Monk, Washington, 1983-91 (current)

Yards Gained
Most Seasons Leading League
7 Don Hutson, Green Bay, 1936, 1938-39, 1941-44
3 Raymond Berry, Baltimore, 1957, 1959-60
Lance Alworth, San Diego, 1965-66, 1968
Jerry Rice, San Francisco, 1986, 1989-90
2 By many players
Most Consecutive Seasons Leading League
4 Don Hutson, Green Bay, 1941-44
2 By many players
Most Yards Gained, Career
13,089 Steve Largent, Seattle, 1976-89
13,035 James Lofton, Green Bay, 1978-86; L.A. Raiders, 1987-88; Buffalo, 1989-91
12,146 Charlie Joiner, Houston, 1969-72; Cincinnati, 1972-75; San Diego, 1976-86
Most Seasons, 1,000 or More Yards, Pass Receiving
8 Steve Largent, Seattle, 1978-81; 1983-86
7 Lance Alworth, San Diego, 1963-69

6 James Lofton, Green Bay, 1980-81, 1983-85; Buffalo, 1991
 Jerry Rice, San Francisco, 1986-91

Most Yards Gained, Season
1,746 Charley Hennigan, Houston, 1961
1,602 Lance Alworth, San Diego, 1965
1,570 Jerry Rice, San Francisco, 1986

Most Yards Gained, Rookie, Season
1,473 Bill Groman, Houston, 1960
1,231 Bill Howton, Green Bay, 1952
1,131 Bill Brooks, Indianapolis, 1986

Most Yards Gained, Game
336 Willie Anderson, L.A. Rams vs. New Orleans, Nov. 26, 1989 (OT)
309 Stephone Paige, Kansas City vs. San Diego, Dec. 22, 1985
303 Jim Benton, Cleveland vs. Detroit, Nov. 22, 1945

Most Games, 200 or More Yards Pass Receiving, Career
5 Lance Alworth, San Diego, 1962-70; Dallas, 1971-72
4 Don Hutson, Green Bay, 1935-45
 Charley Hennigan, Houston, 1960-66
3 Don Maynard, N.Y. Giants, 1958; N.Y. Jets, 1960-72; St. Louis, 1973
 Wes Chandler, New Orleans, 1978-81; San Diego, 1981-87; San Francisco, 1988
 Jerry Rice, San Francisco, 1985-91

Most Games, 200 or More Yards Pass Receiving, Season
3 Charley Hennigan, Houston, 1961
2 Don Hutson, Green Bay, 1942
 Gene Roberts, N.Y. Giants, 1949
 Lance Alworth, San Diego, 1963
 Don Maynard, N.Y. Jets, 1968

Most Games, 100 or More Yards Pass Receiving, Career
50 Don Maynard, N.Y. Giants, 1958; N.Y. Jets, 1960-72; St. Louis, 1973
42 James Lofton, Green Bay, 1978-86; L.A. Raiders, 1987-88; Buffalo, 1989-91
41 Lance Alworth, San Diego, 1962-70; Dallas, 1971-72

Most Games, 100 or More Yards Pass Receiving, Season
10 Charley Hennigan, Houston, 1961
9 Elroy (Crazylegs) Hirsch, Los Angeles, 1951
 Bill Groman, Houston, 1960
 Lance Alworth, San Diego, 1965
 Don Maynard, N.Y. Jets, 1967
 Stanley Morgan, New England, 1986
 Mark Carrier, Tampa Bay, 1989
8 Charley Hennigan, Houston, 1964
 Lance Alworth, San Diego, 1967
 Mark Duper, Miami, 1986
 Jerry Rice, San Francisco, 1989

Most Consecutive Games, 100 or More Yards Pass Receiving
7 Charley Hennigan, Houston, 1961
 Bill Groman, Houston, 1961
6 Raymond Berry, Baltimore, 1960
 Pat Studstill, Detroit, 1966
5 Elroy (Crazylegs) Hirsch, Los Angeles, 1951
 Bob Boyd, Los Angeles, 1954
 Terry Barr, Detroit, 1963
 Lance Alworth, San Diego, 1966

Longest Pass Reception (All TDs except as noted)
99 Andy Farkas (from Filchock), Washington vs. Pittsburgh, Oct. 15, 1939
 Bobby Mitchell (from Izo), Washington vs. Cleveland, Sept. 15, 1963
 Pat Studstill (from Sweetan), Detroit vs. Baltimore, Oct. 16, 1966
 Gerry Allen (from Jurgensen), Washington vs. Chicago, Sept. 15, 1968
 Cliff Branch (from Plunkett), L.A. Raiders vs. Washington, Oct. 2, 1983
 Mike Quick (from Jaworski), Philadelphia vs. Atlanta, Nov. 10, 1985
98 Gaynell Tinsley (from Russell), Chi. Cardinals vs. Cleveland, Nov. 17, 1938
 Dick (Night Train) Lane (from Compton), Chi. Cardinals vs. Green Bay, Nov. 13, 1955
 John Farrington (from Wade), Chicago vs. Detroit, Oct. 8, 1961
 Willard Dewveall (from Lee), Houston vs. San Diego, Nov. 25, 1962
 Homer Jones (from Morrall), N.Y. Giants vs. Pittsburgh, Sept. 11, 1966
 Bobby Moore (from Hart), St. Louis vs. Los Angeles, Dec. 10, 1972 (no TD)
97 Gaynell Tinsley (from Coffee), Chi. Cardinals vs. Chi. Bears, Dec. 5, 1937
 Cloyce Box (from Layne), Detroit vs. Green Bay, Nov. 26, 1953
 Jerry Tarr (from Shaw), Denver vs. Boston, Sept. 21, 1962
 Webster Slaughter (from Kosar), Cleveland vs. Chicago, Oct. 23, 1989
 John Taylor (from Young), San Francisco vs. Atlanta, Nov. 3, 1991

Average Gain
Highest Average Gain, Career (200 receptions)
22.26 Homer Jones, N.Y. Giants, 1964-69; Cleveland, 1970 (224-4,986)
20.83 Buddy Dial, Pittsburgh, 1959-63; Dallas, 1964-66 (261-5,436)
20.35 Willie Gault, Chicago, 1983-87; L.A. Raiders, 1988-91 (298-6,063)

Highest Average Gain, Season (24 receptions)
32.58 Don Currivan, Boston, 1947 (24-782)
31.44 Bucky Pope, Los Angeles, 1964 (25-786)
28.60 Bobby Duckworth, San Diego, 1984 (25-715)

Highest Average Gain, Game (3 receptions)
60.67 Bill Groman, Houston vs. Denver, Nov. 20, 1960 (3-182)
 Homer Jones, N.Y. Giants vs. Washington, Dec. 12, 1965 (3-182)
60.33 Don Currivan, Boston vs. Washington, Nov. 30, 1947 (3-181)
59.67 Bobby Duckworth, San Diego vs. Chicago, Dec. 3, 1984 (3-179)

Touchdowns
Most Seasons Leading League
9 Don Hutson, Green Bay, 1935-38, 1940-44
5 Jerry Rice, San Francisco, 1986-87, 1989-91
3 Lance Alworth, San Diego, 1964-66

Most Consecutive Seasons Leading League
5 Don Hutson, Green Bay, 1940-44
4 Don Hutson, Green Bay, 1935-38
3 Lance Alworth, San Diego, 1964-66
 Jerry Rice, San Francisco, 1989-91

Most Touchdowns, Career
100 Steve Largent, Seattle, 1976-89
99 Don Hutson, Green Bay, 1935-45
93 Jerry Rice, San Francisco, 1985-91

Most Touchdowns, Season
22 Jerry Rice, San Francisco, 1987
18 Mark Clayton, Miami, 1984
17 Don Hutson, Green Bay, 1942
 Elroy (Crazylegs) Hirsch, Los Angeles, 1951
 Bill Groman, Houston, 1961
 Jerry Rice, San Francisco, 1989

Most Touchdowns, Rookie, Season
13 Bill Howton, Green Bay, 1952
 John Jefferson, San Diego, 1979
12 Harlon Hill, Chi. Bears, 1954
 Bill Groman, Houston, 1960
 Mike Ditka, Chicago, 1961
 Bob Hayes, Dallas, 1965
10 Bill Swiacki, N.Y. Giants, 1948
 Bucky Pope, Los Angeles, 1964
 Sammy White, Minnesota, 1976
 Daryl Turner, Seattle, 1984

Most Touchdowns, Game
5 Bob Shaw, Chi. Cardinals vs. Baltimore, Oct. 2, 1950
 Kellen Winslow, San Diego vs. Oakland, Nov. 22, 1981
 Jerry Rice, San Francisco vs. Atlanta, Oct. 14, 1990
4 By many players

Most Consecutive Games, Touchdowns
13 Jerry Rice, San Francisco, 1986-87
11 Elroy (Crazylegs) Hirsch, Los Angeles, 1950-51
 Buddy Dial, Pittsburgh, 1959-60
9 Lance Alworth, San Diego, 1963

Interceptions By
Most Seasons Leading League
3 Everson Walls, Dallas, 1981-82, 1985
2 Dick (Night Train) Lane, Los Angeles, 1952; Chi. Cardinals, 1954
 Jack Christiansen, Detroit, 1953, 1957
 Milt Davis, Baltimore, 1957, 1959
 Dick Lynch, N.Y. Giants, 1961, 1963
 Johnny Robinson, Kansas City, 1966, 1970
 Bill Bradley, Philadelphia, 1971-72
 Emmitt Thomas, Kansas City, 1969, 1974
 Ronnie Lott, San Francisco, 1986; L.A. Raiders, 1991

Most Interceptions By, Career
81 Paul Krause, Washington, 1964-67; Minnesota, 1968-79
79 Emlen Tunnell, N.Y. Giants, 1948-58; Green Bay, 1959-61
68 Dick (Night Train) Lane, Los Angeles, 1952-53; Chi. Cardinals, 1954-59; Detroit, 1960-65

Most Interceptions By, Season
14 Dick (Night Train) Lane, Los Angeles, 1952
13 Dan Sandifer, Washington, 1948
 Orban (Spec) Sanders, N.Y. Yanks, 1950
 Lester Hayes, Oakland, 1980
12 By nine players

Most Interceptions By, Rookie, Season
14 Dick (Night Train) Lane, Los Angeles, 1952
13 Dan Sandifer, Washington, 1948
12 Woodley Lewis, Los Angeles, 1950
 Paul Krause, Washington, 1964

Most Interceptions By, Game
4 Sammy Baugh, Washington vs. Detroit, Nov. 14, 1943
 Dan Sandifer, Washington vs. Boston, Oct. 31, 1948
 Don Doll, Detroit vs. Chi. Cardinals, Oct. 23, 1949
 Bob Nussbaumer, Chi. Cardinals vs. N.Y. Bulldogs, Nov. 13, 1949
 Russ Craft, Philadelphia vs. Chi. Cardinals, Sept. 24, 1950
 Bobby Dillon, Green Bay vs. Detroit, Nov. 26, 1953
 Jack Butler, Pittsburgh vs. Washington, Dec. 13, 1953
 Austin (Goose) Gonsoulin, Denver vs. Buffalo, Sept. 18, 1960
 Jerry Norton, St. Louis vs. Washington, Nov. 20, 1960; vs. Pittsburgh, Nov. 26, 1961
 Dave Baker, San Francisco vs. L.A. Rams, Dec. 4, 1960
 Bobby Ply, Dall. Texans vs. San Diego, Dec. 16, 1962
 Bobby Hunt, Kansas City vs. Houston, Oct. 4, 1964
 Willie Brown, Denver vs. N.Y. Jets, Nov. 15, 1964
 Dick Anderson, Miami vs. Pittsburgh, Dec. 3, 1973
 Willie Buchanon, Green Bay vs. San Diego, Sept. 24, 1978
 Deron Cherry, Kansas City vs. Seattle, Sept. 29, 1985

Most Consecutive Games, Passes Intercepted By
8 Tom Morrow, Oakland, 1962-63
7 Paul Krause, Washington, 1964
 Larry Wilson, St. Louis, 1966
 Ben Davis, Cleveland, 1968
6 Dick (Night Train) Lane, Chi. Cardinals, 1954-55
 Will Sherman, Los Angeles, 1954-55
 Jim Shofner, Cleveland, 1960
 Paul Krause, Minnesota, 1968
 Willie Williams, N.Y. Giants, 1968
 Kermit Alexander, San Francisco, 1968-69
 Mel Blount, Pittsburgh, 1975
 Eric Harris, Kansas City, 1980
 Lester Hayes, Oakland, 1980
 Barry Wilburn, Washington, 1987

Yards Gained
Most Seasons Leading League
2 Dick (Night Train) Lane, Los Angeles, 1952; Chi. Cardinals, 1954
 Herb Adderley, Green Bay, 1965, 1969
 Dick Anderson, Miami, 1968, 1970

Most Yards Gained, Career
1,282 Emlen Tunnell, N.Y. Giants, 1948-58; Green Bay, 1959-61
1,207 Dick (Night Train) Lane, Los Angeles, 1952-53; Chi. Cardinals, 1954-59; Detroit, 1960-65
1,185 Paul Krause, Washington, 1964-67; Minnesota, 1968-79

Most Yards Gained, Season
349 Charlie McNeil, San Diego, 1961

301 Don Doll, Detroit, 1949
298 Dick (Night Train) Lane, Los Angeles, 1952
Most Yards Gained, Rookie, Season
301 Don Doll, Detroit, 1949
298 Dick (Night Train) Lane, Los Angeles, 1952
275 Woodley Lewis, Los Angeles, 1950
Most Yards Gained, Game
177 Charlie McNeil, San Diego vs. Houston, Sept. 24, 1961
167 Dick Jauron, Detroit vs. Chicago, Nov. 18, 1973
151 Tom Myers, New Orleans vs. Minnesota, Sept. 3, 1978
Mike Haynes, L.A. Raiders vs. Miami, Dec. 2, 1984
Longest Return (All TDs)
103 Vencie Glenn, San Diego vs. Denver, Nov. 29, 1987
102 Bob Smith, Detroit vs. Chi. Bears, Nov. 24, 1949
Erich Barnes, N.Y. Giants vs. Dall. Cowboys, Oct. 15, 1961
Gary Barbaro, Kansas City vs. Seattle, Dec. 11, 1977
Louis Breeden, Cincinnati vs. San Diego, Nov. 8, 1981
101 Richie Petitbon, Chicago vs Los Angeles, Dec. 9, 1962
Henry Carr, N.Y. Giants vs. Los Angeles, Nov. 13, 1966
Tony Greene, Buffalo vs. Kansas City, Oct. 3, 1976
Tom Pridemore, Atlanta vs. San Francisco, Sept. 20, 1981

Touchdowns
Most Touchdowns, Career
9 Ken Houston, Houston, 1967-72; Washington, 1973-80
7 Herb Adderley, Green Bay, 1961-69; Dallas, 1970-72
Erich Barnes, Chi. Bears, 1958-60; N.Y. Giants, 1961-64; Cleveland, 1965-70
Lem Barney, Detroit, 1967-77
6 Tom Janik, Denver, 1963-64; Buffalo, 1965-68; Boston, 1969-70; New England, 1971
Miller Farr, Denver, 1965; San Diego, 1965-66; Houston, 1967-69; St. Louis, 1970-72; Detroit, 1973
Bobby Bell, Kansas City, 1963-74
Most Touchdowns, Season
4 Ken Houston, Houston, 1971
Jim Kearney, Kansas City, 1972
3 Dick Harris, San Diego, 1961
Dick Lynch, N.Y. Giants, 1963
Herb Adderley, Green Bay, 1965
Lem Barney, Detroit, 1967
Miller Farr, Houston, 1967
Monte Jackson, Los Angeles, 1976
Rod Perry, Los Angeles, 1978
Ronnie Lott, San Francisco, 1981
Lloyd Burruss, Kansas City, 1986
Wayne Haddix, Tampa Bay, 1990
2 By many players
Most Touchdowns, Rookie, Season
3 Lem Barney, Detroit, 1967
Ronnie Lott, San Francisco, 1981
2 By many players
Most Touchdowns, Game
2 Bill Blackburn, Chi. Cardinals vs. Boston, Oct. 24, 1948
Dan Sandifer, Washington vs. Boston, Oct. 31, 1948
Bob Franklin, Cleveland vs. Chicago, Dec. 11, 1960
Bill Stacy, St. Louis vs. Dall. Cowboys, Nov. 5, 1961
Jerry Norton, St. Louis vs. Pittsburgh, Nov. 26, 1961
Miller Farr, Houston vs. Buffalo, Dec. 7, 1968
Ken Houston, Houston vs. San Diego, Dec. 19, 1971
Jim Kearney, Kansas City vs. Denver, Oct. 1, 1972
Lemar Parrish, Cincinnati vs. Houston, Dec. 17, 1972
Dick Anderson, Miami vs. Pittsburgh, Dec. 3, 1973
Prentice McCray, New England vs. N.Y. Jets, Nov. 21, 1976
Kenny Johnson, Atlanta vs. Green Bay, Nov. 27, 1983 (OT)
Mike Kozlowski, Miami vs. N.Y. Jets, Dec. 16, 1983
Dave Brown, Seattle vs. Kansas City, Nov. 4, 1984
Lloyd Burruss, Kansas City vs. San Diego, Oct. 19, 1986

Punting
Most Seasons Leading League
4 Sammy Baugh, Washington, 1940-43
Jerrel Wilson, Kansas City, 1965, 1968, 1972-73
3 Yale Lary, Detroit, 1959, 1961, 1963
Jim Fraser, Denver, 1962-64
Ray Guy, Oakland, 1974-75, 1977
Rohn Stark, Baltimore, 1983; Indianapolis, 1985-86
2 By many players
Most Consecutive Seasons Leading League
4 Sammy Baugh, Washington, 1940-43
3 Jim Fraser, Denver, 1962-64
2 By many players

Punts
Most Punts, Career
1,154 Dave Jennings, N.Y. Giants, 1974-84; N.Y. Jets, 1985-87
1,083 John James, Atlanta, 1972-81; Detroit, 1982, Houston, 1982-84
1,072 Jerrel Wilson, Kansas City, 1963-77; New England, 1978
Most Punts, Season
114 Bob Parsons, Chicago, 1981
109 John James, Atlanta, 1978
108 John Teltschik, Philadelphia, 1986
Most Punts, Rookie, Season
108 John Teltschik, Philadelphia, 1986
99 Lewis Colbert, Kansas City, 1986
96 Mike Connell, San Francisco, 1978
Chris Norman, Denver, 1984
Most Punts, Game
15 John Teltschik, Philadelphia vs. N.Y. Giants, Dec. 6, 1987 (OT)
14 Dick Nesbitt, Chi. Cardinals vs. Chi. Bears, Nov. 30, 1933
Keith Molesworth, Chi. Bears vs. Green Bay, Dec. 10, 1933
Sammy Baugh, Washington vs. Philadelphia, Nov. 5, 1939
Carl Kinscherf, N.Y. Giants vs. Detroit, Nov. 7, 1943

George Taliaferro, N.Y. Yanks vs. Los Angeles, Sept. 28, 1951
12 By many players. Last time: Bryan Wagner, Cleveland vs. Kansas City, Nov. 19, 1989 (OT)
Longest Punt
98 Steve O'Neal, N.Y. Jets vs. Denver, Sept. 21, 1969
94 Joe Lintzenich, Chi. Bears vs. N.Y. Giants, Nov. 16, 1931
93 Shawn McCarthy, New England vs. Buffalo, Nov. 3, 1991

Average Yardage
Highest Average, Punting, Career (300 punts)
45.10 Sammy Baugh, Washington, 1937-52 (338-15,245)
44.68 Tommy Davis, San Francisco, 1959-69 (511-22,833)
44.29 Yale Lary, Detroit, 1952-53, 1956-64 (503-22,279)
Highest Average, Punting, Season (Qualifiers)
51.40 Sammy Baugh, Washington, 1940 (35-1,799)
48.94 Yale Lary, Detroit, 1963 (35-1,713)
48.73 Sammy Baugh, Washington, 1941 (30-1,462)
Highest Average, Punting, Rookie, Season (Qualifiers)
46.40 Bobby Walden, Minnesota, 1964 (72-3,341)
46.22 Dave Lewis, Cincinnati, 1970 (79-3,651)
45.92 Frank Sinkwich, Detroit, 1943 (12-551)
Highest Average, Punting, Game (4 punts)
61.75 Bob Cifers, Detroit vs. Chi. Bears, Nov. 24, 1946 (4-247)
61.60 Roy McKay, Green Bay vs. Chi. Cardinals, Oct. 28, 1945 (5-308)
59.40 Sammy Baugh, Washington vs. Detroit, Oct. 27, 1940 (5-297)

Punts Had Blocked
Most Consecutive Punts, None Blocked
623 Dave Jennings, N.Y. Giants, 1976-83
619 Ray Guy, Oakland, 1979-81; L.A. Raiders, 1982-86
578 Bobby Walden, Minnesota, 1964-67; Pittsburgh, 1968-72
Most Punts Had Blocked, Career
14 Herman Weaver, Detroit, 1970-76; Seattle, 1977-80
13 Harry Newsome, Pittsburgh, 1985-89; Minnesota, 1990-91
12 Jerrel Wilson, Kansas City, 1963-77; New England, 1978
Tom Blanchard, N.Y. Giants, 1971-73; New Orleans, 1974-78; Tampa Bay, 1979-81
Most Punts Had Blocked, Season
6 Harry Newsome, Pittsburgh, 1988
4 Bryan Wagner, Cleveland, 1990
3 By many players

Punt Returns
Most Seasons Leading League
3 Les (Speedy) Duncan, San Diego, 1965-66; Washington, 1971
Rick Upchurch, Denver, 1976, 1978, 1982
2 Dick Christy, N.Y. Titans, 1961-62
Claude Gibson, Oakland, 1963-64
Billy Johnson, Houston, 1975, 1977
Mel Gray, New Orleans, 1987; Detroit, 1991

Punt Returns
Most Punt Returns, Career
282 Billy Johnson, Houston, 1974-80; Atlanta, 1982-87; Washington, 1988
267 J. T. Smith, Washington, 1978; Kansas City, 1978-84; St. Louis, 1985-87; Phoenix, 1988-90
258 Emlen Tunnell, N.Y. Giants, 1948-58; Green Bay, 1959-61
Most Punt Returns, Season
70 Danny Reece, Tampa Bay, 1979
62 Fulton Walker, Miami-L.A. Raiders, 1985
58 J. T. Smith, Kansas City, 1979
Greg Pruitt, L.A. Raiders, 1983
Leo Lewis, Minnesota, 1988
Most Punt Returns, Rookie, Season
57 Lew Barnes, Chicago, 1986
54 James Jones, Dallas, 1980
53 Louis Lipps, Pittsburgh, 1984
Most Punt Returns, Game
11 Eddie Brown, Washington vs. Tampa Bay, Oct. 9, 1977
10 Theo Bell, Pittsburgh vs. Buffalo, Dec. 16, 1979
Mike Nelms, Washington vs. New Orleans, Dec. 26, 1982
9 Rodger Bird, Oakland vs. Denver, Sept. 10, 1967
Ralph McGill, San Francisco vs. Atlanta, Oct. 29, 1972
Ed Podolak, Kansas City vs. San Diego, Nov. 10, 1974
Anthony Leonard, San Francisco vs. New Orleans, Oct. 17, 1976
Butch Johnson, Dallas vs. Buffalo, Nov. 15, 1976
Larry Marshall, Philadelphia vs. Tampa Bay, Sept. 18, 1977
Nesby Glasgow, Baltimore vs. Kansas City, Sept. 2, 1979
Mike Nelms, Washington vs. St. Louis, Dec. 21, 1980
Leon Bright, N.Y. Giants vs. Philadelphia, Dec. 11, 1982
Pete Shaw, N.Y. Giants vs. Philadelphia, Nov. 20, 1983
Cleotha Montgomery, L.A. Raiders vs. Detroit, Dec. 10, 1984
Phil McConkey, N.Y. Giants vs. Philadelphia, Dec. 6, 1987 (OT)

Fair Catches
Most Fair Catches, Career
102 Willie Wood, Green Bay, 1960-71
99 Phil McConkey, N.Y. Giants, 1984-88; Green Bay, 1986; San Diego, 1989
98 Leo Lewis, Minnesota, 1981-90, 1991; Cleveland, 1990
Most Fair Catches, Season
27 Leo Lewis, Minnesota, 1989
25 Mark Konecny, Philadelphia, 1988
Phil McConkey, N.Y. Giants, 1988
24 Ken Graham, San Diego, 1969
Most Fair Catches, Game
7 Lem Barney, Detroit vs. Chicago, Nov. 21, 1976
Bobby Morse, Philadelphia vs. Buffalo, Dec. 27, 1987
6 Jake Scott, Miami vs. Buffalo, Dec. 20, 1970
Greg Pruitt, L.A. Raiders vs. Seattle, Oct. 7, 1984
Phil McConkey, San Diego vs. Kansas City, Dec. 17, 1989
Gerald McNeil, Houston vs. Pittsburgh, Sept. 16, 1990
5 By many players

Yards Gained

Most Seasons Leading League

- 3   Alvin Haymond, Baltimore, 1965-66; Los Angeles, 1969
- 2   Bill Dudley, Pittsburgh, 1942, 1946
  - Emlen Tunnell, N.Y. Giants, 1951-52
  - Dick Christy, N.Y. Titans, 1961-62
  - Claude Gibson, Oakland, 1963-64
  - Rodger Bird, Oakland, 1966-67
  - J. T. Smith, Kansas City, 1979-80
  - Vai Sikahema, St. Louis, 1986-87
  - David Meggett, N.Y. Giants, 1989-90

Most Yards Gained, Career

- 3,317   Billy Johnson, Houston, 1974-80; Atlanta, 1982-87; Washington, 1988
- 3,008   Rick Upchurch, Denver, 1975-83
- 2,764   J. T. Smith, Washington, 1978; Kansas City, 1978-84; St. Louis, 1985-87; Phoenix, 1988-90

Most Yards Gained, Season

- 692   Fulton Walker, Miami-L.A. Raiders, 1985
- 666   Greg Pruitt, L.A. Raiders, 1983
- 656   Louis Lipps, Pittsburgh, 1984

Most Yards Gained, Rookie, Season

- 656   Louis Lipps, Pittsburgh, 1984
- 655   Neal Colzie, Oakland, 1975
- 608   Mike Haynes, New England, 1976

Most Yards Gained, Game

- 207   LeRoy Irvin, Los Angeles vs. Atlanta, Oct. 11, 1981
- 205   George Atkinson, Oakland vs. Buffalo, Sept. 15, 1968
- 184   Tom Watkins, Detroit vs. San Francisco, Oct. 6, 1963

Longest Punt Return (All TDs)

- 98   Gil LeFebvre, Cincinnati vs. Brooklyn, Dec. 3, 1933
  - Charlie West, Minnesota vs. Washington, Nov. 3, 1968
  - Dennis Morgan, Dallas vs. St. Louis, Oct. 13, 1974
  - Terance Mathis, N.Y. Jets vs. Dallas, Nov. 4, 1990
- 97   Greg Pruitt, L.A. Raiders vs. Washington, Oct. 2, 1983
- 96   Bill Dudley, Washington vs. Pittsburgh, Dec. 3, 1950

Average Yardage

Highest Average, Career (75 returns)

- 12.78   George McAfee, Chi. Bears, 1940-41, 1945-50 (112-1,431)
- 12.75   Jack Christiansen, Detroit, 1951-58 (85-1,084)
- 12.55   Claude Gibson, San Diego, 1961-62; Oakland, 1963-65 (110-1,381)

Highest Average, Season (Qualifiers)

- 23.00   Herb Rich, Baltimore, 1950 (12-276)
- 21.47   Jack Christiansen, Detroit, 1952 (15-322)
- 21.28   Dick Christy, N.Y. Titans, 1961 (18-383)

Highest Average, Rookie, Season (Qualifiers)

- 23.00   Herb Rich, Baltimore, 1950 (12-276)
- 20.88   Jerry Davis, Chi. Cardinals, 1948 (16-334)
- 20.73   Frank Sinkwich, Detroit, 1943 (11-228)

Highest Average, Game (3 returns)

- 47.67   Chuck Latourette, St. Louis vs. New Orleans, Sept. 29, 1968 (3-143)
- 47.33   Johnny Roland, St. Louis vs. Philadelphia, Oct. 2, 1966 (3-142)
- 45.67   Dick Christy, N.Y. Titans vs. Denver, Sept. 24, 1961 (3-137)

Touchdowns

Most Touchdowns, Career

- 8   Jack Christiansen, Detroit, 1951-58
  - Rick Upchurch, Denver, 1975-83
- 6   Billy Johnson, Houston, 1974-80; Atlanta, 1982-87; Washington, 1988
- 5   Emlen Tunnell, N.Y. Giants, 1948-58; Green Bay, 1959-61

Most Touchdowns, Season

- 4   Jack Christiansen, Detroit, 1951
  - Rick Upchurch, Denver, 1976
- 3   Emlen Tunnell, N.Y. Giants, 1951
  - Billy Johnson, Houston, 1975
  - LeRoy Irvin, Los Angeles, 1981
- 2   By many players

Most Touchdowns, Rookie, Season

- 4   Jack Christiansen, Detroit, 1951
- 2   By six players

Most Touchdowns, Game

- 2   Jack Christiansen, Detroit vs. Los Angeles, Oct. 14, 1951; vs. Green Bay, Nov. 22, 1951
  - Dick Christy, N.Y. Titans vs. Denver, Sept. 24, 1961
  - Rick Upchurch, Denver vs. Cleveland, Sept. 26, 1976
  - LeRoy Irvin, Los Angeles vs. Atlanta, Oct. 11, 1981
  - Vai Sikahema, St. Louis vs. Tampa Bay, Dec. 21, 1986

Kickoff Returns

Most Seasons Leading League

- 3   Abe Woodson, San Francisco, 1959, 1962-63
- 2   Lynn Chandnois, Pittsburgh, 1951-52
  - Bobby Jancik, Houston, 1962-63
  - Travis Williams, Green Bay, 1967; Los Angeles, 1971

Kickoff Returns

Most Kickoff Returns, Career

- 275   Ron Smith, Chicago, 1965, 1970-72; Atlanta, 1966-67; Los Angeles, 1968-69; San Diego, 1973; Oakland, 1974
- 243   Bruce Harper, N.Y. Jets, 1977-84
- 199   Ron Brown, L.A. Rams, 1984-89, 1991; L.A. Raiders, 1990

Most Kickoff Returns, Season

- 60   Drew Hill, Los Angeles, 1981
- 55   Bruce Harper, N.Y. Jets, 1978, 1979
  - David Turner, Cincinnati, 1979
  - Stump Mitchell, St. Louis, 1981
- 53   Eddie Payton, Minnesota, 1980
  - Buster Rhymes, Minnesota, 1985

Most Kickoff Returns, Rookie, Season

- 55   Stump Mitchell, St. Louis, 1981
- 53   Buster Rhymes, Minnesota, 1985

- 50   Nesby Glasgow, Baltimore, 1979
  - Dino Hall, Cleveland, 1979

Most Kickoff Returns, Game

- 9   Noland Smith, Kansas City vs. Oakland, Nov. 23, 1967
  - Dino Hall, Cleveland vs. Pittsburgh, Oct. 7, 1979
  - Paul Palmer, Kansas City vs. Seattle, Sept. 20, 1987
- 8   George Taliaferro, N.Y. Yanks vs. N.Y. Giants, Dec. 3, 1950
  - Bobby Jancik, Houston vs. Boston, Dec. 8, 1963
  - Bobby Jancik, Houston vs. Oakland, Dec. 22, 1963
  - Mel Renfro, Dallas vs. Green Bay, Nov. 29, 1964
  - Willie Porter, Boston vs. N.Y. Jets, Sept. 22, 1968
  - Keith Moody, Buffalo vs. Seattle, Oct. 30, 1977
  - Brian Baschnagel, Chicago vs. Houston, Nov. 6, 1977
  - Bruce Harper, N.Y. Jets vs. New England, Oct. 29, 1978
  - Bruce Harper, N.Y. Jets vs. New England, Sept. 9, 1979
  - Dino Hall, Cleveland vs. Pittsburgh, Nov. 25, 1979
  - Terry Metcalf, Washington vs. St. Louis, Sept. 20, 1981
  - Harlan Huckleby, Green Bay vs. Washington, Oct. 17, 1983
  - Gary Ellerson, Green Bay vs. St. Louis, Sept. 29, 1985
  - Bobby Humphrey, N.Y. Jets vs. Cincinnati, Dec. 21, 1986
  - Bobby Joe Edmonds, Seattle vs. L.A. Raiders, Nov. 30, 1987
  - Joe Cribbs, Miami vs. Pittsburgh, Dec. 18, 1988
  - Erric Pegram, Atlanta vs. Washington, Nov. 10, 1991
- 7   By many players

Yards Gained

Most Seasons Leading League

- 3   Bruce Harper, N.Y. Jets, 1977-79
- 2   Marshall Goldberg, Chi. Cardinals, 1941-42
  - Woodley Lewis, Los Angeles, 1953-54
  - Al Carmichael, Green Bay, 1956-57
  - Timmy Brown, Philadelphia, 1961, 1963
  - Bobby Jancik, Houston, 1963, 1966
  - Ron Smith, Atlanta, 1966-67

Most Yards Gained, Career

- 6,922   Ron Smith, Chicago, 1965, 1970-72; Atlanta, 1966-67; Los Angeles, 1968-69; San Diego, 1973; Oakland, 1974
- 5,538   Abe Woodson, San Francisco, 1958-64; St. Louis, 1965-66
- 5,407   Bruce Harper, N.Y. Jets, 1977-84

Most Yards Gained, Season

- 1,345   Buster Rhymes, Minnesota, 1985
- 1,317   Bobby Jancik, Houston, 1963
- 1,314   Dave Hampton, Green Bay, 1971

Most Yards Gained, Rookie, Season

- 1,345   Buster Rhymes, Minnesota, 1985
- 1,292   Stump Mitchell, St. Louis, 1981
- 1,245   Odell Barry, Denver, 1964

Most Yards Gained, Game

- 294   Wally Triplett, Detroit vs. Los Angeles, Oct. 29, 1950
- 247   Timmy Brown, Philadelphia vs. Dallas, Nov. 6, 1966
- 244   Noland Smith, Kansas City vs. San Diego, Oct. 15, 1967

Longest Kickoff Return (All TDs)

- 106   Al Carmichael, Green Bay vs. Chi. Bears, Oct. 7, 1956
  - Noland Smith, Kansas City vs. Denver, Dec. 17, 1967
  - Roy Green, St. Louis vs. Dallas, Oct. 21, 1979
- 105   Frank Seno, Chi. Cardinals vs. N.Y. Giants, Oct. 20, 1946
  - Ollie Matson, Chi. Cardinals vs. Washington, Oct. 14, 1956
  - Abe Woodson, San Francisco vs. Los Angeles, Nov. 8, 1959
  - Timmy Brown, Philadelphia vs. Cleveland, Sept. 17, 1961
  - Jon Arnett, Los Angeles vs. Detroit, Oct. 29, 1961
  - Eugene (Mercury) Morris, Miami vs. Cincinnati, Sept. 14, 1969
  - Travis Williams, Los Angeles vs. New Orleans, Dec. 5, 1971
- 104   By many players

Average Yardage

Highest Average, Career (75 returns)

- 30.56   Gale Sayers, Chicago, 1965-71 (91-2,781)
- 29.57   Lynn Chandnois, Pittsburgh, 1950-56 (92-2,720)
- 28.69   Abe Woodson, San Francisco, 1958-64; St. Louis, 1965-66 (193-5,538)

Highest Average, Season (Qualifiers)

- 41.06   Travis Williams, Green Bay, 1967 (18-739)
- 37.69   Gale Sayers, Chicago, 1967 (16-603)
- 35.50   Ollie Matson, Chi. Cardinals, 1958 (14-497)

Highest Average, Rookie, Season (Qualifiers)

- 41.06   Travis Williams, Green Bay, 1967 (18-739)
- 33.08   Tom Moore, Green Bay, 1960 (12-397)
- 32.88   Duriel Harris, Miami, 1976 (17-559)

Highest Average, Game (3 returns)

- 73.50   Wally Triplett, Detroit vs. Los Angeles, Oct. 29, 1950 (4-294)
- 67.33   Lenny Lyles, San Francisco vs. Baltimore, Dec. 18, 1960 (3-202)
- 65.33   Ken Hall, Houston vs. N.Y. Titans, Oct. 23, 1960 (3-196)

Touchdowns

Most Touchdowns, Career

- 6   Ollie Matson, Chi. Cardinals, 1952, 1954-58; L.A. Rams, 1959-62; Detroit, 1963; Philadelphia, 1964
  - Gale Sayers, Chicago, 1965-71
  - Travis Williams, Green Bay, 1967-70; Los Angeles, 1971
- 5   Bobby Mitchell, Cleveland, 1958-61; Washington, 1962-68
  - Abe Woodson, San Francisco, 1958-64; St. Louis, 1965-66
  - Timmy Brown, Green Bay, 1959; Philadelphia, 1960-67; Baltimore, 1968
- 4   Cecil Turner, Chicago, 1968-73
  - Ron Brown, L.A. Rams, 1984-89, 1991; L.A. Raiders, 1990

Most Touchdowns, Season

- 4   Travis Williams, Green Bay, 1967
  - Cecil Turner, Chicago, 1970
- 3   Verda (Vitamin T) Smith, Los Angeles, 1950
  - Abe Woodson, San Francisco, 1963
  - Gale Sayers, Chicago, 1967
  - Raymond Clayborn, New England, 1977
  - Ron Brown, L.A. Rams, 1985
- 2   By many players

Most Touchdowns, Rookie, Season
- 4 Travis Williams, Green Bay, 1967
- 3 Raymond Clayborn, New England, 1977
- 2 By seven players

Most Touchdowns, Game
- 2 Timmy Brown, Philadelphia vs. Dallas, Nov. 6, 1966
  Travis Williams, Green Bay vs. Cleveland, Nov. 12, 1967
  Ron Brown, L.A. Rams vs. Green Bay, Nov. 24, 1985

Combined Kick Returns

Most Combined Kick Returns, Career
- 510 Ron Smith, Chicago, 1965, 1970-72; Atlanta, 1966-67; Los Angeles, 1968-69; San Diego, 1973; Oakland, 1974 (p-235, k-275)
- 426 Bruce Harper, N.Y. Jets, 1977-84 (p-183, k-243)
- 423 Alvin Haymond, Baltimore, 1964-67; Philadelphia, 1968; Los Angeles, 1969-71; Washington, 1972; Houston, 1973 (p-253, k-170)

Most Combined Kick Returns, Season
- 100 Larry Jones, Washington, 1975 (p-53, k-47)
- 97 Stump Mitchell, St. Louis, 1981 (p-42, k-55)
- 94 Nesby Glasgow, Baltimore, 1979 (p-44, k-50)

Most Combined Kick Returns, Game
- 13 Stump Mitchell, St. Louis vs. Atlanta, Oct. 18, 1981 (p-6, k-7)
- 12 Mel Renfro, Dallas vs. Green Bay, Nov. 29, 1964 (p-4, k-8)
  Larry Jones, Washington vs. Dallas, Dec. 13, 1975 (p-6, k-6)
  Eddie Brown, Washington vs. Tampa Bay, Oct. 9, 1977 (p-11, k-1)
  Nesby Glasgow, Baltimore vs. Denver, Sept. 2, 1979 (p-9, k-3)
- 11 By many players

Yards Gained

Most Yards Returned, Career
- 8,710 Ron Smith, Chicago, 1965, 1970-72; Atlanta, 1966-67; Los Angeles, 1968-69; San Diego, 1973; Oakland, 1974 (p-1,788, k-6,922)
- 7,191 Bruce Harper, N.Y. Jets, 1977-84 (p-1,784, k-5,407)
- 6,740 Les (Speedy) Duncan, San Diego, 1964-70; Washington, 1971-74 (p-2,201, k-4,539)

Most Yards Returned, Season
- 1,737 Stump Mitchell, St. Louis, 1981 (p-445, k-1,292)
- 1,658 Bruce Harper, N.Y. Jets, 1978 (p-378, k-1,280)
- 1,591 Mike Nelms, Washington, 1981 (p-492, k-1,099)

Most Yards Returned, Game
- 294 Wally Triplett, Detroit vs. Los Angeles, Oct. 29, 1950 (k-294)
  Woodley Lewis, Los Angeles vs. Detroit, Oct. 18, 1953 (p-120, k-174)
- 289 Eddie Payton, Detroit vs. Minnesota, Dec. 17, 1977 (p-105, k-184)
- 282 Les (Speedy) Duncan, San Diego vs. N.Y. Jets, Nov. 24, 1968 (p-102, k-180)

Touchdowns

Most Touchdowns, Career
- 9 Ollie Matson, Chi. Cardinals, 1952, 1954-58; Los Angeles, 1959-62; Detroit, 1963; Philadelphia, 1964-66 (p-3, k-6)
- 8 Jack Christiansen, Detroit, 1951-58 (p-8)
  Bobby Mitchell, Cleveland, 1958-61; Washington, 1962-68 (p-3, k-5)
  Gale Sayers, Chicago, 1965-71 (p-2, k-6)
  Rick Upchurch, Denver, 1975-83 (p-8)
  Billy Johnson, Houston, 1974-80; Atlanta, 1982-87; Washington, 1988 (p-6, k-2)
- 7 Abe Woodson, San Francisco, 1958-64; St. Louis, 1965-66 (p-2, k-5)
  Travis Williams, Green Bay, 1967-70; Los Angeles, 1971 (p-1, k-6)

Most Touchdowns, Season
- 4 Jack Christiansen, Detroit, 1951 (p-4)
  Emlen Tunnell, N.Y. Giants, 1951 (p-3, k-1)
  Gale Sayers, Chicago, 1967 (p-1, k-3)
  Travis Williams, Green Bay, 1967 (k-4)
  Cecil Turner, Chicago, 1970 (k-4)
  Billy Johnson, Houston, 1975 (p-3, k-1)
  Rick Upchurch, Denver, 1976 (p-4)
- 3 Verda (Vitamin T) Smith, Los Angeles, 1950 (k-3)
  Abe Woodson, San Francisco, 1963 (k-3)
  Raymond Clayborn, New England, 1977 (k-3)
  Billy Johnson, Houston, 1977 (p-2, k-1)
  LeRoy Irvin, Los Angeles, 1981 (p-3)
  Ron Brown, L.A. Rams, 1985 (k-3)
- 2 By many players

Most Touchdowns, Game
- 2 Jack Christiansen, Detroit vs. Los Angeles, Oct. 14, 1951 (p-2); vs. Green Bay, Nov. 22, 1951 (p-2)
  Jim Patton, N.Y. Giants vs. Washington, Oct. 30, 1955 (p-1, k-1)
  Bobby Mitchell, Cleveland vs. Philadelphia, Nov. 23, 1958 (p-1, k-1)
  Dick Christy, N.Y. Titans vs. Denver, Sept. 24, 1961 (p-2)
  Al Frazier, Denver vs. Boston, Dec. 3, 1961 (p-1, k-1)
  Timmy Brown, Philadelphia vs. Dallas, Nov. 6, 1966 (k-2)
  Travis Williams, Green Bay vs. Cleveland, Nov. 12, 1967 (k-2); vs. Pittsburgh, Nov. 2, 1969 (p-1, k-1)
  Gale Sayers, Chicago vs. San Francisco, Dec. 3, 1967 (p-1, k-1)
  Rick Upchurch, Denver vs. Cleveland, Sept. 26, 1976 (p-2)
  Eddie Payton, Detroit vs. Minnesota, Dec. 17, 1977 (p-1, k-1)
  LeRoy Irvin, Los Angeles vs. Atlanta, Oct. 11, 1981 (p-2)
  Ron Brown, L.A. Rams vs. Green Bay, Nov. 24, 1985 (k-2)
  Vai Sikahema, St. Louis vs. Tampa Bay, Dec. 21, 1986 (p-2)

Fumbles

Most Fumbles, Career
- 108 Dave Krieg, Seattle, 1980-91
- 106 Dan Fouts, San Diego, 1973-87
- 105 Roman Gabriel, Los Angeles, 1962-72; Philadelphia, 1973-77

Most Fumbles, Season
- 18 Dave Krieg, Seattle, 1989
  Warren Moon, Houston, 1990
- 17 Dan Pastorini, Houston, 1973
  Warren Moon, Houston, 1984
  Randall Cunningham, Philadelphia, 1989
- 16 Don Meredith, Dallas, 1964
  Joe Cribbs, Buffalo, 1980
  Steve Fuller, Kansas City, 1980

Paul McDonald, Cleveland, 1984
Phil Simms, N.Y. Giants, 1985

Most Fumbles, Game
- 7 Len Dawson, Kansas City vs. San Diego, Nov. 15, 1964
- 6 Sam Etcheverry, St. Louis vs. N.Y. Giants, Sept. 17, 1961
  Dave Krieg, Seattle vs. Kansas City, Nov. 5, 1989
- 5 Paul Christman, Chi. Cardinals vs. Green Bay, Nov. 10, 1946
  Charlie Conerly, N.Y. Giants vs. San Francisco, Dec. 1, 1957
  Jack Kemp, Buffalo vs. Houston, Oct. 29, 1967
  Roman Gabriel, Philadelphia vs. Oakland, Nov. 21, 1976
  Randall Cunningham, Philadelphia vs. L.A. Raiders, Nov. 30, 1986 (OT)
  Willie Totten, Buffalo vs. Indianapolis, Oct. 4, 1987
  Dave Walter, Cincinnati vs. Seattle, Oct. 11, 1987
  Dave Krieg, Seattle vs. San Diego, Nov. 25, 1990 (OT)

Fumbles Recovered

Most Fumbles Recovered, Career, Own and Opponents'
- 43 Fran Tarkenton, Minnesota, 1961-66, 1972-78; N.Y. Giants, 1967-71 (43 own)
- 39 Warren Moon, Houston, 1984-91 (39 own)
- 38 Jack Kemp, Pittsburgh, 1957; L.A. Chargers, 1960; San Diego, 1961-62; Buffalo, 1962-67, 1969 (38 own)
  Dan Fouts, San Diego, 1973-87 (37 own, 1 opp)

Most Fumbles Recovered, Season, Own and Opponents'
- 9 Don Hultz, Minnesota, 1963 (9 opp)
  Dave Krieg, Seattle, 1989 (9 own)
- 8 Paul Christman, Chi. Cardinals, 1945 (8 own)
  Joe Schmidt, Detroit, 1955 (8 opp)
  Bill Butler, Minnesota, 1963 (8 own)
  Kermit Alexander, San Francisco, 1965 (4 own, 4 opp)
  Jack Lambert, Pittsburgh, 1976 (1 own, 7 opp)
  Danny White, Dallas, 1981 (8 own)
  Dan Marino, Miami, 1988 (7 own, 1 opp)
- 7 By many players

Most Fumbles Recovered, Game, Own and Opponents'
- 4 Otto Graham, Cleveland vs. N.Y. Giants, Oct. 25, 1953 (4 own)
  Sam Etcheverry, St. Louis vs. N.Y. Giants, Sept. 17, 1961 (4 own)
  Roman Gabriel, Los Angeles vs. San Francisco, Oct. 12, 1969 (4 own)
  Joe Ferguson, Buffalo vs. Miami, Sept. 18, 1977 (4 own)
  Randall Cunningham, Philadelphia vs. L.A. Raiders, Nov. 30, 1986 (OT) (4 own)
- 3 By many players

Own Fumbles Recovered

Most Own Fumbles Recovered, Career
- 43 Fran Tarkenton, Minnesota, 1961-66, 1972-78; N.Y. Giants, 1967-71
- 39 Warren Moon, Houston, 1984-91
- 38 Jack Kemp, Pittsburgh, 1957; L.A. Chargers, 1960; San Diego, 1961-62; Buffalo, 1962-67, 1969

Most Own Fumbles Recovered, Season
- 9 Dave Krieg, Seattle, 1989
- 8 Paul Christman, Chi. Cardinals, 1945
  Bill Butler, Minnesota, 1963
  Danny White, Dallas, 1981
- 7 By many players

Most Own Fumbles Recovered, Game
- 4 Otto Graham, Cleveland vs. N.Y. Giants, Oct. 25, 1953
  Sam Etcheverry, St. Louis vs. N.Y. Giants, Sept. 17, 1961
  Roman Gabriel, Los Angeles vs. San Francisco, Oct. 12, 1969
  Joe Ferguson, Buffalo vs. Miami, Sept. 18, 1977
  Randall Cunningham, Philadelphia vs. L.A. Raiders, Nov. 30, 1986 (OT)
- 3 By many players

Opponents' Fumbles Recovered

Most Opponents' Fumbles Recovered, Career
- 29 Jim Marshall, Cleveland, 1960; Minnesota, 1961-79
- 25 Dick Butkus, Chicago, 1965-73
- 23 Carl Eller, Minnesota, 1964-78; Seattle, 1979
  Reggie Williams, Cincinnati, 1976-89

Most Opponents' Fumbles Recovered, Season
- 9 Don Hultz, Minnesota, 1963
- 8 Joe Schmidt, Detroit, 1955
- 7 Alan Page, Minnesota, 1970
  Jack Lambert, Pittsburgh, 1976
  Ray Childress, Houston, 1988
  Rickey Jackson, New Orleans, 1990

Most Opponents' Fumbles Recovered, Game
- 3 Corwin Clatt, Chi. Cardinals vs. Detroit, Nov. 6, 1949
  Vic Sears, Philadelphia vs. Green Bay, Nov. 2, 1952
  Ed Beatty, San Francisco vs. Los Angeles, Oct. 7, 1956
  Ron Carroll, Houston vs. Cincinnati, Oct. 27, 1974
  Maurice Spencer, New Orleans vs. Atlanta, Oct. 10, 1976
  Steve Nelson, New England vs. Philadelphia, Oct. 8, 1978
  Charles Jackson, Kansas City vs. Pittsburgh, Sept. 6, 1981
  Willie Buchanon, San Diego vs. Denver, Sept. 27, 1981
  Joey Browner, Minnesota vs. San Francisco, Sept. 8, 1985
  Ray Childress, Houston vs. Washington, Oct. 30, 1988
- 2 By many players

Yards Returning Fumbles

Longest Fumble Run (All TDs)
- 104 Jack Tatum, Oakland vs. Green Bay, Sept. 24, 1972 (opp)
- 100 Chris Martin, Kansas City vs. Miami, Oct. 13, 1991 (opp)
- 99 Don Griffin, San Francisco vs. Chicago, Dec. 23, 1991 (opp)

Touchdowns

Most Touchdowns, Career (Total)
- 4 Bill Thompson, Denver, 1969-81
- 3 Ralph Heywood, Detroit, 1947-48; Boston, 1948; N.Y. Bulldogs, 1949
  Leo Sugar, Chi. Cardinals, 1954-59; St. Louis, 1960; Philadelphia, 1961; Detroit, 1962
  Bud McFadin, Los Angeles, 1952-56; Denver, 1960-63; Houston, 1964-65
  Doug Cline, Houston, 1960-66; San Diego, 1966
  Bob Lilly, Dall. Cowboys, 1961-74
  Chris Hanburger, Washington, 1965-78

Lemar Parrish, Cincinnati, 1970-77; Washington, 1978-81; Buffalo, 1982
Paul Krause, Washington, 1964-67; Minnesota, 1968-79
Brad Dusek, Washington, 1974-81
David Logan, Tampa Bay, 1979-86; Green Bay, 1987
Thomas Howard, Kansas City, 1977-83; St. Louis, 1984-85
Greg Townsend, L.A. Raiders, 1983-91
Les Miller, San Diego, 1987-90; New Orleans 1991
Chris Martin, New Orleans, 1983; Minnesota, 1984-88; Kansas City 1989-91
Jessie Tuggle, Atlanta, 1987-91
2 By many players

Most Touchdowns, Season (Total)
2 Harold McPhail, Boston, 1934
Harry Ebding, Detroit, 1937
John Morelli, Boston, 1944
Frank Maznicki, Boston, 1947
Fred (Dippy) Evans, Chi. Bears, 1948
Ralph Heywood, Boston, 1948
Art Tait, N.Y. Yanks, 1951
John Dwyer, Los Angeles, 1952
Leo Sugar, Chi. Cardinals, 1957
Doug Cline, Houston, 1961
Jim Bradshaw, Pittsburgh, 1964
Royce Berry, Cincinnati, 1970
Ahmad Rashad, Buffalo, 1974
Tim Gray, Kansas City, 1977
Charles Phillips, Oakland, 1978
Kenny Johnson, Atlanta, 1981
George Martin, N.Y. Giants, 1981
Del Rodgers, Green Bay, 1982
Mike Douglass, Green Bay, 1983
Shelton Robinson, Seattle, 1983
Erik McMillan, N.Y. Jets, 1989
Les Miller, San Diego, 1990
Seth Joyner, Philadelphia, 1991

Most Touchdowns, Career (Own recovered)
2 Ken Kavanaugh, Chi. Bears, 1940-41, 1945-50
Mike Ditka, Chicago, 1961-66; Philadelphia, 1967-68; Dallas, 1969-72
Gail Cogdill, Detroit, 1960-68; Baltimore, 1968; Atlanta, 1969-70
Ahmad Rashad, St. Louis, 1972-73; Buffalo, 1974; Minnesota, 1976-82
Jim Mitchell, Atlanta, 1969-79
Drew Pearson, Dallas, 1973-83
Del Rodgers, Green Bay, 1982, 1984; San Francisco, 1987-88

Most Touchdowns, Season (Own recovered)
2 Ahmad Rashad, Buffalo, 1974
Del Rodgers, Green Bay, 1982
1 By many players

Most Touchdowns, Career (Opponents' recovered)
3 Leo Sugar, Chi. Cardinals, 1954-59; St. Louis, 1960; Philadelphia, 1961; Detroit, 1962
Doug Cline, Houston, 1960-66; San Diego, 1966
Bud McFadin, Los Angeles, 1952-56; Denver, 1960-63; Houston, 1964-65
Bob Lilly, Dall. Cowboys, 1961-74
Chris Hanburger, Washington, 1965-78
Paul Krause, Washington, 1964-67; Minnesota, 1968-79
Lemar Parrish, Cincinnati, 1970-77; Washington, 1978-81; Buffalo, 1982
Bill Thompson, Denver, 1969-81
Brad Dusek, Washington, 1974-81
David Logan, Tampa Bay, 1979-86; Green Bay, 1987
Thomas Howard, Kansas City, 1977-83; St. Louis, 1984-85
Greg Townsend, L.A. Raiders, 1983-91
Les Miller, San Diego, 1987-90; New Orleans, 1991
Chris Martin, New Orleans, 1983; Minnesota, 1984-88; Kansas City, 1989-91
Jessie Tuggle, Atlanta, 1987-91
2 By many players

Most Touchdowns, Season (Opponents' recovered)
2 Harold McPhail, Boston, 1934
Harry Ebding, Detroit, 1937
John Morelli, Boston, 1944
Frank Maznicki, Boston, 1947
Fred (Dippy) Evans, Chi. Bears, 1948
Ralph Heywood, Boston, 1948
Art Tait, N.Y. Yanks, 1951
John Dwyer, Los Angeles, 1952
Leo Sugar, Chi. Cardinals, 1957
Doug Cline, Houston, 1961
Jim Bradshaw, Pittsburgh, 1964
Royce Berry, Cincinnati, 1970
Tim Gray, Kansas City, 1977
Charles Phillips, Oakland, 1978
Kenny Johnson, Atlanta, 1981
George Martin, N.Y. Giants, 1981
Mike Douglass, Green Bay, 1983
Shelton Robinson, Seattle, 1983
Erik McMillan, N.Y. Jets, 1989
Les Miller, San Diego, 1990
Seth Joyner, Philadelphia, 1991

Most Touchdowns, Game (Opponents' recovered)
2 Fred (Dippy) Evans, Chi. Bears vs. Washington, Nov. 28, 1948

Combined Net Yards Gained
Rushing, receiving, interception returns, punt returns, kickoff returns, and fumble returns.
Most Seasons Leading League
5 Jim Brown, Cleveland, 1958-61, 1964
3 Cliff Battles, Boston, 1932-33; Washington, 1937
Gale Sayers, Chicago, 1965-67
Eric Dickerson, L.A. Rams, 1983-84, 1986
2 By many players
Most Consecutive Seasons Leading League
4 Jim Brown, Cleveland, 1958-61
3 Gale Sayers, Chicago, 1965-67
2 Cliff Battles, Boston, 1932-33
Charley Trippi, Chi. Cardinals, 1948-49

Timmy Brown, Philadelphia, 1962-63
Floyd Little, Denver, 1967-68
James Brooks, San Diego, 1981-82
Eric Dickerson, L.A. Rams, 1983-84
Thurman Thomas, Buffalo, 1990-91

Attempts
Most Attempts, Career
4,368 Walter Payton, Chicago, 1975-87
3,351 Tony Dorsett, Dallas, 1977-87; Denver, 1988
3,281 Franco Harris, Pittsburgh, 1972-83; Seattle, 1984
Most Attempts, Season
496 James Wilder, Tampa Bay, 1984
449 Marcus Allen, L.A. Raiders, 1985
442 Eric Dickerson, L.A. Rams, 1983
Most Attempts, Rookie, Season
442 Eric Dickerson, L.A. Rams, 1983
395 George Rogers, New Orleans, 1981
390 Joe Cribbs, Buffalo, 1980
Most Attempts, Game
48 James Wilder, Tampa Bay vs. Pittsburgh, Oct. 30, 1983
47 James Wilder, Tampa Bay vs. Green Bay, Sept. 30, 1984 (OT)
46 Gerald Riggs, Atlanta vs. L.A. Rams, Nov. 17, 1985

Yards Gained
Most Yards Gained, Career
21,803 Walter Payton, Chicago, 1975-87
16,326 Tony Dorsett, Dallas, 1977-87; Denver, 1988
15,459 Jim Brown, Cleveland, 1957-65
Most Yards Gained, Season
2,535 Lionel James, San Diego, 1985
2,462 Terry Metcalf, St. Louis, 1975
2,444 Mack Herron, New England, 1974
Most Yards Gained, Rookie, Season
2,317 Tim Brown, L.A. Raiders, 1988
2,272 Gale Sayers, Chicago, 1965
2,212 Eric Dickerson, L.A. Rams, 1983
Most Yards Gained, Game
373 Billy Cannon, Houston vs. N.Y. Titans, Dec. 10, 1961
345 Lionel James, San Diego vs. L.A. Raiders, Nov. 10, 1985 (OT)
341 Timmy Brown, Philadelphia vs. St. Louis, Dec. 16, 1962

Sacks
Sacks have been compiled since 1982.
Most Sacks, Career
121.5 Lawrence Taylor, N.Y. Giants, 1982-91
110 Reggie White, Philadelphia, 1985-91
103.5 Richard Dent, Chicago, 1983-91
Most Sacks, Season
22 Mark Gastineau, N.Y. Jets, 1984
21 Reggie White, Philadelphia, 1987
Chris Doleman, Minnesota, 1989
20.5 Lawrence Taylor, N.Y. Giants, 1986
Most Sacks, Rookie, Season
12.5 Leslie O'Neal, San Diego, 1986
12 Charles Haley, San Francisco, 1986
11 Vernon Maxwell, Baltimore, 1983
Most Sacks, Game
7 Derrick Thomas, Kansas City vs. Seattle, Nov. 11, 1990
6 Fred Dean, San Francisco vs. New Orleans, Nov. 13, 1983
5.5 William Gay, Detroit vs. Tampa Bay, Sept. 4, 1983

Miscellaneous
Longest Return of Missed Field Goal (All TDs)
101 Al Nelson, Philadelphia vs. Dallas, Sept. 26, 1971
100 Al Nelson, Philadelphia vs. Cleveland, Dec. 11, 1966
Ken Ellis, Green Bay vs. N.Y. Giants, Sept. 19, 1971
99 Jerry Williams, Los Angeles vs. Green Bay, Dec. 16, 1951
Carl Taseff, Baltimore vs. Los Angeles, Dec. 12, 1959
Timmy Brown, Philadelphia vs. St. Louis, Sept. 16, 1962

Team Records

Championships
Most Seasons League Champion
11 Green Bay, 1929-31, 1936, 1939, 1944, 1961-62, 1965-67
9 Chi. Bears, 1921, 1932-33, 1940-41, 1943, 1946, 1963, 1985
6 N.Y. Giants, 1927, 1934, 1938, 1956, 1986, 1990
Most Consecutive Seasons League Champion
3 Green Bay, 1929-31
Green Bay, 1965-67
2 Canton, 1922-23
Chi. Bears, 1932-33
Chi. Bears, 1940-41
Philadelphia, 1948-49
Detroit, 1952-53
Cleveland, 1954-55
Baltimore, 1958-59
Houston, 1960-61
Green Bay, 1961-62
Buffalo, 1964-65
Miami, 1972-73
Pittsburgh, 1974-75
Pittsburgh, 1978-79
San Francisco, 1988-89
Most Times Finishing First, Regular Season (Since 1933)
18 Clev. Browns, 1950-55, 1957, 1964-65, 1967-69, 1971, 1980, 1985-87, 1989
17 N.Y. Giants, 1933-35, 1938-39, 1941, 1944, 1946, 1956, 1958-59, 1961-63, 1986, 1989-90
16 Chi. Bears, 1933-34, 1937, 1940-43, 1946, 1956, 1963, 1984-88, 1990

Most Consecutive Times Finishing First, Regular Season (Since 1933)
   7 Los Angeles, 1973-79
   6 Cleveland, 1950-55
       Dallas, 1966-71
       Minnesota, 1973-78
       Pittsburgh, 1974-79
   5 Oakland, 1972-76
       Chicago, 1984-88
       San Francisco, 1986-90

Games Won

Most Consecutive Games Won
 17 Chi. Bears, 1933-34
 16 Chi. Bears, 1941-42
      Miami, 1971-73
      Miami, 1983-84
 15 L.A. Chargers/San Diego, 1960-61
      San Francisco, 1989-90

Most Consecutive Games Without Defeat
 25 Canton, 1921-23 (won 22, tied 3)
 24 Chi. Bears, 1941-43 (won 23, tied 1)
 23 Green Bay, 1928-30 (won 21, tied 2)

Most Games Won, Season
 15 San Francisco, 1984
      Chicago, 1985
 14 Miami, 1972
      Pittsburgh, 1978
      Washington, 1983
      Miami, 1984
      Chicago, 1986
      N.Y. Giants, 1986
      San Francisco, 1989
      San Francisco, 1990
      Washington, 1991
 13 By many teams

Most Consecutive Games Won, Season
 14 Miami, 1972
 13 Chi. Bears, 1934
 12 Minnesota, 1969
      Chicago, 1985

Most Consecutive Games Won, Start of Season
 14 Miami, 1972, entire season
 13 Chi. Bears, 1934, entire season
 12 Chicago, 1985

Most Consecutive Games Won, End of Season
 14 Miami, 1972, entire season
 13 Chi. Bears, 1934, entire season
 11 Chi. Bears, 1942, entire season
      Cleveland, 1951

Most Consecutive Games Without Defeat, Season
 14 Miami, 1972 (won 14)
 13 Chi. Bears, 1926 (won 11, tied 2)
      Green Bay, 1929 (won 12, tied 1)
      Chi. Bears, 1934 (won 13)
      Baltimore, 1967 (won 11, tied 2)
 12 Canton, 1922 (won 10, tied 2)
      Canton, 1923 (won 11, tied 1)
      Minnesota, 1969 (won 12)
      Chicago, 1985 (won 12)

Most Consecutive Games Without Defeat, Start of Season
 14 Miami, 1972 (won 14), entire season
 13 Chi. Bears, 1926 (won 11, tied 2)
      Green Bay, 1929 (won 12, tied 1), entire season
      Chi. Bears, 1934 (won 13), entire season
      Baltimore, 1967 (won 11, tied 2)
 12 Canton, 1922 (won 10, tied 2), entire season
      Canton, 1923 (won 11, tied 1), entire season
      Chicago, 1985 (won 12)

Most Consecutive Games Without Defeat, End of Season
 14 Miami, 1972 (won 14), entire season
 13 Green Bay, 1929 (won 12, tied 1), entire season
      Chi. Bears, 1934 (won 13), entire season
 12 Canton, 1922 (won 10, tied 2), entire season
      Canton, 1923 (won 11, tied 1), entire season

Most Consecutive Home Games Won
 27 Miami, 1971-74
 20 Green Bay, 1929-32
 18 Oakland, 1968-70
      Dallas, 1979-81

Most Consecutive Home Games Without Defeat
 30 Green Bay, 1928-33 (won 27, tied 3)
 27 Miami, 1971-74 (won 27)
 23 Chi. Bears, 1923-25 (won 19, tied 6)

Most Consecutive Road Games Won
 18 San Francisco, 1988-90
 11 L.A. Chargers/San Diego, 1960-61
      San Francisco, 1987-88
 10 Chi. Bears, 1941-42
      Dallas, 1968-69
      New Orleans, 1987-88

Most Consecutive Road Games Without Defeat
 18 San Francisco, 1988-90 (won 18)
 13 Chi. Bears, 1941-43 (won 12, tied 1)
 12 Green Bay, 1928-30 (won 10, tied 2)

Most Shutout Games Won or Tied, Season
 10 Pottsville, 1926 (won 9, tied 1)
      N.Y. Giants, 1927 (won 9, tied 1)
  9 Akron, 1921 (won 8, tied 1)
      Canton, 1922 (won 7, tied 2)
      Frankford, 1926 (won 9)
      Frankford, 1929 (won 6, tied 3)
  8 By many teams

Most Consecutive Shutout Games Won or Tied
 13 Akron, 1920-21 (won 10, tied 3)
  7 Pottsville, 1926 (won 6, tied 1)
      Detroit, 1934 (won 7)
  6 Buffalo, 1920-21 (won 5, tied 1)
      Frankford, 1926 (won 6)
      Detroit, 1926 (won 4, tied 2)
      N.Y. Giants, 1926-27 (won 5, tied 1)

Games Lost

Most Consecutive Games Lost
 26 Tampa Bay, 1976-77
 19 Chi. Cardinals, 1942-43, 1945
      Oakland, 1961-62
 18 Houston, 1972-73

Most Consecutive Games Without Victory
 26 Tampa Bay, 1976-77 (lost 26)
 23 Rochester, 1922-25 (lost 21, tied 2)
      Washington, 1960-61 (lost 20, tied 3)
 19 Dayton, 1927-29 (lost 18, tied 1)
      Chi. Cardinals, 1942-43, 1945 (lost 19)
      Oakland, 1961-62 (lost 19)

Most Games Lost, Season
 15 New Orleans, 1980
      Dallas, 1989
      New England, 1990
      Indianapolis, 1991
 14 Tampa Bay, 1976
      San Francisco, 1978
      Detroit, 1979
      San Francisco, 1979
      Baltimore, 1981
      New England, 1981
      Houston, 1983
      Tampa Bay, 1983
      Buffalo, 1984
      Buffalo, 1985
      Tampa Bay, 1985
      Tampa Bay, 1986
 13 By many teams

Most Consecutive Games Lost, Season
 14 Tampa Bay, 1976
      New Orleans, 1980
      Baltimore, 1981
      New England, 1990
 13 Oakland, 1962
      Pittsburgh, 1969
      Indianapolis, 1986
 12 Tampa Bay, 1977

Most Consecutive Games Lost, Start of Season
 14 Tampa Bay, 1976, entire season
      New Orleans, 1980
 13 Oakland, 1962
      Indianapolis, 1986
 12 Tampa Bay, 1977

Most Consecutive Games Lost, End of Season
 14 Tampa Bay, 1976, entire season
      New England, 1990
 13 Pittsburgh, 1969
 11 Philadelphia, 1936
      Detroit, 1942, entire season
      Houston, 1972

Most Consecutive Games Without Victory, Season
 14 Tampa Bay, 1976 (lost 14), entire season
      New Orleans, 1980 (lost 14)
      Baltimore, 1981 (lost 14)
      New England, 1990 (lost 14)
 13 Washington, 1961 (lost 12, tied 1)
      Oakland, 1962 (lost 13)
      Pittsburgh, 1969 (lost 13)
      Indianapolis, 1986 (lost 13)
 12 Dall. Cowboys, 1960 (lost 11, tied 1) entire season
      Tampa Bay, 1977 (lost 12)

Most Consecutive Games Without Victory, Start of Season
 14 Tampa Bay, 1976 (lost 14), entire season
      New Orleans, 1980 (lost 14)
 13 Washington, 1961 (lost 12, tied 1)
      Oakland, 1962 (lost 13)
      Indianapolis, 1986 (lost 13)
 12 Dall. Cowboys, 1960 (lost 11, tied 1), entire season
      Tampa Bay, 1977 (lost 12)

Most Consecutive Games Without Victory, End of Season
 14 Tampa Bay, 1976, (lost 14) entire season
      New England, 1990 (lost 14)
 13 Pittsburgh, 1969 (lost 13)
 12 Dall. Cowboys, 1960 (lost 11, tied 1) entire season

Most Consecutive Home Games Lost
 14 Dallas, 1988-89
 13 Houston, 1972-73
      Tampa Bay, 1976-77
 11 Oakland, 1961-62
      Los Angeles, 1961-63

Most Consecutive Home Games Without Victory
 14 Dallas, 1988-89 (lost 14)
 13 Houston, 1972-73 (lost 13)
      Tampa Bay, 1976-77 (lost 13)
 12 Philadelphia, 1936-38 (lost 11, tied 1)

Most Consecutive Road Games Lost
 23 Houston, 1981-84
 22 Buffalo, 1983-86
 19 Tampa Bay, 1983-85
      Atlanta, 1988-91

Most Consecutive Road Games Without Victory

  23 Houston, 1981-84 (lost 23)
  22 Buffalo, 1983-86 (lost 22)
  19 Tampa Bay, 1983-85 (lost 19)
      Atlanta, 1988-91 (lost 19)

Most Shutout Games Lost or Tied, Season

  8 Frankford, 1927 (lost 6, tied 2)
    Brooklyn, 1931 (lost 8)
  7 Dayton, 1925 (lost 6, tied 1)
    Orange, 1929 (lost 4, tied 3)
    Frankford, 1931 (lost 6, tied 1)
  6 By many teams

Most Consecutive Shutout Games Lost or Tied

  8 Rochester, 1922-24 (lost 8)
  7 Hammond, 1922-23 (lost 6, tied 1)
  6 Providence, 1926-27 (lost 5, tied 1)
    Brooklyn, 1942-43 (lost 6)

Tie Games

Most Tie Games, Season

  6 Chi. Bears, 1932
  5 Frankford, 1929
  4 Chi. Bears, 1924
    Orange, 1929
    Portsmouth, 1932

Most Consecutive Tie Games

  3 Chi. Bears, 1932
  2 By many teams

Scoring

Most Seasons Leading League

  10 Chi. Bears, 1932, 1934-35, 1939, 1941-43, 1946-47, 1956
  6 Green Bay, 1931, 1936-38, 1961-62
    L.A. Rams, 1950-52, 1957, 1967, 1973
  5 Oakland, 1967-69, 1974, 1977
    Dallas, 1966, 1968, 1971, 1978, 1980
    San Diego, 1963, 1965, 1981-82, 1985
    San Francisco, 1953, 1965, 1970, 1987, 1989

Most Consecutive Seasons Leading League

  3 Green Bay, 1936-38
    Chi. Bears, 1941-43
    Los Angeles, 1950-52
    Oakland, 1967-69

Points

Most Points, Season

  541 Washington, 1983
  513 Houston, 1961
      Miami, 1984
  485 Washington, 1991

Fewest Points, Season (Since 1932)

  37 Cincinnati/St. Louis, 1934
  38 Cincinnati, 1933
    Detroit, 1942
  51 Pittsburgh, 1934
    Philadelphia, 1936

Most Points, Game

  72 Washington vs. N.Y. Giants, Nov. 27, 1966
  70 Los Angeles vs. Baltimore, Oct. 22, 1950
  65 Chi. Cardinals vs. N.Y. Bulldogs, Nov. 13, 1949
    Los Angeles vs. Detroit, Oct. 29, 1950

Most Points, Both Teams, Game

  113 Washington (72) vs. N.Y. Giants (41), Nov. 27, 1966
  101 Oakland (52) vs. Houston (49), Dec. 22, 1963
  99 Seattle (51) vs. Kansas City (48), Nov. 27, 1983 (OT)

Fewest Points, Both Teams, Game

  0 In many games. Last time: N.Y. Giants vs. Detroit, Nov. 7, 1943

Most Points, Shutout Victory, Game

  64 Philadelphia vs. Cincinnati, Nov. 6, 1934
  62 Akron vs. Oorang, Oct. 29, 1922
  60 Rock Island vs. Evansville, Oct. 15, 1922
    Chi. Cardinals vs. Rochester, Oct. 7, 1923

Fewest Points, Shutout Victory, Game

  2 Green Bay vs. Chi. Bears, Oct. 16, 1932
    Chi. Bears vs. Green Bay, Sept. 18, 1938

Most Points Overcome to Win Game

  28 San Francisco vs. New Orleans, Dec. 7, 1980 (OT) (trailed 7-35, won 38-35)
  25 St. Louis vs. Tampa Bay, Nov. 8, 1987 (trailed 3-28, won 31-28)
  24 Philadelphia vs. Washington, Oct. 27, 1946 (trailed 0-24, won 28-24)
    Detroit vs. Baltimore, Oct. 20, 1957 (trailed 3-27, won 31-27)
    Philadelphia vs. Chi. Cardinals, Oct. 25, 1959 (trailed 0-24, won 28-24)
    Denver vs. Boston, Oct. 23, 1960 (trailed 0-24, won 31-24)
    Miami vs. New England, Dec. 15, 1974 (trailed 0-24, won 34-27)
    Minnesota vs. San Francisco, Dec. 4, 1977 (trailed 0-24, won 28-27)
    Denver vs. Seattle, Sept. 23, 1979 (trailed 10-34, won 37-34)
    Houston vs. Cincinnati, Sept. 23, 1979 (OT) (trailed 0-24, won 30-27)
    L.A. Raiders vs. San Diego, Nov. 22, 1982 (trailed 0-24, won 28-24)
    L.A. Raiders vs. Denver, Sept. 26, 1988 (OT) (trailed 0-24, won 30-27)

Most Points Overcome to Tie Game

  31 Denver vs. Buffalo, Nov. 27, 1960 (trailed 7-38, tied 38-38)
  28 Los Angeles vs. Philadelphia, Oct. 3, 1948 (trailed 0-28, tied 28-28)

Most Points, Each Half

1st: 49 Green Bay vs. Tampa Bay, Oct. 2, 1983
     48 Buffalo vs. Miami, Sept. 18, 1966
     45 Green Bay vs. Cleveland, Nov. 12, 1967
        Indianapolis vs. Denver, Oct. 31, 1988
        Houston vs. Cleveland, Dec. 9, 1990

2nd: 49 Chi. Bears vs. Philadelphia, Nov. 30, 1941
     48 Chi. Cardinals vs. Baltimore, Oct. 2, 1950
        N.Y. Giants vs. Baltimore, Nov. 19, 1950
     45 Cincinnati vs. Houston, Dec. 17, 1972

Most Points, Both Teams, Each Half

1st: 70 Houston (35) vs. Oakland (35), Dec. 22, 1963
     62 N.Y. Jets (41) vs. Tampa Bay (21), Nov. 17, 1985
     59 St. Louis (31) vs. Philadelphia (28), Dec. 16, 1962

2nd: 65 Washington (38) vs. N.Y. Giants (27), Nov. 27, 1966
     62 L.A. Raiders (31) vs. San Diego (31), Jan. 2, 1983
     58 New England (37) vs. Baltimore (21), Nov. 23, 1980
        N.Y. Jets (37) vs. New England (21), Sept. 21, 1987

Most Points, One Quarter

  41 Green Bay vs. Detroit, Oct. 7, 1945 (second quarter)
    Los Angeles vs. Detroit, Oct. 29, 1950 (third quarter)
  37 Los Angeles vs. Green Bay, Sept. 21, 1980 (second quarter)
  35 Chi. Cardinals vs. Boston, Oct. 24, 1948 (third quarter)
    Green Bay vs. Cleveland, Nov. 12, 1967 (first quarter)
    Green Bay vs. Tampa Bay, Oct. 2, 1983 (second quarter)

Most Points, Both Teams, One Quarter

  49 Oakland (28) vs. Houston (21), Dec. 22, 1963 (second quarter)
  48 Green Bay (41) vs. Detroit (7), Oct. 7, 1945 (second quarter)
    Los Angeles (41) vs. Detroit (7), Oct. 29, 1950 (third quarter)
  47 St. Louis (27) vs. Philadelphia (20), Dec. 13, 1964 (second quarter)

Most Points, Each Quarter

1st: 35 Green Bay vs. Cleveland, Nov. 12, 1967
     31 Buffalo vs. Kansas City, Sept. 13, 1964
     28 By six teams

2nd: 41 Green Bay vs. Detroit, Oct. 7, 1945
     37 Los Angeles vs. Green Bay, Sept. 21, 1980
     35 Green Bay vs. Tampa Bay, Oct. 2, 1983

3rd: 41 Los Angeles vs. Detroit, Oct. 29, 1950
     35 Chi. Cardinals vs. Boston, Oct. 24, 1948
     28 By nine teams

4th: 31 Oakland vs. Denver, Dec. 17, 1960
        Oakland vs. San Diego, Dec. 8, 1963
        Atlanta vs. Green Bay, Sept. 13, 1981
     28 By many teams

Most Points, Both Teams, Each Quarter

1st: 42 Green Bay (35) vs. Cleveland (7), Nov. 12, 1967
     35 Dall. Texans (21) vs. N.Y. Titans (14), Nov. 11, 1962
        Dallas (28) vs. Philadelphia (7), Oct. 19, 1969
        Kansas City (21) vs. Seattle (14), Dec. 11, 1977
        Detroit (21) vs. L.A. Raiders (14), Dec. 10, 1990
        Dallas (21) vs. Atlanta (14), Dec. 22, 1991
     34 Los Angeles (21) vs. Baltimore (13), Oct. 22, 1950
        Oakland (21) vs. Atlanta (13), Nov. 30, 1975

2nd: 49 Oakland (28) vs. Houston (21), Dec. 22, 1963
     48 Green Bay (41) vs. Detroit (7), Oct. 7, 1945
     47 St. Louis (27) vs. Philadelphia (20), Dec. 13, 1964

3rd: 48 Los Angeles (41) vs. Detroit (7), Oct. 29, 1950
     42 Washington (28) vs. Philadelphia (14), Oct. 1, 1955
     41 Green Bay (21) vs. N.Y. Yanks (20), Oct. 8, 1950

4th: 42 Chi. Cardinals (28) vs. Philadelphia (14), Dec. 7, 1947
        Green Bay (28) vs. Chi. Bears (14), Nov. 6, 1955
        N.Y. Jets (28) vs. Boston (14), Oct. 27, 1968
        Pittsburgh (21) vs. Cleveland (21), Oct. 18, 1969
     41 Baltimore (27) vs. New England (14), Sept. 18, 1978
        New England (27) vs. Baltimore (14), Nov. 23, 1980
     40 Chicago (21) vs. Tampa Bay (19), Nov. 19, 1989

Most Consecutive Games Scoring

  274 Cleveland, 1950-71
  226 San Francisco, 1977-91 (current)
  218 Dallas, 1970-85

Touchdowns

Most Seasons Leading League, Touchdowns

  13 Chi. Bears, 1932, 1934-35, 1939, 1941-44, 1946-48, 1956, 1965
  7 Dallas, 1966, 1968, 1971, 1977-78, 1980
  6 Oakland, 1967-69, 1972, 1974, 1977
    San Diego, 1963, 1965, 1979, 1981-82, 1985

Most Consecutive Seasons Leading League, Touchdowns

  4 Chi. Bears, 1941-44
    Los Angeles, 1949-52
  3 Chi. Bears, 1946-48
    Baltimore, 1957-59
    Oakland, 1967-69
  2 By many teams

Most Touchdowns, Season

  70 Miami, 1984
  66 Houston, 1961
  64 Los Angeles, 1950

Fewest Touchdowns, Season (Since 1932)

  3 Cincinnati, 1933
  4 Cincinnati/St. Louis, 1934
  5 Detroit, 1942

Most Touchdowns, Game

  10 Philadelphia vs. Cincinnati, Nov. 6, 1934
    Los Angeles vs. Baltimore, Oct. 22, 1950
    Washington vs. N.Y. Giants, Nov. 27, 1966
  9 Chi. Cardinals vs. Rochester, Oct. 7, 1923
    Chi. Cardinals vs. N.Y. Giants, Oct. 17, 1948
    Chi. Cardinals vs. N.Y. Bulldogs, Nov. 13, 1949
    Los Angeles vs. Detroit, Oct. 29, 1950
    Pittsburgh vs. N.Y. Giants, Nov. 30, 1952
    Chicago vs. San Francisco, Dec. 12, 1965
    Chicago vs. Green Bay, Dec. 7, 1980
  8 By many teams.

Most Touchdowns, Both Teams, Game

  16 Washington (10) vs. N.Y. Giants (6), Nov. 27, 1966
  14 Chi. Cardinals (9) vs. N.Y. Giants (5), Oct. 17, 1948
    Los Angeles (10) vs. Baltimore (4), Oct. 22, 1950
    Houston (7) vs. Oakland (7), Dec. 22, 1963
  13 New Orleans (7) vs. St. Louis (6), Nov. 2, 1969
    Kansas City (7) vs. Seattle (6), Nov. 27, 1983 (OT)
    San Diego (8) vs. Pittsburgh (5), Dec. 8, 1985
    N.Y. Jets (7) vs. Miami (6), Sept. 21, 1986 (OT)

Most Consecutive Games Scoring Touchdowns
- 166 Cleveland, 1957-69
- 97 Oakland, 1966-73
- 96 Kansas City, 1963-70

Points After Touchdown
Most Points After Touchdown, Season
- 66 Miami, 1984
- 65 Houston, 1961
- 62 Washington, 1983

Fewest Points After Touchdown, Season
- 2 Chi. Cardinals, 1933
- 3 Cincinnati, 1933
  - Pittsburgh, 1934
- 4 Cincinnati/St. Louis, 1934

Most Points After Touchdown, Game
- 10 Los Angeles vs. Baltimore, Oct. 22, 1950
- 9 Chi. Cardinals vs. N.Y. Giants, Oct. 17, 1948
  - Pittsburgh vs. N.Y. Giants, Nov. 30, 1952
  - Washington vs. N.Y. Giants, Nov. 27, 1966
- 8 By many teams

Most Points After Touchdown, Both Teams, Game
- 14 Chi. Cardinals (9) vs. N.Y. Giants (5), Oct. 17, 1948
  - Houston (7) vs. Oakland (7), Dec. 22, 1963
  - Washington (9) vs. N.Y. Giants (5), Nov. 27, 1966
- 13 Los Angeles (10) vs. Baltimore (3), Oct. 22, 1950
- 12 In many games

Field Goals
Most Seasons Leading League, Field Goals
- 11 Green Bay, 1935-36, 1940-43, 1946-47, 1955, 1972, 1974
- 7 Washington, 1945, 1956, 1971, 1976-77, 1979, 1982
  - N.Y. Giants, 1933, 1937, 1939, 1941, 1944, 1959, 1983
- 5 Portsmouth/Detroit, 1932-33, 1937-38, 1980
  - Kansas City, 1966-67, 1970, 1975, 1990

Most Consecutive Seasons Leading League, Field Goals
- 4 Green Bay, 1940-43
- 3 Cleveland, 1952-54
- 2 By many teams

Most Field Goals Attempted, Season
- 49 Los Angeles, 1966
  - Washington, 1971
- 48 Green Bay, 1972
- 47 N.Y. Jets, 1969
  - Los Angeles, 1973
  - Washington, 1983

Fewest Field Goals Attempted, Season (Since 1938)
- 0 Chi. Bears, 1944
- 2 Cleveland, 1939
  - Card-Pitt, 1944
  - Boston, 1946
  - Chi. Bears, 1947
- 3 Chi. Bears, 1945
  - Cleveland, 1945

Most Field Goals Attempted, Game
- 9 St. Louis vs. Pittsburgh, Sept. 24, 1967
- 8 Pittsburgh vs. St. Louis, Dec. 2, 1962
  - Detroit vs. Minnesota, Nov. 13, 1966
  - N.Y. Jets vs. Buffalo, Nov. 3, 1968
- 7 By many teams

Most Field Goals Attempted, Both Teams, Game
- 11 St. Louis (6) vs. Pittsburgh (5), Nov. 13, 1966
  - Washington (6) vs. Chicago (5), Nov. 14, 1971
  - Green Bay (6) vs. Detroit (5), Sept. 29, 1974
  - Washington (6) vs. N.Y. Giants (5), Nov. 14, 1976
- 10 Denver (5) vs. Boston (5), Nov. 11, 1962
  - Boston (7) vs. San Diego (3), Sept. 20, 1964
  - Buffalo (7) vs. Houston (3), Dec. 5, 1965
  - St. Louis (7) vs. Atlanta (3), Dec. 11, 1966
  - Boston (7) vs. Buffalo (3), Sept. 24, 1967
  - Detroit (7) vs. Minnesota (3), Sept. 20, 1971
  - Washington (7) vs. Houston (3), Oct. 10, 1971
  - Green Bay (5) vs. St. Louis (5), Dec. 5, 1971
  - Kansas City (7) vs. Buffalo (3), Dec. 19, 1971
  - Kansas City (5) vs. San Diego (5), Oct. 29, 1972
  - Minnesota (6) vs. Chicago (4), Sept. 23, 1973
  - Cleveland (7) vs. Denver (3), Oct. 19, 1975
  - Cleveland (5) vs. Denver (5), Oct. 5, 1980
- 9 In many games

Most Field Goals, Season
- 35 N.Y. Giants, 1983
- 34 N.Y. Jets, 1968
  - Kansas City, 1990
- 33 Green Bay, 1972
  - Washington, 1983
  - Pittsburgh, 1985
  - New Orleans, 1987
  - Miami, 1991

Fewest Field Goals, Season (Since 1932)
- 0 Boston, 1932, 1935
  - Chi. Cardinals, 1932, 1945
  - Green Bay, 1932, 1944
  - N.Y. Giants, 1932
  - Brooklyn, 1944
  - Card-Pitt, 1944
  - Chi. Bears, 1944, 1947
  - Boston, 1946
  - Baltimore, 1950
  - Dallas, 1952

Most Field Goals, Game
- 7 St. Louis vs. Pittsburgh, Sept. 24, 1967
  - Minnesota vs. L.A. Rams, Nov. 5, 1989 (OT)
- 6 Boston vs. Denver, Oct. 4, 1964

Detroit vs. Minnesota, Nov. 13, 1966
N.Y. Jets vs. Buffalo, Nov. 3, 1968
Philadelphia vs. Houston, Nov. 12, 1972
N.Y. Jets vs. New Orleans, Dec. 3, 1972
St. Louis vs. Atlanta, Dec. 9, 1973
N.Y. Giants vs. Seattle, Oct. 18, 1981
San Francisco vs. New Orleans, Oct. 16, 1983
Pittsburgh vs. Denver, Oct. 23, 1988
- 5 By many teams

Most Field Goals, Both Teams, Game
- 8 Cleveland (4) vs. St. Louis (4), Sept. 20, 1964
  - Chicago (5) vs. Philadelphia (3), Oct. 20, 1968
  - Washington (5) vs. Chicago (3), Nov. 14, 1971
  - Kansas City (5) vs. Buffalo (3), Dec. 19, 1971
  - Detroit (4) vs. Green Bay (4), Sept. 29, 1974
  - Cleveland (5) vs. Denver (3), Oct. 19, 1975
  - New England (4) vs. San Diego (4), Nov. 9, 1975
  - San Francisco (6) vs. New Orleans (2), Oct. 16, 1983
  - Seattle (5) vs. L.A. Raiders (3), Dec. 18, 1988
- 7 In many games

Most Consecutive Games Scoring Field Goals
- 31 Minnesota, 1968-70
- 28 Washington, 1988-90
- 22 San Francisco, 1988-89

Safeties
Most Safeties, Season
- 4 Cleveland, 1927
  - Detroit, 1962
- 3 By many teams

Most Safeties, Game
- 3 L.A. Rams vs. N.Y. Giants, Sept. 30, 1984
- 2 N.Y. Giants vs. Pottsville, Oct. 30, 1927
  - Chi. Bears vs. Pottsville, Nov. 13, 1927
  - Detroit vs. Brooklyn, Dec. 1, 1935
  - N.Y. Giants vs. Pittsburgh, Sept. 17, 1950
  - N.Y. Giants vs. Washington, Nov. 5, 1961
  - Chicago vs. Pittsburgh, Nov. 9, 1969
  - Dallas vs. Philadelphia, Nov. 19, 1972
  - Los Angeles vs. Green Bay, Oct. 21, 1973
  - Oakland vs. San Diego, Oct. 26, 1975
  - Denver vs. Seattle, Jan. 2, 1983
  - New Orleans vs. Cleveland, Sept. 13, 1987
  - Buffalo vs. Denver, Nov. 8, 1987

Most Safeties, Both Teams, Game
- 3 L.A. Rams (3) vs. N.Y. Giants (0), Sept. 30, 1984
- 2 Chi. Cardinals (1) vs. Frankford (1), Nov. 19, 1927
  - Chi. Cardinals (1) vs. Cincinnati (1), Nov. 12, 1933
  - Chi. Bears (1) vs. San Francisco (1), Oct. 19, 1952
  - Cincinnati (1) vs. Los Angeles (1), Oct. 22, 1972
  - Chi. Bears (1) vs. San Francisco (1), Sept. 19, 1976
  - Baltimore (1) vs. Miami (1), Oct. 29, 1978
  - Atlanta (1) vs. Detroit (1), Oct. 5, 1980
  - Houston (1) vs. Philadelphia (1), Oct. 2, 1988
  - (Also see previous record)

First Downs
Most Seasons Leading League
- 9 Chi. Bears, 1935, 1939, 1941, 1943, 1945, 1947-49, 1955
- 7 San Diego, 1965, 1969, 1980-83, 1985
- 6 L.A. Rams, 1946, 1950-51, 1954, 1957, 1973

Most Consecutive Seasons Leading League
- 4 San Diego, 1980-83
- 3 Chi. Bears, 1947-49
- 2 By many teams

Most First Downs, Season
- 387 Miami, 1984
- 380 San Diego, 1985
- 379 San Diego, 1981

Fewest First Downs, Season
- 51 Cincinnati, 1933
- 64 Pittsburgh, 1935
- 67 Philadelphia, 1937

Most First Downs, Game
- 39 N.Y. Jets vs. Miami, Nov. 27, 1988
  - Washington vs. Detroit, Nov. 4, 1990 (OT)
- 38 Los Angeles vs. N.Y. Giants, Nov. 13, 1966
- 37 Green Bay vs. Philadelphia, Nov. 11, 1962

Fewest First Downs, Game
- 0 N.Y. Giants vs. Green Bay, Oct. 1, 1933
  - Pittsburgh vs. Boston, Oct. 29, 1933
  - Philadelphia vs. Detroit, Sept. 20, 1935
  - N.Y. Giants vs. Washington, Sept. 27, 1942
  - Denver vs. Houston, Sept. 3, 1966

Most First Downs, Both Teams, Game
- 62 San Diego (32) vs. Seattle (30), Sept. 15, 1985
- 59 Miami (31) vs. Buffalo (28), Oct. 9, 1983 (OT)
  - Seattle (33) vs. Kansas City (26), Nov. 27, 1983 (OT)
  - N.Y. Jets (32) vs. Miami (27), Sept. 21, 1986 (OT)
  - N.Y. Jets (39) vs. Miami (20), Nov. 27, 1988
- 58 Los Angeles (30) vs. Chi. Bears (28), Oct. 24, 1954
  - Denver (34) vs. Kansas City (24), Nov. 18, 1974
  - Atlanta (35) vs. New Orleans (23), Sept. 2, 1979 (OT)
  - Pittsburgh (36) vs. Cleveland (22), Nov. 25, 1979 (OT)
  - San Diego (34) vs. Miami (24), Nov. 18, 1984 (OT)
  - Cincinnati (32) vs. San Diego (26), Sept. 22, 1985

Fewest First Downs, Both Teams, Game
- 7 Chi. Cardinals (2) vs. Detroit (5), Sept. 15, 1940
- 9 Pittsburgh (1) vs. Boston (8), Oct. 27, 1935
  - Boston (4) vs. Brooklyn (5), Nov. 24, 1935
  - N.Y. Giants (3) vs. Detroit (6), Nov. 7, 1943
  - Pittsburgh (4) vs. Chi. Cardinals (5), Nov. 11, 1945

N.Y. Bulldogs (1) vs. Philadelphia (8), Sept. 22, 1949
10 N.Y. Giants (4) vs. Washington (6), Dec. 11, 1960

Most First Downs, Rushing, Season
181 New England, 1978
177 Los Angeles, 1973
176 Chicago, 1985

Fewest First Downs, Rushing, Season
36 Cleveland, 1942
Boston, 1944
39 Brooklyn, 1943
40 Philadelphia, 1940
Detroit, 1945

Most First Downs, Rushing, Game
25 Philadelphia vs. Washington, Dec. 2, 1951
23 St. Louis vs. New Orleans, Oct. 5, 1980
21 Cleveland vs. Philadelphia, Dec. 13, 1959
Green Bay vs. Philadelphia, Nov. 11, 1962
Los Angeles vs. New Orleans, Nov. 25, 1973
Pittsburgh vs. Kansas City, Nov. 7, 1976
New England vs. Denver, Nov. 28, 1976
Oakland vs. Green Bay, Sept. 17, 1978

Fewest First Downs, Rushing, Game
0 By many teams. Last time: Houston vs. Philadelphia, Dec. 2, 1991

Most First Downs, Rushing, Both Teams, Game
36 Philadelphia (25) vs. Washington (11), Dec. 2, 1951
31 Detroit (18) vs. Washington (13), Sept. 30, 1951
30 Los Angeles (17) vs. Minnesota (13), Nov. 5, 1961
New Orleans (17) vs. Green Bay (13), Sept. 9, 1979
New Orleans (16) vs. San Francisco (14), Nov. 11, 1979
New England (16) vs. Kansas City (14), Oct. 4, 1981

Fewest First Downs, Rushing, Both Teams, Game
2 Houston (0) vs. Denver (2), Dec. 2, 1962
3 Philadelphia (1) vs. Pittsburgh (2), Oct. 27, 1957
Boston (1) vs. Buffalo (2), Nov. 15, 1964
Los Angeles (0) vs. San Francisco (3), Dec. 6, 1964
Pittsburgh (1) vs. St. Louis (2), Nov. 13, 1966
Seattle (1) vs. New Orleans (2), Sept. 1, 1991
4 In many games

Most First Downs, Passing, Season
259 San Diego, 1985
251 Houston, 1990
250 Miami, 1986

Fewest First Downs, Passing, Season
18 Pittsburgh, 1941
23 Brooklyn, 1942
N.Y. Giants, 1944
24 N.Y. Giants, 1943

Most First Downs, Passing, Game
29 N.Y. Giants vs. Cincinnati, Oct. 13, 1985
27 San Diego vs. Seattle, Sept. 15, 1985
26 Miami vs. Cleveland, Dec. 12, 1988

Fewest First Downs, Passing, Game
0 By many teams. Last time: Houston vs. Kansas City, Oct. 9, 1988

Most First Downs, Passing, Both Teams, Game
43 San Diego (23) vs. Cincinnati (20), Dec. 20, 1982
Miami (24) vs. N.Y. Jets (19), Sept. 21, 1986 (OT)
42 San Francisco (22) vs. San Diego (20), Dec. 11, 1982
41 San Diego (27) vs. Seattle (14), Sept. 15, 1985
Miami (26) vs. Cleveland (15), Dec. 12, 1988

Fewest First Downs, Passing, Both Teams, Game
0 Brooklyn vs. Pittsburgh, Nov. 29, 1942
1 Green Bay (0) vs. Cleveland (1), Sept. 21, 1941
Pittsburgh (0) vs. Brooklyn (1), Oct. 11, 1942
N.Y. Giants (0) vs. Detroit (1), Nov. 7, 1943
Pittsburgh (0) vs. Chi. Cardinals (1), Nov. 11, 1945
N.Y. Bulldogs (0) vs. Philadelphia (1), Sept. 22, 1949
Chicago (0) vs. Buffalo (1), Oct. 7, 1979
2 In many games

Most First Downs, Penalty, Season
42 Chicago, 1987
41 Denver, 1986
39 Seattle, 1978

Fewest First Downs, Penalty, Season
2 Brooklyn, 1940
4 Chi. Cardinals, 1940
N.Y. Giants, 1942, 1944
Washington, 1944
Cleveland, 1952
Kansas City, 1969
5 Brooklyn, 1939
Chi. Bears, 1939
Detroit, 1953
Los Angeles, 1953
Houston, 1982

Most First Downs, Penalty, Game
11 Denver vs. Houston, Oct. 6, 1985
9 Chi. Bears vs. Cleveland, Nov. 25, 1951
Baltimore vs. Pittsburgh, Oct. 30, 1977
N.Y. Jets vs. Houston, Sept. 18, 1988
8 Philadelphia vs. Detroit, Dec. 2, 1979
Cincinnati vs. N.Y. Jets, Oct. 6, 1985
Buffalo vs. Houston, Sept. 20, 1987
Houston vs. Atlanta, Sept. 9, 1990

Fewest First Downs, Penalty, Game
0 By many teams

Most First Downs, Penalty, Both Teams, Game
11 Chi. Bears (9) vs. Cleveland (2), Nov. 25, 1951
Cincinnati (8) vs. N.Y. Jets (3), Oct. 6, 1985
Denver (11) vs. Houston (0), Oct. 6, 1985
Detroit (6) vs. Dallas (5), Nov. 8, 1987
N.Y. Jets (9) vs. Houston (2), Sept. 18, 1988
10 In many games

Net Yards Gained Rushing and Passing

Most Seasons Leading League
12 Chi. Bears, 1932, 1934-35, 1939, 1941-44, 1947, 1949, 1955-56
7 San Diego, 1963, 1965, 1980-83, 1985
6 L.A. Rams, 1946, 1950-51, 1954, 1957, 1973
Baltimore, 1958-60, 1964, 1967, 1976
Dall. Cowboys, 1966, 1968-69, 1971, 1974, 1977

Most Consecutive Seasons Leading League
4 Chi. Bears, 1941-44
San Diego, 1980-83
3 Baltimore, 1958-60
Houston, 1960-62
Oakland, 1968-70
2 By many teams

Most Yards Gained, Season
6,936 Miami, 1984
6,744 San Diego, 1981
6,535 San Diego, 1985

Fewest Yards Gained, Season
1,150 Cincinnati, 1933
1,443 Chi. Cardinals, 1934
1,486 Chi. Cardinals, 1933

Most Yards Gained, Game
735 Los Angeles vs. N.Y. Yanks, Sept. 28, 1951
683 Pittsburgh vs. Chi. Cardinals, Dec. 13, 1958
682 Chi. Bears vs. N.Y. Giants, Nov. 14, 1943

Fewest Yards Gained, Game
−7 Seattle vs. Los Angeles, Nov. 4, 1979
−5 Denver vs. Oakland, Sept. 10, 1967
14 Chi. Cardinals vs. Detroit, Sept. 15, 1940

Most Yards Gained, Both Teams, Game
1,133 Los Angeles (636) vs. N.Y. Yanks (497), Nov. 19, 1950
1,102 San Diego (661) vs. Cincinnati (441), Dec. 20, 1982
1,087 St. Louis (589) vs. Philadelphia (498), Dec. 16, 1962

Fewest Yards Gained, Both Teams, Game
30 Chi. Cardinals (14) vs. Detroit (16), Sept. 15, 1940
136 Chi. Cardinals (50) vs. Green Bay (86), Nov. 18, 1934
154 N.Y. Giants (51) vs. Washington (103), Dec. 11, 1960

Most Consecutive Games, 400 or More Yards Gained
11 San Diego, 1982-83
6 Houston, 1961-62
San Diego, 1981
San Francisco, 1987
5 Chi. Bears, 1947
Philadelphia, 1953
Chi. Bears, 1955
Oakland, 1968
New England, 1981
Cincinnati, 1986

Most Consecutive Games, 300 or More Yards Gained
29 Los Angeles, 1949-51
26 Miami, 1983-85
19 Cleveland, 1978-79
San Diego, 1980-82
San Francisco, 1988-89

Rushing

Most Seasons Leading League
16 Chi. Bears, 1932, 1934-35, 1939-42, 1951, 1955-56, 1968, 1977, 1983-86
6 Cleveland, 1958-59, 1963, 1965-67
Buffalo, 1962, 1964, 1973, 1975, 1982, 1991
4 Green Bay, 1946, 1961-62, 1964
Dall. Texans/Kansas City, 1961, 1966, 1968-69
Detroit, 1936-38, 1981
San Francisco, 1952-54, 1987

Most Consecutive Seasons Leading League
4 Chi. Bears, 1939-42, 1983-86
3 Detroit, 1936-38
San Francisco, 1952-54
Cleveland, 1965-67
2 By many teams

Attempts

Most Rushing Attempts, Season
681 Oakland, 1977
674 Chicago, 1984
671 New England, 1978

Fewest Rushing Attempts, Season
211 Philadelphia, 1982
219 San Francisco, 1982
225 Houston, 1982

Most Rushing Attempts, Game
72 Chi. Bears vs. Brooklyn, Oct. 20, 1935
70 Chi. Cardinals vs. Green Bay, Dec. 5, 1948
69 Chi. Cardinals vs. Green Bay, Dec. 6, 1936
Kansas City vs. Cincinnati, Sept. 3, 1978

Fewest Rushing Attempts, Game
6 Chi. Cardinals vs. Boston, Oct. 29, 1933
7 Oakland vs. Buffalo, Oct. 15, 1963
Houston vs. N.Y. Giants, Dec. 8, 1985
Seattle vs. L.A. Raiders, Nov. 17, 1991
8 Denver vs. Oakland, Dec. 17, 1960
Buffalo vs. St. Louis, Sept. 9, 1984
Detroit vs. San Francisco, Oct. 20, 1991

Most Rushing Attempts, Both Teams, Game
108 Chi. Cardinals (70) vs. Green Bay (38), Dec. 5, 1948
105 Oakland (62) vs. Atlanta (43), Nov. 30, 1975 (OT)
104 Chi. Bears (64) vs. Pittsburgh (40), Oct. 18, 1936

Fewest Rushing Attempts, Both Teams, Game
35 Seattle (15) vs. New Orleans (20), Sept. 1, 1991

36 Houston (15) vs. N.Y. Jets (21), Oct. 13, 1991
37 Atlanta (18) vs. San Francisco (19), Oct. 6, 1985
Houston (11) vs. Philadelphia (26), Dec. 2, 1991

Yards Gained
Most Yards Gained Rushing, Season
3,165 New England, 1978
3,088 Buffalo, 1973
2,986 Kansas City, 1978
Fewest Yards Gained Rushing, Season
298 Philadelphia, 1940
467 Detroit, 1946
471 Boston, 1944
Most Yards Gained Rushing, Game
426 Detroit vs. Pittsburgh, Nov. 4, 1934
423 N.Y. Giants vs. Baltimore, Nov. 19, 1950
420 Boston vs. N.Y. Giants, Oct. 8, 1933
Fewest Yards Gained Rushing, Game
−53 Detroit vs. Chi. Cardinals, Oct. 17, 1943
−36 Philadelphia vs. Chi. Bears, Nov. 19, 1939
−33 Phil-Pitt vs. Brooklyn, Oct. 2, 1943
Most Yards Gained Rushing, Both Teams, Game
595 Los Angeles (371) vs. N.Y. Yanks (224), Nov. 18, 1951
574 Chi. Bears (396) vs. Pittsburgh (178), Oct. 10, 1934
558 Boston (420) vs. N.Y. Giants (138), Oct. 8, 1933
Fewest Yards Gained Rushing, Both Teams, Game
−15 Detroit (−53) vs. Chi. Cardinals (38), Oct. 17, 1943
4 Detroit (−10) vs. Chi. Cardinals (14), Sept. 15, 1940
62 L.A. Rams (15) vs. San Francisco (47), Dec. 6, 1964

Average Gain
Highest Average Gain, Rushing, Season
5.74 Cleveland, 1963
5.65 San Francisco, 1954
5.56 San Diego, 1963
Lowest Average Gain, Rushing, Season
0.94 Philadelphia, 1940
1.45 Boston, 1944
1.55 Pittsburgh, 1935

Touchdowns
Most Touchdowns, Rushing, Season
36 Green Bay, 1962
33 Pittsburgh, 1976
30 Chi. Bears, 1941
New England, 1978
Washington, 1983
Fewest Touchdowns, Rushing, Season
1 Brooklyn, 1934
2 Chi. Cardinals, 1933
Cincinnati, 1933
Pittsburgh, 1934
Philadelphia, 1935
Philadelphia, 1936
Philadelphia, 1937
Philadelphia, 1938
Pittsburgh, 1940
Philadelphia, 1972
3 By many teams
Most Touchdowns, Rushing, Game
7 Los Angeles vs. Atlanta, Dec. 4, 1976
6 By many teams
Most Touchdowns, Rushing, Both Teams, Game
8 Los Angeles (6) vs. N.Y. Yanks (2), Nov. 18, 1951
Chi. Bears (5) vs. Green Bay (3), Nov. 6, 1955
Cleveland (6) vs. Los Angeles (2), Nov. 24, 1957
7 In many games

Passing
Attempts
Most Passes Attempted, Season
709 Minnesota, 1981
667 Houston, 1991
662 San Diego, 1984
Fewest Passes Attempted, Season
102 Cincinnati, 1933
106 Boston, 1933
120 Detroit, 1937
Most Passes Attempted, Game
68 Houston vs. Buffalo, Nov 1, 1964
66 Atlanta vs. Detroit, Dec. 24, 1989
65 San Diego vs. Kansas City, Oct. 19, 1986
Fewest Passes Attempted, Game
0 Green Bay vs. Portsmouth, Oct. 8, 1933
Detroit vs. Cleveland, Sept. 10, 1937
Pittsburgh vs. Brooklyn, Nov. 16, 1941
Pittsburgh vs. Los Angeles, Nov. 13, 1949
Cleveland vs. Philadelphia, Dec. 3, 1950
Most Passes Attempted, Both Teams, Game
104 Miami (55) vs. N.Y. Jets (49), Oct. 18, 1987 (OT)
102 San Francisco (57) vs. Atlanta (45), Oct. 6, 1985
100 Tampa Bay (54) vs. Kansas City (46), Oct. 28, 1984
San Francisco (60) vs. Washington (40), Nov. 17, 1986
Philadelphia (62) vs. Chicago (38), Oct. 2, 1989
Fewest Passes Attempted, Both Teams, Game
4 Chi. Cardinals (1) vs. Detroit (3), Nov. 3, 1935
Detroit (0) vs. Cleveland (4), Sept. 10, 1937
6 Chi. Cardinals (2) vs. Detroit (4), Sept. 15, 1940
8 Brooklyn (2) vs. Philadelphia (6), Oct. 1, 1939

Completions
Most Passes Completed, Season
411 Houston, 1991

401 San Diego, 1984
399 Houston, 1990
Fewest Passes Completed, Season
25 Cincinnati, 1933
33 Boston, 1933
34 Chi. Cardinals, 1934
Detroit, 1934
Most Passes Completed, Game
42 N.Y. Jets vs. San Francisco, Sept. 21, 1980
41 Houston vs. Dallas, Nov. 10, 1991 (OT)
40 Cincinnati vs. San Diego, Dec. 20, 1982
Dallas vs. Detroit, Sept. 15, 1985
N.Y. Giants vs. Cincinnati, Oct. 13, 1985
Fewest Passes Completed, Game
0 By many teams. Last time: Buffalo vs. N.Y. Jets, Sept. 29, 1974
Most Passes Completed, Both Teams, Game
68 San Francisco (37) vs. Atlanta (31), Oct. 6, 1985
66 Cincinnati (40) vs. San Diego (26), Dec. 20, 1982
65 San Diego (33) vs. San Francisco (32), Dec. 11, 1982
San Diego (37) vs. Miami (28), Nov. 18, 1984 (OT)
Houston (41) vs. Dallas (24), Nov. 10, 1991 (OT)
Fewest Passes Completed, Both Teams, Game
1 Chi. Cardinals (0) vs. Philadelphia (1), Nov. 8, 1936
Detroit (0) vs. Cleveland (1), Sept. 10, 1937
Chi. Cardinals (0) vs. Detroit (1), Sept. 15, 1940
Brooklyn (0) vs. Pittsburgh (1), Nov. 29, 1942
2 Chi. Cardinals (0) vs. Detroit (2), Nov. 3, 1935
Buffalo (0) vs. N.Y. Jets (2), Sept. 29, 1974
Chi. Cardinals (0) vs. Green Bay (2), Nov. 18, 1934
3 In seven games

Yards Gained
Most Seasons Leading League, Passing Yardage
10 San Diego, 1965, 1968, 1971, 1978-83, 1985
8 Chi. Bears, 1932, 1939, 1941, 1943, 1945, 1949, 1954, 1964
Washington, 1938, 1940, 1944, 1947-48, 1967, 1974, 1989
6 Clev. Browns, 1951, 1953-55, 1959-60
Dall. Texans/Kansas City, 1962, 1964, 1966-69
San Francisco, 1952, 1957-58, 1965, 1981, 1983
Houston, 1960-61, 1963-64, 1990-91
Most Consecutive Seasons Leading League, Passing Yardage
6 San Diego, 1978-83
4 Green Bay, 1934-37
3 Miami, 1986-88
Most Yards Gained, Passing, Season
5,018 Miami, 1984
4,870 San Diego, 1985
4,805 Houston, 1990
Fewest Yards Gained, Passing, Season
302 Chi. Cardinals, 1934
357 Cincinnati, 1933
459 Boston, 1934
Most Yards Gained, Passing, Game
554 Los Angeles vs. N.Y. Yanks, Sept. 28, 1951
530 Minnesota vs. Baltimore, Sept. 28, 1969
521 Miami vs. N.Y. Jets, Oct. 23, 1988
Fewest Yards Gained, Passing, Game
−53 Denver vs. Oakland, Sept. 10, 1967
−52 Cincinnati vs. Houston, Oct. 31, 1971
−39 Atlanta vs. San Francisco, Oct. 23, 1976
Most Yards Gained, Passing, Both Teams, Game
884 N.Y. Jets (449) vs. Miami (435), Sept. 21, 1986 (OT)
883 San Diego (486) vs. Cincinnati (397), Dec. 20, 1982
849 Minnesota (471) vs. Washington (378), Nov. 2, 1986 (OT)
Fewest Yards Gained, Passing, Both Teams, Game
−11 Green Bay (−10) vs. Dallas (−1), Oct. 24, 1965
1 Chi. Cardinals (0) vs. Philadelphia (1), Nov. 8, 1936
7 Brooklyn (0) vs. Pittsburgh (7), Nov. 29, 1942

Times Sacked
Most Seasons Leading League, Fewest Times Sacked
10 Miami, 1973, 1982-90
4 San Diego, 1963-64, 1967-68
San Francisco, 1964-65, 1970-71
3 N.Y. Jets, 1965-66, 1968
Houston, 1961-62, 1978
St. Louis, 1974-76
Washington, 1966-67, 1991
Most Consecutive Seasons Leading League, Fewest Times Sacked
9 Miami, 1982-90
3 St. Louis, 1974-76
2 By many teams
Most Times Sacked, Season
104 Philadelphia, 1986
72 Philadelphia, 1987
70 Atlanta, 1968
Fewest Times Sacked, Season
7 Miami, 1988
8 San Francisco, 1970
St. Louis, 1975
9 N.Y. Jets, 1966
Washington, 1991
Most Times Sacked, Game
12 Pittsburgh vs. Dallas, Nov. 20, 1966
Baltimore vs. St. Louis, Oct. 26, 1980
Detroit vs. Chicago, Dec. 16, 1984
Houston vs. Dallas, Sept. 29, 1985
11 St. Louis vs. N.Y. Giants, Nov. 1, 1964
Los Angeles vs. Baltimore, Nov. 22, 1964
Denver vs. Buffalo, Dec. 13, 1964
Green Bay vs. Detroit, Nov. 7, 1965
Buffalo vs. Oakland, Oct. 15, 1967
Denver vs. Oakland, Nov. 5, 1967

Atlanta vs. St. Louis, Nov. 24, 1968
Detroit vs. Dallas, Oct. 6, 1975
Philadelphia vs. St. Louis, Dec. 18, 1983
Cleveland vs. Kansas City, Sept. 30, 1984
Minnesota vs. Chicago, Oct. 28, 1984
Atlanta vs. Cleveland, Nov. 18, 1984
Dallas vs. San Diego, Nov. 16, 1986
Philadelphia vs. Detroit, Nov. 16, 1986
Philadelphia vs. L.A. Raiders, Nov. 30, 1986 (OT)
L.A. Raiders vs. Seattle, Dec. 8, 1986
N.Y. Jets vs. Dallas, Oct. 4, 1987
Philadelphia vs. Chicago, Oct. 4, 1987
Dallas vs. Philadelphia, Sept. 15, 1991
10   By many teams

Most Times Sacked, Both Teams, Game
18   Green Bay (10) vs. San Diego (8), Sept. 24, 1978
17   Buffalo (10) vs. N.Y. Titans, Nov. 23, 1961
     Pittsburgh (12) vs. Dallas (5), Nov. 20, 1966
     Atlanta (9) vs. Philadelphia (8), Dec. 16, 1984
     Philadelphia (11) vs. L.A. Raiders (6), Nov. 30, 1986 (OT)
16   Los Angeles (11) vs. Baltimore (5), Nov. 22, 1964
     Buffalo (11) vs. Oakland (5), Oct. 15, 1967

Completion Percentage
Most Seasons Leading League, Completion Percentage
11   Washington, 1937, 1939-40, 1942-45, 1947-48, 1969-70
8   San Francisco, 1952, 1957-58, 1965, 1981, 1983, 1987, 1989
7   Green Bay, 1936, 1941, 1961-62, 1964, 1966, 1968
Most Consecutive Seasons Leading League, Completion Percentage
4   Washington, 1942-45
     Kansas City, 1966-69
3   Cleveland, 1953-55
2   By many teams
Highest Completion Percentage, Season
70.65   Cincinnati, 1982 (310-219)
70.19   San Francisco, 1989 (483-339)
64.34   Buffalo, 1991 (516-332)
Lowest Completion Percentage, Season
22.9   Philadelphia, 1936 (170-39)
24.5   Cincinnati, 1933 (102-25)
25.0   Pittsburgh, 1941 (168-42)

Touchdowns
Most Touchdowns, Passing, Season
49   Miami, 1984
48   Houston, 1961
46   Miami, 1986
Fewest Touchdowns, Passing, Season
0   Cincinnati, 1933
     Pittsburgh, 1945
1   Boston, 1932
     Boston, 1933
     Chi. Cardinals, 1934
     Cincinnati/St. Louis, 1934
     Detroit, 1942
2   Chi. Cardinals, 1932
     Stapleton, 1932
     Chi. Cardinals, 1935
     Brooklyn, 1936
     Pittsburgh, 1942
Most Touchdowns, Passing, Game
7   Chi. Bears vs. N.Y. Giants, Nov. 14, 1943
     Philadelphia vs. Washington, Oct. 17, 1954
     Houston vs. N.Y. Titans, Nov. 19, 1961
     Houston vs. N.Y. Titans, Oct. 14, 1962
     N.Y. Giants vs. Washington, Oct. 28, 1962
     Minnesota vs. Baltimore, Sept. 28, 1969
     San Diego vs. Oakland, Nov. 22, 1981
6   By many teams.
Most Touchdowns, Passing, Both Teams, Game
12   New Orleans (6) vs. St. Louis (6), Nov. 2, 1969
11   N.Y. Giants (7) vs. Washington (4), Oct. 28, 1962
     Oakland (6) vs. Houston (5), Dec. 22, 1963
10   San Diego (5) vs. Seattle (5), Sept. 15, 1985
     Miami (6) vs. N.Y. Jets (4), Sept. 21, 1986 (OT)

Passes Had Intercepted
Most Passes Had Intercepted, Season
48   Houston, 1962
45   Denver, 1961
41   Card-Pitt, 1944
Fewest Passes Had Intercepted, Season
5   Cleveland, 1960
     Green Bay, 1966
     Kansas City, 1990
     N.Y. Giants, 1990
6   Green Bay, 1964
     St. Louis, 1982
7   Los Angeles, 1969
Most Passes Had Intercepted, Game
9   Detroit vs. Green Bay, Oct. 24, 1943
     Pittsburgh vs. Philadelphia, Dec. 12, 1965
8   Green Bay vs. N.Y. Giants, Nov. 21, 1948
     Chi. Cardinals vs. Philadelphia, Sept. 24, 1950
     N.Y. Yanks vs. N.Y. Giants, Dec. 16, 1951
     Denver vs. Houston, Dec. 2, 1962
     Chi. Bears vs. Detroit, Sept. 22, 1968
     Baltimore vs. N.Y. Jets, Sept. 23, 1973
7   By many teams. Last time: Green Bay vs. New Orleans, Sept. 14, 1986
Most Passes Had Intercepted, Both Teams, Game
13   Denver (8) vs. Houston (5), Dec. 2, 1962
11   Philadelphia (7) vs. Boston (4), Nov. 3, 1935
     Boston (6) vs. Pittsburgh (5), Dec. 1, 1935

Cleveland (7) vs. Green Bay (4), Oct. 30, 1938
Green Bay (7) vs. Detroit (4), Oct. 20, 1940
Detroit (7) vs. Chi. Bears (4), Nov. 22, 1942
Detroit (7) vs. Cleveland (4), Nov. 26, 1944
Chi. Cardinals (8) vs. Philadelphia (3), Sept. 24, 1950
Washington (7) vs. N.Y. Giants (4), Dec. 8, 1963
Pittsburgh (9) vs. Philadelphia (2), Dec 12, 1965
10   In many games

Punting
Most Seasons Leading League (Average Distance)
7   Denver, 1962-64, 1966-67, 1982, 1988
6   Washington, 1940-43, 1945, 1958
     Kansas City, 1968, 1971-73, 1979, 1984
4   L.A. Rams, 1946, 1949, 1955-56
     Baltimore/Indianapolis, 1966, 1969, 1983, 1985
Most Consecutive Seasons Leading League (Average Distance)
4   Washington, 1940-43
3   Cleveland, 1950-52
     Denver, 1962-64
     Kansas City, 1971-73
Most Punts, Season
114   Chicago, 1981
113   Boston, 1934
      Brooklyn, 1934
112   Boston, 1935
Fewest Punts, Season
23   San Diego, 1982
31   Cincinnati, 1982
32   Chi. Bears, 1941
Most Punts, Game
17   Chi. Bears vs. Green Bay, Oct. 22, 1933
     Cincinnati vs. Pittsburgh, Oct. 22, 1933
16   Cincinnati vs. Portsmouth, Sept. 17, 1933
     Chi. Cardinals vs. Chi. Bears, Nov. 30, 1933
     Chi. Cardinals vs. Detroit, Sept. 15, 1940
Fewest Punts, Game
0   By many teams. Last time: Kansas City vs. L.A. Raiders, Dec. 22, 1991
Most Punts, Both Teams, Game
31   Chi. Bears (17) vs. Green Bay (14), Oct. 22, 1933
     Cincinnati (17), vs. Pittsburgh (14), Oct. 22, 1933
29   Chi. Cardinals (15) vs. Cincinnati (14), Nov. 12, 1933
     Chi. Cardinals (16) vs. Chi. Bears (13), Nov. 30, 1933
     Chi. Cardinals (16) vs. Detroit (13), Sept. 15, 1940
28   Philadelphia (14) vs. Washington (14), Nov. 5, 1939
Fewest Punts, Both Teams, Game
1   Baltimore (0) vs. Cleveland (1), Nov. 1, 1959
     Dall. Cowboys (0) vs. Cleveland (1), Dec. 3, 1961
     Chicago (0) vs. Detroit (1), Oct. 1, 1972
     San Francisco (0) vs. N.Y. Giants (1), Oct. 15, 1972
     Green Bay (0) vs. Buffalo (1), Dec. 5, 1982
     Miami (0) vs. Buffalo (1), Oct. 12, 1986
     Green Bay (0) vs. Chicago (1), Dec. 17, 1989
2   In many games

Average Yardage
Highest Average Distance, Punting, Season
47.6   Detroit, 1961 (56-2,664)
47.0   Pittsburgh, 1961 (73-3,431)
46.9   Pittsburgh, 1953 (80-3,752)
Lowest Average Distance, Punting, Season
32.7   Card-Pitt, 1944 (60-1,964)
33.8   Cincinnati, 1986 (59-1,996)
33.9   Detroit, 1969 (74-2,510)

Punt Returns
Most Seasons Leading League (Average Return)
9   Detroit, 1943-45, 1951-52, 1962, 1966, 1969, 1991
7   Chi. Cardinals/St. Louis, 1948-49, 1955-56, 1959, 1986-87
5   Cleveland, 1958, 1960, 1964-65, 1967
     Green Bay, 1950, 1953-54, 1961, 1972
     Dall. Texans/Kansas City, 1960, 1968, 1970, 1979-80
Most Consecutive Seasons Leading League (Average Return)
3   Detroit, 1943-45
2   By many teams
Most Punt Returns, Season
71   Pittsburgh, 1976
     Tampa Bay, 1979
     L.A. Raiders, 1985
67   Pittsburgh, 1974
     Los Angeles, 1978
     L.A. Raiders, 1984
65   San Francisco, 1976
Fewest Punt Returns, Season
12   Baltimore, 1981
     San Diego, 1982
14   Los Angeles, 1961
     Philadelphia, 1962
     Baltimore, 1982
15   Houston, 1960
     Washington, 1960
     Oakland, 1961
     N.Y. Giants, 1969
     Philadelphia, 1973
     Kansas City, 1982
Most Punt Returns, Game
12   Philadelphia vs. Cleveland, Dec. 3, 1950
11   Chi. Bears vs. Chi. Cardinals, Oct. 8, 1950
     Washington vs. Tampa Bay, Oct. 9, 1977
10   Philadelphia vs. N.Y. Giants, Nov. 26, 1950
     Philadelphia vs. Tampa Bay, Sept. 18, 1977

Pittsburgh vs. Buffalo, Dec. 16, 1979
Washington vs. New Orleans, Dec. 26, 1982

Most Punt Returns, Both Teams, Game
- 17 Philadelphia (12) vs. Cleveland (5), Dec. 3, 1950
- 16 N.Y. Giants (9) vs. Philadelphia (7), Dec. 12, 1954
  Washington (11) vs. Tampa Bay (5), Oct. 9, 1977
- 15 Detroit (8) vs. Cleveland (7), Sept. 27, 1942
  Los Angeles (8) vs. Baltimore (7), Nov. 27, 1966
  Pittsburgh (8) vs. Houston (7), Dec. 1, 1974
  Philadelphia (10) vs. Tampa Bay (5), Sept. 18, 1977
  Baltimore (9) vs. Kansas City (6), Sept. 2, 1979
  Washington (10) vs. New Orleans (5), Dec. 26, 1982
  L.A. Raiders (8) vs. Cleveland (7), Nov. 16, 1986

Fair Catches

Most Fair Catches, Season
- 34 Baltimore, 1971
- 32 San Diego, 1969
- 30 St. Louis, 1967
  Minnesota, 1971

Fewest Fair Catches, Season
- 0 San Diego, 1975
  New England, 1976
  Tampa Bay, 1976
  Pittsburgh, 1977
  Dallas, 1982
- 1 Cleveland, 1974
  San Francisco, 1975
  Kansas City, 1976
  St. Louis, 1976
  San Diego, 1976
  L.A. Rams, 1982
  St. Louis, 1982
  Tampa Bay, 1982
- 2 By many teams

Most Fair Catches, Game
- 7 Minnesota vs. Dallas, Sept. 25, 1966
  Detroit vs. Chicago, Nov. 21, 1976
  Philadelphia vs. Buffalo, Dec. 27, 1987
- 6 By many teams

Yards Gained

Most Yards, Punt Returns, Season
- 785 L.A. Raiders, 1985
- 781 Chi. Bears, 1948
- 774 Pittsburgh, 1974

Fewest Yards, Punt Returns, Season
- 27 St. Louis, 1965
- 35 N.Y. Giants, 1965
- 37 New England, 1972

Most Yards, Punt Returns, Game
- 231 Detroit vs. San Francisco, Oct. 6, 1963
- 225 Oakland vs. Buffalo, Sept. 15, 1968
- 219 Los Angeles vs. Atlanta, Oct. 11, 1981

Most Yards, Punt Returns, Both Teams, Game
- 282 Los Angeles (219) vs. Atlanta (63), Oct. 11, 1981
- 245 Detroit (231) vs. San Francisco (14), Oct. 6, 1963
- 244 Oakland (225) vs. Buffalo (19), Sept. 15, 1968

Average Yards Returning Punts

Highest Average, Punt Returns, Season
- 20.2 Chi. Bears, 1941 (27-546)
- 19.1 Chi. Cardinals, 1948 (35-669)
- 18.2 Chi. Cardinals, 1949 (30-546)

Lowest Average, Punt Returns, Season
- 1.2 St. Louis, 1965 (23-27)
- 1.5 N.Y. Giants, 1965 (24-35)
- 1.7 Washington, 1970 (27-45)

Touchdowns Returning Punts

Most Touchdowns, Punt Returns, Season
- 5 Chi. Cardinals, 1959
- 4 Chi. Cardinals, 1948
  Detroit, 1951
  N.Y. Giants, 1951
  Denver, 1976
- 3 Washington, 1941
  Detroit, 1952
  Pittsburgh, 1952
  Houston, 1975
  Los Angeles, 1981

Most Touchdowns, Punt Returns, Game
- 2 Detroit vs. Los Angeles, Oct. 14, 1951
  Detroit vs. Green Bay, Nov. 22, 1951
  Chi. Cardinals vs. Pittsburgh, Nov. 1, 1959
  Chi. Cardinals vs. N.Y. Giants, Nov. 22, 1959
  N.Y. Titans vs. Denver, Sept. 24, 1961
  Denver vs. Cleveland, Sept. 26, 1976
  Los Angeles vs. Atlanta, Oct. 11, 1981
  St. Louis vs. Tampa Bay, Dec. 21, 1986

Most Touchdowns, Punt Returns, Both Teams, Game
- 2 Philadelphia (1) vs. Washington (1), Nov. 9, 1952
  Kansas City (1) vs. Buffalo (1), Sept. 11, 1966
  Baltimore (1) vs. New England (1), Nov. 18, 1979
  L.A. Raiders (1) vs. Philadelphia (1), Nov. 30, 1986 (OT)
  (Also see previous record)

Kickoff Returns

Most Seasons Leading League (Average Return)
- 7 Washington, 1942, 1947, 1962-63, 1973-74, 1981
- 6 Chicago Bears, 1943, 1948, 1958, 1966, 1972, 1985
- 5 N.Y. Giants, 1944, 1946, 1949, 1951, 1953

Most Consecutive Seasons Leading League (Average Return)
- 3 Denver, 1965-67
- 2 By many teams

Most Kickoff Returns, Season
- 88 New Orleans, 1980
- 86 Minnesota, 1984
- 84 Baltimore, 1981

Fewest Kickoff Returns, Season
- 17 N.Y. Giants, 1944
- 20 N.Y. Giants, 1941, 1943
  Chi. Bears, 1942
- 23 Washington, 1942

Most Kickoff Returns, Game
- 12 N.Y. Giants vs. Washington, Nov. 27, 1966
- 10 By many teams

Most Kickoff Returns, Both Teams, Game
- 19 N.Y. Giants (12) vs. Washington (7), Nov. 27, 1966
- 18 Houston (10) vs. Oakland (8), Dec. 22, 1963
- 17 Washington (9) vs. Green Bay (8), Oct. 17, 1983
  San Diego (9) vs. Pittsburgh (8), Dec. 8, 1985
  Detroit (9) vs. Green Bay (8), Nov. 27, 1986
  L.A. Raiders (9) vs. Seattle (8), Dec. 18, 1988

Yards Gained

Most Yards, Kickoff Returns, Season
- 1,973 New Orleans, 1980
- 1,824 Houston, 1963
- 1,801 Denver, 1963

Fewest Yards, Kickoff Returns, Season
- 282 N.Y. Giants, 1940
- 381 Green Bay, 1940
- 424 Chicago, 1963

Most Yards, Kickoff Returns, Game
- 362 Detroit vs. Los Angeles, Oct. 29, 1950
- 304 Chi. Bears vs. Green Bay, Nov. 9, 1952
- 295 Denver vs. Boston, Oct. 4, 1964

Most Yards, Kickoff Returns, Both Teams, Game
- 560 Detroit (362) vs. Los Angeles (198), Oct. 29, 1950
- 453 Washington (236) vs. Philadelphia (217), Sept. 28, 1947
- 447 N.Y. Giants (236) vs. Cleveland (211), Dec. 4, 1966

Average Yardage

Highest Average, Kickoff Returns, Season
- 29.4 Chicago, 1972 (52-1,528)
- 28.9 Pittsburgh, 1952 (39-1,128)
- 28.2 Washington, 1962 (61-1,720)

Lowest Average, Kickoff Returns, Season
- 16.1 Cleveland, 1991 (55-888)
- 16.26 Philadelphia, 1991 (47-764)
- 16.27 Chicago, 1990 (54-879)

Touchdowns

Most Touchdowns, Kickoff Returns, Season
- 4 Green Bay, 1967
  Chicago, 1970
- 3 Los Angeles, 1950
  Chi. Cardinals, 1954
  San Francisco, 1963
  Denver, 1966
  Chicago, 1967
  New England, 1977
  L.A. Rams, 1985
- 2 By many teams

Most Touchdowns, Kickoff Returns, Game
- 2 Chi. Bears vs. Green Bay, Sept. 22, 1940
  Chi. Bears vs. Green Bay, Nov. 9, 1952
  Philadelphia vs. Dallas, Nov. 6, 1966
  Green Bay vs. Cleveland, Nov. 12, 1967
  L.A. Rams vs. Green Bay, Nov. 24, 1985

Most Touchdowns, Kickoff Returns, Both Teams, Game
- 2 Washington (1) vs. Philadelphia (1), Nov. 1, 1942
  Washington (1) vs. Philadelphia (1), Sept. 28, 1947
  Los Angeles (1) vs. Detroit (1), Oct. 29, 1950
  N.Y. Yanks (1) vs. N.Y. Giants (1), Nov. 4, 1951 (consecutive)
  Baltimore (1) vs. Chi. Bears (1), Oct. 4, 1958
  Buffalo (1) vs. Boston (1), Nov. 3, 1962
  Pittsburgh (1) vs. Dallas (1), Oct. 30, 1966
  St. Louis (1) vs. Washington (1), Sept. 23, 1973 (consecutive)
  Atlanta (1) vs. San Francisco (1), Dec. 20, 1987 (consecutive)
  Houston (1) vs. Pittsburgh (1), Dec. 4, 1988
  (Also see previous record)

Fumbles

Most Fumbles, Season
- 56 Chi. Bears, 1938
  San Francisco, 1978
- 54 Philadelphia, 1946
- 51 New England, 1973

Fewest Fumbles, Season
- 8 Cleveland, 1959
- 11 Green Bay, 1944
- 12 Brooklyn, 1934
  Detroit, 1943
  Cincinnati, 1982
  Minnesota, 1982

Most Fumbles, Game
- 10 Phil-Pitt vs. New York, Oct. 9, 1943
  Detroit vs. Minnesota, Nov. 12, 1967
  Kansas City vs. Houston, Oct. 12, 1969
  San Francisco vs. Detroit, Dec. 17, 1978
- 9 Philadelphia vs. Green Bay, Oct. 13, 1946
  Kansas City vs. San Diego, Nov. 15, 1964

N.Y. Giants vs. Buffalo, Oct. 20, 1975
St. Louis vs. Washington, Oct. 25, 1976
San Diego vs. Green Bay, Sept. 24, 1978
Pittsburgh vs. Cincinnati, Oct. 14, 1979
Cleveland vs. Seattle, Dec. 20, 1981
Cleveland vs. Pittsburgh, Dec. 23, 1990
8 By many teams

Most Fumbles, Both Teams, Game

14 Washington (8) vs. Pittsburgh (6), Nov. 14, 1937
   Chi. Bears (7) vs. Cleveland (7), Nov. 24, 1940
   St. Louis (8) vs. N.Y. Giants (6), Sept. 17, 1961
   Kansas City (10) vs. Houston (4), Oct. 12, 1969
13 Washington (8) vs. Pittsburgh (5), Nov. 14, 1937
   Philadelphia (7) vs. Boston (6), Dec. 8, 1946
   N.Y. Giants (7) vs. Washington (6), Nov. 5, 1950
   Kansas City (9) vs. San Diego (4), Nov. 15, 1964
   Buffalo (7) vs. Denver (6), Dec. 13, 1964
   N.Y. Jets (7) vs. Houston (6), Sept. 12, 1965
   Houston (8) vs. Pittsburgh (5), Dec. 9, 1973
   St. Louis (9) vs. Washington (4), Oct. 25, 1976
   Cleveland (9) vs. Seattle (4), Dec. 20, 1981
   Green Bay (7) vs. Detroit (6), Oct. 6, 1985
12 In many games

Fumbles Lost

Most Fumbles Lost, Season

36 Chi. Cardinals, 1959
31 Green Bay, 1952
29 Chi. Cardinals, 1946
   Pittsburgh, 1950

Fewest Fumbles Lost, Season

3 Philadelphia, 1938
   Minnesota, 1980
4 San Francisco, 1960
   Kansas City, 1982
5 Chi. Cardinals, 1943
   Detroit, 1943
   N.Y. Giants, 1943
   Cleveland, 1959
   Minnesota, 1982

Most Fumbles Lost, Game

8 St. Louis vs. Washington, Oct. 25, 1976
   Cleveland vs. Pittsburgh, Dec. 23, 1990
7 Cincinnati vs. Buffalo, Nov. 30, 1969
   Pittsburgh vs. Cincinnati, Oct. 14, 1979
   Cleveland vs. Seattle, Dec. 20, 1981
6 By many teams

Fumbles Recovered

Most Fumbles Recovered, Season, Own and Opponents'

58 Minnesota, 1963 (27 own, 31 opp)
51 Chi. Bears, 1938 (37 own, 14 opp)
   San Francisco, 1978 (24 own, 27 opp)
50 Philadelphia, 1987 (23 own, 27 opp)

Fewest Fumbles Recovered, Season, Own and Opponents'

9 San Francisco, 1982 (5 own, 4 opp)
11 Cincinnati, 1982 (5 own, 6 opp)
13 Baltimore, 1967 (5 own, 8 opp)
   N.Y. Jets, 1967 (7 own, 6 opp)
   Philadelphia, 1968 (6 own, 7 opp)
   Miami, 1973 (5 own, 8 opp)
   Chicago, 1982 (6 own, 7 opp)
   Denver, 1982 (6 own, 7 opp)
   Miami, 1982 (5 own, 8 opp)
   N.Y. Giants, 1982 (7 own, 6 opp)

Most Fumbles Recovered, Game, Own and Opponents'

10 Denver vs. Buffalo, Dec. 13, 1964 (5 own, 5 opp)
   Pittsburgh vs. Houston, Dec. 9, 1973 (5 own, 5 opp)
   Washington vs. St. Louis, Oct. 25, 1976 (2 own, 8 opp)
9 St. Louis vs. N.Y. Giants, Sept. 17, 1961 (6 own, 3 opp)
   Houston vs. Cincinnati, Oct. 27, 1974 (4 own, 5 opp)
   Kansas City vs. Dallas, Nov. 10, 1975 (4 own, 5 opp)
   Green Bay vs. Detroit, Oct. 6, 1985 (5 own, 4 opp)
8 By many teams

Most Own Fumbles Recovered, Season

37 Chi. Bears, 1938
28 Pittsburgh, 1987
27 Philadelphia, 1946
   Minnesota, 1963

Fewest Own Fumbles Recovered, Season

2 Washington, 1958
3 Detroit, 1956
   Cleveland, 1959
   Houston, 1982
4 By many teams

Most Opponents' Fumbles Recovered, Season

31 Minnesota, 1963
29 Cleveland, 1951
28 Green Bay, 1946
   Houston, 1977
   Seattle, 1983

Fewest Opponents' Fumbles Recovered, Season

3 Los Angeles, 1974
4 Philadelphia, 1944
   San Francisco, 1982
5 Baltimore, 1982

Most Opponents' Fumbles Recovered, Game

8 Washington vs. St. Louis, Oct. 25, 1976
7 Buffalo vs. Cincinnati, Nov. 30, 1969
   Seattle vs. Cleveland, Dec. 20, 1981
6 By many teams. Last time: New England vs. L.A. Rams, Dec. 11, 1983

Touchdowns

Most Touchdowns, Fumbles Recovered, Season, Own and Opponents'

5 Chi. Bears, 1942 (1 own, 4 opp)
   Los Angeles, 1952 (1 own, 4 opp)
   San Francisco, 1965 (1 own, 4 opp)
   Oakland, 1978 (2 own, 3 opp)
4 Chi. Bears, 1948 (1 own, 3 opp)
   Boston, 1948 (4 opp)
   Denver, 1979 (1 own, 3 opp)
   Atlanta, 1981 (1 own, 3 opp)
   Denver, 1984 (4 opp)
   St. Louis, 1987 (4 opp)
   Minnesota, 1989 (4 opp)
   Atlanta, 1991 (4 opp)
3 By many teams

Most Touchdowns, Own Fumbles Recovered, Season

2 Chi. Bears, 1953
   New England, 1973
   Buffalo, 1974
   Denver, 1975
   Oakland, 1978
   Green Bay, 1982
   New Orleans, 1983
   Cleveland, 1986
   Green Bay, 1989

Most Touchdowns, Opponents' Fumbles Recovered, Season

4 Detroit, 1937
   Chi. Bears, 1942
   Boston, 1948
   Los Angeles, 1952
   San Francisco, 1965
   Denver, 1984
   St. Louis, 1987
   Minnesota, 1989
   Atlanta, 1991
3 By many teams

Most Touchdowns, Fumbles Recovered, Game, Own and Opponents'

2 By many teams

Most Touchdowns, Fumbled Recovered, Game, Both Teams, Own and Opponents'

3 Detroit (2) vs. Minnesota (1), Dec. 9, 1962 (2 own, 1 opp)
   Green Bay (2) vs. Dallas (1), Nov. 29, 1964 (3 opp)
   Oakland (2) vs. Buffalo (1), Dec. 24, 1967 (3 opp)

Most Touchdowns, Own Fumbles Recovered, Game

1 By many teams

Most Touchdowns, Opponents' Fumbles Recovered, Game

2 Detroit vs. Cleveland, Nov. 7, 1937
   Philadelphia vs. N.Y. Giants, Sept. 25, 1938
   Chi. Bears vs. Washington, Nov. 28, 1948
   N.Y. Giants vs. Pittsburgh, Sept. 17, 1950
   Cleveland vs. Dall. Cowboys, Dec. 3, 1961
   Cleveland vs. N.Y. Giants, Oct. 25, 1964
   Green Bay vs. Dallas, Nov. 29, 1964
   San Francisco vs. Detroit, Nov. 14, 1965
   Oakland vs. Buffalo, Dec. 24, 1967
   N.Y. Giants vs. Green Bay, Sept. 19, 1971
   Washington vs. San Diego, Sept. 16, 1973
   New Orleans vs. San Francisco, Oct. 19, 1975
   Cincinnati vs. Pittsburgh, Oct. 14, 1979
   Atlanta vs. Detroit, Oct. 5, 1980
   Kansas City vs. Oakland, Oct. 5, 1980
   New England vs. Baltimore, Nov. 23, 1980
   Denver vs. Green Bay, Oct. 15, 1984
   Miami vs. Kansas City, Oct. 11, 1987
   St. Louis vs. New Orleans, Oct. 11, 1987
   Minnesota vs. Atlanta, Dec. 10, 1989
   Philadelphia vs. Phoenix, Nov. 24, 1991

Most Touchdowns, Opponents' Fumbled Recovered, Game, Both Teams

3 Green Bay (2) vs. Dallas (1), Nov. 29, 1964
   Oakland (2) vs. Buffalo (1), Dec. 24, 1967

Turnovers

(Number of times losing the ball on interceptions and fumbles.)

Most Turnovers, Season

63 San Francisco, 1978
58 Chi. Bears, 1947
   Pittsburgh, 1950
   N.Y. Giants, 1983
57 Green Bay, 1950
   Houston, 1962, 1963
   Pittsburgh, 1965

Fewest Turnovers, Season

12 Kansas City, 1982
14 N.Y. Giants, 1943
   Cleveland, 1959
   N.Y. Giants, 1990
16 San Francisco, 1960
   Cincinnati, 1982
   St. Louis, 1982
   Washington, 1982

Most Turnovers, Game

12 Detroit vs. Chi. Bears, Nov. 22, 1942
   Chi. Cardinals vs. Philadelphia, Sept. 24, 1950
   Pittsburgh vs. Philadelphia, Dec. 12, 1965
11 San Diego vs. Green Bay, Sept. 24, 1978
10 Washington vs. N.Y. Giants, Dec. 4, 1938
   Pittsburgh vs. Green Bay, Nov. 23, 1941
   Detroit vs. Green Bay, Oct. 24, 1943
   Chi. Cardinals vs. Green Bay, Nov. 10, 1946
   Chi. Cardinals vs. N.Y. Giants, Nov. 2, 1952
   Minnesota vs. Detroit, Dec. 9, 1962
   Houston vs. Oakland, Sept. 7, 1963
   Washington vs. N.Y. Giants, Dec. 8, 1963

Chicago vs. Detroit, Sept. 22, 1968
St. Louis vs. Washington, Oct. 25, 1976
N.Y. Jets vs. New England, Nov. 21, 1976
San Francisco vs. Dallas, Oct. 12, 1980
Cleveland vs. Seattle, Dec. 20, 1981
Detroit vs. Denver, Oct. 7, 1984

Most Turnovers, Both Teams, Game
17 Detroit (12) vs. Chi. Bears (5), Nov. 22, 1942
   Boston (9) vs. Philadelphia (8), Dec. 8, 1946
16 Chi. Cardinals (12) vs. Philadelphia (4), Sept. 24, 1950
   Chi. Cardinals (8) vs. Chi. Bears (8), Dec. 7, 1958
   Minnesota (10) vs. Detroit (6), Dec. 9, 1962
   Houston (9) vs. Kansas City (7), Oct. 12, 1969
15 Philadelphia (8) vs. Chi. Cardinals (7), Oct. 3, 1954
   Denver (9) vs. Houston (6), Dec. 2, 1962
   Washington (10) vs. N.Y. Giants (5), Dec. 8, 1963
   St. Louis (9) vs. Kansas City (6), Oct. 2, 1983

Penalties
Most Seasons Leading League, Fewest Penalties
13 Miami, 1968, 1976-84, 1986, 1990-91
9 Pittsburgh, 1946-47, 1950-52, 1954, 1963, 1965, 1968
6 Boston/New England, 1962, 1964-65, 1973, 1987, 1989
Most Consecutive Seasons Leading League, Fewest Penalties
9 Miami, 1976-84
3 Pittsburgh, 1950-52
2 By many teams
Most Seasons Leading League, Most Penalties
16 Chi. Bears, 1941-44, 1946-49, 1951, 1959-61, 1963, 1965, 1968, 1976
8 Oakland/L.A. Raiders, 1963, 1966, 1968-69, 1975, 1982, 1984, 1991
6 L.A. Rams, 1950, 1952, 1962, 1969, 1978, 1980
Most Consecutive Seasons Leading League, Most Penalties
4 Chi. Bears, 1941-44, 1946-49
3 Chi. Cardinals, 1954-56
   Chi. Bears, 1959-61
   Houston, 1988-90
Fewest Penalties, Season
19 Detroit, 1937
21 Boston, 1935
24 Philadelphia, 1936
Most Penalties, Season
149 Houston, 1989
144 Buffalo, 1983
143 L.A. Raiders, 1984
Fewest Penalties, Game
0 By many teams. Last time: Chicago vs. Detroit, Nov. 28, 1991
Most Penalties, Game
22 Brooklyn vs. Green Bay, Sept. 17, 1944
   Chi. Bears vs. Philadelphia, Nov. 26, 1944
21 Cleveland vs. Chi. Bears, Nov. 25, 1951
20 Tampa Bay vs. Seattle, Oct. 17, 1976
Fewest Penalties, Both Teams, Game
0 Brooklyn vs. Pittsburgh, Oct. 28, 1934
   Brooklyn vs. Boston, Sept. 28, 1936
   Cleveland vs. Chi. Bears, Oct. 9, 1938
   Pittsburgh vs. Philadelphia, Nov. 10, 1940
Most Penalties, Both Teams, Game
37 Cleveland (21) vs. Chi. Bears (16), Nov. 25, 1951
35 Tampa Bay (20) vs. Seattle (15), Oct. 17, 1976
33 Brooklyn (22) vs. Green Bay (11), Sept. 17, 1944

Yards Penalized
Most Seasons Leading League, Fewest Yards Penalized
13 Miami, 1967-68, 1973, 1977-84, 1990-91
8 Boston/Washington, 1935, 1953-54, 1956-58, 1970, 1985
7 Pittsburgh, 1946-47, 1950, 1952, 1962, 1965, 1968
Most Consecutive Seasons Leading League, Fewest Yards Penalized
8 Miami, 1977-84
3 Washington, 1956-58
   Boston, 1964-66
2 By many teams
Most Seasons Leading League, Most Yards Penalized
15 Chi. Bears, 1935, 1937, 1939-44, 1946-47, 1949, 1951, 1961-62, 1968
8 Oakland/L.A. Raiders, 1963-64, 1968-69, 1975, 1982, 1984, 1991
6 Buffalo, 1962, 1967, 1970, 1972, 1981, 1983
   Houston, 1961, 1985-86, 1988-90
Most Consecutive Seasons Leading League, Most Yards Penalized
6 Chi. Bears, 1939-44
3 Cleveland, 1976-78
   Houston, 1988-90
2 By many teams
Fewest Yards Penalized, Season
139 Detroit, 1937
146 Philadelphia, 1937
159 Philadelphia, 1936
Most Yards Penalized, Season
1,274 Oakland, 1969
1,239 Baltimore, 1979
1,209 L.A. Raiders, 1984
Fewest Yards Penalized, Game
0 By many teams. Last time: Chicago vs. Detroit, Nov. 28, 1991
Most Yards Penalized, Game
209 Cleveland vs. Chi. Bears, Nov. 25, 1951
190 Tampa Bay vs. Seattle, Oct. 17, 1976
189 Houston vs. Buffalo, Oct. 31, 1965
Fewest Yards Penalized, Both Teams, Game
0 Brooklyn vs. Pittsburgh, Oct. 28, 1934
   Brooklyn vs. Boston, Sept. 28, 1936
   Cleveland vs. Chi. Bears, Oct. 9, 1938
   Pittsburgh vs. Philadelphia, Nov. 10, 1940
Most Yards Penalized, Both Teams, Game
374 Cleveland (209) vs. Chi. Bears (165), Nov. 25, 1951

310 Tampa Bay (190) vs. Seattle (120), Oct. 17, 1976
309 Green Bay (184) vs. Boston (125), Oct. 21, 1945

Defense

Scoring
Most Seasons Leading League, Fewest Points Allowed
9 Chi. Bears, 1932, 1936-37, 1942, 1948, 1963, 1985-86, 1988
   N.Y. Giants, 1935, 1938-39, 1941, 1944, 1958-59, 1961, 1990
6 Cleveland, 1951, 1953-57
5 Green Bay, 1935, 1947, 1962, 1965-66
Most Consecutive Seasons Leading League, Fewest Points Allowed
5 Cleveland, 1953-57
3 Buffalo, 1964-66
   Minnesota, 1969-71
2 By many teams
Fewest Points Allowed, Season (Since 1932)
44 Chi. Bears, 1932
54 Brooklyn, 1933
59 Detroit, 1934
Most Points Allowed, Season
533 Baltimore, 1981
501 N.Y. Giants, 1966
487 New Orleans, 1980
Fewest Touchdowns Allowed, Season (Since 1932)
6 Chi. Bears, 1932
   Brooklyn, 1933
7 Detroit, 1934
8 Green Bay, 1932
Most Touchdowns Allowed, Season
68 Baltimore, 1981
66 N.Y. Giants, 1966
63 Baltimore, 1950

First Downs
Fewest First Downs Allowed Season
77 Detroit, 1935
79 Boston, 1935
82 Washington, 1937
Most First Downs Allowed, Season
406 Baltimore, 1981
371 Seattle, 1981
366 Green Bay, 1983
Fewest First Downs Allowed, Rushing, Season
35 Chi. Bears, 1942
40 Green Bay, 1939
41 Brooklyn, 1944
Most First Downs Allowed, Rushing, Season
179 Detroit, 1985
178 New Orleans, 1980
175 Seattle, 1981
Fewest First Downs Allowed, Passing, Season
33 Chi. Bears, 1943
34 Pittsburgh, 1941
   Washington, 1943
35 Detroit, 1940
   Philadelphia, 1940, 1944
Most First Downs Allowed, Passing, Season
218 San Diego, 1985
216 San Diego, 1981
   N.Y. Jets, 1986
214 Baltimore, 1981
Fewest First Downs Allowed, Penalty, Season
1 Boston, 1944
3 Philadelphia, 1940
   Pittsburgh, 1945
   Washington, 1957
4 Cleveland, 1940
   Green Bay, 1943
   N.Y. Giants, 1943
Most First Downs Allowed, Penalty, Season
48 Houston, 1985
46 Houston, 1986
43 L.A. Raiders, 1984

Net Yards Allowed Rushing and Passing
Most Seasons Leading League, Fewest Yards Allowed
8 Chi. Bears, 1942-43, 1948, 1958, 1963, 1984-86
6 N.Y. Giants, 1938, 1940-41, 1951, 1956, 1959
   Philadelphia, 1944-45, 1949, 1953, 1981, 1991
5 Boston/Washington, 1935-37, 1939, 1946
   Minnesota, 1969-70, 1975, 1988-89
Most Consecutive Seasons Leading League, Fewest Yards Allowed
3 Boston/Washington, 1935-37
   Chicago, 1984-86
2 By many teams
Fewest Yards Allowed, Season
1,539 Chi. Cardinals, 1934
1,703 Chi. Bears, 1942
1,789 Brooklyn, 1933
Most Yards Allowed, Season
6,793 Baltimore, 1981
6,403 Green Bay, 1983
6,352 Minnesota, 1984

Rushing
Most Seasons Leading League, Fewest Yards Allowed
10 Chi. Bears, 1937, 1939, 1942, 1946, 1949, 1963, 1984-85, 1987-88
7 Detroit, 1938, 1950, 1952, 1962, 1970, 1980-81
   Philadelphia, 1944-45, 1947-48, 1953, 1990-91
6 Dallas, 1966-69, 1972, 1978

Most Consecutive Seasons Leading League, Fewest Yards Allowed
- 4 Dallas, 1966-69
- 2 By many teams

Fewest Yards Allowed, Rushing, Season
- 519 Chi. Bears, 1942
- 558 Philadelphia, 1944
- 762 Pittsburgh, 1982

Most Yards Allowed, Rushing, Season
- 3,228 Buffalo, 1978
- 3,106 New Orleans, 1980
- 3,010 Baltimore, 1978

Fewest Touchdowns Allowed, Rushing, Season
- 2 Detroit, 1934
- Dallas, 1968
- Minnesota, 1971
- 3 By many teams

Most Touchdowns Allowed, Rushing, Season
- 36 Oakland, 1961
- 31 N.Y. Giants, 1980
- Tampa Bay, 1986
- 30 Baltimore, 1981

Passing

Most Seasons Leading League, Fewest Yards Allowed
- 8 Green Bay, 1947-48, 1962, 1964-68
- 7 Washington, 1939, 1942, 1945, 1952-53, 1980, 1985
- 6 Chi. Bears, 1938, 1943-44, 1958, 1960, 1963
- Minnesota, 1969-70, 1972, 1975-76, 1989
- Pittsburgh, 1941, 1946, 1951, 1955, 1974, 1990
- Philadelphia, 1934, 1936, 1940, 1949, 1981, 1991

Most Consecutive Seasons Leading League, Fewest Yards Allowed
- 5 Green Bay, 1964-68
- 2 By many teams

Fewest Yards Allowed, Passing, Season
- 545 Philadelphia, 1934
- 558 Portsmouth, 1933
- 585 Chi. Cardinals, 1934

Most Yards Allowed, Passing, Season
- 4,389 N.Y. Jets, 1986
- 4,311 San Diego, 1981
- 4,293 San Diego, 1985

Fewest Touchdowns Allowed, Passing, Season
- 1 Portsmouth, 1932
- Philadelphia, 1934
- 2 Brooklyn, 1933
- Chi. Bears, 1934
- 3 Chi. Bears, 1932
- Green Bay, 1932
- Green Bay, 1934
- Chi. Bears, 1936
- New York, 1939
- New York, 1944

Most Touchdowns Allowed, Passing, Season
- 40 Denver, 1963
- 38 St. Louis, 1969
- 37 Washington, 1961
- Baltimore, 1981

Sacks

Most Seasons Leading League
- 5 Oakland/L.A. Raiders, 1966-68, 1982, 1986
- 4 Boston/New England, 1961, 1963, 1977, 1979
- Dallas, 1966, 1968-69, 1978
- Dallas/Kansas City, 1960, 1965, 1969, 1990
- 3 San Francisco, 1967, 1972, 1976
- L.A. Rams, 1968, 1970, 1988

Most Consecutive Seasons Leading League
- 3 Oakland, 1966-68
- 2 Dallas, 1968-69

Most Sacks, Season
- 72 Chicago, 1984
- 71 Minnesota, 1989
- 70 Chicago, 1987

Fewest Sacks, Season
- 11 Baltimore, 1982
- 12 Buffalo, 1982
- 13 Baltimore, 1981

Most Sacks, Game
- 12 Dallas vs. Pittsburgh, Nov. 20, 1966
- St. Louis vs. Baltimore, Oct. 26, 1980
- Chicago vs. Detroit, Dec. 16, 1984
- Dallas vs. Houston, Sept. 29, 1985
- 11 N.Y. Giants vs. St. Louis, Nov. 1, 1964
- Baltimore vs. Los Angeles, Nov. 22, 1964
- Buffalo vs. Denver, Dec. 13, 1964
- Detroit vs. Green Bay, Nov. 7, 1965
- Oakland vs. Buffalo, Oct. 15, 1967
- Oakland vs. Denver, Nov. 5, 1967
- St. Louis vs. Atlanta, Nov. 24, 1968
- Dallas vs. Detroit, Oct. 6, 1975
- St. Louis vs. Philadelphia, Dec. 18, 1983
- Kansas City vs. Cleveland, Sept. 30, 1984
- Chicago vs. Minnesota, Oct. 28, 1984
- Cleveland vs. Atlanta, Nov. 18, 1984
- Detroit vs. Philadelphia, Nov. 16, 1986
- San Diego vs. Dallas, Nov. 16, 1986
- L.A. Raiders vs. Philadelphia, Nov. 30, 1986 (OT)
- Seattle vs. L.A. Raiders, Dec. 8, 1986
- Chicago vs. Philadelphia, Oct. 4, 1987
- Dallas vs. N.Y. Jets, Oct. 4, 1987
- 10 By many teams

Most Opponents Yards Lost Attempting to Pass, Season
- 666 Oakland, 1967
- 583 Chicago, 1984
- 573 San Francisco, 1976

Fewest Opponents Yards Lost Attempting to Pass, Season
- 75 Green Bay, 1956
- 77 N.Y. Bulldogs, 1949
- 78 Green Bay, 1958

Interceptions By

Most Seasons Leading League
- 9 N.Y. Giants, 1933, 1937-39, 1944, 1948, 1951, 1954, 1961
- 8 Green Bay, 1940, 1942-43, 1947, 1955, 1957, 1962, 1965
- Chi. Bears, 1935-36, 1941-42, 1946, 1963, 1985, 1990
- 6 Kansas City, 1966-70, 1974

Most Consecutive Seasons Leading League
- 5 Kansas City, 1966-70
- 3 N.Y. Giants, 1937-39
- 2 By many teams

Most Passes Intercepted By, Season
- 49 San Diego, 1961
- 42 Green Bay, 1943
- 41 N.Y. Giants, 1951

Fewest Passes Intercepted By, Season
- 3 Houston, 1982
- 5 Baltimore, 1982
- 6 Houston, 1972
- St. Louis, 1982

Most Passes Intercepted By, Game
- 9 Green Bay vs. Detroit, Oct. 24, 1943
- Philadelphia vs. Pittsburgh, Dec. 12, 1965
- 8 N.Y. Giants vs. Green Bay, Nov. 21, 1948
- Philadelphia vs. Chi. Cardinals, Sept. 24, 1950
- N.Y. Giants vs. N.Y. Yanks, Dec. 16, 1951
- Houston vs. Denver, Dec. 2, 1962
- Detroit vs. Chicago, Sept. 22, 1968
- N.Y. Jets vs. Baltimore, Sept. 23, 1973
- 7 By many teams. Last time: New Orleans vs. Green Bay, Sept. 14, 1986

Most Consecutive Games, One or More Interceptions By
- 46 L.A. Chargers/San Diego, 1960-63
- 37 Detroit, 1960-63
- 36 Boston, 1944-47

Most Yards Returning Interceptions, Season
- 929 San Diego, 1961
- 712 Los Angeles, 1952
- 697 Seattle, 1984

Fewest Yards Returning Interceptions, Season
- 5 Los Angeles, 1959
- 37 Dallas, 1989
- 42 Philadelphia, 1982

Most Yards Returning Interceptions, Game
- 325 Seattle vs. Kansas City, Nov. 4, 1984
- 314 Los Angeles vs. San Francisco, Oct. 18, 1964
- 245 Houston vs. N.Y. Jets, Oct. 15, 1967

Most Touchdowns, Returning Interceptions, Season
- 9 San Diego, 1961
- 7 Seattle, 1984
- 6 Cleveland, 1960
- Green Bay, 1966
- Detroit, 1967
- Houston, 1967

Most Touchdowns Returning Interceptions, Game
- 4 Seattle vs. Kansas City, Nov. 4, 1984
- 3 Baltimore vs. Green Bay, Nov. 5, 1950
- Cleveland vs. Chicago, Dec. 11, 1960
- Philadelphia vs. Pittsburgh, Dec. 12, 1965
- Baltimore vs. Pittsburgh, Sept. 29, 1968
- Buffalo vs. N.Y. Jets, Sept. 29, 1968
- Houston vs. San Diego, Dec. 19, 1971
- Cincinnati vs. Houston, Dec. 17, 1972
- Tampa Bay vs. New Orleans, Dec. 11, 1977
- 2 By many teams

Most Touchdowns Returning Interceptions, Both Teams, Game
- 4 Philadelphia (3) vs. Pittsburgh (1), Dec. 12, 1965
- Seattle (4) vs. Kansas City (0), Nov. 4, 1984
- 3 Los Angeles (2) vs. Detroit (1), Nov. 1, 1953
- Cleveland (2) vs. N.Y. Giants (1), Dec. 18, 1960
- Pittsburgh (2) vs. Cincinnati (1), Oct. 10, 1983
- Kansas City (2) vs. San Diego (1), Oct. 19, 1986
- (Also see previous record)

Punt Returns

Fewest Opponents Punt Returns, Season
- 7 Washington, 1962
- San Diego, 1982
- 10 Buffalo, 1982
- 11 Boston, 1962

Most Opponents Punt Returns, Season
- 71 Tampa Bay, 1976, 1977
- 69 N.Y. Giants, 1953
- 68 Cleveland, 1974

Fewest Yards Allowed, Punt Returns, Season
- 22 Green Bay, 1967
- 34 Washington, 1962
- 39 Cleveland, 1959
- Washington, 1972

Most Yards Allowed, Punt Returns, Season
- 932 Green Bay, 1949
- 913 Boston, 1947
- 906 New Orleans, 1974

Lowest Average Allowed, Punt Returns, Season
- 1.20 Chi. Cardinals, 1954 (46-55)

1.22 Cleveland, 1959 (32-39)
1.55 Chi. Cardinals, 1953 (44-68)
Highest Average Allowed, Punt Returns, Season
18.6 Green Bay, 1949 (50-932)
18.0 Cleveland, 1977 (31-558)
17.9 Boston, 1960 (20-357)
Most Touchdowns Allowed, Punt Returns, Season
4 New York, 1959
3 Green Bay, 1949
Chi. Cardinals, 1951
Los Angeles, 1951
Washington, 1952
Dallas, 1952
Pittsburgh, 1959
N.Y. Jets, 1968
Cleveland, 1977
Atlanta, 1986
Tampa Bay, 1986
2 By many teams

Kickoff Returns
Fewest Opponents Kickoff Returns, Season
10 Brooklyn, 1943
15 Detroit, 1942
Brooklyn, 1944
18 Cleveland, 1941
Boston, 1944
Most Opponents Kickoff Returns, Season
91 Washington, 1983
89 New England, 1980
88 San Diego, 1981
Fewest Yards Allowed, Kickoff Returns, Season
225 Brooklyn, 1943
293 Brooklyn, 1944
361 Seattle, 1982
Most Yards Allowed, Kickoff Returns, Season
2,045 Kansas City, 1966
1,827 Chicago, 1985
1,816 N.Y. Giants, 1963
Lowest Average Allowed, Kickoff Returns, Season
14.3 Cleveland, 1980 (71-1,018)
15.0 Seattle, 1982 (24-361)
15.4 N.Y. Jets, 1991 (60-921)
Highest Average Allowed, Kickoff Returns, Season
29.5 N.Y. Jets, 1972 (47-1,386)
29.4 Los Angeles, 1950 (48-1,411)
29.1 New England, 1971 (49-1,427)
Most Touchdowns Allowed, Kickoff Returns, Season
3 Minnesota, 1963, 1970
Dallas, 1966
Detroit, 1980
Pittsburgh, 1986
2 By many teams

Fumbles
Fewest Opponents Fumbles, Season
11 Cleveland, 1956
Baltimore, 1982
13 Los Angeles, 1956
Chicago, 1960
Cleveland, 1963
Cleveland, 1965
Detroit, 1967
San Diego, 1969
14 Baltimore, 1970
Oakland, 1975
Buffalo, 1982
St. Louis, 1982
San Francisco, 1982
Most Opponents Fumbles, Season
50 Minnesota, 1963
San Francisco, 1978
48 N.Y. Giants, 1980
N.Y. Jets, 1986
47 N.Y. Giants, 1977
Seattle, 1984

Turnovers
(Number of times losing the ball on interceptions and fumbles.)
Fewest Opponents Turnovers, Season
11 Baltimore, 1982
13 San Francisco, 1982
15 St. Louis, 1982
Most Opponents Turnovers, Season
66 San Diego, 1961
63 Seattle, 1984
61 Washington, 1983
Most Opponents Turnovers, Game
12 Chi. Bears vs. Detroit, Nov. 22, 1942
Philadelphia vs. Chi. Cardinals, Sept. 24, 1950
Philadelphia vs. Pittsburgh, Dec. 12, 1965
11 Green Bay vs. San Diego, Sept. 24, 1978
10 N.Y. Giants vs. Washington, Dec. 4, 1938
Green Bay vs. Pittsburgh, Nov. 23, 1941
Green Bay vs. Detroit, Oct. 24, 1943
Green Bay vs. Chi. Cardinals, Nov. 10, 1946
N.Y. Giants vs. Chi. Cardinals, Nov. 2, 1952
Detroit vs. Minnesota, Dec. 9, 1962
Oakland vs. Houston, Sept. 7, 1963
N.Y. Giants vs. Washington, Dec. 8, 1963
Detroit vs. Chicago, Sept. 22, 1968
Washington vs. St. Louis, Oct. 25, 1976

New England vs. N.Y. Jets, Nov. 21, 1976
Dallas vs. San Francisco, Oct. 12, 1980
Seattle vs. Cleveland, Dec. 20, 1981
Denver vs. Detroit, Oct. 7, 1984

1,000 Yards Rushing in a Season

Year	Player, Team	Att.	Yards	Avg.	Long	TD
1991	Emmitt Smith, Dallas	365	1,563	4.3	75	12
	Barry Sanders, Detroit[3]	342	1,548	4.5	69	16
	Thurman Thomas, Buffalo[3]	288	1,407	4.9	33	7
	Rodney Hampton, N.Y. Giants	256	1,059	4.1	44	10
	Earnest Byner, Washington[3]	274	1,048	3.8	32	5
	Gaston Green, Denver	261	1,037	4.0	63	4
	Christian Okoye, Kansas City[2]	225	1,031	4.6	48	9
1990	Barry Sanders, Detroit[2]	255	1,304	5.1	45	13
	Thurman Thomas, Buffalo[2]	271	1,297	4.8	80	11
	Marion Butts, San Diego	265	1,225	4.6	52	8
	Earnest Byner, Washington[2]	297	1,219	4.1	22	6
	Bobby Humphrey, Denver[2]	288	1,202	4.2	37	7
	Neal Anderson, Chicago[3]	260	1,078	4.1	52	10
	Barry Word, Kansas City	204	1,015	5.0	53	4
	James Brooks, Cincinnati[3]	195	1,004	5.1	56	5
1989	Christian Okoye, Kansas City	370	1,480	4.0	59	12
	*Barry Sanders, Detroit	280	1,470	5.3	34	14
	Eric Dickerson, Indianapolis[7]	314	1,311	4.2	21	7
	Neal Anderson, Chicago[2]	274	1,275	4.7	73	11
	Dalton Hilliard, New Orleans	344	1,262	3.7	40	13
	Thurman Thomas, Buffalo	298	1,244	4.2	38	6
	James Brooks, Cincinnati[2]	221	1,239	5.6	65	7
	*Bobby Humphrey, Denver	294	1,151	3.9	40	7
	Greg Bell, L.A. Rams[3]	272	1,137	4.2	47	15
	Roger Craig, San Francisco[3]	271	1,054	3.9	27	6
	Ottis Anderson, N.Y. Giants[6]	325	1,023	3.1	36	14
1988	Eric Dickerson, Indianapolis[6]	388	1,659	4.3	41	14
	Herschel Walker, Dallas	361	1,514	4.2	38	5
	Roger Craig, San Francisco[2]	310	1,502	4.8	46	9
	Greg Bell, L.A. Rams[2]	288	1,212	4.2	44	16
	*John Stephens, New England	297	1,168	3.9	52	4
	Gary Anderson, San Diego	225	1,119	5.0	36	3
	Neal Anderson, Chicago	249	1,106	4.4	80	12
	Joe Morris, N.Y. Giants[3]	307	1,083	3.5	27	5
	*Ickey Woods, Cincinnati	203	1,066	5.3	56	15
	Curt Warner, Seattle[4]	266	1,025	3.9	29	10
	John Settle, Atlanta	232	1,024	4.4	62	7
	Mike Rozier, Houston	251	1,002	4.0	28	10
1987	Charles White, L.A. Rams	324	1,374	4.2	58	11
	Eric Dickerson, L.A. Rams-Indianapolis[5]	283	1,288	4.6	57	6
1986	Eric Dickerson, L.A. Rams[4]	404	1,821	4.5	42	11
	Joe Morris, N.Y. Giants[2]	341	1,516	4.4	54	14
	Curt Warner, Seattle[3]	319	1,481	4.6	60	13
	*Rueben Mayes, New Orleans	286	1,353	4.7	50	8
	Walter Payton, Chicago[10]	321	1,333	4.2	41	8
	Gerald Riggs, Atlanta[3]	343	1,327	3.9	31	9
	George Rogers, Washington[4]	303	1,203	4.0	42	18
	James Brooks, Cincinnati	205	1,087	5.3	56	5
1985	Marcus Allen, L.A. Raiders[3]	390	1,759	4.6	61	11
	Gerald Riggs, Atlanta[2]	397	1,719	4.3	50	10
	Walter Payton, Chicago[9]	324	1,551	4.8	40	9
	Joe Morris, N.Y. Giants	294	1,336	4.5	65	21
	Freeman McNeil, N.Y. Jets[2]	294	1,331	4.5	69	3
	Tony Dorsett, Dallas[8]	305	1,307	4.3	60	7
	James Wilder, Tampa Bay[2]	365	1,300	3.6	28	10
	Eric Dickerson, L.A. Rams[3]	292	1,234	4.2	43	12
	Craig James, New England	263	1,227	4.7	65	5
	*Kevin Mack, Cleveland	222	1,104	5.0	61	7
	Curt Warner, Seattle[2]	291	1,094	3.8	38	8
	George Rogers, Washington[3]	231	1,093	4.7	35	7
	Roger Craig, San Francisco	214	1,050	4.9	62	9
	Earnest Jackson, Philadelphia[2]	282	1,028	3.6	59	5
	Stump Mitchell, St. Louis	183	1,006	5.5	64	7
	Earnest Byner, Cleveland	244	1,002	4.1	36	8
1984	Eric Dickerson, L.A. Rams[2]	379	2,105	5.6	66	14
	Walter Payton, Chicago[8]	381	1,684	4.4	72	11
	James Wilder, Tampa Bay	407	1,544	3.8	37	13
	Gerald Riggs, Atlanta	353	1,486	4.2	57	13
	Wendell Tyler, San Francisco[3]	246	1,262	5.1	40	7
	John Riggins, Washington[5]	327	1,239	3.8	24	14
	Tony Dorsett, Dallas[7]	302	1,189	3.9	31	6
	Earnest Jackson, San Diego	296	1,179	4.0	32	8
	Ottis Anderson, St. Louis[5]	289	1,174	4.1	24	6
	Marcus Allen, L.A. Raiders[2]	275	1,168	4.2	52	13
	Sammy Winder, Denver	296	1,153	3.9	24	4
	*Greg Bell, Buffalo	262	1,100	4.2	85	7
	Freeman McNeil, N.Y. Jets	229	1,070	4.7	53	5
1983	*Eric Dickerson, L.A. Rams	390	1,808	4.6	85	18
	William Andrews, Atlanta[4]	331	1,567	4.7	27	7
	*Curt Warner, Seattle	335	1,449	4.3	60	13
	Walter Payton, Chicago[7]	314	1,421	4.5	49	6
	John Riggins, Washington[4]	375	1,347	3.6	44	24
	Tony Dorsett, Dallas[6]	289	1,321	4.6	77	8
	Earl Campbell, Houston[5]	322	1,301	4.0	42	12
	Ottis Anderson, St. Louis[4]	296	1,270	4.3	43	5
	Mike Pruitt, Cleveland[4]	293	1,184	4.0	27	10
	George Rogers, New Orleans[2]	256	1,144	4.5	76	5
	Joe Cribbs, Buffalo[3]	263	1,131	4.3	45	3
	Curtis Dickey, Baltimore	254	1,122	4.4	56	4
	Tony Collins, New England	219	1,049	4.8	50	10
	Billy Sims, Detroit[3]	220	1,040	4.7	41	7
	Marcus Allen, L.A. Raiders	266	1,014	3.8	19	9
	Franco Harris, Pittsburgh[8]	279	1,007	3.6	19	5
1981	*George Rogers, New Orleans	378	1,674	4.4	79	13
	Tony Dorsett, Dallas[5]	342	1,646	4.8	75	4
	Billy Sims, Detroit[2]	296	1,437	4.9	51	13
	Wilbert Montgomery, Philadelphia[3]	286	1,402	4.9	41	8
	Ottis Anderson, St. Louis[3]	328	1,376	4.2	28	9
	Earl Campbell, Houston[4]	361	1,376	3.8	43	10
	William Andrews, Atlanta[3]	289	1,301	4.5	29	10
	Walter Payton, Chicago[6]	339	1,222	3.6	39	6
	Chuck Muncie, San Diego[2]	251	1,144	4.6	73	19
	*Joe Delaney, Kansas City	234	1,121	4.8	82	3
	Mike Pruitt, Cleveland[3]	247	1,103	4.5	21	7
	Joe Cribbs, Buffalo[2]	257	1,097	4.3	35	3
	Pete Johnson, Cincinnati	274	1,077	3.9	39	12
	Wendell Tyler, Los Angeles[2]	260	1,074	4.1	69	12
	Ted Brown, Minnesota	274	1,063	3.9	34	6
1980	Earl Campbell, Houston[3]	373	1,934	5.2	55	13
	Walter Payton, Chicago[5]	317	1,460	4.6	69	6
	Ottis Anderson, St. Louis[2]	301	1,352	4.5	52	9
	William Andrews, Atlanta[2]	265	1,308	4.9	33	4
	*Billy Sims, Detroit	313	1,303	4.2	52	13
	Tony Dorsett, Dallas[4]	278	1,185	4.3	56	11
	*Joe Cribbs, Buffalo	306	1,185	3.9	48	11
	Mike Pruitt, Cleveland[2]	249	1,034	4.2	56	6
1979	Earl Campbell, Houston[2]	368	1,697	4.6	61	19
	Walter Payton, Chicago[4]	369	1,610	4.4	43	14
	*Ottis Anderson, St. Louis	331	1,605	4.8	76	8
	Wilbert Montgomery, Philadelphia[2]	338	1,512	4.5	62	9
	Mike Pruitt, Cleveland	264	1,294	4.9	77	9
	Ricky Bell, Tampa Bay	283	1,263	4.5	49	7
	Chuck Muncie, New Orleans	238	1,198	5.0	69	11
	Franco Harris, Pittsburgh[7]	267	1,186	4.4	71	11
	John Riggins, Washington[3]	260	1,153	4.4	66	9
	Wendell Tyler, Los Angeles	218	1,109	5.1	63	9
	Tony Dorsett, Dallas[3]	250	1,107	4.4	41	6
	*William Andrews, Atlanta	239	1,023	4.3	23	3
1978	*Earl Campbell, Houston	302	1,450	4.8	81	13
	Walter Payton, Chicago[3]	333	1,395	4.2	76	11
	Tony Dorsett, Dallas[2]	290	1,325	4.6	63	7
	Delvin Williams, Miami[2]	272	1,258	4.6	58	8
	Wilbert Montgomery, Philadelphia	259	1,220	4.7	47	9
	Terdell Middleton, Green Bay	284	1,116	3.9	76	11
	Franco Harris, Pittsburgh[6]	310	1,082	3.5	37	8
	Mark van Eeghen, Oakland[3]	270	1,080	4.0	34	9
	*Terry Miller, Buffalo	238	1,060	4.5	60	7
	Tony Reed, Kansas City	206	1,053	5.1	62	5
	John Riggins, Washington[2]	248	1,014	4.1	31	5
1977	Walter Payton, Chicago[2]	339	1,852	5.5	73	14
	Mark van Eeghen, Oakland[2]	324	1,273	3.9	27	7
	Lawrence McCutcheon, Los Angeles[4]	294	1,238	4.2	48	7
	Franco Harris, Pittsburgh[5]	300	1,162	3.9	61	11
	Lydell Mitchell, Baltimore[3]	301	1,159	3.9	64	3
	Chuck Foreman, Minnesota[3]	270	1,112	4.1	51	6
	Greg Pruitt, Cleveland[3]	236	1,086	4.6	78	3
	Sam Cunningham, New England	270	1,015	3.8	31	4
	*Tony Dorsett, Dallas	208	1,007	4.8	84	12
1976	O.J. Simpson, Buffalo[5]	290	1,503	5.2	75	8
	Walter Payton, Chicago	311	1,390	4.5	60	13
	Delvin Williams, San Francisco	248	1,203	4.9	80	7
	Lydell Mitchell, Baltimore[2]	289	1,200	4.2	43	5
	Lawrence McCutcheon, Los Angeles[3]	291	1,168	4.0	40	9
	Chuck Foreman, Minnesota[2]	278	1,155	4.2	46	13
	Franco Harris, Pittsburgh[4]	289	1,128	3.9	30	14
	Mike Thomas, Washington	254	1,101	4.3	28	5
	Rocky Bleier, Pittsburgh	220	1,036	4.7	28	5
	Mark van Eeghen, Oakland	233	1,012	4.3	21	3
	Otis Armstrong, Denver[2]	247	1,008	4.1	31	5
	Greg Pruitt, Cleveland[2]	209	1,000	4.8	64	4
1975	O.J. Simpson, Buffalo[4]	329	1,817	5.5	88	16
	Franco Harris, Pittsburgh[3]	262	1,246	4.8	36	10
	Lydell Mitchell, Baltimore	289	1,193	4.1	70	11
	Jim Otis, St. Louis	269	1,076	4.0	30	5
	Chuck Foreman, Minnesota	280	1,070	3.8	31	13
	Greg Pruitt, Cleveland	217	1,067	4.9	50	8
	John Riggins, N.Y. Jets	238	1,005	4.2	42	8
	Dave Hampton, Atlanta	250	1,002	4.0	22	5
1974	Otis Armstrong, Denver	263	1,407	5.3	43	9
	*Don Woods, San Diego	227	1,162	5.1	56	7
	O.J. Simpson, Buffalo[3]	270	1,125	4.2	41	3
	Lawrence McCutcheon, Los Angeles[2]	236	1,109	4.7	23	3
	Franco Harris, Pittsburgh[2]	208	1,006	4.8	54	5
1973	O.J. Simpson, Buffalo[2]	332	2,003	6.0	80	12
	John Brockington, Green Bay[3]	265	1,144	4.3	53	3
	Calvin Hill, Dallas[2]	273	1,142	4.2	21	6
	Lawrence McCutcheon, Los Angeles	210	1,097	5.2	37	2
	Larry Csonka, Miami[3]	219	1,003	4.6	25	5
1972	O.J. Simpson, Buffalo	292	1,251	4.3	94	6
	Larry Brown, Washington[2]	285	1,216	4.3	38	8
	Ron Johnson, N.Y. Giants[2]	298	1,182	4.0	35	9
	Larry Csonka, Miami[2]	213	1,117	5.2	45	6
	Marv Hubbard, Oakland	219	1,100	5.0	39	4
	*Franco Harris, Pittsburgh	188	1,055	5.6	75	10
	Calvin Hill, Dallas	245	1,036	4.2	26	6
	Mike Garrett, San Diego[2]	272	1,031	3.8	41	6
	John Brockington, Green Bay[2]	274	1,027	3.7	30	8
	Eugene (Mercury) Morris, Miami	190	1,000	5.3	33	12
1971	Floyd Little, Denver	284	1,133	4.0	40	6
	*John Brockington, Green Bay	216	1,105	5.1	52	4
	Larry Csonka, Miami	195	1,051	5.4	28	7
	Steve Owens, Detroit	246	1,035	4.2	23	8
	Willie Ellison, Los Angeles	211	1,000	4.7	80	4
1970	Larry Brown, Washington	237	1,125	4.7	75	5
	Ron Johnson, N.Y. Giants	263	1,027	3.9	68	8

1969	Gale Sayers, Chicago[2]	236	1,032	4.4	28	8
1968	Leroy Kelly, Cleveland[3]	248	1,239	5.0	65	16
	*Paul Robinson, Cincinnati	238	1,023	4.3	87	8
1967	Jim Nance, Boston[2]	269	1,216	4.5	53	7
	Leroy Kelly, Cleveland[2]	235	1,205	5.1	42	11
	Hoyle Granger, Houston	236	1,194	5.1	67	6
	Mike Garrett, Kansas City	236	1,087	4.6	58	9
1966	Jim Nance, Boston	299	1,458	4.9	65	11
	Gale Sayers, Chicago	229	1,231	5.4	58	8
	Leroy Kelly, Cleveland	209	1,141	5.5	70	15
	Dick Bass, Los Angeles[2]	248	1,090	4.4	50	8
1965	Jim Brown, Cleveland[7]	289	1,544	5.3	67	17
	Paul Lowe, San Diego[2]	222	1,121	5.0	59	7
1964	Jim Brown, Cleveland[6]	280	1,446	5.2	71	7
	Jim Taylor, Green Bay[5]	235	1,169	5.0	84	12
	John Henry Johnson, Pittsburgh[2]	235	1,048	4.5	45	7
1963	Jim Brown, Cleveland[5]	291	1,863	6.4	80	12
	Clem Daniels, Oakland	215	1,099	5.1	74	3
	Jim Taylor, Green Bay[4]	248	1,018	4.1	40	9
	Paul Lowe, San Diego	177	1,010	5.7	66	8
1962	Jim Taylor, Green Bay[3]	272	1,474	5.4	51	19
	John Henry Johnson, Pittsburgh	251	1,141	4.5	40	7
	*Cookie Gilchrist, Buffalo	214	1,096	5.1	44	13
	Abner Haynes, Dall. Texans	221	1,049	4.7	71	13
	Dick Bass, Los Angeles	196	1,033	5.3	57	6
	Charlie Tolar, Houston	244	1,012	4.1	25	7
1961	Jim Brown, Cleveland[4]	305	1,408	4.6	38	8
	Jim Taylor, Green Bay[2]	243	1,307	5.4	53	15
1960	Jim Brown, Cleveland[3]	215	1,257	5.8	71	9
	Jim Taylor, Green Bay	230	1,101	4.8	32	11
	John David Crow, St. Louis	183	1,071	5.9	57	6
1959	Jim Brown, Cleveland[2]	290	1,329	4.6	70	14
	J. D. Smith, San Francisco	207	1,036	5.0	73	10
1958	Jim Brown, Cleveland	257	1,527	5.9	65	17
1956	Rick Casares, Chi. Bears	234	1,126	4.8	68	12
1954	Joe Perry, San Francisco[2]	173	1,049	6.1	58	8
1953	Joe Perry, San Francisco	192	1,018	5.3	51	10
1949	Steve Van Buren, Philadelphia[2]	263	1,146	4.4	41	11
	Tony Canadeo, Green Bay	208	1,052	5.1	54	4
1947	Steve Van Buren, Philadelphia	217	1,008	4.6	45	13
1934	*Beattie Feathers, Chi. Bears	119	1,004	8.4	82	8

First year in the league.

200 Yards Rushing in a Game

Date	Player, Team, Opponent	Att.	Yards	TD
Nov. 24, 1991	Barry Sanders, Detroit vs. Minnesota	23	220	4
Dec. 23, 1990	James Brooks, Cincinnati vs. Houston	20	201	1
Oct. 14, 1990	Barry Word, Kansas City vs. Detroit	18	200	2
Sept. 24, 1990	Thurman Thomas, Buffalo vs. N.Y. Jets	18	214	0
Dec. 24, 1989	Greg Bell, L.A. Rams vs. New England	26	210	1
Sept. 24, 1989	Greg Bell, L.A. Rams vs. Green Bay	28	221	2
Sept. 17, 1989	Gerald Riggs, Washington vs. Philadelphia	29	221	1
Dec. 18, 1988	Gary Anderson, San Diego vs. Kansas City	34	217	1
Nov. 30, 1987	*Bo Jackson, L.A. Raiders vs. Seattle	18	221	2
Nov. 15, 1987	Charles White, L.A. Rams vs. St. Louis	34	213	1
Dec. 7, 1986	Rueben Mayes, New Orleans vs. Miami	28	203	2
Oct. 5, 1986	Eric Dickerson, L.A. Rams vs. Tampa Bay (OT)	30	207	2
Dec. 21, 1985	George Rogers, Washington vs. St. Louis	34	206	1
Dec. 21, 1985	Joe Morris, N.Y. Giants vs. Pittsburgh	36	202	3
Dec. 9, 1984	Eric Dickerson, L.A. Rams vs. Houston	27	215	2
Nov. 18, 1984	*Greg Bell, Buffalo vs. Dallas	27	206	1
Nov. 4, 1984	Eric Dickerson, L.A. Rams vs. St. Louis	21	208	0
Sept. 2, 1984	Gerald Riggs, Atlanta vs. New Orleans	35	202	2
Nov. 27, 1983	*Curt Warner, Seattle vs. Kansas City (OT)	32	207	3
Nov. 6, 1983	James Wilder, Tampa Bay vs. Minnesota	31	219	1
Sept. 18, 1983	Tony Collins, New England vs. N.Y. Jets	23	212	3
Sept. 4, 1983	George Rogers, New Orleans vs. St. Louis	24	206	2
Dec. 21, 1980	Earl Campbell, Houston vs. Minnesota	29	203	1
Nov. 16, 1980	Earl Campbell, Houston vs. Chicago	31	206	0
Oct. 26, 1980	Earl Campbell, Houston vs. Cincinnati	27	202	2
Oct. 19, 1980	Earl Campbell, Houston vs. Tampa Bay	33	203	0
Nov. 26, 1978	*Terry Miller, Buffalo vs. N.Y. Giants	21	208	2
Dec. 4, 1977	*Tony Dorsett, Dallas vs. Philadelphia	23	206	2
Nov. 20, 1977	Walter Payton, Chicago vs. Minnesota	40	275	1
Oct. 30, 1977	Walter Payton, Chicago vs. Green Bay	23	205	2
Dec. 5, 1976	O.J. Simpson, Buffalo vs. Miami	24	203	1
Nov. 25, 1976	O.J. Simpson, Buffalo vs. Detroit	29	273	2
Oct. 24, 1976	Chuck Foreman, Minnesota vs. Philadelphia	28	200	2
Dec. 14, 1975	Greg Pruitt, Cleveland vs. Kansas City	26	214	3
Sept. 28, 1975	O.J. Simpson, Buffalo vs. Pittsburgh	28	227	1
Dec. 16, 1973	O.J. Simpson, Buffalo vs. N.Y. Jets	34	200	1
Dec. 9, 1973	O.J. Simpson, Buffalo vs. New England	22	219	1
Sept. 16, 1973	O.J. Simpson, Buffalo vs. New England	29	250	2
Dec. 5, 1971	Willie Ellison, Los Angeles vs. New Orleans	26	247	1
Dec. 20, 1970	John (Frenchy) Fuqua, Pittsburgh vs. Philadelphia	20	218	2
Nov. 3, 1968	Gale Sayers, Chicago vs. Green Bay	24	205	0
Oct. 30, 1966	Jim Nance, Boston vs. Oakland	38	208	2
Oct. 10, 1964	John Henry Johnson, Pittsburgh vs. Cleveland	30	200	3
Dec. 8, 1963	Cookie Gilchrist, Buffalo vs. N.Y. Jets	36	243	5
Nov. 3, 1963	Jim Brown, Cleveland vs. Philadelphia	28	223	1
Oct. 20, 1963	Clem Daniels, Oakland vs. N.Y. Jets	27	200	2
Sept. 22, 1963	Jim Brown, Cleveland vs. Dallas	20	232	2
Dec. 10, 1961	Billy Cannon, Houston vs. N.Y. Titans	25	216	3
Nov. 19, 1961	Jim Brown, Cleveland vs. Philadelphia	34	237	4
Dec. 18, 1960	John David Crow, St. Louis vs. Pittsburgh	24	203	0
Nov. 15, 1959	Bobby Mitchell, Cleveland vs. Washington	14	232	3
Nov. 24, 1957	*Jim Brown, Cleveland vs. Los Angeles	31	237	4
Dec. 16, 1956	*Tom Wilson, Los Angeles vs. Green Bay	23	223	0
Nov. 22, 1953	Dan Towler, Los Angeles vs. Baltimore	14	205	1
Nov. 12, 1950	Gene Roberts, N.Y. Giants vs. Chi. Cardinals	26	218	2
Nov. 27, 1949	Steve Van Buren, Philadelphia vs. Pittsburgh	27	205	0
Oct. 8, 1933	Cliff Battles, Boston vs. N.Y. Giants	16	215	1

First year in the league.

Times 200 or More

57 times by 39 players . . . Simpson 6; Brown, Campbell 4; Bell, Dickerson 3; Payton, Riggs, Rogers 2.

4,000 Yards Passing in a Season

Year	Player, Team	Att.	Comp.	Pct.	Yards	TD	Int.
1991	Warren Moon, Houston[2]	655	404	61.7	4,690	23	21
1990	Warren Moon, Houston	584	362	62.0	4,689	33	13
1989	Don Majkowski, Green Bay	599	353	58.9	4,318	27	20
	Jim Everett, L.A. Rams	518	304	58.7	4,310	29	17
1988	Dan Marino, Miami[4]	606	354	58.4	4,434	28	23
1986	Dan Marino, Miami[3]	623	378	60.7	4,746	44	23
	Jay Schroeder, Washington	541	276	51.0	4,109	22	22
1985	Dan Marino, Miami[2]	567	336	59.3	4,137	30	21
1984	Dan Marino, Miami	564	362	64.2	5,084	48	17
	Neil Lomax, St. Louis	560	345	61.6	4,614	28	16
	Phil Simms, N.Y. Giants	533	286	53.7	4,044	22	18
1983	Lynn Dickey, Green Bay	484	289	59.7	4,458	32	29
	Bill Kenney, Kansas City	603	346	57.4	4,348	24	18
1981	Dan Fouts, San Diego[3]	609	360	59.1	4,802	33	17
1980	Dan Fouts, San Diego[2]	589	348	59.1	4,715	30	24
	Brian Sipe, Cleveland	554	337	60.8	4,132	30	14
1979	Dan Fouts, San Diego	530	332	62.6	4,082	24	24
1967	Joe Namath, N.Y. Jets	491	258	52.5	4,007	26	28

400 Yards Passing in a Game

Date	Player, Team, Opponent	Att.	Comp.	Yards	TD
Nov. 10, 1991	Warren Moon, Houston vs. Dallas (OT)	56	41	432	0
Nov. 10, 1991	Mark Rypien, Washington vs. Atlanta	31	16	442	6
Oct. 13, 1991	Warren Moon, Houston vs. N.Y. Jets	50	35	423	2
Dec. 16, 1990	Warren Moon, Houston vs. Kansas City	45	27	527	3
Nov. 4, 1990	Joe Montana, San Francisco vs. Green Bay	40	25	411	3
Oct. 14, 1990	Joe Montana, San Francisco vs. Atlanta	49	32	476	6
Oct. 7, 1990	Boomer Esiason, Cincinnati vs. L.A. Rams (OT)	45	31	490	3
Dec. 23, 1989	Warren Moon, Houston vs. Cleveland	51	32	414	2
Dec. 11, 1989	Joe Montana, San Francisco vs. L.A. Rams	42	30	458	3
Nov. 26, 1989	Jim Everett, L.A. Rams vs. New Orleans (OT)	51	29	454	1
Nov. 26, 1989	Mark Rypien, Washington vs. Chicago	47	30	401	4
Oct. 2, 1989	Randall Cunningham, Philadelphia vs. Chicago	62	32	401	1
Sept. 24, 1989	Joe Montana, San Francisco vs. Philadelphia	34	25	428	5
Sept. 24, 1989	Dan Marino, Miami vs. N.Y. Jets	55	33	427	3
Sept. 17, 1989	Randall Cunningham, Phil. vs. Washington	46	34	447	5
Dec. 18, 1988	Dave Krieg, Seattle at L.A. Raiders	32	19	410	4
Dec. 12, 1988	Dan Marino, Miami vs. Cleveland	50	30	404	4
Oct. 23, 1988	Dan Marino, Miami vs. N.Y. Jets	60	35	521	3
Oct. 16, 1988	Vinny Testaverde, Tampa Bay at Indianapolis	42	25	469	2
Sept. 11, 1988	Doug Williams, Washington vs. Pittsburgh	52	30	430	2
Nov. 29, 1987	Tom Ramsey, New England vs. Philadelphia	53	34	402	3
Nov. 22, 1987	Boomer Esiason, Cincinnati vs. Pittsburgh	53	30	409	0
Sept. 20, 1987	Neil Lomax, St. Louis vs. San Diego	61	32	457	3
Dec. 21, 1986	Boomer Esiason, Cincinnati vs. N.Y. Jets	30	23	425	5
Dec. 14, 1986	Dan Marino, Miami vs. L.A. Rams (OT)	46	29	403	5
Nov. 23, 1986	Bernie Kosar, Cleveland vs. Pittsburgh (OT)	46	28	414	2
Nov. 17, 1986	Joe Montana, San Francisco vs. Washington	60	33	441	0
Nov. 16, 1986	Dan Marino, Miami vs. Buffalo	54	39	404	4
Nov. 10, 1986	Bernie Kosar, Cleveland vs. Miami	50	32	401	0
Nov. 2, 1986	Tommy Kramer, Minnesota vs. Washington (OT)	35	20	490	4
Nov. 2, 1986	Ken O'Brien, N.Y. Jets vs. Seattle	32	26	431	4
Oct. 27, 1986	Jay Schroeder, Washington vs. N.Y. Giants	40	22	420	1
Oct. 12, 1986	Steve Grogan, New England vs. N.Y. Jets	42	23	401	3
Sept. 21, 1986	Ken O'Brien, N.Y. Jets vs. Miami (OT)	43	29	479	4
Sept. 21, 1986	Dan Marino, Miami vs. N.Y. Jets (OT)	50	30	448	6
Sept. 21, 1986	Tony Eason, New England vs. Seattle	45	26	414	3
Dec. 20, 1985	John Elway, Denver vs. Seattle	42	24	432	1
Nov. 10, 1985	Dan Fouts, San Diego vs. L.A. Raiders (OT)	41	26	436	4
Oct. 13, 1985	Phil Simms, N.Y. Giants vs. Cincinnati	62	40	513	1
Oct. 13, 1985	Dave Krieg, Seattle vs. Atlanta	51	33	405	4
Oct. 6, 1985	Phil Simms, N.Y. Giants vs. Dallas	36	18	432	3
Oct. 6, 1985	Joe Montana, San Francisco vs. Atlanta	57	37	429	5
Sept. 19, 1985	Tommy Kramer, Minnesota vs. Chicago	55	28	436	3
Sept. 15, 1985	Dan Fouts, San Diego vs. Seattle	43	29	440	4
Dec. 16, 1984	Neil Lomax, St. Louis vs. Washington	46	37	468	2
Dec. 9, 1984	Dan Marino, Miami vs. Indianapolis	41	29	404	4
Dec. 2, 1984	Dan Marino, Miami vs. L.A. Raiders	57	35	470	4
Nov. 25, 1984	Dave Krieg, Seattle vs. Denver	44	30	406	3
Nov. 4, 1984	Dan Marino, Miami vs. N.Y. Jets	42	23	422	2
Oct. 21, 1984	Dan Fouts, San Diego vs. L.A. Raiders	45	24	410	3
Sept. 30, 1984	Dan Marino, Miami vs. St. Louis	36	24	429	3
Sept. 2, 1984	Phil Simms, N.Y. Giants vs. Philadelphia	30	23	409	4
Dec. 11, 1983	Bill Kenney, Kansas City vs. San Diego	41	31	411	4
Nov. 20, 1983	Dave Krieg, Seattle vs. Denver	42	31	418	3
Oct. 9, 1983	Joe Ferguson, Buffalo vs. Miami (OT)	55	38	419	5
Oct. 2, 1983	Joe Theismann, Washington vs. L.A. Raiders	39	23	417	3
Sept. 25, 1983	Richard Todd, N.Y. Jets vs. L.A. Rams (OT)	50	37	446	2
Dec. 26, 1982	Vince Ferragamo, L.A. Rams vs. Chicago	46	30	509	3
Dec. 20, 1982	Dan Fouts, San Diego vs. Cincinnati	40	25	435	1
Dec. 20, 1982	Ken Anderson, Cincinnati vs. San Diego	56	40	416	2
Dec. 11, 1982	Dan Fouts, San Diego vs. San Francisco	48	33	444	5
Nov. 21, 1982	Joe Montana, San Francisco vs. St. Louis	39	26	408	3
Nov. 15, 1981	Steve Bartkowski, Atlanta vs. Pittsburgh	50	33	416	2
Oct. 25, 1981	Brian Sipe, Cleveland vs. Baltimore	41	30	444	4
Oct. 25, 1981	David Woodley, Miami vs. Dallas	37	21	408	3
Oct. 11, 1981	Tommy Kramer, Minnesota vs. San Diego	43	27	444	4
Dec. 14, 1980	Tommy Kramer, Minnesota vs. Cleveland	49	38	456	4
Nov. 16, 1980	Doug Williams, Tampa Bay vs. Minnesota	55	30	486	4
Oct. 19, 1980	Dan Fouts, San Diego vs. N.Y. Giants	41	26	444	3
Oct. 12, 1980	Lynn Dickey, Green Bay vs. Tampa Bay (OT)	51	35	418	1
Sept. 21, 1980	Richard Todd, N.Y. Jets vs. San Francisco	60	42	447	3
Oct. 3, 1976	James Harris, Los Angeles vs. Miami	29	17	436	2
Nov. 17, 1975	Ken Anderson, Cincinnati vs. Buffalo	46	30	447	2

Nov. 18, 1974	Charley Johnson, Denver vs. Kansas City	42	28	445	2
Dec. 11, 1972	Joe Namath, N.Y. Jets vs. Oakland	46	25	403	1
Sept. 24, 1972	Joe Namath, N.Y. Jets vs. Baltimore	28	15	496	6
Dec. 21, 1969	Don Horn, Green Bay vs. St. Louis	31	22	410	5
Sept. 28, 1969	Joe Kapp, Minnesota vs. Baltimore	43	28	449	7
Sept. 9, 1968	Pete Beathard, Houston vs. Kansas City	48	23	413	2
Nov. 26, 1967	Sonny Jurgensen, Washington vs. Cleveland	50	32	418	3
Oct. 1, 1967	Joe Namath, N.Y. Jets vs. Miami	39	23	415	3
Sept. 17, 1967	Johnny Unitas, Baltimore vs. Atlanta	32	22	401	2
Nov. 13, 1966	Don Meredith, Dallas vs. Washington	29	21	406	2
Nov. 28, 1965	Sonny Jurgensen, Washington vs. Dallas	43	26	411	3
Oct. 24, 1965	Fran Tarkenton, Minnesota vs. San Francisco	35	21	407	3
Nov. 1, 1964	Len Dawson, Kansas City vs. Denver	38	23	435	6
Oct. 25, 1964	Cotton Davidson, Oakland vs. Denver	36	23	427	5
Oct. 16, 1964	Babe Parilli, Boston vs. Oakland	47	25	422	4
Dec. 22, 1963	Tom Flores, Oakland vs. Houston	29	17	407	6
Nov. 17, 1963	Norm Snead, Washington vs. Pittsburgh	40	23	424	2
Nov. 10, 1963	Don Meredith, Dallas vs. San Francisco	48	30	460	3
Oct. 13, 1963	Charley Johnson, St. Louis vs. Pittsburgh	41	20	428	2
Dec. 16, 1962	Sonny Jurgensen, Philadelphia vs. St. Louis	34	15	419	5
Nov. 18, 1962	Bill Wade, Chicago vs. Dall. Cowboys	46	28	466	2
Oct. 28, 1962	Y.A. Tittle, N.Y. Giants vs. Washington	39	27	505	7
Sept. 15, 1962	Frank Tripucka, Denver vs. Buffalo	56	29	447	2
Dec. 17, 1961	Sonny Jurgensen, Philadelphia vs. Detroit	42	27	403	3
Nov. 19, 1961	George Blanda, Houston vs. N.Y. Titans	32	20	418	7
Oct. 29, 1961	George Blanda, Houston vs. Buffalo	32	18	464	4
Oct. 29, 1961	Sonny Jurgensen, Philadelphia vs. Washington	41	27	436	3
Oct. 13, 1961	Jacky Lee, Houston vs. Boston	41	27	457	2
Dec. 13, 1958	Bobby Layne, Pittsburgh vs. Chi. Cardinals	49	23	409	2
Nov. 8, 1953	Bobby Thomason, Philadelphia vs. N.Y. Giants	44	22	437	4
Oct. 4, 1952	Otto Graham, Cleveland vs. Pittsburgh	49	21	401	3
Sept. 28, 1951	Norm Van Brocklin, Los Angeles vs. N.Y. Yanks	41	27	554	5
Dec. 11, 1949	Johnny Lujack, Chi. Bears vs. Chi. Cardinals	39	24	468	6
Oct. 31, 1948	Sammy Baugh, Washington vs. Boston	24	17	446	4
Oct. 31, 1948	Jim Hardy, Los Angeles vs. Chi. Cardinals	53	28	406	3
Nov. 14, 1943	Sid Luckman, Chi. Bears vs. N.Y. Giants	32	21	433	7

Times 400 or More

109 times by 59 players... Marino 10; Montana 7; Fouts 6; Jurgensen 5; Kramer, Krieg, Moon 4; Esiason, Namath, Simms 3; Anderson, Blanda, Cunningham, Johnson, Kosar, Lomax, Meredith, O'Brien, Rypien, Todd, Williams 2.

1,000 Yards Pass Receiving in a Season

Year	Player, Team	No.	Yards	Avg.	Long	TD
1991	Michael Irvin, Dallas	93	1,523	16.4	66	8
	Gary Clark, Washington[5]	70	1,340	19.1	82	10
	Jerry Rice, San Francisco[6]	80	1,206	15.1	73	14
	Haywood Jeffires, Houston[2]	100	1,181	11.8	44	7
	Michael Haynes, Atlanta	50	1,122	22.4	80	11
	Andre Reed, Buffalo[2]	81	1,113	13.7	55	10
	Drew Hill, Houston[5]	90	1,109	12.3	61	4
	Mark Duper, Miami[4]	70	1,085	15.5	43	5
	James Lofton, Buffalo[6]	57	1,072	18.8	77	8
	Mark Clayton, Miami[5]	70	1,053	15.0	43	12
	Henry Ellard, L.A. Rams[4]	64	1,052	16.4	38	3
	Art Monk, Washington[5]	71	1,049	14.8	64	8
	Irving Fryar, New England	68	1,014	14.9	56	3
	John Taylor, San Francisco[2]	64	1,011	15.8	97	9
	Brian Blades, Seattle[2]	70	1,003	14.3	52	2
1990	Jerry Rice, San Francisco[5]	100	1,502	15.0	64	13
	Henry Ellard, L.A. Rams[3]	76	1,294	17.0	50	4
	Andre Rison, Atlanta	82	1,208	14.7	75	10
	Gary Clark, Washington[4]	75	1,112	14.8	53	8
	Sterling Sharpe, Green Bay[2]	67	1,105	16.5	76	6
	Willie Anderson, L.A. Rams[2]	51	1,097	21.5	55	4
	Haywood Jeffires, Houston	74	1,048	14.2	87	8
	Stephone Paige, Kansas City	65	1,021	15.7	86	5
	Drew Hill, Houston[4]	74	1,019	13.8	57	5
	Anthony Carter, Minnesota[3]	70	1,008	14.4	56	8
1989	Jerry Rice, San Francisco[4]	82	1,483	18.1	68	17
	Sterling Sharpe, Green Bay	90	1,423	15.8	79	12
	Mark Carrier, Tampa Bay	86	1,422	16.5	78	9
	Henry Ellard, L.A. Rams[2]	70	1,382	19.7	53	8
	Andre Reed, Buffalo	88	1,312	14.9	78	9
	Anthony Miller, San Diego	75	1,252	16.7	69	10
	Webster Slaughter, Cleveland	65	1,236	19.0	97	6
	Gary Clark, Washington[3]	79	1,229	15.6	80	9
	Tim McGee, Cincinnati	65	1,211	18.6	74	8
	Art Monk, Washington[4]	86	1,186	13.8	60	8
	Willie Anderson, L.A. Rams	44	1,146	26.0	78	5
	Ricky Sanders, Washington[2]	80	1,138	14.2	68	4
	Vance Johnson, Denver	76	1,095	14.4	69	7
	Richard Johnson, Detroit	70	1,091	15.6	75	8
	Eric Martin, New Orleans[2]	68	1,090	16.0	53	8
	John Taylor, San Francisco	60	1,077	18.0	95	10
	Mervyn Fernandez, L.A. Raiders	57	1,069	18.8	75	9
	Anthony Carter, Minnesota[2]	65	1,066	16.4	50	4
	Brian Blades, Seattle	77	1,063	13.8	60	5
	Mark Clayton, Miami[4]	64	1,011	15.8	78	9
1988	Henry Ellard, L.A. Rams	86	1,414	16.4	68	10
	Jerry Rice, San Francisco[3]	64	1,306	20.4	96	9
	Eddie Brown, Cincinnati	53	1,273	24.0	86	9
	Anthony Carter, Minnesota	72	1,225	17.0	67	6
	Ricky Sanders, Washington	73	1,148	15.7	55	12
	Drew Hill, Houston[3]	72	1,141	15.8	57	10
	Mark Clayton, Miami[3]	86	1,129	13.1	45	14
	Roy Green, Phoenix[3]	68	1,097	16.1	52	7
	Eric Martin, New Orleans	85	1,083	12.7	40	7
	Al Toon, N.Y. Jets[2]	93	1,067	11.5	42	5
	Bruce Hill, Tampa Bay	58	1,040	17.9	42	9
	Lionel Manuel, N.Y. Giants	65	1,029	15.8	46	4
1987	J.T. Smith, St. Louis[2]	91	1,117	12.3	38	8
	Jerry Rice, San Francisco[2]	65	1,078	16.6	57	22
	Gary Clark, Washington[2]	56	1,066	19.0	84	7
	Carlos Carson, Kansas City[3]	55	1,044	19.0	81	7
1986	Jerry Rice, San Francisco	86	1,570	18.3	66	15
	Stanley Morgan, New England[3]	84	1,491	17.8	44	10
	Mark Duper, Miami[3]	67	1,313	19.6	85	11
	Gary Clark, Washington	74	1,265	17.1	55	7
	Al Toon, N.Y. Jets	85	1,176	13.8	62	8
	Todd Christensen, L.A. Raiders[3]	95	1,153	12.1	35	8
	Mark Clayton, Miami[2]	60	1,150	19.2	68	10
	*Bill Brooks, Indianapolis	65	1,131	17.4	84	8
	Drew Hill, Houston[2]	65	1,112	17.1	81	5
	Steve Largent, Seattle[8]	70	1,070	15.3	38	9
	Art Monk, Washington[3]	73	1,068	14.6	69	4
	*Ernest Givins, Houston	61	1,062	17.4	60	3
	Cris Collinsworth, Cincinnati[4]	62	1,024	16.5	46	10
	Wesley Walker, N.Y. Jets[2]	49	1,016	20.7	83	12
	J.T. Smith, St. Louis	80	1,014	12.7	45	6
	Mark Bavaro, N.Y. Giants	66	1,001	15.2	41	4
1985	Steve Largent, Seattle[7]	79	1,287	16.3	43	6
	Mike Quick, Philadelphia[3]	73	1,247	17.1	99	11
	Art Monk, Washington[2]	91	1,226	13.5	53	2
	Wes Chandler, San Diego[4]	67	1,199	17.9	75	10
	Drew Hill, Houston	64	1,169	18.3	57	9
	James Lofton, Green Bay[5]	69	1,153	16.7	56	4
	Louis Lipps, Pittsburgh	59	1,134	19.2	51	12
	Cris Collinsworth, Cincinnati[3]	65	1,125	17.3	71	5
	Tony Hill, Dallas[3]	74	1,113	15.0	53	7
	Lionel James, San Diego	86	1,027	11.9	67	6
	Roger Craig, San Francisco	92	1,016	11.0	73	6
1984	Roy Green, St. Louis[2]	78	1,555	19.9	83	12
	John Stallworth, Pittsburgh[3]	80	1,395	17.4	51	11
	Mark Clayton, Miami	73	1,389	19.0	65	18
	Art Monk, Washington	106	1,372	12.9	72	7
	James Lofton, Green Bay[4]	62	1,361	22.0	79	7
	Mark Duper, Miami[2]	71	1,306	18.4	80	8
	Steve Watson, Denver[3]	69	1,170	17.0	73	7
	Steve Largent, Seattle[6]	74	1,164	15.7	65	12
	Tim Smith, Houston[2]	69	1,141	16.5	75	4
	Stacey Bailey, Atlanta	67	1,138	17.0	61	6
	Carlos Carson, Kansas City[2]	57	1,078	18.9	57	4
	Mike Quick, Philadelphia[2]	61	1,052	17.2	90	9
	Todd Christensen, L.A. Raiders[2]	80	1,007	12.6	38	7
	Kevin House, Tampa Bay[2]	76	1,005	13.2	55	5
	Ozzie Newsome, Cleveland[2]	89	1,001	11.2	52	5
1983	Mike Quick, Philadelphia	69	1,409	20.4	83	13
	Carlos Carson, Kansas City	80	1,351	16.9	50	7
	James Lofton, Green Bay[3]	58	1,300	22.4	74	8
	Todd Christensen, L.A. Raiders	92	1,247	13.6	45	12
	Roy Green, St. Louis	78	1,227	15.7	71	14
	Charlie Brown, Washington	78	1,225	15.7	75	8
	Tim Smith, Houston	83	1,176	14.2	47	6
	Kellen Winslow, San Diego[3]	88	1,172	13.3	46	8
	Earnest Gray, N.Y. Giants	78	1,139	14.6	62	5
	Steve Watson, Denver[2]	59	1,133	19.2	78	5
	Cris Collinsworth, Cincinnati[2]	66	1,130	17.1	63	5
	Steve Largent, Seattle[5]	72	1,074	14.9	46	11
	Mark Duper, Miami	51	1,003	19.7	85	10
1982	Wes Chandler, San Diego[3]	49	1,032	21.1	66	9
1981	Alfred Jenkins, Atlanta[2]	70	1,358	19.4	67	13
	James Lofton, Green Bay[2]	71	1,294	18.2	75	8
	Frank Lewis, Buffalo[2]	70	1,244	17.8	33	4
	Steve Watson, Denver	60	1,244	20.7	95	13
	Steve Largent, Seattle[4]	75	1,224	16.3	57	9
	Charlie Joiner, San Diego[4]	70	1,188	17.0	57	7
	Kevin House, Tampa Bay	56	1,176	21.0	84	9
	Wes Chandler, N.O.-San Diego[2]	69	1,142	16.6	51	6
	Dwight Clark, San Francisco	85	1,105	13.0	78	4
	John Stallworth, Pittsburgh[2]	63	1,098	17.4	55	5
	Kellen Winslow, San Diego[2]	88	1,075	12.2	67	10
	Pat Tilley, St. Louis	66	1,040	15.8	75	3
	Stanley Morgan, New England[2]	44	1,029	23.4	76	6
	Harold Carmichael, Philadelphia[3]	61	1,028	16.9	85	6
	Freddie Scott, Detroit	53	1,022	19.3	48	5
	*Cris Collinsworth, Cincinnati	67	1,009	15.1	74	8
	Joe Senser, Minnesota	79	1,004	12.7	53	8
	Ozzie Newsome, Cleveland	69	1,002	14.5	62	6
	Sammy White, Minnesota	66	1,001	15.2	53	3
1980	John Jefferson, San Diego[3]	82	1,340	16.3	58	13
	Kellen Winslow, San Diego	89	1,290	14.5	65	9
	James Lofton, Green Bay	71	1,226	17.3	47	4
	Charlie Joiner, San Diego[3]	71	1,132	15.9	51	4
	Ahmad Rashad, Minnesota[2]	69	1,095	15.9	76	5
	Steve Largent, Seattle[3]	66	1,064	16.1	67	6
	Tony Hill, Dallas[2]	60	1,055	17.6	58	8
	Alfred Jenkins, Atlanta	57	1,026	18.0	57	6
1979	Steve Largent, Seattle[2]	66	1,237	18.7	55	9
	John Stallworth, Pittsburgh	70	1,183	16.9	65	8
	Ahmad Rashad, Minnesota	80	1,156	14.5	52	9
	John Jefferson, San Diego[2]	61	1,090	17.9	65	10
	Frank Lewis, Buffalo	54	1,082	20.0	55	2
	Wes Chandler, New Orleans	65	1,069	16.4	85	6
	Tony Hill, Dallas	60	1,062	17.7	75	10
	Drew Pearson, Dallas[2]	55	1,026	18.7	56	8
	Wallace Francis, Atlanta	74	1,013	13.7	42	8
	Harold Jackson, New England[3]	45	1,013	22.5	59	7
	Charlie Joiner, San Diego[2]	72	1,008	14.0	39	4
	Stanley Morgan, New England	44	1,002	22.8	63	12

1978	Wesley Walker, N.Y. Jets	48	1,169	24.4	77	8
	Steve Largent, Seattle	71	1,168	16.5	57	8
	Harold Carmichael, Philadelphia[2]	55	1,072	19.5	56	8
	*John Jefferson, San Diego	56	1,001	17.9	46	13
1976	Roger Carr, Baltimore	43	1,112	25.9	79	11
	Cliff Branch, Oakland[2]	46	1,111	24.2	88	12
	Charlie Joiner, San Diego	50	1,056	21.1	81	7
1975	Ken Burrough, Houston	53	1,063	20.1	77	8
1974	Cliff Branch, Oakland	60	1,092	18.2	67	13
	Drew Pearson, Dallas	62	1,087	17.5	50	2
1973	Harold Carmichael, Philadelphia	67	1,116	16.7	73	9
1972	Harold Jackson, Philadelphia[2]	62	1,048	16.9	77	4
	John Gilliam, Minnesota	47	1,035	22.0	66	7
1971	Otis Taylor, Kansas City[2]	57	1,110	19.5	82	7
1970	Gene Washington, San Francisco	53	1,100	20.8	79	12
	Marlin Briscoe, Buffalo	57	1,036	18.2	48	8
	Dick Gordon, Chicago	71	1,026	14.5	69	13
	Gary Garrison, San Diego[2]	44	1,006	22.9	67	12
1969	Warren Wells, Oakland[2]	47	1,260	26.8	80	14
	Harold Jackson, Philadelphia	65	1,116	17.2	65	9
	Roy Jefferson, Pittsburgh[2]	67	1,079	16.1	63	9
	Dan Abramowicz, New Orleans	73	1,015	13.9	49	7
	Lance Alworth, San Diego[7]	64	1,003	15.7	76	4
1968	Lance Alworth, San Diego[6]	68	1,312	19.3	80	10
	Don Maynard, N.Y. Jets[5]	57	1,297	22.8	87	10
	George Sauer, N.Y. Jets[3]	66	1,141	17.3	43	3
	Warren Wells, Oakland	53	1,137	21.5	94	11
	Gary Garrison, San Diego	52	1,103	21.2	84	10
	Roy Jefferson, Pittsburgh	58	1,074	18.5	62	11
	Paul Warfield, Cleveland	50	1,067	21.3	65	12
	Homer Jones, N.Y. Giants[3]	45	1,057	23.5	84	7
	Fred Biletnikoff, Oakland	61	1,037	17.0	82	6
	Lance Rentzel, Dallas	54	1,009	18.7	65	6
1967	Don Maynard, N.Y. Jets[4]	71	1,434	20.2	75	10
	Ben Hawkins, Philadelphia	59	1,265	21.4	87	10
	Homer Jones, N.Y. Giants[2]	49	1,209	24.7	70	13
	Jackie Smith, St. Louis	56	1,205	21.5	76	9
	George Sauer, N.Y. Jets[2]	75	1,189	15.9	61	6
	Lance Alworth, San Diego[5]	52	1,010	19.4	71	9
1966	Lance Alworth, San Diego[4]	73	1,383	18.9	78	13
	Otis Taylor, Kansas City	58	1,297	22.4	89	8
	Pat Studstill, Detroit	67	1,266	18.9	99	5
	Bob Hayes, Dallas[2]	64	1,232	19.3	95	13
	Charlie Frazier, Houston	57	1,129	19.8	79	12
	Charley Taylor, Washington	72	1,119	15.5	86	12
	George Sauer, N.Y. Jets	63	1,081	17.2	77	5
	Homer Jones, N.Y. Giants	48	1,044	21.8	98	8
	Art Powell, Oakland[5]	53	1,026	19.4	46	11
1965	Lance Alworth, San Diego[3]	69	1,602	23.2	85	14
	Dave Parks, San Francisco	80	1,344	16.8	53	12
	Don Maynard, N.Y. Jets[3]	68	1,218	17.9	56	14
	Pete Retzlaff, Philadelphia	66	1,190	18.0	78	10
	Lionel Taylor, Denver[4]	85	1,131	13.3	63	6
	Tommy McDonald, Los Angeles[3]	67	1,036	15.5	51	9
	*Bob Hayes, Dallas	46	1,003	21.8	82	12
1964	Charley Hennigan, Houston[3]	101	1,546	15.3	53	8
	Art Powell, Oakland[4]	76	1,361	17.9	77	11
	Lance Alworth, San Diego[2]	61	1,235	20.2	82	13
	Johnny Morris, Chicago	93	1,200	12.9	63	10
	Elbert Dubenion, Buffalo	42	1,139	27.1	72	10
	Terry Barr, Detroit[2]	57	1,030	18.1	58	9
1963	Bobby Mitchell, Washington[2]	69	1,436	20.8	99	7
	Art Powell, Oakland[3]	73	1,304	17.9	85	16
	Buddy Dial, Pittsburgh[2]	60	1,295	21.6	83	9
	Lance Alworth, San Diego	61	1,205	19.8	85	11
	Del Shofner, N.Y. Giants[4]	64	1,181	18.5	70	9
	Lionel Taylor, Denver[3]	78	1,101	14.1	72	10
	Terry Barr, Detroit	66	1,086	16.5	75	13
	Charley Hennigan, Houston[2]	61	1,051	17.2	83	10
	Sonny Randle, St. Louis[2]	51	1,014	19.9	68	12
	Bake Turner, N.Y. Jets	71	1,009	14.2	53	6
1962	Bobby Mitchell, Washington	72	1,384	19.2	81	11
	Sonny Randle, St. Louis	63	1,158	18.4	86	7
	Tommy McDonald, Philadelphia[2]	58	1,146	19.8	60	10
	Del Shofner, N.Y. Giants[3]	53	1,133	21.4	69	12
	Art Powell, N.Y. Titans[2]	64	1,130	17.7	80	8
	Frank Clarke, Dall. Cowboys	47	1,043	22.2	66	14
	Don Maynard, N.Y. Titans[2]	56	1,041	18.6	86	8
1961	Charley Hennigan, Houston	82	1,746	21.3	80	12
	Lionel Taylor, Denver[2]	100	1,176	11.8	52	4
	Bill Groman, Houston[2]	50	1,175	23.5	80	17
	Tommy McDonald, Philadelphia	64	1,144	17.9	66	13
	Del Shofner, N.Y. Giants[2]	68	1,125	16.5	46	11
	Jim Phillips, Los Angeles	78	1,092	14.0	69	5
	*Mike Ditka, Chicago	56	1,076	19.2	76	12
	Dave Kocourek, San Diego	55	1,055	19.2	76	4
	Buddy Dial, Pittsburgh	53	1,047	19.8	88	12
	R.C. Owens, San Francisco	55	1,032	18.8	54	5
1960	*Bill Groman, Houston	72	1,473	20.5	92	12
	Raymond Berry, Baltimore	74	1,298	17.5	70	10
	Don Maynard, N.Y. Titans	72	1,265	17.6	65	6
	Lionel Taylor, Denver	92	1,235	13.4	80	12
	Art Powell, N.Y. Titans	69	1,167	16.9	76	14
1958	Del Shofner, Los Angeles	51	1,097	21.5	92	8
1956	Bill Howton, Green Bay[2]	55	1,188	21.6	66	12
	Harlon Hill, Chi. Bears[2]	47	1,128	24.0	79	11
1954	Bob Boyd, Los Angeles	53	1,212	22.9	80	6
	*Harlon Hill, Chi. Bears	45	1,124	25.0	76	12
1953	Pete Pihos, Philadelphia	63	1,049	16.7	59	10
1952	*Bill Howton, Green Bay	53	1,231	23.2	90	13
1951	Elroy (Crazylegs) Hirsch, Los Angeles	66	1,495	22.7	91	17
1950	Tom Fears, Los Angeles[2]	84	1,116	13.3	53	7
	Cloyce Box, Detroit	50	1,009	20.2	82	11
1949	Bob Mann, Detroit	66	1,014	15.4	64	4
	Tom Fears, Los Angeles	77	1,013	13.2	51	9
1945	Jim Benton, Cleveland	45	1,067	23.7	84	8
1942	Don Hutson, Green Bay	74	1,211	16.4	73	17

*First year in the league.

250 Yards Pass Receiving in a Game

Date	Player, Team, Opponent	No.	Yards	TD
Dec. 11, 1989	John Taylor, San Francisco vs. L.A. Rams	11	286	2
Nov. 26, 1989	Willie Anderson, L.A. Rams vs. New Orleans (OT)	15	336	1
Oct. 18, 1987	Steve Largent, Seattle vs. Detroit	15	261	3
Oct. 4, 1987	*Anthony Allen, Washington vs. St. Louis	7	255	3
Dec. 22, 1985	Stephone Paige, Kansas City vs. San Diego	8	309	2
Dec. 20, 1982	Wes Chandler, San Diego vs. Cincinnati	10	260	2
Sept. 23, 1979	*Jerry Butler, Buffalo vs. N.Y. Jets	10	255	4
Nov. 4, 1962	Sonny Randle, St. Louis vs. N.Y. Giants	16	256	1
Oct. 28, 1962	Del Shofner, N.Y. Giants vs. Washington	11	269	1
Oct. 13, 1961	Charley Hennigan, Houston vs. Boston	13	272	1
Oct. 21, 1956	Billy Howton, Green Bay vs. Los Angeles	7	257	2
Dec. 3, 1950	Cloyce Box, Detroit vs. Baltimore	12	302	4
Nov. 22, 1945	Jim Benton, Cleveland vs. Detroit	10	303	1

*First year in the league.

2,000 Combined Net Yards Gained in a Season

Year	Player, Team	Rushing Att.-Yds.	Pass Rec.	Punt Ret.	Kickoff Ret.	Fum. Runs	Total Yds.
1991	Thurman Thomas, Buffalo	288-1,407	62-631	0-0	0-0	0-0	350-2,038
1990	Herschel Walker, Minnesota	184-770	35-315	0-0	44-966	4-0	267-2,051
1988	*Tim Brown, L.A. Raiders	14-50	43-725	49-444	41-1,098	7-0	154-2,317
	Roger Craig, San Fran.	310-1,502	76-534	0-0	2-32	2-0	390-2,068
	Eric Dickerson, Indianapolis	388-1,659	36-377	0-0	0-0	1-0	425-2,036
	Herschel Walker, Dallas	361-1,514	53-505	0-0	0-0	3-0	417-2,019
1986	Eric Dickerson, L.A. Rams	404-1,821	26-205	0-0	0-0	2-0	432-2,026
	Gary Anderson, San Diego	127-442	80-871	25-227	24-482	2-0	258-2,022
1985	Lionel James, San Diego	105-516	86-1,027	25-213	36-779	1-0	253-2,535
	Marcus Allen, L.A. Raiders	380-1,759	67-555	0-0	0-0	2-(−6)	449-2,308
	Roger Craig, San Fran.	214-1,050	92-1,016	0-0	0-0	0-0	306-2,066
	Walter Payton, Chicago	324-1,551	49-483	0-0	0-0	1-0	374-2,034
1984	Eric Dickerson, L.A. Rams	379-2,105	21-139	0-0	0-0	4-15	404-2,259
	James Wilder, Tampa Bay	407-1,544	85-685	0-0	0-0	4-0	496-2,229
	Walter Payton, Chicago	381-1,684	45-368	0-0	0-0	1-0	427-2,052
1983	*Eric Dickerson, L.A. Rams	390-1,808	51-404	0-0	0-0	1-0	442-2,212
	William Andrews, Atlanta	331-1,567	59-609	0-0	0-0	2-0	392-2,176
	Walter Payton, Chicago	314-1,421	53-607	0-0	0-0	2-0	369-2,028
1981	*James Brooks, San Diego	109-525	46-329	22-290	40-949	2-0	219-2,093
	William Andrews, Atlanta	289-1,301	81-735	0-0	0-0	0-0	370-2,036
1980	Bruce Harper, N.Y. Jets	45-126	50-634	28-242	49-1,070	3-0	175-2,072
1979	Wilbert Montgomery, Phil.	338-1,512	41-494	0-0	1-6	2-0	382-2,012
1978	Bruce Harper, N.Y. Jets	58-303	13-196	30-378	55-1,280	1-0	157-2,157
1977	Walter Payton, Chicago	339-1,852	27-269	0-0	2-95	5-0	373-2,216
	Terry Metcalf, St. Louis	149-739	34-403	14-108	32-772	1-0	230-2,022
1975	Terry Metcalf, St. Louis	165-816	43-378	23-285	35-960	2-23	268-2,462
	O.J. Simpson, Buffalo	329-1,817	28-426	0-0	0-0	1-0	358-2,243
1974	Mack Herron, New England	231-824	38-474	35-517	28-629	3-0	335-2,444
	Otis Armstrong, Denver	263-1,407	38-405	0-0	16-386	1-0	318-2,198
	Terry Metcalf, St. Louis	152-718	50-377	26-340	20-623	7-0	255-2,058
1973	O.J. Simpson, Buffalo	332-2,003	6-70	0-0	0-0	0-0	338-2,073
1966	Gale Sayers, Chicago	229-1,231	34-447	6-44	23-718	3-0	295-2,440
	Leroy Kelly, Cleveland	209-1,141	32-366	13-104	19-403	0-0	273-2,014
1965	*Gale Sayers, Chicago	166-867	29-507	16-238	21-660	4-0	236-2,272
1963	Timmy Brown, Philadelphia	192-841	36-487	16-152	33-945	2-3	279-2,428
	Jim Brown, Cleveland	291-1,863	24-268	0-0	0-0	0-0	315-2,131
1962	Timmy Brown, Philadelphia	137-545	52-849	6-81	30-831	4-0	229-2,306
	Dick Christy, N.Y. Titans	114-535	62-538	15-250	38-824	2-0	231-2,147
1961	Billy Cannon, Houston	200-948	43-586	9-70	18-439	2-0	272-2,043
1960	*Abner Haynes, Dall. Texans	156-875	55-576	14-215	19-434	4-0	248-2,100

*First year in the league.

300 Combined Net Yards Gained in a Game

Date	Player, Team, Opponent	No.	Yards	TD
Dec. 11, 1989	John Taylor, San Francisco vs. L.A. Rams	14	321	2
Nov. 26, 1989	Willie Anderson, L.A. Rams vs. New Orleans (OT)	15	336	1
Nov. 28, 1988	Tim Brown, L.A. Raiders vs. San Diego	12	306	1
Dec. 22, 1985	Stephone Paige, Kansas City vs. San Diego	8	309	2
Nov. 10, 1985	Lionel James, San Diego vs. L.A. Raiders (OT)	23	345	0
Sept. 22, 1985	Lionel James, San Diego vs. Cincinnati	20	316	2
Dec. 21, 1975	Walter Payton, Chicago vs. New Orleans	32	300	1
Nov. 23, 1975	Greg Pruitt, Cleveland vs. Cincinnati	28	304	2
Nov. 1, 1970	Eugene (Mercury) Morris, Miami vs. Baltimore	17	302	0
Oct. 4, 1970	O. J. Simpson, Buffalo vs. N.Y. Jets	26	303	2
Dec. 6, 1969	Jerry LeVias, Houston vs. N.Y. Jets	18	329	1
Nov. 2, 1969	Travis Williams, Green Bay vs. Pittsburgh	11	314	3
Dec. 18, 1966	Gale Sayers, Chicago vs. Minnesota	20	339	2
Dec. 12, 1965	Gale Sayers, Chicago vs. San Francisco	17	336	6
Nov. 17, 1963	Gary Ballman, Pittsburgh vs. Washington	12	320	2
Dec. 16, 1962	Timmy Brown, Philadelphia vs. St. Louis	19	341	2
Dec. 10, 1961	Billy Cannon, Houston vs. N.Y. Titans	32	373	5
Nov 19, 1961	Jim Brown, Cleveland vs. Philadelphia	38	313	4
Dec. 3, 1950	Cloyce Box, Detroit vs. Baltimore	13	302	4
Oct. 29, 1950	Wally Triplett, Detroit vs. Los Angeles	11	331	1
Nov. 22, 1945	Jim Benton, Cleveland vs. Detroit	10	303	1

Top 20 Scorers

Player	Years	TD	FG	PAT	TP
George Blanda	26	9	335	943	2,002
Jan Stenerud	19	0	373	580	1,699
Pat Leahy	18	0	304	558	1,470
Jim Turner	16	1	304	521	1,439
Mark Moseley	16	0	300	482	1,382
Jim Bakken	17	0	282	534	1,380
Fred Cox	15	0	282	519	1,365

Lou Groza	17	1	234	641	1,349
Nick Lowery	13	0	284	410	1,262
Chris Bahr	14	0	241	490	1,213
Jim Breech	13	0	224	486	1,158
Gino Cappelletti	11	42	176	350	1,130
Ray Wersching	15	0	222	456	1,122
Eddie Murray	12	0	244	381	1,113
Don Cockroft	13	0	216	432	1,080
Garo Yepremian	14	0	210	444	1,074
Matt Bahr	13	0	221	402	1,065
Bruce Gossett	11	0	219	374	1,031
Gary Anderson	10	0	229	323	1,010
Sam Baker	15	2	179	428	977

Cappelletti's total includes four two-point conversions.

Top 20 Touchdown Scorers

Player	Years	Rush	Rec.	Returns	Total TD
Jim Brown	9	106	20	0	126
Walter Payton	13	110	15	0	125
John Riggins	14	104	12	0	116
Lenny Moore	12	63	48	2	113
Don Hutson	11	3	99	3	105
Steve Largent	14	1	100	0	101
Franco Harris	13	91	9	0	100
Jerry Rice	7	4	93	0	97
Marcus Allen	10	77	17	1	95
Eric Dickerson	9	88	5	0	93
Jim Taylor	10	83	10	0	93
Tony Dorsett	12	77	13	1	91
Bobby Mitchell	11	18	65	8	91
Leroy Kelly	10	74	13	3	90
Charley Taylor	13	11	79	0	90
Don Maynard	15	0	88	0	88
Lance Alworth	11	2	85	0	87
Ottis Anderson	13	81	5	0	86
Paul Warfield	13	1	85	0	86
Tommy McDonald	12	0	84	0	85

Top 20 Rushers

Player	Years	Att.	Yards	Avg.	Long	TD
Walter Payton	13	3,838	16,726	4.4	76	110
Tony Dorsett	12	2,936	12,739	4.3	99	77
Eric Dickerson	9	2,783	12,439	4.5	85	88
Jim Brown	9	2,359	12,312	5.2	80	106
Franco Harris	13	2,949	12,120	4.1	75	91
John Riggins	14	2,916	11,352	3.9	66	104
O. J. Simpson	11	2,404	11,236	4.7	94	61
Ottis Anderson	13	2,552	10,242	4.0	76	81
Earl Campbell	8	2,187	9,407	4.3	81	74
Jim Taylor	10	1,941	8,597	4.4	84	83
Joe Perry	14	1,737	8,378	4.8	78	53
Marcus Allen	10	2,023	8,244	4.1	61	77
Gerald Riggs	10	1,989	8,188	4.1	58	69
Larry Csonka	11	1,891	8,081	4.3	54	64
James Brooks	11	1,667	7,918	4.7	65	49
Freeman McNeil	11	1,755	7,904	4.5	69	38
Roger Craig	9	1,848	7,654	4.1	71	51
Mike Pruitt	11	1,844	7,378	4.0	77	51
Leroy Kelly	10	1,727	7,274	4.2	70	74
George Rogers	7	1,692	7,176	4.2	79	54

Top 20 Combined Yards Gained

Player	Years	Tot.	Rush.	Rec.	Int. Ret.	Punt Ret.	Kickoff Ret.	Fumble Ret.
Walter Payton	13	21,803	16,726	4,538	0	0	539	0
Tony Dorsett	12	16,326	12,739	3,554	0	0	0	33
Jim Brown	9	15,459	12,312	2,499	0	0	648	0
James Brooks	11	14,818	7,918	3,622	0	565	2,713	0
Franco Harris	13	14,622	12,120	2,287	0	0	233	−18
Eric Dickerson	9	14,448	12,439	1,994	0	0	0	15
O. J. Simpson	11	14,368	11,236	2,142	0	0	990	0
Bobby Mitchell	11	14,078	2,735	7,954	0	699	2,690	0
John Riggins	14	13,435	11,352	2,090	0	0	0	−7
Steve Largent	14	13,396	83	13,089	0	68	156	0
Ottis Anderson	13	13,333	10,242	3,062	0	0	0	29
James Lofton	14	13,308	246	13,035	0	0	0	27
Greg Pruitt	12	13,262	5,672	3,069	0	2,007	2,514	0
Ollie Matson	14	12,884	5,173	3,285	51	595	3,746	34
Tim Brown	10	12,684	3,862	3,399	0	639	4,781	3
Lenny Moore	12	12,451	5,174	6,039	0	56	1,180	2
Don Maynard	15	12,379	70	11,834	0	132	343	0
Charlie Joiner	18	12,367	22	12,146	0	0	194	5
Drew Hill	12	12,330	19	8,824	0	22	3,460	5
Leroy Kelly	10	12,330	7,274	2,281	0	990	1,784	1

Top 20 Passers

Player	Years	Att.	Comp.	Pct. Comp.	Yards	TD	Pct. TD	Int.	Pct. Int.	Avg. Gain	Rating
Joe Montana	12	4,579	2,914	63.6	34,998	242	5.3	123	2.7	7.64	93.4
Dan Marino	9	4,730	2,798	59.2	35,386	266	5.6	149	3.2	7.48	88.2
Jim Kelly	6	2,562	1,555	60.7	19,574	138	5.4	89	3.5	7.64	88.0
Boomer Esiason	8	3,100	1,753	56.5	24,264	163	5.3	114	3.7	7.83	84.0
Roger Staubach	11	2,958	1,685	57.0	22,700	153	5.2	109	3.7	7.67	83.4
Neil Lomax	8	3,153	1,817	57.6	22,771	136	4.3	90	2.9	7.22	82.7
Sonny Jurgensen	18	4,262	2,433	57.1	32,224	255	6.0	189	4.4	7.56	82.6
Len Dawson	19	3,741	2,136	57.1	28,711	239	6.4	183	4.9	7.67	82.6
Dave Krieg	12	3,576	2,096	58.6	26,132	195	5.5	148	4.1	7.31	82.3
Ken Anderson	16	4,475	2,654	59.3	32,838	197	4.4	160	3.6	7.34	81.9
Danny White	13	2,950	1,761	59.7	21,959	155	5.3	132	4.5	7.44	81.7
Bernie Kosar	7	2,857	1,671	58.5	19,937	103	3.6	71	2.5	6.98	81.6
Ken O'Brien	8	3,367	1,984	58.9	23,744	119	3.5	89	2.6	7.05	81.3
Bart Starr	16	3,149	1,808	57.4	24,718	152	4.8	138	4.4	7.85	80.5
Fran Tarkenton	18	6,467	3,686	57.0	47,003	342	5.3	266	4.1	7.27	80.4
Warren Moon	8	3,680	2,105	57.2	27,679	157	4.3	133	3.6	7.52	80.3
Dan Fouts	15	5,604	3,297	58.8	43,040	254	4.5	242	4.3	7.68	80.2
Tony Eason	8	1,564	911	58.2	11,142	61	3.9	51	3.3	7.12	79.7
Jim Everett	6	2,528	1,431	56.6	18,783	112	4.4	93	3.7	7.43	79.7
Jim McMahon	10	2,151	1,243	57.8	15,637	89	4.1	77	3.6	7.27	79.4

1,500 or more attempts. The passing ratings are based on performance standards established for completion percentage, interception percentage, touchdown percentage, and average gain. Passers are allocated points according to how their marks compare with those standards.

Top 20 Pass Receivers

Player	Years	No.	Yards	Avg.	Long	TD
Steve Largent	14	819	13,089	16.0	74	100
Art Monk	12	801	10,984	13.7	79	60
Charlie Joiner	18	750	12,146	16.2	87	65
James Lofton	14	699	13,035	18.6	80	69
Ozzie Newsome	13	662	7,980	12.1	74	47
Charley Taylor	13	649	9,110	14.0	88	79
Don Maynard	15	633	11,834	18.7	87	88
Raymond Berry	13	631	9,275	14.7	70	68
Harold Carmichael	14	590	8,985	15.2	85	79
Fred Biletnikoff	14	589	8,974	15.2	82	76
Harold Jackson	16	579	10,372	17.9	79	76
Lionel Taylor	10	567	7,195	12.7	80	45
Wes Chandler	11	559	8,966	16.0	85	56
Stanley Morgan	14	557	10,716	19.2	76	72
Roy Green	13	551	8,860	16.1	83	66
J. T. Smith	13	544	6,974	12.8	77	35
Lance Alworth	11	542	10,266	18.9	85	85
Kellen Winslow	9	541	6,741	12.5	67	45
Drew Hill	12	540	8,824	16.3	81	57
John Stallworth	14	537	8,723	16.2	74	63

Top 20 Interceptors

Player	Years	No.	Yards	Avg.	Long	TD
Paul Krause	16	81	1,185	14.6	81	3
Emlen Tunnell	14	79	1,282	16.2	55	4
Dick (Night Train) Lane	14	68	1,207	17.8	80	5
Ken Riley	15	65	596	9.2	66	5
Dick LeBeau	13	62	762	12.3	70	3
Dave Brown	15	62	698	11.3	90	5
Ronnie Lott	11	59	695	11.8	83	5
Emmitt Thomas	13	58	937	16.2	73	5
Bobby Boyd	9	57	994	17.4	74	4
Johnny Robinson	12	57	741	13.0	57	1
Mel Blount	14	57	736	12.9	52	2
Lem Barney	11	56	1,077	19.2	71	7
Pat Fischer	17	56	941	16.8	69	4
Willie Brown	16	54	472	8.7	45	2
Everson Walls	11	54	478	8.9	40	1
Bobby Dillon	8	52	976	18.8	61	5
Jack Butler	9	52	826	15.9	52	4
Larry Wilson	13	52	800	15.4	96	5
Jim Patton	12	52	712	13.7	51	2
Mel Renfro	14	52	626	12.0	90	3

Top 20 Punters

Player	Years	No.	Yards	Avg.	Long	Blk.
Sammy Baugh	16	338	15,245	45.1	85	9
Tommy Davis	11	511	22,833	44.7	82	2
Yale Lary	11	503	22,279	44.3	74	4
Rohn Stark	10	746	32,759	43.9	72	6
Horace Gillom	7	385	16,872	43.8	80	5
Jerry Norton	11	358	15,671	43.8	78	2
Don Chandler	12	660	28,678	43.5	90	4
Reggie Roby	9	520	22,593	43.4	77	3
Sean Landeta	7	440	19,099	43.4	71	1
Jerrel Wilson	16	1,072	46,139	43.0	72	12
Norm Van Brocklin	12	523	22,413	42.9	72	3
Rich Camarillo	11	727	31,109	42.8	76	5
Danny Villanueva	8	488	20,862	42.8	68	2
Bobby Joe Green	14	970	41,317	42.6	75	3
Sam Baker	15	703	29,938	42.6	72	2
Ralf Mojsiejenko	7	413	17,533	42.5	74	5
Bob Waterfield	8	315	13,367	42.4	88	5
Ray Guy	14	1,049	44,493	42.4	74	3
Curley Johnson	10	559	23,651	42.3	73	6
Jim Arnold	9	683	28,774	42.1	69	4

300 or more punts.

Top 20 Punt Returners

Player	Years	No.	Yards	Avg.	Long	TD
George McAfee	8	112	1,431	12.8	74	2
Jack Christiansen	8	85	1,084	12.8	89	8
Claude Gibson	5	110	1,381	12.6	85	3
Mel Gray	6	119	1,479	12.4	80	2
Bill Dudley	9	124	1,515	12.2	96	3
Rick Upchurch	9	248	3,008	12.1	92	8
Billy Johnson	14	282	3,317	11.8	87	6
Mack Herron	3	84	982	11.7	66	0
Billy Thompson	13	157	1,814	11.6	60	0
David Meggett	3	117	1,336	11.4	76	3
Henry Ellard	9	133	1,509	11.3	83	4
Louis Lipps	7	107	1,212	11.3	76	3
Rodger Bird	3	94	1,063	11.3	78	0
Bosh Pritchard	6	95	1,072	11.3	81	2
Bobby Joe Edmonds	4	105	1,178	11.2	75	1
Terry Metcalf	6	84	936	11.1	69	1
Bob Hayes	11	104	1,158	11.1	90	3
Floyd Little	9	81	893	11.0	72	2
Vai Sikahema	6	219	2,391	10.9	76	3
Les (Speedy) Duncan	11	202	2,201	10.9	95	4

75 or more returns.

Top 20 Kickoff Returners

Player	Years	No.	Yards	Avg.	Long	TD
Gale Sayers	7	91	2,781	30.6	103	6
Lynn Chandnois	7	92	2,720	29.6	93	3
Abe Woodson	9	193	5,538	28.7	105	5
Claude (Buddy) Young	6	90	2,514	27.9	104	2
Travis Williams	5	102	2,801	27.5	105	6
Joe Arenas	7	139	3,798	27.3	96	1
Clarence Davis	8	79	2,140	27.1	76	0
Steve Van Buren	8	76	2,030	26.7	98	3
Lenny Lyles	12	81	2,161	26.7	103	3
Eugene (Mercury) Morris	8	111	2,947	26.5	105	3
Bobby Jancik	6	158	4,185	26.5	61	0
Mel Renfro	14	85	2,246	26.4	100	2
Bobby Mitchell	11	102	2,690	26.4	98	5
Ollie Matson	14	143	3,746	26.2	105	6
Alvin Haymond	10	170	4,438	26.1	98	2
Noland Smith	3	82	2,137	26.1	106	1
Al Nelson	9	101	2,625	26.0	78	0
Tim Brown	10	184	4,781	26.0	105	5
Vic Washington	6	129	3,341	25.9	98	1
Dave Hampton	8	113	2,923	25.9	101	3

75 or more returns.

Annual Scoring Leaders

Year	Player, Team	TD	FG	PAT	TP
1991	Chip Lohmiller, Washington, NFC	0	31	56	149
	Pete Stoyanovich, Miami, AFC	0	31	28	121
1990	Nick Lowery, Kansas City, AFC	0	34	37	139
	Chip Lohmiller, Washington, NFC	0	30	41	131
1989	Mike Cofer, San Francisco, NFC	0	29	49	136
	*David Treadwell, Denver, AFC	0	27	39	120
1988	Scott Norwood, Buffalo, AFC	0	32	33	129
	*Mike Cofer, San Francisco, NFC	0	27	40	121
1987	Jerry Rice, San Francisco, NFC	23	0	0	138
	Jim Breech, Cincinnati, AFC	0	24	25	97
1986	Tony Franklin, New England, AFC	0	32	44	140
	Kevin Butler, Chicago, NFC	0	28	36	120
1985	*Kevin Butler, Chicago, NFC	0	31	51	144
	Gary Anderson, Pittsburgh, AFC	0	33	40	139
1984	Ray Wersching, San Francisco, NFC	0	25	56	131
	Gary Anderson, Pittsburgh, AFC	0	24	45	117
1983	Mark Moseley, Washington, NFC	0	33	62	161
	Gary Anderson, Pittsburgh, AFC	0	27	38	119
1982	*Marcus Allen, L.A. Raiders, AFC	14	0	0	84
	Wendell Tyler, L.A. Rams, NFC	13	0	0	78
1981	Ed Murray, Detroit, NFC	0	25	46	121
	Rafael Septien, Dallas, NFC	0	27	40	121
	Jim Breech, Cincinnati, AFC	0	22	49	115
	Nick Lowery, Kansas City, AFC	0	26	37	115
1980	John Smith, New England, AFC	0	26	51	129
	*Ed Murray, Detroit, NFC	0	27	35	116
1979	John Smith, New England, AFC	0	23	46	115
	Mark Moseley, Washington, NFC	0	25	39	114
1978	*Frank Corral, Los Angeles, NFC	0	29	31	118
	Pat Leahy, N.Y. Jets, AFC	0	22	41	107
1977	Errol Mann, Oakland, AFC	0	20	39	99
	Walter Payton, Chicago, NFC	16	0	0	96
1976	Toni Linhart, Baltimore, AFC	0	20	49	109
	Mark Moseley, Washington, NFC	0	22	31	97
1975	O.J. Simpson, Buffalo, AFC	23	0	0	138
	Chuck Foreman, Minnesota, NFC	22	0	0	132
1974	Chester Marcol, Green Bay, NFC	0	25	19	94
	Roy Gerela, Pittsburgh, AFC	0	20	33	93
1973	David Ray, Los Angeles, NFC	0	30	40	130
	Roy Gerela, Pittsburgh, AFC	0	29	36	123
1972	*Chester Marcol, Green Bay, NFC	0	33	29	128
	Bobby Howfield, N.Y. Jets, AFC	0	27	40	121
1971	Garo Yepremian, Miami, AFC	0	28	33	117
	Curt Knight, Washington, NFC	0	29	27	114
1970	Fred Cox, Minnesota, NFC	0	30	35	125
	Jan Stenerud, Kansas City, AFC	0	30	26	116
1969	Jim Turner, N.Y. Jets, AFL	0	32	33	129
	Fred Cox, Minnesota, NFL	0	26	43	121
1968	Jim Turner, N.Y. Jets, AFL	0	34	43	145
	Leroy Kelly, Cleveland, NFL	20	0	0	120
1967	Jim Bakken, St. Louis, NFL	0	27	36	117
	George Blanda, Oakland, AFL	0	20	56	116
1966	Gino Cappelletti, Boston, AFL	6	16	35	119
	Bruce Gossett, Los Angeles, NFL	0	28	29	113
1965	*Gale Sayers, Chicago, NFL	22	0	0	132
	Gino Cappelletti, Boston, AFL	9	17	27	132
1964	Gino Cappelletti, Boston, AFL	7	25	36	#155
	Lenny Moore, Baltimore, NFL	20	0	0	120
1963	Gino Cappelletti, Boston, AFL	2	22	35	113
	Don Chandler, N.Y. Giants, NFL	0	18	52	106
1962	Gene Mingo, Denver, AFL	4	27	32	137
	Jim Taylor, Green Bay, NFL	19	0	0	114
1961	Gino Cappelletti, Boston, AFL	8	17	48	147
	Paul Hornung, Green Bay, NFL	10	15	41	146
1960	Paul Hornung, Green Bay, NFL	15	15	41	176
	*Gene Mingo, Denver, AFL	6	18	33	123
1959	Paul Hornung, Green Bay	7	7	31	94
1958	Jim Brown, Cleveland	18	0	0	108
1957	Sam Baker, Washington	1	14	29	77
	Lou Groza, Cleveland	0	15	32	77
1956	Bobby Layne, Detroit	5	12	33	99
1955	Doak Walker, Detroit	7	9	27	96
1954	Bobby Walston, Philadelphia	11	4	36	114
1953	Gordy Soltau, San Francisco	6	10	48	114
1952	Gordy Soltau, San Francisco	7	6	34	94
1951	Elroy (Crazylegs) Hirsch, Los Angeles	17	0	0	102
1950	*Doak Walker, Detroit	11	8	38	128
1949	Pat Harder, Chi. Cardinals	8	3	45	102
	Gene Roberts, N.Y. Giants	17	0	0	102
1948	Pat Harder, Chi. Cardinals	6	7	53	110
1947	Pat Harder, Chi. Cardinals	7	7	39	102
1946	Ted Fritsch, Green Bay	10	9	13	100
1945	Steve Van Buren, Philadelphia	18	0	2	110
1944	Don Hutson, Green Bay	9	0	31	85
1943	Don Hutson, Green Bay	12	3	36	117
1942	Don Hutson, Green Bay	17	1	33	138
1941	Don Hutson, Green Bay	12	1	20	95
1940	Don Hutson, Green Bay	7	0	15	57
1939	Andy Farkas, Washington	11	0	2	68
1938	Clarke Hinkle, Green Bay	7	3	7	58
1937	Jack Manders, Chi. Bears	5	8	15	69
1936	Earl (Dutch) Clark, Detroit	7	4	19	73
1935	Earl (Dutch) Clark, Detroit	6	1	16	55
1934	Jack Manders, Chi. Bears	3	10	31	79
1933	Ken Strong, N.Y. Giants	6	5	13	64
	Glenn Presnell, Portsmouth	6	6	10	64
1932	Earl (Dutch) Clark, Portsmouth	6	3	10	55

*First year in the league.
#Cappelletti's total includes a two-point conversion.

Annual Passing Touchdown Leaders

Year	Player, Team	TD
1991	Jim Kelly, Buffalo, AFC	33
	Mark Rypien, Washington, NFC	28
1990	Warren Moon, Houston, AFC	33
	Randall Cunningham, Philadelphia, NFC	30
1989	Jim Everett, L.A. Rams, NFC	29
	Boomer Esiason, Cincinnati, AFC	28
1988	Jim Everett, L.A. Rams, NFC	31
	Boomer Esiason, Cincinnati, AFC	28
	Dan Marino, Miami, AFC	28
1987	Joe Montana, San Francisco, NFC	31
	Dan Marino, Miami, AFC	26
1986	Dan Marino, Miami, AFC	44
	Tommy Kramer, Minnesota, NFC	24
1985	Dan Marino, Miami, AFC	30
	Joe Montana, San Francisco, NFC	27
1984	Dan Marino, Miami, AFC	48
	Neil Lomax, St. Louis, NFC	28
	Joe Montana, San Francisco, NFC	28
1983	Lynn Dickey, Green Bay, NFC	32
	Joe Ferguson, Buffalo, AFC	26
	Brian Sipe, Cleveland, AFC	26
1982	Terry Bradshaw, Pittsburgh, AFC	17
	Dan Fouts, San Diego, AFC	17
	Joe Montana, San Francisco, NFC	17
1981	Dan Fouts, San Diego, AFC	33
	Steve Bartkowski, Atlanta, NFC	30
1980	Steve Bartkowski, Atlanta, NFC	31
	Dan Fouts, San Diego, AFC	30
	Brian Sipe, Cleveland, AFC	30
1979	Steve Grogan, New England, AFC	28
	Brian Sipe, Cleveland, AFC	28
	Roger Staubach, Dallas, NFC	27
1978	Terry Bradshaw, Pittsburgh, AFC	28
	Roger Staubach, Dallas, NFC	25
	Fran Tarkenton, Minnesota, NFC	25
1977	Bob Griese, Miami, AFC	22
	Ron Jaworski, Philadelphia, NFC	18
	Roger Staubach, Dallas, NFC	18
1976	Ken Stabler, Oakland, AFC	27
	Jim Hart, St. Louis, NFC	18
1975	Joe Ferguson, Buffalo, AFC	25
	Fran Tarkenton, Minnesota, NFC	25
1974	Ken Stabler, Oakland, AFC	26
	Jim Hart, St. Louis, NFC	20
1973	Roman Gabriel, Philadelphia, NFC	23
	Roger Staubach, Dallas, NFC	23
	Charley Johnson, Denver, AFC	20
1972	Billy Kilmer, Washington, NFC	19
	Joe Namath, N.Y. Jets, AFC	19
1971	John Hadl, San Diego, AFC	21
	John Brodie, San Francisco, NFC	18
1970	John Brodie, San Francisco, NFC	24
	John Hadl, San Diego, AFC	22
	Daryle Lamonica, Oakland, AFC	22
1969	Daryle Lamonica, Oakland, AFL	34
	Roman Gabriel, Los Angeles, NFL	24
1968	John Hadl, San Diego, AFL	27
	Earl Morrall, Baltimore, NFL	26
1967	Sonny Jurgensen, Washington, NFL	31
	Daryle Lamonica, Oakland, AFL	30
1966	Frank Ryan, Cleveland, NFL	29
	Len Dawson, Kansas City, AFL	26
1965	John Brodie, San Francisco, NFL	30
	Len Dawson, Kansas City, AFL	21
1964	Babe Parilli, Boston, AFL	31
	Frank Ryan, Cleveland, NFL	25
1963	Y.A. Tittle, N.Y. Giants, NFL	36
	Len Dawson, Kansas City, AFL	26
1962	Y.A. Tittle, N.Y. Giants, NFL	33
	Len Dawson, Dallas, AFL	29
1961	George Blanda, Houston, AFL	36
	Sonny Jurgensen, Philadelphia, NFL	32
1960	Al Dorow, N.Y. Titans, AFL	26
	Johnny Unitas, Baltimore, NFL	25
1959	Johnny Unitas, Baltimore	32
1958	Johnny Unitas, Baltimore	19
1957	Johnny Unitas, Baltimore	24
1956	Tobin Rote, Green Bay	18
1955	Tobin Rote, Green Bay	17
	Y.A. Tittle, San Francisco	17
1954	Adrian Burk, Philadelphia	23
1953	Robert Thomason, Philadelphia	21
1952	Jim Finks, Pittsburgh	20
	Otto Graham, Cleveland	20
1951	Bobby Layne, Detroit	26
1950	*George Ratterman, N.Y. Yanks	22
1949	Johnny Lujack, Chicago Bears	23
1948	Tommy Thompson, Philadelphia	25
1947	Sammy Baugh, Washington	25
1946	Sid Luckman, Chicago Bears	17
	Bob Waterfield, Los Angeles	17
1945	Sid Luckman, Chicago Bears	14
	*Bob Waterfield, Cleveland	14

Year	Player, Team		
1944	Frank Filchock, Washington		13
1943	Sid Luckman, Chicago Bears		28
1942	Cecil Isbell, Green Bay		24
1941	Cecil Isbell, Green Bay		15
1940	Sammy Baugh, Washington		12
1939	Frank Filchock, Washington		11
1938	Bob Monnett, Green Bay		9
1937	Bernie Masterson, Chicago Bears		9
1936	Arnie Herber, Green Bay		11
1935	Ed Danowski, N.Y. Giants		10
1934	Arnie Herber, Green Bay		8
1933	*Harry Newman, N.Y. Giants		11
1932	Arnie Herber, Green Bay		9

*First year in the league.

Annual Leaders—Most Field Goals Made

Year	Player, Team	Att.	Made	Pct.
1991	Pete Stoyanovich, Miami, AFC	37	31	83.8
	Chip Lohmiller, Washington, NFC	43	31	72.1
1990	Nick Lowery, Kansas City, AFC	34	37	91.9
	Chip Lohmiller, Washington, NFC	30	40	75.0
1989	Rich Karlis, Minnesota, NFC	39	31	79.5
	*David Treadwell, Denver, AFC	33	27	81.8
1988	Scott Norwood, Buffalo, AFC	37	32	86.5
	*Mike Cofer, San Francisco, NFC	38	27	71.1
1987	Morten Andersen, New Orleans, NFC	36	28	77.8
	Dean Biasucci, Indianapolis, AFC	27	24	88.9
	Jim Breech, Cincinnati, AFC	30	24	80.0
1986	Tony Franklin, New England, AFC	41	32	78.0
	Kevin Butler, Chicago, NFC	41	28	68.3
1985	Gary Anderson, Pittsburgh, AFC	42	33	78.6
	Morten Andersen, New Orleans, NFC	35	31	88.6
	*Kevin Butler, Chicago, NFC	37	31	83.8
1984	*Paul McFadden, Philadelphia, NFC	37	30	81.1
	Gary Anderson, Pittsburgh, AFC	32	24	75.0
	Matt Bahr, Cleveland, AFC	32	24	75.0
1983	*Ali Haji-Sheikh, N.Y. Giants, NFC	42	35	83.3
	*Raul Allegre, Baltimore, AFC	35	30	85.7
1982	Mark Moseley, Washington, NFC	21	20	95.2
	Nick Lowery, Kansas City, AFC	24	19	79.2
1981	Rafael Septien, Dallas, NFC	35	27	77.1
	Nick Lowery, Kansas City, AFC	36	26	72.2
1980	*Ed Murray, Detroit, NFC	42	27	64.3
	John Smith, New England, AFC	34	26	76.5
	Fred Steinfort, Denver, AFC	34	26	76.5
1979	Mark Moseley, Washington, NFC	33	25	75.8
	John Smith, New England, AFC	33	23	69.7
1978	*Frank Corral, Los Angeles, NFC	43	29	67.4
	Pat Leahy, N.Y. Jets, AFC	30	22	73.3
1977	Mark Moseley, Washington, NFC	37	21	56.8
	Errol Mann, Oakland, AFC	28	20	71.4
1976	Mark Moseley, Washington, NFC	34	22	64.7
	Jan Stenerud, Kansas City, AFC	38	21	55.3
1975	Jan Stenerud, Kansas City, AFC	32	22	68.8
	Toni Fritsch, Dallas, NFC	35	22	62.9
1974	Chester Marcol, Green Bay, NFC	39	25	64.1
	Roy Gerela, Pittsburgh, AFC	29	20	69.0
1973	David Ray, Los Angeles, NFC	47	30	63.8
	Roy Gerela, Pittsburgh, AFC	43	29	67.4
1972	*Chester Marcol, Green Bay, NFC	48	33	68.8
	Roy Gerela, Pittsburgh, AFC	41	28	68.3
1971	Curt Knight, Washington, NFC	49	29	59.2
	Garo Yepremian, Miami, AFC	40	28	70.0
1970	Jan Stenerud, Kansas City, AFC	42	30	71.4
	Fred Cox, Minnesota, NFC	46	30	65.2
1969	Jim Turner, N.Y. Jets, AFL	47	32	68.1
	Fred Cox, Minnesota, NFL	37	26	70.3
1968	Jim Turner, N.Y. Jets, AFL	46	34	73.9
	Mac Percival, Chicago, NFL	36	25	69.4
1967	Jim Bakken, St. Louis, NFL	39	27	69.2
	Jan Stenerud, Kansas City, AFL	36	21	58.3
1966	Bruce Gossett, Los Angeles, NFL	49	28	57.1
	Mike Mercer, Oakland-Kansas City, AFL	30	21	70.0
1965	Pete Gogolak, Buffalo, AFL	46	28	60.9
	Fred Cox, Minnesota, NFL	35	23	65.7
1964	Jim Bakken, St. Louis, NFL	38	25	65.8
	Gino Cappelletti, Boston, AFL	39	25	64.1
1963	Jim Martin, Baltimore, NFL	39	24	61.5
	Gino Cappelletti, Boston, AFL	38	22	57.9
1962	Gene Mingo, Denver, AFL	39	27	69.2
	Lou Michaels, Pittsburgh, NFL	42	26	61.9
1961	Steve Myhra, Baltimore, NFL	39	21	53.8
	Gino Cappelletti, Boston, AFL	32	17	53.1
1960	Tommy Davis, San Francisco, NFL	32	19	59.4
	*Gene Mingo, Denver, AFL	28	18	64.3
1959	Pat Summerall, New York Giants	29	20	69.0
1958	Paige Cothren, Los Angeles	25	14	56.0
	*Tom Miner, Pittsburgh	28	14	50.0
1957	Lou Groza, Cleveland	22	15	68.2
1956	Sam Baker, Washington	25	17	68.0
1955	Fred Cone, Green Bay	24	16	66.7
1954	Lou Groza, Cleveland	24	16	66.7
1953	Lou Groza, Cleveland	26	23	88.5
1952	Lou Groza, Cleveland	33	19	57.6
1951	Bob Waterfield, Los Angeles	23	13	56.5
1950	*Lou Groza, Cleveland	19	13	68.4
1949	Cliff Patton, Philadelphia	18	9	50.0
	Bob Waterfield, Los Angeles	16	9	56.3
1948	Cliff Patton, Philadelphia	12	8	66.7
1947	Ward Cuff, Green Bay	16	7	43.8
	Pat Harder, Chi. Cardinals	10	7	70.0
	Bob Waterfield, Los Angeles	16	7	43.8
1946	Ted Fritsch, Green Bay	17	9	52.9

1945	Joe Aguirre, Washington	13	7	53.8
1944	Ken Strong, N.Y. Giants	12	6	50.0
1943	Ward Cuff, N.Y. Giants	9	3	33.3
	Don Hutson, Green Bay	5	3	60.0
1942	Bill Daddio, Chi. Cardinals	10	5	50.0
1941	Clarke Hinkle, Green Bay	14	6	42.9
1940	Clarke Hinkle, Green Bay	14	9	64.3
1939	Ward Cuff, N.Y. Giants	16	7	43.8
1938	Ward Cuff, N.Y. Giants	9	5	55.6
	Ralph Kercheval, Brooklyn	13	5	38.5
1937	Jack Manders, Chi. Bears		8	
1936	Jack Manders, Chi. Bears		7	
	Armand Niccolai, Pittsburgh		7	
1935	Armand Niccolai, Pittsburgh		6	
	Bill Smith, Chi. Cardinals		6	
1934	Jack Manders, Chi. Bears		10	
1933	*Jack Manders, Chi. Bears		6	
	Glenn Presnell, Portsmouth		6	
1932	Earl (Dutch) Clark, Portsmouth		3	

*First year in the league.

Annual Rushing Leaders

Year	Player, Team	Att.	Yards	Avg.	TD
1991	Emmitt Smith, Dallas, NFC	365	1,563	4.3	12
	Thurman Thomas, Buffalo, AFC	288	1,407	4.9	7
1990	Barry Sanders, Detroit, NFC	255	1,304	5.1	13
	Thurman Thomas, Buffalo, AFC	271	1,297	4.8	11
1989	Christian Okoye, Kansas City, AFC	370	1,480	4.0	12
	*Barry Sanders, Detroit, NFC	280	1,470	5.3	14
1988	Eric Dickerson, Indianapolis, AFC	388	1,659	4.3	14
	Herschel Walker, Dallas, NFC	361	1,514	4.2	5
1987	Charles White, L.A. Rams, NFC	324	1,374	4.2	11
	Eric Dickerson, Indianapolis, AFC	223	1,011	4.5	5
1986	Eric Dickerson, L.A. Rams, NFC	404	1,821	4.5	11
	Curt Warner, Seattle, AFC	319	1,481	4.6	13
1985	Marcus Allen, L.A. Raiders, AFC	380	1,759	4.6	11
	Gerald Riggs, Atlanta, NFC	397	1,719	4.3	10
1984	Eric Dickerson, L.A. Rams, NFC	379	2,105	5.6	14
	Earnest Jackson, San Diego, AFC	296	1,179	4.0	8
1983	*Eric Dickerson, L.A. Rams, NFC	390	1,808	4.6	18
	*Curt Warner, Seattle, AFC	335	1,449	4.3	13
1982	Freeman McNeil, N.Y. Jets, AFC	151	786	5.2	6
	Tony Dorsett, Dallas, NFC	177	745	4.2	5
1981	*George Rogers, New Orleans, NFC	378	1,674	4.4	13
	Earl Campbell, Houston, AFC	361	1,376	3.8	10
1980	Earl Campbell, Houston, AFC	373	1,934	5.2	13
	Walter Payton, Chicago, NFC	317	1,460	4.6	6
1979	Earl Campbell, Houston, AFC	368	1,697	4.6	19
	Walter Payton, Chicago, NFC	369	1,610	4.4	14
1978	*Earl Campbell, Houston, AFC	302	1,450	4.8	13
	Walter Payton, Chicago, NFC	333	1,395	4.2	11
1977	Walter Payton, Chicago, NFC	339	1,852	5.5	14
	Mark van Eeghen, Oakland, AFC	324	1,273	3.9	7
1976	O.J. Simpson, Buffalo, AFC	290	1,503	5.2	8
	Walter Payton, Chicago, NFC	311	1,390	4.5	13
1975	O.J. Simpson, Buffalo, AFC	329	1,817	5.5	16
	Jim Otis, St. Louis, NFC	269	1,076	4.0	5
1974	Otis Armstrong, Denver, AFC	263	1,407	5.3	9
	Lawrence McCutcheon, Los Angeles, NFC	236	1,109	4.7	3
1973	O.J. Simpson, Buffalo, AFC	332	2,003	6.0	12
	John Brockington, Green Bay, NFC	265	1,144	4.3	3
1972	O.J. Simpson, Buffalo, AFC	292	1,251	4.3	6
	Larry Brown, Washington, NFC	285	1,216	4.3	8
1971	Floyd Little, Denver, AFC	284	1,133	4.0	6
	*John Brockington, Green Bay, NFC	216	1,105	5.1	4
1970	Larry Brown, Washington, NFC	237	1,125	4.7	5
	Floyd Little, Denver, AFC	209	901	4.3	3
1969	Gale Sayers, Chicago, NFL	236	1,032	4.4	8
	Dickie Post, San Diego, AFL	182	873	4.8	6
1968	Leroy Kelly, Cleveland, NFL	248	1,239	5.0	16
	*Paul Robinson, Cincinnati, AFL	238	1,023	4.3	8
1967	Jim Nance, Boston, AFL	269	1,216	4.5	7
	Leroy Kelly, Cleveland, NFL	235	1,205	5.1	11
1966	Jim Nance, Boston, AFL	299	1,458	4.9	11
	Gale Sayers, Chicago, NFL	229	1,231	5.4	8
1965	Jim Brown, Cleveland, NFL	289	1,544	5.3	17
	Paul Lowe, San Diego, AFL	222	1,121	5.0	7
1964	Jim Brown, Cleveland, NFL	280	1,446	5.2	7
	Cookie Gilchrist, Buffalo, AFL	230	981	4.3	6
1963	Jim Brown, Cleveland, NFL	291	1,863	6.4	12
	Clem Daniels, Oakland, AFL	215	1,099	5.1	3
1962	Jim Taylor, Green Bay, NFL	272	1,474	5.4	19
	*Cookie Gilchrist, Buffalo, AFL	214	1,096	5.1	13
1961	Jim Brown, Cleveland, NFL	305	1,408	4.6	8
	Billy Cannon, Houston, AFL	200	948	4.7	6
1960	Jim Brown, Cleveland, NFL	215	1,257	5.8	9
	*Abner Haynes, Dall. Texans, AFL	156	875	5.6	9
1959	Jim Brown, Cleveland	290	1,329	4.6	14
1958	Jim Brown, Cleveland	257	1,527	5.9	17
1957	*Jim Brown, Cleveland	202	942	4.7	9
1956	Rick Casares, Chi. Bears	234	1,126	4.8	12
1955	*Alan Ameche, Baltimore	213	961	4.5	9
1954	Joe Perry, San Francisco	173	1,049	6.1	8
1953	Joe Perry, San Francisco	192	1,018	5.3	10
1952	Dan Towler, Los Angeles	156	894	5.7	10
1951	Eddie Price, N.Y. Giants	271	971	3.6	7
1950	*Marion Motley, Cleveland	140	810	5.8	3
1949	Steve Van Buren, Philadelphia	263	1,146	4.4	11
1948	Steve Van Buren, Philadelphia	201	945	4.7	10
1947	Steve Van Buren, Philadelphia	217	1,008	4.6	13
1946	Bill Dudley, Pittsburgh	146	604	4.1	3
1945	Steve Van Buren, Philadelphia	143	832	5.8	15
1944	Bill Paschal, N.Y. Giants	196	737	3.8	9

1943	*Bill Paschal, N.Y. Giants	147	572	3.9	10
1942	*Bill Dudley, Pittsburgh	162	696	4.3	5
1941	Clarence (Pug) Manders, Brooklyn	111	486	4.4	5
1940	Byron (Whizzer) White, Detroit	146	514	3.5	5
1939	*Bill Osmanski, Chicago	121	699	5.8	7
1938	*Byron (Whizzer) White, Pittsburgh	152	567	3.7	4
1937	Cliff Battles, Washington	216	874	4.0	5
1936	*Alphonse (Tuffy) Leemans, N.Y. Giants	206	830	4.0	2
1935	Doug Russell, Chi. Cardinals	140	499	3.6	0
1934	*Beattie Feathers, Chi. Bears	119	1,004	8.4	8
1933	Jim Musick, Boston	173	809	4.7	5
1932	*Cliff Battles, Boston	148	576	3.9	3

First year in the league.

Annual Passing Leaders

Year	Player, Team	Att.	Comp.	Yards	TD	Int.
1991	Steve Young, San Francisco, NFC	279	180	2,517	17	8
	Jim Kelly, Buffalo, AFC	474	304	3,844	33	17
1990	Jim Kelly, Buffalo, AFC	346	219	2,829	24	9
	Phil Simms, N.Y. Giants, NFC	311	184	2,284	15	4
1989	Joe Montana, San Francisco, NFC	386	271	3,521	26	8
	Boomer Esiason, Cincinnati, AFC	455	258	3,525	28	11
1988	Boomer Esiason, Cincinnati, AFC	388	223	3,572	28	14
	Wade Wilson, Minnesota, NFC	332	204	2,746	15	9
1987	Joe Montana, San Francisco, NFC	398	266	3,054	31	13
	Bernie Kosar, Cleveland, AFC	389	241	3,033	22	9
1986	Tommy Kramer, Minnesota, NFC	372	208	3,000	24	10
	Dan Marino, Miami, AFC	623	378	4,746	44	23
1985	Ken O'Brien, N.Y. Jets, AFC	488	297	3,888	25	8
	Joe Montana, San Francisco, NFC	494	303	3,653	27	13
1984	Dan Marino, Miami, AFC	564	362	5,084	48	17
	Joe Montana, San Francisco, NFC	432	279	3,630	28	10
1983	Steve Bartkowski, Atlanta, NFC	432	274	3,167	22	5
	*Dan Marino, Miami, AFC	296	173	2,210	20	6
1982	Ken Anderson, Cincinnati, AFC	309	218	2,495	12	9
	Joe Theismann, Washington, NFC	252	161	2,033	13	9
1981	Ken Anderson, Cincinnati, AFC	479	300	3,754	29	10
	Joe Montana, San Francisco, NFC	488	311	3,565	19	12
1980	Brian Sipe, Cleveland, AFC	554	337	4,132	30	14
	Ron Jaworski, Philadelphia, NFC	451	257	3,529	27	12
1979	Roger Staubach, Dallas, NFC	461	267	3,586	27	11
	Dan Fouts, San Diego, AFC	530	332	4,082	24	24
1978	Roger Staubach, Dallas, NFC	413	231	3,190	25	16
	Terry Bradshaw, Pittsburgh, AFC	368	207	2,915	28	20
1977	Bob Griese, Miami, AFC	307	180	2,252	22	13
	Roger Staubach, Dallas, NFC	361	210	2,620	18	9
1976	Ken Stabler, Oakland, AFC	291	194	2,737	27	17
	James Harris, Los Angeles, NFC	158	91	1,460	8	6
1975	Ken Anderson, Cincinnati, AFC	377	228	3,169	21	11
	Fran Tarkenton, Minnesota, NFC	425	273	2,994	25	13
1974	Ken Anderson, Cincinnati, AFC	328	213	2,667	18	10
	Sonny Jurgensen, Washington, NFC	167	107	1,185	11	5
1973	Roger Staubach, Dallas, NFC	286	179	2,428	23	15
	Ken Stabler, Oakland, AFC	260	163	1,997	14	10
1972	Norm Snead, N.Y. Giants, NFC	325	196	2,307	17	12
	Earl Morrall, Miami, AFC	150	83	1,360	11	7
1971	Roger Staubach, Dallas, NFC	211	126	1,882	15	4
	Bob Griese, Miami, AFC	263	145	2,089	19	9
1970	John Brodie, San Francisco, NFC	378	223	2,941	24	10
	Daryle Lamonica, Oakland, AFC	356	179	2,516	22	15
1969	Sonny Jurgensen, Washington, NFL	442	274	3,102	22	15
	*Greg Cook, Cincinnati, AFL	197	106	1,854	15	11
1968	Len Dawson, Kansas City, AFL	224	131	2,109	17	9
	Earl Morrall, Baltimore, NFL	317	182	2,909	26	17
1967	Sonny Jurgensen, Washington, NFL	508	288	3,747	31	16
	Daryle Lamonica, Oakland, AFL	425	220	3,228	30	20
1966	Bart Starr, Green Bay, NFL	251	156	2,257	14	3
	Len Dawson, Kansas City, AFL	284	159	2,527	26	10
1965	Rudy Bukich, Chicago, NFL	312	176	2,641	20	9
	John Hadl, San Diego, AFL	348	174	2,798	20	21
1964	Len Dawson, Kansas City, AFL	354	199	2,879	30	18
	Bart Starr, Green Bay, NFL	272	163	2,144	15	4
1963	Y.A. Tittle, N.Y. Giants, NFL	367	221	3,145	36	14
	Tobin Rote, San Diego, AFL	286	170	2,510	20	17
1962	Len Dawson, Dall. Texans, AFL	310	189	2,759	29	17
	Bart Starr, Green Bay, NFL	285	178	2,438	12	9
1961	George Blanda, Houston, AFL	362	187	3,330	36	22
	Milt Plum, Cleveland, NFL	302	177	2,416	18	10
1960	Milt Plum, Cleveland, NFL	250	151	2,297	21	5
	Jack Kemp, L.A. Chargers, AFL	406	211	3,018	20	25
1959	Charlie Conerly, N.Y. Giants	194	113	1,706	14	4
1958	Eddie LeBaron, Washington	145	79	1,365	11	10
1957	Tommy O'Connell, Cleveland	110	63	1,229	9	8
1956	Ed Brown, Chi. Bears	168	96	1,667	11	12
1955	Otto Graham, Cleveland	185	98	1,721	15	8
1954	Norm Van Brocklin, Los Angeles	260	139	2,637	13	21
1953	Otto Graham, Cleveland	258	167	2,722	11	9
1952	Norm Van Brocklin, Los Angeles	205	113	1,736	14	17
1951	Bob Waterfield, Los Angeles	176	88	1,566	13	10
1950	Norm Van Brocklin, Los Angeles	233	127	2,061	18	14
1949	Sammy Baugh, Washington	255	145	1,903	18	14
1948	Tommy Thompson, Philadelphia	246	141	1,965	25	11
1947	Sammy Baugh, Washington	354	210	2,938	25	15
1946	Bob Waterfield, Los Angeles	251	127	1,747	18	17
1945	Sammy Baugh, Washington	182	128	1,669	11	4
	Sid Luckman, Chi. Bears	217	117	1,725	14	10
1944	Frank Filchock, Washington	147	84	1,139	13	9
1943	Sammy Baugh, Washington	239	133	1,754	23	19
1942	Cecil Isbell, Green Bay	268	146	2,021	24	14
1941	Cecil Isbell, Green Bay	206	117	1,479	15	11
1940	Sammy Baugh, Washington	177	111	1,367	12	10
1939	*Parker Hall, Cleveland	208	106	1,227	9	13
1938	Ed Danowski, N.Y. Giants	129	70	848	7	8
1937	*Sammy Baugh, Washington	171	81	1,127	8	14
1936	Arnie Herber, Green Bay	173	77	1,239	11	13
1935	Ed Danowski, N.Y. Giants	113	57	794	10	9
1934	Arnie Herber, Green Bay	115	42	799	8	12
1933	*Harry Newman, N.Y. Giants	136	53	973	11	17
1932	Arnie Herber, Green Bay	101	37	639	9	9

First year in the league.

Annual Touchdown Leaders

Year	Player, Team	TD	Rush	Pass	Ret.
1991	Barry Sanders, Detroit, NFC	17	16	1	0
	Mark Clayton, Miami, AFC	12	0	12	0
	Thurman Thomas, Buffalo, AFC	12	7	5	0
1990	Barry Sanders, Detroit, NFC	16	13	3	0
	Derrick Fenner, Seattle, AFC	15	14	1	0
1989	Dalton Hilliard, New Orleans, NFC	18	13	5	0
	Christian Okoye, Kansas City, AFC	12	12	0	0
	Thurman Thomas, Buffalo, AFC	12	6	6	0
1988	Greg Bell, L.A. Rams, NFC	18	16	2	0
	Eric Dickerson, Indianapolis, AFC	15	14	1	0
	*Ickey Woods, Cincinnati, AFC	15	15	0	0
1987	Jerry Rice, San Francisco, NFC	23	1	22	0
	Johnny Hector, N.Y. Jets, AFC	11	11	0	0
1986	George Rogers, Washington, NFC	18	18	0	0
	Sammy Winder, Denver, AFC	14	9	5	0
1985	Joe Morris, N.Y. Giants, NFC	21	21	0	0
	Louis Lipps, Pittsburgh, AFC	15	1	12	2
1984	Marcus Allen, L.A. Raiders, AFC	18	13	5	0
	Mark Clayton, Miami, AFC	18	0	18	0
	Eric Dickerson, L.A. Rams, NFC	14	14	0	0
	John Riggins, Washington, NFC	14	14	0	0
1983	John Riggins, Washington, NFC	24	24	0	0
	Pete Johnson, Cincinnati, AFC	14	14	0	0
	*Curt Warner, Seattle, AFC	14	13	1	0
1982	*Marcus Allen, L.A. Raiders, AFC	14	11	3	0
	Wendell Tyler, L.A. Rams, NFC	13	9	4	0
1981	Chuck Muncie, San Diego, AFC	19	19	0	0
	Wendell Tyler, Los Angeles, NFC	17	12	5	0
1980	*Billy Sims, Detroit, NFC	16	13	3	0
	Earl Campbell, Houston, AFC	13	13	0	0
	*Curtis Dickey, Baltimore, AFC	13	11	2	0
	John Jefferson, San Diego, AFC	13	0	13	0
1979	Earl Campbell, Houston, AFC	19	19	0	0
	Walter Payton, Chicago, NFC	16	14	2	0
1978	David Sims, Seattle, AFC	15	14	1	0
	Terdell Middleton, Green Bay, NFC	12	11	1	0
1977	Walter Payton, Chicago, NFC	16	14	2	0
	Nat Moore, Miami, AFC	13	1	12	0
1976	Chuck Foreman, Minnesota, NFC	14	13	1	0
	Franco Harris, Pittsburgh, AFC	14	14	0	0
1975	O.J. Simpson, Buffalo, AFC	23	16	7	0
	Chuck Foreman, Minnesota, NFC	22	13	9	0
1974	Chuck Foreman, Minnesota, NFC	15	9	6	0
	Cliff Branch, Oakland, AFC	13	0	13	0
1973	Larry Brown, Washington, NFC	14	8	6	0
	Floyd Little, Denver, AFC	13	12	1	0
1972	Emerson Boozer, N.Y. Jets, AFC	14	11	3	0
	Ron Johnson, N.Y. Giants, NFC	14	9	5	0
1971	Duane Thomas, Dallas, NFC	13	11	2	0
	Leroy Kelly, Cleveland, AFC	12	10	2	0
1970	Dick Gordon, Chicago, NFC	13	0	13	0
	MacArthur Lane, St. Louis, NFC	13	11	2	0
	Gary Garrison, San Diego, AFC	12	0	12	0
1969	Warren Wells, Oakland, AFL	14	0	14	0
	Tom Matte, Baltimore, NFL	13	11	2	0
	Lance Rentzel, Dallas, NFL	13	0	12	1
1968	Leroy Kelly, Cleveland, NFL	20	16	4	0
	Warren Wells, Oakland, AFL	12	1	11	0
1967	Homer Jones, N.Y. Giants, NFL	14	1	13	0
	Emerson Boozer, N.Y. Jets, AFL	13	10	3	0
1966	Leroy Kelly, Cleveland, NFL	16	15	1	0
	Dan Reeves, Dallas, NFL	16	8	8	0
	Lance Alworth, San Diego, AFL	13	0	13	0
1965	*Gale Sayers, Chicago, NFL	22	14	6	2
	Lance Alworth, San Diego, AFL	14	0	14	0
	Don Maynard, N.Y. Jets, AFL	14	0	14	0
1964	Lenny Moore, Baltimore, NFL	20	16	3	1
	Lance Alworth, San Diego, AFL	15	2	13	0
1963	Art Powell, Oakland, AFL	16	0	16	0
	Jim Brown, Cleveland, NFL	15	12	3	0
1962	Abner Haynes, Dallas, AFL	19	13	6	0
	Jim Taylor, Green Bay, NFL	19	19	0	0
1961	Bill Groman, Houston, AFL	18	1	17	0
	Jim Taylor, Green Bay, NFL	16	15	1	0
1960	Paul Hornung, Green Bay, NFL	15	13	2	0
	Sonny Randle, St. Louis, NFL	15	0	15	0
	Art Powell, N.Y. Titans, AFL	14	0	14	0
1959	Raymond Berry, Baltimore	14	0	14	0
	Jim Brown, Cleveland	14	14	0	0
1958	Jim Brown, Cleveland	18	17	1	0
1957	Lenny Moore, Baltimore	11	3	7	1
1956	Rick Casares, Chi. Bears	14	12	2	0
1955	*Alan Ameche, Baltimore	9	9	0	0
	Harlon Hill, Chi. Bears	9	0	9	0
1954	*Harlon Hill, Chi. Bears	12	0	12	0
1953	Joseph Perry, San Francisco	13	10	3	0
1952	Cloyce Box, Detroit	15	0	15	0
1951	Elroy (Crazylegs) Hirsch, Los Angeles	17	0	17	0
1950	Bob Shaw, Chi. Cardinals	12	0	12	0
1949	Gene Roberts, N.Y. Giants	17	9	8	0
1948	Mal Kutner, Chi. Cardinals	15	1	14	0
1947	Steve Van Buren, Philadelphia	14	13	0	1
1946	Ted Fritsch, Green Bay	10	9	1	0

1945	Steve Van Buren, Philadelphia	18	15	2	1
1944	Don Hutson, Green Bay	9	0	9	0
	Bill Paschal, N.Y. Giants	9	9	0	0
1943	Don Hutson, Green Bay	12	0	11	1
	*Bill Paschal, N.Y. Giants	12	10	2	0
1942	Don Hutson, Green Bay	17	0	17	0
1941	Don Hutson, Green Bay	12	2	10	0
	George McAfee, Chi. Bears	12	6	3	3
1940	John Drake, Cleveland	9	9	0	0
	Richard Todd, Washington	9	4	4	1
1939	Andrew Farkas, Washington	11	5	5	1
1938	Don Hutson, Green Bay	9	0	9	0
1937	Cliff Battles, Washington	7	5	1	1
	Clarke Hinkle, Green Bay	7	5	2	0
	Don Hutson, Green Bay	7	0	7	0
1936	Don Hutson, Green Bay	9	0	8	1
1935	*Don Hutson, Green Bay	7	0	6	1
1934	*Beattie Feathers, Chi. Bears	9	8	1	0
1933	*Charlie (Buckets) Goldenberg, Green Bay	7	4	1	2
	John (Shipwreck) Kelly, Brooklyn	7	2	3	2
	*Elvin (Kink) Richards, N.Y. Giants	7	4	3	0
1932	Earl (Dutch) Clark, Portsmouth	6	3	3	0
	Red Grange, Chi. Bears	6	3	3	0

*First year in the league.

1953	Pete Pihos, Philadelphia	63	1,049	16.7	10
1952	Mac Speedie, Cleveland	62	911	14.7	5
1951	Elroy (Crazylegs) Hirsch, Los Angeles	66	1,495	22.7	17
1950	Tom Fears, Los Angeles	84	1,116	13.3	7
1949	Tom Fears, Los Angeles	77	1,013	13.2	9
1948	*Tom Fears, Los Angeles	51	698	13.7	4
1947	Jim Keane, Chi. Bears	64	910	14.2	10
1946	Jim Benton, Los Angeles	63	981	15.6	6
1945	Don Hutson, Green Bay	47	834	17.7	9
1944	Don Hutson, Green Bay	58	866	14.9	9
1943	Don Hutson, Green Bay	47	776	16.5	11
1942	Don Hutson, Green Bay	74	1,211	16.4	17
1941	Don Hutson, Green Bay	58	738	12.7	10
1940	*Don Looney, Philadelphia	58	707	12.2	4
1939	Don Hutson, Green Bay	34	846	24.9	6
1938	Gaynell Tinsley, Chi. Cardinals	41	516	12.6	1
1937	Don Hutson, Green Bay	41	552	13.5	7
1936	Don Hutson, Green Bay	34	536	15.8	8
1935	*Tod Goodwin, N.Y. Giants	26	432	16.6	4
1934	Joe Carter, Philadelphia	16	238	14.9	4
	Morris (Red) Badgro, N.Y. Giants	16	206	12.9	1
1933	John (Shipwreck) Kelly, Brooklyn	22	246	11.2	3
1932	Ray Flaherty, N.Y. Giants	21	350	16.7	3

*First year in the league.

Annual Pass Receiving Leaders

Year	Player, Team	No.	Yards	Avg.	TD
1991	Haywood Jeffires, Houston, AFC	100	1,181	11.8	7
	Michael Irvin, Dallas, NFC	93	1,523	16.4	8
1990	Jerry Rice, San Francisco, NFC	100	1,502	15.0	13
	Haywood Jeffires, Houston, AFC	74	1,048	14.2	8
	Drew Hill, Houston, AFC	74	1,019	13.8	5
1989	Sterling Sharpe, Green Bay, NFC	90	1,423	15.8	12
	Andre Reed, Buffalo, AFC	88	1,312	14.9	9
1988	Al Toon, N.Y. Jets, AFC	93	1,067	11.5	5
	Henry Ellard, L.A. Rams, NFC	86	1,414	16.4	10
1987	J.T. Smith, St. Louis, NFC	91	1,117	12.3	8
	Al Toon, N.Y. Jets, AFC	68	976	14.4	5
1986	Todd Christensen, L.A. Raiders, AFC	95	1,153	12.1	8
	Jerry Rice, San Francisco, NFC	86	1,570	18.3	15
1985	Roger Craig, San Francisco, NFC	92	1,016	11.0	6
	Lionel James, San Diego, AFC	86	1,027	11.9	6
1984	Art Monk, Washington, NFC	106	1,372	12.9	7
	Ozzie Newsome, Cleveland, AFC	89	1,001	11.2	5
1983	Todd Christensen, L.A. Raiders, AFC	92	1,247	13.6	12
	Roy Green, St. Louis, NFC	78	1,227	15.7	14
	Charlie Brown, Washington, NFC	78	1,225	15.7	8
	Earnest Gray, N.Y. Giants, NFC	78	1,139	14.6	5
1982	Dwight Clark, San Francisco, NFC	60	913	15.2	5
	Kellen Winslow, San Diego, AFC	54	721	13.4	6
1981	Kellen Winslow, San Diego, AFC	88	1,075	12.2	10
	Dwight Clark, San Francisco, NFC	85	1,105	13.0	4
1980	Kellen Winslow, San Diego, AFC	89	1,290	14.5	9
	*Earl Cooper, San Francisco, NFC	83	567	6.8	4
1979	Joe Washington, Baltimore, AFC	82	750	9.1	3
	Ahmad Rashad, Minnesota, NFC	80	1,156	14.5	9
1978	Rickey Young, Minnesota, NFC	88	704	8.0	5
	Steve Largent, Seattle, AFC	71	1,168	16.5	8
1977	Lydell Mitchell, Baltimore, AFC	71	620	8.7	4
	Ahmad Rashad, Minnesota, NFC	51	681	13.4	2
1976	MacArthur Lane, Kansas City, AFC	66	686	10.4	1
	Drew Pearson, Dallas, NFC	58	806	13.9	6
1975	Chuck Foreman, Minnesota, NFC	73	691	9.5	9
	Reggie Rucker, Cleveland, AFC	60	770	12.8	3
	Lydell Mitchell, Baltimore, AFC	60	544	9.1	4
1974	Lydell Mitchell, Baltimore, AFC	72	544	7.6	2
	Charles Young, Philadelphia, NFC	63	696	11.0	3
1973	Harold Carmichael, Philadelphia, NFC	67	1,116	16.7	9
	Fred Willis, Houston, AFC	57	371	6.5	1
1972	Harold Jackson, Philadelphia, NFC	62	1,048	16.9	4
	Fred Biletnikoff, Oakland, AFC	58	802	13.8	7
1971	Fred Biletnikoff, Oakland, AFC	61	929	15.2	9
	Bob Tucker, N.Y. Giants, NFC	59	791	13.4	4
1970	Dick Gordon, Chicago, NFC	71	1,026	14.5	13
	Marlin Briscoe, Buffalo, AFC	57	1,036	18.2	8
1969	Dan Abramowicz, New Orleans, NFL	73	1,015	13.9	7
	Lance Alworth, San Diego, AFL	64	1,003	15.7	4
1968	Clifton McNeil, San Francisco, NFL	71	994	14.0	7
	Lance Alworth, San Diego, AFL	68	1,312	19.3	10
1967	George Sauer, N.Y. Jets, AFL	75	1,189	15.9	6
	Charley Taylor, Washington, NFL	70	990	14.1	9
1966	Lance Alworth, San Diego, AFL	73	1,383	18.9	13
	Charley Taylor, Washington, NFL	72	1,119	15.5	12
1965	Lionel Taylor, Denver, AFL	85	1,131	13.3	6
	Dave Parks, San Francisco, NFL	80	1,344	16.8	12
1964	Charley Hennigan, Houston, AFL	101	1,546	15.3	8
	Johnny Morris, Chicago, NFL	93	1,200	12.9	10
1963	Lionel Taylor, Denver, AFL	78	1,101	14.1	10
	Bobby Joe Conrad, St. Louis, NFL	73	967	13.2	10
1962	Lionel Taylor, Denver, AFL	77	908	11.8	4
	Bobby Mitchell, Washington, NFL	72	1,384	19.2	11
1961	Lionel Taylor, Denver, AFL	100	1,176	11.8	4
	Jim (Red) Phillips, Los Angeles, NFL	78	1,092	14.0	5
1960	Lionel Taylor, Denver, AFL	92	1,235	13.4	12
	Raymond Berry, Baltimore, NFL	74	1,298	17.5	10
1959	Raymond Berry, Baltimore	66	959	14.5	14
1958	Raymond Berry, Baltimore	56	794	14.2	9
	Pete Retzlaff, Philadelphia	56	766	13.7	2
1957	Billy Wilson, San Francisco	52	757	14.6	6
1956	Billy Wilson, San Francisco	60	889	14.8	5
1955	Pete Pihos, Philadelphia	62	864	13.9	7
1954	Pete Pihos, Philadelphia	60	872	14.5	10
	Billy Wilson, San Francisco	60	830	13.8	5

Annual Pass Receiving Leaders (Yards)

Year	Player, Team	No.	Yards	Avg.	TD
1991	Michael Irvin, Dallas, NFC	93	1,523	16.4	8
	Haywood Jeffires, Houston, AFC	100	1,181	11.8	7
1990	Jerry Rice, San Francisco, NFC	100	1,502	15.0	13
	Haywood Jeffires, Houston, AFC	74	1,048	14.2	8
1989	Jerry Rice, San Francisco, NFC	82	1,483	18.1	17
	Andre Reed, Buffalo, AFC	88	1,312	14.9	9
1988	Henry Ellard, L.A. Rams, NFC	86	1,414	16.4	10
	Eddie Brown, Cincinnati, AFC	53	1,273	24.0	9
1987	J.T. Smith, St. Louis, NFC	91	1,117	12.3	8
	Carlos Carson, Kansas City, AFC	55	1,044	19.0	7
1986	Jerry Rice, San Francisco, NFC	86	1,570	18.3	15
	Stanley Morgan, New England, AFC	84	1,491	17.8	10
1985	Steve Largent, Seattle, AFC	79	1,287	16.3	6
	Mike Quick, Philadelphia, NFC	73	1,247	17.1	11
1984	Roy Green, St. Louis, NFC	78	1,555	19.9	12
	John Stallworth, Pittsburgh, AFC	80	1,395	17.4	11
1983	Mike Quick, Philadelphia, NFC	69	1,409	20.4	13
	Carlos Carson, Kansas City, AFC	80	1,351	16.9	7
1982	Wes Chandler, San Diego, AFC	49	1,032	21.1	9
	Dwight Clark, San Francisco, NFC	60	913	15.2	5
1981	Alfred Jenkins, Atlanta, NFC	70	1,358	19.4	13
	Frank Lewis, Buffalo, AFC	70	1,244	17.8	4
	Steve Watson, Denver, AFC	60	1,244	20.7	13
1980	John Jefferson, San Diego, AFC	82	1,340	16.3	13
	James Lofton, Green Bay, NFC	71	1,226	17.3	4
1979	Steve Largent, Seattle, AFC	66	1,237	18.7	9
	Ahmad Rashad, Minnesota, NFC	80	1,156	14.5	9
1978	Wesley Walker, N.Y. Jets, AFC	48	1,169	24.4	8
	Harold Carmichael, Philadelphia, NFC	55	1,072	19.5	8
1977	Drew Pearson, Dallas, NFC	48	870	18.1	2
	Ken Burrough, Houston, AFC	43	816	19.0	8
1976	Roger Carr, Baltimore, AFC	43	1,112	25.9	11
	*Sammy White, Minnesota, NFC	51	906	17.8	10
1975	Ken Burrough, Houston, AFC	53	1,063	20.1	8
	Mel Gray, St. Louis, NFC	48	926	19.3	11
1974	Cliff Branch, Oakland, AFC	60	1,092	18.2	13
	Drew Pearson, Dallas, NFC	62	1,087	17.5	2
1973	Harold Carmichael, Philadelphia, NFC	67	1,116	16.7	9
	*Isaac Curtis, Cincinnati, AFC	45	843	18.7	9
1972	Harold Jackson, Philadelphia, NFC	62	1,048	16.9	4
	Rich Caster, N.Y. Jets, AFC	39	833	21.4	10
1971	Otis Taylor, Kansas City, AFC	57	1,110	19.5	7
	Gene Washington, San Francisco, NFC	46	884	19.2	4
1970	Gene Washington, San Francisco, NFC	53	1,100	20.8	12
	Marlin Briscoe, Buffalo, AFC	57	1,036	18.2	8
1969	Warren Wells, Oakland, AFL	47	1,260	26.8	14
	Harold Jackson, Philadelphia, NFL	65	1,116	17.2	9
1968	Lance Alworth, San Diego, AFL	68	1,312	19.3	10
	Roy Jefferson, Pittsburgh, NFL	58	1,074	18.5	11
1967	Don Maynard, N.Y. Jets, AFL	71	1,434	20.3	10
	Ben Hawkins, Philadelphia, NFL	59	1,265	21.4	10
1966	Lance Alworth, San Diego, AFL	73	1,383	18.9	13
	Pat Studstill, Detroit, NFL	67	1,266	18.9	5
1965	Lance Alworth, San Diego, AFL	69	1,602	23.2	14
	Dave Parks, San Francisco, NFL	80	1,344	16.8	12
1964	Charley Hennigan, Houston, AFL	101	1,546	15.3	8
	Johnny Morris, Chicago, NFL	93	1,200	12.9	10
1963	Bobby Mitchell, Washington, NFL	69	1,436	20.8	7
	Art Powell, Oakland, AFL	73	1,304	17.8	16
1962	Bobby Mitchell, Washington, NFL	72	1,384	19.2	11
	Art Powell, N.Y. Titans, AFL	64	1,130	17.6	8
1961	Charley Hennigan, Houston, AFL	82	1,746	21.3	12
	Tommy McDonald, Philadelphia, NFL	64	1,144	17.9	13
1960	*Bill Groman, Houston, AFL	72	1,473	20.5	12
	Raymond Berry, Baltimore, NFL	74	1,298	17.5	10
1959	Raymond Berry, Baltimore	66	959	14.5	14
1958	Del Shofner, Los Angeles	51	1,097	21.5	8
1957	Raymond Berry, Baltimore	47	800	17.0	6
1956	Billy Howton, Green Bay	55	1,188	21.6	12
1955	Pete Pihos, Philadelphia	62	864	13.9	7
1954	Bob Boyd, Los Angeles	53	1,212	22.9	6
1953	Pete Pihos, Philadelphia	63	1,049	16.7	10
1952	*Billy Howton, Green Bay	53	1,231	23.2	13
1951	Elroy (Crazylegs) Hirsch, Los Angeles	66	1,495	22.7	17
1950	Tom Fears, Los Angeles	84	1,116	13.3	7
1949	Bob Mann, Detroit	66	1,014	15.4	4

1948	Mal Kutner, Chi. Cardinals	41	943	23.0	14
1947	Mal Kutner, Chi. Cardinals	43	944	21.9	7
1946	Jim Benton, Los Angeles	63	981	15.5	6
1945	Jim Benton, Cleveland	45	1,067	23.7	8
1944	Don Hutson, Green Bay	58	866	14.6	9
1943	Don Hutson, Green Bay	47	776	16.5	11
1942	Don Hutson, Green Bay	74	1,211	16.4	17
1941	Don Hutson, Green Bay	58	738	12.7	10
1940	*Don Looney, Philadelphia	58	707	12.2	4
1939	Don Hutson, Green Bay	34	846	24.9	6
1938	Don Hutson, Green Bay	32	548	17.1	9
1937	*Gaynell Tinsley, Chi. Cardinals	36	675	18.8	5
1936	Don Hutson, Green Bay	34	526	15.5	8
1935	Charley Malone, Boston	22	433	19.7	2
1934	Harry Ebding, Detroit	9	257	28.6	2
1933	*Paul Moss, Pittsburgh	18	383	21.3	2
1932	Johnny Blood, Green Bay	19	326	17.2	3

First year in the league.

Annual Interception Leaders

Year	Player, Team	No.	Yards	TD
1991	Ronnie Lott, L.A. Raiders, AFC	8	52	0
	Ray Crockett, Detroit, NFC	6	141	1
	Deion Sanders, Atlanta, NFC	6	119	1
	*Aeneas Williams, Phoenix, NFC	6	60	0
	Tim McKyer, Atlanta, NFC	6	24	0
1990	*Mark Carrier, Chicago, NFC	10	39	0
	Richard Johnson, Houston, AFC	8	100	1
1989	Felix Wright, Cleveland, AFC	9	91	1
	Eric Allen, Philadelphia, NFC	8	38	0
1988	Scott Case, Atlanta, NFC	10	47	0
	Erik McMillan, N.Y. Jets, AFC	8	168	2
1987	Barry Wilburn, Washington, NFC	9	135	1
	Mike Prior, Indianapolis, AFC	6	57	0
	Mark Kelso, Buffalo, AFC	6	25	0
	Keith Bostic, Houston, AFC	6	-14	0
1986	Ronnie Lott, San Francisco, NFC	10	134	1
	Deron Cherry, Kansas City, AFC	9	150	0
1985	Everson Walls, Dallas, NFC	9	31	0
	Albert Lewis, Kansas City, AFC	8	59	0
	Eugene Daniel, Indianapolis, AFC	8	53	0
1984	Ken Easley, Seattle, AFC	10	126	2
	*Tom Flynn, Green Bay, NFC	9	106	0
1983	Mark Murphy, Washington, NFC	9	127	0
	Ken Riley, Cincinnati, AFC	8	89	2
	Vann McElroy, L.A. Raiders, AFC	8	68	0
1982	Everson Walls, Dallas, NFC	7	61	0
	Ken Riley, Cincinnati, AFC	5	88	1
	Bobby Jackson, N.Y. Jets, AFC	5	84	1
	Dwayne Woodruff, Pittsburgh, AFC	5	53	0
	Donnie Shell, Pittsburgh, AFC	5	27	0
1981	*Everson Walls, Dallas, NFC	11	133	0
	John Harris, Seattle, AFC	10	155	2
1980	Lester Hayes, Oakland, AFC	13	273	1
	Nolan Cromwell, Los Angeles, NFC	8	140	1
1979	Mike Reinfeldt, Houston, AFC	12	205	0
	Lemar Parrish, Washington, NFC	9	65	0
1978	Thom Darden, Cleveland, AFC	10	200	0
	Ken Stone, St. Louis, NFC	9	139	0
	Willie Buchanon, Green Bay, NFC	9	93	1
1977	Lyle Blackwood, Baltimore, AFC	10	163	0
	Rolland Lawrence, Atlanta, NFC	7	138	0
1976	Monte Jackson, Los Angeles, NFC	10	173	3
	Ken Riley, Cincinnati, AFC	9	141	1
1975	Mel Blount, Pittsburgh, AFC	11	121	0
	Paul Krause, Minnesota, NFC	10	201	0
1974	Emmitt Thomas, Kansas City, AFC	12	214	2
	Ray Brown, Atlanta, NFC	8	164	1
1973	Dick Anderson, Miami, AFC	8	163	2
	Mike Wagner, Pittsburgh, AFC	8	134	0
	Bobby Bryant, Minnesota, NFC	7	105	1
1972	Bill Bradley, Philadelphia, NFC	9	73	0
	Mike Sensibaugh, Kansas City, AFC	8	65	0
1971	Bill Bradley, Philadelphia, NFC	11	248	0
	Ken Houston, Houston, AFC	9	220	4
1970	Johnny Robinson, Kansas City, AFC	10	155	0
	Dick LeBeau, Detroit, NFC	9	96	0
1969	Mel Renfro, Dallas, NFL	10	118	0
	Emmitt Thomas, Kansas City, AFL	9	146	1
1968	Dave Grayson, Oakland, AFL	10	195	1
	Willie Williams, N.Y. Giants, NFL	10	103	0
1967	Miller Farr, Houston, AFL	10	264	3
	*Lem Barney, Detroit, NFL	10	232	3
	Tom Janik, Buffalo, AFL	10	222	2
	Dave Whitsell, New Orleans, NFL	10	178	2
	Dick Westmoreland, Miami, AFL	10	127	1
1966	Larry Wilson, St. Louis, NFL	10	180	2
	Johnny Robinson, Kansas City, AFL	10	136	1
	Bobby Hunt, Kansas City, AFL	10	113	0
1965	W.K. Hicks, Houston, AFL	9	156	0
	Bobby Boyd, Baltimore, NFL	9	78	1
1964	Dainard Paulson, N.Y. Jets, AFL	12	157	1
	*Paul Krause, Washington, NFL	12	140	1
1963	Fred Glick, Houston, AFL	12	180	1
	Dick Lynch, N.Y. Giants, NFL	9	251	3
	Roosevelt Taylor, Chicago, NFL	9	172	1
1962	Lee Riley, N.Y. Titans, AFL	11	122	0
	Willie Wood, Green Bay, NFL	9	132	0
1961	Billy Atkins, Buffalo, AFL	10	158	0
	Dick Lynch, N.Y. Giants, NFL	9	60	0
1960	*Austin (Goose) Gonsoulin, Denver, AFL	11	98	0
	Dave Baker, San Francisco, NFL	10	96	0
	Jerry Norton, St. Louis, NFL	10	96	0
1959	Dean Derby, Pittsburgh	7	127	0
	Milt Davis, Baltimore	7	119	1
	Don Shinnick, Baltimore	7	70	0
1958	Jim Patton, N.Y. Giants	11	183	0
1957	*Milt Davis, Baltimore	10	219	2
	Jack Christiansen, Detroit	10	137	1
	Jack Butler, Pittsburgh	10	85	0
1956	Lindon Crow, Chi. Cardinals	11	170	0
1955	Will Sherman, Los Angeles	11	101	0
1954	Dick (Night Train) Lane, Chi. Cardinals	10	181	0
1953	Jack Christiansen, Detroit	12	238	1
1952	*Dick (Night Train) Lane, Los Angeles	14	298	2
1951	Otto Schnellbacher, N.Y. Giants	11	194	2
1950	*Orban (Spec) Sanders, N.Y. Yanks	13	199	0
1949	Bob Nussbaumer, Chi. Cardinals	12	157	0
1948	*Dan Sandifer, Washington	13	258	2
1947	Frank Reagan, N.Y. Giants	10	203	0
	Frank Seno, Boston	10	100	0
1946	Bill Dudley, Pittsburgh	10	242	1
1945	Roy Zimmerman, Philadelphia	7	90	0
1944	*Howard Livingston, N.Y. Giants	9	172	1
1943	Sammy Baugh, Washington	11	112	0
1942	Clyde (Bulldog) Turner, Chi. Bears	8	96	1
1941	Marshall Goldberg, Chi. Cardinals	7	54	0
1940	Clarence (Ace) Parker, Brooklyn	6	146	1
	Kent Ryan, Detroit	6	65	0
	Don Hutson, Green Bay	6	24	0

First year in the league.

Annual Punting Leaders

Year	Player, Team	No.	Avg.	Long
1991	Reggie Roby, Miami, AFC	54	45.7	64
	Harry Newsome, Minnesota, NFC	68	45.5	65
1990	Mike Horan, Denver, AFC	58	44.4	67
	Sean Landeta, N.Y. Giants, NFC	75	44.1	67
1989	Rich Camarillo, Phoenix, NFC	76	43.4	58
	Greg Montgomery, Houston, AFC	56	43.3	63
1988	Harry Newsome, Pittsburgh, AFC	65	45.4	62
	Jim Arnold, Detroit, NFC	97	42.4	69
1987	Rick Donnelly, Atlanta, NFC	61	44.0	62
	Ralf Mojsiejenko, San Diego, AFC	67	42.9	57
1986	Rohn Stark, Indianapolis, AFC	76	45.2	63
	Sean Landeta, N.Y. Giants, NFC	79	44.8	61
1985	Rohn Stark, Indianapolis, AFC	78	45.9	68
	*Rick Donnelly, Atlanta, NFC	59	43.6	68
1984	Jim Arnold, Kansas City, AFC	98	44.9	63
	*Brian Hansen, New Orleans, NFC	69	43.8	66
1983	Rohn Stark, Baltimore, AFC	91	45.3	68
	*Frank Garcia, Tampa Bay, NFC	95	42.2	64
1982	Luke Prestridge, Denver, AFC	45	45.0	65
	Carl Birdsong, St. Louis, NFC	54	43.8	65
1981	Pat McInally, Cincinnati, AFC	72	45.4	62
	Tom Skladany, Detroit, NFC	64	43.5	74
1980	Dave Jennings, N.Y. Giants, NFC	94	44.8	63
	Luke Prestridge, Denver, AFC	70	43.9	57
1979	*Bob Grupp, Kansas City, AFC	89	43.6	74
	Dave Jennings, N.Y. Giants, NFC	104	42.7	72
1978	Pat McInally, Cincinnati, AFC	91	43.1	65
	*Tom Skladany, Detroit, NFC	86	42.5	63
1977	Ray Guy, Oakland, AFC	59	43.3	74
	Tom Blanchard, New Orleans, NFC	82	42.4	66
1976	Marv Bateman, Buffalo, AFC	86	42.8	78
	John James, Atlanta, NFC	101	42.1	67
1975	Ray Guy, Oakland, AFC	68	43.8	64
	Herman Weaver, Detroit, NFC	80	42.0	61
1974	Ray Guy, Oakland, AFC	74	42.2	66
	Tom Blanchard, New Orleans, NFC	88	42.1	71
1973	Jerrel Wilson, Kansas City, AFC	80	45.5	68
	*Tom Wittum, San Francisco, NFC	79	43.7	62
1972	Jerrel Wilson, Kansas City, AFC	66	44.8	69
	Dave Chapple, Los Angeles, NFC	53	44.2	70
1971	Dave Lewis, Cincinnati, AFC	72	44.8	56
	Tom McNeill, Philadelphia, NFC	73	42.0	64
1970	*Dave Lewis, Cincinnati, AFC	79	46.2	63
	*Julian Fagan, New Orleans, NFC	77	42.5	64
1969	David Lee, Baltimore, NFL	57	45.3	66
	Dennis Partee, San Diego, AFL	71	44.6	62
1968	Jerrel Wilson, Kansas City, AFL	63	45.1	70
	Billy Lothridge, Atlanta, NFL	75	44.3	70
1967	Bob Scarpitto, Denver, AFL	105	44.9	73
	Billy Lothridge, Atlanta, NFL	87	43.7	62
1966	Bob Scarpitto, Denver, AFL	76	45.8	70
	*David Lee, Baltimore, NFL	49	45.6	64
1965	Gary Collins, Cleveland, NFL	65	46.7	71
	Jerrel Wilson, Kansas City, AFL	69	45.4	64
1964	*Bobby Walden, Minnesota, NFL	72	46.4	73
	Jim Fraser, Denver, AFL	73	44.2	67
1963	Yale Lary, Detroit, NFL	35	48.9	73
	Jim Fraser, Denver, AFL	81	44.4	66
1962	Tommy Davis, San Francisco, NFL	48	45.6	82
	Jim Fraser, Denver, AFL	55	43.6	75
1961	Yale Lary, Detroit, NFL	52	48.4	71
	Billy Atkins, Buffalo, AFL	85	44.5	70
1960	Jerry Norton, St. Louis, NFL	39	45.6	62
	*Paul Maguire, L.A. Chargers, AFL	43	40.5	61
1959	Yale Lary, Detroit	45	47.1	67
1958	Sam Baker, Washington	48	45.4	64
1957	Don Chandler, N.Y. Giants	60	44.6	61
1956	Norm Van Brocklin, Los Angeles	48	43.1	72
1955	Norm Van Brocklin, Los Angeles	60	44.6	61
1954	Pat Brady, Pittsburgh	66	43.2	72
1953	Pat Brady, Pittsburgh	80	46.9	64

1952	Horace Gillom, Cleveland	61	45.7	73
1951	Horace Gillom, Cleveland	73	45.5	66
1950	*Fred (Curly) Morrison, Chi. Bears	57	43.3	65
1949	*Mike Boyda, N.Y. Bulldogs	56	44.2	61
1948	Joe Muha, Philadelphia	57	47.3	82
1947	Jack Jacobs, Green Bay	57	43.5	74
1946	Roy McKay, Green Bay	64	42.7	64
1945	Roy McKay, Green Bay	44	41.2	73
1944	Frank Sinkwich, Detroit	45	41.0	73
1943	Sammy Baugh, Washington	50	45.9	81
1942	Sammy Baugh, Washington	37	48.2	74
1941	Sammy Baugh, Washington	30	48.7	75
1940	Sammy Baugh, Washington	35	51.4	85
1939	*Parker Hall, Cleveland	58	40.8	80

**First year in the league.*

Annual Punt Return Leaders

Year	Player, Team	No.	Yards	Avg.	Long	TD
1991	Mel Gray, Detroit, NFC	25	385	15.4	78	1
	Rod Woodson, Pittsburgh, AFC	28	320	11.4	40	0
1990	Clarence Verdin, Indianapolis, AFC	31	396	12.8	36	0
	*Johnny Bailey, Chicago, NFC	36	399	11.1	95	1
1989	Walter Stanley, Detroit, NFC	36	496	13.8	74	0
	Clarence Verdin, Indianapolis, AFC	23	296	12.9	49	1
1988	John Taylor, San Francisco, NFC	44	556	12.6	95	2
	JoJo Townsell, N.Y. Jets, AFC	35	409	11.7	59	1
1987	Mel Gray, New Orleans, NFC	24	352	14.7	80	0
	Bobby Joe Edmonds, Seattle, AFC	20	251	12.6	40	0
1986	*Bobby Joe Edmonds, Seattle, AFC	34	419	12.3	75	1
	*Vai Sikahema, St. Louis, NFC	43	522	12.1	71	2
1985	Irving Fryar, New England, AFC	37	520	14.1	85	2
	Henry Ellard, L.A. Rams, NFC	37	501	13.5	80	1
1984	Mike Martin, Cincinnati, AFC	24	376	15.7	55	0
	Henry Ellard, L.A. Rams, NFC	30	403	13.4	83	2
1983	*Henry Ellard, L.A. Rams, NFC	16	217	13.6	72	1
	Kirk Springs, N.Y. Jets, AFC	23	287	12.5	76	1
1982	Rick Upchurch, Denver, AFC	15	242	16.1	78	2
	Billy Johnson, Atlanta, NFC	24	273	11.4	71	0
1981	LeRoy Irvin, Los Angeles, NFC	46	615	13.4	84	3
	*James Brooks, San Diego, AFC	22	290	13.2	42	0
1980	J. T. Smith, Kansas City, AFC	40	581	14.5	75	2
	*Kenny Johnson, Atlanta, NFC	23	281	12.2	56	0
1979	John Sciarra, Philadelphia, NFC	16	182	11.4	38	0
	*Tony Nathan, Miami, AFC	28	306	10.9	86	1
1978	Rick Upchurch, Denver, AFC	36	493	13.7	75	1
	Jackie Wallace, Los Angeles, NFC	52	618	11.9	58	0
1977	Billy Johnson, Houston, AFC	35	539	15.4	87	2
	Larry Marshall, Philadelphia, NFC	46	489	10.6	48	0
1976	Rick Upchurch, Denver, AFC	39	536	13.7	92	4
	Eddie Brown, Washington, NFC	48	646	13.5	71	1
1975	Billy Johnson, Houston, AFC	40	612	15.3	83	3
	Terry Metcalf, St. Louis, NFC	23	285	12.4	69	1
1974	Lemar Parrish, Cincinnati, AFC	18	338	18.8	90	2
	Dick Jauron, Detroit, NFC	17	286	16.8	58	0
1973	Bruce Taylor, San Francisco, NFC	15	207	13.8	61	0
	Ron Smith, San Diego, AFC	27	352	13.0	84	2
1972	*Ken Ellis, Green Bay, NFC	14	215	15.4	80	1
	Chris Farasopoulos, N.Y. Jets, AFC	17	179	10.5	65	1
1971	Les (Speedy) Duncan, Washington, NFC	22	233	10.6	33	0
	Leroy Kelly, Cleveland, AFC	30	292	9.7	74	0
1970	Ed Podolak, Kansas City, AFC	23	311	13.5	60	0
	*Bruce Taylor, San Francisco, NFC	43	516	12.0	76	0
1969	Alvin Haymond, Los Angeles, NFL	33	435	13.2	52	0
	*Bill Thompson, Denver, AFL	25	288	11.5	40	0
1968	Bob Hayes, Dallas, NFL	15	312	20.8	90	2
	Noland Smith, Kansas City, AFL	18	270	15.0	80	1
1967	Floyd Little, Denver, AFL	16	270	16.9	72	1
	Ben Davis, Cleveland, NFL	18	229	12.7	52	1
1966	Les (Speedy) Duncan, San Diego, AFL	18	238	13.2	81	1
	Johnny Roland, St. Louis, NFL	20	221	11.1	86	1
1965	Leroy Kelly, Cleveland, NFL	17	265	15.6	67	2
	Les (Speedy) Duncan, San Diego, AFL	30	464	15.5	66	2
1964	Bobby Jancik, Houston, AFL	12	220	18.3	82	1
	Tommy Watkins, Detroit, NFL	16	238	14.9	68	2
1963	Dick James, Washington, NFL	16	214	13.4	39	0
	Claude (Hoot) Gibson, Oakland, AFL	26	307	11.8	85	2
1962	Dick Christy, N.Y. Titans, AFL	15	250	16.7	73	2
	Pat Studstill, Detroit, NFL	29	457	15.8	44	0
1961	Dick Christy, N.Y. Titans, AFL	18	383	21.3	70	2
	Willie Wood, Green Bay, NFL	14	225	16.1	72	2
1960	*Abner Haynes, Dall. Texans, AFL	14	215	15.4	46	0
	Abe Woodson, San Francisco, NFL	13	174	13.4	48	0
1959	Johnny Morris, Chi. Bears	14	171	12.2	78	1
1958	Jon Arnett, Los Angeles	18	223	12.4	58	0
1957	Bert Zagers, Washington	14	217	15.5	76	2
1956	Ken Konz, Cleveland	13	187	14.4	65	1
1955	Ollie Matson, Chi. Cardinals	13	245	18.8	78	2
1954	*Veryl Switzer, Green Bay	24	306	12.8	93	1
1953	Charley Trippi, Chi. Cardinals	21	239	11.4	38	0
1952	Jack Christiansen, Detroit	15	322	21.5	79	2
1951	Claude (Buddy) Young, N.Y. Yanks	12	231	19.3	79	1
1950	*Herb Rich, Baltimore	12	276	23.0	86	1
1949	Verda (Vitamin T) Smith, Los Angeles	27	427	15.8	85	1
1948	George McAfee, Chi. Bears	30	417	13.9	60	1
1947	*Walt Slater, Pittsburgh	28	435	15.5	33	0
1946	Bill Dudley, Pittsburgh	27	385	14.3	52	0
1945	*Dave Ryan, Detroit	15	220	14.7	56	0
1944	*Steve Van Buren, Philadelphia	15	230	15.3	55	1
1943	Andy Farkas, Washington	15	168	11.2	33	0
1942	Merlyn Condit, Brooklyn	21	210	10.0	23	0
1941	Byron (Whizzer) White, Detroit	19	262	13.8	64	0

**First year in the league.*

Annual Kickoff Return Leaders

Year	Player, Team	No.	Yards	Avg.	Long	TD
1991	Mel Gray, Detroit, NFC	36	929	25.8	71	0
	Nate Lewis, San Diego, AFC	23	578	25.1	95	1
1990	Kevin Clark, Denver, AFC	20	505	25.3	75	0
	David Meggett, N.Y. Giants, NFC	21	492	23.4	58	0
1989	Rod Woodson, Pittsburgh, AFC	36	982	27.3	84	1
	Mel Gray, Detroit, NFC	24	640	26.7	57	0
1988	*Tim Brown, L.A. Raiders, AFC	41	1,098	26.8	97	1
	Donnie Elder, Tampa Bay, NFC	34	772	22.7	51	0
1987	Sylvester Stamps, Atlanta, NFC	24	660	27.5	97	1
	Paul Palmer, Kansas City, AFC	38	923	24.3	95	2
1986	Dennis Gentry, Chicago, NFC	20	576	28.8	91	1
	*Lupe Sanchez, Pittsburgh, AFC	25	591	23.6	64	0
1985	Ron Brown, L.A. Rams, NFC	28	918	32.8	98	3
	Glen Young, Cleveland, AFC	35	898	25.7	63	0
1984	*Bobby Humphery, N.Y. Jets, AFC	22	675	30.7	97	1
	Barry Redden, L.A. Rams, NFC	23	530	23.0	40	0
1983	Fulton Walker, Miami, AFC	36	962	26.7	78	0
	Darrin Nelson, Minnesota, NFC	18	445	24.7	50	0
1982	*Mike Mosley, Buffalo, AFC	18	487	27.1	66	0
	Alvin Hall, Detroit, NFC	16	426	26.6	96	1
1981	Mike Nelms, Washington, NFC	37	1,099	29.7	84	0
	Carl Roaches, Houston, AFC	28	769	27.5	96	1
1980	Horace Ivory, New England, AFC	36	992	27.6	98	1
	Rich Mauti, New Orleans, NFC	31	798	25.7	52	0
1979	Larry Brunson, Oakland, AFC	17	441	25.9	89	0
	*Jimmy Edwards, Minnesota, NFC	44	1,103	25.1	83	0
1978	Steve Odom, Green Bay, NFC	25	677	27.1	95	1
	*Keith Wright, Cleveland, AFC	30	789	26.3	86	0
1977	*Raymond Clayborn, New England, AFC	28	869	31.0	101	3
	*Wilbert Montgomery, Philadelphia, NFC	23	619	26.9	99	1
1976	*Duriel Harris, Miami, AFC	17	559	32.9	69	0
	Cullen Bryant, Los Angeles, NFC	16	459	28.7	90	1
1975	*Walter Payton, Chicago, NFC	14	444	31.7	70	0
	Harold Hart, Oakland, AFC	17	518	30.5	102	1
1974	Terry Metcalf, St. Louis, NFC	20	623	31.2	94	1
	Greg Pruitt, Cleveland, AFC	22	606	27.5	88	1
1973	Carl Garrett, Chicago, NFC	16	486	30.4	67	0
	*Wallace Francis, Buffalo, AFC	23	687	29.9	101	2
1972	Ron Smith, Chicago, NFC	30	924	30.8	94	1
	*Bruce Laird, Baltimore, AFC	29	843	29.1	73	0
1971	Travis Williams, Los Angeles, NFC	25	743	29.7	105	1
	Eugene (Mercury) Morris, Miami, AFC	15	423	28.2	94	1
1970	Jim Duncan, Baltimore, AFC	20	707	35.4	99	1
	Cecil Turner, Chicago, NFC	23	752	32.7	96	4
1969	Bobby Williams, Detroit, NFL	17	563	33.1	96	1
	*Bill Thompson, Denver, AFL	18	513	28.5	63	0
1968	Preston Pearson, Baltimore, NFL	15	527	35.1	102	2
	*George Atkinson, Oakland, AFL	32	802	25.1	60	0
1967	*Travis Williams, Green Bay, NFL	18	739	41.1	104	4
	*Zeke Moore, Houston, AFL	14	405	28.9	92	1
1966	Gale Sayers, Chicago, NFL	23	718	31.2	93	2
	*Goldie Sellers, Denver, AFL	19	541	28.5	100	2
1965	Tommy Watkins, Detroit, NFL	17	584	34.4	94	0
	Abner Haynes, Denver, AFL	34	901	26.5	60	0
1964	*Clarence Childs, N.Y. Giants, NFL	34	987	29.0	100	1
	Bo Roberson, Oakland, AFL	36	975	27.1	59	0
1963	Abe Woodson, San Francisco, NFL	29	935	32.2	103	3
	Bobby Jancik, Houston, AFL	45	1,317	29.3	53	0
1962	Abe Woodson, San Francisco, NFL	37	1,157	31.3	79	0
	*Bobby Jancik, Houston, AFL	24	826	30.3	61	0
1961	Dick Bass, Los Angeles, NFL	23	698	30.3	64	0
	*Dave Grayson, Dall. Texans, AFL	16	453	28.3	73	0
1960	*Tom Moore, Green Bay, NFL	12	397	33.1	84	0
	Ken Hall, Houston, AFL	19	594	31.3	104	1
1959	Abe Woodson, San Francisco	13	382	29.4	105	1
1958	Ollie Matson, Chi. Cardinals	14	497	35.5	101	2
1957	*Jon Arnett, Los Angeles	18	504	28.0	98	1
1956	*Tom Wilson, Los Angeles	15	477	31.8	103	1
1955	Al Carmichael, Green Bay	14	418	29.9	100	1
1954	Billy Reynolds, Cleveland	14	413	29.5	51	0
1953	Joe Arenas, San Francisco	16	551	34.4	82	0
1952	Lynn Chandnois, Pittsburgh	17	599	35.2	93	2
1951	Lynn Chandnois, Pittsburgh	12	390	32.5	55	0
1950	Verda (Vitamin T) Smith, Los Angeles	22	742	33.7	97	3
1949	*Don Doll, Detroit	21	536	25.5	56	0
1948	*Joe Scott, N.Y. Giants	20	569	28.5	99	1
1947	Eddie Saenz, Washington	29	797	27.5	94	2
1946	Abe Karnofsky, Boston	21	599	28.5	97	1
1945	Steve Van Buren, Philadelphia	13	373	28.7	98	1
1944	Bob Thurbon, Card.-Pitt.	12	291	24.3	55	0
1943	Ken Heineman, Brooklyn	16	444	27.8	69	0
1942	Marshall Goldberg, Chi. Cardinals	15	393	26.2	95	1
1941	Marshall Goldberg, Chi. Cardinals	12	290	24.2	41	0

**First year in the league.*

Points Scored

Year	Team	Points
1991	Washington, NFC	485
	Buffalo, AFC	458
1990	Buffalo, AFC	428
	Philadelphia, NFC	396
1989	San Francisco, NFC	442
	Buffalo, AFC	409
1988	Cincinnati, AFC	448
	L.A. Rams, NFC	407
1987	San Francisco, NFC	459
	Cleveland, AFC	390
1986	Miami, AFC	430
	Minnesota, NFC	398
1985	San Diego, AFC	467
	Chicago, NFC	456
1984	Miami, AFC	513
	San Francisco, NFC	475
1983	Washington, NFC	541
	L.A. Raiders, AFC	442
1982	San Diego, AFC	288
	Dallas, NFC	226
	Green Bay, NFC	226
1981	San Diego, AFC	478
	Atlanta, NFC	426
1980	Dallas, NFC	454
	New England, AFC	441
1979	Pittsburgh, AFC	416
	Dallas, NFC	371
1978	Dallas, NFC	384
	Miami, AFC	372
1977	Oakland, AFC	351

	Dallas, NFC	345
1976	Baltimore, AFC	417
	Los Angeles, NFC	351
1975	Buffalo, AFC	420
	Minnesota, NFC	377
1974	Oakland, AFC	355
	Washington, NFC	320
1973	Los Angeles, NFC	388
	Denver, AFC	354
1972	Miami, AFC	385
	San Francisco, NFC	353
1971	Dallas, NFC	406
	Oakland, AFC	344
1970	San Francisco, NFC	352
	Baltimore, AFC	321
1969	Minnesota, NFL	379
	Oakland, AFL	377
1968	Oakland, AFL	453
	Dallas, NFL	431
1967	Oakland, AFL	468
	Los Angeles, NFL	398
1966	Kansas City, AFL	448
	Dallas, NFL	445
1965	San Francisco, NFL	421
	San Diego, AFL	340
1964	Baltimore, NFL	428
	Buffalo, AFL	400
1963	N.Y. Giants, NFL	448
	San Diego, AFL	399
1962	Green Bay, NFL	415
	Dall. Texans, AFL	389
1961	Houston, AFL	513
	Green Bay, NFL	391
1960	N.Y. Titans, AFL	382
	Cleveland, NFL	362
1959	Baltimore	374
1958	Baltimore	381
1957	Los Angeles	307
1956	Chi. Bears	363
1955	Cleveland	349
1954	Detroit	337
1953	San Francisco	372
1952	Los Angeles	349
1951	Los Angeles	392
1950	Los Angeles	466
1949	Philadelphia	364
1948	Chi. Cardinals	395
1947	Chi. Bears	363
1946	Chi. Bears	289
1945	Philadelphia	272
1944	Philadelphia	267
1943	Chi. Bears	303
1942	Chi. Bears	376
1941	Chi. Bears	396
1940	Washington	245
1939	Chi. Bears	298
1938	Green Bay	223
1937	Green Bay	220
1936	Green Bay	248
1935	Chi. Bears	192
1934	Chi. Bears	286
1933	N.Y. Giants	244
1932	Chicago Bears	160

Total Yards Gained

Year	Team	Yards
1991	Buffalo, AFC	6,252
	San Francisco, NFC	5,858
1990	Houston, AFC	6,222
	San Francisco, NFC	5,895
1989	San Francisco, NFC	6,268
	Cincinnati, AFC	6,101
1988	Cincinnati, AFC	6,057
	San Francisco, NFC	5,900
1987	San Francisco, NFC	5,987
	Denver, AFC	5,624
1986	Cincinnati, AFC	6,490
	San Francisco, NFC	6,082
1985	San Diego, AFC	6,535
	San Francisco, NFC	5,920
1984	Miami, AFC	6,936
	San Francisco, NFC	6,366
1983	San Diego, AFC	6,197
	Green Bay, NFC	6,172
1982	San Diego, AFC	4,048
	San Francisco, NFC	3,242
1981	San Diego, AFC	6,744
	Detroit, NFC	5,933
1980	San Diego, AFC	6,410
	Los Angeles, NFC	6,006
1979	Pittsburgh, AFC	6,258
	Dallas, NFC	5,968
1978	New England, AFC	5,965
	Dallas, NFC	5,959
1977	Dallas, NFC	4,812
	Oakland, AFC	4,736
1976	Baltimore, AFC	5,236
	St. Louis, NFC	5,136
1975	Buffalo, AFC	5,467
	Dallas, NFC	5,025
1974	Dallas, NFC	4,983
	Oakland, AFC	4,718
1973	Los Angeles, NFC	4,906
	Oakland, AFC	4,773
1972	Miami, AFC	5,036
	N.Y. Giants, NFC	4,483
1971	Dallas, NFC	5,035
	San Diego, AFC	4,738
1970	Oakland, AFC	4,829
	San Francisco, NFC	4,503
1969	Dallas, NFL	5,122
	Oakland, AFL	5,036
1968	Oakland, AFL	5,696
	Dallas, NFL	5,117
1967	N.Y. Jets, AFL	5,152
	Baltimore, NFL	5,008
1966	Dallas, NFL	5,145
	Kansas City, AFL	5,114
1965	San Francisco, NFL	5,270
	San Diego, AFL	5,188
1964	Buffalo, AFL	5,206
	Baltimore, NFL	4,779
1963	San Diego, AFL	5,153
	N.Y. Giants, NFL	5,024
1962	N.Y. Giants, NFL	5,005
	Houston, AFL	4,971
1961	Houston, AFL	6,288
	Philadelphia, NFL	5,112
1960	Houston, AFL	4,936
	Baltimore, NFL	4,245
1959	Baltimore	4,458
1958	Baltimore	4,539
1957	Los Angeles	4,143
1956	Chi. Bears	4,537
1955	Chi. Bears	4,316
1954	Los Angeles	5,187
1953	Philadelphia	4,811
1952	Cleveland	4,352
1951	Los Angeles	5,506
1950	Los Angeles	5,420
1949	Chi. Bears	4,873
1948	Chi. Cardinals	4,705
1947	Chi. Bears	5,053
1946	Los Angeles	3,793
1945	Washington	3,549
1944	Chi. Bears	3,239
1943	Chi. Bears	4,045
1942	Chi. Bears	3,900
1941	Chi. Bears	4,265
1940	Green Bay	3,400
1939	Chi. Bears	3,988
1938	Green Bay	3,037
1937	Green Bay	3,201
1936	Detroit	3,703
1935	Chi. Bears	3,454
1934	Chi. Bears	3,900
1933	N.Y. Giants	2,973
1932	Chi. Bears	2,755

Yards Rushing

Year	Team	Yards
1991	Buffalo, AFC	2,381
	Minnesota, NFC	2,201
1990	Philadelphia, NFC	2,556
	San Diego, AFC	2,257
1989	Cincinnati, AFC	2,483
	Chicago, NFC	2,287
1988	Cincinnati, AFC	2,710
	San Francisco, NFC	2,523
1987	San Francisco, NFC	2,237
	L.A. Raiders, AFC	2,197
1986	Chicago, NFC	2,700
	Cincinnati, AFC	2,533
1985	Chicago, NFC	2,761
	Indianapolis, AFC	2,439
1984	Chicago, NFC	2,974
	N.Y. Jets, AFC	2,189
1983	Chicago, NFC	2,727
	Baltimore, AFC	2,695
1982	Buffalo, AFC	1,371
	Dallas, NFC	1,313
1981	Detroit, NFC	2,795
	Kansas City, AFC	2,633
1980	Los Angeles, NFC	2,799
	Houston, AFC	2,635
1979	N.Y. Jets, AFC	2,646
	St. Louis, NFC	2,582
1978	New England, AFC	3,165
	Dallas, NFC	2,783
1977	Chicago, NFC	2,811
	Oakland, AFC	2,627
1976	Pittsburgh, AFC	2,971
	Los Angeles, NFC	2,528
1975	Buffalo, AFC	2,974
	Dallas, NFC	2,432
1974	Dallas, NFC	2,454
	Pittsburgh, AFC	2,417
1973	Buffalo, AFC	3,088
	Los Angeles, NFC	2,925
1972	Miami, AFC	2,960
	Chicago, NFC	2,360
1971	Miami, AFC	2,429
	Detroit, NFC	2,376
1970	Dallas, NFC	2,300
	Miami, AFC	2,082
1969	Dallas, NFL	2,276
	Kansas City, AFL	2,220
1968	Chicago, NFL	2,377
	Kansas City, AFL	2,227
1967	Cleveland, NFL	2,139
	Houston, AFL	2,122
1966	Kansas City, AFL	2,274
	Cleveland, NFL	2,166
1965	Cleveland, NFL	2,331
	San Diego, AFL	2,085
1964	Green Bay, NFL	2,276
	Buffalo, AFL	2,040
1963	Cleveland, NFL	2,639
	San Diego, AFL	2,203
1962	Buffalo, AFL	2,480
	Green Bay, NFL	2,460
1961	Green Bay, NFL	2,350
	Dall. Texans, AFL	2,189
1960	St. Louis, NFL	2,356
	Oakland, AFL	2,056
1959	Cleveland	2,149
1958	Cleveland	2,526
1957	Los Angeles	2,142
1956	Chi. Bears	2,468
1955	Chi. Bears	2,388
1954	San Francisco	2,498
1953	San Francisco	2,230
1952	San Francisco	1,905
1951	Chi. Bears	2,408
1950	N.Y. Giants	2,336
1949	Philadelphia	2,607
1948	Chi. Cardinals	2,560
1947	Los Angeles	2,171
1946	Green Bay	1,765
1945	Cleveland	1,714
1944	Philadelphia	1,661
1943	Phil-Pitt	1,730
1942	Chi. Bears	1,881
1941	Chi. Bears	2,263
1940	Chi. Bears	1,818
1939	Chi. Bears	2,043
1938	Detroit	1,893
1937	Detroit	2,074
1936	Detroit	2,885
1935	Chi. Bears	2,096
1934	Chi. Bears	2,847
1933	Boston	2,260
1932	Chi. Bears	1,770

Yards Passing

Leadership in this category has been based on net yards since 1952.

Year	Team	Yards
1991	Houston, AFC	4,621
	San Francisco, NFC	3,997
1990	Houston, AFC	4,805
	San Francisco, NFC	4,177
1989	Washington, NFC	4,349
	Miami, AFC	4,216
1988	Miami, AFC	4,516
	Washington, NFC	4,136
1987	Miami, AFC	3,876
	San Francisco, NFC	3,750
1986	Miami, AFC	4,779
	San Francisco, NFC	4,096
1985	San Diego, AFC	4,870
	Dallas, NFC	3,861
1984	Miami, AFC	5,018
	St. Louis, NFC	4,257
1983	San Diego, AFC	4,661
	Green Bay, NFC	4,365
1982	San Diego, AFC	2,927
	San Francisco, NFC	2,502
1981	San Diego, AFC	4,739
	Minnesota, NFC	4,333
1980	San Diego, AFC	4,531
	Minnesota, NFC	3,688
1979	San Diego, AFC	3,915
	San Francisco, NFC	3,641
1978	San Diego, AFC	3,375
	Minnesota, NFC	3,243
1977	Buffalo, AFC	2,530
	St. Louis, NFC	2,499
1976	Baltimore, AFC	2,933
	Minnesota, NFC	2,855
1975	Cincinnati, AFC	3,241
	Washington, NFC	2,917
1974	Washington, NFC	2,978
	Cincinnati, AFC	2,804
1973	Philadelphia, NFC	2,998
	Denver, AFC	2,519
1972	N.Y. Jets, AFC	2,777
	San Francisco, NFC	2,735
1971	San Diego, AFC	3,134
	Dallas, NFC	2,786
1970	San Francisco, NFC	2,923
	Oakland, AFC	2,865
1969	Oakland, AFL	3,271
	San Francisco, NFL	3,158
1968	San Diego, AFL	3,623
	Dallas, NFL	3,026
1967	N.Y. Jets, AFL	3,845
	Washington, NFL	3,730
1966	N.Y. Jets, AFL	3,464
	Dallas, NFL	3,023
1965	San Francisco, NFL	3,487
	San Diego, AFL	3,103
1964	Houston, AFL	3,527
	Chicago, NFL	2,841
1963	Baltimore, NFL	3,296
	Houston, AFL	3,222
1962	Denver, AFL	3,404
	Philadelphia, NFL	3,385
1961	Houston, AFL	4,392
	Philadelphia, NFL	3,605
1960	Houston, AFL	3,203
	Baltimore, NFL	2,956
1959	Baltimore	2,753
1958	Pittsburgh	2,752
1957	Baltimore	2,388
1956	Los Angeles	2,419
1955	Philadelphia	2,472
1954	Chi. Bears	3,104
1953	Philadelphia	3,089
1952	Cleveland	2,566
1951	Los Angeles	3,296
1950	Los Angeles	3,709
1949	Chi. Bears	3,055
1948	Washington	2,861
1947	Washington	3,336
1946	Los Angeles	2,080
1945	Chi. Bears	1,857
1944	Washington	2,021
1943	Chi. Bears	2,310
1942	Green Bay	2,407
1941	Chi. Bears	2,002
1940	Washington	1,887
1939	Chi. Bears	1,965
1938	Washington	1,536
1937	Green Bay	1,398
1936	Green Bay	1,629
1935	Green Bay	1,449
1934	Green Bay	1,165
1933	N.Y. Giants	1,348
1932	Chi. Bears	1,013

Fewest Points Allowed

Year	Team	Points
1991	New Orleans, NFC	211
	Denver, AFC	235
1990	N.Y. Giants, NFC	211
	Pittsburgh, AFC	240
1989	Denver, AFC	226
	N.Y. Giants, NFC	252
1988	Chicago, NFC	215
	Buffalo, AFC	237
1987	Indianapolis, AFC	238
	San Francisco, NFC	253
1986	Chicago, NFC	187
	Seattle, AFC	293
1985	Chicago, NFC	198
	N.Y. Jets, AFC	264
1984	San Francisco, NFC	227
	Denver, AFC	241
1983	Miami, AFC	250
	Detroit, NFC	286
1982	Washington, NFC	128
	Miami, AFC	131
1981	Philadelphia, NFC	221
	Miami, AFC	275
1980	Philadelphia, NFC	222
	Houston, AFC	251
1979	Tampa Bay, NFC	237
	San Diego, AFC	246
1978	Pittsburgh, AFC	195
	Dallas, NFC	208
1977	Atlanta, NFC	129
	Denver, AFC	148
1976	Pittsburgh, AFC	138
	Minnesota, NFC	176
1975	Los Angeles, NFC	135
	Pittsburgh, AFC	162
1974	Los Angeles, NFC	181
	Pittsburgh, AFC	189
1973	Miami, AFC	150
	Minnesota, NFC	168
1972	Miami, AFC	171
	Washington, NFC	218
1971	Minnesota, NFC	139
	Baltimore, AFC	140
1970	Minnesota, NFC	143
	Miami, AFC	228
1969	Minnesota, NFL	133
	Kansas City, AFL	177
1968	Baltimore, NFL	144
	Kansas City, AFL	170
1967	Los Angeles, NFL	196
	Houston, AFL	199
1966	Green Bay, NFL	163
	Buffalo, AFL	255
1965	Green Bay, NFL	224
	Buffalo, AFL	226
1964	Baltimore, NFL	225
	Buffalo, AFL	242
1963	Chicago, NFL	144
	San Diego, AFL	255
1962	Green Bay, NFL	148

Year	Team	Points
	Dall. Texans, AFL	233
1961	San Diego, AFL	219
	N.Y. Giants, NFL	220
1960	San Francisco, NFL	205
	Dall. Texans, AFL	253
1959	N.Y. Giants	170
1958	N.Y. Giants	183
1957	Cleveland	172
1956	Cleveland	177
1955	Cleveland	218
1954	Cleveland	162
1953	Cleveland	162
1952	Detroit	192
1951	Cleveland	152
1950	Philadelphia	141
1949	Philadelphia	134
1948	Chi. Bears	151
1947	Green Bay	210
1946	Pittsburgh	117
1945	Washington	121
1944	N.Y. Giants	75
1943	Washington	137
1942	Chi. Bears	84
1941	N.Y. Giants	114
1940	Brooklyn	120
1939	N.Y. Giants	85
1938	N.Y. Giants	79
1937	Chi. Bears	100
1936	Chi. Bears	94
1935	Green Bay	96
	N.Y. Giants	96
1934	Detroit	59
1933	Brooklyn	54
1932	Chi. Bears	44

Fewest Total Yards Allowed

Year	Team	Yards
1991	Philadelphia, NFC	3,549
	Denver, AFC	4,549
1990	Pittsburgh, AFC	4,115
	N.Y. Giants, NFC	4,206
1989	Minnesota, NFC	4,184
	Kansas City, AFC	4,293
1988	Minnesota, NFC	4,091
	Buffalo, AFC	4,578
1987	San Francisco, NFC	4,095
	Cleveland, AFC	4,264
1986	Chicago, NFC	4,130
	L.A. Raiders, AFC	4,804
1985	Chicago, NFC	4,135
	L.A. Raiders, AFC	4,603
1984	Chicago, NFC	3,863
	Cleveland, AFC	4,641
1983	Cincinnati, AFC	4,327
	New Orleans, NFC	4,691
1982	Miami, AFC	2,312
	Tampa Bay, NFC	2,442
1981	Philadelphia, NFC	4,447
	N.Y. Jets, AFC	4,871
1980	Buffalo, AFC	4,101
	Philadelphia, NFC	4,443
1979	Tampa Bay, NFC	3,949
	Pittsburgh, AFC	4,270
1978	Los Angeles, NFC	3,893
	Pittsburgh, AFC	4,168
1977	Dallas, NFC	3,213
	New England, AFC	3,638
1976	Pittsburgh, AFC	3,323
	San Francisco, NFC	3,562
1975	Minnesota, NFC	3,153
	Oakland, AFC	3,629
1974	Pittsburgh, AFC	3,074
	Washington, NFC	3,285
1973	Los Angeles, NFC	2,951
	Oakland, AFC	3,160
1972	Miami, AFC	3,297
	Green Bay, NFC	3,474
1971	Baltimore, AFC	2,852
	Minnesota, NFC	3,406
1970	Minnesota, NFC	2,803
	N.Y. Jets, AFC	3,655
1969	Minnesota, NFL	2,720
	Kansas City, AFL	3,163
1968	Los Angeles, NFL	3,118
	N.Y. Jets, AFL	3,363
1967	Oakland, AFL	3,294
	Green Bay, NFL	3,300
1966	St. Louis, NFL	3,492
	Oakland, AFL	3,910
1965	San Diego, AFL	3,262
	Detroit, NFL	3,557
1964	Green Bay, NFL	3,179
	Buffalo, AFL	3,878
1963	Chicago, NFL	3,176
	Boston, AFL	3,834
1962	Detroit, NFL	3,217
	Dall. Texans, AFL	3,951
1961	San Diego, AFL	3,726
	Baltimore, NFL	3,782
1960	St. Louis, NFL	3,029
	Buffalo, AFL	3,866
1959	N.Y. Giants	2,843
1958	Chi. Bears	3,066
1957	Pittsburgh	2,791
1956	N.Y. Giants	3,081
1955	Cleveland	2,841
1954	Cleveland	2,658
1953	Philadelphia	2,998
1952	Cleveland	3,075
1951	N.Y. Giants	3,250
1950	Cleveland	3,154
1949	Philadelphia	2,831
1948	Chi. Bears	2,931
1947	Green Bay	3,396
1946	Washington	2,451
1945	Philadelphia	2,073
1944	Philadelphia	1,943
1943	Chi. Bears	2,262
1942	Chi. Bears	1,703
1941	N.Y. Giants	2,368
1940	N.Y. Giants	2,219
1939	Washington	2,116
1938	N.Y. Giants	2,029
1937	Washington	2,123
1936	Boston	2,181
1935	Boston	1,996
1934	Chi. Cardinals	1,539
1933	Brooklyn	1,789

Fewest Rushing Yards Allowed

Year	Team	Yards
1991	Philadelphia, NFC	1,136
	N.Y. Jets, AFC	1,442
1990	Philadelphia, NFC	1,169
	San Diego, AFC	1,515
1989	New Orleans, NFC	1,326
	Denver, AFC	1,580
1988	Chicago, NFC	1,326
	Houston, AFC	1,592
1987	Chicago, NFC	1,413
	Cleveland, AFC	1,433
1986	N.Y. Giants, NFC	1,284
	Denver, AFC	1,651
1985	Chicago, NFC	1,319
	N.Y. Jets, AFC	1,516
1984	Chicago, NFC	1,377
	Pittsburgh, AFC	1,617
1983	Washington, NFC	1,289
	Cincinnati, AFC	1,499
1982	Pittsburgh, AFC	762
	Detroit, NFC	854
1981	Detroit, NFC	1,623
	Kansas City, AFC	1,747
1980	Detroit, NFC	1,599
	Cincinnati, AFC	1,680
1979	Denver, AFC	1,693
	Tampa Bay, NFC	1,873
1978	Dallas, NFC	1,721
	Pittsburgh, AFC	1,774
1977	Denver, AFC	1,531
	Dallas, NFC	1,651
1976	Pittsburgh, AFC	1,457
	Los Angeles, NFC	1,564
1975	Minnesota, NFC	1,532
	Houston, AFC	1,680
1974	Los Angeles, NFC	1,302
	New England, AFC	1,587
1973	Los Angeles, NFC	1,270
	Oakland, AFC	1,470
1972	Dallas, NFC	1,515
	Miami, AFC	1,548
1971	Baltimore, AFC	1,113
	Dallas, NFC	1,144
1970	Detroit, NFC	1,152
	N.Y. Jets, AFC	1,283
1969	Dallas, NFL	1,050
	Kansas City, AFL	1,091
1968	Dallas, NFL	1,195
	N.Y. Jets, AFL	1,195
1967	Dallas, NFL	1,081
	Oakland, AFL	1,129
1966	Buffalo, AFL	1,051
	Dallas, NFL	1,176
1965	San Diego, AFL	1,094
	Los Angeles, NFL	1,409
964	Buffalo, AFL	913
	Los Angeles, NFL	1,501
1963	Boston, AFL	1,107
	Chicago, NFL	1,442
1962	Detroit, NFL	1,231
	Dall. Texans, AFL	1,250
1961	Boston, AFL	1,041
	Pittsburgh, NFL	1,463
1960	St. Louis, NFL	1,212
	Dall. Texans, AFL	1,338
1959	N.Y. Giants	1,261
1958	Baltimore	1,291
1957	Baltimore	1,174
1956	N.Y. Giants	1,443
1955	Cleveland	1,189
1954	Cleveland	1,050
1953	Philadelphia	1,117
1952	Detroit	1,145
1951	N.Y. Giants	913
1950	Detroit	1,367
1949	Chi. Bears	1,196
1948	Philadelphia	1,209
1947	Philadelphia	1,329
1946	Chi. Bears	1,060
1945	Philadelphia	817
1944	Philadelphia	558
1943	Phil-Pitt	793
1942	Chi. Bears	519
1941	Washington	1,042
1940	N.Y. Giants	977
1939	Chi. Bears	812
1938	Detroit	1,081
1937	Chi. Bears	933
1936	Boston	1,148
1935	Boston	998
1934	Chi. Cardinals	954
1933	Brooklyn	964

Fewest Passing Yards Allowed

Leadership in this category has been based on net yards since 1952.

Year	Team	Yards
1991	Philadelphia, NFC	2,413
	Denver, AFC	2,755
1990	Pittsburgh, AFC	2,500
	Dallas, NFC	2,639
1989	Minnesota, NFC	2,501
	Kansas City, AFC	2,527
1988	Kansas City, AFC	2,434
	Minnesota, NFC	2,489
1987	San Francisco, NFC	2,484
	L.A. Raiders, AFC	2,727
1986	St. Louis, NFC	2,637
	New England, AFC	2,978
1985	Washington, NFC	2,746
	Pittsburgh, AFC	2,783
1984	New Orleans, NFC	2,453
	Cleveland, AFC	2,696
1983	New Orleans, NFC	2,691
	Cincinnati, AFC	2,828
1982	Miami, AFC	1,027
	Tampa Bay, NFC	1,384
1981	Philadelphia, NFC	2,696
	Buffalo, AFC	2,870
1980	Washington, NFC	2,171
	Buffalo, AFC	2,282
1979	Tampa Bay, NFC	2,076
	Buffalo, AFC	2,530
1978	Buffalo, AFC	1,960
	Los Angeles, NFC	2,048
1977	Atlanta, NFC	1,384
	San Diego, AFC	1,725
1976	Minnesota, NFC	1,575
	Cincinnati, AFC	1,758
1975	Minnesota, NFC	1,621
	Cincinnati, AFC	1,729
1974	Pittsburgh, AFC	1,466
	Atlanta, NFC	1,572
1973	Miami, AFC	1,290
	Atlanta, NFC	1,430
1972	Minnesota, NFC	1,699
	Cleveland, AFC	1,736
1971	Atlanta, NFC	1,638
	Baltimore, AFC	1,739
1970	Minnesota, NFC	1,438
	Kansas City, AFC	2,010
1969	Minnesota, NFL	1,631
	Kansas City, AFL	2,072
1968	Houston, AFL	1,671
	Green Bay, NFL	1,796
1967	Green Bay, NFL	1,377
	Buffalo, AFL	1,825
1966	Green Bay, NFL	1,959
	Oakland, AFL	2,118
1965	Green Bay, NFL	1,981
	San Diego, AFL	2,168
1964	Green Bay, NFL	1,647
	San Diego, AFL	2,518
1963	Chicago, NFL	1,734
	Oakland, AFL	2,589
1962	Green Bay, NFL	1,746
	Oakland, AFL	2,306
1961	Baltimore, NFL	1,913
	San Diego, AFL	2,363
1960	Chicago, NFL	1,388
	Buffalo, AFL	2,124
1959	N.Y. Giants	1,582
1958	Chi. Bears	1,769
1957	Cleveland	1,300
1956	Cleveland	1,103
1955	Pittsburgh	1,295
1954	Cleveland	1,608
1953	Washington	1,751
1952	Washington	1,580
1951	Pittsburgh	1,687
1950	Cleveland	1,581
1949	Philadelphia	1,607
1948	Green Bay	1,626
1947	Green Bay	1,790
1946	Pittsburgh	939
1945	Washington	1,121
1944	Chi. Bears	1,052
1943	Chi. Bears	980
1942	Washington	1,093
1941	Pittsburgh	1,168
1940	Philadelphia	1,012
1939	Washington	1,116
1938	Chi. Bears	897
1937	Detroit	804
1936	Philadelphia	853
1935	Chi. Cardinals	793
1934	Philadelphia	545
1933	Portsmouth	558

Compiled by Elias Sports Bureau

1967: Super Bowl I
1968: Super Bowl II
1969: Super Bowl III
1970: Super Bowl IV
1971: Super Bowl V
1972: Super Bowl VI
1973: Super Bowl VII
1974: Super Bowl VIII
1975: Super Bowl IX

1976: Super Bowl X
1977: Super Bowl XI
1978: Super Bowl XII
1979: Super Bowl XIII
1980: Super Bowl XIV
1981: Super Bowl XV
1982: Super Bowl XVI
1983: Super Bowl XVII
1984: Super Bowl XVIII

1985: Super Bowl XIX
1986: Super Bowl XX
1987: Super Bowl XXI
1988: Super Bowl XXII
1989: Super Bowl XXIII
1990: Super Bowl XXIV
1991: Super Bowl XXV
1992: Super Bowl XXVI

Individual Records

Service
Most Games
- 5 Marv Fleming, Green Bay, 1967-68; Miami, 1972-74
  - Larry Cole, Dallas, 1971-72, 1976, 1978-79
  - Cliff Harris, Dallas, 1971-72, 1976, 1978-79
  - D.D. Lewis, Dallas, 1971-72, 1976, 1978-79
  - Preston Pearson, Baltimore, 1969; Pittsburgh, 1975; Dallas, 1976, 1978-79
  - Charlie Waters, Dallas, 1971-72, 1976, 1978-79
  - Rayfield Wright, Dallas, 1971-72, 1976, 1978-79
- 4 By many players

Most Games, Winning Team
- 4 By many players

Most Games, Coach
- 6 Don Shula, Baltimore, 1969; Miami, 1972-74, 1983, 1985
- 5 Tom Landry, Dallas, 1971-72, 1976, 1978-79
- 4 Bud Grant, Minnesota, 1970, 1974-75, 1977
  - Chuck Noll, Pittsburgh, 1975-76, 1979-80
  - Joe Gibbs, Washington, 1983-84, 1988, 1992

Most Games, Winning Team, Coach
- 4 Chuck Noll, Pittsburgh, 1975-76, 1979-80
- 3 Bill Walsh, San Francisco, 1982, 1985, 1989
  - Joe Gibbs, Washington, 1983, 1988, 1992
- 2 Vince Lombardi, Green Bay, 1967-68
  - Tom Landry, Dallas, 1972, 1978
  - Don Shula, Miami, 1973-74
  - Tom Flores, Oakland, 1981; L.A. Raiders, 1984
  - Bill Parcells, N.Y. Giants, 1987, 1991

Most Games, Losing Team, Coach
- 4 Bud Grant, Minnesota, 1970, 1974-75, 1977
  - Don Shula, Baltimore, 1969; Miami, 1972, 1983, 1985
- 3 Tom Landry, Dallas, 1971, 1976, 1979
  - Dan Reeves, Denver, 1987-88, 1990

Scoring
Points
Most Points, Career
- 24 Franco Harris, Pittsburgh, 4 games (4-td)
  - Roger Craig, San Francisco, 3 games (4-td)
  - Jerry Rice, San Francisco, 2 games (4-td)
- 22 Ray Wersching, San Francisco, 2 games (7-pat, 5-fg)
- 20 Don Chandler, Green Bay, 2 games (8-pat, 4-fg)

Most Points, Game
- 18 Roger Craig, San Francisco vs. Miami, 1985 (3-td)
  - Jerry Rice, San Francisco vs. Denver, 1990 (3-td)
- 15 Don Chandler, Green Bay vs. Oakland, 1968 (3-pat, 4-fg)
- 14 Ray Wersching, San Francisco vs. Cincinnati, 1982 (2-pat, 4-fg)
  - Kevin Butler, Chicago vs. New England, 1986 (5-pat, 3-fg)

Touchdowns
Most Touchdowns, Career
- 4 Franco Harris, Pittsburgh, 4 games (4-r)
  - Roger Craig, San Francisco, 3 games (2-r, 2-p)
  - Jerry Rice, San Francisco, 2 games (4-p)
- 3 John Stallworth, Pittsburgh, 4 games (3-p)
  - Lynn Swann, Pittsburgh, 4 games (3-p)
  - Cliff Branch, Oakland-L.A. Raiders, 3 games (3-p)

Most Touchdowns, Game
- 3 Roger Craig, San Francisco vs. Miami, 1985 (1-r, 2-p)
  - Jerry Rice, San Francisco vs. Denver, 1990 (3-p)
- 2 Max McGee, Green Bay vs. Kansas City, 1967 (2-p)
  - Elijah Pitts, Green Bay vs. Kansas City, 1967 (2-r)
  - Bill Miller, Oakland vs. Green Bay, 1968 (2-p)
  - Larry Csonka, Miami vs. Minnesota, 1974 (2-r)
  - Pete Banaszak, Oakland vs. Minnesota, 1977 (2-r)
  - John Stallworth, Pittsburgh vs. Dallas, 1979 (2-p)
  - Franco Harris, Pittsburgh vs. Los Angeles, 1980 (2-r)
  - Cliff Branch, Oakland vs. Philadelphia, 1981 (2-p)
  - Dan Ross, Cincinnati vs. San Francisco, 1982 (2-p)
  - Marcus Allen, L.A. Raiders vs. Washington, 1984 (2-r)
  - Jim McMahon, Chicago vs. New England, 1986 (2-r)
  - Ricky Sanders, Washington vs. Denver, 1988 (2-p)
  - Timmy Smith, Washington vs. Denver, 1988 (2-r)
  - Tom Rathman, San Francisco vs. Denver, 1990 (2-r)
  - Gerald Riggs, Washington vs. Buffalo, 1992 (2-r)

Points After Touchdown
Most Points After Touchdown, Career
- 9 Mike Cofer, San Francisco, 2 games (10 att)
- 8 Don Chandler, Green Bay, 2 games (8 att)
  - Roy Gerela, Pittsburgh, 3 games (9 att)
  - Chris Bahr, Oakland-L.A. Raiders, 2 games (8 att)
- 7 Ray Wersching, San Francisco, 2 games (7 att)

Most Points After Touchdown, Game
- 7 Mike Cofer, San Francisco vs. Denver, 1990 (8 att)
- 6 Ali Haji-Sheikh, Washington vs. Denver, 1988 (6 att)
- 5 Don Chandler, Green Bay vs. Kansas City, 1967 (5 att)
  - Roy Gerela, Pittsburgh vs. Dallas, 1979 (5 att)

Chris Bahr, L.A. Raiders vs. Washington, 1984 (5 att)
Ray Wersching, San Francisco vs. Miami, 1985 (5 att)
Kevin Butler, Chicago vs. New England, 1986 (5 att)

Field Goals
Field Goals Attempted, Career
- 6 Jim Turner, N.Y. Jets-Denver, 2 games
  - Roy Gerela, Pittsburgh, 3 games
  - Rich Karlis, Denver, 2 games
- 5 Efren Herrera, Dallas, 1 game
  - Ray Wersching, San Francisco, 2 games

Most Field Goals Attempted, Game
- 5 Jim Turner, N.Y. Jets vs. Baltimore, 1969
  - Efren Herrera, Dallas vs. Denver, 1978
- 4 Don Chandler, Green Bay vs. Oakland, 1968
  - Roy Gerela, Pittsburgh vs. Dallas, 1976
  - Ray Wersching, San Francisco vs. Cincinnati, 1982
  - Rich Karlis, Denver vs. N.Y. Giants, 1987
  - Mike Cofer, San Francisco vs. Cincinnati, 1989

Most Field Goals, Career
- 5 Ray Wersching, San Francisco, 2 games (5 att)
- 4 Don Chandler, Green Bay, 2 games (4 att)
  - Jim Turner, N.Y. Jets-Denver, 2 games (6 att)
  - Uwe von Schamann, Miami, 2 games (4 att)
- 3 Mike Clark, Dallas, 2 games (3 att)
  - Jan Stenerud, Kansas City, 1 game (3 att)
  - Chris Bahr, Oakland-L.A. Raiders, 2 games (4 att)
  - Mark Moseley, Washington, 2 games (4 att)
  - Kevin Butler, Chicago, 1 game (3 att)
  - Rich Karlis, Denver, 2 games (6 att)
  - Jim Breech, Cincinnati, 2 games (3 att)
  - Matt Bahr, Pittsburgh-N.Y. Giants, 2 games (3 att)
  - Chip Lohmiller, Washington, 1 game (3 att)

Most Field Goals, Game
- 4 Don Chandler, Green Bay vs. Oakland, 1968
  - Ray Wersching, San Francisco vs. Cincinnati, 1982
- 3 Jim Turner, N.Y. Jets vs. Baltimore, 1969
  - Jan Stenerud, Kansas City vs. Minnesota, 1970
  - Uwe von Schamann, Miami vs. San Francisco, 1985
  - Kevin Butler, Chicago vs. New England, 1986
  - Jim Breech, Cincinnati vs. San Francisco, 1989
  - Chip Lohmiller, Washington, 1992

Longest Field Goal
- 48 Jan Stenerud, Kansas City vs. Minnesota, 1970
  - Rich Karlis, Denver vs. N.Y. Giants, 1987
- 47 Jim Turner, Denver vs. Dallas, 1978
- 46 Chris Bahr, Oakland vs. Philadelphia, 1981

Safeties
Most Safeties, Game
- 1 Dwight White, Pittsburgh vs. Minnesota, 1975
  - Reggie Harrison, Pittsburgh vs. Dallas, 1976
  - Henry Waechter, Chicago vs. New England, 1986
  - George Martin, N.Y. Giants vs. Denver, 1987
  - Bruce Smith, Buffalo vs. N.Y. Giants, 1991

Rushing
Attempts
Most Attempts, Career
- 101 Franco Harris, Pittsburgh, 4 games
- 64 John Riggins, Washington, 2 games
- 57 Larry Csonka, Miami, 3 games

Most Attempts, Game
- 38 John Riggins, Washington vs. Miami, 1983
- 34 Franco Harris, Pittsburgh vs. Minnesota, 1975
- 33 Larry Csonka, Miami vs. Minnesota, 1974

Yards Gained
Most Yards Gained, Career
- 354 Franco Harris, Pittsburgh, 4 games
- 297 Larry Csonka, Miami, 3 games
- 230 John Riggins, Washington, 2 games

Most Yards Gained, Game
- 204 Timmy Smith, Washington vs. Denver, 1988
- 191 Marcus Allen, L.A. Raiders vs. Washington, 1984
- 166 John Riggins, Washington vs. Miami, 1983

Longest Run From Scrimmage
- 74 Marcus Allen, L.A. Raiders vs. Washington, 1984 (TD)
- 58 Tom Matte, Baltimore vs. N.Y. Jets, 1969
  - Timmy Smith, Washington vs. Denver, 1988 (TD)
- 49 Larry Csonka, Miami vs. Washington, 1973

Average Gain
Highest Average Gain, Career (20 attempts)
- 9.6 Marcus Allen, L.A. Raiders, 1 game (20-191)
- 9.3 Timmy Smith, Washington, 1 game (22-204)
- 5.9 Thurman Thomas, Buffalo, 2 games (25-148)

Highest Average Gain, Game (10 attempts)
- 10.5 Tom Matte, Baltimore vs. N.Y. Jets, 1969 (11-116)
- 9.6 Marcus Allen, L.A. Raiders vs. Washington, 1984 (20-191)
- 9.3 Timmy Smith, Washington vs. Denver, 1988 (22-204)

Touchdowns
Most Touchdowns, Career
- 4 Franco Harris, Pittsburgh, 4 games
- 2 Elijah Pitts, Green Bay, 1 game
  - Jim Kiick, Miami, 3 games
  - Larry Csonka, Miami, 3 games
  - Pete Banaszak, Oakland, 2 games
  - Marcus Allen, L.A. Raiders, 1 game
  - John Riggins, Washington, 2 games

Jim McMahon, Chicago, 1 game
Timmy Smith, Washington, 1 game
Roger Craig, San Francisco, 3 games
Tom Rathman, San Francisco, 2 games
John Elway, Denver, 3 games
Ottis Anderson, N.Y. Giants, 2 games
Gerald Riggs, Washington, 1 game
Thurman Thomas, Buffalo, 2 games

Most Touchdowns, Game

2 Elijah Pitts, Green Bay vs. Kansas City, 1967
Larry Csonka, Miami vs. Minnesota, 1974
Pete Banaszak, Oakland vs. Minnesota, 1977
Franco Harris, Pittsburgh vs. Los Angeles, 1980
Marcus Allen, L.A. Raiders vs. Washington, 1984
Jim McMahon, Chicago vs. New England, 1986
Timmy Smith, Washington vs. Denver, 1988
Tom Rathman, San Francisco vs. Denver, 1990
Gerald Riggs, Washington vs. Buffalo, 1992

Passing
Attempts
Most Passes Attempted, Career

122 Joe Montana, San Francisco, 4 games
101 John Elway, Denver, 3 games
98 Roger Staubach, Dallas, 4 games

Most Passes Attempted, Game

58 Jim Kelly, Buffalo vs. Washington, 1992
50 Dan Marino, Miami vs. San Francisco, 1985
38 Ron Jaworski, Philadelphia vs. Oakland, 1981
John Elway, Denver vs. Washington, 1988

Completions
Most Passes Completed, Career

83 Joe Montana, San Francisco, 4 games
61 Roger Staubach, Dallas, 4 games
49 Terry Bradshaw, Pittsburgh, 4 games

Most Passes Completed, Game

29 Dan Marino, Miami vs. San Francisco, 1985
28 Jim Kelly, Buffalo vs. Washington, 1992
25 Ken Anderson, Cincinnati vs. San Francisco, 1982

Most Consecutive Completions, Game

13 Joe Montana, San Francisco vs. Denver, 1990
10 Phil Simms, N.Y. Giants vs. Denver, 1987
8 Len Dawson, Kansas City vs. Green Bay, 1967
Joe Theismann, Washington vs. Miami, 1983

Completion Percentage
Highest Completion Percentage, Career (40 attempts)

68.0 Joe Montana, San Francisco, 4 games (122-83)
63.6 Len Dawson, Kansas City, 2 games (44-28)
63.4 Bob Griese, Miami, 3 games (41-26)

Highest Completion Percentage, Game (20 attempts)

88.0 Phil Simms, N.Y. Giants vs. Denver, 1987 (25-22)
75.9 Joe Montana, San Francisco vs. Denver, 1990 (29-22)
73.5 Ken Anderson, Cincinnati vs. San Francisco, 1982 (34-25)

Yards Gained
Most Yards Gained, Career

1,142 Joe Montana, San Francisco, 4 games
932 Terry Bradshaw, Pittsburgh, 4 games
734 Roger Staubach, Dallas, 4 games

Most Yards Gained, Game

357 Joe Montana, San Francisco vs. Cincinnati, 1989
340 Doug Williams, Washington vs. Denver, 1988
331 Joe Montana, San Francisco vs. Miami, 1985

Longest Pass Completion

80 Jim Plunkett (to King), Oakland vs. Philadelphia, 1981 (TD)
Doug Williams (to Sanders), Washington vs. Denver, 1988 (TD)
76 David Woodley (to Cefalo), Miami vs. Washington, 1983 (TD)
75 Johnny Unitas (to Mackey), Baltimore vs. Dallas, 1971 (TD)
Terry Bradshaw (to Stallworth), Pittsburgh vs. Dallas, 1979 (TD)

Average Gain
Highest Average Gain, Career (40 attempts)

11.10 Terry Bradshaw, Pittsburgh, 4 games (84-932)
9.62 Bart Starr, Green Bay, 2 games (47-452)
9.41 Jim Plunkett, Oakland-L.A. Raiders, 2 games (46-433)

Highest Average Gain, Game (20 attempts)

14.71 Terry Bradshaw, Pittsburgh vs. Los Angeles, 1980 (21-309)
12.80 Jim McMahon, Chicago vs. New England, 1986 (20-256)
12.43 Jim Plunkett, Oakland vs. Philadelphia, 1981 (21-261)

Touchdowns
Most Touchdown Passes, Career

11 Joe Montana, San Francisco, 4 games
9 Terry Bradshaw, Pittsburgh, 4 games
8 Roger Staubach, Dallas, 4 games

Most Touchdown Passes, Game

5 Joe Montana, San Francisco vs. Denver, 1990
4 Terry Bradshaw, Pittsburgh vs. Dallas, 1979
Doug Williams, Washington vs. Denver, 1988
3 Roger Staubach, Dallas vs. Pittsburgh, 1979
Jim Plunkett, Oakland vs. Philadelphia, 1981
Joe Montana, San Francisco vs. Miami, 1985
Phil Simms, N.Y. Giants vs. Denver, 1987

Had Intercepted
Lowest Percentage, Passes Had Intercepted, Career (40 attempts)

0.00 Jim Plunkett, Oakland-L.A. Raiders, 2 games (46-0)
Joe Montana, San Francisco, 4 games (122-0)
2.13 Bart Starr, Green Bay, 2 games (47-1)
4.00 Dan Marino, Miami, 1 game (50-2)

Most Attempts, Without Interception, Game

36 Joe Montana, San Francisco vs. Cincinnati, 1989
35 Joe Montana, San Francisco vs. Miami, 1985
32 Jeff Hostetler, N.Y. Giants vs. Buffalo, 1991

Most Passes Had Intercepted, Career

7 Craig Morton, Dallas-Denver, 2 games
6 Fran Tarkenton, Minnesota, 3 games
John Elway, Denver, 3 games
4 Earl Morrall, Baltimore-Miami, 4 games
Roger Staubach, Dallas, 4 games
Terry Bradshaw, Pittsburgh, 4 games
Joe Theismann, Washington, 2 games
Jim Kelly, Buffalo, 2 games

Most Passes Had Intercepted, Game

4 Craig Morton, Denver vs. Dallas, 1978
Jim Kelly, Buffalo vs. Washington, 1992
3 By eight players

Pass Receiving
Receptions
Most Receptions, Career

20 Roger Craig, San Francisco, 3 games
18 Jerry Rice, San Francisco, 2 games
16 Lynn Swann, Pittsburgh, 4 games

Most Receptions, Game

11 Dan Ross, Cincinnati vs. San Francisco, 1982
Jerry Rice, San Francisco vs. Cincinnati, 1989
10 Tony Nathan, Miami vs. San Francisco, 1985
9 Ricky Sanders, Washington vs. Denver, 1988

Yards Gained
Most Yards Gained, Career

364 Lynn Swann, Pittsburgh, 4 games
363 Jerry Rice, San Francisco, 2 games
268 John Stallworth, Pittsburgh, 4 games

Most Yards Gained, Game

215 Jerry Rice, San Francisco vs. Cincinnati, 1989
193 Ricky Sanders, Washington vs. Denver, 1988
161 Lynn Swann, Pittsburgh vs. Dallas, 1976

Longest Reception

80 Kenny King (from Plunkett), Oakland vs. Philadelphia, 1981 (TD)
Ricky Sanders (from Williams), Washington vs. Denver, 1988 (TD)
76 Jimmy Cefalo (from Woodley), Miami vs. Washington, 1983 (TD)
75 John Mackey (from Unitas), Baltimore vs. Dallas, 1971 (TD)
John Stallworth (from Bradshaw), Pittsburgh vs. Dallas, 1979 (TD)

Average Gain
Highest Average Gain, Career (8 receptions)

24.4 John Stallworth, Pittsburgh, 4 games (11-268)
23.4 Ricky Sanders, Washington, 2 games (10-234)
22.8 Lynn Swann, Pittsburgh, 4 games (16-364)

Highest Average Gain, Game (3 receptions)

40.33 John Stallworth, Pittsburgh vs. Los Angeles, 1980 (3-121)
40.25 Lynn Swann, Pittsburgh vs. Dallas, 1979 (4-161)
38.33 John Stallworth, Pittsburgh vs. Dallas, 1979 (3-115)

Touchdowns
Most Touchdowns, Career

4 Jerry Rice, San Francisco, 2 games
3 John Stallworth, Pittsburgh, 4 games
Lynn Swann, Pittsburgh, 4 games
Cliff Branch, Oakland-L.A. Raiders, 3 games
2 Max McGee, Green Bay, 2 games
Bill Miller, Oakland, 1 game
Butch Johnson, Dallas, 2 games
Dan Ross, Cincinnati, 1 game
Roger Craig, San Francisco, 3 games
Ricky Sanders, Washington, 2 games
John Taylor, San Francisco, 2 games
Gary Clark, Washington, 2 games

Most Touchdowns, Game

3 Jerry Rice, San Francisco vs. Denver, 1990
2 Max McGee, Green Bay vs. Kansas City, 1967
Bill Miller, Oakland vs. Green Bay, 1968
John Stallworth, Pittsburgh vs. Dallas, 1979
Cliff Branch, Oakland vs. Philadelphia, 1981
Dan Ross, Cincinnati vs. San Francisco, 1982
Roger Craig, San Francisco vs. Miami, 1985
Ricky Sanders, Washington vs. Denver, 1988

Interceptions By
Most Interceptions By, Career

3 Chuck Howley, Dallas, 2 games
Rod Martin, Oakland-L.A. Raiders, 2 games
2 Randy Beverly, N.Y. Jets, 1 game
Jake Scott, Miami, 3 games
Mike Wagner, Pittsburgh, 3 games
Mel Blount, Pittsburgh, 4 games
Eric Wright, San Francisco, 4 games
Barry Wilburn, Washington, 1 game
Brad Edwards, Washington, 1 game

Most Interceptions By, Game

3 Rod Martin, Oakland vs. Philadelphia, 1981
2 Randy Beverly, N.Y. Jets vs. Baltimore, 1969
Chuck Howley, Dallas vs. Baltimore, 1971
Jake Scott, Miami vs. Washington, 1973
Barry Wilburn, Washington vs. Denver, 1988
Brad Edwards, Washington vs. Buffalo, 1992

Yards Gained
Most Yards Gained, Career

75 Willie Brown, Oakland, 2 games

63 Chuck Howley, Dallas, 2 games
Jake Scott, Miami, 3 games
60 Herb Adderley, Green Bay-Dallas, 4 games

Most Yards Gained, Game
75 Willie Brown, Oakland vs. Minnesota, 1977
63 Jake Scott, Miami vs. Washington, 1973
60 Herb Adderley, Green Bay vs. Oakland, 1968

Longest Return
75 Willie Brown, Oakland vs. Minnesota, 1977 (TD)
60 Herb Adderley, Green Bay vs. Oakland, 1968 (TD)
55 Jake Scott, Miami vs. Washington, 1973

Touchdowns
Most Touchdowns, Game
1 Herb Adderley, Green Bay vs. Oakland, 1968
Willie Brown, Oakland vs. Minnesota, 1977
Jack Squirek, L.A. Raiders vs. Washington, 1984
Reggie Phillips, Chicago vs. New England, 1986

Punting
Most Punts, Career
17 Mike Eischeid, Oakland-Minnesota, 3 games
15 Larry Seiple, Miami, 3 games
Mike Horan, Denver, 3 games
14 Ron Widby, Dallas, 2 games
Ray Guy, Oakland-L.A. Raiders, 3 games

Most Punts, Game
9 Ron Widby, Dallas vs. Baltimore, 1971
7 By eight players

Longest Punt
63 Lee Johnson, Cincinnati vs. San Francisco, 1989
62 Rich Camarillo, New England vs. Chicago, 1986
61 Jerrel Wilson, Kansas City vs. Green Bay, 1967

Average Yardage
Highest Average, Punting, Career (10 punts)
46.5 Jerrel Wilson, Kansas City, 2 games (11-511)
41.9 Ray Guy, Oakland-L.A. Raiders, 3 games (14-587)
41.3 Larry Seiple, Miami, 3 games (15-620)

Highest Average, Punting, Game (4 punts)
48.5 Jerrel Wilson, Kansas City vs. Minnesota, 1970 (4-194)
46.3 Jim Miller, San Francisco vs. Cincinnati, 1982 (4-185)
45.3 Jerrel Wilson, Kansas City vs. Green Bay, 1967 (7-317)

Punt Returns
Most Punt Returns, Career
6 Willie Wood, Green Bay, 2 games
Jake Scott, Miami, 3 games
Theo Bell, Pittsburgh, 2 games
Mike Nelms, Washington, 1 game
John Taylor, San Francisco, 2 games
5 Dana McLemore, San Francisco, 1 game
4 By seven players

Most Punt Returns, Game
6 Mike Nelms, Washington vs. Miami, 1983
5 Willie Wood, Green Bay vs. Oakland, 1968
Dana McLemore, San Francisco vs. Miami, 1985
4 By six players

Most Fair Catches, Game
3 Ron Gardin, Baltimore vs. Dallas, 1971
Golden Richards, Dallas vs. Pittsburgh, 1976
Greg Pruitt, L.A. Raiders vs. Washington, 1984
Al Edwards, Buffalo vs. N.Y. Giants, 1991
David Meggett, N.Y. Giants vs. Buffalo, 1991

Yards Gained
Most Yards Gained, Career
94 John Taylor, San Francisco, 2 games
52 Mike Nelms, Washington, 1 game
51 Dana McLemore, San Francisco, 1 game

Most Yards Gained, Game
56 John Taylor, San Francisco vs. Cincinnati, 1989
52 Mike Nelms, Washington vs. Miami, 1983
51 Dana McLemore, San Francisco vs. Miami, 1985

Longest Return
45 John Taylor, San Francisco vs. Cincinnati, 1989
34 Darrell Green, Washington vs. L.A. Raiders, 1984
31 Willie Wood, Green Bay vs. Oakland, 1968

Average Yardage
Highest Average, Career (4 returns)
15.7 John Taylor, San Francisco, 2 games (6-94)
10.8 Neal Colzie, Oakland, 1 game (4-43)
10.2 Dana McLemore, San Francisco, 1 game (5-51)

Highest Average, Game (3 returns)
18.7 John Taylor, San Francisco vs. Cincinnati, 1989 (3-56)
12.7 John Taylor, San Francisco vs. Denver, 1990 (3-38)
11.3 Lynn Swann, Pittsburgh vs. Minnesota, 1975 (3-34)

Touchdowns
Most Touchdowns, Game
None

Kickoff Returns
Most Kickoff Returns, Career
10 Ken Bell, Denver, 3 games
8 Larry Anderson, Pittsburgh, 2 games
Fulton Walker, Miami, 2 games
7 Preston Pearson, Baltimore-Pittsburgh-Dallas, 5 games
Stephen Starring, New England, 1 game

Most Kickoff Returns, Game
7 Stephen Starring, New England vs. Chicago, 1986

---

6 Darren Carrington, Denver vs. San Francisco, 1990
5 Larry Anderson, Pittsburgh vs. Los Angeles, 1980
Billy Campfield, Philadelphia vs. Oakland, 1981
David Verser, Cincinnati vs. San Francisco, 1982
Alvin Garrett, Washington vs. L.A. Raiders, 1984
Ken Bell, Denver vs. Washington, 1988

Yards Gained
Most Yards Gained, Career
283 Fulton Walker, Miami, 2 games
207 Larry Anderson, Pittsburgh, 2 games
177 Ken Bell, Denver, 3 games

Most Yards Gained, Game
190 Fulton Walker, Miami vs. Washington, 1983
162 Larry Anderson, Pittsburgh vs. Los Angeles, 1980
153 Stephen Starring, New England vs. Chicago, 1986

Longest Return
98 Fulton Walker, Miami vs. Washington, 1983 (TD)
93 Stanford Jennings, Cincinnati vs. San Francisco, 1989 (TD)
67 Rick Upchurch, Denver vs. Dallas, 1978

Average Yardage
Highest Average, Career (4 returns)
35.4 Fulton Walker, Miami, 2 games (8-283)
25.9 Larry Anderson, Pittsburgh, 2 games (8-207)
24.3 Darren Carrington, Denver, 1 game (6-146)

Highest Average, Game (3 returns)
47.5 Fulton Walker, Miami vs. Washington, 1983 (4-190)
32.4 Larry Anderson, Pittsburgh vs. Los Angeles, 1980 (5-162)
31.3 Rick Upchurch, Denver vs. Dallas, 1978 (3-94)

Touchdowns
Most Touchdowns, Game
1 Fulton Walker, Miami vs. Washington, 1983
Stanford Jennings, Cincinnati vs. San Francisco, 1989

Fumbles
Most Fumbles, Career
5 Roger Staubach, Dallas, 4 games
3 Franco Harris, Pittsburgh, 4 games
Terry Bradshaw, Pittsburgh, 4 games
John Elway, Denver, 3 games
Jim Kelly, Buffalo, 2 games
2 By six players

Most Fumbles, Game
3 Roger Staubach, Dallas vs. Pittsburgh, 1976
Jim Kelly, Buffalo vs. Washington, 1992
2 Franco Harris, Pittsburgh vs. Minnesota, 1975
Butch Johnson, Dallas vs. Denver, 1978
Terry Bradshaw, Pittsburgh vs. Dallas, 1979
Joe Montana, San Francisco vs. Cincinnati, 1989
John Elway, Denver vs. San Francisco, 1990

Recoveries
Most Fumbles Recovered, Career
2 Jake Scott, Miami, 3 games (1 own, 1 opp)
Fran Tarkenton, Minnesota, 3 games (2 own)
Franco Harris, Pittsburgh, 4 games (2 own)
Roger Staubach, Dallas, 4 games (2 own)
Bobby Walden, Pittsburgh, 2 games (2 own)
John Fitzgerald, Dallas, 4 games (2 own)
Randy Hughes, Dallas, 3 games (2 opp)
Butch Johnson, Dallas, 2 games (2 own)
Mike Singletary, Chicago, 1 game (2 opp)
John Elway, Denver, 3 games (2 own)

Most Fumbles Recovered, Game
2 Jake Scott, Miami vs. Minnesota, 1974 (1 own, 1 opp)
Roger Staubach, Dallas vs. Pittsburgh, 1976 (2 own)
Randy Hughes, Dallas vs. Denver, 1978 (2 opp)
Butch Johnson, Dallas vs. Denver, 1978 (2 own)
Mike Singletary, Chicago vs. New England, 1986 (2 opp)

Yards Gained
Most Yards Gained, Game
49 Mike Bass, Washington vs. Miami, 1973 (opp)
37 Mike Hegman, Dallas vs. Pittsburgh, 1979 (opp)
21 Randy Hughes, Dallas vs. Denver, 1978 (opp)

Longest Return
49 Mike Bass, Washington vs. Miami, 1973 (TD)
37 Mike Hegman, Dallas vs. Pittsburgh, 1979 (TD)
19 Randy Hughes, Dallas vs. Denver, 1978

Touchdowns
Most Touchdowns, Game
1 Mike Bass, Washington vs. Miami, 1973 (opp 49 yds)
Mike Hegman, Dallas vs. Pittsburgh, 1979 (opp 37 yds)

Combined Net Yards Gained
(Rushing, receiving, interception returns, punt returns, kickoff returns, and fumble returns)
Attempts
Most Attempts, Career
108 Franco Harris, Pittsburgh, 4 games
73 Roger Craig, San Francisco, 3 games
66 John Riggins, Washington, 2 games

Most Attempts, Game
39 John Riggins, Washington vs. Miami, 1983
35 Franco Harris, Pittsburgh vs. Minnesota, 1975
34 Matt Snell, N.Y. Jets vs. Baltimore, 1969

Yards Gained
Most Yards Gained, Career
468 Franco Harris, Pittsburgh, 4 games

410 Roger Craig, San Francisco, 3 games
391 Lynn Swann, Pittsburgh, 4 games
Most Yards Gained, Game
239 Ricky Sanders, Washington vs. Denver, 1988
220 Jerry Rice, San Francisco vs. Cincinnati, 1989
213 Timmy Smith, Washington vs. Denver, 1988

Sacks
Sacks have been compiled since 1983.
Most Sacks, Game
2 Dwaine Board, San Francisco vs. Miami, 1985
Dennis Owens, New England vs. Chicago, 1986
Otis Wilson, Chicago vs. New England, 1986
Leonard Marshall, N.Y. Giants vs. Denver, 1987
Alvin Walton, Washington vs. Denver, 1988
Charles Haley, San Francisco vs. Cincinnati, 1989
Danny Stubbs, San Francisco, 1990

Team Records

Games, Victories, Defeats
Most Games
5 Dallas, 1971-72, 1976, 1978-79
Miami, 1972-74, 1983, 1985
Washington, 1973, 1983-84, 1988, 1992
4 Minnesota, 1970, 1974-75, 1977
Pittsburgh, 1975-76, 1979-80
Oakland/L.A. Raiders, 1968, 1977, 1981, 1984
Denver, 1978, 1987-88, 1990
San Francisco, 1982, 1985, 1989-90
Most Consecutive Games
3 Miami, 1972-74
2 Green Bay, 1967-68
Dallas, 1971-72
Minnesota, 1974-75
Pittsburgh, 1975-76, 1979-80
Washington, 1983-84
Denver, 1987-88
San Francisco 1989-90
Buffalo 1991-92
Most Games Won
4 Pittsburgh, 1975-76, 1979-80
San Francisco, 1982, 1985, 1989-90
3 Oakland/L.A. Raiders, 1977, 1981, 1984
Washington, 1983, 1988, 1992
2 Green Bay, 1967-68
Miami, 1973-74
Dallas, 1972, 1978
N.Y. Giants, 1987, 1991
Most Consecutive Games Won
2 Green Bay, 1967-68
Miami, 1973-74
Pittsburgh, 1975-76, 1979-80
San Francisco, 1989-90
Most Games Lost
4 Minnesota, 1970, 1974-75, 1977
Denver, 1978, 1987-88, 1990
3 Dallas, 1971, 1976, 1979
Miami, 1972, 1983, 1985
2 Washington, 1973, 1984
Cincinnati, 1982, 1989
Buffalo, 1991-92
Most Consecutive Games Lost
2 Minnesota, 1974-75
Denver, 1987-88
Buffalo, 1991-92

Scoring
Most Points, Game
55 San Francisco vs. Denver, 1990
46 Chicago vs. New England, 1986
42 Washington vs. Denver, 1988
Fewest Points, Game
3 Miami vs. Dallas, 1972
6 Minnesota vs. Pittsburgh, 1975
7 By four teams
Most Points, Both Teams, Game
66 Pittsburgh (35) vs. Dallas (31), 1979
65 San Francisco (55) vs. Denver (10), 1990
61 Washington (37) vs. Buffalo (24), 1992
Fewest Points, Both Teams, Game
21 Washington (7) vs. Miami (14), 1973
22 Minnesota (6) vs. Pittsburgh (16), 1975
23 Baltimore (7) vs. N.Y. Jets (16), 1969
Largest Margin of Victory, Game
45 San Francisco vs. Denver, 1990 (55-10)
36 Chicago vs. New England, 1986 (46-10)
32 Washington vs. Denver, 1988 (42-10)
Most Points, Each Half
1st: 35 Washington vs. Denver, 1988
2nd: 30 N.Y. Giants vs. Denver, 1987
Most Points, Each Quarter
1st: 14 Miami vs. Minnesota, 1974
Oakland vs. Philadelphia, 1981
2nd: 35 Washington vs. Denver, 1988
3rd: 21 Chicago vs. New England, 1986
4th: 14 Pittsburgh vs. Dallas, 1976; vs. Dallas, 1979; vs. Los Angeles, 1980
Dallas vs. Pittsburgh, 1979
Cincinnati vs. San Francisco, 1982
Washington vs. Miami, 1983
San Francisco vs. Cincinnati, 1989; vs. Denver, 1990
Buffalo vs. Washington, 1992

Most Points, Both Teams, Each Half
1st: 45 Washington (35) vs. Denver (10), 1988
2nd: 44 Buffalo (24) vs. Washington (20), 1992
Fewest Points, Both Teams, Each Half
1st: 2 Minnesota (0) vs. Pittsburgh (2), 1975
2nd: 7 Miami (0) vs. Washington (7), 1973
Denver (0) vs. Washington (7), 1988
Most Points, Both Teams, Each Quarter
1st: 17 Miami (10) vs. San Francisco (7), 1985
Denver (10) vs. N.Y. Giants (7), 1987
2nd: 35 Washington (35) vs. Denver (0), 1988
3rd: 24 Washington (14) vs. Buffalo (10), 1992
4th: 28 Dallas (14) vs. Pittsburgh (14), 1979

Touchdowns
Most Touchdowns, Game
8 San Francisco vs. Denver, 1990
6 Washington vs. Denver, 1988
5 Green Bay vs. Kansas City, 1967
Pittsburgh vs. Dallas, 1979
L.A. Raiders vs. Washington, 1984
San Francisco vs. Miami, 1985
Chicago vs. New England, 1986
N.Y. Giants vs. Denver, 1987
Fewest Touchdowns, Game
0 Miami vs. Dallas, 1972
1 By 16 teams
Most Touchdowns, Both Teams, Game
9 Pittsburgh (5) vs. Dallas (4), 1979
San Francisco (8) vs. Denver (1), 1990
7 N.Y. Giants (5) vs. Denver (2), 1987
Washington (6) vs. Denver (1), 1988
Washington (4) vs. Buffalo (3), 1992
6 Green Bay (5) vs. Kansas City (1), 1967
Oakland (4) vs. Minnesota (2), 1977
Pittsburgh (4) vs. Los Angeles (2), 1980
L.A. Raiders (5) vs. Washington (1), 1984
San Francisco (5) vs. Miami (1), 1985
Chicago (5) vs. New England (1), 1986
Fewest Touchdowns, Both Teams, Game
2 Baltimore (1) vs. N.Y. Jets (1), 1969
3 In six games

Points After Touchdown
Most Points After Touchdown, Game
7 San Francisco vs. Denver, 1990
6 Washington vs. Denver, 1988
5 Green Bay vs. Kansas City, 1967
Pittsburgh vs. Dallas, 1979
L.A. Raiders vs. Washington, 1984
San Francisco vs. Miami, 1985
Chicago vs. New England, 1986
Most Points After Touchdown, Both Teams, Game
9 Pittsburgh (5) vs. Dallas (4), 1979
8 San Francisco (7) vs. Denver (1), 1990
7 Washington (6) vs. Denver (1), 1988
Washington (4) vs. Buffalo (3), 1992
Fewest Points After Touchdown, Both Teams, Game
2 Baltimore (1) vs. N.Y. Jets (1), 1969
Baltimore (1) vs. Dallas (1), 1971
Minnesota (0) vs. Pittsburgh (2), 1975

Field Goals
Most Field Goals Attempted, Game
5 N.Y. Jets vs. Baltimore, 1969
Dallas vs. Denver, 1978
4 Green Bay vs. Oakland, 1968
Pittsburgh vs. Dallas, 1976
San Francisco vs. Cincinnati, 1982; 1989
Denver vs. N.Y. Giants, 1987
Most Field Goals Attempted, Both Teams, Game
7 N.Y. Jets (5) vs. Baltimore (2), 1969
San Francisco (4) vs. Cincinnati (3), 1989
6 Dallas (5) vs. Denver (1), 1978
5 Green Bay (4) vs. Oakland (1), 1968
Pittsburgh (4) vs. Dallas (1), 1976
Oakland (3) vs. Philadelphia (2), 1981
Denver (4) vs. N.Y. Giants (1), 1987
Fewest Field Goals Attempted, Both Teams, Game
1 Minnesota (0) vs. Miami (1), 1974
San Francisco (0) vs. Denver (1), 1990
2 Green Bay (0) vs. Kansas City (2), 1967
Miami (1) vs. Washington (1), 1973
Dallas (1) vs. Pittsburgh (1), 1979
Most Field Goals, Game
4 Green Bay vs. Oakland, 1968
San Francisco vs. Cincinnati, 1982
3 N.Y. Jets vs. Baltimore, 1969
Kansas City vs. Minnesota, 1970
Miami vs. San Francisco, 1985
Chicago vs. New England, 1986
Cincinnati vs. San Francisco, 1989
Washington vs. Buffalo, 1992
Most Field Goals, Both Teams, Game
5 Cincinnati (3) vs. San Francisco (2), 1989
4 Green Bay (4) vs. Oakland (0), 1968
San Francisco (4) vs. Cincinnati (0), 1982
Miami (3) vs. San Francisco (1), 1985
Chicago (3) vs. New England (1), 1986
Buffalo (2) vs. N.Y. Giants (2), 1991
Washington (3) vs. Buffalo (1), 1992
3 In eight games

Fewest Field Goals, Both Teams, Game
0 Miami vs. Washington, 1973
  Pittsburgh vs. Minnesota, 1975
1 Green Bay (0) vs. Kansas City (1), 1967
  Minnesota (0) vs. Miami (1), 1974
  Pittsburgh (0) vs. Dallas (1), 1979
  Washington (0) vs. Denver (1), 1988
  San Francisco (0) vs. Denver (1), 1990

Safeties
Most Safeties, Game
1 Pittsburgh vs. Minnesota, 1975; vs. Dallas, 1976
  Chicago vs. New England, 1986
  N.Y. Giants vs. Denver, 1987
  Buffalo vs. N.Y. Giants, 1991

First Downs
Most First Downs, Game
31 San Francisco vs. Miami, 1985
28 San Francisco vs. Denver, 1990
25 Washington vs. Denver, 1988
  Buffalo vs. Washington, 1992
Fewest First Downs, Game
9 Minnesota vs. Pittsburgh, 1975
  Miami vs. Washington, 1983
10 Dallas vs. Baltimore, 1971
  Miami vs. Dallas, 1972
11 Denver vs. Dallas, 1978
Most First Downs, Both Teams, Game
50 San Francisco (31) vs. Miami (19), 1985
49 Buffalo (25) vs. Washington (24), 1992
47 N.Y. Giants (24) vs. Denver (23), 1987
Fewest First Downs, Both Teams, Game
24 Dallas (10) vs. Baltimore (14), 1971
26 Minnesota (9) vs. Pittsburgh (17), 1975
27 Pittsburgh (13) vs. Dallas (14), 1976

Rushing
Most First Downs, Rushing, Game
16 San Francisco vs. Miami, 1985
15 Dallas vs. Miami, 1972
14 Washington vs. Miami, 1983
  San Francisco vs. Denver, 1990
Fewest First Downs, Rushing, Game
1 New England vs. Chicago, 1986
2 Minnesota vs. Kansas City, 1970; vs. Pittsburgh, 1975; vs. Oakland, 1977
  Pittsburgh vs. Dallas, 1979
  Miami vs. San Francisco, 1985
3 Miami vs. Dallas, 1972
  Philadelphia vs. Oakland, 1981
Most First Downs, Rushing, Both Teams, Game
21 Washington (14) vs. Miami (7), 1983
19 Washington (13) vs. Denver (6), 1988
  San Francisco (14) vs. Denver (5), 1990
18 Dallas (15) vs. Miami (3), 1972
  Miami (13) vs. Minnesota (5), 1974
  San Francisco (16) vs. Miami (2), 1985
  N.Y. Giants (10) vs. Buffalo (8), 1991
Fewest First Downs, Rushing, Both Teams, Game
8 Baltimore (4) vs. Dallas (4), 1971
  Pittsburgh (2) vs. Dallas (6), 1979
9 Philadelphia (3) vs. Oakland (6), 1981
10 Minnesota (2) vs. Kansas City (8), 1970

Passing
Most First Downs, Passing, Game
18 Buffalo vs. Washington, 1992
17 Miami vs. San Francisco, 1985
16 Denver vs. N.Y. Giants, 1987
  San Francisco vs. Cincinnati, 1989
Fewest First Downs, Passing, Game
1 Denver vs. Dallas, 1978
2 Miami vs. Washington, 1983
4 Miami vs. Minnesota, 1974
Most First Downs, Passing, Both Teams, Game
32 Miami (17) vs. San Francisco (15), 1985
30 Buffalo (18) vs. Washington (12), 1992
29 Denver (16) vs. N.Y. Giants (13), 1987
Fewest First Downs, Passing, Both Teams, Game
9 Denver (1) vs. Dallas (8), 1978
10 Minnesota (5) vs. Pittsburgh (5), 1975
11 Dallas (5) vs. Baltimore (6), 1971
  Miami (2) vs. Washington (9), 1983

Penalty
Most First Downs, Penalty, Game
4 Baltimore vs. Dallas, 1971
  Miami vs. Minnesota, 1974
  Cincinnati vs. San Francisco, 1982
3 Kansas City vs. Minnesota, 1970
  Minnesota vs. Oakland, 1977
  Buffalo vs. Washington, 1992
Most First Downs, Penalty, Both Teams, Game
6 Cincinnati (4) vs. San Francisco (2), 1982
5 Baltimore (4) vs. Dallas (1), 1971
  Miami (4) vs. Minnesota (1), 1974
  Buffalo (3) vs. Washington (2), 1992
4 Kansas City (3) vs. Minnesota (1), 1970
Fewest First Downs, Penalty, Both Teams, Game
0 Dallas vs. Miami, 1972
  Miami vs. Washington, 1973
  Dallas vs. Pittsburgh, 1976
  Miami vs. San Francisco, 1985

---

1 Green Bay (0) vs. Kansas City (1), 1967
  Miami (0) vs. Washington (1), 1983
  Cincinnati (0) vs. San Francisco (1), 1989
  San Francisco (0) vs. Denver (1), 1990

Net Yards Gained Rushing and Passing
Most Yards Gained, Game
602 Washington vs. Denver, 1988
537 San Francisco vs. Miami, 1985
461 San Francisco vs. Denver, 1990
Fewest Yards Gained, Game
119 Minnesota vs. Pittsburgh, 1975
123 New England vs. Chicago, 1986
156 Denver vs. Dallas, 1978
Most Yards Gained, Both Teams, Game
929 Washington (602) vs. Denver (327), 1988
851 San Francisco (537) vs. Miami (314), 1985
782 Oakland (429) vs. Minnesota (353), 1977
Fewest Yards Gained, Both Teams, Game
452 Minnesota (119) vs. Pittsburgh (333), 1975
481 Washington (228) vs. Miami (253), 1973
  Denver (156) vs. Dallas (325), 1978
497 Minnesota (238) vs. Miami (259), 1974

Rushing
Attempts
Most Attempts, Game
57 Pittsburgh vs. Minnesota, 1975
53 Miami vs. Minnesota, 1974
52 Oakland vs. Minnesota, 1977
  Washington vs. Miami, 1983
Fewest Attempts, Game
9 Miami vs. San Francisco, 1985
11 New England vs. Chicago, 1986
17 Denver vs. Washington, 1988; vs. San Francisco, 1990
Most Attempts, Both Teams, Game
81 Washington (52) vs. Miami (29), 1983
78 Pittsburgh (57) vs. Minnesota (21), 1975
  Oakland (52) vs. Minnesota (26), 1977
77 Miami (53) vs. Minnesota (24), 1974
  Pittsburgh (46) vs. Dallas (31), 1976
Fewest Attempts, Both Teams, Game
49 Miami (9) vs. San Francisco (40), 1985
53 Kansas City (19) vs. Green Bay (34), 1967
55 San Francisco (27) vs. Cincinnati (28), 1989

Yards Gained
Most Yards Gained, Game
280 Washington vs. Denver, 1988
276 Washington vs. Miami, 1983
266 Oakland vs. Minnesota, 1977
Fewest Yards Gained, Game
7 New England vs. Chicago, 1986
17 Minnesota vs. Pittsburgh, 1975
25 Miami vs. San Francisco, 1985
Most Yards Gained, Both Teams, Game
377 Washington (280) vs. Denver (97), 1988
372 Washington (276) vs. Miami (96), 1983
338 N.Y. Giants (172) vs. Buffalo (166), 1991
Fewest Yards Gained, Both Teams, Game
168 Buffalo (43) vs. Washington (125), 1992
171 Baltimore (69) vs. Dallas (102), 1971
174 New England (7) vs. Chicago (167), 1986

Average Gain
Highest Average Gain, Game
7.00 L.A. Raiders vs. Washington, 1984 (33-231)
  Washington vs. Denver, 1988 (40-280)
6.64 Buffalo vs. N.Y. Giants, 1991 (25-166)
6.22 Baltimore vs. N.Y. Jets, 1969 (23-143)
Lowest Average Gain, Game
0.64 New England vs. Chicago, 1986 (11-7)
0.81 Minnesota vs. Pittsburgh, 1975 (21-17)
2.23 Baltimore vs. Dallas, 1971 (31-69)

Touchdowns
Most Touchdowns, Game
4 Chicago vs. New England, 1986
3 Green Bay vs. Kansas City, 1967
  Miami vs. Minnesota, 1974
  San Francisco vs. Denver, 1990
2 Oakland vs. Minnesota, 1977
  Pittsburgh vs. Los Angeles, 1980
  L.A. Raiders vs. Washington, 1984
  San Francisco vs. Miami, 1985
  N.Y. Giants vs. Denver, 1987
  Washington vs. Denver, 1988; vs. Buffalo, 1992
  Buffalo vs. N.Y. Giants, 1991
Fewest Touchdowns, Game
0 By 17 teams
Most Touchdowns, Both Teams, Game
4 Miami (3) vs. Minnesota (1), 1974
  Chicago (4) vs. New England (0), 1986
  San Francisco (3) vs. Denver (1), 1990
3 Green Bay (3) vs. Kansas City (0), 1967
  Pittsburgh (2) vs. Los Angeles (1), 1980
  L.A. Raiders (2) vs. Washington (1), 1984
  N.Y. Giants (2) vs. Denver (1), 1987
  Buffalo (2) vs. N.Y. Giants (1), 1991
  Washington (2) vs. Buffalo (1), 1992
Fewest Touchdowns, Both Teams, Game
0 Pittsburgh vs. Dallas, 1976
  Oakland vs. Philadelphia, 1981

Cincinnati vs. San Francisco, 1989
1   In seven games

Passing
Attempts
Most Passes Attempted, Game
59   Buffalo vs. Washington, 1992
50   Miami vs. San Francisco, 1985
44   Minnesota vs. Oakland, 1977
Fewest Passes Attempted, Game
7   Miami vs. Minnesota, 1974
11   Miami vs. Washington, 1973
14   Pittsburgh vs. Minnesota, 1975
Most Passes Attempted, Both Teams, Game
92   Buffalo (59) vs. Washington (33), 1992
85   Miami (50) vs. San Francisco (35), 1985
70   Baltimore (41) vs. N.Y. Jets (29), 1969
Fewest Passes Attempted, Both Teams, Game
35   Miami (7) vs. Minnesota (28), 1974
39   Miami (11) vs. Washington (28), 1973
40   Pittsburgh (14) vs. Minnesota (26), 1975
Miami (17) vs. Washington (23), 1983

Completions
Most Passes Completed, Game
29   Miami vs. San Francisco, 1985
Buffalo vs. Washington, 1992
26   Denver vs. N.Y. Giants, 1987
25   Cincinnati vs. San Francisco, 1982
Fewest Passes Completed, Game
4   Miami vs. Washington, 1983
6   Miami vs. Minnesota, 1974
8   Miami vs. Washington, 1973
Denver vs. Dallas, 1978
Most Passes Completed, Both Teams, Game
53   Miami (29) vs. San Francisco (24), 1985
48   Denver (26) vs. N.Y. Giants (22), 1987
47   Buffalo (29) vs. Washington (18), 1992
Fewest Passes Completed, Both Teams, Game
19   Miami (4) vs. Washington (15), 1983
20   Pittsburgh (9) vs. Minnesota (11), 1975
22   Miami (8) vs. Washington (14), 1973

Completion Percentage
Highest Completion Percentage, Game (20 attempts)
88.0   N.Y. Giants vs. Denver, 1987 (25-22)
75.0   San Francisco vs. Denver, 1990 (32-24)
73.5   Cincinnati vs. San Francisco, 1982 (34-25)
Lowest Completion Percentage, Game (20 attempts)
32.0   Denver vs. Dallas, 1978 (25-8)
37.9   Denver vs. San Francisco, 1990 (29-11)
38.5   Denver vs. Washington, 1988 (39-15)

Yards Gained
Most Yards Gained, Game
341   San Francisco vs. Cincinnati, 1989
326   San Francisco vs. Miami, 1985
322   Washington vs. Denver, 1988
Fewest Yards Gained, Game
35   Denver vs. Dallas, 1978
63   Miami vs. Minnesota, 1974
69   Miami vs. Washington, 1973
Most Yards Gained, Both Teams, Game
615   San Francisco (326) vs. Miami (289), 1985
583   Denver (320) vs. N.Y. Giants (263), 1987
552   Washington (322) vs. Denver (230), 1988
Fewest Yards Gained, Both Teams, Game
156   Miami (69) vs. Washington (87), 1973
186   Pittsburgh (84) vs. Minnesota (102), 1975
205   Dallas (100) vs. Miami (105), 1972

Times Sacked
Most Times Sacked, Game
7   Dallas vs. Pittsburgh, 1976
New England vs. Chicago, 1986
6   Kansas City vs. Green Bay, 1967
Washington vs. L.A. Raiders, 1984
Denver vs. San Francisco, 1990
5   Dallas vs. Denver, 1978; vs. Pittsburgh, 1979
Cincinnati vs. San Francisco, 1982; 1989
Denver vs. Washington, 1988
Buffalo vs. Washington, 1992
Fewest Times Sacked, Game
0   Baltimore vs. N.Y. Jets, 1969; vs. Dallas, 1971
Minnesota vs. Pittsburgh, 1975
Pittsburgh vs. Los Angeles, 1980
Philadelphia vs. Oakland, 1981
Washington vs. Buffalo, 1992
1   By 10 teams
Most Times Sacked, Both Teams, Game
10   New England (7) vs. Chicago (3), 1986
9   Kansas City (6) vs. Green Bay (3), 1967
Dallas (7) vs. Pittsburgh (2), 1976
Dallas (5) vs. Denver (4), 1978
Dallas (5) vs. Pittsburgh (4), 1979
Cincinnati (5) vs. San Francisco (4), 1989
8   Washington (6) vs. L.A. Raiders (2), 1984
Fewest Times Sacked, Both Teams, Game
1   Philadelphia (0) vs. Oakland (1), 1981
2   Baltimore (0) vs. N.Y. Jets (2), 1969
Baltimore (0) vs. Dallas (2), 1971
Minnesota (0) vs. Pittsburgh (2), 1975
3   In four games

Touchdowns
Most Touchdowns, Game
5   San Francisco vs. Denver, 1990
4   Pittsburgh vs. Dallas, 1979
Washington vs. Denver, 1988
3   Dallas vs. Pittsburgh, 1979
Oakland vs. Philadelphia, 1981
San Francisco vs. Miami, 1985
N.Y. Giants vs. Denver, 1987
Fewest Touchdowns, Game
0   By 14 teams
Most Touchdowns, Both Teams, Game
7   Pittsburgh (4) vs. Dallas (3), 1979
5   Washington (4) vs. Denver (1), 1988
San Francisco (5) vs. Denver (0), 1990
4   Dallas (2) vs. Pittsburgh (2), 1976
Oakland (3) vs. Philadelphia (1), 1981
San Francisco (3) vs. Miami (1), 1985
N.Y. Giants (3) vs. Denver (1), 1987
Washington (2) vs. Buffalo (2), 1992
Fewest Touchdowns, Both Teams, Game
0   N.Y. Jets vs. Baltimore, 1969
Miami vs. Minnesota, 1974
1   In six games

Interceptions By
Most Interceptions By, Game
4   N.Y. Jets vs. Baltimore, 1969
Dallas vs. Denver, 1978
Washington vs. Buffalo, 1992
3   By nine teams
Most Interceptions By, Both Teams, Game
6   Baltimore (3) vs. Dallas (3), 1971
5   Washington (4) vs. Buffalo (1), 1992
4   In six games
Fewest Interceptions By, Both Teams, Game
0   Buffalo vs. N.Y. Giants, 1991
1   Oakland (0) vs. Green Bay (1), 1968
Miami (0) vs. Dallas (1), 1972
Minnesota (0) vs. Miami (1), 1974
N.Y. Giants (0) vs. Denver (1), 1987
San Francisco (1) vs. Cincinnati (0), 1989

Yards Gained
Most Yards Gained, Game
95   Miami vs. Washington, 1973
91   Oakland vs. Minnesota, 1977
89   Pittsburgh vs. Dallas, 1976
Most Yards Gained, Both Teams, Game
95   Miami (95) vs. Washington (0), 1973
91   Oakland (91) vs. Minnesota (0), 1977
89   Pittsburgh (89) vs. Dallas (0), 1976

Touchdowns
Most Touchdowns, Game
1   Green Bay vs. Oakland, 1968
Oakland vs. Minnesota, 1977
L.A. Raiders vs. Washington, 1984
Chicago vs. New England, 1986

Punting
Most Punts, Game
9   Dallas vs. Baltimore, 1971
8   Washington vs. L.A. Raiders, 1984
7   By seven teams
Fewest Punts, Game
2   Pittsburgh vs. Los Angeles, 1980
Denver vs. N.Y. Giants, 1987
3   By nine teams
Most Punts, Both Teams, Game
15   Washington (8) vs. L.A. Raiders (7), 1984
13   Dallas (9) vs. Baltimore (4), 1971
Pittsburgh (7) vs. Minnesota (6), 1975
12   In three games
Fewest Punts, Both Teams, Game
5   Denver (2) vs. N.Y. Giants (3), 1987
6   Oakland (3) vs. Philadelphia (3), 1981
7   In four games

Average Yardage
Highest Average, Game (4 punts)
48.50   Kansas City vs. Minnesota, 1970 (4-194)
46.25   San Francisco vs. Cincinnati, 1982 (4-185)
45.29   Kansas City vs. Green Bay, 1967 (7-317)
Lowest Average, Game (4 punts)
31.20   Washington vs. Miami, 1973 (5-156)
32.38   Washington vs. L.A. Raiders, 1984 (8-259)
32.40   Oakland vs. Minnesota, 1977 (5-162)

Punt Returns
Most Punt Returns, Game
6   Washington vs. Miami, 1983
5   By five teams
Fewest Punt Returns, Game
0   Minnesota vs. Miami, 1974
Buffalo vs. N.Y. Giants, 1991
Washington vs. Buffalo, 1992
1   By 11 teams
Most Punt Returns, Both Teams, Game
9   Pittsburgh (5) vs. Minnesota (4), 1975
8   Green Bay (5) vs. Oakland (3), 1968

Baltimore (5) vs. Dallas (3), 1971
Washington (6) vs. Miami (2), 1983
7   Green Bay (4) vs. Kansas City (3), 1967
Oakland (4) vs. Minnesota (3), 1977
San Francisco (5) vs. Miami (2), 1985

Fewest Punt Returns, Both Teams, Game
2   Dallas (1) vs. Miami (1), 1972
Denver (1) vs. N.Y. Giants (1), 1987
Buffalo (0) vs. N.Y. Giants (2), 1991
3   Kansas City (1) vs. Minnesota (2), 1970
Minnesota (0) vs. Miami (3), 1974
Washington (1) vs. Denver (2), 1988
Washington (0) vs. Buffalo (3), 1992
4   L.A. Raiders (2) vs. Washington (2), 1984
Chicago (2) vs. New England (2), 1986

Yards Gained
Most Yards Gained, Game
56   San Francisco vs. Cincinnati, 1989
52   Washington vs. Miami, 1983
51   San Francisco vs. Miami, 1985

Fewest Yards Gained, Game
−1   Dallas vs. Miami, 1972
0   By seven teams

Most Yards Gained, Both Teams, Game
74   Washington (52) vs. Miami (22), 1983
66   San Francisco (51) vs. Miami (15), 1985
61   San Francisco (56) vs. Cincinnati (5), 1989

Fewest Yards Gained, Both Teams, Game
9   Washington (0) vs. Bufffalo (9), 1992
13   Miami (4) vs. Washington (9), 1973
18   Kansas City (0) vs. Minnesota (18), 1970
Washington (0) vs. Denver (18), 1988

Average Return
Highest Average, Game (3 returns)
18.7   San Francisco vs. Cincinnati, 1989 (3-56)
12.7   San Francisco vs. Denver, 1990 (3-38)
10.8   Oakland vs. Minnesota, 1977 (4-43)

Touchdowns
Most Touchdowns, Game
None

Kickoff Returns
Most Kickoff Returns, Game
9   Denver vs. San Francisco, 1990
7   Oakland vs. Green Bay, 1968
Minnesota vs. Oakland, 1977
Cincinnati vs. San Francisco, 1982
Washington vs. L.A. Raiders, 1984
Miami vs. San Francisco, 1985
New England vs. Chicago, 1986
6   By seven teams

Fewest Kickoff Returns, Game
1   N.Y. Jets vs. Baltimore, 1969
L.A. Raiders vs. Washington, 1984
Washington vs. Buffalo, 1992
2   By six teams

Most Kickoff Returns, Both Teams, Game
12   Denver (9) vs. San Francisco (3), 1990
11   Los Angeles (6) vs. Pittsburgh (5), 1980
Miami (7) vs. San Francisco (4), 1985
New England (7) vs. Chicago (4), 1986
10   Oakland (7) vs. Green Bay (3), 1968

Fewest Kickoff Returns, Both Teams, Game
5   N.Y. Jets (1) vs. Baltimore (4), 1969
Miami (2) vs. Washington (3), 1973
Washington (1) vs. Buffalo (4), 1992
6   In three games

Yards Gained
Most Yards Gained, Game
222   Miami vs. Washington, 1983
196   Denver vs. San Francisco, 1990
173   Denver vs. Dallas, 1978

Fewest Yards Gained, Game
16   Washington vs. Buffalo, 1992
17   L.A. Raiders vs. Washington, 1984
25   N.Y. Jets vs. Baltimore, 1969

Most Yards Gained, Both Teams, Game
279   Miami (222) vs. Washington (57), 1983
245   Denver (196) vs. San Francisco (49), 1990
231   Pittsburgh (162) vs. Los Angeles (79), 1980

Fewest Yards Gained, Both Teams, Game
78   Miami (33) vs. Washington (45), 1973
82   Pittsburgh (32) vs. Minnesota (50), 1975
92   San Francisco (40) vs. Cincinnati (52), 1982

Average Gain
Highest Average, Game (3 returns)
44.0   Cincinnati vs. San Francisco, 1989 (3-132)
37.0   Miami vs. Washington, 1983 (6-222)
32.4   Pittsburgh vs. Los Angeles, 1980 (5-162)

Touchdowns
Most Touchdowns, Game
1   Miami vs. Washington, 1983
Cincinnati vs. San Francisco, 1989

Penalties
Most Penalties, Game
12   Dallas vs. Denver, 1978

10   Dallas vs. Baltimore, 1971
9   Dallas vs. Pittsburgh, 1979

Fewest Penalties, Game
0   Miami vs. Dallas, 1972
Pittsburgh vs. Dallas, 1976
Denver vs. San Francisco, 1990
1   Green Bay vs. Oakland, 1968
Miami vs. Minnesota, 1974; vs. San Francisco, 1985
2   By four teams

Most Penalties, Both Teams, Game
20   Dallas (12) vs. Denver (8), 1978
16   Cincinnati (8) vs. San Francisco (8), 1982
14   Dallas (10) vs. Baltimore (4), 1971
Dallas (9) vs. Pittsburgh (5), 1979

Fewest Penalties, Both Teams, Game
2   Pittsburgh (0) vs. Dallas (2), 1976
3   Miami (0) vs. Dallas (3), 1972
Miami (1) vs. San Francisco (2), 1985
4   Denver (0) vs. San Francisco (4), 1990

Yards Penalized
Most Yards Penalized, Game
133   Dallas vs. Baltimore, 1971
122   Pittsburgh vs. Minnesota, 1975
94   Dallas vs. Denver, 1978

Fewest Yards Penalized, Game
0   Miami vs. Dallas, 1972
Pittsburgh vs. Dallas, 1976
Denver vs. San Francisco, 1990
4   Miami vs. Minnesota, 1974
10   Miami vs. San Francisco, 1985
San Francisco vs. Miami, 1985

Most Yards Penalized, Both Teams, Game
164   Dallas (133) vs. Baltimore (31), 1971
154   Dallas (94) vs. Denver (60), 1978
140   Pittsburgh (122) vs. Minnesota (18), 1975

Fewest Yards Penalized, Both Teams, Game
15   Miami (0) vs. Dallas (15), 1972
20   Pittsburgh (0) vs. Dallas (20), 1976
Miami (10) vs. San Francisco (10), 1985
38   Denver (0) vs. San Francisco (38), 1990

Fumbles
Most Fumbles, Game
6   Dallas vs. Denver, 1978
Buffalo vs. Washington, 1992
5   Baltimore vs. Dallas, 1971
4   By five teams

Fewest Fumbles, Game
0   By 10 teams

Most Fumbles, Both Teams, Game
10   Dallas (6) vs. Denver (4), 1978
8   Dallas (4) vs. Pittsburgh (4), 1976
7   Pittsburgh (4) vs. Minnesota (3), 1975
New England (4) vs. Chicago (3), 1986
Buffalo (6) vs. Washington (1), 1992

Fewest Fumbles, Both Teams, Game
0   Los Angeles vs. Pittsburgh, 1980
1   Oakland (0) vs. Minnesota (1), 1977
Oakland (0) vs. Philadelphia (1), 1981
Denver (0) vs. Washington (1), 1988
N.Y. Giants (0) vs. Buffalo (1), 1991
2   In four games

Most Fumbles Lost, Game
4   Baltimore vs. Dallas, 1971
Denver vs. Dallas, 1978
New England vs. Chicago, 1986
2   In many games

Most Fumbles Lost, Both Teams, Game
6   Denver (4) vs. Dallas (2), 1978
New England (4) vs. Chicago (2), 1986
5   Baltimore (4) vs. Dallas (1), 1971
4   Minnesota (2) vs. Pittsburgh (2), 1975
Dallas (2) vs. Pittsburgh (2), 1979

Fewest Fumbles Lost, Both Teams, Game
0   Green Bay vs. Kansas City, 1967
Dallas vs. Pittsburgh, 1976
Los Angeles vs. Pittsburgh, 1980
Denver vs. N.Y. Giants, 1987
Denver vs. Washington, 1988
Buffalo vs. N.Y. Giants, 1991

Most Fumbles Recovered, Game
8   Dallas vs. Denver, 1978 (4 own, 4 opp)
5   Chicago vs. New England, 1986 (1 own, 4 opp)
4   Pittsburgh vs. Minnesota, 1975 (2 own, 2 opp)
Dallas vs. Pittsburgh, 1976 (4 own)

Turnovers
(Number of times losing the ball on interceptions and fumbles.)
Most Turnovers, Game
8   Denver vs. Dallas, 1978
7   Baltimore vs. Dallas, 1971
6   New England vs. Chicago, 1986

Fewest Turnovers, Game
0   Green Bay vs. Oakland, 1968
Miami vs. Minnesota, 1974
Pittsburgh vs. Dallas, 1976
Oakland vs. Minnesota, 1977; vs. Philadelphia, 1981
N.Y. Giants vs. Denver, 1987; vs. Buffalo, 1991
San Francisco vs. Denver, 1990
Buffalo vs. N.Y. Giants, 1991
1   By many teams

Most Turnovers, Both Teams, Game

11	Baltimore (7) vs. Dallas (4), 1971
10	Denver (8) vs. Dallas (2), 1978
8	New England (6) vs. Chicago (2), 1986

Fewest Turnovers, Both Teams, Game

0	Buffalo vs. N.Y. Giants, 1991
1	N.Y. Giants (0) vs. Denver (1), 1987
2	Green Bay (1) vs. Kansas City (1), 1967
	Miami (0) vs. Minnesota (2), 1974
	Cincinnati (1) vs. San Francisco (1), 1989

Compiled by Elias Sports Bureau

Throughout this all-time postseason record section, the following abbreviations are used to indicate various levels of postseason games:

SB   Super Bowl (1966 to date)
AFC   AFC Championship Game (1970 to date) or AFL Championship Game (1960-69)
NFC   NFC Championship Game (1970 to date) or NFL Championship Game (1933-69)
AFC-D   AFC Divisional Playoff Game (1970 to date), AFC Second-Round Playoff Game (1982), AFL Inter-Divisional Playoff Game (1969), or special playoff game to break tie for AFL Division Championship (1963, 1968)
NFC-D   NFC Divisional Playoff Game (1970 to date), NFC Second-Round Playoff Game (1982), NFL Conference Championship Game (1967-69), or special playoff game to break tie for NFL Division or Conference Championship (1941, 1943, 1947, 1950, 1952, 1957, 1958, 1965)
AFC-FR   AFC First-Round Playoff Game (1978 to date)
NFC-FR   NFC First-Round Playoff Game (1978 to date)

Year references are to the season following which the postseason game occurred, even if the game was played in the next calendar year.

Postseason Game Composite Standings

	W	L	Pct.	Pts.	OP
Green Bay Packers	13	5	.722	416	259
Pittsburgh Steelers	16	9	.640	582	494
San Francisco 49ers	16	9	.640	607	452
Washington Redskins*	20	13	.606	701	598
Los Angeles Raiders**	20	14	.588	790	606
Detroit Lions	7	5	.583	269	255
Miami Dolphins	15	11	.577	586	528
Dallas Cowboys	21	17	.553	828	691
Chicago Bears	13	13	.500	529	490
Denver Broncos	9	9	.500	356	460
Indianapolis Colts***	8	8	.500	285	300
Kansas City Chiefs****	6	6	.500	199	242
Buffalo Bills	8	9	.471	380	351
Philadelphia Eagles	7	8	.467	244	234
Minnesota Vikings	13	15	.464	518	570
New York Jets	5	6	.455	216	200
Houston Oilers	9	11	.450	313	464
New York Giants	13	17	.433	509	539
Seattle Seahawks	3	4	.429	128	139
Cincinnati Bengals	5	7	.417	246	257
New England Patriots†	4	6	.400	195	258
Los Angeles Rams††	13	20	.394	501	697
Cleveland Browns	10	18	.357	567	650
Atlanta Falcons	2	4	.333	119	144
San Diego Chargers†††	4	8	.333	230	279
Tampa Bay Buccaneers	1	3	.250	41	94
Phoenix Cardinals††††	1	4	.200	81	134
New Orleans Saints	0	3	.000	36	87

   * One game played when franchise was in Boston (lost 21-6).
  ** 24 games played when franchise was in Oakland (won 15, lost 9, 587 points scored, 435 points allowed).
 *** 15 games played when franchise was in Baltimore (won 8, lost 7, 264 points scored, 262 points allowed).
**** One game played when franchise was Dallas Texans (won 20-17).
    †Two games played when franchise was in Boston (won 26-8, lost 51-10).
   ††One game played when franchise was in Cleveland (won 15-14).
  †††One game played when franchise was in Los Angeles (lost 24-16).
††††Two games played when franchise was in Chicago (won 28-21, lost 7-0), three games played when franchise was in St. Louis (lost 30-14, lost 35-23, lost 41-16).

Individual Records

Service
Most Games, Career
27   D. D. Lewis, Dallas (SB-5, NFC-9, NFC-D 12, NFC-FR 1)
26   Larry Cole, Dallas (SB-5, NFC-8, NFC-D-12, NFC-FR 1)
25   Charlie Waters, Dallas (SB-5, NFC-9, NFC-D 10, NFC-FR 1)

Scoring
Points
Most Points, Career
115   George Blanda, Chi. Bears-Houston-Oakland, 19 games (49-pat, 22-fg)
102   Franco Harris, Pittsburgh, 19 games (17-td)
 96   Matt Bahr, Pittsburgh-Cleveland-N.Y. Giants, 13 games (39-pat, 19-fg)
Most Points, Game
19   Pat Harder, NFC-D: Detroit vs. Los Angeles, 1952 (2-td, 4-pat, 1-fg)
     Paul Hornung, NFC: Green Bay vs. N.Y. Giants, 1961 (1-td, 4-pat, 3-fg)
18   By 18 players

Touchdowns
Most Touchdowns, Career
17   Franco Harris, Pittsburgh, 19 games (16-r, 1-p)
12   John Riggins, Washington, 9 games (12-r)
     John Stallworth, Pittsburgh, 18 games (12-p)
     Jerry Rice, San Francisco, 11 games (12-p)

10   Fred Biletnikoff, Oakland, 19 games (10-p)
     Larry Csonka, Miami, 12 games (9-r, 1-p)
     Tony Dorsett, Dallas, 17 games (9-r, 1-p)
     Marcus Allen, L.A. Raiders, 10 games (8-r, 2-p)
Most Touchdowns, Game
3   Andy Farkas, NFC-D: Washington vs. N.Y. Giants, 1943 (3-r)
   Tom Fears, NFC-D: Los Angeles vs. Chi. Bears, 1950 (3-p)
   Otto Graham, NFC: Cleveland vs. Detroit, 1954 (3-r)
   Gary Collins, NFC: Cleveland vs. Baltimore, 1964 (3-p)
   Craig Baynham, NFC-D: Dallas vs. Cleveland, 1967 (2-r, 1-p)
   Fred Biletnikoff, AFC-D: Oakland vs. Kansas City, 1968 (3-p)
   Tom Matte, NFC: Baltimore vs. Cleveland, 1968 (3-r)
   Larry Schreiber, NFC-D: San Francisco vs. Dallas, 1972 (3-r)
   Larry Csonka, AFC: Miami vs. Oakland, 1973 (3-r)
   Franco Harris, AFC-D: Pittsburgh vs. Buffalo, 1974 (3-r)
   Preston Pearson, NFC: Dallas vs. Los Angeles, 1975 (3-p)
   Dave Casper, AFC-D: Oakland vs. Baltimore, 1977 (OT) (3-p)
   Alvin Garrett, NFC-FR: Washington vs. Detroit, 1982 (3-p)
   John Riggins, NFC-D: Washington vs. L.A. Rams, 1983 (3-r)
   Roger Craig, SB: San Francisco vs. Miami, 1984 (1-r, 2-p)
   Jerry Rice, NFC-D: San Francisco vs. Minnesota, 1988 (3-p)
   Jerry Rice, SB: San Francisco vs. Denver, 1989 (3-p)
   Kenneth Davis, AFC: Buffalo vs. L.A. Raiders, 1990 (3-r)
Most Consecutive Games Scoring Touchdowns
8   John Stallworth, Pittsburgh, 1978-83
7   John Riggins, Washington, 1982-84
   Marcus Allen, L.A. Raiders, 1982-85
5   Duane Thomas, Dallas, 1970-71
   Franco Harris, Pittsburgh, 1974-75
   Franco Harris, Pittsburgh, 1977-79
   James Lofton, Green Bay-Buffalo, 1982-90

Points After Touchdown
Most Points After Touchdown, Career
49   George Blanda, Chi. Bears-Houston-Oakland, 19 games (49 att)
41   Rafael Septien, L.A. Rams-Dallas, 15 games (41 att)
39   Matt Bahr, Pittsburgh-Cleveland-N.Y. Giants, 13 games (39 att)
Most Points After Touchdown, Game
8   Lou Groza, NFC: Cleveland vs. Detroit, 1954 (8 att)
   Jim Martin, NFC: Detroit vs. Cleveland, 1957 (8 att)
   George Blanda, AFC-D: Oakland vs. Houston, 1969 (8 att)
7   Danny Villanueva, NFC-D: Dallas vs. Cleveland, 1967 (7 att)
   Raul Allegre, NFC-D: N.Y. Giants vs. San Francisco, 1986
   Mike Cofer, SB: San Francisco vs. Denver, 1989 (8 att)
6   George Blair, AFC: San Diego vs. Boston, 1963 (6 att)
   Mark Moseley, NFC-D: Washington vs. L.A. Rams, 1983 (6 att)
   Uwe von Schamann, AFC: Miami vs. Pittsburgh, 1984 (6 att)
   Ali Haji-Sheikh, SB: Washington vs. Denver, 1987 (6 att)
   Scott Norwood, AFC: Buffalo vs. L.A. Raiders, 1990 (7 att)
Most Points After Touchdown, No Misses, Career
49   George Blanda, Chi. Bears-Houston-Oakland, 19 games
41   Rafael Septien, L.A. Rams-Dallas, 14 games
39   Matt Bahr, Pittsburgh-Cleveland-N.Y. Giants, 13 games

Field Goals
Most Field Goals Attempted, Career
39   George Blanda, Chi. Bears-Houston-Oakland, 19 games
31   Mark Moseley, Washington-Cleveland, 11 games
26   Roy Gerela, Houston-Pittsburgh, 15 games
Most Field Goals Attempted, Game
6   George Blanda, AFC: Oakland vs. Houston, 1967
   David Ray, NFC-D: Los Angeles vs. Dallas, 1973
   Mark Moseley, AFC-D: Cleveland vs. N.Y. Jets, 1986 (OT)
   Matt Bahr, NFC: N.Y. Giants vs. San Francisco, 1990
5   Jerry Kramer, NFC: Green Bay vs. N.Y. Giants, 1962
   Gino Cappelletti, AFC-D: Boston vs. Buffalo, 1963
   Pete Gogolak, AFC: Buffalo vs. San Diego, 1965
   Jan Stenerud, AFC-D: Kansas City vs. N.Y. Jets, 1969
   George Blanda, AFC-D: Oakland vs. Pittsburgh, 1973
   Ed Murray, NFC-D: Detroit vs. San Francisco, 1983
   Mark Moseley, NFC: Washington vs. San Francisco, 1983
   Tony Franklin, AFC-FR: New England vs. N.Y. Jets, 1985
   Tony Zendejas, AFC-FR: Houston vs. Seattle, 1987 (OT)
   Chuck Nelson, NFC-D: Minnesota vs. San Francisco, 1987
   Luis Zendejas, NFC-D: Philadelphia vs. Chicago, 1988
4   By many players
Most Field Goals, Career
22   George Blanda, Chi. Bears-Houston-Oakland, 19 games
20   Toni Fritsch, Dallas-Houston, 14 games
19   Matt Bahr, Pittsburgh-Cleveland-N.Y. Giants, 13 games
Most Field Goals, Game
5   Chuck Nelson, NFC-D: Minnesota vs. San Francisco, 1987
   Matt Bahr, NFC: N.Y. Giants vs. San Francisco, 1990
4   Gino Cappelletti, AFC-D: Boston vs. Buffalo, 1963
   George Blanda, AFC: Oakland vs. Houston, 1967
   Don Chandler, SB: Green Bay vs. Oakland, 1967
   Curt Knight, NFC: Washington vs. Dallas, 1972
   George Blanda, AFC-D: Oakland vs. Pittsburgh, 1973
   Ray Wersching, SB: San Francisco vs. Cincinnati, 1981
   Tony Franklin, AFC-FR: New England vs. N.Y. Jets, 1985
   Jess Atkinson, NFC-FR: Washington vs. L.A. Rams, 1986
   Luis Zendejas, NFC-D: Philadelphia vs. Chicago, 1988
   Gary Anderson, AFC-FR: Pittsburgh vs. Houston, 1989 (OT)
3   By many players
Most Consecutive Field Goals
15   Rafael Septien, Dallas, 1978-82
 9   Chuck Nelson, Minnesota, 1987
 8   Tony Fritsch, Houston, 1978-79

Longest Field Goal
58 Pete Stoyanovich, AFC-FR: Miami vs. Kansas City, 1990
54 Ed Murray, NFC-D: Detroit vs. San Francisco, 1983
53 Al Del Greco, AFC-FR: Houston vs. N.Y. Jets, 1991

Safeties
Most Safeties, Game
1 Bill Willis, NFC-D: Cleveland vs. N.Y. Giants, 1950
Carl Eller, NFC-D: Minnesota vs. Los Angeles, 1969
George Andrie, NFC-D: Dallas vs. Detroit, 1970
Alan Page, NFC-D: Minnesota vs. Dallas, 1971
Dwight White, SB: Pittsburgh vs. Minnesota, 1974
Reggie Harrison, SB: Pittsburgh vs. Dallas, 1975
Jim Jensen, NFC-D: Dallas vs. Los Angeles, 1976
Ted Washington, AFC: Houston vs. Pittsburgh, 1978
Randy White, NFC-D: Dallas vs. Los Angeles, 1979
Henry Waechter, SB: Chicago vs. New England, 1985
Rulon Jones, AFC-FR: Denver vs. New England, 1986
George Martin, SB: N.Y. Giants vs. Denver, 1986
D.D. Hoggard, AFC: Cleveland vs. Denver, 1987
Bruce Smith, SB: Buffalo vs. N.Y. Giants, 1990

Rushing
Attempts
Most Attempts, Career
400 Franco Harris, Pittsburgh, 19 games
302 Tony Dorsett, Dallas, 17 games
251 John Riggins, Washington, 9 games
Most Attempts, Game
38 Ricky Bell, NFC-D: Tampa Bay vs. Philadelphia, 1979
John Riggins, SB: Washington vs. Miami, 1982
37 Lawrence McCutcheon, NFC-D: Los Angeles vs. St. Louis, 1975
John Riggins, NFC-D: Washington vs. Minnesota, 1982
36 John Riggins, NFC: Washington vs. Dallas, 1982
John Riggins, NFC: Washington vs. San Francisco, 1983

Yards Gained
Most Yards Gained, Career
1,556 Franco Harris, Pittsburgh, 19 games
1,383 Tony Dorsett, Dallas, 17 games
996 John Riggins, Washington, 9 games
Most Yards Gained, Game
248 Eric Dickerson, NFC-D: L.A. Rams vs. Dallas, 1985
206 Keith Lincoln, AFC: San Diego vs. Boston, 1963
204 Timmy Smith, SB: Washington vs. Denver, 1987
Most Games, 100 or More Yards Rushing, Career
6 John Riggins, Washington, 9 games
5 Franco Harris, Pittsburgh, 19 games
Marcus Allen, L.A. Raiders, 10 games
4 Larry Csonka, Miami, 12 games
Chuck Foreman, Minnesota, 13 games
Thurman Thomas, Buffalo, 9 games
Most Consecutive Games, 100 or More Yards Rushing
6 John Riggins, Washington, 1982-83
4 Thurman Thomas, Buffalo, 1990-91
3 Larry Csonka, Miami, 1973-74
Franco Harris, Pittsburgh, 1974-75
Marcus Allen, L.A. Raiders, 1983
Longest Run From Scrimmage
80 Roger Craig, NFC-D: San Francisco vs. Minnesota, 1988 (TD)
74 Marcus Allen, SB: L.A. Raiders vs. Washington, 1983 (TD)
71 Hugh McElhenny, NFC-D: San Francisco vs. Detroit, 1957
James Lofton, NFC-D: Green Bay vs. Dallas, 1982 (TD)

Average Gain
Highest Average Gain, Career (50 attempts)
6.71 Timmy Smith, Washington, 3 games (51-342)
6.67 Paul Lowe, L.A. Chargers-San Diego, 5 games (57-380)
5.75 Marcus Allen, L.A. Raiders, 10 games (167-961)
Highest Average Gain, Game (10 attempts)
15.90 Elmer Angsman, NFC: Chi. Cardinals vs. Philadelphia, 1947 (10-159)
15.85 Keith Lincoln, AFC: San Diego vs. Boston, 1963 (13-206)
10.90 Bill Osmanski, NFC: Chi. Bears vs. Washington, 1940 (10-109)

Touchdowns
Most Touchdowns, Career
16 Franco Harris, Pittsburgh, 19 games
12 John Riggins, Washington, 9 games
9 Larry Csonka, Miami, 12 games
Tony Dorsett, Dallas, 17 games
Most Touchdowns, Game
3 Andy Farkas, NFC-D: Washington vs. N.Y. Giants, 1943
Otto Graham, NFC: Cleveland vs. Detroit, 1954
Tom Matte, NFC: Baltimore vs. Cleveland, 1968
Larry Schreiber, NFC-D: San Francisco vs. Dallas, 1972
Larry Csonka, AFC: Miami vs. Oakland, 1973
Franco Harris, AFC-D: Pittsburgh vs. Buffalo, 1974
John Riggins, NFC-D: Washington vs. L.A. Rams, 1983
Kenneth Davis, AFC: Buffalo vs. L.A. Raiders, 1990
Most Consecutive Games Rushing for Touchdowns
7 John Riggins, Washington, 1982-84
5 Franco Harris, Pittsburgh, 1974-75
Franco Harris, Pittsburgh, 1977-79
3 By many players

Passing
Passer Rating
Highest Passer Rating, Career (100 attempts)
104.8 Bart Starr, Green Bay, 10 games
98.2 Joe Montana, San Francisco, 19 games
93.3 Ken Anderson, Cincinnati, 6 games

Attempts
Most Passes Attempted, Career
593 Joe Montana, San Francisco, 19 games
456 Terry Bradshaw, Pittsburgh, 19 games
410 Roger Staubach, Dallas, 20 games
Most Passes Attempted, Game
64 Bernie Kosar, AFC-D: Cleveland vs. N.Y. Jets, 1986 (OT)
58 Jim Kelly, SB: Buffalo vs. Washington, 1991
54 Randall Cunningham, NFC-D: Philadelphia vs. Chicago, 1988
Jim Kelly, AFC-D: Buffalo vs. Cleveland, 1989

Completions
Most Passes Completed, Career
375 Joe Montana, San Francisco, 19 games
261 Terry Bradshaw, Pittsburgh, 19 games
223 Roger Staubach, Dallas, 20 games
Most Passes Completed, Game
33 Dan Fouts, AFC-D: San Diego vs. Miami, 1981 (OT)
Bernie Kosar, AFC-D: Cleveland vs. N.Y. Jets, 1986 (OT)
32 Neil Lomax, NFC-FR: St. Louis vs. Green Bay, 1982
Danny White, NFC-FR: Dallas vs. L.A. Rams, 1983
29 Don Strock, AFC-D: Miami vs. San Diego, 1981 (OT)
Dan Marino, SB: Miami vs. San Francisco, 1984
Warren Moon, AFC-FR: Houston vs. Pittsburgh, 1989 (OT)
Erik Kramer, NFC-D: Detroit vs. Dallas, 1991

Completion Percentage
Highest Completion Percentage, Career (100 attempts)
66.3 Ken Anderson, Cincinnati, 6 games (166-110)
63.2 Joe Montana, San Francisco, 19 games (593-375)
62.8 Warren Moon, Houston, 7 games (258-162)
Highest Completion Percentage, Game (15 completions)
88.0 Phil Simms, SB: N.Y. Giants vs. Denver, 1986 (25-22)
86.7 Joe Montana, NFC: San Francisco vs. L.A. Rams, 1989 (30-26)
84.2 David Woodley, AFC-FR: Miami vs. New England, 1982 (19-16)

Yards Gained
Most Yards Gained, Career
4,758 Joe Montana, San Francisco, 19 games
3,833 Terry Bradshaw, Pittsburgh, 19 games
3,019 John Elway, Denver, 13 games
Most Yards Gained, Game
489 Bernie Kosar, AFC-D: Cleveland vs. N.Y. Jets, 1986 (OT)
433 Dan Fouts, AFC-D: San Diego vs. Miami, 1981 (OT)
421 Dan Marino, AFC: Miami vs. Pittsburgh, 1984
Most Games, 300 or More Yards Passing, Career
5 Dan Fouts, San Diego, 7 games
Joe Montana, San Francisco, 19 games
4 Dan Marino, Miami, 6 games
3 Terry Bradshaw, Pittsburgh, 19 games
Danny White, Dallas, 17 games
Most Consecutive Games, 300 or More Yards Passing
4 Dan Fouts, San Diego, 1979-81
3 Jim Kelly, Buffalo 1989-90
2 Daryle Lamonica, Oakland, 1968
Ken Anderson, Cincinnati, 1981-82
Terry Bradshaw, Pittsburgh, 1979-82
Joe Montana, San Francisco, 1983-84
Dan Marino, Miami, 1984
Longest Pass Completion
93 Daryle Lamonica (to Dubenion), AFC-D: Buffalo vs. Boston, 1963 (TD)
88 George Blanda (to Cannon), AFC: Houston vs. L.A. Chargers, 1960 (TD)
86 Don Meredith (to Hayes), NFC-D: Dallas vs. Cleveland, 1967 (TD)

Average Gain
Highest Average Gain, Career (100 attempts)
8.45 Joe Theismann, Washington, 10 games (211-1,782)
8.43 Jim Plunkett, Oakland-L.A. Raiders, 10 games (272-2,293)
8.41 Terry Bradshaw, Pittsburgh, 19 games (456-3,833)
Highest Average Gain, Game (20 attempts)
14.71 Terry Bradshaw, SB: Pittsburgh vs. Los Angeles, 1979 (21-309)
13.33 Bob Waterfield, NFC-D: Los Angeles vs. Chi. Bears, 1950 (21-280)
13.16 Dan Marino, AFC: Miami vs. Pittsburgh, 1984 (32-421)

Touchdowns
Most Touchdown Passes, Career
39 Joe Montana, San Francisco, 19 games
30 Terry Bradshaw, Pittsburgh, 19 games
24 Roger Staubach, Dallas, 20 games
Most Touchdown Passes, Game
6 Daryle Lamonica, AFC-D: Oakland vs. Houston, 1969
5 Sid Luckman, NFC: Chi. Bears vs. Washington, 1943
Daryle Lamonica, AFC-D: Oakland vs. Kansas City, 1968
Joe Montana, SB: San Francisco vs. Denver, 1989
4 Otto Graham, NFC: Cleveland vs. Los Angeles, 1950
Tobin Rote, NFC: Detroit vs. Cleveland, 1957
Bart Starr, NFC: Green Bay vs. Dallas, 1966
Ken Stabler, AFC-D: Oakland vs. Miami, 1974
Roger Staubach, NFC: Dallas vs. Los Angeles, 1975
Terry Bradshaw, SB: Pittsburgh vs. Dallas, 1978
Don Strock, AFC-D: Miami vs. San Diego, 1981 (OT)
Lynn Dickey, NFC-FR: Green Bay vs. St. Louis, 1982
Dan Marino, AFC: Miami vs. Pittsburgh, 1984
Doug Williams, SB: Washington vs. Denver, 1987
Jim Kelly, AFC-D: Buffalo vs. Cleveland, 1989
Joe Montana, NFC-D: San Francisco vs. Minnesota, 1989
Most Consecutive Games, Touchdown Passes
10 Ken Stabler, Oakland, 1973-77
9 John Elway, Denver, 1984-89
8 Terry Bradshaw, Pittsburgh, 1977-82
Joe Montana, San Francisco, 1981-84
Joe Montana, San Francisco, 1988-90 (current)

Had Intercepted
Lowest Percentage, Passes Had Intercepted, Career (100 attempts)
- 1.41 Bart Starr, Green Bay, 16 games (213-3)
- 1.75 Phil Simms, N.Y. Giants, 8 games (228-4)
- 3.07 Jim McMahon, Chicago-Philadelphia, 7 games (130-4)

Most Attempts Without Interception, Game
- 48 Warren Moon, AFC-FR: Houston vs. Pittsburgh, 1989 (OT)
- 47 Daryle Lamonica, AFC: Oakland vs. N.Y. Jets, 1968
- 42 Dan Fouts, AFC-FR: San Diego vs. Pittsburgh, 1982

Most Passes Had Intercepted, Career
- 26 Terry Bradshaw, Pittsburgh, 19 games
- 19 Roger Staubach, Dallas, 20 games
- 17 George Blanda, Chi. Bears-Houston-Oakland, 19 games
  - Fran Tarkenton, Minnesota, 11 games
  - Joe Montana, San Francisco, 19 games
  - John Elway, Denver, 13 games
  - Jim Kelly, Buffalo, 9 games

Most Passes Had Intercepted, Game
- 6 Frank Filchock, NFC: N.Y. Giants vs. Chi. Bears, 1946
  - Bobby Layne, NFC: Detroit vs. Cleveland, 1954
  - Norm Van Brocklin, NFC: Los Angeles vs. Cleveland, 1955
- 5 Frank Filchock, NFC: Washington vs. Chi. Bears, 1940
  - George Blanda, AFC: Houston vs. San Diego, 1961
  - George Blanda, AFC: Houston vs. Dall. Texans, 1962 (OT)
  - Y.A. Tittle, NFC: N.Y. Giants vs. Chicago, 1963
  - Mike Phipps, AFC-D: Cleveland vs. Miami, 1972
  - Dan Pastorini, AFC: Houston vs. Pittsburgh, 1978
  - Dan Fouts, AFC-D: San Diego vs. Houston, 1979
  - Tommy Kramer, NFC-D: Minnesota vs. Philadelphia, 1980
  - Dan Fouts, AFC-D: San Diego vs. Miami, 1982
  - Richard Todd, AFC: N.Y. Jets vs Miami, 1982
  - Gary Danielson, NFC-D: Detroit vs. San Francisco, 1983
  - Jay Schroeder, AFC: L.A. Raiders vs. Buffalo, 1990
- 4 By many players

Pass Receiving
Receptions
Most Receptions, Career
- 73 Cliff Branch, Oakland-L.A. Raiders, 22 games
- 70 Fred Biletnikoff, Oakland, 19 games
- 67 Drew Pearson, Dallas, 22 games

Most Receptions, Game
- 13 Kellen Winslow, AFC-D: San Diego vs. Miami, 1981 (OT)
  - Thurman Thomas, AFC-D: Buffalo vs. Cleveland, 1989
- 12 Raymond Berry, NFC: Baltimore vs. N.Y. Giants, 1958
- 11 Dante Lavelli, NFC: Cleveland vs. Los Angeles, 1950
  - Dan Ross, SB: Cincinnati vs. San Francisco, 1981
  - Franco Harris, AFC-FR: Pittsburgh vs. San Diego, 1982
  - Steve Watson, AFC-D: Denver vs. Pittsburgh, 1984
  - John L. Williams, AFC-D: Seattle vs. Cincinnati, 1988
  - Jerry Rice, SB: San Francisco vs. Cincinnati, 1988
  - Ernest Givins, AFC-FR: Houston vs. Pittsburgh, 1989 (OT)

Most Consecutive Games, Pass Receptions
- 22 Drew Pearson, Dallas, 1973-83
- 18 Paul Warfield, Cleveland-Miami, 1964-74
  - Cliff Branch, Oakland-L.A. Raiders, 1974-83
- 17 John Stallworth, Pittsburgh, 1974-84

Yards Gained
Most Yards Gained, Career
- 1,289 Cliff Branch, Oakland-L.A. Raiders, 22 games
- 1,167 Fred Biletnikoff, Oakland, 19 games
- 1,121 Paul Warfield, Cleveland-Miami, 18 games

Most Yards Gained, Game
- 227 Anthony Carter, NFC-D: Minnesota vs. San Francisco, 1987
- 215 Jerry Rice, SB: San Francisco vs. Cincinnati, 1988
- 198 Tom Fears, NFC-D: Los Angeles vs. Chi. Bears, 1950

Most Games, 100 or More Yards Receiving, Career
- 5 John Stallworth, Pittsburgh, 18 games
- 4 Fred Biletnikoff, Oakland, 19 games
  - Dwight Clark, San Francisco, 7 games
  - Jerry Rice, San Francisco, 11 games
  - Art Monk, Washington, 13 games
- 3 Tom Fears, L.A. Rams, 6 games
  - Cliff Branch, Oakland-L.A. Raiders, 22 games
  - Tony Nathan, Miami, 10 games
  - Mark Duper, Miami, 8 games
  - James Lofton, Green Bay-Buffalo, 9 games
  - Andre Reed, Buffalo, 9 games

Most Consecutive Games, 100 or More Yards Receiving, Career
- 3 Tom Fears, Los Angeles, 1950-51
  - Jerry Rice, San Francisco, 1988-89
- 2 Lenny Moore, Baltimore, 1958-59
  - Fred Biletnikoff, Oakland, 1968
  - Paul Warfield, Miami, 1971
  - Charlie Joiner, San Diego, 1981
  - Dwight Clark, San Francisco, 1981
  - Cris Collinsworth, Cincinnati, 1981-82
  - John Stallworth, Pittsburgh, 1979-82
  - Wesley Walker, N.Y. Jets, 1982
  - Charlie Brown, Washington, 1983
  - Steve Largent, Seattle, 1984-87
  - Andre Reed, Buffalo, 1989-90
  - James Lofton, Buffalo, 1990

Longest Reception
- 93 Elbert Dubenion (from Lamonica), AFC-D: Buffalo vs. Boston, 1963 (TD)
- 88 Billy Cannon (from Blanda), AFC: Houston vs. L.A. Chargers, 1960 (TD)
- 86 Bob Hayes (from Meredith), NFC: Dallas vs. Cleveland, 1967 (TD)

Average Gain
Highest Average Gain, Career (20 receptions)
- 23.7 Willie Gault, Chicago-L.A. Raiders, 10 games (21-497)

- 22.8 Harold Jackson, L.A. Rams-New England-Minnesota-Seattle, 14 games (24-548)
- 21.1 Mark Jackson, Denver, 10 games (20-422)

Highest Average Gain, Game (3 receptions)
- 46.3 Harold Jackson, NFC: Los Angeles vs. Minnesota, 1974 (3-139)
- 42.7 Billy Cannon, AFC: Houston vs. L.A. Chargers, 1960 (3-128)
- 42.0 Lenny Moore, NFC: Baltimore vs. N.Y. Giants, 1959 (3-126)

Touchdowns
Most Touchdowns, Career
- 12 John Stallworth, Pittsburgh, 18 games
  - Jerry Rice, San Francisco, 11 games
- 10 Fred Biletnikoff, Oakland, 19 games
- 9 Lynn Swann, Pittsburgh, 16 games

Most Touchdowns, Game
- 3 Tom Fears, NFC-D: Los Angeles vs. Chi. Bears, 1950
  - Gary Collins, NFC: Cleveland vs. Baltimore, 1964
  - Fred Biletnikoff, AFC-D: Oakland vs. Kansas City, 1968
  - Preston Pearson, NFC: Dallas vs. Los Angeles, 1975
  - Dave Casper, AFC-D: Oakland vs. Baltimore, 1977 (OT)
  - Alvin Garrett, NFC-FR: Washington vs. Detroit, 1982
  - Jerry Rice, NFC-D: San Francisco vs. Minnesota, 1988
  - Jerry Rice, SB: San Francisco vs. Denver, 1989

Most Consecutive Games, Touchdown Passes Caught
- 8 John Stallworth, Pittsburgh, 1978-83
- 5 James Lofton, Green Bay-Buffalo, 1982-90
- 4 Lynn Swann, Pittsburgh, 1978-79
  - Harold Carmichael, Philadelphia, 1978-80
  - Fred Solomon, San Francisco, 1983-84
  - Jerry Rice, San Francisco, 1988-89
  - John Taylor, San Francisco, 1988-89

Interceptions By
Most Interceptions, Career
- 9 Charlie Waters, Dallas, 25 games
  - Bill Simpson, Los Angeles-Buffalo, 11 games
  - Ronnie Lott, San Francisco-L.A. Raiders, 20 games
- 8 Lester Hayes, Oakland-L.A. Raiders, 13 games
- 7 Willie Brown, Oakland, 17 games
  - Dennis Thurman, Dallas, 14 games

Most Interceptions, Game
- 4 Vernon Perry, AFC-D: Houston vs. San Diego, 1979
- 3 Joe Laws, NFC: Green Bay vs. N.Y. Giants, 1944
  - Charlie Waters, NFC-D: Dallas vs. Chicago, 1977
  - Rod Martin, SB: Oakland vs. Philadelphia, 1980
  - Dennis Thurman, NFC-D: Dallas vs. Green Bay, 1982
  - A.J. Duhe, AFC: Miami vs. N.Y. Jets, 1982
- 2 By many players

Most Consecutive Games, Interceptions
- 3 Warren Lahr, Cleveland, 1950-51
  - Ken Gorgal, Cleveland, 1950-53
  - Joe Schmidt, Detroit, 1954-57
  - Emmitt Thomas, Kansas City, 1969
  - Mel Renfro, Dallas, 1970
  - Rick Volk, Baltimore, 1970-71
  - Mike Wagner, Pittsburgh, 1975-76
  - Randy Hughes, Dallas, 1977-78
  - Vernon Perry, Houston, 1979-80
  - Lester Hayes, Oakland, 1980
  - Gerald Small, Miami, 1982
  - Lester Hayes, L.A. Raiders, 1982-83
  - Fred Marion, New England, 1985
  - John Harris, Seattle-Minnesota, 1984-87
  - Felix Wright, Cleveland, 1987-88
  - Kurt Gouveia, Washington, 1991 (current)

Yards Gained
Most Yards Gained, Career
- 196 Willie Brown, Oakland, 17 games
- 187 Ronnie Lott, San Francisco-L.A. Raiders, 20 games
- 151 Glen Edwards, Pittsburgh-San Diego, 17 games

Most Yards Gained, Game
- 98 Darrol Ray, AFC-FR: N.Y. Jets vs. Cincinnati, 1982
- 94 LeRoy Irvin, NFC-FR: L.A. Rams vs. Dallas, 1983
- 88 Walt Sumner, NFC-D: Cleveland vs. Dallas, 1969

Longest Return
- 98 Darrol Ray, AFC-FR: N.Y. Jets vs. Cincinnati, 1982 (TD)
- 94 LeRoy Irvin, NFC-FR: L.A. Rams vs. Dallas, 1983
- 88 Walt Sumner, NFC-D: Cleveland vs. Dallas, 1969 (TD)

Touchdowns
Most Touchdowns, Career
- 3 Willie Brown, Oakland, 17 games
- 2 Lester Hayes, Oakland-L.A. Raiders, 13 games
  - Ronnie Lott, San Francisco-L.A. Raiders, 20 games
  - Darrell Green, Washington, 15 games

Most Touchdowns, Game
- 1 By 49 players

Punting
Most Punts, Career
- 111 Ray Guy, Oakland-L.A. Raiders, 22 games
- 84 Danny White, Dallas, 18 games
- 73 Mike Eischeid, Oakland-Minnesota, 14 games

Most Punts, Game
- 14 Dave Jennings, AFC-D: N.Y. Jets vs. Cleveland, 1986 (OT)
- 12 David Lee, AFC-D: Baltimore vs. Oakland, 1977 (OT)
- 11 Ken Strong, NFC: N.Y. Giants vs. Chi. Bears, 1933
  - Jim Norton, AFC: Houston vs. Oakland, 1967
  - Dale Hatcher, NFC: L.A. Rams vs. Chicago, 1985

Longest Punt
- 76 Ed Danowski, NFC: N.Y. Giants vs. Detroit, 1935
  - Mike Horan, AFC: Denver vs. Buffalo, 1991

72   Charlie Conerly, NFC-D: N. Y. Giants vs. Cleveland, 1950
71   Ray Guy, AFC: Oakland vs. San Diego, 1980

Average Yardage
Highest Average, Career (20 punts)
44.5   Rich Camarillo, New England, 6 games (35-1,559)
44.4   Lee Johnson, Cleveland-Cincinnati, 7 games (28-1,244)
43.4   Jerrel Wilson, Kansas City-New England, 8 games (43-1,866)
Highest Average, Game (4 punts)
56.0   Ray Guy, AFC: Oakland vs. San Diego, 1980 (4-224)
52.5   Sammy Baugh, NFC: Washington vs. Chi. Bears, 1942 (6-315)
51.6   Lee Johnson, AFC-D: Cincinnati vs. L.A. Raiders, 1990 (5-258)

Punt Returns
Most Punt Returns, Career
25   Theo Bell, Pittsburgh-Tampa Bay, 10 games
21   Gerald McNeil, Cleveland-Houston, 8 games
19   Willie Wood, Green Bay, 10 games
      Butch Johnson, Dallas-Denver, 18 games
      Phil McConkey, N. Y. Giants, 5 games
Most Punt Returns, Game
7   Ron Gardin, AFC-D: Baltimore vs. Cincinnati, 1970
     Carl Roaches, AFC-FR: Houston vs. Oakland, 1980
     Gerald McNeil, AFC-D: Cleveland vs. N. Y. Jets, 1986 (OT)
     Phil McConkey, NFC-D: N. Y. Giants vs. San Francisco, 1986
6   George McAfee, NFC-D: Chi. Bears vs. Los Angeles, 1950
     Eddie Brown, NFC-D: Washington vs. Minnesota, 1976
     Theo Bell, AFC: Pittsburgh vs. Houston, 1978
     Eddie Brown, NFC: Los Angeles vs. Tampa Bay, 1979
     John Sciarra, NFC: Philadelphia vs. Dallas, 1980
     Kurt Sohn, AFC: N. Y. Jets vs. Miami, 1982
     Mike Nelms, SB: Washington vs. Miami, 1982
     Anthony Carter, NFC-FR: Minnesota vs. New Orleans, 1987
5   By many players

Yards Gained
Most Yards Gained, Career
237   Anthony Carter, Minnesota, 6 games
221   Neal Colzie, Oakland-Miami-Tampa Bay, 10 games
211   Gerald McNeil, Cleveland-Houston, 8 games
Most Yards Gained, Game
143   Anthony Carter, NFC-FR: Minnesota vs. New Orleans, 1987
141   Bob Hayes, NFC-D: Dallas vs. Cleveland, 1967
102   Charley Trippi, NFC: Chi. Cardinals vs. Philadelphia, 1947
Longest Return
84   Anthony Carter, NFC-FR: Minnesota vs. New Orleans, 1987 (TD)
81   Hugh Gallarneau, NFC-D: Chi. Bears vs. Green Bay, 1941 (TD)
79   Bosh Pritchard, NFC-D: Philadelphia vs. Pittsburgh, 1947 (TD)

Average Yardage
Highest Average, Career (10 returns)
15.8   Anthony Carter, Minnesota, 6 games (15-237)
12.6   Bob Hayes, Dallas, 15 games (12-151)
12.4   Mike Fuller, San Diego-Cincinnati, 7 games (13-161)
Highest Average Gain, Game (3 returns)
47.0   Bob Hayes, NFC-D: Dallas vs. Cleveland, 1967 (3-141)
29.0   George (Butch) Byrd, AFC: Buffalo vs. San Diego, 1965 (3-87)
25.3   Bosh Pritchard, NFC-D: Philadelphia vs. Pittsburgh, 1947 (4-101)

Touchdowns
Most Touchdowns
1   Hugh Gallarneau, NFC-D: Chicago Bears vs. Green Bay, 1941
     Bosh Pritchard, NFC-D: Philadelphia vs. Pittsburgh, 1947
     Charley Trippi, NFC: Chicago Cardinals vs. Philadelphia, 1947
     Verda (Vitamin T) Smith, NFC-D: Los Angeles vs. Detroit, 1952
     George (Butch) Byrd, AFC: Buffalo vs. San Diego, 1965
     Golden Richards, NFC: Dallas vs. Minnesota, 1973
     Wes Chandler, AFC-D: San Diego vs. Miami, 1981 (OT)
     Shaun Gayle, NFC-D: Chicago vs. N. Y. Giants, 1985
     Anthony Carter, NFC-FR: Minnesota vs. New Orleans, 1987
     Darrell Green, NFC-D: Washington vs. Chicago, 1987

Kickoff Returns
Most Kickoff Returns, Career
29   Fulton Walker, Miami-L.A. Raiders, 10 games
21   Ken Bell, Denver, 9 games
19   Preston Pearson, Baltimore-Pittsburgh-Dallas, 22 games
Most Kickoff Returns, Game
8   Marc Logan, AFC-D: Miami vs. Buffalo, 1990
7   Don Bingham, NFC: Chi. Bears vs. N. Y. Giants, 1956
     Reggie Brown, NFC-FR: Atlanta vs. Minnesota, 1982
     David Verser, AFC-FR: Cincinnati vs. N. Y. Jets, 1982
     Del Rodgers, NFC-D: Green Bay vs. Dallas, 1982
     Henry Ellard, NFC-D: L.A. Rams vs. Washington, 1983
     Stephen Starring, SB: New England vs. Chicago, 1985
6   By many players

Yards Gained
Most Yards Gained, Career
677   Fulton Walker, Miami-L.A. Raiders, 10 games
481   Carl Garrett, Oakland, 5 games
458   Cullen Bryant, L.A. Rams-Seattle, 19 games
Most Yards Gained, Game
190   Fulton Walker, SB: Miami vs. Washington, 1982
170   Les (Speedy) Duncan, NFC-D: Washington vs. San Francisco, 1971
169   Carl Garrett, AFC-D: Oakland vs. Baltimore, 1977 (OT)
Longest Return
98   Fulton Walker, SB: Miami vs. Washington, 1982 (TD)
97   Vic Washington, NFC-D: San Francisco vs. Dallas, 1972 (TD)
93   Stanford Jennings, SB: Cincinnati vs. San Francisco, 1988 (TD)

Average Yardage
Highest Average, Career (10 returns)
30.1   Carl Garrett, Oakland, 5 games (16-481)
27.9   George Atkinson, Oakland, 16 games (12-335)
27.7   Eric Metcalf, Cleveland, 2 games (10-277)
Highest Average, Game (3 returns)
56.7   Les (Speedy) Duncan, NFC-D: Washington vs. San Francisco, 1971 (3-170)
51.3   Ed Podolak, AFC-D: Kansas City vs. Miami, 1971 (OT) (3-154)
49.0   Les (Speedy) Duncan, AFC: San Diego vs. Buffalo, 1964 (3-147)

Touchdowns
Most Touchdowns
1   Vic Washington, NFC-D: San Francisco vs. Dallas, 1972
     Nat Moore, AFC-D: Miami vs. Oakland, 1974
     Marshall Johnson, AFC-D: Baltimore vs. Oakland, 1977 (OT)
     Fulton Walker, SB: Miami vs. Washington, 1982
     Stanford Jennings, SB: Cincinnati vs. San Francisco, 1988
     Eric Metcalf, AFC-D: Cleveland vs. Buffalo, 1989

Fumbles
Most Fumbles, Career
13   Tony Dorsett, Dallas, 17 games
10   Franco Harris, Pittsburgh, 19 games
      Terry Bradshaw, Pittsburgh, 19 games
      Roger Staubach, Dallas, 20 games
9   Chuck Foreman, Minnesota, 13 games
     Warren Moon, Houston, 7 games
Most Fumbles, Game
4   Brian Sipe, AFC-D: Cleveland vs. Oakland, 1980
3   By many players

Recoveries
Most Own Fumbles Recovered, Career
6   John Elway, Denver, 13 games
5   Roger Staubach, Dallas, 20 games
     Warren Moon, Houston, 7 games
4   Fran Tarkenton, Minnesota, 11 games
Most Opponents' Fumbles Recovered, Career
4   Cliff Harris, Dallas, 21 games
     Harvey Martin, Dallas, 22 games
     Ted Hendricks, Baltimore-Oakland-L.A. Raiders, 21 games
     Alvin Walton, Washington, 9 games
3   Paul Krause, Minnesota, 19 games
     Jack Lambert, Pittsburgh, 18 games
     Fred Dryer, Los Angeles, 19 games
     Charlie Waters, Dallas, 25 games
     Jack Ham, Pittsburgh, 16 games
     Mike Hegman, Dallas, 16 games
     Tom Jackson, Denver, 10 games
     Mike Singletary, Chicago, 12 games
     Monte Coleman, Washington, 19 games
     Darryl Grant, Washington, 16 games
     Wes Hopkins, Philadelphia, 3 games
     Wilber Marshall, Chicago-Washington, 12 games
2   By many players
Most Fumbles Recovered, Game, Own and Opponents'
3   Jack Lambert, AFC: Pittsburgh vs. Oakland, 1975 (3 opp)
     Ron Jaworski, NFC-FR: Philadelphia vs. N. Y. Giants, 1981 (3 own)
2   By many players

Yards Gained
Longest Return
93   Andy Russell, AFC-D: Pittsburgh vs. Baltimore, 1975 (opp, TD)
60   Mike Curtis, NFC-D: Baltimore vs. Minnesota, 1968 (opp, TD)
      Hugh Green, NFC-FR: Tampa Bay vs. Dallas, 1982 (opp, TD)
52   Wilber Marshall, NFC: Chicago vs. L.A. Rams, 1985 (opp, TD)

Touchdowns
Most Touchdowns
1   By 22 players

Combined Net Yards Gained
Rushing, receiving, interception returns, punt returns, kickoff returns, and fumble returns.
Attempts
Most Attempts, Career
454   Franco Harris, Pittsburgh, 19 games
350   Tony Dorsett, Dallas, 17 games
275   Chuck Foreman, Minnesota, 13 games
Most Attempts, Game
40   Lawrence McCutcheon, NFC-D: Los Angeles vs. St. Louis, 1975
39   John Riggins, SB: Washington vs. Miami, 1982
38   Ricky Bell, NFC-D: Tampa Bay vs. Philadelphia, 1979
     Rob Carpenter, NFC-FR: N. Y. Giants vs. Philadelphia, 1981

Yards Gained
Most Yards Gained, Career
2,060   Franco Harris, Pittsburgh, 19 games
1,786   Tony Dorsett, Dallas, 17 games
1,471   Roger Craig, San Francisco, 16 games
Most Yards Gained, Game
350   Ed Podolak, AFC-D: Kansas City vs. Miami, 1971 (OT)
329   Keith Lincoln, AFC: San Diego vs. Boston, 1963
285   Bob Hayes, NFC-D: Dallas vs. Cleveland, 1967

Sacks

Sacks have been compiled since 1982

Most Sacks, Career
10.5	Richard Dent, Chicago, 10 games	
10	Charles Mann, Washington, 15 games	
8	Dexter Manley, Washington, 14 games	

Most Sacks, Game
3.5	Rich Milot, NFC-D: Washington vs. Chicago, 1984
	Richard Dent, NFC-D: Chicago vs. N.Y. Giants, 1985
3	Richard Dent, NFC-D: Chicago vs. Washington, 1984
	Garin Veris, AFC-FR: New England vs. N.Y. Jets, 1985
	Gary Jeter, NFC-D: L.A. Rams vs. Dallas, 1985
	Carl Hairston, AFC-D: Cleveland vs. N.Y. Jets, 1986 (OT)
	Charles Mann, NFC-D: Washington vs. Chicago, 1987
	Kevin Greene, NFC-FR: L.A. Rams vs. Minnesota, 1988
	Greg Townsend, AFC-D: L.A. Raiders vs. Cincinnati, 1990
	Wilber Marshall, NFC: Washington vs. Detroit, 1991
2.5	Lyle Alzado, AFC-D: L.A. Raiders vs. Pittsburgh, 1983
	Jacob Green, AFC-FR: Seattle vs. L.A. Raiders, 1984
	Larry Roberts, NFC-D: San Francisco vs. Minnesota, 1988

Team Records

Games, Victories, Defeats

Most Seasons Participating in Postseason Games
22	Cleveland/L.A. Rams, 1945, 1949-52, 1955, 1967, 1969, 1973-80, 1983-86, 1988-89
	Cleveland, 1950-55, 1957-58, 1964-65, 1967-69, 1971-72, 1980, 1982, 1985-89
	N.Y. Giants, 1933-35, 1938-39, 1941, 1943-44, 1946, 1950, 1956, 1958-59, 1961-63, 1981, 1984-86, 1989-90
20	Chicago, 1933-34, 1937, 1940-43, 1946, 1950, 1956, 1963, 1977, 1979, 1984-88, 1990-91
19	Dallas, 1966-73, 1975-83, 1985, 1991

Most Consecutive Seasons Participating in Postseason Games
9	Dallas, 1975-83
8	Dallas, 1966-73
	Pittsburgh, 1972-79
	Los Angeles, 1973-80
	San Francisco, 1983-90
6	Cleveland, 1950-55
	Oakland, 1972-77
	Minnesota, 1973-78

Most Games
38	Dallas, 1966-73, 1975-83, 1985, 1991
34	Oakland/L.A. Raiders, 1967-70, 1973-77, 1980, 1982-85, 1990-91
33	Cleveland/L.A. Rams, 1945, 1949-52, 1955, 1967, 1969, 1973-80, 1983-86, 1988-89
	Boston/Washington, 1936-37, 1940, 1942-43, 1945, 1971-74, 1976-77, 1982-84, 1986-87, 1990-91

Most Games Won
21	Dallas, 1967, 1970-73, 1975, 1977-78, 1980-82, 1991
20	Oakland/L.A. Raiders, 1967-70, 1973-77, 1980, 1982-83, 1990
	Washington, 1937, 1942-43, 1972, 1982-83, 1986-87, 1990-91
16	Pittsburgh, 1972, 1974-76, 1978-79, 1984, 1989
	San Francisco, 1970-71, 1981, 1983-84, 1988-90

Most Consecutive Games Won
9	Green Bay, 1961-62, 1965-67
7	Pittsburgh, 1974-76
	San Francisco, 1988-90
6	Miami, 1972-73
	Pittsburgh, 1978-79
	Washington, 1982-83

Most Games Lost
20	L.A. Rams, 1949-50, 1952, 1955, 1967, 1969, 1973-80, 1983-86, 1988-89
18	Cleveland, 1951-53, 1957-58, 1965, 1967-69, 1971-72, 1980, 1982, 1985-89
17	N.Y. Giants, 1933, 1935, 1939, 1941, 1943-44, 1946, 1950, 1958-59, 1961-63, 1981, 1984-85, 1989
	Dallas, 1966-70, 1972-73, 1975-76, 1978-83, 1985, 1991

Most Consecutive Games Lost
6	N.Y. Giants, 1939, 1941, 1943-44, 1946, 1950
	Cleveland, 1969, 1971-72, 1980, 1982, 1985
5	N.Y. Giants, 1958-59, 1961-63
	Los Angeles, 1952, 1955, 1967, 1969, 1973
	Denver, 1977-79, 1983-84
	Baltimore/Indianapolis, 1971, 1975-77, 1987 (current)
	Philadelphia, 1980-81, 1988-90 (current)
4	Washington, 1972-74, 1976
	Miami, 1974, 1978-79, 1981
	Chi. Cardinals/St. Louis, 1948, 1974-75, 1982 (current)
	Boston/New England, 1963, 1976, 1978, 1982

Scoring

Most Points, Game
73	NFC: Chi. Bears vs. Washington, 1940
59	NFC: Detroit vs. Cleveland, 1957
56	NFC: Cleveland vs. Detroit, 1954
	AFC-D: Oakland vs. Houston, 1969

Most Points, Both Teams, Game
79	AFC-D: San Diego (41) vs. Miami (38), 1981 (OT)
78	AFC-D: Buffalo (44) vs. Miami (34), 1990
73	NFC: Chi. Bears (73) vs. Washington (0), 1940
	NFC: Detroit (59) vs. Cleveland (14), 1957
	AFC: Miami (45) vs. Pittsburgh (28), 1984

Fewest Points, Both Teams, Game
5	NFC-D: Detroit (0) vs. Dallas (5), 1970
7	NFC: Chi. Cardinals (0) vs. Philadelphia (7), 1948
9	NFC: Tampa Bay (0) vs. Los Angeles (9), 1979

Largest Margin of Victory, Game
73	NFC: Chi. Bears vs. Washington, 1940 (73-0)
49	AFC-D: Oakland vs. Houston, 1969 (56-7)
48	AFC: Buffalo vs. L.A. Raiders, 1990 (51-3)

Most Points, Shutout Victory, Game
73	NFC: Chi. Bears vs. Washington, 1940
38	AFC-D: Dallas vs. Tampa Bay, 1981
37	NFC: Green Bay vs. N.Y. Giants, 1961

Most Points Overcome to Win Game
20	NFC-D: Detroit vs. San Francisco, 1957 (trailed 7-27, won 31-27)
18	NFC-D: Dallas vs. San Francisco, 1972 (trailed 3-21, won 30-28)
	AFC-D: Miami vs. Cleveland, 1985 (trailed 3-21, won 24-21)
15	AFC-D: Denver vs. Houston, 1991 (trailed 6-21, won 26-24)

Most Points, Each Half
1st:	41	AFC: Buffalo vs. L.A. Raiders, 1990
	38	NFC: Washington vs. L.A. Rams, 1983
	35	NFC: Cleveland vs. Detroit, 1954
		AFC-D: Oakland vs. Houston, 1969
		SB: Washington vs. Denver, 1987
2nd:	45	NFC: Chi. Bears vs. Washington, 1940
	30	SB: N.Y. Giants vs. Denver, 1986
		AFC: Cleveland vs. Denver, 1987
	28	NFC: Chi. Bears vs. N.Y. Giants, 1941
		NFC: Detroit vs. Cleveland, 1957
		NFC-D: Dallas vs. Cleveland, 1967
		NFC-D: Dallas vs. Tampa Bay, 1981
		SB: San Francisco vs. Denver, 1989

Most Points, Each Quarter
1st:	28	AFC-D: Oakland vs. Houston, 1969
	24	AFC-D: San Diego vs. Miami, 1981
	21	NFC: Chi. Bears vs. Washington, 1940
		AFC: San Diego vs. Boston, 1963
		AFC-D: Oakland vs. Kansas City, 1968
		AFC: Oakland vs. San Diego, 1980
		AFC: Buffalo vs. L.A. Raiders, 1990
2nd:	35	SB: Washington vs. Denver, 1987
	26	AFC-D: Pittsburgh vs. Buffalo, 1974
	24	NFC-D: Chi. Bears vs. Green Bay, 1941
		NFC: Green Bay vs. N.Y. Giants, 1961
3rd:	26	NFC: Chi. Bears vs. Washington, 1940
	21	NFC-D: Dallas vs. Cleveland, 1967
		NFC-D: Dallas vs. Tampa Bay, 1981
		AFC-D: L.A. Raiders vs. Pittsburgh, 1983
		SB: Chicago vs. New England, 1985
		NFC-D: N.Y. Giants vs. San Francisco, 1986
		AFC: Cleveland vs. Denver, 1987
		AFC: Cleveland vs. Denver, 1989
	17	NFC: Cleveland vs. Baltimore, 1964
		NFC-D: Dallas vs. Chicago, 1977
		SB: N.Y. Giants vs. Denver, 1986
4th	27	NFC: N.Y. Giants vs. Chi. Bears, 1934
	24	NFC: Baltimore vs. N.Y. Giants, 1959
	21	AFC: Pittsburgh vs. Oakland, 1974
		NFC: Dallas vs. Los Angeles, 1978
		AFC-FR: N. Y. Jets vs. Cincinnati, 1982
		NFC: San Francisco vs. Washington, 1983
OT:	6	NFC: Baltimore vs. N.Y. Giants, 1958
		AFC-D: Oakland vs. Baltimore, 1977
		NFC-D: L.A. Rams vs. N.Y. Giants, 1989

Touchdowns

Most Touchdowns, Game
11	NFC: Chi. Bears vs. Washington, 1940
8	NFC: Cleveland vs. Detroit, 1954
	NFC: Detroit vs. Cleveland, 1957
	AFC-D: Oakland vs. Houston, 1969
	SB: San Francisco vs. Denver, 1989
7	AFC: San Diego vs. Boston, 1963
	NFC-D: Dallas vs. Cleveland, 1967
	NFC-D: N.Y. Giants vs. San Francisco, 1986
	AFC: Buffalo vs. L.A. Raiders, 1990

Most Touchdowns, Both Teams, Game
11	NFC: Chi. Bears (11) vs. Washington (0), 1940
10	NFC: Detroit (8) vs. Cleveland (2), 1957
	AFC-D: Miami (5) vs. San Diego (5), 1981 (OT)
	AFC: Miami (6) vs. Pittsburgh (4), 1984
9	NFC: Chi. Bears (6) vs. Washington (3), 1943
	NFC: Cleveland (8) vs. Detroit (1), 1954
	NFC-D: Dallas (7) vs. Cleveland (2), 1967
	AFC-D: Oakland (8) vs. Houston (1), 1969
	AFC-D: Oakland (5) vs. Baltimore (4), 1977 (OT)
	SB: Pittsburgh (5) vs. Dallas (4), 1978
	AFC: Denver (5) vs. Cleveland (4), 1987
	SB: San Francisco (8) vs. Denver (1), 1989
	AFC-D: Buffalo (5) vs. Miami (4), 1990

Fewest Touchdowns, Both Teams, Game
0	NFC-D: N.Y. Giants vs. Cleveland, 1950
	NFC-D: Dallas vs. Detroit, 1970
	NFC: Los Angeles vs. Tampa Bay, 1979
1	NFC: Chi. Cardinals (0) vs. Philadelphia (1), 1948
	AFC: San Diego (0) vs. Houston (1), 1961
	AFC: N. Y. Jets (0) vs. Kansas City (1), 1969
	NFC-D: Green Bay (0) vs. Washington (1), 1972
	NFC-FR: New Orleans (0) vs. Chicago (1), 1990
	NFC: N.Y. Giants (0) vs. San Francisco (1), 1990
	AFC-FR: L.A. Raiders (0) vs. Kansas City (1), 1991
2	In many games

Points After Touchdown

Most Points After Touchdown, Game
8	NFC: Cleveland vs. Detroit, 1954
	NFC: Detroit vs. Cleveland, 1957
	AFC-D: Oakland vs. Houston, 1969
7	NFC: Chi. Bears vs. Washington, 1940
	NFC-D: Dallas vs. Cleveland, 1967
	NFC-D: N.Y. Giants vs. San Francisco, 1986

SB: San Francisco vs. Denver, 1989
  6 AFC: San Diego vs. Boston, 1963
      NFC-D: Washington vs. L.A. Rams, 1983
      AFC: Miami vs. Pittsburgh, 1984
      AFC: Buffalo vs. L.A. Raiders, 1990

Most Points After Touchdown, Both Teams, Game
 10 NFC: Detroit (8) vs. Cleveland (2), 1957
      AFC-D: Miami (5) vs. San Diego (5), 1981 (OT)
      AFC: Miami (6) vs. Pittsburgh (4), 1984
  9 NFC: Cleveland (8) vs. Detroit (1), 1954
      NFC-D: Dallas (7) vs. Cleveland (2), 1967
      AFC-D: Oakland (8) vs. Houston (1), 1969
      AFC: Denver (5) vs. Cleveland (4), 1987
      AFC-D: Buffalo (5) vs. Miami (4), 1990
  8 In many games

Fewest Points After Touchdown, Both Teams, Game
  0 NFC-D: N.Y. Giants vs. Cleveland, 1950
      NFC-D: Dallas vs. Detroit, 1970
      NFC: Los Angeles vs. Tampa Bay, 1979

Field Goals
Most Field Goals, Game
  5 NFC-D: Minnesota vs. San Francisco, 1987
      NFC: N.Y. Giants vs. San Francisco, 1990
  4 AFC-D: Boston vs. Buffalo, 1963
      AFC: Oakland vs. Houston, 1967
      SB: Green Bay vs. Oakland, 1967
      NFC: Washington vs. Dallas, 1972
      AFC-D: Oakland vs. Pittsburgh, 1973
      SB: San Francisco vs. Cincinnati, 1981
      AFC-FR: New England vs. N.Y. Jets, 1985
      NFC-FR: Washington vs. L.A. Rams, 1986
      NFC-D: Philadelphia vs. Chicago, 1988
      AFC-FR: Pittsburgh vs. Houston, 1989 (OT)
  3 By many teams

Most Field Goals, Both Teams, Game
  7 AFC-FR: Pittsburgh (4) vs. Houston (3), 1989 (OT)
      NFC: N.Y. Giants (5) vs. San Francisco (2), 1990
  6 NFC-D: Minnesota (5) vs. San Francisco (1), 1987
      NFC-D: Philadelphia (4) vs. Chicago (2), 1988
  5 In many games

Most Field Goals Attempted, Game
  6 AFC: Oakland vs. Houston, 1967
      NFC-D: Los Angeles vs. Dallas, 1973
      AFC-D: Cleveland vs. N.Y. Jets, 1986 (OT)
      NFC: N.Y. Giants vs. San Francisco, 1990
  5 By many teams

Most Field Goals Attempted, Both Teams, Game
  9 NFC-D: Philadelphia (5) vs. Chicago (4), 1988
  8 NFC-D: Los Angeles (6) vs. Dallas (2), 1973
      NFC-D: Detroit (5) vs. San Francisco (3), 1983
      AFC-D: Cleveland (6) vs. N.Y. Jets (2), 1986 (OT)
      NFC-D: Minnesota (5) vs. San Francisco (3), 1987
      AFC-FR: Houston (4) vs. Pittsburgh (4), 1989 (OT)
      NFC-FR: Chicago (4) vs. New Orleans (4), 1990
      NFC: N.Y. Giants (6) vs. San Francisco (2), 1990
  7 In many games

Safeties
Most Safeties, Game
  1 By 18 teams

First Downs
Most First Downs, Game
 34 AFC-D: San Diego vs. Miami, 1981 (OT)
 33 AFC-D: Cleveland vs. N.Y. Jets, 1986 (OT)
 31 SB: San Francisco vs. Miami, 1984

Fewest First Downs, Game
  6 NFC: N.Y. Giants vs. Green Bay, 1961
  7 NFC: Green Bay vs. Boston, 1936
      NFC-D: Pittsburgh vs. Philadelphia, 1947
      NFC: Chi. Cardinals vs. Philadelphia, 1948
      NFC: Los Angeles vs. Philadelphia, 1949
      NFC: Cleveland vs. N.Y. Giants, 1958
      AFC-D: Cincinnati vs. Baltimore, 1970
      NFC-D: Detroit vs. Dallas, 1970
  8 By many teams

Most First Downs, Both Teams, Game
 59 AFC-D: San Diego (34) vs. Miami (25), 1981 (OT)
 55 AFC-FR: San Diego (29) vs. Pittsburgh (26), 1982
 51 AFC: Buffalo (30) vs. L.A. Raiders (21), 1990

Fewest First Downs, Both Teams, Game
 15 NFC: Green Bay (7) vs. Boston (8), 1936
 19 NFC: N.Y. Giants (9) vs. Green Bay (10), 1939
      NFC: Washington (9) vs. Chi. Bears (10), 1942
 20 NFC-D: Cleveland (9) vs. N.Y. Giants (11), 1950

Rushing
Most First Downs, Rushing, Game
 19 NFC-FR: Dallas vs. Los Angeles, 1980
 18 AFC-D: Miami vs. Cincinnati, 1973
      AFC-D: Pittsburgh vs. Buffalo, 1974
 17 AFC-D: Cincinnati vs. Seattle, 1988

Fewest First Downs, Rushing, Game
  0 NFC: Los Angeles vs. Philadelphia, 1949
      AFC: Buffalo vs. Boston, 1963
      AFC: Oakland vs. Pittsburgh, 1974
      NFC-FR: New Orleans vs. Minnesota, 1987
      NFC: L.A. Rams vs. San Francisco, 1989
      NFC-D: Chicago vs. N.Y. Giants, 1990
  1 By many teams

Most First Downs, Rushing, Both Teams, Game
 26 AFC: Buffalo (14) vs. L.A. Raiders (12), 1990
 25 NFC-FR: Dallas (19) vs. Los Angeles (6), 1980
 23 NFC: Cleveland (15) vs. Detroit (8), 1952
      AFC-D: Miami (18) vs. Cincinnati (5), 1973
      AFC-D: Pittsburgh (18) vs. Buffalo (5), 1974

Fewest First Downs, Rushing, Both Teams, Game
  5 AFC-D: Buffalo (0) vs. Boston (5), 1963
  6 NFC: Green Bay (2) vs. Boston (4), 1936
      NFC-D: Baltimore (2) vs. Minnesota (4), 1968
      AFC-D: Houston (1) vs. Oakland (5), 1969
      AFC-FR: N.Y. Jets (1) vs. Houston (5), 1991
  7 NFC-D: Washington (2) vs. N.Y. Giants (5), 1943
      NFC: Baltimore (3) vs. N.Y. Giants (4), 1959
      NFC: Washington (3) vs. Dallas (4), 1972
      AFC-FR: N.Y. Jets (3) vs. Buffalo (4), 1981
      NFC-D: Detroit (3) vs. Dallas (4), 1991

Passing
Most First Downs, Passing, Game
 21 AFC-D: Miami vs. San Diego, 1981 (OT)
      AFC-D: San Diego vs. Miami, 1981 (OT)
      AFC-D: Cleveland vs. N.Y. Jets, 1986 (OT)
      NFC-D: Philadelphia vs. Chicago, 1988
 20 NFC-FR: Dallas vs. L.A. Rams, 1983
      AFC-D: Buffalo vs. Cleveland, 1989
 19 NFC-FR: St. Louis vs. Green Bay, 1982
      NFC-FR: Dallas vs. Tampa Bay, 1982
      AFC-FR: Pittsburgh vs. San Diego, 1982
      AFC-FR: San Diego vs. Pittsburgh, 1982
      NFC: Dallas vs. Washington, 1982
      NFC-D: Detroit vs. Dallas, 1991

Fewest First Downs, Passing, Game
  0 NFC: Philadelphia vs. Chi. Cardinals, 1948
  1 NFC-D: N.Y. Giants vs. Washington, 1943
      NFC: Cleveland vs. Detroit, 1953
      SB: Denver vs. Dallas, 1977
  2 By many teams

Most First Downs, Passing, Both Teams, Game
 42 AFC-D: Miami (21) vs. San Diego (21), 1981 (OT)
 38 AFC-FR: Pittsburgh (19) vs. San Diego (19), 1982
 34 NFC: Washington (18) vs. San Francisco (16), 1990

Fewest First Downs, Passing, Both Teams, Game
  2 NFC: Philadelphia (0) vs. Chi. Cardinals (2), 1948
  4 NFC-D: Cleveland (2) vs. N.Y. Giants (2), 1950
  5 NFC: Detroit (2) vs. N.Y. Giants (3), 1935
      NFC: Green Bay (2) vs. N.Y. Giants (3), 1939

Penalty
Most First Downs, Penalty, Game
  7 AFC-D: New England vs. Oakland, 1976
  6 AFC-D: Cleveland vs. N.Y. Jets, 1986 (OT)
  5 AFC-FR: Cleveland vs. L.A. Raiders, 1982

Most First Downs, Penalty, Both Teams, Game
  9 AFC-D: New England (7) vs. Oakland (2), 1976
  8 NFC-FR: Atlanta (4) vs. Minnesota (4), 1982
  7 AFC-D: Baltimore (4) vs. Oakland (3), 1977 (OT)

Net Yards Gained Rushing and Passing
Most Yards Gained, Game
 610 AFC: San Diego vs. Boston, 1963
 602 SB: Washington vs. Denver, 1987
 569 AFC: Miami vs. Pittsburgh, 1984

Fewest Yards Gained, Game
  86 NFC-D: Cleveland vs. N.Y. Giants, 1958
  99 NFC: Chi. Cardinals vs. Philadelphia, 1948
 114 NFC: N.Y. Giants vs. Washington, 1943

Most Yards Gained, Both Teams, Game
 1,036 AFC-D: San Diego (564) vs. Miami (472), 1981 (OT)
 1,024 AFC: Miami (569) vs. Pittsburgh (455), 1984
   929 SB: Washington (602) vs. Denver (327), 1987

Fewest Yards Gained, Both Teams, Game
 331 NFC: Chi. Cardinals (99) vs. Philadelphia (232), 1948
 332 NFC-D: N.Y. Giants (150) vs. Cleveland (182), 1950
 336 NFC: Boston (116) vs. Green Bay (220), 1936

Rushing
Attempts
Most Attempts, Game
 65 NFC: Detroit vs. N.Y. Giants, 1935
 61 NFC: Philadelphia vs. Los Angeles, 1949
 59 AFC: New England vs. Miami, 1985

Fewest Attempts, Game
  9 SB: Miami vs. San Francisco, 1984
 10 NFC: L.A. Rams vs. San Francisco, 1989
 11 SB: New England vs. Chicago, 1985
      AFC-FR: Seattle vs. Houston, 1987 (OT)
      NFC: San Francisco vs. N.Y. Giants, 1990

Most Attempts, Both Teams, Game
 109 NFC: Detroit (65) vs. N.Y. Giants (44), 1935
  97 AFC-D: Baltimore (50) vs. Oakland (47), 1977 (OT)
  91 NFC: Philadelphia (57) vs. Chi. Cardinals (34), 1948

Fewest Attempts, Both Teams, Game
 38 NFC-D: Detroit (16) vs. Dallas (22), 1991
 43 AFC-FR: Houston (20) vs. N.Y. Jets (23), 1991
 44 NFC-FR: Atlanta (22) vs. New Orleans (22), 1991

Yards Gained

Most Yards Gained, Game

382	NFC: Chi. Bears vs. Washington, 1940
338	NFC-FR: Dallas vs. Los Angeles, 1980
318	AFC: San Diego vs. Boston, 1963

Fewest Yards Gained, Game

7	AFC-D: Buffalo vs. Boston, 1963
	SB: New England vs. Chicago, 1985
17	SB: Minnesota vs. Pittsburgh, 1974
18	AFC-D: Seattle vs. Cincinnati, 1988

Most Yards Gained, Both Teams, Game

430	NFC-FR: Dallas (338) vs. Los Angeles (92), 1980
426	NFC: Cleveland (227) vs. Detroit (199), 1952
404	NFC: Chi. Bears (382) vs. Washington (22), 1940

Fewest Yards Gained, Both Teams, Game

90	AFC-D: Buffalo (7) vs. Boston (83), 1963
106	NFC: Boston (39) vs. Green Bay (67), 1936
128	NFC-FR: Philadelphia (53) vs. Atlanta (75), 1978

Average Gain

Highest Average Gain, Game

9.94	AFC: San Diego vs. Boston, 1963 (32-318)
9.29	NFC-D: Green Bay vs. Dallas, 1982 (17-158)
7.35	NFC-FR: Dallas vs. Los Angeles, 1980 (46-338)

Lowest Average Gain, Game

0.58	AFC-D: Buffalo vs. Boston, 1963 (12-7)
0.64	SB: New England vs. Chicago, 1985 (11-7)
0.81	SB: Minnesota vs. Pittsburgh, 1974 (21-17)

Touchdowns

Most Touchdowns, Game

7	NFC: Chi. Bears vs. Washington, 1940
5	NFC: Cleveland vs. Detroit, 1954
4	NFC: Detroit vs. N.Y. Giants, 1935
	AFC: San Diego vs. Boston, 1963
	NFC-D: Dallas vs. Cleveland, 1967
	NFC: Baltimore vs. Cleveland, 1968
	NFC-FR: Dallas vs. Los Angeles, 1980
	AFC-D: L.A. Raiders vs. Pittsburgh, 1983
	SB: Chicago vs. New England, 1985
	AFC: Buffalo vs. L.A. Raiders, 1990

Most Touchdowns, Both Teams, Game

7	NFC: Chi. Bears (7) vs. Washington (0), 1940
6	NFC: Cleveland (5) vs. Detroit (1), 1954
5	NFC: Chi. Cardinals (3) vs. Philadelphia (2), 1947
	AFC: San Diego (4) vs. Boston (1), 1963
	AFC-D: Cincinnati (3) vs. Buffalo (2), 1981

Passing

Attempts

Most Attempts, Game

65	AFC-D: Cleveland vs. N.Y. Jets, 1986 (OT)
59	SB: Buffalo vs. Washington, 1991
55	NFC-D: Philadelphia vs. Chicago, 1988

Fewest Attempts, Game

5	NFC: Detroit vs. N.Y. Giants, 1935
6	AFC: Miami vs. Oakland, 1973
7	SB: Miami vs. Minnesota, 1973

Most Attempts, Both Teams, Game

102	AFC-D: San Diego (54) vs. Miami (48), 1981 (OT)
96	AFC: N.Y. Jets (49) vs. Oakland (47), 1968
95	AFC-D: Cleveland (65) vs. N.Y. Jets (30), 1986 (OT)

Fewest Attempts, Both Teams, Game

18	NFC: Detroit (5) vs. N.Y. Giants (13), 1935
21	NFC: Chi. Bears (7) vs. N.Y. Giants (14), 1933
23	NFC: Chi. Cardinals (11) vs. Philadelphia (12), 1948

Completions

Most Completions, Game

34	AFC-D: Cleveland vs. N.Y. Jets, 1986 (OT)
33	AFC-D: San Diego vs. Miami, 1981 (OT)
32	St. Louis vs. Green Bay, 1982
	NFC-FR: Dallas vs. L.A. Rams, 1983

Fewest Completions, Game

2	NFC: Detroit vs. N.Y. Giants, 1935
	NFC: Philadelphia vs. Chi. Cardinals, 1948
3	NFC: N.Y. Giants vs. Chi. Bears, 1941
	NFC: Green Bay vs. N.Y. Giants, 1944
	NFC: Chi. Cardinals vs. Philadelphia, 1947
	NFC: Chi. Cardinals vs. Philadelphia, 1948
	NFC-D: Cleveland vs. N.Y. Giants, 1950
	NFC-D: N.Y. Giants vs. Cleveland, 1950
	NFC: Cleveland vs. Detroit, 1953
	AFC: Miami vs. Oakland, 1973
4	NFC-D: Dallas vs. Detroit, 1970
	AFC: Miami vs. Baltimore, 1971
	SB: Miami vs. Washington, 1982
	AFC-FR: Seattle vs. L.A. Raiders, 1984

Most Completions, Both Teams, Game

64	AFC-D: San Diego (33) vs. Miami (31), 1981 (OT)
55	AFC-FR: Pittsburgh (28) vs. San Diego (27), 1982
53	SB: Miami (29) vs. San Francisco (24), 1984

Fewest Completions, Both Teams, Game

5	NFC: Philadelphia (2) vs. Chi. Cardinals (3), 1948
6	NFC: Detroit (2) vs. N.Y. Giants (4), 1935
	NFC-D: Cleveland (3) vs. N.Y. Giants (3), 1950
11	NFC: Green Bay (3) vs. N.Y. Giants (8), 1944
	NFC-D: Dallas (4) vs. Detroit (7), 1970

Completion Percentage

Highest Completion Percentage, Game (20 attempts)

88.0	SB: N.Y. Giants vs. Denver, 1986 (25-22)
87.1	NFC: San Francisco vs. L.A. Rams, 1989 (31-27)
80.0	NFC-D: Washington vs. L.A. Rams, 1983 (25-20)

Lowest Completion Percentage, Game (20 attempts)

18.5	NFC: Tampa Bay vs. Los Angeles, 1979 (27-5)
20.0	NFC-D: N.Y. Giants vs. Washington, 1943 (20-4)
25.8	NFC: Chi. Bears vs. Washington, 1937 (31-8)

Yards Gained

Most Yards Gained, Game

483	AFC-D: Cleveland vs. N.Y. Jets, 1986 (OT)
435	AFC: Miami vs. Pittsburgh, 1984
415	AFC-D: San Diego vs. Miami, 1981 (OT)

Fewest Yards Gained, Game

3	NFC: Chi. Cardinals vs. Philadelphia, 1948
7	NFC: Philadelphia vs. Chi. Cardinals, 1948
9	NFC-D: N.Y. Giants vs. Cleveland, 1950
	NFC: Cleveland vs. Detroit, 1953

Most Yards Gained, Both Teams, Game

809	AFC-D: San Diego (415) vs. Miami (394), 1981 (OT)
747	AFC: Miami (435) vs. Pittsburgh (312), 1984
666	AFC-D: Cleveland (483) vs. N.Y. Jets (183), 1986 (OT)

Fewest Yards Gained, Both Teams, Game

10	NFC: Chi. Cardinals (3) vs. Philadelphia (7), 1948
38	NFC-D: N.Y. Giants (9) vs. Cleveland (29), 1950
102	NFC-D: Dallas (22) vs. Detroit (80), 1970

Times Sacked

Most Times Sacked, Game

9	AFC: Kansas City vs. Buffalo, 1966
	NFC: Chicago vs. San Francisco, 1984
	AFC-D: N.Y. Jets vs. Cleveland, 1986 (OT)
8	NFC: Green Bay vs. Dallas, 1967
	NFC: Minnesota vs. Washington, 1987
7	NFC-D: Dallas vs. Los Angeles, 1973
	SB: Dallas vs. Pittsburgh, 1975
	AFC-FR: Houston vs. Oakland, 1980
	NFC-D: Washington vs. Chicago, 1984
	SB: New England vs. Chicago, 1985

Most Times Sacked, Both Teams, Game

13	AFC: Kansas City (9) vs. Buffalo (4), 1966
	AFC-D: N.Y. Jets (9) vs. Cleveland (4), 1986 (OT)
12	NFC-D: Dallas (7) vs. Los Angeles (5), 1973
	NFC-D: Washington (7) vs. Chicago (5), 1984
	NFC: Chicago (9) vs. San Francisco (3), 1984
10	AFC-FR: Houston (7) vs. Oakland (3), 1980
	NFC-D: N.Y. Giants (6) vs. San Francisco (4), 1984
	SB: New England (7) vs. Chicago (3), 1985

Fewest Times Sacked, Both Teams, Game

0	AFC-D: Buffalo vs. Pittsburgh, 1974
	AFC-FR: Pittsburgh vs. San Diego, 1982
	AFC-D: Buffalo vs. Miami, 1990
	AFC-D: Denver vs. Houston, 1991
1	In many games

Touchdowns

Most Touchdowns, Game

6	AFC-D: Oakland vs. Houston, 1969
5	NFC: Chi. Bears vs. Washington, 1943
	NFC: Detroit vs. Cleveland, 1957
	AFC-D: Oakland vs. Kansas City, 1968
	SB: San Francisco vs. Denver, 1989
4	By many teams

Most Touchdowns, Both Teams, Game

7	NFC: Chi. Bears (5) vs. Washington (2), 1943
	AFC-D: Oakland (6) vs. Houston (1), 1969
	SB: Pittsburgh (4) vs. Dallas (3), 1978
	AFC-D: Miami (4) vs. San Diego (3), 1981 (OT)
	AFC: Miami (4) vs. Pittsburgh (3), 1984
	AFC-D: Buffalo (4) vs. Cleveland (3), 1989
6	NFC-FR: Green Bay (4) vs. St. Louis (2), 1982
	AFC: Cleveland (3) vs. Denver (3), 1987
5	In many games

Interceptions By

Most Interceptions By, Game

8	NFC: Chi. Bears vs. Washington, 1940
7	NFC: Cleveland vs. Los Angeles, 1955
6	NFC: Green Bay vs. N.Y. Giants, 1939
	NFC: Chi. Bears vs. N.Y. Giants, 1946
	NFC: Cleveland vs. Detroit, 1954
	AFC: San Diego vs. Houston, 1961
	AFC: Buffalo vs. L.A. Raiders, 1990

Most Interceptions By, Both Teams, Game

10	NFC: Cleveland (7) vs. Los Angeles (3), 1955
	AFC: San Diego (6) vs. Houston (4), 1961
9	NFC: Green Bay (6) vs. N.Y. Giants (3), 1939
8	NFC: Chi. Bears (8) vs. Washington (0), 1940
	NFC: Chi. Bears (6) vs. N.Y. Giants (2), 1946
	NFC: Cleveland (6) vs. Detroit (2), 1954
	AFC-FR: Buffalo (4) vs. N.Y. Jets (4), 1981
	AFC: Miami (5) vs. N.Y. Jets (3), 1982

Yards Gained

Most Yards Gained, Game

138	AFC-FR: N.Y. Jets vs. Cincinnati, 1982
136	AFC: Dall. Texans vs. Houston, 1962 (OT)
130	NFC-D: Los Angeles vs. St. Louis, 1975

Most Yards Gained, Both Teams, Game
     156   NFC: Green Bay (123) vs. N.Y. Giants (33), 1939
     149   NFC: Cleveland (103) vs. Los Angeles (46), 1955
     141   AFC-FR: Buffalo (79) vs. N.Y. Jets (62), 1981

Touchdowns
Most Touchdowns, Game
       3   NFC: Chi. Bears vs. Washington, 1940
       2   NFC-D: Los Angeles vs. St. Louis, 1975
       1   In many games

Punting
Most Punts, Game
      14   AFC-D: N.Y. Jets vs. Cleveland, 1986 (OT)
      13   NFC: N.Y. Giants vs. Chi. Bears, 1933
            AFC-D: Baltimore vs. Oakland, 1977 (OT)
      11   AFC: Houston vs. Oakland, 1967
            AFC-D: Houston vs. Oakland, 1969
            NFC: L.A. Rams vs. Chicago, 1985
Fewest Punts, Game
       0   NFC-FR: St. Louis vs. Green Bay, 1982
            AFC-FR: N.Y. Jets vs. Cincinnati, 1982
       1   NFC-D: Cleveland vs. Dallas, 1969
            AFC: Miami vs. Oakland, 1973
            AFC-D: Oakland vs. Cincinnati, 1975
            AFC-D: Pittsburgh vs. Baltimore, 1976
            AFC: Pittsburgh vs. Houston, 1978
            NFC-FR: Green Bay vs. St. Louis, 1982
            AFC-FR: Miami vs. New England, 1982
            AFC-FR: San Diego vs. Pittsburgh, 1982
            AFC-D: Cleveland vs. Indianapolis, 1987
            AFC-D: Buffalo vs. Miami, 1990
            AFC-FR: L.A. Raiders vs. Kansas City, 1991
            NFC-FR: Atlanta vs. New Orleans, 1991
            NFC-FR: Chicago vs. Dallas, 1991
            AFC-D: Houston vs. Denver, 1991
       2   In many games
Most Punts, Both Teams, Game
      23   NFC: N.Y. Giants (13) vs. Chi. Bears (10), 1933
      22   AFC-D: N.Y. Jets (14) vs. Cleveland (8), 1986 (OT)
      21   AFC-D: Baltimore (13) vs. Oakland (8), 1977 (OT)
            NFC: L.A. Rams (11) vs. Chicago (10), 1985
Fewest Punts, Both Teams, Game
       1   NFC-FR: St. Louis (0) vs. Green Bay (1), 1982
       2   AFC-FR: N.Y. Jets (0) vs. Cincinnati (2), 1982
       3   AFC: Miami (1) vs. Oakland (2), 1973
            AFC-FR: San Diego (1) vs. Pittsburgh (2), 1982
            AFC-D: Buffalo (1) vs. Miami (2), 1990
            AFC-FR: L.A. Raiders (1) vs. Kansas City (2), 1991
            AFC-D: Houston (1) vs. Denver (2), 1991

Average Yardage
Highest Average, Punting, Game (4 punts)
    56.0   AFC: Oakland vs. San Diego, 1980
    52.5   NFC: Washington vs. Chi. Bears, 1942
    51.6   AFC-D: Cincinnati vs. L.A. Raiders, 1990
Lowest Average, Punting, Game (4 punts)
    24.9   NFC: Washington vs. Chi. Bears, 1937
    25.3   AFC-FR: Pittsburgh vs. Houston, 1989
    25.5   NFC: Green Bay vs. N.Y. Giants, 1962

Punt Returns
Most Punt Returns, Game
       8   NFC: Green Bay vs. N.Y. Giants, 1944
       7   By eight teams
Most Punt Returns, Both Teams, Game
      13   AFC-FR: Houston (7) vs. Oakland (6), 1980
      11   NFC: Green Bay (8) vs. N.Y. Giants (3), 1944
            NFC-D: Green Bay (6) vs. Baltimore (5), 1965
      10   In many games
Fewest Punt Returns, Both Teams, Game
       0   NFC: Chi. Bears vs. N.Y. Giants, 1941
            AFC: Boston vs. San Diego, 1963
            NFC-FR: Green Bay vs. St. Louis, 1982
            AFC-FR: Houston vs. N.Y. Jets, 1991
            AFC-D: Denver vs. Houston, 1991
       1   NFC-D: Miami (0) vs. Pittsburgh (1), 1972
            AFC: Cincinnati (0) vs. San Diego (1), 1981
            AFC-FR: Cincinnati (0) vs. N.Y. Jets (1), 1982
            AFC-FR: San Diego (0) vs. Pittsburgh (1), 1982
            NFC-D: Minnesota (0) vs. Washington (1), 1982
            AFC: Seattle (0) vs. L.A. Raiders (1), 1983
            AFC-D: Pittsburgh (0) vs. Denver (1), 1989
            NFC-FR: New Orleans (0) vs. Atlanta (1), 1991
       2   In many games

Yards Gained
Most Yards Gained, Game
     155   NFC-D: Dallas vs. Cleveland, 1967
     150   NFC: Chi. Cardinals vs. Philadelphia, 1947
     143   NFC-FR: Minnesota vs. New Orleans, 1987
Fewest Yards Gained, Game
    −10   NFC: Green Bay vs. Cleveland, 1965
     −9   NFC: Dallas vs. Green Bay, 1966
            AFC: Kansas City vs. Oakland, 1968
     −5   AFC-D: Miami vs. Oakland, 1970
            NFC-D: San Francisco vs. Dallas, 1972
            NFC: Dallas vs. Washington, 1972
Most Yards Gained, Both Teams, Game
     166   NFC-D: Dallas (155) vs. Cleveland (11), 1967
     160   NFC: Chi. Cardinals (150) vs. Philadelphia (10), 1947
     146   NFC-D: Philadelphia (112) vs. Pittsburgh (34), 1947

Fewest Yards Gained, Both Teams, Game
     −9   NFC: Dallas (−9) vs. Green Bay (0), 1966
     −6   AFC-D: Miami (−5) vs. Oakland (−1), 1970
     −3   NFC-D: San Francisco (−5) vs. Dallas (2), 1972

Touchdowns
Most Touchdowns, Game
       1   By 10 teams

Kickoff Returns
Most Kickoff Returns, Game
      10   NFC-D: L.A. Rams vs. Washington, 1983
       9   NFC: Chi. Bears vs. N.Y. Giants, 1956
            AFC: Boston vs. San Diego, 1963
            AFC: Houston vs. Oakland, 1967
            SB: Denver vs. San Francisco, 1989
            AFC-D: Miami vs. Buffalo, 1990
            AFC: L.A. Raiders vs. Buffalo, 1990
       8   By many teams
Most Kickoff Returns, Both Teams, Game
      15   AFC-D: Miami (9) vs. Buffalo (6), 1990
      13   NFC-D: Green Bay (7) vs. Dallas (6), 1982
      12   In many games
Fewest Kickoff Returns, Both Teams, Game
       1   NFC: Green Bay (0) vs. Boston (1), 1936
       2   NFC-D: Los Angeles (0) vs. Chi. Bears (2), 1950
            AFC: Houston (0) vs. San Diego (2), 1961
            AFC-D: Oakland (1) vs. Pittsburgh (1), 1972
            AFC-D: N.Y. Jets (0) vs. L.A. Raiders (2), 1982
            AFC: Miami (1) vs. N.Y. Jets (1), 1982
            NFC: N.Y. Giants (0) vs. Washington (2), 1986
       3   In many games

Yards Gained
Most Yards Gained, Game
     225   NFC: Washington vs. Chi. Bears, 1940
     222   SB: Miami vs. Washington, 1982
     215   AFC: Houston vs. Oakland, 1967
Most Yards Gained, Both Teams, Game
     379   AFC-D: Baltimore (193) vs. Oakland (186), 1977 (OT)
     321   NFC-D: Dallas (173) vs. Green Bay (148), 1982
     318   AFC-D: Miami (183) vs. Oakland (135), 1974
Fewest Yards Gained, Both Teams, Game
      15   NFC: N.Y. Giants (0) vs. Washington (15), 1986
      31   NFC-D: Los Angeles (0) vs. Chi. Bears (31), 1950
      32   NFC: Green Bay (0) vs. Boston (32), 1936

Touchdowns
Most Touchdowns, Game
       1   NFC-D: San Francisco vs. Dallas, 1972
            AFC-D: Miami vs. Oakland, 1974
            AFC-D: Baltimore vs. Oakland, 1977 (OT)
            SB: Miami vs. Washington, 1982
            SB: Cincinnati vs. San Francisco, 1988
            AFC-D: Cleveland vs. Buffalo, 1989

Penalties
Most Penalties, Game
      14   AFC-FR: Oakland vs. Houston, 1980
            NFC-D: San Francisco vs. N.Y. Giants, 1981
      13   AFC-FR: Houston vs. Cleveland, 1988
            AFC-D: Houston vs. Denver, 1991
      12   NFC-D: Chi. Bears vs. Green Bay, 1941
            AFC-D: Pittsburgh vs. Baltimore, 1976
            SB: Dallas vs. Denver, 1977
            AFC-FR: N.Y. Jets vs. Cincinnati, 1982
Fewest Penalties, Game
       0   NFC: Philadelphia vs. Green Bay, 1960
            NFC-D: Detroit vs. Dallas, 1970
            AFC-D: Miami vs. Oakland, 1970
            SB: Miami vs. Dallas, 1971
            NFC-D: Washington vs. Minnesota, 1973
            SB: Pittsburgh vs. Dallas, 1975
            NFC: San Francisco vs. Chicago, 1988
            SB: Denver vs. San Francisco, 1989
            AFC-D: L.A. Raiders vs. Cincinnati, 1990
       1   By many teams
Most Penalties, Both Teams, Game
      22   AFC-FR: Oakland (14) vs. Houston (8), 1980
            NFC-D: San Francisco (14) vs. N.Y. Giants (8), 1981
            AFC-FR: Houston (13) vs. Cleveland (9), 1988
      21   AFC-D: Oakland (11) vs. New England (10), 1976
      20   SB: Dallas (12) vs. Denver (8), 1977
Fewest Penalties, Both Teams, Game
       1   AFC-D: L.A. Raiders (0) vs. Cincinnati (1), 1990
       2   NFC: Washington (1) vs. Chi. Bears (1), 1937
            NFC-D: Washington (0) vs. Minnesota (2), 1973
            SB: Pittsburgh (0) vs. Dallas (2), 1975
       3   AFC: Miami (1) vs. Baltimore (2), 1971
            NFC: San Francisco (1) vs. Dallas (2), 1971
            SB: Miami (0) vs. Dallas (3), 1971
            AFC-D: Pittsburgh (1) vs. Oakland (2), 1972
            AFC-D: Miami (1) vs. Cincinnati (2), 1973
            SB: Miami (1) vs. San Francisco (2), 1984
            NFC: San Francisco (0) vs. Chicago (3), 1988

Yards Penalized
Most Yards Penalized, Game
     145   NFC-D: San Francisco vs. N.Y. Giants, 1981
     133   SB: Dallas vs. Baltimore, 1970
     128   NFC-D: Chi. Bears vs. Green Bay, 1941

Fewest Yards Penalized, Game
   0 By nine teams
Most Yards Penalized, Both Teams, Game
  206 NFC-D: San Francisco (145) vs. N.Y. Giants (61), 1981
  193 AFC-FR: Houston (118) vs. Cleveland (75), 1988
  192 AFC-D: Denver (104) vs. Pittsburgh (88), 1978
Fewest Yards Penalized, Both Teams, Game
   5 AFC-D: L.A. Raiders (0) vs. Cincinnati (5), 1990
   9 NFC-D: Washington (0) vs. Minnesota (9), 1973
  15 SB: Miami (0) vs. Dallas (15), 1971

Fumbles
Most Fumbles, Game
   6 By 11 teams
Most Fumbles, Both Teams, Game
  12 AFC: Houston (6) vs. Pittsburgh (6), 1978
  10 NFC: Chi. Bears (5) vs. N.Y. Giants (5), 1934
      SB: Dallas (6) vs. Denver (4), 1977
   9 NFC-D: San Francisco (6) vs. Detroit (3), 1957
      NFC-D: San Francisco (5) vs. Dallas (4), 1972
      NFC: Dallas (5) vs. Philadelphia (4), 1980
Most Fumbles Lost, Game
   4 NFC: N.Y. Giants vs. Baltimore, 1958 (OT)
      AFC: Kansas City vs. Oakland, 1969
      SB: Baltimore vs. Dallas, 1970
      AFC: Pittsburgh vs. Oakland, 1975
      SB: Denver vs. Dallas, 1977
      AFC: Houston vs. Pittsburgh, 1978
      AFC: Miami vs. New England, 1985
      SB: New England vs. Chicago, 1985
      NFC-FR: L.A. Rams vs. Washington, 1986
   3 By many teams
Fewest Fumbles, Both Teams, Game
   0 NFC: Green Bay vs. Cleveland, 1965
      AFC: Buffalo vs. San Diego, 1965
      AFC-D: Oakland vs. Miami, 1974
      AFC-D: Houston vs. San Diego, 1979
      NFC-D: Dallas vs. Los Angeles, 1979
      SB: Los Angeles vs. Pittsburgh, 1979
      AFC-D: Buffalo vs. Cincinnati, 1981
      AFC-D: Cleveland vs. N.Y. Jets, 1986 (OT)
      AFC-D: Denver vs. New England, 1986
      NFC-D: San Francisco vs. Washington, 1990
   1 In many games

Recoveries
Most Total Fumbles Recovered, Game
   8 SB: Dallas vs. Denver, 1977 (4 own, 4 opp)
   7 NFC: Chi. Bears vs. N.Y. Giants, 1934 (5 own, 2 opp)
      NFC-D: San Francisco vs. Detroit, 1957 (4 own, 3 opp)
      NFC-D: San Francisco vs. Dallas, 1972 (4 own, 3 opp)
      AFC: Pittsburgh vs. Houston, 1978 (3 own, 4 opp)
   6 AFC: Houston vs. San Diego, 1961 (4 own, 2 opp)
      AFC-D: Cleveland vs. Baltimore, 1971 (4 own, 2 opp)
      AFC-D: Cleveland vs. Oakland, 1980 (5 own, 1 opp)
      NFC: Philadelphia vs. Dallas, 1980 (3 own, 3 opp)
Most Own Fumbles Recovered, Game
   5 NFC: Chi. Bears vs. N.Y. Giants, 1934
      AFC-D: Cleveland vs. Oakland, 1980
   4 By many teams

Turnovers
(Numbers of times losing the ball on interceptions and fumbles.)
Most Turnovers, Game
   9 NFC: Washington vs. Chi. Bears, 1940
      NFC: Detroit vs. Cleveland, 1954
      AFC: Houston vs. Pittsburgh, 1978
   8 NFC: N.Y. Giants vs. Chi. Bears, 1946
      NFC: Los Angeles vs. Cleveland, 1955
      NFC: Cleveland vs. Detroit, 1957
      SB: Denver vs. Dallas, 1977
      NFC-D: Minnesota vs. Philadelphia, 1980
   7 AFC: Houston vs. San Diego, 1961
      SB: Baltimore vs. Dallas, 1970
      AFC: Pittsburgh vs. Oakland, 1975
      NFC-D: Chicago vs. Dallas, 1977
      NFC: Los Angeles vs. Dallas, 1978
      AFC-D: San Diego vs. Miami, 1982
      AFC: Buffalo vs. L.A. Raiders, 1990
Fewest Turnovers, Game
   0 By many teams
Most Turnovers, Both Teams, Game
  14 AFC: Houston (9) vs. Pittsburgh (5), 1978
  13 NFC: Detroit (9) vs. Cleveland (4), 1954
      AFC: Houston (7) vs. San Diego (6), 1961
  12 AFC: Pittsburgh (7) vs. Oakland (5), 1975
Fewest Turnovers, Both Teams, Game
   0 SB: Buffalo vs. N.Y. Giants, 1990
   1 AFC-D: Baltimore (0) vs. Cincinnati (1), 1970
      AFC-D: Pittsburgh (0) vs. Buffalo (1), 1974
      AFC: Oakland (0) vs. Pittsburgh (1), 1976
      NFC-D: Minnesota (0) vs. Washington (1), 1982
      NFC-D: Chicago (0) vs. N.Y. Giants (1), 1985
      SB: N.Y. Giants (0) vs. Denver (1), 1986
      NFC: Washington (0) vs. Minnesota (1), 1987
      AFC-D: Cincinnati (0) vs. L.A. Raiders (1), 1990
      NFC: N.Y. Giants (0) vs. San Francisco (1), 1990
   2 In many games

Compiled by Elias Sports Bureau

Individual Records

Service
Most Games
- 10 Lawrence Taylor, N.Y. Giants, 1982-91
  Ronnie Lott, San Francisco, 1982-85, 1987-91; L.A. Raiders 1992
- 9 *Ken Houston, Houston, 1971-73; Washington, 1974-79
  Joe Greene, Pittsburgh, 1971-77, 1979-80
  Jack Lambert, Pittsburgh, 1976-84
  Walter Payton, Chicago, 1977-81, 1984-87
  Harry Carson, N.Y. Giants, 1979-80, 1982-88
  Mike Webster, Pittsburgh, 1979-86, 1988
  **Anthony Muñoz, Cincinnati, 1982-87, 1989-90, 1992
  Mike Singletary, Chicago, 1984-92
- 8 Tom Mack, Los Angeles, 1971-76, 1978-79
  *Franco Harris, Pittsburgh, 1973-76, 1978-81
  Lemar Parrish, Cincinnati, 1971-72, 1975-77; Washington, 1978, 1980-81
  Art Shell, Oakland, 1973-79, 1981
  Ted Hendricks, Baltimore, 1972-74; Green Bay, 1975; Oakland, 1981-82;
    L.A. Raiders, 1983-84
  *John Hannah, New England, 1977, 1979-83, 1985-86
  *Randy White, Dallas, 1978, 1980-86
  *Mike Haynes, New England, 1978-81, 1983; L.A. Raiders, 1985-87
  James Lofton, Green Bay, 1979, 1981-86; Buffalo 1992
  *Also selected, but did not play, in one additional game
  **Also selected, but did not play, in two additional games

Scoring
Points
Most Points, Career
- 30 Jan Stenerud, Kansas City, 1971-72, 1976; Green Bay, 1985 (6-pat, 8-fg)
- 29 Morten Andersen, New Orleans, 1986-89, 1991 (11-pat, 6-fg)
- 22 Eddie Murray, Detroit, 1981, 1990 (4-pat, 6 fg)

Most Points, Game
- 18 John Brockington, Green Bay, 1973 (3-td)
- 15 Garo Yepremian, Miami, 1974 (5-fg)
- 14 Jan Stenerud, Kansas City, 1972 (2-pat, 4-fg)

Touchdowns
Most Touchdowns, Career
- 3 John Brockington, Green Bay, 1972-74 (2-r, 1-p)
  Earl Campbell, Houston, 1979-82, 1984 (3-r)
  Chuck Muncie, New Orleans, 1980; San Diego, 1982-83 (3-r)
  William Andrews, Atlanta, 1981-84 (1-r, 2-p)
  Marcus Allen, L.A. Raiders, 1983, 1985-86, 1988 (2-r, 1-p)
- 2 By 12 players

Most Touchdowns, Game
- 3 John Brockington, Green Bay, 1973 (2-r, 1-p)
- 2 Mel Renfro, Dallas, 1971 (2-ret)
  Earl Campbell, Houston, 1980 (2-r)
  Chuck Muncie, New Orleans, 1980 (2-r)
  William Andrews, Atlanta, 1984 (2-p)
  Herschel Walker, Dallas, 1989 (2-r)
  Johnny Johnson, Phoenix, 1991 (2-r)

Points After Touchdown
Most Points After Touchdown, Career
- 11 Morten Andersen, New Orleans, 1986-89, 1991 (11 att)
- 6 Chester Marcol, Green Bay, 1973, 1975 (6 att)
  Mark Moseley, Washington, 1980, 1983 (7 att)
  Ali Haji-Sheikh, N.Y. Giants, 1984 (6 att)
  Jan Stenerud, Kansas City, 1971-72, 1976; Green Bay, 1985 (6 att)

Most Points After Touchdown, Game
- 6 Ali Haji-Sheikh, N.Y. Giants, 1984 (6 att)
- 4 Chester Marcol, Green Bay, 1973 (4 att)
  Mark Moseley, Washington, 1980 (5 att)
  Morten Andersen, New Orleans, 1986 (4 att), 1989 (4 att)

Field Goals
Most Field Goals Attempted, Career
- 15 Jan Stenerud, Kansas City, 1971-72, 1976; Green Bay, 1985
- 11 Morten Andersen, New Orleans, 1986-89, 1991
- 9 Eddie Murray, Detroit, 1981, 1990

Most Field Goals Attempted, Game
- 6 Jan Stenerud, Kansas City, 1972
  Eddie Murray, Detroit, 1981
  Mark Moseley, Washington, 1983
- 5 Garo Yepremian, Miami, 1974
- 4 Jan Stenerud, Kansas City, 1976
  Nick Lowery, Kansas City, 1991

Most Field Goals, Career
- 8 Jan Stenerud, Kansas City, 1971-72, 1976; Green Bay, 1985
- 6 Morten Andersen, New Orleans, 1986-89, 1991
  Eddie Murray, Detroit, 1981, 1990
- 5 Garo Yepremian, Miami, 1974, 1979

Most Field Goals, Game
- 5 Garo Yepremian, Miami, 1974 (5 att)
- 4 Jan Stenerud, Kansas City, 1972 (6 att)
  Eddie Murray, Detroit, 1981 (6 att)
- 3 Nick Lowery, Kansas City, 1991 (4 att)

Longest Field Goal
- 51 Morten Andersen, New Orleans, 1989
- 48 Jan Stenerud, Kansas City, 1972
  Jeff Jaeger, L.A. Raiders, 1992
- 43 Gary Anderson, Pittsburgh, 1984
  Nick Lowery, Kansas City, 1991

Safeties
Most Safeties, Game
- 1 Art Still, Kansas City, 1983
  Mark Gastineau, N.Y. Jets, 1985
  Greg Townsend, L.A. Raiders, 1992

Rushing
Attempts
Most Attempts, Career
- 81 Walter Payton, Chicago, 1977-81, 1984-87
- 68 O.J. Simpson, Buffalo, 1973-77
- 63 Eric Dickerson, L.A. Rams, 1984-85, 1987; Indianapolis, 1988-90

Most Attempts, Game
- 19 O.J. Simpson, Buffalo, 1974
- 17 Marv Hubbard, Oakland, 1974
- 16 O.J. Simpson, Buffalo, 1973
  Marcus Allen, L.A. Raiders, 1986

Yards Gained
Most Yards Gained, Career
- 368 Walter Payton, Chicago, 1977-81, 1984-87
- 356 O.J. Simpson, Buffalo, 1973-77
- 220 Earl Campbell, Houston, 1979-82, 1984

Most Yards Gained, Game
- 112 O. J. Simpson, Buffalo, 1973
- 104 Marv Hubbard, Oakland, 1974
- 85 Neal Anderson, Chicago, 1989

Longest Run From Scrimmage
- 41 Lawrence McCutcheon, Los Angeles, 1976
- 32 Randall Cunningham, Philadelphia, 1989
- 30 O.J. Simpson, Buffalo, 1975

Average Gain
Highest Average Gain, Career (20 attempts)
- 5.81 Marv Hubbard, Oakland, 1972-74 (36-209)
- 5.71 Wilbert Montgomery, Philadelphia, 1979-80 (21-120)
- 5.36 Larry Csonka, Miami, 1971-72, 1975 (22-118)

Highest Average Gain, Game (10 attempts)
- 7.00 O.J. Simpson, Buffalo, 1973 (16-112)
  Ottis Anderson, St. Louis, 1981 (10-70)
- 6.91 Walter Payton, Chicago, 1985 (11-76)
- 6.90 Earl Campbell, Houston, 1980 (10-69)

Touchdowns
Most Touchdowns, Career
- 3 Earl Campbell, Houston, 1979-82, 1984
  Chuck Muncie, New Orleans, 1980; San Diego, 1982-83
- 2 John Brockington, Green Bay, 1972-74
  O.J. Simpson, Buffalo, 1973-77
  Walter Payton, Chicago, 1977-81, 1984-87
  Marcus Allen, L.A. Raiders, 1983, 1985-86, 1988
  Herschel Walker, Dallas, 1988-89
  Johnny Johnson, Phoenix, 1991

Most Touchdowns, Game
- 2 John Brockington, Green Bay, 1973
  Earl Campbell, Houston, 1980
  Chuck Muncie, New Orleans, 1980
  Herschel Walker, Dallas, 1989
  Johnny Johnson, Phoenix, 1991

Passing
Attempts
Most Attempts, Career
- 120 Dan Fouts, San Diego, 1980-84, 1986
- 88 Bob Griese, Miami, 1971-72, 1974-75, 1977, 1979
- 57 Joe Montana, San Francisco, 1982, 1984-85, 1988

Most Attempts, Game
- 32 Bill Kenney, Kansas City, 1984
- 30 Dan Fouts, San Diego, 1983
- 28 Jim Hart, St. Louis, 1976

Completions
Most Completions, Career
- 63 Dan Fouts, San Diego, 1980-84, 1986
- 44 Bob Griese, Miami, 1971-72, 1974-75, 1977, 1979
- 33 Ken Anderson, Cincinnati, 1976-77, 1982-83

Most Completions, Game
- 21 Joe Theismann, Washington, 1984
- 17 Dan Fouts, San Diego, 1983
- 16 Dan Fouts, San Diego, 1986

Completion Percentage
Highest Completion Percentage, Career (40 attempts)
- 68.9 Joe Theismann, Washington, 1983-84 (45-31)
- 64.4 Jim Kelly, Buffalo, 1988, 1991-92 (45-29)
- 58.9 Ken Anderson, Cincinnati, 1976-77, 1982-83 (56-33)

Highest Completion Percentage, Game (10 attempts)
- 90.0 Archie Manning, New Orleans, 1980 (10-9)
- 77.8 Joe Theismann, Washington, 1984 (27-21)
- 72.2 Jim Everett, L.A. Rams, 1991 (18-13)

Yards Gained
Most Yards Gained, Career
- 890 Dan Fouts, San Diego, 1980-84, 1986
- 554 Bob Griese, Miami, 1971-72, 1974-75, 1977, 1979
- 398 Ken Anderson, Cincinnati, 1976-77, 1982-83

Most Yards Gained, Game
- 274 Dan Fouts, San Diego, 1983
- 242 Joe Theismann, Washington, 1984
- 212 Phil Simms, N.Y. Giants, 1986

Longest Completion
- 64 Dan Pastorini, Houston (to Burrough, Houston), 1976 (TD)
- 59 Randall Cunningham, Philadelphia (to Jackson, Philadelphia [19 yards] lateral to Byner, Washington [40 yards]), 1991
- 57 James Harris, Los Angeles (to Gray, St. Louis), 1975
  - Ken Anderson, Cincinnati (to G. Pruitt, Cleveland), 1977

Average Gain
Highest Average Gain, Career (40 attempts)
- 8.02 Jim Kelly, Buffalo, 1988, 1991-92 (45-361)
- 7.91 Randall Cunningham, Philadelphia, 1989-91 (44-348)
- 7.64 Joe Theismann, Washington, 1983-84 (45-344)

Highest Average Gain, Game (10 attempts)
- 15.27 Randall Cunningham, Philadelphia, 1991 (11-168)
- 11.40 Ken Anderson, Cincinnati, 1977 (10-114)
- 11.20 Archie Manning, New Orleans, 1980 (10-112)

Touchdowns
Most Touchdowns, Career
- 3 Joe Theismann, Washington, 1983-84
  - Joe Montana, San Francisco, 1982, 1984-85, 1988
  - Phil Simms, N.Y. Giants, 1986
  - Jim Kelly, Buffalo, 1988, 1991-92
- 2 James Harris, Los Angeles, 1975
  - Mike Boryla, Philadelphia, 1976
  - Ken Anderson, Cincinnati, 1976-77, 1982-83
  - Mark Rypien, Washington, 1990, 1992

Most Touchdowns, Game
- 3 Joe Theismann, Washington, 1984
  - Phil Simms, N.Y. Giants, 1986
- 2 James Harris, Los Angeles, 1975
  - Mike Boryla, Philadelphia, 1976
  - Ken Anderson, Cincinnati, 1977
  - Jim Kelly, Buffalo, 1991
  - Mark Rypien, Washington, 1992

Had Intercepted
Most Passes Had Intercepted, Career
- 8 Dan Fouts, San Diego, 1980-84, 1986
- 6 Jim Hart, St. Louis, 1975-78
- 5 Ken Stabler, Oakland, 1974-75, 1978

Most Passes Had Intercepted, Game
- 5 Jim Hart, St. Louis, 1977
- 4 Ken Stabler, Oakland, 1974
- 3 Dan Fouts, San Diego, 1986
  - Mark Rypien, Washington, 1990

Most Attempts, Without Interception, Game
- 27 Joe Theismann, Washington, 1984
  - Phil Simms, N.Y. Giants, 1986
- 26 John Brodie, San Francisco, 1971
  - Danny White, Dallas, 1983
- 21 Roman Gabriel, Philadelphia, 1974
  - Dan Marino, Miami, 1985

Percentage, Passes Had Intercepted
Lowest Percentage, Passes Had Intercepted, Career (40 attempts)
- 0.00 Joe Theismann, Washington, 1983-84 (45-0)
- 2.13 Dave Krieg, Seattle, 1985, 1989-90 (47-1)
- 2.22 Jim Kelly, Buffalo, 1988, 1991-92 (45-1)

Pass Receiving
Receptions
Most Receptions, Career
- 18 Walter Payton, Chicago, 1977-81, 1984-87
- 17 Steve Largent, Seattle, 1979, 1982, 1985-88
- 16 Jerry Rice, San Francisco, 1987-88, 1990-92

Most Receptions, Game
- 8 Steve Largent, Seattle, 1986
  - Michael Irvin, Dallas, 1992
- 7 John Stallworth, Pittsburgh, 1983
  - Jerry Rice, San Francisco, 1992
- 6 John Stallworth, Pittsburgh, 1980
  - Kellen Winslow, San Diego, 1982
  - Gary Clark, Washington, 1991

Yards Gained
Most Yards Gained, Career
- 236 Steve Largent, Seattle, 1979, 1982, 1985-88
- 226 Wes Chandler, New Orleans, 1980; San Diego, 1983-84, 1986
- 209 Jerry Rice, San Francisco, 1987-88, 1990-92

Most Yards Gained, Game
- 125 Michael Irvin, Dallas, 1992
- 114 Wes Chandler, San Diego, 1986
- 96 Ken Burrough, Houston, 1976

Longest Reception
- 64 Ken Burrough, Houston (from Pastorini, Houston), 1976 (TD)
- 59 Keith Jackson, Philadelphia (19 yards) lateral to Earnest Byner, Washington (40 yards) (from Cunningham, Philadelphia), 1991
- 57 Mel Gray, St. Louis (from Harris, Los Angeles), 1975
  - Greg Pruitt, Cleveland (from Anderson, Cincinnati), 1977

Touchdowns
Most Touchdowns, Career
- 2 Mel Gray, St. Louis, 1975-78
  - Cliff Branch, Oakland, 1975-78
  - Terry Metcalf, St. Louis, 1975-76, 1978
  - Tony Hill, Dallas, 1979-80, 1986
  - William Andrews, Atlanta, 1981-84

James Lofton, Green Bay, 1979, 1981-86; Buffalo 1992
Jimmie Giles, Tampa Bay, 1981-83, 1986

Most Touchdowns, Game
- 2 William Andrews, Atlanta, 1984

Interceptions By
Most Interceptions By, Career
- 4 Everson Walls, Dallas, 1982-84, 1986
- 3 Ken Houston, Houston, 1971-73; Washington, 1974-79
  - Jack Lambert, Pittsburgh, 1976-84
  - Ted Hendricks, Baltimore, 1972-74; Green Bay, 1975; Oakland, 1981-82; L.A. Raiders, 1983-84
  - Mike Haynes, New England, 1978-81, 1983; L.A. Raiders, 1985-87
- 2 By seven players

Most Interceptions By, Game
- 2 Mel Blount, Pittsburgh, 1977
  - Everson Walls, Dallas, 1982, 1983
  - LeRoy Irvin, L.A. Rams, 1986
  - David Fulcher, Cincinnati, 1990

Yards Gained
Most Yards Gained, Career
- 77 Ted Hendricks, Baltimore, 1972-74; Green Bay, 1975; Oakland, 1981-82; L.A. Raiders, 1983-84
- 51 Jerry Gray, L.A. Rams, 1987-90
- 48 Joey Browner, Minnesota, 1986-90

Most Yards Gained, Game
- 65 Ted Hendricks, Baltimore, 1973
- 51 Jerry Gray, L.A. Rams, 1990
- 48 Joey Browner, Minnesota, 1986

Longest Gain
- 65 Ted Hendricks, Baltimore, 1973
- 51 Jerry Gray, L.A. Rams, 1990 (TD)
- 48 Joey Browner, Minnesota, 1986 (TD)

Touchdowns
Most Touchdowns, Game
- 1 Bobby Bell, Kansas City, 1973
  - Nolan Cromwell, L.A. Rams, 1984
  - Joey Browner, Minnesota, 1986
  - Jerry Gray, L.A. Rams, 1990
  - Mike Johnson, Cleveland, 1990

Punting
Most Punts, Career
- 33 Ray Guy, Oakland, 1974-79, 1981
- 19 Dave Jennings, N.Y. Giants, 1979-81, 1983
- 16 Jerrel Wilson, Kansas City, 1971-73
  - Tom Wittum, San Francisco, 1974-75
  - Rohn Stark, Indianapolis, 1986-87, 1991

Most Punts, Game
- 10 Reggie Roby, Miami, 1985
- 9 Tom Wittum, San Francisco, 1974
  - Rohn Stark, Indianapolis, 1987
- 8 Jerrel Wilson, Kansas City, 1971
  - Tom Skladany, Detroit, 1982

Longest Punt
- 64 Tom Wittum, San Francisco, 1974
- 61 Reggie Roby, Miami, 1985
- 60 Ron Widby, Dallas, 1972

Average Yardage
Highest Average, Career (10 punts)
- 45.25 Jerrel Wilson, Kansas City, 1971-73 (16-724)
- 44.79 Reggie Roby, Miami, 1985, 1990 (14-627)
- 44.64 Ray Guy, Oakland, 1974-79, 1981 (33-1,473)

Highest Average, Game (4 punts)
- 49.57 Jim Arnold, Detroit, 1988 (7-347)
- 49.00 Ray Guy, Oakland, 1974 (4-196)
- 47.75 Bob Grupp, Kansas City, 1980 (4-191)

Punt Returns
Most Punt Returns, Career
- 13 Rick Upchurch, Denver, 1977, 1979-80, 1983
- 11 Vai Sikahema, St. Louis, 1987-88
- 10 Mike Nelms, Washington, 1981-83

Most Punt Returns, Game
- 7 Vai Sikahema, St. Louis, 1987
- 6 Henry Ellard, L.A. Rams, 1985
  - Gerald McNeil, Cleveland, 1988
- 5 Rick Upchurch, Denver, 1980
  - Mike Nelms, Washington, 1981
  - Carl Roaches, Houston, 1982

Most Fair Catches, Game
- 2 Jerry Logan, Baltimore, 1971
  - Dick Anderson, Miami, 1974
  - Henry Ellard, L.A. Rams, 1985

Yards Gained
Most Yards Gained, Career
- 183 Billy Johnson, Houston, 1976, 1978; Atlanta, 1984
- 138 Rick Upchurch, Denver, 1977, 1979-80, 1983
- 119 Mike Nelms, Washington, 1981-83

Most Yards Gained, Game
- 159 Billy Johnson, Houston, 1976
- 138 Mel Renfro, Dallas, 1971
- 117 Wally Henry, Philadelphia, 1980

Longest Punt Return
- 90 Billy Johnson, Houston, 1976 (TD)
- 86 Wally Henry, Philadelphia, 1980 (TD)
- 82 Mel Renfro, Dallas, 1971 (TD)

Touchdowns
Most Touchdowns, Game
- 2 Mel Renfro, Dallas, 1971
- 1 Billy Johnson, Houston, 1976
  -    Wally Henry, Philadelphia, 1980

Kickoff Returns
Most Kickoff Returns, Career
- 10 Rick Upchurch, Denver, 1977, 1979-80, 1983
  -    Greg Pruitt, Cleveland, 1974-75, 1977-78; L.A. Raiders, 1984
- 8 Mike Nelms, Washington, 1981-83
- 7 Mel Gray, Detroit, 1991-92

Most Kickoff Returns, Game
- 6 Greg Pruitt, L.A. Raiders, 1984
- 5 Les (Speedy) Duncan, Washington, 1972
  -    Ron Smith, Chicago, 1973
  -    Herb Mul-Key, Washington, 1974
  -    Mel Gray, Detroit, 1991
- 4 By six players

Yards Gained
Most Yards Gained, Career
- 309 Greg Pruitt, Cleveland, 1974-75, 1977-78; L.A. Raiders, 1984
- 222 Rick Upchurch, Denver, 1977, 1979-80, 1983
- 175 Les (Speedy) Duncan, Washington, 1972

Most Yards Gained, Game
- 192 Greg Pruitt, L.A. Raiders, 1984
- 175 Les (Speedy) Duncan, Washington, 1972
- 152 Ron Smith, Chicago, 1973

Longest Kickoff Return
- 62 Greg Pruitt, L.A. Raiders, 1984
- 61 Eugene (Mercury) Morris, Miami, 1972
- 55 Ron Smith, Chicago, 1973

Touchdowns
Most Touchdowns, Game
-    None

Fumbles
Most Fumbles, Career
- 6 Dan Fouts, San Diego, 1980-84, 1986
- 4 Lawrence McCutcheon, Los Angeles, 1974-78
  -    Franco Harris, Pittsburgh, 1973-76, 1978-81
  -    Jay Schroeder, Washington, 1987
  -    Vai Sikahema, St. Louis, 1987-88
- 3 O.J. Simpson, Buffalo, 1973-77
  -    William Andrews, Atlanta, 1981-84
  -    Joe Montana, San Francisco, 1982, 1984-85, 1988
  -    Walter Payton, Chicago, 1977-81, 1984-87
  -    Neil Lomax, St. Louis, 1985, 1988
  -    Jim Kelly, Buffalo, 1988, 1991-92

Most Fumbles, Game
- 4 Jay Schroeder, Washington, 1987
- 3 Dan Fouts, San Diego, 1982
  -    Vai Sikahema, St. Louis, 1987
- 2 By 11 players

Recoveries
Most Fumbles Recovered, Career
- 3 Harold Jackson, Philadelphia, 1973; Los Angeles, 1974, 1976, 1978 (3-own)
  -    Dan Fouts, San Diego, 1980-84, 1986 (3-own)
  -    Randy White, Dallas, 1978, 1980-86 (3-opp)
- 2 By many players

Most Fumbles Recovered, Game
- 2 Dick Anderson, Miami, 1974 (1-own, 1-opp)
  -    Harold Jackson, Los Angeles, 1974 (2-own)
  -    Dan Fouts, San Diego, 1982 (2-own)
  -    Joey Browner, Minnesota, 1990 (2-opp)

Yardage
Longest Fumble Return
- 83 Art Still, Kansas City, 1985 (TD, opp)
- 51 Phil Villapiano, Oakland, 1974 (opp)
- 37 Sam Mills, New Orleans, 1988 (opp)

Touchdowns
Most Touchdowns, Game
- 1 Art Still, Kansas City, 1985
  -    Keith Millard, Minnesota, 1990

Sacks
Sacks have been compiled since 1983.
Most Sacks, Career
- 8.5 Reggie White, Philadelphia, 1987-92
- 7 Mark Gastineau, N.Y. Jets, 1983-86
  -    Howie Long, L.A. Raiders, 1984-88, 1990

Most Sacks, Game
- 4 Mark Gastineau, N.Y. Jets, 1985
  -    Reggie White, Philadelphia, 1987
- 3 Richard Dent, Chicago, 1985
  -    Bruce Smith, Buffalo, 1991
- 2 By many players

Team Records

Scoring
Most Points, Game
- 45 NFC, 1984
Fewest Points, Game
- 3 AFC, 1984, 1989

Most Points, Both Teams, Game
- 64 NFC (37) vs. AFC (27), 1980
Fewest Points, Both Teams, Game
- 16 NFC (6) vs. AFC (10), 1987

Touchdowns
Most Touchdowns, Game
- 6 NFC, 1984
Fewest Touchdowns, Game
- 0 AFC, 1971, 1974, 1984, 1989
  -    NFC, 1987, 1988
Most Touchdowns, Both Teams, Game
- 8 AFC (4) vs. NFC (4), 1973
  -    NFC (5) vs. AFC (3), 1980
Fewest Touchdowns, Both Teams, Game
- 1 AFC (0) vs. NFC (1), 1974
  -    NFC (0) vs. AFC (1), 1987
  -    NFC (0) vs. AFC (1), 1988

Points After Touchdown
Most Points After Touchdown, Game
- 6 NFC, 1984
Most Points After Touchdown, Both Teams, Game
- 7 NFC (4) vs. AFC (3), 1973
  -    NFC (4) vs. AFC (3), 1980
  -    NFC (4) vs. AFC (3), 1986

Field Goals
Most Field Goals Attempted, Game
- 6 AFC, 1972
  -    NFC, 1981, 1983
Most Field Goals Attempted, Both Teams, Game
- 9 NFC (6) vs. AFC (3), 1983
Most Field Goals, Game
- 5 AFC, 1974
Most Field Goals, Both Teams, Game
- 7 AFC (5) vs. NFC (2), 1974

Net Yards Gained Rushing And Passing
Most Yards Gained, Game
- 466 AFC, 1983
Fewest Yards Gained, Game
- 146 AFC, 1971
Most Yards Gained, Both Teams, Game
- 811 AFC (466) vs. NFC (345), 1983
Fewest Yards Gained, Both Teams, Game
- 424 AFC (202) vs. NFC (222), 1987

Rushing
Attempts
Most Attempts, Game
- 50 AFC, 1974
Fewest Attempts, Game
- 15 AFC, 1989
Most Attempts, Both Teams, Game
- 80 AFC (50) vs. NFC (30), 1974
Fewest Attempts, Both Teams, Game
- 48 AFC (20) vs. NFC (28), 1991

Yards Gained
Most Yards Gained, Game
- 224 NFC, 1976
Fewest Yards Gained, Game
- 28 NFC, 1992
Most Yards Gained, Both Teams, Game
- 425 NFC (224) vs. AFC (201), 1976
Fewest Yards Gained, Both Teams, Game
- 131 NFC (28) vs. AFC (103), 1992

Touchdowns
Most Touchdowns, Game
- 3 NFC, 1989, 1991
Most Touchdowns, Both Teams, Game
- 4 AFC (2) vs. NFC (2), 1973
  -    AFC (2) vs. NFC (2), 1980

Passing
Attempts
Most Attempts, Game
- 50 AFC, 1983
Fewest Attempts, Game
- 17 NFC, 1972
Most Attempts, Both Teams, Game
- 94 AFC (50) vs. NFC (44), 1983
Fewest Attempts, Both Teams, Game
- 42 NFC (17) vs. AFC (25), 1972

Completions
Most Completions, Game
- 31 AFC, 1983
Fewest Completions, Game
- 7 NFC, 1972, 1982
Most Completions, Both Teams, Game
- 55 AFC (31) vs. NFC (24), 1983
Fewest Completions, Both Teams, Game
- 18 NFC (7) vs. AFC (11), 1972

Yards Gained
Most Yards Gained, Game
- 387 AFC, 1983
Fewest Yards Gained, Game
- 42 NFC, 1982

Most Yards Gained, Both Teams, Game
608 AFC (387) vs. NFC (221), 1983
Fewest Yards Gained, Both Teams, Game
215 NFC (89) vs. AFC (126), 1972

Times Sacked
Most Times Sacked, Game
9 NFC, 1985
Fewest Times Sacked, Game
0 NFC, 1971
Most Times Sacked, Both Teams, Game
17 NFC (9) vs. AFC (8), 1985
Fewest Times Sacked, Both Teams, Game
4 AFC (2) vs. NFC (2), 1978

Touchdowns
Most Touchdowns, Game
4 NFC, 1984
Most Touchdowns, Both Teams, Game
5 NFC (3) vs. AFC (2), 1986

Interceptions By
Most Interceptions By, Game
6 AFC, 1977
Most Interceptions By, Both Teams, Game
7 AFC (6) vs. NFC (1), 1977

Yards Gained
Most Yards Gained, Game
78 NFC, 1986
Most Yards Gained, Both Teams, Game
99 NFC (64) vs. AFC (35), 1975

Touchdowns
Most Touchdowns, Game
1 AFC, 1973, 1990
NFC, 1984, 1986, 1990

Punting
Most Punts, Game
10 AFC, 1985
Fewest Punts, Game
0 NFC, 1989
Most Punts, Both Teams, Game
16 AFC (10) vs. NFC (6), 1985
Fewest Punts, Both Teams, Game
4 NFC (1) vs. AFC (3), 1992

Average Yardage
Highest Average, Game
50.50 AFC, 1991 (2-101)

Punt Returns
Most Punt Returns, Game
7 NFC, 1985, 1987
Fewest Punt Returns, Game
0 AFC, 1984, 1989
Most Punt Returns, Both Teams, Game
11 NFC (7) vs. AFC (4), 1985
Fewest Punt Returns, Both Teams, Game
3 AFC (0) vs. NFC (3), 1984
AFC (0) vs. NFC (3), 1989
NFC (1) vs. AFC (2), 1991
NFC (2) vs. AFC (1), 1992

Yards Gained
Most Yards Gained, Game
177 AFC, 1976
Fewest Yards Gained, Game
−1 NFC, 1991
Most Yards Gained, Both Teams, Game
263 AFC (177) vs. NFC (86), 1976
Fewest Yards Gained, Both Teams, Game
16 AFC (0) vs. NFC (16), 1984

Touchdowns
Most Touchdowns, Game
2 NFC, 1971

Kickoff Returns
Most Kickoff Returns, Game
7 AFC, 1984
Fewest Kickoff Returns, Game
1 NFC, 1971, 1984
AFC, 1988, 1991
Most Kickoff Returns, Both Teams, Game
10 AFC (5) vs. NFC (5), 1976
AFC (5) vs. NFC (5), 1986
Fewest Kickoff Returns, Both Teams, Game
5 NFC (2) vs. AFC (3), 1979
AFC (1) vs. NFC (4), 1988
NFC (2) vs. AFC (3), 1992

Yards Gained
Most Yards Gained, Game
215 AFC, 1984
Fewest Yards Gained, Game
6 NFC, 1971
Most Yards Gained, Both Teams, Game
293 NFC (200) vs. AFC (93), 1972
Fewest Yards Gained, Both Teams, Game
99 NFC (48) vs. AFC (51), 1987

Touchdowns
Most Touchdowns, Game
None

Fumbles
Most Fumbles, Game
10 NFC, 1974
Most Fumbles, Both Teams, Game
15 NFC (10) vs. AFC (5), 1974

Recoveries
Most Fumbles Recovered, Game
10 NFC, 1974 (6 own, 4 opp)
Most Fumbles Lost, Game
4 AFC, 1974, 1988
NFC, 1974

Yards Gained
Most Yards Gained, Game
87 AFC, 1985

Touchdowns
Most Touchdowns, Game
1 AFC, 1985
NFC, 1990

Turnovers
(Number of times losing the ball on interceptions and fumbles.)
Most Turnovers, Game
8 AFC, 1974
Fewest Turnovers, Game
0 AFC, 1991
NFC, 1991
Most Turnovers, Both Teams, Game
12 AFC (8) vs. NFC (4), 1974
Fewest Turnovers, Both Teams, Game
0 AFC vs. NFC, 1991

RULES

1992 NFL Roster of Officials 376
Official Signals 378
Digest of Rules 382

1992 NFL Roster of Officials

Jerry Seeman, Director of Officiating
Jack Reader, Assistant Director of Officiating
Leo Miles, Supervisor of Officials
Ron DeSouza, Supervisor of Officials

No.	Name	Position	College	No.	Name	Position	College
25	Alderton, John	Line Judge	Portland State	18	Lewis, Bob	Field Judge	No College
115	Ancich, Hendi	Umpire	Harbor College	49	Look, Dean	Side Judge	Michigan State
81	Anderson, Dave	Head Linesman	Salem College	98	Lovett, Bill	Back Judge	Maryland
34	Austin, Gerald	Referee	Western Carolina	59	Luckett, Phil	Field Judge	Texas-El Paso
22	Baetz, Paul	Back Judge	Heidelberg	82	Mallette, Pat	Field Judge	Nebraska
91	Baker, Ken	Back Judge	Eastern Illinois	9	Markbreit, Jerry	Referee	Illinois
26	Baltz, Mark	Head Linesman	Ohio University	38	Maurer, Bruce	Line Judge	Ohio State
55	Barnes, Tom	Line Judge	Minnesota	48	McCarter, Gordon	Referee	Western Reserve
56	Baynes, Ron	Line Judge	Auburn	95	McElwee, Bob	Referee	Navy
32	Bergman, Jeff	Line Judge	Robert Morris	41	McKenzie, Dick	Line Judge	Ashland
17	Bergman, Jerry	Head Linesman	Duquesne	76	Merrifield, Ed	Field Judge	Missouri
83	Blum, Ron	Line Judge	Marin College	80	Millis, Timmie	Back Judge	Millsaps
90	Borgard, Mike	Side Judge	St. Louis	117	Montgomery, Ben	Line Judge	Morehouse
110	Botchan, Ron	Umpire	Occidental	36	Moore, Bob	Back Judge	Dayton
101	Boylston, Bob	Umpire	Alabama	60	Moore, Tommy	Side Judge	Stephen F. Austin
31	Brown, Chad	Umpire	East Texas State	20	Nemmers, Larry	Referee	Upper Iowa
94	Carey, Mike	Side Judge	Santa Clara	51	Orem, Dale	Line Judge	Louisville
39	Carlsen, Don	Side Judge	Cal State-Chico	77	Orr, Don	Field Judge	Vanderbilt
63	Carollo, Bill	Side Judge	Wisconsin	10	Phares, Ron	Head Linesman	Virginia Tech
43	Cashion, Red	Referee	Texas A&M	79	Pointer, Aaron	Head Linesman	Pacific Lutheran
24	Clymer, Roy	Back Judge	New Mexico State	92	Poole, Jim	Back Judge	San Diego State
65	Coleman, Walt	Line Judge	Arkansas	58	Quinby, Bill	Side Judge	Iowa
27	Conway, Al	Umpire	Army	5	Quirk, Jim	Line Judge	Delaware
71	Coukart, Ed	Umpire	Northwestern	53	Reynolds, Bill	Line Judge	West Chester State
61	Creed, Dick	Side Judge	Louisville	68	Richard, Louis	Back Judge	Southwest Louisiana
75	Daopoulos, Jim	Back Judge	Kentucky	30	Riggs, Dennis	Umpire	Bellarmine
78	Demmas, Art	Umpire	Vanderbilt	121	Rivers, Sanford	Head Linesman	Youngstown State
113	Dorkowski, Don	Field Judge	Cal State-Los Angeles	46	Robison, John	Field Judge	Utah
57	Fiffick, Ed	Umpire	Marquette	33	Roe, Howard	Referee	Wichita State
47	Fincken, Tom	Side Judge	Kansas State	21	Schleyer, John	Head Linesman	Millersville
111	Frantz, Earnie	Head Linesman	No College	122	Schmitz, Bill	Field Judge	Colorado State
50	Gereb, Neil	Umpire	California	109	Semon, Sid	Head Linesman	Southern California
72	Gierke, Terry	Head Linesman	Portland State	118	Sifferman, Tom	Back Judge	Seattle
15	Glass, Bama	Line Judge	Colorado	73	Skelton, Bobby	Field Judge	Alabama
3	Golmont, Van	Side Judge	Miami	29	Slavin, Howard	Side Judge	Southern California
19	Green, Scott	Field Judge	Delaware	88	Spitler, Ron	Side Judge	Panhandle State
23	Grier, Johnny	Referee	University of D.C.	88	Steenson, Scott	Back Judge	North Texas State
40	Haggerty, Pat	Referee	Colorado State	62	Stewart, Charles	Line Judge	No College
96	Hakes, Don	Field Judge	Bradley	103	Stuart, Rex	Umpire	Appalachian State
104	Hamer, Dale	Referee	California, Pa.	4	Toole, Doug	Side Judge	Utah State
42	Hamilton, Dave	Umpire	Utah	37	Upson, Larry	Field Judge	Prince George C.C.
44	Hampton, Donnie	Field Judge	Georgia	93	Vaughan, Jack	Field Judge	Mississippi State
105	Hantak, Dick	Referee	Southeast Missouri	52	Veteri, Tony	Head Linesman	Manhattan College
112	Haynes, Joe	Line Judge	Alcorn State	100	Wagner, Bob	Umpire	Penn State
54	Hayward, George	Head Linesman	Missouri	28	Wedge, Don	Side Judge	Ohio Wesleyan
85	Hochuli, Ed	Back Judge	Texas-El Paso	87	Weidner, Paul	Head Linesman	Cincinnati
114	Johnson, Tom	Head Linesman	Miami, Ohio	89	Wells, Gordon	Umpire	Occidental
97	Jones, Nathan	Side Judge	Lewis & Clark	123	White, Tom	Referee	Temple
106	Jury, Al	Back Judge	San Bernardino Valley	99	Williams, Banks	Back Judge	Houston
107	Kearney, Jim	Back Judge	Pennsylvania	8	Williams, Dale	Head Linesman	Cal St.-Northridge
67	Keck, John	Umpire	Cornell College	84	Wortman, Bob	Field Judge	Findlay
108	Kemp, Stan	Referee	Michigan	16	Wyant, David	Side Judge	Virginia
86	Kukar, Bernie	Referee	St. John's	11	Wyant, Fred	Line Judge	West Virginia
120	Lane, Gary	Referee	Missouri				

Numerical Roster

No.	Name	Position
3	Van Golmont	SJ
4	Doug Toole	SJ
5	Jim Quirk	LJ
8	Dale Williams	HL
9	Jerry Markbreit	R
10	Ron Phares	HL
11	Fred Wyant	LJ
15	Bama Glass	LJ
16	David Wyant	SJ
17	Jerry Bergman	HL
18	Bob Lewis	FJ
19	Scott Green	FJ
20	Larry Nemmers	R
21	John Schleyer	HL
22	Paul Baetz	BJ
23	Johnny Grier	R
24	Roy Clymer	BJ
25	John Alderton	LJ
26	Mark Baltz	HL
27	Al Conway	U
28	Don Wedge	SJ
29	Howard Slavin	SJ
30	Dennis Riggs	U
31	Chad Brown	U
32	Jeff Bergman	LJ
33	Howard Roe	R
34	Gerry Austin	R
36	Bob Moore	BJ
37	Larry Upson	FJ
38	Bruce Maurer	LJ
39	Don Carlsen	SJ
40	Pat Haggerty	R
41	Dick McKenzie	LJ
42	Dave Hamilton	U
43	Red Cashion	R
44	Donnie Hampton	FJ
46	John Robison	FJ
47	Tom Fincken	SJ
48	Gordon McCarter	R
49	Dean Look	SJ
50	Neil Gereb	U
51	Dale Orem	LJ
52	Tony Veteri	HL
53	Bill Reynolds	LJ
54	George Hayward	HL
55	Tom Barnes	LJ
56	Ron Baynes	LJ
57	Ed Fiffick	U
58	Bill Quinby	SJ
59	Phil Luckett	FJ
60	Tommy Moore	SJ
61	Dick Creed	SJ
62	Charles Stewart	LJ
63	Bill Carollo	SJ
65	Walt Coleman	LJ
67	John Keck	U
68	Louis Richard	BJ
71	Ed Coukart	U
72	Terry Gierke	HL
73	Bobby Skelton	FJ
75	Jim Daopoulos	BJ
76	Ed Merrifield	FJ
77	Don Orr	FJ
78	Art Demmas	U
79	Aaron Pointer	HL
80	Timmie Millis	BJ
81	Dave Anderson	HL
82	Pat Mallette	FJ
83	Ron Blum	LJ
84	Bob Wortman	FJ
85	Ed Hochuli	BJ
86	Bernie Kukar	R
87	Paul Weidner	HL
88	Scott Steenson	BJ
89	Gordon Wells	U
90	Mike Borgard	SJ
91	Ken Baker	BJ
92	Jim Poole	BJ
93	Jack Vaughan	FJ
94	Mike Carey	SJ
95	Bob McElwee	R
96	Don Hakes	FJ
97	Nathan Jones	SJ
98	Bill Lovett	BJ
99	Banks Williams	BJ
100	Bob Wagner	U
101	Bob Boylston	U
103	Rex Stuart	U
104	Dale Hamer	R
105	Dick Hantak	R
106	Al Jury	BJ
107	Jim Kearney	BJ
108	Stan Kemp	R
109	Sid Semon	HL
110	Ron Botchan	U
111	Earnie Frantz	HL
112	Joe Haynes	LJ
113	Don Dorkowski	FJ
114	Tom Johnson	HL
115	Hendi Ancich	U
117	Ben Montgomery	LJ
118	Tom Sifferman	BJ
119	Ron Spitler	SJ
120	Gary Lane	R
121	Sanford Rivers	HL
122	Bill Schmitz	FJ
123	Tom White	R

1992 Officials at a Glance

Referees

Gerry Austin, No. 34, Western Carolina, associate superintendent, county schools, 11th year.
Red Cashion, No. 43, Texas A&M, chairman, insurance company, 21st year.
Johnny Grier, No. 23, University of D.C., planning engineer, 12th year.
Pat Haggerty, No. 40, Colorado State, retired educator, 28th year.
Dale Hamer, No. 104, California (Pa.) University, vice president, finance, 15th year.
Dick Hantak, No. 105, Southeast Missouri, educator, 15th year.
Stan Kemp, No. 108, Michigan, independent insurance agent, 7th year.
Bernie Kukar, No. 86, St. John's, owner/director, summer camp for boys, 9th year.
Gary Lane, No. 120, Missouri, vice president, medical supplies, former NFL player, 11th year.
Jerry Markbreit, No. 9, Illinois, trade and barter manager, 17th year.
Gordon McCarter, No. 48, Western Reserve, sales manager, 26th year.
Bob McElwee, No. 95, Navy, owner, heavy construction firm, 17th year.
Larry Nemmers, No. 20, Upper Iowa, high school principal, 8th year.
Howard Roe, No. 33, Wichita State, director, administration and finance, 9th year.
Tom White, No. 123, Temple, president, athletic sportswear, 4th year.

Umpires

Hendi Ancich, No. 115, Harbor, longshoreman, 11th year.
Ron Botchan, No. 110, Occidental, college professor, former AFL player, 13th year.
Bob Boylston, No. 101, Alabama, stockbroker, 15th year.
Chad Brown, No. 31, East Texas State, director, intramural/sports clubs, 1st year.
Al Conway, No. 27, Army, director of manufacturing, 24th year.
Ed Coukart, No. 71, Northwestern, president, commercial bank, 4th year.
Art Demmas, No. 78, Vanderbilt, Southern coordinator College Football Hall of Fame, 25th year.
Ed Fiffick, No. 57, Marquette, podiatric physician, 14th year.
Neil Gereb, No. 50, California, project manager, aircraft company, 12th year.
Dave Hamilton, No. 42, Utah, assistant executive director, 18th year.
John Keck, No. 67, Cornell, petroleum distributor, 21st year.
Dennis Riggs, No. 30, Bellarmine, seminary vice president, 5th year.
Rex Stuart, No. 103, Appalachian State, insurance agent, 9th year.
Bob Wagner, No. 100, Penn State, executive director, cardiovascular institute, 8th year.
Gordon Wells, No. 89, Occidental, college department chairman, 21st year.

Head Linesmen

Dave Anderson, No. 81, Salem, insurance executive, 9th year.
Mark Baltz, No. 26, Ohio University, manufacturer's representative, 4th year.
Jerry Bergman, No. 17, Duquesne, executive director, pension fund, 27th year.
Earnie Frantz, No. 111, vice president and manager, insurance company, 12th year.
Terry Gierke, No. 72, Portland State, real estate broker, 12th year.
George Hayward, No. 54, Missouri, vice president and manager, warehouse company, 2nd year.
Tom Johnson, No. 114, Miami, Ohio, teacher, executive vice president, security company, 11th year.
Ron Phares, No. 10, Virginia Tech, president, construction company, 8th year.
Aaron Pointer, No. 79, Pacific Lutheran, park department administrator, 6th year.
Sanford Rivers, No. 121, Youngstown State, assistant vice president, school administration, 4th year.
John Schleyer, No. 21, Millersville, medical sales, 3rd year.
Sid Semon, No. 109, Southern California, chairman, physical education department, 15th year.
Tony Veteri, No. 52, Manhattan, director of athletics, 1st year.
Paul Weidner, No. 87, Cincinnati, marketing manager, 7th year.
Dale Williams, No. 8, Cal State-Northridge, owner, coin-op laundromats, 13th year.

Line Judges

John Alderton, No. 25, Portland State, vice president, insurance, 4th year.
Tom Barnes, No. 55, Minnesota, manufacturing representative, 7th year.
Ron Baynes, No. 56, Auburn, school administrator, coach, 6th year.
Jeff Bergman, No. 32, Robert Morris, president and chief executive officer, medical services, 2nd year.
Ron Blum, No. 83, Marin College, PGA golf professional, 8th year.
Walt Coleman, No. 65, Arkansas, president, dairy processor, 4th year.
Bama Glass, No. 15, Colorado, owner/manager, retail sales, 14th year.
Joe Haynes, No. 112, Alcorn State, deputy superintendent, public schools, 9th year.
Bruce Maurer, No. 38, Ohio State, administrator/associate director, recreational sports, 6th year.
Dick McKenzie, No. 41, Ashland, financial services, 15th year.
Ben Montgomery, No. 117, Morehouse, school administrator, 11th year.
Dale Orem, No. 51, Louisville, executive director, community foundation, 13th year.
Jim Quirk, No. 5, Delaware, vice president foreign sales, government securities, 5th year.

Bill Reynolds, No. 53, West Chester State, retired teacher, 18th year.
Charles Stewart, No. 62, administrative deputy director, 1st year.
Fred Wyant, No. 11, West Virginia, regional sales manager, former NFL player, 27th year.

Back Judges

Paul Baetz, No. 22, Heidelberg, financial consultant, 15th year.
Ken Baker, No. 91, Eastern Illinois, optician, surgical ophthalmic technician, 2nd year.
Roy Clymer, No. 24, New Mexico State, district marketing manager, gas company, 13th year.
Jim Daopoulos, No. 75, Kentucky, mortgage broker, 4th year.
Ed Hochuli, No. 85, Texas-El Paso, attorney, 3rd year.
Al Jury, No. 106, San Bernardino Valley, state traffic officer, 15th year.
Jim Kearney, No. 107, Pennsylvania, marketing manager, 15th year.
Bill Lovett, No. 98, Maryland, managing partner, financial sales, 3rd year.
Timmie Millis, No. 80, Millsaps, financial investigative consultant, 4th year.
Bob Moore, No. 36, Dayton, attorney, 9th year.
Jim Poole, No. 92, San Diego State, college professor, 18th year.
Louis Richard, No. 68, Southwest Louisiana, sales manager, 7th year.
Tom Sifferman, No. 118, Seattle, manufacturer's representative, 7th year.
Scott Steenson, No. 88, North Texas State, real estate broker, 2nd year.
Banks Williams, No. 99, Houston, vice president, general sales manager, 15th year.

Side Judges

Mike Borgard, No. 90, St. Louis, president/owner, advertising specialties, 3rd year.
Mike Carey, No. 94, Santa Clara, marketing manager, 3rd year.
Don Carlsen, No. 39, Cal State-Chico, budget analyst, comptroller, 4th year.
Bill Carollo, No. 63, Wisconsin, marketing executive, 4th year.
Richard Creed, No. 61, Louisville, manager, real estate, 15th year.
Tom Fincken, No. 47, Emporia State, educator, 9th year.
Van Golmont, No. 3, Miami, regional field promotion manager, 2nd year.
Nathan Jones, No. 97, Lewis and Clark, high school principal, 16th year.
Dean Look, No. 49, Michigan State, director, medical manufacturing, former AFL player, 20th year.
Tommy Moore, No. 60, Stephen F. Austin, marketing, manufacturing representative, 1st year.
Bill Quinby, No. 58, Iowa, retired athletic director, 15th year.
Howard Slavin, No. 29, Southern California, attorney, 6th year.
Ron Spitler, No. 119, Panhandle State, owner, service center, 11th year.
Doug Toole, No. 4, Utah State, physical therapist, orthopedic and sports medicine, 5th year.
Don Wedge, No. 28, Ohio Wesleyan, executive account manager, 21st year.
David Wyant, No. 16, Virginia, research scientist, 2nd year.

Field Judges

Don Dorkowski, No. 113, Cal State-Los Angeles, department head, health and safety, 7th year.
Scott Green, No. 19, Delaware, special advisor, senate judiciary committee, 2nd year.
Don Hakes, No. 96, Bradley, retired educator, 16th year.
Donnie Hampton, No. 44, Georgia, mortgage banker, 5th year.
Bob Lewis, No. 18, retired U.S. government specialist, 17th year.
Phil Luckett, No. 59, Texas-El Paso, computer program analyst, federal civil services, 2nd year.
Pat Mallette, No. 82, Nebraska, real estate broker, 24th year.
Ed Merrifield, No. 76, Missouri, sales representative, 18th year.
Don Orr, No. 77, Vanderbilt, mechanical contractor, 22nd year.
John Robison, No. 46, Utah, high school teacher, 5th year.
Bill Schmitz, No. 122, Colorado State, general sales manager, 4th year.
Bobby Skelton, No. 73, Alabama, industrial representative, 8th year.
Larry Upson, No. 37, Prince George City College, senior personnel management specialist, 2nd year.
Jack Vaughan, No. 93, Mississippi State, financial services, 17th year.
Bob Wortman, No. 84, Findlay, retired supervisor, college basketball officials, 27th year.

1

**TOUCHDOWN, FIELD GOAL,
or SUCCESSFUL TRY**
Both arms extended above head.

2

SAFETY
Palms together above head.

3

FIRST DOWN
Arm pointed toward defensive
team's goal.

4

**CROWD NOISE,
DEAD BALL, or NEUTRAL
ZONE ESTABLISHED**
One arm above head
with an open hand.
With fist closed: **Fourth Down.**

5

**BALL ILLEGALLY
TOUCHED, KICKED,
OR BATTED**
Fingertips tap both shoulders.

6

TIME OUT
Hands crisscrossed above head.
Same signal followed by placing one
hand on top of cap: **Referee's Time Out.**
Same signal followed by arm swung at
side: **Touchback.**

7

**NO TIME OUT or
TIME IN WITH WHISTLE**
Full arm circled to
simulate moving clock.

8

**DELAY OF GAME,
ILLEGAL SUBSTITUTION,
or EXCESS TIME OUT**
Folded arms.

9

FALSE START, ILLEGAL SHIFT, ILLEGAL FORMATION, or KICKOFF OR SAFETY KICK OUT OF BOUNDS
Forearms rotated over and over in front of body.

10

PERSONAL FOUL
One wrist striking the other above head.
Same signal followed by swinging leg:
Roughing Kicker.
Same signal followed by raised arm swinging forward:
Roughing Passer.
Same signal followed by hand striking back of calf: **Clipping.**

11

HOLDING
Grasping one wrist, the fist clenched, in front of chest.

12

ILLEGAL USE OF HANDS, ARMS, OR BODY
Grasping one wrist, the hand open and facing forward, in front of chest.

13

PENALTY REFUSED, INCOMPLETE PASS, PLAY OVER, or MISSED GOAL
Hands shifted in horizontal plane.

14

PASS JUGGLED INBOUNDS AND CAUGHT OUT OF BOUNDS
Hands up and down in front of chest (following incomplete pass signal).

15

ILLEGAL FORWARD PASS
One hand waved behind back followed by loss of down signal (23).

16

INTENTIONAL GROUNDING OF PASS
Parallel arms waved in a diagonal plane across body. Followed by loss of down signal (23).

17

**INTERFERENCE WITH FORWARD
PASS or FAIR CATCH**
Hands open
and extended forward from
shoulders with hands vertical.

18

INVALID FAIR CATCH SIGNAL
One hand waved above head.

19

**INELIGIBLE RECEIVER
OR INELIGIBLE
MEMBER OF KICKING
TEAM DOWNFIELD**
Right hand touching top of cap.

20

ILLEGAL CONTACT
One open hand extended forward.

21

OFFSIDE or ENCROACHING
Hands on hips.

22

ILLEGAL MOTION AT SNAP
Horizontal arc with one hand.

23

LOSS OF DOWN
Both hands held behind head.

24

**CRAWLING, INTERLOCKING
INTERFERENCE, PUSHING, or
HELPING RUNNER**
Pushing movement of hands
to front with arms downward.

25

**TOUCHING A FORWARD
PASS OR SCRIMMAGE KICK**
Diagonal motion of
one hand across another.

26

**UNSPORTSMANLIKE
CONDUCT**
Arms outstretched, palms down.
(Same signal means continuous
action fouls are disregarded.)
Chop block.

27

**ILLEGAL CUT or
BLOCKING BELOW
THE WAIST**
Hand striking front of thigh
preceded by personal foul
signal (10).

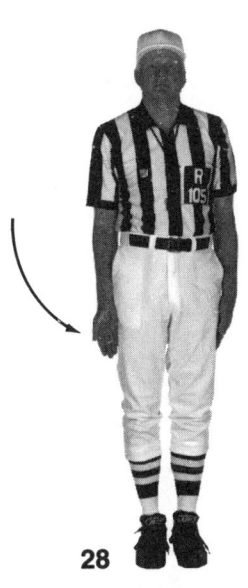

28

ILLEGAL CRACKBACK
Strike of an open right hand
against the right mid thigh
preceded by personal foul
signal (10).

29

PLAYER DISQUALIFIED
Ejection signal.

30

TRIPPING
Repeated action of right foot
in back of left heel.

31

**UNCATCHABLE
FORWARD PASS**
Palm of right hand held
parallel to ground above head.
and moved back and forth.

NFL Digest of Rules

This Digest of Rules of the National Football League has been prepared to aid players, fans, and members of the press, radio, and television media in their understanding of the game.

It is not meant to be a substitute for the official rule book. In any case of conflict between these explanations and the official rules, the rules always have precedence.

In order to make it easier to coordinate the information in this digest the topics discussed generally follow the order of the rule book.

Officials' Jurisdictions, Positions, and Duties

Referee—General oversight and control of game. Gives signals for all fouls and is final authority for rule interpretations. Takes a position in backfield 10 to 12 yards behind line of scrimmage, favors right side (if quarterback is right-handed passer). Determines legality of snap, observes deep back(s) for legal motion. On running play, observes quarterback during and after handoff, remains with him until action has cleared away, then proceeds downfield, checking on runner and contact behind him. When runner is downed, Referee determines forward progress from wing official and, if necessary, adjusts final position of ball.

On pass plays, drops back as quarterback begins to fade back, picks up legality of blocks by near linemen. Changes to complete concentration on quarterback as defenders approach. Primarily responsible to rule on possible roughing action on passer and if ball becomes loose, rules whether ball is free on a fumble or dead on an incomplete pass.

During kicking situations, Referee has primary responsibility to rule on kicker's actions and whether or not any subsequent contact by a defender is legal.

Umpire—Primary responsibility to rule on players' equipment, as well as their conduct and actions on scrimmage line. Lines up approximately four to five yards downfield, varying position from in front of weakside tackle to strongside guard. Looks for possible false start by offensive linemen. Observes legality of contact by both offensive linemen while blocking and by defensive players while they attempt to ward off blockers. Is prepared to call rule infractions if they occur on offense or defense. Moves forward to line of scrimmage when pass play develops in order to insure that interior linemen do not move illegally downfield. If offensive linemen indicate screen pass is to be attempted, Umpire shifts his attention toward screen side, picks up potential receiver in order to insure that he will legally be permitted to run his pattern and continues to rule on action of blockers. Umpire is to assist in ruling on incomplete or trapped passes when ball is thrown overhead or short.

Head Linesman—Primarily responsible for ruling on offside, encroachment, and actions pertaining to scrimmage line prior to or at snap. Keys on closest setback on his side of the field. On pass plays, Linesman is responsible to clear this receiver approximately seven yards downfield as he moves to a point five yards beyond the line. Linesman's secondary responsibility is to rule on any illegal action taken by defenders on any delay receiver moving downfield. Has full responsibility for ruling on sideline plays on his side, e.g., pass receiver or runner in or out of bounds. Together with Referee, Linesman is responsible for keeping track of number of downs and is in charge of mechanics of his chain crew in connection with its duties.

Linesman must be prepared to assist in determining forward progress by a runner on play directed toward middle or into his side zone. He, in turn, is to signal Referee or Umpire what forward point ball has reached. Linesman is also responsible to rule on legality of action involving any receiver who approaches his side zone. He is to call pass interference when the infraction occurs and is to rule on legality of blockers and defenders on plays involving ball carriers, whether it is entirely a running play, a combination pass and run, or a play involving a kick.

Line Judge—Straddles line of scrimmage on side of field opposite Linesman. Keeps time of game as a backup for clock operator. Along with Linesman is responsible for offside, encroachment, and actions pertaining to scrimmage line prior to or at snap. Line Judge keys on closest setback on his side of field. Line Judge is to observe his receiver until he moves at least seven yards downfield. He then moves toward backfield side, being especially alert to rule on any back in motion and on flight of ball when pass is made (he must rule whether forward or backward). Line Judge has primary responsibility to rule whether or not passer is behind or beyond line of scrimmage when pass is made. He also assists in observing actions by blockers and defenders who are on his side of field. After pass is thrown, Line Judge directs attention toward activities that occur in back of Umpire. During punting situations, Line Judge remains at line of scrimmage to be sure that only the end men move downfield until kick has been made. He also rules whether or not the kick crossed line and then observes action by members of the kicking team who are moving downfield to cover the kick.

Back Judge—Operates on same side of field as Line Judge, 20 yards deep. Keys on wide receiver on his side. Concentrates on path of end or back, observing legality of his potential block(s) or of actions taken against him. Is prepared to rule from deep position on holding or illegal use of hands by end or back or on defensive infractions committed by player guarding him. Has primary responsibility to make decisions involving sideline on his side of field, e.g., pass receiver or runner in or out of bounds.

Back Judge makes decisions involving catching, recovery, or illegal touching of a loose ball beyond line of scrimmage; rules on plays involving pass receiver, including legality of catch or pass interference; assists in covering actions of runner, including blocks by teammates and that of defenders; calls clipping on punt returns; and, together with Field Judge, rules whether or not field goal attempts are successful.

Side Judge—Operates on same side of field as Linesman, 20 yards deep. Keys on wide receiver on his side. Concentrates on path of end or back, observing legality of his potential block(s) or of actions taken against him. Is prepared to rule from deep position on holding or illegal use of hands by end or back or on defensive infractions committed by player guarding him. Has primary responsibility to make decisions involving sideline on his side of field, e.g., pass receiver or runner in or out of bounds.

Side Judge makes decisions involving catching, recovery, or illegal touching of a loose ball beyond line of scrimmage; rules on plays involving pass receiver, including legality of catch or pass interference; assists in covering actions of runner, including blocks by teammates and that of defenders; and calls clipping on punt returns.

Field Judge—Takes a position 25 yards downfield. In general, favors the tight end's side of field. Keys on tight end, concentrates on his path and observes legality of tight end's potential block(s) or of actions taken against him. Is prepared to rule from deep position on holding or illegal use of hands by end or back or on defensive infractions committed by player guarding him.

Field Judge times interval between plays on 45/25-second clock plus intermission between two periods of each half; makes decisions involving catching, recovery, or illegal touching of a loose ball beyond line of scrimmage; is responsible to rule on plays involving end line; calls pass interference, fair catch infractions, and clipping on kick returns; and, together with Back Judge, rules whether or not field goals and conversions are successful.

Definitions

1. **Chucking:** Warding off an opponent who is in front of a defender by contacting him with a quick extension of arm or arms, followed by the return of arm(s) to a flexed position, thereby breaking the original contact.
2. **Clipping:** Throwing the body across the back of an opponent's leg or hitting him from the back below the waist while moving up from behind unless the opponent is a runner or the action is in close line play.
3. **Close Line Play:** The area between the positions normally occupied by the offensive tackles, extending three yards on each side of the line of scrimmage.
4. **Crackback:** Eligible receivers who take or move to a position more than two yards outside the tackle may not block an opponent below the waist if they then move back inside to block.
5. **Dead Ball:** Ball not in play.
6. **Double Foul:** A foul by each team during the same down.
7. **Down:** The period of action that starts when the ball is put in play and ends when it is dead.
8. **Encroachment:** When a player enters the neutral zone and makes contact with an opponent before the ball is snapped.
9. **Fair Catch:** An unhindered catch of a kick by a member of the receiving team who must raise one arm a full length above his head while the kick is in flight.
10. **Foul:** Any violation of a playing rule.
11. **Free Kick:** A kickoff, kick after a safety, or kick after a fair catch. It may be a placekick, dropkick, or punt, except a punt may not be used on a kickoff.
12. **Fumble:** The loss of possession of the ball.
13. **Game Clock:** Scoreboard game clock.
14. **Impetus:** The action of a player that gives momentum to the ball.
15. **Live Ball:** A ball legally free kicked or snapped. It continues in play until the down ends.
16. **Loose Ball:** A live ball not in possession of any player.
17. **Muff:** The touching of a loose ball by a player in an unsuccessful attempt to obtain possession.
18. **Neutral Zone:** The space the length of a ball between the two scrimmage lines. The offensive team and defensive team must remain behind their end of the ball.
    Exception: The offensive player who snaps the ball.
19. **Offside:** A player is offside when any part of his body is beyond his scrimmage or free kick line when the ball is snapped.
20. **Own Goal:** The goal a team is guarding.
21. **Play Clock:** 45/25 second clock.
22. **Pocket Area:** Applies from a point two yards outside of either offensive tackle and includes the tight end if he drops off the line of scrimmage to pass protect. Pocket extends longitudinally behind the line back to offensive team's own end line.
23. **Possession:** When a player controls the ball throughout the act of clearly touching both feet, or any other part of his body other than his hand(s), to the ground inbounds.
24. **Post-Possession Foul:** A foul by the receiving team that occurs after a ball is legally kicked from scrimmage prior to possession changing. The ball must cross the line of scrimmage and the receiving team must retain possession of the kicked ball.
25. **Punt:** A kick made when a player drops the ball and kicks it while it is in flight.
26. **Safety:** The situation in which the ball is dead on or behind a team's own goal if the impetus comes from a player on that team. Two points are scored for the opposing team.
27. **Shift:** The movement of two or more offensive players at the same time before the snap.
28. **Striking:** The act of swinging, clubbing, or propelling the arm or forearm in contacting an opponent.
29. **Sudden Death:** The continuation of a tied game into sudden death overtime in which the team scoring first (by safety, field goal, or touchdown) wins.
30. **Touchback:** When a ball is dead on or behind a team's own goal line, provided the impetus came from an opponent and provided it is not a touchdown or a missed field goal.

31. **Touchdown:** When any part of the ball, legally in possession of a player inbounds, is on, above, or over the opponent's goal line, provided it is not a touchback.
32. **Unsportsmanlike Conduct:** Any act contrary to the generally understood principles of sportsmanship.

Summary of Penalties

Automatic First Down
1. Awarded to offensive team on all <u>defensive fouls</u> with these exceptions:
   (a) Offside.
   (b) Encroachment.
   (c) Delay of game.
   (d) Illegal substitution.
   (e) Excessive time out(s).
   (f) Incidental grasp of facemask.
   (g) Prolonged, excessive or premeditated celebrations by individual players or groups of players.
   (h) Running into the kicker.

Loss of Down (No yardage)
1. Second forward pass <u>behind</u> the line.
2. Forward pass strikes ground, goal post, or crossbar.
3. Forward pass goes out of bounds.
4. Forward pass is first touched by eligible receiver who has gone out of bounds and returned.
5. Forward pass touches or is caught by an ineligible receiver on or behind line.
6. Forward pass thrown from behind line of scrimmage after ball once crossed the line.

Five Yards
1. Defensive holding or illegal use of hands (automatic first down).
2. Delay of game.
3. Encroachment.
4. Too many time outs.
5. False start.
6. Illegal formation.
7. Illegal shift.
8. Illegal motion.
9. Illegal substitution.
10. First onside kickoff out of bounds between goal lines and not touched.
11. Invalid fair catch signal.
12. More than 11 players on the field at snap for either team.
13. Less than seven men on offensive line at snap.
14. Offside.
15. Failure to pause one second after shift or huddle.
16. Running into kicker.
17. More than one man in motion at snap.
18. Grasping facemask of opponent.
19. Player out of bounds at snap.
20. Ineligible member(s) of kicking team going beyond line of scrimmage before ball is kicked.
21. Illegal return.
22. Failure to report change of eligibility.
23. Prolonged, excessive or premeditated celebrations by individual players or groups of players.
24. Loss of team time out(s) or five-yard penalty on the defense for excessive crowd noise.

10 Yards
1. Offensive pass interference.
2. Ineligible player downfield during passing down.
3. Holding, illegal use of hands, arms or body by offense.
4. Tripping by a member of either team.
5. Helping the runner.
6. Deliberately batting or punching a loose ball.
7. Deliberately kicking a loose ball.

15 Yards
1. Chop block.
2. Clipping below the waist.
3. Fair catch interference.
4. Illegal crackback block by offense.
5. Piling on (automatic first down).
6. Roughing the kicker (automatic first down).
7. Roughing the passer (automatic first down).
8. Twisting, turning, or pulling an opponent by the facemask.
9. Unnecessary roughness.
10. Unsportsmanlike conduct.
11. Delay of game at start of either half.
12. Illegal blocking below the waist.
13. A tackler using his helmet to butt, spear, or ram an opponent.
14. Any player who uses the top of his helmet unnecessarily.
15. A punter, placekicker, or holder who simulates being roughed by a defensive player.
16. A defender who takes a running start from beyond the line of scrimmage in an attempt to block a field goal or point after touchdown and lands on players.

Five Yards and Loss of Down
1. Forward pass thrown from <u>beyond</u> line of scrimmage.

10 Yards and Loss of Down
1. Intentional grounding of forward pass (safety if passer is in own end zone). If foul occurs more than 10 yards behind line, play results in loss of down at spot of foul.

15 Yards and Loss of Coin Toss Option
1. Team's late arrival on the field prior to scheduled kickoff.
2. Captains not appearing for coin toss.

15 Yards (and disqualification if flagrant)
1. Striking opponent with fist.
2. Kicking or kneeing opponent.
3. Striking opponent on head or neck with forearm, elbow, or hands whether or not the initial contact is made below the neck area.
4. Roughing kicker.
5. Roughing passer.
6. Malicious unnecessary roughness.
7. Unsportsmanlike conduct.
8. Palpably unfair act. (Distance penalty determined by the Referee after consultation with other officials.)

15 Yards and Automatic Disqualification
1. Using a helmet that is not worn as a weapon.

Suspension From Game
1. Illegal equipment. (Player may return after one down when legally equipped.)

Touchdown
1. When Referee determines a palpably unfair act deprived a team of a touchdown. (Example: Player comes off bench and tackles runner apparently en route to touchdown.)

Field
1. Sidelines and end lines are <u>out of bounds</u>. The <u>goal line</u> is <u>actually in the end zone</u>. A player with the ball in his possession scores when the ball is <u>on, above</u>, or <u>over</u> the goal line.
2. The field is rimmed by a white border, a minimum six feet wide, along the sidelines. All of this is <u>out of bounds</u>.
3. The hashmarks (inbound lines) are 70 feet, 9 inches from each sideline.
4. Goal posts must be single-standard type, offset from the end line and painted bright gold. The goal posts must be 18 feet, 6 inches wide and the top face of the crossbar must be 10 feet above the ground. Vertical posts extend at least 30 feet above the crossbar. A ribbon 4 inches by 42 inches long is to be attached to the top of each post. The actual goal is the plane extending indefinitely above the crossbar and between the <u>outer</u> edges of the posts.
5. The field is 360 feet long and 160 feet wide. The end zones are 30 feet deep. The line used in try-for-point plays is two yards out from the goal line.
6. Chain crew members and ball boys must be uniformly identifiable.
7. All clubs must use standardized sideline markers. Pylons must be used for goal line and end line markings.
8. End zone markings and club identification at 50 yard line must be approved by the Commissioner to avoid any confusion as to delineation of goal lines, sidelines, and end lines.

Ball
1. The home club must have 24 balls available for testing by the Referee one hour before game time. In case of bad weather, a playable ball is to be substituted on request of the offensive team captain.

Coin Toss
1. The toss of coin will take place within three minutes of kickoff in center of field. The toss will be called by the visiting captain. The winner may choose one of two privileges and the loser gets the other:
   (a) Receive or kick
   (b) Goal his team will defend
2. Immediately prior to the start of the second half, the captains of both teams must inform the officials of their respective choices. The loser of the original coin toss gets first choice.

Timing
1. The stadium game clock is official. In case it stops or is operating incorrectly, the <u>Line Judge</u> takes over the official timing on the field.
2. Each period is 15 minutes. The intermission between the periods is two minutes. Halftime is 12 minutes, unless otherwise specified.
3. On charged team time outs, the Field Judge starts watch and blows whistle after 1 minute 50 seconds, unless television does not utilize the time for commercial. In this case the length of the time out is reduced to 40 seconds.
4. Referee may allow two minutes for injured player and three minutes for equipment repair.
5. Each team is allowed three time outs each half.
6. Time between plays will be 45 seconds from the end of a given play until the snap of the ball for the next play, or a 25-second interval after certain administrative stoppages and game delays.
7. Clock will start running when ball is snapped following all changes of team possession.
8. With the exception of the last two minutes of the first half and the last five minutes of the second half, the game clock will be restarted following a kickoff return, a player going out of bounds on a play from scrimmage, or after declined penalties when appropriate on the referee's signal.
9. Consecutive team time outs can be taken by opposing teams but the length of the second time out will be reduced to 40 seconds.
10. When, in the judgment of the Referee, the level of crowd noise prevents the offense from hearing its signals, he can institute a series of procedures which can result in a loss of team time outs or a five-yard penalty against the defensive team.

Sudden Death

1. The sudden death system of determining the winner shall prevail when score is tied at the end of the regulation playing time of all NFL games. The team scoring first during overtime play shall be the winner and the game automatically ends upon any score (by safety, field goal, or touchdown) or when a score is awarded by Referee for a palpably unfair act.
2. At the end of regulation time the Referee will immediately toss coin at center of field in accordance with rules pertaining to the usual pregame toss. The captain of the visiting team will call the toss.
3. Following a three-minute intermission after the end of the regulation game, play will be continued in 15-minute periods or until there is a score. There is a two-minute intermission between subsequent periods. The teams change goals at the start of each period. Each team has three time outs and general provisions for play in the last two minutes of a half shall prevail. Disqualified players are not allowed to return.

    Exception: In preseason and regular season games there shall be a maximum of 15 minutes of sudden death with two time outs instead of three. General provisions for play in the last two minutes of a half will be in force.

Timing in Final Two Minutes of Each Half

1. On kickoff, clock does not start until the ball has been legally touched by player of either team in the field of play. (In all other cases, clock starts with kickoff.)
2. A team cannot buy an excess time out for a penalty. However, a fourth time out is allowed without penalty for an injured player, who must be removed immediately. A fifth time out or more is allowed for an injury and a five-yard penalty is assessed if the clock was running. Additionally, if the clock was running and the score is tied or the team in possession is losing, the ball cannot be put in play for at least 10 seconds on the fourth or more time out. The half or game can end while those 10 seconds are run off on the clock.
3. If the defensive team is behind in the score and commits a foul when it has no time outs left in the final 30 seconds of either half, the offensive team can decline the penalty for the foul and have the time on the clock expire.
4. Fouls that occur in the last five minutes of the fourth quarter as well as the last two minutes of the first half will result in the clock starting on the snap.

Try-for-Point

1. After a touchdown, the scoring team is allowed a try-for-point during one scrimmage down. The ball may be spotted anywhere between the inbounds lines, two or more yards from the goal line. The successful conversion counts one point, whether by run, kick, or pass.
2. The defensive team never can score on a try-for-point. As soon as defense gets possession, or the kick is blocked, the ball is dead.
3. Any distance penalty for fouls committed by the defense that prevent the try from being attempted can be enforced on the succeeding kickoff. Any foul committed on a successful try will result in a distance penalty being assessed on the ensuing kickoff.
4. Only the fumbling player may advance a fumble during a try-for-point.

Players-Substitutions

1. Each team is permitted 11 men on the field at the snap.
2. Unlimited substitution is permitted. However, players may enter the field only when the ball is dead. Players who have been substituted for are not permitted to linger on the field. Such lingering will be interpreted as unsportsmanlike conduct.
3. Players leaving the game must be out of bounds on their own side, clearing the field between the end lines, before a snap or free kick. If player crosses end line leaving field, it is delay of game (five-yard penalty).
4. Substitutes who remain in the game must move onto the field as far as the inside of the field numerals before moving to a wide position.

Kickoff

1. The kickoff shall be from the kicking team's 35 yard line at the start of each half and after a field goal and try-for-point. A kickoff is one type of free kick.
2. Either a one-, two-, or three-inch tee may be used (no tee permitted for field goal or try-for-point plays). The ball is put in play by a placekick or dropkick.
3. If the kickoff clears the opponent's goal posts it is not a field goal.
4. A kickoff is illegal unless it travels 10 yards OR is touched by the receiving team. Once the ball is touched by the receiving team it is a free ball. Receivers may recover and advance. Kicking team may recover but NOT advance UNLESS receiver had possession and lost the ball.
5. When a kickoff goes out of bounds between the goal lines without being touched by the receiving team, the ball belongs to the receivers 30 yards from the spot of the kick or at the out-of-bounds spot unless the ball went out-of-bounds the first time an onside kick was attempted. In this case the kicking team is to be penalized five yards and the ball must be kicked again.
6. When a kickoff goes out of bounds between the goal lines and is touched last by receiving team, it is receiver's ball at out-of-bounds spot.

Free Kick

1. In addition to a kickoff, the other free kicks are a kick after a safety and a kick after a fair catch. In both cases, a dropkick, placekick, or punt may be used (a punt may not be used on a kickoff).
2. On a free kick after a fair catch, captain of receiving team has the option to put ball in play by punt, dropkick, or placekick without a tee, or by snap. If the placekick or dropkick goes between the uprights a field goal is scored.

3. On a free kick after a safety, the team scored upon puts ball in play by a punt, dropkick, or placekick without tee. No score can be made on a free kick following a safety, even if a series of penalties places team in position. (A field goal can be scored only on a play from scrimmage or a free kick after a fair catch.)

Field Goal

1. All field goals attempted and missed from scrimmage line beyond the 20 yard line will result in the defensive team taking possession of the ball at the scrimmage line. On any field goal attempted and missed from scrimmage line inside the 20 yard line, ball will revert to defensive team at the 20 yard line.

Safety

1. The important factor in a safety is impetus. Two points are scored for the opposing team when the ball is dead on or behind a team's own goal line if the impetus came from a player on that team.

Examples of Safety:

(a) Blocked punt goes out of kicking team's end zone. Impetus was provided by punting team. The block only changes direction of ball, not impetus.
(b) Ball carrier retreats from field of play into his own end zone and is downed. Ball carrier provides impetus.
(c) Offensive team commits a foul and spot of enforcement is behind its own goal line.
(d) Player on receiving team muffs punt and, trying to get ball, forces or illegally kicks it into end zone where he or a teammate recovers. He has given new impetus to the ball.

Examples of Non-Safety:

(a) Player intercepts a pass with both feet inbounds in the field of play and his momentum carries him into his own end zone. Ball is put in play at spot of interception.
(b) Player intercepts a pass in his own end zone and is downed. Impetus came from passing team, not from defense. (Touchback)
(c) Player passes from behind his own goal line. Opponent bats down ball in end zone. (Incomplete pass)

Measuring

1. The forward point of the ball is used when measuring.

Position of Players at Snap

1. Offensive team must have at least seven players on line.
2. Offensive players, not on line, must be at least one yard back at snap. (**Exception:** player who takes snap.)
3. No interior lineman may move after taking or simulating a three-point stance.
4. No player of either team may invade neutral zone before snap.
5. No player of offensive team may charge or move, after assuming set position, in such manner as to lead defense to believe snap has started.
6. If a player changes his eligibility, the Referee must alert the defensive captain after player has reported to him.
7. All players of offensive team must be stationary at snap, except one back who may be in motion parallel to scrimmage line or backward (not forward).
8. After a shift or huddle all players on offensive team must come to an absolute stop for at least one second with no movement of hands, feet, head, or swaying of body.
9. Quarterbacks can be called for a false start penalty (five yards) if their actions are judged to be an obvious attempt to draw an opponent offside.

Use of Hands, Arms, and Body

1. No player on offense may assist a runner except by blocking for him. There shall be no interlocking interference.
2. A runner may ward off opponents with his hands and arms but no other player on offense may use hands or arms to obstruct an opponent by grasping with hands, pushing, or encircling any part of his body during a block. Hands (open or closed) can be thrust forward to initially contact an opponent on or outside the opponent's frame, but the blocker must work to bring his hands on or inside the frame.

    Note: Pass blocking: Hand(s) thrust forward that slip outside the body of the defender will be legal if blocker worked to bring them back inside. Hand(s) or arm(s) that encircle a defender—i.e., hook an opponent—are to be considered illegal and officials are to call a foul for holding. Blocker cannot use his hands or arms to push from behind, hang onto, or encircle an opponent in a manner that restricts his movement as the play develops.
3. Hands cannot be thrust forward above the frame to contact an opponent on the neck, face or head.

    Note: The frame is defined as the part of the opponent's body below the neck that is presented to the blocker.
4. A defensive player may not tackle or hold an opponent other than a runner. Otherwise, he may use his hands, arms, or body only:
    (a) To defend or protect himself against an obstructing opponent.

        Exception: An eligible receiver is considered to be an obstructing opponent ONLY to a point five yards beyond the line of scrimmage unless the player who receives the snap clearly demonstrates no further intention to pass the ball. Within this five-yard zone, a defensive player may make contact with an eligible receiver that may be maintained as long as it is continuous and unbroken. The defensive player cannot use his hands or arms to push from behind, hang onto, or encircle an eligible receiver in a manner that restricts movement as the play develops. Beyond this five-yard limitation, a defender may use his hands or arms ONLY to defend or protect himself against impend-

ing contact caused by a receiver. In such reaction, the defender may not contact a receiver who attempts to take a path to evade him.

(b) To push or pull opponent out of the way on line of scrimmage.

(c) In actual attempt to get at or tackle runner.

(d) To push or pull opponent out of the way in a legal attempt to recover a loose ball.

(e) During a legal block on an opponent who is not an eligible pass receiver.

(f) When legally blocking an eligible pass receiver above the waist.

Exception: Eligible receivers lined up within two yards of the tackle, whether on or immediately behind the line, may be blocked below the waist at or behind the line of scrimmage. NO eligible receiver may be blocked below the waist after he goes beyond the line.

Note: Once the quarterback hands off or pitches the ball to a back, or if the quarterback leaves the pocket area, the restrictions on the defensive team relative to the offensive receivers will end, provided the ball is not in the air.

5. A defensive player must not contact an opponent above the shoulders with the palm of his hand except to ward him off on the line. This exception is permitted only if it is not a repeated act against the same opponent during any one contact. In all other cases the palms may be used on head, neck, or face only to ward off or push an opponent in legal attempt to get at the ball.

6. Any offensive player who pretends to possess the ball or to whom a teammate pretends to give the ball may be tackled provided he is crossing his scrimmage line between the ends of a normal tight offensive line.

7. An offensive player who lines up more than two yards outside his own tackle or a player who, at the snap, is in a backfield position and subsequently takes a position more than two yards outside a tackle may not clip an opponent anywhere nor may he contact an opponent below the waist if the blocker is moving toward the ball and if contact is made within an area five yards on either side of the line.

8. A player of either team may block at any time provided it is not pass interference, fair catch interference, or unnecessary roughness.

9. A player may not bat or punch:

(a) A loose ball (in field of play) toward his opponent's goal line or in any direction in either end zone.

(b) A ball in player possession or attempt to get possession.

Exception: A forward or backward pass may be batted, tipped, or deflected in any direction at any time by either the offense or the defense.

Note: A pass in flight that is controlled or caught may only be thrown backward.

10. No player may deliberately kick any ball except as a punt, dropkick, or placekick.

Forward Pass

1. A forward pass may be touched or caught by any eligible receiver. All members of the defensive team are eligible. Eligible receivers on the offensive team are players on either end of line (other than center, guard, or tackle) or players at least one yard behind the line at the snap. A T-formation quarterback is not eligible to receive a forward pass during a play from scrimmage.

Exception: T-formation quarterback becomes eligible if pass is previously touched by an eligible receiver.

2. An offensive team may make only one forward pass during each play from scrimmage (Loss of down).

3. The passer must be behind his line of scrimmage (Loss of down and five yards, enforced from the spot of pass).

4. Any eligible offensive player may catch a forward pass. If a pass is touched by one offensive player and touched or caught by a second eligible offensive player, pass completion is legal. Further, all offensive players become eligible once a pass is touched by an eligible receiver or any defensive player.

5. The rules concerning a forward pass and ineligible receivers:

(a) If ball is touched accidentally by an ineligible receiver on or behind his line: loss of down.

(b) If ineligible receiver is illegally downfield: loss of 10 yards.

(c) If touched or caught (intentionally or accidentally) by ineligible receiver beyond the line: loss of 10 yards or loss of down.

6. The player who first controls and continues to maintain control of a pass will be awarded the ball even though his opponent later establishes joint control of the ball.

7. Any forward pass becomes incomplete and ball is dead if:

(a) Pass hits the ground or goes out of bounds.

(b) Hits the goal post or the crossbar of either team.

(c) Is caught by offensive player after touching ineligible receiver.

(d) An illegal pass is caught by the passer.

8. A forward pass is complete when a receiver clearly touches the ground with both feet inbounds while in possession of the ball. If a receiver would have landed inbounds with both feet but is carried or pushed out of bounds while maintaining possession of the ball, pass is complete at the out-of-bounds spot.

9. If an eligible receiver goes out of bounds accidentally or is forced out by a defender and returns to catch a pass, the play is regarded as a pass caught out of bounds. (Loss of down, no yardage.)

10. On a fourth down pass—when the offensive team is inside the opposition's 20 yard line—an incomplete pass results in a loss of down at the line of scrimmage.

11. If a personal foul is committed by the defense prior to the completion of a pass, the penalty is 15 yards from the spot where ball becomes dead.

12. If a personal foul is committed by the offense prior to the completion of a pass, the penalty is 15 yards from the previous line of scrimmage.

Intentional Grounding of Forward Pass

1. Intentional grounding of a forward pass is a foul: loss of down and 10 yards from previous spot if passer is in the field of play or loss of down at the spot of the foul if it occurs more than 10 yards behind the line or safety if passer is in his own end zone when ball is released.

2. It is considered intentional grounding of a forward pass when the ball strikes the ground after the passer throws, tosses, or lobs the ball to prevent a loss of yards by his team.

3. It is not intentional grounding when the defensive rushers have not put sufficient pressure on the passer to prevent him, for strategic purposes, from throwing the ball downfield in a natural and effective motion even though there is no apparent chance of completion.

Protection of Passer

1. By interpretation, a pass begins when the passer—with possession of ball—starts to bring his hand forward. If ball strikes ground after this action has begun, play is ruled an incomplete pass. If passer loses control of ball prior to his bringing his hand forward, play is ruled a fumble.

2. No defensive player may run into a passer of a legal forward pass after the ball has left his hand (15 yards). The Referee must determine whether opponent had a reasonable chance to stop his momentum during an attempt to block the pass or tackle the passer while he still had the ball.

3. No defensive player who has an unrestricted path to the quarterback may hit him flagrantly in the area of the knee(s) when approaching in any direction.

4. Officials are to blow the play dead as soon as the quarterback is clearly in the grasp and control of any tackler, and his safety is in jeopardy.

Pass Interference

1. There shall be no interference with a forward pass thrown from behind the line. The restriction for the passing team starts with the snap. The restriction on the defensive team starts when the ball leaves the passer's hand. Both restrictions end when the ball is touched by anyone.

2. The penalty for defensive pass interference is an automatic first down at the spot of the foul. If interference is in the end zone, it is first down for the offense on the defense's 1 yard line. If previous spot was inside the defense's 1 yard line, penalty is half the distance to the goal line.

3. The penalty for offensive pass interference is 10 yards from the previous spot.

4. It is pass interference by either team when any player movement beyond the offensive line significantly hinders the progress of an eligible player or such player's opportunity to catch the ball during a legal forward pass. When players are competing for position to make a play on the ball, any contact by hands, arms or body shall be considered incidental unless prohibited. Prohibited conduct shall be when a player physically restricts or impedes the opponent in such a manner that is visually evident and materially affects the opponent's opportunity to gain position or retain his position to catch the ball. If a player has gained position, he shall not be considered to have impeded or restricted his opponent in a prohibited manner if all of his actions are a bona fide effort to go to and catch the ball. Provided an eligible player is not interfered with in such a manner, the following exceptions to pass interference will prevail:

(a) If neither player is looking for the ball and there is incidental contact in the act of moving to the ball that does not materially affect the route of an eligible player, there is no interference. If there is any question whether the incidental contact materially affects the route, the ruling shall be no interference.

Note: Inadvertent tripping is not a foul in this situation.

(b) Any eligible player looking for and intent on playing the ball who initiates contact, however severe, while attempting to move to the spot of completion or interception will not be called for interference.

(c) Any eligible player who makes contact, however severe, with one or more eligible players while looking for and making a genuine attempt to catch or bat a reachable ball, will not be called for interference.

(d) It must be remembered that defensive players have as much right to the ball as offensive eligible receivers.

(e) Pass interference by the defense is not to be called when the forward pass is clearly uncatchable.

(f) Note: There is no defensive pass interference behind the line.

Backward Pass

1. Any pass not forward is regarded as a backward pass or lateral. A pass parallel to the line is a backward pass. A runner may pass backward at any time. Any player on either team may catch the pass or recover the ball after it touches the ground.

2. A backward pass that strikes the ground can be recovered and advanced by offensive team.

3. A backward pass that strikes the ground can be recovered but cannot be advanced by the defensive team.

4. A backward pass caught in the air can be advanced by the defensive team.

5. A backward pass in flight may not be batted forward by an offensive player.

Fumble

1. The distinction between a fumble and a muff should be kept in mind in considering rules about fumbles. A fumble is the loss of possession of the ball. A muff is the touching of a loose ball by a player in an unsuccessful attempt to obtain possession.

2. A fumble may be advanced by any player on either team regardless of whether recovered before or after ball hits the ground.

Kicks From Scrimmage

1. Any kick from scrimmage must be made from behind the line to be legal.
2. Any punt or missed field goal that touches a goal post is dead.
3. During a kick from scrimmage, only the end men, as eligible receivers on the line of scrimmage at the time of the snap, are permitted to go beyond the line before the ball is kicked.
   Exception: An eligible receiver who, at the snap, is aligned or in motion behind the line and more than one yard outside the end man on his side of the line, clearly making him the outside receiver, REPLACES that end man as the player eligible to go downfield after the snap. All other members of the kicking team must remain at the line of scrimmage until the ball has been kicked.
4. Any punt that is blocked and does not cross the line of scrimmage can be recovered and advanced by either team. However, if offensive team recovers it must make the yardage necessary for its first down to retain possession if punt was on fourth down.
5. The kicking team may never advance its own kick even though legal recovery is made beyond the line of scrimmage. Possession only.
6. A member of the receiving team may not run into or rough a kicker who kicks from behind his line unless contact is:
   (a) Incidental to and after he had touched ball in flight.
   (b) Caused by kicker's own motions.
   (c) Occurs during a quick kick, or a kick made after a run, or after kicker recovers a loose ball. Ball is loose when kicker muffs snap or snap hits ground.
   (d) Defender is blocked into kicker.
   The penalty for running into the kicker is 5 yards. For roughing the kicker: 15 yards, an automatic first down and disqualification if flagrant.
7. If a member of the kicking team attempting to down the ball on or inside opponent's 5 yard line carries the ball into the end zone, it is a touchback.
8. Fouls during a punt are enforced from the previous spot (line of scrimmage).
   Exception: Illegal touching, illegal fair catch, invalid fair catch signal, and fouls by the receiving team during loose ball after ball is kicked.
9. While the ball is in the air or rolling on the ground following a punt or field goal attempt and receiving team commits a foul before gaining possession, receiving team will retain possession and will be penalized for its foul.
10. It will be illegal for a defensive player to jump or stand on any player, or be picked up by a teammate or to use a hand or hands on a teammate to gain additional height in an attempt to block a kick (Penalty 15 yards, unsportsmanlike conduct).
11. A punted ball remains a kicked ball until it is declared dead or in possession of either team.
12. Any member of the punting team may down the ball anywhere in the field of play. However, it is illegal touching (Official's time out and receiver's ball at spot of illegal touching). This foul does not offset any foul by receivers during the down.
13. Defensive team may advance all kicks from scrimmage (including unsuccessful field goal) whether or not ball crosses defensive team's goal line. Rules pertaining to kicks from scrimmage apply until defensive team gains possession.

Fair Catch

1. The member of the receiving team must raise one arm a full length above his head and wave it from side to side while kick is in flight. (Failure to give proper sign: receivers' ball five yards behind spot of signal.) **Note:** It is legal for the receiver to shield his eyes from the sun by raising one hand no higher than the helmet.
2. No opponent may interfere with the fair catcher, the ball, or his path to the ball. Penalty: 15 yards from spot of foul and fair catch is awarded.
3. A player who signals for a fair catch is not required to catch the ball. However, if a player signals for a fair catch, he may not block or initiate contact with any player on the kicking team until the ball touches a player. Penalty: snap 15 yards behind spot of foul.
4. If ball hits ground or is touched by member of kicking team in flight, fair catch signal is off and all rules for a kicked ball apply.
5. Any undue advance by a fair catch receiver is delay of game. No specific distance is specified for undue advance as ball is dead at spot of catch. If player comes to a reasonable stop, no penalty. For violation, five yards.
6. If time expires while ball is in play and a fair catch is awarded, receiving team may choose to extend the period with one free kick down. However, placekicker may not use tee.

Foul on Last Play of Half or Game

1. On a foul by defense on last play of half or game, the down is replayed if penalty is accepted.
2. On a foul by the offense on last play of half or game, the down is not replayed and the play in which the foul is committed is nullified.
   Exception: Fair catch interference, foul following change of possession, illegal touching. No score by offense counts.
3. On double foul on last play of half or game, down is replayed.

Spot of Enforcement of Foul

1. There are four basic spots at which a penalty for a foul is enforced:
   (a) Spot of foul: The spot where the foul is committed.
   (b) Previous spot: The spot where the ball was put in play.
   (c) Spot of snap, pass, fumble, return kick, or free kick: The spot where the act connected with the foul occurred.
   (d) Succeeding spot: The spot where the ball next would be put in play if no distance penalty were to be enforced.

Exception: If foul occurs after a touchdown and before the whistle for a try-for-point, succeeding spot is spot of next kickoff.

2. All fouls committed by offensive team behind the line of scrimmage and in the field of play shall be penalized from the previous spot.
3. When spot of enforcement for fouls involving defensive holding or illegal use of hands by the defense is behind the line of scrimmage, any penalty yardage to be assessed on that play shall be measured from the line if the foul occurred beyond the line.

Double Foul

1. If there is a double foul during a down in which there is a change of possession, the team last gaining possession may keep the ball unless its foul was committed prior to the change of possession.
2. If double foul occurs after a change of possession, the defensive team retains the ball at the spot of its foul or dead ball spot.
3. If one of the fouls of a double foul involves disqualification, that player must be removed, but no penalty yardage is to be assessed.
4. If the kickers foul during a punt before possession changes and the receivers foul after possession changes, penalties will be offset and the down is replayed.

Penalty Enforced on Following Kickoff

1. When a team scores by touchdown, field goal, extra point, or safety and either team commits a personal foul, unsportsmanlike conduct, or obvious unfair act during the down, the penalty will be assessed on the following kickoff.

Procedures to Terminate or Temporarily Delay Completion of a Game

The National Football League holds to the position that all games should be played to their conclusion. However, if in the opinion of appropriate League authorities, it is impossible to begin or continue a game due to an emergency, or a game is deemed to be imminently threatened by any such emergency— e.g., severely inclement weather, lightning, flooding, power failure, interference by spectators, or other non-participants—then the following procedures will serve as guidelines for the Commissioner and/or his duly appointed representatives. The Commissioner will have the power to review the circumstances of each emergency and to adjust the following procedures in whatever manner he deems appropriate. If, in the Commissioner's opinion, it is reasonable to project that the resumption of an interrupted game would not change its ultimate result, he will be empowered to terminate the game.

1. The League employees vested with the authority to define emergencies under these procedures are the Commissioner, his representatives, and the game Referee. In cases where neither the Commissioner nor his representatives are present, the referee shall have sole authority, but he must make every effort to contact the Commissioner or representative for consultation. In all cases of significant delay, the League authorities will consult with the management of the participating clubs.
2. If, due to an emergency, a regular-season or postseason game is not started at its scheduled time and cannot be played at any later time that same day, the game, nevertheless, must be played on a subsequent date to be determined by the Commissioner.
3. If there is deemed to be a threat of an emergency (e.g., incoming tropical storm) that may occur during the playing of a game, the starting time of such game will not be moved to an earlier time unless there is clearly sufficient time to make an orderly change.
4. If an interrupted regular-season or postseason game cannot be completed on the same day, such game will be rescheduled by the Commissioner and resumed at that point.
5. In instances which require the Commissioner to reschedule a regular-season game, he will make every effort to set the game for no later than two days after its originally scheduled date, and if possible, at its original site. If unable to do so, he will schedule it at the nearest available facility. If it is impossible to schedule the game within two days after its original date, the Commissioner will attempt to schedule it on the Tuesday of the next calendar week in which the two involved clubs play other clubs no earlier than Sunday.
6. If an emergency interrupts a postseason game and such game cannot be resumed on that same date, the Commissioner will make every effort to arrange for its completion as soon as possible. If unable to schedule the game at the same site, he will select an appropriate alternate site. He will terminate the game short of completion only if in his judgment the continuation of the game would not be normally expected to alter the ultimate outcome.
7. In all instances where a game is resumed after interruption, the resumption will begin at the point at which the game was interrupted. The referee will call time out when it is necessary to declare an emergency interruption, and he will make a record of the team possessing the ball, position of the ball on the field, down, distance, time remaining in the period, and any other pertinent information required for an efficient and equitable resumption of play.

Note: In recent history, only two games, both preseason, have been terminated. In 1976, the Chicago College All-Star game was terminated due to thunderstorms with the Steelers leading the All-Stars 24-0, and the 1980 Pro Football Hall of Fame Game at Canton, Ohio, was called with 5:29 remaining due to severe thunder and lightning with the Chargers and Packers tied 0-0.

NOTES

NOTES

NOTES

NOTES

NOTES

NOTES